THE GREAT PANORAMA

THE
HISTORY OF
REDEMPTION

ELLEN G. WHITE

EVERLASTING GOSPEL PUBLISHING ASSOCIATION

Published by

Everlasting Gospel Publishing Association

Seoul, Korea

www.egpa.net / info@egpa.net

Distributed by Pacific Press Publishing Association, Inc.
(North America)
www.adventistbookcenter.com

1350 N. Kings Rd,. Nampa, Idaho, 83653 U. S. A.
Tel : (208)465-2500, Fax : (208)465-2531 / www.pacificpress.com

---

ISBN 89-89268-18-4
Printed in Korea

The

HISTORY OF REDEMPTION

Presented to

_____

on this _____ day of _____

_____

_____

by _____

_____

KEY TO ABBREVIATIONS OF
E. G. WHITE BOOK TITLES

Key	Book Title
AA	The Acts of the Apostles
AH	The Adventist Home
1BC	The Seventh-day Adventist Bible Commentary, vol. 1 (2BC etc.. for vols. 2-7)
CD	Counsels on Diet and Foods
CG	Child Guidance
CH	Counsels on Health
CCh	Counsels for the Church
Chs	Christian Service
CM	Colporteur Ministry
COL	Christ's Object Lessons
CS	Counsels on Stewardship
CSW	Counsels on Sabbath School Work
CT	Counsels to Parents, Teachers, and Students
CW	Counsels to Writers and Editors
DA	The Desire of Ages
Ed	Education
Ev	Evangelism
EW	Early Writings
FE	Fundamentals of Christian Education
GC	The Great Controversy
GW	Gospel Workers
LS	Life Sketches of Ellen G. White
MB	Thoughts From the Mount of Blessing
MH	The Ministry of Healing
ML	My Life Today
MM	Medical Ministry
MYP	Messages to Young People
PK	Prophets and Kings
PP	Patriarchs and Prophets
SC	Steps to Christ
SD	Sons and Daughters of God
1 SG	Spiritual Gifts, vol. 1 (2SG etc.. for vols. 2 and 3)
4 SG-a	Spiritual Gifts, vol. 4, part 1
4 SG-b	Spiritual Gifts, vol. 4, part 2
SL	The Sanctified Life
1 SM	Selected Messages, vol. 1 (2SM etc.. for vols. 2 and 3)
SR	The Story of Redemption
1SP	Spirit of Prophecy 1 (2SP etc.. for vols1-4)
1T	Testimonies, vol. 1 (2T etc.. for vols 2-9)
Te	Temperance
TM	Testimonies to Ministers and Gospel Workers
1TT	Testimony Treasures, vol. 1 (2TT etc.. for vols. 2 and 3)
WM	Welfare Ministry

THE HISTORY OF REDEMPTION SERIES

Book	Abbrev.	Chaps.	Page
○ Patriarchs and Prophets Why Was Sin Permitted? ~ The Last Years of David	PP	73	1
○ Prophets and Kings Solomon ~ Visions of Future Glory	PK	60	297
○ The Desire of Ages "God With Us" ~ "To My Father, and Your Father"	DA	87	497
○ The Mount of Blessing On the Mountainside ~ Not Judging, but Doing	MB	6	797
○ Christ's Object Lessons Teaching in Parables ~ "To Meet the Bridegroom"	COL	29	847
○ The Acts of the Apostles God's Purpose for His Church ~ The Church Triumphant	AA	58	963
○ The Great Controversy The Destruction of Jerusalem ~ The Controversy Ended	GC	42	1131
○ Steps to Christ	SC	13	1389

Development of
The History of Redemption Series

"Ever since the first promise of redemption was spoken in Eden, the life, the character, and the mediatorial work of Christ have been the study of human minds. Yet every mind through whom the Holy Spirit has worked has presented these themes in a light that is fresh and new. The truths of redemption are capable of constant development and expansion. Though old, they are ever new, constantly revealing to the seeker for truth a greater glory and a mightier power.

In every age there is a new development of truth, a message of God to the people of that generation." *COL 127*

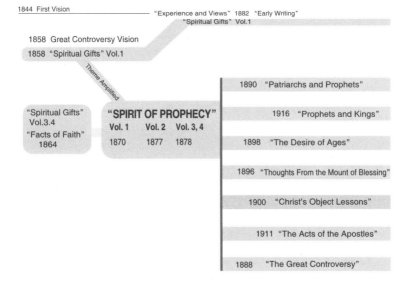

1844 First Vision

"Experience and Views" 1882 "Early Writing"
"Spiritual Gifts" Vol.1

1858 Great Controversy Vision
1858 "Spiritual Gifts" Vol.1

Theme Amplified

"Spiritual Gifts"
Vol.3.4
"Facts of Faith"
1864

"SPIRIT OF PROPHECY"
Vol. 1   Vol. 2   Vol. 3, 4
1870   1877   1878

1890   "Patriarchs and Prophets"

1916   "Prophets and Kings"

1898   "The Desire of Ages"

1896   "Thoughts From the Mount of Blessing"

1900   "Christ's Object Lessons"

1911 "The Acts of the Apostles"

1888   "The Great Controversy"

1844 –1915

1

PATRIARCHS AND PROPHETS

INDEX

SUMMARY	PAGE	SUMMARY	PAGE

PP

INDEX

PAGE	SUMMARY		PAGE	SUMMARY	

PREFACE

The publishers send out this work from a conviction that it throws light upon a subject of paramount importance and universal interest, and one on which light is to be greatly desired; that it presents truths too little known or too widely ignored. the great controversy between truth and error, between light and darkness, between the power of God and the attempted usurpations of the enemy of all righteousness, is the one great spectacle which it is reasonable to suppose must engage the attention of all worlds. that such a controversy exists as the result of sin, that it is to pass through various stages of progress, and end at last in a manner to redound to the glory of God and the higher exaltation of His loyal servants, is as certain as that the Bible is a revelation from God to men. that word reveals the great features of this controversy, a conflict which embraces the redemption of a world; and there are special epochs when these questions assume unwonted interest, and it becomes a matter of the first importance to understand our relation thereto.

Such a time is the present, for all things indicate that we may now confidently cherish the hope that this long controversy is drawing near its close. yet many now seem disposed to relegate to the realm of fable that portion of the record opening to our view the steps by which our world became involved in this great issue; and others, though avoiding this extreme view, seem nevertheless inclined to regard it as obsolete and unimportant, and are thus led to treat it with neglect.

But who would not wish to look into the secret causes of so strange a defection; to discern its spirit, to mark its consequences, and to learn how to avoid its results? With such themes this volume deals. It tends to foster a living interest in those portions of God's word most often neglected. It clothes with new meaning the promises and prophecies of the sacred record, vindicates the ways of God in dealing with rebellion, and shows forth the wonderful grace of God in devising a way of salvation for sinful man. thus we are taken down in the history of this work to a time when the plans and purposes of God had been clearly unfolded to the chosen people.

Though dealing with themes so exalted, themes that stir the heart to its depths and awaken the liveliest emotions of the mind, the style of the book is lucid, and the language plain and direct. We commend this volume to all who take pleasure in studying the divine plan of human redemption and who feel any interest in the relation of their own souls to Christ's atoning work; and to all others we commend it, that it may awaken in them an interest in these things.

That its perusal may be blessed to the good of those who read, and result in turning the feet of many into the way of life, is the earnest prayer of

the Publishers.

INTRODUCTION

This volume treats upon the themes of Bible history, themes not in themselves new, yet here so presented as to give them a new significance, revealing springs of action, showing the important bearing of certain movements, and bringing into stronger light some features that are but briefly mentioned in the Bible. Thus the scenes have a vividness and importance that tend to make new and lasting impressions. Such a light is shed upon the Scripture record as to reveal more fully the character and purposes of God; to make manifest the wiles of Satan and the means by which his power will be finally overthrown; to bring to view the weakness of the human heart, and show how the grace of God has enabled men to conquer in the battle with evil. All this is in harmony with what God has shown to be His purpose in unfolding to men the truths of His word. The agency by which these revelations have been given is seen—when tested by the Scriptures—to be one of the methods God still employs to impart instruction to the children of men.

While it is not now as it was in the beginning, when man in his holiness and innocence had personal instruction from his Maker, still man is not left without a divine teacher which God has provided in His representative, the Holy Spirit. So we hear the apostle Paul declaring that a certain divine "illumination" is the privilege of the followers of Christ; and that they are "enlightened" by being made "partakers of the Holy Ghost." Hebrews 10:32; 6:4. John also says, "Ye have an unction from the Holy One." 1 John 2:20. And Christ promised the disciples, as He was about to leave them, that He would send them the Holy Spirit as a comforter and guide to lead them into all truth. John 14:16, 26.

To show how this promise was to be fulfilled to the church, the apostle Paul, in two of his epistles, presents formal declaration that certain gifts of the Spirit have been placed in the church for its edification and instruction to the end of time. 1 Corinthians 12; Ephesians 4:8-13; Matthew 28:20. Nor is this all: a number of clear and explicit prophecies declare that in the last days there will be a special outpouring of the Holy Spirit, and that the church at the time of Christ's appearing will have had, during its closing experience, "the testimony of Jesus," which is the spirit of prophecy. Acts 2:17-20, 39; 1 Corinthians 1:7; Revelation 12:17; 19:10. In these facts we see an evidence of God's care and love for His people; for the presence of the Holy Spirit as a comforter, teacher, and guide, not only in its ordinary, but in its extraordinary, methods of operation, certainly is needed by the church as it enters the perils of the last days, more than in any other part of its experience.

The Scriptures point out various channels through which the Holy Spirit would operate on the hearts and minds of men to enlighten their understanding and guide their steps. Among these were visions and dreams. In this way God would still communicate with the children of men. Here is His promise on this point: "Hear now My words: If there be a prophet among you, I the Lord will make Myself known unto him in a vision, and will speak unto him in a dream." Numbers 12:6. By this means supernatural knowledge was communicated to Balaam. Thus he says: "Balaam the son of Beor hath said, and the man whose eyes are open hath said: he hath said, which heard the words of God, and knew the knowledge of the Most High, which saw the vision of the Almighty, falling into a trance, but having his eyes open." Numbers 24:15, 16.

It thus becomes a matter of great interest to investigate the testimony of the Scriptures concerning the extent to which the Lord designed that the Spirit should manifest itself in the church during the period of human probation.

After the plan of salvation had been devised, God, as we have seen, could still, through the ministry of His Son and the holy angels, communicate with men across the gulf which sin had made. Sometimes He spoke face to face with them, as in the case of Moses, but more frequently by dreams and visions. Instances of such communication are everywhere prominent upon the sacred record, covering all dispensations. Enoch the seventh from Adam looked forward in the spirit of prophecy to the second advent of Christ in power and glory, and exclaimed, "Behold, the Lord cometh with ten thousands of His saints." Jude 14. "Holy men of God spake as they were moved by the Holy Ghost." 2 Peter 1:21. If the operation of the spirit of prophecy has at times seemed almost to disappear, as the spirituality of the people waned, it has nevertheless marked all the great crises in the experience of the church, and the epochs which witnessed the change from one dispensation to another. When the era marked by the incarnation of Christ was reached, the father of John the Baptist was filled with the Holy Spirit, and prophesied. Luke 1:67. To Simeon it was revealed that he should not see death till he had seen the Lord; and when the parents of Jesus brought Him into the temple that He might be dedicated, Simeon came by the Spirit into the temple, took Him into his arms, and blessed Him while he prophesied concerning Him. And Anna, a prophetess, coming in the same instant, spake of Him to all them that looked for redemption in Jerusalem. Luke 2:26, 36.

The outpouring of the Holy Spirit which was to attend the preaching of the gospel by the followers of Christ was announced by the prophet in these words: "And it shall come to pass afterward, that I will pour out My Spirit upon all flesh; and your sons and your daughters shall prophesy, and your old men shall dream dreams, your young men shall see visions: and also upon the servants and upon the handmaids in those days will I pour out My Spirit. And I will show wonders in the heavens and in the earth, blood, and fire, and pillars of smoke. The sun shall be turned into darkness, and the moon into blood, before the great and the terrible day of the Lord come." Joel 2:28-31.

Peter, on the Day of Pentecost, quoted this prophecy in explanation of the wonderful scene which then occurred. Cloven tongues like as of fire sat upon each of the disciples; they were filled with the Holy Spirit, and spake with other tongues. And when the mockers charged that they were filled with new wine, Peter answered, "These are not drunken, as ye suppose, seeing it is but the third hour of the day. But this is that which was spoken by the prophet Joel." Then he quotes the prophecy substantially as found in Joel (quoted above), only he puts the words "in the last days," in the place of "afterward," making it read, "And it shall come to pass in the last days, saith God, I will pour out of My Spirit," etc.

It is evident that it was that part of the prophecy only which relates to the outpouring of the Spirit, that began to be fulfilled on that day; for there were no old men there dreaming dreams, nor young men and maidens seeing visions and prophesying; and no wonders of blood and fire and pillars of smoke then appeared; and the sun was not darkened and the moon was not turned to blood at that time; and yet what was there witnessed was in fulfillment of the prophecy of Joel. It is equally evident that this part of the prophecy concerning the outpouring of the Spirit was not exhausted in that one manifestation; for the prophecy covers all days from that time on to the coming of the great day of the Lord.

But the Day of Pentecost was in fulfillment of other prophecies besides that of Joel. It fulfilled the words of Christ Himself as well. In His last discourse to His disciples before His crucifixion, He said to them: "I will pray the Father, and He shall give you another Comforter, . . . even the Spirit of truth." John 14:16, 17. "But the Comforter, which is the Holy Ghost, whom the Father will send in My name, He shall teach you all things." Verse 26. "Howbeit when He, the Spirit of truth, is come, He will guide you into all truth." Chapter 16:13. And after Christ had risen from the dead, He said to the disciples, "Behold, I send the promise of My Father upon you: but tarry ye in the city of Jerusalem, until ye be endued with power from on high." Luke 24:49.

On the Day of Pentecost the disciples were thus endued with power from on high. But this promise of Christ's was not, any more than the prophecy of Joel, confined to that occasion. For He gave them the same promise in another form by assuring them that He would be with them always, even to the end of the world. Matthew 28:20. Mark tells us in what sense and what manner the Lord was to be with them. He says, "And they went forth, and preached everywhere, the Lord working with them, and confirming the word with signs following." Mark 16:20. And Peter, on the Day of Pentecost, testified concerning the perpetuity of this operation of the Spirit which they had witnessed. When the convicted Jews said unto the apostles, "What shall we do?" Peter answered, "Repent, and be baptized every one of you in the name of Jesus Christ for the remission of sins, and ye shall receive the gift of the Holy Ghost. For the promise is unto you, and to your children, and to all that are afar off, even as many as the Lord our God shall call." Acts 2:37-39. This certainly provides for the operation of the Holy Spirit in the church, even in its special manifestations, to all coming time, as long as mercy shall invite men to accept the pardoning love of Christ.

Twenty-eight years later in his letter to the Corinthians, Paul set before that church a formal argument on the question. He says (1 Corinthians 12:1), "Now concerning spiritual gifts, brethren, I would not have you ignorant"—so important did he deem it that this subject should be understood in the Christian church. After stating that though the Spirit is one it has diversities of operation, and explaining what those diversities are, he introduces the figure of the human body, with its various members, to show how the church is constituted with its different offices and gifts. And as the body has its various members, each having its particular office to fill, and all working together in unity of purpose to constitute one harmonious whole, so the Spirit was to operate through various channels in the church to constitute a perfect religious body. Paul then continues in these words: "And God hath set some in the church, first apostles, secondarily prophets, thirdly teachers, after that miracles, then gifts of healing, helps, governments, diversities of tongues."

The declaration that God hath set some in the church, etc., implies something more than that the way was left open for the gifts to appear if circumstances should chance to favor. It rather signifies that they were to be permanent parts of the true spiritual constitution of the church, and that if these were not in active operation the church would be in the condition of a human body, some of whose members had, through accident or disease, become crippled and helpless. Having once been set in the church, there these gifts must remain until they are formally removed. But there is no record that they ever have been removed.

Five years later the same apostle writes to the Ephesians relative to the same gifts, plainly stating their object, and thus showing indirectly that they must continue till that object is accomplished. He says (Ephesians 4:8, 11-13): "Wherefore He saith, When He ascended up on high, He led captivity captive, and gave gifts unto men. . . . And He gave some, apostles; and some, prophets; and some, evangelists; and some, pastors and teachers; for the perfecting of the saints, for the work of the ministry, for the edifying of the body of Christ: till we all come in the unity of the faith, and of the knowledge of the Son of God, unto a perfect man, unto the measure of the stature of the fullness of Christ."

The church did not reach the state of unity here contemplated, in the apostolic age; and very soon after that age, the gloom of the great spiritual apostasy began to over-shadow the church; and certainly during that state of declension, this fullness of Christ, and unity of faith, was not reached. Nor will it be reached till the last message of mercy shall have gathered out of every kindred and people, every class of society, and every organization of error, a people complete in all gospel reforms, waiting for the coming of the Son of man. And truly, if ever in her experience the church would need the benefit of every agency ordained for her comfort and guidance, encourage-ment and protection, it would be amid the perils of the last days, when the powers of evil, well-nigh perfected by experience and training for their nefarious work, would, by their masterpieces of imposture, deceive if it were possible even the elect. Very appropriately, therefore, come in the special prophecies of the outpouring of the Spirit for the benefit of the church in the last days.

It is, however, usually taught, in the current literature of the Christian world, that the gifts of the Spirit were only for the apostolic age; that they were given simply for the planting of the gospel; and that the gospel being once established, the gifts were no longer needed, and consequently were suffered soon to disappear from the church. But the apostle Paul warned the Christians of his day that the "mystery of iniquity" was already at work, and that after his departure, grievous wolves would enter in among them, not sparing the flock, and that also of their own selves men would arise, speaking perverse things to draw away disciples after them. Acts 20:29, 30. It cannot therefore be that the gifts, placed in the church to guard against these very evils, were ready, when that time came, to pass away as having accomplished their object; for their presence and help would be needed under these conditions more than when the apostles themselves were on the stage of action.

We find another statement in Paul's letter to the Corinthian church, which shows that the popular conception of the temporary continuance of the gifts cannot be correct. It is his contrast between the present, imperfect state, and the glorious, immortal condition to which the Christian will finally arrive. 1 Corinthians 13. He says (verses 9, 10). "For we know in part, and we prophesy in part. But when that which is perfect is come, then that which is in part shall be done away." He further illustrates this present state by comparing it to the period of childhood with its weakness and immaturity of thought and action; and the perfect state, to the condition of manhood with its clearer vision, maturity, and strength. And he classes the gifts among those things which are needed in this present, imperfect condition, but which we shall have no occasion for when the perfect state is come. "Now," he says (verse 12), "we see through a glass, darkly; but then face to face: now I know in part; but then shall I know even as also I am known." Then he states what graces are adapted to the eternal state, and will there exist, namely, faith, hope, and charity, or love, "these three; but the greatest of these is charity."

This explains the language of verse 8: "Charity never faileth;" that is, charity, the heavenly grace of love, will endure forever; it is the crowning glory of man's future, immortal condition; but "whether there be prophecies, they shall fail;" that is, the time will come when prophecies will be no longer needed, and the gift of prophecy, as one of the helps in the church, will no longer be exercised; "whether there be tongues, they shall cease;" that is, the gift of tongues will no longer be of service; "whether there be knowledge, it shall vanish away;" that is, knowledge, not in the abstract, but as one of the special gifts of the Spirit, will be rendered unnecessary by the perfect knowledge with which we shall be endowed in the eternal world.

Now, if we take the position that the gifts ceased with the apostolic age, because no longer needed, we commit ourselves to the position that the apostolic age was the weak and childish age of the church, when everything was seen through a glass, darkly; but the age that followed, when grievous wolves were to enter in, not sparing the flock, and men were to arise, even in the church, speaking perverse things to draw away disciples after them, was an age of perfect light and knowledge, in which the imperfect and childish and darkened knowledge of apostolic times had passed away! For, be it remembered, the gifts cease only when a perfect state is reached, and because that state is reached, which renders them no longer necessary. But no one, on sober thought, can for a moment seek to maintain the position that the apostolic age was inferior in spiritual elevation to any age which has succeeded it. And if the gifts were needed then, they certainly are needed now.

Among the agencies which the apostle in his letters to both the Corinthians and Ephesians enumerates as "gifts" set in the church, we find "pastors," "teachers," "helps," and "governments;" and all these are acknowledged, on every hand, as still continuing in the church. Why not, then, the others also, including faith, healing, prophecy, etc.? Who is competent to draw the line, and say what gifts have been "set out" of the church, when all were, in the beginning, equally "set" therein?

Revelation 12:17 has been referred to as a prophecy that the gifts would be restored in the last days. An examination of its testimony will confirm this view. The text speaks of the remnant of the woman's seed. The woman being a symbol of the church, her seed would be the individual members composing the church at any one time; and the "remnant" of her seed would be the last generation of Christians, or those living on the earth at the second coming of Christ. The text further declares that these "keep the commandments of God, and have the testimony of Jesus Christ;" and the "testimony of Jesus" is explained in chapter 19:10 to be "the spirit of prophecy," which must be understood as that which among the gifts is called "the gift of prophecy." 1 Corinthians 12:9, 10.

The setting of the gifts in the church does not imply that every individual was to have them in exercise. On this point the apostle (1 Corinthians 12:29) says, "Are all apostles? are all prophets? are all teachers?" etc. The implied answer is No; not all are; but the gifts are divided among the members as it pleases God. 1 Corinthians 12:7, 11. Yet these gifts are said to be "set in the *church,*" and if a gift is bestowed upon even one member of the church, it may be said that that gift is "in the church," or that the church "has" it. So the last generation was to have, and it is believed does now have, the testimony of Jesus, or the gift of prophecy.

Another portion of Scripture evidently written with reference to the last days, brings the same fact plainly to view. 1 Thessalonians 5. The apostle opens the chapter with these words: "But of the times and the seasons, brethren, you have no need that I write unto you. For yourselves know perfectly that the day of the Lord so cometh as a thief in the night." In verse 4 he adds, "But ye, brethren, are not in darkness, that that day should overtake you as a thief." Then he gives them sundry admonitions in view of that event, among which are these (verses 19-21): "Quench not the Spirit. Despise not prophesyings. Prove all things; hold fast that which is good." And in verse 23 he prays that these very ones who were thus to have to do with "prophesyings" may be preserved blameless unto *the coming of the Lord.*

On the strength of these considerations are we not justified in believing that the gift of prophecy will be manifested in the church in the last days, and that through it much light will be imparted, and much timely instruction given?

All things are to be treated according to the apostle's rule: "Prove all things; hold fast that which is good;" and to be tested by the Saviour's standard: "By their fruits ye shall know them." Appealing to this standard in behalf of what claims to be a manifestation of the gift of prophecy, we commend this volume to the consideration of those who believe that the Bible is the word of God, and that the church is the body of which Christ is head.

U. Smith.

CONTENTS

1. Why Was Sin Permitted? 15
2. The Creation 19
3. The Temptation and Fall 22
4. The Plan of Redemption 27
5. Cain and Abel Tested 30
6. Seth and Enoch 33
7. The Flood 37
8. After the Flood 43
9. The Literal Week 45
10. The Tower of Babel 47
11. The Call of Abraham 50
12. Abraham in Canaan 53
13. The Test of Faith 58
14. Destruction of Sodom 62
15. The Marriage of Isaac 68
16. Jacob and Esau 70
17. Jacob's Flight and Exile 73
18. The Night of Wrestling 77
19. The Return to Canaan 80
20. Joseph in Egypt 83
21. Joseph and His Brothers 87
22. Moses 94
23. The Plagues of Egypt 100
24. The Passover 106
25. The Exodus 108
26. From the Red Sea to Sinai 112
27. The Law Given to Israel 116
28. Idolatry at Sinai 122
29. Satan's Enmity Against the Law 128
30. The Tabernacle and Its Services 133
31. The Sin of Nadab and Abihu 138
32. The Law and the Covenants 140
33. From Sinai to Kadesh 145
34. The Twelve Spies 150
35. The Rebellion of Korah 153
36. In the Wilderness 158
37. The Smitten Rock 160
38. The Journey Around Edom 164
39. The Conquest of Bashan 169
40. Balaam 171
41. Apostasy at the Jordan 176
42. The Law Repeated 180
43. The Death of Moses 183
44. Crossing the Jordan 187
45. The Fall of Jericho 189
46. The Blessings and the Curses 193
47. League With the Gibeonites 195
48. The Division of Canaan 197
49. The Last Words of Joshua 202
50. Tithes and Offerings 203
51. God's Care for the Poor 205
52. The Annual Feasts 208
53. The Earlier Judges 211
54. Samson 217
55. The Child Samuel 221
56. Eli and His Sons 223
57. The Ark Taken by the Philistines 226
58. The Schools of the Prophets 230
59. The First King of Israel 234
60. The Presumption of Saul 239
61. Saul Rejected 243
62. The Anointing of David 247
63. David and Goliath 249
64. David a Fugitive 251
65. The Magnanimity of David 256
66. The Death of Saul 261
67. Ancient and Modern Sorcery 264
68. David at Ziklag 266
69. David Called to the Throne 269
70. The Reign of David 271
71. David's Sin and Repentance 277
72. The Rebellion of Absalom 281
73. The Last Years of David 288
Appendix 293

1

Why Was Sin Permitted?

"God is love." 1 John 4:16. His nature, His law, is love. It ever has been; it ever will be. "The high and lofty One that inhabiteth eternity," whose "ways are everlasting," changeth not. With Him "is no variableness, neither shadow of turning." Isaiah 57:15; Habakkuk 3:6; James 1:17.

Every manifestation of creative power is an expression of infinite love. The sovereignty of God involves fullness of blessing to all created beings. The psalmist says:

"Strong is Thy hand, and high is Thy right hand.
Righteousness and judgment are the foundation of Thy throne:
Mercy and truth go before Thy face.
Blessed is the people that know the joyful sound:
They walk, O Lord, in the light of Thy countenance.
In Thy name do they rejoice all the day:
And in Thy righteousness are they exalted.
For Thou art the glory of their strength: . . .
For our shield belongeth unto Jehovah,
And our king to the Holy One."
Psalm 89:13-18, R.V.*

The history of the great conflict between good and evil, from the time it first began in heaven to the final overthrow of rebellion and the total eradication of sin, is also a demonstration of God's unchanging love.

The Sovereign of the universe was not alone in His work of beneficence. He had an associate—a co-worker who could appreciate His purposes, and could share His joy in giving happiness to created beings. "In the beginning was the Word, and the Word was with God, and the Word was God. The same was in the beginning with God." John 1:1, 2. Christ, the Word, the only begotten of God, was one with the eternal Father—one in nature, in character, in purpose—the only being that could enter into all the counsels and purposes of God. "His name shall be called Wonderful, Counselor, The mighty God, The everlasting Father, The Prince of Peace." Isaiah 9:6. His "goings forth have been from of old, from everlasting." Micah 5:2. And the Son of God declares concerning Himself: "The Lord possessed Me in the beginning of His way, before His works of old. I was set up from everlasting. . . . When He appointed the foundations of the earth: then I was by Him, as one brought up with Him: and I

was daily His delight, rejoicing always before Him." Proverbs 8:22-30.

The Father wrought by His Son in the creation of all heavenly beings. "By Him were all things created, . . . whether they be thrones, or dominions, or principalities, or powers: all things were created by Him, and for Him." Colossians 1:16. Angels are God's ministers, radiant with the light ever flowing from His presence and speeding on rapid wing to execute His will. But the Son, the anointed of God, the "express image of His person," "the brightness of His glory," "upholding all things by the word of His power," holds supremacy over them all. Hebrews 1:3. "A glorious high throne from the beginning," was the place of His sanctuary (Jeremiah 17:12); "a scepter of righteousness," the scepter of His kingdom. Hebrews 1:8. "Honor and majesty are before Him: strength and beauty are in His sanctuary." Psalm 96:6. Mercy and truth go before His face. Psalm 89:14.

The law of love being the foundation of the government of God, the happiness of all intelligent beings depends upon their perfect accord with its great principles of righteousness. God desires from all His creatures the service of love—service that springs from an appreciation of His character. He takes no pleasure in a forced obedience; and to all He grants freedom of will, that they may render Him voluntary service.

So long as all created beings acknowledged the allegiance of love, there was perfect harmony throughout the universe of God. It was the joy of the heavenly host to fulfill the purpose of their Creator. They delighted in reflecting His glory and showing forth His praise. And while love to God was supreme, love for one another was confiding and unselfish. There was no note of discord to mar the celestial harmonies. But a change came over this happy state. There was one who perverted the freedom that God had granted to His creatures. Sin originated with him who, next to Christ, had been most honored of God and was highest in power and glory among the inhabitants of heaven. Lucifer, "son of the morning," was first of the covering cherubs, holy and undefiled. He stood in the presence of the great Creator, and the ceaseless beams of glory enshrouding the eternal God rested upon him. "Thus saith the Lord God; Thou sealest up the sum, full of wisdom, and perfect in beauty. Thou hast been in Eden the garden of God; every precious stone was thy covering. . . . Thou art the anointed cherub that covereth; and I have set thee so: thou wast upon the holy mountain of God; thou hast walked up and down in the midst of the stones of fire. Thou wast perfect in thy ways from the day that thou wast created, till iniquity was found in thee." Ezekiel 28:12-15.

---

* In this text and in some other Bible quotations used in this book the word "Jehovah" is employed instead of "Lord," as rendered in the American Supplement to the Revised Version.

Little by little Lucifer came to indulge the desire for self-exaltation. The Scripture says, "Thine heart was lifted up because of thy beauty, thou hast corrupted thy wisdom by reason of thy brightness." Ezekiel 28:17. "Thou hast said in thine heart, . . . I will exalt my throne above the stars of God. . . . I will be like the Most High." Isaiah 14:13, 14. Though all his glory was from God, this mighty angel came to regard it as pertaining to himself. Not content with his position, though honored above the heavenly host, he ventured to covet homage due alone to the Creator. Instead of seeking to make God supreme in the affections and allegiance of all created beings, it was his endeavor to secure their service and loyalty to himself. And coveting the glory with which the infinite Father had invested His Son, this prince of angels aspired to power that was the prerogative of Christ alone.

Now the perfect harmony of heaven was broken. Lucifer's disposition to serve himself instead of his Creator aroused a feeling of apprehension when observed by those who considered that the glory of God should be supreme. In heavenly council the angels pleaded with Lucifer. The Son of God presented before him the greatness, the goodness, and the justice of the Creator, and the sacred, unchanging nature of His law. God Himself had established the order of heaven; and in departing from it, Lucifer would dishonor his Maker and bring ruin upon himself. But the warning, given in infinite love and mercy, only aroused a spirit of resistance. Lucifer allowed his jealousy of Christ to prevail, and became the more determined.

To dispute the supremacy of the Son of God, thus impeaching the wisdom and love of the Creator, had become the purpose of this prince of angels. To this object he was about to bend the energies of that master mind, which, next to Christ's, was first among the hosts of God. But He who would have the will of all His creatures free, left none unguarded to the bewildering sophistry by which rebellion would seek to justify itself. Before the great contest should open, all were to have a clear presentation of His will, whose wisdom and goodness were the spring of all their joy.

The King of the universe summoned the heavenly hosts before Him, that in their presence He might set forth the true position of His Son and show the relation He sustained to all created beings. The Son of God shared the Father's throne, and the glory of the eternal, self-existent One encircled both. About the throne gathered the holy angels, a vast, unnumbered throng—"ten thousand times ten thousand, and thousands of thousands" (Revelation 5:11), the most exalted angels, as ministers and subjects, rejoicing in the light that fell upon

them from the presence of the Deity. Before the assembled inhabitants of heaven the King declared that none but Christ, the Only Begotten of God, could fully enter into His purposes, and to Him it was committed to execute the mighty counsels of His will. The Son of God had wrought the Father's will in the creation of all the hosts of heaven; and to Him, as well as to God, their homage and allegiance were due. Christ was still to exercise divine power, in the creation of the earth and its inhabitants. But in all this He would not seek power or exaltation for Himself contrary to God's plan, but would exalt the Father's glory and execute His purposes of beneficence and love.

The angels joyfully acknowledged the supremacy of Christ, and prostrating themselves before Him, poured out their love and adoration. Lucifer bowed with them, but in his heart there was a strange, fierce conflict. Truth, justice, and loyalty were struggling against envy and jealousy. The influence of the holy angels seemed for a time to carry him with them. As songs of praise ascended in melodious strains, swelled by thousands of glad voices, the spirit of evil seemed vanquished; unutterable love thrilled his entire being; his soul went out, in harmony with the sinless worshipers, in love to the Father and the Son. But again he was filled with pride in his own glory. His desire for supremacy returned, and envy of Christ was once more indulged. The high honors conferred upon Lucifer were not appreciated as God's special gift, and therefore called forth no gratitude to his Creator. He gloried in his brightness and exaltation and aspired to be equal with God. He was beloved and reverenced by the heavenly host, angels delighted to execute his commands, and he was clothed with wisdom and glory above them all. Yet the Son of God was exalted above him, as one in power and authority with the Father. He shared the Father's counsels, while Lucifer did not thus enter into the purposes of God. "Why," questioned this mighty angel, "should Christ have the supremacy? Why is He honored above Lucifer?"

Leaving his place in the immediate presence of the Father, Lucifer went forth to diffuse the spirit of discontent among the angels. He worked with mysterious secrecy, and for a time concealed his real purpose under an appearance of reverence for God. He began to insinuate doubts concerning the laws that governed heavenly beings, intimating that though laws might be necessary for the inhabitants of the worlds, angels, being more exalted, needed no such restraint, for their own wisdom was a sufficient guide. They were not beings that could bring dishonor to God; all their thoughts were holy; it was no more possible for them than for God Himself to err. The exaltation of the Son of God as equal with the Father was represented as an injustice to Lucifer, who, it was claimed, was also entitled to reverence and honor. If this prince of angels could but attain to his true, exalted position, great good would accrue to the entire host of heaven; for it was his object to secure freedom for all. But now even the liberty which they had hitherto enjoyed was at an end; for an absolute Ruler had been appointed them, and to His authority all must pay homage. Such were the subtle deceptions that through the wiles of Lucifer were fast obtaining in the heavenly courts.

38   There had been no change in the position or authority of Christ. Lucifer's envy and misrepresentation and his claims to equality with Christ had made necessary a statement of the true position of the Son of God; but this had been the same from the beginning. Many of the angels were, however, blinded by Lucifer's deceptions.

Taking advantage of the loving, loyal trust reposed in him by the holy beings under his command, he had so artfully instilled into their minds his own distrust and discontent that his agency was not discerned. Lucifer had presented the purposes of God in a false light—misconstruing and distorting them to excite dissent and dissatisfaction. He cunningly drew his hearers on to give utterance to their feelings; then these expressions were repeated by him when it would serve his purpose, as evidence that the angels were not fully in harmony with the government of God. While claiming for himself perfect loyalty to God, he urged that changes in the order and laws of heaven were necessary for the stability of the divine government. Thus while working to excite opposition to the law of God and to instill his own discontent into the minds of the angels under him, he was ostensibly seeking to remove dissatisfaction and to reconcile disaffected angels to the order of heaven. While secretly fomenting discord and rebellion, he with consummate craft caused it to appear as his sole purpose to promote loyalty and to preserve harmony and peace.

The spirit of dissatisfaction thus kindled was doing its baleful work. While there was no open outbreak, division of feeling imperceptibly grew up among the angels. There were some who looked with favor upon Lucifer's insinuations against the government of God. Although they had heretofore been in perfect harmony with the order which God had established, they were now discontented and unhappy because they could not penetrate His unsearchable counsels; they were dissatisfied with His purpose in exalting Christ. These stood ready to second Lucifer's demand for equal authority with the Son of God. But angels who were loyal and true maintained the wisdom and justice of the divine decree and endeavored to reconcile this disaffected being to the will of God. Christ was the Son of God; He had been one with Him before the angels were called into existence. He had ever stood at the right hand of the Father; His supremacy, so full of blessing to all who came under its benignant control, had not heretofore been questioned. The harmony of heaven had never been interrupted; wherefore should there 39 now be discord? The loyal angels could see only terrible consequences from this dissension, and with earnest entreaty they counseled the disaffected ones to renounce their purpose and prove themselves loyal to God by fidelity to His government.

In great mercy, according to His divine character, God bore long with Lucifer. The spirit of discontent and disaffection had never before been known in heaven. It was a new element, strange, mysterious, unaccountable. Lucifer himself had not at first been acquainted with the real nature of his feelings; for a time he had feared to express the workings and imaginings of his mind; yet he did not dismiss them. He did not see whither he was drifting. But such efforts as infinite love and wisdom only could devise, were made to convince him of his error. His disaffection was proved to be without cause, and he was made to see what would be the result of persisting in revolt. Lucifer was convinced that he was in the wrong. He saw that "the Lord is righteous in all His ways, and holy in all His works" (Psalm 145:17); that the divine statutes are just, and that he ought to acknowledge them as such before all heaven. Had he done this, he might have saved himself and many angels. He had not at that time fully cast off his allegiance to God. Though he had left his position as covering cherub, yet if he had been willing to return to God, acknowledging the Creator's wisdom, and satisfied to fill the place appointed him in God's great plan, he would have been reinstated in his office. The time had come for a final decision; he must fully yield to the divine sovereignty or place himself in open rebellion. He nearly reached the decision to return, but pride forbade him. It was too great a sacrifice for one who had been so highly honored to confess that he had been in error, that his imaginings were false, and to yield to the authority which he had been working to prove unjust.

A compassionate Creator, in yearning pity for Lucifer and his followers, was seeking to draw them back from the abyss of ruin into which they were about to plunge. But His mercy was misinterpreted. Lucifer pointed to the long-suffering of God as an evidence of his own superiority, an indication that the King of the universe would yet accede to his terms. If the angels would stand firmly with him, he declared, they could yet gain all that they desired. He persis- 40 tently defended his own course, and fully committed himself to the great controversy against his Maker. Thus it was that Lucifer, "the light bearer," the sharer of God's glory, the attendant of His throne, by transgression became Satan, "the adversary" of God and holy beings and the destroyer of those whom Heaven had committed to his guidance and guardianship.

Rejecting with disdain the arguments and entreaties of the loyal angels, he denounced them as deluded slaves. The preference shown to Christ he declared an act of injustice both to himself and to all the heavenly host, and announced that he would no longer submit to this invasion of his rights and theirs. He would never again acknowledge the supremacy of Christ. He had determined to claim the honor which should have been given him, and take command of all who would become his followers; and he promised those who would enter his ranks a new and better government, under which all would enjoy freedom. Great numbers of the angels signified their purpose to accept him as their leader. Flattered by the favor with which his advances were received, he hoped to win all the angels to his side, to become equal with God Himself, and to be obeyed by the entire host of heaven.

Still the loyal angels urged him and his sympathizers to submit to God; and they set before them the inevitable result should they refuse: He who had created them could overthrow their power and signally punish their rebellious daring. No angel could successfully oppose the law of God, which was as sacred as Himself. They warned all to close their ears against Lucifer's deceptive reasoning, and urged him and his followers to seek the presence of God without delay and confess the error of questioning His wisdom and authority.

Many were disposed to heed this counsel, to repent of their disaffection, and seek to be again received into favor with the Father and His Son. But Lucifer had another deception ready. The mighty revolter now declared that the angels who had united with him had gone too far to return; that he was acquainted with the divine law, and knew that God would not forgive. He declared that all who should submit to the authority of Heaven would be stripped of their honor, degraded from their position. For himself, he was determined never again to acknowledge the authority of Christ. The only course remaining for him and his followers, he said, was to assert their liberty, and gain by force the rights which had not been willingly accorded them.

So far as Satan himself was concerned, it was true that he had now gone too far to return. But not so with those who had been blinded by his deceptions. To them the counsel and entreaties of the loyal angels opened a door of hope; and had they heeded the warning, they might have broken away from the snare of Satan. But pride, love for their leader, and the desire for unrestricted freedom were permitted to bear sway, and the pleadings of divine love and mercy were finally rejected.

God permitted Satan to carry forward his work until the spirit of disaffection ripened into active revolt. It was necessary for his plans to be fully developed, that their true nature and tendency might be seen by all. Lucifer, as the anointed cherub, had been highly exalted; he was greatly loved by the heavenly beings, and his influence over them was strong. God's government included not only the inhabitants of heaven, but of all the worlds that He had created; and Lucifer had concluded that if he could carry the angels of heaven with him in rebellion, he could carry also all the worlds. He had artfully presented his side of the question, employing sophistry and fraud to secure his objects. His power to deceive was very great. By disguising himself in a cloak of falsehood, he had gained an advantage. All his acts were so clothed with mystery that it was difficult to disclose to the angels the true nature of his work. Until fully developed, it could not be made to appear the evil thing it was; his disaffection would not be seen to be rebellion. Even the loyal angels could not fully discern his character or see to what his work was leading.

Lucifer had at first so conducted his temptations that he himself stood uncommitted. The angels whom he could not bring fully to his side, he accused of indifference to the interests of heavenly beings. The very work which he himself was doing, he charged upon the loyal angels. It was his policy to perplex with subtle arguments concerning the purposes of God. Everything that was simple he shrouded in mystery, and by artful perversion cast doubt upon the plainest statements of Jehovah. And his high position, so closely connected with the divine government, gave greater force to his representations.

God could employ only such means as were consistent with truth and righteousness. Satan could use what God could not—flattery and deceit. He had sought to falsify the word of God and had misrepresented His plan of government, claiming that God was not just in imposing laws upon the angels; that in requiring submission and obedience from His creatures, He was seeking merely the exaltation of Himself. It was therefore necessary to demonstrate before the inhabitants of heaven, and of all the worlds, that God's government is just, His law perfect. Satan had made it appear that he himself was seeking to promote the good of the universe. The true character of the usurper and his real object must be understood by all. He must have time to manifest himself by his wicked works.

The discord which his own course had caused in heaven, Satan charged upon the government of God. All evil he declared to be the result of the divine administration. He claimed that it was his own object to improve upon the statutes of Jehovah. Therefore God permitted him to demonstrate the nature of his claims, to show the working out of his proposed changes in the divine law. His own work must condemn him. Satan had claimed from the first that he was not in rebellion. The whole universe must see the deceiver unmasked.

Even when he was cast out of heaven. Infinite Wisdom did not destroy Satan. Since only the service of love can be acceptable to God, the allegiance of His creatures must rest upon a conviction of His justice and benevolence. The inhabitants of heaven and of the worlds, being unprepared to comprehend the nature or consequences of sin, could not then have seen the justice of God in the destruction of Satan. Had he been immediately blotted out of existence, some would have served God from fear rather than from love. The influence of the deceiver would not have been fully destroyed, nor would the spirit of rebellion have been utterly eradicated. For the good of the entire universe through ceaseless ages, he must more fully develop his principles, that his charges against the divine government might be seen in their true light by all created beings, and that the justice and mercy of God and the immutability of His law might be forever placed beyond all question.

Satan's rebellion was to be a lesson to the universe through all coming ages—a perpetual testimony to the nature of sin and its terrible
43 results. The working out of Satan's rule, its effects upon both men and angels, would show what must be the fruit of setting aside the divine authority. It would testify that with the existence of God's government is bound up the well-being of all the creatures He has made. Thus the history of this terrible experiment of rebellion was to be a perpetual safeguard to all holy beings, to prevent them from being deceived as to the nature of transgression, to save them from committing sin, and suffering its penalty.

He that ruleth in the heavens is the one who sees the end from the beginning—the one before whom the mysteries of the past and the future are alike outspread, and who, beyond the woe and darkness and ruin that sin has wrought, beholds the accomplishment of His own purposes of love and blessing. Though "clouds and darkness are round about Him: righteousness and judgment are the foundation of His throne." Psalm 97:2, R.V. And this the inhabitants of the universe, both loyal and disloyal, will one day understand. "His work is perfect: for all His ways are judgment: a God of truth and without iniquity, just and right is He." Deuteronomy 32:4.

2

The Creation

44

"By the word of the Lord were the heavens made; and all the host of them by the breath of His mouth." "For He spake, and it was;" "He commanded, and it stood fast." Psalm 33:6, 9. He "laid the foundations of the earth, that it should not be removed forever." Psalm 104:5.

As the earth came forth from the hand of its Maker, it was exceedingly beautiful. Its surface was diversified with mountains, hills, and plains, interspersed with noble rivers and lovely lakes; but the hills and mountains were not abrupt and rugged, abounding in terrific steeps and frightful chasms, as they now do; the sharp, ragged edges of earth's rocky framework were buried beneath the fruitful soil, which everywhere produced a luxuriant growth of verdure. There were no loathsome swamps or barren deserts. Graceful shrubs and delicate flowers greeted the eye at every turn. The heights were crowned with trees more majestic than any that now exist. The air, untainted by foul miasma, was clear and healthful. The entire landscape outvied in beauty the decorated grounds of the proudest palace. The angelic host viewed the scene with delight, and rejoiced at the wonderful works of God.

After the earth with its teeming animal and vegetable life had been called into existence, man, the crowning work of the Creator, and the one for whom the beautiful earth had been fitted up, was brought upon the stage of action. To him was given dominion over all that his eye could behold; for "God said, Let Us make man in Our image, after Our likeness: and let them have dominion over . . . all the earth. . . . So God created man in His own image; . . . male and female created He them." Here is clearly set forth the origin of the human race; and the divine record is so plainly stated that there is no occasion for erroneous conclusions. God created 45 man in His own image. Here is no mystery. There is no ground for the supposition that man was evolved by slow degrees of development from the lower forms of animal or vegetable life. Such teaching lowers the great work of the Creator to the level of man's narrow, earthly conceptions. Men are so intent upon excluding God from the sovereignty of the universe that they degrade man and defraud him of the dignity of his origin. He who set the starry worlds on high and tinted with delicate skill the flowers of the field, who filled the earth and the heavens with the wonders of His power, when He came to crown His glorious work, to place one in the midst to stand as ruler of the fair earth, did not

This chapter is based on Genesis 1 and 2.

fail to create a being worthy of the hand that gave him life. The genealogy of our race, as given by inspiration, traces back its origin, not to a line of developing germs, mollusks, and quadrupeds, but to the great Creator. Though formed from the dust, Adam was "the son of God."

He was placed, as God's representative, over the lower orders of being. They cannot understand or acknowledge the sovereignty of God, yet they were made capable of loving and serving man. The psalmist says, "Thou madest him to have dominion over the works of Thy hands; Thou hast put all things under his feet: . . . the beasts of the field; the fowl of the air, . . . and whatsoever passeth through the paths of the seas." Psalm 8:6-8.

Man was to bear God's image, both in outward resemblance and in character. Christ alone is "the express image" (Hebrews 1:3) of the Father; but man was formed in the likeness of God. His nature was in harmony with the will of God. His mind was capable of comprehending divine things. His affections were pure; his appetites and passions were under the control of reason. He was holy and happy in bearing the image of God and in perfect obedience to His will.

As man came forth from the hand of his Creator, he was of lofty stature and perfect symmetry. His countenance bore the ruddy tint of health and glowed with the light of life and joy. Adam's height was much greater than that of men who now inhabit the earth. Eve was somewhat less in stature; yet her form was noble, and full of beauty. The sinless pair wore no artificial garments; they were clothed with a covering of light and glory, such as the angels wear. So long as they lived in obedience to God, this robe of light continued to enshroud them.

46   After the creation of Adam every living creature was brought before him to receive its name; he saw that to each had been given a companion, but among them "there was not found an help meet for him." Among all the creatures that God had made on the earth, there was not one equal to man. And God said, "It is not good that the man should be alone; I will make him an help meet for him." Man was not made to dwell in solitude; he was to be a social being. Without companionship the beautiful scenes and delightful employments of Eden would have failed to yield perfect happiness. Even communion with angels could not have satisfied his desire for sympathy and companionship. There was none of the same nature to love and to be loved.

God Himself gave Adam a companion. He provided "an help meet for him"—a helper corresponding to him—one who was fitted to be his companion, and who could be one with him in love and sympathy. Eve was created from a rib taken from the side of Adam, signifying that she was not to control him as the head, nor to be trampled under his feet as an inferior, but to stand by his side as an equal, to be loved and protected by him. A part of man, bone of his bone, and flesh of his flesh, she was his second self, showing the close union and the affectionate attachment that should exist in this relation. "For no man ever yet hated his own flesh; but nourisheth and cherisheth it." Ephesians 5:29. "Therefore shall a man leave his father and his mother, and shall cleave unto his wife; and they shall be one."

God celebrated the first marriage. Thus the institution has for its originator the Creator of the universe. "Marriage is honorable" (Hebrews 13:4); it was one of the first gifts of God to man, and it is one of the two institutions that, after the Fall, Adam brought with him beyond the gates of Paradise. When the divine principles are recognized and obeyed in this relation, marriage is a blessing; it guards the purity and happiness of the race, it provides for man's social needs, it elevates the physical, the intellectual, and the moral nature.

"And the Lord God planted a garden eastward in Eden; and there He put the man whom He had formed." Everything that God had made was the perfection of beauty, and nothing seemed wanting that could contribute to the happiness of the holy pair; yet the Creator gave   47 them still another token of His love, by preparing a garden especially for their home. In this garden were trees of every variety, many of them laden with fragrant and delicious fruit. There were lovely vines, growing upright, yet presenting a most graceful appearance, with their branches drooping under their load of tempting fruit of the richest and most varied hues. It was the work of Adam and Eve to train the branches of the vine to form bowers, thus making for themselves a dwelling from living trees covered with foliage and fruit. There were fragrant flowers of every hue in rich profusion. In the midst of the garden stood the tree of life, surpassing in glory all other trees. Its fruit appeared like apples of gold and silver, and had the power to perpetuate life.

The creation was now complete. "The heavens and the earth were finished, and all the host of them." "And God saw everything that He had made, and, behold, it was very good." Eden bloomed on earth. Adam and Eve had free access to the tree of life. No taint of sin or shadow of death marred the fair creation. "The morning stars sang together, and all the sons of God shouted for joy." Job 38:7.

The great Jehovah had laid the foundations of the earth; He had dressed the whole world in the garb of beauty and had filled it with things useful to man; He had created all the wonders of the land and of the sea. In six days the great work of creation had been accomplished. And

God "rested on the seventh day from all His work which He had made. And God blessed the seventh day, and sanctified it: because that in it He had rested from all His work which God created and made." God looked with satisfaction upon the work of His hands. All was perfect, worthy of its divine Author, and He rested, not as one weary, but as well pleased with the fruits of His wisdom and goodness and the manifestations of His glory.

After resting upon the seventh day, God sanctified it, or set it apart, as a day of rest for man. Following the example of the Creator, man was to rest upon this sacred day, that as he should look upon the heavens and the earth, he might reflect upon God's great work of creation; and that as he should behold the evidences of God's wisdom and goodness, his heart might be filled with love and reverence for his Maker.

48   In Eden, God set up the memorial of His work of creation, in placing His blessing upon the seventh day. The Sabbath was committed to Adam, the father and representative of the whole human family. Its observance was to be an act of grateful acknowledgment, on the part of all who should dwell upon the earth, that God was their Creator and their rightful Sovereign; that they were the work of His hands and the subjects of His authority. Thus the institution was wholly commemorative, and given to all mankind. There was nothing in it shadowy or of restricted application to any people.

God saw that a Sabbath was essential for man, even in Paradise. He needed to lay aside his own interests and pursuits for one day of the seven, that he might more fully contemplate the works of God and meditate upon His power and goodness. He needed a Sabbath to remind him more vividly of God and to awaken gratitude because all that he enjoyed and possessed came from the beneficent hand of the Creator.

God designs that the Sabbath shall direct the minds of men to the contemplation of His created works. Nature speaks to their senses, declaring that there is a living God, the Creator, the Supreme Ruler of all. "The heavens declare the glory of God; and the firmament showeth His handiwork. Day unto day uttereth speech, and night unto night showeth knowledge." Psalm 19:1, 2. The beauty that clothes the earth is a token of God's love. We may behold it in the everlasting hills, in the lofty trees, in the opening buds and the delicate flowers. All speak to us of God. The Sabbath, ever pointing to Him who made them all, bids men open the great book of nature and trace therein the wisdom, the power, and the love of the Creator.

Our first parents, though created innocent and holy, were not placed beyond the possibility of wrongdoing. God made them free moral agents, capable of appreciating the wisdom and benevolence of His character and the justice of His requirements, and with full liberty to yield or to withhold obedience. They were to enjoy communion with God and with holy angels; but before they could be rendered eternally secure, their loyalty must be tested. At the very beginning of man's existence a check was placed upon the desire for self-indulgence, the fatal passion that lay at the foundation of Satan's fall. The tree of knowledge, which stood near the tree of life in the midst of the garden, was to be 49 a test of the obedience, faith, and love of our first parents. While permitted to eat freely of every other tree, they were forbidden to taste of this, on pain of death. They were also to be exposed to the temptations of Satan; but if they endured the trial, they would finally be placed beyond his power, to enjoy perpetual favor with God.

God placed man under law, as an indispensable condition of his very existence. He was a subject of the divine government, and there can be no government without law. God might have created man without the power to transgress His law; He might have withheld the hand of Adam from touching the forbidden fruit; but in that case man would have been, not a free moral agent, but a mere automaton. Without freedom of choice, his obedience would not have been voluntary, but forced. There could have been no development of character. Such a course would have been contrary to God's plan in dealing with the inhabitants of other worlds. It would have been unworthy of man as an intelligent being, and would have sustained Satan's charge of God's arbitrary rule.

God made man upright; He gave him noble traits of character, with no bias toward evil. He endowed him with high intellectual powers, and presented before him the strongest possible inducements to be true to his allegiance. Obedience, perfect and perpetual, was the condition of eternal happiness. On this condition he was to have access to the tree of life.

The home of our first parents was to be a pattern for other homes as their children should go forth to occupy the earth. That home, beautified by the hand of God Himself, was not a gorgeous palace. Men, in their pride, delight in magnificent and costly edifices and glory in the works of their own hands; but God placed Adam in a garden. This was his dwelling. The blue heavens were its dome; the earth, with its delicate flowers and carpet of living green, was its floor; and the leafy branches of the goodly trees were its canopy. Its walls were hung with the most magnificent adornings—the handiwork of the great Master Artist. In the surroundings of the holy pair was a lesson for all time—that true happiness is found, not in the indulgence of pride and luxury, but in communion with God through His created works. If men would give less attention to the artificial, and would culti-

vate greater simplicity, they would come far
nearer to answering the purpose of God in their
creation. Pride and ambition are never satisfied,
but those who are truly wise will find substantial and elevating pleasure in the sources of
enjoyment that God has placed within the reach
of all.

To the dwellers in Eden was committed the
care of the garden, "to dress it and to keep it."
Their occupation was not wearisome, but pleasant and invigorating. God appointed labor as a
blessing to man, to occupy his mind, to
strengthen his body, and to develop his faculties. In mental and physical activity Adam
found one of the highest pleasures of his holy
existence. And when, as a result of his disobedience, he was driven from his beautiful home,
and forced to struggle with a stubborn soil to
gain his daily bread, that very labor, although
widely different from his pleasant occupation in
the garden, was a safeguard against temptation
and a source of happiness. Those who regard
work as a curse, attended though it be with
weariness and pain, are cherishing an error. The
rich often look down with contempt upon the
working classes, but this is wholly at variance
with God's purpose in creating man. What are
the possessions of even the most wealthy in
comparison with the heritage given to the lordly
Adam? Yet Adam was not to be idle. Our Creator, who understands what is for man's happiness, appointed Adam his work. The true joy of
life is found only by the working men and
women. The angels are diligent workers; they
are the ministers of God to the children of men.
The Creator has prepared no place for the stag-
nating practice of indolence.

While they remained true to God, Adam and
his companion were to bear rule over the earth.
Unlimited control was given them over every
living thing. The lion and the lamb sported
peacefully around them or lay down together at
their feet. The happy birds flitted about them
without fear; and as their glad songs ascended to
the praise of their Creator, Adam and Eve united with them in thanksgiving to the Father and
the Son.

The holy pair were not only children under the
fatherly care of God but students receiving
instruction from the all-wise Creator. They were
visited by angels, and were granted communion
with their Maker, with no obscuring veil
between. They were full of the vigor imparted
by the tree of life, and their intellectual power
was but little less than that of the angels. The
mysteries of the visible universe—"the wondrous works of Him which is perfect in knowledge" (Job 37:16)—afforded them an exhaustless source of instruction and delight. The laws
and operations of nature, which have engaged
men's study for six thousand years, were opened
to their minds by the infinite Framer and

Upholder of all. They held converse with leaf
and flower and tree, gathering from each the
secrets of its life. With every living creature,
from the mighty leviathan that playeth among
the waters to the insect mote that floats in the
sunbeam, Adam was familiar. He had given to
each its name, and he was acquainted with the
nature and habits of all. God's glory in the heavens, the innumerable worlds in their orderly revolutions, "the balancings of the clouds," the
mysteries of light and sound, of day and night—
all were open to the study of our first parents. On
every leaf of the forest or stone of the mountains,
in every shining star, in earth and air and sky,
God's name was written. The order and harmony of creation spoke to them of infinite wisdom
and power. They were ever discovering some
attraction that filled their hearts with deeper love
and called forth fresh expressions of gratitude.

So long as they remained loyal to the divine
law, their capacity to know, to enjoy, and to
love would continually increase. They would be
constantly gaining new treasures of knowledge,
discovering fresh springs of happiness, and
obtaining clearer and yet clearer conceptions of
the immeasurable, unfailing love of God.

3

The Temptation and Fall

No longer free to stir up rebellion in heaven,
Satan's enmity against God found a new field in
plotting the ruin of the human race. In the happiness and peace of the holy pair in Eden he
beheld a vision of the bliss that to him was forever lost. Moved by envy, he determined to
incite them to disobedience, and bring upon
them the guilt and penalty of sin. He would
change their love to distrust and their songs of
praise to reproaches against their Maker. Thus
he would not only plunge these innocent beings
into the same misery which he was himself
enduring, but would cast dishonor upon God,
and cause grief in heaven.

Our first parents were not left without a warning of the danger that threatened them. Heavenly messengers opened to them the history of
Satan's fall and his plots for their destruction,
unfolding more fully the nature of the divine
government, which the prince of evil was trying
to overthrow. It was by disobedience to the just
commands of God that Satan and his host had
fallen. How important, then, that Adam and Eve
should honor that law by which alone it was
possible for order and equity to be maintained.

The law of God is as sacred as God Himself.
It is a revelation of His will, a transcript of His
character, the expression of divine love and wisdom. The harmony of creation depends upon

the perfect conformity of all beings, of everything, animate and inanimate, to the law of the Creator. God has ordained laws for the government, not only of living beings, but of all the operations of nature. Everything is under fixed laws, which cannot be disregarded. But while everything in nature is governed by natural laws, man alone, of all that inhabits the earth, is amenable to moral law. To man, the crowning work of creation, God has given power to understand His requirements, to comprehend the justice and beneficence of His law, and its sacred claims upon him; and of man unswerving obedience is required.

53   Like the angels, the dwellers in Eden had been placed upon probation; their happy estate could be retained only on condition of fidelity to the Creator's law. They could obey and live, or disobey and perish. God had made them the recipients of rich blessings; but should they disregard His will, He who spared not the angels that sinned, could not spare them; transgression would forfeit His gifts and bring upon them misery and ruin.

The angels warned them to be on their guard against the devices of Satan, for his efforts to ensnare them would be unwearied. While they were obedient to God the evil one could not harm them; for, if need be, every angel in heaven would be sent to their help. If they steadfastly repelled his first insinuations, they would be as secure as the heavenly messengers. But should they once yield to temptation, their nature would become so depraved that in themselves they would have no power and no disposition to resist Satan.

The tree of knowledge had been made a test of their obedience and their love to God. The Lord had seen fit to lay upon them but one prohibition as to the use of all that was in the garden; but if they should disregard His will in this particular, they would incur the guilt of transgression. Satan was not to follow them with continual temptations; he could have access to them only at the forbidden tree. Should they attempt to investigate its nature, they would be exposed to his wiles. They were admonished to give careful heed to the warning which God had sent them and to be content with the instruction which He had seen fit to impart.

In order to accomplish his work unperceived, Satan chose to employ as his medium the serpent—a disguise well adapted for his purpose of deception. The serpent was then one of the wisest and most beautiful creatures on the earth. It had wings, and while flying through the air presented an appearance of dazzling brightness, having the color and brilliancy of burnished gold. Resting in the rich-laden branches of the forbidden tree and regaling itself with the delicious fruit, it was an object to arrest the attention and delight the eye of the beholder. Thus in the garden of peace lurked the destroyer, watching for his prey.

The angels had cautioned Eve to beware of separating herself from her husband while occupied in their daily labor in the garden; with him she would be in less danger from temptation than if she were alone. But absorbed in her pleasing task, she unconsciously wandered from his side. On perceiving that she was alone, she 54 felt an apprehension of danger, but dismissed her fears, deciding that she had sufficient wisdom and strength to discern evil and to withstand it. Unmindful of the angels' caution, she soon found herself gazing with mingled curiosity and admiration upon the forbidden tree. The fruit was very beautiful, and she questioned with herself why God had withheld it from them. Now was the tempter's opportunity. As if he were able to discern the workings of her mind, he addressed her: "Yea, hath God said, Ye shall not eat of every tree of the garden?" Eve was surprised and startled as she thus seemed to hear the echo of her thoughts. But the serpent continued, in a musical voice, with subtle praise of her surpassing loveliness; and his words were not displeasing. Instead of fleeing from the spot she lingered wonderingly to hear a serpent speak. Had she been addressed by a being like the angels, her fears would have been excited; but she had no thought that the fascinating serpent could become the medium of the fallen foe.

To the tempter's ensnaring question she replied: "We may eat of the fruit of the trees of the garden: but of the fruit of the tree which is in the midst of the garden, God hath said, Ye shall not eat of it, neither shall ye touch it, lest ye die. And the serpent said unto the woman, Ye shall not surely die: for God doth know that in the day ye eat thereof, then your eyes shall be opened, and ye shall be as gods, knowing good and evil."

By partaking of this tree, he declared, they would attain to a more exalted sphere of existence and enter a broader field of knowledge. He himself had eaten of the forbidden fruit, and as a result had acquired the power of speech. And he insinuated that the Lord jealously desired to withhold it from them, lest they should be exalted to equality with Himself. It was because of its wonderful properties, imparting wisdom and power, that He had prohibited them from tasting or even touching it. The tempter intimated that the divine warning was not to be actually fulfilled; it was designed merely to intimidate them. How could it be possible for them to die? Had they not eaten of the tree of life? God had been seeking to prevent them from reaching a nobler development and finding greater happiness.

Such has been Satan's work from the days of Adam to the present, and he has pursued it with great success. He tempts men to distrust God's love and to doubt His wisdom. He is constantly seeking to excite a spirit of irreverent curiosity, a restless, inquisitive desire to penetrate the secrets of divine wisdom and power. In their efforts to search out what God has been pleased to withhold, multitudes overlook the truths which He has revealed, and which are essential to salvation. Satan tempts men to disobedience by leading them to believe they are entering a wonderful field of knowledge. But this is all a deception. Elated with their ideas of progression, they are, by trampling on God's requirements, setting their feet in the path that leads to degradation and death.

Satan represented to the holy pair that they would be gainers by breaking the law of God. Do we not today hear similar reasoning? Many talk of the narrowness of those who obey God's commandments, while they themselves claim to have broader ideas and to enjoy greater liberty. What is this but an echo of the voice from Eden, "In the day ye eat thereof"—transgress the divine requirement—"ye shall be as gods"? Satan claimed to have received great good by eating of the forbidden fruit, but he did not let it appear that by transgression he had become an outcast from heaven. Though he had found sin to result in infinite loss, he concealed his own misery in order to draw others into the same position. So now the transgressor seeks to disguise his true character; he may claim to be holy; but his exalted profession only makes him the more dangerous as a deceiver. He is on the side of Satan, trampling upon the law of God, and leading others to do the same, to their eternal ruin.

Eve really believed the words of Satan, but her belief did not save her from the penalty of sin. She disbelieved the words of God, and this was what led to her fall. In the judgment men will not be condemned because they conscientiously believed a lie, but because they did not believe the truth, because they neglected the opportunity of learning what is truth. Notwithstanding the sophistry of Satan to the contrary, it is always disastrous to disobey God. We must set our hearts to know what is truth. All the lessons which God has caused to be placed on record in His word are for our warning and instruction. They are given to save us from deception. Their neglect will result in ruin to ourselves. Whatever contradicts God's word, we may be sure proceeds from Satan.

The serpent plucked the fruit of the forbidden tree and placed it in the hands of the half-reluctant Eve. Then he reminded her of her own words, that God had forbidden them to touch it, lest they die. She would receive no more harm from eating the fruit, he declared, than from touching it. Perceiving no evil results from what she had done, Eve grew bolder. When she "saw

that the tree was good for food, and that it was pleasant to the eyes, and a tree to be desired to make one wise, she took of the fruit thereof, and did eat." It was grateful to the taste, and as she ate, she seemed to feel a vivifying power, and imagined herself entering upon a higher state of existence. Without a fear she plucked and ate. And now, having herself transgressed, she became the agent of Satan in working the ruin of her husband. In a state of strange, unnatural excitement, with her hands filled with the forbidden fruit, she sought his presence, and related all that had occurred.

An expression of sadness came over the face of Adam. He appeared astonished and alarmed. To the words of Eve he replied that this must be the foe against whom they had been warned; and by the divine sentence she must die. In answer she urged him to eat, repeating the words of the serpent, that they should not surely die. She reasoned that this must be true, for she felt no evidence of God's displeasure, but on the contrary realized a delicious, exhilarating influence, thrilling every faculty with new life, such, she imagined, as inspired the heavenly messengers.

Adam understood that his companion had transgressed the command of God, disregarded the only prohibition laid upon them as a test of their fidelity and love. There was a terrible struggle in his mind. He mourned that he had permitted Eve to wander from his side. But now the deed was done; he must be separated from her whose society had been his joy. How could he have it thus? Adam had enjoyed the companionship of God and of holy angels. He had looked upon the glory of the Creator. He understood the high destiny opened to the human race should they remain faithful to God. Yet all these blessings were lost sight of in the fear of losing that one gift which in his eyes outvalued every other. Love, gratitude, loyalty to the Creator— all were overborne by love to Eve. She was a part of himself, and he could not endure the thought of separation. He did not realize that the same Infinite Power who had from the dust of the earth created him, a living, beautiful form, and had in love given him a companion, could supply her place. He resolved to share her fate; if she must die, he would die with her. After all, he reasoned, might not the words of the wise serpent be true? Eve was before him, as beautiful and apparently as innocent as before this act of disobedience. She expressed greater love for him than before. No sign of death appeared in her, and he decided to brave the consequences. He seized the fruit and quickly ate.

After his transgression Adam at first imagined himself entering upon a higher state of existence. But soon the thought of his sin filled him with terror. The air, which had hitherto been of a mild and uniform temperature, seemed to chill the guilty pair. The love and peace which had been theirs was gone, and in its place they felt a sense of sin, a dread of the future, a nakedness of soul. The robe of light which had enshrouded them, now disappeared, and to supply its place they endeavored to fashion for themselves a covering; for they could not, while unclothed, meet the eye of God and holy angels.

They now began to see the true character of their sin. Adam reproached his companion for her folly in leaving his side and permitting herself to be deceived by the serpent; but they both flattered themselves that He who had given them so many evidences of His love, would pardon this one transgression, or that they would not be subjected to so dire a punishment as they had feared.

Satan exulted in his success. He had tempted the woman to distrust God's love, to doubt His wisdom, and to transgress His law, and through her he had caused the overthrow of Adam.

But the great Lawgiver was about to make known to Adam and Eve the consequences of their transgression. The divine presence was manifested in the garden. In their innocence and holiness they had joyfully welcomed the approach of their Creator; but now they fled in terror, and sought to hide in the deepest recesses of the garden. But "the Lord God called unto Adam, and said unto him, Where art thou? And he said, I heard Thy voice in the garden, and I was afraid, because I was naked; and I hid myself. And He said, Who told thee that thou wast naked? Hast thou eaten of the tree, whereof I commanded thee that thou shouldest not eat?"

Adam could neither deny nor excuse his sin; but instead of manifesting penitence, he endeavored to cast the blame upon his wife, and thus upon God Himself: "The woman whom *Thou gavest* to be with me, she gave me of the tree, and I did eat." He who, from love to Eve, had deliberately chosen to forfeit the approval of God, his home in Paradise, and an eternal life of joy, could now, after his fall, endeavor to make his companion, and even the Creator Himself, responsible for the transgression. So terrible is the power of sin.

When the woman was asked, "What is this that thou hast done?" she answered, "The serpent beguiled me, and I did eat." "Why didst Thou create the serpent? Why didst Thou suffer him to enter Eden?"—these were the questions implied in her excuse for her sin. Thus, like Adam, she charged God with the responsibility of their fall. The spirit of self-justification originated in the father of lies; it was indulged by our first parents as soon as they yielded to the influence of Satan, and has been exhibited by all the sons and daughters of Adam. Instead of humbly confessing their sins, they try to shield themselves by casting the blame upon others, upon circumstances, or upon God—making even His blessings an occasion of murmuring against Him.

The Lord then passed sentence upon the serpent: "Because thou hast done this, thou art cursed above all cattle, and above every beast of the field; upon thy belly shalt thou go, and dust shalt thou eat all the days of thy life." Since it had been employed as Satan's medium, the serpent was to share the visitation of divine judgment. From the most beautiful and admired of the creatures of the field, it was to become the most groveling and detested of them all, feared and hated by both man and beast. The words next addressed to the serpent applied directly to Satan himself, pointing forward to his ultimate defeat and destruction: "I will put enmity between thee and the woman, and between thy seed and her seed; it shall bruise thy head, and thou shalt bruise his heel."

Eve was told of the sorrow and pain that must henceforth be her portion. And the Lord said, "Thy desire shall be to thy husband, and he shall rule over thee." In the creation God had made her the equal of Adam. Had they remained obedient to God—in harmony with His great law of love—they would ever have been in harmony with each other; but sin had brought discord, and now their union could be maintained and harmony preserved only by submission on the part of the one or the other. Eve had been the first in transgression; and she had fallen into temptation by separating from her companion, contrary to the divine direction. It was by her solicitation that Adam sinned, and she was now placed in subjection to her husband. Had the principles enjoined in the law of God been cherished by the fallen race, this sentence, though growing out of the results of sin, would have proved a blessing to them; but man's abuse of the supremacy thus given him has too often rendered the lot of woman very bitter and made her life a burden.

Eve had been perfectly happy by her husband's side in her Eden home; but, like restless modern Eves, she was flattered with the hope of entering a higher sphere than that which God had assigned her. In attempting to rise above her original position, she fell far below it. A similar result will be reached by all who are unwilling to take up cheerfully their life duties in accordance with God's plan. In their efforts to reach positions for which He has not fitted them, many are leaving vacant the place where they might be a blessing. In their desire for a higher sphere, many have sacrificed true womanly dignity and nobility of character, and have left undone the very work that Heaven appointed them.

To Adam the Lord declared: "Because thou hast hearkened unto the voice of thy wife, and hast eaten of the tree, of which I commanded thee, saying, Thou shalt not eat of it: cursed is the ground for thy sake; in sorrow shalt thou eat of it all the days of thy life; thorns also and thistles shall it bring forth to thee; and thou shalt eat the herb of the field; in the sweat of thy face shalt thou eat bread, till thou return unto the ground; for out of it wast thou taken: for dust thou art, and unto dust shalt thou return."

It was not the will of God that the sinless pair should know aught of evil. He had freely given them the good, and had withheld the evil. But, contrary to His command, they had eaten of the forbidden tree, and now they would continue to eat of it—they would have the knowledge of evil—all the days of their life. From that time the race would be afflicted by Satan's temptations. Instead of the happy labor heretofore appointed them, anxiety and toil were to be their lot. They would be subject to disappointment, grief, and pain, and finally to death.

Under the curse of sin all nature was to witness to man of the character and results of rebellion against God. When God made man He made him ruler over the earth and all living creatures. So long as Adam remained loyal to Heaven, all nature was in subjection to him. But when he rebelled against the divine law, the inferior creatures were in rebellion against his rule. Thus the Lord, in His great mercy, would show men the sacredness of His law, and lead them, by their own experience, to see the danger of setting it aside, even in the slightest degree.

And the life of toil and care which was henceforth to be man's lot was appointed in love. It was a discipline rendered needful by his sin, to place a check upon the indulgence of appetite and passion, to develop habits of self-control. It was a part of God's great plan for man's recovery from the ruin and degradation of sin.

The warning given to our first parents—"In the day that thou eatest thereof thou shalt surely die" (Genesis 2:17)—did not imply that they were to die on the very day when they partook of the forbidden fruit. But on that day the irrevocable sentence would be pronounced. Immortality was promised them on condition of obedience; by transgression they would forfeit eternal life. That very day they would be doomed to death.

In order to possess an endless existence, man must continue to partake of the tree of life. Deprived of this, his vitality would gradually diminish until life should become extinct. It was Satan's plan that Adam and Eve should by disobedience incur God's displeasure; and then, if they failed to obtain forgiveness, he hoped that they would eat of the tree of life, and thus perpetuate an existence of sin and misery. But after man's fall, holy angels were immediately commissioned to guard the tree of life. Around these angels flashed beams of light having the appearance of a glittering sword. None of the family of Adam were permitted to pass that barrier to partake of the life-giving fruit; hence there is not an immortal sinner.

The tide of woe that flowed from the transgression of our first parents is regarded by many as too awful a consequence for so small a sin, and they impeach the wisdom and justice of God in His dealings with man. But if they would look more deeply into this question, they might discern their error. God created man after His own likeness, free from sin. The earth was to be peopled with beings only a little lower than the angels; but their obedience must be tested; for God would not permit the world to be filled with those who would disregard His law. Yet, in His great mercy, He appointed Adam no severe test. And the very lightness of the prohibition made the sin exceedingly great. If Adam could not bear the smallest of tests, he could not have endured a greater trial had he been entrusted with higher responsibilities.

Had some great test been appointed Adam, then those whose hearts incline to evil would have excused themselves by saying, "This is a trivial matter, and God is not so particular about little things." And there would be continual transgression in things looked upon as small, and which pass unrebuked among men. But the Lord has made it evident that sin in any degree is offensive to HIM.

To Eve it seemed a small thing to disobey God by tasting the fruit of the forbidden tree, and to tempt her husband also to transgress; but their sin opened the floodgates of woe upon the world. Who can know, in the moment of temptation, the terrible consequences that will result from one wrong step?

Many who teach that the law of God is not binding upon man, urge that it is impossible for him to obey its precepts. But if this were true, why did Adam suffer the penalty of transgression? The sin of our first parents brought guilt and sorrow upon the world, and had it not been for the goodness and mercy of God, would have plunged the race into hopeless despair. Let none deceive themselves. "The wages of sin is death." Romans 6:23. The law of God can no more be transgressed with impunity now than when sentence was pronounced upon the father of mankind.

After their sin Adam and Eve were no longer to dwell in Eden. They earnestly entreated that they might remain in the home of their innocence and joy. They confessed that they had forfeited all right to that happy abode, but pledged themselves for the future to yield strict obedience to God. But they were told that their nature had become depraved by sin; they had lessened their strength to resist evil and had opened the way for Satan to gain more ready access to them. In their innocence they had yielded to temptation; and now, in a state of conscious guilt, they would have less power to maintain their integrity.

In humility and unutterable sadness they bade farewell to their beautiful home and went forth to dwell upon the earth, where rested the curse of sin. The atmosphere, once so mild and uniform in temperature, was now subject to marked changes, and the Lord mercifully provided them with a garment of skins as a protection from the extremes of heat and cold.

As they witnessed in drooping flower and falling leaf the first signs of decay, Adam and his companion mourned more deeply than men now mourn over their dead. The death of the frail, delicate flowers was indeed a cause of sorrow; but when the goodly trees cast off their leaves, the scene brought vividly to mind the stern fact that death is the portion of every living thing.

The Garden of Eden remained upon the earth long after man had become an outcast from its pleasant paths. The fallen race were long permitted to gaze upon the home of innocence, their entrance barred only by the watching angels. At the cherubim-guarded gate of Paradise the divine glory was revealed. Hither came Adam and his sons to worship God. Here they renewed their vows of obedience to that law the transgression of which had banished them from Eden. When the tide of iniquity overspread the world, and the wickedness of men determined their destruction by a flood of waters, the hand that had planted Eden withdrew it from the earth. But in the final restitution, when there shall be "a new heaven and a new earth" (Revelation 21:1), it is to be restored more gloriously adorned than at the beginning.

Then they that have kept God's commandments shall breathe in immortal vigor beneath the tree of life; and through unending ages the inhabitants of sinless worlds shall behold, in that garden of delight, a sample of the perfect work of God's creation, untouched by the curse of sin—a sample of what the whole earth would have become, had man but fulfilled the Creator's glorious plan.

4

The Plan of Redemption

The fall of man filled all heaven with sorrow. The world that God had made was blighted with the curse of sin and inhabited by beings doomed to misery and death. There appeared no escape for those who had transgressed the law. Angels ceased their songs of praise. Throughout the heavenly courts there was mourning for the ruin that sin had wrought.

The Son of God, heaven's glorious Commander, was touched with pity for the fallen race. His heart was moved with infinite compassion as the woes of the lost world rose up before Him. But divine love had conceived a plan whereby man might be redeemed. The broken law of God demanded the life of the sinner. In all the universe there was but one who could, in behalf of man, satisfy its claims. Since the divine law is as sacred as God Himself, only one equal with God could make atonement for its transgression. None but Christ could redeem fallen man from the curse of the law and bring him again into harmony with Heaven. Christ would take upon Himself the guilt and shame of sin—sin so offensive to a holy God that it must separate the Father and His Son. Christ would reach to the depths of misery to rescue the ruined race.

Before the Father He pleaded in the sinner's behalf, while the host of heaven awaited the result with an intensity of interest that words cannot express. Long continued was that mysterious communing—"the counsel of peace" (Zechariah 6:13) for the fallen sons of men. The plan of salvation had been laid before the creation of the earth; for Christ is "the Lamb slain from the foundation of the world" (Revelation 13:8); yet it was a struggle, even with the King of the universe, to yield up His Son to die for the guilty race. But "God so loved the world, that He gave His only-begotten Son, that whosoever believeth in Him should not perish, but have everlasting life." John 3:16. Oh, the mystery of redemption! the love of God for a world that did not love Him! Who can know the depths of that love which "passeth knowledge"? Through endless ages immortal minds, seeking to comprehend the mystery of that incomprehensible love, will wonder and adore.

God was to be manifest in Christ, "reconciling the world unto Himself." 2 Corinthians 5:19. Man had become so degraded by sin that it was impossible for him, in himself, to come into harmony with Him whose nature is purity and goodness. But Christ, after having redeemed man from the condemnation of the law, could impart divine power to unite with human effort. Thus by repentance toward God and faith in Christ the fallen children of Adam might once more become "sons of God." 1 John 3:2.

The plan by which alone man's salvation could be secured, involved all heaven in its infinite sacrifice. The angels could not rejoice as Christ opened before them the plan of redemption, for they saw that man's salvation must cost their loved Commander unutterable woe. In grief and wonder they listened to His words as He told them how He must descend from heaven's purity and peace, its joy and glory and immortal life, and come in contact with the degradation of earth, to endure its sorrow, shame, and death. He was to stand between the sinner and the penalty of sin; yet few would receive Him as the Son of God. He would leave His high position as the Majesty of heaven, appear upon earth and humble Himself as a man, and by His own experience become acquainted with the sorrows and temptations which man would have to endure. All this would be necessary in order that He might be able to succor them that should be tempted. Hebrews 2:18. When His mission as a teacher should be ended, He must be delivered into the hands of wicked men and be subjected to every insult and torture that Satan could inspire them to inflict. He must die the cruelest of deaths, lifted up between the heavens and the earth as a guilty sinner. He must pass long hours of agony so terrible that angels could not look upon it, but would veil their faces from the sight. He must endure anguish of soul, the hiding of His Father's face, while the guilt of transgression— the weight of the sins of the whole world— should be upon Him.

The angels prostrated themselves at the feet of their Commander and offered to become a sacrifice for man. But an angel's life could not pay the debt; only He who created man had power to redeem him. Yet the angels were to have a part to act in the plan of redemption. Christ was to be made "a little lower than the angels for the suffering of death." Hebrews 2:9. As He should take human nature upon Him, His strength would not be equal to theirs, and they were to minister to Him, to strengthen and soothe Him under His sufferings. They were also to be ministering spirits, sent forth to minister for them who should be heirs of salvation. Hebrews 1:14. They would guard the subjects of grace from the power of evil angels and from the darkness constantly thrown around them by Satan.

When the angels should witness the agony and humiliation of their Lord, they would be filled with grief and indignation and would wish to deliver Him from His murderers; but they were not to interpose in order to prevent anything which they should behold. It was a part of the plan of redemption that Christ should suffer the scorn and abuse of wicked men, and He consented to all this when He became the Redeemer of man.

Christ assured the angels that by His death He would ransom many, and would destroy him who had the power of death. He would recover the kingdom which man had lost by transgression, and the redeemed were to inherit it with Him, and dwell therein forever. Sin and sinners would be blotted out, nevermore to disturb the peace of heaven or earth. He bade the angelic host to be in accord with the plan that His Father had accepted, and rejoice that, through His death, fallen man could be reconciled to God.

Then joy, inexpressible joy, filled heaven.

The glory and blessedness of a world redeemed, outmeasured even the anguish and sacrifice of the Prince of life. Through the celestial courts echoed the first strains of that song which was to ring out above the hills of Bethlehem—"Glory to God in the highest, and on earth peace, good will toward men." Luke 2:14. With a deeper gladness now than in the rapture of the new creation, "the morning stars sang together, and all the sons of God shouted for joy." Job 38:7.

To man the first intimation of redemption was communicated in the sentence pronounced upon Satan in the garden. The Lord declared, "I will put enmity between thee and the woman, and between thy seed and her seed; it shall bruise thy head, and thou shalt bruise his heel." Genesis 3:15. This sentence, uttered in the hearing of our first parents, was to them a promise. While it foretold war between man and Satan, it declared that the power of the great adversary would finally be broken. Adam and Eve stood as criminals before the righteous Judge, awaiting the sentence which transgression had incurred; but before they heard of the life of toil and sorrow which must be their portion, or of the decree that they must return to dust, they listened to words that could not fail to give them hope. Though they must suffer from the power of their mighty foe, they could look forward to final victory.

When Satan heard that enmity should exist between himself and the woman, and between his seed and her seed, he knew that his work of depraving human nature would be interrupted; that by some means man would be enabled to resist his power. Yet as the plan of salvation was more fully unfolded, Satan rejoiced with his angels that, having caused man's fall, he could bring down the Son of God from His exalted position. He declared that his plans had thus far been successful upon the earth, and that when Christ should take upon Himself human nature, He also might be overcome, and thus the redemption of the fallen race might be prevented.

Heavenly angels more fully opened to our first parents the plan that had been devised for their salvation. Adam and his companion were assured that notwithstanding their great sin, they were not to be abandoned to the control of Satan. The Son of God had offered to atone, with His own life, for their transgression. A period of probation would be granted them, and through repentance and faith in Christ they might again become the children of God.

The sacrifice demanded by their transgression revealed to Adam and Eve the sacred character of the law of God; and they saw, as they had never seen before, the guilt of sin and its dire results. In their remorse and anguish they pleaded that the penalty might not fall upon Him whose love had been the source of all their joy; rather let it descend upon them and their posterity.

They were told that since the law of Jehovah is the foundation of His government in heaven as well as upon the earth, even the life of an angel could not be accepted as a sacrifice for its transgression. Not one of its precepts could be abrogated or changed to meet man in his fallen condition; but the Son of God, who had created man, could make an atonement for him. As Adam's transgression had brought wretchedness and death, so the sacrifice of Christ would bring life and immortality.

Not only man but the earth had by sin come under the power of the wicked one, and was to be restored by the plan of redemption. At his creation Adam was placed in dominion over the earth. But by yielding to temptation, he was brought under the power of Satan. "Of whom a man is overcome, of the same is he brought in bondage." 2 Peter 2:19. When man became Satan's captive, the dominion which he held, passed to his conqueror. Thus Satan became "the god of this world." 2 Corinthians 4:4. He had usurped that dominion over the earth which had been originally given to Adam. But Christ, by His sacrifice paying the penalty of sin, would not only redeem man, but recover the dominion which he had forfeited. All that was lost by the first Adam will be restored by the second. Says the prophet, "O tower of the flock, the stronghold of the daughter of Zion, unto thee shall it come, even the first dominion." Micah 4:8. And the apostle Paul points forward to the "redemption of the purchased possession." Ephesians 1:14. God created the earth to be the abode of holy, happy beings. The Lord "formed the earth and made it; He hath established it, He created it not in vain, He formed it to be inhabited." Isaiah 45:18. That purpose will be fulfilled, when, renewed by the power of God, and freed from sin and sorrow, it shall become the eternal abode of the redeemed. "The righteous shall inherit the land, and dwell therein forever." "And there shall be no more curse: but the throne of God and of the Lamb shall be in it; and His servants shall serve Him." Psalm 37:29; Revelation 22:3.

Adam, in his innocence, had enjoyed open communion with his Maker; but sin brought separation between God and man, and the atonement of Christ alone could span the abyss and make possible the communication of blessing or salvation from heaven to earth. Man was still cut off from direct approach to his Creator, but God would communicate with him through Christ and angels.

Thus were revealed to Adam important events in the history of mankind, from the time when the divine sentence was pronounced in Eden, to the Flood, and onward to the first advent of the Son of God. He was shown that while the sacrifice of Christ would be of sufficient value to save the whole world, many would choose a life of sin rather than of repentance and obedience. Crime would increase through successive generations, and the curse of sin would rest more and more heavily upon the human race, upon the beasts, and upon the earth. The days of man would be shortened by his own course of sin; he would deteriorate in physical stature and endurance and in moral and intellectual power, until the world would be filled with misery of every type. Through the indulgence of appetite and passion men would become incapable of appreciating the great truths of the plan of redemption. Yet Christ, true to the purpose for which He left heaven, would continue His interest in men, and still invite them to hide their weakness and deficiencies in Him. He would supply the needs of all who would come unto Him in faith. And there would ever be a few who would preserve the knowledge of God and would remain unsullied amid the prevailing iniquity.

The sacrificial offerings were ordained by God to be to man a perpetual reminder and a penitential acknowledgment of his sin and a confession of his faith in the promised Redeemer. They were intended to impress upon the fallen race the solemn truth that it was sin that caused death. To Adam, the offering of the first sacrifice was a most painful ceremony. His hand must be raised to take life, which only God could give. It was the first time he had ever witnessed death, and he knew that had he been obedient to God, there would have been no death of man or beast. As he slew the innocent victim, he trembled at the thought that his sin must shed the blood of the spotless Lamb of God. This scene gave him a deeper and more vivid sense of the greatness of his transgression, which nothing but the death of God's dear Son could expiate. And he marveled at the infinite goodness that would give such a ransom to save the guilty. A star of hope illumined the dark and terrible future and relieved it of its utter desolation.

But the plan of redemption had a yet broader and deeper purpose than the salvation of man. It was not for this alone that Christ came to the earth; it was not merely that the inhabitants of this little world might regard the law of God as it should be regarded; but it was to vindicate the character of God before the universe. To this result of His great sacrifice—its influence upon the intelligences of other worlds, as well as upon man—the Saviour looked forward when just before His crucifixion He said: "Now is the judgment of this world: now shall the prince of this world be cast out. And I, if I be lifted up from the earth, will draw all men unto Me." John 12:31, 32. The act of Christ in dying for the salvation of man would not only make heaven accessible to men, but before all the universe it would justify God and His Son in their dealing with the rebellion of Satan. It would establish the perpetuity of the law of God and would reveal the nature and the results of sin.

From the first the great controversy had been upon the law of God. Satan had sought to prove that God was unjust, that His law was faulty, and that the good of the universe required it to be changed. In attacking the law he aimed to overthrow the authority of its Author. In the controversy it was to be shown whether the divine statutes were defective and subject to change, or perfect and immutable.

When Satan was thrust out of heaven, he determined to make the earth his kingdom. When he tempted and overcame Adam and Eve, he thought that he had gained possession of this world; "because," said he, "they have chosen me as their ruler." He claimed that it was impossible that forgiveness should be granted to the sinner, and therefore the fallen race were his rightful subjects, and the world was his. But God gave His own dear Son—one equal with Himself—to bear the penalty of transgression, and thus He provided a way by which they might be restored to His favor, and brought back to their Eden home. Christ undertook to redeem man and to rescue the world from the grasp of Satan. The great controversy begun in heaven was to be decided in the very world, on the very same field, that Satan claimed as his.

It was the marvel of all the universe that Christ should humble Himself to save fallen man. That He who had passed from star to star, from world to world, superintending all, by His providence supplying the needs of every order of being in His vast creation—that He should consent to leave His glory and take upon Himself human nature, was a mystery which the sinless intelligences of other worlds desired to understand. When Christ came to our world in the form of humanity, all were intensely interested in following Him as He traversed, step by step, the bloodstained path from the manger to Calvary. Heaven marked the insult and mockery that He received, and knew that it was at Satan's instigation. They marked the work of counteragencies going forward; Satan constantly pressing darkness, sorrow, and suffering upon the race, and Christ counteracting it. They watched the battle between light and darkness as it [70] waxed stronger. And as Christ in His expiring agony upon the cross cried out, "It is finished" (John 19:30), a shout of triumph rang through every world and through heaven itself. The great contest that had been so long in progress in this world was now decided, and Christ was conqueror. His death had answered the question whether the Father and the Son had sufficient love for man to exercise self-denial and a spirit

of sacrifice. Satan had revealed his true character as a liar and a murderer. It was seen that the very same spirit with which he had ruled the children of men who were under his power, he would have manifested if permitted to control the intelligences of heaven. With one voice the loyal universe united in extolling the divine administration.

If the law could be changed, man might have been saved without the sacrifice of Christ; but the fact that it was necessary for Christ to give His life for the fallen race, proves that the law of God will not release the sinner from its claims upon him. It is demonstrated that the wages of sin is death. When Christ died, the destruction of Satan was made certain. But if the law was abolished at the cross, as many claim, then the agony and death of God's dear Son were endured only to give to Satan just what he asked; then the prince of evil triumphed, his charges against the divine government were sustained. The very fact that Christ bore the penalty of man's transgression is a mighty argument to all created intelligences that the law is changeless; that God is righteous, merciful, and self-denying; and that infinite justice and mercy unite in the administration of His government.

5

Cain and Abel Tested

Cain and Abel, the sons of Adam, differed widely in character. Abel had a spirit of loyalty to God; he saw justice and mercy in the Creator's dealings with the fallen race, and gratefully accepted the hope of redemption. But Cain cherished feelings of rebellion, and murmured against God because of the curse pronounced upon the earth and upon the human race for Adam's sin. He permitted his mind to run in the same channel that led to Satan's fall—indulging the desire for self-exaltation and questioning the divine justice and authority.

These brothers were tested, as Adam had been tested before them, to prove whether they would believe and obey the word of God. They were acquainted with the provision made for the salvation of man, and understood the system of offerings which God had ordained. They knew that in these offerings they were to express faith in the Saviour whom the offerings typified, and at the same time to acknowledge their total dependence on Him for pardon; and they knew that by thus conforming to the divine plan for their redemption, they were giving proof of their obedience to the will of God. Without the shedding of blood there could be no remission of sin; and they were to show their faith in the blood of Christ as the promised atonement by

This chapter is based on Genesis 4:1-15.

offering the firstlings of the flock in sacrifice. Besides this, the first fruits of the earth were to be presented before the Lord as a thank offering.

The two brothers erected their altars alike, and each brought an offering. Abel presented a sacrifice from the flock, in accordance with the Lord's directions. "And the Lord had respect unto Abel and to his offering." Fire flashed from heaven and consumed the sacrifice. But Cain, disregarding the Lord's direct and explicit command, presented only an offering of fruit. There was no token from heaven to show that it was accepted. Abel pleaded with his brother to approach God in the divinely prescribed way, but his entreaties only made Cain the more determined to follow his own will. As the eldest, he felt above being admonished by his brother, and despised his counsel.

Cain came before God with murmuring and infidelity in his heart in regard to the promised sacrifice and the necessity of the sacrificial offerings. His gift expressed no penitence for sin. He felt, as many now feel, that it would be an acknowledgment of weakness to follow the exact plan marked out by God, of trusting his salvation wholly to the atonement of the promised Saviour. He chose the course of self-dependence. He would come in his own merits. He would not bring the lamb, and mingle its blood with his offering, but would present *his* fruits, the products of *his* labor. He presented his offering as a favor done to God, through which he expected to secure the divine approval. Cain obeyed in building an altar, obeyed in bringing a sacrifice; but he rendered only a partial obedience. The essential part, the recognition of the need of a Redeemer, was left out.

So far as birth and religious instruction were concerned, these brothers were equal. Both were sinners, and both acknowledged the claims of God to reverence and worship. To outward appearance their religion was the same up to a certain point, but beyond this the difference between the two was great.

"By faith Abel offered unto God a more excellent sacrifice than Cain." Hebrews 11:4. Abel grasped the great principles of redemption. He saw himself a sinner, and he saw sin and its penalty, death, standing between his soul and communion with God. He brought the slain victim, the sacrificed life, thus acknowledging the claims of the law that had been transgressed. Through the shed blood he looked to the future sacrifice, Christ dying on the cross of Calvary; and trusting in the atonement that was there to be made, he had the witness that he was righteous, and his offering accepted.

Cain had the same opportunity of learning and accepting these truths as had Abel. He was not the victim of an arbitrary purpose. One brother was not elected to be accepted of God, and the other to be rejected. Abel chose faith and obedience; Cain, unbelief and rebellion. Here the whole matter rested.

Cain and Abel represent two classes that will exist in the world till the close of time. One class avail themselves of the appointed sacrifice for sin; the other venture to depend upon their own merits; theirs is a sacrifice without the virtue of divine mediation, and thus it is not able to bring man into favor with God. It is only through the merits of Jesus that our transgressions can be pardoned. Those who feel no need of the blood of Christ, who feel that without divine grace they can by their own works secure the approval of God, are making the same mistake as did Cain. If they do not accept the cleansing blood, they are under condemnation. There is no other provision made whereby they can be released from the thralldom of sin.

The class of worshipers who follow the example of Cain includes by far the greater portion of the world; for nearly every false religion has been based on the same principle—that man can depend upon his own efforts for salvation. It is claimed by some that the human race is in need, not of redemption, but of development— that it can refine, elevate, and regenerate itself. As Cain thought to secure the divine favor by an offering that lacked the blood of a sacrifice, so do these expect to exalt humanity to the divine standard, independent of the atonement. The history of Cain shows what must be the result. It shows what man will become apart from Christ. Humanity has no power to regenerate itself. It does not tend upward, toward the divine, but downward, toward the satanic. Christ is our only hope. "There is none other name under heaven given among men, whereby we must be saved." "Neither is there salvation in any other." Acts 4:12.

True faith, which relies wholly upon Christ, will be manifested by obedience to all the requirements of God. From Adam's day to the present time the great controversy has been concerning obedience to God's law. In all ages there have been those who claimed a right to the favor of God even while they were disregarding some of His commands. But the Scriptures declare that by works is "faith made perfect;" and that, without the works of obedience, faith "is dead." James 2:22, 17. He that professes to know God, "and keepeth not His commandments, is a liar, and the truth is not in him." 1 John 2:4.

When Cain saw that his offering was rejected, he was angry with the Lord and with Abel; he was angry that God did not accept man's substitute in place of the sacrifice divinely ordained, and angry with his brother for choosing to obey God instead of joining in rebellion against Him. Notwithstanding Cain's disregard of the divine command, God did not leave him to himself; but He condescended to reason with the man who had shown himself so unreasonable. And the Lord said unto Cain, "Why art thou wroth? and why is thy countenance fallen?" Through an angel messenger the divine warning was conveyed: "If thou doest well, shalt thou not be accepted? And if thou doest not well, sin lieth at the door." The choice lay with Cain himself. If he would trust to the merits of the promised Saviour, and would obey God's requirements, he would enjoy His favor. But should he persist in unbelief and transgression, he would have no ground for complaint because he was rejected by the Lord.

But instead of acknowledging his sin, Cain continued to complain of the injustice of God and to cherish jealousy and hatred of Abel. He angrily reproached his brother, and attempted to draw him into controversy concerning God's dealings with them. In meekness, yet fearlessly and firmly, Abel defended the justice and goodness of God. He pointed out Cain's error, and tried to convince him that the wrong was in himself. He pointed to the compassion of God in sparing the life of their parents when He might have punished them with instant death, and urged that God loved them, or He would not have given His Son, innocent and holy, to suffer the penalty which they had incurred. All this caused Cain's anger to burn the hotter. Reason and conscience told him that Abel was in the right; but he was enraged that one who had been wont to heed his counsel should now presume to disagree with him, and that he could gain no sympathy in his rebellion. In the fury of his passion he slew his brother.

Cain hated and killed his brother, not for any wrong that Abel had done, but "because his own works were evil, and his brother's righteous." 1 John 3:12. So in all ages the wicked have hated those who were better than themselves. Abel's life of obedience and unswerving faith was to Cain a perpetual reproof. "Everyone that doeth evil hateth the light, neither cometh to the light, lest his deeds should be reproved." John 3:20. The brighter the heavenly light that is reflected from the character of God's faithful servants, the more clearly the sins of the ungodly are revealed, and the more determined will be their efforts to destroy those who disturb their peace.

77 The murder of Abel was the first example of the enmity that God had declared would exist between the serpent and the seed of the woman—between Satan and his subjects and Christ and His followers. Through man's sin, Satan had gained control of the human race, but Christ would enable them to cast off his yoke. Whenever, through faith in the Lamb of God, a soul renounces the service of sin, Satan's wrath is kindled. The holy life of Abel testified against Satan's claim that it is impossible for man to keep God's law. When Cain, moved by the spirit of the wicked one, saw that he could not control Abel, he was so enraged that he destroyed his life. And wherever there are any who will stand in vindication of the righteousness of the law of God, the same spirit will be manifested against them. It is the spirit that through all the ages has set up the stake and kindled the burning pile for the disciples of Christ. But the cruelties heaped upon the follower of Jesus are instigated by Satan and his hosts because they cannot force him to submit to their control. It is the rage of a vanquished foe. Every martyr of Jesus has died a conqueror. Says the prophet, "They overcame him ["that old serpent, called the devil, and Satan"] by the blood of the Lamb, and by the word of their testimony; and they loved not their lives unto the death." Revelation 12:11, 9.

Cain the murderer was soon called to answer for his crime. "The Lord said unto Cain, Where is Abel thy brother? And he said, I know not: Am I my brother's keeper?" Cain had gone so far in sin that he had lost a sense of the continual presence of God and of His greatness and omniscience. So he resorted to falsehood to conceal his guilt.

Again the Lord said to Cain, "What hast thou done? The voice of thy brother's blood crieth unto Me from the ground." God had given Cain an opportunity to confess his sin. He had had time to reflect. He knew the enormity of the deed he had done, and of the falsehood he had uttered to conceal it; but he was rebellious still, and sentence was no longer deferred. The divine voice that had been heard in entreaty and admonition pronounced the terrible words: "And now art thou cursed from the earth, which hath opened her mouth to receive thy brother's blood from thy hand. When thou tillest the ground, it shall not henceforth yield unto thee her strength; a fugitive and a vagabond shalt thou be in the earth."

Notwithstanding that Cain had by his crimes 78 merited the sentence of death, a merciful Creator still spared his life, and granted him opportunity for repentance. But Cain lived only to harden his heart, to encourage rebellion against the divine authority, and to become the head of a line of bold, abandoned sinners. This one apostate, led on by Satan, became a tempter to others; and his example and influence exerted their demoralizing power, until the earth became so corrupt and filled with violence as to call for its destruction.

In sparing the life of the first murderer, God presented before the whole universe a lesson bearing upon the great controversy. The dark history of Cain and his descendants was an illustration of what would have been the result of permitting the sinner to live on forever, to carry out his rebellion against God. The forbearance of God only rendered the wicked more bold and defiant in their iniquity. Fifteen centuries after the sentence pronounced upon Cain, the universe witnessed the fruition of his influence and example, in the crime and pollution that flooded the earth. It was made manifest that the sentence of death pronounced upon the fallen race for the transgression of God's law was both just and merciful. The longer men lived in sin, the more abandoned they became. The divine sentence cutting short a career of unbridled iniquity, and freeing the world from the influence of those who had become hardened in rebellion, was a blessing rather than a curse.

Satan is constantly at work, with intense energy and under a thousand disguises, to misrepresent the character and government of God. With extensive, well-organized plans and marvelous power, he is working to hold the inhabitants of the world under his deceptions. God, the One infinite and all-wise, sees the end from the beginning, and in dealing with evil His plans were far-reaching and comprehensive. It was His purpose, not merely to put down the rebellion, but to demonstrate to all the universe the nature of the rebellion. God's plan was unfolding, showing both His justice and His mercy, and fully vindicating His wisdom and righteousness in His dealings with evil.

The holy inhabitants of other worlds were watching with the deepest interest the events taking place on the earth. In the condition of the world that existed before the Flood they saw illustrated the results of the administration which Lucifer had endeavored to establish in heaven, in rejecting the authority of Christ and casting aside the law of God. In those highhanded sinners of the antediluvian world they saw the subjects over whom Satan held sway. The thoughts of men's hearts were only evil continually. Genesis 6:5. Every emotion, every impulse and imagination, was at war with the divine principles of purity and peace and love. It was an example of the awful depravity resulting from Satan's policy to remove from God's creatures the restraint of His holy law.

By the facts unfolded in the progress of the great controversy, God will demonstrate the principles of His rules of government, which have been falsified by Satan and by all whom he has deceived. His justice will finally be acknowledged by the whole world, though the acknowledgment will be made too late to save the rebellious. God carries with Him the sympathy and approval of the whole universe as step by step His great plan advances to its complete fulfillment. He will carry it with Him in the final eradication of rebellion. It will be seen that all who have forsaken the divine precepts have placed themselves on the side of Satan, in warfare against Christ. When the prince of this world shall be judged, and all who have united

with him shall share his fate, the whole universe as witnesses to the sentence will declare, "Just and true are Thy ways, Thou King of saints." Revelation 15:3.

6

Seth and Enoch

To Adam was given another son, to be the inheritor of the divine promise, the heir of the spiritual birthright. The name Seth, given to this son, signified "appointed," or "compensation;" "for," said the mother, "God hath appointed me another seed instead of Abel, whom Cain slew." Seth was of more noble stature than Cain or Abel, and resembled Adam more closely than did his other sons. He was a worthy character, following in the steps of Abel. Yet he inherited no more natural goodness than did Cain. Concerning the creation of Adam it is said, "In the likeness of God made He him;" but man, after the Fall, "begat a son in his *own* likeness, after *his* image." While Adam was created sinless, in the likeness of God, Seth, like Cain, inherited the fallen nature of his parents. But he received also the knowledge of the Redeemer and instruction in righteousness. By divine grace he served and honored God; and he labored, as Abel would have done, had he lived, to turn the minds of sinful men to revere and obey their Creator.

"To Seth, to him also there was born a son; and he called his name Enos: then began men to call upon the name of Jehovah." The faithful had worshiped God before; but as men increased, the distinction between the two classes became more marked. There was an open profession of loyalty to God on the part of one, as there was of contempt and disobedience on the part of the other.

Before the Fall our first parents had kept the Sabbath, which was instituted in Eden; and after their expulsion from Paradise they continued its observance. They had tasted the bitter fruits of disobedience, and had learned what every one that tramples upon God's commandments will sooner or later learn—that the divine precepts are sacred and immutable, and that the penalty of transgression will surely be inflicted. The Sabbath was honored by all the children of Adam that remained loyal to God. But Cain and his descendants did not respect the day upon which God had rested. They chose their own time for labor and for rest, regardless of Jehovah's express command.

Upon receiving the curse of God, Cain had withdrawn from his father's household. He had first chosen his occupation as a tiller of the soil, and he now founded a city, calling it after the name of his eldest son. He had gone out from

This chapter is based on Genesis 4:25 to 6:2.

the presence of the Lord, cast away the promise of the restored Eden, to seek his possessions and enjoyment in the earth under the curse of sin, thus standing at the head of that great class of men who worship the god of this world. In that which pertains to mere earthly and material progress, his descendants became distinguished. But they were regardless of God, and in opposition to His purposes for man. To the crime of murder, in which Cain had led the way, Lamech, the fifth in descent, added polygamy, and, boastfully defiant, he acknowledged God, only to draw from the avenging of Cain an assurance of his own safety. Abel had led a pastoral life, dwelling in tents or booths, and the descendants of Seth followed the same course, counting themselves "strangers and pilgrims on the earth," seeking "a better country, that is, an heavenly." Hebrews 11:13, 16.

For some time the two classes remained separate. The race of Cain, spreading from the place of their first settlement, dispersed over the plains and valleys where the children of Seth had dwelt; and the latter, in order to escape from their contaminating influence, withdrew to the mountains, and there made their home. So long as this separation continued, they maintained the worship of God in its purity. But in the lapse of time they ventured, little by little, to mingle with the inhabitants of the valleys. This association was productive of the worst results. "The sons of God saw the daughters of men that they were fair." The children of Seth, attracted by the beauty of the daughters of Cain's descendants, displeased the Lord by intermarrying with them. Many of the worshipers of God were beguiled into sin by the allurements that were now constantly before them, and they lost their peculiar, holy character. Mingling with the depraved, they became like them in spirit and in deeds; the restrictions of the seventh commandment were disregarded, "and they took them wives of all which they chose." The children of Seth went 82 "in the way of Cain" (Jude 11); they fixed their minds upon worldly prosperity and enjoyment and neglected the commandments of the Lord. Men "did not like to retain God in their knowledge;" they "became vain in their imaginations, and their foolish heart was darkened." Romans 1:21. Therefore "God gave them over to a mind void of judgment." Verse 28, margin. Sin spread abroad in the earth like a deadly leprosy.

For nearly a thousand years Adam lived among men, a witness to the results of sin. Faithfully he sought to stem the tide of evil. He had been commanded to instruct his posterity in the way of the Lord; and he carefully treasured what God had revealed to him, and repeated it to succeeding generations. To his children and children's children, to the ninth generation, he described man's holy and happy estate in Paradise, and repeated the history of his fall, telling

them of the sufferings by which God had taught him the necessity of strict adherence to His law, and explaining to them the merciful provisions for their salvation. Yet there were but few who gave heed to his words. Often he was met with bitter reproaches for the sin that had brought such woe upon his posterity.

Adam's life was one of sorrow, humility, and contrition. When he left Eden, the thought that he must die thrilled him with horror. He was first made acquainted with the reality of death in the human family when Cain, his first-born son, became the murderer of his brother. Filled with the keenest remorse for his own sin, and doubly bereaved in the death of Abel and the rejection of Cain, Adam was bowed down with anguish. He witnessed the wide-spreading corruption that was finally to cause the destruction of the world by a flood; and though the sentence of death pronounced upon him by his Maker had at first appeared terrible, yet after beholding for nearly a thousand years the results of sin, he felt that it was merciful in God to bring to an end a life of suffering and sorrow.

Notwithstanding the wickedness of the antediluvian world, that age was not, as has often been supposed, an era of ignorance and barbarism. The people were granted the opportunity of reaching a high standard of moral and intellectual attainment. They possessed great physical and mental strength, and their advantages for acquiring both religious and scientific knowledge were unrivaled. It is a mistake to suppose that because they lived to a great age 83 their minds matured late; their mental powers were early developed, and those who cherished the fear of God and lived in harmony with His will continued to increase in knowledge and wisdom throughout their life. Could illustrious scholars of our time be placed in contrast with men of the same age who lived before the Flood, they would appear as greatly inferior in mental as in physical strength. As the years of man have decreased, and his physical strength has diminished, so his mental capacities have lessened. There are men who now apply themselves to study during a period of from twenty to fifty years, and the world is filled with admiration of their attainments. But how limited are these acquirements in comparison with those of men whose mental and physical powers were developing for centuries!

It is true that the people of modern times have the benefit of the attainments of their predecessors. The men of masterly minds, who planned and studied and wrote, have left their work for those who follow. But even in this respect, and so far as merely human knowledge is concerned, how much greater the advantages of the men of that olden time! They had among them for hundreds of years him who was formed in God's image, whom the Creator Himself pronounced "good"—the man whom God had instructed in all the wisdom pertaining to the material world. Adam had learned from the Creator the history of creation; he himself witnessed the events of nine centuries; and he imparted his knowledge to his descendants. The antediluvians were without books, they had no written records; but with their great physical and mental vigor, they had strong memories, able to grasp and to retain that which was communicated to them, and in turn to transmit it unimpaired to their posterity. And for hundreds of years there were seven generations living upon the earth contemporaneously, having the opportunity of consulting together and profiting each by the knowledge and experience of all.

The advantages enjoyed by men of that age to gain a knowledge of God through His works have never been equaled since. And so far from being an era of religious darkness, that was an age of great light. All the world had opportunity to receive instruction from Adam, and those who feared the Lord had also Christ and angels for their teachers. And they had a silent witness to the truth, in the garden of God, which for so many centuries remained among men. At the 84 cherubim-guarded gate of Paradise the glory of God was revealed, and hither came the first worshipers. Here their altars were reared, and their offerings presented. It was here that Cain and Abel had brought their sacrifices, and God had condescended to communicate with them.

Skepticism could not deny the existence of Eden while it stood just in sight, its entrance barred by watching angels. The order of creation, the object of the garden, the history of its two trees so closely connected with man's destiny, were undisputed facts. And the existence and supreme authority of God, the obligation of His law, were truths which men were slow to question while Adam was among them.

Notwithstanding the prevailing iniquity, there was a line of holy men who, elevated and ennobled by communion with God, lived as in the companionship of heaven. They were men of massive intellect, of wonderful attainments. They had a great and holy mission—to develop a character of righteousness, to teach a lesson of godliness, not only to the men of their time, but for future generations. Only a few of the most prominent are mentioned in the Scriptures; but all through the ages God had faithful witnesses, truehearted worshipers.

Of Enoch it is written that he lived sixty-five years, and begat a son. After that he walked with God three hundred years. During these earlier years Enoch had loved and feared God and had kept His commandments. He was one of the holy line, the preservers of the true faith, the progenitors of the promised seed. From the lips of Adam he had learned the dark story of the Fall, and the cheering one of God's grace as seen in the promise; and he relied upon the Redeemer to come. But after the birth of his first son, Enoch reached a higher experience; he was drawn into a closer relationship with God. He realized more fully his own obligations and responsibility as a son of God. And as he saw the child's love for its father, its simple trust in his protection; as he felt the deep, yearning tenderness of his own heart for that firstborn son, he learned a precious lesson of the wonderful love of God to men in the gift of His Son, and the confidence which the children of God may repose in their heavenly Father. The infinite, unfathomable love of God through Christ became the subject of his meditations day and night; and with all the fervor of his soul he sought to reveal that love to the people among whom he dwelt.

Enoch's walk with God was not in a trance or 85 a vision, but in all the duties of his daily life. He did not become a hermit, shutting himself entirely from the world; for he had a work to do for God in the world. In the family and in his intercourse with men, as a husband and father, a friend, a citizen, he was the steadfast, unwavering servant of the Lord.

His heart was in harmony with God's will; for "can two walk together, except they be agreed?" Amos 3:3. And this holy walk was continued for three hundred years. There are few Christians who would not be far more earnest and devoted if they knew that they had but a short time to live, or that the coming of Christ was about to take place. But Enoch's faith waxed the stronger, his love became more ardent, with the lapse of centuries.

Enoch was a man of strong and highly cultivated mind and extensive knowledge; he was honored with special revelations from God; yet being in constant communion with Heaven, with a sense of the divine greatness and perfection ever before him, he was one of the humblest of men. The closer the connection with God, the deeper was the sense of his own weakness and imperfection.

Distressed by the increasing wickedness of the ungodly, and fearing that their infidelity might lessen his reverence for God, Enoch avoided constant association with them, and spent much time in solitude, giving himself to meditation and prayer. Thus he waited before the Lord, seeking a clearer knowledge of His will, that he might perform it. To him prayer was as the breath of the soul; he lived in the very atmosphere of heaven.

Through holy angels God revealed to Enoch His purpose to destroy the world by a flood, and He also opened more fully to him the plan of redemption. By the spirit of prophecy He carried him down through the generations that should live after the Flood, and showed him the great events connected with the second coming of Christ and the end of the world.

Enoch had been troubled in regard to the dead. It had seemed to him that the righteous and the wicked would go to the dust together, and that this would be their end. He could not see the life of the just beyond the grave. In prophetic vision he was instructed concerning the death of Christ, and was shown His coming in glory, attended by all the holy angels, to ransom His people from the grave. He also saw the corrupt state of the world when Christ should appear the second time—that there would be a boastful, presumptuous, self-willed generation, denying the only God and the Lord Jesus Christ, trampling upon the law, and despising the atonement. He saw the righteous crowned with glory and honor, and the wicked banished from the presence of the Lord, and destroyed by fire.

Enoch became a preacher of righteousness, making known to the people what God had revealed to him. Those who feared the Lord sought out this holy man, to share his instruction and his prayers. He labored publicly also, bearing God's messages to all who would hear the words of warning. His labors were not restricted to the Sethites. In the land where Cain had sought to flee from the divine Presence, the prophet of God made known the wonderful scenes that had passed before his vision. "Behold," he declared, "the Lord cometh with ten thousands of His saints, to execute judgment upon all, and to convince all that are ungodly among them of all their ungodly deeds." Jude 14, 15.

He was a fearless reprover of sin. While he preached the love of God in Christ to the people of his time, and pleaded with them to forsake their evil ways, he rebuked the prevailing iniquity and warned the men of his generation that judgment would surely be visited upon the transgressor. It was the Spirit of Christ that spoke through Enoch; that Spirit is manifested, not alone in utterances of love, compassion, and entreaty; it is not smooth things only that are spoken by holy men. God puts into the heart and lips of His messengers truths to utter that are keen and cutting as a two-edged sword.

The power of God that wrought with His servant was felt by those who heard. Some gave heed to the warning, and renounced their sins; but the multitudes mocked at the solemn message, and went on more boldly in their evil ways. The servants of God are to bear a similar message to the world in the last days, and it will also be received with unbelief and mockery. The antediluvian world rejected the warning words of him who walked with God. So will the last generation make light of the warnings of the Lord's messengers.

In the midst of a life of active labor, Enoch steadfastly maintained his communion with God. The greater and more pressing his labors, the more constant and earnest were his prayers. He continued to exclude himself, at certain periods, from all society. After remaining for a time among the people, laboring to benefit them by instruction and example, he would withdraw, to spend a season in solitude, hungering and thirsting for that divine knowledge which God alone can impart. Communing thus with God, Enoch came more and more to reflect the divine image. His face was radiant with a holy light, even the light that shineth in the face of Jesus. As he came forth from these divine communings, even the ungodly beheld with awe the impress of heaven upon his countenance.

The wickedness of men had reached such a height that destruction was pronounced against them. As year after year passed on, deeper and deeper grew the tide of human guilt, darker and darker gathered the clouds of divine judgment. Yet Enoch, the witness of faith, held on his way, warning, pleading, entreating, striving to turn back the tide of guilt and to stay the bolts of vengeance. Though his warnings were disregarded by a sinful, pleasure-loving people, he had the testimony that God approved, and he continued to battle faithfully against the prevailing evil, until God removed him from a world of sin to the pure joys of heaven.

The men of that generation had mocked the folly of him who sought not to gather gold or silver or to build up possessions here. But Enoch's heart was upon eternal treasures. He had looked upon the celestial city. He had seen the King in His glory in the midst of Zion. His mind, his heart, his conversation, were in heaven. The greater the existing iniquity, the more earnest was his longing for the home of God. While still on earth, he dwelt, by faith, in the realms of light.

"Blessed are the pure in heart: for they shall see God." Matthew 5:8. For three hundred years Enoch had been seeking purity of soul, that he might be in harmony with Heaven. For three centuries he had walked with God. Day by day he had longed for a closer union; nearer and nearer had grown the communion, until God took him to Himself. He had stood at the threshold of the eternal world, only a step between him and the land of the blest; and now the portals opened, the walk with God, so long pursued on earth, continued, and he passed through the gates of the Holy City—the first from among men to enter there.

His loss was felt on earth. The voice that had been heard day after day in warning and instruction was missed. There were some, both of the righteous and the wicked, who had witnessed his departure; and hoping that he might have been conveyed to some one of his places of retirement, those who loved him made diligent search, as afterward the sons of the prophets searched for Elijah; but without avail. They reported that he was not, for God had taken him.

By the translation of Enoch the Lord designed to teach an important lesson. There was danger that men would yield to discouragement, because of the fearful results of Adam's sin. Many were ready to exclaim, "What profit is it that we have feared the Lord and have kept His ordinances, since a heavy curse is resting upon the race, and death is the portion of us all?" But the instructions which God gave to Adam, and which were repeated by Seth, and exemplified by Enoch, swept away the gloom and darkness, and gave hope to man, that as through Adam came death, so through the promised Redeemer would come life and immortality. Satan was urging upon men the belief that there was no reward for the righteous or punishment for the wicked, and that it was impossible for men to obey the divine statutes. But in the case of Enoch, God declares "that He is, and that He is a rewarder of them that diligently seek Him." Hebrews 11:6. He shows what He will do for those who keep His commandments. Men were taught that it is possible to obey the law of God; that even while living in the midst of the sinful and corrupt, they were able, by the grace of God, to resist temptation, and become pure and holy. They saw in his example the blessedness of such a life; and his translation was an evidence of the truth of his prophecy concerning the hereafter, with its award of joy and glory and immortal life to the obedient, and of condemnation, woe, and death to the transgressor.

By faith Enoch "was translated that he should not see death; . . . for before his translation he had this testimony, that he pleased God." Hebrews 11:5. In the midst of a world by its iniquity doomed to destruction, Enoch lived a life of such close communion with God that he was not permitted to fall under the power of death. The godly character of this prophet represents the state of holiness which must be attained by those who shall be "redeemed from the earth" (Revelation 14:3) at the time of Christ's second advent. Then, as in the world before the Flood, iniquity will prevail. Following the promptings of their corrupt hearts and the teachings of a deceptive philosophy, men will rebel against the authority of Heaven. But like Enoch, God's people will seek for purity of heart and conformity to His will, until they shall reflect the likeness of Christ. Like Enoch, they will warn the world of the Lord's second coming and of the judgments to be visited upon transgression, and by their holy conversation and example they will condemn the sins of the ungodly. As Enoch was translated to heaven before the destruction of the world by water, so the living righteous will be translated from the earth before its destruction by fire. Says the apostle: "We shall not all sleep, but we shall all be changed, in a moment, in the twinkling of an

eye, at the last trump." "For the Lord Himself shall descend from heaven with a shout, with the voice of the Archangel, and with the trump of God;" "the trumpet shall sound, and the dead shall be raised incorruptible, and we shall be changed." "The dead in Christ shall rise first: then we which are alive and remain shall be caught up together with them in the clouds, to meet the Lord in the air: and so shall we ever be with the Lord. Wherefore comfort one another with these words." 1 Corinthians 15:51, 52; 1 Thessalonians 4:16-18.

7
The Flood

In the days of Noah a double curse was resting upon the earth in consequence of Adam's transgression and of the murder committed by Cain. Yet this had not greatly changed the face of nature. There were evident tokens of decay, but the earth was still rich and beautiful in the gifts of God's providence. The hills were crowned with majestic trees supporting the fruitladen branches of the vine. The vast, gardenlike plains were clothed with verdure, and sweet with the fragrance of a thousand flowers. The fruits of the earth were in great variety, and almost without limit. The trees far surpassed in size, beauty, and perfect proportion any now to be found; their wood was of fine grain and hard substance, closely resembling stone, and hardly less enduring. Gold, silver, and precious stones existed in abundance.

The human race yet retained much of its early vigor. But a few generations had passed since Adam had access to the tree which was to prolong life; and man's existence was still measured by centuries. Had that long-lived people, with their rare powers to plan and execute, devoted themselves to the service of God, they would have made their Creator's name a praise in the earth, and would have answered the purpose for which He gave them life. But they failed to do this. There were many giants, men of great stature and strength, renowned for wisdom, skillful in devising the most cunning and wonderful works; but their guilt in giving loose rein to iniquity was in proportion to their skill and mental ability.

God bestowed upon these antediluvians many and rich gifts; but they used His bounties to glorify themselves, and turned them into a curse by fixing their affections upon the gifts instead of the Giver. They employed the gold and silver, the precious stones and the choice wood, in the construction of habitations for themselves, and endeavored to excel one another in beautifying their dwellings with the most skillful workman-

91 ship. They sought only to gratify the desires of their own proud hearts, and reveled in scenes of pleasure and wickedness. Not desiring to retain God in their knowledge, they soon came to deny His existence. They adored nature in place of the God of nature. They glorified human genius, worshiped the works of their own hands, and taught their children to bow down to graven images.

In the green fields and under the shadow of the goodly trees they set up the altars of their idols. Extensive groves, that retained their foliage throughout the year, were dedicated to the worship of false gods. With these groves were connected beautiful gardens, their long, winding avenues overhung with fruit-bearing trees of all descriptions, adorned with statuary, and furnished with all that could delight the senses or minister to the voluptuous desires of the people, and thus allure them to participate in the idolatrous worship.

Men put God out of their knowledge and worshiped the creatures of their own imagination; and as the result, they became more and more debased. The psalmist describes the effect produced upon the worshiper by the adoration of idols. He says, "They that make them are like unto them; so is every one that trusteth in them." Psalm 115:8. It is a law of the human mind that by beholding we become changed. Man will rise no higher than his conceptions of truth, purity, and holiness. If the mind is never exalted above the level of humanity, if it is not uplifted by faith to contemplate infinite wisdom and love, the man will be constantly sinking lower and lower. The worshipers of false gods clothed their deities with human attributes and passions, and thus their standard of character was degraded to the likeness of sinful humanity. They were defiled in consequence. "God saw that the wickedness of man was great in the earth, and that every imagination of the thoughts of his heart was only evil continually. . . . The earth also was corrupt before God; and the earth was filled with violence." God had given men His commandments as a rule of life, but His law was transgressed, and every conceivable sin was the result. The wickedness of men was open and daring, justice was trampled in the dust, and the cries of the oppressed reached unto heaven.

Polygamy had been early introduced, contrary to the divine arrangement at the beginning. 92 The Lord gave to Adam one wife, showing His order in that respect. But after the Fall, men chose to follow their own sinful desires; and as the result, crime and wretchedness rapidly increased. Neither the marriage relation nor the rights of property were respected. Whoever coveted the wives or the possessions of his neighbor, took them by force, and men exulted in their deeds of violence. They delighted in destroying the life of animals; and the use of flesh for food rendered them still more cruel and bloodthirsty, until they came to regard human life with astonishing indifference.

The world was in its infancy; yet iniquity had become so deep and widespread that God could no longer bear with it; and He said, "I will destroy man whom I have created from the face of the earth." He declared that His Spirit should not always strive with the guilty race. If they did not cease to pollute with their sins the world and its rich treasures, He would blot them from His creation, and would destroy the things with which He had delighted to bless them; He would sweep away the beasts of the field, and the vegetation which furnished such an abundant supply of food, and would transform the fair earth into one vast scene of desolation and ruin.

Amid the prevailing corruption, Methuselah, Noah, and many others labored to keep alive the knowledge of the true God and to stay the tide of moral evil. A hundred and twenty years before the Flood, the Lord by a holy angel declared to Noah His purpose, and directed him to build an ark. While building the ark he was to preach that God would bring a flood of water upon the earth to destroy the wicked. Those who would believe the message, and would prepare for that event by repentance and reformation, should find pardon and be saved. Enoch had repeated to his children what God had shown him in regard to the Flood, and Methuselah and his sons, who lived to hear the preaching of Noah, assisted in building the ark.

God gave Noah the exact dimensions of the ark and explicit directions in regard to its construction in every particular. Human wisdom could not have devised a structure of so great strength and durability. God was the designer, and Noah the master builder. It was constructed like the hull of a ship, that it might float upon the water, but in some respects it more nearly resembled a house. It was three stories high, with but one door, which was in the side. The 95 light was admitted at the top, and the different apartments were so arranged that all were lighted. The material employed in the construction of the ark was the cypress, or gopher wood, which would be untouched by decay for hundreds of years. The building of this immense structure was a slow and laborious process. On account of the great size of the trees and the nature of the wood, much more labor was required then than now to prepare timber, even with the greater strength which men then possessed. All that man could do was done to render the work perfect, yet the ark could not of itself have withstood the storm which was to come upon the earth. God alone could preserve His servants upon the tempestuous waters.

"By faith Noah, being warned of God of things not seen as yet, moved with fear, prepared an ark to the saving of his house; by the which he condemned the world, and became heir of the righteousness which is by faith." Hebrews 11:7. While Noah was giving his warning message to the world, his works testified of his sincerity. It was thus that his faith was perfected and made evident. He gave the world an example of believing just what God says. All that he possessed, he invested in the ark. As he began to construct that immense boat on dry ground, multitudes came from every direction to see the strange sight and to hear the earnest, fervent words of the singular preacher. Every blow struck upon the ark was a witness to the people.

Many at first appeared to receive the warning; yet they did not turn to God with true repentance. They were unwilling to renounce their sins. During the time that elapsed before the coming of the Flood, their faith was tested, and they failed to endure the trial. Overcome by the prevailing unbelief, they finally joined their former associates in rejecting the solemn message. Some were deeply convicted, and would have heeded the words of warning; but there were so many to jest and ridicule, that they partook of the same spirit, resisted the invitations of mercy, and were soon among the boldest and most defiant scoffers; for none are so reckless and go to such lengths in sin as do those who have once had light, but have resisted the convicting Spirit of God.

The men of that generation were not all, in the fullest acceptation of the term, idolaters. 96 Many professed to be worshipers of God. They claimed that their idols were representations of the Deity, and that through them the people could obtain a clearer conception of the divine Being. This class were foremost in rejecting the preaching of Noah. As they endeavored to represent God by material objects, their minds were blinded to His majesty and power; they ceased to realize the holiness of His character, or the sacred, unchanging nature of His requirements. As sin became general, it appeared less and less sinful, and they finally declared that the divine law was no longer in force; that it was contrary to the character of God to punish transgression; and they denied that His judgments were to be visited upon the earth. Had the men of that generation obeyed the divine law, they would have recognized the voice of God in the warning of His servant; but their minds had become so blinded by rejection of light that they really believed Noah's message to be a delusion.

It was not multitudes or majorities that were on the side of right. The world was arrayed against God's justice and His laws, and Noah was regarded as a fanatic. Satan, when tempting Eve to disobey God, said to her, "Ye shall not surely die." Genesis 3:4. Great men, worldly, honored, and wise men, repeated the same. "The threatenings of God," they said, "are for the purpose of intimidating, and will never be verified. You need not be alarmed. Such an event as the destruction of the world by the God who made it, and the punishment of the beings He has created, will never take place. Be at peace; fear not. Noah is a wild fanatic." The world made merry at the folly of the deluded old man. Instead of humbling the heart before God, they continued their disobedience and wickedness, the same as though God had not spoken to them through His servant.

But Noah stood like a rock amid the tempest. Surrounded by popular contempt and ridicule, he distinguished himself by his holy integrity and unwavering faithfulness. A power attended his words, for it was the voice of God to man through His servant. Connection with God made him strong in the strength of infinite power, while for one hundred and twenty years his solemn voice fell upon the ears of that generation in regard to events, which, so far as human wisdom could judge, were impossible.

The world before the Flood reasoned that for centuries the laws of nature had been fixed. The recurring seasons had come in their order. Heretofore rain had never fallen; the earth had been watered by a mist or dew. The rivers had 97 never yet passed their boundaries, but had borne their waters safely to the sea. Fixed decrees had kept the waters from overflowing their banks. But these reasoners did not recognize the hand of Him who had stayed the waters, saying, "Hitherto shalt thou come, but no further." Job 38:11.

As time passed on, with no apparent change in nature, men whose hearts had at times trembled with fear, began to be reassured. They reasoned, as many reason now, that nature is above the God of nature, and that her laws are so firmly established that God Himself could not change them. Reasoning that if the message of Noah were correct, nature would be turned out of her course, they made that message, in the minds of the world, a delusion—a grand deception. They manifested their contempt for the warning of God by doing just as they had done before the warning was given. They continued their festivities and their gluttonous feasts; they ate and drank, planted and builded, laying their plans in reference to advantages they hoped to gain in the future; and they went to greater lengths in wickedness, and in defiant disregard of God's requirements, to testify that they had no fear of the Infinite One. They asserted that if there were any truth in what Noah had said, the men of renown—the wise, the prudent, the great men—would understand the matter.

Had the antediluvians believed the warning, and repented of their evil deeds, the Lord would have turned aside His wrath, as He afterward did from Nineveh. But by their obstinate resistance to the reproofs of conscience and the warnings of God's prophet, that generation filled up the measure of their iniquity, and became ripe for destruction.

The period of their probation was about to expire. Noah had faithfully followed the instructions which he had received from God. The ark was finished in every part as the Lord had directed, and was stored with food for man and beast. And now the servant of God made his last solemn appeal to the people. With an agony of desire that words cannot express, he entreated them to seek a refuge while it might be found. Again they rejected his words, and raised their voices in jest and scoffing. Suddenly a silence fell upon the mocking throng. Beasts of every description, the fiercest as well as the most gentle, were seen coming from mountain and forest and quietly making their way toward the ark. A noise as of a rushing wind was heard, and lo,
98 birds were flocking from all directions, their numbers darkening the heavens, and in perfect order they passed to the ark. Animals obeyed the command of God, while men were disobedient. Guided by holy angels, they "went in two and two unto Noah into the ark," and the clean beasts by sevens. The world looked on in wonder, some in fear. Philosophers were called upon to account for the singular occurrence, but in vain. It was a mystery which they could not fathom. But men had become so hardened by their persistent rejection of light that even this scene produced but a momentary impression. As the doomed race beheld the sun shining in its glory, and the earth clad in almost Eden beauty, they banished their rising fears by boisterous merriment, and by their deeds of violence they seemed to invite upon themselves the visitation of the already awakened wrath of God.

God commanded Noah, "Come thou and all thy house into the ark; for thee have I seen righteous before Me in this generation." Noah's warnings had been rejected by the world, but his influence and example resulted in blessings to his family. As a reward for his faithfulness and integrity, God saved all the members of his family with him. What encouragement to parental fidelity!

Mercy had ceased its pleadings for the guilty race. The beasts of the field and the birds of the air had entered the place of refuge. Noah and his household were within the ark, "and the Lord shut him in." A flash of dazzling light was seen, and a cloud of glory more vivid than the lightning descended from heaven and hovered before the entrance of the ark. The massive door, which it was impossible for those within to close, was slowly swung to its place by unseen hands. Noah was shut in, and the rejecters of God's mercy were shut out. The seal of Heaven was on that door; God had shut it, and God alone could open it. So when Christ shall cease His intercession for guilty men,

before His coming in the clouds of heaven, the door of mercy will be shut. Then divine grace will no longer restrain the wicked, and Satan will have full control of those who have rejected mercy. They will endeavor to destroy God's people; but as Noah was shut into the ark, so the righteous will be shielded by divine power.

For seven days after Noah and his family entered the ark, there appeared no sign of the coming storm. During this period their faith was tested. It was a time of triumph to the world without. The apparent delay confirmed them in the belief that Noah's message was a 99 delusion, and that the Flood would never come. Notwithstanding the solemn scenes which they had witnessed—the beasts and birds entering the ark, and the angel of God closing the door—they still continued their sport and revelry, even making a jest of these signal manifestations of God's power. They gathered in crowds about the ark, deriding its inmates with a daring violence which they had never ventured upon before.

But upon the eighth day dark clouds overspread the heavens. There followed the muttering of thunder and the flash of lightning. Soon large drops of rain began to fall. The world had never witnessed anything like this, and the hearts of men were struck with fear. All were secretly inquiring, "Can it be that Noah was in the right, and that the world is doomed to destruction?" Darker and darker grew the heavens, and faster came the falling rain. The beasts were roaming about in the wildest terror, and their discordant cries seemed to moan out their own destiny and the fate of man. Then "the fountains of the great deep" were "broken up, and the windows of heaven were opened." Water appeared to come from the clouds in mighty cataracts. Rivers broke away from their boundaries, and overflowed the valleys. Jets of water burst from the earth with indescribable force, throwing massive rocks hundreds of feet into the air, and these, in falling, buried themselves deep in the ground.

The people first beheld the destruction of the works of their own hands. Their splendid buildings, and the beautiful gardens and groves where they had placed their idols, were destroyed by lightning from heaven, and the ruins were scattered far and wide. The altars on which human sacrifices had been offered were torn down, and the worshipers were made to tremble at the power of the living God, and to know that it was their corruption and idolatry which had called down their destruction.

As the violence of the storm increased, trees, buildings, rocks, and earth were hurled in every direction. The terror of man and beast was beyond description. Above the roar of the tempest was heard the wailing of a people that had despised the authority of God. Satan himself, who was compelled to remain in the midst of the warring elements, feared for his own existence. He had delighted to control so powerful a race, and desired them to live to practice their abominations and continue their rebellion against the Ruler of heaven. He now uttered imprecations against God, charging Him with injustice and cruelty. Many of the people, like Satan, blasphemed God, and had they been able, they would have torn Him from the throne of power. Others were frantic with fear, stretching their hands toward the ark and pleading for admittance. But their entreaties were in vain. Conscience was at last aroused to know that there is a God who ruleth in the heavens. They called upon Him earnestly, but His ear was not open to their cry. In that terrible hour they saw that the transgression of God's law had caused their ruin. Yet while, through fear of punishment, they acknowledged their sin, they felt no true contrition, no abhorrence of evil. They would have returned to their defiance of Heaven, had the judgment been removed. So when God's judgments shall fall upon the earth before its deluge by fire, the impenitent will know just where and what their sin is—the despising of His holy law. Yet they will have no more true repentance than did the old-world sinners.

Some in their desperation endeavored to break into the ark, but the firm-made structure withstood their efforts. Some clung to the ark until they were borne away by the surging waters, or their hold was broken by collision with rocks and trees. The massive ark trembled in every fiber as it was beaten by the merciless winds and flung from billow to billow. The cries of the beasts within expressed their fear and pain. But amid the warring elements it continued to ride safely. Angels that excel in strength were commissioned to preserve it.

The beasts, exposed to the tempest, rushed toward man, as though expecting help from him. Some of the people bound their children and themselves upon powerful animals, knowing that these were tenacious of life, and would climb to the highest points to escape the rising waters. Some fastened themselves to lofty trees on the summit of hills or mountains; but the trees were uprooted, and with their burden of living beings were hurled into the seething billows. One spot after another that promised safety was abandoned. As the waters rose higher and higher, the people fled for refuge to the loftiest mountains. Often man and beast would struggle together for a foothold, until both were swept away.

From the highest peaks men looked abroad upon a shoreless ocean. The solemn warnings of God's servant no longer seemed a subject for ridicule and scorning. How those doomed sinners longed for the opportunities which they had slighted! How they pleaded for one hour's probation, one more privilege of mercy, one call from the lips of Noah! But the sweet voice of mercy was no more to be heard by them. Love, no less than justice, demanded that God's judgments should put a check on sin. The avenging waters swept over the last retreat, and the despisers of God perished in the black depths.

"By the word of God . . . the world that then was, being overflowed with water, perished: but the heavens and the earth, which are now, by the same word are kept in store, reserved unto fire against the day of judgment and perdition of ungodly men." 2 Peter 3:5-7. Another storm is coming. The earth will again be swept by the desolating wrath of God, and sin and sinners will be destroyed.

The sins that called for vengeance upon the antediluvian world exist today. The fear of God is banished from the hearts of men, and His law is treated with indifference and contempt. The intense worldliness of that generation is equaled by that of the generation now living. Said Christ, "As in the days that were before the Flood they were eating and drinking, marrying and giving in marriage, until the day that Noah entered into the ark, and knew not until the Flood came, and took them all away; so shall also the coming of the Son of man be." Matthew 24:38, 39. God did not condemn the antediluvians for eating and drinking; He had given them the fruits of the earth in great abundance to supply their physical wants. Their sin consisted in taking these gifts without gratitude to the Giver, and debasing themselves by indulging appetite without restraint. It was lawful for them to marry. Marriage was in God's order; it was one of the first institutions which He established. He gave special directions concerning this ordinance, clothing it with sanctity and beauty; but these directions were forgotten, and marriage was perverted and made to minister to passion.

A similar condition of things exists now. That which is lawful in itself is carried to excess. Appetite is indulged without restraint. Professed followers of Christ are today eating and drinking with the drunken, while their names stand in honored church records. Intemperance benumbs the moral and spiritual powers and prepares the way for indulgence of the lower passions. Multitudes feel under no moral obligation to curb their sensual desires, and they become the slaves of lust. Men are living for the pleasures of sense; for this world and this life alone. Extravagance pervades all circles of society. Integrity is sacrificed for luxury and display. They that make haste to be rich pervert justice and oppress the poor, and "slaves and souls of men" are still bought and sold. Fraud and bribery and theft stalk unrebuked in high places and in low. The issues of the press teem with records of murder—crimes so cold-blooded and causeless that it seems as though every instinct of humanity were blotted out. And these atrocities have become of so common occurrence that they hardly elicit a comment or awaken surprise. The spirit of anarchy is permeating all nations, and the outbreaks that from time to time excite the horror of the world are but indications of the pent-up fires of passion and lawlessness that, having once escaped control, will fill the earth with woe and desolation. The picture which Inspiration has given of the antediluvian world represents too truly the condition to which modern society is fast hastening. Even now, in the present century, and in professedly Christian lands, there are crimes daily perpetrated as black and terrible as those for which the old-world sinners were destroyed.

Before the Flood God sent Noah to warn the world, that the people might be led to repentance, and thus escape the threatened destruction. As the time of Christ's second appearing draws near, the Lord sends His servants with a warning to the world to prepare for that great event. Multitudes have been living in transgression of God's law, and now He in mercy calls them to obey its sacred precepts. All who will put away their sins by repentance toward God and faith in Christ are offered pardon. But many feel that it requires too great a sacrifice to put away sin. Because their life does not harmonize with the pure principles of God's moral government, they reject His warnings and deny the authority of His law.

Of the vast population of the earth before the Flood, only eight souls believed and obeyed God's word through Noah. For a hundred and twenty years the preacher of righteousness warned the world of the coming destruction, but his message was rejected and despised. So it will be now. Before the Lawgiver shall come to punish the disobedient, transgressors are warned to repent, and return to their allegiance; but with the majority these warnings will be in vain. Says the apostle Peter, "There shall come in the last days scoffers, walking after their own lusts, and saying, Where is the promise of His coming? for since the fathers fell asleep, all things continue as they were from the beginning." 2 Peter 3:3, 4. Do we not hear these very words repeated, not merely by the openly ungodly, but by many who occupy the pulpits of our land? "There is no cause for alarm," they cry. "Before Christ shall come, all the world is to be converted, and righteousness is to reign for a thousand years. Peace, peace! all things continue as they were from the beginning. Let none be disturbed by the exciting message of these alarmists." But this doctrine of the millennium does not harmonize with the teachings of Christ and His apostles. Jesus asked the significant question, "When the Son of man cometh, shall He find faith on the earth?" Luke 18:8. And, as we have seen, He declares that the state of the world will be as in the days of Noah. Paul warns us that we may look for wickedness

to increase as the end draws near: "The Spirit speaketh expressly, that in the latter times some shall depart from the faith, giving heed to seducing spirits, and doctrines of devils." 1 Timothy 4:1. The apostle says that "in the last days perilous times shall come." 2 Timothy 3:1. And he gives a startling list of sins that will be found among those who have a form of godliness.

As the time of their probation was closing, the antediluvians gave themselves up to exciting amusements and festivities. Those who possessed influence and power were bent on keeping the minds of the people engrossed with mirth and pleasure, lest any should be impressed by the last solemn warning. Do we not see the same repeated in our day? While God's servants are giving the message that the end of all things is at hand, the world is absorbed in amusements and pleasure seeking. There is a constant round of excitement that causes indifference to God and prevents the people from being impressed by the truths which alone can save them from the coming destruction.

In Noah's day philosophers declared that it was impossible for the world to be destroyed by water; so now there are men of science who endeavor to show that the world cannot be destroyed by fire—that this would be inconsistent with the laws of nature. But the God of nature, the Maker and Controller of her laws, can use the works of His hands to serve His own purpose.

When great and wise men had proved to their satisfaction that it was impossible for the world to be destroyed by water, when the fears of the people were quieted, when all regarded Noah's prophecy as a delusion, and looked upon him as a fanatic—then it was that God's time had come. "The fountains of the great deep" were "broken up, and the windows of heaven were opened," and the scoffers were overwhelmed in the waters of the Flood. With all their boasted philosophy, men found too late that their wisdom was foolishness, that the Lawgiver is greater than the laws of nature, and that Omnipotence is at no loss for means to accomplish His purposes. "As it was in the days of Noah," "even thus shall it be in the days when the Son of man is revealed." Luke 17:26, 30. "The day of the Lord will come as a thief in the night; in the which the heavens shall pass away with a great noise, and the elements shall melt with fervent heat, the earth also and the works that are therein shall be burned up." 2 Peter 3:10. When the reasoning of philosophy has banished the fear of God's judgments; when religious teachers are pointing forward to long ages of peace and prosperity, and the world are absorbed in their rounds of business and pleasure, planting and building, feasting and merrymaking, rejecting God's warnings and mocking His messengers—then it is that sudden destruction cometh upon them, and they shall not escape. 1 Thessalonians 5:3.

105

8

After the Flood

The waters rose fifteen cubits above the highest mountains. It often seemed to the family within the ark that they must perish, as for five long months their boat was tossed about, apparently at the mercy of wind and wave. It was a trying ordeal; but Noah's faith did not waver, for he had the assurance that the divine hand was upon the helm.

As the waters began to subside, the Lord caused the ark to drift into a spot protected by a group of mountains that had been preserved by His power. These mountains were but a little distance apart, and the ark moved about in this quiet haven, and was no longer driven upon the boundless ocean. This gave great relief to the weary, tempest-tossed voyagers.

Noah and his family anxiously waited for the decrease of the waters, for they longed to go forth again upon the earth. Forty days after the tops of the mountains became visible, they sent out a raven, a bird of quick scent, to discover whether the earth had become dry. This bird, finding nothing but water, continued to fly to and from the ark. Seven days later a dove was sent forth, which, finding no footing, returned to the ark. Noah waited seven days longer, and again sent forth the dove. When she returned at evening with an olive leaf in her mouth, there was great rejoicing. Later "Noah removed the covering of the ark, and looked, and, behold, the face of the ground was dry." Still he waited patiently within the ark. As he had entered at God's command, he waited for special directions to depart.

At last an angel descended from heaven, opened the massive door, and bade the patriarch and his household go forth upon the earth and take with them every living thing. In the joy of their release Noah did not forget Him by whose gracious care they had been preserved. His first

106 act after leaving the ark was to build an altar and offer from every kind of clean beast and fowl a sacrifice, thus manifesting his gratitude to God for deliverance and his faith in Christ, the great sacrifice. This offering was pleasing to the Lord; and a blessing resulted, not only to the patriarch and his family, but to all who should live upon the earth. "The Lord smelled a sweet savor; and the Lord said in His heart, I will not again curse the ground any more for man's sake. . . . While the earth remaineth, seedtime and harvest, and cold and heat, and summer and winter, and day and night shall not cease." Here was a lesson for all succeeding generations. Noah had come forth upon a desolate earth, but

This chapter is based on Genesis 7:20 to 9:17.

before preparing a house for himself he built an altar to God. His stock of cattle was small, and had been preserved at great expense; yet he cheerfully gave a part to the Lord as an acknowledgment that all was His. In like manner it should be our first care to render our freewill offerings to God. Every manifestation of His mercy and love toward us should be gratefully acknowledged, both by acts of devotion and by gifts to His cause.

Lest the gathering clouds and falling rain should fill men with constant terror, from fear of another flood, the Lord encouraged the family of Noah by a promise: "I will establish My covenant with you; . . . neither shall there any more be a flood to destroy the earth. . . . I do set My bow in the cloud, and it shall be for a token of a covenant between Me and the earth. And it shall come to pass, when I bring a cloud over the earth, that the bow shall be seen in the cloud. . . . And I will look upon it, that I may remember the everlasting covenant between God and every living creature."

How great the condescension of God and His compassion for His erring creatures in thus placing the beautiful rainbow in the clouds as a token of His covenant with men! The Lord declares that when He looks upon the bow, He will remember His covenant. This does not imply that He would ever forget; but He speaks to us in our own language, that we may better understand Him. It was God's purpose that as the children of after generations should ask the meaning of the glorious arch which spans the heavens, their parents should repeat the story of the Flood, and tell them that the Most High had bended the bow and placed it in the clouds as an assurance that the waters should never again overflow the earth. Thus from generation to generation it would testify of divine love to man 107 and would strengthen his confidence in God.

In heaven the semblance of a rainbow encircles the throne and overarches the head of Christ. The prophet says, "As the appearance of the bow that is in the cloud in the day of rain, so was the appearance of the brightness round about [the throne]. This was the appearance of the likeness of the glory of Jehovah." Ezekiel 1:28. The revelator declares, "Behold, a throne was set in heaven, and one sat on the throne. . . . There was a rainbow round about the throne, in sight like unto an emerald." Revelation 4:2, 3. When man by his great wickedness invites the divine judgments, the Saviour, interceding with the Father in his behalf, points to the bow in the clouds, to the rainbow around the throne and above His own head, as a token of the mercy of God toward the repentant sinner.

With the assurance given to Noah concerning the Flood, God Himself has linked one of the most precious promises of His grace: "As I have sworn that the waters of Noah should no more go over the earth; so have I sworn that I would not be wroth with thee, nor rebuke thee. For the mountains shall depart, and the hills be removed; but My kindness shall not depart from thee, neither shall the covenant of My peace be removed, saith Jehovah that hath mercy on thee." Isaiah 54:9, 10.

As Noah looked upon the powerful beasts of prey that came forth with him from the ark, he feared that his family, numbering only eight persons, would be destroyed by them. But the Lord sent an angel to His servant with the assuring message: "The fear of you and the dread of you shall be upon every beast of the earth, and upon every fowl of the air, upon all that moveth upon the earth, and upon all the fishes of the sea; into your hand are they delivered. Every moving thing that liveth shall be meat for you; even as the green herb have I given you all things." Before this time God had given man no permission to eat animal food; He intended that the race should subsist wholly upon the productions of the earth; but now that every green thing had been destroyed. He allowed them to eat the flesh of the clean beasts that had been preserved in the ark.

The entire surface of the earth was changed at the Flood. A third dreadful curse rested upon it in consequence of sin. As the water began to subside, the hills and mountains were surround108 ed by a vast, turbid sea. Everywhere were strewn the dead bodies of men and beasts. The Lord would not permit these to remain to decompose and pollute the air, therefore He made of the earth a vast burial ground. A violent wind which was caused to blow for the purpose of drying up the waters, moved them with great force, in some instances even carrying away the tops of the mountains and heaping up trees, rocks, and earth above the bodies of the dead. By the same means the silver and gold, the choice wood and precious stones, which had enriched and adorned the world before the Flood, and which the inhabitants had idolized, were concealed from the sight and search of men, the violent action of the waters piling earth and rocks upon these treasures, and in some cases even forming mountains above them. God saw that the more He enriched and prospered sinful men, the more they would corrupt their ways before Him. The treasures that should have led them to glorify the bountiful Giver had been worshiped, while God had been dishonored and despised.

The earth presented an appearance of confusion and desolation impossible to describe. The mountains, once so beautiful in their perfect symmetry, had become broken and irregular. Stones, ledges, and ragged rocks were now scattered upon the surface of the earth. In many places hills and mountains had disappeared, leaving no trace where they once stood; and

plains had given place to mountain ranges. These changes were more marked in some places than in others. Where once had been earth's richest treasures of gold, silver, and precious stones, were seen the heaviest marks of the curse. And upon countries that were not inhabited, and those where there had been the least crime, the curse rested more lightly.

At this time immense forests were buried. These have since been changed to coal, forming the extensive coal beds that now exist, and also yielding large quantities of oil. The coal and oil frequently ignite and burn beneath the surface of the earth. Thus rocks are heated, limestone is burned, and iron ore melted. The action of the water upon the lime adds fury to the intense heat, and causes earthquakes, volcanoes, and fiery issues. As the fire and water come in contact with ledges of rock and ore, there are heavy explosions underground, which sound like muffled thunder. The air is hot and suffocating. Volcanic eruptions follow; and these often failing to give sufficient vent to the heated elements, the earth itself is convulsed, the ground heaves and swells like the waves of the sea, great fissures appear, and sometimes cities, villages, and burning mountains are swallowed up. These wonderful manifestations will be more and more frequent and terrible just before the second coming of Christ and the end of the world, as signs of its speedy destruction. 109

The depths of the earth are the Lord's arsenal, whence were drawn weapons to be employed in the destruction of the old world. Waters gushing from the earth united with the waters from heaven to accomplish the work of desolation. Since the Flood, fire as well as water has been God's agent to destroy very wicked cities. These judgments are sent that those who lightly regard God's law and trample upon His authority may be led to tremble before His power and to confess His just sovereignty. As men have beheld burning mountains pouring forth fire and flames and torrents of melted ore, drying up rivers, overwhelming populous cities, and everywhere spreading ruin and desolation, the stoutest heart has been filled with terror and infidels and blasphemers have been constrained to acknowledge the infinite power of God.

Said the prophets of old, referring to scenes like these: "Oh that Thou wouldest rend the heavens, that Thou wouldest come down, that the mountains might flow down at Thy presence, as when the melting fire burneth, the fire causeth the waters to boil, to make Thy name known to Thine adversaries, that the nations may tremble at Thy presence! When Thou didst terrible things which we looked not for, Thou camest down, the mountains flowed down at Thy presence." Isaiah 64:1-3. "The Lord hath His way in the whirlwind and in the storm, and the clouds are the dust of His feet. He rebuketh the sea, and maketh it dry, and drieth up all the rivers." Nahum 1:3, 4.

More terrible manifestations than the world has ever yet beheld, will be witnessed at the second advent of Christ. "The mountains quake at Him, and the hills melt, and the earth is burned at His presence, yea, the world, and all that dwell therein. Who can stand before His indignation? and who can abide in the fierceness of His anger?" Nahum 1:5, 6. "Bow Thy heavens, O Lord, and come down: touch the mountains, and they shall smoke. Cast forth lightning, and scatter them: shoot out Thine arrows, and destroy them." Psalm 144:5, 6.

110 "I will show wonders in heaven above, and signs in the earth beneath; blood, and fire, and vapor of smoke." Acts 2:19. "And there were voices, and thunders, and lightnings; and there was a great earthquake, such as was not since men were upon the earth, so mighty an earthquake, and so great." "And every island fled away, and the mountains were not found. And there fell upon men a great hail out of heaven, every stone about the weight of a talent." Revelation 16:18, 20, 21.

As lightnings from heaven unite with the fire in the earth, the mountains will burn like a furnace, and will pour forth terrific streams of lava, overwhelming gardens and fields, villages and cities. Seething molten masses thrown into the rivers will cause the waters to boil, sending forth massive rocks with indescribable violence and scattering their broken fragments upon the land. Rivers will be dried up. The earth will be convulsed; everywhere there will be dreadful earthquakes and eruptions.

Thus God will destroy the wicked men off the earth. But the righteous will be preserved in the midst of these commotions, as Noah was preserved in the ark. God will be their refuge, and under His wings shall they trust. Says the psalmist: "Because thou hast made the Lord, which is my refuge, even the Most High, thy habitation; there shall no evil befall thee." Psalm 91:9, 10. "In the time of trouble He shall hide me in His pavilion: in the secret of His tabernacle shall He hide me." Psalm 27:5. God's promise is, "Because he hath set his love upon Me, therefore will I deliver him: I will set him on high, because he hath known My name." Psalm 91:14.

111

9

The Literal Week

Like the Sabbath, the week originated at creation, and it has been preserved and brought down to us through Bible history. God Himself measured off the first week as a sample for successive weeks to the close of time. Like every other, it consisted of seven literal days. Six days were employed in the work of creation; upon the seventh, God rested, and He then blessed this day and set it apart as a day of rest for man.

In the law given from Sinai, God recognized the week, and the facts upon which it is based. After giving the command, "Remember the Sabbath day, to keep it holy," and specifying what shall be done on the six days, and what shall not be done on the seventh, He states the reason for thus observing the week, by pointing back to His own example: "For in six days the Lord made heaven and earth, the sea, and all that in them is, and rested the seventh day: wherefore the Lord blessed the Sabbath day, and hallowed it." Exodus 20:8-11. This reason appears beautiful and forcible when we understand the days of creation to be literal. The first six days of each week are given to man for labor, because God employed the same period of the first week in the work of creation. On the seventh day man is to refrain from labor, in commemoration of the Creator's rest.

But the assumption that the events of the first week required thousands upon thousands of years, strikes directly at the foundation of the fourth commandment. It represents the Creator as commanding men to observe the week of literal days in commemoration of vast, indefinite periods. This is unlike His method of dealing with His creatures. It makes indefinite and obscure that which He has made very plain. It is infidelity in its most insidious and hence most dangerous form; its real character is so disguised that it is held and taught by many who profess to believe the Bible.

"By the word of the Lord were the heavens 112 made; and all the host of them by the breath of His mouth." "For He spake, and it was done; He commanded, and it stood fast." Psalm 33:6, 9. The Bible recognizes no long ages in which the earth was slowly evolved from chaos. Of each successive day of creation, the sacred record declares that it consisted of the evening and the morning, like all other days that have followed. At the close of each day is given the result of the Creator's work. The statement is made at the close of the first week's record, "These are the generations of the heavens and of the earth when they were created." Genesis 2:4. But this does not convey the idea that the days of creation were other than literal days. Each day was called a generation, because that in it God generated, or produced, some new portion of His work.

Geologists claim to find evidence from the earth itself that it is very much older than the Mosaic record teaches. Bones of men and animals, as well as instruments of warfare, petrified trees, et cetera, much larger than any that now exist, or that have existed for thousands of years, have been discovered, and from this it is inferred that the earth was populated long before the time brought to view in the record of creation, and by a race of beings vastly superior in size to any men now living. Such reasoning has led many professed Bible believers to adopt the position that the days of creation were vast, indefinite periods.

But apart from Bible history, geology can prove nothing. Those who reason so confidently upon its discoveries have no adequate conception of the size of men, animals, and trees before the Flood, or of the great changes which then took place. Relics found in the earth do give evidence of conditions differing in many respects from the present, but the time when these conditions existed can be learned only from the Inspired Record. In the history of the Flood, inspiration has explained that which geology alone could never fathom. In the days of Noah, men, animals, and trees, many times larger than now exist, were buried, and thus preserved as an evidence to later generations that the antediluvians perished by a flood. God designed that the discovery of these things should establish faith in inspired history; but men, with their vain reasoning, fall into the same error as did the people before the Flood— the things which God gave them as a benefit, they turn into a curse by making a wrong use of them.

113 It is one of Satan's devices to lead the people to accept the fables of infidelity; for he can thus obscure the law of God, in itself very plain, and embolden men to rebel against the divine government. His efforts are especially directed against the fourth commandment, because it so clearly points to the living God, the Maker of the heavens and the earth.

There is a constant effort made to explain the work of creation as the result of natural causes; and human reasoning is accepted even by professed Christians, in opposition to plain Scripture facts. There are many who oppose the investigation of the prophecies, especially those of Daniel and the Revelation, declaring them to be so obscure that we cannot understand them; yet these very persons eagerly receive the suppositions of geologists, in contradiction of the Mosaic record. But if that which God has revealed is so difficult to understand, how inconsistent it is to accept mere suppositions in regard to that which He has not revealed!

"The secret things belong unto the Lord our God: but those things which are revealed belong unto us and to our children forever." Deuteronomy 29:29. Just how God accomplished the work of creation He has never revealed to men; human science cannot search out the secrets of the Most High. His creative power is as incomprehensible as His existence.

God has permitted a flood of light to be poured upon the world in both science and art; but when professedly scientific men treat upon these subjects from a merely human point of view, they will assuredly come to wrong conclusions. It may be innocent to speculate beyond what God's word has revealed, if our theories do not contradict facts found in the Scriptures; but those who leave the word of God, and seek to account for His created works upon scientific principles, are drifting without chart or compass upon an unknown ocean. The greatest minds, if not guided by the word of God in their research, become bewildered in their attempts to trace the relations of science and revelation. Because the Creator and His works are so far beyond their comprehension that they are unable to explain them by natural laws, they regard Bible history as unreliable. Those who doubt the reliability of the records of the Old and New Testaments, will be led to go a step further, and doubt the existence of God; and then, having lost their anchor, they are left to beat about upon the rocks of infidelity.

These persons have lost the simplicity of 114 faith. There should be a settled belief in the divine authority of God's Holy Word. The Bible is not to be tested by men's ideas of science. Human knowledge is an unreliable guide. Skeptics who read the Bible for the sake of caviling, may, through an imperfect comprehension of either science or revelation, claim to find contradictions between them; but rightly understood, they are in perfect harmony. Moses wrote under the guidance of the Spirit of God, and a correct theory of geology will never claim discoveries that cannot be reconciled with his statements. All truth, whether in nature or in revelation, is consistent with itself in all its manifestations.

In the word of God many queries are raised that the most profound scholars can never answer. Attention is called to these subjects to show us how much there is, even among the common things of everyday life, that finite minds, with all their boasted wisdom, can never fully understand.

Yet men of science think that they can comprehend the wisdom of God, that which He has done or can do. The idea largely prevails that He is restricted by His own laws. Men either deny or ignore His existence, or think to explain everything, even the operation of His Spirit upon the human heart; and they no longer reverence His name or fear His power. They do not believe in the supernatural, not understanding God's laws or His infinite power to work His will through them. As commonly used, the term "laws of nature" comprises what men have been able to discover with regard to the laws that govern the physical world; but how limited is their knowledge, and how vast the field in which the Creator can work in harmony with

His own laws and yet wholly beyond the comprehension of finite beings!

Many teach that matter possesses vital power—that certain properties are imparted to matter, and it is then left to act through its own inherent energy; and that the operations of nature are conducted in harmony with fixed laws, with which God Himself cannot interfere. This is false science, and is not sustained by the word of God. Nature is the servant of her Creator. God does not annul His laws or work contrary to them, but He is continually using them as His instruments. Nature testifies of an intelligence, a presence, an active energy, that works in and through her laws. There is in nature the continual working of the Father and the Son. Christ says, "My Father worketh hitherto, and I work." John 5:17.

115   The Levites, in their hymn recorded by Nehemiah, sang, "Thou, even Thou, art Lord alone; Thou hast made heaven, the heaven of heavens, with all their host, the earth, and all things therein, . . . and Thou *preservest* them all." Nehemiah 9:6. As regards this world, God's work of creation is completed. For "the works were finished from the foundation of the world." Hebrews 4:3. But His energy is still exerted in upholding the objects of His creation. It is not because the mechanism that has once been set in motion continues to act by its own inherent energy that the pulse beats and breath follows breath; but every breath, every pulsation of the heart, is an evidence of the all-pervading care of Him in whom "we live, and move, and have our being." Acts 17:28. It is not because of inherent power that year by year the earth produces her bounties and continues her motion around the sun. The hand of God guides the planets and keeps them in position in their orderly march through the heavens. He "bringeth out their host by number: He calleth them all by names by the greatness of His might, for that He is strong in power; not one faileth." Isaiah 40:26. It is through His power that vegetation flourishes, that the leaves appear and the flowers bloom. He "maketh grass to grow upon the mountains" (Psalm 147:8), and by Him the valleys are made fruitful. "All the beasts of the forest . . . seek their meat from God," and every living creature, from the smallest insect up to man, is daily dependent upon His providential care. In the beautiful words of the psalmist, "These wait all upon Thee. . . . That Thou givest them they gather: Thou openest Thine hand, they are filled with good." Psalm 104:20, 21, 27, 28. His word controls the elements; He covers the heavens with clouds and prepares rain for the earth. "He giveth snow like wool: He scattereth the hoarfrost like ashes." Psalm 147:16. "When He uttereth His voice, there is a multitude of waters in the heavens, and He causeth the vapors to ascend from the ends of the earth; He maketh lightnings with rain, and bringeth forth the wind out of His treasuries." Jeremiah 10:13.

God is the foundation of everything. All true science is in harmony with His works; all true education leads to obedience to His government. Science opens new wonders to our view; she soars high, and explores new depths; but she brings nothing from her research that conflicts with divine revelation. Ignorance may seek to support false views of God by appeals to science, but the book of nature and the written word shed light upon each other. We are thus   116 led to adore the Creator and to have an intelligent trust in His word.

No finite mind can fully comprehend the existence, the power, the wisdom, or the works of the Infinite One. Says the sacred writer: "Canst thou by searching find out God? canst thou find out the Almighty unto perfection? It is as high as heaven; what canst thou do? deeper than hell; what canst thou know? The measure thereof is longer than the earth, and broader than the sea." Job 11:7-9. The mightiest intellects of earth cannot comprehend God. Men may be ever searching, ever learning, and still there is an infinity beyond.

Yet the works of creation testify of God's power and greatness. "The heavens declare the glory of God; and the firmament showeth His handiwork." Psalm 19:1. Those who take the written word as their counselor will find in science an aid to understand God. "The invisible things of Him from the creation of the world are clearly seen, being understood by the things that are made, even His eternal power and Godhead." Romans 1:20.

10   117

The Tower of Babel

To repeople the desolate earth, which the Flood had so lately swept from its moral corruption, God had preserved but one family, the household of Noah, to whom He had declared, "Thee have I seen righteous before Me in this generation." Genesis 7:1. Yet in the three sons of Noah was speedily developed the same great distinction seen in the world before the Flood. In Shem, Ham, and Japheth, who were to be the founders of the human race, was foreshadowed the character of their posterity.

Noah, speaking by divine inspiration, foretold the history of the three great races to spring from these fathers of mankind. Tracing the descendants of Ham, through the son rather than the father, he declared, "Cursed be Canaan; a servant of servants shall he be unto his brethren." The unnatural crime of Ham declared

This chapter is based on Genesis 9:25-27; 11:1-9.

that filial reverence had long before been cast from his soul, and it revealed the impiety and vileness of his character. These evil characteristics were perpetuated in Canaan and his posterity, whose continued guilt called upon them the judgments of God.

On the other hand, the reverence manifested by Shem and Japheth for their father, and thus for the divine statutes, promised a brighter future for their descendants. Concerning these sons it was declared: "Blessed be Jehovah, God of Shem; and Canaan shall be his servant. God shall enlarge Japheth, and he shall dwell in the tents of Shem; and Canaan shall be his servant." The line of Shem was to be that of the chosen people, of God's covenant, of the promised Redeemer. Jehovah was the God of Shem. From him would descend Abraham, and the people of Israel, through whom Christ was to come. "Happy is that people, whose God is the Lord." Psalm 144:15. And Japheth "shall dwell in the tents of Shem." In the blessings of the gospel the descendants of Japheth were especially to share.

118

The posterity of Canaan descended to the most degrading forms of heathenism. Though the prophetic curse had doomed them to slavery, the doom was withheld for centuries. God bore with their impiety and corruption until they passed the limits of divine forbearance. Then they were dispossessed, and became bondmen to the descendants of Shem and Japheth.

The prophecy of Noah was no arbitrary denunciation of wrath or declaration of favor. It did not fix the character and destiny of his sons. But it showed what would be the result of the course of life they had severally chosen and the character they had developed. It was an expression of God's purpose toward them and their posterity in view of their own character and conduct. As a rule, children inherit the dispositions and tendencies of their parents, and imitate their example; so that the sins of the parents are practiced by the children from generation to generation. Thus the vileness and irreverence of Ham were reproduced in his posterity, bringing a curse upon them for many generations. "One sinner destroyeth much good." Ecclesiastes 9:18.

On the other hand, how richly rewarded was Shem's respect for his father; and what an illustrious line of holy men appears in his posterity! "The Lord knoweth the days of the upright," "and his seed is blessed." Psalm 37:18, 26. "Know therefore that the Lord thy God He is God, the faithful God, which keepeth covenant and mercy with them that love Him and keep His commandments to a thousand generations." Deuteronomy 7:9.

For a time the descendants of Noah continued to dwell among the mountains where the ark had rested. As their numbers increased, apostasy

soon led to division. Those who desired to forget their Creator and to cast off the restraint of His law felt a constant annoyance from the teaching and example of their God-fearing associates, and after a time they decided to separate from the worshipers of God. Accordingly they journeyed to the plain of Shinar, on the banks of the river Euphrates. They were attracted by the beauty of the situation and the fertility of the soil, and upon this plain they determined to make their home.

Here they decided to build a city, and in it a tower of such stupendous height as should render it the wonder of the world. These enterprises were designed to prevent the people from scattering abroad in colonies. God had directed men to disperse throughout the earth, to replenish and subdue it; but these Babel builders determined to keep their community united in one body, and to found a monarchy that should eventually embrace the whole earth. Thus their city would become the metropolis of a universal empire; its glory would command the admiration and homage of the world and render the founders illustrious. The magnificent tower, reaching to the heavens, was intended to stand as a monument of the power and wisdom of its builders, perpetuating their fame to the latest generations.

119

The dwellers on the plain of Shinar disbelieved God's covenant that He would not again bring a flood upon the earth. Many of them denied the existence of God and attributed the Flood to the operation of natural causes. Others believed in a Supreme Being, and that it was He who had destroyed the antediluvian world; and their hearts, like that of Cain, rose up in rebellion against Him. One object before them in the erection of the tower was to secure their own safety in case of another deluge. By carrying the structure to a much greater height than was reached by the waters of the Flood, they thought to place themselves beyond all possibility of danger. And as they would be able to ascend to the region of the clouds, they hoped to ascertain the cause of the Flood. The whole undertaking was designed to exalt still further the pride of its projectors and to turn the minds of future generations away from God and lead them into idolatry.

When the tower had been partially completed, a portion of it was occupied as a dwelling place for the builders; other apartments, splendidly furnished and adorned, were devoted to their idols. The people rejoiced in their success, and praised the gods of silver and gold, and set themselves against the Ruler of heaven and earth. Suddenly the work that had been advancing so prosperously was checked. Angels were sent to bring to naught the purpose of the builders. The tower had reached a lofty height, and it was impossible for the workmen at the top to communicate directly with those at the base; therefore men were stationed at different points, each to receive and report to the one next below him the orders for needed material or other directions concerning the work. As messages were thus passing from one to another the language was confounded, so that material was 120 called for which was not needed, and the directions delivered were often the reverse of those that had been given. Confusion and dismay followed. All work came to a standstill. There could be no further harmony or co-operation. The builders were wholly unable to account for the strange misunderstandings among them, and in their rage and disappointment they reproached one another. Their confederacy ended in strife and bloodshed. Lightnings from heaven, as an evidence of God's displeasure, broke off the upper portion of the tower and cast it to the ground. Men were made to feel that there is a God who ruleth in the heavens.

Up to this time all men had spoken the same language; now those that could understand one another's speech united in companies; some went one way, and some another. "The Lord scattered them abroad from thence upon the face of all the earth." This dispersion was the means of peopling the earth, and thus the Lord's purpose was accomplished through the very means that men had employed to prevent its fulfillment.

But at what a loss to those who had set themselves against God! It was His purpose that as men should go forth to found nations in different parts of the earth they should carry with them a knowledge of His will, that the light of truth might shine undimmed to succeeding generations. Noah, the faithful preacher of righteousness, lived for three hundred and fifty years after the Flood, Shem for five hundred years, and thus their descendants had an opportunity to become acquainted with the requirements of God and the history of His dealings with their fathers. But they were unwilling to listen to these unpalatable truths; they had no desire to retain God in their knowledge; and by the confusion of tongues they were, in a great measure, shut out from intercourse with those who might have given them light.

The Babel builders had indulged the spirit of murmuring against God. Instead of gratefully remembering His mercy to Adam and His gracious covenant with Noah, they had complained of His severity in expelling the first pair from Eden and destroying the world by a flood. But while they murmured against God as arbitrary and severe, they were accepting the rule of the cruelest of tyrants. Satan was seeking to bring contempt upon the sacrificial offerings that prefigured the death of Christ; and as the minds of the people were darkened by idolatry, he led them to counterfeit these offerings and sacrifice

their own children upon the altars of their gods. 123 As men turned away from God, the divine attributes—justice, purity, and love—were supplanted by oppression, violence, and brutality.

The men of Babel had determined to establish a government that should be independent of God. There were some among them, however, who feared the Lord, but who had been deceived by the pretensions of the ungodly and drawn into their schemes. For the sake of these faithful ones the Lord delayed His judgments and gave the people time to reveal their true character. As this was developed, the sons of God labored to turn them from their purpose; but the people were fully united in their Heaven-daring undertaking. Had they gone on unchecked, they would have demoralized the world in its infancy. Their confederacy was founded in rebellion; a kingdom established for self-exaltation, but in which God was to have no rule or honor. Had this confederacy been permitted, a mighty power would have borne sway to banish righteousness—and with it peace, happiness, and security—from the earth. For the divine statutes, which are "holy and just and good" (Romans 7:12), men were endeavoring to substitute laws to suit the purpose of their own selfish and cruel hearts.

Those who feared the Lord cried unto Him to interpose. "And the Lord came down to see the city and the tower, which the children of men builded." In mercy to the world He defeated the purpose of the tower builders and overthrew the memorial of their daring. In mercy He confounded their speech, thus putting a check on their purposes of rebellion. God bears long with the perversity of men, giving them ample opportunity for repentance; but He marks all their devices to resist the authority of His just and holy law. From time to time the unseen hand that holds the scepter of government is stretched out to restrain iniquity. Unmistakable evidence is given that the Creator of the universe, the One infinite in wisdom and love and truth, is the Supreme Ruler of heaven and earth, and that none can with impunity defy His power.

The schemes of the Babel builders ended in shame and defeat. The monument to their pride became the memorial of their folly. Yet men are continually pursuing the same course—depending upon self, and rejecting God's law. It is the principle that Satan tried to carry out in heaven; the same that governed Cain in presenting his offering.

There are tower builders in our time. Infidels construct their theories from the supposed 124 deductions of science, and reject the revealed word of God. They presume to pass sentence upon God's moral government; they despise His law and boast of the sufficiency of human reason. Then, "because sentence against an evil work is not executed speedily, therefore the heart of the sons of men is fully set in them to do evil." Ecclesiastes 8:11.

In the professedly Christian world many turn away from the plain teachings of the Bible and build up a creed from human speculations and pleasing fables, and they point to their tower as a way to climb up to heaven. Men hang with admiration upon the lips of eloquence while it teaches that the transgressor shall not die, that salvation may be secured without obedience to the law of God. If the professed followers of Christ would accept God's standard, it would bring them into unity; but so long as human wisdom is exalted above His Holy Word, there will be divisions and dissension. The existing confusion of conflicting creeds and sects is fitly represented by the term "Babylon," which prophecy (Revelation 14:8; 18:2) applies to the world-loving churches of the last days.

Many seek to make a heaven for themselves by obtaining riches and power. They "speak wickedly concerning oppression: they speak loftily" (Psalm 73:8), trampling upon human rights and disregarding divine authority. The proud may be for a time in great power, and may see success in all that they undertake; but in the end they will find only disappointment and wretchedness.

The time of God's investigation is at hand. The Most High will come down to see that which the children of men have builded. His sovereign power will be revealed; the works of human pride will be laid low. "The Lord looketh from heaven; He beholdeth all the sons of men. From the place of His habitation He looketh upon all the inhabitants of the earth." "The Lord bringeth the counsel of the heathen to nought: He maketh the devices of the people of none effect. The counsel of the Lord standeth forever, the thoughts of His heart to all generations." Psalm 33:13, 14, 10, 11.

11

The Call of Abraham

After the dispersion from Babel idolatry again became well-nigh universal, and the Lord finally left the hardened transgressors to follow their evil ways, while He chose Abraham, of the line of Shem, and made him the keeper of His law for future generations. Abraham had grown up in the midst of superstition and heathenism. Even his father's household, by whom the knowledge of God had been preserved, were yielding to the seductive influences surrounding them, and they "served other gods" than Jehovah. But the true faith was not to become extinct. God has ever preserved a remnant to

serve Him. Adam, Seth, Enoch, Methuselah, Noah, Shem, in unbroken line, had preserved from age to age the precious revealings of His will. The son of Terah became the inheritor of this holy trust. Idolatry invited him on every side, but in vain. Faithful among the faithless, uncorrupted by the prevailing apostasy, he steadfastly adhered to the worship of the one true God. "The Lord is nigh unto all them that call upon Him, to all that call upon Him in truth." Psalm 145:18. He communicated His will to Abraham, and gave him a distinct knowledge of the requirements of His law and of the salvation that would be accomplished through Christ.

There was given to Abraham the promise, especially dear to the people of that age, of a numerous posterity and of national greatness: "I will make of thee a great nation, and I will bless thee, and make thy name great; and thou shalt be a blessing." And to this was added the assurance, precious above every other to the inheritor of faith, that of his line the Redeemer of the world should come: "In thee shall all families of the earth be blessed." Yet, as the first condition of fulfillment, there was to be a test of faith; a sacrifice was demanded.

The message of God came to Abraham, "Get thee out of thy country, and from thy kindred, and from thy father's house, unto a land that I will show thee." In order that God might qualify him for his great work as the keeper of the sacred oracles, Abraham must be separated from the associations of his early life. The influence of kindred and friends would interfere with the training which the Lord purposed to give His servant. Now that Abraham was, in a special sense, connected with heaven, he must dwell among strangers. His character must be peculiar, differing from all the world. He could not even explain his course of action so as to be understood by his friends. Spiritual things are spiritually discerned, and his motives and actions were not comprehended by his idolatrous kindred.

"By faith Abraham, when he was called to go out into a place which he should after receive for an inheritance, obeyed; and he went out, not knowing whither he went." Hebrews 11:8. Abraham's unquestioning obedience is one of the most striking evidences of faith to be found in all the Bible. To him, faith was "the substance of things hoped for, the evidence of things not seen." Verse 1. Relying upon the divine promise, without the least outward assurance of its fulfillment, he abandoned home and kindred and native land, and went forth, he knew not whither, to follow where God should lead. "By faith he became a sojourner in the land of promise, as in a land not his own, dwelling in tents, with Isaac and Jacob, the heirs with him of the same promise." Hebrews

This chapter is based on Genesis 12.

11:9, R.V.

It was no light test that was thus brought upon Abraham, no small sacrifice that was required of him. There were strong ties to bind him to his country, his kindred, and his home. But he did not hesitate to obey the call. He had no question to ask concerning the land of promise—whether the soil was fertile and the climate healthful; whether the country afforded agreeable surroundings and would afford opportunities for amassing wealth. God had spoken, and His servant must obey; the happiest place on earth for him was the place where God would have him to be.

Many are still tested as was Abraham. They do not hear the voice of God speaking directly from the heavens, but He calls them by the teachings of His word and the events of His providence. They may be required to abandon a career that promises wealth and honor, to leave 127 congenial and profitable associations, and separate from kindred, to enter upon what appears to be only a path of self-denial, hardship, and sacrifice. God has a work for them to do; but a life of ease and the influence of friends and kindred would hinder the development of the very traits essential for its accomplishment. He calls them away from human influences and aid, and leads them to feel the need of His help, and to depend upon Him alone, that He may reveal Himself to them. Who is ready at the call of Providence to renounce cherished plans and familiar associations? Who will accept new duties and enter untried fields, doing God's work with firm and willing heart, for Christ's sake counting his losses gain? He who will do this has the faith of Abraham, and will share with him that "far more exceeding and eternal weight of glory," with which "the sufferings of this present time are not worthy to be compared." 2 Corinthians 4:17; Romans 8:18.

The call from heaven first came to Abraham while he dwelt in "Ur of the Chaldees" and in obedience to it he removed to Haran. Thus far his father's family accompanied him, for with their idolatry they united the worship of the true God. Here Abraham remained till the death of Terah. But from his father's grave the divine Voice bade him go forward. His brother Nahor with his household clung to their home and their idols. Besides Sarah, the wife of Abraham, only Lot, the son of Haran long since dead, chose to share the patriarch's pilgrim life. Yet it was a large company that set out from Mesopotamia. Abraham already possessed extensive flocks and herds, the riches of the East, and he was surrounded by a numerous body of servants and retainers. He was departing from the land of his fathers, never to return, and he took with him all that he had, "their substance that they had gathered, and the souls that they had gotten in Haran." Among these were many led by higher considerations than those of service and self-interest. During their stay in Haran, both Abraham and Sarah had led others to the worship and service of the true God. These attached themselves to the patriarch's household, and accompanied him to the land of promise. "And they went forth to go into the land of Canaan; and into the land of Canaan they came."

The place where they first tarried was Shechem. Under the shade of the oaks of Moreh, in a wide, grassy valley, with its olive groves and gushing springs, between Mount Ebal on the one side and Mount Gerizim on the 128 other, Abraham made his encampment. It was a fair and goodly country that the patriarch had entered—"a land of brooks of water, of fountains and depths that spring out of valleys and hills; a land of wheat, and barley, and vines, and fig trees, and pomegranates; a land of oil olive, and honey." Deuteronomy 8:7, 8. But to the worshiper of Jehovah, a heavy shadow rested upon wooded hill and fruitful plain. "The Canaanite was then in the land." Abraham had reached the goal of his hopes to find a country occupied by an alien race and overspread with idolatry. In the groves were set up the altars of false gods, and human sacrifices were offered upon the neighboring heights. While he clung to the divine promise, it was not without distressful forebodings that he pitched his tent. Then "the Lord appeared unto Abram, and said, Unto thy seed will I give this land." His faith was strengthened by this assurance that the divine presence was with him, that he was not left to the mercy of the wicked. "And there builded he an altar unto the Lord, who appeared unto him." Still a wayfarer, he soon removed to a spot near Bethel, and again erected an altar, and called upon the name of the Lord.

Abraham, "the friend of God," set us a worthy example. His was a life of prayer. Wherever he pitched his tent, close beside it was set up his altar, calling all within his encampment to the morning and evening sacrifice. When his tent was removed, the altar remained. In following years, there were those among the roving Canaanites who received instruction from Abraham; and whenever one of these came to that altar, he knew who had been there before him; and when he had pitched his tent, he repaired the altar, and there worshiped the living God.

Abraham continued to journey southward, 129 and again his faith was tested. The heavens withheld their rain, the brooks ceased to flow in the valleys, and the grass withered on the plains. The flocks and herds found no pasture, and starvation threatened the whole encampment. Did not the patriarch now question the leadings of Providence? Did he not look back with longing to the plenty of the Chaldean plains? All were eagerly watching to see what Abraham would do, as trouble after trouble came upon him. So long as his confidence appeared unshaken, they felt that there was hope; they were assured that God was his Friend, and that He was still guiding him.

Abraham could not explain the leadings of Providence; he had not realized his expectations; but he held fast the promise, "I will bless thee, and make thy name great; and thou shalt be a blessing." With earnest prayer he considered how to preserve the life of his people and his flocks, but he would not allow circumstances to shake his faith in God's word. To escape the famine he went down into Egypt. He did not forsake Canaan, or in his extremity turn back to the Chaldean land from which he came, where there was no scarcity of bread; but he sought a temporary refuge as near as possible to the Land of Promise, intending shortly to return where God had placed him.

The Lord in His providence had brought this trial upon Abraham to teach him lessons of submission, patience, and faith—lessons that were to be placed on record for the benefit of all who should afterward be called to endure affliction. God leads His children by a way that they know not, but He does not forget or cast off those who put their trust in Him. He permitted affliction to come upon Job, but He did not forsake him. He allowed the beloved John to be exiled to lonely Patmos, but the Son of God met him there, and his vision was filled with scenes of immortal glory. God permits trials to assail His people, that by their constancy and obedience they themselves may be spiritually enriched, and that their example may be a source of strength to others. "I know the thoughts that I think toward you, saith the Lord, thoughts of peace, and not of evil." Jeremiah 29:11. The very trials that task our faith most severely and make it seem that God has forsaken us, are to lead us closer to Christ, that we may lay all our burdens at His feet and experience the peace which He will give us in exchange.

God has always tried His people in the furnace of affliction. It is in the heat of the furnace that the dross is separated from the true gold of the Christian character. Jesus watches the test; He knows what is needed to purify the precious metal, that it may reflect the radiance of His love. It is by close, testing trials that God disciplines His servants. He sees that some have powers which may be used in the advancement of His work, and He puts these persons upon trial; in His providence He brings them into positions that test their character and reveal defects and weaknesses that have been hidden 130 from their own knowledge. He gives them opportunity to correct these defects and to fit themselves for His service. He shows them their own weakness, and teaches them to lean upon Him; for He is their only help and safeguard. Thus His object is attained. They are educated,

trained, and disciplined, prepared to fulfill the grand purpose for which their powers were given them. When God calls them to action, they are ready, and heavenly angels can unite with them in the work to be accomplished on the earth.

During his stay in Egypt, Abraham gave evidence that he was not free from human weakness and imperfection. In concealing the fact that Sarah was his wife, he betrayed a distrust of the divine care, a lack of that lofty faith and courage so often and nobly exemplified in his life. Sarah was fair to look upon, and he doubted not that the dusky Egyptians would covet the beautiful stranger, and that in order to secure her, they would not scruple to slay her husband. He reasoned that he was not guilty of falsehood in representing Sarah as his sister, for she was the daughter of his father, though not of his mother. But this concealment of the real relation between them was deception. No deviation from strict integrity can meet God's approval. Through Abraham's lack of faith, Sarah was placed in great peril. The king of Egypt, being informed of her beauty, caused her to be taken to his palace, intending to make her his wife. But the Lord, in His great mercy, protected Sarah by sending judgments upon the royal household. By this means the monarch learned the truth in the matter, and, indignant at the deception practiced upon him, he reproved Abraham and restored to him his wife, saying, "What is this that thou hast done unto me? . . . Why saidst thou, She is my sister? So I might have taken her to me to wife. Now therefore behold thy wife, take her, and go thy way."

Abraham had been greatly favored by the king; even now Pharaoh would permit no harm to be done him or his company, but ordered a guard to conduct them in safety out of his dominions. At this time laws were made prohibiting the Egyptians from intercourse with foreign shepherds in any such familiarity as eating or drinking with them. Pharaoh's dismissal of Abraham was kind and generous; but he bade him leave Egypt, for he dared not permit him to remain. He had ignorantly been about to do him a serious injury, but God had interposed, and saved the monarch from committing so great a 131 sin. Pharaoh saw in this stranger a man whom the God of heaven honored, and he feared to have in his kingdom one who was so evidently under divine favor. Should Abraham remain in Egypt, his increasing wealth and honor would be likely to excite the envy or covetousness of the Egyptians, and some injury might be done him, for which the monarch would be held responsible, and which might again bring judgments upon the royal house.

The warning that had been given to Pharaoh proved a protection to Abraham in his after-intercourse with heathen peoples; for the matter could not be kept secret, and it was seen that the God whom Abraham worshiped would protect His servant, and that any injury done him would be avenged. It is a dangerous thing to wrong one of the children of the King of heaven. The psalmist refers to this chapter in Abraham's experience when he says, in speaking of the chosen people, that God "reproved kings for their sakes; saying, Touch not Mine anointed, and do My prophets no harm." Psalm 105:14, 15.

There is an interesting similarity between Abraham's experience in Egypt and that of his posterity, centuries later. Both went down into Egypt on account of a famine, and both sojourned there. Through the manifestation of divine judgments in their behalf, the fear of them fell upon the Egyptians; and, enriched by the gifts of the heathen, they went out with great substance.

12

Abraham in Canaan

Abraham returned to Canaan "very rich in cattle, in silver, and in gold." Lot was still with him, and again they came to Bethel, and pitched their tents by the altar which they had before erected. They soon found that increased possessions brought increased trouble. In the midst of hardships and trials they had dwelt together in harmony, but in their prosperity there was danger of strife between them. The pasturage was not sufficient for the flocks and herds of both, and the frequent disputes among the herdsmen were brought for settlement to their masters. It was evident that they must separate. Abraham was Lot's senior in years, and his superior in relation, in wealth, and in position; yet he was the first to propose plans for preserving peace. Although the whole land had been given him by God Himself, he courteously waived this right.

"Let there be no strife," he said, "between me and thee, and between my herdmen and thy herdmen; for we be brethren. Is not the whole land before thee? separate thyself, I pray thee, from me: if thou wilt take the left hand, then I will go to the right; or if thou depart to the right hand, then I will go to the left."

Here the noble, unselfish spirit of Abraham was displayed. How many under similar circumstances would, at all hazards, cling to their individual rights and preferences! How many households have thus been rent asunder! How many churches have been divided, making the cause of truth a byword and a reproach among the wicked! "Let there be no strife between me and thee," said Abraham, "for we be brethren;" not only by natural relationship, but as wor-

shipers of the true God. The children of God the world over are one family, and the same spirit of love and conciliation should govern them. "Be kindly affectioned one to another with brotherly love; in honor preferring one another" (Romans 12:10), is the teaching of our Saviour. The cultivation of a uniform courtesy, a willingness to do to others as we would wish them to do to us, would annihilate half the ills of life. The spirit of self-aggrandizement is the spirit of Satan; but the heart in which the love of Christ is cherished, will possess that charity which seeketh not her own. Such will heed the divine injunction, "Look not every man on his own things, but every man also on the things of others." Philippians 2:4.

Although Lot owed his prosperity to his connection with Abraham, he manifested no gratitude to his benefactor. Courtesy would have dictated that he yield the choice to Abraham, but instead of this he selfishly endeavored to grasp all its advantages. He "lifted up his eyes, and beheld all the plain of Jordan, that it was well watered everywhere, . . . even as the garden of the Lord, like the land of Egypt, as thou comest unto Zoar." The most fertile region in all Palestine was the Jordan Valley, reminding the beholders of the lost Paradise and equaling the beauty and productiveness of the Nile-enriched plains they had so lately left. There were cities also, wealthy and beautiful, inviting to profitable traffic in their crowded marts. Dazzled with visions of worldly gain, Lot overlooked the moral and spiritual evils that would be encountered there. The inhabitants of the plain were "sinners before the Lord exceedingly;" but of this he was ignorant, or, knowing, gave it but little weight. He "chose him all the plain of Jordan," and "pitched his tent toward Sodom." How little did he foresee the terrible results of that selfish choice!

After the separation from Lot, Abraham again received from the Lord a promise of the whole country. Soon after this he removed to Hebron, pitching his tent under the oaks of Mamre and erecting beside it an altar to the Lord. In the free air of those upland plains, with their olive groves and vineyards, their fields of waving grain, and the wide pasture grounds of the encircling hills, he dwelt, well content with his simple, patriarchal life, and leaving to Lot the perilous luxury of the vale of Sodom.

Abraham was honored by the surrounding nations as a mighty prince and a wise and able chief. He did not shut away his influence from his neighbors. His life and character, in their marked contrast with those of the worshipers of idols, exerted a telling influence in favor of the true faith. His allegiance to God was unswerving, while his affability and benevolence inspired confidence and friendship and his unaffected greatness commanded respect and honor.

This chapter is based on Genesis 13 to 15; 17:1-16; 18.

His religion was not held as a precious treasure to be jealously guarded and enjoyed solely by the possessor. True religion cannot be thus held, for such a spirit is contrary to the principles of the gospel. While Christ is dwelling in the heart it is impossible to conceal the light of His presence, or for that light to grow dim. On the contrary, it will grow brighter and brighter as day by day the mists of selfishness and sin that envelop the soul are dispelled by the bright beams of the Sun of Righteousness.

The people of God are His representatives upon the earth, and He intends that they shall be lights in the moral darkness of this world. Scattered all over the country, in the towns, cities, and villages, they are God's witnesses, the channels through which He will communicate to an unbelieving world the knowledge of His will and the wonders of His grace. It is His plan that all who are partakers of the great salvation shall be missionaries for Him. The piety of the Christian constitutes the standard by which worldlings judge the gospel. Trials patiently borne, blessings gratefully received, meekness, kindness, mercy, and love, habitually exhibited, are the lights that shine forth in the character before the world, revealing the contrast with the darkness that comes of the selfishness of the natural heart.

Rich in faith, noble in generosity, unfaltering in obedience, and humble in the simplicity of his pilgrim life, Abraham was also wise in diplomacy and brave and skillful in war. Notwithstanding he was known as the teacher of a new religion, three royal brothers, rulers of the Amorite plains in which he dwelt, manifested their friendship by inviting him to enter into an alliance with them for greater security; for the country was filled with violence and oppression. An occasion soon arose for him to avail himself of this alliance.

Chedorlaomer, king of Elam, had invaded Canaan fourteen years before, and made it tributary to him. Several of the princes now revolted, and the Elamite king, with four allies, again marched into the country to reduce them to submission. Five kings of Canaan joined their forces and met the invaders in the vale of Siddim, but only to be completely overthrown. A 135 large part of the army was cut to pieces, and those who escaped fled for safety to the mountains. The victors plundered the cities of the plain and departed with rich spoil and many captives, among whom were Lot and his family.

Abraham, dwelling in peace in the oak groves at Mamre, learned from one of the fugitives the story of the battle and the calamity that had befallen his nephew. He had cherished no unkind memory of Lot's ingratitude. All his affection for him was awakened, and he determined that he should be rescued. Seeking, first of all, divine counsel, Abraham prepared for war. From his own encampment he summoned three hundred and eighteen trained servants, men trained in the fear of God, in the service of their master, and in the practice of arms. His confederates, Mamre, Eschol, and Aner, joined him with their bands, and together they started in pursuit of the invaders. The Elamites and their allies had encamped at Dan, on the northern border of Canaan. Flushed with victory, and having no fear of an assault from their vanquished foes, they had given themselves up to reveling. The patriarch divided his force so as to approach from different directions, and came upon the encampment by night. His attack, so vigorous and unexpected, resulted in speedy victory. The king of Elam was slain and his panic-stricken forces were utterly routed. Lot and his family, with all the prisoners and their goods, were recovered, and a rich booty fell into the hands of the victors. To Abraham, under God, the triumph was due. The worshiper of Jehovah had not only rendered a great service to the country, but had proved himself a man of valor. It was seen that righteousness is not cowardice, and that Abraham's religion made him courageous in maintaining the right and defending the oppressed. His heroic act gave him a widespread influence among the surrounding tribes. On his return, the king of Sodom came out with his retinue to honor the conqueror. He bade him take the goods, begging only that the prisoners should be restored. By the usage of war, the spoils belonged to the conquerors; but Abraham had undertaken this expedition with no purpose of gain, and he refused to take advantage of the unfortunate, only stipulating that his confederates should receive the portion to which they were entitled.

Few, if subjected to such a test, would have shown themselves as noble as did Abraham. Few would have resisted the temptation to 136 secure so rich a booty. His example is a rebuke to self-seeking, mercenary spirits. Abraham regarded the claims of justice and humanity. His conduct illustrates the inspired maxim, "Thou shalt love thy neighbor as thyself." Leviticus 19:18. "I have lifted up my hand," he said, "unto the Lord, the most high God, the possessor of heaven and earth, that I will not take from a thread even to a shoe latchet, and that I will not take anything that is thine, lest thou shouldest say, I have made Abram rich." He would give them no occasion to think that he had engaged in warfare for the sake of gain, or to attribute his prosperity to their gifts or favor. God had promised to bless Abraham, and to Him the glory should be ascribed.

Another who came out to welcome the victorious patriarch was Melchizedek, king of Salem, who brought forth bread and wine for the refreshment of his army. As "priest of the most high God," he pronounced a blessing upon

Abraham, and gave thanks to the Lord, who had wrought so great a deliverance by His servant. And Abraham "gave him tithes of all."

Abraham gladly returned to his tents and his flocks, but his mind was disturbed by harassing thoughts. He had been a man of peace, so far as possible shunning enmity and strife; and with horror he recalled the scene of carnage he had witnessed. But the nations whose forces he had defeated would doubtless renew the invasion of Canaan, and make him the special object of their vengeance. Becoming thus involved in national quarrels, the peaceful quiet of his life would be broken. Furthermore, he had not entered upon the possession of Canaan, nor could he now hope for an heir, to whom the promise might be fulfilled.

In a vision of the night the divine Voice was again heard. "Fear not, Abram," were the words of the Prince of princes; "I am thy shield, and thy exceeding great reward." But his mind was so oppressed by forebodings that he could not now grasp the promise with unquestioning confidence as heretofore. He prayed for some tangible evidence that it would be fulfilled. And how was the covenant promise to be realized, while the gift of a son was withheld? "What wilt thou give me," he said, "seeing I go childless?" "And, lo, one born in my house is mine heir." He proposed to make his trusty servant Eliezer his son by adoption, and the inheritor of his possessions. But he was assured that a child of his own was to be his heir. Then he was led outside his tent, and told to look up to the unnumbered stars glittering in the heavens; and as he did so, the words were spoken, "So shall thy seed be." "Abraham believed God, and it was counted unto him for righteousness." Romans 4:3.

Still the patriarch begged for some visible token as a confirmation of his faith and as an evidence to after-generations that God's gracious purposes toward them would be accomplished. The Lord condescended to enter into a covenant with His servant, employing such forms as were customary among men for the ratification of a solemn engagement. By divine direction, Abraham sacrificed a heifer, a she-goat, and a ram, each three years old, dividing the bodies and laying the pieces a little distance apart. To these he added a turtledove and a young pigeon, which, however, were not divided. This being done, he reverently passed between the parts of the sacrifice, making a solemn vow to God of perpetual obedience. Watchful and steadfast, he remained beside the carcasses till the going down of the sun, to guard them from being defiled or devoured by birds of prey. About sunset he sank into a deep sleep; and, "lo, a horror of great darkness fell upon him." And the voice of God was heard, bidding him not to expect immediate possession of the Promised Land, and pointing forward to

the sufferings of his posterity before their establishment in Canaan. The plan of redemption was here opened to him, in the death of Christ, the great sacrifice, and His coming in glory. Abraham saw also the earth restored to its Eden beauty, to be given him for an everlasting possession, as the final and complete fulfillment of the promise.

As a pledge of this covenant of God with men, a smoking furnace and a burning lamp, symbols of the divine presence, passed between the severed victims, totally consuming them. And again a voice was heard by Abraham, confirming the gift of the land of Canaan to his descendants, "from the river of Egypt unto the great river, the river Euphrates."

When Abraham had been nearly twenty-five years in Canaan, the Lord appeared unto him, and said, "I am the Almighty God; walk before Me, and be thou perfect." In awe, the patriarch fell upon his face, and the message continued: "Behold, My covenant is with thee, and thou shalt be a father of many nations." In token of the fulfillment of this covenant, his name, heretofore called Abram, was changed to Abraham, which signifies, "father of a great multitude." Sarai's name became Sarah—"princess;" for, said the divine Voice, "she shall be a mother of nations; kings of people shall be of her."

At this time the rite of circumcision was given to Abraham as "a seal of the righteousness of the faith which he had yet being uncircumcised." Romans 4:11. It was to be observed by the patriarch and his descendants as a token that they were devoted to the service of God and thus separated from idolaters, and that God accepted them as His peculiar treasure. By this rite they were pledged to fulfill, on their part, the conditions of the covenant made with Abraham. They were not to contract marriages with the heathen; for by so doing they would lose their reverence for God and His holy law; they would be tempted to engage in the sinful practices of other nations, and would be seduced into idolatry.

God conferred great honor upon Abraham. Angels of heaven walked and talked with him as friend with friend. When judgments were about to be visited upon Sodom, the fact was not hidden from him, and he became an intercessor with God for sinners. His interview with the angels presents also a beautiful example of hospitality.

In the hot summer noontide the patriarch was sitting in his tent door, looking out over the quiet landscape, when he saw in the distance three travelers approaching. Before reaching his tent, the strangers halted, as if consulting as to their course. Without waiting for them to solicit favors, Abraham rose quickly, and as they were apparently turning in another direction, he hastened after them, and with the utmost courtesy urged them to honor him by tarrying for refreshment. With his own hands he brought water that they might wash the dust of travel from their feet. He himself selected their food, and while they were at rest under the cooling shade, an entertainment was made ready, and he stood respectfully beside them while they partook of his hospitality. This act of courtesy God regarded of sufficient importance to record in His word; and a thousand years later it was referred to by an inspired apostle: "Be not forgetful to entertain strangers: for thereby some have entertained angels unawares." Hebrews 13:2.

139 Abraham had seen in his guests only three tired wayfarers, little thinking that among them was One whom he might worship without sin. But the true character of the heavenly messengers was now revealed. Though they were on their way as ministers of wrath, yet to Abraham, the man of faith, they spoke first of blessings. Though God is strict to mark iniquity and to punish transgression, He takes no delight in vengeance. The work of destruction is a "strange work" to Him who is infinite in love.

"The secret of the Lord is with them that fear Him." Psalm 25:14. Abraham had honored God, and the Lord honored him, taking him into His counsels, and revealing to him His purposes. "Shall I hide from Abraham that thing which I do?" said the Lord. "The cry of Sodom and Gomorrah is great, and because their sin is very grievous, I will go down now, and see whether they have done altogether according to the cry of it, which is come unto me; and if not, I will know." God knew well the measure of Sodom's guilt; but He expressed Himself after the manner of men, that the justice of His dealings might be understood. Before bringing judgment upon the transgressors He would go Himself, to institute an examination of their course; if they had not passed the limits of divine mercy, He would still grant them space for repentance.

Two of the heavenly messengers departed, leaving Abraham alone with Him whom he now knew to be the Son of God. And the man of faith pleaded for the inhabitants of Sodom. Once he had saved them by his sword, now he endeavored to save them by prayer. Lot and his household were still dwellers there; and the unselfish love that prompted Abraham to their rescue from the Elamites, now sought to save them, if it were God's will, from the storm of divine judgment.

With deep reverence and humility he urged his plea: "I have taken upon me to speak unto the Lord, which am but dust and ashes." There was no self-confidence, no boasting of his own righteousness. He did not claim favor on the ground of his obedience, or of the sacrifices he had made in doing God's will. Himself a sinner, he pleaded in the sinner's behalf. Such a spirit all who approach God should possess. Yet

Abraham manifested the confidence of a child pleading with a loved father. He came close to the heavenly Messenger, and fervently urged his petition. Though Lot had become a dweller in Sodom, he did not partake in the iniquity of its inhabitants. Abraham thought that in that populous city there must be other worshipers of the true God. And in view of this he pleaded, "That 140 be far from Thee, to do after this manner, to slay the righteous with the wicked: . . . that be far from Thee: Shall not the Judge of all the earth do right?" Abraham asked not once merely, but many times. Waxing bolder as his requests were granted, he continued until he gained the assurance that if even ten righteous persons could be found in it, the city would be spared.

Love for perishing souls inspired Abraham's prayer. While he loathed the sins of that corrupt city, he desired that the sinners might be saved. His deep interest for Sodom shows the anxiety that we should feel for the impenitent. We should cherish hatred of sin, but pity and love for the sinner. All around us are souls going down to ruin as hopeless, as terrible, as that which befell Sodom. Every day the probation of some is closing. Every hour some are passing beyond the reach of mercy. And where are the voices of warning and entreaty to bid the sinner flee from this fearful doom? Where are the hands stretched out to draw him back from death? Where are those who with humility and persevering faith are pleading with God for him?

The spirit of Abraham was the spirit of Christ. The Son of God is Himself the great Intercessor in the sinner's behalf. He who has paid the price for its redemption knows the worth of the human soul. With an antagonism to evil such as can exist only in a nature spotlessly pure, Christ manifested toward the sinner a love which infinite goodness alone could conceive. In the agonies of the crucifixion, Himself burdened with the awful weight of the sins of the whole world, He prayed for His revilers and murderers, "Father, forgive them; for they know not what they do." Luke 23:34.

Of Abraham it is written that "he was called the friend of God," "the father of all them that believe." James 2:23; Romans 4:11. The testimony of God concerning this faithful patriarch is, "Abraham obeyed My voice, and kept My charge, My commandments, My statutes, and My laws." And again, "I know him, that he will command his children and his household after him, and they shall keep the way of the Lord, to do justice and judgment; that the Lord may bring upon Abraham that which He hath spoken of him." It was a high honor to which Abraham was called, that of being the father of the people who for centuries were the guardians and preservers of the truth of God for the world—of 141 that people through whom all the nations of the earth should be blessed in the advent of the promised Messiah. But He who called the patriarch judged him worthy. It is God that speaks. He who understands the thoughts afar off, and places the right estimate upon men, says, "I know him." There would be on the part of Abraham no betraying of the truth for selfish purposes. He would keep the law and deal justly and righteously. And he would not only fear the Lord himself, but would cultivate religion in his home. He would instruct his family in righteousness. The law of God would be the rule in his household.

Abraham's household comprised more than a thousand souls. Those who were led by his teachings to worship the one God, found a home in his encampment; and here, as in a school, they received such instruction as would prepare them to be representatives of the true faith. Thus a great responsibility rested upon him. He was training heads of families, and his methods of government would be carried out in the households over which they should preside.

In early times the father was the ruler and priest of his own family, and he exercised authority over his children, even after they had families of their own. His descendants were taught to look up to him as their head, in both religious and secular matters. This patriarchal system of government Abraham endeavored to perpetuate, as it tended to preserve the knowledge of God. It was necessary to bind the members of the household together, in order to build up a barrier against the idolatry that had become so widespread and so deep-seated. Abraham sought by every means in his power to guard the inmates of his encampment against mingling with the heathen and witnessing their idolatrous practices, for he knew that familiarity with evil would insensibly corrupt the principles. The greatest care was exercised to shut out every form of false religion and to impress the mind with the majesty and glory of the living God as the true object of worship.

It was a wise arrangement, which God Himself had made, to cut off His people, so far as possible, from connection with the heathen, making them a people dwelling alone, and not reckoned among the nations. He had separated Abraham from his idolatrous kindred, that the patriarch might train and educate his family apart from the seductive influences which 142 would have surrounded them in Mesopotamia, and that the true faith might be preserved in its purity by his descendants from generation to generation.

Abraham's affection for his children and his household led him to guard their religious faith, to impart to them a knowledge of the divine statutes, as the most precious legacy he could transmit to them, and through them to the world. All were taught that they were under the rule of

the God of heaven. There was to be no oppression on the part of parents and no disobedience on the part of children. God's law had appointed to each his duties, and only in obedience to it could any secure happiness or prosperity.

His own example, the silent influence of his daily life, was a constant lesson. The unswerving integrity, the benevolence and unselfish courtesy, which had won the admiration of kings, were displayed in the home. There was a fragrance about the life, a nobility and loveliness of character, which revealed to all that he was connected with Heaven. He did not neglect the soul of the humblest servant. In his household there was not one law for the master and another for the servant; a royal way for the rich and another for the poor. All were treated with justice and compassion, as inheritors with him of the grace of life.

"He will command his . . . household." There would be no sinful neglect to restrain the evil propensities of his children, no weak, unwise, indulgent favoritism; no yielding of his conviction of duty to the claims of mistaken affection. Abraham would not only give right instruction, but he would maintain the authority of just and righteous laws.

How few there are in our day who follow this example! On the part of too many parents there is a blind and selfish sentimentalism, miscalled love, which is manifested in leaving children, with their unformed judgment and undisciplined passions, to the control of their own will. This is the veriest cruelty to the youth and a great wrong to the world. Parental indulgence causes disorder in families and in society. It confirms in the young the desire to follow inclination, instead of submitting to the divine requirements. Thus they grow up with a heart averse to doing God's will, and they transmit their irreligious, insubordinate spirit to their children and children's children. Like Abraham, parents should command their households after them. Let obedience to parental authority be taught and 143 enforced as the first step in obedience to the authority of God.

The light esteem in which the law of God is held, even by religious leaders, has been productive of great evil. The teaching which has become so widespread, that the divine statutes are no longer binding upon men, is the same as idolatry in its effect upon the morals of the people. Those who seek to lessen the claims of God's holy law are striking directly at the foundation of the government of families and nations. Religious parents, failing to walk in His statutes, do not command their household to keep the way of the Lord. The law of God is not made the rule of life. The children, as they make homes of their own, feel under no obligation to teach their children what they themselves have never been taught. And this is why there are so many godless families; this is why depravity is so deep and widespread.

Not until parents themselves walk in the law of the Lord with perfect hearts will they be prepared to command their children after them. A reformation in this respect is needed—a reformation which shall be deep and broad. Parents need to reform; ministers need to reform; they need God in their households. If they would see a different state of things, they must bring His word into their families and must make it their counselor. They must teach their children that it is the voice of God addressed to them, and is to be implicitly obeyed. They should patiently instruct their children, kindly and untiringly teach them how to live in order to please God. The children of such a household are prepared to meet the sophistries of infidelity. They have accepted the Bible as the basis of their faith, and they have a foundation that cannot be swept away by the incoming tide of skepticism.

In too many households prayer is neglected. Parents feel that they have no time for morning and evening worship. They cannot spare a few moments to be spent in thanksgiving to God for His abundant mercies—for the blessed sunshine and the showers of rain, which cause vegetation to flourish, and for the guardianship of holy angels. They have no time to offer prayer for divine help and guidance and for the abiding presence of Jesus in the household. They go forth to labor as the ox or the horse goes, without one thought of God or heaven. They have souls so precious that rather than permit them to be hopelessly lost, the Son of God gave His life 144 to ransom them; but they have little more appreciation of His great goodness than have the beasts that perish.

Like the patriarchs of old, those who profess to love God should erect an altar to the Lord wherever they pitch their tent. If ever there was a time when every house should be a house of prayer, it is now. Fathers and mothers should often lift up their hearts to God in humble supplication for themselves and their children. Let the father, as priest of the household, lay upon the altar of God the morning and evening sacrifice, while the wife and children unite in prayer and praise. In such a household Jesus will love to tarry.

From every Christian home a holy light should shine forth. Love should be revealed in action. It should flow out in all home intercourse, showing itself in thoughtful kindness, in gentle, unselfish courtesy. There are homes where this principle is carried out—homes where God is worshiped and truest love reigns. From these homes morning and evening prayer ascends to God as sweet incense, and His mercies and blessings descend upon the suppliants like the morning dew.

A well-ordered Christian household is a powerful argument in favor of the reality of the Christian religion—an argument that the infidel cannot gainsay. All can see that there is an influence at work in the family that affects the children, and that the God of Abraham is with them. If the homes of professed Christians had a right religious mold, they would exert a mighty influence for good. They would indeed be the "light of the world." The God of heaven speaks to every faithful parent in the words addressed to Abraham: "I know him, that he will command his children and his household after him, and they shall keep the way of the Lord, to do justice and judgment; that the Lord may bring upon Abraham that which He hath spoken of him."

13

The Test of Faith

Abraham had accepted without question the promise of a son, but he did not wait for God to fulfill His word in His own time and way. A delay was permitted, to test his faith in the power of God; but he failed to endure the trial. Thinking it impossible that a child should be given her in her old age, Sarah suggested, as a plan by which the divine purpose might be fulfilled, that one of her handmaidens should be taken by Abraham as a secondary wife. Polygamy had become so widespread that it had ceased to be regarded as a sin, but it was no less a violation of the law of God, and was fatal to the sacredness and peace of the family relation. Abraham's marriage with Hagar resulted in evil, not only to his own household, but to future generations.

Flattered with the honor of her new position as Abraham's wife, and hoping to be the mother of the great nation to descend from him, Hagar became proud and boastful, and treated her mistress with contempt. Mutual jealousies disturbed the peace of the once happy home. Forced to listen to the complaints of both, Abraham vainly endeavored to restore harmony. Though it was at Sarah's earnest entreaty that he had married Hagar, she now reproached him as the one at fault. She desired to banish her rival; but Abraham refused to permit this; for Hagar was to be the mother of his child, as he fondly hoped, the son of promise. She was Sarah's servant, however, and he still left her to the control of her mistress. Hagar's haughty spirit would not brook the harshness which her insolence had provoked. "When Sarai dealt hardly with her, she fled from her face."

She made her way to the desert, and as she rested beside a fountain, lonely and friendless, an angel of the Lord, in human form, appeared

This chapter is based on Genesis 16; 17:18-20; 21:1-14; 22:1-19.

to her. Addressing her as "Hagar, Sarai's maid," to remind her of her position and her duty, he bade her, "Return to thy mistress, and submit thyself under her hands." Yet with the reproof there were mingled words of comfort. "The Lord hath heard thy affliction." "I will multiply thy seed exceedingly, that it shall not be numbered for multitude." And as a perpetual reminder of His mercy, she was bidden to call her child Ishmael, "God shall hear."

When Abraham was nearly one hundred years old, the promise of a son was repeated to him, with the assurance that the future heir should be the child of Sarah. But Abraham did not yet understand the promise. His mind at once turned to Ishmael, clinging to the belief that through him God's gracious purposes were to be accomplished. In his affection for his son he exclaimed, "O that Ishmael might live before Thee!" Again the promise was given, in words that could not be mistaken: "Sarah thy wife shall bear thee a son indeed; and thou shalt call his name Isaac: and I will establish My covenant with him." Yet God was not unmindful of the father's prayer. "As for Ishmael," He said, "I have heard thee: Behold, I have blessed him, . . . and I will make him a great nation."

The birth of Isaac, bringing, after a lifelong waiting, the fulfillment of their dearest hopes, filled the tents of Abraham and Sarah with gladness. But to Hagar this event was the overthrow of her fondly cherished ambitions. Ishmael, now a youth, had been regarded by all in the encampment as the heir of Abraham's wealth and the inheritor of the blessings promised to his descendants. Now he was suddenly set aside; and in their disappointment, mother and son hated the child of Sarah. The general rejoicing increased their jealousy, until Ishmael dared openly to mock the heir of God's promise. Sarah saw in Ishmael's turbulent disposition a perpetual source of discord, and she appealed to Abraham, urging that Hagar and Ishmael be sent away from the encampment. The patriarch was thrown into great distress. How could he banish Ishmael his son, still dearly beloved? In his perplexity he pleaded for divine guidance. The Lord, through a holy angel, directed him to grant Sarah's desire; his love for Ishmael or Hagar ought not to stand in the way, for only thus could he restore harmony and happiness to his family. And the angel gave him the consoling promise that though separated from his father's home, Ishmael should not be forsaken by God; his life should be preserved, and he should become the father of a great nation. Abraham obeyed the angel's word, but it was not without keen suffering. The father's heart was heavy with unspoken grief as he sent away Hagar and his son.

The instruction given to Abraham touching the sacredness of the marriage relation was to be a lesson for all ages. It declares that the rights and happiness of this relation are to be carefully guarded, even at a great sacrifice. Sarah was the only true wife of Abraham. Her rights as a wife and mother no other person was entitled to share. She reverenced her husband, and in this she is presented in the New Testament as a worthy example. But she was unwilling that Abraham's affections should be given to another, and the Lord did not reprove her for requiring the banishment of her rival. Both Abraham and Sarah distrusted the power of God, and it was this error that led to the marriage with Hagar.

God had called Abraham to be the father of the faithful, and his life was to stand as an example of faith to succeeding generations. But his faith had not been perfect. He had shown distrust of God in concealing the fact that Sarah was his wife, and again in his marriage with Hagar. That he might reach the highest standard, God subjected him to another test, the closest which man was ever called to endure. In a vision of the night he was directed to repair to the land of Moriah, and there offer up his son as a burnt offering upon a mountain that should be shown him.

At the time of receiving this command, Abraham had reached the age of a hundred and twenty years. He was regarded as an old man, even in his generation. In his earlier years he had been strong to endure hardship and to brave danger, but now the ardor of his youth had passed away. One in the vigor of manhood may with courage meet difficulties and afflictions that would cause his heart to fail later in life, when his feet are faltering toward the grave. But God had reserved His last, most trying test for Abraham until the burden of years was heavy upon him, and he longed for rest from anxiety and toil.

The patriarch was dwelling at Beersheba, surrounded by prosperity and honor. He was very rich, and was honored as a mighty prince by the rulers of the land. Thousands of sheep and cattle covered the plains that spread out beyond his encampment. On every side were the tents of his retainers, the home of hundreds of faithful servants. The son of promise had grown up to manhood by his side. Heaven seemed to have crowned with its blessing a life of sacrifice in patient endurance of hope deferred.

In the obedience of faith, Abraham had forsaken his native country—had turned away from the graves of his fathers and the home of his kindred. He had wandered as a stranger in the land of his inheritance. He had waited long for the birth of the promised heir. At the command of God he had sent away his son Ishmael. And now, when the child so long desired was entering upon manhood, and the patriarch seemed able to discern the fruition of his hopes, a trial greater than all others was before him.

The command was expressed in words that must have wrung with anguish that father's heart: "Take now thy son, thine only son Isaac, whom thou lovest, . . . and offer him there for a burnt offering." Isaac was the light of his home, the solace of his old age, above all else the inheritor of the promised blessing. The loss of such a son by accident or disease would have been heart rending to the fond father; it would have bowed down his whitened head with grief; but he was commanded to shed the blood of that son with his own hand. It seemed to him a fearful impossibility.

Satan was at hand to suggest that he must be deceived, for the divine law commands, "Thou shalt not kill," and God would not require what He had once forbidden. Going outside his tent, Abraham looked up to the calm brightness of the unclouded heavens, and recalled the promise made nearly fifty years before, that his seed should be innumerable as the stars. If this promise was to be fulfilled through Isaac, how could he be put to death? Abraham was tempted to believe that he might be under a delusion. In his doubt and anguish he bowed upon the earth, and prayed, as he had never prayed before, for some confirmation of the command if he must perform this terrible duty. He remembered the angels sent to reveal to him God's purpose to destroy Sodom, and who bore to him the promise of this same son Isaac, and he went to the place where he had several times met the heavenly messengers, hoping to meet them again, and receive some further direction; but none came to his relief. Darkness seemed to shut him in; but the command of God was sounding in his ears, "Take now thy son, thine only son Isaac, whom thou lovest." That command must be obeyed, and he dared not delay. Day was approaching, and he must be on his journey.

Returning to his tent, he went to the place where Isaac lay sleeping the deep, untroubled 151 sleep of youth and innocence. For a moment the father looked upon the dear face of his son, then turned tremblingly away. He went to the side of Sarah, who was also sleeping. Should he awaken her, that she might once more embrace her child? Should he tell her of God's requirement? He longed to unburden his heart to her, and share with her this terrible responsibility; but he was restrained by the fear that she might hinder him. Isaac was her joy and pride; her life was bound up in him, and the mother's love might refuse the sacrifice.

Abraham at last summoned his son, telling him of the command to offer sacrifice upon a distant mountain. Isaac had often gone with his father to worship at some one of the various altars that marked his wanderings, and this summons excited no surprise. The preparations for the journey were quickly completed. The wood was made ready and put upon the ass, and with two menservants they set forth.

Side by side the father and the son journeyed in silence. The patriarch, pondering his heavy secret, had no heart for words. His thoughts were of the proud, fond mother, and the day when he should return to her alone. Well he knew that the knife would pierce her heart when it took the life of her son.

That day—the longest that Abraham had ever experienced—dragged slowly to its close. While his son and the young men were sleeping, he spent the night in prayer, still hoping that some heavenly messenger might come to say that the trial was enough, that the youth might return unharmed to his mother. But no relief came to his tortured soul. Another long day, another night of humiliation and prayer, while ever the command that was to leave him childless was ringing in his ears. Satan was near to whisper doubts and unbelief, but Abraham resisted his suggestions. As they were about to begin the journey of the third day, the patriarch, looking northward, saw the promised sign, a cloud of glory hovering over Mount Moriah, and he knew that the voice which had spoken to him was from heaven.

Even now he did not murmur against God, but strengthened his soul by dwelling upon the evidences of the Lord's goodness and faithfulness. This son had been unexpectedly given; and had not He who bestowed the precious gift a right to recall His own? Then faith repeated the promise, "In Isaac shall thy seed be called"—a seed numberless as the grains of sand upon the shore. Isaac was the child of a miracle, and could not the power that gave him 152 life restore it? Looking beyond that which was seen, Abraham grasped the divine word, "accounting that God was able to raise him up, even from the dead." Hebrews 11:19.

Yet none but God could understand how great was the father's sacrifice in yielding up his son to death; Abraham desired that none but God should witness the parting scene. He bade his servants remain behind, saying, "I and the lad will go yonder and worship, and come again to you." The wood was laid upon Isaac, the one to be offered, the father took the knife and the fire, and together they ascended toward the mountain summit, the young man silently wondering whence, so far from folds and flocks, the offering was to come. At last he spoke, "My father," "behold the fire and the wood: but where is the lamb for a burnt offering?" Oh, what a test was this! How the endearing words, "my father," pierced Abraham's heart! Not yet—he could not tell him now. "My son," he said, "God will provide Himself a lamb for a burnt offering."

At the appointed place they built the altar and laid the wood upon it. Then, with trembling voice, Abraham unfolded to his son the divine message. It was with terror and amazement that Isaac learned his fate, but he offered no resistance. He could have escaped his doom, had he chosen to do so; the grief-stricken old man, exhausted with the struggle of those three terrible days, could not have opposed the will of the vigorous youth. But Isaac had been trained from childhood to ready, trusting obedience, and as the purpose of God was opened before him, he yielded a willing submission. He was a sharer in Abraham's faith, and he felt that he was honored in being called to give his life as an offering to God. He tenderly seeks to lighten the father's grief, and encourages his nerveless hands to bind the cords that confine him to the altar.

And now the last words of love are spoken, the last tears are shed, the last embrace is given. The father lifts the knife to slay his son, when suddenly his arm is stayed. An angel of God calls to the patriarch out of heaven, "Abraham, Abraham!" He quickly answers, "Here am I." And again the voice is heard, "Lay not thine hand upon the lad, neither do thou any thing unto him for now I know that thou fearest God, seeing thou hast not withheld thy son, thine only son, from Me."

153 Then Abraham saw "a ram caught in a thicket," and quickly bringing the new victim, he offered it "in the stead of his son." In his joy and gratitude Abraham gave a new name to the sacred spot—"Jehovah-jireh," "the Lord will provide."

On Mount Moriah, God again renewed His covenant, confirming with a solemn oath the blessing to Abraham and to his seed through all coming generations: "By Myself have I sworn, saith Jehovah, for because thou hast done this thing, and hast not withheld thy son, thine only son, that in blessing I will bless thee, and in multiplying I will multiply thy seed as the stars of the heaven, and as the sand which is upon the seashore; and thy seed shall possess the gate of his enemies; and in thy seed shall all the nations of the earth be blessed; because thou hast obeyed My voice."

Abraham's great act of faith stands like a pillar of light, illuminating the pathway of God's servants in all succeeding ages. Abraham did not seek to excuse himself from doing the will of God. During that three days' journey he had sufficient time to reason, and to doubt God, if he was disposed to doubt. He might have reasoned that the slaying of his son would cause him to be looked upon as a murderer, a second Cain; that it would cause his teaching to be rejected and despised, and thus destroy his power to do good to his fellow men. He might have pleaded that age should excuse him from obedience. But the patriarch did not take refuge in any of these excuses. Abraham was human;

his passions and attachments were like ours; but he did not stop to question how the promise could be fulfilled if Isaac should be slain. He did not stay to reason with his aching heart. He knew that God is just and righteous in all His requirements, and he obeyed the command to the very letter.

"Abraham believed God, and it was imputed unto him for righteousness: and he was called the friend of God." James 2:23. And Paul says, "They which are of faith, the same are the children of Abraham." Galatians 3:7. But Abraham's faith was made manifest by his works. "Was not Abraham our father justified by works, when he had offered Isaac his son upon the altar? Seest thou how faith wrought with his works, and by works was faith made perfect?" James 2:21, 22. There are many who fail to understand the relation of faith and works. They say, "Only believe in Christ, and you are safe. You have nothing to do with keeping the law." 154 But genuine faith will be manifest in obedience. Said Christ to the unbelieving Jews, "If ye were Abraham's children, ye would do the works of Abraham." John 8:39. And concerning the father of the faithful the Lord declares, "Abraham obeyed My voice, and kept My charge, My commandments, My statutes, and My laws." Genesis 26:5. Says the apostle James, "Faith, if it hath not works, is dead, being alone." James 2:17. And John, who dwells so fully upon love, tells us, "This is the love of God, that we keep His commandments." 1 John 5:3.

Through type and promise God "preached before the gospel unto Abraham." Galatians 3:8. And the patriarch's faith was fixed upon the Redeemer to come. Said Christ to the Jews, "Your father Abraham rejoiced that he should see My day; and he saw it, and was glad." John 8:56, R.V., margin. The ram offered in the place of Isaac represented the Son of God, who was to be sacrificed in our stead. When man was doomed to death by transgression of the law of God, the Father, looking upon His Son, said to the sinner, "Live: I have found a ransom."

It was to impress Abraham's mind with the reality of the gospel, as well as to test his faith, that God commanded him to slay his son. The agony which he endured during the dark days of that fearful trial was permitted that he might understand from his own experience something of the greatness of the sacrifice made by the infinite God for man's redemption. No other test could have caused Abraham such torture of soul as did the offering of his son. God gave His Son to a death of agony and shame. The angels who witnessed the humiliation and soul anguish of the Son of God were not permitted to interpose, as in the case of Isaac. There was no voice to cry, "It is enough." To save the fallen race, the King of glory yielded up His life. What stronger proof can be given of the infinite compassion and love of God? "He that spared not His own Son, but delivered Him up for us all, how shall He not with Him also freely give us all things?" Romans 8:32.

The sacrifice required of Abraham was not alone for his own good, nor solely for the benefit of succeeding generations; but it was also for the instruction of the sinless intelligences of heaven and of other worlds. The field of the controversy between Christ and Satan—the field on which the plan of redemption is wrought out—is the lesson book of the universe. Because Abraham had shown a lack of faith in God's promises, Satan had accused him before the angels and before God of having failed to comply with the conditions of the covenant, and as unworthy of its blessings. God desired to prove the loyalty of His servant before all heaven, to demonstrate that nothing less than perfect obedience can be accepted, and to open more fully before them the plan of salvation.

Heavenly beings were witnesses of the scene as the faith of Abraham and the submission of Isaac were tested. The trial was far more severe than that which had been brought upon Adam. Compliance with the prohibition laid upon our first parents involved no suffering, but the command to Abraham demanded the most agonizing sacrifice. All heaven beheld with wonder and admiration Abraham's unfaltering obedience. All heaven applauded his fidelity. Satan's accusations were shown to be false. God declared to His servant, "Now I know that thou fearest God [notwithstanding Satan's charges], seeing thou hast not withheld thy son, thine only son from Me." God's covenant, confirmed to Abraham by an oath before the intelligences of other worlds, testified that obedience will be rewarded.

It had been difficult even for the angels to grasp the mystery of redemption—to comprehend that the Commander of heaven, the Son of God, must die for guilty man. When the command was given to Abraham to offer up his son, the interest of all heavenly beings was enlisted. With intense earnestness they watched each step in the fulfillment of this command. When to Isaac's question, "Where is the lamb for a burnt offering?" Abraham made answer, "God will provide Himself a lamb;" and when the father's hand was stayed as he was about to slay his son, and the ram which God had provided was offered in the place of Isaac—then light was shed upon the mystery of redemption, and even the angels understood more clearly the wonderful provision that God had made for man's salvation. 1 Peter 1:12.

14
Destruction of Sodom

Fairest among the cities of the Jordan Valley was Sodom, set in a plain which was "as the garden of the Lord" in its fertility and beauty. Here the luxuriant vegetation of the tropics flourished. Here was the home of the palm tree, the olive, and the vine; and flowers shed their fragrance throughout the year. Rich harvests clothed the fields, and flocks and herds covered the encircling hills. Art and commerce contributed to enrich the proud city of the plain. The treasures of the East adorned her palaces, and the caravans of the desert brought their stores of precious things to supply her marts of trade. With little thought or labor, every want of life could be supplied, and the whole year seemed one round of festivity.

The profusion reigning everywhere gave birth to luxury and pride. Idleness and riches make the heart hard that has never been oppressed by want or burdened by sorrow. The love of pleasure was fostered by wealth and leisure, and the people gave themselves up to sensual indulgence. "Behold," says the prophet, "this was the iniquity of thy sister Sodom, pride, fullness of bread, and abundance of idleness was in her and in her daughters, neither did she strengthen the hand of the poor and needy. And they were haughty, and committed abomination before Me: therefore I took them away as I saw good." Ezekiel 16:49, 50. There is nothing more desired among men than riches and leisure, and yet these gave birth to the sins that brought destruction upon the cities of the plain. Their useless, idle life made them a prey to Satan's temptations, and they defaced the image of God, and became satanic rather than divine. Idleness is the greatest curse that can fall upon man, for vice and crime follow in its train. It enfeebles the mind, perverts the understanding, and debases the soul. Satan lies in ambush, ready to destroy those who are unguarded, whose leisure gives him opportunity to insinuate himself under some attractive disguise. He is never more successful than when he comes to men in their idle hours.

In Sodom there was mirth and revelry, feasting and drunkenness. The vilest and most brutal passions were unrestrained. The people openly defied God and His law and delighted in deeds of violence. Though they had before them the example of the antediluvian world, and knew how the wrath of God had been manifested in their destruction, yet they followed the same course of wickedness.

At the time of Lot's removal to Sodom, cor-

This chapter is based on Genesis 19.

ruption had not become universal, and God in His mercy permitted rays of light to shine amid the moral darkness. When Abraham rescued the captives from the Elamites, the attention of the people was called to the true faith. Abraham was not a stranger to the people of Sodom, and his worship of the unseen God had been a matter of ridicule among them; but his victory over greatly superior forces, and his magnanimous disposition of the prisoners and spoil, excited wonder and admiration. While his skill and valor were extolled, none could avoid the conviction that a divine power had made him conqueror. And his noble and unselfish spirit, so foreign to the self-seeking inhabitants of Sodom, was another evidence of the superiority of the religion which he had honored by his courage and fidelity.

Melchizedek, in bestowing the benediction upon Abraham, had acknowledged Jehovah as the source of his strength and the author of the victory: "Blessed be Abram of the most high God, possessor of heaven and earth: and blessed be the most high God, which hath delivered thine enemies into thy hand." Genesis 14:19, 20. God was speaking to that people by His providence, but the last ray of light was rejected as all before had been.

And now the last night of Sodom was approaching. Already the clouds of vengeance cast their shadows over the devoted city. But men perceived it not. While angels drew near on their mission of destruction, men were dreaming of prosperity and pleasure. The last day was like every other that had come and gone. Evening fell upon a scene of loveliness and security. A landscape of unrivaled beauty was bathed in the rays of the declining sun. The coolness of eventide had called forth the inhabitants of the city, and the pleasure-seeking throngs were passing to and fro, intent upon the enjoyment of the hour.

In the twilight two strangers drew near to the city gate. They were apparently travelers coming in to tarry for the night. None could discern in those humble wayfarers the mighty heralds of divine judgment, and little dreamed the gay, careless multitude that in their treatment of these heavenly messengers that very night they would reach the climax of the guilt which doomed their proud city. But there was one man who manifested kindly attention toward the strangers and invited them to his home. Lot did not know their true character, but politeness and hospitality were habitual with him; they were a part of his religion—lessons that he had learned from the example of Abraham. Had he not cultivated a spirit of courtesy, he might have been left to perish with the rest of Sodom. Many a household, in closing its doors against a stranger, has shut out God's messenger, who would have brought blessing and hope and

peace.

Every act of life, however small, has its bearing for good or for evil. Faithfulness or neglect in what are apparently the smallest duties may open the door for life's richest blessings or its greatest calamities. It is little things that test the character. It is the unpretending acts of daily self-denial, performed with a cheerful, willing heart, that God smiles upon. We are not to live for self, but for others. And it is only by self-forgetfulness, by cherishing a loving, helpful spirit, that we can make our life a blessing. The little attentions, the small, simple courtesies, go far to make up the sum of life's happiness, and the neglect of these constitutes no small share of human wretchedness.

Seeing the abuse to which strangers were exposed in Sodom, Lot made it one of his duties to guard them at their entrance, by offering them entertainment at his own house. He was sitting at the gate as the travelers approached, and upon observing them, he rose from his place to meet them, and bowing courteously, said, "Behold now, my lords, turn in, I pray you, into your servant's house, and tarry all night." They seemed to decline his hospitality, saying, "Nay; but we will abide in the street." Their object in this answer was twofold—to test the sincerity of Lot and also to appear ignorant of the character of the men of Sodom, as if they supposed it safe to remain in the street at night. Their answer made Lot the more determined not to leave them to the mercy of the rabble. He pressed his invitation until they yielded, and accompanied him to his house.

He had hoped to conceal his intention from the idlers at the gate by bringing the strangers to his home by a circuitous route; but their hesitation and delay, and his persistent urging, caused them to be observed, and before they had retired for the night, a lawless crowd gathered about the house. It was an immense company, youth and aged men alike inflamed by the vilest passions. The strangers had been making inquiry in regard to the character of the city, and Lot had warned them not to venture out of his door that night, when the hooting and jeers of the mob were heard, demanding that the men be brought out to them.

Knowing that if provoked to violence they could easily break into his house, Lot went out to try the effect of persuasion upon them. "I pray you, brethren," he said, "do not so wickedly," using the term "brethren" in the sense of neighbors, and hoping to conciliate them and make them ashamed of their vile purposes. But his words were like oil upon the flames. Their rage became like the roaring of a tempest. They mocked Lot as making himself a judge over them, and threatened to deal worse with him than they had purposed toward his guests. They rushed upon him, and would have torn him in pieces had he not been rescued by the angels of God. The heavenly messengers "put forth their hand, and pulled Lot into the house to them, and shut to the door." The events that followed, revealed the character of the guests he had entertained. "They smote the men that were at the door of the house with blindness, both small and great: so that they wearied themselves to find the door." Had they not been visited with double blindness, being given up to hardness of heart, the stroke of God upon them would have caused them to fear, and to desist from their evil work. That last night was marked by no greater sins than many others before it; but mercy, so long slighted, had at last ceased its pleading. The inhabitants of Sodom had passed the limits of divine forbearance—"the hidden boundary between God's patience and His wrath." The fires of His vengeance were about to be kindled in the vale of Siddim.

The angels revealed to Lot the object of their mission: "We will destroy this place, because the cry of them is waxen great before the face of the Lord; and the Lord hath sent us to destroy 160 it." The strangers whom Lot had endeavored to protect, now promised to protect him, and to save also all the members of his family who would flee with him from the wicked city. The mob had wearied themselves out and departed, and Lot went out to warn his children. He repeated the words of the angels, "Up, get you out of this place; for the Lord will destroy this city." But he seemed to them as one that mocked. They laughed at what they called his superstitious fears. His daughters were influenced by their husbands. They were well enough off where they were. They could see no evidence of danger. Everything was just as it had been. They had great possessions, and they could not believe it possible that beautiful Sodom would be destroyed.

Lot returned sorrowfully to his home and told the story of his failure. Then the angels bade him arise and take his wife and the two daughters who were yet in his house and leave the city. But Lot delayed. Though daily distressed at beholding deeds of violence, he had no true conception of the debasing and abominable iniquity practiced in that vile city. He did not realize the terrible necessity for God's judgments to put a check on sin. Some of his children clung to Sodom, and his wife refused to depart without them. The thought of leaving those whom he held dearest on earth seemed more than he could bear. It was hard to forsake his luxurious home and all the wealth acquired by the labors of his whole life, to go forth a destitute wanderer. Stupefied with sorrow, he lingered, loath to depart. But for the angels of God, they would all have perished in the ruin of Sodom. The heavenly messengers took him and his wife and daughters by the hand and led them out of the city.

Here the angels left them, and turned back to Sodom to accomplish their work of destruction. Another—He with whom Abraham had pleaded—drew near to Lot. In all the cities of the plain, even ten righteous persons had not been found; but in answer to the patriarch's prayer, the one man who feared God was snatched from destruction. The command was given with startling vehemence: "Escape for thy life; look not behind thee, neither stay thou in all the plain; escape to the mountain, lest thou be consumed." Hesitancy or delay now would be fatal. To cast one lingering look upon the devoted city, to tarry for one moment from regret to leave so beautiful a home, would have cost their life. The 161 storm of divine judgment was only waiting that these poor fugitives might make their escape.

But Lot, confused and terrified, pleaded that he could not do as he was required lest some evil should overtake him and he should die. Living in that wicked city, in the midst of unbelief, his faith had grown dim. The Prince of heaven was by his side, yet he pleaded for his own life as though God, who had manifested such care and love for him, would not still preserve him. He should have trusted himself wholly to the divine Messenger, giving his will and his life into the Lord's hands without a doubt or a question. But like so many others, he endeavored to plan for himself: "Behold now, this city is near to flee unto, and it is a little one: O, let me escape thither, (is it not a little one?) and my soul shall live." The city here mentioned was Bela, afterward called Zoar. It was but a few miles from Sodom, and, like it, was corrupt and doomed to destruction. But Lot asked that it might be spared, urging that this was but a small request; and his desire was granted. The Lord assured him, "I have accepted thee concerning this thing also, that I will not overthrow this city, for the which thou hast spoken." Oh, how great the mercy of God toward His erring creatures!

Again the solemn command was given to hasten, for the fiery storm would be delayed but little longer. But one of the fugitives ventured to cast a look backward to the doomed city, and she became a monument of God's judgment. If Lot himself had manifested no hesitancy to obey the angels' warning, but had earnestly fled toward the mountains, without one word of pleading or remonstrance, his wife also would have made her escape. The influence of his example would have saved her from the sin that sealed her doom. But his hesitancy and delay caused her to lightly regard the divine warning. While her body was upon the plain, her heart clung to Sodom, and she perished with it. She rebelled against God because His judgments involved her possessions and her children in the ruin. Although so greatly favored in being called out from the wicked city, she felt that she was severely dealt with, because the wealth that it had taken years to accumulate must be left to destruction. Instead of thankfully accepting deliverance, she presumptuously looked back to desire the life of those who had rejected the divine warning. Her sin showed her to be unworthy of life, for the preservation of which she felt so little gratitude.

We should beware of treating lightly God's gracious provisions for our salvation. There are Christians who say, "I do not care to be saved unless my companion and children are saved with me." They feel that heaven would not be heaven to them without the presence of those who are so dear. But have those who cherish this feeling a right conception of their own relation to God, in view of His great goodness and mercy toward them? Have they forgotten that they are bound by the strongest ties of love and honor and loyalty to the service of their Creator and Redeemer? The invitations of mercy are addressed to all; and because our friends reject the Saviour's pleading love, shall we also turn away? The redemption of the soul is precious. Christ has paid an infinite price for our salvation, and no one who appreciates the value of this great sacrifice or the worth of the soul will despise God's offered mercy because others choose to do so. The very fact that others are ignoring His just claims should arouse us to greater diligence, that we may honor God ourselves, and lead all whom we can influence, to accept His love.

"The sun was risen upon the earth when Lot entered into Zoar." The bright rays of the morning seemed to speak only prosperity and peace to the cities of the plain. The stir of active life began in the streets; men were going their various ways, intent on the business or the pleasures of the day. The sons-in-law of Lot were making merry at the fears and warnings of the weak-minded old man. Suddenly and unexpectedly as would be a thunder peal from an unclouded sky, the tempest broke. The Lord rained brimstone and fire out of heaven upon the cities and the fruitful plain; its palaces and temples, costly dwellings, gardens and vineyards, and the gay, pleasure-seeking throngs that only the night before had insulted the messengers of heaven— all were consumed. The smoke of the conflagration went up like the smoke of a great furnace. And the fair vale of Siddim became a desolation, a place never to be built up or inhabited—a witness to all generations of the certainty of God's judgments upon transgression.

The flames that consumed the cities of the plain shed their warning light down even to our time. We are taught the fearful and solemn lesson that while God's mercy bears long with the transgressor, there is a limit beyond which men may not go on in sin. When that limit is reached, then the offers of mercy are withdrawn, and the ministration of judgment begins.

The Redeemer of the world declares that there are greater sins than that for which Sodom and Gomorrah were destroyed. Those who hear the gospel invitation calling sinners to repentance, and heed it not, are more guilty before God than were the dwellers in the vale of Siddim. And still greater sin is theirs who profess to know God and to keep His commandments, yet who deny Christ in their character and their daily life. In the light of the Saviour's warning, the fate of Sodom is a solemn admonition, not merely to those who are guilty of outbreaking sin, but to all who are trifling with Heaven-sent light and privileges.

Said the True Witness to the church at Ephesus: "I have somewhat against thee, because thou hast left thy first love. Remember therefore from whence thou art fallen, and repent, and do the first works; or else I will come unto thee quickly, and will remove thy candlestick out of his place, except thou repent." Revelation 2:4, 5. The Saviour watches for a response to His offers of love and forgiveness, with a more tender compassion than that which moves the heart of an earthly parent to forgive a wayward, suffering son. He cries after the wanderer, "Return unto Me, and I will return unto you." Malachi 3:7. But if the erring one persistently refuses to heed the voice that calls him with pitying, tender love, he will at last be left in darkness. The heart that has long slighted God's mercy, becomes hardened in sin, and is no longer susceptible to the influence of the grace of God. Fearful will be the doom of that soul of whom the pleading Saviour shall finally declare, he "is joined to idols: let him alone." Hosea 4:17. It will be more tolerable in the day of judgment for the cities of the plain than for those who have known the love of Christ, and yet have turned away to choose the pleasures of a world of sin.

You who are slighting the offers of mercy, think of the long array of figures accumulating against you in the books of heaven; for there is a record kept of the impieties of nations, of families, of individuals. God may bear long while the account goes on, and calls to repentance and offers of pardon may be given; yet a time will come when the account will be full; when the soul's decision has been made; when by his own choice man's destiny has been fixed. Then the signal will be given for judgment to be executed.

There is cause for alarm in the condition of the religious world today. God's mercy has been trifled with. The multitudes make void the law of Jehovah, "teaching for doctrines the commandments of men." Matthew 15:9. Infidelity prevails in many of the churches in our land; not infidelity in its broadest sense—an open denial of the Bible—but an infidelity that is robed in the garb of Christianity, while it is undermining faith in the Bible as a revelation from God. Fervent devotion and vital piety have given place to hollow formalism. As the result, apostasy and sensualism prevail. Christ declared, "As it was in the days of Lot, . . . even thus shall it be in the day when the Son of man is revealed." Luke 17:28, 30. The daily record of passing events testifies to the fulfillment of His words. The world is fast becoming ripe for destruction. Soon the judgments of God are to be poured out, and sin and sinners are to be consumed.

Said our Saviour: "Take heed to yourselves, lest at any time your hearts be overcharged with surfeiting, and drunkenness, and cares of this life, and so that day come upon you unawares. For as a snare shall it come on all them that dwell on the face of the whole earth"—upon all whose interests are centered in this world. "Watch ye therefore, and pray always, that ye may be accounted worthy to escape all these things that shall come to pass, and to stand before the Son of man." Luke 21:34-36.

Before the destruction of Sodom, God sent a message to Lot, "Escape for thy life; look not behind thee, neither stay thou in all the plain; escape to the mountain, lest thou be consumed." The same voice of warning was heard by the disciples of Christ before the destruction of Jerusalem: "When ye shall see Jerusalem compassed with armies, then know that the desolation thereof is nigh. Then let them which are in Judea flee to the mountains." Luke 21:20, 21. They must not tarry to secure anything from their possessions, but must make the most of the opportunity to escape.

There was a coming out, a decided separation from the wicked, an escape for life. So it was in the days of Noah; so with Lot; so with the disciples prior to the destruction of Jerusalem; and so it will be in the last days. Again the voice of God is heard in a message of warning, bidding His people separate themselves from the prevailing iniquity.

167   The state of corruption and apostasy that in the last days would exist in the religious world, was presented to the prophet John in the vision of Babylon, "that great city, which reigneth over the kings of the earth." Revelation 17:18. Before its destruction the call is to be given from heaven, "Come out of her, My people, that ye be not partakers of her sins, and that ye receive not of her plagues." Revelation 18:4. As in the days of Noah and Lot, there must be a marked separation from sin and sinners. There can be no compromise between God and the world, no turning back to secure earthly treasures. "Ye cannot serve God and mammon." Matthew 6:24.

Like the dwellers in the vale of Siddim, the people are dreaming of prosperity and peace. "Escape for thy life," is the warning from the angels of God; but other voices are heard saying, "Be not excited; there is no cause for alarm." The multitudes cry, "Peace and safety," while Heaven declares that swift destruction is about to come upon the transgressor. On the night prior to their destruction, the cities of the plain rioted in pleasure and derided the fears and warnings of the messenger of God; but those scoffers perished in the flames; that very night the door of mercy was forever closed to the wicked, careless inhabitants of Sodom. God will not always be mocked; He will not long be trifled with. "Behold, the day of the Lord cometh, cruel both with wrath and fierce anger, to lay the land desolate: and He shall destroy the sinners thereof out of it." Isaiah 13:9. The great mass of the world will reject God's mercy, and will be overwhelmed in swift and irretrievable ruin. But those who heed the warning shall dwell "in the secret place of the Most High," and "abide under the shadow of the Almighty." His truth shall be their shield and buckler. For them is the promise, "With long life will I satisfy him, and show him My salvation." Psalm 91:1, 4, 16.

Lot dwelt but a short time in Zoar. Iniquity prevailed there as in Sodom, and he feared to remain, lest the city should be destroyed. Not long after, Zoar was consumed, as God had purposed. Lot made his way to the mountains, and abode in a cave, stripped of all for which he had dared to subject his family to the influences of a wicked city. But the curse of Sodom followed him even here. The sinful conduct of his daughters was the result of the evil associations of that vile place. Its moral corruption had become so 168 interwoven with their character that they could not distinguish between good and evil. Lot's only posterity, the Moabites and Ammonites, were vile, idolatrous tribes, rebels against God and bitter enemies of His people.

In how wide contrast to the life of Abraham was that of Lot! Once they had been companions, worshiping at one altar, dwelling side by side in their pilgrim tents; but how widely separated now! Lot had chosen Sodom for its pleasure and profit. Leaving Abraham's altar and its daily sacrifice to the living God, he had permitted his children to mingle with a corrupt and idolatrous people; yet he had retained in his heart the fear of God, for he is declared in the Scriptures to have been a "just" man; his righteous soul was vexed with the vile conversation that greeted his ears daily and the violence and crime he was powerless to prevent. He was saved at last as "a brand plucked out of the fire" (Zechariah 3:2), yet stripped of his possessions, bereaved of his wife and children, dwelling in caves, like the wild beasts, covered with infamy in his old age; and he gave to the world, not a race of righteous men, but two idolatrous nations, at enmity with God and warring upon His people, until, their cup of iniquity being full, they were appointed to destruction. How terrible were the results that followed one unwise step!

Says the wise man, "Labor not to be rich: cease from thine own wisdom." "He that is greedy of gain troubleth his own house; but he that hateth gifts shall live." Proverbs 23:4; 15:27. And the apostle Paul declares, "They that will be rich fall into temptation and a snare, and into many foolish and hurtful lusts, which drown men in destruction and perdition." 1 Timothy 6:9.

When Lot entered Sodom he fully intended to keep himself free from iniquity and to command his household after him. But he signally failed. The corrupting influences about him had an effect upon his own faith, and his children's connection with the inhabitants of Sodom bound up his interest in a measure with theirs. The result is before us.

Many are still making a similar mistake. In selecting a home they look more to the temporal advantages they may gain than to the moral and social influences that will surround themselves and their families. They choose a beautiful and fertile country, or remove to some flourishing 169 city, in the hope of securing greater prosperity; but their children are surrounded by temptation, and too often they form associations that are unfavorable to the development of piety and the formation of a right character. The atmosphere of lax morality, of unbelief, of indifference to religious things, has a tendency to counteract the influence of the parents. Examples of rebellion against parental and divine authority are ever before the youth; many form attachments for infidels and unbelievers, and cast in their lot with the enemies of God.

In choosing a home, God would have us consider, first of all, the moral and religious influences that will surround us and our families. We may be placed in trying positions, for many cannot have their surroundings what they would; and whenever duty calls us, God will enable us to stand uncorrupted, if we watch and pray, trusting in the grace of Christ. But we should not needlessly expose ourselves to influences that are unfavorable to the formation of Christian character. When we voluntarily place ourselves in an atmosphere of worldliness and unbelief, we displease God and drive holy angels from our homes.

Those who secure for their children worldly wealth and honor at the expense of their eternal interests, will find in the end that these advantages are a terrible loss. Like Lot, many see their children ruined, and barely save their own souls. Their lifework is lost; their life is a sad failure. Had they exercised true wisdom, their children might have had less of worldly prosperity, but they would have made sure of a title to the immortal inheritance.

The heritage that God has promised to His people is not in this world. Abraham had no possession in the earth, "no, not so much as to set his foot on." Acts 7:5. He possessed great substance, and he used it to the glory of God and the good of his fellow men; but he did not look upon this world as his home. The Lord had called him to leave his idolatrous countrymen, with the promise of the land of Canaan as an everlasting possession; yet neither he nor his son nor his son's son received it. When Abraham desired a burial place for his dead, he had to buy it of the Canaanites. His sole possession in the Land of Promise was that rock-hewn tomb in the cave of Machpelah.

But the word of God had not failed; neither did it meet its final accomplishment in the occupation of Canaan by the Jewish people. "To Abraham and his seed were the promises made." Galatians 3:16. Abraham himself was to 170 share the inheritance. The fulfillment of God's promise may seem to be long delayed—for "one day is with the Lord as a thousand years, and a thousand years as one day" (2 Peter 3:8); it may appear to tarry; but at the appointed time "it will surely come, it will not tarry." Habakkuk 2:3. The gift to Abraham and his seed included not merely the land of Canaan, but the whole earth. So says the apostle, "The promise, that he should be the heir of the world, was not to Abraham, or to his seed, through the law, but through the righteousness of faith." Romans 4:13. And the Bible plainly teaches that the promises made to Abraham are to be fulfilled through Christ. All that are Christ's are "Abraham's seed, and heirs according to the promise"—heirs to "an inheritance incorruptible, and undefiled, and that fadeth not away"— the earth freed from the curse of sin. Galatians 3:29; 1 Peter 1:4. For "the kingdom and dominion, and the greatness of the kingdom under the whole heaven, shall be given to the people of the saints of the Most High;" and "the meek shall inherit the earth; and shall delight themselves in the abundance of peace." Daniel 7:27; Psalm 37:11.

God gave to Abraham a view of this immortal inheritance, and with this hope he was content. "By faith he sojourned in the Land of Promise, as in a strange country, dwelling in tabernacles with Isaac and Jacob, the heirs with him of the same promise: for he looked for a city which hath foundations, whose builder and maker is God." Hebrews 11:9, 10.

Of the posterity of Abraham it is written, "These all died in faith, not having received the promises, but having seen them afar off, and were persuaded of them, and embraced them, and confessed that they were strangers and pilgrims on the earth." Verse 13. We must dwell as pilgrims and strangers here if we would gain "a better country, that is, an heavenly." Verse 16. Those who are children of Abraham will be seeking the city which he looked for, "whose builder and maker is God."

15
The Marriage of Isaac

Abraham had become an old man, and expected soon to die; yet one act remained for him to do in securing the fulfillment of the promise to his posterity. Isaac was the one divinely appointed to succeed him as the keeper of the law of God and the father of the chosen people, but he was yet unmarried. The inhabitants of Canaan were given to idolatry, and God had forbidden intermarriage between His people and them, knowing that such marriages would lead to apostasy. The patriarch feared the effect of the corrupting influences surrounding his son. Abraham's habitual faith in God and submission to His will were reflected in the character of Isaac; but the young man's affections were strong, and he was gentle and yielding in disposition. If united with one who did not fear God, he would be in danger of sacrificing principle for the sake of harmony. In the mind of Abraham the choice of a wife for his son was a matter of grave importance; he was anxious to have him marry one who would not lead him from God.

In ancient times marriage engagements were generally made by the parents, and this was the custom among those who worshiped God. None were required to marry those whom they could not love; but in the bestowal of their affections the youth were guided by the judgment of their experienced, God-fearing parents. It was regarded as a dishonor to parents, and even a crime, to pursue a course contrary to this.

Isaac, trusting to his father's wisdom and affection, was satisfied to commit the matter to him, believing also that God Himself would direct in the choice made. The patriarch's thoughts turned to his father's kindred in the land of Mesopotamia. Though not free from idolatry, they cherished the knowledge and the worship of the true God. Isaac must not leave Canaan to go to them, but it might be that among them could be found one who would leave her home and unite with him in maintaining the pure worship of the living God. Abraham committed the important matter to "his eldest servant," a man of piety, experience, and sound judgment, who had rendered him long and faithful service. He required this servant to make a solemn oath before the Lord, that he would not take a wife for Isaac of the Canaanites, but would choose a maiden from the family of Nahor in Mesopotamia. He charged him not to take Isaac thither. If a damsel could not be found who would leave her kindred, then the messenger would be released from his oath. The patriarch encouraged him in his difficult and delicate undertaking with the assurance that God would crown his mission with success. "The Lord God of heaven," he said, "which took me from my father's house, and from the land of my kindred, . . . He shall send His angel before thee."

The messenger set out without delay. Taking with him ten camels for the use of his own company and the bridal party that might return with him, provided also with gifts for the intended wife and her friends, he made the long journey beyond Damascus, and onward to the rich plains that border on the great river of the East. Arrived at Haran, "the city of Nahor," he halted outside the walls, near the well to which the women of the place came at evening for water. It was a time of anxious thought with him. Important results, not only to his master's household, but to future generations, might follow from the choice he made; and how was he to choose wisely among entire strangers? Remembering the words of Abraham, that God would send His angel with him, he prayed earnestly for positive guidance. In the family of his master he was accustomed to the constant exercise of kindness and hospitality, and he now asked that an act of courtesy might indicate the maiden whom God had chosen.

Hardly was the prayer uttered before the answer was given. Among the women who were gathered at the well, the courteous manners of one attracted his attention. As she came from the well, the stranger went to meet her, asking for some water from the pitcher upon her shoulder. The request received a kindly answer, with an offer to draw water for the camels also, a service which it was customary even for the daughters of princes to perform for their fathers' flocks and herds. Thus the desired sign was given. The maiden "was very fair to look upon," and her ready courtesy gave evidence of a kind heart and an active, energetic nature. Thus far the divine hand had been with him. After acknowledging her kindness by rich gifts, the messenger asked her parentage, and on learning that she was the daughter of Bethuel, Abraham's nephew, he "bowed down his head, and worshiped the Lord."

The man had asked for entertainment at her father's house, and in his expressions of thanksgiving had revealed the fact of his connection with Abraham. Returning home, the maiden told what had happened, and Laban, her brother, at once hastened to bring the stranger and his attendants to share their hospitality.

Eliezer would not partake of food until he had told his errand, his prayer at the well, with all

This chapter is based on Genesis 24.

the circumstances attending it. Then he said, "And now, if ye will deal kindly and truly with my master, tell me: and if not, tell me; that I may turn to the right hand, or to the left." The answer was, "The thing proceedeth from the Lord: we cannot speak unto thee bad or good. Behold, Rebekah is before thee; take her, and go, and let her be thy master's son's wife, as the Lord hath spoken."

After the consent of the family had been obtained, Rebekah herself was consulted as to whether she would go to so great a distance from her father's house, to marry the son of Abraham. She believed, from what had taken place, that God had selected her to be Isaac's wife, and she said, "I will go."

The servant, anticipating his master's joy at the success of his mission, was impatient to be gone; and with the morning they set out on the homeward journey. Abraham dwelt at Beersheba, and Isaac, who had been attending to the flocks in the adjoining country, had returned to his father's tent to await the arrival of the messenger from Haran. "And Isaac went out to meditate in the field at the eventide: and he lifted up his eyes, and saw, and, behold, the camels were coming. And Rebekah lifted up her eyes, and when she saw Isaac, she lighted off the camel. For she had said unto the servant, What man is that that walketh in the field to meet us? And the servant had said, It is my master: therefore she took a veil, and covered herself. And the servant told Isaac all things that he had done. And Isaac brought her into his mother Sarah's tent, and took Rebekah, and she became his wife; and he loved her: and Isaac was comforted after his mother's death."

Abraham had marked the result of the intermarriage of those who feared God and those 174 who feared Him not, from the days of Cain to his own time. The consequences of his own marriage with Hagar, and of the marriage connections of Ishmael and Lot, were before him. The lack of faith on the part of Abraham and Sarah had resulted in the birth of Ishmael, the mingling of the righteous seed with the ungodly. The father's influence upon his son was counteracted by that of the mother's idolatrous kindred and by Ishmael's connection with heathen wives. The jealousy of Hagar, and of the wives whom she chose for Ishmael, surrounded his family with a barrier that Abraham endeavored in vain to overcome.

Abraham's early teachings had not been without effect upon Ishmael, but the influence of his wives resulted in establishing idolatry in his family. Separated from his father, and embittered by the strife and contention of a home destitute of the love and fear of God, Ishmael was driven to choose the wild, marauding life of the desert chief, "his hand" "against every man, and every man's hand against him." Genesis 16:12.

In his latter days he repented of his evil ways and returned to his father's God, but the stamp of character given to his posterity remained. The powerful nation descended from him were a turbulent, heathen people, who were ever an annoyance and affliction to the descendants of Isaac.

The wife of Lot was a selfish, irreligious woman, and her influence was exerted to separate her husband from Abraham. But for her, Lot would not have remained in Sodom, deprived of the counsel of the wise, God-fearing patriarch. The influence of his wife and the associations of that wicked city had led him to apostatize from God had it not been for the faithful instruction he had early received from Abraham. The marriage of Lot and his choice of Sodom for a home were the first links in a chain of events fraught with evil to the world for many generations.

No one who fears God can without danger connect himself with one who fears Him not. "Can two walk together, except they be agreed?" Amos 3:3. The happiness and prosperity of the marriage relation depend upon the unity of the parties; but between the believer and the unbeliever there is a radical difference of tastes, inclinations, and purposes. They are serving two masters, between whom there can be no concord. However pure and correct one's principles may be, the influence of an unbelieving companion will have a tendency to lead away from God.

He who has entered the marriage relation 175 while unconverted, is by his conversion placed under stronger obligation to be faithful to his companion, however widely they may differ in regard to religious faith; yet the claims of God should be placed above every earthly relationship, even though trials and persecution may be the result. With the spirit of love and meekness, this fidelity may have an influence to win the unbelieving one. But the marriage of Christians with the ungodly is forbidden in the Bible. The Lord's direction is, "Be ye not unequally yoked together with unbelievers." 2 Corinthians 6:14, 17, 18.

Isaac was highly honored by God in being made inheritor of the promises through which the world was to be blessed; yet when he was forty years of age he submitted to his father's judgment in appointing his experienced, God-fearing servant to choose a wife for him. And the result of that marriage, as presented in the Scriptures, is a tender and beautiful picture of domestic happiness: "Isaac brought her into his mother Sarah's tent, and took Rebekah, and she became his wife; and he loved her: and Isaac was comforted after his mother's death."

What a contrast between the course of Isaac and that pursued by the youth of our time, even among professed Christians! Young people too often feel that the bestowal of their affections is a matter in which self alone should be consulted—a matter that neither God nor their parents should in any wise control. Long before they have reached manhood or womanhood they think themselves competent to make their own choice, without the aid of their parents. A few years of married life are usually sufficient to show them their error, but often too late to prevent its baleful results. For the same lack of wisdom and self-control that dictated the hasty choice is permitted to aggravate the evil, until the marriage relation becomes a galling yoke. Many have thus wrecked their happiness in this life and their hope of the life to come.

If there is any subject which should be carefully considered and in which the counsel of older and more experienced persons should be sought, it is the subject of marriage; if ever the Bible was needed as a counselor, if ever divine guidance should be sought in prayer, it is before taking a step that binds persons together for life.

176 Parents should never lose sight of their own responsibility for the future happiness of their children. Isaac's deference to his father's judgment was the result of the training that had taught him to live a life of obedience. While Abraham required his children to respect parental authority, his daily life testified that that authority was not a selfish or arbitrary control, but was founded in love, and had their welfare and happiness in view.

Fathers and mothers should feel that a duty devolves upon them to guide the affections of the youth, that they may be placed upon those who will be suitable companions. They should feel it a duty, by their own teaching and example, with the assisting grace of God, to so mold the character of the children from their earliest years that they will be pure and noble and will be attracted to the good and true. Like attracts like; like appreciates like. Let the love for truth and purity and goodness be early implanted in the soul, and the youth will seek the society of those who possess these characteristics.

Let parents seek, in their own character and in their home life, to exemplify the love and beneficence of the heavenly Father. Let the home be full of sunshine. This will be worth far more to your children than lands or money. Let the home love be kept alive in their hearts, that they may look back upon the home of their childhood as a place of peace and happiness next to heaven. The members of the family do not all have the same stamp of character, and there will be frequent occasion for the exercise of patience and forbearance; but through love and self-discipline all may be bound together in the closest union.

True love is a high and holy principle, altogether different in character from that love which is awakened by impulse and which suddenly dies when severely tested. It is by faithfulness to duty in the parental home that the youth are to prepare themselves for homes of their own. Let them here practice self-denial and manifest kindness, courtesy, and Christian sympathy. Thus love will be kept warm in the heart, and he who goes out from such a household to stand at the head of a family of his own will know how to promote the happiness of her whom he has chosen as a companion for life. Marriage, instead of being the end of love, will be only its beginning.

16   177

Jacob and Esau

Jacob and Esau, the twin sons of Isaac, present a striking contrast, both in character and in life. This unlikeness was foretold by the angel of God before their birth. When in answer to Rebekah's troubled prayer he declared that two sons would be given her, he opened to her their future history, that each would become the head of a mighty nation, but that one would be greater than the other, and that the younger would have the pre-eminence.

Esau grew up loving self-gratification and centering all his interest in the present. Impatient of restraint, he delighted in the wild freedom of the chase, and early chose the life of a hunter. Yet he was the father's favorite. The quiet, peace-loving shepherd was attracted by the daring and vigor of this elder son, who fearlessly ranged over mountain and desert, returning home with game for his father and with exciting accounts of his adventurous life. Jacob, thoughtful, diligent, and care-taking, ever thinking more of the future than the present, was content to dwell at home, occupied in the care of the flocks and the tillage of the soil. His patient perseverance, thrift, and foresight were valued by the mother. His affections were deep and strong, and his gentle, unremitting attentions added far more to her happiness than did the boisterous and occasional kindnesses of Esau. To Rebekah, Jacob was the dearer son.

The promises made to Abraham and confirmed to his son were held by Isaac and Rebekah as the great object of their desires and hopes. With these promises Esau and Jacob were familiar. They were taught to regard the birthright as a matter of great importance, for it included not only an inheritance of worldly wealth but spiritual pre-eminence. He who received it was to be the priest of his family, and in the line of his posterity the Redeemer of the world would come. On the other hand, there were obligations resting upon the possessor of the birthright. He who   178 should inherit its blessings must devote his life to

This chapter is based on Genesis 25:19-34; 27.

71

16. Jacob and Esau

the service of God. Like Abraham, he must be obedient to the divine requirements. In marriage, in his family relations, in public life, he must consult the will of God.

Isaac made known to his sons these privileges and conditions, and plainly stated that Esau, as the eldest, was the one entitled to the birthright. But Esau had no love for devotion, no inclination to a religious life. The requirements that accompanied the spiritual birthright were an unwelcome and even hateful restraint to him. The law of God, which was the condition of the divine covenant with Abraham, was regarded by Esau as a yoke of bondage. Bent on self-indulgence, he desired nothing so much as liberty to do as he pleased. To him power and riches, feasting and reveling, were happiness. He gloried in the unrestrained freedom of his wild, roving life. Rebekah remembered the words of the angel, and she read with clearer insight than did her husband the character of their sons. She was convinced that the heritage of divine promise was intended for Jacob. She repeated to Isaac the angel's words; but the father's affections were centered upon the elder son, and he was unshaken in his purpose.

Jacob had learned from his mother of the divine intimation that the birthright should fall to him, and he was filled with an unspeakable desire for the privileges which it would confer. It was not the possession of his father's wealth that he craved; the spiritual birthright was the object of his longing. To commune with God as did righteous Abraham, to offer the sacrifice of atonement for his family, to be the progenitor of the chosen people and of the promised Messiah, and to inherit the immortal possessions embraced in the blessings of the covenant— here were the privileges and honors that kindled his most ardent desires. His mind was ever reaching forward to the future, and seeking to grasp its unseen blessings.

With secret longing he listened to all that his father told concerning the spiritual birthright; he carefully treasured what he had learned from his mother. Day and night the subject occupied his thoughts, until it became the absorbing interest of his life. But while he thus esteemed eternal above temporal blessings, Jacob had not an experimental knowledge of the God whom he revered. His heart had not been renewed by divine grace. He believed that the promise concerning himself could not be fulfilled so long as Esau retained the rights of the first-born, and he constantly studied to devise some way whereby he might secure the blessing which his brother held so lightly, but which was so precious to himself.

When Esau, coming home one day faint and weary from the chase, asked for the food that Jacob was preparing, the latter, with whom one thought was ever uppermost, seized upon his advantage, and offered to satisfy his brother's hunger at the price of the birthright. "Behold, I am at the point to die," cried the reckless, self-indulgent hunter, "and what profit shall this birthright do to me?" And for a dish of red pottage he parted with his birthright, and confirmed the transaction by an oath. A short time at most would have secured him food in his father's tents, but to satisfy the desire of the moment he carelessly bartered the glorious heritage that God Himself had promised to his fathers. His whole interest was in the present. He was ready to sacrifice the heavenly to the earthly, to exchange a future good for a momentary indulgence.

"Thus Esau despised his birthright." In disposing of it he felt a sense of relief. Now his way was unobstructed; he could do as he liked. For this wild pleasure, miscalled freedom, how many are still selling their birthright to an inheritance pure and undefiled, eternal in the heavens!

Ever subject to mere outward and earthly attractions, Esau took two wives of the daughters of Heth. They were worshipers of false gods, and their idolatry was a bitter grief to Isaac and Rebekah. Esau had violated one of the conditions of the covenant, which forbade intermarriage between the chosen people and the heathen; yet Isaac was still unshaken in his determination to bestow upon him the birthright. The reasoning of Rebekah, Jacob's strong desire for the blessing, and Esau's indifference to its obligations had no effect to change the father's purpose.

Years passed on, until Isaac, old and blind, and expecting soon to die, determined no longer to delay the bestowal of the blessing upon his elder son. But knowing the opposition of Rebekah and Jacob, he decided to perform the solemn ceremony in secret. In accordance with the custom of making a feast upon such occasions, the patriarch bade Esau, "Go out to the field, and take me some venison; and make me savory meat, . . . that my soul may bless thee before I die."

Rebekah divined his purpose. She was confident that it was contrary to what God had revealed as His will. Isaac was in danger of incurring the divine displeasure and of debarring his younger son from the position to which God had called him. She had in vain tried the effect of reasoning with Isaac, and she determined to resort to stratagem.

No sooner had Esau departed on his errand than Rebekah set about the accomplishment of her purpose. She told Jacob what had taken place, urging the necessity of immediate action to prevent the bestowal of the blessing, finally and irrevocably, upon Esau. And she assured her son that if he would follow her directions, he might obtain it as God had promised. Jacob did not readily consent to the plan that she proposed. The thought of deceiving his father caused him great distress. He felt that such a sin would bring a curse rather than a blessing. But his scruples were overborne, and he proceeded to carry out his mother's suggestions. It was not his intention to utter a direct falsehood, but once in the presence of his father he seemed to have gone too far to retreat, and he obtained by fraud the coveted blessing.

Jacob and Rebekah succeeded in their purpose, but they gained only trouble and sorrow by their deception. God had declared that Jacob should receive the birthright, and His word would have been fulfilled in His own time had they waited in faith for Him to work for them. But like many who now profess to be children of God, they were unwilling to leave the matter in His hands. Rebekah bitterly repented the wrong counsel she had given her son; it was the means of separating him from her, and she never saw his face again. From the hour when he received the birthright, Jacob was weighed down with self-condemnation. He had sinned against his father, his brother, his own soul, and against God. In one short hour he had made work for a lifelong repentance. This scene was vivid before him in afteryears, when the wicked course of his own sons oppressed his soul.

No sooner had Jacob left his father's tent than Esau entered. Though he had sold his birthright, and confirmed the transfer by a solemn oath, he was now determined to secure its blessings, regardless of his brother's claim. With the spiritual was connected the temporal birthright, which would give him the headship of the family and possession of a double portion of his father's wealth. These were blessings that he could value. "Let my father arise," he said, "and eat of his son's venison, that thy soul may bless me."

Trembling with astonishment and distress, the blind old father learned the deception that had been practiced upon him. His long and fondly cherished hopes had been thwarted, and he keenly felt the disappointment that must come upon his elder son. Yet the conviction flashed upon him that it was God's providence which had defeated his purpose and brought about the very thing he had determined to prevent. He remembered the words of the angel to Rebekah, and notwithstanding the sin of which Jacob was now guilty, he saw in him the one best fitted to accomplish the purposes of God. While the words of blessing were upon his lips, he had felt the Spirit of inspiration upon him; and now, knowing all the circumstances, he ratified the benediction unwittingly pronounced upon Jacob: "I have blessed him; yea, and he shall be blessed."

Esau had lightly valued the blessing while it seemed within his reach, but he desired to possess it now that it was gone from him forever. All the strength of his impulsive, passionate nature was aroused, and his grief and rage were terrible. He cried with an exceeding bitter cry, "Bless me, even me also, O my father!" "Hast thou not reserved a blessing for me?" But the promise given was not to be recalled. The birthright which he had so carelessly bartered he could not now regain. "For one morsel of meat," for a momentary gratification of appetite that had never been restrained, Esau sold his inheritance; but when he saw his folly, it was too late to recover the blessing. "He found no place of repentance, though he sought it carefully with tears." Hebrews 12:16, 17. Esau was not shut out from the privilege of seeking God's favor by repentance, but he could find no means of recovering the birthright. His grief did not spring from conviction of sin; he did not desire to be reconciled to God. He sorrowed because of the results of his sin, but not for the sin itself.

Because of his indifference to the divine blessings and requirements, Esau is called in Scripture "a profane person." Verse 16. He represents those who lightly value the redemption purchased for them by Christ, and are ready to sacrifice their heirship to heaven for the perishable things of earth. Multitudes live for the present, with no thought or care for the future. Like Esau they cry, "Let us eat and drink; for tomorrow we die." 1 Corinthians 15:32. They are controlled by inclination; and rather than practice self-denial, they will forgo the most valuable considerations. If one must be relinquished, the gratification of a depraved appetite or the heavenly blessings promised only to the self-denying and God-fearing, the claims of appetite prevail, and God and heaven are virtually despised. How many, even of professed Christians, cling to indulgences that are injurious to health and that benumb the sensibilities of the soul. When the duty is presented of cleansing themselves from all filthiness of the flesh and spirit, perfecting holiness in the fear of God, they are offended. They see that they cannot retain these hurtful gratifications and yet secure heaven, and they conclude that since the way to eternal life is so strait, they will no longer walk therein.

Multitudes are selling their birthright for sensual indulgence. Health is sacrificed, the mental faculties are enfeebled, and heaven is forfeited; and all for a mere temporary pleasure—an indulgence at once both weakening and debasing in its character. As Esau awoke to see the folly of his rash exchange when it was too late to recover his loss, so it will be in the day of God with those who have bartered their heirship to heaven for selfish gratifications.

183

17

Jacob's Flight and Exile

Threatened with death by the wrath of Esau, Jacob went out from his father's home a fugitive; but he carried with him the father's blessing; Isaac had renewed to him the covenant promise, and had bidden him, as its inheritor, to seek a wife of his mother's family in Mesopotamia. Yet it was with a deeply troubled heart that Jacob set out on his lonely journey. With only his staff in his hand he must travel hundreds of miles through a country inhabited by wild, roving tribes. In his remorse and timidity he sought to avoid men, lest he should be traced by his angry brother. He feared that he had lost forever the blessing that God had purposed to give him; and Satan was at hand to press temptations upon him.

The evening of the second day found him far away from his father's tents. He felt that he was an outcast, and he knew that all this trouble had been brought upon him by his own wrong course. The darkness of despair pressed upon his soul, and he hardly dared to pray. But he was so utterly lonely that he felt the need of protection from God as he had never felt it before. With weeping and deep humiliation he confessed his sin, and entreated for some evidence that he was not utterly forsaken. Still his burdened heart found no relief. He had lost all confidence in himself, and he feared that the God of his fathers had cast him off.

But God did not forsake Jacob. His mercy was still extended to His erring, distrustful servant. The Lord compassionately revealed just what Jacob needed—a Saviour. He had sinned, but his heart was filled with gratitude as he saw revealed a way by which he could be restored to the favor of God.

Wearied with his journey, the wanderer lay down upon the ground, with a stone for his pillow. As he slept he beheld a ladder, bright and shining, whose base rested upon the earth, while the top reached to heaven. Upon this ladder angels were ascending and descending; above it 184 was the Lord of glory, and from the heavens His voice was heard: "I am the Lord God of Abraham thy father, and the God of Isaac." The land whereon he lay as an exile and fugitive was promised to him and to his posterity, with the assurance, "In thee and in thy seed shall all the families of the earth be blessed." This promise had been given to Abraham and to Isaac, and now it was renewed to Jacob. Then in special regard to his present loneliness and distress, the words of comfort and encouragement were spoken: "Behold, I am with thee, and will keep thee

in all places whither thou goest, and will bring thee again into this land; for I will not leave thee, until I have done that which I have spoken to thee of."

The Lord knew the evil influences that would surround Jacob, and the perils to which he would be exposed. In mercy He opened up the future before the repentant fugitive, that he might understand the divine purpose with reference to himself, and be prepared to resist the temptations that would surely come to him when alone amid idolaters and scheming men. There would be ever before him the high standard at which he must aim; and the knowledge that through him the purpose of God was reaching its accomplishment, would constantly prompt him to faithfulness.

In this vision the plan of redemption was presented to Jacob, not fully, but in such parts as were essential to him at that time. The mystic ladder revealed to him in his dream was the same to which Christ referred in His conversation with Nathanael. Said He, "Ye shall see heaven open, and the angels of God ascending and descending upon the Son of man." John 1:51. Up to the time of man's rebellion against the government of God, there had been free communion between God and man. But the sin of Adam and Eve separated earth from heaven, so that man could not have communion with his Maker. Yet the world was not left in solitary hopelessness. The ladder represents Jesus, the appointed medium of communication. Had He not with His own merits bridged the gulf that sin had made, the ministering angels could have held no communion with fallen man. Christ connects man in his weakness and helplessness with the source of infinite power.

All this was revealed to Jacob in his dream. Although his mind at once grasped a part of the revelation, its great and mysterious truths were the study of his lifetime, and unfolded to his understanding more and more.

Jacob awoke from his sleep in the deep stillness of night. The shining forms of his vision had disappeared. Only the dim outline of the lonely hills, and above them the heavens bright with stars, now met his gaze. But he had a solemn sense that God was with him. An unseen presence filled the solitude. "Surely the Lord is in this place," he said, "and I knew it not. This is none other but the house of God, and this is the gate of heaven."

"And Jacob rose up early in the morning, and took the stone that he had put for his pillows, and set it up for a pillar, and poured oil upon the top of it." In accordance with the custom of commemorating important events, Jacob set up a memorial of God's mercy, that whenever he should pass that way he might tarry at this sacred spot to worship the Lord. And he called the place Bethel, or the "house of God." With

187

This chapter is based on Genesis 28 to 31.

deep gratitude he repeated the promise that God's presence would be with him; and then he made the solemn vow, "If God will be with me, and will keep me in this way that I go, and will give me bread to eat, and raiment to put on, so that I come again to my father's house in peace; then shall the Lord be my God: and this stone, which I have set for a pillar, shall be God's house: and of all that Thou shalt give me I will surely give the tenth unto Thee."

Jacob was not here seeking to make terms with God. The Lord had already promised him prosperity, and this vow was the outflow of a heart filled with gratitude for the assurance of God's love and mercy. Jacob felt that God had claims upon him which he must acknowledge, and that the special tokens of divine favor granted him demanded a return. So does every blessing bestowed upon us call for a response to the Author of all our mercies. The Christian should often review his past life and recall with gratitude the precious deliverances that God has wrought for him, supporting him in trial, opening ways before him when all seemed dark and forbidding, refreshing him when ready to faint. He should recognize all of them as evidences of the watchcare of heavenly angels. In view of these innumerable blessings he should often ask, with subdued and grateful heart, "What shall I render unto the Lord for all His benefits toward me?" Psalm 116:12.

Our time, our talents, our property, should be sacredly devoted to Him who has given us these blessings in trust. Whenever a special deliverance is wrought in our behalf, or new and unexpected favors are granted us, we should acknowledge God's goodness, not only by expressing our gratitude in words, but, like Jacob, by gifts and offerings to His cause. As we are continually receiving the blessings of God, so we are to be continually giving.

"Of all that Thou shalt give me," said Jacob, "I will surely give the tenth unto Thee." Shall we who enjoy the full light and privileges of the gospel be content to give less to God than was given by those who lived in the former, less favored dispensation? Nay, as the blessings we enjoy are greater, are not our obligations correspondingly increased? But how small the estimate; how vain the endeavor to measure with mathematical rules, time, money, and love, against a love so immeasurable and a gift of such inconceivable worth. Tithes for Christ! Oh, meager pittance, shameful recompense for that which cost so much! From the cross of Calvary, Christ calls for an unreserved consecration. All that we have, all that we are, should be devoted to God.

With a new and abiding faith in the divine promises, and assured of the presence and guardianship of heavenly angels, Jacob pursued his journey to "the land of the children of the East." Genesis 29:1, margin. But how different his arrival from that of Abraham's messenger nearly a hundred years before! The servant had come with a train of attendants riding upon camels, and with rich gifts of gold and silver; the son was a lonely, footsore traveler, with no possession save his staff. Like Abraham's servant, Jacob tarried beside a well, and it was here that he met Rachel, Laban's younger daughter. It was Jacob now who rendered service, rolling the stone from the well and watering the flocks. On making known his kinship, he was welcomed to the home of Laban. Though he came portionless and unattended, a few weeks showed the worth of his diligence and skill, and he was urged to tarry. It was arranged that he should render Laban seven years' service for the hand of Rachel.

In early times custom required the bridegroom, before the ratification of a marriage engagement, to pay a sum of money or its equivalent in other property, according to his circumstances, to the father of his wife. This was regarded as a safeguard to the marriage relation. Fathers did not think it safe to trust the happiness of their daughters to men who had not made provision for the support of a family. If they had not sufficient thrift and energy to manage business and acquire cattle or lands, it was feared that their life would prove worthless. But provision was made to test those who had nothing to pay for a wife. They were permitted to labor for the father whose daughter they loved, the length of time being regulated by the value of the dowry required. When the suitor was faithful in his services, and proved in other respects worthy, he obtained the daughter as his wife; and generally the dowry which the father had received was given her at her marriage. In the case of both Rachel and Leah, however, Laban selfishly retained the dowry that should have been given them; they referred to this when they said, just before the removal from Mesopotamia, "He hath sold us, and hath quite devoured also our money."

The ancient custom, though sometimes abused, as by Laban, was productive of good results. When the suitor was required to render service to secure his bride, a hasty marriage was prevented, and there was opportunity to test the depth of his affections, as well as his ability to provide for a family. In our time many evils result from pursuing an opposite course. It is often the case that persons before marriage have little opportunity to become acquainted with each other's habits and disposition, and, so far as everyday life is concerned, they are virtually strangers when they unite their interests at the altar. Many find, too late, that they are not adapted to each other, and lifelong wretchedness is the result of their union. Often the wife and children suffer from the indolence and inefficiency or the vicious habits of the husband and father. If the character of the suitor had been tested before marriage, according to the ancient custom, great unhappiness might have been prevented.

Seven years of faithful service Jacob gave for Rachel, and the years that he served "seemed unto him but a few days, for the love he had to her." But the selfish and grasping Laban, desiring to retain so valuable a helper, practiced a cruel deception in substituting Leah for Rachel. The fact that Leah herself was a party to the cheat, caused Jacob to feel that he could not love her. His indignant rebuke to Laban was met with the offer of Rachel for another seven years' service. But the father insisted that Leah should not be discarded, since this would bring disgrace upon the family. Jacob was thus placed in a most painful and trying position; he finally decided to retain Leah and marry Rachel. Rachel was ever the one best loved; but his preference for her excited envy and jealousy, and his life was embittered by the rivalry between the sister-wives.

For twenty years Jacob remained in Mesopotamia, laboring in the service of Laban, who, disregarding the ties of kinship, was bent upon securing to himself all the benefits of their connection. Fourteen years of toil he demanded for his two daughters; and during the remaining period, Jacob's wages were ten times changed. Yet Jacob's service was diligent and faithful. His words to Laban in their last interview vividly describe the untiring vigilance which he had given to the interests of his exacting master: "This twenty years have I been with thee; thy ewes and thy she-goats have not cast their young, and the rams of thy flock have I not eaten. That which was torn of beasts I brought not unto thee; I bare the loss of it; of my hand didst thou require it, whether stolen by day, or stolen by night. Thus I was; in the day the drought consumed me, and the frost by night; and my sleep departed from mine eyes."

It was necessary for the shepherd to watch his flocks day and night. They were in danger from robbers, and also from wild beasts, which were numerous and bold, often committing great havoc in flocks that were not faithfully guarded. Jacob had many assistants in caring for the extensive flocks of Laban, but he himself was held responsible for them all. During some portions of the year it was necessary for him to be constantly with the flocks in person, to guard them in the dry season against perishing from thirst, and during the coldest months from becoming chilled with the heavy night frosts. Jacob was the chief shepherd; the servants in his employ were the undershepherds. If any of the sheep were missing, the chief shepherd suffered the loss; and he called the servants to whom he entrusted the care of the flock to a strict account

if it was not found in a flourishing condition.

The shepherd's life of diligence and care-taking, and his tender compassion for the helpless creatures entrusted to his charge, have been employed by the inspired writers to illustrate some of the most precious truths of the gospel. Christ, in His relation to His people, is compared to a shepherd. After the Fall He saw His sheep doomed to perish in the dark ways of sin. To save these wandering ones He left the honors and glories of His Father's house. He says, "I will seek that which was lost, and bring again that which was driven away, and will bind up that which was broken, and will strengthen that which was sick." I will "save My flock, and they shall no more be a prey." "Neither shall the beast of the land devour them." Ezekiel 34:16, 22, 28. His voice is heard calling them to His fold, "a shadow in the daytime from the heat, and for a place of refuge, and for a covert from storm and from rain." Isaiah 4:6. His care for the flock is unwearied. He strengthens the weak, relieves the suffering, gathers the lambs in His arms, and carries them in His bosom. His sheep love Him. "And a stranger will they not follow, but will flee from him; for they know not the voice of strangers." John 10:5.

Christ says, "The good shepherd giveth his life for the sheep. But he that is an hireling, and not the shepherd, whose own the sheep are not, seeth the wolf coming, and leaveth the sheep, and fleeth; and the wolf catcheth them, and scattereth the sheep. The hireling fleeth, because he is an hireling, and careth not for the sheep. I am the Good Shepherd, and know My sheep, and am known of Mine." Verses 11-14.

Christ, the Chief Shepherd, has entrusted the care of His flock to His ministers as undershepherds; and He bids them have the same interest that He has manifested, and feel the sacred responsibility of the charge He has entrusted to them. He has solemnly commanded them to be faithful, to feed the flock, to strengthen the weak, to revive the fainting, and to shield them from devouring wolves.

To save His sheep, Christ laid down His own life; and He points His shepherds to the love thus manifested, as their example. But "he that is an hireling, . . . whose own the sheep are not," has no real interest in the flock. He is laboring merely for gain, and he cares only for himself. He studies his own profit instead of the interest of his charge; and in time of peril or danger he will flee, and leave the flock.

The apostle Peter admonishes the undershepherds: "Feed the flock of God which is among you, taking the oversight thereof, not by constraint, but willingly; not for filthy lucre, but of a ready mind; neither as being lords over God's heritage, but being ensamples to the flock." 1 Peter 5:2, 3. Paul says, "Take heed therefore unto yourselves, and to all the flock, over the

192 which the Holy Ghost hath made you overseers, to feed the church of God, which He hath purchased with His own blood. For I know this, that after my departing shall grievous wolves enter in among you, not sparing the flock." Acts 20:28, 29.

All who regard as an unwelcome task the care and burdens that fall to the lot of the faithful shepherd, are reproved by the apostle: "Not by constraint, but willingly; not for filthy lucre, but of a ready mind." 1 Peter 5:2. All such unfaithful servants the Chief Shepherd would willingly release. The church of Christ has been purchased with His blood, and every shepherd should realize that the sheep under his care cost an infinite sacrifice. He should regard them each as of priceless worth, and should be unwearied in his efforts to keep them in a healthy, flourishing condition. The shepherd who is imbued with the spirit of Christ will imitate His self-denying example, constantly laboring for the welfare of his charge; and the flock will prosper under his care.

All will be called to render a strict account of their ministry. The Master will demand of every shepherd, "Where is the flock that was given thee, thy beautiful flock?" Jeremiah 13:20. He that is found faithful, will receive a rich reward. "When the Chief Shepherd shall appear," says the apostle, "ye shall receive a crown of glory that fadeth not away." 1 Peter 5:4.

When Jacob, growing weary of Laban's service, proposed to return to Canaan, he said to his father-in-law, "Send me away, that I may go unto mine own place, and to my country. Give me my wives and my children, for whom I have served thee, and let me go: for thou knowest my service which I have done thee." But Laban urged him to remain, declaring, "I have learned by experience that the Lord hath blessed me for thy sake." He saw that his property was increasing under the care of his son-in-law.

Said Jacob, "It was little which thou hadst before I came, and it is now increased unto a multitude." But as time passed on, Laban became envious of the greater prosperity of Jacob, who "increased exceedingly, and had much cattle, and maidservants, and menservants, and camels, and asses." Laban's sons shared their father's jealousy, and their malicious speeches came to Jacob's ears: He "hath taken away all that was our father's, and of that which was our father's hath he gotten all this 193 glory. And Jacob beheld the countenance of Laban, and, behold, it was not toward him as before."

Jacob would have left his crafty kinsman long before but for the fear of encountering Esau. Now he felt that he was in danger from the sons of Laban, who, looking upon his wealth as their own, might endeavor to secure it by violence. He was in great perplexity and distress, not knowing which way to turn. But mindful of the gracious Bethel promise, he carried his case to God, and sought direction from Him. In a dream his prayer was answered: "Return unto the land of thy fathers, and to thy kindred; and I will be with thee."

Laban's absence afforded opportunity for departure. The flocks and herds were speedily gathered and sent forward, and with his wives, children, and servants, Jacob crossed the Euphrates, urging his way toward Gilead, on the borders of Canaan. After three days Laban learned of their flight, and set forth in pursuit, overtaking the company on the seventh day of their journey. He was hot with anger, and bent on forcing them to return, which he doubted not he could do, since his band was much the stronger. The fugitives were indeed in great peril.

That he did not carry out his hostile purpose was due to the fact that God Himself had interposed for the protection of His servant. "It is in the power of my hand to do you hurt," said Laban, "but the God of your father spake unto me yesternight, saying, Take thou heed that thou speak not to Jacob either good or bad;" that is, he should not force him to return, or urge him by flattering inducements.

Laban had withheld the marriage dowry of his daughters and had ever treated Jacob with craft and harshness; but with characteristic dissimulation he now reproached him for his secret departure, which had given the father no opportunity to make a parting feast or even to bid farewell to his daughters and their children.

In reply Jacob plainly set forth Laban's selfish and grasping policy, and appealed to him as a witness to his own faithfulness and honesty. "Except the God of my father, the God of Abraham, and the fear of Isaac, had been with me," said Jacob, "surely thou hadst sent me away now empty. God hath seen mine affliction, and the labor of my hands, and rebuked thee yesternight."

Laban could not deny the facts brought forward, and he now proposed to enter into a 194 covenant of peace. Jacob consented to the proposal, and a pile of stones was erected as a token of the compact. To this pillar Laban gave the name Mizpah, "watchtower," saying, "The Lord watch between me and thee, when we are absent one from another."

"And Laban said to Jacob, Behold this heap, and behold this pillar, which I have cast betwixt me and thee; this heap be witness, and this pillar be witness, that I will not pass over this heap to thee, and that thou shalt not pass over this heap and this pillar unto me, for harm. The God of Abraham, and the God of Nahor, the God of their father, judge betwixt us. And Jacob sware by the fear of his father Isaac." To confirm the treaty, the parties held a feast. The night was spent in friendly communing; and at the dawn of day, Laban and his company departed. With this separation ceased all trace of connection between the children of Abraham and the dwellers in Mesopotamia.

195

18

The Night of Wrestling

Though Jacob had left Padan-aram in obedience to the divine direction, it was not without many misgivings that he retraced the road which he had trodden as a fugitive twenty years before. His sin in the deception of his father was ever before him. He knew that his long exile was the direct result of that sin, and he pondered over these things day and night, the reproaches of an accusing conscience making his journey very sad. As the hills of his native land appeared before him in the distance, the heart of the patriarch was deeply moved. All the past rose vividly before him. With the memory of his sin came also the thought of God's favor toward him, and the promises of divine help and guidance.

As he drew nearer his journey's end, the thought of Esau brought many a troubled foreboding. After the flight of Jacob, Esau had regarded himself as the sole heir of their father's possessions. The news of Jacob's return would excite the fear that he was coming to claim the inheritance. Esau was now able to do his brother great injury, if so disposed, and he might be moved to violence against him, not only by the desire for revenge, but in order to secure undisturbed possession of the wealth which he had so long looked upon as his own.

Again the Lord granted Jacob a token of the divine care. As he traveled southward from Mount Gilead, two hosts of heavenly angels seemed to encompass him behind and before, advancing with his company, as if for their protection. Jacob remembered the vision at Bethel so long before, and his burdened heart grew lighter at this evidence that the divine messengers who had brought him hope and courage at his flight from Canaan were to be the guardians of his return. And he said, "This is God's host: and he called the name of that place Mahanaim"—"two hosts, or, camps."

Yet Jacob felt that he had something to do to secure his own safety. He therefore dispatched 196 messengers with a conciliatory greeting to his brother. He instructed them as to the exact words in which they were to address Esau. It had been foretold before the birth of the two brothers that the elder should serve the younger, and, lest the memory of this should be a cause of bitterness, Jacob told the servants they were sent to "my lord Esau;" when brought before him, they were

to refer to their master as "thy servant Jacob;" and to remove the fear that he was returning, a destitute wanderer, to claim the paternal inheritance, Jacob was careful to state in his message, "I have oxen, and asses, flocks, and menservants, and womenservants; and I have sent to tell my lord, that I may find grace in thy sight."

But the servants returned with the tidings that Esau was approaching with four hundred men, and no response was sent to the friendly message. It appeared certain that he was coming to seek revenge. Terror pervaded the camp. "Jacob was greatly afraid and distressed." He could not go back, and he feared to advance. His company, unarmed and defenseless, were wholly unprepared for a hostile encounter. He accordingly divided them into two bands, so that if one should be attacked, the other might have an opportunity to escape. He sent from his vast flocks generous presents to Esau, with a friendly message. He did all in his power to atone for the wrong to his brother and to avert the threatened danger, and then in humiliation and repentance he pleaded for divine protection: Thou "saidst unto me, Return unto thy country, and to thy kindred, and I will deal well with thee: I am not worthy of the least of all the mercies, and of all the truth, which Thou hast showed unto Thy servant; for with my staff I passed over this Jordan; and now I am become two bands. Deliver me, I pray Thee, from the hand of my brother, from the hand of Esau: for I fear him, lest he will come and smite me, and the mother with the children."

They had now reached the river Jabbok, and as night came on, Jacob sent his family across the ford of the river, while he alone remained behind. He had decided to spend the night in prayer, and he desired to be alone with God. God could soften the heart of Esau. In Him was the patriarch's only hope.

It was in a lonely, mountainous region, the haunt of wild beasts and the lurking place of robbers and murderers. Solitary and unprotected, Jacob bowed in deep distress upon the earth. It was midnight. All that made life dear to him were at a distance, exposed to danger and death. 197 Bitterest of all was the thought that it was his own sin which had brought this peril upon the innocent. With earnest cries and tears he made his prayer before God. Suddenly a strong hand was laid upon him. He thought that an enemy was seeking his life, and he endeavored to wrest himself from the grasp of his assailant. In the darkness the two struggled for the mastery. Not a word was spoken, but Jacob put forth all his strength, and did not relax his efforts for a moment. While he was thus battling for his life, the sense of his guilt pressed upon his soul; his sins rose up before him, to shut him out from God. But in his terrible extremity he remembered God's promises, and his whole heart went

This chapter is based on Genesis 32 and 33.

out in entreaty for His mercy. The struggle continued until near the break of day, when the stranger placed his finger upon Jacob's thigh, and he was crippled instantly. The patriarch now discerned the character of his antagonist. He knew that he had been in conflict with a heavenly messenger, and this was why his almost superhuman effort had not gained the victory. It was Christ, "the Angel of the covenant," who had revealed Himself to Jacob. The patriarch was now disabled and suffering the keenest pain, but he would not loosen his hold. All penitent and broken, he clung to the Angel; "he wept, and made supplication" (Hosea 12:4), pleading for a blessing. He must have the assurance that his sin was pardoned. Physical pain was not sufficient to divert his mind from this object. His determination grew stronger, his faith more earnest and persevering, until the very last. The Angel tried to release Himself; He urged, "Let Me go, for the day breaketh;" but Jacob answered, "I will not let Thee go, except Thou bless me." Had this been a boastful, presumptuous confidence, Jacob would have been instantly destroyed; but his was the assurance of one who confesses his own unworthiness, yet trusts the faithfulness of a covenant-keeping God.

Jacob "had power over the Angel, and prevailed." Hosea 12:4. Through humiliation, repentance, and self-surrender, this sinful, erring mortal prevailed with the Majesty of heaven. He had fastened his trembling grasp upon the promises of God, and the heart of Infinite Love could not turn away the sinner's plea.

198 The error that had led to Jacob's sin in obtaining the birthright by fraud was now clearly set before him. He had not trusted God's promises, but had sought by his own efforts to bring about that which God would have accomplished in His own time and way. As an evidence that he had been forgiven, his name was changed from one that was a reminder of his sin, to one that commemorated his victory. "Thy name," said the Angel, "shall be called no more Jacob [the supplanter], but Israel: for as a prince hast thou power with God and with men, and hast prevailed."

Jacob had received the blessing for which his soul had longed. His sin as a supplanter and deceiver had been pardoned. The crisis in his life was past. Doubt, perplexity, and remorse had embittered his existence, but now all was changed; and sweet was the peace of reconciliation with God. Jacob no longer feared to meet his brother. God, who had forgiven his sin, could move the heart of Esau also to accept his humiliation and repentance.

While Jacob was wrestling with the Angel, another heavenly messenger was sent to Esau. In a dream, Esau beheld his brother for twenty years an exile from his father's house; he witnessed his grief at finding his mother dead; he saw him encompassed by the hosts of God. This dream was related by Esau to his soldiers, with the charge not to harm Jacob, for the God of his father was with him.

The two companies at last approached each other, the desert chief leading his men of war, and Jacob with his wives and children, attended by shepherds and handmaidens, and followed by long lines of flocks and herds. Leaning upon his staff, the patriarch went forward to meet the band of soldiers. He was pale and disabled from his recent conflict, and he walked slowly and painfully, halting at every step; but his countenance was lighted up with joy and peace.

At sight of that crippled sufferer, "Esau ran to meet him, and embraced him, and fell on his neck, and kissed him: and they wept." As they looked upon the scene, even the hearts of Esau's rude soldiers were touched. Notwithstanding he had told them of his dream, they could not account for the change that had come over their captain. Though they beheld the patriarch's infirmity, they little thought that this his weakness had been made his strength.

201 In his night of anguish beside the Jabbok, when destruction seemed just before him, Jacob had been taught how vain is the help of man, how groundless is all trust in human power. He saw that his only help must come from Him against whom he had so grievously sinned. Helpless and unworthy, he pleaded God's promise of mercy to the repentant sinner. That promise was his assurance that God would pardon and accept him. Sooner might heaven and earth pass than that word could fail; and it was this that sustained him through that fearful conflict.

Jacob's experience during that night of wrestling and anguish represents the trial through which the people of God must pass just before Christ's second coming. The prophet Jeremiah, in holy vision looking down to this time, said, "We have heard a voice of trembling, of fear, and not of peace. . . . All faces are turned into paleness. Alas! for that day is great, so that none is like it: it is even the time of Jacob's trouble; but he shall be saved out of it." Jeremiah 30:5-7.

When Christ shall cease His work as mediator in man's behalf, then this time of trouble will begin. Then the case of every soul will have been decided, and there will be no atoning blood to cleanse from sin. When Jesus leaves His position as man's intercessor before God, the solemn announcement is made, "He that is unjust, let him be unjust still: and he which is filthy, let him be filthy still: and he that is righteous, let him be righteous still: and he that is holy, let him be holy still." Revelation 22:11. Then the restraining Spirit of God is withdrawn from the earth. As Jacob was threatened with death by his angry brother, so the people of God will be in peril from the wicked who are seeking to destroy them. And as the patriarch wrestled all night for deliverance from the hand of Esau, so the righteous will cry to God day and night for deliverance from the enemies that surround them.

Satan had accused Jacob before the angels of God, claiming the right to destroy him because of his sin; he had moved upon Esau to march against him; and during the patriarch's long night of wrestling, Satan endeavored to force upon him a sense of his guilt, in order to discourage him, and break his hold upon God. When in his distress Jacob laid hold of the Angel, and made supplication with tears, the heavenly Messenger, in order to try his faith, also reminded him of his sin, and endeavored to escape from him. But Jacob would not be turned away. He had learned that God is merciful, and he cast himself upon His mercy. He pointed back to his repentance for his sin, and pleaded for deliverance. As he reviewed his life, he was driven almost to despair; but he held fast the Angel, and with earnest, agonizing cries urged his petition until he prevailed.

202

Such will be the experience of God's people in their final struggle with the powers of evil. God will test their faith, their perseverance, their confidence in His power to deliver them. Satan will endeavor to terrify them with the thought that their cases are hopeless; that their sins have been too great to receive pardon. They will have a deep sense of their shortcomings, and as they review their lives their hopes will sink. But remembering the greatness of God's mercy, and their own sincere repentance, they will plead His promises made through Christ to helpless, repenting sinners. Their faith will not fail because their prayers are not immediately answered. They will lay hold of the strength of God, as Jacob laid hold of the Angel, and the language of their souls will be, "I will not let Thee go, except Thou bless me."

Had not Jacob previously repented of his sin in obtaining the birthright by fraud, God could not have heard his prayer and mercifully preserved his life. So in the time of trouble, if the people of God had unconfessed sins to appear before them while tortured with fear and anguish, they would be overwhelmed; despair would cut off their faith, and they could not have confidence to plead with God for deliverance. But while they have a deep sense of their unworthiness, they will have no concealed wrongs to reveal. Their sins will have been blotted out by the atoning blood of Christ, and they cannot bring them to remembrance.

Satan leads many to believe that God will overlook their unfaithfulness in the minor affairs of life; but the Lord shows in His dealing with Jacob that He can in no wise sanction or tolerate evil. All who endeavor to excuse or conceal their sins, and permit them to remain upon the books of heaven, unconfessed and unforgiven, will be overcome by Satan. The more exalted their profession, and the more honorable the position which they hold, the more grievous is their course in the sight of God, and the more certain the triumph of the great adversary.

Yet Jacob's history is an assurance that God will not cast off those who have been betrayed into sin, but who have returned unto Him with true repentance. It was by self-surrender and confiding faith that Jacob gained what he had failed to gain by conflict in his own strength. God thus taught His servant that divine power and grace alone could give him the blessing he craved. Thus it will be with those who live in the last days. As dangers surround them, and despair seizes upon the soul, they must depend solely upon the merits of the atonement. We can do nothing of ourselves. In all our helpless unworthiness we must trust in the merits of the crucified and risen Saviour. None will ever perish while they do this. The long, black catalogue of our delinquencies is before the eye of the Infinite. The register is complete; none of our offenses are forgotten. But He who listened to the cries of His servants of old, will hear the prayer of faith and pardon our transgressions. He has promised, and He will fulfill His word.

203

Jacob prevailed because he was persevering and determined. His experience testifies to the power of importunate prayer. It is now that we are to learn this lesson of prevailing prayer, of unyielding faith. The greatest victories to the church of Christ or to the individual Christian are not those that are gained by talent or education, by wealth or the favor of men. They are those victories that are gained in the audience chamber with God, when earnest, agonizing faith lays hold upon the mighty arm of power.

Those who are unwilling to forsake every sin and to seek earnestly for God's blessing, will not obtain it. But all who will lay hold of God's promises as did Jacob, and be as earnest and persevering as he was, will succeed as he succeeded. "Shall not God avenge His own elect, which cry day and night unto Him, though He bear long with them? I tell you that He will avenge them speedily." Luke 18:7, 8.

204

19
The Return to Canaan

Crossing the Jordan, "Jacob came in peace to the city of Shechem, which is in the land of Canaan." Genesis 33:18, R.V. Thus the patriarch's prayer at Bethel, that God would bring him again in peace to his own land, had been granted. For a time he dwelt in the vale of Shechem. It was here that Abraham, more than a hundred years before, had made his first encampment and erected his first altar in the Land of Promise. Here Jacob "bought the parcel of ground where he had spread his tent, at the hand of the children of Hamor, Shechem's father, for a hundred pieces of money. And he erected there an altar, and called it El-elohe-Israel" (verses 19, 20)—"God, the God of Israel." Like Abraham, Jacob set up beside his tent an altar unto the Lord, calling the members of his household to the morning and the evening sacrifice. It was here also that he dug the well to which, seventeen centuries later, came Jacob's Son and Saviour, and beside which, resting during the noontide heat, He told His wondering hearers of that "well of water springing up into everlasting life." John 4:14.

The tarry of Jacob and his sons at Shechem ended in violence and bloodshed. The one daughter of the household had been brought to shame and sorrow, two brothers were involved in the guilt of murder, a whole city had been given to ruin and slaughter, in retaliation for the lawless deed of one rash youth. The beginning that led to results so terrible was the act of Jacob's daughter, who "went out to see the daughters of the land," thus venturing into association with the ungodly. He who seeks pleasure among those that fear not God is placing himself on Satan's ground and inviting his temptations.

The treacherous cruelty of Simeon and Levi was not unprovoked; yet in their course toward the Shechemites they committed a grievous sin. They had carefully concealed from Jacob their

205

intentions, and the tidings of their revenge filled him with horror. Heartsick at the deceit and violence of his sons, he only said, "Ye have troubled me to make me to stink among the inhabitants of the land: . . . and I being few in number, they shall gather themselves together against me, and slay me; and I shall be destroyed, I and my house." But the grief and abhorrence with which he regarded their bloody deed is shown by the words in which, nearly fifty years later, he referred to it, as he lay upon his deathbed in Egypt: "Simeon and Levi are brethren; instruments of cruelty are in their habitations. O my soul, come not thou into their secret; unto their assembly, mine honor, be not thou united. . . . Cursed be their anger, for it was fierce; and their wrath, for it was cruel." Genesis 49:5-7.

Jacob felt that there was cause for deep humiliation. Cruelty and falsehood were manifest in the character of his sons. There were false gods in the camp, and idolatry had to some extent gained a foothold even in his household. Should the Lord deal with them according to their deserts, would He not leave them to the vengeance of the surrounding nations?

While Jacob was thus bowed down with trouble, the Lord directed him to journey southward to Bethel. The thought of this place reminded the patriarch not only of his vision of the angels and of God's promises of mercy, but also of the vow which he had made there, that the Lord should be his God. He determined that before going to this sacred spot his household should be freed from the defilement of idolatry. He therefore gave direction to all in the encampment, "Put away the strange gods that are among you, and be clean, and change your garments: and let us arise, and go up to Bethel; and I will make there an altar unto God, who answered me in the day of my distress, and was with me in the way which I went."

With deep emotion Jacob repeated the story of his first visit to Bethel, when he left his father's tent a lonely wanderer, fleeing for his life, and how the Lord had appeared to him in the night vision. As he reviewed the wonderful dealings of God with him, his own heart was softened, his children also were touched by a subduing power; he had taken the most effectual way to prepare them to join in the worship of God when they should arrive at Bethel. "And they gave unto Jacob all the strange gods which were in their hand, and all their earrings which were in their ears; and Jacob hid them under the oak which was by Shechem."

206

God caused a fear to rest upon the inhabitants of the land, so that they made no attempt to avenge the slaughter at Shechem. The travelers reached Bethel unmolested. Here the Lord again appeared to Jacob and renewed to him the covenant promise. "And Jacob set up a pillar in the place where He talked with him, even a pillar of stone."

At Bethel, Jacob was called to mourn the loss of one who had long been an honored member of his father's family—Rebekah's nurse, Deborah, who had accompanied her mistress from Mesopotamia to the land of Canaan. The presence of this aged woman had been to Jacob a precious tie that bound him to his early life, and especially to the mother whose love for him had been so strong and tender. Deborah was buried with expressions of so great sorrow that the oak under which her grave was made, was called "the oak of weeping." It should not be passed

This chapter is based on Genesis 34; 35; 37.

unnoticed that the memory of her life of faithful service and of the mourning over this household friend has been accounted worthy to be preserved in the word of God.

From Bethel it was only a two days' journey to Hebron, but it brought to Jacob a heavy grief in the death of Rachel. Twice seven years' service he had rendered for her sake, and his love had made the toil but light. How deep and abiding that love had been, was shown when long afterward, as Jacob in Egypt lay near his death, Joseph came to visit his father, and the aged patriarch, glancing back upon his own life, said, "As for me, when I came from Padan, Rachel died by me in the land of Canaan in the way, when yet there was but a little way to come unto Ephrath: and I buried her there in the way of Ephrath." Genesis 48:7. In the family history of his long and troubled life the loss of Rachel was alone recalled.

Before her death Rachel gave birth to a second son. With her parting breath she named the child Benoni, "son of my sorrow." But his father called him Benjamin, "son of my right hand," or "my strength." Rachel was buried where she died, and a pillar was raised upon the spot to perpetuate her memory.

On the way to Ephrath another dark crime stained the family of Jacob, causing Reuben, the first-born son, to be denied the privileges and honors of the birthright.

207   At last Jacob came to his journey's end, "unto Isaac his father unto Mamre, . . . which is Hebron, where Abraham and Isaac sojourned." Here he remained during the closing years of his father's life. To Isaac, infirm and blind, the kind attentions of this long-absent son were a comfort during years of loneliness and bereavement.

Jacob and Esau met at the deathbed of their father. Once the elder brother had looked forward to this event as an opportunity for revenge, but his feelings had since greatly changed. And Jacob, well content with the spiritual blessings of the birthright, resigned to the elder brother the inheritance of their father's wealth—the only inheritance that Esau sought or valued. They were no longer estranged by jealousy or hatred, yet they parted, Esau removing to Mount Seir. God, who is rich in blessing, had granted to Jacob worldly wealth, in addition to the higher good that he had sought. The possessions of the two brothers "were more than that they might dwell together; and the land wherein they were strangers could not bear them because of their cattle." This separation was in accordance with the divine purpose concerning Jacob. Since the brothers differed so greatly in regard to religious faith, it was better for them to dwell apart.

Esau and Jacob alike been instructed in the knowledge of God, and both were free to walk in His commandments and to receive His favor; but they had not both chosen to do this.

The two brothers had walked in different ways, and their paths would continue to diverge more and more widely.

There was no arbitrary choice on the part of God by which Esau was shut out from the blessings of salvation. The gifts of His grace through Christ are free to all. There is no election but one's own by which any may perish. God has set forth in His word the conditions upon which every soul will be elected to eternal life—obedience to His commandments, through faith in Christ. God has elected a character in harmony with His law, and anyone who shall reach the standard of His requirement will have an entrance into the kingdom of glory. Christ Himself said, "He that believeth on the Son hath everlasting life: and he that believeth not the Son shall not see life." John 3:36. "Not everyone that saith unto Me, Lord, Lord, shall enter into the kingdom of heaven; but he that *doeth the will of My Father* which is in heaven." Matthew 7:21. And in the Revelation He declares, "Blessed are they that do His commandments, that they may have right to the tree of life, and may enter in through the gates into the city." Revelation 22:14. As regards man's final salvation, this is the only election brought to view in the word of God.   208

Every soul is elected who will work out his own salvation with fear and trembling. He is elected who will put on the armor and fight the good fight of faith. He is elected who will watch unto prayer, who will search the Scriptures, and flee from temptation. He is elected who will have faith continually, and who will be obedient to every word that proceedeth out of the mouth of God. The *provisions* of redemption are free to all; the *results* of redemption will be enjoyed by those who have complied with the conditions.

Esau had despised the blessings of the covenant. He had valued temporal above spiritual good, and he had received that which he desired. It was by his own deliberate choice that he was separated from the people of God. Jacob had chosen the inheritance of faith. He had endeavored to obtain it by craft, treachery, and falsehood; but God had permitted his sin to work out its correction. Yet through all the bitter experience of his later years, Jacob had never swerved from his purpose or renounced his choice. He had learned that in resorting to human skill and craft to secure the blessing, he had been warring against God. From that night of wrestling beside the Jabbok, Jacob had come forth a different man. Self-confidence had been uprooted. Henceforth the early cunning was no longer seen. In place of craft and deception, his life was marked by simplicity and truth. He had learned the lesson of simple reliance upon the Almighty Arm, and amid trial and affliction he bowed in humble submission to the will of God.

The baser elements of character were consumed in the furnace fire, the true gold was refined, until the faith of Abraham and Isaac appeared undimmed in Jacob.

The sin of Jacob, and the train of events to which it led, had not failed to exert an influence for evil—an influence that revealed its bitter fruit in the character and life of his sons. As these sons arrived at manhood they developed serious faults. The results of polygamy were manifest in the household. This terrible evil tends to dry up the very springs of love, and its influence weakens the most sacred ties. The jealousy of the several mothers had embittered the family relation, the children had grown up contentious and impatient of control, and the father's life was darkened with anxiety and grief.

There was one, however, of a widely different character—the elder son of Rachel, Joseph, whose rare personal beauty seemed but to reflect an inward beauty of mind and heart. Pure, active, and joyous, the lad gave evidence also of moral earnestness and firmness. He listened to his father's instructions, and loved to obey God. The qualities that afterward distinguished him in Egypt—gentleness, fidelity, and truthfulness—were already manifest in his daily life. His mother being dead, his affections clung the more closely to the father, and Jacob's heart was bound up in this child of his old age. He "loved Joseph more than all his children."

But even this affection was to become a cause of trouble and sorrow. Jacob unwisely manifested his preference for Joseph, and this excited the jealousy of his other sons. As Joseph witnessed the evil conduct of his brothers, he was greatly troubled; he ventured gently to remonstrate with them, but only aroused still further their hatred and resentment. He could not endure to see them sinning against God, and he laid the matter before his father, hoping that his authority might lead them to reform.

Jacob carefully avoided exciting their anger by harshness or severity. With deep emotion he expressed his solicitude for his children, and implored them to have respect for his gray hairs, and not to bring reproach upon his name, and above all not to dishonor God by such disregard of His precepts. Ashamed that their wickedness was known, the young men seemed to be repentant, but they only concealed their real feelings, which were rendered more bitter by this exposure.

The father's injudicious gift to Joseph of a costly coat, or tunic, such as was usually worn by persons of distinction, seemed to them another evidence of his partiality, and excited a suspicion that he intended to pass by his elder children, to bestow the birthright upon the son of Rachel. Their malice was still further increased as the boy one day told them of a dream that he

had had. "Behold," he said, "we were binding sheaves in the field, and, lo, my sheaf arose, and also stood upright; and, behold, your sheaves stood round about, and made obeisance to my sheaf."

"Shalt thou indeed reign over us? or shalt thou indeed have dominion over us?" exclaimed his brothers in envious anger.

Soon he had another dream, of similar import, which he also related: "Behold, the sun and the moon and the eleven stars made obeisance to me." This dream was interpreted as readily as the first. The father, who was present, spoke reprovingly—"What is this dream that thou hast dreamed? Shall I and thy mother and thy brethren indeed come to bow down ourselves to thee to the earth?" Notwithstanding the apparent severity of his words, Jacob believed that the Lord was revealing the future to Joseph.

As the lad stood before his brothers, his beautiful countenance lighted up with the Spirit of inspiration, they could not withhold their admiration; but they did not choose to renounce their evil ways, and they hated the purity that reproved their sins. The same spirit that actuated Cain was kindling in their hearts.

The brothers were obliged to move from place to place to secure pasturage for their flocks, and frequently they were absent from home for months together. After the circumstances just related, they went to the place which their father had bought at Shechem. Some time passed, bringing no tidings from them, and the father began to fear for their safety, on account of their former cruelty toward the Shechemites. He therefore sent Joseph to find them, and bring him word as to their welfare. Had Jacob known the real feeling of his sons toward Joseph, he would not have trusted him alone with them; but this they had carefully concealed.

With a joyful heart, Joseph parted from his father, neither the aged man nor the youth dreaming of what would happen before they should meet again. When, after his long and solitary journey, Joseph arrived at Shechem, his brothers and their flocks were not to be found. Upon inquiring for them, he was directed to Dothan. He had already traveled more than fifty miles, and now an additional distance of fifteen lay before him, but he hastened on, forgetting his weariness in the thought of relieving the anxiety of his father, and meeting the brothers, whom, despite their unkindness, he still loved.

His brothers saw him approaching; but no thought of the long journey he had made to meet them, of his weariness and hunger, of his claims upon their hospitality and brotherly love, softened the bitterness of their hatred. The sight of the coat, the token of their father's love, filled them with frenzy. "Behold, this dreamer cometh," they cried in mockery. Envy and revenge, long secretly cherished, now controlled them. "Let us slay him," they said, "and cast him into some pit, and we will say, Some evil beast hath devoured him; and we shall see what will become of his dreams."

They would have executed their purpose but for Reuben. He shrank from participating in the murder of his brother, and proposed that Joseph be cast alive into a pit, and left there to perish; secretly intending, however, to rescue him and return him to his father. Having persuaded all to consent to this plan, Reuben left the company, fearing that he might fail to control his feelings, and that his real intentions would be discovered.

Joseph came on, unsuspicious of danger, and glad that the object of his long search was accomplished; but instead of the expected greeting, he was terrified by the angry and revengeful glances which he met. He was seized and his coat stripped from him. Taunts and threats revealed a deadly purpose. His entreaties were unheeded. He was wholly in the power of those maddened men. Rudely dragging him to a deep pit, they thrust him in, and having made sure that there was no possibility of his escape, they left him there to perish from hunger, while they "sat down to eat bread."

But some of them were ill at ease; they did not feel the satisfaction they had anticipated from their revenge. Soon a company of travelers was seen approaching. It was a caravan of Ishmaelites from beyond Jordan, on their way to Egypt with spices and other merchandise. Judah now proposed to sell their brother to these heathen traders instead of leaving him to die. While he would be effectually put out of their way, they would remain clear of his blood; "for," he urged, "he is our brother and our flesh." To this proposition all agreed, and Joseph was quickly drawn out of the pit.

As he saw the merchants the dreadful truth flashed upon him. To become a slave was a fate more to be feared than death. In an agony of terror he appealed to one and another of his brothers, but in vain. Some were moved with pity, but fear of derision kept them silent; all felt that they had now gone too far to retreat. If Joseph were spared, he would doubtless report them to 212 the father, who would not overlook their cruelty toward his favorite son. Steeling their hearts against his entreaties, they delivered him into the hands of the heathen traders. The caravan moved on, and was soon lost to view.

Reuben returned to the pit, but Joseph was not there. In alarm and self-reproach he rent his garments, and sought his brothers, exclaiming, "The child is not; and I, whither shall I go?" Upon learning the fate of Joseph, and that it would now be impossible to recover him, Reuben was induced to unite with the rest in the attempt to conceal their guilt. Having killed a kid, they dipped Joseph's coat in its blood, and

took it to their father, telling him that they had found it in the fields, and that they feared it was their brother's. "Know now," they said, "whether it be thy son's coat or no." They had looked forward to this scene with dread, but they were not prepared for the heart-rending anguish, the utter abandonment of grief, which they were compelled to witness. "It is my son's coat," said Jacob; "an evil beast hath devoured him. Joseph is without doubt rent in pieces." Vainly his sons and daughters attempted to comfort him. He "rent his clothes, and put sackcloth upon his loins, and mourned for his son many days." Time seemed to bring no alleviation of his grief. "I will go down into the grave unto my son mourning," was his despairing cry. The young men, terrified at what they had done, yet dreading their father's reproaches, still hid in their own hearts the knowledge of their guilt, which even to themselves seemed very great.

20

213

Joseph in Egypt

Meanwhile, Joseph with his captors was on the way to Egypt. As the caravan journeyed southward toward the borders of Canaan, the boy could discern in the distance the hills among which lay his father's tents. Bitterly he wept at thought of that loving father in his loneliness and affliction. Again the scene at Dothan came up before him. He saw his angry brothers and felt their fierce glances bent upon him. The stinging, insulting words that had met his agonized entreaties were ringing in his ears. With a trembling heart he looked forward to the future. What a change in situation—from the tenderly cherished son to the despised and helpless slave! Alone and friendless, what would be his lot in the strange land to which he was going? For a time Joseph gave himself up to uncontrolled grief and terror.

But, in the providence of God, even this experience was to be a blessing to him. He had learned in a few hours that which years might not otherwise have taught him. His father, strong and tender as his love had been, had done him wrong by his partiality and indulgence. This unwise preference had angered his brothers and provoked them to the cruel deed that had separated him from his home. Its effects were manifest also in his own character. Faults had been encouraged that were now to be corrected. He was becoming self-sufficient and exacting. Accustomed to the tenderness of his father's care, he felt that he was unprepared to cope with the difficulties before him, in the bitter, uncared-for life of a stranger and a slave.

Then his thoughts turned to his father's God.

This chapter is based on Genesis 39 to 41.

In his childhood he had been taught to love and fear Him. Often in his father's tent he had listened to the story of the vision that Jacob saw as he fled from his home an exile and a fugitive. He had been told of the Lord's promises to Jacob, and how they had been fulfilled—how, in the hour of need, the angels of God had come 214 to instruct, comfort, and protect him. And he had learned of the love of God in providing for men a Redeemer. Now all these precious lessons came vividly before him. Joseph believed that the God of his fathers would be his God. He then and there gave himself fully to the Lord, and he prayed that the Keeper of Israel would be with him in the land of his exile.

His soul thrilled with the high resolve to prove himself true to God—under all circumstances to act as became a subject of the King of heaven. He would serve the Lord with undivided heart; he would meet the trials of his lot with fortitude and perform every duty with fidelity. One day's experience had been the turning point in Joseph's life. Its terrible calamity had transformed him from a petted child to a man, thoughtful, courageous, and self-possessed.

Arriving in Egypt, Joseph was sold to Potiphar, captain of the king's guard, in whose service he remained for ten years. He was here exposed to temptations of no ordinary character. He was in the midst of idolatry. The worship of false gods was surrounded by all the pomp of royalty, supported by the wealth and culture of the most highly civilized nation then in existence. Yet Joseph preserved his simplicity and his fidelity to God. The sights and sounds of vice were all about him, but he was as one who saw and heard not. His thoughts were not permitted to linger upon forbidden subjects. The desire to gain the favor of the Egyptians could not cause him to conceal his principles. Had he attempted to do this, he would have been overcome by temptation; but he was not ashamed of the religion of his fathers, and he made no effort to hide the fact that he was a worshiper of Jehovah.

"And the Lord was with Joseph, and he was a prosperous man. . . . And his master saw that the Lord was with him, and that the Lord made all that he did to prosper in his hand." Potiphar's confidence in Joseph increased daily, and he finally promoted him to be his steward, with full control over all his possessions. "And he left all that he had in Joseph's hand; and he knew not aught he had, save the bread which he did eat."

The marked prosperity which attended everything placed under Joseph's care was not the result of a direct miracle; but his industry, care, and energy were crowned with the divine blessing. Joseph attributed his success to the favor of God, and even his idolatrous master accepted 217 this as the secret of his unparalleled prosperity. Without steadfast, well-directed effort, howev-

er, success could never have been attained. God was glorified by the faithfulness of His servant. It was His purpose that in purity and uprightness the believer in God should appear in marked contrast to the worshipers of idols—that thus the light of heavenly grace might shine forth amid the darkness of heathenism.

Joseph's gentleness and fidelity won the heart of the chief captain, who came to regard him as a son rather than a slave. The youth was brought in contact with men of rank and learning, and he acquired a knowledge of science, of languages, and of affairs—an education needful to the future prime minister of Egypt.

But Joseph's faith and integrity were to be tested by fiery trials. His master's wife endeavored to entice the young man to transgress the law of God. Heretofore he had remained untainted by the corruption teeming in that heathen land; but this temptation, so sudden, so strong, so seductive—how should it be met? Joseph knew well what would be the consequence of resistance. On the one hand were concealment, favor, and rewards; on the other, disgrace, imprisonment, perhaps death. His whole future life depended upon the decision of the moment. Would principle triumph? Would Joseph still be true to God? With inexpressible anxiety, angels looked upon the scene.

Joseph's answer reveals the power of religious principle. He would not betray the confidence of his master on earth, and, whatever the consequences, he would be true to his Master in heaven. Under the inspecting eye of God and holy angels many take liberties of which they would not be guilty in the presence of their fellow men, but Joseph's first thought was of God. "How . . . can I do this great wickedness, and sin against God?" he said.

If we were to cherish an habitual impression that God sees and hears all that we do and say and keeps a faithful record of our words and actions, and that we must meet it all, we would fear to sin. Let the young ever remember that wherever they are, and whatever they do, they are in the presence of God. No part of our conduct escapes observation. We cannot hide our ways from the Most High. Human laws, though sometimes severe, are often transgressed without detection, and hence with impunity. But not so with the law of God. The deepest midnight is no cover for the guilty one. He may think himself alone, but to every deed there is an unseen 218 witness. The very motives of his heart are open to divine inspection. Every act, every word, every thought, is as distinctly marked as though there were only one person in the whole world, and the attention of heaven were centered upon him.

Joseph suffered for his integrity, for his tempter revenged herself by accusing him of a foul crime, and causing him to be thrust into prison. Had Potiphar believed his wife's charge against Joseph, the young Hebrew would have lost his life; but the modesty and uprightness that had uniformly characterized his conduct were proof of his innocence; and yet, to save the reputation of his master's house, he was abandoned to disgrace and bondage.

At the first Joseph was treated with great severity by his jailers. The psalmist says, "His feet they hurt with fetters; he was laid in chains of iron: until the time that his word came to pass; the word of the Lord tried him." Psalm 105:18, 19, R.V. But Joseph's real character shines out, even in the darkness of the dungeon. He held fast his faith and patience; his years of faithful service had been most cruelly repaid, yet this did not render him morose or distrustful. He had the peace that comes from conscious innocence, and he trusted his case with God. He did not brood upon his own wrongs, but forgot his sorrow in trying to lighten the sorrows of others. He found a work to do, even in the prison. God was preparing him in the school of affliction for greater usefulness, and he did not refuse the needful discipline. In the prison, witnessing the results of oppression and tyranny and the effects of crime, he learned lessons of justice, sympathy, and mercy, that prepared him to exercise power with wisdom and compassion.

Joseph gradually gained the confidence of the keeper of the prison, and was finally entrusted with the charge of all the prisoners. It was the part he acted in the prison—the integrity of his daily life and his sympathy for those who were in trouble and distress—that opened the way for his future prosperity and honor. Every ray of light that we shed upon others is reflected upon ourselves. Every kind and sympathizing word spoken to the sorrowful, every act to relieve the oppressed, and every gift to the needy, if prompted by a right motive, will result in blessings to the giver.

219 The chief baker and chief butler of the king had been cast into prison for some offense, and they came under Joseph's charge. One morning, observing that they appeared very sad, he kindly inquired the cause and was told that each had had a remarkable dream, of which they were anxious to learn the significance. "Do not interpretations belong to God?" said Joseph, "tell me them, I pray you." As each related his dream, Joseph made known its import: In three days the butler was to be reinstated in his position, and give the cup into Pharaoh's hand as before, but the chief baker would be put to death by the king's command. In both cases the event occurred as foretold.

The king's cupbearer had professed the deepest gratitude to Joseph, both for the cheering interpretation of his dream and for many acts of kind attention; and in return the latter, referring in a most touching manner to his own unjust captivity, entreated that his case be brought before the king. "Think on me," he said, "when it shall be well with thee, and show kindness, I pray thee, unto me, and make mention of me unto Pharaoh, and bring me out of this house: for indeed I was stolen away out of the land of the Hebrews: and here also have I done nothing that they should put me into the dungeon." The chief butler saw the dream fulfilled in every particular; but when restored to royal favor, he thought no more of his benefactor. For two years longer Joseph remained a prisoner. The hope that had been kindled in his heart gradually died out, and to all other trials was added the bitter sting of ingratitude.

But a divine hand was about to open the prison gates. The king of Egypt had in one night two dreams, apparently pointing to the same event and seeming to foreshadow some great calamity. He could not determine their significance, yet they continued to trouble his mind. The magicians and wise men of his realm could give no interpretation. The king's perplexity and distress increased, and terror spread throughout his palace. The general agitation recalled to the chief butler's mind the circumstances of his own dream; with it came the memory of Joseph, and a pang of remorse for his forgetfulness and ingratitude. He at once informed the king how his own dream and that of the chief baker had been interpreted by a Hebrew captive, and how the predictions had been fulfilled.

It was humiliating to Pharaoh to turn away 220 from the magicians and wise men of his kingdom to consult an alien and a slave, but he was ready to accept the lowliest service if his troubled mind might find relief. Joseph was immediately sent for; he put off his prison attire, and shaved himself, for his hair had grown long during the period of his disgrace and confinement. He was then conducted to the presence of the king.

"And Pharaoh said unto Joseph, I have dreamed a dream, and there is none that can interpret it: and I have heard say of thee, that thou canst understand a dream to interpret it. And Joseph answered Pharaoh, saying, It is not in me: God shall give Pharaoh an answer of peace." Joseph's reply to the king reveals his humility and his faith in God. He modestly disclaims the honor of possessing in himself superior wisdom. "It is not in me." God alone can explain these mysteries.

Pharaoh then proceeded to relate his dreams: "Behold, I stood upon the bank of the river: and, behold, there came up out of the river seven kine, fat-fleshed and well-favored; and they fed in a meadow: and, behold, seven other kine came up after them, poor and very ill-favored and lean-fleshed, such as I never saw in all the land of Egypt for badness: and the lean and the ill-favored kine did eat up the first seven fat kine: and when they had eaten them up, it could not be known that they had eaten them; but they were still ill-favored, as at the beginning. So I awoke. And I saw in my dream, and, behold, seven ears came up in one stalk, full and good: and, behold, seven ears, withered, thin, and blasted with the east wind, sprung up after them: and the thin ears devoured the seven good ears: and I told this unto the magicians; but there was none that could declare it to me."

"The dream of Pharaoh is one," said Joseph. "God hath showed Pharaoh what He is about to do." There were to be seven years of great plenty. Field and garden would yield more abundantly than ever before. And this period was to be followed by seven years of famine. "And the plenty shall not be known in the land by reason of that famine following; for it shall be very grievous." The repetition of the dream was evidence both of the certainty and nearness of the fulfillment. "Now therefore," he continued, "let Pharaoh look out a man discreet and wise, and set him over the land of Egypt. Let Pharaoh do this, and let him appoint officers over the land, and take up the fifth part of the land of Egypt in the seven plenteous years. And let them gather all the food of those good years that come, and lay up corn under the hand of Pharaoh, and let them keep food in the cities. And that food shall be for store to the land against the seven years of famine."

The interpretation was so reasonable and consistent, and the policy which it recommended was so sound and shrewd, that its correctness could not be doubted. But who was to be entrusted with the execution of the plan? Upon the wisdom of this choice depended the nation's preservation. The king was troubled. For some time the matter of the appointment was under consideration. Through the chief butler the monarch had learned of the wisdom and prudence displayed by Joseph in the management of the prison; it was evident that he possessed administrative ability in a pre-eminent degree. The cupbearer, now filled with self-reproach, endeavored to atone for his former ingratitude, by the warmest praise of his benefactor; and further inquiry by the king proved the correctness of his report. In all the realm Joseph was the only man gifted with wisdom to point out the danger that threatened the kingdom and the preparation necessary to meet it; and the king was convinced that he was the one best qualified to execute the plans which he had proposed. It was evident that a divine power was with him, and that there were none among the king's officers of state so well qualified to conduct the affairs of the nation at this crisis. The fact that he was a Hebrew and a slave was of little moment when weighed against his evident wisdom and sound judgment. "Can we find such a one as this is, a man in whom the Spirit

of God is?" said the king to his counselors.

The appointment was decided upon, and to Joseph the astonishing announcement was made, "Forasmuch as God hath showed thee all this, there is none so discreet and wise as thou art: thou shalt be over my house, and according unto thy word shall all my people be ruled: only in the throne will I be greater than thou." The king proceeded to invest Joseph with the insignia of his high office. "And Pharaoh took off his ring from his hand, and put it upon Joseph's hand, and arrayed him in vestures of fine linen, and put a gold chain about his neck; and he made him to ride in the second chariot which he had; and they cried before him, Bow the knee."

"He made him lord of his house, and ruler of all his substance: to bind his princes at his pleasure; and teach his senators wisdom." Psalm 105:21, 22. From the dungeon Joseph was exalted to be ruler over all the land of Egypt. It was a position of high honor, yet it was beset with difficulty and peril. One cannot stand upon a lofty height without danger. As the tempest leaves unharmed the lowly flower of the valley, while it uproots the stately tree upon the mountaintop, so those who have maintained their integrity in humble life may be dragged down to the pit by the temptations that assail worldly success and honor. But Joseph's character bore the test alike of adversity and prosperity. The same fidelity to God was manifest when he stood in the palace of the Pharaohs as when in a prisoner's cell. He was still a stranger in a heathen land, separated from his kindred, the worshipers of God; but he fully believed that the divine hand had directed his steps, and in constant reliance upon God he faithfully discharged the duties of his position. Through Joseph the attention of the king and great men of Egypt was directed to the true God; and though they adhered to their idolatry, they learned to respect the principles revealed in the life and character of the worshiper of Jehovah.

How was Joseph enabled to make such a record of firmness of character, uprightness, and wisdom?—In his early years he had consulted duty rather than inclination; and the integrity, the simple trust, the noble nature, of the youth bore fruit in the deeds of the man. A pure and simple life had favored the vigorous development of both physical and intellectual powers. Communion with God through His works and the contemplation of the grand truths entrusted to the inheritors of faith had elevated and ennobled his spiritual nature, broadening and strengthening the mind as no other study could do. Faithful attention to duty in every station, from the lowliest to the most exalted, had been training every power for its highest service. He who lives in accordance with the Creator's will is securing to himself the truest and noblest development of character. "The fear of the Lord, that is wisdom; and to depart from evil is understanding." Job 28:28.

223   There are few who realize the influence of the little things of life upon the development of character. Nothing with which we have to do is really small. The varied circumstances that we meet day by day are designed to test our faithfulness and to qualify us for greater trusts. By adherence to principle in the transactions of ordinary life, the mind becomes accustomed to hold the claims of duty above those of pleasure and inclination. Minds thus disciplined are not wavering between right and wrong, like the reed trembling in the wind; they are loyal to duty because they have trained themselves to habits of fidelity and truth. By faithfulness in that which is least they acquire strength to be faithful in greater matters.

An upright character is of greater worth than the gold of Ophir. Without it none can rise to an honorable eminence. But character is not inherited. It cannot be bought. Moral excellence and fine mental qualities are not the result of accident. The most precious gifts are of no value unless they are improved. The formation of a noble character is the work of a lifetime and must be the result of diligent and persevering effort. God gives opportunities; success depends upon the use made of them.

224

21
Joseph and His Brothers

At the very opening of the fruitful years began the preparation for the approaching famine. Under the direction of Joseph, immense storehouses were erected in all the principal places throughout the land of Egypt, and ample arrangements were made for preserving the surplus of the expected harvest. The same policy was continued during the seven years of plenty, until the amount of grain laid in store was beyond computation.

And now the seven years of dearth began to come, according to Joseph's prediction. "And the dearth was in all lands; but in all the land of Egypt there was bread. And when all the land of Egypt was famished, the people cried to Pharaoh for bread: and Pharaoh said unto all the Egyptians, Go unto Joseph; what he saith to you, do. And the famine was over all the face of the earth: and Joseph opened all the storehouses, and sold unto the Egyptians."

The famine extended to the land of Canaan and was severely felt in that part of the country where Jacob dwelt. Hearing of the abundant provision made by the king of Egypt, ten of Jacob's sons journeyed thither to purchase

grain. On their arrival they were directed to the king's deputy, and with other applicants they came to present themselves before the ruler of the land. And they "bowed down themselves before him with their faces to the earth." "Joseph knew his brethren, but they knew not him." His Hebrew name had been exchanged for the one bestowed upon him by the king, and there was little resemblance between the prime minister of Egypt and the stripling whom they had sold to the Ishmaelites. As Joseph saw his brothers stooping and making obeisance, his dreams came to his mind, and the scenes of the past rose vividly before him. His keen eye, surveying the group, discovered that Benjamin was not among them. Had he also fallen a victim to   225 the treacherous cruelty of those savage men? He determined to learn the truth. "Ye are spies," he said sternly; "to see the nakedness of the land ye are come."

They answered, "Nay, my lord, but to buy food are thy servants come. We are all one man's sons; we are true men; thy servants are no spies." He wished to learn if they possessed the same haughty spirit as when he was with them, and also to draw from them some information in regard to their home; yet he well knew how deceptive their statements might be. He repeated the charge, and they replied, "Thy servants are twelve brethren, the sons of one man in the land of Canaan; and, behold, the youngest is this day with our father, and one is not."

Professing to doubt the truthfulness of their story, and to still look upon them as spies, the governor declared that he would prove them, by requiring them to remain in Egypt till one of their number should go and bring their youngest brother down. If they would not consent to this, they were to be treated as spies. But to such an arrangement the sons of Jacob could not agree, since the time required for carrying it out would cause their families to suffer for food; and who among them would undertake the journey alone, leaving his brothers in prison? How could he meet his father under such circumstances? It appeared probable that they were to be put to death or to be made slaves; and if Benjamin were brought, it might be only to share their fate. They decided to remain and suffer together, rather than bring additional sorrow upon their father by the loss of his only remaining son. They were accordingly cast into prison, where they remained three days.

During the years since Joseph had been separated from his brothers, these sons of Jacob had changed in character. Envious, turbulent, deceptive, cruel, and revengeful they had been; but now, when tested by adversity, they were shown to be unselfish, true to one another, devoted to their father, and, themselves middle-aged men, subject to his authority.

This chapter is based on Genesis 41:54-56; 42 to 50.

The three days in the Egyptian prison were days of bitter sorrow as the brothers reflected upon their past sins. Unless Benjamin could be produced their conviction as spies appeared certain, and they had little hope of gaining their father's consent to Benjamin's absence. On the third day Joseph caused the brothers to be brought before him. He dared not detain them longer. Already his father and the families with him might be suffering for food. "This do, and live," he said; "for I fear God; if ye be true men, let one of your brethren be bound in the house of your prison: go ye, carry corn for the famine of your houses: but bring your youngest brother unto me; so shall your words be verified, and ye shall not die." This proposition they agreed to accept, though expressing little hope that their father would let Benjamin return with them. Joseph had communicated with them through an interpreter, and having no thought that the governor understood them, they conversed freely with one another in his presence. They accused themselves in regard to their treatment of Joseph: "We are verily guilty concerning our brother, in that we saw the anguish of his soul, when he besought us, and we would not hear; therefore is this distress come upon us." Reuben, who had formed the plan for delivering him at Dothan, added, "Spake I not unto you, saying, Do not sin against the child; and ye would not hear? therefore, behold, also his blood is required." Joseph, listening, could not control his emotions, and he went out and wept. On his return he commanded that Simeon be bound before them and again committed to prison. In the cruel treatment of their brother, Simeon had been the instigator and chief actor, and it was for this reason that the choice fell upon him.

Before permitting his brothers to depart, Joseph gave directions that they should be supplied with grain, and also that each man's money should be secretly placed in the mouth of his sack. Provender for the beasts on the homeward journey was also supplied. On the way one of the company, opening his sack, was surprised to find his bag of silver. On his making known the fact to the others, they were alarmed and perplexed, and said one to another, "What is this that God hath done unto us?"— should they regard it as a token of good from the Lord, or had He suffered it to occur to punish them for their sins and plunge them still deeper in affliction? They acknowledged that God had seen their sins, and that He was now punishing them.

Jacob was anxiously awaiting the return of his sons, and on their arrival the whole encampment gathered eagerly around them as they related to their father all that had occurred. Alarm and apprehension filled every heart. The conduct of the Egyptian governor seemed to imply some evil design, and their fears were confirmed, when, as they opened their sacks, the owner's money was found in each. In his distress the aged father exclaimed, "Me have ye bereaved of my children: Joseph is not, and Simeon is not, and ye will take Benjamin away: all these things are against me." Reuben answered, "Slay my two sons, if I bring him not to thee: deliver him into my hand, and I will bring him to thee again." This rash speech did not relieve the mind of Jacob. His answer was, "My son shall not go down with you; for his brother is dead, and he is left alone: if mischief befall him by the way in the which ye go, then shall ye bring down my gray hairs with sorrow to the grave."

But the drought continued, and in process of time the supply of grain that had been brought from Egypt was nearly exhausted. The sons of Jacob well knew that it would be in vain to return to Egypt without Benjamin. They had little hope of changing their father's resolution, and they awaited the issue in silence. Deeper and deeper grew the shadow of approaching famine; in the anxious faces of all in the encampment the old man read their need; at last he said, "Go again, buy us a little food."

Judah answered, "The man did solemnly protest unto us, saying, Ye shall not see my face, except your brother be with you. If thou wilt send our brother with us, we will go down and buy thee food: but if thou wilt not send him, we will not go down: for the man said unto us, Ye shall not see my face, except your brother be with you." Seeing that his father's resolution began to waver, he added, "Send the lad with me, and we will arise and go; that we may live, and not die, both we, and thou, and also our little ones;" and he offered to be surety for his brother and to bear the blame forever if he failed to restore Benjamin to his father.

Jacob could no longer withhold his consent, and he directed his sons to prepare for the journey. He bade them also take to the ruler a present of such things as the famine-wasted country afforded—"a little balm, and a little honey, spices and myrrh, nuts and almonds," also a double quantity of money. "Take also your brother," he said, "and arise, go again unto the man." As his sons were about to depart on their doubtful journey the aged father arose, and raising his hands to heaven, uttered the prayer, "God Almighty give you mercy before the man, that he may send away your other brother, and Benjamin. If I be bereaved of my children, I am bereaved."

Again they journeyed to Egypt and presented themselves before Joseph. As his eye fell upon Benjamin, his own mother's son, he was deeply moved. He concealed his emotion, however, but ordered that they be taken to his house, and that preparation be made for them to dine with him.

Upon being conducted to the governor's palace, the brothers were greatly alarmed, fearing that they were to be called to account for the money found in their sacks. They thought that it might have been intentionally placed there, to furnish occasion for making them slaves. In their distress they consulted with the steward of the house, relating to him the circumstances of their visit to Egypt; and in proof of their innocence informed him that they had brought back the money found in their sacks, also other money to buy food; and they added, "We cannot tell who put our money in our sacks." The man replied, "Peace be to you, fear not: your God, and the God of your father, hath given you treasure in your sacks: I had your money." Their anxiety was relieved, and when Simeon, who had been released from prison, joined them, they felt that God was indeed gracious unto them.

When the governor again met them they presented their gifts and humbly "bowed themselves to him to the earth." Again his dreams came to his mind, and after saluting his guests he hastened to ask, "Is your father well, the old man of whom ye spake? Is he yet alive?" "Thy servant our father is in good health, he is yet alive," was the answer, as they again made obeisance. Then his eye rested upon Benjamin, and he said, "Is this your younger brother, of whom ye spake unto me?" "God be gracious unto thee, my son;" but, overpowered by feelings of tenderness, he could say no more. "He entered into his chamber, and wept there."

Having recovered his self-possession, he returned, and all proceeded to the feast. By the laws of caste the Egyptians were forbidden to eat with people of any other nation. The sons of Jacob had therefore a table by themselves, while the governor, on account of his high rank, ate by himself, and the Egyptians also had separate tables. When all were seated the brothers were surprised to see that they were arranged in exact order, according to their ages. Joseph "sent messes unto them from before him;" but Benjamin's was five times as much as any of theirs. By this token of favor to Benjamin he hoped to ascertain if the youngest brother was regarded with the envy and hatred that had been manifested toward himself. Still supposing that 229 Joseph did not understand their language, the brothers freely conversed with one another; thus he had a good opportunity to learn their real feelings. Still he desired to test them further, and before their departure he ordered that his own drinking cup of silver should be concealed in the sack of the youngest.

Joyfully they set out on their return. Simeon and Benjamin were with them, their animals were laden with grain, and all felt that they had safely escaped the perils that had seemed to surround them. But they had only reached the outskirts of the city when they were overtaken by the governor's steward, who uttered the scathing inquiry, "Wherefore have ye rewarded evil for good? Is not this it in which my lord drinketh, and whereby indeed he divineth? ye have done evil in so doing." This cup was supposed to possess the power of detecting any poisonous substance placed therein. At that day cups of this kind were highly valued as a safeguard against murder by poisoning.

To the steward's accusation the travelers answered, "Wherefore saith my lord these words? God forbid that thy servants should do according to this thing: behold, the money, which we found in our sacks' mouths, we brought again unto thee out of the land of Canaan: how then should we steal out of thy lord's house silver or gold? With whomsoever of thy servants it be found, both let him die, and we also will be my lord's bondmen."

"Now also let it be according unto your words," said the steward; "he with whom it is found shall be my servant; and ye shall be blameless."

The search began immediately. "They speedily took down every man his sack to the ground," and the steward examined each, beginning with Reuben's, and taking them in order down to that of the youngest. In Benjamin's sack the cup was found.

The brothers rent their garments in token of utter wretchedness, and slowly returned to the city. By their own promise Benjamin was doomed to a life of slavery. They followed the steward to the palace, and finding the governor yet there, they prostrated themselves before him. "What deed is this that ye have done?" he said. "Wot ye not that such a man as I can certainly divine?" Joseph designed to draw from them an acknowledgment of their sin. He had never claimed the power of divination, but was willing to have them believe that he could read the secrets of their lives.

Judah answered, "What shall we say unto my lord? what shall we speak? or how shall we 230 clear ourselves? God hath found out the iniquity of thy servants: behold, we are my lord's servants, both we, and he also with whom the cup is found."

"God forbid that I should do so," was the reply; "but the man in whose hand the cup is found, he shall be my servant; and as for you, get you up in peace unto your father."

In his deep distress Judah now drew near to the ruler and exclaimed, "O my lord, let thy servant, I pray thee, speak a word in my lord's ears, and let not thine anger burn against thy servant: for thou art even as Pharaoh." In words of touching eloquence he described his father's grief at the loss of Joseph and his reluctance to let Benjamin come with them to Egypt, as he was the only son left of his mother, Rachel, whom Jacob so dearly loved. "Now therefore," he said, "when I come to thy servant my father, and the lad be not with us; seeing that his life is bound up in the lad's life; it shall come to pass, when he seeth that the lad is not with us, that he will die: and thy servants shall bring down the gray hairs of thy servant our father with sorrow to the grave. For thy servant became surety for the lad unto my father, saying, If I bring him not unto thee, then I shall bear the blame to my father forever. Now therefore, I pray thee, let thy servant abide instead of the lad a bondman to my lord; and let the lad go up with his brethren. For how shall I go up to my father, and the lad be not with me? lest peradventure I see the evil that shall come on my father."

Joseph was satisfied. He had seen in his brothers the fruits of true repentance. Upon hearing Judah's noble offer he gave orders that all but these men should withdraw; then, weeping aloud, he cried, "I am Joseph; doth my father yet live?"

His brothers stood motionless, dumb with fear and amazement. The ruler of Egypt their brother Joseph, whom they had envied and would have murdered, and finally sold as a slave! All their ill treatment of him passed before them. They remembered how they had despised his dreams and had labored to prevent their fulfillment. Yet they had acted their part in fulfilling these dreams; and now that they were completely in his power he would, no doubt, avenge the wrong that he had suffered.

Seeing their confusion, he said kindly, "Come near to me, I pray you;" and as they came near, he continued, "I am Joseph your brother, whom 231 ye sold into Egypt. Now therefore be not grieved, nor angry with yourselves, that ye sold me hither: for God did send me before you to preserve life." Feeling that they had already suffered enough for their cruelty toward him, he nobly sought to banish their fears and lessen the bitterness of their self-reproach.

"For these two years," he continued, "hath the famine been in the land: and yet there are five years, in the which there shall neither be earing nor harvest. And God sent me before you to preserve you a posterity in the earth, and to save your lives by a great deliverance. So now it was not you that sent me hither, but God: and He hath made me a father to Pharaoh, and lord of all his house, and a ruler throughout all the land of Egypt. Haste ye, and go up to my father, and say unto him, Thus saith thy son Joseph, God hath made me lord of all Egypt: come down unto me, tarry not: and thou shalt dwell in the land of Goshen, and thou shalt be near unto me, thou, and thy children, and thy children's children, and thy flocks, and thy herds, and all that thou hast: and there will I nourish thee; for yet there are five years of famine; lest thou, and thy household, and all that thou hast, come to poverty. And, behold, your eyes see, and the eyes of my brother Benjamin, that it is my mouth that speaketh unto you." "And he fell upon his brother Benjamin's neck, and wept; and Benjamin wept upon his neck. Moreover he kissed all his brethren, and wept upon them: and after that his brethren talked with him." They humbly confessed their sin and entreated his forgiveness. They had long suffered anxiety and remorse, and now they rejoiced that he was still alive.

The news of what had taken place was quickly carried to the king, who, eager to manifest his gratitude to Joseph, confirmed the governor's invitation to his family, saying, "The good of all the land of Egypt is yours." The brothers were sent away abundantly supplied with provision and carriages and everything necessary for the removal of all their families and attendants to Egypt. On Benjamin, Joseph bestowed more valuable gifts than upon the others. Then, fearing that disputes would arise among them on the homeward journey, he gave them, as they were about to leave him, the charge, "See that ye fall not out by the way."

The sons of Jacob returned to their father with the joyful tidings, "Joseph is yet alive, and he is governor over all the land of Egypt." At first the aged man was overwhelmed; he could not believe what he heard; but when he saw the 232 long train of wagons and loaded animals, and when Benjamin was with him once more, he was convinced, and in the fullness of his joy exclaimed, "It is enough; Joseph my son is yet alive: I will go and see him before I die."

Another act of humiliation remained for the ten brothers. They now confessed to their father the deceit and cruelty that for so many years had embittered his life and theirs. Jacob had not suspected them of so base a sin, but he saw that all had been overruled for good, and he forgave and blessed his erring children.

The father and his sons, with their families, their flocks and herds, and numerous attendants, were soon on the way to Egypt. With gladness of heart they pursued their journey, and when they came to Beersheba the patriarch offered grateful sacrifices and entreated the Lord to grant them an assurance that He would go with them. In a vision of the night the divine word came to him: "Fear not to go down into Egypt; for I will there make of thee a great nation. I will go down with thee into Egypt; and I will also surely bring thee up again."

The assurance, "Fear not to go down into Egypt; for I will *there* make of thee a great nation," was significant. The promise had been given to Abraham of a posterity numberless as the stars, but as yet the chosen people had increased but slowly. And the land of Canaan now offered no field for the development of such a nation as had been foretold. It was in the possession of powerful heathen tribes, that were not to be dispossessed until "the fourth generation." If the descendants of Israel were here to become a numerous people, they must either drive out the inhabitants of the land or disperse themselves among them. The former, according to the divine arrangement, they could not do; and should they mingle with the Canaanites, they would be in danger of being seduced into idolatry. Egypt, however, offered the conditions necessary to the fulfillment of the divine purpose. A section of country well-watered and fertile was open to them there, affording every advantage for their speedy increase. And the antipathy they must encounter in Egypt on account of their occupation—for every shepherd was "an abomination unto the Egyptians"—would enable them to remain a distinct and separate people and would thus serve to shut them out from participation in the idolatry of Egypt.

233　Upon reaching Egypt the company proceeded directly to the land of Goshen. Thither came Joseph in his chariot of state, attended by a princely retinue. The splendor of his surroundings and the dignity of his position were alike forgotten; one thought alone filled his mind, one longing thrilled his heart. As he beheld the travelers approaching, the love whose yearnings had for so many long years been repressed, would no longer be controlled. He sprang from his chariot and hastened forward to bid his father welcome. "And he fell on his neck, and wept on his neck a good while. And Israel said unto Joseph, Now let me die, since I have seen thy face, because thou art yet alive."

Joseph took five of his brothers to present to Pharaoh and receive from him the grant of land for their future home. Gratitude to his prime minister would have led the monarch to honor them with appointments to offices of state; but Joseph, true to the worship of Jehovah, sought to save his brothers from the temptations to which they would be exposed at a heathen court; therefore he counseled them, when questioned by the king, to tell him frankly their occupation. The sons of Jacob followed this counsel, being careful also to state that they had come to sojourn in the land, not to become permanent dwellers there, thus reserving the right to depart if they chose. The king assigned them a home, as offered, in "the best of the land," the country of Goshen.

Not long after their arrival Joseph brought his father also to be presented to the king. The patriarch was a stranger in royal courts; but amid the sublime scenes of nature he had communed with a mightier Monarch; and now, in conscious superiority, he raised his hands and blessed Pharaoh.

In his first greeting to Joseph, Jacob had spoken as if, with this joyful ending to his long anxiety and sorrow, he was ready to die. But seventeen years were yet to be granted him in the peaceful retirement of Goshen. These years were in happy contrast to those that had preceded them. He saw in his sons evidence of true repentance; he saw his family surrounded by all the conditions needful for the development of a great nation; and his faith grasped the sure promise of their future establishment in Canaan. He himself was surrounded with every token of love and favor that the prime minister of Egypt could bestow; and happy in the society of his long-lost son, he passed down gently and peacefully to the grave.

As he felt death approaching, he sent for 234 Joseph. Still holding fast the promise of God respecting the possession of Canaan, he said, "Bury me not, I pray thee, in Egypt: but I will lie with my fathers, and thou shalt carry me out of Egypt, and bury me in their burying place." Joseph promised to do so, but Jacob was not satisfied; he exacted a solemn oath to lay him beside his fathers in the cave of Machpelah.

Another important matter demanded attention; the sons of Joseph were to be formally instated among the children of Israel. Joseph, coming for a last interview with his father, brought with him Ephraim and Manasseh. These youths were connected, through their mother, with the highest order of the Egyptian priesthood; and the position of their father opened to them the avenues to wealth and distinction, should they choose to connect themselves with the Egyptians. It was Joseph's desire, however, that they should unite with their own people. He manifested his faith in the covenant promise, in behalf of his sons renouncing all the honors that the court of Egypt offered, for a place among the despised shepherd tribes, to whom had been entrusted the oracles of God.

Said Jacob, "Thy two sons, Ephraim and Manasseh, which were born unto thee in the land of Egypt, before I came unto thee into Egypt, are mine; as Reuben and Simeon, they shall be mine." They were to be adopted as his own, and to become the heads of separate tribes. Thus one of the birthright privileges, which Reuben had forfeited, was to fall to Joseph—a double portion in Israel.

Jacob's eyes were dim with age, and he had not been aware of the presence of the young men; but now, catching the outline of their forms, he said, "Who are these?" On being told, he added, "Bring them, I pray thee, unto me, and I will bless them." As they came nearer, the patriarch embraced and kissed them, solemnly laying his hands upon their heads in benediction. Then he uttered the prayer, "God, before whom my fathers Abraham and Isaac did walk, the God which fed me all my life long unto this day, the Angel which redeemed me from all evil, bless the lads." There was no spirit of self-dependence, no reliance upon human power or cunning now. God had been his preserver and support. There was no complaint of the evil days in the past. Its trials and sorrows were no longer regarded as things that were "against" him. Memory recalled only His mercy and loving-kindness who had been with him throughout his pilgrimage.

The blessing ended, Jacob gave his son the assurance—leaving for the generations to come, through long years of bondage and sorrow, this testimony to his faith—"Behold, I die; but God shall be with you, and bring you again unto the land of your fathers."

At the last all the sons of Jacob were gathered about his dying bed. And Jacob called unto his sons, and said, "Gather yourselves together, and hear, ye sons of Jacob; and hearken unto Israel your father," "that I may tell you that which shall befall you in the last days." Often and anxiously he had thought of their future, and had endeavored to picture to himself the history of the different tribes. Now as his children waited to receive his last blessing the Spirit of Inspiration rested upon him, and before him in prophetic vision the future of his descendants was unfolded. One after another the names of his sons were mentioned, the character of each was described, and the future history of the tribe was briefly foretold.

"Reuben, thou art my first-born,
My might, and the beginning of my strength,
The excellency of dignity, and the excellency
of power."

Thus the father pictured what should have been the position of Reuben as the first-born son; but his grievous sin at Edar had made him unworthy of the birthright blessing. Jacob continued—

"Unstable as water,
Thou shalt not excel."

The priesthood was apportioned to Levi, the kingdom and the Messianic promise to Judah, and the double portion of the inheritance to Joseph. The tribe of Reuben never rose to any eminence in Israel; it was not so numerous as Judah, Joseph, or Dan, and was among the first that were carried into captivity.

Next in age to Reuben were Simeon and Levi. They had been united in their cruelty toward the Shechemites, and they had also been the most guilty in the selling of Joseph. Concerning them it was declared—

"I will divide them in Jacob,
And scatter them in Israel."

At the numbering of Israel, just before their entrance to Canaan, Simeon was the smallest tribe. Moses, in his last blessing, made no reference to Simeon. In the settlement of Canaan this tribe had only a small portion of Judah's lot, and such families as afterward became powerful formed different colonies and settled in territory outside the borders of the Holy Land. Levi also received no inheritance except forty-eight cities scattered in different parts of the land. In the case of this tribe, however, their fidelity to Jehovah when the other tribes apostatized, secured their appointment to the sacred service of the sanctuary, and thus the curse was changed into a blessing.

The crowning blessings of the birthright were transferred to Judah. The significance of the name—which denotes praise—is unfolded in the prophetic history of this tribe:

"Judah, thou art he whom thy brethren shall
praise:
Thy hand shall be in the neck of thine ene-
mies;
Thy father's children shall bow down before
thee.
Judah is a lion's whelp:
From the prey, my son, thou art gone up:
He stooped down, he couched as a lion,
And as an old lion: who shall rouse him up?
The scepter shall not depart from Judah,
Nor a lawgiver from between his feet,
Until Shiloh come;
And unto Him shall the gathering of the peo-
ple be."

The lion, king of the forest, is a fitting symbol of this tribe, from which came David, and the Son of David, Shiloh, the true "Lion of the tribe of Judah," to whom all powers shall finally bow and all nations render homage.

For most of his children Jacob foretold a prosperous future. At last the name of Joseph was reached, and the father's heart overflowed as he invoked blessings upon "the head of him that was separate from his brethren":

"Joseph is a fruitful bough,
Even a fruitful bough by a well;
Whose branches run over the wall:
The archers have sorely grieved him,
And shot at him, and hated him:
But his bow abode in strength,
And the arms of his hands were made strong
By the hands of the mighty God of Jacob;
(From thence is the shepherd, the stone of
Israel;)
Even by the God of thy father, who shall
help thee;
And by the Almighty, who shall bless thee
With blessings of heaven above,
Blessings of the deep that lieth under,
Blessings of the breasts, and of the womb:
The blessings of thy father have prevailed

Above the blessings of my progenitors
Unto the utmost bound of the everlasting
   hills:
They shall be on the head of Joseph,
And on the crown of the head of him that
   was separate from his brethren."

Jacob had ever been a man of deep and ardent
affection; his love for his sons was strong and
tender, and his dying testimony to them was not
the utterance of partiality or resentment. He had
forgiven them all, and he loved them to the last.
His paternal tenderness would have found
expression only in words of encouragement and
hope; but the power of God rested upon him,
and under the influence of Inspiration he was
constrained to declare the truth, however
painful.

   The last blessings pronounced, Jacob repeated the charge concerning his burial place: "I am
to be gathered unto my people: bury me with
my fathers . . . in the cave that is in the field of
Machpelah." "There they buried Abraham and
Sarah his wife; there they buried Isaac and
Rebekah his wife; and there I buried Leah."
Thus the last act of his life was to manifest his
faith in God's promise.

   Jacob's last years brought an evening of tranquillity and repose after a troubled and weary
day. Clouds had gathered dark above his path,
yet his sun set clear, and the radiance of heaven
illumined his parting hours. Says the Scripture,
"At evening time it shall be light." Zechariah
14:7. "Mark the perfect man, and behold the
upright: for the end of that man is peace." Psalm
37:37.

   Jacob had sinned, and had deeply suffered.
Many years of toil, care, and sorrow had been
his since the day when his great sin caused him
to flee from his father's tents. A homeless fugitive, separated from his mother, whom he never
saw again; laboring seven years for her whom
he loved, only to be basely cheated; toiling
twenty years in the service of a covetous and
grasping kinsman; seeing his wealth increasing,
and sons rising around him, but finding little joy
in the contentious and divided household; distressed by his daughter's shame, by her broth-
238 ers' revenge, by the death of Rachel, by the
unnatural crime of Reuben, by Judah's sin, by
the cruel deception and malice practiced toward
Joseph—how long and dark is the catalogue of
evils spread out to view! Again and again he
had reaped the fruit of that first wrong deed.
Over and over he saw repeated among his sons
the sins of which he himself had been guilty.
But bitter as had been the discipline, it had
accomplished its work. The chastening, though
grievous, had yielded "the peaceable fruit of
righteousness." Hebrews 12:11.

   Inspiration faithfully records the faults of
good men, those who were distinguished by the
favor of God; indeed, their faults are more fully
presented than their virtues. This has been a
subject of wonder to many, and has given the
infidel occasion to scoff at the Bible. But it is
one of the strongest evidences of the truth of
Scripture, that facts are not glossed over, nor the
sins of its chief characters suppressed. The
minds of men are so subject to prejudice that it
is not possible for human histories to be
absolutely impartial. Had the Bible been written
by uninspired persons, it would no doubt have
presented the character of its honored men in a
more flattering light. But as it is, we have a correct record of their experiences.

   Men whom God favored, and to whom He
entrusted great responsibilities, were sometimes
overcome by temptation and committed sin,
even as we at the present day strive, waver, and
frequently fall into error. Their lives, with all
their faults and follies, are open before us, both
for our encouragement and warning. If they had
been represented as without fault, we, with our
sinful nature, might despair at our own mistakes
and failures. But seeing where others struggled
through discouragements like our own, where
they fell under temptation as we have done, and
yet took heart again and conquered through the
grace of God, we are encouraged in our striving
after righteousness. As they, though sometimes
beaten back, recovered their ground, and were
blessed of God, so we too may be overcomers
in the strength of Jesus. On the other hand, the
record of their lives may serve as a warning to
us. It shows that God will by no means clear the
guilty. He sees sin in His most favored ones,
and He deals with it in them even more strictly
than in those who have less light and responsibility.

   After the burial of Jacob fear again filled the 239
hearts of Joseph's brothers. Notwithstanding his
kindness toward them, conscious guilt made
them distrustful and suspicious. It might be that
he had but delayed his revenge, out of regard to
their father, and that he would now visit upon
them the long-deferred punishment for their
crime. They dared not appear before him in person, but sent a message: "Thy father did command before he died, saying, So shall ye say
unto Joseph, Forgive, I pray thee now, the trespass of thy brethren, and their sin; for they did
unto thee evil: and now, we pray thee, forgive
the trespass of the servants of the God of thy
father." This message affected Joseph to tears,
and, encouraged by this, his brothers came and
fell down before him, with the words, "Behold,
we be thy servants." Joseph's love for his brothers was deep and unselfish, and he was pained
at the thought that they could regard him as
cherishing a spirit of revenge toward them.
"Fear not," he said; "for am I in the place of
God? But as for you, ye thought evil against me;
but God meant it unto good, to bring to pass, as

it is this day, to save much people alive. Now therefore fear ye not: I will nourish you, and your little ones."

The life of Joseph illustrates the life of Christ. It was envy that moved the brothers of Joseph to sell him as a slave; they hoped to prevent him from becoming greater than themselves. And when he was carried to Egypt, they flattered themselves that they were to be no more troubled with his dreams, that they had removed all possibility of their fulfillment. But their own course was overruled by God to bring about the very event that they designed to hinder. So the Jewish priests and elders were jealous of Christ, fearing that He would attract the attention of the people from them. They put Him to death, to prevent Him from becoming king, but they were thus bringing about this very result.

Joseph, through his bondage in Egypt, became a savior to his father's family; yet this fact did not lessen the guilt of his brothers. So the crucifixion of Christ by His enemies made Him the Redeemer of mankind, the Saviour of the fallen race, and Ruler over the whole world; but the crime of His murderers was just as heinous as though God's providential hand had not controlled events for His own glory and the good of man.

240 As Joseph was sold to the heathen by his own brothers, so Christ was sold to His bitterest enemies by one of His disciples. Joseph was falsely accused and thrust into prison because of his virtue; so Christ was despised and rejected because His righteous, self-denying life was a rebuke to sin; and though guilty of no wrong, He was condemned upon the testimony of false witnesses. And Joseph's patience and meekness under injustice and oppression, his ready forgiveness and noble benevolence toward his unnatural brothers, represent the Saviour's uncomplaining endurance of the malice and abuse of wicked men, and His forgiveness, not only of His murderers, but of all who have come to Him confessing their sins and seeking pardon.

Joseph outlived his father fifty-four years. He lived to see "Ephraim's children of the third generation: the children also of Machir the son of Manasseh were brought up upon Joseph's knees." He witnessed the increase and prosperity of his people, and through all the years his faith in God's restoration of Israel to the Land of Promise was unshaken.

When he saw that his end was near, he summoned his kinsmen about him. Honored as he had been in the land of the Pharaohs, Egypt was to him but the place of his exile; his last act was to signify that his lot was cast with Israel. His last words were, "God will surely visit you, and bring you out of this land unto the land which He sware to Abraham, to Isaac, and to Jacob." And he took a solemn oath of the children of

Israel that they would carry up his bones with them to the land of Canaan. "So Joseph died, being an hundred and ten years old: and they embalmed him, and he was put in a coffin in Egypt." And through the centuries of toil which followed, that coffin, a reminder of the dying words of Joseph, testified to Israel that they were only sojourners in Egypt, and bade them keep their hopes fixed upon the Land of Promise, for the time of deliverance would surely come.

22
241

Moses

The people of Egypt, in order to supply themselves with food during the famine, had sold to the crown their cattle and lands, and had finally bound themselves to perpetual serfdom. Joseph wisely provided for their release; he permitted them to become royal tenants, holding their lands of the king, and paying an annual tribute of one fifth of the products of their labor.

But the children of Jacob were not under the necessity of making such conditions. On account of the service that Joseph had rendered the Egyptian nation, they were not only granted a part of the country as a home, but were exempted from taxation, and liberally supplied with food during the continuance of the famine. The king publicly acknowledged that it was through the merciful interposition of the God of Joseph that Egypt enjoyed plenty while other nations were perishing from famine. He saw, too, that Joseph's management had greatly enriched the kingdom, and his gratitude surrounded the family of Jacob with royal favor.

But as time rolled on, the great man to whom Egypt owed so much, and the generation blessed by his labors, passed to the grave. And "there arose up a new king over Egypt, which knew not Joseph." Not that he was ignorant of Joseph's services to the nation, but he wished to make no recognition of them, and, so far as possible, to bury them in oblivion. "And he said unto his people, Behold, the people of the children of Israel are more and mightier than we: come on, let us deal wisely with them; lest they multiply, and it come to pass, that, when there falleth out any war, they join also unto our enemies, and fight against us, and so get them up out of the land."

The Israelites had already become very numerous; they "were fruitful, and increased abundantly, and multiplied, and waxed exceeding mighty; and the land was filled with them." Under Joseph's fostering care, and the favor of the king who was then ruling, they had spread rapidly over the land. But they had kept them- 242

This chapter is based on Exodus 1 to 4.

selves a distinct race, having nothing in common with the Egyptians in customs or religion; and their increasing numbers now excited the fears of the king and his people, lest in case of war they should join themselves with the enemies of Egypt. Yet policy forbade their banishment from the country. Many of them were able and understanding workmen, and they added greatly to the wealth of the nation; the king needed such laborers for the erection of his magnificent palaces and temples. Accordingly he ranked them with the Egyptians who had sold themselves with their possessions to the kingdom. Soon taskmasters were set over them, and their slavery became complete. "And the Egyptians made the children of Israel to serve with rigor: and they made their lives bitter with hard bondage, in mortar, and in brick, and in all manner of service in the field: all their service, wherein they made them serve, was with rigor." "But the more they afflicted them, the more they multiplied and grew."

The king and his counselors had hoped to subdue the Israelites with hard labor, and thus decrease their numbers and crush out their independent spirit. Failing to accomplish their purpose, they proceeded to more cruel measures. Orders were issued to the women whose employment gave them opportunity for executing the command, to destroy the Hebrew male children at their birth. Satan was the mover in this matter. He knew that a deliverer was to be raised up among the Israelites; and by leading the king to destroy their children he hoped to defeat the divine purpose. But the women feared God, and dared not execute the cruel mandate. The Lord approved their course, and prospered them. The king, angry at the failure of his design, made the command more urgent and extensive. The whole nation was called upon to hunt out and slaughter his helpless victims. "And Pharaoh charged all his people, saying, Every son that is born ye shall cast into the river, and every daughter ye shall save alive."

While this decree was in full force a son was born to Amram and Jochebed, devout Israelites of the tribe of Levi. The babe was "a goodly child;" and the parents, believing that the time of Israel's release was drawing near, and that God would raise up a deliverer for His people, 243 determined that their little one should not be sacrificed. Faith in God strengthened their hearts, "and they were not afraid of the king's commandment." Hebrews 11:23.

The mother succeeded in concealing the child for three months. Then, finding that she could no longer keep him safely, she prepared a little ark of rushes, making it watertight by means of slime and pitch; and laying the babe therein, she placed it among the flags at the river's brink. She dared not remain to guard it, lest the child's life and her own should be forfeited; but his sister, Miriam, lingered near, apparently indifferent, but anxiously watching to see what would become of her little brother. And there were other watchers. The mother's earnest prayers had committed her child to the care of God; and angels, unseen, hovered above his lowly resting place. Angels directed Pharaoh's daughter thither. Her curiosity was excited by the little basket, and as she looked upon the beautiful child within, she read the story at a glance. The tears of the babe awakened her compassion, and her sympathies went out to the unknown mother who had resorted to this means to preserve the life of her precious little one. She determined that he should be saved; she would adopt him as her own.

Miriam had been secretly noting every movement; perceiving that the child was tenderly regarded, she ventured nearer, and at last said, "Shall I go and call to thee a nurse of the Hebrew women, that she may nurse the child for thee?" And permission was given.

The sister hastened to her mother with the happy news, and without delay returned with her to the presence of Pharaoh's daughter. "Take this child away, and nurse it for me, and I will give thee thy wages," said the princess.

God had heard the mother's prayers; her faith had been rewarded. It was with deep gratitude that she entered upon her now safe and happy task. She faithfully improved her opportunity to educate her child for God. She felt confident that he had been preserved for some great work, and she knew that he must soon be given up to his royal mother, to be surrounded with influences that would tend to lead him away from God. All this rendered her more diligent and careful in his instruction than in that of her other children. She endeavored to imbue his mind with the fear of God and the love of truth and justice, and earnestly prayed that he might be 244 preserved from every corrupting influence. She showed him the folly and sin of idolatry, and early taught him to bow down and pray to the living God, who alone could hear him and help him in every emergency.

She kept the boy as long as she could, but was obliged to give him up when he was about twelve years old. From his humble cabin home he was taken to the royal palace, to the daughter of Pharaoh, "and he became her son." Yet even here he did not lose the impressions received in childhood. The lessons learned at his mother's side could not be forgotten. They were a shield from the pride, the infidelity, and the vice that flourished amid the splendor of the court.

How far-reaching in its results was the influence of that one Hebrew woman, and she an exile and a slave! The whole future life of Moses, the great mission which he fulfilled as the leader of Israel, testifies to the importance of the work of the Christian mother. There is no other work that can equal this. To a very great extent the mother holds in her own hands the destiny of her children. She is dealing with developing minds and characters, working not alone for time, but for eternity. She is sowing seed that will spring up and bear fruit, either for good or for evil. She has not to paint a form of beauty upon canvas or to chisel it from marble, but to impress upon a human soul the image of the divine. Especially during their early years the responsibility rests upon her of forming the character of her children. The impressions now made upon their developing minds will remain with them all through life. Parents should direct the instruction and training of their children while very young, to the end that they may be Christians. They are placed in our care to be trained, not as heirs to the throne of an earthly empire, but as kings unto God, to reign through unending ages.

Let every mother feel that her moments are priceless; her work will be tested in the solemn day of accounts. Then it will be found that many of the failures and crimes of men and women have resulted from the ignorance and neglect of those whose duty it was to guide their childish feet in the right way. Then it will be found that many who have blessed the world with the light of genius and truth and holiness, owe the principles that were the mainspring of their influence and success to a praying, Christian mother.

245 At the court of Pharaoh, Moses received the highest civil and military training. The monarch had determined to make his adopted grandson his successor on the throne, and the youth was educated for his high station. "And Moses was learned in all the wisdom of the Egyptians, and was mighty in words and in deeds." Acts 7:22. His ability as a military leader made him a favorite with the armies of Egypt, and he was generally regarded as a remarkable character. Satan had been defeated in his purpose. The very decree condemning the Hebrew children to death had been overruled by God for the training and education of the future leader of His people.

The elders of Israel were taught by angels that the time for their deliverance was near, and that Moses was the man whom God would employ to accomplish this work. Angels instructed Moses also that Jehovah had chosen him to break the bondage of His people. He, supposing that they were to obtain their freedom by force of arms, expected to lead the Hebrew host against the armies of Egypt, and having this in view, he guarded his affections, lest in his attachment to his foster mother or to Pharaoh he would not be free to do the will of God.

By the laws of Egypt all who occupied the throne of the Pharaohs must become members of the priestly caste; and Moses, as the heir apparent, was to be initiated into the mysteries of the national religion. This duty was committed to the priests. But while he was an ardent and untiring student, he could not be induced to participate in the worship of the gods. He was threatened with the loss of the crown, and warned that he would be disowned by the princess should his adherence in his adherence to the Hebrew faith. But he was unshaken in his determination to render homage to none save the one God, the Maker of heaven and earth. He reasoned with priests and worshipers, showing the folly of their superstitious veneration of senseless objects. None could refute his arguments or change his purpose, yet for the time his firmness was tolerated on account of his high position and the favor with which he was regarded by both the king and the people.

"By faith Moses, when he was come to years, refused to be called the son of Pharaoh's daughter; choosing rather to suffer affliction with the people of God, than to enjoy the pleasures of sin for a season; esteeming the reproach of Christ greater riches than the treasures in Egypt: for he 246 had respect unto the recompense of the reward." Hebrews 11:24-26. Moses was fitted to take pre-eminence among the great of the earth, to shine in the courts of its most glorious kingdom, and to sway the scepter of its power. His intellectual greatness distinguishes him above the great men of all ages. As historian, poet, philosopher, general of armies, and legislator, he stands without a peer. Yet with the world before him, he had the moral strength to refuse the flattering prospects of wealth and greatness and fame, "choosing rather to suffer affliction with the people of God, than to enjoy the pleasures of sin for a season."

Moses had been instructed in regard to the final reward to be given to the humble and obedient servants of God, and worldly gain sank to its proper insignificance in comparison. The magnificent palace of Pharaoh and the monarch's throne were held out as an inducement to Moses; but he knew that the sinful pleasures that make men forget God were in its lordly courts. He looked beyond the gorgeous palace, beyond a monarch's crown, to the high honors that will be bestowed on the saints of the Most High in a kingdom untainted by sin. He saw by faith an imperishable crown that the King of heaven would place on the brow of the overcomer. This faith led him to turn away from the lordly ones of earth and join the humble, poor, despised nation that had chosen to obey God rather than to serve sin.

Moses remained at court until he was forty years of age. His thoughts often turned upon the abject condition of his people, and he visited his brethren in their servitude, and encouraged them with the assurance that God would work for their deliverance. Often, stung to resentment by the sight of injustice and oppression, he burned to avenge their wrongs. One day, while thus abroad, seeing an Egyptian smiting an Israelite, he sprang forward and slew the Egyptian. Except the Israelite, there had been no witness to the deed, and Moses immediately buried the body in the sand. He had now shown himself ready to maintain the cause of his people, and he hoped to see them rise to recover their liberty. "He supposed his brethren would have understood how that God by his hand would deliver them; but they understood not." Acts 7:25. They were not yet prepared for freedom. On the following day Moses saw two Hebrews

247 striving together, one of them evidently at fault. Moses reproved the offender, who at once retaliated upon the reprover, denying his right to interfere, and basely accusing him of crime: "Who made thee a prince and a judge over us?" he said. "Intendest thou to kill me, as thou killedst the Egyptian?"

The whole matter was quickly made known to the Egyptians, and, greatly exaggerated, soon reached the ears of Pharaoh. It was represented to the king that this act meant much; that Moses designed to lead his people against the Egyptians, to overthrow the government, and to seat himself upon the throne; and that there could be no security for the kingdom while he lived. It was at once determined by the monarch that he should die; but, becoming aware of his danger, he made his escape and fled toward Arabia.

The Lord directed his course, and he found a home with Jethro, the priest and prince of Midian, who was also a worshiper of God. After a time Moses married one of the daughters of Jethro; and here, in the service of his father-in-law, as keeper of his flocks, he remained forty years.

In slaying the Egyptian, Moses had fallen into the same error so often committed by his fathers, of taking into their own hands the work that God had promised to do. It was not God's will to deliver His people by warfare, as Moses thought, but by His own mighty power, that the glory might be ascribed to Him alone. Yet even this rash act was overruled by God to accomplish His purposes. Moses was not prepared for his great work. He had yet to learn the same lesson of faith that Abraham and Jacob had been taught—not to rely upon human strength or wisdom, but upon the power of God for the fulfillment of His promises. And there were other lessons that, amid the solitude of the mountains, Moses was to receive. In the school of self-denial and hardship he was to learn patience, to temper his passions. Before he could govern wisely, he must be trained to obey. His own heart must be fully in harmony with God before he could teach the knowledge of His will to Israel. By his own experience he must be prepared to exercise a fatherly care over all who needed his help.

Man would have dispensed with that long period of toil and obscurity, deeming it a great loss of time. But Infinite Wisdom called him who was to become the leader of his people to spend forty years in the humble work of a shepherd. 248 The habits of caretaking, of self-forgetfulness and tender solicitude for his flock, thus developed, would prepare him to become the compassionate, longsuffering shepherd of Israel. No advantage that human training or culture could bestow, could be a substitute for this experience.

Moses had been learning much that he must unlearn. The influences that had surrounded him in Egypt—the love of his foster mother, his own high position as the king's grandson, the dissipation on every hand, the refinement, the subtlety, and the mysticism of a false religion, the splendor of idolatrous worship, the solemn grandeur of architecture and sculpture—all had left deep impressions upon his developing mind and had molded, to some extent, his habits and character. Time, change of surroundings, and communion with God could remove these impressions. It would require on the part of Moses himself a struggle as for life to renounce error and accept truth, but God would be his helper when the conflict should be too severe for human strength.

In all who have been chosen to accomplish a work for God the human element is seen. Yet they have not been men of stereotyped habits and character, who were satisfied to remain in that condition. They earnestly desired to obtain wisdom from God and to learn to work for Him. Says the apostle, "If any of you lack wisdom, let him ask of God, that giveth to all men liberally, and upbraideth not; and it shall be given him." James 1:5. But God will not impart to men divine light while they are content to remain in darkness. In order to receive God's help, man must realize his weakness and deficiency; he must apply his own mind to the great change to be wrought in himself; he must be aroused to earnest and persevering prayer and effort. Wrong habits and customs must be shaken off; and it is only by determined endeavor to correct these errors and to conform to right principles that the victory can be gained. Many never attain to the position that they might occupy, because they wait for God to do for them that which He has given them power to do for themselves. All who are fitted for usefulness must be trained by the severest mental and moral discipline, and God will assist them by uniting divine power with human effort.

Shut in by the bulwarks of the mountains, Moses was alone with God. The magnificent 251 temples of Egypt no longer impressed his mind with their superstition and falsehood. In the solemn grandeur of the everlasting hills he beheld the majesty of the Most High, and in contrast realized how powerless and insignificant were the gods of Egypt. Everywhere the Creator's name was written. Moses seemed to stand in His presence and to be overshadowed by His power. Here his pride and self-sufficiency were swept away. In the stern simplicity of his wilderness life, the results of the ease and luxury of Egypt disappeared. Moses became patient, reverent, and humble, "very meek, above all the men which were upon the face of the earth" (Numbers 12:3), yet strong in faith in the mighty God of Jacob.

As the years rolled on, and he wandered with his flocks in solitary places, pondering upon the oppressed condition of his people, he recounted the dealings of God with his fathers and the promises that were the heritage of the chosen nation, and his prayers for Israel ascended by day and by night. Heavenly angels shed their light around him. Here, under the inspiration of the Holy Spirit, he wrote the book of Genesis. The long years spent amid the desert solitudes were rich in blessing, not alone to Moses and his people, but to the world in all succeeding ages.

"And it came to pass in process of time, that the king of Egypt died: and the children of Israel sighed by reason of the bondage, and they cried, and their cry came up unto God by reason of the bondage. And God heard their groaning, and God remembered His covenant with Abraham, with Isaac, and with Jacob. And God looked upon the children of Israel, and God had respect unto them." The time for Israel's deliverance had come. But God's purpose was to be accomplished in a manner to pour contempt on human pride. The deliverer was to go forth as a humble shepherd, with only a rod in his hand; but God would make that rod the symbol of His power. Leading his flocks one day near Horeb, "the mountain of God," Moses saw a bush in flames, branches, foliage, and trunk, all burning, yet seeming not to be consumed. He drew near to view the wonderful sight, when a voice from out of the flame called him by name. With trembling lips he answered, "Here am I." He was warned not to approach irreverently: "Put off thy shoes from off thy feet; for the place whereon thou standest is holy ground. . . . I am the 252 God of thy father, the God of Abraham, the God of Isaac, and the God of Jacob." It was He who, as the Angel of the covenant, had revealed Himself to the fathers in ages past. "And Moses hid his face; for he was afraid to look upon God."

Humility and reverence should characterize the deportment of all who come into the presence of God. In the name of Jesus we may come before Him with confidence, but we must not approach Him with the boldness of presumption, as though He were on a level with ourselves. There are those who address the great and all-powerful and holy God, who dwelleth in light unapproachable, as they would address an equal, or even an inferior. There are those who conduct themselves in His house as they would not presume to do in the audience chamber of an earthly ruler. These should remember that they are in His sight whom angels adore, before whom angels veil their faces. God is greatly to be reverenced; all who truly realize His presence will bow in humility before Him, and, like Jacob beholding the vision of God, they will cry out, "How dreadful is this place! This is none other but the house of God, and this is the gate of heaven."

As Moses waited in reverent awe before God the words continued: "I have surely seen the affliction of My people which are in Egypt, and have heard their cry by reason of their taskmasters; for I know their sorrows; and I am come down to deliver them out of the hand of the Egyptians, and to bring them up out of that land unto a good land and a large, unto a land flowing with milk and honey. . . . Come now therefore, and I will send thee unto Pharaoh, that thou mayest bring forth My people the children of Israel out of Egypt."

Amazed and terrified at the command, Moses drew back, saying, "Who am I, that I should go unto Pharaoh, and that I should bring forth the children of Israel out of Egypt?" The reply was, "Certainly I will be with thee; and this shall be a token unto thee, that I have sent thee: When thou hast brought forth the people out of Egypt, ye shall serve God upon this mountain."

Moses thought of the difficulties to be encountered, of the blindness, ignorance, and unbelief of his people, many of whom were almost destitute of a knowledge of God. "Behold," he said, "when I come unto the children of Israel, and shall say unto them, The God 253 of your fathers hath sent me unto you; and they shall say to me, What is His name? what shall I say unto them?" The answer was—

"I AM THAT I AM." "Thus shalt thou say unto the children of Israel, I AM hath sent me unto you."

Moses was commanded first to assemble the elders of Israel, the most noble and righteous among them, who had long grieved because of their bondage, and to declare to them a message from God, with a promise of deliverance. Then he was to go with the elders before the king, and say to him—

"The Lord God of the Hebrews hath met with us: and now let us go, we beseech thee, three days' journey into the wilderness, that we may sacrifice to the Lord our God."

Moses was forewarned that Pharaoh would resist the appeal to let Israel go. Yet the courage of God's servant must not fail; for the Lord would make this the occasion to manifest His power before the Egyptians and before His people. "And I will stretch out My hand, and smite

Egypt with all My wonders which I will do in the midst thereof: and after that he will let you go."

Direction was also given concerning the provision they were to make for the journey. The Lord declared, "It shall come to pass, that, when ye go, ye shall not go empty: but every woman shall borrow of her neighbor, and of her that sojourneth in her house, jewels of silver, and jewels of gold, and raiment." The Egyptians had been enriched by the labor unjustly exacted from the Israelites, and as the latter were to start on the journey to their new home, it was right for them to claim the reward of their years of toil. They were to ask for articles of value, such as could be easily transported, and God would give them favor in the sight of the Egyptians. The mighty miracles wrought for their deliverance would strike terror to the oppressors, so that the requests of the bondmen would be granted.

Moses saw before him difficulties that seemed insurmountable. What proof could he give his people that God had indeed sent him? "Behold," he said, "they will not believe me, nor hearken unto my voice: for they will say, The Lord hath not appeared unto thee." Evidence that appealed to his own senses was now given. He was told to cast his rod upon the ground. As he did so, "it became a serpent; and Moses fled from before it." He was commanded 254 to seize it, and in his hand it became a rod. He was bidden to put his hand into his bosom. He obeyed, and "when he took it out, behold, his hand was leprous as snow." Being told to put it again into his bosom, he found on withdrawing it that it had become like the other. By these signs the Lord assured Moses that His own people, as well as Pharaoh, should be convinced that One mightier than the king of Egypt was manifest among them.

But the servant of God was still overwhelmed by the thought of the strange and wonderful work before him. In his distress and fear he now pleaded as an excuse a lack of ready speech: "O my Lord, I am not eloquent, neither heretofore, nor since Thou hast spoken unto Thy servant; but I am slow of speech, and of a slow tongue." He had been so long away from the Egyptians that he had not so clear knowledge and ready use of their language as when he was among them.

The Lord said unto him, "Who hath made man's mouth? or who maketh the dumb, or deaf, or the seeing, or the blind? have not I the Lord?" To this was added another assurance of divine aid: "Now therefore go, and I will be with thy mouth, and teach thee what thou shalt say." But Moses still entreated that a more competent person be selected. These excuses at first proceeded from humility and diffidence; but after the Lord had promised to remove all diffi-

culties, and to give him final success, then any further shrinking back and complaining of his unfitness showed distrust of God. It implied a fear that God was unable to qualify him for the great work to which He had called him, or that He had made a mistake in the selection of the man.

Moses was now directed to Aaron, his elder brother, who, having been in daily use of the language of the Egyptians, was able to speak it perfectly. He was told that Aaron was coming to meet him. The next words from the Lord were an unqualified command:

"Thou shalt speak unto him, and put words in his mouth: and I will be with thy mouth, and with his mouth, and will teach you what ye shall do. And he shall be thy spokesman unto the people: and he shall be, even he shall be to thee instead of a mouth, and thou shalt be to him instead of God. And thou shalt take this rod in thine hand, wherewith thou shalt do signs." He could make no further resistance, for all ground for excuse was removed.

The divine command given to Moses found 255 him self-distrustful, slow of speech, and timid. He was overwhelmed with a sense of his incapacity to be a mouthpiece for God to Israel. But having once accepted the work, he entered upon it with his whole heart, putting all his trust in the Lord. The greatness of his mission called into exercise the best powers of his mind. God blessed his ready obedience, and he became eloquent, hopeful, self-possessed, and well fitted for the greatest work ever given to man. This is an example of what God does to strengthen the character of those who trust Him fully and give themselves unreservedly to His commands.

A man will gain power and efficiency as he accepts the responsibilities that God places upon him, and with his whole soul seeks to qualify himself to bear them aright. However humble his position or limited his ability, that man will attain true greatness who, trusting to divine strength, seeks to perform his work with fidelity. Had Moses relied upon his own strength and wisdom, and eagerly accepted the great charge, he would have evinced his entire unfitness for such a work. The fact that a man feels his weakness is at least some evidence that he realizes the magnitude of the work appointed him, and that he will make God his counselor and his strength.

Moses returned to his father-in-law and expressed his desire to visit his brethren in Egypt. Jethro's consent was given, with his blessing, "Go in peace." With his wife and children, Moses set forth on the journey. He had not dared to make known the object of his mission, lest they should not be allowed to accompany him. Before reaching Egypt, however, he himself thought it best for their own safety to send them back to the home in Midian.

A secret dread of Pharaoh and the Egyptians, whose anger had been kindled against him forty years before, had rendered Moses still more reluctant to return to Egypt; but after he had set out to obey the divine command, the Lord revealed to him that his enemies were dead.

On the way from Midian, Moses received a startling and terrible warning of the Lord's displeasure. An angel appeared to him in a threatening manner, as if he would immediately destroy him. No explanation was given; but Moses remembered that he had disregarded one of God's requirements; yielding to the persuasion of his wife, he had neglected to perform the rite of circumcision upon their youngest son. He had failed to comply with the condition by which his child could be entitled to the blessings of God's covenant with Israel; and such a neglect on the part of their chosen leader could not but lessen the force of the divine precepts upon the people. Zipporah, fearing that her husband would be slain, performed the rite herself, and the angel then permitted Moses to pursue his journey. In his mission to Pharaoh, Moses was to be placed in a position of great peril; his life could be preserved only through the protection of holy angels. But while living in neglect of a known duty, he would not be secure; for he could not be shielded by the angels of God.

In the time of trouble just before the coming of Christ, the righteous will be preserved through the ministration of heavenly angels; but there will be no security for the transgressor of God's law. Angels cannot then protect those who are disregarding one divine precepts.

256

257

23

The Plagues of Egypt

Aaron, being instructed by angels, went forth to meet his brother, from whom he had been so long separated; and they met amid the desert solitudes, near Horeb. Here they communed together, and Moses told Aaron "all the words of the Lord who had sent him, and all the signs which He had commanded him." Exodus 4:28. Together they journeyed to Egypt; and having reached the land of Goshen, they proceeded to assemble the elders of Israel. Aaron repeated to them all the dealings of God with Moses, and then the signs which God had given Moses were shown before the people. "The people believed: and when they heard that the Lord had visited the children of Israel, and that He had looked upon their affliction, then they bowed their heads and worshiped." Verse 31.

Moses had been charged also with a message for the king. The two brothers entered the palace of the Pharaohs as ambassadors from the King of kings, and they spoke in His name: "Thus saith Jehovah, God of Israel, Let My people go, that they may hold a feast unto Me in the wilderness."

"Who is Jehovah, that I should obey His voice to let Israel go?" demanded the monarch; "I know not Jehovah, neither will I let Israel go."

Their answer was, "The God of the Hebrews hath met with us: let us go, we pray thee, three days' journey into the desert, and sacrifice unto the Lord our God; lest He fall upon us with pestilence, or with the sword."

Tidings of them and of the interest they were exciting among the people had already reached the king. His anger was kindled. "Wherefore do ye, Moses and Aaron, let [hinder] the people from their works?" he said. "Get you unto your burdens." Already the kingdom had suffered loss by the interference of these strangers. At thought of this he added, "Behold, the people of the land now are many, and ye make them rest from their burdens."

258

In their bondage the Israelites had to some extent lost the knowledge of God's law, and they had departed from its precepts. The Sabbath had been generally disregarded, and the exactions of their taskmasters made its observance apparently impossible. But Moses had shown his people that obedience to God was the first condition of deliverance; and the efforts made to restore the observance of the Sabbath had come to the notice of their oppressors.*

The king, thoroughly roused, suspected the Israelites of a design to revolt from his service. Disaffection was the result of idleness; he would see that no time was left them for dangerous scheming. And he at once adopted measures to tighten their bonds and crush out their independent spirit. The same day orders were issued that rendered their labor still more cruel and oppressive. The most common building material of that country was sun-dried brick; the walls of the finest edifices were made of this, and then faced with stone; and the manufacture of brick employed great numbers of the bondmen. Cut straw being intermixed with the clay, to hold it together, large quantities of straw were required for the work; the king now directed that no more straw be furnished; the laborers must find it for themselves, while the same amount of brick should be exacted.

This order produced great distress among the Israelites throughout the land. The Egyptian taskmasters had appointed Hebrew officers to oversee the work of the people, and these officers were responsible for the labor performed by those under their charge. When the requirement of the king was put in force, the people scattered themselves throughout the land, to gather stubble instead of straw; but they found it impossible to accomplish the usual amount of labor. For this

---

This chapter is based on Exodus 5 to 10.   * See Appendix, Note 1.

failure the Hebrew officers were cruelly beaten.

These officers supposed that their oppression came from their taskmasters, and not from the king himself; and they went to him with their grievances. Their remonstrance was met by Pharaoh with a taunt: "Ye are idle, ye are idle: therefore ye say, Let us go and do sacrifice to the Lord." They were ordered back to their work, with the declaration that their burdens were in no case to be lightened. Returning, they met Moses and Aaron, and cried out to them, "The Lord look upon you, and judge; because ye have made our savor to be abhorred in the eyes of Pharaoh, and in the eyes of his servants, to put a sword in their hand to slay us."

259 As Moses listened to these reproaches he was greatly distressed. The sufferings of the people had been much increased. All over the land a cry of despair went up from old and young, and all united in charging upon him the disastrous change in their condition. In bitterness of soul he went before God, with the cry, "Lord, wherefore hast Thou so evil entreated this people? why is it that Thou hast sent me? For since I came to Pharaoh to speak in Thy name, he hath done evil to this people; neither hast Thou delivered Thy people at all." The answer was, "Now shalt thou see what I will do to Pharaoh: for with a strong hand shall he let them go, and with a strong hand shall he drive them out of his land." Again he was pointed back to the covenant which God had made with the fathers, and was assured that it would be fulfilled.

During all the years of servitude in Egypt there had been among the Israelites some who adhered to the worship of Jehovah. These were sorely troubled as they saw their children daily witnessing the abominations of the heathen, and even bowing down to their false gods. In their distress they cried unto the Lord for deliverance from the Egyptian yoke, that they might be freed from the corrupting influence of idolatry. They did not conceal their faith, but declared to the Egyptians that the object of their worship was the Maker of heaven and earth, the only true and living God. They rehearsed the evidences of His existence and power, from creation down to the days of Jacob. The Egyptians thus had an opportunity to become acquainted with the religion of the Hebrews; but disdaining to be instructed by their slaves, they tried to seduce the worshipers of God by promises of reward, and, this failing, by threats and cruelty.

The elders of Israel endeavored to sustain the sinking faith of their brethren by repeating the promises made to their fathers, and the prophetic words of Joseph before his death, foretelling their deliverance from Egypt. Some would listen and believe. Others, looking at the circumstances that surrounded them, refused to hope. The Egyptians, being informed of what was reported among their bondmen, derided their expectations and scornfully denied the power of their God. They pointed to their situation as a nation of slaves, and tauntingly said, "If your God is just and merciful, and possesses power above that of the Egyptian gods, why does He not make you a free people?" They called attention to their own condition. They worshiped deities termed by the Israelites false gods, yet they were a rich and powerful nation. They 260 declared that their gods had blessed them with prosperity, and had given them the Israelites as servants, and they gloried in their power to oppress and destroy the worshipers of Jehovah. Pharaoh himself boasted that the God of the Hebrews could not deliver them from his hand.

Words like these destroyed the hopes of many of the Israelites. The case appeared to them very much as the Egyptians had represented. It was true that they were slaves, and must endure whatever their cruel taskmasters might choose to inflict. Their children had been hunted and slain, and their own lives were a burden. Yet they were worshiping the God of heaven. If Jehovah were indeed above all gods, surely He would not thus leave them in bondage to idolaters. But those who were true to God understood that it was because of Israel's departure from Him—because of their disposition to marry with heathen nations, thus being led into idolatry—that the Lord had permitted them to become bondmen; and they confidently assured their brethren that He would soon break the yoke of the oppressor.

The Hebrews had expected to obtain their freedom without any special trial of their faith or any real suffering or hardship. But they were not yet prepared for deliverance. They had little faith in God, and were unwilling patiently to endure their afflictions until He should see fit to work for them. Many were content to remain in bondage rather than meet the difficulties attending removal to a strange land; and the habits of some had become so much like those of the Egyptians that they preferred to dwell in Egypt. Therefore the Lord did not deliver them by the first manifestation of His power before Pharaoh. He overruled events more fully to develop the tyrannical spirit of the Egyptian king and also to reveal Himself to His people. Beholding His justice, His power, and His love, they would choose to leave Egypt and give themselves to His service. The task of Moses would have been much less difficult had not many of the Israelites become so corrupted that they were unwilling to leave Egypt.

The Lord directed Moses to go again to the people and repeat the promise of deliverance, with a fresh assurance of divine favor. He went as he was commanded; but they would not listen. Says the Scripture, "They hearkened not . . . for anguish of spirit, and for cruel bondage." Again the divine message came to Moses, "Go 263 in, speak unto Pharaoh king of Egypt, that he let the children of Israel go out of his land." In discouragement he replied, "Behold, the children of Israel have not hearkened unto me; how then shall Pharaoh hear me?" He was told to take Aaron with him and go before Pharaoh, and again demand "that he send the children of Israel out of his land."

He was informed that the monarch would not yield until God should visit judgments upon Egypt and bring out Israel by the signal manifestation of His power. Before the infliction of each plague, Moses was to describe its nature and effects, that the king might save himself from it if he chose. Every punishment rejected would be followed by one more severe, until his proud heart would be humbled, and he would acknowledge the Maker of heaven and earth as the true and living God. The Lord would give the Egyptians an opportunity to see how vain was the wisdom of their mighty men, how feeble the power of their gods, when opposed to the commands of Jehovah. He would punish the people of Egypt for their idolatry and silence their boasting of the blessings received from their senseless deities. God would glorify His own name, that other nations might hear of His power and tremble at His mighty acts, and that His people might be led to turn from their idolatry and render Him pure worship.

Again Moses and Aaron entered the lordly halls of the king of Egypt. There, surrounded by lofty columns and glittering adornments, by the rich paintings and sculptured images of heathen gods, before the monarch of the most powerful kingdom then in existence, stood the two representatives of the enslaved race, to repeat the command from God for Israel's release. The king demanded a miracle, in evidence of their divine commission. Moses and Aaron had been directed how to act in case such a demand should be made, and Aaron now took the rod and cast it down before Pharaoh. It became a serpent. The monarch sent for his "wise men and the sorcerers," who "cast down every man his rod and they became serpents: but Aaron's rod swallowed up their rods." Then the king, more determined than before, declared his magicians equal in power with Moses and Aaron; he denounced the servants of the Lord as impostors, and felt himself secure in resisting their demands. Yet while he despised their message, he was restrained by divine power from doing them harm.

264   It was the hand of God, and no human influence or power possessed by Moses and Aaron, that wrought the miracles which they showed before Pharaoh. Those signs and wonders were designed to convince Pharaoh that the great "I AM" had sent Moses, and that it was the duty of the king to let Israel go, that they might serve the living God. The magicians also showed signs and wonders; for they wrought not by their own skill alone, but by the power of their god, Satan, who assisted them in counterfeiting the work of Jehovah.

The magicians did not really cause their rods to become serpents; but by magic, aided by the great deceiver, they were able to produce this appearance. It was beyond the power of Satan to change the rods to living serpents. The prince of evil, though possessing all the wisdom and might of an angel fallen, has not power to create, or to give life; this is the prerogative of God alone. But all that was in Satan's power to do, he did; he produced a counterfeit. To human sight the rods were changed to serpents. Such they were believed to be by Pharaoh and his court. There was nothing in their appearance to distinguish them from the serpent produced by Moses. Though the Lord caused the real serpent to swallow up the spurious ones, yet even this was regarded by Pharaoh, not as a work of God's power, but as the result of a kind of magic superior to that of his servants.

Pharaoh desired to justify his stubbornness in resisting the divine command, and hence he was seeking some pretext for disregarding the miracles that God had wrought through Moses. Satan gave him just what he wanted. By the work that he wrought through the magicians he made it appear to the Egyptians that Moses and Aaron were only magicians and sorcerers, and that the message they brought could not claim respect as coming from a superior being. Thus Satan's counterfeit accomplished its purpose of emboldening the Egyptians in their rebellion and causing Pharaoh to harden his heart against conviction. Satan hoped also to shake the faith of Moses and Aaron in the divine origin of their mission, that his instruments might prevail. He was unwilling that the children of Israel should be released from bondage to serve the living God.

But the prince of evil had a still deeper object in manifesting his wonders through the magicians. He well knew that Moses, in breaking the yoke of bondage from off the children of Israel, pre-figured Christ, who was to break the reign of sin over the human family. He knew that 265 when Christ should appear, mighty miracles would be wrought as an evidence to the world that God had sent Him. Satan trembled for his power. By counterfeiting the work of God through Moses, he hoped not only to prevent the deliverance of Israel, but to exert an influence through future ages to destroy faith in the miracles of Christ. Satan is constantly seeking to counterfeit the work of Christ and to establish his own power and claims. He leads men to account for the miracles of Christ by making them appear to be the result of human skill and power. In many minds he thus destroys faith in Christ as the Son of God, and leads them to reject the gracious offers of mercy through the plan of redemption.

Moses and Aaron were directed to visit the riverside next morning, where the king was accustomed to repair. The overflowing of the Nile being the source of food and wealth for all Egypt, the river was worshiped as a god, and the monarch came thither daily to pay his devotions. Here the two brothers again repeated the message to him, and then they stretched out the rod and smote upon the water. The sacred stream ran blood, the fish died, and the river became offensive to the smell. The water in the houses, the supply preserved in cisterns, was likewise changed to blood. But "the magicians of Egypt did so with their enchantments," and "Pharaoh turned and went into his house, neither did he set his heart to this also." For seven days the plague continued, but without effect.

Again the rod was stretched out over the waters, and frogs came up from the river and spread over the land. They overran the houses, took possession of the bed chambers, and even the ovens and kneading troughs. The frog was regarded as sacred by the Egyptians, and they would not destroy it; but the slimy pests had now become intolerable. They swarmed even in the palace of the Pharaohs, and the king was impatient to have them removed. The magicians had appeared to produce frogs, but they could not remove them. Upon seeing this, Pharaoh was somewhat humbled. He sent for Moses and Aaron, and said, "Entreat the Lord, that He may take away the frogs from me, and from my people; and I will let the people go, that they may do sacrifice unto the Lord." After reminding the king of his former boasting, they requested him to appoint a time when they should pray for the removal of the plague. He set the next day, secretly hoping that in the interval the frogs 266 might disappear of themselves, and thus save him from the bitter humiliation of submitting to the God of Israel. The plague, however, continued till the time specified, when throughout all Egypt the frogs died, but their putrid bodies, which remained, polluted the atmosphere.

The Lord could have caused them to return to dust in a moment; but He did not do this lest after their removal the king and his people should pronounce it the result of sorcery or enchantment, like the work of the magicians. The frogs died, and were then gathered together in heaps. Here the king and all Egypt had evidence which their vain philosophy could not gainsay, that this work was not accomplished by magic, but was a judgment from the God of heaven.

"When Pharaoh saw that there was respite, he hardened his heart." At the command of God, Aaron stretched out his hand, and the dust of the earth became lice throughout all the land of Egypt. Pharaoh called upon the magicians to do the same, but they could not. The work of God was thus shown to be superior to that of Satan. The magicians themselves acknowledged, "This is the finger of God." But the king was still unmoved.

Appeal and warning were ineffectual, and another judgment was inflicted. The time of its occurrence was foretold, that it might not be said to have come by chance. Flies filled the houses and swarmed upon the ground, so that "the land was corrupted by reason of the swarms of flies." These flies were large and venomous, and their bite was extremely painful to man and beast. As had been foretold, this visitation did not extend to the land of Goshen.

Pharaoh now offered the Israelites permission to sacrifice in Egypt, but they refused to accept such conditions. "It is not meet," said Moses; "lo, shall we sacrifice the abomination of the Egyptians before their eyes, and will they not stone us?" The animals which the Hebrews would be required to sacrifice were among those regarded as sacred by the Egyptians; and such was the reverence in which these creatures were held, that to slay one, even accidentally, was a crime punishable with death. It would be impossible for the Hebrews to worship in Egypt without giving offense to their masters. Moses again proposed to go three days' journey into the wilderness. The monarch consented, and begged the servants of God to entreat that the plague might be removed. They promised to do this, but warned him against dealing deceitfully 267 with them. The plague was stayed, but the king's heart had become hardened by persistent rebellion, and he still refused to yield.

A more terrible stroke followed—murrain upon all the Egyptian cattle that were in the field. Both the sacred animals and the beasts of burden—kine and oxen and sheep, horses and camels and asses—were destroyed. It had been distinctly stated that the Hebrews were to be exempt; and Pharaoh, on sending messengers to the home of the Israelites, proved the truth of this declaration of Moses. "Of the cattle of the children of Israel died not one." Still the king was obstinate.

Moses was next directed to take ashes of the furnace, and "sprinkle it toward heaven in the sight of Pharaoh." This act was deeply significant. Four hundred years before, God had shown to Abraham the future oppression of His people, under the figure of a smoking furnace and a burning lamp. He had declared that He would visit judgments upon their oppressors, and would bring forth the captives with great substance. In Egypt, Israel had long languished in the furnace of affliction. This act of Moses was an assurance to them that God was mindful of His covenant, and that the time for their deliverance had come.

As the ashes were sprinkled toward heaven,

the fine particles spread over all the land of Egypt, and wherever they settled, produced boils "breaking forth with blains upon man, and upon beast." The priests and magicians had hitherto encouraged Pharaoh in his stubbornness, but now a judgment had come that reached even them. Smitten with a loathsome and painful disease, their vaunted power only making them contemptible, they were no longer able to contend against the God of Israel. The whole nation was made to see the folly of trusting in the magicians, when they were not able to protect even their own persons.

Still the heart of Pharaoh grew harder. And now the Lord sent a message to him, declaring, "I will at this time send all My plagues upon thy heart, and upon thy servants, and upon thy people; that thou mayest know that there is none like Me in all the earth. . . . And in very deed for this cause have I raised thee up, for to show in thee My power." Not that God had given him an existence for this purpose, but His providence had overruled events to place him upon the throne at the very time appointed for Israel's deliverance. Though this haughty tyrant had by 268 his crimes forfeited the mercy of God, yet his life had been preserved that through his stubbornness the Lord might manifest His wonders in the land of Egypt. The disposing of events is of God's providence. He could have placed upon the throne a more merciful king, who would not have dared to withstand the mighty manifestations of divine power. But in that case the Lord's purposes would not have been accomplished. His people were permitted to experience the grinding cruelty of the Egyptians, that they might not be deceived concerning the debasing influence of idolatry. In His dealing with Pharaoh, the Lord manifested His hatred of idolatry and His determination to punish cruelty and oppression.

God had declared concerning Pharaoh, "I will harden his heart, that he shall not let the people go." Exodus 4:21. There was no exercise of supernatural power to harden the heart of the king. God gave to Pharaoh the most striking evidence of divine power, but the monarch stubbornly refused to heed the light. Every display of infinite power rejected by him, rendered him the more determined in his rebellion. The seeds of rebellion that he sowed when he rejected the first miracle, produced their harvest. As he continued to venture on in his own course, going from one degree of stubbornness to another, his heart became more and more hardened, until he was called to look upon the cold, dead faces of the first-born.

God speaks to men through His servants, giving cautions and warnings, and rebuking sin. He gives to each an opportunity to correct his errors before they become fixed in the character; but if one refuses to be corrected, divine power does not interpose to counteract the tendency of his own action. He finds it more easy to repeat the same course. He is hardening the heart against the influence of the Holy Spirit. A further rejection of light places him where a far stronger influence will be ineffectual to make an abiding impression.

He who has once yielded to temptation will yield more readily the second time. Every repetition of the sin lessens his power of resistance, blinds his eyes, and stifles conviction. Every seed of indulgence sown will bear fruit. God works no miracle to prevent the harvest. "Whatsoever a man soweth, that shall he also reap." Galatians 6:7. He who manifests an infidel hardihood, a stolid indifference to divine truth, is but reaping the harvest of that which he has 269 himself sown. It is thus that multitudes come to listen with stoical indifference to the truths that once stirred their very souls. They sowed neglect and resistance to the truth, and such is the harvest which they reap.

Those who are quieting a guilty conscience with the thought that they can change a course of evil when they choose, that they can trifle with the invitations of mercy, and yet be again and again impressed, take this course at their peril. They think that after casting all their influence on the side of the great rebel, in a moment of utmost extremity, when danger compasses them about, they will change leaders. But this is not so easily done. The experience, the education, the discipline of a life of sinful indulgence, has so thoroughly molded the character that they cannot then receive the image of Jesus. Had no light shone upon their pathway, the case would have been different. Mercy might interpose, and give them an opportunity to accept her overtures; but after light has been long rejected and despised, it will be finally withdrawn.

A plague of hail was next threatened upon Pharaoh, with the warning, "Send therefore now, and gather thy cattle, and all that thou hast in the field; for upon every man and beast which shall be found in the field, and shall not be brought home, the hail shall come down upon them, and they shall die." Rain or hail was unusual in Egypt, and such a storm as was foretold had never been witnessed. The report spread rapidly, and all who believed the word of the Lord gathered in their cattle, while those who despised the warning left them in the field. Thus in the midst of judgment the mercy of God was displayed, the people were tested, and it was shown how many had been led to fear God by the manifestation of His power.

The storm came as predicted—thunder and hail, and fire mingled with it, "very grievous, such as there was none like it in all the land of Egypt since it became a nation. And the hail smote throughout all the land of Egypt all that was in the field, both man and beast; and the hail smote every herb of the field, and brake every tree of the field." Ruin and desolation marked the path of the destroying angel. The land of Goshen alone was spared. It was demonstrated to the Egyptians that the earth is under the control of the living God, that the elements obey His voice, and that the only safety is in obedience to Him.

270   All Egypt trembled before the awful outpouring of divine judgment. Pharaoh hastily sent for the two brothers, and cried out, "I have sinned this time: the Lord is righteous, and I and my people are wicked. Entreat the Lord (for it is enough) that there be no more mighty thunderings and hail; and I will let you go, and ye shall stay no longer." The answer was, "As soon as I am gone out of the city, I will spread abroad my hands unto the Lord; and the thunder shall cease, neither shall there be any more hail; that thou mayest know how that the earth is the Lord's. But as for thee and thy servants, I know that ye will not yet fear the Lord God."

Moses knew that the contest was not ended. Pharaoh's confessions and promises were not the effect of any radical change in his mind or heart, but were wrung from him by terror and anguish. Moses promised, however, to grant his request; for he would give him no occasion for further stubbornness. The prophet went forth, unheeding the fury of the tempest, and Pharaoh and all his host were witnesses to the power of Jehovah to preserve His messenger. Having passed without the city, Moses "spread abroad his hands unto the Lord: and the thunders and hail ceased, and the rain was not poured upon the earth." But no sooner had the king recovered from his fears than his heart returned to its perversity.

Then the Lord said unto Moses, "Go in unto Pharaoh: for I have hardened his heart, and the heart of his servants, that I might show these My signs before him; and that thou mayest tell in the ears of thy son, and of thy son's son, what things I have wrought in Egypt, and My signs which I have done among them; that ye may know how that I am Jehovah." The Lord was manifesting His power, to confirm the faith of Israel in Him as the only true and living God. He would give unmistakable evidence of the difference He placed between them and the Egyptians, and would cause all nations to know that the Hebrews, whom they had despised and oppressed, were under the protection of the God of heaven.

Moses warned the monarch that if he still remained obstinate, a plague of locusts would be sent, which would cover the face of the earth and eat up every green thing that remained; they would fill the houses, even the palace itself; such a scourge, he said, as "neither thy fathers, nor thy fathers' fathers have seen, since

the day that they were upon the earth unto this day."

The counselors of Pharaoh stood aghast. The   271 nation had sustained great loss in the death of their cattle. Many of the people had been killed by the hail. The forests were broken down and the crops destroyed. They were fast losing all that had been gained by the labor of the Hebrews. The whole land was threatened with starvation. Princes and courtiers pressed about the king and angrily demanded, "How long shall this man be a snare unto us? let the men go, that they may serve the Lord their God: knowest thou not yet that Egypt is destroyed?"

Moses and Aaron were again summoned, and the monarch said to them, "Go, serve the Lord your God: but who are they that shall go?"

The answer was, "We will go with our young and with our old, with our sons and with our daughters, with our flocks and with our herds will we go; for we must hold a feast unto the Lord."

The king was filled with rage. "Let the Lord be so with you," he cried, "as I will let you go, and your little ones: look to it; for evil is before you. Not so: go now ye that are men, and serve the Lord; for that ye did desire. And they were driven out from Pharaoh's presence." Pharaoh had endeavored to destroy the Israelites by hard labor, but he now pretended to have a deep interest in their welfare and a tender care for their little ones. His real object was to keep the women and children as surety for the return of the men.

Moses now stretched forth his rod over the land, and an east wind blew, and brought locusts. "Very grievous were they; before them there were no such locusts as they, neither after them shall be such." They filled the sky till the land was darkened, and devoured every green thing remaining. Pharaoh sent for the prophets in haste, and said, "I have sinned against the Lord your God, and against you. Now therefore forgive, I pray thee, my sin only this once, and entreat the Lord your God, that He may take away from me this death only." They did so, and a strong west wind carried away the locusts toward the Red Sea. Still the king persisted in his stubborn resolution.

The people of Egypt were ready to despair. The scourges that had already fallen upon them seemed almost beyond endurance, and they were filled with fear for the future. The nation had worshiped Pharaoh as a representative of their god, but many were now convinced that he   272 was opposing himself to One who made all the powers of nature the ministers of His will. The Hebrew slaves, so miraculously favored, were becoming confident of deliverance. Their taskmasters dared not oppress them as heretofore. Throughout Egypt there was a secret fear that the enslaved race would rise and avenge their wrongs. Everywhere men were asking with bated breath, What will come next?

Suddenly a darkness settled upon the land, so thick and black that it seemed a "darkness which may be felt." Not only were the people deprived of light, but the atmosphere was very oppressive, so that breathing was difficult. "They saw not one another, neither rose any from his place for three days: but all the children of Israel had light in their dwellings." The sun and moon were objects of worship to the Egyptians; in this mysterious darkness the people and their gods alike were smitten by the power that had undertaken the cause of the bondmen.* Yet fearful as it was, this judgment is an evidence of God's compassion and His unwillingness to destroy. He would give the people time for reflection and repentance before bringing upon them the last and most terrible of the plagues.

Fear at last wrung from Pharaoh a further concession. At the end of the third day of darkness he summoned Moses, and consented to the departure of the people, provided the flocks and herds were permitted to remain. "There shall not an hoof be left behind," replied the resolute Hebrew. "We know not with what we must serve the Lord, until we come thither." The king's anger burst forth beyond control. "Get thee from me," he cried, "take heed to thyself, see my face no more; for in that day thou seest my face thou shalt die."

The answer was, "Thou hast spoken well, I will see thy face again no more."

"The man Moses was very great in the land of Egypt, in the sight of Pharaoh's servants, and in the sight of the people." Moses was regarded with awe by the Egyptians. The king dared not harm him, for the people looked upon him as alone possessing power to remove the plagues. They desired that the Israelites might be permitted to leave Egypt. It was the king and the priests that opposed to the last the demands of Moses.

273

24

The Passover

When the demand for Israel's release had been first presented to the king of Egypt, the warning of the most terrible of the plagues had been given. Moses was directed to say to Pharaoh, "Thus saith the Lord, Israel is My son, even My first-born: and I say unto thee, Let My son go, that he may serve Me: and if thou refuse to let him go, behold, I will slay thy son, even thy first-born." Exodus 4:22, 23. Though despised by the Egyptians, the Israelites had been honored by God, in that they were singled

out to be the depositaries of His law. In the special blessings and privileges accorded them, they had pre-eminence among the nations, as the first-born son had among brothers.

The judgment of which Egypt had first been warned, was to be the last visited. God is long-suffering and plenteous in mercy. He has a tender care for the beings formed in His image. If the loss of their harvests and their flocks and herds had brought Egypt to repentance, the children would not have been smitten; but the nation had stubbornly resisted the divine command, and now the final blow was about to fall.

Moses had been forbidden, on pain of death, to appear again in Pharaoh's presence; but a last message from God was to be delivered to the rebellious monarch, and again Moses came before him, with the terrible announcement: "Thus saith the Lord, About midnight will I go out into the midst of Egypt: and all the first-born in the land of Egypt shall die, from the first-born of Pharaoh that sitteth upon his throne, even unto the first-born of the maidservant that is behind the mill; and all the first-born of beasts. And there shall be a great cry throughout all the land of Egypt, such as there was none like it, nor shall be like it any more. But against any of the children of Israel shall not a dog move his tongue, against man or beast: that ye may know how that the Lord doth put a differ- 274 ence between the Egyptians and Israel. And all these thy servants shall come down unto me, and bow down themselves unto me, saying, Get thee out, and all the people that follow thee: and after that I will go out."

Before the execution of this sentence the Lord through Moses gave direction to the children of Israel concerning their departure from Egypt, and especially for their preservation from the coming judgment. Each family, alone or in connection with others, was to slay a lamb or a kid "without blemish," and with a bunch of hyssop sprinkle its blood on "the two side posts and on the upper doorpost" of the house, that the destroying angel, coming at midnight, might not enter that dwelling. They were to eat the flesh roasted, with unleavened bread and bitter herbs, at night, as Moses said, "with your loins girded, your shoes on your feet, and your staff in your hand; and ye shall eat it in haste: it is the Lord's Passover."

The Lord declared: "I will pass through the land of Egypt this night, and will smite all the first-born in the land of Egypt, both man and beast; and against all the gods of Egypt I will execute judgment. . . . And the blood shall be to you for a token upon the houses where ye are: and when I see the blood, I will pass over you, and the plague shall not be upon you to destroy you, when I smite the land of Egypt."

In commemoration of this great deliverance a feast was to be observed yearly by the people of

---

* See Appendix, Note 2.   This chapter is based on Exodus 11; 12:1-32.

Israel in all future generations. "This day shall be unto you for a memorial; and ye shall keep it a feast to the Lord throughout your generations: ye shall keep it a feast by an ordinance forever." As they should keep the feast in future years, they were to repeat to their children the story of this great deliverance, as Moses bade them: "Ye shall say, It is the sacrifice of the Lord's Passover, who passed over the houses of the children of Israel in Egypt, when He smote the Egyptians, and delivered our houses."

Furthermore, the first-born of both man and beast were to be the Lord's, to be brought back only by a ransom, in acknowledgment that when the first-born in Egypt perished, that of Israel, though graciously preserved, had been justly exposed to the same doom but for the atoning sacrifice. "All the first-born are Mine," the Lord declared; "for on the day that I smote all the first-born in the land of Egypt, I hallowed unto Me all the first-born in Israel, both man and beast: Mine they shall be." Numbers 3:13. After the institution of the tabernacle service the Lord chose unto Himself the tribe of Levi for the work of the sanctuary, instead of the first-born of the people. "They are wholly given unto Me from among the children of Israel," He said. "Instead of the first-born of all the children of Israel, have I taken them unto Me." Numbers 8:16. All the people were, however, still required, in acknowledgment of God's mercy, to pay a redemption price for the first-born son. Numbers 18:15, 16.

The Passover was to be both commemorative and typical, not only pointing back to the deliverance from Egypt, but forward to the greater deliverance which Christ was to accomplish in freeing His people from the bondage of sin. The sacrificial lamb represents "the Lamb of God," in whom is our only hope of salvation. Says the apostle, "Christ our Passover is sacrificed for us." 1 Corinthians 5:7. It was not enough that the paschal lamb be slain; its blood must be sprinkled upon the doorposts; so the merits of Christ's blood must be applied to the soul. We must believe, not only that He died for the world, but that He died for us individually. We must appropriate to ourselves the virtue of the atoning sacrifice.

The hyssop used in sprinkling the blood was the symbol of purification, being thus employed in the cleansing of the leper and of those defiled by contact with the dead. In the psalmist's prayer also its significance is seen: "Purge me with hyssop, and I shall be clean: wash me, and I shall be whiter than snow." Psalm 51:7.

The lamb was to be prepared whole, not a bone of it being broken; so not a bone was to be broken of the Lamb of God, who was to die for us. John 19:36. Thus was also represented the completeness of Christ's sacrifice.

The flesh was to be eaten. It is not enough even that we believe on Christ for the forgiveness of sin; we must by faith be constantly receiving spiritual strength and nourishment from Him through His word. Said Christ, "Except ye eat the flesh of the Son of man, and drink His blood, ye have no life in you. Whoso eateth My flesh, and drinketh My blood, hath eternal life." John 6:53, 54. And to explain His meaning He said, "The words that I speak unto you, they are spirit, and they are life." Verse 63. Jesus accepted His Father's law, wrought out its principles in His life, manifested its spirit, and showed its beneficent power in the heart. Says John, "The Word was made flesh, and dwelt among us, (and we beheld His glory, the glory as of the only begotten of the Father,) full of grace and truth." John 1:14. The followers of Christ must be partakers of His experience. They must receive and assimilate the word of God so that it shall become the motive power of life and action. By the power of Christ they must be changed into His likeness, and reflect the divine attributes. They must eat the flesh and drink the blood of the Son of God, or there is no life in them. The spirit and work of Christ must become the spirit and work of His disciples.

The lamb was to be eaten with bitter herbs, as pointing back to the bitterness of the bondage in Egypt. So when we feed upon Christ, it should be with contrition of heart, because of our sins. The use of unleavened bread also was significant. It was expressly enjoined in the law of the Passover, and as strictly observed by the Jews in their practice, that no leaven should be found in their houses during the feast. In like manner the leaven of sin must be put away from all who would receive life and nourishment from Christ. So Paul writes to the Corinthian church, "Purge out therefore the old leaven, that ye may be a new lump. . . . For even Christ our Passover is sacrificed for us: therefore let us keep the feast, not with old leaven, neither with the leaven of malice and wickedness; but with the unleavened bread of sincerity and truth." 1 Corinthians 5:7, 8.

Before obtaining freedom, the bondmen must show their faith in the great deliverance about to be accomplished. The token of blood must be placed upon their houses, and they must separate themselves and their families from the Egyptians, and gather within their own dwellings. Had the Israelites disregarded in any particular the directions given them, had they neglected to separate their children from the Egyptians, had they slain the lamb, but failed to strike the doorpost with blood, or had any gone out of their houses, they would not have been secure. They might have honestly believed that they had done all that was necessary, but their sincerity would not have saved them. All who failed to heed the Lord's directions would lose

279 their first-born by the hand of the destroyer.

By obedience the people were to give evidence of their faith. So all who hope to be saved by the merits of the blood of Christ should realize that they themselves have something to do in securing their salvation. While it is Christ only that can redeem us from the penalty of transgression, we are to turn from sin to obedience. Man is to be saved by faith, not by works; yet his faith must be shown by his works. God has given His Son to die as a propitiation for sin, He has manifested the light of truth, the way of life, He has given facilities, ordinances, and privileges; and now man must co-operate with these saving agencies; he must appreciate and use the helps that God has provided—believe and obey all the divine requirements.

As Moses rehearsed to Israel the provisions of God for their deliverance, "the people bowed the head and worshiped." The glad hope of freedom, the awful knowledge of the impending judgment upon their oppressors, the cares and labors incident to their speedy departure—all were for the time swallowed up in gratitude to their gracious Deliverer. Many of the Egyptians had been led to acknowledge the God of the Hebrews as the only true God, and these now begged to be permitted to find shelter in the homes of Israel when the destroying angel should pass through the land. They were gladly welcomed, and they pledged themselves henceforth to serve the God of Jacob and to go forth from Egypt with His people.

The Israelites obeyed the directions that God had given. Swiftly and secretly they made their preparations for departure. Their families were gathered, the paschal lamb slain, the flesh roasted with fire, the unleavened bread and bitter herbs prepared. The father and priest of the household sprinkled the blood upon the doorpost, and joined his family within the dwelling. In haste and silence the paschal lamb was eaten. In awe the people prayed and watched, the heart of the eldest born, from the strong man down to the little child, throbbing with indefinable dread. Fathers and mothers clasped in their arms their loved first-born as they thought of the fearful stroke that was to fall that night. But no dwelling of Israel was visited by the death-dealing angel. The sign of blood—the sign of a Saviour's protection—was on their doors, and the destroyer entered not.

280 At midnight "there was a great cry in Egypt: for there was not a house where there was not one dead." All the first-born in the land, "from the firstborn of Pharaoh that sat on his throne unto the firstborn of the captive that was in the dungeon; and all the firstborn of cattle" had been smitten by the destroyer. Throughout the vast realm of Egypt the pride of every household had been laid low. The shrieks and wails of the mourners filled the air. King and courtiers,

with blanched faces and trembling limbs, stood aghast at the overmastering horror. Pharaoh remembered how he had once exclaimed, "Who is Jehovah, that I should obey His voice to let Israel go? I know not Jehovah, neither will I let Israel go." Now, his heaven-daring pride humbled in the dust, he "called for Moses and Aaron by night, and said, Rise up, and get you forth from among my people, both ye and the children of Israel; and go, serve the Lord, as ye have said. Also take your flocks and your herds, as ye have said. . . . And be gone; and bless me also." The royal counselors also and the people entreated the Israelites to depart "out of the land in haste; for they said, We be all dead men."

281 **25**

The Exodus

With their loins girt, with sandaled feet, and staff in hand, the people of Israel had stood, hushed, awed, yet expectant, awaiting the royal mandate that should bid them go forth. Before the morning broke, they were on their way. During the plagues, as the manifestation of God's power had kindled faith in the hearts of the bondmen and had struck terror to their oppressors, the Israelites had gradually assembled themselves in Goshen; and notwithstanding the suddenness of their flight, some provision had already been made for the necessary organization and control of the moving multitudes, they being divided into companies, under appointed leaders.

And they went out, "about six hundred thousand on foot that were men, beside children. And a mixed multitude went up also with them." In this multitude were not only those who were actuated by faith in the God of Israel, but also a far greater number who desired only to escape from the plagues, or who followed in the wake of the moving multitudes merely from excitement and curiosity. This class were ever a hindrance and a snare to Israel.

The people took also with them "flocks, and herds, even very much cattle." These were the property of the Israelites, who had never sold their possessions to the king, as had the Egyptians. Jacob and his sons had brought their flocks and herds with them to Egypt, where they had greatly increased. Before leaving Egypt, the people, by the direction of Moses, claimed a recompense for their unpaid labor; and the Egyptians were too eager to be freed from their presence to refuse them. The bondmen went forth laden with the spoil of their oppressors.

That day completed the history revealed to Abraham in prophetic vision centuries before: "Thy seed shall be a stranger in a land that is not

This chapter is based on Exodus 12:34-51; 13 to 15.

theirs, and shall serve them; and they shall afflict them four hundred years; and also that **282** nation, whom they shall serve, will I judge: and afterward shall they come out with great substance." Genesis 15:13, 14.* The four hundred years had been fulfilled. "And it came to pass the selfsame day, that the Lord did bring the children of Israel out of the land of Egypt by their armies." In their departure from Egypt the Israelites bore with them a precious legacy, in the bones of Joseph, which had so long awaited the fulfillment of God's promise, and which, during the dark years of bondage, had been a reminder of Israel's deliverance.

Instead of pursuing the direct route to Canaan, which lay through the country of the Philistines, the Lord directed their course southward, toward the shores of the Red Sea. "For God said, Lest peradventure the people repent when they see war, and they return to Egypt." Had they attempted to pass through Philistia, their progress would have been opposed; for the Philistines, regarding them as slaves escaping from their masters, would not have hesitated to make war upon them. The Israelites were poorly prepared for an encounter with that powerful and warlike people. They had little knowledge of God and little faith in Him, and they would have become terrified and disheartened. They were unarmed and unaccustomed to war, their spirits were depressed by long bondage, and they were encumbered with women and children, flocks and herds. In leading them by the way of the Red Sea, the Lord revealed Himself as a God of compassion as well as of judgment.

"And they took their journey from Succoth, and encamped in Etham, in the edge of the wilderness. And the Lord went before them by day in a pillar of cloud, to lead them the way; and by night in a pillar of fire, to give them light; to go by day and night. He took not away the pillar of the cloud by day, nor the pillar of fire by night, from before the people." Says the psalmist, "He spread a cloud for a covering; and fire to give light in the night." Psalm 105:39. See also 1 Corinthians 10:1, 2. The standard of their invisible Leader was ever with them. By day the cloud directed their journeyings or spread as a canopy above the host. It served as a protection from the burning heat, and by its coolness and moisture afforded grateful refreshment in the parched, thirsty desert. By night it became a pillar of fire, illuminating their encampment and constantly assuring them of the divine presence.

283 In one of the most beautiful and comforting passages of Isaiah's prophecy, reference is made to the pillar of cloud and of fire to represent God's care for His people in the great final struggle with the powers of evil: "The Lord will create upon every dwelling place of Mount Zion, and upon her assemblies, a cloud and smoke by day, and the shining of a flaming fire by night: for above all the glory shall be a covering. And there shall be a tabernacle for a shadow in the daytime from the heat, and for a place of refuge, and for a covert from storm and from rain." Isaiah 4:5, 6, margin.

Across a dreary, desertlike expanse they journeyed. Already they began to wonder whither their course would lead; they were becoming weary with the toilsome way, and in some hearts began to arise a fear of pursuit by the Egyptians. But the cloud went forward, and they followed. And now the Lord directed Moses to turn aside into a rocky defile, and encamp beside the sea. It was revealed to him that Pharaoh would pursue them, but that God would be honored in their deliverance.

In Egypt the report was spread that the children of Israel, instead of tarrying to worship in the desert, were pressing on toward the Red Sea. Pharaoh's counselors declared to the king that their bondmen had fled, never to return. The people deplored their folly in attributing the death of the first-born to the power of God. Their great men, recovering from their fears, accounted for the plagues as the result of natural causes. "Why have we done this, that we have let Israel go from serving us?" was the bitter cry.

Pharaoh collected his forces, "six hundred chosen chariots, and all the chariots of Egypt," horsemen, captains, and foot soldiers. The king himself, attended by the great men of his realm, headed the attacking army. To secure the favor of the gods, and thus ensure the success of their undertaking, the priests also accompanied them. The king was resolved to intimidate the Israelites by a grand display of his power. The Egyptians feared lest their forced submission to the God of Israel should subject them to the derision of other nations; but if they should now go forth with a great show of power and bring back the fugitives, they would redeem their glory, as well as recover the services of their bondmen.

The Hebrews were encamped beside the sea, whose waters presented a seemingly impassable **284** barrier before them, while on the south a rugged mountain obstructed their further progress. Suddenly they beheld in the distance the flashing armor and moving chariots betokening the advance guard of a great army. As the force drew nearer, the hosts of Egypt were seen in full pursuit. Terror filled the hearts of Israel. Some cried unto the Lord, but far the greater part hastened to Moses with their complaints: "Because there were no graves in Egypt, hast thou taken us away to die in the wilderness? wherefore hast thou dealt thus with us, to carry us forth out of Egypt? Is not this the word that we did tell thee in Egypt, saying, Let us alone, that we may serve the Egyptians? For it had been better for

---

* See Appendix, Note 3.

us to serve the Egyptians, than that we should die in the wilderness."

Moses was greatly troubled that his people should manifest so little faith in God, notwithstanding they had repeatedly witnessed the manifestation of His power in their behalf. How could they charge upon him the dangers and difficulties of their situation, when he had followed the express command of God? True, there was no possibility of deliverance unless God Himself should interpose for their release; but having been brought into this position in obedience to the divine direction, Moses felt no fear of the consequences. His calm and assuring reply to the people was, "Fear ye not, stand still, and see the salvation of the Lord, which He will show to you today: for the Egyptians whom ye have seen today, ye shall see them again no more forever. The Lord shall fight for you, and ye shall hold your peace."

It was not an easy thing to hold the hosts of Israel in waiting before the Lord. Lacking discipline and self-control, they became violent and unreasonable. They expected speedily to fall into the hands of their oppressors, and their wailings and lamentations were loud and deep. The wonderful pillar of cloud had been followed as the signal of God to go forward; but now they questioned among themselves if it might not foreshadow some great calamity; for had it not led them on the wrong side of the mountain, into an impassable way? Thus the angel of God appeared to their deluded minds as the harbinger of disaster.

But now, as the Egyptian host approached them, expecting to make them an easy prey, the cloudy column rose majestically into the heavens, passed over the Israelites, and descended between them and the armies of Egypt. A wall of darkness interposed between the pursued and their pursuers. The Egyptians could no longer discern the camp of the Hebrews, and were forced to halt. But as the darkness of night deepened, the wall of cloud became a great light to the Hebrews, flooding the entire encampment with the radiance of day.

Then hope returned to the hearts of Israel. And Moses lifted up his voice unto the Lord. "And the Lord said unto Moses, Wherefore criest thou unto Me? speak unto the children of Israel, that they go forward. But lift thou up thy rod, and stretch out thine hand over the sea, and divide it: and the children of Israel shall go on dry ground through the midst of the sea."

The psalmist, describing the passage of the sea by Israel, sang, "Thy way was in the sea, and Thy paths in the great waters, and Thy footsteps were not known. Thou leddest Thy people like a flock, by the hand of Moses and Aaron." Psalm 77:19, 20, R.V. As Moses stretched out his rod the waters parted, and Israel went into the midst of the sea, upon dry ground, while the

waters stood like a wall upon each side. The light from God's pillar of fire shone upon the foam-capped billows, and lighted the road that was cut like a mighty furrow through the waters of the sea, and was lost in the obscurity of the farther shore.

"The Egyptians pursued, and went in after them to the midst of the sea, even all Pharaoh's horses, his chariots, and his horsemen. And it came to pass, that in the morning watch the Lord looked unto the host of the Egyptians through the pillar of fire and of the cloud, and troubled the host of the Egyptians." The mysterious cloud changed to a pillar of fire before their astonished eyes. The thunders pealed and the lightnings flashed. "The clouds poured out water; the skies sent out a sound: Thine arrows also went abroad. The voice of Thy thunder was in the whirlwind; the lightning lightened the world: the earth trembled and shook." Psalm 77:17, 18, R.V.

The Egyptians were seized with confusion and dismay. Amid the wrath of the elements, in which they heard the voice of an angry God, they endeavored to retrace their steps and flee to the shore they had quitted. But Moses stretched out his rod, and the piled-up waters, hissing, roaring, and eager for their prey, rushed together and swallowed the Egyptian army in their black depths.

As morning broke it revealed to the multitudes of Israel all that remained of their mighty foes—the mail-clad bodies cast upon the shore. From the most terrible peril, one night had brought complete deliverance. That vast, helpless throng—bondmen unused to battle, women, children, and cattle, with the sea before them, and the mighty armies of Egypt pressing behind—had seen their path opened through the waters and their enemies overwhelmed in the moment of expected triumph. Jehovah alone had brought them deliverance, and to Him their hearts were turned in gratitude and faith. Their emotion found utterance in songs of praise. The Spirit of God rested upon Moses, and he led the people in a triumphant anthem of thanksgiving, the earliest and one of the most sublime that are known to man.

"I will sing unto Jehovah, for He hath triumphed gloriously;
The horse and his rider hath He thrown into the sea.
The Lord is my strength and my song,
And He is become my salvation:
This is my God, and I will praise Him;
My father's God, and I will exalt Him.
The Lord is a man of war:
Jehovah is His name.
Pharaoh's chariots and his host hath He cast into the sea:
And his chosen captains are sunk in the Red

Sea.
The deeps cover them:
They went down into the depths like a stone.
Thy right hand, O Lord, is glorious in power,
Thy right hand, O Lord, dasheth in pieces the
   enemy. . . .
Who is like unto Thee, O Lord, among the
   gods?
Who is like Thee, glorious in holiness,
Fearful in praises, doing wonders? . . .
Thou in Thy mercy hast led the people which
   Thou hast redeemed:
Thou hast guided them in Thy strength to
   Thy holy habitation.
The peoples have heard, they tremble . . . .
Terror and dread falleth upon them;
By the greatness of Thine arm they are as
   still as a stone;
Till Thy people pass over, O Lord,
Till the people pass over which Thou hast
   purchased.
Thou shalt bring them in, and plant them in
   the mountain of Thine inheritance,
The place, O Lord, which Thou hast made
   for Thee to dwell in."
                                    Exodus 15:1-17, R.V.

Like the voice of the great deep, rose from
the vast hosts of Israel that sublime ascription. It
was taken up by the women of Israel, Miriam,
the sister of Moses, leading the way, as they
went forth with timbrel and dance. Far over
desert and sea rang the joyous refrain, and the
mountains re-echoed the words of their praise—
"Sing ye to Jehovah, for He hath triumphed gloriously."

This song and the great deliverance which it
commemorates, made an impression never to be
effaced from the memory of the Hebrew people.
From age to age it was echoed by the prophets
and singers of Israel, testifying that Jehovah is
the strength and deliverance of those who trust
in Him. That song does not belong to the Jewish
people alone. It points forward to the destruction of all the foes of righteousness and the final
victory of the Israel of God. The prophet of Patmos beholds the white-robed multitude that
have "gotten the victory," standing on the "sea
of glass mingled with fire," having "the harps of
God. And they sing the song of Moses the servant of God, and the song of the Lamb." Revelation 15:2, 3.

"Not unto us, O Lord, not unto us, but unto
Thy name give glory, for Thy mercy, and for
Thy truth's sake." Psalm 115:1. Such was the
spirit that pervaded Israel's song of deliverance,
and it is the spirit that should dwell in the hearts
of all who love and fear God. In freeing our
souls from the bondage of sin, God has wrought
for us a deliverance greater than that of the
Hebrews at the Red Sea. Like the Hebrew host,
we should praise the Lord with heart and soul

and voice for His "wonderful works to the children of men." Those who dwell upon God's
great mercies, and are not unmindful of His
lesser gifts, will put on the girdle of gladness
and make melody in their hearts to the Lord.
The daily blessings that we receive from the
hand of God, and above all else the death of
Jesus to bring happiness and heaven within our
reach, should be a theme for constant gratitude.
What compassion, what matchless love, has
God shown to us, lost sinners, in connecting us
with Himself, to be to Him a peculiar treasure!
What a sacrifice has been made by our
Redeemer, that we may be called children of
God! We should praise God for the blessed
hope held out before us in the great plan of
redemption, we should praise Him for the heavenly inheritance and for His rich promises;
praise Him that Jesus lives to intercede for us.

"Whoso offereth praise," says the Creator,
"glorifieth Me." Psalm 50:23. All the inhabitants of heaven unite in praising God. Let us
learn the song of the angels now, that we may
sing it when we join their shining ranks. Let us
say with the psalmist, "While I live will I praise
the Lord: I will sing praises unto my God while
I have any being." "Let the people praise Thee,
O God; let all the people praise Thee." Psalms
146:2; 67:5.

God in His providence brought the Hebrews
into the mountain fastnesses before the sea, that
He might manifest His power in their deliverance and signally humble the pride of their
oppressors. He might have saved them in any
other way, but He chose this method in order to
test their faith and strengthen their trust in Him.
The people were weary and terrified, yet if they
had held back when Moses bade them advance,
God would never have opened the path for
them. It was "by faith" that "they passed
through the Red Sea as by dry land." Hebrews
11:29. In marching down to the very water, they
showed that they believed the word of God as
spoken by Moses. They did all that was in their
power to do, and then the Mighty One of Israel
divided the sea to make a path for their feet.

The great lesson here taught is for all time.
Often the Christian life is beset by dangers, and
duty seems hard to perform. The imagination
pictures impending ruin before and bondage or
death behind. Yet the voice of God speaks
clearly, "Go forward." We should obey this
command, even though our eyes cannot penetrate the darkness, and we feel the cold waves
about our feet. The obstacles that hinder our
progress will never disappear before a halting,
doubting spirit. Those who defer obedience till
every shadow of uncertainty disappears and
there remains no risk of failure or defeat, will
never obey at all. Unbelief whispers, "Let us
wait till the obstructions are removed, and we
can see our way clearly;" but faith courageously

urges an advance, hoping all things, believing all things.

The cloud that was a wall of darkness to the Egyptians was to the Hebrews a great flood of light, illuminating the whole camp, and shedding brightness upon the path before them. So the dealings of Providence bring to the unbelieving, darkness and despair, while to the trusting soul they are full of light and peace. The path where God leads the way may lie through the desert or the sea, but it is a safe path.

26

From the Red Sea to Sinai

From the Red Sea the hosts of Israel again set forth on their journey, under the guidance of the pillar of cloud. The scene around them was most dreary—bare, desolate-looking mountains, barren plains, and the sea stretching far away, its shores strewn with the bodies of their enemies; yet they were full of joy in the consciousness of freedom, and every thought of discontent was hushed.

But for three days, as they journeyed, they could find no water. The supply which they had taken with them was exhausted. There was nothing to quench their burning thirst as they dragged wearily over the sun-burnt plains. Moses, who was familiar with this region, knew what the others did not, that at Marah, the nearest station where springs were to be found, the water was unfit for use. With intense anxiety he watched the guiding cloud. With a sinking heart he heard the glad shout, "Water! water!" echoed along the line. Men, women, and children in joyous haste crowded to the fountain, when, lo, a cry of anguish burst forth from the host—the water was bitter.

In their horror and despair they reproached Moses for having led them in such a way, not remembering that the divine presence in that mysterious cloud had been leading him as well as them. In his grief at their distress Moses did what they had forgotten to do; he cried earnestly to God for help. "And the Lord showed him a tree, which when he had cast into the waters, the waters were made sweet." Here the promise was given to Israel through Moses, "If thou wilt diligently hearken to the voice of the Lord thy God, and wilt do that which is right in His sight, and wilt give ear to His commandments, and keep all His statutes, I will put none of these diseases upon thee, which I have brought upon the Egyptians: for I am the Lord that healeth thee."

From Marah the people journeyed to Elim, where they found "twelve wells of water, and threescore and ten palm trees." Here they remained several days before entering the wilderness of Sin. When they had been a month absent from Egypt, they made their first encampment in the wilderness. Their store of provisions had now begun to fail. There was scanty herbage in the wilderness, and their flocks were diminishing. How was food to be supplied for these vast multitudes? Doubts filled their hearts, and again they murmured. Even the rulers and elders of the people joined in complaining against the leaders of God's appointment: "Would to God we had died by the hand of the Lord in the land of Egypt, when we sat by the fleshpots, and when we did eat bread to the full; for ye have brought us forth into this wilderness, to kill this whole assembly with hunger."

They had not as yet suffered from hunger; their present wants were supplied, but they feared for the future. They could not understand how these vast multitudes were to subsist in their travels through the wilderness, and in imagination they saw their children famishing. The Lord permitted difficulties to surround them, and their supply of food to be cut short, that their hearts might turn to Him who had hitherto been their Deliverer. If in their want they would call upon Him, He would still grant them manifest tokens of His love and care. He had promised that if they would obey His commandments, no disease should come upon them, and it was sinful unbelief on their part to anticipate that they or their children might die of hunger.

God had promised to be their God, to take them to Himself as a people, and to lead them to a large and good land; but they were ready to faint at every obstacle encountered in the way to that land. In a marvelous manner He had brought them out from their bondage in Egypt, that He might elevate and ennoble them and make them a praise in the earth. But it was necessary for them to encounter difficulties and to endure privations. God was bringing them from a state of degradation and fitting them to occupy an honorable place among the nations and to receive important and sacred trusts. Had they possessed faith in Him, in view of all that He had wrought for them, they would cheerfully have borne inconvenience, privation, and even real suffering; but they were unwilling to trust the Lord any further than they could witness the continual evidences of His power. They forgot their bitter service in Egypt. They forgot the goodness and power of God displayed in their behalf in their deliverance from bondage. They forgot how their children had been spared when the destroying angel slew all the first-born of Egypt. They forgot the grand exhibition of divine power at the Red Sea. They forgot that while they had crossed safely in the path that had been opened for them, the armies of their enemies, attempting to follow them, had been

This chapter is based on Exodus 15:22-27; 16 to 18.

overwhelmed by the waters of the sea. They saw and felt only their present inconveniences and trials; and instead of saying, "God has done great things for us; whereas we were slaves, He is making of us a great nation," they talked of the hardness of the way, and wondered when their weary pilgrimage would end.

The history of the wilderness life of Israel was chronicled for the benefit of the Israel of God to the close of time. The record of God's dealings with the wanderers of the desert in all their marchings to and fro, in their exposure to hunger, thirst, and weariness, and in the striking manifestations of His power for their relief, is fraught with warning and instruction for His people in all ages. The varied experience of the Hebrews was a school of preparation for their promised home in Canaan. God would have His people in these days review with a humble heart and teachable spirit the trials through which ancient Israel passed, that they may be instructed in their preparation for the heavenly Canaan.

Many look back to the Israelites, and marvel at their unbelief and murmuring, feeling that they themselves would not have been so ungrateful; but when their faith is tested, even by little trials, they manifest no more faith or patience than did ancient Israel. When brought into strait places, they murmur at the process by which God has chosen to purify them. Though their present needs are supplied, many are unwilling to trust God for the future, and they are in constant anxiety lest poverty shall come upon them, and their children shall be left to suffer. Some are always anticipating evil or magnifying the difficulties that really exist, so that their eyes are blinded to the many blessings which demand their gratitude. The obstacles they encounter, instead of leading them to seek help from God, the only Source of strength, separate them from Him, because they awaken unrest and repining.

294

Do we well to be thus unbelieving? Why should we be ungrateful and distrustful? Jesus is our friend; all heaven is interested in our welfare; and our anxiety and fear grieve the Holy Spirit of God. We should not indulge in a solicitude that only frets and wears us, but does not help us to bear trials. No place should be given to that distrust of God which leads us to make a preparation against future want the chief pursuit of life, as though our happiness consisted in these earthly things. It is not the will of God that His people should be weighed down with care. But our Lord does not tell us that there are no dangers in our path. He does not propose to take His people out of the world of sin and evil, but He points us to a never-failing refuge. He invites the weary and care-laden, "Come unto Me, all ye that labor and are heavy-laden, and I will give you rest." Lay off the yoke of anxiety and worldly care that you have placed on your own neck, and "take My yoke upon you, and learn of Me; for I am meek and lowly in heart; and ye shall find rest unto your souls." Matthew 11:28, 29. We may find rest and peace in God, casting all our care upon Him; for He careth for us. See 1 Peter 5:7.

Says the apostle Paul, "Take heed, brethren, lest there be in any of you an evil heart of unbelief, in departing from the living God." Hebrews 3:12. In view of all that God has wrought for us, our faith should be strong, active, and enduring. Instead of murmuring and complaining, the language of our hearts should be, "Bless the Lord, O my soul: and all that is within me, bless His holy name. Bless the Lord, O my soul, and forget not all His benefits." Psalm 103:1, 2.

God was not unmindful of the wants of Israel. He said to their leader, "I will rain bread from heaven for you." And directions were given that the people gather a daily supply, with a double amount on the sixth day, that the sacred observance of the Sabbath might be maintained.

Moses assured the congregation that their wants were to be supplied: "The Lord shall give you in the evening flesh to eat, and in the morning bread to the full." And he added, "What are we? your murmurings are not against us, but against the Lord." He further bade Aaron say to them, "Come near before the Lord: for He hath heard your murmurings." While Aaron was speaking, "they looked toward the wilderness, and, behold, the glory of the Lord appeared in the cloud." A splendor such as they had never witnessed symbolized the divine Presence. Through manifestations addressed to their senses, they were to obtain a knowledge of God. They must be taught that the Most High, and not merely the man Moses, was their leader, that they might fear His name and obey His voice.

295

At nightfall the camp was surrounded by vast flocks of quails, enough to supply the entire company. In the morning there lay upon the surface of the ground "a small round thing, as small as the hoarfrost." "It was like coriander seed, white." The people called it "manna." Moses said, "This is the bread which the Lord hath given you to eat." The people gathered the manna, and found that there was an abundant supply for all. They "ground it in mills, or beat it in a mortar, and baked it in pans, and made cakes of it." Numbers 11:8. "And the taste of it was like wafers made with honey." They were directed to gather daily an omer for every person; and they were not to leave of it until the morning. Some attempted to keep a supply until the next day, but it was then found to be unfit for food. The provision for the day must be gathered in the morning; for all that remained upon the ground was melted by the sun.

In the gathering of the manna it was found that some obtained more and some less than the stipulated amount; but "when they did mete it

114

with an omer, he that gathered much had nothing over, and he that gathered little had no lack." An explanation of this scripture, as well as a practical lesson from it, is given by the apostle Paul in his second epistle to the Corinthians. He says, "I mean not that other men be eased, and ye burdened: but by an equality, that now at this time your abundance may be a supply for their want, that their abundance also may be a supply for your want: that there may be equality: as it is written, He that had gathered much had nothing over; and he that had gathered little had no lack." 2 Corinthians 8:13-15.

On the sixth day the people gathered two omers for every person. The rulers hastened to acquaint Moses with what had been done. His answer was, "This is that which the Lord hath 296 said, Tomorrow is the rest of the holy Sabbath unto the Lord: bake that which ye will bake today, and seethe that ye will seethe; and that which remaineth over lay up for you to be kept until the morning." They did so, and found that it remained unchanged. "And Moses said, Eat that today; for today is a Sabbath unto the Lord: today ye shall not find it in the field. Six days ye shall gather it; but on the seventh day, which is the Sabbath, in it there shall be none."

God requires that His holy day be as sacredly observed now as in the time of Israel. The command given to the Hebrews should be regarded by all Christians as an injunction from Jehovah to them. The day before the Sabbath should be made a day of preparation, that everything may be in readiness for its sacred hours. In no case should our own business be allowed to encroach upon holy time. God has directed that the sick and suffering be cared for; the labor required to make them comfortable is a work of mercy, and no violation of the Sabbath; but all unnecessary work should be avoided. Many carelessly put off till the beginning of the Sabbath little things that might have been done on the day of preparation. This should not be. Work that is neglected until the beginning of the Sabbath should remain undone until it is past. This course might help the memory of these thoughtless ones, and make them careful to do their own work on the six working days.

Every week during their long sojourn in the wilderness the Israelites witnessed a threefold miracle, designed to impress their minds with the sacredness of the Sabbath: a double quantity of manna fell on the sixth day, none on the seventh, and the portion needed for the Sabbath was preserved sweet and pure, when if any were kept over at any other time it became unfit for use.

In the circumstances connected with the giving of the manna, we have conclusive evidence that the Sabbath was not instituted, as many claim, when the law was given at Sinai. Before the Israelites came to Sinai they understood the Sabbath to be obligatory upon them. In being obliged to gather every Friday a double portion of manna in preparation for the Sabbath, when none would fall, the sacred nature of the day of rest was continually impressed upon them. And when some of the people went out on the Sab- 297 bath to gather manna, the Lord asked, "How long *refuse ye* to keep My commandments and My laws?"

"The children of Israel did eat manna forty years, until they came to a land inhabited: they did eat manna, until they came unto the borders of the land of Canaan." For forty years they were daily reminded by this miraculous provision, of God's unfailing care and tender love. In the words of the psalmist, God gave them "of the corn of heaven. Man did eat angels' food" (Psalm 78:24, 25)—that is, food provided for them by the angels. Sustained by "the corn of heaven," they were daily taught that, having God's promise, they were as secure from want as if surrounded by fields of waving grain on the fertile plains of Canaan.

The manna, falling from heaven for the sustenance of Israel, was a type of Him who came from God to give life to the world. Said Jesus, "I am that Bread of life. Your fathers did eat manna in the wilderness, and are dead. This is the bread which cometh down from heaven. . . . If any man eat of this bread, he shall live forever: and the bread that I will give is My flesh, which I will give for the life of the world." John 6:48-51. And among the promises of blessing to God's people in the future life it is written, "To him that overcometh will I give to eat of the hidden manna." Revelation 2:17.

After leaving the wilderness of Sin, the Israelites encamped in Rephidim. Here there was no water, and again they distrusted the providence of God. In their blindness and presumption the people came to Moses with the demand, "Give us water that we may drink." But his patience failed not. "Why chide ye with me?" he said; "wherefore do ye tempt the Lord?" They cried in anger, "Wherefore is this, that thou hast brought us up out of Egypt, to kill us and our children and our cattle with thirst?" When they had been so abundantly supplied with food, they remembered with shame their unbelief and murmurings, and promised to trust the Lord in the future; but they soon forgot their promise, and failed at the first trial of their faith. The pillar of cloud that was leading them seemed to veil a fearful mystery. And Moses—who was he? they questioned, and what could be his object in bringing them from Egypt? Suspicion and distrust filled their hearts, and they boldly accused him of designing to kill them and their children by privations and hardships 298 that he might enrich himself with their possessions. In the tumult of rage and indignation they were about to stone him.

In distress Moses cried to the Lord, "What shall I do unto this people?" He was directed to take the elders of Israel and the rod wherewith he had wrought wonders in Egypt, and to go on before the people. And the Lord said unto him, "Behold, I will stand before thee there upon the rock in Horeb; and thou shalt smite the rock, and there shall come water out of it, that the people may drink." He obeyed, and the waters burst forth in a living stream that abundantly supplied the encampment. Instead of commanding Moses to lift up his rod and call down some terrible plague, like those on Egypt, upon the leaders in this wicked murmuring, the Lord in His great mercy made the rod His instrument to work their deliverance.

"He clave the rocks in the wilderness, and gave them drink as out of the great depths. He brought streams also out of the rock, and caused waters to run down like rivers." Psalm 78:15, 16. Moses smote the rock, but it was the Son of God who, veiled in the cloudy pillar, stood beside Moses, and caused the lifegiving water to flow. Not only Moses and the elders, but all the congregation who stood at a distance, beheld the glory of the Lord; but had the cloud been removed, they would have been slain by the terrible brightness of Him who abode therein.

In their thirst the people had tempted God, saying, "Is the Lord among us, or not?"—"If God has brought us here, why does He not give us water as well as bread?" The unbelief thus manifested was criminal, and Moses feared that the judgments of God would rest upon them. And he called the name of the place Massah, "temptation," and Meribah, "chiding," as a memorial of their sin.

A new danger now threatened them. Because of their murmuring against Him, the Lord suffered them to be attacked by their enemies. The Amalekites, a fierce, warlike tribe inhabiting that region, came out against them and smote those who, faint and weary, had fallen into the rear. Moses, knowing that the masses of the people were unprepared for battle, directed Joshua to choose from the different tribes a body of soldiers, and lead them on the morrow 299 against the enemy, while he himself would stand on an eminence near by with the rod of God in his hand. Accordingly the next day Joshua and his company attacked the foe, while Moses and Aaron and Hur were stationed on a hill overlooking the battlefield. With arms outstretched toward heaven, and holding the rod of God in his right hand, Moses prayed for the success of the armies of Israel. As the battle progressed, it was observed that so long as his hands were reaching upward, Israel prevailed, but when they were lowered, the enemy was victorious. As Moses became weary, Aaron and Hur stayed up his hands until the going down of the sun, when the enemy was put to flight.

As Aaron and Hur supported the hands of Moses, they showed the people their duty to sustain him in his arduous work while he should receive the word from God to speak to them. And the act of Moses also was significant, showing that God held their destiny in His hands; while they made Him their trust, He would fight for them and subdue their enemies; but when they should let go their hold upon Him, and trust in their own power, they would be even weaker than those who had not the knowledge of God, and their foes would prevail against them.

As the Hebrews triumphed when Moses was reaching his hands toward heaven and interceding in their behalf, so the Israel of God prevail when they by faith take hold upon the strength of their mighty Helper. Yet divine strength is to be combined with human effort. Moses did not believe that God would overcome their foes while Israel remained inactive. While the great leader was pleading with the Lord, Joshua and his brave followers were putting forth their utmost efforts to repulse the enemies of Israel and of God.

After the defeat of the Amalekites, God directed Moses, "Write this for a memorial in a book, and rehearse it in the ears of Joshua: for I will utterly put out the remembrance of Amalek from under heaven." Just before his death the great leader delivered to his people the solemn charge: "Remember what Amalek did unto thee by the way, when ye were come forth out of Egypt; how he met thee by the way, and smote the hindmost of thee, even all that were feeble behind thee, when thou wast faint and weary; and he feared not God. . . . Thou shalt blot out the remembrance of Amalek from under heav- 300 en; thou shalt not forget it." Deuteronomy 25:17-19. Concerning this wicked people the Lord declared, "The hand of Amalek is against the throne of Jehovah." Exodus 17:16, margin.

The Amalekites were not ignorant of God's character or of His sovereignty, but instead of fearing before Him, they had set themselves to defy His power. The wonders wrought by Moses before the Egyptians were made a subject of mockery by the people of Amalek, and the fears of surrounding nations were ridiculed. They had taken oath by their gods that they would destroy the Hebrews, so that not one should escape, and they boasted that Israel's God would be powerless to resist them. They had not been injured or threatened by the Israelites. Their assault was wholly unprovoked. It was to manifest their hatred and defiance of God that they sought to destroy His people. The Amalekites had long been high-handed sinners, and their crimes had cried to God for vengeance, yet His mercy had still called them to repentance; but when the men of Amalek fell upon the wearied and defenseless ranks of

116

Israel, they sealed their nation's doom. The care of God is over the weakest of His children. No act of cruelty or oppression toward them is unmarked by Heaven. Over all who love and fear Him, His hand extends as a shield; let men beware that they smite not that hand; for it wields the sword of justice.

Not far distant from where the Israelites were now encamped was the home of Jethro, the father-in-law of Moses. Jethro had heard of the deliverance of the Hebrews, and he now set out to visit them, and restore to Moses his wife and two sons. The great leader was informed by messengers of their approach, and he went out with joy to meet them, and, the first greetings over, conducted them to his tent. He had sent back his family when on his way to the perils of leading Israel from Egypt, but now he could again enjoy the relief and comfort of their society. To Jethro he recounted the wonderful dealings of God with Israel, and the patriarch rejoiced and blessed the Lord, and with Moses and the elders he united in offering sacrifice and holding a solemn feast in commemoration of God's mercy.

As Jethro remained in the camp, he soon saw how heavy were the burdens that rested upon Moses. To maintain order and discipline among that vast, ignorant, and untrained multitude was indeed a stupendous task. Moses was their rec
301 ognized leader and magistrate, and not only the general interests and duties of the people, but the controversies that arose among them, were referred to him. He had permitted this, for it gave him an opportunity to instruct them; as he said, "I do make them know the statutes of God, and His laws." But Jethro remonstrated against this, saying, "This thing is too heavy for thee; thou art not able to perform it thyself alone." "Thou wilt surely wear away," and he counseled Moses to appoint proper persons as rulers of thousands, and others as rulers of hundreds, and others of tens. They should be "able men, such as fear God, men of truth, hating covetousness." These were to judge in all matters of minor consequence, while the most difficult and important cases should still be brought before Moses, who was to be to the people, said Jethro, "to God-ward, that thou mayest bring the causes unto God: and thou shalt teach them ordinances and laws, and shalt show them the way wherein they must walk, and the work that they must do." This counsel was accepted, and it not only brought relief to Moses, but resulted in establishing more perfect order among the people.

The Lord had greatly honored Moses, and had wrought wonders by his hand; but the fact that he had been chosen to instruct others did not lead him to conclude that he himself needed no instruction. The chosen leader of Israel listened gladly to the suggestions of the godly priest of Midian, and adopted his plan as a wise

arrangement.

From Rephidim the people continued their journey, following the movement of the cloudy pillar. Their route had led across barren plains, over steep ascents, and through rocky defiles. Often as they had traversed the sandy wastes, they had seen before them rugged mountains, like huge bulwarks, piled up directly across their course, and seeming to forbid all further progress. But as they approached, openings here and there appeared in the mountain wall, and beyond, another plain opened to view. Through one of the deep, gravelly passes they were now led. It was a grand and impressive scene. Between the rocky cliffs rising hundreds of feet on either side, flowed in a living tide, far as the eye could reach, the hosts of Israel with their flocks and herds. And now before them in solemn majesty Mount Sinai lifted its massive front. The cloudy pillar rested upon its summit, and the people spread their tents upon the plain beneath. Here was to be their home for nearly a year. At night the pillar of fire assured them of 302 the divine protection, and while they were locked in slumber, the bread of heaven fell gently upon the encampment.

The dawn gilded the dark ridges of the mountains, and the sun's golden rays pierced the deep gorges, seeming to these weary travelers like beams of mercy from the throne of God. On every hand vast, rugged heights seemed in their solitary grandeur to speak of eternal endurance and majesty. Here the mind was impressed with solemnity and awe. Man was made to feel his ignorance and weakness in the presence of Him who "weighed the mountains in scales, and the hills in a balance." Isaiah 40:12. Here Israel was to receive the most wonderful revelation ever made by God to men. Here the Lord had gathered His people that He might impress upon them the sacredness of His requirements by declaring with His own voice His holy law. Great and radical changes were to be wrought in them; for the degrading influences of servitude and a long-continued association with idolatry had left their mark upon habits and character. God was working to lift them to a higher moral level by giving them a knowledge of Himself.

27

The Law Given to Israel

Soon after the encampment at Sinai, Moses was called up into the mountain to meet with God. Alone he climbed the steep and rugged path, and drew near to the cloud that marked the place of Jehovah's presence. Israel was now to be taken into a close and peculiar relation to the Most High—to be incorporated as a church and

303

This chapter is based on Exodus 19 to 24.

a nation under the government of God. The message to Moses for the people was:

"Ye have seen what I did unto the Egyptians, and how I bare you on eagles' wings, and brought you unto Myself. Now therefore, if ye will obey My voice indeed, and keep My covenant, then ye shall be a peculiar treasure unto Me above all people: for all the earth is Mine: and ye shall be unto Me a kingdom of priests, and an holy nation."

Moses returned to the camp, and having summoned the elders of Israel, he repeated to them the divine message. Their answer was, "All that the Lord hath spoken we will do." Thus they entered into a solemn covenant with God, pledging themselves to accept Him as their ruler, by which they became, in a special sense, the subjects of His authority.

Again their leader ascended the mountain, and the Lord said unto him, "Lo, I come unto thee in a thick cloud, that the people may hear when I speak with thee, and believe thee forever." When they met with difficulties in the way, they were disposed to murmur against Moses and Aaron, and accuse them of leading the hosts of Israel from Egypt to destroy them. The Lord would honor Moses before them, that they might be led to confide in his instructions.

God purposed to make the occasion of speaking His law a scene of awful grandeur, in keeping with its exalted character. The people were to be impressed that everything connected with the service of God must be regarded with the 304 greatest reverence. The Lord said to Moses, "Go unto the people, and sanctify them today and tomorrow, and let them wash their clothes, and be ready against the third day: for the third day the Lord will come down in the sight of all the people upon Mount Sinai." During these intervening days all were to occupy the time in solemn preparation to appear before God. Their person and their clothing must be freed from impurity. And as Moses should point out their sins, they were to devote themselves to humiliation, fasting, and prayer, that their hearts might be cleansed from iniquity.

The preparations were made, according to the command; and in obedience to a further injunction, Moses directed that a barrier be placed about the mount, that neither man nor beast might intrude upon the sacred precinct. If any ventured so much as to touch it, the penalty was instant death.

On the morning of the third day, as the eyes of all the people were turned toward the mount, its summit was covered with a thick cloud, which grew more black and dense, sweeping downward until the entire mountain was wrapped in darkness and awful mystery. Then a sound as of a trumpet was heard, summoning the people to meet with God; and Moses led them forth to the base of the mountain. From the thick darkness flashed vivid lightnings, while peals of thunder echoed and re-echoed among the surrounding heights. "And Mount Sinai was altogether on a smoke, because the Lord descended upon it in fire: and the smoke thereof ascended as the smoke of a furnace, and the whole mount quaked greatly." "The glory of the Lord was like devouring fire on the top of the mount" in the sight of the assembled multitude. And "the voice of the trumpet sounded long, and waxed louder and louder." So terrible were the tokens of Jehovah's presence that the hosts of Israel shook with fear, and fell upon their faces before the Lord. Even Moses exclaimed, "I exceedingly fear and quake." Hebrews 12:21.

And now the thunders ceased; the trumpet was no longer heard; the earth was still. There was a period of solemn silence, and then the voice of God was heard. Speaking out of the thick darkness that enshrouded Him, as He stood upon the mount, surrounded by a retinue of angels, the Lord made known His law. Moses, describing the scene, says: "The Lord came from Sinai, and rose up from Seir unto 305 them; He shined forth from Mount Paran, and He came with ten thousands of saints: from His right hand went a fiery law for them. Yea, He loved the people; all His saints are in Thy hand: and they sat down at Thy feet; every one shall receive of Thy words." Deuteronomy 33:2, 3.

Jehovah revealed Himself, not alone in the awful majesty of the judge and lawgiver, but as the compassionate guardian of His people: "I am the Lord thy God, which have brought thee out of the land of Egypt, out of the house of bondage." He whom they had already known as their Guide and Deliverer, who had brought them forth from Egypt, making a way for them through the sea, and overthrowing Pharaoh and his hosts, who had thus shown Himself to be above all the gods of Egypt—He it was who now spoke His law.

The law was not spoken at this time exclusively for the benefit of the Hebrews. God honored them by making them the guardians and keepers of His law, but it was to be held as a sacred trust for the whole world. The precepts of the Decalogue are adapted to all mankind, and they were given for the instruction and government of all. Ten precepts, brief, comprehensive, and authoritative, cover the duty of man to God and to his fellow man; and all based upon the great fundamental principle of love. "Thou shalt love the Lord thy God with all thy heart, and with all thy soul, and with all thy strength, and with all thy mind; and thy neighbor as thyself." Luke 10:27. See also Deuteronomy 6:4, 5; Leviticus 19:18. In the Ten Commandments these principles are carried out in detail, and made applicable to the condition and circumstances of man.

"Thou shalt have no other gods before Me."

Jehovah, the eternal, self-existent, uncreated One, Himself the Source and Sustainer of all, is alone entitled to supreme reverence and worship. Man is forbidden to give to any other object the first place in his affections or his service. Whatever we cherish that tends to lessen our love for God or to interfere with the service due Him, of that do we make a god.

"Thou shalt not make unto thee any graven image, or any likeness of anything that is in heaven above, or that is in the earth beneath, or that is in the water under the earth: thou shalt not bow down thyself to them, nor serve them."

The second commandment forbids the worship of the true God by images or similitudes. Many heathen nations claimed that their images were mere figures or symbols by which the Deity was worshiped, but God has declared such worship to be sin. The attempt to represent the Eternal One by material objects would lower man's conception of God. The mind, turned away from the infinite perfection of Jehovah, would be attracted to the creature rather than to the Creator. And as his conceptions of God were lowered, so would man become degraded.

"I the Lord thy God am a jealous God." The close and sacred relation of God to His people is represented under the figure of marriage. Idolatry being spiritual adultery, the displeasure of God against it is fitly called jealousy.

"Visiting the iniquity of the fathers upon the children unto the third and fourth generation of them that hate Me." It is inevitable that children should suffer from the consequences of parental wrongdoing, but they are not punished in their parents' guilt, except as they participate in their sins. It is usually the case, however, that children walk in the steps of their parents. By inheritance and example the sons become partakers of the father's sin. Wrong tendencies, perverted appetites, and debased morals, as well as physical disease and degeneracy, are transmitted as a legacy from father to son, to the third and fourth generation. This fearful truth should have a solemn power to restrain men from following a course of sin.

"Showing mercy unto thousands of them that love Me, and keep My commandments." In prohibiting the worship of false gods, the second commandment by implication enjoins the worship of the true God. And to those who are faithful in His service, mercy is promised, not merely to the third and fourth generation as is the wrath threatened against those who hate Him, but to *thousands* of generations.

"Thou shalt not take the name of the Lord thy God in vain: for the Lord will not hold him guiltless that taketh His name in vain."

This commandment not only prohibits false oaths and common swearing, but it forbids us to use the name of God in a light or careless manner, without regard to its awful significance. By the thoughtless mention of God in common conversation, by appeals to Him in trivial matters, and by the frequent and thoughtless repetition of His name, we dishonor Him. "Holy and reverend is His name." Psalm 111:9. All should meditate upon His majesty, His purity and holiness, that the heart may be impressed with a sense of His exalted character; and His holy name should be uttered with reverence and solemnity.

"Remember the Sabbath day, to keep it holy. Six days shalt thou labor, and do all thy work: but the seventh day is the Sabbath of the Lord thy God: in it thou shalt not do any work, thou, nor thy son, nor thy daughter, thy manservant, nor thy maidservant, nor thy cattle, nor thy stranger that is within thy gates: for in six days the Lord made heaven and earth, the sea, and all that in them is, and rested the seventh day: wherefore the Lord blessed the Sabbath day, and hallowed it."

The Sabbath is not introduced as a new institution but as having been founded at creation. It is to be remembered and observed as the memorial of the Creator's work. Pointing to God as the Maker of the heavens and the earth, it distinguishes the true God from all false gods. All who keep the seventh day signify by this act that they are worshipers of Jehovah. Thus the Sabbath is the sign of man's allegiance to God as long as there are any upon the earth to serve Him. The fourth commandment is the only one of all the ten in which are found both the name and the title of the Lawgiver. It is the only one that shows by whose authority the law is given. Thus it contains the seal of God, affixed to His law as evidence of its authenticity and binding force.

God has given men six days wherein to labor, and He requires that their own work be done in the six working days. Acts of necessity and mercy are permitted on the Sabbath, the sick and suffering are at all times to be cared for; but unnecessary labor is to be strictly avoided. "Turn away thy foot from the Sabbath, from doing thy pleasure on My holy day; and call the Sabbath a delight, the holy of the Lord, honorable; and . . . honor Him, not doing thine own ways, nor finding thine own pleasure." Isaiah 58:13. Nor does the prohibition end here. "Nor speaking thine own words," says the prophet. Those who discuss business matters or lay plans on the Sabbath are regarded by God as though engaged in the actual transaction of business. To keep the Sabbath holy, we should not even allow our minds to dwell upon things of a worldly character. And the commandment includes all within our gates. The inmates of the house are to lay aside their worldly business during the sacred hours. All should unite to honor God by willing service upon His holy day.

"Honor thy father and thy mother: that thy days may be long upon the land which the Lord thy God giveth thee."

Parents are entitled to a degree of love and respect which is due to no other person. God Himself, who has placed upon them a responsibility for the souls committed to their charge, has ordained that during the earlier years of life, parents shall stand in the place of God to their children. And he who rejects the rightful authority of his parents is rejecting the authority of God. The fifth commandment requires children not only to yield respect, submission, and obedience to their parents, but also to give them love and tenderness, to lighten their cares, to guard their reputation, and to succor and comfort them in old age. It also enjoins respect for ministers and rulers and for all others to whom God has delegated authority.

This, says the apostle, "is the first commandment with promise." Ephesians 6:2. To Israel, expecting soon to enter Canaan, it was a pledge to the obedient, of long life in that good land; but it has a wider meaning, including all the Israel of God, and promising eternal life upon the earth when it shall be freed from the curse of sin.

"Thou shalt not kill."

All acts of injustice that tend to shorten life; the spirit of hatred and revenge, or the indulgence of any passion that leads to injurious acts toward others, or causes us even to wish them harm (for "whosoever hateth his brother is a murderer"); a selfish neglect of caring for the needy or suffering; all self-indulgence or unnecessary deprivation or excessive labor that tends to injure health—all these are, to a greater or less degree, violations of the sixth commandment.

"Thou shalt not commit adultery."

This commandment forbids not only acts of impurity, but sensual thoughts and desires, or any practice that tends to excite them. Purity is demanded not only in the outward life but in the secret intents and emotions of the heart. Christ, who taught the far-reaching obligation of the law of God, declared the evil thought or look to be as truly sin as is the unlawful deed.

"Thou shalt not steal."

309 Both public and private sins are included in this prohibition. The eighth commandment condemns manstealing and slave dealing, and forbids wars of conquest. It condemns theft and robbery. It demands strict integrity in the minutest details of the affairs of life. It forbids overreaching in trade, and requires the payment of just debts or wages. It declares that every attempt to advantage oneself by the ignorance, weakness, or misfortune of another is registered as fraud in the books of heaven.

"Thou shalt not bear false witness against thy neighbor."

False speaking in any matter, every attempt or purpose to deceive our neighbor, is here included. An intention to deceive is what constitutes falsehood. By a glance of the eye, a motion of the hand, an expression of the countenance, a falsehood may be told as effectually as by words. All intentional overstatement, every hint or insinuation calculated to convey an erroneous or exaggerated impression, even the statement of facts in such a manner as to mislead, is falsehood. This precept forbids every effort to injure our neighbor's reputation by misrepresentation or evil surmising, by slander or tale bearing. Even the intentional suppression of truth, by which injury may result to others, is a violation of the ninth commandment.

"Thou shalt not covet thy neighbor's house, thou shalt not covet thy neighbor's wife, nor his manservant, nor his maidservant, nor his ox, nor his ass, nor anything that is thy neighbor's."

The tenth commandment strikes at the very root of all sins, prohibiting the selfish desire, from which springs the sinful act. He who in obedience to God's law refrains from indulging even a sinful desire for that which belongs to another will not be guilty of an act of wrong toward his fellow creatures.

Such were the sacred precepts of the Decalogue, spoken amid thunder and flame, and with a wonderful display of the power and majesty of the great Lawgiver. God accompanied the proclamation of His law with exhibitions of His power and glory, that His people might never forget the scene, and that they might be impressed with profound veneration for the Author of the law, the Creator of heaven and earth. He would also show to all men the sacredness, the importance, and the permanence of His law.

The people of Israel were overwhelmed with terror. The awful power of God's utterances seemed more than their trembling hearts could bear. For as God's great rule of right was presented before them, they realized as never 310 before the offensive character of sin, and their own guilt in the sight of a holy God. They shrank away from the mountain in fear and awe. The multitude cried out to Moses, "Speak thou with us, and we will hear: but let not God speak with us, lest we die." The leader answered, "Fear not: for God is come to prove you, and that His fear may be before your faces, that ye sin not." The people, however, remained at a distance, gazing in terror upon the scene, while Moses "drew near unto the thick darkness where God was."

The minds of the people, blinded and debased by slavery and heathenism, were not prepared to appreciate fully the far-reaching principles of God's ten precepts. That the obligations of the Decalogue might be more fully understood and enforced, additional precepts were given, illustrating and applying the principles of the Ten Commandments. These laws were called judgments, both because they were framed in infinite wisdom and equity and because the magistrates were to give judgment according to them. Unlike the Ten Commandments, they were delivered privately to Moses, who was to communicate them to the people.

The first of these laws related to servants. In ancient times criminals were sometimes sold into slavery by the judges; in some cases, debtors were sold by their creditors; and poverty even led persons to sell themselves or their children. But a Hebrew could not be sold as a slave for life. His term of service was limited to six years; on the seventh he was to be set at liberty. Manstealing, deliberate murder, and rebellion against parental authority were to be punished with death. The holding of slaves not of Israelitish birth was permitted, but their life and person were strictly guarded. The murderer of a slave was to be punished; an injury inflicted upon one by his master, though no more than the loss of a tooth, entitled him to his freedom.

The Israelites had lately been servants themselves, and now that they were to have servants under them, they were to beware of indulging the spirit of cruelty and exaction from which they had suffered under their Egyptian taskmasters. The memory of their own bitter servitude should enable them to put themselves in the servant's place, leading them to be kind and compassionate, to deal with others as they would wish to be dealt with.

The rights of widows and orphans were specially guarded, and a tender regard for their 311 helpless condition was enjoined. "If thou afflict them in any wise," the Lord declared, "and they cry at all unto Me, I will surely hear their cry; and My wrath shall wax hot, and I will kill you with the sword; and your wives shall be widows, and your children fatherless." Aliens who united themselves with Israel were to be protected from wrong or oppression. "Thou shalt not oppress a stranger: for ye know the heart of a stranger, seeing ye were strangers in the land of Egypt."

The taking of usury from the poor was forbidden. A poor man's raiment or blanket taken as a pledge, must be restored to him at nightfall. He who was guilty of theft was required to restore double. Respect for magistrates and rulers was enjoined, and judges were warned against perverting judgment, aiding a false cause, or receiving bribes. Calumny and slander were prohibited, and acts of kindness enjoined, even toward personal enemies.

Again the people were reminded of the sacred obligation of the Sabbath. Yearly feasts were appointed, at which all the men of the nation were to assemble before the Lord, bringing to Him their offerings of gratitude and the first fruits of His bounties. The object of all these regulations was stated: they proceeded from no exercise of mere arbitrary sovereignty; all were given for the good of Israel. The Lord said, "Ye shall be holy men unto Me"—worthy to be acknowledged by a holy God.

These laws were to be recorded by Moses, and carefully treasured as the foundation of the national law, and, with the ten precepts which they were given to illustrate, the condition of the fulfillment of God's promises to Israel.

The message was now given them from Jehovah: "Behold, I send an Angel before thee, to keep thee in the way, and to bring thee into the place which I have prepared. Beware of Him, and obey His voice, provoke Him not; for He will not pardon your transgressions: for My name is in Him. But if thou shalt indeed obey His voice, and do all that I speak; then I will be an enemy unto thine enemies, and an adversary unto thine adversaries." During all the wanderings of Israel, Christ, in the pillar of cloud and of fire, was their Leader. While there were types pointing to a Saviour to come, there was also a present Saviour, who gave commands to Moses for the people, and who was set forth before them as the only channel of blessing.

Upon descending from the mountain, "Moses came and told the people all the words of the Lord, and all the judgments: and all the people 312 answered with one voice, and said, All the words which the Lord hath said will we do." This pledge, together with the words of the Lord which it bound them to obey, was written by Moses in a book.

Then followed the ratification of the covenant. An altar was built at the foot of the mountain, and beside it twelve pillars were set up, "according to the twelve tribes of Israel," as a testimony to their acceptance of the covenant. Sacrifices were then presented by young men chosen for the service.

Having sprinkled the altar with the blood of the offerings, Moses "took the book of the covenant, and read in the audience of the people." Thus the conditions of the covenant were solemnly repeated, and all were at liberty to choose whether or not they would comply with them. They had at the first promised to obey the voice of God; but they had since heard His law proclaimed; and its principles had been particularized, that they might know how much this covenant involved. Again the people answered with one accord, "All that the Lord hath said will we do, and be obedient." "When Moses had spoken every precept to all the people according to the law, he took the blood, . . . and sprinkled both the book and all the people, saying, This is the blood of the testament which God hath enjoined unto you." Hebrews 9:19, 20.

Arrangements were now to be made for the full establishment of the chosen nation under

Jehovah as their king. Moses had received the command, "Come up unto the Lord, thou, and Aaron, Nadab, and Abihu, and seventy of the elders of Israel; and worship ye afar off. And Moses alone shall come near the Lord." While the people worshiped at its foot, these chosen men were called up into the mount. The seventy elders were to assist Moses in the government of Israel, and God put upon them His Spirit, and honored them with a view of His power and greatness. "And they saw the God of Israel: and there was under His feet as it were a paved work of a sapphire stone, and as it were the body of heaven in his clearness." They did not behold the Deity, but they saw the glory of His presence. Before this they could not have endured such a scene; but the exhibition of God's power had awed them to repentance; they had been contemplating His glory, purity, and mercy, until they could approach nearer to Him who was the subject of their meditations.

313　　Moses and "his minister Joshua" were now summoned to meet with God. And as they were to be some time absent, the leader appointed Aaron and Hur, assisted by the elders, to act in his stead. "And Moses went up into the mount, and a cloud covered the mount. And the glory of the Lord abode upon Mount Sinai." For six days the cloud covered the mountain as a token of God's special presence; yet there was no revelation of Himself or communication of His will. During this time Moses remained in waiting for a summons to the presence chamber of the Most High. He had been directed, "Come up to Me into the mount, and be there," and though his patience and obedience were tested, he did not grow weary of watching, or forsake his post. This period of waiting was to him a time of preparation, of close self-examination. Even this favored servant of God could not at once approach into His presence and endure the exhibitions of His glory. Six days must be employed in devoting himself to God by searching of heart, meditation, and prayer before he could be prepared for direct communication with his Maker.

Upon the seventh day, which was the Sabbath, Moses was called up into the cloud. The thick cloud opened in the sight of all Israel, and the glory of the Lord broke forth like devouring fire. "And Moses went into the midst of the cloud, and gat him up into the mount; and Moses was in the mount forty days and forty nights." The forty days' tarry in the mount did not include the six days of preparation. During the six days Joshua was with Moses, and together they ate of the manna and drank of "the brook that descended out of the mount." But Joshua did not enter with Moses into the cloud. He remained without, and continued to eat and drink daily while awaiting the return of Moses, but Moses fasted during the entire forty days.

During his stay in the mount, Moses received directions for the building of a sanctuary in which the divine presence would be specially manifested. "Let them make Me a sanctuary; that I may dwell among them" (Exodus 25:8), was the command of God. For the third time the observance of the Sabbath was enjoined. "It is a sign between Me and the children of Israel forever," the Lord declared, "that ye may know that I am Jehovah that doth sanctify you. Ye shall keep the Sabbath therefore; for it is holy unto you. . . . Whosoever doeth any work therein, that soul shall be cut off from among his people." Exodus 31:17, 13, 14. Directions had　314 just been given for the immediate erection of the tabernacle for the service of God; and now the people might conclude, because the object had in view was the glory of God, and also because of their great need of a place of worship, that they would be justified in working at the building upon the Sabbath. To guard them from this error, the warning was given. Even the sacredness and urgency of that special work for God must not lead them to infringe upon His holy rest day.

Henceforth the people were to be honored with the abiding presence of their King. "I will dwell among the children of Israel, and will be their God," "and the tabernacle shall be sanctified by My glory" (Exodus 29:45, 43), was the assurance given to Moses. As the symbol of God's authority and the embodiment of His will, there was delivered to Moses a copy of the Decalogue engraved by the finger of God Himself upon two tables of stone (Deuteronomy 9:10; Exodus 32:15, 16), to be sacredly enshrined in the sanctuary, which, when made, was to be the visible center of the nation's worship.

From a race of slaves the Israelites had been exalted above all peoples to be the peculiar treasure of the King of kings. God had separated them from the world, that He might commit to them a sacred trust. He had made them the depositaries of His law, and He purposed, through them, to preserve among men the knowledge of Himself. Thus the light of heaven was to shine out to a world enshrouded in darkness, and a voice was to be heard appealing to all peoples to turn from their idolatry to serve the living God. If the Israelites would be true to their trust, they would become a power in the world. God would be their defense, and He would exalt them above all other nations. His light and truth would be revealed through them, and they would stand forth under His wise and holy rule as an example of the superiority of His worship over every form of idolatry.

315

28

Idolatry at Sinai

While Moses was absent it was a time of waiting and suspense to Israel. The people knew that he had ascended the mount with Joshua, and had entered the cloud of thick darkness which could be seen from the plain below, resting on the mountain peak, illuminated from time to time with the lightnings of the divine Presence. They waited eagerly for his return. Accustomed as they had been in Egypt to material representations of deity, it had been hard for them to trust in an invisible being, and they had come to rely upon Moses to sustain their faith. Now he was taken from them. Day after day, week after week passed, and still he did not return. Notwithstanding the cloud was still in view, it seemed to many in the camp that their leader had deserted them, or that he had been consumed by the devouring fire.

During this period of waiting, there was time for them to meditate upon the law of God which they had heard, and to prepare their hearts to receive the further revelations that He might make to them. They had none too much time for this work; and had they been thus seeking a clearer understanding of God's requirements, and humbling their hearts before Him, they would have been shielded from temptation. But they did not do this, and they soon became careless, inattentive, and lawless. Especially was this the case with the mixed multitude. They were impatient to be on their way to the Land of Promise—the land flowing with milk and honey. It was only on condition of obedience that the goodly land was promised them, but they had lost sight of this. There were some who suggested a return to Egypt, but whether forward to Canaan or backward to Egypt, the masses of the people were determined to wait no longer for Moses.

316 Feeling their helplessness in the absence of their leader, they returned to their old superstitions. The "mixed multitude" had been the first to indulge murmuring and impatience, and they were the leaders in the apostasy that followed. Among the objects regarded by the Egyptians as symbols of deity was the ox or calf; and it was at the suggestion of those who had practiced this form of idolatry in Egypt that a calf was now made and worshiped. The people desired some image to represent God, and to go before them in the place of Moses. God had given no manner of similitude of Himself, and He had prohibited any material representation for such a purpose. The mighty miracles in Egypt and at the Red Sea were designed to establish faith in Him

as the invisible, all-powerful Helper of Israel, the only true God. And the desire for some visible manifestation of His presence had been granted in the pillar of cloud and of fire that guided their hosts, and in the revealing of His glory upon Mount Sinai. But with the cloud of the Presence still before them, they turned back in their hearts to the idolatry of Egypt, and represented the glory of the invisible God by the similitude of an ox!

In the absence of Moses, the judicial authority had been delegated to Aaron, and a vast crowd gathered about his tent, with the demand, "Make us gods, which shall go before us; for as for this Moses, the man that brought us up out of the land of Egypt, we wot not what is become of him."* The cloud, they said, that had heretofore led them, now rested permanently upon the mount; it would no longer direct their travels. They must have an image in its place; and if, as had been suggested, they should decide to return to Egypt, they would find favor with the Egyptians by bearing this image before them and acknowledging it as their god.

Such a crisis demanded a man of firmness, decision, and unflinching courage; one who held the honor of God above popular favor, personal safety, or life itself. But the present leader of Israel was not of this character. Aaron feebly remonstrated with the people, but his wavering and timidity at the critical moment only rendered them the more determined. The tumult increased. A blind, unreasoning frenzy seemed to take possession of the multitude. There were some who remained true to their covenant with God, but the greater part of the people joined in the apostasy. A few who ventured to denounce the proposed image making as idolatry, were set 317 upon and roughly treated, and in the confusion and excitement they finally lost their lives.

Aaron feared for his own safety; and instead of nobly standing up for the honor of God, he yielded to the demands of the multitude. His first act was to direct that the golden earrings be collected from all the people and brought to him, hoping that pride would lead them to refuse such a sacrifice. But they willingly yielded up their ornaments; and from these he made a molten calf, in imitation of the gods of Egypt. The people proclaimed, "These be thy gods, O Israel, which brought thee up out of the land of Egypt." And Aaron basely permitted this insult to Jehovah. He did more. Seeing with what satisfaction the golden god was received, he built an altar before it, and made proclamation, "Tomorrow is a feast to the Lord." The announcement was heralded by trumpeters from company to company throughout the camp. "And they rose up early on the morrow, and offered burnt offerings, and brought peace offerings; and the people sat down to eat and to drink, and rose up to play." Under the pretense

---

This chapter is based on Exodus 32 to 34.   * See Appendix, Note 4.

of holding "a feast to the Lord," they gave themselves up to gluttony and licentious reveling.

How often, in our own day, is the love of pleasure disguised by a "form of godliness"! A religion that permits men, while observing the rites of worship, to devote themselves to selfish or sensual gratification, is as pleasing to the multitudes now as in the days of Israel. And there are still pliant Aarons, who, while holding positions of authority in the church, will yield to the desires of the unconsecrated, and thus encourage them in sin.

Only a few days had passed since the Hebrews had made a solemn covenant with God to obey His voice. They had stood trembling with terror before the mount, listening to the words of the Lord, "Thou shalt have no other gods before Me." The glory of God still hovered above Sinai in the sight of the congregation; but they turned away, and asked for other gods. "They made a calf in Horeb, and worshiped the molten image. Thus they changed their glory into the similitude of an ox." Psalm 106:19, 20. How could greater ingratitude have been shown, or more daring insult offered, to Him who had revealed Himself to them as a tender father and an all-powerful king!

318 Moses in the mount was warned of the apostasy in the camp and was directed to return without delay. "Go, get thee down," were the words of God; "thy people, which thou broughtest out of the land of Egypt, have corrupted themselves: they have turned aside quickly out of the way which I commanded them. They have made them a molten calf, and have worshiped it." God might have checked the movement at the outset; but He suffered it to come to this height that He might teach all a lesson in His punishment of treason and apostasy.

God's covenant with His people had been disannulled, and He declared to Moses, "Let Me alone, that My wrath may wax hot against them, and that I may consume them: and I will make of thee a great nation." The people of Israel, especially the mixed multitude, would be constantly disposed to rebel against God. They would also murmur against their leader, and would grieve him by their unbelief and stubbornness, and it would be a laborious and soul-trying work to lead them through to the Promised Land. Their sins had already forfeited the favor of God, and justice called for their destruction. The Lord therefore proposed to destroy them, and make of Moses a mighty nation.

"Let Me alone, . . . that I may consume them," were the words of God. If God had purposed to destroy Israel, who could plead for them? How few but would have left the sinners to their fate! How few but would have gladly exchanged a lot of toil and burden and sacrifice,

repaid with ingratitude and murmuring, for a position of ease and honor, when it was God Himself that offered the release.

But Moses discerned ground for hope where there appeared only discouragement and wrath. The words of God, "Let Me alone," he understood not to forbid but to encourage intercession, implying that nothing but the prayers of Moses could save Israel, but that if thus entreated, God would spare His people. He "besought the Lord his God, and said, Lord, why doth Thy wrath wax hot against Thy people, which Thou hast brought forth out of the land of Egypt with great power, and with a mighty hand?"

God had signified that He disowned His people. He had spoken of them to Moses as "thy people, which thou broughtest out of Egypt." But Moses humbly disclaimed the leadership of Israel. They were not his, but God's—"Thy people, which Thou hast brought forth . . . with great power, and with a mighty hand. Where- 319 fore," he urged, "should the Egyptians speak, and say, For mischief did He bring them out, to slay them in the mountains, and to consume them from the face of the earth?"

During the few months since Israel left Egypt, the report of their wonderful deliverance had spread to all the surrounding nations. Fear and terrible foreboding rested upon the heathen. All were watching to see what the God of Israel would do for His people. Should they now be destroyed, their enemies would triumph, and God would be dishonored. The Egyptians would claim that their accusations were true—instead of leading His people into the wilderness to sacrifice, He had caused them to be sacrificed. They would not consider the sins of Israel; the destruction of the people whom He had so signally honored, would bring reproach upon His name. How great the responsibility resting upon those whom God has highly honored, to make His name a praise in the earth! With what care should they guard against committing sin, to call down His judgments and cause His name to be reproached by the ungodly!

As Moses interceded for Israel, his timidity was lost in his deep interest and love for those for whom he had, in the hands of God, been the means of doing so much. The Lord listened to his pleadings, and granted his unselfish prayer. God had proved His servant; He had tested his faithfulness and his love for that erring, ungrateful people, and nobly had Moses endured the trial. His interest in Israel sprang from no selfish motive. The prosperity of God's chosen people was dearer to him than personal honor, dearer than the privilege of becoming the father of a mighty nation. God was pleased with his faithfulness, his simplicity of heart, and his integrity, and He committed to him, as a faithful shepherd, the great charge of leading Israel to the

Promised Land.

As Moses and Joshua came down from the mount, the former bearing the "tables of the testimony," they heard the shouts and outcries of the excited multitude, evidently in a state of wild uproar. To Joshua the soldier, the first thought was of an attack from their enemies. "There is a noise of war in the camp," he said. But Moses judged more truly the nature of the commotion. The sound was not that of combat, but of revelry. "It is not the voice of them that shout for mastery, neither is it the voice of them that cry for being overcome; but the noise of them that sing do I hear."

320 As they drew near the encampment, they beheld the people shouting and dancing around their idol. It was a scene of heathen riot, an imitation of the idolatrous feasts of Egypt; but how unlike the solemn and reverent worship of God! Moses was overwhelmed. He had just come from the presence of God's glory, and though he had been warned of what was taking place, he was unprepared for that dreadful exhibition of the degradation of Israel. His anger was hot. To show his abhorrence of their crime, he threw down the tables of stone, and they were broken in the sight of all the people, thus signifying that as they had broken their covenant with God, so God had broken His covenant with them.

Entering the camp, Moses passed through the crowds of revelers, and seizing upon the idol, cast it into the fire. He afterward ground it to powder, and having strewed it upon the stream that descended from the mount, he made the people drink of it. Thus was shown the utter worthlessness of the god which they had been worshiping.

The great leader summoned his guilty brother and sternly demanded, "What did this people unto thee, that thou hast brought so great a sin upon them?" Aaron endeavored to shield himself by relating the clamors of the people; that if he had not complied with their wishes, he would have been put to death. "Let not the anger of my lord wax hot," he said; "thou knowest the people, that they are set on mischief. For they said unto me, Make us gods, which shall go before us: for as for this Moses, the man that brought us up out of the land of Egypt, we wot not what is become of him. And I said unto them, Whosoever hath any gold, let them break it off. So they gave it me: then I cast it into the fire, and there came out this calf." He would lead Moses to believe that a miracle had been wrought—that the gold had been cast into the fire, and by supernatural power changed to a calf. But his excuses and prevarications were of no avail. He was justly dealt with as the chief offender.

The fact that Aaron had been blessed and honored so far above the people was what made his sin so heinous. It was Aaron "the saint of the Lord" (Psalm 106:16), that had made the idol and announced the feast. It was he who had been appointed as spokesman for Moses, and concerning whom God Himself had testified, "I know that he can speak well" (Exodus 4:14), that had failed to check the idolaters in their heaven-daring purpose. He by whom God had 323 wrought in bringing judgments both upon the Egyptians and upon their gods, had heard unmoved the proclamation before the molten image, "These be thy gods, O Israel, which brought thee up out of the land of Egypt." It was he who had been with Moses on the mount, and had there beheld the glory of the Lord, who had seen that in the manifestation of that glory there was nothing of which an image could be made—it was he who had changed that glory into the similitude of an ox. He to whom God had committed the government of the people in the absence of Moses, was found sanctioning their rebellion. "The Lord was very angry with Aaron to have destroyed him." Deuteronomy 9:20. But in answer to the earnest intercession of Moses, his life was spared; and in penitence and humiliation for his great sin, he was restored to the favor of God.

If Aaron had had courage to stand for the right, irrespective of consequences, he could have prevented that apostasy. If he had unswervingly maintained his own allegiance to God, if he had cited the people to the perils of Sinai, and had reminded them of their solemn covenant with God to obey His law, the evil would have been checked. But his compliance with the desires of the people and the calm assurance with which he proceeded to carry out their plans, emboldened them to go to greater lengths in sin than had before entered their minds.

When Moses, on returning to the camp, confronted the rebels, his severe rebukes and the indignation he displayed in breaking the sacred tables of the law were contrasted by the people with his brother's pleasant speech and dignified demeanor, and their sympathies were with Aaron. To justify himself, Aaron endeavored to make the people responsible for his weakness in yielding to their demand; but notwithstanding this, they were filled with admiration of his gentleness and patience. But God seeth not as man sees. Aaron's yielding spirit and his desire to please had blinded his eyes to the enormity of the crime he was sanctioning. His course in giving his influence to sin in Israel cost the life of thousands. In what contrast with this was the course of Moses, who, while faithfully executing God's judgments, showed that the welfare of Israel was dearer to him than prosperity or honor or life.

Of all the sins that God will punish, none are more grievous in His sight than those that encourage others to do evil. God would have 324

His servants prove their loyalty by faithfully rebuking transgression, however painful the act may be. Those who are honored with a divine commission are not to be weak, pliant time-servers. They are not to aim at self-exaltation, or to shun disagreeable duties, but to perform God's work with unswerving fidelity.

Though God had granted the prayer of Moses in sparing Israel from destruction, their apostasy was to be signally punished. The lawlessness and insubordination into which Aaron had permitted them to fall, if not speedily crushed, would run riot in wickedness, and would involve the nation in irretrievable ruin. By terrible severity the evil must be put away. Standing in the gate of the camp, Moses called to the people, "Who is on the Lord's side? let him come unto me." Those who had not joined in the apostasy were to take their position at the right of Moses; those who were guilty but repentant, at the left. The command was obeyed. It was found that the tribe of Levi had taken no part in the idolatrous worship. From among other tribes there were great numbers who, although they had sinned, now signified their repentance. But a large company, mostly of the mixed multitude that instigated the making of the calf, stubbornly persisted in their rebellion. In the name of "the Lord God of Israel," Moses now commanded those upon his right hand, who had kept themselves clear of idolatry, to gird on their swords and slay all who persisted in rebellion. "And there fell of the people that day about three thousand men." Without regard to position, kindred, or friendship, the ringleaders in wickedness were cut off; but all who repented and humbled themselves were spared.

Those who performed this terrible work of judgment were acting by divine authority, executing the sentence of the King of heaven. Men are to beware how they, in their human blindness, judge and condemn their fellow men; but when God commands them to execute His sentence upon iniquity, He is to be obeyed. Those who performed this painful act, thus manifested their abhorrence of rebellion and idolatry, and consecrated themselves more fully to the service of the true God. The Lord honored their faithfulness by bestowing special distinction upon the tribe of Levi.

The Israelites had been guilty of treason, and that against a King who had loaded them with benefits and whose authority they had voluntarily pledged themselves to obey. That the divine 325 government might be maintained justice must be visited upon the traitors. Yet even here God's mercy was displayed. While He maintained His law, He granted freedom of choice and opportunity for repentance to all. Only those were cut off who persisted in rebellion.

It was necessary that this sin should be punished, as a testimony to surrounding nations of God's displeasure against idolatry. By executing justice upon the guilty, Moses, as God's instrument, must leave on record a solemn and public protest against their crime. As the Israelites should hereafter condemn the idolatry of the neighboring tribes, their enemies would throw back upon them the charge that the people who claimed Jehovah as their God had made a calf and worshiped it in Horeb. Then though compelled to acknowledge the disgraceful truth, Israel could point to the terrible fate of the transgressors, as evidence that their sin had not been sanctioned or excused.

Love no less than justice demanded that for this sin judgment should be inflicted. God is the guardian as well as the sovereign of His people. He cuts off those who are determined upon rebellion, that they may not lead others to ruin. In sparing the life of Cain, God had demonstrated to the universe what would be the result of permitting sin to go unpunished. The influence exerted upon his descendants by his life and teaching led to the state of corruption that demanded the destruction of the whole world by a flood. The history of the antediluvians testifies that long life is not a blessing to the sinner; God's great forbearance did not repress their wickedness. The longer men lived, the more corrupt they became.

So with the apostasy at Sinai. Unless punishment had been speedily visited upon transgression, the same results would again have been seen. The earth would have become as corrupt as in the days of Noah. Had these transgressors been spared, evils would have followed, greater than resulted from sparing the life of Cain. It was the mercy of God that thousands should suffer, to prevent the necessity of visiting judgments upon millions. In order to save the many, He must punish the few. Furthermore, as the people had cast off their allegiance to God, they had forfeited the divine protection, and, deprived of their defense, the whole nation was exposed to the power of their enemies. Had not the evil been promptly put away, they would soon have fallen a prey to their numerous and powerful foes. It was necessary for the good of 326 Israel, and also as a lesson to all succeeding generations, that crime should be promptly punished. And it was no less a mercy to the sinners themselves that they should be cut short in their evil course. Had their life been spared, the same spirit that led them to rebel against God would have been manifested in hatred and strife among themselves, and they would eventually have destroyed one another. It was in love to the world, in love to Israel, and even to the transgressors, that crime was punished with swift and terrible severity.

As the people were roused to see the enormity of their guilt, terror pervaded the entire encampment. It was feared that every offender was to be cut off. Pitying their distress, Moses promised to plead once more with God for them.

"Ye have sinned a great sin," he said, "and now I will go up unto the Lord; peradventure I shall make an atonement for your sin." He went, and in his confession before God he said, "Oh, this people have sinned a great sin, and have made them gods of gold. Yet now if Thou wilt forgive their sin—; and if not, blot me, I pray Thee, out of Thy book which Thou hast written." The answer was, "Whosoever hath sinned against Me, him will I blot out of My book. Therefore now go, lead the people into the place of which I have spoken unto thee: behold, Mine Angel shall go before thee: nevertheless, in the day when I visit, I will visit their sin upon them."

In the prayer of Moses our minds are directed to the heavenly records in which the names of all men are inscribed, and their deeds, whether good or evil, are faithfully registered. The book of life contains the names of all who have ever entered the service of God. If any of these depart from Him, and by stubborn persistence in sin become finally hardened against the influences of His Holy Spirit, their names will in the judgment be blotted from the book of life, and they themselves will be devoted to destruction. Moses realized how dreadful would be the fate of the sinner; yet if the people of Israel were to be rejected by the Lord, he desired his name to be blotted out with theirs; he could not endure to see the judgments of God fall upon those who had been so graciously delivered. The intercession of Moses in behalf of Israel illustrates the mediation of Christ for sinful men. But the Lord did not permit Moses to bear, as did Christ, the 327 guilt of the transgressor. "Whosoever hath sinned against Me," He said, "him will I blot out of My book."

In deep sadness the people had buried their dead. Three thousand had fallen by the sword; a plague had soon after broken out in the encampment; and now the message came to them that the divine Presence would no longer accompany them in their journeyings. Jehovah had declared, "I will not go up in the midst of thee; for thou art a stiffnecked people: lest I consume thee in the way." And the command was given, "Put off thy ornaments from thee, that I may know what to do unto thee." Now there was mourning throughout the encampment. In penitence and humiliation "the children of Israel stripped themselves of their ornaments by the mount Horeb."

By the divine direction the tent that had served as a temporary place of worship was removed "afar off from the camp." This was still further evidence that God had withdrawn His presence from them. He would reveal Himself to Moses, but not to such a people. The rebuke was keenly felt, and to the conscience-smitten multitudes it seemed a foreboding of greater calamity. Had not the Lord separated Moses from the camp that He might utterly destroy them? But they were not left without hope. The tent was pitched without the encampment, but Moses called it "the tabernacle of the congregation." All who were truly penitent, and desired to return to the Lord, were directed to repair thither to confess their sins and seek His mercy. When they returned to their tents Moses entered the tabernacle. With agonizing interest the people watched for some token that his intercessions in their behalf were accepted. If God should condescend to meet with him, they might hope that they were not to be utterly consumed. When the cloudy pillar descended, and stood at the entrance of the tabernacle, the people wept for joy, and they "rose up and worshiped, every man in his tent door."

Moses knew well the perversity and blindness of those who were placed under his care; he knew the difficulties with which he must contend. But he had learned that in order to prevail with the people, he must have help from God. He pleaded for a clearer revelation of God's will and for an assurance of His presence: "See, Thou sayest unto me, Bring up this people: and Thou hast not let me know whom Thou wilt send with me. Yet Thou hast said, I know thee 328 by name, and thou hast also found grace in My sight. Now therefore, I pray Thee, if I have found grace in Thy sight, show me now Thy way, that I may know Thee, that I may find grace in Thy sight: and consider that this nation is Thy people."

The answer was, "My presence shall go with thee, and I will give thee rest." But Moses was not yet satisfied. There pressed upon his soul a sense of the terrible results should God leave Israel to hardness and impenitence. He could not endure that his interests should be separated from those of his brethren, and he prayed that the favor of God might be restored to His people, and that the token of His presence might continue to direct their journeyings: "If Thy presence go not with me, carry us not up hence. For wherein shall it be known here that I and Thy people have found grace in Thy sight? is it not in that Thou goest with us? So shall we be separated, I and Thy people, from all the people that are upon the face of the earth."

And the Lord said, "I will do this thing also that thou hast spoken: for thou hast found grace in My sight, and I know thee by name." Still the prophet did not cease pleading. Every prayer had been answered, but he thirsted for greater tokens of God's favor. He now made a request that no human being had ever made before: "I beseech Thee, show me Thy glory."

God did not rebuke his request as presumptuous; but the gracious words were spoken, "I will make all My goodness pass before thee." The unveiled glory of God, no man in this mortal state can look upon and live; but Moses was assured that he should behold as much of the divine glory as he could endure. Again he was summoned to the mountain summit; then the hand that made the world, that hand that "removeth the mountains, and they know not" (Job 9:5), took this creature of the dust, this mighty man of faith, and placed him in a cleft of the rock, while the glory of God and all His goodness passed before him.

This experience—above all else the promise that the divine Presence would attend him—was to Moses an assurance of success in the work before him; and he counted it of infinitely greater worth than all the learning of Egypt or all his attainments as a statesman or a military leader. No earthly power or skill or learning can supply the place of God's abiding presence.

329 To the transgressor it is a fearful thing to fall into the hands of the living God; but Moses stood alone in the presence of the Eternal One, and he was not afraid; for his soul was in harmony with the will of his Maker. Says the psalmist, "If I regard iniquity in my heart, the Lord will not hear me." Psalm 66:18. But "the secret of the Lord is with them that fear Him; and He will show them His covenant." Psalm 25:14.

The Deity proclaimed Himself, "The Lord, The Lord God, merciful and gracious, long-suffering, and abundant in goodness and truth, keeping mercy for thousands, forgiving iniquity and transgression and sin, and that will by no means clear the guilty."

"Moses made haste, and bowed his head toward the earth, and worshiped." Again he entreated that God would pardon the iniquity of His people, and take them for His inheritance. His prayer was granted. The Lord graciously promised to renew His favor to Israel, and in their behalf to do marvels such as had not been done "in all the earth, nor in any nation."

Forty days and nights Moses remained in the mount; and during all this time, as at the first, he was miraculously sustained. No man had been permitted to go up with him, nor during the time of his absence were any to approach the mount. At God's command he had prepared two tables of stone, and had taken them with him to the summit; and again the Lord "wrote upon the tables the words of the covenant, the Ten Commandments."*

During that long time spent in communion with God, the face of Moses had reflected the glory of the divine Presence; unknown to himself his face shone with a dazzling light when he descended from the mountain. Such a light illumined the countenance of Moses when brought before his judges; "and all that sat in the council, looking steadfastly on him, saw his

face as it had been the face of an angel." Acts 6:15. Aaron as well as the people shrank away from Moses, and "they were afraid to come nigh him." Seeing their confusion and terror, but ignorant of the cause, he urged them to come near. He held out to them the pledge of God's reconciliation, and assured them of His restored favor. They perceived in his voice nothing but love and entreaty, and at last one ventured to approach him. Too awed to speak, he silently pointed to the countenance of Moses, and then toward heaven. The great leader understood his 330 meaning. In their conscious guilt, feeling themselves still under the divine displeasure, they could not endure the heavenly light, which, had they been obedient to God, would have filled them with joy. There is fear in guilt. The soul that is free from sin will not wish to hide from the light of heaven.

Moses had much to communicate to them; and compassionating their fear, he put a veil upon his face, and continued to do so thereafter whenever he returned from communion with God.

By this brightness God designed to impress upon Israel the sacred, exalted character of His law, and the glory of the gospel revealed through Christ. While Moses was in the mount, God presented to him, not only the tables of the law, but also the plan of salvation. He saw that the sacrifice of Christ was prefigured by all the types and symbols of the Jewish age; and it was the heavenly light streaming from Calvary, no less than the glory of the law of God, that shed such a radiance upon the face of Moses. That divine illumination symbolized the glory of the dispensation of which Moses was the visible mediator, a representative of the one true Intercessor.

The glory reflected in the countenance of Moses illustrates the blessings to be received by God's commandment-keeping people through the mediation of Christ. It testifies that the closer our communion with God, and the clearer our knowledge of His requirements, the more fully shall we be conformed to the divine image, and the more readily do we become partakers of the divine nature.

Moses was a type of Christ. As Israel's intercessor veiled his countenance, because the people could not endure to look upon its glory, so Christ, the divine Mediator, veiled His divinity with humanity when He came to earth. Had He come clothed with the brightness of heaven, he could not have found access to men in their sinful state. They could not have endured the glory of His presence. Therefore He humbled Himself, and was made "in the likeness of sinful flesh"(Romans 8:3), that He might reach the fallen race, and lift them up.

---

* See Appendix, Note 5.

331

29
Satan's Enmity Against the Law

The very first effort of Satan to overthrow God's law—undertaken among the sinless inhabitants of heaven—seemed for a time to be crowned with success. A vast number of the angels were seduced; but Satan's apparent triumph resulted in defeat and loss, separation from God, and banishment from heaven.

When the conflict was renewed upon the earth, Satan again won a seeming advantage. By transgression, man became his captive, and man's kingdom also was betrayed into the hands of the archrebel. Now the way seemed open for Satan to establish an independent kingdom, and to defy the authority of God and His Son. But the plan of salvation made it possible for man again to be brought into harmony with God, and to render obedience to His law, and for both man and the earth to be finally redeemed from the power of the wicked one.

Again Satan was defeated, and again he resorted to deception, in the hope of converting his defeat into a victory. To stir up rebellion in the fallen race, he now represented God as unjust in having permitted man to transgress His law. "Why," said the artful tempter, "when God knew what would be the result, did He permit man to be placed on trial, to sin, and bring in misery and death?" And the children of Adam, forgetful of the long-suffering mercy that had granted man another trial, regardless of the amazing, the awful sacrifice which his rebellion had cost the King of heaven, gave ear to the tempter, and murmured against the only Being who could save them from the destructive power of Satan.

There are thousands today echoing the same rebellious complaint against God. They do not see that to deprive man of the freedom of choice would be to rob him of his prerogative as an intelligent being, and make him a mere automaton. It is not God's purpose to coerce the will.

332 Man was created a free moral agent. Like the inhabitants of all other worlds, he must be subjected to the test of obedience; but he is never brought into such a position that yielding to evil becomes a matter of necessity. No temptation or trial is permitted to come to him which he is unable to resist. God made such ample provision that man need never have been defeated in the conflict with Satan.

As men increased upon the earth, almost the whole world joined the ranks of rebellion. Once more Satan seemed to have gained the victory. But omnipotent power again cut short the working of iniquity, and the earth was cleansed by the Flood from its moral pollution.

Says the prophet, "When Thy judgments are in the earth, the inhabitants of the world will learn righteousness. Let favor be showed to the wicked, yet will he not learn righteousness, . . . and will not behold the majesty of Jehovah." Isaiah 26:9, 10. Thus it was after the Flood. Released from His judgments, the inhabitants of the earth again rebelled against the Lord. Twice God's covenant and His statutes had been rejected by the world. Both the people before the Flood and the descendants of Noah cast off the divine authority. Then God entered into covenant with Abraham, and took to Himself a people to become the depositaries of His law. To seduce and destroy this people, Satan began at once to lay his snares. The children of Jacob were tempted to contract marriages with the heathen and to worship their idols. But Joseph was faithful to God, and his fidelity was a constant testimony to the true faith. It was to quench this light that Satan worked through the envy of Joseph's brothers to cause him to be sold as a slave in a heathen land. God overruled events, however, so that the knowledge of Himself should be given to the people of Egypt. Both in the house of Potiphar and in the prison Joseph received an education and training that, with the fear of God, prepared him for his high position as prime minister of the nation. From the palace of the Pharaohs his influence was felt throughout the land, and the knowledge of God spread far and wide. The Israelites in Egypt also became prosperous and wealthy, and such as were true to God exerted a widespread influence. The idolatrous priests were filled with alarm as they saw the new religion finding favor. Inspired by Satan with his own enmity toward the God of heaven, they set themselves to quench the light. To the priests was committed the education of the heir to the throne, and it 333 was this spirit of determined opposition to God and zeal for idolatry that molded the character of the future monarch, and led to cruelty and oppression toward the Hebrews.

During the forty years after the flight of Moses from Egypt, idolatry seemed to have conquered. Year by year the hopes of the Israelites grew fainter. Both king and people exulted in their power, and mocked the God of Israel. This grew until it culminated in the Pharaoh who was confronted by Moses. When the Hebrew leader came before the king with a message from "Jehovah, God of Israel," it was not ignorance of the true God, but defiance of His power, that prompted the answer, "Who is Jehovah, that I should obey His voice? . . . . I know not Jehovah." From first to last, Pharaoh's opposition to the divine command was not the result of ignorance, but of hatred and defiance.

Though the Egyptians had so long rejected the knowledge of God, the Lord still gave them opportunity for repentance. In the days of Joseph, Egypt had been an asylum for Israel; God had been honored in the kindness shown His people; and now the long-suffering One, slow to anger, and full of compassion, gave each judgment time to do its work; the Egyptians, cursed through the very objects they had worshiped, had evidence of the power of Jehovah, and all who would, might submit to God and escape His judgments. The bigotry and stubbornness of the king resulted in spreading the knowledge of God, and bringing many of the Egyptians to give themselves to His service.

It was because the Israelites were so disposed to connect themselves with the heathen and imitate their idolatry that God had permitted them to go down into Egypt, where the influence of Joseph was widely felt, and where circumstances were favorable for them to remain a distinct people. Here also the gross idolatry of the Egyptians and their cruelty and oppression during the latter part of the Hebrew sojourn should have inspired in them an abhorrence of idolatry, and should have led them to flee for refuge to the God of their fathers. This very providence Satan made a means to serve his purpose, darkening the minds of the Israelites and leading them to imitate the practices of their heathen masters. On account of the superstitious veneration in which animals were held by the Egyptians, the Hebrews were not permitted, during their bondage, to present the sacrificial offerings. Thus their minds were not directed by this service to the great Sacrifice, and their faith was weakened. When the time came for Israel's deliverance, Satan set himself to resist the purposes of God. It was his determination that that great people, numbering more than two million souls, should be held in ignorance and superstition. The people whom God had promised to bless and multiply, to make a power in the earth, and through whom He was to reveal the knowledge of His will—the people whom He was to make the keepers of His law—this very people Satan was seeking to keep in obscurity and bondage, that he might obliterate from their minds the remembrance of God.

When the miracles were wrought before the king, Satan was on the ground to counteract their influence and prevent Pharaoh from acknowledging the supremacy of God and obeying His mandate. Satan wrought to the utmost of his power to counterfeit the work of God and resist His will. The only result was to prepare the way for greater exhibitions of the divine power and glory, and to make more apparent, both to the Israelites and to all Egypt, the existence and sovereignty of the true and living God.

God delivered Israel with the mighty manifestations of His power, and with judgments upon all the gods of Egypt. "He brought forth His people with joy, and His chosen with gladness: . . . that they might observe His statutes, and keep His laws." Psalm 105:43-45. He rescued them from their servile state, that He might bring them to a good land—a land which in His providence had been prepared for them as a refuge from their enemies, where they might dwell under the shadow of His wings. He would bring them to Himself, and encircle them in His everlasting arms; and in return for all His goodness and mercy to them they were required to have no other gods before Him, the living God, and to exalt His name and make it glorious in the earth.

During the bondage in Egypt many of the Israelites had, to a great extent, lost the knowledge of God's law, and had mingled its precepts with heathen customs and traditions. God brought them to Sinai, and there with His own voice declared His law.

Satan and evil angels were on the ground. Even while God was proclaiming His law to His people, Satan was plotting to tempt them to sin. This people whom God had chosen, he would wrench away, in the very face of Heaven. By leading them into idolatry, he would destroy the efficacy of all worship; for how can man be elevated by adoring what is no higher than himself and may be symbolized by his own handiwork? If men could become so blinded to the power, the majesty, and the glory of the infinite God as to represent Him by a graven image, or even by a beast or reptile; if they could so forget their own divine relationship, formed in the image of their Maker as to bow down to these revolting and senseless objects—then the way was open for foul license; the evil passions of the heart would be unrestrained, and Satan would have full sway.

At the very foot of Sinai, Satan began to execute his plans for overthrowing the law of God, thus carrying forward the same work he had begun in heaven. During the forty days while Moses was in the mount with God, Satan was busy exciting doubt, apostasy, and rebellion. While God was writing down His law, to be committed to His covenant people, the Israelites, denying their loyalty to Jehovah, were demanding gods of gold! When Moses came from the awful presence of the divine glory, with the precepts of the law which they had pledged themselves to obey, he found them, in open defiance of its commands, bowing in adoration before a golden image.

By leading Israel to this daring insult and blasphemy to Jehovah, Satan had planned to cause their ruin. Since they had proved themselves to be so utterly degraded, so lost to all sense of the privileges and blessings that God

334

335

had offered them, and to their own solemn and repeated pledges of loyalty, the Lord would, he believed, divorce them from Himself and devote them to destruction. Thus would be secured the extinction of the seed of Abraham, that seed of promise that was to preserve the knowledge of the living God, and through whom He was to come—the true Seed, that was to conquer Satan. The great rebel had planned to destroy Israel, and thus thwart the purposes of God. But again he was defeated. Sinful as they were, the people of Israel were not destroyed. While those who stubbornly ranged themselves on the side of Satan were cut off, the people, humbled and repentant, were mercifully pardoned. The history of this sin was to stand as a perpetual testimony to the guilt and punishment of idolatry, and the justice and long-suffering mercy of God.

The whole universe had been witness to the scenes at Sinai. In the working out of the two 336 administrations was seen the contrast between the government of God and that of Satan. Again the sinless inhabitants of other worlds beheld the results of Satan's apostasy, and the kind of government he would have established in heaven had he been permitted to bear sway.

By causing men to violate the second commandment, Satan aimed to degrade their conceptions of the Divine Being. By setting aside the fourth, he would cause them to forget God altogether. God's claim to reverence and worship, above the gods of the heathen, is based upon the fact that He is the Creator, and that to Him all other beings owe their existence. Thus it is presented in the Bible. Says the prophet Jeremiah: "The Lord is the true God, He is the living God, and an everlasting King. . . . The gods that have not made the heavens and the earth, even they shall perish from the earth, and from under these heavens. He hath made the earth by His power, He hath established the world by His wisdom, and hath stretched out the heavens by His discretion." "Every man is brutish in his knowledge: every founder is confounded by the graven image: for his molten image is falsehood, and there is no breath in them. They are vanity, and the work of errors: in the time of their visitation they shall perish. The portion of Jacob is not like them: for He is the former of all things." Jeremiah 10:10-12, 14-16. The Sabbath, as a memorial of God's creative power, points to Him as the maker of the heavens and the earth. Hence it is a constant witness to His existence and a reminder of His greatness, His wisdom, and His love. Had the Sabbath always been sacredly observed, there could never have been an atheist or an idolater.

The Sabbath institution, which originated in Eden, is as old as the world itself. It was observed by all the patriarchs, from creation down. During the bondage in Egypt, the Israelites were forced by their taskmasters to violate the Sabbath, and to a great extent they lost the knowledge of its sacredness. When the law was proclaimed at Sinai the very first words of the fourth commandment were, "Remember the Sabbath day, to keep it holy"—showing that the Sabbath was not then instituted; we are pointed back for its origin to creation. In order to obliterate God from the minds of men, Satan aimed to tear down this great memorial. If men could be led to forget their Creator, they would make no effort to resist the power of evil, and Satan would be sure of his prey.

Satan's enmity against God's law had 337 impelled him to war against every precept of the Decalogue. To the great principle of love and loyalty to God, the Father of all, the principle of filial love and obedience is closely related. Contempt for parental authority will soon lead to contempt for the authority of God. Hence Satan's efforts to lessen the obligation of the fifth commandment. Among heathen peoples the principle enjoined in this precept was little heeded. In many nations parents were abandoned or put to death as soon as age had rendered them incapable of providing for themselves. In the family the mother was treated with little respect, and upon the death of her husband she was required to submit to the authority of her eldest son. Filial obedience was enjoined by Moses; but as the Israelites departed from the Lord, the fifth commandment, with others, came to be disregarded.

Satan was "a murderer from the beginning" (John 8:44); and as soon as he had obtained power over the human race, he not only prompted them to hate and slay one another, but, the more boldly to defy the authority of God, he made the violation of the sixth commandment a part of their religion.

By perverted conceptions of divine attributes, heathen nations were led to believe human sacrifices necessary to secure the favor of their deities; and the most horrible cruelties have been perpetrated under the various forms of idolatry. Among these was the practice of causing their children to pass through the fire before their idols. When one of them came through this ordeal unharmed, the people believed that their offerings were accepted; the one thus delivered was regarded as specially favored by the gods, was loaded with benefits, and ever afterward held in high esteem; and however aggravated his crimes, he was never punished. But should one be burned in passing through the fire, his fate was sealed; it was believed that the anger of the gods could be appeased only by taking the life of the victim, and he was accordingly offered as a sacrifice. In times of great apostasy these abominations prevailed, to some extent, among the Israelites.

The violation of the seventh commandment

also was early practiced in the name of religion. The most licentious and abominable rites were made a part of the heathen worship. The gods themselves were represented as impure, and their worshipers gave the rein to the baser passions. Unnatural vices prevailed and the religious festivals were characterized by universal and open impurity.

Polygamy was practiced at an early date. It was one of the sins that brought the wrath of God upon the antediluvian world. Yet after the Flood it again became widespread. It was Satan's studied effort to pervert the marriage institution, to weaken its obligations and lessen its sacredness; for in no surer way could he deface the image of God in man and open the door to misery and vice.

From the opening of the great controversy it has been Satan's purpose to misrepresent God's character and to excite rebellion against His law, and this work appears to be crowned with success. The multitudes give ear to Satan's deceptions and set themselves against God. But amid the working of evil, God's purposes move steadily forward to their accomplishment; to all created intelligences He is making manifest His justice and benevolence. Through Satan's temptations the whole human race have become transgressors of God's law, but by the sacrifice of His Son a way is opened whereby they may return to God. Through the grace of Christ they may be enabled to render obedience to the Father's law. Thus in every age, from the midst of apostasy and rebellion, God gathers out a people that are true to Him—a people "in whose heart is His law." Isaiah 51:7.

It was by deception that Satan seduced angels; thus he has in all ages carried forward his work among men, and he will continue this policy to the last. Should he openly profess to be warring against God and His law, men would beware; but he disguises himself, and mixes truth with error. The most dangerous falsehoods are those that are mingled with truth. It is thus that errors are received that captivate and ruin the soul. By this means Satan carries the world with him. But a day is coming when his triumph will be forever ended.

God's dealings with rebellion will result in fully unmasking the work that has so long been carried on under cover. The results of Satan's rule, the fruits of setting aside the divine statutes, will be laid open to the view of all created intelligences. The law of God will stand fully vindicated. It will be seen that all the dealings of God have been conducted with reference to the eternal good of His people, and the good of all the worlds that He has created. Satan himself, in the presence of the witnessing universe, will confess the justice of God's government and the righteousness of His law.

The time is not far distant when God will arise to vindicate His insulted authority. "The Lord cometh out of His place to punish the inhabitants of the earth for their iniquity." Isaiah 26:21. "But who may abide the day of His coming? and who shall stand when He appeareth?" Malachi 3:2. The people of Israel, because of their sinfulness, were forbidden to approach the mount when God was about to descend upon it to proclaim His law, lest they should be consumed by the burning glory of His presence. If such manifestations of His power marked the place chosen for the proclamation of God's law, how terrible must be His tribunal when He comes for the execution of these sacred statutes. How will those who have trampled upon His authority endure His glory in the great day of final retribution? The terrors of Sinai were to represent to the people the scenes of the judgment. The sound of a trumpet summoned Israel to meet with God. The voice of the Archangel and the trump of God shall summon, from the whole earth, both the living and the dead to the presence of their Judge. The Father and the Son, attended by a multitude of angels, were present upon the mount. At the great judgment day Christ will come "in the glory of His Father with His angels." Matthew 16:27. He shall then sit upon the throne of His glory, and before Him shall be gathered all nations.

When the divine Presence was manifested upon Sinai, the glory of the Lord was like devouring fire in the sight of all Israel. But when Christ shall come in glory with His holy angels the whole earth shall be ablaze with the terrible light of His presence. "Our God shall come, and shall not keep silence: a fire shall devour before Him, and it shall be very tempestuous round about Him. He shall call to the heavens from above, and to the earth, that He may judge His people." Psalm 50:3, 4. A fiery stream shall issue and come forth from before Him, which shall cause the elements to melt with fervent heat, the earth also, and the works that are therein shall be burned up. "The Lord Jesus shall be revealed from heaven with His mighty angels, in flaming fire taking vengeance on them that know not God, and that obey not the gospel." 2 Thessalonians 1:7, 8.

Never since man was created had there been witnessed such a manifestation of divine power as when the law was proclaimed from Sinai. "The earth shook, the heavens also dropped at the presence of God: even Sinai itself was moved at the presence of God, the God of Israel." Psalm 68:8. Amid the most terrific convulsions of nature the voice of God, like a trumpet, was heard from the cloud. The mountain was shaken from base to summit, and the hosts of Israel, pale and trembling with terror, lay upon their faces upon the earth. He whose voice then shook the earth has declared, "Yet once more I shake not the earth only, but also heaven." Hebrews 12:26. Says the Scripture, "The Lord shall roar from on high, and utter His voice from His holy habitation;" "and the heavens and the earth shall shake." Jeremiah 25:30; Joel 3:16. In that great coming day, the heaven itself shall depart "as a scroll when it is rolled together." Revelation 6:14. And every mountain and island shall be moved out of its place. "The earth shall reel to and fro like a drunkard, and shall be removed like a cottage; and the transgression thereof shall be heavy upon it; and it shall fall, and not rise again." Isaiah 24:20.

"Therefore shall all hands be faint," all faces shall be "turned into paleness," "and every man's heart shall melt. And they shall be afraid: pangs and sorrows shall take hold of them." "And I will punish the world for their evil," saith the Lord, "and I will cause the arrogancy of the proud to cease, and will lay low the haughtiness of the terrible." Isaiah 13:7, 8, 11; Jeremiah 30:6.

When Moses came from the divine Presence in the mount, where he had received the tables of the testimony, guilty Israel could not endure the light that glorified his countenance. How much less can transgressors look upon the Son of God when He shall appear in the glory of His Father, surrounded by all the heavenly host, to execute judgment upon the transgressors of His law and the rejecters of His atonement. Those who have disregarded the law of God and trodden under foot the blood of Christ, "the kings of the earth, and the great men, and the rich men, and the chief captains, and the mighty men," shall hide themselves "in the dens and in the 341 rocks of the mountains," and they shall say to the mountains and rocks, "Fall on us, and hide us from the face of Him that sitteth on the throne, and from the wrath of the Lamb: for the great day of His wrath is come; and who shall be able to stand?" Revelation 6:15-17. "In that day a man shall cast his idols of silver, and his idols of gold, . . . to the moles and to the bats; to go into the clefts of the rocks, and into the tops of the ragged rocks, for fear of the Lord, and for the glory of His majesty, when He ariseth to shake terribly the earth." Isaiah 2:20, 21.

Then it will be seen that Satan's rebellion against God has resulted in ruin to himself and to all that chose to become his subjects. He has represented that great good would result from transgression; but it will be seen that "the wages of sin is death." "For, behold, the day cometh, that shall burn as an oven; and all the proud, yea, and all that do wickedly, shall be stubble: and the day that cometh shall burn them up, saith the Lord of hosts, that it shall leave them neither root nor branch." Malachi 4:1. Satan, the root of every sin, and all evil workers, who are his branches, shall be utterly cut off. An end will be made of sin, with all the woe and ruin that have resulted from it. Says the psalmist,

"Thou hast destroyed the wicked, thou hast put out their name forever and ever. O thou enemy, destructions are come to a perpetual end." Psalm 9:5, 6.

But amid the tempest of divine judgment the children of God will have no cause for fear. "The Lord will be the hope of His people, and the strength of the children of Israel." Joel 3:16. The day that brings terror and destruction to the transgressors of God's law will bring to the obedient "joy unspeakable and full of glory." "Gather My saints together unto Me," saith the Lord, "those that have made a covenant with Me by sacrifice. And the heavens shall declare His righteousness: for God is Judge Himself."

"Then shall ye return, and discern between the righteous and the wicked, between him that serveth God and him that serveth Him not." Malachi 3:18. "Hearken unto Me, ye that know righteousness, *the people in whose heart is My law.*" "Behold, I have taken out of thine hand the cup of trembling, . . . thou shalt no more drink it again." "I, even I, am He that comforteth you." Isaiah 51:7, 22, 12. "For the mountains shall depart, and the hills be removed; but My kindness shall not depart from thee, neither 342 shall the covenant of My peace be removed, saith the Lord that hath mercy on thee." Isaiah 54:10.

The great plan of redemption results in fully bringing back the world into God's favor. All that was lost by sin is restored. Not only man but the earth is redeemed, to be the eternal abode of the obedient. For six thousand years Satan has struggled to maintain possession of the earth. Now God's original purpose in its creation is accomplished. "The saints of the Most High shall take the kingdom, and possess the kingdom forever, even forever and ever." Daniel 7:18.

"From the rising of the sun unto the going down of the same the Lord's name is to be praised." Psalm 113:3. "In that day shall there be one Lord, and His name one." "And Jehovah shall be king over all the earth." Zechariah 14:9. Says the Scripture, "Forever, O Lord, Thy word is settled in heaven." "All His commandments are sure. They stand fast forever and ever." Psalms 119:89; 111:7, 8. The sacred statutes which Satan has hated and sought to destroy, will be honored throughout a sinless universe. And "as the earth bringeth forth her bud, and as the garden causeth the things that are sown in it to spring forth; so the Lord God will cause righteousness and praise to spring forth before all nations." Isaiah 61:11.

343

30

The Tabernacle and Its Services

The command was communicated to Moses while in the mount with God, "Let them make Me a sanctuary; that I may dwell among them;" and full directions were given for the construction of the tabernacle. By their apostasy the Israelites forfeited the blessing of the divine Presence, and for the time rendered impossible the erection of a sanctuary for God among them. But after they were again taken into favor with Heaven, the great leader proceeded to execute the divine command.

Chosen men were especially endowed by God with skill and wisdom for the construction of the sacred building. God Himself gave to Moses the plan of that structure, with particular directions as to its size and form, the materials to be employed, and every article of furniture which it was to contain. The holy places made with hands were to be "figures of the true," "patterns of things in the heavens" (Hebrews 9:24, 23)—a miniature representation of the heavenly temple where Christ, our great High Priest, after offering His life as a sacrifice, was to minister in the sinner's behalf. God presented before Moses in the mount a view of the heavenly sanctuary, and commanded him to make all things according to the pattern shown him. All these directions were carefully recorded by Moses, who communicated them to the leaders of the people.

For the building of the sanctuary great and expensive preparations were necessary; a large amount of the most precious and costly material was required; yet the Lord accepted only freewill offerings. "Of every man that giveth it willingly with his heart ye shall take My offering" was the divine command repeated by Moses to the congregation. Devotion to God and a spirit of sacrifice were the first requisites in preparing a dwelling place for the Most High.

344 All the people responded with one accord. "They came, every one whose heart stirred him up, and every one whom his spirit made willing, and they brought the Lord's offering to the work of the tabernacle of the congregation, and for all His service, and for the holy garments. And they came, both men and women, as many as were willinghearted, and brought bracelets, and earrings, and rings, and tablets, all jewels of gold: and every man that offered, offered an offering of gold unto the Lord."

"And every man with whom was found blue, and purple, and scarlet, and fine linen, and goats' hair, and rams' skins dyed red, and sealskins, brought them. Everyone that did offer an offering of silver and brass brought the Lord's offering: and every man, with whom was found acacia wood for any work of the service, brought it.

"And all the women that were wisehearted did spin with their hands, and brought that which they had spun, the blue, and the purple, the scarlet, and the fine linen. And all the women whose heart stirred them up in wisdom spun the goats' hair.

"And the rulers brought the onyx stones, and the stones to be set, for the ephod, and for the breastplate; and the spice, and the oil; for the light, and for the anointing oil, and for the sweet incense." Exodus 35:23-28, R.V.

While the building of the sanctuary was in progress the people, old and young—men, women, and children—continued to bring their offerings, until those in charge of the work found that they had enough, and even more than could be used. And Moses caused to be proclaimed throughout the camp, "Let neither man nor woman make any more work for the offering of the sanctuary. So the people were restrained from bringing." The murmurings of the Israelites and the visitations of God's judgments because of their sins are recorded as a warning to after-generations. And their devotion, their zeal and liberality, are an example worthy of imitation. All who love the worship of God and prize the blessing of His sacred presence will manifest the same spirit of sacrifice in preparing a house where He may meet with them. They will desire to bring to the Lord an offering of the very best that they possess. A house built for God should not be left in debt, for He is thereby dishonored. An amount sufficient to accomplish the work should be freely given, that the workmen may be able to say, as 347 did the builders of the tabernacle, "Bring no more offerings."

The tabernacle was so constructed that it could be taken apart and borne with the Israelites in all their journeyings. It was therefore small, being not more than fifty-five feet in length, and eighteen in breadth and height. Yet it was a magnificent structure. The wood employed for the building and its furniture was that of the acacia tree, which was less subject to decay than any other to be obtained at Sinai. The walls consisted of upright boards, set in silver sockets, and held firm by pillars and connecting bars; and all were overlaid with gold, giving to the building the appearance of solid gold. The roof was formed of four sets of curtains, the innermost of "fine twined linen, and blue, and purple, and scarlet: with cherubim of cunning work;" the other three respectively were of goats' hair, rams' skins dyed red, and

This chapter is based on Exodus 25 to 40; Leviticus 4 and 16.

sealskins, so arranged as to afford complete protection.

The building was divided into two apartments by a rich and beautiful curtain, or veil, suspended from gold-plated pillars; and a similar veil closed the entrance of the first apartment. These, like the inner covering, which formed the ceiling, were of the most gorgeous colors, blue, purple, and scarlet, beautifully arranged, while inwrought with threads of gold and silver were cherubim to represent the angelic host who are connected with the work of the heavenly sanctuary and who are ministering spirits to the people of God on earth.

The sacred tent was enclosed in an open space called the court, which was surrounded by hangings, or screens, of fine linen, suspended from pillars of brass. The entrance to this enclosure was at the eastern end. It was closed by curtains of costly material and beautiful workmanship, though inferior to those of the sanctuary. The hangings of the court being only about half as high as the walls of the tabernacle, the building could be plainly seen by the people without. In the court, and nearest the entrance, stood the brazen altar of burnt offering. Upon this altar were consumed all the sacrifices made by fire unto the Lord, and its horns were sprinkled with the atoning blood. Between the altar and the door of the tabernacle was the laver, which was also of brass, made from the mirrors that had been the freewill offering of the women of Israel. At the laver the priests were to wash 348 their hands and their feet whenever they went into the sacred apartments, or approached the altar to offer a burnt offering unto the Lord.

In the first apartment, or holy place, were the table of shewbread, the candlestick, or lampstand, and the altar of incense. The table of shewbread stood on the north. With its ornamental crown, it was overlaid with pure gold. On this table the priests were each Sabbath to place twelve cakes, arranged in two piles, and sprinkled with frankincense. The loaves that were removed, being accounted holy, were to be eaten by the priests. On the south was the seven-branched candlestick, with its seven lamps. Its branches were ornamented with exquisitely wrought flowers, resembling lilies, and the whole was made from one solid piece of gold. There being no windows in the tabernacle, the lamps were never all extinguished at one time, but shed their light by day and by night. Just before the veil separating the holy place from the most holy and the immediate presence of God, stood the golden altar of incense. Upon this altar the priest was to burn incense every morning and evening; its horns were touched with the blood of the sin offering, and it was sprinkled with blood upon the great Day of Atonement. The fire upon this altar was kindled by God Himself and was sacredly cherished.

Day and night the holy incense diffused its fragrance throughout the sacred apartments, and without, far around the tabernacle.

Beyond the inner veil was the holy of holies, where centered the symbolic service of atonement and intercession, and which formed the connecting link between heaven and earth. In this apartment was the ark, a chest of acacia wood, overlaid within and without with gold, and having a crown of gold about the top. It was made as a depository for the tables of stone, upon which God Himself had inscribed the Ten Commandments. Hence it was called the ark of God's testament, or the ark of the covenant, since the Ten Commandments were the basis of the covenant made between God and Israel.

The cover of the sacred chest was called the mercy seat. This was wrought of one solid piece of gold, and was surmounted by golden cherubim, one standing on each end. One wing of each angel was stretched forth on high, while the other was folded over the body (see Ezekiel 1:11) in token of reverence and humility. The position of the cherubim, with their faces turned toward each other, and looking reverently 349 downward toward the ark, represented the reverence with which the heavenly host regard the law of God and their interest in the plan of redemption.

Above the mercy seat was the Shekinah, the manifestation of the divine Presence; and from between the cherubim, God made known His will. Divine messages were sometimes communicated to the high priest by a voice from the cloud. Sometimes a light fell upon the angel at the right, to signify approval or acceptance, or a shadow or cloud rested upon the one at the left to reveal disapproval or rejection.

The law of God, enshrined within the ark, was the great rule of righteousness and judgment. That law pronounced death upon the transgressor; but above the law was the mercy seat, upon which the presence of God was revealed, and from which, by virtue of the atonement, pardon was granted to the repentant sinner. Thus in the work of Christ for our redemption, symbolized by the sanctuary service, "mercy and truth are met together; righteousness and peace have kissed each other." Psalm 85:10.

No language can describe the glory of the scene presented within the sanctuary—the gold-plated walls reflecting the light from the golden candlestick, the brilliant hues of the richly embroidered curtains with their shining angels, the table, and the altar of incense, glittering with gold; beyond the second veil the sacred ark, with its mystic cherubim, and above it the holy Shekinah, the visible manifestation of Jehovah's presence; all but a dim reflection of the glories of the temple of God in heaven, the great center of the work for man's redemption.

A period of about half a year was occupied in the building of the tabernacle. When it was completed, Moses examined all the work of the builders, comparing it with the pattern shown him in the mount and the directions he had received from God. "As the Lord had commanded, even so had they done it: and Moses blessed them." With eager interest the multitudes of Israel crowded around to look upon the sacred structure. While they were contemplating the scene with reverent satisfaction, the pillar of cloud floated over the sanctuary and, descending, enveloped it. "And the glory of the Lord filled the tabernacle." There was a revealing of the divine majesty, and for a time even Moses 350 could not enter. With deep emotion the people beheld the token that the work of their hands was accepted. There were no loud demonstrations of rejoicing. A solemn awe rested upon all. But the gladness of their hearts welled up in tears of joy, and they murmured low, earnest words of gratitude that God had condescended to abide with them.

By divine direction the tribe of Levi was set apart for the service of the sanctuary. In the earliest times every man was the priest of his own household. In the days of Abraham the priesthood was regarded as the birthright of the eldest son. Now, instead of the first-born of all Israel, the Lord accepted the tribe of Levi for the work of the sanctuary. By this signal honor He manifested His approval of their fidelity, both in adhering to His service and in executing His judgments when Israel apostatized in the worship of the golden calf. The priesthood, however, was restricted to the family of Aaron. Aaron and his sons alone were permitted to minister before the Lord; the rest of the tribe were entrusted with the charge of the tabernacle and its furniture, and they were to attend upon the priests in their ministration, but they were not to sacrifice, to burn incense, or to see the holy things till they were covered.

In accordance with their office, a special dress was appointed for the priests. "Thou shalt make holy garments for Aaron thy brother, for glory and for beauty," was the divine direction to Moses. The robe of the common priest was of white linen, and woven in one piece. It extended nearly to the feet and was confined about the waist by a white linen girdle embroidered in blue, purple, and red. A linen turban, or miter, completed his outer costume. Moses at the burning bush was directed to put off his sandals, for the ground whereon he stood was holy. So the priests were not to enter the sanctuary with shoes upon their feet. Particles of dust cleaving to them would desecrate the holy place. They were to leave their shoes in the court before entering the sanctuary, and also to wash both their hands and their feet before ministering in the tabernacle or at the altar of burnt offering.

Thus was constantly taught the lesson that all defilement must be put away from those who would approach into the presence of God.

The garments of the high priest were of costly material and beautiful workmanship, befitting his exalted station. In addition to the linen dress 351 of the common priest, he wore a robe of blue, also woven in one piece. Around the skirt it was ornamented with golden bells, and pomegranates of blue, purple, and scarlet. Outside of this was the ephod, a shorter garment of gold, blue, purple, scarlet, and white. It was confined by a girdle of the same colors, beautifully wrought. The ephod was sleeveless, and on its gold-embroidered shoulder pieces were set two onyx stones, bearing the names of the twelve tribes of Israel.

Over the ephod was the breastplate, the most sacred of the priestly vestments. This was of the same material as the ephod. It was in the form of a square, measuring a span, and was suspended from the shoulders by a cord of blue from golden rings. The border was formed of a variety of precious stones, the same that form the twelve foundations of the City of God. Within the border were twelve stones set in gold, arranged in rows of four, and, like those in the shoulder pieces, engraved with the names of the tribes. The Lord's direction was, "Aaron shall bear the names of the children of Israel in the breastplate of judgment upon his heart, when he goeth in unto the holy place, for a memorial before the Lord continually." Exodus 28:29. So Christ, the great High Priest, pleading His blood before the Father in the sinner's behalf, bears upon His heart the name of every repentant, believing soul. Says the psalmist, "I am poor and needy; yet the Lord thinketh upon me." Psalm 40:17.

At the right and left of the breastplate were two large stones of great brilliancy. These were known as the Urim and Thummim. By them the will of God was made known through the high priest. When questions were brought for decision before the Lord, a halo of light encircling the precious stone at the right was a token of the divine consent or approval, while a cloud shadowing the stone at the left was an evidence of denial or disapprobation.

The miter of the high priest consisted of the white linen turban, having attached to it by a lace of blue, a gold plate bearing the inscription, "Holiness to Jehovah." Everything connected with the apparel and deportment of the priests was to be such as to impress the beholder with a sense of the holiness of God, the sacredness of His worship, and the purity required of those who came into His presence.

Not only the sanctuary itself, but the ministration of the priests, was to "serve unto the example and shadow of heavenly things." Hebrews 352 8:5. Thus it was of great importance; and the

Lord, through Moses, gave the most definite and explicit instruction concerning every point of this typical service. The ministration of the sanctuary consisted of two divisions, a daily and a yearly service. The daily service was performed at the altar of burnt offering in the court of the tabernacle and in the holy place; while the yearly service was in the most holy.

No mortal eye but that of the high priest was to look upon the inner apartment of the sanctuary. Only once a year could the priest enter there, and that after the most careful and solemn preparation. With trembling he went in before God, and the people in reverent silence awaited his return, their hearts uplifted in earnest prayer for the divine blessing. Before the mercy seat the high priest made the atonement for Israel; and in the cloud of glory, God met with him. His stay here beyond the accustomed time filled them with fear, lest because of their sins or his own he had been slain by the glory of the Lord.

The daily service consisted of the morning and evening burnt offering, the offering of sweet incense on the golden altar, and the special offerings for individual sins. And there were also offerings for sabbaths, new moons, and special feasts.

Every morning and evening a lamb of a year old was burned upon the altar, with its appropriate meat offering, thus symbolizing the daily consecration of the nation to Jehovah, and their constant dependence upon the atoning blood of Christ. God expressly directed that every offering presented for the service of the sanctuary should be "without blemish." Exodus 12:5. The priests were to examine all animals brought as a sacrifice, and were to reject every one in which a defect was discovered. Only an offering "without blemish" could be a symbol of His perfect purity who was to offer Himself as "a lamb without blemish and without spot." 1 Peter 1:19. The apostle Paul points to these sacrifices as an illustration of what the followers of Christ are to become. He says, "I beseech you therefore, brethren, by the mercies of God, that ye present your bodies a living sacrifice, holy, acceptable unto God, which is your reasonable service." Romans 12:1. We are to give ourselves to the service of God, and we should seek to make the offering as nearly perfect as possible. God will not be pleased with anything less than the best we can offer. Those who love Him with all the heart, will desire to give Him the best service of the life, and they will be constantly seeking to bring every power of their being into harmony with the laws that will promote their ability to do His will.

353 In the offering of incense the priest was brought more directly into the presence of God than in any other act of the daily ministration. As the inner veil of the sanctuary did not extend to the top of the building, the glory of God, which was manifested above the mercy seat, was partially visible from the first apartment. When the priest offered incense before the Lord, he looked toward the ark; and as the cloud of incense arose, the divine glory descended upon the mercy seat and filled the most holy place, and often so filled both apartments that the priest was obliged to retire to the door of the tabernacle. As in that typical service the priest looked by faith to the mercy seat which he could not see, so the people of God are now to direct their prayers to Christ, their great High Priest, who, unseen by human vision, is pleading in their behalf in the sanctuary above.

The incense, ascending with the prayers of Israel, represents the merits and intercession of Christ, His perfect righteousness, which through faith is imputed to His people, and which can alone make the worship of sinful beings acceptable to God. Before the veil of the most holy place was an altar of perpetual intercession, before the holy, an altar of continual atonement. By blood and by incense God was to be approached—symbols pointing to the great Mediator, through whom sinners may approach Jehovah, and through whom alone mercy and salvation can be granted to the repentant, believing soul.

As the priests morning and evening entered the holy place at the time of incense, the daily sacrifice was ready to be offered upon the altar in the court without. This was a time of intense interest to the worshipers who assembled at the tabernacle. Before entering into the presence of God through the ministration of the priest, they were to engage in earnest searching of heart and confession of sin. They united in silent prayer, with their faces toward the holy place. Thus their petitions ascended with the cloud of incense, while faith laid hold upon the merits of the promised Saviour prefigured by the atoning sacrifice. The hours appointed for the morning and the evening sacrifice were regarded as 354 sacred, and they came to be observed as the set time for worship throughout the Jewish nation. And when in later times the Jews were scattered as captives in distant lands, they still at the appointed hour turned their faces toward Jerusalem and offered up their petitions to the God of Israel. In this custom Christians have an example for morning and evening prayer. While God condemns a mere round of ceremonies, without the spirit of worship, He looks with great pleasure upon those who love Him, bowing morning and evening to seek pardon for sins committed and to present their requests for needed blessings.

The shewbread was kept ever before the Lord as a perpetual offering. Thus it was a part of the daily sacrifice. It was called shewbread, or "bread of the presence," because it was ever before the face of the Lord. It was an acknowledgment of man's dependence upon God for both temporal and spiritual food, and that it is received only through the mediation of Christ. God had fed Israel in the wilderness with bread from heaven, and they were still dependent upon His bounty, both for temporal food and spiritual blessings. Both the manna and the shewbread pointed to Christ, the living Bread, who is ever in the presence of God for us. He Himself said, "I am the living Bread which came down from heaven." John 6:48-51. Frankincense was placed upon the loaves. When the bread was removed every Sabbath, to be replaced by fresh loaves, the frankincense was burned upon the altar as a memorial before God.

The most important part of the daily ministration was the service performed in behalf of individuals. The repentant sinner brought his offering to the door of the tabernacle, and, placing his hand upon the victim's head, confessed his sins, thus in figure transferring them from himself to the innocent sacrifice. By his own hand the animal was then slain, and the blood was carried by the priest into the holy place and sprinkled before the veil, behind which was the ark containing the law that the sinner had transgressed. By this ceremony the sin was, through the blood, transferred in figure to the sanctuary. In some cases the blood was not taken into the holy place;* but the flesh was then to be eaten by the priest, as Moses directed the sons of Aaron, saying, "God hath given it you to bear the iniquity of 355 the congregation." Leviticus 10:17. Both ceremonies alike symbolized the transfer of the sin from the penitent to the sanctuary.

Such was the work that went on day by day throughout the year. The sins of Israel being thus transferred to the sanctuary, the holy places were defiled, and a special work became necessary for the removal of the sins. God commanded that an atonement be made for each of the sacred apartments, as for the altar, to "cleanse it, and hallow it from the uncleanness of the children of Israel." Leviticus 16:19.

Once a year, on the great Day of Atonement, the priest entered the most holy place for the cleansing of the sanctuary. The work there performed completed the yearly round of ministration.

On the Day of Atonement two kids of the goats were brought to the door of the tabernacle, and lots were cast upon them, "one lot for the Lord, and the other lot for the scapegoat." The goat upon which the first lot fell was to be slain as a sin offering for the people. And the priest was to bring his blood within the veil, and sprinkle it upon the mercy seat. "And he shall make an atonement for the holy place, because of the uncleanness of the children of Israel, and because of their transgressions in all their sins: and so shall he do for the tabernacle of the con-

gregation, that remaineth among them in the midst of their uncleanness."

"And Aaron shall lay both his hands upon the head of the live goat, and confess over him all the iniquities of the children of Israel, and all their transgressions in all their sins, putting them upon the head of the goat, and shall send him away by the hand of a fit man into the wilderness: and the goat shall bear upon him all their iniquities unto a land not inhabited." Not until the goat had been thus sent away did the people regard themselves as freed from the burden of their sins. Every man was to afflict his soul while the work of atonement was going forward. All business was laid aside, and the whole congregation of Israel spent the day in solemn humiliation before God, with prayer, fasting, and deep searching of heart.

Important truths concerning the atonement were taught the people by this yearly service. In the sin offerings presented during the year, a substitute had been accepted in the sinner's stead; but the blood of the victim had not made full atonement for the sin. It had only provided a means by which the sin was transferred to the 356 sanctuary. By the offering of blood, the sinner acknowledged the authority of the law, confessed the guilt of his transgression, and expressed his faith in Him who was to take away the sin of the world; but he was not entirely released from the condemnation of the law. On the Day of Atonement the high priest, having taken an offering for the congregation, went into the most holy place with the blood and sprinkled it upon the mercy seat, above the tables of the law. Thus the claims of the law, which demanded the life of the sinner, were satisfied. Then in his character of mediator priest took the sins upon himself, and, leaving the sanctuary, he bore with him the burden of Israel's guilt. At the door of the tabernacle he laid his hands upon the head of the scapegoat and confessed over him "all the iniquities of the children of Israel, and all their transgressions in all their sins, putting them upon the head of the goat." And as the goat bearing these sins was sent away, they were, with him, regarded as forever separated from the people. Such was the service performed "unto the example and shadow of heavenly things." Hebrews 8:5.

As has been stated, the earthly sanctuary was built by Moses according to the pattern shown him in the mount. It was "a figure for the time then present, in which were offered both gifts and sacrifices;" its two holy places were "patterns of things in the heavens;" Christ, our great High Priest, is "a minister of the sanctuary, and of the true tabernacle, which the Lord pitched, and not man." Hebrews 9:9, 23; 8:2. As in vision the apostle John was granted a view of the temple of God in heaven, he beheld there "seven lamps of fire burning before the throne."

---

* See Appendix, Note 6.

He saw an angel "having a golden censer; and there was given unto him much incense, that he should offer it with the prayers of all saints upon the golden altar which was before the throne." Revelation 4:5; 8:3. Here the prophet was permitted to behold the first apartment of the sanctuary in heaven; and he saw there the "seven lamps of fire" and the "golden altar" represented by the golden candlestick and the altar of incense in the sanctuary on earth. Again, "the temple of God was opened" (Revelation 11:19), and he looked within the inner veil, upon the holy of holies. Here he beheld "the ark of His testament" (Revelation 11:19), represented by the sacred chest constructed by Moses to contain the law of God.

357 Moses made the earthly sanctuary, "according to the fashion that he had seen." Paul declares that "the tabernacle, and all the vessels of the ministry," when completed, were "the patterns of things in the heavens." Acts 7:44; Hebrews 9:21, 23. And John says that he saw the sanctuary in heaven. That sanctuary, in which Jesus ministers in our behalf, is the great original, of which the sanctuary built by Moses was a copy.

The heavenly temple, the abiding place of the King of kings, where "thousand thousands ministered unto Him, and ten thousand times ten thousand stood before Him" (Daniel 7:10), that temple filled with the glory of the eternal throne, where seraphim, its shining guardians, veil their faces in adoration—no earthly structure could represent its vastness and its glory. Yet important truths concerning the heavenly sanctuary and the great work there carried forward for man's redemption were to be taught by the earthly sanctuary and its services.

After His ascension, our Saviour was to begin His work as our High Priest. Says Paul, "Christ is not entered into the holy places made with hands, which are the figures of the true; but into heaven itself, now to appear in the presence of God for us." Hebrews 9:24. As Christ's ministration was to consist of two great divisions, each occupying a period of time and having a distinctive place in the heavenly sanctuary, so the typical ministration consisted of two divisions, the daily and the yearly service, and to each a department of the tabernacle was devoted.

As Christ at His ascension appeared in the presence of God to plead His blood in behalf of penitent believers, so the priest in the daily ministration sprinkled the blood of the sacrifice in the holy place in the sinner's behalf.

The blood of Christ, while it was to release the repentant sinner from the condemnation of the law, was not to cancel the sin; it would stand on record in the sanctuary until the final atonement; so in the type the blood of the sin offering removed the sin from the penitent, but it rested in the sanctuary until the Day of Atonement.

In the great day of final award, the dead are to be "judged out of those things which were written in the books, according to their works." Revelation 20:12. Then by virtue of the atoning blood of Christ, the sins of all the truly penitent will be blotted from the books of heaven. Thus the sanctuary will be freed, or cleansed, from 358 the record of sin. In the type, this great work of atonement, or blotting out of sins, was represented by the services of the Day of Atonement—the cleansing of the earthly sanctuary, which was accomplished by the removal, by virtue of the blood of the sin offering, of the sins by which it had been polluted.

As in the final atonement the sins of the truly penitent are to be blotted from the records of heaven, no more to be remembered or come into mind, so in the type they were borne away into the wilderness, forever separated from the congregation.

Since Satan is the originator of sin, the direct instigator of all the sins that caused the death of the Son of God, justice demands that Satan shall suffer the final punishment. Christ's work for the redemption of men and the purification of the universe from sin will be closed by the removal of sin from the heavenly sanctuary and the placing of these sins upon Satan, who will bear the final penalty. So in the typical service, the yearly round of ministration closed with the purification of the sanctuary, and the confessing of the sins on the head of the scapegoat.

Thus in the ministration of the tabernacle, and of the temple that afterward took its place, the people were taught each day the great truths relative to Christ's death and ministration, and once each year their minds were carried forward to the closing events of the great controversy between Christ and Satan, the final purification of the universe from sin and sinners.

31

359

The Sin of Nadab and Abihu

After the dedication of the tabernacle, the priests were consecrated to their sacred office. These services occupied seven days, each marked by special ceremonies. On the eighth day they entered upon their ministration. Assisted by his sons, Aaron offered the sacrifices that God required, and he lifted up his hands and blessed the people. All had been done as God commanded, and He accepted the sacrifice, and revealed His glory in a remarkable manner; fire came from the Lord and consumed the offering upon the altar. The people looked upon this wonderful manifestation of divine power with awe and intense interest. They saw in it a token

This chapter is based on Leviticus 10:1-11.

of God's glory and favor, and they raised a universal shout of praise and adoration and fell on their faces as if in the immediate presence of Jehovah.

But soon afterward a sudden and terrible calamity fell upon the family of the high priest. At the hour of worship, as the prayers and praise of the people were ascending to God, two of the sons of Aaron took each his censer and burned fragrant incense thereon, to rise as a sweet odor before the Lord. But they transgressed His command by the use of "strange fire." For burning the incense they took common instead of the sacred fire which God Himself had kindled, and which He had commanded to be used for this purpose. For this sin a fire went out from the Lord and devoured them in the sight of the people.

Next to Moses and Aaron, Nadab and Abihu had stood highest in Israel. They had been especially honored by the Lord, having been permitted with the seventy elders to behold His glory in the mount. But their transgression was not therefore to be excused or lightly regarded. All this rendered their sin more grievous. Because men have received great light, because they have, like the princes of Israel, ascended to the mount, and been privileged to have communion 360 with God, and to dwell in the light of His glory, let them not flatter themselves that they can afterward sin with impunity, that because they have been thus honored, God will not be strict to punish their iniquity. This is a fatal deception. The great light and privileges bestowed require returns of virtue and holiness corresponding to the light given. Anything short of this, God cannot accept. Great blessings or privileges should never lull to security or carelessness. They should never give license to sin or cause the recipients to feel that God will not be exact with them. All the advantages which God has given are His means to throw ardor into the spirit, zeal into effort, and vigor into the carrying out of His holy will.

Nadab and Abihu had not in their youth been trained to habits of self-control. The father's yielding disposition, his lack of firmness for right, had led him to neglect the discipline of his children. His sons had been permitted to follow inclination. Habits of self-indulgence, long cherished, obtained a hold upon them which even the responsibility of the most sacred office had not power to break. They had not been taught to respect the authority of their father, and they did not realize the necessity of exact obedience to the requirements of God. Aaron's mistaken indulgence of his sons prepared them to become the subjects of the divine judgments.

God designed to teach the people that they must approach Him with reverence and awe, and in His own appointed manner. He cannot accept partial obedience. It was not enough that in this solemn season of worship *nearly* everything was done as He had directed. God has pronounced a curse upon those who depart from His commandments, and put no difference between common and holy things. He declares by the prophet: "Woe unto them that call evil good, and good evil; that put darkness for light, and light for darkness! . . . Woe unto them that are wise in their own eyes, and prudent in their own sight! . . . which justify the wicked for reward, and take away the righteousness of the righteous from him! . . . They have cast away the law of the Lord of hosts, and despised the word of the Holy One of Israel." Isaiah 5:20-24. Let no one deceive himself with the belief that a part of God's commandments are nonessential, or that He will accept a substitute for that which He has required. Said the prophet Jeremiah, "Who is he that saith, and it cometh to pass, when the Lord commandeth it not?" Lamentations 3:37. God has placed in His word no command which men may obey or disobey at will 361 and not suffer the consequences. If men choose any other path than that of strict obedience, they will find that "the end thereof are the ways of death." Proverbs 14:12.

"Moses said unto Aaron, and unto Eleazar and unto Ithamar, his sons, Uncover not your heads, neither rend your clothes; lest ye die, . . . for the anointing oil of the Lord is upon you." The great leader reminded his brother of the words of God, "I will be sanctified in them that come nigh Me, and before all the people I will be glorified." Aaron was silent. The death of his sons, cut down without warning, in so terrible a sin—a sin which he now saw to be the result of his own neglect of duty—wrung the father's heart with anguish, but he gave his feelings no expression. By no manifestation of grief must he seem to sympathize with sin. The congregation must not be led to murmur against God.

The Lord would teach His people to acknowledge the justice of His corrections, that others may fear. There were those in Israel whom the warning of this terrible judgment might save from presuming upon God's forbearance until they, too, should seal their own destiny. The divine rebuke is upon that false sympathy for the sinner which endeavors to excuse his sin. It is the effect of sin to deaden the moral perceptions, so that the wrongdoer does not realize the enormity of transgression, and without the convicting power of the Holy Spirit he remains in partial blindness to his sin. It is the duty of Christ's servants to show these erring ones their peril. Those who destroy the effect of the warning by blinding the eyes of sinners to the real character and results of sin often flatter themselves that they thus give evidence of their charity; but they are working directly to oppose and hinder the work of God's Holy Spirit; they are lulling the sinner to rest on the brink of destruction; they are making themselves partakers in his guilt and incurring a fearful responsibility for his impenitence. Many, many, have gone down to ruin as the result of this false and deceptive sympathy.

Nadab and Abihu would never have committed that fatal sin had they not first become partially intoxicated by the free use of wine. They understood that the most careful and solemn preparation was necessary before presenting themselves in the sanctuary, where the divine Presence was manifested; but by intemperance they were disqualified for their holy office. Their minds became confused and their moral perceptions dulled so that they could not discern the difference between the sacred and the common. To Aaron and his surviving sons was given the warning: "Do not drink wine nor strong drink, thou, nor thy sons with thee, when ye go into the tabernacle of the congregation, lest ye die: it shall be a statute forever throughout your generations: and that ye may put difference between holy and unholy, and between unclean and clean; and that ye may teach the children of Israel all the statutes which the Lord hath spoken." The use of spirituous liquors has the effect to weaken the body, confuse the mind, and debase the morals. It prevents men from realizing the sacredness of holy things or the binding force of God's requirements. All who occupied positions of sacred responsibility were to be men of strict temperance, that their minds might be clear to discriminate between right and wrong, that they might possess firmness of principle, and wisdom to administer justice and to show mercy.

The same obligation rests upon every follower of Christ. The apostle Peter declares, "Ye are a chosen generation, a royal priesthood, an holy nation, a peculiar people." 1 Peter 2:9. We are required by God to preserve every power in the best possible condition, that we may render acceptable service to our Creator. When intoxicants are used, the same effects will follow as in the case of those priests of Israel. The conscience will lose its sensibility to sin, and a process of hardening to iniquity will most certainly take place, till the common and the sacred will lose all difference of significance. How can we then meet the standard of the divine requirements. "Know ye not that your body is the temple of the Holy Ghost which is in you, which ye have of God, and ye are not your own? For ye are bought with a price: therefore glorify God in your body, and in your spirit, which are God's." 1 Corinthians 6:19, 20. "Whether therefore ye eat, or drink, or whatsoever ye do, do all to the glory of God." 1 Corinthians 10:31. To the church of Christ in all ages is addressed the solemn and fearful warning, "If any man defile the temple of God, him shall God destroy; for the temple of God is holy, which temple ye are." 1 Corinthians 3:17.

32

The Law and the Covenants

Adam and Eve, at their creation, had a knowledge of the law of God; they were acquainted with its claims upon them; its precepts were written upon their hearts. When man fell by transgression the law was not changed, but a remedial system was established to bring him back to obedience. The promise of a Saviour was given, and sacrificial offerings pointing forward to the death of Christ as the great sin offering were established. But had the law of God never been transgressed, there would have been no death, and no need of a Saviour; consequently there would have been no need of sacrifices.

Adam taught his descendants the law of God, and it was handed down from father to son through successive generations. But notwithstanding the gracious provision for man's redemption, there were few who accepted it and rendered obedience. By transgression the world became so vile that it was necessary to cleanse it by the Flood from its corruption. The law was preserved by Noah and his family, and Noah taught his descendants the Ten Commandments. As men again departed from God, the Lord chose Abraham, of whom He declared, "Abraham obeyed My voice, and kept My charge, My commandments, My statutes, and My laws." Genesis 26:5. To him was given the rite of circumcision, which was a sign that those who received it were devoted to the service of God— a pledge that they would remain separate from idolatry, and would obey the law of God. The failure of Abraham's descendants to keep this pledge, as shown in their disposition to form alliances with the heathen and adopt their practices, was the cause of their sojourn and bondage in Egypt. But in their intercourse with idolaters, and their forced submission to the Egyptians, the divine precepts became still further corrupted with the vile and cruel teachings of heathenism. Therefore when the Lord brought them forth from Egypt, He came down upon Sinai, enshrouded in glory and surrounded by His angels, and in awful majesty spoke His law in the hearing of all the people.

He did not even then trust His precepts to the memory of a people who were prone to forget His requirements, but wrote them upon tables of stone. He would remove from Israel all possibility of mingling heathen traditions with His holy precepts, or of confounding His requirements with human ordinances or customs. But He did not stop with giving them the precepts of the Decalogue. The people had shown themselves so easily led astray that He would leave no door of temptation unguarded. Moses was commanded to write, as God should bid him, judgments and laws giving minute instruction as to what was required. These directions relating to the duty of the people to God, to one another, and to the stranger were only the principles of the Ten Commandments amplified and given in a specific manner, that none need err. They were designed to guard the sacredness of the ten precepts engraved on the tables of stone.

If man had kept the law of God, as given to Adam after his fall, preserved by Noah, and observed by Abraham, there would have been no necessity for the ordinance of circumcision. And if the descendants of Abraham had kept the covenant, of which circumcision was a sign, they would never have been seduced into idolatry, nor would it have been necessary for them to suffer a life of bondage in Egypt; they would have kept God's law in mind, and there would have been no necessity for it to be proclaimed from Sinai or engraved upon the tables of stone. And had the people practiced the principles of the Ten Commandments, there would have been no need of the additional directions given to Moses.

The sacrificial system, committed to Adam, was also perverted by his descendants. Superstition, idolatry, cruelty, and licentiousness corrupted the simple and significant service that God had appointed. Through long intercourse with idolaters the people of Israel had mingled many heathen customs with their worship; therefore the Lord gave them at Sinai definite instruction concerning the sacrificial service. After the completion of the tabernacle He communicated with Moses from the cloud of glory above the mercy seat, and gave him full directions concerning the system of offerings and the 365 forms of worship to be maintained in the sanctuary. The ceremonial law was thus given to Moses, and by him written in a book. But the law of Ten Commandments spoken from Sinai had been written by God Himself on the tables of stone, and was sacredly preserved in the ark.

There are many who try to blend these two systems, using the texts that speak of the ceremonial law to prove that the moral law has been abolished; but this is a perversion of the Scriptures. The distinction between the two systems is broad and clear. The ceremonial system was made up of symbols pointing to Christ, to His sacrifice and His priesthood. This ritual law, with its sacrifices and ordinances, was to be performed by the Hebrews until type met antitype in the death of Christ, the Lamb of God that taketh away the sin of the world. Then all the sacrificial offerings were to cease. It is this law that Christ "took . . . out of the way, nailing it to

His cross." Colossians 2:14. But concerning the law of Ten Commandments the psalmist declares, "Forever, O Lord, Thy word is settled in heaven." Psalm 119:89. And Christ Himself says, "Think not that I am come to destroy the law. . . . Verily I say unto you"—making the assertion as emphatic as possible—"Till heaven and earth pass, one jot or one tittle shall in no wise pass from the law, till all be fulfilled." Matthew 5:17, 18. Here He teaches, not merely what the claims of God's law had been, and were then, but that these claims should hold as long as the heavens and the earth remain. The law of God is as immutable as His throne. It will maintain its claims upon mankind in all ages.

Concerning the law proclaimed from Sinai, Nehemiah says, "Thou camest down also upon Mount Sinai, and spakest with them from heaven, and gavest them right judgments, and true laws, good statutes and commandments." Nehemiah 9:13. And Paul, "the apostle to the Gentiles," declares, "The law is holy, and the commandment holy, and just, and good." Romans 7:12. This can be no other than the Decalogue; for it is the law that says, "Thou shalt not covet." Verse 7.

While the Saviour's death brought to an end the law of types and shadows, it did not in the least detract from the obligation of the moral law. On the contrary, the very fact that it was necessary for Christ to die in order to atone for the transgression of that law, proves it to be immutable.

Those who claim that Christ came to abrogate the law of God and to do away with the Old 366 Testament, speak of the Jewish age as one of darkness, and represent the religion of the Hebrews as consisting of mere forms and ceremonies. But this is an error. All through the pages of sacred history, where the dealings of God with His chosen people are recorded, there are burning traces of the great I AM. Never has He given to the sons of men more open manifestations of His power and glory than when He alone was acknowledged as Israel's ruler, and gave the law to His people. Here was a scepter swayed by no human hand; and the stately goings forth of Israel's invisible King were unspeakably grand and awful.

In all these revelations of the divine presence the glory of God was manifested through Christ. Not alone at the Saviour's advent, but through all the ages after the Fall and the promise of redemption, "God was in Christ, reconciling the world unto Himself." 2 Corinthians 5:19. Christ was the foundation and center of the sacrificial system in both the patriarchal and the Jewish age. Since the sin of our first parents there has been no direct communication between God and man. The Father has given the world into the hands of Christ, that through His mediatorial work He may redeem man and vindicate the authority and holiness of the law of God. All the communion between heaven and the fallen race has been through Christ. It was the Son of God that gave to our first parents the promise of redemption. It was He who revealed Himself to the patriarchs. Adam, Noah, Abraham, Isaac, Jacob, and Moses understood the gospel. They looked for salvation through man's Substitute and Surety. These holy men of old held communion with the Saviour who was to come to our world in human flesh; and some of them talked with Christ and heavenly angels face to face.

Christ was not only the leader of the Hebrews in the wilderness—the Angel in whom was the name of Jehovah, and who, veiled in the cloudy pillar, went before the host—but it was He who gave the law to Israel.* Amid the awful glory of Sinai, Christ declared in the hearing of all the people the ten precepts of His Father's law. It was He who gave to Moses the law engraved upon the tables of stone.

367 It was Christ that spoke to His people through the prophets. The apostle Peter, writing to the Christian church, says that the prophets "prophesied of the grace that should come unto you: searching what, or what manner of time the *Spirit of Christ* which was in them did signify, when it testified beforehand the sufferings of Christ and the glory that should follow." 1 Peter 1:10, 11. It is the voice of Christ that speaks to us through the Old Testament. "The testimony of Jesus is the spirit of prophecy." Revelation 19:10.

In His teachings while personally among men Jesus directed the minds of the people to the Old Testament. He said to the Jews, "Ye search the Scriptures, because ye think that in them ye have eternal life; and these are they which bear witness of Me." John 5:39, R.V. At this time the books of the Old Testament were the only part of the Bible in existence. Again the Son of God declared, "They have Moses and the prophets; let them hear them." And He added, "If they hear not Moses and the prophets, neither will they be persuaded, though one rose from the dead." Luke 16:29, 31.

The ceremonial law was given by Christ. Even after it was no longer to be observed, Paul presented it before the Jews in its true position and value, showing its place in the plan of redemption and its relation to the work of Christ; and the great apostle pronounces this law glorious, worthy of its divine Originator. The solemn service of the sanctuary typified the grand truths that were to be revealed through successive generations. The cloud of incense ascending with the prayers of Israel represents His righteousness that alone can make the sinner's prayer acceptable to God; the bleeding victim on the altar of sacrifice testified of a Redeemer to come; and from the holy of holies

the visible token of the divine Presence shone forth. Thus through age after age of darkness and apostasy faith was kept alive in the hearts of men until the time came for the advent of the promised Messiah.

Jesus was the light of His people—the Light of the world—before He came to earth in the form of humanity. The first gleam of light that pierced the gloom in which sin had wrapped the world, came from Christ. And from Him has come every ray of heaven's brightness that has fallen upon the inhabitants of the earth. In the plan of redemption Christ is the Alpha and the Omega—the First and the Last.

Since the Saviour shed His blood for the remission of sins, and ascended to heaven "to appear in the presence of God for us" (Hebrews 368 9:24), light has been streaming from the cross of Calvary and from the holy places of the sanctuary above. But the clearer light granted us should not cause us to despise that which in earlier times was received through the types pointing to the coming Saviour. The gospel of Christ sheds light upon the Jewish economy and gives significance to the ceremonial law. As new truths are revealed, and that which has been known from the beginning is brought into clearer light, the character and purposes of God are made manifest in His dealings with His chosen people. Every additional ray of light that we receive gives us a clearer understanding of the plan of redemption, which is the working out of the divine will in the salvation of man. We see new beauty and force in the inspired word, and we study its pages with a deeper and more absorbing interest.

The opinion is held by many that God placed a separating wall between the Hebrews and the outside world; that His care and love, withdrawn to a great extent from the rest of mankind, were centered upon Israel. But God did not design that His people should build up a wall of partition between themselves and their fellow men. The heart of Infinite Love was reaching out toward all the inhabitants of the earth. Though they had rejected Him, He was constantly seeking to reveal Himself to them and make them partakers of His love and grace. His blessing was granted to the chosen people, that they might bless others.

God called Abraham, and prospered and honored him; and the patriarch's fidelity was a light to the people in all the countries of his sojourn. Abraham did not shut himself away from the people around him. He maintained friendly relations with the kings of the surrounding nations, by some of whom he was treated with great respect; and his integrity and unselfishness, his valor and benevolence, were representing the character of God. In Mesopotamia, in Canaan, in Egypt, and even to the inhabitants of Sodom, the God of heaven was revealed through His

---

* See Appendix, Note 7.

representative.

So to the people of Egypt and of all the nations connected with that powerful kingdom, God manifested Himself through Joseph. Why did the Lord choose to exalt Joseph so highly among the Egyptians? He might have provided some other way for the accomplishment of His purposes toward the children of Jacob; but He desired to make Joseph a light, and He placed 369 him in the palace of the king, that the heavenly illumination might extend far and near. By his wisdom and justice, by the purity and benevolence of his daily life, by his devotion to the interests of the people—and that people a nation of idolaters—Joseph was a representative of Christ. In their benefactor, to whom all Egypt turned with gratitude and praise, that heathen people were to behold the love of their Creator and Redeemer. So in Moses also God placed a light beside the throne of the earth's greatest kingdom, that all who would, might learn of the true and living God. And all this light was given to the Egyptians before the hand of God was stretched out over them in judgments.

In the deliverance of Israel from Egypt a knowledge of the power of God spread far and wide. The warlike people of the stronghold of Jericho trembled. "As soon as we had heard these things," said Rahab, "our hearts did melt, neither did there remain any more courage in any man, because of you: for Jehovah your God, He is God in heaven above, and in earth beneath." Joshua 2:11. Centuries after the exodus the priests of the Philistines reminded their people of the plagues of Egypt, and warned them against resisting the God of Israel.

God called Israel, and blessed and exalted them, not that by obedience to His law they alone might receive His favor and become the exclusive recipients of His blessings, but in order to reveal Himself through them to all the inhabitants of the earth. It was for the accomplishment of this very purpose that He commanded them to keep themselves distinct from the idolatrous nations around them.

Idolatry and all the sins that followed in its train were abhorrent to God, and He commanded His people not to mingle with other nations, to "*do after their works*," and forget God. He forbade their marriage with idolaters, lest their hearts should be led away from Him. It was just as necessary then as it is now that God's people should be pure, "unspotted from the world." They must keep themselves free from its spirit, because it is opposed to truth and righteousness. But God did not intend that His people, in self-righteous exclusiveness, should shut themselves away from the world, so that they could have no influence upon it.

Like their Master, the followers of Christ in every age were to be the light of the world. The 370 Saviour said, "A city that is set on an hill cannot be hid. Neither do men light a candle, and put it under a bushel, but on a candlestick; and it giveth light unto all that are in the house"—that is, in the world. And He adds, "Let your light so shine before men, that they may see your good works, and glorify your Father which is in heaven." Matthew 5:14-16. This is just what Enoch, and Noah, Abraham, Joseph, and Moses did. It is just what God designed that His people Israel should do.

It was their own evil heart of unbelief, controlled by Satan, that led them to hide their light, instead of shedding it upon surrounding peoples; it was that same bigoted spirit that caused them either to follow the iniquitous practices of the heathen or to shut themselves away in proud exclusiveness, as if God's love and care were over them alone.

As the Bible presents two laws, one changeless and eternal, the other provisional and temporary, so there are two covenants. The covenant of grace was first made with man in Eden, when after the Fall there was given a divine promise that the seed of the woman should bruise the serpent's head. To all men this covenant offered pardon and the assisting grace of God for future obedience through faith in Christ. It also promised them eternal life on condition of fidelity to God's law. Thus the patriarchs received the hope of salvation.

This same covenant was renewed to Abraham in the promise, "In thy seed shall all the nations of the earth be blessed." Genesis 22:18. This promise pointed to Christ. So Abraham understood it (see Galatians 3:8, 16), and he trusted in Christ for the forgiveness of sins. It was this faith that was accounted unto him for righteousness. The covenant with Abraham also maintained the authority of God's law. The Lord appeared unto Abraham, and said, "I am the Almighty God; walk before Me, and be thou perfect." Genesis 17:1. The testimony of God concerning His faithful servant was, "Abraham obeyed My voice, and kept My charge, My commandments, My statutes, and My laws." Genesis 26:5. And the Lord declared to him, "I will establish My covenant between Me and thee and thy seed after thee in their generations, for an *everlasting covenant*, to be a God unto thee and to thy seed after thee." Genesis 17:7.

Though this covenant was made with Adam and renewed to Abraham, it could not be ratified until the death of Christ. It had existed by 371 the promise of God since the first intimation of redemption had been given; it had been accepted by faith; yet when ratified by Christ, it is called a *new* covenant. The law of God was the basis of this covenant, which was simply an arrangement for bringing men again into harmony with the divine will, placing them where they could obey God's law.

Another compact—called in Scripture the

"old" covenant—was formed between God and Israel at Sinai, and was then ratified by the blood of a sacrifice. The Abrahamic covenant was ratified by the blood of Christ, and it is called the "second," or "new," covenant, because the blood by which it was sealed was shed after the blood of the first covenant. That the new covenant was valid in the days of Abraham is evident from the fact that it was then confirmed both by the promise and by the oath of God—the "two immutable things, in which it was impossible for God to lie." Hebrews 6:18.

But if the Abrahamic covenant contained the promise of redemption, why was another covenant formed at Sinai? In their bondage the people had to a great extent lost the knowledge of God and of the principles of the Abrahamic covenant. In delivering them from Egypt, God sought to reveal to them His power and His mercy, that they might be led to love and trust Him. He brought them down to the Red Sea—where, pursued by the Egyptians, escape seemed impossible—that they might realize their utter helplessness, their need of divine aid; and then He wrought deliverance for them. Thus they were filled with love and gratitude to God and with confidence in His power to help them. He had bound them to Himself as their deliverer from temporal bondage.

But there was a still greater truth to be impressed upon their minds. Living in the midst of idolatry and corruption, they had no true conception of the holiness of God, of the exceeding sinfulness of their own hearts, their utter inability, in themselves, to render obedience to God's law, and their need of a Saviour. All this they must be taught.

God brought them to Sinai; He manifested His glory; He gave them His law, with the promise of great blessings on condition of obedience: "If ye will obey My voice indeed, and keep My covenant, then . . . ye shall be unto Me a kingdom of priests, and an holy nation." Exodus 19:5, 6. The people did not realize the sinfulness of their own hearts, and that without Christ it was impossible for them to keep God's law; and they readily entered into covenant with God. Feeling that they were able to establish their own righteousness, they declared, "All that the Lord hath said will we do, and be obedient." Exodus 24:7. They had witnessed the proclamation of the law in awful majesty, and had trembled with terror before the mount; and yet only a few weeks passed before they broke their covenant with God, and bowed down to worship a graven image. They could not hope for the favor of God through a covenant which they had broken; and now, seeing their sinfulness and their need of pardon, they were brought to feel their need of the Saviour revealed in the Abrahamic covenant and shadowed forth in the sacrificial offerings. Now by faith and love they

were bound to God as their deliverer from the bondage of sin. Now they were prepared to appreciate the blessings of the new covenant.

The terms of the "old covenant" were, Obey and live: "If a man do, he shall even live in them" (Ezekiel 20:11; Leviticus 18:5); but "cursed be he that confirmeth not all the words of this law to do them." Deuteronomy 27:26. The "new covenant" was established upon "better promises"—the promise of forgiveness of sins and of the grace of God to renew the heart and bring it into harmony with the principles of God's law. "This shall be the covenant that I will make with the house of Israel; After those days, saith the Lord, I will put my law in their inward parts, and write it in their hearts. . . . I will forgive their iniquity, and I will remember their sin no more." Jeremiah 31:33, 34.

The same law that was engraved upon the tables of stone is written by the Holy Spirit upon the tables of the heart. Instead of going about to establish our own righteousness we accept the righteousness of Christ. His blood atones for our sins. His obedience is accepted for us. Then the heart renewed by the Holy Spirit will bring forth "the fruits of the Spirit." Through the grace of Christ we shall live in obedience to the law of God written upon our hearts. Having the Spirit of Christ, we shall walk even as He walked. Through the prophet He declared of Himself, "I delight to do Thy will, O My God: yea, Thy law is within My heart." Psalm 40:8. And when among men He said, "The Father hath not left Me alone; for I do always those things that please Him." John 8:29.

The apostle Paul clearly presents the relation between faith and the law under the new covenant. He says: "Being justified by faith, we have peace with God through our Lord Jesus Christ." "Do we then make void the law through faith? God forbid: yea, we establish the law." "For what the law could not do, in that it was weak through the flesh"—it could not justify man, because in his sinful nature he could not keep the law—"God sending His own Son in the likeness of sinful flesh, and for sin, condemned sin in the flesh: that the righteousness of the law might be fulfilled in us, who walk not after the flesh, but after the Spirit." Romans 5:1; 3:31; 8:3, 4.

God's work is the same in all time, although there are different degrees of development and different manifestations of His power, to meet the wants of men in the different ages. Beginning with the first gospel promise, and coming down through the patriarchal and Jewish ages, and even to the present time, there has been a gradual unfolding of the purposes of God in the plan of redemption. The Saviour typified in the rites and ceremonies of the Jewish law is the very same that is revealed in the gospel. The clouds that enveloped His divine form have rolled back; the mists and shades have disappeared; and Jesus, the world's Redeemer, stands revealed. He who proclaimed the law from Sinai, and delivered to Moses the precepts of the ritual law, is the same that spoke the Sermon on the Mount. The great principles of love to God, which He set forth as the foundation of the law and the prophets, are only a reiteration of what He had spoken through Moses to the Hebrew people: "Hear, O Israel: The Lord our God is one Lord: and thou shalt love the Lord thy God with all thine heart, and with all thy soul, and with all thy might." Deuteronomy 6:4, 5. "Thou shalt love thy neighbor as thyself." Leviticus 19:18. The teacher is the same in both dispensations. God's claims are the same. The principles of His government are the same. For all proceed from Him "with whom is no variableness, neither shadow of turning." James 1:17.

374

33

From Sinai to Kadesh

The building of the tabernacle was not begun for some time after Israel arrived at Sinai; and the sacred structure was first set up at the opening of the second year from the Exodus. This was followed by the consecration of the priests, the celebration of the Passover, the numbering of the people, and the completion of various arrangements essential to their civil or religious system, so that nearly a year was spent in the encampment at Sinai. Here their worship had taken a more definite form, the laws had been given for the government of the nation, and a more efficient organization had been effected preparatory to their entrance into the land of Canaan.

The government of Israel was characterized by the most thorough organization, wonderful alike for its completeness and its simplicity. The order so strikingly displayed in the perfection and arrangement of all God's created works was manifest in the Hebrew economy. God was the center of authority and government, the sovereign of Israel. Moses stood as their visible leader, by God's appointment, to administer the laws in His name. From the elders of the tribes a council of seventy was afterward chosen to assist Moses in the general affairs of the nation. Next came the priests, who consulted the Lord in the sanctuary. Chiefs, or princes, ruled over the tribes. Under these were "captains over thousands, and captains over hundreds, and captains over fifties, and captains over tens," and, lastly, officers who might be employed for special duties. Deuteronomy 1:15.

This chapter is based on Numbers 11 and 12.

The Hebrew camp was arranged in exact order. It was separated into three great divisions, each having its appointed position in the encampment. In the center was the tabernacle, the abiding place of the invisible King. Around it were stationed the priests and Levites. Beyond 375 these were encamped all the other tribes.

To the Levites was committed the charge of the tabernacle and all that pertained thereto, both in the camp and on the journey. When the camp set forward they were to strike the sacred tent; when a halting place was reached they were to set it up. No person of another tribe was allowed to come near, on pain of death. The Levites were separated into three divisions, the descendants of the three sons of Levi, and each was assigned its special position and work. In front of the tabernacle, and nearest to it, were the tents of Moses and Aaron. On the south were the Kohathites, whose duty it was to care for the ark and the other furniture; on the north the Merarites, who were placed in charge of the pillars, sockets, boards, etc.; in the rear the Gershonites, to whom the care of the curtains and hangings was committed.

The position of each tribe also was specified. Each was to march and to encamp beside its own standard, as the Lord had commanded: "Every man of the children of Israel shall pitch by his own standard, with the ensign of their father's house: far off about the tabernacle of the congregation shall they pitch." "As they encamp, so shall they set forward, every man in his place by their standards." Numbers 2:2, 17. The mixed multitude that had accompanied Israel from Egypt were not permitted to occupy the same quarters with the tribes, but were to abide upon the outskirts of the camp; and their offspring were to be excluded from the community until the third generation. Deuteronomy 23:7, 8.

Scrupulous cleanliness as well as strict order throughout the encampment and its environs was enjoined. Thorough sanitary regulations were enforced. Every person who was unclean from any cause was forbidden to enter the camp. These measures were indispensable to the preservation of health among so vast a multitude; and it was necessary also that perfect order and purity be maintained, that Israel might enjoy the presence of a holy God. Thus He declared: "The Lord thy God walketh in the midst of thy camp, to deliver thee, and to give up thine enemies before thee; therefore shall thy camp be holy."

In all the journeyings of Israel, "the ark of the covenant of the Lord went before them, . . . to search out a resting place for them." Numbers 376 10:33. Borne by the sons of Kohath, the sacred chest containing God's holy law was to lead the van. Before it went Moses and Aaron; and the priests, bearing silver trumpets, were stationed near. These priests received directions from Moses, which they communicated to the people by the trumpets. It was the duty of the leaders of each company to give definite directions concerning all the movements to be made, as indicated by the trumpets. Whoever neglected to comply with the directions given was punished with death.

God is a God of order. Everything connected with heaven is in perfect order; subjection and thorough discipline mark the movements of the angelic host. Success can only attend order and harmonious action. God requires order and system in His work now no less than in the days of Israel. All who are working for Him are to labor intelligently, not in a careless, haphazard manner. He would have His work done with faith and exactness, that He may place the seal of His approval upon it.

God Himself directed the Israelites in all their travels. The place of their encampment was indicated by the descent of the pillar of cloud; and so long as they were to remain in camp, the cloud rested over the tabernacle. When they were to continue their journey it was lifted high above the sacred tent. A solemn invocation marked both the halt and the departure. "It came to pass, when the ark set forward, that Moses said, Rise up, Lord, and let Thine enemies be scattered; and let them that hate Thee flee before Thee. And when it rested, he said, Return, O Lord, unto the many thousands of Israel." Numbers 10:35, 36.

A distance of only eleven days' journey lay between Sinai and Kadesh, on the borders of Canaan; and it was with the prospect of speedily entering the goodly land that the hosts of Israel resumed their march when the cloud at last gave the signal for an onward movement. Jehovah had wrought wonders in bringing them from Egypt, and what blessings might they not expect now that they had formally covenanted to accept Him as their Sovereign, and had been acknowledged as the chosen people of the Most High?

Yet it was almost with reluctance that many left the place where they had so long encamped. They had come almost to regard it as their home. Within the shelter of those granite walls 377 God had gathered His people, apart from all other nations, to repeat to them His holy law. They loved to look upon the sacred mount, on whose hoary peaks and barren ridges the divine glory had so often been displayed. The scene was so closely associated with the presence of God and holy angels that it seemed too sacred to be left thoughtlessly, or even gladly.

At the signal from the trumpeters, however, the entire camp set forward, the tabernacle borne in the midst, and each tribe in its appointed position, under its own standard. All eyes were turned anxiously to see in what direction the cloud would lead. As it moved toward the east, where were only mountain masses huddled together, black and desolate, a feeling of sadness and doubt arose in many hearts.

As they advanced, the way became more difficult. Their route lay through stony ravine and barren waste. All around them was the great wilderness—"a land of deserts and of pits," "a land of drought, and of the shadow of death," "a land that no man passed through, and where no man dwelt." Jeremiah 2:6. The rocky gorges, far and near, were thronged with men, women, and children, with beasts and wagons, and long lines of flocks and herds. Their progress was necessarily slow and toilsome; and the multitudes, after their long encampment, were not prepared to endure the perils and discomforts of the way.

After three days' journey open complaints were heard. These originated with the mixed multitude, many of whom were not fully united with Israel, and were continually watching for some cause of censure. The complainers were not pleased with the direction of the march, and they were continually finding fault with the way in which *Moses* was leading them, though they well knew that he, as well as they, was following the guiding cloud. Dissatisfaction is contagious, and it soon spread in the encampment.

Again they began to clamor for flesh to eat. Though abundantly supplied with manna, they were not satisfied. The Israelites, during their bondage in Egypt, had been compelled to subsist on the plainest and simplest food; but the keen appetite induced by privation and hard labor had made it palatable. Many of the Egyptians, however, who were now among them, had been accustomed to a luxurious diet; and these were the first to complain. At the giving of the 378 manna, just before Israel reached Sinai, the Lord had granted them flesh in answer to their clamors; but it was furnished them for only one day.

God might as easily have provided them with flesh as with manna, but a restriction was placed upon them for their good. It was His purpose to supply them with food better suited to their wants than the feverish diet to which many had become accustomed in Egypt. The perverted appetite was to be brought into a more healthy state, that they might enjoy the food originally provided for man—the fruits of the earth, which God gave to Adam and Eve in Eden. It was for this reason that the Israelites had been deprived, in a great measure, of animal food.

Satan tempted them to regard this restriction as unjust and cruel. He caused them to lust after forbidden things, because he saw that the unrestrained indulgence of appetite would tend to produce sensuality, and by this means the people could be more easily brought under his control. The author of disease and misery will assail men where he can have the greatest success.

Through temptations addressed to the appetite he has, to a large extent, led men into sin from the time when he induced Eve to eat of the forbidden fruit. It was by this same means that he led Israel to murmur against God. Intemperance in eating and drinking, leading as it does to the indulgence of the lower passions, prepares the way for men to disregard all moral obligations. When assailed by temptation, they have little power of resistance.

God brought the Israelites from Egypt, that He might establish them in the land of Canaan, a pure, holy, and happy people. In the accomplishment of this object He subjected them to a course of discipline, both for their own good and for the good of their posterity. Had they been willing to deny appetite, in obedience to His wise restrictions, feebleness and disease would have been unknown among them. Their descendants would have possessed both physical and mental strength. They would have had clear perceptions of truth and duty, keen discrimination, and sound judgment. But their unwillingness to submit to the restrictions and requirements of God, prevented them, to a great extent, from reaching the high standard which He desired them to attain, and from receiving the blessings which He was ready to bestow upon them.

379 Says the psalmist: "They tempted God in their heart by asking meat for their lust. Yea, they spake against God; they said, Can God furnish a table in the wilderness? Behold, He smote the rock, that the waters gushed out, and the streams overflowed; can He give bread also? can He provide flesh for His people? Therefore the Lord heard this, and was wroth." Psalm 78:18-21. Murmuring and tumults had been frequent during the journey from the Red Sea to Sinai, but in pity for their ignorance and blindness God had not then visited the sin with judgments. But since that time He had revealed Himself to them at Horeb. They had received great light, as they had been witnesses to the majesty, the power, and the mercy of God; and their unbelief and discontent incurred the greater guilt. Furthermore, they had covenanted to accept Jehovah as their king and to obey His authority. Their murmuring was now rebellion, and as such it must receive prompt and signal punishment, if Israel was to be preserved from anarchy and ruin. "The fire of Jehovah burnt among them, and consumed them that were in the uttermost parts of the camp." The most guilty of the complainers were slain by lightning from the cloud.

The people in terror besought Moses to entreat the Lord for them. He did so, and the fire was quenched. In memory of this judgment he called the name of the place Taberah, "a burning."

But the evil was soon worse than before.

Instead of leading the survivors to humiliation and repentance, this fearful judgment seemed only to increase their murmurings. In all directions the people were gathered at the door of their tents, weeping and lamenting. "The mixed multitude that was among them fell a lusting: and the children of Israel also wept again, and said, Who shall give us flesh to eat? We remember the fish, which we did eat in Egypt freely; the cucumbers, and the melons, and the leeks, and the onions, and the garlic: but now our soul is dried away: there is nothing at all, beside this manna, before our eyes." Thus they manifested their discontent with the food provided for them by their Creator. Yet they had constant evidence that it was adapted to their wants; for notwithstanding the hardships they endured, there was not a feeble one in all their tribes.

The heart of Moses sank. He had pleaded that Israel should not be destroyed, even though his own posterity might then become a great nation. In his love for them he had prayed that his name 380 might be blotted from the book of life rather than that they should be left to perish. He had imperiled all for them, and this was their response. All their hardships, even their imaginary sufferings, they charged upon him; and their wicked murmurings made doubly heavy the burden of care and responsibility under which he staggered. In his distress he was tempted even to distrust God. His prayer was almost a complaint. "Wherefore hast Thou afflicted Thy servant? and wherefore have I not found favor in Thy sight, that Thou layest the burden of all this people upon me? . . . Whence should I have flesh to give unto all this people? for they weep unto me, saying, Give us flesh, that we may eat. I am not able to bear all this people alone, because it is too heavy for me."

The Lord hearkened to his prayer, and directed him to summon seventy men of the elders of Israel—men not only advanced in years, but possessing dignity, sound judgment, and experience. "And bring them unto the tabernacle of the congregation," He said, "that they may stand there with thee. And I will come down and talk with thee there: and I will take of the spirit which is upon thee, and will put it upon them; and they shall bear the burden of the people with thee, that thou bear it not thyself alone."

The Lord permitted Moses to choose for himself the most faithful and efficient men to share the responsibility with him. Their influence would assist in holding in check the violence of the people, and quelling insurrection; yet serious evils would eventually result from their promotion. They would never have been chosen had Moses manifested faith corresponding to the evidences he had witnessed of God's power and goodness. But he had magnified his own burdens and services, almost losing sight of the fact that he was only the instrument by which

God had wrought. He was not excusable in indulging, in the slightest degree, the spirit of murmuring that was the curse of Israel. Had he relied fully upon God, the Lord would have guided him continually and would have given him strength for every emergency.

Moses was directed to prepare the people for what God was about to do for them. "Sanctify yourselves against tomorrow, and ye shall eat flesh: for ye have wept in the ears of the Lord, saying, Who shall give us flesh to eat? for it was well with us in Egypt: therefore the Lord will 381 give you flesh, and ye shall eat. Ye shall not eat one day, nor two days, nor five days, neither ten days, nor twenty days; but even a whole month, until it come out at your nostrils, and it be loathsome unto you: because that ye have despised the Lord which is among you, and have wept before Him, saying, Why came we forth out of Egypt?"

"The people, among whom I am," exclaimed Moses, "are six hundred thousand footmen; and Thou hast said, I will give them flesh, that they may eat a whole month. Shall the flocks and the herds be slain for them, to suffice them? or shall all the fish of the sea be gathered together for them?"

He was reproved for his distrust: "Is the Lord's hand waxed short? thou shalt see now whether My word shall come to pass unto thee or not."

Moses repeated to the congregation the words of the Lord, and announced the appointment of the seventy elders. The great leader's charge to these chosen men might well serve as a model of judicial integrity for the judges and legislators of modern times: "Hear the causes between your brethren, and judge righteously between every man and his brother, and the stranger that is with him. Ye shall not respect persons in judgment; but ye shall hear the small as well as the great; ye shall not be afraid of the face of man; for the judgment is God's." Deuteronomy 1:16, 17.

Moses now summoned the seventy to the tabernacle. "And the Lord came down in a cloud, and spake unto him, and took of the spirit that was upon him, and gave it unto the seventy elders: and it came to pass, that, when the spirit rested upon them, they prophesied, and did not cease." Like the disciples on the Day of Pentecost, they were endued with "power from on high." It pleased the Lord thus to prepare them for their work, and to honor them in the presence of the congregation, that confidence might be established in them as men divinely chosen to unite with Moses in the government of Israel.

Again evidence was given of the lofty, unselfish spirit of the great leader. Two of the seventy, humbly counting themselves unworthy of so responsible a position, had not joined their brethren at the tabernacle; but the Spirit of God came upon them where they were, and they, too, exercised the prophetic gift. On being informed of this, Joshua desired to check such irregularity, fearing that it might tend to division. Jealous for the honor of his master, "My lord Moses," 382 he said, "forbid them." The answer was, "Enviest thou for my sake? would God that all the Lord's people were prophets, and that the Lord would put His Spirit upon them."

A strong wind blowing from the sea now brought flocks of quails, "about a day's journey on this side, and a day's journey on the other side, round about the camp, and about two cubits above the face of the earth." Numbers 11:31, R.V. All that day and night, and the following day, the people labored in gathering the food miraculously provided. Immense quantities were secured. "He that gathered least gathered ten homers." All that was not needed for present use was preserved by drying, so that the supply, as promised, was sufficient for a whole month.

God gave the people that which was not for their highest good, because they persisted in desiring it; they would not be satisfied with those things that would prove a benefit to them. Their rebellious desires were gratified, but they were left to suffer the result. They feasted without restraint, and their excesses were speedily punished. "The Lord smote the people with a very great plague." Large numbers were cut down by burning fevers, while the most guilty among them were smitten as soon as they tasted the food for which they had lusted.

At Hazeroth, the next encampment after leaving Taberah, a still more bitter trial awaited Moses. Aaron and Miriam had occupied a position of high honor and leadership in Israel. Both were endowed with the prophetic gift, and both had been divinely associated with Moses in the deliverance of the Hebrews. "I sent before thee Moses, Aaron, and Miriam" (Micah 6:4), are the words of the Lord by the prophet Micah. Miriam's force of character had been early displayed when as a child she watched beside the Nile the little basket in which was hidden the infant Moses. Her self-control and tact God had made instrumental in preserving the deliverer of His people. Richly endowed with the gifts of poetry and music, Miriam had led the women of Israel in song and dance on the shore of the Red Sea. In the affections of the people and the honor of Heaven she stood second only to Moses and Aaron. But the same evil that first brought discord in heaven sprang up in the heart of this woman of Israel, and she did not fail to find a sympathizer in her dissatisfaction.

In the appointment of the seventy elders Miriam and Aaron had not been consulted, and their 383 jealousy was excited against Moses. At the time of Jethro's visit, while the Israelites were on the way to Sinai, the ready acceptance by Moses of the counsel of his father-in-law had aroused in

Aaron and Miriam a fear that his influence with the great leader exceeded theirs. In the organization of the council of elders they felt that their position and authority had been ignored. Miriam and Aaron had never known the weight of care and responsibility which had rested upon Moses; yet because they had been chosen to aid him they regarded themselves as sharing equally with him the burden of leadership, and they regarded the appointment of further assistants as uncalled for.

Moses felt the importance of the great work committed to him as no other man had ever felt it. He realized his own weakness, and he made God his counselor. Aaron esteemed himself more highly, and trusted less in God. He had failed when entrusted with responsibility, giving evidence of the weakness of his character by his base compliance in the matter of the idolatrous worship at Sinai. But Miriam and Aaron, blinded by jealousy and ambition, lost sight of this. Aaron had been highly honored by God in the appointment of his family to the sacred office of the priesthood; yet even this now added to the desire for self-exaltation. "And they said, Hath the Lord indeed spoken only by Moses? hath He not spoken also by us?" Regarding themselves as equally favored by God, they felt that they were entitled to the same position and authority.

Yielding to the spirit of dissatisfaction, Miriam found cause of complaint in events that God had especially overruled. The marriage of Moses had been displeasing to her. That he should choose a woman of another nation, instead of taking a wife from among the Hebrews, was an offense to her family and national pride. Zipporah was treated with ill-disguised contempt.

Though called a "Cushite woman" (Numbers 12:1, R.V.), the wife of Moses was a Midianite, and thus a descendant of Abraham. In personal appearance she differed from the Hebrews in being of a somewhat darker complexion. Though not an Israelite, Zipporah was a worshiper of the true God. She was of a timid, retiring disposition, gentle and affectionate, and greatly distressed at the sight of suffering; and it was for this reason that Moses, when on the way to Egypt, had consented to her return to Midian. He desired to spare her the pain of witnessing the judgments that were to fall on the Egyptians.

When Zipporah rejoined her husband in the wilderness, she saw that his burdens were wearing away his strength, and she made known her fears to Jethro, who suggested measures for his relief. Here was the chief reason for Miriam's antipathy to Zipporah. Smarting under the supposed neglect shown to herself and Aaron, she regarded the wife of Moses as the cause, concluding that her influence had prevented him from taking them into his counsels as formerly.

Had Aaron stood up firmly for the right, he might have checked the evil; but instead of showing Miriam the sinfulness of her conduct, he sympathized with her, listened to her words of complaint, and thus came to share her jealousy.

Their accusations were borne by Moses in uncomplaining silence. It was the experience gained during the years of toil and waiting in Midian—the spirit of humility and long-suffering there developed—that prepared Moses to meet with patience the unbelief and murmuring of the people and the pride and envy of those who should have been his unswerving helpers. Moses "was very meek, above all the men which were upon the face of the earth," and this is why he was granted divine wisdom and guidance above all others. Says the Scripture, "The meek will He guide in judgment: and the meek will He teach His way." Psalm 25:9. The meek are guided by the Lord, because they are teachable, willing to be instructed. They have a sincere desire to know and to do the will of God. The Saviour's promise is, "If any man will do His will, he shall know of the doctrine." John 7:17. And He declares by the apostle James, "If any of you lack wisdom, let him ask of God, that giveth to all men liberally, and upbraideth not; and it shall be given him." James 1:5. But His promise is only to those who are willing to follow the Lord wholly. God does not force the will of any; hence He cannot lead those who are too proud to be taught, who are bent upon having their own way. Of the double-minded man—he who seeks to follow his own will, while professing to do the will of God—it is written, "Let not that man think that he shall receive anything of the Lord." James 1:7.

God had chosen Moses, and had put His Spirit upon him; and Miriam and Aaron, by their murmurings, were guilty of disloyalty, not only to their appointed leader, but to God Himself. The seditious whisperers were summoned to the tabernacle, and brought face to face with Moses. "And Jehovah came down in the pillar of the cloud, and stood in the door of the tabernacle, and called Aaron and Miriam." Their claim to the prophetic gift was not denied; God might have spoken to them in visions and dreams. But to Moses, whom the Lord Himself declared "faithful in all Mine house," a nearer communion had been granted. With *him* God spake mouth to mouth. "Wherefore then were ye not afraid to speak against My servant Moses? And the anger of the Lord was kindled against them; and He departed." The cloud disappeared from the tabernacle in token of God's displeasure, and Miriam was smitten. She "became leprous, white as snow." Aaron was spared, but he was severely rebuked in Miriam's punishment. Now, their pride humbled in the dust, Aaron confessed their sin, and entreated that his sister

384

385

428 might not be left to perish by that loathsome and deadly scourge. In answer to the prayers of Moses the leprosy was cleansed. Miriam was, however, shut out of the camp for seven days. Not until she was banished from the encampment did the symbol of God's favor again rest upon the tabernacle. In respect for her high position, and in grief at the blow that had fallen upon her, the whole company abode in Hazeroth, awaiting her return.

This manifestation of the Lord's displeasure was designed to be a warning to all Israel, to check the growing spirit of discontent and insubordination. If Miriam's envy and dissatisfaction had not been signally rebuked, it would have resulted in great evil. Envy is one of the most satanic traits that can exist in the human heart, and it is one of the most baleful in its effects. Says the wise man, "Wrath is cruel, and anger is outrageous; but who is able to stand before envy?" Proverbs 27:4. It was envy that first caused discord in heaven, and its indulgence has wrought untold evil among men. "Where envying and strife is, there is confusion and every evil work." James 3:16.

It should not be regarded as a light thing to speak evil of others or to make ourselves judges of their motives or actions. "He that speaketh evil of his brother, and judgeth his brother, speaketh evil of the law, and judgeth the law: but if thou judge the law, thou art not a doer of the law, but a judge." James 4:11. There is but one judge—He "who both will bring to light the 386 hidden things of darkness, and will make manifest the counsels of the hearts." 1 Corinthians 4:5. And whoever takes it upon himself to judge and condemn his fellow men is usurping the prerogative of the Creator.

The Bible specially teaches us to beware of lightly bringing accusation against those whom God has called to act as His ambassadors. The apostle Peter, describing a class who are abandoned sinners, says, "Presumptuous are they, self-willed, they are not afraid to speak evil of dignities. Whereas angels, which are greater in power and might, bring not railing accusation against them before the Lord." 2 Peter 2:10, 11. And Paul, in his instruction for those who are placed over the church, says, "Against an elder receive not an accusation, but before two or three witnesses." 1 Timothy 5:19. He who has placed upon men the heavy responsibility of leaders and teachers of His people will hold the people accountable for the manner in which they treat His servants. We are to honor those whom God has honored. The judgment visited upon Miriam should be a rebuke to all who yield to jealousy, and murmur against those upon whom God lays the burden of His work.

34

387

The Twelve Spies

Eleven days after leaving Mount Horeb the Hebrew host encamped at Kadesh, in the wilderness of Paran, which was not far from the borders of the Promised Land. Here it was proposed by the people that spies be sent up to survey the country. The matter was presented before the Lord by Moses, and permission was granted, with the direction that one of the rulers of each tribe should be selected for this purpose. The men were chosen as had been directed, and Moses bade them go and see the country, what it was, its situation and natural advantages; and the people that dwelt therein, whether they were strong or weak, few or many; also to observe the nature of the soil and its productiveness and to bring of the fruit of the land.

They went, and surveyed the whole land, entering at the southern border and proceeding to the northern extremity. They returned after an absence of forty days. The people of Israel were cherishing high hopes and were waiting in eager expectancy. The news of the spies' return was carried from tribe to tribe and was hailed with rejoicing. The people rushed out to meet the messengers, who had safely escaped the dangers of their perilous undertaking. The spies brought specimens of the fruit, showing the fertility of the soil. It was in the time of ripe grapes, and they brought a cluster of grapes so large that it was carried between two men. They also brought of the figs and pomegranates which grew there in abundance.

The people rejoiced that they were to come into possession of so goodly a land, and they listened intently as the report was brought to Moses, that not a word should escape them. "We came unto the land whither thou sentest us," the spies began, "and surely it floweth with milk and honey; and this is the fruit of it." The people were enthusiastic; they would eagerly obey the voice of the Lord, and go up at once to possess the land. But after describing the beauty 388 and fertility of the land, all but two of the spies enlarged upon the difficulties and dangers that lay before the Israelites should they undertake the conquest of Canaan. They enumerated the powerful nations located in various parts of the country, and said that the cities were walled and very great, and the people who dwelt therein were strong, and it would be impossible to conquer them. They also stated that they had seen giants, the sons of Anak, there, and it was useless to think of possessing the land.

Now the scene changed. Hope and courage gave place to cowardly despair, as the spies

This chapter is based on Numbers 13 and 14.

uttered the sentiments of their unbelieving hearts, which were filled with discouragement prompted by Satan. Their unbelief cast a gloomy shadow over the congregation, and the mighty power of God, so often manifested in behalf of the chosen nation, was forgotten. The people did not wait to reflect; they did not reason that He who had brought them thus far would certainly give them the land; they did not call to mind how wonderfully God had delivered them from their oppressors, cutting a path through the sea and destroying the pursuing hosts of Pharaoh. They left God out of the question, and acted as though they must depend solely on the power of arms.

In their unbelief they limited the power of God and distrusted the hand that had hitherto safely guided them. And they repeated their former error of murmuring against Moses and Aaron. "This, then, is the end of our high hopes," they said. "This is the land we have traveled all the way from Egypt to possess." They accused their leaders of deceiving the people and bringing trouble upon Israel.

The people were desperate in their disappointment and despair. A wail of agony arose and mingled with the confused murmur of voices. Caleb comprehended the situation, and, bold to stand in defense of the word of God, he did all in his power to counteract the evil influence of his unfaithful associates. For an instant the people were stilled to listen to his words of hope and courage respecting the goodly land. He did not contradict what had already been said; the walls were high and the Canaanites strong. But God had promised the land to Israel. "Let us go up at once and possess it," urged Caleb; "for we are well able to overcome it."

But the ten, interrupting him, pictured the obstacles in darker colors than at first. "We be 389 not able to go up against the people," they declared; "for they are stronger than we. . . . All the people that we saw in it are men of a great stature. And there we saw the giants, the sons of Anak, which come of the giants: and we were in our own sight as grasshoppers, and so we were in their sight."

These men, having entered upon a wrong course, stubbornly set themselves against Caleb and Joshua, against Moses, and against God. Every advance step rendered them the more determined. They were resolved to discourage all effort to gain possession of Canaan. They distorted the truth in order to sustain their baleful influence. It "is a land that eateth up the inhabitants thereof," they said. This was not only an evil report, but it was also a lying one. It was inconsistent with itself. The spies had declared the country to be fruitful and prosperous, and the people of giant stature, all of which would be impossible if the climate were so unhealthful that the land could be said to "eat up

the inhabitants." But when men yield their hearts to unbelief they place themselves under the control of Satan, and none can tell to what lengths he will lead them.

"And all the congregation lifted up their voice, and cried; and the people wept that night." Revolt and open mutiny quickly followed; for Satan had full sway, and the people seemed bereft of reason. They cursed Moses and Aaron, forgetting that God hearkened to their wicked speeches, and that, enshrouded in the cloudy pillar, the Angel of His presence was witnessing their terrible outburst of wrath. In bitterness they cried out, "Would God that we had died in the land of Egypt! or would God we had died in this wilderness!" Then their feelings rose against God: "Wherefore hath the Lord brought us unto this land, to fall by the sword, that our wives and our children should be a prey? were it not better for us to return into Egypt? And they said one to another, Let us make a captain, and let us return into Egypt." Thus they accused not only Moses, but God Himself, of deception, in promising them a land which they were not able to possess. And they went so far as to appoint a captain to lead them back to the land of their suffering and bondage, from which they had been delivered by the strong arm of Omnipotence.

In humiliation and distress "Moses and Aaron fell on their faces before all the assembly of the congregation of the children of Israel," not knowing what to do to turn them from their rash and passionate purpose. Caleb and Joshua attempted to quiet the tumult. With their gar- 390 ments rent in token of grief and indignation, they rushed in among the people, and their ringing voices were heard above the tempest of lamentation and rebellious grief: "The land, which we passed through to search it, is an exceeding good land. If the Lord delight in us, then He will bring us into this land, and give it us; a land which floweth with milk and honey. Only rebel not ye against the Lord, neither fear ye the people of the land; for they are bread for us: their defense is departed from them, and the Lord is with us: fear them not."

The Canaanites had filled up the measure of their iniquity, and the Lord would no longer bear with them. His protection being removed, they would be an easy prey. By the covenant of God the land was ensured to Israel. But the false report of the unfaithful spies was accepted, and through it the whole congregation were deluded. The traitors had done their work. If only the two men had brought the evil report, and all the ten had encouraged them to possess the land in the name of the Lord, they would still have taken the advice of the two in preference to the ten, because of their wicked unbelief. But there were only two advocating the right, while ten were on the side of rebellion.

The unfaithful spies were loud in denunciation of Caleb and Joshua, and the cry was raised to stone them. The insane mob seized missiles with which to slay those faithful men. They rushed forward with yells of madness, when suddenly the stones dropped from their hands, a hush fell upon them, and they shook with fear. God had interposed to check their murderous design. The glory of His presence, like a flaming light, illuminated the tabernacle. All the people beheld the signal of the Lord. A mightier one than they had revealed Himself, and none dared continue their resistance. The spies who brought the evil report crouched terror-stricken, and with bated breath sought their tents.

Moses now arose and entered the tabernacle. The Lord declared to him, "I will smite them with the pestilence, and disinherit them, and will make of thee a greater nation." But again Moses pleaded for his people. He could not consent to have them destroyed, and he himself made a mightier nation. Appealing to the mercy of God, he said: "I beseech Thee, let the power of my Lord be great according as Thou hast spoken, saying, The Lord is long-suffering, and of great mercy. . . . Pardon, I beseech Thee, the iniquity of this people according to the greatness of Thy mercy, and as Thou hast forgiven 391 this people, from Egypt even until now."

The Lord promised to spare Israel from immediate destruction; but because of their unbelief and cowardice He could not manifest His power to subdue their enemies. Therefore in His mercy He bade them, as the only safe course, to turn back toward the Red Sea.

In their rebellion the people had exclaimed, "Would God we had died in this wilderness!" Now this prayer was to be granted. The Lord declared: "As ye have spoken in Mine ears, so will I do to you: your carcasses shall fall in this wilderness, and all that were numbered of you, according to your whole number, from twenty years old and upward. . . . But your little ones, which ye said should be a prey, them will I bring in, and they shall know the land which ye have despised." And of Caleb He said, "My servant Caleb, because he had another spirit with him, and hath followed Me fully, him will I bring into the land whereinto he went; and his seed shall possess it." As the spies had spent forty days in their journey, so the hosts of Israel were to wander in the wilderness forty years.

When Moses made known to the people the divine decision, their rage was changed to mourning. They knew that their punishment was just. The ten unfaithful spies, divinely smitten by the plague, perished before the eyes of all Israel; and in their fate the people read their own doom.

Now they seemed sincerely to repent of their sinful conduct; but they sorrowed because of the result of their evil course rather than from a sense of their ingratitude and disobedience. When they found that the Lord did not relent in His decree, their self-will again arose, and they declared that they would not return into the wilderness. In commanding them to retire from the land of their enemies, God tested their apparent submission and proved that it was not real. They knew that they had deeply sinned in allowing their rash feelings to control them and in seeking to slay the spies who had urged them to obey God; but they were only terrified to find that they had made a fearful mistake, the consequences of which would prove disastrous to themselves. Their hearts were unchanged, and they only needed an excuse to occasion a similar outbreak. This presented itself when Moses, by the authority of God, commanded them to go back into the wilderness.

The decree that Israel was not to enter 392 Canaan for forty years was a bitter disappointment to Moses and Aaron, Caleb and Joshua; yet without a murmur they accepted the divine decision. But those who had been complaining of God's dealings with them, and declaring that they would return to Egypt, wept and mourned greatly when the blessings which they had despised were taken from them. They had complained at nothing, and now God gave them cause to weep. Had they mourned for their sin when it was faithfully laid before them, this sentence would not have been pronounced; but they mourned for the judgment; their sorrow was not repentance, and could not secure a reversing of their sentence.

The night was spent in lamentation, but with the morning came a hope. They resolved to redeem their cowardice. When God had bidden them go up and take the land, they had refused; and now when He directed them to retreat they were equally rebellious. They determined to seize upon the land and possess it; it might be that God would accept their work and change His purpose toward them.

God had made it their privilege and their duty to enter the land at the time of His appointment, but through their willful neglect that permission had been withdrawn. Satan had gained his object in preventing them from entering Canaan; and now he urged them on to do the very thing, in the face of the divine prohibition, which they had refused to do when God required it. Thus the great deceiver gained the victory by leading them to rebellion the second time. They had distrusted the power of God to work with their efforts in gaining possession of Canaan; yet now they presumed upon their own strength to accomplish the work independent of divine aid. "We have sinned against the Lord," they cried; "we will go up and fight, according to all that the Lord our God commanded us." Deuteronomy 1:41. So terribly blinded had they become by transgression. The Lord had never commanded them to "go up and fight." It was not His purpose that they should gain the land by warfare, but by strict obedience to His commands.

Though their hearts were unchanged, the people had been brought to confess the sinfulness and folly of their rebellion at the report of the spies. They now saw the value of the blessing which they had so rashly cast away. They confessed that it was their own unbelief which had shut them out from Canaan. "We have sinned," they said, acknowledging that the fault was in themselves, and not in God, whom they had so wickedly charged with failing to fulfill His promises to them. Though their confession did not spring from true repentance, it served to vindicate the justice of God in His dealings with them.

The Lord still works in a similar manner to glorify His name by bringing men to acknowledge His justice. When those who profess to love Him complain of His providence, despise His promises, and, yielding to temptation, unite with evil angels to defeat the purposes of God, the Lord often so overrules circumstances as to bring these persons where, though they may have no real repentance, they will be convinced of their sin and will be constrained to acknowledge the wickedness of their course and the justice and goodness of God in His dealings with them. It is thus that God sets counteragencies at work to make manifest the works of darkness. And though the spirit which prompted to the evil course is not radically changed, confessions are made that vindicate the honor of God and justify His faithful reprovers, who have been opposed and misrepresented. Thus it will be when the wrath of God shall be finally poured out. When "the Lord cometh with ten thousand of His saints, to execute judgment upon all," He will also "convince all that are ungodly among them of all their ungodly deeds." Jude 14, 15. Every sinner will be brought to see and acknowledge the justice of his condemnation.

Regardless of the divine sentence, the Israelites prepared to undertake the conquest of Canaan. Equipped with armor and weapons of war, they were, in their own estimation, fully prepared for conflict; but they were sadly deficient in the sight of God and His sorrowful servants. When, nearly forty years later, the Lord directed Israel to go up and take Jericho, He promised to go with them. The ark containing His law was borne before their armies. His appointed leaders were to direct their movements, under the divine supervision. With such guidance, no harm could come to them. But now, contrary to the command of God and the solemn prohibition of their leaders, without the ark, and without Moses, they went out to meet the armies of the enemy.

The trumpet sounded an alarm, and Moses hastened after them with the warning, "Wherefore now do ye transgress the commandment of the Lord? but it shall not prosper. Go not up, for the Lord is not among you; that ye be not smitten before your enemies. For the Amalekites and the Canaanites are there before you, and ye shall fall by the sword."

The Canaanites had heard of the mysterious power that seemed to be guarding this people and of the wonders wrought in their behalf, and they now summoned a strong force to repel the invaders. The attacking army had no leader. No prayer was offered that God would give them the victory. They set forth with the desperate purpose to reverse their fate or to die in battle. Though untrained in war, they were a vast multitude of armed men, and they hoped by a sudden and fierce assault to bear down all opposition. They presumptuously challenged the foe that had not dared to attack them.

The Canaanites had stationed themselves upon a rocky tableland reached only by difficult passes and a steep and dangerous ascent. The immense numbers of the Hebrews could only render their defeat more terrible. They slowly threaded the mountain paths, exposed to the deadly missiles of their enemies above. Massive rocks came thundering down, marking their path with the blood of the slain. Those who reached the summit, exhausted with their ascent, were fiercely repulsed, and driven back with great loss. The field of carnage was strewn with the bodies of the dead. The army of Israel was utterly defeated. Destruction and death was the result of that rebellious experiment.

Forced to submission at last, the survivors "returned, and wept before the Lord;" but "the Lord would not hearken" to their voice. Deuteronomy 1:45. By their signal victory the enemies of Israel, who had before awaited with trembling the approach of that mighty host, were inspired with confidence to resist them. All the reports they had heard concerning the marvelous things that God had wrought for His people, they now regarded as false, and they felt that there was no cause for fear. That first defeat of Israel, by inspiring the Canaanites with courage and resolution, had greatly increased the difficulties of the conquest. Nothing remained for Israel but to fall back from the face of their victorious foes, into the wilderness, knowing that here must be the grave of a whole generation.

35

The Rebellion of Korah

The judgments visited upon the Israelites served for a time to restrain their murmuring and insubordination, but the spirit of rebellion was still in the heart and eventually brought forth the bitterest fruits. The former rebellions had been mere popular tumults, arising from the sudden impulse of the excited multitude; but now a deep-laid conspiracy was formed, the result of a determined purpose to overthrow the authority of the leaders appointed by God Himself.

Korah, the leading spirit in this movement, was a Levite, of the family of Kohath, and a cousin of Moses; he was a man of ability and influence. Though appointed to the service of the tabernacle, he had become dissatisfied with his position and aspired to the dignity of the priesthood. The bestowal upon Aaron and his house of the priestly office, which had formerly devolved upon the first-born son of every family, had given rise to jealousy and dissatisfaction, and for some time Korah had been secretly opposing the authority of Moses and Aaron, though he had not ventured upon any open act of rebellion. He finally conceived the bold design of overthrowing both the civil and the religious authority. He did not fail to find sympathizers. Close to the tents of Korah and the Kohathites, on the south side of the tabernacle, was the encampment of the tribe of Reuben, the tents of Dathan and Abiram, two princes of this tribe, being near that of Korah. These princes readily joined in his ambitious schemes. Being descendants from the eldest son of Jacob, they claimed that the civil authority belonged to them, and they determined to divide with Korah the honors of the priesthood.

The state of feeling among the people favored the designs of Korah. In the bitterness of their disappointment, their former doubts, jealousy, and hatred had returned, and again their complaints were directed against their patient leader. 396 The Israelites were continually losing sight of the fact that they were under divine guidance. They forgot that the Angel of the covenant was their invisible leader, that, veiled by the cloudy pillar, the presence of Christ went before them, and that from Him Moses received all his directions.

They were unwilling to submit to the terrible sentence that they must all die in the wilderness, and hence they were ready to seize upon every pretext for believing that it was not God but Moses who was leading them and who had pronounced their doom. The best efforts of the meekest man upon the earth could not quell the insubordination of this people; and although the marks of God's displeasure at their former perverseness were still before them in their broken ranks and missing numbers, they did not take the lesson to heart. Again they were overcome by temptation.

The humble shepherd's life of Moses had been far more peaceful and happy than his present position as leader of that vast assembly of turbulent spirits. Yet Moses dared not choose. In place of a shepherd's crook a rod of power had been given him, which he could not lay down until God should release him.

He who reads the secrets of all hearts had marked the purposes of Korah and his companions and had given His people such warning and instruction as might have enabled them to escape the deception of these designing men. They had seen the judgment of God fall upon Miriam because of her jealousy and complaints against Moses. The Lord had declared that Moses was greater than a prophet. "With him will I speak mouth to mouth." "Wherefore, then," He added, "were ye not afraid to speak against My servant Moses?" Numbers 12:8. These instructions were not intended for Aaron and Miriam alone, but for all Israel.

Korah and his fellow conspirators were men who had been favored with special manifestations of God's power and greatness. They were of the number who went up with Moses into the mount and beheld the divine glory. But since that time a change had come. A temptation, slight at first, had been harbored, and had strengthened as it was encouraged, until their minds were controlled by Satan, and they ventured upon their work of disaffection. Professing great interest in the prosperity of the people, they first whispered their discontent to one another and then to leading men of Israel. Their insinuations were so readily received that they 397 ventured still further, and at last they really believed themselves to be actuated by zeal for God.

They were successful in alienating two hundred and fifty princes, men of renown in the congregation. With these strong and influential supporters they felt confident of making a radical change in the government and greatly improving upon the administration of Moses and Aaron.

Jealousy had given rise to envy, and envy to rebellion. They had discussed the question of the right of Moses to so great authority and honor, until they had come to regard him as occupying a very enviable position, which any of them could fill as well as he. And they deceived themselves and one another into thinking that Moses and Aaron had themselves assumed the positions they held. The discontented ones said that these leaders had exalted themselves above the congregation of the Lord, in taking upon them the priesthood and government, but their house was not entitled to distinction above others in Israel; they were no more holy than the people, and it should be enough for them to be on a level with their brethren, who were equally favored with God's special presence and protection.

The next work of the conspirators was with

the people. To those who are in the wrong, and deserving of reproof, there is nothing more pleasing than to receive sympathy and praise. And thus Korah and his associates gained the attention and enlisted the support of the congregation. The charge that the murmurings of the people had brought upon them the wrath of God was declared to be a mistake. They said that the congregation were not at fault, since they desired nothing more than their rights; but that Moses was an overbearing ruler; that he had reproved the people as sinners, when they were a holy people, and the Lord was among them.

Korah reviewed the history of their travels through the wilderness, where they had been brought into strait places, and many had perished because of their murmuring and disobedience. His hearers thought they saw clearly that their troubles might have been prevented if Moses had pursued a different course. They decided that all their disasters were chargeable to him, and that their exclusion from Canaan was in consequence of the mismanagement of Moses and Aaron; that if Korah would be their leader, and would encourage them by dwelling 398 upon their good deeds instead of reproving their sins, they would have a very peaceful, prosperous journey; instead of wandering to and fro in the wilderness, they would proceed directly to the Promised Land.

In this work of disaffection there was greater union and harmony among the discordant elements of the congregation than had ever before existed. Korah's success with the people increased his confidence and confirmed him in his belief that the usurpation of authority by Moses, if unchecked, would be fatal to the liberties of Israel; he also claimed that God had opened the matter to him, and had authorized him to make a change in the government before it should be too late. But many were not ready to accept Korah's accusations against Moses. The memory of his patient, self-sacrificing labors came up before them, and conscience was disturbed. It was therefore necessary to assign some selfish motive for his deep interest for Israel; and the old charge was reiterated, that he had led them out to perish in the wilderness, that he might seize upon their possessions.

For a time this work was carried on secretly. As soon, however, as the movement had gained sufficient strength to warrant an open rupture, Korah appeared at the head of the faction, and publicly accused Moses and Aaron of usurping authority which Korah and his associates were equally entitled to share. It was charged, further, that the people had been deprived of their liberty and independence. "Ye take too much upon you," said the conspirators, "seeing all the congregation are holy, every one of them, and the Lord is among them: wherefore then lift ye up yourselves above the congregation of the Lord?"

Moses had not suspected this deep-laid plot, and when its terrible significance burst upon him, he fell upon his face in silent appeal to God. He arose sorrowful indeed, but calm and strong. Divine guidance had been granted him. "Even tomorrow," he said, "the Lord will show who are His, and who is holy; and will cause him to come near unto Him: even him whom He hath chosen will He cause to come near unto Him." The test was to be deferred until the morrow, that all might have time for reflection. Then those who aspired to the priesthood were to come each with a censer, and offer incense at the tabernacle in the presence of the congregation. The law was very explicit that only those who had been ordained to the sacred office should minister in the sanctuary. And even the priests, Nadab and Abihu, had been destroyed 399 for venturing to offer "strange fire," in disregard of a divine command. Yet Moses challenged his accusers, if they dared enter upon so perilous an appeal, to refer the matter to God.

Singling out Korah and his fellow Levites, Moses said, "Seemeth it but a small thing unto you, that the God of Israel hath separated you from the congregation of Israel, to bring you near to Himself to do the service of the tabernacle of the Lord, and to stand before the congregation to minister unto them? And He hath brought thee near to Him, and all thy brethren the sons of Levi with thee: and seek ye the priesthood also? for which cause both thou and all thy company are gathered together against the Lord. And what is Aaron, that ye murmur against him?"

Dathan and Abiram had not taken so bold a stand as had Korah; and Moses, hoping that they might have been drawn into the conspiracy without having become wholly corrupted, summoned them to appear before him, that he might hear their charges against him. But they would not come, and they insolently refused to acknowledge his authority. Their reply, uttered in the hearing of the congregation, was, "Is it a small thing that thou hast brought us up out of a land that floweth with milk and honey, to kill us in the wilderness, except thou make thyself altogether a prince over us? Moreover thou hast not brought us into a land that floweth with milk and honey, or given us inheritance of fields and vineyards: wilt thou put out the eyes of these men? We will not come up."

Thus they applied to the scene of their bondage the very language in which the Lord had described the promised inheritance. They accused Moses of pretending to act under divine guidance, as a means of establishing his authority; and they declared that they would no longer submit to be led about like blind men, now toward Canaan, and now toward the wilderness, as best suited his ambitious designs. Thus he who had been as a tender father, a patient shepherd, was represented in the blackest character of a tyrant and usurper. The exclusion from Canaan, in punishment of their own sins, was charged upon him.

It was evident that the sympathies of the people were with the disaffected party; but Moses made no effort at self-vindication. He solemnly appealed to God, in the presence of the congregation, as a witness to the purity of his motives and the uprightness of his conduct, and implored Him to be his judge.

400   On the morrow, the two hundred and fifty princes, with Korah at their head, presented themselves, with their censers. They were brought into the court of the tabernacle, while the people gathered without, to await the result. It was not Moses who assembled the congregation to behold the defeat of Korah and his company, but the rebels, in their blind presumption, had called them together to witness their victory. A large part of the congregation openly sided with Korah, whose hopes were high of carrying his point against Aaron.

As they were thus assembled before God, "the glory of the Lord appeared unto all the congregation." The divine warning was communicated to Moses and Aaron, "Separate yourselves from among this congregation, that I may consume them in a moment." But they fell upon their faces, with the prayer, "O God, the God of the spirits of all flesh, shall one man sin, and wilt Thou be wroth with all the congregation?"

Korah had withdrawn from the assembly to join Dathan and Abiram when Moses, accompanied by the seventy elders, went down with a last warning to the men who had refused to come to him. The multitudes followed, and before delivering his message, Moses, by divine direction, bade the people, "Depart, I pray you, from the tents of these wicked men, and touch nothing of theirs, lest ye be consumed in all their sins." The warning was obeyed, for an apprehension of impending judgment rested upon all. The chief rebels saw themselves abandoned by those whom they had deceived, but their hardihood was unshaken. They stood with their families in the door of their tents, as if in defiance of the divine warning.

In the name of the God of Israel, Moses now declared, in the hearing of the congregation: "Hereby ye shall know that the Lord hath sent me to do all these works; for I have not done them of mine own mind. If these men die the common death of all men, or if they be visited after the visitation of all men, then the Lord hath not sent me. But if the Lord make a new thing, and the earth open her mouth, and swallow them up, with all that appertain unto them, and they go down quick into the pit, then ye shall understand that these men have provoked the Lord."

The eyes of all Israel were fixed upon Moses as they stood, in terror and expectation, awaiting the event. As he ceased speaking, the solid earth parted, and the rebels went down alive into the 401 pit, with all that pertained to them, and "they perished from among the congregation." The people fled, self-condemned as partakers in the sin.

But the judgments were not ended. Fire flashing from the cloud consumed the two hundred and fifty princes who had offered incense. These men, not being the first in rebellion, were not destroyed with the chief conspirators. They were permitted to see their end, and to have an opportunity for repentance; but their sympathies were with the rebels, and they shared their fate.

When Moses was entreating Israel to flee from the coming destruction, the divine judgment might even then have been stayed, if Korah and his company had repented and sought forgiveness. But their stubborn persistence sealed their doom. The entire congregation were sharers in their guilt, for all had, to a greater or less degree, sympathized with them. Yet God in His great mercy made a distinction between the leaders in rebellion and those whom they had led. The people who had permitted themselves to be deceived were still granted space for repentance. Overwhelming evidence had been given that they were wrong, and that Moses was right. The signal manifestation of God's power had removed all uncertainty.

Jesus, the Angel who went before the Hebrews, sought to save them from destruction. Forgiveness was lingering for them. The judgment of God had come very near, and appealed to them to repent. A special, irresistible interference from heaven had arrested their rebellion. Now, if they would respond to the interposition of God's providence, they might be saved. But while they fled from the judgments, through fear of destruction, their rebellion was not cured. They returned to their tents that night terrified, but not repentant.

They had been flattered by Korah and his company until they really believed themselves to be very good people, and that they had been wronged and abused by Moses. Should they admit that Korah and his company were wrong, and Moses right, then they would be compelled to receive as the word of God the sentence that they must die in the wilderness. They were not willing to submit to this, and they tried to believe that Moses had deceived them. They had fondly cherished the hope that a new order of things was about to be established, in which praise would be substituted for reproof, and ease for anxiety and conflict. The men who had per- 402 ished had spoken flattering words and had professed great interest and love for them, and the people concluded that Korah and his companions must have been good men, and that Moses had by some means been the cause of their destruction.

It is hardly possible for men to offer greater insult to God than to despise and reject the instrumentalities He would use for their salvation. The Israelites had not only done this, but had purposed to put both Moses and Aaron to death. Yet they did not realize the necessity of seeking pardon of God for their grievous sin. That night of probation was not passed in repentance and confession, but in devising some way to resist the evidences which showed them to be the greatest of sinners. They still cherished hatred of the men of God's appointment, and braced themselves to resist their authority. Satan was at hand to pervert their judgment and lead them blindfold to destruction.

All Israel had fled in alarm at the cry of the doomed sinners who went down into the pit, for they said, "Lest the earth swallow us up also." "But on the morrow all the congregation of the children of Israel murmured against Moses and against Aaron, saying, Ye have killed the people of the Lord." And they were about to proceed to violence against their faithful, self-sacrificing leaders.

A manifestation of the divine glory was seen in the cloud above the tabernacle, and a voice from the cloud spoke to Moses and Aaron, "Get you up from among this congregation, that I may consume them as in a moment."

The guilt of sin did not rest upon Moses, and hence he did not fear and did not hasten away and leave the congregation to perish. Moses lingered, in this fearful crisis manifesting the true shepherd's interest for the flock of his care. He pleaded that the wrath of God might not utterly destroy the people of His choice. By his intercession he stayed the arm of vengeance, that a full end might not be made of disobedient, rebellious Israel.

But the minister of wrath had gone forth; the plague was doing its work of death. By his brother's direction, Aaron took a censer and hastened into the midst of the congregation to "make an atonement for them." "And he stood between the dead and the living." As the smoke of the incense ascended, the prayers of Moses in the tabernacle went up to God; and the plague was stayed; but not until fourteen thousand of 403 Israel lay dead, an evidence of the guilt of murmuring and rebellion.

But further evidence was given that the priesthood had been established in the family of Aaron. By divine direction each tribe prepared a rod and wrote upon it the name of the tribe. The name of Aaron was upon that of Levi. The rods were laid up in the tabernacle, "before the testimony." The blossoming of any rod was to be a token that the Lord had chosen that tribe for the priesthood. On the morrow, "behold, the rod of

Aaron for the house of Levi was budded, and brought forth buds, and bloomed blossoms, and yielded almonds." It was shown to the people, and afterward laid up in the tabernacle as a witness to succeeding generations. This miracle effectually settled the question of the priesthood.

It was now fully established that Moses and Aaron had spoken by divine authority, and the people were compelled to believe the unwelcome truth that they were to die in the wilderness. "Behold," they exclaimed, "we die, we perish, we all perish." They confessed that they had sinned in rebelling against their leaders, and that Korah and his company had suffered from the just judgment of God.

In the rebellion of Korah is seen the working out, upon a narrower stage, of the same spirit that led to the rebellion of Satan in heaven. It was pride and ambition that prompted Lucifer to complain of the government of God, and to seek the overthrow of the order which had been established in heaven. Since his fall it has been his object to infuse the same spirit of envy and discontent, the same ambition for position and honor, into the minds of men. He thus worked upon the minds of Korah, Dathan, and Abiram, to arouse the desire for self-exaltation and excite envy, distrust, and rebellion. Satan caused them to reject God as their leader, by rejecting the men of God's appointment. Yet while in their murmuring against Moses and Aaron they blasphemed God, they were so deluded as to think themselves righteous, and to regard those who had faithfully reproved their sins as actuated by Satan.

Do not the same evils still exist that lay at the foundation of Korah's ruin? Pride and ambition are widespread; and when these are cherished, they open the door to envy, and a striving for supremacy; the soul is alienated from God, and unconsciously drawn into the ranks of Satan. 404 Like Korah and his companions, many, even of the professed followers of Christ, are thinking, planning, and working so eagerly for self-exaltation that in order to gain the sympathy and support of the people they are ready to pervert the truth, falsifying and misrepresenting the Lord's servants, and even charging them with the base and selfish motives that inspire their own hearts. By persistently reiterating falsehood, and that against all evidence, they at last come to believe it to be truth. While endeavoring to destroy the confidence of the people in the men of God's appointment, they really believe that they are engaged in a good work, verily doing God service.

The Hebrews were not willing to submit to the directions and restrictions of the Lord. They were restless under restraint, and unwilling to receive reproof. This was the secret of their murmuring against Moses. Had they been left free to do as they pleased, there would have been fewer complaints against their leader. All through the history of the church God's servants have had the same spirit to meet.

It is by sinful indulgence that men give Satan access to their minds, and they go from one stage of wickedness to another. The rejection of light darkens the mind and hardens the heart, so that it is easier for them to take the next step in sin and to reject still clearer light, until at last their habits of wrongdoing become fixed. Sin ceases to appear sinful to them. He who faithfully preaches God's word, thereby condemning their sins, too often incurs their hatred. Unwilling to endure the pain and sacrifice necessary to reform, they turn upon the Lord's servant and denounce his reproofs as uncalled for and severe. Like Korah, they declare that the people are not at fault; it is the reprover that causes all the trouble. And soothing their consciences with this deception, the jealous and disaffected combine to sow discord in the church and weaken the hands of those who would build it up.

Every advance made by those whom God has called to lead in His work has excited suspicion; every act has been misrepresented by the jealous and faultfinding. Thus it was in the time of Luther, of the Wesleys and other reformers. Thus it is today.

Korah would not have taken the course he did had he *known* that all the directions and reproofs communicated to Israel were from God. But he might have known this. God had given over-whelming evidence that He was leading Israel. But Korah and his companions rejected light until they became so blinded that the most striking manifestations of His power were not sufficient to convince them; they attributed them all to human or satanic agency. The same thing was done by the people, who the day after the destruction of Korah and his company came to Moses and Aaron, saying, "Ye have killed the people of the Lord." Notwithstanding they had had the most convincing evidence of God's displeasure at their course, in the destruction of the men who had deceived them, they dared to attribute His judgments to Satan, declaring that through the power of the evil one, Moses and Aaron had caused the death of good and holy men. It was this act that sealed their doom. They had committed the sin against the Holy Spirit, a sin by which man's heart is effectually hardened against the influence of divine grace. "Whoso-ever speaketh a word against the Son of man," said Christ, "it shall be forgiven him: but whosoever speaketh against the Holy Ghost, it shall not be forgiven him." Matthew 12:32. These words were spoken by our Saviour when the gracious works which He had performed through the power of God were attributed by the Jews to Beelzebub. It is through the agency of the Holy Spirit that God communicates with

man; and those who deliberately reject this agency as satanic, have cut off the channel of communication between the soul and Heaven.

God works by the manifestation of His Spirit to reprove and convict the sinner; and if the Spirit's work is finally rejected, there is no more that God can do for the soul. The last resource of divine mercy has been employed. The transgressor has cut himself off from God, and sin has no remedy to cure itself. There is no reserved power by which God can work to convict and convert the sinner. "Let him alone" (Hosea 4:17) is the divine command. Then "there remaineth no more sacrifice for sins, but a certain fearful looking for of judgment and fiery indignation, which shall devour the adversaries." Hebrews 10:26, 27.

36

In the Wilderness

For nearly forty years the children of Israel are lost to view in the obscurity of the desert. "The space," says Moses, "in which we came from Kadesh-barnea, until we were come over the brook Zered, was thirty and eight years; until all the generation of the men of war were wasted out from among the host, as the Lord sware unto them. For indeed the hand of the Lord was against them, to destroy them from among the host, until they were consumed." Deuteronomy 2:14, 15.

During these years the people were constantly reminded that they were under the divine rebuke. In the rebellion at Kadesh they had rejected God, and God had for the time rejected them. Since they had proved unfaithful to His covenant, they were not to receive the sign of the covenant, the rite of circumcision. Their desire to return to the land of slavery had shown them to be unworthy of freedom, and the ordinance of the Passover, instituted to commemorate the deliverance from bondage, was not to be observed.

Yet the continuance of the tabernacle service testified that God had not utterly forsaken His people. And His providence still supplied their wants. "The Lord thy God hath blessed thee in all the works of thy hand," said Moses, in rehearsing the history of their wanderings. "He knoweth thy walking through this great wilderness; these forty years the Lord thy God hath been with thee; thou hast lacked nothing." And the Levites' hymn, recorded by Nehemiah, vividly pictures God's care for Israel, even during these years of rejection and banishment: "Thou in Thy manifold mercies forsookest them not in the wilderness: the pillar of the cloud departed not from them by day, to lead them in the way; neither the pillar of fire by night, to show them light, and the way wherein they should go. Thou gavest also Thy good Spirit to instruct them, and withheldest not Thy manna from their mouth, and gavest them water for their thirst. Yea, forty years didst Thou sustain them in the wilderness; . . . their clothes waxed not old, and their feet swelled not." Nehemiah 9:19-21.

The wilderness wandering was not only ordained as a judgment upon the rebels and murmurers, but it was to serve as a discipline for the rising generation, preparatory to their entrance into the Promised Land. Moses declared to them, "As a man chasteneth his son, so the Lord thy God chasteneth thee," "to humble thee, and to prove thee, to know what was in thine heart, whether thou wouldest keep His commandments, or no. And He . . . suffered thee to hunger, and fed thee with manna, which thou knewest not, neither did thy fathers know; that He might make thee know that man doth not live by bread only, but by every word that proceedeth out of the mouth of the Lord doth man live." Deuteronomy 8:5, 2, 3.

"He found him in a desert land, and in the waste howling wilderness; He led him about, He instructed him, He kept him as the apple of His eye." "In all their affliction He was afflicted, and the Angel of His presence saved them; in His love and in His pity He redeemed them; and He bare them, and carried them all the days of old." Deuteronomy 32:10; Isaiah 63:9.

Yet the only records of their wilderness life are instances of rebellion against the Lord. The revolt of Korah had resulted in the destruction of fourteen thousand of Israel. And there were isolated cases that showed the same spirit of contempt for the divine authority.

On one occasion the son of an Israelitish woman and of an Egyptian, one of the mixed multitude that had come up with Israel from Egypt, left his own part of the camp, and entering that of the Israelites, claimed the right to pitch his tent there. This the divine law forbade him to do, the descendants of an Egyptian being excluded from the congregation until the third generation. A dispute arose between him and an Israelite, and the matter being referred to the judges was decided against the offender.

Enraged at this decision, he cursed the judge, and in the heat of passion blasphemed the name of God. He was immediately brought before Moses. The command had been given, "He that curseth his father, or his mother, shall surely be put to death" (Exodus 21:17); but no provision had been made to meet this case. So terrible was the crime that there was felt to be a necessity for special direction from God. The man was placed in ward until the will of the Lord could be ascertained. God Himself pronounced the sentence; by the divine direction the blasphemer

was conducted outside the camp and stoned to death. Those who had been witnesses to the sin placed their hands upon his head, thus solemnly testifying to the truth of the charge against him. Then they threw the first stones, and the people who stood by afterward joined in executing the sentence.

This was followed by the announcement of a law to meet similar offenses: "Thou shalt speak unto the children of Israel, saying, Whosoever curseth his God shall bear his sin. And he that blasphemeth the name of the Lord, he shall surely be put to death, and all the congregation shall certainly stone him: as well the stranger, as he that is born in the land, when he blasphemeth the name of the Lord, shall be put to death." Leviticus 24:15, 16.

There are those who will question God's love and His justice in visiting so severe punishment for words spoken in the heat of passion. But both love and justice require it to be shown that utterances prompted by malice against God are a great sin. The retribution visited upon the first offender would be a warning to others, that God's name is to be held in reverence. But had this man's sin been permitted to pass unpunished, others would have been demoralized; and as the result many lives must eventually have been sacrificed.

The mixed multitude that came up with the Israelites from Egypt were a source of continual temptation and trouble. They professed to have renounced idolatry and to worship the true God; but their early education and training had molded their habits and character, and they were more or less corrupted with idolatry and with irreverence for God. They were oftenest the ones to stir up strife and were the first to complain, and they leavened the camp with their idolatrous practices and their murmurings against God.

Soon after the return into the wilderness, an instance of Sabbath violation occurred, under circumstances that rendered it a case of peculiar guilt. The Lord's announcement that He would disinherit Israel had roused a spirit of rebellion. One of the people, angry at being excluded from Canaan, and determined to show his defiance of God's law, ventured upon the open transgression of the fourth commandment by going out to gather sticks upon the Sabbath. During the sojourn in the wilderness the kindling of fires upon the seventh day had been strictly prohibited. The prohibition was not to extend to the land of Canaan, where the severity of the climate would often render fires a necessity; but in the wilderness, fire was not needed for warmth. The act of this man was a willful and deliberate violation of the fourth commandment—a sin, not of thoughtlessness or ignorance, but of presumption.

He was taken in the act and brought before

Moses. It had already been declared that Sabbathbreaking should be punished with death, but it had not yet been revealed how the penalty was to be inflicted. The case was brought by Moses before the Lord, and the direction was given, "The man shall be surely put to death: all the congregation shall stone him with stones without the camp." Numbers 15:35. The sins of blasphemy and willful Sabbathbreaking received the same punishment, being equally an expression of contempt for the authority of God.

In our day there are many who reject the creation Sabbath as a Jewish institution and urge that if it is to be kept, the penalty of death must be inflicted for its violation; but we see that blasphemy received the same punishment as did Sabbathbreaking. Shall we therefore conclude that the third commandment also is to be set aside as applicable only to the Jews? Yet the argument drawn from the death penalty applies to the third, the fifth, and indeed to nearly all the ten precepts, equally with the fourth. Though God may not now punish the transgression of His law with temporal penalties, yet His word declares that the wages of sin is death; and in the final execution of the judgment it will be found that death is the portion of those who violate His sacred precepts.

During the entire forty years in the wilderness, the people were every week reminded of the sacred obligation of the Sabbath, by the miracle of the manna. Yet even this did not lead them to obedience. Though they did not venture upon so open and bold transgression as had 410 received such signal punishment, yet there was great laxness in the observance of the fourth commandment. God declares through His prophet, "My Sabbaths they greatly polluted." Ezekiel 20:13-24. And this is enumerated among the reasons for the exclusion of the first generation from the Promised Land. Yet their children did not learn the lesson. Such was their neglect of the Sabbath during the forty years' wandering, that though God did not prevent them from entering Canaan, He declared that they should be scattered among the heathen after the settlement in the Land of Promise.

From Kadesh the children of Israel had turned back into the wilderness; and the period of their desert sojourn being ended, they came, "even the whole congregation, into the desert of Zin in the first month: and the people abode in Kadesh." Numbers 20:1.

Here Miriam died and was buried. From that scene of rejoicing on the shores of the Red Sea, when Israel went forth with song and dance to celebrate Jehovah's triumph, to the wilderness grave which ended a lifelong wandering—such had been the fate of millions who with high hopes had come forth from Egypt. Sin had dashed from their lips the cup of blessing. Would the next generation learn the lesson?

"For all this they sinned still, and believed not for His wondrous works. . . . When He slew them, then they sought Him: and they returned and inquired early after God. And they remembered that God was their Rock, and the high God their Redeemer." Psalm 78:32-35. Yet they did not turn to God with a sincere purpose. Though when afflicted by their enemies they sought help from Him who alone could deliver, yet "their heart was not right with Him, neither were they steadfast in His covenant. But He, being full of compassion, forgave their iniquity, and destroyed them not: yea, many a time turned He His anger away. . . . For He remembered that they were but flesh; a wind that passeth away, and cometh not again." Verses 37-39.

37

The Smitten Rock

From the smitten rock in Horeb first flowed the living stream that refreshed Israel in the desert. During all their wanderings, wherever the need existed, they were supplied with water by a miracle of God's mercy. The water did not, however, continue to flow from Horeb. Wherever in their journeyings they wanted water, there from the clefts of the rock it gushed out beside their encampment.

It was Christ, by the power of His word, that caused the refreshing stream to flow for Israel. "They drank of that spiritual Rock that followed them: and that Rock was Christ." 1 Corinthians 10:4. He was the source of all temporal as well as spiritual blessings. Christ, the true Rock, was with them in all their wanderings. "They thirsted not when He led them through the deserts: He caused the waters to flow out of the rock for them; He clave the rock also, and the waters gushed out." "They ran in the dry places like a river." Isaiah 48:21; Psalm 105:41.

The smitten rock was a figure of Christ, and through this symbol the most precious spiritual truths are taught. As the life-giving waters flowed from the smitten rock, so from Christ, "smitten of God," "wounded for our transgressions," "bruised for our iniquities" (Isaiah 53:4, 5), the stream of salvation flows for a lost race. As the rock had been once smitten, so Christ was to be "once offered to bear the sins of many." Hebrews 9:28. Our Saviour was not to be sacrificed a second time; and it is only necessary for those who seek the blessings of His grace to ask in the name of Jesus, pouring forth the heart's desire in penitential prayer. Such prayer will bring before the Lord of hosts the wounds of Jesus, and then will flow forth afresh the life-giving blood, symbolized by the flowing

This chapter is based on Numbers 20:1-13.

of the living water for Israel.

412 The flowing of the water from the rock in the desert was celebrated by the Israelites, after their establishment in Canaan, with demonstrations of great rejoicing. In the time of Christ this celebration had become a most impressive ceremony. It took place on the occasion of the Feast of Tabernacles, when the people from all the land were assembled at Jerusalem. On each of the seven days of the feast the priests went out with music and the choir of Levites to draw water in a golden vessel from the spring of Siloam. They were followed by multitudes of the worshipers, as many as could get near the stream drinking of it, while the jubilant strains arose, "With joy shall ye draw water out of the wells of salvation." Isaiah 12:3. Then the water drawn by the priests was borne to the temple amid the sounding of trumpets and the solemn chant, "Our feet shall stand within thy gates, O Jerusalem." Psalm 122:2. The water was poured out upon the altar of burnt offering, while songs of praise rang out, the multitudes joining in triumphant chorus with musical instruments and deep-toned trumpets.

The Saviour made use of this symbolic service to direct the minds of the people to the blessings that He had come to bring them. "In the last day, that great day of the feast," His voice was heard in tones that rang through the temple courts, "If any man thirst, let him come unto Me, and drink. He that believeth on Me, as the Scripture hath said, out of his belly shall flow rivers of living water." "This," said John, "spake He of the Spirit, which they that believe on Him should receive." John 7:37-39. The refreshing water, welling up in a parched and barren land, causing the desert place to blossom, and flowing out to give life to the perishing, is an emblem of the divine grace which Christ alone can bestow, and which is as the living water, purifying, refreshing, and invigorating the soul. He in whom Christ is abiding has within him a never-failing fountain of grace and strength. Jesus cheers the life and brightens the path of all who truly seek Him. His love, received into the heart, will spring up in good works unto eternal life. And not only does it bless the soul in which it springs, but the living stream will flow out in words and deeds of righteousness, to refresh the thirsting around him.

The same figure Christ had employed in His conversation with the woman of Samaria at Jacob's well: "Whosoever drinketh of the water that I give him shall never thirst; but the 413 water that I shall give him shall be in him a well of water springing up into everlasting life." John 4:14. Christ combines the two types. He is the rock, He is the living water.

The same beautiful and expressive figures are carried throughout the Bible. Centuries before the advent of Christ, Moses pointed to Him as the rock of Israel's salvation (Deuteronomy 32:15); the psalmist sang of Him as "my Redeemer," "the rock of my strength," "the rock that is higher than I," "a rock of habitation," "rock of my heart," "rock of my refuge." In David's song His grace is pictured also as the cool, "still waters," amid green pastures, beside which the heavenly Shepherd leads His flock. Again, "Thou shalt make them," he says, "drink of the river of Thy pleasures. For with Thee is the fountain of life." Psalms 19:14; 62:7; 61:2; 71:3 (margin); 73:26 (margin); 94:22; 23:2; 36:8, 9. And the wise man declares, "The wellspring of wisdom [is] as a flowing brook." Proverbs 18:4. To Jeremiah, Christ is "the fountain of living waters;" to Zechariah, "a fountain opened . . . for sin and for uncleanness." Jeremiah 2:13; Zechariah 13:1.

Isaiah describes Him as the "rock of ages," and "the shadow of a great rock in a weary land." Isaiah 26:4 (margin); 32:2. And he records the precious promise, bringing vividly to mind the living stream that flowed for Israel: "When the poor and needy seek water, and there is none, and their tongue faileth for thirst, I the Lord will hear them, I the God of Israel will not forsake them." "I will pour water upon him that is thirsty, and floods upon the dry ground;" "in the wilderness shall waters break out, and streams in the desert." The invitation is given, "Ho, every one that thirsteth, come ye to the waters." Isaiah 41:17; 44:3; 35:6; 55:1. And in the closing pages of the Sacred Word this invitation is echoed. The river of the water of life, "clear as crystal," proceeds from the throne of God and the Lamb; and the gracious call is ringing down through the ages, "Whosoever will, let him take the water of life freely." Revelation 22:17.

Just before the Hebrew host reached Kadesh, the living stream ceased that for so many years had gushed out beside their encampment. It was the Lord's purpose again to test His people. He would prove whether they would trust His providence or imitate the unbelief of their fathers.

They were now in sight of the hills of Canaan. A few days' march would bring them 414 to the borders of the Promised Land. They were but a little distance from Edom, which belonged to the descendants of Esau, and through which lay the appointed route to Canaan. The direction had been given to Moses, "Turn you northward. And command thou the people, saying, Ye are to pass through the coast of your brethren the children of Esau, which dwell in Seir; and they shall be afraid of you. . . . Ye shall buy meat of them for money, that ye may eat; and ye shall also buy water of them for money, that ye may drink." Deuteronomy 2:3-6. These directions should have been sufficient to explain why their supply of water had been cut off; they were

162

about to pass through a well-watered, fertile country, in a direct course to the land of Canaan. God had promised them an unmolested passage through Edom, and an opportunity to purchase food, and also water sufficient to supply the host. The cessation of the miraculous flow of water should therefore have been a cause of rejoicing, a token that the wilderness wandering was ended. Had they not been blinded by their unbelief, they would have understood this. But that which should have been an evidence of the fulfillment of God's promise was made the occasion of doubt and murmuring. The people seemed to have given up all hope that God would bring them into possession of Canaan, and they clamored for the blessings of the wilderness.

Before God permitted them to enter Canaan, they must show that they believed His promise. The water ceased before they had reached Edom. Here was an opportunity for them, for a little time, to walk by faith instead of sight. But the first trial developed the same turbulent, unthankful spirit that had been manifested by their fathers. No sooner was the cry for water heard in the encampment than they forgot the hand that had for so many years supplied their wants, and instead of turning to God for help, they murmured against Him, in their desperation exclaiming, "Would God that we had died when our brethren died before the Lord!" (Numbers 20:1-13); that is, they wished they had been of the number who were destroyed in the rebellion of Korah.

Their cries were directed against Moses and Aaron: "Why have ye brought up the congregation of the Lord into this wilderness, that we and our cattle should die there? And wherefore have ye made us to come up out of Egypt, to bring us in unto this evil place? it is no place of seed, or of figs, or of vines, or of pomegranates; neither is there any water to drink."

The leaders went to the door of the tabernacle and fell upon their faces. Again "the glory of the Lord appeared," and Moses was directed, "Take the rod, and gather thou the assembly together, thou and Aaron thy brother, and speak ye unto the rock before their eyes; and it shall give forth his water, and thou shalt bring forth to them water out of the rock."

The two brothers went on before the multitude, Moses with the rod of God in his hand. They were now aged men. Long had they borne with the rebellion and obstinacy of Israel; but now, at last, even the patience of Moses gave way. "Hear now, ye rebels," he cried; "must we fetch you water out of this rock?" and instead of speaking to the rock, as God had commanded him, he smote it twice with the rod.

The water gushed forth in abundance to satisfy the host. But a great wrong had been done. Moses had spoken from irritated feeling; his words were an expression of human passion rather than of holy indignation because God had been dishonored. "Hear now, ye rebels," he said. This accusation was true, but even truth is not to be spoken in passion or impatience. When God had bidden Moses to charge upon Israel their rebellion, the words had been painful to him, and hard for them to bear, yet God had sustained him in delivering the message. But when he took it upon himself to accuse them, he grieved the Spirit of God and wrought only harm to the people. His lack of patience and self-control was evident. Thus the people were given occasion to question whether his past course had been under the direction of God, and to excuse their own sins. Moses, as well as they, had offended God. His course, they said, had from the first been open to criticism and censure. They had now found the pretext which they desired for rejecting all the reproofs that God had sent them through His servant.

Moses manifested distrust of God. "Shall we bring water?" he questioned, as if the Lord would not do what He promised. "Ye believed Me not," the Lord declared to the two brothers, "to sanctify Me in the eyes of the children of Israel." At the time when the water failed, their own faith in the fulfillment of God's promise had been shaken by the murmuring and rebellion of the people. The first generation had been condemned to perish in the wilderness because of their unbelief, yet the same spirit appeared in their children. Would these also fail of receiving the promise? Wearied and disheartened, Moses and Aaron had made no effort to stem the current of popular feeling. Had they themselves manifested unwavering faith in God, they might have set the matter before the people in such a light as would have enabled them to bear this test. By prompt, decisive exercise of the authority vested in them as magistrates, they might have quelled the murmuring. It was their duty to put forth every effort in their power to bring about a better state of things before asking God to do the work for them. Had the murmuring at Kadesh been promptly checked, what a train of evil might have been prevented!

By his rash act Moses took away the force of the lesson that God purposed to teach. The rock, being a symbol of Christ, had been once smitten, as Christ was to be once offered. The second time it was needful only to speak to the rock, as we have only to ask for blessings in the name of Jesus. By the second smiting of the rock the significance of this beautiful figure of Christ was destroyed.

More than this, Moses and Aaron had assumed power that belongs only to God. The necessity for divine interposition made the occasion one of great solemnity, and the leaders of Israel should have improved it to impress the people with reverence for God and to strengthen their faith in His power and goodness. When they angrily cried, "Must we fetch you water out of this rock?" they put themselves in God's place, as though the power lay with themselves, men possessing human frailties and passions. Wearied with the continual murmuring and rebellion of the people, Moses had lost sight of his Almighty Helper, and without the divine strength he had been left to mar his record for an exhibition of human weakness. The man who might have stood pure, firm, and unselfish to the close of his work had been overcome at last. God had been dishonored before the congregation of Israel, when He should have been magnified and exalted.

God did not on this occasion pronounce judgments upon those whose wicked course had so provoked Moses and Aaron. All the reproof fell upon the leaders. Those who stood as God's representatives had not honored Him. Moses and Aaron had felt themselves aggrieved, losing sight of the fact that the murmuring of the people was not against them but against God. It was 419 by looking to themselves, appealing to their own sympathies, that they unconsciously fell into sin, and failed to set before the people their great guilt before God.

Bitter and deeply humiliating was the judgment immediately pronounced. "The Lord spake unto Moses and Aaron, Because ye believed Me not, to sanctify Me in the eyes of the children of Israel, therefore ye shall not bring this congregation into the land which I have given them." With rebellious Israel they must die before the crossing of the Jordan. Had Moses and Aaron been cherishing self-esteem or indulging a passionate spirit in the face of divine warning and reproof, their guilt would have been far greater. But they were not chargeable with willful or deliberate sin; they had been overcome by a sudden temptation, and their contrition was immediate and heartfelt. The Lord accepted their repentance, though because of the harm their sin might do among the people, He could not remit its punishment.

Moses did not conceal his sentence, but told the people that since he had failed to ascribe glory to God, he could not lead them into the Promised Land. He bade them mark the severe punishment visited upon him, and then consider how God must regard their murmurings in charging upon a mere man the judgments which they had by their sins brought upon themselves. He told them how he had pleaded with God for a remission of the sentence, and had been refused. "The Lord was wroth with me for your sakes," he said, "and would not hear me." Deuteronomy 3:26.

On every occasion of difficulty or trial the Israelites had been ready to charge Moses with having led them from Egypt, as though God had had no agency in the matter. Throughout their journeyings, as they had complained of the difficulties in the way, and murmured against their leaders, Moses had told them, "Your murmurings are against God. It is not I, but God, who has wrought in your deliverance." But his hasty words before the rock, "shall we bring water?" were a virtual admission of their charge, and would thus confirm them in their unbelief and justify their murmurings. The Lord would remove this impression forever from their minds, by forbidding Moses to enter the Promised Land. Here was unmistakable evidence that their leader was not Moses, but the mighty Angel of whom the Lord had said, "Behold, I send an Angel before thee, to keep thee in the way, and to bring thee into the place which I have prepared. Beware of Him, and obey His voice: . . . for My name is in Him." Exodus 23:20, 21.

"The Lord was wroth with me for your 420 sakes," said Moses. The eyes of all Israel were upon Moses, and his sin cast a reflection upon God, who had chosen him as the leader of His people. The transgression was known to the whole congregation; and had it been passed by lightly, the impression would have been given that unbelief and impatience under great provocation might be excused in those in responsible positions. But when it was declared that because of that one sin Moses and Aaron were not to enter Canaan, the people knew that God is no respecter of persons, and that He will surely punish the transgressor.

The history of Israel was to be placed on record for the instruction and warning of coming generations. Men of all future time must see the God of heaven as an impartial ruler, in no case justifying sin. But few realize the exceeding sinfulness of sin. Men flatter themselves that God is too good to punish the transgressor. But in the light of Bible history it is evident that God's goodness and His love engage Him to deal with sin as an evil fatal to the peace and happiness of the universe.

Not even the integrity and faithfulness of Moses could avert the retribution of his fault. God had forgiven the people greater transgressions, but He could not deal with sin in the leaders as in those who were led. He had honored Moses above every other man upon the earth. He had revealed to him His glory, and through him He had communicated His statutes to Israel. The fact that Moses had enjoyed so great light and knowledge made his sin more grievous. Past faithfulness will not atone for one wrong act. The greater the light and privileges granted to man, the greater is his responsibility, the more aggravated his failure, and the heavier his punishment.

Moses was not guilty of a great crime, as men would view the matter; his sin was one of common occurrence. The psalmist says that "he spake unadvisedly with his lips." Psalm 106:33. To human judgment this may seem a light thing; but if God dealt so severely with this sin in His most faithful and honored servant, He will not excuse it in others. The spirit of self-exaltation, the disposition to censure our brethren, is displeasing to God. Those who indulge in these evils cast doubt upon the work of God, and give the skeptical an excuse for their unbelief. The more important one's position, and the greater his influence, the greater is the necessity that he should cultivate patience and humility.

421 If the children of God, especially those who stand in positions of responsibility, can be led to take to themselves the glory that is due to God, Satan exults. He has gained a victory. It was thus that he fell. Thus he is most successful in tempting others to ruin. It is to place us on our guard against his devices that God has given in His word so many lessons teaching the danger of self-exaltation. There is not an impulse of our nature, not a faculty of the mind or an inclination of the heart, but needs to be, moment by moment, under the control of the Spirit of God. There is not a blessing which God bestows upon man, nor a trial which He permits to befall him, but Satan both can and will seize upon it to tempt, to harass and destroy the soul, if we give him the least advantage. Therefore however great one's spiritual light, however much he may enjoy of the divine favor and blessing, he should ever walk humbly before the Lord, pleading in faith that God will direct every thought and control every impulse.

All who profess godliness are under the most sacred obligation to guard the spirit, and to exercise self-control under the greatest provocation. The burdens placed upon Moses were very great; few men will ever be so severely tried as he was; yet this was not allowed to excuse his sin. God has made ample provision for His people; and if they rely upon His strength, they will never become the sport of circumstances. The strongest temptation cannot excuse sin. However great the pressure brought to bear upon the soul, transgression is our own act. It is not in the power of earth or hell to compel anyone to do evil. Satan attacks us at our weak points, but we need not be overcome. However severe or unexpected the assault, God has provided help for us, and in His strength we may conquer.

422 **38**
The Journey Around Edom

The encampment of Israel at Kadesh was but a short distance from the borders of Edom, and both Moses and the people greatly desired to follow the route through this country to the Promised Land; accordingly they sent a message, as God had directed them, to the Edomite king—

"Thus saith thy brother Israel, Thou knowest all the travail that hath befallen us: how our fathers went down into Egypt, and we have dwelt in Egypt a long time; and the Egyptians vexed us, and our fathers: and when we cried unto the Lord, He heard our voice, and sent an Angel, and hath brought us forth out of Egypt: and, behold, we are in Kadesh, a city in the uttermost of thy border. Let us pass, I pray thee, through thy country: we will not pass through the fields, or through the vineyards, neither will we drink of the water of the wells: we will go by the king's highway, we will not turn to the right hand nor to the left, until we have passed thy borders."

To this courteous request a threatening refusal was returned: "Thou shalt not pass by me, lest I come out against thee with the sword."

Surprised at this repulse, the leaders of Israel sent a second appeal to the king, with the promise, "We will go by the highway: and if I and my cattle drink of thy water, then I will pay for it: I will only, without doing anything else, go through on my feet."

"Thou shalt not go through," was the answer. Armed bands of Edomites were already posted at the difficult passes, so that any peaceful advance in that direction was impossible, and the Hebrews were forbidden to resort to force. They must make the long journey around the land of Edom.

Had the people, when brought into trial, trusted in God, the Captain of the Lord's host would have led them through Edom, and the fear of 423 them would have rested upon the inhabitants of the land, so that, instead of manifesting hostility, they would have shown them favor. But the Israelites did not act promptly upon God's word, and while they were complaining and murmuring, the golden opportunity passed. When they were at last ready to present their request to the king, it was refused. Ever since they left Egypt, Satan had been steadily at work to throw hindrances and temptations in their way, that they might not inherit Canaan. And by their own unbelief they had repeatedly opened the door for him to resist the purpose of God.

It is important to believe God's word and act upon it promptly, while His angels are waiting to work for us. Evil angels are ready to contest every step of advance. And when God's providence bids His children go forward, when He is ready to do great things for them, Satan tempts them to displease the Lord by hesitation and delay; he seeks to kindle a spirit of strife or to arouse murmuring or unbelief, and thus deprive them of the blessings that God desired to

This chapter is based on Numbers 20:14-29; 21:1-9.

bestow. God's servants should be minutemen, ever ready to move as fast as His providence opens the way. Any delay on their part gives time for Satan to work to defeat them.

In the directions first given to Moses concerning their passage through Edom, after declaring that the Edomites should be afraid of Israel, the Lord had forbidden His people to make use of this advantage against them. Because the power of God was engaged for Israel, and the fears of the Edomites would make them an easy prey, the Hebrews were not therefore to prey upon them. The command given them was, "Take ye good heed unto yourselves therefore: meddle not with them; for I will not give you of their land, no, not so much as a foot breadth; because I have given Mount Seir unto Esau for a possession." Deuteronomy 2:4, 5. The Edomites were descendants of Abraham and Isaac, and for the sake of these His servants, God had shown favor to the children of Esau. He had given them Mount Seir for a possession, and they were not to be disturbed unless by their sins they should place themselves beyond the reach of His mercy. The Hebrews were to dispossess and utterly destroy the inhabitants of Canaan, who had filled up the measure of their iniquity; but the Edomites were still probationers, and as such were to be mercifully dealt with. God delights in mercy, and He manifests His compassion before He inflicts His judgments. He **424** teaches Israel to spare the people of Edom, before requiring them to destroy the inhabitants of Canaan.

The ancestors of Edom and Israel were brothers, and brotherly kindness and courtesy should exist between them. The Israelites were forbidden, either then or at any future time, to revenge the affront given them in the refusal of passage through the land. They must not expect to possess any part of the land of Edom. While the Israelites were the chosen and favored people of God, they must heed the restrictions which He placed upon them. God had promised them a goodly inheritance; but they were not to feel that they alone had any rights in the earth, and seek to crowd out all others. They were directed, in all their intercourse with the Edomites, to beware of doing them injustice. They were to trade with them, buying such supplies as were needed, and promptly paying for all they received. As an encouragement to Israel to trust in God and obey His word they were reminded, "The Lord thy God hath blessed thee; . . . thou hast lacked nothing." Deuteronomy 2:7. They were not dependent upon the Edomites, for they had a God rich in resources. They must not by force or fraud seek to obtain anything pertaining to them; but in all their intercourse they should exemplify the principle of the divine law, "Thou shalt love thy neighbor as thyself."

Had they in this manner passed through

Edom, as God had purposed, the passage would have proved a blessing, not only to themselves, but to the inhabitants of the land; for it would have given them an opportunity to become acquainted with God's people and His worship and to witness how the God of Jacob prospered those who loved and feared Him. But all this the unbelief of Israel had prevented. God had given the people water in answer to their clamors, but He permitted their unbelief to work out its punishment. Again they must traverse the desert and quench their thirst from the miraculous spring, which, had they but trusted in Him, they would no longer have needed.

Accordingly the hosts of Israel again turned toward the south, and made their way over sterile wastes, that seemed even more dreary after a glimpse of the green spots among the hills and valleys of Edom. From the mountain range overlooking this gloomy desert, rises Mount Hor, whose summit was to be the place of Aaron's death and burial. When the Israelites came to this mountain, the divine command was addressed to Moses—

"Take Aaron and Eleazar his son, and bring **425** them up unto Mount Hor: and strip Aaron of his garments, and put them upon Eleazar his son: and Aaron shall be gathered unto his people, and shall die there."

Together these two aged men and the younger one toiled up the mountain height. The heads of Moses and Aaron were white with the snows of sixscore winters. Their long and eventful lives had been marked with the deepest trials and the greatest honors that had ever fallen to the lot of man. They were men of great natural ability, and all their powers had been developed, exalted, and dignified by communion with the Infinite One. Their life had been spent in unselfish labor for God and their fellow men; their countenances gave evidence of great intellectual power, firmness and nobility of purpose, and strong affections.

Many years Moses and Aaron had stood side by side in their cares and labors. Together they had breasted unnumbered dangers, and had shared together the signal blessing of God; but the time was at hand when they must be separated. They moved on very slowly, for every moment in each other's society was precious. The ascent was steep and toilsome; and as they often paused to rest, they communed together of the past and the future. Before them, as far as the eye could reach, was spread out the scene of their desert wanderings. In the plain below were encamped the vast hosts of Israel, for whom these chosen men had spent the best portion of their lives; for whose welfare they had felt so deep an interest, and made so great sacrifices. Somewhere beyond the mountains of Edom was the path leading to the Promised Land—that land whose blessings Moses and Aaron were not to enjoy. No rebellious feelings found a place in their hearts, no expression of murmuring escaped their lips; yet a solemn sadness rested upon their countenances as they remembered what had debarred them from the inheritance of their fathers.

Aaron's work for Israel was done. Forty years before, at the age of eighty-three, God had called him to unite with Moses in his great and important mission. He had co-operated with his brother in leading the children of Israel from Egypt. He had held up the great leader's hands when the Hebrew hosts gave battle to Amalek. He had been permitted to ascend Mount Sinai, to approach into the presence of God, and to behold the divine glory. The Lord had conferred upon the family of Aaron the office of the priesthood, and had honored him with the sacred consecration of high priest. He had sustained him in the holy office by the terrible manifestations of divine judgment in the destruction of Korah and his company. It was through Aaron's intercession that the plague was stayed. When his two sons were slain for disregarding God's express command, he did not rebel or even murmur. Yet the record of his noble life had been marred. Aaron committed a grievous sin when he yielded to the clamors of the people and made the golden calf at Sinai; and again, when he united with Miriam in envy and murmuring against Moses. And he, with Moses, offended the Lord at Kadesh by disobeying the command to speak to the rock that it might give forth its water.

God intended that these great leaders of His people should be representatives of Christ. Aaron bore the names of Israel upon his breast. He communicated to the people the will of God. He entered the most holy place on the Day of Atonement, "not without blood," as a mediator for all Israel. He came forth from that work to bless the congregation, as Christ will come forth to bless His waiting people when His work of atonement in their behalf shall be ended. It was the exalted character of that sacred office as representative of our great High Priest that made Aaron's sin at Kadesh of so great magnitude.

With deep sorrow Moses removed from Aaron the holy vestments, and placed them upon Eleazar, who thus became his successor by divine appointment. For his sin at Kadesh, Aaron was denied the privilege of officiating as God's high priest in Canaan—of offering the first sacrifice in the goodly land, and thus consecrating the inheritance of Israel. Moses was to continue to bear his burden in leading the people to the very borders of Canaan. He was to come within sight of the Promised Land, but was not to enter it. Had these servants of God, when they stood before the rock at Kadesh, borne unmurmuringly the test there brought upon them, how different would have been their future! A wrong act can never be undone. It may be that the work of a lifetime will not recover what has been lost in a single moment of temptation or even thoughtlessness.

The absence from the camp of the two great leaders, and the fact that they had been accompanied by Eleazar, who, it was well known, was to be Aaron's successor in holy office, awakened a feeling of apprehension, and their return was anxiously awaited. As the people looked about them, upon their vast congregation, they saw that nearly all the adults who left Egypt had perished in the wilderness. All felt a foreboding of evil as they remembered the sentence pronounced against Moses and Aaron. Some were aware of the object of that mysterious journey to the summit of Mount Hor, and their solicitude for their leaders was heightened by bitter memories and self-accusings.

The forms of Moses and Eleazar were at last discerned, slowly descending the mountainside, but Aaron was not with them. Upon Eleazar were the sacerdotal garments, showing that he had succeeded his father in the sacred office. As the people with heavy hearts gathered about their leader, Moses told them that Aaron had died in his arms upon Mount Hor, and that they there buried him. The congregation broke forth in mourning and lamentation, for they all loved Aaron, though they had so often caused him sorrow. "They mourned for Aaron thirty days, even all the house of Israel."

Concerning the burial of Israel's high priest, the Scriptures give only the simple record, "There Aaron died, and there he was buried." Deuteronomy 10:6. In what striking contrast to the customs of the present day was this burial, conducted according to the express command of God. In modern times the funeral services of a man of high position are often made the occasion of ostentatious and extravagant display. When Aaron died, one of the most illustrious men that ever lived, there were only two of his nearest friends to witness his death and to attend his burial. And that lonely grave upon Mount Hor was forever hidden from the sight of Israel. God is not honored in the great display so often made over the dead, and the extravagant expense incurred in returning their bodies to the dust.

The whole congregation sorrowed for Aaron, yet they could not feel the loss so keenly as did Moses. The death of Aaron forcibly reminded Moses that his own end was near; but short as the time of his stay on earth must be, he deeply felt the loss of his constant companion—the one who had shared his joys and sorrows, his hopes and fears, for so many long years. Moses must now continue the work alone; but he knew that God was his friend, and upon Him he leaned more heavily.

Soon after leaving Mount Hor the Israelites

428 suffered defeat in an engagement with Arad, one of the Canaanite kings. But as they earnestly sought help from God, divine aid was granted them, and their enemies were routed. This victory, instead of inspiring gratitude and leading the people to feel their dependence upon God, made them boastful and self-confident. Soon they fell into the old habit of murmuring. They were now dissatisfied because the armies of Israel had not been permitted to advance upon Canaan immediately after their rebellion at the report of the spies nearly forty years before. They pronounced their long sojourn in the wilderness an unnecessary delay, reasoning that they might have conquered their enemies as easily heretofore as now.

As they continued their journey toward the south, their route lay through a hot, sandy valley, destitute of shade or vegetation. The way seemed long and difficult, and they suffered from weariness and thirst. Again they failed to endure the test of their faith and patience. By continually dwelling on the dark side of their experiences, they separated themselves farther and farther from God. They lost sight of the fact that but for their murmuring when the water ceased at Kadesh, they would have been spared the journey around Edom. God had purposed better things for them. Their hearts should have been filled with gratitude to Him that He had punished their sin so lightly. But instead of this, they flattered themselves that if God and Moses had not interfered, they might now have been in possession of the Promised Land. After bringing trouble upon themselves, making their lot altogether harder than God designed, they charged all their misfortunes upon Him. Thus they cherished bitter thoughts concerning His dealings with them, and finally they became discontented with everything. Egypt looked brighter and more desirable than liberty and the land to which God was leading them.

As the Israelites indulged the spirit of discontent, they were disposed to find fault even with their blessings. "And the people spake against God, and against Moses, Wherefore have ye brought us up out of Egypt to die in the wilderness? for there is no bread, neither is there any water; and our soul loatheth this light bread."

Moses faithfully set before the people their great sin. It was God's power alone that had preserved them in "that great and terrible wilderness, wherein were fiery serpents, and 429 scorpions, and drought, where there was no water." Deuteronomy 8:15. Every day of their travels they had been kept by a miracle of divine mercy. In all the way of God's leading they had found water to refresh the thirsty, bread from heaven to satisfy their hunger, and peace and safety under the shadowy cloud by day and the pillar of fire by night. Angels had ministered to them as they climbed the rocky

heights or threaded the rugged paths of the wilderness. Notwithstanding the hardships they had endured, there was not a feeble one in all their ranks. Their feet had not swollen in their long journeys, neither had their clothes grown old. God had subdued before them the fierce beasts of prey and the venomous reptiles of the forest and the desert. If with all these tokens of His love the people still continued to complain, the Lord would withdraw His protection until they should be led to appreciate His merciful care, and return to Him with repentance and humiliation.

Because they had been shielded by divine power they had not realized the countless dangers by which they were continually surrounded. In their ingratitude and unbelief they had anticipated death, and now the Lord permitted death to come upon them. The poisonous serpents that infested the wilderness were called fiery serpents, on account of the terrible effects produced by their sting, it causing violent inflammation and speedy death. As the protecting hand of God was removed from Israel, great numbers of the people were attacked by these venomous creatures.

Now there was terror and confusion throughout the encampment. In almost every tent were the dying or the dead. None were secure. Often the silence of night was broken by piercing cries that told of fresh victims. All were busy in ministering to the sufferers, or with agonizing care endeavoring to protect those who were not yet stricken. No murmuring now escaped their lips. When compared with the present suffering, their former difficulties and trials seemed unworthy of a thought.

The people now humbled themselves before God. They came to Moses with their confessions and entreaties. "We have sinned," they said, "for we have spoken against the Lord, and against thee." Only a little before, they had accused him of being their worst enemy, the cause of all their distress and afflictions. But even when the words were upon their lips, they knew that the charge was false; and as soon as real trouble came they fled to him as the only 430 one who could intercede with God for them. "Pray unto the Lord," was their cry, "that He take away the serpents from us."

Moses was divinely commanded to make a serpent of brass resembling the living ones, and to elevate it among the people. To this, all who had been bitten were to look, and they would find relief. He did so, and the joyful news was sounded throughout the encampment that all who had been bitten might look upon the brazen serpent and live. Many had already died, and when Moses raised the serpent upon the pole, some would not believe that merely gazing upon that metallic image would heal them; these perished in their unbelief. Yet there were many who had faith in the provision which God had made. Fathers, mothers, brothers, and sisters were anxiously engaged in helping their suffering, dying friends to fix their languid eyes upon the serpent. If these, though faint and dying, could only once look, they were perfectly restored.

The people well knew that there was no power in the serpent of brass to cause such a change in those who looked upon it. The healing virtue was from God alone. In His wisdom He chose this way of displaying His power. By this simple means the people were made to realize that this affliction had been brought upon them by their sins. They were also assured that while obeying God they had no reason to fear, for He would preserve them.

The lifting up of the brazen serpent was to teach Israel an important lesson. They could not save themselves from the fatal effect of the poison in their wounds. God alone was able to heal them. Yet they were required to show their faith in the provision which He had made. They must look in order to live. It was their faith that was acceptable with God, and by looking upon the serpent their faith was shown. They knew that there was no virtue in the serpent itself, but it was a symbol of Christ; and the necessity of faith in His merits was thus presented to their minds. Heretofore many had brought their offerings to God, and had felt that in so doing they made ample atonement for their sins. They did not rely upon the Redeemer to come, of whom these offerings were only a type. The Lord would now teach them that their sacrifices, in themselves, had no more power or virtue than the serpent of brass, but were, like that, to lead their minds to Christ, the great sin offering.

431 "As Moses lifted up the serpent in the wilderness," even so was the Son of man "lifted up: that whosoever believeth in Him should not perish, but have eternal life." John 3:14, 15. All who have ever lived upon the earth have felt the deadly sting of "that old serpent, called the devil, and Satan." Revelation 12:9. The fatal effects of sin can be removed only by the provision that God has made. The Israelites saved their lives by looking upon the uplifted serpent. That look implied faith. They lived because they believed God's word, and trusted in the means provided for their recovery. So the sinner may look to Christ, and live. He receives pardon through faith in the atoning sacrifice. Unlike the inert and lifeless symbol, Christ has power and virtue in Himself to heal the repenting sinner.

While the sinner cannot save himself, he still has something to do to secure salvation. "Him that cometh to Me," says Christ, "I will in no wise cast out." John 6:37. But we must *come* to Him; and when we repent of our sins, we must believe that He accepts and pardons us. Faith is the gift of God, but the power to exercise it is

ours. Faith is the hand by which the soul takes hold upon the divine offers of grace and mercy.

Nothing but the righteousness of Christ can entitle us to one of the blessings of the covenant of grace. There are many who have long desired and tried to obtain these blessings, but have not received them, because they have cherished the idea that they could do something to make themselves worthy of them. They have not looked away from self, believing that Jesus is an all-sufficient Saviour. We must not think that our own merits will save us; Christ is our only hope of salvation. "For there is none other name under heaven given among men, whereby we must be saved." Acts 4:12.

When we trust God fully, when we rely upon the merits of Jesus as a sin-pardoning Saviour, we shall receive all the help that we can desire. Let none look to self, as though they had power to save themselves. Jesus died for us because we were helpless to do this. In Him is our hope, our justification, our righteousness. When we see our sinfulness we should not despond and fear that we have no Saviour, or that He has no thoughts of mercy toward us. At this very time He is inviting us to come to Him in our helplessness and be saved.

Many of the Israelites saw no help in the rem- 432 edy which Heaven had appointed. The dead and dying were all around them, and they knew that, without divine aid, their own fate was certain; but they continued to lament their wounds, their pains, their sure death, until their strength was gone, and their eyes were glazed, when they might have had instant healing. If we are conscious of our needs, we should not devote all our powers to mourning over them. While we realize our helpless condition without Christ, we are not to yield to discouragement, but rely upon the merits of a crucified and risen Saviour. Look and live. Jesus has pledged His word; He will save all who come unto Him. Though millions who need to be healed will reject His offered mercy, not one who trusts in His merits will be left to perish.

Many are unwilling to accept of Christ until the whole mystery of the plan of salvation shall be made plain to them. They refuse the look of faith, although they see that thousands have looked, and have felt the efficacy of looking, to the cross of Christ. Many wander in the mazes of philosophy, in search of reasons and evidence which they will never find, while they reject the evidence which God has been pleased to give. They refuse to walk in the light of the Sun of Righteousness, until the reason of its shining shall be explained. All who persist in this course will fail to come to a knowledge of the truth. God will never remove every occasion for doubt. He gives sufficient evidence on which to base faith, and if this is not accepted, the mind is left in darkness. If those who were bitten by the serpents had stopped to doubt and question before they would consent to look, they would have perished. It is our duty, first, to look; and the look of faith will give us life.

433

39

The Conquest of Bashan

After passing to the south of Edom, the Israelites turned northward, and again set their faces toward the Promised Land. Their route now lay over a vast, elevated plain, swept by cool, fresh breezes from the hills. It was a welcome change from the parched valley through which they had been traveling, and they pressed forward, buoyant and hopeful. Having crossed the brook Zered, they passed to the east of the land of Moab; for the command had been given, "Distress not the Moabites, neither contend with them in battle: for I will not give thee of their land for a possession; because I have given Ar unto the children of Lot." And the same direction was repeated concerning the Ammonites, who were also descendants of Lot.

Still pushing northward, the hosts of Israel soon reached the country of the Amorites. This strong and warlike people originally occupied the southern part of the land of Canaan; but, increasing in numbers, they crossed the Jordan, made war upon the Moabites, and gained possession of a portion of their territory. Here they had settled, holding undisputed sway over all the land from the Arnon as far north as the Jabbok. The route to the Jordan which the Israelites desired to pursue lay directly through this territory, and Moses sent a friendly message to Sihon, the Amorite king, at his capital: "Let me pass through thy land: I will go along by the highway, I will neither turn unto the right hand nor to the left. Thou shalt sell me meat for money, that I may eat; and give me water for money, that I may drink: only I will pass through on my feet." The answer was a decided refusal, and all the hosts of the Amorites were summoned to oppose the progress of the invaders. This formidable army struck terror to the Israelites, who were poorly prepared for an encounter with well-

434 armed and well-disciplined forces. So far as skill in warfare was concerned, their enemies had the advantage. To all human appearance, a speedy end would be made of Israel.

But Moses kept his gaze fixed upon the cloudy pillar, and encouraged the people with the thought that the token of God's presence was still with them. At the same time he directed them to do all that human power could do in preparing for war. Their enemies were eager for battle, and confident that they would blot out the unprepared Israelites from the land. But

from the Possessor of all lands the mandate had gone forth to the leader of Israel: "Rise ye up, take your journey, and pass over the river Arnon: behold, I have given into thine hand Sihon the Amorite, king of Heshbon, and his land: begin to possess it, and contend with him in battle. This day will I begin to put the dread of thee and the fear of thee upon the nations that are under the whole heaven, who shall hear report of thee, and shall tremble, and be in anguish because of thee."

These nations on the borders of Canaan would have been spared, had they not stood, in defiance of God's word, to oppose the progress of Israel. The Lord had shown Himself to be long-suffering, of great kindness and tender pity, even to these heathen peoples. When Abraham was shown in vision that his seed, the children of Israel, should be strangers in a strange land four hundred years, the Lord gave him the promise, "In the fourth generation they shall come hither again: for the iniquity of the Amorites is not yet full." Genesis 15:16. Although the Amorites were idolaters, whose life was justly forfeited by their great wickedness, God spared them four hundred years to give them unmistakable evidence that He was the only true God, the Maker of heaven and earth. All His wonders in bringing Israel from Egypt were known to them. Sufficient evidence was given; they might have known the truth, had they been willing to turn from their idolatry and licentiousness. But they rejected the light and clung to their idols.

When the Lord brought His people a second time to the borders of Canaan, additional evidence of His power was granted to those heathen nations. They saw that God was with Israel in the victory gained over King Arad and the Canaanites, and in the miracle wrought to save those who were perishing from the sting of the serpents. Although the Israelites had been refused a passage through the land of Edom, thus being compelled to take the long and diffi- 435 cult route by the Red Sea, yet in all their journeyings and encampments, past the land of Edom, of Moab and Ammon, they had shown no hostility, and had done no injury to the people or their possessions. On reaching the border of the Amorites, Israel had asked permission only to travel directly through the country, promising to observe the same rules that had governed their intercourse with other nations. When the Amorite king refused this courteous solicitation, and defiantly gathered his hosts for battle, their cup of iniquity was full, and God would now exercise His power for their overthrow.

The Israelites crossed the river Arnon and advanced upon the foe. An engagement took place, in which the armies of Israel were victorious; and, following up the advantage gained, they were soon in possession of the country of

This chapter is based on Deuteronomy 2; 3:1-11.

the Amorites. It was the Captain of the Lord's host who vanquished the enemies of His people; and He would have done the same thirty-eight years before had Israel trusted in Him.

Filled with hope and courage, the army of Israel eagerly pressed forward, and, still journeying northward, they soon reached a country that might well test their courage and their faith in God. Before them lay the powerful and populous kingdom of Bashan, crowded with great stone cities that to this day excite the wonder of the world—"threescore cities . . . with high walls, gates, and bars; besides unwalled towns a great many." Deuteronomy 3:1-11. The houses were constructed of huge black stones, of such stupendous size as to make the buildings absolutely impregnable to any force that in those times could have been brought against them. It was a country filled with wild caverns, lofty precipices, yawning gulfs, and rocky strongholds. The inhabitants of this land, descendants from a giant race, were themselves of marvelous size and strength, and so distinguished for violence and cruelty as to be the terror of all surrounding nations; while Og, the king of the country, was remarkable for size and prowess, even in a nation of giants.

But the cloudy pillar moved forward, and following its guidance the Hebrew hosts advanced to Edrei, where the giant king, with his forces, awaited their approach. Og had skillfully chosen the place of battle. The city of Edrei was situated upon the border of a tableland rising abruptly from the plain, and covered with jagged, volcanic rocks. It could be approached only by narrow pathways, steep and difficult of ascent. In case of defeat, his forces could find refuge in that wilderness of rocks, where it would be impossible for strangers to follow them.

Confident of success, the king came forth with an immense army upon the open plain, while shouts of defiance were heard from the tableland above, where might be seen the spears of thousands, eager for the fray. When the Hebrews looked upon the lofty form of that giant of giants towering above the soldiers of his army; when they saw the hosts that surrounded him, and beheld the seemingly impregnable fortress, behind which unseen thousands were entrenched, the hearts of many in Israel quaked with fear. But Moses was calm and firm; the Lord had said concerning the king of Bashan, "Fear him not: for I will deliver him, and all his people, and his land, into thy hand; and thou shalt do unto him as thou didst unto Sihon king of the Amorites, which dwelt at Heshbon."

The calm faith of their leader inspired the people with confidence in God. They trusted all to His omnipotent arm, and He did not fail them. Not mighty giants nor walled cities, armed hosts nor rocky fortresses, could stand

before the Captain of the Lord's host. The Lord led the army; the Lord discomfited the enemy; the Lord conquered in behalf of Israel. The giant king and his army were destroyed, and the Israelites soon took possession of the whole country. Thus was blotted from the earth that strange people who had given themselves up to iniquity and abominable idolatry.

In the conquest of Gilead and Bashan there were many who recalled the events which nearly forty years before had, in Kadesh, doomed Israel to the long desert wandering. They saw that the report of the spies concerning the Promised Land was in many respects correct. The cities were walled and very great, and were inhabited by giants, in comparison with whom the Hebrews were mere pygmies. But they could now see that the fatal mistake of their fathers had been in distrusting the power of God. This alone had prevented them from at once entering the goodly land.

When they were at the first preparing to enter Canaan, the undertaking was attended with far less difficulty than now. God had promised His people that if they would obey His voice He would go before them and fight for them; and He would also send hornets to drive out the inhabitants of the land. The fears of the nations had not been generally aroused, and little preparation had been made to oppose their progress. But when the Lord now bade Israel go forward, they must advance against alert and powerful foes, and must contend with large and well-trained armies that had been preparing to resist their approach.

In their contest with Og and Sihon the people were brought to the same test beneath which their fathers had so signally failed. But the trial was now far more severe than when God had commanded Israel to go forward. The difficulties in their way had greatly increased since they refused to advance when bidden to do so in the name of the Lord. It is thus that God still tests His people. And if they fail to endure the trial, He brings them again to the same point, and the second time the trial will come closer, and be more severe than the preceding. This is continued until they bear the test, or, if they are still rebellious, God withdraws His light from them and leaves them in darkness.

The Hebrews now remembered how once before, when their forces had gone to battle, they had been routed, and thousands slain. But they had then gone in direct opposition to the command of God. They had gone out without Moses, God's appointed leader, without the cloudy pillar, the symbol of the divine presence, and without the ark. But now Moses was with them, strengthening their hearts with words of hope and faith; the Son of God, enshrined in the cloudy pillar, led the way; and the sacred ark accompanied the host. This experience has a lesson for us. The mighty God of Israel is our God. In Him we may trust, and if we obey His requirements He will work for us in as signal a manner as He did for His ancient people. Everyone who seeks to follow the path of duty will at times be assailed by doubt and unbelief. The way will sometimes be so barred by obstacles, apparently insurmountable, as to dishearten those who will yield to discouragement; but God is saying to such, Go forward. Do your duty at any cost. The difficulties that seem so formidable, that fill your soul with dread, will vanish as you move forward in the path of obedience, humbly trusting in God.

40

Balaam

Returning to the Jordan from the conquest of Bashan, the Israelites, in preparation for the immediate invasion of Canaan, encamped beside the river, and just opposite the plain of Jericho. They were upon the very borders of Moab, and the Moabites were filled with terror at the close proximity of the invaders.

The people of Moab had not been molested by Israel, yet they had watched with troubled forebodings all that had taken place in the surrounding countries. The Amorites, before whom they had been forced to retreat, had been conquered by the Hebrews, and the territory which the Amorites had wrested from Moab was now in the possession of Israel. The hosts of Bashan had yielded before the mysterious power enshrouded in the cloudy pillar, and the giant strongholds were occupied by the Hebrews. The Moabites dared not risk an attack upon them; an appeal to arms was hopeless in face of the supernatural agencies that wrought in their behalf. But they determined, as Pharaoh had done, to enlist the power of sorcery to counteract the work of God. They would bring a curse upon Israel.

The people of Moab were closely connected with the Midianites, both by the ties of nationality and religion. And Balak, the king of Moab, aroused the fears of the kindred people, and secured their co-operation in his designs against Israel by the message, "Now shall this company lick up all that are round about us, as the ox licketh up the grass of the field." Balaam, an inhabitant of Mesopotamia, was reported to possess supernatural powers, and his fame had reached to the land of Moab. It was determined to call him to their aid. Accordingly, messengers of "the elders of Moab and the elders of Midian," were sent to secure his divinations and enchantments against Israel.

The ambassadors at once set out on their long journey over the mountains and across the deserts to Mesopotamia; and upon finding Balaam, they delivered to him the message of their king: "Behold, there is a people come out from Egypt: behold, they cover the face of the earth, and they abide over against me: come now therefore, I pray thee, curse me this people; for they are too mighty for me: peradventure I shall prevail, that we may smite them, and that I may drive them out of the land: for I wot that he whom thou blessest is blessed, and he whom thou cursest is cursed."

Balaam was once a good man and a prophet of God; but he had apostatized, and had given himself up to covetousness; yet he still professed to be a servant of the Most High. He was not ignorant of God's work in behalf of Israel; and when the messengers announced their errand, he well knew that it was his duty to refuse the rewards of Balak and to dismiss the ambassadors. But he ventured to dally with temptation, and urged the messengers to tarry with him that night, declaring that he could give no decided answer till he had asked counsel of the Lord. Balaam knew that his curse could not harm Israel. God was on their side, and so long as they were true to Him no adverse power of earth or hell could prevail against them. But his pride was flattered by the words of the ambassadors, "He whom thou blessest is blessed, and he whom thou cursest is cursed." The bribe of costly gifts and prospective exaltation excited his covetousness. He greedily accepted the offered treasures, and then, while professing strict obedience to the will of God, he tried to comply with the desires of Balak.

In the night season the angel of God came to Balaam with the message, "Thou shalt not go with them; thou shalt not curse the people: for they are blessed."

In the morning Balaam reluctantly dismissed the messengers, but he did not tell them what the Lord had said. Angry that his visions of gain and honor had been suddenly dispelled, he petulantly exclaimed, "Get you into your land: for the Lord refuseth to give me leave to go with you."

Balaam "loved the wages of unrighteousness." 2 Peter 2:15. The sin of covetousness, which God declares to be idolatry, had made him a timeserver, and through this one fault Satan gained entire control of him. It was this that caused his ruin. The tempter is ever presenting worldly gain and honor to entice men from the service of God. He tells them it is their overconscientiousness that keeps them from prosperity. Thus many are induced to venture out of the path of strict integrity. One wrong step makes the next easier, and they become more and more presumptuous. They will do and dare most terrible things when once they have given themselves to the control of avarice and a desire

This chapter is based on Numbers 22 to 24.

for power. Many flatter themselves that they can depart from strict integrity for a time, for the sake of some worldly advantage, and that having gained their object, they can change their course when they please. Such are entangling themselves in the snare of Satan, and it is seldom that they escape.

When the messengers reported to Balak the prophet's refusal to accompany them, they did not intimate that God had forbidden him. Supposing that Balaam's delay was merely to secure a richer reward, the king sent princes more in number and more honorable than the first, with promises of higher honors, and with authority to concede to any terms that Balaam might demand. Balak's urgent message to the prophet was, "Let nothing, I pray thee, hinder thee from coming unto me: for I will promote thee unto very great honor, and I will do whatsoever thou sayest unto me: come therefore, I pray thee, curse me this people."

A second time Balaam was tested. In response to the solicitations of the ambassadors he professed great conscientiousness and integrity, assuring them that no amount of gold and silver could induce him to go contrary to the will of God. But he longed to comply with the king's request; and although the will of God had already been definitely made known to him, he urged the messengers to tarry, that he might further inquire of God; as though the Infinite One were a man, to be persuaded.

In the night season the Lord appeared to Balaam and said, "If the men come to call thee, rise up, and go with them; but yet the word which I shall say unto thee, that shalt thou do." Thus far the Lord would permit Balaam to follow his own will, because he was determined upon it. He did not seek to do the will of God, but chose his own course, and then endeavored to secure the sanction of the Lord.

441   There are thousands at the present day who are pursuing a similar course. They would have no difficulty in understanding their duty if it were in harmony with their inclinations. It is plainly set before them in the Bible or is clearly indicated by circumstances and reason. But because these evidences are contrary to their desires and inclinations they frequently set them aside and presume to go to God to learn their duty. With great apparent conscientiousness they pray long and earnestly for light. But God will not be trifled with. He often permits such persons to follow their own desires and to suffer the result. "My people would not hearken to My voice. . . . So I gave them up unto their own hearts' lust: and they walked in their own counsels." Psalm 81:11, 12. When one clearly sees a duty, let him not presume to go to God with the prayer that he may be excused from performing it. He should rather, with a humble, submissive spirit, ask for divine strength and wisdom to meet its claims.

The Moabites were a degraded, idolatrous people; yet according to the light which they had received their guilt was not so great in the sight of Heaven as was that of Balaam. As he professed to be God's prophet, however, all he should say would be supposed to be uttered by divine authority. Hence he was not to be permitted to speak as he chose, but must deliver the message which God should give him. "The word which I shall say unto thee, that shalt thou do," was the divine command.

Balaam had received permission to go with the messengers from Moab if they came in the morning to call him. But, annoyed at his delay, and expecting another refusal, they set out on their homeward journey without further consultation with him. Every excuse for complying with the request of Balak had now been removed. But Balaam was determined to secure the reward; and, taking the beast upon which he was accustomed to ride, he set out on the journey. He feared that even now the divine permission might be withdrawn, and he pressed eagerly forward, impatient lest he should by some means fail to gain the coveted reward.

But "the angel of the Lord stood in the way for an adversary against him." The animal saw the divine messenger, who was unperceived by the man, and turned aside from the highway into a field. With cruel blows Balaam brought the beast back into the path; but again, in a narrow place shut in by walls, the angel appeared, and the animal, trying to avoid the menacing figure, crushed her master's foot against the wall. Balaam was blinded to the heavenly interposition, and knew not that God was obstructing his path. The man became exasperated, and beating the ass unmercifully, forced it to proceed.   442

Again, "in a narrow place, where was no way to turn either to the right hand or to the left," the angel appeared, as before, in a threatening attitude; and the poor beast, trembling with terror, made a full stop, and fell to the earth under its rider. Balaam's rage was unbounded, and with his staff he smote the animal more cruelly than before. God now opened its mouth, and by "the dumb ass speaking with man's voice," He "forbade the madness of the prophet." 2 Peter 2:16. "What have I done unto thee," it said, "that thou hast smitten me these three times?"

Furious at being thus hindered in his journey, Balaam answered the beast as he would have addressed an intelligent being—"Because thou hast mocked me: I would there were a sword in mine hand, for now would I kill thee." Here was a professed magician, on his way to pronounce a curse upon a whole people with the intent to paralyze their strength, while he had not power even to slay the animal upon which he rode!

The eyes of Balaam were now opened, and he beheld the angel of God standing with drawn sword ready to slay him. In terror "he bowed down his head, and fell flat on his face." The angel said to him, "Wherefore hast thou smitten thine ass these three times? Behold, I went out to withstand thee, because thy way is perverse before me: and the ass saw me, and turned from me these three times: unless she had turned from me surely now also I had slain thee, and saved her alive."

Balaam owed the preservation of his life to the poor animal that he had treated so cruelly. The man who claimed to be a prophet of the Lord, who declared that his eyes were open, and he saw the "vision of the Almighty," was so blinded by covetousness and ambition that he could not discern the angel of God visible to his beast. "The god of this world hath blinded the minds of them which believe not." 2 Corinthians 4:4. How many are thus blinded! They rush on in forbidden paths, transgressing the divine law, and cannot discern that God and His angels are against them. Like Balaam they are angry at those who would prevent their ruin.

Balaam had given evidence of the spirit that controlled him, by his treatment of his beast. "A righteous man regardeth the life of his beast: but the tender mercies of the wicked are cruel." Proverbs 12:10. Few realize as they should the sinfulness of abusing animals or leaving them to suffer from neglect. He who created man made the lower animals also, and "His tender mercies are over all His works." Psalm 145:9. The animals were created to serve man, but he has no right to cause them pain by harsh treatment or cruel exaction.

It is because of man's sin that "the whole creation groaneth and travaileth in pain together." Romans 8:22. Suffering and death were thus entailed, not only upon the human race, but upon the animals. Surely, then, it becomes man to seek to lighten, instead of increasing, the weight of suffering which his transgression has brought upon God's creatures. He who will abuse animals because he has them in his power is both a coward and a tyrant. A disposition to cause pain, whether to our fellow men or to the brute creation, is satanic. Many do not realize that their cruelty will ever be known, because the poor dumb animals cannot reveal it. But could the eyes of these men be opened, as were those of Balaam, they would see an angel of God standing as a witness, to testify against them in the courts above. A record goes up to heaven, and a day is coming when judgment will be pronounced against those who abuse God's creatures.

When he beheld the messenger of God, Balaam exclaimed in terror, "I have sinned; for I knew not that thou stoodest in the way against me: now therefore, if it displease thee, I will get me back again." The Lord suffered him to proceed on his journey, but gave him to understand that his words should be controlled by divine power. God would give evidence to Moab that the Hebrews were under the guardianship of Heaven, and this He did effectually when He showed them how powerless Balaam was even to utter a curse against them without divine permission.

The king of Moab, being informed of the approach of Balaam, went out with a large retinue to the borders of his kingdom, to receive him. When he expressed his astonishment at Balaam's delay, in view of the rich rewards awaiting him, the prophet's answer was, "Lo, I am come unto thee: have I now any power at all to say anything? the word that God putteth in my mouth, that shall I speak." Balaam greatly regretted this restriction; he feared that his purpose could not be carried out, because the Lord's controlling power was upon him.

With great pomp the king, with the chief dignitaries of his kingdom, escorted Balaam to "the high places of Baal," from which he could survey the Hebrew host. Behold the prophet as he stands upon the lofty height, looking down over the encampment of God's chosen people. How little do the Israelites know of what is taking place so near them! How little do they know of the care of God, extended over them by day and by night! How dull are the perceptions of God's people! How slow are they, in every age, to comprehend His great love and mercy! If they could discern the wonderful power of God constantly exerted in their behalf, would not their hearts be filled with gratitude for His love, and with awe at the thought of His majesty and power?

Balaam had some knowledge of the sacrificial offerings of the Hebrews, and he hoped that by surpassing them in costly gifts he might secure the blessing of God and ensure the accomplishment of his sinful projects. Thus the sentiments of the idolatrous Moabites were gaining control of his mind. His wisdom had become foolishness; his spiritual vision was beclouded; he had brought blindness upon himself by yielding to the power of Satan.

By Balaam's direction seven altars were erected, and he offered a sacrifice upon each. He then withdrew to a "high place," to meet with God, promising to make known to Balak whatever the Lord should reveal.

With the nobles and princes of Moab the king stood beside the sacrifice, while around them gathered the eager multitude, watching for the return of the prophet. He came at last, and the people waited for the words that should paralyze forever that strange power exerted in behalf of the hated Israelites. Balaam said:

"The king of Moab hath brought me from Aram,
Out of the mountains of the east,

Saying, Come, curse me Jacob,
And come, defy Israel.
How shall I curse, whom God hath not
    cursed?
Or how shall I defy, whom the Lord hath not
    defied?
For from the top of the rocks I see him,
And from the hills I behold him:
Lo, the people shall dwell alone,
And shall not be reckoned among the nations.
Who can count the dust of Jacob,
And the number of the fourth part of Israel?
Let me die the death of the righteous,
And let my last end be like his!"

447   Balaam confessed that he came with the purpose of cursing Israel, but the words he uttered
were directly contrary to the sentiments of his
heart. He was constrained to pronounce blessings, while his soul was filled with curses.

As Balaam looked upon the encampment of
Israel he beheld with astonishment the evidence
of their prosperity. They had been represented
to him as a rude, disorganized multitude, infest-
ing the country in roving bands that were a pest
and terror to the surrounding nations; but their
appearance was the reverse of all this. He saw
the vast extent and perfect arrangement of their
camp, everything bearing the marks of thorough
discipline and order. He was shown the favor
with which God regarded Israel, and their distinctive character as His chosen people. They
were not to stand upon a level with other
nations, but to be exalted above them all. "The
people shall dwell alone, and shall not be reckoned among the nations." At the time when
these words were spoken the Israelites had no
permanent settlement, and their peculiar character, their manners and customs, were not familiar to Balaam. But how strikingly was this
prophecy fulfilled in the afterhistory of Israel!
Through all the years of their captivity, through
all the ages since they were dispersed among the
nations, they have remained a distinct people.
So the people of God—the true Israel—though
scattered throughout all nations, are on earth but
sojourners, whose citizenship is in heaven.

Not only was Balaam shown the history of
the Hebrew people as a nation, but he beheld the
increase and prosperity of the true Israel of God
to the close of time. He saw the special favor of
the Most High attending those who love and
fear Him. He saw them supported by His arm as
they enter the dark valley of the shadow of
death. And he beheld them coming forth from
their graves, crowned with glory, honor, and
immortality. He saw the redeemed rejoicing in
the unfading glories of the earth made new.
Gazing upon the scene, he exclaimed, "Who can
count the dust of Jacob, and the number of the
fourth part of Israel?" And as he saw the crown
of glory on every brow, the joy beaming from

every countenance, and looked forward to that
endless life of unalloyed happiness, he uttered
the solemn prayer, "Let me die the death of the
righteous, and let my last end be like his!"

If Balaam had had a disposition to accept the   448
light that God had given, he would now have
made true his words; he would at once have
severed all connection with Moab. He would no
longer have presumed upon the mercy of God,
but would have returned to Him with deep
repentance. But Balaam loved the wages of
unrighteousness, and these he was determined
to secure.

Balak had confidently expected a curse that
would fall like a withering blight upon Israel;
and at the words of the prophet he passionately
exclaimed, "What hast thou done unto me? I
took thee to curse mine enemies, and, behold,
thou hast blessed them altogether." Balaam,
seeking to make a virtue of necessity, professed
to have spoken from a conscientious regard for
the will of God the words that had been forced
from his lips by divine power. His answer was,
"Must I not take heed to speak that which the
Lord hath put in my mouth?"

Balak could not even now relinquish his purpose. He decided that the imposing spectacle
presented by the vast encampment of the
Hebrews had so intimidated Balaam that he
dared not practice his divinations against them.
The king determined to take the prophet to some
point where only a small part of the host might
be seen. If Balaam could be induced to curse
them in detached parties, the whole camp would
soon be devoted to destruction. On the top of an
elevation called Pisgah another trial was made.
Again seven altars were erected, whereon were
placed the same offerings as at the first. The king
and his princes remained by the sacrifices, while
Balaam retired to meet with God. Again the
prophet was entrusted with a divine message,
which he was powerless to alter or withhold.

When he appeared to the anxious, expectant
company the question was put to him, "What
hath the Lord spoken?" The answer, as before,
struck terror to the heart of king and princes:

"God is not a man, that He should lie;
Neither the son of man, that He should
    repent:
Hath He said, and shall He not do it?
Or hath He spoken, and shall He not make it
    good?
Behold, I have received commandment to
    bless:
And He hath blessed; and I cannot reverse it.
He hath not beheld iniquity in Jacob,
Neither hath He seen perverseness in Israel:
The Lord his God is with him,
And the shout of a king is among them."

Awed by these revelations, Balaam   449

exclaimed, "Surely there is no enchantment against Jacob, neither is there any divination against Israel." The great magician had tried his power of enchantment, in accordance with the desire of the Moabites; but concerning this very occasion it should be said of Israel, "What hath God wrought!" While they were under the divine protection, no people or nation, though aided by all the power of Satan, should be able to prevail against them. All the world should wonder at the marvelous work of God in behalf of His people—that a man determined to pursue a sinful course should be so controlled by divine power as to utter, instead of imprecations, the richest and most precious promises, in the language of sublime and impassioned poetry. And the favor of God at this time manifested toward Israel was to be an assurance of His protecting care for His obedient, faithful children in all ages. When Satan should inspire evil men to misrepresent, harass, and destroy God's people, this very occurrence would be brought to their remembrance, and would strengthen their courage and their faith in God.

The king of Moab, disheartened and distressed, exclaimed, "Neither curse them at all, nor bless them at all." Yet a faint hope still lingered in his heart, and he determined to make another trial. He now conducted Balaam to Mount Peor, where was a temple devoted to the licentious worship of Baal, their god. Here the same number of altars were erected as before, and the same number of sacrifices were offered; but Balaam went not alone, as at other times, to learn God's will. He made no pretense of sorcery, but standing beside the altars, he looked abroad upon the tents of Israel. Again the Spirit of God rested upon him, and the divine message came from his lips:

> "How goodly are thy tents, O Jacob,
> And thy tabernacles, O Israel!
> As the valleys they spread forth, as gardens by the river's side,
> As the trees of lignaloes which the Lord hath planted, and as cedar trees beside the waters.
> He shall pour the water out of his buckets, and his seed shall be in many waters,
> And his King shall be higher than Agag, and his kingdom shall be exalted....
> He couched, he lay down as a lion, and as a great lion: who shall stir him up?
> Blessed is he that blesseth thee, and cursed is he that curseth thee."

The prosperity of God's people is here represented by some of the most beautiful figures to be found in nature. The prophet likens Israel to fertile valleys covered with abundant harvests; to flourishing gardens watered by never-failing springs; to the fragrant sandal tree and the stately cedar. The figure last mentioned is one of the most strikingly beautiful and appropriate to be found in the inspired word. The cedar of Lebanon was honored by all the people of the East. The class of trees to which it belongs is found wherever man has gone throughout the earth. From the arctic regions to the tropic zone they flourish, rejoicing in the heat, yet braving the cold; springing in rich luxuriance by the riverside, yet towering aloft upon the parched and thirsty waste. They plant their roots deep among the rocks of the mountains and boldly stand in defiance of the tempest. Their leaves are fresh and green when all else has perished at the breath of winter. Above all other trees the cedar of Lebanon is distinguished for its strength, its firmness, its undecaying vigor; and this is used as a symbol of those whose life is "hid with Christ in God." Colossians 3:3. Says the Scripture, "The righteous . . . shall grow like a cedar." Psalm 92:12. The divine hand has exalted the cedar as king over the forest. "The fir trees were not like his boughs, and the chestnut trees were not like his branches" (Ezekiel 31:8); nor any tree in the garden of God. The cedar is repeatedly employed as an emblem of royalty, and its use in Scripture to represent the righteous shows how Heaven regards those who do the will of God.

Balaam prophesied that Israel's King would be greater and more powerful than Agag. This was the name given to the kings of the Amalekites, who were at this time a very powerful nation; but Israel, if true to God, would subdue all her enemies. The King of Israel was the Son of God; and His throne was one day to be established in the earth, and His power to be exalted above all earthly kingdoms.

As he listened to the prophet's words Balak was overwhelmed with disappointed hope, with fear and rage. He was indignant that Balaam could have given him the least encouragement of a favorable response, when everything was determined against him. He regarded with scorn the prophet's compromising, deceptive course. The king exclaimed fiercely, "Therefore now flee thou to thy place: I thought to promote thee unto great honor; but, lo, the Lord hath kept thee back from honor." The answer was that the king had been forewarned that Balaam could speak only the message given him from God.

Before returning to his people, Balaam uttered a most beautiful and sublime prophecy of the world's Redeemer and the final destruction of the enemies of God:

> "I shall see Him, but not now: I shall behold Him, but not nigh:
> There shall come a Star out of Jacob, and a Scepter shall rise out of Israel,
> And shall smite the corners of Moab, and destroy all the children of Sheth."

And he closed by predicting the complete destruction of Moab and Edom, of Amalek and the Kenites, thus leaving to the Moabitish king no ray of hope.

Disappointed in his hopes of wealth and promotion, in disfavor with the king, and conscious that he had incurred the displeasure of God, Balaam returned from his self-chosen mission. After he had reached his home the controlling power of the Spirit of God left him, and his covetousness, which had been merely held in check, prevailed. He was ready to resort to any means to gain the reward promised by Balak. Balaam knew that the prosperity of Israel depended upon their obedience to God, and that there was no way to cause their overthrow but by seducing them into sin. He now decided to secure Balak's favor by advising the Moabites of the course to be pursued to bring a curse upon Israel.

He immediately returned to the land of Moab and laid his plans before the king. The Moabites themselves were convinced that so long as Israel remained true to God, He would be their shield. The plan proposed by Balaam was to separate them from God by enticing them into idolatry. If they could be led to engage in the licentious worship of Baal and Ashtaroth, their omnipotent Protector would become their enemy, and they would soon fall a prey to the fierce, warlike nations around them. This plan was readily accepted by the king, and Balaam himself remained to assist in carrying it into effect.

Balaam witnessed the success of his diabolical scheme. He saw the curse of God visited upon His people, and thousands falling under His judgments; but the divine justice that punished sin in Israel did not permit the tempters to escape. In the war of Israel against the Midianites, Balaam was slain. He had felt a presentiment that his own end was near when he 452 exclaimed, "Let me die the death of the righteous, and let my last end be like his!" But he had not chosen to live the life of the righteous, and his destiny was fixed with the enemies of God.

The fate of Balaam was similar to that of Judas, and their characters bear a marked resemblance to each other. Both these men tried to unite the service of God and mammon, and met with signal failure. Balaam acknowledged the true God, and professed to serve Him; Judas believed in Jesus as the Messiah, and united with His followers. But Balaam hoped to make the service of Jehovah the steppingstone to the acquirement of riches and worldly honor; and failing in this he stumbled and fell and was broken. Judas expected by his connection with Christ to secure wealth and promotion in that worldly kingdom which, as he believed, the Messiah was about to set up. The failure of his hopes drove him to apostasy and ruin. Both Balaam and Judas had received great light and enjoyed special privileges, but a single cherished sin poisoned the entire character and caused their destruction.

It is a perilous thing to allow an unchristian trait to live in the heart. One cherished sin will, little by little, debase the character, bringing all its nobler powers into subjection to the evil desire. The removal of one safeguard from the conscience, the indulgence of one evil habit, one neglect of the high claims of duty, breaks down the defenses of the soul and opens the way for Satan to come in and lead us astray. The only safe course is to let our prayers go forth daily from a sincere heart, as did David, "Hold up my goings in Thy paths, that my footsteps slip not." Psalm 17:5.

41 453

Apostasy at the Jordan

With joyful hearts and renewed faith in God, the victorious armies of Israel had returned from Bashan. They had already gained possession of a valuable territory, and they were confident of the immediate conquest of Canaan. Only the river Jordan lay between them and the Promised Land. Just across the river was a rich plain, covered with verdure, watered with streams from copious fountains, and shaded by luxuriant palm trees. On the western border of the plain rose the towers and palaces of Jericho, so embosomed in its palm-tree groves that it was called "the city of palm trees."

On the eastern side of Jordan, between the river and the high tableland which they had been traversing, was also a plain, several miles in width and extending some distance along the river. This sheltered valley had the climate of the tropics; here flourished the shittim, or acacia, tree, giving to the plain the name, "Vale of Shittim." It was here that the Israelites encamped, and in the acacia groves by the riverside they found an agreeable retreat.

But amid these attractive surroundings they were to encounter an evil more deadly than mighty hosts of armed men or the wild beasts of the wilderness. That country, so rich in natural advantages, had been defiled by the inhabitants. In the public worship of Baal, the leading deity, the most degrading and iniquitous scenes were constantly enacted. On every side were places noted for idolatry and licentiousness, the very names being suggestive of the vileness and corruption of the people.

These surroundings exerted a polluting influence upon the Israelites. Their minds became familiar with the vile thoughts constantly suggested; their life of ease and inaction produced its demoralizing effect; and almost unconsciously to themselves they were departing from God 454

This chapter is based on Numbers 25.

and coming into a condition where they would fall an easy prey to temptation.

During the time of their encampment beside Jordan, Moses was preparing for the occupation of Canaan. In this work the great leader was fully employed; but to the people this time of suspense and expectation was most trying, and before many weeks had elapsed their history was marred by the most frightful departures from virtue and integrity.

At first there was little intercourse between the Israelites and their heathen neighbors, but after a time Midianitish women began to steal into the camp. Their appearance excited no alarm, and so quietly were their plans conducted that the attention of Moses was not called to the matter. It was the object of these women, in their association with the Hebrews, to seduce them into transgression of the law of God, to draw their attention to heathen rites and customs, and lead them into idolatry. These motives were studiously concealed under the garb of friendship, so that they were not suspected, even by the guardians of the people.

At Balaam's suggestion, a grand festival in honor of their gods was appointed by the king of Moab, and it was secretly arranged that Balaam should induce the Israelites to attend. He was regarded by them as a prophet of God, and hence had little difficulty in accomplishing his purpose. Great numbers of the people joined him in witnessing the festivities. They ventured upon the forbidden ground, and were entangled in the snare of Satan. Beguiled with music and dancing, and allured by the beauty of heathen vestals, they cast off their fealty to Jehovah. As they united in mirth and feasting, indulgence in wine beclouded their senses and broke down the barriers of self-control. Passion had full sway; and having defiled their consciences by lewdness, they were persuaded to bow down to idols. They offered sacrifice upon heathen altars and participated in the most degrading rites.

It was not long before the poison had spread, like a deadly infection, through the camp of Israel. Those who would have conquered their enemies in battle were overcome by the wiles of heathen women. The people seemed to be infatuated. The rulers and the leading men were among the first to transgress, and so many of the people were guilty that the apostasy became national. "Israel joined himself unto Baalpeor." When Moses was aroused to perceive the evil, the plots of their enemies had been so successful that not only were the Israelites participating in the licentious worship at Mount Peor, but the heathen rites were coming to be observed in the camp of Israel. The aged leader was filled with indignation, and the wrath of God was kindled.

Their iniquitous practices did that for Israel which all the enchantments of Balaam could not do—they separated them from God. By swift-

coming judgments the people were awakened to the enormity of their sin. A terrible pestilence broke out in the camp, to which tens of thousands speedily fell a prey. God commanded that the leaders in this apostasy be put to death by the magistrates. This order was promptly obeyed. The offenders were slain, then their bodies were hung up in sight of all Israel that the congregation, seeing the leaders so severely dealt with, might have a deep sense of God's abhorrence of their sin and the terror of His wrath against them.

All felt that the punishment was just, and the people hastened to the tabernacle, and with tears and deep humiliation confessed their sin. While they were thus weeping before God, at the door of the tabernacle, while the plague was still doing its work of death, and the magistrates were executing their terrible commission, Zimri, one of the nobles of Israel, came boldly into the camp, accompanied by a Midianitish harlot, a princess "of a chief house in Midian," whom he escorted to his tent. Never was vice bolder or more stubborn. Inflamed with wine, Zimri declared his "sin as Sodom," and gloried in his shame. The priests and leaders had prostrated themselves in grief and humiliation, weeping "between the porch and the altar," and entreating the Lord to spare His people, and give not His heritage to reproach, when this prince in Israel flaunted his sin in the sight of the congregation, as if to defy the vengeance of God and mock the judges of the nation. Phinehas, the son of Eleazar the high priest, rose up from among the congregation, and seizing a javelin, "he went after the man of Israel into the tent," and slew them both. Thus the plague was stayed, while the priest who had executed the divine judgment was honored before all Israel, and the priesthood was confirmed to him and to his house forever.

Phinehas "hath turned My wrath away from the children of Israel," was the divine message; "wherefore say, Behold, I give unto him My covenant of peace: and he shall have it, and his seed after him, even the covenant of an everlasting priesthood; because he was zealous for His God, and made an atonement for the children of Israel."

The judgments visited upon Israel for their sin at Shittim, destroyed the survivors of that vast company, who, nearly forty years before, had incurred the sentence, "They shall surely die in the wilderness." The numbering of the people by divine direction, during their encampment on the plains of Jordan, showed that "of them whom Moses and Aaron the priest numbered, when they numbered the children of Israel in the wilderness of Sinai, . . . there was not left a man of them, save Caleb the son of Jephunneh, and Joshua the son of Nun." Numbers 26:64, 65.

God had sent judgments upon Israel for yielding to the enticements of the Midianites; but the tempters were not to escape the wrath of divine justice. The Amalekites, who had attacked Israel at Rephidim, falling upon those who were faint and weary behind the host, were not punished till long after; but the Midianites who seduced them into sin were speedily made to feel God's judgments, as being the more dangerous enemies. "Avenge the children of Israel of the Midianites" (Numbers 31:2), was the command of God to Moses; "afterward shalt thou be gathered unto thy people." This mandate was immediately obeyed. One thousand men were chosen from each of the tribes and sent out under the leadership of Phinehas. "And they warred against the Midianites, as the Lord commanded Moses. . . . And they slew the kings of Midian, beside the rest of them that were slain; . . . five kings of Midian: Balaam also the son of Beor they slew with the sword." Verses 7, 8. The women also, who had been made captives by the attacking army, were put to death at the command of Moses, as the most guilty and most dangerous of the foes of Israel.

Such was the end of them that devised mischief against God's people. Says the psalmist: "The heathen are sunk down in the pit that they made: in the net which they hid is their own foot taken." Psalm 9:15. "For the Lord will not cast off His people, neither will He forsake His inheritance. But judgment shall return unto righteousness." When men "gather themselves together against the soul of the righteous," the Lord "shall bring upon them their own iniquity, and shall cut them off in their own wickedness." Psalm 94:14, 15, 21, 23.

457 When Balaam was called to curse the Hebrews he could not, by all his enchantments, bring evil upon them; for the Lord had not "beheld iniquity in Jacob," neither had He "seen perverseness in Israel." Numbers 23:21, 23. But when through yielding to temptation they transgressed God's law, their defense departed from them. When the people of God are faithful to His commandments, "there is no enchantment against Jacob, neither is there any divination against Israel." Hence all the power and wily arts of Satan are exerted to seduce them into sin. If those who profess to be the depositaries of God's law become transgressors of its precepts, they separate themselves from God, and they will be unable to stand before their enemies.

The Israelites, who could not be overcome by the arms or by the enchantments of Midian, fell a prey to her harlots. Such is the power that woman, enlisted in the service of Satan, has exerted to entrap and destroy souls. "She hath cast down many wounded: yea, many strong men have been slain by her." Proverbs 7:26. It was thus that the children of Seth were seduced from their integrity, and the holy seed became corrupt. It was thus that Joseph was tempted.

Thus Samson betrayed his strength, the defense of Israel, into the hands of the Philistines. Here David stumbled. And Solomon, the wisest of kings, who had thrice been called the beloved of his God, became a slave of passion, and sacrificed his integrity to the same bewitching power.

"Now all these things happened unto them for ensamples: and they are written for our admonition, upon whom the ends of the world are come. Wherefore let him that thinketh he standeth take heed lest he fall." 1 Corinthians 10:11, 12. Satan well knows the material with which he has to deal in the human heart. He knows—for he has studied with fiendish intensity for thousands of years—the points most easily assailed in every character; and through successive generations he has wrought to overthrow the strongest men, princes in Israel, by the same temptations that were so successful at Baalpeor. All along through the ages there are strewn wrecks of character that have been stranded upon the rocks of sensual indulgence. As we approach the close of time, as the people of God stand upon the borders of the heavenly Canaan, Satan will, as of old, redouble his efforts to prevent them from entering the goodly land. He lays his snares for every soul. It is not the ignorant and uncultured merely that need to 458 be guarded; he will prepare his temptations for those in the highest positions, in the most holy office; if he can lead them to pollute their souls, he can through them destroy many. And he employs the same agents now as he employed three thousand years ago. By worldly friendships, by the charms of beauty, by pleasure seeking, mirth, feasting, or the wine cup, he tempts to the violation of the seventh commandment.

Satan seduced Israel into licentiousness before leading them to idolatry. Those who will dishonor God's image and defile His temple in their own persons will not scruple at any dishonor to God that will gratify the desire of their depraved hearts. Sensual indulgence weakens the mind and debases the soul. The moral and intellectual powers are benumbed and paralyzed by the gratification of the animal propensities; and it is impossible for the slave of passion to realize the sacred obligation of the law of God, to appreciate the atonement, or to place a right value upon the soul. Goodness, purity, and truth, reverence for God, and love for sacred things—all those holy affections and noble desires that link men with the heavenly world—are consumed in the fires of lust. The soul becomes a blackened and desolate waste, the habitation of evil spirits, and the "cage of every unclean and hateful bird." Beings formed in the image of God are dragged down to a level with the brutes.

It was by associating with idolaters and joining in their festivities that the Hebrews were led to transgress God's law and bring His judgments upon the nation. So now it is by leading the followers of Christ to associate with the ungodly and unite in their amusements that Satan is most successful in alluring them into sin. "Come out from among them, and be ye separate, saith the Lord, and touch not the unclean." 2 Corinthians 6:17. God requires of His people now as great a distinction from the world, in customs, habits, and principles, as He required of Israel anciently. If they faithfully follow the teachings of His word, this distinction will exist; it cannot be otherwise. The warnings given to the Hebrews against assimilating with the heathen were not more direct or explicit than are those forbidding Christians to conform to the spirit and customs of the ungodly. Christ speaks to us, "Love not the world, neither the things that are in the world. If any man love the world, the love of the Father is not in him." 1 John 2:15. "The friendship of the world is enmity with God; whosoever therefore will be 459 a friend of the world is the enemy of God." James 4:4. The followers of Christ are to separate themselves from sinners, choosing their society only when there is opportunity to do them good. We cannot be too decided in shunning the company of those who exert an influence to draw us away from God. While we pray, "Lead us not into temptation," we are to shun temptation, so far as possible.

It was when the Israelites were in a condition of outward ease and security that they were led into sin. They failed to keep God ever before them, they neglected prayer and cherished a spirit of self-confidence. Ease and self-indulgence left the citadel of the soul unguarded, and debasing thoughts found entrance. It was the traitors within the walls that overthrew the strongholds of principle and betrayed Israel into the power of Satan. It is thus that Satan still seeks to compass the ruin of the soul. A long preparatory process, unknown to the world, goes on in the heart before the Christian commits open sin. The mind does not come down at once from purity and holiness to depravity, corruption, and crime. It takes time to degrade those formed in the image of God to the brutal or the satanic. By beholding we become changed. By the indulgence of impure thoughts man can so educate his mind that sin which he once loathed will become pleasant to him.

Satan is using every means to make crime and debasing vice popular. We cannot walk the streets of our cities without encountering flaring notices of crime presented in some novel, or to be acted at some theater. The mind is educated to familiarity with sin. The course pursued by the base and vile is kept before the people in the periodicals of the day, and everything that can excite passion is brought before them in excit-

ing stories. They hear and read so much of debasing crime that the once tender conscience, which would have recoiled with horror from such scenes, becomes hardened, and they dwell upon these things with greedy interest.

Many of the amusements popular in the world today, even with those who claim to be Christians, tend to the same end as did those of the heathen. There are indeed few among them that Satan does not turn to account in destroying souls. Through the drama he has worked for ages to excite passion and glorify vice. The opera, with its fascinating display and bewildering music, the masquerade, the dance, the card 460 table, Satan employs to break down the barriers of principle and open the door to sensual indulgence. In every gathering for pleasure where pride is fostered or appetite indulged, where one is led to forget God and lose sight of eternal interests, there Satan is binding his chains about the soul.

"Keep thy heart with all diligence," is the counsel of the wise man; "for out of it are the issues of life." Proverbs 4:23. As man "thinketh in his heart, so is he." Proverbs 23:7. The heart must be renewed by divine grace, or it will be in vain to seek for purity of life. He who attempts to build up a noble, virtuous character independent of the grace of Christ is building his house upon the shifting sand. In the fierce storms of temptation it will surely be overthrown. David's prayer should be the petition of every soul: "Create in me a clean heart, O God; and renew a right spirit within me." Psalm 51:10. And having become partakers of the heavenly gift, we are to go on unto perfection, being "kept by the power of God through faith." 1 Peter 1:5.

Yet we have a work to do to resist temptation. Those who would not fall a prey to Satan's devices must guard well the avenues of the soul; they must avoid reading, seeing, or hearing that which will suggest impure thoughts. The mind should not be left to wander at random upon every subject that the adversary of souls may suggest. "Girding up the loins of your mind," says the apostle Peter, "be sober, . . . not fashioning yourselves according to your former lusts in . . . your ignorance: but like as He which called you is holy, be ye yourselves also holy in all manner of living." 1 Peter 1:13-15, R.V. Says Paul, "Whatsoever things are true, whatsoever things are honest, whatsoever things are just, whatsoever things are pure, whatsoever things are lovely, whatsoever things are of good report; if there be any virtue, and if there be any praise, think on these things." Philippians 4:8. This will require earnest prayer and unceasing watchfulness. We must be aided by the abiding influence of the Holy Spirit, which will attract the mind upward, and habituate it to dwell on pure and holy things. And we must give diligent study to the word of God. "Wherewithal shall a young man cleanse his way? by taking heed thereto according to Thy word." "Thy word," says the psalmist, "have I hid in mine heart, that I might not sin against Thee." Psalm 119:9, 11.

461   Israel's sin at Beth-peor brought the judgments of God upon the nation, and though the same sins may not now be punished as speedily, they will as surely meet retribution. "If any man defile the temple of God, him shall God destroy." 1 Corinthians 3:17. Nature has affixed terrible penalties to these crimes—penalties which, sooner or later, will be inflicted upon every transgressor. It is these sins more than any other that have caused the fearful degeneracy of our race, and the weight of disease and misery with which the world is cursed. Men may succeed in concealing their transgression from their fellow men, but they will no less surely reap the result, in suffering, disease, imbecility, or death. And beyond this life stands the tribunal of the judgment, with its award of eternal penalties. "They which do such things shall not inherit the kingdom of God," but with Satan and evil angels shall have their part in that "lake of fire" which "is the second death." Galatians 5:21; Revelation 20:14.

    "The lips of a strange woman drop as an honeycomb, and her mouth is smoother than oil: but her end is bitter as wormwood, sharp as a two-edged sword." Proverbs 5:3, 4. "Remove thy way far from her, and come not nigh the door of her house: lest thou give thine honor unto others, and thy years unto the cruel: lest strangers be filled with thy wealth; and thy labors be in the house of a stranger; and thou mourn at the last, when thy flesh and thy body are consumed." Verses 8-11. "Her house inclineth unto death." "None that go unto her return again." Proverbs 2:18, 19. "Her guests are in the depths of hell." Proverbs 9:18.

462

42

The Law Repeated

    The Lord announced to Moses that the appointed time for the possession of Canaan was at hand; and as the aged prophet stood upon the heights overlooking the river Jordan and the Promised Land, he gazed with deep interest upon the inheritance of his people. Would it be possible that the sentence pronounced against him for his sin at Kadesh might be revoked? With deep earnestness he pleaded, "O Lord God, Thou hast begun to show Thy servant Thy greatness, and Thy mighty hand; for what god is there in heaven or in earth, that can do according to Thy works, and according to Thy might? I pray Thee, let me go over, and see the good land that is beyond Jordan, that goodly moun-

tain, and Lebanon." Deuteronomy 3:24-27.

    The answer was, "Let it suffice thee; speak no more unto Me of this matter. Get thee up into the top of Pisgah, and lift up thine eyes westward, and northward, and southward, and eastward, and behold it with thine eyes; for thou shalt not go over this Jordan."

    Without a murmur Moses submitted to the decree of God. And now his great anxiety was for Israel. Who would feel the interest for their welfare that he had felt? From a full heart he poured forth the prayer, "Let the Lord, the God of the spirits of all flesh, set a man over the congregation, which may go out before them, and which may go in before them, and which may lead them out, and which may bring them in; that the congregation of the Lord be not as sheep which have no shepherd." Numbers 27:16, 17.

    The Lord hearkened to the prayer of His servant; and the answer came, "Take thee Joshua, the son of Nun, a man in whom is the Spirit, and lay thine hand upon him; and set him before Eleazar the priest, and before all the congregation; and give him a charge in their sight. And thou shalt put some of thine honor upon him, that all the congregation of the people of Israel may be obedient." Verses 18-20. Joshua had long attended Moses; and being a man of wisdom, ability, and faith, he was chosen to succeed him.   463

    Through the laying on of hands by Moses, accompanied by a most impressive charge, Joshua was solemnly set apart as the leader of Israel. He was also admitted to a present share in the government. The words of the Lord concerning Joshua came through Moses to the congregation, "He shall stand before Eleazar the priest, who shall ask counsel for him, after the judgment of Urim before the Lord. At his word shall they go out, and at his word they shall come in, both he, and all the children of Israel with him, even all the congregation." Verses 21-23.

    Before relinquishing his position as the visible leader of Israel, Moses was directed to rehearse to them the history of their deliverance from Egypt and their journeyings in the wilderness, and also to recapitulate the law spoken from Sinai. When the law was given, but few of the present congregation were old enough to comprehend the awful solemnity of the occasion. As they were soon to pass over Jordan and take possession of the Promised Land, God would present before them the claims of His law and enjoin upon them obedience as the condition of prosperity.

    Moses stood before the people to repeat his last warnings and admonitions. His face was illumined with a holy light. His hair was white with age; but his form was erect, his countenance expressed the unabated vigor of health,

This chapter is based on Deuteronomy 4 to 6; 28.

and his eye was clear and undimmed. It was an important occasion, and with deep feeling he portrayed the love and mercy of their Almighty Protector:

"Ask now of the days that are past, which were before thee, since the day that God created man upon the earth, and ask from the one side of heaven unto the other, whether there hath been any such thing as this great thing is, or hath been heard like it? Did ever people hear the voice of God speaking out of the midst of the fire, as thou hast heard, and live? or hath God assayed to go and take Him a nation from the midst of another nation, by temptations, by signs, and by wonders, and by war, and by a mighty hand, and by a stretched-out arm, and by great terrors, according to all that the Lord your God did for you in Egypt before your eyes? Unto thee it was showed, that thou mightest know that the Lord He is God; there is none else beside Him."

464   "The Lord did not set His love upon you, nor choose you, because ye were more in number than any people; for ye were the fewest of all people: but because the Lord loved you, and because He would keep the oath which He had sworn unto your fathers, hath the Lord brought you out with a mighty hand, and redeemed you out of the house of bondmen, from the hand of Pharaoh king of Egypt. Know therefore that Jehovah thy God, He is God, the faithful God, which keepeth covenant and mercy with them that love Him and keep His commandments to a thousand generations." Deuteronomy 7:7-9.

The people of Israel had been ready to ascribe their troubles to Moses; but now their suspicions that he was controlled by pride, ambition, or selfishness, were removed, and they listened with confidence to his words. Moses faithfully set before them their errors and the transgressions of their fathers. They had often felt impatient and rebellious because of their long wandering in the wilderness; but the Lord had not been chargeable with this delay in possessing Canaan; He was more grieved than they because He could not bring them into immediate possession of the Promised Land, and thus display before all nations His mighty power in the deliverance of His people. With their distrust of God, with their pride and unbelief, they had not been prepared to enter Canaan. They would in no way represent that people whose God is the Lord; for they did not bear His character of purity, goodness, and benevolence. Had their fathers yielded in faith to the direction of God, being governed by His judgments and walking in His ordinances, they would long before have been settled in Canaan, a prosperous, holy, happy people. Their delay to enter the goodly land dishonored God and detracted from His glory in the sight of surrounding nations.

Moses, who understood the character and value of the law of God, assured the people that no other nation had such wise, righteous, and merciful rules as had been given to the Hebrews. "Behold," he said, "I have taught you statutes and judgments, even as the Lord my God commanded me, that ye should do so in the land whither ye go to possess it. Keep therefore and do them; for this is your wisdom and your understanding in the sight of the nations, which shall hear all these statutes, and say, Surely this great nation is a wise and understanding people."

Moses called their attention to the "day that 465 thou stoodest before the Lord thy God in Horeb." And he challenged the Hebrew host: "What nation is there so great, who hath God so nigh unto them, as the Lord our God is in all things that we call upon Him for? And what nation is there so great, that hath statutes and judgments so righteous as all this law, which I set before you this day?" Today the challenge to Israel might be repeated. The laws which God gave His ancient people were wiser, better, and more humane than those of the most civilized nations of the earth. The laws of the nations bear marks of the infirmities and passions of the unrenewed heart; but God's law bears the stamp of the divine.

"The Lord hath taken you, and brought you forth out of the iron furnace," declared Moses, "to be unto Him a people of inheritance." The land which they were soon to enter, and which was to be theirs on condition of obedience to the law of God, was thus described to them—and how must these words have moved the hearts of Israel, as they remembered that he who so glowingly pictured the blessings of the goodly land had been, through their sin, shut out from sharing the inheritance of his people:

"The Lord thy God bringeth thee into a good land," "not as the land of Egypt, from whence ye came out, where thou sowedst thy seed, and wateredst it with thy foot, as a garden of herbs: but the land, whither ye go to possess it, is a land of hills and valleys, and drinketh water of the rain of heaven;" "a land of brooks of water, of fountains and depths that spring out of valleys and hills; a land of wheat, and barley, and vines, and fig trees, and pomegranates; a land of oil olive, and honey; a land wherein thou shalt eat bread without scarceness, thou shalt not lack anything in it; a land whose stones are iron, and out of whose hills thou mayest dig brass;" "a land which the Lord thy God careth for: the eyes of the Lord thy God are always upon it, from the beginning of the year even unto the end of the year." Deuteronomy 8:7-9; 11:10-12.

"And it shall be, when the Lord thy God shall have brought thee into the land which He sware unto thy fathers, to Abraham, to Isaac, and to Jacob, to give thee great and goodly cities, which thou buildedst not, and houses full of all

good things, which thou filledst not, and wells digged, which thou diggedst not, vineyards and olive trees, which thou plantedst not; when thou
466 shalt have eaten and be full; then beware lest thou forget the Lord." "Take heed unto yourselves, lest ye forget the covenant of the Lord your God. . . . For the Lord thy God is a consuming fire, even a jealous God." If they should do evil in the sight of the Lord, then, said Moses, "Ye shall soon utterly perish from off the land whereunto ye go over Jordan to possess it."

After the public rehearsal of the law, Moses completed the work of writing all the laws, the statutes, and the judgments which God had given him, and all the regulations concerning the sacrificial system. The book containing these was placed in charge of the proper officers, and was for safe keeping deposited in the side of the ark. Still the great leader was filled with fear that the people would depart from God. In a most sublime and thrilling address he set before them the blessings that would be theirs on condition of obedience, and the curses that would follow upon transgression:

"If thou shalt hearken diligently unto the voice of the Lord thy God, to observe and to do all His commandments which I command thee this day," "blessed shalt thou be in the city, and blessed shalt thou be in the field," in "the fruit of thy body, and the fruit of thy ground, and the fruit of thy cattle. . . . Blessed shall be thy basket and thy store. Blessed shalt thou be when thou comest in, and blessed shalt thou be when thou goest out. The Lord shall cause thine enemies that rise up against thee to be smitten before thy face. . . . The Lord shall command the blessing upon thee in thy storehouses, and in all that thou settest thine hand unto."

"But it shall come to pass, if thou wilt not hearken unto the voice of the Lord thy God, to observe to do all His commandments and His statutes which I command thee this day; that all these curses shall come upon thee," "and thou shalt become an astonishment, a proverb, and a byword, among all nations whither the Lord shall lead thee." "And the Lord shall scatter thee among all people, from the one end of the earth even unto the other; and there thou shalt serve other gods, which neither thou nor thy fathers have known, even wood and stone. And among these nations shalt thou find no ease, neither shall the sole of thy foot have rest: but the Lord shall give thee there a trembling heart, and failing of eyes, and sorrow of mind: and thy life shall hang in doubt before thee; and thou shalt
467 fear day and night, and shalt have none assurance of thy life: in the morning thou shalt say, Would God it were even! and at even thou shalt say, Would God it were morning! for the fear of thine heart wherewith thou shalt fear, and for the sight of thine eyes which thou shalt see."

By the Spirit of Inspiration, looking far down the ages, Moses pictured the terrible scenes of Israel's final overthrow as a nation, and the destruction of Jerusalem by the armies of Rome: "The Lord shall bring a nation against thee from far, from the end of the earth, as swift as the eagle flieth; a nation whose tongue thou shalt not understand; a nation of fierce countenance, which shall not regard the person of the old, nor show favor to the young."

The utter wasting of the land and the horrible suffering of the people during the siege of Jerusalem under Titus centuries later, were vividly portrayed: "He shall eat the fruit of thy cattle, and the fruit of thy land, until thou be destroyed. . . . And he shall besiege thee in all thy gates, until thy high and fenced walls come down, wherein thou trustedst, throughout all thy land. . . . Thou shalt eat the fruit of thine own body, the flesh of thy sons and of thy daughters, which the Lord thy God hath given thee, in the siege, and in the straitness, wherewith thine enemies shall distress thee." "The tender and delicate woman among you, which would not adventure to set the sole of her foot upon the ground for delicateness and tenderness, her eye shall be evil toward the husband of her bosom, . . . and toward her children which she shall bear: for she shall eat them for want of all things secretly in the siege and straitness, wherewith thine enemy shall distress thee in thy gates."

Moses closed with these impressive words: "I call heaven and earth to record this day against you, that I have set before you life and death, blessing and cursing: therefore choose life, that both thou and thy seed may live: that thou mayest love the Lord thy God, and that thou mayest obey His voice, and that thou mayest cleave unto Him: for He is thy life, and the length of thy days: that thou mayest dwell in the land which the Lord sware unto thy fathers, to Abraham, to Isaac, and to Jacob, to give them." Deuteronomy 30:19, 20.

The more deeply to impress these truths upon all minds, the great leader embodied them in
468 sacred verse. This song was not only historical, but prophetic. While it recounted the wonderful dealings of God with His people in the past, it also foreshadowed the great events of the future, the final victory of the faithful when Christ shall come the second time in power and glory. The people were directed to commit to memory this poetic history, and to teach it to their children and children's children. It was to be chanted by the congregation when they assembled for worship, and to be repeated by the people as they went about their daily labors. It was the duty of parents to so impress these words upon the susceptible minds of their children that they might never be forgotten.

Since the Israelites were to be, in a special sense, the guardians and keepers of God's law, the significance of its precepts and the importance of obedience were especially to be impressed upon them, and through them, upon their children and children's children. The Lord commanded concerning His statutes: "Thou shalt teach them diligently unto thy children, and shalt talk of them when thou sittest in thine house, and when thou walkest by the way, and when thou liest down, and when thou risest up. . . . And thou shalt write them upon the posts of thy house, and on thy gates."

When their children should ask in time to come, "What mean the testimonies, and the statutes, and the judgments, which the Lord our God hath commanded you?" then the parents were to repeat the history of God's gracious dealings with them—how the Lord had wrought for their deliverance that they might obey His law—and to declare to them, "The Lord commanded us to do all these statutes, to fear the Lord our God, for our good always, that He might preserve us alive, as it is at this day. And it shall be our righteousness, if we observe to do all these commandments before the Lord our God as He hath commanded us."

43

The Death of Moses

In all the dealings of God with His people there is, mingled with His love and mercy, the most striking evidence of His strict and impartial justice. This is exemplified in the history of the Hebrew people. God had bestowed great blessings upon Israel. His loving-kindness toward them is touchingly portrayed: "As an eagle stirreth up her nest, fluttereth over her young, spreadeth abroad her wings, taketh them, beareth them on her wings: so the Lord alone did lead him." And yet what swift and severe retribution was visited upon them for their transgressions!

The infinite love of God has been manifested in the gift of His only-begotten Son to redeem a lost race. Christ came to the earth to reveal to men the character of His Father, and His life was filled with deeds of divine tenderness and compassion. And yet Christ Himself declares, "Till heaven and earth pass, one jot or one title shall in no wise pass from the law." Matthew 5:18. The same voice that with patient, loving entreaty invites the sinner to come to Him and find pardon and peace, will in the judgment bid the rejecters of His mercy, "Depart from Me, ye cursed." Matthew 25:41. In all the Bible, God is represented not only as a tender father but as a righteous judge. Though He delights in showing mercy, and "forgiving iniquity and transgression and sin," yet He "will by no means clear the

guilty." Exodus 34:7.

The great Ruler of nations had declared that Moses was not to lead the congregation of Israel into the goodly land, and the earnest pleading of God's servant could not secure a reversing of His sentence. He knew that he must die. Yet he had not for a moment faltered in his care for Israel. He had faithfully sought to prepare the congregation to enter upon the promised inheritance. At the divine command Moses and Joshua repaired to the tabernacle, while the pillar of cloud came and stood over the door. Here the people were solemnly committed to the charge of Joshua. The work of Moses as leader of Israel was ended. Still he forgot himself in his interest for his people. In the presence of the assembled multitude Moses, in the name of God, addressed to his successor these words of holy cheer: "Be strong and of a good courage: for thou shalt bring the children of Israel into the land which I sware unto them: and I will be with thee." He then turned to the elders and officers of the people, giving them a solemn charge to obey faithfully the instructions he had communicated to them from God.

As the people gazed upon the aged man, so soon to be taken from them, they recalled, with a new and deeper appreciation, his parental tenderness, his wise counsels, and his untiring labors. How often, when their sins had invited the just judgments of God, the prayers of Moses had prevailed with Him to spare them! Their grief was heightened by remorse. They bitterly remembered that their own perversity had provoked Moses to the sin for which he must die.

The removal of their beloved leader would be a far stronger rebuke to Israel than any which they could have received had his life and mission been continued. God would lead them to feel that they were not to make the life of their future leader as trying as they had made that of Moses. God speaks to His people in blessings bestowed; and when these are not appreciated, He speaks to them in blessings removed, that they may be led to see their sins, and return to Him with all the heart.

That very day there came to Moses the command, "Get thee up . . . unto Mount Nebo, . . . and behold the land of Canaan, which I give unto the children of Israel for a possession: and die in the mount whither thou goest up, and be gathered unto thy people." Moses had often left the camp, in obedience to the divine summons, to commune with God; but he was now to depart on a new and mysterious errand. He must go forth to resign his life into the hands of his Creator. Moses knew that he was to die alone; no earthly friend would be permitted to minister to him in his last hours. There was a mystery and awfulness about the scene before him, from which his heart shrank. The severest trial was his separation from the people of his care and

469

470

This chapter is based on Deuteronomy 31 to 34.

love—the people with whom his interest and his life had so long been united. But he had learned to trust in God, and with unquestioning faith he committed himself and his people to His love and mercy.

For the last time Moses stood in the assembly of his people. Again the Spirit of God rested upon him, and in the most sublime and touching language he pronounced a blessing upon each of the tribes, closing with a benediction upon them all:

"There is none like unto God, O Jeshurun,
Who rideth upon the heaven for thy help,
And in His excellency on the skies.
The eternal God is thy dwelling place,
And underneath are the everlasting arms;
And He thrust out the enemy from before thee,
And said, Destroy.
And Israel dwelleth in safety,
The fountain of Jacob alone,
In a land of corn and wine;
Yea, His heavens drop down dew.
Happy art thou, O Israel:
Who is like unto thee, a people saved by Jehovah,
The shield of thy help."

Deuteronomy 33:26-29, R.V.

Moses turned from the congregation, and in silence and alone made his way up the mountainside. He went to "the mountain of Nebo, to the top of Pisgah." Upon that lonely height he stood, and gazed with undimmed eye upon the scene spread out before him. Far away to the west lay the blue waters of the Great Sea; in the north, Mount Hermon stood out against the sky; to the east was the tableland of Moab, and beyond lay Bashan, the scene of Israel's triumph; and away to the south stretched the desert of their long wanderings.

In solitude Moses reviewed his life of vicissitudes and hardships since he turned from courtly honors and from a prospective kingdom in Egypt, to cast in his lot with God's chosen people. He called to mind those long years in the desert with the flocks of Jethro, the appearance of the Angel in the burning bush, and his own call to deliver Israel. Again he beheld the mighty miracles of God's power displayed in behalf of the chosen people, and His long-suffering mercy during the years of their wandering and rebellion. Notwithstanding all that God had wrought for them, notwithstanding his own prayers and labors, only two of all the adults in the vast army that left Egypt had been found so faithful that they could enter the Promised Land. As Moses reviewed the result of his labors, his life of trial and sacrifice seemed to have been almost in vain.

Yet he did not regret the burdens he had borne. He knew that his mission and work were of God's own appointing. When first called to become the leader of Israel from bondage, he shrank from the responsibility; but since he had taken up the work he had not cast aside the burden. Even when the Lord had proposed to release him, and destroy rebellious Israel, Moses could not consent. Though his trials had been great, he had enjoyed special tokens of God's favor; he had obtained a rich experience during the sojourn in the wilderness, in witnessing the manifestations of God's power and glory, and in the communion of His love; he felt that he had made a wise decision in choosing to suffer affliction with the people of God, rather than to enjoy the pleasures of sin for a season.

As he looked back upon his experience as a leader of God's people, one wrong act marred the record. If that transgression could be blotted out, he felt that he would not shrink from death. He was assured that repentance, and faith in the promised Sacrifice, were all that God required, and again Moses confessed his sin and implored pardon in the name of Jesus.

And now a panoramic view of the Land of Promise was presented to him. Every part of the country was spread out before him, not faint and uncertain in the dim distance, but standing out clear, distinct, and beautiful to his delighted vision. In this scene it was presented, not as it then appeared, but as it would become, with God's blessing upon it, in the possession of Israel. He seemed to be looking upon a second Eden. There were mountains clothed with cedars of Lebanon, hills gray with olives and fragrant with the odor of the vine, wide green plains bright with flowers and rich in fruitfulness, here the palm trees of the tropics, there waving fields of wheat and barley, sunny valleys musical with the ripple of brooks and the song of birds, goodly cities and fair gardens, lakes rich in "the abundance of the seas," grazing flocks upon the hillsides, and even amid the rocks the wild bee's hoarded treasures. It was indeed such a land as Moses, inspired by the Spirit of God, had described to Israel: "Blessed of the Lord . . . for the precious things of heaven, for the dew, and for the deep that coucheth beneath, and for the precious fruits brought forth by the sun, . . . and for the chief things of the ancient mountains, . . . and for the precious things of the earth and fullness thereof."

Moses saw the chosen people established in Canaan, each of the tribes in its own possession. He had a view of their history after the settlement of the Promised Land; the long, sad story of their apostasy and its punishment was spread out before him. He saw them, because of their sins, dispersed among the heathen, the glory departed from Israel, her beautiful city in ruins, and her people captives in strange lands. He saw them restored to the land of their fathers, and at last brought under the dominion of Rome.

He was permitted to look down the stream of time and behold the first advent of our Saviour. He saw Jesus as a babe in Bethlehem. He heard the voices of the angelic host break forth in the glad song of praise to God and peace on earth. He beheld in the heavens the star guiding the Wise Men of the East to Jesus, and a great light flooded his mind as he recalled those prophetic words, "There shall come a Star out of Jacob, and a Scepter shall rise out of Israel." Numbers 24:17. He beheld Christ's humble life in Nazareth, His ministry of love and sympathy and healing, His rejection by a proud, unbelieving nation. Amazed he listened to their boastful exaltation of the law of God, while they despised and rejected Him by whom the law was given. He saw Jesus upon Olivet as with weeping He bade farewell to the city of His love. As Moses beheld the final rejection of that people so highly blessed of Heaven—that people for whom he had toiled and prayed and sacrificed, for whom he had been willing that his own name should be blotted from the book of life; as he listened to those fearful words, "Behold your house is left unto you desolate" (Matthew 23:38), his heart was wrung with anguish, and bitter tears fell from his eyes, in sympathy with the sorrow of the Son of God.

He followed the Saviour to Gethsemane, and beheld the agony in the garden, the betrayal, the mockery and scourging—the crucifixion. Moses saw that as he had lifted up the serpent in the wilderness, so the Son of God must be lifted up, that whosoever would believe on Him 476 "should not perish, but have eternal life." John 3:15. Grief, indignation, and horror filled the heart of Moses as he viewed the hypocrisy and satanic hatred manifested by the Jewish nation against their Redeemer, the mighty Angel who had gone before their fathers. He heard Christ's agonizing cry, "My God, My God, why hast Thou forsaken Me?" Mark 15:34. He saw Him lying in Joseph's new tomb. The darkness of hopeless despair seemed to enshroud the world. But he looked again, and beheld Him coming forth a conqueror, and ascending to heaven escorted by adoring angels and leading a multitude of captives. He saw the shining gates open to receive Him, and the host of heaven with songs of triumph welcoming their Commander. And it was there revealed to him that he himself would be one who should attend the Saviour, and open to Him the everlasting gates. As he looked upon the scene, his countenance shone with a holy radiance. How small appeared the trials and sacrifices of his life when compared with those of the Son of God! how light in contrast with the "far more exceeding and eternal weight of glory"! 2 Corinthians 4:17. He rejoiced that he had been permitted, even in a small measure, to be a par-

taker in the sufferings of Christ.

Moses beheld the disciples of Jesus as they went forth to carry His gospel to the world. He saw that though the people of Israel "according to the flesh" had failed of the high destiny to which God had called them, in their unbelief had failed to become the light of the world, though they had despised God's mercy and forfeited their blessings as His chosen people—yet God had not cast off the seed of Abraham; the glorious purposes which He had undertaken to accomplish through Israel were to be fulfilled. All who through Christ should become the children of faith were to be counted as Abraham's seed; they were inheritors of the covenant promises; like Abraham, they were called to guard and to make known to the world the law of God and the gospel of His Son. Moses saw the light of the gospel shining out through the disciples of Jesus to them "which sat in darkness" (Matthew 4:16), and thousands from the lands of the Gentiles flocking to the brightness of its rising. And beholding, he rejoiced in the increase and prosperity of Israel.

And now another scene passed before him. He had been shown the work of Satan in leading the Jews to reject Christ, while they professed to honor His Father's law. He now saw the Christ- 477 ian world under a similar deception in professing to accept Christ while they rejected God's law. He had heard from the priests and elders the frenzied cry, "Away with Him!" "Crucify Him, crucify Him!" and now he heard from professedly Christian teachers the cry, "Away with the law!" He saw the Sabbath trodden under foot, and a spurious institution established in its place. Again Moses was filled with astonishment and horror. How could those who believed in Christ reject the law spoken by His own voice upon the sacred mount? How could any that feared God set aside the law which is the foundation of His government in heaven and earth? With joy Moses saw the law of God still honored and exalted by a faithful few. He saw the last great struggle of earthly powers to destroy those who keep God's law. He looked forward to the time when God shall arise to punish the inhabitants of the earth for their iniquity, and those who have feared His name shall be covered and hid in the day of His anger. He heard God's covenant of peace with those who have kept His law, as He utters His voice from His holy habitation and the heavens and the earth do shake. He saw the second coming of Christ in glory, the righteous dead raised to immortal life, and the living saints translated without seeing death, and together ascending with songs of gladness to the City of God.

Still another scene opens to his view—the earth freed from the curse, lovelier than the fair Land of Promise so lately spread out before him. There is no sin, and death cannot enter.

There the nations of the saved find their eternal home. With joy unutterable Moses looks upon the scene—the fulfillment of a more glorious deliverance than his brightest hopes have ever pictured. Their earthly wanderings forever past, the Israel of God have at last entered the goodly land.

Again the vision faded, and his eyes rested upon the land of Canaan as it spread out in the distance. Then, like a tired warrior, he lay down to rest. "So Moses the servant of the Lord died there in the land of Moab, according to the word of the Lord. And He buried him in a valley in the land of Moab, over against Beth-peor: but no man knoweth of his sepulcher." Many who had been unwilling to heed the counsels of Moses while he was with them would have been 478 in danger of committing idolatry over his dead body had they known the place of his burial. For this reason it was concealed from men. But angels of God buried the body of His faithful servant and watched over the lonely grave.

"There arose not a prophet since in Israel like unto Moses, whom Jehovah knew face to face, in all the signs and the wonders which Jehovah sent him to do . . . and in all that mighty hand, and in all the great terror which Moses showed in the sight of all Israel."

Had not the life of Moses been marred with that one sin, in failing to give God the glory of bringing water from the rock at Kadesh, he would have entered the Promised Land, and would have been translated to heaven without seeing death. But he was not long to remain in the tomb. Christ Himself, with the angels who had buried Moses, came down from heaven to call forth the sleeping saint. Satan had exulted at his success in causing Moses to sin against God, and thus come under the dominion of death. The great adversary declared that the divine sentence—"Dust thou art, and unto dust shalt thou return" (Genesis 3:19)—gave him possession of the dead. The power of the grave had never been broken, and all who were in the tomb he claimed as his captives, never to be released from his dark prison house.

For the first time Christ was about to give life to the dead. As the Prince of life and the shining ones approached the grave, Satan was alarmed for his supremacy. With his evil angels he stood to dispute an invasion of the territory that he claimed as his own. He boasted that the servant of God had become his prisoner. He declared that even Moses was not able to keep the law of God; that he had taken to himself the glory due to Jehovah—the very sin which had caused Satan's banishment from heaven—and by transgression had come under the dominion of Satan. The archtraitor reiterated the original charges that he had made against the divine government, and repeated his complaints of God's injustice toward him.

Christ did not stoop to enter into controversy with Satan. He might have brought against him the cruel work which his deceptions had wrought in heaven, causing the ruin of a vast number of its inhabitants. He might have pointed to the falsehoods told in Eden, that had led to 479 Adam's sin and brought death upon the human race. He might have reminded Satan that it was his own work in tempting Israel to murmuring and rebellion, which had wearied the long-suffering patience of their leader, and in an unguarded moment had surprised him into the sin for which he had fallen under the power of death. But Christ referred all to His Father, saying, "The Lord rebuke thee." Jude 9. The Saviour entered into no dispute with His adversary, but He then and there began His work of breaking the power of the fallen foe, and bringing the dead to life. Here was an evidence that Satan could not controvert, of the supremacy of the Son of God. The resurrection was forever made certain. Satan was despoiled of his prey; the righteous dead would live again.

In consequence of sin Moses had come under the power of Satan. In his own merits he was death's lawful captive; but he was raised to immortal life, holding his title in the name of the Redeemer. Moses came forth from the tomb glorified, and ascended with his Deliverer to the City of God.

Never, till exemplified in the sacrifice of Christ, were the justice and the love of God more strikingly displayed than in His dealings with Moses. God shut Moses out of Canaan, to teach a lesson which should never be forgotten—that He requires exact obedience, and that men are to beware of taking to themselves the glory which is due to their Maker. He could not grant the prayer of Moses that he might share the inheritance of Israel, but He did not forget or forsake His servant. The God of heaven understood the suffering that Moses had endured; He had noted every act of faithful service through those long years of conflict and trial. On the top of Pisgah, God called Moses to an inheritance infinitely more glorious than the earthly Canaan.

Upon the mount of transfiguration Moses was present with Elijah, who had been translated. They were sent as bearers of light and glory from the Father to His Son. And thus the prayer of Moses, uttered so many centuries before, was at last fulfilled. He stood upon the "goodly mountain," within the heritage of his people, bearing witness to Him in whom all the promises to Israel centered. Such is the last scene revealed to mortal vision in the history of that man so highly honored of Heaven.

Moses was a type of Christ. He himself had 480 declared to Israel, "The Lord thy God will raise up unto thee a Prophet from the midst of thee, of thy brethren, like unto me; unto Him ye shall hearken." Deuteronomy 18:15. God saw fit to discipline Moses in the school of affliction and poverty before he could be prepared to lead the hosts of Israel to the earthly Canaan. The Israel of God, journeying to the heavenly Canaan, have a Captain who needed no human teaching to prepare Him for His mission as a divine leader; yet He was made perfect through sufferings; and "in that He Himself hath suffered being tempted, He is able to succor them that are tempted." Hebrews 2:10, 18. Our Redeemer manifested no human weakness or imperfection; yet He died to obtain for us an entrance into the Promised Land.

"And Moses verily was faithful in all his house as a servant, for a testimony of those things which were to be spoken after; but Christ as a son over His own house; whose house are we, if we hold fast the confidence and the rejoicing of the hope firm unto the end." Hebrews 3:5, 6.

481

44

Crossing the Jordan

The Israelites deeply mourned for their departed leader, and thirty days were devoted to special services in honor of his memory. Never till he was taken from them had they so fully realized the value of his wise counsels, his parental tenderness, and his unswerving faith. With a new and deeper appreciation they recalled the precious lessons he had given while still with them.

Moses was dead, but his influence did not die with him. It was to live on, reproducing itself in the hearts of his people. The memory of that holy, unselfish life would long be cherished, with silent, persuasive power molding the lives even of those who had neglected his living words. As the glow of the descending sun lights up the mountain peaks long after the sun itself has sunk behind the hills, so the works of the pure, the holy, and the good shed light upon the world long after the actors themselves have passed away. Their works, their words, their example, will forever live. "The righteous shall be in everlasting remembrance." Psalm 112:6.

While they were filled with grief at their great loss, the people knew that they were not left alone. The pillar of cloud rested over the tabernacle by day, and the pillar of fire by night, an assurance that God would still be their guide and helper if they would walk in the way of His commandments.

Joshua was now the acknowledged leader of Israel. He had been known chiefly as a warrior, and his gifts and virtues were especially valuable at this stage in the history of his people.

Courageous, resolute, and persevering, prompt, incorruptible, unmindful of selfish interests in his care for those committed to his charge, and, above all, inspired by a living faith in God—such was the character of the man divinely chosen to conduct the armies of Israel in their entrance upon the Promised Land. During the sojourn in the wilderness he had acted as prime minister to Moses, and by his quiet, unpretending fidelity, his steadfastness when others wavered, his firmness to maintain the truth in the midst of danger, he had given evidence of his fitness to succeed Moses, even before he was called to the position by the voice of God.

482

It was with great anxiety and self-distrust that Joshua had looked forward to the work before him; but his fears were removed by the assurance of God, "As I was with Moses, so I will be with thee: I will not fail thee, nor forsake thee. . . . Unto this people shalt thou divide for an inheritance the land, which I sware unto their fathers to give them." "Every place that the sole of your foot shall tread upon, that have I given unto you, as I said unto Moses." To the heights of Lebanon in the far distance, to the shores of the Great Sea, and away to the banks of the Euphrates in the east—all was to be theirs.

To this promise was added the injunction, "Only be thou strong and very courageous, that thou mayest observe to do according to all the law, which Moses My servant commanded." The Lord's direction was, "This book of the law shall not depart out of thy mouth; but thou shalt meditate therein day and night;" "turn not from it to the right hand or to the left;" "for then thou shalt make thy way prosperous, and then thou shalt have good success."

The Israelites were still encamped on the east side of Jordan, which presented the first barrier to the occupation of Canaan. "Arise," had been the first message of God to Joshua, "go over this Jordan, thou, and all this people, unto the land which I do give to them." No instruction was given as to the way in which they were to make the passage. Joshua knew, however, that whatever God should command, He would make a way for His people to perform, and in this faith the intrepid leader at once began his arrangements for an advance.

A few miles beyond the river, just opposite the place where the Israelites were encamped, was the large and strongly fortified city of Jericho. This city was virtually the key to the whole country, and it would present a formidable obstacle to the success of Israel. Joshua therefore sent two young men as spies to visit this city and ascertain something as to its population, its resources, and the strength of its fortifications. The inhabitants of the city, terrified and suspicious, were constantly on the alert, and the messengers were in great danger. They were, however, preserved by Rahab, a woman of Jeri-

483

This chapter is based on Joshua 1 to 5:12.

cho, at the peril of her own life. In return for her kindness they gave her a promise of protection when the city should be taken.

The spies returned in safety with the tidings, "Truly the Lord hath delivered into our hands all the land; for even all the inhabitants of the country do faint because of us." It had been declared to them in Jericho, "We have heard how the Lord dried up the water of the Red Sea for you, when ye came out of Egypt; and what ye did unto the two kings of the Amorites, that were on the other side Jordan, Sihon and Og, whom ye utterly destroyed. And as soon as we had heard these things, our hearts did melt, neither did there remain any more courage in any man, because of you: for the Lord your God, He is God in heaven above, and in earth beneath."

Orders were now issued to make ready for an advance. The people were to prepare a three days' supply of food, and the army was to be put in readiness for battle. All heartily acquiesced in the plans of their leader and assured him of their confidence and support: "All that thou commandest us we will do, and whithersoever thou sendest us, we will go. According as we hearkened unto Moses in all things, so will we hearken unto thee: only the Lord thy God be with thee, as He was with Moses."

Leaving their encampment in the acacia groves of Shittim, the host descended to the border of the Jordan. All knew, however, that without divine aid they could not hope to make the passage. At this time of the year—in the spring season—the melting snows of the mountains had so raised the Jordan that the river overflowed its banks, making it impossible to cross at the usual fording places. God willed that the passage of Israel over Jordan should be miraculous. Joshua, by divine direction, commanded the people to sanctify themselves; they must put away their sins and free themselves from all outward impurity; "for tomorrow," he said, "the Lord will do wonders among you." The "ark of the covenant" was to lead the way before the host. When they should see the token of Jehovah's presence, borne by the priests, remove from its place in the center of the camp, and advance toward the river, then they were to remove from their place, "and go after it." The circumstances of the passage were minutely foretold; and said Joshua, "Hereby ye shall know that the living God is among you, and that He will without fail drive out from before you the Canaanites. . . . Behold, the ark of the covenant of the Lord of all the earth passeth over before you into Jordan."

At the appointed time began the onward movement, the ark, borne upon the shoulders of the priests, leading the van. The people had been directed to fall back, so that there was a vacant space of more than half a mile about the ark. All watched with deep interest as the priests

484

advanced down the bank of the Jordan. They saw them with the sacred ark move steadily forward toward the angry, surging stream, till the feet of the bearers were dipped into the waters. Then suddenly the tide above was swept back, while the current below flowed on, and the bed of the river was laid bare.

At the divine command the priests advanced to the middle of the channel and stood there while the entire host descended and crossed to the farther side. Thus was impressed upon the minds of all Israel the fact that the power that stayed the waters of Jordan was the same that had opened the Red Sea to their fathers forty years before. When the people had all passed over, the ark itself was borne to the western shore. No sooner had it reached a place of security, and "the soles of the priests' feet were lifted up unto the dry land," than the imprisoned waters, being set free, rushed down, a resistless flood, in the natural channel of the stream.

Coming generations were not to be without a witness to this great miracle. While the priests bearing the ark were still in the midst of Jordan, twelve men previously chosen, one from each tribe, took up each a stone from the river bed where the priests were standing, and carried it over to the western side. These stones were to be set up as a monument in the first camping place beyond the river. The people were bidden to repeat to their children and children's children the story of the deliverance that God had wrought for them, as Joshua said, "That all the people of the earth might know the hand of the Lord, that it is mighty; that ye might fear the Lord your God forever."

The influence of this miracle, both upon the Hebrews and upon their enemies, was of great importance. It was an assurance to Israel of God's continued presence and protection—an evidence that He would work for them through Joshua as He had wrought through Moses. Such an assurance was needed to strengthen their hearts as they entered upon the conquest of the land—the stupendous task that had staggered the faith of their fathers forty years before. The Lord had declared to Joshua before the crossing, "This day will I begin to magnify thee in the sight of all Israel, that they may know that, as I was with Moses, so I will be with thee." And the result fulfilled the promise. "On that day the Lord magnified Joshua in the sight of all Israel; and they feared him, as they feared Moses, all the days of his life."

This exercise of divine power in behalf of Israel was designed also to increase the fear with which they were regarded by the surrounding nations, and thus prepare the way for their easier and complete triumph. When the tidings that God had stayed the waters of Jordan before the children of Israel, reached the kings of the Amorites and of the Canaanites, their hearts

485

melted with fear. The Hebrews had already slain the five kings of Midian, the powerful Sihon, king of the Amorites, and Og of Bashan, and now the passage over the swollen and impetuous Jordan filled all the surrounding nations with terror. To the Canaanites, to all Israel, and to Joshua himself, unmistakable evidence had been given that the living God, the King of heaven and earth, was among His people, and that He would not fail them nor forsake them.

A short distance from Jordan the Hebrews made their first encampment in Canaan. Here Joshua "circumcised the children of Israel;" "and the children of Israel encamped in Gilgal, and kept the Passover." The suspension of the rite of circumcision since the rebellion at Kadesh had been a constant witness to Israel that their covenant with God, of which it was the appointed symbol, had been broken. And the discontinuance of the Passover, the memorial of their deliverance from Egypt, had been an evidence of the Lord's displeasure at their desire to return to the land of bondage. Now, however, the years of rejection were ended. Once more God acknowledged Israel as His people, and the sign of the covenant was restored. The rite of circumcision was performed upon all the people who had been born in the wilderness. And the Lord declared to Joshua, "This day have I rolled away the reproach of Egypt from off you," and in allusion to this the place of their encampment was called Gilgal, "a rolling away," or "rolling off."

Heathen nations had reproached the Lord and His people because the Hebrews had failed to take possession of Canaan, as they expected, soon after leaving Egypt. Their enemies had triumphed because Israel had wandered so long in the wilderness, and they had mockingly declared that the God of the Hebrews was not able to bring them into the Promised Land. The Lord had now signally manifested His power and favor in opening the Jordan before His people, and their enemies could no longer reproach them.

"On the fourteenth day of the month at even," the Passover was celebrated on the plains of Jericho. "And they did eat of the old corn of the land on the morrow after the Passover, unleavened cakes, and parched corn in the selfsame day. And the manna ceased on the morrow after they had eaten of the old corn of the land; neither had the children of Israel manna any more; but they did eat of the fruit of the land of Canaan." The long years of their desert wanderings were ended. The feet of Israel were at last treading the Promised Land.

45

The Fall of Jericho

The Hebrews had entered Canaan, but they had not subdued it; and to human appearance the struggle to gain possession of the land must be long and difficult. It was inhabited by a powerful race, who stood ready to oppose the invasion of their territory. The various tribes were bound together by the fear of a common danger. Their horses and iron battle chariots, their knowledge of the country, and their training in war, would give them great advantage. Furthermore, the country was guarded by fortresses— "cities great and fenced up to heaven." Deuteronomy 9:1. Only in the assurance of a strength not their own could the Israelites hope for success in the impending conflict.

One of the strongest fortresses in the land— the large and wealthy city of Jericho—lay just before them, but a little distance from their camp at Gilgal. On the border of a fertile plain abounding with the rich and varied productions of the tropics, its palaces and temples the abode of luxury and vice, this proud city, behind its massive battlements, offered defiance to the God of Israel. Jericho was one of the principal seats of idol worship, being especially devoted to Ashtaroth, the goddess of the moon. Here centered all that was vilest and most degrading in the religion of the Canaanites. The people of Israel, in whose minds were fresh the fearful results of their sin at Beth-peor, could look upon this heathen city only with disgust and horror.

To reduce Jericho was seen by Joshua to be the first step in the conquest of Canaan. But first of all he sought an assurance of divine guidance, and it was granted him. Withdrawing from the encampment to meditate and to pray that the God of Israel would go before His people, he beheld an armed warrior, of lofty stature and commanding presence, "with his sword drawn in his hand." To Joshua's challenge, "Art thou for us, or for our adversaries?" the answer was given, "As Captain of the host of the Lord am I now come." The same command given to Moses in Horeb, "Loose thy shoe from off thy foot; for the place whereon thou standest is holy," revealed the true character of the mysterious stranger. It was Christ, the Exalted One, who stood before the leader of Israel. Awestricken, Joshua fell upon his face and worshiped, and heard the assurance, "I have given into thine hand Jericho, and the king thereof, and the mighty men of valor," and he received instruction for the capture of the city.

In obedience to the divine command Joshua marshaled the armies of Israel. No assault was to be made. They were simply to make the circuit of the city, bearing the ark of God and blowing upon trumpets. First came the warriors, a body of chosen men, not now to conquer by their own skill and prowess, but by obedience to the directions given them from God. Seven priests with trumpets followed. Then the ark of God, surrounded by a halo of divine glory, was borne by priests clad in the dress denoting their sacred office. The army of Israel followed, each tribe under its standard. Such was the procession that compassed the doomed city. No sound was heard but the tread of that mighty host and the solemn peal of the trumpets, echoing among the hills and resounding through the streets of Jericho. The circuit completed, the army returned in silence to their tents, and the ark was restored to its place in the tabernacle.

With wonder and alarm the watchmen of the city marked every move, and reported to those in authority. They knew not the meaning of all this display; but when they beheld that mighty host marching around their city once each day, with the sacred ark and the attendant priests, the mystery of the scene struck terror to the hearts of priest and people. Again they would inspect their strong defenses, feeling certain they could successfully resist the most powerful attack. Many ridiculed the thought that any harm could come to them through these singular demonstrations. Others were awed as they beheld the procession that each day wound about the city. They remembered that the Red Sea had once parted before this people, and that a passage had just been opened for them through the river Jordan. They knew not what further wonders God might work for them.

For six days the host of Israel made the circuit of the city. The seventh day came, and with the first dawn of light, Joshua marshaled the armies of the Lord. Now they were directed to march seven times around Jericho, and at a mighty peal from the trumpets to shout with a loud voice, for God had given them the city.

491

The vast army marched solemnly around the devoted walls. All was silent, save the measured tread of many feet, and the occasional sound of the trumpet, breaking the stillness of the early morning. The massive walls of solid stone seemed to defy the siege of men. The watchers on the walls looked on with rising fear, as, the first circuit ended, there followed a second, then a third, a fourth, a fifth, a sixth. What could be the object of these mysterious movements? What mighty event was impending? They had not long to wait. As the seventh circuit was completed, the long procession paused. The trumpets, which for an interval had been silent, now broke forth in a blast that shook the very earth. The walls of solid stone, with their massive towers and battlements, tottered and heaved from their foundations, and with a crash fell in

ruin to the earth. The inhabitants of Jericho were paralyzed with terror, and the hosts of Israel marched in and took possession of the city.

The Israelites had not gained the victory by their own power; the conquest had been wholly the Lord's; and as the first fruits of the land, the city, with all that it contained, was to be devoted as a sacrifice to God. It was to be impressed upon Israel that in the conquest of Canaan they were not to fight for themselves, but simply as instruments to execute the will of God; not to seek for riches or self-exaltation, but the glory of Jehovah their King. Before the capture the command had been given, "The city shall be accursed, even it, and all that are therein." "Keep yourselves from the accursed thing, lest ye make yourselves accursed . . . and make the camp of Israel a curse, and trouble it."

All the inhabitants of the city, with every living thing that it contained, "both man and woman, young and old, and ox, and sheep, and ass," were put to the sword. Only faithful Rahab, with her household, was spared, in fulfillment of the promise of the spies. The city itself was burned; its palaces and temples, its magnificent dwellings with all their luxurious appointments, the rich draperies and the costly garments, were given to the flames. That which could not be destroyed by fire, "the silver, and the gold, and the vessels of brass and of iron," was to be devoted to the service of the tabernacle. The very site of the city was accursed; Jericho was never to be rebuilt as a stronghold; judgments were threatened upon anyone who should presume to restore the walls that divine power had cast down. The solemn declaration was made in the presence of all Israel, "Cursed be the man before the Lord, that riseth up and buildeth this city Jericho: he shall lay the foundation thereof in his first-born, and in his youngest son shall he set up the gates of it."

492

The utter destruction of the people of Jericho was but a fulfillment of the commands previously given through Moses concerning the inhabitants of Canaan: "Thou shalt smite them, and utterly destroy them." Deuteronomy 7:2. "Of the cities of these people, . . . thou shalt save alive nothing that breatheth." Deuteronomy 20:16. To many these commands seem to be contrary to the spirit of love and mercy enjoined in other portions of the Bible, but they were in truth the dictates of infinite wisdom and goodness. God was about to establish Israel in Canaan, to develop among them a nation and government that should be a manifestation of His kingdom upon the earth. They were not only to be inheritors of the true religion, but to disseminate its principles throughout the world. The Canaanites had abandoned themselves to the foulest and most debasing heathenism, and it was necessary that the land should be cleared of what would so surely prevent the fulfillment of

God's gracious purposes.

The inhabitants of Canaan had been granted ample opportunity for repentance. Forty years before, the opening of the Red Sea and the judgments upon Egypt had testified to the supreme power of the God of Israel. And now the overthrow of the kings of Midian, of Gilead and Bashan, had further shown that Jehovah was above all gods. The holiness of His character and His abhorrence of impurity had been evinced in the judgments visited upon Israel for their participation in the abominable rites of Baalpeor. All these events were known to the inhabitants of Jericho, and there were many who shared Rahab's conviction, though they refused to obey it, that Jehovah, the God of Israel, "is God in heaven above, and upon the earth beneath." Like the men before the Flood, the Canaanites lived only to blaspheme Heaven and defile the earth. And both love and justice demanded the prompt execution of these rebels against God and foes to man.

493 How easily the armies of heaven brought down the walls of Jericho, that proud city whose bulwarks, forty years before, had struck terror to the unbelieving spies! The Mighty One of Israel had said, "I have given into thine hand Jericho." Against that word human strength was powerless.

"By faith the walls of Jericho fell down." Hebrews 11:30. The Captain of the Lord's host communicated only with Joshua; He did not reveal Himself to all the congregation, and it rested with them to believe or doubt the words of Joshua, to obey the commands given by him in the name of the Lord, or to deny his authority. *They* could not see the host of angels who attended them under the leadership of the Son of God. They might have reasoned: "What unmeaning movements are these, and how ridiculous the performance of marching daily around the walls of the city, blowing trumpets of rams' horns. This can have no effect upon those towering fortifications." But the very plan of continuing this ceremony through so long a time prior to the final overthrow of the walls afforded opportunity for the development of faith among the Israelites. It was to be impressed upon their minds that their strength was not in the wisdom of man, nor in his might, but only in the God of their salvation. They were thus to become accustomed to relying wholly upon their divine Leader.

God will do great things for those who trust in Him. The reason why His professed people have no greater strength is that they trust so much to their own wisdom, and do not give the Lord an opportunity to reveal His power in their behalf. He will help His believing children in every emergency if they will place their entire confidence in Him and faithfully obey Him.

Soon after the fall of Jericho, Joshua determined to attack Ai, a small town among the ravines a few miles to the west of the Jordan Valley. Spies sent to this place brought back the report that the inhabitants were but few, and that only a small force would be needed to overthrow it.

The great victory that God had gained for them had made the Israelites self-confident. Because He had promised them the land of Canaan they felt secure, and failed to realize that divine help alone could give them success. Even Joshua laid his plans for the conquest of Ai without seeking counsel from God.

The Israelites had begun to exalt their own strength and to look with contempt upon their foes. An easy victory was expected, and three thousand men were thought sufficient to take the place. These rushed to the attack without the 494 assurance that God would be with them. They advanced nearly to the gate of the city, only to encounter the most determined resistance. Panic-stricken at the numbers and thorough preparation of their enemies, they fled in confusion down the steep descent. The Canaanites were in hot pursuit; "they chased them from before the gate, . . . and smote them in the going down." Though the loss was small as to numbers—but thirty-six men being slain—the defeat was disheartening to the whole congregation. "The hearts of the people melted, and became as water." This was the first time they had met the Canaanites in actual battle, and if put to flight before the defenders of this little town, what would be the result in the greater conflicts before them? Joshua looked upon their ill success as an expression of God's displeasure, and in distress and apprehension he "rent his clothes, and fell to the earth upon his face before the ark of the Lord until the eventide, he and the elders of Israel, and put dust upon their heads."

"Alas, O Lord God," he cried, "wherefore hast Thou at all brought this people over Jordan, to deliver us into the hand of the Amorites, to destroy us? . . . O Lord, what shall I say, when Israel turneth their backs before their enemies! For the Canaanites and all the inhabitants of the land shall hear of it, and shall environ us round, and cut off our name from the earth: and what wilt Thou do unto Thy great name?"

The answer from Jehovah was, "Get thee up; wherefore liest thou thus upon thy face? Israel hath . . . transgressed My covenant which I commanded them." It was a time for prompt and decided action, and not for despair and lamentation. There was secret sin in the camp, and it must be searched out and put away before the presence and blessing of the Lord could be with His people. "Neither will I be with you any more, except ye destroy the accursed from among you."

God's command had been disregarded by one

of those appointed to execute His judgments. And the nation was held accountable for the guilt of the transgressor: "*They* have even taken of the accursed thing, and have also stolen, and dissembled also." Instruction was given to Joshua for the discovery and punishment of the criminal. The lot was to be employed for the detection of the guilty. The sinner was not directly pointed out, the matter being left in doubt for a time, that the people might feel their responsibility for the sins existing among them, and thus be led to searching of heart and humiliation before God.

Early in the morning, Joshua gathered the people together by their tribes, and the solemn and impressive ceremony began. Step by step the investigation went on. Closer and still closer came the fearful test. First the tribe, then the family, then the household, then the man was taken, and Achan the son of Carmi, of the tribe of Judah, was pointed out by the finger of God as the troubler of Israel.

To establish his guilt beyond all question, leaving no ground for the charge that he had been unjustly condemned, Joshua solemnly adjured Achan to acknowledge the truth. The wretched man made full confession of his crime: "Indeed I have sinned against the Lord God of Israel. . . . When I saw among the spoils a goodly Babylonish garment, and two hundred shekels of silver, and a wedge of gold of fifty shekels' weight, then I coveted them, and took them; and, behold, they are hid in the earth in the midst of my tent." Messengers were immediately dispatched to the tent, where they removed the earth at the place specified, and "behold, it was hid in his tent, and the silver under it. And they took them out of the midst of the tent, and brought them unto Joshua, . . . and laid them out before the Lord."

Sentence was pronounced and immediately executed. "Why hast thou troubled us?" said Joshua, "the Lord shall trouble thee this day." As the people had been held responsible for Achan's sin, and had suffered from its consequences, they were, through their representatives, to take part in its punishment. "All Israel stoned him with stones."

Then there was raised over him a great pile of stones—a witness to the sin and its punishment. "Wherefore the name of that place was called, The valley of Achor," that is, "trouble." In the book of Chronicles his memorial is written—"Achar, the troubler of Israel." 1 Chronicles 2:7.

Achan's sin was committed in defiance of the most direct and solemn warnings and the most mighty manifestations of God's power. "Keep yourselves from the accursed thing, lest ye make yourselves accursed," had been the proclamation to all Israel. The command was given immediately after the miraculous passage of the Jordan, and the recognition of God's

covenant by the circumcision of the people—after the observance of the Passover, and the appearance of the Angel of the covenant, the Captain of the Lord's host. It had been followed by the overthrow of Jericho, giving evidence of the destruction which will surely overtake all transgressors of God's law. The fact that divine power alone had given the victory to Israel, that they had not come into possession of Jericho by their own strength, gave solemn weight to the command prohibiting them from partaking of the spoils. God, by the might of His own word, had overthrown this stronghold; the conquest was His, and to Him alone the city with all that it contained was to be devoted.

Of the millions of Israel there was but one man who, in that solemn hour of triumph and of judgment, had dared to transgress the command of God. Achan's covetousness was excited by the sight of that costly robe of Shinar; even when it had brought him face to face with death he called it "a *goodly* Babylonish garment." One sin had led to another, and he appropriated the gold and silver devoted to the treasury of the Lord—he robbed God of the first fruits of the land of Canaan.

The deadly sin that led to Achan's ruin had its root in covetousness, of all sins one of the most common and the most lightly regarded. While other offenses meet with detection and punishment, how rarely does the violation of the tenth commandment so much as call forth censure. The enormity of this sin, and its terrible results, are the lessons of Achan's history.

Covetousness is an evil of gradual development. Achan had cherished greed of gain until it became a habit, binding him in fetters well-nigh impossible to break. While fostering this evil, he would have been filled with horror at the thought of bringing disaster upon Israel; but his perceptions were deadened by sin, and when temptation came, he fell an easy prey.

Are not similar sins still committed, in the face of warnings as solemn and explicit? We are as directly forbidden to indulge covetousness as was Achan to appropriate the spoils of Jericho. God has declared it to be idolatry. We are warned, "Ye cannot serve God and mammon." Matthew 6:24. "Take heed, and beware of covetousness." Luke 12:15. "Let it not be once named among you." Ephesians 5:3. We have before us the fearful doom of Achan, of Judas, of Ananias and Sapphira. Back of all these we have that of Lucifer, the "son of the morning," who, coveting a higher state, forfeited forever the brightness and bliss of heaven. And yet, notwithstanding all these warnings, covetousness abounds.

Everywhere its slimy track is seen. It creates discontent and dissension in families; it excites envy and hatred in the poor against the rich; it prompts the grinding oppression of the rich toward the poor. And this evil exists not in the world alone, but in the church. How common even here to find selfishness, avarice, over-reaching, neglect of charities, and robbery of God "in tithes and offerings." Among church members "in good and regular standing" there are, alas! many Achans. Many a man comes stately to church, and sits at the table of the Lord, while among his possessions are hidden unlawful gains, the things that God has cursed. For a goodly Babylonish garment, multitudes sacrifice the approval of conscience and their hope of heaven. Multitudes barter their integrity, and their capabilities for usefulness, for a bag of silver shekels. The cries of the suffering poor are unheeded; the gospel light is hindered in its course; the scorn of worldlings is kindled by practices that give the lie to the Christian profession; and yet the covetous professor continues to heap up treasures. "Will a man rob God? Yet ye have robbed Me" (Malachi 3:8), saith the Lord.

Achan's sin brought disaster upon the whole nation. For one man's sin the displeasure of God will rest upon His church till the transgression is searched out and put away. The influence most to be feared by the church is not that of open opposers, infidels, and blasphemers, but of inconsistent professors of Christ. These are the ones that keep back the blessing of the God of Israel and bring weakness upon His people.

When the church is in difficulty, when coldness and spiritual declension exist, giving occasion for the enemies of God to triumph, then, instead of folding their hands and lamenting their unhappy state, let its members inquire if there is not an Achan in the camp. With humiliation and searching of heart, let each seek to discover the hidden sins that shut out God's presence.

Achan acknowledged his guilt, but when it was too late for the confession to benefit himself. He had seen the armies of Israel return from Ai defeated and disheartened; yet he did not come forward and confess his sin. He had seen Joshua and the elders of Israel bowed to the earth in grief too great for words. Had he then made confession, he would have given some proof of true penitence; but he still kept silence. He had listened to the proclamation that a great crime had been committed, and had even heard its character definitely stated. But his lips were sealed. Then came the solemn investigation. How his soul thrilled with terror as he saw his tribe pointed out, then his family and his household! But still he uttered no confession, until the finger of God was placed upon him. Then, when his sin could no longer be concealed, he admitted the truth. How often are similar confessions made. There is a vast difference between admitting facts after they have been proved and confessing sins known only to

498

ourselves and to God. Achan would not have confessed had he not hoped by so doing to avert the consequences of his crime. But his confession only served to show that his punishment was just. There was no genuine repentance for sin, no contrition, no change of purpose, no abhorrence of evil.

So confessions will be made by the guilty when they stand before the bar of God, after every case has been decided for life or death. The consequences to result to himself will draw from each an acknowledgment of his sin. It will be forced from the soul by an awful sense of condemnation and a fearful looking for of judgment. But such confessions cannot save the sinner.

So long as they can conceal their transgressions from their fellow men, many, like Achan, feel secure, and flatter themselves that God will not be strict to mark iniquity. All too late their sins will find them out in that day when they shall not be purged with sacrifice or offering forever. When the records of heaven shall be opened, the Judge will not in words declare to man his guilt, but will cast one penetrating, convicting glance, and every deed, every transaction of life, will be vividly impressed upon the memory of the wrongdoer. The person will not, as in Joshua's day, need to be hunted out from tribe to family, but his own lips will confess his shame. The sins hidden from the knowledge of men will then be proclaimed to the whole world.

46   499

The Blessings and the Curses

After the execution of the sentence upon Achan, Joshua was commanded to marshal all the men of war and again advance against Ai. The power of God was with His people, and they were soon in possession of the city.

Military operations were now suspended, that all Israel might engage in a solemn religious service. The people were eager to obtain a settlement in Canaan; as yet they had not homes or lands for their families, and in order to gain these they must drive out the Canaanites; but this important work must be deferred, for a higher duty demanded their first attention.

Before taking possession of their inheritance, they must renew their covenant of loyalty to God. In the last instructions of Moses, direction had been twice given for a convocation of the tribes upon Mounts Ebal and Gerizim, at Shechem, for the solemn recognition of the law of God. In obedience to these injunctions the whole people, not only men, but "the women, and the little ones, and the strangers that were

This chapter is based on Joshua 8.

conversant among them" left their camp at Gilgal, and marched through the country of their enemies, to the vale of Shechem, near the center of the land. Though surrounded by unconquered foes, they were safe under the protection of God as long as they were faithful to Him. Now, as in the days of Jacob, "the terror of God was upon the cities that were round about them" (Genesis 35:5), and the Hebrews were unmolested.

The place appointed for this solemn service was one already sacred from its association with the history of their fathers. It was here that Abraham raised his first altar to Jehovah in the land of Canaan. Here both Abraham and Jacob had pitched their tents. Here the latter bought the field in which the tribes were to bury the body of Joseph. Here also was the well that Jacob had dug, and the oak under which he had 500 buried the idolatrous images of his household.

The spot chosen was one of the most beautiful in all Palestine, and worthy to be the theater where this grand and impressive scene was to be enacted. The lovely valley, its green fields dotted with olive groves, watered with brooks from living fountains, and gemmed with wild flowers, spread out invitingly between the barren hills. Ebal and Gerizim, upon opposite sides of the valley, nearly approach each other, their lower spurs seeming to form a natural pulpit, every word spoken on one being distinctly audible on the other, while the mountainsides, receding, afford space for a vast assemblage.

According to the directions given by Moses, a monument of great stones was erected upon Mount Ebal. Upon these stones, previously prepared by a covering of plaster, the law was inscribed—not only the ten precepts spoken from Sinai and engraved on the tables of stone, but the laws communicated to Moses, and by him written in a book. Beside this monument was built an altar of unhewn stone, upon which sacrifices were offered unto the Lord. The fact that the altar was set up on Mount Ebal, the mountain upon which the curse was put, was significant, denoting that because of their transgressions of God's law, Israel had justly incurred His wrath, and that it would be at once visited, but for the atonement of Christ, represented by the altar of sacrifice.

Six of the tribes—all descended from Leah and Rachel—were stationed upon Mount Gerizim; while those that descended from the handmaids, together with Reuben and Zebulun, took their position on Ebal, the priests with the ark occupying the valley between them. Silence was proclaimed by the sound of the signal trumpet; and then in the deep stillness, and in the presence of this vast assembly, Joshua, standing beside the sacred ark, read the blessings that were to follow obedience to God's law. All the tribes on Gerizim responded by an Amen. He then read the curses, and the tribes on Ebal in

like manner gave their assent, thousands upon thousands of voices uniting as the voice of one man in the solemn response. Following this came the reading of the law of God, together with the statutes and judgments that had been delivered to them by Moses.

Israel had received the law directly from the mouth of God at Sinai; and its sacred precepts, written by His own hand, were still preserved in 503 the ark. Now it had been again written where all could read it. All had the privilege of seeing for themselves the conditions of the covenant under which they were to hold possession of Canaan. All were to signify their acceptance of the terms of the covenant and give their assent to the blessings or curses for its observance or neglect. The law was not only written upon the memorial stones, but was read by Joshua himself in the hearing of all Israel. It had not been many weeks since Moses gave the whole book of Deuteronomy in discourses to the people, yet now Joshua read the law again.

Not alone the men of Israel, but "all the women and the little ones" listened to the reading of the law; for it was important that they also should know and do their duty. God had commanded Israel concerning His statutes: "Therefore shall ye lay up these My words in your heart and in your soul, and bind them for a sign upon your hand, that they may be as frontlets between your eyes. And ye shall teach them your children, ... that your days may be multiplied, and the days of your children, in the land which the Lord sware unto your fathers to give them, as the days of heaven upon the earth." Deuteronomy 11:18-21.

Every seventh year the whole law was to be read in the assembly of all Israel, as Moses commanded: "At the end of every seven years, in the solemnity of the year of release, in the feast of tabernacles, when all Israel is come to appear before the Lord thy God in the place which He shall choose, thou shalt read this law before all Israel in their hearing. Gather the people together, men, and women, and children, and thy stranger that is within thy gates, that they may hear, and that they may learn, and fear the Lord your God, and observe to do all the words of this law: and that their children, which have not known anything, may hear, and learn to fear the Lord your God, as long as ye live in the land whither ye go over Jordan to possess it." Deuteronomy 31:10-13.

Satan is ever at work endeavoring to pervert what God has spoken, to blind the mind and darken the understanding, and thus lead men into sin. This is why the Lord is so explicit, making His requirements so very plain that none need err. God is constantly seeking to draw men close under His protection, that Satan may not practice his cruel, deceptive power upon them. He has condescended to speak to

504 them with His own voice, to write with His own hand the living oracles. And these blessed words, all instinct with life and luminous with truth, are committed to men as a perfect guide. Because Satan is so ready to catch away the mind and divert the affections from the Lord's promises and requirements, the greater diligence is needed to fix them in the mind and impress them upon the heart.

Greater attention should be given by religious teachers to instructing the people in the facts and lessons of Bible history and the warnings and requirements of the Lord. These should be presented in simple language, adapted to the comprehension of children. It should be a part of the work both of ministers and parents to see that the young are instructed in the Scriptures.

Parents can and should interest their children in the varied knowledge found in the sacred pages. But if they would interest their sons and daughters in the word of God, they must be interested in it themselves. They must be familiar with its teachings, and, as God commanded Israel, speak of it, "when thou sittest in thine house, and when thou walkest by the way, when thou liest down, and when thou risest up." Deuteronomy 11:19. Those who desire their children to love and reverence God must talk of His goodness, His majesty, and His power, as revealed in His word and in the works of creation.

Every chapter and every verse of the Bible is a communication from God to men. We should bind its precepts as signs upon our hands and as frontlets between our eyes. If studied and obeyed, it would lead God's people, as the Israelites were led, by the pillar of cloud by day and the pillar of fire by night.

505

47

League With the Gibeonites

From Shechem the Israelites returned to their encampment at Gilgal. Here they were soon after visited by a strange deputation, who desired to enter into treaty with them. The ambassadors represented that they had come from a distant country, and this seemed to be confirmed by their appearance. Their clothing was old and worn, their sandals were patched, their provisions moldy, and the skins that served them for wine bottles were rent and bound up, as if hastily repaired on the journey.

In their far-off home—professedly beyond the limits of Palestine—their fellow countrymen, they said, had heard of the wonders which God had wrought for His people, and had sent them to make a league with Israel. The Hebrews had been specially warned against entering into

any league with the idolaters of Canaan, and a doubt as to the truth of the strangers' words arose in the minds of the leaders. "Peradventure ye dwell among us," they said. To this the ambassadors only replied, "We are thy servants." But when Joshua directly demanded of them, "Who are ye? and from whence come ye?" they reiterated their former statement, and added, in proof of their sincerity, "This our bread we took hot for our provision out of our houses on the day we came forth to go unto you; but now, behold, it is dry, and it is moldy: and these bottles of wine, which we filled, were new; and, behold, they be rent: and these our garments and our shoes are become old by reason of the very long journey."

These representations prevailed. The Hebrews "asked not counsel at the mouth of the Lord. And Joshua made peace with them, and made a league with them, to let them live: and the princes of the congregation sware unto them." Thus the treaty was entered into. Three days afterward the truth was discovered. "They heard that they were their neighbors, and that they dwelt among them." Knowing that it was 506 impossible to resist the Hebrews, the Gibeonites had resorted to stratagem to preserve their lives.

Great was the indignation of the Israelites as they learned the deception that had been practiced upon them. And this was heightened when, after three days' journey, they reached the cities of the Gibeonites, near the center of the land. "All the congregation murmured against the princes;" but the latter refused to break the treaty, though secured by fraud, because they had "sworn unto them by the Lord God of Israel." "And the children of Israel smote them not." The Gibeonites had pledged themselves to renounce idolatry, and accept the worship of Jehovah; and the preservation of their lives was not a violation of God's command to destroy the idolatrous Canaanites. Hence the Hebrews had not by their oath pledged themselves to commit sin. And though the oath had been secured by deception, it was not to be disregarded. The obligation to which one's word is pledged—if it do not bind him to perform a wrong act—should be held sacred. No consideration of gain, of revenge, or of self-interest can in any way affect the inviolability of an oath or pledge. "Lying lips are abomination to the Lord." Proverbs 12:22. He that "shall ascend into the hill of the Lord," and "stand in His holy place," is "he that sweareth to his own hurt, and changeth not." Psalms 24:3; 15:4.

The Gibeonites were permitted to live, but were attached as bondmen to the sanctuary, to perform all menial services. "Joshua made them that day hewers of wood and drawers of water for the congregation, and for the altar of the Lord." These conditions they gratefully accepted, conscious that they had been at fault, and

This chapter is based on Joshua 9 and 10.

glad to purchase life on any terms. "Behold, we are in thine hand," they said to Joshua; "as it seemeth good and right unto thee to do unto us, do." For centuries their descendants were connected with the service of the sanctuary.

The territory of the Gibeonites comprised four cities. The people were not under the rule of a king, but were governed by elders, or senators. Gibeon, the most important of their towns, "was a great city, as one of the royal cities," "and all the men thereof were mighty." It is a striking evidence of the terror with which the Israelites had inspired the inhabitants of Canaan, that the people of such a city should have resorted to so humiliating an expedient to save their lives.

507 But it would have fared better with the Gibeonites had they dealt honestly with Israel. While their submission to Jehovah secured the preservation of their lives, their deception brought them only disgrace and servitude. God had made provision that all who would renounce heathenism, and connect themselves with Israel, should share the blessings of the covenant. They were included under the term, "the stranger that sojourneth among you," and with few exceptions this class were to enjoy equal favors and privileges with Israel. The Lord's direction was—

"If a stranger sojourn with thee in your land, ye shall not vex him. But the stranger that dwelleth with you shall be unto you as one born among you, and thou shalt love him as thyself." Leviticus 19:33, 34. Concerning the Passover and the offering of sacrifices it was commanded, "One ordinance shall be both for you and for the stranger that sojourneth with you: . . . as ye are, so shall the stranger be before the Lord." Numbers 15:15.

Such was the footing on which the Gibeonites might have been received, but for the deception to which they had resorted. It was no light humiliation to those citizens of a "royal city," "all the men whereof were mighty," to be made hewers of wood and drawers of water throughout their generations. But they had adopted the garb of poverty for the purpose of deception, and it was fastened upon them as a badge of perpetual servitude. Thus through all their generations their servile condition would testify to God's hatred of falsehood.

The submission of Gibeon to the Israelites filled the kings of Canaan with dismay. Steps were at once taken for revenge upon those who had made peace with the invaders. Under the leadership of Adonizedek, king of Jerusalem, five of the Canaanite kings entered into a confederacy against Gibeon. Their movements were rapid. The Gibeonites were unprepared for defense, and they sent a message to Joshua at Gilgal: "Slack not thy hand from thy servants; come up to us quickly, and save us, and help us: for all the kings of the Amorites that dwell in the mountains are gathered together against us." The danger threatened not the people of Gibeon alone, but also Israel. This city commanded the passes to central and southern Palestine, and it must be held if the country was to be conquered.

Joshua prepared to go at once to the relief of Gibeon. The inhabitants of the besieged city had feared that he would reject their appeal, because 508 of the fraud which they had practiced; but since they had submitted to the control of Israel, and had accepted the worship of God, he felt himself under obligation to protect them. He did not this time move without divine counsel, and the Lord encouraged him in the undertaking. "Fear them not," was the divine message; "for I have delivered them into thine hand; there shall not a man of them stand before thee." "So Joshua ascended from Gilgal, he, and all the people of war with him, and all the mighty men of valor."

By marching all night he brought his forces before Gibeon in the morning. Scarcely had the confederate princes mustered their armies about the city when Joshua was upon them. The attack resulted in the utter discomfiture of the assailants. The immense host fled before Joshua up the mountain pass to Beth-horon; and having gained the height, they rushed down the precipitous descent upon the other side. Here a fierce hailstorm burst upon them. "The Lord cast down great stones from heaven: . . . they were more which died with hailstones than they whom the children of Israel slew with the sword."

While the Amorites were continuing their headlong flight, intent on finding refuge in the mountain strongholds, Joshua, looking down from the ridge above, saw that the day would be too short for the accomplishment of his work. If not fully routed, their enemies would again rally, and renew the struggle. "Then spake Joshua to the Lord, . . . and he said in the sight of Israel, Sun, stand thou still upon Gibeon; and thou, Moon, in the valley of Ajalon. And the sun stood still, and the moon stayed, until the people had avenged themselves upon their enemies. . . . The sun stood still in the midst of heaven, and hasted not to go down about a whole day."

Before the evening fell, God's promise to Joshua had been fulfilled. The entire host of the enemy had been given into his hand. Long were the events of that day to remain in the memory of Israel. "There was no day like that before it or after it, that Jehovah hearkened unto the voice of a man: for the Lord fought for Israel." "The sun and moon stood still in their habitation: at the light of Thine arrows they went, and at the shining of Thy glittering spear. Thou didst march through the land in indignation, Thou didst thresh the heathen in anger. Thou wentest forth for the salvation of Thy people." Habakkuk 3:11-13.

The Spirit of God inspired Joshua's prayer, 509 that evidence might again be given of the power of Israel's God. Hence the request did not show presumption on the part of the great leader. Joshua had received the promise that God would surely overthrow these enemies of Israel, yet he put forth as earnest effort as though success depended upon the armies of Israel alone. He did all that human energy could do, and then he cried in faith for divine aid. The secret of success is the union of divine power with human effort. Those who achieve the greatest results are those who rely most implicitly upon the Almighty Arm. The man who commanded, "Sun, stand thou still upon Gibeon; and thou, Moon, in the valley of Ajalon," is the man who for hours lay prostrate upon the earth in prayer in the camp at Gilgal. The men of prayer are the men of power.

This mighty miracle testifies that the creation is under the control of the Creator. Satan seeks to conceal from men the divine agency in the physical world—to keep out of sight the unwearied working of the first great cause. In this miracle all who exalt nature above the God of nature stand rebuked.

At His own will God summons the forces of nature to overthrow the might of His enemies—"fire, and hail; snow, and vapor; stormy wind fulfilling His word." Psalm 148:8. When the heathen Amorites had set themselves to resist His purposes, God interposed, casting down "great stones from heaven" upon the enemies of Israel. We are told of a greater battle to take place in the closing scenes of earth's history, when "Jehovah hath opened His armory, and hath brought forth the weapons of His indignation." Jeremiah 50:25. "Hast thou," he inquires, "entered into the treasures of the snow? or hast thou seen the treasures of the hail, which I have reserved against the time of trouble, against the day of battle and war?" Job 38:22, 23.

The revelator describes the destruction that is to take place when the "great voice out of the temple of heaven" announces, "It is done." He says, "There fell upon men a great hail out of heaven, every stone about the weight of a talent." Revelation 16:17, 21.

510

48

The Division of Canaan

The victory at Beth-horon was speedily followed by the conquest of southern Canaan. "Joshua smote all the country of the hills, and of the south, and of the vale. . . . And all these kings and their land did Joshua take at one time, because the Lord God of Israel fought for Israel. And Joshua returned, and all Israel with him, unto the camp at Gilgal."

The tribes of northern Palestine, terrified at the success which had attended the armies of Israel, now entered into a league against them.

At the head of this confederacy was Jabin, king of Hazor, a territory to the west of Lake Merom. "And they went out, they and all their hosts with them." This army was much larger than any that the Israelites had before encountered in Canaan—"much people, even as the sand that is upon the seashore in multitude, with horses and chariots very many. And when all these kings were met together, they came and pitched together at the waters of Merom, to fight against Israel." Again a message of encouragement was given to Joshua: "Be not afraid because of them: for tomorrow about this time will I deliver them up all slain before Israel."

Near Lake Merom he fell upon the camp of the allies and utterly routed their forces. "The Lord delivered them into the hand of Israel, who smote them, and chased them . . . until they left them none remaining." The chariots and horses that had been the pride and boast of the Canaanites were not to be appropriated by Israel. At the command of God the chariots were burned, and the horses lamed, and thus rendered unfit for use in battle. The Israelites were not to put their trust in chariots or horses, but "in the name of the Lord their God."

One by one the cities were taken, and Hazor, the stronghold of the confederacy, was burned. The war was continued for several years, but its close found Joshua master of Canaan. "And the land had rest from war."

511

But though the power of the Canaanites had been broken, they had not been fully dispossessed. On the west the Philistines still held a fertile plain along the seacoast, while north of them was the territory of the Sidonians. Lebanon also was in the possession of the latter people; and to the south, toward Egypt, the land was still occupied by the enemies of Israel.

Joshua was not, however, to continue the war. There was another work for the great leader to perform before he should relinquish the command of Israel. The whole land, both the parts already conquered and that which was yet unsubdued, was to be apportioned among the tribes. And it was the duty of each tribe to fully subdue its own inheritance. If the people should prove faithful to God, He would drive out their enemies from before them; and He promised to give them still greater possessions if they would but be true to His covenant.

To Joshua, with Eleazar the high priest, and the heads of the tribes, the distribution of the land was committed, the location of each tribe being determined by lot. Moses himself had fixed the bounds of the country as it was to be divided among the tribes when they should come in possession of Canaan, and had appointed a prince from each tribe to attend to the distribution. The tribe of Levi, being devoted to the sanctuary service, was not counted in this allotment; but forty-eight cities in different parts of the country were assigned the Levites as their inheritance.

Before the distribution of the land had been entered upon, Caleb, accompanied by the heads of his tribe, came forward with a special claim. Except Joshua, Caleb was now the oldest man in Israel. Caleb and Joshua were the only ones among the spies who had brought a good report of the Land of Promise, encouraging the people to go up and possess it in the name of the Lord. Caleb now reminded Joshua of the promise then made, as the reward of his faithfulness: "The land whereon thy feet have trodden shall be thine inheritance, and thy children's forever, because thou hast wholly followed the Lord." He therefore presented a request that Hebron be given him for a possession. Here had been for many years the home of Abraham, Isaac, and Jacob; and here, in the cave of Machpelah, they 512 were buried. Hebron was the seat of the dreaded Anakim, whose formidable appearance had so terrified the spies, and through them destroyed the courage of all Israel. This, above all others, was the place which Caleb, trusting in the strength of God, chose for his inheritance.

"Behold, the Lord hath kept me alive," he said, "these forty and five years, even since the Lord spake this word unto Moses: . . . and now, lo, I am this day fourscore and five years old. As yet I am as strong this day as I was in the day that Moses sent me: as my strength was then, even so is my strength now, for war, both to go out, and to come in. Now therefore give me this mountain, whereof the Lord spake in that day; for thou heardest in that day how the Anakim were there, and that the cities were great and fenced: if so be the Lord will be with me, then I shall be able to drive them out, as the Lord said." This request was supported by the chief men of Judah. Caleb himself being the one appointed from this tribe to apportion the land, he had chosen to unite these men with him in presenting his claim, that there might be no appearance of having employed his authority for selfish advantage.

His claim was immediately granted. To none could the conquest of this giant stronghold be more safely entrusted. "Joshua blessed him, and gave unto Caleb the son of Jephunneh Hebron for an inheritance," "because that he wholly followed the Lord God of Israel." Caleb's faith now was just what it was when his testimony had contradicted the evil report of the spies. He had believed God's promise that He would put His people in possession of Canaan, and in this he had followed the Lord fully. He had endured with his people the long wandering in the wilderness, thus sharing the disappointments and burdens of the guilty; yet he made no complaint of this, but exalted the mercy of God that had preserved him in the wilderness when his brethren were cut off. Amid all the hardships,

perils, and plagues of the desert wanderings, and during the years of warfare since entering Canaan, the Lord had preserved him; and now at upwards of fourscore his vigor was unabated. He did not ask for himself a land already conquered, but the place which above all others the spies had thought it impossible to subdue. By the help of God he would wrest his stronghold from the very giants whose power had staggered the faith of Israel. It was no desire for honor or aggrandizement that prompted Caleb's request. The brave old warrior was desirous of giving to 513 the people an example that would honor God, and encourage the tribes fully to subdue the land which their fathers had deemed unconquerable.

Caleb obtained the inheritance upon which his heart had been set for forty years, and, trusting in God to be with him, he "drove thence the three sons of Anak." Having thus secured a possession for himself and his house, his zeal did not abate; he did not settle down to enjoy his inheritance, but pushed on to further conquests for the benefit of the nation and the glory of God.

The cowards and rebels had perished in the wilderness, but the righteous spies ate of the grapes of Eschol. To each was given according to his faith. The unbelieving had seen their fears fulfilled. Notwithstanding God's promise, they had declared that it was impossible to inherit Canaan, and they did not possess it. But those who trusted in God, looking not so much to the difficulties to be encountered as to the strength of their Almighty Helper, entered the goodly land. It was through faith that the ancient worthies "subdued kingdoms, . . . escaped the edge of the sword, out of weakness were made strong, waxed valiant in fight, turned to flight the armies of the aliens." Hebrews 11:33, 34. "This is the victory that overcometh the world, even our faith." 1 John 5:4.

Another claim concerning the division of the land revealed a spirit widely different from that of Caleb. It was presented by the children of Joseph, the tribe of Ephraim with the half tribe of Manasseh. In consideration of their superior numbers, these tribes demanded a double portion of territory. The lot designated for them was the richest in the land, including the fertile plain of Sharon; but many of the principal towns in the valley were still in possession of the Canaanites, and the tribes shrank from the toil and danger of conquering their possessions, and desired an additional portion in territory already subdued. The tribe of Ephraim was one of the largest in Israel, as well as the one to which Joshua himself belonged, and its members naturally regarded themselves as entitled to special consideration. "Why hast thou given me but one lot and one portion to inherit," they said, "seeing I am a great people?" But no departure from strict justice could be won from the inflexible leader.

His answer was, "If thou be a great people,

then get thee up to the wood country, and cut down for thyself there in the land of the Perizzites and of the giants, if Mount Ephraim be too narrow for thee."

Their reply showed the real cause of complaint. They lacked faith and courage to drive out the Canaanites. "The hill is not enough for us," they said; "and all the Canaanites that dwell in the land of the valley have chariots of iron."

The power of the God of Israel had been pledged to His people, and had the Ephraimites possessed the courage and faith of Caleb, no enemy could have stood before them. Their evident desire to shun hardship and danger was firmly met by Joshua. "Thou art a great people, and hast great power," he said; "thou shalt drive out the Canaanites, though they have iron chariots, and though they be strong." Thus their own arguments were turned against them. Being a great people, as they claimed, they were fully able to make their own way, as did their brethren. With the help of God they need not fear the chariots of iron.

Heretofore Gilgal had been the headquarters of the nation and the seat of the tabernacle. But now the tabernacle was to be removed to the place chosen for its permanent location. This was Shiloh, a little town in the lot of Ephraim. It was near the center of the land, and was easy of access to all the tribes. Here a portion of country had been thoroughly subdued, so that the worshipers would not be molested. "And the whole congregation of the children of Israel assembled together at Shiloh, and set up the tabernacle of the congregation there." The tribes that were still encamped when the tabernacle was removed from Gilgal followed it, and pitched near Shiloh. Here these tribes remained until they dispersed to their possessions.

The ark remained at Shiloh for three hundred years, until, because of the sins of Eli's house, it fell into the hands of the Philistines, and Shiloh was ruined. The ark was never returned to the tabernacle here, the sanctuary service was finally transferred to the temple at Jerusalem, and Shiloh fell into insignificance. There are only ruins to mark the spot where it once stood. Long afterward its fate was made use of as a warning to Jerusalem. "Go ye now unto My place which was in Shiloh," the Lord declared by the prophet Jeremiah, "where I set My name at the first, and see what I did to it for the wickedness of My people Israel. . . . Therefore will I do unto this house, which is called by My name, wherein ye trust, and unto the place which I gave to you and to your fathers, as I have done to Shiloh." Jeremiah 7:12-14.

"When they had made an end of dividing the land," and all the tribes had been allotted their inheritance, Joshua presented his claim. To him, as to Caleb, a special promise of inheritance had been given; yet he asked for no extensive

province, but only a single city. "They gave him the city which he asked, . . . and he built the city, and dwelt therein." The name given to the city was Timnathserah, "the portion that remains"—a standing testimony to the noble character and unselfish spirit of the conqueror, who, instead of being the first to appropriate the spoils of conquest, deferred his claim until the humblest of his people had been served.

Six of the cities assigned to the Levites—three on each side the Jordan—were appointed as cities of refuge, to which the manslayer might flee for safety. The appointment of these cities had been commanded by Moses, "that the slayer may flee thither, which killeth any person at unawares. And they shall be unto you cities for refuge," he said, "that the manslayer die not, until he stand before the congregation in judgment." Numbers 35:11, 12. This merciful provision was rendered necessary by the ancient custom of private vengeance, by which the punishment of the murderer devolved on the nearest relative or the next heir of the deceased. In cases where guilt was clearly evident it was not necessary to wait for a trial by the magistrates. The avenger might pursue the criminal anywhere and put him to death wherever he should be found. The Lord did not see fit to abolish this custom at that time, but He made provision to ensure the safety of those who should take life unintentionally.

The cities of refuge were so distributed as to be within a half day's journey of every part of the land. The roads leading to them were always to be kept in good repair; all along the way signposts were to be erected bearing the word "Refuge" in plain, bold characters, that the fleeing one might not be delayed for a moment. Any person—Hebrew, stranger, or sojourner—might avail himself of this provision. But while the guiltless were not to be rashly slain, neither were the guilty to escape punishment. The case of the fugitive was to be fairly tried by the proper authorities, and only when found innocent of intentional murder was he to be protected in the city of refuge. The guilty were given up to the avenger. And those who were entitled to protection could receive it only on condition of remaining within the appointed refuge. Should one wander away beyond the prescribed limits, and be found by the avenger of blood, his life would pay the penalty of his disregard of the Lord's provision. At the death of the high priest, however, all who had sought shelter in the cities of refuge were at liberty to return to their possessions.

In a trial for murder the accused was not to be condemned on the testimony of one witness, even though circumstantial evidence might be strong against him. The Lord's direction was, "Whoso killeth any person, the murderer shall be put to death by the mouth of witnesses: but one witness shall not testify against any person to cause him to die." Numbers 35:30. It was Christ who gave to Moses these directions for Israel; and when personally with His disciples on earth, as He taught them how to treat the erring, the Great Teacher repeated the lesson that one man's testimony is not to acquit or condemn. One man's views and opinions are not to settle disputed questions. In all these matters two or more are to be associated, and together they are to bear the responsibility, "that in the mouth of two or three witnesses every word may be established." Matthew 18:16.

If the one tried for murder were proved guilty, no atonement or ransom could rescue him. "Whoso sheddeth man's blood, by man shall his blood be shed." Genesis 9:6. "Ye shall take no satisfaction for the life of a murderer, which is guilty of death: but he shall be surely put to death." "Thou shalt take him from Mine altar, that he may die," was the command of God; "the land cannot be cleansed of the blood that is shed therein, but by the blood of him that shed it." Numbers 35:31, 33; Exodus 21:14. The safety and purity of the nation demanded that the sin of murder be severely punished. Human life, which God alone could give, must be sacredly guarded.

The cities of refuge appointed for God's ancient people were a symbol of the refuge provided in Christ. The same merciful Saviour who appointed those temporal cities of refuge has by the shedding of His own blood provided for the transgressors of God's law a sure retreat, in which they may flee for safety from the second death. No power can take out of His hands the souls that go to Him for pardon. "There is therefore now no condemnation to them which are in Christ Jesus." "Who is he that condemneth? It is Christ that died, yea rather, that is risen again, who is even at the right hand of God, who also maketh intercession for us;" that "we might have a strong consolation, who have fled for refuge to lay hold upon the hope set before us." Romans 8:1, 34; Hebrews 6:18.

He who fled to the city of refuge could make no delay. Family and employment were left behind. There was no time to say farewell to loved ones. His life was at stake, and every other interest must be sacrificed to the one purpose—to reach the place of safety. Weariness was forgotten, difficulties were unheeded. The fugitive dared not for one moment slacken his pace until he was within the wall of the city.

The sinner is exposed to eternal death, until he finds a hiding place in Christ; and as loitering and carelessness might rob the fugitive of his only chance for life, so delays and indifference may prove the ruin of the soul. Satan, the great adversary, is on the track of every transgressor of God's holy law, and he who is not sensible of his danger, and does not earnestly seek shelter in the eternal refuge, will fall a prey to the destroyer.

The prisoner who at any time went outside the city of refuge was abandoned to the avenger of blood. Thus the people were taught to adhere to the methods which infinite wisdom appointed for their security. Even so, it is not enough that the sinner *believe* in Christ for the pardon of sin; he must, by faith and obedience, abide in Him. "For if we sin willfully after that we have received the knowledge of the truth, there remaineth no more sacrifice for sins, but a certain fearful looking for of judgment and fiery indignation, which shall devour the adversaries." Hebrews 10:26, 27.

Two of the tribes of Israel, Gad and Reuben, with half the tribe of Manasseh, had received their inheritance before crossing the Jordan. To a pastoral people, the wide upland plains and rich forests of Gilead and Bashan, offering extensive grazing land for their flocks and herds, had attractions which were not to be found in Canaan itself, and the two and a half tribes, desiring to settle here, had pledged themselves to furnish their proportion of armed men to accompany their brethren across the Jordan and to share their battles till they also should enter upon their inheritance. The obligation had been faithfully discharged. When the ten tribes entered Canaan forty thousand of "the children of Reuben, and the children of Gad, and half the tribe of Manasseh . . . prepared for war passed over before the Lord unto battle, to the plains of Jericho." Joshua 4:12, 13. For years they had fought bravely by the side of their brethren. Now the time had come for them to get unto the land of their possession. As they had united with their brethren in the conflicts, so they had shared the spoils; and they returned "with much riches . . . and with very much cattle, with silver, and with gold, and with brass, and with iron, and with very much raiment," all of which they were to share with those who had remained with the families and flocks.

They were now to dwell at a distance from the sanctuary of the Lord, and it was with an anxious heart that Joshua witnessed their departure, knowing how strong would be the temptations, in their isolated and wandering life, to fall into the customs of the heathen tribes that dwelt upon their borders.

While the minds of Joshua and other leaders were still oppressed with anxious forebodings, strange tidings reached them. Beside the Jordan, near the place of Israel's miraculous passage of the river, the two and a half tribes had erected a great altar, similar to the altar of burnt offering at Shiloh. The law of God prohibited, on pain of death, the establishment of another worship than that at the sanctuary. If such was the object of this altar, it would, if permitted to remain, lead the people away from the true faith.

The representatives of the people assembled

at Shiloh, and in the heat of their excitement and indignation proposed to make war at once upon the offenders. Through the influence of the more cautious, however, it was decided to send first a delegation to obtain from the two and a half tribes an explanation of their conduct. Ten princes, one from each tribe, were chosen. At their head was Phinehas, who had distinguished himself by his zeal in the matter of Peor.

The two and a half tribes had been at fault in entering, without explanation, upon an act open to such grave suspicions. The ambassadors, taking it for granted that their brethren were guilty, met them with sharp rebuke. They accused them of rebelling against the Lord, and bade them remember how judgments had been visited upon Israel for joining themselves to Baalpeor. 519 In behalf of all Israel, Phinehas stated to the children of Gad and Reuben that if they were unwilling to abide in that land without an altar for sacrifice, they would be welcome to a share in the possessions and privileges of their brethren on the other side.

In reply the accused explained that their altar was not intended for sacrifice, but simply as a witness that, although separated by the river, they were of the same faith as their brethren in Canaan. They had feared that in future years their children might be excluded from the tabernacle, as having no part in Israel. Then this altar, erected after the pattern of the altar of the Lord at Shiloh, would be a witness that its builders were also worshipers of the living God.

With great joy the ambassadors accepted this explanation, and immediately carried back the tidings to those who sent them. All thoughts of war were dismissed, and the people united in rejoicing, and praise to God.

The children of Gad and Reuben now placed upon their altar an inscription pointing out the purpose for which it was erected; and they said, "It shall be a witness between us that Jehovah is God." Thus they endeavored to prevent future misapprehension and to remove what might be a cause of temptation.

How often serious difficulties arise from a simple misunderstanding, even among those who are actuated by the worthiest motives; and without the exercise of courtesy and forbearance, what serious and even fatal results may follow. The ten tribes remembered how, in Achan's case, God had rebuked the lack of vigilance to discover the sins existing among them. Now they resolved to act promptly and earnestly; but in seeking to shun their first error, they had gone to the opposite extreme. Instead of making courteous inquiry to learn the facts in the case, they had met their brethren with censure and condemnation. Had the men of Gad and Reuben retorted in the same spirit, war would have been the result. While it is impor-

tant on the one hand that laxness in dealing with sin be avoided, it is equally important on the other to shun harsh judgment and groundless suspicion.

While very sensitive to the least blame in regard to their own course, many are too severe in dealing with those whom they suppose to be in error. No one was ever reclaimed from a wrong position by censure and reproach; but many are thus driven further from the right path 520 and led to harden their hearts against conviction. A spirit of kindness, a courteous, forbearing deportment may save the erring and hide a multitude of sins.

The wisdom displayed by the Reubenites and their companions is worthy of imitation. While honestly seeking to promote the cause of true religion, they were misjudged and severely censured; yet they manifested no resentment. They listened with courtesy and patience to the charges of their brethren before attempting to make their defense, and then fully explained their motives and showed their innocence. Thus the difficulty which had threatened such serious consequences was amicably settled.

Even under false accusation those who are in the right can afford to be calm and considerate. God is acquainted with all that is misunderstood and misinterpreted by men, and we can safely leave our case in His hands. He will as surely vindicate the cause of those who put their trust in Him as He searched out the guilt of Achan. Those who are actuated by the spirit of Christ will possess that charity which suffers long and is kind.

It is the will of God that union and brotherly love should exist among His people. The prayer of Christ just before His crucifixion was that His disciples might be one as He is one with the Father, that the world might believe that God had sent Him. This most touching and wonderful prayer reaches down the ages, even to our day; for His words were, "Neither pray I for these alone, but for them also which shall believe on Me through their word." John 17:20. While we are not to sacrifice one principle of truth, it should be our constant aim to reach this state of unity. This is the evidence of our discipleship. Said Jesus, "By this shall all men know that ye are My disciples, if ye have love one to another." John 13:35. The apostle Peter exhorts the church, "Be ye all of one mind, having compassion one of another; love as brethren, be pitiful, be courteous: not rendering evil for evil, or railing for railing: but contrariwise blessing; knowing that ye are thereunto called, that ye should inherit a blessing." 1 Peter 3:8, 9.

49

The Last Words of Joshua

The wars and conquest ended, Joshua had withdrawn to the peaceful retirement of his home at Timnathserah. "And it came to pass, a long time after that the Lord had given rest unto Israel from all their enemies round about, that Joshua . . . called for all Israel, and for their elders, and for their heads, and for their judges, and for their officers."

Some years had passed since the people had settled in their possessions, and already could be seen cropping out the same evils that had heretofore brought judgments upon Israel. As Joshua felt the infirmities of age stealing upon him, and realized that his work must soon close, he was filled with anxiety for the future of his people. It was with more than a father's interest that he addressed them, as they gathered once more about their aged chief. "Ye have seen," he said, "all that the Lord your God hath done unto all these nations because of you; for the Lord your God is He that hath fought for you." Although the Canaanites had been subdued, they still possessed a considerable portion of the land promised to Israel, and Joshua exhorted his people not to settle down at ease and forget the Lord's command to utterly dispossess these idolatrous nations.

The people in general were slow to complete the work of driving out the heathen. The tribes had dispersed to their possessions, the army had disbanded, and it was looked upon as a difficult and doubtful undertaking to renew the war. But Joshua declared: "The Lord your God, He shall expel them from before you, and drive them from out of your sight; and ye shall possess their land, as the Lord your God hath promised unto you. Be ye therefore very courageous to keep and to do all that is written in the book of the law of Moses, that ye turn not aside therefrom to the right hand or to the left."

Joshua appealed to the people themselves as witnesses that, so far as they had complied with the conditions, God had faithfully fulfilled His promises to them. "Ye know in all your hearts and in all your souls," he said, "that not one thing hath failed of all the good things which the Lord your God spake concerning you; all are come to pass unto you, and not one thing hath failed thereof." He declared to them that as the Lord had fulfilled His promises, so He would fulfill His threatenings. "It shall come to pass, that as all good things are come upon you, which the Lord your God promised you; so shall the Lord bring upon you all evil things. . . . When ye have transgressed the covenant of the

Lord, . . . then shall the anger of the Lord be kindled against you, and ye shall perish quickly from off the good land which He hath given unto you."

Satan deceives many with the plausible theory that God's love for His people is so great that He will excuse sin in them; he represents that while the threatenings of God's word are to serve a certain purpose in His moral government, they are never to be literally fulfilled. But in all His dealings with His creatures God has maintained the principles of righteousness by revealing sin in its true character—by demonstrating that its sure result is misery and death. The unconditional pardon of sin never has been, and never will be. Such pardon would show the abandonment of the principles of righteousness, which are the very foundation of the government of God. It would fill the unfallen universe with consternation. God has faithfully pointed out the results of sin, and if these warnings were not true, how could we be sure that His promises would be fulfilled? That so-called benevolence which would set aside justice is not benevolence but weakness.

God is the life-giver. From the beginning all His laws were ordained to life. But sin broke in upon the order that God had established, and discord followed. So long as sin exists, suffering and death are inevitable. It is only because the Redeemer has borne the curse of sin in our behalf that man can hope to escape, in his own person, its dire results.

Before the death of Joshua the heads and representatives of the tribes, obedient to his summons, again assembled at Shechem. No spot in all the land possessed so many sacred associations, carrying their minds back to God's covenant with Abraham and Jacob, and recalling also their own solemn vows upon their entrance into Canaan. Here were the mountains Ebal and Gerizim, the silent witnesses of those vows which now, in the presence of their dying leader, they had assembled to renew. On every side were evidences of what God had wrought for them; how He had given them a land for which they did not labor, and cities which they built not, vineyards and oliveyards which they planted not. Joshua reviewed once more the history of Israel, recounting the wonderful works of God, that all might have a sense of His love and mercy and might serve Him "in sincerity and in truth."

By Joshua's direction the ark had been brought from Shiloh. The occasion was one of great solemnity, and this symbol of God's presence would deepen the impression he wished to make upon the people. After presenting the goodness of God toward Israel, he called upon them, in the name of Jehovah, to choose whom they would serve. The worship of idols was still to some extent secretly practiced, and Joshua

This chapter is based on Joshua 23 and 24.

endeavored now to bring them to a decision that should banish this sin from Israel. "If it seem evil unto you to serve Jehovah," he said, "choose you this day whom ye will serve." Joshua desired to lead them to serve God, not by compulsion, but willingly. Love to God is the very foundation of religion. To engage in His service merely from hope of reward or fear of punishment would avail nothing. Open apostasy would not be more offensive to God than hypocrisy and mere formal worship.

The aged leader urged the people to consider, in all its bearings, what he had set before them, and to decide if they really desired to live as did the degraded idolatrous nations around them. If it seemed evil to them to serve Jehovah, the source of power, the fountain of blessing, let them that day choose whom they would serve— "the gods which your fathers served," from whom Abraham was called out, "or the gods of the Amorites, in whose land ye dwell." These last words were a keen rebuke to Israel. The gods of the Amorites had not been able to protect their worshipers. Because of their abominable and debasing sins, that wicked nation had been destroyed, and the good land which they once possessed had been given to God's people. What folly for Israel to choose the deities for whose worship the Amorites had been destroyed! "As for me and my house," said Joshua, "we will serve Jehovah." The same holy zeal that inspired the leader's heart was communicated to the people. His appeals called forth the unhesitating response, "God forbid that we should forsake Jehovah, to serve other gods."

"Ye cannot serve the Lord," said Joshua: "for He is a holy God; . . . He will not forgive your transgressions nor your sins." Before there could be any permanent reformation the people must be led to feel their utter inability in themselves to render obedience to God. They had broken His law, it condemned them as transgressors, and it provided no way of escape. While they trusted in their own strength and righteousness, it was impossible for them to secure the pardon of sin; they could not meet the claims of God's perfect law, and it was in vain that they pledged themselves to serve God. It was only by faith in Christ that they could secure pardon of sin and receive strength to obey God's law. They must cease to rely upon their own efforts for salvation, they must trust wholly in the merits of the promised Saviour, if they would be accepted of God.

Joshua endeavored to lead his hearers to weigh well their words, and refrain from vows which they would be unprepared to fulfill. With deep earnestness they repeated the declaration: "Nay; but we will serve the Lord." Solemnly consenting to the witness against themselves that they had chosen Jehovah, they once more reiterated their pledge of loyalty: "The Lord our God will we serve, and His voice will we obey.

"So Joshua made a covenant with the people that day, and set them a statute and an ordinance in Shechem." Having written an account of this solemn transaction, he placed it, with the book of the law, in the side of the ark. And he set up a pillar as a memorial, saying, "Behold, this stone shall be a witness unto us; for it hath heard all the words of the Lord which He spake unto us; it shall be therefore a witness unto you, lest ye deny your God. So Joshua let the people depart, every man unto his inheritance."

Joshua's work for Israel was done. He had "wholly followed the Lord;" and in the book of God he is written, "The servant of Jehovah." The noblest testimony to his character as a public leader is the history of the generation that had enjoyed his labors: "Israel served the Lord all the days of Joshua, and all the days of the elders that overlived Joshua."

50

Tithes and Offerings

In the Hebrew economy one tenth of the income of the people was set apart to support the public worship of God. Thus Moses declared to Israel: "All the tithe of the land, whether of the seed of the land, or of the fruit of the tree, is the Lord's: it is holy unto the Lord." "And concerning the tithe of the herd, or of the flock, . . . the tenth shall be holy unto the Lord." Leviticus 27:30, 32.

But the tithing system did not originate with the Hebrews. From the earliest times the Lord claimed a tithe as His, and this claim was recognized and honored. Abraham paid tithes to Melchizedek, the priest of the most high God. Genesis 14:20. Jacob, when at Bethel, an exile and a wanderer, promised the Lord, "Of all that Thou shalt give me I will surely give the tenth unto Thee." Genesis 28:22. As the Israelites were about to be established as a nation, the law of tithing was reaffirmed as one of the divinely ordained statutes upon obedience to which their prosperity depended.

The system of tithes and offerings was intended to impress the minds of men with a great truth—that God is the source of every blessing to His creatures, and that to Him man's gratitude is due for the good gifts of His providence.

"He giveth to all life, and breath, and all things." Acts 17:25. The Lord declares, "Every beast of the forest is Mine, and the cattle upon a thousand hills." Psalm 50:10. "The silver is Mine, and the gold is Mine." Haggai 2:8. And it is God who gives men power to get wealth. Deuteronomy 8:18. As an acknowledgment that all things came from Him, the Lord directed that a portion of His bounty should be returned to Him in gifts and offerings to sustain His worship.

"The tithe . . . is the Lord's." Here the same form of expression is employed as in the law of the Sabbath. "The seventh day is the sabbath of the Lord thy God." Exodus 20:10. God reserved to Himself a specified portion of man's time and of his means, and no man could, without guilt, appropriate either for his own interests.

The tithe was to be exclusively devoted to the use of the Levites, the tribe that had been set apart for the service of the sanctuary. But this was by no means the limit of the contributions for religious purposes. The tabernacle, as afterward the temple, was erected wholly by freewill offerings; and to provide for necessary repairs and other expenses, Moses directed that as often as the people were numbered, each should contribute a half shekel for "the service of the tabernacle." In the time of Nehemiah a contribution was made yearly for this purpose. See Exodus 30:12-16; 2 Kings 12:4, 5; 2 Chronicles 24:4-13; Nehemiah 10:32, 33. From time to time sin offerings and thank offerings were brought to God. These were presented in great numbers at the annual feasts. And the most liberal provision was made for the poor.

Even before the tithe could be reserved there had been an acknowledgment of the claims of God. The first that ripened of every product of the land was consecrated to Him. The first of the wool when the sheep were shorn, of the grain when the wheat was threshed, the first of the oil and the wine, were set apart for God. So also were the first-born of all animals; and a redemption price was paid for the first-born son. The first fruits were to be presented before the Lord at the sanctuary, and were then devoted to the use of the priests.

Thus the people were constantly reminded that God was the true proprietor of their fields, their flocks, and their herds; that He sent them sunshine and rain for their seedtime and harvest, and that everything they possessed was of His creation, and He had made them stewards of His goods.

As the men of Israel, laden with the first fruits of field and orchard and vineyard, gathered at the tabernacle, there was made a public acknowledgment of God's goodness. When the priest accepted the gift, the offerer, speaking as in the presence of Jehovah, said, "A Syrian ready to perish was my father;" and he described the sojourn in Egypt and the affliction from which God had delivered Israel "with an outstretched arm, and with great terribleness, and with signs, and with wonders." And he said, "He hath brought us into this place, and hath given us this land, even a land that floweth with milk and honey. And now, behold, I have brought the firstfruits of the land, which Thou, Jehovah, hast given me." Deuteronomy 26:5, 8-11.

The contributions required of the Hebrews for religious and charitable purposes amounted to fully one fourth of their income. So heavy a tax upon the resources of the people might be expected to reduce them to poverty; but, on the contrary, the faithful observance of these regulations was one of the conditions of their prosperity. On condition of their obedience God made them this promise: "I will rebuke the devourer for your sakes, and he shall not destroy the fruits of your ground; neither shall your vine cast her fruit before the time in the field. . . . And all nations shall call you blessed: for ye shall be a delightsome land, saith the Lord of hosts." Malachi 3:11.

A striking illustration of the results of selfishly withholding even freewill offerings from the cause of God was given in the days of the prophet Haggai. After their return from the captivity in Babylon, the Jews undertook to rebuild the temple of the Lord; but meeting determined opposition from their enemies, they discontinued the work; and a severe drought, by which they were reduced to actual want, convinced them that it was impossible to complete the building of the temple. "The time is not come," they said, "the time that the Lord's house should be built." But a message was sent them by the Lord's prophet: "Is it time for you, O ye, to dwell in your ceiled houses, and this house lie waste? Now therefore thus saith the Lord of hosts; Consider your ways. Ye have sown much, and bring in little; ye eat, but ye have not enough; ye drink, but ye are not filled with drink; ye clothe you, but there is none warm; and he that earneth wages, earneth wages to put it into a bag with holes." Haggai 1:2-6. And then the reason is given: "Ye looked for much, and, lo, it came to little; and when ye brought it home, I did blow upon it. Why? saith the Lord of hosts. Because of Mine house that is waste, and ye run every man unto his own house. Therefore the heaven over you is stayed from dew, and the earth is stayed from her fruit. And I called for a drought upon the land, and upon the mountains, and upon the corn, and upon the new wine, and upon the oil, and upon that which the ground bringeth forth, and upon men, and upon cattle, and upon all the labor of the hands." Verses 9-12. "When one came to a heap of twenty measures, there were but ten: when one came to the pressfat for to draw out fifty vessels out of the press, there were but twenty. I smote you with blasting and with mildew and with hail in all the labors of your hands." Haggai 2:16, 19.

Roused by these warnings, the people set themselves to build the house of God. Then the word of the Lord came to them: "Consider now from this day and upward, from the four and twentieth day of the ninth month, even from the day that the foundation of the Lord's temple was laid, . . . from this day will I bless you." Verses 18, 19.

Says the wise man, "There is that scattereth, and yet increaseth; and there is that withholdeth more than is meet, but it tendeth to poverty." Proverbs 11:24. And the same lesson is taught in the New Testament by the apostle Paul: "He which soweth sparingly shall reap also sparingly; and he which soweth bountifully shall reap also bountifully." "God is able to make all grace abound toward you; that ye, always having all sufficiency in all things, may abound to every good work." 2 Corinthians 9:6, 8.

God intended that His people Israel should be light bearers to all the inhabitants of the earth. In maintaining His public worship they were bearing a testimony to the existence and sovereignty of the living God. And this worship it was their privilege to sustain, as an expression of their loyalty and their love to Him. The Lord has ordained that the diffusion of light and truth in the earth shall be dependent upon the efforts and offerings of those who are partakers of the heavenly gift. He might have made angels the ambassadors of His truth; He might have made known His will, as He proclaimed the law from Sinai, with His own voice; but in His infinite love and wisdom He called men to become colaborers with Himself, by choosing them to do this work.

In the days of Israel the tithe and freewill offerings were needed to maintain the ordinances of divine service. Should the people of God give less in this age? The principle laid down by Christ is that our offerings to God should be in proportion to the light and privileges enjoyed. "Unto whomsoever much is given, of him shall be much required." Luke 12:48. Said the Saviour to His disciples as He sent them forth, "Freely ye have received, freely give." Matthew 10:8. As our blessings and privileges are increased—above all, as we have before us the unparalleled sacrifice of the glorious Son of God—should not our gratitude find expression in more abundant gifts to extend to others the message of salvation? The work of the gospel, as it widens, requires greater provision to sustain it than was called for anciently; and this makes the law of tithes and offerings of even more urgent necessity now than under the Hebrew economy. If His people were liberally to sustain His cause by their voluntary gifts, instead of resorting to unchristian and unhallowed methods to fill the treasury, God would be honored, and many more souls would be won to Christ.

The plan of Moses to raise means for the building of the tabernacle was highly successful. No urging was necessary. Nor did he employ any of the devices to which churches in our day so often resort. He made no grand feast. He did not invite the people to scenes of gaiety, dancing, and general amusement; neither did he institute lotteries, nor anything of this profane order, to obtain means to erect the tabernacle for God. The Lord directed Moses to invite the children of Israel to bring their offerings. He was to accept gifts from everyone that gave willingly, from his heart. And the offerings came in so great abundance that Moses bade the people cease bringing, for they had supplied more than could be used.

God has made men His stewards. The property which He has placed in their hands is the means that He has provided for the spread of the gospel. To those who prove themselves faithful stewards He will commit greater trusts. Saith the Lord, "Them that honor Me I will honor." 1 Samuel 2:30. "God loveth a cheerful giver," and when His people, with grateful hearts, bring their gifts and offerings to Him, "not grudgingly, or of necessity," His blessing will attend them, as He has promised. "Bring ye all the tithes into the storehouse, that there may be meat in Mine house, and prove Me now herewith, saith the Lord of hosts, if I will not open you the windows of heaven, and pour you out a blessing, that there shall not be room enough to receive it." Malachi 3:10.

51

530

God's Care for the Poor

To promote the assembling of the people for religious service, as well as to provide for the poor, a second tithe of all the increase was required. Concerning the first tithe, the Lord had declared, "I have given the children of Levi *all the tenth* in Israel." Numbers 18:21. But in regard to the second He commanded, "Thou shalt eat before the Lord thy God, in the place which He shall choose to place His name there, the tithe of thy corn, of thy wine, and of thine oil, and the firstlings of thy herds and of thy flocks; that thou mayest learn to fear the Lord thy God always." Deuteronomy 14:23, 29; 16:11-14. This tithe, or its equivalent in money, they were for two years to bring to the place where the sanctuary was established. After presenting a thank offering to God, and a specified portion to the priest, the offerers were to use the remainder for a religious feast, in which the Levite, the stranger, the fatherless, and the widow should participate. Thus provision was made for the thank offerings and feasts at the yearly festivals, and the people were drawn to

529

the society of the priests and Levites, that they might receive instruction and encouragement in the service of God.

Every third year, however, this second tithe was to be used at home, in entertaining the Levite and the poor, as Moses said, "That they may eat within thy gates, and be filled." Deuteronomy 26:12. This tithe would provide a fund for the uses of charity and hospitality.

And further provision was made for the poor. There is nothing, after their recognition of the claims of God, that more distinguishes the laws given by Moses than the liberal, tender, and hospitable spirit enjoined toward the poor. Although God had promised greatly to bless His people, it was not His design that poverty should be wholly unknown among them. He declared that the poor should never cease out of the land. There would ever be those among His people who would call into exercise their sympathy, tenderness, and benevolence. Then, as now, persons were subject to misfortune, sickness, and loss of property; yet so long as they followed the instruction given by God, there were no beggars among them, neither any who suffered for food.

The law of God gave the poor a right to a certain portion of the produce of the soil. When hungry, a man was at liberty to go to his neighbor's field or orchard or vineyard, and eat of the grain or fruit to satisfy his hunger. It was in accordance with this permission that the disciples of Jesus plucked and ate of the standing grain as they passed through a field upon the Sabbath day.

All the gleanings of harvest field, orchard, and vineyard, belonged to the poor. "When thou cuttest down thine harvest in thy field," said Moses, "and hast forgot a sheaf in the field, thou shalt not go again to fetch it. . . . When thou beatest thine olive tree, thou shalt not go over the boughs again. . . . When thou gatherest the grapes of thy vineyard, thou shalt not glean it afterward: it shall be for the stranger, for the fatherless, and for the widow. And thou shalt remember that thou wast a bondman in the land of Egypt." Deuteronomy 24:19-22; Leviticus 19:9, 10.

Every seventh year special provision was made for the poor. The sabbatical year, as it was called, began at the end of the harvest. At the seedtime, which followed the ingathering, the people were not to sow; they should not dress the vineyard in the spring; and they must expect neither harvest nor vintage. Of that which the land produced spontaneously they might eat while fresh, but they were not to lay up any portion of it in their storehouses. The yield of this year was to be free for the stranger, the fatherless, and the widow, and even for the creatures of the field. Exodus 23:10, 11; Leviticus 25:5.

But if the land ordinarily produced only enough to supply the wants of the people, how were they to subsist during the year when no crops were gathered? For this the promise of God made ample provision. "I will command My blessing upon you in the sixth year," He said, "and it shall bring forth fruit for three years. And ye shall sow the eighth year, and eat yet of old fruit until the ninth year; until her fruits come in ye shall eat of the old store." Leviticus 25:21, 22.

The observance of the sabbatical year was to be a benefit to both the land and the people. The soil, lying untilled for one season, would afterward produce more plentifully. The people were released from the pressing labors of the field; and while there were various branches of work that could be followed during this time, all enjoyed greater leisure, which afforded opportunity for the restoration of their physical powers for the exertions of the following years. They had more time for meditation and prayer, for acquainting themselves with the teachings and requirements of the Lord, and for the instruction of their households.

In the sabbatical year the Hebrew slaves were to be set at liberty, and they were not to be sent away portionless. The Lord's direction was: "When thou sendest him out free from thee, thou shalt not let him go away empty. Thou shalt furnish him liberally out of thy flock, and out of thy floor, and out of thy winepress: of that wherewith the Lord thy God hath blessed thee thou shalt give unto him." Deuteronomy 15:13, 14.

The hire of a laborer was to be promptly paid: "Thou shalt not oppress a hired servant that is poor and needy, whether he be of thy brethren, or of thy strangers that are in thy land: . . . at his day thou shalt give him his hire, neither shall the sun go down upon it; for he is poor, and setteth his heart upon it." Deuteronomy 24:14, 15.

Special directions were also given concerning the treatment of fugitives from service: "Thou shalt not deliver unto his master the servant which is escaped from his master unto thee. He shall dwell with thee, even among you, in that place which he shall choose in one of thy gates, where it liketh him best: thou shalt not oppress him." Deuteronomy 23:15, 16.

To the poor, the seventh year was a year of release from debt. The Hebrews were enjoined at all times to assist their needy brethren by lending them money without interest. To take usury from a poor man was expressly forbidden: "If thy brother be waxen poor, and fallen in decay with thee; then thou shalt relieve him: yea, though he be a stranger, or a sojourner; that he may live with thee. Take thou no usury of him, or increase: but fear thy God; that thy brother may live with thee. Thou shalt not give him thy money upon usury, nor lend him thy victuals for increase." Leviticus 25:35-37. If the

533 debt remained unpaid until the year of release, the principal itself could not be recovered. The people were expressly warned against withholding from their brethren needed assistance on account of this: "If there be among you a poor man of one of thy brethren, . . . thou shalt not harden thine heart, nor shut thine hand from thy poor brother. . . . Beware that there be not a thought in thy wicked heart, saying, The seventh year, the year of release, is at hand; and thine eye be evil against thy poor brother, and thou givest him nought; and he cry unto the Lord against thee, and it be sin unto thee." "The poor shall never cease out of the land; therefore I command thee, saying, Thou shalt open thine hand wide unto thy brother, to thy poor, and to thy needy, in thy land," "and shalt surely lend him sufficient for his need, in that which he wanteth." Deuteronomy 15:7-9, 11, 8.

None need fear that their liberality would bring them to want. Obedience to God's commandments would surely result in prosperity. "Thou shalt lend unto many nations," He said, "but thou shalt not borrow; and thou shalt reign over many nations, but they shall not reign over thee." Deuteronomy 15:6.

After "seven sabbaths of years," "seven times seven years," came that great year of release—the jubilee. "Then shalt thou cause the trumpet of the jubilee to sound . . . throughout all your land. And ye shall hallow the fiftieth year, and proclaim liberty throughout all the land unto all the inhabitants thereof: it shall be a jubilee unto you; and ye shall return every man unto his possession, and ye shall return every man unto his family." Leviticus 25:9, 10.

"On the tenth day of the seventh month, in the Day of Atonement," the trumpet of the jubilee was sounded. Throughout the land, wherever the Jewish people dwelt, the sound was heard, calling upon all the children of Jacob to welcome the year of release. On the great Day of Atonement satisfaction was made for the sins of Israel, and with gladness of heart the people would welcome the jubilee.

As in the sabbatical year, the land was not to be sown or reaped, and all that it produced was to be regarded as the rightful property of the poor. Certain classes of Hebrew slaves—all who did not receive their liberty in the sabbatical year—were now set free. But that which especially distinguished the year of jubilee was the reversion of all landed property to the family 534 of the original possessor. By the special direction of God the land had been divided by lot. After the division was made no one was at liberty to trade his estate. Neither was he to sell his land unless poverty compelled him to do so, and then, whenever he or any of his kindred might desire to redeem it, the purchaser must not refuse to sell it; and if unredeemed, it would revert to its first possessor or his heirs in the

year of jubilee.

The Lord declared to Israel: "The land shall not be sold forever: for the land is Mine; for ye are strangers and sojourners with Me." Leviticus 25:23. The people were to be impressed with the fact that it was God's land which they were permitted to possess for a time; that He was the rightful owner, the original proprietor, and that He would have special consideration made for the poor and unfortunate. It was to be impressed upon the minds of all that the poor have as much right to a place in God's world as have the more wealthy.

Such were the provisions made by our merciful Creator, to lessen suffering, to bring some ray of hope, to flash some gleam of sunshine, into the life of the destitute and distressed.

The Lord would place a check upon the inordinate love of property and power. Great evils would result from the continued accumulation of wealth by one class, and the poverty and degradation of another. Without some restraint the power of the wealthy would become a monopoly, and the poor, though in every respect fully as worthy in God's sight, would be regarded and treated as inferior to their more prosperous brethren. The sense of this oppression would arouse the passions of the poorer class. There would be a feeling of despair and desperation which would tend to demoralize society and open the door to crimes of every description. The regulations that God established were designed to promote social equality. The provisions of the sabbatical year and the jubilee would, in a great measure, set right that which during the interval had gone wrong in the social and political economy of the nation.

These regulations were designed to bless the rich no less than the poor. They would restrain avarice and a disposition for self-exaltation, and would cultivate a noble spirit of benevolence; and by fostering good will and confidence between all classes, they would promote social order, the stability of government. We are all woven together in the great web of humanity, and whatever we can do to benefit and uplift 535 others will reflect in blessing upon ourselves. The law of mutual dependence runs through all classes of society. The poor are not more dependent upon the rich than are the rich upon the poor. While the one class ask a share in the blessings which God has bestowed upon their wealthier neighbors, the other need the faithful service, the strength of brain and bone and muscle, that are the capital of the poor.

Great blessings were promised to Israel on condition of obedience to the Lord's directions. "I will give you rain in due season," He declared, "and the land shall yield her increase, and the trees of the field shall yield their fruit. And your threshing shall reach unto the vintage, and the vintage shall reach unto the sowing time: and ye shall eat your bread to the full, and dwell in your land safely. And I will give peace in the land, and ye shall lie down, and none shall make you afraid: and I will rid evil beasts out of the land, neither shall the sword go through your land. . . . I will walk among you, and will be your God, and ye shall be My people. . . . But if ye will not hearken unto Me, and will not do all these commandments; and. . . ye break My covenant: . . . ye shall sow your seed in vain, for your enemies shall eat it. And I will set My face against you, and ye shall be slain before your enemies: they that hate you shall reign over you; and ye shall flee when none pursueth you." Leviticus 26:4-17.

There are many who urge with great enthusiasm that all men should have an equal share in the temporal blessings of God. But this was not the purpose of the Creator. A diversity of condition is one of the means by which God designs to prove and develop character. Yet He intends that those who have worldly possessions shall regard themselves merely as stewards of His goods, as entrusted with means to be employed for the benefit of the suffering and the needy.

Christ has said that we shall have the poor always with us, and He unites His interests with that of His suffering people. The heart of our Redeemer sympathizes with the poorest and lowliest of His earthly children. He tells us that they are His representatives on earth. He has placed them among us to awaken in our hearts the love that He feels toward the suffering and oppressed. Pity and benevolence shown to them 536 are accepted by Christ as if shown to Himself. An act of cruelty or neglect toward them is regarded as though done to Him.

If the law given by God for the benefit of the poor had continued to be carried out, how different would be the present condition of the world, morally, spiritually, and temporally! Selfishness and self-importance would not be manifested as now, but each would cherish a kind regard for the happiness and welfare of others; and such widespread destitution as is now seen in many lands would not exist.

The principles which God has enjoined, would prevent the terrible evils that in all ages have resulted from the oppression of the rich toward the poor and the suspicion and hatred of the poor toward the rich. While they might hinder the amassing of great wealth and the indulgence of unbounded luxury, they would prevent the consequent ignorance and degradation of tens of thousands whose ill-paid servitude is required to build up these colossal fortunes. They would bring a peaceful solution of those problems that now threaten to fill the world with anarchy and bloodshed.

52 537

The Annual Feasts

There were three annual assemblies of all Israel for worship at the sanctuary. Exodus 23:14-16. Shiloh was for a time the place of these gatherings; but Jerusalem afterward became the center of the nation's worship, and here the tribes convened for the solemn feasts.

The people were surrounded by fierce, warlike tribes, that were eager to seize upon their lands; yet three times every year all the able-bodied men and all the people who could make the journey were directed to leave their homes and repair to the place of assembly, near the center of the land. What was to hinder their enemies from sweeping down upon those unprotected households, to lay them waste with fire and sword? What was to prevent an invasion of the land, that would bring Israel into captivity to some foreign foe? God had promised to be the protector of His people. "The angel of Jehovah encampeth round about them that fear Him, and delivereth them." Psalm 34:7. While the Israelites went up to worship, divine power would place a restraint upon their enemies. God's promise was, "I will cast out the nations before thee, and enlarge thy borders: neither shall any man desire thy land, when thou shalt go up to appear before the Lord thy God thrice in the year." Exodus 34:24.

The first of these festivals, the Passover, the feast of unleavened bread, occurred in Abib, the first month of the Jewish year, corresponding to the last of March and the beginning of April. The cold of winter was past, the latter rain had ended, and all nature rejoiced in the freshness and beauty of the springtime. The grass was green on the hills and valleys, and wild flowers everywhere brightened the fields. The moon, now approaching the full, made the evenings delightful. It was the season so beautifully pictured by the sacred singer:

"The winter is past, 538
The rain is over and gone;
The flowers appear on the earth;
The time of the singing of birds is come,
And the voice of the turtle is heard in our
  land;
The fig tree ripeneth her green figs,
And the vines are in blossom,
  They give forth their fragrance." Song of
      Solomon 2:11-13, R.V.

Throughout the land bands of pilgrims were making their way toward Jerusalem. The shepherds from their flocks, the herdsmen from the mountains, fishers from the Sea of Galilee, the husbandmen from their fields, and sons of the prophets from the sacred schools—all turned their steps toward the place where God's presence was revealed. They journeyed by short stages, for many went on foot. The caravans were constantly receiving accessions, and often became very large before reaching the Holy City.

Nature's gladness awakened joy in the hearts of Israel and gratitude to the Giver of all good. The grand Hebrew psalms were chanted, exalting the glory and majesty of Jehovah. At the sound of the signal trumpet, with the music of cymbals, the chorus of thanksgiving arose, swelled by hundreds of voices:

"I was glad when they said unto me,
Let us go unto the house of the Lord.
Our feet are standing
Within thy gates, O Jerusalem. . . .
Whither the tribes go up, even the tribes of
the Lord, . . .
To give thanks unto the name of Jehovah. . . .
Pray for the peace of Jerusalem:
They shall prosper that love thee."
Psalm 122:1-6, R.V.

As they saw around them the hills where the heathen had been wont to kindle their altar fires, the children of Israel sang:

"Shall I lift up mine eyes to the hills?
Whence should my help come?
My help cometh from Jehovah,
Which made heaven and earth."
Psalm 121:1, 2 (margin).

"They that trust in the Lord
Are as Mount Zion, which cannot be moved,
but abideth forever.
As the mountains are round about Jerusalem,
So the Lord is round about His people,
From this time forth and forevermore."
Psalm 125:1, 2, R.V.

539 Surmounting the hills in view of the Holy City, they looked with reverent awe upon the throngs of worshipers wending their way to the temple. They saw the smoke of the incense ascending, and as they heard the trumpets of the Levites heralding the sacred service, they caught the inspiration of the hour, and sang:

"Great is the Lord, and greatly to be praised
In the city of our God, in the mountain of His
holiness.
Beautiful for situation, the joy of the whole
earth,
Is Mount Zion, on the sides of the north,
The city of the great King."
Psalm 48:1, 2.

"Peace be within thy walls,
And prosperity within thy palaces."
"Open to me the gates of righteousness:
I will go into them, and I will praise the
Lord."
"I will pay my vows unto the Lord
Now in the presence of all His people,
In the courts of the Lord's house,
In the midst of thee, O Jerusalem,
Praise ye the Lord."
Psalm 122:7; 118:19; 116:18, 19.

All the houses in Jerusalem were thrown open to the pilgrims, and rooms were furnished free; but this was not sufficient for the vast assembly, and tents were pitched in every available space in the city and upon the surrounding hills.

On the fourteenth day of the month, at even, the Passover was celebrated, its solemn, impressive ceremonies commemorating the deliverance from bondage in Egypt, and pointing forward to the sacrifice that should deliver from the bondage of sin. When the Saviour yielded up His life on Calvary, the significance of the Passover ceased, and the ordinance of the Lord's Supper was instituted as a memorial of the same event of which the Passover had been a type.

The Passover was followed by the seven days' feast of unleavened bread. The first and the seventh day were days of holy convocation, when no servile work was to be performed. On the second day of the feast, the first fruits of the year's harvest were presented before God. Barley was the earliest grain in Palestine, and at the opening of the feast it was beginning to ripen. A sheaf of this grain was waved by the priest before the altar of God, as an acknowledgment that all was His. Not until this ceremony had been performed was the harvest to be gathered.

Fifty days from the offering of first fruits, 540 came the Pentecost, called also the feast of harvest and the feast of weeks. As an expression of gratitude for the grain prepared as food, two loaves baked with leaven were presented before God. The Pentecost occupied but one day, which was devoted to religious service.

In the seventh month came the Feast of Tabernacles, or of ingathering. This feast acknowledged God's bounty in the products of the orchard, the olive grove, and the vineyard. It was the crowning festal gathering of the year. The land had yielded its increase, the harvests had been gathered into the granaries, the fruits, the oil, and the wine had been stored, the first fruits had been reserved, and now the people came with their tributes of thanksgiving to God, who had thus richly blessed them. This feast was to be pre-eminently an occasion of rejoicing. It occurred just after the great

Day of Atonement, when the assurance had been given that their iniquity should be remembered no more. At peace with God, they now came before Him to acknowledge His goodness and to praise Him for His mercy. The labors of the harvest being ended, and the toils of the new year not yet begun, the people were free from care, and could give themselves up to the sacred, joyous influences of the hour. Though only the fathers and sons were commanded to appear at the feasts, yet, so far as possible, all the household were to attend them, and to their hospitality the servants, the Levites, the stranger, and the poor were made welcome.

Like the Passover, the Feast of Tabernacles was commemorative. In memory of their pilgrim life in the wilderness the people were now to leave their houses and dwell in booths, or arbors, formed from the green branches "of goodly trees, branches of palm trees, and the boughs of thick trees, and willows of the brook." Leviticus 23:40, 42, 43.

The first day was a holy convocation, and to the seven days of the feast an eighth day was added, which was observed in like manner.

At these yearly assemblies the hearts of old and young would be encouraged in the service of God, while the association of the people from the different quarters of the land would strengthen the ties that bound them to God and to one another. Well would it be for the people of God 541 at the present time to have a Feast of Tabernacles—a joyous commemoration of the blessings of God to them. As the children of Israel celebrated the deliverance that God had wrought for their fathers, and His miraculous preservation of them during their journeyings from Egypt, so should we gratefully call to mind the various ways He has devised for bringing us out from the world, and from the darkness of error, into the precious light of His grace and truth.

With those who lived at a distance from the tabernacle, more than a month of every year must have been occupied in attendance upon the annual feasts. This example of devotion to God should emphasize the importance of religious worship and the necessity of subordinating our selfish, worldly interests to those that are spiritual and eternal. We sustain a loss when we neglect the privilege of associating together to strengthen and encourage one another in the service of God. The truths of His word lose their vividness and importance in our minds. Our hearts cease to be enlightened and aroused by the sanctifying influence, and we decline in spirituality. In our intercourse as Christians we lose much by lack of sympathy with one another. He who shuts himself up to himself is not filling the position that God designed he should. We are all children of one Father, dependent upon one another for happiness. The claims of God and of humanity are upon us. It is the proper cultivation of the social elements of our nature that brings us into sympathy with our brethren and affords us happiness in our efforts to bless others.

The Feast of Tabernacles was not only commemorative but typical. It not only pointed back to the wilderness sojourn, but, as the feast of harvest, it celebrated the ingathering of the fruits of the earth, and pointed forward to the great day of final ingathering, when the Lord of the harvest shall send forth His reapers to gather the tares together in bundles for the fire, and to gather the wheat into His garner. At that time the wicked will all be destroyed. They will become "as though they had not been." Obadiah 16. And every voice in the whole universe will unite in joyful praise to God. Says the revelator, "Every creature which is in heaven, and on the earth, and under the earth, and such as are in the sea, and all that are in them, heard I saying, Blessing, and honor, and glory, and power, be unto Him that sitteth upon the throne, and unto the Lamb forever and ever." Revelation 5:13.

The people of Israel praised God at the Feast 542 of Tabernacles, as they called to mind His mercy in their deliverance from the bondage of Egypt and His tender care for them during their pilgrim life in the wilderness. They rejoiced also in the consciousness of pardon and acceptance, through the service of the Day of Atonement, just ended. But when the ransomed of the Lord shall have been safely gathered into the heavenly Canaan, forever delivered from the bondage of the curse, under which "the whole creation groaneth and travaileth in pain together until now" (Romans 8:22), they will rejoice with joy unspeakable and full of glory. Christ's great work of atonement for men will then have been completed, and their sins will have been forever blotted out.

"The wilderness and the solitary place shall
    be glad for them;
And the desert shall rejoice, and blossom as
    the rose.
It shall blossom abundantly, and rejoice even
    with joy and singing:
The glory of Lebanon shall be given unto it,
The excellency of Carmel and Sharon;
They shall see the glory of the Lord, and the
    excellency of our God.

"Then the eyes of the blind shall be opened,
And the ears of the deaf shall be unstopped.
Then shall the lame man leap as an hart,
And the tongue of the dumb sing:

"For in the wilderness shall waters break out,
And streams in the desert.
And the parched ground shall become a
    pool,
And the thirsty land springs of water: . . .

"And an highway shall be there, and a way,

And it shall be called The way of holiness;
The unclean shall not pass over it;
But it shall be for those:
The wayfaring men, though fools, shall not
    err therein.

"No lion shall be there,
Nor any ravenous beast shall go up thereon,
It shall not be found there;
But the redeemed shall walk there:

"And the ransomed of the Lord shall return,
And come to Zion with songs
And everlasting joy upon their heads:
They shall obtain joy and gladness,
And sorrow and sighing shall flee away."
                                Isaiah 35:1, 2, 5-10.

⁵⁴³

53
The Earlier Judges

After the settlement in Canaan the tribes made no vigorous effort to complete the conquest of the land. Satisfied with the territory already gained, their zeal soon flagged, and the war was discontinued. "When Israel was strong, . . . they put the Canaanites to tribute, and did not utterly drive them out." Judges 1:28.

The Lord had faithfully fulfilled, on His part, the promises made to Israel; Joshua had broken the power of the Canaanites, and had distributed the land to the tribes. It only remained for them, trusting in the assurance of divine aid, to complete the work of dispossessing the inhabitants of the land. But this they failed to do. By entering into league with the Canaanites they directly transgressed the command of God, and thus failed to fulfill the condition on which He had promised to place them in possession of Canaan.

From the very first communication of God with them at Sinai, they had been warned against idolatry. Immediately after the proclamation of the law the message was sent them by Moses concerning the nations of Canaan: "Thou shalt not bow down to their gods, nor serve them, nor do after their works: but thou shalt utterly overthrow them, and quite break down their images. And ye shall serve the Lord your God, and He shall bless thy bread, and thy water; and I will take sickness away from the midst of thee." Exodus 23:24, 25. The assurance was given that so long as they remained obedient, God would subdue their enemies before them: "I will send My fear before thee, and will destroy all the people to whom thou shalt come; and I will make all thine enemies turn their backs unto thee. And I will send hornets before thee, which shall drive out the Hivite, the Canaanite, and the Hittite, from before thee. I will not drive them out from

before thee in one year; lest the land become desolate, and the beast of the field multiply against thee. By little and little I will drive them out from before thee, until thou be increased, and inherit the land. . . . I will deliver the inhabitants of the land into your hand; and thou shalt drive them out before thee. Thou shalt make no covenant with them, nor with their gods. They shall not dwell in thy land, lest they make thee sin against Me: for if thou serve their gods, it will surely be a snare unto thee." Exodus 23:27-33. These directions were reiterated in the most solemn manner by Moses before his death, and they were repeated by Joshua. ⁵⁴⁴

God had placed His people in Canaan as a mighty breastwork to stay the tide of moral evil, that it might not flood the world. If faithful to Him, God intended that Israel should go on conquering and to conquer. He would give into their hands nations greater and more powerful than the Canaanites. The promise was: "If ye shall diligently keep all these commandments which I command you, . . . then will the Lord drive out all these nations from before you, and ye shall possess greater nations and mightier than yourselves. Every place whereon the soles of your feet shall tread shall be yours: from the wilderness and Lebanon, from the river, the river Euphrates, even unto the uttermost sea shall your coast be. There shall no man be able to stand before you: for the Lord your God shall lay the fear of you and the dread of you upon all the land that ye shall tread upon, as He hath said unto you." Deuteronomy 11:22-25.

But regardless of their high destiny, they chose the course of ease and self-indulgence; they let slip their opportunities for completing the conquest of the land; and for many generations they were afflicted by the remnant of these idolatrous peoples, that were, as the prophet had foretold, as "pricks" in their eyes, and as "thorns" in their sides. Numbers 33:55.

The Israelites were "mingled among the heathen, and learned their works." Psalm 106:35. They intermarried with the Canaanites, and idolatry spread like a plague throughout the land. "They served their idols: which were a snare unto them. Yea, they sacrificed their sons and their daughters unto devils: . . . and the land was polluted with blood. . . . Therefore was the wrath of the Lord kindled against His people, insomuch that He abhorred His own inheritance." Psalm 106:36-40.

Until the generation that had received instruction from Joshua became extinct, idolatry made little headway; but the parents had prepared the ⁵⁴⁵ way for the apostasy of their children. The disregard of the Lord's restrictions on the part of those who came in possession of Canaan sowed seeds of evil that continued to bring forth bitter fruit for many generations. The simple habits of the Hebrews had secured them physical health;

This chapter is based on Judges 6 to 8; 10.

212

but association with the heathen led to the indulgence of appetite and passion, which gradually lessened physical strength and enfeebled the mental and moral powers. By their sins the Israelites were separated from God; His strength was removed from them, and they could no longer prevail against their enemies. Thus they were brought into subjection to the very nations that through God they might have subdued.

"They forsook the Lord God of their fathers, which brought them out of the land of Egypt," "and guided them in the wilderness like a flock." "They provoked Him to anger with their high places, and moved Him to jealousy with their graven images." Therefore the Lord "forsook the tabernacle of Shiloh, the tent which He placed among them; and delivered His strength into captivity, and His glory into the enemy's hand." Judges 2:12; Psalm 78:52, 58, 60, 61. Yet He did not utterly forsake His people. There was ever a remnant who were true to Jehovah; and from time to time the Lord raised up faithful and valiant men to put down idolatry and to deliver the Israelites from their enemies. But when the deliverer was dead, and the people were released from his authority, they would gradually return to their idols. And thus the story of backsliding and chastisement, of confession and deliverance, was repeated again and again.

The king of Mesopotamia, the king of Moab, and after them the Philistines, and the Canaanites of Hazor, led by Sisera, in turn became the oppressors of Israel. Othniel, Shamgar, and Ehud, Deborah and Barak, were raised up as deliverers of their people. But again "the children of Israel did evil in the sight of the Lord; and the Lord delivered them into the hand of Midian." Heretofore the hand of the oppressor had fallen but lightly on the tribes dwelling east of the Jordan, but in the present calamities they were the first sufferers.

The Amalekites on the south of Canaan, as well as the Midianites on its eastern border, and in the deserts beyond, were still the unrelenting enemies of Israel. The latter nation had been nearly destroyed by the Israelites in the days of 546 Moses, but they had since increased greatly, and had become numerous and powerful. They had thirsted for revenge; and now that the protecting hand of God was withdrawn from Israel, the opportunity had come. Not alone the tribes east of Jordan, but the whole land suffered from their ravages. The wild, fierce inhabitants of the desert, "as locusts for multitude" (Judges 6:5, R.V.), came swarming into the land, with their flocks and herds. Like a devouring plague they spread over the country, from the river Jordan to the Philistine plain. They came as soon as the harvests began to ripen, and remained until the last fruits of the earth had been gathered. They stripped the fields of their increase and robbed and maltreated the inhabitants and then returned to the deserts. Thus the Israelites dwelling in the open country were forced to abandon their homes, and to congregate in walled towns, to seek refuge in fortresses, or even to find shelter in caves and rocky fastnesses among the mountains. For seven years this oppression continued, and then, as the people in their distress gave heed to the Lord's reproof, and confessed their sins, God again raised up a helper for them.

Gideon was the son of Joash, of the tribe of Manasseh. The division to which this family belonged held no leading position, but the household of Joash was distinguished for courage and integrity. Of his brave sons it is said, "Each one resembled the children of a king." All but one had fallen in the struggles against the Midianites, and he had caused his name to be feared by the invaders. To Gideon came the divine call to deliver his people. He was engaged at the time in threshing wheat. A small quantity of grain had been concealed, and not daring to beat it out on the ordinary threshing floor, he had resorted to a spot near the winepress; for the season of ripe grapes being still far off, little notice was now taken of the vineyards. As Gideon labored in secrecy and silence, he sadly pondered upon the condition of Israel and considered how the oppressor's yoke might be broken from off his people.

Suddenly the "Angel of the Lord" appeared and addressed him with the words, "Jehovah is with thee, thou mighty man of valor."

"O my Lord," was his answer, "if the Lord be with us, why then is all this befallen us? and where be all His miracles which our fathers told us of, saying, Did not the Lord bring us up from Egypt? but now the Lord hath forsaken us, and delivered us into the hands of the Midianites." 547

The Messenger of heaven replied, "Go in this thy might, and thou shalt save Israel from the hand of the Midianites: have not I sent thee?"

Gideon desired some token that the one now addressing him was the Covenant Angel, who in time past had wrought for Israel. Angels of God, who communed with Abraham, had once tarried to share his hospitality; and Gideon now entreated the divine Messenger to remain as his guest. Hastening to his tent, he prepared from his scanty store a kid and unleavened cakes, which he brought forth and set before Him. But the Angel bade him, "Take the flesh and the unleavened cakes, and lay them upon this rock, and pour out the broth." Gideon did so, and then the sign which he had desired was given: with the staff in His hand, the Angel touched the flesh and the unleavened cakes, and a flame bursting from the rock consumed the sacrifice. Then the Angel vanished from his sight.

Gideon's father, Joash, who shared in the apostasy of his countrymen, had erected at Ophrah, where he dwelt, a large altar to Baal, at which the people of the town worshiped.

Gideon was commanded to destroy this altar and to erect an altar to Jehovah over the rock on which the offering had been consumed, and there to present a sacrifice to the Lord. The offering of sacrifice to God had been committed to the priests, and had been restricted to the altar at Shiloh; but He who had established the ritual service, and to whom all its offerings pointed, had power to change its requirements. The deliverance of Israel was to be preceded by a solemn protest against the worship of Baal. Gideon must declare war upon idolatry before going out to battle with the enemies of his people.

The divine direction was faithfully carried out. Knowing that he would be opposed if it were attempted openly, Gideon performed the work in secret; with the aid of his servants, accomplishing the whole in one night. Great was the rage of the men of Ophrah when they came next morning to pay their devotions to Baal. They would have taken Gideon's life had not Joash—who had been told of the Angel's visit—stood in defense of his son. "Will ye plead for Baal?" said Joash. "Will ye save him? he that will plead for him, let him be put to death whilst it is yet morning: if he be a god, let him plead for himself, because one hath cast down his altar." If Baal could not defend his own altar, how could he be trusted to protect his worshipers?

All thoughts of violence toward Gideon were dismissed; and when he sounded the trumpet of war, the men of Ophrah were among the first to gather to his standard. Heralds were dispatched to his own tribe of Manasseh, and also to Asher, Zebulun, and Naphtali, and all answered to the call.

Gideon dared not place himself at the head of the army without still further evidence that God had called him to this work, and that He would be with him. He prayed, "If Thou wilt save Israel by mine hand, as Thou hast said, behold, I will put a fleece of wool in the floor; and if the dew be on the fleece only, and it be dry upon all the earth besides, then shall I know that Thou wilt save Israel by mine hand, as Thou hast said." In the morning the fleece was wet, while the ground was dry. But now a doubt arose, since wool naturally absorbs moisture when there is any in the air; the test might not be decisive. Hence he asked that the sign be reversed, pleading that his extreme caution might not displease the Lord. His request was granted.

Thus encouraged, Gideon led out his forces to give battle to the invaders. "All the Midianites and the Amalekites and the children of the east were gathered together, and went over, and pitched in the valley of Jezreel." The entire force under Gideon's command numbered only thirty-two thousand men; but with the vast host of the enemy spread out before him, the word of

the Lord came to him: "The people that are with thee are too many for Me to give the Midianites into their hands, lest Israel vaunt themselves against Me, saying, Mine own hand hath saved me. Now therefore go to, proclaim in the ears of the people, saying, Whosoever is fearful and afraid, let him return and depart early from Mount Gilead." Those who were unwilling to face danger and hardships, or whose worldly interests would draw their hearts from the work of God, would add no strength to the armies of Israel. Their presence would prove only a cause of weakness.

It had been made a law in Israel that before they went to battle the following proclamation should be made throughout the army: "What man is there that hath built a new house, and hath not dedicated it? let him go and return to his house, lest he die in the battle, and another man dedicate it. And what man is he that hath planted a vineyard, and hath not yet eaten of it? let him also go and return unto his house, lest he die in the battle, and another man eat of it. And what man is there that hath betrothed a wife, and hath not taken her? let him go and return unto his house, lest he die in the battle, and another man take her." And the officers were to speak further to the people, saying, "What man is there that is fearful and fainthearted? let him go and return unto his house, lest his brethren's heart faint as well as his heart." Deuteronomy 20:5-8.

Because his numbers were so few compared with those of the enemy, Gideon had refrained from making the usual proclamation. He was filled with astonishment at the declaration that his army was too large. But the Lord saw the pride and unbelief existing in the hearts of His people. Aroused by the stirring appeals of Gideon, they had readily enlisted; but many were filled with fear when they saw the multitudes of the Midianites. Yet, had Israel triumphed, those very ones would have taken the glory to themselves instead of ascribing the victory to God.

Gideon obeyed the Lord's direction, and with a heavy heart he saw twenty-two thousand, or more than two thirds of his entire force, depart for their homes. Again the word of the Lord came to him: "The people are yet too many; bring them down unto the water, and I will try them for thee there: and it shall be, that of whom I say unto thee, This shall go with thee, the same shall go with thee; and of whomsoever I say unto thee, This shall not go with thee, the same shall not go." The people were led down to the waterside, expecting to make an immediate advance upon the enemy. A few hastily took a little water in the hand and sucked it up as they went on; but nearly all bowed upon their knees, and leisurely drank from the surface of the stream. Those who took of the water in their hands were but three hundred out of ten thousand; yet these were selected; all the rest were permitted to return to their homes.

By the simplest means character is often tested. Those who in time of peril were intent upon supplying their own wants were not the men to be trusted in an emergency. The Lord has no place in His work for the indolent and self-indulgent. The men of His choice were the few who would not permit their own wants to delay them in the discharge of duty. The three hundred chosen men not only possessed courage and self-control, but they were men of faith. They had not defiled themselves with idolatry. God could direct them, and through them He could work deliverance for Israel. Success does not depend upon numbers. God can deliver by few as well as by many. He is honored not so much by the great numbers as by the character of those who serve Him.

The Israelites were stationed on the brow of a hill overlooking the valley where the hosts of the invaders lay encamped. "And the Midianites and the Amalekites and all the children of the east lay along in the valley like locusts for multitude; and their camels were without number, as the sand which is upon the seashore for multitude." Judges 7:12, R.V. Gideon trembled as he thought of the conflict of the morrow. But the Lord spoke to him in the night season and bade him, with Phurah his attendant, go down to the camp of the Midianites, intimating that he would there hear something for his encouragement. He went, and, waiting in the darkness and silence, he heard a soldier relating a dream to his companion: "Lo, a cake of barley bread tumbled into the host of Midian, and came unto a tent, and smote it that it fell, and overturned it, that the tent lay along." The other answered in words that stirred the heart of that unseen listener, "This is nothing else save the sword of Gideon the son of Joash, a man of Israel: for into his hand hath God delivered Midian, and all the host." Gideon recognized the voice of God speaking to him through those Midianitish strangers. Returning to the few men under his command, he said, "Arise; for the Lord hath delivered into your hand the host of Midian."

By divine direction a plan of attack was suggested to him, which he immediately set out to execute. The three hundred men were divided into three companies. To every man were given a trumpet, and a torch concealed in an earthen pitcher. The men were stationed in such a manner as to approach the Midianite camp from different directions. In the dead of night, at a signal from Gideon's war horn, the three companies sounded their trumpets; then, breaking their pitchers and displaying the blazing torches, they rushed upon the enemy with the terrible war cry, "The sword of the Lord, and of Gideon!" The sleeping army was suddenly aroused.

Upon every side was seen the light of the flaming torches. In every direction was heard the sound of trumpets, with the cry of the assailants. Believing themselves at the mercy of an overwhelming force, the Midianites were panic-stricken. With wild cries of alarm they fled for life, and, mistaking their own companions for enemies, they slew one another. As news of the victory spread, thousands of the men of Israel who had been dismissed to their homes returned and joined in pursuit of their fleeing enemies. The Midianites were making their way toward the Jordan, hoping to reach their own territory, beyond the river. Gideon sent messengers to the tribe of Ephraim, rousing them to intercept the fugitives at the southern fords. Meanwhile, with his three hundred, "faint, yet pursuing," Gideon crossed the stream hard after those who had already gained the farther side. The two princes, Zebah and Zalmunna, who had been over the entire host, and who had escaped with an army of fifteen thousand men, were overtaken by Gideon, their force completely scattered, and the leaders captured and slain.

In this signal defeat not less than one hundred and twenty thousand of the invaders perished. The power of the Midianites was broken, so that they were never again able to make war upon Israel. The tidings spread swiftly far and wide, that Israel's God had again fought for His people. No words can describe the terror of the surrounding nations when they learned what simple means had prevailed against the power of a bold, warlike people.

The leader whom God chose to overthrow the Midianites occupied no prominent position in Israel. He was not a ruler, a priest, or a Levite. He thought himself the least in his father's house. But God saw in him a man of courage and integrity. He was distrustful of himself and willing to follow the guidance of the Lord. God does not always choose for His work men of the greatest talents, but He selects those whom He can best use. "Before honor is humility." Proverbs 15:33. The Lord can work most effectually through those who are most sensible of their own insufficiency, and who will rely upon Him as their leader and source of strength. He will make them strong by uniting their weakness to His might, and wise by connecting their ignorance with His wisdom.

If they would cherish true humility, the Lord could do much more for His people; but there are few who can be trusted with any large measure of responsibility or success without becoming self-confident and forgetful of their dependence upon God. This is why, in choosing the instruments for His work, the Lord passes by those whom the world honors as great, talented, and brilliant. They are too often proud and self-sufficient. They feel competent to act without counsel from God.

The simple act of blowing a blast upon the trumpet by the army of Joshua around Jericho, and by Gideon's little band about the hosts of Midian, was made effectual, through the power of God, to overthrow the might of His enemies. The most complete system that men have ever devised, apart from the power and wisdom of God, will prove a failure, while the most unpromising methods will succeed when divinely appointed and entered upon with humility and faith. Trust in God and obedience to His will are as essential to the Christian in the spiritual warfare as to Gideon and Joshua in their battles with the Canaanites. By the repeated manifestations of His power in behalf of Israel, God would lead them to have faith in Him— with confidence to seek His help in every emergency. He is just as willing to work with the efforts of His people now and to accomplish great things through weak instrumentalities. All heaven awaits our demand upon its wisdom and strength. God is "able to do exceeding abundantly above all that we ask or think." Ephesians 3:20.

Gideon returned from pursuing the enemies of the nation, to meet censure and accusation from his own countrymen. When at his call the men of Israel had rallied against the Midianites, the tribe of Ephraim had remained behind. They looked upon the effort as a perilous undertaking; and as Gideon sent them no special summons, they availed themselves of this excuse not to join their brethren. But when the news of Israel's triumph reached them, the Ephraimites were envious because they had not shared it. After the rout of the Midianites, the men of Ephraim had, by Gideon's direction, seized the fords of the Jordan, thus preventing the escape of the fugitives. By this means a large number of the enemy were slain, among whom were two princes, Oreb and Zeeb. Thus the men of Ephraim followed up the battle, and helped complete the victory. Nevertheless, they were jealous and angry, as though Gideon had been led by his own will and judgment. They did not discern God's hand in the triumph of Israel, they did not appreciate His power and mercy in their deliverance; and this very fact showed them unworthy to be chosen as His special instruments.

Returning with the trophies of victory, they angrily reproached Gideon: "Why hast thou served us thus, that thou calledst us not, when thou wentest to fight with the Midianites?"

"What have I done now, in comparison of you?" said Gideon. "Is not the *gleaning* of the grapes of Ephraim better than the *vintage* of Abiezer? *God* hath delivered into your hands the princes of Midian, Oreb and Zeeb: and what was I able to do in comparison of you?"

The spirit of jealousy might easily have been fanned into a quarrel that would have caused strife and bloodshed; but Gideon's modest answer soothed the anger of the men of Ephraim, and they returned in peace to their homes. Firm and uncompromising where principle was concerned, and in war a "mighty man of valor," Gideon displayed also a spirit of courtesy that is rarely witnessed.

The people of Israel, in their gratitude at deliverance from the Midianites, proposed to Gideon that he should become their king, and that the throne should be confirmed to his descendants. This proposition was in direct violation of the principles of the theocracy. God was the king of Israel, and for them to place a man upon the throne would be a rejection of their Divine Sovereign. Gideon recognized this fact; his answer shows how true and noble were his motives. "I will not rule over you," he declared; "neither shall my son rule over you: the Lord shall rule over you."

But Gideon was betrayed into another error, which brought disaster upon his house and upon all Israel. The season of inactivity that succeeds a great struggle is often fraught with greater danger than is the period of conflict. To this danger Gideon was now exposed. A spirit of unrest was upon him. Hitherto he had been content to fulfill the directions given him from God; but now, instead of waiting for divine guidance, he began to plan for himself. When the armies of the Lord have gained a signal victory, Satan will redouble his efforts to overthrow the work of God. Thus thoughts and plans were suggested to the mind of Gideon, by which the people of Israel were led astray.

Because he had been commanded to offer sacrifice upon the rock where the Angel appeared to him, Gideon concluded that he had been appointed to officiate as a priest. Without waiting for the divine sanction, he determined to provide a suitable place, and to institute a system of worship similar to that carried on at the tabernacle. With the strong popular feeling in his favor he found no difficulty in carrying out his plan. At his request all the earrings of gold taken from the Midianites were given him as his share of the spoil. The people also collected many other costly materials, together with the richly adorned garments of the princes of Midian. From the material thus furnished, Gideon constructed an ephod and a breastplate, in imitation of those worn by the high priest. His course proved a snare to himself and his family, as well as to Israel. The unauthorized worship led many of the people finally to forsake the Lord altogether, to serve idols. After Gideon's death great numbers, among whom were his own family, joined in this apostasy. The people were led away from God by the very man who had once overthrown their idolatry.

There are few who realize how far-reaching is the influence of their words and acts. How often the errors of parents produce the most disastrous effects upon their children and children's children, long after the actors themselves have been laid in the grave. Everyone is exerting an influence upon others, and will be held accountable for the result of that influence. Words and actions have a telling power, and the long hereafter will show the effect of our life here. The impression made by our words and deeds will surely react upon ourselves in blessing or in cursing. This thought gives an awful solemnity to life, and should draw us to God in humble prayer that He will guide us by His wisdom.

Those who stand in the highest positions may lead astray. The wisest err; the strongest may falter and stumble. There is need that light from above should be constantly shed upon our pathway. Our only safety lies in trusting our way implicitly to Him who has said, "Follow Me."

After the death of Gideon "the children of Israel remembered not the Lord their God, who had delivered them out of the hands of all their enemies on every side: neither showed they kindness to the house of Jerubbaal, namely, Gideon, according to all the goodness which he had showed unto Israel." Forgetful of all that they owed to Gideon, their judge and deliverer, the people of Israel accepted his baseborn son 557 Abimelech as their king, who, to sustain his power, murdered all but one of Gideon's lawful children. When men cast off the fear of God they are not long in departing from honor and integrity. An appreciation of the Lord's mercy will lead to an appreciation of those who, like Gideon, have been employed as instruments to bless His people. The cruel course of Israel toward the house of Gideon was what might be expected from a people who manifested so great ingratitude to God.

After the death of Abimelech the rule of judges who feared the Lord served for a time to put a check upon idolatry, but erelong the people returned to the practices of the heathen communities around them. Among the northern tribes the gods of Syria and Sidon had many worshipers. On the southwest the idols of the Philistines, and on the east those of Moab and Ammon, had turned the hearts of Israel from the God of their fathers. But apostasy speedily brought its punishment. The Ammonites subdued the eastern tribes and, crossing the Jordan, invaded the territory of Judah and Ephraim. On the west the Philistines came up from their plain beside the sea, burning and pillaging far and near. Again Israel seemed to be abandoned to the power of relentless foes.

Again the people sought help from Him whom they had so forsaken and insulted. "The children of Israel cried unto the Lord, saying, We have sinned against Thee, both because we have forsaken our God, and also served Baalim." But sorrow had not worked true repen-

tance. The people mourned because their sins had brought suffering upon themselves, but not because they had dishonored God by transgression of His holy law. True repentance is more than sorrow for sin. It is a resolute turning away from evil.

The Lord answered them through one of His prophets: "Did I not deliver you from the Egyptians, and from the Amorites, from the children of Ammon, and from the Philistines? The Zidonians also, and the Amalekites, and the Maonites, did oppress you; and ye cried to Me, and I delivered you out of their hand. Yet ye have forsaken Me, and served other gods: wherefore I will deliver you no more. Go and cry unto the gods which ye have chosen; let them deliver you in the time of your tribulation."

These solemn and fearful words carry the mind forward to another scene—the great day of final judgment—when the rejecters of God's 558 mercy and the despisers of His grace shall be brought face to face with His justice. At that tribunal must they render an account who have devoted their God-given talents of time, of means, or of intellect, to serving the gods of this world. They have forsaken their true and loving Friend, to follow the path of convenience and worldly pleasure. They intended at some time to return to God; but the world with its follies and deceptions absorbed the attention. Frivolous amusements, pride of dress, indulgence of appetite, hardened the heart and benumbed the conscience, so that the voice of truth was not heard. Duty was despised. Things of infinite value were lightly esteemed, until the heart lost all desire to sacrifice for Him who has given so much for man. But in the reaping time they will gather that which they have sown.

Saith the Lord: "I have called, and ye refused; I have stretched out My hand, and no man regarded; but ye have set at nought all My counsel, and would none of My reproof: . . . when your fear cometh as desolation, and your destruction cometh as a whirlwind; when distress and anguish cometh upon you. Then shall they call upon Me, but I will not answer; they shall seek Me early, but they shall not find Me: for that they hated knowledge, and did not choose the fear of the Lord: they would none of My counsel: they despised all My reproof. Therefore shall they eat of the fruit of their own way, and be filled with their own devices." "But whoso hearkeneth unto Me shall dwell safely, and shall be quiet from fear of evil." Proverbs 1:24-31, 33.

The Israelites now humbled themselves before the Lord. "And they put away the strange gods from among them, and served Jehovah." And the Lord's heart of love was grieved—"*was grieved* for the misery of Israel." Oh, the long-suffering mercy of our God! When His people put away the sins that had shut out His presence, He heard their prayers and at once began to work for them.

A deliverer was raised up in the person of Jephthah, a Gileadite, who made war upon the Ammonites and effectually destroyed their power. For eighteen years at this time Israel had suffered under the oppression of her foes, yet again the lesson taught by suffering was forgotten.

559 As His people returned to their evil ways, the Lord permitted them to be still oppressed by their powerful enemies, the Philistines. For many years they were constantly harassed, and at times completely subjugated, by this cruel and warlike nation. They had mingled with these idolaters, uniting with them in pleasure and in worship, until they seemed to be one with them in spirit and interest. Then these professed friends of Israel became their bitterest enemies and sought by every means to accomplish their destruction.

Like Israel, Christians too often yield to the influence of the world and conform to its principles and customs, in order to secure the friendship of the ungodly; but in the end it will be found that these professed friends are the most dangerous of foes. The Bible plainly teaches that there can be no harmony between the people of God and the world. "Marvel not, my brethren, if the world hate you." 1 John 3:13. Our Saviour says, "Ye know that it hated Me before it hated you." John 15:18. Satan works through the ungodly, under cover of a pretended friendship, to allure God's people into sin, that he may separate them from Him; and when their defense is removed, then he will lead his agents to turn against them and seek to accomplish their destruction.

560

54

Samson

Amid the widespread apostasy the faithful worshipers of God continued to plead with Him for the deliverance of Israel. Though there was apparently no response, though year after year the power of the oppressor continued to rest more heavily upon the land, God's providence was preparing help for them. Even in the early years of the Philistine oppression a child was born through whom God designed to humble the power of these mighty foes.

On the border of the hill country overlooking the Philistine plain was the little town of Zorah. Here dwelt the family of Manoah, of the tribe of Dan, one of the few households that amid the general defection had remained true to Jehovah. To the childless wife of Manoah "the Angel of

This chapter is based on Judges 13 to 16.

Jehovah" appeared with the message that she should have a son, through whom God would begin to deliver Israel. In view of this the Angel gave her instruction concerning her own habits, and also for the treatment of her child: "Now therefore beware, I pray thee, and drink not wine nor strong drink, and eat not any unclean thing." And the same prohibition was to be imposed, from the first, upon the child, with the addition that his hair should not be cut; for he was to be consecrated to God as a Nazarite from his birth.

The woman sought her husband, and, after describing the Angel, she repeated His message. Then, fearful that they should make some mistake in the important work committed to them, the husband prayed, "Let the Man of God which Thou didst send come again unto us, and teach us what we shall do unto the child that shall be born."

When the Angel again appeared, Manoah's anxious inquiry was, "How shall we order the child, and how shall we do unto him?" The previous instruction was repeated—"Of all that I said unto the woman let her beware. She may 561 not eat of anything that cometh of the vine, neither let her drink wine or strong drink, nor eat any unclean thing: all that I commanded her let her observe."

God had an important work for the promised child of Manoah to do, and it was to secure for him the qualifications necessary for this work that the habits of both the mother and the child were to be carefully regulated. "Neither let her drink wine or strong drink," was the Angel's instruction for the wife of Manoah, "nor eat any unclean thing. All that I commanded her let her observe." The child will be affected for good or for evil by the habits of the mother. She must herself be controlled by principle and must practice temperance and self-denial, if she would seek the welfare of her child. Unwise advisers will urge upon the mother the necessity of gratifying every wish and impulse, but such teaching is false and mischievous. The mother is by the command of God Himself placed under the most solemn obligation to exercise self-control.

And fathers as well as mothers are involved in this responsibility. Both parents transmit their own characteristics, mental and physical, their dispositions and appetites, to their children. As the result of parental intemperance children often lack physical strength and mental and moral power. Liquor drinkers and tobacco users may, and do, transmit their insatiable craving, their inflamed blood and irritable nerves, to their children. The licentious often bequeath their unholy desires, and even loathsome diseases, as a legacy to their offspring. And as the children have less power to resist temptation than had the parents, the tendency is for each generation to fall lower and lower. To a great degree parents are responsible not only for the violent passions and perverted appetites of their children but for the infirmities of the thousands born deaf, blind, diseased, or idiotic.

The inquiry of every father and mother should be, "What shall we do unto the child that shall be born unto us?" The effect of prenatal influences has been by many lightly regarded; but the instruction sent from heaven to those Hebrew parents, and twice repeated in the most explicit and solemn manner, shows how this matter is looked upon by our Creator.

And it was not enough that the promised child should receive a good legacy from the parents. This must be followed by careful training and the formation of right habits. God directed that the future judge and deliverer of Israel should be trained to strict temperance from infancy. He was to be a Nazarite from his birth, thus being placed under a perpetual prohibition against the use of wine or strong drink. The lessons of temperance, self-denial, and self-control are to be taught to children even from babyhood.

The Angel's prohibition included "every unclean thing." The distinction between articles of food as clean and unclean was not a merely ceremonial and arbitrary regulation, but was based upon sanitary principles. To the observance of this distinction may be traced, in a great degree, the marvelous vitality which for thousands of years has distinguished the Jewish people. The principles of temperance must be carried further than the mere use of spirituous liquors. The use of stimulating and indigestible food is often equally injurious to health, and in many cases sows the seeds of drunkenness. True temperance teaches us to dispense entirely with everything hurtful and to use judiciously that which is healthful. There are few who realize as they should how much their habits of diet have to do with their health, their character, their usefulness in this world, and their eternal destiny. The appetite should ever be in subjection to the moral and intellectual powers. The body should be servant to the mind, and not the mind to the body.

The divine promise to Manoah was in due time fulfilled in the birth of a son, to whom the name of Samson was given. As the boy grew up it became evident that he possessed extraordinary physical strength. This was not, however, as Samson and his parents well knew, dependent upon his well-knit sinews, but upon his condition as a Nazarite, of which his unshorn hair was a symbol. Had Samson obeyed the divine commands as faithfully as his parents had done, his would have been a nobler and happier destiny. But association with idolaters corrupted him. The town of Zorah being near the country of the Philistines, Samson came to mingle with them on friendly terms. Thus in his youth intimacies sprang up, the influence of which darkened his whole life. A young woman dwelling in the Philistine town of Timnath engaged Samson's affections, and he determined to make her his wife. To his God-fearing parents, who endeavored to dissuade him from his purpose, his only answer was, "She pleaseth me well." The parents at last yielded to his wishes, and the marriage took place.

Just as he was entering upon manhood, the time when he must execute his divine mission—the time above all others when he should have been true to God—Samson connected himself with the enemies of Israel. He did not ask whether he could better glorify God when united with the object of his choice, or whether he was placing himself in a position where he could not fulfill the purpose to be accomplished by his life. To all who seek first to honor Him, God has promised wisdom; but there is no promise to those who are bent upon self-pleasing.

How many are pursuing the same course as did Samson! How often marriages are formed between the godly and the ungodly, because inclination governs in the selection of husband or wife! The parties do not ask counsel of God, nor have His glory in view. Christianity ought to have a controlling influence upon the marriage relation, but it is too often the case that the motives which lead to this union are not in keeping with Christian principles. Satan is constantly seeking to strengthen his power over the people of God by inducing them to enter into alliance with his subjects; and in order to accomplish this he endeavors to arouse unsanctified passions in the heart. But the Lord has in His word plainly instructed His people not to unite themselves with those who have not His love abiding in them. "What concord hath Christ with Belial? or what part hath he that believeth with an infidel? and what agreement hath the temple of God with idols?" 2 Corinthians 6:15, 16.

At his marriage feast Samson was brought into familiar association with those who hated the God of Israel. Whoever voluntarily enters into such relations will feel it necessary to conform, to some degree, to the habits and customs of his companions. The time thus spent is worse than wasted. Thoughts are entertained and words are spoken that tend to break down the strongholds of principle and to weaken the citadel of the soul.

The wife, to obtain whom Samson had transgressed the command of God, proved treacherous to her husband before the close of the marriage feast. Incensed at her perfidy, Samson forsook her for the time, and went alone to his home at Zorah. When, afterward relenting, he returned for his bride, he found her the wife of another. His revenge, in the wasting of all the fields and vineyards of the Philistines, provoked them to murder her, although their threats had driven her to the deceit with which the trouble began. Samson had already given evidence of his marvelous strength by slaying, singlehanded, a young lion, and by killing thirty of the men of Askelon. Now, moved to anger by the barbarous murder of his wife, he attacked the Philistines and smote them "with a great slaughter." Then, wishing a safe retreat from his enemies, he withdrew to "the rock Etam," in the tribe of Judah.

To this place he was pursued by a strong force, and the inhabitants of Judah, in great alarm, basely agreed to deliver him to his enemies. Accordingly three thousand men of Judah went up to him. But even at such odds they would not have dared approach him had they not felt assured that he would not harm his own countrymen. Samson consented to be bound and delivered to the Philistines, but first exacted from the men of Judah a promise not to attack him themselves, and thus compel him to destroy them. He permitted them to bind him with two new ropes, and he was led into the camp of his enemies amid demonstrations of great joy. But while their shouts were waking the echoes of the hills, "the Spirit of Jehovah came mightily upon him." He burst asunder the strong new cords as if they had been flax burned in the fire. Then seizing the first weapon at hand, which, though only the jawbone of an ass, was rendered more effective than sword or spear, he smote the Philistines until they fled in terror, leaving a thousand men dead upon the field.

Had the Israelites been ready to unite with Samson and follow up the victory, they might at this time have freed themselves from the power of their oppressors. But they had become dispirited and cowardly. They had neglected the work which God commanded them to perform, in dispossessing the heathen, and had united with them in their degrading practices, tolerating their cruelty, and, so long as it was not directed against themselves, even countenancing their injustice. When themselves brought under the power of the oppressor, they tamely submitted to the degradation which they might have escaped, had they only obeyed God. Even when the Lord raised up a deliverer for them, they would, not infrequently, desert him and unite with their enemies.

After his victory the Israelites made Samson judge, and he ruled Israel for twenty years. But one wrong step prepares the way for another. Samson had transgressed the command of God by taking a wife from the Philistines, and again he ventured among them—now his deadly enemies—in the indulgence of unlawful passion. Trusting to his great strength, which had inspired the Philistines with such terror, he went boldly to Gaza, to visit a harlot of that place. The inhabitants of the city learned of his presence, and they were eager for revenge. Their enemy was shut safely within the walls of the most strongly fortified of all their cities; they felt sure of their prey, and only waited till the morning to complete their triumph. At midnight Samson was aroused. The accusing voice of conscience filled him with remorse, as he remembered that he had broken his vow as a Nazarite. But notwithstanding his sin, God's mercy had not forsaken him. His prodigious strength again served to deliver him. Going to the city gate, he wrenched it from its place and carried it, with its posts and bars, to the top of a hill on the way to Hebron.

But even this narrow escape did not stay his evil course. He did not again venture among the Philistines, but he continued to seek those sensuous pleasures that were luring him to ruin. "He loved a woman in the valley of Sorek," not far from his own birthplace. Her name was Delilah, "the consumer." The vale of Sorek was celebrated for its vineyards; these also had a temptation for the wavering Nazarite, who had already indulged in the use of wine, thus breaking another tie that bound him to purity and to God. The Philistines kept a vigilant watch over the movements of their enemy, and when he degraded himself by this new attachment, they determined, through Delilah, to accomplish his ruin.

A deputation consisting of one leading man from each of the Philistine provinces was sent to the vale of Sorek. They dared not attempt to seize him while in possession of his great strength, but it was their purpose to learn, if possible, the secret of his power. They therefore bribed Delilah to discover and reveal it.

As the betrayer plied Samson with her questions, he deceived her by declaring that the weakness of other men would come upon him if certain processes were tried. When she put the matter to the test, the cheat was discovered. Then she accused him of falsehood, saying, "How canst thou say, I love thee, when thine heart is not with me? Thou hast mocked me these three times, and hast not told me wherein thy great strength lieth." Three times Samson had the clearest evidence that the Philistines had leagued with his charmer to destroy him; but when her purpose failed, she treated the matter as a jest, and he blindly banished fear.

Day by day Delilah urged him, until "his soul was vexed unto death;" yet a subtle power kept him by her side. Overcome at last, Samson made known the secret: "There hath not come a razor upon mine head; for I have been a Nazarite unto God from my mother's womb: if I be shaven, then my strength will go from me, and I shall become weak, and be like any other man." A messenger was immediately dispatched to the lords of the Philistines, urging them to come to her without delay. While the warrior slept, the heavy masses of his hair were severed from his head. Then, as she had done three times before, she called, "The Philistines be upon thee, Samson!" Suddenly awaking, he thought to exert his strength as before and destroy them; but his powerless arms refused to do his bidding, and he knew that "Jehovah was departed from him." When he had been shaven, Delilah began to annoy him and cause him pain, thus making a trial of his strength; for the Philistines dared not approach him till fully convinced that his power was gone. Then they seized him and, having put out both his eyes, they took him to Gaza. Here he was bound with fetters in their prison house and confined to hard labor.

What a change to him who had been the judge and champion of Israel!—now weak, blind, imprisoned, degraded to the most menial service! Little by little he had violated the conditions of his sacred calling. God had borne long with him; but when he had so yielded himself to the power of sin as to betray his secret, the Lord departed from him. There was no virtue in his long hair merely, but it was a token of his loyalty to God; and when the symbol was sacrificed in the indulgence of passion, the blessings of which it was a token were also forfeited.

In suffering and humiliation, a sport for the Philistines, Samson learned more of his own weakness than he had ever known before; and his afflictions led him to repentance. As his hair grew, his power gradually returned; but his enemies, regarding him as a fettered and helpless prisoner, felt no apprehensions.

The Philistines ascribed their victory to their gods; and, exulting, they defied the God of Israel. A feast was appointed in honor of Dagon, the fish god, "the protector of the sea." From town and country throughout the Philistine plain the people and their lords assembled. Throngs of worshipers filled the vast temple and crowded the galleries about the roof. It was a scene of festivity and rejoicing. There was the pomp of the sacrificial service, followed by music and feasting. Then, as the crowning trophy of Dagon's power, Samson was brought in. Shouts of exultation greeted his appearance. People and rulers mocked his misery and adored the god who had overthrown "the destroyer of their country." After a time, as if weary, Samson asked permission to rest against the two central pillars which supported the temple roof. Then he silently uttered the prayer, "O Lord God, remember me, I pray Thee, and strengthen me, I pray Thee, only this once, O God, that I may be at once avenged of the Philistines." With these words he encircled the pillars with his mighty arms; and crying, "Let me die with the Philistines!" he bowed himself, and the roof

fell, destroying at one crash all that vast multitude. "So the dead which he slew at his death were more than they which he slew in his life."

The idol and its worshipers, priest and peasant, warrior and noble, were buried together beneath the ruins of Dagon's temple. And among them was the giant form of him whom God had chosen to be the deliverer of His people. Tidings of the terrible overthrow were carried to the land of Israel, and Samson's kinsmen came down from their hills, and, unopposed, rescued the body of the fallen hero. And they "brought him up, and buried him between Zorah and Eshtaol, in the burying place of Manoah his father."

God's promise that through Samson He would "begin to deliver Israel out of the hand of the Philistines" was fulfilled; but how dark and terrible the record of that life which might have been a praise to God and a glory to the nation! Had Samson been true to his divine calling, the purpose of God could have been accomplished in his honor and exaltation. But he yielded to temptation and proved untrue to his trust, and his mission was fulfilled in defeat, bondage, and death.

Physically, Samson was the strongest man upon the earth; but in self-control, integrity, and firmness, he was one of the weakest of men. Many mistake strong passions for a strong character, but the truth is that he who is mastered by his passions is a weak man. The real greatness of the man is measured by the power of the feelings that he controls, not by those that control him.

God's providential care had been over Samson, that he might be prepared to accomplish the work which he was called to do. At the very outset of life he was surrounded with favorable conditions for physical strength, intellectual vigor, and moral purity. But under the influence of wicked associates he let go that hold upon God which is man's only safeguard, and he was swept away by the tide of evil. Those who in the way of duty are brought into trial may be sure that God will preserve them; but if men willfully place themselves under the power of temptation, they will fall, sooner or later.

The very ones whom God purposes to use as His instruments for a special work, Satan employs his utmost power to lead astray. He attacks us at our weak points, working through defects in the character to gain control of the whole man; and he knows that if these defects are cherished, he will succeed. But none need be overcome. Man is not left alone to conquer the power of evil by his own feeble efforts. Help is at hand and will be given to every soul who really desires it. Angels of God, that ascend and descend the ladder which Jacob saw in vision, will help every soul who will, to climb even to the highest heaven.

55

The Child Samuel

Elkanah, a Levite of Mount Ephraim, was a man of wealth and influence, and one who loved and feared the Lord. His wife, Hannah, was a woman of fervent piety. Gentle and unassuming, her character was marked with deep earnestness and a lofty faith.

The blessing so earnestly sought by every Hebrew was denied this godly pair; their home was not gladdened by the voice of childhood; and the desire to perpetuate his name led the husband—as it had led many others—to contract a second marriage. But this step, prompted by a lack of faith in God, did not bring happiness. Sons and daughters were added to the household; but the joy and beauty of God's sacred institution had been marred and the peace of the family was broken. Peninnah, the new wife, was jealous and narrow-minded, and she bore herself with pride and insolence. To Hannah, hope seemed crushed and life a weary burden; yet she met the trial with uncomplaining meekness.

Elkanah faithfully observed the ordinances of God. The worship at Shiloh was still maintained, but on account of irregularities in the ministration his services were not required at the sanctuary, to which, being a Levite, he was to give attendance. Yet he went up with his family to worship and sacrifice at the appointed gatherings.

Even amid the sacred festivities connected with the service of God the evil spirit that had cursed his home intruded. After presenting the thank offerings, all the family, according to the established custom, united in a solemn yet joyous feast. Upon these occasions Elkanah gave the mother of his children a portion for herself and for each of her sons and daughters; and in token of regard for Hannah, he gave her a double portion, signifying that his affection for her was the same as if she had had a son. Then the second wife, fired with jealousy, claimed the precedence as one highly favored of God, and taunted Hannah with her childless state as evidence of the Lord's displeasure. This was repeated from year to year, until Hannah could endure it no longer. Unable to hide her grief, she wept without restraint, and withdrew from the feast. Her husband vainly sought to comfort her. "Why weepest thou? and why eatest thou not? and why is thy heart grieved?" he said; "am I not better to thee than ten sons?"

Hannah uttered no reproach. The burden which she could share with no earthly friend she cast upon God. Earnestly she pleaded that He would take away her reproach and grant her the precious gift of a son to nurture and train for Him. And she made a solemn vow that if her request were granted, she would dedicate her child to God, even from its birth. Hannah had drawn near to the entrance of the tabernacle, and in the anguish of her spirit she "prayed, . . . and wept sore." Yet she communed with God in silence, uttering no sound. In those evil times such scenes of worship were rarely witnessed. Irreverent feasting and even drunkenness were not uncommon, even at the religious festivals; and Eli the high priest, observing Hannah, supposed that she was overcome with wine. Thinking to administer a deserved rebuke, he said sternly, "How long wilt thou be drunken? put away thy wine from thee."

Pained and startled, Hannah answered gently, "No, my lord, I am a woman of a sorrowful spirit: I have drunk neither wine nor strong drink, but have poured out my soul before the Lord. Count not thine handmaid for a daughter of Belial: for out of the abundance of my complaint and grief have I spoken hitherto."

The high priest was deeply moved, for he was a man of God; and in place of rebuke he uttered a blessing: "Go in peace: and the God of Israel grant thee thy petition that thou hast asked of Him."

Hannah's prayer was granted; she received the gift for which she had so earnestly entreated. As she looked upon the child, she called him Samuel—"asked of God." As soon as the little one was old enough to be separated from his mother, she fulfilled her vow. She loved her child with all the devotion of a mother's heart; day by day, as she watched his expanding powers and listened to his childish prattle, her affections entwined about him more closely. He was her only son, the special gift of Heaven; but she had received him as a treasure consecrated to God, and she would not withhold from the Giver His own.

Once more Hannah journeyed with her husband to Shiloh and presented to the priest, in the name of God, her precious gift, saying, "For this child I prayed; and the Lord hath given me my petition which I asked of Him: therefore also I have lent him to the Lord; as long as he liveth he shall be lent to the Lord." Eli was deeply impressed by the faith and devotion of this woman of Israel. Himself an overindulgent father, he was awed and humbled as he beheld this mother's great sacrifice in parting with her only child, that she might devote him to the service of God. He felt reproved for his own selfish love, and in humiliation and reverence he bowed before the Lord and worshiped.

The mother's heart was filled with joy and praise, and she longed to pour forth her gratitude to God. The Spirit of Inspiration came

This chapter is based on 1 Samuel 1; 2:1-11.

upon her; "and Hannah prayed, and said:

"My heart rejoiceth in the Lord;
Mine horn is exalted in the Lord;
My mouth is enlarged over mine enemies;
Because I rejoice in Thy salvation.
There is none holy as the Lord:
For there is none beside Thee:
Neither is there any rock like our God.
Talk no more so exceeding proudly;
Let not arrogancy come out of your mouth;
For Jehovah is a God of knowledge,
And by Him actions are weighed. . . .
The Lord killeth, and maketh alive:
He bringeth down to the grave, and bringeth
up.
The Lord maketh poor, and maketh rich:
He bringeth low, and lifteth up.
He raiseth up the poor out of the dust,
And lifteth up the beggar from the dunghill,
To set them among princes,
And to make them inherit the throne of
glory:
For the pillars of the earth are the Lord's,
And He hath set the world upon them.
He will keep the feet of His saints,
And the wicked shall be silent in darkness;
For by strength shall no man prevail.
The adversaries of the Lord shall be broken
to pieces;
Out of heaven shall He thunder upon them:
The Lord shall judge the ends of the earth;
And He shall give strength unto His king,
And exalt the horn of His anointed."

572

Hannah's words were prophetic, both of David, who should reign as king of Israel, and of the Messiah, the Lord's Anointed. Referring first to the boasting of an insolent and contentious woman, the song points to the destruction of the enemies of God and the final triumph of His redeemed people.

From Shiloh, Hannah quietly returned to her home at Ramah, leaving the child Samuel to be trained for service in the house of God, under the instruction of the high priest. From the earliest dawn of intellect she had taught her son to love and reverence God and to regard himself as the Lord's. By every familiar object surrounding him she had sought to lead his thoughts up to the Creator. When separated from her child, the faithful mother's solicitude did not cease. Every day he was the subject of her prayers. Every year she made, with her own hands, a robe of service for him; and as she went up with her husband to worship at Shiloh, she gave the child this reminder of her love. Every fiber of the little garment had been woven with a prayer that he might be pure, noble, and true. She did not ask for her son worldly greatness, but she earnestly pleaded that he might attain that greatness which Heaven values—that he might honor

God and bless his fellow men.

What a reward was Hannah's! and what an encouragement to faithfulness is her example! There are opportunities of inestimable worth, interests infinitely precious, committed to every mother. The humble round of duties which women have come to regard as a wearisome task should be looked upon as a grand and noble work. It is the mother's privilege to bless the world by her influence, and in doing this she will bring joy to her own heart. She may make straight paths for the feet of her children, through sunshine and shadow, to the glorious heights above. But it is only when she seeks, in her own life, to follow the teachings of Christ that the mother can hope to form the character of her children after the divine pattern. The world teems with corrupting influences. Fashion and custom exert a strong power over the young. If the mother fails in her duty to instruct, guide, and restrain, her children will naturally accept the evil, and turn from the good. Let every mother go often to her Saviour with the prayer, "Teach us, how shall we order the child, and what shall we do unto him?" Let her heed the instruction which God has given in His word, and wisdom will be given her as she shall have need.

573

"The child Samuel grew on, and was in favor both with the Lord, and also with men." Though Samuel's youth was passed at the tabernacle devoted to the worship of God, he was not free from evil influences or sinful example. The sons of Eli feared not God, nor honored their father; but Samuel did not seek their company nor follow their evil ways. It was his constant endeavor to become what God would have him. This is the privilege of every youth. God is pleased when even little children give themselves to His service.

Samuel had been placed under the care of Eli, and the loveliness of his character drew forth the warm affection of the aged priest. He was kind, generous, obedient, and respectful. Eli, pained by the waywardness of his own sons, found rest and comfort and blessing in the presence of his charge. Samuel was helpful and affectionate, and no father ever loved his child more tenderly than did Eli this youth. It was a singular thing that between the chief magistrate of the nation and the simple child so warm an affection should exist. As the infirmities of age came upon Eli, and he was filled with anxiety and remorse by the profligate course of his own sons, he turned to Samuel for comfort.

It was not customary for the Levites to enter upon their peculiar services until they were twenty-five years of age, but Samuel had been an exception to this rule. Every year saw more important trusts committed to him; and while he was yet a child, a linen ephod was placed upon him as a token of his consecration to the work of the sanctuary. Young as he was when brought to minister in the tabernacle, Samuel had even then duties to perform in the service of God, according to his capacity. These were at first very humble, and not always pleasant; but they were performed to the best of his ability, and with a willing heart. His religion was carried into every duty of life. He regarded himself as God's servant, and his work as God's work. His efforts were accepted, because they were prompted by love to God and a sincere desire to do His will. It was thus that Samuel became a co-worker with the Lord of heaven and earth. And God fitted him to accomplish a great work for Israel.

If children were taught to regard the humble round of everyday duties as the course marked out for them by the Lord, as a school in which they were to be trained to render faithful and efficient service, how much more pleasant and honorable would their work appear. To perform every duty as unto the Lord, throws a charm around the humblest employment and links the workers on earth with the holy beings who do God's will in heaven.

Success in this life, success in gaining the future life, depends upon a faithful, conscientious attention to the little things. Perfection is seen in the least, no less than in the greatest, of the works of God. The hand that hung the worlds in space is the hand that wrought with delicate skill the lilies of the field. And as God is perfect in His sphere, so we are to be perfect in ours. The symmetrical structure of a strong, beautiful character is built up by individual acts of duty. And faithfulness should characterize our life in the least as well as in the greatest of its details. Integrity in little things, the performance of little acts of fidelity and little deeds of kindness, will gladden the path of life; and when our work on earth is ended, it will be found that every one of the little duties faithfully performed has exerted an influence for good—an influence that can never perish.

The youth of our time may become as precious in the sight of God as was Samuel. By faithfully maintaining their Christian integrity, they may exert a strong influence in the work of reform. Such men are needed at this time. God has a work for every one of them. Never did men achieve greater results for God and humanity than may be achieved in this our day by those who will be faithful to their God-given trust.

56

Eli and His Sons

Eli was priest and judge in Israel. He held the highest and most responsible positions among the people of God. As a man divinely chosen for the sacred duties of the priesthood, and set over the land as the highest judicial authority, he was looked up to as an example, and he wielded a great influence over the tribes of Israel. But although he had been appointed to govern the people, he did not rule his own household. Eli was an indulgent father. Loving peace and ease, he did not exercise his authority to correct the evil habits and passions of his children. Rather than contend with them or punish them, he would submit to their will and give them their own way. Instead of regarding the education of his sons as one of the most important of his responsibilities, he treated the matter as of little consequence. The priest and judge of Israel had not been left in darkness as to the duty of restraining and governing the children that God had given to his care. But Eli shrank from this duty, because it involved crossing the will of his sons, and would make it necessary to punish and deny them. Without weighing the terrible consequences that would follow his course, he indulged his children in whatever they desired and neglected the work of fitting them for the service of God and the duties of life.

God had said of Abraham, "I know him, that he will *command* his children and his household after him, and they shall keep the way of the Lord, to do justice and judgment." Genesis 18:19. But Eli allowed his children to control him. The father became subject to the children. The curse of transgression was apparent in the corruption and evil that marked the course of his sons. They had no proper appreciation of the character of God or of the sacredness of His law. His service was to them a common thing. From childhood they had been accustomed to the sanctuary and its service; but instead of becoming more reverent, they had lost all sense of its holiness and significance. The father had not corrected their want of reverence for his authority, had not checked their disrespect for the solemn services of the sanctuary; and when they reached manhood, they were full of the deadly fruits of skepticism and rebellion.

Though wholly unfit for the office, they were placed as priests in the sanctuary to minister before God. The Lord had given the most specific directions in regard to offering sacrifices; but these wicked men carried their disregard of authority into the service of God, and did not give attention to the law of the offerings, which were to be made in the most solemn manner. The sacrifices, pointing forward to the death of Christ, were designed to preserve in the hearts of the people faith in the Redeemer to come; hence it was of the greatest importance that the Lord's directions concerning them should be strictly heeded. The peace offerings were especially an expression of thanksgiving to God. In these offerings the fat alone was to be burned

This chapter is based on 1 Samuel 2:12-36.

upon the altar; a certain specified portion was reserved for the priests, but the greater part was returned to the offerer, to be eaten by him and his friends in a sacrificial feast. Thus all hearts were to be directed, in gratitude and faith, to the great Sacrifice that was to take away the sin of the world.

The sons of Eli, instead of realizing the solemnity of this symbolic service, only thought how they could make it a means of self-indulgence. Not content with the part of the peace offerings allotted them, they demanded an additional portion; and the great number of these sacrifices presented at the annual feasts gave the priests an opportunity to enrich themselves at the expense of the people. They not only demanded more than their right, but refused to wait even until the fat had been burned as an offering to God. They persisted in claiming whatever portion pleased them, and, if denied, threatened to take it by violence.

This irreverence on the part of the priests soon robbed the service of its holy and solemn significance, and the people "abhorred the offering of the Lord." The great antitypical sacrifice to which they were to look forward was no longer recognized. "Wherefore the sin of the young men was very great before the Lord."

These unfaithful priests also transgressed God's law and dishonored their sacred office by their vile and degrading practices; yet they continued to pollute by their presence the tabernacle of God. Many of the people, filled with indignation at the corrupt course of Hophni and Phinehas, ceased to come up to the appointed place of worship. Thus the service which God had ordained was despised and neglected because associated with the sins of wicked men, while those whose hearts were inclined to evil were emboldened in sin. Ungodliness, profligacy, and even idolatry prevailed to a fearful extent.

Eli had greatly erred in permitting his sons to minister in holy office. By excusing their course, on one pretext and another, he became blinded to their sins; but at last they reached a pass where he could no longer hide his eyes from the crimes of his sons. The people complained of their violent deeds, and the high priest was grieved and distressed. He dared remain silent no longer. But his sons had been brought up to think of no one but themselves, and now they cared for no one else. They saw the grief of their father, but their hard hearts were not touched. They heard his mild admonitions, but they were not impressed, nor would they change their evil course though warned of the consequences of their sin. Had Eli dealt justly with his wicked sons, they would have been rejected from the priestly office and punished with death. Dreading thus to bring public disgrace and condemnation upon them, he sustained them in the most sacred positions of trust.

He still permitted them to mingle their corruption with the holy service of God and to inflict upon the cause of truth an injury which years could not efface. But when the judge of Israel neglected his work, God took the matter in hand.

"There came a man of God unto Eli, and said unto him, Thus saith the Lord, Did I plainly appear unto the house of thy father, when they were in Egypt in Pharaoh's house? And did I choose him out of all the tribes of Israel to be My priest, to offer upon Mine altar, to burn incense, to wear an ephod before Me? and did I give unto the house of thy father all the offerings made by fire of the children of Israel? Wherefore kick ye at My sacrifice and at Mine offering, which I have commanded in My habitation; and honorest thy sons above Me, to make yourselves fat with the chiefest of all the offerings of Israel My people? Wherefore the Lord God of Israel saith, I said indeed that thy house, and the house of thy father, should walk before Me forever: but now the Lord saith, Be it far from Me; for them that honor Me I will honor, and they that despise Me shall be lightly esteemed. . . . And I will raise Me up a faithful priest, that shall do according to that which is in Mine heart and in My mind: and I will build him a sure house; and he shall walk before Mine anointed forever."

God charged Eli with honoring his sons above the Lord. Eli had permitted the offering appointed by God as a blessing to Israel to be made a thing of abhorrence, rather than bring his sons to shame for their impious and abominable practices. Those who follow their own inclination, in blind affection for their children, indulging them in the gratification of their selfish desires, and do not bring to bear the authority of God to rebuke sin and correct evil, make it manifest that they are honoring their wicked children more than they honor God. They are more anxious to shield their reputation than to glorify God; more desirous to please their children than to please the Lord and to keep His service from every appearance of evil.

God held Eli, as a priest and judge of Israel, accountable for the moral and religious standing of his people, and in a special sense for the character of his sons. He should first have attempted to restrain evil by mild measures; but if these did not avail, he should have subdued the wrong by the severest means. He incurred the Lord's displeasure by not reproving sin and executing justice upon the sinner. He could not be depended upon to keep Israel pure. Those who have too little courage to reprove wrong, or who through indolence or lack of interest make no earnest effort to purify the family or the church of God, are held accountable for the evil that may result from their neglect of duty. We are just as responsible for evils that we might have checked in others by exercise of parental or pastoral authority as if the acts had been our own.

Eli did not manage his household according to God's rules for family government. He followed his own judgment. The fond father overlooked the faults and sins of his sons in their childhood, flattering himself that after a time they would outgrow their evil tendencies. Many are now making a similar mistake. They think they know a better way of training their children than that which God has given in His word. They foster wrong tendencies in them, urging as an excuse, "They are too young to be punished. Wait till they become older, and can be reasoned with." Thus wrong habits are left to strengthen until they become second nature. The children grow up without restraint, with traits of character that are a lifelong curse to them and are liable to be reproduced in others.

There is no greater curse upon households than to allow the youth to have their own way. When parents regard every wish of their children and indulge them in what they know is not for their good, the children soon lose all respect for their parents, all regard for the authority of God or man, and are led captive at the will of Satan. The influence of an ill-regulated family is widespread and disastrous to all society. It accumulates in a tide of evil that affects families, communities, and governments.

Because of Eli's position, his influence was more extended than if he had been an ordinary man. His family life was imitated throughout Israel. The baleful results of his negligent, ease-loving ways were seen in thousands of homes that were molded by his example. If children are indulged in evil practices, while the parents make a profession of religion, the truth of God is brought into reproach. The best test of the Christianity of a home is the type of character begotten by its influence. Actions speak louder than the most positive profession of godliness. If professors of religion, instead of putting forth earnest, persistent, and painstaking effort to bring up a well-ordered household as a witness to the benefits of faith in God, are lax in their government and indulgent to the evil desires of their children, they are doing as did Eli, and are bringing disgrace on the cause of Christ and ruin upon themselves and their households. But great as are the evils of parental unfaithfulness under any circumstances, they are tenfold greater when they exist in the families of those appointed as teachers of the people. When these fail to control their own households, they are, by their wrong example, misleading many. Their guilt is as much greater than that of others as their position is more responsible.

The promise had been made that the house of Aaron should walk before God forever; but this promise had been made on condition that they should devote themselves to the work of the sanctuary with singleness of heart and honor God in all their ways, not serving self nor following their own perverse inclinations. Eli and his sons had been tested, and the Lord had found them wholly unworthy of the exalted position of priests in His service. And God declared, "Be it far from Me." He could not accomplish the good that He had meant to do them, because they failed to do their part.

The example of those who minister in holy things should be such as to impress the people with reverence for God and with fear to offend Him. When men, standing "in Christ's stead" (2 Corinthians 5:20) to speak to the people God's message of mercy and reconciliation, use their sacred calling as a cloak for selfish or sensual gratification, they make themselves the most effective agents of Satan. Like Hophni and Phinehas, they cause men to "abhor the offering of the Lord." They may pursue their evil course in secret for a time; but when at last their true character is exposed, the faith of the people receives a shock that often results in destroying their confidence in religion. There is left upon the mind a distrust of all who profess to teach the word of God. The message of the true servant of Christ is doubtfully received. The question constantly arises, "Will not this man prove to be like the one we thought so holy, and found so corrupt?" Thus the word of God loses its power upon the souls of men.

In Eli's reproof to his sons are words of solemn and fearful import—words that all who minister in sacred things would do well to ponder: "If one man sin against another, the judge shall judge him; but if a man sin against the Lord, who shall entreat for him?" Had their crimes injured only their fellow men, the judge might have made reconciliation by appointing a penalty and requiring restitution; and thus the offenders might have been pardoned. Or had they not been guilty of a presumptuous sin, a sin offering might have been presented for them. But their sins were so interwoven with their ministration as priests of the Most High, in offering sacrifice for sin, the work of God was so profaned and dishonored before the people, that no expiation could be accepted for them. Their own father, though himself high priest, dared not make intercession in their behalf; he could not shield them from the wrath of a holy God. Of all sinners, those are most guilty who cast contempt upon the means that Heaven has provided for man's redemption—who "crucify to themselves the Son of God afresh, and put Him to an open shame." Hebrews 6:6.

579 (margin)
580 (margin)

581

57

The Ark Taken by
the Philistines

Another warning was to be given to Eli's house. God could not communicate with the high priest and his sons; their sins, like a thick cloud, had shut out the presence of His Holy Spirit. But in the midst of evil the child Samuel remained true to Heaven, and the message of condemnation to the house of Eli was Samuel's commission as a prophet of the Most High.

"The word of the Lord was precious in those days; there was no open vision. And it came to pass at that time, when Eli was laid down in his place, and his eyes began to wax dim, that he could not see; and ere the lamp of God went out in the temple of the Lord, where the ark of God was, and Samuel was laid down to sleep; that the Lord called Samuel." Supposing the voice to be that of Eli, the child hastened to the bedside of the priest, saying, "Here am I; for thou calledst me." The answer was, "I called not, my son; lie down again." Three times Samuel was called, and thrice he responded in like manner. And then Eli was convinced that the mysterious call was the voice of God. The Lord had passed by His chosen servant, the man of hoary hairs, to commune with a child. This in itself was a bitter yet deserved rebuke to Eli and his house.

No feeling of envy or jealousy was awakened in Eli's heart. He directed Samuel to answer, if again called, "Speak, Lord; for Thy servant heareth." Once more the voice was heard, and the child answered, "Speak; for Thy servant heareth." So awed was he at the thought that the great God should speak to him that he could not remember the exact words which Eli bade him say.

"And the Lord said to Samuel, Behold, I will do a thing in Israel, at which both the ears of everyone that heareth it shall tingle. In that day I will perform against Eli all things which I have spoken concerning his house: when I begin, I will also make an end. For I have told him that I will judge his house forever for the iniquity which he knoweth; because his sons made themselves vile, and he restrained them not. And therefore I have sworn unto the house of Eli, that the iniquity of Eli's house shall not be purged with sacrifice nor offering forever."

Before receiving this message from God, "Samuel did not yet know the Lord, neither was the word of the Lord yet revealed unto him;" that is, he was not acquainted with such direct manifestations of God's presence as were grant-

582

ed to the prophets. It was the Lord's purpose to reveal Himself in an unexpected manner, that Eli might hear of it through the surprise and inquiry of the youth.

Samuel was filled with fear and amazement at the thought of having so terrible a message committed to him. In the morning he went about his duties as usual, but with a heavy burden upon his young heart. The Lord had not commanded him to reveal the fearful denunciation, hence he remained silent, avoiding, as far as possible, the presence of Eli. He trembled, lest some question should compel him to declare the divine judgments against one whom he loved and reverenced. Eli was confident that the message foretold some great calamity to him and his house. He called Samuel, and charged him to relate faithfully what the Lord had revealed. The youth obeyed, and the aged man bowed in humble submission to the appalling sentence. "It is the Lord," he said: "let Him do what seemeth Him good."

Yet Eli did not manifest the fruits of true repentance. He confessed his guilt, but failed to renounce the sin. Year after year the Lord delayed His threatened judgments. Much might have been done in those years to redeem the failures of the past, but the aged priest took no effective measures to correct the evils that were polluting the sanctuary of the Lord and leading thousands in Israel to ruin. The forbearance of God caused Hophni and Phinehas to harden their hearts and to become still bolder in transgression. The messages of warning and reproof to his house were made known by Eli to the whole nation. By this means he hoped to counteract, in some measure, the evil influence of his past neglect. But the warnings were disregarded by the people, as they had been by the priests. The people of surrounding nations also, who were not ignorant of the iniquities openly practiced in Israel, became still bolder in their idolatry and crime. They felt no sense of guilt for their sins, as they would have felt had the 583 Israelites preserved their integrity. But a day of retribution was approaching. God's authority had been set aside, and His worship neglected and despised, and it became necessary for Him to interpose, that the honor of His name might be maintained.

"Now Israel went out against the Philistines to battle, and pitched beside Ebenezer: and the Philistines pitched in Aphek." This expedition was undertaken by the Israelites without counsel from God, without the concurrence of high priest or prophet. "And the Philistines put themselves in array against Israel: and when they joined battle, Israel was smitten before the Philistines: and they slew of the army in the field about four thousand men." As the shattered and disheartened force returned to their encampment, "the elders of Israel said, Wherefore hath

This chapter is based on 1 Samuel 3 to 7.

the Lord smitten us today before the Philistines?" The nation was ripe for the judgments of God, yet they did not see that their own sins had been the cause of this terrible disaster. And they said, "Let us fetch the ark of the covenant of the Lord out of Shiloh unto us, that, when it cometh among us, it may save us out of the hand of our enemies." The Lord had given no command or permission that the ark should come into the army; yet the Israelites felt confident that victory would be theirs, and uttered a great shout when it was borne into the camp by the sons of Eli.

The Philistines looked upon the ark as the god of Israel. All the mighty works that Jehovah had wrought for His people were attributed to its power. As they heard the shouts of joy at its approach, they said, "What meaneth the noise of this great shout in the camp of the Hebrews? And they understood that the ark of the Lord was come into the camp. And the Philistines were afraid; for they said, God has come into the camp. And they said, Woe unto us! for there hath not been such a thing heretofore. Woe unto us! who shall deliver us out of the hand of these mighty Gods? These are the Gods that smote the Egyptians with all the plagues in the wilderness. Be strong, and quit yourselves like men, O ye Philistines, that ye be not servants unto the Hebrews, as they have been to you: quit yourselves like men, and fight."

The Philistines made a fierce assault, which resulted in the defeat of Israel, with great slaughter. Thirty thousand men lay dead upon the field, and the ark of God was taken, the two sons of Eli having fallen while fighting to 584 defend it. Thus again was left upon the page of history a testimony for all future ages—that the iniquity of God's professed people will not go unpunished. The greater the knowledge of God's will, the greater the sin of those who disregard it.

The most terrifying calamity that could occur had befallen Israel. The ark of God had been captured, and was in the possession of the enemy. The glory had indeed departed from Israel when the symbol of the abiding presence and power of Jehovah was removed from the midst of them. With this sacred chest were associated the most wonderful revelations of God's truth and power. In former days miraculous victories had been achieved whenever it appeared. It was shadowed by the wings of the golden cherubim, and the unspeakable glory of the Shekinah, the visible symbol of the most high God, had rested over it in the holy of holies. But now it had brought no victory. It had not proved a defense on this occasion, and there was mourning throughout Israel.

They had not realized that their faith was only a nominal faith, and had lost its power to prevail with God. The law of God, contained in the ark,

was also a symbol of His presence; but they had cast contempt upon the commandments, had despised their requirements, and had grieved the Spirit of the Lord from among them. When the people obeyed the holy precepts, the Lord was with them to work for them by His infinite power; but when they looked upon the ark, and did not associate it with God, nor honor His revealed will by obedience to His law, it could avail them little more than a common box. They looked to the ark as the idolatrous nations looked to their gods, as if it possessed in itself the elements of power and salvation. They transgressed the law it contained; for their very worship of the ark led to formalism, hypocrisy, and idolatry. Their sin had separated them from God, and He could not give them the victory until they had repented of and forsaken their iniquity.

It was not enough that the ark and the sanctuary were in the midst of Israel. It was not enough that the priests offered sacrifices, and that the people were called the children of God. The Lord does not regard the request of those who cherish iniquity in the heart; it is written that "he that turneth away his ear from hearing the law, even his prayer shall be abomination." Proverbs 28:9.

When the army went out to battle, Eli, blind 585 and old, had tarried at Shiloh. It was with troubled forebodings that he awaited the result of the conflict; "for his heart trembled for the ark of God." Taking his position outside the gate of the tabernacle, he sat by the highway side day after day, anxiously expecting the arrival of a messenger from the battlefield.

At length a Benjamite from the army, "with his clothes rent, and with earth upon his head," came hurrying up the ascent leading to the city. Passing heedlessly on to the town, he repeated to eager throngs the tidings of defeat and loss.

The sound of wailing and lamentation reached the watcher beside the tabernacle. The messenger was brought to him. And the man said unto Eli, "Israel is fled before the Philistines, and there hath been also a great slaughter among the people, and thy two sons also, Hophni and Phinehas, are dead." Eli could endure all this, terrible as it was, for he had expected it. But when the messenger added, "And the ark of God is taken," a look of unutterable anguish passed over his countenance. The thought that his sin had thus dishonored God and caused Him to withdraw His presence from Israel was more than he could bear; his strength was gone, he fell, "and his neck brake, and he died."

The wife of Phinehas, notwithstanding the impiety of her husband, was a woman who feared the Lord. The death of her father-in-law and her husband, and above all, the terrible tidings that the ark of God was taken, caused her death. She felt that the last hope of Israel was gone; and she named the child born in this hour of adversity, Ichabod, or "inglorious;" with her dying breath mournfully repeating the words, "The glory is departed from Israel: for the ark of God is taken."

But the Lord had not wholly cast aside His people, nor would He long suffer the exultation of the heathen. He had used the Philistines as the instrument to punish Israel, and He employed the ark to punish the Philistines. In time past the divine Presence had attended it, to be the strength and glory of His obedient people. That invisible Presence would still attend it, to bring terror and destruction to the transgressors of His holy law. The Lord often employs His bitterest enemies to punish the unfaithfulness of His professed people. The wicked may triumph for a time as they see Israel suffering 586 chastisement, but the time will come when they, too, must meet the sentence of a holy, sin-hating God. Wherever iniquity is cherished, there, swift and unerring, the divine judgments will follow.

The Philistines removed the ark in triumph to Ashdod, one of their five principal cities, and placed it in the house of their god Dagon. They imagined that the power which had hitherto attended the ark would be theirs, and that this, united with the power of Dagon, would render them invincible. But upon entering the temple on the following day, they beheld a sight which filled them with consternation. Dagon had fallen upon his face to the earth before the ark of Jehovah. The priests reverently lifted the idol and restored it to its place. But the next morning they found it, strangely mutilated, again lying upon the earth before the ark. The upper part of this idol was like that of a man, and the lower part was in the likeness of a fish. Now every part that resembled the human form had been cut off, and only the body of the fish remained. Priests and people were horror-struck; they looked upon this mysterious event as an evil omen, foreboding destruction to themselves and their idols before the God of the Hebrews. They now removed the ark from their temple and placed it in a building by itself.

The inhabitants of Ashdod were smitten with a distressing and fatal disease. Remembering the plagues that were inflicted upon Egypt by the God of Israel, the people attributed their afflictions to the presence of the ark among them. It was decided to convey it to Gath. But the plague followed close upon its removal, and the men of that city sent it to Ekron. Here the people received it with terror, crying, "They have brought about the ark of the God of Israel to us, to slay us and our people." They turned to their gods for protection, as the people of Gath and Ashdod had done; but the work of the destroyer went on, until, in their distress, "the cry of the city went up to heaven." Fearing longer to retain the ark among the homes of men, the people next placed it in the open field. There followed a plague of mice, which infested the land, destroying the products of the soil, both in the storehouse and in the field. Utter destruction, by disease or famine, now threatened the nation.

For seven months the ark remained in Philistia, and during all this time the Israelites made no effort for its recovery. But the Philistines were now as anxious to free themselves from its presence as they had been to obtain it. Instead of 587 being a source of strength to them, it was a great burden and a heavy curse. Yet they knew not what course to pursue; for wherever it went the judgments of God followed. The people called for the princes of the nation, with the priests and diviners, and eagerly inquired, "What shall we do to the ark of Jehovah? tell us wherewith we shall send it to his place?" They were advised to return it with a costly trespass offering. "Then," said the priests, "ye shall be healed, and it shall be known to you why His hand is not removed from you."

To ward off or to remove a plague, it was anciently the custom among the heathen to make an image in gold, silver, or other material, of that which caused the destruction, or of the object or part of the body specially affected. This was set up on a pillar or in some conspicuous place, and was supposed to be an effectual protection against the evils thus represented. A similar practice still exists among some heathen peoples. When a person suffering from disease goes for cure to the temple of his idol, he carries with him a figure of the part affected, which he presents as an offering to his god.

It was in accordance with the prevailing superstition that the Philistine lords directed the people to make representations of the plagues by which they had been afflicted—"five golden emerods, and five golden mice, according to the number of the lords of the Philistines: for," said they, "one plague was on you all, and on your lords."

These wise men acknowledged a mysterious power accompanying the ark—a power which they had no wisdom to meet. Yet they did not counsel the people to turn from their idolatry to serve the Lord. They still hated the God of Israel, though compelled by overwhelming judgments to submit to His authority. Thus sinners may be convinced by the judgments of God that it is in vain to contend against Him. They may be compelled to submit to His power, while at heart they rebel against His control. Such submission cannot save the sinner. The heart must be yielded to God—must be subdued by divine grace—before man's repentance can be accepted.

How great is the long-suffering of God toward the wicked! The idolatrous Philistines and backsliding Israel had alike enjoyed the gifts of His providence. Ten thousand unnoticed mercies were silently falling in the pathway of ungrateful, rebellious men. Every blessing spoke to them of the Giver, but they were indifferent to His love. The forbearance of God was very great toward the children of men; but when they stubbornly persisted in their impenitence, He removed from them His protecting hand. They refused to listen to the voice of God in His created works, and in the warnings, counsels, and reproofs of His word, and thus He was forced to speak to them through judgments.

There were some among the Philistines who stood ready to oppose the return of the ark to its own land. Such an acknowledgment of the power of Israel's God would be humiliating to the pride of Philistia. But "the priests and the diviners" admonished the people not to imitate the stubbornness of Pharaoh and the Egyptians, and thus bring upon themselves still greater afflictions. A plan which won the consent of all was now proposed, and immediately put in execution. The ark, with the golden trespass offering, was placed upon a new cart, thus precluding all danger of defilement; to this cart, or car, were attached two kine upon whose necks a yoke had never been placed. Their calves were shut up at home, and the cows were left free to go where they pleased. If the ark should thus be returned to the Israelites by the way of Beth-shemesh, the nearest city of the Levites, the Philistines would accept this as evidence that the God of Israel had done unto them this great evil; "but if not," they said, "then we shall know that it is not His hand that smote us; it was a chance that happened to us."

On being set free, the kine turned from their young and, lowing as they went, took the direct road to Beth-shemesh. Guided by no human hand, the patient animals kept on their way. The divine Presence accompanied the ark, and it passed on safely to the very place designated.

It was now the time of wheat harvest, and the men of Beth-shemesh were reaping in the valley. "And they lifted up their eyes, and saw the ark, and rejoiced to see it. And the cart came into the field of Joshua, a Beth-shemite, and stood there, where there was a great stone: and they clave the wood of the cart, and offered the kine a burnt-offering unto the Lord." The lords of the Philistines, who had followed the ark "unto the border of Beth-shemesh," and had witnessed its reception, now returned to Ekron. The plague had ceased, and they were convinced that their calamities had been a judgment from the God of Israel.

The men of Beth-shemesh quickly spread the tidings that the ark was in their possession, and the people from the surrounding country flocked to welcome its return. The ark had been placed upon the stone that first served for an altar, and before it additional sacrifices were offered unto the Lord. Had the worshipers repented of their sins, God's blessing would have attended them. But they were not faithfully obeying His law; and while they rejoiced at the return of the ark as a harbinger of good, they had no true sense of its sacredness. Instead of preparing a suitable place for its reception, they permitted it to remain in the harvest field. As they continued to gaze upon the sacred chest and to talk of the wonderful manner in which it had been restored, they began to conjecture wherein lay its peculiar power. At last, overcome by curiosity, they removed the coverings and ventured to open it.

All Israel had been taught to regard the ark with awe and reverence. When required to remove it from place to place the Levites were not so much as to look upon it. Only once a year was the high priest permitted to behold the ark of God. Even the heathen Philistines had not dared to remove its coverings. Angels of heaven, unseen, ever attended it in all its journeyings. The irreverent daring of the people at Beth-shemesh was speedily punished. Many were smitten with sudden death.

The survivors were not led by this judgment to repent of their sin, but only to regard the ark with superstitious fear. Eager to be free from its presence, yet not daring to remove it, the Beth-shemites sent a message to the inhabitants of Kirjath-jearim, inviting them to take it away. With great joy the men of this place welcomed the sacred chest. They knew that it was the pledge of divine favor to the obedient and faithful. With solemn gladness they brought it to their city and placed it in the house of Abinadab, a Levite. This man appointed his son Eleazar to take charge of it, and it remained there for many years.

During the years since the Lord first manifested Himself to the son of Hannah, Samuel's call to the prophetic office had come to be acknowledged by the whole nation. By faithfully delivering the divine warning to the house of Eli, painful and trying as the duty had been, Samuel had given proof of his fidelity as Jehovah's messenger; "and the Lord was with him, and did let none of his words fall to the ground. And all Israel from Dan even to Beersheba knew that Samuel was established to be a prophet of the Lord."

The Israelites as a nation still continued in a state of irreligion and idolatry, and as a punishment they remained in subjection to the Philistines. During this time Samuel visited the cities and villages throughout the land, seeking to turn the hearts of the people to the God of their fathers; and his efforts were not without good results. After suffering the oppression of their enemies for twenty years, the Israelites "mourned after the Lord." Samuel counseled them, "If ye do return unto the Lord with all your hearts, then put away the strange gods and Ashtaroth from among you, and prepare your hearts unto the Lord, and serve Him only." Here we see that practical piety, heart religion, was taught in the days of Samuel as taught by Christ when He was upon the earth. Without the grace of Christ the outward forms of religion were valueless to ancient Israel. They are the same to modern Israel.

There is need today of such a revival of true heart religion as was experienced by ancient Israel. Repentance is the first step that must be taken by all who would return to God. No one can do this work for another. We must individually humble our souls before God and put away our idols. When we have done all that we can do, the Lord will manifest to us His salvation.

With the co-operation of the heads of the tribes, a large assembly was gathered at Mizpeh. Here a solemn fast was held. With deep humiliation the people confessed their sins; and as an evidence of their determination to obey the instructions they had heard, they invested Samuel with the authority of judge.

The Philistines interpreted this gathering to be a council of war, and with a strong force set out to disperse the Israelites before their plans could be matured. The tidings of their approach caused great terror in Israel. The people entreated Samuel, "Cease not to cry unto the Lord our God for us, that He will save us out of the hand of the Philistines."

591 While Samuel was in the act of presenting a lamb as a burnt offering, the Philistines drew near for battle. Then the Mighty One who had descended upon Sinai amid fire and smoke and thunder, who had parted the Red Sea and made a way through Jordan for the children of Israel, again manifested His power. A terrible storm burst upon the advancing host, and the earth was strewn with the dead bodies of mighty warriors.

The Israelites had stood in silent awe, trembling with hope and fear. When they beheld the slaughter of their enemies, they knew that God had accepted their repentance. Though unprepared for battle, they seized the weapons of the slaughtered Philistines and pursued the fleeing host to Beth-car. This signal victory was gained upon the very field where, twenty years before, Israel had been smitten before the Philistines, the priests slain, and the ark of God taken. For nations as well as for individuals, the path of obedience to God is the path of safety and happiness, while that of transgression leads only to disaster and defeat. The Philistines were now so completely subdued that they surrendered the strongholds which had been taken from Israel and refrained from acts of hostility for many

years. Other nations followed this example, and the Israelites enjoyed peace until the close of Samuel's sole administration.

That the occasion might never be forgotten, Samuel set up, between Mizpeh and Shen, a great stone as a memorial. He called the name of it Ebenezer, "the stone of help," saying to the people, "hitherto hath Jehovah helped us."

58

The Schools of the Prophets

592

The Lord Himself directed the education of Israel. His care was not restricted to their religious interests; whatever affected their mental or physical well-being was also the subject of divine providence, and came within the sphere of divine law.

God had commanded the Hebrews to teach their children His requirements and to make them acquainted with all His dealings with their fathers. This was one of the special duties of every parent—one that was not to be delegated to another. In the place of stranger lips the loving hearts of the father and mother were to give instruction to their children. Thoughts of God were to be associated with all the events of daily life. The mighty works of God in the deliverance of His people and the promises of the Redeemer to come were to be often recounted in the homes of Israel; and the use of figures and symbols caused the lessons given to be more firmly fixed in the memory. The great truths of God's providence and of the future life were impressed on the young mind. It was trained to see God alike in the scenes of nature and the words of revelation. The stars of heaven, the trees and flowers of the field, the lofty mountains, the rippling brooks—all spoke of the Creator. The solemn service of sacrifice and worship at the sanctuary and the utterances of the prophets were a revelation of God.

Such was the training of Moses in the lowly cabin home in Goshen; of Samuel, by the faithful Hannah; of David, in the hill dwelling at Bethlehem; of Daniel, before the scenes of the captivity separated him from the home of his fathers. Such, too, was the early life of Christ at Nazareth; such the training by which the child Timothy learned from the lips of his grandmother Lois, and his mother Eunice (2 Timothy 1:5; 3:15), the truths of Holy Writ.

Further provision was made for the instruction of the young, by the establishment of the schools of the prophets. If a youth desired to search deeper into the truths of the word of God and to seek wisdom from above, that he might become a teacher in Israel, these schools were open to him. The schools of the prophets were

593

founded by Samuel to serve as a barrier against the widespread corruption, to provide for the moral and spiritual welfare of the youth, and to promote the future prosperity of the nation by furnishing it with men qualified to act in the fear of God as leaders and counselors. In the accomplishment of this object Samuel gathered companies of young men who were pious, intelligent, and studious. These were called the sons of the prophets. As they communed with God and studied His word and His works, wisdom from above was added to their natural endowments. The instructors were men not only well versed in divine truth, but those who had themselves enjoyed communion with God and had received the special endowment of His Spirit. They enjoyed the respect and confidence of the people, both for learning and piety.

In Samuel's day there were two of these schools—one at Ramah, the home of the prophet, and the other at Kirjath-jearim, where the ark then was. Others were established in later times.

The pupils of these schools sustained themselves by their own labor in tilling the soil or in some mechanical employment. In Israel this was not thought strange or degrading; indeed, it was regarded a crime to allow children to grow up in ignorance of useful labor. By the command of God every child was taught some trade, even though he was to be educated for holy office. Many of the religious teachers supported themselves by manual labor. Even so late as the time of the apostles, Paul and Aquila were no less honored because they earned a livelihood by their trade of tentmaking.

The chief subjects of study in these schools were the law of God, with the instructions given to Moses, sacred history, sacred music, and poetry. The manner of instruction was far different from that in the theological schools of the present day, from which many students graduate with less real knowledge of God and religious truth than when they entered. In those schools of the olden time it was the grand object of all 594 study to learn the will of God and man's duty toward Him. In the records of sacred history were traced the footsteps of Jehovah. The great truths set forth by the types were brought to view, and faith grasped the central object of all that system—the Lamb of God that was to take away the sin of the world.

A spirit of devotion was cherished. Not only were students taught the duty of prayer, but they were taught how to pray, how to approach their Creator, how to exercise faith in Him, and how to understand and obey the teachings of His Spirit. Sanctified intellects brought forth from the treasure house of God things new and old, and the Spirit of God was manifested in prophecy and sacred song.

Music was made to serve a holy purpose, to lift the thoughts to that which is pure, noble, and elevating, and to awaken in the soul devotion and gratitude to God. What a contrast between the ancient custom and the uses to which music is now too often devoted! How many employ this gift to exalt self, instead of using it to glorify God! A love for music leads the unwary to unite with world lovers in pleasure gatherings where God has forbidden His children to go. Thus that which is a great blessing when rightly used, becomes one of the most successful agencies by which Satan allures the mind from duty and from the contemplation of eternal things.

Music forms a part of God's worship in the courts above, and we should endeavor, in our songs of praise, to approach as nearly as possible to the harmony of the heavenly choirs. The proper training of the voice is an important feature in education and should not be neglected. Singing, as a part of religious service, is as much an act of worship as is prayer. The heart must feel the spirit of the song to give it right expression.

How wide the difference between those schools taught by the prophets of God and our modern institutions of learning! How few schools are to be found that are not governed by the maxims and customs of the world! There is a deplorable lack of proper restraint and judicious discipline. The existing ignorance of God's word among a people professedly Christian is alarming. Superficial talk, mere sentimentalism, passes for instruction in morals and religion. The justice and mercy of God, the beauty of holiness and the sure reward of rightdoing, the heinous character of sin and the certainty of its terrible results, are not impressed upon the 595 minds of the young. Evil associates are instructing the youth in the ways of crime, dissipation, and licentiousness.

Are there not some lessons which the educators of our day might learn with profit from the ancient schools of the Hebrews? He who created man has provided for his development in body and mind and soul. Hence, real success in education depends upon the fidelity with which men carry out the Creator's plan.

The true object of education is to restore the image of God in the soul. In the beginning God created man in His own likeness. He endowed him with noble qualities. His mind was well balanced, and all the powers of his being were harmonious. But the Fall and its effects have perverted these gifts. Sin has marred and well-nigh obliterated the image of God in man. It was to restore this that the plan of salvation was devised, and a life of probation was granted to man. To bring him back to the perfection in which he was first created is the great object of life—the object that underlies every other. It is the work of parents and teachers, in the education of the youth, to co-operate with the divine purpose; and in so doing they are "laborers together with God." 1 Corinthians 3:9.

All the varied capabilities that men possess—of mind and soul and body—are given them by God, to be so employed as to reach the highest possible degree of excellence. But this cannot be a selfish and exclusive culture; for the character of God, whose likeness we are to receive, is benevolence and love. Every faculty, every attribute, with which the Creator has endowed us is to be employed for His glory and for the uplifting of our fellow men. And in this employment is found its purest, noblest, and happiest exercise.

Were this principle given the attention which its importance demands, there would be a radical change in some of the current methods of education. Instead of appealing to pride and selfish ambition, kindling a spirit of emulation, teachers would endeavor to awaken the love for goodness and truth and beauty—to arouse the desire for excellence. The student would seek the development of God's gifts in himself, not to excel others, but to fulfill the purpose of the Creator and to receive His likeness. Instead of being directed to mere earthly standards, or 596 being actuated by the desire for self-exaltation, which in itself dwarfs and belittles, the mind would be directed to the Creator, to know Him and to become like Him.

"The fear of the Lord is the beginning of wisdom: and *the knowledge of the Holy* is understanding." Proverbs 9:10. The great work of life is character building, and a knowledge of God is the foundation of all true education. To impart this knowledge and to mold the character in harmony with it should be the object of the teacher's work. The law of God is a reflection of His character. Hence the psalmist says, "All Thy commandments are righteousness;" and "through Thy precepts I get understanding." Psalm 119:172, 104. God has revealed Himself to us in His word and in the works of creation. Through the volume of inspiration and the book of nature we are to obtain a knowledge of God.

It is a law of the mind that it gradually adapts itself to the subjects upon which it is trained to dwell. If occupied with commonplace matters only, it will become dwarfed and enfeebled. If never required to grapple with difficult problems, it will after a time almost lose the power of growth. As an educating power the Bible is without a rival. In the word of God the mind finds subject for the deepest thought, the loftiest aspiration. The Bible is the most instructive history that men possess. It came fresh from the fountain of eternal truth, and a divine hand has preserved its purity through all the ages. It lights up the far-distant past, where human research seeks vainly to penetrate. In God's word we behold the power that laid the foundation of the earth and that stretched out the heavens. Here only can we find a history of our race unsullied by human prejudice or human pride. Here are recorded the struggles, the defeats, and the victories of the greatest men this world has ever known. Here the great problems of duty and destiny are unfolded. The curtain that separates the visible from the invisible world is lifted, and we behold the conflict of the opposing forces of good and evil, from the first entrance of sin to the final triumph of righteousness and truth; and all is but a revelation of the character of God. In the reverent contemplation of the truths presented in His word the mind of the student is brought into communion with the infinite mind. Such a study will not only refine and ennoble the character, but it cannot fail to expand and 599 invigorate the mental powers.

The teaching of the Bible has a vital bearing upon man's prosperity in all the relations of this life. It unfolds the principles that are the cornerstone of a nation's prosperity—principles with which is bound up the well-being of society, and which are the safeguard of the family—principles without which no man can attain usefulness, happiness, and honor in this life, or can hope to secure the future, immortal life. There is no position in life, no phase of human experience, for which the teaching of the Bible is not an essential preparation. Studied and obeyed, the word of God would give to the world men of stronger and more active intellect than will the closest application to all the subjects that human philosophy embraces. It would give men of strength and solidity of character, of keen perception and sound judgment—men who would be an honor to God and a blessing to the world.

In the study of the sciences also we are to obtain a knowledge of the Creator. All true science is but an interpretation of the handwriting of God in the material world. Science brings from her research only fresh evidences of the wisdom and power of God. Rightly understood, both the book of nature and the written word make us acquainted with God by teaching us something of the wise and beneficent laws through which He works.

The student should be led to see God in all the works of creation. Teachers should copy the example of the Great Teacher, who from the familiar scenes of nature drew illustrations that simplified His teachings and impressed them more deeply upon the minds of His hearers. The birds caroling in the leafy branches, the flowers of the valley, the lofty trees, the fruitful lands, the springing grain, the barren soil, the setting sun gilding the heavens with its golden beams—all served as means of instruction. He connected the visible works of the Creator with the words of life which He spoke, that whenever these objects should be presented to the eyes of His hearers, their thoughts might revert to the lessons of truth He had linked with them.

The impress of Deity, manifest in the pages of revelation, is seen upon the lofty mountains, the fruitful valleys, the broad, deep ocean. The things of nature speak to man of his Creator's love. He has linked us to Himself by unnumbered tokens in heaven and in earth. This world is not all sorrow and misery. "God is love," is written upon every opening bud, upon the petals of every flower, and upon every spire of grass. Though the curse of sin has caused the earth to bring forth thorns and thistles, there are flowers upon the thistles and the thorns are hidden by roses. All things in nature testify to the tender, fatherly care of our God and to His desire to make His children happy. His prohibitions and injunctions are not intended merely to display His authority, but in all that He does He has the well-being of His children in view. He does not require them to give up anything that it would be for their best interest to retain.

The opinion which prevails in some classes of society, that religion is not conducive to health or to happiness in this life, is one of the most mischievous of errors. The Scripture says: "The fear of the Lord tendeth to life: and he that hath it shall abide satisfied." Proverbs 19:23. "What man is he that desireth life, and loveth many days, that he may see good? Keep thy tongue from evil, and thy lips from speaking guile. Depart from evil, and do good; seek peace, and pursue it." Psalm 34:12-14. The words of wisdom "are life unto those that find them, and health to all their flesh." Proverbs 4:22.

True religion brings man into harmony with the laws of God, physical, mental, and moral. It teaches self-control, serenity, temperance. Religion ennobles the mind, refines the taste, and sanctifies the judgment. It makes the soul a partaker of the purity of heaven. Faith in God's love and overruling providence lightens the burdens of anxiety and care. It fills the heart with joy and contentment in the highest or the lowliest lot. Religion tends directly to promote health, to lengthen life, and to heighten our enjoyment of all its blessings. It opens to the soul a never-failing fountain of happiness. Would that all who have not chosen Christ might realize that He has something vastly better to offer them than they are seeking for themselves. Man is doing the greatest injury and injustice to his own soul when he thinks and acts contrary to the will of God. No real joy can be found in the path forbidden by Him who knows what is best, and who plans for the good of His creatures. The path of transgression leads to misery and destruction; but wisdom's "ways are ways of pleasantness, and all her paths are peace." Proverbs 3:17.

The physical as well as the religious training practiced in the schools of the Hebrews may be profitably studied. The worth of such training is not appreciated. There is an intimate relation between the mind and the body, and in order to reach a high standard of moral and intellectual attainment the laws that control our physical being must be heeded. To secure a strong, well-balanced character, both the mental and the physical powers must be exercised and developed. What study can be more important for the young than that which treats of this wonderful organism that God has committed to us, and of the laws by which it may be preserved in health?

And now, as in the days of Israel, every youth should be instructed in the duties of practical life. Each should acquire a knowledge of some branch of manual labor by which, if need be, he may obtain a livelihood. This is essential, not only as a safeguard against the vicissitudes of life, but from its bearing upon physical, mental, and moral development. Even if it were certain that one would never need to resort to manual labor for his support, still he should be taught to work. Without physical exercise, no one can have a sound constitution and vigorous health; and the discipline of well-regulated labor is no less essential to the securing of a strong and active mind and a noble character.

Every student should devote a portion of each day to active labor. Thus habits of industry would be formed and a spirit of self-reliance encouraged, while the youth would be shielded from many evil and degrading practices that are so often the result of idleness. And this is all in keeping with the primary object of education, for in encouraging activity, diligence, and purity we are coming into harmony with the Creator.

Let the youth be led to understand the object of their creation, to honor God and bless their fellow men; let them see the tender love which the Father in heaven has manifested toward them, and the high destiny for which the discipline of this life is to prepare them, the dignity and honor to which they are called, even to become the sons of God, and thousands would turn with contempt and loathing from the low and selfish aims and the frivolous pleasures that have hitherto engrossed them. They would learn to hate sin and to shun it, not merely from hope of reward or fear of punishment, but from a sense of its inherent baseness, because it would be a degrading of their God-given powers, a stain upon their Godlike manhood.

God does not bid the youth to be less aspiring. The elements of character that make a man successful and honored among men—the irrepressible desire for some greater good, the indomitable will, the strenuous exertion, the untiring perseverance—are not to be crushed out. By the grace of God they are to be directed to objects as much higher than mere selfish and temporal interests as the heavens are higher than the earth. And the education begun in this life will be continued in the life to come. Day by day the wonderful works of God, the evidences of His wisdom and power in creating and sustaining the universe, the infinite mystery of love and wisdom in the plan of redemption, will open to the mind in new beauty. "Eye hath not seen, nor ear heard, neither have entered into the heart of man, the things which God hath prepared for them that love Him." 1 Corinthians 2:9. Even in this life we may catch glimpses of His presence and may taste the joy of communion with Heaven, but the fullness of its joy and blessing will be reached in the hereafter. Eternity alone can reveal the glorious destiny to which man, restored to God's image, may attain.

59

The First King of Israel

The government of Israel was administered in the name and by the authority of God. The work of Moses, of the seventy elders, of the rulers and judges, was simply to enforce the laws that God had given; they had no authority to legislate for the nation. This was, and continued to be, the condition of Israel's existence as a nation. From age to age men inspired by God were sent to instruct the people and to direct in the enforcement of the laws.

The Lord foresaw that Israel would desire a king, but He did not consent to a change in the principles upon which the state was founded. The king was to be the vicegerent of the Most High. God was to be recognized as the Head of the nation, and His law was to be enforced as the supreme law of the land.*

When the Israelites first settled in Canaan they acknowledged the principles of the theocracy, and the nation prospered under the rule of Joshua. But increase of population and intercourse with other nations brought a change. The people adopted many of the customs of their heathen neighbors and thus sacrificed to a great degree their own peculiar, holy character. Gradually they lost their reverence for God and ceased to prize the honor of being His chosen people. Attracted by the pomp and display of heathen monarchs, they tired of their own simplicity. Jealousy and envy sprang up between the tribes. Internal dissensions made them weak; they were continually exposed to the invasion of their heathen foes, and the people were coming to believe that in order to maintain their standing among the nations, the tribes must be united under a strong central government. As they departed from obedience to God's law, they desired to be freed from the rule of their divine Sovereign; and thus the demand for a monarchy became widespread throughout Israel.

Since the days of Joshua the government had never been conducted with so great wisdom and success as under Samuel's administration. Divinely invested with the threefold office of judge, prophet, and priest, he had labored with untiring and disinterested zeal for the welfare of his people, and the nation had prospered under his wise control. Order had been restored, and godliness promoted, and the spirit of discontent was checked for the time. But with advancing years the prophet was forced to share with others the cares of government, and he appointed his two sons to act as his assistants. While Samuel continued the duties of his office at Ramah, the young men were stationed at Beersheba, to administer justice among the people near the southern border of the land.

It was with the full assent of the nation that Samuel had appointed his sons to office, but they did not prove themselves worthy of their father's choice. The Lord had, through Moses, given special directions to His people that the rulers of Israel should judge righteously, deal justly with the widow and the fatherless, and receive no bribes. But the sons of Samuel "turned aside after lucre, and took bribes, and perverted judgment." The sons of the prophet had not heeded the precepts which he had sought to impress upon their minds. They had not copied the pure, unselfish life of their father. The warning given to Eli had not exerted the influence upon the mind of Samuel that it should have done. He had been to some extent too indulgent with his sons, and the result was apparent in their character and life.

The injustice of these judges caused much dissatisfaction, and a pretext was thus furnished for urging the change that had long been secretly desired. "All the elders of Israel gathered themselves together, and came to Samuel unto Ramah, and said unto him, Behold, thou art old, and thy sons walk not in thy ways: now make us a king to judge us like all the nations." The cases of abuse among the people had not been referred to Samuel. Had the evil course of his sons been known to him, he would have removed them without delay; but this was not what the petitioners desired. Samuel saw that their real motive was discontent and pride, and that their demand was the result of a deliberate and determined purpose. No complaint had been made against Samuel. All acknowledged the integrity and wisdom of his administration; but the aged prophet looked upon the request as a censure upon himself, and a direct effort to set him aside. He did not, however, reveal his feelings; he uttered no reproach, but carried the matter to the Lord in prayer and sought counsel from Him alone.

And the Lord said unto Samuel: "Hearken unto the voice of the people in all that they say unto thee: for they have not rejected thee, but they have rejected Me, that I should not reign

---

* See Appendix, Note 8.   This chapter is based on 1 Samuel 8 to 12.

over them. According to all the works which they have done since the day that I brought them up out of Egypt even unto this day, wherewith they have forsaken Me, and served other gods, so do they also unto thee." The prophet was reproved for grieving at the conduct of the people toward himself as an individual. They had not manifested disrespect for him, but for the authority of God, who had appointed the rulers of His people. Those who despise and reject the faithful servant of God show contempt, not merely for the man, but for the Master who sent him. It is God's words, His reproofs and counsel, that are set at nought; it is His authority that is rejected.

The days of Israel's greatest prosperity had been those in which they acknowledged Jehovah as their King—when the laws and the government which He had established were regarded as superior to those of all other nations. Moses had declared to Israel concerning the commandments of the Lord: "This is your wisdom and your understanding in the sight of the nations, which shall hear all these statutes, and say, Surely this great nation is a wise and understanding people." Deuteronomy 4:6. But by departing from God's law the Hebrews had failed to become the people that God desired to make them, and then all the evils which were the result of their own sin and folly they charged upon the government of God. So completely had they become blinded by sin.

The Lord had, through His prophets, foretold that Israel would be governed by a king; but it does not follow that this form of government was best for them or according to His will. He permitted the people to follow their own choice, because they refused to be guided by His counsel. Hosea declares that God gave them a king in His anger. Hosea 13:11. When men choose to have their own way, without seeking counsel from God, or in opposition to His revealed will, He often grants their desires, in order that, 606 through the bitter experience that follows, they may be led to realize their folly and to repent of their sin. Human pride and wisdom will prove a dangerous guide. That which the heart desires contrary to the will of God will in the end be found a curse rather than a blessing.

God desired His people to look to Him alone as their Lawgiver and their Source of strength. Feeling their dependence upon God, they would be constantly drawn nearer to Him. They would become elevated and ennobled, fitted for the high destiny to which He had called them as His chosen people. But when a man was placed upon the throne, it would tend to turn the minds of the people from God. They would trust more to human strength, and less to divine power, and the errors of their king would lead them into sin and separate the nation from God.

Samuel was instructed to grant the request of the people, but to warn them of the Lord's disapproval, and also make known what would be the result of their course. "And Samuel told all the words of the Lord unto the people that asked of him a king." He faithfully set before them the burdens that would be laid upon them, and showed the contrast between such a state of oppression and their present comparatively free and prosperous condition. Their king would imitate the pomp and luxury of other monarchs, to support which, grievous exactions upon their persons and property would be necessary. The goodliest of their young men he would require for his service. They would be made charioteers and horsemen and runners before him. They must fill the ranks of his army, and they would be required to till *his* fields, to reap *his* harvests, and to manufacture implements of war for his service. The daughters of Israel would be taken for confectioners and bakers for the royal household. To support his kingly state he would seize upon the best of their lands, bestowed upon the people by Jehovah Himself. The most valuable of their servants also, and of their cattle, he would take, and "put them to his work." Besides all this, the king would require a tenth of all their income, the profits of their labor, or the products of the soil. "Ye shall be his servants," concluded the prophet. "And ye shall cry out in that day because of your king which ye shall have chosen you; and the Lord will not hear you in that day." However burdensome its exactions should be found, when once a monarchy was established, they could not set it aside at pleasure.

But the people returned the answer, "Nay; but 607 we will have a king over us; that we also may be like all the nations; and that our king may judge us, and go out before us, and fight our battles."

"Like all the nations." The Israelites did not realize that to be in this respect unlike other nations was a special privilege and blessing. God had separated the Israelites from every other people, to make them His own peculiar treasure. But they, disregarding this high honor, eagerly desired to imitate the example of the heathen! And still the longing to conform to worldly practices and customs exists among the professed people of God. As they depart from the Lord they become ambitious for the gains and honors of the world. Christians are constantly seeking to imitate the practices of those who worship the god of this world. Many urge that by uniting with worldlings and conforming to their customs they might exert a stronger influence over the ungodly. But all who pursue this course thereby separate from the Source of their strength. Becoming the friends of the world, they are the enemies of God. For the sake of earthly distinction they sacrifice the unspeakable honor to which God has called them, of showing forth the praises of Him who hath called us out of darkness into His marvelous light. 1 Peter 2:9.

With deep sadness Samuel listened to the words of the people; but the Lord said unto him, "Hearken unto their voice, and make them a king." The prophet had done his duty. He had faithfully presented the warning, and it had been rejected. With a heavy heart he dismissed the people, and himself departed to prepare for the great change in the government.

Samuel's life of purity and unselfish devotion was a perpetual rebuke both to self-serving priests and elders and to the proud, sensual congregation of Israel. Although he assumed no pomp and made no display, his labors bore the signet of Heaven. He was honored by the world's Redeemer, under whose guidance he ruled the Hebrew nation. But the people had become weary of his piety and devotion; they despised his humble authority and rejected him for a man who should rule them as a king.

In the character of Samuel we see reflected the likeness of Christ. It was the purity of our Saviour's life that provoked the wrath of Satan. That life was the light of the world, and 608 revealed the hidden depravity in the hearts of men. It was the holiness of Christ that stirred up against Him the fiercest passions of falsehearted professors of godliness. Christ came not with the wealth and honors of earth, yet the works which He wrought showed Him to possess power greater than that of any human prince. The Jews looked for the Messiah to break the oppressor's yoke, yet they cherished the sins that had bound it upon their necks. Had Christ cloaked their sins and applauded their piety, they would have accepted Him as their king; but they would not bear His fearless rebuke of their vices. The loveliness of a character in which benevolence, purity, and holiness reigned supreme, which entertained no hatred except for sin, they despised. Thus it has been in every age of the world. The light from heaven brings condemnation on all who refuse to walk in it. When rebuked by the example of those who hate sin, hypocrites will become agents of Satan to harass and persecute the faithful. "All that will live godly in Christ Jesus shall suffer persecution." 2 Timothy 3:12.

Though a monarchical form of government for Israel had been foretold in prophecy, God had reserved to Himself the right to choose their king. The Hebrews so far respected the authority of God as to leave the selection entirely to Him. The choice fell upon Saul, a son of Kish, of the tribe of Benjamin.

The personal qualities of the future monarch were such as to gratify that pride of heart which prompted the desire for a king. "There was not among the children of Israel a goodlier person than he." 1 Samuel 9:2. Of noble and dignified

bearing, in the prime of life, comely and tall, he appeared like one born to command. Yet with these external attractions, Saul was destitute of those higher qualities that constitute true wisdom. He had not in youth learned to control his rash, impetuous passions; he had never felt the renewing power of divine grace.

Saul was the son of a powerful and wealthy chief, yet in accordance with the simplicity of the times he was engaged with his father in the humble duties of a husbandman. Some of his father's animals having strayed upon the mountains, Saul went with a servant to seek for them. For three days they searched in vain, when, as they were not far from Ramah,* the home of Samuel, the servant proposed that they should inquire of the prophet concerning the missing property. "I have here at hand the fourth part of 609 a shekel of silver," he said: "that will I give to the man of God, to tell us our way." This was in accordance with the custom of the times. A person approaching a superior in rank or office made him a small present, as an expression of respect.

As they drew near to the city they met some young maidens who had come out to draw water, and inquired of them for the seer. In reply they were told that a religious service was about to take place, that the prophet had already arrived, there was to be an offering upon "the high place," and after that a sacrificial feast. A great change had taken place under Samuel's administration. When the call of God first came to him the services of the sanctuary were held in contempt. "Men abhorred the offering of the Lord." 1 Samuel 2:17. But the worship of God was now maintained throughout the land, and the people manifested an interest in religious services. There being no ministration in the tabernacle, sacrifices were for the time offered elsewhere; and the cities of the priests and Levites, where the people resorted for instruction, were chosen for this purpose. The highest points in these cities were usually selected as the place of sacrifice, and hence were called "the high places."

At the gate of the city Saul was met by the prophet himself. God had revealed to Samuel that at that time the chosen king of Israel would present himself before him. As they now stood face to face, the Lord said to Samuel, "Behold the man whom I spake to thee of! this same shall reign over My people."

To the request of Saul, "Tell me, I pray thee, where the seer's house is," Samuel replied, "I am the seer." Assuring him also that the lost animals had been found, he urged him to tarry and attend the feast, at the same time giving some intimation of the great destiny before him: "On whom is all the desire of Israel? Is it not on thee, and on all thy father's house?" The listener's heart thrilled at the prophet's words. He

---

* See Appendix, Note 9.

could not but perceive something of their significance, for the demand for a king had become a matter of absorbing interest to the whole nation. Yet with modest self-depreciation Saul replied, "Am not I a Benjamite, of the smallest of the tribes of Israel? and my family the least of all the families of the tribe of Benjamin? wherefore then speakest thou so to me?"

610 Samuel conducted the stranger to the place of assembly, where the principal men of the town were gathered. Among them, at the prophet's direction, the place of honor was given to Saul, and at the feast the choicest portion was set before him. The services over, Samuel took his guest to his own home, and there upon the housetop he communed with him, setting forth the great principles on which the government of Israel had been established, and thus seeking to prepare him, in some measure, for his high station.

When Saul departed, early next morning, the prophet went forth with him. Having passed through the town, he directed the servant to go forward. Then he bade Saul stand still to receive a message sent him from God. "Then Samuel took a vial of oil, and poured it upon his head, and kissed him, and said, Is it not because Jehovah hath anointed thee to be captain over His inheritance?" As evidence that this was done by divine authority, he foretold the incidents that would occur on the homeward journey and assured Saul that he would be qualified by the Spirit of God for the station awaiting him. "The Spirit of Jehovah will come upon thee," said the prophet, and thou "shalt be turned into another man. And let it be, when these signs are come unto thee, that thou do as occasion serve thee; for God is with thee."

As Saul went on his way, all came to pass as the prophet had said. Near the border of Benjamin he was informed that the lost animals had been found. In the plain of Tabor he met three men who were going to worship God at Bethel. One of them carried three kids for sacrifice, another three loaves of bread, and the third a bottle of wine, for the sacrificial feast. They gave Saul the usual salutation and also presented him with two of the three loaves of bread. At Gibeah, his own city, a band of prophets returning from "the high place" were singing the praise of God to the music of the pipe and the harp, the psaltery and the tabret. As Saul approached them the Spirit of the Lord came upon him also, and he joined in their song of praise, and prophesied with them. He spoke with so great fluency and wisdom, and joined so earnestly in the service, that those who had known him exclaimed in astonishment, "What is this that is come unto the son of Kish? Is Saul also among the prophets?"

As Saul united with the prophets in their worship, a great change was wrought in him by the Holy Spirit. The light of divine purity and holiness shone in upon the darkness of the natural heart. He saw himself as he was before God. He saw the beauty of holiness. He was now called to begin the warfare against sin and Satan, and he was made to feel that in this conflict his strength must come wholly from God. The plan of salvation, which had before seemed dim and uncertain, was opened to his understanding. The Lord endowed him with courage and wisdom for his high station. He revealed to him the Source of strength and grace, and enlightened his understanding as to the divine claims and his own duty.   611

The anointing of Saul as king had not been made known to the nation. The choice of God was to be publicly manifested by lot. For this purpose Samuel convoked the people at Mizpeh. Prayer was offered for divine guidance; then followed the solemn ceremony of casting the lot. In silence the assembled multitude awaited the issue. The tribe, the family, and the household were successively designated, and then Saul, the son of Kish, was pointed out as the individual chosen. But Saul was not in the assembly. Burdened with a sense of the great responsibility about to fall upon him, he had secretly withdrawn. He was brought back to the congregation, who observed him with pride and satisfaction that he was of kingly bearing and noble form, being "higher than any of the people from his shoulders and upward." Even Samuel, when presenting him to the assembly, exclaimed, "See ye him whom the Lord hath chosen, that there is none like him among all the people?" And in response arose from the vast throng one long, loud shout of joy, "God save the king!"

Samuel then set before the people "the manner of the kingdom," stating the principles upon which the monarchical government was based, and by which it should be controlled. The king was not to be an absolute monarch, but was to hold his power in subjection to the will of the Most High. This address was recorded in a book, wherein were set forth the prerogatives of the prince and the rights and privileges of the people. Though the nation had despised Samuel's warning, the faithful prophet, while forced to yield to their desires, still endeavored, as far as possible, to guard their liberties.

While the people in general were ready to acknowledge Saul as their king, there was a large party in opposition. For a monarch to be chosen from Benjamin, the smallest of the tribes of Israel—and that to the neglect of both Judah and Ephraim, the largest and most powerful—was a slight which they could not brook. They refused to profess allegiance to Saul or to bring him the customary presents. Those who had   612 been most urgent in their demand for a king were the very ones that refused to accept with gratitude the man of God's appointment. The members of each faction had their favorite, whom they wished to see placed on the throne, and several among the leaders had desired the honor for themselves. Envy and jealousy burned in the hearts of many. The efforts of pride and ambition had resulted in disappointment and discontent.

In this condition of affairs Saul did not see fit to assume the royal dignity. Leaving Samuel to administer the government as formerly, he returned to Gibeah. He was honorably escorted thither by a company, who, seeing the divine choice in his selection, were determined to sustain him. But he made no attempt to maintain by force his right to the throne. In his home among the uplands of Benjamin he quietly occupied himself in the duties of a husbandman, leaving the establishment of his authority entirely to God.

Soon after Saul's appointment the Ammonites, under their king, Nahash, invaded the territory of the tribes east of Jordan and threatened the city of Jabesh-gilead. The inhabitants tried to secure terms of peace by offering to become tributary to the Ammonites. To this the cruel king would not consent but on condition that he might put out the right eye of every one of them, thus making them abiding witnesses to his power.

The people of the besieged city begged a respite of seven days. To this the Ammonites consented, thinking thus to heighten the honor of their expected triumph. Messengers were at once dispatched from Jabesh, to seek help from the tribes west of Jordan. They carried the tidings to Gibeah, creating widespread terror. Saul, returning at night from following the oxen in the field, heard the loud wail that told of some great calamity. He said, "What aileth the people that they weep?" When the shameful story was repeated, all his dormant powers were roused. "The Spirit of God came upon Saul. . . . And he took a yoke of oxen, and hewed them in pieces, and sent them throughout all the coasts of Israel by the hands of messengers, saying, Whosoever cometh not forth after Saul and after Samuel, so shall it be done unto his oxen."

Three hundred and thirty thousand men gathered on the plain of Bezek, under the command 613 of Saul. Messengers were immediately sent to the besieged city with the assurance that they might expect help on the morrow, the very day on which they were to submit to the Ammonites. By a rapid night march Saul and his army crossed the Jordan and arrived before Jabesh in "the morning watch." Like Gideon, dividing his force into three companies, he fell upon the Ammonite camp at that early hour, when, not suspecting danger, they were least secure. In the panic that followed they were routed with great slaughter. And "they which remained were scattered, so that two of them were not left together."

The promptness and bravery of Saul, as well as the generalship shown in the successful conduct of so large a force, were qualities which the people of Israel had desired in a monarch, that they might be able to cope with other nations. They now greeted him as their king, attributing the honor of the victory to human agencies and forgetting that without God's special blessing all their efforts would have been in vain. In their enthusiasm some proposed to put to death those who had at first refused to acknowledge the authority of Saul. But the king interfered, saying, "There shall not a man be put to death this day: for today the Lord hath wrought salvation in Israel." Here Saul gave evidence of the change that had taken place in his character. Instead of taking honor to himself, he gave the glory to God. Instead of showing a desire for revenge, he manifested a spirit of compassion and forgiveness. This is unmistakable evidence that the grace of God dwells in the heart.

Samuel now proposed that a national assembly should be convoked at Gilgal, that the kingdom might there be publicly confirmed to Saul. It was done; "and there they sacrificed sacrifices of peace offerings before the Lord; and there Saul and all the men of Israel rejoiced greatly."

Gilgal had been the place of Israel's first encampment in the Promised Land. It was here that Joshua, by divine direction, set up the pillar of twelve stones to commemorate the miraculous passage of the Jordan. Here circumcision had been renewed. Here they had kept the first Passover after the sin at Kadesh and the desert sojourn. Here the manna ceased. Here the Captain of the Lord's host had revealed Himself as chief in command of the armies of Israel. From this place they marched to the overthrow of Jericho and the conquest of Ai. Here Achan met the penalty of his sin, and here was made that treaty 614 with the Gibeonites which punished Israel's neglect to ask counsel of God. Upon this plain, linked with so many thrilling associations, stood Samuel and Saul; and when the shouts of welcome to the king had died away, the aged prophet gave his parting words as ruler of the nation.

"Behold," he said, "I have hearkened unto your voice in all that ye said unto me, and have made a king over you. And now, behold, the king walketh before you: and I am old and grayheaded; . . . and I have walked before you from my childhood unto this day. Behold, here I am: witness against me before the Lord, and before His anointed: whose ox have I taken? or whose ass have I taken? or whom have I defrauded? whom have I oppressed? or of whose hand have I received any bribe to blind mine eyes therewith? and I will restore it you."

With one voice the people answered, "Thou

hast not defrauded us, nor oppressed us, neither hast thou taken ought of any man's hand."

Samuel was not seeking merely to justify his own course. He had previously set forth the principles that should govern both the king and the people, and he desired to add to his words the weight of his own example. From childhood he had been connected with the work of God, and during his long life one object had been ever before him—the glory of God and the highest good of Israel.

Before there could be any hope of prosperity for Israel they must be led to repentance before God. In consequence of sin they had lost their faith in God and their discernment of His power and wisdom to rule the nation—lost their confidence in His ability to vindicate His cause. Before they could find true peace they must be led to see and confess the very sin of which they had been guilty. They had declared the object of the demand for a king to be, "That our king may judge us, and go out before us, and fight our battles." Samuel recounted the history of Israel, from the day when God brought them from Egypt. Jehovah, the King of kings, had gone out before them and had fought their battles. Often their sins had sold them into the power of their enemies, but no sooner did they turn from their evil ways than God's mercy raised up a deliverer. The Lord sent Gideon and Barak, and "Jeph-thah, and Samuel, and delivered you out of the hand of your enemies on every side, and ye dwelt safe." Yet when threatened with danger they had declared, "A king shall reign over us," when, said the prophet, "Jehovah your God was your King."

"Now therefore," continued Samuel, "stand and see this great thing, which the Lord will do before your eyes. Is it not wheat harvest today? I will call unto the Lord, and He shall send thunder and rain; that ye may perceive and see that your wickedness is great, which ye have done in the sight of the Lord, in asking you a king. So Samuel called unto the Lord; and the Lord sent thunder and rain that day." At the time of wheat harvest, in May and June, no rain fell in the East. The sky was cloudless, and the air serene and mild. So violent a storm at this season filled all hearts with fear. In humiliation the people now confessed their sin—the very sin of which they had been guilty: "Pray for thy servants unto the Lord thy God, that we die not: for we have added unto all our sins this evil, to ask us a king."

Samuel did not leave the people in a state of discouragement, for this would have prevented all effort for a better life. Satan would lead them to look upon God as severe and unforgiving, and they would thus be exposed to manifold temptations. God is merciful and forgiving, ever desiring to show favor to His people when they will obey His voice. "Fear not," was the mes-sage of God by His servant: "ye have done all this wickedness: yet turn not aside from follow-ing the Lord, but serve the Lord with all your heart; and turn ye not aside: for then should ye go after vain things, which cannot profit nor deliver; for they are vain. For the Lord will not forsake His people."

Samuel said nothing of the slight which had been put upon himself; he uttered no reproach for the ingratitude with which Israel had repaid his lifelong devotion; but he assured them of his unceasing interest for them: "God forbid that I should sin against the Lord in ceasing to pray for you: but I will teach you the good and the right way: only fear the Lord, and serve Him in truth with all your heart: for consider how great things He hath done for you. But if ye shall still do wickedly, ye shall be consumed, both ye and your king."

60

The Presumption of Saul

After the assembly at Gilgal, Saul disbanded the army that had at his call arisen to overthrow the Ammonites, reserving only two thousand men to be stationed under his command at Michmash and one thousand to attend his son Jonathan at Gibeah. Here was a serious error. His army was filled with hope and courage by the recent victory; and had he proceeded at once against other enemies of Israel, a telling blow might have been struck for the liberties of the nation.

Meanwhile their warlike neighbors, the Philistines, were active. After the defeat at Ebenezer they had still retained possession of some hill fortresses in the land of Israel, and now they established themselves in the very heart of the country. In facilities, arms, and equipments the Philistines had great advantage over Israel. During the long period of their oppressive rule they had endeavored to strength-en their power by forbidding the Israelites to practice the trade of smiths, lest they should make weapons of war. After the conclusion of peace the Hebrews had still resorted to the Philistine garrisons for such work as needed to be done. Controlled by love of ease and the abject spirit induced by long oppression, the men of Israel had, to a great extent, neglected to provide themselves with weapons of war. Bows and slings were used in warfare, and these the Israelites could obtain; but there were none among them, except Saul and his son Jonathan, who possessed a spear or a sword.

It was not until the second year of Saul's reign that an attempt was made to subdue the Philistines. The first blow was struck by

This chapter is based on 1 Samuel 13; 14.

Jonathan, the king's son, who attacked and overcame their garrison at Geba. The Philistines, exasperated by this defeat, made ready for a speedy attack upon Israel. Saul now caused war to be proclaimed by the sound of the trumpet throughout the land, calling upon all the men of war, including the tribes across the Jordan, to assemble at Gilgal. This summons was obeyed.

The Philistines had gathered an immense force at Michmash—"thirty thousand chariots, and six thousand horsemen, and people as the sand which is on the seashore in multitude." When the tidings reached Saul and his army at Gilgal, the people were appalled at thought of the mighty forces they would have to encounter in battle. They were not prepared to meet the enemy, and many were so terrified that they dared not come to the test of an encounter. Some crossed the Jordan, while others hid themselves in caves and pits and amid the rocks that abounded in that region. As the time for the encounter drew near, the number of desertions rapidly increased, and those who did not withdraw from the ranks were filled with foreboding and terror.

When Saul was first anointed king of Israel, he had received from Samuel explicit directions concerning the course to be pursued at this time. "Thou shalt go down before me to Gilgal," said the prophet; "and, behold, I will come down unto thee, to offer burnt offerings, and to sacrifice sacrifices of peace offerings: seven days shalt thou tarry, till I come to thee, and show thee what thou shalt do." 1 Samuel 10:8.

Day after day Saul tarried, but without making decided efforts toward encouraging the people and inspiring confidence in God. Before the time appointed by the prophet had fully expired, he became impatient at the delay and allowed himself to be discouraged by the trying circumstances that surrounded him. Instead of faithfully seeking to prepare the people for the service that Samuel was coming to perform, he indulged in unbelief and foreboding. The work of seeking God by sacrifice was a most solemn and important work; and God required that His people should search their hearts and repent of their sins, that the offering might be made with acceptance before Him, and that His blessing might attend their efforts to conquer the enemy. But Saul had grown restless; and the people, instead of trusting in God for help, were looking to the king whom they had chosen, to lead and direct them.

Yet the Lord still cared for them and did not give them up to the disasters that would have come upon them if the frail arm of flesh had become their only support. He brought them into close places, that they might be convinced of the folly of depending on man, and that they might turn to Him as their only help. The time

for the proving of Saul had come. He was now to show whether or not he would depend on God and patiently wait according to His command, thus revealing himself as one whom God could trust in trying places as the ruler of His people, or whether he would be vacillating and unworthy of the sacred responsibility that had devolved upon him. Would the king whom Israel had chosen, listen to the Ruler of all kings? Would he turn the attention of his fainthearted soldiers to the One in whom is everlasting strength and deliverance?

With growing impatience he awaited the arrival of Samuel and attributed the confusion and distress and desertion of his army to the absence of the prophet. The appointed time came, but the man of God did not immediately appear. God's providence had detained His servant. But Saul's restless, impulsive spirit would no longer be restrained. Feeling that something must be done to calm the fears of the people, he determined to summon an assembly for religious service, and by sacrifice entreat the divine aid. God had directed that only those consecrated to the office should present sacrifices before Him. But Saul commanded, "Bring hither a burnt offering;" and, equipped as he was with armor and weapons of war, he approached the altar and offered sacrifice before God.

"And it came to pass, that as soon as he had made an end of offering the burnt offering, behold, Samuel came; and Saul went out to meet him, that he might salute him." Samuel saw at once that Saul had gone contrary to the express directions that had been given him. The Lord had spoken by His prophet that at this time He would reveal what Israel must do in this crisis. If Saul had fulfilled the conditions upon which divine help was promised, the Lord would have wrought a marvelous deliverance for Israel, with the few who were loyal to the king. But Saul was so well satisfied with himself and his work that he went out to meet the prophet as one who should be commended rather than disapproved.

Samuel's countenance was full of anxiety and trouble; but to his inquiry, "What hast thou done?" Saul offered excuses for his presumptuous act. He said: "I saw that the people were scattered from me, and that thou camest not within the days appointed, and that the Philistines gathered themselves together at Michmash; therefore said I, The Philistines will come down now upon me to Gilgal, and I have not made supplication unto the Lord: I forced myself therefore, and offered a burnt offering.

"And Samuel said to Saul, Thou hast done foolishly: thou hast not kept the commandment of the Lord thy God, which He commanded thee: for now would the Lord have established thy kingdom upon Israel forever. But now thy kingdom shall not continue: the Lord hath sought Him a man after His own heart, and the Lord hath commanded him to be captain over His people. . . . And Samuel arose, and gat him up from Gilgal unto Gibeah of Benjamin."

Either Israel must cease to be the people of God, or the principle upon which the monarchy was founded must be maintained, and the nation must be governed by a divine power. If Israel would be wholly the Lord's, if the will of the human and earthly were held in subjection to the will of God, He would continue to be the Ruler of Israel. So long as the king and the people would conduct themselves as subordinate to God, so long He could be their defense. But in Israel no monarchy could prosper that did not in all things acknowledge the supreme authority of God.

If Saul had shown a regard for the requirements of God in this time of trial, God could have worked His will through him. His failure now proved him unfit to be the vicegerent of God to His people. He would mislead Israel. His will, rather than the will of God, would be the controlling power. If Saul had been faithful, his kingdom would have been established forever; but since he had failed, the purpose of God must be accomplished by another. The government of Israel must be committed to one who would rule the people according to the will of Heaven.

We do not know what great interests may be at stake in the proving of God. There is no safety except in strict obedience to the word of God. All His promises are made upon condition of faith and obedience, and a failure to comply with His commands cuts off the fulfillment to us of the rich provisions of the Scriptures. We should not follow impulse, nor rely on the judgment of men; we should look to the revealed will of God and walk according to His definite commandment, no matter what circumstances may surround us. God will take care of the results; by faithfulness to His word we may in time of trial prove before men and angels that the Lord can trust us in difficult places to carry out His will, honor His name, and bless His people.

Saul was in disfavor with God, and yet unwilling to humble his heart in penitence. What he lacked in real piety he would try to make up by his zeal in the forms of religion. Saul was not ignorant of Israel's defeat when the ark of God was brought into the camp by Hophni and Phinehas; and yet, knowing all this, he determined to send for the sacred chest and its attendant priest. Could he by this means inspire confidence in the people, he hoped to reassemble his scattered army and give battle to the Philistines. He would now dispense with Samuel's presence and support, and thus free himself from the prophet's unwelcome criticisms and reproofs.

The Holy Spirit had been granted to Saul to enlighten his understanding and soften his heart. He had received faithful instruction and reproof from the prophet of God. And yet how great was his perversity! The history of Israel's first king presents a sad example of the power of early wrong habits. In his youth Saul did not love and fear God; and that impetuous spirit, not early trained to submission, was ever ready to rebel against divine authority. Those who in their youth cherish a sacred regard for the will of God, and who faithfully perform the duties of their position, will be prepared for higher service in afterlife. But men cannot for years pervert the powers that God has given them, and then, when they choose to change, find these powers fresh and free for an entirely opposite course.

Saul's efforts to arouse the people proved unavailing. Finding his force reduced to six hundred men, he left Gilgal and retired to the fortress at Geba, lately taken from the Philistines. This stronghold was on the south side of a deep, rugged valley, or gorge, a few miles north of the site of Jerusalem. On the north side of the same valley, at Michmash, the Philistine force lay encamped while detachments of troops went out in different directions to ravage the country.

God had permitted matters to be thus brought to a crisis that He might rebuke the perversity of Saul and teach His people a lesson of humility and faith. Because of Saul's sin in his presumptuous offering, the Lord would not give him the honor of vanquishing the Philistines. Jonathan, the king's son, a man who feared the Lord, was chosen as the instrument to deliver Israel. Moved by a divine impulse, he proposed to his armor-bearer that they should make a secret attack upon the enemy's camp. "It may be," he urged, "that the Lord will work for us: for there is no restraint to the Lord to save by many or by few."

The armor-bearer, who also was a man of faith and prayer, encouraged the design, and together they withdrew from the camp, secretly, lest their purpose should be opposed. With earnest prayer to the Guide of their fathers, they agreed upon a sign by which they might determine how to proceed. Then passing down into the gorge separating the two armies, they silently threaded their way, under the shadow of the cliff, and partially concealed by the mounds and ridges of the valley. Approaching the Philistine fortress, they were revealed to the view of their enemies, who said, tauntingly, "Behold, the Hebrews come forth out of the holes where they had hid themselves," then challenged them, "Come up to us, and we will show you a thing," meaning that they would punish the two Israelites for their daring. This challenge was the token that Jonathan and his companion had agreed to accept as evidence that the Lord would prosper their undertaking. Passing now from the sight of the Philistines, and choosing a secret and difficult path, the warriors made their way to the summit of a cliff that had been deemed inaccessible, and was not very strongly guarded. Thus they penetrated the enemy's camp and slew the sentinels, who, overcome with surprise and fear, offered no resistance.

Angels of heaven shielded Jonathan and his attendant, angels fought by their side, and the Philistines fell before them. The earth trembled as though a great multitude with horsemen and chariots were approaching. Jonathan recognized the tokens of divine aid, and even the Philistines knew that God was working for the deliverance of Israel. Great fear seized upon the host, both in the field and in the garrison. In the confusion, mistaking their own soldiers for enemies, the Philistines began to slay one another.

624   Soon the noise of the battle was heard in the camp of Israel. The king's sentinels reported that there was great confusion among the Philistines, and that their numbers were decreasing. Yet it was not known that any part of the Hebrew army had left the camp. Upon inquiry it was found that none were absent except Jonathan and his armor-bearer. But seeing that the Philistines were meeting with a repulse, Saul led his army to join the assault. The Hebrews who had deserted to the enemy now turned against them; great numbers also came out of their hiding places, and as the Philistines fled, discomfited, Saul's army committed terrible havoc upon the fugitives.

Determined to make the most of his advantage, the king rashly forbade his soldiers to partake of food for the entire day, enforcing his command by the solemn imprecation, "Cursed be the man that eateth any food until evening, that I may be avenged on mine enemies." The victory had already been gained, without Saul's knowledge or co-operation, but he hoped to distinguish himself by the utter destruction of the vanquished army. The command to refrain from food was prompted by selfish ambition, and it showed the king to be indifferent to the needs of his people when these conflicted with his desire for self-exaltation. To confirm his prohibition by a solemn oath showed Saul to be both rash and profane. The very words of the curse give evidence that Saul's zeal was for himself, and not for the honor of God. He declared his object to be, not "that the Lord may be avenged on *His* enemies," but "that *I* may be avenged on *mine* enemies."

The prohibition resulted in leading the people to transgress the command of God. They had been engaged in warfare all day, and were faint for want of food; and as soon as the hours of restriction were over, they fell upon the spoil and devoured the flesh with the blood, thus vio-lating the law that forbade the eating of blood.

During the day's battle Jonathan, who had not heard of the king's command, unwittingly offended by eating a little honey as he passed through a wood. Saul learned of this at evening. He had declared that the violation of his edict should be punished with death; and though Jonathan had not been guilty of a willful sin, though God had miraculously preserved his life and had wrought deliverance through him, the king declared that the sentence must be execut-ed. To spare the life of his son would have been 625 an acknowledgment on the part of Saul that he had sinned in making so rash a vow. This would have been humiliating to his pride. "God do so, and more also," was his terrible sentence: "thou shalt surely die, Jonathan."

Saul could not claim the honor of the victory, but he hoped to be honored for his zeal in main-taining the sacredness of his oath. Even at the sacrifice of his son, he would impress upon his subjects the fact that the royal authority must be maintained. At Gilgal, but a short time before, Saul had presumed to officiate as priest, con-trary to the command of God. When reproved by Samuel, he had stubbornly justified himself. Now, when his own command was disobeyed—though the command was unreasonable and had been violated through ignorance—the king and father sentenced his son to death.

The people refused to allow the sentence to be executed. Braving the anger of the king, they declared, "Shall Jonathan die, who hath wrought this great salvation in Israel? God for-bid: as the Lord liveth, there shall not one hair of his head fall to the ground; for he hath wrought with God this day." The proud monarch dared not disregard this unanimous verdict, and the life of Jonathan was preserved.

Saul could not but feel that his son was pre-ferred before him, both by the people and by the Lord. Jonathan's deliverance was a severe reproof to the king's rashness. He felt a presen-timent that his curses would return upon his own head. He did not longer continue the war with the Philistines, but returned to his home, moody and dissatisfied.

Those who are most ready to excuse or justify themselves in sin are often most severe in judg-ing and condemning others. Many, like Saul, bring upon themselves the displeasure of God, but they reject counsel and despise reproof. Even when convinced that the Lord is not with them, they refuse to see in themselves the cause of their trouble. They cherish a proud, boastful spirit, while they indulge in cruel judgment or severe rebuke of others who are better than they. Well would it be for such self-constituted judges to ponder those words of Christ: "With what judgment ye judge, ye shall be judged: and with what measure ye mete, it shall be measured to you again." Matthew 7:2.

Often those who are seeking to exalt themselves are brought into positions where their true character is revealed. So it was in the case of Saul. His own course convinced the people that kingly honor and authority were dearer to him than justice, mercy, or benevolence. Thus the people were led to see their error in rejecting the government that God had given them. They had exchanged the pious prophet, whose prayers had brought down blessings, for a king who in his blind zeal had prayed for a curse upon them.

Had not the men of Israel interposed to save the life of Jonathan, their deliverer would have perished by the king's decree. With what misgivings must that people afterward have followed Saul's guidance! How bitter the thought that he had been placed upon the throne by their own act! The Lord bears long with the waywardness of men, and to all He grants opportunity to see and forsake their sins; but while He may seem to prosper those who disregard His will and despise His warnings, He will, in His own time, surely make manifest their folly.

61

Saul Rejected

Saul had failed to bear the test of faith in the trying situation at Gilgal, and had brought dishonor upon the service of God; but his errors were not yet irretrievable, and the Lord would grant him another opportunity to learn the lesson of unquestioning faith in His word and obedience to His commands.

When reproved by the prophet at Gilgal, Saul saw no great sin in the course he had pursued. He felt that he had been treated unjustly, and endeavored to vindicate his actions and offered excuses for his error. From that time he had little intercourse with the prophet. Samuel loved Saul as his own son, while Saul, bold and ardent in temper, had held the prophet in high regard; but he resented Samuel's rebuke, and thenceforth avoided him so far as possible.

But the Lord sent His servant with another message to Saul. By obedience he might still prove his fidelity to God and his worthiness to walk before Israel. Samuel came to the king and delivered the word of the Lord. That the monarch might realize the importance of heeding the command, Samuel expressly declared that he spoke by divine direction, by the same authority that had called Saul to the throne. The prophet said, "Thus saith the Lord of hosts, I remember that which Amalek did to Israel, how he laid wait for him in the way, when he came up from Egypt. Now go and smite Amalek, and utterly destroy all that they have, and spare them not; but slay both man and woman, infant and

suckling, ox and sheep, camel and ass." The Amalekites had been the first to make war upon Israel in the wilderness; and for this sin, together with their defiance of God and their debasing idolatry, the Lord, through Moses, had pronounced sentence upon them. By divine direction the history of their cruelty toward Israel had been recorded, with the command, "Thou shalt blot out the remembrance of Amalek from under heaven; thou shalt not forget it." Deuteronomy 25:19. For four hundred years the execution of this sentence had been deferred; but the Amalekites had not turned from their sins. The Lord knew that this wicked people would, if it were possible, blot out His people and His worship from the earth. Now the time had come for the sentence, so long delayed, to be executed.

The forbearance that God has exercised toward the wicked, emboldens men in transgression; but their punishment will be none the less certain and terrible for being long delayed. "The Lord shall rise up as in Mount Perazim, He shall be wroth as in the valley of Gibeon, that He may do His work, His strange work; and bring to pass His act, His strange act." Isaiah 28:21. To our merciful God the act of punishment is a strange act. "As I live, saith the Lord God, I have no pleasure in the death of the wicked; but that the wicked turn from his way and live." Ezekiel 33:11. The Lord is "merciful and gracious, long-suffering, and abundant in goodness and truth, . . . forgiving iniquity and transgression and sin." Yet He will "by no means clear the guilty." Exodus 34:6, 7. While He does not delight in vengeance, He will execute judgment upon the transgressors of His law. He is forced to do this, to preserve the inhabitants of the earth from utter depravity and ruin. In order to save some He must cut off those who have become hardened in sin. "The Lord is slow to anger, and great in power, and will not at all acquit the wicked." Nahum 1:3. By terrible things in righteousness He will vindicate the authority of His downtrodden law. And the very fact of His reluctance to execute justice testifies to the enormity of the sins that call forth His judgments and to the severity of the retribution awaiting the transgressor.

But while inflicting judgment, God remembered mercy. The Amalekites were to be destroyed, but the Kenites, who dwelt among them, were spared. This people, though not wholly free from idolatry, were worshipers of God and were friendly to Israel. Of this tribe was the brother-in-law of Moses, Hobab, who had accompanied the Israelites in their travels through the wilderness, and by his knowledge of the country had rendered them valuable assistance.

Since the defeat of the Philistines at Michmash, Saul had made war against Moab,

629 Ammon, and Edom, and against the Amalekites and the Philistines; and wherever he turned his arms, he gained fresh victories. On receiving the commission against the Amalekites, he at once proclaimed war. To his own authority was added that of the prophet, and at the call to battle the men of Israel flocked to his standard. The expedition was not to be entered upon for the purpose of self-aggrandizement; the Israelites were not to receive either the honor of the conquest or the spoils of their enemies. They were to engage in the war solely as an act of obedience to God, for the purpose of executing His judgment upon the Amalekites. God intended that all nations should behold the doom of that people that had defied His sovereignty, and should mark that they were destroyed by the very people whom they had despised.

"Saul smote the Amalekites from Havilah until thou comest to Shur, that is over against Egypt. And he took Agag the king of the Amalekites alive, and utterly destroyed all the people with the edge of the sword. But Saul and the people spared Agag, and the best of the sheep, and of the oxen, and of the fatlings, and the lambs, and all that was good, and would not utterly destroy them: but everything that was vile and refuse, that they destroyed utterly."

This victory over the Amalekites was the most brilliant victory that Saul had ever gained, and it served to rekindle the pride of heart that was his greatest peril. The divine edict devoting the enemies of God to utter destruction was but partially fulfilled. Ambitious to heighten the honor of his triumphal return by the presence of a royal captive, Saul ventured to imitate the customs of the nations around him and spared Agag, the fierce and warlike king of the Amalekites. The people reserved for themselves the finest of the flocks, herds, and beasts of burden, excusing their sin on the ground that the cattle were reserved to be offered as sacrifices to the Lord. It was their purpose, however, to use these merely as a substitute, to save their own cattle.

Saul had now been subjected to the final test. His presumptuous disregard of the will of God, showing his determination to rule as an independent monarch, proved that he could not be trusted with royal power as the vicegerent of the Lord. While Saul and his army were marching home in the flush of victory, there was deep anguish in the home of Samuel the prophet. He had received a message from the Lord denounc-

630 ing the course of the king: "It repenteth Me that I have set up Saul to be king: for he is turned back from following Me, and hath not performed My commandments." The prophet was deeply grieved over the course of the rebellious king, and he wept and prayed all night for a reversing of the terrible sentence.

God's repentance is not like man's repen-tance. "The Strength of Israel will not lie nor repent: for He is not a man, that He should repent." Man's repentance implies a change of mind. God's repentance implies a change of circumstances and relations. Man may change his relation to God by complying with the conditions upon which he may be brought into the divine favor, or he may, by his own action, place himself outside the favoring condition; but the Lord is the same "yesterday, and today, and forever." Hebrews 13:8. Saul's disobedience changed his relation to God; but the conditions of acceptance with God were unaltered—God's requirements were still the same, for with Him there "is no variableness, neither shadow of turning." James 1:17.

With an aching heart the prophet set forth the next morning to meet the erring king. Samuel cherished a hope that, upon reflection, Saul might become conscious of his sin, and by repentance and humiliation be again restored to the divine favor. But when the first step is taken in the path of transgression the way becomes easy. Saul, debased by his disobedience, came to meet Samuel with a lie upon his lips. He exclaimed, "Blessed be thou of the Lord: I have performed the commandment of the Lord."

The sounds that fell on the prophet's ears disproved the statement of the disobedient king. To the pointed question, "What meaneth then this bleating of the sheep in mine ears, and the lowing of the oxen which I hear?" Saul made answer, "They have brought them from the Amalekites: for the people spared the best of the sheep and of the oxen, to sacrifice unto the Lord thy God; and the rest we have utterly destroyed." The people had obeyed Saul's directions; but in order to shield himself, he was willing to charge upon them the sin of his disobedience.

The message of Saul's rejection brought unspeakable grief to the heart of Samuel. It had to be delivered before the whole army of Israel, when they were filled with pride and triumphal rejoicing over a victory that was accredited to the valor and generalship of their king, for Saul 631 had not associated God with the success of Israel in this conflict; but when the prophet saw the evidence of Saul's rebellion, he was stirred with indignation that he, who had been so highly favored of God, should transgress the commandment of Heaven and lead Israel into sin. Samuel was not deceived by the subterfuge of the king. With mingled grief and indignation he declared, "Stay, and I will tell thee what the Lord hath said to me this night. . . . When thou wast little in thine own sight, wast thou not made the head of the tribes of Israel, and the Lord anointed thee king over Israel?" He repeated the command of the Lord concerning Amalek, and demanded the reason of the king's disobedience.

Saul persisted in self-justification: "Yea, I have obeyed the voice of the Lord, and have gone the way which the Lord sent me, and have brought Agag the king of Amalek, and have utterly destroyed the Amalekites. But the people took of the spoil, sheep and oxen, the chief of the things which should have been utterly destroyed, to sacrifice unto the Lord thy God in Gilgal."

In stern and solemn words the prophet swept away the refuge of lies and pronounced the irrevocable sentence: "Hath the Lord as great delight in burnt offerings and sacrifices, as in obeying the voice of the Lord? Behold, to obey is better than sacrifice, and to hearken than the fat of rams. For rebellion is as the sin of witchcraft, and stubbornness is as iniquity and idolatry. Because thou hast rejected the word of the Lord, He hath also rejected thee from being king."

As the king heard this fearful sentence he cried out, "I have sinned: for I have transgressed the commandment of the Lord, and thy words: because I feared the people, and obeyed their voice." Terrified by the denunciation of the prophet, Saul acknowledged his guilt, which he had before stubbornly denied; but he still persisted in casting blame upon the people, declaring that he had sinned through fear of them.

It was not sorrow for sin, but fear of its penalty, that actuated the king of Israel as he entreated Samuel, "I pray thee, pardon my sin, and turn again with me, that I may worship the Lord." If Saul had had true repentance, he would have made public confession of his sin; but it was his chief anxiety to maintain his authority and retain the allegiance of the people. He desired the honor of Samuel's presence in order to strengthen his own influence with the nation.

632   "I will not return with thee," was the answer of the prophet: "for thou hast rejected the word of the Lord, and the Lord hath rejected thee from being king over Israel." As Samuel turned to depart, the king, in an agony of fear, laid hold of his mantle to hold him back, but it rent in his hands. Upon this, the prophet declared, "The Lord hath rent the kingdom of Israel from thee this day, and hath given it to a neighbor of thine, that is better than thou."

Saul was more disturbed by the alienation of Samuel than by the displeasure of God. He knew that the people had greater confidence in the prophet than in himself. Should another by divine command be now anointed king, Saul felt that it would be impossible to maintain his own authority. He feared an immediate revolt should Samuel utterly forsake him. Saul entreated the prophet to honor him before the elders and the people by publicly uniting with him in a religious service. By divine direction Samuel yielded to the king's request, that no occasion might be given for a revolt. But he remained only as a silent witness of the service.

An act of justice, stern and terrible, was yet to be performed. Samuel must publicly vindicate the honor of God and rebuke the course of Saul. He commanded that the king of the Amalekites be brought before him. Above all who had fallen by the sword of Israel, Agag was the most guilty and merciless; one who had hated and sought to destroy the people of God, and whose influence had been strongest to promote idolatry. He came at the prophet's command, flattering himself that the danger of death was past. Samuel declared: "As thy sword hath made women childless, so shall thy mother be childless among women. And Samuel hewed Agag in pieces before the Lord." This done, Samuel returned to his home at Ramah, Saul to his at Gibeah. Only once thereafter did the prophet and the king ever meet each other.

When called to the throne, Saul had a humble opinion of his own capabilities, and was willing to be instructed. He was deficient in knowledge and experience and had serious defects of character. But the Lord granted him the Holy Spirit as a guide and helper, and placed him in a position where he could develop the qualities requisite for a ruler of Israel. Had he remained humble, seeking constantly to be guided by divine wisdom, he would have been enabled to discharge the duties of his high position with success and honor. Under the influence of divine grace every good quality would have been gaining strength, while evil tendencies would have lost their power. This is the work which the Lord proposes to do for all who consecrate themselves to Him. There are many whom He has called to positions in His work because they have a humble and teachable spirit. In His providence He places them where they may learn of Him. He will reveal to them their defects of character, and to all who seek His aid He will give strength to correct their errors.

But Saul presumed upon his exaltation, and dishonored God by unbelief and disobedience. Though when first called to the throne he was humble and self-distrustful, success made him self-confident. The very first victory of his reign had kindled that pride of heart which was his greatest danger. The valor and military skill displayed in the deliverance of Jabesh-gilead had roused the enthusiasm of the whole nation. The people honored their king, forgetting that he was but the agent by whom God had wrought; and though at first Saul ascribed the glory to God, he afterward took honor to himself. He lost sight of his dependence upon God, and in heart departed from the Lord. Thus the way was prepared for his sin of presumption and sacrilege at Gilgal. The same blind self-confidence led him to reject Samuel's reproof. Saul acknowledged Samuel to be a prophet sent from God; hence he should have accepted the reproof, though he could not himself see that he had sinned. Had he been willing to see and confess his error, this bitter experience would have proved a safeguard for the future.

If the Lord had then separated Himself entirely from Saul, He would not have again spoken to him through His prophet, entrusting him with a definite work to perform, that he might correct the errors of the past. When one who professes to be a child of God becomes careless in doing His will, thereby influencing others to be irreverent and unmindful of the Lord's injunctions, it is still possible for his failures to be turned into victories if he will but accept reproof with true contrition of soul and return to God in humility and faith. The humiliation of defeat often proves a blessing by showing us our inability to do the will of God without His aid.

When Saul turned away from the reproof sent 634 him by God's Holy Spirit, and persisted in his stubborn self-justification, he rejected the only means by which God could work to save him from himself. He had willfully separated himself from God. He could not receive divine help or guidance until he should return to God by confession of his sin.

At Gilgal, Saul had made an appearance of great conscientiousness, as he stood before the army of Israel offering up a sacrifice to God. But his piety was not genuine. A religious service performed in direct opposition to the command of God only served to weaken Saul's hands, placing him beyond the help that God was so willing to grant him.

In his expedition against Amalek, Saul thought he had done all that was essential of that which the Lord had commanded him; but the Lord was not pleased with partial obedience, nor willing to pass over what had been neglected through so plausible a motive. God has given men no liberty to depart from His requirements. The Lord had declared to Israel, "Ye shall not do . . . every man whatsoever is right in his own eyes;" but ye shall "observe and hear all these words which I command thee." Deuteronomy 12:8, 28. In deciding upon any course of action we are not to ask whether we can see that harm will result from it, but whether it is in keeping with the will of God. "There is a way which seemeth right unto a man; but the end thereof are the ways of death." Proverbs 14:12.

"To obey is better than sacrifice." The sacrificial offerings were in themselves of no value in the sight of God. They were designed to express on the part of the offerer penitence for sin and faith in Christ and to pledge future obedience to the law of God. But without penitence, faith, and an obedient heart, the offerings were worthless. When, in direct violation of God's command, Saul proposed to present a sacrifice of that which God had devoted to destruction, open contempt was shown for the divine authority.

The service would have been an insult to Heaven. Yet with the sin of Saul and its result before us, how many are pursuing a similar course. While they refuse to believe and obey some requirement of the Lord, they persevere in offering up to God their formal services of religion. There is no response of the Spirit of God to such service. No matter how zealous men may be in their observance of religious ceremonies, the Lord cannot accept them if they persist in willful violation of one of His commands.

"Rebellion is as the sin of witchcraft, and stubbornness is as iniquity and idolatry." Rebellion 635 originated with Satan, and all rebellion against God is directly due to satanic influence. Those who set themselves against the government of God have entered into an alliance with the archapostate, and he will exercise his power and cunning to captivate the senses and mislead the understanding. He will cause everything to appear in a false light. Like our first parents, those who are under his bewitching spell see only the great benefits to be received by transgression.

No stronger evidence can be given of Satan's delusive power than that many who are thus led by him deceive themselves with the belief that they are in the service of God. When Korah, Dathan, and Abiram rebelled against the authority of Moses, they thought they were opposing only a human leader, a man like themselves; and they came to believe that they were verily doing God service. But in rejecting God's chosen instrument they rejected Christ; they insulted the Spirit of God. So, in the days of Christ, the Jewish scribes and elders, who professed great zeal for the honor of God, crucified His Son. The same spirit still exists in the hearts of those who set themselves to follow their own will in opposition to the will of God.

Saul had had the most ample proof that Samuel was divinely inspired. His venturing to disregard the command of God through the prophet was against the dictates of reason and sound judgment. His fatal presumption must be attributed to satanic sorcery. Saul had manifested great zeal in suppressing idolatry and witchcraft; yet in his disobedience to the divine command he had been actuated by the same spirit of opposition to God and had been as really inspired by Satan as are those who practice sorcery; and when reproved, he had added stubbornness to rebellion. He could have offered no greater insult to the Spirit of God had he openly united with idolaters.

It is a perilous step to slight the reproofs and warnings of God's word or of His Spirit. Many, like Saul, yield to temptation until they become blind to the true character of sin. They flatter themselves that they have had some good object in view, and have done no wrong in departing from the Lord's requirements. Thus they do despite to the Spirit of grace, until its voice is no longer heard, and they are left to the delusions which they have chosen.

636   In Saul, God had given to Israel a king after their own heart, as Samuel said when the kingdom was confirmed to Saul at Gilgal, "Behold the king whom ye have chosen, and whom ye have desired." 1 Samuel 12:13. Comely in person, of noble stature and princely bearing, his appearance accorded with their conceptions of royal dignity; and his personal valor and his ability in the conduct of armies were the qualities which they regarded as best calculated to secure respect and honor from other nations. They felt little solicitude that their king should possess those higher qualities which alone could fit him to rule with justice and equity. They did not ask for one who had true nobility of character, who possessed the love and fear of God. They had not sought counsel from God as to the qualities a ruler should possess, in order to preserve their distinctive, holy character as His chosen people. They were not seeking God's way, but their own way. Therefore God gave them such a king as they desired—one whose character was a reflection of their own. Their hearts were not in submission to God, and their king also was unsubdued by divine grace. Under the rule of this king they would obtain the experience necessary in order that they might see their error, and return to their allegiance to God.

Yet the Lord, having placed on Saul the responsibility of the kingdom, did not leave him to himself. He caused the Holy Spirit to rest upon Saul to reveal to him his own weakness and his need of divine grace; and had Saul relied upon God, God would have been with him. So long as his will was controlled by the will of God, so long as he yielded to the discipline of His Spirit, God could crown his efforts with success. But when Saul chose to act independently of God, the Lord could no longer be his guide, and was forced to set him aside. Then He called to the throne "a man after His own heart" (1 Samuel 13:14)—not one who was faultless in character, but who, instead of trusting to himself, would rely upon God, and be guided by His Spirit; who, when he sinned, would submit to reproof and correction.

637

62

The Anointing of David

A few miles south of Jerusalem, "the city of the great King," is Bethlehem, where David, the son of Jesse, was born more than a thousand years before the infant Jesus was cradled in the manger and worshiped by the Wise Men from the East. Centuries before the advent of the Saviour, David, in the freshness of boyhood, kept

This chapter is based on 1 Samuel 16:1-13.

watch of his flocks as they grazed on the hills surrounding Bethlehem. The simple shepherd boy sang the songs of his own composing, and the music of his harp made a sweet accompaniment to the melody of his fresh young voice. The Lord had chosen David, and was preparing him, in his solitary life with his flocks, for the work He designed to commit to his trust in after years.

While David was thus living in the retirement of his humble shepherd's life, the Lord God was speaking about him to the prophet Samuel. "And the Lord said unto Samuel, How long wilt thou mourn for Saul, seeing I have rejected him from reigning over Israel? fill thine horn with oil, and go, I will send thee to Jesse the Bethlehemite: for I have provided Me a king among his sons. . . . Take an heifer with thee, and say, I am come to sacrifice to the Lord. And call Jesse to the sacrifice, and I will show thee what thou shalt do: and thou shalt anoint unto Me him whom I name unto thee. And Samuel did that which the Lord spake, and came to Bethlehem. And the elders of the town trembled at his coming, and said, Comest thou peaceably? And he said, Peaceably." The elders accepted an invitation to the sacrifice, and Samuel called also Jesse and his sons. The altar was built and the sacrifice was ready. All the household of Jesse were present, with the exception of David, the youngest son, who had been left to guard the sheep, for it was not safe to leave the flocks unprotected.

When the sacrifice was ended, and before partaking of the offering feast, Samuel began his prophetic inspection of the noble-appearing sons of Jesse. Eliab was the eldest, and more nearly resembled Saul for stature and beauty than the others. His comely features and finely developed form attracted the attention of the prophet. As Samuel looked upon his princely bearing, he thought, "This is indeed the man whom God has chosen as successor to Saul," and he waited for the divine sanction that he might anoint him. But Jehovah did not look upon the outward appearance. Eliab did not fear the Lord. Had he been called to the throne, he would have been a proud, exacting ruler. The Lord's word to Samuel was, "Look not on his countenance, or on the height of his stature; because I have refused him: for the Lord seeth not as man seeth; for man looketh on the outward appearance, but the Lord looketh on the heart." No outward beauty can recommend the soul to God. The wisdom and excellence revealed in the character and deportment, express the true beauty of the man; and it is the inner worth, the excellency of the heart, that determines our acceptance with the Lord of hosts. How deeply should we feel this truth in the judgment of ourselves and others. We may learn from the mistake of Samuel how vain is the estimation that rests on beauty of face or nobility of stature. We may see how incapable is man's wisdom of understanding the secrets of

638

the heart or of comprehending the counsels of God without special enlightenment from heaven. The thoughts and ways of God in relation to His creatures are above our finite minds; but we may be assured that His children will be brought to fill the very place for which they are qualified, and will be enabled to accomplish the very work committed to their hands, if they will but submit their will to God, that His beneficent plans may not be frustrated by the perversity of man.

Eliab passed from the inspection of Samuel, and the six brothers who were in attendance at the service followed in succession to be observed by the prophet; but the Lord did not signify His choice of any one of them. With painful suspense Samuel had looked upon the last of the young men; the prophet was perplexed and bewildered. He inquired of Jesse, "Are here all thy children?" The father answered, "There remaineth yet the youngest, and behold, he keepeth the sheep." Samuel directed that he should be summoned, saying, "We will not sit down till he come hither."

641 The lonely shepherd was startled by the unexpected call of the messenger, who announced that the prophet had come to Bethlehem and had sent for him. With surprise he questioned why the prophet and judge of Israel should desire to see him; but without delay he obeyed the call. "Now he was ruddy, and withal of a beautiful countenance, and goodly to look to." As Samuel beheld with pleasure the handsome, manly, modest shepherd boy, the voice of the Lord spoke to the prophet, saying, "Arise, anoint him: for this is he." David had proved himself brave and faithful in the humble office of a shepherd, and now God had chosen him to be captain of His people. "Then Samuel took the horn of oil, and anointed him in the midst of [from among] his brethren: and the Spirit of the Lord came upon David from that day forward." The prophet had accomplished his appointed work, and with a relieved heart he returned to Ramah.

Samuel had not made known his errand, even to the family of Jesse, and the ceremony of anointing David had been performed in secret. It was an intimation to the youth of the high destiny awaiting him, that amid all the varied experiences and perils of his coming years, this knowledge might inspire him to be true to the purpose of God to be accomplished by his life.

The great honor conferred upon David did not serve to elate him. Notwithstanding the high position which he was to occupy, he quietly continued his employment, content to await the development of the Lord's plans in His own time and way. As humble and modest as before his anointing, the shepherd boy returned to the hills and watched and guarded his flocks as tenderly as ever. But with new inspiration he composed his melodies and played upon his harp. Before him spread a landscape of rich and varied beauty.

The vines, with their clustering fruit, brightened in the sunshine. The forest trees, with their green foliage, swayed in the breeze. He beheld the sun flooding the heavens with light, coming forth as a bridegroom out of his chamber and rejoicing as a strong man to run a race. There were the bold summits of the hills reaching toward the sky; in the faraway distance rose the barren cliffs of the mountain wall of Moab; above all spread the tender blue of the overarching heavens. And beyond was God. He could not see Him, but His works were full of His praise. The light of day, gilding forest and mountain, meadow and stream, carried the mind up to behold the Father of lights, the Author of every good and perfect gift. Daily rev- 642 elations of the character and majesty of his Creator filled the young poet's heart with adoration and rejoicing. In contemplation of God and His works the faculties of David's mind and heart were developing and strengthening for the work of his afterlife. He was daily coming into a more intimate communion with God. His mind was constantly penetrating into new depths for fresh themes to inspire his song and to wake the music of his harp. The rich melody of his voice poured out upon the air, echoed from the hills as if responsive to the rejoicing of the angels' songs in heaven.

Who can measure the results of those years of toil and wandering among the lonely hills? The communion with nature and with God, the care of his flocks, the perils and deliverances, the griefs and joys, of his lowly lot, were not only to mold the character of David and to influence his future life, but through the psalms of Israel's sweet singer they were in all coming ages to kindle love and faith in the hearts of God's people, bringing them nearer to the ever-loving heart of Him in whom all His creatures live.

David, in the beauty and vigor of his young manhood, was preparing to take a high position with the noblest of the earth. His talents, as precious gifts from God, were employed to extol the glory of the divine Giver. His opportunities of contemplation and meditation served to enrich him with that wisdom and piety that made him beloved of God and angels. As he contemplated the perfections of his Creator, clearer conceptions of God opened before his soul. Obscure themes were illuminated, difficulties were made plain, perplexities were harmonized, and each ray of new light called forth fresh bursts of rapture, and sweeter anthems of devotion, to the glory of God and the Redeemer. The love that moved him, the sorrows that beset him, the triumphs that attended his active thought; and as he beheld the love of God in all the providences of his life, his heart throbbed with more fervent adoration and gratitude, his voice rang out in a richer melody, his harp was swept with more exultant joy; and the shepherd boy proceeded from strength to strength, from knowledge to knowledge; for the Spirit of the Lord was upon him.

63

David and Goliath

When King Saul realized that he had been rejected by God, and when he felt the force of the words of denunciation that had been addressed to him by the prophet, he was filled with bitter rebellion and despair. It was not true repentance that had bowed the proud head of the king. He had no clear perception of the offensive character of his sin, and did not arouse to the work of reforming his life, but brooded over what he thought was the injustice of God in depriving him of the throne of Israel and in taking the succession away from his posterity. He was ever occupied in anticipating the ruin that had been brought upon his house. He felt that the valor which he had displayed in encountering his enemies should offset his sin of disobedience. He did not accept with meekness the chastisement of God; but his haughty spirit became desperate, until he was on the verge of losing his reason. His counselors advised him to seek for the services of a skillful musician, in the hope that the soothing notes of a sweet instrument might calm his troubled spirit. In the providence of God, David, as a skillful performer upon the harp, was brought before the king. His lofty and heaven-inspired strains had the desired effect. The brooding melancholy that had settled like a dark cloud over the mind of Saul was charmed away.

When his services were not required at the court of Saul, David returned to his flocks among the hills and continued to maintain his simplicity of spirit and demeanor. Whenever it was necessary, he was recalled to minister before the king, to soothe the mind of the troubled monarch till the evil spirit should depart from him. But although Saul expressed delight in David and his music, the young shepherd went from the king's house to the fields and hills of his pasture with a sense of relief and gladness.

David was growing in favor with God and man. He had been instructed in the way of the Lord, and he now set his heart more fully to do the will of God than ever before. He had new themes for thought. He had been in the court of the king and had seen the responsibilities of royalty. He had discovered some of the temptations that beset the soul of Saul and had penetrated some of the mysteries in the character and dealings of Israel's first king. He had seen the glory of royalty shadowed with a dark cloud of sorrow, and he knew that the household of Saul, in

their private life, were far from happy. All these things served to bring troubled thoughts to him who had been anointed to be king over Israel. But while he was absorbed in deep meditation, and harassed by thoughts of anxiety, he turned to his harp, and called forth strains that elevated his mind to the Author of every good, and the dark clouds that seemed to shadow the horizon of the future were dispelled.

God was teaching David lessons of trust. As Moses was trained for his work, so the Lord was fitting the son of Jesse to become the guide of His chosen people. In his watchcare for his flocks, he was gaining an appreciation of the care that the Great Shepherd has for the sheep of His pasture.

The lonely hills and the wild ravines where David wandered with his flocks were the lurking place of beasts of prey. Not infrequently the lion from the thickets by the Jordan, or the bear from his lair among the hills, came, fierce with hunger, to attack the flocks. According to the custom of his time, David was armed only with his sling and shepherd's staff; yet he early gave proof of his strength and courage in protecting his charge. Afterward describing these encounters, he said: "When there came a lion, or a bear, and took a lamb out of the flock, I went out after him, and smote him, and delivered it out of his mouth: and when he arose against me, I caught him by his beard, and smote him, and slew him." 1 Samuel 17:34, 35, R.V. His experience in these matters proved the heart of David and developed in him courage and fortitude and faith.

Even before he was summoned to the court of Saul, David had distinguished himself by deeds of valor. The officer who brought him to the notice of the king declared him to be "a mighty valiant man, and a man of war, and prudent in matters," and he said, "The Lord is with him."

When war was declared by Israel against the Philistines, three of the sons of Jesse joined the army under Saul; but David remained at home. After a time, however, he went to visit the camp of Saul. By his father's direction he was to carry a message and a gift to his elder brothers and to learn if they were still in safety and health. But, unknown to Jesse, the youthful shepherd had been entrusted with a higher mission. The armies of Israel were in peril, and David had been directed by an angel to save his people.

As David drew near to the army, he heard the sound of commotion, as if an engagement was about to begin. And "the host was going forth to the fight, and shouted for the battle." Israel and the Philistines were drawn up in array, army against army. David ran to the army, and came and saluted his brothers. While he was talking with them, Goliath, the champion of the Philistines, came forth, and with insulting language defied Israel and challenged them to provide a man from their ranks who would meet

This chapter is based on 1 Samuel 16:14-23; 17.

him in single combat. He repeated his challenge, and when David saw that all Israel were filled with fear, and learned that the Philistine's defiance was hurled at them day after day, without arousing a champion to silence the boaster, his spirit was stirred within him. He was fired with zeal to preserve the honor of the living God and the credit of His people.

The armies of Israel were depressed. Their courage failed. They said one to another, "Have ye seen this man that is come up? surely to defy Israel is he come up." In shame and indignation, David exclaimed, "Who is this uncircumcised Philistine, that he should defy the armies of the living God?"

Eliab, David's eldest brother, when he heard these words, knew well the feelings that were stirring the young man's soul. Even as a shepherd, David had manifested daring, courage, and strength but rarely witnessed; and the mysterious visit of Samuel to their father's house, and his silent departure, had awakened in the minds of the brothers suspicions of the real object of his visit. Their jealousy had been aroused as they saw David honored above them, and they did not regard him with the respect and love due to his integrity and brotherly tenderness. They looked upon him as merely a stripling shepherd, and now the question which he asked was regarded by Eliab as a censure upon his own cowardice in making no attempt to silence the giant of the Philistines. The elder brother exclaimed angrily, 646 "Why camest thou down hither? and with whom hast thou left those few sheep in the wilderness? I know thy pride, and the naughtiness of thine heart; for thou art come down that thou mightest see the battle." David's answer was respectful but decided: "What have I now done? Is there not a cause?"

The words of David were repeated to the king, who summoned the youth before him. Saul listened with astonishment to the words of the shepherd, as he said, "Let no man's heart fail because of him; thy servant will go and fight with this Philistine." Saul strove to turn David from his purpose, but the young man was not to be moved. He replied in a simple, unassuming way, relating his experiences while guarding his father's flocks. And he said, "The Lord that delivered me out of the paw of the lion, and out of the paw of the bear, He will deliver me out of the hand of this Philistine. And Saul said unto David, Go, and the Lord be with thee."

For forty days the host of Israel had trembled before the haughty challenge of the Philistine giant. Their hearts failed within them as they looked upon his massive form, in height measuring six cubits and a span. Upon his head was a helmet of brass, he was clothed with a coat of mail that weighed five thousand shekels, and he had greaves of brass upon his legs. The coat was made of plates of brass that overlaid one another, like the scales of a fish, and they were so closely joined that no dart or arrow could possibly penetrate the armor. At his back the giant bore a huge javelin, or lance, also of brass. "The staff of his spear was like a weaver's beam; and his spear's head weighed six hundred shekels of iron; and one bearing a shield went before him."

Morning and evening Goliath had approached the camp of Israel, saying with a loud voice, "Why are ye come out to set your battle in array? am not I a Philistine, and ye servants to Saul? choose you a man for you, and let him come down to me. If he be able to fight with me, and to kill me, then will we be your servants: but if I prevail against him, and kill him, then shall ye be our servants, and serve us. And the Philistine said, I defy the armies of Israel this day; give me a man, that we may fight together."

Though Saul had given David permission to accept Goliath's challenge, the king had small hope that David would be successful in his 647 courageous undertaking. Command was given to clothe the youth in the king's own armor. The heavy helmet of brass was put upon his head, and the coat of mail was placed upon his body; the monarch's sword was at his side. Thus equipped, he started upon his errand, but erelong began to retrace his steps. The first thought in the minds of the anxious spectators was that David had decided not to risk his life in meeting an antagonist in so unequal an encounter. But this was far from the thought of the brave young man. When he returned to Saul he begged permission to lay aside the heavy armor, saying, "I cannot go with these; for I have not proved them." He laid off the king's armor, and in its stead took only his staff in his hand, with his shepherd's scrip and a simple sling. Choosing five smooth stones out of the brook, he put them in his bag, and, with his sling in his hand, drew near to the Philistine. The giant strode boldly forward, expecting to meet the mightiest of the warriors of Israel. His armor-bearer walked before him, and he looked as if nothing could withstand him. As he came nearer to David he saw but a stripling, called a boy because of his youth. David's countenance was ruddy with health, and his well-knit form, unprotected by armor, was displayed to advantage; yet between its youthful outline and the massive proportions of the Philistine, there was a marked contrast.

Goliath was filled with amazement and anger. "Am I a dog," he exclaimed, "that thou comest to me with staves?" Then he poured upon David the most terrible curses by all the gods of his knowledge. He cried in derision, "Come to me, and I will give thy flesh unto the fowls of the air, and to the beasts of the field."

David did not weaken before the champion of the Philistines. Stepping forward, he said to his antagonist: "Thou comest to me with a sword, and with a spear, and with a shield: but I come to thee in the name of the Lord of hosts, the God of the armies of Israel, whom thou hast defied. This day will the Lord deliver thee into mine hand; and I will smite thee, and take thine head from thee; and I will give the carcasses of the host of the Philistines this day unto the fowls of the air, and to the wild beasts of the earth; that all the earth may know that there is a God in Israel. And all this assembly shall know that the Lord saveth not with sword and spear: for the battle is the Lord's, and He will give you into our hands."

648   There was a ring of fearlessness in his tone, a look of triumph and rejoicing upon his fair countenance. This speech, given in a clear, musical voice, rang out on the air, and was distinctly heard by the listening thousands marshaled for war. The anger of Goliath was roused to the very highest heat. In his rage he pushed up the helmet that protected his forehead and rushed forward to wreak vengeance upon his opponent. The son of Jesse was preparing for his foe. "And it came to pass, when the Philistine arose, and came and drew nigh to meet David, that David hasted, and ran toward the army to meet the Philistine. And David put his hand in his bag, and took thence a stone, and slang it, and smote the Philistine in the forehead, that the stone sunk into his forehead; and he fell upon his face to the earth."

Amazement spread along the lines of the two armies. They had been confident that David would be slain; but when the stone went whizzing through the air, straight to the mark, they saw the mighty warrior tremble, and reach forth his hands, as if he were struck with sudden blindness. The giant reeled, and staggered, and like a smitten oak, fell to the ground. David did not wait an instant. He sprang upon the prostrate form of the Philistine, and with both hands laid hold of Goliath's heavy sword. A moment before, the giant had boasted that with it he would sever the youth's head from his shoulders and give his body to the fowls of the air. Now it was lifted in the air, and then the head of the boaster rolled from his trunk, and a shout of exultation went up from the camp of Israel.

The Philistines were smitten with terror, and the confusion which ensued resulted in a precipitate retreat. The shouts of the triumphant Hebrews echoed along the summits of the mountains, as they rushed after their fleeing enemies; and they "pursued the Philistines, until thou come to the valley, and to the gates of Ekron. And the wounded of the Philistines fell down by the way to Shaaraim, even unto Gath, and unto Ekron. And the children of Israel returned from chasing after the Philistines, and they spoiled their tents. And David took the

head of the Philistine, and brought it to Jerusalem; but he put his armor in his tent."

64

David a Fugitive

649

After the slaying of Goliath, Saul kept David with him, and would not permit him to return to his father's house. And it came to pass that "the soul of Jonathan was knit with the soul of David, and Jonathan loved him as his own soul." Jonathan and David made a covenant to be united as brethren, and the king's son "stripped himself of the robe that was upon him, and gave it to David, and his garments, even to his sword, and to his bow, and to his girdle." David was entrusted with important responsibilities, yet he preserved his modesty, and won the affection of the people as well as of the royal household.

"David went out whithersoever Saul sent him, and behaved himself wisely: and Saul set him over the men of war." David was prudent and faithful, and it was evident that the blessing of God was with him. Saul at times realized his own unfitness for the government of Israel, and he felt that the kingdom would be more secure if there could be connected with him one who received instruction from the Lord. Saul hoped also that his connection with David would be a safeguard to himself. Since David was favored and shielded by the Lord, his presence might be a protection to Saul when he went out with him to war.

It was the providence of God that had connected David with Saul. David's position at court would give him a knowledge of affairs, in preparation for his future greatness. It would enable him to gain the confidence of the nation. The vicissitudes and hardships which befell him, through the enmity of Saul, would lead him to feel his dependence upon God, and to put his whole trust in Him. And the friendship of Jonathan for David was also of God's providence, to preserve the life of the future ruler of Israel. In all these things God was working out His gracious purposes, both for David and for the people of Israel.

Saul, however, did not long remain friendly   650 to David. When Saul and David were returning from battle with the Philistines, "the women came out of all cities of Israel, singing and dancing, to meet King Saul, with tabrets, with joy, and with instruments of music." One company sang, "Saul hath slain his thousands," while another company took up the strain, and responded, "And David his ten thousands." The demon of jealousy entered the heart of the king. He was angry because David was exalted above himself in the song of the women of Israel. In place of subduing these envious feelings, he displayed the weakness of his character, and exclaimed, "They have ascribed unto David ten thousands, and to me they have ascribed but thousands: and what can he have more but the kingdom?"

One great defect in the character of Saul was his love of approbation. This trait had had a controlling influence over his actions and thoughts; everything was marked by his desire for praise and self-exaltation. His standard of right and wrong was the low standard of popular applause. No man is safe who lives that he may please men, and does not seek first for the approbation of God. It was the ambition of Saul to be first in the estimation of men; and when this song of praise was sung, a settled conviction entered the mind of the king that David would obtain the hearts of the people and reign in his stead.

Saul opened his heart to the spirit of jealousy by which his soul was poisoned. Notwithstanding the lessons which he had received from the prophet Samuel, instructing him that God would accomplish whatsoever He chose, and that no one could hinder it, the king made it evident that he had no true knowledge of the plans or power of God. The monarch of Israel was opposing his will to the will of the Infinite One. Saul had not learned, while ruling the kingdom of Israel, that he should rule his own spirit. He allowed his impulses to control his judgment, until he was plunged into a fury of passion. He had paroxysms of rage, when he was ready to take the life of any who dared oppose his will. From this frenzy he would pass into a state of despondency and self-contempt, and remorse would take possession of his soul.

He loved to hear David play upon his harp, and the evil spirit seemed to be charmed away for the time; but one day when the youth was ministering before him, and bringing sweet music from his instrument, accompanying his 651 voice as he sang the praises of God, Saul suddenly threw his spear at the musician, for the purpose of putting an end to his life. David was preserved by the interposition of God, and without injury fled from the rage of the maddened king.

As Saul's hatred of David increased, he became more and more watchful to find an opportunity to take his life; but none of his plans against the anointed of the Lord were successful. Saul gave himself up to the control of the wicked spirit that ruled over him; while David trusted in Him who is mighty in counsel, and strong to deliver. "The fear of the Lord is the beginning of wisdom" (Proverbs 9:10), and David's prayer was continually directed to God, that he might walk before Him in a perfect way.

Desiring to be freed from the presence of his rival, the king "removed him from him, and made him his captain over a thousand. . . . But all Israel and Judah loved David." The people were not slow to see that David was a competent person, and that the affairs entrusted to his hands were managed with wisdom and skill. The counsels of the young man were of a wise and discreet character, and proved to be safe to follow; while the judgment of Saul was at times unreliable, and his decisions were not wise.

Though Saul was ever on the alert for an opportunity to destroy David, he stood in fear of him, since it was evident that the Lord was with him. David's blameless character aroused the wrath of the king; he deemed that the very life and presence of David cast a reproach upon him, since by contrast it presented his own character to disadvantage. It was envy that made Saul miserable and put the humble subject of his throne in jeopardy. What untold mischief has this evil trait of character worked in our world! The same enmity existed in the heart of Saul that stirred the heart of Cain against his brother Abel, because Abel's works were righteous, and God honored him, and his own works were evil, and the Lord could not bless him. Envy is the offspring of pride, and if it is entertained in the heart, it will lead to hatred, and eventually to revenge and murder. Satan displayed his own character in exciting the fury of Saul against him who had never done him harm.

The king kept a strict watch upon David, hoping to find some occasion of indiscretion or rashness that might serve as an excuse to bring him into disgrace. He felt that he could not be satisfied until he could take the young man's 652 life and still be justified before the nation for his evil act. He laid a snare for the feet of David, urging him to conduct the war against the Philistines with still greater vigor, and promising, as a reward of his valor, an alliance with the eldest daughter of the royal house. To this proposal David's modest answer was, "Who am I? and what is my life, or my father's family in Israel, that I should be son-in-law to the king?" The monarch manifested his insincerity by wedding the princess to another.

An attachment for David on the part of Michal, Saul's youngest daughter, afforded the king another opportunity to plot against his rival. Michal's hand was offered the young man on condition that evidence should be given of the defeat and slaughter of a specified number of their national foes. "Saul thought to make David fall by the hand of the Philistines," but God shielded His servant. David returned a victor from the battle, to become the king's son-in-law. "Michal Saul's daughter loved him," and the monarch, enraged, saw that his plots had resulted in the elevation of him whom he sought to destroy. He was still more assured that this was the man whom the Lord had said was better than he, and who should reign on the throne of Israel in his place. Throwing off all disguise, he issued a command to Jonathan and to the officers of the court to take the life of the one he hated.

Jonathan revealed the king's intention to David and bade him conceal himself while he would plead with his father to spare the life of the deliverer of Israel. He presented before the king what David had done to preserve the honor and even the life of the nation, and what terrible guilt would rest upon the murderer of the one whom God had used to scatter their enemies. The conscience of the king was touched, and his heart was softened. "And Saul sware, As the Lord liveth,' he shall not be slain." David was brought to Saul, and he ministered in his presence, as he had done in the past.

Again war was declared between the Israelites and the Philistines, and David led the army against their enemies. A great victory was gained by the Hebrews, and the people of the realm praised his wisdom and heroism. This served to stir up the former bitterness of Saul against him. While the young man was playing before the king, filling the palace with sweet 653 harmony, Saul's passion overcame him, and he hurled a javelin at David, thinking to pin the musician to the wall; but the angel of the Lord turned aside the deadly weapon. David escaped and fled to his own house. Saul sent spies that they might take him as he should come out in the morning, and put an end to his life.

Michal informed David of the purpose of her father. She urged him to flee for his life, and let him down from the window, thus enabling him to make his escape. He fled to Samuel at Ramah, and the prophet, fearless of the king's displeasure, welcomed the fugitive. The home of Samuel was a peaceful place in contrast with the royal palace. It was here, amid the hills, that the honored servant of the Lord continued his work. A company of seers was with him, and they studied closely the will of God and listened reverently to the words of instruction that fell from the lips of Samuel. Precious were the lessons that David learned from the teacher of Israel. David believed that the troops of Saul would not be ordered to invade this sacred place, but no place seemed to be sacred to the darkened mind of the desperate king. David's connection with Samuel aroused the jealousy of the king, lest he who was revered as a prophet of God throughout all Israel should lend his influence to the advancement of Saul's rival. When the king learned where David was, he sent officers to bring him to Gibeah, where he intended to carry out his murderous design.

The messengers went on their way, intent upon taking David's life; but One greater than Saul controlled them. They were met by unseen angels, as was Balaam when he was on his way to curse Israel. They began to utter prophetic sayings of what would occur in the future, and proclaimed the glory and majesty of Jehovah. Thus God overruled the wrath of man and manifested His power to restrain evil, while He walled in His servant by a guard of angels.

The tidings reached Saul as he eagerly waited to have David in his power; but instead of feeling the rebuke of God, he was still more exasperated, and sent other messengers. These also were overpowered by the Spirit of God, and united with the first in prophesying. The third embassage was sent by the king; but when they came into the company of the prophets, the divine influence fell upon them also, and they prophesied. Saul then decided that he himself would go, for his fierce enmity had become 654 uncontrollable. He was determined to wait for no further chance to kill David; as soon as he should come within reach of him, he intended with his own hand to slay him, whatever might be the consequences.

But an angel of God met him on the way and controlled him. The Spirit of God held him in Its power, and he went forward uttering prayers to God, interspersed with predictions and sacred melodies. He prophesied of the coming Messiah as the world's Redeemer. When he came to the prophet's home in Ramah, he laid aside the outer garments that betokened his rank, and all day and all night he lay before Samuel and his pupils, under the influence of the divine Spirit. The people were drawn together to witness this strange scene, and the experience of the king was reported far and wide. Thus again, near the close of his reign, it became a proverb in Israel that Saul also was among the prophets.

Again the persecutor was defeated in his purpose. He assured David that he was at peace with him, but David had little confidence in the king's repentance. He took this opportunity to escape, lest the mood of the king should change, as formerly. His heart was wounded within him, and he longed to see his friend Jonathan once more. Conscious of his innocence, he sought the king's son and made a most touching appeal. "What have I done?" he asked, "what is mine iniquity? and what is my sin before thy father, that he seeketh my life?" Jonathan believed that his father had changed his purpose and no longer intended to take the life of David. And Jonathan said unto him, "God forbid; thou shalt not die: behold, my father will do nothing either great or small, but that he will show it me: and why should my father hide this thing from me? It is not so." After the remarkable exhibition of the power of God, Jonathan could not believe that his father would still harm David, since this would be manifest rebellion against God. But David was not convinced. With intense earnestness he declared to Jonathan, "As the Lord liveth, and as thy soul liveth, there is but a step between me and death."

At the time of the new moon a sacred festival was celebrated in Israel. This festival recurred upon the day following the interview between David and Jonathan. At this feast it was expected that both the young men would appear at the king's table; but David feared to be present, and it was arranged that he should visit his brothers in Bethlehem. On his return he was to hide himself in a field not far from the banqueting hall, for three days absenting himself from the presence of the king; and Jonathan would note the effect upon Saul. If inquiry should be made as to the whereabouts of the son of Jesse, Jonathan was to say that he had gone home to attend the sacrifice offered by his father's household. If no angry demonstrations were made by the king, but he should answer, "It is well," then it would be safe for David to return to the court. But if he should become enraged at his absence, it would decide the matter of David's flight.

On the first day of the feast the king made no inquiry concerning the absence of David; but when his place was vacant the second day, he questioned, "Wherefore cometh not the son of Jesse to meat, neither yesterday nor today? And Jonathan answered Saul, David earnestly asked leave of me to go to Bethlehem: and he said, Let me go, I pray thee; for our family hath a sacrifice in the city; and my brother, he hath commanded me to be there: and now, if I have found favor in thine eyes, let me get away, I pray thee, and see my brethren. Therefore he cometh not unto the king's table." When Saul heard these words, his anger was ungovernable. He declared that as long as David lived, Jonathan could not come to the throne of Israel, and he demanded that David should be sent for immediately, that he might be put to death. Jonathan again made intercession for his friend, pleading, "Wherefore shall he be slain? what hath he done?" This appeal to the king only made him more satanic in his fury, and the spear which he had intended for David he now hurled at his own son.

The prince was grieved and indignant, and leaving the royal presence, he was no more a guest at the feast. His soul was bowed down with sorrow as he repaired at the appointed time to the spot where David was to learn the king's intentions toward him. Each fell upon the other's neck, and they wept bitterly. The dark passion of the king cast its shadow upon the life of the young man, and their grief was too intense for expression. Jonathan's last words fell upon the ear of David as they separated to pursue their different paths, "Go in peace, forasmuch as we have sworn both of us in the name of the Lord, saying, The Lord be between me and thee, and between my seed and thy seed forever."

The king's son returned to Gibeah, and David

hastened to reach Nob, a city but a few miles distant, and also belonging to the tribe of Benjamin. The tabernacle had been taken to this place from Shiloh, and here Ahimelech the high priest ministered. David knew not whither to flee for refuge, except to the servant of God. The priest looked upon him with astonishment, as he came in haste and apparently alone, with a countenance marked by anxiety and sorrow. He inquired what had brought him there. The young man was in constant fear of discovery, and in his extremity he resorted to deception. David told the priest that he had been sent by the king on a secret errand, one which required the utmost expedition. Here he manifested a want of faith in God, and his sin resulted in causing the death of the high priest. Had the facts been plainly stated, Ahimelech would have known what course to pursue to preserve his life. God requires that truthfulness shall mark His people, even in the greatest peril. David asked the priest for five loaves of bread. There was nothing but hallowed bread in the possession of the man of God, but David succeeded in removing his scruples, and obtained the bread to satisfy his hunger.

A new danger now presented itself. Doeg, the chief of Saul's herdsmen, who had professed the faith of the Hebrews, was now paying his vows in the place of worship. At sight of this man David determined to make haste to secure another place of refuge, and to obtain some weapon with which to defend himself if defense should become necessary. He asked Ahimelech for a sword, and was told that he had none except the sword of Goliath, which had been kept as a relic in the tabernacle. David replied, "There is none like that; give it me." His courage revived as he grasped the sword that he had once used in destroying the champion of the Philistines.

David fled to Achish, the king of Gath; for he felt that there was more safety in the midst of the enemies of his people than in the dominions of Saul. But it was reported to Achish that David was the man who had slain the Philistine champion years before; and now he who had sought refuge with the foes of Israel found himself in great peril. But, feigning madness, he deceived his enemies and thus made his escape.

The first error of David was his distrust of God at Nob, and his second mistake was his deception before Achish. David had displayed noble traits of character, and his moral worth had won him favor with the people; but as trial came upon him, his faith was shaken, and human weakness appeared. He saw in every man a spy and a betrayer. In a great emergency David had looked up to God with a steady eye of faith, and had vanquished the Philistine giant. He believed in God, he went in His name. But as he had been hunted and persecuted, perplexity and distress had nearly hidden his heavenly Father from his sight.

Yet this experience was serving to teach David wisdom; for it led him to realize his weakness and the necessity of constant dependence upon God. Oh, how precious is the sweet influence of the Spirit of God as it comes to depressed or despairing souls, encouraging the fainthearted, strengthening the feeble, and imparting courage and help to the tried servants of the Lord! Oh, what a God is ours, who deals gently with the erring and manifests His patience and tenderness in adversity, and when we are overwhelmed with some great sorrow!

Every failure on the part of the children of God is due to their lack of faith. When shadows encompass the soul, when we want light and guidance, we must look up; there is light beyond the darkness. David ought not to have distrusted God for one moment. He had cause for trusting in Him: he was the Lord's anointed, and in the midst of danger he had been protected by the angels of God; he had been armed with courage to do wonderful things; and if he had but removed his mind from the distressing situation in which he was placed, and had thought of God's power and majesty, he would have been at peace even in the midst of the shadows of death; he could with confidence have repeated the promise of the Lord, "The mountains shall depart, and the hills be removed; but My kindness shall not depart from thee, neither shall the covenant of My peace be removed." Isaiah 54:10.

Among the mountains of Judah, David sought refuge from the pursuit of Saul. He made good his escape to the cave of Adullam, a place that, with a small force, could be held against a large army. "And when his brethren and all his father's house heard it, they went down thither to him." The family of David could not feel secure, knowing that at any time the unreasonable suspicions of Saul might be directed against them on account of their relation to David. They had now learned—what was coming to be generally known in Israel—that God had chosen David as the future ruler of His people; and they believed that they would be safer with him, even though he was a fugitive in a lonely cave, than they could be while exposed to the insane madness of a jealous king.

In the cave of Adullam the family were united in sympathy and affection. The son of Jesse could make melody with voice and harp as he sang, "Behold, how good and how pleasant it is for brethren to dwell together in unity!" Psalm 133:1. He had tasted the bitterness of distrust on the part of his own brothers; and the harmony that had taken the place of discord brought joy to the exile's heart. It was here that David composed the fifty-seventh psalm.

It was not long before David's company was joined by others who desired to escape the exactions of the king. There were many who had lost confidence in the ruler of Israel, for they could see that he was no longer guided by the Spirit of the Lord. "And everyone that was in distress, and everyone that was in debt, and everyone that was discontented," resorted to David, "and he became a captain over them: and there were with him about four hundred men." Here David had a little kingdom of his own, and in it order and discipline prevailed. But even in his retreat in the mountains he was far from feeling secure, for he received continual evidence that the king had not relinquished his murderous purpose.

He found a refuge for his parents with the king of Moab, and then, at a warning of danger from a prophet of the Lord, he fled from his hiding place to the forest of Hareth. The experience through which David was passing was not unnecessary or fruitless. God was giving him a course of discipline to fit him to become a wise general as well as a just and merciful king. With his band of fugitives he was gaining a preparation to take up the work that Saul, because of his murderous passion and blind indiscretion, was becoming wholly unfitted to do. Men cannot depart from the counsel of God and still retain that calmness and wisdom which will enable them to act with justice and discretion. There is no insanity so dreadful, so hopeless, as that of following human wisdom, unguided by the wisdom of God.

Saul had been preparing to ensnare and capture David in the cave of Adullam, and when it was discovered that David had left this place of refuge, the king was greatly enraged. The flight of David was a mystery to Saul. He could account for it only by the belief that there had been traitors in his camp, who had informed the son of Jesse of his proximity and design. 659

He affirmed to his counselors that a conspiracy had been formed against him, and with the offer of rich gifts and positions of honor he bribed them to reveal who among his people had befriended David. Doeg the Edomite turned informer. Moved by ambition and avarice, and by hatred of the priest, who had reproved his sins, Doeg reported David's visit to Ahimelech, representing the matter in such a light as to kindle Saul's anger against the man of God. The words of that mischievous tongue, set on fire of hell, stirred up the worst passions in Saul's heart. Maddened with rage, he declared that the whole family of the priest should perish. And the terrible decree was executed. Not only Ahimelech, but the members of his father's house—"fourscore and five persons that did wear a linen ephod"—were slain at the king's command, by the murderous hand of Doeg.

"And Nob, the city of the priests, smote he with the edge of the sword, both men and women, children and sucklings, and oxen, and

658

asses, and sheep." This is what Saul could do under the control of Satan. When God had said that the iniquity of the Amalekites was full, and had commanded him to destroy them utterly, he thought himself too compassionate to execute the divine sentence, and he spared that which was devoted to destruction; but now, without a command from God, under the guidance of Satan, he could slay the priests of the Lord and bring ruin upon the inhabitants of Nob. Such is the perversity of the human heart that has refused the guidance of God.

This deed filled all Israel with horror. It was the king whom they had chosen that had committed this outrage, and he had only done after the manner of the kings of other nations that feared not God. The ark was with them, but the priests of whom they had inquired were slain with the sword. What would come next?

660

65

The Magnanimity of David

After Saul's atrocious slaughter of the priests of the Lord, "one of the sons of Ahimelech the son of Ahitub, named Abiathar, escaped, and fled after David. And Abiathar showed David that Saul had slain the Lord's priests. And David said unto Abiathar, I knew it that day, when Doeg the Edomite was there, that he would surely tell Saul: I have occasioned the death of all the persons of thy father's house. Abide thou with me, fear not: for he that seeketh my life seeketh thy life: but with me thou shalt be in safeguard."

Still hunted by the king, David found no place of rest or security. At Keilah his brave band saved the town from capture by the Philistines, but they were not safe, even among the people whom they had delivered. From Keilah they repaired to the wilderness of Ziph.

At this time, when there were so few bright spots in the path of David, he was rejoiced to receive an unexpected visit from Jonathan, who had learned the place of his refuge. Precious were the moments which these two friends passed in each other's society. They related their varied experiences, and Jonathan strengthened the heart of David, saying, "Fear not: for the hand of Saul my father shall not find thee; and thou shalt be king over Israel, and I shall be next unto thee; and that also Saul my father knoweth." As they talked of the wonderful dealings of God with David, the hunted fugitive was greatly encouraged. "And they two made a covenant before the Lord: and David abode in the wood, and Jonathan went to his house."

After the visit of Jonathan, David encouraged

his soul with songs of praise, accompanying his voice with his harp as he sang:

"In the Lord put I my trust: 661
How say ye to my soul,
Flee as a bird to your mountain?
For, lo, the wicked bend their bow,
They make ready their arrow upon the string,
That they may privily shoot at the upright in heart.
If the foundations be destroyed,
What can the righteous do?
The Lord is in His holy temple,
The Lord's throne is in heaven:
His eyes behold, His eyelids try, the children of men.
The Lord trieth the righteous:
But the wicked and him that loveth violence
His soul hateth."

Psalm 11:1-5.

The Ziphites, into whose wild regions David went from Keilah, sent word to Saul in Gibeah that they knew where David was hiding, and that they would guide the king to his retreat. But David, warned of their intentions, changed his position, seeking refuge in the mountains between Maon and the Dead Sea.

Again word was sent to Saul, "Behold, David is in the wilderness of Engedi. Then Saul took three thousand chosen men out of all Israel, and went to seek David and his men upon the rocks of the wild goats." David had only six hundred men in his company, while Saul advanced against him with an army of three thousand. In a secluded cave the son of Jesse and his men waited for the guidance of God as to what should be done. As Saul was pressing his way up the mountains, he turned aside, and entered, alone, the very cavern in which David and his band were hidden. When David's men saw this they urged their leader to kill Saul. The fact that the king was now in his power was interpreted by them as certain evidence that God Himself had delivered the enemy into their hand, that they might destroy him. David was tempted to take this view of the matter; but the voice of conscience spoke to him, saying, "Touch not the anointed of the Lord."

David's men were still unwilling to leave Saul in peace, and they reminded their commander of the words of God, "Behold, I will deliver thine enemy into thine hand, that thou mayest do to him as it shall seem good unto thee. Then David arose, and cut off the skirt of Saul's robe privily." But his conscience smote him afterward, because he had even marred the garment of the king.

Saul rose up and went out of the cave to con- 662 tinue his search, when a voice fell upon his startled ears, saying, "My lord the king." He turned to see who was addressing him, and lo! it was

This chapter is based on 1 Samuel 22:20-23; 23 to 27.

the son of Jesse, the man whom he had so long
desired to have in his power that he might kill
him. David bowed himself to the king, acknowledging him as his master. Then he addressed
Saul in these words: "Wherefore hearest thou
men's words, saying, Behold, David seeketh thy
hurt? Behold, this day thine eyes have seen how
that the Lord hath delivered thee today into
mine hand in the cave: and some bade me kill
thee; but mine eye spared thee; and I said, I will
not put forth mine hand against my lord; for he
is the Lord's anointed. Moreover, my father,
see, yea, see the skirt of thy robe in my hand:
for in that I cut off the skirt of thy robe, and
killed thee not, know thou and see that there is
neither evil nor transgression in mine hand, and
I have not sinned against thee; yet thou huntest
my soul to take it."

When Saul heard the words of David he was
humbled, and could not but admit their truthfulness. His feelings were deeply moved as he
realized how completely he had been in the
power of the man whose life he sought. David
stood before him in conscious innocence. With
a softened spirit, Saul exclaimed, "Is this thy
voice, my son David? And Saul lifted up his
voice, and wept." Then he declared to David:
"Thou art more righteous than I: for thou hast
rewarded me good, whereas I have rewarded
thee evil. . . . For if a man find his enemy, will
he let him go well away? wherefore the Lord
reward thee good for that thou hast done unto
me this day. And now, behold, I know well that
thou shalt surely be king, and that the kingdom
of Israel shall be established in thine hand." And
David made a covenant with Saul that when this
should take place he would favorably regard the
house of Saul, and not cut off his name.

Knowing what he did of Saul's past course,
David could put no confidence in the assurances
of the king, nor hope that his penitent condition
would long continue. So when Saul returned to
his home David remained in the strongholds of
the mountains.

The enmity that is cherished toward the servants of God by those who have yielded to the
power of Satan changes at times to a feeling of
reconciliation and favor, but the change does
not always prove to be lasting. After evil-mind-
ed men have engaged in doing and saying
663 wicked things against the Lord's servants, the
conviction that they have been in the wrong
sometimes takes deep hold upon their minds.
The Spirit of the Lord strives with them, and
they humble their hearts before God, and before
those whose influence they have sought to
destroy, and they may change their course
toward them. But as they again open the door to
the suggestions of the evil one, the old doubts
are revived, the old enmity is awakened, and
they return to engage in the same work which
they repented of, and for a time abandoned.

Again they speak evil, accusing and condemning in the bitterest manner the very ones to
whom they made their most humble confession.
Satan can use such souls with far greater power
after such a course has been pursued than he
could before, because they have sinned against
greater light.

"And Samuel died; and all the Israelites were
gathered together, and lamented him, and buried
him in his house at Ramah." The death of
Samuel was regarded as an irreparable loss by
the nation of Israel. A great and good prophet
and an eminent judge had fallen in death, and
the grief of the people was deep and heartfelt.
From his youth up Samuel had walked before
Israel in the integrity of his heart; although Saul
had been the acknowledged king, Samuel had
wielded a more powerful influence than he,
because his record was one of faithfulness, obedience, and devotion. We read that he judged
Israel all the days of his life.

As the people contrasted the course of Saul
with that of Samuel, they saw what a mistake
they had made in desiring a king that they might
not be different from the nations around them.
Many looked with alarm at the condition of
society, fast becoming leavened with irreligion
and godlessness. The example of their ruler was
exerting a widespread influence, and well might
Israel mourn that Samuel, the prophet of the
Lord, was dead.

The nation had lost the founder and president
of its sacred schools, but that was not all. It had
lost him to whom the people had been accustomed to go with their great troubles—lost one
who had constantly interceded with God in
behalf of the best interests of its people. The
intercession of Samuel had given a feeling of
security; for "the effectual fervent prayer of a
righteous man availeth much." James 5:16. The
people felt now that God was forsaking them.
The king seemed little less than a madman. Justice was perverted, and order was turned to confusion.

It was when the nation was racked with inter- 664
nal strife, when the calm, God-fearing counsel
of Samuel seemed to be most needed, that God
gave His aged servant rest. Bitter were the
reflections of the people as they looked upon his
quiet resting place, and remembered their folly
in rejecting him as their ruler; for he had had so
close a connection with Heaven that he seemed
to bind all Israel to the throne of Jehovah. It was
Samuel who had taught them to love and obey
God; but now that he was dead, the people felt
that they were left to the mercies of a king who
was joined to Satan, and who would divorce the
people from God and heaven.

David could not be present at the burial of
Samuel, but he mourned for him as deeply and
tenderly as a faithful son could mourn for a
devoted father. He knew that Samuel's death

had broken another bond of restraint from the actions of Saul, and he felt less secure than when the prophet lived. While the attention of Saul was engaged in mourning for the death of Samuel, David took the opportunity to seek a place of greater security; so he fled to the wilderness of Paran. It was here that he composed the one hundred and twentieth and twenty-first psalms. In these desolate wilds, realizing that the prophet was dead, and the king was his enemy, he sang:

"My help cometh from the Lord,
Which made heaven and earth.
He will not suffer thy foot to be moved:
He that keepeth thee will not slumber.
Behold, He that keepeth Israel
Shall neither slumber nor sleep. . . .
The Lord shall preserve thee from all evil:
He shall preserve thy soul.
The Lord shall preserve thy going out and
    thy coming in
From this time forth, and even forevermore."
                                   Psalm 121:2-8.

While David and his men were in the wilderness of Paran, they protected from the depredations of marauders the flocks and herds of a wealthy man named Nabal, who had vast possessions in that region. Nabal was a descendant of Caleb, but his character was churlish and niggardly.

It was the time of sheepshearing, a season of hospitality. David and his men were in sore need of provisions; and in accordance with the custom of the times, the son of Jesse sent ten 665 young men to Nabal, bidding them greet him in their master's name; and he added: "Thus shall ye say to him that liveth in prosperity, Peace be both to thee, and peace be to thine house, and peace be unto all that thou hast. And now I have heard that thou hast shearers: now thy shepherds which were with us, we hurt them not, neither was there aught missing unto them, all the while they were in Carmel.* Ask thy young men, and they will show thee. Wherefore let the young men find favor in thine eyes; for we come in a good day: give, I pray thee, whatsoever cometh to thine hand unto thy servants, and to thy son David."

David and his men had been like a wall of protection to the shepherds and flocks of Nabal; and now this rich man was asked to furnish from his abundance some relief to the necessities of those who had done him such valuable service. David and his men might have helped themselves from the flocks and herds, but they did not. They behaved themselves in an honest way. Their kindness, however, was lost upon Nabal. The answer he returned to David was indicative of his character: "Who is David? and who is the son of Jesse? There be many servants

nowadays that break away every man from his master. Shall I then take my bread, and my water, and my flesh that I have killed for my shearers, and give it unto men, whom I know not whence they be?"

When the young men returned empty-handed and related the affair to David, he was filled with indignation. He commanded his men to equip themselves for an encounter; for he had determined to punish the man who had denied him what was his right, and had added insult to injury. This impulsive movement was more in harmony with the character of Saul than with that of David, but the son of Jesse had yet to learn lessons of patience in the school of affliction.

One of Nabal's servants hastened to Abigail, the wife of Nabal, after he had dismissed David's young men, and told her what had happened. "Behold," he said, "David sent messengers out of the wilderness to salute our master; and he railed on them. But the men were very good unto us, and we were not hurt, neither missed we anything, as long as we were conversant with them, when we were in the fields. They were a wall unto us both by night and day, 666 all the while we were with them keeping the sheep. Now therefore know and consider what thou wilt do; for evil is determined against our master, and against all his household."

Without consulting her husband or telling him of her intention, Abigail made up an ample supply of provisions, which, laded upon asses, she sent forward in the charge of servants, and herself started out to meet the band of David. She met them in a covert of a hill. "And when Abigail saw David, she hasted, and lighted off the ass, and fell before David on her face, and bowed herself to the ground, and fell at his feet, and said, Upon me, my lord, upon me let this iniquity be: and let thine handmaid, I pray thee, speak in thine audience." Abigail addressed David with as much reverence as though speaking to a crowned monarch. Nabal had scornfully exclaimed, "Who is David?" but Abigail called him, "my lord." With kind words she sought to sooth his irritated feelings, and she pleaded with him in behalf of her husband. With nothing of ostentation or pride, but full of the wisdom and love of God, Abigail revealed the strength of her devotion to her household; and she made it plain to David that the unkind course of her husband was in no wise premeditated against him as a personal affront, but was simply the outburst of an unhappy and selfish nature.

"Now therefore, my lord, as the Lord liveth, and as thy soul liveth, seeing the Lord hath withholden thee from coming to shed blood, and from avenging thyself with thine own hand, now let thine enemies, and they that seek evil to my lord, be as Nabal." Abigail did not take to herself the credit of this reasoning to turn David from his hasty purpose, but gave to God the

---

* Not Mount Carmel, but a place in the territory of Judah, near the hill town of Maon.

honor and the praise. She then offered her rich provision as a peace offering to the men of David, and still pleaded as if she herself were the one who had so excited the resentment of the chief.

"I pray thee," she said, "forgive the trespass of thine handmaid; for the Lord will certainly make my lord a sure house; because my lord fighteth the battles of the Lord, and evil hath not been found in thee all thy days." Abigail presented by implication the course that David ought to pursue. He should fight the battles of the Lord. He was not to seek revenge for personal wrongs, even though persecuted as a traitor. She continued: "Though man be risen up to 667 pursue thee, and to seek thy soul, yet the soul of my lord shall be bound in the bundle of life with the Lord thy God. . . . And it shall come to pass, when the Lord shall have done to my lord according to all the good that He hath spoken concerning thee, and shall have appointed thee prince over Israel; that this shall be no grief unto thee, nor offense of heart unto my lord, either that thou hast shed blood causeless, or that my lord hath avenged himself: and when the Lord shall have dealt well with my lord, then remember thine handmaid." 1 Samuel 25:29-31, R.V.

These words could have come only from the lips of one who had partaken of the wisdom from above. The piety of Abigail, like the fragrance of a flower, breathed out all unconsciously in face and word and action. The Spirit of the Son of God was abiding in her soul. Her speech, seasoned with grace, and full of kindness and peace, shed a heavenly influence. Better impulses came to David, and he trembled as he thought what might have been the consequences of his rash purpose. "Blessed are the peacemakers: for they shall be called the children of God." Matthew 5:9. Would that there were many more like this woman of Israel, who would soothe the irritated feelings, prevent rash impulses, and quell great evils by words of calm and well-directed wisdom.

A consecrated Christian life is ever shedding light and comfort and peace. It is characterized by purity, tact, simplicity, and usefulness. It is controlled by that unselfish love that sanctifies the influence. It is full of Christ, and leaves a track of light wherever its possessor may go. Abigail was a wise reprover and counselor. David's passion died away under the power of her influence and reasoning. He was convinced that he had taken an unwise course and had lost control of his own spirit.

With a humble heart he received the rebuke, in harmony with his own words, "Let the righteous smite me; it shall be a kindness: and let him reprove me; it shall be an excellent oil." Psalm 141:5. He gave thanks and blessings because she advised him righteously. There are many who, when they are reproved, think it praiseworthy if they receive the rebuke without becoming impatient; but how few take reproof with gratitude of heart and bless those who seek to save them from pursuing an evil course.

When Abigail returned home she found Nabal and his guests in the enjoyment of a great feast, which they had converted into a scene of 668 drunken revelry. Not until the next morning did she relate to her husband what had occurred in her interview with David. Nabal was a coward at heart; and when he realized how near his folly had brought him to a sudden death, he seemed smitten with paralysis. Fearful that David would still pursue his purpose of revenge, he was filled with horror, and sank down in a condition of helpless insensibility. After ten days he died. The life that God had given him had been only a curse to the world. In the midst of his rejoicing and making merry, God had said to him, as He said to the rich man of the parable, "This night thy soul shall be required of thee." Luke 12:20.

David afterward married Abigail. He was already the husband of one wife, but the custom of the nations of his time had perverted his judgment and influenced his actions. Even great and good men have erred in following the practices of the world. The bitter result of marrying many wives was sorely felt throughout all the life of David.

After the death of Samuel, David was left in peace for a few months. Again he repaired to the solitude of the Ziphites; but these enemies, hoping to secure the favor of the king, informed him of David's hiding place. This intelligence aroused the demon of passion that had been slumbering in Saul's breast. Once more he summoned his men of arms and led them out in pursuit of David. But friendly spies brought tidings to the son of Jesse that Saul was again pursuing him; and with a few of his men, David started out to learn the location of his enemy. It was night when, cautiously advancing, they came upon the encampment, and saw before them the tents of the king and his attendants. They were unobserved, for the camp was quiet in slumber. David called upon his friends to go with him into the very midst of the foe. In answer to his question, "Who will go down with me to Saul to the camp?" Abishai promptly responded, "I will go down with thee."

Hidden by the deep shadows of the hills, David and his attendant entered the encampment of the enemy. As they sought to ascertain the exact number of their foes, they came upon Saul sleeping, his spear stuck in the ground, and a cruse of water at his head. Beside him lay Abner, his chief commander, and all around them were the soldiers, locked in slumber. Abishai raised his spear, and said to David, "God hath delivered thine enemy into thine hand this day: now therefore let me smite him, I 671 pray thee, with the spear even to the earth at once, and I will not smite him the second time." He waited for the word of permission; but there fell upon his ear the whispered words: "Destroy him not: for who can stretch forth his hand against the Lord's anointed, and be guiltless? . . . As the Lord liveth, the Lord shall smite him; or his day shall come to die; or he shall descend into battle, and perish. The Lord forbid that I should stretch forth mine hand against the Lord's anointed: but, I pray thee, take thou now the spear that is at his bolster, and the cruse of water, and let us go. So David took the spear and the cruse of water from Saul's bolster; and they gat them away, and no man saw it, nor knew it, neither awaked: for they were all asleep; because a deep sleep from the Lord was fallen upon them." How easily the Lord can weaken the strongest, remove prudence from the wisest, and baffle the skill of the most watchful!

When David was at a safe distance from the camp he stood on the top of a hill and cried with a loud voice to the people and to Abner, saying, "Art not thou a valiant man? and who is like to thee in Israel? wherefore then hast thou not kept thy lord the king? for there came one of the people in to destroy the king thy lord. This thing is not good that thou hast done. As the Lord liveth, ye are worthy to die, because ye have not kept your master, the Lord's anointed. And now see where the king's spear is, and the cruse of water that was at his bolster. And Saul knew David's voice, and said, Is this thy voice, my son David? And David said, It is my voice, my lord, O king. And he said, Wherefore doth my lord thus pursue after his servant? for what have I done? or what evil is in mine hand? Now therefore, I pray thee, let my lord the king hear the words of his servant." Again the acknowledgment fell from the lips of the king, "I have sinned: return, my son David; for I will no more do thee harm, because my soul was precious in thine eyes this day: behold, I have played the fool, and have erred exceedingly. And David answered and said, Behold the king's spear! and let one of the young men come over and fetch it." Although Saul had made the promise, "I will no more do thee harm," David did not place himself in his power.

This second instance of David's respect for his sovereign's life made a still deeper impression upon the mind of Saul and brought from him a more humble acknowledgment of his 672 fault. He was astonished and subdued at the manifestation of such kindness. In parting from David, Saul exclaimed, "Blessed be thou, my son David: thou shalt both do great things, and also shalt still prevail." But the son of Jesse had no hope that the king would long continue in this frame of mind.

David despaired of a reconciliation with Saul.

It seemed inevitable that he should at last fall a victim to the malice of the king, and he determined again to seek refuge in the land of the Philistines. With the six hundred men under his command, he passed over to Achish, the king of Gath.

David's conclusion that Saul would certainly accomplish his murderous purpose was formed without the counsel of God. Even while Saul was plotting and seeking to accomplish his destruction, the Lord was working to secure David the kingdom. God works out His plans, though to human eyes they are veiled in mystery. Men cannot understand the ways of God; and, looking at appearances, they interpret the trials and tests and provings that God permits to come upon them as things that are against them, and that will only work their ruin. Thus David looked on appearances, and not at the promises of God. He doubted that he would ever come to the throne. Long trials had wearied his faith and exhausted his patience.

The Lord did not send David for protection to the Philistines, the most bitter foes of Israel. This very nation would be among his worst enemies to the last, and yet he had fled to them for help in his time of need. Having lost all confidence in Saul and in those who served him, he threw himself upon the mercies of the enemies of his people. David was a brave general, and had proved himself a wise and successful warrior; but he was working directly against his own interests when he went to the Philistines. God had appointed him to set up his standard in the land of Judah, and it was want of faith that led him to forsake his post of duty without a command from the Lord.

God was dishonored by David's unbelief. The Philistines had feared David more than they had feared Saul and his armies; and by placing himself under the protection of the Philistines, David discovered to them the weakness of his own people. Thus he encouraged these relentless foes to oppress Israel. David had been anointed to stand in defense of the people of God; and the Lord would not have His servants give encouragement to the wicked by disclosing 673 the weakness of His people or by an appearance of indifference to their welfare. Furthermore, the impression was received by his brethren that he had gone to the heathen to serve their gods. By this act he gave occasion for misconstruing his motives, and many were led to hold prejudice against him. The very thing that Satan desired to have him do he was led to do; for, in seeking refuge among the Philistines, David caused great exultation to the enemies of God and His people. David did not renounce his worship of God nor cease his devotion to His cause; but he sacrificed his trust in Him to his personal safety, and thus tarnished the upright and faithful character that God requires His servants to possess.

David was cordially received by the king of the Philistines. The warmth of this reception was partly due to the fact that the king admired him and partly to the fact that it was flattering to his vanity to have a Hebrew seek his protection. David felt secure from betrayal in the dominions of Achish. He brought his family, his household, and his possessions, as did also his men; and to all appearance he had come to settle permanently in the land of Philistia. All this was gratifying to Achish, who promised to protect the fugitive Israelites.

At David's request for a residence in the country, removed from the royal city, the king graciously granted Ziklag as a possession. David realized that it would be dangerous for himself and his men to be under the influence of idolaters. In a town wholly separated for their use they might worship God with more freedom than they could if they remained in Gath, where the heathen rites could not but prove a source of evil and annoyance.

While dwelling in this isolated town David made war upon the Geshurites, the Gezrites, and the Amalekites, and he left none alive to bring tidings to Gath. When he returned from battle he gave Achish to understand that he had been warring against those of his own nation, the men of Judah. By this dissembling he was the means of strengthening the hand of the Philistines; for the king said, "He hath made his people Israel utterly to abhor him; therefore he shall be my servant forever." David knew that it was the will of God that those heathen tribes should be destroyed, and he knew that he was appointed to do this work; but he was not walking in the counsel of God when he practiced deception.

"And it came to pass in those days, that the 674 Philistines gathered their armies together for warfare, to fight with Israel. And Achish said unto David, Know thou assuredly, that thou shalt go out with me to battle, thou and thy men." David had no intention of lifting his hand against his people; but he was not certain as to what course he would pursue, until circumstances should indicate his duty. He answered the king evasively, and said, "Surely thou shalt know what thy servant can do." Achish understood these words as a promise of assistance in the approaching war, and pledged his word to bestow upon David great honor, and give him a high position at the Philistine court.

But although David's faith had staggered somewhat at the promises of God, he still remembered that Samuel had anointed him king of Israel. He recalled the victories that God had given him over his enemies in the past. He reviewed the great mercy of God in preserving him from the hand of Saul, and determined not to betray a sacred trust. Even though the king of

Israel had sought his life, he would not join his forces with the enemies of his people.

66

675

The Death of Saul

Again war was declared between Israel and the Philistines. "The Philistines gathered themselves together, and came and pitched in Shunem," on the northern edge of the plain of Jezreel; while Saul and his forces encamped but a few miles distant, at the foot of Mount Gilboa, on the southern border of the plain. It was on this plain that Gideon, with three hundred men, had put to flight the hosts of Midian. But the spirit that inspired Israel's deliverer was widely different from that which now stirred the heart of the king. Gideon went forth strong in faith in the mighty God of Jacob; but Saul felt himself to be alone and defenseless, because God had forsaken him. As he looked abroad upon the Philistine host, "he was afraid, and his heart greatly trembled."

Saul had learned that David and his force were with the Philistines, and he expected that the son of Jesse would take this opportunity to revenge the wrongs he had suffered. The king was in sore distress. It was his own unreasoning passion, spurring him on to destroy the chosen of God, that had involved the nation in so great peril. While he had been engrossed in pursuing David he had neglected the defense of his kingdom. The Philistines, taking advantage of its unguarded condition, had penetrated into the very heart of the country. Thus while Satan had been urging Saul to employ every energy in hunting David, that he might destroy him, the same malignant spirit had inspired the Philistines to seize their opportunity to work Saul's ruin and overthrow the people of God. How often is the same policy still employed by the archenemy! He moves upon some unconsecrated heart to kindle envy and strife in the church, and then, taking advantage of the divided condition of God's people, he stirs up his agents to work their ruin.

On the morrow Saul must engage the Philistines in battle. The shadows of impending doom gathered dark about him; he longed for 676 help and guidance. But it was in vain that he sought counsel from God. "The Lord answered him not, neither by dreams, nor by Urim, nor by prophets." The Lord never turned away a soul that came to Him in sincerity and humility. Why did He turn Saul away unanswered? The king had by his own act forfeited the benefits of all the methods of inquiring of God. He had rejected the counsel of Samuel the prophet; he had exiled David, the chosen of God; he had slain

This chapter is based on 1 Samuel 28 ; 31.

the priests of the Lord. Could he expect to be answered by God when he had cut off the channels of communication that Heaven had ordained? He had sinned away the Spirit of grace, and could he be answered by dreams and revelations from the Lord? Saul did not turn to God with humility and repentance. It was not pardon for sin and reconciliation with God, that he sought, but deliverance from his foes. By his own stubbornness and rebellion he had cut himself off from God. There could be no return but by the way of penitence and contrition; but the proud monarch, in his anguish and despair, determined to seek help from another source.

"Then said Saul unto his servants, Seek me a woman that hath a familiar spirit, that I may go to her, and inquire of her." Saul had a full knowledge of the character of necromancy. It had been expressly forbidden by the Lord, and the sentence of death was pronounced against all who practiced its unholy arts. During the life of Samuel, Saul had commanded that all wizards and those that had familiar spirits should be put to death; but now, in the rashness of desperation, he had recourse to that oracle which he had condemned as an abomination.

It was told the king that a woman who had a familiar spirit was living in concealment at Endor. This woman had entered into covenant with Satan to yield herself to his control, to fulfill his purposes; and in return, the prince of evil wrought wonders for her and revealed secret things to her.

Disguising himself, Saul went forth by night with but two attendants, to seek the retreat of the sorceress. Oh, pitiable sight! the king of Israel led captive by Satan at his will! What path so dark for human feet to tread as that chosen by one who has persisted in having his own way, resisting the holy influences of the Spirit of God! What bondage so terrible as that of him who is given over to the control of the worst of tyrants—himself! Trust in God and obedience to His will were the only conditions upon which Saul could be king of Israel. Had he complied with these conditions throughout his reign, his kingdom would have been secure; God would have been his guide, the Omnipotent his shield. God had borne long with Saul; and although his rebellion and obstinacy had well-nigh silenced the divine voice in the soul, there was still opportunity for repentance. But when in his peril he turned from God to obtain light from a confederate of Satan, he had cut the last tie that bound him to his Maker; he had placed himself fully under the control of that demoniac power which for years had been exercised upon him, and which had brought him to the verge of destruction.

Under the cover of darkness Saul and his attendants made their way across the plain, and, safely passing the Philistine host, they crossed the mountain ridge, to the lonely home of the sorceress of Endor. Here the woman with a familiar spirit had hidden herself away that she might secretly continue her profane incantations. Disguised as he was, Saul's lofty stature and kingly port declared that he was no common soldier. The woman suspected that her visitor was Saul, and his rich gifts strengthened her suspicions. To his request, "I pray thee, divine unto me by the familiar spirit, and bring me him up, whom I shall name unto thee," the woman answered, "Behold, thou knowest what Saul hath done, how he hath cut off those that have familiar spirits, and the wizards, out of the land: wherefore then layest thou a snare for my life, to cause me to die?" Then "Saul sware to her by the Lord, saying, As the Lord liveth, there shall no punishment happen to thee for this thing." And when she said, "Whom shall I bring up unto thee?" he answered, "Samuel."

After practicing her incantations, she said, "I saw gods ascending out of the earth. . . . An old man cometh up; and he is covered with a mantle. And Saul perceived that it was Samuel, and he stooped with his face to the ground, and bowed himself."

It was not God's holy prophet that came forth at the spell of a sorcerer's incantation. Samuel was not present in that haunt of evil spirits. That supernatural appearance was produced solely by the power of Satan. He could as easily assume the form of Samuel as he could assume that of an angel of light, when he tempted Christ in the wilderness.

The woman's first words under the spell of her incantation had been addressed to the king, "Why hast thou deceived me? for thou art Saul." Thus the first act of the evil spirit which personated the prophet was to communicate secretly with this wicked woman, to warn her of the deception that had been practiced upon her. The message to Saul from the pretended prophet was, "Why hast thou disquieted me, to bring me up? And Saul answered, I am sore distressed; for the Philistines make war against me, and God is departed from me, and answereth me no more, neither by prophets, nor by dreams: therefore I have called thee, that thou mayest make known unto me what I shall do."

When Samuel was living, Saul had despised his counsel and had resented his reproofs. But now, in the hour of his distress and calamity, he felt that the prophet's guidance was his only hope, and in order to communicate with Heaven's ambassador he vainly had recourse to the messenger of hell! Saul had placed himself fully in the power of Satan; and now he whose only delight is in causing misery and destruction, made the most of his advantage, to work the ruin of the unhappy king. In answer to Saul's agonized entreaty came the terrible message, professedly from the lips of Samuel:

"Wherefore then dost thou ask of me, seeing the Lord is departed from thee, and is become thine enemy? And the Lord hath done to him, as he spake by me: for the Lord hath rent the kingdom out of thine hand, and given it to thy neighbor, even to David: because thou obeyedst not the voice of the Lord, nor executedst His fierce wrath upon Amalek, therefore hath the Lord done this thing unto thee this day. Moreover the Lord will also deliver Israel with thee into the hand of the Philistines."

All through his course of rebellion Saul had been flattered and deceived by Satan. It is the tempter's work to belittle sin, to make the path of transgression easy and inviting, to blind the mind to the warnings and threatenings of the Lord. Satan, by his bewitching power, had led Saul to justify himself in defiance of Samuel's reproofs and warning. But now, in his extremity, he turned upon him, presenting the enormity of his sin and the hopelessness of pardon, that he might goad him to desperation. Nothing could have been better chosen to destroy his courage and confuse his judgment, or to drive him to despair and self-destruction.

Saul was faint with weariness and fasting; he was terrified and conscience-stricken. As the fearful prediction fell upon his ear, his form swayed like an oak before the tempest, and he fell prostrate to the earth.

The sorceress was filled with alarm. The king of Israel lay before her like one dead. Should he perish in her retreat, what would be the consequences to herself? She besought him to arise and partake of food, urging that since she had imperiled her life in granting his desire, he should yield to her request for the preservation of his own. His servants joining their entreaties, Saul yielded at last, and the woman set before him the fatted calf and unleavened bread hastily prepared. What a scene!—In the wild cave of the sorceress, which but a little before had echoed with the words of doom—in the presence of Satan's messenger—he who had been anointed of God as king over Israel sat down to eat, in preparation for the day's deadly strife.

Before the break of day he returned with his attendants to the camp of Israel to make ready for the conflict. By consulting that spirit of darkness Saul had destroyed himself. Oppressed by the horror of despair, it would be impossible for him to inspire his army with courage. Separated from the Source of strength, he could not lead the minds of Israel to look to God as their helper. Thus the prediction of evil would work its own accomplishment.

On the plain of Shunem and the slopes of Mount Gilboa the armies of Israel and the hosts of the Philistines closed in mortal combat. Though the fearful scene in the cave of Endor had driven all hope from his heart, Saul fought with desperate valor for his throne and his kingdom. But it was in vain. "The men of Israel fled from before the Philistines, and fell down slain in Mount Gilboa." Three brave sons of the king died at his side. The archers pressed upon Saul. He had seen his soldiers falling around him and his princely sons cut down by the sword. Himself wounded, he could neither fight nor fly. Escape was impossible, and determined not to be taken alive by the Philistines, he bade his armor-bearer, "Draw thy sword, and thrust me through therewith." When the man refused to lift his hand against the Lord's anointed, Saul took his own life by falling upon his sword.

Thus the first king of Israel perished, with the guilt of self-murder upon his soul. His life had been a failure, and he went down in dishonor and despair, because he had set up his own perverse will against the will of God.

The tidings of defeat spread far and wide, carrying terror to all Israel. The people fled from the cities, and the Philistines took undisturbed possession. Saul's reign, independent of God, had well-nigh proved the ruin of his people.

On the day following the engagement, the Philistines, searching the battlefield to rob the slain, discovered the bodies of Saul and his three sons. To complete their triumph, they cut off the head of Saul and stripped him of his armor; then the head and the armor, reeking with blood, were sent to the country of the Philistines as a trophy of victory, "to publish it in the house of their idols, and among the people." The armor was finally put in "the house of Ashtaroth," while the head was fastened in the temple of Dagon. Thus the glory of the victory was ascribed to the power of these false gods, and the name of Jehovah was dishonored.

The dead bodies of Saul and his sons were dragged to Beth-shan, a city not far from Gilboa, and near the river Jordan. Here they were hung up in chains, to be devoured by birds of prey. But the brave men of Jabesh-gilead, remembering Saul's deliverance of their city in his earlier and happier years, now manifested their gratitude by rescuing the bodies of the king and princes, and giving them honorable burial. Crossing the Jordan by night, they "took the body of Saul and the bodies of his sons from the wall of Beth-shan, and came to Jabesh, and burnt them there. And they took their bones, and buried them under a tree at Jabesh, and fasted seven days." Thus the noble deed performed forty years before, secured for Saul and his sons burial by tender and pitying hands in that dark hour of defeat and dishonor.

683

67

Ancient and Modern Sorcery

The Scripture account of Saul's visit to the woman of Endor has been a source of perplexity to many students of the Bible. There are some who take the position that Samuel was actually present at the interview with Saul, but the Bible itself furnishes sufficient ground for a contrary conclusion. If, as claimed by some, Samuel was in heaven, he must have been summoned thence, either by the power of God or by that of Satan. None can believe for a moment that Satan had power to call the holy prophet of God from heaven to honor the incantations of an abandoned woman. Nor can we conclude that God summoned him to the witch's cave; for the Lord had already refused to communicate with Saul, by dreams, by Urim, or by prophets. 1 Samuel 28:6. These were God's own appointed mediums of communication, and He did not pass them by to deliver the message through the agent of Satan.

The message itself is sufficient evidence of its origin. Its object was not to lead Saul to repentance, but to urge him on to ruin; and this is not the work of God, but of Satan. Furthermore, the act of Saul in consulting a sorceress is cited in Scripture as one reason why he was rejected by God and abandoned to destruction: "Saul died for his transgression which he committed against the Lord, even against the word of the Lord, which he kept not, and also for asking counsel of one that had a familiar spirit, *to inquire of it*; and inquired not of the Lord: therefore He slew him, and turned the kingdom unto David the son of Jesse." 1 Chronicles 10:13, 14. Here it is distinctly stated that Saul inquired of the familiar spirit, not of the Lord. He did not communicate with Samuel, the prophet of God; but through the sorceress he held intercourse with Satan. Satan could not present the real Samuel, but he did present a counterfeit, that served his purpose of deception.

684   Nearly all forms of ancient sorcery and witchcraft were founded upon a belief in communion with the dead. Those who practiced the arts of necromancy claimed to have intercourse with departed spirits, and to obtain through them a knowledge of future events. This custom of consulting the dead is referred to in the prophecy of Isaiah: "When they shall say unto you, Seek unto them that have familiar spirits, and unto wizards that peep and that mutter: should not a people seek unto their God? *for the living to the dead*?" Isaiah 8:19.

This same belief in communion with the dead formed the cornerstone of heathen idolatry. The

gods of the heathen were believed to be the deified spirits of departed heroes. Thus the religion of the heathen was a worship of the dead. This is evident from the Scriptures. In the account of the sin of Israel at Bethpeor, it is stated: "Israel abode in Shittim, and the people began to commit whoredom with the daughters of Moab. And they called the people unto the sacrifices of their gods: and the people did eat, and bowed down to their gods. And Israel joined himself unto Baalpeor." Numbers 25:1-3. The psalmist tells us to what kind of gods these sacrifices were offered. Speaking of the same apostasy of the Israelites, he says, "They joined themselves also unto Baalpeor, and *ate the sacrifices of the dead*" (Psalm 106:28); that is, sacrifices that had been offered to the dead.

The deification of the dead has held a prominent place in nearly every system of heathenism, as has also the supposed communion with the dead. The gods were believed to communicate their will to men, and also, when consulted, to give them counsel. Of this character were the famous oracles of Greece and Rome.

The belief in communion with the dead is still held, even in professedly Christian lands. Under the name of spiritualism the practice of communicating with beings claiming to be the spirits of the departed has become widespread. It is calculated to take hold of the sympathies of those who have laid their loved ones in the grave. Spiritual beings sometimes appear to persons in the form of their deceased friends, and relate incidents connected with their lives and perform acts which they performed while living. In this way they lead men to believe that their dead friends are angels, hovering over them and communicating with them. Those who thus assume   685 to be the spirits of the departed are regarded with a certain idolatry, and with many their word has greater weight than the word of God.

There are many, however, who regard spiritualism as a mere imposture. The manifestations by which it supports its claims to a supernatural character are attributed to fraud on the part of the medium. But while it is true that the results of trickery have often been palmed off as genuine manifestations, there have also been marked evidences of supernatural power. And many who reject spiritualism as the result of human skill or cunning will, when confronted with manifestations which they cannot account for upon this ground, be led to acknowledge its claims.

Modern spiritualism and the forms of ancient witchcraft and idol worship—all having communion with the dead as their vital principle—are founded upon that first lie by which Satan beguiled Eve in Eden: "Ye shall not surely die: for God doth know that in the day ye eat thereof, . . . ye shall be as gods." Genesis 3:4, 5. Alike based upon falsehood and perpetuating the same, they are alike from the father of lies.

The Hebrews were expressly forbidden to engage in any manner in pretended communion with the dead. God closed this door effectually when He said: "The dead know not anything. . . . Neither have they any more a portion forever in anything that is done under the sun." Ecclesiastes 9:5, 6. "His breath goeth forth, he returneth to his earth; in that very day his thoughts perish." Psalm 146:4. And the Lord declared to Israel: "The soul that turneth after such as have familiar spirits, and after wizards, to go a whoring after them, I will even set My face against that soul, and will cut him off from among his people." Leviticus 20:6.

The "familiar spirits" were not the spirits of the dead, but evil angels, the messengers of Satan. Ancient idolatry, which, as we have seen, comprises both worship of the dead and pretended communion with them, is declared by the Bible to have been demon worship. The apostle Paul, in warning his brethren against participating, in any manner, in the idolatry of their heathen neighbors, says, "The things which the Gentiles sacrifice, they sacrifice to devils, and not to God, and I would not that ye should have fellowship with devils." 1 Corinthians 10:20. The psalmist, speaking of Israel, says that "they sacrificed their sons and their daughters unto devils," and in the next verse he explains that they sacrificed them "unto the idols of Canaan." Psalm 106:37, 38. In their supposed worship of dead men they were in reality worshiping demons.

Modern spiritualism, resting upon the same foundation, is but a revival in a new form of the witchcraft and demon worship that God condemned and prohibited of old. It is foretold in the Scriptures, which declare that "in the latter times some shall depart from the faith, giving heed to seducing spirits, and doctrines of devils." 1 Timothy 4:1. Paul, in his second letter to the Thessalonians, points to the special working of Satan in spiritualism as an event to take place immediately before the second advent of Christ. Speaking of Christ's second coming, he declares that it is "after the working of Satan with all power and signs and lying wonders." 2 Thessalonians 2:9. And Peter, describing the dangers to which the church was to be exposed in the last days, says that as there were false prophets who led Israel into sin, so there will be false teachers, "who privily shall bring in damnable heresies, even denying the Lord that bought them. . . . And many shall follow their pernicious ways." 2 Peter 2:1, 2. Here the apostle has pointed out one of the marked characteristics of spiritualist teachers. They refuse to acknowledge Christ as the Son of God. Concerning such teachers the beloved John declares: "Who is a liar but he that denieth that Jesus is the Christ? He is antichrist, that denieth the

Father and the Son. Whosoever denieth the Son, the same hath not the Father." 1 John 2:22, 23. Spiritualism, by denying Christ, denies both the Father and the Son, and the Bible pronounces it the manifestation of antichrist.

By the prediction of Saul's doom, given through the woman of Endor, Satan planned to ensnare the people of Israel. He hoped that they would be inspired with confidence in the sorceress, and would be led to consult her. Thus they would turn from God as their counselor and would place themselves under the guidance of Satan. The lure by which spiritualism attracts the multitudes is its pretended power to draw aside the veil from the future and reveal to men what God has hidden. God has in His word opened before us the great events of the future—all that it is essential for us to know—and He has given us a safe guide for our feet amid all its perils; but it is Satan's purpose to destroy men's confidence in God, to make them dissatisfied with their condition in life, and to lead them to seek a knowledge of what God has wisely veiled from them, and to despise what He has revealed in His Holy Word.

There are many who become restless when they cannot know the definite outcome of affairs. They cannot endure uncertainty, and in their impatience they refuse to wait to see the salvation of God. Apprehended evils drive them nearly distracted. They give way to their rebellious feelings, and run hither and thither in passionate grief, seeking intelligence concerning that which has not been revealed. If they would but trust in God, and watch unto prayer, they would find divine consolation. Their spirit would be calmed by communion with God. The weary and the heavy-laden would find rest unto their souls if they would only go to Jesus; but when they neglect the means that God has ordained for their comfort, and resort to other sources, hoping to learn what God has withheld, they commit the error of Saul, and thereby gain only a knowledge of evil.

God is not pleased with this course, and has expressed it in the most explicit terms. This impatient haste to tear away the veil from the future reveals a lack of faith in God and leaves the soul open to the suggestions of the master deceiver. Satan leads men to consult those that have familiar spirits; and by revealing hidden things of the past, he inspires confidence in his power to foretell things to come. By experience gained through the long ages he can reason from cause to effect and often forecast, with a degree of accuracy, some of the future events of man's life. Thus he is enabled to deceive poor, misguided souls and bring them under his power and lead them captive at his will.

God has given us the warning by His prophet: "When they shall say unto you, Seek unto them that have familiar spirits, and unto wizards that peep and that mutter: should not a people seek unto their God? for the living to the dead? To the law and to the testimony: if they speak not according to this word, it is because there is no light in them." Isaiah 8:19, 20.

688 Shall those who have a holy God, infinite in wisdom and power, go unto wizards, whose knowledge comes from intimacy with the enemy of our Lord? God Himself is the light of His people; He bids them fix their eyes by faith upon the glories that are veiled from human sight. The Sun of Righteousness sends its bright beams into their hearts; they have light from the throne of heaven, and they have no desire to turn away from the source of light to the messengers of Satan.

The demon's message to Saul, although it was a denunciation of sin and a prophecy of retribution, was not meant to reform him, but to goad him to despair and ruin. Oftener, however, it serves the tempter's purpose best to lure men to destruction by flattery. The teaching of the demon gods in ancient times fostered the vilest license. The divine precepts condemning sin and enforcing righteousness were set aside; truth was lightly regarded, and impurity was not only permitted but enjoined. Spiritualism declares that there is no death, no sin, no judgment, no retribution; that "men are unfallen demigods;" that desire is the highest law; and that man is accountable only to himself. The barriers that God has erected to guard truth, purity, and reverence are broken down, and many are thus emboldened in sin. Does not such teaching suggest an origin similar to that of demon worship?

The Lord presented before Israel the results of holding communion with evil spirits, in the abominations of the Canaanites: they were without natural affection, idolaters, adulterers, murderers, and abominable by every corrupt thought and revolting practice. Men do not know their own hearts; for "the heart is deceitful above all things, and desperately wicked." Jeremiah 17:9. But God understands the tendencies of the depraved nature of man. Then, as now, Satan was watching to bring about conditions favorable to rebellion, that the people of Israel might make themselves as abhorrent to God as were the Canaanites. The adversary of souls is ever on the alert to open channels for the unrestrained flow of evil in us; for he desires that we may be ruined, and be condemned before God.

Satan was determined to keep his hold on the land of Canaan, and when it was made the habitation of the children of Israel, and the law of God was made the law of the land, he hated Israel with a cruel and malignant hatred and
689 plotted their destruction. Through the agency of evil spirits strange gods were introduced; and because of transgression, the chosen people were finally scattered from the Land of Promise.

This history Satan is striving to repeat in our day. God is leading His people out from the abominations of the world, that they may keep His law; and because of this, the rage of "the accuser of our brethren" knows no bounds. "The devil is come down unto you, having great wrath, because he knoweth that he hath but a short time." Revelation 12:10, 12. The antitypical land of promise is just before us, and Satan is determined to destroy the people of God and cut them off from their inheritance. The admonition, "Watch ye and pray, lest ye enter into temptation" (Mark 14:38), was never more needed than now.

The word of the Lord to ancient Israel is addressed also to His people in this age: "Regard not them that have familiar spirits, neither seek after wizards, to be defiled by them;" "for all that do these things are an abomination unto the Lord." Leviticus 19:31; Deuteronomy 18:12.

68

690

David at Ziklag

David and his men had not taken part in the battle between Saul and the Philistines, though they had marched with the Philistines to the field of conflict. As the two armies prepared to join battle the son of Jesse found himself in a situation of great perplexity. It was expected that he would fight for the Philistines. Should he in the engagement quit the post assigned him and retire from the field, he would not only brand himself with cowardice, but with ingratitude and treachery to Achish, who had protected him and confided in him. Such an act would cover his name with infamy, and would expose him to the wrath of enemies more to be feared than Saul. Yet he could not for a moment consent to fight against Israel. Should he do this, he would become a traitor to his country—the enemy of God and of His people. It would forever bar his way to the throne of Israel; and should Saul be slain in the engagement, his death would be charged upon David.

David was caused to feel that he had missed his path. Far better would it have been for him to find refuge in God's strong fortresses of the mountains than with the avowed enemies of Jehovah and His people. But the Lord in His great mercy did not punish this error of His servant by leaving him to himself in his distress and perplexity; for though David, losing his grasp on divine power, had faltered and turned aside from the path of strict integrity, it was still the purpose of his heart to be true to God. While Satan and his host were busy helping the adversaries of God and of Israel to plan against a king

This chapter is based on 1 Samuel 29; 30 ; 2 Samuel 1.

who had forsaken God, the angels of the Lord were working to deliver David from the peril into which he had fallen. Heavenly messengers moved upon the Philistine princes to protest against the presence of David and his force with the army in the approaching conflict.

691   "What do these Hebrews here?" cried the Philistine lords, pressing about Achish. The latter, unwilling to part with so important an ally, answered, "Is not this David, the servant of Saul the king of Israel, which hath been with me these days, or these years, and I have found no fault in him since he fell unto me unto this day?"

But the princes angrily persisted in their demand: "Make this fellow return, that he may go again to his place which thou hast appointed him, and let him not go down with us to battle, lest in the battle he be an adversary to us: for wherewith should he reconcile himself unto his master? should it not be with the heads of these men? Is not this David, of whom they sang one to another in dances, saying, Saul slew his thousands, and David his ten thousands?" The slaughter of their famed champion and the triumph of Israel upon that occasion were still fresh in the memory of the Philistine lords. They did not believe that David would fight against his own people; and should he, in the heat of battle, take sides with them, he could inflict greater harm on the Philistines than would the whole of Saul's army.

Thus Achish was forced to yield, and calling David, said unto him, "Surely as Jehovah liveth, thou hast been upright, and thy going out and thy coming in with me in the host is good in my sight: for I have not found evil in thee since the day of thy coming unto me unto this day. Nevertheless the lords favor thee not. Wherefore now return, and go in peace, that thou displease not the lords of the Philistines."

David, fearing to betray his real feelings, answered, "But what have I done? and what hast thou found in thy servant so long as I have been with thee unto this day, that I may not go fight against the enemies of my lord the king?"

The reply of Achish must have sent a thrill of shame and remorse through David's heart, as he thought how unworthy of a servant of Jehovah were the deceptions to which he had stooped. "I know that thou art good in my sight, as an angel of God," said the king: "notwithstanding, the princes of the Philistines have said, He shall not go up with us to the battle. Wherefore now rise up early in the morning with thy master's servants that are come with thee: and as soon as ye be up early in the morning, and have light, depart." Thus the snare in which David had become entangled was broken, and he was set free.

692   After three days' travel David and his band of six hundred men reached Ziklag, their Philistine home. But a scene of desolation met their view. The Amalekites, taking advantage of David's absence, with his force, had avenged themselves for his incursions into their territory. They had surprised the city while it was left unguarded, and having sacked and burned it, had departed, taking all the women and children as captives, with much spoil.

Dumb with horror and amazement, David and his men for a little time gazed in silence upon the blackened and smoldering ruins. Then as a sense of their terrible desolation burst upon them, those battle-scarred warriors "lifted up their voice and wept, until they had no more power to weep."

Here again David was chastened for the lack of faith that had led him to place himself among the Philistines. He had opportunity to see how much safety could be found among the foes of God and His people. David's followers turned upon him as the cause of their calamities. He had provoked the vengeance of the Amalekites by his attack upon them; yet, too confident of security in the midst of his enemies, he had left the city unguarded. Maddened with grief and rage, his soldiers were now ready for any desperate measures, and they threatened even to stone their leader.

David seemed to be cut off from every human support. All that he held dear on earth had been swept from him. Saul had driven him from his country; the Philistines had driven him from the camp; the Amalekites had plundered his city; his wives and children had been made prisoners; and his own familiar friends had banded against him, and threatened him even with death. In this hour of utmost extremity David, instead of permitting his mind to dwell upon these painful circumstances, looked earnestly to God for help. He "encouraged himself in the Lord." He reviewed his past eventful life. Wherein had the Lord ever forsaken him? His soul was refreshed in recalling the many evidences of God's favor. The followers of David, by their discontent and impatience, made their affliction doubly grievous; but the man of God, having even greater cause for grief, bore himself with fortitude. "What time I am afraid, I will trust in Thee" (Psalm 56:3), was the language of his heart. Though he himself could not discern a way out 693 of the difficulty, God could see it, and would teach him what to do.

Sending for Abiathar the priest, the son of Ahimelech, David inquired of the Lord, saying, If I pursue after this troop, shall I overtake them?" The answer was, "Pursue: for thou shalt surely overtake them, and shalt without fail recover all." 1 Samuel 30:8, R.V.

At these words the tumult of grief and passion ceased. David and his soldiers at once set out in pursuit of their fleeing foe. So rapid was their march, that upon reaching the brook Besor, which empties near Gaza into the Mediterranean Sea, two hundred of the band were compelled by exhaustion to remain behind. But David with the remaining four hundred pressed forward, nothing daunted.

Advancing, they came upon an Egyptian slave apparently about to perish from weariness and hunger. Upon receiving food and drink, however, he revived, and they learned that he had been left to die by his cruel master, an Amalekite belonging to the invading force. He told the story of the raid and pillage; and then, having exacted a promise that he should not be slain or delivered to his master, he consented to lead David's company to the camp of their enemies.

As they came in sight of the encampment a scene of revelry met their gaze. The victorious host were holding high festival. "They were spread abroad upon all the earth, eating and drinking, and dancing, because of all the great spoil that they had taken out of the land of the Philistines, and out of the land of Judah." An immediate attack was ordered, and the pursuers rushed fiercely upon their prey. The Amalekites were surprised and thrown into confusion. The battle was continued all that night and the following day, until nearly the entire host was slain. Only a band of four hundred men, mounted upon camels, succeeded in making their escape. The word of the Lord was fulfilled. "David recovered all that the Amalekites had carried away: and David rescued his two wives. And there was nothing lacking to them, neither small nor great, neither sons nor daughters, neither spoil, nor anything that they had taken to them: David recovered all."

694 When David had invaded the territory of the Amalekites, he had put to the sword all the inhabitants that fell into his hands. But for the restraining power of God the Amalekites would have retaliated by destroying the people of Ziklag. They decided to spare the captives, desiring to heighten the honor of the triumph by leading home a large number of prisoners, and intending afterward to sell them as slaves. Thus, unwittingly, they fulfilled God's purpose, keeping the prisoners unharmed, to be restored to their husbands and fathers.

All earthly powers are under the control of the Infinite One. To the mightiest ruler, to the most cruel oppressor, He says, "Hitherto shalt thou come, but no further." Job 38:11. God's power is constantly exercised to counteract the agencies of evil; He is ever at work among men, not for their destruction, but for their correction and preservation.

With great rejoicing the victors took up their homeward march. Upon reaching their companions who had remained behind, the more selfish and unruly of the four hundred urged that those who had had no part in the battle should not

share the spoils; that it was enough for them to recover each his wife and children. But David would permit no such arrangement. "Ye shall not do so, my brethren," he said, "with that which the Lord hath given us. . . . As his part is that goeth down to the battle, so shall his part be that tarrieth by the stuff; they shall part alike." Thus the matter was settled, and it afterward became a statute in Israel that all who were honorably connected with a military campaign should share the spoils equally with those who engaged in actual combat.

Besides recovering all the spoil that had been taken from Ziklag, David and his band had captured extensive flocks and herds belonging to the Amalekites. These were called "David's spoil;" and upon returning to Ziklag, he sent from this spoil presents to the elders of his own tribe of Judah. In this distribution all those were remembered who had befriended him and his followers in the mountain fastnesses, when he had been forced to flee from place to place for his life. Their kindness and sympathy, so precious to the hunted fugitive, were thus gratefully acknowledged.

It was the third day since David and his warriors returned to Ziklag. As they labored to restore their ruined homes, they watched with anxious hearts for tidings of the battle which they knew must have been fought between 695 Israel and the Philistines. Suddenly a messenger entered the town, "with his clothes rent, and earth upon his head." He was at once brought to David, before whom he bowed with reverence, expressing recognition of him as a powerful prince, whose favor he desired. David eagerly inquired how the battle had gone. The fugitive reported Saul's defeat and death, and the death of Jonathan. But he went beyond a simple statement of facts. Evidently supposing that David must cherish enmity toward his relentless persecutor, the stranger hoped to secure honor to himself as the slayer of the king. With an air of boasting the man went on to relate that during the battle he found the monarch of Israel wounded, and sore pressed by his foes, and that at his own request the messenger had slain him. The crown from his head and the golden bracelets from his arm he had brought to David. He confidently expected that these tidings would be hailed with joy, and that a rich reward would be his for the part that he had acted.

But "David took hold on his clothes, and rent them; and likewise all the men that were with him: and they mourned, and wept, and fasted until even, for Saul, and for Jonathan his son, and for the people of the Lord, and for the house of Israel; because they were fallen by the sword."

The first shock of the fearful tidings past, David's thoughts returned to the stranger herald, and the crime of which, according to his own statement, he was guilty. The chief demanded of the young man, "Whence art thou?" And he answered, "I am the son of a stranger, an Amalekite. And David said unto him, How wast thou not afraid to stretch forth thine hand to destroy the Lord's anointed?" Twice David had had Saul in his power; but when urged to slay him, he had refused to lift his hand against him who had been consecrated by the command of God to rule over Israel. Yet the Amalekite feared not to boast that he had slain the king of Israel. He had accused himself of a crime worthy of death, and the penalty was inflicted at once. David said, "Thy blood be upon thy head; for thy mouth hath testified against thee, saying, I have slain the Lord's anointed."

David's grief at the death of Saul was sincere and deep, evincing the generosity of a noble nature. He did not exult in the fall of his enemy. The obstacle that had barred his access to the throne of Israel was removed, but at this he did not rejoice. Death had obliterated the remembrance of Saul's distrust and cruelty, and now nothing in his history was thought of but that which was noble and kingly. The name of Saul was linked with that of Jonathan, whose friendship had been so true and so unselfish.

The song in which David gave utterance to the feelings of his heart became a treasure to his nation, and to the people of God in all subsequent ages:

"Thy glory, O Israel, is slain upon thy high places!
How are the mighty fallen!
Tell it not in Gath,
Publish it not in the streets of Ashkelon;
Lest the daughters of the Philistines rejoice,
Lest the daughters of the uncircumcised triumph.
Ye mountains of Gilboa,
Let there be no dew nor rain upon you, neither fields of offerings:
For there the shield of the mighty was vilely cast away,
The shield of Saul as of one not anointed with oil. . . .
Saul and Jonathan were lovely and pleasant in their lives,
And in their death they were not divided;
They were swifter than eagles,
They were stronger than lions.
Ye daughters of Israel, weep over Saul,
Who clothed you in scarlet delicately,
Who put ornaments of gold upon your apparel.
How are the mighty fallen in the midst of the battle!
Jonathan is slain upon thy high places.
I am distressed for thee, my brother Jonathan:
Very pleasant hast thou been unto me:

Thy love to me was wonderful,
Passing the love of women.
How are the mighty fallen,
And the weapons of war perished!"
2 Samuel 1:19-27, R.V.

69

David Called to the Throne

The death of Saul removed the dangers that had made David an exile. The way was now open for him to return to his own land. When the days of mourning for Saul and Jonathan were ended, "David inquired of the Lord, saying, Shall I go up into any of the cities of Judah? And the Lord said unto him, Go up. And David said, Whither shall I go up? And He said, Unto Hebron."

Hebron was twenty miles north from Beersheba, and about midway between that city and the future site of Jerusalem. It was originally called Kirjath-arba, the city of Arba, the father of Anak. Later it was called Mamre, and here was the burial place of the patriarchs, "the cave of Machpelah." Hebron had been the possession of Caleb and was now the chief city of Judah. It lies in a valley surrounded by fertile hill country and fruitful lands. The most beautiful vineyards of Palestine were on its borders, together with numerous plantations of olive and other fruit trees.

David and his followers immediately prepared to obey the instruction which they had received from God. The six hundred armed men, with their wives and children, their flocks and herds, were soon on the way to Hebron. As the caravan entered the city the men of Judah were waiting to welcome David as the future king of Israel. Arrangements were at once made for his coronation. "And there they anointed David king over the house of Judah." But no effort was made to establish his authority by force over the other tribes.

One of the first acts of the new-crowned monarch was to express his tender regard for the memory of Saul and Jonathan. Upon learning of the brave deed of the men of Jabesh-gilead in rescuing the bodies of the fallen leaders and giving them honorable burial, David sent an embassy to Jabesh with the message, "Blessed be ye of the Lord, that ye have showed this kindness unto your lord, even unto Saul, and have buried him. And now the Lord show kindness and truth unto you: and I also will requite you this kindness." And he announced his own accession to the throne of Judah and invited the allegiance of those who had proved themselves so truehearted.

The Philistines did not oppose the action of

This chapter is based on 2 Samuel 2 to 5:5.

Judah in making David king. They had befriended him in his exile, in order to harass and weaken the kingdom of Saul, and now they hoped that because of their former kindness to David the extension of his power would, in the end, work to their advantage. But David's reign was not to be free from trouble. With his coronation began the dark record of conspiracy and rebellion. David did not sit upon a traitor's throne; God had chosen him to be king of Israel, and there had been no occasion for distrust or opposition. Yet hardly had his authority been acknowledged by the men of Judah, when through the influence of Abner, Ishbosheth, the son of Saul, was proclaimed king, and set upon a rival throne in Israel.

Ishbosheth was but a weak and incompetent representative of the house of Saul, while David was pre-eminently qualified to bear the responsibilities of the kingdom. Abner, the chief agent in raising Ishbosheth to kingly power, had been commander-in-chief of Saul's army, and was the most distinguished man in Israel. Abner knew that David had been appointed by the Lord to the throne of Israel, but having so long hunted and pursued him, he was not now willing that the son of Jesse should succeed to the kingdom over which Saul had reigned.

The circumstances under which Abner was placed served to develop his real character and showed him to be ambitious and unprincipled. He had been intimately associated with Saul and had been influenced by the spirit of the king to despise the man whom God had chosen to reign over Israel. His hatred had been increased by the cutting rebuke that David had given him at the time when the cruse of water and the spear of the king had been taken from the side of Saul as he slept in the camp. He remembered how David had cried in the hearing of the king and the people of Israel, "Art not thou a valiant man? and who is like to thee in Israel? wherefore then hast thou not kept thy lord the king? . . . This thing is not good that thou hast done. As 699 the Lord liveth, ye are worthy to die, because ye have not kept your master, the Lord's anointed." This reproof had rankled in his breast, and he determined to carry out his revengeful purpose and create division in Israel, whereby he himself might be exalted. He employed the representative of departed royalty to advance his own selfish ambitions and purposes. He knew that the people loved Jonathan. His memory was cherished, and Saul's first successful campaigns had not been forgotten by the army. With determination worthy a better cause, this rebellious leader went forward to carry out his plans.

Mahanaim, on the farther side of Jordan, was chosen as the royal residence, since it offered the greatest security against attack, either from David or from the Philistines. Here the coronation of Ishbosheth took place. His reign was first accepted by the tribes east of Jordan, and was finally extended over all Israel except Judah. For two years the son of Saul enjoyed his honors in his secluded capital. But Abner, intent upon extending his power over all Israel, prepared for aggressive warfare. And "there was long war between the house of Saul and the house of David: but David waxed stronger and stronger, and the house of Saul waxed weaker and weaker."

At last treachery overthrew the throne that malice and ambition had established. Abner, becoming incensed against the weak and incompetent Ishbosheth, deserted to David, with the offer to bring over to him all the tribes of Israel. His proposals were accepted by the king, and he was dismissed with honor to accomplish his purpose. But the favorable reception of so valiant and famed a warrior excited the jealousy of Joab, the commander-in-chief of David's army. There was a blood feud between Abner and Joab, the former having slain Asahel, Joab's brother, during the war between Israel and Judah. Now Joab, seeing an opportunity to avenge his brother's death and rid himself of a prospective rival, basely took occasion to waylay and murder Abner.

David, upon hearing of this treacherous assault, exclaimed, "I and my kingdom are guiltless before the Lord forever from the blood of Abner the son of Ner. Let it rest on the head of Joab; and on all his father's house." In view of the unsettled state of the kingdom, and the power and position of the murderers—for Joab's brother Abishai had been united with him—David could not visit the crime with just retribution, yet he publicly manifested his 700 abhorrence of the bloody deed. The burial of Abner was attended with public honors. The army, with Joab at their head, were required to take part in the services of mourning, with rent garments and clothed in sackcloth. The king manifested his grief by keeping a fast upon the day of burial; he followed the bier as chief mourner; and at the grave he pronounced an elegy which was a cutting rebuke of the murderers. "The king lamented over Abner, and said:

"Died Abner as a fool dieth?
Thy hands were not bound,
Nor thy feet put into fetters:
As a man falleth before wicked men,
So fellest thou."

David's magnanimous recognition of one who had been his bitter enemy won the confidence and admiration of all Israel. "All the people took notice of it, and it pleased them: as whatsoever the king did pleased all the people. For all the people and all Israel understood that day that it was not of the king to slay Abner the son of Ner." In the private circle of his trusted counselors and attendants the king spoke of the crime, and recognizing his own inability to punish the murderers as he desired, he left them to the justice of God: "Know ye not that there is a prince and a great man fallen this day in Israel? And I am this day weak, though anointed king; and these men the sons of Zeruiah be too hard for me: the Lord shall reward the doer of evil according to his wickedness."

Abner had been sincere in his offers and representations to David, yet his motives were base and selfish. He had persistently opposed the king of God's appointment, in the expectation of securing honor to himself. It was resentment, wounded pride, and passion that led him to forsake the cause he had so long served; and in deserting to David he hoped to receive the highest position of honor in his service. Had he succeeded in his purpose, his talents and ambition, his great influence and want of godliness, would have endangered the throne of David and the peace and prosperity of the nation.

701 "When Saul's son heard that Abner was dead in Hebron, his hands were feeble, and all the Israelites were troubled." It was evident that the kingdom could not long be maintained. Soon another act of treachery completed the downfall of the waning power. Ishbosheth was foully murdered by two of his captains, who, cutting off his head, hastened with it to the king of Judah, hoping thus to ingratiate themselves in his favor.

They appeared before David with the gory witness to their crime, saying, "Behold the head of Ishbosheth the son of Saul thine enemy, which sought thy life; and the Lord hath avenged my lord the king this day of Saul, and of his seed." But David, whose throne God Himself had established, and whom God had delivered from his adversaries, did not desire the aid of treachery to establish his power. He told these murderers of the doom visited upon him who boasted of slaying Saul. "How much more," he added, "when wicked men have slain a righteous person in his own house upon his bed? shall I not therefore now require his blood of your hand, and take you away from the earth? And David commanded his young men, and they slew them. . . . But they took the head of Ishbosheth and buried it in the sepulchre of Abner in Hebron."

After the death of Ishbosheth there was a general desire among the leading men of Israel that David should become king of all the tribes. "Then came all the tribes of Israel to David unto Hebron, and spake, saying, Behold, we are thy bone and thy flesh." They declared, "Thou wast he that leddest out and broughtest in Israel: and the Lord said to thee, Thou shalt feed My people Israel, and thou shalt be a captain over Israel. So all the elders of Israel came to the king to Hebron; and King David made a league

with them in Hebron before the Lord." Thus through the providence of God the way had been opened for him to come to the throne. He had no personal ambition to gratify, for he had not sought the honor to which he had been brought.

More than eight thousand of the descendants of Aaron and of the Levites waited upon David. The change in the sentiments of the people was marked and decisive. The revolution was quiet and dignified, befitting the great work they were doing. Nearly half a million souls, the former subjects of Saul, thronged Hebron and its environs. The very hills and valleys were alive with the multitudes. The hour for the coronation was appointed; the man who had been expelled from the court of Saul, who had fled to the mountains and hills and to the caves of 702 the earth to preserve his life, was about to receive the highest honor that can be conferred upon man by his fellow man. Priests and elders, clothed in the garments of their sacred office, officers and soldiers with glittering spear and helmet, and strangers from long distances, stood to witness the coronation of the chosen king. David was arrayed in the royal robe. The sacred oil was put upon his brow by the high priest, for the anointing by Samuel had been prophetic of what would take place at the inauguration of the king. The time had come, and David, by solemn rite, was consecrated to his office as God's vicegerent. The scepter was placed in his hands. The covenant of his righteous sovereignty was written, and the people gave their pledges of loyalty. The diadem was placed upon his brow, and the coronation ceremony was over. Israel had a king by divine appointment. He who had waited patiently for the Lord, beheld the promise of God fulfilled. "And David went on, and grew great, and the Lord God of hosts was with him." 2 Samuel 5:10.

70   703

The Reign of David

As soon as David was established on the throne of Israel he began to seek a more appropriate location for the capital of his realm. Twenty miles from Hebron a place was selected as the future metropolis of the kingdom. Before Joshua had led the armies of Israel over Jordan it had been called Salem. Near this place Abraham had proved his loyalty to God. Eight hundred years before the coronation of David it had been the home of Melchizedek, the priest of the most high God. It held a central and elevated position in the country and was protected by an environment of hills. Being on the border

This chapter is based on 2 Samuel 5:6-25 ; 6 ; 7 ; 9 ; 10.

between Benjamin and Judah, it was in close proximity to Ephraim and was easy of access to the other tribes.

In order to secure this location the Hebrews must dispossess a remnant of the Canaanites, who held a fortified position on the mountains of Zion and Moriah. This stronghold was called Jebus, and its inhabitants were known as Jebusites. For centuries Jebus had been looked upon as impregnable; but it was besieged and taken by the Hebrews under the command of Joab, who, as the reward of his valor, was made commander-in-chief of the armies of Israel. Jebus now became the national capital, and its heathen name was changed to Jerusalem.

Hiram, king of the wealthy city of Tyre, on the Mediterranean Sea, now sought an alliance with the king of Israel, and lent his aid to David in the work of erecting a palace at Jerusalem. Ambassadors were sent from Tyre, accompanied by architects and workmen and long trains laden with costly wood, cedar trees, and other valuable material.

The increasing strength of Israel in its union under David, the acquisition of the stronghold of Jebus, and the alliance with Hiram, king of Tyre, excited the hostility of the Philistines, and they again invaded the country with a strong force, taking up their position in the valley of Rephaim, but a short distance from Jerusalem. David with his men of war retired to the stronghold of Zion, to await divine direction. "And David inquired of the Lord, saying, Shall I go up to the Philistines? wilt thou deliver them into mine hand? And the Lord said unto David, Go up: for I will doubtless deliver the Philistines into thine hand."

David advanced upon the enemy at once, defeated and destroyed them, and took from them the gods which they had brought with them to ensure their victory. Exasperated by the humiliation of their defeat, the Philistines gathered a still larger force, and returned to the conflict. And again they "spread themselves in the valley of Rephaim." Again David sought the Lord and the great I AM took the direction of the armies of Israel.

God instructed David, saying, "Thou shalt not go up; but fetch a compass behind them, and come upon them over against the mulberry trees. And let it be, when thou hearest the sound of a going in the tops of the mulberry trees, that then thou shalt bestir thyself: for then shall the Lord go out before thee, to smite the host of the Philistines." If David, like Saul, had chosen his own way, success would not have attended him. But he did as the Lord had commanded, and he "smote the host of the Philistines from Gibeon even to Gazer. And the fame of David went out into all lands; and the Lord brought the fear of him upon all nations." 1 Chronicles 14:16, 17.

Now that David was firmly established upon

the throne and free from the invasions of foreign foes, he turned to the accomplishment of a cherished purpose—to bring up the ark of God to Jerusalem. For many years the ark had remained at Kirjath-jearim, nine miles distant; but it was fitting that the capital of the nation should be honored with the token of the divine Presence.

David summoned thirty thousand of the leading men of Israel, for it was his purpose to make the occasion a scene of great rejoicing and imposing display. The people responded gladly to the call. The high priest, with his brethren in sacred office and the princes and leading men of the tribes, assembled at Kirjath-jearim. David was aglow with holy zeal. The ark was brought out from the house of Abinadab and placed upon a new cart drawn by oxen, while two of the sons of Abinadab attended it.

The men of Israel followed with exultant shouts and songs of rejoicing, a multitude of voices joining in melody with the sound of musical instruments; "David and all the house of Israel played before the Lord . . . on harps, and on psalteries, and on timbrels, and on cornets, and on cymbals." It had been long since Israel had witnessed such a scene of triumph. With solemn gladness the vast procession wound its way along the hills and valleys toward the Holy City.

But "when they came to Nachon's threshing floor, Uzzah put forth his hand to the ark of God, and took hold of it; for the oxen shook it. And the anger of the Lord was kindled against Uzzah, and God smote him there for his rashness;* and there he died by the ark of God." A sudden terror fell upon the rejoicing throng. David was astonished and greatly alarmed, and in his heart he questioned the justice of God. He had been seeking to honor the ark as the symbol of the divine presence. Why, then, had that fearful judgment been sent to turn the season of gladness into an occasion of grief and mourning? Feeling that it would be unsafe to have the ark near him, David determined to let it remain where it was. A place was found for it nearby, at the house of Obed-edom the Gittite.

The fate of Uzzah was a divine judgment upon the violation of a most explicit command. Through Moses the Lord had given special instruction concerning the transportation of the ark. None but the priests, the descendants of Aaron, were to touch it, or even to look upon it uncovered. The divine direction was, "The sons of Kohath shall come to bear it: but they shall not touch any holy thing, lest they die." Numbers 4:15. The priests were to cover the ark, and then the Kohathites must lift it by the staves, which were placed in rings upon each side of the ark and were never removed. To the Gershonites and Merarites, who had in charge the curtains and boards and pillars of the tabernacle, Moses gave carts and oxen for the transportation of that

---

* Marginal reading

which was committed to them. "But unto the sons of Kohath he gave none: because the service of the sanctuary belonging unto them was that they should bear *upon their shoulders.*" Numbers 7:9. Thus in the bringing of the ark from Kirjath-jearim there had been a direct and inexcusable disregard of the Lord's directions.

David and his people had assembled to perform a sacred work, and they had engaged in it with glad and willing hearts; but the Lord could not accept the service, because it was not performed in accordance with His directions. The Philistines, who had not a knowledge of God's law, had placed the ark upon a cart when they returned it to Israel, and the Lord accepted the effort which they made. But the Israelites had in their hands a plain statement of the will of God in all these matters, and their neglect of these instructions was dishonoring to God. Upon Uzzah rested the greater guilt of presumption. Transgression of God's law had lessened his sense of its sacredness, and with unconfessed sins upon him he had, in face of the divine prohibition, presumed to touch the symbol of God's presence. God can accept no partial obedience, no lax way of treating His commandments. By the judgment upon Uzzah He designed to impress upon all Israel the importance of giving strict heed to His requirements. Thus the death of that one man, by leading the people to repentance, might prevent the necessity of inflicting judgments upon thousands.

Feeling that his own heart was not wholly right with God, David, seeing the stroke upon Uzzah, had feared the ark, lest some sin on his part should bring judgments upon him. But Obed-edom, though he rejoiced with trembling, welcomed the sacred symbol as the pledge of God's favor to the obedient. The attention of all Israel was now directed to the Gittite and his household; all watched to see how it would fare with them. "And the Lord blessed Obed-edom, and all his household."

Upon David the divine rebuke accomplished its work. He was led to realize as he had never realized before the sacredness of the law of God and the necessity of strict obedience. The favor shown to the house of Obed-edom led David again to hope that the ark might bring a blessing to him and to his people.

At the end of three months he resolved to make another attempt to remove the ark, and he now gave earnest heed to carry out in every particular the directions of the Lord. Again the chief men of the nation were summoned, and a vast assemblage gathered about the dwelling place of the Gittite. With reverent care the ark was now placed upon the shoulders of men of divine appointment, the multitude fell into line, and with trembling hearts the vast procession again set forth. After advancing six paces the trumpet sounded a halt. By David's direction

sacrifices of "oxen and fatlings" were to be offered. Rejoicing now took the place of trembling and terror. The king had laid aside his royal robes and had attired himself in a plain linen ephod, such as was worn by the priests. He did not by this act signify that he assumed priestly functions, for the ephod was sometimes worn by others besides the priests. But in this holy service he would take his place as, before God, on an equality with his subjects. Upon that day Jehovah was to be adored. He was to be the sole object of reverence.

Again the long train was in motion, and the music of harp and cornet, trumpet and cymbal, floated heavenward, blended with the melody of many voices. "And David danced before the Lord," in his gladness keeping time to the measure of the song.

David's dancing in reverent joy before God has been cited by pleasure lovers in justification of the fashionable modern dance, but there is no ground for such an argument. In our day dancing is associated with folly and midnight reveling. Health and morals are sacrificed to pleasure. By the frequenters of the ballroom God is not an object of thought and reverence; prayer or the song of praise would be felt to be out of place in their assemblies. This test should be decisive. Amusements that have a tendency to weaken the love for sacred things and lessen our joy in the service of God are not to be sought by Christians. The music and dancing in joyful praise to God at the removal of the ark had not the faintest resemblance to the dissipation of modern dancing. The one tended to the remembrance of God and exalted His holy name. The other is a device of Satan to cause men to forget God and to dishonor Him.

The triumphal procession approached the capital, following the sacred symbol of their invisible King. Then a burst of song demanded of the watchers upon the walls that the gates of the Holy City should be thrown open:

"Lift up your heads, O ye gates;
And be ye lift up, ye everlasting doors;
And the King of glory shall come in."

A band of singers and players answered:

"Who is this King of glory?"

From another company came the response:

"The Lord strong and mighty,
The Lord mighty in battle."

Then hundreds of voices, uniting, swelled the triumphal chorus:

"Lift up your heads, O ye gates;
Even lift them up, ye everlasting doors;

706

707

708

And the King of glory shall come in."

Again the joyful interrogation was heard, "Who is this King of glory?" And the voice of the great multitude, like "the sound of many waters," was heard in the rapturous reply:

"The Lord of hosts,
He is the King of glory."
Psalm 24:7-10.

Then the gates were opened wide, the procession entered, and with reverent awe the ark was deposited in the tent that had been prepared for its reception. Before the sacred enclosure altars for sacrifice were erected; the smoke of peace offerings and burnt offerings, and the clouds of incense, with the praises and supplications of Israel, ascended to heaven. The service ended, the king himself pronounced a benediction upon his people. Then with regal bounty he caused gifts of food and wine to be distributed for their refreshment.

All the tribes had been represented in this service, the celebration of the most sacred event that had yet marked the reign of David. The Spirit of divine inspiration had rested upon the king, and now as the last beams of the setting sun bathed the tabernacle in a hallowed light, his heart was uplifted in gratitude to God that the blessed symbol of His presence was now so near the throne of Israel.

Thus musing, David turned toward his palace, "to bless his household." But there was one who had witnessed the scene of rejoicing with a spirit widely different from that which moved the heart of David. "As the ark of the Lord came into the city of David, Michal Saul's daughter looked through a window, and saw King David leaping and dancing before the Lord; and she despised him in her heart." In the bitterness of her passion she could not await David's return to the palace, but went out to meet him, and to his kindly greeting poured forth a torrent of bitter words. Keen and cutting was the irony of her speech:

"How glorious was the king of Israel today, who uncovered himself today in the eyes of the handmaids of his servants, as one of the vain fellows shamelessly uncovereth himself!"

711 David felt that it was the service of God which Michal had despised and dishonored, and he sternly answered: "It was before the Lord, which chose me before thy father, and before all his house, to appoint me ruler over the people of the Lord, over Israel: therefore will I play before the Lord. And I will yet be more vile than thus, and will be base in mine own sight: and of the maidservants which thou hast spoken of, of them shall I be had in honor." To David's rebuke was added that of the Lord: because of her pride and arrogance, Michal "had no child

unto the day of her death."

The solemn ceremonies attending the removal of the ark had made a lasting impression upon the people of Israel, arousing a deeper interest in the sanctuary service and kindling anew their zeal for Jehovah. David endeavored by every means in his power to deepen these impressions. The service of song was made a regular part of religious worship, and David composed psalms, not only for the use of the priests in the sanctuary service, but also to be sung by the people in their journeys to the national altar at the annual feasts. The influence thus exerted was far-reaching, and it resulted in freeing the nation from idolatry. Many of the surrounding peoples, beholding the prosperity of Israel, were led to think favorably of Israel's God, who had done such great things for His people.

The tabernacle built by Moses, with all that appertained to the sanctuary service, except the ark, was still at Gibeah. It was David's purpose to make Jerusalem the religious center of the nation. He had erected a palace for himself, and he felt that it was not fitting for the ark of God to rest within a tent. He determined to build for it a temple of such magnificence as should express Israel's appreciation of the honor granted the nation in the abiding presence of Jehovah their King. Communicating his purpose to the prophet Nathan, he received the encouraging response, "Do all that is in thine heart; for the Lord is with thee."

But that same night the word of the Lord came to Nathan, giving him a message for the king. David was to be deprived of the privilege of building a house for God, but he was granted an assurance of the divine favor to him, to his posterity, and to the kingdom of Israel: "Thus 712 saith Jehovah of hosts; I took thee from the sheepcote, from following the sheep, to be ruler over My people, over Israel; and I was with thee whithersoever thou wentest, and have cut off all thine enemies out of thy sight, and have made thee a great name, like unto the name of the great men that are in the earth. Moreover I will appoint a place for My people Israel, and will plant them, that they may dwell in a place of their own, and move no more; neither shall the children of wickedness afflict them any more, as beforetime."

As David had desired to build a house for God, the promise was given, "The Lord telleth thee that He will make thee a house. . . . I will set up thy seed after thee. . . . He shall build a house for My name, and I will stablish the throne of his kingdom forever."

The reason why David was not to build the temple was declared: "Thou hast shed blood abundantly, and hast made great wars: thou shalt not build a house unto My name. . . . Behold, a son shall be born to thee, who shall be a man of rest; and I will give him rest from all his enemies: . . . his name shall be Solomon [peaceable], and I will give peace and quietness unto Israel in his days. He shall build a house for My name." 1 Chronicles 22:8-10.

Though the cherished purpose of his heart had been denied, David received the message with gratitude. "Who am I, O Lord God?" he exclaimed, "and what is my house, that Thou hast brought me hitherto? And this was yet a small thing in Thy sight, O Lord God; but Thou hast spoken also of Thy servant's house for a great while to come;" and he then renewed his covenant with God.

David knew that it would be an honor to his name and would bring glory to his government to perform the work that he had purposed in his heart to do, but he was ready to submit his will to the will of God. The grateful resignation thus manifested is rarely seen, even among Christians. How often do those who have passed the strength of manhood cling to the hope of accomplishing some great work upon which their hearts are set, but which they are unfitted to perform! God's providence may speak to them, as did His prophet to David, declaring that the work which they so much desire is not committed to them. It is theirs to prepare the way for another to accomplish it. But instead of gratefully submitting to the divine direction, 713 many fall back as if slighted and rejected, feeling that if they cannot do the one thing which they desire to do, they will do nothing. Many cling with desperate energy to responsibilities which they are incapable of bearing, and vainly endeavor to accomplish a work for which they are insufficient, while that which they might do, lies neglected. And because of this lack of co-operation on their part the greater work is hindered or frustrated.

David, in his covenant with Jonathan, had promised that when he should have rest from his enemies he would show kindness to the house of Saul. In his prosperity, mindful of this covenant, the king made inquiry, "Is there yet any that is left of the house of Saul, that I may show him kindness for Jonathan's sake?" He was told of a son of Jonathan, Mephibosheth, who had been lame from childhood. At the time of Saul's defeat by the Philistines at Jezreel, the nurse of this child, attempting to flee with him, had let him fall, thus making him a lifelong cripple. David now summoned the young man to court and received him with great kindness. The private possessions of Saul were restored to him for the support of his household; but the son of Jonathan was himself to be the constant guest of the king, sitting daily at the royal table. Through reports from the enemies of David, Mephibosheth had been led to cherish a strong prejudice against him as a usurper; but the monarch's generous and courteous reception of him and his continued kindness won the heart of the young man; he became strongly attached to David, and, like his father Jonathan, he felt that his interest was one with that of the king whom God had chosen.

After David's establishment upon the throne of Israel the nation enjoyed a long interval of peace. The surrounding peoples, seeing the strength and unity of the kingdom, soon thought it prudent to desist from open hostilities; and David, occupied with the organization and upbuilding of his kingdom, refrained from aggressive war. At last, however, he made war upon Israel's old enemies, the Philistines, and upon the Moabites, and succeeded in overcoming both and making them tributary.

Then there was formed against the kingdom of David a vast coalition of the surrounding nations, out of which grew the greatest wars and victories of his reign and the most extensive accessions to his power. This hostile alliance, which really sprang from jealousy of David's increasing power, had been wholly unprovoked 714 by him. The circumstances that led to its rise were these:

Tidings were received at Jerusalem announcing the death of Nahash, king of the Ammonites—a monarch who had shown kindness to David when he was a fugitive from the rage of Saul. Now, desiring to express his grateful appreciation of the favor shown him in his distress, David sent ambassadors with a message of sympathy to Hanun, the son and successor of the Ammonite king. "Said David, I will show kindness unto Hanun the son of Nahash, as his father showed kindness unto me."

But his courteous act was misinterpreted. The Ammonites hated the true God and were the bitter enemies of Israel. The apparent kindness of Nahash to David had been prompted wholly by hostility to Saul as king of Israel. The message of David was misconstrued by Hanun's counselors. They "said unto Hanun their lord, Thinkest thou that David doth honor thy father, that he hath sent comforters unto thee? hath not David rather sent his servants unto thee, to search the city, and to spy it out, and to overthrow it?" It was by the advice of his counselors that Nahash, half a century before, had been led to make the cruel condition required of the people of Jabesh-gilead, when, besieged by the Ammonites, they sued for a covenant of peace. Nahash had demanded the privilege of thrusting out all their right eyes. The Ammonites still vividly remembered how the king of Israel had foiled their cruel design, and had rescued the people whom they would have humbled and mutilated. The same hatred of Israel still prompted them. They could have no conception of the generous spirit that had inspired David's message. When Satan controls the minds of men he will excite envy and suspicion which will misconstrue the very best intentions. Listening to his counselors, Hanun regarded David's messengers as spies, and loaded them with scorn and insult.

The Ammonites had been permitted to carry out the evil purposes of their hearts without restraint, that their real character might be revealed to David. It was not God's will that Israel should enter into a league with this treacherous heathen people.

In ancient times, as now, the office of ambassador was held sacred. By the universal law of nations it ensured protection from personal violence or insult. The ambassador standing as a representative of his sovereign, any indignity offered to him demanded prompt retaliation. The Ammonites, knowing that the insult offered to Israel would surely be avenged, made preparation for war. "When the children of Ammon saw that they had made themselves odious to David, Hanun and the children of Ammon sent a thousand talents of silver to hire them chariots and horsemen out of Mesopotamia, and out of Syria-maachah, and out of Zobah. So they hired thirty and two thousand chariots. . . . And the children of Ammon gathered themselves together from their cities, and came to battle." 1 Chronicles 19:6, 7.

It was indeed a formidable alliance. The inhabitants of the region lying between the river Euphrates and the Mediterranean Sea had leagued with the Ammonites. The north and east of Canaan was encircled with armed foes, banded together to crush the kingdom of Israel.

The Hebrews did not wait for the invasion of their country. Their forces, under Joab, crossed the Jordan and advanced toward the Ammonite capital. As the Hebrew captain led his army to the field he sought to inspire them for the conflict, saying, "Be of good courage, and let us behave ourselves valiantly for our people, and for the cities of our God: and let the Lord do that which is good in His sight." 1 Chronicles 19:13. The united forces of the allies were overcome in the first engagement. But they were not yet willing to give over the contest, and the next year renewed the war. The king of Syria gathered his forces, threatening Israel with an immense army. David, realizing how much depended upon the result of this contest, took the field in person, and by the blessing of God inflicted upon the allies a defeat so disastrous that the Syrians, from Lebanon to the Euphrates, not only gave up the war, but became tributary to Israel. Against the Ammonites David pushed the war with vigor, until their strongholds fell and the whole region came under the dominion of Israel.

The dangers which had threatened the nation with utter destruction proved, through the providence of God, to be the very means by which it rose to unprecedented greatness. In commemorating his remarkable deliverances, David sings:

"The Lord liveth; and blessed be my rock; and exalted be the God of my salvation: Even the God that executeth vengeance for me, and subdueth peoples under me. He rescueth me from mine enemies: Yea, Thou liftest me up above them that rise up against me: Thou deliverest me from the violent man. Therefore I will give thanks unto Thee, O Lord, among the nations, And will sing praises unto Thy name. Great deliverance giveth He to His king; And sheweth loving-kindness to His anointed, To David and to his seed, forevermore." Psalm 18:46-50, R.V.

And throughout the songs of David the thought was impressed on his people that Jehovah was their strength and deliverer:

"There is no king saved by the multitude of a host: A mighty man is not delivered by much strength. A horse is a vain thing for safety: Neither shall he deliver any by his great strength." Psalm 33:16, 17.

"Thou art my King, O God: Command deliverances for Jacob. Through Thee will we push down our enemies: Through Thy name will we tread them under that rise up against us. For I will not trust in my bow, Neither shall my sword save me. But Thou hast saved us from our enemies, And hast put them to shame that hated us." Psalm 44:4-7.

"Some trust in chariots, and some in horses: But we will remember the name of Jehovah our God." Psalm 20:7.

The kingdom of Israel had now reached in extent the fulfillment of the promise given to Abraham, and afterward repeated to Moses: "Unto thy seed have I given this land, from the river of Egypt unto the great river, the river Euphrates." Genesis 15:18. Israel had become a mighty nation, respected and feared by surrounding peoples. In his own realm David's power had become very great. He commanded, as few sovereigns in any age have been able to command, the affections and allegiance of his people. He had honored God, and God was now honoring him.

But in the midst of prosperity lurked danger. In the time of his greatest outward triumph

David was in the greatest peril, and met his most humiliating defeat.

71

David's Sin and Repentance

The Bible has little to say in praise of men. Little space is given to recounting the virtues of even the best men who have ever lived. This silence is not without purpose; it is not without a lesson. All the good qualities that men possess are the gift of God; their good deeds are performed by the grace of God through Christ. Since they owe all to God the glory of whatever they are or do belongs to Him alone; they are but instruments in His hands. More than this—as all the lessons of Bible history teach—it is a perilous thing to praise or exalt men; for if one comes to lose sight of his entire dependence on God, and to trust to his own strength, he is sure to fall. Man is contending with foes who are stronger than he. "We wrestle not against flesh and blood, but against principalities, against powers, against the rulers of the darkness of this world, against wicked spirits in high places." Ephesians 6:12, margin. It is impossible for us in our own strength to maintain the conflict; and whatever diverts the mind from God, whatever leads to self-exaltation or to self-dependence, is surely preparing the way for our overthrow. The tenor of the Bible is to inculcate distrust of human power and to encourage trust in divine power.

It was the spirit of self-confidence and self-exaltation that prepared the way for David's fall. Flattery and the subtle allurements of power and luxury were not without effect upon him. Intercourse with surrounding nations also exerted an influence for evil. According to the customs prevailing among Eastern rulers, crimes not to be tolerated in subjects were uncondemned in the king; the monarch was not under obligation to exercise the same self-restraint as the subject. All this tended to lessen David's sense of the exceeding sinfulness of sin. And instead of relying in humility upon the power of Jehovah, he began to trust to his own wisdom and might. As soon as Satan can separate the soul from God, the only Source of strength, he will seek to arouse the unholy desires of man's carnal nature. The work of the enemy is not abrupt; it is not, at the outset, sudden and startling; it is a secret undermining of the strongholds of principle. It begins in apparently small things—the neglect to be true to God and to rely upon Him wholly, the disposition to follow the customs and practices of the world.

Before the conclusion of the war with the Ammonites, David, leaving the conduct of the army to Joab, returned to Jerusalem. The Syrians had already submitted to Israel, and the complete overthrow of the Ammonites appeared certain. David was surrounded by the fruits of victory and the honors of his wise and able rule. It was now, while he was at ease and unguarded, that the tempter seized the opportunity to occupy his mind. The fact that God had taken David into so close connection with Himself and had manifested so great favor toward him, should have been to him the strongest of incentives to preserve his character unblemished. But when in ease and self-security he let go his hold upon God, David yielded to Satan and brought upon his soul the stain of guilt. He, the Heaven-appointed leader of the nation, chosen by God to execute His law, himself trampled upon its precepts. He who should have been a terror to evildoers, by his own act strengthened their hands.

Amid the perils of his earlier life David in conscious integrity could trust his case with God. The Lord's hand had guided him safely past the unnumbered snares that had been laid for his feet. But now, guilty and unrepentant, he did not ask help and guidance from Heaven, but sought to extricate himself from the dangers in which sin had involved him. Bathsheba, whose fatal beauty had proved a snare to the king, was the wife of Uriah the Hittite, one of David's bravest and most faithful officers. None could foresee what would be the result should the crime become known. The law of God pronounced the adulterer guilty of death, and the proud-spirited soldier, so shamefully wronged, might avenge himself by taking the life of the king or by exciting the nation to revolt.

Every effort which David made to conceal his guilt proved unavailing. He had betrayed himself into the power of Satan; danger surrounded him, dishonor more bitter than death was before him. There appeared but one way of escape, and in his desperation he was hurried on to add murder to adultery. He who had compassed the destruction of Saul was seeking to lead David also to ruin. Though the temptations were different, they were alike in leading to transgression of God's law. David reasoned that if Uriah were slain by the hand of enemies in battle, the guilt of his death could not be traced home to the king, Bathsheba would be free to become David's wife, suspicion could be averted, and the royal honor would be maintained.

Uriah was made the bearer of his own death warrant. A letter sent by his hand to Joab from the king commanded, "Set ye Uriah in the fore-front of the hottest battle, and retire ye from him, that he may be smitten, and die." Joab, already stained with the guilt of one wanton murder, did not hesitate to obey the king's instructions, and Uriah fell by the sword of the children of Ammon.

This chapter is based on 2 Samuel 11; 12.

Heretofore David's record as a ruler had been such as few monarchs have ever equaled. It is written of him that he "executed judgment and justice unto all his people." 2 Samuel 8:15. His integrity had won the confidence and fealty of the nation. But as he departed from God and yielded himself to the wicked one, he became for the time the agent of Satan; yet he still held the position and authority that God had given him, and because of this, claimed obedience that would imperil the soul of him who should yield it. And Joab, whose allegiance had been given to the king rather than to God, transgressed God's law because the king commanded it.

David's power had been given him by God, but to be exercised only in harmony with the divine law. When he commanded that which was contrary to God's law, it became sin to obey. "The powers that be are ordained of God" (Romans 13:1), but we are not to obey them contrary to God's law. The apostle Paul, writing to the Corinthians, sets forth the principle by which we should be governed. He says, "Be ye followers of me, even as I also am of Christ." 1 Corinthians 11:1.

An account of the execution of his order was sent to David, but so carefully worded as not to implicate either Joab or the king. Joab "charged the messenger saying, When thou hast made an end of telling the matters of the war unto the 720 king, and if so be that the king's wrath arise, . . . then say thou, Thy servant Uriah the Hittite is dead also. So the messenger went, and came and showed David all that Joab had sent him for."

The king's answer was, "Thus shalt thou say unto Joab, Let not this thing displease thee, for the sword devoureth one as well as another: make thy battle more strong against the city, and overthrow it: and encourage thou him."

Bathsheba observed the customary days of mourning for her husband; and at their close "David sent and fetched her to his house, and she became his wife." He whose tender conscience and high sense of honor would not permit him, even when in peril of his life, to put forth his hand against the Lord's anointed, had so fallen that he could wrong and murder one of his most faithful and most valiant soldiers, and hope to enjoy undisturbed the reward of his sin. Alas! how had the fine gold become dim! how had the most fine gold changed!

From the beginning Satan has portrayed to men the gains to be won by transgression. Thus he seduced angels. Thus he tempted Adam and Eve to sin. And thus he is still leading multitudes away from obedience to God. The path of transgression is made to appear desirable; "but the end thereof are the ways of death." Proverbs 14:12. Happy they who, having ventured in this way, learn how bitter are the fruits of sin, and turn from it betimes. God in His mercy did not leave David to be lured to utter ruin by the deceitful rewards of sin.

For the sake of Israel also there was a necessity for God to interpose. As time passed on, David's sin toward Bathsheba became known, and suspicion was excited that he had planned the death of Uriah. The Lord was dishonored. He had favored and exalted David, and David's sin misrepresented the character of God and cast reproach upon His name. It tended to lower the standard of godliness in Israel, to lessen in many minds the abhorrence of sin; while those who did not love and fear God were by it emboldened in transgression.

Nathan the prophet was bidden to bear a message of reproof to David. It was a message terrible in its severity. To few sovereigns could such a reproof be given but at the price of certain death to the reprover. Nathan delivered the divine sentence unflinchingly, yet with such heaven-born wisdom as to engage the sympa- 721 thies of the king, to arouse his conscience, and to call from his lips the sentence of death upon himself. Appealing to David as the divinely appointed guardian of his people's rights, the prophet repeated a story of wrong and oppression that demanded redress.

"There were two men in one city," he said, "the one rich, and the other poor. The rich man had exceeding many flocks and herds: but the poor man had nothing, save one little ewe lamb, which he had bought and nourished up: and it grew up together with him, and with his children; it did eat of his own meat, and drank of his own cup, and lay in his bosom, and was unto him as a daughter. And there came a traveler unto the rich man, and he spared to take of his own flock and of his own herd, to dress for the wayfaring man that was come unto him; but took the poor man's lamb, and dressed it for the man that was come to him."

The anger of the king was roused, and he exclaimed, "As the Lord liveth, the man that hath done this thing is worthy to die. And he shall restore the lamb fourfold, because he did this thing, and because he had no pity." 2 Samuel 12:5, 6, margin.

Nathan fixed his eyes upon the king; then, lifting his right hand to heaven, he solemnly declared, "Thou art the man." "Wherefore," he continued, "hast thou despised the commandment of the Lord, to do evil in His sight?" The guilty may attempt, as David had done, to conceal their crime from men; they may seek to bury the evil deed forever from human sight or knowledge; but "all things are naked and opened unto the eyes of Him with whom we have to do." Hebrews 4:13. "There is nothing covered, that shall not be revealed; and hid, that shall not be known." Matthew 10:26.

Nathan declared: "Thus saith the Lord God of Israel, I anointed thee king over Israel, and I delivered thee out of the hand of Saul. . . . Wherefore hast thou despised the commandment of the Lord, to do evil in His sight? thou hast killed Uriah the Hittite with the sword, and hast taken his wife to be thy wife, and hast slain him with the sword of the children of Ammon. Now therefore the sword shall never depart from thine house. . . . Behold, I will raise up evil against thee out of thine own house, and I will take thy wives before thine eyes, and give them unto thy neighbor. . . . For thou didst it secretly; but I will do this thing before all Israel, and before the sun."

722 The prophet's rebuke touched the heart of David; conscience was aroused; his guilt appeared in all its enormity. His soul was bowed in penitence before God. With trembling lips he said, "I have sinned against the Lord." All wrong done to others reaches back from the injured one to God. David had committed a grievous sin, toward both Uriah and Bathsheba, and he keenly felt this. But infinitely greater was his sin against God.

Though there would be found none in Israel to execute the sentence of death upon the anointed of the Lord, David trembled, lest, guilty and unforgiven, he should be cut down by the swift judgment of God. But the message was sent him by the prophet, "The Lord also hath put away thy sin; thou shalt not die." Yet justice must be maintained. The sentence of death was transferred from David to the child of his sin. Thus the king was given opportunity for repentance; while to him the suffering and death of the child, as a part of his punishment, was far more bitter than his own death could have been. The prophet said, "Because by this deed thou hast given great occasion to the enemies of the Lord to blaspheme, the child also that is born unto thee shall surely die."

When his child was stricken, David, with fasting and deep humiliation, pleaded for its life. He put off his royal robes, he laid aside his crown, and night after night he lay upon the earth, in heartbroken grief interceding for the innocent one suffering for his guilt. "The elders of his house arose, and went to him, to raise him up from the earth: but he would not." Often when judgments had been pronounced upon persons or cities, humiliation and repentance had turned aside the blow, and the Ever-Merciful, swift to pardon, had sent messengers of peace. Encouraged by this thought, David persevered in his supplication so long as the child was spared. Upon learning that it was dead, he quietly submitted to the decree of God. The first stroke had fallen of that retribution which he himself had declared just; but David, trusting in God's mercy, was not without comfort.

Very many, reading the history of David's fall, have inquired, "Why has this record been made public? Why did God see fit to throw open to the world this dark passage in the life of one so highly honored of Heaven?" The prophet, in his reproof to David, had declared concerning his sin, "By this deed thou hast given great occasion to the enemies of the Lord to blaspheme." Through successive generations infidels have pointed to the character of David, 723 bearing this dark stain, and have exclaimed in triumph and derision, "This is the man after God's own heart!" Thus a reproach has been brought upon religion, God and His word have been blasphemed, souls have been hardened in unbelief, and many, under a cloak of piety, have become bold in sin.

But the history of David furnishes no countenance to sin. It was when he was walking in the counsel of God that he was called a man after God's own heart. When he sinned, this ceased to be true of him until by repentance he had returned to the Lord. The word of God plainly declares, "The thing that David had done was evil in the eyes of the Lord." 2 Samuel 11:27, margin. And the Lord said to David by the prophet, "Wherefore hast thou despised the commandment of the Lord, to do evil in His sight? . . . Now therefore the sword shall never depart from thine house; because thou hast despised Me." Though David repented of his sin and was forgiven and accepted by the Lord, he reaped the baleful harvest of the seed he himself had sown. The judgments upon him and upon his house testify to God's abhorrence of the sin.

Heretofore God's providence had preserved David against all the plottings of his enemies, and had been directly exercised to restrain Saul. But David's transgression had changed his relation to God. The Lord could not in any wise sanction iniquity. He could not exercise His power to protect David from the results of his sin as he had protected him from the enmity of Saul.

There was a great change in David himself. He was broken in spirit by the consciousness of his sin and its far-reaching results. He felt humbled in the eyes of his subjects. His influence was weakened. Hitherto his prosperity had been attributed to his conscientious obedience to the commandments of the Lord. But now his subjects, having a knowledge of his sin, would be led to sin more freely. His authority in his own household, his claim to respect and obedience from his sons, was weakened. A sense of his guilt kept him silent when he should have condemned sin; it made his arm feeble to execute justice in his house. His evil example exerted its influence upon his sons, and God would not interpose to prevent the result. He would permit things to take their natural course, and thus David was severely chastised.

For a whole year after his fall David lived in apparent security; there was no outward evidence of God's displeasure. But the divine sen- 724 tence was hanging over him. Swiftly and surely a day of judgment and retribution was approaching, which no repentance could avert, agony and shame that would darken his whole earthly life. Those who, by pointing to the example of David, try to lessen the guilt of their own sins, should learn from the Bible record that the way of transgression is hard. Though like David they should turn from their evil course, the results of sin, even in this life, will be found bitter and hard to bear.

God intended the history of David's fall to serve as a warning that even those whom He has greatly blessed and favored are not to feel secure and neglect watchfulness and prayer. And thus it has proved to those who in humility have sought to learn the lesson that God designed to teach. From generation to generation thousands have thus been led to realize their own danger from the tempter's power. The fall of David, one so greatly honored by the Lord, has awakened in them distrust of self. They have felt that God alone could keep them by His power through faith. Knowing that in Him was their strength and safety, they have feared to take the first step on Satan's ground.

Even before the divine sentence was pronounced against David he had begun to reap the fruit of transgression. His conscience was not at rest. The agony of spirit which he then endured is brought to view in the thirty-second psalm. He says:

"Blessed is he whose transgression is forgiven, whose sin is covered.
Blessed is the man unto whom the Lord imputeth not iniquity,
And in whose spirit there is no guile.
When I kept silence, my bones waxed old
Through my roaring all the day long.
For day and night Thy hand was heavy upon me:
My moisture was changed as with the drought of summer."
Psalm 32:1-4, R.V.

And the fifty-first psalm is an expression of David's repentance, when the message of reproof came to him from God:

"Have mercy upon me, O God, according to Thy loving-kindness:
According unto the multitude of Thy tender mercies blot out my transgressions.
725   Wash me thoroughly from mine iniquity, and cleanse me from my sin.
For I acknowledge my transgressions: and my sin is ever before me. . . .
Purge me with hyssop, and I shall be clean: wash me, and I shall be whiter than snow.
Make me to hear joy and gladness;
That the bones which Thou hast broken may

rejoice.
Hide Thy face from my sins,
And blot out all mine iniquities.
Create in me a clean heart, O God;
And renew a right spirit within me.
Cast me not away from Thy presence;
And take not Thy Holy Spirit from me.
Restore unto me the joy of Thy salvation;
And uphold me with Thy free Spirit.
Then will I teach transgressors Thy ways;
And sinners shall be converted unto Thee.
Deliver me from bloodguiltiness, O God,
Thou God of my salvation:
And my tongue shall sing aloud of Thy righteousness."
Psalm 51:1-14.

Thus in a sacred song to be sung in the public assemblies of his people, in the presence of the court—priests and judges, princes and men of war—and which would preserve to the latest generation the knowledge of his fall, the king of Israel recounted his sin, his repentance, and his hope of pardon through the mercy of God. Instead of endeavoring to conceal his guilt he desired that others might be instructed by the sad history of his fall.

David's repentance was sincere and deep. There was no effort to palliate his crime. No desire to escape the judgments threatened, inspired his prayer. But he saw the enormity of his transgression against God; he saw the defilement of his soul; he loathed his sin. It was not for pardon only that he prayed, but for purity of heart. David did not in despair give over the struggle. In the promises of God to repentant sinners he saw the evidence of his pardon and acceptance.

"For Thou desirest not sacrifice; else would I give it:
Thou delightest not in burnt offering.
The sacrifices of God are a broken spirit:
A broken and a contrite heart, O God, Thou wilt not despise."
Psalm 51:16, 17.

Though David had fallen, the Lord lifted him 726 up. He was now more fully in harmony with God and in sympathy with his fellow men than before he fell. In the joy of his release he sang:

"I acknowledged my sin unto Thee, and mine iniquity have I not hid.
I said, I will confess my transgressions unto the Lord;
And Thou forgavest the iniquity of my sin. . . .
Thou art my hiding place; Thou shalt preserve me from trouble;
Thou shalt compass me about with songs of deliverance."
Psalm 32:5-7.

Many have murmured at what they called God's injustice in sparing David, whose guilt was so great, after having rejected Saul for what appear to them to be far less flagrant sins. But David humbled himself and confessed his sin, while Saul despised reproof and hardened his heart in impenitence.

This passage in David's history is full of significance to the repenting sinner. It is one of the most forcible illustrations given us of the struggles and temptations of humanity, and of genuine repentance toward God and faith in our Lord Jesus Christ. Through all the ages it has proved a source of encouragement to souls that, having fallen into sin, were struggling under the burden of their guilt. Thousands of the children of God, who have been betrayed into sin, when ready to give up to despair have remembered how David's sincere repentance and confession were accepted by God, notwithstanding he suffered for his transgression; and they also have taken courage to repent and try again to walk in the way of God's commandments.

Whoever under the reproof of God will humble the soul with confession and repentance, as did David, may be sure that there is hope for him. Whoever will in faith accept God's promises, will find pardon. The Lord will never cast away one truly repentant soul. He has given this promise: "Let him take hold of My strength, that he may make peace with Me; and he shall make peace with Me." Isaiah 27:5. "Let the wicked forsake his way, and the unrighteous man his thoughts: and let him return unto the Lord, and He will have mercy upon him; and to our God, for He will *abundantly* pardon." Isaiah 55:7.

72

The Rebellion of Absalom

"He shall restore fourfold," had been David's unwitting sentence upon himself, on listening to the prophet Nathan's parable; and according to his own sentence he was to be judged. Four of his sons must fall, and the loss of each would be a result of the father's sin.

The shameful crime of Amnon, the first-born, was permitted by David to pass unpunished and unrebuked. The law pronounced death upon the adulterer, and the unnatural crime of Amnon made him doubly guilty. But David, self-condemned for his own sin, failed to bring the offender to justice. For two full years Absalom, the natural protector of the sister so foully wronged, concealed his purpose of revenge, but only to strike more surely at the last. At a feast of the king's sons the drunken, incestuous Amnon was slain by his brother's command.

Twofold judgment had been meted out to David. The terrible message was carried to him, "Absalom hath slain all the king's sons, and there is not one of them left. Then the king arose, and tare his garments, and lay on the earth; and all his servants stood by with their clothes rent." The king's sons, returning in alarm to Jerusalem, revealed to their father the truth; Amnon alone had been slain; and they "lifted up their voice and wept: and the king also and all his servants wept very sore." But Absalom fled to Talmai, the king of Geshur, his mother's father.

Like other sons of David, Amnon had been left to selfish indulgence. He had sought to gratify every thought of his heart, regardless of the requirements of God. Notwithstanding his great sin, God had borne long with him. For two years he had been granted opportunity for repentance; but he continued in sin, and with his guilt upon him, he was cut down by death, to await the awful tribunal of the judgment.

David had neglected the duty of punishing the crime of Amnon, and because of the unfaithfulness of the king and father and the impenitence of the son, the Lord permitted events to take their natural course, and did not restrain Absalom. When parents or rulers neglect the duty of punishing iniquity, God Himself will take the case in hand. His restraining power will be in a measure removed from the agencies of evil, so that a train of circumstances will arise which will punish sin with sin.

The evil results of David's unjust indulgence toward Amnon were not ended, for it was here that Absalom's alienation from his father began. After he fled to Geshur, David, feeling that the crime of his son demanded some punishment, refused him permission to return. And this had a tendency to increase rather than to lessen the inextricable evils in which the king had come to be involved. Absalom, energetic, ambitious, and unprincipled, shut out by his exile from participation in the affairs of the kingdom, soon gave himself up to dangerous scheming.

At the close of two years Joab determined to effect a reconciliation between the father and his son. And with this object in view he secured the services of a woman of Tekoah, reputed for wisdom. Instructed by Joab, the woman represented herself to David as a widow whose two sons had been her only comfort and support. In a quarrel one of these had slain the other, and now all the relatives of the family demanded that the survivor should be given up to the avenger of blood. "And so," said the mother, "they shall quench my coal which is left, and shall not leave to my husband neither name nor remainder upon the earth." The king's feelings were touched by this appeal, and he assured the woman of the royal protection for her son.

This chapter is based on 2 Samuel 13 to 19.

After drawing from him repeated promises for the young man's safety, she entreated the king's forbearance, declaring that he had spoken as one at fault, in that he did not fetch home again his banished. "For," she said, "we must needs die, and are as water spilt on the ground, which cannot be gathered up again; neither doth God respect any person; yet doth *He devise means, that His banished be not expelled from Him.*" This tender and touching portrayal of the love of God toward the sinner—coming as it did from Joab, the rude soldier—is a striking evidence of the familiarity of the Israelites with the great truths of redemption. The king, feeling his own need of God's mercy, could not resist this appeal. To Joab the command was given, "Go therefore, bring the young man Absalom again."

729

Absalom was permitted to return to Jerusalem, but not to appear at court or to meet his father. David had begun to see the evil effects of his indulgence toward his children; and tenderly as he loved this beautiful and gifted son, he felt it necessary, as a lesson both to Absalom and to the people, that abhorrence for such a crime should be manifested. Absalom lived two years in his own house, but banished from the court. His sister dwelt with him, and her presence kept alive the memory of the irreparable wrong she had suffered. In the popular estimation the prince was a hero rather than an offender. And having this advantage, he set himself to gain the hearts of the people. His personal appearance was such as to win the admiration of all beholders. "In all Israel there was none to be so much praised as Absalom for his beauty: from the sole of his foot even to the crown of his head there was no blemish in him." It was not wise for the king to leave a man of Absalom's character—ambitious, impulsive, and passionate—to brood for two years over supposed grievances. And David's action in permitting him to return to Jerusalem, and yet refusing to admit him to his presence, enlisted in his behalf the sympathies of the people.

With the memory ever before him of his own transgression of the law of God, David seemed morally paralyzed; he was weak and irresolute, when before his sin he had been courageous and decided. His influence with the people had been weakened. And all this favored the designs of his unnatural son.

Through the influence of Joab, Absalom was again admitted to his father's presence; but though there was an outward reconciliation, he continued his ambitious scheming. He now assumed an almost royal state, having chariots and horses, and fifty men to run before him. And while the king was more and more inclined to desire retirement and solitude, Absalom sedulously courted the popular favor.

The influence of David's listlessness and irresolution extended to his subordinates; negligence and delay characterized the administration of justice. Absalom artfully turned every cause of dissatisfaction to his own advantage. Day by day this man of noble mien might be seen at the gate of the city, where a crowd of suppliants waited to present their wrongs for redress. Absalom mingled with them and listened to their grievances, expressing sympathy with their sufferings and regret at the inefficiency of the government. Having thus listened to the story of a man of Israel, the prince would reply, "Thy matters are good and right; but there is no man deputed of the king to hear thee;" adding, "O that I were made judge in the land, that every man which hath any suit or cause might come unto me, and I would do him justice! And it was so, that when any man came nigh to him to do him obeisance, he put forth his hand, and took him, and kissed him."

730

Fomented by the artful insinuations of the prince, discontent with the government was fast spreading. The praise of Absalom was on the lips of all. He was generally regarded as heir to the kingdom; the people looked upon him with pride as worthy of this high station, and a desire was kindled that he might occupy the throne. "So Absalom stole the hearts of the men of Israel." Yet the king, blinded by affection for his son, suspected nothing. The princely state which Absalom had assumed, was regarded by David as intended to do honor to his court—as an expression of joy at the reconciliation.

The minds of the people being prepared for what was to follow, Absalom secretly sent picked men throughout the tribes, to concert measures for a revolt. And now the cloak of religious devotion was assumed to conceal his traitorous designs. A vow made long before while he was in exile must be paid in Hebron. Absalom said to the king, "I pray thee, let me go and pay my vow, which I have vowed unto the Lord, in Hebron. For thy servant vowed a vow while I abode at Geshur in Syria, saying, If the Lord shall bring me again indeed to Jerusalem, then I will serve the Lord." The fond father, comforted with this evidence of piety in his son, dismissed him with his blessing. The conspiracy was now fully matured. Absalom's crowning act of hypocrisy was designed not only to blind the king but to establish the confidence of the people, and thus to lead them on to rebellion against the king whom God had chosen.

Absalom set forth for Hebron, and there went with him "two hundred men out of Jerusalem, that were called; and they went in their simplicity, and they knew not anything." These men went with Absalom, little thinking that their love for the son was leading them into rebellion against the father. Upon arriving at Hebron, Absalom immediately summoned Ahithophel, one of the chief counselors of David, a man in

731

high repute for wisdom, whose opinion was thought to be as safe and wise as that of an oracle. Ahithophel joined the conspirators, and his support made the cause of Absalom appear certain of success, attracting to his standard many influential men from all parts of the land. As the trumpet of revolt was sounded, the prince's spies throughout the country spread the tidings that Absalom was king, and many of the people gathered to him.

Meanwhile the alarm was carried to Jerusalem, to the king. David was suddenly aroused, to see rebellion breaking out close beside his throne. His own son—the son whom he had loved and trusted—had been planning to seize his crown and doubtless to take his life. In his great peril David shook off the depression that had so long rested upon him, and with the spirit of his earlier years he prepared to meet this terrible emergency. Absalom was mustering his forces at Hebron, only twenty miles away. The rebels would soon be at the gates of Jerusalem.

From his palace David looked out upon his capital—"beautiful for situation, the joy of the whole earth, . . . the city of the great King." Psalm 48:2. He shuddered at the thought of exposing it to carnage and devastation. Should he call to his help the subjects still loyal to his throne, and make a stand to hold his capital? Should he permit Jerusalem to be deluged with blood? His decision was taken. The horrors of war should not fall upon the chosen city. He would leave Jerusalem, and then test the fidelity of his people, giving them an opportunity to rally to his support. In this great crisis it was his duty to God and to his people to maintain the authority with which Heaven had invested him. The issue of the conflict he would trust with God.

In humility and sorrow David passed out of the gate of Jerusalem—driven from his throne, from his palace, from the ark of God, by the insurrection of his cherished son. The people followed in long, sad procession, like a funeral train. David's bodyguard of Cherethites, Pelethites, and six hundred Gittites from Gath, under the command of Ittai, accompanied the king. But David, with characteristic unselfishness, could not consent that these strangers who had sought his protection should be involved in his calamity. He expressed surprise that they should be ready to make this sacrifice for him. Then said the king to Ittai the Gittite, "Where-732 fore goest thou also with us? return to thy place, and abide with the king: for thou art a stranger, and also an exile. Whereas thou camest but yesterday, should I this day make thee go up and down with us? seeing I go whither I may, return thou, and take back thy brethren: mercy and truth be with thee."

Ittai answered, "As the Lord liveth, and as my lord the king liveth, surely in what place my lord the king shall be, whether in death or life, even there also will thy servant be." These men had been converted from paganism to the worship of Jehovah, and nobly they now proved their fidelity to their God and their king. David, with grateful heart, accepted their devotion to his apparently sinking cause, and all passed over the brook Kidron on the way toward the wilderness.

Again the procession halted. A company clad in holy vestments was approaching. "And lo Zadok also, and all the Levites were with him, bearing the ark of the covenant of God." The followers of David looked upon this as a happy omen. The presence of that sacred symbol was to them a pledge of their deliverance and ultimate victory. It would inspire the people with courage to rally to the king. Its absence from Jerusalem would bring terror to the adherents of Absalom.

At sight of the ark joy and hope for a brief moment thrilled the heart of David. But soon other thoughts came to him. As the appointed ruler of God's heritage he was under solemn responsibility. Not personal interests, but the glory of God and the good of his people, were to be uppermost in the mind of Israel's king. God, who dwelt between the cherubim, had said of Jerusalem, "This is My rest" (Psalm 132:14); and without divine authority neither priest nor king had a right to remove therefrom the symbol of His presence. And David knew that his heart and life must be in harmony with the divine precepts, else the ark would be the means of disaster rather than of success. His great sin was ever before him. He recognized in this conspiracy the just judgment of God. The sword that was not to depart from his house had been unsheathed. He knew not what the result of the struggle might be. It was not for him to remove from the capital of the nation the sacred statutes which embodied the will of their divine Sovereign, which were the constitution of the realm and the foundation of its prosperity.

He commanded Zadok, "Carry back the ark 735 of God into the city: if I shall find favor in the eyes of the Lord, He will bring me again, and show me both it and His habitation: but if He thus say, I have no delight in thee; behold, here am I, let Him do to me as seemeth good unto Him."

David added, "Art not thou a seer?"—a man appointed of God to instruct the people. "Return into the city in peace, and your two sons with you, Ahimaaz thy son, and Jonathan the son of Abiathar. See, I will tarry in the plain of the wilderness, until there come word from you to certify me." In the city the priests might do him good service by learning the movements and purposes of the rebels, and secretly communicating them to the king by their sons, Ahimaaz and Jonathan.

As the priests turned back toward Jerusalem a deeper shadow fell upon the departing throng. Their king a fugitive, themselves outcasts, forsaken even by the ark of God—the future was dark with terror and foreboding. "And David went up by the ascent of Mount Olivet, and wept as he went up, and had his head covered, and he went barefoot: and all the people that was with him covered every man his head, and they went up, weeping as they went up. And one told David, saying, Ahithophel is among the conspirators with Absalom." Again David was forced to recognize in his calamities the results of his own sin. The defection of Ahithophel, the ablest and most wily of political leaders, was prompted by revenge for the family disgrace involved in the wrong to Bathsheba, who was his granddaughter.

"And David said, O Lord, I pray Thee, turn the counsel of Ahithophel into foolishness." Upon reaching the top of the mount, the king bowed in prayer, casting upon God the burden of his soul and humbly supplicating divine mercy. His prayer seemed to be at once answered. Hushai the Archite, a wise and able counselor, who had proved himself a faithful friend to David, now came to him with his robes rent and with earth upon his head, to cast in his fortunes with the dethroned and fugitive king. David saw, as by a divine enlightenment, that this man, faithful and truehearted, was the one needed to serve the interests of the king in the councils at the capital. At David's request Hushai returned to Jerusalem to offer his services to Absalom and defeat the crafty counsel of Ahithophel.

736 With this gleam of light in the darkness, the king and his followers pursued their way down the eastern slope of Olivet, through a rocky and desolate waste, through wild ravines, and along stony and precipitous paths, toward the Jordan. "And when King David came to Bahurim, behold, thence came out a man of the family of the house of Saul, whose name was Shimei, the son of Gera: he came forth, and cursed still as he came. And he cast stones at David, and at all the servants of King David: and all the people and all the mighty men were on his right hand and on his left. And thus said Shimei when he cursed, Come out, come out, thou bloody man, and thou man of Belial. The Lord hath returned upon thee all the blood of the house of Saul, in whose stead thou hast reigned; and the Lord hath delivered the kingdom into the hand of Absalom thy son: and, behold, thou art taken in thy mischief, because thou art a bloody man."

In David's prosperity Shimei had not shown by word or act that he was not a loyal subject. But in the affliction of the king this Benjamite revealed his true character. He had honored David upon his throne, but he cursed him in his humiliation. Base and selfish, he looked upon others as of the same character as himself, and, inspired by Satan, he wreaked his hatred upon him whom God had chastened. The spirit that leads man to triumph over, to revile or distress, one who is in affliction is the spirit of Satan.

Shimei's accusations against David were utterly false—a baseless and malignant slander. David had not been guilty of wrong toward Saul or his house. When Saul was wholly in his power, and he could have slain him, he merely cut the skirt of his robe, and he reproached himself for showing even this disrespect for the Lord's anointed.

Of David's sacred regard for human life, striking evidence had been given, even while he himself was hunted like a beast of prey. One day while he was hidden in the cave of Adullam, his thoughts turning back to the untroubled freedom of his boyhood life, the fugitive exclaimed, "Oh that one would give me drink of the water of the well of Bethlehem, which is by the gate!" 2 Samuel 23:13-17. Bethlehem was at that time in the hands of the Philistines; but three mighty men of David's band broke through the guard, and brought of the water of Bethlehem to their master. David could not drink it. "Be it far from me," he cried; "is not 737 this the blood of the men that went in jeopardy of their lives?" And he reverently poured out the water as an offering to God. David had been a man of war, much of his life had been spent amid scenes of violence; but of all who have passed through such an ordeal, few indeed have been so little affected by its hardening, demoralizing influence as was David.

David's nephew, Abishai, one of the bravest of his captains, could not listen patiently to Shimei's insulting words. "Why," he exclaimed, "should this dead dog curse my lord the king? let me go over, I pray thee, and take off his head." But the king forbade him. "Behold," he said, "my son . . . seeketh my life: how much more now may this Benjamite do it? let him alone, and let him curse; for the Lord hath bidden him. It may be that the Lord will look on mine affliction, and that the Lord will requite me good for his cursing this day."

Conscience was uttering bitter and humiliating truths to David. While his faithful subjects wondered at his sudden reverse of fortune, it was no mystery to the king. He had often had forebodings of an hour like this. He had wondered that God had so long borne with his sins, and had delayed the merited retribution, and now in his hurried and sorrowful flight, his feet bare, his royal robes changed for sackcloth, the lamentations of his followers awaking the echoes of the hills, he thought of his loved capital—of the place which had been the scene of his sin—and as he remembered the goodness and long-suffering of God, he was not altogether without hope. He felt that the Lord would still deal with him in mercy.

Many a wrongdoer has excused his own sin by pointing to David's fall, but how few there are who manifest David's penitence and humility. How few would bear reproof and retribution with the patience and fortitude that he manifested. He had confessed his sin, and for years had sought to do his duty as a faithful servant of God; he had labored for the upbuilding of his kingdom, and under his rule it had attained to strength and prosperity never reached before. He had gathered rich stores of material for the building of the house of God, and now was all the labor of his life to be swept away? Must the results of years of consecrated toil, the work of genius and devotion and statesmanship, pass into the hands of his reckless and traitorous son, who regarded not the honor of God nor the prosperity of Israel? How natural it would have seemed for David to murmur against God in this great affliction!

But he saw in his own sin the cause of his trouble. The words of the prophet Micah breathe the spirit that inspired David's heart. "When I sit in darkness, the Lord shall be a light unto me. I will bear the indignation of the Lord, because I have sinned against Him, until He plead my cause, and execute judgment for me." Micah 7:8, 9. And the Lord did not forsake David. This chapter in his experience, when, under cruelest wrong and insult, he shows himself to be humble, unselfish, generous, and submissive, is one of the noblest in his whole experience. Never was the ruler of Israel more truly great in the sight of heaven than at this hour of his deepest outward humiliation.

Had God permitted David to go on unrebuked in sin, and while transgressing the divine precepts, to remain in peace and prosperity upon his throne, the skeptic and infidel might have had some excuse for citing the history of David as a reproach to the religion of the Bible. But in the experience through which He caused David to pass, the Lord shows that He cannot tolerate or excuse sin. And David's history enables us to see also the great ends which God has in view in His dealings with sin; it enables us to trace, even through darkest judgments, the working out of His purposes of mercy and beneficence. He caused David to pass under the rod, but He did not destroy him; the furnace is to purify, but not to consume. The Lord says, "If they break My statutes, and keep not My commandments; then will I visit their transgression with the rod, and their iniquity with stripes. Nevertheless My loving-kindness will I not utterly take from him, nor suffer My faithfulness to fail." Psalm 89:31-33.

Soon after David left Jerusalem, Absalom and his army entered, and without a struggle took possession of the stronghold of Israel. Hushai was among the first to greet the new-crowned monarch, and the prince was surprised and gratified at the accession of his father's old friend and counselor. Absalom was confident of success. Thus far his schemes had prospered, and eager to strengthen his throne and secure the confidence of the nation, he welcomed Hushai to his court.

Absalom was now surrounded by a large force, but it was mostly composed of men untrained for war. As yet they had not been brought into conflict. Ahithophel well knew that David's situation was far from hopeless. A large part of the nation were still true to him; he was surrounded by tried warriors, who were faithful to their king, and his army was commanded by able and experienced generals. Ahithophel knew that after the first burst of enthusiasm in favor of the new king, a reaction would come. Should the rebellion fail, Absalom might be able to secure a reconciliation with his father; then Ahithophel, as his chief counselor, would be held most guilty for the rebellion; upon him the heaviest punishment would fall. To prevent Absalom from retracing his steps, Ahithophel counseled him to an act that in the eyes of the whole nation would make reconciliation impossible. With hellish cunning this wily and unprincipled statesman urged Absalom to add the crime of incest to that of rebellion. In the sight of all Israel he was to take to himself his father's concubines, according to the custom of oriental nations, thus declaring that he succeeded to his father's throne. And Absalom carried out the vile suggestion. Thus was fulfilled the word of God to David by the prophet, "Behold, I will raise up evil against thee out of thine own house, and I will take thy wives before thine eyes, and give them unto thy neighbor. . . . For thou didst it secretly: but I will do this thing before all Israel, and before the sun." 2 Samuel 12:11, 12. Not that God prompted these acts of wickedness, but because of David's sin He did not exercise His power to prevent them.

Ahithophel had been held in high esteem for his wisdom, but he was destitute of the enlightenment which comes from God. "The fear of the Lord is the beginning of wisdom" (Proverbs 9:10); and this, Ahithophel did not possess, or he could hardly have based the success of treason upon the crime of incest. Men of corrupt hearts plot wickedness, as if there were no overruling Providence to cross their designs; but "He that sitteth in the heavens shall laugh: the Lord shall have them in derision." Psalm 2:4. The Lord declares: "They would none of My counsel: they despised all My reproof. Therefore shall they eat of the fruit of their own way, and be filled with their own devices. For the turning away of the simple shall slay them, and the prosperity of fools shall destroy them."

Proverbs 1:30-32.

Having succeeded in the plot for securing his own safety, Ahithophel urged upon Absalom the necessity of immediate action against David. "Let me now choose out twelve thousand men," he said, "and I will arise and pursue after David this night: and I will come upon him while he is weary and weak-handed, and will make him afraid: and all the people that are with him shall flee; and I will smite the king only: and I will bring back all the people unto thee." This plan was approved by the king's counselors. Had it been followed, David would surely have been slain, unless the Lord had directly interposed to save him. But a wisdom higher than that of the renowned Ahithophel was directing events. "The Lord had appointed to defeat the good counsel of Ahithophel, to the intent that the Lord might bring evil upon Absalom."

Hushai had not been called to the council, and he would not intrude himself unasked, lest suspicion should be drawn upon him as a spy; but after the assembly had dispersed, Absalom, who had a high regard for the judgment of his father's counselor, submitted to him the plan of Ahithophel. Hushai saw that if the proposed plan were followed, David would be lost. And he said, "The counsel that Ahithophel hath given is not good at this time. For, said Hushai, thou knowest thy father and his men, that they be mighty men, and they be chafed in their minds, as a bear robbed of her whelps in the field: and thy father is a man of war, and will not lodge with the people. Behold, he is hid now in some pit, or in some other place;" he argued that, if Absalom's forces should pursue David, they would not capture the king; and should they suffer a reverse, it would tend to dishearten them and work great harm to Absalom's cause. "For," he said, "all Israel knoweth that thy father is a mighty man, and they which be with him are valiant men." And he suggested a plan attractive to a vain and selfish nature, fond of the show of power: "I counsel that all Israel be generally gathered unto thee, from Dan even to Beer-sheba, as the sand that is by the sea for multitude; and that thou go to battle in thine own person. So shall we come upon him in some place where he shall be found, and we will light upon him as the dew falleth on the ground: and of him and of all the men that are with him there shall not be left so much as one. Moreover, if he be gotten into a city, then shall all Israel bring ropes to that city, and we will draw it into the river, until there be not one small stone found there."

741   "And Absalom and all the men of Israel said, The counsel of Hushai the Archite is better than the counsel of Ahithophel." But there was one who was not deceived—one who clearly foresaw the result of this fatal mistake of Absalom's. Ahithophel knew that the cause of the rebels was lost. And he knew that whatever might be the fate of the prince, there was no hope for the counselor who had instigated his greatest crimes. Ahithophel had encouraged Absalom in rebellion; he had counseled him to the most abominable wickedness, to the dishonor of his father; he had advised the slaying of David and had planned its accomplishment; he had cut off the last possibility of his own reconciliation with the king; and now another was preferred before him, even by Absalom. Jealous, angry, and desperate, Ahithophel "gat him home to his house, to his city, and put his household in order, and hanged himself, and died." Such was the result of the wisdom of one, who, with all his high endowments, did not make God his counselor. Satan allures men with flattering promises, but in the end it will be found by every soul, that the "wages of sin is death." Romans 6:23.

Hushai, not certain that his counsel would be followed by the fickle king, lost no time in warning David to escape beyond Jordan without delay. To the priests, who were to forward it by their sons, Hushai sent the message: "Thus and thus did Ahithophel counsel Absalom and the elders of Israel; and thus and thus have I counseled. Now therefore . . . lodge not this night in the plains of the wilderness, but speedily pass over; lest the king be swallowed up, and all the people that are with him."

The young men were suspected and pursued, yet they succeeded in performing their perilous mission. David, spent with toil and grief after that first day of flight, received the message that he must cross the Jordan that night, for his son was seeking his life.

What were the feelings of the father and king, so cruelly wronged, in this terrible peril? "A mighty valiant man," a man of war, a king, whose word was law, betrayed by his son whom he had loved and indulged and unwisely trusted, wronged and deserted by subjects bound to him by the strongest ties of honor and fealty—in what words did David pour out the feelings of his soul? In the hour of his darkest trial David's heart was stayed upon God, and he sang:

"Lord, how are they increased that trouble   742
    me!
Many are they that rise up against me.
Many there be which say of my soul,
There is no help for him in God.
But Thou, O Lord, art a shield for me;
My glory, and the lifter up of mine head.
I cried unto the Lord with my voice,
And He heard me out of His holy hill.
I laid me down and slept;
I awaked; for the Lord sustained me.
I will not be afraid of ten thousands of people,
That have set themselves against me round
    about. . . .

Salvation belongeth unto the Lord:
Thy blessing is upon Thy people."
                            Psalm 3:1-8.

David and all his company—warriors and statesmen, old men and youth, the women and the little children—in the darkness of night crossed the deep and swift-flowing river. "By the morning light there lacked not one of them that was not gone over Jordan."

David and his forces fell back to Mahanaim, which had been the royal seat of Ishbosheth. This was a strongly fortified city, surrounded by a mountainous district favorable for retreat in case of war. The country was well-provisioned, and the people were friendly to the cause of David. Here many adherents joined him, while wealthy tribesmen brought abundant gifts of provision, and other needed supplies.

Hushai's counsel had achieved its object, gaining for David opportunity for escape; but the rash and impetuous prince could not be long restrained, and he soon set out in pursuit of his father. "And Absalom passed over Jordan, he and all the men of Israel with him." Absalom made Amasa, the son of David's sister Abigail, commander-in-chief of his forces. His army was large, but it was undisciplined and poorly prepared to cope with the tried soldiers of his father.

David divided his forces into three battalions under the command of Joab, Abishai, and Ittai the Gittite. It had been his purpose himself to lead his army in the field; but against this the officers of the army, the counselors, and the people vehemently protested. "Thou shalt not go forth," they said: "for if we flee away, they will not care for us; neither if half of us die, will they care for us: but thou art worth ten thousand 743 of us: therefore now it is better that thou be ready to succour us out of the city. And the king said unto them, What seemeth you best I will do." 2 Samuel 18:3, 4, R.V.

From the walls of the city the long lines of the rebel army were in full view. The usurper was accompanied by a vast host, in comparison with which David's force seemed but a handful. But as the king looked upon the opposing forces, the thought uppermost in his mind was not of the crown and the kingdom, nor of his own life, that depended upon the wage of battle. The father's heart was filled with love and pity for his rebellious son. As the army filed out from the city gates David encouraged his faithful soldiers, bidding them go forth trusting that the God of Israel would give them the victory. But even here he could not repress his love for Absalom. As Joab, leading the first column, passed his king, the conqueror of a hundred battlefields stooped his proud head to hear the monarch's last message, as with trembling voice he said, "Deal gently for my sake with the young man,

even with Absalom." And Abishai and Ittai received the same charge—"Deal gently *for my sake* with the young man, even with Absalom." But the king's solicitude, seeming to declare that Absalom was dearer to him than his kingdom, dearer even than the subjects faithful to his throne, only increased the indignation of the soldiers against the unnatural son.

The place of battle was a wood near the Jordan, in which the great numbers of Absalom's army were only a disadvantage to him. Among the thickets and marshes of the forest these undisciplined troops became confused and unmanageable. And "the people of Israel were slain before the servants of David, and there was there a great slaughter that day of twenty thousand men." Absalom, seeing that the day was lost, had turned to flee, when his head was caught between the branches of a widespreading tree, and his mule going out from under him, he was left helplessly suspended, a prey to his enemies. In this condition he was found by a soldier, who, for fear of displeasing the king, spared Absalom, but reported to Joab what he had seen. Joab was restrained by no scruples. He had befriended Absalom, having twice secured his reconciliation with David, and the trust had been shamelessly betrayed. But for the advantages gained by Absalom through Joab's intercession, this rebellion, with all its horrors, could never have occurred. Now it was in Joab's power at one blow to destroy the instiga- 744 tor of all this evil. "And he took three darts in his hand, and thrust them through the heart of Absalom. . . . And they took Absalom, and cast him into a great pit in the wood, and laid a very great heap of stones upon him."

Thus perished the instigators of rebellion in Israel. Ahithophel had died by his own hand. The princely Absalom, whose glorious beauty had been the pride of Israel, had been cut down in the vigor of his youth, his dead body thrust into a pit, and covered with a heap of stones, in token of everlasting reproach. During his lifetime Absalom had reared for himself a costly monument in the king's dale, but the only memorial which marked his grave was that heap of stones in the wilderness.

The leader of the rebellion being slain, Joab by the sound of the trumpet recalled his army from the pursuit of the fleeing host, and messengers were at once dispatched to bear the tidings to the king.

The watchman upon the city wall, looking out toward the battlefield, discovered a man running alone. Soon a second came in sight. As the first drew nearer, the watchman said to the king, who was waiting beside the gate, "Me thinketh the running of the foremost is like the running of Ahimaaz the son of Zadok. And the king said, He is a good man, and cometh with good tidings. And Ahimaaz called, and said unto the king, All is well. And he fell down to the earth upon his face before the king, and said, Blessed be the Lord thy God, which hath delivered up the men that lifted up their hand against my lord the king." To the king's eager inquiry, "Is the young man Absalom safe?" Ahimaaz returned an evasive answer.

The second messenger came, crying, "Tidings, my lord the king: for the Lord hath avenged this day of all them that rose up against thee." Again from the father's lips came the absorbing question, "Is the young man Absalom safe?" Unable to conceal the heavy tidings, the herald answered, "The enemies of my lord the king, and all that rise against thee to do thee hurt, be as that young man is." It was enough. David questioned no further, but with bowed head he "went up to the chamber over the gate, and wept: and as he went, thus he said, O my son Absalom! my son, my son Absalom! would God I had died for thee, O Absalom, my son, my son!"

745   The victorious army, returning from the field, approached the city, their shouts of triumph awaking the echoes of the hills. But as they entered the city gate the shout died away, their banners drooped in their hands, and with downcast gaze they advanced more like those who had suffered defeat than like conquerors. For the king was not waiting to bid them welcome, but from the chamber above the gate his wailing cry was heard, "O my son Absalom! my son, my son Absalom! would God I had died for thee, O Absalom, my son, my son!"

"The victory that day was turned into mourning unto all the people; for the people heard say that day how the king was grieved for his son. And the people gat them by stealth that day into the city, as people being ashamed steal away when they flee in battle."

Joab was filled with indignation. God had given them reason for triumph and gladness; the greatest rebellion that had ever been known in Israel had been crushed; and yet this great victory was turned to mourning for him whose crime had cost the blood of thousands of brave men. The rude, blunt captain pushed his way into the presence of the king, and boldly said, "Thou hast shamed this day the faces of all thy servants, which this day have saved thy life, and the lives of thy sons and of thy daughters; . . . in that thou lovest thine enemies, and hatest thy friends. For thou hast declared this day, that thou regardest neither princes nor servants: for this day I perceive, that if Absalom had lived, and all we had died this day, then it had pleased thee well. Now therefore arise, go forth, and speak comfortably unto thy servants: for I swear by the Lord, if thou go not forth, there will not tarry one with thee this night: and that will be worse unto thee than all the evil that befell thee from thy youth until now."

Harsh and even cruel as was the reproof to the heart-stricken king, David did not resent it. Seeing that his general was right, he went down to the gate, and with words of courage and commendation greeted his brave soldiers as they marched past him.

73
746

The Last Years of David

The overthrow of Absalom did not at once bring peace to the kingdom. So large a part of the nation had joined in revolt that David would not return to his capital and resume his authority without an invitation from the tribes. In the confusion that followed Absalom's defeat there was no prompt and decided action to recall the king, and when at last Judah undertook to bring back David, the jealousy of the other tribes was roused, and a counterrevolution followed. This, however, was speedily quelled, and peace returned to Israel.

The history of David affords one of the most impressive testimonies ever given to the dangers that threaten the soul from power and riches and worldly honor—those things that are most eagerly desired among men. Few have ever passed through an experience better adapted to prepare them for enduring such a test. David's early life as a shepherd, with its lessons of humility, of patient toil, and of tender care for his flocks; the communion with nature in the solitude of the hills, developing his genius for music and poetry, and directing his thoughts to the Creator; the long discipline of his wilderness life, calling into exercise courage, fortitude, patience, and faith in God, had been appointed by the Lord as a preparation for the throne of Israel. David had enjoyed precious experiences of the love of God, and had been richly endowed with His Spirit; in the history of Saul he had seen the utter worthlessness of mere human wisdom. And yet worldly success and honor so weakened the character of David that he was repeatedly overcome by the tempter.

Intercourse with heathen peoples led to a desire to follow their national customs and kindled ambition for worldly greatness. As the people of Jehovah, Israel was to be honored; but as pride and self-confidence increased, the Israelites were not content with this pre-eminence. They cared rather for their standing among other nations. This spirit could not fail to invite temptation. With a view to extending his conquests among foreign nations, David determined to increase his army by requiring military service from all who were of proper age. To effect this, it became necessary to take a census of the population. It was pride and ambition that

747

This chapter is based on 2 Samuel 24; 1 Kings 1; 1 Chronicles 21; 28 ; 29.

prompted this action of the king. The numbering of the people would show the contrast between the weakness of the kingdom when David ascended the throne and its strength and prosperity under his rule. This would tend still further to foster the already too great self-confidence of both king and people. The Scripture says, "Satan stood up against Israel, and provoked David to number Israel." The prosperity of Israel under David had been due to the blessing of God rather than to the ability of her king or the strength of her armies. But the increasing of the military resources of the kingdom would give the impression to surrounding nations that Israel's trust was in her armies, and not in the power of Jehovah.

Though the people of Israel were proud of their national greatness, they did not look with favor upon David's plan for so greatly extending the military service. The proposed enrollment caused much dissatisfaction; consequently it was thought necessary to employ the military officers in place of the priests and magistrates, who had formerly taken the census. The object of the undertaking was directly contrary to the principles of a theocracy. Even Joab remonstrated, unscrupulous as he had heretofore shown himself. He said, "The Lord make His people a hundred times so many more as they be: but, my lord the king, are they not all my lord's servants? why then doth my lord require this thing? why will he be a cause of trespass to Israel? Nevertheless the king's word prevailed against Joab. Wherefore Joab departed, and went throughout all Israel, and came to Jerusalem." The numbering was not finished when David was convicted of his sin. Self-condemned, he "said unto God, I have sinned greatly, because I have done this thing: but now, I beseech Thee, do away the iniquity of Thy servant; for I have done very foolishly." The next morning a message was brought to David by the prophet Gad: "Thus saith the Lord, Choose thee either three years' famine; or three months to be destroyed 748 before thy foes, while that the sword of thine enemies overtaketh thee; or else three days the sword of the Lord, even the pestilence, in the land, and the angel of the Lord destroying throughout all the coasts of Israel. Now therefore," said the prophet, "advise thyself what word I shall bring again to Him that sent me."

The king's answer was, "I am in a great strait: let us fall now into the hand of the Lord; for His mercies are great: and let me not fall into the hand of man."

The land was smitten with pestilence, which destroyed seventy thousand in Israel. The scourge had not yet entered the capital, when "David lifted up his eyes, and saw the angel of the Lord stand between the earth and the heaven, having a drawn sword in his hand stretched out over Jerusalem. Then David and the elders of Israel, who were clothed in sackcloth, fell upon their faces." The king pleaded with God in behalf of Israel: "Is it not I that commanded the people to be numbered? even I it is that have sinned and done evil indeed; but as for these sheep, what have they done? let Thine hand, I pray Thee, O Lord my God, be on me, and on my father's house; but not on Thy people, that they should be plagued."

The taking of the census had caused disaffection among the people; yet they had themselves cherished the same sins that prompted David's action. As the Lord through Absalom's sin visited judgment upon David, so through David's error He punished the sins of Israel.

The destroying angel had stayed his course outside Jerusalem. He stood upon Mount Moriah, "in the threshing floor of Ornan the Jebusite." Directed by the prophet, David went to the mountain, and there built an altar to the Lord, "and offered burnt offerings and peace offerings, and called upon the Lord; and He answered him from heaven by fire upon the altar of burnt offering." "So the Lord was entreated for the land, and the plague was stayed from Israel."

The spot upon which the altar was erected, henceforth ever to be regarded as holy ground, was tendered to the king by Ornan as a gift. But the king declined thus to receive it. "I will verily buy it for the full price," he said; "for I will not take that which is thine for the Lord, nor offer burnt offerings without cost. So David gave to Ornan for the place six hundred shekels of gold 749 by weight." This spot, memorable as the place where Abraham had built the altar to offer up his son, and now hallowed by this great deliverance, was afterward chosen as the site of the temple erected by Solomon.

Still another shadow was to gather over the last years of David. He had reached the age of threescore and ten. The hardships and exposures of his early wanderings, his many wars, the cares and afflictions of his later years, had sapped the fountain of life. Though his mind retained its clearness and strength, feebleness and age, with their desire for seclusion, prevented a quick apprehension of what was passing in the kingdom, and again rebellion sprang up in the very shadow of the throne. Again the fruit of David's parental indulgence was manifest. The one who now aspired to the throne was Adonijah, "a very goodly man" in person and bearing, but unprincipled and reckless. In his youth he had been subjected to but little restraint; for "his father had not displeased him at any time in saying, Why hast thou done so?" He now rebelled against the authority of God, who had appointed Solomon to the throne. Both by natural endowments and religious character Solomon was better qualified than his elder brother to become ruler of Israel; yet although the choice of God had been clearly indicated, Adonijah did not fail to find sympathizers. Joab, though guilty of many crimes, had heretofore been loyal to the throne; but he now joined the conspiracy against Solomon, as did also Abiathar the priest.

The rebellion was ripe; the conspirators had assembled at a great feast just without the city to proclaim Adonijah king, when their plans were thwarted by the prompt action of a few faithful persons, chief among whom were Zadok the priest, Nathan the prophet, and Bathsheba the mother of Solomon. They represented the state of affairs to the king, reminding him of the divine direction that Solomon should succeed to the throne. David at once abdicated in favor of Solomon, who was immediately anointed and proclaimed king. The conspiracy was crushed. Its chief actors had incurred the penalty of death. Abiathar's life was spared, out of respect to his office and his former fidelity to David; but he was degraded from the office of high priest, which passed to the line of Zadok. Joab and Adonijah were spared for the time, but after the death of David they suffered the penalty of their crime. The execution of the sentence upon the son of David completed the fourfold judgment that testified to God's abhorrence of the father's sin.

From the very opening of David's reign one of his most cherished plans had been that of erecting a temple to the Lord. Though he had not been permitted to execute this design, he had manifested no less zeal and earnestness in its behalf. He had provided an abundance of the most costly material—gold, silver, onyx stones, and stones of divers colors; marble, and the most precious woods. And now these valuable treasures that he had collected must be committed to others; for other hands must build the house for the ark, the symbol of God's presence.

Seeing that his end was near, the king summoned the princes of Israel, with representative men from all parts of the kingdom, to receive this legacy in trust. He desired to commit to them his dying charge and secure their concurrence and support in the great work to be accomplished. Because of his physical weakness, it had not been expected that he would attend to this transfer in person; but the inspiration of God came upon him, and with more than his wonted fervor and power, he was able, for the last time, to address his people. He told them of his own desire to build the temple, and of the Lord's command that the work should be committed to Solomon his son. The divine assurance was, "Solomon thy son, he shall build My house and My courts; for I have chosen him to be My son, and I will be his Father. Moreover I will establish his kingdom forever, if he be constant to do My commandments and My judgments, as at this day." "Now therefore," David said, "in the sight of all Israel the congregation of the Lord, and in the audience of our God, keep and seek for all the commandments of the Lord your God: that ye may possess this good land, and leave it for an inheritance for your children after you forever."

David had learned by his own experience how hard is the path of him who departs from God. He had felt the condemnation of the broken law, and had reaped the fruits of transgression; and his whole soul was moved with solicitude that the leaders of Israel should be true to God, and that Solomon should obey God's law, shunning the sins that had weakened his father's authority, embittered his life, and dishonored God. David knew that it would require humility of heart, a constant trust in God, and unceasing watchfulness to withstand the temptations that would surely beset Solomon in his exalted station; for such prominent characters are a special mark for the shafts of Satan. Turning to his son, already acknowledged as his successor on the throne, David said: "And thou, Solomon my son, know thou the God of thy father, and serve Him with a perfect heart and with a willing mind: for the Lord searcheth all hearts, and understandeth all the imaginations of the thoughts: if thou seek Him, He will be found of thee; but if thou forsake Him, He will cast thee off forever. Take heed now; for the Lord hath chosen thee to build a house for the sanctuary: be strong, and do it."

David gave Solomon minute directions for building the temple, with patterns of every part, and of all its instruments of service, as had been revealed to him by divine inspiration. Solomon was still young, and shrank from the weighty responsibilities that would devolve upon him in the erection of the temple and in the government of God's people. David said to his son, "Be strong and of good courage, and do it: fear not, nor be dismayed, for the Lord God, even my God, will be with thee; He will not fail thee, nor forsake thee."

Again David appealed to the congregation: "Solomon my son, whom alone God hath chosen, is yet young and tender, and the work is great: for the palace is not for man, but for the Lord God." He said, "I have prepared with all my might for the house of my God," and he went on to enumerate the materials he had gathered. More than this, he said, "I have set my affection to the house of my God, I have of mine own proper good, of gold and silver, which I have given to the house of my God, over and above all that I have prepared for the holy house, even three thousand talents of gold, of the gold of Ophir, and seven thousand talents of refined silver, to overlay the walls of the houses withal." "Who then," he asked of the assembled multitude that had brought their liberal gifts—"who then is willing to consecrate his *service* this day unto the Lord?"

There was a ready response from the assembly. "The chief of the fathers and princes of the tribes of Israel, and the captains of thousands and of hundreds, with the rulers of the king's work, offered willingly, and gave, for the service of the house of God, of gold five thousand talents and ten thousand drams, and of silver ten thousand talents, and of brass eighteen thousand talents, and one hundred thousand talents of iron. And they with whom precious stones were found gave them to the treasure of the house of the Lord. . . . Then the people rejoiced, for that they offered willingly, because with perfect heart they offered willingly to the Lord: and David the king also rejoiced with great joy.

"Wherefore David blessed the Lord before all the congregation: and David said, Blessed be Thou, Lord God of Israel our father, forever and ever. Thine, O Lord, is the greatness, and the power, and the glory, and the victory, and the majesty: for all that is in the heaven and in the earth is Thine; Thine is the kingdom, O Lord, and Thou art exalted as head above all. Both riches and honor come of Thee, and Thou reignest over all; and in Thine hand is power and might; and in Thine hand it is to make great, and to give strength unto all. Now therefore, our God, we thank Thee, and praise Thy glorious name. But who am I, and what is my people, that we should be able to offer so willingly after this sort? for all things come of Thee, and of Thine own have we given Thee. For we are strangers before Thee, and sojourners, as were all our fathers: our days on the earth are as a shadow, and there is none abiding. O Lord our God, all this store that we have prepared to build Thee an house for Thine holy name cometh of Thine hand, and is all Thine own. I know also, my God, that Thou triest the heart, and hast pleasure in uprightness.

"As for me, in the uprightness of mine heart I have willingly offered all these things: and now have I seen with joy Thy people, which are present here, to offer willingly unto Thee. O Lord God of Abraham, Isaac and of Israel, our fathers, keep this forever in the imagination of the thoughts of the heart of Thy people, and prepare their heart unto Thee: and give unto Solomon my son a perfect heart, to keep Thy commandments, Thy testimonies, and Thy statutes, and to do all these things, and to build the palace, for the which I have made provision. And David said to all the congregation, Now bless the Lord your God. And all the congregation blessed the Lord God of their fathers, and bowed down their heads, and worshiped the Lord."

With deepest interest the king had gathered the rich material for building and beautifying the temple. He had composed the glorious anthems that in afteryears should echo through its courts. Now his heart was made glad in God,

as the chief of the fathers and the princes of Israel so nobly responded to his appeal, and offered themselves to the important work before them. And as they gave their service, they were disposed to do more. They swelled the offerings, giving of their own possessions into the treasury. David had felt deeply his own unworthiness in gathering the material for the house of God, and the expression of loyalty in the ready response of the nobles of his kingdom, as with willing hearts they dedicated their treasures to Jehovah and devoted themselves to His service, filled him with joy. But it was God alone who had imparted this disposition to His people. He, not man, must be glorified. It was He who had provided the people with the riches of earth, and His Spirit had made them willing to bring their precious things for the temple. It was all of the Lord; if His love had not moved upon the hearts of the people, the king's efforts would have been vain, and the temple would never have been erected.

All that man receives of God's bounty still belongs to God. Whatever God has bestowed in the valuable and beautiful things of earth is placed in the hands of men to test them—to sound the depths of their love for Him and their appreciation of His favors. Whether it be the treasures of wealth or of intellect, they are to be laid, a willing offering, at the feet of Jesus; the giver saying, meanwhile, with David, "All things come of Thee, and of Thine own have we given Thee."

When he felt that death was approaching, the burden of David's heart was still for Solomon and for the kingdom of Israel, whose prosperity must so largely depend upon the fidelity of her king. "And he charged Solomon his son, saying, I go the way of all the earth: be thou strong therefore, and show thyself a man; and keep the charge of the Lord thy God, to walk in His ways, to keep His statutes, and His commandments, and His judgments, and His testimonies, . . . that thou mayest prosper in all that thou doest, and whithersoever thou turnest thyself: that the Lord may continue His word which He spake concerning me, saying, If thy children take heed to their way, to walk before Me in truth with all their heart and with all their soul, there shall not fail thee (said He) a man on the throne of Israel." 1 Kings 2:1-4.

David's "last words," as recorded, are a song—a song of trust, of loftiest principle, and undying faith:

"David the son of Jesse saith,
And the man who was raised on high saith,
The anointed of the God of Jacob,
And the sweet psalmist of Israel:
The Spirit of Jehovah spake by me: . . .
One that ruleth over men righteously,
That ruleth in the fear of God,

He shall be as the light of the morning, when
    the sun riseth,
A morning without clouds;
When the tender grass springeth out of the
    earth,
Through clear shining after rain.
Verily my house is not so with God;
Yet He hath made me an everlasting
    covenant,
Ordered in all things, and sure:
For it is all my salvation, and all my desire."
               2 Samuel 23:1-5, R.V.

Great had been David's fall, but deep was his
repentance, ardent was his love, and strong his
faith. He had been forgiven much, and therefore
he loved much. Luke 7:47.

The psalms of David pass through the whole
range of experience, from the depths of conscious guilt and self-condemnation to the loftiest faith and the most exalted communing with
God. His life record declares that sin can bring
only shame and woe, but that God's love and
mercy can reach to the deepest depths, that faith
will lift up the repenting soul to share the adoption of the sons of God. Of all the assurances
which His word contains, it is one of the
strongest testimonies to the faithfulness, the justice, and the covenant mercy of God.

Man "fleeth also as a shadow, and continueth
not," "but the word of our God shall stand forever." "The mercy of Jehovah is from everlasting to everlasting upon them that fear Him, and
His righteousness unto children's children; to
such as keep His covenant, and to those that
remember His commandments to do them." Job
14:2; Isaiah 40:8; Psalm 103:17, 18.

"Whatsoever God doeth, it shall be forever."
Ecclesiastes 3:14.

Glorious are the promises made to David and
his house, promises that look forward to the
eternal ages, and find their complete fulfillment
in Christ. The Lord declared:

755 "I have sworn unto David My servant . . .
with whom My hand shall be established: Mine

arm also shall strengthen him. . . . My faithfulness and My mercy shall be with him: and in
My name shall his horn be exalted. I will set his
hand also in the sea, and his right hand in the
rivers. He shall cry unto Me, Thou art my
Father, my God, and the Rock of my salvation.
Also I will make him My first-born, higher than
the kings of the earth. My mercy will I keep for
him forevermore, and My covenant shall stand
fast with him." Psalm 89:3-28.

"His seed also will I make to endure forever,
    And his throne as the days of heaven."
               Psalm 89:29.

"He shall judge the poor of the people,
    He shall save the children of the needy,
    And shall break in pieces the oppressor.
They shall fear thee while the sun endureth,
    And so long as the moon, throughout all gen-
      erations. . . .
In his days shall the righteous flourish;
    And abundance of peace, till the moon be no
      more.
He shall have dominion also from sea to sea,
    And from the river unto the ends of the
      earth."
"His name shall endure forever:
    His name shall be continued as long as the
      sun:
And men shall be blessed in him:
    All nations shall call him blessed."
            Psalm 72:4-8, R.V., 17.

"For unto us a Child is born, unto us a Son is
given: and the government shall be upon His
shoulder: and His name shall be called Wonderful, Counselor, The mighty God, The everlasting Father, The Prince of Peace." "He shall be
great, and shall be called the Son of the Highest;
and the Lord God shall give unto Him the
throne of His father David: and He shall reign
over the house of Jacob forever; and of His
kingdom there shall be no end." Isaiah 9:6;
Luke 1:32, 33.

APPENDIX

Note I. Page 258. In the command for Israel's release, the Lord said to Pharaoh, "Israel is My son, even My first-born. . . . Let My son go, that he may serve Me." Exodus 4:22, 23. The psalmist tells us why God delivered Israel from Egypt: "He brought forth His people with joy, and His chosen with gladness: and gave them the lands of the heathen: and they inherited the labor of the people; that they might observe His statutes, and keep His laws." Psalm 105:43-45. Here we learn that the Hebrews could not serve God in Egypt.

In Deuteronomy 5:14, 15 we find special emphasis given to that portion of the fourth commandment which requires the manservant and the maidservant to rest, and the Israelite was told to remember that he had been a servant in the land of Egypt. The Lord said, "The seventh day is the Sabbath of the Lord thy God: in it thou shalt not do any work, thou, nor thy son, nor thy daughter, nor thy manservant, nor thy maidservant, nor thine ox, nor thine ass, nor any of thy cattle, nor thy stranger that is within thy gates; that thy manservant and thy maidservant may rest as well as thou. And remember that thou wast a servant in the land of Egypt, and that the Lord thy God brought thee out thence through a mighty hand and by a stretched-out arm: therefore the Lord thy God commanded thee to keep the Sabbath day." In Exodus 5:5 we learn that Moses and Aaron made the people "*rest* from their burdens."

From these facts we may conclude that the Sabbath was one of the things in which they could not serve the Lord in Egypt; and when Moses and Aaron came with the message of God (Exodus 4:29-31), they attempted a reform, which only increased the oppression. The Israelites were delivered that they might observe the statutes of the Lord, including the fourth commandment, and this placed upon them an additional obligation to keep the Sabbath strictly, as well as to keep all the commandments. Thus in Deuteronomy 24:17, 18 the fact of their deliverance from Egypt is cited as placing them under special obligation to show kindness to the widow and the fatherless: "Thou shalt not pervert the judgment of the stranger, nor of the fatherless; nor take a widow's raiment to pledge: but thou shalt remember that thou wast a bondman in Egypt, and the Lord thy God redeemed thee thence: therefore I command thee to do this thing."

Note 2. Page 272. That the plagues were designed to destroy the confidence of the Egyptians in the power and protection of their idols, and even made their gods to appear as cruel tormentors of their worshipers, can be seen from a study of the Egyptian religion. A few examples may serve to illustrate this fact. The first plague, turning the water of the river Nile and of all canals into blood (Exodus 7:19), was directed against the source of Egypt's very existence. The river Nile was regarded with religious reverence, and at several places sacrifices were offered to the Nile as to a god.

The second plague brought frogs over Egypt. Exodus 8:6. Frogs were held sacred by the Egyptians, and one of their deities, Heqa, was a frog-headed goddess thought to possess creative power. When the frogs, as the result of Moses' command, multiplied to the extent that they filled the land from one end to the other, the Egyptians may have wondered why Heqa was tormenting her ardent worshipers instead of protecting them. In this way the Egyptians were not only punished by the second plague, but witnessed also contempt heaped upon them, as they supposed, by one of their gods (Exodus 9:3), of which many represented powerful gods in the Egyptian pantheon. To mention only a few, we find that the Apis bull was dedicated to Ptah, the father of all the gods, the cow was sacred to Hathor, one of the most widely worshiped of all female deities of the Nile country, while the ram represented several gods like Khnemu, and the ram-headed Amen, who was Egypt's chief god in the New Empire period. Hence, the disease which slew the animals dedicated to their deities revealed to the Egyptians the impotence of their gods in the presence of the God of the despised Hebrews.

The ninth plague (Exodus 10:21) dealt a heavy blow to one of the greatest gods of Egypt, the sun god Ra, who had been continuously worshiped from the earliest times of that country's known history. In a land which hardly ever saw clouds in the sky, the sun was recognized as a never-failing power which provided warmth, light, life, and growth to the whole world. Every Egyptian king considered himself as a "son of Ra," and carried this expression in his titulary. When Amen of Thebes became chief god of Egypt during the eighteenth dynasty, the power of the sun-god Ra was recognized as so great that a compromise was made by combining Amen and Ra to make one god —Amen-Ra. A few years after the Exodus, when Ikhnaton introduced a short-lived monotheism, the only god retained was Aton, the sun disk. Seeing how entrenched sunworship was in the religious life of the Egyptians, and how highly the sun-god Ra, Amen-Ra, or Aton was revered, we can understand why the plague directed against the god was brought upon Egypt toward the culmination of the fight between the God of the Hebrews and His Egyptian adversaries.

Also the tenth plague, the slaughtering of the first-born (Exodus 12:29), was striking at least one god, and that was the king, who was considered to be Horus, the son of Osiris. As the ruler of the Nile country, he was addressed by his subjects as "the good god." Hence, the last plague crowned the actions wrought by the miracle-working power of the Hebrew God. So far gods controlling the forces of nature or animals had been disgraced, but now a god living in a visible form among the Egyptians was also humiliated by the despised God of the Hebrew slaves, of whom the proud Pharaoh once had said, "Who is the Lord,

that I should obey His voice to let Israel go? I know not the Lord, neither will I let Israel go." Exodus 5:2.

Note 3. Page 282. In Genesis 15:13 we read that the Lord said to Abraham, "Know of a surety that thy seed shall be a stranger in a land that is not theirs, and shall serve them; and they shall afflict them four hundred years." This text raises the questions whether the 400 years refer to the time of affliction or sojourning, or both, and what the relation of the 400 years is to the 430 years of Exodus 12:40, 41, and Galatians 3:16, 17.

The statement in Exodus 12:40, that "the sojourning of the children of Israel, who dwelt in Egypt, was four hundred and thirty years," gives the impression that the Israelites, from Jacob's entry into Egypt to the Exodus, actually spent 430 years in the country of the Nile. That this impression cannot be correct is obvious from Paul's inspired interpretation presented in Galatians 3:16, 17, where the 430 years are said to cover the period beginning when God made His covenant with Abraham until the law was promulgated at Sinai. Paul seems to refer to the first promise made by God to Abraham when he was called to leave Haran. Genesis 12:1-3. At that time the 430 years began, when Abraham was seventy-five years old (chapter 12:4), while the 400 years of the prophecy of Genesis 15:13 began thirty years later, when Abraham was 105 and his son Isaac five years old (chapter 21:5). At that time Ishmael, who "was born after the flesh persecuted him [Isaac] that was born after the Spirit" (Galatians 4:29; Genesis 21:9-11), beginning a time of affliction of Abraham's seed which intermittently would be continued until the time of the Exodus. Isaac had not only troubles with his half brother Ishmael, but also with the Philistines (Genesis 26:15, 20, 21); Jacob fled for his life from Esau (Genesis 27: 41-43), and later from Laban (Genesis 31:21), and then was again in jeopardy from Esau (Genesis 32:8); Joseph was sold into slavery by his brethren (Genesis 37:28), and the children of Israel were oppressed by the Egyptians for many decades (Exodus 1:14).

The time from Abraham's call to Jacob's entry into Egypt was 215 years, being the total of (1) twenty-five years lying between Abraham's call and the birth of Isaac (Genesis 12:4; 21:5), (2) sixty years lying between Isaac's birth and Jacob's birth (Genesis 25:26), and (3) the age of Jacob at the time of his migration into Egypt (Genesis 47:9). This leaves the remaining 215 years of the 430 as the actual time the Hebrews spent in Egypt. Hence the 430 years of Exodus 12:40 includes the sojourn of the patriarchs in Canaan as well as their stay in Egypt. Since in the time of Moses, Palestine was part of the Egyptian Empire, it is not strange to find an author of that period including Canaan in the term "Egypt." The translators of the Septuagint, knowing that the 430 years included the sojourn of the patriarchs in Canaan, made this point clear in their rendering of this passage: "And the sojourning of the children of Israel, while they sojourned in the land of Egypt and the land of

Canaan, was four hundred and thirty years." An additional corroboration of the interpretation of the 430 years given above is found in the prophecy that the fourth generation of those who had entered Egypt would leave it (Genesis 15:16), and its recorded fulfillment in Exodus 6:16-20.

Note 4. Page 316. The Israelites, in their adoration of the golden calf, *professed* to be worshiping God. Thus Aaron, when inaugurating the worship of the idol, proclaimed, "Tomorrow is a feast unto Jehovah." They proposed to worship God, as the Egyptians worshiped Osiris, under the semblance of the image. But God could not accept the service. Though offered in His name, the sun-god, and not Jehovah, was the real object of their adoration.

The worship of Apis was accompanied with the grossest licentiousness, and the Scripture record indicates that the calf worship by the Israelites was attended with all the license usual in heathen worship. We read: "They rose up early on the morrow, and offered burnt offerings, and brought peace offerings; and the people sat down to eat and to drink, and rose up to play." Exodus 32:6. The Hebrew word rendered "to play" signifies playing with leaping, singing, and dancing. This dancing, especially among the Egyptians, was sensual and indecent. The word rendered "corrupted" in the next verse, where it is said, "Thy people, which thou broughtest out of the land of Egypt, have corrupted themselves," is the same that is used in Genesis 6:11, 12, where we read that the earth was corrupt, "for all flesh had corrupted his way upon the earth." This explains the terrible anger of the Lord, and why He desired to consume the people at once.

Note 5. Page 329. The Ten Commandments were the "covenant" to which the Lord referred when, in proposing a covenant with Israel, He said, "If ye will obey My voice indeed, and keep *My* covenant," etc. Exodus 19:5. The Ten Commandments were termed God's "covenant" before the covenant was made with Israel. They were *not an agreement* made, but something which God *commanded them to perform.* Thus the Ten Commandments—God's covenant—became the *basis* of the covenant made between Him and Israel. The Ten Commandments in all their details are "all these words," *concerning which* the covenant was made. See Exodus 24:8.

Note 6. Page 354. When a sin offering was presented for a priest or for the whole congregation, the blood was carried into the holy place and sprinkled before the veil and placed upon the horns of the golden altar. The fat was consumed upon the altar of burnt offering in the court, but the body of the victim was burned without the camp. See Leviticus 4:1-21.

When, however, the offering was for a ruler or for one of the people, the blood was not taken into the holy place, but the flesh was to be eaten by the priest, as the Lord directed Moses: "The priest that offereth it for sin shall eat it: in a holy place shall it be eaten, in

295

the court of the tent of meeting." Leviticus 6:26, R.V. See also Leviticus 4:22-35.

Note 7. Page 366. That the One who spoke the law, who called Moses into the mount and talked with him, was our Lord Jesus Christ, is evident from the following considerations:

Christ is the one through whom God has at all times revealed Himself to man. "But to us there is but one God, the Father, of whom are all things, and we in Him; and one Lord Jesus Christ, *by whom are all things*, and we by Him." 1 Corinthians 8:6. "This is he [Moses], that was in the church in the wilderness with the Angel which spake to him in the mount Sinai, and with our fathers: who received the lively oracles to give unto us." Acts 7:38. This angel was the Angel of God's presence (Isaiah 63:9), the Angel in whom was the name of the great Jehovah (Exodus 23:20-23). The expression can refer to no other than the Son of God.

Again: Christ is called the Word of God. John 1:1-3. He is so called because God gave His revelations to man in all ages through Christ. It was His Spirit that inspired the prophets. 1 Peter 1:10, 11. He was revealed to them as the Angel of Jehovah, the Captain of the Lord's host, Michael the Archangel.

Note 8. Page 603. The question has been raised, and is now much agitated, if a theocracy was good in the time of Israel, why would not a theocratical form of government be equally good for this time? The answer is easy:

A theocracy is a government which derives its power immediately from God. The government of Israel was a true theocracy. That was really a government of God. At the burning bush, God commissioned Moses to lead His people out of Egypt. By signs and wonders and mighty miracles multiplied, God delivered Israel from Egypt and led them through the wilderness and finally into the Promised Land. There He ruled them by judges "until Samuel the prophet," to whom, when he was a child, God spoke, and by whom He made known His will. In the days of Samuel the people asked that they might have a king. This was allowed, and God chose Saul, and Samuel anointed him king of Israel. Saul failed to do the will of God; and as he rejected the word of the Lord, the Lord rejected him from being king and sent Samuel to anoint David king of Israel; and David's throne God established forevermore. When Solomon succeeded to the kingdom in the place of David his father, the record is: "Then Solomon sat on the throne of the Lord as king instead of David his father." 1 Chronicles 29:23. David's throne was the throne of the Lord, and Solomon sat on the throne of the Lord as king over the earthly kingdom of God. The succession to the throne descended in David's line to Zedekiah, who was made subject to the king of Babylon, and who entered into a solemn covenant before God that he would loyally render allegiance to the king of Babylon. But Zedekiah broke his covenant, and then God said to him:

"Thou, profane wicked prince of Israel, whose day

is come, when iniquity shall have an end, thus saith the Lord God; Remove the diadem, and take off the crown: this shall not be the same: exalt him that is low, and abase him that is high. I will overturn, overturn, overturn, it: and it shall be no more, until He come whose right it is; and I will give it Him." Ezekiel 21:25-27. See also chapter 17:1-21.

The kingdom was then subject to Babylon. When Babylon fell, and Medo-Persia succeeded, it was overturned the first time. When Medo-Persia fell and was succeeded by Greece, it was overturned the second time. When the Greek Empire gave way to Rome, it was overturned the third time. And then says the word, "It shall be no more, until He come whose right it is; and I will give it Him." Who is He whose right it is? "Thou . . . shalt call His name Jesus. He shall be great, and shall be called the Son of the Highest: and the Lord God shall give unto Him the throne of His father David: and He shall reign over the house of Jacob forever; and of His kingdom there shall be no end." Luke 1:31-33. And while He was here as "that Prophet," a Man of Sorrows and acquainted with grief, the night in which He was betrayed He Himself declared, "My kingdom is not of this world." Thus the throne of the Lord has been removed from this world and will "be no more, until He come whose right it is," And then it will be given Him. And that time is the end of this world, and the beginning of "the world to come."

To the twelve apostles the Saviour said, "I appoint unto you a kingdom, as My Father hath appointed unto Me; that ye may eat and drink at My table in My kingdom, and sit on thrones, judging the twelve tribes of Israel." Luke 22:29, 30. From Matthew's account of Christ's promise to the Twelve we learn when it will be fulfilled: "In the regeneration when the Son of man shall sit in the throne of His glory, ye also shall sit upon twelve thrones, judging the twelve tribes of Israel." Matthew 19:28. In the parable of the talents, Christ represents Himself under the figure of a nobleman who "went into a far country to receive for himself a kingdom, and to return." Luke 19:12. And He Himself has told us when He will sit upon the throne of His glory: "When the Son of man shall come in His glory, and all the holy angels with Him, then shall He sit upon the throne of His glory: and before Him shall be gathered all nations." Matthew 25:31, 32.

To this time the revelator looks forward when he says, "The kingdoms of this world are become the kingdoms of our Lord, and of His Christ; and He shall reign forever and ever." Revelation 11:15. The context clearly shows when this will take place: "The nations were angry, and Thy wrath is come, and the time of the dead, that they should be judged, and that Thou shouldest give reward unto Thy servants the prophets, and to the saints, and them that fear Thy name, small and great; and shouldest destroy them which destroy the earth." Verse 18. It is at the time of the final judgment, the reward of the righteous, and the punishment of the wicked that the kingdom of Christ will be set up. When all who oppose the sovereignty of Christ have been destroyed, the kingdoms of this world become the kingdoms of our Lord and of His Christ.

Then Christ will reign, "King of kings, and Lord of lords." Revelation 19:16. "And the kingdom and dominion, and the greatness of the kingdom under the whole heaven, shall be given to the people of the saints of the Most High." And "the saints of the Most High shall take the kingdom, and possess the kingdom forever, even forever and ever." Daniel 7:27, 18.

Until that time the kingdom of Christ cannot be established on the earth. His kingdom is not of this world. His followers are to account themselves "strangers and pilgrims on the earth." Paul says, "Our citizenship is in heaven; from whence also we wait for a Saviour, the Lord Jesus Christ." Hebrews 11:13; Philippians 3:20, R.V.

Since the kingdom of Israel passed away, God has never delegated authority to any man or body of men to execute His laws as such. "Vengeance is Mine; I will repay, saith the Lord." Romans 12:19. Civil governments have to do with the relations of man with man; but they have nothing whatever to do with the duties that grow out of man's relation to God.

Except the kingdom of Israel, no government has ever existed on the earth in which God by inspired men directed the affairs of state. Whenever men have endeavored to form such a government as that of Israel, they have, of necessity, taken it upon themselves to interpret and enforce the law of God. They have assumed the right to control the conscience, and thus have usurped the prerogative of God.

In the former dispensation, while sins against God were visited with temporal penalties, the judgments executed were not only by divine sanction, but under His direct control, and by His command. Sorcerers were to be put to death. Idolaters were to be slain. Profanity and sacrilege were punished with death. Whole nations of idolaters were to be exterminated. But the infliction of these penalties was directed by Him who reads the hearts of men, who knows the measure of their guilt, and who deals with His creatures in wisdom and mercy. When men, with human frailties and passions, undertake to do this work, it needs no argument to show that the door is opened to unrestrained injustice and cruelty. The most inhuman crimes will be perpetrated, and all in the sacred name of Christ.

From the laws of Israel, which punished offenses against God, arguments have been drawn to prove the duty of punishing similar sins in this age. All persecutors have employed them to justify their deeds. The principle that God has delegated to human authority the right to control the conscience is the very foundation of religious tyranny and persecution. But all who reason thus lose sight of the fact that we are now living in a different dispensation, under conditions wholly different from those of Israel; that the kingdom of Israel was a type of the kingdom of Christ, which will not be set up until His second coming; and that the duties which pertain to man's relation to God are not to be regulated or enforced by human authority.

Note 9. Page 608. Concerning the identity of the Ramah of Samuel with the Ramah of Benjamin, Dr. Edersheim says: "These two points seem established: Saul's residence was at Gibeah, and he first met Samuel in Ramah. But if so, it seems impossible, in view of 1 Samuel 10:2, to identify the Ramah of Samuel with the Ramah of Benjamin, or to regard it as the modern Neby Samuel, four miles northwest of Jerusalem."

2

PROPHETS AND KINGS

INDEX

SUMMARY	PAGE	SUMMARY	PAGE

PK

INDEX

PAGE	SUMMARY	PAGE	SUMMARY

PK

FOREWORD

The Story of Prophets and Kings is the second in a series of five outstanding volumes spanning sacred history. It was, however, the last book of the series to be written, and the last of many rich works to come from the gifted pen of Ellen G. White. Through her seventy years of speaking and writing in America and abroad, Mrs. White ever kept before the public the larger significance of the events of history, revealing that in the affairs of men are to be detected the unseen influences of righteousness and evil—the *hand* of God and the *work* of the great adversary.

The author with deep insight in providential workings draws the curtain aside and reveals a philosophy of history by which the events of the past take on eternal significance. she expressed this philosophy in this way:

"The strength of nations and of individuals is not found in the opportunities and facilities that appear to make them invincible; it is not found in their boasted greatness. that which alone can make them great or strong is the power and purpose of god. they themselves by their attitude toward his purpose, decide their own destiny.

"Human histories relate man's achievements, his victories in battle, his success in climbing to worldly greatness. God's history describes man as heaven views him."

This volume, *Prophets and Kings*, opens with the account of Solomon's glorious reign over Israel, a united kingdom, with the temple of Jehovah—the center of true worship. Here are traced the vicissitudes of a favored and chosen people, torn between allegiance to God and serving the gods of the nations about them. And here are seen vividly, through a crucial period of this world's history, the dramatic evidences of the raging conflict between Christ and Satan for the hearts and allegiance of men.

The book abounds in fascinating character studies—the wise Solomon, whose wisdom did not keep him from transgression; Jeroboam, the self-serving man of policy, and the evil results which followed his reign; the mighty and fearless Elijah; Elisha, the prophet of peace and healing; Ahaz, the fearful and wicked; Hezekiah, the loyal and good-hearted; Daniel, the beloved of God; Jeremiah, the prophet of sorrow; Haggai, Zechariah, and Malachi, prophets of the restoration. Beyond them all rises in glory the coming King, the lamb of God, the only-begotten son, in whom the typical sacrifices find fulfillment.

Patriarchs and Prophets, the first book of the series, spans world history from creation to the close of David's reign; *The Desire of Ages*, the third book, treats of the life and ministry of Christ; this volume, *Prophets and Kings* fits between these two. *The*

Acts of the Apostles, the fourth, portrays the history of the early Christian church, and *The Great Controversy*, the last in the series, traces the conflict story to our day and then on in a prophetic vein to the earth made new.

The story of prophets and kings, having enjoyed a circulation which has demanded many printings since its first appearance, is now presented to the public in attractive form with type reset, but with no change of text or pagination. this new edition is embellished with attractive illustrations, many of them original paintings designed especially for this work.

That this volume with its rich lessons of faith in god and his son, the saviour of the world, and the stories of his providence in the lives of great men and women of Old Testament times may deepen the religious experience and enlighten the minds of all who read its pages is the sincere wish of the publishers and

INTRODUCTION

The Vineyard of the Lord

It was for the purpose of bringing the best gifts of Heaven to all the peoples of earth that God called Abraham out from his idolatrous kindred and bade him dwell in the land of Canaan. "I will make of thee a great nation," He said, "and I will bless thee, and make thy name great; and thou shalt be a blessing." Genesis 12:2. It was a high honor to which Abraham was called—that of being the father of the people who for centuries were to be the guardians and preservers of the truth of God to the world, the people through whom all the nations of the earth should be blessed in the advent of the promised Messiah.

Men had well-nigh lost the knowledge of the true God. Their minds were darkened by idolatry. For the divine statutes, which are "holy, and just, and good" (Romans 7:12), men were endeavoring to substitute laws in harmony with the purposes of their own cruel, selfish hearts. Yet God in His mercy did not blot them out of existence. He purposed to give them opportunity for becoming acquainted with Him through His church. He designed that the principles revealed through His people should be the means of restoring the moral image of God in man.

God's law must be exalted, His authority maintained; and to the house of Israel was given this great and noble work. God separated them from the world, that He might commit to them a sacred trust. He made them the depositaries of His law, and He purposed through them to preserve among men the knowledge of Himself. Thus the light of heaven was to shine out to a world enshrouded in darkness, and a voice was to be heard appealing to all peoples to turn from idolatry to serve the living God.

"With great power, and with a mighty hand," God brought His chosen people out of the land of Egypt. Exodus 32:11. "He sent Moses His servant; and Aaron whom He had chosen. They showed His signs among them, and wonders in the land of Ham." "He rebuked the Red Sea also, and it was dried up: so He led them through the depths." Psalms 105:26, 27; 106:9. He rescued them from their servile state, that He might bring them to a good land, a land which in His providence He had prepared for them as a refuge from their enemies. He would bring them to Himself and encircle them in His everlasting arms; and in return for His goodness and mercy they were to exalt His name and make it glorious in the earth.

"The Lord's portion is His people; Jacob is the lot of His inheritance. He found him in a desert land, and in the waste howling wilderness; He led him about, He instructed him, He kept him as the apple of His eye. As an eagle stirreth up her nest, fluttereth over her young, spreadeth abroad her wings, taketh them, beareth them on her wings: so the Lord alone did lead him, and there was no strange god with him." Deuteronomy 32:9-12. Thus He brought the Israelites unto Himself, that they might dwell as under the shadow of the Most High. Miraculously preserved from the perils of the wilderness wandering, they were finally established in the Land of Promise as a favored nation.

By means of a parable, Isaiah has told with touching pathos the story of Israel's call and training to stand in the world as Jehovah's representatives, fruitful in every good work:

"Now will I sing to my well-beloved a song of my beloved touching His vineyard. My well-beloved hath a vineyard in a very fruitful hill: and He fenced it, and gathered out the stones thereof, and planted it with the choicest vine, and built a tower in the midst of it, and also made a wine press therein: and He looked that it should bring forth grapes." Isaiah 5:1, 2.

Through the chosen nation, God had purposed to bring blessing to all mankind. "The vineyard of the Lord of hosts," the prophet declared, "is the house of Israel, and the men of Judah His pleasant plant." Isaiah 5:7.

To this people were committed the oracles of God. They were hedged about by the precepts of His law, the everlasting principles of truth, justice, and purity. Obedience to these principles was to be their protection, for it would save them from destroying themselves by sinful practices. And as the tower in the vineyard, God placed in the midst of the land His holy temple.

Christ was their instructor. As He had been with them in the wilderness, so He was still to be their teacher and guide. In the tabernacle and the temple His glory dwelt in the holy Shekinah above the mercy seat. In their behalf He constantly manifested the riches of His love and patience.

Through Moses the purpose of God was set before them and the terms of their prosperity made plain. "Thou art an holy people unto the Lord thy God," he said; "the Lord thy God hath chosen thee to be a special people unto Himself, above all people that are upon the face of the earth."

"Thou hast avouched the Lord this day to be thy God, and to walk in His ways, and to keep His statutes, and His commandments, and His judgments, and to hearken unto His voice: and the Lord hath avouched thee this day to be His peculiar people, as He hath promised thee, and that thou shouldest keep all His commandments; and to make thee high above all nations which He hath made, in praise, and in name, and in honor; and that thou mayest be an holy people unto the Lord thy God, as He hath spoken." Deuteronomy 7:6; 26:17-19.

The children of Israel were to occupy all the territory which God appointed them.

Those nations that rejected the worship and service of the true God were to be dispossessed. But it was God's purpose that by the revelation of His character through Israel men should be drawn unto Him. To all the world the gospel invitation was to be given. Through the teaching of the sacrificial service, Christ was to be uplifted before the nations, and all who would look unto Him should live. All who, like Rahab the Canaanite and Ruth the Moabitess, turned from idolatry to the worship of the true God were to unite themselves with His chosen people. As the numbers of Israel increased, they were to enlarge their borders until their kingdom should embrace the world.

But ancient Israel did not fulfill God's purpose. The Lord declared, "I had planted thee a noble vine, wholly a right seed: how then art thou turned into the degenerate plant of a strange vine unto Me?" "Israel is an empty vine, he bringeth forth fruit unto himself." "And now, O inhabitants of Jerusalem, and men of Judah, judge, I pray you, betwixt Me and My vineyard. What could have been done more to My vineyard, that I have not done in it? Wherefore, when I looked that it should bring forth grapes, brought it forth wild grapes? And now go to; I will tell you what I will do to My vineyard: I will take away the hedge thereof, and it shall be eaten up; and break down the wall thereof, and it shall be trodden down: and I will lay it waste: it shall not be pruned, nor digged; but there shall come up briers and thorns: I will also command the clouds that they rain no rain upon it. For . . . He looked for judgment, but behold oppression; for righteousness, but behold a cry." Jeremiah 2:21; Hosea 10:1; Isaiah 5:3-7.

The Lord had through Moses set before His people the result of unfaithfulness. By refusing to keep His covenant, they would cut themselves off from the life of God, and His blessing could not come upon them. At times these warnings were heeded, and rich blessings were bestowed upon the Jewish nation and through them upon surrounding peoples. But more often in their history they forgot God and lost sight of their high privilege as His representatives. They robbed Him of the service He required of them, and they robbed their fellow men of religious guidance and a holy example. They desired to appropriate to themselves the fruits of the vineyard over which they had been made stewards. Their covetousness and greed caused them to be despised even by the heathen. Thus the Gentile world was given occasion to misinterpret the character of God and the laws of His kingdom.

With a father's heart, God bore with His people. He pleaded with them by mercies given and mercies withdrawn. Patiently He set their sins before them and in forbearance waited for their acknowledgment. Prophets and messengers were sent to urge His claim upon the husbandmen; but, instead of being welcomed, these men of discernment and spiritual power were treated as enemies. The husbandmen persecuted and killed them. God sent still other messengers, but they received the same treatment as the first, only that the husbandmen showed still more determined hatred.

The withdrawal of divine favor during the period of the Exile led many to repentance, yet after their return to the Land of Promise the Jewish people repeated the mistakes of former generations and brought themselves into political conflict with surrounding nations. The prophets whom God sent to correct the prevailing evils were received with the same suspicion and scorn that had been accorded the messengers of earlier times; and thus, from century to century, the keepers of the vineyard added to their guilt.

The goodly vine planted by the divine Husbandman upon the hills of Palestine was despised by the men of Israel and was finally cast over the vineyard wall; they bruised it and trampled it under their feet and hoped that they had destroyed it forever. The Husbandman removed the vine and concealed it from their sight. Again He planted it, but on the other side of the wall and in such a manner that the stock was no longer visible. The branches hung over the wall, and grafts might be joined to it; but the stem itself was placed beyond the power of men to reach or harm.

Of special value to God's church on earth today—the keepers of His vineyard—are the messages of counsel and admonition given through the prophets who have made plain His eternal purpose in behalf of mankind. In the teachings of the prophets, His love for the lost race and His plan for their salvation are clearly revealed. The story of Israel's call, of their successes and failures, of their restoration to divine favor, of their rejection of the Master of the vineyard, and of the carrying out of the plan of the ages by a goodly remnant to whom are to be fulfilled all the covenant promises—this has been the theme of God's messengers to His church throughout the centuries that have passed. And today God's message to His church—to those who are occupying His vineyard as faithful husbandmen—is none other than that spoken through the prophet of old:

"Sing ye unto her, A vineyard of red wine. I the Lord do keep it; I will water it every moment: lest any hurt it, I will keep it night and day." Isaiah 27:2, 3.

Let Israel hope in God. The Master of the vineyard is even now gathering from among men of all nations and peoples the precious fruits for which He has long been waiting. Soon He will come unto His own; and in that glad day His eternal purpose for the house of Israel will finally be fulfilled. "He shall cause them that come of Jacob to take root: Israel shall blossom and bud, and fill the face of the world with fruit." Verse 6.

CONTENTS

Introduction—The Vineyard of the Lord   306

Section I—From Strength to Weakness
1. Solomon   311
2. The Temple and Its Dedication   314
3. Pride of Prosperity   318
4. Results of Transgression   321
5. Solomon's Repentance   324
6. The Rending of the Kingdom   328
7. Jeroboam   331
8. National Apostasy   333

Section II—Prophets of the Northern Kingdom
9. Elijah the Tishbite   336
10. The Voice of Stern Rebuke   338
11. Carmel   342
12. From Jezreel to Horeb   345
13. "What Doest Thou Here?"   348
14. "In the Spirit and Power of Elias"   351
15. Jehoshaphat   354
16. The Fall of the House of Ahab   358
17. The Call of Elisha   361
18. The Healing of the Waters   365
19. A Prophet of Peace   366
20. Naaman   369
21. Elisha's Closing Ministry   371
22. "Nineveh, That Great City"   374
23. The Assyrian Captivity   378
24. "Destroyed for Lack of Knowledge"   381

Section III—A Preacher of Righteousness
25. The Call of Isaiah   383
26. "Behold Your God!"   386
27. Ahaz   388
28. Hezekiah   391
29. The Ambassadors From Babylon   393
30. Deliverance From Assyria   395
31. Hope for the Heathen   400

Section IV—National Retribution
32. Manasseh and Josiah   404
33. The Book of the Law   407
34. Jeremiah   410
35. Approaching Doom   414
36. The Last King of Judah   419
37. Carried Captive Into Babylon   422
38. Light Through Darkness   426

Section V—In the Lands of the Heathen
39. In the Court of Babylon   429
40. Nebuchadnezzar's Dream   432
41. The Fiery Furnace   435
42. True Greatness   438
43. The Unseen Watcher   440
44. In the Lions' Den   445

Section VI—After the Exile
45. The Return of the Exiles   447
46. "The Prophets of God Helping Them"   451
47. Joshua and the Angel   456
48. "Not by Might, nor by Power"   459
49. In the Days of Queen Esther   460
50. Ezra, the Priest and Scribe   462
51. A Spiritual Revival   465
52. A Man of Opportunity   468
53. The Builders on the Wall   469
54. A Rebuke Against Extortion   472
55. Heathen Plots   474
56. Instructed in the Law of God   476
57. Reformation   478

Section VII—Light at Eventide
58. The Coming of a Deliverer   480
59. "The House of Israel"   487
60. Visions of Future Glory   492

SECTION I

FROM
STRENGTH TO WEAKNESS

"Thus saith the Lord, Let not the wise man glory in his wisdom, neither let the mighty man glory in his might, let not the rich man glory in his riches: but let him that glorieth glory in this, that he understandeth and knoweth Me, that I am the Lord which exercise loving-kindness, judgment, and righteousness, in the earth: for in these things I delight, saith the Lord."

Jeremiah 9:23, 24.

1

Solomon

In the reign of David and Solomon, Israel became strong among the nations and had many opportunities to wield a mighty influence in behalf of truth and the right. The name of Jehovah was exalted and held in honor, and the purpose for which the Israelites had been established in the Land of Promise bade fair of meeting with fulfillment. Barriers were broken down, and seekers after truth from the lands of the heathen were not turned away unsatisfied. Conversions took place, and the church of God on earth was enlarged and prospered.

Solomon was anointed and proclaimed king in the closing years of his father David, who abdicated in his favor. His early life was bright with promise, and it was God's purpose that he should go on from strength to strength, from glory to glory, ever approaching nearer the similitude of the character of God, and thus inspiring His people to fulfill their sacred trust as the depositaries of divine truth.

David knew that God's high purpose for Israel could be met only as rulers and people should seek with unceasing vigilance to attain to the standard placed before them. He knew that in order for his son Solomon to fulfill the trust with which God was pleased to honor him, the youthful ruler must be not merely a warrior, a statesman, and a sovereign, but a strong, good man, a teacher of righteousness, an example of fidelity.

With tender earnestness David entreated

Solomon to be manly and noble, to show mercy and loving-kindness to his subjects, and in all his dealings with the nations of earth to honor and glorify the name of God and to make manifest the beauty of holiness. The many trying and remarkable experiences through which David had passed during his lifetime had taught him the value of the nobler virtues and led him to declare in his dying charge to Solomon: "He that ruleth over men must be just, ruling in the fear of God. And he shall be as the light of the morning, when the sun riseth, even a morning without clouds; as the tender grass springing out of the earth by clear shining after rain." 2 Samuel 23:3, 4.

Oh, what an opportunity was Solomon's! Should he follow the divinely inspired instruction of his father, his reign would be a reign of righteousness, like that described in the seventy-second psalm:

"Give the king Thy judgments, O God,
And Thy righteousness unto the king's son.
He shall judge Thy people with righteousness,
And Thy poor with judgment. . . .
He shall come down like rain upon the mown grass:
As showers that water the earth.
In his days shall the righteous flourish;
And abundance of peace so long as the moon endureth.
He shall have dominion also from sea to sea,
And from the river unto the ends of the earth. . . .
The kings of Tarshish and of the isles shall bring presents:
The kings of Sheba and Seba shall offer gifts.
Yea, all kings shall fall down before him:
All nations shall serve him.
For he shall deliver the needy when he crieth;
The poor also, and him that hath no helper. . . .
Prayer also shall be made for him continually;
And daily shall he be praised. . . .
His name shall endure forever:
His name shall be continued as long as the sun:
And men shall be blessed in him:
All nations shall call him blessed.

"Blessed be the Lord God, the God of Israel,
Who only doeth wondrous things.
And blessed be His glorious name forever:
And let the whole earth be filled with His glory;
Amen, and Amen."

In his youth Solomon made David's choice his own, and for many years he walked uprightly, his life marked with strict obedience to God's commands. Early in his reign he went with his counselors of state to Gibeon, where the tabernacle that had been built in the wilderness still was, and there he united with his chosen advisers, "the captains of thousands and of hundreds," "the judges," and "every governor in all Israel, the chief of the fathers," in offering sacrifices to God and in consecrating themselves fully to the Lord's service. 2 Chronicles 1:2. Comprehending something of the magnitude of the duties connected with the kingly office, Solomon knew that those bearing heavy burdens must seek the Source of Wisdom for guidance, if they would fulfill their responsibilities acceptably. This led him to encourage his counselors to unite with him heartily in making sure of their acceptance with God.

Above every earthly good, the king desired wisdom and understanding for the accomplishment of the work God had given him to do. He longed for quickness of mind, for largeness of heart, for tenderness of spirit. That night the Lord appeared to Solomon in a dream and said, "Ask what I shall give thee." In his answer the young and inexperienced ruler gave utterance to his feeling of helplessness and his desire for aid. "Thou hast showed unto Thy servant David my father great mercy," he said, "according as he walked before Thee in truth, and in righteousness, and in uprightness of heart with Thee; and Thou hast kept for him this great kindness, that Thou hast given him a son to sit on his throne, as it is this day.

"And now, O Lord my God, Thou hast made Thy servant king instead of David my father: and I am but a little child: I know not how to go out or come in. And Thy servant is in the midst of Thy people which Thou hast chosen, a great people, that cannot be numbered nor counted for multitude. Give therefore Thy servant an understanding heart to judge Thy people, that I may discern between good and bad: for who is able to judge this Thy so great a people?

"And the speech pleased the Lord, that Solomon had asked this thing.

"Because this was in thine heart," God said to Solomon, "and thou hast not asked riches, wealth, or honor, nor the life of thine enemies, neither yet hast asked long life; but hast asked wisdom and knowledge for thyself, that thou mayest judge My people," "behold, I have done according to thy words: lo, I have given thee a wise and an understanding heart; so that there was none like thee before thee, neither after thee shall any arise like unto thee. And I have also given thee that which thou hast not asked, both riches, and honor," "such as none of the kings have had that have been before thee, neither shall there any after thee have the like."

"And if thou wilt walk in My ways, to keep My statutes and My commandments, as thy father David did walk, then I will lengthen thy days." 1 Kings 3:5-14; 2 Chronicles 1:7-12.

God promised that as He had been with David, so He would be with Solomon. If the king would walk before the Lord in uprightness, if he would do what God had commanded him, his throne would be established and his reign would be the means of exalting Israel as "a wise and understanding people," the light of the surrounding nations. Deuteronomy 4:6.

The language used by Solomon while praying to God before the ancient altar at Gibeon reveals his humility and his strong desire to honor God. He realized that without divine aid he was as helpless as a little child to fulfill the responsibilities resting on him. He knew that he lacked discernment, and it was a sense of his great need that led him to seek God for wisdom. In his heart there was no selfish aspiration for a knowledge that would exalt him above others. He desired to discharge faithfully the duties devolving upon him, and he chose the gift that would be the means of causing his reign to bring glory to God. Solomon was never so rich or so wise or so truly great as when he confessed, "I am but a little child: I know not how to go out or come in."

Those who today occupy positions of trust should seek to learn the lesson taught by Solomon's prayer. The higher the position a man occupies, the greater the responsibility that he has to bear, the wider will be the influence that he exerts and the greater his need of dependence on God. Ever should he remember that with the call to work comes the call to walk circumspectly before his fellow men. He is to stand before God in the attitude of a learner. Position does not give holiness of character. It is by honoring God and obeying His commands that a man is made truly great.

The God whom we serve is no respecter of persons. He who gave to Solomon the spirit of wise discernment is willing to impart the same blessing to His children today. "If any of you lack wisdom," His word declares, "let him ask of God, that giveth to all men liberally, and upbraideth not; and it shall be given him." James 1:5. When a burden bearer desires wisdom more than he desires wealth, power, or fame, he will not be disappointed. Such a one will learn from the Great Teacher not only what to do, but how to do it in a way that will meet with the divine approval.

So long as he remains consecrated, the man whom God has endowed with discernment and ability will not manifest an eagerness for high position, neither will he seek to rule or control. Of necessity men must bear responsibilities; but instead of striving for the supremacy, he who is a true leader will pray for an understanding heart, to discern between good and evil.

The path of men who are placed as leaders is not an easy one. But they are to see in every difficulty a call to prayer. Never are they to fail of consulting the great Source of all wisdom. Strengthened and enlightened by the Master Worker, they will be enabled to stand firm against unholy influences and to discern right from wrong, good from evil. They will approve that which God approves, and will strive earnestly against the introduction of wrong principles into His cause.

The wisdom that Solomon desired above riches, honor, or long life, God gave him. His petition for a quick mind, a large heart, and a tender spirit was granted. "God gave Solomon wisdom and understanding exceeding much, and largeness of heart, even as the sand that is on the seashore. And Solomon's wisdom excelled the wisdom of all the children of the east country, and all the wisdom of Egypt. For he was wiser than all men; . . . and his fame was in all nations round about." 1 Kings 4:29-31.

"And all Israel . . . feared the king: for they saw that the wisdom of God was in him, to do judgment." 1 Kings 3:28. The hearts of the people were turned toward Solomon, as they had been toward David, and they obeyed him in all things. "Solomon . . . was strengthened in his kingdom, and the Lord his God was with him, and magnified him exceedingly." 2 Chronicles 1:1.

For many years Solomon's life was marked with devotion to God, with uprightness and firm principle, and with strict obedience to God's commands. He directed in every important enterprise and managed wisely the business matters connected with the kingdom. His wealth and wisdom, the magnificent buildings and public works that he constructed during the early years of his reign, the energy, piety, justice, and magnanimity that he revealed in word and deed, won the loyalty of his subjects and the admiration and homage of the rulers of many lands.

The name of Jehovah was greatly honored during the first part of Solomon's reign. The wisdom and righteousness revealed by the king bore witness to all nations of the excellency of the attributes of the God whom he served. For a time Israel was as the light of the world, showing forth the greatness of Jehovah. Not in the surpassing wisdom, the fabulous riches, the far-reaching power and fame that were his, lay the real glory of Solomon's early reign; but in the honor that he brought to the name of the God of Israel through a wise use of the gifts of Heaven.

As the years went by and Solomon's fame increased, he sought to honor God by adding to his mental and spiritual strength, and by continuing to impart to others the blessings he received. None understood better than he that it was through the favor of Jehovah that he had come into possession of power and wisdom and understanding, and that these gifts were bestowed that he might give to the world a knowledge of the King of kings.

Solomon took an especial interest in natural history, but his researches were not confined to any one branch of learning. Through a diligent study of all created things, both animate and inanimate, he gained a clear conception of the Creator. In the forces of nature, in the mineral and the animal world, and in every tree and shrub and flower, he saw a revelation of God's wisdom; and as he sought to learn more and more, his knowledge of God and his love for Him constantly increased.

Solomon's divinely inspired wisdom found expression in songs of praise and in many proverbs. "He spake three thousand proverbs: and his songs were a thousand and five. And he spake of trees, from the cedar tree that is in Lebanon even unto the hyssop that springeth out of the wall: he spake also of beasts, and of fowl, and of creeping things, and of fishes." 1 Kings 4:32, 33.

In the proverbs of Solomon are outlined principles of holy living and high endeavor, principles that are heaven-born and that lead to godliness, principles that should govern every act of life. It was the wide dissemination of these principles, and the recognition of God as the One to whom all praise and honor belong, that made Solomon's early reign a time of moral uplift as well as of material prosperity.

"Happy is the man that findeth wisdom," he wrote, "and the man that getteth understanding. For the merchandise of it is better than the merchandise of silver, and the gain thereof than fine gold. She is more precious than rubies: and all the things thou canst desire are not to be compared unto her. Length of days is in her right hand; and in her left hand riches and honor. Her ways are ways of pleasantness, and all her paths are peace. She is a tree of life to them that lay hold upon her: and happy is every one that retaineth her." Proverbs 3:13-18.

"Wisdom is the principal thing; therefore get wisdom: and with all thy getting get understanding." Proverbs 4:7. "The fear of the Lord is the beginning of wisdom." Psalm 111:10. "The fear of the Lord is to hate evil: pride, and arrogancy, and the evil way, and the froward mouth, do I hate." Proverbs 8:13.

O that in later years Solomon had heeded these wonderful words of wisdom! O that he who had declared, "The lips of the wise disperse knowledge" (Proverbs 15:7), and who had himself taught the kings of the earth to render to the King of kings the praise they desired to give to an earthly ruler, had never with a "froward mouth," in "pride and arrogancy," taken to himself the glory due to God alone!

35

2

The Temple and Its Dedication

The long-cherished plan of David to erect a temple to the Lord, Solomon wisely carried out. For seven years Jerusalem was filled with busy workers engaged in leveling the chosen site, in building vast retaining walls, in laying broad foundations,—"great stones, costly stones, and hewed stones,"—in shaping the heavy timbers brought from the Lebanon forests, and in erecting the magnificent sanctuary. 1 Kings 5:17.

Simultaneously with the preparation of wood and stone, to which task many thousands were bending their energies, the manufacture of the furnishings for the temple was steadily progressing under the leadership of Hiram of Tyre, "a cunning man, endued with understanding, . . . skillful to work in gold, and in silver, in brass, in iron, in stone, and in timber, in purple, in blue, and in fine linen, and in crimson." 2 Chronicles 2:13, 14.

Thus as the building on Mount Moriah was
36 noiselessly upreared with "stone made ready before it was brought thither: so that there was neither hammer nor ax nor any tool of iron heard in the house, while it was in building," the beautiful fittings were perfected according to the patterns committed by David to his son, "all the vessels that were for the house of God." 1 Kings 6:7; 2 Chronicles 4:19. These included the altar of incense, the table of shewbread, the candlestick and lamps, with the vessels and instruments connected with the ministrations of the priests in the holy place, all "of gold, and that perfect gold." 2 Chronicles 4:21. The brazen furniture,—the altar of burnt offering, the great laver supported by twelve oxen, the lavers of smaller size, with many other vessels,—"in the plain of Jordan did the king cast them, in the clay ground between Succoth and Zeredathah." 2 Chronicles 4:17. These furnishings were provided in abundance, that there should be no lack.

Of surpassing beauty and unrivaled splendor was the palatial building which Solomon and his associates erected for God and His worship. Garnished with precious stones, surrounded by spacious courts with magnificent approaches, and lined with carved cedar and burnished gold, the temple structure, with its broidered hangings and rich furnishings, was a fit emblem of the living church of God on earth, which through the ages has been building in accordance with the divine pattern, with materials that have been likened to "gold, silver, precious stones," "polished after the similitude of a palace." 1 Corinthians 3:12; Psalm 144:12. Of this spiritu-

al temple Christ is "the chief Cornerstone; in whom all the building fitly framed together groweth unto an holy temple in the Lord." Ephesians 2:20, 21.

At last the temple planned by King David, 37 and built by Solomon his son, was completed. "All that came into Solomon's heart to make in the house of the Lord," he had "prosperously effected." 2 Chronicles 7:11. And now, in order that the palace crowning the heights of Mount Moriah might indeed be, as David had so much desired, a dwelling place "not for man, but for the Lord God" (1 Chronicles 29:1), there remained the solemn ceremony of formally dedicating it to Jehovah and His worship.

The spot on which the temple was built had long been regarded as a consecrated place. It was here that Abraham, the father of the faithful, had revealed his willingness to sacrifice his only son in obedience to the command of Jehovah. Here God had renewed with Abraham the covenant of blessing, which included the glorious Messianic promise to the human race of deliverance through the sacrifice of the Son of the Most High. See Genesis 22:9, 16-18. Here it was that when David offered burnt offerings and peace offerings to stay the avenging sword of the destroying angel, God had answered him by fire from heaven. See 1 Chronicles 21. And now once more the worshipers of Jehovah were here to meet their God and renew their vows of allegiance to Him.

The time chosen for the dedication was a most favorable one—the seventh month, when the people from every part of the kingdom were accustomed to assemble at Jerusalem to celebrate the Feast of Tabernacles. This feast was preeminently an occasion of rejoicing. The labors of the harvest being ended and the toils of the new year not yet begun, the people were free from care and could give themselves up to the sacred, joyous influences of the hour.

At the appointed time the hosts of Israel, with 38 richly clad representatives from many foreign nations, assembled in the temple courts. The scene was one of unusual splendor. Solomon, with the elders of Israel and the most influential men among the people, had returned from another part of the city, whence they had brought the ark of the testament. From the sanctuary on the heights of Gibeon had been transferred the ancient "tabernacle of the congregation, and all the holy vessels that were in the tabernacle" (2 Chronicles 5:5); and these cherished reminders of the earlier experiences of the children of Israel during their wanderings in the wilderness and their conquest of Canaan, now found a permanent home in the splendid building that had been erected to take the place of the portable structure.

In bringing to the temple the sacred ark containing the two tables of stone on which were written by the finger of God the precepts of the Decalogue, Solomon had followed the example of his father David. Every six paces he sacrificed. With singing and with music and with great ceremony, "the priests brought in the ark of the covenant of the Lord unto his place, to the oracle of the house, into the most holy place." Verse 7. As they came out of the inner sanctuary, they took the positions assigned them. The singers—Levites arrayed in white linen, having cymbals and psalteries and harps—stood at the east end of the altar, and with them a hundred and twenty priests sounding with trumpets. See verse 12.

39   "It came even to pass, as the trumpeters and singers were as one, to make one sound to be heard in praising and thanking the Lord; and when they lifted up their voice with the trumpets and cymbals and instruments of music, and praised the Lord, saying, For He is good; for His mercy endureth forever: that then the house was filled with a cloud, even the house of the Lord; so that the priests could not stand to minister by reason of the cloud: for the glory of the Lord had filled the house of God." Verses 13, 14.

Realizing the significance of this cloud, Solomon declared: "The Lord hath said that He would dwell in the thick darkness. But I have built an house of habitation for Thee, and a place for Thy dwelling forever." 2 Chronicles 6:1, 2.

"The Lord reigneth;
Let the people tremble:
He sitteth between the cherubims;
Let the earth be moved.

"The Lord is great in Zion;
And He is high above all the people.
Let them praise Thy great and terrible name;
For it is holy. . . .

"Exalt ye the Lord our God,
And worship at His footstool;
For He is holy."

Psalm 99:1-5.

"In the midst of the court" of the temple had been erected "a brazen scaffold," or platform, "five cubits long, and five cubits broad, and three cubits high." Upon this Solomon stood and with uplifted hands blessed the vast multitude before him. "And all the congregation of Israel stood." 2 Chronicles 6:13, 3.

"Blessed be the Lord God of Israel," Solomon exclaimed, "who hath with His hands 40   fulfilled that which He spake with His mouth to my father David, saying, ... I have chosen Jerusalem, that My name might be there." Verses 4-6.

Solomon then knelt upon the platform, and in the hearing of all the people offered the dedicatory prayer. Lifting his hands toward heaven, while the congregation were bowed with their faces to the ground, the king pleaded: "Lord God of Israel, there is no God like Thee in the heaven, nor in the earth; which keepest covenant, and showest mercy unto Thy servants, that walk before Thee with all their heart."

"Will God in very deed dwell with men on the earth? Behold, heaven and the heaven of heavens cannot contain Thee; how much less this house which I have built? Have respect therefore to the prayer of Thy servant, and to his supplication, O Lord my God, to hearken unto the cry and the prayer which Thy servant prayeth before Thee: that Thine eyes may be open upon this house day and night, upon the place whereof Thou hast said that Thou wouldest put Thy name there; to hearken unto the prayer which Thy servant prayeth toward this place. Hearken therefore unto the supplications of Thy servant, and of Thy people Israel, which they shall make toward this place: hear Thou from Thy dwelling place, even from heaven; and when Thou hearest, forgive. . . .

"If Thy people Israel be put to the worse before the enemy, because they have sinned against Thee; and shall return and confess Thy name, and pray and make supplication before Thee in this house; then hear Thou from the heavens, and forgive the sin of Thy people Israel, and bring them again unto the land which Thou gavest to them and to their fathers.

"When the heaven is shut up, and there is no 41 rain, because they have sinned against Thee; yet if they pray toward this place, and confess Thy name, and turn from their sin, when Thou dost afflict them; then hear Thou from heaven, and forgive the sin of Thy servants, and of Thy people Israel, when Thou hast taught them the good way, wherein they should walk; and send rain upon Thy land, which Thou hast given unto Thy people for an inheritance.

"If there be dearth in the land, if there be pestilence, if there be blasting, or mildew, locusts, or caterpillars; if their enemies besiege them in the cities of their land; whatsoever sore or whatsoever sickness there be: then what prayer or what supplication soever shall be made of any man, or of all Thy people Israel, when everyone shall know his own sore and his own grief, and shall spread forth his hands in this house: then hear Thou from heaven Thy dwelling place, and forgive, and render unto every man according unto all his ways, whose heart Thou knowest; . . . that they may fear Thee, to walk in Thy ways, so long as they live in the land which Thou gavest unto our fathers.

"Moreover concerning the stranger, which is not of Thy people Israel, but is come from a far country for Thy great name's sake, and Thy mighty hand, and Thy stretched-out arm; if they come and pray in this house; then hear Thou from the heavens, even from Thy dwelling place, and do according to all that the stranger calleth to Thee for; that all people of the earth may know Thy name, and fear Thee, as doth Thy people Israel, and may know that this house which I have built is called by Thy name.

42 "If Thy people go out to war against their enemies by the way that Thou shalt send them, and they pray unto Thee toward this city which Thou hast chosen, and the house which I have built for Thy name; then hear Thou from the heavens their prayer and their supplication, and maintain their cause.

"If they sin against Thee, (for there is no man which sinneth not,) and Thou be angry with them, and deliver them over before their enemies, and they carry them away captives unto a land far off or near; yet if they bethink themselves in the land whither they are carried captive, and turn and pray unto Thee in the land of their captivity, saying, We have sinned, we have done amiss, and have dealt wickedly; if they return to thee with all their heart and with all their soul in the land of their captivity, whither they have carried them captives, and pray toward their land, which Thou gavest unto their fathers, and toward the city which Thou hast chosen, and toward the house which I have built for Thy name: then hear Thou from the heavens, even from Thy dwelling place, their prayer and their supplications, and maintain their cause, and forgive Thy people which have sinned against Thee.

"Now, my God, let, I beseech Thee, Thine eyes be open, and let Thine ears be attent unto the prayer that is made in this place. Now therefore arise, O Lord God, into Thy resting place, Thou, and the ark of Thy strength: let Thy priests, O Lord God, be clothed with salvation, and let Thy saints rejoice in goodness. O Lord God, turn not away the face of Thine anointed: remember the mercies of David Thy servant." Verses 14-42.

45 As Solomon ended his prayer, "fire came down from heaven, and consumed the burnt offering and the sacrifices." The priests could not enter the temple because "the glory of the Lord had filled the Lord's house." "When all the children of Israel saw . . . the glory of the Lord upon the house, they bowed themselves with their faces to the ground upon the pavement, and worshiped, and praised the Lord, saying, For He is good; for His mercy endureth forever."

Then king and people offered sacrifices before the Lord. "So the king and all the people dedicated the house of God." 2 Chronicles 7:1-5. For seven days the multitudes from every part of the kingdom, from the borders "of Hamath unto the river of Egypt," "a very great congregation," kept a joyous feast. The week following was spent by the happy throng in observing the Feast of Tabernacles. At the close of the season of reconsecration and rejoicing the people returned to their homes, "glad and merry in heart for the goodness that the Lord had showed unto David, and to Solomon, and to Israel His people." Verses 8, 10.

The king had done everything within his power to encourage the people to give themselves wholly to God and His service, and to magnify His holy name. And now once more, as at Gibeon early in his reign, Israel's ruler was given evidence of divine acceptance and blessing. In a night vision the Lord appeared to him with the message: "I have heard thy prayer, and have chosen this place to Myself for an house of sacrifice. If I shut up heaven that there be no rain, or if I command the locusts to devour the land, or if I send pestilence among My people; 46 if My people, which are called by My name, shall humble themselves, and pray, and seek My face, and turn from their wicked ways; then will I hear from heaven, and will forgive their sin, and will heal their land. Now Mine eyes shall be open, and Mine ears attent unto the prayer that is made in this place. For now have I chosen and sanctified this house, that My name may be there forever: and Mine eyes and Mine heart shall be there perpetually." Verses 12-16.

Had Israel remained true to God, this glorious building would have stood forever, a perpetual sign of God's especial favor to His chosen people. "The sons of the stranger," God declared, "that join themselves to the Lord, to serve Him, and to love the name of the Lord, to be His servants, everyone that keepeth the Sabbath from polluting it, and taketh hold of My covenant; even them will I bring to My holy mountain, and make them joyful in My house of prayer: their burnt offerings and their sacrifices shall be accepted upon Mine altar; for Mine house shall be called an house of prayer for all people." Isaiah 56:6, 7.

In connection with these assurances of acceptance, the Lord made very plain the path of duty before the king. "As for thee," He declared, "if thou wilt walk before Me, as David thy father walked, and do according to all that I have commanded thee, and shalt observe My statutes and My judgments; then will I establish the throne of thy kingdom, according as I have covenanted with David thy father, saying, There shall not fail thee a man to be ruler in Israel." 2 Chronicles 7:17, 18.

Had Solomon continued to serve the Lord in 47 humility, his entire reign would have exerted a powerful influence for good over the surrounding nations, nations that had been so favorably impressed by the reign of David his father and by the wise words and the magnificent works of the earlier years of his own reign. Foreseeing the terrible temptations that attend prosperity and worldly honor, God warned Solomon against the evil of apostasy and foretold the awful results of sin. Even the beautiful temple that had just been dedicated, He declared, would become "a proverb and a byword among all nations" should the Israelites forsake "the Lord God of their fathers" and persist in idolatry. Verses 20, 22.

Strengthened in heart and greatly cheered by the message from heaven that his prayer in behalf of Israel had been heard, Solomon now entered upon the most glorious period of his reign, when "all the kings of the earth" began to seek his presence, "to hear his wisdom, that God had put in his heart." 2 Chronicles 9:23. Many came to see the manner of his government and to receive instruction regarding the conduct of difficult affairs.

As these people visited Solomon, he taught them of God as the Creator of all things, and they returned to their homes with clearer conceptions of the God of Israel and of His love for the human race. In the works of nature they now beheld an expression of His love and a revelation of His character; and many were led to worship Him as their God.

The humility of Solomon at the time he began to bear the burdens of state, when he acknowledged before God, "I am but a little child" (1 Kings 3:7), his marked love of God, his profound reverence for things divine, his distrust of self, and his exaltation of the infinite Creator of all—all these traits of character, so worthy of emulation, were revealed during the services connected with the completion of the temple, when during his dedicatory prayer he knelt in the humble position of a petitioner. Christ's followers today should guard against the tendency to lose the spirit of reverence and godly fear. The Scriptures teach men how they should approach their Maker—with humility and awe, through faith in a divine Mediator. The psalmist has declared:

> "The Lord is a great God,
> And a great King above all gods. . . .
> O come, let us worship and bow down:
> Let us kneel before the Lord our Maker."
> Psalm 95:3-6.

Both in public and in private worship it is our privilege to bow on our knees before God when we offer our petitions to Him. Jesus, our example, "kneeled down, and prayed." Luke 22:41. Of His disciples it is recorded that they, too, "kneeled down, and prayed." Acts 9:40. Paul declared, "I bow my knees unto the Father of our Lord Jesus Christ." Ephesians 3:14. In confessing before God the sins of Israel, Ezra knelt. See Ezra 9:5. Daniel "kneeled upon his knees three times a day, and prayed, and gave thanks

before his God." Daniel 6:10.

True reverence for God is inspired by a sense of His infinite greatness and a realization of His presence. With this sense of the Unseen, every heart should be deeply impressed. The hour and place of prayer are sacred, because God is there. And as reverence is manifested in attitude and demeanor, the feeling that inspires it will be deepened. "Holy and reverend is His name," the psalmist declares. Psalm 111:9. Angels, when they speak that name, veil their faces. With what reverence, then, should we, who are fallen and sinful, take it upon our lips!

Well would it be for old and young to ponder those words of Scripture that show how the place marked by God's special presence should be regarded. "Put off thy shoes from off thy feet," He commanded Moses at the burning bush, "for the place whereon thou standest is holy ground." Exodus 3:5. Jacob, after beholding the vision of the angel, exclaimed, "The Lord is in this place; and I knew it not. . . . This is none other but the house of God, and this is the gate of heaven." Genesis 28:16, 17.

In that which was said during the dedicatory services, Solomon had sought to remove from the minds of those present the superstitions in regard to the Creator, that had beclouded the minds of the heathen. The God of heaven is not, like the gods of the heathen, confined to temples made with hands; yet He would meet with His people by His Spirit when they should assemble at the house dedicated to His worship.

Centuries later Paul taught the same truth in the words: "God that made the world and all things therein, seeing that He is Lord of heaven and earth, dwelleth not in temples made with hands; neither is worshiped with men's hands, as though He needed anything, seeing He giveth to all life, and breath, and all things; . . . that they should seek the Lord, if haply they might feel after Him, and find Him, though He be not far from every one of us: for in Him we live, and move, and have our being." Acts 17:24-28.

> "Blessed is the nation whose God is the Lord;
> And the people whom He hath chosen for His own inheritance.
> The Lord looketh from heaven;
> He beholdeth all the sons of men.
> From the place of His habitation
> He looketh upon all the inhabitants of the earth."

> "The Lord hath prepared His throne in the heavens;
> And His kingdom ruleth over all."

> "Thy way, O God, is in the sanctuary:
> Who is so great a God as our God?
> Thou art the God that doest wonders:

48

49

50

Thou hast declared Thy strength among the people."
Psalms 33:12-14; 103:19; 77:13, 14.

Although God dwells not in temples made with hands, yet He honors with His presence the assemblies of His people. He has promised that when they come together to seek Him, to acknowledge their sins, and to pray for one another, He will meet with them by His Spirit. But those who assemble to worship Him should put away every evil thing. Unless they worship Him in spirit and truth and in the beauty of holiness, their coming together will be of no avail. Of such the Lord declares, "This people draweth nigh unto Me with their mouth, and honoreth Me with their lips; but their heart is far from Me." Matthew 15:8, 9. Those who worship God must worship Him "in spirit and in truth: for the Father seeketh such to worship Him." John 4:23.

"The Lord is in His holy temple: let all the earth keep silence before Him." Habakkuk 2:20.

51

3
Pride of Prosperity

While Solomon exalted the law of heaven, God was with him, and wisdom was given him to rule over Israel with impartiality and mercy. At first, as wealth and worldly honor came to him, he remained humble, and great was the extent of his influence. "Solomon reigned over all kingdoms from the river [Euphrates] unto the land of the Philistines, and unto the border of Egypt." "He . . . had peace on all sides round about him. And Judah and Israel dwelt safely, every man under his vine and under his fig tree, . . . all the days of Solomon." 1 Kings 4:21, 24, 25.

But after a morning of great promise his life was darkened by apostasy. History records the melancholy fact that he who had been called Jedidiah,—"Beloved of the Lord" (2 Samuel 12:25, margin),—he who had been honored by God with tokens of divine favor so remarkable that his wisdom and uprightness gained for him world-wide fame, he who had led others to

52 ascribe honor to the God of Israel, turned from the worship of Jehovah to bow before the idols of the heathen.

Hundreds of years before Solomon came to the throne, the Lord, foreseeing the perils that would beset those who might be chosen as rulers of Israel, gave Moses instruction for their guidance. Directions were given that he who should sit on the throne of Israel should "write him a copy" of the statutes of Jehovah "in a book out of that which is before the priests the

Levites." "It shall be with him," the Lord said, "and shall read therein all the days of his life: that he may learn to fear the Lord his God, to keep all the words of this law and these statutes, to do them: that his heart be not lifted up above his brethren, and that he turn not aside from the commandment, to the right hand, or to the left: to the end that he may prolong his days in his kingdom, he, and his children, in the midst of Israel." Deuteronomy 17:18-20.

In connection with this instruction the Lord particularly cautioned the one who might be anointed king not to "multiply wives to himself, that his heart turn not away: neither shall he greatly multiply to himself silver and gold." Verse 17.

With these warnings Solomon was familiar, and for a time he heeded them. His greatest desire was to live and rule in accordance with the statutes given at Sinai. His manner of conducting the affairs of the kingdom was in striking contrast with the customs of the nations of his time—nations who feared not God and whose rulers trampled underfoot His holy law.

In seeking to strengthen his relations with the   53
powerful kingdom lying to the southward of Israel, Solomon ventured upon forbidden ground. Satan knew the results that would attend obedience; and during the earlier years of Solomon's reign—years glorious because of the wisdom, the beneficence, and the uprightness of the king—he sought to bring in influences that would insidiously undermine Solomon's loyalty to principle and cause him to separate from God. That the enemy was successful in this effort, we know from the record: "Solomon made affinity with Pharaoh king of Egypt, and took Pharaoh's daughter, and brought her into the City of David." 1 Kings 3:1.

From a human point of view, this marriage, though contrary to the teachings of God's law, seemed to prove a blessing; for Solomon's heathen wife was converted and united with him in the worship of the true God. Furthermore, Pharaoh rendered signal service to Israel by taking Gezer, slaying "the Canaanites that dwelt in the city," and giving it "for a present unto his daughter, Solomon's wife." 1 Kings 9:16. This city Solomon rebuilt and thus apparently greatly strengthened his kingdom along the Mediterranean seacoast. But in forming an alliance with a heathen nation, and sealing the compact by marriage with an idolatrous princess, Solomon rashly disregarded the wise provision that God had made for maintaining the purity of His people. The hope that his Egyptian wife might be converted was but a feeble excuse for the sin.

For a time God in His compassionate mercy overruled this terrible mistake; and the king, by a wise course, could have checked at least in a   54
large measure the evil forces that his imprudence had set in operation. But Solomon had

begun to lose sight of the Source of his power and glory. As inclination gained the ascendancy over reason, self-confidence increased, and he sought to carry out the Lord's purpose in his own way. He reasoned that political and commercial alliances with the surrounding nations would bring these nations to a knowledge of the true God; and he entered into unholy alliance with nation after nation. Often these alliances were sealed by marriages with heathen princesses. The commands of Jehovah were set aside for the customs of surrounding peoples.

Solomon flattered himself that his wisdom and the power of his example would lead his wives from idolatry to the worship of the true God, and also that the alliances thus formed would draw the nations round about into close touch with Israel. Vain hope! Solomon's mistake in regarding himself as strong enough to resist the influence of heathen associates was fatal. And fatal, too, the deception that led him to hope that notwithstanding a disregard of God's law on his part, others might be led to revere and obey its sacred precepts.

The king's alliances and commercial relations with heathen nations brought him renown, honor, and the riches of this world. He was enabled to bring gold from Ophir and silver from Tarshish in great abundance. "The king made silver and gold at Jerusalem as plenteous as stones, and cedar trees made he as the sycamore trees that are in the vale for abundance." 2 Chronicles 1:15. Wealth, with all its attendant temptations, came in Solomon's day to an increasingly large number of people; but the fine gold of character was dimmed and marred.

So gradual was Solomon's apostasy that before he was aware of it, he had wandered far from God. Almost imperceptibly he began to trust less and less in divine guidance and blessing, and to put confidence in his own strength. Little by little he withheld from God that unswerving obedience which was to make Israel a peculiar people, and he conformed more and more closely to the customs of the surrounding nations. Yielding to the temptations incident to his success and his honored position, he forgot the Source of his prosperity. An ambition to excel all other nations in power and grandeur led him to pervert for selfish purposes the heavenly gifts hitherto employed for the glory of God. The money which should have been held in sacred trust for the benefit of the worthy poor and for the extension of principles of holy living throughout the world, was selfishly absorbed in ambitious projects.

Engrossed in an overmastering desire to surpass other nations in outward display, the king overlooked the need of acquiring beauty and perfection of character. In seeking to glorify himself before the world, he sold his honor and

integrity. The enormous revenues acquired through commerce with many lands were supplemented by heavy taxes. Thus pride, ambition, prodigality, and indulgence bore fruit in cruelty and exaction. The conscientious, considerate spirit that had marked his dealings with the people during the early part of his reign, was now changed. From the wisest and most merciful of rulers, he degenerated into a tyrant. Once the compassionate, God-fearing guardian of the people, he became oppressive and despotic. Tax after tax was levied upon the people, that means might be forthcoming to support the luxurious court.

The people began to complain. The respect and admiration they had once cherished for their king was changed into disaffection and abhorrence.

As a safeguard against dependence on the arm of flesh, the Lord had warned those who should rule over Israel not to multiply horses to themselves. But in utter disregard of this command, "Solomon had horses brought out of Egypt." "And they brought unto Solomon horses out of Egypt, and out of all lands." "Solomon gathered together chariots and horsemen: and he had a thousand and four hundred chariots, and twelve thousand horsemen, whom he bestowed in the cities for chariots, and with the king at Jerusalem." 2 Chronicles 1:16; 9:28; 1 Kings 10:26.

More and more the king came to regard luxury, self-indulgence, and the favor of the world as indications of greatness. Beautiful and attractive women were brought from Egypt, Phoenicia, Edom, Moab, and from many other places. These women were numbered by hundreds. Their religion was idol worship, and they had been taught to practice cruel and degrading rites. Infatuated with their beauty, the king neglected his duties to God and to his kingdom.

His wives exerted a strong influence over him and gradually prevailed on him to unite with them in their worship. Solomon had disregarded the instruction that God had given to serve as a barrier against apostasy, and now he gave himself up to the worship of false gods. "It came to pass, when Solomon was old, that his wives turned away his heart after other gods: and his heart was not perfect with the Lord his God, as was the heart of David his father. For Solomon went after Ashtoreth the goddess of the Zidonians, and after Milcom the abomination of the Ammonites." 1 Kings 11:4, 5.

On the southern eminence of the Mount of Olives, opposite Mount Moriah, where stood the beautiful temple of Jehovah, Solomon erected an imposing pile of buildings to be used as idolatrous shrines. To please his wives, he placed huge idols, unshapely images of wood and stone, amidst the groves of myrtle and olive. There, before the altars of heathen deities,

"Chemosh, the abomination of Moab," and "Molech, the abomination of the children of Ammon," were practiced the most degrading rites of heathenism. Verse 7.

Solomon's course brought its sure penalty. His separation from God through communication with idolaters was his ruin. As he cast off his allegiance to God, he lost the mastery of himself. His moral efficiency was gone. His fine sensibilities became blunted, his conscience seared. He who in his early reign had displayed so much wisdom and sympathy in restoring a helpless babe to its unfortunate mother (see 1 Kings 3:16-28), fell so low as to consent to the erection of an idol to whom living children were offered as sacrifices. He who in his youth was endowed with discretion and understanding, and who in his strong manhood had been inspired to write, "There is a way which seemeth right unto a man, but the end thereof are the ways of death" (Proverbs 14:12), in later years departed so far from purity as to countenance licentious, revolting rites connected with the worship of Chemosh and Ashtoreth. He who at the dedication of the temple had said to his people, "Let your heart therefore be perfect with the Lord our God" (1 Kings 8:61), became himself an offender, in heart and life denying his own words. He mistook license for liberty. He tried—but at what cost!—to unite light with darkness, good with evil, purity with impurity, Christ with Belial.

From being one of the greatest kings that ever wielded a scepter, Solomon became a profligate, the tool and slave of others. His character, once noble and manly, became enervated and effeminate. His faith in the living God was supplanted by atheistic doubts. Unbelief marred his happiness, weakened his principles, and degraded his life. The justice and magnanimity of his early reign were changed to despotism and tyranny. Poor, frail human nature! God can do little for men who lose their sense of dependence upon Him.

During these years of apostasy, the spiritual decline of Israel progressed steadily. How could it be otherwise when their king had united his interests with satanic agencies? Through these agencies the enemy worked to confuse the minds of the Israelites in regard to true and false worship, and they became an easy prey. Commerce with other nations brought them into intimate contact with those who had no love for God, and their own love for Him was greatly lessened. Their keen sense of the high, holy character of God was deadened. Refusing to follow in the path of obedience, they transferred their allegiance to the enemy of righteousness. It came to be a common practice to intermarry with idolaters, and the Israelites rapidly lost their abhorrence of idol worship. Polygamy was countenanced. Idolatrous mothers brought their children up to observe heathen rites. In the lives of some, the pure religious service instituted by God was replaced by idolatry of the darkest hue.

Christians are to keep themselves distinct and separate from the world, its spirit, and its influences. God is fully able to keep us in the world, but we are not to be of the world. His love is not uncertain and fluctuating. Ever He watches over His children with a care that is measureless. But He requires undivided allegiance. "No man can serve two masters: for either he will hate the one, and love the other; or else he will hold to the one, and despise the other. Ye cannot serve God and mammon." Matthew 6:24.

Solomon was endued with wonderful wisdom, but the world drew him away from God. Men today are no stronger than he; they are as prone to yield to the influences that caused his downfall. As God warned Solomon of his danger, so today He warns His children not to imperil their souls by affinity with the world. "Come out from among them," He pleads, "and be ye separate, . . . and touch not the unclean thing, and I will receive you, and will be a Father unto you, and ye shall be My sons and daughters, saith the Lord Almighty." 2 Corinthians 6:17, 18.

In the midst of prosperity lurks danger. Throughout the ages, riches and honor have ever been attended with peril to humility and spirituality. It is not the empty cup that we have difficulty in carrying; it is the cup full to the brim that must be carefully balanced. Affliction and adversity may cause sorrow, but it is prosperity that is most dangerous to spiritual life. Unless the human subject is in constant submission to the will of God, unless he is sanctified by the truth, prosperity will surely arouse the natural inclination to presumption.

In the valley of humiliation, where men depend on God to teach them and to guide their every step, there is comparative safety. But the men who stand, as it were, on a lofty pinnacle, and who, because of their position, are supposed to possess great wisdom—these are in gravest peril. Unless such men make God their dependence, they will surely fall.

Whenever pride and ambition are indulged, the life is marred, for pride, feeling no need, closes the heart against the infinite blessings of Heaven. He who makes self-glorification his aim will find himself destitute of the grace of God, through whose efficiency the truest riches and the most satisfying joys are won. But he who gives all and does all for Christ will know the fulfillment of the promise, "The blessing of the Lord, it maketh rich, and He addeth no sorrow with it." Proverbs 10:22. With the gentle touch of grace the Saviour banishes from the soul unrest and unholy ambition, changing enmity to love and unbelief to confidence. When He speaks to the soul, saying, "Follow

Me," the spell of the world's enchantment is broken. At the sound of His voice the spirit of greed and ambition flees from the heart, and men arise, emancipated, to follow Him.

4

Results of Transgression

Prominent among the primary causes that led Solomon into extravagance and oppression was his failure to maintain and foster the spirit of self-sacrifice.

When, at the foot of Sinai, Moses told the people of the divine command, "Let them make Me a sanctuary; that I may dwell among them," the response of the Israelites was accompanied by the appropriate gifts. "They came, everyone whose heart stirred him up, and everyone whom his spirit made willing," and brought offerings. Exodus 25:8; 35:21. For the building of the sanctuary, great and extensive preparations were necessary; a large amount of the most precious and costly material was required, but the Lord accepted only freewill offerings. "Of every man that giveth it willingly with his heart ye shall take My offering," was the command repeated by Moses to the congregation. Exodus 25:2. Devotion to God and a spirit of sacrifice are the first requisites in preparing a dwelling place for the Most High.

A similar call to self-sacrifice was made when David turned over to Solomon the responsibility of building the temple. Of the assembled multitude David asked, "Who then is willing to consecrate his service this day unto the Lord?" 1 Chronicles 29:5. This call to consecration and willing service should ever have been kept in mind by those who had to do with the erection of the temple.

For the construction of the wilderness tabernacle, chosen men were endowed by God with special skill and wisdom. "Moses said unto the children of Israel, See, the Lord hath called by name Bezaleel, . . . of the tribe of Judah; and He hath filled him with the Spirit of God, in wisdom, in understanding, and in knowledge, and in all manner of workmanship. . . . And He hath put in his heart that he may teach, both he, and Aholiab, . . . of the tribe of Dan. Them hath He filled with wisdom of heart, to work all manner of work, of the engraver, and of the cunning workman, and of the embroiderer, . . . and of the weaver, even of them that do any work. . . . Then wrought Bezaleel and Aholiab, and every wisehearted man, in whom the Lord put wisdom and understanding." Exodus 35:30-35; 36:1. Heavenly intelligences co-operated with the workmen whom God Himself had chosen.

The descendants of these workmen inherited to a large degree the talents conferred on their forefathers. For a time these men of Judah and Dan remained humble and unselfish; but gradually, almost imperceptibly, they lost their hold upon God and their desire to serve Him unselfishly. They asked higher wages for their services, because of their superior skill as workmen in the finer arts. In some instances their request was granted, but more often they found employment in the surrounding nations. In place of the noble spirit of self-sacrifice that had filled the hearts of their illustrious ancestors, they indulged a spirit of covetousness, of grasping for more and more. That their selfish desires might be gratified, they used their God-given skill in the service of heathen kings, and lent their talent to the perfecting of works which were a dishonor to their Maker.

It was among these men that Solomon looked for a master workman to superintend the construction of the temple on Mount Moriah. Minute specifications, in writing, regarding every portion of the sacred structure, had been entrusted to the king; and he could have looked to God in faith for consecrated helpers, to whom would have been granted special skill for doing with exactness the work required. But Solomon lost sight of this opportunity to exercise faith in God. He sent to the king of Tyre for a man "cunning to work in gold, and in silver, and in brass, and in iron, and in purple, and crimson, and blue, and that can skill to grave with the cunning men . . . in Judah and in Jerusalem." 2 Chronicles 2:7.

The Phoenician king responded by sending Huram, "the son of a woman of the daughters of Dan, and his father was a man of Tyre." Verse 14. Huram was a descendant, on his mother's side, of Aholiab, to whom, hundreds of years before, God had given special wisdom for the construction of the tabernacle.

Thus at the head of Solomon's company of workmen there was placed a man whose efforts were not prompted by an unselfish desire to render service to God. He served the god of this world, mammon. The very fibers of his being were inwrought with the principles of selfishness.

Because of his unusual skill, Huram demanded large wages. Gradually the wrong principles that he cherished came to be accepted by his associates. As they labored with him day after day, they yielded to the inclination to compare his wages with their own, and they began to lose sight of the holy character of their work. The spirit of self-denial left them, and in its place came the spirit of covetousness. The result was a demand for higher wages, which was granted.

The baleful influences thus set in operation permeated all branches of the Lord's service, and extended throughout the kingdom. The high wages demanded and received gave to many an opportunity to indulge in luxury and extravagance. The poor were oppressed by the rich; the spirit of self-sacrifice was well-nigh lost. In the far-reaching effects of these influences may be traced one of the principal causes of the terrible apostasy of him who once was numbered among the wisest of mortals.

The sharp contrast between the spirit and motives of the people building the wilderness tabernacle, and of those engaged in erecting Solomon's temple, has a lesson of deep significance. The self-seeking that characterized the workers on the temple finds its counterpart today in the selfishness that rules in the world. The spirit of covetousness, of seeking for the highest position and the highest wage, is rife.

65 The willing service and joyous self-denial of the tabernacle workers is seldom met with. But this is the only spirit that should actuate the followers of Jesus. Our divine Master has given an example of how His disciples are to work. To those whom He bade, "Follow Me, and I will make you fishers of men" (Matthew 4:19), He offered no stated sum as a reward for their services. They were to share with Him in self-denial and sacrifice.

Not for the wages we receive are we to labor. The motive that prompts us to work for God should have in it nothing akin to self-serving. Unselfish devotion and a spirit of sacrifice have always been and always will be the first requisite of acceptable service. Our Lord and Master designs that not one thread of selfishness shall be woven into His work. Into our efforts we are to bring the tact and skill, the exactitude and wisdom, that the God of perfection required of the builders of the earthly tabernacle; yet in all our labors we are to remember that the greatest talents or the most splendid services are acceptable only when self is laid upon the altar, a living, consuming sacrifice.

Another of the deviations from right principles that finally led to the downfall of Israel's king was his yielding to the temptation to take to himself the glory that belongs to God alone.

From the day that Solomon was entrusted with the work of building the temple, to the time of its completion, his avowed purpose was "to build an house for the name of the Lord God of Israel." 2 Chronicles 6:7. This purpose was fully recognized before the assembled hosts of Israel

66 at the time of the dedication of the temple. In his prayer the king acknowledged that Jehovah had said, "My name shall be there." 1 Kings 8:29.

One of the most touching portions of Solomon's dedicatory prayer was his plea to God for the strangers that should come from countries afar to learn more of Him whose fame had been spread abroad among the nations. "They shall hear," the king pleaded, "of Thy great name, and of Thy strong hand, and of Thy stretched-out arm." In behalf of every one of these stranger worshipers Solomon had peti-

tioned: "Hear Thou, . . . and do according to all that the stranger calleth to Thee for: that all people of the earth may know Thy name; to fear Thee, as do Thy people Israel; and that they may know that this house, which I have builded, is called by Thy name." Verses 42, 43.

At the close of the service, Solomon had exhorted Israel to be faithful and true to God, in order that "all the people of the earth may know," he said, "that the Lord is God, and that there is none else." Verse 60.

A Greater than Solomon was the designer of the temple; the wisdom and glory of God stood there revealed. Those who were unacquainted with this fact naturally admired and praised Solomon as the architect and builder; but the king disclaimed any honor for its conception or erection.

Thus it was when the Queen of Sheba came to visit Solomon. Hearing of his wisdom and of the magnificent temple he had built, she determined "to prove him with hard questions" and to see for herself his famous works. Attended by a retinue of servants, and with camels bearing "spices, and gold in abundance, and precious 67 stones," she made the long journey to Jerusalem. "And when she was come to Solomon, she communed with him of all that was in her heart." She talked with him of the mysteries of nature; and Solomon taught her of the God of nature, the great Creator, who dwells in the highest heaven and rules over all. "Solomon told her all her questions: there was not anything hid from the king, which he told her not." 1 Kings 10:1-3; 2 Chronicles 9:1, 2.

"When the Queen of Sheba had seen all Solomon's wisdom, and the house that he had built, . . . there was no more spirit in her." "It was a true report," she acknowledged, "which I heard in mine own land of thine acts, and of thy wisdom: howbeit I believed not their words, until I came, and mine eyes had seen it:" "and, behold, the half was not told me: thy wisdom and prosperity exceedeth the fame which I heard. Happy are thy men, happy are these thy servants, which stand continually before thee, and that hear thy wisdom." 1 Kings 10:4-8; 2 Chronicles 9:3-6.

By the time of the close of her visit the queen had been so fully taught by Solomon as to the source of his wisdom and prosperity that she was constrained, not to extol the human agent, but to exclaim, "Blessed be the Lord thy God, which delighted in thee, to set thee on the throne of Israel: because the Lord loved Israel forever, therefore made He thee king, to do judgment and justice." 1 Kings 10:9. This is the impression that God designed should be made upon all peoples. And when "all the kings of the earth sought the presence of Solomon, to hear his wisdom, that God had put in his heart" (2 68 Chronicles 9:23), Solomon for a time honored

God by reverently pointing them to the Creator of the heavens and the earth, the Ruler of the universe, the All-wise.

Had Solomon continued in humility of mind to turn the attention of men from himself to the One who had given him wisdom and riches and honor, what a history might have been his! But while the pen of inspiration records his virtues, it also bears faithful witness to his downfall. Raised to a pinnacle of greatness and surrounded with the gifts of fortune, Solomon became dizzy, lost his balance, and fell. Constantly extolled by men of the world, he was at length unable to withstand the flattery offered him. The wisdom entrusted to him that he might glorify the Giver, filled him with pride. He finally permitted men to speak of him as the one most worthy of praise for the matchless splendor of the building planned and erected for the honor of "the name of the Lord God of Israel."

Thus it was that the temple of Jehovah came to be known throughout the nations as "Solomon's temple." The human agent had taken to himself the glory that belonged to the One "higher than the highest." Ecclesiastes 5:8. Even to this day the temple of which Solomon declared, "This house which I have built is called by Thy name" (2 Chronicles 6:33), is oftenest spoken of, not as the temple of Jehovah, but as "Solomon's temple."

Man cannot show greater weakness than by allowing men to ascribe to him the honor for gifts that are Heaven-bestowed. The true Christian will make God first and last and best in everything. No ambitious motives will chill his love for God; steadily, perseveringly, will he cause honor to redound to his heavenly Father. It is when we are faithful in exalting the name of God that our impulses are under divine supervision, and we are enabled to develop spiritual and intellectual power.

Jesus, the divine Master, ever exalted the name of His heavenly Father. He taught His disciples to pray, "Our Father who art in heaven, hallowed be Thy name." Matthew 6:9, A.R.V. And they were not to forget to acknowledge, "Thine is . . . the glory." Verse 13. So careful was the great Healer to direct attention from Himself to the Source of His power, that the wondering multitude, "when they saw the dumb to speak, the maimed to be whole, the lame to walk, and the blind to see," did not glorify Him, but "glorified the God of Israel." Matthew 15:31. In the wonderful prayer that Christ offered just before His crucifixion, He declared, "I have glorified Thee on the earth." "Glorify Thy Son," He pleaded, "that Thy Son also may glorify Thee." "O righteous Father, the world hath not known Thee: but I have known Thee, and these have known that Thou hast sent Me. And I have declared unto them Thy name, and will declare it: that the love wherewith Thou hast loved Me may be in them, and I in them." John 17:1, 4, 25, 26.

"Thus saith the Lord, Let not the wise man glory in his wisdom, neither let the mighty man glory in his might, let not the rich man glory in his riches: but let him that glorieth glory in this, that he understandeth and knoweth Me, that I am the Lord which exercise loving-kindness, judgment, and righteousness, in the earth: for in these things I delight, saith the Lord." Jeremiah 9:23, 24.

"I will praise the name of God, . . .
And will magnify Him with thanksgiving."

"Thou art worthy, O Lord, to receive glory and honor and power."

"I will praise Thee, O Lord my God, with all my heart:
And I will glorify Thy name forevermore."

"O magnify the Lord with me,
And let us exalt His name together."
Psalm 69:30; Revelation 4:11;
Psalms 86:12; 34:3.

The introduction of principles leading away from a spirit of sacrifice and tending toward self-glorification, was accompanied by yet another gross perversion of the divine plan for Israel. God had designed that His people should be the light of the world. From them was to shine forth the glory of His law as revealed in the life practice. For the carrying out of this design, He had caused the chosen nation to occupy a strategic position among the nations of earth.

In the days of Solomon the kingdom of Israel extended from Hamath on the north to Egypt on the south, and from the Mediterranean Sea to the river Euphrates. Through this territory ran many natural highways of the world's commerce, and caravans from distant lands were constantly passing to and fro. Thus there was given to Solomon and his people opportunity to reveal to men of all nations the character of the King of kings, and to teach them to reverence and obey Him. To all the world this knowledge was to be given. Through the teaching of the sacrificial offerings, Christ was to be uplifted before the nations, that all who would might live.

Placed at the head of a nation that had been set as a beacon light to the surrounding nations, Solomon should have used his God-given wisdom and power of influence in organizing and directing a great movement for the enlightenment of those who were ignorant of God and His truth. Thus multitudes would have been won to allegiance to the divine precepts, Israel would have been shielded from the evils practiced by the heathen, and the Lord of glory would have been greatly honored. But Solomon lost sight of this high purpose. He failed of improving his splendid opportunities for enlightening those who were continually passing through his territory or tarrying at the principal cities.

The missionary spirit that God had implanted in the heart of Solomon and in the hearts of all true Israelites was supplanted by a spirit of commercialism. The opportunities afforded by contact with many nations were used for personal aggrandizement. Solomon sought to strengthen his position politically by building fortified cities at the gateways of commerce. He rebuilt Gezer, near Joppa, lying along the road between Egypt and Syria; Beth-horon, to the westward of Jerusalem, commanding the passes of the highway leading from the heart of Judea to Gezer and the seacoast; Megiddo, situated on the caravan road from Damascus to Egypt, and from Jerusalem to the northward; and "Tadmor in the wilderness" (2 Chronicles 8:4), along the route of caravans from the east. All these cities were strongly fortified. The commercial advantages of an outlet at the head of the Red Sea were developed by the construction of "a navy of ships in Ezion-geber, . . . on the shore of the Red Sea, in the land of Edom." Trained sailors from Tyre, "with the servants of Solomon," manned these vessels on voyages "to Ophir, and fetched from thence gold," and "great plenty of almug trees, and precious stones." Verse 18; 1 Kings 9:26, 28; 10:11.

The revenue of the king and of many of his subjects was greatly increased, but at what a cost! Through the cupidity and shortsightedness of those to whom had been entrusted the oracles of God, the countless multitudes who thronged the highways of travel were allowed to remain in ignorance of Jehovah.

In striking contrast to the course pursued by Solomon was the course followed by Christ when He was on this earth. The Saviour, though possessing "all power," never used this power for self-aggrandizement. No dream of earthly conquest, of worldly greatness, marred the perfection of His service for mankind. "Foxes have holes, and the birds of the air have nests," He said; "but the Son of man hath not where to lay His head." Matthew 8:20. Those who, in response to the call of the hour, have entered the service of the Master Worker, may well study His methods. He took advantage of the opportunities to be found along the great thoroughfares of travel.

In the intervals of His journeys to and fro, Jesus dwelt at Capernaum, which came to be known as "His own city." Matthew 9:1. Situated on the highway from Damascus to Jerusalem and Egypt and to the Mediterranean Sea, it was well adapted to be the center of the Saviour's work. People from many lands passed through the city or tarried for rest. There Jesus met with those of all nations and all ranks, and thus His lessons were carried to other countries and into many households. By this means interest was aroused in the prophecies pointing forward to the Messiah, attention was directed to the Saviour, and His mission was brought before the world.

In this our day the opportunities for coming into contact with men and women of all classes and many nationalities are much greater than in the days of Israel. The thoroughfares of travel have multiplied a thousandfold.

Like Christ, the messengers of the Most High today should take their position in these great thoroughfares, where they can meet the passing multitudes from all parts of the world. Like Him, hiding self in God, they are to sow the gospel seed, presenting before others the precious truths of Holy Scripture that will take deep root in mind and heart, and spring up unto life eternal.

Solemn are the lessons of Israel's failure during the years when ruler and people turned from the high purpose they had been called to fulfill. Wherein they were weak, even to the point of failure, the Israel of God today, the representatives of heaven that make up the true church of Christ, must be strong; for upon them devolves the task of finishing the work that has been committed to man, and of ushering in the day of final awards. Yet the same influences that prevailed against Israel in the time when Solomon reigned are to be met with still. The forces of the enemy of all righteousness are strongly entrenched; only by the power of God can the victory be gained. The conflict before us calls for the exercise of a spirit of self-denial, for distrust of self and for dependence on God alone, for the wise use of every opportunity for the saving of souls. The Lord's blessing will attend His church as they advance unitedly, revealing to a world lying in the darkness of error the beauty of holiness as manifested in a Christlike spirit of self-sacrifice, in an exaltation of the divine rather than the human, and in loving and untiring service for those so much in need of the blessings of the gospel.

5

Solomon's Repentance

Twice during Solomon's reign the Lord had appeared to him with words of approval and counsel—in the night vision at Gibeon, when the promise of wisdom, riches, and honor was accompanied by an admonition to remain humble and obedient; and after the dedication of the temple, when once more the Lord exhorted him to faithfulness. Plain were the admonitions, wonderful the promises, given to Solomon; yet of him who in circumstances, in character, and in life seemed abundantly fitted to heed the charge and meet the expectation of Heaven, it is recorded: "He kept not that which the Lord commanded." "His heart was turned from the Lord God of Israel, which had appeared unto him twice, and had commanded him concerning this thing, that he should not go after other gods." 1 Kings 11:9, 10. And so complete was his apostasy, so hardened his heart in transgression, that his case seemed well-nigh hopeless.

76   From the joy of divine communion, Solomon turned to find satisfaction in the pleasures of sense. Of this experience he says:

"I made me great works; I builded me houses; I planted me vineyards: I made me gardens and orchards: . . . I got me servants and maidens: . . . I gathered me also silver and of gold, and the peculiar treasure of kings and of the provinces: I gat me men singers and women singers, and the delights of the sons of men, as musical instruments, and that of all sorts. So I was great, and increased more than all that were before me in Jerusalem. . . .

"And whatsoever mine eyes desired I kept not from them, I withheld not my heart from any joy; for my heart rejoiced in all my labor. . . . Then I looked on all the works that my hands had wrought, and on the labor that I had labored to do: and, behold, all was vanity and vexation of spirit, and there was no profit under the sun.

"And I turned myself to behold wisdom, and madness, and folly: for what can the man do that cometh after the king? even that which hath been already done. . . . I hated life. . . . Yea, I hated all my labor which I had taken under the sun." Ecclesiastes 2:4-18.

By his own bitter experience, Solomon learned the emptiness of a life that seeks in earthly things its highest good. He erected altars to heathen gods, only to learn how vain is their promise of rest to the spirit. Gloomy and soul-harassing thoughts troubled him night and day. For him there was no longer any joy of life or peace of mind, and the future was dark with despair.

77   Yet the Lord forsook him not. By messages of reproof and by severe judgments, He sought to arouse the king to a realization of the sinfulness of his course. He removed His protecting care and permitted adversaries to harass and weaken the kingdom. "The Lord stirred up an adversary unto Solomon, Hadad the Edomite. . . . And God stirred him up another adversary, Rezon, . . . captain over a band," who "abhorred Israel, and reigned over Syria. And Jeroboam, . . . Solomon's servant," "a mighty man of valor," "even he lifted up his hand against the king." 1 Kings 11:14-28.

At last the Lord, through a prophet, delivered to Solomon the startling message: "Forasmuch as this is done of thee, and thou hast not kept My covenant and My statutes, which I have commanded thee, I will surely rend the kingdom from thee, and will give it to thy servant. Notwithstanding in thy days I will not do it for David thy father's sake: but I will rend it out of the hand of thy son." Verses 11, 12.

Awakened as from a dream by this sentence of judgment pronounced against him and his house, Solomon with quickened conscience began to see his folly in its true light. Chastened in spirit, with mind and body enfeebled, he turned wearied and thirsting from earth's broken cisterns, to drink once more at the fountain of life. For him at last the discipline of suffering had accomplished its work. Long had he been harassed by the fear of utter ruin because of inability to turn from folly; but now he discerned in the message given him a ray of hope. God had not utterly cut him off, but stood ready to deliver him from a bondage more cruel than   78 the grave, and from which he had had no power to free himself.

In gratitude Solomon acknowledged the power and the loving-kindness of the One who is "higher than the highest" (Ecclesiastes 5:8); in penitence he began to retrace his steps toward the exalted plane of purity and holiness from whence he had fallen so far. He could never hope to escape the blasting results of sin, he could never free his mind from all remembrance of the self-indulgent course he had been pursuing, but he would endeavor earnestly to dissuade others from following after folly. He would humbly confess the error of his ways and lift his voice in warning lest others be lost irretrievably because of the influences for evil he had been setting in operation.

The true penitent does not put his past sins from his remembrance. He does not, as soon as he has obtained peace, grow unconcerned in regard to the mistakes he has made. He thinks of those who have been led into evil by his course, and tries in every possible way to lead them back into the true path. The clearer the light that he has entered into, the stronger is his desire to set the feet of others in the right way. He does not gloss over his wayward course, making his wrong a light thing, but lifts the danger signal, that others may take warning.

Solomon acknowledged that "the heart of the sons of men is full of evil, and madness is in their heart." Ecclesiastes 9:3. And again he declared, "Because sentence against an evil work is not executed speedily, therefore the heart of the sons of men is fully set in them to do evil. Though a sinner do evil an hundred times, and his days be prolonged, yet surely I   79 know that it shall be well with them that fear God, which fear before Him: but it shall not be well with the wicked, neither shall he prolong his days, which are as a shadow; because he feareth not before God." Ecclesiastes 8:11-13.

By the spirit of inspiration the king recorded for after generations the history of his wasted years with their lessons of warning. And thus, although the seed of his sowing was reaped by his people in harvests of evil, his lifework was not wholly lost. With meekness and lowliness Solomon in his later years "taught the people knowledge; yea, he gave good heed, and sought out, and set in order many proverbs." He "sought to find out acceptable words: and that which was written was upright, even words of truth." "The words of the wise are as goads, and as nails fastened by the masters of assemblies, which are given from one shepherd. And further, by these, my son, be admonished." Ecclesiastes 12:9-12.

"Let us hear the conclusion of the whole matter," he wrote: "Fear God, and keep His commandments: for this is the whole duty of man. For God shall bring every work into judgment, with every secret thing, whether it be good, or whether it be evil." Verses 13, 14.

Solomon's later writings reveal that as he realized more and still more the wickedness of his course, he gave special attention to warning the youth against falling into the errors that had led him to squander for nought Heaven's choicest gifts. With sorrow and shame he confessed that in the prime of manhood, when he should have found God his comfort, his support, his life, he turned from the light of Heaven and the wisdom of God, and put idolatry in the place of the worship of Jehovah. And now, having learned through sad experience the folly of such a life, his yearning desire was to save others from entering into the bitter experience through which he had passed.

With touching pathos he wrote concerning the privileges and responsibilities before the youth in God's service:

"Truly the light is sweet, and a pleasant thing it is for the eyes to behold the sun: but if a man live many years, and rejoice in them all; yet let him remember the days of darkness; for they shall be many. All that cometh is vanity. Rejoice, O young man, in thy youth; and let thy heart cheer thee in the days of thy youth, and walk in the ways of thine heart, and in the sight of thine eyes: but know thou, that for all these things God will bring thee into judgment. Therefore remove sorrow from thy heart, and put away evil from thy flesh: for childhood and youth are vanity." Ecclesiastes 11:7-10.

"Remember now thy Creator in the days of thy
      youth,
   While the evil days come not,
   Nor the years draw nigh,
   When thou shalt say, I have no pleasure in
      them;

"While the sun,

Or the light,
Or the moon,
Or the stars,
Be not darkened,
Nor the clouds return after the rain:

"In the day when the keepers of the house
      shall tremble,
And the strong men shall bow themselves,
And the grinders cease because they are few,
And those that look out of the windows be
      darkened,
And the doors shall be shut in the streets,

"When the sound of the grinding is low,
And he shall rise up at the voice of the bird,
And all the daughters of music shall be
      brought low;

"Also when they shall be afraid of that which
      is high,
And fears shall be in the way,

"And the almond tree shall flourish,
   And the grasshopper shall be a burden,
   And desire shall fail:

"Because man goeth to his long home,
And the mourners go about the streets:

"Or ever the silver cord be loosed,
   Or the golden bowl be broken,
   Or the pitcher be broken at the fountain,
   Or the wheel broken at the cistern.

"Then shall the dust return to the earth
As it was:
And the spirit shall return unto God
Who gave it."
                                   Ecclesiastes 12:1-7.

Not only to the youth, but to those of mature years, and to those who are descending the hill of life and facing the western sun, the life of Solomon is full of warning. We see and hear of unsteadiness in youth, the young wavering between right and wrong, and the current of evil passions proving too strong for them. In those of maturer years, we do not look for this unsteadiness and unfaithfulness; we expect the character to be established, the principles firmly rooted. But this is not always so. When Solomon should have been in character as a sturdy oak, he fell from his steadfastness under the power of temptation. When his strength should have been the firmest, he was found to be the weakest.

From such examples we should learn that in watchfulness and prayer is the only safety for both young and old. Security does not lie in exalted position and great privileges. One may for many years have enjoyed a genuine Christian experience, but he is still exposed to Satan's attacks. In the battle with inward sin and outward temptation, even the wise and powerful Solomon was vanquished. His failure teaches us that, whatever a man's intellectual qualities may be, and however faithfully he may have served God in the past, he can never with safety trust in his own wisdom and integrity.

In every generation and in every land the true foundation and pattern for character building have been the same. The divine law, "Thou shalt love the Lord thy God with all thy heart, . . . and thy neighbor as thyself," the great principle made manifest in the character and life of our Saviour, is the only secure foundation, the only sure guide. Luke 10:27. "Wisdom and knowledge shall be the stability of thy times, and strength of salvation," the wisdom and knowledge which God's word alone can impart. Isaiah 33:6.

It is as true now as when the words were spoken to Israel of obedience to His commandments: "This is your wisdom and your understanding in the sight of the nations." Deuteronomy 4:6. Here is the only safeguard for individual integrity, for the purity of the home, the well-being of society, or the stability of the nation. Amidst all life's perplexities and dangers and conflicting claims, the one safe and sure rule is to do what God says. "The statutes of the Lord are right," and "he that doeth these things shall never be moved." Psalms 19:8; 15:5.

Those who heed the warning of Solomon's apostasy will shun the first approach of those sins that overcame him. Only obedience to the requirements of Heaven will keep man from apostasy. God has bestowed upon man great light and many blessings; but unless this light and these blessings are accepted, they are no security against disobedience and apostasy. When those whom God has exalted to positions of high trust turn from Him to human wisdom, their light becomes darkness. Their entrusted capabilities become a snare.

Till the conflict is ended, there will be those who will depart from God. Satan will so shape circumstances that unless we are kept by divine power, they will almost imperceptibly weaken the fortifications of the soul. We need to inquire at every step, "Is this the way of the Lord?" So long as life shall last, there will be need of guarding the affections and the passions with a firm purpose. Not one moment can we be secure except as we rely upon God, the life hidden with Christ. Watchfulness and prayer are the safeguards of purity.

All who enter the City of God will enter through the strait gate—by agonizing effort; for "there shall in no wise enter into it anything that defileth." Revelation 21:27. But none who have fallen need give up to despair. Aged men, once honored of God, may have defiled their souls, sacrificing virtue on the altar of lust; but if they repent, forsake sin, and turn to God, there is still hope for them. He who declares, "Be thou faithful unto death, and I will give thee a crown of life," also gives the invitation, "Let the wicked forsake his way, and the unrighteous man his thoughts: and let him return unto the Lord, and He will have mercy upon him; and to our God, for He will abundantly pardon." Revelation 2:10; Isaiah 55:7. God hates sin, but He loves the sinner. "I will heal their backsliding," He declares; "I will love them freely." Hosea 14:4.

Solomon's repentance was sincere; but the harm that his example of evil-doing had wrought could not be undone. During his apostasy there were in the kingdom men who remained true to their trust, maintaining their purity and loyalty. But many were led astray; and the forces of evil set in operation by the introduction of idolatry and worldly practices could not easily be stayed by the penitent king. His influence for good was greatly weakened. Many hesitated to place full confidence in his leadership. Though the king confessed his sin and wrote out for the benefit of after generations a record of his folly and repentance, he could never hope entirely to destroy the baleful influence of his wrong deeds. Emboldened by his apostasy, many continued to do evil, and evil only. And in the downward course of many of the rulers who followed him may be traced the sad influence of the prostitution of his God-given powers.

In the anguish of bitter reflection on the evil of his course, Solomon was constrained to declare, "Wisdom is better than weapons of war: but one sinner destroyeth much good." "There is an evil which I have seen under the sun, as an error which proceedeth from the ruler: folly is set in great dignity."

"Dead flies cause the ointment of the apothecary to send forth a stinking savor: so doth a little folly him that is in reputation for wisdom and honor." Ecclesiastes 9:18; 10:5, 6, 1.

Among the many lessons taught by Solomon's life, none is more strongly emphasized than the power of influence for good or for ill. However contracted may be our sphere, we still exert an influence for weal or woe. Beyond our knowledge or control, it tells upon others in blessing or cursing. It may be heavy with the gloom of discontent and selfishness, or poisonous with the deadly taint of some cherished sin; or it may be charged with the life-giving power of faith, courage, and hope, and sweet with the fragrance of love. But potent for good or for ill it will surely be.

That our influence should be a savor of death unto death is a fearful thought, yet it is possible. One soul misled, forfeiting eternal bliss—who can estimate the loss! And yet one rash act, one thoughtless word, on our part may exert so deep an influence on the life of another that it will prove the ruin of his soul. One blemish on the character may turn many away from Christ.

As the seed sown produces a harvest, and this in turn is sown, the harvest is multiplied. In our relation to others, this law holds true. Every act, every word, is a seed that will bear fruit. Every deed of thoughtful kindness, of obedience, of self-denial, will reproduce itself in others, and through them in still others. So every act of envy, malice, or dissension is a seed that will spring up in a "root of bitterness" whereby many shall be defiled. Hebrews 12:15. And how much larger number will the "many" poison! Thus the sowing of good and evil goes on for time and for eternity.

6

The Rending of the Kingdom

"Solomon slept with his fathers, and was buried in the City of David his father: and Rehoboam his son reigned in his stead." 1 Kings 11:43.

Soon after his accession to the throne, Rehoboam went to Shechem, where he expected to receive formal recognition from all the tribes. "To Shechem were all Israel come to make him king." 2 Chronicles 10:1.

Among those present was Jeroboam the son of Nebat—the same Jeroboam who during Solomon's reign had been known as "a mighty man of valor," and to whom the prophet Ahijah the Shilonite had delivered the startling message, "Behold, I will rend the kingdom out of the hand of Solomon, and will give ten tribes to thee." 1 Kings 11:28, 31.

The Lord through His messenger had spoken plainly to Jeroboam regarding the necessity of dividing the kingdom. This division must take place, He had declared, "because that they have forsaken Me, and have worshiped Ashtoreth the goddess of the Zidonians, Chemosh the god of the Moabites, and Milcom the god of the children of Ammon, and have not walked in My ways, to do that which is right in Mine eyes, and to keep My statutes and My judgments, as did David." Verse 33.

Jeroboam had been further instructed that the kingdom was not to be divided before the close of Solomon's reign. "I will not take the whole kingdom out of his hand," the Lord had declared; "but I will make him prince all the days of his life for David My servant's sake, whom I chose, because he kept My commandments and My statutes: but I will take the kingdom out of his son's hand, and will give it unto thee, even ten tribes." Verses 34, 35.

Although Solomon had longed to prepare the mind of Rehoboam, his chosen successor, to

meet with wisdom the crisis foretold by the prophet of God, he had never been able to exert a strong molding influence for good over the mind of his son, whose early training had been so grossly neglected. Rehoboam had received from his mother, an Ammonitess, the stamp of a vacillating character. At times he endeavored to serve God and was granted a measure of prosperity; but he was not steadfast, and at last he yielded to the influences for evil that had surrounded him from infancy. In the mistakes of Rehoboam's life and in his final apostasy is revealed the fearful result of Solomon's union with idolatrous women.

The tribes had long suffered grievous wrongs under the oppressive measures of their former ruler. The extravagance of Solomon's reign during his apostasy had led him to tax the people heavily and to require of them much menial service. Before going forward with the coronation of a new ruler, the leading men from among the tribes determined to ascertain whether or not it was the purpose of Solomon's son to lessen these burdens. "So Jeroboam and all Israel came and spake to Rehoboam, saying, Thy father made our yoke grievous: now therefore ease thou somewhat the grievous servitude of thy father, and his heavy yoke that he put upon us, and we will serve thee."

Desirous of taking counsel with his advisers before outlining his policy, Rehoboam answered, "Come again unto me after three days. And the people departed.

"And King Rehoboam took counsel with the old men that had stood before Solomon his father while he yet lived, saying, What counsel give ye me to return answer to this people? And they spake unto him, saying, If thou be kind to this people, and please them, and speak good words to them, they will be thy servants forever." 2 Chronicles 10:3-7.

Dissatisfied, Rehoboam turned to the younger men with whom he had associated during his youth and early manhood, and inquired of them, "What counsel give ye that we may answer this people, who have spoken to me, saying, Make the yoke which thy father did put upon us lighter?" 1 Kings 12:9. The young men suggested that he deal sternly with the subjects of his kingdom and make plain to them that from the very beginning he would brook no interference with his personal wishes.

Flattered by the prospect of exercising supreme authority, Rehoboam determined to disregard the counsel of the older men of his realm, and to make the younger men his advisers. Thus it came to pass that on the day appointed, when "Jeroboam and all the people came to Rehoboam" for a statement concerning the policy he intended to pursue, Rehoboam "answered the people roughly, . . . saying, My father made your yoke heavy, and I will add to your yoke:

my father also chastised you with whips, but I will chastise you with scorpions." Verses 12-14.

Had Rehoboam and his inexperienced counselors understood the divine will concerning Israel, they would have listened to the request of the people for decided reforms in the administration of the government. But in the hour of opportunity that came to them during the meeting in Shechem, they failed to reason from cause to effect, and thus forever weakened their influence over a large number of the people. Their expressed determination to perpetuate and add to the oppression introduced during Solomon's reign was in direct conflict with God's plan for Israel, and gave the people ample occasion to doubt the sincerity of their motives. In this unwise and unfeeling attempt to exercise power, the king and his chosen counselors revealed the pride of position and authority.

The Lord did not allow Rehoboam to carry out the policy he had outlined. Among the tribes were many thousands who had become thoroughly aroused over the oppressive measures of Solomon's reign, and these now felt that they could not do otherwise than rebel against the house of David. "When all Israel saw that the king hearkened not unto them, the people answered the king, saying, What portion have we in David? neither have we inheritance in the son of Jesse: to your tents, O Israel: now see to thine own house, David. So Israel departed unto their tents." Verse 16.

The breach created by the rash speech of Rehoboam proved irreparable. Thenceforth the twelve tribes of Israel were divided, the tribes of Judah and Benjamin composing the lower or southern kingdom of Judah, under the rulership of Rehoboam; while the ten northern tribes formed and maintained a separate government, known as the kingdom of Israel, with Jeroboam as their ruler. Thus was fulfilled the prediction of the prophet concerning the rending of the kingdom. "The cause was from the Lord." Verse 15.

When Rehoboam saw the ten tribes withdrawing their allegiance from him, he was aroused to action. Through one of the influential men of his kingdom, "Adoram, who was over the tribute," he made an effort to conciliate them. But the ambassador of peace received treatment which bore witness to the feeling against Rehoboam. "All Israel stoned him with stones, that he died." Startled by this evidence of the strength of revolt, "King Rehoboam made speed to get him up to his chariot, to flee to Jerusalem." Verse 18.

At Jerusalem "he assembled all the house of Judah, with the tribe of Benjamin, an hundred and forscore thousand chosen men, which were warriors, to fight against the house of Israel, to bring the kingdom again to Rehoboam the son

of Solomon. But the word of God came unto Shemaiah the man of God, saying, Speak unto Rehoboam, the son of Solomon, king of Judah, and unto all the house of Judah and Benjamin, and to the remnant of the people, saying, Thus saith the Lord, Ye shall not go up, nor fight against your brethren the children of Israel: return every man to his house; for this thing is from Me. They hearkened therefore to the word of the Lord, and returned to depart, according to the word of the Lord." Verses 21-24.

For three years Rehoboam tried to profit by his sad experience at the beginning of his reign; and in this effort he was prospered. He "built cities for defense in Judah," and "fortified the strongholds, and put captains in them, and store of victual, and of oil and wine." He was careful to make these fortified cities "exceeding strong." 2 Chronicles 11:5, 11, 12. But the secret of Judah's prosperity during the first years of Rehoboam's reign lay not in these measures. It was their recognition of God as the Supreme Ruler that placed the tribes of Judah and Benjamin on vantage ground. To their number were added many God-fearing men from the northern tribes. "Out of all the tribes of Israel," the record reads, "such as set their hearts to seek the Lord God of Israel came to Jerusalem, to sacrifice unto the Lord God of their fathers. So they strengthened the kingdom of Judah, and made Rehoboam the son of Solomon strong, three years: for three years they walked in the way of David and Solomon." Verses 16, 17.

In continuing this course lay Rehoboam's opportunity to redeem in large measure the mistakes of the past and to restore confidence in his ability to rule with discretion. But the pen of inspiration has traced the sad record of Solomon's successor as one who failed to exert a strong influence for loyalty to Jehovah. Naturally headstrong, confident, self-willed, and inclined to idolatry, nevertheless, had he placed his trust wholly in God, he would have developed strength of character, steadfast faith, and submission to the divine requirements. But as time passed, the king put his trust in the power of position and in the strongholds he had fortified. Little by little he gave way to inherited weaknesses, until he threw his influence wholly on the side of idolatry. "It came to pass, when Rehoboam had established the kingdom, and had strengthened himself, he forsook the law of the Lord, and all Israel with him." 2 Chronicles 12:1.

How sad, how filled with significance, the words, "And all Israel with him"! The people whom God had chosen to stand as a light to the surrounding nations were turning from their Source of strength and seeking to become like the nations about them. As with Solomon, so with Rehoboam—the influence of wrong example led many astray. And as with them, so to a greater or less degree is it today with everyone who gives himself up to work evil—the influence of wrongdoing is not confined to the doer. No man liveth unto himself. None perish alone in their iniquity. Every life is a light that brightens and cheers the pathway of others, or a dark and desolating influence that tends toward despair and ruin. We lead others either upward to happiness and immortal life, or downward to sorrow and eternal death. And if by our deeds we strengthen or force into activity the evil powers of those around us, we share their sin.

God did not allow the apostasy of Judah's ruler to remain unpunished. "In the fifth year of King Rehoboam Shishak king of Egypt came up against Jerusalem, because they had transgressed against the Lord, with twelve hundred chariots, and three score thousand horsemen: and the people were without number that came with him out of Egypt. . . . And he took the fenced cities which pertained to Judah, and came to Jerusalem.

"Then came Shemaiah the prophet to Rehoboam, and to the princes of Judah, that were gathered together to Jerusalem because of Shishak, and said unto them, Thus saith the Lord, Ye have forsaken Me, and therefore have I also left you in the hand of Shishak." Verses 2-5.

The people had not yet gone to such lengths in apostasy that they despised the judgments of God. In the losses sustained by the invasion of Shishak, they recognized the hand of God and for a time humbled themselves. "The Lord is righteous," they acknowledged.

"And when the Lord saw that they humbled themselves, the word of the Lord came to Shemaiah, saying, They have humbled themselves; therefore I will not destroy them, but I will grant them some deliverance; and My wrath shall not be poured out upon Jerusalem by the hand of Shishak. Nevertheless they shall be his servants; that they may know My service, and the service of the kingdoms of the countries.

"So Shishak king of Egypt came up against Jerusalem, and took away the treasures of the house of the Lord, and the treasures of the king's house; he took all: he carried away also the shields of gold which Solomon had made. Instead of which King Rehoboam made shields of brass, and committed them to the hands of the chief of the guard, that kept the entrance of the king's house. . . . And when he humbled himself, the wrath of the Lord turned from him, that He would not destroy him altogether: and also in Judah things went well." Verses 6-12.

But as the hand of affliction was removed, and the nation prospered once more, many forgot their fears and turned again to idolatry. Among these was King Rehoboam himself. Though humbled by the calamity that had befallen him, he failed to make this experi-

ence a decisive turning point in his life. Forgetting the lesson that God had endeavored to teach him, he relapsed into the sins that had brought judgments on the nation. After a few inglorious years, during which the king "did evil, because he prepared not his heart to seek the Lord," "Rehoboam slept with his fathers, and was buried in the City of David: and Abijah his son reigned in his stead." Verses 14, 16.

With the rending of the kingdom early in Rehoboam's reign the glory of Israel began to depart, never again to be regained in its fullness. At times during the centuries that followed, the throne of David was occupied by men of moral worth and far-seeing judgment, and under the rulership of these sovereigns the blessings resting upon the men of Judah were extended to the surrounding nations. At times the name of Jehovah was exalted above every false god, and His law was held in reverence. From time to time mighty prophets arose to strengthen the hands of the rulers and to encourage the people to continued faithfulness. But the seeds of evil already springing up when Rehoboam ascended the throne were never to be wholly uprooted; and at times the once-favored people of God were to fall so low as to become a byword among the heathen.

Yet notwithstanding the perversity of those who leaned toward idolatrous practices, God in mercy would do everything in His power to save the divided kingdom from utter ruin. And as the years rolled on and His purpose concerning Israel seemed to be utterly thwarted by the devices of men inspired by satanic agencies, He still manifested His beneficent designs through the captivity and restoration of the chosen nation.

The rending of the kingdom was but the beginning of a wonderful history, wherein are revealed the long-sufferance and tender mercy of God. From the crucible of affliction through which they were to pass because of hereditary and cultivated tendencies to evil, those whom God was seeking to purify unto Himself a peculiar people, zealous of good works, were finally to acknowledge:

"There is none like unto Thee, O Lord; Thou art great, and Thy name is great in might. Who would not fear Thee, O King of nations? . . . Among all the wise men of the nations, and in all their kingdoms, there is none like unto Thee." "The Lord is the true God, He is the living God, and an everlasting King." Jeremiah 10:6, 7, 10.

And the worshipers of idols were at last to learn the lesson that false gods are powerless to uplift and save. "The gods that have not made the heavens and the earth, even they shall perish from the earth, and from under these heavens." Verse 11. Only in allegiance to the living God, the Creator of all and the Ruler over all, can man find rest and peace.

With one accord the chastened and penitent of Israel and Judah were at last to renew their covenant relationship with Jehovah of hosts, the God of their fathers; and of Him they were to declare:

> "He hath made the earth by His power,
> He hath established the world by His wisdom,
> And hath stretched out the heavens by His discretion.

98
> "When He uttereth His voice, there is a multitude of waters in the heavens,
> And He causeth the vapors to ascend from the ends of the earth;
> He maketh lightnings with rain, and bringeth forth the wind out of His treasures.

> "Every man is brutish in his knowledge:
> Every founder is confounded by the graven image:
> For his molten image is falsehood, and there is no breath in them.

> "They are vanity, and the work of errors:
> In the time of their visitation they shall perish.
> The portion of Jacob is not like them:

> "For He is the former of all things;
> And Israel is the rod of His inheritance:
> The Lord of hosts is His name."
>
> Verses 12-16.

99

7

Jeroboam

Placed on the throne by the ten tribes of Israel who had rebelled against the house of David, Jeroboam, the former servant of Solomon, was in a position to bring about wise reforms in both civil and religious affairs. Under the rulership of Solomon he had shown aptitude and sound judgment; and the knowledge he had gained during years of faithful service fitted him to rule with discretion. But Jeroboam failed to make God his trust.

Jeroboam's greatest fear was that at some future time the hearts of his subjects might be won over by the ruler occupying the throne of David. He reasoned that if the ten tribes should be permitted to visit often the ancient seat of the Jewish monarchy, where the services of the temple were still conducted as in the years of Solomon's reign, many might feel inclined to renew their allegiance to the government centering at Jerusalem. Taking counsel with his advisers, Jeroboam determined by one bold

stroke to lessen, so far as possible, the proba- 100 bility of a revolt from his rule. He would bring this about by creating within the borders of his newly formed kingdom two centers of worship, one at Bethel and the other at Dan. In these places the ten tribes should be invited to assemble, instead of at Jerusalem, to worship God.

In arranging this transfer, Jeroboam thought to appeal to the imagination of the Israelites by setting before them some visible representation to symbolize the presence of the invisible God. Accordingly he caused to be made two calves of gold, and these were placed within shrines at the appointed centers of worship. In this effort to represent the Deity, Jeroboam violated the plain command of Jehovah: "Thou shalt not make unto thee any graven image. . . . Thou shalt not bow down thyself to them, nor serve them." Exodus 20:4, 5.

So strong was Jeroboam's desire to keep the ten tribes away from Jerusalem that he lost sight of the fundamental weakness of his plan. He failed to take into consideration the great peril to which he was exposing the Israelites by setting before them the idolatrous symbol of the deity with which their ancestors had been so familiar during the centuries of Egyptian bondage. Jeroboam's recent residence in Egypt should have taught him the folly of placing before the people such heathen representations. But his set purpose of inducing the northern tribes to discontinue their annual visits to the Holy City led him to adopt the most imprudent of measures. "It is too much for you to go up to Jerusalem," he urged; "behold thy gods, O Israel, which brought thee up out of the land of Egypt." 1 Kings 12:28. Thus 101 they were invited to bow down before the golden images and adopt strange forms of worship.

The king tried to persuade the Levites, some of whom were living within his realm, to serve as priests in the newly erected shrines at Bethel and Dan; but in this effort he met with failure. He was therefore compelled to elevate to the priesthood men from "the lowest of the people." Verse 31. Alarmed over the prospect, many of the faithful, including a great number of the Levites, fled to Jerusalem, where they might worship in harmony with the divine requirements.

"Jeroboam ordained a feast in the eighth month, on the fifteenth day of the month, like unto the feast that is in Judah, and he offered upon the altar. So did he in Bethel, sacrificing unto the calves that he had made: and he placed in Bethel the priests of the high places which he had made." Verse 32.

The king's bold defiance of God in thus setting aside divinely appointed institutions was not allowed to pass unrebuked. Even while he was officiating and burning incense during the dedication of the strange altar he had set up at Bethel, there appeared before him a man of God from the kingdom of Judah, sent to denounce him for presuming to introduce new forms of worship. The prophet "cried against the altar, . . . and said, O altar, altar, thus saith the Lord; Behold, a child shall be born unto the house of David, Josiah by name; and upon thee shall he offer the priests of the high places that burn incense upon thee, and men's bones shall be burnt upon thee.

"And he gave a sign the same day, saying, This is the sign which the Lord hath spoken; Behold, the altar shall be rent, and the ashes that are upon it shall be poured out." Immediately the altar "was rent, and the ashes poured out from the altar, according to the sign which the man of God had given by the word of the Lord." 1 Kings 13:2, 3, 5.

On seeing this, Jeroboam was filled with a spirit of defiance against God and attempted to restrain the one who had delivered the message. In wrath "he put forth his hand from the altar" and cried out, "Lay hold on him." His impetuous act met with swift rebuke. The hand outstretched against the messenger of Jehovah suddenly became powerless and withered, and could not be withdrawn.

Terror-stricken, the king appealed to the prophet to intercede with God in his behalf. "Entreat now the face of the Lord thy God," he pleaded, "and pray for me, that my hand may be restored me again. And the man of God besought the Lord, and the king's hand was restored him again, and became as it was before." Verses 4, 6.

Vain had been Jeroboam's effort to invest with solemnity the dedication of a strange altar, respect for which would have led to disrespect for the worship of Jehovah in the temple at Jerusalem. By the message of the prophet, the king of Israel should have been led to repent and to renounce his wicked purposes, which were turning the people away from the true worship of God. But he hardened his heart and determined to follow a way of his own choosing.

At the time of the feast at Bethel the hearts of the Israelites were not fully hardened. Many were susceptible to the influence of the Holy Spirit. The Lord designed that those who were taking rapid steps in apostasy should be checked in their course before it should be too late. He sent His messenger to interrupt the idolatrous proceedings and to reveal to king and people what the outworking of this apostasy would be. The rending of the altar was a sign of God's displeasure at the abomination that was being wrought in Israel.

The Lord seeks to save, not to destroy. He delights in the rescue of sinners. "As I live, saith the Lord God, I have no pleasure in the death of the wicked." Ezekiel 33:11. By warnings and entreaties He calls the wayward to cease from their evil-doing and to turn to Him and live. He gives His chosen messengers a holy boldness, that those who hear may fear and be brought to repentance. How firmly the man of God rebuked the king! And this firmness was essential; in no other way could the existing evils have been rebuked. The Lord gave His servant boldness, that an abiding impression might be made on those who heard. The messengers of the Lord are never to fear the face of man, but are to stand unflinchingly for the right. So long as they put their trust in God, they need not fear; for He who gives them their commission gives them also the assurance of His protecting care.

Having delivered his message, the prophet was about to return, when Jeroboam said to him, "Come home with me, and refresh thyself, and I will give thee a reward." "If thou wilt give me half thine house," the prophet replied, "I will not go in with thee, neither will I eat bread nor drink water in this place: for so was it charged me by the word of the Lord, saying, Eat no bread, nor drink water, nor turn again by the same way that thou camest." 1 Kings 13:7-9.

Well would it have been for the prophet had he adhered to his purpose to return to Judea without delay. While traveling homeward by another route, he was overtaken by an aged man who claimed to be a prophet and who made false representations to the man of God, declaring, "I am a prophet also as thou art; and an angel spake unto me by the word of the Lord, saying, Bring him back with thee into thine house, that he may eat bread and drink water." Again and again the lie was repeated and the invitation urged until the man of God was persuaded to return.

Because the true prophet allowed himself to take a course contrary to the line of duty, God permitted him to suffer the penalty of transgression. While he and the one who had invited him to return to Bethel were sitting together at the table, the inspiration of the Almighty came upon the false prophet, "and he cried unto the man of God that came from Judah, saying, Thus saith the Lord, Forasmuch as thou hast disobeyed the mouth of the Lord, and hast not kept the commandment which the Lord thy God commanded thee, . . . thy carcass shall not come unto the sepulcher of thy fathers." Verses 18-22.

This prophecy of doom was soon literally fulfilled. "It came to pass, after he had eaten bread, and after he had drunk, that he saddled for him the ass. . . . And when he was gone, a lion met him by the way, and slew him: and his carcass was cast in the way, and the ass stood by it, the lion also stood by the carcass. And, behold, men passed by, and saw the carcass cast in the way, . . . and they came and told it in the city where the old prophet dwelt. And when the prophet that brought him back from the way heard thereof, he said, It is the man of God, who was disobedient unto the word of the Lord." Verses 23-26.

The penalty that overtook the unfaithful messenger was a still further evidence of the truth of the prophecy uttered over the altar. If, after disobeying the word of the Lord, the prophet had been permitted to go on in safety, the king would have used this fact in an attempt to vindicate his own disobedience. In the rent altar, in the palsied arm, and in the terrible fate of the one who dared disobey an express command of Jehovah, Jeroboam should have discerned the swift displeasure of an offended God, and these judgments should have warned him not to persist in wrongdoing. But, far from repenting, Jeroboam "made again of the lowest of the people priests of the high places: whosoever would, he consecrated him, and he became one of the priests of the high places." Thus he not only sinned greatly himself, but "made Israel to sin;" and "this thing became sin unto the house of Jeroboam, even to cut it off, and to destroy it from off the face of the earth." Verses 33, 34; 14:16.

Toward the close of a troubled reign of twenty-two years, Jeroboam met with a disastrous defeat in a war with Abijah, the successor of Rehoboam. "Neither did Jeroboam recover strength again in the days of Abijah: and the Lord struck him, and he died." 2 Chronicles 13:20.

The apostasy introduced during Jeroboam's reign became more and more marked, until finally it resulted in the utter ruin of the kingdom of Israel. Even before the death of Jeroboam, Ahijah, the aged prophet at Shiloh who many years before had predicted the elevation of Jeroboam to the throne, declared: "The Lord shall smite Israel, as a reed is shaken in the water, and He shall root up Israel out of this good land, which He gave to their fathers, and shall scatter them beyond the river, because they have made their groves, provoking the Lord to anger. And He shall give Israel up because of the sins of Jeroboam, who did sin, and who made Israel to sin." 1 Kings 14:15, 16.

Yet the Lord did not give Israel up without first doing all that could be done to lead them back to their allegiance to Him. Through long, dark years when ruler after ruler stood up in bold defiance of Heaven and led Israel deeper and still deeper into idolatry, God sent message after message to His backslidden people. Through His prophets He gave them every opportunity to stay the tide of apostasy and to return to Him. During the years that were to follow the rending of the kingdom, Elijah and Elisha were to live and labor, and the tender appeals of Hosea and Amos and Obadiah were to be heard in the land. Never was the kingdom

of Israel to be left without noble witnesses to the mighty power of God to save from sin. Even in the darkest hours some would remain true to their divine Ruler and in the midst of idolatry would live blameless in the sight of a holy God. These faithful ones were numbered among the goodly remnant through whom the eternal purpose of Jehovah was finally to be fulfilled.

8

National Apostasy

From the time of Jeroboam's death to Elijah's appearance before Ahab the people of Israel suffered a steady spiritual decline. Ruled by men who did not fear Jehovah and who encouraged strange forms of worship, the larger number of the people rapidly lost sight of their duty to serve the living God and adopted many of the practices of idolatry.

Nadab, the son of Jeroboam, occupied the throne of Israel for only a few months. His career of evil was suddenly stopped by a conspiracy headed by Baasha, one of his generals, to gain control of the government. Nadab was slain, with all his kindred in the line of succession, "according unto the saying of the Lord, which He spake by His servant Ahijah the Shilonite: because of the sins of Jeroboam which he sinned, and which he made Israel sin." 1 Kings 15:29, 30.

Thus perished the house of Jeroboam. The idolatrous worship introduced by him had brought upon the guilty offenders the retributive judgments of Heaven; and yet the rulers who followed—Baasha, Elah, Zimri, and Omri—during a period of nearly forty years, continued in the same fatal course of evil-doing.

During the greater part of this time of apostasy in Israel, Asa was ruling in the kingdom of Judah. For many years "Asa did that which was good and right in the eyes of the Lord his God: for he took away the altars of the strange gods, and the high places, and brake down the images, and cut down the groves: and commanded Judah to seek the Lord God of their fathers, and to do the law and the commandment. Also he took away out of all the cities of Judah the high places and the sun [margin] images: and the kingdom was quiet before him." 2 Chronicles 14:2-5.

The faith of Asa was put to a severe test when "Zerah the Ethiopian with an host of a thousand thousand, and three hundred chariots," invaded his kingdom. Verse 9. In this crisis Asa did not put his trust in the "fenced cities in Judah" that he had built, with "walls, and towers, gates, and bars," nor in the "mighty men of valor" in his carefully trained army. Verses 6-8. The king's trust was in Jehovah of hosts, in whose name marvelous deliverances had been wrought in behalf of Israel of old. Setting his forces in battle array, he sought the help of God.

The opposing armies now stood face to face. It was a time of test and trial to those who served the Lord. Had every sin been confessed? Had the men of Judah full confidence in God's power to deliver? Such thoughts as these were in the minds of the leaders. From every human viewpoint the vast host from Egypt would sweep everything before it. But in time of peace Asa had not been giving himself to amusement and pleasure; he had been preparing for any emergency. He had an army trained for conflict; he had endeavored to lead his people to make their peace with God. And now, although his forces were fewer in number than the enemy, his faith in the One whom he had made his trust did not weaken.

Having sought the Lord in the days of prosperity, the king could now rely upon Him in the day of adversity. His petitions showed that he was not a stranger to God's wonderful power. "It is nothing with Thee to help," he pleaded, "whether with many, or with them that have no power: help us, O Lord our God; for we rest on Thee, and in Thy name we go against this multitude. O Lord, Thou art our God; let not man prevail against Thee." Verse 11.

The prayer of Asa is one that every Christian believer may fittingly offer. We fight in a warfare, not against flesh and blood, but against principalities and powers, and against spiritual wickedness in high places. See Ephesians 6:12. In life's conflict we must meet evil agencies that have arrayed themselves against the right. Our hope is not in man, but in the living God. With full assurance of faith we may expect that He will unite His omnipotence with the efforts of human instrumentalities, for the glory of His name. Clad with the armor of His righteousness, we may gain the victory over every foe.

King Asa's faith was signally rewarded. "The Lord smote the Ethiopians before Asa, and before Judah; and the Ethiopians fled. And Asa and the people that were with him pursued them unto Gerar: and the Ethiopians were overthrown, that they could not recover themselves; for they were destroyed before the Lord, and before His host." 2 Chronicles 14:12, 13.

As the victorious armies of Judah and Benjamin were returning to Jerusalem, "the Spirit of God came upon Azariah the son of Oded: and he went out to meet Asa, and said unto him, Hear ye me, Asa, and all Judah and Benjamin; The Lord is with you, while ye be with Him; and if ye seek Him, He will be found of you; but if ye forsake Him, He will forsake you." "Be ye strong therefore, and let not your hands be weak: for your work shall be rewarded." 2 Chronicles 15:1, 2, 7.

Greatly encouraged by these words, Asa soon led out in a second reformation in Judah. He "put away the abominable idols out of all the land of Judah and Benjamin, and out of the cities which he had taken from Mount Ephraim, and renewed the altar of the Lord, that was before the porch of the Lord.

"And he gathered all Judah and Benjamin, and the strangers with them out of Ephraim and Manasseh, and out of Simeon: for they fell to him out of Israel in abundance, when they saw that the Lord his God was with him. So they gathered themselves together at Jerusalem in the third month, in the fifteenth year of the reign of Asa. And they offered unto the Lord the same time, of the spoil which they had brought, seven hundred oxen and seven thousand sheep. And they entered into a covenant to seek the Lord God of their fathers with all their heart and with all their soul." "And He was found of them: and the Lord gave them rest round about." Verses 8-12, 15.

Asa's long record of faithful service was marred by some mistakes, made at times when he failed to put his trust fully in God. When, on one occasion, the king of Israel entered the kingdom of Judah and seized Ramah, a fortified city only five miles from Jerusalem, Asa sought deliverance by forming an alliance with Benhadad, king of Syria. This failure to trust God alone in time of need was sternly rebuked by Hanani the prophet, who appeared before Asa with the message:

"Because thou hast relied on the king of Syria, and not relied on the Lord thy God, therefore is the host of the king of Syria escaped out of thine hand. Were not the Ethiopians and the Lubims a huge host, with very many chariots and horsemen? yet, because thou didst rely on the Lord, He delivered them into thine hand. For the eyes of the Lord run to and fro throughout the whole earth, to show Himself strong in the behalf of them whose heart is perfect toward Him. Herein thou hast done foolishly: therefore from henceforth thou shalt have wars." 2 Chronicles 16:7-9.

Instead of humbling himself before God because of his mistake, "Asa was wroth with the seer, and put him in a prison house; for he was in a rage with him because of this thing. And Asa oppressed some of the people the same time." Verse 10.

"In the thirty and ninth year of his reign," Asa was "diseased in his feet, until his disease was exceeding great: yet in his disease he sought not to the Lord, but to the physicians." Verse 12. The king died in the forty-first year of his reign and was succeeded by Jehoshaphat, his son.

Two years before the death of Asa, Ahab began to rule in the kingdom of Israel. From the beginning his reign was marked by a strange and terrible apostasy. His father, Omri, the founder of Samaria, had "wrought evil in the eyes of the Lord, and did worse than all that were before him" (1 Kings 16:25); but the sins of Ahab were even greater. He "did more to provoke the Lord God of Israel to anger than all the kings of Israel that were before him," acting "as if it had been a light thing for him to walk in the sins of Jeroboam the son of Nebat." Verses 33, 31. Not content with encouraging the forms of religious service followed at Bethel and Dan, he boldly led the people into the grossest heathenism, by setting aside the worship of Jehovah for Baal worship.

Taking to wife Jezebel, "the daughter of Ethbaal king of the Zidonians" and high priest of Baal, Ahab "served Baal, and worshiped him. And he reared up an altar for Baal in the house of Baal, which he had built in Samaria." Verses 31, 32.

Not only did Ahab introduce Baal worship at the capital city, but under the leadership of Jezebel he erected heathen altars in many "high places," where in the shelter of surrounding groves the priests and others connected with this seductive form of idolatry exerted their baleful influence, until well-nigh all Israel were following after Baal. "There was none like unto Ahab," who "did sell himself to work wickedness in the sight of the Lord, whom Jezebel his wife stirred up. And he did very abominably in following idols, according to all things as did the Amorites, whom the Lord cast out before the children of Israel." 1 Kings 21:25, 26.

Ahab was weak in moral power. His union by marriage with an idolatrous woman of decided character and positive temperament resulted disastrously both to himself and to the nation. Unprincipled, and with no high standard of rightdoing, his character was easily molded by the determined spirit of Jezebel. His selfish nature was incapable of appreciating the mercies of God to Israel and his own obligations as the guardian and leader of the chosen people.

Under the blighting influence of Ahab's rule, Israel wandered far from the living God and corrupted their ways before Him. For many years they had been losing their sense of reverence and godly fear; and now it seemed as if there were none who dared expose their lives by openly standing forth in opposition to the prevailing blasphemy. The dark shadow of apostasy covered the whole land. Images of Baalim and Ashtoreth were everywhere to be seen. Idolatrous temples and consecrated groves, wherein were worshiped the works of men's hands, were multiplied. The air was polluted with the smoke of the sacrifices offered to false gods. Hill and vale resounded with the drunken cries of a heathen priesthood who sacrificed to the sun, moon, and stars.

Through the influence of Jezebel and her impious priests, the people were taught that the idol gods that had been set up were deities, ruling by their mystic power the elements of earth, fire, and water. All the bounties of heaven—the running brooks, the streams of living water, the gentle dew, the showers of rain which refreshed the earth and caused the fields to bring forth abundantly—were ascribed to the favor of Baal and Ashtoreth, instead of to the Giver of every good and perfect gift. The people forgot that the hills and valleys, the streams and fountains, were in the hand of the living God, that He controlled the sun, the clouds of heaven, and all the powers of nature.

Through faithful messengers the Lord sent repeated warnings to the apostate king and the people, but in vain were these words of reproof. In vain did the inspired messengers assert Jehovah's right to be the only God in Israel; in vain did they exalt the laws that He had entrusted to them. Captivated by the gorgeous display and the fascinating rites of idol worship, the people followed the example of the king and his court, and gave themselves up to the intoxicating, degrading pleasures of a sensual worship. In their blind folly they chose to reject God and His worship. The light so graciously given them had become darkness. The fine gold had become dim.

Alas, how had the glory of Israel departed! Never before had the chosen people of God fallen so low in apostasy. Of "the prophets of Baal" there were "four hundred and fifty," besides four hundred "prophets of the groves." 1 Kings 18:19. Nothing short of the miracle-working power of God could preserve the nation from utter destruction. Israel had voluntarily separated herself from Jehovah, yet the Lord in compassion still yearned after those who had been led into sin, and He was about to send to them one of the mightiest of His prophets, through whom many were to be led back to allegiance to the God of their fathers.

SECTION II

PROPHETS OF THE NORTHERN KINGDOM

"Who is wise, and he shall understand
these things?
Prudent, and he shall know them?
For the ways of the Lord are right,
And the just shall walk in them:
But the transgressors shall fall therein."
Hosea 14:9.

9

Elijah the Tishbite

Among the mountains of Gilead, east of the Jordan, there dwelt in the days of Ahab a man of faith and prayer whose fearless ministry was destined to check the rapid spread of apostasy in Israel. Far removed from any city of renown, and occupying no high station in life, Elijah the Tishbite nevertheless entered upon his mission confident in God's purpose to prepare the way before him and to give him abundant success. The word of faith and power was upon his lips, and his whole life was devoted to the work of reform. His was the voice of one crying in the wilderness to rebuke sin and press back the tide of evil. And while he came to the people as a reprover of sin, his message offered the balm of Gilead to the sin-sick souls of all who desired to be healed.

As Elijah saw Israel going deeper and deeper into idolatry, his soul was distressed and his indignation aroused. God had done great things for His people. He had delivered them from bondage and given them "the lands of the heathen, . . . that they might observe His statutes, and keep His laws." Psalm 105:44, 45. But the beneficent designs of Jehovah were now well-nigh forgotten. Unbelief was fast separating the chosen nation from the Source of their strength. Viewing this apostasy from his mountain retreat, Elijah was overwhelmed with sorrow. In anguish of soul he besought God to arrest the once-favored people in their wicked course, to visit them with judgments, if need be, that they might be led to see in its true light their departure from Heaven. He longed to see them brought to repentance before they should go to such lengths in evil-doing as to provoke the Lord to destroy them utterly.

This chapter is based on 1 Kings 17:1-7.

Elijah's prayer was answered. Oft-repeated appeals, remonstrances, and warnings had failed to bring Israel to repentance. The time had come when God must speak to them by means of judgments. Inasmuch as the worshipers of Baal claimed that the treasures of heaven, the dew and the rain, came not from Jehovah, but from the ruling forces of nature, and that it was through the creative energy of the sun that the earth was enriched and made to bring forth abundantly, the curse of God was to rest heavily upon the polluted land. The apostate tribes of Israel were to be shown the folly of trusting to the power of Baal for temporal blessings. Until they should turn to God with repentance, and acknowledge Him as the source of all blessing, there should fall upon the land neither dew nor rain.

To Elijah was entrusted the mission of delivering to Ahab Heaven's message of judgment. He did not seek to be the Lord's messenger; the word of the Lord came to him. And jealous for the honor of God's cause, he did not hesitate to obey the divine summons, though to obey seemed to invite swift destruction at the hand of the wicked king. The prophet set out at once and traveled night and day until he reached Samaria. At the palace he solicited no admission, nor waited to be formally announced. Clad in the coarse garments usually worn by the prophets of that time, he passed the guards, apparently unnoticed, and stood for a moment before the astonished king.

Elijah made no apology for his abrupt appearance. A Greater than the ruler of Israel had commissioned him to speak; and, lifting his hand toward heaven, he solemnly affirmed by the living God that the judgments of the Most High were about to fall upon Israel. "As the Lord God of Israel liveth, before whom I stand," he declared, "there shall not be dew nor rain these years, but according to my word."

It was only by the exercise of strong faith in the unfailing power of God's word that Elijah delivered his message. Had he not possessed implicit confidence in the One whom he served, he would never have appeared before Ahab. On his way to Samaria, Elijah had passed by ever-flowing streams, hills covered with verdure, and stately forests that seemed beyond the reach of drought. Everything on which the eye rested was clothed with beauty. The prophet might have wondered how the streams that had never ceased their flow could become dry, or how those hills and valleys could be burned with drought. But he gave no place to unbelief. He fully believed that God would humble apostate Israel, and that through judgments they would be brought to repentance. The fiat of Heaven had gone forth; God's word could not fail; and at the peril of his life Elijah fearlessly fulfilled his commission. Like a thunderbolt from a clear sky, the message of impending judgment fell upon the ears of the wicked king; but before Ahab could recover from his astonishment, or frame a reply, Elijah disappeared as abruptly as he had come, without waiting to witness the effect of his message. And the Lord went before him, making plain the way. "Turn thee eastward," the prophet was bidden, "and hide thyself by the brook Cherith, that is before Jordan. And it shall be, that thou shalt drink of the brook; and I have commanded the ravens to feed thee."

The king made diligent inquiry, but the prophet was not to be found. Queen Jezebel, angered over the message that had locked up the treasures of heaven, lost no time in conferring with the priests of Baal, who united with her in cursing the prophet and in defying the wrath of Jehovah. But notwithstanding their desire to find him who had uttered the word of woe, they were destined to meet with disappointment. Nor could they conceal from others a knowledge of the judgment pronounced in consequence of the prevailing apostasy. Tidings of Elijah's denunciation of the sins of Israel, and of his prophecy of swift-coming punishment, quickly spread throughout the land. The fears of some were aroused, but in general the heavenly message was received with scorn and ridicule.

The prophet's words went into immediate effect. Those who were at first inclined to scoff at the thought of calamity, soon had occasion for serious reflection; for after a few months the earth, unrefreshed by dew or rain, became dry, and vegetation withered. As time passed, streams that had never been known to fail began to decrease, and brooks began to dry up. Yet the people were urged by their leaders to have confidence in the power of Baal and to set aside as idle words the prophecy of Elijah. The priests still insisted that it was through the power of Baal that the showers of rain fell. Fear not the God of Elijah, nor tremble at His word, they urged, it is Baal that brings forth the harvest in its season and provides for man and beast.

God's message to Ahab gave Jezebel and her priests and all the followers of Baal and Ashtoreth opportunity to test the power of their gods, and, if possible, to prove the word of Elijah false. Against the assurances of hundreds of idolatrous priests, the prophecy of Elijah stood alone. If, notwithstanding the prophet's declaration, Baal could still give dew and rain, causing the streams to continue to flow and vegetation to flourish, then let the king of Israel worship him and the people say that he is God.

Determined to keep the people in deception, the priests of Baal continue to offer sacrifices to their gods and to call upon them night and day to refresh the earth. With costly offerings the priests attempt to appease the anger of their gods; with a zeal and a perseverance worthy of a better cause they linger round their pagan altars and pray earnestly for rain. Night after night, throughout the doomed land, their cries and entreaties arise. But no clouds appear in the heavens by day to hide the burning rays of the sun. No dew or rain refreshes the thirsty earth. The word of Jehovah stands unchanged by anything the priests of Baal can do.

A year passes, and yet there is no rain. The earth is parched as if with fire. The scorching heat of the sun destroys what little vegetation has survived. Streams dry up, and lowing herds and bleating flocks wander hither and thither in distress. Once-flourishing fields have become like burning desert sands, a desolate waste. The groves dedicated to idol worship are leafless; the forest trees, gaunt skeletons of nature, afford no shade. The air is dry and suffocating; dust storms blind the eyes and nearly stop the breath. Once-prosperous cities and villages have become places of mourning. Hunger and thirst are telling upon man and beast with fearful mortality. Famine, with all its horrors, comes closer and still closer.

Yet notwithstanding these evidences of God's power, Israel repented not, nor learned the lesson that God would have them learn. They did not see that He who created nature controls her laws, and can make of them instruments of blessing or of destruction. Proudhearted, enamored of their false worship, they were unwilling to humble themselves under the mighty hand of God, and they began to cast about for some other cause to which to attribute their sufferings.

Jezebel utterly refused to recognize the drought as a judgment from Jehovah. Unyielding in her determination to defy the God of heaven, she, with nearly the whole of Israel, united in denouncing Elijah as the cause of all their misery. Had he not borne testimony against their forms of worship? If only he could be put out of the way, she argued, the anger of their gods would be appeased, and their troubles would end.

Urged on by the queen, Ahab instituted a most diligent search for the hiding place of the prophet. To the surrounding nations, far and near, he sent messengers to seek for the man whom he hated, yet feared; and in his anxiety to make the search as thorough as possible, he required of these kingdoms and nations an oath that they knew nothing of the whereabouts of the prophet. But the search was in vain. The prophet was safe from the malice of the king whose sins had brought upon the land the denunciation of an offended God.

Failing in her efforts against Elijah, Jezebel determined to avenge herself by slaying all the prophets of Jehovah in Israel. Not one should be left alive. The infuriated woman carried out her purpose in the massacre of many of God's servants. Not all, however, perished. Obadiah, the governor of Ahab's house, yet faithful to God, "took an hundred prophets," and at the risk of his own life, "hid them by fifty in a cave, and fed them with bread and water." 1 Kings 18:4.

The second year of famine passed, and still the pitiless heavens gave no sign of rain.

Drought and famine continued their devastation throughout the kingdom. Fathers and mothers, powerless to relieve the sufferings of their children, were forced to see them die. Yet still apostate Israel refused to humble their hearts before God and continued to murmur against the man by whose word these terrible judgments had been brought upon them. They seemed unable to discern in their suffering and distress a call to repentance, a divine interposition to save them from taking the fatal step beyond the boundary of Heaven's forgiveness.

The apostasy of Israel was an evil more dreadful than all the multiplied horrors of famine. God was seeking to free the people from their delusion and lead them to understand their accountability to the One to whom they owed their life and all things. He was trying to help them to recover their lost faith, and He must needs bring upon them great affliction.

"Have I any pleasure at all that the wicked should die? saith the Lord God: and not that he should return from his ways, and live?" "Cast away from you all your transgressions, whereby ye have transgressed; and make you a new heart and a new spirit: for why will ye die, O house of Israel? For I have no pleasure in the death of him that dieth, saith the Lord God: wherefore turn yourselves, and live ye." "Turn ye, turn ye from your evil ways; for why will ye die, O house of Israel?" Ezekiel 18:23, 31, 32; 33:11.

God had sent messengers to Israel, with appeals to return to their allegiance. Had they heeded these appeals, had they turned from Baal to the living God, Elijah's message of judgment would never have been given. But the warnings that might have been a savor of life unto life had proved to them a savor of death unto death. Their pride had been wounded, their anger had been aroused against the messengers, and now they regarded with intense hatred the prophet Elijah. If only he should fall into their hands, gladly they would deliver him to Jezebel—as if by silencing his voice they could stay the fulfillment of his words! In the face of calamity they continued to stand firm in their idolatry. Thus they were adding to the guilt that had brought the judgments of Heaven upon the land.

For stricken Israel there was but one remedy—a turning away from the sins that had brought upon them the chastening hand of the Almighty, and a turning to the Lord with full purpose of heart. To them had been given the assurance, "If I shut up heaven that there be no rain, or if I command the locusts to devour the land, or if I send pestilence among My people; if My people, which are called by My name, shall humble themselves, and pray, and seek My face, and turn from their wicked ways; then will I hear from heaven, and will forgive their sin, and will heal their land." 2 Chronicles 7:13, 14. It was to bring to pass this blessed result that God continued to withhold from them the dew and the rain until a decided reformation should take place.

10

The Voice of Stern Rebuke

For a time Elijah remained hidden in the mountains by the brook Cherith. There for many months he was miraculously provided with food. Later on, when, because of the continued drought, the brook became dry, God bade His servant find refuge in a heathen land. "Arise," He bade him, "get thee to Zarephath, [known in New Testament times as Sarepta], which belongeth to Zidon, and dwell there: behold, I have commanded a widow woman there to sustain thee."

This woman was not an Israelite. She had never had the privileges and blessings that the chosen people of God had enjoyed; but she was a believer in the true God and had walked in all the light that was shining on her pathway. And now, when there was no safety for Elijah in the land of Israel, God sent him to this woman to find an asylum in her home.

"So he arose and went to Zarephath. And when he came to the gate of the city, behold, the widow woman was there gathering of sticks: and he called to her, and said, Fetch me, I pray thee, a little water in a vessel, that I may drink. And as she was going to fetch it, he called to her, and said, Bring me, I pray thee, a morsel of bread in thine hand."

In this poverty-stricken home the famine pressed sore, and the pitifully meager fare seemed about to fail. The coming of Elijah on the very day when the widow feared that she must give up the struggle to sustain life tested to the utmost her faith in the power of the living God to provide for her necessities. But even in her dire extremity she bore witness to her faith by a compliance with the request of the stranger who was asking her to share her last morsel with him.

In response to Elijah's request for food and drink, the widow said, "As the Lord thy God liveth, I have not a cake, but an handful of meal in a barrel, and a little oil in a cruse: and, behold, I am gathering two sticks, that I may go in and dress it for me and my son, that we may eat it, and die." Elijah said to her, "Fear not; go and do as thou hast said: but make me thereof a little cake first, and bring it unto me, and after make for thee and for thy son. For thus saith the Lord God of Israel, The barrel of meal shall not waste, neither shall the cruse of oil fail, until the day that the Lord sendeth rain upon the earth."

No greater test of faith than this could have been required. The widow had hitherto treated all strangers with kindness and liberality. Now,

This chapter is based on 1 Kings 17:8-24; 18:1-19.

regardless of the suffering that might result to herself and child, and trusting in the God of 131 Israel to supply her every need, she met this supreme test of hospitality by doing "according to the saying of Elijah."

Wonderful was the hospitality shown to God's prophet by this Phoenician woman, and wonderfully were her faith and generosity rewarded. "She, and he, and her house, did eat many days. And the barrel of meal wasted not, neither did the cruse of oil fail, according to the word of the Lord, which He spake by Elijah.

"And it came to pass after these things, that the son of the woman, the mistress of the house, fell sick; and his sickness was so sore, that there was no breath left in him. And she said unto Elijah, What have I to do with thee, O thou man of God? art thou come unto me to call my sin to remembrance, and to slay my son?

"And he said unto her, Give me thy son. And he took him out of her bosom, and carried him up into a loft, where he abode, and laid him upon his own bed. . . . And he stretched himself upon the child three times, and cried unto the Lord. . . . And the Lord heard the voice of Elijah; and the soul of the child came into him again, and he revived.

"And Elijah took the child, and brought him down out of the chamber into the house, and delivered him unto his mother: and Elijah said, See, thy son liveth. And the woman said to Elijah, Now by this I know that thou art a man of God, and that the word of the Lord in thy mouth is truth."

The widow of Zarephath shared her morsel with Elijah, and in return her life and that of her son were preserved. And to all who, in time of 132 trial and want, give sympathy and assistance to others more needy, God has promised great blessing. He has not changed. His power is no less now than in the days of Elijah. No less sure now than when spoken by our Saviour is the promise, "He that receiveth a prophet in the name of a prophet shall receive a prophet's reward." Matthew 10:41.

"Be not forgetful to entertain strangers: for thereby some have entertained angels unawares." Hebrews 13:2. These words have lost none of their force through the lapse of time. Our heavenly Father still continues to place in the pathway of His children opportunities that are blessings in disguise; and those who improve these opportunities find great joy. "If thou draw out thy soul to the hungry, and satisfy the afflicted soul; then shall thy light rise in obscurity, and thy darkness be as the noonday: and the Lord shall guide thee continually, and satisfy thy soul in drought, and make fat thy bones: and thou shalt be like a watered garden, and like a spring of water, whose waters fail not." Isaiah 58:10, 11.

To His faithful servants today Christ says, "He that receiveth you receiveth Me, and he that receiveth Me receiveth Him that sent Me." No act of kindness shown in His name will fail to be recognized and rewarded. And in the same tender recognition Christ includes even the feeblest and lowliest of the family of God. "Whosoever shall give to drink," He says, "unto one of these little ones"—those who are as children in their faith and their knowledge of Christ—"a cup of cold water only in the name of a disciple, verily I say unto you, he shall in no wise lose his reward." Matthew 10:40, 42.

Through the long years of drought and 133 famine, Elijah prayed earnestly that the hearts of Israel might be turned from idolatry to allegiance to God. Patiently the prophet waited, while the hand of the Lord rested heavily on the stricken land. As he saw evidences of suffering and want multiplying on every side, his heart was wrung with sorrow, and he longed for power to bring about a reformation quickly. But God Himself was working out His plan, and all that His servant could do was to pray on in faith and await the time for decided action.

The apostasy prevailing in Ahab's day was the result of many years of evil-doing. Step by step, year after year, Israel had been departing from the right way. For generation after generation they had refused to make straight paths for their feet, and at last the great majority of the people had yielded themselves to the leadership of the powers of darkness.

About a century had passed since, under the rulership of King David, Israel had joyfully united in chanting hymns of praise to the Most High, in recognition of their entire dependence on Him for daily mercies. Listen to their words of adoration as then they sang:

"O God of our salvation, . . .
Thou makest the outgoings of the morning
    and evening to rejoice.
Thou visitest the earth, and waterest it:
Thou greatly enrichest it with the river of
    God, which is full of water:
Thou preparest them corn, when Thou hast so
    provided for it.
Thou waterest the ridges thereof abundantly: 134
    Thou causest rain to descend into the fur-
    rows thereof:
Thou makest it soft with showers: Thou bless-
    est the springing thereof.
Thou crownest the year with Thy goodness;
And Thy paths drop fatness.
They drop upon the pastures of the wilder-
    ness:
And the little hills rejoice on every side.
The pastures are clothed with flocks;
The valleys also are covered over with corn;
They shout for joy, they also sing."
           Psalm 65:5, 8-13, margin.

Israel had then recognized God as the One who "laid the foundations of the earth." In expression of their faith they had sung:

"Thou coveredst it with the deep as with a garment:
The waters stood above the mountains.
At Thy rebuke they fled;
At the voice of Thy thunder they hasted away.
They go up by the mountains; they go down by the valleys
Unto the place which Thou hast founded for them.
Thou hast set a bound that they may not pass over;
That they turn not again to cover the earth."
Psalm 104:5-9.

It is by the mighty power of the Infinite One that the elements of nature in earth and sea and sky are kept within bounds. And these elements He uses for the happiness of His creatures. "His good treasure" is freely expended "to give the rain . . . in his season, and to bless all the work" of man's hands. Deuteronomy 28:12.

"He sendeth the springs into the valleys,
Which run among the hills.
They give drink to every beast of the field:
The wild asses quench their thirst.
By them shall the fowls of the heaven have their habitation,
Which sing among the branches. . . .
He causeth the grass to grow for the cattle,
135 And herb for the service of man:
That He may bring forth food out of the earth;
And wine that maketh glad the heart of man,
And oil to make his face to shine,
And bread which strengtheneth man's heart. .

"O Lord, how manifold are Thy works!
In wisdom hast Thou made them all:
The earth is full of Thy riches.
So is this great and wide sea,
Wherein are things creeping innumerable,
Both small and great beasts. . . .
These wait all upon Thee;
That Thou mayest give them their meat in due season.
That Thou givest them they gather:

"Thou openest Thine hand,
They are filled with good."
Psalm 104:10-15, 24-28.

Israel had had abundant occasion for rejoicing. The land to which the Lord had brought them was a land flowing with milk and honey. During the wilderness wandering, God had assured them that He was guiding them to a country where they need never suffer for lack of rain. "The land, whither thou goest in to possess it," He had told them, "is not as the land of Egypt, from whence ye came out, where thou sowedst thy seed, and wateredst it with thy foot, as a garden of herbs:

but the land, whither ye go to possess it, is a land of hills and valleys, and drinketh water of the rain of heaven: a land which the Lord thy God careth for: the eyes of the Lord thy God are always upon it, from the beginning of the year even unto the end of the year."

136 The promise of abundance of rain had been given on condition of obedience. "It shall come to pass," the Lord had declared, "if ye shall hearken diligently unto My commandments which I command you this day, to love the Lord your God, and to serve Him with all your heart and with all your soul, that I will give you the rain of your land in his due season, the first rain and the latter rain, that thou mayest gather in thy corn, and thy wine, and thine oil. And I will send grass in thy fields for thy cattle, that thou mayest eat and be full.

"Take heed to yourselves," the Lord had admonished His people, "that your heart be not deceived, and ye turn aside, and serve other gods, and worship them; and then the Lord's wrath be kindled against you, and He shut up the heaven, that there be no rain, and that the land yield not her fruit; and lest ye perish quickly from off the good land which the Lord giveth you." Deuteronomy 11:10-17.

"If thou wilt not hearken unto the voice of the Lord thy God, to observe to do all His commandments and His statutes," the Israelites had been warned, "thy heaven that is over thy head shall be brass, and the earth that is under thee shall be iron. The Lord shall make the rain of thy land powder and dust: from heaven shall it come down upon thee, until thou be destroyed." Deuteronomy 28:15, 23, 24.

These were among the wise counsels of Jehovah to ancient Israel. "Lay up these My words in your heart and in your soul," He had commanded His chosen people, "and bind them for a sign upon your hand, that they may be as frontlets between your eyes. And ye shall teach them your children, speaking of them when thou sittest in thine house, and when thou walkest by 137 the way, when thou liest down, and when thou risest up." Deuteronomy 11:18, 19. Plain were these commands, yet as the centuries passed, and generation after generation lost sight of the provisions made for their spiritual welfare, the ruinous influences of apostasy threatened to sweep aside every barrier of divine grace.

Thus it had come to pass that God was now visiting His people with the severest of His judgments. The prediction of Elijah was meeting with terrible fulfillment. For three years the messenger of woe was sought for in city after city and nation after nation. At the mandate of Ahab, many rulers had given their oath of honor that the strange prophet could not be found in their dominions. Yet the search was continued, for Jezebel and the prophets of Baal hated Elijah with a deadly hatred, and they spared no effort to bring him within reach of their power. And still there was no rain.

At last, "after many days," the word of the Lord came to Elijah, "Go, show thyself unto Ahab; and I will send rain upon the earth."

In obedience to the command, "Elijah went to show himself unto Ahab." About the time that the prophet set forth on his journey to Samaria, Ahab had proposed to Obadiah, the governor of his household, that they make thorough search for springs and brooks of water, in the hope of finding pasture for their starving flocks and herds. Even in the royal court the effect of the long-continued drought was keenly felt. The king, deeply concerned over the outlook for his household, decided to unite personally with his servant in a search for some favored spots where pasture might be had. "So they divided the land between them to pass throughout it: Ahab went one way by himself, and Obadiah went another way by himself."

"As Obadiah was in the way, behold, Elijah met him: and he knew him, and fell on his face, and said, Art thou that my lord Elijah?"

During the apostasy of Israel, Obadiah had remained faithful. His master, the king, had been unable to turn him from his allegiance to the living God. Now he was honored with a commission from Elijah, who said, "Go, tell thy lord, Behold, Elijah is here."

Greatly terrified, Obadiah exclaimed, "What have I sinned, that thou wouldest deliver thy servant into the hand of Ahab, to slay me?" To take such a message as this to Ahab was to court certain death. "As the Lord thy God liveth," he explained to the prophet, "there is no nation or kingdom, whither my lord hath not sent to seek thee: and when they said, He is not there; he took an oath of the kingdom and nation, that they found thee not. And now thou sayest, Go, tell thy lord, Behold, Elijah is here. And it shall come to pass, as soon as I am gone from thee, that the Spirit of the Lord shall carry thee whither I know not; and so when I come and tell Ahab, and he cannot find thee, he shall slay me."

Earnestly Obadiah pleaded with the prophet not to urge him. "I thy servant," he urged, "fear the Lord from my youth. Was it not told my lord what I did when Jezebel slew the prophets of the Lord, how I hid an hundred men of the Lord's prophets by fifty in a cave, and fed them with bread and water? And now thou sayest, Go, tell thy lord, Behold, Elijah is here: and he shall slay me."

With a solemn oath Elijah promised Obadiah that the errand should not be in vain. "As the Lord of hosts liveth, before whom I stand," he declared, "I will surely show myself unto him today." Thus assured, "Obadiah went to meet Ahab, and told him."

In astonishment mingled with terror the king listened to the message from the man whom he feared and hated, and for whom he had sought so untiringly. Well he knew that Elijah would not endanger his life merely for the sake of meeting him. Could it be possible that the prophet was about to utter another woe against Israel? The king's heart was seized with dread. He remembered the withered arm of Jeroboam. Ahab could not avoid obeying the summons, neither dared he lift up his hand against the messenger of God. And so, accompanied by a bodyguard of soldiers, the trembling monarch went to meet the prophet.

The king and the prophet stand face to face. Though Ahab is filled with passionate hatred, yet in the presence of Elijah he seems unmanned, powerless. In his first faltering words, "Art thou he that troubleth Israel?" he unconsciously reveals the inmost feelings of his heart. Ahab knew that it was by the word of God that the heavens had become as brass, yet he sought to cast upon the prophet the blame for the heavy judgments resting on the land.

It is natural for the wrongdoer to hold the messengers of God responsible for the calamities that come as the sure result of a departure from the way of righteousness. Those who place themselves in Satan's power are unable to see things as God sees them. When the mirror of truth is held up before them, they become indignant at the thought of receiving reproof. Blinded by sin, they refuse to repent; they feel that God's servants have turned against them and are worthy of severest censure.

Standing in conscious innocence before Ahab, Elijah makes no attempt to excuse himself or to flatter the king. Nor does he seek to evade the king's wrath by the good news that the drought is almost over. He has no apology to offer. Indignant, and jealous for the honor of God, he casts back the imputation of Ahab, fearlessly declaring to the king that it is *his* sins, and the sins of *his* fathers, that have brought upon Israel this terrible calamity. "I have not troubled Israel," Elijah boldly asserts, "but thou, and thy father's house, in that ye have forsaken the commandments of the Lord, and thou hast followed Baalim."

Today there is need of the voice of stern rebuke; for grievous sins have separated the people from God. Infidelity is fast becoming fashionable. "We will not have this man to reign over us," is the language of thousands. Luke 19:14. The smooth sermons so often preached make no lasting impression; the trumpet does not give a certain sound. Men are not cut to the heart by the plain, sharp truths of God's word.

There are many professed Christians who, if they should express their real feelings, would say, What need is there of speaking so plainly? They might as well ask, Why need John the Baptist have said to the Pharisees, "O generation of vipers, who hath warned you to flee from the wrath to come?" Luke 3:7. Why need he have provoked the anger of Herodias by telling Herod that it was unlawful for him to live with his brother's wife? The forerunner of Christ lost his life by his plain speaking. Why could he not have moved along without incurring the displeasure of those who were living in sin?

So men who should be standing as faithful guardians of God's law have argued, till policy has taken the place of faithfulness, and sin is allowed to go unreproved. When will the voice of faithful rebuke be heard once more in the church?

"Thou art the man." 2 Samuel 12:7. Words as unmistakably plain as these spoken by Nathan to David are seldom heard in the pulpits of today, seldom seen in the public press. If they were not so rare, we should see more of the power of God revealed among men. The Lord's messengers should not complain that their efforts are without fruit until they repent of their own love of approbation and their desire to please men, which leads them to suppress truth.

Those ministers who are men pleasers, who cry, Peace, peace, when God has not spoken peace, might well humble their hearts before God, asking pardon for their insincerity and their lack of moral courage. It is not from love for their neighbor that they smooth down the message entrusted to them, but because they are self-indulgent and ease-loving. True love seeks first the honor of God and the salvation of souls. Those who have this love will not evade the truth to save themselves from the unpleasant results of plain speaking. When souls are in peril, God's ministers will not consider self, but will speak the word given them to speak, refusing to excuse or palliate evil.

Would that every minister might realize the sacredness of his office and the holiness of his work, and show the courage that Elijah showed! As divinely appointed messengers, ministers are in a position of awful responsibility. They are to "reprove, rebuke, exhort with all long-suffering." 2 Timothy 4:2. In Christ's stead they are to labor as stewards of the mysteries of heaven, encouraging the obedient and warning the disobedient. With them worldly policy is to have no weight. Never are they to swerve from the path in which Jesus has bidden them walk. They are to go forward in faith, remembering that they are surrounded by a cloud of witnesses. They are not to speak their own words, but words which One greater than the potentates of earth has bidden them speak. Their message is to be, "Thus saith the Lord." God calls for men like Elijah, Nathan, and John the Baptist—men who will bear His message with faithfulness, regardless of the consequences; men who will speak the truth bravely, though it call for the sacrifice of all they have.

God cannot use men who, in time of peril, when the strength, courage, and influence of all are needed, are afraid to take a firm stand for the right. He calls for men who will do faithful battle against wrong, warring against principalities and powers, against the rulers of the darkness of this world, against spiritual wickedness in high places. It is to such as these that He will speak the words: "Well done, good and faithful servant; . . . enter thou into the joy of thy Lord." Matthew 25:23.

11

Carmel

Standing before Ahab, Elijah demanded that all Israel be assembled to meet him and the prophets of Baal and Ashtoreth on Mount Carmel. "Send," he commanded, "and gather to me all Israel unto Mount Carmel, and the prophets of Baal four hundred and fifty, and the prophets of the groves four hundred, which eat at Jezebel's table."

The command was issued by one who seemed to stand in the very presence of Jehovah; and Ahab obeyed at once, as if the prophet were monarch, and the king a subject. Swift messengers were sent throughout the kingdom with the summons to meet Elijah and the prophets of Baal and Ashtoreth. In every town and village the people prepared to assemble at the appointed time. As they journeyed toward the place, the hearts of many were filled with strange forebodings. Something unusual was about to happen; else why this summons to gather at Carmel? What new calamity was about to fall upon the people and the land?

Before the drought, Mount Carmel had been a place of beauty, its streams fed from never-failing springs, and its fertile slopes covered with fair flowers and flourishing groves. But now its beauty languished under a withering curse. The altars erected to the worship of Baal and Ashtoreth stood now in leafless groves. On the summit of one of the highest ridges, in sharp contrast with these was the broken-down altar of Jehovah.

Carmel overlooked a wide expanse of country; its heights were visible from many parts of the kingdom of Israel. At the foot of the mount there were vantage points from which could be seen much of what took place above. God had been signally dishonored by the idolatrous worship carried on under cover of its wooded slopes; and Elijah chose this elevation as the most conspicuous place for the display of God's power and for the vindication of the honor of His name.

Early on the morning of the day appointed, the hosts of apostate Israel, in eager expectancy, gather near the top of the mountain. Jezebel's prophets march up in imposing array. In regal

This chapter is based on 1 Kings 18:19-40.

pomp the king appears and takes his position at the head of the priests, and the idolaters shout his welcome. But there is apprehension in the hearts of the priests as they remember that at the word of the prophet the land of Israel for three years and a half has been destitute of dew and rain. Some fearful crisis is at hand, they feel sure. The gods in whom they have trusted have been unable to prove Elijah a false prophet. To their frantic cries, their prayers, their tears, their humiliation, their revolting ceremonies, their costly and ceaseless sacrifices, the objects of their worship have been strangely indifferent. [147]

Facing King Ahab and the false prophets, and surrounded by the assembled hosts of Israel, Elijah stands, the only one who has appeared to vindicate the honor of Jehovah. He whom the whole kingdom has charged with its weight of woe is now before them, apparently defenseless in the presence of the monarch of Israel, the prophets of Baal, the men of war, and the surrounding thousands. But Elijah is not alone. Above and around him are the protecting hosts of heaven, angels that excel in strength.

Unashamed, unterrified, the prophet stands before the multitude, fully aware of his commission to execute the divine command. His countenance is lighted with an awful solemnity. In anxious expectancy the people wait for him to speak. Looking first upon the broken-down altar of Jehovah, and then upon the multitude, Elijah cries out in clear, trumpetlike tones, "How long halt ye between two opinions? if the Lord be God, follow Him: but if Baal, then follow him."

The people answer him not a word. Not one in that vast assembly dare reveal loyalty to Jehovah. Like a dark cloud, deception and blindness had overspread Israel. Not all at once had this fatal apostasy closed about them, but gradually, as from time to time they had failed to heed the words of warning and reproof that the Lord sent them. Each departure from rightdoing, each refusal to repent, had deepened their guilt and driven them farther from Heaven. And now, in this crisis, they persisted in refusing to take their stand for God.

The Lord abhors indifference and disloyalty in a time of crisis in His work. The whole universe is watching with inexpressible interest the closing scenes of the great controversy between good and evil. The people of God are nearing the borders of the eternal world; what can be of more importance to them than that they be loyal to the God of heaven? All through the ages, God has had moral heroes, and He has them now—those who, like Joseph and Elijah and Daniel, are not ashamed to acknowledge themselves His peculiar people. His special blessing accompanies the labors of men of action, men who will not be swerved from the straight line of duty, but who with divine energy will inquire, "Who is on the Lord's side?" (Exodus [148]

32:26), men who will not stop merely with the inquiry, but who will demand that those who choose to identify themselves with the people of God shall step forward and reveal unmistakably their allegiance to the King of kings and Lord of lords. Such men make their wills and plans subordinate to the law of God. For love of Him they count not their lives dear unto themselves. Their work is to catch the light from the Word and let it shine forth to the world in clear, steady rays. Fidelity to God is their motto.

While Israel on Carmel doubt and hesitate, the voice of Elijah again breaks the silence: "I, even I only, remain a prophet of the Lord; but Baal's prophets are four hundred and fifty men. Let them therefore give us two bullocks; and let them choose one bullock for themselves, and cut it in pieces, and lay it on wood, and put no fire under: and I will dress the other bullock, and lay it on wood, and put no fire under: and call ye on the name of your gods, and I will call on the name of the Lord: and the God that answereth by fire, let him be God." [149]

The proposal of Elijah is so reasonable that the people cannot well evade it, so they find courage to answer, "It is well spoken." The prophets of Baal dare not lift their voices in dissent; and, addressing them, Elijah directs, "Choose you one bullock for yourselves, and dress it first; for ye are many; and call on the name of your gods, but put no fire under."

Outwardly bold and defiant, but with terror in their guilty hearts, the false priests prepare their altar, laying on the wood and the victim; and then they begin their incantations. Their shrill cries echo and re-echo through the forests and the surrounding heights, as they call on the name of their god, saying, "O Baal, hear us." The priests gather about their altar, and with leaping and writhing and screaming, with tearing of hair and cutting of flesh, they beseech their god to help them.

The morning passes, noon comes, and yet there is no evidence that Baal hears the cries of his deluded followers. There is no voice, no reply to their frantic prayers. The sacrifice remains unconsumed.

As they continue their frenzied devotions, the crafty priests are continually trying to devise some means by which they may kindle a fire upon the altar and lead the people to believe that the fire has come direct from Baal. But Elijah watches every movement; and the priests, hoping against hope for some opportunity to deceive, continue to carry on their senseless ceremonies.

"It came to pass at noon, that Elijah mocked them, and said, Cry aloud: for he is a god; either he is talking, or he is pursuing, or he is in a journey, or peradventure he sleepeth, and must be awaked. And they cried aloud, and cut themselves after their manner with knives and [150] lancets, till the blood gushed out upon them. And it came to pass, when midday was past, and they prophesied until the time of the offering of the evening sacrifice, that there was neither voice, nor any to answer, nor any that regarded."

Gladly would Satan have come to the help of those whom he had deceived, and who were devoted to his service. Gladly would he have sent the lightning to kindle their sacrifice. But Jehovah has set Satan's bounds, restrained his power, and not all the enemy's devices can convey one spark to Baal's altar.

At last, their voices hoarse with shouting, their garments stained with blood from self-inflicted wounds, the priests become desperate. With unabated frenzy they now mingle with their pleading terrible cursings of their sun-god, and Elijah continues to watch intently; for he knows that if by any device the priests should succeed in kindling their altar fire, he would instantly be torn in pieces.

Evening draws on. The prophets of Baal are weary, faint, confused. One suggests one thing, and another something else, until finally they cease their efforts. Their shrieks and curses no longer resound over Carmel. In despair they retire from the contest.

All day long the people have witnessed the demonstrations of the baffled priests. They have beheld their wild leaping round the altar, as if they would grasp the burning rays of the sun to 151 serve their purpose. They have looked with horror on the frightful, self-inflicted mutilations of the priests, and have had opportunity to reflect on the follies of idol worship. Many in the throng are weary of the exhibitions of demonism, and they now await with deepest interest the movements of Elijah.

It is the hour of the evening sacrifice, and Elijah bids the people, "Come near unto me." As they tremblingly draw near, he turns to the broken-down altar where once men worshiped the God of heaven, and repairs it. To him this heap of ruins is more precious than all the magnificent altars of heathendom.

In the reconstruction of this ancient altar, Elijah revealed his respect for the covenant that the Lord made with Israel when they crossed the Jordan into the Promised Land. Choosing "twelve stones, according to the number of the tribes of the sons of Jacob, . . . he built an altar in the name of the Lord."

The disappointed priests of Baal, exhausted by their vain efforts, wait to see what Elijah will do. They hate the prophet for proposing a test that has exposed the weakness and inefficiency of their gods; yet they fear his power. The people, fearful also, and almost breathless with expectancy, watch while Elijah continues his preparations. The calm demeanor of the prophet stands out in sharp contrast with the fanatical, senseless frenzy of the followers of Baal.

The altar completed, the prophet makes a trench about it, and, having put the wood in order and prepared the bullock, he lays the victim on the altar and commands the people to flood the sacrifice and the altar with water. "Fill four barrels," he directed, "and pour it on the 152 burnt sacrifice, and on the wood. And he said, Do it the second time. And they did it the second time. And he said, Do it the third time. And they did it the third time. And the water ran round about the altar; and he filled the trench also with water."

Reminding the people of the long-continued apostasy that has awakened the wrath of Jehovah, Elijah calls upon them to humble their hearts and turn to the God of their fathers, that the curse upon the land of Israel may be removed. Then, bowing reverently before the unseen God, he raises his hands toward heaven and offers a simple prayer. Baal's priests have screamed and foamed and leaped, from early morning until late in the afternoon; but as Elijah prays, no senseless shrieks resound over Carmel's height. He prays as if he knows Jehovah is there, a witness to the scene, a listener to his appeal. The prophets of Baal have prayed wildly, incoherently. Elijah prays simply and fervently, asking God to show His superiority over Baal, that Israel may be led to turn to Him.

"Lord God of Abraham, Isaac, and of Israel," the prophet pleads, "let it be known this day that Thou art God in Israel, and that I am Thy servant, and that I have done all these things at Thy word. Hear me, O Lord, hear me, that this people may know that Thou art the Lord God, and that Thou hast turned their heart back again."

A silence, oppressive in its solemnity, rests upon all. The priests of Baal tremble with terror. Conscious of their guilt, they look for swift retribution.

No sooner is the prayer of Elijah ended than flames of fire, like brilliant flashes of lightning, 153 descend from heaven upon the upreared altar, consuming the sacrifice, licking up the water in the trench, and consuming even the stones of the altar. The brilliancy of the blaze illumines the mountain and dazzles the eyes of the multitude. In the valleys below, where many are watching in anxious suspense the movements of those above, the descent of fire is clearly seen, and all are amazed at the sight. It resembles the pillar of fire which at the Red Sea separated the children of Israel from the Egyptian host.

The people on the mount prostrate themselves in awe before the unseen God. They dare not continue to look upon the Heaven-sent fire. They fear that they themselves will be consumed; and, convicted of their duty to acknowledge the God of Elijah as the God of their fathers, to whom they owe allegiance, they cry out together as with one voice, "The Lord, He is the God; the Lord, He is the God." With startling distinctness the cry resounds over the mountain and echoes in the plain below. At last Israel is aroused, undeceived, penitent. At last the people see how greatly they have dishonored God. The character of Baal worship, in contrast with the reasonable service required by the true God, stands fully revealed. The people recognize God's justice and mercy in withholding the dew and the rain until they have been brought to confess His name. They are ready now to admit that the God of Elijah is above every idol.

¹⁵⁴ The priests of Baal witness with consternation the wonderful revelation of Jehovah's power. Yet even in their discomfiture and in the presence of divine glory, they refuse to repent of their evil-doing. They would still remain the prophets of Baal. Thus they showed themselves ripe for destruction. That repentant Israel may be protected from the allurements of those who have taught them to worship Baal, Elijah is directed by the Lord to destroy these false teachers. The anger of the people has already been aroused against the leaders in transgression; and when Elijah gives the command, "Take the prophets of Baal; let not one of them escape," they are ready to obey. They seize the priests, and take them to the brook Kishon, and there, before the close of the day that marked the beginning of decided reform, the ministers of Baal are slain. Not one is permitted to live.

¹⁵⁵

12

From Jezreel to Horeb

With the slaying of the prophets of Baal, the way was opened for carrying forward a mighty spiritual reformation among the ten tribes of the northern kingdom. Elijah had set before the people their apostasy; he had called upon them to humble their hearts and turn to the Lord. The judgments of Heaven had been executed; the people had confessed their sins, and had acknowledged the God of their fathers as the living God; and now the curse of Heaven was to be withdrawn, and the temporal blessings of life renewed. The land was to be refreshed with rain. "Get thee up, eat and drink," Elijah said to Ahab; "for there is a sound of abundance of rain." Then the prophet went to the top of the mount to pray.

It was not because of any outward evidence that the showers were about to fall, that Elijah could so confidently bid Ahab prepare for rain. The prophet saw no clouds in the heavens; he ¹⁵⁶ heard no thunder. He simply spoke the word that the Spirit of the Lord had moved him to speak in response to his own strong faith.

Throughout the day he had unflinchingly performed the will of God and had revealed his implicit confidence in the prophecies of God's word; and now, having done all that was in his power to do, he knew that Heaven would freely bestow the blessings foretold. The same God who had sent the drought had promised an abundance of rain as the reward of rightdoing; and now Elijah waited for the promised outpouring. In an attitude of humility, "his face between his knees," he interceded with God in behalf of penitent Israel.

Again and again Elijah sent his servant to a point overlooking the Mediterranean, to learn whether there were any visible token that God had heard his prayer. Each time the servant returned with the word, "There is nothing." The prophet did not become impatient or lose faith, but continued his earnest pleading. Six times the servant returned with the word that there was no sign of rain in the brassy heavens. Undaunted, Elijah sent him forth once more; and this time the servant returned with the word, "Behold, there ariseth a little cloud out of the sea, like a man's hand."

This was enough. Elijah did not wait for the heavens to gather blackness. In that small cloud he beheld by faith an abundance of rain; and he acted in harmony with his faith, sending his servant quickly to Ahab with the message, "Prepare thy chariot, and get thee down, that the rain stop thee not."

It was because Elijah was a man of large faith that God could use him in this grave crisis in the history of Israel. As he prayed, his faith reached ¹⁵⁷ out and grasped the promises of Heaven, and he persevered in prayer until his petitions were answered. He did not wait for the full evidence that God had heard him, but was willing to venture all on the slightest token of divine favor. And yet what he was enabled to do under God, all may do in their sphere of activity in God's service; for of the prophet from the mountains of Gilead it is written: "Elias was a man subject to like passions as we are, and he prayed earnestly that it might not rain: and it rained not on the earth by the space of three years and six months." James 5:17.

Faith such as this is needed in the world today—faith that will lay hold on the promises of God's word and refuse to let go until Heaven hears. Faith such as this connects us closely with Heaven, and brings us strength for coping with the powers of darkness. Through faith God's children have "subdued kingdoms, wrought righteousness, obtained promises, stopped the mouths of lions, quenched the violence of fire, escaped the edge of the sword, out of weakness were made strong, waxed valiant in fight, turned to flight the armies of the aliens." Hebrews 11:33, 34. And through faith we today are to reach the heights of God's purpose for us.

This chapter is based on 1 Kings 18:41-46; 19:1-8.

"If thou canst believe, all things are possible to him that believeth." Mark 9:23.

Faith is an essential element of prevailing prayer. "He that cometh to God must believe that He is, and that He is a rewarder of them that diligently seek Him." "If we ask anything according to His will, He heareth us: and if we know that He hear us, whatsoever we ask, we 158 know that we have the petitions that we desired of Him." Hebrews 11:6; 1 John 5:14, 15. With the persevering faith of Jacob, with the unyielding persistence of Elijah, we may present our petitions to the Father, claiming all that He has promised. The honor of His throne is staked for the fulfillment of His word.

The shades that impart were gathering about Mount Carmel as Ahab prepared for the descent. "It came to pass in the meanwhile, that the heaven was black with clouds and wind, and there was a great rain. And Ahab rode, and went to Jezreel." As he journeyed toward the royal city through the darkness and the blinding rain, Ahab was unable to see his way before him. Elijah, who, as the prophet of God, had that day humiliated Ahab before his subjects and slain his idolatrous priests, still acknowledged him as Israel's king; and now, as an act of homage, and strengthened by the power of God, he ran before the royal chariot, guiding the king to the entrance of the city.

In this gracious act of God's messenger shown to a wicked king is a lesson for all who claim to be servants of God, but who are exalted in their own estimation. There are those who feel above performing duties that to them appear menial. They hesitate to perform even needful service, fearing that they will be found doing the work of a servant. These have much to learn from the example of Elijah. By his word the treasures of heaven had been for three years withheld from the earth; he had been signally honored of God as, in answer to his prayer on Carmel, fire had flashed from heaven and con-
159 sumed the sacrifice; his hand had executed the judgment of God in slaying the idolatrous prophets; his petition for rain had been granted. And yet, after the signal triumphs with which God had been pleased to honor his public ministry, he was willing to perform the service of a menial.

At the gate of Jezreel, Elijah and Ahab separated. The prophet, choosing to remain outside the walls, wrapped himself in his mantle, and lay down upon the bare earth to sleep. The king, passing within, soon reached the shelter of his palace and there related to his wife the wonderful events of the day and the marvelous revelation of divine power that had proved to Israel that Jehovah is the true God and Elijah His chosen messenger. As Ahab told the queen of the slaying of the idolatrous prophets, Jezebel, hardened and impenitent, became infuriated. She refused to recognize in the events on Carmel the overruling providence of God, and, still defiant, she boldly declared that Elijah should die.

That night a messenger aroused the weary prophet and delivered to him the word of Jezebel: "So let the gods do to me, and more also, if I make not thy life as the life of one of them by tomorrow about this time."

It would seem that after showing courage so undaunted, after triumphing so completely over king and priests and people, Elijah could never afterward have given way to despondency nor been awed into timidity. But he who had been blessed with so many evidences of God's loving care was not above the frailties of mankind, and in this dark hour his faith and courage forsook 160 him. Bewildered, he started from his slumber. The rain was pouring from the heavens, and darkness was on every side. Forgetting that three years before, God had directed his course to a place of refuge from the hatred of Jezebel and the search of Ahab, the prophet now fled for his life. Reaching Beersheba, he "left his servant there. But he himself went a day's journey into the wilderness."

Elijah should not have fled from his post of duty. He should have met the threat of Jezebel with an appeal for protection to the One who had commissioned him to vindicate the honor of Jehovah. He should have told the messenger that the God in whom he trusted would protect him against the hatred of the queen. Only a few hours had passed since he had witnessed a wonderful manifestation of divine power, and this should have given him assurance that he would not now be forsaken. Had he remained where he was, had he made God his refuge and strength, standing steadfast for the truth, he would have been shielded from harm. The Lord would have given him another signal victory by sending His judgments on Jezebel; and the impression made on the king and the people would have wrought a great reformation.

Elijah had expected much from the miracle wrought on Carmel. He had hoped that after this display of God's power, Jezebel would no longer have influence over the mind of Ahab, and that there would be a speedy reform throughout Israel. All day on Carmel's height he had toiled without food. Yet when he guided the chariot of Ahab to the gate of Jezreel, his courage was strong, despite the physical strain under which he had labored.

But a reaction such as frequently follows high 161 faith and glorious success was pressing upon Elijah. He feared that the reformation begun on Carmel might not be lasting; and depression seized him. He had been exalted to Pisgah's top; now he was in the valley. While under the inspiration of the Almighty, he had stood the severest trial of faith; but in this time of discouragement, with Jezebel's threat sounding in his ears, 162 and Satan still apparently prevailing through the plotting of this wicked woman, he lost his hold on God. He had been exalted above measure, and the reaction was tremendous. Forgetting God, Elijah fled on and on, until he found himself in a dreary waste, alone. Utterly wearied, he sat down to rest under a juniper tree. And sitting there, he requested for himself that he might die. "It is enough; now, O Lord," he said, "take away my life; for I am not better than my fathers." A fugitive, far from the dwelling places of men, his spirits crushed by bitter disappointment, he desired never again to look upon the face of man. At last, utterly exhausted, he fell asleep.

Into the experience of all there come times of keen disappointment and utter discouragement—days when sorrow is the portion, and it is hard to believe that God is still the kind benefactor of His earthborn children; days when troubles harass the soul, till death seems preferable to life. It is then that many lose their hold on God and are brought into the slavery of doubt, the bondage of unbelief. Could we at such times discern with spiritual insight the meaning of God's providences we should see angels seeking to save us from ourselves, striving to plant our feet upon a foundation more firm than the everlasting hills, and new faith, new life, would spring into being.

The faithful Job, in the day of his affliction and darkness, declared:

"Let the day perish wherein I was born."
"O that my grief were throughly weighed,
And my calamity laid in the balances together!"

163   "O that I might have my request;
And that God would grant me the thing that I long for!
Even that it would please God to destroy me;
That He would let loose His hand, and cut me off!
Then should I yet have comfort."
"I will not refrain my mouth;
I will speak in the anguish of my spirit;
I will complain in the bitterness of my soul."

"My soul chooseth . . . death rather than my life.
I loathe it;
I would not live alway:
Let me alone;
For my days are vanity."
     Job 3:3; 6:2, 8-10; 7:11, 15, 16.

But though weary of life, Job was not allowed to die. To him were pointed out the possibilities of the future, and there was given him the message of hope:

"Thou shalt be steadfast, and shalt not fear:
Because thou shalt forget thy misery,
And remember it as waters that pass away:
And thine age shall be clearer than the noonday;
Thou shalt shine forth, thou shalt be as the morning.
And thou shalt be secure,
Because there is hope. . . .
Thou shalt lie down,
And none shall make thee afraid;
Yea, many shall make suit unto thee.
But the eyes of the wicked shall fail,
And they shall not escape,
And their hope shall be as the giving up of the ghost."
           Job 11:15-20.

From the depths of discouragement and despondency Job rose to the heights of implicit trust in the mercy and the saving power of God. Triumphantly he declared:

"Though He slay me, yet will I trust in Him: . . .   164
He also shall be my salvation."

"I know that my Redeemer liveth,
And that He shall stand at the latter day upon the earth:
And though after my skin worms destroy this body,
Yet in my flesh shall I see God:
Whom I shall see for myself,
And mine eyes shall behold, and not another."
     Job 13:15, 16; 19:25-27.

"The Lord answered Job out of the whirlwind" (Job 38:1), and revealed to His servant the might of His power. When Job caught a glimpse of his Creator, he abhorred himself and repented in dust and ashes. Then the Lord was able to bless him abundantly and to make his last years the best of his life.

Hope and courage are essential to perfect service for God. These are the fruit of faith. Despondency is sinful and unreasonable. God is able and willing "more abundantly" (Hebrews 6:17) to bestow upon His servants the strength they need for test and trial. The plans of the enemies of His work may seem to be well laid and firmly established, but God can overthrow the strongest of these. And this He does in His own time and way, when He sees that the faith of His servants has been sufficiently tested.

For the disheartened there is a sure remedy—faith, prayer, work. Faith and activity will impart assurance and satisfaction that will increase day by day. Are you tempted to give way to feelings of anxious foreboding or utter despondency? In the darkest days, when appearances seem most forbidding, fear not.

165 Have faith in God. He knows your need. He has all power. His infinite love and compassion never weary. Fear not that He will fail of fulfilling His promise. He is eternal truth. Never will He change the covenant He has made with those who love Him. And He will bestow upon His faithful servants the measure of efficiency that their need demands. The apostle Paul has testified: "He said unto me, My grace is sufficient for thee: for My strength is made perfect in weakness. . . . Therefore I take pleasure in infirmities, in reproaches, in necessities, in persecutions, in distresses for Christ's sake: for when I am weak, then am I strong." 2 Corinthians 12:9, 10.

166 Did God forsake Elijah in his hour of trial? Oh, no! He loved His servant no less when Elijah felt himself forsaken of God and man than when, in answer to his prayer, fire flashed from heaven and illuminated the mountaintop. And now, as Elijah slept, a soft touch and a pleasant voice awoke him. He started up in terror, as if to flee, fearing that the enemy had discovered him. But the pitying face bending over him was not the face of an enemy, but of a friend. God had sent an angel from heaven with food for His servant. "Arise and eat," the angel said. "And he looked, and, behold, there was a cake baken on the coals, and a cruse of water at his head."

After Elijah had partaken of the refreshment prepared for him, he slept again. A second time the angel came. Touching the exhausted man, he said with pitying tenderness, "Arise and eat; because the journey is too great for thee." "And he arose, and did eat and drink;" and in the strength of that food he was able to journey "forty days and forty nights unto Horeb the mount of God," where he found refuge in a cave.

167

13

"What Doest Thou Here?"

Elijah's retreat on Mount Horeb, though hidden from man, was known to God; and the weary and discouraged prophet was not left to struggle alone with the powers of darkness that were pressing upon him. At the entrance to the cave wherein Elijah had taken refuge, God met with him, through a mighty angel sent to inquire into his needs and to make plain the divine purpose for Israel.

Not until Elijah had learned to trust wholly in God could he complete his work for those who had been seduced into Baal worship. The signal triumph on the heights of Carmel had opened the way for still greater victories; yet from the wonderful opportunities opening before him, Elijah had been turned away by the threat of

Jezebel. The man of God must be made to understand the weakness of his present position as compared with the vantage ground the Lord would have him occupy.

God met His tried servant with the inquiry, 168 "What doest thou here, Elijah? I sent you to the brook Cherith and afterward to the widow of Sarepta. I commissioned you to return to Israel and to stand before the idolatrous priests on Carmel, and I girded you with strength to guide the chariot of the king to the gate of Jezreel. But who sent you on this hasty flight into the wilderness? What errand have you here?"

In bitterness of soul Elijah mourned out his complaint: "I have been very jealous for the Lord God of hosts: for the children of Israel have forsaken Thy covenant, thrown down Thine altars, and slain Thy prophets with the sword; and I, even I only, am left; and they seek my life, to take it away."

Calling upon the prophet to leave the cave, the angel bade him stand before the Lord on the mount, and listen to His word. "And, behold, the Lord passed by, and a great and strong wind rent the mountains, and brake in pieces the rocks before the Lord; but the Lord was not in the wind: and after the wind an earthquake; but the Lord was not in the earthquake: and after the earthquake a fire; but the Lord was not in the fire: and after the fire a still small voice. And it was so, when Elijah heard it, that he wrapped his face in his mantle, and went out, and stood in the entering in of the cave."

Not in mighty manifestations of divine power, but by "a still small voice," did God choose to reveal Himself to His servant. He desired to teach Elijah that it is not always the work that makes the greatest demonstration that is most successful in accomplishing His purpose. While Elijah waited for the revelation of 169 the Lord, a tempest rolled, the lightnings flashed, and a devouring fire swept by; but God was not in all this. Then there came a still, small voice, and the prophet covered his head before the presence of the Lord. His petulance was silenced, his spirit softened and subdued. He now knew that a quiet trust, a firm reliance on God, would ever find for him a present help in time of need.

It is not always the most learned presentation of God's truth that convicts and converts the soul. Not by eloquence or logic are men's hearts reached, but by the sweet influences of the Holy Spirit, which operate quietly yet surely in transforming and developing character. It is the still, small voice of the Spirit of God that has power to change the heart.

"What doest thou here, Elijah?" the voice inquired; and again the prophet answered, "I have been very jealous for the Lord God of hosts: because the children of Israel have forsaken Thy covenant, thrown down Thine altars,

This chapter is based on 1 Kings 19:9-18.

and slain Thy prophets with the sword; and I, even I only, am left; and they seek my life, to take it away."

The Lord answered Elijah that the wrongdoers in Israel should not go unpunished. Men were to be especially chosen to fulfill the divine purpose in the punishment of the idolatrous kingdom. There was stern work to be done, that all might be given opportunity to take their position on the side of the true God. Elijah himself was to return to Israel, and share with others the burden of bringing about a reformation.

"Go," the Lord commanded Elijah, "return on thy way to the wilderness of Damascus: and when thou comest, anoint Hazael to be king over Syria: and Jehu the son of Nimshi shalt thou anoint to be king over Israel: and Elisha the son of Shaphat of Abel-meholah shalt thou anoint to be prophet in thy room. And it shall come to pass, that him that escapeth the sword of Hazael shall Jehu slay: and him that escapeth from the sword of Jehu shall Elisha slay."

Elijah had thought that he alone in Israel was a worshiper of the true God. But He who reads the hearts of all revealed to the prophet that there were many others who, through the long years of apostasy, had remained true to Him. "I have left Me," God said, "seven thousand in Israel, all the knees which have not bowed unto Baal, and every mouth which hath not kissed him."

From Elijah's experience during those days of discouragement and apparent defeat there are many lessons to be drawn, lessons invaluable to the servants of God in this age, marked as it is by general departure from right. The apostasy prevailing today is similar to that which in the prophet's day overspread Israel. In the exaltation of the human above the divine, in the praise of popular leaders, in the worship of mammon, and in the placing of the teachings of science above the truths of revelation, multitudes today are following after Baal. Doubt and unbelief are exercising their baleful influence over mind and heart, and many are substituting for the oracles of God the theories of men. It is publicly taught that we have reached a time when human reason should be exalted above the teachings of the Word. The law of God, the divine standard of righteousness, is declared to be of no effect. The enemy of all truth is working with deceptive power to cause men and women to place human institutions where God should be, and to forget that which was ordained for the happiness and salvation of mankind.

Yet this apostasy, widespread as it has come to be, is not universal. Not all in the world are lawless and sinful; not all have taken sides with the enemy. God has many thousands who have not bowed the knee to Baal, many who long to understand more fully in regard to Christ and the law, many who are hoping against hope that Jesus will come soon to end the reign of sin and death. And there are many who have been worshiping Baal ignorantly, but with whom the Spirit of God is still striving.

These need the personal help of those who have learned to know God and the power of His word. In such a time as this, every child of God should be actively engaged in helping others. As those who have an understanding of Bible truth try to seek out the men and women who are longing for light, angels of God will attend them. And where angels go, none need fear to move forward. As a result of the faithful efforts of consecrated workers, many will be turned from idolatry to the worship of the living God. Many will cease to pay homage to man-made institutions and will take their stand fearlessly on the side of God and His law.

Much depends on the unceasing activity of those who are true and loyal, and for this reason Satan puts forth every possible effort to thwart the divine purpose to be wrought out through the obedient. He causes some to lose sight of their high and holy mission, and to become satisfied with the pleasures of this life. He leads them to settle down at ease, or, for the sake of greater worldly advantages, to remove from places where they might be a power for good. Others he causes to flee in discouragement from duty, because of opposition or persecution. But all such are regarded by Heaven with tenderest pity. To every child of God whose voice the enemy of souls had succeeded in silencing, the question is addressed, "What doest thou here?" I commissioned you to go into all the world and preach the gospel, to prepare a people for the day of God. Why are you here? Who sent you?

The joy set before Christ, the joy that sustained Him through sacrifice and suffering, was the joy of seeing sinners saved. This should be the joy of every follower of His, the spur to his ambition. Those who realize, even in a limited degree, what redemption means to them and to their fellow men, will comprehend in some measure the vast needs of humanity. Their hearts will be moved to compassion as they see the moral and spiritual destitution of thousands who are under the shadow of a terrible doom, in comparison with which physical suffering fades into nothingness.

Of families, as of individuals, the question is asked, "What doest thou here?" In many churches there are families well instructed in the truths of God's word, who might widen the sphere of their influence by moving to places in need of the ministry they are capable of giving. God calls for Christian families to go into the dark places of the earth and work wisely and perseveringly for those who are enshrouded in spiritual gloom. To answer this call requires self-sacrifice. While many are waiting to have every obstacle removed, souls are dying, without hope and without God. For the sake of worldly advantage, for the sake of acquiring scientific knowledge, men are willing to venture into pestilential regions and to endure hardship and privation. Where are those who are willing to do as much for the sake of telling others of the Saviour?

If, under trying circumstances, men of spiritual power, pressed beyond measure, become discouraged and desponding, if at times they see nothing desirable in life, that they should choose it, this is nothing strange or new. Let all such remember that one of the mightiest of the prophets fled for his life before the rage of an infuriated woman. A fugitive, weary and travelworn, bitter disappointment crushing his spirits, he asked that he might die. But it was when hope was gone and his lifework seemed threatened with defeat, that he learned one of the most precious lessons of his life. In the hour of his greatest weakness he learned the need and the possibility of trusting God under circumstances the most forbidding.

Those who, while spending their life energies in self-sacrificing labor, are tempted to give way to despondency and distrust, may gather courage from the experience of Elijah. God's watchful care, His love, His power, are especially manifest in behalf of His servants whose zeal is misunderstood or unappreciated, whose counsels and reproofs are slighted, and whose efforts toward reform are repaid with hatred and opposition.

174 It is at the time of greatest weakness that Satan assails the soul with the fiercest temptations. It was thus that he hoped to prevail over the Son of God; for by this policy he had gained many victories over man. When the will power weakened and faith failed, then those who had stood long and valiantly for the right yielded to temptation. Moses, wearied with forty years of wandering and unbelief, lost for a moment his hold on Infinite Power. He failed just on the borders of the Promised Land. So with Elijah. He who had maintained his trust in Jehovah during the years of drought and famine, he who had stood undaunted before Ahab, he who throughout that trying day on Carmel had stood before the whole nation of Israel the sole witness to the true God, in a moment of weariness allowed the fear of death to overcome his faith in God.

And so it is today. When we are encompassed with doubt, perplexed by circumstances, or afflicted by poverty or distress, Satan seeks to shake our confidence in Jehovah. It is then that he arrays before us our mistakes and tempts us to distrust God, to question His love. He hopes to discourage the soul and break our hold on God.

Those who, standing in the forefront of the conflict, are impelled by the Holy Spirit to do a special work, will frequently feel a reaction when the pressure is removed. Despondency may shake the most heroic faith and weaken the most steadfast will. But God understands, and He still pities and loves. He reads the motives and the purposes of the heart. To wait patiently, to trust when everything looks dark, is the lesson that the leaders in God's work need to learn. Heaven will not fail them in their day of adversity. Nothing is apparently more helpless, yet 175 really more invincible, than the soul that feels its nothingness and relies wholly on God.

Not alone for men in positions of large responsibility is the lesson of Elijah's experience in learning anew how to trust God in the hour of trial. He who was Elijah's strength is strong to uphold every struggling child of His, no matter how weak. Of everyone He expects loyalty, and to everyone He grants power according to the need. In his own strength man is strengthless; but in the might of God he may be strong to overcome evil and to help others to overcome. Satan can never gain advantage of him who makes God his defense. "Surely, shall one say, in the Lord have I righteousness and strength." Isaiah 45:24.

Fellow Christian, Satan knows your weakness; therefore cling to Jesus. Abiding in God's love, you may stand every test. The righteousness of Christ alone can give you power to stem the tide of evil that is sweeping over the world. Bring faith into your experience. Faith lightens every burden, relieves every weariness. Providences that are now mysterious you may solve by continued trust in God. Walk by faith in the path He marks out. Trials will come, but go forward. This will strengthen your faith and fit you for service. The records of sacred history are written, not merely that we may read and wonder, but that the same faith which wrought in God's servants of old may work in us. In no less marked manner will the Lord work now, wherever there are hearts of faith to be channels of His power.

To us, as to Peter, the word is spoken, "Satan hath desired to have you, that he may sift you as 176 wheat: but I have prayed for thee, that thy faith fail not." Luke 22:31, 32. Christ will never abandon those for whom He has died. We may leave Him and be overwhelmed with temptation, but Christ can never turn from one for whom He has paid the ransom of His own life. Could our spiritual vision be quickened, we should see souls bowed under oppression and burdened with grief, pressed as a cart beneath sheaves, and ready to die in discouragement. We should see angels flying quickly to the aid of these tempted ones, forcing back the hosts of evil that encompass them, and placing their feet on the sure foundation. The battles waging between the two armies are as real as those fought by the armies of this world, and on the issue of the spiritual conflict eternal destinies depend.

In the vision of the prophet Ezekiel there was the appearance of a hand beneath the wings of the cherubim. This is to teach God's servants that it is divine power that gives success. Those whom God employs as His messengers are not to feel that His work is dependent on them. Finite beings are not left to carry this burden of responsibility. He who slumbers not, who is continually at work for the accomplishment of His designs, will carry forward His work. He will thwart the purposes of wicked men and will bring to confusion the counsels of those who plot mischief against His people. He who is the King, the Lord of hosts, sitteth between the cherubim, and amidst the strife and tumult of nations. He guards His children still. When the strongholds of kings shall be overthrown, when the arrows of wrath shall strike through the hearts of His enemies, His people will be safe in His hands.

14

"In the Spirit and Power of Elias"

Through the long centuries that have passed since Elijah's time, the record of his lifework has brought inspiration and courage to those who have been called to stand for the right in the midst of apostasy. And for us, "upon whom the ends of the world are come" (1 Corinthians 10:11), it has special significance. History is being repeated. The world today has its Ahabs and its Jezebels. The present age is one of idolatry, as verily as was that in which Elijah lived. No outward shrine may be visible; there may be no image for the eye to rest upon; yet thousands are following after the gods of this world—after riches, fame, pleasure, and the pleasing fables that permit man to follow the inclinations of the unregenerate heart. Multitudes have a wrong conception of God and His attributes, and are as truly serving a false god as were the worshipers of Baal. Many even of those who claim to be Christians have allied themselves with influences that are unalterably opposed to God and His truth. Thus they are led to turn away from the divine and to exalt the human.

The prevailing spirit of our time is one of infidelity and apostasy—a spirit of avowed illumination because of a knowledge of truth, but in reality of the blindest presumption. Human theories are exalted and placed where God and His law should be. Satan tempts men and women to disobey, with the promise that in disobedience they will find liberty and freedom that will make them as gods. There is seen a spirit of opposition to the plain word of God, of idolatrous exaltation of human wisdom above divine revelation. Men have allowed their minds to become so darkened and confused by conformity to worldly customs and influences that they seem to have lost all power to discriminate between light and darkness, truth and error. So far have they departed from the right way that they hold the opinions of a few philosophers, so-called, to be more trustworthy than the truths of the Bible. The entreaties and promises of God's word, its threatenings against disobedience and idolatry—these seem powerless to melt their hearts. A faith such as actuated Paul, Peter, and John they regard as old-fashioned, mystical, and unworthy of the intelligence of modern thinkers.

In the beginning, God gave His law to mankind as a means of attaining happiness and eternal life. Satan's only hope of thwarting the purpose of God is to lead men and women to disobey this law, and his constant effort has been to misrepresent its teachings and belittle its importance. His master stroke has been an attempt to change the law itself, so as to lead men to violate its precepts while professing to obey it.

One writer has likened the attempt to change the law of God to an ancient mischievous practice of turning in a wrong direction a signpost erected at an important junction where two roads met. The perplexity and hardship which this practice often caused was great.

A signpost was erected by God for those journeying through this world. One arm of this signpost pointed out willing obedience to the Creator as the road to felicity and life, while the other arm indicated disobedience as the path to misery and death. The way to happiness was as clearly defined as was the way to the city of refuge under the Jewish dispensation. But in an evil hour for our race, the great enemy of all good turned the signpost around, and multitudes have mistaken the way.

Through Moses the Lord instructed the Israelites: "Verily My Sabbaths ye shall keep: for it is a sign between Me and you throughout your generations; that ye may know that I am the Lord that doth sanctify you. Ye shall keep the Sabbath therefore; for it is holy unto you: everyone that defileth it shall surely be put to death: for whosoever doeth any work. . . in the Sabbath day, he shall surely be put to death. Wherefore the children of Israel shall keep the Sabbath, to observe the Sabbath throughout their generations, for a perpetual covenant. It is a sign between Me and the children of Israel forever: for in six days the Lord made heaven and earth, and on the seventh day He rested, and was refreshed." Exodus 31:13-17.

In these words the Lord clearly defined obedience as the way to the City of God; but the man of sin has changed the signpost, making it [180] point in the wrong direction. He has set up a false sabbath and has caused men and women to think that by resting on it they were obeying the command of the Creator.

God has declared that the seventh day is the Sabbath of the Lord. When "the heavens and the earth were finished," He exalted this day as a memorial of His creative work. Resting on the seventh day "from all His work which He had made," "God blessed the seventh day, and sanctified it." Genesis 2:1-3.

At the time of the Exodus from Egypt, the Sabbath institution was brought prominently before the people of God. While they were still in bondage, their taskmasters had attempted to [181] force them to labor on the Sabbath by increasing the amount of work required each week. Again and again the conditions of labor had been made harder and more exacting. But the Israelites were delivered from bondage and brought to a place where they might observe unmolested all the precepts of Jehovah. At Sinai the law was spoken; and a copy of it, on two tables of stone, "written with the finger of God" was delivered to Moses. Exodus 31:18. And through nearly forty years of wandering the Israelites were constantly reminded of God's appointed rest day, by the withholding of the manna every seventh day and the miraculous preservation of the double portion that fell on the preparation day.

[182] Before entering the Promised Land, the Israelites were admonished by Moses to "keep the Sabbath day to sanctify it." Deuteronomy 5:12. The Lord designed that by a faithful observance of the Sabbath command, Israel should continually be reminded of their accountability to Him as their Creator and their Redeemer. While they should keep the Sabbath in the proper spirit, idolatry could not exist; but should the claims of this precept of the Decalogue be set aside as no longer binding, the Creator would be forgotten and men would worship other gods. "I gave them My Sabbaths," God declared, "to be a sign between Me and them, that they might know that I am the Lord that sanctify them." Yet "they despised My judgments, and walked not in My statutes, but polluted My Sabbaths: for their heart went after their idols." And in His appeal to them to return to Him, He called their attention anew to the importance of keeping the Sabbath holy. "I am the Lord your God," He said; "walk in My statutes, and keep My judgments, and do them; and hallow My Sabbaths; and they shall be a sign between Me and you, that ye may know that I am the Lord your God." Ezekiel 20:12, 16, 19, 20.

In calling the attention of Judah to the sins that finally brought upon them the Babylonian Captivity, the Lord declared: "Thou hast. . . pro-faned My Sabbaths." "Therefore have I poured out Mine indignation upon them; I have consumed them with the fire of My wrath: their own way have I recompensed upon their heads." Ezekiel 22:8, 31.

At the restoration of Jerusalem, in the days of Nehemiah, Sabbathbreaking was met with the stern inquiry, "Did not your fathers thus, and did not our God bring all this evil upon us, and [183] upon this city? yet ye bring more wrath upon Israel by profaning the Sabbath." Nehemiah 13:18.

Christ, during His earthly ministry, emphasized the binding claims of the Sabbath; in all His teaching He showed reverence for the institution He Himself had given. In His days the Sabbath had become so perverted that its observance reflected the character of selfish and arbitrary men rather than the character of God. Christ set aside the false teaching by which those who claimed to know God had misrepresented Him. Although followed with merciless hostility by the rabbis, He did not even appear to conform to their requirements, but went straight forward keeping the Sabbath according to the law of God.

In unmistakable language He testified to His regard for the law of Jehovah. "Think not that I am come to destroy the law, or the prophets," He said; "I am not come to destroy, but to fulfill. For verily I say unto you, Till heaven and earth pass, one jot or one tittle shall in no wise pass from the law, till all be fulfilled. Whosoever therefore shall break one of these least commandments, and shall teach men so, he shall be called the least in the kingdom of heaven: but whosoever shall do and teach them, the same shall be called great in the kingdom of heaven." Matthew 5:17-19.

During the Christian dispensation, the great enemy of man's happiness has made the Sabbath of the fourth commandment an object of special attack. Satan says, "I will work at cross purposes with God. I will empower my followers to set aside God's memorial, the seventh-day Sabbath. Thus I will show the world that the day sanctified and blessed by God has been [184] changed. That day shall not live in the minds of the people. I will obliterate the memory of it. I will place in its stead a day that does not bear the credentials of God, a day that cannot be a sign between God and His people. I will lead those who accept this day to place upon it the sanctity that God placed upon the seventh day.

"Through my vicegerent, I will exalt myself. The first day will be extolled, and the Protestant world will receive this spurious sabbath as genuine. Through the nonobservance of the Sabbath that God instituted, I will bring His law into contempt. The words, 'A sign between Me and you throughout your generations,' I will make to serve on the side of my sabbath.

"Thus the world will become mine. I will be the ruler of the earth, the prince of the world. I will so control the minds under my power that God's Sabbath shall be a special object of contempt. A sign? I will make the observance of the seventh day a sign of disloyalty to the authorities of earth. Human laws will be made so stringent that men and women will not dare to observe the seventh-day Sabbath. For fear of wanting food and clothing, they will join with the world in transgressing God's law. The earth will be wholly under my dominion."

Through the setting up of a false sabbath, the enemy thought to change times and laws. But has he really succeeded in changing God's law? The words of the thirty-first chapter of Exodus are the answer. He who is the same yesterday, today, and forever, has declared of the seventh-day Sabbath: "It is a sign between Me and you 185 throughout your generations." "It is a sign . . . forever." Exodus 31:13, 17. The changed signpost is pointing the wrong way, but God has not changed. He is still the mighty God of Israel. "Behold, the nations are as a drop of a bucket, and are counted as the small dust of the balance: behold, He taketh up the isles as a very little thing. And Lebanon is not sufficient to burn, nor the beasts thereof sufficient for a burnt offering. All nations before Him are as nothing; and they are counted to Him less than nothing, and vanity." Isaiah 40:15-17. And He is just as jealous for His law now as He was in the days of Ahab and Elijah.

But how is that law disregarded! Behold the world today in open rebellion against God. This is in truth a froward generation, filled with ingratitude, formalism, insincerity, pride, and apostasy. Men neglect the Bible and hate truth. Jesus sees His law rejected, His love despised, His ambassadors treated with indifference. He has spoken by His mercies, but these have been unacknowledged; He has spoken by warnings, but these have been unheeded. The temple courts of the human soul have been turned into places of unholy traffic. Selfishness, envy, pride, malice—all are cherished.

Many do not hesitate to sneer at the word of God. Those who believe that word just as it reads are held up to ridicule. There is a growing contempt for law and order, directly traceable to a violation of the plain commands of Jehovah. Violence and crime are the result of turning aside from the path of obedience. Behold the wretchedness and misery of multitudes who worship at the shrine of idols and who seek in vain for happiness and peace.

186 Behold the well-nigh universal disregard of the Sabbath commandment. Behold also the daring impiety of those who, while enacting laws to safeguard the supposed sanctity of the first day of the week, at the same time are making laws legalizing the liquor traffic. Wise above that which is written, they attempt to coerce the consciences of men, while lending their sanction to an evil that brutalizes and destroys the beings created in the image of God. It is Satan himself who inspires such legislation. He well knows that the curse of God will rest on those who exalt human enactments above the divine, and he does all in his power to lead men into the broad road that ends in destruction.

So long have men worshiped human opinions and human institutions that almost the whole world is following after idols. And he who has endeavored to change God's law is using every deceptive artifice to induce men and women to array themselves against God and against the sign by which the righteous are known. But the Lord will not always suffer His law to be broken and despised with impunity. There is a time coming when "the lofty looks of man shall be humbled, and the haughtiness of men shall be bowed down, and the Lord alone shall be exalted in that day." Isaiah 2:11. Skepticism may treat the claims of God's law with jest, scoffing, and denial. The spirit of worldliness may contaminate the many and control the few, the cause of God may hold its ground only by great exertion and continual sacrifice, yet in the end the truth will triumph gloriously.

In the closing work of God in the earth, the standard of His law will be again exalted. False religion may prevail, iniquity may abound, the 187 love of many may wax cold, the cross of Calvary may be lost sight of, and darkness, like the pall of death, may spread over the world; the whole force of the popular current may be turned against the truth; plot after plot may be formed to overthrow the people of God; but in the hour of greatest peril the God of Elijah will raise up human instrumentalities to bear a message that will not be silenced. In the populous cities of the land, and in the places where men have gone to the greatest lengths in speaking against the Most High, the voice of stern rebuke will be heard. Boldly will men of God's appointment denounce the union of the church with the world. Earnestly will they call upon men and women to turn from the observance of a man-made institution to the observance of the true Sabbath. "Fear God, and give glory to Him," they will proclaim to every nation; "for the hour of His judgment is come: and worship Him that made heaven, and earth, and the sea, and the fountains of waters. . . . If any man worship the beast and his image, and receive his mark in his forehead, or in his hand, the same shall drink of the wine of the wrath of God, which is poured out without mixture into the cup of His indignation." Revelation 14:7-10.

God will not break His covenant, nor alter the thing that has gone out of His lips. His word will stand fast forever as unalterable as His throne. At the judgment this covenant will be brought forth, plainly written with the finger of God, and the world will be arraigned before the bar of Infinite Justice to receive sentence.

188 Today, as in the days of Elijah, the line of demarcation between God's commandment-keeping people and the worshipers of false gods is clearly drawn. "How long halt ye between two opinions?" Elijah cried; "if the Lord be God, follow Him: but if Baal, then follow him." 1 Kings 18:21. And the message for today is: "Babylon the great is fallen, is fallen. . . . Come out of her, My people, that ye be not partakers of her sins, and that ye receive not of her plagues. For her sins have reached unto heaven, and God hath remembered her iniquities." Revelation 18:2, 4, 5.

The time is not far distant when the test will come to every soul. The observance of the false sabbath will be urged upon us. The contest will be between the commandments of God and the commandments of men. Those who have yielded step by step to worldly demands and conformed to worldly customs will then yield to the powers that be, rather than subject themselves to derision, insult, threatened imprisonment, and death. At that time the gold will be separated from the dross. True godliness will be clearly distinguished from the appearance and tinsel of it. Many a star that we have admired for its brilliance will then go out in darkness. Those who have assumed the ornaments of the sanctuary, but are not clothed with Christ's righteousness, will then appear in the shame of their own nakedness.

Among earth's inhabitants, scattered in every land, there are those who have not bowed the knee to Baal. Like the stars of heaven, which appear only at night, these faithful ones will shine forth when darkness covers the earth and gross darkness the people. In heathen Africa, in the Catholic lands of Europe and of South 189 America, in China, in India, in the islands of the sea, and in all the dark corners of the earth, God has in reserve a firmament of chosen ones that will yet shine forth amidst the darkness, revealing clearly to an apostate world the transforming power of obedience to His law. Even now they are appearing in every nation, among every tongue and people; and in the hour of deepest apostasy, when Satan's supreme effort is made to cause "all, both small and great, rich and poor, free and bond," to receive, under penalty of death, the sign of allegiance to a false rest day, these faithful ones, "blameless and harmless, the sons of God, without rebuke," will "shine as lights in the world." Revelation 13:16; Philippians 2:15. The darker the night, the more brilliantly will they shine.

What strange work Elijah would have done in numbering Israel at the time when God's judgments were falling upon the backsliding people! He could count only one on the Lord's side. But when he said, "I, even I only, am left; and they seek my life," the word of the Lord surprised him, "Yet I have left Me seven thousand in Israel, all the knees which have not bowed unto Baal." 1 Kings 19:14, 18.

Then let no man attempt to number Israel today, but let everyone have a heart of flesh, a heart of tender sympathy, a heart that, like the heart of Christ, reaches out for the salvation of a lost world.

15

190

Jehoshaphat

Until called to the throne at the age of thirty-five, Jehoshaphat had before him the example of good King Asa, who in nearly every crisis had done "that which was right in the eyes of the Lord." 1 Kings 15:11. During a prosperous reign of twenty-five years, Jehoshaphat sought to walk "in all the ways of Asa his father; he turned not aside."

In his efforts to rule wisely, Jehoshaphat endeavored to persuade his subjects to take a firm stand against idolatrous practices. Many of the people in his realm "offered and burnt incense yet in the high places." 1 Kings 22:43. The king did not at once destroy these shrines; but from the beginning he tried to safeguard Judah from the sins characterizing the northern kingdom under the rule of Ahab, of whom he was a contemporary for many years. Jehoshaphat himself was loyal to God. He "sought not unto Baalim; but sought to the Lord 191 God of his father, and walked in His commandments, and not after the doings of Israel." Because of his integrity, the Lord was with him, and "stablished the kingdom in his hand." 2 Chronicles 17:3-5.

"All Judah brought to Jehoshaphat presents; and he had riches and honor in abundance. And his heart was lifted up in the ways of the Lord." As time passed and reformations were wrought, the king "took away the high places and groves out of Judah." Verses 5, 6. "And the remnant of the Sodomites, which remained in the days of his father Asa, he took out of the land." 1 Kings 22:46. Thus gradually the inhabitants of Judah were freed from many of the perils that had been threatening to retard seriously their spiritual development.

Throughout the kingdom the people were in need of instruction in the law of God. In an understanding of this law lay their safety; by conforming their lives to its requirements they would become loyal both to God and to man. Knowing this, Jehoshaphat took steps to ensure to his people thorough instruction in the Holy Scriptures. The princes in charge of the different portions of his realm were directed to arrange for the faithful ministry of teaching priests. By royal appointment these instructors, working under the direct supervision of the princes, "went about throughout all the cities of Judah, and taught the people." 2 Chronicles 17:7-9. And as many endeavored to understand God's requirements and to put away sin, a revival was effected.

192

To this wise provision for the spiritual needs of his subjects, Jehoshaphat owed much of his prosperity as a ruler. In obedience to God's law there is great gain. In conformity to the divine requirements there is a transforming power that brings peace and good will among men. If the teachings of God's word were made the controlling influence in the life of every man and woman, if mind and heart were brought under its restraining power, the evils that now exist in national and in social life would find no place. From every home would go forth an influence that would make men and women strong in spiritual insight and in moral power, and thus nations and individuals would be placed on vantage ground.

For many years Jehoshaphat lived in peace, unmolested by surrounding nations. "The fear of the Lord fell upon all the kingdoms of the lands that were round about Judah." Verse 10. From Philistia he received tribute money and presents; from Arabia, large flocks of sheep and goats. "Jehoshaphat waxed great exceedingly; and he built in Judah castles, and cities of store. . . . Men of war, mighty men of valor, . . . waited on the king, beside those whom the king put in the fenced cities throughout all Judah." Verses 12-19. Blessed abundantly with "riches and honor," he was enabled to wield a mighty influence for truth and righteousness. 2 Chronicles 18:1.

Some years after coming to the throne, Jehoshaphat, now in the height of his prosperity, consented to the marriage of his son, Jehoram, to Athaliah, daughter of Ahab and Jezebel. By 195 this union there was formed between the kingdoms of Judah and Israel an alliance which was not in the order of God and which in a time of crisis brought disaster to the king and to many of his subjects.

On one occasion Jehoshaphat visited the king of Israel at Samaria. Special honor was shown the royal guest from Jerusalem, and before the close of his visit he was persuaded to unite with the king of Israel in war against the Syrians. Ahab hoped that by joining his forces with those of Judah he might regain Ramoth, one of the old cities of refuge, which, he contended, rightfully belonged to the Israelites.

Although Jehoshaphat in a moment of weakness had rashly promised to join the king of Israel in his war against the Syrians, yet his better judgment led him to seek to learn the will of God concerning the undertaking. "Inquire, I

pray thee, at the word of the Lord today," he suggested to Ahab. In response, Ahab called together four hundred of the false prophets of Samaria, and asked of them, "Shall we go to Ramothgilead to battle, or shall I forbear?" And they answered, "Go up; for God will deliver it into the king's hand." Verses 4, 5.

Unsatisfied, Jehoshaphat sought to learn for a certainty the will of God. "Is there not here a prophet of the Lord," he asked, "that we might inquire of him?" Verse 6. "There is yet one man, Micaiah the son of Imlah, by whom we may inquire of the Lord," Ahab answered; "but I hate him; for he doth not prophesy good concerning me, but evil." 1 Kings 22:8. Jehoshaphat was firm in his request that the man of God be called; and upon appearing before them and being adjured by Ahab to tell "nothing but that which is true in the name of the Lord," 196 Micaiah said: "I saw all Israel scattered upon the hills, as sheep that have not a shepherd: and the Lord said, These have no master: let them return every man to his house in peace." Verses 16, 17.

The words of the prophet should have been enough to show the kings that their project was not favored by Heaven, but neither ruler felt inclined to heed the warning. Ahab had marked out his course, and he was determined to follow it. Jehoshaphat had given his word of honor, "We will be with thee in the war;" and after making such a promise, he was reluctant to withdraw his forces. 2 Chronicles 18:3. "So the king of Israel and Jehoshaphat the king of Judah went up to Ramothgilead." 1 Kings 22:29.

During the battle that followed, Ahab was shot by an arrow, and at eventide he died. "About the going down of the sun," "there went a proclamation throughout the host," "Every man to his city, and every man to his own country." Verse 36. Thus was fulfilled the word of the prophet.

From this disastrous battle Jehoshaphat returned to Jerusalem. As he approached the city, the prophet Jehu met him with the reproof: "Shouldest thou help the ungodly, and love them that hate the Lord? therefore is wrath upon thee from before the Lord. Nevertheless there are good things found in thee, in that thou hast taken away the groves out of the land, and hast prepared thine heart to seek God." 2 Chronicles 19:2, 3.

The later years of Jehoshaphat's reign were largely spent in strengthening the national and spiritual defenses of Judah. He "went out again 197 through the people from Beersheba to Mount Ephraim, and brought them back unto the Lord God of their fathers." Verse 4.

One of the important steps taken by the king was the establishment and maintenance of efficient courts of justice. He "set judges in the land throughout all the fenced cities of Judah, city by city;" and in the charge given them he urged: "Take heed what ye do: for ye judge not for man, but for the Lord, who is with you in the judgment. Wherefore now let the fear of the Lord be upon you; take heed and do it: for there is no iniquity with the Lord our God, nor respect of persons, nor taking of gifts." Verses 5-7.

The judicial system was perfected by the founding of a court of appeal at Jerusalem, where Jehoshaphat "set of the Levites, and of the priests, and of the chief of the fathers of Israel, for the judgment of the Lord, and for controversies." Verse 8.

The king exhorted these judges to be faithful. "Thus shall ye do in the fear of the Lord, faithfully, and with a perfect heart," he charged them. "And what cause soever shall come to you of your brethren that dwell in their cities, between blood and blood, between law and commandment, statutes and judgments, ye shall even warn them that they trespass not against the Lord, and so wrath come upon you, and upon your brethren: this do, and ye shall not trespass.

"And, behold, Amariah the chief priest is over you in all matters of the Lord; and Zebadiah the son of Ishmael, the ruler of the house of Judah, for all the king's matters: also the Levites shall be officers before you.

"Deal courageously, and the Lord shall be with the good." Verses 9-11.

In his careful safeguarding of the rights and liberties of his subjects, Jehoshaphat emphasized the consideration that every member of the human family receives from the God of justice, who rules over all. "God standeth in the congregation of the mighty; He judgeth among the gods." And those who are appointed to act as judges under Him, are to "defend the poor and fatherless;" they are to "do justice to the afflicted and needy," and "rid them out of the hand of the wicked." Psalm 82:1, 3, 4.

Toward the close of Jehoshaphat's reign the kingdom of Judah was invaded by an army before whose approach the inhabitants of the land had reason to tremble. "The children of Moab, and the children of Ammon, and with them other beside the Ammonites, came against Jehoshaphat to battle." Tidings of this invasion reached the king through a messenger, who appeared with the startling word, "There cometh a great multitude against thee from beyond the sea on this side Syria; and, behold, they be in Hazazon-tamar, which is Engedi." 2 Chronicles 20:1, 2.

Jehoshaphat was a man of courage and valor. For years he had been strengthening his armies and his fortified cities. He was well prepared to meet almost any foe; yet in this crisis he put not his trust in the arm of flesh. Not by disciplined armies and fenced cities, but by a living faith in the God of Israel, could he hope to gain the victory over these heathen who boasted of their power to humble Judah in the eyes of the nations.

"Jehoshaphat feared, and set himself to seek the Lord, and proclaimed a fast throughout all Judah. And Judah gathered themselves together, to ask help of the Lord: even out of all the cities of Judah they came to seek the Lord."

Standing in the temple court before his people, Jehoshaphat poured out his soul in prayer, pleading God's promises, with confession of Israel's helplessness. "O Lord God of our fathers," he petitioned, "art not Thou God in heaven? and rulest not Thou over all the kingdoms of the heathen? and in Thine hand is there not power and might, so that none is able to withstand Thee? Art not Thou our God, who didst drive out the inhabitants of this land before Thy people Israel, and gavest it to the seed of Abraham Thy friend forever? And they dwelt therein, and have built Thee a sanctuary therein for Thy name, saying, If, when evil cometh upon us, as the sword, judgment, or pestilence, or famine, we stand before this house, and in Thy presence, (for Thy name is in this house,) and cry unto Thee in our affliction, then Thou wilt hear and help.

"And now, behold, the children of Ammon and Moab and Mount Seir, whom Thou wouldest not let Israel invade, when they came out of the land of Egypt, but they turned from them, and destroyed them not; behold, I say, how they reward us, to come to cast us out of Thy possession, which Thou hast given us to inherit. O our God, wilt Thou not judge them? for we have no might against this great company that cometh against us; neither know we what to do: but our eyes are upon Thee." Verses 3-12.

With confidence Jehoshaphat could say to the Lord, "Our eyes are upon Thee." For years he had taught the people to trust in the One who in past ages had so often interposed to save His chosen ones from utter destruction; and now, when the kingdom was in peril, Jehoshaphat did not stand alone; "all Judah stood before the Lord, with their little ones, their wives, and their children." Verse 13. Unitedly they fasted and prayed; unitedly they besought the Lord to put their enemies to confusion, that the name of Jehovah might be glorified.

"Keep not Thou silence, O God:
Hold not Thy peace, and be not still, O God.
For, lo, Thine enemies make a tumult:
And they that hate Thee have lifted up the head.
They have taken crafty counsel against Thy people,
And consulted against Thy hidden ones.
They have said, Come, and let us cut them off from

being a nation;
That the name of Israel may be no more in
remembrance.
For they have consulted together with one
consent:
They are confederate against Thee:
The tabernacles of Edom, and the Ishmaelites;
Of Moab, and the Hagarenes;
Gebal, and Ammon, and Amalek. . . .
Do unto them as unto the Midianites;
As to Sisera, as to Jabin, at the brook of
Kison: . . .
Let them be confounded and troubled forever;
Yea, let them be put to shame, and perish;
That men may know that Thou, whose name
alone is Jehovah,
Art the Most High over all the earth."
Psalm 83.

201   As the people joined with their king in humbling themselves before God, and asking Him
for help, the Spirit of the Lord came upon
Jahaziel, "a Levite of the sons of Asaph," and
he said:

"Hearken ye, all Judah, and ye inhabitants of
Jerusalem, and thou King Jehoshaphat, Thus
saith the Lord unto you, Be not afraid nor dismayed by reason of this great multitude; for the
battle is not yours, but God's. Tomorrow go ye
down against them: behold, they come up by the
cliff of Ziz; and ye shall find them at the end of
the brook, before the wilderness of Jeruel. Ye
shall not need to fight in this battle: set yourselves, stand ye still, and see the salvation of the
Lord with you, O Judah and Jerusalem: fear not,
nor be dismayed; tomorrow go out against
them: for the Lord will be with you."

"Jehoshaphat bowed his head with his face to
the ground: and all Judah and the inhabitants of
Jerusalem fell before the Lord, worshiping the
Lord. And the Levites, of the children of the
Kohathites, and of the children of the Korhites,
stood up to praise the Lord God of Israel with a
loud voice on high."

Early in the morning they rose and went into
the wilderness of Tekoa. As they advanced to the
battle, Jehoshaphat said, "Hear me, O Judah, and
ye inhabitants of Jerusalem; Believe in the Lord
your God, so shall ye be established; believe His
prophets, so shall ye prosper." "And when he had
consulted with the people, he appointed singers
unto the Lord, and that should praise the beauty
of holiness." 2 Chronicles 20:14-21. These
singers went before the army, lifting their voices
in praise to God for the promise of victory.

202   It was a singular way of going to battle
against the enemy's army—praising the Lord
with singing, and exalting the God of Israel.
This was their battle song. They possessed the
beauty of holiness. If more praising of God
were engaged in now, hope and courage and
faith would steadily increase. And would not

this strengthen the hands of the valiant soldiers
who today are standing in defense of truth?

"The Lord set ambushments against the children of Ammon, Moab, and Mount Seir, which
were come against Judah; and they were smitten. For the children of Ammon and Moab stood
up against the inhabitants of Mount Seir, utterly
to slay and destroy them: and when they had
made an end of the inhabitants of Seir, everyone
helped to destroy another.

"And when Judah came toward the watchtower in the wilderness, they looked unto the
multitude, and, behold, they were dead bodies
fallen to the earth, and none escaped." Verses
22-24.

God was the strength of Judah in this crisis, and
He is the strength of His people today. We are not
to trust in princes, or to set men in the place of
God. We are to remember that human beings are
fallible and erring, and that He who has all
power is our strong tower of defense. In every
emergency we are to feel that the battle is His.
His resources are limitless, and apparent impossibilities will make the victory all the greater.

"Save us, O God of our salvation,
And gather us together,
And deliver us from the heathen,
That we may give thanks to Thy holy name,
And glory in Thy praise."
1 Chronicles 16:35.

Laden with spoil, the armies of Judah   203
returned "with joy; for the Lord had made them
to rejoice over their enemies. And they came to
Jerusalem with psalteries and harps and trumpets unto the house of the Lord." 2 Chronicles
20:27, 28. Great was their cause for rejoicing. In
obedience to the command, "Stand ye still, and
see the salvation of the Lord: . . . fear not, nor be
dismayed," they had put their trust wholly in
God, and He had proved to be their fortress and
their deliverer. Verse 17. Now they could sing
with understanding the inspired hymns of
David:

"God is our refuge and strength,
A very present help in trouble. . . .
He breaketh the bow, and cutteth the spear in
sunder;
He burneth the chariot in the fire.
Be still, and know that I am God:
I will be exalted among the heathen, I will be
exalted in the earth.
The Lord of hosts is with us;
The God of Jacob is our refuge."
Psalm 46.

"According to Thy name, O God,
So is Thy praise unto the ends of the earth:
Thy right hand is full of righteousness.
Let Mount Zion rejoice,

Let the daughters of Judah be glad,
Because of Thy judgments. . . .

"This God is our God for ever and ever:
He will be our guide even unto death."

Psalm 48:10-14.

Through the faith of Judah's ruler and of his armies "the fear of God was on all the kingdoms of those countries, when they had heard that the Lord fought against the enemies of Israel. So the realm of Jehoshaphat was quiet: for his God gave him rest." 2 Chronicles 20:29, 30.

204

16

The Fall of the House of Ahab

The evil influence that Jezebel had exercised from the first over Ahab continued during the later years of his life and bore fruit in deeds of shame and violence such as have seldom been equaled in sacred history. "There was none like unto Ahab, which did sell himself to work wickedness in the sight of the Lord, whom Jezebel his wife stirred up."

Naturally of a covetous disposition, Ahab, strengthened and sustained in wrongdoing by Jezebel, had followed the dictates of his evil heart until he was fully controlled by the spirit of selfishness. He could brook no refusal of his wishes; the things he desired he felt should by right be his.

This dominant trait in Ahab, which influenced so disastrously the fortunes of the kingdom under his successors, is revealed in an incident which took place while Elijah was still a prophet in Israel. Hard by the palace of the king 205 was a vineyard belonging to Naboth, a Jezreelite. Ahab set his heart on possessing this vineyard, and he proposed to buy it or else to give in exchange for it another piece of land. "Give me thy vineyard," he said to Naboth, "that I may have it for a garden of herbs, because it is near unto my house: and I will give thee for it a better vineyard than it; or, if it seem good to thee, I will give thee the worth of it in money."

Naboth valued his vineyard highly because it had belonged to his fathers, and he refused to part with it. "The Lord forbid it me," he said to Ahab, "that I should give the inheritance of my fathers unto thee." According to the Levitical code no land could be transferred permanently by sale or exchange; every one of the children of Israel must "keep himself to the inheritance of the tribe of his fathers." Numbers 36:7.

Naboth's refusal made the selfish monarch ill. "Ahab came into his house heavy and displeased because of the word which Naboth the Jezreelite had spoken to him. . . . And he laid him down upon his bed, and turned away his

face, and would eat no bread."

Jezebel soon learned the particulars, and, indignant that anyone should refuse the request of the king, she assured Ahab that he need no longer be sad. "Dost thou now govern the kingdom of Israel?" she said. "Arise, and eat bread, and let thine heart be merry: I will give thee the vineyard of Naboth the Jezreelite."

Ahab cared not by what means his wife might accomplish the desired object, and Jezebel immediately proceeded to carry out her wicked purpose. She wrote letters in the name of the king, sealed them with his signet, and sent them 206 to the elders and nobles of the city where Naboth dwelt, saying: "Proclaim a fast, and set Naboth on high among the people: and set two men, sons of Belial, before him, to bear witness against him, saying, Thou didst blaspheme God and the king. And then carry him out, and stone him, that he may die."

The command was obeyed. "The men of his city, even the elders and the nobles, . . . did as Jezebel had . . . written in the letters which she had sent unto them." Then Jezebel went to the king and bade him arise and take the vineyard. And Ahab, heedless of the consequences, blindly followed her counsel and went down to take possession of the coveted property.

The king was not allowed to enjoy unrebuked that which he had gained by fraud and bloodshed. "The word of the Lord came to Elijah the Tishbite, saying, Arise, go down to meet Ahab king of Israel, which is in Samaria: behold, he is in the vineyard of Naboth, whither he is gone down to possess it. And thou shalt speak unto him, saying, Thus saith the Lord, Hast thou killed, and also taken possession?" And the Lord further instructed Elijah to pronounce upon Ahab a terrible judgment.

The prophet hastened to carry out the divine command. The guilty ruler, meeting the stern messenger of Jehovah face to face in the vineyard, gave voice to his startled fear in the words, "Hast thou found me, O mine enemy?"

Without hesitation the messenger of the Lord replied, "I have found thee: because thou hast sold thyself to work evil in the sight of the Lord. Behold, I will bring evil upon thee, and will take away thy posterity." No mercy was to be 207 shown. The house of Ahab was to be utterly destroyed, "like the house of Jeroboam the son of Nebat, and like the house of Baasha the son of Ahijah," the Lord declared through His servant, "for the provocation wherewith thou hast provoked Me to anger, and made Israel to sin."

And of Jezebel the Lord declared, "The dogs shall eat Jezebel by the wall of Jezreel. Him that dieth of Ahab in the city the dogs shall eat; and him that dieth in the field shall the fowls of the air eat."

When the king heard this fearful message, "he rent his clothes, and put sackcloth upon his

This chapter is based on 1 Kings 21; 2 Kings 1.

flesh, and fasted, and lay in sackcloth, and went softly.

"And the word of the Lord came to Elijah the Tishbite, saying, Seest thou how Ahab humbleth himself before Me? because he humbleth himself before Me, I will not bring the evil in his days: but in his son's days will I bring the evil upon his house."

It was less than three years later that King Ahab met his death at the hands of the Syrians. Ahaziah, his successor, "did evil in the sight of the Lord, and walked in the way of his father, and in the way of his mother, and in the way of Jeroboam." "He served Baal, and worshipped him, and provoked to anger the Lord God of Israel," as his father Ahab had done. 1 Kings 22:52, 53. But judgments followed close upon the sins of the rebellious king. A disastrous war with Moab, and then an accident by which his own life was threatened, attested to God's wrath against him.

Having fallen "through a lattice in his upper chamber," Ahaziah, seriously injured, and fearful of the possible outcome, sent some of his 208 servants to make inquiry of Baalzebub, the god of Ekron, whether he should recover or not. The god of Ekron was supposed to give information, through the medium of its priests, concerning future events. Large numbers of people went to inquire of it; but the predictions there uttered, and the information given, proceeded from the prince of darkness.

Ahaziah's servants were met by a man of God, who directed them to return to the king with the message: "Is it because there is no God in Israel, that ye go to inquire of Baal-zebub, the god of Ekron? Now therefore thus saith Jehovah, Thou shalt not come down from the bed whither thou art gone up, but shalt surely die." Having delivered his message, the prophet departed.

The astonished servants hastened back to the king, and repeated to him the words of the man of God. The king inquired, "What manner of man was he?" They answered, "He was an hairy man, and girt with a girdle of leather about his loins." "It is Elijah the Tishbite," Ahaziah exclaimed. He knew that if the stranger whom his messengers had met was indeed Elijah, the words of doom pronounced would surely come to pass. Anxious to avert, if possible, the threatened judgment, he determined to send for the prophet.

Twice Ahaziah sent a company of soldiers to intimidate the prophet, and twice the wrath of God fell upon them in judgment. The third company of soldiers humbled themselves before God; and their captain, as he approached the Lord's messenger, "fell on his knees before Elijah, and besought him, and said unto him, O 209 man of God, I pray thee, let my life, and the life of these fifty thy servants, be precious in thy sight."

"The angel of Jehovah said unto Elijah, Go down with him: be not afraid of him. And he arose, and went down with him unto the king. And he said unto him, Thus saith Jehovah, Forasmuch as thou hast sent messengers to inquire of Baal-zebub, the god of Ekron, is it because there is no God in Israel to inquire of His word? therefore thou shalt not come down from the bed whither thou art gone up, but shalt surely die."

During his father's reign, Ahaziah had witnessed the wondrous works of the Most High. He had seen the terrible evidences that God had given apostate Israel of the way in which He regards those who set aside the binding claims of His law. Ahaziah had acted as if these awful realities were but idle tales. Instead of humbling his heart before the Lord, he had followed after 210 Baal, and at last he had ventured upon this, his most daring act of impiety. Rebellious, and unwilling to repent, Ahaziah died, "according to the word of the Lord which Elijah had spoken."

The history of King Ahaziah's sin and its punishment has in it a warning which none can disregard with impunity. Men today may not pay homage to heathen gods, yet thousands are worshiping at Satan's shrine as verily as did the king of Israel. The spirit of idolatry is rife in the world today, although, under the influence of science and education, it has assumed forms more refined and attractive than in the days when Ahaziah sought to the god of Ekron. Every day adds its sorrowful evidence that faith in the sure word of prophecy is decreasing, and that in its stead superstition and satanic witchery are captivating the minds of many.

Today the mysteries of heathen worship are replaced by the secret associations and seances, the obscurities and wonders, of spiritistic mediums. The disclosures of these mediums are eagerly received by thousands who refuse to accept light from God's word or through His Spirit. Believers in spiritism may speak with scorn of the magicians of old, but the great deceiver laughs in triumph as they yield to his arts under a different form.

There are many who shrink with horror from the thought of consulting spirit mediums, but who are attracted by more pleasing forms of spiritism. Others are led astray by the teachings of Christian Science, and by the mysticism of Theosophy and other Oriental religions.

The apostles of nearly all forms of spiritism 211 claim to have power to heal. They attribute this power to electricity, magnetism, the so-called "sympathetic remedies," or to latent forces within the mind of man. And there are not a few, even in this Christian age, who go to these healers, instead of trusting in the power of the living God and the skill of well-qualified physicians. The mother, watching by the sickbed of her child, exclaims, "I can do no more. Is there no physician who has power to restore my child?" She is told of the wonderful cures performed by some clairvoyant or magnetic healer, and she trusts her dear one to his charge, placing it as verily in the hand of Satan as if he were standing by her side. In many instances the future life of the child is controlled by a satanic power which it seems impossible to break.

God had cause for displeasure at Ahaziah's impiety. What had He not done to win the hearts of the people of Israel and to inspire them with confidence in Himself? For ages He had been giving His people manifestations of unexampled kindness and love. From the beginning He had shown that His "delights were with the sons of men." Proverbs 8:31. He had been a very present help to all who sought Him in sincerity. Yet now the king of Israel, turning from God to ask help of the worst enemy of his people, proclaimed to the heathen that he had more confidence in their idols than in the God of heaven. In the same manner do men and women dishonor Him when they turn from the Source of strength and wisdom to ask help or counsel from the powers of darkness. If God's wrath [212] was kindled by Ahaziah's act, how does He regard those who, having still greater light, choose to follow a similar course?

Those who give themselves up to the sorcery of Satan, may boast of great benefit received; but does this prove their course to be wise or safe? What if life should be prolonged? What if temporal gain should be secured? Will it pay in the end to have disregarded the will of God? All such apparent gain will prove at last an irrecoverable loss. We cannot with impunity break down a single barrier which God has erected to guard His people from Satan's power.

As Ahaziah had no son, he was succeeded by Jehoram, his brother, who reigned over the ten tribes for twelve years. Throughout these years his mother, Jezebel, was still living, and she continued to exercise her evil influence over the affairs of the nation. Idolatrous customs were still practiced by many of the people. Jehoram himself "wrought evil in the sight of the Lord; but not like his father, and like his mother: for he put away the image of Baal that his father had made. Nevertheless he cleaved unto the sins of Jeroboam the son of Nebat, which made Israel to sin; he departed not therefrom." 2 Kings 3:2, 3.

It was during Jehoram's reign over Israel that Jehoshaphat died, and Jehoshaphat's son, also named Jehoram, ascended the throne of the kingdom of Judah. By his marriage with the daughter of Ahab and Jezebel, Jehoram of Judah was closely connected with the king of Israel; and in his reign he followed after Baal, "like as did the house of Ahab." "Moreover he made high places in the mountains of Judah,

and caused the inhabitants of Jerusalem to com- [213] mit fornication, and compelled Judah thereto." 2 Chronicles 21:6, 11.

The king of Judah was not permitted to continue his terrible apostasy unreproved. The prophet Elijah had not yet been translated, and he could not remain silent while the kingdom of Judah was pursuing the same course that had brought the northern kingdom to the verge of ruin. The prophet sent to Jehoram of Judah a written communication, in which the wicked king read the awful words:

"Thus saith the Lord God of David thy father, Because thou hast not walked in the ways of Jehoshaphat thy father, nor in the ways of Asa king of Judah, but hast walked in the way of the kings of Israel, and hast made Judah and the inhabitants of Jerusalem to go a whoring, like to the whoredoms of the house of Ahab, and also hast slain thy brethren of thy father's house, which were better than thyself: behold, with a great plague will the Lord smite thy people, and thy children, and thy wives, and all thy goods: and thou shalt have great sickness."

In fulfillment of this prophecy "the Lord stirred up against Jehoram the spirit of the Philistines, and of the Arabians, that were near the Ethiopians: and they came up into Judah, and brake into it, and carried away all the substance that was found in the king's house, and his sons also, and his wives; so that there was never a son left him, save Jehoahaz [Ahaziah, Azariah], the youngest of his sons.

"And after all this the Lord smote him in his bowels with an incurable disease. And it came to pass, that in process of time, after the end of two years, ... he died of sore diseases." "And [214] Ahaziah [Jehoahaz] his son reigned in his stead." Verses 12-19; 2 Kings 8:24.

Jehoram the son of Ahab was still reigning in the kingdom of Israel when his nephew, Ahaziah, came to the throne of Judah. Ahaziah ruled only one year, and during this time, influenced by his mother, Athaliah, "his counselor to do wickedly," "he walked in the way of the house of Ahab, and did evil in the sight of the Lord." 2 Chronicles 22:3, 4; 2 Kings 8:27. Jezebel, his grandmother, was still living, and he allied himself boldly with Jehoram of Israel, his uncle.

Ahaziah of Judah soon met a tragic end. The surviving members of the house of Ahab were indeed "his counselors after the death of his father to his destruction." 2 Chronicles 22:3, 4. While Ahaziah was visiting his uncle at Jezreel, the prophet Elisha was divinely directed to send one of the sons of the prophets to Ramothgilead to anoint Jehu king of Israel. The combined forces of Judah and Israel were at that time engaged in a military campaign against the Syrians of Ramothgilead. Jehoram had been wounded in battle, and had returned to Jezreel, leaving Jehu in charge of the royal armies.

In anointing Jehu, the messenger of Elisha declared, "I have anointed thee king over the people of the Lord, even over Israel." And then he solemnly charged Jehu with a special commission from heaven. "Thou shalt smite the house of Ahab thy master," the Lord declared through His messenger, "that I may avenge the blood of My servants the prophets, and at the hand
215 blood of all the servants of the Lord, at the hand of Jezebel. For the whole house of Ahab shall perish." 2 Kings 9:6-8.

After he had been proclaimed king by the army, Jehu hastened to Jezreel, where he began his work of execution on those who had deliberately chosen to continue in sin and to lead others into sin. Jehoram of Israel, Ahaziah of Judah, and Jezebel the queen mother, with "all that remained of the house of Ahab in Jezreel, and all his great men, and his kinsfolks, and his priests," were slain. "All the prophets of Baal, all his servants, and all his priests" dwelling at the center of Baal worship near Samaria, were put to the sword. The idolatrous images were broken down and burned, and the temple of Baal was laid in ruins. "Thus Jehu destroyed Baal out of Israel." 2 Kings 10:11, 19, 28.

Tidings of this general execution reached Athaliah, Jezebel's daughter, who still occupied a commanding position in the kingdom of Judah. When she saw that her son, the king of Judah, was dead, "she arose and destroyed all the seed royal of the house of Judah." In this massacre all the descendants of David who were eligible to the throne were destroyed, save one, a babe named Joash, whom the wife of Jehoiada the high priest hid within the precincts of the temple. For six years the child remained hidden, while "Athaliah reigned over the land." 2 Chronicles 22:10, 12.

At the end of this time, "the Levites and all Judah" (2 Chronicles 23:8) united with Jehoiada the high priest in crowning and anointing the child Joash and acclaiming him their king. "And they clapped their hands, and said, God save the king." 2 Kings 11:12.
216 "Now when Athaliah heard the noise of the people running and praising the king, she came to the people into the house of the Lord." 2 Chronicles 23:12. "And when she looked, behold, the king stood by a pillar, as the manner was, and the princes and the trumpeters by the king, and all the people of the land rejoiced, and blew with trumpets."

"Athaliah rent her clothes, and cried, Treason, Treason." 2 Kings 11:14. But Jehoiada commanded the officers to lay hold of Athaliah and all her followers and lead them out of the temple to a place of execution, where they were to be slain.

Thus perished the last member of the house of Ahab. The terrible evil that had been wrought through his alliance with Jezebel, continued till the last of his descendants was destroyed. Even in the land of Judah, where the worship of the true God had never been formally set aside, Athaliah had succeeded in seducing many. Immediately after the execution of the impenitent queen "all the people of the land went into the house of Baal, and brake it down; his altars and his images brake they in pieces thoroughly, and slew Mattan the priest of Baal before the altars." Verse 18.

A reformation followed. Those who took part in acclaiming Joash king, had solemnly covenanted "that they should be the Lord's people." And now that the evil influence of the daughter of Jezebel had been removed from the kingdom of Judah, and the priests of Baal had been slain and their temple destroyed, "all the people of the land rejoiced: and the city was quiet." 2 Chronicles 23:16, 21.

17   217

The Call of Elisha

God had bidden Elijah anoint another to be prophet in his stead. "Elisha the son of Shaphat . . . shalt thou anoint to be prophet in thy room" (1 Kings 19:16), He had said; and in obedience to the command, Elijah went to find Elisha. As he journeyed northward, how changed was the scene from what it had been only a short while before! Then the ground was parched, the farming districts unworked, for neither dew nor rain had fallen for three and a half years. Now on every hand vegetation was springing up as if to redeem the time of drought and famine.

Elisha's father was a wealthy farmer, a man whose household were among the number that in a time of almost universal apostasy had not bowed the knee to Baal. Theirs was a home where God was honored and where allegiance to the faith of ancient Israel was the rule of daily life. In such surroundings the early years of Elisha were passed. In the quietude of country life, under the teaching of God and nature and 218 the discipline of useful work, he received the training in habits of simplicity and of obedience to his parents and to God that helped to fit him for the high position he was afterward to occupy.

The prophetic call came to Elisha while, with his father's servants, he was plowing in the field. He had taken up the work that lay nearest. He possessed both the capabilities of a leader among men and the meekness of one who is ready to serve. Of a quiet and gentle spirit, he was nevertheless energetic and steadfast. Integrity, fidelity, and the love and fear of God were his, and in the humble round of daily toil he gained strength of purpose and nobleness of character, constantly increasing in grace and knowledge. While co-operating with his father in the home-life duties, he was learning to co-operate with God.

By faithfulness in little things, Elisha was preparing for weightier trusts. Day by day, through practical experience, he gained a fitness for a broader, higher work. He learned to serve; and in learning this, he learned also how to instruct and lead. The lesson is for all. None can know what may be God's purpose in His discipline; but all may be certain that faithfulness in little things is the evidence of fitness for greater responsibilities. Every act of life is a revelation of character, and he only who in small duties proves himself "a workman that needeth not to be ashamed" can be honored by God with higher service. 2 Timothy 2:15.

He who feels that it is of no consequence how he performs the smaller tasks proves himself unfit for a more honored position. He may think himself fully competent to take up the larger duties; but God looks deeper than the surface. After test and trial, there is written against him the sentence, "Thou art weighed in the balances, and art found wanting." His unfaithfulness reacts upon himself. He fails of gaining the grace, the power, the force of character, which is received through unreserved surrender.

Because they are not connected with some directly religious work, many feel that their lives are useless, that they are doing nothing for the advancement of God's kingdom. If they could do some great thing how gladly they would undertake it! But because they can serve only in little things, they think themselves justified in doing nothing. In this they err. A man may be in the active service of God while engaged in the ordinary, everyday duties—while felling trees, clearing the ground, or following the plow. The mother who trains her children for Christ is as truly working for God as is the minister in the pulpit.

Many long for special talent with which to do a wonderful work, while the duties lying close at hand, the performance of which would make the life fragrant, are lost sight of. Let such ones take up the duties lying directly in their pathway. Success depends not so much on talent as on energy and willingness. It is not the possession of splendid talents that enables us to render acceptable service, but the conscientious performance of daily duties, the contented spirit, the unaffected, sincere interest in the welfare of others. In the humblest lot true excellence may be found. The commonest tasks, wrought with loving faithfulness, are beautiful in God's sight.

As Elijah, divinely directed in seeking a successor, passed the field in which Elisha was plowing, he cast upon the young man's shoulders the mantle of consecration. During the famine the family of Shaphat had become familiar with the work and mission of Elijah, and now the Spirit of God impressed Elisha's heart as to the meaning of the prophet's act. To him it was the signal that God had called him to be the successor of Elijah.

"And he left the oxen, and ran after Elijah, and said, Let me, I pray thee, kiss my father and my mother, and then I will follow thee." "Go back again," was Elijah's answer, "for what have I done to thee?" This was not a repulse, but a test of faith. Elisha must count the cost—decide for himself to accept or reject the call. If his desires clung to his home and its advantages, he was at liberty to remain there. But Elisha understood the meaning of the call. He knew it was from God, and he did not hesitate to obey. Not for any worldly advantage would he forgo the opportunity of becoming God's messenger or sacrifice the privilege of association with His servant. He "took a yoke of oxen, and slew them, and boiled their flesh with the instruments of the oxen, and gave unto the people, and they did eat. Then he arose, and went after Elijah, and ministered unto him." 1 Kings 19:20, 21. Without hesitation he left a home where he was beloved, to attend the prophet in his uncertain life.

Had Elisha asked Elijah what was expected of him,—what would be his work,—he would have been answered: God knows; He will make it known to you. If you wait upon the Lord, He will answer your every question. You may come with me if you have evidence that God has called you. Know for yourself that God stands back of me, and that it is His voice you hear. If you can count everything but dross that you may win the favor of God, come.

Similar to the call that came to Elisha was the answer given by Christ to the young ruler who asked Him the question, "What good thing shall I do, that I may have eternal life?" "If thou wilt be perfect," Christ replied, "go and sell that thou hast, and give to the poor, and thou shalt have treasure in heaven: and come and follow Me." Matthew 19:16, 21.

Elisha accepted the call to service, casting no backward glance at the pleasures and comforts he was leaving. The young ruler, when he heard the Saviour's words, "went away sorrowful: for he had great possessions." Verse 22. He was not willing to make the sacrifice. His love for his possessions was greater than his love for God. By his refusal to renounce all for Christ, he proved himself unworthy of a place in the Master's service.

The call to place all on the altar of service comes to each one. We are not all asked to serve as Elisha served, nor are we all bidden to sell everything we have; but God asks us to give His service the first place in our lives, to allow no day to pass without doing something to advance His work in the earth. He does not expect from all the same kind of service. One may be called to ministry in a foreign land; another may be asked to give of his means for the support of gospel work. God accepts the offering of each. It is the consecration of the life and all its interests, that is necessary. Those who make this consecration will hear and obey the call of Heaven.

222 To everyone who becomes a partaker of His grace, the Lord appoints a work for others. Individually we are to stand in our lot, saying, "Here am I; send me." Whether a man be a minister of the Word or a physician, whether he be merchant or farmer, professional man or mechanic, the responsibility rests upon him. It is his work to reveal to others the gospel of their salvation. Every enterprise in which he engages should be a means to this end.

It was no great work that was at first required of Elisha; commonplace duties still constituted his discipline. He is spoken of as pouring water on the hands of Elijah, his master. He was willing to do anything that the Lord directed, and at every step he learned lessons of humility and service. As the prophet's personal attendant, he continued to prove faithful in little things, while with daily strengthening purpose he devoted himself to the mission appointed him by God.

Elisha's life after uniting with Elijah was not without temptations. Trials he had in abundance; but in every emergency he relied on God. He was tempted to think of the home that he had left, but to this temptation he gave no heed. Having put his hand to the plow, he was resolved not to turn back, and through test and trial he proved true to his trust.

Ministry comprehends far more than preaching the word. It means training young men as Elijah trained Elisha, taking them from their ordinary duties, and giving them responsibilities to bear in God's work—small responsibilities at first, and larger ones as they gain strength and experience. There are in the ministry men of 223 faith and prayer, men who can say, "That which was from the beginning, which we have heard, which we have seen with our eyes, which we have looked upon, and our hands have handled, of the Word of life; . . . that which we have seen and heard declare we unto you." 1 John 1:1-3. Young, inexperienced workers should be trained by actual labor in connection with these experienced servants of God. Thus they will learn how to bear burdens.

Those who undertake this training of young workers are doing noble service. The Lord Himself co-operates with their efforts. And the young men to whom the word of consecration has been spoken, whose privilege it is to be brought into close association with earnest, godly workers, should make the most of their opportunity. God has honored them by choosing them for His service and by placing them where they can gain greater fitness for it, and they should be humble, faithful, obedient, and willing to sacrifice. If they submit to God's discipline, carrying out His directions and choosing His servants as their counselors, they will develop into righteous, high-principled, steadfast men, whom God can entrust with responsibilities.

As the gospel is proclaimed in its purity, men will be called from the plow and from the common commercial business vocations that largely occupy the mind and will be educated in connection with men of experience. As they learn to labor effectively, they will proclaim the truth with power. Through most wonderful workings of divine providence, mountains of difficulty will be removed and cast into the sea. The message that means so much to the dwellers upon the earth will be heard and understood. Men will know what is truth. Onward and still 224 onward the work will advance until the whole earth shall have been warned, and then shall the end come.

For several years after the call of Elisha, Elijah and Elisha labored together, the younger man daily gaining greater preparedness for his work. Elijah had been God's instrument for the overthrow of gigantic evils. The idolatry which, supported by Ahab and the heathen Jezebel, had seduced the nation, had been given a decided check. Baal's prophets had been slain. The whole people of Israel had been deeply stirred, and many were returning to the worship of God. As Elijah's successor, Elisha, by careful, patient instruction, must endeavor to guide Israel in safe paths. His association with Elijah, the greatest prophet since the days of Moses, prepared him for the work that he was soon to take up alone.

During these years of united ministry, Elijah from time to time was called upon to meet flagrant evils with stern rebuke. When wicked Ahab seized Naboth's vineyard, it was the voice of Elijah that prophesied his doom and the doom of all his house. And when Ahaziah, after the death of his father Ahab, turned from the living God to Baal-zebub, the god of Ekron, it was Elijah's voice that was heard once more in earnest protest.

The schools of the prophets, established by Samuel, had fallen into decay during the years of Israel's apostasy. Elijah re-established these schools, making provision for young men to gain an education that would lead them to magnify the law and make it honorable. Three of these schools, one at Gilgal, one at Bethel, and one at Jericho, are mentioned in the record. Just 225 before Elijah was taken to heaven, he and Elisha visited these centers of training. The lessons that the prophet of God had given them on former visits, he now repeated. Especially did he instruct them concerning their high privilege of loyally maintaining their allegiance to the God of heaven. He also impressed upon their minds the importance of letting simplicity mark every feature of their education. Only in this way could they receive the mold of heaven and go forth to work in the ways of the Lord.

The heart of Elijah was cheered as he saw what was being accomplished by means of these schools. The work of reformation was not complete, but he could see throughout the kingdom a verification of the word of the Lord, "Yet I have left Me seven thousand in Israel, all the knees which have not bowed unto Baal." 1 Kings 19:18.

As Elisha accompanied the prophet on his round of service from school to school, his faith and resolution were once more tested. At Gilgal, and again at Bethel and Jericho, he was invited by the prophet to turn back. "Tarry here, I pray thee," Elijah said; "for the Lord hath sent me to Bethel." But in his early labor of guiding the plow, Elisha had learned not to fail or to become discouraged, and now that he had set his hand to the plow in another line of duty he would not be diverted from his purpose. He would not be parted from his master, so long as opportunity remained for gaining a further fitting up for service. Unknown to Elijah, the revelation that he was to be translated had been made known to his disciples in the schools of the prophets, and in particular to Elisha. And now the tried servant of the man of God kept 226 close beside him. As often as the invitation to turn back was given, his answer was, "As the Lord liveth, and as thy soul liveth, I will not leave thee."

"And they two went on. . . . And they two stood by Jordan. And Elijah took his mantle, and wrapped it together, and smote the waters, and they were divided hither and thither, so that they two went over on dry ground. And it came to pass, when they were gone over, that Elijah said unto Elisha, Ask what I shall do for thee, before I be taken away from thee."

Elisha asked not for worldly honor, or for a high place among the great men of earth. That 227 which he craved was a large measure of the Spirit that God had bestowed so freely upon the one about to be honored with translation. He knew that nothing but the Spirit which had rested upon Elijah could fit him to fill the place in Israel to which God had called him, and so he asked, "I pray thee, let a double portion of thy Spirit be upon me."

In response to this request, Elijah said, "Thou hast asked a hard thing: nevertheless, if thou see me when I am taken from thee, it shall be so unto thee; but if not, it shall not be so. And it came to pass, as they still went on, and talked, that, behold, there appeared a chariot of fire, and horses of fire, and parted them both asunder; and Elijah went up by a whirlwind into heaven."

See 2 Kings 2:1-11.

Elijah was a type of the saints who will be living on the earth at the time of the second advent of Christ and who will be "changed, in a moment, in the twinkling of an eye, at the last trump," without tasting of death. 1 Corinthians 15:51, 52. It was as a representative of those who shall be thus translated that Elijah, near the close of Christ's earthly ministry, was permitted to stand with Moses by the side of the Saviour on the mount of transfiguration. In these glorified ones, the disciples saw in miniature a representation of the kingdom of the redeemed. They beheld Jesus clothed with the light of heaven; they heard the "voice out of the cloud" (Luke 9:35), acknowledging Him as the Son of God; they saw Moses, representing those who will be raised from the dead at the time of the second advent; and there also stood Elijah, representing those who at the close of earth's history will be changed from mortal to immortal and be translated to heaven without seeing death.

In the desert, in loneliness and discouragement, Elijah had said that he had had enough of 238 life and had prayed that he might die. But the Lord in His mercy had not taken him at his word. There was yet a great work for Elijah to do; and when his work was done, he was not to perish in discouragement and solitude. Not for him the descent into the tomb, but the ascent with God's angels to the presence of His glory.

"And Elisha saw it, and he cried, My father, my father, the chariot of Israel, and the horsemen thereof. And he saw him no more: and he took hold of his own clothes, and rent them in two pieces. He took up also the mantle of Elijah that fell from him, and went back, and stood by the bank of Jordan; and he took the mantle of Elijah that fell from him, and smote the waters, and said, Where is the Lord God of Elijah? and when he also had smitten the waters, they parted hither and thither: and Elisha went over. And when the sons of the prophets which were to view at Jericho saw him, they said, The Spirit of Elijah doth rest on Elisha. And they came to meet him, and bowed themselves to the ground before him." 2 Kings 2:12-15.

When the Lord in His providence sees fit to remove from His work those to whom He has given wisdom, He helps and strengthens their successors, if they will look to Him for aid and will walk in His ways. They may be even wiser than their predecessors; for they may profit by their experience and learn wisdom from their mistakes.

Henceforth Elisha stood in Elijah's place. He who had been faithful in that which was least was to prove himself faithful also in much.

229

18

The Healing of the Waters

In patriarchal times the Jordan Valley was "well watered everywhere, . . . even as the garden of the Lord." It was in this fair valley that Lot chose to make his home when he "pitched his tent toward Sodom." Genesis 13:10, 12. At the time that the cities of the plain were destroyed, the region round about became a desolate waste, and it has since formed a part of the wilderness of Judea.

A portion of the beautiful valley remained, with its life-giving springs and streams, to gladden the heart of man. In this valley, rich with fields of grain and forests of date palms and other fruit-bearing trees, the hosts of Israel had encamped after crossing the Jordan and had first partaken of the fruits of the Promised Land. Before them had stood the walls of Jericho, a heathen stronghold, the center of the worship of Ashtoreth, vilest and most degrading of all Canaanitish forms of idolatry. Soon its walls
230 were thrown down and its inhabitants slain, and at the time of its fall the solemn declaration was made, in the presence of all Israel: "Cursed be the man before the Lord, that riseth up and buildeth this city Jericho: he shall lay the foundation thereof in his first-born, and in his youngest son shall he set up the gates of it." Joshua 6:26.

Five centuries passed. The spot lay desolate, accursed of God. Even the springs that had made residence in this portion of the valley so desirable suffered the blighting effects of the curse. But in the days of Ahab's apostasy, when through Jezebel's influence the worship of Ashtoreth was revived, Jericho, the ancient seat of this worship, was rebuilt, though at a fearful cost to the builder. Hiel the Bethelite "laid the foundation thereof in Abiram his first-born, and set up the gates thereof in his youngest son Segub, according to the word of the Lord." 1 Kings 16:34.

Not far from Jericho, in the midst of fruitful groves, was one of the schools of the prophets, and thither, after the ascension of Elijah, Elisha went. During his sojourn among them the men of the city came to the prophet and said, "Behold, I pray thee, the situation of this city is pleasant, as my lord seeth: but the water is nought, and the ground barren." The spring that in former years had been pure and life-giving, and had contributed largely to the water supply of the city and the surrounding district, was now unfit for use.

In response to the plea of the men of Jericho, Elisha said, "Bring me a new cruse, and put salt

therein." Having received this, "he went forth unto the spring of the waters, and cast the salt in 231 there, and said, Thus saith the Lord, I have healed these waters; there shall not be from thence any more death or barren land." 2 Kings 2:19-21.

The healing of the waters of Jericho was accomplished, not by any wisdom of man, but by the miraculous interposition of God. Those who had rebuilt the city were undeserving of the favor of Heaven; yet He who "maketh His sun to rise on the evil and on the good, and sendeth rain on the just and on the unjust," saw fit in this instance to reveal, through this token of compassion, His willingness to heal Israel of their spiritual maladies. Matthew 5:45.

The restoration was permanent; "the waters were healed unto this day, according to the saying of Elisha which he spake." 2 Kings 2:22. From age to age the waters have flowed on, making that portion of the valley an oasis of beauty.

Many are the spiritual lessons to be gathered from the story of the healing of the waters. The new cruse, the salt, the spring—all are highly symbolic.

In casting salt into the bitter spring, Elisha taught the same spiritual lesson imparted centuries later by the Saviour to His disciples when He declared, "Ye are the salt of the earth." Matthew 5:13. The salt mingling with the polluted spring purified its waters and brought life and blessing where before had been blighting and death. When God compares His children to salt, He would teach them that His purpose in making them the subjects of His grace is that they may become agents in saving others. The object of God in choosing a people before all the world was not only that He might adopt 232 them as His sons and daughters, but that through them the world might receive the grace that bringeth salvation. When the Lord chose Abraham, it was not simply to be the special friend of God, but to be a medium of the peculiar privileges the Lord desired to bestow upon the nations.

The world needs evidences of sincere Christianity. The poison of sin is at work at the heart of society. Cities and towns are steeped in sin and moral corruption. The world is full of sickness, suffering, and iniquity. Nigh and afar off are souls in poverty and distress, weighed down with a sense of guilt and perishing for want of a saving influence. The gospel of truth is kept ever before them, yet they perish because the example of those who should be a savor of life to them is a savor of death. Their souls drink in bitterness because the springs are poisoned, when they should be like a well of water springing up unto everlasting life.

Salt must be mingled with the substance to which it is added; it must penetrate, infuse it, that it may be preserved. So it is through personal contact and association that men are reached by the saving power of the gospel. They are not saved as masses, but as individuals. Personal influence is a power. It is to work with the influence of Christ, to lift where Christ lifts, to impart correct principles, and to stay the progress of the world's corruption. It is to diffuse that grace which Christ alone can impart. It is to uplift, to sweeten the lives and characters of others by the power of a pure example united with earnest faith and love.

233 Of the hitherto polluted spring at Jericho, the Lord declared, "I have healed these waters; there shall not be from thence any more death or barren land." The polluted stream represents the soul that is separate from God. Sin not only shuts away from God, but destroys in the human soul both the desire and the capacity for knowing Him. Through sin, the whole human organism is deranged, the mind is perverted, the imagination corrupted; the faculties of the soul are degraded. There is an absence of pure religion, of heart holiness. The converting power of God has not wrought in transforming the character. The soul is weak, and for want of moral force to overcome, is polluted and debased.

To the heart that has become purified, all is changed. Transformation of character is the testimony to the world of an indwelling Christ. The Spirit of God produces a new life in the soul, bringing the thoughts and desires into obedience to the will of Christ; and the inward man is renewed in the image of God. Weak and erring men and women show to the world that the redeeming power of grace can cause the faulty character to develop into symmetry and abundant fruitfulness.

The heart that receives the word of God is not as a pool that evaporates, not like a broken cistern that loses its treasure. It is like the mountain stream, fed by unfailing springs, whose cool, sparkling waters leap from rock to rock, refreshing the weary, the thirsty, the heavy-laden. It is like a river constantly flowing and, as it advances, becoming deeper and wider, until its 234 life-giving waters are spread over all the earth. The stream that goes singing on its way leaves behind its gift of verdure and fruitfulness. The grass on its banks is a fresher green, the trees have a richer verdure, the flowers are more abundant. When the earth lies bare and brown under the summer's scorching heat, a line of verdure marks the river's course.

So it is with the true child of God. The religion of Christ reveals itself as a vitalizing, pervading principle, a living, working, spiritual energy. When the heart is opened to the heavenly influence of truth and love, these principles will flow forth again like streams in the desert, causing fruitfulness to appear where now are barrenness and dearth.

As those who have been cleansed and sanctified through a knowledge of Bible truth engage heartily in the work of soulsaving, they will become indeed a savor of life unto life. And as daily they drink of the inexhaustible fountain of grace and knowledge, they will find that their own hearts are filled to overflowing with the Spirit of their Master, and that through their unselfish ministry many are benefited physically, mentally, and spiritually. The weary are refreshed, the sick restored to health, and the sin-burdened relieved. In far-off countries thanksgiving is heard from the lips of those whose hearts are turned from the service of sin unto righteousness.

"Give, and it shall be given unto you;" for the word of God is "a fountain of gardens, a well of living waters, and streams from Lebanon." Luke 6:38; Song of Solomon 4:15.

19

235

A Prophet of Peace

The work of Elisha as a prophet was in some respects very different from that of Elijah. To Elijah had been committed messages of condemnation and judgment; his was the voice of fearless reproof, calling king and people to turn from their evil ways. Elisha's was a more peaceful mission; his it was to build up and strengthen the work that Elijah had begun; to teach the people the way of the Lord. Inspiration pictures him as coming into personal touch with the people, surrounded by the sons of the prophets, bringing by his miracles and his ministry healing and rejoicing.

Elisha was a man of mild and kindly spirit; but that he could also be stern is shown by his course when, on the way to Bethel, he was mocked by ungodly youth who had come out of the city. These youth had heard of Elijah's ascension, and they made this solemn event the subject of their jeers, saying to Elisha, "Go up, thou bald head; go up, thou bald head." At the 236 sound of their mocking words the prophet turned back, and under the inspiration of the Almighty he pronounced a curse upon them. The awful judgment that followed was of God. "There came forth two she-bears out of the wood, and tare forty and two" of them. 2 Kings 2:23, 24.

Had Elisha allowed the mockery to pass unnoticed, he would have continued to be ridiculed and reviled by the rabble, and his mission to instruct and save in a time of grave national peril might have been defeated. This one instance of terrible severity was sufficient to command respect throughout his life. For fifty years he went in and out of the gate of Bethel,

This chapter is based on 2 Kings 4.

and to and fro in the land, from city to city, passing through crowds of idle, rude, dissolute youth; but none mocked him or made light of his qualifications as the prophet of the Most High.

Even kindness should have its limits. Authority must be maintained by a firm severity, or it will be received by many with mockery and contempt. The so-called tenderness, the coaxing and indulgence, used toward youth by parents and guardians, is one of the worst evils which can come upon them. In every family, firmness, decision, positive requirements, are essential.

237 Reverence, in which the youth who mocked Elisha were so lacking, is a grace that should be carefully cherished. Every child should be taught to show true reverence for God. Never should His name be spoken lightly or thoughtlessly. Angels, as they speak it, veil their faces. With what reverence should we, who are fallen and sinful, take it upon our lips!

Reverence should be shown for God's representatives—for ministers, teachers, and parents, who are called to speak and act in His stead. In the respect shown them, God is honored.

Courtesy, also, is one of the graces of the Spirit and should be cultivated by all. It has power to soften natures which without it would grow hard and rough. Those who profess to be followers of Christ, and are at the same time rough, unkind, and uncourteous, have not learned of Jesus. Their sincerity may not be doubted, their uprightness may not be questioned; but sincerity and uprightness will not atone for a lack of kindness and courtesy.

The kindly spirit that enabled Elisha to exert a powerful influence over the lives of many in Israel, is revealed in the story of his friendly relations with a family dwelling at Shunem. In his journeyings to and fro throughout the kingdom "it fell on a day, that Elisha passed to Shunem, where was a great woman; and she constrained him to eat bread. And so it was, that as oft as he passed by, he turned in thither to eat bread." The mistress of the house perceived that Elisha was "an holy man of God," and she said to her husband: "Let us make a little chamber, I pray thee, on the wall; and let us set for him there a bed, and a table, and a stool, and a candlestick: and it shall be, when he cometh to us, that he shall turn in thither." To this retreat Elisha often came, thankful for its quiet peace. Nor was God unmindful of the woman's kindness. Her home had been childless; and now the Lord rewarded her hospitality by the gift of a son.

238 Years passed. The child was old enough to be out in the field with the reapers. One day he was stricken down by the heat, "and he said unto his father, My head, my head." The father bade a lad carry the child to his mother; "and when he had taken him, and brought him to his mother, he sat on her knees till noon, and then died. And she went up, and laid him on the bed of the man of God, and shut the door upon him, and went out."

In her distress, the Shunammite determined to go to Elisha for help. The prophet was then at Mount Carmel, and the woman, accompanied by her servant, set forth immediately. "And it came to pass, when the man of God saw her afar off, that he said to Gehazi his servant, Behold, yonder is that Shunammite: run now, I pray thee, to meet her, and say unto her, Is it well with thee? is it well with thy husband? is it well with the child?" The servant did as he was bidden, but not till she had reached Elisha did the stricken mother reveal the cause of her sorrow. Upon hearing of her loss, Elisha bade Gehazi: "Gird up thy loins, and take my staff in thine hand, and go thy way: if thou meet any man, salute him not; and if any salute thee, answer him not again: and lay my staff upon the face of the child."

But the mother would not be satisfied till Elisha himself came with her. "As the Lord liveth, and as thy soul liveth, I will not leave thee," she declared. "And he arose, and followed her. And Gehazi passed on before them, and laid the staff upon the face of the child; but there was neither voice, nor hearing. Wherefore he went again to meet him, and told him, saying, The child is not awaked."

When they reached the house, Elisha went 239 into the room where the dead child lay, "and shut the door upon them twain, and prayed unto the Lord. And he went up, and lay upon the child, and put his mouth upon his mouth, and his eyes upon his eyes, and his hands upon his hands: and he stretched himself upon the child; and the flesh of the child waxed warm. Then he returned, and walked in the house to and fro; and went up, and stretched himself upon him: and the child sneezed seven times, and the child opened his eyes."

Calling Gehazi, Elisha bade him send the mother to him. "And when she was come in unto him, he said, Take up thy son. Then she went in, and fell at his feet, and bowed herself to the ground, and took up her son, and went out."

So was the faith of this woman rewarded. Christ, the great Life-giver, restored her son to her. In like manner will His faithful ones be rewarded, when, at His coming, death loses its sting and the grave is robbed of the victory it has claimed. Then will He restore to His servants the children that have been taken from them by death. "Thus saith the Lord; A voice was heard in Ramah, lamentation, and bitter weeping; Rachel weeping for her children refused to be comforted for her children, because they were not. Thus saith the Lord; Refrain thy voice from weeping, and thine eyes from tears: for thy work shall be rewarded, . . . and they shall come again from the land of the enemy. And there is hope in thine end, saith the Lord, that thy children shall come again to their own border." Jeremiah 31:15-17.

240 Jesus comforts our sorrow for the dead with a message of infinite hope: "I will ransom them from the power of the grave; I will redeem them from death: O death, I will be thy plagues; O grave, I will be thy destruction." Hosea 13:14. "I am He that liveth, and was dead; and, behold, I am alive for evermore, . . . and have the keys of hell and of death." Revelation 1:18. "The Lord Himself shall descend from heaven with a shout, with the voice of the Archangel, and with the trump of God: and the dead in Christ shall rise first: then we which are alive and remain shall be caught up together with them in the clouds, to meet the Lord in the air: and so shall we ever be with the Lord." 1 Thessalonians 4:16, 17.

Like the Saviour of mankind, of whom he was a type, Elisha in his ministry among men combined the work of healing with that of teaching. Faithfully, untiringly, throughout his long and effective labors, Elisha endeavored to foster and advance the important educational work carried on by the schools of the prophets. In the providence of God his words of instruction to the earnest groups of young men assembled were confirmed by the deep movings of the Holy Spirit, and at times by other unmistakable evidences of his authority as a servant of Jehovah.

It was on the occasion of one of his visits to the school established at Gilgal that he healed the poisoned pottage. "There was a dearth in the land; and the sons of the prophets were sitting before him: and he said unto his servant, Set on the great pot, and seethe pottage for the sons of the prophets. And one went out into the field to gather herbs, and found a wild vine, and gath- 241 ered thereof wild gourds his lap full, and came and shred them into the pot of pottage: for they knew them not. So they poured out for the men to eat. And it came to pass, as they were eating of the pottage, that they cried out, and said, O thou man of God, there is death in the pot. And they could not eat thereof. But he said, Then bring meal. And he cast it into the pot; and he said, Pour out for the people, that they may eat. And there was no harm in the pot."

At Gilgal, also, while the dearth was still in the land, Elisha fed one hundred men with the present brought to him by "a man from Baal-shalisha," "bread of the first fruits, twenty loaves of barley, and full ears of corn in the husk thereof." There were those with him who were sorely in need of food. When the offering came, he said to his servant, "Give unto the people, that they may eat. And his servitor said, What, should I set this before an hundred men? He said again, Give the people, that they may

eat: for thus saith the Lord, They shall eat, and shall leave thereof. So he set it before them, and they did eat, and left thereof, according to the word of the Lord."

What condescension it was on the part of Christ, through His messenger, to work this miracle to satisfy hunger! Again and again since that time, though not always in so marked and perceptible a manner, has the Lord Jesus worked to supply human need. If we had clearer spiritual discernment we would recognize more readily than we do God's compassionate dealing with the children of men.

It is the grace of God on the small portion that makes it all-sufficient. God's hand can multiply it a hundredfold. From His resources He can 242 spread a table in the wilderness. By the touch of His hand He can increase the scanty provision and make it sufficient for all. It was His power that increased the loaves and corn in the hands of the sons of the prophets.

In the days of Christ's earthly ministry, when He performed a similar miracle in feeding the multitudes, the same unbelief was manifested as was shown by those associated with the prophet 243 of old. "What!" said Elisha's servant; "should I set this before an hundred men?" And when Jesus bade His disciples give the multitude to eat, they answered, "We have no more but five loaves and two fishes; except we should go and buy meat for all this people." Luke 9:13. What is that among so many?

The lesson is for God's children in every age. When the Lord gives a work to be done, let not men stop to inquire into the reasonableness of the command or the probable result of their efforts to obey. The supply in their hands may seem to fall short of the need to be filled; but in the hands of the Lord it will prove more than sufficient. The servitor "set it before them, and they did eat, and left thereof, according to the word of the Lord."

A fuller sense of God's relationship to those whom He has purchased with the gift of His Son, a greater faith in the onward progress of His cause in the earth—this is the great need of the church today. Let none waste time in deploring the scantiness of their visible resources. The outward appearance may be unpromising, but energy and trust in God will develop resources. The gift brought to Him with thanksgiving and with prayer for His blessing, He will multiply as He multiplied the food given to the sons of the prophets and to the weary multitude.

20

Naaman

"Now Naaman, captain of the host of the king of Syria, was a great man with his master, and honorable, because by him the Lord had given deliverance unto Syria: he was also a mighty man in valor, but he was a leper."

Ben-hadad, king of Syria, had defeated the armies of Israel in the battle which resulted in the death of Ahab. Since that time the Syrians had maintained against Israel a constant border warfare, and in one of their raids they had carried away a little maid who, in the land of her captivity, "waited on Naaman's wife." A slave, far from her home, this little maid was nevertheless one of God's witnesses, unconsciously fulfilling the purpose for which God had chosen Israel as His people. As she ministered in that heathen home, her sympathies were aroused in behalf of her master; and, remembering the wonderful miracles of healing wrought through Elisha, she said to her mistress, "Would God my lord were with the prophet that is in Samaria! for he would recover him of his leprosy." She knew that the power of Heaven was with Elisha, and she believed that by this power Naaman could be healed.

The conduct of the captive maid, the way that she bore herself in that heathen home, is a strong witness to the power of early home training. There is no higher trust than that committed to fathers and mothers in the care and training of their children. Parents have to do with the very foundations of habit and character. By their example and teaching the future of their children is largely decided.

Happy are the parents whose lives are a true reflection of the divine, so that the promises and commands of God awaken in the child gratitude and reverence; the parents whose tenderness and justice and long-suffering interpret to the child the love and justice and long-suffering of God, and who by teaching the child to love and trust and obey them, are teaching him to love and trust and obey his Father in heaven. Parents who impart to the child such a gift have endowed him with a treasure more precious than the wealth of all the ages, a treasure as enduring as eternity.

We know not in what line our children may be called to serve. They may spend their lives within the circle of the home; they may engage in life's common vocations, or go as teachers of the gospel to heathen lands; but all are alike called to be missionaries for God, ministers of mercy to the world. They are to obtain an education that will help them to stand by the side of Christ in unselfish service.

The parents of that Hebrew maid, as they taught her of God, did not know the destiny that would be hers. But they were faithful to their trust; and in the home of the captain of the Syrian host, their child bore witness to the God whom she had learned to honor.

Naaman heard of the words that the maid had spoken to her mistress; and, obtaining permission from the king, he went forth to seek healing, taking with him "ten talents of silver, and six thousand pieces of gold, and ten changes of raiment." He also carried a letter from the king of Syria to the king of Israel, in which was written the message, "Behold, I have . . . sent Naaman my servant to thee, that thou mayest recover him of his leprosy." When the king of Israel read the letter, "he rent his clothes, and said, Am I God, to kill and to make alive, that this man doth send unto me to recover a man of his leprosy? wherefore consider, I pray you, and see how he seeketh a quarrel against me."

Tidings of the matter reached Elisha, and he sent word to the king, saying, "Wherefore has thou rent thy clothes? let him come now to me, and he shall know that there is a prophet in Israel."

"So Naaman came with his horses and with his chariot, and stood at the door of the house of Elisha." Through a messenger the prophet bade him, "Go and wash in Jordan seven times, and thy flesh shall come again to thee, and thou shalt be clean."

Naaman had expected to see some wonderful manifestation of power from heaven. "I thought," he said, "he will surely come out to me, and stand, and call on the name of the Lord his God, and strike his hand over the place, and recover the leper." When told to wash in the Jordan, his pride was touched, and in mortification and disappointment he exclaimed, "Are not Abana and Pharpar, rivers of Damascus, better than all the waters of Israel? may I not wash in them, and be clean?" "So he turned and went away in a rage."

The proud spirit of Naaman rebelled against following the course outlined by Elisha. The rivers mentioned by the Syrian captain were beautified by surrounding groves, and many flocked to the banks of these pleasant streams to worship their idol gods. It would have cost Naaman no great humiliation of soul to descend into one of those streams. But it was only through following the specific directions of the prophet that he could find healing. Willing obedience alone would bring the desired result.

Naaman's servants entreated him to carry out Elisha's directions: "If the prophet had bid thee do some great thing," they urged, "wouldest thou not have done it? how much rather then, when he saith to thee, Wash, and be clean?" The faith of Naaman was being tested, while pride

This chapter is based on 2 Kings 5.

struggled for the mastery. But faith conquered, and the haughty Syrian yielded his pride of heart and bowed in submission to the revealed will of Jehovah. Seven times he dipped himself in Jordan, "according to the saying of the man of God." And his faith was honored; "his flesh came again like unto the flesh of a little child, and he was clean."

Gratefully "he returned to the man of God, he and all his company," with the acknowledgment, "Behold, now I know that there is no God in all the earth, but in Israel."

250

In accordance with the custom of the times, Naaman now asked Elisha to accept a costly present. But the prophet refused. It was not for him to take payment for a blessing that God had in mercy bestowed. "As the Lord liveth," he said, "I will receive none." The Syrian "urged him to take it; but he refused.

"And Naaman said, Shall there not then, I pray thee, be given to thy servant two mules' burden of earth? for thy servant will henceforth offer neither burnt offering nor sacrifice unto other gods, but unto the Lord. In this thing the Lord pardon thy servant, that when my master goeth into the house of Rimmon to worship there, and he leaneth on my hand, and I bow myself in the house of Rimmon: when I bow down myself in the house of Rimmon, the Lord pardon thy servant in this thing.

"And he said unto him, Go in peace. So he departed from him a little way."

Gehazi, Elisha's servant, had had opportunity during the years to develop the spirit of self-denial characterizing his master's lifework. It had been his privilege to become a noble standard-bearer in the army of the Lord. The best gifts of Heaven had long been within his reach; yet, turning from these, he had coveted instead the base alloy of worldly wealth. And now the hidden longings of his avaricious spirit led him to yield to an overmastering temptation. "Behold," he reasoned within himself, "my master hath spared Naaman this Syrian, in not receiving at his hands that which he brought:

251

but . . . I will run after him, and take somewhat of him." And thus it came about that in secrecy "Gehazi followed after Naaman."

"When Naaman saw him running after him, he lighted down from the chariot to meet him, and said, Is all well? And he said, All is well." Then Gehazi uttered a deliberate lie. "My master," he said, "hath sent me, saying, Behold, even now there be come to me from Mount Ephraim two young men of the sons of the prophets: give them, I pray thee, a talent of silver, and two changes of garments." To the request Naaman gladly acceded, pressing upon Gehazi two talents of silver instead of one, "with two changes of garments," and commissioning servants to bear the treasure back.

As Gehazi neared Elisha's home, he dismissed the servants and placed the silver and the garments in hiding. This accomplished, "he went in, and stood before his master;" and, to shield himself from censure, he uttered a second lie. In response to the inquiry of the prophet, "Whence comest thou?" Gehazi answered, "Thy servant went no whither."

Then came the stern denunciation, showing that Elisha knew all. "Went not mine heart with thee," he asked, "when the man turned again from his chariot to meet thee? Is it a time to receive money, and to receive garments, and olive yards, and vineyards, and sheep, and oxen, and menservants, and maidservants? The leprosy therefore of Naaman shall cleave unto thee, and unto thy seed forever." Swift was the retribution that overtook the guilty man. He went out from Elisha's presence "a leper as white as snow."

Solemn are the lessons taught by this experi- 252 ence of one to whom had been given high and holy privileges. The course of Gehazi was such as to place a stumbling block in the pathway of Naaman, upon whose mind had broken a wonderful light, and who was favorably disposed toward the service of the living God. For the deception practiced by Gehazi there could be pleaded no excuse. To the day of his death he remained a leper, cursed of God and shunned by his fellow men.

"A false witness shall not be unpunished, and he that speaketh lies shall not escape." Proverbs 19:5. Men may think to hide their evil deeds from human eyes, but they cannot deceive God. "All things are naked and opened unto the eyes of Him with whom we have to do." Heb. 4:13. Gehazi thought to deceive Elisha, but God revealed to His prophet the words that Gehazi had spoken to Naaman, and every detail of the scene between the two men.

Truth is of God; deception in all its myriad forms is of Satan, and whoever in any way departs from the straight line of truth is betraying himself into the power of the wicked one. Those who have learned of Christ will "have no fellowship with the unfruitful works of darkness." Ephesians 5:11. In speech, as in life, they will be simple, straightforward, and true, for they are preparing for the fellowship of those holy ones in whose mouth is found no guile. See Revelation 14:5.

Centuries after Naaman returned to his Syrian home, healed in body and converted in spirit, his wonderful faith was referred to and commended by the Saviour as an object lesson for 253 all who claim to serve God. "Many lepers were in Israel in the time of Eliseus the prophet," the Saviour declared; "and none of them was cleansed, saving Naaman the Syrian." Luke 4:27. God passed over the many lepers in Israel because their unbelief closed the door of good to them. A heathen nobleman who had been true to his convictions of right, and who felt his need of help, was in the sight of God more worthy of His blessing than were the afflicted in Israel, who had slighted and despised their God-given privileges. God works for those who appreciate His favors and respond to the light given them from heaven.

Today in every land there are those who are honest in heart, and upon these the light of heaven is shining. If they continue faithful in following that which they understand to be duty, they will be given increased light, until, like Naaman of old, they will be constrained to acknowledge that "there is no God in all the earth," save the living God, the Creator.

To every sincere soul "that walketh in darkness, and hath no light," is given the invitation, "Let him trust in the name of the Lord, and stay upon his God." "For since the beginning of the world men have not heard, nor perceived by the ear, neither hath the eye seen, O God, beside Thee, what He hath prepared for him that waiteth for Him. Thou meetest him that rejoiceth and worketh righteousness, those that remember Thee in Thy ways." Isaiah 50:10; 64:4, 5.

254

21

Elisha's Closing Ministry

Called to the prophetic office while Ahab was still reigning, Elisha had lived to see many changes take place in the kingdom of Israel. Judgment upon judgment had befallen the Israelites during the reign of Hazael the Syrian, who had been anointed to be the scourge of the apostate nation. The stern measures of reform instituted by Jehu had resulted in the slaying of all the house of Ahab. In continued wars with the Syrians, Jehoahaz, Jehu's successor, had lost some of the cities lying east of the Jordan. For a time it had seemed as if the Syrians might gain control of the entire kingdom. But the reformation begun by Elijah and carried forward by Elisha had led many to inquire after God. The altars of Baal were being forsaken, and slowly yet surely God's purpose was being fulfilled in the lives of those who chose to serve Him with all the heart.

It was because of His love for erring Israel that God permitted the Syrians to scourge them.
255 It was because of His compassion for those whose moral power was weak that He raised up Jehu to slay wicked Jezebel and all the house of Ahab. Once more, through a merciful providence, the priests of Baal and of Ashtoreth were set aside and their heathen altars thrown down. God in His wisdom foresaw that if temptation were removed, some would forsake heathenism and turn their faces heavenward, and this is why

He permitted calamity after calamity to befall them. His judgments were tempered with mercy; and when His purpose was accomplished, He turned the tide in favor of those who had learned to inquire after Him.

While influences for good and for evil were striving for the ascendancy, and Satan was doing all in his power to complete the ruin he had wrought during the reign of Ahab and Jezebel, Elisha continued to bear his testimony. He met with opposition, yet none could gainsay his words. Throughout the kingdom he was honored and venerated. Many came to him for counsel. While Jezebel was still living, Joram, the king of Israel, sought his advice; and once, when in Damascus, he was visited by messengers from Benhadad, king of Syria, who desired to learn whether a sickness then upon him would result in death. To all the prophet bore faithful witness in a time when, on every hand, truth was being perverted and the great majority of the people were in open rebellion against Heaven.

And God never forsook His chosen messenger. On one occasion, during a Syrian invasion, the king of Syria sought to destroy Elisha because of his activity in apprising the king of Israel of the plans of the enemy. The Syrian king had taken counsel with his servants, saying, "In such and such a place shall be my camp." This plan was revealed by the Lord to Elisha, who "sent unto the king of Israel, saying, Beware that thou pass not such a place; for thither the Syrians are come down. And the king of Israel sent to the place which the man of God told him and warned him of, and saved himself there, not once nor twice.

"Therefore the heart of the king of Syria was sore troubled for this thing; and he called his servants, and said unto them, Will ye not show me which of us is for the king of Israel? And one of his servants said, None, my lord, O king: but Elisha, the prophet that is in Israel, telleth the king of Israel the words that thou speakest in thy bedchamber."

Determined to make way with the prophet, the Syrian king commanded, "Go and spy where he is, that I may send and fetch him." The prophet was in Dothan; and, learning this, the king sent thither "horses, and chariots, and a great host: and they came by night, and compassed the city about. And when the servant of the man of God was risen early, and gone forth, behold, an host compassed the city both with horses and chariots."

In terror Elisha's servant sought him with the tidings. "Alas, my master!" he said, "how shall we do?"

"Fear not," was the answer of the prophet; "for they that be with us are more than they that be with them." And then, that the servant might know this for himself, "Elisha prayed, and said,

Lord, I pray Thee, open his eyes, that he may see." "The Lord opened the eyes of the young 257 man; and he saw: and, behold, the mountain was full of horses and chariots of fire round about Elisha." Between the servant of God and the hosts of armed foemen was an encircling band of heavenly angels. They had come down in mighty power, not to destroy, not to exact homage, but to encamp round about and minister to the Lord's weak and helpless ones.

When the people of God are brought into strait places, and apparently there is no escape for them, the Lord alone must be their dependence.

As the company of Syrian soldiers boldly advanced, ignorant of the unseen hosts of heaven, "Elisha prayed unto the Lord, and said, Smite this people, I pray Thee, with blindness. And He smote them with blindness according to the word of Elisha. And Elisha said unto them, This is not the way, neither is this the city: follow me, and I will bring you to the man whom ye seek. But he led them to Samaria.

"And it came to pass, when they were come into Samaria, that Elisha said, Lord, open the eyes of these men, that they may see. And the Lord opened their eyes, and they saw; and, behold, they were in the midst of Samaria. And the king of Israel said unto Elisha, when he saw them, My father, shall I smite them? shall I smite them? And he answered, Thou shalt not smite them: wouldest thou smite those whom thou hast taken captive with thy sword and with thy bow? set bread and water before them, that they may eat and drink, and go to their master. And he prepared great provision for them: and 258 when they had eaten and drunk, he sent them away, and they went to their master." See 2 Kings 6.

For a time after this, Israel was free from the attacks of the Syrians. But later, under the energetic direction of a determined king, Hazael, the Syrian hosts surrounded Samaria and besieged it. Never had Israel been brought into so great a strait as during this siege. The sins of the fathers were indeed being visited upon the children and the children's children. The horrors of prolonged famine were driving the king of Israel to desperate measures, when Elisha predicted deliverance the following day.

As the next morning was about to dawn, the Lord "made the host of the Syrians to hear a noise of chariots, and a noise of horses, even the noise of a great host;" and they, seized with fear, "arose and fled in the twilight," leaving "their tents, and their horses, and their asses, even the camp as it was," with rich stores of food. They "fled for their life," not tarrying until after the Jordan had been crossed.

During the night of the flight, four leprous men at the gate of the city, made desperate by hunger, had proposed to visit the Syrian camp and throw themselves upon the mercy of the besiegers, hoping thereby to arouse sympathy and obtain food. What was their astonishment when, entering the camp, they found "no man there." With none to molest or forbid, "they went into one tent, and did eat and drink, and carried thence silver, and gold, and raiment, and went and hid it; and came again, and entered into another tent, and carried thence also, and went and hid it. Then they said one to another, We do not well: this day is a day of good tidings, and we hold our peace." Quickly they 259 returned to the city with the glad news.

Great was the spoil; so abundant were the supplies that on that day "a measure of fine flour was sold for a shekel, and two measures of barley for a shekel," as had been foretold by Elisha the day before. Once more the name of God was exalted before the heathen "according to the word of the Lord" through His prophet in Israel. See 2 Kings 7:5-16.

Thus the man of God continued to labor from year to year, drawing close to the people in faithful ministry, and in times of crisis standing by the side of kings as a wise counselor. The long years of idolatrous backsliding on the part of rulers and people had wrought their baleful work; the dark shadow of apostasy was still everywhere apparent, yet here and there were those who had steadfastly refused to bow the knee to Baal. As Elisha continued his work of reform, many were reclaimed from heathenism, and these learned to rejoice in the service of the true God. The prophet was cheered by these miracles of divine grace, and he was inspired with a great longing to reach all who were honest in heart. Wherever he was he endeavored to be a teacher of righteousness.

From a human point of view the outlook for the spiritual regeneration of the nation was as hopeless as is the outlook today before God's servants who are laboring in the dark places of the earth. But the church of Christ is God's agency for the proclamation of truth; she is empowered by Him to do a special work; and if she is loyal to God, obedient to His commandments, there will dwell within her the excellency of divine power. If she will be true to her allegiance, there is no power that can stand 260 against her. The forces of the enemy will be no more able to overwhelm her than is the chaff to resist the whirlwind.

There is before the church the dawn of a bright, glorious day, if she will put on the robe of Christ's righteousness, withdrawing from all allegiance to the world.

God calls upon His faithful ones, who believe in Him, to talk courage to those who are unbelieving and hopeless. Turn to the Lord, ye prisoners of hope. Seek strength from God, the living God. Show an unwavering, humble faith in His power and His willingness to save. When in faith we take hold of His strength, He will change, wonderfully change, the most hopeless, discouraging outlook. He will do this for the glory of His name.

So long as Elisha was able to journey from place to place throughout the kingdom of Israel, he continued to take an active interest in the upbuilding of the schools of the prophets. Wherever he was, God was with him, giving him words to speak and power to work miracles. On one occasion "the sons of the prophets said unto Elisha, Behold now, the place where we dwell with thee is too strait for us. Let us go, we pray thee, unto Jordan, and take thence every man a beam, and let us make us a place there, where we may dwell." 2 Kings 6:1, 2. Elisha went with them to Jordan, encouraging them by his presence, giving them instruction, and even performing a miracle to aid them in their work. "As one was felling a beam, the axhead fell into the water: and he cried, and said, Alas, master! for it was borrowed. And the man of God said, 261 Where fell it? And he showed him the place. And he cut down a stick, and cast it in thither; and the iron did swim. Therefore said he, Take it up to thee. And he put out his hand, and took it." Verses 5-7.

So effectual had been his ministry and so widespread his influence that, as he lay upon his deathbed, even the youthful King Joash, an idolater with but little respect for God, recognized in the prophet a father in Israel, and acknowledged that his presence among them was of more value in time of trouble than the possession of an army of horses and chariots. The record reads: "Now Elisha was fallen sick of his sickness whereof he died. And Joash the king of Israel came down unto him, and wept over his face, and said, O my father, my father, the chariot of Israel, and the horsemen thereof." 2 Kings 13:14.

To many a troubled soul in need of help the prophet had acted the part of a wise, sympathetic father. And in this instance he turned not from the godless youth before him, so unworthy of the position of trust he was occupying, and yet so greatly in need of counsel. God in His providence was bringing to the king an opportunity to redeem the failures of the past and to place his kingdom on vantage ground. The Syrian foe, now occupying the territory east of the Jordan, was to be repulsed. Once more the power of God was to be manifested in behalf of erring Israel.

The dying prophet bade the king, "Take bow and arrows." Joash obeyed. Then the prophet said, "Put thine hand upon the bow." Joash "put his hand upon it: and Elisha put his hands upon 262 the king's hands. And he said, Open the window eastward"—toward the cities beyond the Jordan in possession of the Syrians. The king having opened the latticed window, Elisha bade

him shoot. As the arrow sped on its way, the prophet was inspired to say, "The arrow of the Lord's deliverance, and the arrow of deliverance from Syria: for thou shalt smite the Syrians in Aphek, till thou have consumed them."

And now the prophet tested the faith of the king. Bidding Joash take up the arrows, he said, "Smite upon the ground." Thrice the king smote the ground, and then he stayed his hand. "Thou shouldest have smitten five or six times," Elisha exclaimed in dismay; "then hadst thou smitten Syria till thou hadst consumed it: whereas now 263 thou shalt smite Syria but thrice." 2 Kings 13:15-19.

The lesson is for all in positions of trust. When God opens the way for the accomplishment of a certain work and gives assurance of success, the chosen instrumentality must do all in his power to bring about the promised result. In proportion to the enthusiasm and perseverance with which the work is carried forward will be the success given. God can work miracles for His people only as they act their part with untiring energy. He calls for men of devotion to His work, men of moral courage, with ardent love for souls, and with a zeal that never flags. Such workers will find no task too arduous, no prospect too hopeless; they will labor on, undaunted, until apparent defeat is turned into glorious victory. Not even prison walls nor the martyr's stake beyond, will cause them to swerve from their purpose of laboring together with God for the upbuilding of His kingdom.

With the counsel and encouragement given Joash, the work of Elisha closed. He upon whom had fallen in full measure the spirit resting upon Elijah, had proved faithful to the end. Never had he wavered. Never had he lost his trust in the power of Omnipotence. Always, when the way before him seemed utterly closed, he had still advanced by faith, and God had honored his confidence and opened the way before him.

It was not given Elisha to follow his master in a fiery chariot. Upon him the Lord permitted to come a lingering illness. During the long hours of human weakness and suffering his faith laid 264 fast hold on the promises of God, and he beheld ever about him heavenly messengers of comfort and peace. As on the heights of Dothan he had seen the encircling hosts of heaven, the fiery chariots of Israel and the horsemen thereof, so now he was conscious of the presence of sympathizing angels, and he was sustained. Throughout all his life he had exercised strong faith, and as he had advanced in a knowledge of God's providences and of His merciful kindness, faith had ripened into an abiding trust in his God, and when death called him he was ready to rest from his labors.

"Precious in the sight of the Lord is the death of His saints." Psalm 116:15. "The righteous hath hope in his death." Proverbs 14:32. With the psalmist, Elisha could say in all confidence, "God will redeem my soul from the power of the grave: for He shall receive me." Psalm 49:15. And with rejoicing he could testify, "I know that my Redeemer liveth, and that He shall stand at the latter day upon the earth." Job 19:25. "As for me, I will behold Thy face in righteousness: I shall be satisfied, when I awake, with Thy likeness." Psalm 17:15.

265

22

"Nineveh, That Great City"

Among the cities of the ancient world in the days of divided Israel one of the greatest was Nineveh, the capital of the Assyrian realm. Founded on the fertile bank of the Tigris, soon after the dispersion from the tower of Babel, it had flourished through the centuries until it had become "an exceeding great city of three days' journey." Jonah 3:3.

In the time of its temporal prosperity Nineveh was a center of crime and wickedness. Inspiration has characterized it as "the bloody city, . . . full of lies and robbery." In figurative language the prophet Nahum compared the Ninevites to a cruel, ravenous lion. "Upon whom," he inquired, "hath not thy wickedness passed continually?" Nahum 3:1, 19.

Yet Nineveh, wicked though it had become, was not wholly given over to evil. He who "beholdeth all the sons of men" (Psalm 33:13) and "seeth every precious thing" (Job 28:10) perceived in that city many who were reaching out after something better and higher, and who, if granted opportunity to learn of the living God, would put away their evil deeds and worship Him. And so in His wisdom God revealed Himself to them in an unmistakable manner, to lead them, if possible, to repentance.

The instrument chosen for this work was the prophet Jonah, the son of Amittai. To him came the word of the Lord, "Arise, go to Nineveh, that great city, and cry against it; for their wickedness is come up before Me." Jonah 1:1, 2.

As the prophet thought of the difficulties and seeming impossibilities of this commission, he was tempted to question the wisdom of the call. From a human viewpoint it seemed as if nothing could be gained by proclaiming such a message in that proud city. He forgot for the moment that the God whom he served was all-wise and all-powerful. While he hesitated, still doubting, Satan overwhelmed him with discouragement. The prophet was seized with a great dread, and he "rose up to flee unto Tarshish." Going to Joppa, and finding there a ship ready to sail, "he paid the fare thereof and went down into it, to go with them." Verse 3.

In the charge given him, Jonah had been entrusted with a heavy responsibility; yet He who had bidden him go was able to sustain His servant and grant him success. Had the prophet obeyed unquestioningly, he would have been spared many bitter experiences, and in would have been blessed abundantly. Yet in the hour of Jonah's despair the Lord did not desert him. Through a series of trials and strange providences, the prophet's confidence in God and in His infinite power to save was to be revived.

If, when the call first came to him, Jonah had stopped to consider calmly, he might have known how foolish would be any effort on his part to escape the responsibility placed upon him. But not for long was he permitted to go on undisturbed in his mad flight. "The Lord sent out a great wind into the sea, and there was a mighty tempest in the sea, so that the ship was like to be broken. Then the mariners were afraid, and cried every man unto his god, and cast forth the wares that were in the ship into the sea, to lighten it of them. But Jonah had gone down into the sides of the ship; and he lay, and was fast asleep." Verses 4, 5.

As the mariners were beseeching their heathen gods for help, the master of the ship, distressed beyond measure, sought out Jonah and said, "What meanest thou, O sleeper? arise, call upon thy God, if so be that God will think upon us, that we perish not." Verse 6.

But the prayers of the man who had turned aside from the path of duty brought no help. The mariners, impressed with the thought that the strange violence of the storm betokened the anger of their gods, proposed as a last resort the casting of lots, "that we may know," they said, "for whose cause this evil is upon us. So they cast lots, and the lot fell upon Jonah. Then said they unto him, Tell us, we pray thee, for whose cause this evil is upon us; what is thine occupation? and whence comest thou? what is thy country? and of what people art thou?

"And he said unto them, I am an Hebrew; and I fear the Lord, the God of heaven, which hath made the sea and the dry land.

"Then were the men exceedingly afraid, and said unto him, Why hast thou done this? For the men knew that he fled from the presence of the Lord, because he had told them.

"Then said they unto him, What shall we do unto thee, that the sea may be calm unto us? for the sea wrought, and was tempestuous. And he said unto them, Take me up, and cast me forth into the sea; so shall the sea be calm unto you: for I know that for my sake this great tempest is upon you.

"Nevertheless the men rowed hard to bring it to the land; but they could not: for the sea wrought, and was tempestuous against them. Wherefore they cried unto the Lord, and said, We beseech Thee, O Lord, we beseech Thee, let us not perish for this man's life, and lay not upon us innocent blood: for Thou, O Lord, hast done as it pleased Thee. So they took up Jonah, and cast him forth into the sea: and the sea ceased from her raging. Then the men feared the Lord exceedingly, and offered a sacrifice unto the Lord, and made vows.

"Now the Lord had prepared a great fish to swallow up Jonah. And Jonah was in the belly of the fish three days and three nights.

"Then Jonah prayed unto the Lord his God out of the fish's belly, and said:

"I cried by reason of mine affliction unto the Lord,
And He heard me;
Out of the belly of hell cried I,
And Thou heardest my voice.

269   "For Thou hadst cast me into the deep,
In the midst of the seas;
And the floods compassed me about:
All Thy billows and Thy waves passed over me.

"Then I said, I am cast out of Thy sight;
Yet I will look again toward Thy holy temple.
The waters compassed me about,
Even to the soul:

"The depth closed me round about,
The weeds were wrapped about my head.
I went down to the bottoms of the mountains;
The earth with her bars was about me forever:

"Yet hast Thou brought up my life from corruption, O Lord my God.
When my soul fainted within me I remembered the Lord:
And my prayer came in unto Thee,
Into Thine holy temple.

"They that observe lying vanities forsake their own mercy.
But I will sacrifice unto Thee with the voice of thanksgiving;
I will pay that that I have vowed.
Salvation is of the Lord."

Verse 7 to 2:9.

At last Jonah had learned that "salvation belongeth unto the Lord." Psalm 3:8. With penitence and a recognition of the saving grace of God, came deliverance. Jonah was released from the perils of the mighty deep and was cast upon the dry land.

Once more the servant of God was commissioned to warn Nineveh. "The word of the Lord came unto Jonah the second time, saying, Arise, go unto Nineveh, that great city, and preach unto it the preaching that I bid thee." This time he did

not stop to question or doubt, but obeyed unhesitatingly. He "arose, and went unto Nineveh, according to the word of the Lord." Jonah 3:1-3. 270

As Jonah entered the city, he began at once to "cry against" it the message, "Yet forty days, and Nineveh shall be overthrown." Verse 4. From street to street he went, sounding the note of warning.

The message was not in vain. The cry that rang through the streets of the godless city was passed from lip to lip until all the inhabitants had heard the startling announcement. The Spirit of God pressed the message home to every heart and caused multitudes to tremble because of their sins and to repent in deep humiliation.

"The people of Nineveh believed God, and proclaimed a fast, and put on sackcloth, from the greatest of them even to the least of them. For word came unto the king of Nineveh, and he arose from his throne, and he laid his robe from him, and covered him with sackcloth, and sat in ashes. And he caused it to be proclaimed and published through Nineveh by the decree of the king and his nobles, saying, Let neither man nor beast, herd nor flock, taste anything: let them not feed, nor drink water: but let man and beast be covered with sackcloth, and cry mightily unto God: yea, let them turn everyone from his evil way, and from the violence that is in their hands. Who can tell if God will turn and repent, and turn away from His fierce anger, that we perish not?" Verses 5-9.

As king and nobles, with the common people, the high and the low, "repented at the preaching of Jonas" (Matthew 12:41) and united in crying to the God of heaven, His mercy was granted 271 them. He "saw their works, that they turned from their evil way; and God repented of the evil, that He had said that He would do unto them; and He did it not." Jonah 3:10. Their doom was averted, the God of Israel was exalted and honored throughout the heathen world, and His law was revered. Not until many years later was Nineveh to fall a prey to the surrounding nations through forgetfulness of God and through boastful pride. [For an account of the downfall of Assyria, see chapter 30.]

When Jonah learned of God's purpose to spare the city that, notwithstanding its wickedness, had been led to repent in sackcloth and ashes, he should have been the first to rejoice because of God's amazing grace; but instead he allowed his mind to dwell upon the possibility of his being regarded as a false prophet. Jealous of his reputation, he lost sight of the infinitely greater value of the souls in that wretched city. The compassion shown by God toward the repentant Ninevites "displeased Jonah exceedingly, and he was very angry." "Was not this my saying," he inquired of the Lord, "when I was yet in my country? Therefore I fled before unto Tarshish: for I knew that Thou art a gracious God, and merciful, slow to anger, and of great kindness, and repentest Thee of the evil." Jonah 4:1, 2.

Once more he yielded to his inclination to question and doubt, and once more he was overwhelmed with discouragement. Losing sight of the interests of others, and feeling as if he would rather die than live to see the city spared, in his dissatisfaction he exclaimed, "Now, O Lord, take, I beseech Thee, my life from me; for it is better for me to die than to live."

272 "Doest thou well to be angry?" the Lord inquired. "So Jonah went out of the city, and sat on the east side of the city, and there made him a booth, and sat under it in the shadow, till he might see what would become of the city. And the Lord God prepared a gourd, and made it to come up over Jonah, that it might be a shadow over his head, to deliver him from his grief. So Jonah was exceeding glad of the gourd." Verses 3-6.

Then the Lord gave Jonah an object lesson. He "prepared a worm when the morning rose the next day, and it smote the gourd that it withered. And it came to pass, when the sun did arise, that God prepared a vehement east wind; and the sun beat upon the head of Jonah, that he fainted, and wished in himself to die, and said, It is better for me to die than to live."

Again God spoke to His prophet, "Doest thou well to be angry for the gourd?" And he said, "I do well to be angry, even unto death."

"Then said the Lord, Thou hast had pity on the gourd, for the which thou hast not labored, neither madest it grow; which came up in a night, and perished in a night: and should not I spare Nineveh, that great city, wherein are more than sixscore thousand persons that cannot discern between their right hand and their left hand; and also much cattle?" Verses 7-11.

Confused, humiliated, and unable to understand God's purpose in sparing Nineveh, Jonah nevertheless had fulfilled the commission given him to warn that great city; and though the event predicted did not come to pass, yet the 273 message of warning was nonetheless from God. And it accomplished the purpose God designed it should. The glory of His grace was revealed among the heathen. Those who had long been sitting "in darkness and in the shadow of death, being bound in affliction and iron," "cried unto the Lord in their trouble," and "He saved them out of their distresses. He brought them out of darkness and the shadow of death, and brake their bands in sunder." "He sent His word, and healed them, and delivered them from their destructions." Psalm 107:10, 13, 14, 20.

Christ during His earthly ministry referred to the good wrought by the preaching of Jonah in Nineveh, and compared the inhabitants of that 274 heathen center with the professed people of God in His day. "The men of Nineveh," He declared,

"shall rise in judgment with this generation, and shall condemn it: because they repented at the preaching of Jonas; and, behold, a greater than Jonas is here." Matthew 12:40, 41. Into the busy world, filled with the din of commerce and the altercation of trade, where men were trying to get all they could for self, Christ had come; and above the confusion His voice, like the trump of God, was heard: "What shall it profit a man, if he shall gain the whole world, and lose his own soul? or what shall a man give in exchange for his soul?" Mark 8:36, 37.

As the preaching of Jonah was a sign to the Ninevites, so Christ's preaching was a sign to His generation. But what a contrast in the reception of the word! Yet in the face of indifference and scorn the Saviour labored on and on, until He had accomplished His mission.

The lesson is for God's messengers today, when the cities of the nations are as verily in need of a knowledge of the attributes and purposes of the true God as were the Ninevites of old. Christ's ambassadors are to point men to the nobler world, which has largely been lost sight of. According to the teaching of the Holy Scriptures, the only city that will endure is the city whose builder and maker is God. With the eye of faith man may behold the threshold of heaven, flushed with God's living glory. Through His ministering servants the Lord Jesus is calling upon men to strive with sanctified ambition to secure the immortal inheritance. He urges them to lay up treasure beside the throne of God.

There is coming rapidly and surely an almost 275 universal guilt upon the inhabitants of the cities, because of the steady increase of determined wickedness. The corruption that prevails is beyond the power of the human pen to describe. Every day brings fresh revelations of strife, bribery, and fraud; every day brings its heartsickening record of violence and lawlessness, of indifference to human suffering, of brutal, fiendish destruction of human life. Every day testifies to the increase of insanity, murder, and suicide.

From age to age Satan has sought to keep men in ignorance of the beneficent designs of Jehovah. He has endeavored to remove from their sight the great things of God's law—the principles of justice, mercy, and love therein set forth. Men boast of the wonderful progress and enlightenment of the age in which we are now living; but God sees the earth filled with iniquity and violence. Men declare that the law of God has been abrogated, that the Bible is not authentic; and as a result, a tide of evil, such as has not been seen since the days of Noah and of apostate Israel, is sweeping over the world. Nobility of soul, gentleness, piety, are bartered away to gratify the lust for forbidden things. The black record of crime committed for the sake of gain is enough to chill the blood and fill the soul with horror.

Our God is a God of mercy. With long-sufferance and tender compassion He deals with the transgressors of His law. And yet, in this our day, when men and women have so many opportunities for becoming familiar with the divine law as revealed in Holy Writ, the great Ruler of the universe cannot behold with any 276 satisfaction the wicked cities, where reign violence and crime. The end of God's forbearance with those who persist in disobedience is approaching rapidly.

Ought men to be surprised over a sudden and unexpected change in the dealings of the Supreme Ruler with the inhabitants of a fallen world? Ought they to be surprised when punishment follows transgression and increasing crime? Ought they to be surprised that God should bring destruction and death upon those whose ill-gotten gains have been obtained through deception and fraud? Notwithstanding the fact that increasing light regarding God's requirements has been shining on their pathway, many have refused to recognize Jehovah's rulership, and have chosen to remain under the black banner of the originator of all rebellion against the government of heaven.

The forbearance of God has been very great—so great that when we consider the continuous insult to His holy commandments, we marvel. The Omnipotent One has been exerting a restraining power over His own attributes. But He will certainly arise to punish the wicked, who so boldly defy the just claims of the Decalogue.

God allows men a period of probation; but there is a point beyond which divine patience is exhausted, and the judgments of God are sure to follow. The Lord bears long with men, and with cities, mercifully giving warnings to save them from divine wrath; but a time will come when pleadings for mercy will no longer be heard, and the rebellious element that continues to reject the light of truth will be blotted out, in mercy to themselves and to those who would otherwise be influenced by their example.

277 The time is at hand when there will be sorrow in the world that no human balm can heal. The Spirit of God is being withdrawn. Disasters by sea and by land follow one another in quick succession. How frequently we hear of earthquakes and tornadoes, of destruction by fire and flood, with great loss of life and property! Apparently these calamities are capricious outbreaks of disorganized, unregulated forces of nature, wholly beyond the control of man; but in them all, God's purpose may be read. They are among the agencies by which He seeks to arouse men and women to a sense of their danger.

God's messengers in the great cities are not to become discouraged over the wickedness, the injustice, the depravity, which they are called upon to face while endeavoring to proclaim the glad tidings of salvation. The Lord would cheer every such worker with the same message that He gave to the apostle Paul in wicked Corinth: "Be not afraid, but speak, and hold not thy peace: for I am with thee, and no man shall set on thee to hurt thee: for I have much people in this city." Acts 18:9, 10. Let those engaged in soul-saving ministry remember that while there are many who will not heed the counsel of God in His word, the whole world will not turn from light and truth, from the invitations of a patient, forbearing Saviour. In every city, filled though it may be with violence and crime, there are many who with proper teaching may learn to become followers of Jesus. Thousands may thus be reached with saving truth and be led to receive Christ as a personal Saviour.

God's message for the inhabitants of earth 278 today is, "Be ye also ready: for in such an hour as ye think not the Son of man cometh." Matthew 24:44. The conditions prevailing in society, and especially in the great cities of the nations, proclaim in thunder tones that the hour of God's judgment is come and that the end of all things earthly is at hand. We are standing on the threshold of the crisis of the ages. In quick succession the judgments of God will follow one another—fire, and flood, and earthquake, with war and bloodshed. We are not to be surprised at this time by events both great and decisive; for the angel of mercy cannot remain much longer to shelter the impenitent.

"Behold, the Lord cometh out of His place to punish the inhabitants of the earth for their iniquity: the earth also shall disclose her blood, and shall no more cover her slain." Isaiah 26:21. The storm of God's wrath is gathering; and those only will stand who respond to the invitations of mercy, as did the inhabitants of Nineveh under the preaching of Jonah, and become sanctified through obedience to the laws of the divine Ruler. The righteous alone shall be hid with Christ in God till the desolation be overpast. Let the language of the soul be:

"Other refuge have I none,
  Hangs my helpless soul on Thee;
  Leave, O, leave me not alone!
  Still support and comfort me.

"Hide me, O my Saviour, hide!
  Till the storm of life is past;
  Safe into the haven guide,
  O receive my soul at last!"

279

23

The Assyrian Captivity

The closing years of the ill-fated kingdom of Israel were marked with violence and bloodshed such as had never been witnessed even in the worst periods of strife and unrest under the house of Ahab. For two centuries and more the rulers of the ten tribes had been sowing the wind; now they were reaping the whirlwind. King after king was assassinated to make way for others ambitious to rule. "They have set up kings," the Lord declared of these godless usurpers, "but not by Me: they have made princes, and I knew it not." Hosea 8:4. Every principle of justice was set aside; those who should have stood before the nations of earth as the depositaries of divine grace, "dealt treacherously against the Lord" and with one another. Hosea 5:7.

With the severest reproofs, God sought to arouse the impenitent nation to a realization of its imminent danger of utter destruction. 280 Through Hosea and Amos He sent the ten tribes message after message, urging full and complete repentance, and threatening disaster as the result of continued transgression. "Ye have plowed wickedness," declared Hosea, "ye have reaped iniquity; ye have eaten the fruit of lies: because thou didst trust in thy way, in the multitude of thy mighty men. Therefore shall a tumult arise among thy people, and all thy fortresses shall be spoiled. . . . In a morning shall the king of Israel utterly be cut off." Hosea 10:13-15.

Of Ephraim the prophet testified, "Strangers have devoured his strength, and he knoweth it not: yea, gray hairs are here and there upon him, yet he knoweth not." [The prophet Hosea often referred to Ephraim, a leader in apostasy among the tribes of Israel, as a symbol of the apostate nation.] "Israel hath cast off the thing that is good." "Broken in judgment," unable to discern the disastrous outcome of their evil course, the ten tribes were soon to be "wanderers among the nations." Hosea 7:9; 8:3; 5:11; 9:17.

Some of the leaders in Israel felt keenly their loss of prestige and wished that this might be regained. But instead of turning away from those practices which had brought weakness to the kingdom, they continued in iniquity, flattering themselves that when occasion arose, they would attain to the political power they desired by allying themselves with the heathen. "When Ephraim saw his sickness, and Judah saw his wound, then went Ephraim to the Assyrian." "Ephraim also is like a silly dove without heart: they call to Egypt, they go to Assyria." "They

do make a covenant with the Assyrians." Hosea 5:13; 7:11; 12:1.

Through the man of God that had appeared 281 before the altar at Bethel, through Elijah and Elisha, through Amos and Hosea, the Lord had repeatedly set before the ten tribes the evils of disobedience. But notwithstanding reproof and entreaty, Israel had sunk lower and still lower in apostasy. "Israel slideth back as a backsliding heifer," the Lord declared; "My people are bent to backsliding from Me." Hosea 4:16; 11:7.

There were times when the judgments of Heaven fell very heavily on the rebellious people. "I hewed them by the prophets," God declared; "I have slain them by the words of My mouth: and thy judgments are as the light that goeth forth. For I desired mercy, and not sacrifice; and the knowledge of God more than burnt offerings. But they like men have transgressed the covenant: there have they dealt treacherously against Me." Hosea 6:5-7.

"Hear the word of the Lord, ye children of Israel," was the message that finally came to them: "Seeing thou hast forgotten the law of thy God, I will also forget thy children. As they were increased, so they sinned against Me: therefore will I change their glory into shame. . . . I will punish them for their ways, and reward them their doings." Hosea 4:1, 6-9.

The iniquity in Israel during the last half century before the Assyrian captivity was like that of the days of Noah, and of every other age when men have rejected God and have given themselves wholly to evil-doing. The exaltation of nature above the God of nature, the worship of the creature instead of the Creator, has always resulted in the grossest of evils. Thus 282 when the people of Israel, in their worship of Baal and Ashtoreth, paid supreme homage to the forces of nature, they severed their connection with all that is uplifting and ennobling, and fell an easy prey to temptation. With the defenses of the soul broken down, the misguided worshipers had no barrier against sin and yielded themselves to the evil passions of the human heart.

Against the marked oppression, the flagrant injustice, the unwonted luxury and extravagance, the shameless feasting and drunkenness, the gross licentiousness and debauchery, of their age, the prophets lifted their voices; but in vain were their protests, in vain their denunciation of sin. "Him that rebuketh in the gate," declared Amos, "they hate, . . . and they abhor him that speaketh uprightly." "They afflict the just, they take a bribe, and they turn aside the poor in the gate from their right." Amos 5:10, 12.

Such were some of the results that had followed the setting up of the two calves of gold by Jeroboam. The first departure from established forms of worship had led to the introduction of grosser forms of idolatry, until finally nearly all the inhabitants of the land had given themselves over to the alluring practices of nature worship. Forgetting their Maker, Israel "deeply corrupted themselves." Hosea 9:9.

The prophets continued to protest against these evils and to plead for rightdoing. "Sow to yourselves in righteousness, reap in mercy," Hosea urged; "break up your fallow ground: for it is time to seek the Lord, till He come and rain righteousness upon you." "Turn thou to thy God: keep mercy and judgment, and wait on thy God continually." "O Israel, return unto the Lord thy God; for thou hast fallen by thine iniquity: . . . say unto Him, Take away all iniquity, and receive us graciously." Hosea 10:12; 12:6; 14:1, 2.

The transgressors were given many opportunities to repent. In their hour of deepest apostasy and greatest need, God's message to them was one of forgiveness and hope. "O Israel," He declared, "thou hast destroyed thyself; but in Me is thine help. I will be thy King: where is any other that may save thee?" Hosea 13:9, 10.

"Come, and let us return unto the Lord," the prophet entreated; "for He hath torn, and He will heal us; He hath smitten, and He will bind us up. After two days will He revive us: in the third day He will raise us up, and we shall live in His sight. Then shall we know, if we follow on to know the Lord: His going forth is prepared as the morning; and He shall come unto us as the rain, as the latter and former rain unto the earth." Hosea 6:1-3.

To those who had lost sight of the plan of the ages for the deliverance of sinners ensnared by the power of Satan, the Lord offered restoration and peace. "I will heal their backsliding, I will love them freely," He declared: "for Mine anger is turned away from him. I will be as the dew unto Israel: he shall grow as the lily, and cast forth his roots as Lebanon. His branches shall spread, and his beauty shall be as the olive tree, and his smell as Lebanon. They that dwell under His shadow shall return; they shall revive as the corn, and grow as the vine: the scent thereof shall be as the wine of Lebanon. Ephraim shall say, What have I to do any more with idols? I have heard him, and observed him: I am like a green fir tree. From Me is thy fruit found.

"Who is wise, and he shall understand these things?
Prudent, and he shall know them?
For the ways of the Lord are right,
And the just shall walk in them:
But the transgressors shall fall therein."
Hosea 14:4-9.

The benefits of seeking God were strongly urged. "Seek ye Me," the Lord invited, "and ye shall live: but seek not Bethel, nor enter into Gilgal, and pass not to Beersheba: for Gilgal shall surely go into captivity, and Bethel shall come to nought."

"Seek good, and not evil, that ye may live: and so the Lord, the God of hosts, shall be with you, as ye have spoken. Hate the evil, and love the good, and establish judgment in the gate: it may be that the Lord God of hosts will be gracious unto the remnant of Joseph." Amos 5:4, 5, 14, 15.

By far the greater number of those who heard these invitations refused to profit by them. So contrary to the evil desires of the impenitent were the words of God's messengers, that the idolatrous priest at Bethel sent to the ruler in Israel, saying, "Amos hath conspired against thee in the midst of the house of Israel: the land is not able to bear all his words." Amos 7:10.

Through Hosea the Lord declared, "When I would have healed Israel, then the iniquity of Ephraim was discovered, and the wickedness of Samaria." "The pride of Israel testifieth to his face: and they do not return to the Lord their God, nor seek Him for all this." Hosea 7:1, 10.

From generation to generation the Lord had borne with His wayward children, and even now, in the face of defiant rebellion, He still longed to reveal Himself to them as willing to save. "O Ephraim," He cried, "what shall I do unto thee? O Judah, what shall I do unto thee? for your goodness is as a morning cloud, and as the early dew it goeth away." Hosea 6:4.

The evils that had overspread the land had become incurable; and upon Israel was pronounced the dread sentence: "Ephraim is joined to idols: let him alone." "The days of visitation are come, the days of recompense are come; Israel shall know it." Hosea 4:17; 9:7.

The ten tribes of Israel were now to reap the fruitage of the apostasy that had taken form with the setting up of the strange altars at Bethel and at Dan. God's message to them was: "Thy calf, O Samaria, hath cast thee off; Mine anger is kindled against them: how long will it be ere they attain to innocency? For from Israel was it also: the workman made it; therefore it is not God: but the calf of Samaria shall be broken in pieces." "The inhabitants of Samaria shall fear because of the calves of Beth-aven: for the people thereof shall mourn over it, and the priests thereof that rejoiced on it. . . . It shall be also carried unto Assyria for a present to King Jareb" (Sennacherib). Hosea 8:5, 6; 10:5, 6.

"Behold, the eyes of the Lord God are upon the sinful kingdom, and I will destroy it from off the face of the earth; saying that I will not utterly destroy the house of Jacob, saith the Lord. For, lo, I will command, and I will sift the house of Israel among all nations, like as corn is sifted in a sieve, yet shall not the least grain fall upon the earth. All the sinners of My people shall die by the sword, which say, The evil shall not overtake nor prevent us."

"The houses of ivory shall perish, and the great houses shall have an end, saith the Lord." "The Lord God of hosts is He that toucheth the land, and it shall melt, and all that dwell therein shall mourn." "Thy sons and thy daughters shall fall by the sword, and thy land shall be divided by line; and thou shalt die in a polluted land: and Israel shall surely go into captivity forth of his land." "Because I will do this unto thee, prepare to meet thy God, O Israel." Amos 9:8-10; 3:15; 9:5; 7:17; 4:12.

For a season these predicted judgments were stayed, and during the long reign of Jeroboam II the armies of Israel gained signal victories; but this time of apparent prosperity wrought no change in the hearts of the impenitent, and it was finally decreed, "Jeroboam shall die by the sword, and Israel shall surely be led away captive out of their own land." Amos 7:11.

The boldness of this utterance was lost on king and people, so far had they gone in impenitence. Amaziah, a leader among the idolatrous priests at Bethel, stirred by the plain words spoken by the prophet against the nation and their king, said to Amos, "O thou seer, go, flee thee away into the land of Judah, and there eat bread, and prophesy there: but prophesy not again any more at Bethel: for it is the king's chapel, and it is the king's court." Verses 12, 13.

To this the prophet firmly responded: "Thus saith the Lord, . . . Israel shall surely go into captivity." Verse 17.

287   The words spoken against the apostate tribes were literally fulfilled; yet the destruction of the kingdom came gradually. In judgment the Lord remembered mercy, and at first, when "Pul the king of Assyria came against the land," Menahem, then king of Israel, was not taken captive, but was permitted to remain on the throne as a vassal of the Assyrian realm. "Menahem gave Pul a thousand talents of silver, that his hand might be with him to confirm the kingdom in his hand. And Menahem exacted the money of Israel, even of all the mighty men of wealth, of each man fifty shekels of silver, to give to the king of Assyria." 2 Kings 15:19, 20. The Assyrians, having humbled the ten tribes, returned for a season to their own land.

Menahem, far from repenting of the evil that had wrought ruin in his kingdom, continued in "the sins of Jeroboam the son of Nebat, who made Israel to sin." Pekahiah and Pekah, his successors, also "did that which was evil in the sight of the Lord." Verses 18, 24, 28. "In the days of Pekah," who reigned twenty years, Tiglath-pileser, king of Assyria, invaded Israel and carried away with him a multitude of captives from among the tribes living in Galilee and east of the Jordan. "The Reubenites, and the Gadites, and the half tribe of Manasseh," with others of the inhabitants of "Gilead, and Galilee, all the land of Naphtali" (1 Chronicles 5:26; 2

Kings 15:29), were scattered among the heathen in lands far removed from Palestine.

From this terrible blow the northern kingdom never recovered. The feeble remnant continued the forms of government, though no longer possessed of power. Only one more ruler, Hoshea, was to follow Pekah. Soon the kingdom was to 288 be swept away forever. But in that time of sorrow and distress God still remembered mercy, and gave the people another opportunity to turn from idolatry. In the third year of Hoshea's reign, good King Hezekiah began to rule in Judah and as speedily as possible instituted important reforms in the temple service at Jerusalem. A Passover celebration was arranged for, and to this feast were invited not only the tribes of Judah and Benjamin, over which Hezekiah had been anointed king, but all the northern tribes as well. A proclamation was sounded "throughout all Israel, from Beersheba even to Dan, that they should come to keep the Passover unto the Lord God of Israel at Jerusalem: for they had not done it of a long time in such sort as it was written.

"So the posts went with the letters from the king and his princes throughout all Israel and Judah," with the pressing invitation, "Ye children of Israel, turn again unto the Lord God of Abraham, Isaac, and Israel, and He will return to the remnant of you, that are escaped out of the hand of the kings of Assyria. . . . Be ye not stiff-necked, as your fathers were, but yield yourselves unto the Lord, and enter into His sanctuary, which He hath sanctified forever: and serve the Lord your God, that the fierceness of His wrath may turn away from you. For if ye turn again unto the Lord, your brethren and your children shall find compassion before them that lead them captive, so that they shall come again into this land: for the Lord your God is gracious and merciful, and will not turn away His face from you, if ye return unto Him." 2 Chronicles 30:5-9.

"From city to city through the country of 291 Ephraim and Manasseh even unto Zebulun," the couriers sent out by Hezekiah carried the message. Israel should have recognized in this invitation an appeal to repent and turn to God. But the remnant of the ten tribes still dwelling within the territory of the once-flourishing northern kingdom treated the royal messengers from Judah with indifference and even with contempt. "They laughed them to scorn, and mocked them." There were a few, however, who gladly responded. "Divers of Asher and Manasseh and of Zebulun humbled themselves, and came to Jerusalem, . . . to keep the feast of unleavened bread." Verses 10-13.

About two years later, Samaria was invested by the hosts of Assyria under Shalmaneser; and in the siege that followed, multitudes perished miserably of hunger and disease as well as by the sword. The city and nation fell, and the broken remnant of the ten tribes were carried away captive and scattered in the provinces of the Assyrian realm.

The destruction that befell the northern kingdom was a direct judgment from Heaven. The Assyrians were merely the instruments that God used to carry out His purpose. Through Isaiah, who began to prophesy shortly before the fall of Samaria, the Lord referred to the Assyrian hosts as "the rod of Mine anger." "The staff in their hand," He said, "is Mine indignation." Isaiah 10:5.

Grievously had the children of Israel "sinned against the Lord their God, . . . and wrought wicked things." "They would not hear, but . . . rejected His statutes; and His covenant that He made with their fathers, and His testimonies which He testified against them." It was because they had "left all the commandments of the Lord their God, and made them molten images, even two calves, and made a grove, and worshiped all the host of heaven, and served Baal," and refused steadfastly to repent, that the Lord "afflicted them, and delivered them into the hand of spoilers, until He had cast them out of His sight," in harmony with the plain warnings He had sent them "by all His servants the prophets."

"So was Israel carried away out of their own land to Assyria," "because they obeyed not the voice of the Lord their God, but transgressed His covenant, and all that Moses the servant of the Lord commanded." 2 Kings 17:7, 11, 14-16, 20, 23; 18:12.

In the terrible judgments brought upon the ten tribes the Lord had a wise and merciful purpose. That which He could no longer do through them in the land of their fathers He would seek to accomplish by scattering them among the heathen. His plan for the salvation of all who should choose to avail themselves of pardon through the Saviour of the human race must yet be fulfilled; and in the afflictions brought upon Israel, He was preparing the way for His glory to be revealed to the nations of earth. Not all who were carried captive were impenitent. Among them were some who had remained true to God, and others who had humbled themselves before Him. Through these, "the sons of the living God" (Hosea 1:10), He would bring multitudes in the Assyrian realm to a knowledge of the attributes of His character and the beneficence of His law.

24

"Destroyed for Lack of Knowledge"

God's favor toward Israel had always been conditional on their obedience. At the foot of Sinai they had entered into covenant relationship with Him as His "peculiar treasure . . . above all people." Solemnly they had promised to follow in the path of obedience. "All that the Lord hath spoken we will do," they had said. Exodus 19:5, 8. And when, a few days afterward, God's law was spoken from Sinai, and additional instruction in the form of statutes and judgments was communicated through Moses, the Israelites with one voice had again promised, "All the words which the Lord hath said will we do." At the ratification of the covenant, the people had once more united in declaring, "All that the Lord hath said will we do, and be obedient." Exodus 24:3, 7. God had chosen Israel as His people, and they had chosen Him as their King.

Near the close of the wilderness wandering the conditions of the covenant had been repeated. At Baalpeor, on the very borders of the Promised Land, where many fell a prey to subtle temptation, those who remained faithful renewed their vows of allegiance. Through Moses they were warned against the temptations that would assail them in the future; and they were earnestly exhorted to remain separate from the surrounding nations and to worship God alone.

"Now therefore hearken," Moses had instructed Israel, "unto the statutes and unto the judgments, which I teach you, for to do them, that ye may live, and go in and possess the land which the Lord God of your fathers giveth you. Ye shall not add unto the word which I command you, neither shall ye diminish aught from it, that ye may keep the commandments of the Lord your God which I command you. . . . Keep therefore and do them; for this is your wisdom and your understanding in the sight of the nations, which shall hear all these statutes, and say, Surely this great nation is a wise and understanding people." Deuteronomy 4:1-6.

The Israelites had been specially charged not to lose sight of the commandments of God, in obedience to which they would find strength and blessing. "Take heed to thyself, and keep thy soul diligently," had been the word of the Lord to them through Moses, "lest thou forget the things which thine eyes have seen, and lest they depart from thy heart all the days of thy life: but teach them thy sons, and thy sons' sons." Verse 9. The awe-inspiring scenes connected with the giving of the law at Sinai were never to be forgotten. Plain and decided were the warnings that had been given Israel against the idolatrous customs prevailing among the neighboring nations. "Take ye . . . good heed unto yourselves," was the counsel given; "lest ye corrupt yourselves, and make you a graven image, the similitude of any figure," "and lest thou lift up thine eyes unto heaven, and when thou seest the sun, and the moon, and the stars, even all the host of heaven, shouldest be driven to worship them, and serve them, which the Lord thy God hath divided unto all nations under the whole heaven." "Take heed unto yourselves, lest ye forget the covenant of the Lord your God, which He made with you, and make you a graven image, or the likeness of anything, which the Lord thy God hath forbidden thee." Verses 15, 16, 19, 23.

Moses traced the evils that would result from a departure from the statutes of Jehovah. Calling heaven and earth to witness, he declared that if, after having dwelt long in the Land of Promise, the people should introduce corrupt forms of worship and bow down to graven images and should refuse to return to the worship of the true God, the anger of the Lord would be aroused, and they would be carried away captive and scattered among the heathen. "Ye shall soon utterly perish from off the land whereunto ye go over Jordan to possess it," he warned them; "ye shall not prolong your days upon it, but shall utterly be destroyed. And the Lord shall scatter you among the nations, and ye shall be left few in number among the heathen, whither the Lord shall lead you. And there ye shall serve gods, the work of men's hands, wood and stone, which neither see, nor hear, nor eat, nor smell." Verses 26-28.

This prophecy, fulfilled in part in the time of the judges, met a more complete and literal fulfillment in the captivity of Israel in Assyria and of Judah in Babylon.

The apostasy of Israel had developed gradually. From generation to generation, Satan had made repeated attempts to cause the chosen nation to forget "the commandments, the statutes, and the judgments" that they had promised to keep forever. Deuteronomy 6:1. He knew that if he could only lead Israel to forget God, and to "walk after other gods, and serve them, and worship them," they would "surely perish." Deuteronomy 8:19.

The enemy of God's church upon the earth had not, however, taken fully into account the compassionate nature of Him who "will by no means clear the guilty," yet whose glory it is to be "merciful and gracious, long-suffering, and abundant in goodness and truth, keeping mercy for thousands, forgiving iniquity and transgression and sin." Exodus 34:6, 7. Despite the efforts of Satan to thwart God's purpose for Israel, nevertheless even in some of the darkest hours of their history, when it seemed as if the forces of evil were about to gain the victory, the Lord graciously revealed Himself. He spread before Israel the things that were for the welfare of the nation. "I have written to him the great things of My law," He declared through Hosea, "but they were counted as a strange thing. "I taught Ephraim also to go, taking them by their arms; but they knew not that I healed them." Hosea 8:12; 11:3. Tenderly had the Lord dwelt with them, instructing them by His prophets line upon line, precept upon precept.

Had Israel heeded the messages of the prophets, they would have been spared the humiliation that followed. It was because they had persisted in turning aside from His law that God was compelled to let them go into captivity. "My people are destroyed for lack of knowledge," was His message to them through Hosea. "Because thou hast rejected knowledge, I will also reject thee: . . . seeing thou hast forgotten the law of thy God." Hosea 4:6.

In every age, transgression of God's law has been followed by the same result. In the days of Noah, when every principle of rightdoing was violated, and iniquity became so deep and widespread that God could no longer bear with it, the decree went forth, "I will destroy man whom I have created from the face of the earth." Genesis 6:7. In Abraham's day the people of Sodom openly defied God and His law; and there followed the same wickedness, the same corruption, the same unbridled indulgence, that had marked the antediluvian world. The inhabitants of Sodom passed the limits of divine forbearance, and there was kindled against them the fire of God's vengeance.

The time preceding the captivity of the ten tribes of Israel was one of similar disobedience and of similar wickedness. God's law was counted as a thing of nought, and this opened the floodgates of iniquity upon Israel. "The Lord hath a controversy with the inhabitants of the land," Hosea declared, "because there is no truth, nor mercy, nor knowledge of God in the land. By swearing, and lying, and killing, and stealing, and committing adultery, they break out, and blood toucheth blood." Hosea 4:1, 2.

The prophecies of judgment delivered by Amos and Hosea were accompanied by predictions of future glory. To the ten tribes, long rebellious and impenitent, was given no promise of complete restoration to their former power in Palestine. Until the end of time, they were to be "wanderers among the nations." But through Hosea was given a prophecy that set before them the privilege of having a part in the final restoration that is to be made to the people of God at the close of earth's history, when Christ shall appear as King of kings and Lord of lords. "Many days," the prophet declared, the ten tribes were to abide "without a king, and without a prince, and without a sacrifice, and without an image, and without an ephod, and without teraphim." "Afterward," the prophet continued, "shall the children of Israel return, and seek the Lord their God, and David their king; and shall fear the Lord and His goodness in the latter days." Hosea 3:4, 5.

In symbolic language Hosea set before the ten tribes God's plan of restoring to every penitent soul who would unite with His church on earth, the blessings granted Israel in the days of their loyalty to Him in the Promised Land. Referring to Israel as one to whom He longed to show mercy, the Lord declared, "I will allure her, and bring her into the wilderness, and speak comfortably unto her. And I will give her her vineyards from thence, and the valley of Achor for a door of hope: and she shall sing there, as in the days of her youth, and as in the day when she came up out of the land of Egypt. And it shall be at that day, saith the Lord, that thou shalt call 299 Me Ishi ["My husband," margin]; and shalt call Me no more Baali ["My lord," margin]. For I will take away the names of Baalim out of her mouth, and they shall no more be remembered by their name." Hosea 2:14-17.

In the last days of this earth's history, God's covenant with His commandment-keeping people is to be renewed. "In that day will I make a covenant for them with the beasts of the field, and with the fowls of heaven, and with the creeping things of the ground: and I will break the bow and the sword and the battle out of the earth, and will make them to lie down safely. And I will betroth thee unto Me forever; yea, I will betroth thee unto Me in righteousness, and in judgment, and in loving-kindness, and in mercies. I will even betroth thee unto Me in faithfulness: and thou shalt know the Lord.

"And it shall come to pass in that day, I will hear, saith the Lord, I will hear the heavens, and they shall hear the earth; and the earth shall hear the corn, and the wine, and the oil; and they shall hear Jezreel; and I will sow her unto Me in the earth; and I will have mercy upon her that had not obtained mercy; and I will say to them which were not My people, Thou art My people; and they shall say, Thou art my God." Verses 18-23.

"In that day" "the remnant of Israel, and such as are escaped of the house of Jacob, . . . shall stay upon the Lord, the Holy One of Israel, in truth." Isaiah 10:20. From "every nation, and kindred, and tongue, and people" there will be some who will gladly respond to the message, "Fear God, and give glory to Him; for the hour of His judgment is come." They will turn from 300 every idol that binds them to earth, and will "worship Him that made heaven, and earth, and the sea, and the fountains of waters." They will

free themselves from every entanglement and will stand before the world as monuments of God's mercy. Obedient to the divine requirements, they will be recognized by angels and by men as those that have kept "the commandments of God, and the faith of Jesus." Revelation 14:6, 7, 12.

"Behold, the days come, saith the Lord, that the plowman shall overtake the reaper, and the treader of grapes him that soweth seed; and the mountains shall drop sweet wine, and all the hills shall melt. And I will bring again the captivity of My people of Israel, and they shall build the waste cities, and inhabit them; and they shall plant vineyards, and drink the wine thereof; they shall also make gardens, and eat the fruit of them. And I will plant them upon their land, and they shall no more be pulled up out of their land which I have given them, saith the Lord thy God." Amos 9:13-15.

SECTION III

A PREACHER OF
RIGHTEOUSNESS

"Shall the prey be taken from the mighty, or the lawful captive delivered?" "Thus saith the Lord, Even the captives of the mighty shall be taken away, and the prey of the terrible shall be delivered." "They shall be greatly ashamed, that trust in graven images, that say to the molten images, Ye are our gods." Isaiah 49:24, 25; 42:17.

25
303

The Call of Isaiah

The long reign of Uzziah [also known as Azariah] in the land of Judah and Benjamin was characterized by a prosperity greater than that of any other ruler since the death of Solomon, nearly two centuries before. For many years the king ruled with discretion. Under the blessing of Heaven his armies regained some of the territory that had been lost in former years. Cities were rebuilt and fortified, and the position of the nation among the surrounding peoples was greatly strengthened. Commerce revived, and the riches of the nations flowed into Jerusalem. Uzziah's name "spread far abroad; for he was marvellously helped, till he was strong." 2 Chronicles 26:15.

This outward prosperity, however, was not accompanied by a corresponding revival of spiritual power. The temple services were continued as in former years, and multitudes assembled to worship the living God; but pride and formality gradually took the place of humility and sincerity. Of Uzziah himself it is written: "When he was strong, his heart was lifted up to his destruction: for he transgressed against the Lord his God." Verse 16.

The sin that resulted so disastrously to Uzziah was one of presumption. In violation of a plain command of Jehovah, that none but the descendants of Aaron should officiate as priests, the king entered the sanctuary "to burn incense upon the altar." Azariah the high priest and his associates remonstrated, and pleaded with him to turn from his purpose. "Thou hast trespassed," they urged; "neither shall it be for thine honor." Verses 16, 18.

Uzziah was filled with wrath that he, the king, should be thus rebuked. But he was not permitted to profane the sanctuary against the united protest of those in authority. While standing there, in wrathful rebellion, he was suddenly smitten with a divine judgment. Leprosy appeared on his forehead. In dismay he fled, never again to enter the temple courts. Unto the day of his death, some years later, Uzziah remained a leper—a living example of the folly of departing from a plain "Thus saith the Lord." Neither his exalted position nor his long life of service could be pleaded as an excuse for the presumptuous sin by which he marred the closing years of his reign, and brought upon himself the judgment of Heaven.

God is no respecter of persons. "The soul that doeth aught presumptuously, whether he be born in the land, or a stranger, the same reproacheth the Lord; and that soul shall be cut off from among his people." Numbers 15:30.

The judgment that befell Uzziah seemed to have a restraining influence on his son. Jotham bore heavy responsibilities during the later years of his father's reign and succeeded to the throne after Uzziah's death. Of Jotham it is written: "He did that which was right in the sight of the Lord: he did according to all that his father Uzziah had done. Howbeit the high places were not removed: the people sacrificed and burned incense still in the high places." 2 Kings 15:34, 35.

The reign of Uzziah was drawing to a close, and Jotham was already bearing many of the burdens of state, when Isaiah, of the royal line, was called, while yet a young man, to the prophetic mission. The times in which Isaiah was to labor were fraught with peculiar peril to the people of God. The prophet was to witness the invasion of Judah by the combined armies of northern Israel and of Syria; he was to behold the Assyrian hosts encamped before the chief cities of the kingdom. During his lifetime, Samaria was to fall, and the ten tribes of Israel were to be scattered among the nations. Judah was again and again to be invaded by the Assyrian armies, and Jerusalem was to suffer a siege that would have resulted in her downfall had not God miraculously interposed. Already grave perils were threatening the peace of the southern kingdom. The divine protection was being removed, and the Assyrian forces were about to overspread the land of Judah.

But the dangers from without, overwhelming though they seemed, were not so serious as the dangers from within. It was the perversity of his people that brought to the Lord's servant the greatest perplexity and the deepest depression. By their apostasy and rebellion those who should have been standing as light bearers among the nations were inviting the judgments of God. Many of the evils which were hastening the swift destruction of the northern kingdom, and which had recently been denounced in unmistakable terms by Hosea and Amos, were fast corrupting the kingdom of Judah.

The outlook was particularly discouraging as regards the social conditions of the people. In their desire for gain, men were adding house to house and field to field. See Isaiah 5:8. Justice was perverted, and no pity was shown the poor. Of these evils God declared, "The spoil of the poor is in your houses." "Ye beat My people to pieces, and grind the faces of the poor." Isaiah 3:14, 15. Even the magistrates, whose duty it was to protect the helpless, turned a deaf ear to the cries of the poor and needy, the widows and the fatherless. See Isaiah 10:1, 2.

With oppression and wealth came pride and love of display, gross drunkenness, and a spirit of revelry. See Isaiah 2:11, 12; 3:16, 18-23; 5:22, 11, 12. And in Isaiah's day idolatry itself no longer provoked surprise. See Isaiah 2:8, 9. Iniquitous practices had become so prevalent among all classes that the few who remained true to God were often tempted to lose heart and to give way to discouragement and despair. It seemed as if God's purpose for Israel were about to fail and that the rebellious nation was to suffer a fate similar to that of Sodom and Gomorrah.

In the face of such conditions it is not surprising that when, during the last year of Uzziah's reign, Isaiah was called to bear to Judah God's messages of warning and reproof, he shrank from the responsibility. He well knew that he would encounter obstinate resistance. As he realized his own inability to meet the situation and thought of the stubbornness and unbelief of the people for whom he was to labor, his task seemed hopeless. Should he in despair relinquish his mission and leave Judah undisturbed to their idolatry? Were the gods of Nineveh to rule the earth in defiance of the God of heaven?

Such thoughts as these were crowding through Isaiah's mind as he stood under the portico of the temple. Suddenly the gate and the inner veil of the temple seemed to be uplifted or withdrawn, and he was permitted to gaze within, upon the holy of holies, where even the prophet's feet might not enter. There rose up before him a vision of Jehovah sitting upon a throne high and lifted up, while the train of His glory filled the temple. On each side of the throne hovered the seraphim, their faces veiled in adoration, as they ministered before their Maker and united in the solemn invocation, "Holy, holy, holy, is the Lord of hosts: the whole earth is full of His glory," until post and pillar and cedar gate seemed shaken with the sound, and the house was filled with their tribute of praise. Isaiah 6:3.

As Isaiah beheld this revelation of the glory and majesty of his Lord, he was overwhelmed with a sense of the purity and holiness of God. How sharp the contrast between the matchless perfection of his Creator, and the sinful course of those who, with himself, had long been numbered among the chosen people of Israel and Judah! "Woe is me!" he cried; "for I am undone; because I am a man of unclean lips, and I dwell in the midst of a people of unclean lips: for mine eyes have seen the King, the Lord of hosts." Verse 5. Standing, as it were, in the full light of the divine presence within the inner sanctuary, he realized that if left to his own imperfection and inefficiency, he would be utterly unable to accomplish the mission to which he had been called. But a seraph was sent to relieve him of his distress and to fit him for his great mission. A living coal from the altar was laid upon his lips, with the words, "Lo, this hath touched thy lips; and thine iniquity is taken away, and thy sin purged." Then the voice of God was heard saying, "Whom shall I send, and who will go for Us?" and Isaiah responded, "Here am I; send me." Verses 7, 8.

The heavenly visitant bade the waiting messenger, "Go, and tell this people,

"Hear ye indeed, but understand not;
And see ye indeed, but perceive not.
Make the heart of this people fat,
And make their ears heavy, and shut their eyes;
Lest they see with their eyes, and hear with their ears,
And understand with their heart,
And convert, and be healed."

Verses 9, 10.

The prophet's duty was plain; he was to lift his voice in protest against the prevailing evils. But he dreaded to undertake the work without some assurance of hope. "Lord, how long?" he inquired. Verse 11. Are none of Thy chosen people ever to understand and repent and be healed?

His burden of soul in behalf of erring Judah was not to be borne in vain. His mission was not to be wholly fruitless. Yet the evils that had been multiplying for many generations could not be removed in his day. Throughout his lifetime he must be a patient, courageous teacher— a prophet of hope as well as of doom. The divine purpose finally accomplished, the full fruitage of his efforts, and of the labors of all God's faithful messengers, would appear. A remnant should be saved. That this might be brought about, the messages of warning and entreaty were to be delivered to the rebellious nation, the Lord declared:

"Until the cities be wasted without inhabitant,
And the houses without man,
And the land be utterly desolate,
And the Lord have removed men far away,
And there be a great forsaking in the midst of the land."

Verses 11, 12.

The heavy judgments that were to befall the impenitent,—war, exile, oppression, the loss of power and prestige among the nations,—all these were to come in order that those who would recognize in them the hand of an offended God might be led to repent. The ten tribes of the northern kingdom were soon to be scattered among the nations and their cities left desolate; the destroying armies of hostile nations were to sweep over their land again and again; even Jerusalem was finally to fall, and Judah was to be carried away captive; yet the Promised Land was not to remain wholly forsaken forever. The assurance of the heavenly visitant to Isaiah was:

"In it shall be a tenth,
And it shall return, and shall be eaten:
As a teil tree, and as an oak,
Whose substance is in them, when they cast their leaves:
So the holy seed shall be the substance thereof."

Verse 13.

This assurance of the final fulfillment of God's purpose brought courage to the heart of Isaiah. What though earthly powers array themselves against Judah? What though the Lord's messenger meet with opposition and resistance? Isaiah had seen the King, the Lord of hosts; he had heard the song of the seraphim, "The whole earth is full of His glory;" he had the promise that the messages of Jehovah to backsliding Judah would be accompanied by the convicting power of the Holy Spirit; and the prophet was nerved for the work before him. Verse 3. Throughout his long and arduous mission he carried with him the memory of this vision. For sixty years or more he stood before the children of Judah as a prophet of hope, waxing bolder and still bolder in his predictions of the future triumph of the church.

26

"Behold Your God!"

In Isaiah's day the spiritual understanding of mankind was dark through misapprehension of God. Long had Satan sought to lead men to look upon their Creator as the author of sin and suffering and death. Those whom he had thus deceived, imagined that God was hard and exacting. They regarded Him as watching to denounce and condemn, unwilling to receive the sinner so long as there was a legal excuse for not helping him. The law of love by which heaven is ruled had been misrepresented by the archdeceiver as a restriction upon men's happiness, a burdensome yoke from which they should be glad to escape. He declared that its precepts could not be obeyed and that the penalties of transgression were bestowed arbitrarily.

In losing sight of the true character of Jehovah, the Israelites were without excuse. Often had God revealed Himself to them as one "full of compassion, and gracious, long-suffering, and plenteous in mercy and truth." Psalm 86:15. "When Israel was a child," He testified, "then I loved him, and called My son out of Egypt." Hosea 11:1.

Tenderly had the Lord dealt with Israel in their deliverance from Egyptian bondage and in their journey to the Promised Land. "In all their affliction He was afflicted, and the angel of His presence saved them: in His love and in His pity He redeemed them; and He bare them, and carried them all the days of old." Isaiah 63:9.

"My presence shall go with thee," was the promise given during the journey through the wilderness. Exodus 33:14. This assurance was accompanied by a marvelous revelation of Jehovah's character, which enabled Moses to proclaim to all Israel the goodness of God, and to instruct them fully concerning the attributes of their invisible King. "The Lord passed by before him, and proclaimed, The Lord, The Lord God, merciful and gracious, long-suffering, and abundant in goodness and truth, keeping mercy for thousands, forgiving iniquity and transgression and sin, and that will by no means clear the guilty." Exodus 34:6, 7.

It was upon his knowledge of the long-sufferance of Jehovah and of His infinite love and mercy, that Moses based his wonderful plea for the life of Israel when, on the borders of the Promised Land, they refused to advance in obedience to the command of God. At the height of their rebellion the Lord had declared, "I will smite them with the pestilence, and disinherit them;" and He had proposed to make of the descendants of Moses "a greater nation and mightier than they." Numbers 14:12. But the prophet pleaded the marvelous providences and promises of God in behalf of the chosen nation. And then, as the strongest of all pleas, he urged the love of God for fallen man. See verses 17-19.

Graciously the Lord responded, "I have pardoned according to thy word." And then He imparted to Moses, in the form of a prophecy, a knowledge of His purpose concerning the final triumph of Israel. "As truly as I live," He declared, "all the earth shall be filled with the glory of the Lord." Verses 20, 21. God's glory, His character, His merciful kindness and tender love—that which Moses had pleaded in behalf of Israel—were to be revealed to all mankind. And this promise of Jehovah was made doubly sure; it was confirmed by an oath. As surely as God lives and reigns, His glory should be declared "among the heathen, His wonders among all people." Psalm 96:3.

It was concerning the future fulfillment of this prophecy that Isaiah had heard the shining seraphim singing before the throne, "The whole earth is full of His glory." Isaiah 6:3. The prophet, confident of the certainty of these words, himself afterward boldly declared of those who were bowing down to images of wood and stone, "They shall see the glory of the Lord, and the excellency of our God." Isaiah 35:2.

Today this prophecy is meeting rapid fulfillment. The missionary activities of the church of God on earth are bearing rich fruitage, and soon the gospel message will have been proclaimed to all nations. "To the praise of the glory of His grace," men and women from every kindred, tongue, and people are being made "accepted in the Beloved," "that in the ages to come He might show the exceeding riches of His grace in His kindness toward us through Christ Jesus." Ephesians 1:6; 2:7. "Blessed be the Lord God, the God of Israel, who only doeth wondrous things. And blessed be His glorious name forever: and let the whole earth be filled with His glory." Psalm 72:18, 19.

In the vision that came to Isaiah in the temple court, he was given a clear view of the character of the God of Israel. "The high and lofty One that inhabiteth eternity, whose name is Holy," had appeared before him in great majesty; yet the prophet was made to understand the compassionate nature of his Lord. He who dwells "in the high and holy place" dwells "with him also that is of a contrite and humble spirit, to revive the spirit of the humble, and to revive the heart of the contrite ones." Isaiah 57:15. The angel commissioned to touch Isaiah's lips had brought to him the message, "Thine iniquity is taken away, and thy sin purged." Isaiah 6:7.

In beholding his God, the prophet, like Saul of Tarsus at the gate of Damascus, had not only been given a view of his own unworthiness; there had come to his humbled heart the assurance of forgiveness, full and free; and he had arisen a changed man. He had seen his Lord. He had caught a glimpse of the loveliness of the divine character. He could testify of the transformation wrought through beholding Infinite Love. Henceforth he was inspired with longing desire to see erring Israel set free from the burden and penalty of sin. "Why should ye be stricken any more?" the prophet inquired. "Come now, and let us reason together, saith the Lord: though your sins be as scarlet, they shall be as white as snow; though they be red like crimson, they shall be as wool." "Wash you, make you clean; put away the evil of your doings from before Mine eyes; cease to do evil; learn to do well." Isaiah 1:5, 18, 16, 17.

The God whom they had been claiming to serve, but whose character they had misunderstood, was set before them as the great Healer of spiritual disease. What though the whole head was sick and the whole heart faint? what though from the sole of the foot even unto the crown of the head there was no soundness, but wounds, and bruises, and putrefying sores? See Isaiah 1:6. He who had been walking frowardly in the way of his heart might find healing by turning to the Lord. "I have seen his ways," the Lord declared, "and will heal him: I will lead him also, and restore comforts unto him. . . . Peace, peace to him that is far off, and to him that is near, saith the Lord; and I will heal him." Isaiah 57:18, 19.

The prophet exalted God as Creator of all. His message to the cities of Judah was, "Behold your God!" Isaiah 40:9. "Thus saith God the Lord, He that created the heavens, and stretched them out; He that spread forth the earth, and that which cometh out of it;" "I am the Lord that maketh all things;" "I form the light, and create darkness;" "I have made the earth, and created man upon it: I, even My hands, have stretched out the heavens, and all their host have I commanded." Isaiah 42:5; 44:24; 45:7, 12. "To whom then will ye liken Me, or shall I be equal? saith the Holy One. Lift up your eyes on high, and behold who hath created these things, that bringeth out their host by number: He calleth them all by names by the greatness of His might, for that He is strong in power; not one faileth." Isaiah 40:25, 26.

To those who feared they would not be received if they should return to God, the prophet declared:

"Why sayest thou, O Jacob, and speakest, O Israel, My way is hid from the Lord, and my judgment is passed over from my God? Hast thou not known? hast thou not heard, that the everlasting God, the Lord, the Creator of the ends of the earth, fainteth not, neither is weary? there is no searching of His understanding. He giveth power to the faint; and to them that have no might He increaseth strength. Even the youths shall faint and be weary, and the young men shall utterly fall: but they that wait upon the Lord shall renew their strength; they shall mount up with wings as eagles; they shall run, and not be weary; and they shall walk, and not faint." Verses 27-31.

The heart of Infinite Love yearns after those who feel powerless to free themselves from the snares of Satan; and He graciously offers to strengthen them to live for Him. "Fear thou not," He bids them; "for I am with thee: be not dismayed; for I am thy God: I will strengthen thee; yea, I will help thee; yea, I will uphold thee with the right hand of My righteousness." "I the Lord thy God will hold thy right hand, saying unto thee, Fear not; I will help thee. Fear not, thou worm Jacob, and ye men of Israel; I will help thee, saith the Lord, and thy Redeemer, the Holy One of Israel." Isaiah 41:10, 13, 14.

The inhabitants of Judah were all undeserving, yet God would not give them up. By them His name was to be exalted among the heathen. Many who were wholly unacquainted with His attributes were yet to behold the glory of the divine character. It was for the purpose of making plain His merciful designs that He kept sending His servants the prophets with the message, "Turn ye again now everyone from his evil way." Jeremiah 25:5. "For My name's sake," He declared through Isaiah, "will I defer Mine anger, and for My praise will I refrain for thee, that I cut thee not off." "For Mine own sake, even for Mine own sake, will I do it: for how should My name be polluted? and I will not give My glory unto another." Isaiah 48:9, 11.

The call to repentance was sounded with unmistakable clearness, and all were invited to return. "Seek ye the Lord while He may be found," the prophet pleaded; "call ye upon Him while He is near: let the wicked forsake his way, and the unrighteous man his thoughts: and let him return unto the Lord, and He will have mercy upon him; and to our God, for He will abundantly pardon." Isaiah 55:6, 7.

Have you, reader, chosen your own way? Have you wandered far from God? Have you sought to feast upon the fruits of transgression, only to find them turn to ashes upon your lips? And now, your life plans thwarted and your hopes dead, do you sit alone and desolate? That voice which has long been speaking to your heart, but to which you would not listen, comes to you distinct and clear, "Arise ye, and depart; for this is not your rest: because it is polluted, it shall destroy you, even with a sore destruction."

Micah 2:10. Return to your Father's house. He invites you, saying, "Return unto Me; for I have redeemed thee." "Come unto Me: hear, and your soul shall live; and I will make an everlasting covenant with you, even the sure mercies of David." Isaiah 44:22; 55:3.

Do not listen to the enemy's suggestion to stay away from Christ until you have made yourself better, until you are good enough to come to God. If you wait until then you will never come. When Satan points to your filthy garments, repeat the promise of the Saviour, "Him that cometh to Me I will in no wise cast out." John 6:37. Tell the enemy that the blood of Jesus Christ cleanses from all sin. Make the prayer of David your own: "Purge me with hyssop, and I shall be clean: wash me, and I shall be whiter than snow." Psalm 51:7.

The exhortations of the prophet to Judah to behold the living God, and to accept His gracious offers, were not in vain. There were some who gave earnest heed, and who turned from their idols to the worship of Jehovah. They learned to see in their Maker love and mercy and tender compassion. And in the dark days that were to come in the history of Judah, when only a remnant were to be left in the land, the prophet's words were to continue bearing fruit in decided reformation. "At that day," declared Isaiah, "shall a man look to his Maker, and his eyes shall have respect to the Holy One of Israel. And he shall not look to the altars, the work of his hands, neither shall respect that which his fingers have made, either the groves, or the images." Isaiah 17:7, 8.

321   Many were to behold the One altogether lovely, the chiefest among ten thousand. "Thine eyes shall see the King in His beauty," was the gracious promise made them. Isaiah 33:17. Their sins were to be forgiven, and they were to make their boast in God alone. In that glad day of redemption from idolatry they would exclaim, "The glorious Lord will be unto us a place of broad rivers and streams. . . . The Lord is our judge, the Lord is our lawgiver, the Lord is our king; He will save us." Verses 21, 22.

The messages borne by Isaiah to those who chose to turn from their evil ways were full of comfort and encouragement. Hear the word of the Lord through His prophet:

"Remember these, O Jacob and Israel;
For thou art My servant:
I have formed thee; thou art My servant:
O Israel, thou shalt not be forgotten of Me.
I have blotted out, as a thick cloud, thy transgressions,
And, as a cloud, thy sins:
Return unto Me; for I have redeemed thee."
                                        Isaiah 44:21, 22.

"In that day thou shalt say,
O Lord, I will praise Thee:
Though Thou wast angry with me,
Thine anger is turned away, and Thou comfortedst me.

"Behold, God is my salvation;
I will trust, and not be afraid:
For the Lord Jehovah is my strength and my song;
He also is become my salvation. . . .

"Sing unto the Lord; for He hath done excellent things:
This is known in all the earth.
Cry out and shout, thou inhabitant of Zion:
For great is the Holy One of Israel in the midst of thee."
                                        Isaiah 12.

27

Ahaz

The accession of Ahaz to the throne brought Isaiah and his associates face to face with conditions more appalling than any that had hitherto existed in the realm of Judah. Many who had formerly withstood the seductive influence of idolatrous practices were now being persuaded to take part in the worship of heathen deities. Princes in Israel were proving untrue to their trust; false prophets were arising with messages to lead astray; even some of the priests were teaching for hire. Yet the leaders in apostasy still kept up the forms of divine worship and claimed to be numbered among the people of God.

The prophet Micah, who bore his testimony during those troublous times, declared that sinners in Zion, while claiming to "lean upon the Lord," and blasphemously boasting, "Is not the Lord among us? none evil can come upon us," continued to "build up Zion with blood, and Jerusalem with iniquity." Micah 3:11, 10. Against these evils the prophet Isaiah lifted his voice in stern rebuke: "Hear the word of the Lord, ye rulers of Sodom; give ear unto the law of our God, ye people of Gomorrah. To what purpose is the multitude of your sacrifices unto Me? saith the Lord. . . . When ye come to appear before Me, who hath required this at your hand, to tread My courts?" Isaiah 1:10-12.

Inspiration declares, "The sacrifice of the wicked is abomination: how much more, when he bringeth it with a wicked mind?" Proverbs 21:27. The God of heaven is "of purer eyes than to behold evil," and cannot "look on iniquity." Habakkuk 1:13. It is not because He is unwilling to forgive that He turns from the transgressor; it is because the sinner refuses to make use of the abundant provisions of grace, that God is unable to deliver from sin. "The Lord's hand is not shortened, that it cannot save; neither His ear heavy, that it cannot hear: but your iniquities have separated between you and your God, and your sins have hid His face from you, that He will not hear." Isaiah 59:1, 2.

Solomon had written, "Woe to thee, O land, when thy king is a child!" Ecclesiastes 10:16. Thus it was with the land of Judah. Through continued transgression her rulers had become as children. Isaiah called the attention of the people to the weakness of their position among the nations of earth, and he showed that this was the result of wickedness in high places. "Behold," he said, "the Lord, the Lord of hosts, doth take away from Jerusalem and from Judah the stay and the staff, the whole stay of bread, and the whole stay of water, the mighty man, and the man of war, the judge, and the prophet, 324 and the prudent, and the ancient, the captain of fifty, and the honorable man, and the counselor, and the cunning artificer, and the eloquent orator. And I will give children to be their princes, and babes shall rule over them." "For Jerusalem is ruined, and Judah is fallen: because their tongue and their doings are against the Lord." Isaiah 3:1-4, 8.

"They which lead thee," the prophet continued, "cause thee to err, and destroy the way of thy paths." Verse 12. During the reign of Ahaz this was literally true; for of him it is written: "He walked in the ways of the kings of Israel, and made also molten images for Baalim. Moreover he burnt incense in the valley of the son of Hinnom;" "yea, and made his son to pass through the fire, according to the abominations of the heathen, whom the Lord cast out from before the children of Israel." 2 Chron. 28:2, 3; 2 Kings 16:3.

This was indeed a time of great peril for the chosen nation. Only a few short years, and the ten tribes of the kingdom of Israel were to be scattered among the nations of heathendom. And in the kingdom of Judah also the outlook was dark. The forces for good were rapidly diminishing, the forces for evil multiplying. The prophet Micah, viewing the situation, was constrained to exclaim: "The good man is perished out of the earth: and there is none upright among men." "The best of them is as a brier: the most upright is sharper than a thorn hedge." Micah 7:2, 4. "Except the Lord of hosts had left unto us a very small remnant," declared Isaiah, "we should have been as Sodom, and . . . Gomorrah." Isaiah 1:9.

In every age, for the sake of those who have remained true, as well as because of His infinite 325 love for the erring, God has borne long with the rebellious, and has urged them to forsake their course of evil and return to Him. "Precept upon precept; line upon line, . . . here a little, and there a little," through men of His appointment, He has taught transgressors the way of righteousness. Isaiah 28:10.

And thus it was during the reign of Ahaz. Invitation upon invitation was sent to erring Israel to return to their allegiance to Jehovah. Tender were the pleadings of the prophets; and as they stood before the people, earnestly exhorting to repentance and reformation, their words bore fruit to the glory of God.

Through Micah came the wonderful appeal, "Hear ye now what the Lord saith; Arise, contend thou before the mountains, and let the hills hear thy voice. Hear ye, O mountains, the Lord's controversy, and ye strong foundations of the earth: for the Lord hath a controversy with His people, and He will plead with Israel.

"O My people, what have I done unto thee? and wherein have I wearied thee? testify against Me. For I brought thee up out of the land of Egypt, and redeemed thee out of the house of servants; and I sent before thee Moses, Aaron, and Miriam.

"O My people, remember now what Balak king of Moab consulted, and what Balaam the son of Beor answered him from Shittim unto Gilgal; that ye may know the righteousness of the Lord." Micah 6:1-5.

The God whom we serve is long-suffering; "His compassions fail not." Lamentations 3:22. Throughout the period of probationary time His Spirit is entreating men to accept the gift of life. 326 "As I live, saith the Lord God, I have no pleasure in the death of the wicked; but that the wicked turn from his way and live: turn ye, turn ye from your evil ways; for why will ye die?" Ezekiel 33:11. It is Satan's special device to lead man into sin and then leave him there, helpless and hopeless, fearing to seek for pardon. But God invites, "Let him take hold of My strength, that he may make peace with Me; and he shall make peace with Me." Isaiah 27:5. In Christ every provision has been made, every encouragement offered.

In the days of apostasy in Judah and Israel, many were inquiring: "Wherewith shall I come before the Lord, and bow myself before the high God? shall I come before Him with burnt offerings, with calves of a year old? will the Lord be pleased with thousands of rams, or with ten thousands of rivers of oil?" The answer is plain and positive: "He hath showed thee, O man, what is good; and what doth the Lord require of thee, but to do justly, and to love mercy, and to walk humbly with thy God?" Micah 6:6-8.

In urging the value of practical godliness, the prophet was only repeating the counsel given Israel centuries before. Through Moses, as they were about to enter the Promised Land, the word of the Lord had been: "And now, Israel, what doth the Lord thy God require of thee, but to fear the Lord thy God, to walk in all His ways, and to love Him, and to serve the Lord thy God with all thy heart and with all thy soul, to keep the commandments of the Lord, and His statutes, which I command thee this day for thy good?" Deuteronomy 10:12, 13. From age to age these counsels were repeated by the servants of Jehovah to those who were in danger of falling into habits of formalism and of forgetting to show mercy. When Christ Himself, during His earthly ministry, was approached by a lawyer with the question, "Master, which is the great commandment in the law?" Jesus said to him, "Thou shalt love the Lord thy God with all thy heart, and with all thy soul, and with all thy mind. This is the first and great commandment. And the second is like unto it, Thou shalt love thy neighbor as thyself. On these two commandments hang all the law and the prophets." Matthew 22:36-40.

These plain utterances of the prophets and of the Master Himself, should be received by us as the voice of God to every soul. We should lose no opportunity of performing deeds of mercy, of tender forethought and Christian courtesy, for the burdened and the oppressed. If we can do no more, we may speak words of courage and hope to those who are unacquainted with God, and who can be approached most easily by the avenue of sympathy and love.

Rich and abundant are the promises made to those who are watchful of opportunities to bring joy and blessing into the lives of others. "If thou draw out thy soul to the hungry, and satisfy the afflicted soul; then shall thy light rise in obscurity, and thy darkness be as the noonday: and the Lord shall guide thee continually, and satisfy thy soul in drought, and make fat thy bones: and thou shalt be like a watered garden, and like a spring of water, whose waters fail not." Isaiah 58:10, 11.

The idolatrous course of Ahaz, in the face of the earnest appeals of the prophets, could have but one result. "The wrath of the Lord was upon Judah and Jerusalem, and He . . . delivered them to trouble, to astonishment, and to hissing." 2 Chronicles 29:8. The kingdom suffered a rapid decline, and its very existence was soon imperiled by invading armies. "Rezin king of Syria and Pekah son of Remaliah king of Israel came up to Jerusalem to war: and they besieged Ahaz." 2 Kings 16:5.

Had Ahaz and the chief men of his realm been true servants of the Most High, they would have had no fear of so unnatural an alliance as had been formed against them. But repeated transgression had shorn them of strength. Stricken with a nameless dread of the retributive judgments of an offended God, the heart of the king "was moved, and the heart of his people, as the trees of the wood are moved with the wind."

Isaiah 7:2. In this crisis the word of the Lord came to Isaiah, bidding him meet the trembling king and say:

"Take heed, and be quiet; fear not, neither be fainthearted . . . . Because Syria, Ephraim, and the son of Remaliah, have taken evil counsel against thee, saying, Let us go up against Judah, and vex it, and let us make a breach therein for us, and set a king in the midst of it: . . . thus saith the Lord God, It shall not stand, neither shall it come to pass." The prophet declared that the kingdom of Israel, and Syria as well, would soon come to an end. "If ye will not believe," he concluded, "surely ye shall not be established." Verses 4-7, 9.

Well would it have been for the kingdom of Judah had Ahaz received this message as from heaven. But choosing to lean on the arm of flesh, he sought help from the heathen. In desperation he sent word to Tiglath-pileser, king of Assyria: "I am thy servant and thy son: come up, and save me out of the hand of the king of Syria, and out of the hand of the king of Israel, which rise up against me." 2 Kings 16:7. The request was accompanied by a rich present from the king's treasure and from the temple storehouse.

The help asked for was sent, and King Ahaz was given temporary relief, but at what a cost to Judah! The tribute offered aroused the cupidity of Assyria, and that treacherous nation soon threatened to overflow and spoil Judah. Ahaz and his unhappy subjects were now harassed by the fear of falling completely into the hands of the cruel Assyrians.

"The Lord brought Judah low" because of continued transgression. In this time of chastisement Ahaz, instead of repenting, trespassed "yet more against the Lord: . . . for he sacrificed unto the gods of Damascus." "Because the gods of the kings of Syria help them," he said, "therefore will I sacrifice to them, that they may help me." 2 Chronicles 28:19, 22, 23.

As the apostate king neared the end of his reign, he caused the doors of the temple to be closed. The sacred services were interrupted. No longer were the candlesticks kept burning before the altar. No longer were offerings made for the sins of the people. No longer did sweet incense ascend on high at the time of the morning and the evening sacrifice. Deserting the courts of the house of God and locking fast its doors, the inhabitants of the godless city boldly set up altars for the worship of heathen deities on the street corners throughout Jerusalem. Heathenism had seemingly triumphed; the powers of darkness had well-nigh prevailed.

But in Judah there dwelt some who maintained their allegiance to Jehovah, steadfastly refusing to be led into idolatry. It was to these that Isaiah and Micah and their associates looked in hope as they surveyed the ruin wrought during the last years of Ahaz. Their sanctuary was closed, but the faithful ones were assured: "God is with us." "Sanctify the Lord of hosts Himself; and let Him be your fear, and let Him be your dread. And He shall be for a sanctuary." Isaiah 8:10, 13, 14.

331

28

Hezekiah

In sharp contrast with the reckless rule of Ahaz was the reformation wrought during the prosperous reign of his son. Hezekiah came to the throne determined to do all in his power to save Judah from the fate that was overtaking the northern kingdom. The messages of the prophets offered no encouragement to halfway measures. Only by most decided reformation could the threatened judgments be averted.

In the crisis, Hezekiah proved to be a man of opportunity. No sooner had he ascended the throne than he began to plan and to execute. He first turned his attention to the restoration of the temple services, so long neglected; and in this work he earnestly solicited the co-operation of a band of priests and Levites who had remained true to their sacred calling. Confident of their loyal support, he spoke with them freely concerning his desire to institute immediate and far-reaching reforms. "Our fathers have trespassed," he confessed, "and done that which was evil in the eyes of the Lord our God, and have forsaken Him, and have turned away their faces from the habitation of the Lord." "Now it is in mine heart to make a covenant with the Lord God of Israel, that His fierce wrath may turn away from us." 2 Chronicles 29:6, 10.

332

In a few well-chosen words the king reviewed the situation they were facing—the closed temple and the cessation of all services within its precincts; the flagrant idolatry practiced in the streets of the city and throughout the kingdom; the apostasy of multitudes who might have remained true to God had the leaders in Judah set before them a right example; and the decline of the kingdom and loss of prestige in the estimation of surrounding nations. The northern kingdom was rapidly crumbling to pieces; many were perishing by the sword; a multitude had already been carried away captive; soon Israel would fall completely into the hands of the Assyrians, and be utterly ruined; and this fate would surely befall Judah as well, unless God should work mightily through chosen representatives.

Hezekiah appealed directly to the priests to unite with him in bringing about the necessary reforms; "Be not now negligent," he exhorted them; "for the Lord hath chosen you to stand before Him, to serve Him, and that ye should minister unto Him, and burn incense." "Sanctify now yourselves, and sanctify the house of the Lord God of your fathers." Verses 11, 5.

It was a time for quick action. The priests began at once. Enlisting the co-operation of others of their number who had not been present during this conference, they engaged heartily in the work of cleansing and sanctifying the temple. Because of the years of desecration and neglect, this was attended with many difficulties; but the priests and the Levites labored untiringly, and within a remarkably short time they were able to report their task completed. The temple doors had been repaired and thrown open; the sacred vessels had been assembled and put into place; and all was in readiness for the re-establishment of the sanctuary services.

333

In the first service held, the rulers of the city united with King Hezekiah and with the priests and Levites in seeking forgiveness for the sins of the nation. Upon the altar were placed sin offerings "to make an atonement for all Israel." "And when they had made an end of offering, the king and all that were present with him bowed themselves, and worshiped." Once more the temple courts resounded with words of praise and adoration. The songs of David and of Asaph were sung with joy, as the worshipers realized that they were being delivered from the bondage of sin and apostasy. "Hezekiah rejoiced, and all the people, that God had prepared the people: for the thing was done suddenly." Verses 24, 29, 36.

God had indeed prepared the hearts of the chief men of Judah to lead out in a decided reformatory movement, that the tide of apostasy might be stayed. Through His prophets He had sent to His chosen people message after message of earnest entreaty—messages that had been despised and rejected by the ten tribes of the kingdom of Israel, now given over to the enemy. But in Judah there remained a goodly remnant, and to these the prophets continued to appeal. Hear Isaiah urging, "Turn ye unto Him from whom the children of Israel have deeply revolted." Isaiah 31:6. Hear Micah declaring with confidence: "I will look unto the Lord; I will wait for the God of my salvation: my God will hear me. Rejoice not against me, O mine enemy: when I fall, I shall arise; when I sit in darkness, the Lord shall be a light unto me. I will bear the indignation of the Lord, because I have sinned against Him, until He plead my cause, and execute judgment for me: He will bring me forth to the light, and I shall behold His righteousness." Micah 7:7-9.

334

These and other like messages revealing the willingness of God to forgive and accept those who turned to Him with full purpose of heart, had brought hope to many a fainting soul in the dark years when the temple doors remained closed; and now, as the leaders began to institute a reform, a multitude of the people, weary of the thralldom of sin, were ready to respond.

Those who entered the temple courts to seek forgiveness and to renew their vows of allegiance to Jehovah, had wonderful encouragement offered them in the prophetic portions of Scripture. The solemn warnings against idolatry, spoken through Moses in the hearing of all Israel, had been accompanied by prophecies of God's willingness to hear and forgive those who in times of apostasy should seek Him with all the heart. "If thou turn to the Lord thy God," Moses had said, "and shalt be obedient unto His voice; (for the Lord thy God is a merciful God;) He will not forsake thee, neither destroy thee, nor forget the covenant of thy fathers which He sware unto them." Deuteronomy 4:30, 31.

335   And in the prophetic prayer offered at the dedication of the temple whose services Hezekiah and his associates were now restoring, Solomon had prayed, "When Thy people Israel be smitten down before the enemy, because they have sinned against Thee, and shall turn again to Thee, and confess Thy name, and pray, and make supplication unto Thee in this house: then hear Thou in heaven, and forgive the sin of Thy people Israel." 1 Kings 8:33, 34. The seal of divine approval had been placed upon this prayer; for at its close fire had come down from heaven to consume the burnt offering and the sacrifices, and the glory of the Lord had filled the temple. See 2 Chronicles 7:1. And by night the Lord had appeared to Solomon to tell him that his prayer had been heard, and that mercy would be shown those who should worship there. The gracious assurance was given: "If My people, which are called by My name, shall humble themselves, and pray, and seek My face, and turn from their wicked ways; then will I hear from heaven, and will forgive their sin, and will heal their land." Verse 14.

These promises met abundant fulfillment during the reformation under Hezekiah.

The good beginning made at the time of the purification of the temple was followed by a broader movement, in which Israel as well as Judah participated. In his zeal to make the temple services a real blessing to the people, Hezekiah determined to revive the ancient custom of gathering the Israelites together for the celebration of the Passover feast.

For many years the Passover had not been observed as a national festival. The division of
336   the kingdom after the close of Solomon's reign had made this seem impracticable. But the terrible judgments befalling the ten tribes were awakening in the hearts of some a desire for better things; and the stirring messages of the prophets were having their effect. By royal couriers the invitation to the Passover at Jerusalem was heralded far and wide, "from city to city through the country of Ephraim and

Manasseh even unto Zebulun." The bearers of
337   the gracious invitation were usually repulsed. The impenitent turned lightly aside; nevertheless some, eager to seek God for a clearer knowledge of His will, "humbled themselves, and came to Jerusalem." 2 Chronicles 30:10, 11.

In the land of Judah the response was very general; for upon them was "the hand of God," "to give them one heart to do the commandment of the king and of the princes"—a command in accord with the will of God as revealed through His prophets. Verses 22, 21.

The occasion was one of the greatest profit to the multitudes assembled. The desecrated streets of the city were cleared of the idolatrous shrines placed there during the reign of Ahaz. On the appointed day the Passover was observed, and the week was spent by the people in offering peace offerings and in learning what God would have them do. Daily the Levites "taught the good knowledge of the Lord;" and those who had prepared their hearts to seek God, found pardon. A great gladness took possession of the worshiping multitude; "the Levites and the priests praised the Lord day by day, singing with loud instruments;" all were united in their desire to praise Him who had proved so gracious and merciful. Verse 12.

The seven days usually allotted to the Passover feast passed all too quickly, and the worshipers determined to spend another seven days in learning more fully the way of the Lord. The teaching priests continued their work of instruction from the book of the law; daily the people assembled at the temple to offer their tribute of praise and thanksgiving; and as the great meeting drew to a close, it was evident
338   that God had wrought marvelously in the conversion of backsliding Judah and in stemming the tide of idolatry which threatened to sweep all before it. The solemn warnings of the prophets had not been uttered in vain. "There was great joy in Jerusalem: for since the time of Solomon the son of David king of Israel there was not the like in Jerusalem." Verse 26.

The time had come for the return of the worshipers to their homes. "The priests the Levites arose and blessed the people: and their voice was heard, and their prayer came up to His holy dwelling place, even unto heaven." Verse 27. God had accepted those who with broken hearts had confessed their sins and with resolute purpose had turned to Him for forgiveness and help.

There now remained an important work in which those who were returning to their homes must take an active part, and the accomplishment of this work bore evidence to the genuineness of the reformation wrought. The record reads: "All Israel that were present went out to the cities of Judah, and brake the images in pieces, and cut down the groves, and threw down the high places and the altars out of all Judah and Benjamin, in Ephraim also and Manasseh, until they had utterly destroyed them all. Then all the children of Israel returned, every man to his possession, into their own cities." 2 Chronicles 31:1.

Hezekiah and his associates instituted various reforms for the upbuilding of the spiritual and temporal interests of the kingdom. "Throughout all Judah" the king "wrought that which was good and right and truth before the Lord his God. And in every work that he began, . . . he did it with all his heart, and prospered." "He trusted in the Lord God of Israel, . . . and departed not from following Him, but kept His commandments, which the Lord commanded Moses. And the Lord was with him; and he prospered." Verses 20, 21; 2 Kings 18:5-7.

The reign of Hezekiah was characterized by a series of remarkable providences which revealed to the surrounding nations that the God of Israel was with His people. The success of the Assyrians in capturing Samaria and in scattering the shattered remnant of the ten tribes among the nations, during the earlier portion of his reign, was leading many to question the power of the God of the Hebrews. Emboldened by their successes, the Ninevites had long since set aside the message of Jonah and had become defiant in their opposition to the purposes of Heaven. A few years after the fall of Samaria the victorious armies reappeared in Palestine, this time directing their forces against the fenced cities of Judah, with some measure of success; but they withdrew for a season because of difficulties arising in other portions of their realm. Not until some years later, toward the close of Hezekiah's reign, was it to be demonstrated before the nations of the world whether the gods of the heathen were finally to prevail.

29

The Ambassadors From Babylon

In the midst of his prosperous reign King Hezekiah was suddenly stricken with a fatal malady. "Sick unto death," his case was beyond the power of man to help. And the last vestige of hope seemed removed when the prophet Isaiah appeared before him with the message, "Thus saith the Lord, Set thine house in order: for thou shalt die, and not live." Isaiah 38:1.

The outlook seemed utterly dark; yet the king could still pray to the One who had hitherto been his "refuge and strength, a very present help in trouble." Psalm 46:1. And so "he turned his face to the wall, and prayed unto the Lord, saying, I beseech Thee, O Lord, remember now how I have walked before Thee in truth and with a perfect heart, and have done that which is good in Thy sight. And Hezekiah wept sore." 2 Kings 20:2, 3.

Since the days of David there had reigned no king who had wrought so mightily for the upbuilding of the kingdom of God in a time of apostasy and discouragement as had Hezekiah. The dying ruler had served his God faithfully, and had strengthened the confidence of the people in Jehovah as their Supreme Ruler. And, like David, he could now plead:

"Let my prayer come before Thee:
Incline Thine ear unto my cry;
For my soul is full of troubles:
And my life draweth nigh unto the grave."
Psalm 88:2, 3.

"Thou art my hope, O Lord God:
Thou art my trust from my youth.
By Thee have I been holden up."
"Forsake me not when my strength faileth."
"O God, be not far from me:
O my God, make haste for my help."
"O God, forsake me not;
Until I have showed Thy strength unto this generation,
And Thy power to everyone that is to come."
Psalm 71:5, 6, 9, 12, 18.

He whose "compassions fail not," heard the prayer of His servant. Lamentations 3:22. "It came to pass, afore Isaiah was gone out into the middle court, that the word of the Lord came to him, saying, Turn again, and tell Hezekiah the captain of My people, Thus saith the Lord, the God of David thy father, I have heard thy prayer, I have seen thy tears: behold, I will heal thee: on the third day thou shalt go up unto the house of the Lord. And I will add unto thy days fifteen years; and I will deliver thee and this city out of the hand of the king of Assyria; and I will defend this city for Mine own sake, and for My servant David's sake." 2 Kings 20:4-6.

Gladly the prophet returned with the words of assurance and hope. Directing that a lump of figs be laid upon the diseased part, Isaiah delivered to the king the message of God's mercy and protecting care.

Like Moses in the land of Midian, like Gideon in the presence of the heavenly messenger, like Elisha just before the ascension of his master, Hezekiah pleaded for some sign that the message was from heaven. "What shall be the sign," he inquired of the prophet, "that the Lord will heal me, and that I shall go up into the house of the Lord the third day?"

"This sign shalt thou have of the Lord," the prophet answered, "that the Lord will do the thing that He hath spoken: shall the shadow go forward ten degrees, or go back ten degrees?"

"It is a light thing," Hezekiah replied, "for the shadow to go down ten degrees: nay, but let the shadow return backward ten degrees."

Only by the direct interposition of God could the shadow on the sundial be made to turn back ten degrees; and this was to be the sign to Hezekiah that the Lord had heard his prayer. Accordingly, "the prophet cried unto the Lord: and He brought the shadow ten degrees backward, by which it had gone down in the dial of Ahaz." Verses 8-11.

Restored to his wonted strength, the king of Judah acknowledged in words of song the mercies of Jehovah, and vowed to spend his remaining days in willing service to the King of kings. His grateful recognition of God's compassionate dealing with him is an inspiration to all who desire to spend their years to the glory of their Maker.

343 "I said
In the cutting off of my days,
I shall go to the gates of the grave:
I am deprived of the residue of my years.

"I said,
I shall not see the Lord, even the Lord, in the land of the living:
I shall behold man no more with the inhabitants of the world.

"Mine age is departed,
And is removed from me as a shepherd's tent:

"I have cut off like a weaver my life:
He will cut me off with pining sickness:

"From day even to night wilt Thou make an end of me.
I reckoned till morning, that,
As a lion, so will He break all my bones:

"From day even to night wilt Thou make an end of me.
Like a crane or a swallow, so did I chatter:
I did mourn as a dove:
Mine eyes fail with looking upward:
O Lord, I am oppressed; undertake for me.

"What shall I say?
He hath both spoken unto me,
And Himself hath done it:
I shall go softly all my years in the bitterness of my soul.

"O Lord, by these things men live,
And in all these things is the life of my spirit:
So wilt Thou recover me, and make me to live.

"Behold, for peace I had great bitterness:
But Thou hast in love to my soul delivered it

from the pit of corruption:
For Thou hast cast all my sins behind Thy back.

"For the grave cannot praise Thee,
Death cannot celebrate Thee:
They that go down into the pit cannot hope for Thy truth.

"The living, the living, he shall praise Thee, 344
As I do this day:
The father to the children shall make known Thy truth.

"The Lord was ready to save me:
Therefore we will sing my songs to the stringed instruments
All the days of our life in the house of the Lord."

Isaiah 38:10-20.

In the fertile valleys of the Tigris and the Euphrates there dwelt an ancient race which, though at that time subject to Assyria, was destined to rule the world. Among its people were wise men who gave much attention to the study of astronomy; and when they noticed that the shadow on the sundial had been turned back ten degrees, they marveled greatly. Their king, Merodachbaladan, upon learning that this miracle had been wrought as a sign to the king of Judah that the God of heaven had granted him a new lease of life, sent ambassadors to Hezekiah to congratulate him on his recovery and to learn, if possible, more of the God who was able to perform so great a wonder.

The visit of these messengers from the ruler of a faraway land gave Hezekiah an opportunity to extol the living God. How easy it would have been for him to tell them of God, the upholder of all created things, through whose favor his own life had been spared when all other hope had fled! What momentous transformations might have taken place had these seekers after truth from the plains of Chaldea been led to acknowledge the supreme sovereignty of the living God!

But pride and vanity took possession of Hezekiah's heart, and in self-exaltation he laid open to covetous eyes the treasures with which 345 God had enriched His people. The king "showed them the house of his precious things, the silver, and the gold, and the spices, and the precious ointment, and all the house of his armor, and all that was found in his treasures: there was nothing in his house, nor in all his dominion, that Hezekiah showed them not." Isaiah 39:2. Not to glorify God did he do this, but to exalt himself in the eyes of the foreign princes. He did not stop to consider that these men were representatives of a powerful nation that had not the fear nor the love of God in their hearts, and that it was imprudent to make them his confidants concerning the temporal riches of the nation.

The visit of the ambassadors to Hezekiah was a test of his gratitude and devotion. The record says, "Howbeit in the business of the ambassadors of the princes of Babylon, who sent unto him to inquire of the wonder that was done in the land, God left him, to try him, that He might know all that was in his heart." 2 Chronicles 32:31. Had Hezekiah improved the opportunity given him to bear witness to the power, the goodness, the compassion, of the God of Israel, the report of the ambassadors would have been as light piercing darkness. But he magnified himself above the Lord of hosts. He "rendered not again according to the benefit done unto him; for his heart was lifted up." Verse 25.

How disastrous the results which were to follow! To Isaiah it was revealed that the returning ambassadors were carrying with them a report of the riches they had seen, and that the king of Babylon and his counselors would plan to enrich their own country with the treasures of Jerusalem. Hezekiah had grievously sinned; "therefore there was wrath upon him, and upon Judah and Jerusalem." Verse 25.

"Then came Isaiah the prophet unto King Hezekiah, and said unto him, What said these men? and from whence came they unto thee? And Hezekiah said, They are come from a far country unto me, even from Babylon. Then said he, What have they seen in thine house? And Hezekiah answered, All that is in mine house have they seen: there is nothing among my treasures that I have not showed them.

"Then said Isaiah to Hezekiah, Hear the word of the Lord of hosts: Behold, the days come, that all that is in thine house, and that which thy fathers have laid up in store until this day, shall be carried to Babylon: nothing shall be left, saith the Lord. And of thy sons that shall issue from thee, which thou shalt beget, shall they take away; and they shall be eunuchs in the palace of the king of Babylon.

"Then said Hezekiah to Isaiah, Good is the word of the Lord which thou hast spoken." Isaiah 39:3-8.

Filled with remorse, "Hezekiah humbled himself for the pride of his heart, both he and the inhabitants of Jerusalem, so that the wrath of the Lord came not upon them in the days of Hezekiah." 2 Chronicles 32:26. But the evil seed had been sown and in time was to spring up and yield a harvest of desolation and woe. During his remaining years the king of Judah was to have much prosperity because of his steadfast purpose to redeem the past and to bring honor to the name of the God whom he served; yet his faith was to be severely tried, and he was to learn that only by putting his trust fully in Jehovah could he hope to triumph over the powers of darkness that were plotting his ruin and the utter destruction of his people.

The story of Hezekiah's failure to prove true to his trust at the time of the visit of the ambassadors is fraught with an important lesson for all. Far more than we do, we need to speak of the precious chapters in our experience, of the mercy and loving-kindness of God, of the matchless depths of the Saviour's love. When mind and heart are filled with the love of God, it will not be difficult to impart that which enters into the spiritual life. Great thoughts, noble aspirations, clear perceptions of truth, unselfish purposes, yearnings for piety and holiness, will find expression in words that reveal the character of the heart treasure.

Those with whom we associate day by day need our help, our guidance. They may be in such a condition of mind that a word spoken in season will be as a nail in a sure place. Tomorrow some of these souls may be where we can never reach them again. What is our influence over these fellow travelers?

Every day of life is freighted with responsibilities which we must bear. Every day, our words and acts are making impressions upon those with whom we associate. How great the need that we set a watch upon our lips and guard carefully our steps! One reckless movement, one imprudent step, and the surging waves of some strong temptation may sweep a soul into the downward path. We cannot gather up the thoughts we have planted in human minds. If they have been evil, we may have set in motion a train of circumstances, a tide of evil, which we are powerless to stay.

On the other hand, if by our example we aid others in the development of good principles, we give them power to do good. In their turn they exert the same beneficial influence over others. Thus hundreds and thousands are helped by our unconscious influence. The true follower of Christ strengthens the good purposes of all with whom he comes in contact. Before an unbelieving, sin-loving world he reveals the power of God's grace and the perfection of His character.

30

Deliverance From Assyria

In a time of grave national peril, when the hosts of Assyria were invading the land of Judah and it seemed as if nothing could save Jerusalem from utter destruction, Hezekiah rallied the forces of his realm to resist with unfailing courage their heathen oppressors and to trust in the power of Jehovah to deliver. "Be strong and courageous, be not afraid nor dismayed for the king of Assyria, nor for all the multitude that is with him," Hezekiah exhorted the men of Judah; "for there be more with us than with him: with him is an arm of flesh; but with us is the Lord our God to help us, and to fight our battles." 2 Chronicles 32:7, 8.

It was not without reason that Hezekiah could speak with certainty of the outcome. The boastful Assyrian, while used by God for a season as the rod of His anger for the punishment of the nations, was not always to prevail. See Isaiah 10:5. "Be not afraid of the Assyrian," had been the message of the Lord through Isaiah some years before to those that dwelt in Zion; "for yet a very little while, . . . and the Lord of hosts shall stir up a scourge for him according to the slaughter of Midian at the rock of Oreb: and as His rod was upon the sea, so shall He lift it up after the manner of Egypt. And it shall come to pass in that day, that his burden shall be taken away from off thy shoulder, and his yoke from off thy neck, and the yoke shall be destroyed because of the anointing." Verses 24-27.

In another prophetic message, given "in the year that King Ahaz died," the prophet had declared: "The Lord of hosts hath sworn, saying, Surely as I have thought, so shall it come to pass; and as I have purposed, so shall it stand: that I will break the Assyrian in My land, and upon My mountains tread him underfoot: then shall his yoke depart from off them, and his burden depart from off their shoulders. This is the purpose that is purposed upon the whole earth: and this is the hand that is stretched out upon all the nations. For the Lord of hosts hath purposed, and who shall disannul it? and His hand is stretched out, and who shall turn it back?" Isaiah 14:28, 24-27.

The power of the oppressor was to be broken. Yet Hezekiah, in the earlier years of his reign, had continued to pay tribute to Assyria, in harmony with the agreement entered into by Ahaz. Meanwhile the king had taken "counsel with his princes and his mighty men," and had done everything possible for the defense of his kingdom. He had made sure of a bountiful supply of water within the walls of Jerusalem, while without the city there should be a scarcity. "Also he strengthened himself, and built up all the wall that was broken, and raised it up to the towers, and another wall without, and repaired Millo in the city of David, and made darts and shields in abundance. And he set captains of war over the people." 2 Chronicles 32:3, 5, 6. Nothing had been left undone that could be done in preparation for a siege.

At the time of Hezekiah's accession to the throne of Judah, the Assyrians had already carried captive a large number of the children of Israel from the northern kingdom; and a few years after he had begun to reign, and while he

was still strengthening the defenses of Jerusalem, the Assyrians besieged and captured Samaria and scattered the ten tribes among the many provinces of the Assyrian realm. The borders of Judah were only a few miles distant, with Jerusalem less than fifty miles away; and the rich spoils to be found within the temple would tempt the enemy to return.

But the king of Judah had determined to do his part in preparing to resist the enemy; and, having accomplished all that human ingenuity and energy could do, he had assembled his forces and had exhorted them to be of good courage. "Great is the Holy One of Israel in the midst of thee" had been the message of the prophet Isaiah to Judah; and the king with unwavering faith now declared, "With us is the Lord our God to help us, and to fight our battles." Isaiah 12:6; 2 Chronicles 32:8.

Nothing more quickly inspires faith than the exercise of faith. The king of Judah had prepared for the coming storm; and now, confident that the prophecy against the Assyrians would be fulfilled, he stayed his soul upon God. "And the people rested themselves upon the words of Hezekiah." 2 Chronicles 32:8. What though the armies of Assyria, fresh from the conquest of the greatest nations of earth, and triumphant over Samaria in Israel, should now turn their forces against Judah? What though they should boast, "As my hand hath found the kingdoms of the idols, and whose graven images did excel them of Jerusalem and of Samaria; shall I not, as I have done unto Samaria and her idols, so do to Jerusalem and her idols?" Isaiah 10:10, 11. Judah had nothing to fear; for their trust was in Jehovah.

The long-expected crisis finally came. The forces of Assyria, advancing from triumph to triumph, appeared in Judea. Confident of victory, the leaders divided their forces into two armies, one of which was to meet the Egyptian army to the southward, while the other was to besiege Jerusalem.

Judah's only hope was now in God. All possible help from Egypt had been cut off, and no other nations were near to lend a friendly hand.

The Assyrian officers, sure of the strength of their disciplined forces, arranged for a conference with the chief men of Judah, during which they insolently demanded the surrender of the city. This demand was accompanied by blasphemous revilings against the God of the Hebrews. Because of the weakness and apostasy of Israel and Judah, the name of God was no longer feared among the nations, but had become a subject for continual reproach. See Isaiah 52:5.

"Speak ye now to Hezekiah," said Rabshakeh, one of Sennacherib's chief officers, "Thus saith the great king, the king of Assyria, What confidence is this wherein thou trustest? Thou sayest, (but they are but vain words,) I have counsel and strength for the war. Now on whom dost thou trust, that thou rebellest against me?" 2 Kings 18:19, 20.

The officers were conferring outside the gates of the city, but within the hearing of the sentries on the wall; and as the representatives of the Assyrian king loudly urged their proposals upon the chief men of Judah, they were requested to speak in the Syrian rather than the Jewish language, in order that those upon the wall might not have knowledge of the proceedings of the conference. Rabshakeh, scorning this suggestion, lifted his voice still higher, and, continuing to speak in the Jewish language, said:

"Hear ye the words of the great king, the king of Assyria. Thus saith the king, Let not Hezekiah deceive you: for he shall not be able to deliver you. Neither let Hezekiah make you trust in the Lord, saying, The Lord will surely deliver us: this city shall not be delivered into the hand of the king of Assyria.

"Hearken not to Hezekiah: for thus saith the king of Assyria, Make an agreement with me by a present, and come out to me: and eat ye every-one of his vine, and everyone of his fig tree, and drink ye everyone the waters of his own cistern; until I come and take you away to a land like your own land, a land of corn and wine, a land of bread and vineyards.

"Beware lest Hezekiah persuade you, saying, The Lord will deliver us. Hath any of the gods of the nations delivered his land out of the hand of the king of Assyria? Where are the gods of Hamath and Arphad? where are the gods of Sepharvaim? and have they delivered Samaria out of my hand? Who are they among all the 354 gods of these lands, that have delivered their land out of my hand, that the Lord should deliver Jerusalem out of my hand?" Isaiah 36:13-20.

To these taunts the children of Judah "answered him not a word." The conference was at an end. The Jewish representatives returned to Hezekiah "with their clothes rent, and told him the words of Rabshakeh." Verses 21, 22. The king, upon learning of the blasphemous challenge, "rent his clothes, and covered himself with sackcloth, and went into the house of the Lord." 2 Kings 19:1.

A messenger was dispatched to Isaiah to inform him of the outcome of the conference. "This day is a day of trouble, and of rebuke, and blasphemy," was the word the king sent. "It may be the Lord thy God will hear all the words of Rabshakeh, whom the king of Assyria his master hath sent to reproach the living God; and will reprove the words which the Lord thy God hath heard: wherefore lift up thy prayer for the remnant that are left." Verses 3, 4.

"For this cause Hezekiah the king, and the prophet Isaiah the son of Amoz, prayed and cried to Heaven." 2 Chronicles 32:20.

God answered the prayers of His servants. To Isaiah was given the message for Hezekiah:

"Thus saith the Lord, Be not afraid of the words which thou hast heard, with which the servants of the king of Assyria have blasphemed Me. Behold, I will send a blast upon him, and he shall hear a rumor, and shall return to his own land; and I will cause him to fall by the sword in his own land." 2 Kings 19:6, 7.

The Assyrian representatives, after taking leave of the chief men of Judah, communicated direct with their king, who was with the division 355 of his army guarding the approach from Egypt. Upon hearing the report, Sennacherib wrote "letters to rail on the Lord God of Israel, and to speak against Him, saying, As the gods of the nations of other lands have not delivered their people out of mine hand, so shall not the God of Hezekiah deliver His people out of mine hand." 2 Chronicles 32:17.

The boastful threat was accompanied by the message: "Let not thy God in whom thou trustest deceive thee, saying, Jerusalem shall not be delivered into the hand of the king of Assyria. Behold, thou hast heard what the kings of Assyria have done to all lands, by destroying them utterly: and shalt thou be delivered? Have the gods of the nations delivered them which my fathers have destroyed; as Gozan, and Haran, and Rezeph, and the children of Eden which were in Thelasar? Where is the king of Hamath, and the king of Arpad, and the king of the city of Sepharvaim, of Hena, and Ivah?" 2 Kings 19:10-13.

When the king of Judah received the taunting letter, he took it into the temple and "spread it before the Lord" and prayed with strong faith for help from heaven, that the nations of earth might know that the God of the Hebrews still lived and reigned. Verse 14. The honor of Jehovah was at stake; He alone could bring deliverance.

"O Lord God of Israel, which dwellest between the cherubims," Hezekiah pleaded, "Thou art the God, even Thou alone, of all the kingdoms of the earth; Thou hast made heaven and earth. Lord, bow down Thine ear, and hear: open, Lord, Thine eyes, and see: and hear the words of Sennacherib, which hath sent him to 356 reproach the living God. Of a truth, Lord, the kings of Assyria have destroyed the nations and their lands, and have cast their gods into the fire: for they were no gods, but the work of men's hands, wood and stone: therefore they have destroyed them. Now therefore, O Lord our God, I beseech Thee, save Thou us out of his hand, that all the kingdoms of the earth may know that Thou art the Lord God, even Thou only." 2 Kings 19:15-19.

"Give ear, O Shepherd of Israel,
Thou that leadest Joseph like a flock;
Thou that dwellest between the cherubims,
shine forth.

Before Ephraim and Benjamin and Manasseh
stir up Thy strength,
And come and save us.
Turn us again, O God,
And cause Thy face to shine; and we shall be
saved.

"O Lord God of hosts,
How long wilt Thou be angry against the
prayer of Thy people?
Thou feedest them with the bread of tears;
And givest them tears to drink in great mea-
sure.
Thou makest us a strife unto our neighbors:
And our enemies laugh among themselves.
Turn us again, O God of hosts,
And cause Thy face to shine; and we shall be
saved.

"Thou hast brought a vine out of Egypt:
Thou hast cast out the heathen, and planted it.
Thou preparedst room before it,
And didst cause it to take deep root, and it
filled the land.
The hills were covered with the shadow of it,
And the boughs thereof were like the goodly
cedars.
She sent out her boughs unto the sea,
And her branches unto the river.

359 "Why hast Thou then broken down her
hedges,
So that all they which pass by the way do
pluck her?
The boar out of the wood doth waste it,
And the wild beast of the field doth devour it.
Return, we beseech Thee, O God of hosts:
Look down from heaven, and behold, and
visit this vine;
And the vineyard which Thy right hand hath
planted,
And the branch that Thou madest strong for
Thyself. . . .

"Quicken us, and we will call upon Thy name.
Turn us again, O Lord God of hosts,
Cause Thy face to shine; and we shall be
saved."

Psalm 80.

Hezekiah's pleadings in behalf of Judah
and of the honor of their Supreme Ruler were
in harmony with the mind of God. Solomon,
in his benediction at the dedication of the
temple, had prayed the Lord to maintain "the
cause of His people Israel at all times, as the
matter shall require: that all the people of the
earth may know that the Lord is God, and that
there is none else." 1 Kings 8:59, 60. Especially was the Lord to show favor when, in
times of war or of oppression by an army, the
chief men of Israel should enter the house of
prayer and plead for deliverance. Verses 33,
34.

Hezekiah was not left without hope. Isaiah
sent to him, saying, "Thus saith the Lord God of
Israel, That which thou hast prayed to Me
against Sennacherib king of Assyria I have
heard. This is the word that the Lord hath spoken concerning him:
"The virgin the daughter of Zion hath
despised thee, and laughed thee to scorn; the
daughter of Jerusalem hath shaken her head at
thee.
"Whom hast thou reproached and blasphemed? and against whom hast thou exalted
thy voice, and lifted up thine eyes on high? even
against the Holy One of Israel. By thy messen- 360
gers thou hast reproached the Lord, and hast
said, With the multitude of my chariots I am
come up to the height of the mountains, to the
sides of Lebanon, and will cut down the tall
cedar trees thereof, and the choice fir trees
thereof: and I will enter into the lodgings of his
borders, and into the forest of his Carmel. I have
digged and drunk strange waters, and with the
sole of my feet have I dried up all the rivers of
besieged places.
"Hast thou not heard long ago how I have
done it, and of ancient times that I have formed
it? now have I brought it to pass, that thou
shouldest be to lay waste fenced cities into
ruinous heaps. Therefore their inhabitants were
of small power, they were dismayed and confounded; they were as the grass of the field,
and as the green herb, as the grass on the
housetops, and as corn blasted before it be
grown up.
"But I know thy abode, and thy going out,
and thy coming in, and thy rage against Me.
Because thy rage against Me and thy tumult is
come up into Mine ears, therefore I will put My
hook in thy nose, and My bridle in thy lips, and
I will turn thee back by the way by which thou
camest." 2 Kings 19:20-28.
The land of Judah had been laid waste by the
army of occupation, but God had promised to
provide miraculously for the needs of the people. To Hezekiah came the message: "This shall
be a sign unto thee, Ye shall eat this year such
things as grow of themselves, and in the second
year that which springeth of the same; and in
the third year sow ye, and reap, and plant vineyards, and eat the fruits thereof. And the remnant that is escaped of the house of Judah shall 361
yet again take root downward, and bear fruit
upward. For out of Jerusalem shall go forth a
remnant, and they that escape out of Mount
Zion: the zeal of the Lord of hosts shall do this.
"Therefore thus saith the Lord concerning the
king of Assyria, He shall not come into this city,
nor shoot an arrow there, nor come before it
with shield, nor cast a bank against it. By the
way that he came, by the same shall he return,

and shall not come into this city, saith the Lord. For I will defend this city, to save it, for Mine own sake, and for My servant David's sake." Verses 29-34.

That very night deliverance came. "The angel of the Lord went out, and smote in the camp of the Assyrians an hundred fourscore and five thousand." Verse 35. "All the mighty men of valor, and the leaders and captains in the camp of the king of Assyria," were slain. 2 Chronicles 32:21.

Tidings of this terrible judgment upon the army that had been sent to take Jerusalem, soon reached Sennacherib, who was still guarding the approach to Judea from Egypt. Stricken with fear, the Assyrian king hasted to depart and "returned with shame of face to his own land." Verse 21. But he had not long to reign. In harmony with the prophecy that had been uttered concerning his sudden end, he was assassinated by those of his own home, "and Esarhaddon his son reigned in his stead." Isaiah 37:38.

The God of the Hebrews had prevailed over the proud Assyrian. The honor of Jehovah was vindicated in the eyes of the surrounding nations. In Jerusalem the hearts of the people were filled with holy joy. Their earnest entreaties for deliverance had been mingled with confession of sin and with many tears. In their great need they had trusted wholly in the power of God to save, and He had not failed them. Now the temple courts resounded with songs of solemn praise.

"In Judah is God known:
His name is great in Israel.
In Salem also is His tabernacle,
And His dwelling place in Zion.
There brake He the arrows of the bow,
The shield, and the sword, and the battle.

"Thou art more glorious and excellent
Than the mountains of prey.
The stouthearted are spoiled, they have slept
their sleep:
And none of the men of might have found
their hands.
At Thy rebuke, O God of Jacob,
Both the chariot and horse are cast into a dead
sleep.

"Thou, even Thou, art to be feared:
And who may stand in Thy sight when once
Thou art angry?
Thou didst cause judgment to be heard from
heaven;
The earth feared, and was still,
When God arose to judgment,
To save all the meek of the earth.

"Surely the wrath of man shall praise Thee:

The remainder of wrath shalt Thou restrain.
Vow, and pay unto the Lord your God:
Let all that be round about Him bring presents
unto Him
that ought to be feared.
He shall cut off the spirit of princes:
He is terrible to the kings of the earth."
                                        Psalm 76.

The rise and fall of the Assyrian Empire is rich in lessons for the nations of earth today. Inspiration has likened the glory of Assyria at the height of her prosperity to a noble tree in the garden of God, towering above the surrounding trees.

"The Assyrian was a cedar in Lebanon with fair branches, and with a shadowing shroud, and of an high stature; and his top was among the thick boughs. . . . Under his shadow dwelt all great nations. Thus was he fair in his greatness, in the length of his branches: for his root was by great waters. The cedars in the garden of God could not hide him: the fir trees were not like his boughs, and the chestnut trees were not like his branches; nor any tree in the garden of God was like unto him in his beauty. . . . All the trees of Eden, that were in the garden of God, envied him." Ezekiel 31:3-9.

But the rulers of Assyria, instead of using their unusual blessings for the benefit of mankind, became the scourge of many lands. Merciless, with no thought of God or their fellow men, they pursued the fixed policy of causing all nations to acknowledge the supremacy of the gods of Nineveh, whom they exalted above the Most High. God had sent Jonah to them with a message of warning, and for a season they humbled themselves before the Lord of hosts and sought forgiveness. But soon they turned again to idol worship and to the conquest of the world.

The prophet Nahum, in his arraignment of the evildoers in Nineveh, exclaimed:

"Woe to the bloody city!
It is all full of lies and robbery;
The prey departeth not;

"The noise of a whip, and the noise of the rattling of the wheels,
And of the prancing horses, and of the jump-
ing chariots.
The horseman lifteth up both the bright sword
and the glittering spear:
And there is a multitude of slain. . . .

"Behold, I am against thee,
Saith the Lord of hosts."
                                        Nahum 3:1-5.

With unerring accuracy the Infinite One still keeps account with the nations. While His mercy is tendered, with calls to repentance, this account remains open; but when the figures reach a certain amount which God has fixed, the ministry of His wrath begins. The account is closed. Divine patience ceases. Mercy no longer pleads in their behalf.

"The Lord is slow to anger, and great in power, and will not at all acquit the wicked: the Lord hath His way in the whirlwind and in the storm, and the clouds are the dust of His feet. He rebuketh the sea, and maketh it dry, and drieth up all the rivers: Bashan languisheth, and Carmel, and the flower of Lebanon languisheth. The mountains quake at Him, and the hills melt, and the earth is burned at His presence, yea, the world, and all that dwell therein. Who can stand before His indignation? and who can abide in the fierceness of His anger? His fury is poured out like fire, and the rocks are thrown down by Him." Nahum 1:3-6.

It was thus that Nineveh, "the rejoicing city that dwelt carelessly, that said in her heart, I am, and there is none beside me," became a desolation, "empty, and void, and waste," "the dwelling of the lions, and the feeding place of the young lions, where the lion, even the old lion, walked, and the lion's whelp, and none made them afraid." Zephaniah 2:15; Nahum 2:10, 11.

365 Looking forward to the time when the pride of Assyria should be brought low, Zephaniah prophesied of Nineveh: "Flocks shall lie down in the midst of her, all the beasts of the nations: both the cormorant and the bittern shall lodge in the upper lintels of it; their voice shall sing in the windows; desolation shall be in the thresholds: for He shall uncover the cedar work." Zephaniah 2:14.

Great was the glory of the Assyrian realm; great was its downfall. The prophet Ezekiel, carrying farther the figure of a noble cedar tree, plainly foretold the fall of Assyria because of its pride and cruelty. He declared:

"Thus saith the Lord God; . . . He hath shot up his top among the thick boughs, and his heart is lifted up in his height; I have therefore delivered him into the hand of the mighty one of the heathen; he shall surely deal with him: I have driven him out for his wickedness. And strangers, the terrible of the nations, have cut him off, and have left him: upon the mountains and in all the valleys his branches are fallen, and his boughs are broken by all the rivers of the land; and all the people of the earth are gone down from his shadow, and have left him. Upon his ruin shall all the fowls of the heaven remain, and all the beasts of the field shall be upon his branches: *to the end that none of all the trees by the waters exalt themselves* for their height. . . .

"Thus saith the Lord God; In the day when he went down to the grave I caused a mourning: . . . and all the trees of the field fainted for him. I made the nations to shake at the sound of his fall." Ezekiel 31:10-16.

The pride of Assyria and its fall are to serve as an object lesson to the end of time. Of the nations of earth today who in arrogance and pride array themselves against Him, God inquires, "To whom art thou thus like in glory and in greatness among the trees of Eden? yet shalt thou be brought down with the trees of Eden unto the nether parts of the earth." Verse 18.

"The Lord is good, a stronghold in the day of trouble; and He knoweth them that trust in Him. But with an overrunning flood He will make an utter end" of all who endeavor to exalt themselves above the Most High. Nahum 1:7, 8.

"The pride of Assyria shall be brought down, 366 and the scepter of Egypt shall depart away." Zechariah 10:11. This is true not only of the nations that arrayed themselves against God in ancient times, but also of nations today who fail of fulfilling the divine purpose. In the day of final awards, when the righteous Judge of all the earth shall "sift the nations" (Isaiah 30:28), and those that have kept the truth shall be permitted to enter the City of God, heaven's arches will ring with the triumphant songs of the redeemed. "Ye shall have a song," the prophet declares, "as in the night when a holy solemnity is kept; and gladness of heart, as when one goeth with a pipe to come into the mountain of the Lord, to the Mighty One of Israel. And the Lord shall cause His glorious voice to be heard. . . . Through the voice of the Lord shall the Assyrian be beaten down, which smote with a rod. And in every place where the grounded staff shall pass, which the Lord shall lay upon him, it shall be with tabrets and harps." Verses 29-32.

31
367

Hope for the Heathen

Throughout his ministry Isaiah bore a plain testimony concerning God's purpose for the heathen. Other prophets had made mention of the divine plan, but their language was not always understood. To Isaiah it was given to make very plain to Judah the truth that among the Israel of God were to be numbered many who were not descendants of Abraham after the flesh. This teaching was not in harmony with the theology of his age, yet he fearlessly proclaimed the messages given him of God and brought hope to many a longing heart reaching out after the spiritual blessings promised to the seed of Abraham.

The apostle to the Gentiles, in his letter to the believers in Rome, calls attention to this characteristic of Isaiah's teaching. "Isaiah is very bold," Paul declares, "and saith, I was found of them that sought Me not; I was made manifest unto them that asked not after Me." Romans 10:20.

Often the Israelites seemed unable or unwilling to understand God's purpose for the heathen. Yet it was this very purpose that had made them a separate people and had established them as an independent nation among the nations of the earth. Abraham, their father, to whom the covenant promise was first given, had been called to go forth from his kindred, to the regions beyond, that he might be a light bearer to the heathen. Although the promise to him included a posterity as numerous as the sand by the sea, yet it was for no selfish purpose that he was to become the founder of a great nation in the land of Canaan. God's covenant with him embraced all the nations of earth. "I will bless thee," Jehovah declared, "and make thy name great; and thou shalt be a blessing: and I will bless them that bless thee, and curse him that curseth thee: and in thee shall all families of the earth be blessed." Genesis 12:2, 3.

In the renewal of the covenant shortly before the birth of Isaac, God's purpose for mankind was again made plain. "All the nations of the earth shall be blessed in him," was the assurance of the Lord concerning the child of promise. Genesis 18:18. And later the heavenly visitant once more declared, "In thy seed shall all the nations of the earth be blessed." Genesis 22:18.

The all-embracing terms of this covenant were familiar to Abraham's children and to his children's children. It was in order that the Israelites might be a blessing to the nations, and that God's name might be made known "throughout all the earth" (Exodus 9:16), that they were delivered from Egyptian bondage. If obedient to His requirements, they were to be placed far in advance of other peoples in wisdom and understanding; but this supremacy was to be reached and maintained only in order that through them the purpose of God for "all nations of the earth" might be fulfilled.

The marvelous providences connected with Israel's deliverance from Egyptian bondage and with their occupancy of the Promised Land led many of the heathen to recognize the God of Israel as the Supreme Ruler. "The Egyptians shall know," had been the promise, "that I am the Lord, when I stretch forth Mine hand upon Egypt, and bring out the children of Israel from among them." Exodus 7:5. Even proud Pharaoh was constrained to acknowledge Jehovah's power. "Go, serve the Lord," he urged Moses and Aaron, "and bless me also." Exodus 12:31, 32.

The advancing hosts of Israel found that knowledge of the mighty workings of the God of the Hebrews had gone before them, and that

some among the heathen were learning that He alone was the true God. In wicked Jericho the testimony of a heathen woman was, "The Lord your God, He is God in heaven above, and in earth beneath." Joshua 2:11. The knowledge of Jehovah that had thus come to her, proved her salvation. By faith "Rahab perished not with them that believed not." Hebrews 11:31. And her conversion was not an isolated case of God's mercy toward idolaters who acknowledged His divine authority. In the midst of the land a numerous people—the Gibeonites—renounced their heathenism and united with Israel, sharing in the blessings of the covenant.

No distinction on account of nationality, race, or caste, is recognized by God. He is the Maker of all mankind. All men are of one family by creation, and all are one through redemption. Christ came to demolish every wall of partition, to throw open every compartment of the temple courts, that every soul may have free access to God. His love is so broad, so deep, so full, that it penetrates everywhere. It lifts out of Satan's influence those who have been deluded by his deceptions, and places them within reach of the throne of God, the throne encircled by the rainbow of promise. In Christ there is neither Jew nor Greek, bond nor free.

In the years that followed the occupation of the Promised Land, the beneficent designs of Jehovah for the salvation of the heathen were almost wholly lost sight of, and it became necessary for Him to set forth His plan anew. "All the ends of the world," the psalmist was inspired to sing, "shall remember and turn unto the Lord: and all the kindreds of the nations shall worship before Thee." "Princes shall come out of Egypt; Ethiopia shall soon stretch out her hands unto God." "The heathen shall fear the name of the Lord, and all the kings of the earth Thy glory." "This shall be written for the generation to come: and the people which shall be created shall praise the Lord. For He hath looked down from the height of His sanctuary; from heaven did the Lord behold the earth; to hear the groaning of the prisoner; to loose those that are appointed to death; to declare the name of the Lord in Zion, and His praise in Jerusalem; when the people are gathered together, and the kingdoms, to serve the Lord." Psalms 22:27; 68:31; 102:15, 18-22.

Had Israel been true to her trust, all the nations of earth would have shared in her blessings. But the hearts of those to whom had been entrusted a knowledge of saving truth, were untouched by the needs of those around them. As God's purpose was lost sight of, the heathen came to be looked upon as beyond the pale of His mercy. The light of truth was withheld, and darkness prevailed. The nations were overspread with a veil of ignorance; the love of God was little known; error and superstition flourished.

Such was the prospect that greeted Isaiah when he was called to the prophetic mission; yet he was not discouraged, for ringing in his ears was the triumphal chorus of the angels surrounding the throne of God, "The whole earth is full of His glory." Isaiah 6:3. And his faith was strengthened by visions of glorious conquests by the church of God, when "the earth shall be full of the knowledge of the Lord, as the waters cover the sea." Isaiah 11:9. "The face of the covering cast over all people, and the veil that is spread over all nations," was finally to be destroyed. Isaiah 25:7. The Spirit of God was to be poured out upon all flesh. Those who hunger and thirst after righteousness were to be numbered among the Israel of God. "They shall spring up as among the grass, as willows by the watercourses," said the prophet. "One shall say, I am the Lord's; and another shall call himself by the name of Jacob; and another shall subscribe with his hand unto the Lord, and surname himself by the name of Israel." Isaiah 44:4, 5.

To the prophet was given a revelation of the beneficent design of God in scattering impenitent Judah among the nations of earth. "My people shall know My name," the Lord declared; "they shall know in that day that I am He that doth speak." Isaiah 52:6. And not only were they themselves to learn the lesson of obedience and trust; in their places of exile they were also to impart to others a knowledge of the living God. Many from among the sons of the strangers were to learn to love Him as their Creator and their Redeemer; they were to begin the observance of His holy Sabbath day as a memorial of His creative power; and when He should make "bare His holy arm in the eyes of all the nations," to deliver His people from captivity, "all the ends of the earth" should see of the salvation of God. Verse 10. Many of these converts from heathenism would wish to unite themselves fully with the Israelites and accompany them on the return journey to Judea. None of these were to say, "The Lord hath utterly separated me from His people" (Isaiah 56:3), for the word of God through His prophet to those who should yield themselves to Him and observe His law was that they should thenceforth be numbered among spiritual Israel—His church on earth.

"The sons of the stranger, that join themselves to the Lord, to serve Him, and to love the name of the Lord, to be His servants, everyone that keepeth the Sabbath from polluting it, and taketh hold of My covenant; even them will I bring to My holy mountain, and make them joyful in My house of prayer: their burnt offerings and their sacrifices shall be accepted upon Mine altar; for Mine house shall be called an house of prayer for all people. The Lord God which gathereth the outcasts of Israel saith, Yet will I gather others to Him, beside those that are gathered unto Him." Verses 6-8.

The prophet was permitted to look down the centuries to the time of the advent of the promised Messiah. At first he beheld only "trouble and darkness, dimness of anguish." Isaiah 8:22. Many who were longing for the light of truth were being led astray by false teachers into the bewildering mazes of philosophy and spiritism; others were placing their trust in a form of godliness, but were not bringing true holiness into the life practice. The outlook seemed hopeless; but soon the scene changed, and before the eyes of the prophet was spread a wondrous vision. He saw the Sun of Righteousness arise with healing in His wings; and, lost in admiration, he exclaimed: "The dimness shall not be such as was in her vexation, when at the first He lightly afflicted the land of Zebulun and the land of Naphtali, and afterward did more grievously afflict her by the way of the sea, beyond Jordan, in Galilee of the nations. The people that walked in darkness have seen a great light: they that dwell in the land of the shadow of death, upon them hath the light shined." Isaiah 9:1, 2.

This glorious Light of the world was to bring salvation to every nation, kindred, tongue, and people. Of the work before Him, the prophet heard the eternal Father declare: "It is a light thing that Thou shouldest be My servant to raise up the tribes of Jacob, and to restore the preserved of Israel: I will also give Thee for a light to the Gentiles, that Thou mayest be My salvation unto the end of the earth." "In an acceptable time have I heard Thee, and in a day of salvation have I helped Thee: and I will preserve Thee, and give Thee for a covenant of the people, to establish the earth, to cause to inherit the desolate heritages; that Thou mayest say to the prisoners, Go forth; to them that are in darkness, Show yourselves." "Behold, these shall come from far: and, lo, these from the north and from the west; and these from the land of Sinim." Isaiah 49:6, 8, 9, 12.

Looking on still farther through the ages, the prophet beheld the literal fulfillment of these glorious promises. He saw the bearers of the glad tidings of salvation going to the ends of the earth, to every kindred and people. He heard the Lord saying of the gospel church, "Behold, I will extend peace to her like a river, and the glory of the Gentiles like a flowing stream;" and he heard the commission, "Enlarge the place of thy tent, and let them stretch forth the curtains of thine habitations: spare not, lengthen thy cords, and strengthen thy stakes; for thou shalt break forth on the right hand and on the left; and thy seed shall inherit the Gentiles." Isaiah 66:12; 54:2, 3.

Jehovah declared to the prophet that He would send His witnesses "unto the nations, to Tarshish, Pul, and Lud, . . . to Tubal, and Javan, to the isles afar off." Isaiah 66:19.

"How beautiful upon the mountains
Are the feet of him that bringeth good tidings,
That publisheth peace;
That bringeth good tidings of good,
That publisheth salvation;
That saith unto Zion, Thy God reigneth!"
Isaiah 52:7.

375   The prophet heard the voice of God calling
His church to her appointed work, that the way
might be prepared for the ushering in of His
everlasting kingdom. The message was unmistakably plain:

"Arise, shine; for thy light is come,
And the glory of the Lord is risen upon thee.

"For, behold, the darkness shall cover the
earth,
And gross darkness the people:
But the Lord shall arise upon thee,
And His glory shall be seen upon thee.
And the Gentiles shall come to thy light,
And kings to the brightness of thy rising.

"Lift up thine eyes round about, and see:
All they gather themselves together, they
come to thee:
Thy sons shall come from far,
And thy daughters shall be nursed at thy
side."

"And the sons of strangers shall build up thy
walls,
And their kings shall minister unto thee:
For in My wrath I smote thee,
But in My favor have I had mercy on thee.
Therefore thy gates shall be open continually;
They shall not be shut day nor night;
That men may bring unto thee the forces of
the Gentiles,
And that their kings may be brought."

"Look unto Me, and be ye saved, all the ends
of the earth:
For I am God, and there is none else."
Isaiah 60:1-4, 10, 11; 45:22.

These prophecies of a great spiritual awakening in a time of gross darkness are today meeting fulfillment in the advancing lines of mission
stations that are reaching out into the benighted
regions of earth. The groups of missionaries in
heathen lands have been likened by the prophet
376 to ensigns set up for the guidance of those who
are looking for the light of truth.

"In that day," says Isaiah, "there shall be a
root of Jesse, which shall stand for an ensign of
the people; to it shall the Gentiles seek: and his
rest shall be glorious. And it shall come to pass

in that day, that the Lord shall set His hand
again the second time to recover the remnant of
His people. . . . And He shall set up an ensign
for the nations, and shall assemble the outcasts
of Israel, and gather together the dispersed of
Judah from the four corners of the earth." Isaiah
11:10-12.

The day of deliverance is at hand. "The eyes
of the Lord run to and fro throughout the whole
earth, to show Himself strong in the behalf of
them whose heart is perfect toward Him." 2
Chronicles 16:9. Among all nations, kindreds,
and tongues, He sees men and women who are
praying for light and knowledge. Their souls are
unsatisfied: long have they fed on ashes. See
Isaiah 44:20. The enemy of all righteousness
has turned them aside, and they grope as blind
men. But they are honest in heart and desire to
learn a better way. Although in the depths of
heathenism, with no knowledge of the written
law of God nor of His Son Jesus, they have
revealed in manifold ways the working of a
divine power on mind and character.

At times those who have no knowledge of
God aside from that which they have received
under the operations of divine grace have been
kind to His servants, protecting them at the risk
of their own lives. The Holy Spirit is implanting
the grace of Christ in the heart of many a noble
seeker after truth, quickening his sympathies   377
contrary to his nature, contrary to his former
education. The "Light, which lighteth every
man that cometh into the world" (John 1:9), is
shining in his soul; and this Light, if heeded,
will guide his feet to the kingdom of God. The
prophet Micah said: "When I sit in darkness, the
Lord shall be a light unto me. . . . He will bring
me forth to the light, and I shall behold His
righteousness." Micah 7:8, 9.

Heaven's plan of salvation is broad enough to
embrace the whole world. God longs to breathe
into prostrate humanity the breath of life. And
He will not permit any soul to be disappointed   378
who is sincere in his longing for something
higher and nobler than anything the world can
offer. Constantly He is sending His angels to
those who, while surrounded by circumstances
the most discouraging, pray in faith for some
power higher than themselves to take possession of them and bring deliverance and peace.
In various ways God will reveal Himself to
them and will place them in touch with providences that will establish their confidence in the
One who has given Himself a ransom for all,
"that they might set their hope in God, and not
forget the works of God, but keep His commandments." Psalm 78:7.

"Shall the prey be taken from the mighty, or
the lawful captive delivered?" "Thus saith the
Lord, Even the captives of the mighty shall be
taken away, and the prey of the terrible shall be
delivered." Isaiah 49:24, 25. "They shall be

greatly ashamed, that trust in graven images, that say to the molten images, Ye are our gods." Isaiah 42:17.

"Happy is he that hath the God of Jacob for his help, whose hope is in the Lord his God!" Psalm 146:5. "Turn you to the stronghold, ye prisoners of hope!" Zechariah 9:12. Unto all the honest in heart in heathen lands—"the upright" in the sight of Heaven—"there ariseth light in the darkness." Psalm 112:4. God hath spoken: "I will bring the blind by a way that they knew not; I will lead them in paths that they have not known: I will make darkness light before them, and crooked things straight. These things will I do unto them, and not forsake them." Isaiah 42:16.

SECTION IV

NATIONAL RETRIBUTION

"I will correct thee in measure, and will not leave thee altogether unpunished." Jeremiah 30:11

32

Manasseh and Josiah

The kingdom of Judah, prosperous throughout the times of Hezekiah, was once more brought low during the long years of Manasseh's wicked reign, when paganism was revived, and many of the people were led into idolatry. "Manasseh made Judah and the inhabitants of Jerusalem to err, and to do worse than the heathen." 2 Chronicles 33:9. The glorious light of former generations was followed by the darkness of superstition and error. Gross evils sprang up and flourished—tyranny, oppression, hatred of all that is good. Justice was perverted; violence prevailed.

Yet those evil times were not without witnesses for God and the right. The trying experiences through which Judah had safely passed during Hezekiah's reign had developed, in the hearts of many, a sturdiness of character that now served as a bulwark against the prevailing iniquity. Their testimony in behalf of truth and righteousness aroused the anger of Manasseh
and his associates in authority, who endeavored to establish themselves in evil-doing by silencing every voice of disapproval. "Manasseh shed innocent blood very much, till he had filled Jerusalem from one end to another." 2 Kings 21:16.

One of the first to fall was Isaiah, who for over half a century had stood before Judah as the appointed messenger of Jehovah. "Others had trial of cruel mockings and scourgings, yea, moreover of bonds and imprisonment: they were stoned, they were sawn asunder, were tempted, were slain with the sword: they wandered about in sheepskins and goatskins; being destitute, afflicted, tormented; (of whom the world was not worthy:) they wandered in deserts, and in mountains, and in dens and caves of the earth." Hebrews 11:36-38.

Some of those who suffered persecution during Manasseh's reign were commissioned to bear special messages of reproof and of judgment. The king of Judah, the prophets declared, "hath done wickedly above all . . . which were before him." Because of this wickedness, his kingdom was nearing a crisis; soon the inhabitants of the land were to be carried captive to Babylon, there to become "a prey and a spoil to all their enemies." 2 Kings 21:11, 14. But the Lord would not utterly forsake those who in a strange land should acknowledge Him as their Ruler; they might suffer great tribulation, yet He would bring deliverance to them in His appointed time and way. Those who should put their trust wholly in Him would find a sure refuge.

Faithfully the prophets continued their warnings and their exhortations; fearlessly they spoke to Manasseh and to his people; but the messages were scorned; backsliding Judah would not heed. As an earnest of what would befall the people should they continue impenitent, the Lord permitted their king to be captured by a band of Assyrian soldiers, who "bound him with fetters, and carried him to Babylon," their temporary capital. This affliction brought the king to his senses; "he besought the Lord his God, and humbled himself greatly before the God of his fathers, and prayed unto Him: and He was entreated of him, and heard his supplication, and brought him again to Jerusalem into his kingdom. Then Manasseh knew that the Lord He was God." 2 Chronicles 33:11-13. But this repentance, remarkable though it was, came too late to save the kingdom from the corrupting influence of years of idolatrous practices. Many had stumbled and fallen, never again to rise.

Among those whose life experience had been shaped beyond recall by the fatal apostasy of Manasseh, was his own son, who came to the throne at the age of twenty-two. Of King Amon it is written: "He walked in all the way that his father walked in, and served the idols that his father served, and worshiped them: and he forsook the Lord God of his fathers" (2 Kings 21:21, 22); he "humbled not himself before the Lord, as Manasseh his father had humbled himself; but Amon trespassed more and more." The wicked king was not permitted to reign long. In the midst of his daring impiety, only two years from the time he ascended the throne, he was slain in the palace by his own servants; and "the people of the land made Josiah his son king in his stead." 2 Chronicles 33:23, 25.

384   With the accession of Josiah to the throne, where he was to rule for thirty-one years, those who had maintained the purity of their faith began to hope that the downward course of the kingdom was checked; for the new king, though only eight years old, feared God, and from the very beginning "he did that which was right in the sight of the Lord, and walked in all the way of David his father, and turned not aside to the right hand or to the left." 2 Kings 22:2. Born of a wicked king, beset with temptations to follow in his father's steps, and with few counselors to encourage him in the right way, Josiah nevertheless was true to the God of Israel. Warned by the errors of past generations, he chose to do right, instead of descending to the low level of sin and degradation to which his father and his grandfather had fallen. He "turned not aside to the right hand or to the left." As one who was to occupy a position of trust, he resolved to obey the instruction that had been given for the guidance of Israel's rulers, and his obedience made it possible for God to use him as a vessel unto honor.

At the time Josiah began to rule, and for many years before, the truehearted in Judah were questioning whether God's promises to ancient Israel could ever be fulfilled. From a human point of view the divine purpose for the chosen nation seemed almost impossible of accomplishment. The apostasy of former centuries had gathered strength with the passing years; ten of the tribes had been scattered among the heathen; only the tribes of Judah and Benjamin remained, and even these now

385   seemed on the verge of moral and national ruin. The prophets had begun to foretell the utter destruction of their fair city, where stood the temple built by Solomon, and where all their earthly hopes of national greatness had centered. Could it be that God was about to turn aside from His avowed purpose of bringing deliverance to those who should put their trust in Him? In the face of the long-continued persecution of the righteous, and of the apparent prosperity of the wicked, could those who had remained true to God hope for better days?

These anxious questionings were voiced by the prophet Habakkuk. Viewing the situation of the faithful in his day, he expressed the burden of his heart in the inquiry: "O Lord, how long shall I cry, and Thou wilt not hear! even cry out unto Thee of violence, and Thou wilt not save! Why dost Thou show me iniquity, and cause me to behold grievance? for spoiling and violence are before me: and there are that raise up strife and contention. Therefore the law is slacked,

and judgment doth never go forth: for the wicked doth compass about the righteous; therefore wrong judgment proceedeth." Habakkuk 1:2-4.

God answered the cry of His loyal children. Through His chosen mouthpiece He revealed His determination to bring chastisement upon the nation that had turned from Him to serve the gods of the heathen. Within the lifetime of some who were even then making inquiry regarding the future, He would miraculously shape the affairs of the ruling nations of earth and bring the Babylonians into the ascendancy. These Chaldeans, "terrible and dreadful," were to fall suddenly upon the land of Judah as a divinely appointed scourge. Verse 7. The princes of 386 Judah and the fairest of the people were to be carried captive to Babylon; the Judean cities and villages and the cultivated fields were to be laid waste; nothing was to be spared.

Confident that even in this terrible judgment the purpose of God for His people would in some way be fulfilled, Habakkuk bowed in submission to the revealed will of Jehovah. "Art Thou not from everlasting, O Lord my God, mine Holy One?" he exclaimed. And then, his faith reaching out beyond the forbidding prospect of the immediate future, and laying fast hold on the precious promises that reveal God's love for His trusting children, the prophet added, "We shall not die." Verse 12. With this declaration of faith he rested his case, and that of every believing Israelite, in the hands of a compassionate God.

This was not Habakkuk's only experience in the exercise of strong faith. On one occasion, when meditating concerning the future, he said, "I will stand upon my watch, and set me upon the tower, and will watch to see what He will say unto me." Graciously the Lord answered him: "Write the vision, and make it plain upon tables, that he may run that readeth it. For the vision is yet for an appointed time, but at the end it shall speak, and not lie: though it tarry, wait for it; because it will surely come, it will not tarry. Behold, his soul which is lifted up is not upright in him: but *the just shall live by his faith.*" Habakkuk 2:1-4.

The faith that strengthened Habakkuk and all the holy and the just in those days of deep trial was the same faith that sustains God's people today. In the darkest hours, under circumstances the most forbidding, the Christian believer may 387 keep his soul stayed upon the source of all light and power. Day by day, through faith in God, his hope and courage may be renewed. "The just shall live by his faith." In the service of God there need be no despondency, no wavering, no fear. The Lord will more than fulfill the highest expectations of those who put their trust in Him. He will give them the wisdom their varied necessities demand.

Of the abundant provision made for every tempted soul, the apostle Paul bears eloquent testimony. To him was given the divine assurance, "My grace is sufficient for thee: for My strength is made perfect in weakness." In gratitude and confidence the tried servant of God responded: "Most gladly therefore will I rather glory in my infirmities, that the power of Christ may rest upon me. Therefore I take pleasure in infirmities, in reproaches, in necessities, in persecutions, in distresses for Christ's sake: for when I am weak, then am I strong." 2 Corinthians 12:9, 10.

We must cherish and cultivate the faith of which prophets and apostles have testified—the faith that lays hold on the promises of God and waits for deliverance in His appointed time and way. The sure word of prophecy will meet its final fulfillment in the glorious advent of our Lord and Saviour Jesus Christ, as King of kings and Lord of lords. The time of waiting may seem long, the soul may be oppressed by discouraging circumstances, many in whom confidence has been placed may fall by the way; but with the prophet who endeavored to encourage Judah in a time of unparalleled apostasy, let us confidently declare, "The Lord is in His holy temple: let all the earth keep silence before Him." Habakkuk 2:20. Let us ever hold in remembrance the cheering message, "The vision is yet for an appointed time, but at the end it shall speak, and not lie: though it tarry, wait for it; because it will surely come, it will not tarry. . . . The just shall live by his faith." Verses 3, 4.

> "O Lord, revive Thy work in the midst of the years,
> In the midst of the years make known;
> In wrath remember mercy.

> "God came from Teman,
> And the Holy One from Mount Paran.
> His glory covered the heavens,
> And the earth was full of His praise.
> And His brightness was as the light;
> He had bright beams out of His side:
> And there was the hiding of His power.
> Before Him went the pestilence,
> And burning coals went forth at His feet.
> He stood, and measured the earth:
> He beheld, and drove asunder the nations;
> And the everlasting mountains were scattered,
> The perpetual hills did bow:
> His ways are everlasting."

> "Thou wentest forth for the salvation of Thy people,
> Even for salvation with Thine anointed."

> "Although the fig tree shall not blossom,

> Neither shall fruit be in the vines;
> The labor of the olive shall fail,
> And the fields shall yield no meat;
> The flock shall be cut off from the fold,
> And there shall be no herd in the stalls:
> Yet I will rejoice in the Lord,
> I will joy in the God of my salvation.
> The Lord God is my strength."
> Habakkuk 3:2-6, 13, 17-19, margin.

Habakkuk was not the only one through whom was given a message of bright hope and of future triumph as well as of present judgment. During the reign of Josiah the word of the Lord came to Zephaniah, specifying plainly the results of continued apostasy, and calling the attention of the true church to the glorious prospect beyond. His prophecies of impending judgment upon Judah apply with equal force to the judgments that are to fall upon an impenitent world at the time of the second advent of Christ:

> "The great day of the Lord is near,
> It is near, and hasteth greatly,
> Even the voice of the day of the Lord:
> The mighty man shall cry there bitterly.

> "That day is a day of wrath,
> A day of trouble and distress,
> A day of wasteness and desolation,
> A day of darkness and gloominess,

> "A day of clouds and thick darkness,
> A day of the trumpet and alarm
> Against the fenced cities,
> And against the high towers."
> Zephaniah 1:14-16.

"I will bring distress upon men, that they shall walk like blind men, because they have sinned against the Lord: and their blood shall be poured out as dust. . . . Neither their silver nor their gold shall be able to deliver them in the day of the Lord's wrath; but the whole land shall be devoured by the fire of His jealousy: for He shall make even a speedy riddance of all them that dwell in the land." Verses 17, 18.

> "Gather yourselves together, yea, gather together,
> O nation not desired;
> Before the decree bring forth,
> Before the day pass as the chaff,
> Before the fierce anger of the Lord come upon you,
> Before the day of the Lord's anger come upon you.

> "Seek ye the Lord, all ye meek of the earth,
> Which have wrought His judgment;
> Seek righteousness,
> Seek meekness:

388

389

390

It may be ye shall be hid
In the day of the Lord's anger."
Zephaniah 2:1-3.

391   "Behold, at that time I will deal with all them that afflict thee: and I will save her that halteth, and gather her that was driven away; and I will make them a praise and a name, whose shame hath been in all the earth. At that time will I bring you in, and at that time will I gather you: for I will make you a name and a praise among all the peoples of the earth, when I bring again your captivity before your eyes, saith the Lord." Zephaniah 3:19, 20, R.V.

"Sing, O daughter of Zion; shout, O Israel;
Be glad and rejoice with all the heart,
    O daughter of Jerusalem.
The Lord hath taken away thy judgments,
He hath cast out thine enemy:
The King of Israel, even the Lord,
Is in the midst of thee:
Thou shalt not see evil any more.

"In that day it shall be said to Jerusalem, Fear thou not:
And to Zion, Let not thine hands be slack.
The Lord thy God in the midst of thee
    Is mighty; He will save,
He will rejoice over thee with joy;
    He will rest in His love,
He will joy over thee with singing."
Verses 14-17.

392

33

The Book of the Law

The silent yet powerful influences set in operation by the messages of the prophets regarding the Babylonian Captivity did much to prepare the way for a reformation that took place in the eighteenth year of Josiah's reign. This reform movement, by which threatened judgments were averted for a season, was brought about in a wholly unexpected manner through the discovery and study of a portion of Holy Scripture that for many years had been strangely misplaced and lost.

Nearly a century before, during the first Passover celebrated by Hezekiah, provision had been made for the daily public reading of the book of the law to the people by teaching priests. It was the observance of the statutes recorded by Moses, especially those given in the book of the covenant, which forms a part of Deuteronomy, that had made the reign of Hezekiah so prosperous. But Manasseh had dared set aside these statutes; and during his 393 reign the temple copy of the book of the law, through careless neglect, had become lost. Thus

for many years the people generally were deprived of its instruction.

The long-lost manuscript was found in the temple by Hilkiah, the high priest, while the building was undergoing extensive repairs in harmony with King Josiah's plan for the preservation of the sacred structure. The high priest handed the precious volume to Shaphan, a learned scribe, who read it and then took it to the king with the story of its discovery.

Josiah was deeply stirred as he heard read for the first time the exhortations and warnings recorded in this ancient manuscript. Never before had he realized so fully the plainness with which God had set before Israel "life and death, blessing and cursing" (Deuteronomy 30:19); and how repeatedly they had been urged to choose the way of life, that they might become a praise in the earth, a blessing to all nations. "Be strong and of a good courage, fear not, nor be afraid," Israel had been exhorted through Moses; "for the Lord thy God, He it is that doth go with thee; He will not fail thee, nor forsake thee." Deuteronomy 31:6.

The book abounded in assurances of God's willingness to save to the uttermost those who should place their trust fully in Him. As He had wrought in their deliverance from Egyptian bondage, so would He work mightily in establishing them in the Land of Promise and in placing them at the head of the nations of earth.

The encouragements offered as the reward of obedience were accompanied by prophecies of judgments against the disobedient; and as the king heard the inspired words, he recognized, in 394 the picture set before him, conditions that were similar to those actually existing in his kingdom. In connection with these prophetic portrayals of departure from God, he was startled to find plain statements to the effect that the day of calamity would follow swiftly and that there would be no remedy. The language was plain; there could be no mistaking the meaning of the words. And at the close of the volume, in a summary of God's dealings with Israel and a rehearsal of the events of the future, these matters were made doubly plain. In the hearing of all Israel, Moses had declared:

"Give ear, O ye heavens, and I will speak;
And hear, O earth, the words of my mouth.
My doctrine shall drop as the rain,
My speech shall distill as the dew,
As the small rain upon the tender herb,
And as the showers upon the grass:
Because I will publish the name of the Lord:
Ascribe ye greatness unto our God.
He is the Rock, His work is perfect:
For all His ways are judgment:
A God of truth and without iniquity,
Just and right is He."
Deuteronomy 32:1-4.

"Remember the days of old,
Consider the years of many generations:
Ask thy father, and he will show thee;
Thy elders, and they will tell thee.
When the Most High divided to the nations
    their inheritance,
When He separated the sons of Adam,
He set the bounds of the people
According to the number of the children of
    Israel.
For the Lord's portion is His people;
Jacob is the lot of His inheritance.
He found him in a desert land,
And in the waste howling wilderness;
395 He led him about, He instructed him,
He kept him as the apple of His eye."
              Verses 7-10.

But Israel "forsook God which made him,
And lightly esteemed the Rock of his salva-
    tion.
They provoked Him to jealousy with strange
    gods,
With abominations provoked they Him to
    anger.
They sacrificed unto devils, not to God;
To gods whom they knew not,
To new gods that came newly up,
Whom your fathers feared not.
Of the Rock that begat thee thou art unmind-
    ful,
And hast forgotten God that formed thee.

"And when the Lord saw it, He abhorred them,
Because of the provoking of His sons, and of
    His daughters.
And He said, I will hide My face from them,
I will see what their end shall be:
For they are a very froward generation,
Children in whom is no faith.
They have moved Me to jealousy with that
    which is not God;
They have provoked Me to anger with their
    vanities:
And I will move them to jealousy with those
    which are not a people;
I will provoke them to anger with a foolish
    nation."

"I will heap mischiefs upon them;
I will spend Mine arrows upon them.
They shall be burnt with hunger, and
    devoured with burning heat,
And with bitter destruction."
"For they are a nation void of counsel,
Neither is there any understanding in them.
O that they were wise, that they understood
    this,
That they would consider their latter end!
396 How should one chase a thousand,
And two put ten thousand to flight,
Except their rock had sold them,

And the Lord had shut them up?
For their rock is not as our Rock,
Even our enemies themselves being judges."

"Is not this laid up in store with Me,
And sealed up among My treasures?
To Me belongeth vengeance, and recom-
    pense;
Their foot shall slide in due time:
For the day of their calamity is at hand,
And the things that shall come upon them
    make haste."
        Verses 15-21, 23, 24, 28-31, 34, 35.

These and similar passages revealed to Josiah God's love for His people and His abhorrence of sin. As the king read the prophecies
of swift judgment upon those who should persist in rebellion, he trembled for the future.
The perversity of Judah had been great; what
was to be the outcome of their continued apostasy?

In former years the king had not been indifferent to the prevailing idolatry. "In the eighth
year of his reign, while he was yet young," he
had consecrated himself fully to the service of
God. Four years later, at the age of twenty, he
had made an earnest effort to remove temptation from his subjects by purging "Judah and
Jerusalem from the high places, and the
groves, and the carved images, and the molten
images." "They brake down the altars of Baalim in his presence; and the images, that were
on high above them, he cut down; and the
groves, and the carved images, and the molten
images, he brake in pieces, and made dust of
them, and strowed it upon the graves of them
that had sacrificed unto them. And he burnt the
bones of the priests upon their altars, and 397
cleansed Judah and Jerusalem." 2 Chronicles
34:3-5.

Not content with doing thorough work in the
land of Judah, the youthful ruler had extended
his efforts to the portions of Palestine formerly
occupied by the ten tribes of Israel, only a feeble remnant of which now remained. "So did
he," the record reads, "in the cities of Manasseh,
and Ephraim, and Simeon, even unto Naphtali."
Not until he had traversed the length and
breadth of this region of ruined homes, and "had
broken down the altars and the groves, and had 398
beaten the graven images into powder, and cut
down all the idols throughout all the land of
Israel," did he return to Jerusalem. Verses 6, 7.

Thus Josiah, from his earliest manhood, had
endeavored to take advantage of his position as
king to exalt the principles of God's holy law.
And now, while Shaphan the scribe was reading
to him out of the book of the law, the king discerned in this volume a treasure of knowledge, a
powerful ally, in the work of reform he so much
desired to see wrought in the land. He resolved

to walk in the light of its counsels, and also to do all in his power to acquaint his people with its teachings and to lead them, if possible, to cultivate reverence and love for the law of heaven.

But was it possible to bring about the needed reform? Israel had almost reached the limit of divine forbearance; soon God would arise to punish those who had brought dishonor upon His name. Already the anger of the Lord was kindled against the people. Overwhelmed with sorrow and dismay, Josiah rent his garments and bowed before God in agony of spirit, seeking pardon for the sins of an impenitent nation.

At that time the prophetess Huldah was living in Jerusalem, near the temple. The mind of the king, filled with anxious foreboding, reverted to her, and he determined to inquire of the Lord through this chosen messenger to learn, if possible, whether by any means within his power he might save erring Judah, now on the verge of ruin.

399 The gravity of the situation and the respect in which he held the prophetess led him to choose as his messengers to her the first men of the kingdom. "Go ye," he bade them, "inquire of the Lord for me, and for the people, and for all Judah, concerning the words of this book that is found: for great is the wrath of the Lord that is kindled against us, because our fathers have not hearkened unto the words of this book, to do according unto all that which is written concerning us." 2 Kings 22:13.

Through Huldah the Lord sent Josiah word that Jerusalem's ruin could not be averted. Even should the people now humble themselves before God, they could not escape their punishment. So long had their senses been deadened by wrongdoing that, if judgment should not come upon them, they would soon return to the same sinful course. "Tell the man that sent you to me," the prophetess declared, "Thus saith the Lord, Behold, I will bring evil upon this place, and upon the inhabitants thereof, even all the words of the book which the king of Judah hath read: because they have forsaken Me, and have burned incense unto other gods, that they might provoke Me to anger with all the works of their hands; therefore My wrath shall be kindled against this place, and shall not be quenched." Verses 15-17.

But because the king had humbled his heart before God, the Lord would acknowledge his promptness in seeking forgiveness and mercy. To him was sent the message: "Because thine heart was tender, and thou hast humbled thyself before the Lord, when thou heardest what I spake against this place, and against the inhabitants thereof, that they should become a desolation and a curse, and hast rent thy clothes, and wept before Me; I also have heard thee, saith the Lord. Behold therefore, I will gather thee unto thy fathers, and thou shalt be gathered into thy grave in peace; and thine eyes shall not see all the evil which I will bring upon this place." 400 Verses 19, 20.

The king must leave with God the events of the future; he could not alter the eternal decrees of Jehovah. But in announcing the retributive judgments of Heaven, the Lord had not withdrawn opportunity for repentance and reformation; and Josiah, discerning in this a willingness on the part of God to temper His judgments with mercy, determined to do all in his power to bring about decided reforms. He arranged at once for a great convocation, to which were invited the elders and magistrates in Jerusalem and Judah, together with the common people. These, with the priests and Levites, met the king in the court of the temple.

To this vast assembly the king himself read "all the words of the book of the covenant which was found in the house of the Lord." 2 Kings 23:2. The royal reader was deeply affected, and he delivered his message with the pathos of a broken heart. His hearers were profoundly moved. The intensity of feeling revealed in the countenance of the king, the solemnity of the message itself, the warning of judgments impending—all these had their effect, and many determined to join with the king in seeking forgiveness.

Josiah now proposed that those highest in authority unite with the people in solemnly covenanting before God to co-operate with one another in an effort to institute decided changes. "The king stood by a pillar, and made a covenant before the Lord, to walk after the Lord, and to keep His commandments and His 401 testimonies and His statutes with all their heart and all their soul, to perform the words of this covenant that were written in this book." The response was more hearty than the king had dared hope for: "All the people stood to the covenant." Verse 3.

In the reformation that followed, the king turned his attention to the destruction of every vestige of idolatry that remained. So long had the inhabitants of the land followed the customs of the surrounding nations in bowing down to images of wood and stone, that it seemed almost beyond the power of man to remove every trace of these evils. But Josiah persevered in his effort to cleanse the land. Sternly he met idolatry by slaying "all the priests of the high places;" "moreover the workers with familiar spirits, and the wizards, and the images, and the idols, and all the abominations that were spied in the land of Judah and in Jerusalem, did Josiah put away, that he might perform the words of the law which were written in the book that Hilkiah the priest found in the house of the Lord." Verses

20, 24.

In the days of the rending of the kingdom, centuries before, when Jeroboam the son of Nebat, in bold defiance of the God whom Israel had served, was endeavoring to turn the hearts of the people away from the services of the temple in Jerusalem to new forms of worship, he had set up an unconsecrated altar at Bethel. During the dedication of this altar, where many in years to come were to be seduced into idolatrous practices, there had suddenly appeared a man of God from Judea, with words of condemnation for the sacrilegious proceedings. He had "cried against the altar," declaring:

"O altar, altar, thus saith the Lord; Behold, a child shall be born unto the house of David, Josiah by name; and upon thee shall he offer the priests of the high places that burn incense upon thee, and men's bones shall be burnt upon thee." 1 Kings 13:2. This announcement had been accompanied by a sign that the word spoken was of the Lord.

Three centuries had passed. During the reformation wrought by Josiah, the king found himself in Bethel, where stood this ancient altar. The prophecy uttered so many years before in the presence of Jeroboam, was now to be literally fulfilled.

"The altar that was at Bethel, and the high place which Jeroboam the son of Nebat, who made Israel to sin, had made, both that altar and the high place he brake down, and burned the high place, and stamped it small to powder, and burned the grove.

"And as Josiah turned himself, he spied the sepulchers that were there in the mount, and sent, and took the bones out of the sepulchers, and burned them upon the altar, and polluted it, according to the word of the Lord which the man of God proclaimed, who proclaimed these words.

"Then he said, What title is that that I see? And the men of the city told him, It is the sepulcher of the man of God, which came from Judah, and proclaimed these things that thou hast done against the altar of Bethel. And he said, Let him alone; let no man move his bones. So they let his bones alone, with the bones of the prophet that came out of Samaria." 2 Kings 23:15-18.

On the southern slopes of Olivet, opposite the beautiful temple of Jehovah on Mount Moriah, were the shrines and images that had been placed there by Solomon to please his idolatrous wives. See 1 Kings 11:6-8. For upwards of three centuries the great, misshapen images had stood on the "Mount of Offense," mute witnesses to the apostasy of Israel's wisest king. These, too, were removed and destroyed by Josiah.

The king sought further to establish the faith of Judah in the God of their fathers by holding a great Passover feast, in harmony with the provisions made in the book of the law. Preparation was made by those having the sacred services in charge, and on the great day of the feast, offerings were freely made. "There was not holden such a Passover from the days of the judges that judged Israel, nor in all the days of the kings of Israel, nor of the kings of Judah." 2 Kings 23:22. But the zeal of Josiah, acceptable though it was to God, could not atone for the sins of past generations; nor could the piety displayed by the king's followers effect a change of heart in many who stubbornly refused to turn from idolatry to the worship of the true God.

For more than a decade following the celebration of the Passover, Josiah continued to reign. At the age of thirty-nine he met death in battle with the forces of Egypt, "and was buried in one of the sepulchers of his fathers." "All Judah and Jerusalem mourned for Josiah. And Jeremiah lamented for Josiah: and all the singing men and the singing women spake of Josiah in their lamentations to this day, and made them an ordinance in Israel: and, behold, they are written in the lamentations." 2 Chronicles 35:24, 25. Like unto Josiah "was there no king before him, that turned to the Lord with all his heart, and with all his soul, and with all his might, according to all the law of Moses; neither after him arose there any like him. Notwithstanding the Lord turned not from the fierceness of His great wrath, . . . because of all the provocations that Manasseh had provoked Him withal." 2 Kings 23:25, 26. The time was rapidly approaching when Jerusalem was to be utterly destroyed and the inhabitants of the land carried captive to Babylon, there to learn the lessons they had refused to learn under circumstances more favorable.

34

Jeremiah

Among those who had hoped for a permanent spiritual revival as the result of the reformation under Josiah was Jeremiah, called of God to the prophetic office while still a youth, in the thirteenth year of Josiah's reign. A member of the Levitical priesthood, Jeremiah had been trained from childhood for holy service. In those happy years of preparation he little realized that he had been ordained from birth to be "a prophet unto the nations;" and when the divine call came, he was overwhelmed with a sense of his unworthiness. "Ah, Lord God!" he exclaimed, "behold, I cannot speak: for I am a child." Jeremiah 1:5, 6.

In the youthful Jeremiah, God saw one who would be true to his trust and who would stand for the right against great opposition. In childhood he had proved faithful; and now he was to endure hardness, as a good soldier of the cross. "Say not, I am a child," the Lord bade His chosen messenger; "for thou shalt go to all that I shall send thee, and whatsoever I command thee thou shalt speak. Be not afraid of their faces: for I am with thee to deliver thee." "Gird up thy loins, and arise, and speak unto them all that I command thee: be not dismayed at their faces, lest I confound thee before them. For, behold, I have made thee this day a defensed city, and an iron pillar, and brazen walls against the whole land, against the kings of Judah, against the princes thereof, against the priests thereof, and against the people of the land. And they shall fight against thee; but they shall not prevail against thee; for I am with thee, saith the Lord, to deliver thee." Verses 7, 8, 17-19.

For forty years Jeremiah was to stand before the nation as a witness for truth and righteousness. In a time of unparalleled apostasy he was to exemplify in life and character the worship of the only true God. During the terrible sieges of Jerusalem he was to be the mouthpiece of Jehovah. He was to predict the downfall of the house of David and the destruction of the beautiful temple built by Solomon. And when imprisoned because of his fearless utterances, he was still to speak plainly against sin in high places. Despised, hated, rejected of men, he was finally to witness the literal fulfillment of his own prophecies of impending doom, and share in the sorrow and woe that should follow the destruction of the fated city.

Yet amid the general ruin into which the nation was rapidly passing, Jeremiah was often permitted to look beyond the distressing scenes of the present to the glorious prospects of the future, when God's people should be ransomed from the land of the enemy and planted again in Zion. He foresaw the time when the Lord would renew His covenant relationship with them. "Their soul shall be as a watered garden; and they shall not sorrow any more at all." Jeremiah 31:12.

Of his call to the prophetic mission, Jeremiah himself wrote: "The Lord put forth His hand, and touched my mouth. And the Lord said unto me, Behold, I have put My words in thy mouth. See, I have this day set thee over the nations and over the kingdoms, to root out, and to pull down, and to destroy, and to throw down, to build, and to plant." Jeremiah 1:9, 10.

Thank God for the words, "to build, and to plant." By these words Jeremiah was assured of the Lord's purpose to restore and to heal. Stern were the messages to be borne in the years that were to follow. Prophecies of swift-coming judgments were to be fearlessly delivered. From the plains of Shinar "an evil" was to "break forth upon all the inhabitants of the land." "I will utter My judgments against them," the Lord declared, "touching all their wickedness, who

have forsaken Me." Verses 14, 16. Yet the prophet was to accompany these messages with assurances of forgiveness to all who should turn from their evil-doing.

As a wise master builder, Jeremiah at the very beginning of his lifework sought to encourage the men of Judah to lay the foundations of their spiritual life broad and deep, by making thorough work of repentance. Long had they been building with material likened by the apostle Paul to wood, hay, and stubble, and by Jeremiah himself to dross. "Refuse silver shall men call them," he declared of the impenitent nation, "because the Lord hath rejected them." Jeremiah 6:30, margin. Now they were urged to begin building wisely and for eternity, casting aside the rubbish of apostasy and unbelief, and using as foundation material the pure gold, the refined silver, the precious stones—faith and obedience and good works—which alone are acceptable in the sight of a holy God.

Through Jeremiah the word of the Lord to His people was: "Return, thou backsliding Israel, . . . and I will not cause Mine anger to fall upon you: for I am merciful, saith the Lord, and I will not keep anger forever. Only acknowledge thine iniquity, that thou hast transgressed against the Lord thy God. . . . Turn, O backsliding children, saith the Lord; for I am married unto you." "Thou shalt call Me, My Father; and shalt not turn away from Me." "Return, ye backsliding children, and I will heal your backslidings." Jeremiah 3:12-14, 19, 22.

And in addition to these wonderful pleadings, the Lord gave His erring people the very words with which they might turn to Him. They were to say: "Behold, we come unto Thee; for Thou art the Lord our God. Truly in vain is salvation hoped for from the hills, and from the multitude of mountains: truly in the Lord our God is the salvation of Israel. . . . We lie down in our shame, and our confusion covereth us: for we have sinned against the Lord our God, we and our fathers, from our youth even unto this day, and have not obeyed the voice of the Lord our God." Verses 22-25.

The reformation under Josiah had cleansed the land of the idolatrous shrines, but the hearts of the multitude had not been transformed. The seeds of truth that had sprung up and given promise of an abundant harvest had been choked by thorns. Another such backsliding would be fatal; and the Lord sought to arouse the nation to a realization of their danger. Only as they should prove loyal to Jehovah could they hope for the divine favor and for prosperity.

Jeremiah called their attention repeatedly to the counsels given in Deuteronomy. More than any other of the prophets, he emphasized the teachings of the Mosaic law and showed how these might bring the highest spiritual blessing to the nation and to every individual heart. "Ask for the old paths, where is the good way, and walk therein," he pleaded, "and ye shall find rest for your souls." Jeremiah 6:16.

On one occasion, by command of the Lord, the prophet took his position at one of the principal entrances to the city and there urged the importance of keeping holy the Sabbath day. The inhabitants of Jerusalem were in danger of losing sight of the sanctity of the Sabbath, and they were solemnly warned against following their secular pursuits on that day. A blessing was promised on condition of obedience. "If ye diligently hearken unto Me," the Lord declared, and "hallow the Sabbath day, to do no work therein; then shall there enter into the gates of this city kings and princes sitting upon the throne of David, riding in chariots and on horses, they, and their princes, the men of Judah, and the inhabitants of Jerusalem: and this city shall remain forever." Jeremiah 17:24, 25.

This promise of prosperity as the reward of allegiance was accompanied by a prophecy of the terrible judgments that would befall the city should its inhabitants prove disloyal to God and His law. If the admonitions to obey the Lord God of their fathers and to hallow His Sabbath day were not heeded, the city and its palaces would be utterly destroyed by fire.

Thus the prophet stood firmly for the sound principles of right living so clearly outlined in the book of the law. But the conditions prevailing in the land of Judah were such that only by the most decided measures could a change for the better be brought about; therefore he labored most earnestly in behalf of the impenitent. "Break up your fallow ground," he pleaded, "and sow not among thorns." "O Jerusalem, wash thine heart from wickedness, that thou mayest be saved." Jeremiah 4:3, 14.

But by the great mass of the people the call to repentance and reformation was unheeded. Since the death of good King Josiah, those who ruled the nation had been proving untrue to their trust and had been leading many astray. Jehoahaz, deposed by the interference of the king of Egypt, had been followed by Jehoiakim, an older son of Josiah. From the beginning of Jehoiakim's reign, Jeremiah had little hope of saving his beloved land from destruction and the people from captivity. Yet he was not permitted to remain silent while utter ruin threatened the kingdom. Those who had remained loyal to God must be encouraged to persevere in rightdoing, and sinners must, if possible, be induced to turn from iniquity.

The crisis demanded a public and far-reaching effort. Jeremiah was commanded by the Lord to stand in the court of the temple and speak to all the people of Judah who might pass in and out. From the messages given him he must diminish not a word, that sinners in Zion might have the fullest possible opportunity to hearken and to turn from their evil ways.

The prophet obeyed; he stood in the gate of the Lord's house and there lifted his voice in warning and entreaty. Under the inspiration of the Almighty he declared:

"Hear the word of the Lord, all ye of Judah, that enter in at these gates to worship the Lord. Thus saith the Lord of hosts, the God of Israel, Amend your ways and your doings, and I will cause you to dwell in this place. Trust ye not in lying words, saying, The temple of the Lord, The temple of the Lord, The temple of the Lord, are these. For if ye thoroughly amend your ways and your doings; if ye thoroughly execute judgment between a man and his neighbor; if ye oppress not the stranger, the fatherless, and the widow, and shed not innocent blood in this place, neither walk after other gods to your hurt: then will I cause you to dwell in this place, in the land that I gave to your fathers, forever and ever." Jeremiah 7:2-7.

The unwillingness of the Lord to chastise is here vividly shown. He stays His judgments that He may plead with the impenitent. He who exercises "loving-kindness, judgment, and righteousness, in the earth" yearns over His erring children; in every way possible He seeks to teach them the way of life everlasting. Jeremiah 9:24. He had brought the Israelites out of bondage that they might serve Him, the only true and living God. Though they had wandered long in idolatry and had slighted His warnings, yet He now declares His willingness to defer chastisement and grant yet another opportunity for repentance. He makes plain the fact that only by the most thorough heart reformation could the impending doom be averted. In vain would be the trust they might place in the temple and its services. Rites and ceremonies could not atone for sin. Notwithstanding their claim to be the chosen people of God, reformation of heart and of the life practice alone could save them from the inevitable result of continued transgression.

Thus it was that "in the cities of Judah, and in the streets of Jerusalem" the message of Jeremiah to Judah was, "Hear ye the words of this covenant,"—the plain precepts of Jehovah as recorded in the Sacred Scriptures,—"and do them." Jeremiah 11:6. And this is the message he proclaimed as he stood in the temple courts in the beginning of the reign of Jehoiakim.

Israel's experience from the days of the Exodus was briefly reviewed. God's covenant with them had been, "Obey My voice, and I will be your God, and ye shall be My people: and walk ye in all the ways that I have commanded you, that it may be well unto you." Shamelessly and repeatedly had this covenant been broken. The chosen nation had "walked in the counsels and in the imagination of their evil heart, and went backward, and not forward." Jeremiah 7:23, 24.

"Why," the Lord inquired, "is this people of Jerusalem slidden back by a perpetual backsliding?" Jeremiah 8:5. In the language of the prophet it was because they had obeyed not the voice of the Lord their God and had refused to be corrected. See Jeremiah 5:3. "Truth is perished," he mourned, "and is cut off from their mouth." "The stork in the heaven knoweth her appointed times; and the turtle and the crane and
415 the swallow observe the time of their coming; but My people know not the judgment of the Lord." "Shall I not visit them for these things? saith the Lord: shall not My soul be avenged on such a nation as this?" Jeremiah 7:28; 8:7; 9:9.

The time had come for deep heart searching. While Josiah had been their ruler, the people had had some ground for hope. But no longer could he intercede in their behalf, for he had fallen in battle. The sins of the nation were such that the time for intercession had all but passed by. "Though Moses and Samuel stood before Me," the Lord declared, "yet My mind could not be toward this people: cast them out of My sight, and let them go forth. And it shall come to pass, if they say unto thee, Whither shall we go forth? then thou shalt tell them, Thus saith the Lord; Such as are for death, to death; and such as are for the sword, to the sword; and such as are for the famine, to the famine; and such as are for the captivity, to the captivity." Jeremiah 15:1, 2.

A refusal to heed the invitation of mercy that God was now offering would bring upon the impenitent nation the judgments that had befallen the northern kingdom of Israel over a century before. The message to them now was: "If ye will not hearken to Me, to walk in My law, which I have set before you, to hearken to the words of My servants the prophets, whom I sent unto you, both rising up early, and sending them, but ye have not hearkened; then will I make this house like Shiloh, and will make this city a curse to all the nations of the earth." Jeremiah 26:4-6.

Those who stood in the temple court listening to Jeremiah's discourse understood clearly this
416 reference to Shiloh, and to the time in the days of Eli when the Philistines had overcome Israel and carried away the ark of the testament.

The sin of Eli had consisted in passing lightly over the iniquity of his sons in sacred office, and over the evils prevailing throughout the land. His neglect to correct these evils had brought upon Israel a fearful calamity. His sons had fallen in battle, Eli himself had lost his life, the ark of God had been taken from the land of Israel, thirty thousand of the people had been slain—and all because sin had been allowed to flourish unrebuked and unchecked. Israel had vainly thought that, notwithstanding their sinful practices, the presence of the ark would ensure

them victory over the Philistines. In like manner, during the days of Jeremiah, the inhabitants of Judah were prone to believe that a strict observance of the divinely appointed services of the temple would preserve them from a just punishment for their wicked course.

What a lesson is this to men holding positions of responsibility today in the church of God! What a solemn warning to deal faithfully with wrongs that bring dishonor to the cause of truth! Let none who claim to be the depositaries of God's law flatter themselves that the regard they may outwardly show toward the commandments will preserve them from the exercise of divine justice. Let none refuse to be reproved for evil, nor charge the servants of God with being too zealous in endeavoring to cleanse the camp from evil-doing. A sin-hating God calls upon those who claim to keep His law to depart from all iniquity. A neglect to repent and to render willing obedience will bring upon men and women today as serious consequences as came upon ancient Israel. There is a limit beyond 417 which the judgments of Jehovah can no longer be delayed. The desolation of Jerusalem in the days of Jeremiah is a solemn warning to modern Israel, that the counsels and admonitions given them through chosen instrumentalities cannot be disregarded with impunity.

Jeremiah's message to priests and people aroused the antagonism of many. With boisterous denunciation they cried out, "Why hast thou prophesied in the name of the Lord, saying, This house shall be like Shiloh, and this city shall be desolate without an inhabitant? And all the people were gathered against Jeremiah in the house of the Lord." Jeremiah 26:9. Priests, false prophets, and people turned in wrath upon him who would not speak to them smooth things or prophesy deceit. Thus was the message of God despised, and His servant threatened with death.

Tidings of the words of Jeremiah were carried to the princes of Judah, and they hastened from the palace of the king to the temple, to learn for themselves the truth of the matter. "Then spake the priests and the prophets unto the princes and to all the people, saying, This man is worthy to die; for he hath prophesied against this city, as ye have heard with your ears." Verse 11. But Jeremiah stood boldly before the princes and the people, declaring: "The Lord sent me to prophesy against this house and against this city all the words that ye have heard. Therefore now amend your ways and your doings, and obey the voice of the Lord your God; and the Lord will repent Him of the evil that He hath pronounced against you. As for me, behold, I am in your hand: do with me as seemeth good and meet unto you. But know ye for certain, that if ye put 418 me to death, ye shall surely bring innocent blood upon yourselves, and upon this city, and upon the inhabitants thereof: for of a truth the

Lord hath sent me unto you to speak all these words in your ears." Verses 12-15.

Had the prophet been intimidated by the threatening attitude of those high in authority, his message would have been without effect, and he would have lost his life; but the courage with which he delivered the solemn warning commanded the respect of the people and turned the princes of Israel in his favor. They reasoned with the priests and false prophets, showing them how unwise would be the extreme measures they advocated, and their words produced a reaction in the minds of the people. Thus God raised up defenders for His servant.

The elders also united in protesting against the decision of the priests regarding the fate of Jeremiah. They cited the case of Micah, who had prophesied judgments upon Jerusalem, saying, "Zion shall be plowed like a field, and Jerusalem shall become heaps, and the mountain of the house as the high places of a forest." And they asked: "Did Hezekiah king of Judah and all Judah put him at all to death? did he not fear the Lord, and besought the Lord, and the Lord repented Him of the evil which He had pronounced against them? Thus might we procure great evil against our souls." Verses 18, 19.

Through the pleading of these men of influence the prophet's life was spared, although many of the priests and false prophets, unable to
419 endure the condemning truths he uttered, would gladly have seen him put to death on the plea of sedition.

From the day of his call to the close of his ministry, Jeremiah stood before Judah as "a tower and a fortress" against which the wrath of man could not prevail. "They shall fight against thee," the Lord had forewarned His servant, "but they shall not prevail against thee: for I am with thee to save thee and to deliver thee, saith the Lord. And I will deliver thee out of the hand of the wicked, and I will redeem thee out of the hand of the terrible." Jeremiah 6:27; 15:20, 21.

Naturally of a timid and shrinking disposition, Jeremiah longed for the peace and quiet of
420 a life of retirement, where he need not witness the continued impenitence of his beloved nation. His heart was wrung with anguish over the ruin wrought by sin. "O that my head were waters, and mine eyes a fountain of tears," he mourned, "that I might weep day and night for the slain of the daughter of my people! O that I had in the wilderness a lodging place of wayfaring men; that I might leave my people, and go from them." Jeremiah 9:1, 2.

Cruel were the mockings he was called upon to endure. His sensitive soul was pierced through and through by the arrows of derision hurled at him by those who despised his messages and made light of his burden for their conversion. "I was a derision to all my people," he declared, "and their song all the day." "I am in derision daily, everyone mocketh me." "All my familiars watched for my halting, saying, Peradventure he will be enticed, and we shall prevail against him, and we shall take our revenge on him." Lamentations 3:14; Jeremiah 20:7, 10.

But the faithful prophet was daily strengthened to endure. "The Lord is with me as a mighty terrible One," he declared in faith; "therefore my persecutors shall stumble, and they shall not prevail: they shall be greatly ashamed; for they shall not prosper: their everlasting confusion shall never be forgotten." "Sing unto the Lord, praise ye the Lord: for He hath delivered the soul of the poor from the hand of evildoers." Jeremiah 20:11, 13.

The experiences through which Jeremiah passed in the days of his youth and also in the later years of his ministry, taught him the lesson that "the way of man is not in himself: it is not 421 in man that walketh to direct his steps." He learned to pray, "O Lord, correct me, but with judgment; not in Thine anger, lest Thou bring me to nothing." Jeremiah 10:23, 24.

When called to drink of the cup of tribulation and sorrow, and when tempted in his misery to say, "My strength and my hope is perished from the Lord," he recalled the providences of God in his behalf and triumphantly exclaimed, "It is of the Lord's mercies that we are not consumed, because His compassions fail not. They are new every morning: great is Thy faithfulness. The Lord is my portion, saith my soul; therefore will I hope in Him. The Lord is good unto them that wait for Him, to the soul that seeketh Him. It is good that a man should both hope and quietly wait for the salvation of the Lord." Lamentations 3:18, 22-26.

35
422

Approaching Doom

The first years of Jehoiakim's reign were filled with warnings of approaching doom. The word of the Lord spoken by the prophets was about to be fulfilled. The Assyrian power to the northward, long supreme, was no longer to rule the nations. Egypt on the south, in whose power the king of Judah was vainly placing his trust, was soon to receive a decided check. All unexpectedly a new world power, the Babylonian Empire, was rising to the eastward and swiftly overshadowing all other nations.

Within a few short years the king of Babylon was to be used as the instrument of God's wrath upon impenitent Judah. Again and again Jerusalem was to be invested and entered by the besieging armies of Nebuchadnezzar. Company after company—at first a few only, but later on thousands and tens of thousands—were to be taken captive to the land of Shinar, there to dwell in enforced exile. Jehoiakim, Jehoiachin, Zedekiah—all these Jewish kings were in turn to become vassals of the Babylonian ruler, and all in turn were to rebel. Severer and yet more severe chastisements were to be inflicted upon the rebellious nation, until at last the entire land was to become a desolation, Jerusalem was to be laid waste and burned with fire, the temple that Solomon had built was to be destroyed, and the kingdom of Judah was to fall, never again to occupy its former position among the nations of earth.

Those times of change, so fraught with peril to the Israelitish nation, were marked with many messages from Heaven through Jeremiah. Thus the Lord gave the children of Judah ample opportunity of freeing themselves from entangling alliances with Egypt, and of avoiding controversy with the rulers of Babylon. As the threatened danger came closer, he taught the people by means of a series of acted parables, hoping thus to arouse them to a sense of their obligation to God, and also to encourage them to maintain friendly relations with the Babylonian government.

To illustrate the importance of yielding implicit obedience to the requirements of God, Jeremiah gathered some Rechabites into one of the chambers of the temple and set wine before them, inviting them to drink. As was to have been expected, he met with remonstrance and absolute refusal. "We will drink no wine," the Rechabites firmly declared, "for Jonadab the son of Rechab our father commanded us, saying, Ye shall drink no wine, neither ye, nor your sons forever."

"Then came the word of the Lord unto Jeremiah, saying, Thus saith the Lord of hosts, the God of Israel; Go and tell the men of Judah and the inhabitants of Jerusalem, Will ye not receive instruction to hearken to My words? saith the Lord. The words of Jonadab the son of Rechab, that he commanded his sons not to drink wine, are performed; for unto this day they drink none, but obey their father's commandment." Jeremiah 35:6, 12-14.

God sought thus to bring into sharp contrast the obedience of the Rechabites with the disobedience and rebellion of His people. The Rechabites had obeyed the command of their father and now refused to be enticed into transgression. But the men of Judah had hearkened not to the words of the Lord, and were in consequence about to suffer His severest judgments.

"I have spoken unto you, rising early and speaking," the Lord declared, "but ye hearkened not unto Me. I have sent also unto you all My servants the prophets, rising up early and sending them, saying, Return ye now every man from his evil way, and amend your doings, and go not after other gods to serve them, and ye shall dwell in the land which I have given to you and to your fathers: but ye have not inclined your ear, nor hearkened unto Me. Because the sons of Jonadab the son of Rechab have performed the commandment of their father, which he commanded them; but this people hath not hearkened unto Me: therefore thus saith the Lord God of hosts, the God of Israel; Behold, I will bring upon Judah and upon all the inhabitants of Jerusalem all the evil that I have pronounced against them: because I have spoken unto them, but they have not heard; and I have called unto them, but they have not answered." Verses 14-17.

When men's hearts are softened and subdued by the constraining influence of the Holy Spirit, they will give heed to counsel; but when they turn from admonition until their hearts become hardened, the Lord permits them to be led by other influences. Refusing the truth, they accept falsehood, which becomes a snare to their own destruction.

God had pleaded with Judah not to provoke Him to anger, but they had hearkened not. Finally sentence was pronounced against them. They were to be led away captive to Babylon. The Chaldeans were to be used as the instrument by which God would chastise His disobedient people. The sufferings of the men of Judah were to be in proportion to the light they had had and to the warnings they had despised and rejected. Long had God delayed His judgments, but now He would visit His displeasure upon them as a last effort to check them in their evil course.

Upon the house of the Rechabites was pronounced a continued blessing. The prophet declared, "Because ye have obeyed the commandment of Jonadab your father, and kept all his precepts, and done according unto all that he hath commanded you: therefore thus saith the Lord of hosts, the God of Israel; Jonadab the son of Rechab shall not want a man to stand before Me forever." Verses 18, 19. Thus God taught His people that faithfulness and obedience would be reflected back upon Judah in blessing, even as the Rechabites were blessed for obedience to their father's command.

The lesson is for us. If the requirements of a good and wise father, who took the best and most effectual means to secure his posterity against the evils of intemperance, were worthy of strict obedience, surely God's authority should be held in as much greater reverence as He is holier than man. Our Creator and our Commander, infinite in power, terrible in judgment, seeks by every means to bring men to see and repent of their sins. By the mouth of His servants He predicts the dangers of disobedience; He sounds the note of warning and faithfully reproves sin. His people are kept in prosperity only by His mercy, through the vigilant watchcare of chosen instrumentalities. He cannot uphold and guard a people who reject His counsel and despise His reproofs. For a time He may withhold His retributive judgments; yet He cannot always stay His hand.

The children of Judah were numbered among those of whom God had declared, "Ye shall be unto Me a kingdom of priests, and an holy nation." Exodus 19:6. Never did Jeremiah in his ministry lose sight of the vital importance of heart holiness in the varied relationships of life, and especially in the service of the most high God. Plainly he foresaw the downfall of the kingdom and a scattering of the inhabitants of Judah among the nations; but with the eye of faith he looked beyond all this to the times of restoration. Ringing in his ears was the divine promise: "I will gather the remnant of My flock out of all countries whither I have driven them, and will bring them again to their folds. . . . Behold, the days come, saith the Lord, that I will raise unto David a righteous Branch, and a King shall reign and prosper, and shall execute judgment and justice in the earth. In His days 427 Judah shall be saved, and Israel shall dwell safely: and this is His name whereby He shall be called, THE LORD OUR RIGHTEOUSNESS." Jeremiah 23:3-6.

Thus prophecies of oncoming judgment were mingled with promises of final and glorious deliverance. Those who should choose to make their peace with God and live holy lives amid the prevailing apostasy, would receive strength for every trial and be enabled to witness for Him with mighty power. And in the ages to come the deliverance wrought in their behalf would exceed in fame that wrought for the children of Israel at the time of the Exodus. The days were coming, the Lord declared through His prophet, when "they shall no more say, The Lord liveth, which brought up the children of Israel out of the land of Egypt; but, The Lord liveth, which brought up and which led the seed of the house of Israel out of the north country, and from all countries whither I had driven them; and they shall dwell in their own land." Verses 7, 8. Such were the wonderful prophecies uttered by Jeremiah during the closing years of the history of the kingdom of Judah, when the Babylonians were coming unto universal rule, and were even then bringing their besieging armies against the walls of Zion.

Like sweetest music these promises of deliverance fell upon the ears of those who were steadfast in their worship of Jehovah. In the homes of the high and the lowly, where the counsels of a covenant-keeping God were still held in reverence, the words of the prophet were repeated again and again. Even the children were mightily stirred, and upon their young and receptive minds lasting impressions were made. 428 It was their conscientious observance of the

commands of Holy Scripture, that in the days of Jeremiah's ministry brought to Daniel and his fellows opportunities to exalt the true God before the nations of earth. The instruction these Hebrew children had received in the homes of their parents, made them strong in faith and constant in their service of the living God, the Creator of the heavens and the earth. When, early in the reign of Jehoiakim, Nebuchadnezzar for the first time besieged and captured Jerusalem, and carried away Daniel and his companions, with others specially chosen for service in the court of Babylon, the faith of the Hebrew captives was tried to the utmost. But those who had learned to place their trust in the promises of God found these all-sufficient in every experience through which they were called to pass during their sojourn in a strange land. The Scriptures proved to them a guide and a stay.

As an interpreter of the meaning of the judgments beginning to fall upon Judah, Jeremiah stood nobly in defense of the justice of God and of His merciful designs even in the severest chastisements. Untiringly the prophet labored. Desirous of reaching all classes, he extended the sphere of his influence beyond Jerusalem to the surrounding districts by frequent visits to various parts of the kingdom.

In his testimonies to the church, Jeremiah constantly referred to the teachings of the book of the law that had been so greatly honored and exalted during Josiah's reign. He emphasized anew the importance of maintaining a covenant relationship with the all-merciful and compassionate Being who upon the heights of Sinai had 429 spoken the precepts of the Decalogue. Jeremiah's words of warning and entreaty reached every part of the kingdom, and all had opportunity to know the will of God concerning the nation.

The prophet made plain the fact that our heavenly Father allows His judgments to fall, "that the nations may know themselves to be but men." Psalm 9:20. "If ye walk contrary unto Me, and will not hearken unto Me," the Lord had forewarned His people, "I, even I, . . . will scatter you among the heathen, and will draw out a sword after you: and your land shall be desolate, and your cities waste." Leviticus 26:21, 28, 33.

At the very time messages of impending doom were urged upon princes and people, their ruler, Jehoiakim, who should have been a wise spiritual leader, foremost in confession of sin and in reformation and good works, was spending his time in selfish pleasure. "I will build me a wide house and large chambers," he proposed; and this house, "ceiled with cedar, and painted with vermilion" (Jeremiah 22:14), was built with money and labor secured through fraud and oppression.

The wrath of the prophet was aroused, and he was inspired to pronounce judgment upon the faithless ruler. "Woe unto him that buildeth his house by unrighteousness, and his chambers by wrong," he declared; "that useth his neighbor's service without wages, and giveth him not for his work. . . . Shalt thou reign, because thou closest thyself in cedar? Did not thy father eat and drink, and do judgment and justice, and then it was well with him? He judged the cause of the poor and needy; then it was well with him: was not this to know Me? saith the Lord. But thine eyes and thine heart are not but for thy covetousness, and for to shed innocent blood, and for oppression, and for violence, to do it.

"Therefore thus saith the Lord concerning Jehoiakim the son of Josiah king of Judah; They shall not lament for him, saying, Ah my brother! or, Ah sister! they shall not lament for him, saying, Ah lord! or, Ah his glory! He shall be buried with the burial of an ass, drawn and cast forth beyond the gates of Jerusalem." Verses 13-19.

Within a few years this terrible judgment was to be visited upon Jehoiakim; but first the Lord in mercy informed the impenitent nation of His set purpose. In the fourth year of Jehoiakim's reign "Jeremiah the prophet spake unto all the people of Judah, and to all the inhabitants of Jerusalem," pointing out that for over a score of years, "from the thirteenth year of Josiah, . . . even unto this day," he had borne witness of God's desire to save, but that his messages had been despised. Jeremiah 25:2, 3. And now the word of the Lord to them was:

"Thus saith the Lord of hosts; Because ye have not heard My words, behold, I will send and take all the families of the north, saith the Lord, and Nebuchadnezzar the king of Babylon, My servant, and will bring them against this land, and against the inhabitants thereof, and against all these nations round about, and will utterly destroy them, and make them an astonishment, and an hissing, and perpetual desolations. Moreover I will take from them the voice of mirth, and the voice of gladness, the voice of the bridegroom, and the voice of the bride, the sound of the millstones, and the light of the candle. And this whole land shall be a desolation, and an astonishment; and these nations shall serve the king of Babylon seventy years." Verses 8-11.

Although the sentence of doom had been clearly pronounced, its awful import could scarcely be understood by the multitudes who heard. That deeper impressions might be made, the Lord sought to illustrate the meaning of the words spoken. He bade Jeremiah liken the fate of the nation to the draining of a cup filled with the wine of divine wrath. Among the first to drink of this cup of woe were to be "Jerusalem, and the cities of Judah, and the kings thereof."

Others were to partake of the same cup—"Pharaoh king of Egypt, and his servants, and his princes, and all his people," and many other nations of earth—until God's purpose should have been fulfilled. See Jeremiah 25.

To illustrate further the nature of the swift-coming judgments, the prophet was bidden to "take of the ancients of the people, and of the ancients of the priests; and go forth unto the valley of the son of Hinnom," and there, after reviewing the apostasy of Judah, he was to dash to pieces "a potter's earthen bottle," and declare in behalf of Jehovah, whose servant he was, "Even so will I break this people and this city, as one breaketh a potter's vessel, that cannot be made whole again."

The prophet did as he was commanded. Then, returning to the city, he stood in the court of the temple and declared in the hearing of all the people, "Thus saith the Lord of hosts, the God of Israel; Behold, I will bring upon this city and upon all her towns all the evil that I have pronounced against it, because they have hardened their necks, that they might not hear My words." See Jeremiah 19.

The prophet's words, instead of leading to confession and repentance, aroused the anger of those high in authority, and as a consequence Jeremiah was deprived of his liberty. Imprisoned, and placed in the stocks, the prophet nevertheless continued to speak the messages of Heaven to those who stood by. His voice could not be silenced by persecution. The word of truth, he declared, "was in mine heart as a burning fire shut up in my bones, and I was weary with forbearing, and I could not stay." Jeremiah 20:9.

It was about this time that the Lord commanded Jeremiah to commit to writing the messages he desired to bear to those for whose salvation his heart of pity was continually yearning. "Take thee a roll of a book," the Lord bade His servant, "and write therein all the words that I have spoken unto thee against Israel, and against Judah, and against all the nations, from the day I spake unto thee, from the days of Josiah, even unto this day. It may be that the house of Judah will hear all the evil which I purpose to do unto them; that they may return every man from his evil way; that I may forgive their iniquity and their sin." Jeremiah 36:2, 3.

In obedience to this command, Jeremiah called to his aid a faithful friend, Baruch the scribe, and dictated "all the words of the Lord, which He had spoken unto him." Verse 4. These were carefully written out on a roll of parchment and constituted a solemn reproof for sin, a warning of the sure result of continual apostasy, and an earnest appeal for the renunciation of all evil.

When the writing was completed, Jeremiah, who was still a prisoner, sent Baruch to read the roll to the multitudes who were assembling at the temple on the occasion of a national fast day, "in the fifth year of Jehoiakim the son of Josiah king of Judah, in the ninth month." "It may be," the prophet said, "they will present their supplication before the Lord, and will return everyone from his evil way: for great is the anger and the fury that the Lord hath pronounced against this people." Verses 9, 7.

Baruch obeyed, and the roll was read before all the people of Judah. Afterward the scribe was summoned before the princes to read the words to them. They listened with great interest and promised to inform the king concerning all they had heard, but counseled the scribe to hide himself, for they feared the king would reject the testimony and seek to slay those who had prepared and delivered the message.

When King Jehoiakim was told by the princes what Baruch had read, he immediately ordered the roll brought before him and read in his hearing. One of the royal attendants, Jehudi by name, fetched the roll and began reading the words of reproof and warning. It was the time of winter, and the king and his companions of state, the princes of Judah, were gathered about an open fire. Only a small portion had been 434 read, when the king, far from trembling at the danger hanging over himself and his people, seized the roll and in a frenzy of rage "cut it with the penknife and cast it into the fire that was on the hearth, until all the roll was consumed." Verse 23.

Neither the king nor his princes were afraid "nor rent their garments." Certain of the princes, however, "had made intercession to the king that he would not burn the roll: but he would not hear them." The writing having been destroyed, the wrath of the wicked king rose against Jeremiah and Baruch, and he forthwith sent for them to be taken; "but the Lord hid them." Verses 24-26.

435 In bringing to the attention of the temple worshipers, and of the princes and king, the written admonitions contained in the inspired roll, God was graciously seeking to warn the men of Judah for their good. "It may be," He said, "the house of Judah will hear all the evil which I purpose to do unto them; that they may return every man from his evil way; that I may forgive their iniquity and their sin." Verse 3. God pities men struggling in the blindness of perversity; He seeks to enlighten the darkened understanding by sending reproofs and threatenings designed to cause the most exalted to feel their ignorance and to deplore their errors. He endeavors to help the self-complacent to become dissatisfied with their vain attainments and to seek for spiritual blessing through a close connection with heaven.

God's plan is not to send messengers who will please and flatter sinners; He delivers no messages of peace to lull the unsanctified into carnal security. Instead, He lays heavy burdens upon the conscience of the wrongdoer and pierces his soul with sharp arrows of conviction. Ministering angels present to him the fearful judgments of God, to deepen the sense of need and to prompt the agonizing cry, "What must I do to be saved?" Acts 16:30. But the Hand that humbles to the dust, rebukes sin, and puts pride and ambition to shame, is the Hand that lifts up the penitent, stricken one. With deepest sympathy He who permits the chastisement to fall, inquires, "What wilt thou that I shall do unto thee?"

When man has sinned against a holy and merciful God, he can pursue no course so noble as to repent sincerely and confess his errors in 436 tears and bitterness of soul. This God requires of him; He accepts nothing less than a broken heart and a contrite spirit. But King Jehoiakim and his lords, in their arrogance and pride, refused the invitation of God. They would not heed the warning, and repent. The gracious opportunity proffered them at the time of the burning of the sacred roll, was their last. God had declared that if at that time they refused to hear His voice, He would inflict upon them fearful retribution. They did refuse to hear, and He pronounced His final judgments upon Judah, and He would visit with special wrath the man who had proudly lifted himself up against the Almighty.

"Thus saith the Lord of Jehoiakim king of Judah; He shall have none to sit upon the throne of David: and his dead body shall be cast out in the day to the heat, and in the night to the frost. And I will punish him and his seed and his servants for their iniquity; and I will bring upon them, and upon the inhabitants of Jerusalem, and upon the men of Judah, all the evil that I have pronounced against them." Jeremiah 36:30, 31.

The burning of the roll was not the end of the matter. The written words were more easily disposed of than the reproof and warning they contained and the swift-coming punishment God had pronounced against rebellious Israel. But even the written roll was reproduced. "Take thee again another roll," the Lord commanded His servant, "and write in it all the former words that were in the first roll, which Jehoiakim the king of Judah hath burned." The record of the prophecies concerning Judah and Jerusalem had been reduced to ashes; but the words were still 437 living in the heart of Jeremiah, "as a burning fire," and the prophet was permitted to reproduce that which the wrath of man would fain have destroyed.

Taking another roll, Jeremiah gave it to Baruch, "who wrote therein from the mouth of Jeremiah all the words of the book which Jehoiakim king of Judah had burned in the fire: and there were added besides unto them many like words." Verses 28, 32. The wrath of man had sought to prevent the labors of the prophet of God; but the very means by which Jehoiakim had endeavored to limit the influence of the servant of Jehovah, gave further opportunity for making plain the divine requirements.

The spirit of opposition to reproof, that led to the persecution and imprisonment of Jeremiah, exists today. Many refuse to heed repeated warnings, preferring rather to listen to false teachers who flatter their vanity and overlook their evil-doing. In the day of trouble such will have no sure refuge, no help from heaven. God's chosen servants should meet with courage and patience the trials and sufferings that befall them through reproach, neglect, and misrepresentation. They should continue to discharge faithfully the work God has given them to do, ever remembering that the prophets of old and the Saviour of mankind and His apostles also endured abuse and persecution for the Word's sake.

It was God's purpose that Jehoiakim should heed the counsels of Jeremiah and thus win favor in the eyes of Nebuchadnezzar and save himself much sorrow. The youthful king had sworn allegiance to the Babylonian ruler, and had he remained true to his promise he would have commanded the respect of the heathen, and this would have led to precious opportunities for the conversion of souls.

Scorning the unusual privileges granted him, Judah's king willfully followed a way of his own choosing. He violated his word of honor to the Babylonian ruler, and rebelled. This brought him and his kingdom into a very strait place. Against him were sent "bands of the Chaldees, and bands of the Syrians, and bands of the Moabites, and bands of the children of Ammon," and he was powerless to prevent the land from being overrun by these marauders. 2 Kings 24:2. Within a few years he closed his disastrous reign in ignominy, rejected of Heaven, unloved by his people, and despised by the rulers of Babylon whose confidence he had betrayed—and all as the result of his fatal mistake in turning from the purpose of God as revealed through His appointed messenger.

Jehoiachin [also known as Jeconiah, and Coniah], the son of Jehoiakim, occupied the throne only three months and ten days, when he surrendered to the Chaldean armies which, because of the rebellion of Judah's ruler, were once more besieging the fated city. On this occasion Nebuchadnezzar "carried away Jehoiachin to Babylon, and the king's mother, and the king's wives, and his officers, and the mighty of the land," several thousand in number, together with "craftsmen and smiths a thousand." With these the king of Babylon took "all the treasures of the house of the Lord, and the treasures of the king's house." 2 Kings 24:15, 16, 13.

The kingdom of Judah, broken in power and robbed of its strength both in men and in treasure, was nevertheless still permitted to exist as a separate government. At its head Nebuchadnezzar placed Mattaniah, a younger son of Josiah, changing his name to Zedekiah.

36

The Last King of Judah

Zedekiah at the beginning of his reign was trusted fully by the king of Babylon and had as a tried counselor the prophet Jeremiah. By pursuing an honorable course toward the Babylonians and by paying heed to the messages from the Lord through Jeremiah, he could have kept the respect of many in high authority and have had opportunity to communicate to them a knowledge of the true God. Thus the captive exiles already in Babylon would have been placed on vantage ground and granted many liberties; the name of God would have been honored far and wide; and those that remained in the land of Judah would have been spared the terrible calamities that finally came upon them.

Through Jeremiah, Zedekiah and all Judah, including those taken to Babylon, were counseled to submit quietly to the temporary rule of their conquerors. It was especially important that those in captivity should seek the peace of the land into which they had been carried. This, however, was contrary to the inclinations of the human heart; and Satan, taking advantage of the circumstances, caused false prophets to arise among the people, both in Jerusalem and in Babylon, who declared that the yoke of bondage would soon be broken and the former prestige of the nation restored.

The heeding of such flattering prophecies would have led to fatal moves on the part of the king and the exiles, and would have frustrated the merciful designs of God in their behalf. Lest an insurrection be incited and great suffering ensue, the Lord commanded Jeremiah to meet the crisis without delay, by warning the king of Judah of the sure consequence of rebellion. The captives also were admonished, by written communications, not to be deluded into believing their deliverance near. "Let not your prophets and your diviners, that be in the midst of you, deceive you," he urged. Jeremiah 29:8. In this connection mention was made of the Lord's purpose to restore Israel at the close of the seventy years of captivity foretold by His messengers.

With what tender compassion did God inform His captive people of His plans for Israel! He knew that should they be persuaded by false prophets to look for a speedy deliverance, their

438

439

440

441

position in Babylon would be made very diffi-cult. Any demonstration or insurrection on their part would awaken the vigilance and severity of the Chaldean authorities and would lead to a further restriction of their liberties. Suffering and disaster would result. He desired them to submit quietly to their fate and make their servi-tude as pleasant as possible; and his counsel to them was: "Build ye houses, and dwell in them; and plant gardens, and eat the fruit of them; . . . and seek the peace of the city whither I have caused you to be carried away captives, and pray unto the Lord for it: for in the peace there-of shall ye have peace." Verses 5-7.

Among the false teachers in Babylon were two men who claimed to be holy, but whose lives were corrupt. Jeremiah had condemned the evil course of these men and had warned them of their danger. Angered by reproof, they sought to oppose the work of the true prophet by stir-ring up the people to discredit his words and to act contrary to the counsel of God in the matter of subjecting themselves to the king of Babylon. The Lord testified through Jeremiah that these false prophets should be delivered into the hands of Nebuchadnezzar and slain before his eyes. Not long afterward, this prediction was lit-erally fulfilled.

To the end of time, men will arise to create confusion and rebellion among those who claim to be representatives of the true God. Those who prophesy lies will encourage men to look upon sin as a light thing. When the terrible results of their evil deeds are made manifest, they will seek, if possible, to make the one who has faithfully warned them, responsible for their difficulties, even as the Jews charged Jeremiah with their evil fortunes. But as surely as the words of Jehovah through His prophet were vin-dicated anciently, so surely will the certainty of His messages be established today.

From the first, Jeremiah had followed a con-sistent course in counseling submission to the Babylonians. This counsel was given not only to Judah, but to many of the surrounding nations. In the earlier portion of Zedekiah's reign, ambassadors from the rulers of Edom, Moab, Tyre, and other nations visited the king of Judah to learn whether in his judgment the time was opportune for a united revolt and whether he would join them in battling against the king of Babylon. While these ambassadors were awaiting a response, the word of the Lord came to Jeremiah, saying, "Make thee bonds and yokes, and put them upon thy neck, and send them to the king of Edom, and to the king of Moab, and to the king of the Ammonites, and to the king of Tyrus, and to the king of Zidon, by the hand of the messengers which come to Jerusalem unto Zedekiah king of Judah." Jere-miah 27:2, 3.

Jeremiah was commanded to instruct the ambassadors to inform their rulers that God had given them all into the hand of Nebuchadnez-zar, the king of Babylon, and that they were to "serve him, and his son, and his son's son, until the very time of his land come." Verse 7.

The ambassadors were further instructed to declare to their rulers that if they refused to serve the Babylonian king they should be pun-ished "with the sword, and with the famine, and with the pestilence" till they were consumed. Especially were they to turn from the teaching of false prophets who might counsel otherwise. "Hearken not ye to your prophets," the Lord declared, "nor to your diviners, nor to your dreamers, nor to your enchanters, nor to your sorcerers, which speak unto you, saying, Ye shall not serve the king of Babylon: for they prophesy a lie unto you, to remove you far from your land; and that I should drive you out, and ye should perish. But the nations that bring their neck under the yoke of the king of Babylon, and serve him, those will I let remain still in their own land, saith the Lord; and they shall till it, and dwell therein." Verses 8-11. The lightest punishment that a merciful God could inflict upon so rebellious a people was submission to the rule of Babylon, but if they warred against this decree of servitude they were to feel the full rigor of His chastisement.

The amazement of the assembled council of nations knew no bounds when Jeremiah, carry-ing the yoke of subjection about his neck, made known to them the will of God.

Against determined opposition Jeremiah stood firmly for the policy of submission. Prominent among those who presumed to gain-say the counsel of the Lord was Hananiah, one of the false prophets against whom the people had been warned. Thinking to gain the favor of the king and of the royal court, he lifted his voice in protest, declaring that God had given him words of encouragement for the Jews. Said he: "Thus speaketh the Lord of hosts, the God of Israel, saying, I have broken the yoke of the king of Babylon. Within two full years will I bring again into this place all the vessels of the Lord's house, that Nebuchadnezzar king of Babylon took away from this place, and carried them to Babylon: and I will bring again to this place Jeconiah the son of Jehoiakim king of Judah, with all the captives of Judah, that went into Babylon, saith the Lord: for I will break the yoke of the king of Babylon." Jeremiah 28:2-4.

Jeremiah, in the presence of the priests and people, earnestly entreated them to submit to the king of Babylon for the time the Lord had speci-fied. He cited the men of Judah to the prophe-cies of Hosea, Habakkuk, Zephaniah, and others whose messages of reproof and warning had been similar to his own. He referred them to events which had taken place in fulfillment of prophecies of retribution for unrepented sin. In the past the judgments of God had been visited upon the impenitent in exact fulfillment of His purpose as revealed through His messengers.

"The prophet which prophesieth of peace," Jeremiah proposed in conclusion, "when the word of the prophet shall come to pass, then shall the prophet be known, that the Lord hath truly sent him." Verse 9. If Israel chose to run the risk, future developments would effectually decide which was the true prophet.

446 The words of Jeremiah counseling submission aroused Hananiah to a daring challenge of the reliability of the message delivered. Taking the symbolic yoke from Jeremiah's neck, Hananiah broke it, saying, "Thus saith the Lord; Even so will I break the yoke of Nebuchadnezzar king of Babylon from the neck of all nations within the space of two full years.

"And the prophet Jeremiah went his way." Verse 11. Apparently he could do nothing more than to retire from the scene of conflict. But Jeremiah was given another message. "Go and tell Hananiah," he was bidden, "Thus saith the Lord; Thou hast broken the yokes of wood; but thou shalt make for them yokes of iron. For thus saith the Lord of hosts, the God of Israel; I have put a yoke of iron upon the neck of all these nations, that they may serve Nebuchadnezzar king of Babylon; and they shall serve him. . . .

"Then said the prophet Jeremiah unto Hananiah the prophet, Hear now, Hananiah; The Lord hath not sent thee: but thou makest this people to trust in a lie. Therefore thus saith the Lord; Behold, I will cast thee from off the face of the earth: this year thou shalt die, because thou hast taught rebellion against the Lord. So Hananiah the prophet died the same year in the seventh month." Verses 13-17.

The false prophet had strengthened the unbelief of the people in Jeremiah and his message. He had wickedly declared himself the Lord's messenger, and he suffered death in consequence. In the fifth month Jeremiah prophesied the death of Hananiah, and in the seventh month his words were proved true by their fulfillment.

447 The unrest caused by the representations of the false prophets brought Zedekiah under suspicion of treason, and only by quick and decisive action on his part was he permitted to continue reigning as a vassal. Opportunity for such action was taken advantage of shortly after the return of the ambassadors from Jerusalem to the surrounding nations, when the king of Judah accompanied Seraiah, "a quiet prince," on an important mission to Babylon. Jeremiah 51:59. During this visit to the Chaldean court, Zedekiah renewed his oath of allegiance to Nebuchadnezzar.

Through Daniel and others of the Hebrew captives, the Babylonian monarch had been made acquainted with the power and supreme authority of the true God; and when Zedekiah once more solemnly promised to remain loyal, Nebuchadnezzar required him to swear to this promise in the name of the Lord God of Israel. Had Zedekiah respected this renewal of his covenant oath, his loyalty would have had a profound influence on the minds of many who were watching the conduct of those who claimed to reverence the name and to cherish the honor of the God of the Hebrews.

But Judah's king lost sight of his high privilege of bringing honor to the name of the living God. Of Zedekiah it is recorded: "He did that which was evil in the sight of the Lord his God, and humbled not himself before Jeremiah the prophet speaking from the mouth of the Lord. And he also rebelled against King Nebuchadnezzar, who had made him swear by God: but he stiffened his neck, and hardened his heart from turning unto the Lord God of Israel." 2 Chronicles 36:12, 13.

While Jeremiah continued to bear his testimony in the land of Judah, the prophet Ezekiel was raised up from among the captives in Babylon, to warn and to comfort the exiles, and also to confirm the word of the Lord that was being spoken through Jeremiah. During the years that remained of Zedekiah's reign, Ezekiel made very plain the folly of trusting to the false predictions of those who were causing the captives to hope for an early return to Jerusalem. He was also instructed to foretell, by means of a variety of symbols and solemn messages, the siege and utter destruction of Jerusalem. 448

In the sixth year of the reign of Zedekiah, the Lord revealed to Ezekiel in vision some of the abominations that were being practiced in Jerusalem, and within the gate of the Lord's house, and even in the inner court. The chambers of images, and the pictured idols, "every form of creeping things, and abominable beasts, and all the idols of the house of Israel"—all these in rapid succession passed before the astonished gaze of the prophet. Ezekiel 8:10.

Those who should have been spiritual leaders among the people, "the ancients of the house of Israel," to the number of seventy, were seen offering incense before the idolatrous representations that had been introduced into hidden chambers within the sacred precincts of the temple court. "The Lord seeth us not," the men of Judah flattered themselves as they engaged in their heathenish practices; "the Lord hath forsaken the earth," they blasphemously declared. Verses 11, 12.

There were still "greater abominations" for the prophet to behold. At a gate leading from the outer to the inner court he was shown 449 "women weeping for Tammuz," and within "the inner court of the Lord's house, . . . at the door of the temple of the Lord, between the porch and the altar, were about five and twenty men, with their backs toward the temple of the Lord, and their faces toward the east; and they worshiped the sun toward the east." Verses 13-16.

And now the glorious Being who accompanied Ezekiel throughout this astonishing vision of wickedness in high places in the land of Judah, inquired of the prophet: "Hast thou seen this, O son of man? Is it a light thing to the house of Judah that they commit the abominations which they commit here? for they have filled the land with violence, and have returned to provoke Me to anger: and, lo, they put the branch to their nose. Therefore will I also deal in fury: Mine eye shall not spare, neither will I have pity: and though they cry in Mine ears with a loud voice, yet will I not hear them." Verses 17, 18.

Through Jeremiah the Lord had declared of the wicked men who presumptuously dared to stand before the people in His name: "Both prophet and priest are profane; yea, in My house have I found their wickedness." Jeremiah 23:11. In the terrible arraignment of Judah as recorded in the closing narrative of the chronicler of Zedekiah's reign, this charge of violating the sanctity of the temple was repeated. "Moreover," the sacred writer declared, "all the chief of the priests, and the people, transgressed very much after all the abominations of the heathen; and polluted the house of the Lord which He had hallowed in Jerusalem." 2 Chronicles 36:14.

450 The day of doom for the kingdom of Judah was fast approaching. No longer could the Lord set before them the hope of averting the severest of His judgments. "Should ye be utterly unpunished?" He inquired. "Ye shall not be unpunished." Jeremiah 25:29.

Even these words were received with mocking derision. "The days are prolonged, and every vision faileth," declared the impenitent. But through Ezekiel this denial of the sure word of prophecy was sternly rebuked. "Tell them," the Lord declared, "I will make this proverb to cease, and they shall no more use it as a proverb in Israel; but say unto them, The days are at hand, and the effect of every vision. For there shall be no more any vain vision nor flattering divination within the house of Israel. For I am the Lord: I will speak, and the word that I shall speak shall come to pass; it shall be no more prolonged: for in your days, O rebellious house, will I say the word, and will perform it, saith the Lord God.

"Again," testifies Ezekiel, "the word of the Lord came to me, saying, Son of man, behold, they of the house of Israel say, The vision that he seeth is for many days to come, and he prophesieth of the times that are far off. Therefore say unto them, Thus saith the Lord God; There shall none of My words be prolonged any more, but the word which I have spoken shall be done, saith the Lord God." Ezekiel 12:22-28.

Foremost among those who were rapidly leading the nation to ruin was Zedekiah their king. Forsaking utterly the counsels of the Lord as given through the prophets, forgetting the debt of gratitude he owed Nebuchadnezzar, vio- 451 lating his solemn oath of allegiance taken in the name of the Lord God of Israel, Judah's king rebelled against the prophets, against his benefactor, and against his God. In the vanity of his own wisdom he turned for help to the ancient enemy of Israel's prosperity, "sending his ambassadors into Egypt, that they might give him horses and much people."

"Shall he prosper?" the Lord inquired concerning the one who had thus basely betrayed every sacred trust; "shall he escape that doeth such things? or shall he break the covenant, and be delivered? As I live, saith the Lord God, surely in the place where the king dwelleth that made him king, whose oath he despised, and whose covenant he brake, even with him in the midst of Babylon he shall die. Neither shall Pharaoh with his mighty army and great company make for him in the war: . . . . seeing he despised the oath by breaking the covenant, when, lo, he had given his hand, and hath done all these things, he shall not escape." Ezekiel 17:15-18.

To the "profane wicked prince" had come the day of final reckoning. "Remove the diadem," the Lord decreed, "and take off the crown." Not until Christ Himself should set up His kingdom was Judah again to be permitted to have a king. "I will overturn, overturn, overturn, it," was the divine edict concerning the throne of the house of David; "and it shall be no more, until He come whose right it is; and I will give it Him." Ezekiel 21:25-27.

37 452

Carried Captive Into Babylon

In the ninth year of Zedekiah's reign "Nebuchadnezzar king of Babylon came, he, and all his host, against Jerusalem," to besiege the city. 2 Kings 25:1. The outlook for Judah was hopeless. "Behold, I am against thee," the Lord Himself declared through Ezekiel. "I the Lord have drawn forth My sword out of his sheath: it shall not return any more. . . . Every heart shall melt, and all hands shall be feeble, and every spirit shall faint, and all knees shall be weak as water." "I will pour out Mine indignation upon thee, I will blow against thee in the fire of My wrath, and deliver thee into the hand of brutish men, and skillful to destroy." Ezekiel 21:3, 5-7, 31.

The Egyptians endeavored to come to the rescue of the beleaguered city; and the Chaldeans, in order to keep them back, abandoned for a time their siege of the Judean capital. Hope sprang up in the heart of Zedekiah, and he sent a messenger to Jeremiah, asking him to pray to God in behalf of the Hebrew nation.

The prophet's fearful answer was that the Chaldeans would return and destroy the city. The fiat had gone forth; no longer could the impenitent nation avert the divine judgments. "Deceive not yourselves," the Lord warned His people. "The Chaldeans . . . shall not depart. For though ye had smitten the whole army of the Chaldeans that fight against you, and there remained but wounded men among them, yet should they rise up every man in his tent, and burn this city with fire." Jeremiah 37:9, 10. The remnant of Judah were to go into captivity, to learn through adversity the lessons they had refused to learn under circumstances more favorable. From this decree of the holy Watcher there could be no appeal.

Among the righteous still in Jerusalem, to whom had been made plain the divine purpose, were some who determined to place beyond the reach of ruthless hands the sacred ark containing the tables of stone on which had been traced the precepts of the Decalogue. This they did. With mourning and sadness they secreted the ark in a cave, where it was to be hidden from the people of Israel and Judah because of their sins, and was to be no more restored to them. That sacred ark is yet hidden. It has never been disturbed since it was secreted.

For many years Jeremiah had stood before the people as a faithful witness for God; and now, as the fated city was about to pass into the hands of the heathen, he considered his work done and attempted to leave, but was prevented by a son of one of the false prophets, who reported that Jeremiah was about to join the Babylonians, to whom he had repeatedly urged the men of Judah to submit. The prophet denied the lying charge, but nevertheless "the princes were wroth with Jeremiah, and smote him, and put him in prison." Verse 15.

The hopes that had sprung up in the hearts of princes and people when the armies of Nebuchadnezzar turned south to meet the Egyptians, were soon dashed to the ground. The word of the Lord had been, "Behold, I am against thee, Pharaoh king of Egypt." The might of Egypt was but a broken reed. "All the inhabitants of Egypt," Inspiration had declared, "shall know that I am the Lord, because they have been a staff of reed to the house of Israel." "I will strengthen the arms of the king of Babylon, and the arms of Pharaoh shall fall down; and they shall know that I am the Lord, when I shall put My sword into the hand of the king of Babylon, and he shall stretch it out upon the land of Egypt." Ezekiel 29:3, 6; 30:25, 26.

While the princes of Judah were still vainly looking toward Egypt for help, King Zedekiah with anxious foreboding was thinking of the prophet of God that had been thrust into prison. After many days the king sent for him and asked him secretly, "Is there any word from the Lord?" Jeremiah answered, "There is: for, said He, thou shalt be delivered into the hand of the king of Babylon.

"Moreover Jeremiah said unto King Zedekiah, What have I offended against thee, or against thy servants, or against this people, that ye have put me in prison? Where are now your prophets which prophesied unto you, saying, The king of Babylon shall not come against you, nor against this land? Therefore hear now, I pray thee, O my lord the king: let my supplication, I pray thee, be accepted before thee; that thou cause me not to return to the house of Jonathan the scribe, lest I die there." Jeremiah 37:17-20.

At this Zedekiah commanded that they "commit Jeremiah into the court of the prison, and that they should give him daily a piece of bread out of the bakers' street, until all the bread in the city were spent. Thus Jeremiah remained in the court of the prison." Verse 21.

The king dared not openly manifest any faith in Jeremiah. Though his fear drove him to seek information of him privately, yet he was too weak to brave the disapprobation of his princes and of the people by submitting to the will of God as declared by the prophet.

From the court of the prison Jeremiah continued to advise submission to the Babylonian rule. To offer resistance would be to invite sure death. The message of the Lord to Judah was: "He that remaineth in this city shall die by the sword, by the famine, and by the pestilence: but he that goeth forth to the Chaldeans shall live; for he shall have his life for a prey, and shall live." Plain and positive were the words spoken. In the name of the Lord the prophet boldly declared, "This city shall surely be given into the hand of the king of Babylon's army, which shall take it." Jeremiah 38:2, 3.

At last the princes, enraged over the repeated counsels of Jeremiah, which were contrary to their set policy of resistance, made a vigorous protest before the king, urging that the prophet was an enemy to the nation, and that his words had weakened the hands of the people and brought misfortune upon them; therefore he should be put to death.

The cowardly king knew that the charges were false; but in order to propitiate those who occupied high and influential positions in the nation, he feigned to believe their falsehoods and gave Jeremiah into their hands to do with him as they pleased. The prophet was cast "into the dungeon of Malchiah the son of Hammelech, that was in the court of the prison: and they let down Jeremiah with cords. And in the dungeon there was no water, but mire: so Jeremiah sunk in the mire." Verse 6. But God raised up friends for him, who besought the king in his behalf, and had him again removed to the court of the prison.

Once more the king sent privately for Jeremiah, and bade him faithfully relate the purpose of God toward Jerusalem. In response, Jeremiah inquired, "If I declare it unto thee, wilt thou not surely put me to death? and if I give thee counsel, wilt thou not hearken unto me?" The king entered into a secret compact with the prophet. "As the Lord liveth, that made us this soul," Zedekiah promised, "I will not put thee to death, neither will I give thee into the hand of these men that seek thy life." Verses 15, 16.

There was still opportunity for the king to reveal a willingness to heed the warnings of Jehovah, and thus to temper with mercy the judgments even now falling on city and nation. "If thou wilt assuredly go forth unto the king of Babylon's princes," was the message given the king, "then thy soul shall live, and this city shall not be burned with fire; and thou shalt live, and thine house: but if thou wilt not go forth to the king of Babylon's princes, then shall this city be given into the hand of the Chaldeans, and they shall burn it with fire, and thou shalt not escape out of their hand."

"I am afraid of the Jews that are fallen to the Chaldeans," the king replied, "lest they deliver me into their hand, and they mock me." But the prophet promised, "They shall not deliver thee." And he added the earnest entreaty, "Obey, I beseech thee, the voice of the Lord, which I speak unto thee: so it shall be well unto thee, and thy soul shall live." Verses 17-20.

Thus even to the last hour, God made plain His willingness to show mercy to those who should choose to submit to His just requirements. Had the king chosen to obey, the lives of the people might have been spared, and the city saved from conflagration; but he thought he had gone too far to retrace his steps. He was afraid of the Jews, afraid of ridicule, afraid for his life. After years of rebellion against God, Zedekiah thought it too humiliating to say to his people, I accept the word of the Lord, as spoken through the prophet Jeremiah; I dare not venture to war against the enemy in the face of all these warnings.

With tears Jeremiah entreated Zedekiah to save himself and his people. With anguish of spirit he assured him that unless he should heed the counsel of God, he could not escape with his life, and all his possessions would fall to the Babylonians. But the king had started on the wrong course, and he would not retrace his steps. He decided to follow the counsel of the false prophets, and of the men whom he really despised, and who ridiculed his weakness in yielding so readily to their wishes. He sacrificed the noble freedom of his manhood and became a cringing slave to public opinion. With no fixed purpose to do evil, he was also without resolution to stand boldly for the right. Convicted though he was of the value of the counsel given by Jeremiah, he had not the moral stamina to obey; and as a consequence he advanced steadily in the wrong direction.

The king was even too weak to be willing that his courtiers and people should know that he had held a conference with Jeremiah, so fully had the fear of man taken possession of his soul. If Zedekiah had stood up bravely and declared that he believed the words of the prophet, already half fulfilled, what desolation might have been averted! He should have said, I will obey the Lord, and save the city from utter ruin. I dare not disregard the commands of God because of the fear or favor of man. I love the truth, I hate sin, and I will follow the counsel of the Mighty One of Israel.

Then the people would have respected his courageous spirit, and those who were wavering between faith and unbelief would have taken a firm stand for the right. The very fearlessness and justice of this course would have inspired his subjects with admiration and loyalty. He would have had ample support, and Judah would have been spared the untold woe of carnage and famine and fire.

The weakness of Zedekiah was a sin for which he paid a fearful penalty. The enemy swept down like a resistless avalanche and devastated the city. The Hebrew armies were beaten back in confusion. The nation was conquered. Zedekiah was taken prisoner, and his sons were slain before his eyes. The king was led away from Jerusalem a captive, his eyes were put out, and after arriving in Babylon he perished miserably. The beautiful temple that for more than four centuries had crowned the summit of Mount Zion was not spared by the Chaldeans. "They burnt the house of God, and brake down the wall of Jerusalem, and burnt all the palaces thereof with fire, and destroyed all the goodly vessels thereof." 2 Chronicles 36:19.

At the time of the final overthrow of Jerusalem by Nebuchadnezzar, many had escaped the horrors of the long siege, only to perish by the sword. Of those who still remained, some, notably the chief of the priests and officers and the princes of the realm, were taken to Babylon and there executed as traitors. Others were carried captive, to live in servitude to Nebuchadnezzar and to his sons "until the reign of the kingdom of Persia: to fulfill the word of the Lord by the mouth of Jeremiah." Verses 20, 21.

Of Jeremiah himself it is recorded: "Nebuchadnezzar king of Babylon gave charge concerning Jeremiah to Nebuzar-adan the captain of the guard, saying, Take him, and look well to him, and do him no harm; but do unto him even as he shall say unto thee." Jeremiah 39:11, 12.

Released from prison by the Babylonian officers, the prophet chose to cast in his lot with the feeble remnant, "certain poor of the land" left by the Chaldeans to be "vinedressers and husbandmen." Over these the Babylonians set Gedaliah as governor. Only a few months passed before the newly appointed governor was treacherously slain. The poor people, after passing through many trials, were finally persuaded by their leaders to take refuge in the land of Egypt. Against this move, Jeremiah lifted his voice in protest. "Go ye not into Egypt," he pleaded. But the inspired counsel was not heeded, and "all the remnant of Judah, . . . even men, and women, and children," took flight into Egypt. "They obeyed not the voice of the Lord: thus came they even to Tahpanhes." Jeremiah 43:5-7.

The prophecies of doom pronounced by Jeremiah upon the remnant that had rebelled against Nebuchadnezzar by fleeing to Egypt were mingled with promises of pardon to those who should repent of their folly and stand ready to return. While the Lord would not spare those 461 who turned from His counsel to the seductive influences of Egyptian idolatry, yet He would show mercy to those who should prove loyal and true. "A small number that escape the sword shall return out of the land of Egypt into the land of Judah," He declared; "and all the remnant of Judah, that are gone into the land of Egypt to sojourn there, shall know whose words shall stand, Mine, or theirs." Jeremiah 44:28.

The sorrow of the prophet over the utter perversity of those who should have been the spiritual light of the world, his sorrow over the fate of Zion and of the people carried captive to Babylon, is revealed in the lamentations he has left on record as a memorial of the folly of turning from the counsels of Jehovah to human wisdom. Amid the ruin wrought, Jeremiah could still declare, "It is of the Lord's mercies that we are not consumed;" and his constant prayer was, "Let us search and try our ways, and turn again to the Lord." Lamentations 3:22, 40. While Judah was still a kingdom among the nations, he had inquired of his God, "Hast Thou utterly rejected Judah? hath Thy soul loathed Zion?" and he had made bold to plead, "Do not abhor us, for Thy name's sake." Jeremiah 14:19, 21. The prophet's absolute faith in God's eternal purpose to bring order out of confusion, and to demonstrate to the nations of earth and to the entire universe His attributes of justice and love, now led him to plead confidently in behalf of those who might turn from evil to righteousness.

But now Zion was utterly destroyed; the people of God were in their captivity. Over- 462 whelmed with grief, the prophet exclaimed:

"How doth the city sit solitary, that was full of people! how is she become as a widow! she that was great among the nations, and princess among the provinces, how is she become tributary! She weepeth sore in the night, and her tears are on her cheeks: among all her lovers she hath none to comfort her: all her friends have dealt treacherously with her, they are become her enemies.

"Judah is gone into captivity because of affliction, and because of great servitude: she dwelleth among the heathen, she findeth no rest: all her persecutors overtook her between the straits. The ways of Zion do mourn, because none come to the solemn feasts: all her gates are desolate: her priests sigh, her virgins are afflicted, and she is in bitterness. Her adversaries are the chief, her enemies prosper; for the Lord hath afflicted her for the multitude of her transgressions: her children are gone into captivity before the enemy."

"How hath the Lord covered the daughter of Zion with a cloud in His anger, and cast down from heaven unto the earth the beauty of Israel, and remembered not His footstool in the day of His anger! The Lord hath swallowed up all the habitations of Jacob, and hath not pitied: He hath thrown down in His wrath the strongholds of the daughter of Judah; He hath brought them down to the ground: He hath polluted the kingdom and the princes thereof. He hath cut off in His fierce anger all the horn of Israel: He hath drawn back His right hand from before the enemy, and He burned against Jacob like a flaming fire, which devoureth round about. He hath bent His bow like an enemy: He stood with His right hand as an adversary, and slew all that 463 were pleasant to the eye in the tabernacle of the daughter of Zion: He poured out His fury like fire."

"What thing shall I take to witness for thee? what thing shall I liken to thee, O daughter of Jerusalem? what shall I equal to thee, that I may comfort thee, O virgin daughter of Zion? for thy breach is great like the sea: who can heal thee?"

"Remember, O Lord, what is come upon us: consider, and behold our reproach. Our inheritance is turned to strangers, our houses to aliens. We are orphans and fatherless, our mothers are as widows. . . . Our fathers have sinned, and are not; and we have borne their iniquities. Servants have ruled over us: there is none that doth deliver us out of their hand. . . . For this our heart is faint; for these things our eyes are dim."

"Thou, O Lord, remainest forever; Thy throne from generation to generation. Wherefore dost Thou forget us forever, and forsake us so long time? Turn Thou us unto Thee, O Lord, and we shall be turned; renew our days as of old." Lamentations 1:1-5; 2:1-4, 13; 5:1-3, 7, 8, 17, 19-21.

38

Light Through Darkness

The dark years of destruction and death marking the end of the kingdom of Judah would have brought despair to the stoutest heart had it not been for the encouragements in the prophetic utterances of God's messengers. Through Jeremiah in Jerusalem, through Daniel in the court of Babylon, through Ezekiel on the banks of the Chebar, the Lord in mercy made clear His eternal purpose and gave assurance of His willingness to fulfill to His chosen people the promises recorded in the writings of Moses. That which He had said He would do for those who should prove true to Him, He would surely bring to pass. "The word of God . . . liveth and abideth forever." 1 Peter 1:23.

In the days of the wilderness wandering the Lord had made abundant provision for His children to keep in remembrance the words of His law. After the settlement in Canaan the divine precepts were to be repeated daily in every home; they were to be written plainly upon the doorposts and gates, and spread upon memorial tablets. They were to be set to music and chanted by young and old. Priests were to teach these holy precepts in public assemblies, and the rulers of the land were to make them their daily study. "Meditate therein day and night," the Lord commanded Joshua concerning the book of the law, "that thou mayest observe to do according to all that is written therein: for then thou shalt make thy way prosperous, and then thou shalt have good success." Joshua 1:8.

The writings of Moses were taught by Joshua to all Israel. "There was not a word of all that Moses commanded, which Joshua read not before all the congregation of Israel, with the women, and the little ones, and the strangers that were conversant among them." Joshua 8:35. This was in harmony with the express command of Jehovah providing for a public rehearsal of the words of the book of the law every seven years, during the Feast of Tabernacles. "Gather the people together, men, and women, and children, and thy stranger that is within thy gates," the spiritual leaders of Israel had been instructed, "that they may hear, and that they may learn, and fear the Lord your God, and observe to do all the words of this law: and that their children, which have not known anything, may hear, and learn to fear the Lord your God, as long as ye live in the land whither ye go over Jordan to possess it." Deuteronomy 31:12, 13.

Had this counsel been heeded through the centuries that followed, how different would have been Israel's history! Only as a reverence for God's Holy Word was cherished in the hearts of the people, could they hope to fulfill the divine purpose. It was regard for the law of God that gave Israel strength during the reign of David and the earlier years of Solomon's rule; it was through faith in the living word that reformation was wrought in the days of Elijah and of Josiah. And it was to these same Scriptures of truth, Israel's richest heritage, that Jeremiah appealed in his efforts toward reform. Wherever he ministered he met the people with the earnest plea, "Hear ye the words of this covenant," words which would bring them a full understanding of God's purpose to extend to all nations a knowledge of saving truth. Jeremiah 11:2.

In the closing years of Judah's apostasy the exhortations of the prophets were seemingly of but little avail; and as the armies of the Chaldeans came for the third and last time to besiege Jerusalem, hope fled from every heart. Jeremiah predicted utter ruin; and it was because of his insistence on surrender that he had finally been thrown into prison. But God left not to hopeless despair the faithful remnant who were still in the city. Even while Jeremiah was kept under close surveillance by those who scorned his messages, there came to him fresh revelations concerning Heaven's willingness to forgive and to save, which have been an unfailing source of comfort to the church of God from that day to this.

Laying fast hold on the promises of God, Jeremiah, by means of an acted parable, illustrated before the inhabitants of the fated city his strong faith in the ultimate fulfillment of God's purpose for His people. In the presence of witnesses, and with careful observance of all necessary legal forms, he purchased for seventeen shekels of silver an ancestral field situated in the neighboring village of Anathoth.

From every human point of view this purchase of land in territory already under the control of the Babylonians, appeared to be an act of folly. The prophet himself had been foretelling the destruction of Jerusalem, the desolation of Judea, and the utter ruin of the kingdom. He had been prophesying a long period of captivity in faraway Babylon. Already advanced in years, he could never hope to receive personal benefit from the purchase he had made. However, his study of the prophecies that were recorded in the Scriptures had created within his heart a firm conviction that the Lord purposed to restore to the children of the captivity their ancient possession of the Land of Promise. With the eye of faith Jeremiah saw the exiles returning at the end of the years of affliction and reoccupying the land of their fathers. Through the purchase of the Anathoth estate he would do what he could to inspire others with the hope that brought so much comfort to his own heart.

Having signed the deeds of transfer and secured the countersignatures of witnesses, Jeremiah charged Baruch his secretary: "Take these evidences, this evidence of the purchase, both which is sealed, and this evidence which is open; and put them in an earthen vessel, that they may continue many days. For thus saith the Lord of hosts, the God of Israel; Houses and fields and vineyards shall be possessed again in this land." Jeremiah 32:14, 15.

So discouraging was the outlook for Judah at the time of this extraordinary transaction that immediately after perfecting the details of the purchase and arranging for the preservation of the written records, the faith of Jeremiah, unshaken though it had been, was now sorely tried. Had he, in his endeavor to encourage Judah, acted presumptuously? In his desire to establish confidence in the promises of God's word, had he given ground for false hope? Those who had entered into covenant relationship with God had long since scorned the provisions made in their behalf. Could the promises to the chosen nation ever meet with complete fulfillment?

Perplexed in spirit, bowed down with sorrow over the sufferings of those who had refused to repent of their sins, the prophet appealed to God for further enlightenment concerning the divine purpose for mankind.

"Ah Lord God!" he prayed, "behold, Thou hast made the heaven and the earth by Thy great power and stretched-out arm, and there is nothing too hard for Thee: Thou showest lovingkindness unto thousands, and recompensest the iniquity of the fathers into the bosom of their children after them: the great, the mighty God, the Lord of hosts, is His name, great in counsel, and mighty in work: for Thine eyes are open upon all the ways of the sons of men: to give everyone according to his ways, and according to the fruit of his doings: which hast set signs and wonders in the land of Egypt, even unto this day, and in Israel, and among other men; and hast made Thee a name, as at this day; and hast brought forth Thy people Israel out of the land of Egypt with signs, and with wonders, and with a strong hand, and with a stretched-out arm, and with great terror; and hast given them this land, which Thou didst swear to their fathers to give them, a land flowing with milk and honey; and they came in, and possessed it; but they obeyed not Thy voice, neither walked in Thy law; they have done nothing of all that Thou commandedst them to do: therefore Thou hast caused all this evil to come upon them." Verses 17-23.

Nebuchadnezzar's armies were about to take the walls of Zion by storm. Thousands were perishing in a last desperate defense of the city. Many thousands more were dying of hunger and disease. The fate of Jerusalem was already sealed. The besieging towers of the enemy's forces were already overlooking the walls. "Behold the mounts," the prophet continued in his prayer to God; "they are come unto the city to take it; and the city is given into the hand of the Chaldeans, that fight against it, because of the sword, and of the famine, and of the pestilence: and what Thou hast spoken is come to pass; and, behold, Thou seest it. And Thou hast said unto me, O Lord God, Buy thee the field for money, and take witnesses; for the city is given into the hand of the Chaldeans." Verses 24, 25.

The prayer of the prophet was graciously answered. "The word of the Lord unto Jeremiah" in that hour of distress, when the faith of the messenger of truth was being tried as by fire, was: "Behold, I am the Lord, the God of all flesh: is there anything too hard for Me?" Verses 26, 27. The city was soon to fall into the hand of the Chaldeans; its gates and palaces were to be set on fire and burned; but, notwithstanding the fact that destruction was imminent and the inhabitants of Jerusalem were to be carried away captive, nevertheless the eternal purpose of Jehovah for Israel was yet to be fulfilled. In further answer to the prayer of His servant, the Lord declared concerning those upon whom His chastisements were falling:

"Behold, I will gather them out of all countries, whither I have driven them in Mine anger, and in My fury, and in great wrath; and I will bring them again unto this place, and I will cause them to dwell safely: and they shall be My people, and I will be their God: and I will give them one heart, and one way, that they may fear Me forever, for the good of them, and of their children after them: and I will make an everlasting covenant with them, that I will not turn away from them, to do them good; but I will put My fear in their hearts, that they shall not depart from Me. Yea, I will rejoice over them to do them good, and I will plant them in this land assuredly with My whole heart and with My whole soul.

"For thus saith the Lord; Like as I have brought all this great evil upon this people, so will I bring upon them all the good that I have promised them. And fields shall be bought in this land, whereof ye say, It is desolate without man or beast; it is given into the hand of the Chaldeans. Men shall buy fields for money, and subscribe evidences, and seal them, and take witnesses in the land of Benjamin, and in the places about Jerusalem, and in the cities of Judah, and in the cities of the mountains, and in the cities of the valley, and in the cities of the south: for I will cause their captivity to return, saith the Lord." Verses 37-44.

In confirmation of these assurances of deliverance and restoration, "the word of the Lord came unto Jeremiah the second time, while he was yet

473 shut up in the court of the prison, saying,

"Thus saith the Lord the Maker thereof, the Lord that formed it, to establish it; the Lord is His name; Call unto Me, and I will answer thee, and show thee great and mighty things, which thou knowest not. For thus saith the Lord, the God of Israel, concerning the houses of this city, and concerning the houses of the kings of Judah, which are thrown down by the mounts, and by the sword; . . . . Behold, I will bring it health and cure, and I will cure them, and will reveal unto them the abundance of peace and truth. And I will cause the captivity of Judah and the captivity of Israel to return, and will build them, as at the first. And I will cleanse them from all their iniquity, whereby they have sinned against Me; and I will pardon all their iniquities. . . . And it shall be to Me a name of joy, a praise and an honor before all the nations of the earth, which shall hear all the good that I do unto them: and they shall fear and tremble for all the goodness and for all the prosperity that I procure unto it.

"Thus saith the Lord; Again there shall be heard in this place, which ye say shall be desolate without man and without beast, even in the cities of Judah, and in the streets of Jerusalem, . . . the voice of joy, and the voice of gladness, the voice of the bridegroom, and the voice of the bride, the voice of them that shall say, Praise the Lord of hosts: for the Lord is good; for His mercy endureth forever: and of them that shall bring the sacrifice of praise into the house of the Lord. For I will cause to return the captivity of the land, as at the first, saith the Lord.

474 "Thus saith the Lord of hosts; Again in this place, which is desolate without man and without beast, and in all the cities thereof, shall be an habitation of shepherds causing their flocks to lie down. In the cities of the mountains, and in the cities of the vale, and in the cities of the south, and in the land of Benjamin, and in the places about Jerusalem, and in the cities of Judah, shall the flocks pass again under the hands of him that telleth them, saith the Lord.

"Behold, the days come, saith the Lord, that I will perform that good thing which I have promised unto the house of Israel and to the house of Judah." Jeremiah 33:1-14.

Thus was the church of God comforted in one of the darkest hours of her long conflict with the forces of evil. Satan had seemingly triumphed in his efforts to destroy Israel; but the Lord was overruling the events of the present, and during the years that were to follow, His people were to have opportunity to redeem the past. His message to the church was:

"Fear thou not, O My servant Jacob; . . . neither be dismayed, O Israel: for, lo, I will save thee from afar, and thy seed from the land of their captivity; and Jacob shall return, and shall be in rest, and be quiet, and none shall make him afraid. For I am with thee, saith the Lord, to save thee." "I will restore health unto thee, and I will heal thee of thy wounds." Jeremiah 30:10, 11, 17.

In the glad day of restoration the tribes of divided Israel were to be reunited as one people. The Lord was to be acknowledged as ruler over "all the families of Israel." "They shall be My people," He declared. "Sing with gladness for Jacob, and shout among the chief of the nations: publish ye, praise ye, and say, O Lord, save Thy people, the remnant of Israel. Behold, I will 475 bring them from the north country, and gather them from the coasts of the earth, and with them the blind and the lame; . . . they shall come with weeping, and with supplications will I lead them: I will cause them to walk by the rivers of waters in a straight way, wherein they shall not stumble: for I am a Father to Israel, and Ephraim is My first-born." Jeremiah 31:1, 7-9.

Humbled in the sight of the nations, those who once had been recognized as favored of Heaven above all other peoples of the earth were to learn in exile the lesson of obedience so necessary for their future happiness. Until they had learned this lesson, God could not do for them all that He desired to do. "I will correct thee in measure, and will not leave thee altogether unpunished," He declared in explanation of His purpose to chastise them for their spiritual good. Jeremiah 30:11. Yet those who had been the object of His tender love were not forever set aside; before all the nations of earth He would demonstrate His plan to bring victory out of apparent defeat, to save rather than to destroy. To the prophet was given the message:

"He that scattered Israel will gather him, and keep him, as a shepherd doth his flock. For the Lord hath redeemed Jacob, and ransomed him from the hand of him that was stronger than he. Therefore they shall come and sing in the height of Zion, and shall flow together to the goodness of the Lord, for wheat, and for wine, and for oil, and for the young of the flock and of the herd: and their soul shall be as a watered garden; and they shall not sorrow any more at all. . . . I will 476 turn their mourning into joy, and will comfort them, and make them rejoice from their sorrow. And I will satiate the soul of the priests with fatness, and My people shall be satisfied with My goodness, saith the Lord."

"Thus saith the Lord of hosts, the God of Israel; As yet they shall use this speech in the land of Judah and in the cities thereof, when I shall bring again their captivity; The Lord bless thee, O habitation of justice, and mountain of holiness. And there shall dwell in Judah itself, and in all the cities thereof together, husbandmen, and they that go forth with flocks. For I have satiated the weary soul, and I have replenished every sorrowful soul."

"Behold, the days come, saith the Lord, that I will make a new covenant with the house of

Israel, and with the house of Judah: not according to the covenant that I made with their fathers in the day that I took them by the hand to bring them out of the land of Egypt; which My covenant they brake, although I was an husband unto them, saith the Lord: but this shall be the covenant that I will make with the house of Israel; After those days, saith the Lord, I will put My law in their inward parts, and write it in their hearts; and will be their God, and they shall be My people. And they shall teach no more every man his neighbor, and every man his brother, saying, Know the Lord: for they shall all know Me, from the least of them unto the greatest of them, saith the Lord: for I will forgive their iniquity, and I will remember their sin no more." Jeremiah 31:10-14, 23-25, 31-34.

SECTION V

IN THE LANDS OF THE HEATHEN

"Ye are My witnesses, saith the Lord, and My servant whom I have chosen." Isaiah 43:10.

479

39

In the Court of Babylon

Among the children of Israel who were carried captive to Babylon at the beginning of the seventy years' captivity were Christian patriots, men who were as true as steel to principle, who would not be corrupted by selfishness, but who would honor God at the loss of all things. In the land of their captivity these men were to carry out God's purpose by giving to heathen nations the blessings that come through a knowledge of Jehovah. They were to be His representatives. Never were they to compromise with idolaters; their faith and their name as worshipers of the living God they were to bear as a high honor. And this they did. In prosperity and adversity they honored God, and God honored them.

The fact that these men, worshipers of Jehovah, were captives in Babylon, and that the vessels of God's house had been placed in the temple of the Babylonish gods, was boastfully cited

480 by the victors as evidence that their religion and customs were superior to the religion and customs of the Hebrews. Yet through the very humiliations that Israel's departure from Him had invited, God gave Babylon evidence of His supremacy, of the holiness of His requirements, and of the sure results of obedience. And this testimony He gave, as alone it could be given,

through those who were loyal to Him.

Among those who maintained their allegiance to God were Daniel and his three companions—illustrious examples of what men may become who unite with the God of wisdom and power. From the comparative simplicity of their Jewish home, these youth of royal line were taken to the most magnificent of cities and into the court of the world's greatest monarch. Nebuchadnezzar "spake unto Ashpenaz the master of his eunuchs, that he should bring certain of the children of Israel, and of the king's seed, and of the princes; children in whom was no blemish, but well favored, and skillful in all wisdom, and cunning in knowledge, and understanding science, and such as had ability in them to stand in the king's palace. . . .

"Now among these were of the children of Judah, Daniel, Hananiah, Mishael, and Azariah." Seeing in these youth the promise of remarkable ability, Nebuchadnezzar determined that they should be trained to fill important positions in his kingdom. That they might be fully qualified for their lifework, he arranged for them to learn the language of the Chaldeans and for three years to be granted the unusual educational advantages afforded princes of the realm.

The names of Daniel and his companions were changed to names representing Chaldean deities. 481 Great significance was attached to the names given by Hebrew parents to their children. Often these stood for traits of character that the parent desired to see developed in the child. The prince in whose charge the captive youth were placed, "gave unto Daniel the name of Belteshazzar; and to Hananiah, of Shadrach; and to Mishael, of Meshach; and to Azariah, of Abednego."

The king did not compel the Hebrew youth to renounce their faith in favor of idolatry, but he hoped to bring this about gradually. By giving them names significant of idolatry, by bringing them daily into close association with idolatrous customs, and under the influence of the seductive rites of heathen worship, he hoped to induce them to renounce the religion of their nation and to unite with the worship of the Babylonians.

At the very outset of their career there came to them a decisive test of character. It was provided that they should eat of the food and drink of the wine that came from the king's table. In this the king thought to give them an expression of his favor and of his solicitude for their welfare. But a portion having been offered to idols, the food from the king's table was consecrated to idolatry; and one partaking of it would be regarded as offering homage to the gods of Babylon. In such homage, loyalty to Jehovah forbade Daniel and his companions to join. Even a mere pretense of eating the food or drinking the wine would be a denial of their faith. To do this would be to array themselves with heathenism and to dishonor the principles

This chapter is based on Daniel 1.

of the law of God.

482 Nor dared they risk the enervating effect of luxury and dissipation on physical, mental, and spiritual development. They were acquainted with the history of Nadab and Abihu, the record of whose intemperance and its results had been preserved in the parchments of the Pentateuch; and they knew that their own physical and mental power would be injuriously affected by the use of wine.

Daniel and his associates had been trained by their parents to habits of strict temperance. They had been taught that God would hold them accountable for their capabilities, and that they must never dwarf or enfeeble their powers. This education was to Daniel and his companions the means of their preservation amidst the demoralizing influences of the court of Babylon. Strong were the temptations surrounding them in that corrupt and luxurious court, but they remained uncontaminated. No power, no influence, could sway them from the principles they had learned in early life by a study of the word and works of God.

Had Daniel so desired, he might have found in his surroundings a plausible excuse for departing from strictly temperate habits. He might have argued that, dependent as he was on the king's favor and subject to his power, there was no other course for him to pursue than to eat of the king's food and drink of his wine; for should he adhere to the divine teaching, he would offend the king and probably lose his position and his life. Should he disregard the commandment of the Lord he would retain the favor of the king and secure for himself intellectual advantages and flattering worldly prospects.

483 But Daniel did not hesitate. The approval of God was dearer to him than the favor of the most powerful earthly potentate—dearer than life itself. He determined to stand firm in his integrity, let the result be what it might. He "purposed in his heart that he would not defile himself with the portion of the king's meat, nor with the wine which he drank." And in this resolve he was supported by his three companions.

In reaching this decision, the Hebrew youth did not act presumptuously, but in firm reliance upon God. They did not choose to be singular, but they would be so rather than dishonor God. Should they compromise with wrong in this instance by yielding to the pressure of circumstances, their departure from principle would weaken their sense of right and their abhorrence of wrong. The first wrong step would lead to others, until their connection with Heaven severed, they would be swept away by temptation.

"God had brought Daniel into favor and tender love with the prince of the eunuchs," and the request that he might not defile himself was received with respect. Yet the prince hesitated to grant it. "I fear my lord the king, who hath appointed your meat and your drink," he explained to Daniel; "for why should he see your faces worse liking than the children which are of your sort? then shall ye make me endanger my head to the king."

Daniel then appealed to Melzar, the officer in special charge of the Hebrew youth, requesting 484 that they might be excused from eating the king's meat and drinking his wine. He asked that the matter be tested by a ten days' trial, the Hebrew youth during this time being supplied with simple food, while their companions ate of the king's dainties.

Melzar, though fearful that by complying with this request he would incur the displeasure of the king, nevertheless consented; and Daniel knew that his case was won. At the end of the ten days' trial the result was found to be the opposite of the prince's fears. "Their countenances appeared fairer and fatter in flesh than all the children which did eat the portion of the king's meat." In personal appearance the Hebrew youth showed a marked superiority over their companions. As a result, Daniel and his associates were permitted to continue their simple diet during their entire course of training.

For three years the Hebrew youth studied to acquire "the learning and the tongue of the Chaldeans." During this time they held fast their allegiance to God and depended constantly upon His power. With their habits of self-denial they united earnestness of purpose, diligence, and steadfastness. It was not pride or ambition that had brought them into the king's court, into companionship with those who neither knew nor feared God; they were captives in a strange land, placed there by Infinite Wisdom. Separated from home influences and sacred associations, they sought to acquit themselves creditably, for the honor of their downtrodden people, and for the glory of Him whose servants they were.

The Lord regarded with approval the firmness and self-denial of the Hebrew youth, and their purity of motive; and His blessing attended them. He "gave them knowledge and skill in all learning and wisdom: and Daniel had understanding in all visions and dreams." The promise 485 was fulfilled, "Them that honor Me I will honor." 1 Samuel 2:30. As Daniel clung to God with unwavering trust, the spirit of prophetic power came upon him. While receiving instruction from man in the duties of court life, he was being taught by God to read the mysteries of the future and to record for coming generations, through figures and symbols, events covering the history of this world till the close of time.

When the time came for the youth in training to be tested, the Hebrews were examined, with other candidates, for the service of the kingdom. But "among them all was found none like Daniel, Hananiah, Mishael, and Azariah." Their keen comprehension, their wide knowledge, their choice and exact language, testified to the unimpaired strength and vigor of their mental powers. "In all matters of wisdom and understanding, that the king inquired of them, he found them ten times better than all the magicians and astrologers that were in all his realm;" "therefore stood they before the king."

At the court of Babylon were gathered representatives from all lands, men of the highest talent, men the most richly endowed with natural gifts, and possessed of the broadest culture that the world could bestow; yet among them all, the Hebrew youth were without a peer. In physical strength and beauty, in mental vigor and literary attainment, they stood unrivaled. The erect form, the firm, elastic step, the fair countenance, the undimmed senses, the untainted breath—all were so many certificates of good habits, insignia of the nobility with which nature honors those who are obedient to her laws.

486   In acquiring the wisdom of the Babylonians, Daniel and his companions were far more successful than their fellow students; but their learning did not come by chance. They obtained their knowledge by the faithful use of their powers, under the guidance of the Holy Spirit. They placed themselves in connection with the Source of all wisdom, making the knowledge of God the foundation of their education. In faith they prayed for wisdom, and they lived their prayers. They placed themselves where God could bless them. They avoided that which would weaken their powers, and improved every opportunity to become intelligent in all lines of learning. They followed the rules of life that could not fail to give them strength of intellect. They sought to acquire knowledge for one purpose—that they might honor God. They realized that in order to stand as representatives of true religion amid the false religions of heathenism they must have clearness of intellect and must perfect a Christian character. And God Himself was their teacher. Constantly praying, conscientiously studying, keeping in touch with the Unseen, they walked with God as did Enoch.

True success in any line of work is not the result of chance or accident or destiny. It is the outworking of God's providences, the reward of faith and discretion, of virtue and perseverance. Fine mental qualities and a high moral tone are not the result of accident. God gives opportunities; success depends upon the use made of them.

While God was working in Daniel and his companions "to will and to do of His good pleasure," they were working out their own salvation. Philippians 2:13. Herein is revealed the outworking of the divine principle of co-opera-487 tion, without which no true success can be attained. Human effort avails nothing without divine power; and without human endeavor, divine effort is with many of no avail. To make

God's grace our own, we must act our part. His grace is given to work in us to will and to do, but never as a substitute for our effort.

As the Lord co-operated with Daniel and his fellows, so He will co-operate with all who strive to do His will. And by the impartation of His Spirit He will strengthen every true purpose, every noble resolution. Those who walk in the path of obedience will encounter many hindrances. Strong, subtle influences may bind them to the world; but the Lord is able to render futile every agency that works for the defeat of His chosen ones; in His strength they may overcome every temptation, conquer every difficulty.

God brought Daniel and his associates into connection with the great men of Babylon, that in the midst of a nation of idolaters they might represent His character. How did they become fitted for a position of so great trust and honor? It was faithfulness in little things that gave complexion to their whole life. They honored God in the smallest duties, as well as in the larger responsibilities.

As God called Daniel to witness for Him in Babylon, so He calls us to be His witnesses in the world today. In the smallest as well as the largest affairs of life, He desires us to reveal to men the principles of His kingdom. Many are waiting for some great work to be brought to them, while daily they lose opportunities for revealing faithfulness to God. Daily they fail of 488 discharging with wholeheartedness the little duties of life. While they wait for some large work in which they may exercise supposedly great talents, and thus satisfy their ambitious longings, their days pass away.

In the life of the true Christian there are no nonessentials; in the sight of Omnipotence every duty is important. The Lord measures with exactness every possibility for service. The unused capabilities are just as much brought into account as those that are used. We shall be judged by what we ought to have done, but did not accomplish because we did not use our powers to glorify God.

A noble character is not the result of accident; it is not due to special favors or endowments of Providence. It is the result of self-discipline, of subjection of the lower to the higher nature, of the surrender of self to the service of God and man.

Through the fidelity to the principles of temperance shown by the Hebrew youth God is speaking to the youth of today. There is need of men who like Daniel will do and dare for the cause of right. Pure hearts, strong hands, fearless courage, are needed; for the warfare between vice and virtue calls for ceaseless vigilance. To every soul Satan comes with temptation in many alluring forms on the point of indulgence of appetite.

The body is a most important medium through

which the mind and the soul are developed for the upbuilding of character. Hence it is that the adversary of souls directs his temptations to the enfeebling and degrading of the physical powers. His success here often means the surrender
489 of the whole being to evil. The tendencies of the physical nature, unless under the dominion of a higher power, will surely work ruin and death. The body is to be brought into subjection to the higher powers of the being. The passions are to be controlled by the will, which is itself to be under the control of God. The kingly power of reason, sanctified by divine grace, is to bear sway in the life. Intellectual power, physical stamina, and the length of life depend upon immutable laws. Through obedience to these laws, man may stand conqueror of himself, conqueror of his own inclinations, conqueror of principalities and powers, of "the rulers of the darkness of this world," and of "spiritual wickedness in high places." Ephesians 6:12.

In that ancient ritual which is the gospel in symbol, no blemished offering could be brought to God's altar. The sacrifice that was to represent Christ must be spotless. The word of God points to this as an illustration of what His children are to be—"a living sacrifice," "holy and without blemish." Romans 12:1; Ephesians 5:27.

The Hebrew worthies were men of like passions with ourselves; yet, notwithstanding the seductive influences of the court of Babylon, they stood firm, because they depended upon a strength that is infinite. In them a heathen nation beheld an illustration of the goodness and beneficence of God, and of the love of Christ. And in their experience we have an instance of the triumph of principle over temptation, of purity over depravity, of devotion and loyalty over atheism and idolatry.

The spirit that possessed Daniel, the youth of today may have; they may draw from the same
490 source of strength, possess the same power of self-control, and reveal the same grace in their lives, even under circumstances as unfavorable. Though surrounded by temptations to self-indulgence, especially in our large cities, where every form of sensual gratification is made easy and inviting, yet by divine grace their purpose to honor God may remain firm. Through strong resolution and vigilant watchfulness they may withstand every temptation that assails the soul. But only by him who determines to do right because it is right will the victory be gained.

What a lifework was that of these noble Hebrews! As they bade farewell to their childhood home, little did they dream what a high destiny was to be theirs. Faithful and steadfast, they yielded to the divine guiding, so that through them God could fulfill His purpose.

The same mighty truths that were revealed through these men, God desires to reveal through the youth and children today. The life of Daniel and his fellows is a demonstration of what He will do for those who yield themselves to Him and with the whole heart seek to accomplish His purpose.

40 491

Nebuchadnezzar's Dream

Soon after Daniel and his companions entered the service of the king of Babylon, events occurred that revealed to an idolatrous nation the power and faithfulness of the God of Israel. Nebuchadnezzar had a remarkable dream, by which "his spirit was troubled, and his sleep brake from him." But although the king's mind was deeply impressed, he found it impossible, when he awoke, to recall the particulars.

In his perplexity, Nebuchadnezzar assembled his wise men—"the magicians, and the astrologers, and the sorcerers"—and besought their help. "I have dreamed a dream," he said, "and my spirit was troubled to know the dream." With this statement of his perplexity he requested them to reveal to him that which would bring relief to his mind.

To this the wise men responded, "O king, live forever: tell thy servants the dream, and we will show the interpretation."

Dissatisfied with their evasive answer, and 492 suspicious because, despite their pretentious claims to reveal the secrets of men, they nevertheless seemed unwilling to grant him help, the king commanded his wise men, with promises of wealth and honor on the one hand, and threats of death on the other, to tell him not only the interpretation of the dream, but the dream itself. "The thing is gone from me," he said; "if ye will not make known unto me the dream, with the interpretation thereof, ye shall be cut in pieces, and your houses shall be made a dunghill. But if ye show the dream, and the interpretation thereof, ye shall receive of me gifts and rewards and great honor."

Still the wise men returned the answer, "Let the king tell his servants the dream, and we will show the interpretation of it."

Nebuchadnezzar, now thoroughly aroused and angered by the apparent perfidy of those in whom he had trusted, declared: "I know of certainty that ye would gain the time, because ye see the thing is gone from me. But if ye will not make known unto me the dream, there is but one decree for you: for ye have prepared lying and corrupt words to speak before me, till the time be changed: therefore tell me the dream, and I shall know that ye can show me the interpretation thereof."

Filled with fear for the consequences of their

This chapter is based on Daniel 2.

failure, the magicians endeavored to show the king that his request was unreasonable and his test beyond that which had ever been required of any man. "There is not a man upon the earth," they remonstrated, "that can show the king's matter: therefore there is no king, lord, nor ruler, that asked such things at any magician, or astrologer, or Chaldean. And it is a rare thing that the king requireth, and there is none other that can show it before the king, except the gods, whose dwelling is not with flesh."

Then "the king was angry and very furious, and commanded to destroy all the wise men of Babylon."

Among those sought for by the officers who were preparing to fulfill the provisions of the royal decree, were Daniel and his friends. When told that according to the decree they also must die, "with counsel and wisdom" Daniel inquired of Arioch, the captain of the king's guard, "Why is the decree so hasty from the king?" Arioch told him the story of the king's perplexity over his remarkable dream, and of his failure to secure help from those in whom he had hitherto placed fullest confidence. Upon hearing this, Daniel, taking his life in his hands, ventured into the king's presence and begged that time be granted, that he might petition his God to reveal to him the dream and its interpretation.

To this request the monarch acceded. "Then Daniel went to his house, and made the thing known to Hananiah, Mishael, and Azariah, his companions." Together they sought for wisdom from the Source of light and knowledge. Their faith was strong in the consciousness that God had placed them where they were, that they were doing His work and meeting the demands of duty. In times of perplexity and danger they had always turned to Him for guidance and protection, and He had proved an ever-present help. Now with contrition of heart they submitted themselves anew to the Judge of the earth, pleading that He would grant them deliverance in this their time of special need. And they did not plead in vain. The God whom they had honored, now honored them. The Spirit of the Lord rested upon them, and to Daniel, "in a night vision," was revealed the king's dream and its meaning.

Daniel's first act was to thank God for the revelation given him. "Blessed be the name of God forever and ever," he exclaimed; "for wisdom and might are His: and He changeth the times and the seasons: He removeth kings, and setteth up kings: He giveth wisdom unto the wise, and knowledge to them that know understanding: He revealeth the deep and secret things: He knoweth what is in the darkness, and the light dwelleth with Him. I thank Thee, and praise Thee, O Thou God of my fathers, who hast given me wisdom and might, and hast made known unto me now what we desired of

Thee: for Thou hast now made known unto us the king's matter."

Going immediately to Arioch, whom the king had commanded to destroy the wise men, Daniel said, "Destroy not the wise men of Babylon: bring me in before the king, and I will show unto the king the interpretation." Quickly the officer ushered Daniel in before the king, with the words, "I have found a man of the captives of Judah, that will make known unto the king the interpretation."

Behold the Jewish captive, calm and self-possessed, in the presence of the monarch of the world's most powerful empire. In his first words he disclaimed honor for himself and exalted God as the source of all wisdom. To the anxious inquiry of the king, "Art thou able to make known unto me the dream which I have seen, and the interpretation thereof?" he replied: "The secret which the king hath demanded cannot the wise men, the astrologers, the magicians, the soothsayers, show unto the king; but there is a God in heaven that revealeth secrets, and maketh known to the king Nebuchadnezzar what shall be in the latter days.

"Thy dream," Daniel declared, "and the visions of thy head upon thy bed, are these; As for thee, O king, thy thoughts came into thy mind upon thy bed, what should come to pass hereafter: and He that revealeth secrets maketh known to thee what shall come to pass. But as for me, this secret is not revealed to me for any wisdom that I have more than any living, but for their sakes that shall make known the interpretation to the king, and that thou mightest know the thoughts of thy heart.

"Thou, O king, sawest, and behold a great image. This great image, whose brightness was excellent, stood before thee; and the form thereof was terrible. This image's head was of fine gold, his breast and his arms of silver, his belly and his thighs of brass, his legs of iron, his feet part of iron and part of clay.

"Thou sawest till that a stone was cut out without hands, which smote the image upon his feet that were of iron and clay, and brake them to pieces. Then was the iron, the clay, the brass, the silver, and the gold, broken to pieces together, and became like the chaff of the summer threshing floors; and the wind carried them away, that no place was found for them: and the stone that smote the image became a great mountain, and filled the whole earth.

"This is the dream," confidently declared Daniel; and the king, listening with closest attention to every particular, knew it was the very dream over which he had been so troubled. Thus his mind was prepared to receive with favor the interpretation. The King of kings was about to communicate great truth to the Babylonian monarch. God would reveal that He has power over the kingdoms of the world, power to enthrone and to dethrone kings. Nebuchadnezzar's mind was to be awakened, if possible, to a sense of his responsibility to Heaven. The events of the future, reaching down to the end of time, were to be opened before him.

"Thou, O king, art a king of kings," Daniel continued, "for the God of heaven hath given thee a kingdom, power, and strength, and glory. And wheresoever the children of men dwell, the beasts of the field and fowls of the heaven hath He given into thine hand, and hath made thee ruler over them all. Thou art this head of gold.

"And after thee shall arise another kingdom inferior to thee, and another third kingdom of brass, which shall bear rule over all the earth.

"And the fourth kingdom shall be strong as iron: forasmuch as iron breaketh in pieces and subdueth all things: and as iron that breaketh all these, shall it break in pieces and bruise.

"And whereas thou sawest the feet and toes, part of potters' clay, and part of iron, the kingdom shall be divided; but there shall be in it of the strength of the iron, forasmuch as thou sawest the iron mixed with miry clay. And as the toes of the feet were part of iron, and part of clay, so the kingdom shall be partly strong, and partly broken. And whereas thou sawest iron mixed with miry clay, they shall mingle themselves with the seed of men: but they shall not cleave one to another, even as iron is not mixed with clay."

"In the days of these kings shall the God of heaven set up a kingdom, which shall never be destroyed: and the kingdom shall not be left to other people, but it shall break in pieces and consume all these kingdoms, and it shall stand forever. Forasmuch as thou sawest that the stone was cut out of the mountain without hands, and that it brake in pieces the iron, the brass, the clay, the silver, and the gold; the great God hath made known to the king what shall come to pass hereafter: and the dream is certain, and the interpretation thereof sure."

The king was convinced of the truth of the interpretation, and in humility and awe he "fell upon his face, and worshiped," saying, "Of a truth it is, that your God is a God of gods, and a Lord of kings, and a revealer of secrets, seeing thou couldest reveal this secret."

Nebuchadnezzar revoked the decree for the destruction of the wise men. Their lives were spared because of Daniel's connection with the Revealer of secrets. And "the king made Daniel a great man, and gave him many great gifts, and made him ruler over the whole province of Babylon, and chief of the governors over all the wise men of Babylon. Then Daniel requested of the king, and he set Shadrach, Meshach, and Abednego, over the affairs of the province of Babylon: but Daniel sat in the gate of the king."

In the annals of human history, the growth of nations, the rise and fall of empires, appear as if dependent on the will and prowess of man; the shaping of events seems, to a great degree, to be determined by his power, ambition, or caprice. But in the word of God the curtain is drawn aside, and we behold, above, behind, and through all the play and counterplay of human interest and power and passions, the agencies of the All-merciful One, silently, patiently working out the counsels of His own will.

In words of matchless beauty and tenderness, the apostle Paul set before the sages of Athens the divine purpose in the creation and distribution of races and nations. "God that made the world and all things therein," declared the apostle, "hath made of one blood all nations of men for to dwell on all the face of the earth, and hath determined the times before appointed, and the bounds of their habitation; that they should seek the Lord, if haply they might feel after Him, and find Him." Acts 17:24-27.

God has made plain that whosoever will, may come "into the bond of the covenant." Ezekiel 20:37. In the creation it was His purpose that the earth should be inhabited by beings whose existence would be a blessing to themselves and to one another, and an honor to their Creator. All who will may identify themselves with this purpose. Of them it is spoken, "This people have I formed for Myself; they shall show forth My praise." Isaiah 43:21.

In His law God has made known the principles that underlie all true prosperity, both of nations and of individuals. To the Israelites Moses declared of this law: "This is your wisdom and your understanding." "It is not a vain thing for you; because it is your life." Deuteronomy 4:6; 32:47. The blessings thus assured to Israel are, on the same conditions and in the same degree, assured to every nation and to every individual under the broad heavens.

Hundreds of years before certain nations came upon the stage of action, the Omniscient One looked down the ages and predicted the rise and fall of the universal kingdoms. God declared to Nebuchadnezzar that the kingdom of Babylon should fall, and a second kingdom would arise, which also would have its period of trial. Failing to exalt the true God, its glory would fade, and a third kingdom would occupy its place. This also would pass away; and a fourth, strong as iron, would subdue the nations of the world.

Had the rulers of Babylon—that richest of all earthly kingdoms—kept always before them the fear of Jehovah, they would have been given wisdom and power which would have bound them to Him and kept them strong. But they made God their refuge only when harassed and perplexed. At such times, failing to find help in their great men, they sought it from men like Daniel—men who they knew honored the living God and were honored by Him. To these men they appealed to unravel the mysteries of Providence; for though the rulers of proud Babylon were men of the highest intellect, they had separated themselves so far from God by transgression that they could not understand the revelations and the warnings given them concerning the future.

In the history of nations the student of God's word may behold the literal fulfillment of divine prophecy. Babylon, shattered and broken at last, passed away because in prosperity its rulers had regarded themselves as independent of God, and had ascribed the glory of their kingdom to human achievement. The Medo-Persian realm was visited by the wrath of Heaven because in it God's law had been trampled underfoot. The fear of the Lord had found no place in the hearts of the vast majority of the people. Wickedness, blasphemy, and corruption prevailed. The kingdoms that followed were even more base and corrupt; and these sank lower and still lower in the scale of moral worth.

The power exercised by every ruler on the earth is Heaven-imparted; and upon his use of the power thus bestowed, his success depends. To each the word of the divine Watcher is, "I girded thee, though thou hast not known Me." Isaiah 45:5. And to each the words spoken to Nebuchadnezzar of old are the lesson of life: "Break off thy sins by righteousness, and thine iniquities by showing mercy to the poor; if it may be a lengthening of thy tranquillity." Daniel 4:27.

To understand these things,—to understand that "righteousness exalteth a nation;" that "the throne is established by righteousness," and "upholden by mercy;" to recognize the outworking of these principles in the manifestation of His power who "removeth kings, and setteth up kings,"—this is to understand the philosophy of history. Proverbs 14:34; 16:12; 20:28; Daniel 2:21.

In the word of God only is this clearly set forth. Here it is shown that the strength of nations, as of individuals, is not found in the opportunities or facilities that appear to make them invincible; it is not found in their boasted greatness. It is measured by the fidelity with which they fulfill God's purpose.

41

The Fiery Furnace

The dream of the great image, opening before Nebuchadnezzar events reaching to the close of time, had been given that he might understand the part he was to act in the world's history, and the relation that his kingdom should sustain to the kingdom of heaven. In the interpretation of

This chapter is based on Daniel 3.

the dream, he had been plainly instructed regarding the establishment of God's everlasting kingdom. "In the days of these kings," Daniel had declared, "shall the God of heaven set up a kingdom, which shall never be destroyed: and the kingdom shall not be left to other people, but it shall break in pieces and consume all these kingdoms, and it shall stand forever. . . . The dream is certain, and the interpretation thereof sure." Daniel 2:44, 45.

The king had acknowledged the power of God, saying to Daniel, "Of a truth it is, that your God is a God of gods, . . . and a revealer of secrets." Verse 47. For a time afterward, Nebuchadnezzar was influenced by the fear of God; but his heart was not yet cleansed from worldly ambition and a desire for self-exaltation. The prosperity attending his reign filled him with pride. In time he ceased to honor God, and resumed his idol worship with increased zeal and bigotry.

The words, "Thou art this head of gold," had made a deep impression upon the ruler's mind. Verse 38. The wise men of his realm, taking advantage of this and of his return to idolatry, proposed that he make an image similar to the one seen in his dream, and set it up where all might behold the head of gold, which had been interpreted as representing his kingdom.

Pleased with the flattering suggestion, he determined to carry it out, and to go even farther. Instead of reproducing the image as he had seen it, he would excel the original. His image should not deteriorate in value from the head to the feet, but should be entirely of gold—symbolic throughout of Babylon as an eternal, indestructible, all-powerful kingdom, which should break in pieces all other kingdoms and stand forever.

The thought of establishing the empire and a dynasty that should endure forever, appealed very strongly to the mighty ruler before whose arms the nations of earth had been unable to stand. With an enthusiasm born of boundless ambition and selfish pride, he entered into counsel with his wise men as to how to bring this about. Forgetting the remarkable providences connected with the dream of the great image; forgetting also that the God of Israel through His servant Daniel had made plain the significance of the image, and that in connection with this interpretation the great men of the realm had been saved an ignominious death; forgetting all except their desire to establish their own power and supremacy, the king and his counselors of state determined that by every means possible they would endeavor to exalt Babylon as supreme, and worthy of universal allegiance.

The symbolic representation by which God had revealed to king and people His purpose for the nations of earth, was now to be made to serve for the glorification of human power.

Daniel's interpretation was to be rejected and forgotten; truth was to be misinterpreted and misapplied. The symbol designed of Heaven to unfold to the minds of men important events of the future, was to be used to hinder the spread of the knowledge that God desired the world to receive. Thus through the devisings of ambitious men, Satan was seeking to thwart the divine purpose for the human race. The enemy of mankind knew that truth unmixed with error is a power mighty to save; but that when used to exalt self and to further the projects of men, it becomes a power for evil.

From his rich store of treasure, Nebuchadnezzar caused to be made a great golden image, similar in its general features to that which had been seen in vision, save in the one particular of the material of which it was composed. Accustomed as they were to magnificent representations of their heathen deities, the Chaldeans had never before produced anything so imposing and majestic as this resplendent statue, threescore cubits in height and six cubits in breadth. And it is not surprising that in a land where idol worship was of universal prevalence, the beautiful and priceless image on the plain of Dura, representing the glory of Babylon and its magnificence and power, should be consecrated as an object of worship. This was accordingly provided for, and a decree went forth that on the day of the dedication all should show their supreme loyalty to the Babylonian power by bowing before the image.

The appointed day came, and a vast concourse from all "people, nations, and languages," assembled on the plain of Dura. In harmony with the king's command, when the sound of music was heard, the whole company "fell down and worshiped the golden image." On that eventful day the powers of darkness seemed to be gaining a signal triumph; the worship of the golden image bade fair to become connected permanently with the established forms of idolatry recognized as the state religion of the land. Satan hoped thereby to defeat God's purpose of making the presence of captive Israel in Babylon a means of blessing to all the nations of heathendom.

But God decreed otherwise. Not all had bowed the knee to the idolatrous symbol of human power. In the midst of the worshiping multitude there were three men who were firmly resolved not thus to dishonor the God of heaven. Their God was King of kings and Lord of lords; they would bow to none other.

To Nebuchadnezzar, flushed with triumph, was brought the word that among his subjects there were some who dared disobey his mandate. Certain of the wise men, jealous of the honors that had been bestowed upon the faithful companions of Daniel, now reported to the king their flagrant violation of his wishes. "O king,

live forever," they exclaimed. "There are certain Jews whom thou hast set over the affairs of the province of Babylon, Shadrach, Meshach, and Abednego; these men, O king, have not regarded thee: they serve not thy gods, nor worship the golden image which thou hast set up."

The king commanded that the men be brought before him. "Is it true," he inquired, "do not ye serve my gods, nor worship the golden image which I have set up?" He endeavored by threats to induce them to unite with the multitude. Pointing to the fiery furnace, he reminded them of the punishment awaiting them if they should persist in their refusal to obey his will. But firmly the Hebrews testified to their allegiance to the God of heaven, and their faith in His power to deliver. The act of bowing to the image was understood by all to be an act of worship. Such homage they could render to God alone.

As the three Hebrews stood before the king, he was convinced that they possessed something the other wise men of his kingdom did not have. They had been faithful in the performance of every duty. He would give them another trial. If only they would signify their willingness to unite with the multitude in worshiping the image, all would be well with them; "but if ye worship not," he added, "ye shall be cast the same hour into the midst of a burning fiery furnace." Then with his hand stretched upward in defiance, he demanded, "Who is that God that shall deliver you out of my hands?"

In vain were the king's threats. He could not turn the men from their allegiance to the Ruler of the universe. From the history of their fathers they had learned that disobedience to God results in dishonor, disaster, and death; and that the fear of the Lord is the beginning of wisdom, the foundation of all true prosperity. Calmly facing the furnace, they said, "O Nebuchadnezzar, we are not careful to answer thee in this matter. If it be so [if this is your decision], our God whom we serve is able to deliver us from the burning fiery furnace, and He will deliver us out of thine hand, O king." Their faith strengthened as they declared that God would be glorified by delivering them, and with triumphant assurance born of implicit trust in God, they added, "But if not, be it known unto thee, O king, that we will not serve thy gods, nor worship the golden image which thou hast set up."

The king's wrath knew no bounds. "Full of fury," "the form of his visage was changed" against Shadrach, Meshach, and Abednego, representatives of a despised and captive race. Directing that the furnace be heated seven times hotter than its wont, he commanded the mighty men of his army to bind the worshipers of Israel's God, preparatory to summary execution.

"Then these men were bound in their coats, their hosen, and their hats, and their other garments, and were cast into the midst of the burning fiery furnace. Therefore because the king's commandment was urgent, and the furnace exceeding hot, the flame of the fire slew those men that took up Shadrach, Meshach, and Abednego."

But the Lord did not forget His own. As His witnesses were cast into the furnace, the Saviour 509 revealed Himself to them in person, and together they walked in the midst of the fire. In the presence of the Lord of heat and cold, the flames lost their power to consume.

From his royal seat the king looked on, expecting to see the men who had defied him utterly destroyed. But his feelings of triumph suddenly changed. The nobles standing near saw his face grow pale as he started from the throne and looked intently into the glowing flames. In alarm the king, turning to his lords, asked, "Did not we cast three men bound into the midst of the fire? . . . Lo, I see four men loose, walking in the midst of the fire, and they have no hurt; and the form of the fourth is like the Son of God."

How did that heathen king know what the Son of God was like? The Hebrew captives filling positions of trust in Babylon had in life and character represented before him the truth. When asked for a reason of their faith, they had given it without hesitation. Plainly and simply they had presented the principles of righteousness, thus teaching those around them of the God whom they worshiped. They had told of Christ, the Redeemer to come; and in the form of the fourth in the midst of the fire the king recognized the Son of God.

And now, his own greatness and dignity forgotten, Nebuchadnezzar descended from his throne and, going to the mouth of the furnace, cried out, "Ye servants of the most high God, come forth, and come hither."

Then Shadrach, Meshach, and Abednego came forth before the vast multitude, showing themselves unhurt. The presence of their Saviour had guarded them from harm, and only their fetters had been burned. "And the princes, 510 governors, and captains, and the king's counselors, being gathered together, saw these men, upon whose bodies the fire had no power, nor was an hair of their head singed, neither were their coats changed, nor the smell of fire had passed on them."

Forgotten was the great golden image, set up with such pomp. In the presence of the living God, men feared and trembled. "Blessed be the God of Shadrach, Meshach, and Abednego," the humbled king was constrained to acknowledge, "who hath sent His angel, and delivered His servants that trusted in Him, and have changed the king's word, and yielded their bodies, that they might not serve nor worship any god, except their own God."

The experiences of that day led Nebuchadnezzar to issue a decree, "that every people, nation, and language, which speak anything amiss against the God of Shadrach, Meshach, and Abednego, shall be cut in pieces, and their houses shall be made a dunghill." "There is no other god," he urged as the reason for the decree, "that can deliver after this sort."

In these and like words the king of Babylon endeavored to spread abroad before all the peoples of earth his conviction that the power and authority of the God of the Hebrews was worthy of supreme adoration. And God was pleased with the effort of the king to show Him reverence, and to make the royal confession of allegiance as widespread as was the Babylonian realm.

It was right for the king to make public confession, and to seek to exalt the God of heaven above all other gods; but in endeavoring to force his subjects to make a similar confession of 511 faith and to show similar reverence, Nebuchadnezzar was exceeding his right as a temporal sovereign. He had no more right, either civil or moral, to threaten men with death for not worshiping God, than he had to make the decree consigning to the flames all who refused to worship the golden image. God never compels the obedience of man. He leaves all free to choose whom they will serve.

By the deliverance of His faithful servants, the Lord declared that He takes His stand with the oppressed, and rebukes all earthly powers that rebel against the authority of Heaven. The 512 three Hebrews declared to the whole nation of Babylon their faith in Him whom they worshiped. They relied on God. In the hour of their trial they remembered the promise, "When thou passest through the waters, I will be with thee; and through the rivers, they shall not overflow thee: when thou walkest through the fire, thou shalt not be burned; neither shall the flame kindle upon thee." Isaiah 43:2. And in a marvelous manner their faith in the living Word had been honored in the sight of all. The tidings of their wonderful deliverance were carried to many countries by the representatives of the different nations that had been invited by Nebuchadnezzar to the dedication. Through the faithfulness of His children, God was glorified in all the earth.

Important are the lessons to be learned from the experience of the Hebrew youth on the plain of Dura. In this our day, many of God's servants, though innocent of wrongdoing, will be given over to suffer humiliation and abuse at the hands of those who, inspired by Satan, are filled with envy and religious bigotry. Especially will the wrath of man be aroused against those who hallow the Sabbath of the fourth commandment; and at last a universal decree will denounce these as deserving of death.

The season of distress before God's people will call for a faith that will not falter. His children must make it manifest that He is the only object of their worship, and that no consideration, not even that of life itself, can induce them to make the least concession to false worship. To the loyal heart the commands of sinful, finite 513 men will sink into insignificance beside the word of the eternal God. Truth will be obeyed though the result be imprisonment or exile or death.

As in the days of Shadrach, Meshach, and Abednego, so in the closing period of earth's history the Lord will work mightily in behalf of those who stand steadfastly for the right. He who walked with the Hebrew worthies in the fiery furnace will be with His followers wherever they are. His abiding presence will comfort and sustain. In the midst of the time of trouble—trouble such as has not been since there was a nation—His chosen ones will stand unmoved. Satan with all the hosts of evil cannot destroy the weakest of God's saints. Angels that excel in strength will protect them, and in their behalf Jehovah will reveal Himself as a "God of gods," able to save to the uttermost those who have put their trust in Him.

514

42

True Greatness

Exalted to the pinnacle of worldly honor, and acknowledged even by Inspiration as "a king of kings" (Ezekiel 26:7), Nebuchadnezzar nevertheless at times had ascribed to the favor of Jehovah the glory of his kingdom and the splendor of his reign. Such had been the case after his dream of the great image. His mind had been profoundly influenced by this vision and by the thought that the Babylonian Empire, universal though it was, was finally to fall; and other kingdoms were to bear sway, until at last all earthly powers were to be superseded by a kingdom set up by the God of heaven, which kingdom was never to be destroyed.

Nebuchadnezzar's noble conception of God's purpose concerning the nations was lost sight of later in his experience; yet when his proud spirit was humbled before the multitude on the plain of Dura, he once more had acknowledged that God's kingdom is "an everlasting kingdom, and His dominion is from generation to generation." 515 An idolater by birth and training, and at the head of an idolatrous people, he had nevertheless an innate sense of justice and right, and God was able to use him as an instrument for the punishment of the rebellious and for the fulfillment of the divine purpose. "The terrible of the nations" (Ezekiel 28:7), it was given Neb-

uchadnezzar, after years of patient and wearing labor, to conquer Tyre; Egypt also fell a prey to his victorious armies; and as he added nation after nation to the Babylonian realm, he added more and more to his fame as the greatest ruler of the age.

It is not surprising that the successful monarch, so ambitious and so proud-spirited, should be tempted to turn aside from the path of humility, which alone leads to true greatness. In the intervals between his wars of conquest he gave much thought to the strengthening and beautifying of his capital, until at length the city of Babylon became the chief glory of his kingdom, "the golden city," "the praise of the whole earth." His passion as a builder, and his signal success in making Babylon one of the wonders of the world, ministered to his pride, until he was in grave danger of spoiling his record as a wise ruler whom God could continue to use as an instrument for the carrying out of the divine purpose.

In mercy God gave the king another dream, to warn him of his peril and of the snare that had been laid for his ruin. In a vision of the night, Nebuchadnezzar saw a great tree growing in the midst of the earth, its top towering to the heavens and its branches stretching to the ends of the earth. Flocks and herds from the mountains and hills enjoyed shelter beneath its shadow, and the birds of the air built their nests in its boughs. 516 "The leaves thereof were fair, and the fruit thereof much, and in it was meat for all: . . . and all flesh was fed of it."

As the king gazed upon the lofty tree, he beheld "a Watcher," even "an Holy One," who approached the tree and in a loud voice cried:

"Hew down the tree, and cut off his branches, shake off his leaves, and scatter his fruit: let the beasts get away from under it, and the fowls from his branches: nevertheless leave the stump of his roots in the earth, even with a band of iron and brass, in the tender grass of the field; and let it be wet with the dew of heaven, and let his portion be with the beasts in the grass of the earth: let his heart be changed from man's, and let a beast's heart be given unto him; and let seven times pass over him. This matter is by the decree of the watchers, and the demand by the word of the holy ones: to the intent that the living may know that the Most High ruleth in the kingdom of men, and giveth it to whomsoever He will, and setteth up over it the basest of men."

Greatly troubled by the dream, which was evidently a prediction of adversity, the king repeated it to "the magicians, the astrologers, the Chaldeans, and the soothsayers;" but although the dream was very explicit, none of the wise men could interpret it.

Once more in this idolatrous nation, testimony was to be borne to the fact that only those

This chapter is based on Daniel 4.

who love and fear God can understand the mysteries of the kingdom of heaven. The king in his perplexity sent for his servant Daniel, a man esteemed for his integrity and constancy and for his unrivaled wisdom.

517 When Daniel, in response to the royal summons, stood in the king's presence, Nebuchadnezzar said, "O Belteshazzar, master of the magicians, because I know that the spirit of the holy gods is in thee, and no secret troubleth thee, tell me the visions of my dream that I have seen, and the interpretation thereof." After relating the dream, Nebuchadnezzar said: "O Belteshazzar, declare the interpretation thereof, forasmuch as all the wise men of my kingdom are not able to make known unto me the interpretation: but thou art able; for the spirit of the holy gods is in thee."

To Daniel the meaning of the dream was plain, and its significance startled him. He "was astonied for one hour, and his thoughts troubled him." Seeing Daniel's hesitation and distress, the king expressed sympathy for his servant. "Belteshazzar," he said, "let not the dream, or the interpretation thereof, trouble thee."

"My lord," Daniel answered, "the dream be to them that hate thee, and the interpretation thereof to thine enemies." The prophet realized that upon him God had laid the solemn duty of revealing to Nebuchadnezzar the judgment that was about to fall upon him because of his pride and arrogance. Daniel must interpret the dream in language the king could understand; and although its dreadful import had made him hesitate in dumb amazement, yet he must state the truth, whatever the consequences to himself.

Then Daniel made known the mandate of the Almighty. "The tree that thou sawest," he said, "which grew, and was strong, whose height reached unto the heaven, and the sight thereof to

518 all the earth; whose leaves were fair, and the fruit thereof much, and in it was meat for all; under which the beasts of the field dwelt, and upon whose branches the fowls of the heaven had their habitation: it is thou, O king, that art grown and become strong: for thy greatness is grown, and reacheth unto heaven, and thy dominion to the end of the earth.

"And whereas the king saw a Watcher and an Holy One coming down from heaven, and saying, Hew the tree down, and destroy it; yet leave the stump of the roots thereof in the earth, even with a band of iron and brass, in the tender grass of the field; and let it be wet with the dew of heaven, and let his portion be with the beasts of the field, till seven times pass over him; this is the interpretation, O king, and this is the decree of the Most High, which is come upon my lord the king: that they shall drive thee from men, and thy dwelling shall be with the beasts of the field, and they shall make thee to eat grass as oxen, and they shall wet thee with the dew of

heaven, and seven times shall pass over thee, till thou know that the Most High ruleth in the kingdom of men, and giveth it to whomsoever He will. And whereas they commanded to leave the stump of the tree roots; thy kingdom shall be sure unto thee, after that thou shalt have known that the Heavens do rule."

Having faithfully interpreted the dream, Daniel urged the proud monarch to repent and turn to God, that by rightdoing he might avert the threatened calamity. "O king," the prophet pleaded, "let my counsel be acceptable unto thee, and break off thy sins by righteousness, and thine iniquities by showing mercy to the 519 poor; if it may be a lengthening of thy tranquillity."

For a time the impression of the warning and the counsel of the prophet was strong upon Nebuchadnezzar; but the heart that is not transformed by the grace of God soon loses the impressions of the Holy Spirit. Self-indulgence and ambition had not yet been eradicated from the king's heart, and later on these traits reappeared. Notwithstanding the instruction so graciously given him, and the warnings of past experience, Nebuchadnezzar again allowed himself to be controlled by a spirit of jealousy against the kingdoms that were to follow. His rule, which heretofore had been to a great degree just and merciful, became oppressive. Hardening his heart, he used his God-given talents for self-glorification, exalting himself above the God who had given him life and power.

For months the judgment of God lingered. But instead of being led to repentance by this forbearance, the king indulged his pride until he lost confidence in the interpretation of the dream, and jested at his former fears.

A year from the time he had received the warning, Nebuchadnezzar, walking in his palace and thinking with pride of his power as a ruler and of his success as a builder, exclaimed, "Is not this great Babylon, that I have built for the house of the kingdom by the might of my power, and for the honor of my majesty?"

While the proud boast was yet on the king's lips, a voice from heaven announced that God's appointed time of judgment had come. Upon his 520 ears fell the mandate of Jehovah: "O King Nebuchadnezzar, to thee it is spoken; The kingdom is departed from thee. And they shall drive thee from men, and thy dwelling shall be with the beasts of the field: they shall make thee to eat grass as oxen, and seven times shall pass over thee, until thou know that the Most High ruleth in the kingdom of men, and giveth it to whomsoever He will."

In a moment the reason that God had given him was taken away; the judgment that the king thought perfect, the wisdom on which he prided himself, was removed, and the once mighty ruler was a maniac. His hand could no longer sway the scepter. The messages of warning had been unheeded; now, stripped of the power his Creator had given him, and driven from men, Nebuchadnezzar "did eat grass as oxen, and his body was wet with the dew of heaven, till his hairs were grown like eagles' feathers, and his nails like birds' claws."

For seven years Nebuchadnezzar was an astonishment to all his subjects; for seven years he was humbled before all the world. Then his reason was restored and, looking up in humility to the God of heaven, he recognized the divine hand in his chastisement. In a public proclamation he acknowledged his guilt and the great mercy of God in his restoration. "At the end of the days," he said, "I Nebuchadnezzar lifted up mine eyes unto heaven, and mine understanding returned unto me, and I blessed the Most High, and I praised and honored Him that liveth forever, whose dominion is an everlasting dominion, and His kingdom is from generation to generation: and all the inhabitants of the earth are reputed as nothing: and He doeth according to His will in the army of heaven, and among the inhabitants of the earth: and none can stay His hand, or say unto Him, What doest Thou?

"At the same time my reason returned unto me; and for the glory of my kingdom, mine honor and brightness returned unto me; and my counselors and my lords sought unto me; and I was established in my kingdom, and excellent majesty was added unto me."

The once proud monarch had become a humble child of God; the tyrannical, overbearing ruler, a wise and compassionate king. He who had defied and blasphemed the God of heaven, now acknowledged the power of the Most High and earnestly sought to promote the fear of Jehovah and the happiness of his subjects. Under the rebuke of Him who is King of kings and Lord of lords, Nebuchadnezzar had learned at last the lesson which all rulers need to learn— that true greatness consists in true goodness. He acknowledged Jehovah as the living God, saying, "I Nebuchadnezzar praise and extol and honor the King of heaven, all whose works are truth, and His ways judgment: and those that walk in pride He is able to abase."

God's purpose that the greatest kingdom in the world should show forth His praise was now fulfilled. This public proclamation, in which Nebuchadnezzar acknowledged the mercy and goodness and authority of God, was the last act of his life recorded in sacred history.

⁵²¹

43

The Unseen Watcher

⁵²²

Toward the close of Daniel's life great changes were taking place in the land to which, over threescore years before, he and his Hebrew companions had been carried captive. Nebuchadnezzar, "the terrible of the nations" (Ezekiel 28:7), had died, and Babylon, "the praise of the whole earth" (Jeremiah 51:41), had passed under the unwise rule of his successors, and gradual but sure dissolution was resulting.

Through the folly and weakness of Belshazzar, the grandson of Nebuchadnezzar, proud Babylon was soon to fall. Admitted in his youth to a share in kingly authority, Belshazzar gloried in his power and lifted up his heart against the God of heaven. Many had been his opportunities to know the divine will and to understand his responsibility of rendering obedience thereto. He had known of his grandfather's banishment, by the decree of God, from the society of men; and he was familiar with Nebuchadnezzar's conversion and miraculous restoration. But Belshazzar allowed the love of pleasure and ⁵²³ self-glorification to efface the lessons that he should never have forgotten. He wasted the opportunities graciously granted him, and neglected to use the means within his reach for becoming more fully acquainted with truth. That which Nebuchadnezzar had finally gained at the cost of untold suffering and humiliation, Belshazzar passed by with indifference.

It was not long before reverses came. Babylon was besieged by Cyrus, nephew of Darius the Mede, and commanding general of the combined armies of the Medes and Persians. But within the seemingly impregnable fortress, with its massive walls and its gates of brass, protected by the river Euphrates, and stocked with provision in abundance, the voluptuous monarch felt safe and passed his time in mirth and revelry.

In his pride and arrogancy, with a reckless feeling of security, Belshazzar "made a great feast to a thousand of his lords, and drank wine before the thousand." All the attractions that wealth and power could command, added splendor to the scene. Beautiful women with their enchantments were among the guests in attendance at the royal banquet. Men of genius and education were there. Princes and statesmen drank wine like water and reveled under its maddening influence.

With reason dethroned through shameless intoxication, and with lower impulses and passions now in the ascendancy, the king himself took the lead in the riotous orgy. As the feast

This chapter is based on Daniel 5.

progressed, he "commanded to bring the golden and silver vessels which . . . Nebuchadnezzar had taken out of the temple which was in Jerusalem; that the king, and his princes, his wives, and his concubines, might drink therein." The king would prove that nothing was too sacred for his hands to handle. "They brought the golden vessels; . . . and the king, and his princes, his wives, and his concubines, drank in them. They drank wine, and praised the gods of gold, and of silver, of brass, of iron, of wood, and of stone."

Little did Belshazzar think that there was a heavenly Witness to his idolatrous revelry; that a divine Watcher, unrecognized, looked upon the scene of profanation, heard the sacrilegious mirth, beheld the idolatry. But soon the uninvited Guest made His presence felt. When the revelry was at its height a bloodless hand came forth and traced upon the walls of the palace characters that gleamed like fire—words which, though unknown to the vast throng, were a portent of doom to the now conscience-stricken king and his guests.

Hushed was the boisterous mirth, while men and women, seized with nameless terror, watched the hand slowly tracing the mysterious characters. Before them passed, as in panoramic view, the deeds of their evil lives; they seemed to be arraigned before the judgment bar of the eternal God, whose power they had just defied. Where but a few moments before had been hilarity and blasphemous witticism, were pallid faces and cries of fear. When God makes men fear, they cannot hide the intensity of their terror.

Belshazzar was the most terrified of them all. He it was who above all others had been responsible for the rebellion against God which that night had reached its height in the Babylonian realm. In the presence of the unseen Watcher, the representative of Him whose power had been challenged and whose name had been blasphemed, the king was paralyzed with fear. Conscience was awakened. "The joints of his loins were loosed, and his knees smote one against another." Belshazzar had impiously lifted himself up against the God of heaven and had trusted in his own might, not supposing that any would dare say, "Why doest thou thus?" but now he realized that he must render an account of the stewardship entrusted him, and that for his wasted opportunities and his defiant attitude he could offer no excuse.

In vain the king tried to read the burning letters. But here was a secret he could not fathom, a power he could neither understand nor gainsay. In despair he turned to the wise men of his realm for help. His wild cry rang out in the assembly, calling upon the astrologers, the Chaldeans, and the soothsayers to read the writing. "Whosoever shall read this writing," he promised, "and show me the interpretation thereof, shall be clothed with scarlet, and have a chain of gold about his neck, and shall be the third ruler in the kingdom." But of no avail was his appeal to his trusted advisers, with offers of rich awards. Heavenly wisdom cannot be bought or sold. "All the king's wise men . . . could not read the writing, nor make known to the king the interpretation thereof." They were no more able to read the mysterious characters than had been the wise men of a former generation to interpret the dreams of Nebuchadnezzar.

Then the queen mother remembered Daniel, who, over half a century before, had made known to King Nebuchadnezzar the dream of the great image and its interpretation. "O king, live forever," she said. "Let not thy thoughts trouble thee, nor let thy countenance be changed: there is a man in thy kingdom, in whom is the spirit of the holy gods; and in the days of thy father light and understanding and wisdom, like the wisdom of the gods, was found in him; whom the king Nebuchadnezzar . . . made master of the magicians, astrologers, Chaldeans, and soothsayers; forasmuch as an excellent spirit, and knowledge, and understanding, interpreting of dreams, and showing of hard sentences, and dissolving of doubts, were found in the same Daniel, whom the king named Belteshazzar: now let Daniel be called, and he will show the interpretation.

"Then was Daniel brought in before the king." Making an effort to regain his composure, Belshazzar said to the prophet: "Art thou that Daniel, which art of the children of the captivity of Judah, whom the king my father brought out of Jewry? I have even heard of thee, that the spirit of the gods is in thee, and that light and understanding and excellent wisdom is found in thee. And now the wise men, the astrologers, have been brought in before me, that they should read this writing, and make known unto me the interpretation thereof: but they could not show the interpretation of the thing: and I have heard of thee, that thou canst make interpretations, and dissolve doubts: now if thou canst read the writing, and make known to me the interpretation thereof, thou shalt be clothed with scarlet, and have a chain of gold about thy neck, and shalt be the third ruler in the kingdom."

Before that terror-stricken throng, Daniel, unmoved by the promises of the king, stood in the quiet dignity of a servant of the Most High, not to speak words of flattery, but to interpret a message of doom. "Let thy gifts be to thyself," he said, "and give thy rewards to another; yet I will read the writing unto the king, and make known to him the interpretation."

The prophet first reminded Belshazzar of matters with which he was familiar, but which had not taught him the lesson of humility that might have saved him. He spoke of Nebuchadnezzar's sin and fall, and of the Lord's dealings with him—the dominion and glory bestowed upon him, the divine judgment for his pride, and his subsequent acknowledgment of the power and mercy of the God of Israel; and then in bold and emphatic words he rebuked Belshazzar for his great wickedness. He held the king's sin up before him, showing him the lessons he might have learned but did not. Belshazzar had not read aright the experience of his grandfather, nor heeded the warning of events so significant to himself. The opportunity of knowing and obeying the true God had been given him, but had not been taken to heart, and he was about to reap the consequence of his rebellion.

"Thou, . . . O Belshazzar," the prophet declared, "hast not humbled thine heart, though thou knewest all this; but hast lifted up thyself against the Lord of heaven; and they have brought the vessels of His house before thee, and thou, and thy lords, thy wives, and thy concubines, have drunk wine in them; and thou hast praised the gods of silver, and gold, of brass, iron, wood, and stone, which see not, nor hear, nor know: and the God in whose hand thy 530 breath is, and whose are all thy ways, hast thou not glorified: then was the part of the hand sent from Him; and this writing was written."

Turning to the Heaven-sent message on the wall, the prophet read, "MENE, MENE, TEKEL, UPHARSIN." The hand that had traced the characters was no longer visible, but these four words were still gleaming forth with terrible distinctness; and now with bated breath the people listened while the aged prophet declared:

"This is the interpretation of the thing: MENE; God hath numbered thy kingdom, and finished it. TEKEL; Thou art weighed in the balances, and art found wanting. PERES; Thy kingdom is divided, and given to the Medes and Persians."

In that last night of mad folly, Belshazzar and his lords had filled up the measure of their guilt and the guilt of the Chaldean kingdom. No longer could God's restraining hand ward off the impending evil. Through manifold providences, God had sought to teach them reverence for His law. "We would have healed Babylon," He declared of those whose judgment was now reaching unto heaven, "but she is not healed." Jeremiah 51:9. Because of the strange perversity of the human heart, God had at last found it necessary to pass the irrevocable sentence. Belshazzar was to fall, and his kingdom was to pass into other hands.

As the prophet ceased speaking, the king commanded that he be awarded the promised honors; and in harmony with this, "they clothed Daniel with scarlet, and put a chain of gold about his neck, and made a proclamation concerning him, that he should be the third ruler in the kingdom."

More than a century before, Inspiration had 531 foretold that "the night of . . . pleasure" during which king and counselors would vie with one another in blasphemy against God, would suddenly be changed into a season of fear and destruction. And now, in rapid succession, momentous events followed one another exactly as had been portrayed in the prophetic scriptures years before the principals in the drama had been born.

While still in the festal hall, surrounded by those whose doom had been sealed, the king is informed by a messenger that "his city is taken" by the enemy against whose devices he had felt so secure; "that the passages are stopped, . . . and the men of war are affrighted." Verses 31, 32. Even while he and his nobles were drinking from the sacred vessels of Jehovah, and praising their gods of silver and of gold, the Medes and the Persians, having turned the Euphrates out of its channel, were marching into the heart of the unguarded city. The army of Cyrus now stood under the walls of the palace; the city was filled with the soldiers of the enemy, "as with caterpillars" (verse 14); and their triumphant shouts could be heard above the despairing cries of the astonished revelers.

"In that night was Belshazzar the king of the Chaldeans slain," and an alien monarch sat upon the throne.

Clearly had the Hebrew prophets spoken concerning the manner in which Babylon should fall. As in vision God had revealed to them the events of the future, they had exclaimed: "How is Sheshach taken! and how is the praise of the whole earth surprised! how is Babylon become an astonishment among the nations!" "How is the hammer of the whole earth cut asunder and 532 broken! how is Babylon become a desolation among the nations!" "At the noise of the taking of Babylon the earth is moved, and the cry is heard among the nations."

"Babylon is suddenly fallen and destroyed." "The spoiler is come upon her, even upon Babylon, and her mighty men are taken, every one of their bows is broken: for the Lord God of recompenses shall surely requite. And I will make drunk her princes, and her wise men, her captains, and her rulers, and her mighty men: and they shall sleep a perpetual sleep, and not wake, saith the King, whose name is the Lord of hosts."

"I have laid a snare for thee, and thou art also taken, O Babylon, and thou wast not aware: thou art found, and also caught, because thou hast striven against the Lord. The Lord hath opened His armory, and hath brought forth the weapons of His indignation: for this is the work of the Lord God of hosts in the land of the Chaldeans."

"Thus saith the Lord of hosts; The children of Israel and the children of Judah were oppressed together: and all that took them captives held them fast; they refused to let them go. Their Redeemer is strong; the Lord of hosts is His name: He shall throughly plead their cause, that He may give rest to the land, and disquiet the inhabitants of Babylon." Jeremiah 51:41; 50:23, 46; 51:8, 56, 57; 50:24, 25, 33, 34.

Thus "the broad walls of Babylon" became "utterly broken, and her high gates . . . burned with fire." Thus did Jehovah of hosts "cause the arrogancy of the proud to cease," and lay 533 low "the haughtiness of the terrible." Thus did "Babylon, the glory of kingdoms, the beauty of the Chaldees' excellency," become as Sodom and Gomorrah—a place forever accursed. "It shall never be inhabited," Inspiration has declared, "neither shall it be dwelt in from generation to generation: neither shall the Arabian pitch tent there; neither shall the shepherds make their fold there. But wild beasts of the desert shall lie there; and their houses shall be full of doleful creatures; and owls shall dwell there, and satyrs shall dance there. And the wild beasts of the islands shall cry in their desolate houses, and dragons in their pleasant palaces." "I will also make it a possession for the bittern, and pools of water: and I will sweep it with the besom of destruction, saith the Lord of hosts." Jeremiah 51:58; Isaiah 13:11, 19-22; 14:23.

To the last ruler of Babylon, as in type to its first, had come the sentence of the divine Watcher: "O king, . . . to thee it is spoken; The kingdom is departed from thee." Daniel 4:31.

"Come down, and sit in the dust, O virgin daughter of Babylon,

Sit on the ground: there is no throne. . . .

Sit thou silent,

And get thee into darkness, O daughter of the Chaldeans:

For thou shalt no more be called, The lady of kingdoms.

"I was wroth with My people,

I have polluted Mine inheritance, and given them into

thine hand:

Thou didst show them no mercy; . . .

"And thou saidst, I shall be a lady forever:

So that thou didst not lay these things to thy heart,

Neither didst remember the latter end of it.

534 "Therefore hear now this,

Thou that art given to pleasures,

That dwellest carelessly,

That sayest in thine heart,

I am, and none else beside me;

I shall not sit as a widow,

Neither shall I know the loss of children: . . .

"These two things shall come to thee in a moment in one day,

The loss of children, and widowhood:

They shall come upon thee in their perfection for the multitude of thy sorceries, and for the great abundance of thine enchantments.

For thou hast trusted in thy wickedness:

Thou hast said, None seeth me.

"Thy wisdom and thy knowledge, it hath perverted thee;

And thou hast said in thine heart,

I am, and none else beside me.

Therefore shall evil come upon thee;

Thou shalt not know from whence it riseth:

And mischief shall fall upon thee;

Thou shalt not be able to put it off:

And desolation shall come upon thee suddenly, which thou shalt not know.

"Stand now with thine enchantments, and with the multitude of thy sorceries, wherein thou hast labored from thy youth;

If so be thou shalt be able to profit,

If so be thou mayest prevail.

"Thou art wearied in the multitude of thy counsels.

Let now the astrologers, the stargazers, the monthly prognosticators,

Stand up, and save thee from these things that shall come upon thee.

Behold, they shall be as stubble; . . .

They shall not deliver themselves from the power of the flame: . . .

None shall save thee." Isaiah 47:1-15.

Every nation that has come upon the stage of 535 action has been permitted to occupy its place on the earth, that the fact might be determined whether it would fulfill the purposes of the Watcher and the Holy One. Prophecy has traced the rise and progress of the world's great empires—Babylon, Medo-Persia, Greece, and Rome. With each of these, as with the nations of less power, history has repeated itself. Each has had its period of test; each has failed, its glory faded, its power departed.

While nations have rejected God's principles, and in this rejection have wrought their own ruin, yet a divine, overruling purpose has manifestly been at work throughout the ages. It was this that the prophet Ezekiel saw in the wonderful representation given him during his exile in the land of the Chaldeans, when before his astonished gaze were portrayed the symbols that revealed an overruling Power that has to do with the affairs of earthly rulers.

Upon the banks of the river Chebar, Ezekiel

beheld a whirlwind seeming to come from the north, "a great cloud, and a fire infolding itself, and a brightness was about it, and out of the midst thereof as the color of amber." A number of wheels intersecting one another were moved by four living beings. High above all these "was the likeness of a throne, as the appearance of a sapphire stone: and upon the likeness of the throne was the likeness as the appearance of a man above upon it." "And there appeared in the cherubims the form of a man's hand under their wings." Ezekiel 1:4, 26; 10:8. The wheels were so complicated in arrangement that at first sight they appeared to be in confusion; yet they moved in perfect harmony. Heavenly beings, sustained and guided by the hand beneath the wings of the cherubim, were impelling those wheels; above them, upon the sapphire throne, was the Eternal One; and round about the throne was a rainbow, the emblem of divine mercy.

As the wheellike complications were under the guidance of the hand beneath the wings of the cherubim, so the complicated play of human events is under divine control. Amidst the strife and tumult of nations He that sitteth above the cherubim still guides the affairs of this earth.

The history of nations speaks to us today. To every nation and to every individual God has assigned a place in His great plan. Today men and nations are being tested by the plummet in the hand of Him who makes no mistake. All are by their own choice deciding their destiny, and God is overruling all for the accomplishment of His purposes.

The prophecies which the great I AM has given in His word, uniting link after link in the chain of events, from eternity in the past to eternity in the future, tell us where we are today in the procession of the ages and what may be expected in the time to come. All that prophecy has foretold as coming to pass, until the present time, has been traced on the pages of history, and we may be assured that all which is yet to come will be fulfilled in its order.

Today the signs of the times declare that we are standing on the threshold of great and solemn events. Everything in our world is in agitation. Before our eyes is fulfilling the Saviour's prophecy of the events to precede His coming: "Ye shall hear of wars and rumors of wars. . . . Nation shall rise against nation, and kingdom against kingdom: and there shall be famines, and pestilences, and earthquakes, in divers places." Matthew 24:6, 7.

The present is a time of overwhelming interest to all living. Rulers and statesmen, men who occupy positions of trust and authority, thinking men and women of all classes, have their attention fixed upon the events taking place about us. They are watching the relations that exist among the nations. They observe the intensity that is taking possession of every earthly ele-ment, and they recognize that something great and decisive is about to take place—that the world is on the verge of a stupendous crisis.

The Bible, and the Bible only, gives a correct view of these things. Here are revealed the great final scenes in the history of our world, events that already are casting their shadows before, the sound of their approach causing the earth to tremble and men's hearts to fail them for fear.

"Behold, the Lord maketh the earth empty, and maketh it waste, and turneth it upside down, and scattereth abroad the inhabitants thereof; . . . because they have transgressed the laws, changed the ordinance, broken the everlasting covenant. Therefore hath the curse devoured the earth, and they that dwell therein are desolate." Isaiah 24:1-6.

"Alas for the day! for the day of the Lord is at hand, and as a destruction from the Almighty shall it come. . . . The seed is rotten under their clods, the garners are laid desolate, the barns are broken down; for the corn is withered. How do the beasts groan! the herds of cattle are per-plexed, because they have no pasture; yea, the flocks of sheep are made desolate." "The vine is dried up, and the fig tree languisheth; the pome-granate tree, the palm tree also, and the apple tree, even all the trees of the field, are withered: because joy is withered away from the sons of men." Joel 1:15-18, 12.

"I am pained at my very heart; . . . I cannot hold my peace, because thou hast heard, O my soul, the sound of the trumpet, the alarm of war. Destruction upon destruction is cried; for the whole land is spoiled." Jeremiah 4:19, 20.

"Alas! for that day is great, so that none is like it: it is even the time of Jacob's trouble; but he shall be saved out of it." Jeremiah 30:7.

"Because thou hast made the Lord, which is
  my refuge,
Even the Most High, thy habitation;
There shall no evil befall thee,
Neither shall any plague come nigh thy
  dwelling."
                              Psalm 91:9, 10.

"O daughter of Zion, . . . the Lord shall redeem thee from the hand of thine enemies. Now also many nations are gathered against thee, that say, Let her be defiled, and let our eye look upon Zion. But they know not the thoughts of the Lord, neither understand they His coun-sel." Micah 4:10-12. God will not fail His church in the hour of her greatest peril. He has promised deliverance. "I will bring again the captivity of Jacob's tents," He has declared, "and have mercy on his dwelling places." Jere-miah 30:18.

Then will the purpose of God be fulfilled; the principles of His kingdom will be honored by all beneath the sun.

44

In the Lions' Den

When Darius the Median took the throne formerly occupied by the Babylonian rulers, he at once proceeded to reorganize the government. He "set over the kingdom an hundred and twenty princes; . . . and over these three presidents; of whom Daniel was first: that the princes might give accounts unto them, and the king should have no damage. Then this Daniel was preferred above the presidents and princes, because an excellent spirit was in him; and the king thought to set him over the whole realm."

The honors bestowed upon Daniel excited the jealousy of the leading men of the kingdom, and they sought for occasion of complaint against him. But they could find none, "forasmuch as he was faithful, neither was there any error or fault found in him."

Daniel's blameless conduct excited still further the jealousy of his enemies. "We shall not find any occasion against this Daniel," they were constrained to acknowledge, "except we find it against him concerning the law of his God."

Thereupon the presidents and princes, counseling together, devised a scheme whereby they hoped to accomplish the prophet's destruction. They determined to ask the king to sign a decree which they should prepare, forbidding any person in the realm to ask anything of God or man, except of Darius the king, for the space of thirty days. A violation of this decree should be punished by casting the offender into a den of lions.

Accordingly, the princes prepared such a decree, and presented it to Darius for his signature. Appealing to his vanity, they persuaded him that the carrying out of this edict would add greatly to his honor and authority. Ignorant of the subtle purpose of the princes, the king did not discern their animosity as revealed in the decree, and, yielding to their flattery, he signed it.

The enemies of Daniel left the presence of Darius, rejoicing over the snare now securely laid for the servant of Jehovah. In the conspiracy thus formed, Satan had played an important part. The prophet was high in command in the kingdom, and evil angels feared that his influence would weaken their control over its rulers. It was these satanic agencies who had stirred the princes to envy and jealousy; it was they who had inspired the plan for Daniel's destruction; and the princes, yielding themselves as instruments of evil, carried it into effect.

The prophet's enemies counted on Daniel's firm adherence to principle for the success of their plan. And they were not mistaken in their estimate of his character. He quickly read their malignant purpose in framing the decree, but he did not change his course in a single particular. Why should he cease to pray now, when he most needed to pray? Rather would he relinquish life itself, than his hope of help in God. With calmness he performed his duties as chief of the princes; and at the hour of prayer he went to his chamber, and with his windows open toward Jerusalem, in accordance with his usual custom, he offered his petition to the God of heaven. He did not try to conceal his act. Although he knew full well the consequences of his fidelity to God, his spirit faltered not. Before those who were plotting his ruin, he would not allow it even to appear that his connection with Heaven was severed. In all cases where the king had a right to command, Daniel would obey; but neither the king nor his decree could make him swerve from allegiance to the King of kings.

Thus the prophet boldly yet quietly and humbly declared that no earthly power has a right to interpose between the soul and God. Surrounded by idolaters, he was a faithful witness to this truth. His dauntless adherence to right was a bright light in the moral darkness of that heathen court. Daniel stands before the world today a worthy example of Christian fearlessness and fidelity.

For an entire day the princes watched Daniel. Three times they saw him go to his chamber, and three times they heard his voice lifted in earnest intercession to God. The next morning they laid their complaint before the king. Daniel, his most honored and faithful statesman, had set the royal decree at defiance. "Hast thou not signed a decree," they reminded him, "that every man that shall ask a petition of any god or man within thirty days, save of thee, O king, shall be cast into the den of lions?"

"The thing is true," the king answered, "according to the law of the Medes and Persians, which altereth not."

Exultantly they now informed Darius of the conduct of his most trusted adviser. "That Daniel, which is of the children of the captivity of Judah," they exclaimed, "regardeth not thee, O king, nor the decree that thou hast signed, but maketh his petition three times a day."

When the monarch heard these words, he saw at once the snare that had been set for his faithful servant. He saw that it was not zeal for kingly glory and honor, but jealousy against Daniel, that had led to the proposal for a royal decree. "Sore displeased with himself" for his part in the evil that had been wrought, he "labored till the going down of the sun" to deliver his friend. The princes, anticipating this effort on the part of the king, came to him with the words, "Know, O king, that the law of the Medes and Persians is, that no decree nor statute which the king establisheth may be changed." The decree, though rashly made, was unalterable and must be carried into effect.

"Then the king commanded, and they brought Daniel, and cast him into the den of lions. Now the king spake and said unto Daniel, Thy God whom thou servest continually, He will deliver thee." A stone was laid on the mouth of the den, and the king himself "sealed it with his own signet, and with the signet of his lords; that the purpose might not be changed concerning Daniel. Then the king went to his palace, and passed the night fasting: neither were instruments of music brought before him: and his sleep went from him."

God did not prevent Daniel's enemies from casting him into the lions' den; He permitted evil angels and wicked men thus far to accomplish their purpose; but it was that He might make the deliverance of His servant more marked, and the defeat of the enemies of truth 544 and righteousness more complete. "Surely the wrath of man shall praise Thee" (Psalm 76:10), the psalmist has testified. Through the courage of this one man who chose to follow right rather than policy, Satan was to be defeated, and the name of God was to be exalted and honored.

Early the next morning King Darius hastened to the den and "cried with a lamentable voice," "O Daniel, servant of the living God, is thy God, whom thou servest continually, able to deliver thee from the lions?"

The voice of the prophet replied: "O king, live forever. My God hath sent His angel, and hath shut the lions' mouths, that they have not hurt me: forasmuch as before Him innocency was found in me; and also before thee, O king, have I done no hurt."

"Then was the king exceeding glad for him, and commanded that they should take Daniel up out of the den. So Daniel was taken up out of the den, and no manner of hurt was found upon him, because he believed in his God.

"And the king commanded, and they brought those men which had accused Daniel, and they cast them into the den of lions, them, their children, and their wives; and the lions had the mastery of them, and brake all their bones in pieces or ever they came at the bottom of the den."

Once more a proclamation was issued by a heathen ruler, exalting the God of Daniel as the true God. "King Darius wrote unto all people, nations, and languages, that dwell in all the earth; Peace be multiplied unto you. I make a decree, that in every dominion of my kingdom men tremble and fear before the God of Daniel: for He is the living God, and steadfast forever, 545 and His kingdom that which shall not be destroyed, and His dominion shall be even unto the end. He delivereth and rescueth, and He worketh signs and wonders in heaven and in earth, who hath delivered Daniel from the power of the lions."

The wicked opposition to God's servant was now completely broken. "Daniel prospered in the reign of Darius, and in the reign of Cyrus the Persian." And through association with him, these heathen monarchs were constrained to acknowledge his God as "the living God, and steadfast forever, and His kingdom that which shall not be destroyed."

From the story of Daniel's deliverance we may learn that in seasons of trial and gloom God's children should be just what they were when their prospects were bright with hope and their surroundings all that they could desire. Daniel in the lions' den was the same Daniel who stood before the king as chief among the ministers of state and as a prophet of the Most High. A man whose heart is stayed upon God will be the same in the hour of his greatest trial as he is in prosperity, when the light and favor of God and of man beam upon him. Faith reaches to the unseen, and grasps eternal realities.

Heaven is very near those who suffer for righteousness' sake. Christ identifies His interests with the interests of His faithful people; He suffers in the person of His saints, and whoever touches His chosen ones touches Him. The power that is near to deliver from physical harm or distress is also near to save from the greater evil, making it possible for the servant of God to maintain his integrity under all circumstances, and to triumph through divine grace.

The experience of Daniel as a statesman in 546 the kingdoms of Babylon and Medo-Persia reveals the truth that a businessman is not necessarily a designing, policy man, but that he may be a man instructed by God at every step. Daniel, the prime minister of the greatest of earthly kingdoms, was at the same time a prophet of God, receiving the light of heavenly inspiration. A man of like passions as ourselves, the pen of inspiration describes him as without fault. His business transactions, when subjected to the closest scrutiny of his enemies, were found to be without one flaw. He was an example of what every businessman may become when his heart is converted and consecrated, and when his motives are right in the sight of God.

Strict compliance with the requirements of Heaven brings temporal as well as spiritual blessings. Unwavering in his allegiance to God, unyielding in his mastery of self, Daniel, by his noble dignity and unswerving integrity, while yet a young man, won the "favor and tender love" of the heathen officer in whose charge he had been placed. Daniel 1:9. The same characteristics marked his afterlife. He rose speedily to the position of prime minister of the kingdom of Babylon. Through the reign of successive monarchs, the downfall of the nation, and the establishment of another world empire, such were his wisdom and statesmanship, so perfect his tact, his courtesy, his genuine goodness of heart, his fidelity to principle, that even his enemies were forced to the confession that "they could find none occasion nor fault; forasmuch as he was faithful."

547   Honored by men with the responsibilities of state and with the secrets of kingdoms bearing universal sway, Daniel was honored by God as His ambassador, and was given many revelations of the mysteries of ages to come. His wonderful prophecies, as recorded by him in chapters 7 to 12 of the book bearing his name, were not fully understood even by the prophet himself; but before his life labors closed, he was given the blessed assurance that "at the end of the days"—in the closing period of this world's history—he would again be permitted to stand in his lot and place. It was not given him to understand all that God had revealed of the divine purpose. "Shut up the words, and seal the book," he was directed concerning his prophetic writings; these were to be sealed "even to the time of the end." "Go thy way, Daniel," the angel once more directed the faithful messenger of Jehovah; "for the words are closed up and sealed till the time of the end. . . . Go thou thy way till the end be: for thou shalt rest, and stand in thy lot at the end of the days." Daniel 12:4, 9, 13.

As we near the close of this world's history, the prophecies recorded by Daniel demand our special attention, as they relate to the very time in which we are living. With them should be linked the teachings of the last book of the New Testament Scriptures. Satan has led many to believe that the prophetic portions of the writings of Daniel and of John the revelator cannot be understood. But the promise is plain that special blessing will accompany the study of these prophecies. "The wise shall understand" (verse 10), was spoken of the visions of Daniel that

548   were to be unsealed in the latter days; and of the revelation that Christ gave to His servant John for the guidance of God's people all through the centuries, the promise is, "Blessed is he that readeth, and they that hear the words of this prophecy, and keep those things which are written therein." Revelation 1:3.

From the rise and fall of nations as made plain in the books of Daniel and the Revelation, we need to learn how worthless is mere outward and worldly glory. Babylon, with all its power and magnificence, the like of which our world has never since beheld,—power and magnificence which to the people of that day seemed so stable and enduring,—how completely has it passed away! As "the flower of the grass," it has perished. James 1:10. So perished the Medo-Persian kingdom, and the kingdoms of Grecia and Rome. And so perishes all that has not God for its foundation. Only that which is bound up

with His purpose, and expresses His character, can endure. His principles are the only steadfast things our world knows.

A careful study of the working out of God's purpose in the history of nations and in the revelation of things to come, will help us to estimate at their true value things seen and things unseen, and to learn what is the true aim of life. Thus, viewing the things of time in the light of eternity, we may, like Daniel and his fellows, live for that which is true and noble and enduring. And learning in this life the principles of the kingdom of our Lord and Saviour, that blessed kingdom which is to endure for ever and ever, we may be prepared at His coming to enter with Him into its possession.

SECTION VI

AFTER THE EXILE

"The Lord rebuke thee, O Satan; even the Lord that hath chosen Jerusalem rebuke thee: is not this a brand plucked out of the fire?" Zechariah 3:2.

45

551

The Return of the Exiles

The advent of the army of Cyrus before the walls of Babylon was to the Jews a sign that their deliverance from captivity was drawing nigh. More than a century before the birth of Cyrus, Inspiration had mentioned him by name, and had caused a record to be made of the actual work he should do in taking the city of Babylon unawares, and in preparing the way for the release of the children of the captivity. Through Isaiah the word had been spoken:

"Thus saith the Lord to His anointed, to Cyrus, whose right hand I have holden, to subdue nations before him; . . . to open before him the two-leaved gates; and the gates shall not be shut; I will go before thee, and make the crooked places straight: I will break in pieces the gates of brass, and cut in sunder the bars of iron: and I will give thee the treasures of darkness, and hidden riches of secret places, that thou mayest know that I, the Lord, which call thee by thy name, am the God of Israel." Isaiah 45:1-3.

In the unexpected entry of the army of the   552
Persian conqueror into the heart of the Babylonian capital by way of the channel of the river whose waters had been turned aside, and

through the inner gates that in careless security had been left open and unprotected, the Jews had abundant evidence of the literal fulfillment of Isaiah's prophecy concerning the sudden overthrow of their oppressors. And this should have been to them an unmistakable sign that God was shaping the affairs of nations in their behalf; for inseparably linked with the prophecy outlining the manner of Babylon's capture and fall were the words:

"Cyrus, he is My shepherd, and shall perform all My pleasure: even saying to Jerusalem, Thou shalt be built; and to the temple, Thy foundation shall be laid." "I have raised him up in righteousness, and I will direct all his ways: he shall build My city, and he shall let go My captives, not for price nor reward, saith the Lord of hosts." Isaiah 44:28; 45:13.

Nor were these the only prophecies upon which the exiles had opportunity to base their hope of speedy deliverance. The writings of Jeremiah were within their reach, and in these was plainly set forth the length of time that should elapse before the restoration of Israel from Babylon. "When seventy years are accomplished," the Lord had foretold through His messenger, "I will punish the king of Babylon, and that nation, saith the Lord, for their iniquity, and the land of the Chaldeans, and will make it perpetual desolations." Jeremiah 25:12. Favor would be shown the remnant of Judah, in 553 answer to fervent prayer. "I will be found of you, saith the Lord: and I will turn away your captivity, and I will gather you from all the nations, and from all the places whither I have driven you, saith the Lord; and I will bring you again into the place whence I caused you to be carried away captive." Jeremiah 29:14.

Often had Daniel and his companions gone over these and similar prophecies outlining God's purpose for His people. And now, as the rapid course of events betokened the mighty hand of God at work among the nations, Daniel gave special thought to the promises made to Israel. His faith in the prophetic word led him to enter into experiences foretold by the sacred writers. "After seventy years be accomplished at Babylon," the Lord had declared, "I will visit you, and perform My good word toward you, in causing you to return. . . . I know the thoughts that I think toward you, saith the Lord, thoughts of peace, and not of evil, to give you an expected end. Then shall ye call upon Me, and ye shall go and pray unto Me, and I will hearken unto you. And ye shall seek Me, and find Me, when ye shall search for Me with all your heart." Verses 10-13.

Shortly before the fall of Babylon, when Daniel was meditating on these prophecies and seeking God for an understanding of the times, a series of visions was given him concerning the rise and fall of kingdoms. With the first vision, as recorded in the seventh chapter of the book of Daniel, an interpretation was given; yet not all was made clear to the prophet. "My cogitations much troubled me," he wrote of his experience at the time, "and my countenance 554 changed in me: but I kept the matter in my heart." Daniel 7:28.

Through another vision further light was thrown upon the events of the future; and it was at the close of this vision that Daniel heard "one saint speaking, and another saint said unto that certain saint which spake, How long shall be the vision?" Daniel 8:13. The answer that was given, "Unto two thousand and three hundred days; then shall the sanctuary be cleansed" (verse 14), filled him with perplexity. Earnestly he sought for the meaning of the vision. He could not understand the relation sustained by the seventy years' captivity, as foretold through Jeremiah, to the twenty-three hundred years that in vision he heard the heavenly visitant declare should elapse before the cleansing of God's sanctuary. The angel Gabriel gave him a partial interpretation; yet when the prophet heard the words, "The vision . . . shall be for many days," he fainted away. "I Daniel fainted," he records of his experience, "and was sick certain days; afterward I rose up, and did the king's business; and I was astonished at the vision, but none understood it." Verses 26, 27.

Still burdened in behalf of Israel, Daniel studied anew the prophecies of Jeremiah. They were very plain—so plain that he understood by these testimonies recorded in books "the number of the years, whereof the word of the Lord came to Jeremiah the prophet, that He would accomplish seventy years in the desolations of Jerusalem." Daniel 9:2.

With faith founded on the sure word of prophecy, Daniel pleaded with the Lord for the speedy fulfillment of these promises. He plead- 555 ed for the honor of God to be preserved. In his petition he identified himself fully with those who had fallen short of the divine purpose, confessing their sins as his own.

"I set my face unto the Lord God," the prophet declared, "to seek by prayer and supplications, with fasting, and sackcloth, and ashes: and I prayed unto the Lord my God, and made my confession." Verses 3, 4. Though Daniel had long been in the service of God, and had been spoken of by heaven as "greatly beloved," yet he now appeared before God as a sinner, urging the great need of the people he loved. His prayer was eloquent in its simplicity, and intensely earnest. Hear him pleading:

"O Lord, the great and dreadful God, keeping the covenant and mercy to them that love Him, and to them that keep His commandments; we have sinned, and have committed iniquity, and have done wickedly, and have rebelled, even by departing from Thy precepts and from Thy judgments; neither have we hearkened unto Thy servants the prophets, which spake in Thy name to our kings, our princes, and our fathers, and to all the people of the land.

"O Lord, righteousness belongeth unto Thee, but unto us confusion of faces, as at this day; to the men of Judah, and to the inhabitants of Jerusalem, and unto all Israel, that are near, and that are far off, through all the countries whither Thou hast driven them, because of their trespass that they have trespassed against Thee. . . .

"To the Lord our God belong mercies and forgivenesses, though we have rebelled against Him." "O Lord, according to all Thy righteousness, I beseech Thee, let Thine anger and Thy fury be turned away from Thy city Jerusalem, Thy holy mountain: because for our sins, and for the iniquities of our fathers, Jerusalem and Thy people are become a reproach to all that are about us.

"Now therefore, O our God, hear the prayer of Thy servant, and his supplications, and cause Thy face to shine upon Thy sanctuary that is desolate, for the Lord's sake. O my God, incline Thine ear, and hear; open Thine eyes, and behold our desolations, and the city which is called by Thy name: for we do not present our supplications before Thee for our righteousnesses, but for Thy great mercies.

"O Lord, hear; O Lord, forgive; O Lord, hearken and do; defer not, for Thine own sake, O my God: for Thy city and Thy people are called by Thy name." Verses 4-9, 16-19.

Heaven was bending low to hear the earnest supplication of the prophet. Even before he had finished his plea for pardon and restoration, the mighty Gabriel again appeared to him, and called his attention to the vision he had seen prior to the fall of Babylon and the death of Belshazzar. And then the angel outlined before him in detail the period of the seventy weeks, which was to begin at the time of "the going forth of the commandment to restore and to build Jerusalem." Verse 25.

Daniel's prayer had been offered "in the first year of Darius" (verse 1), the Median monarch whose general, Cyrus, had wrested from Babylonia the scepter of universal rule. The reign of Darius was honored of God. To him was sent the angel Gabriel, "to confirm and to strengthen him." Daniel 11:1. Upon his death, within about two years of the fall of Babylon, Cyrus succeeded to the throne, and the beginning of his reign marked the completion of the seventy years since the first company of Hebrews had been taken by Nebuchadnezzar from their Judean home to Babylon.

The deliverance of Daniel from the den of lions had been used of God to create a favorable impression upon the mind of Cyrus the Great. The sterling qualities of the man of God as a statesman of farseeing ability led the Persian ruler to show him marked respect and to honor his judgment. And now, just at the time God had said He would cause His temple at Jerusalem to be rebuilt, He moved upon Cyrus as His agent to discern the prophecies concerning himself, with which Daniel was so familiar, and to grant the Jewish people their liberty.

As the king saw the words foretelling, more than a hundred years before his birth, the manner in which Babylon should be taken; as he read the message addressed to him by the Ruler of the universe, "I girded thee, though thou hast not known Me; that they may know from the rising of the sun, and from the west, that there is none beside Me;" as he saw before his eyes the declaration of the eternal God, "For Jacob My servant's sake, and Israel Mine elect, I have even called thee by thy name: I have surnamed thee, though thou hast not known Me;" as he traced the inspired record, "I have raised him up in righteousness, and I will direct all his ways: he shall build My city, and he shall let go My captives, not for price nor reward," his heart was profoundly moved, and he determined to fulfill his divinely appointed mission. Isaiah 45:5, 6, 4, 13. He would let the Judean captives go free; he would help them restore the temple of Jehovah.

In a written proclamation published "throughout all his kingdom," Cyrus made known his desire to provide for the return of the Hebrews and for the rebuilding of their temple. "The Lord God of heaven hath given me all the kingdoms of the earth," the king gratefully acknowledged in this public proclamation; "and He hath charged me to build Him an house at Jerusalem, which is in Judah. Who is there among you of all His people? his God be with him, and let him go up to Jerusalem, . . . and build the house of the Lord God of Israel, (He is the God,) which is in Jerusalem. And whosoever remaineth in any place where he sojourneth, let the men of his place help him with silver, and with gold, and with goods, and with beasts, beside the freewill offering." Ezra 1:1-4.

"Let the house be builded," he further directed regarding the temple structure, "the place where they offered sacrifices, and let the foundations thereof be strongly laid; the height thereof threescore cubits, and the breadth thereof threescore cubits; with three rows of great stones, and a row of new timber: and let the expenses be given out of the king's house: and also let the golden and silver vessels of the house of God, which Nebuchadnezzar took forth out of the temple which is at Jerusalem, and brought unto Babylon, be restored, and brought again unto the temple which is at Jerusalem." Ezra 6:3-5.

Tidings of this decree reached the farthermost provinces of the king's realm, and everywhere among the children of the dispersion there was great rejoicing. Many, like Daniel, had been

559 studying the prophecies, and had been seeking God for His promised intervention in behalf of Zion. And now their prayers were being answered; and with heartfelt joy they could unite in singing:

"When the Lord turned again the captivity of Zion,
We were like them that dream.
Then was our mouth filled with laughter,
And our tongue with singing:
Then said they among the heathen,
The Lord hath done great things for them.
The Lord hath done great things for us;
Whereof we are glad."

Psalm 126:1-3.

"The chief of the fathers of Judah and Benjamin, and the priests, and the Levites, with all them whose spirit God had raised"—these were the goodly remnant, about fifty thousand strong, from among the Jews in the lands of exile, who determined to take advantage of the wonderful opportunity offered them "to go up to build the house of the Lord which is in Jerusalem." Their friends did not permit them to go empty-handed. "All they that were about them strengthened their hands with vessels of silver, with gold, with goods, and with beasts, and with precious things." And to these and many other voluntary offerings were added "the vessels of the house of the Lord, which Nebuchadnezzar had brought forth out of Jerusalem; . . . even those did Cyrus king of Persia bring forth by the hand of Mithredath the treasurer, . . . five thousand and four hundred" in number, for use in the temple that was to be rebuilt. Ezra 1:5-11.

560 Upon Zerubbabel (known also as Sheshbazzar), a descendant of King David, Cyrus placed the responsibility of acting as governor of the company returning to Judea; and with him was associated Joshua the high priest. The long journey across the desert wastes was accomplished in safety, and the happy company, grateful to God for His many mercies, at once undertook the work of re-establishing that which had been broken down and destroyed. "The chief of the fathers" led out in offering of their substance to help defray the expense of rebuilding the temple; and the people, following their example, gave freely of their meager store. See Ezra 2:64-70.

As speedily as possible, an altar was erected on the site of the ancient altar in the temple court. To the exercises connected with the dedication of this altar, the people had "gathered themselves together as one man;" and there they united in re-establishing the sacred services that had been interrupted at the time of the destruction of Jerusalem by Nebuchadnezzar. Before separating to dwell in the homes they were endeavoring to restore, "they kept also the Feast of Tabernacles." Ezra 3:1-6.

The setting up of the altar of daily burnt offerings greatly cheered the faithful remnant. Heartily they entered into the preparations necessary for the rebuilding of the temple, gathering courage as these preparations advanced from month to month. They had for many years been deprived of the visible tokens of God's presence. And now, surrounded as they were by many sad reminders of the apostasy of their fathers, they longed for some abiding token of divine forgiveness and favor. Above the regaining of personal property and ancient privileges, they valued the approval of God. Wonderfully had He wrought in their behalf, and they felt the 563 assurance of His presence with them; yet they desired greater blessings still. With joyous anticipation they looked forward to the time when, with temple rebuilt, they might behold the shining forth of His glory from within.

The workmen engaged in the preparation of the building material, found among the ruins some of the immense stones brought to the temple site in the days of Solomon. These were made ready for use, and much new material was provided; and soon the work was advanced to the point where the foundation stone must be laid. This was done in the presence of many thousands who had assembled to witness the progress of the work and to give expression to their joy in having a part in it. While the cornerstone was being set in position, the people, accompanied by the trumpets of the priests and the cymbals of the sons of Asaph, "sang together by course in praising and giving thanks unto the Lord; because He is good, for His mercy endureth forever toward Israel." Verse 11.

The house that was about to be rebuilt had been the subject of many prophecies concerning the favor that God desired to show Zion, and all who were present at the laying of the cornerstone should have entered heartily into the spirit of the occasion. Yet mingled with the music and the shouts of praise that were heard on that glad day, was a discordant note. "Many of the priests and Levites and chief of the fathers, who were ancient men, that had seen the first house, when the foundation of this house was laid before their eyes, wept with a loud voice." Verse 12.

It was natural that sadness should fill the 564 hearts of these aged men, as they thought of the results of long-continued impenitence. Had they and their generation obeyed God, and carried out His purpose for Israel, the temple built by Solomon would not have been destroyed and the captivity would not have been necessary. But because of ingratitude and disloyalty they had been scattered among the heathen.

Conditions were now changed. In tender mercy the Lord had again visited His people and allowed them to return to their own land. Sadness because of the mistakes of the past should have given way to feelings of great joy. God had moved upon the heart of Cyrus to aid them in rebuilding the temple, and this should have called forth expressions of profound gratitude. But some failed of discerning God's opening providences. Instead of rejoicing, they cherished thoughts of discontent and discouragement. They had seen the glory of Solomon's temple, and they lamented because of the inferiority of the building now to be erected.

The murmuring and complaining, and the unfavorable comparisons made, had a depressing influence on the minds of many and weakened the hands of the builders. The workmen were led to question whether they should proceed with the erection of a building that at the beginning was so freely criticized and was the cause of so much lamentation.

There were many in the congregation, however, whose larger faith and broader vision did not lead them to view this lesser glory with such dissatisfaction. "Many shouted aloud for joy: so that the people could not discern the noise of the shout of joy from the noise of the weeping of the people: for the people shouted with a loud shout, and the noise was heard afar off." Verses 12, 13.

Could those who failed to rejoice at the laying of the foundation stone of the temple have foreseen the results of their lack of faith on that day, they would have been appalled. Little did they realize the weight of their words of disapproval and disappointment; little did they know how much their expressed dissatisfaction would delay the completion of the Lord's house.

The magnificence of the first temple, and the imposing rites of its religious services, had been a source of pride to Israel before their captivity; but their worship had ofttimes been lacking in those qualities which God regards as most essential. The glory of the first temple, the splendor of its service, could not recommend them to God; for that which is alone of value in His sight, they did not offer. They did not bring Him the sacrifice of a humble and contrite spirit.

It is when the vital principles of the kingdom of God are lost sight of, that ceremonies become multitudinous and extravagant. It is when the character building is neglected, when the adornment of the soul is lacking, when the simplicity of godliness is despised, that pride and love of display demand magnificent church edifices, splendid adornings, and imposing ceremonials. But in all this God is not honored. He values His church, not for its external advantages, but for the sincere piety which distinguishes it from the world. He estimates it according to the growth of its members in the knowledge of Christ, according to their progress in spiritual experience. He looks for the principles of love and goodness. Not all the beauty of art can bear comparison with the beauty of temper and character to be revealed in those who are Christ's representatives.

A congregation may be the poorest in the land. It may be without the attractions of any outward show; but if the members possess the principles of the character of Christ, angels will unite with them in their worship. The praise and thanksgiving from grateful hearts will ascend to God as a sweet oblation.

"Give thanks unto the Lord, for He is good:
For His mercy endureth forever.
Let the redeemed of the Lord say so,
Whom He hath redeemed from the hand of the enemy."

"Sing unto Him, sing psalms unto Him:
Talk ye of all His wondrous works.
Glory ye in His holy name:
Let the heart of them rejoice that seek the Lord."

"For He satisfieth the longing soul,
And filleth the hungry soul with goodness."
Psalms 107:1, 2; 105:2, 3; 107:9.

46

"The Prophets of God Helping Them"

Close by the Israelites who had set themselves to the task of rebuilding the temple, dwelt the Samaritans, a mixed race that had sprung up through the intermarriage of heathen colonists from the provinces of Assyria with the remnant of the ten tribes which had been left in Samaria and Galilee. In later years the Samaritans claimed to worship the true God, but in heart and practice they were idolaters. It is true, they held that their idols were but to remind them of the living God, the Ruler of the universe; nevertheless the people were prone to reverence graven images.

During the period of the restoration, these Samaritans came to be known as "the adversaries of Judah and Benjamin." Hearing that "the children of the captivity builded the temple unto the Lord God of Israel," "they came to Zerubbabel, and to the chief of the fathers," and expressed a desire to unite with them in its erection. "Let us build with you," they proposed; "for we seek your God, as ye do; and we do sacrifice unto Him since the days of Esarhaddon king of Assur, which brought us up hither." But the privilege they asked was refused them. "Ye have nothing to do with us to build an house unto our God," the leaders of the Israelites declared; "but we ourselves together will build unto the Lord God of Israel, as King Cyrus the king of Persia hath commanded us." Ezra 4:1-3.

Only a remnant had chosen to return from Babylon; and now, as they undertake a work seemingly beyond their strength, their nearest neighbors come with an offer of help. The Samaritans refer to their worship of the true God, and express a desire to share the privileges and blessings connected with the temple service. "We seek your God, as ye do," they declare. "Let us build with you." But had the Jewish leaders accepted this offer of assistance, they would have opened a door for the entrance of idolatry. They discerned the insincerity of the Samaritans. They realized that help gained through an alliance with these men would be as nothing in comparison with the blessing they might expect to receive by following the plain commands of Jehovah.

Regarding the relation that Israel should sustain to surrounding peoples, the Lord had declared through Moses: "Thou shalt make no covenant with them, nor show mercy unto them: neither shalt thou make marriages with them; . . . for they will turn away thy son from following Me, that they may serve other gods: so will the anger of the Lord be kindled against you, and destroy thee suddenly." "Thou art an holy people unto the Lord thy God, and the Lord hath 569 chosen thee to be a peculiar people unto Himself, above all the nations that are upon the earth." Deuteronomy 7:2-4; 14:2.

The result that would follow an entrance into covenant relation with surrounding nations was plainly foretold. "The Lord shall scatter thee among all people, from the one end of the earth even unto the other," Moses had declared; "and there thou shalt serve other gods, which neither thou nor thy fathers have known, even wood and stone. And among these nations shalt thou find no ease, neither shall the sole of thy foot have rest: but the Lord shall give thee there a trembling heart, and failing of eyes, and sorrow of mind: and thy life shall hang in doubt before thee; and thou shalt fear day and night, and shalt have none assurance of thy life: in the morning thou shalt say, Would God it were even! and at even thou shalt say, Would God it were morning! for the fear of thine heart wherewith thou shalt fear, and for the sight of thine eyes which thou shalt see." Deuteronomy 28:64-67. "But if from thence thou shalt seek the Lord thy God," the promise had been, "thou shalt find Him, if thou seek Him with all thy heart and with all thy soul." Deuteronomy 4:29.

Zerubbabel and his associates were familiar with these and many like scriptures; and in the recent captivity they had evidence after evidence of their fulfillment. And now, having repented of the evils that had brought upon them and their fathers the judgments foretold so plainly through Moses; having turned with all the heart to God, and renewed their covenant relationship with Him, they had been permitted 570 to return to Judea, that they might restore that which had been destroyed. Should they, at the very beginning of their undertaking, enter into a covenant with idolaters?

"Thou shalt make no covenant with them," God had said; and those who had recently rededicated themselves to the Lord at the altar set up before the ruins of His temple, realized that the line of demarcation between His people and the world is ever to be kept unmistakably distinct. They refused to enter into alliance with those who, though familiar with the requirements of God's law, would not yield to its claims.

The principles set forth in Deuteronomy for the instruction of Israel are to be followed by God's people to the end of time. True prosperity is dependent on the continuance of our covenant relationship with God. Never can we afford to compromise principle by entering into alliance with those who do not fear Him.

There is constant danger that professing Christians will come to think that in order to have influence with worldlings, they must to a certain extent conform to the world. But though such a course may appear to afford great advantages, it always ends in spiritual loss. Against every subtle influence that seeks entrance by means of flattering inducements from the enemies of truth, God's people must strictly guard. They are pilgrims and strangers in this world, traveling a path beset with danger. To the ingenious subterfuges and alluring inducements held out to tempt from allegiance, they must give no heed.

It is not the open and avowed enemies of the cause of God that are most to be feared. Those 571 who, like the adversaries of Judah and Benjamin, come with smooth words and fair speeches, apparently seeking for friendly alliance with God's children, have greater power to deceive. Against such every soul should be on the alert, lest some carefully concealed and masterly snare take him unaware. And especially today, while earth's history is closing, the Lord requires of His children a vigilance that knows no relaxation. But though the conflict is a ceaseless one, none are left to struggle alone. Angels help and protect those who walk humbly before God. Never will our Lord betray one who trusts in Him. As His children draw near to Him for protection from evil, in pity and love He lifts up for them a standard against the enemy. Touch them not, He says; for they are Mine. I have graven them upon the palms of My hands.

Untiring in their opposition, the Samaritans "weakened the hands of the people of Judah, and troubled them in building, and hired counselors against them, to frustrate their purpose, all the days of Cyrus king of Persia, even until the reign of Darius." Ezra 4:4, 5. By false reports they aroused suspicion in minds easily led to suspect. But for many years the powers of evil were held in check, and the people in Judea had liberty to continue their work.

While Satan was striving to influence the highest powers in the kingdom of Medo-Persia to show disfavor to God's people, angels worked in behalf of the exiles. The controversy was one in which all heaven was interested. Through the prophet Daniel we are given a glimpse of this mighty struggle between the 572 forces of good and the forces of evil. For three weeks Gabriel wrestled with the powers of darkness, seeking to counteract the influences at work on the mind of Cyrus; and before the contest closed, Christ Himself came to Gabriel's aid. "The prince of the kingdom of Persia withstood me one and twenty days," Gabriel declares; "but, lo, Michael, one of the chief princes, came to help me; and I remained there with the kings of Persia." Daniel 10:13. All that heaven could do in behalf of the people of God was done. The victory was finally gained; the forces of the enemy were held in check all the days of Cyrus, and all the days of his son Cambyses, who reigned about seven and a half years.

This was a time of wonderful opportunity for the Jews. The highest agencies of heaven were working on the hearts of kings, and it was for the people of God to labor with the utmost activity to carry out the decree of Cyrus. They should have spared no effort to restore the temple and its services, and to re-establish themselves in their Judean homes. But in the day of God's power many proved unwilling. The opposition of their enemies was strong and determined, and gradually the builders lost heart. Some could not forget the scene at the laying of the cornerstone, when many had given expression to their lack of confidence in the enterprise. And as the Samaritans grew more bold, many of the Jews questioned whether, after all, the time had come to rebuild. The feeling soon became widespread. Many of the workmen, discouraged and disheartened, returned to their homes to take up the ordinary pursuits of life.

During the reign of Cambyses the work on the temple progressed slowly. And during the 573 reign of the false Smerdis (called Artaxerxes in Ezra 4:7) the Samaritans induced the unscrupulous impostor to issue a decree forbidding the Jews to rebuild their temple and city.

For over a year the temple was neglected and well-nigh forsaken. The people dwelt in their homes and strove to attain temporal prosperity, but their situation was deplorable. Work as they might they did not prosper. The very elements of nature seemed to conspire against them. Because they had let the temple lie waste, the Lord sent upon their substance a wasting drought. God had bestowed upon them the fruits of field and garden, the corn and the wine and the oil, as a token of His favor; but because they had used these bountiful gifts so selfishly, the blessings were removed.

Such were the conditions existing during the early part of the reign of Darius Hystaspes. Spiritually as well as temporally, the Israelites were in a pitiable state. So long had they murmured and doubted; so long had they chosen to make personal interests first, while viewing with apathy the Lord's temple in ruins, that many had lost sight of God's purpose in restoring them to Judea; and these were saying, "The time is not come, the time that the Lord's house should be built." Haggai 1:2.

But even this dark hour was not without hope for those whose trust was in God. The prophets Haggai and Zechariah were raised up to meet the crisis. In stirring testimonies these appointed messengers revealed to the people the cause of their troubles. The lack of temporal prosperity was the result of a neglect to put God's interests first, the prophets declared. Had the Israelites honored God, had they shown Him due respect and courtesy, by making the building of His 574 house their first work, they would have invited His presence and blessing.

To those who had become discouraged, Haggai addressed the searching inquiry, "Is it time for you, O ye, to dwell in your ceiled houses, and this house lie waste? Now therefore thus saith the Lord of hosts; Consider your ways." Why have you done so little? Why do you feel concern for your own buildings and unconcern for the Lord's building? Where is the zeal you once felt for the restoration of the Lord's house? What have you gained by serving self? The desire to escape poverty has led you to neglect the temple, but this neglect has brought upon you that which you feared. "Ye have sown much, and bring in little; ye eat, but ye have not enough; ye drink, but ye are not filled with drink; ye clothe you, but there is none warm; and he that earneth wages earneth wages to put it into a bag with holes." Verses 4-6.

And then, in words that they could not fail to understand, the Lord revealed the cause that had brought them to want: "Ye looked for much, and, lo, it came to little; and when ye brought it home, I did blow upon it. Why? saith the Lord of hosts. Because of Mine house that is waste, and ye run every man unto his own house. Therefore the heaven over you is stayed from dew, and the earth is stayed from her fruit. And I called for a drought upon the land, and upon the mountains, and upon the corn, and upon the new wine, and upon the oil, and upon that which the ground bringeth forth, and upon men, and upon cattle, and upon all the labor of the hands." Verses 9-11.

575 "Consider your ways," the Lord urged. "Go up to the mountain, and bring wood, and build the house; and I will take pleasure in it, and I will be glorified." Verses 7, 8.

The message of counsel and reproof given through Haggai was taken to heart by the leaders and people of Israel. They felt that God was in earnest with them. They dared not disregard the repeated instruction sent them—that their prosperity, both temporal and spiritual, was dependent on faithful obedience to God's commands. Aroused by the warnings of the prophet, Zerubbabel and Joshua, "with all the remnant of the people, obeyed the voice of the Lord their God, and the words of Haggai the prophet." Verse 12.

As soon as Israel decided to obey, the words of reproof were followed by a message of encouragement. "Then spake Haggai . . . unto the people, saying, I am with you, saith the Lord. And the Lord stirred up the spirit of Zerubbabel" and of Joshua, and "of all the remnant of the people; and they came and did work in the house of the Lord of hosts, their God." Verses 13, 14.

In less than a month after the work on the temple was resumed, the builders received another comforting message. "Be strong, O Zerubbabel," the Lord Himself urged through His prophet; "be strong, O Joshua; . . . and be strong, all ye people of the land, saith the Lord, and work: for I am with you, saith the Lord of hosts." Haggai 2:4.

To Israel encamped before Mount Sinai the Lord had declared: "I will dwell among the chil-
576 dren of Israel, and will be their God. And they shall know that I am the Lord their God, that brought them forth out of the land of Egypt, that I may dwell among them: I am the Lord their God." Exodus 29:45, 46. And now, notwithstanding the fact that they had repeatedly "rebelled, and vexed His Holy Spirit" (Isaiah 63:10), God once more, through the messages of His prophet, was stretching out His hand to save. As a recognition of their co-operation with His purpose, He was renewing His covenant that His Spirit should remain among them; and He bade them, "Fear not."

To His children today the Lord declares, "Be strong, . . . and work: for I am with you." The Christian always has a strong helper in the Lord. The way of the Lord's helping we may not know; but this we do know: He will never fail those who put their trust in Him. Could Christians realize how many times the Lord has ordered their way, that the purposes of the enemy concerning them might not be accomplished, they would not stumble along complainingly. Their faith would be stayed on God, and no trial would have power to move them.

They would acknowledge Him as their wisdom and efficiency, and He would bring to pass that which He desires to work out through them.

The earnest pleadings and the encouragements given through Haggai were emphasized and added to by Zechariah, whom God raised up to stand by his side in urging Israel to carry out the command to arise and build. Zechariah's first message was an assurance that God's word never fails and a promise of blessing to those who would hearken to the sure word of prophecy.

With fields lying waste, with their scant store 577 of provisions rapidly failing, and surrounded as they were by unfriendly peoples, the Israelites nevertheless moved forward by faith in response to the call of God's messengers, and labored diligently to restore the ruined temple. It was a work requiring firm reliance upon God. As the people endeavored to do their part, and sought for a renewal of God's grace in heart and life, message after message was given them through Haggai and Zechariah, with assurances that their faith would be richly rewarded and that the word of God concerning the future glory of the temple whose walls were rearing would not fail. In this very building would appear, in the fullness of time, the Desire of all nations as the Teacher and Saviour of mankind.

Thus the builders were not left to struggle alone; "with them were the prophets of God helping them;" and the Lord of hosts Himself had declared, "Be strong, . . . and work: for I am with you." Ezra 5:2; Haggai 2:4.

With heartfelt repentance and a willingness to advance by faith, came the promise of temporal prosperity. "From this day," the Lord declared, "will I bless you." Verse 19.

To Zerubbabel their leader—he who, through all the years since their return from Babylon, had been so sorely tried—was given a most precious message. The day was coming, the Lord declared, when all the enemies of His chosen people would be cast down. "In that day, saith the Lord of hosts, will I take thee, O Zerubbabel, My servant, . . . and will make thee as a signet: for I have chosen thee." Verse 23. Now the governor of Israel could see the meaning of 578 the providence that had led him through discouragement and perplexity; he could discern God's purpose in it all.

This personal word to Zerubbabel has been left on record for the encouragement of God's children in every age. God has a purpose in sending trial to His children. He never leads them otherwise than they would choose to be led if they could see the end from the beginning, and discern the glory of the purpose that they are fulfilling. All that He brings upon them in test and trial comes that they may be strong to do and to suffer for Him.

The messages delivered by Haggai and Zechariah roused the people to put forth every possible effort for the rebuilding of the temple; but, as they worked, they were sadly harassed by the Samaritans and others who devised many hindrances. On one occasion the provincial officers of the Medo-Persian realm visited Jerusalem and requested the name of the one who had authorized the restoration of the building. If at that time the Jews had not been trusting in the Lord for guidance, this inquiry might have resulted disastrously to them. "But the eye of their God was upon the elders of the Jews, that they could not cause them to cease, till the matter came to Darius." Ezra 5:5. The officers were answered so wisely that they decided to write a letter to Darius Hystaspes, then the ruler of Medo-Persia, directing his attention to the original decree made by Cyrus, which commanded that the house of God at Jerusalem be rebuilt, and that the expenses for the same be paid from the king's treasury.

579   Darius searched for this decree, and found it; whereupon he directed those who had made the inquiry to allow the rebuilding of the temple to proceed. "Let the work of this house of God alone," he commanded; "let the governor of the Jews and the elders of the Jews build this house of God in his place.

"Moreover," Darius continued, "*I make a decree* what ye shall do to the elders of these Jews for the building of this house of God: that of the king's goods, even of the tribute beyond the river, forthwith expenses be given unto these men, that they be not hindered. And that which they have need of, both young bullocks, and rams, and lambs, for the burnt offerings of the God of heaven, wheat, salt, wine, and oil, according to the appointment of the priests which are at Jerusalem, let it be given them day by day without fail: that they may offer sacrifices of sweet savors unto the God of heaven, and pray for the life of the king, and of his sons." Ezra 6:7-10.

The king further decreed that severe penalties be meted out to those who should in any wise alter the decree; and he closed with the remarkable statement: "The God that hath caused His name to dwell there destroy all kings and people, that shall put to their hand to alter and to destroy this house of God which is at Jerusalem. I Darius have made a decree; let it be done with speed." Verse 12. Thus the Lord prepared the way for the completion of the temple.

For months before this decree was made, the Israelites had kept on working by faith, the prophets of God still helping them by means of 580 timely messages, through which the divine purpose for Israel was kept before the workers. Two months after Haggai's last recorded message was delivered, Zechariah had a series of visions regarding the work of God in the earth. These messages, given in the form of parables and symbols, came at a time of great uncertainty

and anxiety, and were of peculiar significance to the men who were advancing in the name of the God of Israel. It seemed to the leaders as if the permission granted the Jews to rebuild was about to be withdrawn; the future appeared very dark. God saw that His people were in need of being sustained and cheered by a revelation of His infinite compassion and love.

In vision Zechariah heard the angel of the Lord inquiring, "O Lord of hosts, how long wilt Thou not have mercy on Jerusalem and on the cities of Judah, against which Thou hast had indignation these threescore and ten years? And the Lord answered the angel that talked with me," Zechariah declared, "with good words and comfortable words.

"So the angel that communed with me said unto me, Cry thou, saying, Thus saith the Lord of hosts; I am jealous for Jerusalem and for Zion with a great jealousy. And I am very sore displeased with the heathen that are at ease: for I was but a little displeased, and they helped forward the affliction. Therefore thus saith the Lord; I am returned to Jerusalem with mercies: My house shall be built in it, . . . and a line shall be stretched forth upon Jerusalem." Zechariah 1:12-16.

The prophet was now directed to predict, "Thus saith the Lord of hosts; My cities through 581 prosperity shall yet be spread abroad; and the Lord shall yet comfort Zion, and shall yet choose Jerusalem." Verse 17.

Zechariah then saw the powers that had "scattered Judah, Israel, and Jerusalem," symbolized by four horns. Immediately afterward he saw four carpenters, representing the agencies used by the Lord in restoring His people and the house of His worship. See verses 18-21.

"I lifted up mine eyes again," Zechariah said, "and looked, and behold a man with a measuring line in his hand. Then said I, Whither goest thou? And he said unto me, To measure Jerusalem, to see what is the breadth thereof, and what is the length thereof. And, behold, the angel that talked with me went forth, and another angel went out to meet him, and said unto him, Run, speak to this young man, saying, Jerusalem shall be inhabited as towns without walls for the multitude of men and cattle therein: for I, saith the Lord, will be unto her a wall of fire round about, and will be the glory in the midst of her." Zechariah 2:1-5.

God had commanded that Jerusalem be rebuilt; the vision of the measuring of the city was an assurance that He would give comfort and strength to His afflicted ones, and fulfill to them the promises of His everlasting covenant. His protecting care, He declared, would be like "a wall of fire round about;" and through them His glory would be revealed to all the sons of men. That which He was accomplishing for His people was to be known in all the earth. "Cry

456

out and shout, thou inhabitant of Zion: for great is the Holy One of Israel in the midst of thee." Isaiah 12:6.

47

Joshua and the Angel

The steady advancement made by the builders of the temple greatly discomfited and alarmed the hosts of evil. Satan determined to put forth still further effort to weaken and discourage God's people by holding before them their imperfections of character. If those who had long suffered because of transgression could again be induced to disregard God's commandments, they would be brought once more under the bondage of sin.

Because Israel had been chosen to preserve the knowledge of God in the earth, they had ever been the special objects of Satan's enmity; he was determined to cause their destruction. While they were obedient, he could do them no harm; therefore he had bent all his power and cunning to entice them into sin. Ensnared by his temptations, they had transgressed the law of God and had been left to become the prey of their enemies.

Yet though they were carried as captives to Babylon, God did not forsake them. He sent His prophets to them with reproofs and warnings, and aroused them to see their guilt. When they humbled themselves before God and returned to Him with true repentance, He sent them messages of encouragement, declaring that He would deliver them from captivity, restore them to His favor, and once more establish them in their own land. And now that this work of restoration had begun, and a remnant of Israel had already returned to Judea, Satan was determined to frustrate the carrying out of the divine purpose, and to this end he was seeking to move upon the heathen nations to destroy them utterly.

But in this crisis the Lord strengthened His people "with good words and comfortable words." Zechariah 1:13. Through an impressive illustration of the work of Satan and the work of Christ, He showed the power of their Mediator to vanquish the accuser of His people.

In vision the prophet beholds "Joshua the high priest," "clothed with filthy garments" (Zechariah 3:1, 3), standing before the Angel of the Lord, entreating God's mercy in behalf of his afflicted people. As he pleads for the fulfillment of God's promises, Satan stands up boldly to resist him. He points to the transgressions of Israel as a reason why they should not be restored to the favor of God. He claims them as his prey, and demands that they be given into his hands.

The high priest cannot defend himself or his people from Satan's accusations. He does not claim that Israel is free from fault. In filthy garments, symbolizing the sins of the people, which he bears as their representative, he stands before the Angel, confessing their guilt, yet pointing to their repentance and humiliation, and relying upon the mercy of a sin-pardoning Redeemer. In faith he claims the promises of God.

Then the Angel, who is Christ Himself, the Saviour of sinners, puts to silence the accuser of His people, declaring, "The Lord rebuke thee, O Satan; even the Lord that hath chosen Jerusalem rebuke thee: is not this a brand plucked out of the fire?" Verse 2. Long had Israel remained in the furnace of affliction. Because of their sins they had been well-nigh consumed in the flame kindled by Satan and his agents for their destruction, but God had now set His hand to bring them forth.

As the intercession of Joshua is accepted, the command is given, "Take away the filthy garments from him;" and to Joshua the Angel says, "Behold, I have caused thine iniquity to pass from thee, and I will clothe thee with change of raiment." "So they set a fair miter upon his head, and clothed him with garments." Verses 4, 5. His own sins and those of his people were pardoned. Israel was clothed with "change of raiment"—the righteousness of Christ imputed to them. The miter placed upon Joshua's head was such as was worn by the priests, and bore the inscription, "Holiness to the Lord" (Exodus 28:36), signifying that notwithstanding his former transgressions, he was now qualified to minister before God in His sanctuary.

The Angel now declared to Joshua: "Thus saith the Lord of hosts; If thou wilt walk in My ways, and if thou wilt keep My charge, then thou shalt also judge My house, and shalt also keep My courts, and I will give thee places to walk among these that stand by." Zechariah 3:7. If obedient, he should be honored as the judge, or ruler, over the temple and all its services; he should walk among attending angels, even in this life; and at last he should join the glorified throng around the throne of God.

"Hear now, O Joshua the high priest, thou, and thy fellows that sit before thee: for they are men wondered at: for, behold, I will bring forth My Servant the Branch." Verse 8. In the Branch, the Deliverer to come, lay the hope of Israel. It was by faith in the coming Saviour that Joshua and his people had received pardon. Through faith in Christ they had been restored to God's favor. By virtue of His merits, if they walked in His ways and kept His statutes, they would be "men wondered at," honored as the chosen of Heaven among the nations of the earth.

As Satan accused Joshua and his people, so in all ages he accuses those who seek the mercy and favor of God. He is "the accuser of our brethren, . . . which accused them before our God day and night." Revelation 12:10. Over every soul that is rescued from the power of evil, and whose name is registered in the Lamb's book of life, the controversy is repeated. Never is one received into the family of God without exciting the determined resistance of the enemy. But He who was the hope of Israel then, their defense, their justification and redemption, is the hope of the church today.

586   Satan's accusations against those who seek the Lord are not prompted by displeasure at their sins. He exults in their defective characters; for he knows that only through their transgression of God's law can he obtain power over them. His accusations arise solely from his enmity to Christ. Through the plan of salvation, Jesus is breaking Satan's hold upon the human family and rescuing souls from his power. All the hatred and malignity of the archrebel is stirred as he beholds the evidences of Christ's supremacy; and with fiendish power and cunning he works to wrest from Him the children of men who have accepted salvation. He leads men into skepticism, causing them to lose confidence in God and to separate from His love; he tempts them to break the law and then claims them as his captives, contesting Christ's right to take them from him.

Satan knows that those who ask God for pardon and grace will obtain it; therefore he presents their sins before them to discourage them. Against those who are trying to obey God, he is constantly seeking occasion for complaint. Even their best and most acceptable service he seeks to make appear corrupt. By countless devices, the most subtle and the most cruel, he endeavors to secure their condemnation.

In his own strength, man cannot meet the charges of the enemy. In sin-stained garments, confessing his guilt, he stands before God. But Jesus, our Advocate, presents an effectual plea in behalf of all who by repentance and faith have committed the keeping of their souls to Him. He pleads their cause, and by the mighty arguments of Calvary, vanquishes their accuser. His perfect obedience to God's law has given Him all power in heaven and in earth, and He claims from His Father mercy and reconciliation for guilty man. To the accuser of His peo-
587   ple He declares: "The Lord rebuke thee, O Satan. These are the purchase of My blood, brands plucked from the burning." And to those who rely on Him in faith, He gives the assurance, "Behold, I have caused thine iniquity to pass from thee, and I will clothe thee with change of raiment." Zechariah 3:4.

All who have put on the robe of Christ's righteousness will stand before Him as chosen and faithful and true. Satan has no power to pluck them out of the hand of the Saviour. Not one soul who in penitence and faith has claimed His protection will Christ permit to pass under the enemy's power. His word is pledged: "Let him take hold of My strength, that he may make peace with Me; and he shall make peace with Me." Isaiah 27:5. The promise given to Joshua is given to all: "If thou wilt keep My charge, . . . I will give thee places to walk among these that stand by." Zechariah 3:7. Angels of God will walk on either side of them, even in this world, and they will stand at last among the angels that surround the throne of God.

Zechariah's vision of Joshua and the Angel applies with peculiar force to the experience of God's people in the closing scenes of the great day of atonement. The remnant church will then be brought into great trial and distress. Those who keep the commandments of God and the faith of Jesus will feel the ire of the dragon and his hosts. Satan numbers the world as his subjects; he has gained control even of many professing Christians. But here is a little company who are resisting his supremacy. If he could blot them from the earth, his triumph would be complete. As he influenced the heathen nations   588 to destroy Israel, so in the near future he will stir up the wicked powers of earth to destroy the people of God. Men will be required to render obedience to human edicts in violation of the divine law.

Those who are true to God will be menaced, denounced, proscribed. They will be "betrayed both by parents, and brethren, and kinsfolks, and friends," even unto death. Luke 21:16. Their only hope is in the mercy of God; their only defense will be prayer. As Joshua pleaded before the Angel, so the remnant church, with brokenness of heart and unfaltering faith, will plead for pardon and deliverance through Jesus, their Advocate. They are fully conscious of the sinfulness of their lives, they see their weakness and unworthiness; and they are ready to despair.

The tempter stands by to accuse them, as he stood by to resist Joshua. He points to their filthy garments, their defective characters. He presents their weakness and folly, their sins of ingratitude, their unlikeness to Christ, which has dishonored their Redeemer. He endeavors to affright them with the thought that their case is hopeless, that the stain of their defilement will never be washed away. He hopes so to destroy their faith that they will yield to his temptations, and turn from their allegiance to God.

Satan has an accurate knowledge of the sins that he has tempted God's people to commit, and he urges his accusations against them, declaring that by their sins they have forfeited divine protection, and claiming that he has the right to destroy them. He pronounces them just as deserving as himself of exclusion from the

458

589 favor of God. "Are these," he says, "the people who are to take my place in heaven, and the place of the angels who united with me? They profess to obey the law of God; but have they kept its precepts? Have they not been lovers of self more than lovers of God? Have they not placed their own interests above His service? Have they not loved the things of the world? Look at the sins that have marked their lives. Behold their selfishness, their malice, their hatred of one another. Will God banish me and my angels from His presence, and yet reward those who have been guilty of the same sins? Thou canst not do this, O Lord, in justice. Justice demands that sentence be pronounced against them."

But while the followers of Christ have sinned, they have not given themselves up to be controlled by the satanic agencies. They have repented of their sins and have sought the Lord in humility and contrition, and the divine Advocate pleads in their behalf. He who has been most abused by their ingratitude, who knows their sin and also their penitence, declares: "The Lord rebuke thee, O Satan. I gave My life for these souls. They are graven upon the palms of My hands. They may have imperfections of character; they may have failed in their endeavors; but they have repented, and I have forgiven and accepted them."

The assaults of Satan are strong, his delusions are subtle; but the Lord's eye is upon His people. Their affliction is great, the flames of the furnace seem about to consume them; but Jesus will bring them forth as gold tried in the fire. Their earthliness will be removed, that through them the image of Christ may be perfectly revealed.

590 At times the Lord may seem to have forgotten the perils of His church and the injury done her by her enemies. But God has not forgotten. Nothing in this world is so dear to the heart of God as His church. It is not His will that worldly policy shall corrupt her record. He does not leave His people to be overcome by Satan's temptations. He will punish those who misrepresent Him, but He will be gracious to all who sincerely repent. To those who call upon Him for strength for the development of Christian character, He will give all needed help.

In the time of the end the people of God will sigh and cry for the abominations done in the land. With tears they will warn the wicked of their danger in trampling upon the divine law, and with unutterable sorrow they will humble themselves before the Lord in penitence. The wicked will mock their sorrow and ridicule their solemn appeals. But the anguish and humiliation of God's people is unmistakable evidence that they are regaining the strength and nobility of character lost in consequence of sin. It is because they are drawing nearer to Christ, because their eyes are fixed on His perfect purity, that they discern so clearly the exceeding sinfulness of sin. Meekness and lowliness are the conditions of success and victory. A crown of glory awaits those who bow at the foot of the cross.

God's faithful, praying ones are, as it were, shut in with Him. They themselves know not how securely they are shielded. Urged on by Satan, the rulers of this world are seeking to destroy them; but could the eyes of God's children be opened, as were the eyes of Elisha's servant at Dothan, they would see angels of God 591 encamped about them, holding in check the hosts of darkness.

As the people of God afflict their souls before Him, pleading for purity of heart, the command is given, "Take away the filthy garments," and the encouraging words are spoken, "Behold, I have caused thine iniquity to pass from thee, and I will clothe thee with change of raiment." Zechariah 3:4. The spotless robe of Christ's righteousness is placed upon the tried, tempted, faithful children of God. The despised remnant are clothed in glorious apparel, nevermore to be defiled by the corruptions of the world. Their names are retained in the Lamb's book of life, enrolled among the faithful of all ages. They have resisted the wiles of the deceiver; they have not been turned from their loyalty by the dragon's roar. Now they are eternally secure from the tempter's devices. Their sins are transferred to the originator of sin. A "fair miter" is set upon their heads.

While Satan has been urging his accusations, holy angels, unseen, have been passing to and fro, placing upon the faithful ones the seal of the living God. These are they that stand upon Mount Zion with the Lamb, having the Father's name written in their foreheads. They sing the new song before the throne, that song which no man can learn save the hundred and forty and four thousand which were redeemed from the earth. "These are they which follow the Lamb whithersoever He goeth. These were redeemed from among men, being the first fruits unto God and to the Lamb. And in their mouth was found no guile: for they are without fault before the throne of God." Revelation 14:4, 5.

Now is reached the complete fulfillment of 592 the words of the Angel: "Hear now, O Joshua the high priest, thou, and thy fellows that sit before thee: for they are men wondered at: for, behold, I will bring forth My Servant the Branch." Zechariah 3:8. Christ is revealed as the Redeemer and Deliverer of His people. Now indeed are the remnant "men wondered at," as the tears and humiliation of their pilgrimage give place to joy and honor in the presence of God and the Lamb. "In that day shall the branch of the Lord be beautiful and glorious, and the fruit of the earth shall be excellent and comely for them that are escaped of Israel. And it shall come to pass, that he that is left in Zion, and he that remaineth in Jerusalem, shall be called holy, even everyone that is written among the living in Jerusalem." Isaiah 4:2, 3.

48

"Not by Might, nor by Power"

Immediately after Zechariah's vision of Joshua and the Angel, the prophet received a message regarding the work of Zerubbabel. "The Angel that talked with me," Zechariah declares, "came again, and waked me, as a man that is wakened out of his sleep, and said unto me, What seest thou? And I said, I have looked, and behold a candlestick all of gold, with a bowl upon the top of it, and his seven lamps thereon, and seven pipes to the seven lamps, which are upon the top thereof: and two olive trees by it, one upon the right side of the bowl, and the other upon the left side thereof.

"So I answered and spake to the Angel that talked with me, saying, What are these, my Lord? . . . Then He answered and spake unto me, saying, This is the word of the Lord unto Zerubbabel, saying, Not by might, nor by power, but by My Spirit, saith the Lord of hosts."

"Then answered I, and said unto Him, What are these two olive trees upon the right side of the candlestick and upon the left side thereof? And I answered again, and said unto Him, What be these two olive branches which through the two golden pipes empty the golden oil out of themselves? . . . Then said He, These are the two anointed ones, that stand by the Lord of the whole earth." Zechariah 4:1-6, 11-14.

In this vision the two olive trees which stand before God are represented as emptying the golden oil out of themselves through golden tubes into the bowl of the candlestick. From this the lamps of the sanctuary are fed, that they may give a bright, continuous light. So from the anointed ones that stand in God's presence the fullness of divine light and love and power is imparted to His people, that they may impart to others light and joy and refreshing. Those who are thus enriched are to enrich others with the treasure of God's love.

In rebuilding the house of the Lord, Zerubbabel had labored in the face of manifold difficulties. From the beginning, adversaries had "weakened the hands of the people of Judah, and troubled them in building," "and made them to cease by force and power." Ezra 4:4, 23. But the Lord had interposed in behalf of the builders, and now He spoke through His prophet to Zerubbabel, saying, "Who art thou, O great mountain? before Zerubbabel thou shalt become a plain: and he shall bring forth the headstone thereof with shoutings, crying, Grace, grace unto it." Zechariah 4:7.

Throughout the history of God's people great mountains of difficulty, apparently insurmountable, have loomed up before those who were trying to carry out the purposes of Heaven. Such obstacles are permitted by the Lord as a test of faith. When we are hedged about on every side, this is the time above all others to trust in God and in the power of His Spirit. The exercise of a living faith means an increase of spiritual strength and the development of an unfaltering trust. It is thus that the soul becomes a conquering power. Before the demand of faith, the obstacles placed by Satan across the pathway of the Christian will disappear; for the powers of heaven will come to his aid. "Nothing shall be impossible unto you." Matthew 17:20.

The way of the world is to begin with pomp and boasting. God's way is to make the day of small things the beginning of the glorious triumph of truth and righteousness. Sometimes He trains His workers by bringing to them disappointment and apparent failure. It is His purpose that they shall learn to master difficulties.

Often men are tempted to falter before the perplexities and obstacles that confront them. But if they will hold the beginning of their confidence steadfast unto the end, God will make the way clear. Success will come to them as they struggle against difficulties. Before the intrepid spirit and unwavering faith of a Zerubbabel, great mountains of difficulty will become a plain; and he whose hands have laid the foundation, even "his hands shall also finish it." "He shall bring forth the headstone thereof with shoutings, crying, Grace, grace unto it." Zechariah 4:9, 7.

Human power and human might did not establish the church of God, and neither can they destroy it. Not on the rock of human strength, but on Christ Jesus, the Rock of Ages, was the church founded, "and the gates of hell shall not prevail against it." Matthew 16:18. The presence of God gives stability to His cause. "Put not your trust in princes, nor in the son of man," is the word that comes to us. Psalm 146:3. "In quietness and in confidence shall be your strength." Isaiah 30:15. God's glorious work, founded on the eternal principles of right, will never come to nought. It will go on from strength to strength, "not by might, nor by power, but by My Spirit, saith the Lord of hosts." Zechariah 4:6.

The promise, "The hands of Zerubbabel have laid the foundation of this house; his hands shall also finish it," was literally fulfilled. Verse 9. "The elders of the Jews builded, and they prospered through the prophesying of Haggai the prophet and Zechariah the son of Iddo. And they builded, and finished it, according to the commandment of the God of Israel, and according to the commandment of Cyrus, and Darius, and Artaxerxes king of Persia. And this house was finished on the third day of the month Adar [the twelfth month], which was in the sixth year of the reign of Darius the king." Ezra 6:14, 15.

Shortly afterward the restored temple was dedicated. "The children of Israel, the priests, and the Levites, and the rest of the children of the captivity, kept the dedication of this house of God with joy;" and "upon the fourteenth day of the first month" they "kept the Passover." Verses 16, 17, 19.

The second temple did not equal the first in magnificence, nor was it hallowed by those visible tokens of the divine presence which pertained to the first temple. There was no manifestation of supernatural power to mark its dedication. No cloud of glory was seen to fill the newly erected sanctuary. No fire from heaven descended to consume the sacrifice upon its altar. The Shekinah no longer abode between the cherubim in the most holy place; the ark, the mercy seat, and the tables of testimony were not found there. No sign from heaven made known to the inquiring priest the will of Jehovah.

And yet this was the building concerning which the Lord had declared by the prophet Haggai: "The glory of this latter house shall be greater than of the former." "I will shake all nations, and the Desire of all nations shall come: and I will fill this house with glory, saith the Lord of hosts." Haggai 2:9, 7. For centuries learned men have endeavored to show wherein the promise of God, given to Haggai, has been fulfilled; yet in the advent of Jesus of Nazareth, the Desire of all nations, who by His personal presence hallowed the precincts of the temple, many have steadfastly refused to see any special significance. Pride and unbelief have blinded their minds to the true meaning of the prophet's words.

The second temple was honored, not with the cloud of Jehovah's glory, but with the presence of the One in whom dwelt "all the fullness of the Godhead bodily"—God Himself "manifest in the flesh." Colossians 2:9; 1 Timothy 3:16. In being honored with the personal presence of Christ during His earthly ministry, and in this alone, did the second temple exceed the first in glory. The "Desire of all nations" had indeed come to His temple, when the Man of Nazareth taught and healed in the sacred courts.

had taken advantage of the decree permitting their return. These, however, in comparison with the hundreds of thousands scattered throughout the provinces of Medo-Persia, were but a mere remnant. The great majority of the Israelites had chosen to remain in the land of their exile rather than undergo the hardships of the return journey and the re-establishment of their desolated cities and homes.

A score or more of years passed by, when a second decree, quite as favorable as the first, was issued by Darius Hystaspes, the monarch then ruling. Thus did God in mercy provide another opportunity for the Jews in the Medo-Persian realm to return to the land of their fathers. The Lord foresaw the troublous times that were to follow during the reign of Xerxes,—the Ahasuerus of the book of Esther,—and He not only wrought a change of feeling in the hearts of men in authority, but also inspired Zechariah to plead with the exiles to return.

"Ho, ho, come forth, and flee from the land of the north," was the message given the scattered tribes of Israel who had become settled in many lands far from their former home. "I have spread you abroad as the four winds of the heaven, saith the Lord. Deliver thyself, O Zion, that dwellest with the daughter of Babylon. For thus saith the Lord of hosts; After the glory hath He sent me unto the nations which spoiled you: for he that toucheth you toucheth the apple of His eye. For, behold, I will shake mine hand upon them, and they shall be a spoil to their servants: and ye shall know that the Lord of hosts hath sent me." Zechariah 2:6-9.

It was still the Lord's purpose, as it had been from the beginning, that His people should be a praise in the earth, to the glory of His name. During the long years of their exile He had given them many opportunities to return to their allegiance to Him. Some had chosen to listen and to learn; some had found salvation in the midst of affliction. Many of these were to be numbered among the remnant that should return. They were likened by Inspiration to "the highest branch of the high cedar," which was to be planted "upon an high mountain and eminent: in the mountain of the height of Israel." Ezekiel 17:22, 23.

It was those "whose spirit God had raised" (Ezra 1:5) who had returned under the decree of Cyrus. But God ceased not to plead with those who voluntarily remained in the land of their exile, and through manifold agencies He made it possible for them also to return. The large number, however, of those who failed to respond to the decree of Cyrus, remained unimpressible to later influences; and even when Zechariah warned them to flee from Babylon without further delay, they did not heed the invitation.

49

In the Days of Queen Esther

Under the favor shown them by Cyrus, nearly fifty thousand of the children of the captivity

Meanwhile conditions in the Medo-Persian realm were rapidly changing. Darius Hystaspes, under whose reign the Jews had been shown marked favor, was succeeded by Xerxes the Great. It was during his reign that those of the Jews who had failed of heeding the message to flee were called upon to face a terrible crisis. Having refused to take advantage of the way of escape God had provided, now they were brought face to face with death.

Through Haman the Agagite, an unscrupulous man high in authority in Medo-Persia, Satan worked at this time to counterwork the purposes of God. Haman cherished bitter malice against Mordecai, a Jew. Mordecai had done Haman no harm, but had simply refused to show him worshipful reverence. Scorning to "lay hands on Mordecai alone," Haman plotted "to destroy all the Jews that were throughout the whole kingdom of Ahasuerus, even the people of Mordecai." Esther 3:6.

Misled by the false statements of Haman, Xerxes was induced to issue a decree providing for the massacre of all the Jews "scattered abroad and dispersed among the people in all the provinces" of the Medo-Persian kingdom. Verse 8. A certain date was appointed on which the Jews were to be destroyed and their property confiscated. Little did the king realize the far-reaching results that would have accompanied the complete carrying out of this decree. Satan himself, the hidden instigator of the scheme, was trying to rid the earth of those who preserved the knowledge of the true God.

601

"In every province, whithersoever the king's commandment and his decree came, there was great mourning among the Jews, and fasting, and weeping, and wailing; and many lay in sackcloth and ashes." Esther 4:3. The decree of the Medes and Persians could not be revoked; apparently there was no hope; all the Israelites were doomed to destruction.

But the plots of the enemy were defeated by a Power that reigns among the children of men. In the providence of God, Esther, a Jewess who feared the Most High, had been made queen of the Medo-Persian kingdom. Mordecai was a near relative of hers. In their extremity they decided to appeal to Xerxes in behalf of their people. Esther was to venture into his presence as an intercessor. "Who knoweth," said Mordecai, "whether thou art come to the kingdom for such a time as this?" Verse 14.

The crisis that Esther faced demanded quick, earnest action; but both she and Mordecai realized that unless God should work mightily in their behalf, their own efforts would be unavailing. So Esther took time for communion with God, the source of her strength. "Go," she directed Mordecai, "gather together all the Jews that are present in Shushan, and fast ye for me, and neither eat nor drink three days, night or day: I also and my maidens will fast likewise; and so will I go in unto the king, which is not according to the law: and if I perish, I perish." Verse 16.

The events that followed in rapid succession,—the appearance of Esther before the king, the marked favor shown her, the banquets of the king and queen with Haman as the only guest, the troubled sleep of the king, the public honor shown Mordecai, and the humiliation and fall of Haman upon the discovery of his wicked plot,—all these are parts of a familiar story. God wrought marvelously for His penitent people; and a counter decree issued by the king, allowing them to fight for their lives, was rapidly communicated to every part of the realm by mounted couriers, who were "hastened and pressed on by the king's commandment." "And in every province, and in every city, whithersoever the king's commandment and his decree came, the Jews had joy and gladness, a feast and a good day. And many of the people of the land became Jews; for the fear of the Jews fell upon them." Esther 8:14, 17.

602

On the day appointed for their destruction, "the Jews gathered themselves together in their cities throughout all the provinces of the king Ahasuerus, to lay hand on such as sought their hurt: and no man could withstand them; for the fear of them fell upon all people." Angels that excel in strength had been commissioned by God to protect His people while they "stood for their lives." Esther 9:2, 16.

Mordecai was given the position of honor formerly occupied by Haman. He "was next unto King Ahasuerus, and great among the Jews, and accepted of the multitude of his brethren" (Esther 10:3); and he sought to promote the welfare of Israel. Thus did God bring His chosen people once more into favor at the Medo-Persian court, making possible the carrying out of His purpose to restore them to their own land. But it was not until several years later, in the seventh year of Artaxerxes I, the successor of Xerxes the Great, that any considerable number returned to Jerusalem, under Ezra.

605

The trying experiences that came to God's people in the days of Esther were not peculiar to that age alone. The revelator, looking down the ages to the close of time, has declared, "The dragon was wroth with the woman, and went to make war with the remnant of her seed, which keep the commandments of God, and have the testimony of Jesus Christ." Revelation 12:17. Some who today are living on the earth will see these words fulfilled. The same spirit that in ages past led men to persecute the true church, will in the future lead to the pursuance of a similar course toward those who maintain their loyalty to God. Even now preparations are being made for this last great conflict.

The decree that will finally go forth against

the remnant people of God will be very similar to that issued by Ahasuerus against the Jews. Today the enemies of the true church see in the little company keeping the Sabbath commandment, a Mordecai at the gate. The reverence of God's people for His law is a constant rebuke to those who have cast off the fear of the Lord and are trampling on His Sabbath.

Satan will arouse indignation against the minority who refuse to accept popular customs and traditions. Men of position and reputation will join with the lawless and the vile to take counsel against the people of God. Wealth, genius, education, will combine to cover them 606 with contempt. Persecuting rulers, ministers, and church members will conspire against them. With voice and pen, by boasts, threats, and ridicule, they will seek to overthrow their faith. By false representations and angry appeals, men will stir up the passions of the people. Not having a "Thus saith the Scriptures" to bring against the advocates of the Bible Sabbath, they will resort to oppressive enactments to supply the lack. To secure popularity and patronage, legislators will yield to the demand for Sunday laws. But those who fear God, cannot accept an institution that violates a precept of the Decalogue. On this battlefield will be fought the last great conflict in the controversy between truth and error. And we are not left in doubt as to the issue. Today, as in the days of Esther and Mordecai, the Lord will vindicate His truth and His people.

607

50

Ezra, the Priest and Scribe

About seventy years after the return of the first company of exiles under Zerubbabel and Joshua, Artaxerxes Longimanus came to the throne of Medo-Persia. The name of this king is connected with sacred history by a series of remarkable providences. It was during his reign that Ezra and Nehemiah lived and labored. He is the one who in 457 B.C. issued the third and final decree for the restoration of Jerusalem. His reign saw the return of a company of Jews under Ezra, the completion of the walls of Jerusalem by Nehemiah and his associates, the reorganization of the temple services, and the great religious reformations instituted by Ezra and Nehemiah. During his long rule he often showed favor to God's people, and in his trusted and well-beloved Jewish friends, Ezra and Nehemiah, he recognized men of God's appointment, raised up for a special work.

The experience of Ezra while living among the Jews who remained in Babylon was so unusual that it attracted the favorable notice of King Artaxerxes, with whom he talked freely 608 regarding the power of the God of heaven, and the divine purpose in restoring the Jews to Jerusalem.

Born of the sons of Aaron, Ezra had been given a priestly training; and in addition to this he had acquired a familiarity with the writings of the magicians, the astrologers, and the wise men of the Medo-Persian realm. But he was not satisfied with his spiritual condition. He longed to be in full harmony with God; he longed for wisdom to carry out the divine will. And so he "prepared his heart to seek the law of the Lord, and to do it." Ezra 7:10. This led him to apply himself diligently to a study of the history of God's people, as recorded in the writings of prophets and kings. He searched the historical and poetical books of the Bible to learn why the Lord had permitted Jerusalem to be destroyed and His people carried captive into a heathen land.

To the experiences of Israel from the time the promise was made to Abraham, Ezra gave special thought. He studied the instruction given at Mount Sinai and through the long period of wilderness wandering. As he learned more and still more concerning God's dealings with His children, and comprehended the sacredness of the law given at Sinai, Ezra's heart was stirred. He experienced a new and thorough conversion and determined to master the records of sacred history, that he might use this knowledge to bring blessing and light to his people.

Ezra endeavored to gain a heart preparation for the work he believed was before him. He sought God earnestly, that he might be a wise teacher in Israel. As he learned to yield mind and will to divine control, there were brought into his life the principles of true sanctification, 609 which, in later years, had a molding influence, not only upon the youth who sought his instruction, but upon all others associated with him.

God chose Ezra to be an instrument of good to Israel, that He might put honor upon the priesthood, the glory of which had been greatly eclipsed during the captivity. Ezra developed into a man of extraordinary learning and became "a ready scribe in the law of Moses." Verse 6. These qualifications made him an eminent man in the Medo-Persian kingdom.

Ezra became a mouthpiece for God, educating those about him in the principles that govern heaven. During the remaining years of his life, whether near the court of the king of Medo-Persia or at Jerusalem, his principal work was that of a teacher. As he communicated to others the truths he learned, his capacity for labor increased. He became a man of piety and zeal. He was the Lord's witness to the world of the power of Bible truth to ennoble the daily life.

The efforts of Ezra to revive an interest in the study of the Scriptures were given permanency by his painstaking, lifelong work of preserving and multiplying the Sacred Writings. He gathered all the copies of the law that he could find and had these transcribed and distributed. The pure word, thus multiplied and placed in the hands of many people, gave knowledge that was of inestimable value.

Ezra's faith that God would do a mighty work for His people, led him to tell Artaxerxes of his desire to return to Jerusalem to revive an interest in the study of God's word and to assist his brethren in restoring the Holy City. As Ezra declared his perfect trust in the God of Israel as one abundantly able to protect and care for His people, the king was deeply impressed. He well understood that the Israelites were returning to Jerusalem that they might serve Jehovah; yet so great was the king's confidence in the integrity of Ezra that he showed him marked favor, granting his request and bestowing on him rich gifts for the temple service. He made him a special representative of the Medo-Persian kingdom and conferred on him extensive powers for the carrying out of the purposes that were in his heart.

The decree of Artaxerxes Longimanus for the restoring and building of Jerusalem, the third issued since the close of the seventy years' captivity, is remarkable for its expressions regarding the God of heaven, for its recognition of the attainments of Ezra, and for the liberality of the grants made to the remnant people of God. Artaxerxes refers to Ezra as "the priest, the scribe, even a scribe of the words of the commandments of the Lord, and of His statutes to Israel;" "a scribe of the law of the God of heaven." The king united with his counselors in offering freely "unto the God of Israel, whose habitation is in Jerusalem;" and in addition he made provision for meeting many heavy expenses by ordering that they be paid "out of the king's treasure house." Verses 11, 12, 15, 20.

"Thou art sent of the king, and of his seven counselors," Artaxerxes declared to Ezra, "to inquire concerning Judah and Jerusalem, according to the law of thy God which is in thine hand." And he further decreed: "Whatsoever is commanded by the God of heaven, let it be diligently done for the house of the God of heaven: for why should there be wrath against the realm of the king and his sons?" Verses 14, 23.

In giving permission to the Israelites to return, Artaxerxes arranged for the restoration of the members of the priesthood to their ancient rites and privileges. "We certify you," he declared, "that touching any of the priests and Levites, singers, porters, Nethinims, or ministers of this house of God, it shall not be lawful to impose toll, tribute, or custom, upon them." He also arranged for the appointment of civil officers to govern the people justly in accordance with the Jewish code of laws. "Thou, Ezra, after the wisdom of thy God, that is in thine hand," he directed, "set magistrates and judges, which may judge all the people that are beyond the river, all such as know the laws of thy God; and teach ye them that know them not. And whosoever will not do the law of thy God, and the law of the king, let judgment be executed speedily upon him, whether it be unto death, or to banishment, or to confiscation of goods, or to imprisonment." Verses 24-26.

Thus, "according to the good hand of his God upon him," Ezra had persuaded the king to make abundant provision for the return of all the people of Israel and of the priests and Levites in the Medo-Persian realm, who were minded "of their own free will to go up to Jerusalem." Verses 9, 13. Thus again the children of the dispersion were given opportunity to return to the land with the possession of which were linked the promises to the house of Israel. This decree brought great rejoicing to those who had been uniting with Ezra in a study of God's purposes concerning His people. "Blessed be the Lord God of our fathers," Ezra exclaimed, "which hath put such a thing as this in the king's heart, to beautify the house of the Lord which is in Jerusalem: and hath extended mercy unto me before the king, and his counselors, and before all the king's mighty princes." Verses 27, 28.

In the issuing of this decree by Artaxerxes, God's providence was manifest. Some discerned this and gladly took advantage of the privilege of returning under circumstances so favorable. A general place of meeting was named, and at the appointed time those who were desirous of going to Jerusalem assembled for the long journey. "I gathered them together to the river that runneth to Ahava," Ezra says, "and there abode we in tents three days." Ezra 8:15.

Ezra had expected that a large number would return to Jerusalem, but the number who responded to the call was disappointingly small. Many who had acquired houses and lands had no desire to sacrifice these possessions. They loved ease and comfort and were well satisfied to remain. Their example proved a hindrance to others who otherwise might have chosen to cast in their lot with those who were advancing by faith.

As Ezra looked over the company assembled, he was surprised to find none of the sons of Levi. Where were the members of the tribe that had been set apart for the sacred service of the temple? To the call, Who is on the Lord's side? the Levites should have been the first to respond. During the captivity, and afterward, they had been granted many privileges. They had enjoyed the fullest liberty to minister to the spiritual needs of their brethren in exile. Synagogues had been built, in which the priests conducted the worship of God and instructed the people. The observance of the Sabbath, and the performance of the sacred rites peculiar to the Jewish faith, had been freely allowed.

614 But with the passing of the years after the close of the captivity, conditions changed, and many new responsibilities rested upon the leaders in Israel. The temple at Jerusalem had been rebuilt and dedicated, and more priests were needed to carry on its services. There was pressing need of men of God to act as teachers of the people. And besides, the Jews remaining in Babylon were in danger of having their religious liberty restricted. Through the prophet Zechariah, as well as by their recent experience during the troublous times of Esther and Mordecai, the Jews in Medo-Persia had been plainly warned to return to their own land. The time had come when it was perilous for them to dwell longer in the midst of heathen influences. In view of these changed conditions, the priests in Babylon should have been quick to discern in the issuance of the decree a special call to them to return to Jerusalem.

The king and his princes had done more than their part in opening the way for the return. They had provided abundant means, but where were the men? The sons of Levi failed at a time when the influence of a decision to accompany their brethren would have led others to follow their example. Their strange indifference is a sad revelation of the attitude of the Israelites in Babylon toward God's purpose for His people.

Once more Ezra appealed to the Levites, sending them an urgent invitation to unite with his company. To emphasize the importance of quick action, he sent with his written plea several of his "chief men" and "men of understanding." Ezra 7:28; 8:16.

615 While the travelers tarried with Ezra, these trusted messengers hastened back with the plea, "Bring unto us ministers for the house of our God." Ezra 8:17. The appeal was heeded; some who had been halting, made final decision to return. In all, about forty priests and two hundred and twenty Nethinim—men upon whom Ezra could rely as wise ministers and good teachers and helpers—were brought to the camp.

All were now ready to set forth. Before them was a journey that would occupy several months. The men were taking with them their wives and children, and their substance, besides large treasure for the temple and its service. Ezra was aware that enemies lay in wait by the way, ready to plunder and destroy him and his company; yet he had asked from the king no armed force for protection. "I was ashamed," he has explained, "to require of the king a band of soldiers and horsemen to help us against the enemy in the way: because we had spoken unto

the king, saying, The hand of our God is upon all them for good that seek Him; but His power and His wrath is against all them that forsake Him." Verse 22.

In this matter, Ezra and his companions saw an opportunity to magnify the name of God before the heathen. Faith in the power of the living God would be strengthened if the Israelites themselves should now reveal implicit faith in their divine Leader. They therefore determined to put their trust wholly in Him. They would ask for no guard of soldiers. They would give the heathen no occasion to ascribe to the strength of man the glory that belongs to God alone. They could not afford to arouse in the minds of their heathen friends one doubt as to the sincerity of their dependence on God as His people. 616 Strength would be gained, not through wealth, not through the power and influence of idolatrous men, but through the favor of God. Only by keeping the law of the Lord before them, and striving to obey it, would they be protected.

This knowledge of the conditions under which they would continue to enjoy the prospering hand of God, lent more than ordinary solemnity to the consecration service that was held by Ezra and his company of faithful souls just before their departure. "I proclaimed a fast there, at the river of Ahava," Ezra has declared of this experience, "that we might afflict ourselves before our God, to seek Him a right way for us, and for our little ones, and for all our substance." "So we fasted and besought our God for this: and He was entreated of us." Verses 21, 23.

The blessing of God, however, did not make unnecessary the exercise of prudence and forethought. As a special precaution in safeguarding the treasure, Ezra "separated twelve of the chief of the priests"—men whose faithfulness and fidelity had been proved—"and weighed unto them the silver, and the gold, and the vessels, even the offering of the house of our God, which the king, and his counselors, and his lords, and all Israel there present, had offered." These men were solemnly charged to act as vigilant stewards over the treasure entrusted to their care. "Ye are holy unto the Lord," Ezra declared; "the vessels are holy also; and the silver and the gold are a freewill offering unto the Lord God of your fathers. Watch ye, and keep them, until ye weigh them before the chief of the priests and the Levites, and chief of the 617 fathers of Israel, at Jerusalem, in the chambers of the house of the Lord." Verses 24, 25, 28, 29.

The care exercised by Ezra in providing for the transportation and safety of the Lord's treasure, teaches a lesson worthy of thoughtful study. Only those whose trustworthiness had been proved were chosen, and they were instructed plainly regarding the responsibility resting on them. In the appointment of faithful officers to act as treasurers of the Lord's goods, Ezra recognized the necessity and value of order and organization in connection with the work of God.

During the few days that the Israelites tarried at the river, every provision was completed for the long journey. "We departed," Ezra writes, "on the twelfth day of the first month, to go unto Jerusalem: and the hand of our God was upon us, and He delivered us from the hand of the enemy, and of such as lay in wait by the way." Verse 31. About four months were occupied on the journey, the multitude that accompanied Ezra, several thousand in all, including women and children, necessitating slow progress. But all were preserved in safety. Their enemies were restrained from harming them. Their journey was a prosperous one, and on the first day of the fifth month, in the seventh year of Artaxerxes, they reached Jerusalem.

51

A Spiritual Revival

Ezra's arrival in Jerusalem was opportune. There was great need of the influence of his presence. His coming brought courage and hope to the hearts of many who had long labored under difficulties. Since the return of the first company of exiles under the leadership of Zerubbabel and Joshua, over seventy years before, much had been accomplished. The temple had been finished, and the walls of the city had been partially repaired. Yet much remained undone.

Among those who had returned to Jerusalem in former years, there were many who had remained true to God as long as they lived; but a considerable number of the children and the children's children lost sight of the sacredness of God's law. Even some of the men entrusted with responsibilities were living in open sin. Their course was largely neutralizing the efforts made by others to advance the cause of God; for so long as flagrant violations of the law were allowed to go unrebuked, the blessing of Heaven could not rest upon the people.

It was in the providence of God that those who returned with Ezra had had special seasons of seeking the Lord. The experiences through which they had just passed, on their journey from Babylon, unprotected as they had been by any human power, had taught them rich spiritual lessons. Many had grown strong in faith; and as these mingled with the discouraged and the indifferent in Jerusalem, their influence was a powerful factor in the reform soon afterward instituted.

On the fourth day after the arrival, the trea-

sures of silver and gold, with the vessels for the service of the sanctuary, were delivered by the treasurers into the hands of the temple officers, in the presence of witnesses, and with the utmost exactitude. Every article was examined "by number and by weight." Ezra 8:34.

The children of the captivity who had returned with Ezra "offered burnt offerings unto the God of Israel" for a sin offering and as a token of their gratitude and thanksgiving for the protection of holy angels during the journey. "And they delivered the king's commissions unto the king's lieutenants, and to the governors on this side the river: and they furthered the people, and the house of God." Verses 35, 36.

Very soon thereafter a few of the chief men of Israel approached Ezra with a serious complaint. Some of "the people of Israel, and the priests, and the Levites" had so far disregarded the holy commands of Jehovah as to intermarry with the surrounding peoples. "They have taken of their daughters for themselves, and for their sons," Ezra was told, "so that the holy seed have mingled themselves with the people" of heathen lands; "yea, the hand of the princes and rulers hath been chief in this trespass." Ezra 9:1, 2.

In his study of the causes leading to the Babylonish captivity, Ezra had learned that Israel's apostasy was largely traceable to their mingling with heathen nations. He had seen that if they had obeyed God's command to keep separate from the nations surrounding them, they would have been spared many sad and humiliating experiences. Now when he learned that notwithstanding the lessons of the past, men of prominence had dared transgress the laws given as a safeguard against apostasy, his heart was stirred within him. He thought of God's goodness in again giving His people a foothold in their native land, and he was overwhelmed with righteous indignation and with grief at their ingratitude. "When I heard this thing," he says, "I rent my garment and my mantle, and plucked off the hair of my head and of my beard, and sat down astonied.

"Then were assembled unto me everyone that trembled at the words of the God of Israel, because of the transgression of those that had been carried away; and I sat astonied until the evening sacrifice." Verses 3, 4.

At the time of the evening sacrifice Ezra rose, and, once more rending his garment and his mantle, he fell upon his knees and unburdened his soul in supplication to Heaven. Spreading out his hands unto the Lord, he exclaimed, "O my God, I am ashamed and blush to lift up my face to Thee, my God: for our iniquities are increased over our head, and our trespass is grown up unto the heavens.

"Since the days of our fathers," the suppliant continued, "have we been in a great trespass unto this day; and for our iniquities have we, our kings, and our priests, been delivered into the hand of the kings of the lands, to the sword, to captivity, and to a spoil, and to confusion of face, as it is this day. And now for a little space grace hath been showed from the Lord our God, to leave us a remnant to escape, and to give us a nail in His holy place, that our God may lighten our eyes, and give us a little reviving in our bondage. For we were bondmen; yet our God hath not forsaken us in our bondage, but hath extended mercy unto us in the sight of the kings of Persia, to give us a reviving, to set up the house of our God, and to repair the desolations thereof, and to give us a wall in Judah and in Jerusalem.

"And now, O our God, what shall we say after this? for we have forsaken Thy commandments, which Thou hast commanded by Thy servants the prophets. . . . And after all that is come upon us for our evil deeds, and for our great trespass, seeing that Thou our God hast punished us less than our iniquities deserve, and hast given us such deliverance as this; should we again break Thy commandments, and join in affinity with the people of these abominations? wouldest not Thou be angry with us till Thou hadst consumed us, so that there should be no remnant nor escaping? O Lord God of Israel, Thou art righteous: for we remain yet escaped, as it is this day: behold, we are before Thee in our trespasses: for we cannot stand before Thee because of this." Verses 6-15.

622   The sorrow of Ezra and his associates over the evils that had insidiously crept into the very heart of the Lord's work, wrought repentance. Many of those who had sinned were deeply affected. "The people wept very sore." Ezra 10:1. In a limited degree they began to realize the heinousness of sin and the horror with which God regards it. They saw the sacredness of the law spoken at Sinai, and many trembled at the thought of their transgressions.

One of those present, Shechaniah by name, acknowledged as true all the words spoken by Ezra. "We have trespassed against our God," he confessed, "and have taken strange wives of the people of the land: yet now there is hope in Israel concerning this thing." Shechaniah proposed that all who had transgressed should make a covenant with God to forsake their sin and to be adjudged "according to the law." "Arise," he bade Ezra; "for this matter belongeth unto thee: we also will be with thee: be of good courage." "Then arose Ezra, and made the chief priests, the Levites, and all Israel, to swear that they should do according to this word." Verses 2-5.

This was the beginning of a wonderful reformation. With infinite patience and tact, and with a careful consideration for the rights and welfare of every individual concerned, Ezra and his associates strove to lead the penitent Israel into the right way. Above all else, Ezra was a teacher of the law; and as he gave personal attention to the examination of every case, he sought to impress the people with the holiness of this law and the blessings to be gained through obedience.

Wherever Ezra labored, there sprang up a 623 revival in the study of the Holy Scriptures. Teachers were appointed to instruct the people; the law of the Lord was exalted and made honorable. The books of the prophets were searched, and the passages foretelling the coming of the Messiah brought hope and comfort to many a sad and weary heart.

More than two thousand years have passed since Ezra "prepared his heart to seek the law of the Lord, and to do it" (Ezra 7:10), yet the lapse of time has not lessened the influence of his pious example. Through the centuries the record of his life of consecration has inspired many with the determination "to seek the law of the Lord, and to do it."

Ezra's motives were high and holy; in all that he did he was actuated by a deep love for souls. The compassion and tenderness that he revealed toward those who had sinned, either willfully or through ignorance, should be an object lesson to all who seek to bring about reforms. The servants of God are to be as firm as a rock where right principles are involved; and yet, withal, they are to manifest sympathy and forbearance. Like Ezra, they are to teach transgressors the way of life by inculcating principles that are the foundation of all rightdoing.

In this age of the world, when Satan is seeking, through manifold agencies, to blind the eyes of men and women to the binding claims of the law of God, there is need of men who can cause many to "tremble at the commandment of our God." Ezra 10:3. There is need of true reformers, who will point transgressors to the great Lawgiver and teach them that "the law of the Lord is perfect, converting the soul." Psalm 624 19:7. There is need of men mighty in the Scriptures, men whose every word and act exalts the statutes of Jehovah, men who seek to strengthen faith. Teachers are needed, oh, so much, who will inspire hearts with reverence and love for the Scriptures.

The widespread iniquity prevalent today may in a great degree be attributed to a failure to study and obey the Scriptures, for when the word of God is set aside, its power to restrain the evil passions of the natural heart is rejected. Men sow to the flesh and of the flesh reap corruption.

With the setting aside of the Bible has come a turning away from God's law. The doctrine that men are released from obedience to the divine precepts, has weakened the force of moral obligation and opened the floodgates of iniquity upon the world. Lawlessness, dissipation, and corruption are sweeping in like an overwhelming flood. Everywhere are seen envy, evil surmising, hypocrisy, estrangement, emulation, strife, betrayal of sacred trusts, indulgence of lust. The whole system of religious principles and doctrines, which should form the foundation and framework of social life, seems to be a tottering mass, ready to fall in ruins.

In the last days of this earth's history the voice that spoke from Sinai is still declaring, "Thou shalt have no other gods before Me." Exodus 20:3. Man has set his will against the will of God, but he cannot silence the word of command. The human mind cannot evade its obligation to a higher power. Theories and speculations may abound; men may try to set science in opposition to revelation, and thus do 625 away with God's law; but stronger and still stronger comes the command, "*Thou shalt worship the Lord thy God, and Him only shalt thou serve.*" Matthew 4:10.

There is no such thing as weakening or strengthening the law of Jehovah. As it has been, so it is. It always has been, and always will be, holy, just, and good, complete in itself. It cannot be repealed or changed. To "honor" or "dishonor" it is but the speech of men.

Between the laws of men and the precepts of Jehovah will come the last great conflict of the controversy between truth and error. Upon this battle we are now entering—a battle not between rival churches contending for the supremacy, but between the religion of the Bible and the religions of fable and tradition. The agencies which have united against truth are now actively at work. God's Holy Word, which has been handed down to us at so great a cost of suffering and bloodshed, is little valued. There are few who really accept it as the rule of life. Infidelity prevails to an alarming extent, not in the world only, but in the church. Many have come to deny doctrines which are the very pillars of the Christian faith. The great facts of creation as presented by the inspired writers, the fall of man, the atonement, the perpetuity of the law—these all are practically rejected by a large share of the professedly Christian world. Thousands who pride themselves on their knowledge regard it as an evidence of weakness to place implicit confidence in the Bible, and a proof of learning to cavil at the Scriptures and to spiritualize and explain away their most important truths.

626 Christians should be preparing for what is soon to break upon the world as an overwhelming surprise, and this preparation they should make by diligently studying the word of God and striving to conform their lives to its precepts. The tremendous issues of eternity demand of us something besides an imaginary religion, a religion of words and forms, where truth is kept in the outer court. God calls for a revival and a reformation. The words of the Bible, and the Bible alone, should be heard from the pulpit. But the Bible has been robbed of its power, and the result is seen in a lowering of the tone of spiritual life. In many sermons of today there is not that divine manifestation which awakens the conscience and brings life to the soul. The hearers cannot say, "Did not our heart burn within us, while He talked with us by the way, and while He opened to us the Scriptures?" Luke 24:32. There are many who are crying out for the living God, longing for the divine presence. Let the word of God speak to the heart. Let those who have heard only tradition and human theories and maxims, hear the voice of Him who can renew the soul unto eternal life.

Great light shone forth from patriarchs and prophets. Glorious things were spoken of Zion, the City of God. Thus the Lord designs that the light shall shine forth through His followers today. If the saints of the Old Testament bore so bright a testimony of loyalty, should not those upon whom is shining the accumulated light of centuries, bear a still more signal witness to the power of truth? The glory of the prophecies sheds their light upon our pathway. Type has 627 met antitype in the death of God's Son. Christ has risen from the dead, proclaiming over the rent sepulcher, "I am the resurrection, and the life." John 11:25. He has sent His Spirit into the world to bring all things to our remembrance. By a miracle of power He has preserved His written word through the ages.

The Reformers whose protest has given us the name of Protestant, felt that God had called them to give the light of the gospel to the world; and in the effort to do this they were ready to sacrifice their possessions, their liberty, even life itself. In the face of persecution and death the gospel was proclaimed far and near. The word of God was carried to the people; and all classes, high and low, rich and poor, learned and ignorant, eagerly studied it for themselves. Are we, in this last conflict of the great controversy, as faithful to our trust as the early Reformers were to theirs?

"Blow the trumpet in Zion, sanctify a fast, call a solemn assembly: gather the people, sanctify the congregation, assemble the elders, gather the children: . . . let the priests, the ministers of the Lord, weep between the porch and the altar, and let them say, Spare Thy people, O Lord, and give not Thine heritage to reproach." "Turn ye even to Me with all your heart, and with fasting, and with weeping, and with mourning: and rend your heart, and not your garments, and turn unto the Lord your God: for He is gracious and merciful, slow to anger, and of great kindness, and repenteth Him of the evil. Who knoweth if He will return and repent, and leave a blessing behind Him?" Joel 2:15-17, 12-14.

52

A Man of Opportunity

Nehemiah, one of the Hebrew exiles, occupied a position of influence and honor in the Persian court. As cupbearer to the king he was admitted freely to the royal presence. By virtue of his position, and because of his abilities and fidelity, he had become the monarch's friend and counselor. The recipient of royal favor, however, though surrounded by pomp and splendor, did not forget his God nor his people. With deepest interest his heart turned toward Jerusalem; his hopes and joys were bound up with her prosperity. Through this man, prepared by his residence in the Persian court for the work to which he was to be called, God purposed to bring blessing to His people in the land of their fathers.

By messengers from Judea the Hebrew patriot learned that days of trial had come to Jerusalem, the chosen city. The returned exiles were suffering affliction and reproach. The temple and portions of the city had been rebuilt; but

629 the work of restoration was hindered, the temple services were disturbed, and the people kept in constant alarm by the fact that the walls of the city were still largely in ruins.

Overwhelmed with sorrow, Nehemiah could neither eat nor drink; he "wept, and mourned certain days, and fasted." In his grief he turned to the divine Helper. "I . . . prayed," he said, "before the God of heaven." Faithfully he made confession of his sins and the sins of his people. He pleaded that God would maintain the cause of Israel, restore their courage and strength, and help them to build up the waste places of Judah.

As Nehemiah prayed, his faith and courage grew strong. His mouth was filled with holy arguments. He pointed to the dishonor that would be cast upon God, if His people, now that they had returned to Him, should be left in weakness and oppression; and he urged the Lord to bring to pass His promise: "If ye turn unto Me, and keep My commandments, and do them; though there were of you cast out unto the uttermost part of the heaven, yet will I gather them from thence, and will bring them unto the place that I have chosen to set My name there." See Deuteronomy 4:29-31. This promise had been given to Israel through Moses before they had entered Canaan, and during the centuries it had stood unchanged. God's people had now returned to Him in penitence and faith, and His promise would not fail.

Nehemiah had often poured out his soul in behalf of his people. But now as he prayed a holy purpose formed in his mind. He resolved

that if he could obtain the consent of the king, and the necessary aid in procuring implements and material, he would himself undertake the 630 task of rebuilding the walls of Jerusalem and restoring Israel's national strength. And he asked the Lord to grant him favor in the sight of the king, that this plan might be carried out. "Prosper, I pray Thee, Thy servant this day," he entreated, "and grant him mercy in the sight of this man."

Four months Nehemiah waited for a favorable opportunity to present his request to the king. During this time, though his heart was heavy with grief, he endeavored to bear himself with cheerfulness in the royal presence. In those halls of luxury and splendor all must appear lighthearted and happy. Distress must not cast its shadow over the countenance of any attendant of royalty. But in Nehemiah's seasons of retirement, concealed from human sight, many were the prayers, the confessions, the tears, heard and witnessed by God and angels.

At length the sorrow that burdened the patriot's heart could no longer be concealed. Sleepless nights and care-filled days left their trace upon his countenance. The king, jealous for his own safety, was accustomed to read countenances and to penetrate disguises, and he saw that some secret trouble was preying upon his cupbearer. "Why is thy countenance sad," he inquired, "seeing thou art not sick? this is nothing else but sorrow of heart."

The question filled Nehemiah with apprehension. Would not the king be angry to hear that while outwardly engaged in his service, the courtier's thoughts had been far away with his afflicted people? Would not the offender's life be forfeited? His cherished plan for restoring the strength of Jerusalem—was it about to be over- 631 thrown? "Then," he writes, "I was very sore afraid." With trembling lips and tearful eyes he revealed the cause of his sorrow. "Let the king live forever," he answered. "Why should not my countenance be sad, when the city, the place of my fathers' sepulchers, lieth waste, and the gates thereof are consumed with fire?"

The recital of the condition of Jerusalem awakened the sympathy of the monarch without arousing his prejudices. Another question gave the opportunity for which Nehemiah had long waited: "For what dost thou make request?" But the man of God did not venture to reply till he had sought direction from One higher than Artaxerxes. He had a sacred trust to fulfill, in which he required help from the king; and he realized that much depended upon his presenting the matter in such a way as to win his approval and enlist his aid. "I prayed," he said, "to the God of heaven." In that brief prayer Nehemiah pressed into the presence of the King of kings and won to his side a power that can turn hearts as the rivers of waters are turned.

To pray as Nehemiah prayed in his hour of need is a resource at the command of the Christian under circumstances when other forms of prayer may be impossible. Toilers in the busy walks of life, crowded and almost overwhelmed with perplexity, can send up a petition to God for divine guidance. Travelers by sea and land, when threatened with some great danger, can thus commit themselves to Heaven's protection. In times of sudden difficulty or peril the heart may send up its cry for help to One who has pledged Himself to come to the aid of His faithful, believing ones whenever they call upon Him. In every circumstance, under every condition, the soul weighed down with grief and care, or fiercely assailed by temptation, may find assurance, support, and succor in the unfailing love and power of a covenant-keeping God.

Nehemiah, in that brief moment of prayer to the King of kings, gathered courage to tell Artaxerxes of his desire to be released for a time from his duties at the court, and he asked for authority to build up the waste places of Jerusalem and to make it once more a strong and defensed city. Momentous results to the Jewish nation hung upon this request. "And," Nehemiah declares, "the king granted me, according to the good hand of my God upon me."

Having secured the help he sought, Nehemiah with prudence and forethought proceeded to make the arrangements necessary to ensure the success of the enterprise. He neglected no precaution that would tend to its accomplishment. Not even to his own countrymen did he reveal his purpose. While he knew that many would rejoice in his success, he feared that some, by acts of indiscretion, might arouse the jealousy of their enemies and perhaps bring about the defeat of the undertaking.

His request to the king had been so favorably received that Nehemiah was encouraged to ask for still further assistance. To give dignity and authority to his mission, as well as to provide protection on the journey, he asked for and secured a military escort. He obtained royal letters to the governors of the provinces beyond the Euphrates, the territory through which he must pass on his way to Judea; and he obtained, also, a letter to the keeper of the king's forest in the mountains of Lebanon, directing him to furnish such timber as would be needed. That there might be no occasion for complaint that he had exceeded his commission, Nehemiah was careful to have the authority and privileges accorded him, clearly defined.

This example of wise forethought and resolute action should be a lesson to all Christians. God's children are not only to pray in faith, but to work with diligent and provident care. They encounter many difficulties and often hinder the working of Providence in their behalf, because they regard prudence and painstaking effort as having little to do with religion. Nehemiah did not regard his duty done when he had wept and prayed before the Lord. He united his petitions with holy endeavor, putting forth earnest, prayerful efforts for the success of the enterprise in which he was engaged. Careful consideration and well-matured plans are as essential to the carrying forward of sacred enterprises today as in the time of the rebuilding of Jerusalem's walls.

Nehemiah did not depend upon uncertainty. The means that he lacked he solicited from those who were able to bestow. And the Lord is still willing to move upon the hearts of those in possession of His goods, in behalf of the cause of truth. Those who labor for Him are to avail themselves of the help that He prompts men to give. These gifts may open ways by which the light of truth shall go to many benighted lands. The donors may have no faith in Christ, no acquaintance with His word; but their gifts are not on this account to be refused.

53

The Builders on the Wall

Nehemiah's journey to Jerusalem was accomplished in safety. The royal letters to the governors of the provinces along his route secured him honorable reception and prompt assistance. No enemy dared molest the official who was guarded by the power of the Persian king and treated with marked consideration by the provincial rulers. His arrival in Jerusalem, however, with a military escort, showing that he had come on some important mission, excited the jealousy of the heathen tribes living near the city, who had so often indulged their enmity against the Jews by heaping upon them injury and insult. Foremost in this evil work were certain chiefs of these tribes, Sanballat the Horonite, Tobiah the Ammonite, and Geshem the Arabian. From the first these leaders watched with critical eyes the movements of Nehemiah and endeavored by every means in their power to thwart his plans and hinder his work.

Nehemiah continued to exercise the same caution and prudence that had hitherto marked his course. Knowing that bitter and determined enemies stood ready to oppose him, he concealed the nature of his mission from them until a study of the situation should enable him to form his plans. Thus he hoped to secure the cooperation of the people and set them at work before the opposition of his enemies should be aroused.

Choosing a few men whom he knew to be

worthy of confidence, Nehemiah told them of the circumstances that had led them to come to Jerusalem, the object that he wished to accomplish, and the plans he proposed to follow. Their interest in his undertaking was at once enlisted and their assistance secured.

On the third night after his arrival Nehemiah rose at midnight and with a few trusted companions went out to view for himself the desolation of Jerusalem. Mounted on his mule, he passed from one part of the city to another, surveying the broken-down walls and gates of the city of his fathers. Painful reflections filled the mind of the Jewish patriot as with sorrow-stricken heart he gazed upon the ruined defenses of his beloved Jerusalem. Memories of Israel's past greatness stood out in sharp contrast with the evidences of her humiliation.

In secrecy and silence Nehemiah completed his circuit of the walls. "The rulers knew not whither I went," he declares, "or what I did; neither had I as yet told it to the Jews, nor to the priests, nor to the nobles, nor to the rulers, nor to the rest that did the work." The remainder of 637 the night he spent in prayer; for he knew that the morning would call for earnest effort to arouse and unite his dispirited and divided countrymen.

Nehemiah bore a royal commission requiring the inhabitants to co-operate with him in rebuilding the walls of the city, but he did not depend upon the exercise of authority. He sought rather to gain the confidence and sympathy of the people, knowing that a union of hearts as well as of hands was essential in the great work before him. When on the morrow he called the people together he presented such arguments as were calculated to arouse their dormant energies and unite their scattered numbers.

Nehemiah's hearers did not know, neither did he tell them, of his midnight circuit of the night before. But the fact that he had made this circuit contributed greatly to his success; for he was able to speak of the condition of the city with an accuracy and a minuteness that astonished his hearers. The impression made upon him as he had looked upon the weakness and degradation of Jerusalem, gave earnestness and power to his words.

Nehemiah presented before the people their reproach among the heathen—their religion dishonored, their God blasphemed. He told them that in a distant land he had heard of their affliction, that he had entreated the favor of Heaven in their behalf, and that, as he was praying, he had determined to ask permission from the king to come to their assistance. He had asked God that the king might not only grant this permission, but might also invest him with the authori-638 ty and give him the help needed for the work; and his prayer had been answered in such a way as to show that the plan was of the Lord.

All this he related, and then, having shown that he was sustained by the combined authority of the God of Israel and the Persian king, Nehemiah asked the people directly whether they would take advantage of this opportunity and arise and build the wall.

The appeal went straight to their hearts. The thought of how Heaven's favor had been manifested toward them put their fears to shame, and with new courage they said with one voice, "Let us rise up and build." "So they strengthened their hands for this good work."

Nehemiah's whole soul was in the enterprise he had undertaken. His hope, his energy, his enthusiasm, his determination, were contagious, inspiring others with the same high courage and lofty purpose. Each man became a Nehemiah in his turn and helped to make stronger the heart and hand of his neighbor.

When the enemies of Israel heard what the Jews were hoping to accomplish, they laughed them to scorn, saying, "What is this thing that ye do? will ye rebel against the king?" But Nehemiah answered, "The God of heaven, He will prosper us; therefore will we His servants arise and build: but ye have no portion, nor right, nor memorial, in Jerusalem."

Among the first to catch Nehemiah's spirit of zeal and earnestness were the priests. Because of their influential position, these men could do much to advance or hinder the work; and their ready co-operation, at the very outset, contributed not a little to its success. The majority 639 of the princes and rulers of Israel came up nobly to their duty, and these faithful men have honorable mention in the book of God. There were a few, the Tekoite nobles, who "put not their necks to the work of their Lord." The memory of these slothful servants is branded with shame and has been handed down as a warning to all future generations.

In every religious movement there are some who, while they cannot deny that the cause is God's, still hold themselves aloof, refusing to make any effort to help. It were well for such ones to remember the record kept on high—that book in which there are no omissions, no mistakes, and out of which they will be judged. There every neglected opportunity to do service for God is recorded; and there, too, every deed of faith and love is held in everlasting remembrance.

Against the inspiring influence of Nehemiah's presence the example of the Tekoite nobles had little weight. The people in general were animated by patriotism and zeal. Men of ability and influence organized the various classes of citizens into companies, each leader making himself responsible for the erection of a certain part of the wall. And of some it is written that they builded "everyone over against his house."

Nor did Nehemiah's energy abate, now that

the work was actually begun. With tireless vigilance he superintended the building, directing the workmen, noting the hindrances, and providing for emergencies. Along the whole extent of that three miles of wall his influence was constantly felt. With timely words he encouraged the fearful, aroused the laggard, and approved the diligent. And ever he watched the movements of their enemies, who from time to time collected at a distance and engaged in conversation, as if plotting mischief, and then, drawing nearer the workmen, attempted to divert their attention.

In his many activities Nehemiah did not forget the source of his strength. His heart was constantly uplifted to God, the great Overseer of all. "The God of heaven," he exclaimed, "He will prosper us;" and the words, echoed and reechoed, thrilled the hearts of all the workers on the wall.

But the restoration of the defenses of Jerusalem did not go forward unhindered. Satan was working to stir up opposition and bring discouragement. Sanballat, Tobiah, and Geshem, his principal agents in this movement, now set themselves to hinder the work of rebuilding. They endeavored to cause division among the workmen. They ridiculed the efforts of the builders, declaring the enterprise an impossibility and predicting failure.

"What do these feeble Jews?" exclaimed Sanballat mockingly; "will they fortify themselves? . . . will they revive the stones out of the heaps of the rubbish which are burned?" Tobiah, still more contemptuous, added, "Even that which they build, if a fox go up, he shall even break down their stone wall."

The builders were soon beset by more active opposition. They were compelled to guard continually against the plots of their adversaries, who, professing friendliness, sought in various ways to cause confusion and perplexity, and to arouse distrust. They endeavored to destroy the courage of the Jews; they formed conspiracies to draw Nehemiah into their toils; and falsehearted Jews were found ready to aid the treacherous undertaking. The report was spread that Nehemiah was plotting against the Persian monarch, intending to exalt himself as a king over Israel, and that all who aided him were traitors.

But Nehemiah continued to look to God for guidance and support, and "the people had a mind to work." The enterprise went forward until the gaps were filled and the entire wall built up to half its intended height.

As the enemies of Israel saw how unavailing were their efforts, they were filled with rage. Hitherto they had not dared employ violent measures, for they knew that Nehemiah and his companions were acting under the king's commission, and they feared that active opposition

against him might bring upon them the monarch's displeasure. But now in their anger they themselves became guilty of the crime of which they had accused Nehemiah. Assembling for counsel, they "conspired all of them together to come and to fight against Jerusalem."

At the same time that the Samaritans were plotting against Nehemiah and his work, some of the leading men among the Jews, becoming disaffected, sought to discourage him by exaggerating the difficulties attending the enterprise. "The strength of the bearers of burdens is decayed," they said, "and there is much rubbish; so that we are not able to build the wall."

Discouragement came from still another source. "The Jews which dwelt by," those who were taking no part in the work, gathered up the statements and reports of their enemies and used these to weaken courage and create disaffection.

But taunts and ridicule, opposition and threats, seemed only to inspire Nehemiah with firmer determination and to arouse him to greater watchfulness. He recognized the dangers that must be met in this warfare with their enemies, but his courage was undaunted. "We made our prayer unto our God," he declares, "and set a watch against them day and night." "Therefore set I in the lower places behind the wall, and on the higher places, I even set the people after their families with their swords, their spears, and their bows. And I looked, and rose up, and said unto the nobles, and to the rulers, and to the rest of the people, Be not ye afraid of them: remember the Lord, which is great and terrible, and fight for your brethren, your sons, and your daughters, your wives, and your houses.

"And it came to pass, when our enemies heard that it was known unto us, and God had brought their counsel to nought, that we returned all of us to the wall, everyone unto his work. And it came to pass from that time forth, that the half of my servants wrought in the work, and the other half of them held both the spears, the shields, and the bows, and the habergeons. . . . They which builded on the wall, and they that bare burdens, with those that laded, everyone with one of his hands wrought in the work, and with the other hand held a weapon. For the builders, everyone had his sword girded by his side, and so builded."

Beside Nehemiah stood a trumpeter, and on different parts of the wall were stationed priests bearing the sacred trumpets. The people were scattered in their labors, but on the approach of danger at any point a signal was given for them to repair thither without delay. "So we labored in the work," Nehemiah says, "and half of them held the spears from the rising of the morning till the stars appeared."

Those who had been living in towns and villages outside Jerusalem were now required to lodge within the walls, both to guard the work and to be ready for duty in the morning. This would prevent unnecessary delay, and would cut off the opportunity which the enemy would otherwise improve, of attacking the workmen as they went to and from their homes. Nehemiah and his companions did not shrink from hardship or trying service. Neither by day nor night, not even during the short time given to sleep, did they put off their clothing or lay aside their armor.

The opposition and discouragement that the builders in Nehemiah's day met from open enemies and pretended friends is typical of the experience that those today will have who work for God. Christians are tried, not only by the anger, contempt, and cruelty of enemies, but by the indolence, inconsistency, lukewarmness, and treachery of avowed friends and helpers. Derision and reproach are hurled at them. And the same enemy that leads to contempt, at a favorable opportunity uses more cruel and violent measures.

Satan takes advantage of every unconsecrated element for the accomplishment of his purposes. Among those who profess to be the supporters of God's cause there are those who unite with His enemies and thus lay His cause open to the attacks of His bitterest foes. Even some who desire the work of God to prosper will yet weaken the hands of His servants by hearing, reporting, and half believing the slanders, boasts, and menaces of His adversaries. Satan works with marvelous success through his agents, and all who yield to their influence are subject to a bewitching power that destroys the wisdom of the wise and the understanding of the prudent. But, like Nehemiah, God's people are neither to fear nor to despise their enemies. Putting their trust in God, they are to go steadily forward, doing His work with unselfishness, and committing to His providence the cause for which they stand.

Amidst great discouragement, Nehemiah made God his trust, his sure defense. And He who was the support of His servant then has been the dependence of His people in every age. In every crisis His people may confidently declare, "If God be for us, who can be against us?" Romans 8:31. However craftily the plots of Satan and his agents may be laid, God can detect them, and bring to nought all their counsels. The response of faith today will be the response made by Nehemiah, "Our God shall fight for us;" for God is in the work, and no man can prevent its ultimate success.

54

A Rebuke Against Extortion

The wall of Jerusalem had not yet been completed when Nehemiah's attention was called to the unhappy condition of the poorer classes of the people. In the unsettled state of the country, tillage had been to some extent neglected. Furthermore, because of the selfish course pursued by some who had returned to Judea, the Lord's blessing was not resting upon their land, and there was a scarcity of grain.

In order to obtain food for their families, the poor were obliged to buy on credit and at exorbitant prices. They were also compelled to raise money by borrowing on interest to pay the heavy taxes imposed upon them by the kings of Persia. To add to the distress of the poor, the more wealthy among the Jews had taken advantage of their necessities, thus enriching themselves.

The Lord had commanded Israel, through Moses, that every third year a tithe be raised for the benefit of the poor; and a further provision had been made in the suspension of agricultural labor every seventh year, the land lying fallow, its spontaneous products being left to those in need. Faithfulness in devoting these offerings to the relief of the poor and to other benevolent uses would have tended to keep fresh before the people the truth of God's ownership of all, and their opportunity to be channels of blessing. It was Jehovah's purpose that the Israelites should have a training that would eradicate selfishness, and develop breadth and nobility of character.

God had also instructed through Moses: "If thou lend money to any of My people that is poor by thee, thou shalt not be to him as an usurer." "Thou shalt not lend upon usury to thy brother; usury of money, usury of victuals, usury of anything that is lent upon usury." Exodus 22:25; Deuteronomy 23:19. Again He had said, "If there be among you a poor man of one of thy brethren within any of thy gates in thy land which the Lord thy God giveth thee, thou shalt not harden thine heart, nor shut thine hand from thy poor brother: but thou shalt open thine hand wide unto him, and shalt surely lend him sufficient for his need, in that which he wanteth." "For the poor shall never cease out of the land: therefore I command thee, saying, Thou shalt open thine hand wide unto thy brother, to thy poor, and to thy needy, in thy land." Deuteronomy 15:7, 8, 11.

At times following the return of the exiles from Babylon, the wealthy Jews had gone directly contrary to these commands. When the poor were obliged to borrow to pay tribute to

This chapter is based on Nehemiah 5.

the king, the wealthy had lent them money, but had exacted a high rate of interest. By taking mortgages on the lands of the poor, they had gradually reduced the unfortunate debtors to the deepest poverty. Many had been forced to sell their sons and daughters into servitude; and there seemed no hope of improving their condition, no way to redeem either their children or their lands, no prospect before them but ever-increasing distress, with perpetual want and bondage. Yet they were of the same nation, children of the same covenant, as their more favored brethren.

At length the people presented their condition before Nehemiah. "Lo," they said, "we bring into bondage our sons and our daughters to be servants, and some of our daughters are brought into bondage already: neither is it in our power to redeem them; for other men have our lands and vineyards."

As Nehemiah heard of this cruel oppression, his soul was filled with indignation. "I was very angry," he says, "when I heard their cry and these words." He saw that if he succeeded in breaking up the oppressive custom of exaction he must take a decided stand for justice. With characteristic energy and determination he went to work to bring relief to his brethren.

The fact that the oppressors were men of wealth, whose support was greatly needed in the work of restoring the city, did not for a moment influence Nehemiah. He sharply rebuked the nobles and rulers, and when he had gathered a great assembly of the people he set before them the requirements of God touching the case.

He called their attention to events that had occurred in the reign of King Ahaz. He repeated the message which God had at that time sent to Israel to rebuke their cruelty and oppression. The children of Judah, because of their idolatry, had been delivered into the hands of their still more idolatrous brethren, the people of Israel. The latter had indulged their enmity by slaying in battle many thousands of the men of Judah and had seized all the women and children, intending to keep them as slaves or to sell them into bondage to the heathen.

Because of the sins of Judah, the Lord had not interposed to prevent the battle; but by the prophet Oded He rebuked the cruel design of the victorious army: "Ye purpose to keep under the children of Judah and Jerusalem for bond-men and bondwomen unto you: but are there not with you, even with you, sins against the Lord your God?" 2 Chronicles 28:10. Oded warned the people of Israel that the anger of the Lord was kindled against them, and that their course of injustice and oppression would call down His judgments. Upon hearing these words, the armed men left the captives and the spoil before the princes and all the congregation. Then certain leading men of the tribe of Ephraim "took the captives, and with the spoil clothed all that were naked among them, and arrayed them, and shod them, and gave them to eat and to drink, and anointed them, and carried all the feeble of them upon asses, and brought them to Jericho, the city of palm trees, to their brethren." Verse 15.

Nehemiah and others had ransomed certain of the Jews who had been sold to the heathen, and he now placed this course in contrast with the conduct of those who for the sake of worldly gain were enslaving their brethren. "It is not good that ye do," he said; "ought ye not to walk in the fear of our God because of the reproach of the heathen our enemies?"

Nehemiah showed them that he himself, being invested with authority from the Persian king, might have demanded large contributions for his personal benefit. But instead of this he had not taken even that which justly belonged to him, but had given liberally to relieve the poor in their need. He urged those among the Jewish rulers who had been guilty of extortion, to cease this iniquitous work; to restore the lands of the poor, and also the increase of money which they had exacted from them; and to lend to them without security or usury.

These words were spoken in the presence of the whole congregation. Had the rulers chosen to justify themselves, they had opportunity to do so. But they offered no excuse. "We will restore them," they declared, "and will require nothing of them; so will we do as thou sayest." At this, Nehemiah in the presence of the priests "took an oath of them, that they should do according to this promise." "And all the congregation said, Amen, and praised the Lord. And the people did according to this promise."

This record teaches an important lesson. "The love of money is the root of all evil." 1 Timothy 6:10. In this generation the desire for gain is the absorbing passion. Wealth is often obtained by fraud. There are multitudes struggling with poverty, compelled to labor hard for small wages, unable to secure even the barest necessities of life. Toil and deprivation, with no hope of better things, make their burden heavy. Care-worn and oppressed, they know not where to turn for relief. And all this that the rich may support their extravagance or indulge their desire to hoard!

Love of money and love of display have made this world as a den of thieves and robbers. The Scriptures picture the greed and oppression that will prevail just before Christ's second coming. "Go to now, ye rich men," James writes; "ye have heaped treasure together for the last days. Behold, the hire of the laborers who have reaped down your fields, which is of you kept back by fraud, crieth: and the cries of them which have reaped are entered into the ears of the Lord of Sabaoth. Ye have lived in pleasure on the earth, and been wanton; ye have nourished your hearts, as in a day of slaughter. Ye have condemned and killed the just; and he doth not resist you." James 5:1, 3-6.

Even among those who profess to be walking in the fear of the Lord, there are some who are acting over again the course pursued by the nobles of Israel. Because it is in their power to do so, they exact more than is just, and thus become oppressors. And because avarice and treachery are seen in the lives of those who have named the name of Christ, because the church retains on her books the names of those who have gained their possessions by injustice, the religion of Christ is held in contempt. Extravagance, overreaching, extortion, are corrupting the faith of many and destroying their spirituality. The church is in a great degree responsible for the sins of her members. She gives countenance to evil if she fails to lift her voice against it.

652 The customs of the world are no criterion for the Christian. He is not to imitate its sharp practices, its overreaching, its extortion. Every unjust act toward a fellow being is a violation of the golden rule. Every wrong done to the children of God is done to Christ Himself in the person of His saints. Every attempt to take advantage of the ignorance, weakness, or misfortune of another is registered as fraud in the ledger of heaven. He who truly fears God, would rather toil day and night, and eat the bread of poverty, than to indulge the passion for gain that oppresses the widow and fatherless or turns the stranger from his right.

The slightest departure from rectitude breaks down the barriers and prepares the heart to do greater injustice. Just to that extent that a man would gain advantage for himself at the disadvantage of another, will his soul become insensible to the influence of the Spirit of God. Gain obtained at such a cost is a fearful loss.

We were all debtors to divine justice, but we had nothing with which to pay the debt. Then the Son of God, who pitied us, paid the price of our redemption. He became poor that through His poverty we might be rich. By deeds of liberality toward His poor we may prove the sincerity of our gratitude for the mercy extended to us. "Let us do good unto all men," the apostle Paul enjoins, "especially unto them who are of the household of faith." Galatians 6:10. And his words accord with those of the Saviour: "Ye have the poor with you always, and whensoever ye will ye may do them good." "Whatsoever ye would that men should do to you, do ye even so to them: for this is the law and the prophets." Mark 14:7; Matthew 7:12.

653

55
Heathen Plots

Sanballat and his confederates dared not make open war upon the Jews; but with increasing malice they continued their secret efforts to discourage, perplex, and injure them. The wall about Jerusalem was rapidly approaching completion. When it should be finished and its gates set up, these enemies of Israel could not hope to force an entrance into the city. They were the more eager, therefore, to stop the work without further delay. At last they devised a plan by which they hoped to draw Nehemiah from his station, and while they had him in their power, to kill or imprison him.

Pretending to desire a compromise of the opposing parties, they sought a conference with Nehemiah, and invited him to meet them in a village on the plain of Ono. But enlightened by the Holy Spirit as to their real purpose, he refused. "I sent messengers unto them," he writes, "saying, I am doing a great work, so that 654 I cannot come down: why should the work cease, whilst I leave it, and come down to you?" But the tempters were persistent. Four times they sent a message of similar import, and each time they received the same answer.

Finding this scheme unsuccessful, they resorted to a more daring stratagem. Sanballat sent Nehemiah a messenger bearing an open letter which said: "It is reported among the heathen, and Gashmu saith it, that thou and the Jews think to rebel: for which cause thou buildest the wall, that thou mayest be their king. . . . And thou hast also appointed prophets to preach of thee at Jerusalem, saying, There is a king in Judah: and now shall it be reported to the king according to these words. Come now therefore, and let us take counsel together."

Had the reports mentioned been actually circulated, there would have been cause for apprehension; for they would soon have been carried to the king, whom a slight suspicion might provoke to the severest measures. But Nehemiah was convinced that the letter was wholly false, written to arouse his fears and draw him into a snare. This conclusion was strengthened by the fact that the letter was sent open, evidently that the people might read the contents, and become alarmed and intimidated.

He promptly returned the answer, "There are no such things done as thou sayest, but thou feignest them out of thine own heart." Nehemiah was not ignorant of Satan's devices. He knew that these attempts were made in order to weaken the hands of the builders and thus frustrate their efforts.

This chapter is based on Nehemiah 6.

Again and again had Satan been defeated; and now, with deeper malice and cunning, he laid a still more subtle and dangerous snare for the servant of God. Sanballat and his companions hired men who professed to be the friends of Nehemiah, to give him evil counsel as the word of the Lord. The chief one engaged in this iniquitous work was Shemaiah, a man previously held in good repute by Nehemiah. This man shut himself up in a chamber near the sanctuary as if fearing that his life was in danger. The temple was at this time protected by walls and gates, but the gates of the city were not yet set up. Professing great concern for Nehemiah's safety, Shemaiah advised him to seek shelter in the temple. "Let us meet together in the house of God, within the temple," he proposed, "and let us shut the doors of the temple: for they will come to slay thee; yea, in the night will they come to slay thee."

Had Nehemiah followed this treacherous counsel, he would have sacrificed his faith in God, and in the eyes of the people he would have appeared cowardly and contemptible. In view of the important work that he had undertaken, and the confidence that he professed to have in the power of God, it would have been altogether inconsistent for him to hide as if in fear. The alarm would have spread among the people, each would have sought his own safety, and the city would have been left unprotected, to fall a prey to its enemies. That one unwise move on the part of Nehemiah would have been a virtual surrender of all that had been gained.

Nehemiah was not long in penetrating the true character and object of his counselor. "I perceived that God had not sent him," he says, "but that he pronounced this prophecy against me: for Tobiah and Sanballat had hired him. Therefore was he hired, that I should be afraid, and do so, and sin, and that they might have matter for an evil report, that they might reproach me."

The infamous counsel given by Shemaiah was seconded by more than one man of high reputation, who, while professing to be Nehemiah's friends, were secretly in league with his enemies. But it was to no avail that they laid their snare. Nehemiah's fearless answer was: "Should such a man as I flee? and who is there that, being as I am, would go into the temple to save his life? I will not go in."

Notwithstanding the plots of enemies, open and secret, the work of building went steadily forward, and in less than two months from the time of Nehemiah's arrival in Jerusalem the city was girded with its defenses and the builders could walk upon the walls and look down upon their defeated and astonished foes. "When all our enemies heard thereof, and all the heathen that were about us saw these things," Nehemiah writes, "they were much cast down in their own eyes: for they perceived that this work was wrought of our God."

Yet even this evidence of the Lord's controlling hand was not sufficient to restrain discontent, rebellion, and treachery among the Israelites. "The nobles of Judah sent many letters unto Tobiah, and the letters of Tobiah came unto them. For there were many in Judah sworn unto him, because he was the son-in-law of Shechaniah." Here are seen the evil results of intermarriage with idolaters. A family of Judah had become connected with the enemies of God, and the relation had proved a snare. Many others had done the same. These, like the mixed multitude that came up with Israel from Egypt, were a source of constant trouble. They were not wholehearted in His service; and when God's work demanded a sacrifice, they were ready to violate their solemn oath of co-operation and support.

Some who had been foremost in plotting mischief against the Jews, now professed a desire to be on friendly terms with them. The nobles of Judah who had become entangled in idolatrous marriages, and who had held traitorous correspondence with Tobiah and taken oath to serve him, now represented him as a man of ability and foresight, an alliance with whom would be greatly to the advantage of the Jews. At the same time they betrayed to him Nehemiah's plans and movements. Thus the work of God's people was laid open to the attacks of their enemies, and opportunity was given to misconstrue Nehemiah's words and acts, and to hinder his work.

When the poor and oppressed had appealed to Nehemiah for redress of their wrongs, he had stood boldly in their defense and had caused the wrongdoers to remove the reproach that rested on them. But the authority that he had exercised in behalf of his downtrodden countrymen he did not now exercise in his own behalf. His efforts had been met by some with ingratitude and treachery, but he did not use his power to bring the traitors to punishment. Calmly and unselfishly he went forward in his service for the people, never slackening his efforts or allowing his interest to grow less.

Satan's assaults have ever been directed against those who have sought to advance the work and cause of God. Though often baffled, he as often renews his attacks with fresh vigor, using means hitherto untried. But it is his secret working through those who avow themselves the friends of God's work, that is most to be feared. Open opposition may be fierce and cruel, but it is fraught with far less peril to God's cause than is the secret enmity of those who, while professing to serve God, are at heart the servants of Satan. These have it in their power to place every advantage in the hands of those who will use their knowledge to hinder the work of God and injure His servants.

Every device that the prince of darkness can suggest will be employed to induce God's servants to form a confederacy with the agents of

Satan. Repeated solicitations will come to call them from duty; but, like Nehemiah, they should steadfastly reply, "I am doing a great work, so that I cannot come down." God's workers may safely keep on with their work, letting their efforts refute the falsehoods that malice may coin for their injury. Like the builders on the walls of Jerusalem they must refuse to be diverted from their work by threats or mockery or falsehood. Not for one moment are they to relax their watchfulness or vigilance, for enemies are continually on their track. Ever they must make their prayer to God "and set a watch against them day and night." Nehemiah 4:9.

As the time of the end draws near, Satan's temptations will be brought to bear with greater power upon God's workers. He will employ human agents to mock and revile those who "build the wall." But should the builders come down to meet the attacks of their foes, this would but retard the work. They should endeavor to defeat the purposes of their adversaries, but they should not allow anything to call them from their work. Truth is stronger than error, and right will prevail over wrong.

Neither should they allow their enemies to gain their friendship and sympathy, and thus lure them from their post of duty. He who by any unguarded act exposes the cause of God to reproach, or weakens the hands of his fellow workers, brings upon his own character a stain not easily removed, and places a serious obstacle in the way of his future usefulness.

660 "They that forsake the law praise the wicked." Proverbs 28:4. When those who are uniting with the world, yet claiming great purity, plead for union with those who have ever been the opposers of the cause of truth, we should fear and shun them as decidedly as did Nehemiah. Such counsel is prompted by the enemy of all good. It is the speech of time-servers, and should be resisted as resolutely today as then. Whatever influence would tend to unsettle the faith of God's people in His guiding power, should be steadfastly withstood.

In Nehemiah's firm devotion to the work of God, and his equally firm reliance on God, lay the reason of the failure of his enemies to draw him into their power. The soul that is indolent falls an easy prey to temptation; but in the life that has a noble aim, an absorbing purpose, evil finds little foothold. The faith of him who is constantly advancing does not weaken; for above, beneath, beyond, he recognizes Infinite Love, working out all things to accomplish His good purpose. God's true servants work with a determination that will not fail because the throne of grace is their constant dependence.

God has provided divine assistance for all the emergencies to which our human resources are unequal. He gives the Holy Spirit to help in every strait, to strengthen our hope and assurance, to illuminate our minds and purify our hearts. He provides opportunities and opens channels of working. If His people are watching the indications of His providence, and are ready to co-operate with Him, they will see mighty results.

56

661

Instructed in the Law of God

It was the time of the Feast of Trumpets. Many were gathered at Jerusalem. The scene was one of mournful interest. The wall of Jerusalem had been rebuilt and the gates set up, but a large part of the city was still in ruins.

On a platform of wood, erected in one of the broadest streets, and surrounded on every hand by the sad reminders of Judah's departed glory, stood Ezra, now an aged man. At his right and left were gathered his brother Levites. Looking down from the platform, their eyes swept over a sea of heads. From all the surrounding country the children of the covenant had assembled. "And Ezra blessed the Lord, the great God. And all the people answered, Amen: . . . and they bowed their heads, and worshiped the Lord with their faces to the ground."

Yet even here was evidence of the sin of Israel. Through the intermarriage of the people with other nations, the Hebrew language had 662 become corrupted, and great care was necessary on the part of the speakers to explain the law in the language of the people, that it might be understood by all. Certain of the priests and Levites united with Ezra in explaining the principles of the law. "They read in the book in the law of God distinctly, and gave the sense, and caused them to understand the reading."

"And the ears of all the people were attentive unto the book of the law." They listened, intent and reverent, to the words of the Most High. As the law was explained, they were convinced of their guilt, and they mourned because of their transgressions. But this day was a festival, a day of rejoicing, a holy convocation, a day which the Lord had commanded the people to keep with joy and gladness; and in view of this they were bidden to restrain their grief and to rejoice because of God's great mercy toward them. "This day is holy unto the Lord your God," Nehemiah said. "Mourn not, nor weep. . . . Go your way, eat the fat, and drink the sweet, and send portions unto them for whom nothing is prepared: for this day is holy unto our Lord: neither be ye sorry; for the joy of the Lord is your strength."

The earlier part of the day was devoted to religious exercises, and the people spent the remainder of the time in gratefully recounting the blessings of God and in enjoying the boun-

This chapter is based on Nehemiah 8; 9; to 10

ties that He had provided. Portions were also sent to the poor, who had nothing to prepare. There was great rejoicing because the words of the law had been read and understood.

On the following day the reading and explaining of the law were continued. And at the time appointed—on the tenth day of the seventh month—the solemn services of the Day of Atonement were performed according to the command of God.

From the fifteenth to the twenty-second of the same month the people and their rulers kept once more the Feast of Tabernacles. It was proclaimed "in all their cities, and in Jerusalem, saying, Go forth unto the mount, and fetch olive branches, and pine branches, and myrtle branches, and palm branches, and branches of thick trees, to make booths, as it is written. So the people went forth, and brought them, and made themselves booths, everyone upon the roof of his house, and in their courts, and in the courts of the house of God. . . . And there was very great gladness. Also day by day, from the first day unto the last day, he [Ezra] read in the book of the law of God."

As they had listened from day to day to the words of the law, the people had been convicted of their transgressions, and of the sins of their nation in past generations. They saw that it was because of a departure from God that His protecting care had been withdrawn and that the children of Abraham had been scattered in foreign lands, and they determined to seek His mercy and to pledge themselves to walk in His commandments. Before entering upon this solemn service, held on the second day after the close of the Feast of Tabernacles, they separated themselves from the heathen among them.

As the people prostrated themselves before the Lord, confessing their sins and pleading for pardon, their leaders encouraged them to believe that God, according to His promise, heard their prayers. They must not only mourn and weep, and repent, but they must believe that God pardoned them. They must show their faith by recounting His mercies and praising Him for His goodness. "Stand up," said these teachers, "and bless the Lord your God for ever and ever."

Then from the assembled throng, as they stood with outstretched hands toward heaven, there arose the song:

"Blessed be Thy glorious name,
Which is exalted above all blessing and praise.
Thou, even Thou, art Lord alone;
Thou hast made heaven, the heaven of heavens,
with all their host,
The earth, and all things that are therein,
The seas, and all that is therein,
And Thou preservest them all;
And the host of heaven worshipeth Thee."

The song of praise ended, the leaders of the congregation related the history of Israel, showing how great had been God's goodness toward them, and how great their ingratitude. Then the whole congregation entered into a covenant to keep all the commandments of God. They had suffered punishment for their sins; now they acknowledged the justice of God's dealings with them and pledged themselves to obey His law. And that this might be "a sure covenant," and be preserved in permanent form, as a memorial of the obligation they had taken upon themselves, it was written out, and the priests, Levites, and princes signed it. It was to serve as a reminder of duty and a barrier against temptation. The people took a solemn oath "to walk in God's law, which was given by Moses the servant of God, and to observe and do all the commandments of the Lord our God, and His judgments and His statutes." The oath taken at this time included a promise not to intermarry with the people of the land.

Before the day of fasting ended, the people still further manifested their determination to return to the Lord, by pledging themselves to cease from desecrating the Sabbath. Nehemiah did not at this time, as at a later date, exercise his authority to prevent heathen traders from coming into Jerusalem; but in an effort to save the people from yielding to temptation, he bound them, by a solemn covenant, not to transgress the Sabbath law by purchasing from these venders, hoping that this would discourage the traders and put an end to the traffic.

Provision was also made to support the public worship of God. In addition to the tithe the congregation pledged themselves to contribute yearly a stated sum for the service of the sanctuary. "We cast the lots," Nehemiah writes, "to bring the first fruits of our ground, and the first fruits of all fruit of all trees, year by year, unto the house of the Lord: also the first-born of our sons, and of our cattle, as it is written in the law, and the firstlings of our herds and of our flocks."

Israel had returned to God with deep sorrow for backsliding. They had made confession with mourning and lamentation. They had acknowledged the righteousness of God's dealings with them, and had covenanted to obey His law. Now they must manifest faith in His promises. God had accepted their repentance; they were now to rejoice in the assurance of sins forgiven and their restoration to divine favor.

Nehemiah's efforts to restore the worship of the true God had been crowned with success. As long as the people were true to the oath they had taken, as long as they were obedient to God's word, so long would the Lord fulfill His promise by pouring rich blessings upon them.

For those who are convicted of sin and weighed down with a sense of their unworthiness, there are lessons of faith and encouragement in this record. The Bible faithfully presents the result of Israel's apostasy; but it portrays also the deep humiliation and repentance, the earnest devotion and generous sacrifice, that marked their seasons of return to the Lord.

Every true turning to the Lord brings abiding joy into the life. When a sinner yields to the influence of the Holy Spirit, he sees his own guilt and defilement in contrast with the holiness of the great Searcher of hearts. He sees himself condemned as a transgressor. But he is not, because of this, to give way to despair; for his pardon has already been secured. He may rejoice in the sense of sins forgiven, in the love of a pardoning heavenly Father. It is God's glory to encircle sinful, repentant human beings in the arms of His love, to bind up their wounds, to cleanse them from sin, and to clothe them with the garments of salvation.

669

57
Reformation

Solemnly and publicly the people of Judah had pledged themselves to obey the law of God. But when the influence of Ezra and Nehemiah was for a time withdrawn, there were many who departed from the Lord. Nehemiah had returned to Persia. During his absence from Jerusalem, evils crept in that threatened to pervert the nation. Idolaters not only gained a foothold in the city, but contaminated by their presence the very precincts of the temple. Through intermarriage, a friendship had been brought about between Eliashib the high priest and Tobiah the Ammonite, Israel's bitter enemy. As a result of this unhallowed alliance, Eliashib had permitted Tobiah to occupy an apartment connected with the temple, which heretofore had been used as a storeroom for tithes and offerings of the people.

670 Because of the cruelty and treachery of the Ammonites and Moabites toward Israel, God had declared through Moses that they should be forever shut out from the congregation of His people. See Deuteronomy 23:3-6. In defiance of this word, the high priest had cast out the offerings stored in the chamber of God's house, to make a place for this representative of a proscribed race. Greater contempt for God could not have been shown than to confer such a favor on this enemy of God and His truth.

On returning from Persia, Nehemiah learned of the bold profanation and took prompt measures to expel the intruder. "It grieved me sore," he declares; "therefore I cast forth all the household stuff of Tobiah out of the chamber. Then I commanded, and they cleansed the chambers: and thither brought I again the vessels of the house of God, with the meat offering and the frankincense."

Not only had the temple been profaned, but the offerings had been misapplied. This had tended to discourage the liberalities of the people. They had lost their zeal and fervor, and were reluctant to pay their tithes. The treasuries of the Lord's house were poorly supplied; many of the singers and others employed in the temple service, not receiving sufficient support, had left the work of God to labor elsewhere.

Nehemiah set to work to correct these abuses. He gathered together those who had left the service of the Lord's house, "and set them in their place." This inspired the people with confidence, and all Judah brought "the tithe of the corn and the new wine and the oil." Men who "were counted faithful" were made "treasurers over the treasuries," "and their office was to distribute unto their brethren."

Another result of intercourse with idolaters 671 was a disregard of the Sabbath, the sign distinguishing the Israelites from all other nations as worshipers of the true God. Nehemiah found that heathen merchants and traders from the surrounding country, coming to Jerusalem, had induced many among the Israelites to engage in traffic on the Sabbath. There were some who could not be persuaded to sacrifice principle, but others transgressed and joined with the heathen in their efforts to overcome the scruples of the more conscientious. Many dared openly to violate the Sabbath. "In those days," Nehemiah writes, "saw I in Judah some treading wine presses on the Sabbath, and bringing in sheaves, and lading asses; as also wine, grapes, and figs, and all manner of burdens, which they brought into Jerusalem on the Sabbath day. . . . There dwelt men of Tyre also therein, which brought fish, and all manner of ware, and sold on the Sabbath unto the children of Judah."

This state of things might have been prevented had the rulers exercised their authority; but a desire to advance their own interests had led them to favor the ungodly. Nehemiah fearlessly rebuked them for their neglect of duty. "What evil thing is this that ye do, and profane the Sabbath day?" he sternly demanded. "Did not your fathers thus, and did not our God bring all this evil upon us, and upon this city? yet ye bring more wrath upon Israel by profaning the Sabbath." He then gave command that "when the gates of Jerusalem began to be dark before the Sabbath," they should be shut, and not opened again till the Sabbath was past; and having more confidence in his own servants than in those that 672 the magistrates of Jerusalem might appoint, he stationed them at the gates to see that his orders were enforced.

This chapter is based on Nehemiah 13.

Not inclined to abandon their purpose, "the merchants and sellers of all kind of ware lodged without Jerusalem once or twice," hoping to find opportunity for traffic, with either the citizens or the country people. Nehemiah warned them that they would be punished if they continued this practice. "Why lodge ye about the wall?" he demanded; "if ye do so again, I will lay hands on you." "From that time forth came they no more on the Sabbath." He also directed the Levites to guard the gates, knowing that they would command greater respect than the common people, while from their close connection with the service of God it was reasonable to expect that they would be more zealous in enforcing obedience to His law.

And now Nehemiah turned his attention to the danger that again threatened Israel from intermarriage and association with idolaters. "In those days," he writes, "saw I Jews that had married wives of Ashdod, of Ammon, and of Moab: and their children spake half in the speech of Ashdod, and could not speak in the Jews' language, but according to the language of each people."

These unlawful alliances were causing great confusion in Israel; for some who entered into them were men in high position, rulers to whom the people had a right to look for counsel and a safe example. Foreseeing the ruin before the nation if this evil were allowed to continue, Nehemiah reasoned earnestly with the wrongdoers. Pointing to the case of Solomon, he reminded them that among all the nations there had risen no king like this man, to whom God had given great wisdom; yet idolatrous women had turned his heart from God, and his example had corrupted Israel. "Shall we then hearken unto you," Nehemiah sternly demanded, "to do all this great evil?" "Ye shall not give your daughters unto their sons, nor take their daughters unto your sons, or for yourselves."

As he set before them God's commands and threatenings, and the fearful judgments visited on Israel in the past for this very sin, their consciences were aroused, and a work of reformation was begun that turned away God's threatened anger and brought His approval and blessing.

There were some in sacred office who pleaded for their heathen wives, declaring that they could not bring themselves to separate from them. But no distinction was made; no respect was shown for rank or position. Whoever among the priests or rulers refused to sever his connection with idolaters was immediately separated from the service of the Lord. A grandson of the high priest, having married a daughter of the notorious Sanballat, was not only removed from office, but promptly banished from Israel. "Remember them, O my God," Nehemiah prayed, "because they have defiled the priesthood, and the covenant of the priesthood, and of the Levites."

How much anguish of soul this needed severity cost the faithful worker for God the judgment alone will reveal. There was a constant struggle with opposing elements, and only by fasting, humiliation, and prayer was advancement made.

Many who had married idolaters chose to go with them into exile, and these, with those who had been expelled from the congregation, joined the Samaritans. Hither some who had occupied high positions in the work of God found their way and after a time cast in their lot fully with them. Desiring to strengthen this alliance, the Samaritans promised to adopt more fully the Jewish faith and customs, and the apostates, determined to outdo their former brethren, erected a temple on Mount Gerizim in opposition to the house of God at Jerusalem. Their religion continued to be a mixture of Judaism and heathenism, and their claim to be the people of God was the source of schism, emulation, and enmity between the two nations, from generation to generation.

In the work of reform to be carried forward today, there is need of men who, like Ezra and Nehemiah, will not palliate or excuse sin, nor shrink from vindicating the honor of God. Those upon whom rests the burden of this work will not hold their peace when wrong is done, neither will they cover evil with a cloak of false charity. They will remember that God is no respecter of persons, and that severity to a few may prove mercy to many. They will remember also that in the one who rebukes evil the spirit of Christ should ever be revealed.

In their work, Ezra and Nehemiah humbled themselves before God, confessing their sins and the sins of their people, and entreating pardon as if they themselves were the offenders. Patiently they toiled and prayed and suffered. That which made their work most difficult was not the open hostility of the heathen, but the secret opposition of pretended friends, who, by lending their influence to the service of evil, increased tenfold the burden of God's servants. These traitors furnished the Lord's enemies with material to use in their warfare upon His people. Their evil passions and rebellious wills were ever at war with the plain requirements of God.

The success attending Nehemiah's efforts shows what prayer, faith, and wise, energetic action will accomplish. Nehemiah was not a priest; he was not a prophet; he made no pretension to high title. He was a reformer raised up for an important time. It was his aim to set his people right with God. Inspired with a great purpose, he bent every energy of his being to its accomplishment. High, unbending integrity marked his efforts. As he came into contact with evil and opposition to right he took so determined a stand that the people were roused to labor with fresh zeal and courage. They could not but recognize his loyalty, his patriotism, and his deep love for God; and, seeing this, they were willing to follow where he led.

Industry in a God-appointed duty is an important part of true religion. Men should seize circumstances as God's instruments with which to work His will. Prompt and decisive action at the right time will gain glorious triumphs, while delay and neglect result in failure and dishonor to God. If the leaders in the cause of truth show no zeal, if they are indifferent and purposeless, the church will be careless, indolent, and pleasure-loving; but if they are filled with a holy purpose to serve God and Him alone, the people will be united, hopeful, eager.

The word of God abounds in sharp and striking contrasts. Sin and holiness are placed side by side, that, beholding, we may shun the one and accept the other. The pages that describe the hatred, falsehood, and treachery of Sanballat and Tobiah, describe also the nobility, devotion, and self-sacrifice of Ezra and Nehemiah. We are left free to copy either, as we choose. The fearful results of transgressing God's commands are placed over against the blessings resulting from obedience. We ourselves must decide whether we will suffer the one or enjoy the other.

677 The work of restoration and reform carried on by the returned exiles, under the leadership of Zerubbabel, Ezra, and Nehemiah, presents a picture of a work of spiritual restoration that is to be wrought in the closing days of this earth's history. The remnant of Israel were a feeble people, exposed to the ravages of their enemies; but through them God purposed to preserve in the earth a knowledge of Himself and of His law. They were the guardians of the true worship, the keepers of the holy oracles. Varied were the experiences that came to them as they rebuilt the temple and the wall of Jerusalem; strong was the opposition that they had to meet. Heavy were the burdens borne by the leaders in this work; but these men moved forward in unwavering confidence, in humility of spirit, and in firm reliance upon God, believing that He would cause His truth to triumph. Like King Hezekiah, Nehemiah "clave to the Lord, and departed not from following Him, but kept His commandments. . . . And the Lord was with him." 2 Kings 18:6, 7.

The spiritual restoration of which the work carried forward in Nehemiah's day was a symbol, is outlined in the words of Isaiah: "They shall build the old wastes, they shall raise up the former desolations, and they shall repair the waste cities." "They that shall be of thee shall build the old waste places: thou shalt raise up the foundations of many generations; and thou shalt be called, The repairer of the breach, The restorer of paths to dwell in." Isaiah 61:4; 58:12.

The prophet here describes a people who, in a time of general departure from truth and righteousness, are seeking to restore the principles 678 that are the foundation of the kingdom of God. They are repairers of a breach that has been made in God's law—the wall that He has placed around His chosen ones for their protection, and obedience to whose precepts of justice, truth, and purity is to be their perpetual safeguard.

In words of unmistakable meaning the prophet points out the specific work of this remnant people who build the wall. "If thou turn away thy foot from the Sabbath, from doing thy pleasure on My holy day; and call the Sabbath a delight, the holy of the Lord, honorable; and shalt honor Him, not doing thine own ways, nor finding thine own pleasure, nor speaking thine own words: then shalt thou delight thyself in the Lord; and I will cause thee to ride upon the high places of the earth, and feed thee with the heritage of Jacob thy father: for the mouth of the Lord hath spoken it." Isaiah 58:13, 14.

In the time of the end every divine institution is to be restored. The breach made in the law at the time the Sabbath was changed by man, is to be repaired. God's remnant people, standing before the world as reformers, are to show that the law of God is the foundation of all enduring reform and that the Sabbath of the fourth commandment is to stand as a memorial of creation, a constant reminder of the power of God. In clear, distinct lines they are to present the necessity of obedience to all the precepts of the Decalogue. Constrained by the love of Christ, they are to co-operate with Him in building up the waste places. They are to be repairers of the breach, restorers of paths to dwell in. See verse 12.

SECTION VII

LIGHT AT EVENTIDE

"The kingdom and dominion, and the greatness of the kingdom under the whole heaven, shall be given to the people of the saints of the Most High, whose kingdom is an everlasting kingdom." Daniel 7:27.

58

The Coming of a Deliverer

681

Through the long centuries of "trouble and darkness" and "dimness of anguish" (Isaiah 8:22) marking the history of mankind from the day our first parents lost their Eden home, to the time the Son of God appeared as the Saviour of sinners, the hope of the fallen race was centered in the coming of a Deliverer to free men and women from the bondage of sin and the grave.

The first intimation of such a hope was given to Adam and Eve in the sentence pronounced upon the serpent in Eden when the Lord declared to Satan in their hearing, "I will put enmity between thee and the woman, and between thy seed and her seed; it shall bruise thy head, and thou shalt bruise his heel." Genesis 3:15.

As the guilty pair listened to these words, they were inspired with hope; for in the prophecy concerning the breaking of Satan's power they discerned a promise of deliverance from the ruin wrought through transgression. Though they must suffer from the power of their adversary because they had fallen under his seductive influence and had chosen to disobey the plain command of Jehovah, yet they need not yield to utter despair. The Son of God was offering to atone with His own lifeblood for their transgression. To them was to be granted a period of probation, during which, through faith in the power of Christ to save, they might become once more the children of God.

Satan, by means of his success in turning man aside from the path of obedience, became "the god of this world." 2 Corinthians 4:4. The dominion that once was Adam's passed to the usurper. But the Son of God proposed to come to this earth to pay the penalty of sin, and thus not only redeem man, but recover the dominion forfeited. It is of this restoration that Micah prophesied when he said, "O Tower of the flock, the stronghold of the daughter of Zion, unto Thee shall it come, even the first dominion." Micah 4:8. The apostle Paul has referred to it as "the redemption of the purchased possession." Ephesians 1:14. And the psalmist had in mind the same final restoration of man's original inheritance when he declared, "The righteous shall inherit the land, and dwell therein forever." Psalm 37:29.

This hope of redemption through the advent of the Son of God as Saviour and King, has never become extinct in the hearts of men. From the beginning there have been some whose faith has reached out beyond the shadows of the present to the realities of the future. Adam, Seth, Enoch, Methuselah, Noah, Shem, Abraham, Isaac, and Jacob—through these and other worthies the Lord has preserved the precious revealings of His will. And it was thus that to the children of Israel, the chosen people through whom was to be given to the world the promised Messiah, God imparted a knowledge of the requirements of His law, and of the salvation to be accomplished through the atoning sacrifice of His beloved Son.

The hope of Israel was embodied in the promise made at the time of the call of Abraham, and afterward repeated again and again to his posterity, "In thee shall all families of the earth be blessed." Genesis 12:3. As the purpose of God for the redemption of the race was unfolded to Abraham, the Sun of Righteousness shone upon his heart, and his darkness was scattered. And when, at last, the Saviour Himself walked and talked among the sons of men, He bore witness to the Jews of the patriarch's bright hope of deliverance through the coming of a Redeemer. "Your father Abraham rejoiced to see My day," Christ declared; "and he saw it, and was glad." John 8:56.

This same blessed hope was foreshadowed in the benediction pronounced by the dying patriarch Jacob upon his son Judah:

"Judah, thou art he whom thy brethren shall praise:

Thy hand shall be in the neck of thine enemies;

Thy father's children shall bow down before thee. . . .

The scepter shall not depart from Judah,

Nor a lawgiver from between his feet,

Until Shiloh come;

And unto Him shall the gathering of the people be."

Genesis 49:8-10.

Again, on the borders of the Promised Land, the coming of the world's Redeemer was foretold in the prophecy uttered by Balaam:

"I shall see Him, but not now: I shall behold Him, but not nigh:

There shall come a Star out of Jacob, and a Scepter shall rise out of Israel,

And shall smite the corners of Moab, and destroy all the children of Sheth."

Numbers 24:17.

Through Moses, God's purpose to send His Son as the Redeemer of the fallen race, was kept before Israel. On one occasion, shortly before his death, Moses declared, "The Lord thy God will raise up unto thee a Prophet from the midst of thee, of thy brethren, like unto me; unto Him ye shall hearken." Plainly had Moses been instructed for Israel concerning the work of the Messiah to come. "I will raise them up a Prophet from among their brethren, like unto thee," was the word of Jehovah to His servant; "and will put My words in His mouth; and He shall speak unto them all that I shall command Him." Deuteronomy 18:15, 18.

In patriarchal times the sacrificial offerings

connected with divine worship constituted a perpetual reminder of the coming of a Saviour, and thus it was with the entire ritual of the sanctuary services throughout Israel's history. In the ministration of the tabernacle, and of the temple that afterward took its place, the people were taught each day, by means of types and shadows, the great truths relative to the advent of Christ as Redeemer, Priest, and King; and once each year their minds were carried forward to the closing events of the great controversy between Christ and Satan, the final purification of the universe from sin and sinners. The sacrifices and offerings of the Mosaic ritual were ever pointing toward a better service, even a heavenly. The earthly sanctuary was "a figure for the time then present," in which were offered both gifts and sacrifices; its two holy places were "patterns of things in the heavens;" for Christ, our great High Priest, is today "a minister of the sanctuary, and of the true tabernacle, which the Lord pitched, and not man." Hebrews 9:9, 23; 8:2.

From the day the Lord declared to the serpent in Eden, "I will put enmity between thee and the woman, and between thy seed and her seed" (Genesis 3:15), Satan has known that he can never hold absolute sway over the inhabitants of this world. When Adam and his sons began to offer the ceremonial sacrifices ordained by God as a type of the coming Redeemer, Satan discerned in these a symbol of communion between earth and heaven. During the long centuries that have followed, it has been his constant effort to intercept this communion. Untiringly has he sought to misrepresent God and to misinterpret the rites pointing to the Saviour, and with a great majority of the members of the human family he has been successful.

While God has desired to teach men that from His own love comes the Gift which reconciles them to Himself, the archenemy of mankind has endeavored to represent God as one who delights in their destruction. Thus the sacrifices and the ordinances designed of Heaven to reveal divine love have been perverted to serve as means whereby sinners have vainly hoped to propitiate, with gifts and good works, the wrath of an offended God. At the same time, Satan has sought to arouse and strengthen the evil passions of men in order that through repeated transgression multitudes might be led on and on, far from God, and hopelessly bound with the fetters of sin.

When God's written word was given through the Hebrew prophets, Satan studied with diligence the messages concerning the Messiah. Carefully he traced the words that outlined with unmistakable clearness Christ's work among men as a suffering sacrifice and as a conquering king. In the parchment rolls of the Old Testament Scriptures he read that the One who was to

appear was to be "brought as a lamb to the slaughter," "His visage . . . so marred more than any man, and His form more than the sons of men." Isaiah 53:7; 52:14. The promised Saviour of humanity was to be "despised and rejected of men; a man of sorrows, and acquainted with grief; . . . smitten of God, and afflicted;" yet He was also to exercise His mighty power in order to "judge the poor of the people." He was to "save the children of the needy," and "break in pieces the oppressor." Isaiah 53:3, 4; Psalm 72:4. These prophecies caused Satan to fear and tremble; yet he relinquished not his purpose to thwart, if possible, the merciful provisions of Jehovah for the redemption of the lost race. He determined to blind the eyes of the people, so far as might be possible, to the real significance of the Messianic prophecies, in order to prepare the way for the rejection of Christ at His coming.

During the centuries immediately preceding the Flood, success had attended Satan's efforts to bring about a worldwide prevalence of rebellion against God. And even the lessons of the Deluge were not long held in remembrance. With artful insinuations Satan again led the children of men step by step into bold rebellion. Again he seemed about to triumph, but God's purpose for fallen man was not thus to be set aside. Through the posterity of faithful Abraham, of the line of Shem, a knowledge of Jehovah's beneficent designs was to be preserved for the benefit of future generations. From time to time divinely appointed messengers of truth were to be raised up to call attention to the meaning of the sacrificial ceremonies, and especially to the promise of Jehovah concerning the advent of the One toward whom all the ordinances of the sacrificial system pointed. Thus the world was to be kept from universal apostasy.

Not without the most determined opposition was the divine purpose carried out. In every way possible the enemy of truth and righteousness worked to cause the descendants of Abraham to forget their high and holy calling, and to turn aside to the worship of false gods. And often his efforts were all but successful. For centuries preceding Christ's first advent, darkness covered the earth, and gross darkness the people. Satan was throwing his hellish shadow athwart the pathway of men, that he might prevent them from gaining a knowledge of God and of the future world. Multitudes were sitting in the shadow of death. Their only hope was for this gloom to be lifted, that God might be revealed.

With prophetic vision David, the anointed of God, had foreseen that the coming of Christ should be "as the light of the morning, when the sun riseth, even a morning without clouds." 2 Samuel 23:4. And Hosea testified, "His going forth is prepared as the morning." Hosea 6:3. Quietly and gently the daylight breaks upon the earth, dispelling the shadow of darkness and waking the earth to life. So was the Sun of Righteousness to arise, "with healing in His wings." Malachi 4:2. The multitudes dwelling "in the land of the shadow of death" were to see "a great light." Isaiah 9:2.

The prophet Isaiah, looking with rapture upon this glorious deliverance, exclaimed:

"Unto us a Child is born,
Unto us a Son is given:
And the government shall be upon His shoulder:
And His name shall be called
Wonderful, Counselor, The mighty God,
The everlasting Father, The Prince of Peace.
Of the increase of His government and peace there shall be no end,
Upon the throne of David,
And upon His kingdom,
To order it, and to establish it
With judgment and with justice
From henceforth even forever.
The zeal of the Lord of hosts will perform this."

Verses 6, 7.

In the later centuries of Israel's history prior to the first advent it was generally understood [689] that the coming of the Messiah was referred to in the prophecy, "It is a light thing that Thou shouldest be My servant to raise up the tribes of Jacob, and to restore the preserved of Israel: I will also give Thee for a light to the Gentiles, that Thou mayest be My salvation unto the end of the earth." "The glory of the Lord shall be revealed," the prophet had foretold, "and all flesh shall see it together." Isaiah 49:6; 40:5. It was of this light of men that John the Baptist afterward testified so boldly, when he proclaimed, "I am the voice of one crying in the wilderness, Make straight the way of the Lord, as said the prophet Esaias." John 1:23.

It was to Christ that the prophetic promise was given: "Thus saith the Lord, the Redeemer of Israel, and His Holy One, to Him whom man despiseth, to Him whom the nation abhorreth, . . . thus saith the Lord, . . . I will preserve Thee, and give Thee for a covenant of the people, to establish the earth, to cause to inherit the desolate heritages; that Thou mayest say to the prisoners, Go forth; to them that are in darkness, Show yourselves. . . . They shall not hunger nor thirst; neither shall the heat nor sun smite them: for He that hath mercy on them shall lead them, even by the springs of water shall He guide them." Isaiah 49:7-10.

The steadfast among the Jewish nation, descendants of that holy line through whom a knowledge of God had been preserved,

strengthened their faith by dwelling on these and similar passages. With exceeding joy they read how the Lord would anoint One "to preach good tidings unto the meek," "to bind up the brokenhearted, to proclaim liberty to the captives," and to declare "the acceptable year of the Lord." Isaiah 61:1, 2. Yet their hearts were [690] filled with sadness as they thought of the sufferings He must endure in order to fulfill the divine purpose. With deep humiliation of soul they traced the words in the prophetic roll:

"Who hath believed our report?
And to whom is the arm of the Lord revealed?

"For He shall grow up before Him as a tender plant,
And as a root out of a dry ground:
He hath no form nor comeliness;
And when we shall see Him,
There is no beauty that we should desire Him.

"He is despised and rejected of men;
A Man of Sorrows, and acquainted with grief:
And we hid as it were our faces from Him;
He was despised, and we esteemed Him not.

"Surely He hath borne our griefs,
And carried our sorrows:
Yet we did esteem Him stricken,
Smitten of God, and afflicted.

"But He was wounded for our transgressions,
He was bruised for our iniquities:
The chastisement of our peace was upon Him;
And with His stripes we are healed.

"All we like sheep have gone astray;
We have turned everyone to his own way;
And the Lord hath laid on Him
The iniquity of us all.

"He was oppressed, and He was afflicted,
Yet He opened not His mouth: [691]
He is brought as a lamb to the slaughter,
And as a sheep before her shearers is dumb,
So He openeth not His mouth.

"He was taken from prison and from judgment:
And who shall declare His generation?
For He was cut off out of the land of the living:
For the transgression of My people was He stricken.

"And He made His grave with the wicked,
And with the rich in His death;
Because He had done no violence,
Neither was any deceit in His mouth."
Isaiah 53:1-9.

Of the suffering Saviour Jehovah Himself declared through Zechariah, "Awake, O sword, against My Shepherd, and against the Man that is My Fellow." Zechariah 13:7. As the substitute and surety for sinful man, Christ was to suffer under divine justice. He was to understand what justice meant. He was to know what it means for sinners to stand before God without an intercessor.

Through the psalmist the Redeemer had prophesied of Himself:

"Reproach hath broken My heart;
And I am full of heaviness:
And I looked for some to take pity,
But there was none;
And for comforters,
But I found none.
They gave Me also gall for My meat;
And in My thirst they gave Me vinegar to drink."

Psalm 69:20, 21.

Of the treatment He was to receive, He prophesied, "Dogs have compassed Me: the assembly of the wicked have enclosed Me: they pierced My hands and My feet. I may tell all My bones: they look and stare upon Me. They part My garments among them, and cast lots upon My vesture." Psalm 22:16-18.

692 These portrayals of the bitter suffering and cruel death of the Promised One, sad though they were, were rich in promise; for of Him whom "it pleased the Lord to bruise" and to put to grief, in order that He might become "an offering for sin," Jehovah declared:

"He shall see His seed, He shall prolong His days,
And the pleasure of the Lord shall prosper in His hand.
He shall see of the travail of His soul, and shall be satisfied:

"By His knowledge shall My righteous Servant justify many;
For He shall bear their iniquities.
Therefore will I divide Him a portion with the great,
And He shall divide the spoil with the strong;
Because He hath poured out His soul unto death:
And He was numbered with the transgressors;
And He bare the sin of many,
And made intercession for the transgressors."

Isaiah 53:10-12.

It was love for sinners that led Christ to pay the price of redemption. "He saw that there was no man, and wondered that there was no intercessor;" none other could ransom men and women from the power of the enemy; "therefore His arm brought salvation unto him; and His righteousness, it sustained him." Isaiah 59:16.

"Behold My Servant, whom I uphold;
Mine Elect, in whom My soul delighteth;
I have put My Spirit upon Him:
He shall bring forth judgment to the Gentiles."

Isaiah 42:1.

In His life no self-assertion was to be mingled. The homage which the world gives to position, to wealth, and to talent, was to be foreign to the Son of God. None of the means that men employ to win allegiance or to command homage, was the Messiah to use. His utter 693 renunciation of self was foreshadowed in the words:

"He shall not cry,
Nor lift up,
Nor cause His voice to be heard in the street.
A bruised reed shall He not break,
And the smoking flax shall He not quench."

Verses 2, 3.

In marked contrast to the teachers of His day was the Saviour to conduct Himself among men. In His life no noisy disputation, no ostentatious worship, no act to gain applause, was ever to be witnessed. The Messiah was to be hid in God, and God was to be revealed in the character of His Son. Without a knowledge of God, humanity would be eternally lost. Without divine help, men and women would sink lower and lower. Life and power must be imparted by Him who made the world. Man's necessities could be met in no other way.

It was further prophesied of the Messiah: "He shall not fail nor be discouraged, till He have set judgment in the earth: and the isles shall wait for His law." The Son of God was to "magnify the law, and make it honorable." Verses 4, 21. He was not to lessen its importance and binding claims; He was rather to exalt it. At the same time He was to free the divine precepts from those burdensome exactions placed upon them by man, whereby many were brought to discouragement in their efforts to serve God acceptably.

Of the mission of the Saviour the word of Jehovah was: "I the Lord have called Thee in righteousness, and will hold Thine hand, and will keep Thee, and give Thee for a covenant of 694 the people, for a light of the Gentiles; to open the blind eyes, to bring out the prisoners from the prison, and them that sit in darkness out of the prison house. I am the Lord: that is My name: and My glory will I not give to another, neither My praise to graven images. Behold, the former things are come to pass, and new things do I declare: before they spring forth I tell you of them." Verses 6-9.

695 Through the promised Seed, the God of Israel was to bring deliverance to Zion. "There shall come forth a Rod out of the stem of Jesse, and a Branch shall grow out of his roots." "Behold, a virgin shall conceive, and bear a Son, and shall call His name Immanuel. Butter and honey shall He eat, that He may know to refuse the evil, and choose the good." Isaiah 11:1; 7:14, 15.

"And the Spirit of the Lord shall rest upon Him, the Spirit of wisdom and understanding, the Spirit of counsel and might, the Spirit of knowledge and of the fear of the Lord; and shall make Him of quick understanding in the fear of the Lord: and He shall not judge after the sight of His eyes, neither reprove after the hearing of His ears: but with righteousness shall He judge the poor, and reprove with equity for the meek of the earth: and He shall smite the earth with the rod of His mouth, and with the breath of His lips shall He slay the wicked. And righteousness shall be the girdle of His loins, and faithfulness the girdle of His reins." "And in that day there shall be a Root of Jesse, which shall stand for an ensign of the people; to it shall the Gentiles seek: and His rest shall be glorious." Isaiah 11:2-5, 10.

"Behold the Man whose name is the Branch; . . . He shall build the temple of the Lord; and He shall bear the glory, and shall sit and rule upon His throne; and He shall be a priest upon His throne." Zechariah 6:12, 13.

A fountain was to be opened "for sin and for uncleanness" (Zechariah 13:1); the sons of men were to hear the blessed invitation:

696 "Ho, everyone that thirsteth, come ye to the waters,
And he that hath no money; come ye, buy, and eat;
Yea, come, buy wine and milk
Without money and without price.

"Wherefore do ye spend money for that which is not bread?
And your labor for that which satisfieth not?
Hearken diligently unto Me, and eat ye that which is good,
And let your soul delight itself in fatness.

"Incline your ear, and come unto Me:
Hear, and your soul shall live;
And I will make an everlasting covenant with you,
Even the sure mercies of David."
Isaiah 55:1-3.

To Israel the promise was made: "Behold, I have given Him for a witness to the people, a leader and commander to the people. Behold, thou shalt call a nation that thou knowest not, and nations that knew not thee shall run unto thee because of the Lord thy God, and for the Holy One of Israel; for He hath glorified thee." Verses 4, 5.

"I bring near My righteousness; it shall not be far off, and My salvation shall not tarry: and I will place salvation in Zion for Israel My glory." Isaiah 46:13.

In word and in deed the Messiah, during His earthly ministry, was to reveal to mankind the glory of God the Father. Every act of His life, every word spoken, every miracle wrought, was to make known to fallen humanity the infinite love of God.

"O Zion, that bringest good tidings,
Get thee up into the high mountain;
O Jerusalem, that bringest good tidings,
Lift up thy voice with strength;
Lift it up, be not afraid;
Say unto the cities of Judah, Behold your God!

"Behold, the Lord God will come with strong 697 hand,
And His arm shall rule for Him:
Behold, His reward is with Him,
And His work before Him.
He shall feed His flock like a shepherd:
He shall gather the lambs with His arm,
And carry them in His bosom,
And shall gently lead those that are with young."
Isaiah 40:9-11.

"And in that day shall the deaf hear the words of the Book,
And the eyes of the blind shall see out of obscurity, and out of darkness.
The meek also shall increase their joy in the Lord,
And the poor among men shall rejoice in the Holy One of Israel.

"They also that erred in spirit shall come to understanding,
And they that murmured shall learn doctrine."
Isaiah 29:18, 19, 24.

Thus, through patriarchs and prophets, as well as through types and symbols, God spoke to the world concerning the coming of a Deliverer from sin. A long line of inspired prophecy pointed to the advent of "the Desire of all nations." Haggai 2:7. Even the very place of His birth and the time of His appearance were minutely specified.

The Son of David must be born in David's city. Out of Bethlehem, said the prophet, "shall He come forth . . . that is to be ruler in Israel; whose goings forth have been from of old, from the days of eternity." Micah 5:2, margin.

"And thou Bethlehem, land of Judah,

Art in no wise least among the princes of
  Judah:
For out of thee shall come forth a Governor,
  Which shall be Shepherd of My people
  Israel."

Matthew 2:6, R.V.

"70 WEEKS ARE DECREED ["CUT OFF"] UPON THY PEOPLE"

490 YEARS

B.C. 457	B.C. 408	A.D. 27	A.D. 31	A.D. 34
			$3^{1}/_{2}$	$3^{1}/_{2}$
7 WEEKS, OR **49 YEARS**	3 SCORE AND 2(62) WEEKS, OR **434 YEARS**	1 WEEKS, OR **7 YEARS**		

A Chart of the "seventh weeks" which were
decreed to God's people. Christ's advent proved
the prophecy true.

The time of the first advent and of some of the
chief events clustering about the Saviour's lifework was made known by the angel Gabriel to
Daniel. "Seventy weeks," said the angel, "are
determined upon thy people and upon thy holy
city, to finish the transgression, and to make an
end of sins, and to make reconciliation for iniquity, and to bring in everlasting righteousness, and
to seal up the vision and prophecy, and to anoint
the most holy." Daniel 9:24. A day in prophecy
stands for a year. See Numbers 14:34; Ezekiel
4:6. The seventy weeks, or four hundred and
ninety days, represent four hundred and ninety
years. A starting point for this period is given:
"Know therefore and understand, that from the
going forth of the commandment to restore and
to build Jerusalem unto the Messiah the Prince
shall be seven weeks, and threescore and two
weeks" (Daniel 9:25), sixty-nine weeks, or four
hundred and eighty-three years. The commandment to restore and build Jerusalem, as completed by the decree of Artaxerxes Longimanus,
went into effect in the autumn of 457 B.C. See
Ezra 6:14; 7:1, 9. From this time four hundred
and eighty-three years extend to the autumn of
A.D. 27. According to the prophecy, this period
was to reach to the Messiah, the Anointed One.
In A.D. 27, Jesus at His baptism received the
anointing of the Holy Spirit and soon afterward
began His ministry. Then the message was proclaimed, "The time is fulfilled." Mark 1:15.

Then, said the angel, "He shall confirm the
covenant with many for one week [seven
years]." For seven years after the Saviour
entered on His ministry, the gospel was to be
preached especially to the Jews; for three and a
half years by Christ Himself, and afterward by
the apostles. "In the midst of the week He shall
cause the sacrifice and the oblation to cease."
Daniel 9:27. In the spring of A.D. 31, Christ, the

true Sacrifice, was offered on Calvary. Then the
veil of the temple was rent in twain, showing
that the sacredness and significance of the sacrificial service had departed. The time had come
for the earthly sacrifice and oblation to cease.

The one week—seven years—ended in A.D.
34. Then by the stoning of Stephen the Jews finally sealed their rejection of the gospel; the disciples
who were scattered abroad by persecution "went
everywhere preaching the word" (Acts 8:4); and
shortly after, Saul the persecutor was converted
and became Paul the apostle to the Gentiles.

The many prophecies concerning the Saviour's advent led the Hebrews to live in an attitude of constant expectancy. Many died in the
faith, not having received the promises. But having seen them afar off, they believed and confessed that they were strangers and pilgrims on
the earth. From the days of Enoch the promises
repeated through patriarchs and prophets had
kept alive the hope of His appearing.

Not at first had God revealed the exact time
of the first advent; and even when the prophecy
of Daniel made this known, not all rightly interpreted the message.

Century after century passed away; finally the
voices of the prophets ceased. The hand of the
oppressor was heavy upon Israel. As the Jews
departed from God, faith grew dim, and hope
well-nigh ceased to illuminate the future. The
words of the prophets were uncomprehended by
many; and those whose faith should have continued strong were ready to exclaim, "The days
are prolonged, and every vision faileth." Ezekiel
12:22. But in heaven's council the hour for the
coming of Christ had been determined; and
"when the fullness of the time was come, God
sent forth His Son, . . . to redeem them that were
under the law, that we might receive the adoption of sons." Galatians 4:4, 5.

Lessons must be given to humanity in the language of humanity. The Messenger of the
covenant must speak. His voice must be heard
in His own temple. He, the author of truth, must
separate truth from the chaff of man's utterance,
which had made it of no effect. The principles
of God's government and the plan of redemption must be clearly defined. The lessons of the
Old Testament must be fully set before men.

When the Saviour finally appeared "in the
likeness of men" (Philippians 2:7), and began His
ministry of grace, Satan could but bruise the heel,
while by every act of humiliation or suffering
Christ was bruising the head of His adversary.
The anguish that sin has brought was poured into
the bosom of the Sinless; yet while Christ
endured the contradiction of sinners against Himself, He was paying the debt for sinful man and
breaking the bondage in which humanity had
been held. Every pang of anguish, every insult,
was working out the deliverance of the race.

Could Satan have induced Christ to yield to a

single temptation, could he have led Him by one act or even thought to stain His perfect purity, the prince of darkness would have triumphed over man's Surety and would have gained the whole human family to himself. But while Satan could distress, he could not contaminate. He could cause agony, but not defilement. He made the life of Christ one long scene of conflict and trial, yet with every attack he was losing his hold upon humanity.

In the wilderness of temptation, in the Garden of Gethsemane, and on the cross, our Saviour measured weapons with the prince of darkness. His wounds became the trophies of His victory in behalf of the race. When Christ hung in agony upon the cross, while evil spirits rejoiced and evil men reviled, then indeed His heel was bruised by Satan. But that very act was crushing the serpent's head. Through death He destroyed "him that had the power of death, that is, the devil." Hebrews 2:14. This act decided the destiny of the rebel chief, and made forever sure the plan of salvation. In death He gained the victory over its power; in rising again, He opened the gates of the grave to all His followers. In that last great contest we see fulfilled the prophecy, "It shall bruise thy head, and thou shall bruise his heel." Genesis 3:15.

"Beloved, now are we the sons of God, and it doth not yet appear what we shall be: but we know that, when He shall appear, we shall be like Him; for we shall see Him as He is." 1 John 3:2. Our Redeemer has opened the way, so that the most sinful, the most needy, the most oppressed and despised, may find access to the Father.

"O Lord, Thou art my God;
I will exalt Thee,
I will praise Thy name;
For Thou hast done wonderful things;
Thy counsels of old are faithfulness and truth."

Isaiah 25:1.

59

"The House of Israel"

In proclaiming the truths of the everlasting gospel to every nation, kindred, tongue, and people, God's church on earth today is fulfilling the ancient prophecy, "Israel shall blossom and bud, and fill the face of the world with fruit." Isaiah 27:6. The followers of Jesus, in co-operation with heavenly intelligences, are rapidly occupying the waste places of the earth; and, as the result of their labors, an abundant fruitage of precious souls is developing. Today, as never before, the dissemination of Bible truth by

means of a consecrated church is bringing to the sons of men the benefits foreshadowed centuries ago in the promise to Abraham and to all Israel,—to God's church on earth in every age,—"I will bless thee, . . . and thou shalt be a blessing." Genesis 12:2.

This promise of blessing should have met fulfillment in large measure during the centuries following the return of the Israelites from the lands of their captivity. It was God's design that the whole earth be prepared for the first advent of Christ, even as today the way is preparing for His second coming. At the end of the years of humiliating exile, God graciously gave to His people Israel, through Zechariah, the assurance: "I am returned unto Zion, and will dwell in the midst of Jerusalem: and Jerusalem shall be called a city of truth; and the mountain of the Lord of hosts the holy mountain." And of His people He said, "Behold, . . . I will be their God, in truth and in righteousness." Zechariah 8:3, 7, 8.

These promises were conditional on obedience. The sins that had characterized the Israelites prior to the captivity, were not to be repeated. "Execute true judgment," the Lord exhorted those who were engaged in rebuilding; "and show mercy and compassions every man to his brother: and oppress not the widow, nor the fatherless, the stranger, nor the poor; and let none of you imagine evil against his brother." "Speak ye every man the truth to his neighbor; execute the judgment of truth and peace in your gates." Zechariah 7:9, 10; 8:16.

Rich were the rewards, both temporal and spiritual, promised those who should put into practice these principles of righteousness. "The seed shall be prosperous," the Lord declared; "the vine shall give her fruit, and the ground shall give her increase, and the heavens shall give their dew; and I will cause the remnant of this people to possess all these things. And it shall come to pass, that as ye were a curse among the heathen, O house of Judah, and house of Israel; so I will save you, and ye shall be a blessing." Zechariah 8:12, 13.

By the Babylonish captivity the Israelites were effectually cured of the worship of graven images. After their return, they gave much attention to religious instruction and to the study of that which had been written in the book of the law and in the prophets concerning the worship of the true God. The restoration of the temple enabled them to carry out fully the ritual services of the sanctuary. Under the leadership of Zerubbabel, of Ezra, and of Nehemiah they repeatedly covenanted to keep all the commandments and ordinances of Jehovah. The seasons of prosperity that followed gave ample evidence of God's willingness to accept and forgive, and yet with fatal shortsightedness they turned again and again from their glorious destiny and selfishly appropriated to themselves that which would have brought healing and spiritual life to countless multitudes.

This failure to fulfill the divine purpose was very apparent in Malachi's day. Sternly the Lord's messenger dealt with the evils that were robbing Israel of temporal prosperity and spiritual power. In his rebuke against transgressors the prophet spared neither priests nor people. "The burden of the word of the Lord to Israel" through Malachi was that the lessons of the past be not forgotten and that the covenant made by Jehovah with the house of Israel be kept with fidelity. Only by heartfelt repentance could the blessing of God be realized. "I pray you," the prophet pleaded, "beseech God that He will be gracious unto us." Malachi 1:1, 9.

Not by any temporary failure of Israel, however, was the plan of the ages for the redemption of mankind to be frustrated. Those to whom the prophet was speaking might not heed the message given, but the purposes of Jehovah were nevertheless to move steadily forward to their complete fulfillment. "From the rising of the sun even unto the going down of the same," the Lord declared through His messenger, "My name shall be great among the Gentiles; and in every place incense shall be offered unto My name, and a pure offering: for My name shall be great among the heathen." Malachi 1:11.

The covenant of "life and peace" God had made with the sons of Levi—the covenant which, if kept, would have brought untold blessing—the Lord now offered to renew with those who once had been spiritual leaders, but who through transgression had become "contemptible and base before all the people." Malachi 2:5, 9.

Solemnly evildoers were warned of the day of judgment to come and of Jehovah's purpose to visit with swift destruction every transgressor. Yet none were left without hope; Malachi's prophecies of judgment were accompanied by invitations to the impenitent to make their peace with God. "Return unto Me," the Lord urged; "and I will return unto you." Malachi 3:7.

It seems as if every heart must respond to such an invitation. The God of heaven is pleading with His erring children to return to Him, that they may again co-operate with Him in carrying forward His work in the earth. The Lord holds out His hand to take the hand of Israel and to help them to the narrow path of self-denial and self-sacrifice, to share with Him the heirship as sons of God. Will they be entreated? Will they discern their only hope?

How sad the record, that in Malachi's day the Israelites hesitated to yield their proud hearts in prompt and loving obedience and hearty co-operation! Self-vindication is apparent in their response, "Wherein shall we return?"

The Lord reveals to His people one of their special sins. "Will a man rob God?" He asks. "Yet ye have robbed Me." Still unconvicted of sin, the disobedient inquire, "Wherein have we robbed Thee?"

Definite indeed is the Lord's answer: "In tithes and offerings. Ye are cursed with a curse: for ye have robbed Me, even this whole nation. Bring ye all the tithes into the storehouse, that there may be meat in Mine house, and prove Me now herewith, saith the Lord of hosts, if I will not open you the windows of heaven, and pour you out a blessing, that there shall not be room enough to receive it. And I will rebuke the devourer for your sakes, and he shall not destroy the fruits of your ground; neither shall your vine cast her fruit before the time in the field, saith the Lord of hosts. And all nations shall call you blessed: for ye shall be a delightsome land, saith the Lord of hosts." Verses 7-12.

God blesses the work of men's hands, that they may return to Him His portion. He gives them the sunshine and the rain; He causes vegetation to flourish; He gives health and ability to acquire means. Every blessing comes from His bountiful hand, and He desires men and women to show their gratitude by returning Him a portion in tithes and offerings—in thank offerings, in freewill offerings, in trespass offerings. They are to devote their means to His service, that His vineyard may not remain a barren waste. They are to study what the Lord would do were He in their place. They are to take all difficult matters to Him in prayer. They are to reveal an unselfish interest in the building up of His work in all parts of the world.

Through messages such as those borne by Malachi, the last of the Old Testament prophets, as well as through oppression from heathen foes, the Israelites finally learned the lesson that true prosperity depends upon obedience to the law of God. But with many of the people, obedience was not the outflow of faith and love. Their motives were selfish. Outward service was rendered as a means of attaining to national greatness. The chosen people did not become the light of the world, but shut themselves away from the world as a safeguard against being seduced into idolatry. The restrictions which God had given, forbidding intermarriage between His people and the heathen, and prohibiting Israel from joining in the idolatrous practices of surrounding nations, were so perverted as to build up a wall of partition between the Israelites and all other peoples, thus shutting from others the very blessings which God had commissioned Israel to give to the world.

At the same time the Jews were, by their sins, separating themselves from God. They were unable to discern the deep spiritual significance of their symbolic service. In their self-righteousness they trusted to their own works, to the sac-

706

707

708

rifices and ordinances themselves, instead of relying upon the merits of Him to whom all these things pointed. Thus "going about to establish their own righteousness" (Romans 10:3), they built themselves up in a self-sufficient formalism. Wanting the Spirit and grace of God, they tried to make up for the lack by a rigorous observance of religious ceremonies and rites. Not content with the ordinances which God Himself had appointed, they encumbered the divine commands with countless exactions of their own devising. The greater their distance from God, the more rigorous they were in the observance of these forms.

With all these minute and burdensome exactions it was a practical impossibility for the people to keep the law. The great principles of righteousness set forth in the Decalogue, and the glorious truths shadowed in the symbolic service, were alike obscured, buried under a mass of human tradition and enactment. Those who were really desirous of serving God, and who tried to observe the whole law as enjoined by the priests and rulers, groaned under a heavy burden.

As a nation, the people of Israel, while desiring the advent of the Messiah, were so far separated from God in heart and life that they could have no true conception of the character or mission of the promised Redeemer. Instead of desiring redemption from sin, and the glory and peace of holiness, their hearts were fixed upon deliverance from their national foes, and restoration to worldly power. They looked for Messiah to come as a conqueror, to break every yoke, and exalt Israel to dominion over all nations. Thus Satan had succeeded in preparing the hearts of the people to reject the Saviour when He should appear. Their own pride of heart, and their false conceptions of His character and mission, would prevent them from honestly weighing the evidences of His Messiahship.

For more than a thousand years the Jewish people had waited the coming of the promised Saviour. Their brightest hopes had rested upon this event. For a thousand years, in song and prophecy, in temple rite and household prayer, His name had been enshrined; and yet when He came, they did not recognize Him as the Messiah for whom they had so long waited. "He came unto His own, and His own received Him not." John 1:11. To their world-loving hearts the Beloved of heaven was "as a root out of a dry ground." In their eyes He had "no form nor comeliness;" they discerned in Him no beauty that they should desire Him. Isaiah 53:2.

The whole life of Jesus of Nazareth among the Jewish people was a reproof to their selfishness, as revealed in their unwillingness to recognize the just claims of the Owner of the vineyard over which they had been placed as hus-

bandmen. They hated His example of truthfulness and piety; and when the final test came, the test which meant obedience unto eternal life or disobedience unto eternal death, they rejected the Holy One of Israel and became responsible for His crucifixion on Calvary's cross.

In the parable of the vineyard, Christ near the close of His earthly ministry called the attention of the Jewish teachers to the rich blessings bestowed upon Israel, and in these showed God's claim to their obedience. Plainly He set before them the glory of God's purpose, which through obedience they might have fulfilled. Withdrawing the veil from the future, He showed how, by failure to fulfill His purpose, the whole nation was forfeiting His blessing and bringing ruin upon itself.

"There was a certain householder," Christ said, "which planted a vineyard, and hedged it round about, and digged a wine press in it, and built a tower, and let it out to husbandmen, and went into a far country." Matthew 21:33.

Thus the Saviour referred to "the vineyard of the Lord of hosts," which the prophet Isaiah centuries before had declared to be "the house of Israel." Isaiah 5:7.

"And when the time of the fruit drew near," Christ continued, the owner of the vineyard "sent his servants to the husbandmen, that they might receive the fruits of it. And the husbandmen took his servants, and beat one, and killed another, and stoned another. Again, he sent other servants more than the first: and they did unto them likewise. But last of all he sent unto them his son, saying, They will reverence my son. But when the husbandmen saw the son, they said among themselves, This is the heir; come, let us kill him, and let us seize on his inheritance. And they caught him, and cast him out of the vineyard, and slew him."

Having portrayed before the priests their crowning act of wickedness, Christ now put to them the question, "When the lord therefore of the vineyard cometh, what will he do unto those husbandmen?" The priests had been following the narrative with deep interest; and without considering the relation of the subject to themselves, they joined with the people in answering, "He will miserably destroy those wicked men, and will let out his vineyard unto other husbandmen, which shall render him the fruits in their seasons."

Unwittingly they had pronounced their own doom. Jesus looked upon them, and under His searching gaze they knew that He read the secrets of their hearts. His divinity flashed out before them with unmistakable power. They saw in the husbandmen a picture of themselves, and they involuntarily exclaimed, "God forbid!"

Solemnly and regretfully Christ asked: "Did ye never read in the Scriptures, The stone which the builders rejected, the same is become the head of the corner: this is the Lord's doing, and it is marvelous in our eyes? Therefore say I unto you, The kingdom of God shall be taken from you, and given to a nation bringing forth the fruits thereof. And whosoever shall fall on this stone shall be broken: but on whomsoever it shall fall, it will grind him to powder." Matthew 21:34-44.

Christ would have averted the doom of the Jewish nation if the people had received Him. But envy and jealousy made them implacable. They determined that they would not receive Jesus of Nazareth as the Messiah. They rejected the Light of the world, and henceforth their lives were surrounded with darkness as the darkness of midnight. The doom foretold came upon the Jewish nation. Their own fierce passions, uncontrolled, wrought their ruin. In their blind rage they destroyed one another. Their rebellious, stubborn pride brought upon them the 713 wrath of their Roman conquerors. Jerusalem was destroyed, the temple laid in ruins, and its site plowed like a field. The children of Judah perished by the most horrible forms of death. Millions were sold to serve as bondmen in heathen lands.

That which God purposed to do for the world through Israel, the chosen nation, He will finally accomplish through His church on earth today. 714 He has "let out His vineyard unto other husbandmen," even to His covenant-keeping people, who faithfully "render Him the fruits in their seasons." Never has the Lord been without true representatives on this earth who have made His interests their own. These witnesses for God are numbered among the spiritual Israel, and to them will be fulfilled all the covenant promises made by Jehovah to His ancient people.

Today the church of God is free to carry forward to completion the divine plan for the salvation of a lost race. For many centuries God's people suffered a restriction of their liberties. The preaching of the gospel in its purity was prohibited, and the severest of penalties were visited upon those who dared disobey the mandates of men. As a consequence, the Lord's great moral vineyard was almost wholly unoccupied. The people were deprived of the light of God's word. The darkness of error and superstition threatened to blot out a knowledge of true religion. God's church on earth was as verily in captivity during this long period of relentless persecution as were the children of Israel held captive in Babylon during the period of the exile.

But, thank God, His church is no longer in bondage. To spiritual Israel have been restored the privileges accorded the people of God at the time of their deliverance from Babylon. In every part of the earth, men and women which John the revelator prophesied would be proclaimed prior to the second coming of Christ: "Fear God, and give glory to Him; for the hour of His judgment is come." Revelation 14:7.

No longer have the hosts of evil power to 715 keep the church captive; for "Babylon is fallen, is fallen, that great city," which hath "made all nations drink of the wine of the wrath of her fornication;" and to spiritual Israel is given the message, "Come out of her, My people, that ye be not partakers of her sins, and that ye receive not of her plagues." Verse 8; 18:4. As the captive exiles heeded the message, "Flee out of the midst of Babylon" (Jeremiah 51:6), and were restored to the Land of Promise, so those who fear God today are heeding the message to withdraw from spiritual Babylon, and soon they are to stand as trophies of divine grace in the earth made new, the heavenly Canaan.

In Malachi's day the mocking inquiry of the impenitent, "Where is the God of judgment?" met with the solemn response: "The Lord . . . shall suddenly come to His temple, even the Messenger of the covenant. . . . But who may abide the day of His coming? and who shall stand when He appeareth? for He is like a refiner's fire, and like fullers' soap: and He shall sit as a refiner and purifier of silver: and He shall purify the sons of Levi, and purge them as gold and silver, that they may offer unto the Lord an offering in righteousness. Then shall the offering of Judah and Jerusalem be pleasant unto the Lord, as in the days of old, and as in former years." Malachi 2:17; 3:1-4.

When the promised Messiah was about to appear, the message of the forerunner of Christ was: Repent, publicans and sinners; repent, Pharisees and Sadducees; "for the kingdom of heaven is at hand." Matthew 3:2.

Today, in the spirit and power of Elias and 716 of John the Baptist, messengers of God's appointment are calling the attention of a judgment-bound world to the solemn events soon to take place in connection with the closing hours of probation and the appearance of Christ Jesus as King of kings and Lord of lords. Soon every man is to be judged for the deeds done in the body. The hour of God's judgment has come, and upon the members of His church on earth rests the solemn responsibility of giving warning to those who are standing as it were on the very brink of eternal ruin. To every human being in the wide world who will give heed must be made plain the principles at stake in the great controversy being waged, principles upon which hang the destinies of all mankind.

In these final hours of probation for the sons of men, when the fate of every soul is so soon to be decided forever, the Lord of heaven and earth expects His church to arouse to action as never before. Those who have been made free in Christ through a knowledge of precious truth, are regarded by the Lord Jesus as His chosen ones, favored above all other people on the face of the earth; and He is counting on them to show forth the praises of Him who hath called them out of darkness into marvelous light. The blessings which are so liberally bestowed are to be communicated to others. The good news of salvation is to go to every nation, kindred, tongue, and people.

In the visions of the prophets of old the Lord of glory was represented as bestowing special light upon His church in the days of darkness and unbelief preceding His second coming. As the Sun of Righteousness, He was to arise upon His church, "with healing in His wings." Malachi 4:2. And from every true disciple was to be diffused an influence for life, courage, helpfulness, and true healing.

The coming of Christ will take place in the darkest period of this earth's history. The days of Noah and of Lot picture the condition of the world just before the coming of the Son of man. The Scriptures, pointing forward to this time, declare that Satan will work with all power and "with all deceivableness of unrighteousness." 2 Thessalonians 2:9, 10. His working is plainly revealed by the rapidly increasing darkness, the multitudinous errors, heresies, and delusions of these last days. Not only is Satan leading the world captive, but his deceptions are leavening the professed churches of our Lord Jesus Christ. The great apostasy will develop into darkness deep as midnight. To God's people it will be a night of trial, a night of weeping, a night of persecution for the truth's sake. But out of that night of darkness God's light will shine.

He causes "the light to shine out of darkness." 2 Corinthians 4:6. When "the earth was without form, and void; and darkness was upon the face of the deep," "the Spirit of God moved upon the face of the waters. And God said, Let there be light: and there was light." Genesis 1:2, 3. So in the night of spiritual darkness, God's word goes forth, "Let there be light." To His people He says, "Arise, shine; for thy light is come, and the glory of the Lord is risen upon thee." Isaiah 60:1.

"Behold," says the Scripture, "the darkness shall cover the earth, and gross darkness the people: but the Lord shall arise upon thee, and His glory shall be seen upon thee." Verse 2. Christ, the outshining of the Father's glory, came to the world as its light. He came to represent God to men, and of Him it is written that He was anointed "with the Holy Ghost and with power," and "went about doing good." Acts 10:38. In the synagogue at Nazareth He said, "The Spirit of the Lord is upon Me, because He hath anointed Me to preach the gospel to the poor; He hath sent Me to heal the brokenhearted, to preach deliverance to the captives, and recovering of sight to the blind, to set at liberty them that are bruised, to preach the acceptable year of the Lord." Luke 4:18, 19. This was the work He commissioned His disciples to do. "Ye are the light of the world," He said. "Let your light so shine before men, that they may see your good works, and glorify your Father which is in heaven." Matthew 5:14, 16.

This is the work which the prophet Isaiah describes when he says: "Is it not to deal thy bread to the hungry, and that thou bring the poor that are cast out to thy house? when thou seest the naked, that thou cover him; and that thou hide not thyself from thine own flesh? Then shall thy light break forth as the morning, and thine health shall spring forth speedily: and thy righteousness shall go before thee; the glory of the Lord shall be thy rereward." Isaiah 58:7, 8.

Thus in the night of spiritual darkness God's glory is to shine forth through His church in lifting up the bowed down and comforting those that mourn.

All around us are heard the wails of a world's sorrow. On every hand are the needy and distressed. It is ours to aid in relieving and softening life's hardships and misery. The wants of the soul only the love of Christ can satisfy. If Christ is abiding in us, our hearts will be full of divine sympathy. The sealed fountains of earnest, Christlike love will be unsealed.

There are many from whom hope has departed. Bring back the sunshine to them. Many have lost their courage. Speak to them words of cheer. Pray for them. There are those who need the bread of life. Read to them from the word of God. Upon many is a soul sickness which no earthly balm can reach nor physician heal. Pray for these souls. Bring them to Jesus. Tell them that there is a balm in Gilead and a Physician there.

Light is a blessing, a universal blessing, pouring forth its treasures on a world unthankful, unholy, demoralized. So it is with the light of the Sun of Righteousness. The whole earth, wrapped as it is in the darkness of sin and sorrow and pain, is to be lighted with the knowledge of God's love. From no sect, rank, or class of people is the light shining from heaven's throne to be excluded.

The message of hope and mercy is to be carried to the ends of the earth. Whosoever will, may reach forth and take hold of God's strength and make peace with Him, and he shall make peace. No longer are the heathen to be wrapped in midnight darkness. The gloom is to disappear before the bright beams of the Sun of Righteousness.

Christ has made every provision that His church shall be a transformed body, illumined with the Light of the world, possessing the glory of Immanuel. It is His purpose that every Christian shall be surrounded with a spiritual atmosphere of light and peace. He desires that we shall reveal His own joy in our lives.

"Arise, shine; for thy light is come, and the glory of the Lord is risen upon thee." Isaiah 60:1. Christ is coming with power and great glory. He is coming with His own glory and with the glory of the Father. And the holy angels will attend Him on His way. While all the world is plunged in darkness, there will be light in every dwelling of the saints. They will catch the first light of His second appearing. The unsullied light will shine from His splendor, and Christ the Redeemer will be admired by all who have served Him. While the wicked flee, Christ's followers will rejoice in His presence.

Then it is that the redeemed from among men will receive their promised inheritance. Thus God's purpose for Israel will meet with literal fulfillment. That which God purposes, man is powerless to disannul. Even amid the working of evil, God's purposes have been moving steadily forward to their accomplishment. It was thus with the house of Israel throughout the history of the divided monarchy; it is thus with spiritual Israel today.

The seer of Patmos, looking down through the ages to the time of this restoration of Israel in the earth made new, testified:

"I beheld, and, lo, a great multitude, which no man could number, of all nations, and kindreds, 721 and people, and tongues, stood before the throne, and before the Lamb, clothed with white robes, and palms in their hands; and cried with a loud voice, saying, Salvation to our God which sitteth upon the throne, and unto the Lamb.

"And all the angels stood round about the throne, and about the elders and the four beasts ["living creatures," R.V.], and fell before the throne on their faces, and worshiped God, saying, Amen: Blessing, and glory, and wisdom, and thanksgiving, and honor, and power, and might, be unto our God forever and ever."

"And I heard as it were the voice of a great multitude, and as the voice of many waters, and as the voice of mighty thunderings, saying, Alleluia: for the Lord God omnipotent reigneth. Let us be glad and rejoice, and give honor to Him." "He is Lord of lords, and King of kings: and they that are with Him are called, and chosen, and faithful." Revelation 7:9-12; 19:6, 7; 17:14.

722 **60**

Visions of Future Glory

In the darkest days of her long conflict with evil, the church of God has been given revelations of the eternal purpose of Jehovah. His people have been permitted to look beyond the trials of the present to the triumphs of the future, when, the warfare having been accomplished, the redeemed will enter into possession of the promised land. These visions of future glory, scenes pictured by the hand of God, should be dear to His church today, when the controversy of the ages is rapidly closing and the promised blessings are soon to be realized in all their fullness.

Many were the messages of comfort given the church by the prophets of old. "Comfort ye, comfort ye My people" (Isaiah 40:1), was Isaiah's commission from God; and with the commission were given wonderful visions that have been the believers' hope and joy through all the centuries that have followed. Despised of men, persecuted, forsaken, God's children in every 723 age have nevertheless been sustained by His sure promises. By faith they have looked forward to the time when He will fulfill to His church the assurance, "I will make thee an eternal excellency, a joy of many generations." Isaiah 60:15.

Often the church militant is called upon to suffer trial and affliction; for not without severe conflict is the church to triumph. "The bread of adversity," "the water of affliction" (Isaiah 30:20), these are the common lot of all; but none who put their trust in the One mighty to deliver will be utterly overwhelmed. "Thus saith the Lord that created thee, O Jacob, and He that formed thee, O Israel, Fear not: for I have redeemed thee, I have called thee by thy name; thou art Mine. When thou passest through the waters, I will be with thee; and through the rivers, they shall not overflow thee: when thou walkest through the fire, thou shalt not be burned; neither shall the flame kindle upon thee. For I am the Lord thy God, the Holy One of Israel, thy Saviour: I gave Egypt for thy ransom, Ethiopia and Seba for thee. Since thou wast precious in My sight, thou hast been honorable, and I have loved thee: therefore will I give men for thee, and people for thy life." Isaiah 43:1-4.

There is forgiveness with God; there is acceptance full and free through the merits of Jesus, our crucified and risen Lord. Isaiah heard the Lord declaring to His chosen ones: "I, even I, am He that blotteth out thy transgressions for Mine own sake, and will not remember thy sins. Put Me in remembrance: let us plead together: declare thou, that thou mayest be justified." "Thou shalt know that I the Lord am thy Sav- 724 iour and thy Redeemer, the Mighty One of Jacob." Verses 25, 26; 60:16.

"The rebuke of His people shall He take away," the prophet declared. "They shall call them, The holy people, The redeemed of the Lord." He hath appointed "to give unto them beauty for ashes, the oil of joy for mourning, the garment of praise for the spirit of heaviness; that they might be called trees of righteousness, the planting of the Lord, that He might be glorified."

"Awake, awake; put on thy strength, O Zion;
Put on thy beautiful garments, O Jerusalem, the Holy City:
For henceforth there shall no more come unto thee the uncircumcised and the unclean.

"Shake thyself from the dust;
Arise, and sit down, O Jerusalem:
Loose thyself from the bands of thy neck, O captive daughter of Zion."

"O thou afflicted, tossed with tempest, and not comforted,
Behold, I will lay thy stones with fair colors,
And lay thy foundations with sapphires.

"And I will make thy windows of agates,
And thy gates of carbuncles,
And all thy borders of pleasant stones.

"And all thy children shall be taught of the Lord;
And great shall be the peace of thy children.
In righteousness shalt thou be established:

"Thou shalt be far from oppression; for thou shalt not fear:
And from terror; for it shall not come near thee.
Behold, they shall surely gather together, but not by Me:
Whosoever shall gather together against thee shall fall for thy sake. . . .

725 "No weapon that is formed against thee shall prosper;
And every tongue that shall rise against thee in judgment thou shalt condemn.
This is the heritage of the servants of the Lord,
And their righteousness is of Me, saith the Lord."
Isaiah 25:8; 62:12; 61:3; 52:1, 2; 54:11-17.

Clad in the armor of Christ's righteousness, the church is to enter upon her final conflict. "Fair as the moon, clear as the sun, and terrible as an army with banners" (Song of Solomon 6:10), she is to go forth into all the world, conquering and to conquer.

The darkest hour of the church's struggle with the powers of evil is that which immediately precedes the day of her final deliverance. But none who trust in God need fear; for "when the blast of the terrible ones is as a storm against the wall," God will be to His church "a refuge from the storm." Isaiah 25:4.

In that day only the righteous are promised deliverance. "The sinners in Zion are afraid; fearfulness hath surprised the hypocrites. Who among us shall dwell with the devouring fire? who among us shall dwell with everlasting burnings? He that walketh righteously, and speaketh uprightly; he that despiseth the gain of oppressions, that shaketh his hands from holding of bribes, that stoppeth his ears from hearing of blood, and shutteth his eyes from seeing evil; he shall dwell on high: his place of defense shall be the munitions of rocks: bread shall be given him; his waters shall be sure." Isaiah 33:14-16.

The word of the Lord to His faithful ones is: "Come, My people, enter thou into thy chambers, and shut thy doors about thee: hide thyself 726 as it were for a little moment, until the indignation be overpast. For, behold, the Lord cometh out of His place to punish the inhabitants of the earth for their iniquity." Isaiah 26:20, 21.

In visions of the great judgment day the inspired messengers of Jehovah were given glimpses of the consternation of those unprepared to meet their Lord in peace.

"Behold, the Lord maketh the earth empty, and maketh it waste, and turneth it upside down, and scattereth abroad the inhabitants thereof; . . . because they have transgressed the laws, changed the ordinance, broken the everlasting covenant. Therefore hath the curse devoured the earth, and they that dwell therein are desolate. . . . The mirth of tabrets ceaseth, the noise of them that rejoice endeth, the joy of the harp ceaseth." Isaiah 24:1-8.

"Alas for the day! for the day of the Lord is at hand, and as a destruction from the Almighty shall it come. . . . The seed is rotten under their clods, the garners are laid desolate, the barns are broken down; for the corn is withered. How do the beasts groan! the herds of cattle are perplexed, because they have no pasture; yea, the flocks of sheep are made desolate." "The vine is dried up, and the fig tree languisheth; the pomegranate tree, the palm tree also, and the apple tree, even all the trees of the field, are withered: because joy is withered away from the sons of men." Joel 1:15-18, 12.

"I am pained at my very heart," Jeremiah exclaims as he beholds the desolations wrought during the closing scenes of earth's history. "I cannot hold my peace, because thou hast heard, 727 O my soul, the sound of the trumpet, the alarm of war. Destruction upon destruction is cried; for the whole land is spoiled." Jeremiah 4:19, 20.

"The loftiness of man shall be bowed down," declares Isaiah of the day of God's vengeance, "and the haughtiness of men shall be made low: and the Lord alone shall be exalted in that day. And the idols He shall utterly abolish. . . . In that day a man shall cast his idols of silver, and his idols of gold, which they made each one for himself to worship, to the moles and to the bats; to go into the clefts of the rocks, and into the tops of the ragged rocks, for fear of the Lord, and for the glory of His majesty, when He ariseth to shake terribly the earth." Isaiah 2:17-21.

Of those times of transition, when the pride of man shall be laid low, Jeremiah testifies: "I beheld the earth, and, lo, it was without form, and void; and the heavens, and they had no light. I beheld the mountains, and, lo, they trembled, and all the hills moved lightly. I beheld, and, lo, there was no man, and all the birds of the heavens were fled. I beheld, and, lo, the fruitful place was a wilderness, and all the cities thereof were broken down." Jeremiah 4:23-26; 30:7.

The day of wrath to the enemies of God is the day of final deliverance to His church. The prophet declares:

"Strengthen ye the weak hands,
And confirm the feeble knees.
728 Say to them that are of a fearful heart, Be strong, fear not:
Behold, your God will come with vengeance,
Even God with a recompense;
He will come and save you."

"He will swallow up death in victory; and the Lord God will wipe away tears from off all faces; and the rebuke of His people shall He take away from off all the earth: for the Lord hath spoken it." Isaiah 35:3, 4; 25:8. And as the prophet beholds the Lord of glory descending from heaven, with all the holy angels, to gather the remnant church from among the nations of earth, he hears the waiting ones unite in the exultant cry:

"Lo, this is our God;
We have waited for Him,
And He will save us:
This is the Lord;
We have waited for Him,
We will be glad and rejoice in His salvation."

Isaiah 25:9.

The voice of the Son of God is heard calling forth the sleeping saints, and as the prophet beholds them coming from the prison house of death, he exclaims, "Thy dead men shall live, together with my dead body shall they arise. Awake and sing, ye that dwell in dust: for thy dew is as the dew of herbs, and the earth shall cast out the dead."

"Then the eyes of the blind shall be opened,
And the ears of the deaf shall be unstopped.

Then shall the lame man leap as an hart,
And the tongue of the dumb sing."
Isaiah 26:19; 35:5, 6.

In the visions of the prophet, those who have triumphed over sin and the grave are now seen happy in the presence of their Maker, talking freely with Him as man talked with God in the beginning. "Be ye glad," the Lord bids them, "and rejoice forever in that which I create: for, behold, I create Jerusalem a rejoicing, and her people a joy. And I will rejoice in Jerusalem, and joy in My people: and the voice of weeping shall be no more heard in her, nor the voice of crying." "The inhabitant shall not say, I am sick: the people that dwell therein shall be forgiven their iniquity."

"In the wilderness shall waters break out,
And streams in the desert.
And the parched ground shall become a pool,
And the thirsty land springs of water."

"Instead of the thorn shall come up the fir tree,
And instead of the brier shall come up the myrtle tree."

"And an highway shall be there, and a way,
And it shall be called The way of holiness;
The unclean shall not pass over it;
But it shall be for those:
The wayfaring men, though fools, shall not err therein."

"Speak ye comfortably to Jerusalem, and cry unto her, that her warfare is accomplished, that her iniquity is pardoned: for she hath received of the Lord's hand double for all her sins." Isaiah 65:18, 19; 33:24; 35:6, 7; 55:13; 35:8; 40:2.

As the prophet beholds the redeemed dwelling in the City of God, free from sin and from all marks of the curse, in rapture he exclaims, "Rejoice ye with Jerusalem, and be glad with her, all ye that love her: rejoice for joy with her."

"Violence shall no more be heard in thy land,   730
Wasting nor destruction within thy borders;
But thou shalt call thy walls Salvation,
And thy gates Praise.

"The sun shall be no more thy light by day;
Neither for brightness shall the moon give light unto thee:
But the Lord shall be unto thee an everlasting light,
And thy God thy glory.

"Thy sun shall no more go down;
Neither shall thy moon withdraw itself:
For the Lord shall be thine everlasting light,

And the days of thy mourning shall be ended.

"Thy people also shall be all righteous:
They shall inherit the land forever,
The branch of My planting,
The work of My hands,
That I may be glorified."
                    Isaiah 66:10; 60:18-21.

The prophet caught the sound of music there, and song, such music and song as, save in the visions of God, no mortal ear has heard or mind conceived. "The ransomed of the Lord shall return, and come to Zion with songs and everlasting joy upon their heads: they shall obtain joy and gladness, and sorrow and sighing shall flee away." "Joy and gladness shall be found therein, thanksgiving, and the voice of melody." "As well the singers as the players on instruments shall be there." "They shall lift up their voice, they shall sing for the majesty of the Lord." Isaiah 35:10; 51:3; Psalm 87:7; Isaiah 24:14.

In the earth made new, the redeemed will engage in the occupations and pleasures that brought happiness to Adam and Eve in the beginning. The Eden life will be lived, the life in garden and field. "They shall build houses, and inhabit them; and they shall plant vineyards, and eat the fruit of them. They shall not build, and another inhabit; they shall not plant, and another eat: for as the days of a tree are the days of My people, and Mine elect shall long enjoy the work of their hands." Isaiah 65:21, 22.

There every power will be developed, every capability increased. The grandest enterprises will be carried forward, the loftiest aspirations will be reached, the highest ambitions realized. And still there will appear new heights to surmount, new wonders to admire, new truths to comprehend, fresh objects of study to call forth the powers of body and mind and soul.

The prophets to whom these great scenes were revealed longed to understand their full import. They "inquired and searched diligently: . . . searching what, or what manner of time the Spirit of Christ which was in them did signify. . . . Unto whom it was revealed, that not unto themselves, but unto us they did minister the things, which are now reported unto you." 1 Peter 1:10-12.

To us who are standing on the very verge of their fulfillment, of what deep moment, what living interest, are these delineations of the things to come—events for which, since our first parents turned their steps from Eden, God's children have watched and waited, longed and prayed!

Fellow pilgrim, we are still amid the shadows and turmoil of earthly activities; but soon our Saviour is to appear to bring deliverance and rest. Let us by faith behold the blessed hereafter as pictured by the hand of God. He who died for the sins of the world is opening wide the gates of Paradise to all who believe on Him. Soon the battle will have been fought, the victory won. Soon we shall see Him in whom our hopes of eternal life are centered. And in His presence the trials and sufferings of this life will seem as nothingness. The former things "shall not be remembered, nor come into mind." "Cast not away therefore your confidence, which hath great recompense of reward. For ye have need of patience, that, after ye have done the will of God, ye might receive the promise. For yet a little while, and He that shall come will come, and will not tarry." "Israel shall be saved . . . with an everlasting salvation: ye shall not be ashamed nor confounded world without end." Isaiah 65:17; Hebrews 10:35-37; Isaiah 45:17.

Look up, look up, and let your faith continually increase. Let this faith guide you along the narrow path that leads through the gates of the city into the great beyond, the wide, unbounded future of glory that is for the redeemed. "Be patient therefore, brethren, unto the coming of the Lord. Behold, the husbandman waiteth for the precious fruit of the earth, and hath long patience for it, until he receive the early and latter rain. Be ye also patient; stablish your hearts: for the coming of the Lord draweth nigh." James 5:7, 8.

The nations of the saved will know no other law than the law of heaven. All will be a happy, united family, clothed with the garments of praise and thanksgiving. Over the scene the morning stars will sing together, and the sons of God will shout for joy, while God and Christ will unite in proclaiming, "There shall be no more sin, neither shall there be any more death."

"And it shall come to pass, that from one new moon to another, and from one Sabbath to another, shall all flesh come to worship before Me, saith the Lord." "The glory of the Lord shall be revealed, and all flesh shall see it together." "The Lord God will cause righteousness and praise to spring forth before all the nations." "In that day shall the Lord of hosts be for a crown of glory, and for a diadem of beauty, unto the residue of His people."

"The Lord shall comfort Zion: He will comfort all her waste places; and He will make her wilderness like Eden, and her desert like the garden of the Lord." "The glory of Lebanon shall be given unto it, the excellency of Carmel and Sharon." "Thou shalt no more be termed Forsaken; neither shall thy land any more be termed Desolate: but thou shalt be called My Delight, and thy land Beulah. . . . As the bridegroom rejoiceth over the bride, so shall thy God rejoice over thee." Isaiah 66:23; 40:5; 61:11; 28:5; 51:3; 35:2; 62:4, 5, margin.

3

THE DESIRE OF AGES

INDEX

SUMMARY	PAGE	SUMMARY	PAGE

DA

PREFACE

In the hearts of all mankind, of whatever race or station in life, there are inexpressible longings for something they do not now possess. This longing is implanted in the very constitution of man by a merciful God, that man may not be satisfied with his present conditions or attainments, whether bad, or good, or better. God desires that the human shall seek the best, and find it to the eternal blessing of his soul.

Satan, by wily scheme and craft, has perverted these longings of the human heart. He makes men believe that this desire may be satisfied by pleasure, by wealth, by ease, by fame, by power; but those who have been thus deceived by him (and they number myriads) find all these things pall upon the sense, leaving the soul as barren and unsatisfied as before.

It is God's design that this longing of the human heart should lead to the One who alone is able to satisfy it. The desire is of Him that it may lead to Him, the fullness and fulfillment of that desire. That fullness is found in Jesus the Christ, the Son of the Eternal God. "For it was the good pleasure of the Father that in Him should all the fullness dwell;" "for in Him dwelleth all the fullness of the Godhead bodily." And it is also true that "in Him ye are made full" with respect to every desire divinely implanted and normally followed.

Haggai calls Him "the Desire of all nations," and we may well call Him "*the Desire of all ages*," even as He is "the King of ages."

It is the purpose of this book to set forth Jesus Christ as the One in whom every longing may be satisfied. There is many a "Life of Christ" written, excellent books, large funds of information, elaborate essays on chronology and contemporaneous history, customs, and events, with much of the teaching and many glimpses of the many-sided life of Jesus of Nazareth. Yet it may be truly said, "The half has never been told."

It is not, however, the purpose of this work to set forth a harmony of the Gospels, or even to give in strictly chronological order the important events and wonderful lessons of the life of Christ; its purpose is to present the love of God as revealed in His Son, the divine beauty of the life of Christ, of which all may partake, and not to satisfy the desires of the merely curious nor the questionings of critics. But even as by the attraction of His own goodness of character Jesus drew His disciples unto Himself, and by His personal presence, by His sympathetic touch and feeling in all their infirmities and needs, and by His constant association, transformed their characters from the earthly to the heavenly, from the selfish to the sacrificing, from smallhearted ignorance and prejudice to largehearted knowledge and profound love for souls of all nations and races, even so it is the purpose of this book so to present the blessed Redeemer as to help the reader to come to Him face to face, heart to heart, and find in Him, even as did the disciples of old, Jesus the Mighty One, who saves "to the uttermost," and transforms to His own divine image all those who come unto God by Him. Yet how impossible it is to reveal His Life! It is like attempting to put upon canvas the living rainbow; into characters of black and white the sweetest music.

In the following pages the author, a woman of large and deep and long experience in the things of God, has set forth new beauties from the life of Jesus. She has brought many new gems from the precious casket. She opens before the reader undreamed-of riches from this infinite treasure house. New and glorious light flashes forth from many a familiar passage, the depth of which the reader supposed he had long before fathomed. to state it in brief, Jesus Christ is revealed as the Fullness of the Godhead, the infinitely merciful Saviour of sinners, the Sun of Righteousness, the merciful High Priest, the Healer of all human maladies and diseases, the tender, compassionate Friend, the constant, ever-present and helpful Companion, the Prince of the House of David, the Shield of His people, the Prince of Peace, the Coming King, the Everlasting Father, the culmination and fruition of the desires and hopes of all the ages.

Under the blessing of God this book is given to the world with the prayer that the Lord by His Spirit will make the words of this book words of life to many souls whose longings and desires are yet unsatisfied; that they "may know Him, and the power of His resurrection, and the fellowship of His sufferings," and finally, throughout a blessed eternity, at His right hand, share in "that fullness of joy," and "pleasures forevermore," which will be the ripened fruitage of all those who find in Him the all in all, "the Chiefest among ten thousand," and "the One altogether lovely."

Publishers.

51. "The Light of Life"
52. The Divine Shepherd
53. The Last Journey From Galilee
54. The Good Samaritan

CONTENTS

1. "God With Us" 506
2. The Chosen People 509
3. "The Fullness of the Time" 510
4. Unto You a Saviour 513
5. The Dedication 514
6. "We Have Seen His Star" 517
7. As a Child 520
8. The Passover Visit 523
9. Days of Conflict 526
10. The Voice in the Wilderness 529
11. The Baptism 533
12. The Temptation 535
13. The Victory 539
14. "We Have Found the Messias" 542
15. At the Marriage Feast 546
16. In His Temple 550
17. Nicodemus 554
18. "He Must Increase" 558
19. At Jacob's Well 560
20. "Except Ye See Signs and Wonders" 564
21. Bethesda and the Sanhedrin 566
22. Imprisonment and Death of John 571
23. "The Kingdom of God Is at Hand" 576
24. "Is Not This the Carpenter's Son?" 578
25. The Call by the Sea 581
26. At Capernaum 584
27. "Thou Canst Make Me Clean" 588
28. Levi-Matthew 592
29. The Sabbath 596
30. "He Ordained Twelve" 599
31. The Sermon on the Mount 602

32. The Centurion 609
33. Who Are My Brethren? 611
34. The Invitation 614
35. "Peace, Be Still" 615
36. The Touch of Faith 619
37. The First Evangelists 621
38. Come Rest Awhile 625
39. "Give Ye Them to Eat" 627
40. A Night on the Lake 630
41. The Crisis in Galilee 633
42. Tradition 638
43. Barriers Broken Down 639
44. The True Sign 642
45. The Foreshadowing of the Cross 644
46. He Was Transfigured 648
47. Ministry 650
48. Who Is the Greatest? 652
49. At the Feast of Tabernacles 656
50. Among Snares 659
51. "The Light of Life" 663
52. The Divine Shepherd 668
53. The Last Journey From Galilee 671
54. The Good Samaritan 675
55. Not With Outward Show 678
56. Blessing the Children 680
57. "One Thing Thou Lackest" 682
58. "Lazarus, Come Forth" 684
59. Priestly Plottings 688
60. The Law of the New Kingdom 691
61. Zacchaeus 693
62. The Feast at Simon's House 694

63. "Thy King Cometh"	699	76. Judas	753
64. A Doomed People	703	77. In Pilate's Judgment Hall	756
65. The Temple Cleansed Again	705	78. Calvary	763
66. Controversy	711	79. "It Is Finished"	769
67. Woes on the Pharisees	714	80. In Joseph's Tomb	772
68. In the Outer Court	719	81. "The Lord Is Risen"	777
69. On the Mount of Olives	721	82. "Why Weepest Thou?"	779
70. "The Least of These My Brethren"	725	83. The Walk to Emmaus	782
71. A Servant of Servants	727	84. "Peace Be Unto You"	784
72. "In Remembrance of Me"	731	85. By the Sea Once More	786
73. "Let Not Your Heart Be Troubled"	735	86. Go Teach All Nations	789
74. Gethsemane	742	87. "To My Father, and Your Father"	794
75. Before Annas and the Court of Caiaphas	746		

1

"God With Us"

"His name shall be called Immanuel, . . . God with us."

"The light of the knowledge of the glory of God" is seen "in the face of Jesus Christ." From the days of eternity the Lord Jesus Christ was one with the Father; He was "the image of God," the image of His greatness and majesty, "the outshining of His glory." It was to manifest this glory that He came to our world. To this sin-darkened earth He came to reveal the light of God's love,—to be "God with us." Therefore it was prophesied of Him, "His name shall be called Immanuel."

By coming to dwell with us, Jesus was to reveal God both to men and to angels. He was the Word of God,—God's thought made audible. In His prayer for His disciples He says, "I have declared unto them Thy name,"—"merciful and gracious, long-suffering, and abundant in goodness and truth,"—"that the love wherewith Thou hast loved Me may be in them, and I in them." But not alone for His earthborn children was this revelation given. Our little world is the lesson book of the universe. God's wonderful purpose of grace, the mystery of redeeming love, is the theme into which "angels desire to look," and it will be their study throughout endless ages. Both the redeemed and the unfallen beings will find in the cross of Christ their science and their song. It will be seen that the glory shining in the face of Jesus is the glory of self-sacrificing love. In the light from Calvary it will be seen that the law of self-renouncing love is the law of life for earth and heaven; that the love which "seeketh not her own" has its source in the heart of God; and that in the meek and lowly One is manifested the character of Him who dwelleth in the light which no man can approach unto.

In the beginning, God was revealed in all the works of creation. It was Christ that spread the heavens, and laid the foundations of the earth. It was His hand that hung the worlds in space, and fashioned the flowers of the field. "His strength setteth fast the mountains." "The sea is His, and He made it." Ps. 65:6; 95:5. It was He that filled the earth with beauty, and the air with song. And upon all things in earth, and air, and sky, He wrote the message of the Father's love.

Now sin has marred God's perfect work, yet that handwriting remains. Even now all created things declare the glory of His excellence. There is nothing, save the selfish heart of man, that lives unto itself. No bird that cleaves the air, no animal that moves upon the ground, but ministers to some other life. There is no leaf of the forest, or lowly blade of grass, but has its ministry. Every tree and shrub and leaf pours forth that element of life without which neither man nor animal could live; and man and animal, in turn, minister to the life of tree and shrub and leaf. The flowers breathe fragrance and unfold their beauty in blessing to the world. The sun sheds its light to gladden a thousand worlds. The ocean, itself the source of all our springs and fountains, receives the streams from every land, but takes to give. The mists ascending from its bosom fall in showers to water the earth, that it may bring forth and bud.

The angels of glory find their joy in giving,—giving love and tireless watchcare to souls that are fallen and unholy. Heavenly beings woo the hearts of men; they bring to this dark world light from the courts above; by gentle and patient ministry they move upon the human spirit, to bring the lost into a fellowship with Christ which is even closer than they themselves can know.

But turning from all lesser representations, we behold God in Jesus. Looking unto Jesus we see that it is the glory of our God to give. "I do nothing of Myself," said Christ; "the living Father hath sent Me, and I live by the Father." "I seek not Mine own glory," but the glory of Him that sent Me. John 8:28; 6:57; 8:50; 7:18. In these words is set forth the great principle which is the law of life for the universe. All things Christ received from God, but He took to give. So in the heavenly courts, in His ministry for all created beings: through the beloved Son, the Father's life flows out to all; through the Son it returns, in praise and joyous service, a tide of love, to the great Source of all. And thus through Christ the circuit of beneficence is complete, representing the character of the great Giver, the law of life.

In heaven itself this law was broken. Sin originated in self-seeking. Lucifer, the covering cherub, desired to be first in heaven. He sought to gain control of heavenly beings, to draw them away from their Creator, and to win their homage to himself. Therefore he misrepresented God, attributing to Him the desire for self-exaltation. With his own evil characteristics he sought to invest the loving Creator. Thus he deceived angels. Thus he deceived men. He led them to doubt the word of God, and to distrust His goodness. Because God is a God of justice and terrible majesty, Satan caused them to look upon Him as severe and unforgiving. Thus he drew men to join him in rebellion against God, and the night of woe settled down upon the world.

The earth was dark through misapprehension of God. That the gloomy shadows might be lightened, that the world might be brought back to God, Satan's deceptive power was to be broken. This could not be done by force. The exercise of force is contrary to the principles of God's government; He desires only the service of love; and love cannot be commanded; it cannot be won by force or authority. Only by love is love awakened. To know God is to love Him; His character must be manifested in contrast to the character of Satan. This work only one Being in all the universe could do. Only He who knew the height and depth of the love of God could make it known. Upon the world's dark night the Sun of Righteousness must rise, "with healing in His wings." Mal. 4:2.

The plan for our redemption was not an afterthought, a plan formulated after the fall of Adam. It was a revelation of "the mystery which hath been kept in silence through times eternal." Rom. 16:25, R. V. It was an unfolding of the principles that from eternal ages have been the foundation of God's throne. From the beginning, God and Christ knew of the apostasy of Satan, and of the fall of man through the deceptive power of the apostate. God did not ordain that sin should exist, but He foresaw its existence, and made provision to meet the terrible emergency. So great was His love for the world, that He covenanted to give His only-begotten Son, "that whosoever believeth in Him should not perish, but have everlasting life." John 3:16.

Lucifer had said, "I will exalt my throne above the stars of God: . . . I will be like the Most High." Isa. 14:13, 14. But Christ, "being in the form of God, counted it not a thing to be grasped to be on an equality with God, but emptied Himself, taking the form of a servant, being made in the likeness of men." Phil. 2:6, 7, R. V., margin.

This was a voluntary sacrifice. Jesus might have remained at the Father's side. He might have retained the glory of heaven, and the homage of the angels. But He chose to give

23 back the scepter into the Father's hands, and to step down from the throne of the universe, that He might bring light to the benighted, and life to the perishing.

Nearly two thousand years ago, a voice of mysterious import was heard in heaven, from the throne of God, "Lo, I come." "Sacrifice and offering Thou wouldest not, but a body hast Thou prepared Me. . . . Lo, I come (in the volume of the Book it is written of Me,) to do Thy will, O God." Heb. 10:5-7. In these words is announced the fulfillment of the purpose that had been hidden from eternal ages. Christ was about to visit our world, and to become incarnate. He says, "A body hast Thou prepared Me." Had He appeared with the glory that was His with the Father before the world was, we could not have endured the light of His presence. That we might behold it and not be destroyed, the manifestation of His glory was

shrouded. His divinity was veiled with humanity,—the invisible glory in the visible human form.

This great purpose had been shadowed forth in types and symbols. The burning bush, in which Christ appeared to Moses, revealed God. The symbol chosen for the representation of the Deity was a lowly shrub, that seemingly had no attractions. This enshrined the Infinite. The all-merciful God shrouded His glory in a most humble type, that Moses could look upon it and live. So in the pillar of cloud by day and the pillar of fire by night, God communicated with Israel, revealing to men His will, and imparting to them His grace. God's glory was subdued, and His majesty veiled, that the weak vision of finite men might behold it. So Christ was to come in "the body of our humiliation" (Phil. 3:21, R. V.), "in the likeness of men." In the eyes of the world He possessed no beauty that they should desire Him; yet He was the incarnate God, the light of heaven and earth. His glory was veiled, His greatness and majesty were hidden, that He might draw near to sorrowful, tempted men.

God commanded Moses for Israel, "Let them make Me a sanctuary; that I may dwell among them" (Ex. 25:8), and He abode in the sanctuary, in the midst of His people. Through all their weary wandering in the desert, the symbol of His presence was with them. So Christ set up His tabernacle in the midst of our human encampment. He pitched His tent by the side of the tents of men, that He might dwell among us, and make us familiar with His divine character and life. "The Word became flesh, and tabernacled among us (and we beheld His glory, glory as of the Only Begotten from the Father), full of 24 grace and truth." John 1:14, R. V., margin.

Since Jesus came to dwell with us, we know that God is acquainted with our trials, and sympathizes with our griefs. Every son and daughter of Adam may understand that our Creator is the friend of sinners. For in every doctrine of grace, every promise of joy, every deed of love, every divine attraction presented in the Saviour's life on earth, we see "God with us."

Satan represents God's law of love as a law of selfishness. He declares that it is impossible for us to obey its precepts. The fall of our first parents, with all the woe that has resulted, he charges upon the Creator, leading men to look upon God as the author of sin, and suffering, and death. Jesus was to unveil this deception. As one of us He was to give an example of obedience. For this He took upon Himself our nature, and passed through our experiences. "In all things it behooved Him to be made like unto His brethren." Heb. 2:17. If we had to bear anything which Jesus did not endure, then upon this point Satan would represent the power of God as insufficient for us. Therefore Jesus was "in all points tempted like as we are." Heb. 4:15. He endured every trial to which we are subject. And He exercised in His own behalf no power that is not freely offered to us. As man, He met temptation, and overcame in the strength given Him from God. He says, "I delight to do Thy will, O My God: yea, Thy law is within My heart." Ps. 40:8. As He went about doing good, and healing all who were afflicted by Satan, He made plain to men the character of God's law and the nature of His service. His life testifies that it is possible for us also to obey the law of God.

By His humanity, Christ touched humanity; by His divinity, He lays hold upon the throne of God. As the Son of man, He gave us an example of obedience; as the Son of God, He gives us power to obey. It was Christ who from the bush on Mount Horeb spoke to Moses saying, "I AM THAT I AM. . . . Thus shalt thou say unto the children of Israel, I AM hath sent me unto you." Ex. 3:14. This was the pledge of Israel's deliverance. So when He came "in the likeness of men," He declared Himself the I AM. The Child of Bethlehem, the meek and lowly Saviour, is God "manifest in the flesh." 1 Tim. 3:16. And to us He says: "I AM the Good Shepherd." "I AM the living Bread." "I AM the

25 Way, the Truth, and the Life." "All power is given unto Me in heaven and in earth." John 10:11; 6:51; 14:6; Matt. 28:18. I AM the assurance of every promise. I AM; be not afraid. "God with us" is the surety of our deliverance from sin, the assurance of our power to obey the law of heaven.

In stooping to take upon Himself humanity, Christ revealed a character the opposite of the character of Satan. But He stepped still lower in the path of humiliation. "Being found in fashion as a man, He humbled Himself, and became obedient unto death, even the death of the cross." Phil. 2:8. As the high priest laid aside his gorgeous pontifical robes, and officiated in the white linen dress of the common priest, so Christ took the form of a servant, and offered sacrifice, Himself the priest, Himself the victim. "He was wounded for our transgressions, He was bruised for our iniquities: the chastisement of our peace was upon Him." Isa. 53:5.

Christ was treated as we deserve, that we might be treated as He deserves. He was condemned for our sins, in which He had no share, that we might be justified by His righteousness, in which we had no share. He suffered the death which was ours, that we might receive the life which was His. "With His stripes we are healed."

By His life and His death, Christ has achieved even more than recovery from the ruin wrought through sin. It was Satan's purpose to bring about an eternal separation between God and man; but in Christ we become more closely united to God

than if we had never fallen. In taking our nature, the Saviour has bound Himself to humanity by a tie that is never to be broken. Through the eternal ages He is linked with us. "God so loved the world, that He gave His only-begotten Son." John 3:16. He gave Him not only to bear our sins, and to die as our sacrifice; He gave Him to the fallen race. To assure us of His immutable counsel of peace, God gave His only-begotten Son to become one of the human family, forever to retain His human nature. This is the pledge that God will fulfill His word. "Unto *us* a child is born, unto *us* a son is given: and the government shall be upon His shoulder." God has adopted human nature in the person of His Son, and has carried the same into the highest heaven. It is the "Son of man" who shares the throne of the universe. It is the "Son of man" whose name shall be called, "Wonderful, Counselor, The mighty God, The everlasting Father, The Prince of Peace." Isa. 9:6. The I AM is the Daysman between God and humanity, laying His hand upon both. He who is "holy, harmless, undefiled, separate from sinners," is not ashamed to call us brethren. Heb. 7:26; 2:11. In Christ the family of earth and the family of heaven are bound together. Christ glori- 26 fied is our brother. Heaven is enshrined in humanity, and humanity is enfolded in the bosom of Infinite Love.

Of His people God says, "They shall be as the stones of a crown, lifted up as an ensign upon His land. For how great is His goodness, and how great is His beauty!" Zech. 9:16, 17. The exaltation of the redeemed will be an eternal testimony to God's mercy. "In the ages to come," He will "show the exceeding riches of His grace in His kindness toward us through Christ Jesus." "To the intent that . . . unto the principalities and the powers in the heavenly places might be made known . . . the manifold wisdom of God, according to the eternal purpose which He purposed in Christ Jesus our Lord." Eph. 2:7; 3:10, 11, R. V.

Through Christ's redeeming work the government of God stands justified. The Omnipotent One is made known as the God of love. Satan's charges are refuted, and his character unveiled. Rebellion can never again arise. Sin can never again enter the universe. Through eternal ages all are secure from apostasy. By love's self-sacrifice, the inhabitants of earth and heaven are bound to their Creator in bonds of indissoluble union.

The work of redemption will be complete. In the place where sin abounded, God's grace much more abounds. The earth itself, the very field that Satan claims as his, is to be not only ransomed but exalted. Our little world, under the curse of sin the one dark blot in His glorious creation, will be honored above all other worlds in the universe of God. Here, where the Son of God tabernacled in humanity; where the King of glory lived and suffered and died,—here, when He shall make all things new, the tabernacle of God shall be with men, "and He will dwell with them, and they shall be His people, and God Himself shall be with them, and be their God." And through endless ages as the redeemed walk in the light of the Lord, they will praise Him for His unspeakable Gift,—

Immanuel, "God with us."

2

The Chosen People

For more than a thousand years the Jewish people had awaited the Saviour's coming. Upon this event they had rested their brightest hopes. In song and prophecy, in temple rite and household prayer, they had enshrined His name. And yet at His coming they knew Him not. The Beloved of heaven was to them "as a root out of a dry ground;" He had "no form nor comeliness;" and they saw in Him no beauty that they should desire Him. "He came unto His own, and His own received Him not." Isa. 53:2; John 1:11.

Yet God had chosen Israel. He had called them to preserve among men the knowledge of His law, and of the symbols and prophecies that pointed to the Saviour. He desired them to be as wells of salvation to the world. What Abraham was in the land of his sojourn, what Joseph was in Egypt, and Daniel in the courts of Babylon, the Hebrew people were to be among the nations. They were to reveal God to men.

In the call of Abraham the Lord had said, "I will bless thee; . . . and thou shalt be a blessing: . . . and in thee shall all families of the earth be blessed." Gen. 12:2, 3. The same teaching was repeated through the prophets. Even after Israel had been wasted by war and captivity, the promise was theirs, "The remnant of Jacob shall be in the midst of many people as a dew from the Lord, as the showers upon the grass, that tarrieth not for man, nor waiteth for the sons of men." Micah 5:7. Concerning the temple at Jerusalem, the Lord declared through Isaiah, "Mine house shall be called an house of prayer for all peoples." Isa. 56:7, R. V.

But the Israelites fixed their hopes upon worldly greatness. From the time of their entrance to the land of Canaan, they departed from the commandments of God, and followed the ways of the heathen. It was in vain that God sent them warning by His prophets. In vain they suffered the chastisement of heathen oppression. Every reformation was followed by deeper apostasy.

Had Israel been true to God, He could have accomplished His purpose through their honor and exaltation. If they had walked in the ways of obedience, He would have made them "high above all nations which He hath made, in praise, and in name, and in honor." "All people of the earth," said Moses, "shall see that thou art called by the name of the Lord; and they shall be afraid of thee." "The nations which shall hear all these statutes" shall say, "Surely this great nation is a wise and understanding people." Deut. 26:19; 28:10; 4:6. But because of their unfaithfulness, God's purpose could be wrought out only through continued adversity and humiliation.

They were brought into subjection to Babylon, and scattered through the lands of the heathen. In affliction many renewed their faithfulness to His covenant. While they hung their harps upon the willows, and mourned for the holy temple that was laid waste, the light of truth shone out through them, and a knowledge of God was spread among the nations. The heathen systems of sacrifice were a perversion of the system that God had appointed; and many a sincere observer of heathen rites learned from the Hebrews the meaning of the service divinely ordained, and in faith grasped the promise of a Redeemer.

Many of the exiles suffered persecution. Not a few lost their lives because of their refusal to disregard the Sabbath and to observe the heathen festivals. As idolaters were roused to crush out the truth, the Lord brought His servants face to face with kings and rulers, that they and their people might receive the light. Time after time the greatest monarchs were led to proclaim the supremacy of the God whom their Hebrew captives worshiped.

By the Babylonish captivity the Israelites were effectually cured of the worship of graven images. During the centuries that followed, they suffered from the oppression of heathen foes, until the conviction became fixed that their prosperity depended upon their obedience to the law of God. But with too many of the people obedience was not prompted by love. The motive was selfish. They rendered outward service to God as the means of attaining to national greatness. They did not become the light of the world, but shut themselves away from the world in order to escape temptation to idolatry. In the instruction given through Moses, God had placed restrictions upon their association with idolaters; but this teaching had been misinterpreted. It was intended to prevent them from conforming to the practices of the heathen. But it was used to build up a wall of separation between Israel and all other nations. The Jews looked upon Jerusalem as their heaven, and they were actually jealous lest the Lord should show mercy to the Gentiles.

After the return from Babylon, much attention was given to religious instruction. All over the country, synagogues were erected, where the law was expounded by the priests and scribes. And schools were established, which, together with the arts and sciences, professed to teach the principles of righteousness. But these agencies became corrupted. During the captivity, many of the people had received heathen ideas and customs, and these were brought into their religious service. In many things they conformed to the practices of idolaters.

As they departed from God, the Jews in a great degree lost sight of the teaching of the ritual service. That service had been instituted by Christ Himself. In every part it was a symbol of Him; and it had been full of vitality and spiritual beauty. But the Jews lost the spiritual life from their ceremonies, and clung to the dead forms. They trusted to the sacrifices and ordinances themselves, instead of resting upon Him to whom they pointed. In order to supply the place of that which they had lost, the priests and rabbis multiplied requirements of their own; and the more rigid they grew, the less of the love of God was manifested. They measured their holiness by the multitude of their ceremonies, while their hearts were filled with pride and hypocrisy.

With all their minute and burdensome injunctions, it was an impossibility to keep the law. Those who desired to serve God, and who tried to observe the rabbinical precepts, toiled under a heavy burden. They could find no rest from the accusings of a troubled conscience. Thus Satan worked to discourage the people, to lower their conception of the character of God, and to bring the faith of Israel into contempt. He hoped to establish the claim put forth when he rebelled in heaven,—that the requirements of God were unjust, and could not be obeyed. Even Israel, he declared, did not keep the law.

30   While the Jews desired the advent of the Messiah, they had no true conception of His mission. They did not seek redemption from sin, but deliverance from the Romans. They looked for the Messiah to come as a conqueror, to break the oppressor's power, and exalt Israel to universal dominion. Thus the way was prepared for them to reject the Saviour.

At the time of the birth of Christ the nation was chafing under the rule of her foreign masters, and racked with internal strife. The Jews had been permitted to maintain the form of a separate government; but nothing could disguise the fact that they were under the Roman yoke, or reconcile them to the restriction of their power. The Romans claimed the right of appointing and removing the high priest, and the office was often secured by fraud, bribery, and even murder. Thus the priesthood became more and more corrupt. Yet the priests still possessed great power, and they employed it for selfish and mercenary ends. The people were subjected

to their merciless demands, and were also heavily taxed by the Romans. This state of affairs caused widespread discontent. Popular outbreaks were frequent. Greed and violence, distrust and spiritual apathy, were eating out the very heart of the nation.

Hatred of the Romans, and national and spiritual pride, led the Jews still to adhere rigorously to their forms of worship. The priests tried to maintain a reputation for sanctity by scrupulous attention to the ceremonies of religion. The people, in their darkness and oppression, and the rulers, thirsting for power, longed for the coming of One who would vanquish their enemies and restore the kingdom to Israel. They had studied the prophecies, but without spiritual insight. Thus they overlooked those scriptures that point to the humiliation of Christ's first advent, and misapplied those that speak of the glory of His second coming. Pride obscured their vision. They interpreted prophecy in accordance with their selfish desires.

3

"The Fullness of the Time"

"When the fullness of the time was come, God sent forth His Son, . . . to redeem them that were under the law, that we might receive the adoption of sons." Gal. 4:4, 5.

The Saviour's coming was foretold in Eden. When Adam and Eve first heard the promise, they looked for its speedy fulfillment. They joyfully welcomed their first-born son, hoping that he might be the Deliverer. But the fulfillment of the promise tarried. Those who first received it died without the sight. From the days of Enoch the promise was repeated through patriarchs and prophets, keeping alive the hope of His appearing, and yet He came not. The prophecy of Daniel revealed the time of His advent, but not all rightly interpreted the message. Century after century passed away; the voices of the prophets ceased. The hand of the oppressor was heavy upon Israel, and many were ready to exclaim, "The days are prolonged, and every vision faileth." Ezek. 12:22.

But like the stars in the vast circuit of their 32 appointed path, God's purposes know no haste and no delay. Through the symbols of the great darkness and the smoking furnace, God had revealed to Abraham the bondage of Israel in Egypt, and had declared that the time of their sojourning should be four hundred years. "Afterward," He said, "shall they come out with great substance." Gen. 15:14. Against that word, all the power of Pharaoh's proud empire battled in vain. On "the selfsame day" appointed in the divine promise, "it came to pass, that all the hosts of the Lord went out from the land of Egypt." Ex. 12:41. So in heaven's council the hour for the coming of Christ had been determined. When the great clock of time pointed to that hour, Jesus was born in Bethlehem.

"When the fullness of the time was come, God sent forth His Son." Providence had directed the movements of nations, and the tide of human impulse and influence, until the world was ripe for the coming of the Deliverer. The nations were united under one government. One language was widely spoken, and was everywhere recognized as the language of literature. From all lands the Jews of the dispersion gathered to Jerusalem to the annual feasts. As these returned to the places of their sojourn, they could spread throughout the world the tidings of the Messiah's coming.

At this time the systems of heathenism were losing their hold upon the people. Men were weary of pageant and fable. They longed for a religion that could satisfy the heart. While the light of truth seemed to have departed from among men, there were souls who were looking for light, and who were filled with perplexity and sorrow. They were thirsting for a knowledge of the living God, for some assurance of a life beyond the grave.

As the Jews had departed from God, faith had grown dim, and hope had well-nigh ceased to illuminate the future. The words of the prophets were uncomprehended. To the masses of the people, death was a dread mystery; beyond was uncertainty and gloom. It was not alone the wailing of the mothers of Bethlehem, but the cry from the great heart of humanity, that was borne to the prophet across the centuries,—the voice heard in Ramah, "lamentation, and weeping, and great mourning, Rachel weeping for her children, and would not be comforted, because they are not." Matt. 2:18. In "the region and shadow of death," men sat unsolaced. With 33 longing eyes they looked for the coming of the Deliverer, when the darkness should be dispelled, and the mystery of the future should be made plain.

Outside of the Jewish nation there were men who foretold the appearance of a divine instructor. These men were seeking for truth, and to them the Spirit of Inspiration was imparted. One after another, like stars in the darkened heavens, such teachers had arisen. Their words of prophecy had kindled hope in the hearts of thousands of the Gentile world.

For hundreds of years the Scriptures had been translated into the Greek language, then widely spoken throughout the Roman Empire. The Jews were scattered everywhere, and their expectation of the Messiah's coming was to some extent shared by the Gentiles. Among those whom the Jews styled heathen were men who had a better understanding of the Scripture prophecies concerning the Messiah than had the teachers in Israel. There were some who hoped for His coming as a deliverer from sin. Philosophers endeavored to study into the mystery of the Hebrew economy. But the bigotry of the Jews hindered the spread of the light. Intent on maintaining the separation between themselves and other nations, they were unwilling to impart the knowledge they still possessed concerning the symbolic service. The true Interpreter must 34 come. The One whom all these types prefigured must explain their significance.

Through nature, through types and symbols, through patriarchs and prophets, God had spoken to the world. Lessons must be given to humanity in the language of humanity. The Messenger of the covenant must speak. His voice must be heard in His own temple. Christ must come to utter words which should be clearly and definitely understood. He, the author of truth, must separate truth from the chaff of man's utterance, which had made it of no effect. The principles of God's government and the plan of redemption must be clearly defined. The lessons of the Old Testament must be fully set before men.

Among the Jews there were yet steadfast souls, descendants of that holy line through whom a knowledge of God had been preserved. These still looked for the hope of the promise made unto the fathers. They strengthened their faith by dwelling upon the assurance given through Moses, "A Prophet shall the Lord your God raise up unto you of your brethren, like unto me; Him shall ye hear in all things whatsoever He shall say unto you." Acts 3:22. Again, they read how the Lord would anoint One "to preach good tidings unto the meek," "to bind up the brokenhearted, to proclaim liberty to the captives," and to declare the "acceptable year of the Lord." Isa. 61:1, 2. They read how He would "set judgment in the earth," how the isles should "wait for His law," how the Gentiles should come to His light, and kings to the brightness of His rising. Isa. 42:4; 60:3.

The dying words of Jacob filled them with hope: "The scepter shall not depart from Judah, nor a lawgiver from between his feet, until Shiloh come." Gen. 49:10. The waning power of Israel testified that the Messiah's coming was at hand. The prophecy of Daniel pictured the glory of His reign over an empire which should succeed all earthly kingdoms; and, said the prophet, "It shall stand forever." Dan. 2:44. While few understood the nature of Christ's mission, there was a widespread expectation of a mighty prince who should establish his kingdom in Israel, and who should come as a deliverer to the nations.

The fullness of the time had come. Humanity, becoming more degraded through ages of transgression, called for the coming of the

Redeemer. Satan had been working to make the gulf deep and impassable between earth and heaven. By his falsehoods he had emboldened men in sin. It was his purpose to wear out the forbearance of God, and to extinguish His love for man, so that He would abandon the world to satanic jurisdiction.

Satan was seeking to shut out from men a knowledge of God, to turn their attention from the temple of God, and to establish his own kingdom. His strife for supremacy had seemed to be almost wholly successful. It is true that in every generation God had His agencies. Even among the heathen there were men through whom Christ was working to uplift the people from their sin and degradation. But these men were despised and hated. Many of them suffered a violent death. The dark shadow that Satan had cast over the world grew deeper and deeper.

Through heathenism, Satan had for ages turned men away from God; but he won his great triumph in perverting the faith of Israel. By contemplating and worshiping their own conceptions, the heathen had lost a knowledge of God, and had become more and more corrupt. So it was with Israel. The principle that man can save himself by his own works lay at the foundation of every heathen religion; it had now become the principle of the Jewish religion. Satan had implanted this principle. Wherever it is held, men have no barrier against sin.

The message of salvation is communicated to men through human agencies. But the Jews had sought to make a monopoly of the truth which is eternal life. They had hoarded the living manna, and it had turned to corruption. The religion which they tried to shut up to themselves became an offense. They robbed God of His glory, and defrauded the world by a counterfeit of the gospel. They had refused to surrender themselves to God for the salvation of the world, and they became agents of Satan for its destruction.

The people whom God had called to be the pillar and ground of the truth had become representatives of Satan. They were doing the work that he desired them to do, taking a course to misrepresent the character of God, and cause the world to look upon Him as a tyrant. The very priests who ministered in the temple had lost sight of the significance of the service they performed. They had ceased to look beyond the symbol to the thing signified. In presenting the sacrificial offerings they were as actors in a play. The ordinances which God Himself had appointed were made the means of blinding the mind and hardening the heart. God could do no more for man through these channels. The whole system must be swept away.

The deception of sin had reached its height. All the agencies for depraving the souls of men had been put in operation. The Son of God, looking upon the world, beheld suffering and misery. With pity He saw how men had become victims of satanic cruelty. He looked with compassion upon those who were being corrupted, murdered, and lost. They had chosen a ruler who chained them to his car as captives. Bewildered and deceived, they were moving on in gloomy procession toward eternal ruin,—to death in which is no hope of life, toward night to which comes no morning. Satanic agencies were incorporated with men. The bodies of human beings, made for the dwelling place of God, had become the habitation of demons. The senses, the nerves, the passions, the organs of men, were worked by supernatural agencies in the indulgence of the vilest lust. The very stamp of demons was impressed upon the countenances of men. Human faces reflected the expression of the legions of evil with which they were possessed. Such was the prospect upon which the world's Redeemer looked. What a spectacle for Infinite Purity to behold!

Sin had become a science, and vice was consecrated as a part of religion. Rebellion had struck its roots deep into the heart, and the hostility of man was most violent against heaven. It was demonstrated before the universe that, apart from God, humanity could not be uplifted. A new element of life and power must be imparted by Him who made the world.

With intense interest the unfallen worlds had watched to see Jehovah arise, and sweep away the inhabitants of the earth. And if God should do this, Satan was ready to carry out his plan for securing to himself the allegiance of heavenly beings. He had declared that the principles of God's government make forgiveness impossible. Had the world been destroyed, he would have claimed that his accusations were proved true. He was ready to cast blame upon God, and to spread his rebellion to the worlds above. But instead of destroying the world, God sent His Son to save it. Though corruption and defiance might be seen in every part of the alien province, a way for its recovery was provided. At the very crisis, when Satan seemed about to triumph, the Son of God came with the embassage of divine grace. Through every age, through every hour, the love of God had been exercised toward the fallen race. Notwithstanding the perversity of men, the signals of mercy had been continually exhibited. And when the fullness of the time had come, the Deity was glorified by pouring upon the world a flood of healing grace that was never to be obstructed or withdrawn till the plan of salvation should be fulfilled.

Satan was exulting that he had succeeded in debasing the image of God in humanity. Then Jesus came to restore in man the image of his Maker. None but Christ can fashion anew the character that has been ruined by sin. He came to expel the demons that had controlled the will. He came to lift us up from the dust, to reshape the marred character after the pattern of His divine character, and to make it beautiful with His own glory.

4

Unto You a Saviour

The King of glory stooped low to take humanity. Rude and forbidding were His earthly surroundings. His glory was veiled, that the majesty of His outward form might not become an object of attraction. He shunned all outward display. Riches, worldly honor, and human greatness can never save a soul from death; Jesus purposed that no attraction of an earthly nature should call men to His side. Only the beauty of heavenly truth must draw those who would follow Him. The character of the Messiah had long been foretold in prophecy, and He desired men to accept Him upon the testimony of the word of God.

The angels had wondered at the glorious plan of redemption. They watched to see how the people of God would receive His Son, clothed in the garb of humanity. Angels came to the land of the chosen people. Other nations were dealing in fables and worshiping false gods. To the land where the glory of God had been revealed, and the light of prophecy had shone, the angels came. They came unseen to Jerusalem, to the appointed expositors of the Sacred Oracles, and the ministers of God's house. Already to Zacharias the priest, as he ministered before the altar, the nearness of Christ's coming had been announced. Already the forerunner was born, his mission attested by miracle and prophecy. The tidings of his birth and the wonderful significance of his mission had been spread abroad. Yet Jerusalem was not preparing to welcome her Redeemer.

With amazement the heavenly messengers beheld the indifference of that people whom God had called to communicate to the world the light of sacred truth. The Jewish nation had been preserved as a witness that Christ was to be born of the seed of Abraham and of David's line; yet they knew not that His coming was now at hand. In the temple the morning and the evening sacrifice daily pointed to the Lamb of God; yet even here there was no preparation to receive Him. The priests and teachers of the nation knew not that the greatest event of the ages was about to take place. They rehearsed their meaningless prayers, and performed the rites of worship to be seen by men, but in their strife for riches and worldly honor they were not prepared for the revelation of the Messiah. The same indifference pervaded the land of Israel. Hearts selfish and world-engrossed were untouched by the joy that thrilled all heaven. Only a few were longing to behold the Unseen. To these heaven's embassy was sent.

Angels attend Joseph and Mary as they journey from their home in Nazareth to the city of David. The decree of imperial Rome for the enrollment of the peoples of her vast dominion has extended to the dwellers among the hills of Galilee. As in old time Cyrus was called to the throne of the world's empire that he might set free the captives of the Lord, so Caesar Augustus is made the agent for the fulfillment of God's purpose in bringing the mother of Jesus to Bethlehem. She is of the lineage of David, and the Son of David must be born in David's city. Out of Bethlehem, said the prophet, "shall He come forth . . . that is to be ruler in Israel; whose goings forth have been from of old, from the days of eternity." Micah 5:2, margin. But in the city of their royal line, Joseph and Mary are unrecognized and unhonored. Weary and homeless, they traverse the entire length of the narrow street, from the gate of the city to the eastern extremity of the town, vainly seeking a resting place for the night. There is no room for them at the crowded inn. In a rude building where the beasts are sheltered, they at last find refuge, and here the Redeemer of the world is born.

Men know it not, but the tidings fill heaven with rejoicing. With a deeper and more tender interest the holy beings from the world of light are drawn to the earth. The whole world is brighter for His presence. Above the hills of Bethlehem are gathered an innumerable throng of angels. They wait the signal to declare the glad news to the world. Had the leaders in Israel been true to their trust, they might have shared the joy of heralding the birth of Jesus. But now they are passed by.

God declares, "I will pour water upon him that is thirsty, and floods upon the dry ground." "Unto the upright there ariseth light in the darkness." Isa. 44:3; Ps. 112:4. To those who are seeking for light, and who accept it with gladness, the bright rays from the throne of God will shine.

In the fields where the boy David had led his flock, shepherds were still keeping watch by night. Through the silent hours they talked together of the promised Saviour, and prayed for the coming of the King to David's throne. "And, lo, the angel of the Lord came upon them, and the glory of the Lord shone round about them: and they were sore afraid. And the angel said unto them, Fear not: for, behold, I bring you good tidings of great joy, which shall be to all people. For unto you is born this day in the city of David a Saviour, which is Christ the Lord."

This chapter is based on Luke 2:1-20.

At these words, visions of glory fill the minds of the listening shepherds. The Deliverer has come to Israel! Power, exaltation, triumph, are associated with His coming. But the angel must prepare them to recognize their Saviour in poverty and humiliation. "This shall be a sign unto you," he says; "Ye shall find the babe wrapped in swaddling clothes, lying in a manger."

The heavenly messenger had quieted their fears. He had told them how to find Jesus. With tender regard for their human weakness, he had given them time to become accustomed to the divine radiance. Then the joy and glory could no longer be hidden. The whole plain was lighted up with the bright shining of the hosts of God. Earth was hushed, and heaven stooped to listen to the song,—

"Glory to God in the highest,
And on earth peace, good will toward men."

Oh that today the human family could recognize that song! The declaration then made, the note then struck, will swell to the close of time, and resound to the ends of the earth. When the Sun of Righteousness shall arise, with healing in His wings, that song will be re-echoed by the voice of a great multitude, as the voice of many waters, saying, "Alleluia: for the Lord God omnipotent reigneth." Rev. 19:6.

As the angels disappeared, the light faded away, and the shadows of night once more fell on the hills of Bethlehem. But the brightest picture ever beheld by human eyes remained in the memory of the shepherds. "And it came to pass, as the angels were gone away from them into heaven, the shepherds said one to another, Let us now go even unto Bethlehem, and see this thing which is come to pass, which the Lord hath made known unto us. And they came with haste, and found Mary, and Joseph, and the babe lying in a manger."

Departing with great joy, they made known the things they had seen and heard. "And all they that heard it wondered at those things which were told them by the shepherds. But Mary kept all these things, and pondered them in her heart. And the shepherds returned, glorifying and praising God."

Heaven and earth are no wider apart today than when shepherds listened to the angels' song. Humanity is still as much the object of heaven's solicitude as when common men of common occupations met angels at noonday, and talked with the heavenly messengers in the vineyards and the fields. To us in the common walks of life, heaven may be very near. Angels from the courts above will attend the steps of those who come and go at God's command.

The story of Bethlehem is an exhaustless theme. In it is hidden "the depth of the riches both of the wisdom and knowledge of God." Rom. 11:33. We marvel at the Saviour's sacrifice in exchanging the throne of heaven for the manger, and the companionship of adoring angels for the beasts of the stall. Human pride and self-sufficiency stand rebuked in His presence. Yet this was but the beginning of His wonderful condescension. It would have been an almost infinite humiliation for the Son of God to take man's nature, even when Adam stood in his innocence in Eden. But Jesus accepted humanity when the race had been weakened by four thousand years of sin. Like every child of Adam He accepted the results of the working of the great law of heredity. What these results were is shown in the history of His earthly ancestors. He came with such a heredity to share our sorrows and temptations, and to give us the example of a sinless life.

Satan in heaven had hated Christ for His position in the courts of God. He hated Him the more when he himself was dethroned. He hated Him who pledged Himself to redeem a race of sinners. Yet into the world where Satan claimed dominion God permitted His Son to come, a helpless babe, subject to the weakness of humanity. He permitted Him to meet life's peril in common with every human soul, to fight the battle as every child of humanity must fight it, at the risk of failure and eternal loss.

The heart of the human father yearns over his son. He looks into the face of his little child, and trembles at the thought of life's peril. He longs to shield his dear one from Satan's power, to hold him back from temptation and conflict. To meet a bitterer conflict and a more fearful risk, God gave His only-begotten Son, that the path of life might be made sure for our little ones. "Herein is love." Wonder, O heavens! and be astonished, O earth!

5

The Dedication

About forty days after the birth of Christ, Joseph and Mary took Him to Jerusalem, to present Him to the Lord, and to offer sacrifice. This was according to the Jewish law, and as man's substitute Christ must conform to the law in every particular. He had already been subjected to the rite of circumcision, as a pledge of His obedience to the law.

As an offering for the mother, the law required a lamb of the first year for a burnt offering, and a young pigeon or a turtledove for a sin offering. But the law provided that if the parents were too poor to bring a lamb, a pair of turtledoves or two young pigeons, one for a burnt offering, the other for a sin offering, might

This chapter is based on Luke 2:21-38.

be accepted.

The offerings presented to the Lord were to be without blemish. These offerings represented Christ, and from this it is evident that Jesus Himself was free from physical deformity. He was the "lamb without blemish and without spot." 1 Peter 1:19. His physical structure was not marred by any defect; His body was strong and healthy. And throughout His lifetime He lived in conformity to nature's laws. Physically as well as spiritually, He was an example of what God designed all humanity to be through obedience to His laws.

The dedication of the first-born had its origin in the earliest times. God had promised to give the First-born of heaven to save the sinner. This gift was to be acknowledged in every household by the consecration of the first-born son. He was to be devoted to the priesthood, as a representative of Christ among men.

In the deliverance of Israel from Egypt, the dedication of the first-born was again commanded. While the children of Israel were in bondage to the Egyptians, the Lord directed Moses to go to Pharaoh, king of Egypt, and say, "Thus saith the Lord, Israel is My son, even My first-born: and I say unto thee, Let My son go, that he may serve Me: and if thou refuse to let him go, behold, I will slay thy son, even thy first-born." Ex. 4:22, 23.

Moses delivered his message; but the proud king's answer was, "Who is the Lord, that I should obey His voice to let Israel go? I know not the Lord, neither will I let Israel go." Ex. 5:2. The Lord worked for His people by signs and wonders, sending terrible judgments upon Pharaoh. At length the destroying angel was bidden to slay the first-born of man and beast among the Egyptians. That the Israelites might be spared, they were directed to place upon their doorposts the blood of a slain lamb. Every house was to be marked, that when the angel came on his mission of death, he might pass over the homes of the Israelites.

After sending this judgment upon Egypt, the Lord said to Moses, "Sanctify unto Me all the first-born, . . . both of man and of beast: it is Mine;" "for on the day that I smote all the first-born in the land of Egypt I hallowed unto Me all the first-born in Israel, both man and beast: Mine shall they be: I am the Lord." Ex. 13:2; Num. 3:13. After the tabernacle service was established, the Lord chose the tribe of Levi in the place of the first-born of all Israel to minister in the sanctuary. But the first-born were still to be regarded as the Lord's, and were to be bought back by a ransom.

Thus the law for the presentation of the first-born was made particularly significant. While it was a memorial of the Lord's wonderful deliverance of the children of Israel, it prefigured a greater deliverance, to be wrought out by the only-begotten Son of God. As the blood sprinkled on the doorposts had saved the first-born of Israel, so the blood of Christ has power to save the world.

What meaning then was attached to Christ's [52] presentation! But the priest did not see through the veil; he did not read the mystery beyond. The presentation of infants was a common scene. Day after day the priest received the redemption money as the babes were presented to the Lord. Day after day he went through the routine of his work, giving little heed to the parents or children, unless he saw some indication of the wealth or high rank of the parents. Joseph and Mary were poor; and when they came with their child, the priests saw only a man and woman dressed as Galileans, and in the humblest garments. There was nothing in their appearance to attract attention, and they presented only the offering made by the poorer classes.

The priest went through the ceremony of his official work. He took the child in his arms, and held it up before the altar. After handing it back to its mother, he inscribed the name "Jesus" on the roll of the first-born. Little did he think, as the babe lay in his arms, that it was the Majesty of heaven, the King of glory. The priest did not think that this babe was the One of whom Moses had written, "A Prophet shall the Lord your God raise up unto you of your brethren, like unto me; Him shall ye hear in all things whatsoever He shall say unto you." Acts 3:22. He did not think that this babe was He whose glory Moses had asked to see. But One greater than Moses lay in the priest's arms; and when he enrolled the child's name, he was enrolling the name of One who was the foundation of the whole Jewish economy. That name was to be its death warrant; for the system of sacrifices and offerings was waxing old; the type had almost reached its antitype, the shadow its substance.

The Shekinah had departed from the sanctuary, but in the Child of Bethlehem was veiled the glory before which angels bow. This unconscious babe was the promised seed, to whom the first altar at the gate of Eden pointed. This was Shiloh, the peace giver. It was He who declared Himself to Moses as the I AM. It was He who in the pillar of cloud and of fire had been the guide of Israel. This was He whom seers had long foretold. He was the Desire of all nations, the Root and the Offspring of David, and the Bright and Morning Star. The name of that helpless little babe, inscribed in the roll of Israel, declaring Him our brother, was the hope of fallen humanity. The child for whom the redemption money had been paid was He who was to pay the ransom for the sins of the whole world. He was the true "high priest over the house of God," the head of "an unchangeable priesthood," the intercessor at "the right hand of [55] the Majesty on high." Heb. 10:21; 7:24; 1:3.

Spiritual things are spiritually discerned. In the temple the Son of God was dedicated to the work He had come to do. The priest looked upon Him as he would upon any other child. But though he neither saw nor felt anything unusual, God's act in giving His Son to the world was acknowledged. This occasion did not pass without some recognition of Christ. "There was a man in Jerusalem, whose name was Simeon; and the same man was just and devout, waiting for the Consolation of Israel: and the Holy Ghost was upon him. And it was revealed unto him by the Holy Ghost, that he should not see death, before he had seen the Lord's Christ."

As Simeon enters the temple, he sees a family presenting their first-born son before the priest. Their appearance bespeaks poverty; but Simeon understands the warnings of the Spirit, and he is deeply impressed that the infant being presented to the Lord is the Consolation of Israel, the One he has longed to see. To the astonished priest, Simeon appears like a man enraptured. The child has been returned to Mary, and he takes it in his arms and presents it to God, while a joy that he has never before felt enters his soul. As he lifts the infant Saviour toward heaven, he says, "Lord, now lettest Thou Thy servant depart in peace, according to Thy word: for mine eyes have seen Thy salvation, which Thou hast prepared before the face of all people; a light to lighten the Gentiles, and the glory of Thy people Israel."

The spirit of prophecy was upon this man of God, and while Joseph and Mary stood by, wondering at his words, he blessed them, and said unto Mary, "Behold, this child is set for the fall and rising again of many in Israel; and for a sign which shall be spoken against; (yea, a sword shall pierce through thy own soul also,) that the thoughts of many hearts may be revealed."

Anna also, a prophetess, came in and confirmed Simeon's testimony concerning Christ. As Simeon spoke, her face lighted up with the glory of God, and she poured out her heartfelt thanks that she had been permitted to behold Christ the Lord.

These humble worshipers had not studied the prophecies in vain. But those who held positions as rulers and priests in Israel, though they too had before them the precious utterances of prophecy, were not walking in the way of the Lord, and their eyes were not open to behold the Light of life.

56 So it is still. Events upon which the attention of all heaven is centered are undiscerned, their very occurrence is unnoticed, by religious leaders, and worshipers in the house of God. Men acknowledge Christ in history, while they turn away from the living Christ. Christ in His word calling to self-sacrifice, in the poor and suffering who plead for relief, in the righteous cause that involves poverty and toil and reproach, is no more readily received today than He was eighteen hundred years ago.

Mary pondered the broad and far-reaching prophecy of Simeon. As she looked upon the child in her arms, and recalled the words spoken by the shepherds of Bethlehem, she was full of grateful joy and bright hope. Simeon's words called to her mind the prophetic utterances of Isaiah: "There shall come forth a rod out of the stem of Jesse, and a Branch shall grow out of his roots: and the Spirit of the Lord shall rest upon Him, the spirit of wisdom and understanding, the spirit of counsel and might, the spirit of knowledge and of the fear of the Lord. . . . And righteousness shall be the girdle of His loins, and faithfulness the girdle of His reins." "The people that walked in darkness have seen a great light: they that dwell in the land of the shadow of death, upon them hath the light shined. . . . For unto us a child is born, unto us a son is given: and the government shall be upon His shoulder: and His name shall be called Wonderful, Counselor, The mighty God, The everlasting Father, The Prince of Peace." Isa. 11:1-5; 9:2-6.

Yet Mary did not understand Christ's mission. Simeon had prophesied of Him as a light to lighten the Gentiles, as well as a glory to Israel. Thus the angels had announced the Saviour's birth as tidings of joy to all peoples. God was seeking to correct the narrow, Jewish conception of the Messiah's work. He desired men to behold Him, not merely as the deliverer of Israel, but as the Redeemer of the world. But many years must pass before even the mother of Jesus would understand His mission.

Mary looked forward to the Messiah's reign on David's throne, but she saw not the baptism of suffering by which it must be won. Through Simeon it is revealed that the Messiah is to have no unobstructed passage through the world. In the words to Mary, "A sword shall pierce through thy own soul also," God in His tender mercy gives to the mother of Jesus an intimation of the anguish that already for His sake she had begun to bear.

"Behold," Simeon had said, "this child is set for the fall and rising again of many in Israel; and for a sign which shall be spoken against." They must fall who would rise again. We must 57 fall upon the Rock and be broken before we can be uplifted in Christ. Self must be dethroned, pride must be humbled, if we would know the glory of the spiritual kingdom. The Jews would not accept the honor that is reached through humiliation. Therefore they would not receive their Redeemer. He was a sign that was spoken against.

"That the thoughts of many hearts may be revealed." In the light of the Saviour's life, the hearts of all, even from the Creator to the prince of darkness, are revealed. Satan has represented

God as selfish and oppressive, as claiming all, and giving nothing, as requiring the service of His creatures for His own glory, and making no sacrifice for their good. But the gift of Christ reveals the Father's heart. It testifies that the thoughts of God toward us are "thoughts of peace, and not of evil." Jer. 29:11. It declares that while God's hatred of sin is as strong as death, His love for the sinner is stronger than death. Having undertaken our redemption, He will spare nothing, however dear, which is necessary to the completion of His work. No truth essential to our salvation is withheld, no miracle of mercy is neglected, no divine agency is left unemployed. Favor is heaped upon favor, gift upon gift. The whole treasury of heaven is open to those He seeks to save. Having collected the riches of the universe, and laid open the resources of infinite power, He gives them all into the hands of Christ, and says, All these are for man. Use these gifts to convince him that there is no love greater than Mine in earth or heaven. His greatest happiness will be found in loving Me.

At the cross of Calvary, love and selfishness stood face to face. Here was their crowning manifestation. Christ had lived only to comfort and bless, and in putting Him to death, Satan manifested the malignity of his hatred against God. He made it evident that the real purpose of his rebellion was to dethrone God, and to destroy Him through whom the love of God was shown.

By the life and the death of Christ, the thoughts of men also are brought to view. From the manger to the cross, the life of Jesus was a call to self-surrender, and to fellowship in suffering. It unveiled the purposes of men. Jesus came with the truth of heaven, and all who were listening to the voice of the Holy Spirit were drawn to Him. The worshipers of self belonged to Satan's kingdom. In their attitude toward Christ, all would show on which side they stood. And thus everyone passes judgment on himself.

58   In the day of final judgment, every lost soul will understand the nature of his own rejection of truth. The cross will be presented, and its real bearing will be seen by every mind that has been blinded by transgression. Before the vision of Calvary with its mysterious Victim, sinners will stand condemned. Every lying excuse will be swept away. Human apostasy will appear in its heinous character. Men will see what their choice has been. Every question of truth and error in the long-standing controversy will then have been made plain. In the judgment of the universe, God will stand clear of blame for the existence or continuance of evil. It will be demonstrated that the divine decrees are not accessory to sin. There was no defect in God's government, no cause for disaffection. When the thoughts of all hearts shall be revealed, both

the loyal and the rebellious will unite in declaring, "Just and true are Thy ways, Thou King of saints. Who shall not fear Thee, O Lord, and glorify Thy name? . . . for Thy judgments are made manifest." Rev. 15:3, 4.

6   59

"We Have Seen His Star"

"Now when Jesus was born in Bethlehem of Judea in the days of Herod the king, behold, there came wise men from the East to Jerusalem, saying, Where is He that is born King of the Jews? for we have seen His star in the East, and are come to worship Him."

The wise men from the East were philosophers. They belonged to a large and influential class that included men of noble birth, and comprised much of the wealth and learning of their nation. Among these were many who imposed on the credulity of the people. Others were upright men who studied the indications of Providence in nature, and who were honored for their integrity and wisdom. Of this character were the wise men who came to Jesus.

The light of God is ever shining amid the darkness of heathenism. As these magi studied the starry heavens, and sought to fathom the mystery hidden in their bright paths, they beheld the glory of the Creator. Seeking clearer knowledge, they turned to the Hebrew Scriptures. In their own land were treasured prophetic writings that predicted the coming of a divine teacher. Balaam belonged to the magicians, though at one time a prophet of God; by the Holy Spirit he had foretold the prosperity of Israel and the appearing of the Messiah; and his prophecies had been handed down by tradition from century to century. But in the Old Testament the Saviour's advent was more clearly revealed. The magi learned with joy that His coming was near, and that the whole world was to be filled with a knowledge of the glory of the Lord.

The wise men had seen a mysterious light in the heavens upon that night when the glory of God flooded the hills of Bethlehem. As the light faded, a luminous star appeared, and lingered in the sky. It was not a fixed star nor a planet, and the phenomenon excited the keenest interest. That star was a distant company of shining angels, but of this the wise men were ignorant. Yet they were impressed that the star was of special import to them. They consulted priests and philosophers, and searched the scrolls of the ancient records. The prophecy of Balaam had declared, "There shall come a Star out of Jacob, and a Scepter shall rise out of Israel." Num. 24:17. Could this strange star have been sent as a harbinger of the Promised One? The magi had

This chapter is based on Matthew 2.

welcomed the light of heaven-sent truth; now it was shed upon them in brighter rays. Through dreams they were instructed to go in search of the newborn Prince.

As by faith Abraham went forth at the call of God, "not knowing whither he went" (Heb. 11:8); as by faith Israel followed the pillar of cloud to the Promised Land, so did these Gentiles go forth to find the promised Saviour. The Eastern country abounded in precious things, and the magi did not set out empty-handed. It was the custom to offer presents as an act of homage to princes or other personages of rank, and the richest gifts the land afforded were borne as an offering to Him in whom all the families of the earth were to be blessed. It was necessary to journey by night in order to keep the star in view; but the travelers beguiled the hours by repeating traditional sayings and prophetic utterances concerning the One they sought. At every pause for rest they searched the prophecies; and the conviction deepened that they were divinely guided. While they had the star before them as an outward sign, they had also the inward evidence of the Holy Spirit, which was impressing their hearts, and inspiring them with hope. The journey, though long, was a happy one to them.

They have reached the land of Israel, and are descending the Mount of Olives, with Jerusalem in sight, when, lo, the star that has guided them all the weary way rests above the temple, and after a season fades from their view. With eager steps they press onward, confidently expecting the Messiah's birth to be the joyful burden of every tongue. But their inquiries are in vain. Entering the holy city, they repair to the temple. To their amazement they find none who seem to have a knowledge of the newborn king. Their questions call forth no expressions of joy, but rather of surprise and fear, not unmingled with contempt.

The priests are rehearsing traditions. They extol their religion and their own piety, while they denounce the Greeks and Romans as heathen, and sinners above others. The wise men are not idolaters, and in the sight of God they stand far higher than do these, His professed worshipers; yet they are looked upon by the Jews as heathen. Even among the appointed guardians of the Holy Oracles their eager questionings touch no chord of sympathy.

The arrival of the magi was quickly noised throughout Jerusalem. Their strange errand created an excitement among the people, which penetrated to the palace of King Herod. The wily Edomite was aroused at the intimation of a possible rival. Countless murders had stained his pathway to the throne. Being of alien blood, he was hated by the people over whom he ruled. His only security was the favor of Rome. But this new Prince had a higher claim. He was born

to the kingdom.

Herod suspected the priests of plotting with the strangers to excite a popular tumult and unseat him from the throne. He concealed his mistrust, however, determined to thwart their schemes by superior cunning. Summoning the chief priests and the scribes, he questioned them as to the teaching of their sacred books in regard to the place of the Messiah's birth.

This inquiry from the usurper of the throne, and made at the request of strangers, stung the pride of the Jewish teachers. The indifference with which they turned to the rolls of prophecy enraged the jealous tyrant. He thought them trying to conceal their knowledge of the matter. With an authority they dared not disregard, he commanded them to make close search, and to declare the birthplace of their expected King. "And they said unto him, In Bethlehem of Judea: for thus it is written by the prophet,

"And thou Bethlehem, land of Judah,
Art in nowise least among the princes of Judah:
For out of thee shall come forth a governor,
Which shall be shepherd of My people Israel."

R. V.

Herod now invited the magi to a private interview. A tempest of wrath and fear was raging in his heart, but he preserved a calm exterior, and received the strangers courteously. He inquired at what time the star had appeared, and professed to hail with joy the intimation of the birth of Christ. He bade his visitors, "Search diligently for the young child; and when ye have found Him, bring me word again, that I may come and worship Him also." So saying, he dismissed them to go on their way to Bethlehem.

The priests and elders of Jerusalem were not as ignorant concerning the birth of Christ as they pretended. The report of the angels' visit to the shepherds had been brought to Jerusalem, but the rabbis had treated it as unworthy of their notice. They themselves might have found Jesus, and might have been ready to lead the magi to His birthplace; but instead of this, the wise men came to call their attention to the birth of the Messiah. "Where is He that is born King of the Jews?" they said; "for we have seen His star in the East, and are come to worship Him."

Now pride and envy closed the door against the light. If the reports brought by the shepherds and the wise men were credited, they would place the priests and rabbis in a most unenviable position, disproving their claim to be the exponents of the truth of God. These learned teachers would not stoop to be instructed by those whom they termed heathen. It could not be, they said, that God had passed them by, to communicate with ignorant shepherds or uncircumcised

Gentiles. They determined to show their contempt for the reports that were exciting King Herod and all Jerusalem. They would not even go to Bethlehem to see whether these things were so. And they led the people to regard the interest in Jesus as a fanatical excitement. Here began the rejection of Christ by the priests and rabbis. From this point their pride and stubbornness grew into a settled hatred of the Saviour. While God was opening the door to the Gentiles, the Jewish leaders were closing the door to themselves.

The wise men departed alone from Jerusalem. The shadows of night were falling as they left the gates, but to their great joy they again saw the star, and were directed to Bethlehem. They had received no such intimation of the lowly estate of Jesus as was given to the shepherds. After the long journey they had been disappointed by the indifference of the Jewish leaders, and had left Jerusalem less confident than when they entered the city. At Bethlehem they found no royal guard stationed to protect the newborn King. None of the world's honored men were in attendance. Jesus was cradled in a manger. His parents, uneducated peasants, were His only guardians. Could this be He of whom it was written, that He should "raise up the tribes of Jacob," and "restore the preserved of Israel;" that He should be "a light to the Gentiles," and for "salvation unto the end of the earth"? Isa. 49:6.

"When they were come into the house, they saw the young child with Mary His mother, and fell down, and worshiped Him." Beneath the lowly guise of Jesus, they recognized the presence of Divinity. They gave their hearts to Him as their Saviour, and then poured out their gifts,—"gold, and frankincense, and myrrh."

64 What a faith was theirs! It might have been said of the wise men from the East, as afterward of the Roman centurion, "I have not found so great faith, no, not in Israel." Matt. 8:10.

The wise men had not penetrated Herod's design toward Jesus. When the object of their journey was accomplished, they prepared to return to Jerusalem, intending to acquaint him with their success. But in a dream they received a divine message to hold no further communication with him. Avoiding Jerusalem, they set out for their own country by another route.

In like manner Joseph received warning to flee into Egypt with Mary and the child. And the angel said, "Be thou there until I bring thee word: for Herod will seek the young child to destroy Him." Joseph obeyed without delay, setting out on the journey by night for greater security.

Through the wise men, God had called the attention of the Jewish nation to the birth of His Son. Their inquiries in Jerusalem, the popular interest excited, and even the jealousy of Herod, which compelled the attention of the priests and rabbis, directed minds to the prophecies concerning the Messiah, and to the great event that had just taken place.

Satan was bent on shutting out the divine 65 light from the world, and he used his utmost cunning to destroy the Saviour. But He who never slumbers nor sleeps was watching over His beloved Son. He who had rained manna from heaven for Israel and had fed Elijah in the time of famine provided in a heathen land a refuge for Mary and the child Jesus. And through the gifts of the magi from a heathen country, the Lord supplied the means for the journey into Egypt and the sojourn in a land of strangers.

The magi had been among the first to welcome the Redeemer. Their gift was the first that was laid at His feet. And through that gift, what privilege of ministry was theirs! The offering from the heart that loves, God delights to honor, giving it highest efficiency in service for Him. If we have given our hearts to Jesus, we also shall bring our gifts to Him. Our gold and silver, our most precious earthly possessions, our highest mental and spiritual endowments, will be freely devoted to Him who loved us, and gave Himself for us.

Herod in Jerusalem impatiently awaited the return of the wise men. As time passed, and they did not appear, his suspicions were roused. The unwillingness of the rabbis to point out the Messiah's birthplace seemed to indicate that they had penetrated his design, and that the magi had purposely avoided him. He was maddened at the thought. Craft had failed, but there was left the resort to force. He would make an example of this child-king. Those haughty Jews should see what they might expect in their attempts to place a monarch on the throne.

Soldiers were at once sent to Bethlehem, with orders to put to death all the children of two years and under. The quiet homes of the city of David witnessed those scenes of horror that, six hundred years before, had been opened to the prophet. "In Ramah was there a voice heard, lamentation, and weeping, and great mourning, Rachel weeping for her children, and would not be comforted, because they are not."

This calamity the Jews had brought upon themselves. If they had been walking in faithfulness and humility before God, He would in a signal manner have made the wrath of the king harmless to them. But they had separated themselves from God by their sins, and had rejected the Holy Spirit, which was their only shield. They had not studied the Scriptures with a desire to conform to the will of God. They had searched for prophecies which could be interpreted to exalt themselves, and to show how God despised all other nations. It was their proud boast that the Messiah was to come as a 66 king, conquering His enemies, and treading down the heathen in His wrath. Thus they had excited the hatred of their rulers. Through their misrepresentation of Christ's mission, Satan had purposed to compass the destruction of the Saviour; but instead of this, it returned upon their own heads.

This act of cruelty was one of the last that darkened the reign of Herod. Soon after the slaughter of the innocents, he was himself compelled to yield to that doom which none can turn aside. He died a fearful death.

Joseph, who was still in Egypt, was now bidden by an angel of God to return to the land of Israel. Regarding Jesus as the heir of David's throne, Joseph desired to make his home in Bethlehem; but learning that Archelaus reigned in Judea in his father's stead, he feared that the father's designs against Christ might be carried out by the son. Of all the sons of Herod, Archelaus most resembled him in character. Already his succession to the government had been marked by a tumult in Jerusalem, and the slaughter of thousands of Jews by the Roman guards.

Again Joseph was directed to a place of safety. He returned to Nazareth, his former home, and here for nearly thirty years Jesus dwelt, "that it might be fulfilled which was spoken by the prophets, He shall be called a Nazarene." Galilee was under the control of a son of Herod, but it had a much larger admixture of foreign inhabitants than Judea. Thus there was less interest in matters relating especially to the Jews, and the claims of Jesus would be less likely to excite the jealousy of those in power.

Such was the Saviour's reception when He came to the earth. There seemed to be no place of rest or safety for the infant Redeemer. God could not trust His beloved Son with men, even while carrying forward His work for their salvation. He commissioned angels to attend Jesus and protect Him till He should accomplish His mission on earth, and die by the hands of those whom He came to save.

7

As a Child

The childhood and youth of Jesus were spent in a little mountain village. There was no place on earth that would not have been honored by His presence. The palaces of kings would have been privileged in receiving Him as a guest. But He passed by the homes of wealth, the courts of royalty, and the renowned seats of learning, to make His home in obscure and despised Nazareth.

Wonderful in its significance is the brief record of His early life: "The child grew, and waxed strong in spirit, filled with wisdom: and the grace of God was upon Him." In the sunlight of His Father's countenance, Jesus "increased in wisdom and stature, and in favor with God and man." Luke 2:52. His mind was active and penetrating, with a thoughtfulness and wisdom beyond His years. Yet His character was beautiful in its symmetry. The powers of mind and body developed gradually, in keeping with the laws of childhood.

As a child, Jesus manifested a peculiar loveliness of disposition. His willing hands were ever ready to serve others. He manifested a patience that nothing could disturb, and a truthfulness that would never sacrifice integrity. In principle firm as a rock, His life revealed the grace of unselfish courtesy.

With deep earnestness the mother of Jesus watched the unfolding of His powers, and beheld the impress of perfection upon His character. With delight she sought to encourage that bright, receptive mind. Through the Holy Spirit she received wisdom to co-operate with the heavenly agencies in the development of this child, who could claim only God as His Father.

From the earliest times the faithful in Israel had given much care to the education of the youth. The Lord had directed that even from babyhood the children should be taught of His goodness and His greatness, especially as revealed in His law, and shown in the history of Israel. Song and prayer and lessons from the Scriptures were to be adapted to the opening mind. Fathers and mothers were to instruct their children that the law of God is an expression of His character, and that as they received the principles of the law into the heart, the image of God was traced on mind and soul. Much of the teaching was oral; but the youth also learned to read the Hebrew writings; and the parchment rolls of the Old Testament Scriptures were open to their study.

In the days of Christ the town or city that did not provide for the religious instruction of the young was regarded as under the curse of God. Yet the teaching had become formal. Tradition had in a great degree supplanted the Scriptures. True education would lead the youth to "seek the Lord, if haply they might feel after Him, and find Him." Acts 17:27. But the Jewish teachers gave their attention to matters of ceremony. The mind was crowded with material that was worthless to the learner, and that would not be recognized in the higher school of the courts above. The experience which is obtained through a personal acceptance of God's word had no place in the educational system. Absorbed in the round of externals, the students found no quiet hours to spend with God. They did not hear His voice speaking to the heart. In their search after knowledge, they turned away

This chapter is based on Luke 2:39, 40.

from the Source of wisdom. The great essentials of the service of God were neglected. The principles of the law were obscured. That which was regarded as superior education was the greatest hindrance to real development. Under the training of the rabbis the powers of the youth were repressed. Their minds became cramped and narrow.

70 The child Jesus did not receive instruction in the synagogue schools. His mother was His first human teacher. From her lips and from the scrolls of the prophets, He learned of heavenly things. The very words which He Himself had spoken to Moses for Israel He was now taught at His mother's knee. As He advanced from childhood to youth, He did not seek the schools of the rabbis. He needed not the education to be obtained from such sources; for God was His instructor.

The question asked during the Saviour's ministry, "How knoweth this man letters, having never learned?" does not indicate that Jesus was unable to read, but merely that He had not received a rabbinical education. John 7:15. Since He gained knowledge as we may do, His intimate acquaintance with the Scriptures shows how diligently His early years were given to the study of God's word. And spread out before Him was the great library of God's created works. He who had made all things studied the lessons which His own hand had written in earth and sea and sky. Apart from the unholy ways of the world, He gathered stores of scientific knowledge from nature. He studied the life of plants and animals, and the life of man. From His earliest years He was possessed of one purpose; He lived to bless others. For this He found resources in nature; new ideas of ways and means flashed into His mind as He studied plant life and animal life. Continually He was seeking to draw from things seen illustrations by which to present the living oracles of God. The parables by which, during His ministry, He loved to teach His lessons of truth show how open His spirit was to the influences of nature, and how He had gathered the spiritual teaching from the surroundings of His daily life.

Thus to Jesus the significance of the word and the works of God was unfolded, as He was trying to understand the reason of things. Heavenly beings were His attendants, and the culture of holy thoughts and communings was His. From the first dawning of intelligence He was constantly growing in spiritual grace and knowledge of truth.

Every child may gain knowledge as Jesus did. As we try to become acquainted with our heavenly Father through His word, angels will draw near, our minds will be strengthened, our characters will be elevated and refined. We shall become more like our Saviour. And as we behold the beautiful and grand in nature, our

affections go out after God. While the spirit is awed, the soul is invigorated by coming in contact with the Infinite through His works. Communion with God through prayer develops the 71 mental and moral faculties, and the spiritual powers strengthen as we cultivate thoughts upon spiritual things.

The life of Jesus was a life in harmony with God. While He was a child, He thought and spoke as a child; but no trace of sin marred the image of God within Him. Yet He was not exempt from temptation. The inhabitants of Nazareth were proverbial for their wickedness. The low estimate in which they were generally held is shown by Nathanael's question, "Can there any good thing come out of Nazareth?" John 1:46. Jesus was placed where His character would be tested. It was necessary for Him to be constantly on guard in order to preserve His purity. He was subject to all the conflicts which we have to meet, that He might be an example to us in childhood, youth, and manhood.

Satan was unwearied in his efforts to overcome the Child of Nazareth. From His earliest years Jesus was guarded by heavenly angels, yet His life was one long struggle against the powers of darkness. That there should be upon the earth one life free from the defilement of evil was an offense and a perplexity to the prince of darkness. He left no means untried to ensnare Jesus. No child of humanity will ever be called to live a holy life amid so fierce a conflict with temptation as was our Saviour.

The parents of Jesus were poor, and depen- 72 dent upon their daily toil. He was familiar with poverty, self-denial, and privation. This experience was a safeguard to Him. In His industrious life there were no idle moments to invite temptation. No aimless hours opened the way for corrupting associations. So far as possible, He closed the door to the tempter. Neither gain nor pleasure, applause nor censure, could induce Him to consent to a wrong act. He was wise to discern evil, and strong to resist it.

Christ was the only sinless one who ever dwelt on earth; yet for nearly thirty years He lived among the wicked inhabitants of Nazareth. This fact is a rebuke to those who think themselves dependent upon place, fortune, or prosperity, in order to live a blameless life. Temptation, poverty, adversity, is the very discipline needed to develop purity and firmness.

Jesus lived in a peasant's home, and faithfully and cheerfully acted His part in bearing the burdens of the household. He had been the Commander of heaven, and angels had delighted to fulfill His word; now He was a willing servant, a loving, obedient son. He learned a trade, and with His own hands worked in the carpenter's shop with Joseph. In the simple garb of a common laborer He walked the streets of the little town, going to and returning from His humble work. He did not employ His divine power to lessen His burdens or to lighten His toil.

As Jesus worked in childhood and youth, mind and body were developed. He did not use His physical powers recklessly, but in such a way as to keep them in health, that He might do the best work in every line. He was not willing to be defective, even in the handling of tools. He was perfect as a workman, as He was perfect in character. By His own example He taught that it is our duty to be industrious, that our work should be performed with exactness and thoroughness, and that such labor is honorable. The exercise that teaches the hands to be useful and trains the young to bear their share of life's burdens gives physical strength, and develops every faculty. All should find something to do that will be beneficial to themselves and helpful to others. God appointed work as a blessing, and only the diligent worker finds the true glory and joy of life. The approval of God rests with loving assurance upon children and youth who cheerfully take their part in the duties of the household, sharing the burdens of father and mother. Such children will go out from the home to be useful members of society.

73   Throughout His life on earth, Jesus was an earnest and constant worker. He expected much; therefore He attempted much. After He had entered on His ministry, He said, "I must work the works of Him that sent Me, while it is day: the night cometh, when no man can work." John 9:4. Jesus did not shirk care and responsibility, as do many who profess to be His followers. It is because they seek to evade this discipline that so many are weak and inefficient. They may possess precious and amiable traits, but they are nerveless and almost useless when difficulties are to be met or obstacles surmounted. The positiveness and energy, the solidity and strength of character, manifested in Christ are to be developed in us, through the same discipline that He endured. And the grace that He received is for us.

So long as He lived among men, our Saviour shared the lot of the poor. He knew by experience their cares and hardships, and He could comfort and encourage all humble workers. Those who have a true conception of the teaching of His life will never feel that a distinction must be made between classes, that the rich are to be honored above the worthy poor.

Jesus carried into His labor cheerfulness and tact. It requires much patience and spirituality to bring Bible religion into the home life and into the workshop, to bear the strain of worldly business, and yet keep the eye single to the glory of God. This is where Christ was a helper. He was never so full of worldly care as to have no time or thought for heavenly things. Often He expressed the gladness of His heart by singing psalms and heavenly songs. Often the dwellers in Nazareth heard His voice raised in praise and thanksgiving to God. He held communion with heaven in song; and as His companions complained of weariness from labor, they were cheered by the sweet melody from His lips. His praise seemed to banish the evil angels, and, like incense, fill the place with fragrance. The minds of His hearers were carried away from their earthly exile, to the heavenly home.

Jesus was the fountain of healing mercy for 74 the world; and through all those secluded years at Nazareth, His life flowed out in currents of sympathy and tenderness. The aged, the sorrowing, and the sin-burdened, the children at play in their innocent joy, the little creatures of the groves, the patient beasts of burden,—all were happier for His presence. He whose word of power upheld the worlds would stoop to relieve a wounded bird. There was nothing beneath His notice, nothing to which He disdained to minister.

Thus as He grew in wisdom and stature, Jesus increased in favor with God and man. He drew the sympathy of all hearts by showing Himself capable of sympathizing with all. The atmosphere of hope and courage that surrounded Him made Him a blessing in every home. And often in the synagogue on the Sabbath day He was called upon to read the lesson from the prophets, and the hearts of the hearers thrilled as a new light shone out from the familiar words of the sacred text.

Yet Jesus shunned display. During all the years of His stay in Nazareth, He made no exhibition of His miraculous power. He sought no high position and assumed no titles. His quiet and simple life, and even the silence of the Scriptures concerning His early years, teach an important lesson. The more quiet and simple the life of the child,—the more free from artificial excitement, and the more in harmony with nature,—the more favorable is it to physical and mental vigor and to spiritual strength.

Jesus is our example. There are many who dwell with interest upon the period of His public ministry, while they pass unnoticed the teaching of His early years. But it is in His home life that He is the pattern for all children and youth. The Saviour condescended to poverty, that He might teach how closely we in a humble lot may walk with God. He lived to please, honor, and glorify His Father in the common things of life. His work began in consecrating the lowly trade of the craftsmen who toil for their daily bread. He was doing God's service just as much when laboring at the carpenter's bench as when working miracles for the multitude. And every youth who follows Christ's example of faithfulness and obedience in His lowly home may claim those words spoken of Him by the Father through the Holy Spirit, "Behold My Servant, whom I uphold; Mine Elect, in whom My soul delighteth." Isa. 42:1.

8

The Passover Visit

Among the Jews the twelfth year was the dividing line between childhood and youth. On completing this year a Hebrew boy was called a son of the law, and also a son of God. He was given special opportunities for religious instruction, and was expected to participate in the sacred feasts and observances. It was in accordance with this custom that Jesus in His boyhood made the Passover visit to Jerusalem. Like all devout Israelites, Joseph and Mary went up every year to attend the Passover; and when Jesus had reached the required age, they took Him with them.

There were three annual feasts, the Passover, the Pentecost, and the Feast of Tabernacles, at which all the men of Israel were commanded to appear before the Lord at Jerusalem. Of these feasts the Passover was the most largely attended. Many were present from all countries where the Jews were scattered. From every part of Palestine the worshipers came in great numbers. The journey from Galilee occupied several days, and the travelers united in large companies for companionship and protection. The women and aged men rode upon oxen or asses over the steep and rocky roads. The stronger men and the youth journeyed on foot. The time of the Passover corresponded to the close of March or the beginning of April, and the whole land was bright with flowers, and glad with the song of birds. All along the way were spots memorable in the history of Israel, and fathers and mothers recounted to their children the wonders that God had wrought for His people in ages past. They beguiled their journey with song and music, and when at last the towers of Jerusalem came into view, every voice joined in the triumphant strain,—

"Our feet shall stand
Within thy gates, O Jerusalem. . . .
Peace be within thy walls,
And prosperity within thy palaces."
Ps. 122:2-7.

The observance of the Passover began with the birth of the Hebrew nation. On the last night of their bondage in Egypt, when there appeared no token of deliverance, God commanded them to prepare for an immediate release. He had warned Pharaoh of the final judgment on the Egyptians, and He directed the Hebrews to gather their families within their own dwellings.

Having sprinkled the doorposts with the blood of the slain lamb, they were to eat the lamb, roasted, with unleavened bread and bitter herbs. "And thus shall ye eat it," He said, "with your loins girded, your shoes on your feet, and your staff in your hand; and ye shall eat it in haste: it is the Lord's passover." Ex. 12:11. At midnight all the first-born of the Egyptians were slain. Then the king sent to Israel the message, "Rise up, and get you forth from among my people; . . . and go, serve the Lord, as ye have said." Ex. 12:31. The Hebrews went out from Egypt an independent nation. The Lord had commanded that the Passover should be yearly kept. "It shall come to pass," He said, "when your children shall say unto you, What mean ye by this service? that ye shall say, It is the sacrifice of the Lord's passover, who passed over the houses of the children of Israel in Egypt, when He smote the Egyptians." Thus from generation to generation the story of this wonderful deliverance was to be repeated.

The Passover was followed by the seven days' feast of unleavened bread. On the second day of the feast, the first fruits of the year's harvest, a sheaf of barley, was presented before the Lord. All the ceremonies of the feast were types of the work of Christ. The deliverance of Israel from Egypt was an object lesson of redemption, which the Passover was intended to keep in memory. The slain lamb, the unleavened bread, the sheaf of first fruits, represented the Saviour.

With most of the people in the days of Christ, the observance of this feast had degenerated into formalism. But what was its significance to the Son of God!

For the first time the child Jesus looked upon the temple. He saw the white-robed priests performing their solemn ministry. He beheld the bleeding victim upon the altar of sacrifice. With the worshipers He bowed in prayer, while the cloud of incense ascended before God. He witnessed the impressive rites of the paschal service. Day by day He saw their meaning more clearly. Every act seemed to be bound up with His own life. New impulses were awakening within Him. Silent and absorbed, He seemed to be studying out a great problem. The mystery of His mission was opening to the Saviour.

Rapt in the contemplation of these scenes, He did not remain beside His parents. He sought to be alone. When the paschal services were ended, He still lingered in the temple courts; and when the worshipers departed from Jerusalem, He was left behind.

In this visit to Jerusalem, the parents of Jesus wished to bring Him in connection with the great teachers in Israel. While He was obedient in every particular to the word of God, He did not conform to the rabbinical rites and usages. Joseph and Mary hoped that He might be led to reverence the learned rabbis, and give more dili-

This chapter is based on Luke 2:41-51.

gent heed to their requirements. But Jesus in the temple had been taught by God. That which He had received, He began at once to impart.

At that day an apartment connected with the temple was devoted to a sacred school, after the manner of the schools of the prophets. Here leading rabbis with their pupils assembled, and hither the child Jesus came. Seating Himself at the feet of these grave, learned men, He listened to their instruction. As one seeking for wisdom, He questioned these teachers in regard to the prophecies, and to events then taking place that pointed to the advent of the Messiah.

Jesus presented Himself as one thirsting for a knowledge of God. His questions were suggestive of deep truths which had long been obscured, yet which were vital to the salvation of souls. While showing how narrow and superficial was the wisdom of the wise men, every question put before them a divine lesson, and placed truth in a new aspect. The rabbis spoke of the wonderful elevation which the Messiah's coming would bring to the Jewish nation; but Jesus presented the prophecy of Isaiah, and asked them the meaning of those scriptures that point to the suffering and death of the Lamb of God.

The doctors turned upon Him with questions, and they were amazed at His answers. With the humility of a child He repeated the words of
79 Scripture, giving them a depth of meaning that the wise men had not conceived of. If followed, the lines of truth He pointed out would have worked a reformation in the religion of the day. A deep interest in spiritual things would have been awakened; and when Jesus began His ministry, many would have been prepared to receive Him.

80 The rabbis knew that Jesus had not been instructed in their schools; yet His understanding of the prophecies far exceeded theirs. In this thoughtful Galilean boy they discerned great promise. They desired to gain Him as a student, that He might become a teacher in Israel. They wanted to have charge of His education, feeling that a mind so original must be brought under their molding.

The words of Jesus had moved their hearts as they had never before been moved by words from human lips. God was seeking to give light to those leaders in Israel, and He used the only means by which they could be reached. In their pride they would have scorned to admit that they could receive instruction from anyone. If Jesus had appeared to be trying to teach them, they would have disdained to listen. But they flattered themselves that they were teaching Him, or at least testing His knowledge of the Scriptures. The youthful modesty and grace of Jesus disarmed their prejudices. Unconsciously their minds were opened to the word of God, and the Holy Spirit spoke to their hearts.

They could not but see that their expectation in regard to the Messiah was not sustained by prophecy; but they would not renounce the theories that had flattered their ambition. They would not admit that they had misapprehended the Scriptures they claimed to teach. From one to another passed the inquiry, How hath this youth knowledge, having never learned? The light was shining in darkness; but "the darkness apprehended it not." John 1:5, R. V.

Meanwhile Joseph and Mary were in great perplexity and distress. In the departure from Jerusalem they had lost sight of Jesus, and they knew not that He had tarried behind. The country was then densely populated, and the caravans from Galilee were very large. There was much confusion as they left the city. On the way the pleasure of traveling with friends and acquaintances absorbed their attention, and they did not notice His absence till night came on. Then as they halted for rest, they missed the helpful hand of their child. Supposing Him to be with their company, they had felt no anxiety. Young as He was, they had trusted Him implicitly, expecting that when needed, He would be ready to assist them, anticipating their wants as He had always done. But now their fears were roused. They searched for Him throughout their company, but in vain. Shuddering they remembered how Herod had tried to destroy Him in His infancy. Dark forebodings filled their hearts. They bitterly reproached themselves.

Returning to Jerusalem, they pursued their 81 search. The next day, as they mingled with the worshipers in the temple, a familiar voice arrested their attention. They could not mistake it; no other voice was like His, so serious and earnest, yet so full of melody.

In the school of the rabbis they found Jesus. Rejoiced as they were, they could not forget their grief and anxiety. When He was with them again, the mother said, in words that implied reproof, "Son, why hast Thou thus dealt with us? Behold, Thy father and I have sought Thee sorrowing."

"How is it that ye sought Me?" answered Jesus. "Wist ye not that I must be about My Father's business?" And as they seemed not to understand His words, He pointed upward. On His face was a light at which they wondered. Divinity was flashing through humanity. On finding Him in the temple, they had listened to what was passing between Him and the rabbis, and they were astonished at His questions and answers. His words started a train of thought that would never be forgotten.

And His question to them had a lesson. "Wist ye not," He said, "that I must be about My Father's business?" Jesus was engaged in the work that He had come into the world to do; but Joseph and Mary had neglected theirs. God had shown them high honor in committing to them

His Son. Holy angels had directed the course of Joseph in order to preserve the life of Jesus. But for an entire day they had lost sight of Him whom they should not have forgotten for a moment. And when their anxiety was relieved, they had not censured themselves, but had cast the blame upon Him.

It was natural for the parents of Jesus to look upon Him as their own child. He was daily with them, His life in many respects was like that of other children, and it was difficult for them to realize that He was the Son of God. They were in danger of failing to appreciate the blessing granted them in the presence of the world's Redeemer. The grief of their separation from Him, and the gentle reproof which His words conveyed, were designed to impress them with the sacredness of their trust.

In the answer to His mother, Jesus showed for the first time that He understood His relation to God. Before His birth the angel had said to Mary, "He shall be great, and shall be called the Son of the Highest: and the Lord God shall give
82 unto Him the throne of His father David: and He shall reign over the house of Jacob forever." Luke 1:32, 33. These words Mary had pondered in her heart; yet while she believed that her child was to be Israel's Messiah, she did not comprehend His mission. Now she did not understand His words; but she knew that He had disclaimed kinship to Joseph, and had declared His Sonship to God.

Jesus did not ignore His relation to His earthly parents. From Jerusalem He returned home with them, and aided them in their life of toil. He hid in His own heart the mystery of His mission, waiting submissively for the appointed time for Him to enter upon His work. For eighteen years after He had recognized that He was the Son of God, He acknowledged the tie that bound Him to the home at Nazareth, and performed the duties of a son, a brother, a friend, and a citizen.

As His mission had opened to Jesus in the temple, He shrank from contact with the multitude. He wished to return from Jerusalem in quietness, with those who knew the secret of His life. By the paschal service, God was seeking to call His people away from their worldly cares, and to remind them of His wonderful work in their deliverance from Egypt. In this work He desired them to see a promise of deliverance from sin. As the blood of the slain lamb sheltered the homes of Israel, so the blood of Christ was to save their souls; but they could be saved through Christ only as by faith their should make His life their own. There was virtue in the symbolic service only as it directed the worshipers to Christ as their personal Saviour. God desired that they should be led to prayerful study and meditation in regard to Christ's mission. But as the multitudes left

Jerusalem, the excitement of travel and social intercourse too often absorbed their attention, and the service they had witnessed was forgotten. The Saviour was not attracted to their company.

As Joseph and Mary should return from Jerusalem alone with Jesus, He hoped to direct their minds to the prophecies of the suffering Saviour. Upon Calvary He sought to lighten His mother's grief. He was thinking of her now. Mary was to witness His last agony, and Jesus desired her to understand His mission, that she might be strengthened to endure, when the sword should pierce through her soul. As Jesus had been separated from her, and she had sought Him sorrowing three days, so when He should be offered up for the sins of the world, He would again be lost to her for three days. And as He should come forth from the tomb, her sorrow would again be turned to joy. But how much better she could have borne the   83
anguish of His death if she had understood the Scriptures to which He was now trying to turn her thoughts!

If Joseph and Mary had stayed their minds upon God by meditation and prayer, they would have realized the sacredness of their trust, and would not have lost sight of Jesus. By one day's neglect they lost the Saviour; but it cost them three days of anxious search to find Him. So with us; by idle talk, evilspeaking, or neglect of prayer, we may in one day lose the Saviour's presence, and it may take many days of sorrowful search to find Him, and regain the peace that we have lost.

In our association with one another, we should take heed lest we forget Jesus, and pass along unmindful that He is not with us. When we become absorbed in worldly things so that we have no thought for Him in whom our hope of eternal life is centered, we separate ourselves from Jesus and from the heavenly angels. These holy beings cannot remain where the Saviour's presence is not desired, and His absence is not marked. This is why discouragement so often exists among the professed followers of Christ.

Many attend religious services, and are refreshed and comforted by the word of God; but through neglect of meditation, watchfulness, and prayer, they lose the blessing, and find themselves more destitute than before they received it. Often they feel that God has dealt hardly with them. They do not see that the fault is their own. By separating themselves from Jesus, they have shut away the light of His presence.

It would be well for us to spend a thoughtful hour each day in contemplation of the life of Christ. We should take it point by point, and let the imagination grasp each scene, especially the closing ones. As we thus dwell upon His great sacrifice for us, our confidence in Him will be more constant, our love will be quickened, and we shall be more deeply imbued with His spirit. If we would be saved at last, we must learn the lesson of penitence and humiliation at the foot of the cross.

As we associate together, we may be a blessing to one another. If we are Christ's, our sweetest thoughts will be of Him. We shall love to talk of Him; and as we speak to one another of His love, our hearts will be softened by divine influences. Beholding the beauty of His character, we shall be "changed into the same image from glory to glory." 2 Cor. 3:18.

9

Days of Conflict

From its earliest years the Jewish child was surrounded with the requirements of the rabbis. Rigid rules were prescribed for every act, down to the smallest details of life. Under the synagogue teachers the youth were instructed in the countless regulations which as orthodox Israelites they were expected to observe. But Jesus did not interest Himself in these matters. From childhood He acted independently of the rabbinical laws. The Scriptures of the Old Testament were His constant study, and the words, "Thus saith the Lord," were ever upon His lips.

As the condition of the people began to open to His mind, He saw that the requirements of society and the requirements of God were in constant collision. Men were departing from the word of God, and exalting theories of their own invention. They were observing traditional rites that possessed no virtue. Their service was a mere round of ceremonies; the sacred truths it was designed to teach were hidden from the worshipers. He saw that in their faithless services they found no peace. They did not know the freedom of spirit that would come to them by serving God in truth. Jesus had come to teach the meaning of the worship of God, and He could not sanction the mingling of human requirements with the divine precepts. He did not attack the precepts or practices of the learned teachers; but when reproved for His own simple habits, He presented the word of God in justification of His conduct.

In every gentle and submissive way, Jesus tried to please those with whom He came in contact. Because He was so gentle and unobtrusive, the scribes and elders supposed that He would be easily influenced by their teaching. They urged Him to receive the maxims and traditions that had been handed down from the ancient rabbis, but He asked for their authority in Holy Writ. He would hear every word that proceeds from the mouth of God; but He could not obey the inventions of men. Jesus seemed to know the Scriptures from beginning to end, and He presented them in their true import. The rabbis were ashamed to be instructed by a child. They claimed that it was their office to explain the Scriptures, and that it was His place to accept their interpretation. They were indignant that He should stand in opposition to their word.

They knew that no authority could be found in Scripture for their traditions. They realized that in spiritual understanding Jesus was far in advance of them. Yet they were angry because He did not obey their dictates. Failing to convince Him, they sought Joseph and Mary, and set before them His course of noncompliance. Thus He suffered rebuke and censure.

At a very early age, Jesus had begun to act for Himself in the formation of His character, and not even respect and love for His parents could turn Him from obedience to God's word. "It is written" was His reason for every act that varied from the family customs. But the influence of the rabbis made His life a bitter one. Even in His youth He had to learn the hard lesson of silence and patient endurance.

His brothers, as the sons of Joseph were called, sided with the rabbis. They insisted that the traditions must be heeded, as if they were the requirements of God. They even regarded the precepts of men more highly than the word of God, and they were greatly annoyed at the clear penetration of Jesus in distinguishing between the false and the true. His strict obedience to the law of God they condemned as stubbornness. They were surprised at the knowledge and wisdom He showed in answering the rabbis. They knew that He had not received instruction from the wise men, yet they could not but see that He was an instructor to them. They recognized that His education was of a higher type than their own. But they did not discern that He had access to the tree of life, a source of knowledge of which they were ignorant.

Christ was not exclusive, and He had given special offense to the Pharisees by departing in this respect from their rigid rules. He found the domain of religion fenced in by high walls of seclusion, as too sacred a matter for everyday life. These walls of partition He overthrew. In His contact with men He did not ask, What is your creed? To what church do you belong? He exercised His helping power in behalf of all who needed help. Instead of secluding Himself in a hermit's cell in order to show His heavenly character, He labored earnestly for humanity. He inculcated the principle that Bible religion does not consist in the mortification of the body. He taught that pure and undefiled religion is not meant only for set times and special occasions. At all times and in all places He manifested a loving interest in men, and shed about Him the light of a cheerful piety. All this was a rebuke to the Pharisees. It showed that religion does not consist in selfishness, and that their morbid devotion to personal interest was far from being true godliness. This had roused their enmity against Jesus, so that they tried to enforce His conformity to their regulations.

87   Jesus worked to relieve every case of suffering that He saw. He had little money to give, but He often denied Himself of food in order to relieve those who appeared more needy than He. His brothers felt that His influence went far to counteract theirs. He possessed a tact which none of them had, or desired to have. When they spoke harshly to poor, degraded beings, Jesus sought out these very ones, and spoke to them words of encouragement. To those who were in need He would give a cup of cold water, and would quietly place His own meal in their hands. As He relieved their sufferings, the truths He taught were associated with His acts of mercy, and were thus riveted in the memory.

All this displeased His brothers. Being older than Jesus, they felt that He should be under their dictation. They charged Him with thinking Himself superior to them, and reproved Him for setting Himself above their teachers and the priests and rulers of the people. Often they threatened and tried to intimidate Him; but He passed on, making the Scriptures His guide.

Jesus loved His brothers, and treated them with unfailing kindness; but they were jealous of Him, and manifested the most decided unbelief and contempt. They could not understand His conduct. Great contradictions presented themselves in Jesus. He was the divine Son of

88 God, and yet a helpless child. The Creator of the worlds, the earth was His possession, and yet poverty marked His life experience at every step. He possessed a dignity and individuality wholly distinct from earthly pride and assumption; He did not strive for worldly greatness, and in even the lowliest position He was content. This angered His brothers. They could not account for His constant serenity under trial and deprivation. They did not know that for our sake He had become poor, that we "through His poverty might be rich." 2 Cor. 8:9. They could understand the mystery of His mission no more than the friends of Job could understand his humiliation and suffering.

Jesus was misunderstood by His brothers because He was not like them. His standard was not their standard. In looking to men they had turned away from God, and they had not His power in their lives. The forms of religion which they observed could not transform the character. They paid "tithe of mint and anise and cummin," but omitted "the weightier matters of the law, judgment, mercy, and faith." Matt. 23:23. The example of Jesus was to them a continual irritation. He hated but one thing in the world, and that was sin. He could not witness a wrong act without pain which it was

impossible to disguise. Between the formalists, whose sanctity of appearance concealed the love of sin, and a character in which zeal for God's glory was always paramount, the contrast was unmistakable. Because the life of Jesus condemned evil, He was opposed, both at home and abroad. His unselfishness and integrity were commented on with a sneer. His forbearance and kindness were termed cowardice.

Of the bitterness that falls to the lot of humanity, there was no part which Christ did not taste. There were those who tried to cast contempt upon Him because of His birth, and even in His childhood He had to meet their scornful looks and evil whisperings. If He had responded by an impatient word or look, if He had conceded to His brothers by even one wrong act, He would have failed of being a perfect example. Thus He would have failed of carrying out the plan for our redemption. Had He even admitted that there could be an excuse for sin, Satan would have triumphed, and the world would have been lost. This is why the tempter worked to make His life as trying as possible, that He might be led to sin.

But to every temptation He had one answer, "It is written." He rarely rebuked any wrongdoing of His brothers, but He had a word from 89 God to speak to them. Often He was accused of cowardice for refusing to unite with them in some forbidden act; but His answer was, It is written, "The fear of the Lord, that is wisdom; and to depart from evil is understanding." Job 28:28.

There were some who sought His society, feeling at peace in His presence; but many avoided Him, because they were rebuked by His stainless life. Young companions urged Him to do as they did. He was bright and cheerful; they enjoyed His presence, and welcomed His ready suggestions; but they were impatient at His scruples, and pronounced Him narrow and strait-laced. Jesus answered, It is written, "Wherewithal shall a young man cleanse his way? by taking heed thereto according to Thy word." "Thy word have I hid in mine heart, that I might not sin against Thee." Ps. 119:9, 11.

Often He was asked, Why are you bent on being so singular, so different from us all? It is written, He said, "Blessed are the undefiled in the way, who walk in the law of the Lord. Blessed are they that keep His testimonies, and that seek Him with the whole heart. They also do no iniquity: they walk in His ways." Ps. 119:1-3.

When questioned why He did not join in the frolics of the youth of Nazareth, He said, It is written, "I have rejoiced in the way of Thy testimonies, as much as in all riches. I will meditate in Thy precepts, and have respect unto Thy ways. I will delight myself in Thy statutes: I will not forget Thy word." Ps. 119:14-16.

Jesus did not contend for His rights. Often His work was made unnecessarily severe because He was willing and uncomplaining. Yet He did not fail nor become discouraged. He lived above these difficulties, as if in the light of God's countenance. He did not retaliate when roughly used, but bore insult patiently.

Again and again He was asked, Why do You submit to such despiteful usage, even from Your brothers? It is written, He said, "My son, forget not My law; but let thine heart keep My commandments: for length of days, and long life, and peace, shall they add to thee. Let not mercy and truth forsake thee: bind them about thy neck; write them upon the table of thine heart: so shalt thou find favor and good understanding in the sight of God and man." Prov. 3:1-4.

From the time when the parents of Jesus found Him in the temple, His course of action was a mystery to them. He would not enter into controversy, yet His example was a constant 90 lesson. He seemed as one who was set apart. His hours of happiness were found when alone with nature and with God. Whenever it was His privilege, He turned aside from the scene of His labor, to go into the fields, to meditate in the green valleys, to hold communion with God on the mountainside or amid the trees of the forest. The early morning often found Him in some secluded place, meditating, searching the Scriptures, or in prayer. From these quiet hours He would return to His home to take up His duties again, and to give an example of patient toil.

The life of Christ was marked with respect and love for His mother. Mary believed in her heart that the holy child born of her was the long-promised Messiah, yet she dared not express her faith. Throughout His life on earth she was a partaker in His sufferings. She witnessed with sorrow the trials brought upon Him in His childhood and youth. By her vindication of what she knew to be right in His conduct, she herself was brought into trying positions. She looked upon the associations of the home, and the mother's tender watchcare over her children, as of vital importance in the formation of character. The sons and daughters of Joseph knew this, and by appealing to her anxiety, they tried to correct the practices of Jesus according to their standard.

Mary often remonstrated with Jesus, and urged Him to conform to the usages of the rabbis. But He could not be persuaded to change His habits of contemplating the works of God and seeking to alleviate the suffering of men or even of dumb animals. When the priests and teachers required Mary's aid in controlling Jesus, she was greatly troubled; but peace came to her heart as He presented the statements of Scripture upholding His practices.

At times she wavered between Jesus and His brothers, who did not believe that He was the Sent of God; but evidence was abundant that His was a divine character. She saw Him sacrificing Himself for the good of others. His presence brought a purer atmosphere into the home, and His life was as leaven working amid the elements of society. Harmless and undefiled, He walked among the thoughtless, the rude, the uncourteous; amid the unjust publicans, the reckless prodigals, the unrighteous Samaritans, the heathen soldiers, the rough peasants, and the mixed multitude. He spoke a word of sympathy here and a word there, as He saw men weary, yet compelled to bear heavy burdens. He shared their burdens, and repeated to them the lessons He had learned from nature, of the love, the kindness, the goodness of God.

He taught all to look upon themselves as 91 endowed with precious talents, which if rightly employed would secure for them eternal riches. He weeded all vanity from life, and by His own example taught that every moment of time is fraught with eternal results; that it is to be cherished as a treasure, and to be employed for holy purposes. He passed by no human being as worthless, but sought to apply the saving remedy to every soul. In whatever company He found Himself, He presented a lesson that was appropriate to the time and the circumstances. He sought to inspire with hope the most rough and unpromising, setting before them the assurance that they might become blameless and harmless, attaining such a character as would make them manifest as the children of God. Often He met those who had drifted under Satan's control, and who had no power to break from his snare. To such a one, discouraged, sick, tempted, and fallen, Jesus would speak words of tenderest pity, words that were needed and could be understood. Others He met who 92 were fighting a hand-to-hand battle with the adversary of souls. These He encouraged to persevere, assuring them that they would win; for angels of God were on their side, and would give them the victory. Those whom He thus helped were convinced that here was One in whom they could trust with perfect confidence. He would not betray the secrets they poured into His sympathizing ear.

Jesus was the healer of the body as well as of the soul. He was interested in every phase of suffering that came under His notice, and to every sufferer He brought relief, His kind words having a soothing balm. None could say that He had worked a miracle; but virtue—the healing power of love—went out from Him to the sick and distressed. Thus in an unobtrusive way He worked for the people from His very childhood. And this was why, after His public ministry began, so many heard Him gladly.

Yet through childhood, youth, and manhood, Jesus walked alone. In His purity and His faithfulness, He trod the wine press alone, and of the people there was none with Him. He carried the awful weight of responsibility for the salvation of men. He knew that unless there was a decided change in the principles and purposes of the human race, all would be lost. This was the burden of His soul, and none could appreciate the weight that rested upon Him. Filled with intense purpose, He carried out the design of His life that He Himself should be the light of men.

10

The Voice in the Wilderness

From among the faithful in Israel, who had long waited for the coming of the Messiah, the forerunner of Christ arose. The aged priest Zacharias and his wife Elisabeth were "both righteous before God;" and in their quiet and holy lives the light of faith shone out like a star amid the darkness of those evil days. To this godly pair was given the promise of a son, who should "go before the face of the Lord to prepare His ways."

Zacharias dwelt in "the hill country of Judea," but he had gone up to Jerusalem to minister for one week in the temple, a service required twice a year from the priests of each course. "And it came to pass, that while he executed the priest's office before God in the order of his course, according to the custom of the priest's office, his lot was to burn incense when he went into the temple of the Lord."

He was standing before the golden altar in the holy place of the sanctuary. The cloud of incense with the prayers of Israel was ascending before God. Suddenly he became conscious of a divine presence. An angel of the Lord was "standing on the right side of the altar." The position of the angel was an indication of favor, but Zacharias took no note of this. For many years he had prayed for the coming of the Redeemer; now heaven had sent its messenger to announce that these prayers were about to be answered; but the mercy of God seemed too great for him to credit. He was filled with fear and self-condemnation.

But he was greeted with the joyful assurance: "Fear not, Zacharias: for thy prayer is heard; and thy wife Elisabeth shall bear thee a son, and thou shalt call his name John. And thou shalt have joy and gladness; and many shall rejoice at his birth. For he shall be great in the sight of the Lord, and shall drink neither wine nor strong drink; and he shall be filled with the Holy Ghost. . . . And many of the children of Israel shall he turn to the Lord their God. And he shall go before Him in the spirit and power of Elias, to turn the hearts of the fathers to the children, and the disobedient to the wisdom of the just; to

make ready a people prepared for the Lord. And Zacharias said unto the angel, Whereby shall I know this? for I am an old man, and my wife well stricken in years."

Zacharias well knew how to Abraham in his old age a child was given because he believed Him faithful who had promised. But for a moment the aged priest turns his thought to the weakness of humanity. He forgets that what God has promised, He is able to perform. What a contrast between this unbelief and the sweet, childlike faith of Mary, the maiden of Nazareth, whose answer to the angel's wonderful announcement was, "Behold the handmaid of the Lord; be it unto me according to thy word"! Luke 1:38.

The birth of a son to Zacharias, like the birth of the child of Abraham, and that of Mary, was to teach a great spiritual truth, a truth that we are slow to learn and ready to forget. In ourselves we are incapable of doing any good thing; but that which we cannot do will be wrought by the power of God in every submissive and believing soul. It was through faith that the child of promise was given. It is through faith that spiritual life is begotten, and we are enabled to do the works of righteousness.

To the question of Zacharias, the angel said, "I am Gabriel, that stand in the presence of God; and am sent to speak unto thee, and to show thee these glad tidings." Five hundred years before, Gabriel had made known to Daniel the prophetic period which was to extend to the coming of Christ. The knowledge that the end of this period was near had moved Zacharias to pray for the Messiah's advent. Now the very messenger through whom the prophecy was given had come to announce its fulfillment.

The words of the angel, "I am Gabriel, that stand in the presence of God," show that he holds a position of high honor in the heavenly courts. When he came with a message to Daniel, he said, "There is none that holdeth with me in these things, but Michael [Christ] your Prince." Dan. 10:21. Of Gabriel the Saviour speaks in the Revelation, saying that "He sent and signified it by His angel unto His servant John." Rev. 1:1. And to John the angel declared, "I am a fellow servant with thee and with thy brethren the prophets." Rev. 22:9, R. V. Wonderful thought—that the angel who stands next in honor to the Son of God is the one chosen to open the purposes of God to sinful men.

Zacharias had expressed doubt of the angel's words. He was not to speak again until they were fulfilled. "Behold," said the angel, "thou shalt be dumb, . . . until the day that these things shall be performed, because thou believest not my words, which shall be fulfilled in their season." It was the duty of the priest in this service to pray for the pardon of public and national sins, and for the coming of the Messiah; but when Zacharias attempted to do this, he could

This chapter is based on Luke 1:5-23, 57-80; 3:1-18; Matthew 3:1-12; Mark 1:1-8.

not utter a word.

Coming forth to bless the people, "he beckoned unto them, and remained speechless." They had waited long, and had begun to fear, lest he had been cut down by the judgment of God. But as he came forth from the holy place, his face was shining with the glory of God, "and they perceived that he had seen a vision in the temple." Zacharias communicated to them what he had seen and heard; and "as soon as the days of his ministration were accomplished, he departed to his own house."

Soon after the birth of the promised child, the father's tongue was loosed, "and he spake, and praised God. And fear came on all that dwelt round about them: and all these sayings were noised abroad throughout all the hill country of Judea. And all they that heard them laid them up in their hearts, saying, What manner of child shall this be!" All this tended to call attention to the Messiah's coming, for which John was to prepare the way.

The Holy Spirit rested upon Zacharias, and in these beautiful words he prophesied of the mission of his son:

"Thou, child, shalt be called the prophet of the Highest:
For thou shalt go before the face of the Lord to prepare His ways;
To give knowledge of salvation unto His people
By the remission of their sins,
Through the tender mercy of our God;
Whereby the Dayspring from on high hath visited us,
To give light to them that sit in darkness and in the shadow of death,
To guide our feet into the way of peace."

"And the child grew, and waxed strong in spirit, and was in the deserts till the day of his showing unto Israel." Before the birth of John, the angel had said, "He shall be great in the sight of the Lord, and shall drink neither wine nor strong drink; and he shall be filled with the Holy Ghost." God had called the son of Zacharias to a great work, the greatest ever committed to men. In order to accomplish this work, he must have the Lord to work with him. And the Spirit of God would be with him if he heeded the instruction of the angel.

John was to go forth as Jehovah's messenger, to bring to men the light of God. He must give a new direction to their thoughts. He must impress them with the holiness of God's requirements, and their need of His perfect righteousness. Such a messenger must be holy. He must be a temple for the indwelling Spirit of God. In order to fulfill his mission, he must have a sound physical constitution, and mental and spiritual strength. Therefore it would be necessary for him to control the appetites and passions. He must be able so to control all his powers that he could stand among men as unmoved by surrounding circumstances as the rocks and mountains of the wilderness.

In the time of John the Baptist, greed for riches, and the love of luxury and display had become widespread. Sensuous pleasures, feasting and drinking, were causing physical disease and degeneracy, benumbing the spiritual perceptions, and lessening the sensibility to sin. John was to stand as a reformer. By his abstemious life and plain dress he was to rebuke the excesses of his time. Hence the directions given to the parents of John,—a lesson of temperance by an angel from the throne of heaven.

In childhood and youth the character is most impressible. The power of self-control should then be acquired. By the fireside and at the family board influences are exerted whose results are as enduring as eternity. More than any natural endowment, the habits established in early years decide whether a man will be victorious or vanquished in the battle of life. Youth is the sowing time. It determines the character of the harvest, for this life and for the life to come.

As a prophet, John was "to turn the hearts of the fathers to the children, and the disobedient to the wisdom of the just; to make ready a people prepared for the Lord." In preparing the way for Christ's first advent, he was a representative of those who are to prepare a people for our Lord's second coming. The world is given to self-indulgence. Errors and fables abound. Satan's snares for destroying souls are multiplied. All who would perfect holiness in the fear of God must learn the lessons of temperance and self-control. The appetites and passions must be held in subjection to the higher powers of the mind. This self-discipline is essential to that mental strength and spiritual insight which will enable us to understand and to practice the sacred truths of God's word. For this reason temperance finds its place in the work of preparation for Christ's second coming.

In the natural order of things, the son of Zacharias would have been educated for the priesthood. But the training of the rabbinical schools would have unfitted him for his work. God did not send him to the teachers of theology to learn how to interpret the Scriptures. He called him to the desert, that he might learn of nature and nature's God.

It was a lonely region where he found his home, in the midst of barren hills, wild ravines, and rocky caves. But it was his choice to forgo the enjoyments and luxuries of life for the stern discipline of the wilderness. Here his surroundings were favorable to habits of simplicity and self-denial. Uninterrupted by the clamor of the world, he could here study the lessons of nature, of revelation, and of Providence. The words of the angel to Zacharias had been often repeated to John by his God-fearing parents. From childhood his mission had been kept before him, and he had accepted the holy trust. To him the solitude of the desert was a welcome escape from society in which suspicion, unbelief, and impurity had become well-nigh all-pervading. He 102 distrusted his own power to withstand temptation, and shrank from constant contact with sin, lest he should lose the sense of its exceeding sinfulness.

Dedicated to God as a Nazarite from his birth, he made the vow his own in a life-long consecration. His dress was that of the ancient prophets, a garment of camel's hair, confined by a leather girdle. He ate the "locusts and wild honey" found in the wilderness, and drank the pure water from the hills.

But the life of John was not spent in idleness, in ascetic gloom, or in selfish isolation. From time to time he went forth to mingle with men; and he was ever an interested observer of what was passing in the world. From his quiet retreat he watched the unfolding of events. With vision illuminated by the divine Spirit he studied the characters of men, that he might understand how to reach their hearts with the message of heaven. The burden of his mission was upon him. In solitude, by meditation and prayer, he sought to gird up his soul for the lifework before him.

Although in the wilderness, he was not exempt from temptation. So far as possible, he closed every avenue by which Satan could enter, yet he was still assailed by the tempter. But his spiritual perceptions were clear; he had developed strength and decision of character, and through the aid of the Holy Spirit he was able to detect Satan's approaches, and to resist his power.

John found in the wilderness his school and his sanctuary. Like Moses amid the mountains of Midian, he was shut in by God's presence, and surrounded by the evidences of His power. It was not his lot to dwell, as did Israel's great leader, amid the solemn majesty of the mountain solitudes; but before him were the heights of Moab, beyond Jordan, speaking of Him who had set fast the mountains, and girded them with strength. The gloomy and terrible aspect of nature in his wilderness home vividly pictured the condition of Israel. The fruitful vineyard of the Lord had become a desolate waste. But above the desert the heavens bent bright and beautiful. The clouds that gathered, dark with tempest, were arched by the rainbow of promise. So above Israel's degradation shone the promised glory of the Messiah's reign. The clouds of wrath were spanned by the rainbow of His covenant-mercy.

Alone in the silent night he read God's promise to Abraham of a seed numberless as the stars. The light of dawn, gilding the mountains of Moab, told of Him who should be as "the light of the morning, when the sun riseth, even a 103 morning without clouds." 2 Sam. 23:4. And in the brightness of noontide he saw the splendor of His manifestation, when "the glory of the Lord shall be revealed, and all flesh shall see it together." Isa. 40:5.

With awed yet exultant spirit he searched in the prophetic scrolls the revelations of the Messiah's coming,—the promised seed that should bruise the serpent's head; Shiloh, "the peace giver," who was to appear before a king should cease to reign on David's throne. Now the time had come. A Roman ruler sat in the palace upon Mount Zion. By the sure word of the Lord, already the Christ was born.

Isaiah's rapt portrayals of the Messiah's glory were his study by day and by night,—the Branch from the root of Jesse; a King to reign in righteousness, judging "with equity for the meek of the earth;" "a covert from the tempest; . . . the shadow of a great rock in a weary land;" Israel no longer to be termed "Forsaken," nor her land "Desolate," but to be called of the Lord, "My Delight," and her land "Beulah." Isa. 11:4; 32:2; 62:4, margin. The heart of the lonely exile was filled with the glorious vision.

He looked upon the King in His beauty, and self was forgotten. He beheld the majesty of holiness, and felt himself to be inefficient and unworthy. He was ready to go forth as Heaven's messenger, unawed by the human, because he had looked upon the Divine. He could stand erect and fearless in the presence of earthly monarchs, because he had bowed low before the King of kings.

John did not fully understand the nature of the Messiah's kingdom. He looked for Israel to be delivered from her national foes; but the coming of a King in righteousness, and the establishment of Israel as a holy nation, was the great object of his hope. Thus he believed would be accomplished the prophecy given at his birth,—

"To remember His holy covenant; . . .
That we being delivered out of the hand of
     our enemies
Might serve Him without fear,
In holiness and righteousness before Him, all
     the days of our life."

He saw his people deceived, self-satisfied, and asleep in their sins. He longed to rouse them to a holier life. The message that God had given him to bear was designed to startle them from their lethargy, and cause them to tremble 104 because of their great wickedness. Before the seed of the gospel could find lodgment, the soil of the heart must be broken up. Before they would seek healing from Jesus, they must be awakened to their danger from the wounds of sin.

God does not send messengers to flatter the sinner. He delivers no message of peace to lull the unsanctified into fatal security. He lays heavy burdens upon the conscience of the wrongdoer, and pierces the soul with arrows of conviction. The ministering angels present to him the fearful judgments of God to deepen the sense of need, and prompt the cry, "What must I do to be saved?" Then the hand that has humbled in the dust, lifts up the penitent. The voice that has rebuked sin, and put to shame pride and ambition, inquires with tenderest sympathy, "What wilt thou that I shall do unto thee?"

When the ministry of John began, the nation was in a state of excitement and discontent verging on revolution. At the removal of Archelaus, Judea had been brought directly under the control of Rome. The tyranny and extortion of the Roman governors, and their determined efforts to introduce the heathen symbols and customs, kindled revolt, which had been quenched in the blood of thousands of the bravest of Israel. All this intensified the national hatred against Rome, and increased the longing to be freed from her power.

Amid discord and strife, a voice was heard from the wilderness, a voice startling and stern, yet full of hope: "Repent ye; for the kingdom of heaven is at hand." With a new, strange power it moved the people. Prophets had foretold the coming of Christ as an event far in the future; but here was an announcement that it was at hand. John's singular appearance carried the minds of his hearers back to the ancient seers. In his manner and dress he resembled the prophet Elijah. With the spirit and power of Elijah he denounced the national corruption, and rebuked the prevailing sins. His words were plain, pointed, and convincing. Many believed him to be one of the prophets risen from the dead. The whole nation was stirred. Multitudes flocked to the wilderness.

John proclaimed the coming of the Messiah, and called the people to repentance. As a symbol of cleansing from sin, he baptized them in the waters of the Jordan. Thus by a significant object lesson he declared that those who claimed to be the chosen people of God were defiled by sin, and that without purification of heart and life they could have no part in the Messiah's kingdom.

105 Princes and rabbis, soldiers, publicans, and peasants came to hear the prophet. For a time the solemn warning from God alarmed them. Many were brought to repentance, and received baptism. Persons of all ranks submitted to the requirement of the Baptist, in order to participate in the kingdom he announced.

Many of the scribes and Pharisees came confessing their sins, and asking for baptism. They had exalted themselves as better than other men, and had led the people to entertain a high opinion of their piety; now the guilty secrets of their lives were unveiled. But John was impressed by the Holy Spirit that many of these men had no real conviction of sin. They were timeservers. As friends of the prophet, they hoped to find favor with the coming Prince. And by receiving baptism at the hands of this popular young teacher, they thought to strengthen their influence with the people.

John met them with the scathing inquiry, "O generation of vipers, who hath warned you to flee from the wrath to come? Bring forth therefore fruits meet for repentance: and think not to say within yourselves, We have Abraham to our 106 father: for I say unto you, that God is able of these stones to raise up children unto Abraham."

The Jews had misinterpreted God's promise of eternal favor to Israel: "Thus saith the Lord, which giveth the sun for a light by day, and the ordinances of the moon and of the stars for a light by night, which divideth the sea when the waves thereof roar; The Lord of hosts is His name: If those ordinances depart from before Me, saith the Lord, then the seed of Israel also shall cease from being a nation before Me forever. Thus saith the Lord; If heaven above can be measured, and the foundations of the earth searched out beneath, I will also cast off all the seed of Israel for all that they have done, saith the Lord." Jer. 31:35-37. The Jews regarded their natural descent from Abraham as giving them a claim to this promise. But they overlooked the conditions which God had specified. Before giving the promise, He had said, "I will put My law in their inward parts, and write it in their hearts; and will be their God, and they shall be My people. . . . For I will forgive their iniquity, and I will remember their sin no more." Jer. 31:33, 34.

To a people in whose hearts His law is written, the favor of God is assured. They are one with Him. But the Jews had separated themselves from God. Because of their sins they were suffering under His judgments. This was the cause of their bondage to a heathen nation. Their minds were darkened by transgression, and because in times past the Lord had shown them so great favor, they excused their sins. They flattered themselves that they were better than other men, and entitled to His blessings.

These things "are written for our admonition, upon whom the ends of the world are come." 1 Cor. 10:11. How often we misinterpret God's blessings, and flatter ourselves that we are favored on account of some goodness in us! God cannot do for us that which He longs to do. His gifts are used to increase our self-satisfaction, and to harden our hearts in unbelief and sin.

John declared to the teachers of Israel that

their pride, selfishness, and cruelty showed them to be a generation of vipers, a deadly curse to the people, rather than the children of just and obedient Abraham. In view of the light they had received from God, they were even worse than the heathen, to whom they felt so much superior. They had forgotten the rock whence they were hewn, and the hole of the pit from which they had been digged. God was not dependent [107] upon them for the fulfilling of His purpose. As He had called Abraham out from a heathen people, so He could call others to His service. Their hearts might now appear as lifeless as the stones of the desert, but His Spirit could quicken them to do His will, and receive the fulfillment of His promise.

"And now also," said the prophet, "the ax is laid unto the root of the trees: therefore every tree which bringeth not forth good fruit is hewn down, and cast into the fire." Not by its name, but by its fruit, is the value of a tree determined. If the fruit is worthless, the name cannot save the tree from destruction. John declared to the Jews that their standing before God was to be decided by their character and life. Profession was worthless. If their life and character were not in harmony with God's law, they were not His people.

Under his heart-searching words, his hearers were convicted. They came to him with the inquiry, "What shall we do then?" He answered, "He that hath two coats, let him impart to him that hath none; and he that hath meat, let him do likewise." And he warned the publicans against injustice, and the soldiers against violence.

All who became the subjects of Christ's kingdom, he said, would give evidence of faith and repentance. Kindness, honesty, and fidelity would be seen in their lives. They would minister to the needy, and bring their offerings to God. They would shield the defenseless, and give an example of virtue and compassion. So the followers of Christ will give evidence of the transforming power of the Holy Spirit. In the daily life, justice, mercy, and the love of God will be seen. Otherwise they are like the chaff that is given to the fire.

"I indeed baptize you in water unto repentance," said John; "but He that cometh after me is mightier than I, whose shoes I am not worthy to bear: He shall baptize you with the Holy Ghost and with fire." Matt. 3:11, R. V., margin. The prophet Isaiah had declared that the Lord would cleanse His people from their iniquities "by the spirit of judgment, and by the spirit of burning." The word of the Lord to Israel was, "I will turn My hand upon thee, and purely purge away thy dross, and take away all thy tin." Isa. 4:4; 1:25. To sin, wherever found, "our God is a consuming fire." Heb. 12:29. In all who submit to His power the Spirit of God will consume sin. But if men cling to sin, they become identified

with it. Then the glory of God, which destroys sin, must destroy them. Jacob, after his night of wrestling with the Angel, exclaimed, "I have seen God face to face, and my life is preserved." Gen. 32:30. Jacob had been guilty of a great sin [108] in his conduct toward Esau; but he had repented. His transgression had been forgiven, and his sin purged; therefore he could endure the revelation of God's presence. But wherever men came before God while willfully cherishing evil, they were destroyed. At the second advent of Christ the wicked shall be consumed "with the Spirit of His mouth," and destroyed "with the brightness of His coming." 2 Thess. 2:8. The light of the glory of God, which imparts life to the righteous, will slay the wicked.

In the time of John the Baptist, Christ was about to appear as the revealer of the character of God. His very presence would make manifest to men their sin. Only as they were willing to be purged from sin could they enter into fellowship with Him. Only the pure in heart could abide in His presence.

Thus the Baptist declared God's message to Israel. Many gave heed to his instruction. Many sacrificed all in order to obey. Multitudes followed this new teacher from place to place, and not a few cherished the hope that he might be the Messiah. But as John saw the people turning to him, he sought every opportunity of directing their faith to Him who was to come.

11

The Baptism

Tidings of the wilderness prophet and his wonderful announcement spread throughout Galilee. The message reached the peasants in the remotest hill towns, and the fisher folk by the sea, and in these simple, earnest hearts found its truest response. In Nazareth it was told in the carpenter shop that had been Joseph's, and One recognized the call. His time had come. Turning from His daily toil, He bade farewell to His mother, and followed in the steps of His countrymen who were flocking to the Jordan.

Jesus and John the Baptist were cousins, and closely related by the circumstances of their birth; yet they had had no direct acquaintance with each other. The life of Jesus had been spent at Nazareth in Galilee; that of John, in the wilderness of Judea. Amid widely different surroundings they had lived in seclusion, and had had no communication with each other. Providence had ordered this. No occasion was to be given for the charge that they had conspired together to support each other's claims.

John was acquainted with the events that had

marked the birth of Jesus. He had heard of the visit to Jerusalem in His boyhood, and of what had passed in the school of the rabbis. He knew of His sinless life, and believed Him to be the Messiah; but of this he had no positive assurance. The fact that Jesus had for so many years remained in obscurity, giving no special evidence of His mission, gave occasion for doubt as to whether He could be the Promised One. The Baptist, however, waited in faith, believing that in God's own time all would be made plain. It had been revealed to him that the Messiah would seek baptism at his hands, and that a sign of His divine character should then be given. Thus he would be enabled to present Him to the people.

When Jesus came to be baptized, John recognized in Him a purity of character that he had never before perceived in any man. The very atmosphere of His presence was holy and awe-inspiring. Among the multitudes that had gathered about him at the Jordan, John had heard dark tales of crime, and had met souls bowed down with the burden of myriad sins; but never had he come in contact with a human being from whom there breathed an influence so divine. All this was in harmony with what had been revealed to John regarding the Messiah. Yet he shrank from granting the request of Jesus. How could he, a sinner, baptize the Sinless One? And why should He who needed no repentance submit to a rite that was a confession of guilt to be washed away?

As Jesus asked for baptism, John drew back, exclaiming, "I have need to be baptized of Thee, and comest Thou to me?" With firm yet gentle authority, Jesus answered, "Suffer it to be so now: for thus it becometh us to fulfill all righteousness." And John, yielding, led the Saviour down into the Jordan, and buried Him beneath the water. "And straightway coming up out of the water," Jesus "saw the heavens opened, and the Spirit like a dove descending upon Him."

Jesus did not receive baptism as a confession of guilt on His own account. He identified Himself with sinners, taking the steps that we are to take, and doing the work that we must do. His life of suffering and patient endurance after His baptism was also an example to us.

Upon coming up out of the water, Jesus bowed in prayer on the river bank. A new and important era was opening before Him. He was now, upon a wider stage, entering on the conflict of His life. Though He was the Prince of Peace, His coming must be as the unsheathing of a sword. The kingdom He had come to establish was the opposite of that which the Jews desired. He who was the foundation of the ritual and economy of Israel would be looked upon as its enemy and destroyer. He who had proclaimed the law upon Sinai would be condemned as a transgressor. He who had come to break the power of Satan would be denounced as Beelzebub. No one upon earth had understood Him, and during His ministry He must still walk alone. Throughout His life His mother and His brothers did not comprehend His mission. Even His disciples did not understand Him. He had dwelt in eternal light, as one with God, but His life on earth must be spent in solitude.

As one with us, He must bear the burden of our guilt and woe. The Sinless One must feel the shame of sin. The peace lover must dwell with strife, the truth must abide with falsehood, purity with vileness. Every sin, every discord, every defiling lust that transgression had brought, was torture to His spirit.

Alone He must tread the path; alone He must bear the burden. Upon Him who had laid off His glory and accepted the weakness of humanity the redemption of the world must rest. He saw and felt it all, but His purpose remained steadfast. Upon His arm depended the salvation of the fallen race, and He reached out His hand to grasp the hand of Omnipotent Love.

The Saviour's glance seems to penetrate heaven as He pours out His soul in prayer. Well He knows how sin has hardened the hearts of men, and how difficult it will be for them to discern His mission, and accept the gift of salvation. He pleads with the Father for power to overcome their unbelief, to break the fetters with which Satan has enthralled them, and in their behalf to conquer the destroyer. He asks for the witness that God accepts humanity in the person of His Son.

Never before have the angels listened to such a prayer. They are eager to bear to their loved Commander a message of assurance and comfort. But no; the Father Himself will answer the petition of His Son. Direct from the throne issue the beams of His glory. The heavens are opened, and upon the Saviour's head descends a dovelike form of purest light,—fit emblem of Him, the meek and lowly One.

Of the vast throng at the Jordan, few except John discerned the heavenly vision. Yet the solemnity of the divine Presence rested upon the assembly. The people stood silently gazing upon Christ. His form was bathed in the light that ever surrounds the throne of God. His upturned face was glorified as they had never before seen the face of man. From the open heavens a voice was heard saying, "This is My beloved Son, in whom I am well pleased."

These words of confirmation were given to inspire faith in those who witnessed the scene, and to strengthen the Saviour for His mission. Notwithstanding that the sins of a guilty world were laid upon Christ, notwithstanding the humiliation of taking upon Himself our fallen nature, the voice from heaven declared Him to be the Son of the Eternal.

John had been deeply moved as he saw Jesus

bowed as a suppliant, pleading with tears for the approval of the Father. As the glory of God encircled Him, and the voice from heaven was heard, John recognized the token which God had promised. He knew that it was the world's Redeemer whom he had baptized. The Holy Spirit rested upon him, and with outstretched hand pointing to Jesus, he cried, "Behold the Lamb of God, which taketh away the sin of the world."

None among the hearers, and not even the speaker himself, discerned the import of these words, "the Lamb of God." Upon Mount Moriah, Abraham had heard the question of his son, "My father, . . . where is the lamb for a burnt offering?" The father answered, "My son, God will provide Himself a lamb for a burnt offering." Gen. 22:7, 8. And in the ram divinely provided in the place of Isaac, Abraham saw a symbol of Him who was to die for the sins of men. The Holy Spirit through Isaiah, taking up the illustration, prophesied of the Saviour, "He is
113 brought as a lamb to the slaughter," "and the Lord hath laid on Him the iniquity of us all" (Isa. 53:7, 6); but the people of Israel had not understood the lesson. Many of them regarded the sacrificial offerings much as the heathen looked upon their sacrifices,—as gifts by which they themselves might propitiate the Deity. God desired to teach them that from His own love comes the gift which reconciles them to Himself.

And the word that was spoken to Jesus at the Jordan, "This is My beloved Son, in whom I am well pleased," embraces humanity. God spoke to Jesus as our representative. With all our sins and weaknesses, we are not cast aside as worthless. "He hath made us accepted in the Beloved." Eph. 1:6. The glory that rested upon Christ is a pledge of the love of God for us. It tells us of the power of prayer,—how the human voice may reach the ear of God, and our petitions find acceptance in the courts of heaven. By sin, earth was cut off from heaven, and alienated from its communion; but Jesus has connected it again with the sphere of glory. His love has encircled man, and reached the highest heaven. The light which fell from the open portals upon the head of our Saviour will fall upon us as we pray for help to resist temptation. The voice which spoke to Jesus says to every believing soul, This is My beloved child, in whom I am well pleased.

"Beloved, now are we the sons of God, and it doth not yet appear what we shall be: but we know that, when He shall appear, we shall be like Him; for we shall see Him as He is." 1 John 3:2. Our Redeemer has opened the way so that the most sinful, the most needy, the most oppressed and despised, may find access to the Father. All may have a home in the mansions which Jesus has gone to prepare. "These things saith He that is holy, He that is true, He that

hath the key of David, He that openeth, and no man shutteth; and shutteth, and no man openeth; . . . behold, I have set before thee an open door, and no man can shut it." Rev. 3:7, 8.

12

114

The Temptation

"And Jesus being full of the Holy Ghost returned from Jordan, and was led by the Spirit into the wilderness." The words of Mark are still more significant. He says, "Immediately the Spirit driveth Him into the wilderness. And He was there in the wilderness forty days, tempted of Satan; and was with the wild beasts." "And in those days He did eat nothing."

When Jesus was led into the wilderness to be tempted, He was led by the Spirit of God. He did not invite temptation. He went to the wilderness to be alone, to contemplate His mission and work. By fasting and prayer He was to brace Himself for the bloodstained path He must travel. But Satan knew that the Saviour had gone into the wilderness, and he thought this the best time to approach Him.

Mighty issues for the world were at stake in the conflict between the Prince of light and the leader of the kingdom of darkness. After tempting man to sin, Satan claimed the earth as his, and styled himself the prince of this world. Having conformed to his own nature the father and mother of our race, he thought to establish here his empire. He declared that men had chosen him as their sovereign. Through his control of 115 men, he held dominion over the world. Christ had come to disprove Satan's claim. As the Son of man, Christ would stand loyal to God. Thus it would be shown that Satan had not gained complete control of the human race, and that his claim to the world was false. All who desired deliverance from his power would be set free. The dominion that Adam had lost through sin would be recovered.

Since the announcement to the serpent in Eden, "I will put enmity between thee and the woman, and between thy seed and her seed" (Gen. 3:15), Satan had known that he did not hold absolute sway over the world. There was seen in men the working of a power that withstood his dominion. With intense interest he watched the sacrifices offered by Adam and his sons. In these ceremonies he discerned a symbol of communion between earth and heaven. He set himself to intercept this communion. He misrepresented God, and misinterpreted the rites that pointed to the Saviour. Men were led to fear God as one who delighted in their destruction. The sacrifices that should have revealed His love were offered only to appease His wrath.

This chapter is based on Matthew 4:1-11; Mark 1:12, 13; Luke 4:1-13.

Satan excited the evil passions of men, in order to fasten his rule upon them. When God's written word was given, Satan studied the prophecies of the Saviour's advent. From generation to generation he worked to blind the people to these prophecies, that they might reject Christ at His coming.

At the birth of Jesus, Satan knew that One had come with a divine commission to dispute his dominion. He trembled at the angel's message attesting the authority of the newborn King. Satan well knew the position that Christ had held in heaven as the Beloved of the Father. That the Son of God should come to this earth as a man filled him with amazement and with apprehension. He could not fathom the mystery of this great sacrifice. His selfish soul could not understand such love for the deceived race. The glory and peace of heaven, and the joy of communion with God, were but dimly comprehend-116 ed by men; but they were well known to Lucifer, the covering cherub. Since he had lost heaven, he was determined to find revenge by causing others to share his fall. This he would do by causing them to undervalue heavenly things, and to set the heart upon things of earth.

Not without hindrance was the Commander of heaven to win the souls of men to His kingdom. From the time when He was a babe in Bethlehem, He was continually assailed by the evil one. The image of God was manifest in Christ, and in the councils of Satan it was determined that He should be overcome. No human being had come into the world and escaped the power of the deceiver. The forces of the confederacy of evil were set upon His track to engage in warfare against Him, and if possible to prevail over Him.

At the Saviour's baptism, Satan was among the witnesses. He saw the Father's glory overshadowing His Son. He heard the voice of Jehovah testifying to the divinity of Jesus. Ever since Adam's sin, the human race had been cut off from direct communion with God; the intercourse between heaven and earth had been through Christ; but now that Jesus had come "in the likeness of sinful flesh" (Rom. 8:3), the Father Himself spoke. He had before communicated with humanity *through* Christ; now He communicated with humanity *in* Christ. Satan had hoped that God's abhorrence of evil would bring an eternal separation between heaven and earth. But now it was manifest that the connection between God and man had been restored.

Satan saw that he must either conquer or be conquered. The issues of the conflict involved too much to be entrusted to his confederate angels. He must personally conduct the warfare. All the energies of apostasy were rallied against the Son of God. Christ was made the mark of every weapon of hell.

Many look on this conflict between Christ and Satan as having no special bearing on their own life; and for them it has little interest. But within the domain of every human heart this controversy is repeated. Never does one leave the ranks of evil for the service of God without encountering the assaults of Satan. The enticements which Christ resisted were those that we find it so difficult to withstand. They were urged upon Him in as much greater degree as His character is superior to ours. With the terrible weight of the sins of the world upon Him, Christ withstood the test upon appetite, upon the love of the world, and upon that love of display which leads to presumption. These were the temptations that overcame Adam and Eve, and 117 that so readily overcome us.

Satan had pointed to Adam's sin as proof that God's law was unjust, and could not be obeyed. In our humanity, Christ was to redeem Adam's failure. But when Adam was assailed by the tempter, none of the effects of sin were upon him. He stood in the strength of perfect manhood, possessing the full vigor of mind and body. He was surrounded with the glories of Eden, and was in daily communion with heavenly beings. It was not thus with Jesus when He entered the wilderness to cope with Satan. For four thousand years the race had been decreasing in physical strength, in mental power, and in moral worth; and Christ took upon Him the infirmities of degenerate humanity. Only thus could He rescue man from the lowest depths of his degradation.

Many claim that it was impossible for Christ to be overcome by temptation. Then He could not have been placed in Adam's position; He could not have gained the victory that Adam failed to gain. If we have in any sense a more trying conflict than had Christ, then He would not be able to succor us. But our Saviour took humanity, with all its liabilities. He took the nature of man, with the possibility of yielding to temptation. We have nothing to bear which He has not endured.

With Christ, as with the holy pair in Eden, appetite was the ground of the first great temptation. Just where the ruin began, the work of our redemption must begin. As by the indulgence of appetite Adam fell, so by the denial of appetite Christ must overcome. "And when He had fasted forty days and forty nights, He was afterward an hungred. And when the tempter came to Him, he said, If Thou be the Son of God, command that these stones be made bread. But He answered and said, It is written, Man shall not live by bread alone, but by every word that proceedeth out of the mouth of God."

From the time of Adam to that of Christ, self-indulgence had increased the power of the appetites and passions, until they had almost unlimited control. Thus men had become debased and diseased, and of themselves it was impossible for them to overcome. In man's behalf, Christ conquered by enduring the severest test. For our sake He exercised a self-control stronger than hunger or death. And in this first victory were involved other issues that enter into all our conflicts with the powers of darkness.

When Jesus entered the wilderness, He was shut in by the Father's glory. Absorbed in communion with God, He was lifted above human weakness. But the glory departed, and He was left to battle with temptation. It was pressing upon Him every moment. His human nature shrank from the conflict that awaited Him. For forty days He fasted and prayed. Weak and emaciated from hunger, worn and haggard with mental agony, "His visage was so marred more than any man, and His form more than the sons of men." Isa. 52:14. Now was Satan's opportunity. Now he supposed that he could overcome Christ.

There came to the Saviour, as if in answer to His prayers, one in the guise of an angel from heaven. He claimed to have a commission from God to declare that Christ's fast was at an end. As God had sent an angel to stay the hand of Abraham from offering Isaac, so, satisfied with Christ's willingness to enter the bloodstained path, the Father had sent an angel to deliver Him; this was the message brought to Jesus. The Saviour was faint from hunger, He was craving for food, when Satan came suddenly upon Him. Pointing to the stones which strewed the desert, and which had the appearance of loaves, the tempter said, "If Thou be the Son of God, command that these stones be made bread."

Though he appears as an angel of light, these first words betray his character. "If Thou be the Son of God." Here is the insinuation of distrust. Should Jesus do what Satan suggests, it would be an acceptance of the doubt. The tempter plans to overthrow Christ by the same means that were so successful with the human race in the beginning. How artfully had Satan approached Eve in Eden! "Yea, hath God said, Ye shall not eat of every tree of the garden?" Gen. 3:1. Thus far the tempter's words were truth; but in his manner of speaking them there was a disguised contempt for the words of God. There was a covert negative, a doubt of the divine truthfulness. Satan sought to instill into the mind of Eve the thought that God would not do as He had said; that the withholding of such beautiful fruit was a contradiction of His love and compassion for man. So now the tempter seeks to inspire Christ with his own sentiments. "If Thou be the Son of God." The words rankle with bitterness in His mind. In the tones of his voice is an expression of utter incredulity. Would God treat His own Son thus? Would He leave Him in the desert with wild beasts, without food, without companions, without comfort? He insinuates that God never meant His Son to be in such a state as this. "If Thou be the Son of God," show Thy power by relieving Thyself of this pressing hunger. Command that this stone be made bread.

The words from heaven, "This is My beloved Son, in whom I am well pleased" (Matt. 3:17), were still sounding in the ears of Satan. But he was determined to make Christ disbelieve this testimony. The word of God was Christ's assurance of His divine mission. He had come to live as a man among men, and it was the word that declared His connection with heaven. It was Satan's purpose to cause Him to doubt that word. If Christ's confidence in God could be shaken, Satan knew that the victory in the whole controversy would be his. He could overcome Jesus. He hoped that under the force of despondency and extreme hunger, Christ would lose faith in His Father, and work a miracle in His own behalf. Had He done this, the plan of salvation would have been broken.

When Satan and the Son of God first met in conflict, Christ was the commander of the heavenly hosts; and Satan, the leader of revolt in heaven, was cast out. Now their condition is apparently reversed, and Satan makes the most of his supposed advantage. One of the most powerful of the angels, he says, has been banished from heaven. The appearance of Jesus indicates that He is that fallen angel, forsaken by God, and deserted by man. A divine being would be able to sustain his claim by working a miracle; "if Thou be the Son of God, command this stone that it be made bread." Such an act of creative power, urges the tempter, would be conclusive evidence of divinity. It would bring the controversy to an end.

Not without a struggle could Jesus listen in silence to the archdeceiver. But the Son of God was not to prove His divinity to Satan, or to explain the reason of His humiliation. By conceding to the demands of the rebel, nothing for the good of man or the glory of God would be gained. Had Christ complied with the suggestion of the enemy, Satan would still have said, Show me a sign that I may believe you to be the Son of God. Evidence would have been worthless to break the power of rebellion in his heart. And Christ was not to exercise divine power for His own benefit. He had come to bear trial as we must do, leaving us an example of faith and submission. Neither here nor at any subsequent time in His earthly life did He work a miracle in His own behalf. His wonderful works were all for the good of others. Though Jesus recognized Satan from the beginning, He was not provoked to enter into controversy with him. Strengthened with the memory of the voice from heaven, He rested in His Father's love. He would not parley with temptation.

Jesus met Satan with the words of Scripture. "It is written," He said. In every temptation the weapon of His warfare was the word of God. Satan demanded of Christ a miracle as a sign of His divinity. But that which is greater than all miracles, a firm reliance upon a "Thus saith the Lord," was a sign that could not be controverted. So long as Christ held to this position, the tempter could gain no advantage.

It was in the time of greatest weakness that Christ was assailed by the fiercest temptations. Thus Satan thought to prevail. By this policy he had gained the victory over men. When strength failed, and the will power weakened, and faith ceased to repose in God, then those who had stood long and valiantly for the right were overcome. Moses was wearied with the forty years' wandering of Israel, when for the moment his faith let go its hold upon infinite power. He failed just upon the borders of the Promised Land. So with Elijah, who had stood undaunted before King Ahab, who had faced the whole nation of Israel, with the four hundred and fifty prophets of Baal at their head. After that terrible day upon Carmel, when the false prophets had been slain, and the people had declared their allegiance to God, Elijah fled for his life before the threats of the idolatrous Jezebel. Thus Satan has taken advantage of the weakness of humanity. And he will still work in the same way. Whenever one is encompassed with clouds, perplexed by circumstances, or afflicted by poverty or distress, Satan is at hand to tempt and annoy. He attacks our weak points of character. He seeks to shake our confidence in God, who suffers such a condition of things to exist. We are tempted to distrust God, to question His love. Often the tempter comes to us as he came to 121 Christ, arraying before us our weakness and infirmities. He hopes to discourage the soul, and to break our hold on God. Then he is sure of his prey. If we would meet him as Jesus did, we should escape many a defeat. By parleying with the enemy, we give him an advantage.

When Christ said to the tempter, "Man shall not live by bread, but by every word that proceedeth out of the mouth of God," He repeated the words that, more than fourteen hundred years before, He had spoken to Israel: "The Lord thy God led thee these forty years in the wilderness. . . . And He humbled thee, and suffered thee to hunger, and fed thee with manna, which thou knewest not, neither did thy fathers know; that He might make thee know that man doth not live by bread only, but by every word that proceedeth out of the mouth of the Lord doth man live." Deut. 8:2, 3. In the wilderness, when all means of sustenance failed, God sent His people manna from heaven; and a sufficient and constant supply was given. This provision was to teach them that while they trusted in God and walked in His ways He

would not forsake them. The Saviour now practiced the lesson He had taught to Israel. By the word of God succor had been given to the Hebrew host, and by the same word it would be given to Jesus. He awaited God's time to bring relief. He was in the wilderness in obedience to God, and He would not obtain food by following the suggestions of Satan. In the presence of the witnessing universe, He testified that it is a less calamity to suffer whatever may befall than to depart in any manner from the will of God.

"Man shall not live by bread alone, but by every word of God." Often the follower of Christ is brought where he cannot serve God and carry forward his worldly enterprises. Perhaps it appears that obedience to some plain requirement of God will cut off his means of support. Satan would make him believe that he must sacrifice his conscientious convictions. But the only thing in our world upon which we can rely is the word of God. "Seek ye first the kingdom of God, and His righteousness; and all these things shall be added unto you." Matt. 6:33. Even in this life it is not for our good to depart from the will of our Father in heaven. When we learn the power of His word, we shall not follow the suggestions of Satan in order to obtain food or to save our lives. Our only questions will be, What is God's command? and what His promise? Knowing these, we shall obey the one, and trust the other.

In the last great conflict of the controversy with Satan those who are loyal to God will see every earthly support cut off. Because they refuse to break His law in obedience to earthly 122 powers, they will be forbidden to buy or sell. It will finally be decreed that they shall be put to death. See Rev. 13:11-17. But to the obedient is given the promise, "He shall dwell on high: his place of defense shall be the munitions of rocks: bread shall be given him; his waters shall be sure." Isa. 33:16. By this promise the children of God will live. When the earth shall be wasted with famine, they shall be fed. "They shall not be ashamed in the evil time: and in the days of famine they shall be satisfied." Ps. 37:19. To that time of distress the prophet Habakkuk looked forward, and his words express the faith of the church: "Although the fig tree shall not blossom, neither shall fruit be in the vines; the labor of the olive shall fail, and the fields shall yield no meat; the flock shall be cut off from the fold, and there shall be no herd in the stalls: yet I will rejoice in the Lord, I will joy in the God of my salvation." Hab. 3:17, 18.

Of all the lessons to be learned from our Lord's first great temptation none is more important than that bearing upon the control of the appetites and passions. In all ages, temptations appealing to the physical nature have been most effectual in corrupting and degrading mankind. Through intemperance, Satan works to destroy the mental and moral powers that God gave to man as a priceless endowment. Thus it becomes impossible for men to appreciate things of eternal worth. Through sensual indulgence, Satan seeks to blot from the soul every trace of likeness to God.

The uncontrolled indulgence and consequent disease and degradation that existed at Christ's first advent will again exist, with intensity of evil, before His second coming. Christ declares that the condition of the world will be as in the days before the Flood, and as in Sodom and Gomorrah. Every imagination of the thoughts of the heart will be evil continually. Upon the very verge of that fearful time we are now living, and to us should come home the lesson of the Saviour's fast. Only by the inexpressible anguish which Christ endured can we estimate the evil of unrestrained indulgence. His example declares that our only hope of eternal life is through bringing the appetites and passions into subjection to the will of God.

In our own strength it is impossible for us to deny the clamors of our fallen nature. Through this channel Satan will bring temptation upon us. Christ knew that the enemy would come to every human being, to take advantage of hereditary weakness, and by his false insinuations to ensnare all whose trust is not in God. And by passing over the ground which man must travel, our Lord has prepared the way for us to overcome. It is not His will that we should be placed at a disadvantage in the conflict with Satan. He would not have us intimidated and discouraged by the assaults of the serpent. "Be of good cheer," He says; "I have overcome the world." John 16:33.

Let him who is struggling against the power of appetite look to the Saviour in the wilderness of temptation. See Him in His agony upon the cross, as He exclaimed, "I thirst." He has endured all that it is possible for us to bear. His victory is ours.

Jesus rested upon the wisdom and strength of His heavenly Father. He declares, "The Lord God will help Me; therefore shall I not be confounded: . . . and I know that I shall not be ashamed. . . . Behold, the Lord God will help Me." Pointing to His own example, He says to us, "Who is among you that feareth the Lord, . . . that walketh in darkness, and hath no light? let him trust in the name of the Lord, and stay upon his God." Isa. 50:7-10.

"The prince of this world cometh," said Jesus, "and hath nothing in Me." John 14:30. There was in Him nothing that responded to Satan's sophistry. He did not consent to sin. Not even by a thought did He yield to temptation. So it may be with us. Christ's humanity was united with divinity; He was fitted for the conflict by the indwelling of the Holy Spirit. And He came

to make us partakers of the divine nature. So long as we are united to Him by faith, sin has no more dominion over us. God reaches for the hand of faith in us to direct it to lay fast hold upon the divinity of Christ, that we may attain to perfection of character.

And how this is accomplished, Christ has shown us. By what means did He overcome in the conflict with Satan? By the word of God. Only by the word could He resist temptation. "It is written," He said. And unto us are given "exceeding great and precious promises: that by these ye might be partakers of the divine nature, having escaped the corruption that is in the world through lust." 2 Peter 1:4. Every promise in God's word is ours. "By every word that proceedeth out of the mouth of God" are we to live. When assailed by temptation, look not to circumstances or to the weakness of self, but to the power of the word. All its strength is yours. "Thy word," says the psalmist, "have I hid in mine heart, that I might not sin against Thee." "By the word of Thy lips I have kept me from the paths of the destroyer." Ps. 119:11; 17:4.

13

The Victory

"Then the devil taketh Him up into the holy city, and setteth Him on a pinnacle of the temple, and saith unto Him, If Thou be the Son of God, cast Thyself down: for it is written,—

"He shall give His angels charge concerning Thee:
And in their hands they shall bear Thee up,
Lest at any time Thou dash Thy foot against a stone."

Satan now supposes that he has met Jesus on His own ground. The wily foe himself presents words that proceeded from the mouth of God. He still appears as an angel of light, and he makes it evident that he is acquainted with the Scriptures, and understands the import of what is written. As Jesus before used the word of God to sustain His faith, the tempter now uses it to countenance his deception. He claims that he has been only testing the fidelity of Jesus, and he now commends His steadfastness. As the Saviour has manifested trust in God, Satan urges Him to give still another evidence of His faith.

But again the temptation is prefaced with the insinuation of distrust, "If Thou be the Son of God." Christ was tempted to answer the "if;" but He refrained from the slightest acceptance of the doubt. He would not imperil His life in order to give evidence to Satan.

This chapter is based on Matthew 4:5-11; Mark 1:12, 13; Luke 4:5-13.

The tempter thought to take advantage of Christ's humanity, and urge Him to presumption. But while Satan can solicit, he cannot compel to sin. He said to Jesus, "Cast Thyself down," knowing that he could not cast Him down; for God would interpose to deliver Him. Nor could Satan force Jesus to cast Himself down. Unless Christ should consent to temptation, He could not be overcome. Not all the power of earth or hell could force Him in the slightest degree to depart from the will of His Father.

125 The tempter can never compel us to do evil. He cannot control minds unless they are yielded to his control. The will must consent, faith must let go its hold upon Christ, before Satan can exercise his power upon us. But every sinful desire we cherish affords him a foothold. Every point in which we fail of meeting the divine standard is an open door by which he can enter to tempt and destroy us. And every failure or defeat on our part gives occasion for him to reproach Christ.

When Satan quoted the promise, "He shall give His angels charge over Thee," he omitted the words, "to keep Thee in all Thy ways;" that is, in all the ways of God's choosing. Jesus refused to go outside the path of obedience. While manifesting perfect trust in His Father, He would not place Himself, unbidden, in a position that would necessitate the interposition of His Father to save Him from death. He would not force Providence to come to His rescue, and thus fail of giving man an example of trust and submission.

Jesus declared to Satan, "It is written again, Thou shalt not tempt the Lord thy God." These words were spoken by Moses to the children of Israel when they thirsted in the desert, and demanded that Moses should give them water,
126 exclaiming, "Is the Lord among us, or not?" Exodus 17:7. God had wrought marvelously for them; yet in trouble they doubted Him, and demanded evidence that He was with them. In their unbelief they sought to put Him to the test. And Satan was urging Christ to do the same thing. God had already testified that Jesus was His Son; and now to ask for proof that He was the Son of God would be putting God's word to the test,—tempting Him. And the same would be true of asking for that which God had not promised. It would manifest distrust, and be really proving, or tempting, Him. We should not present our petitions to God to prove whether He will fulfill His word, but because He will fulfill it; not to prove that He loves us, but because He loves us. "Without faith it is impossible to please Him: for he that cometh to God must believe that He is, and that He is a rewarder of them that diligently seek Him." Heb. 11:6.

But faith is in no sense allied to presumption.

Only he who has true faith is secure against presumption. For presumption is Satan's counterfeit of faith. Faith claims God's promises, and brings forth fruit in obedience. Presumption also claims the promises, but uses them as Satan did, to excuse transgression. Faith would have led our first parents to trust the love of God, and to obey His commands. Presumption led them to transgress His law, believing that His great love would save them from the consequence of their sin. It is not faith that claims the favor of Heaven without complying with the conditions on which mercy is to be granted. Genuine faith has its foundation in the promises and provisions of the Scriptures.

Often when Satan has failed of exciting distrust, he succeeds in leading us to presumption. If he can cause us to place ourselves unnecessarily in the way of temptation, he knows that the victory is his. God will preserve all who walk in the path of obedience; but to depart from it is to venture on Satan's ground. There we are sure to fall. The Saviour has bidden us, "Watch ye and pray, lest ye enter into temptation." Mark 14:38. Meditation and prayer would keep us from rushing unbidden into the way of danger, and thus we should be saved from many a defeat.

Yet we should not lose courage when assailed by temptation. Often when placed in a trying situation we doubt that the Spirit of God has been leading us. But it was the Spirit's leading that brought Jesus into the wilderness to be tempted by Satan. When God brings us into trial, He has a purpose to accomplish for our good. Jesus did not presume on God's promises by going unbidden into temptation, neither did
129 He give up to despondency when temptation came upon Him. Nor should we. "God is faithful, who will not suffer you to be tempted above that ye are able; but will with the temptation also make a way to escape, that ye may be able to bear it." He says, "Offer unto God thanksgiving; and pay thy vows unto the Most High: and call upon Me in the day of trouble: I will deliver thee, and thou shalt glorify Me." 1 Cor. 10:13; Ps. 50:14, 15.

Jesus was victor in the second temptation, and now Satan manifests himself in his true character. But he does not appear as a hideous monster, with cloven feet and bat's wings. He is a mighty angel, though fallen. He avows himself the leader of rebellion and the god of this world.

Placing Jesus upon a high mountain, Satan caused the kingdoms of the world, in all their glory, to pass in panoramic view before Him. The sunlight lay on templed cities, marble palaces, fertile fields, and fruit-laden vineyards. The traces of evil were hidden. The eyes of Jesus, so lately greeted by gloom and desolation, now gazed upon a scene of unsurpassed loveliness and prosperity. Then the tempter's voice was heard: "All this power will I give Thee, and the glory of them: for that is delivered unto me; and to whomsoever I will I give it. If Thou therefore wilt worship me, all shall be Thine."

Christ's mission could be fulfilled only through suffering. Before Him was a life of sorrow, hardship, and conflict, and an ignominious death. He must bear the sins of the whole world. He must endure separation from His Father's love. Now the tempter offered to yield up the power he had usurped. Christ might deliver Himself from the dreadful future by acknowledging the supremacy of Satan. But to do this was to yield the victory in the great controversy. It was in seeking to exalt himself above the Son of God that Satan had sinned in heaven. Should he prevail now, it would be the triumph of rebellion.

When Satan declared to Christ, The kingdom and glory of the world are delivered unto me, and to whomsoever I will I give it, he stated what was true only in part, and he declared it to serve his own purpose of deception. Satan's dominion was that wrested from Adam, but Adam was the vicegerent of the Creator. His was not an independent rule. The earth is God's, and He has committed all things to His Son. Adam was to reign subject to Christ. When Adam betrayed his sovereignty into Satan's hands, Christ still remained the rightful King. Thus the Lord had said to King Nebuchadnez-130 zar, "The Most High ruleth in the kingdom of men, and giveth it to whomsoever He will." Dan. 4:17. Satan can exercise his usurped authority only as God permits.

When the tempter offered to Christ the kingdom and glory of the world, he was proposing that Christ should yield up the real kingship of the world, and hold dominion subject to Satan. This was the same dominion upon which the hopes of the Jews were set. They desired the kingdom of this world. If Christ had consented to offer them such a kingdom, they would gladly have received Him. But the curse of sin, with all its woe, rested upon it. Christ declared to the tempter, "Get thee behind Me, Satan: for it is written, Thou shalt worship the Lord thy God, and Him only shalt thou serve."

By the one who had revolted in heaven the kingdoms of this world were offered Christ, to buy His homage to the principles of evil; but He would not be bought; He had come to establish a kingdom of righteousness, and He would not abandon His purpose. With the same temptation Satan approaches men, and here he has better success than with Christ. To men he offers the kingdom of this world on condition that they will acknowledge his supremacy. He requires that they sacrifice integrity, disregard conscience, indulge selfishness. Christ bids them

seek first the kingdom of God, and His righteousness; but Satan walks by their side and says: Whatever may be true in regard to life eternal, in order to make a success in this world you must serve me. I hold your welfare in my hands. I can give you riches, pleasures, honor, and happiness. Hearken to my counsel. Do not allow yourselves to be carried away with whimsical notions of honesty or self-sacrifice. I will prepare the way before you. Thus multitudes are deceived. They consent to live for the service of self, and Satan is satisfied. While he allures them with the hope of worldly dominion, he gains dominion over the soul. But he offers that which is not his to bestow, and which is soon to be wrested from him. In return he beguiles them of their title to the inheritance of the sons of God.

Satan had questioned whether Jesus was the Son of God. In his summary dismissal he had proof that he could not gainsay. Divinity flashed through suffering humanity. Satan had no power to resist the command. Writhing with humiliation and rage, he was forced to withdraw from the presence of the world's Redeemer. Christ's victory was as complete as had been the failure of Adam.

So we may resist temptation, and force Satan to depart from us. Jesus gained the victory through submission and faith in God, and by the 131 apostle He says to us, "Submit yourselves therefore to God. Resist the devil, and he will flee from you. Draw nigh to God, and He will draw nigh to you." James 4:7, 8. We cannot save ourselves from the tempter's power; he has conquered humanity, and when we try to stand in our own strength, we shall become a prey to his devices; but "the name of the Lord is a strong tower: the righteous runneth into it, and is safe." Prov. 18:10. Satan trembles and flees before the weakest soul who finds refuge in that mighty name.

After the foe had departed, Jesus fell exhausted to the earth, with the pallor of death upon His face. The angels of heaven had watched the conflict, beholding their loved Commander as He passed through inexpressible suffering to make a way of escape for us. He had endured the test, greater than we shall ever be called to endure. The angels now ministered to the Son of God as He lay like one dying. He was strengthened with food, comforted with the message of His Father's love and the assurance that all heaven triumphed in His victory. Warming to life again, His great heart goes out in sympathy for man, and He goes forth to complete the work He has begun; to rest not until the foe is vanquished, and our fallen race redeemed.

Never can the cost of our redemption be realized until the redeemed shall stand with the Redeemer before the throne of God. Then as the glories of the eternal home burst upon our enraptured senses we shall remember that Jesus left all this for us, that He not only became an exile from the heavenly courts, but for us took the risk of failure and eternal loss. Then we shall cast our crowns at His feet, and raise the song, "Worthy is the Lamb that was slain to receive power, and riches, and wisdom, and strength, and honor, and glory, and blessing." Rev. 5:12.

132

14

"We Have Found the Messias"

John the Baptist was now preaching and baptizing at Bethabara, beyond Jordan. It was not far from this spot that God had stayed the river in its flow until Israel had passed over. A little distance from here the stronghold of Jericho had been overthrown by the armies of heaven. The memory of these events was at this time revived, and gave a thrilling interest to the Baptist's message. Would not He who had wrought so wonderfully in ages past again manifest His power for Israel's deliverance? Such was the thought stirring the hearts of the people who daily thronged the banks of the Jordan.

The preaching of John had taken so deep a hold on the nation as to demand the attention of the religious authorities. The danger of insurrection caused every popular gathering to be looked upon with suspicion by the Romans, and whatever pointed toward an uprising of the people excited the fears of the Jewish rulers. John had not recognized the authority of the Sanhedrin by seeking their sanction for his work; 133 and he had reproved rulers and people, Pharisees and Sadducees alike. Yet the people followed him eagerly. The interest in his work seemed to be continually increasing. Though he had not deferred to them, the Sanhedrin accounted that, as a public teacher, he was under their jurisdiction.

This body was made up of members chosen from the priesthood, and from the chief rulers and teachers of the nation. The high priest was usually the president. All its members were to be men advanced in years, though not aged; men of learning, not only versed in Jewish religion and history, but in general knowledge. They were to be without physical blemish, and must be married men, and fathers, as being more likely than others to be humane and considerate. Their place of meeting was an apartment connected with the temple at Jerusalem. In the days of Jewish independence the Sanhedrin was the supreme court of the nation, possessing secular as well as ecclesiastical authority. Though now subordinated by the Roman governors, it still exercised a strong influence in civil as well as religious matters.

The Sanhedrin could not well defer an investigation of John's work. There were some who recalled the revelation made to Zacharias in the temple, and the father's prophecy that had pointed to his child as the Messiah's herald. In the tumults and changes of thirty years, these things had in a great measure been lost sight of. They were now called to mind by the excitement concerning the ministry of John.

It was long since Israel had had a prophet, long since such a reformation as was now in progress had been witnessed. The demand for confession of sin seemed new and startling. Many among the leaders would not go to hear John's appeals and denunciations, lest they should be led to disclose the secrets of their own lives. Yet his preaching was a direct announcement of the Messiah. It was well known that the seventy weeks of Daniel's prophecy, covering the Messiah's advent, were nearly ended; and all were eager to share in that era of national glory which was then expected. Such was the popular enthusiasm that the Sanhedrin would soon be forced either to sanction or to reject John's work. Already their power over the people was waning. It was becoming a serious question how to maintain their position. In the hope of arriving at some conclusion, they dispatched to the Jordan a deputation of priests and Levites to confer with the new teacher.

A multitude were gathered, listening to his words, when the delegates approached. With an air of authority designed to impress the people and to command the deference of the prophet 134 the haughty rabbis came. With a movement of respect, almost of fear, the crowd opened to let them pass. The great men, in their rich robes, in the pride of rank and power, stood before the prophet of the wilderness.

"Who art thou?" they demanded.

Knowing what was in their thoughts, John answered, "I am not the Christ."

"What then? Art thou Elias?"

"I am not."

"Art thou that prophet?"

"No."

"Who art thou? that we may give an answer to them that sent us. What sayest thou of thyself?"

"I am the voice of one crying in the wilderness, Make straight the way of the Lord, as said the prophet Esaias."

The scripture to which John referred is that beautiful prophecy of Isaiah: "Comfort ye, comfort ye My people, saith your God. Speak ye 135 comfortably to Jerusalem, and cry unto her, that her appointed time is accomplished, that her iniquity is pardoned. . . . The voice of him that crieth in the wilderness, Prepare ye the way of the Lord, make straight in the desert a highway for our God. Every valley shall be exalted, and every mountain and hill shall be made low: and

This chapter is based on John 1:19-51.

the crooked shall be made straight, and the rough places plain: and the glory of the Lord shall be revealed, and all flesh shall see it together." Isa. 40:1-5, margin.

Anciently, when a king journeyed through the less frequented parts of his dominion, a company of men was sent ahead of the royal chariot to level the steep places and to fill up the hollows, that the king might travel in safety and without hindrance. This custom is employed by the prophet to illustrate the work of the gospel. "Every valley shall be exalted, and every mountain and hill shall be made low." When the Spirit of God, with its marvelous awakening power, touches the soul, it abases human pride. Worldly pleasure and position and power are seen to be worthless. "Imaginations, and every high thing that exalteth itself against the knowledge of God" are cast down; every thought is brought into captivity "to the obedience of Christ." 2 Cor. 10:5. Then humility and self-sacrificing love, so little valued among men, are exalted as alone of worth. This is the work of the gospel, of which John's message was a part.

The rabbis continued their questioning: "Why baptizest thou then, if thou be not that Christ, nor Elias, neither that prophet?" The words "that prophet" had reference to Moses. The Jews had been inclined to the belief that Moses would be raised from the dead, and taken to heaven. They did not know that he had already been raised. When the Baptist began his ministry, many thought that he might be the prophet Moses risen from the dead, for he seemed to have a thorough knowledge of the prophecies and of the history of Israel.

It was believed also that before the Messiah's advent, Elijah would personally appear. This expectation John met in his denial; but his words had a deeper meaning. Jesus afterward said, referring to John, "If ye are willing to receive it, this is Elijah, which is to come." Matt. 11:14, R. V. John came in the spirit and power of Elijah, to do such a work as Elijah did. If the Jews had received him, it would have been accomplished for them. But they did not receive his message. To them he was not Elijah. He could not fulfill for them the mission he came to accomplish.

136   Many of those gathered at the Jordan had been present at the baptism of Jesus; but the sign then given had been manifest to but few among them. During the preceding months of the Baptist's ministry, many had refused to heed the call to repentance. Thus they had hardened their hearts and darkened their understanding. When Heaven bore testimony to Jesus at His baptism, they perceived it not. Eyes that had never turned in faith to Him that is invisible beheld not the revelation of the glory of God; ears that had never listened to His voice heard not the words of witness. So it is now.

Often the presence of Christ and the ministering angels is manifest in the assemblies of the people, and yet there are many who know it not. They discern nothing unusual. But to some the Saviour's presence is revealed. Peace and joy animate their hearts. They are comforted, encouraged, and blessed.

The deputies from Jerusalem had demanded of John, "Why baptizest thou?" and they were awaiting his answer. Suddenly, as his glance swept over the throng, his eye kindled, his face was lighted up, his whole being was stirred with deep emotion. With outstretched hands he cried, "I baptize in water: in the midst of you standeth One whom ye know not, even He that cometh after me, the latchet of whose shoe I am not worthy to unloose." John 1:26, 27, R. V., margin.

The message was distinct and unequivocal, to be carried back to the Sanhedrin. The words of John could apply to no other than the long-promised One. The Messiah was among them! In amazement priests and rulers gazed about them, hoping to discover Him of whom John had spoken. But He was not distinguishable among the throng.

When at the baptism of Jesus, John pointed to Him as the Lamb of God, a new light was shed upon the Messiah's work. The prophet's mind was directed to the words of Isaiah, "He is brought as a lamb to the slaughter." Isa. 53:7. During the weeks that followed, John with new interest studied the prophecies and the teaching of the sacrificial service. He did not distinguish clearly the two phases of Christ's work,—as a suffering sacrifice and a conquering king,—but he saw that His coming had a deeper signifi- 137 cance than priests or people had discerned. When he beheld Jesus among the throng on His return from the desert, he confidently looked for Him to give the people some sign of His true character. Almost impatiently he waited to hear the Saviour declare His mission; but no word was spoken, no sign given. Jesus did not respond to the Baptist's announcement of Him, but mingled with the disciples of John, giving no outward evidence of His special work, and taking no measures to bring Himself to notice.

The next day John sees Jesus coming. With the light of the glory of God resting upon him, the prophet stretches out his hands, declaring, "Behold, the Lamb of God, which taketh away the sin of the world! This is He of whom I said, After me cometh a man which is become before me. . . . And I knew Him not; but that He should be made manifest to Israel, for this cause came I baptizing in water. . . . I have beheld the Spirit descending as a dove out of heaven; and it abode upon Him. And I knew Him not: but He that sent me to baptize in water, He said unto me, Upon whomsoever thou shalt see the Spirit descending, and abiding upon Him, the same is He that baptizeth with the Holy Spirit. And I have seen, and have borne witness that this is the Son of God." John 1:29-34, R. V., margin.

Was this the Christ? With awe and wonder the people looked upon the One just declared to be the Son of God. They had been deeply moved by the words of John. He had spoken to them in the name of God. They had listened to him day after day as he reproved their sins, and daily the conviction that he was sent of Heaven had strengthened. But who was this One greater than John the Baptist? In His dress and bearing there was nothing that betokened rank. He was apparently a simple personage, clad like themselves in the humble garments of the poor.

There were in the throng some who at Christ's baptism had beheld the divine glory, and had heard the voice of God. But since that time the Saviour's appearance had greatly changed. At His baptism they had seen His countenance transfigured in the light of heaven; now, pale, worn, and emaciated, He had been recognized only by the prophet John.

But as the people looked upon Him, they saw a face where divine compassion was blended with conscious power. Every glance of the eye, every feature of the countenance, was marked with humility, and expressive of unutterable 138 love. He seemed to be surrounded by an atmosphere of spiritual influence. While His manners were gentle and unassuming, He impressed men with a sense of power that was hidden, yet could not be wholly concealed. Was this the One for whom Israel had so long waited?

Jesus came in poverty and humiliation, that He might be our example as well as our Redeemer. If He had appeared with kingly pomp, how could He have taught humility? how could He have presented such cutting truths as in the Sermon on the Mount? Where would have been the hope of the lowly in life had Jesus come to dwell as a king among men?

To the multitude, however, it seemed impossible that the One designated by John should be associated with their lofty anticipations. Thus many were disappointed, and greatly perplexed.

The words which the priests and rabbis so much desired to hear, that Jesus would now restore the kingdom to Israel, had not been spoken. For such a king they had been waiting and watching; such a king they were ready to receive. But one who sought to establish in their hearts a kingdom of righteousness and peace, they would not accept.

On the following day, while two disciples were standing near, John again saw Jesus among the people. Again the face of the prophet was lighted up with glory from the Unseen, as he cried, "Behold the Lamb of God!" The words thrilled the hearts of the disciples. They did not fully understand them. What meant the name that John had given Him,—"the Lamb of God"? John himself had not explained it.

Leaving John, they went to seek Jesus. One of the two was Andrew, the brother of Simon; the other was John the evangelist. These were Christ's first disciples. Moved by an irresistible impulse, they followed Jesus,—anxious to speak with Him, yet awed and silent, lost in the overwhelming significance of the thought, "Is this the Messiah?"

Jesus knew that the disciples were following Him. They were the first fruits of His ministry, and there was joy in the heart of the divine Teacher as these souls responded to His grace. Yet turning, He asked only, "What seek ye?" He would leave them free to turn back or to speak of their desire.

Of one purpose only were they conscious. One presence filled their thought. They exclaimed, "Rabbi, . . . where dwellest Thou?" In a brief interview by the wayside they could not receive that for which they longed. They desired to be alone with Jesus, to sit at His feet, and hear His words.

"He saith unto them, Come and see. They 139 came and saw where He dwelt, and abode with Him that day."

If John and Andrew had possessed the unbelieving spirit of the priests and rulers, they would not have been found as learners at the feet of Jesus. They would have come to Him as critics, to judge His words. Many thus close the door to the most precious opportunities. But not so did these first disciples. They had responded to the Holy Spirit's call in the preaching of John the Baptist. Now they recognized the voice of the heavenly Teacher. To them the words of Jesus were full of freshness and truth and beauty. A divine illumination was shed upon the teaching of the Old Testament Scriptures. The many-sided themes of truth stood out in new light.

It is contrition and faith and love that enable the soul to receive wisdom from heaven. Faith working by love is the key of knowledge, and everyone that loveth "knoweth God." 1 John 4:7.

The disciple John was a man of earnest and deep affection, ardent, yet contemplative. He had begun to discern the glory of Christ,—not the worldly pomp and power for which he had been taught to hope, but "the glory as of the Only-begotten of the Father, full of grace and truth." John 1:14. He was absorbed in contemplation of the wondrous theme.

Andrew sought to impart the joy that filled his heart. Going in search of his brother Simon, he cried, "We have found the Messias." Simon waited for no second bidding. He also had heard the preaching of John the Baptist, and he hastened to the Saviour. The eye of Christ rested upon him, reading his character and his life history. His impulsive nature, his loving, sympathetic heart, his ambition and self-confidence, the history of his fall, his repentance, his labors, and his martyr death,—the Saviour read it all, and He said, "Thou art Simon the son of Jona: thou shalt be called Cephas, which is by interpretation, A stone."

"The day following Jesus would go forth into Galilee, and findeth Philip, and saith unto him, Follow Me." Philip obeyed the command, and straightway he also became a worker for Christ.

Philip called Nathanael. The latter had been among the throng when the Baptist pointed to Jesus as the Lamb of God. As Nathanael looked upon Jesus, he was disappointed. Could this man, who bore the marks of toil and poverty, be the Messiah? Yet Nathanael could not decide to reject Jesus, for the message of John had brought conviction to his heart.

140   At the time when Philip called him, Nathanael had withdrawn to a quiet grove to meditate upon the announcement of John and the prophecies concerning the Messiah. He prayed that if the one announced by John was the deliverer, it might be made known to him, and the Holy Spirit rested upon him with assurance that God had visited His people and raised up a horn of salvation for them. Philip knew that his friend was searching the prophecies, and while Nathanael was praying under a fig tree, Philip discovered his retreat. They had often prayed together in this secluded spot hidden by the foliage.

The message, "We have found Him, of whom Moses in the law, and the prophets, did write," seemed to Nathanael a direct answer to his prayer. But Philip had yet a trembling faith. He added doubtfully, "Jesus of Nazareth, the son of Joseph." Again prejudice arose in Nathanael's heart. He exclaimed, "Can there any good thing come out of Nazareth?"

Philip entered into no controversy. He said, "Come and see. Jesus saw Nathanael coming to Him, and saith of him, Behold an Israelite indeed, in whom is no guile!" In surprise Nathanael exclaimed, "Whence knowest Thou me? Jesus answered and said unto him, Before that Philip called thee, when thou wast under the fig tree, I saw thee."

It was enough. The divine Spirit that had borne witness to Nathanael in his solitary prayer under the fig tree now spoke to him in the words of Jesus. Though in doubt, and yielding somewhat to prejudice, Nathanael had come to Christ with an honest desire for truth, and now his desire was met. His faith went beyond that of the one who had brought him to Jesus. He answered and said, "Rabbi, Thou art the Son of God; Thou art the King of Israel."

If Nathanael had trusted to the rabbis for guidance, he would never have found Jesus. It was by seeing and judging for himself that he 141   became a disciple. So in the case of many today whom prejudice withholds from good. How dif-

ferent would be the result if they would "come and see"!

While they trust to the guidance of human authority, none will come to a saving knowledge of the truth. Like Nathanael, we need to study God's word for ourselves, and pray for the enlightenment of the Holy Spirit. He who saw Nathanael under the fig tree will see us in the secret place of prayer. Angels from the world of light are near to those who in humility seek for divine guidance.

With the calling of John and Andrew and Simon, of Philip and Nathanael, began the foundation of the Christian church. John directed two of his disciples to Christ. Then one of these, Andrew, found his brother, and called him to the Saviour. Philip was then called, and he went in search of Nathanael. These examples should teach us the importance of personal effort, of making direct appeals to our kindred, friends, and neighbors. There are those who for a lifetime have professed to be acquainted with Christ, yet who have never made a personal effort to bring even one soul to the Saviour. They leave all the work for the minister. He may be well qualified for his calling, but he cannot do that which God has left for the members of the church.

There are many who need the ministration of loving Christian hearts. Many have gone down to ruin who might have been saved if their neighbors, common men and women, had put forth personal effort for them. Many are waiting to be personally addressed. In the very family, the neighborhood, the town, where we live, there is work for us to do as missionaries for Christ. If we are Christians, this work will be our delight. No sooner is one converted than there is born within him a desire to make known to others what a precious friend he has found in Jesus. The saving and sanctifying truth cannot be shut up in his heart.

All who are consecrated to God will be channels of light. God makes them His agents to communicate to others the riches of His grace. His promise is, "I will make them and the places round about My hill a blessing; and I will cause the shower to come down in his season; there shall be showers of blessing." Ezek. 34:26.

Philip said to Nathanael, "Come and see." He did not ask him to accept another's testimony, but to behold Christ for himself. Now that Jesus has ascended to heaven, His disciples are His representatives among men, and one of the most effective ways of winning souls to Him is in exemplifying His character in our daily life. Our 142   influence upon others depends not so much upon what we say as upon what we are. Men may combat and defy our logic, they may resist our appeals; but a life of disinterested love is an argument they cannot gainsay. A consistent life, characterized by the meekness of Christ, is a power in the world.

The teaching of Christ was the expression of an inwrought conviction and experience, and those who learn of Him become teachers after the divine order. The word of God, spoken by one who is himself sanctified through it, has a life-giving power that makes it attractive to the hearers, and convicts them that it is a living reality. When one has received the truth in the love of it, he will make this manifest in the persuasion of his manner and the tones of his voice. He makes known that which he himself has heard, seen, and handled of the word of life, that others may have fellowship with him through the knowledge of Christ. His testimony, from lips touched with a live coal from off the altar, is truth to the receptive heart, and works sanctification upon the character.

And he who seeks to give light to others will himself be blessed. "There shall be showers of blessing." "He that watereth shall be watered also himself." Prov. 11:25. God could have reached His object in saving sinners without our aid; but in order for us to develop a character like Christ's, we must share in His work. In order to enter into His joy,—the joy of seeing souls redeemed by His sacrifice,—we must participate in His labors for their redemption.

Nathanael's first expression of his faith, so full and earnest and sincere, fell like music on the ears of Jesus. And He "answered and said unto him, Because I said unto thee, I saw thee under the fig tree, believest thou? Thou shalt see greater things than these." The Saviour looked forward with joy to His work in preaching good tidings to the meek, binding up the brokenhearted, and proclaiming liberty to the captives of Satan. At thought of the precious blessings He had brought to men, Jesus added, "Verily, verily, I say unto you, Hereafter ye shall see heaven open, and the angels of God ascending and descending upon the Son of man."

Here Christ virtually says, On the bank of the Jordan the heavens were opened, and the Spirit descended like a dove upon Me. That scene was but a token that I am the Son of God. If you believe on Me as such, your faith shall be quickened. You shall see that the heavens are opened, and are never to be closed. I have opened them 143 to you. The angels of God are ascending, bearing the prayers of the needy and distressed to the Father above, and descending, bringing blessing and hope, courage, help, and life, to the children of men.

The angels of God are ever passing from earth to heaven, and from heaven to earth. The miracles of Christ for the afflicted and suffering were wrought by the power of God through the ministration of the angels. And it is through Christ, by the ministration of His heavenly messengers, that every blessing comes from God to us. In taking upon Himself humanity, our Saviour unites His interests with those of the fallen sons and daughters of Adam, while through His divinity He grasps the throne of God. And thus Christ is the medium of communication of men with God, and of God with men.

15

144

At the Marriage Feast

Jesus did not begin His ministry by some great work before the Sanhedrin at Jerusalem. At a household gathering in a little Galilean village His power was put forth to add to the joy of a wedding feast. Thus He showed His sympathy with men, and His desire to minister to their happiness. In the wilderness of temptation He Himself had drunk the cup of woe. He came forth to give to men the cup of blessing, by His benediction to hallow the relations of human life.

From the Jordan, Jesus had returned to Galilee. There was to be a marriage at Cana, a little town not far from Nazareth; the parties were relatives of Joseph and Mary; and Jesus, knowing of this family gathering, went to Cana, and with His disciples was invited to the feast.

Again He met His mother, from whom He had for some time been separated. Mary had heard of the manifestation at the Jordan, at His baptism. The tidings had been carried to Nazareth, and had brought to her mind afresh the scenes that for so many years had been hidden in her heart. In common with all Israel, Mary was deeply stirred by the mission of John the Baptist. Well she remembered the prophecy given at his birth. Now his connection with Jesus kindled her hopes anew. But tidings had 145 reached her also of the mysterious departure of Jesus to the wilderness, and she was oppressed with troubled forebodings.

From the day when she heard the angel's announcement in the home at Nazareth Mary had treasured every evidence that Jesus was the Messiah. His sweet, unselfish life assured her that He could be no other than the Sent of God. Yet there came to her also doubts and disappointments, and she had longed for the time when His glory should be revealed. Death had separated her from Joseph, who had shared her knowledge of the mystery of the birth of Jesus. Now there was no one to whom she could confide her hopes and fears. The past two months had been very sorrowful. She had been parted from Jesus, in whose sympathy she found comfort; she pondered upon the words of Simeon, "A sword shall pierce through thy own soul also" (Luke 2:35); she recalled the three days of agony when she thought Jesus lost to her forever; and with an anxious heart she awaited His return.

This chapter is based on John 2:1-11.

At the marriage feast she meets Him, the same tender, dutiful son. Yet He is not the same. His countenance is changed. It bears the traces of His conflict in the wilderness, and a new expression of dignity and power gives evidence of His heavenly mission. With Him is a group of young men, whose eyes follow Him with reverence, and who call Him Master. These companions recount to Mary what they have seen and heard at the baptism and elsewhere. They conclude by declaring, "We have found Him, of whom Moses in the law, and the prophets, did write." John 1:45.

As the guests assemble, many seem to be preoccupied with some topic of absorbing interest. A suppressed excitement pervades the company. Little groups converse together in eager but quiet tones, and wondering glances are turned upon the Son of Mary. As Mary had heard the disciples' testimony in regard to Jesus, she had been gladdened with the assurance that her long-cherished hopes were not in vain. Yet she would have been more than human if there had not mingled with this holy joy a trace of the fond mother's natural pride. As she saw the many glances bent upon Jesus, she longed to have Him prove to the company that He was really the Honored of God. She hoped there might be opportunity for Him to work a miracle before them.

It was the custom of the times for marriage festivities to continue several days. On this occasion, before the feast ended it was found that the supply of wine had failed. This discovery caused much perplexity and regret. It was unusual to dispense with wine on festive occasions, and its absence would seem to indicate a want of hospitality. As a relative of the parties, Mary had assisted in the arrangements for the feast, and she now spoke to Jesus, saying, "They have no wine." These words were a suggestion that He might supply their need. But Jesus answered, "Woman, what have I to do with thee? Mine hour is not yet come."

This answer, abrupt as it seems to us, expressed no coldness or discourtesy. The Saviour's form of address to His mother was in accordance with Oriental custom. It was used toward persons to whom it was desired to show respect. Every act of Christ's earthly life was in harmony with the precept He Himself had given, "Honor thy father and thy mother." Ex. 20:12. On the cross, in His last act of tenderness toward His mother, He again addressed her in the same way, as He committed her to the care of His best-loved disciple. Both at the marriage feast and upon the cross, the love expressed in tone and look and manner interpreted His words.

At His visit to the temple in His boyhood, as the mystery of His lifework opened before Him, Christ had said to Mary, "Wist ye not that I must be about My Father's business?" Luke 2:49. These words struck the keynote of His [147] whole life and ministry. Everything was held in abeyance to His work, the great work of redemption which He had come into the world to accomplish. Now He repeated the lesson. There was danger that Mary would regard her relationship to Jesus as giving her a special claim upon Him, and the right, in some degree, to direct Him in His mission. For thirty years He had been to her a loving and obedient son, and His love was unchanged; but He must now go about His Father's work. As Son of the Most High, and Saviour of the world, no earthly ties must hold Him from His mission, or influence His conduct. He must stand free to do the will of God. This lesson is also for us. The claims of God are paramount even to the ties of human relationship. No earthly attraction should turn our feet from the path in which He bids us walk.

The only hope of redemption for our fallen race is in Christ; Mary could find salvation only through the Lamb of God. In herself she possessed no merit. Her connection with Jesus placed her in no different spiritual relation to Him from that of any other human soul. This is indicated in the Saviour's words. He makes clear the distinction between His relation to her as the Son of man and as the Son of God. The tie of kinship between them in no way placed her on an equality with Him.

The words, "Mine hour is not yet come," point to the fact that every act of Christ's life on earth was in fulfillment of the plan that had existed from the days of eternity. Before He came to earth, the plan lay out before Him, perfect in all its details. But as He walked among men, He was guided, step by step, by the Father's will. He did not hesitate to act at the appointed time. With the same submission He waited until the time had come.

In saying to Mary that His hour had not yet come, Jesus was replying to her unspoken thought,—to the expectation she cherished in common with her people. She hoped that He would reveal Himself as the Messiah, and take the throne of Israel. But the time had not come. Not as a King, but as "a Man of Sorrows, and acquainted with grief," had Jesus accepted the lot of humanity.

But though Mary had not a right conception of Christ's mission, she trusted Him implicitly. To this faith Jesus responded. It was to honor Mary's trust, and to strengthen the faith of His disciples, that the first miracle was performed. The disciples were to encounter many and great temptations to unbelief. To them the prophecies had made it clear beyond all controversy that [148] Jesus was the Messiah. They looked for the religious leaders to receive Him with confidence even greater than their own. They declared among the people the wonderful works of Christ and their own confidence in His mission, but they were amazed and bitterly disappointed by the unbelief, the deep-seated prejudice, and the enmity to Jesus, displayed by the priests and rabbis. The Saviour's early miracles strengthened the disciples to stand against this opposition.

In nowise disconcerted by the words of Jesus, Mary said to those serving at table, "Whatsoever He saith unto you, do it." Thus she did what she could to prepare the way for the work of Christ.

Beside the doorway stood six large stone water jars, and Jesus bade the servants fill these with water. It was done. Then as the wine was wanted for immediate use, He said, "Draw out now, and bear unto the governor of the feast." Instead of the water with which the vessels had been filled, there flowed forth wine. Neither the ruler of the feast nor the guests generally were aware that the supply of wine had failed. Upon tasting that which the servants brought, the ruler found it superior to any he had ever before drunk, and very different from that served at the beginning of the feast. Turning to the bridegroom, he said, "Every man at the beginning doth set forth good wine; and when men have well drunk, then that which is worse: but thou hast kept the good wine until now."

As men set forth the best wine first, then afterward that which is worse, so does the world with its gifts. That which it offers may please the eye and fascinate the senses, but it proves to be unsatisfying. The wine turns to bitterness, the gaiety to gloom. That which was begun with songs and mirth ends in weariness and disgust. But the gifts of Jesus are ever fresh and new. The feast that He provides for the soul never fails to give satisfaction and joy. Each new gift increases the capacity of the receiver to appreciate and enjoy the blessings of the Lord. He gives grace for grace. There can be no failure of supply. If you abide in Him, the fact that you receive a rich gift today insures the reception of a richer gift tomorrow. The words of Jesus to Nathanael express the law of God's dealing with the children of faith. With every fresh revelation of His love, He declares to the receptive heart, "Believest thou? thou shalt see greater things than these." John 1:50.

The gift of Christ to the marriage feast was a symbol. The water represented baptism into His 149 death; the wine, the shedding of His blood for the sins of the world. The water to fill the jars was brought by human hands, but the word of Christ alone could impart to it life-giving virtue. So with the rites which point to the Saviour's death. It is only by the power of Christ, working through faith, that they have efficacy to nourish the soul.

The word of Christ supplied ample provision for the feast. So abundant is the provision of His grace to blot out the iniquities of men, and to renew and sustain the soul.

At the first feast He attended with His disciples, Jesus gave them the cup that symbolized His work for their salvation. At the last supper He gave it again, in the institution of that sacred rite by which His death was to be shown forth "till He come." 1 Cor. 11:26. And the sorrow of the disciples at parting from their Lord was comforted with the promise of reunion, as He said, "I will not drink henceforth of this fruit of the vine, until that day when I drink it new with you in My Father's kingdom." Matt. 26:29.

The wine which Christ provided for the feast, and that which He gave to the disciples as a symbol of His own blood, was the pure juice of the grape. To this the prophet Isaiah refers when he speaks of the new wine "in the cluster," and says, "Destroy it not; for a blessing is in it." Isa. 65:8.

It was Christ who in the Old Testament gave the warning to Israel, "Wine is a mocker, strong drink is raging: and whosoever is deceived thereby is not wise." Prov. 20:1. And He Himself provided no such beverage. Satan tempts men to indulgence that will becloud reason and benumb the spiritual perceptions, but Christ teaches us to bring the lower nature into subjection. His whole life was an example of self-denial. In order to break the power of appetite, He suffered in our behalf the severest test that humanity could endure. It was Christ who directed that John the Baptist should drink neither wine nor strong drink. It was He who enjoined similar abstinence upon the wife of Manoah. And He pronounced a curse upon the man who should put the bottle to his neighbor's lips. Christ did not contradict His own teaching. The unfermented wine which He provided for the wedding guests was a wholesome and refreshing drink. Its effect was to bring the taste into harmony with a healthful appetite.

As the guests at the feast remarked upon the quality of the wine, inquiries were made that drew from the servants an account of the miracle. The company were for a time too much amazed to think of Him who had performed the wonderful work. When at length they looked for Him, it was found that He had withdrawn so quietly as to be unnoticed even by His disciples. 150

The attention of the company was now turned to the disciples. For the first time they had the opportunity of acknowledging their faith in Jesus. They told what they had seen and heard at the Jordan, and there was kindled in many hearts the hope that God had raised up a deliverer for His people. The news of the miracle spread through all that region, and was carried to Jerusalem. With new interest the priests and elders searched the prophecies pointing to Christ's coming. There was eager desire to learn the mission of this new teacher, who appeared among the people in so unassuming a manner.

The ministry of Christ was in marked contrast to that of the Jewish elders. Their regard for tradition and formalism had destroyed all real freedom of thought or action. They lived in continual dread of defilement. To avoid contact with the "unclean," they kept aloof, not only from the Gentiles, but from the majority of their own people, seeking neither to benefit them nor to win their friendship. By dwelling constantly on these matters, they had dwarfed their minds and narrowed the orbit of their lives. Their example encouraged egotism and intolerance among all classes of the people.

Jesus began the work of reformation by coming into close sympathy with humanity. While He showed the greatest reverence for the law of God, He rebuked the pretentious piety of the Pharisees, and tried to free the people from the senseless rules that bound them. He was seeking to break down the barriers which separated the different classes of society, that He might bring men together as children of one family. His attendance at the marriage feast was designed to be a step toward effecting this.

God had directed John the Baptist to dwell in the wilderness, that he might be shielded from the influence of the priests and rabbis, and be prepared for a special mission. But the austerity and isolation of his life were not an example for the people. John himself had not directed his hearers to forsake their former duties. He bade them give evidence of their repentance by faithfulness to God in the place where He had called them.

Jesus reproved self-indulgence in all its forms, yet He was social in His nature. He accepted the hospitality of all classes, visiting 151 the homes of the rich and the poor, the learned and the ignorant, and seeking to elevate their thoughts from questions of commonplace life to those things that are spiritual and eternal. He gave no license to dissipation, and no shadow of worldly levity marred His conduct; yet He found pleasure in scenes of innocent happiness, and by His presence sanctioned the social gathering. A Jewish marriage was an impressive occasion, and its joy was not displeasing to the Son of man. By attending this feast, Jesus honored marriage as a divine institution.

In both the Old and the New Testament, the marriage relation is employed to represent the tender and sacred union that exists between Christ and His people. To the mind of Jesus the gladness of the wedding festivities pointed forward to the rejoicing of that day when He shall bring home His bride to the Father's house, and the redeemed with the Redeemer shall sit down to the marriage supper of the Lamb. He says, "As the bridegroom rejoiceth over the bride, so shall thy God rejoice over thee." "Thou shalt no more be termed Forsaken; . . . but thou shalt be called My Delight; . . . for the Lord delighteth in thee." "He will rejoice over thee with joy; He will rest in His love, He will joy over thee with singing." Isa. 62:5, 4, margin; Zeph. 3:17. When the vision of heavenly things was granted to John the apostle, he wrote: "I heard as it were the voice of a great multitude, and as the voice of many waters, and as the voice of mighty thunderings, saying, Alleluia: for the Lord God omnipotent reigneth. Let us be glad and rejoice, and give honor to Him: for the marriage of the Lamb is come, and His wife hath made herself ready." "Blessed are they which are called unto the marriage supper of the Lamb." Rev. 19:6, 7, 9.

Jesus saw in every soul one to whom must be given the call to His kingdom. He reached the hearts of the people by going among them as one who desired their good. He sought them in the public streets, in private houses, on the boats, in the synagogue, by the shores of the lake, and at the marriage feast. He met them at their daily vocations, and manifested an interest in their secular affairs. He carried His instruction into the household, bringing families in their own homes under the influence of His divine presence. His strong personal sympathy helped to win hearts. He often repaired to the mountains for solitary prayer, but this was a preparation for His labor among men in active life. From these seasons He came forth to relieve the sick, to instruct the ignorant, and to break the chains from the captives of Satan.

It was by personal contact and association 152 that Jesus trained His disciples. Sometimes He taught them, sitting among them on the mountainside; sometimes beside the sea, or walking with them by the way, He revealed the mysteries of the kingdom of God. He did not sermonize as men do today. Wherever hearts were open to receive the divine message, He unfolded the truths of the way of salvation. He did not command His disciples to do this or that, but said, "Follow Me." On His journeys through country and cities He took them with Him, that they might see how He taught the people. He linked their interest with His, and they united with Him in the work.

The example of Christ in linking Himself with the interests of humanity should be followed by all who preach His word, and by all who have received the gospel of His grace. We are not to renounce social communion. We should not seclude ourselves from others. In order to reach all classes, we must meet them where they are. They will seldom seek us of their own accord. Not alone from the pulpit are the hearts of men touched by divine truth. There is another field of labor, humbler, it may be, but fully as promising. It is found in the home of the lowly, and in the mansion of the great; at the hospitable board, and in gatherings for innocent social enjoyment.

As disciples of Christ we shall not mingle with the world from a mere love of pleasure, to unite with them in folly. Such associations can result only in harm. We should never give sanction to sin by our words or our deeds, our silence or our presence. Wherever we go, we are to carry Jesus with us, and to reveal to others the preciousness of our Saviour. But those who try to preserve their religion by hiding it within stone walls lose precious opportunities of doing good. Through the social relations, Christianity comes in contact with the world. Everyone who has received the divine illumination is to brighten the pathway of those who know not the Light of life.

We should all become witnesses for Jesus. Social power, sanctified by the grace of Christ, must be improved in winning souls to the Saviour. Let the world see that we are not selfishly absorbed in our own interests, but that we desire others to share our blessings and privileges. Let them see that our religion does not make us unsympathetic or exacting. Let all who profess to have found Christ, minister as He did for the benefit of men.

We should never give to the world the false impression that Christians are a gloomy, unhappy people. If our eyes are fixed on Jesus, we 153 shall see a compassionate Redeemer, and shall catch light from His countenance. Wherever His Spirit reigns, there peace abides. And there will be joy also, for there is a calm, holy trust in God.

Christ is pleased with His followers when they show that, though human, they are partakers of the divine nature. They are not statues, but living men and women. Their hearts, refreshed by the dews of divine grace, open and expand to the Sun of Righteousness. The light that shines upon them they reflect upon others in works that are luminous with the love of Christ.

154

16

In His Temple

"After this He went down to Capernaum, He, and His mother, and His brethren, and His disciples: and they continued there not many days. And the Jews' Passover was at hand, and Jesus went up to Jerusalem."

In this journey, Jesus joined one of the large companies that were making their way to the capital. He had not yet publicly announced His mission, and He mingled unnoticed with the throng. Upon these occasions, the coming of the Messiah, to which such prominence had been given by the ministry of John, was often the theme of conversation. The hope of national greatness was dwelt upon with kindling enthusiasm. Jesus knew that this hope was to be disappointed, for it was founded on a misinterpretation of the Scriptures. With deep earnestness He explained the prophecies, and tried to arouse the people to a closer study of God's word.

The Jewish leaders had instructed the people that at Jerusalem they were to be taught to worship God. Here during the Passover week large numbers assembled, coming from all parts of Palestine, and even from distant lands. The temple courts were filled with a promiscuous throng. Many were unable to bring with them the sacrifices that were to be offered up as typi- 155 fying the one great Sacrifice. For the convenience of these, animals were bought and sold in the outer court of the temple. Here all classes of people assembled to purchase their offerings. Here all foreign money was exchanged for the coin of the sanctuary.

Every Jew was required to pay yearly a half shekel as "a ransom for his soul;" and the money thus collected was used for the support of the temple. Ex. 30:12-16. Besides this, large sums were brought as freewill offerings, to be deposited in the temple treasury. And it was required that all foreign coin should be changed for a coin called the temple shekel, which was accepted for the service of the sanctuary. The money changing gave opportunity for fraud and extortion, and it had grown into a disgraceful traffic, which was a source of revenue to the priests.

The dealers demanded exorbitant prices for the animals sold, and they shared their profits with the priests and rulers, who thus enriched themselves at the expense of the people. The worshipers had been taught to believe that if they did not offer sacrifice, the blessing of God would not rest on their children or their lands. Thus a high price for the animals could be secured; for after coming so far, the people would not return to their homes without performing the act of devotion for which they had come.

A great number of sacrifices were offered at the time of the Passover, and the sales at the temple were very large. The consequent confusion indicated a noisy cattle market rather than the sacred temple of God. There could be heard sharp bargaining, the lowing of cattle, the bleating of sheep, the cooing of doves, mingled with the chinking of coin and angry disputation. So great was the confusion that the worshipers were disturbed, and the words addressed to the Most High were drowned in the uproar that invaded the temple. The Jews were exceedingly proud of their piety. They rejoiced over their temple, and regarded a word spoken in its disfavor as blasphemy; they were very rigorous in

This chapter is based on John 2:12-22.

the performance of ceremonies connected with it; but the love of money had overruled their scruples. They were scarcely aware how far they had wandered from the original purpose of the service instituted by God Himself.

When the Lord descended upon Mount Sinai, the place was consecrated by His presence. Moses was commanded to put bounds around the mount and sanctify it, and the word of the
156 Lord was heard in warning: "Take heed to yourselves, that ye go not up into the mount, or touch the border of it: whosoever toucheth the mount shall be surely put to death: there shall not an hand touch it, but he shall surely be stoned, or shot through; whether it be beast or man, it shall not live." Ex. 19:12, 13. Thus was taught the lesson that wherever God manifests His presence, the place is holy. The precincts of God's temple should have been regarded as sacred. But in the strife for gain, all this was lost sight of.

The priests and rulers were called to be the representatives of God to the nation; they should have corrected the abuses of the temple
157 court. They should have given to the people an example of integrity and compassion. Instead of studying their own profit, they should have considered the situation and needs of the worshipers, and should have been ready to assist those who were not able to buy the required sacrifices. But this they did not do. Avarice had hardened their hearts.

There came to this feast those who were suffering, those who were in want and distress. The blind, the lame, the deaf, were there. Some were brought on beds. Many came who were too poor to purchase the humblest offering for the Lord, too poor even to buy food with which to satisfy their own hunger. These were greatly distressed by the statements of the priests. The priests boasted of their piety; they claimed to be the guardians of the people; but they were without sympathy or compassion. The poor, the sick, the dying, made their vain plea for favor. Their suffering awakened no pity in the hearts of the priests.

As Jesus came into the temple, He took in the whole scene. He saw the unfair transactions. He saw the distress of the poor, who thought that without shedding of blood there would be no forgiveness for their sins. He saw the outer court of His temple converted into a place of unholy traffic. The sacred enclosure had become one vast exchange.

Christ saw that something must be done. Numerous ceremonies were enjoined upon the people without the proper instruction as to their import. The worshipers offered their sacrifices without understanding that they were typical of the only perfect Sacrifice. And among them, unrecognized and unhonored, stood the One symbolized by all their service. He had given

directions in regard to the offerings. He understood their symbolical value, and He saw that they were now perverted and misunderstood. Spiritual worship was fast disappearing. No link bound the priests and rulers to their God. Christ's work was to establish an altogether different worship.

With searching glance, Christ takes in the scene before Him as He stands upon the steps of the temple court. With prophetic eye He looks into futurity, and sees not only years, but centuries and ages. He sees how priests and rulers will turn the needy from their right, and forbid that the gospel shall be preached to the poor. He sees how the love of God will be concealed from sinners, and men will make merchandise of His grace. As He beholds the scene, indignation, authority, and power are expressed in His countenance. The attention of the people is attracted to Him. The eyes of those engaged in their unholy traffic are riveted upon His face. They cannot withdraw their gaze. They feel that this Man reads their inmost thoughts, and discovers their hidden motives. Some attempt to conceal their faces, as if their evil deeds were written upon their countenances, to be scanned by those searching eyes.
158

The confusion is hushed. The sound of traffic and bargaining has ceased. The silence becomes painful. It is as if they were arraigned before the tribunal of God to answer for their deeds. Looking upon Christ, they behold divinity flash through the garb of humanity. The Majesty of heaven stands as the Judge will stand at the last day,—not now encircled with the glory that will then attend Him, but with the same power to read the soul. His eye sweeps over the multitude, taking in every individual. His form seems to rise above them in commanding dignity, and a divine light illuminates His countenance. He speaks, and His clear, ringing voice—the same that upon Mount Sinai proclaimed the law that priests and rulers are transgressing—is heard echoing through the arches of the temple: "Take these things hence; make not My Father's house an house of merchandise."

Slowly descending the steps, and raising the scourge of cords gathered up on entering the enclosure, He bids the bargaining company depart from the precincts of the temple. With a zeal and severity He has never before manifested, He overthrows the tables of the money-changers. The coin falls, ringing sharply upon the marble pavement. None presume to question His authority. None dare stop to gather up their ill-gotten gain. Jesus does not smite them with the whip of cords, but in His hand that simple scourge seems terrible as a flaming sword. Officers of the temple, speculating priests, brokers and cattle traders, with their sheep and oxen, rush from the place, with the one thought of escaping from the condemnation of His presence.

A panic sweeps over the multitude, who feel the overshadowing of His divinity. Cries of terror escape from hundreds of blanched lips. Even the disciples tremble. They are awestruck by the words and manner of Jesus, so unlike His usual demeanor. They remember that it is written of Him, "The zeal of Thine house hath eaten Me up." Ps. 69:9. Soon the tumultuous throng with their merchandise are far removed from the temple of the Lord. The courts are free from unholy traffic, and a deep silence and solemnity settles upon the scene of confusion. The presence of the Lord, that of old sanctified the mount, has now made sacred the temple reared in His honor.

In the cleansing of the temple, Jesus was announcing His mission as the Messiah, and entering upon His work. That temple, erected for the abode of the divine Presence, was designed to be an object lesson for Israel and for the world. From eternal ages it was God's purpose that every created being, from the bright and holy seraph to man, should be a temple for the indwelling of the Creator. Because of sin, humanity ceased to be a temple for God. Darkened and defiled by evil, the heart of man no longer revealed the glory of the Divine One. But by the incarnation of the Son of God, the purpose of Heaven is fulfilled. God dwells in humanity, and through saving grace the heart of man becomes again His temple. God designed that the temple at Jerusalem should be a continual witness to the high destiny open to every soul. But the Jews had not understood the significance of the building they regarded with so much pride. They did not yield themselves as holy temples for the Divine Spirit. The courts of the temple at Jerusalem, filled with the tumult of unholy traffic, represented all too truly the temple of the heart, defiled by the presence of sensual passion and unholy thoughts. In cleansing the temple from the world's buyers and sellers, Jesus announced His mission to cleanse the heart from the defilement of sin,—from the earthly desires, the selfish lusts, the evil habits, that corrupt the soul. "The Lord, whom ye seek, shall suddenly come to His temple, even the Messenger of the covenant, whom ye delight in: behold, He shall come, saith the Lord of hosts. But who may abide the day of His coming? and who shall stand when He appeareth? for He is like a refiner's fire, and like fullers' soap: and He shall sit as a refiner and purifier of silver: and He shall purify the sons of Levi, and purge them as gold and silver." Mal. 3:1-3.

"Know ye not that ye are the temple of God, and that the Spirit of God dwelleth in you? If any man defile the temple of God, him shall God destroy; for the temple of God is holy, which temple ye are." 1 Cor. 3:16, 17. No man can of himself cast out the evil throng that have taken possession of the heart. Only Christ can cleanse the soul temple. But He will not force an entrance. He comes not into the heart as to the temple of old; but He says, "Behold, I stand at the door, and knock: if any man hear My voice, and open the door, I will come in to him." Rev. 3:20. He will come, not for one day merely; for He says, "I will dwell in them, and walk in them; . . . and they shall be My people." "He will subdue our iniquities; and Thou wilt cast all their sins into the depths of the sea." 2 Cor. 6:16; Micah 7:19. His presence will cleanse and sanctify the soul, so that it may be a holy temple unto the Lord, and "an habitation of God through the Spirit." Eph. 2:21, 22.

Overpowered with terror, the priests and rulers had fled from the temple court, and from the searching glance that read their hearts. In their flight they met others on their way to the temple, and bade them turn back, telling them what they had seen and heard. Christ looked upon the fleeing men with yearning pity for their fear, and their ignorance of what constituted true worship. In this scene He saw symbolized the dispersion of the whole Jewish nation for their wickedness and impenitence.

And why did the priests flee from the temple? Why did they not stand their ground? He who commanded them to go was a carpenter's son, a poor Galilean, without earthly rank or power. Why did they not resist Him? Why did they leave the gain so ill acquired, and flee at the command of One whose outward appearance was so humble?

Christ spoke with the authority of a king, and in His appearance, and in the tones of His voice, there was that which they had no power to resist. At the word of command they realized, as they had never realized before, their true position as hypocrites and robbers. When divinity flashed through humanity, not only did they see indignation on Christ's countenance; they realized the import of His words. They felt as if before the throne of the eternal Judge, with their sentence passed on them for time and for eternity. For a time they were convinced that Christ was a prophet; and many believed Him to be the Messiah. The Holy Spirit flashed into their minds the utterances of the prophets concerning Christ. Would they yield to this conviction?

Repent they would not. They knew that Christ's sympathy for the poor had been aroused. They knew that they had been guilty of extortion in their dealings with the people. Because Christ discerned their thoughts they hated Him. His public rebuke was humiliating to their pride, and they were jealous of His growing influence with the people. They determined to challenge Him as to the power by which He had driven them forth, and who gave Him this power.

Slowly and thoughtfully, but with hate in their hearts, they returned to the temple. But what a change had taken place during their 163 absence! When they fled, the poor remained behind; and these were now looking to Jesus, whose countenance expressed His love and sympathy. With tears in His eyes, He said to the trembling ones around Him: Fear not; I will deliver thee, and thou shalt glorify Me. For this cause came I into the world.

The people pressed into Christ's presence with urgent, pitiful appeals: Master, bless me. His ear heard every cry. With pity exceeding that of a tender mother He bent over the suffering little ones. All received attention. Everyone was healed of whatever disease he had. The dumb opened their lips in praise; the blind beheld the face of their Restorer. The hearts of the sufferers were made glad.

As the priests and temple officials witnessed this great work, what a revelation to them were the sounds that fell on their ears! The people were relating the story of the pain they had suffered, of their disappointed hopes, of painful days and sleepless nights. When the last spark of hope seemed to be dead, Christ had healed them. The burden was so heavy, one said; but I have found a helper. He is the Christ of God, and I will devote my life to His service. Parents said to their children, He has saved your life; lift up your voice and praise Him. The voices of children and youth, fathers and mothers, friends and spectators, blended in thanksgiving and praise. Hope and gladness filled their hearts. Peace came to their minds. They were restored soul and body, and they returned home, proclaiming everywhere the matchless love of Jesus.

At the crucifixion of Christ, those who had thus been healed did not join with the rabble throng in crying, "Crucify Him, crucify Him." Their sympathies were with Jesus; for they had felt His great sympathy and wonderful power. They knew Him to be their Saviour; for He had given them health of body and soul. They listened to the preaching of the apostles, and the entrance of God's word into their hearts gave them understanding. They became agents of God's mercy, and instruments of His salvation.

The crowd that had fled from the temple court after a time slowly drifted back. They had partially recovered from the panic that had seized them, but their faces expressed irresolution and timidity. They looked with amazement on the works of Jesus, and were convicted that in Him the prophecies concerning the Messiah were fulfilled. The sin of the desecration of the temple rested, in a great degree, upon the 164 priests. It was by their arrangement that the court had been turned into a market place. The people were comparatively innocent. They were impressed by the divine authority of Jesus; but with them the influence of the priests and rulers was paramount. They regarded Christ's mission as an innovation, and questioned His right to interfere with what was permitted by the authorities of the temple. They were offended because the traffic had been interrupted, and they stifled the convictions of the Holy Spirit.

Above all others the priests and rulers should have seen in Jesus the anointed of the Lord; for in their hands were the sacred scrolls that described His mission, and they knew that the cleansing of the temple was a manifestation of more than human power. Much as they hated Jesus, they could not free themselves from the thought that He might be a prophet sent by God to restore the sanctity of the temple. With a deference born of this fear, they went to Him with the inquiry, "What sign showest Thou unto us, seeing that Thou doest these things?"

Jesus had shown them a sign. In flashing light into their hearts, and in doing before them the works which the Messiah was to do, He had given convincing evidence of His character. Now when they asked for a sign, He answered them by a parable, showing that He read their malice, and saw to what lengths it would lead them. "Destroy this temple," He said, "and in three days I will raise it up."

In these words His meaning was twofold. He referred not only to the destruction of the Jewish temple and worship, but to His own death,—the destruction of the temple of His body. This the Jews were already plotting. As the priests and rulers returned to the temple, they had proposed to kill Jesus, and thus rid themselves of the troubler. Yet when He set before them their purpose, they did not understand Him. They took His words as applying only to the temple at Jerusalem, and with indignation exclaimed, "Forty and six years was this temple in building, and wilt Thou rear it up in three days?" Now they felt that Jesus had justified their unbelief, and they were confirmed in their rejection of Him.

Christ did not design that His words should be understood by the unbelieving Jews, nor even by His disciples at this time. He knew that they would be misconstrued by His enemies, and would be turned against Him. At His trial they would be brought as an accusation, and on Calvary they would be flung at Him as a taunt. But to explain them now would give His disciples a knowledge of His sufferings, and bring upon them sorrow which as yet they were not 165 able to bear. And an explanation would prematurely disclose to the Jews the result of their prejudice and unbelief. Already they had entered upon a path which they would steadily pursue until He should be led as a lamb to the slaughter.

It was for the sake of those who should believe on Him that these words of Christ were spoken. He knew that they would be repeated. Being spoken at the Passover, they would come to the ears of thousands, and be carried to all parts of the world. After He had risen from the dead, their meaning would be made plain. To many they would be conclusive evidence of His divinity.

Because of their spiritual darkness, even the disciples of Jesus often failed of comprehending His lessons. But many of these lessons were made plain to them by subsequent events. When He walked no more with them, His words were a stay to their hearts.

As referring to the temple at Jerusalem, the Saviour's words, "Destroy this temple, and in three days I will raise it up," had a deeper meaning than the hearers perceived. Christ was the foundation and life of the temple. Its services were typical of the sacrifice of the Son of God. The priesthood was established to represent the mediatorial character and work of Christ. The entire plan of sacrificial worship was a foreshadowing of the Saviour's death to redeem the world. There would be no efficacy in these offerings when the great event toward which they had pointed for ages was consummated.

Since the whole ritual economy was symbolical of Christ, it had no value apart from Him. When the Jews sealed their rejection of Christ by delivering Him to death, they rejected all that gave significance to the temple and its services. Its sacredness had departed. It was doomed to destruction. From that day sacrificial offerings and the service connected with them were meaningless. Like the offering of Cain, they did not express faith in the Saviour. In putting Christ to death, the Jews virtually destroyed their temple. When Christ was crucified, the inner veil of the temple was rent in twain from top to bottom, signifying that the great final sacrifice had been made, and that the system of sacrificial offerings was forever at an end.

"In three days I will raise it up." In the Saviour's death the powers of darkness seemed to prevail, and they exulted in their victory. But from the rent sepulcher of Joseph, Jesus came forth a conqueror. "Having spoiled principalities and powers, He made a show of them openly, triumphing over them." Col. 2:15. By virtue of His death and resurrection He became the minister of the "true tabernacle, which the Lord pitched, and not man." Heb. 8:2. Men reared the Jewish tabernacle; men builded the Jewish temple; but the sanctuary above, of which the earthly was a type, was built by no human architect. "Behold the Man whose name is The Branch; . . . He shall build the temple of the Lord; and He shall bear the glory, and shall sit and rule upon His throne; and He shall be a priest upon His throne." Zech. 6:12, 13.

The sacrificial service that had pointed to Christ passed away; but the eyes of men were turned to the true sacrifice for the sins of the world. The earthly priesthood ceased; but we look to Jesus, the minister of the new covenant, and "to the blood of sprinkling, that speaketh better things than that of Abel." "The way into the holiest of all was not yet made manifest, while as the first tabernacle was yet standing: . . . but Christ being come an high priest of good things to come, by a greater and more perfect tabernacle, not made with hands, ... by His own blood He entered in once into the holy place, having obtained eternal redemption for us." Heb. 12:24; 9:8-12.

"Wherefore He is able also to save them to the uttermost that come unto God by Him, seeing He ever liveth to make intercession for them." Heb. 7:25. Though the ministration was to be removed from the earthly to the heavenly temple; though the sanctuary and our great high priest would be invisible to human sight, yet the disciples were to suffer no loss thereby. They would realize no break in their communion, and no diminution of power because of the Saviour's absence. While Jesus ministers in the sanctuary above, He is still by His Spirit the minister of the church on earth. He is withdrawn from the eye of sense, but His parting promise is fulfilled, "Lo, I am with you alway, even unto the end of the world." Matt. 28:20. While He delegates His power to inferior ministers, His energizing presence is still with His church.

"Seeing then that we have a great high priest, . . . Jesus, the Son of God, let us hold fast our profession. For we have not an high priest which cannot be touched with the feeling of our infirmities; but was in all points tempted like as we are, yet without sin. Let us therefore come boldly unto the throne of grace, that we may obtain mercy, and find grace to help in time of need." Heb. 4:14-16.

17

Nicodemus

Nicodemus held a high position of trust in the Jewish nation. He was highly educated, and possessed talents of no ordinary character, and he was an honored member of the national council. With others, he had been stirred by the teaching of Jesus. Though rich, learned, and honored, he had been strangely attracted by the humble Nazarene. The lessons that had fallen from the Saviour's lips had greatly impressed him, and he desired to learn more of these wonderful truths.

Christ's exercise of authority in the cleansing of the temple had roused the determined hatred of the priests and rulers. They feared the power

This chapter is based on John 3:1-17.

of this stranger. Such boldness on the part of an obscure Galilean was not to be tolerated. They were bent on putting an end to His work. But not all were agreed in this purpose. There were some that feared to oppose One who was so evidently moved upon by the Spirit of God. They remembered how prophets had been slain for rebuking the sins of the leaders in Israel. They knew that the bondage of the Jews to a heathen nation was the result of their stubbornness in rejecting reproofs from God. They feared that in plotting against Jesus the priests and rulers were following in the steps of their fathers, and would bring fresh calamities upon the nation. Nicodemus shared these feelings. In a council of the Sanhedrin, when the course to be pursued toward Jesus was considered, Nicodemus advised caution and moderation. He urged that if Jesus was really invested with authority from God, it would be perilous to reject His warnings. The priests dared not disregard this counsel, and for the time they took no open measures against the Saviour.

Since hearing Jesus, Nicodemus had anxiously studied the prophecies relating to the Messiah; and the more he searched, the stronger was his conviction that this was the One who was to come. With many others in Israel he had been greatly distressed by the profanation of the temple He was a witness of the scene when Jesus drove out the buyers and the sellers; he beheld the wonderful manifestation of divine power; he saw the Saviour receiving the poor and healing the sick; he saw their looks of joy, and heard their words of praise; and he could not doubt that Jesus of Nazareth was the Sent of God.

He greatly desired an interview with Jesus, but shrank from seeking Him openly. It would be too humiliating for a ruler of the Jews to acknowledge himself in sympathy with a teacher as yet so little known. And should his visit come to the knowledge of the Sanhedrin, it would draw upon him their scorn and denunciation. He resolved upon a secret interview, excusing this on the ground that if he were to go openly, others might follow his example. Learning by special inquiry the Saviour's place of retirement in the Mount of Olives, he waited until the city was hushed in slumber, and then sought Him.

In the presence of Christ, Nicodemus felt a strange timidity, which he endeavored to conceal under an air of composure and dignity. "Rabbi," he said, "we know that Thou art a teacher come from God: for no man can do these miracles that Thou doest, except God be with him." By speaking of Christ's rare gifts as a teacher, and also of His wonderful power to perform miracles, he hoped to pave the way for his interview. His words were designed to express and to invite confidence; but they really expressed unbelief. He did not acknowledge

Jesus to be the Messiah, but only a teacher sent from God.

Instead of recognizing this salutation, Jesus bent His eyes upon the speaker, as if reading his very soul. In His infinite wisdom He saw before Him a seeker after truth. He knew the object of this visit, and with a desire to deepen the conviction already resting upon His listener's mind, He came directly to the point, saying solemnly, yet kindly, "Verily, verily, I say unto thee, Except a man be born from above, he cannot see the kingdom of God." John 3:3, margin.

Nicodemus had come to the Lord thinking to enter into a discussion with Him, but Jesus laid bare the foundation principles of truth. He said to Nicodemus, It is not theoretical knowledge you need so much as spiritual regeneration. You need not to have your curiosity satisfied, but to have a new heart. You must receive a new life from above before you can appreciate heavenly things. Until this change takes place, making all things new, it will result in no saving good for you to discuss with Me My authority or My mission.

Nicodemus had heard the preaching of John the Baptist concerning repentance and baptism, and pointing the people to One who should baptize with the Holy Spirit. He himself had felt that there was a lack of spirituality among the Jews, that, to a great degree, they were controlled by bigotry and worldly ambition. He had hoped for a better state of things at the Messiah's coming. Yet the heart-searching message of the Baptist had failed to work in him conviction of sin. He was a strict Pharisee, and prided himself on his good works. He was widely esteemed for his benevolence and his liberality in sustaining the temple service, and he felt secure of the favor of God. He was startled at the thought of a kingdom too pure for him to see in his present state.

The figure of the new birth, which Jesus had used, was not wholly unfamiliar to Nicodemus. Converts from heathenism to the faith of Israel were often compared to children just born. Therefore he must have perceived that the words of Christ were not to be taken in a literal sense. But by virtue of his birth as an Israelite he regarded himself as sure of a place in the kingdom of God. He felt that he needed no change. Hence his surprise at the Saviour's words. He was irritated by their close application to himself. The pride of the Pharisee was struggling against the honest desire of the seeker after truth. He wondered that Christ should speak to him as He did, not respecting his position as ruler in Israel.

Surprised out of his self-possession, he answered Christ in words full of irony, "How can a man be born when he is old?" Like many others when cutting truth is brought home to the conscience, he revealed the fact that the natural man receiveth not the things of the Spirit of God. There is in him nothing that responds to spiritual things; for spiritual things are spiritually discerned.

But the Saviour did not meet argument with argument. Raising His hand with solemn, quiet dignity, He pressed the truth home with greater 172 assurance, "Verily, verily, I say unto thee, Except a man be born of water and of the Spirit, he cannot enter into the kingdom of God." Nicodemus knew that Christ here referred to water baptism and the renewing of the heart by the Spirit of God. He was convinced that he was in the presence of the One whom John the Baptist had foretold.

Jesus continued: "That which is born of the flesh is flesh; and that which is born of the Spirit is spirit." By nature the heart is evil, and "who can bring a clean thing out of an unclean? not one." Job 14:4. No human invention can find a remedy for the sinning soul. "The carnal mind is enmity against God: for it is not subject to the law of God, neither indeed can be." "Out of the heart proceed evil thoughts, murders, adulteries, fornications, thefts, false witness, blasphemies." Rom. 8:7; Matt. 15:19. The fountain of the heart must be purified before the streams can become pure. He who is trying to reach heaven by his own works in keeping the law is attempting an impossibility. There is no safety for one who has merely a legal religion, a form of godliness. The Christian's life is not a modification or improvement of the old, but a transformation of nature. There is a death to self and sin, and a new life altogether. This change can be brought about only by the effectual working of the Holy Spirit.

Nicodemus was still perplexed, and Jesus used the wind to illustrate His meaning: "The wind bloweth where it listeth, and thou hearest the sound thereof, but canst not tell whence it cometh, and whither it goeth: so is everyone that is born of the Spirit."

The wind is heard among the branches of the trees, rustling the leaves and flowers; yet it is invisible, and no man knows whence it comes or whither it goes. So with the work of the Holy Spirit upon the heart. It can no more be explained than can the movements of the wind. A person may not be able to tell the exact time or place, or to trace all the circumstances in the process of conversion; but this does not prove him to be unconverted. By an agency as unseen as the wind, Christ is constantly working upon the heart. Little by little, perhaps unconsciously to the receiver, impressions are made that tend to draw the soul to Christ. These may be received through meditating upon Him, through reading the Scriptures, or through hearing the word from the living preacher. Suddenly, as the Spirit comes with more direct appeal, the soul gladly surrenders itself to Jesus. By many this is called sudden conversion; but it is the result of long wooing by the Spirit of God,—a patient, protracted process.

While the wind is itself invisible, it produces 173 effects that are seen and felt. So the work of the Spirit upon the soul will reveal itself in every act of him who has felt its saving power. When the Spirit of God takes possession of the heart, it transforms the life. Sinful thoughts are put away, evil deeds are renounced; love, humility, and peace take the place of anger, envy, and strife. Joy takes the place of sadness, and the countenance reflects the light of heaven. No one sees the hand that lifts the burden, or beholds the light descend from the courts above. The blessing comes when by faith the soul surrenders itself to God. Then that power which no human eye can see creates a new being in the image of God.

It is impossible for finite minds to comprehend the work of redemption. Its mystery exceeds human knowledge; yet he who passes from death to life realizes that it is a divine reality. The beginning of redemption we may know here through a personal experience. Its results reach through the eternal ages.

While Jesus was speaking, some gleams of truth penetrated the ruler's mind. The softening, subduing influence of the Holy Spirit impressed his heart. Yet he did not fully understand the Saviour's words. He was not so much impressed by the necessity of the new birth as by the manner of its accomplishment. He said wonderingly, "How can these things be?"

"Art thou a master of Israel, and knowest not these things?" Jesus asked. Surely one entrusted with the religious instruction of the people should not be ignorant of truths so important. His words conveyed the lesson that instead of feeling irritated over the plain words of truth, Nicodemus should have had a very humble opinion of himself, because of his spiritual ignorance. Yet Christ spoke with such solemn dignity, and both look and tone expressed such earnest love, that Nicodemus was not offended as he realized his humiliating condition.

But as Jesus explained that His mission on earth was to establish a spiritual instead of a temporal kingdom, His hearer was troubled. Seeing this, Jesus added, "If I have told you earthly things, and ye believe not, how shall ye believe, if I tell you of heavenly things?" If Nicodemus could not receive Christ's teaching, illustrating the work of grace upon the heart, how could he comprehend the nature of His glorious heavenly kingdom? Not discerning the nature of Christ's work on earth, he could not understand His work in heaven.

The Jews whom Jesus had driven from the temple claimed to be children of Abraham, but they fled from the Saviour's presence because they could not endure the glory of God which 174 was manifested in Him. Thus they gave evidence that they were not fitted by the grace of God to participate in the sacred services of the temple. They were zealous to maintain an appearance of holiness, but they neglected holiness of heart. While they were sticklers for the letter of the law, they were constantly violating its spirit. Their great need was that very change which Christ had been explaining to Nicodemus,—a new moral birth, a cleansing from sin, and a renewing of knowledge and holiness.

There was no excuse for the blindness of Israel in regard to the work of regeneration. Under the inspiration of the Holy Spirit, Isaiah had written, "We are all as an unclean thing, and all our righteousnesses are as filthy rags." David had prayed, "Create in me a clean heart, O God; and renew a right spirit within me." And through Ezekiel the promise had been given, "A new heart also will I give you, and a new spirit will I put within you: and I will take away the stony heart out of your flesh, and I will give you an heart of flesh. And I will put My Spirit within you, and cause you to walk in My statutes." Isa. 64:6; Ps. 51:10; Ezek. 36:26, 27.

Nicodemus had read these scriptures with a clouded mind; but he now began to comprehend their meaning. He saw that the most rigid obedience to the mere letter of the law as applied to the outward life could entitle no man to enter the kingdom of heaven. In the estimation of men, his life had been just and honorable; but in the presence of Christ he felt that his heart was unclean, and his life unholy.

Nicodemus was being drawn to Christ. As the Saviour explained to him concerning the new birth, he longed to have this change wrought in himself. By what means could it be accomplished? Jesus answered the unspoken question: "As Moses lifted up the serpent in the wilderness, even so must the Son of man be lifted up: that whosoever believeth in Him should not perish, but have eternal life."

Here was ground with which Nicodemus was familiar. The symbol of the uplifted serpent made plain to him the Saviour's mission. When the people of Israel were dying from the sting of the fiery serpents, God directed Moses to make a serpent of brass, and place it on high in the midst of the congregation. Then the word was sounded throughout the encampment that all who would look upon the serpent should live. The people well knew that in itself the serpent had no power to help them. It was a symbol of Christ. As the image made in the likeness of the 175 destroying serpents was lifted up for their healing, so One made "in the likeness of sinful flesh" was to be their Redeemer. Rom. 8:3. Many of the Israelites regarded the sacrificial service as having in itself virtue to set them free from sin. God desired to teach them that it had no more value than that serpent of brass. It was

to lead their minds to the Saviour. Whether for the healing of their wounds or the pardon of their sins, they could do nothing for themselves but show their faith in the Gift of God. They were to look and live.

Those who had been bitten by the serpents might have delayed to look. They might have questioned how there could be efficacy in that brazen symbol. They might have demanded a scientific explanation. But no explanation was given. They must accept the word of God to them through Moses. To refuse to look was to perish.

Not through controversy and discussion is the soul enlightened. We must look and live. Nicodemus received the lesson, and carried it with him. He searched the Scriptures in a new way, not for the discussion of a theory, but in order to receive life for the soul. He began to see the kingdom of heaven as he submitted himself to the leading of the Holy Spirit.

There are thousands today who need to learn the same truth that was taught to Nicodemus by the uplifted serpent. They depend on their obedience to the law of God to commend them to His favor. When they are bidden to look to Jesus, and believe that He saves them solely through His grace, they exclaim, "How can these things be?"

Like Nicodemus, we must be willing to enter into life in the same way as the chief of sinners. Than Christ, "there is none other name under heaven given among men, whereby we must be saved." Acts 4:12. Through faith we receive the grace of God; but faith is not our Saviour. It earns nothing. It is the hand by which we lay hold upon Christ, and appropriate His merits, the remedy for sin. And we cannot even repent without the aid of the Spirit of God. The Scripture says of Christ, "Him hath God exalted with His right hand to be a Prince and a Saviour, for to give repentance to Israel, and forgiveness of sins." Acts 5:31. Repentance comes from Christ as truly as does pardon.

How, then, are we to be saved? "As Moses lifted up the serpent in the wilderness," so the Son of man has been lifted up, and everyone who has been deceived and bitten by the serpent may look and live. "Behold the Lamb of God, which taketh away the sin of the world." John 176 1:29. The light shining from the cross reveals the love of God. His love is drawing us to Himself. If we do not resist this drawing, we shall be led to the foot of the cross in repentance for the sins that have crucified the Saviour. Then the Spirit of God through faith produces a new life in the soul. The thoughts and desires are brought into obedience to the will of Christ. The heart, the mind, are created anew in the image of Him who works in us to subdue all things to Himself. Then the law of God is written in the mind and heart, and we can say with Christ, "I delight to do Thy will, O my God." Ps. 40:8.

In the interview with Nicodemus, Jesus unfolded the plan of salvation and His mission to the world. In none of His subsequent discourses did He explain so fully, step by step, the work necessary to be done in the hearts of all who would inherit the kingdom of heaven. At the very beginning of His ministry He opened the truth to a member of the Sanhedrin, to the mind that was most receptive, and to an appointed teacher of the people. But the leaders of Israel did not welcome the light. Nicodemus hid the truth in his heart, and for three years there was little apparent fruit.

But Jesus was acquainted with the soil into which He cast the seed. The words spoken at night to one listener in the lonely mountain were not lost. For a time Nicodemus did not publicly acknowledge Christ, but he watched His life, and pondered His teachings. In the Sanhedrin council he repeatedly thwarted the schemes of the priests to destroy Him. When at last Jesus was lifted up on the cross, Nicodemus remembered the teaching upon Olivet: "As Moses lifted up the serpent in the wilderness, even so must the Son of man be lifted up: that whosoev-
177　er believeth in Him should not perish, but have eternal life." The light from that secret interview illumined the cross upon Calvary, and Nicodemus saw in Jesus the world's Redeemer.

After the Lord's ascension, when the disciples were scattered by persecution, Nicodemus came boldly to the front. He employed his wealth in sustaining the infant church that the Jews had expected to be blotted out at the death of Christ. In the time of peril he who had been so cautious and questioning was firm as a rock, encouraging the faith of the disciples, and furnishing means to carry forward the work of the gospel. He was scorned and persecuted by those who had paid him reverence in other days. He became poor in this world's goods; yet he faltered not in the faith which had its beginning in that night conference with Jesus.

Nicodemus related to John the story of that interview, and by his pen it was recorded for the instruction of millions. The truths there taught are as important today as they were on that solemn night in the shadowy mountain, when the Jewish ruler came to learn the way of life from the lowly Teacher of Galilee.

178

18

"He Must Increase"

For a time the Baptist's influence over the nation had been greater than that of its rulers, priests, or princes. If he had announced himself as the Messiah, and raised a revolt against

Rome, priests and people would have flocked to his standard. Every consideration that appeals to the ambition of the world's conquerors Satan had stood ready to urge upon John the Baptist. But with the evidence before him of his power, he had steadfastly refused the splendid bribe. The attention which was fixed upon him he had directed to Another.

Now he saw the tide of popularity turning away from himself to the Saviour. Day by day the crowds about him lessened. When Jesus came from Jerusalem to the region about Jordan, the people flocked to hear Him. The number of His disciples increased daily. Many came for baptism, and while Christ Himself did not baptize, He sanctioned the administration of the ordinance by His disciples. Thus He set His seal upon the mission of His forerunner. But the disciples of John looked with jealousy upon the growing popularity of Jesus. They stood ready to criticize His work, and it was not long before they found occasion. A question arose between them and the Jews as to whether baptism availed to cleanse the soul from sin; they maintained that the baptism of Jesus differed essentially from that of John. Soon they were in dispute with Christ's disciples in regard to the form of words proper to use at baptism, and finally as to the right of the latter to baptize at all.

The disciples of John came to him with their　179 grievances, saying, "Rabbi, He that was with thee beyond Jordan, to whom thou bearest witness, behold, the same baptizeth, and all men come to Him." Through these words, Satan brought temptation upon John. Though John's mission seemed about to close, it was still possible for him to hinder the work of Christ. If he had sympathized with himself, and expressed grief or disappointment at being superseded, he would have sown the seeds of dissension, would have encouraged envy and jealousy, and would seriously have impeded the progress of the gospel.

John had by nature the faults and weaknesses common to humanity, but the touch of divine love had transformed him. He dwelt in an atmosphere uncontaminated with selfishness and ambition, and far above the miasma of jealousy. He manifested no sympathy with the dissatisfaction of his disciples, but showed how clearly he understood his relation to the Messiah, and how gladly he welcomed the One for whom he had prepared the way.

He said, "A man can receive nothing, except it be given him from heaven. Ye yourselves bear me witness, that I said, I am not the Christ, but that I am sent before Him. He that hath the bride is the bridegroom: but the friend of the bridegroom, which standeth and heareth him, rejoiceth greatly because of the bridegroom's voice." John represented himself as the friend who acted as a messenger between the betrothed

This chapter is based on John 3:22-36.

parties, preparing the way for the marriage. When the bridegroom had received his bride, the mission of the friend was fulfilled. He rejoiced in the happiness of those whose union he had promoted. So John had been called to direct the people to Jesus, and it was his joy to witness the success of the Saviour's work. He said, "This my joy therefore is fulfilled. He must increase, but I must decrease."

Looking in faith to the Redeemer, John had risen to the height of self-abnegation. He sought not to attract men to himself, but to lift their thoughts higher and still higher, until they should rest upon the Lamb of God. He himself had been only a voice, a cry in the wilderness. Now with joy he accepted silence and obscurity, that the eyes of all might be turned to the Light of life.

Those who are true to their calling as messengers for God will not seek honor for themselves. Love for self will be swallowed up in love for Christ. No rivalry will mar the precious cause of the gospel. They will recognize that it is their work to proclaim, as did John the Baptist, [180] "Behold the Lamb of God, which taketh away the sin of the world." John 1:29. They will lift up Jesus, and with Him humanity will be lifted up. "Thus saith the high and lofty One that inhabiteth eternity, whose name is Holy; I dwell in the high and holy place, with him also that is of a contrite and humble spirit, to revive the spirit of the humble, and to revive the heart of the contrite ones." Isa. 57:15.

The soul of the prophet, emptied of self, was filled with the light of the divine. As he witnessed to the Saviour's glory, his words were almost a counterpart of those that Christ Himself had spoken in His interview with Nicodemus. John said, "He that cometh from above is above all: he that is of the earth is earthly, and speaketh of the earth: He that cometh from heaven is above all. . . . For He whom God hath sent speaketh the words of God: for God giveth not the Spirit by measure unto Him." Christ could say, "I seek not Mine own will, but the will of the Father which hath sent Me." John 5:30. To Him it is declared, "Thou hast loved righteousness, and hated iniquity; therefore God, even Thy God, hath anointed Thee with the oil of gladness above Thy fellows." Heb. 1:9. The Father "giveth not the Spirit by measure unto Him."

[181] So with the followers of Christ. We can receive of heaven's light only as we are willing to be emptied of self. We cannot discern the character of God, or accept Christ by faith, unless we consent to the bringing into captivity of every thought to the obedience of Christ. To all who do this the Holy Spirit is given without measure. In Christ "dwelleth all the fullness of the Godhead bodily, and in Him ye are made full." Col. 2:9, 10, R. V.

The disciples of John had declared that all men were coming to Christ; but with clearer insight, John said, "No man receiveth His witness;" so few were ready to accept Him as the Saviour from sin. But "he that hath received His witness hath set his seal to this, that God is true." John 3:33, R. V. "He that believeth on the Son hath everlasting life." No need of disputation as to whether Christ's baptism or John's purified from sin. It is the grace of Christ that gives life to the soul. Apart from Christ, baptism, like any other service, is a worthless form. "He that believeth not the Son shall not see life."

The success of Christ's work, which the Baptist had received with such joy, was reported also to the authorities at Jerusalem. The priests and rabbis had been jealous of John's influence as they saw the people leaving the synagogues and flocking to the wilderness; but here was One who had still greater power to attract the multitudes. Those leaders in Israel were not willing to say with John, "He must increase, but I must decrease." They arose with a new determination to put an end to the work that was drawing the people away from them.

Jesus knew that they would spare no effort to create a division between His own disciples and those of John. He knew that the storm was gathering which would sweep away one of the greatest prophets ever given to the world. Wishing to avoid all occasion for misunderstanding or dissension, He quietly ceased His labors, and withdrew to Galilee. We also, while loyal to truth, should try to avoid all that may lead to discord and misapprehension. For whenever these arise, they result in the loss of souls. Whenever circumstances occur that threaten to cause division, we should follow the example of Jesus and of John the Baptist.

John had been called to lead out as a reformer. Because of this, his disciples were in danger of fixing their attention upon him, feeling that the success of the work depended upon his labors, and losing sight of the fact that he was only an instrument through which God had wrought. But the work of John was not sufficient to lay the foundation of the Christian [182] church. When he had fulfilled his mission, another work was to be done, which his testimony could not accomplish. His disciples did not understand this. When they saw Christ coming in to take the work, they were jealous and dissatisfied.

The same dangers still exist. God calls a man to do a certain work; and when he has carried it as far as he is qualified to take it, the Lord brings in others, to carry it still farther. But, like John's disciples, many feel that the success of the work depends upon the first laborer. Attention is fixed upon the human instead of the divine, jealousy comes in, and the work of God is marred. The one thus unduly honored is tempted to cherish self-confidence. He does not realize his dependence on God. The people are taught to rely on man for guidance, and thus they fall into error, and are led away from God.

The work of God is not to bear the image and superscription of man. From time to time the Lord will bring in different agencies, through whom His purpose can best be accomplished. Happy are they who are willing for self to be humbled, saying with John the Baptist, "He must increase, but I must decrease."

183

19

At Jacob's Well

On the way to Galilee Jesus passed through Samaria. It was noon when He reached the beautiful Vale of Shechem. At the opening of this valley was Jacob's well. Wearied with His journey, He sat down here to rest while His disciples went to buy food.

The Jews and the Samaritans were bitter enemies, and as far as possible avoided all dealing with each other. To trade with the Samaritans in case of necessity was indeed counted lawful by the rabbis; but all social intercourse with them was condemned. A Jew would not borrow from a Samaritan, nor receive a kindness, not even a morsel of bread or a cup of water. The disciples, in buying food, were acting in harmony with the custom of their nation. But beyond this they did not go. To ask a favor of the Samaritans, or in any way seek to benefit them, did not enter into the thought of even Christ's disciples.

As Jesus sat by the well side, He was faint from hunger and thirst. The journey since morning had been long, and now the sun of noontide beat upon Him. His thirst was increased by the thought of the cool, refreshing water so near, yet inaccessible to Him; for He had no rope nor water jar, and the well was deep. The lot of humanity was His, and He waited for someone to come to draw.

A woman of Samaria approached, and seeming unconscious of His presence, filled her pitcher with water. As she turned to go away, Jesus asked her for a drink. Such a favor no Oriental would withhold. In the East, water was called "the gift of God." To offer a drink to the thirsty traveler was held to be a duty so sacred 184 that the Arabs of the desert would go out of their way in order to perform it. The hatred between Jews and Samaritans prevented the woman from offering a kindness to Jesus; but the Saviour was seeking to find the key to this heart, and with the tact born of divine love, He asked, not offered, a favor. The offer of a kindness might have been rejected; but trust awakens trust. The King of heaven came to this outcast soul, asking a service at her hands. He who made the ocean, who controls the waters of the great deep, who opened the springs and channels of the earth, rested from His weariness at Jacob's well, and was dependent upon a stranger's kindness for even the gift of a drink of water.

The woman saw that Jesus was a Jew. In her surprise she forgot to grant His request, but tried to learn the reason for it. "How is it," she said, "that Thou, being a Jew, askest drink of me, which am a woman of Samaria?"

Jesus answered, "If thou knewest the gift of God, and who it is that saith to thee, Give Me to drink; thou wouldest have asked of Him, and He would have given thee living water." You wonder that I should ask of you even so small a favor as a draught of water from the well at our feet. Had you asked of Me, I would have given you to drink of the water of everlasting life.

The woman had not comprehended the words of Christ, but she felt their solemn import. Her light, bantering manner began to change. Supposing that Jesus spoke of the well before them, she said, "Sir, Thou hast nothing to draw with, and the well is deep: from whence then hast Thou that living water? Art Thou greater than our father Jacob, which gave us the well, and drank thereof himself?" She saw before her only a thirsty traveler, wayworn and dusty. In her mind she compared Him with the honored patriarch Jacob. She cherished the feeling, which is so natural, that no other well could be equal to that provided by the fathers. She was looking backward to the fathers, forward to the Messiah's coming, while the Hope of the fathers, the Messiah Himself, was beside her, and she knew Him not. How many thirsting souls are today close by the living fountain, yet looking far away for the wellsprings of life! "Say not in thine heart, Who shall ascend into heaven? (that is, to bring Christ down from above:) or, Who shall descend into the deep? (that is, to bring up Christ again from the dead.) . . . The word is nigh thee, even in thy mouth, and in thy heart: . . . if thou shalt confess with thy mouth the Lord Jesus, and shalt believe in thine heart that God hath raised Him from the dead, thou shalt be saved." Rom. 10:6-9.

Jesus did not immediately answer the question in regard to Himself, but with solemn 187 earnestness He said, "Whosoever drinketh of this water shall thirst again: but whosoever drinketh of the water that I shall give him shall never thirst; but the water that I shall give him shall be in him a well of water springing up into everlasting life."

He who seeks to quench his thirst at the fountains of this world will drink only to thirst again. Everywhere men are unsatisfied. They long for something to supply the need of the soul. Only One can meet that want. The need of the world,

This chapter is based on John 4:1-42.

"The Desire of all nations," is Christ. The divine grace which He alone can impart, is as living water, purifying, refreshing, and invigorating the soul.

Jesus did not convey the idea that merely one draft of the water of life would suffice the receiver. He who tastes of the love of Christ will continually long for more; but he seeks for nothing else. The riches, honors, and pleasures of the world do not attract him. The constant cry of his heart is, More of Thee. And He who reveals to the soul its necessity is waiting to satisfy its hunger and thirst. Every human resource and dependence will fail. The cisterns will be emptied, the pools become dry; but our Redeemer is an inexhaustible fountain. We may drink, and drink again, and ever find a fresh supply. He in whom Christ dwells has within himself the fountain of blessing,—"a well of water springing up into everlasting life." From this source he may draw strength and grace sufficient for all his needs.

As Jesus spoke of the living water, the woman looked upon Him with wondering attention. He had aroused her interest, and awakened a desire for the gift of which He spoke. She perceived that it was not the water of Jacob's well to which He referred; for of this she used continually, drinking, and thirsting again. "Sir," she said, "give me this water, that I thirst not, neither come hither to draw."

Jesus now abruptly turned the conversation. Before this could receive the gift He longed to bestow, she must be brought to recognize her sin and her Saviour. He "saith unto her, Go, call thy husband, and come hither." She answered, "I have no husband." Thus she hoped to prevent all questioning in that direction. But the Saviour continued, "Thou hast well said, I have no husband: for thou hast had five husbands; and he whom thou now hast is not thy husband: in that saidst thou truly."

The listener trembled. A mysterious hand was turning the pages of her life history, bringing to 188 view that which she had hoped to keep forever hidden. Who was He that could read the secrets of her life? There came to her thoughts of eternity, of the future judgment, when all that is now hidden shall be revealed. In its light, conscience was awakened.

She could deny nothing; but she tried to evade all mention of a subject so unwelcome. With deep reverence, she said, "Sir, I perceive that Thou art a prophet." Then, hoping to silence conviction, she turned to points of religious controversy. If this was a prophet, surely He could give her instruction concerning these matters that had been so long disputed.

Patiently Jesus permitted her to lead the conversation whither she would. Meanwhile He watched for the opportunity of again bringing the truth home to her heart. "Our fathers worshiped in this mountain," she said, "and ye say, that in Jerusalem is the place where men ought to worship." Just in sight was Mount Gerizim. Its temple was demolished, and only the altar remained. The place of worship had been a subject of contention between the Jews and the Samaritans. Some of the ancestors of the latter people had once belonged to Israel; but because of their sins, the Lord suffered them to be overcome by an idolatrous nation. For many generations they were intermingled with idolaters, whose religion gradually contaminated their own. It is true they held that their idols were only to remind them of the living God, the Ruler of the universe; nevertheless the people were led to reverence their graven images.

When the temple at Jerusalem was rebuilt in the days of Ezra, the Samaritans wished to join the Jews in its erection. This privilege was refused them, and a bitter animosity sprang up between the two peoples. The Samaritans built a rival temple on Mount Gerizim. Here they worshiped in accordance with the Mosaic ritual, though they did not wholly renounce idolatry. But disasters attended them, their temple was destroyed by their enemies, and they seemed to be under a curse; yet they still clung to their traditions and their forms of worship. They would not acknowledge the temple at Jerusalem as the house of God, nor admit that the religion of the Jews was superior to their own.

In answer to the woman, Jesus said, "Believe Me, the hour cometh, when ye shall neither in this mountain, nor yet at Jerusalem, worship the Father. Ye worship ye know not what: we know what we worship: for salvation is of the Jews." Jesus had shown that He was free from Jewish prejudice against the Samaritans. Now He sought to break down the prejudice of this 189 Samaritan against the Jews. While referring to the fact that the faith of the Samaritans was corrupted with idolatry, He declared that the great truths of redemption had been committed to the Jews, and that from among them the Messiah was to appear. In the Sacred Writings they had a clear presentation of the character of God and the principles of His government. Jesus classed Himself with the Jews as those to whom God had given a knowledge of Himself.

He desired to lift the thoughts of His hearer above matters of form and ceremony, and questions of controversy. "The hour cometh," He said, "and now is, when the true worshipers shall worship the Father in spirit and in truth: for the Father seeketh such to worship Him. God is a Spirit: and they that worship Him must worship Him in spirit and in truth."

Here is declared the same truth that Jesus had revealed to Nicodemus when He said, "Except a man be born from above, he cannot see the kingdom of God." John 3:3, margin. Not by seeking a holy mountain or a sacred temple are men brought into communion with heaven. Religion is not to be confined to external forms and ceremonies. The religion that comes from God is the only religion that will lead to God. In order to serve Him aright, we must be born of the divine Spirit. This will purify the heart and renew the mind, giving us a new capacity for knowing and loving God. It will give us a willing obedience to all His requirements. This is true worship. It is the fruit of the working of the Holy Spirit. By the Spirit every sincere prayer is indited, and such prayer is acceptable to God. Wherever a soul reaches out after God, there the Spirit's working is manifest, and God will reveal Himself to that soul. For such worshipers He is seeking. He waits to receive them, and to make them His sons and daughters.

As the woman talked with Jesus, she was impressed with His words. Never had she heard such sentiments from the priests of her own people or from the Jews. As the past of her life had been spread out before her, she had been made sensible of her great want. She realized her soul thirst, which the waters of the well of Sychar could never satisfy. Nothing that had hitherto come in contact with her had so awakened her to a higher need. Jesus had convinced her that He read the secrets of her life; yet she felt that He was her friend, pitying and loving her. While the very purity of His presence condemned her sin, He had spoken no word of denunciation, but had told her of His grace, that could renew the soul. She began to have some 190 conviction of His character. The question arose in her mind, Might not this be the long-looked-for Messiah? She said to Him, "I know that Messias cometh, which is called Christ: when He is come, He will tell us all things." Jesus answered, "I that speak unto thee am He."

As the woman heard these words, faith sprang up in her heart. She accepted the wonderful announcement from the lips of the divine Teacher.

This woman was in an appreciative state of mind. She was ready to receive the noblest revelation; for she was interested in the Scriptures, and the Holy Spirit had been preparing her mind to receive more light. She had studied the Old Testament promise, "The Lord thy God will raise up unto thee a Prophet from the midst of thee, of thy brethren, like unto me; unto Him ye shall hearken." Deut. 18:15. She longed to understand this prophecy. Light was already flashing into her mind. The water of life, the spiritual life which Christ gives to every thirsty soul, had begun to spring up in her heart. The Spirit of the Lord was working with her.

The plain statement made by Christ to this woman could not have been made to the self-righteous Jews. Christ was far more reserved when He spoke to them. That which had been withheld from the Jews, and which the disciples were afterward enjoined to keep secret, was revealed to her. Jesus saw that she would make use of her knowledge in bringing others to share His grace.

When the disciples returned from their errand, they were surprised to find their Master speaking with the woman. He had not taken the refreshing draught that He desired, and He did not stop to eat the food His disciples had brought. When the woman had gone, the disciples entreated Him to eat. They saw Him silent, absorbed, as in rapt meditation. His face was beaming with light, and they feared to interrupt His communion with heaven. But they knew that He was faint and weary, and thought it their duty to remind Him of His physical necessities. Jesus recognized their loving interest, and He said, "I have meat to eat that ye know not of."

The disciples wondered who could have brought Him food; but He explained, "My meat is to do the will of Him that sent Me, and to accomplish His work." John 4:34, R. V. As His words to the woman had aroused her conscience, Jesus rejoiced. He saw her drinking of the water of life, and His own hunger and thirst 191 were satisfied. The accomplishment of the mission which He had left heaven to perform strengthened the Saviour for His labor, and lifted Him above the necessities of humanity. To minister to a soul hungering and thirsting for the truth was more grateful to Him than eating or drinking. It was a comfort, a refreshment, to Him. Benevolence was the life of His soul.

Our Redeemer thirsts for recognition. He hungers for the sympathy and love of those whom He has purchased with His own blood. He longs with inexpressible desire that they should come to Him and have life. As the mother watches for the smile of recognition from her little child, which tells of the dawning of intelligence, so does Christ watch for the expression of grateful love, which shows that spiritual life is begun in the soul.

The woman had been filled with joy as she listened to Christ's words. The wonderful revelation was almost overpowering. Leaving her waterpot, she returned to the city, to carry the message to others. Jesus knew why she had gone. Leaving her waterpot spoke unmistakably as to the effect of His words. It was the earnest desire of her soul to obtain the living water; and she forgot her errand to the well, she forgot the Saviour's thirst, which she had purposed to supply. With heart overflowing with gladness, she hastened on her way, to impart to others the precious light she had received.

"Come, see a man, which told me all things that ever I did," she said to the men of the city. "Is not this the Christ?" Her words touched their hearts. There was a new expression on her face, a change in her whole appearance. They were interested to see Jesus. "Then they went out of the city, and came unto Him."

As Jesus still sat at the well side, He looked over the fields of grain that were spread out before Him, their tender green touched by the golden sunlight. Pointing His disciples to the scene, He employed it as a symbol: "Say not ye, There are yet four months, and then cometh harvest? behold, I say unto you, Lift up your eyes, and look on the fields; for they are white already to harvest." And as He spoke, He looked on the groups that were coming to the well. It was four months to the time for harvesting the grain, but here was a harvest ready for the reaper.

"He that reapeth," He said, "receiveth wages, and gathereth fruit unto life eternal: that both he that soweth and he that reapeth may rejoice 192 together. And herein is that saying true, One soweth, and another reapeth." Here Christ points out the sacred service owed to God by those who receive the gospel. They are to be His living agencies. He requires their individual service. And whether we sow or reap, we are working for God. One scatters the seed; another gathers in the harvest; and both the sower and the reaper receive wages. They rejoice together in the reward of their labor.

Jesus said to the disciples, "I sent you to reap that whereon ye bestowed no labor: other men labored, and ye are entered into their labors." The Saviour was here looking forward to the great ingathering on the day of Pentecost. The disciples were not to regard this as the result of their own efforts. They were entering into other men's labors. Ever since the fall of Adam Christ had been committing the seed of the word to His chosen servants, to be sown in human hearts. And an unseen agency, even an omnipotent power, had worked silently but effectually to produce the harvest. The dew and rain and sunshine of God's grace had been given, to refresh and nourish the seed of truth. Christ was about to water the seed with His own blood. His disciples were privileged to be laborers together with God. They were coworkers with Christ and with the holy men of old. By the outpouring of the Holy Spirit at Pentecost, thousands were to be converted in a day. This was the result of Christ's sowing, the harvest of His work.

In the words spoken to the woman at the well, good seed had been sown, and how quickly the harvest was received. The Samaritans came and heard Jesus, and believed on Him. Crowding about Him at the well, they plied Him with questions, and eagerly received His explanations of many things that had been obscure to them. As they listened, their perplexity began to clear away. They were like a people in great darkness tracing up a sudden ray of light till they had found the day. But they were not satisfied with this short conference. They were anxious to hear more, and to have their friends also listen to this wonderful teacher. They invited Him to their city, and begged Him to remain with them. For two days He tarried in Samaria, and many more believed on Him.

The Pharisees despised the simplicity of Jesus. They ignored His miracles, and demanded a sign that He was the Son of God. But the Samaritans asked no sign, and Jesus performed no miracles among them, save in revealing the secrets of her life to the woman at the well. Yet many received Him. In their new joy they said to the woman, "Now we believe, not because of 193 thy saying: for we have heard Him ourselves, and know that this is indeed the Christ, the Saviour of the world."

The Samaritans believed that the Messiah was to come as the Redeemer, not only of the Jews, but of the world. The Holy Spirit through Moses had foretold Him as a prophet sent from God. Through Jacob it had been declared that unto Him should the gathering of the people be; and through Abraham, that in Him all the nations of the earth should be blessed. On these scriptures the people of Samaria based their faith in the Messiah. The fact that the Jews had misinterpreted the later prophets, attributing to the first advent the glory of Christ's second coming, had led the Samaritans to discard all the sacred writings except those given through Moses. But as the Saviour swept away these false interpretations, many accepted the later prophecies and the words of Christ Himself in regard to the kingdom of God.

Jesus had begun to break down the partition wall between Jew and Gentile, and to preach salvation to the world. Though He was a Jew, He mingled freely with the Samaritans, setting at nought the Pharisaic customs of His nation. In face of their prejudices He accepted the hospitality of this despised people. He slept under their roofs, ate with them at their tables,—partaking of the food prepared and served by their hands,—taught in their streets, and treated them with the utmost kindness and courtesy.

In the temple at Jerusalem a low wall separated the outer court from all other portions of the sacred building. Upon this wall were inscriptions in different languages, stating that none but Jews were allowed to pass this boundary. Had a Gentile presumed to enter the inner enclosure, he would have desecrated the temple, and would have paid the penalty with his life. But Jesus, the originator of the temple and its service, drew the Gentiles to Him by the tie of human sympathy, while His divine grace brought to them the salvation which the Jews rejected.

The stay of Jesus in Samaria was designed to be a blessing to His disciples, who were still under the influence of Jewish bigotry. They felt that loyalty to their own nation required them to cherish enmity toward the Samaritans. They wondered at the conduct of Jesus. They could not refuse to follow His example, and during the two days in Samaria, fidelity to Him kept their prejudices under control; yet in heart they were unreconciled. They were slow to learn that their contempt and hatred must give place to pity and sympathy. But after the Lord's ascension, His lessons came back to them with a new meaning. After the outpouring of the Holy Spirit, they recalled the Saviour's look, His words, the respect and tenderness of His bearing toward these despised strangers. When Peter went to preach in Samaria, he brought the same spirit into his own work. When John was called to Ephesus and Smyrna, he remembered the experience at Shechem, and was filled with gratitude to the divine Teacher, who, foreseeing the difficulties they must meet, had given them help in His own example.

The Saviour is still carrying forward the same work as when He proffered the water of life to the woman of Samaria. Those who call themselves His followers may despise and shun the outcast ones; but no circumstance of birth or nationality, no condition of life, can turn away His love from the children of men. To every soul, however sinful, Jesus says, If thou hadst asked of Me, I would have given thee living water.

The gospel invitation is not to be narrowed down, and presented only to a select few, who, we suppose, will do us honor if they accept it. The message is to be given to all. Wherever hearts are open to receive the truth, Christ is ready to instruct them. He reveals to them the Father, and the worship acceptable to Him who reads the heart. For such He uses no parables. To them, as to the woman at the well, He says, "I that speak unto thee am He."

When Jesus sat down to rest at Jacob's well, He had come from Judea, where His ministry had produced little fruit. He had been rejected by the priests and rabbis, and even the people who professed to be His disciples had failed of perceiving His divine character. He was faint and weary; yet He did not neglect the opportunity of speaking to one woman, though she was a stranger, an alien from Israel, and living in open sin.

The Saviour did not wait for congregations to assemble. Often He began His lessons with only a few gathered about Him, but one by one the passers-by paused to listen, until a multitude heard with wonder and awe the words of God through the heaven-sent Teacher. The worker for Christ should not feel that he cannot speak with the same earnestness to a few hearers as to a larger company. There may be only one to hear the message; but who can tell how far-reaching will be its influence? It seemed a small matter, even to His disciples, for the Saviour to spend His time upon a woman of Samaria. But He reasoned more earnestly and eloquently with

her than with kings, councilors, or high priests. The lessons He gave to that woman have been repeated to the earth's remotest bounds.

As soon as she had found the Saviour the Samaritan woman brought others to Him. She proved herself a more effective missionary than His own disciples. The disciples saw nothing in Samaria to indicate that it was an encouraging field. Their thoughts were fixed upon a great work to be done in the future. They did not see that right around them was a harvest to be gathered. But through the woman whom they despised, a whole cityful were brought to hear the Saviour. She carried the light at once to her countrymen.

This woman represents the working of a practical faith in Christ. Every true disciple is born into the kingdom of God as a missionary. He who drinks of the living water becomes a fountain of life. The receiver becomes a giver. The grace of Christ in the soul is like a spring in the desert, welling up to refresh all, and making those who are ready to perish eager to drink of the water of life.

20

"Except Ye See Signs and Wonders"

The Galileans who returned from the Passover brought back the report of the wonderful works of Jesus. The judgment passed upon His acts by the dignitaries at Jerusalem opened His way in Galilee. Many of the people lamented the abuse of the temple and the greed and arrogance of the priests. They hoped that this Man, who had put the rulers to flight, might be the looked-for Deliverer. Now tidings had come that seemed to confirm their brightest anticipations. It was reported that the prophet had declared Himself to be the Messiah.

But the people of Nazareth did not believe on Him. For this reason, Jesus did not visit Nazareth on His way to Cana. The Saviour declared to His disciples that a prophet has no honor in his own country. Men estimate character by that which they themselves are capable of appreciating. The narrow and worldly-minded judged of Christ by His humble birth, His lowly garb, and daily toil. They could not appreciate the purity of that spirit upon which was no stain of sin.

The news of Christ's return to Cana soon spread throughout Galilee, bringing hope to the suffering and distressed. In Capernaum the tidings attracted the attention of a Jewish nobleman who was an officer in the king's service. A son of the officer was suffering from what

This chapter is based on John 4:43-54.

seemed to be an incurable disease. Physicians had given him up to die; but when the father heard of Jesus, he determined to seek help from Him. The child was very low, and, it was feared, might not live till his return; yet the nobleman felt that he must present the case in person. He hoped that a father's prayers might awaken the sympathy of the Great Physician.

On reaching Cana he found a throng surrounding Jesus. With an anxious heart he pressed through to the Saviour's presence. His faith faltered when he saw only a plainly dressed man, dusty and worn with travel. He doubted that this Person could do what he had come to ask of Him; yet he secured an interview with Jesus, told his errand, and besought the Saviour to accompany him to his home. But 198 already his sorrow was known to Jesus. Before the officer had left his home, the Saviour had beheld his affliction.

But He knew also that the father had, in his own mind, made conditions concerning his belief in Jesus. Unless his petition should be granted, he would not receive Him as the Messiah. While the officer waited in an agony of suspense, Jesus said, "Except ye see signs and wonders, ye will not believe."

Notwithstanding all the evidence that Jesus was the Christ, the petitioner had determined to make his belief in Him conditional on the granting of his own request. The Saviour contrasted this questioning unbelief with the simple faith of the Samaritans, who asked for no miracle or sign. His word, the ever-present evidence of His divinity, had a convincing power that reached their hearts. Christ was pained that His own people, to whom the Sacred Oracles had been committed, should fail to hear the voice of God speaking to them in His Son.

Yet the nobleman had a degree of faith; for he had come to ask what seemed to him the most precious of all blessings. Jesus had a greater gift to bestow. He desired, not only to heal the child, but to make the officer and his household sharers in the blessings of salvation, and to kindle a light in Capernaum, which was so soon to be the field of His own labors. But the nobleman must realize his need before he would desire the grace of Christ. This courtier represented many of his nation. They were interested in Jesus from selfish motives. They hoped to receive some special benefit through His power, and they staked their faith on the granting of this temporal favor; but they were ignorant as to their spiritual disease, and saw not their need of divine grace.

Like a flash of light, the Saviour's words to the nobleman laid bare his heart. He saw that his motives in seeking Jesus were selfish. His vacillating faith appeared to him in its true character. In deep distress he realized that his doubt might cost the life of his son. He knew that he was in the presence of One who could read the thoughts, and to whom all things were possible. In an agony of supplication he cried, "Sir, come down ere my child die." His faith took hold upon Christ as did Jacob, when, wrestling with the Angel, he cried, "I will not let Thee go, except Thou bless me." Gen. 32:26.

Like Jacob he prevailed. The Saviour cannot withdraw from the soul that clings to Him, pleading its great need. "Go thy way," He said; "thy son liveth." The nobleman left the Saviour's presence with a peace and joy he had 199 never known before. Not only did he believe that his son would be restored, but with strong confidence he trusted in Christ as the Redeemer.

At the same hour the watchers beside the dying child in the home at Capernaum beheld a sudden and mysterious change. The shadow of death was lifted from the sufferer's face. The flush of fever gave place to the soft glow of returning health. The dim eyes brightened with intelligence, and strength returned to the feeble, emaciated frame. No signs of his malady lingered about the child. His burning flesh had become soft and moist, and he sank into a quiet sleep. The fever had left him in the very heat of the day. The family were amazed, and great was the rejoicing.

Cana was not so far from Capernaum but that the officer might have reached his home on the evening after his interview with Jesus; but he did not hasten on the homeward journey. It was not until the next morning that he reached Capernaum. What a homecoming was that! When he went to find Jesus, his heart was heavy with sorrow. The sunshine seemed cruel to him, the songs of the birds a mockery. How different his feelings now! All nature wears a new aspect. He sees with new eyes. As he journeys in the quiet of the early morning, all nature seems to be praising God with him. While he is still some distance from his own dwelling, servants come out to meet him, anxious to relieve the suspense they are sure he must feel. He shows no surprise at the news they bring, but with a depth of interest they cannot know he asks at what hour the child began to mend. They answer, "Yesterday at the seventh hour the fever left him." At the very moment when the father's faith grasped the assurance, "Thy son liveth." divine love touched the dying child.

The father hurries on to greet his son. He 200 clasps him to his heart as one restored from the dead, and thanks God again and again for this wonderful restoration.

The nobleman longed to know more of Christ. As he afterward heard His teaching, he and all his household became disciples. Their affliction was sanctified to the conversion of the entire family. Tidings of the miracle spread; and in Capernaum, where so many of His mighty works were performed, the way was prepared for Christ's personal ministry.

He who blessed the nobleman at Capernaum is just as desirous of blessing us. But like the afflicted father, we are often led to seek Jesus by the desire for some earthly good; and upon the granting of our request we rest our confidence in His love. The Saviour longs to give us a greater blessing than we ask; and He delays the answer to our request that He may show us the evil of our own hearts, and our deep need of His grace. He desires us to renounce the selfishness that leads us to seek Him. Confessing our helplessness and bitter need, we are to trust ourselves wholly to His love.

The nobleman wanted to *see* the fulfillment of his prayer before he should believe; but he had to accept the word of Jesus that his request was heard and the blessing granted. This lesson we also have to learn. Not because we see or feel that God hears us are we to believe. We are to trust in His promises. When we come to Him in faith, every petition enters the heart of God. When we have asked for His blessing, we should believe that we receive it, and thank Him that we *have* received it. Then we are to go about our duties, assured that the blessing will be realized when we need it most. When we have learned to do this, we shall know that our prayers are answered. God will do for us "exceeding abundantly," "according to the riches of His glory," and "the working of His mighty power." Eph. 3:20, 16; 1:19.

21

Bethesda and the Sanhedrin

"Now there is at Jerusalem by the sheep market a pool, which is called in the Hebrew tongue Bethesda, having five porches. In these lay a great multitude of impotent folk, of blind, halt, withered, waiting for the moving of the water."

At certain seasons the waters of this pool were agitated, and it was commonly believed that this was the result of supernatural power, and that whoever first after the troubling of the pool stepped into the waters, would be healed of whatever disease he had. Hundreds of sufferers visited the place; but so great was the crowd when the water was troubled that they rushed forward, trampling underfoot men, women, and children, weaker than themselves. Many could not get near the pool. Many who had succeeded in reaching it died upon its brink. Shelters had been erected about the place, that the sick might be protected from the heat by day and the chilliness of the night. There were some who spent the night in these porches, creeping to the edge of the pool day after day, in the vain hope of relief.

This chapter is based on John 5.

Jesus was again at Jerusalem. Walking alone, in apparent meditation and prayer, He came to the pool. He saw the wretched sufferers watching for that which they supposed to be their only chance of cure. He longed to exercise His healing power, and make every sufferer whole. But it was the Sabbath day. Multitudes were going to the temple for worship, and He knew that such an act of healing would so excite the prejudice of the Jews as to cut short His work.

But the Saviour saw one case of supreme wretchedness. It was that of a man who had been a helpless cripple for thirty-eight years. His disease was in a great degree the result of his own sin, and was looked upon as a judgment from God. Alone and friendless, feeling that he was shut out from God's mercy, the sufferer had passed long years of misery. At the time when it was expected that the waters would be troubled, those who pitied his helplessness would bear him to the porches. But at the favored moment he had no one to help him in. He had seen the rippling of the water, but had never been able to get farther than the edge of the pool. Others stronger than he would plunge in before him. He could not contend successfully with the selfish, scrambling crowd. His persistent efforts toward the one object, and his anxiety and continual disappointment, were fast wearing away the remnant of his strength.

The sick man was lying on his mat, and occasionally lifting his head to gaze at the pool, when a tender, compassionate face bent over him, and the words, "Wilt thou be made whole?" arrested his attention. Hope came to his heart. He felt that in some way he was to have help. But the glow of encouragement soon faded. He remembered how often he had tried to reach the pool, and now he had little prospect of living till it should again be troubled. He turned away wearily, saying, "Sir, I have no man, when the water is troubled, to put me into the pool: but while I am coming, another steppeth down before me."

Jesus does not ask this sufferer to exercise faith in Him. He simply says, "Rise, take up thy bed, and walk." But the man's faith takes hold upon that word. Every nerve and muscle thrills with new life, and healthful action comes to his crippled limbs. Without question he sets his will to obey the command of Christ, and all his muscles respond to his will. Springing to his feet, he finds himself an active man.

Jesus had given him no assurance of divine help. The man might have stopped to doubt, and lost his one chance of healing. But he believed Christ's word, and in acting upon it he received strength.

Through the same faith we may receive spiritual healing. By sin we have been severed from the life of God. Our souls are palsied. Of ourselves we are no more capable of living a holy life than was the impotent man capable of walking. There are many who realize their helplessness, and who long for that spiritual life which will bring them into harmony with God; they are vainly striving to obtain it. In despair they cry, "O wretched man that I am! who shall deliver me from this body of death?" Rom. 7:24, margin. Let these desponding, struggling ones look up. The Saviour is bending over the purchase of His blood, saying with inexpressible tenderness and pity, "Wilt thou be made whole?" He bids you arise in health and peace. Do not wait to feel that you are made whole. Believe His word, and it will be fulfilled. Put your will on the side of Christ. Will to serve Him, and in acting upon His word you will receive strength. Whatever may be the evil practice, the master passion which through long indulgence binds both soul and body, Christ is able and longs to deliver. He will impart life to the soul that is "dead in trespasses." Eph. 2:1. He will set free the captive that is held by weakness and misfortune and the chains of sin.

The restored paralytic stooped to take up his bed, which was only a rug and a blanket, and as he straightened himself again with a sense of delight, he looked around for his Deliverer; but Jesus was lost in the crowd. The man feared that he would not know Him if he should see Him again. As he hurried on his way with firm, free step, praising God and rejoicing in his newfound strength, he met several of the Pharisees, and immediately told them of his cure. He was surprised at the coldness with which they listened to his story.

With lowering brows they interrupted him, asking why he was carrying his bed on the Sabbath day. They sternly reminded him that it was not lawful to bear burdens on the Lord's day. In his joy the man had forgotten that it was the Sabbath; yet he felt no condemnation for obeying the command of One who had such power 204 from God. He answered boldly, "He that made me whole, the same said unto me, Take up thy bed, and walk." They asked who it was that had done this, but he could not tell. These rulers knew well that only One had shown Himself able to perform this miracle; but they wished for direct proof that it was Jesus, that they might condemn Him as a Sabbath-breaker. In their judgment He had not only broken the law in healing the sick man on the Sabbath, but had committed sacrilege in bidding him bear away his bed.

The Jews had so perverted the law that they made it a yoke of bondage. Their meaningless requirements had become a byword among other nations. Especially was the Sabbath hedged in by all manner of senseless restrictions. It was not to them a delight, the holy of the Lord, and honorable. The scribes and Pharisees had made its observance an intolerable burden. A Jew was not allowed to kindle a fire nor even to light a candle on the Sabbath. As a consequence the people were dependent upon the Gentiles for many services which their rules forbade them to do for themselves. They did not reflect that if these acts were sinful, those who employed others to perform them were as guilty as if they had done the work themselves. They thought that salvation was restricted to the Jews, and that the condition of all others, being already hopeless, could be made no worse. But God has given no commandments which cannot be obeyed by all. His laws sanction no unreasonable or selfish restrictions.

In the temple Jesus met the man who had been healed. He had come to bring a sin offering and also a thank offering for the great mercy he had received. Finding him among the worshipers, Jesus made Himself known, with the warning words, "Behold, thou art made whole: sin no more, lest a worse thing come unto thee."

The healed man was overjoyed at meeting his Deliverer. Ignorant of the enmity toward Jesus, he told the Pharisees who had questioned him, that this was He who had performed the cure. "Therefore did the Jews persecute Jesus, and sought to slay Him, because He had done these things on the Sabbath day."

Jesus was brought before the Sanhedrin to answer the charge of Sabbathbreaking. Had the Jews at this time been an independent nation, such a charge would have served their purpose for putting Him to death. This their subjection to the Romans prevented. The Jews had not the power to inflict capital punishment, and the accusations brought against Christ would have 205 no weight in a Roman court. There were other objects, however, which they hoped to secure. Notwithstanding their efforts to counteract His work, Christ was gaining, even in Jerusalem, an influence over the people greater than their own. Multitudes who were not interested in the harangues of the rabbis were attracted by His teaching. They could understand His words, and their hearts were warmed and comforted. He spoke of God, not as an avenging judge, but as a tender father, and He revealed the image of God as mirrored in Himself. His words were like balm to the wounded spirit. Both by His words and by His works of mercy He was breaking the oppressive power of the old traditions and manmade commandments, and presenting the love of God in its exhaustless fullness.

In one of the earliest prophecies of Christ it is written, "The scepter shall not depart from Judah, nor a lawgiver from between his feet, until Shiloh come; and unto Him shall the gathering of the people be." Gen. 49:10. The people were gathering to Christ. The sympathetic hearts of the multitude accepted lessons of love and benevolence in preference to the rigid ceremonies required by the priests. If the priests and rabbis had not interposed, His teaching would have wrought such a reformation as this world has never witnessed. But in order to maintain their own power, these leaders determined to break down the influence of Jesus. His arraignment before the Sanhedrin, and an open condemnation of His teachings, would aid in effecting this; for the people still had great reverence for their religious leaders. Whoever dared to condemn the rabbinical requirements, or attempt to lighten the burdens they had brought upon the people, was regarded as guilty, not only of blasphemy, but of treason. On this ground the rabbis hoped to excite suspicion of Christ. They represented Him as trying to overthrow the established customs, thus causing division among the people, and preparing the way for complete subjugation by the Romans.

But the plans which these rabbis were working so zealously to fulfill originated in another council than that of the Sanhedrin. After Satan had failed to overcome Christ in the wilderness, he combined his forces to oppose Him in His ministry, and if possible to thwart His work. What he could not accomplish by direct, personal effort, he determined to effect by strategy. No sooner had he withdrawn from the conflict in the wilderness than in council with his confederate angels he matured his plans for still further blinding the minds of the Jewish people, 206 that they might not recognize their Redeemer. He planned to work through his human agencies in the religious world, by imbuing them with his own enmity against the champion of truth. He would lead them to reject Christ and to make His life as bitter as possible, till He have set age Him in His mission. And the leaders in Israel became instruments of Satan in warring against the Saviour.

Jesus had come to "magnify the law, and make it honorable." He was not to lessen its dignity, but to exalt it. The scripture says, "He shall not fail nor be discouraged, till He have set judgment in the earth." Isa. 42:21, 4. He had come to free the Sabbath from those burdensome requirements that had made it a curse instead of a blessing.

For this reason He had chosen the Sabbath upon which to perform the act of healing at Bethesda. He could have healed the sick man as well on any other day of the week; or He might simply have cured him, without bidding him bear away his bed. But this would not have given Him the opportunity He desired. A wise purpose underlay every act of Christ's life on earth. Everything He did was important in itself and in its teaching. Among the afflicted ones at the pool He selected the worst case upon whom to exercise His healing power, and bade the man carry his bed through the city in order to publish the great work that had been wrought upon him. This would raise the question of what it was

lawful to do on the Sabbath, and would open the way for Him to denounce the restrictions of the Jews in regard to the Lord's day, and to declare their traditions void.

Jesus stated to them that the work of relieving the afflicted was in harmony with the Sabbath law. It was in harmony with the work of God's angels, who are ever descending and ascending between heaven and earth to minister to suffering humanity. Jesus declared, "My Father worketh hitherto, and I work." All days are God's, in which to carry out His plans for the human race. If the Jews' interpretation of the law was correct, then Jehovah was at fault, whose work has quickened and upheld every living thing since first He laid the foundations of the earth; then He who pronounced His work good, and instituted the Sabbath to commemorate its completion, must put a period to His labor, and stop the never-ending routine of the universe.

Should God forbid the sun to perform its office upon the Sabbath, cut off its genial rays from warming the earth and nourishing vegetation? Must the system of worlds stand still through that holy day? Should He command the 207 brooks to stay from watering the fields and forests, and bid the waves of the sea still their ceaseless ebbing and flowing? Must the wheat and corn stop growing, and the ripening cluster defer its purple bloom? Must the trees and flowers put forth no bud nor blossom on the Sabbath?

In such a case, men would miss the fruits of the earth, and the blessings that make life desirable. Nature must continue her unvarying course. God could not for a moment stay His hand, or man would faint and die. And man also has a work to perform on this day. The necessities of life must be attended to, the sick must be cared for, the wants of the needy must be supplied. He will not be held guiltless who neglects to relieve suffering on the Sabbath. God's holy rest day was made for man, and acts of mercy are in perfect harmony with its intent. God does not desire His creatures to suffer an hour's pain that may be relieved on the Sabbath or any other day.

The demands upon God are even greater upon the Sabbath than upon other days. His people then leave their usual employment, and spend the time in meditation and worship. They ask more favors of Him on the Sabbath than upon other days. They demand His special attention. They crave His choicest blessings. God does not wait for the Sabbath to pass before He grants these requests. Heaven's work never ceases, and men should never rest from doing good. The Sabbath is not intended to be a period of useless inactivity. The law forbids secular labor on the rest day of the Lord; the toil that gains a livelihood must cease; no labor for worldly pleasure or profit is lawful upon that day; but as God ceased His labor of creating, and rested upon the Sabbath and blessed it, so man is to leave the occupations of his daily life, and devote those sacred hours to healthful rest, to worship, and to holy deeds. The work of Christ in healing the sick was in perfect accord with the law. It honored the Sabbath.

Jesus claimed equal rights with God in doing a work equally sacred, and of the same character with that which engaged the Father in heaven. But the Pharisees were still more incensed. He had not only broken the law, according to their understanding, but in calling God "His own Father" had declared Himself equal with God. John 5:18, R. V.

The whole nation of the Jews called God their Father, therefore they would not have been so enraged if Christ had represented Himself as standing in the same relation to God. But they accused Him of blasphemy, showing that they understood Him as making this claim in the highest sense.

These adversaries of Christ had no arguments with which to meet the truths He brought home to their consciences. They could only cite their customs and traditions, and these seemed weak and vapid when compared with the arguments Jesus had drawn from the word of God and the unceasing round of nature. Had the rabbis felt any desire to receive light, they would have been convinced that Jesus spoke the truth. But they evaded the points He made concerning the Sabbath, and sought to stir up anger against Him because He claimed to be equal with God. The fury of the rulers knew no bounds. Had they not feared the people, the priests and rabbis would have slain Jesus on the spot. But the popular sentiment in His favor was strong. Many recognized in Jesus the friend who had healed their diseases and comforted their sorrows, and they justified His healing of the sufferer at Bethesda. So for the time the leaders were obliged to restrain their hatred.

Jesus repelled the charge of blasphemy. My authority, He said, for doing the work of which you accuse Me, is that I am the Son of God, one with Him in nature, in will, and in purpose. In all His works of creation and providence, I cooperate with God. "The Son can do nothing of Himself, but what He seeth the Father do." The priests and rabbis were taking the Son of God to task for the very work He had been sent into the world to do. By their sins they had separated themselves from God, and in their pride were moving independently of Him. They felt sufficient in themselves for all things, and realized no need of a higher wisdom to direct their acts. But the Son of God was surrendered to the Father's will, and dependent upon His power. So utterly was Christ emptied of self that He made no plans for Himself. He accepted God's plans for Him, and day by day the Father

unfolded His plans. So should we depend upon God, that our lives may be the simple outworking of His will.

When Moses was about to build the sanctuary as a dwelling place for God, he was directed to make all things according to the pattern shown him in the mount. Moses was full of zeal to do God's work; the most talented, skillful men were at hand to carry out his suggestions. Yet he was not to make a bell, a pomegranate, a tassel, a fringe, a curtain, or any vessel of the sanctuary, except according to the pattern shown him. God called him into the mount, and revealed to him the heavenly things. The Lord covered him with His own glory, that he might see the pattern, and according to it all things were made. So to Israel, whom He desired to make His dwelling place, He had revealed His glorious ideal of character. The pattern was shown them in the mount when the law was given from Sinai, and when the Lord passed by before Moses and proclaimed, "The Lord, The Lord God, merciful and gracious, long-suffering, and abundant in goodness and truth, keeping mercy for thousands, forgiving iniquity and transgression and sin." Ex. 34:6, 7.

Israel had chosen their own ways. They had not builded according to the pattern; but Christ, the true temple for God's indwelling, molded every detail of His earthly life in harmony with God's ideal. He said, "I delight to do Thy will, O My God: yea, Thy law is within My heart." Ps. 40:8. So our characters are to be builded "for an habitation of God through the Spirit." Eph. 2:22. And we are to "make all things according to the pattern," even Him who "suffered for us, leaving us an example, that ye should follow His steps." Heb. 8:5; 1 Peter 2:21.

The words of Christ teach that we should regard ourselves as inseparably bound to our Father in heaven. Whatever our position, we are dependent upon God, who holds all destinies in His hands. He has appointed us our work, and has endowed us with faculties and means for that work. So long as we surrender the will to God, and trust in His strength and wisdom, we shall be guided in safe paths, to fulfill our appointed part in His great plan. But the one who depends upon his own wisdom and power is separating himself from God. Instead of working in unison with Christ, he is fulfilling the purpose of the enemy of God and man.

The Saviour continued: "What things soever He [the Father] doeth, these also doeth the Son likewise. . . . As the Father raiseth up the dead, and quickeneth them; even so the Son quickeneth whom He will." The Sadducees held that there would be no resurrection of the body; but Jesus tells them that one of the greatest works of His Father is raising the dead, and that He Himself has power to do the same work. "The hour is coming, and now is, when the dead shall hear the voice of the Son of God: and they that hear shall live." The Pharisees believed in the resurrection of the dead. Christ declares that even now the power which gives life to the dead is among them, and they are to behold its manifestation. This same resurrection power is that which gives life to the soul "dead in trespasses and sins." Eph. 2:1. That spirit of life in Christ Jesus, "the power of His resurrection," sets men "free from the law of sin and death." Phil. 3:10; Rom. 8:2. The dominion of evil is broken, and through faith the soul is kept from sin. He who opens his heart to the Spirit of Christ becomes a partaker of that mighty power which shall bring forth his body from the grave.

The humble Nazarene asserts His real nobility. He rises above humanity, throws off the guise of sin and shame, and stands revealed, the Honored of the angels, the Son of God, One with the Creator of the universe. His hearers are spellbound. No man has ever spoken words like His, or borne himself with such a kingly majesty. His utterances are clear and plain, fully declaring His mission, and the duty of the world. "For the Father judgeth no man, but hath committed all judgment unto the Son: that all men should honor the Son, even as they honor the Father. He that honoreth not the Son honoreth not the Father which hath sent Him. . . . For as the Father hath life in Himself; so hath He given to the Son to have life in Himself; and hath given Him authority to execute judgment also, because He is the Son of man."

The priests and rulers had set themselves up as judges to condemn Christ's work, but He declared Himself their judge, and the judge of all the earth. The world has been committed to Christ, and through Him has come every blessing from God to the fallen race. He was the Redeemer before as after His incarnation. As soon as there was sin, there was a Saviour. He has given light and life to all, and according to the measure of light given, each is to be judged. And He who has given the light, He who has followed the soul with tenderest entreaty, seeking to win it from sin to holiness, is in one its advocate and judge. From the opening of the great controversy in heaven, Satan has maintained his cause through deception; and Christ has been working to unveil his schemes and to break his power. It is He who has encountered the deceiver, and who through all the ages has been seeking to wrest the captives from his grasp, who will pass judgment upon every soul.

And God "hath given Him authority to execute judgment also, because He is the Son of man." Because He has tasted the very dregs of human affliction and temptation, and understands the frailties and sins of men; because in our behalf He has victoriously withstood the temptations of Satan, and will deal justly and tenderly with the souls that His own blood has

been poured out to save,—because of this, the Son of man is appointed to execute the judgment.

But Christ's mission was not for judgment, but for salvation. "God sent not His Son into the world to condemn the world; but that the world through Him might be saved." John 3:17. And before the Sanhedrin Jesus declared, "He that heareth My word, and believeth Him that sent Me, hath eternal life, and cometh not into judgment, but hath passed out of death into life." John 5:24, R. V.

Bidding His hearers marvel not, Christ opened before them, in still wider view, the mystery of the future. "The hour cometh," He said, "in which all that are in the tombs shall hear His voice, and shall come forth; they that have done good, unto the resurrection of life; and they that have done ill, unto the resurrection of judgment." John 5:28, 29, R. V.

This assurance of the future life was that for which Israel had so long waited, and which they had hoped to receive at the Messiah's advent. The only light that can lighten the gloom of the grave was shining upon them. But self-will is blind. Jesus had violated the traditions of the rabbis, and disregarded their authority, and they would not believe.

The time, the place, the occasion, the intensity of feeling that pervaded the assembly, all combined to make the words of Jesus before the Sanhedrin the more impressive. The highest religious authorities of the nation were seeking the life of Him who declared Himself the restorer of Israel. The Lord of the Sabbath was arraigned before an earthly tribunal to answer the charge of breaking the Sabbath law. When He so fearlessly declared His mission, His judges looked upon Him with astonishment and rage; but His words were unanswerable. They could not condemn Him. He denied the right of the priests and rabbis to question Him, or to interfere with His work. They were invested with no such authority. Their claims were based upon their own pride and arrogance. He refused to plead guilty of their charges, or to be catechized by them.

Instead of apologizing for the act of which they complained, or explaining His purpose in doing it, Jesus turned upon the rulers, and the accused became the accuser. He rebuked them for the hardness of their hearts, and their ignorance of the Scriptures. He declared that they had rejected the word of God, inasmuch as they had rejected Him whom God had sent. "Ye search the Scriptures, because ye think that in them ye have eternal life; and these are they which bear witness of Me." John 5:39, R. V.

In every place, whether history, or precept, or prophecy, the Old Testament Scriptures are irradiated with the glory of the Son of God. So far as it was of divine institution, the entire system of Judaism was a compacted prophecy of the gospel. To Christ "give all the prophets witness." Acts 10:43. From the promise given to Adam, down through the patriarchal line and the legal economy, heaven's glorious light made plain the footsteps of the Redeemer. Seers beheld the Star of Bethlehem, the Shiloh to come, as future things swept before them in mysterious procession. In every sacrifice Christ's death was shown. In every cloud of incense His righteousness ascended. By every jubilee trumpet His name was sounded. In the awful mystery of the holy of holies His glory dwelt.

The Jews had the Scriptures in their possession, and supposed that in their mere outward knowledge of the word they had eternal life. But Jesus said, "Ye have not His word abiding in you." Having rejected Christ in His word, they rejected Him in person. "Ye will not come to Me," He said, "that ye might have life."

The Jewish leaders had studied the teachings of the prophets concerning the kingdom of the Messiah; but they had done this, not with a sincere desire to know the truth, but with the purpose of finding evidence to sustain their ambitious hopes. When Christ came in a manner contrary to their expectations, they would not receive Him; and in order to justify themselves, they tried to prove Him a deceiver. When once they had set their feet in this path, it was easy for Satan to strengthen their opposition to Christ. The very words that should have been received as evidence of His divinity were interpreted against Him. Thus they turned the truth of God into a lie, and the more directly the Saviour spoke to them in His works of mercy, the more determined they were in resisting the light.

Jesus said, "I receive not honor from men." It was not the influence of the Sanhedrin, it was not their sanction He desired. He could receive no honor from their approbation. He was invested with the honor and authority of Heaven. Had He desired it, angels would have come to do Him homage; the Father would again have testified to His divinity. But for their own sake, for the sake of the nation whose leaders they were, He desired the Jewish rulers to discern His character, and receive the blessings He came to bring them.

"I am come in My Father's name, and ye receive Me not: if another shall come in his own name, him ye will receive." Jesus came by the authority of God, bearing His image, fulfilling His word, and seeking His glory; yet He was not accepted by the leaders in Israel; but when others should come, assuming the character of Christ, but actuated by their own will and seeking their own glory, they would be received. And why? Because he who is seeking his own glory appeals to the desire for self-exaltation in others. To such appeals the Jews could respond.

They would receive the false teacher because he flattered their pride by sanctioning their cherished opinions and traditions. But the teaching of Christ did not coincide with their ideas. It was spiritual, and demanded the sacrifice of self; therefore they would not receive it. They were not acquainted with God, and to them His voice through Christ was the voice of a stranger.

Is not the same thing repeated in our day? Are there not many, even religious leaders, who are hardening their hearts against the Holy Spirit, making it impossible for them to recognize the voice of God? Are they not rejecting the word of God, that they may keep their own traditions?

"Had ye believed Moses," said Jesus, "ye would have believed Me: for he wrote of Me. But if ye believe not his writings, how shall ye believe My words?" It was Christ who had spoken to Israel through Moses. If they had listened to the divine voice that spoke through their great leader, they would have recognized it in the teachings of Christ. Had they believed Moses, they would have believed Him of whom Moses wrote.

Jesus knew that the priests and rabbis were determined to take His life; yet He clearly explained to them His unity with the Father, and His relation to the world. They saw that their opposition to Him was without excuse, yet their murderous hatred was not quenched. Fear seized them as they witnessed the convincing power that attended His ministry; but they resisted His appeals, and locked themselves in darkness.

They had signally failed to subvert the authority of Jesus or to alienate the respect and attention of the people, many of whom were convicted by His words. The rulers themselves had felt deep condemnation as He had pressed their guilt home upon their consciences; yet this only made them the more bitter against Him. They were determined to take His life. They sent messengers all over the country to warn the people against Jesus as an impostor. Spies were sent to watch Him, and report what He said and did. The precious Saviour was now most surely standing under the shadow of the cross.

22

Imprisonment and Death of John

John the Baptist had been first in heralding Christ's kingdom, and he was first also in suffering. From the free air of the wilderness and the vast throngs that had hung upon his words, he was now shut in by the walls of a dungeon cell. He had become a prisoner in the fortress of

This chapter is based on Matthew 11:1-11; 14:1-11; Mark 6:17-28; Luke 7:19-28.

Herod Antipas. In the territory east of Jordan, which was under the dominion of Antipas, much of John's ministry had been spent. Herod himself had listened to the preaching of the Baptist. The dissolute king had trembled under the call to repentance. "Herod feared John, knowing that he was a just man and an holy; . . . and when he heard him, he did many things, and heard him gladly." John dealt with him faithfully, denouncing his iniquitous alliance with Herodias, his brother's wife. For a time Herod feebly sought to break the chain of lust that bound him; but Herodias fastened him the more firmly in her toils, and found revenge upon the Baptist by inducing Herod to cast him into prison.

The life of John had been one of active labor, and the gloom and inaction of his prison life weighed heavily upon him. As week after week passed, bringing no change, despondency and doubt crept over him. His disciples did not forsake him. They were allowed access to the prison, and they brought him tidings of the works of Jesus, and told how the people were flocking to Him. But they questioned why, if this new teacher was the Messiah, He did nothing to effect John's release. How could He permit His faithful herald to be deprived of liberty and perhaps of life?

These questions were not without effect. Doubts which otherwise would never have arisen were suggested to John. Satan rejoiced to hear the words of these disciples, and to see how they bruised the soul of the Lord's messenger. Oh, how often those who think themselves the friends of a good man, and who are eager to show their fidelity to him, prove to be his most dangerous enemies! How often, instead of strengthening his faith, their words depress and dishearten!

Like the Saviour's disciples, John the Baptist did not understand the nature of Christ's kingdom. He expected Jesus to take the throne of David; and as time passed, and the Saviour made no claim to kingly authority, John became perplexed and troubled. He had declared to the people that in order for the way to be prepared before the Lord, the prophecy of Isaiah must be fulfilled; the mountains and hills must be brought low, the crooked made straight, and the rough places plain. He had looked for the high places of human pride and power to be cast down. He had pointed to the Messiah as the One whose fan was in His hand, and who would thoroughly purge His floor, who would gather the wheat into His garner, and burn up the chaff with unquenchable fire. Like the prophet Elijah, in whose spirit and power he had come to Israel, he looked for the Lord to reveal Himself as a God that answereth by fire.

In his mission the Baptist had stood as a fearless reprover of iniquity, both in high places and in low. He had dared to face King Herod with the plain rebuke of sin. He had not counted his life dear unto himself, that he might fulfill his appointed work. And now from his dungeon he watched for the Lion of the tribe of Judah to cast down the pride of the oppressor, and to deliver the poor and him that cried. But Jesus seemed to content Himself with gathering disciples about Him, and healing and teaching the people. He was eating at the tables of the publicans, while every day the Roman yoke rested more heavily upon Israel, while King Herod and his vile paramour worked their will, and the cries of the poor and suffering went up to heaven.

To the desert prophet all this seemed a mystery beyond his fathoming. There were hours when the whisperings of demons tortured his spirit, and the shadow of a terrible fear crept over him. Could it be that the long-hoped-for Deliverer had not yet appeared? Then what meant the message that he himself had been impelled to bear? John had been bitterly disappointed in the result of his mission. He had expected that the message from God would have the same effect as when the law was read in the days of Josiah and of Ezra (2 Chronicles 34; Nehemiah 8, 9); that there would follow a deep-seated work of repentance and returning unto the Lord. For the success of this mission his whole life had been sacrificed. Had it been in vain?

John was troubled to see that through love for him, his own disciples were cherishing unbelief in regard to Jesus. Had his work for them been fruitless? Had he been unfaithful in his mission, that he was now cut off from labor? If the promised Deliverer had appeared, and John had been found true to his calling, would not Jesus now overthrow the oppressor's power, and set free His herald?

But the Baptist did not surrender his faith in Christ. The memory of the voice from heaven and the descending dove, the spotless purity of Jesus, the power of the Holy Spirit that had rested upon John as he came into the Saviour's presence, and the testimony of the prophetic scriptures,—all witnessed that Jesus of Nazareth was the Promised One.

John would not discuss his doubts and anxieties with his companions. He determined to send a message of inquiry to Jesus. This he entrusted to two of his disciples, hoping that an interview with the Saviour would confirm their faith, and bring assurance to their brethren. And he longed for some word from Christ spoken directly for himself.

The disciples came to Jesus with their message, "Art Thou He that should come, or do we look for another?"

How short the time since the Baptist had pointed to Jesus, and proclaimed, "Behold the

Lamb of God, which taketh away the sin of the world." "He it is, who coming after me is preferred before me." John 1:29, 27. And now the question, "Art Thou He that should come?" It was keenly bitter and disappointing to human nature. If John, the faithful forerunner, failed to discern Christ's mission, what could be expected from the self-seeking multitude?

The Saviour did not at once answer the disciples' question. As they stood wondering at His silence, the sick and afflicted were coming to Him to be healed. The blind were groping their way through the crowd; diseased ones of all classes, some urging their own way, some borne by their friends, were eagerly pressing into the presence of Jesus. The voice of the mighty Healer penetrated the deaf ear. A word, a touch of His hand, opened the blind eyes to behold the light of day, the scenes of nature, the faces of friends, and the face of the Deliverer. Jesus rebuked disease and banished fever. His voice reached the ears of the dying, and they arose in health and vigor. Paralyzed demoniacs obeyed His word, their madness left them, and they worshiped Him. While He healed their diseases, He taught the people. The poor peasants and laborers, who were shunned by the rabbis as unclean, gathered close about Him, and He spoke to them the words of eternal life.

Thus the day wore away, the disciples of John seeing and hearing all. At last Jesus called them to Him, and bade them go and tell John what they had witnessed, adding, "Blessed is he, whosoever shall find none occasion of stumbling in Me." Luke 7:23, R. V. The evidence of His divinity was seen in its adaptation to the needs of suffering humanity. His glory was shown in His condescension to our low estate.

The disciples bore the message, and it was enough. John recalled the prophecy concerning the Messiah, "The Lord hath anointed Me to preach good tidings unto the meek; He hath sent Me to bind up the brokenhearted, to proclaim liberty to the captives, and the opening of the prison to them that are bound; to proclaim the acceptable year of the Lord." Isa. 61:1, 2. The works of Christ not only declared Him to be the Messiah, but showed in what manner His kingdom was to be established. To John was opened the same truth that had come to Elijah in the desert, when "a great and strong wind rent the mountains, and brake in pieces the rocks before the Lord; but the Lord was not in the wind: and after the wind an earthquake; but the Lord was not in the earthquake: and after the earthquake a fire; but the Lord was not in the fire:" and after the fire, God spoke to the prophet by "a still small voice." 1 Kings 19:11, 12. So Jesus was to do His work, not with the clash of arms and the overturning of thrones and kingdoms, but through speaking to the hearts of men by a life of mercy and self-sacrifice.

The principle of the Baptist's own life of self-abnegation was the principle of the Messiah's kingdom. John well knew how foreign all this was to the principles and hopes of the leaders in Israel. That which was to him convincing evidence of Christ's divinity would be no evidence to them. They were looking for a Messiah who had not been promised. John saw that the Saviour's mission could win from them only hatred and condemnation. He, the forerunner, was but drinking of the cup which Christ Himself must drain to its dregs.

The Saviour's words, "Blessed is he, whosoever shall find none occasion of stumbling in Me," were a gentle reproof to John. It was not lost upon him. Understanding more clearly now the nature of Christ's mission, he yielded himself to God for life or for death, as should best serve the interests of the cause he loved.

After the messengers had departed, Jesus spoke to the people concerning John. The Saviour's heart went out in sympathy to the faithful witness now buried in Herod's dungeon. He would not leave the people to conclude that God had forsaken John, or that his faith had failed in the day of trial. "What went ye out into the wilderness to see?" He said. "A reed shaken with the wind?"

The tall reeds that grew beside the Jordan, bending before every breeze, were fitting representatives of the rabbis who had stood as critics and judges of the Baptist's mission. They were swayed this way and that by the winds of popular opinion. They would not humble themselves to receive the heart-searching message of the Baptist, yet for fear of the people they dared not openly oppose his work. But God's messenger was of no such craven spirit. The multitudes who were gathered about Christ had been witnesses to the work of John. They had heard his fearless rebuke of sin. To the self-righteous Pharisees, the priestly Sadducees, King Herod and his court, princes and soldiers, publicans and peasants, John had spoken with equal plainness. He was no trembling reed, swayed by the winds of human praise or prejudice. In the prison he was the same in his loyalty to God and his zeal for righteousness as when he preached God's message in the wilderness. In his faithfulness to principle he was as firm as a rock.

Jesus continued, "But what went ye out for to see? A man clothed in soft raiment? Behold, they which are gorgeously apparelled, and live delicately, are in kings' courts." John had been called to reprove the sins and excesses of his time, and his plain dress and self-denying life were in harmony with the character of his mission. Rich apparel and the luxuries of this life are not the portion of God's servants, but of those who live "in kings' courts," the rulers of this world, to whom pertain its power and its riches. Jesus wished to direct attention to the contrast between the clothing of John, and that worn by the priests and rulers. These officials arrayed themselves in rich robes and costly ornaments. They loved display, and hoped to dazzle the people, and thus command greater consideration. They were more anxious to gain the admiration of men than to obtain the purity of heart which would win the approval of God. Thus they revealed that their allegiance was not given to God, but to the kingdom of this world.

"But what," said Jesus, "went ye out for to see? A prophet? yea, I say unto you, and more than a prophet. For this is he, of whom it is written,—

"Behold, I send My messenger before Thy face,
Which shall prepare Thy way before Thee.

"Verily I say unto you, Among them that are born of women there hath not risen a greater than John the Baptist." In the announcement to Zacharias before the birth of John, the angel had declared, "He shall be great in the sight of the Lord." Luke 1:15. In the estimation of Heaven, what is it that constitutes greatness? Not that which the world accounts greatness; not wealth, or rank, or noble descent, or intellectual gifts, in themselves considered. If intellectual greatness, apart from any higher consideration, is worthy of honor, then our homage is due to Satan, whose intellectual power no man has ever equaled. But when perverted to self-serving, the greater the gift, the greater curse it becomes. It is moral worth that God values. Love and purity are the attributes He prizes most. John was great in the sight of the Lord, when, before the messengers from the Sanhedrin, before the people, and before his own disciples, he refrained from seeking honor for himself, but pointed all to Jesus as the Promised One. His unselfish joy in the ministry of Christ presents the highest type of nobility ever revealed in man.

The witness borne of him after his death, by those who had heard his testimony to Jesus, was, "John did no miracle: but all things that John spake of this Man were true." John 10:41. It was not given to John to call down fire from 220 heaven, or to raise the dead, as Elijah did, nor to wield Moses' rod of power in the name of God. He was sent to herald the Saviour's advent, and to call upon the people to prepare for His coming. So faithfully did he fulfill his mission, that as the people recalled what he had taught them of Jesus, they could say, "All things that John spake of this Man were true." Such witness to Christ every disciple of the Master is called upon to bear.

As the Messiah's herald, John was "much more than a prophet." For while prophets had seen from afar Christ's advent, to John it was given to behold Him, to hear the testimony from heaven to His Messiahship, and to present Him to Israel as the Sent of God. Yet Jesus said, "He that is least in the kingdom of heaven is greater than he."

The prophet John was the connecting link between the two dispensations. As God's representative he stood forth to show the relation of the law and the prophets to the Christian dispensation. He was the lesser light, which was to be followed by a greater. The mind of John was illuminated by the Holy Spirit, that he might shed light upon his people; but no other light ever has shone or ever will shine so clearly upon fallen man as that which emanated from the teaching and example of Jesus. Christ and His mission had been but dimly understood as typified in the shadowy sacrifices. Even John had not fully comprehended the future, immortal life through the Saviour.

Aside from the joy that John found in his mission, his life had been one of sorrow. His voice had been seldom heard except in the wilderness. His was a lonely lot. And he was not permitted to see the result of his own labors. It was not his privilege to be with Christ and witness the manifestation of divine power attending the greater light. It was not for him to see the blind restored to sight, the sick healed, and the dead raised to life. He did not behold the light that shone through every word of Christ, shedding glory upon the promises of prophecy. The least disciple who saw Christ's mighty works and heard His words was in this sense more highly privileged than John the Baptist, and therefore is said to have been greater than he.

Through the vast throngs that had listened to John's preaching, his fame had spread throughout the land. A deep interest was felt as to the result of his imprisonment. Yet his blameless life, and the strong public sentiment in his favor, led to the belief that no violent measures would be taken against him.

Herod believed John to be a prophet of God, and he fully intended to set him at liberty. But 221 he delayed his purpose from fear of Herodias.

Herodias knew that by direct measures she could never win Herod's consent to the death of John, and she resolved to accomplish her purpose by stratagem. On the king's birthday an entertainment was to be given to the officers of state and the nobles of the court. There would be feasting and drunkenness. Herod would thus be thrown off his guard, and might then be influenced according to her will.

When the great day arrived, and the king with his lords was feasting and drinking, Herodias sent her daughter into the banqueting hall to dance for the entertainment of the guests. Salome was in the first flush of womanhood, and her voluptuous beauty captivated the senses of the lordly revelers. It was not customary for the ladies of the court to appear at these festivities, and a flattering compliment was paid to Herod when this daughter of Israel's priests and princes danced for the amusement of his guests.

The king was dazed with wine. Passion held sway, and reason was dethroned. He saw only the hall of pleasure, with its reveling guests, the banquet table, the sparkling wine and the flashing lights, and the young girl dancing before him. In the recklessness of the moment, he desired to make some display that would exalt him before the great men of his realm. With an oath he promised to give the daughter of Herodias whatever she might ask, even to the half of his kingdom.

Salome hastened to her mother, to know what she should ask. The answer was ready,—the head of John the Baptist. Salome knew not of the thirst for revenge in her mother's heart, and she shrank from presenting the request; but the determination of Herodias prevailed. The girl returned with the terrible petition, "I will that thou forthwith give me in a charger the head of John the Baptist." Mark 6:25, R. V.

Herod was astonished and confounded. The riotous mirth ceased, and an ominous silence settled down upon the scene of revelry. The king was horror-stricken at the thought of taking the life of John. Yet his word was pledged, and he was unwilling to appear fickle or rash. The oath had been made in honor of his guests, and if one of them had offered a word against the fulfillment of his promise, he would gladly have spared the prophet. He gave them opportunity to speak in the prisoner's behalf. They had traveled long distances in order to hear the preaching of John, and they knew him to be a man without crime, and a servant of God. But though 222 shocked at the girl's demand, they were too besotted to interpose a remonstrance. No voice was raised to save the life of Heaven's messenger. These men occupied high positions of trust in the nation, and upon them rested grave responsibilities; yet they had given themselves up to feasting and drunkenness until the senses were benumbed. Their heads were turned with the giddy scene of music and dancing, and conscience lay dormant. By their silence they pronounced the sentence of death upon the prophet of God to satisfy the revenge of an abandoned woman.

Herod waited in vain to be released from his oath; then he reluctantly commanded the execution of the prophet. Soon the head of John was brought in before the king and his guests. Forever sealed were those lips that had faithfully warned Herod to turn from his life of sin. Never more would that voice be heard calling men to repentance. The revels of one night had cost the life of one of the greatest of the prophets.

Oh, how often has the life of the innocent been sacrificed through the intemperance of those who should have been guardians of jus-

tice! He who puts the intoxicating cup to his lips makes himself responsible for all the injustice he may commit under its besotting power. By benumbing his senses he makes it impossible for him to judge calmly or to have a clear perception of right and wrong. He opens the way for Satan to work through him in oppressing and destroying the innocent. "Wine is a mocker, strong drink is raging: and whosoever is deceived thereby is not wise." Prov. 20:1. Thus it is that "judgment is turned away backward, . . . and he that departeth from evil maketh himself a prey." Isa. 59:14, 15. Those who have jurisdiction over the lives of their fellow men should be held guilty of a crime when they yield to intemperance. All who execute the laws should be lawkeepers. They should be men of self-control. They need to have full command of their physical, mental, and moral powers, that they may possess vigor of intellect, and a high sense of justice.

The head of John the Baptist was carried to Herodias, who received it with fiendish satisfaction. She exulted in her revenge, and flattered herself that Herod's conscience would no longer be troubled. But no happiness resulted to her from her sin. Her name became notorious and abhorred, while Herod was more tormented by remorse than he had been by the warnings of the prophet. The influence of John's teachings was not silenced; it was to extend to every generation till the close of time.

Herod's sin was ever before him. He was 223 constantly seeking to find relief from the accusings of a guilty conscience. His confidence in John was unshaken. As he recalled his life of self-denial, his solemn, earnest appeals, his sound judgment in counsel, and then remembered how he had come to his death, Herod could find no rest. Engaged in the affairs of the state, receiving honors from men, he bore a smiling face and dignified mien, while he concealed an anxious heart, ever oppressed with the fear that a curse was upon him.

Herod had been deeply impressed by the words of John, that nothing can be hidden from God. He was convinced that God was present in every place, that He had witnessed the revelry of the banqueting room, that He had heard the command to behead John, and had seen the exultation of Herodias, and the insult she offered to the severed head of her reprover. And many things that Herod had heard from the lips of the prophet now spoke to his conscience more distinctly than had the preaching in the wilderness.

When Herod heard of the works of Christ, he was exceedingly troubled. He thought that God had raised John from the dead, and sent him forth with still greater power to condemn sin. He was in constant fear that John would avenge his death by passing condemnation upon him and his house. Herod was reaping that which God had declared to be the result of a course of sin,—"a trembling heart, and failing of eyes, and sorrow of mind: and thy life shall hang in doubt before thee; and thou shalt fear day and night, and shalt have none assurance of thy life: in the morning thou shalt say, Would God it were even! and at even thou shalt say, Would God it were morning! for the fear of thine heart wherewith thou shalt fear, and for the sight of thine eyes which thou shalt see." Deut. 28:65-67. The sinner's own thoughts are his accusers; and there can be no torture keener than the stings of a guilty conscience, which give him no rest day nor night.

To many minds a deep mystery surrounds the fate of John the Baptist. They question why he should have been left to languish and die in prison. The mystery of this dark providence our human vision cannot penetrate; but it can never shake our confidence in God when we remember that John was but a sharer in the sufferings of Christ. All who follow Christ will wear the crown of sacrifice. They will surely be misunderstood by selfish men, and will be made a mark for the fierce assaults of Satan. It is this principle of self-sacrifice that his kingdom is established to destroy, and he will war against it wherever manifested.

224 The childhood, youth, and manhood of John had been characterized by firmness and moral power. When his voice was heard in the wilderness saying, "Prepare ye the way of the Lord, make His paths straight" (Matt. 3:3), Satan feared for the safety of his kingdom. The sinfulness of sin was revealed in such a manner that men trembled. Satan's power over many who had been under his control was broken. He had been unwearied in his efforts to draw away the Baptist from a life of unreserved surrender to God; but he had failed. And he had failed to overcome Jesus. In the temptation in the wilderness, Satan had been defeated, and his rage was great. Now he determined to bring sorrow upon Christ by striking John. The One whom he could not entice to sin he would cause to suffer.

Jesus did not interpose to deliver His servant. He knew that John would bear the test. Gladly would the Saviour have come to John, to brighten the dungeon gloom with His own presence. But He was not to place Himself in the hands of enemies and imperil His own mission. Gladly would He have delivered His faithful servant. But for the sake of thousands who in after years must pass from prison to death, John was to drink the cup of martyrdom. As the followers of Jesus should languish in lonely cells, or perish by the sword, the rack, or the fagot, apparently forsaken by God and man, what a stay to their hearts would be the thought that John the Baptist, to whose faithfulness Christ Himself had borne witness, had passed through a similar experience!

Satan was permitted to cut short the earthly life of God's messenger; but that life which "is hid with Christ in God," the destroyer could not reach. Col. 3:3. He exulted that he had brought sorrow upon Christ, but he had failed of conquering John. Death itself only placed him forever beyond the power of temptation. In this warfare, Satan was revealing his own character. Before the witnessing universe he made manifest his enmity toward God and man.

Though no miraculous deliverance was granted John, he was not forsaken. He had always the companionship of heavenly angels, who opened to him the prophecies concerning Christ, and the precious promises of Scripture. These were his stay, as they were to be the stay of God's people through the coming ages. To John the Baptist, as to those that came after him, was given the assurance, "Lo, I am with you all the days, even unto the end." Matt. 28:20, R. V., margin.

God never leads His children otherwise than they would choose to be led, if they could see the end from the beginning, and discern the glory of the purpose which they are fulfilling 225 as co-workers with Him. Not Enoch, who was translated to heaven, not Elijah, who ascended in a chariot of fire, was greater or more honored than John the Baptist, who perished alone in the dungeon. "Unto you it is given in the behalf of Christ, not only to believe on Him, but also to suffer for His sake." Phil. 1:29. And of all the gifts that Heaven can bestow upon men, fellowship with Christ in His sufferings is the most weighty trust and the highest honor.

23

231

"The Kingdom of God Is at Hand"

"Jesus came into Galilee, preaching the gospel of the kingdom of God, and saying, The time is fulfilled, and the kingdom of God is at hand: repent ye, and believe the gospel." Mark 1:14, 15.

The Messiah's coming had been first announced in Judea. In the temple at Jerusalem the birth of the forerunner had been foretold to Zacharias as he ministered before the altar. On the hills of Bethlehem the angels had proclaimed the birth of Jesus. To Jerusalem the magi had come in search of Him. In the temple Simeon and Anna had testified to His divinity. "Jerusalem, and all Judea" had listened to the preaching of John the Baptist; and the deputation from the Sanhedrin, with the multitude, had heard his testimony concerning Jesus. In Judea, Christ had received His first disciples. Here much of His early ministry had been spent. The flashing forth of His divinity in the cleansing of the temple, His miracles of healing, and the lessons of divine truth that fell from His lips, all proclaimed that which after the healing at Bethesda He had declared before the Sanhedrin,—His Sonship to the Eternal.

If the leaders in Israel had received Christ, He would have honored them as His messengers to carry the gospel to the world. To them first was given the opportunity to become heralds of the kingdom and grace of God. But Israel knew not the time of her visitation. The jealousy and distrust of the Jewish leaders had ripened into open hatred, and the hearts of the people were turned away from Jesus.

The Sanhedrin had rejected Christ's message and was bent upon His death; therefore Jesus departed from Jerusalem, from the priests, the temple, the religious leaders, the people who had been instructed in the law, and turned to another class to proclaim His message, and to gather out those who should carry the gospel to all nations.

As the light and life of men was rejected by the ecclesiastical authorities in the days of Christ, so it has been rejected in every succeeding generation. Again and again the history of Christ's withdrawal from Judea has been repeated. When the Reformers preached the word of God, they had no thought of separating themselves from the established church; but the religious leaders would not tolerate the light, and those that bore it were forced to seek another class, who were longing for the truth. In our day few of the professed followers of the Reformers are actuated by their spirit. Few are listening for the voice of God, and ready to accept truth in whatever guise it may be presented. Often those who follow in the steps of the Reformers are forced to turn away from the churches they love, in order to declare the plain teaching of the word of God. And many times those who are seeking for light are by the same teaching obliged to leave the church of their fathers, that they may render obedience.

The people of Galilee were despised by the rabbis of Jerusalem as rude and unlearned, yet they presented a more favorable field for the Saviour's work. They were more earnest and sincere; less under the control of bigotry; their minds were more open for the reception of truth. In going to Galilee, Jesus was not seeking seclusion or isolation. The province was at this time the home of a crowded population, with a much larger admixture of people of other nations than was found in Judea.

As Jesus traveled through Galilee, teaching and healing, multitudes flocked to Him from the cities and villages. Many came even from Judea and the adjoining provinces. Often He was obliged to hide Himself from the people. The enthusiasm ran so high that it was necessary to take precautions lest the Roman authorities should be aroused to fear an insurrection. Never before had there been such a period as this for the world. Heaven was brought down to men. Hungering and thirsting souls that had waited long for the redemption of Israel now feasted upon the grace of a merciful Saviour.

The burden of Christ's preaching was, "The time is fulfilled, and the kingdom of God is at hand: repent ye, and believe the gospel." Thus the gospel message, as given by the Saviour Himself, was based on the prophecies. The "time" which He declared to be fulfilled was the period made known by the angel Gabriel to Daniel. "Seventy weeks," said the angel, "are determined upon thy people and upon thy holy city, to finish the transgression, and to make an end of sins, and to make reconciliation for iniquity, and to bring in everlasting righteousness, and to seal up the vision and prophecy, and to anoint the most holy." Dan. 9:24. A day in prophecy stands for a year. See Num. 14:34; Ezek. 4:6. The seventy weeks, or four hundred and ninety days, represent four hundred and ninety years. A starting point for this period is given: "Know therefore and understand, that from the going forth of the commandment to restore and to build Jerusalem unto the Messiah the Prince shall be seven weeks, and threescore and two weeks," sixty-nine weeks, or four hundred and eighty-three years. Dan. 9:25. The commandment to restore and build Jerusalem, as completed by the decree of Artaxerxes Longimanus (see Ezra 6:14; 7:1, 9, margin), went into effect in the autumn of B. C. 457. From this time four hundred and eighty-three years extend to the autumn of A. D. 27. According to the prophecy, this period was to reach to the Messiah, the Anointed One. In A. D. 27, Jesus at His baptism received the anointing of the Holy Spirit, and soon afterward began His ministry. Then the message was proclaimed, "The time is fulfilled."

Then, said the angel, "He shall confirm the covenant with many for one week [seven years]." For seven years after the Saviour entered on His ministry, the gospel was to be preached especially to the Jews; for three and a half years by Christ Himself; and afterward by the apostles. "In the midst of the week He shall cause the sacrifice and the oblation to cease." Dan. 9:27. In the spring of A. D. 31, Christ the true sacrifice was offered on Calvary. Then the veil of the temple was rent in twain, showing that the sacredness and significance of the sacrificial service had departed. The time had come for the earthly sacrifice and oblation to cease.

The one week—seven years—ended in A. D. 34. Then by the stoning of Stephen the Jews finally sealed their rejection of the gospel; the disciples who were scattered abroad by persecution "went everywhere preaching the word" (Acts 8:4); and shortly after, Saul the persecutor was converted, and became Paul, the apostle to the Gentiles.

234 The time of Christ's coming, His anointing by the Holy Spirit, His death, and the giving of the gospel to the Gentiles, were definitely pointed out. It was the privilege of the Jewish people to understand these prophecies, and to recognize their fulfillment in the mission of Jesus. Christ urged upon His disciples the importance of prophetic study. Referring to the prophecy given to Daniel in regard to their time, He said, "Whoso readeth, let him understand." Matt. 24:15. After His resurrection He explained to the disciples in "all the prophets" "the things concerning Himself." Luke 24:27. The Saviour had spoken through all the prophets. "The Spirit of Christ which was in them" "testified beforehand the sufferings of Christ, and the glory that should follow." 1 Peter 1:11.

It was Gabriel, the angel next in rank to the Son of God, who came with the divine message to Daniel. It was Gabriel, "His angel," whom Christ sent to open the future to the beloved John; and a blessing is pronounced on those who read and hear the words of the prophecy, and keep the things written therein. Rev. 1:3.

"The Lord God will do nothing, but He revealeth His secret unto His servants the prophets." While "the secret things belong unto the Lord our God," "those things which are revealed belong unto us and to our children forever." Amos 3:7; Deut. 29:29. God has given these things to us, and His blessing will attend the reverent, prayerful study of the prophetic scriptures.

As the message of Christ's first advent announced the kingdom of His grace, so the message of His second advent announces the kingdom of His glory. And the second message, like the first, is based on the prophecies. The words of the angel to Daniel relating to the last days were to be understood in the time of the end. At that time, "many shall run to and fro, and knowledge shall be increased." "The wicked shall do wickedly: and none of the wicked shall understand; but the wise shall understand." Dan. 12:4, 10. The Saviour Himself has given signs of His coming, and He says, "When ye see these things come to pass, know ye that the kingdom of God is nigh at hand." "And take heed to yourselves, lest at any time your hearts be overcharged with surfeiting, and drunkenness, and cares of this life, and so that day come upon you unawares." "Watch ye therefore, and pray always, that ye may be accounted worthy to escape all these things that

shall come to pass, and to stand before the Son of man." Luke 21:31, 34, 36.

We have reached the period foretold in these 235 scriptures. The time of the end is come, the visions of the prophets are unsealed, and their solemn warnings point us to our Lord's coming in glory as near at hand.

The Jews misinterpreted and misapplied the word of God, and they knew not the time of their visitation. The years of the ministry of Christ and His apostles,—the precious last years of grace to the chosen people,—they spent in plotting the destruction of the Lord's messengers. Earthly ambitions absorbed them, and the offer of the spiritual kingdom came to them in vain. So today the kingdom of this world absorbs men's thoughts, and they take no note of the rapidly fulfilling prophecies and the tokens of the swift-coming kingdom of God.

"But ye, brethren, are not in darkness, that that day should overtake you as a thief. Ye are all the children of light, and the children of the day: we are not of the night, nor of darkness." While we are not to know the hour of our Lord's return, we may know when it is near. "Therefore let us not sleep, as do others; but let us watch and be sober." 1 Thess. 5:4-6.

24

236

"Is Not This the Carpenter's Son?"

Across the bright days of Christ's ministry in Galilee, one shadow lay. The people of Nazareth rejected Him. "Is not this the carpenter's son?" they said.

During His childhood and youth, Jesus had worshiped among His brethren in the synagogue at Nazareth. Since the opening of His ministry He had been absent from them, but they had not been ignorant of what had befallen Him. As He again appeared among them, their interest and expectation were excited to the highest pitch. Here were the familiar forms and faces of those whom He had known from infancy. Here were His mother, His brothers and sisters, and all eyes were turned upon Him as He entered the synagogue upon the Sabbath day, and took His place among the worshipers.

In the regular service for the day, the elder read from the prophets, and exhorted the people still to hope for the Coming One, who would bring in a glorious reign, and banish all oppression. He sought to encourage his hearers by rehearsing the evidence that the Messiah's coming was near. He described the glory of His advent, keeping prominent the thought that He would appear at the head of armies to deliver

This chapter is based on Luke 4:16-30.

Israel.

When a rabbi was present at the synagogue, he was expected to deliver the sermon, and any Israelite might give the reading from the prophets. Upon this Sabbath Jesus was requested to take part in the service. He "stood up to read. And there was delivered unto Him a roll of the prophet Isaiah." Luke 4:16, 17, R. V., margin. The scripture which He read was one that was understood as referring to the Messiah:

237

"The Spirit of the Lord is upon Me,
Because He hath anointed Me to preach the gospel to the poor;
He hath sent Me to heal the brokenhearted,
To preach deliverance to the captives,
And recovering of sight to the blind,
To set at liberty them that are bruised,
To preach the acceptable year of the Lord."

"And He closed the roll, and gave it back to the attendant: . . . and the eyes of all in the synagogue were fastened on Him. . . . And all bare Him witness, and wondered at the words of grace which proceeded out of His mouth." Luke 4:20-22, R. V., margin.

Jesus stood before the people as a living expositor of the prophecies concerning Himself. Explaining the words He had read, He spoke of the Messiah as a reliever of the oppressed, a liberator of captives, a healer of the afflicted, restoring sight to the blind, and revealing to the world the light of truth. His impressive manner and the wonderful import of His words thrilled the hearers with a power they had never felt before. The tide of divine influence broke every barrier down; like Moses, they beheld the Invisible. As their hearts were moved upon by the Holy Spirit, they responded with fervent amens and praises to the Lord.

But when Jesus announced, "This day is this scripture fulfilled in your ears," they were suddenly recalled to think of themselves, and of the claims of Him who had been addressing them. They, Israelites, children of Abraham, had been represented as in bondage. They had been addressed as prisoners to be delivered from the power of evil; as in darkness, and needing the light of truth. Their pride was offended, and their fears were roused. The words of Jesus indicated that His work for them was to be altogether different from what they desired. Their deeds might be investigated too closely. Notwithstanding their exactness in outward ceremonies, they shrank from inspection by those clear, searching eyes.

Who is this Jesus? they questioned. He who had claimed for Himself the glory of the Messiah was the son of a carpenter, and had worked at His trade with His father Joseph. They had seen Him toiling up and down the hills, they were acquainted with His brothers and sisters, and knew His life and labors. They had seen Him develop from childhood to youth, and from youth to manhood. Although His life had been spotless, they would not believe that He was the Promised One.

What a contrast between His teaching in regard to the new kingdom and that which they had heard from their elder! Jesus had said nothing of delivering them from the Romans. They had heard of His miracles, and had hoped that His power would be exercised for their advantage, but they had seen no indication of such purpose. 238

As they opened the door to doubt, their hearts became so much the harder for having been momentarily softened. Satan was determined that blind eyes should not that day be opened, nor souls bound in slavery be set at liberty. With intense energy he worked to fasten them in unbelief. They made no account of the sign already given, when they had been stirred by the conviction that it was their Redeemer who addressed them.

But Jesus now gave them an evidence of His divinity by revealing their secret thoughts. "He said unto them, Doubtless ye will say unto Me this parable, Physician, heal thyself: whatsoever we have heard done at Capernaum, do also here in Thine own country. And He said, Verily I say unto you, No prophet is acceptable in his own country. But of a truth I say unto you, There were many widows in Israel in the days of Elijah, when the heaven was shut up three years and six months, when there came a great famine over all the land; and unto none of them was Elijah sent, but only to Zarephath, in the land of Sidon, unto a woman that was a widow. And there were many lepers in Israel in the time of Elisha the prophet; and none of them was cleansed, but only Naaman, the Syrian." Luke 4:23-27, R. V.

By this relation of events in the lives of the prophets, Jesus met the questionings of His hearers. The servants whom God had chosen for a special work were not allowed to labor for a hardhearted and unbelieving people. But those who had hearts to feel and faith to believe were especially favored with evidences of His power through the prophets. In the days of Elijah, Israel had departed from God. They clung to their sins, and rejected the warnings of the Spirit through the Lord's messengers. Thus they cut themselves off from the channel by which God's blessing could come to them. The Lord passed by the homes of Israel, and found a refuge for His servant in a heathen land, with a woman who did not belong to the chosen people. But this woman was favored because she had followed the light she had received, and her heart was open to the greater light that God sent her through His prophet.

It was for the same reason that in Elisha's 239

time the lepers of Israel were passed by. But Naaman, a heathen nobleman, had been faithful to his convictions of right, and had felt his great need of help. He was in a condition to receive the gifts of God's grace. He was not only cleansed from his leprosy, but blessed with a knowledge of the true God.

Our standing before God depends, not upon the amount of light we have received, but upon the use we make of what we have. Thus even the heathen who choose the right as far as they can distinguish it are in a more favorable condition than are those who have had great light, and profess to serve God, but who disregard the light, and by their daily life contradict their profession.

The words of Jesus to His hearers in the synagogue struck at the root of their self-righteousness, pressing home upon them the bitter truth that they had departed from God and forfeited their claim to be His people. Every word cut like a knife as their real condition was set before them. They now scorned the faith with which Jesus had at first inspired them. They would not admit that He who had sprung from poverty and lowliness was other than a common man.

Their unbelief bred malice. Satan controlled them, and in wrath they cried out against the Saviour. They had turned from Him whose mission it was to heal and restore; now they manifested the attributes of the destroyer.

240 When Jesus referred to the blessings given to the Gentiles, the fierce national pride of His hearers was aroused, and His words were drowned in a tumult of voices. These people had prided themselves on keeping the law; but now that their prejudices were offended, they were ready to commit murder. The assembly broke up, and laying hands upon Jesus, they thrust Him from the synagogue, and out of the city. All seemed eager for His destruction. They hurried Him to the brow of a precipice, intending to cast Him down headlong. Shouts and maledictions filled the air. Some were casting stones at Him, when suddenly He disappeared from among them. The heavenly messengers who had been by His side in the synagogue were with Him in the midst of that maddened throng. They shut Him in from His enemies, and conducted Him to a place of safety.

So angels protected Lot, and led him out safely from the midst of Sodom. So they protected Elisha in the little mountain city. When the encircling hills were filled with the horses and chariots of the king of Syria, and the great host of his armed men, Elisha beheld the nearer hill slopes covered with the armies of God,—horses and chariots of fire round about the servant of the Lord.

So, in all ages, angels have been near to Christ's faithful followers. The vast confederacy of evil is arrayed against all who would over-

come; but Christ would have us look to the things which are not seen, to the armies of heaven encamped about all who love God, to deliver them. From what dangers, seen and unseen, we have been preserved through the interposition of the angels, we shall never know, until in the light of eternity we see the providences of God. Then we shall know that the whole family of heaven was interested in the family here below, and that messengers from the throne of God attended our steps from day to day.

When Jesus in the synagogue read from the prophecy, He stopped short of the final specification concerning the Messiah's work. Having read the words, "To proclaim the acceptable year of the Lord," He omitted the phrase, "and the day of vengeance of our God." Isa. 61:2. This was just as much truth as was the first of the prophecy, and by His silence Jesus did not deny the truth. But this last expression was that upon which His hearers delighted to dwell, and which they were desirous of fulfilling. They denounced judgments against the heathen, not discerning that their own guilt was even greater 241 than that of others. They themselves were in deepest need of the mercy they were so ready to deny to the heathen. That day in the synagogue, when Jesus stood among them, was their opportunity to accept the call of Heaven. He who "delighteth in mercy" (Micah 7:18) would fain have saved them from the ruin which their sins were inviting.

Not without one more call to repentance could He give them up. Toward the close of His ministry in Galilee, He again visited the home of His childhood. Since His rejection there, the fame of His preaching and His miracles had filled the land. None now could deny that He possessed more than human power. The people of Nazareth knew that He went about doing good, and healing all that were oppressed by Satan. About them were whole villages where there was not a moan of sickness in any house; for He had passed through them, and healed all their sick. The mercy revealed in every act of His life testified to His divine anointing.

Again as they listened to His words the Nazarenes were moved by the Divine Spirit. But even now they would not admit that this Man, who had been brought up among them, was other or greater than themselves. Still there rankled the bitter memory that while He had claimed for Himself to be the Promised One, He had really denied them a place with Israel; for He had shown them to be less worthy of God's favor than a heathen man and woman. Hence though they questioned, "Whence hath this Man this wisdom, and these mighty works?" they would not receive Him as the Christ of God. Because of their unbelief, the Saviour could not work many miracles among them. Only a few hearts were open to His blessing, and reluctantly

He departed, never to return.

Unbelief, having once been cherished, continued to control the men of Nazareth. So it controlled the Sanhedrin and the nation. With priests and people, the first rejection of the demonstration of the Holy Spirit's power was the beginning of the end. In order to prove that their first resistance was right, they continued ever after to cavil at the words of Christ. Their rejection of the Spirit culminated in the cross of Calvary, in the destruction of their city, in the scattering of the nation to the winds of heaven.

Oh, how Christ longed to open to Israel the precious treasures of the truth! But such was their spiritual blindness that it was impossible to reveal to them the truths relating to His kingdom. They clung to their creed and their useless ceremonies when the truth of Heaven awaited their acceptance. They spent their money for chaff and husks, when the bread of life was within their reach. Why did they not go to the word of God, and search diligently to know whether they were in error? The Old Testament Scriptures stated plainly every detail of Christ's ministry, and again and again He quoted from the prophets, and declared, "This day is this scripture fulfilled in your ears." If they had honestly searched the Scriptures, bringing their theories to the test of God's word, Jesus need not have wept over their impenitence. He need not have declared, "Behold, your house is left unto you desolate." Luke 13:35. They might have been acquainted with the evidence of His Messiahship, and the calamity that laid their proud city in ruins might have been averted. But the minds of the Jews had become narrowed by their unreasoning bigotry. The lessons of Christ revealed their deficiencies of character, and demanded repentance. If they accepted His teachings, their practices must be changed, and their cherished hopes relinquished. In order to be honored by Heaven, they must sacrifice the honor of men. If they obeyed the words of this new rabbi, they must go contrary to the opinions of the great thinkers and teachers of the time.

Truth was unpopular in Christ's day. It is unpopular in our day. It has been unpopular ever since Satan first gave man a disrelish for it by presenting fables that lead to self-exaltation. Do we not today meet theories and doctrines that have no foundation in the word of God? Men cling as tenaciously to them as did the Jews to their traditions.

The Jewish leaders were filled with spiritual pride. Their desire for the glorification of self manifested itself even in the service of the sanctuary. They loved the highest seats in the synagogue. They loved greetings in the market places, and were gratified with the sound of their titles on the lips of men. As real piety declined, they became more jealous for their traditions and ceremonies.

Because their understanding was darkened by selfish prejudice, they could not harmonize the power of Christ's convicting words with the humility of His life. They did not appreciate the fact that real greatness can dispense with outward show. This Man's poverty seemed wholly inconsistent with His claim to be the Messiah. They questioned, If He was what He claimed to be, why was He so unpretending? If He was satisfied to be without the force of arms, what would become of their nation? How could the power and glory so long anticipated bring the nations as subjects to the city of the Jews? Had not the priests taught that Israel was to bear rule over all the earth? and could it be possible that the great religious teachers were in error?

But it was not simply the absence of outward glory in His life that led the Jews to reject Jesus. He was the embodiment of purity, and they were impure. He dwelt among men an example of spotless integrity. His blameless life flashed light upon their hearts. His sincerity revealed their insincerity. It made manifest the hollowness of their pretentious piety, and discovered iniquity to them in its odious character. Such a light was unwelcome.

If Christ had called attention to the Pharisees, and had extolled their learning and piety, they would have hailed Him with joy. But when He spoke of the kingdom of heaven as a dispensation of mercy for all mankind, He was presenting a phase of religion they would not tolerate. Their own example and teaching had never been such as to make the service of God seem desirable. When they saw Jesus giving attention to the very ones they hated and repulsed, it stirred up the worst passions of their proud hearts. Notwithstanding their boast that under the "Lion of the tribe of Judah" (Rev. 5:5), Israel should be exalted to pre-eminence over all nations, they could have borne the disappointment of their ambitious hopes better than they could bear Christ's reproof of their sins, and the reproach they felt even from the presence of His purity.

25

The Call by the Sea

Day was breaking over the Sea of Galilee. The disciples, weary with a night of fruitless toil, were still in their fishing boats on the lake. Jesus had come to spend a quiet hour by the waterside. In the early morning He hoped for a little season of rest from the multitude that followed Him day after day. But soon the people began to gather about Him. Their numbers rapidly increased, so that He was pressed upon all sides. Meanwhile the disciples had come to

This chapter is based on Matthew 4:18-22; Mark 1:16-20; Luke 5:1-11.

land. In order to escape the pressure of the multitude, Jesus stepped into Peter's boat, and bade him pull out a little from the shore. Here Jesus could be better seen and heard by all, and from the boat He taught the multitude on the beach.

What a scene was this for angels to contemplate; their glorious Commander, sitting in a fisherman's boat, swayed to and fro by the restless waves, and proclaiming the good news of salvation to the listening throng that were pressing down to the water's edge! He who was the Honored of heaven was declaring the great things of His kingdom in the open air, to the common people. Yet He could have had no more fitting scene for His labors. The lake, the mountains, the spreading fields, the sunlight flooding the earth, all furnished objects to illustrate His lessons and impress them upon the mind. And no lesson of Christ's fell fruitless. Every message from His lips came to some soul as the word of eternal life.

Every moment added to the multitude upon the shore. Aged men leaning upon their staffs, hardy peasants from the hills, fishermen from their toil on the lake, merchants and rabbis, the rich and learned, old and young, bringing their sick and suffering ones, pressed to hear the words of the divine Teacher. To such scenes as this the prophets had looked forward, and they wrote:

"The land of Zebulon and the land of Naphtali,
Toward the sea, beyond Jordan,
Galilee of the Gentiles,
The people which sat in darkness
Saw a great light,
And to them which sat in the region and shadow of death,
To them did light spring up."
R. V.

Beside the throng on the shores of Gennesaret, Jesus in His sermon by the sea had other audiences before His mind. Looking down the ages, He saw His faithful ones in prison and judgment hall, in temptation and loneliness and affliction. Every scene of joy and conflict and perplexity was open before Him. In the words spoken to those gathered about Him, He was speaking also to these other souls the very words that would come to them as a message of hope in trial, of comfort in sorrow, and heavenly light in darkness. Through the Holy Spirit, that voice which was speaking from the fisherman's boat on the Sea of Galilee would be heard speaking peace to human hearts to the close of time.

The discourse ended, Jesus turned to Peter, and bade him launch out into the sea, and let down his net for a draught. But Peter was disheartened. All night he had taken nothing. During the lonely hours he had thought of the fate of John the Baptist, who was languishing alone in his dungeon. He had thought of the prospect before Jesus and His followers, of the ill success of the mission to Judea, and the malice of the priests and rabbis. Even his own occupation had failed him; and as he watched by the empty nets, the future had seemed dark with discouragement. "Master," he said, "we have toiled all the night, and have taken nothing: nevertheless at Thy word I will let down the net."

Night was the only favorable time for fishing with nets in the clear waters of the lake. After toiling all night without success, it seemed hopeless to cast the net by day; but Jesus had given the command, and love for their Master moved the disciples to obey. Simon and his brother together let down the net. As they attempted to draw it in, so great was the quantity of fish enclosed that it began to break. They were obliged to summon James and John to their aid. When the catch was secured, both the boats were so heavily laden that they were in danger of sinking.

But Peter was unmindful now of boats or lading. This miracle, above any other he had ever witnessed, was to him a manifestation of divine power. In Jesus he saw One who held all nature under His control. The presence of divinity revealed His own unholiness. Love for his Master, shame for his own unbelief, gratitude for the condescension of Christ, above all, the sense of his uncleanness in the presence of infinite purity, overwhelmed him. While his companions were securing the contents of the net, Peter fell at the Saviour's feet, exclaiming, "Depart from me; for I am a sinful man, O Lord."

It was the same presence of divine holiness that had caused the prophet Daniel to fall as one dead before the angel of God. He said, "My comeliness was turned in me into corruption, and I retained no strength." So when Isaiah beheld the glory of the Lord, he exclaimed, "Woe is me! for I am undone; because I am a man of unclean lips, and I dwell in the midst of a people of unclean lips: for mine eyes have seen the King, the Lord of hosts." Dan. 10:8; Isa. 6:5. Humanity, with its weakness and sin, was brought in contrast with the perfection of divinity, and he felt altogether deficient and unholy. Thus it has been with all who have been granted a view of God's greatness and majesty.

Peter exclaimed, "Depart from me; for I am a sinful man;" yet he clung to the feet of Jesus, feeling that he could not be parted from Him. The Saviour answered, "Fear not; from henceforth thou shalt catch men." It was after Isaiah had beheld the holiness of God and his own unworthiness that he was entrusted with the divine message. It was after Peter had been led to self-renunciation and dependence upon divine power that he received the call to his work for Christ.

Until this time none of the disciples had fully united as colaborers with Jesus. They had witnessed many of His miracles, and had listened to His teaching; but they had not entirely forsaken their former employment. The imprisonment of John the Baptist had been to them all a bitter disappointment. If such were to be the outcome of John's mission, they could have little hope for their Master, with all the religious leaders combined against Him. Under the circumstances it was a relief to them to return for a short time to their fishing. But now Jesus called them to forsake their former life, and unite their interests with His. Peter had accepted the call. Upon reaching the shore, Jesus bade the three other disciples, "Follow Me, and I will make you fishers of men." Immediately they left all, and followed Him.

Before asking them to leave their nets and fishing boats, Jesus had given them the assurance that God would supply their needs. The use of Peter's boat for the work of the gospel had been richly repaid. He who is "rich unto all that call upon Him," has said, "Give, and it shall be given unto you; good measure, pressed down, and shaken together, and running over." Rom. 10:12; Luke 6:38. In this measure He had rewarded the disciple's service. And every sacrifice that is made in His ministry will be recompensed according to "the exceeding riches of His grace." Eph. 3:20; 2:7.

During that sad night on the lake, when they were separated from Christ, the disciples were pressed hard by unbelief, and weary with fruitless toil. But His presence kindled their faith, and brought them joy and success. So it is with us; apart from Christ, our work is fruitless, and it is easy to distrust and murmur. But when He is near, and we labor under His direction, we rejoice in the evidence of His power. It is Satan's work to discourage the soul; it is Christ's work to inspire with faith and hope.

The deeper lesson which the miracle conveyed for the disciples is a lesson for us also,—that He whose word could gather the fishes from the sea could also impress human hearts, and draw them by the cords of His love, so that His servants might become "fishers of men."

They were humble and unlearned men, those fishers of Galilee; but Christ, the light of the world, was abundantly able to qualify them for the position for which He had chosen them. The Saviour did not despise education; for when controlled by the love of God, and devoted to His service, intellectual culture is a blessing. But He passed by the wise men of His time, because they were so self-confident that they could not sympathize with suffering humanity, and become colaborers with the Man of Nazareth. In their bigotry they scorned to be taught by Christ. The Lord Jesus seeks the cooperation of those who will become unobstructed channels for the communication of His grace. The first thing to be learned by all who would become workers together with God is the lesson of self-distrust; then they are prepared to have imparted to them the character of Christ. This is not to be gained through education in the most scientific schools. It is the fruit of wisdom that is obtained from the divine Teacher alone.

Jesus chose unlearned fishermen because they had not been schooled in the traditions and erroneous customs of their time. They were men of native ability, and they were humble and teachable,—men whom He could educate for His work. In the common walks of life there is many a man patiently treading the round of daily toil, unconscious that he possesses powers which, if called into action, would raise him to an equality with the world's most honored men. The touch of a skillful hand is needed to arouse those dormant faculties. It was such men that Jesus called to be His colaborers; and He gave them the advantage of association with Himself. Never had the world's great men such a teacher. When the disciples came forth from the Saviour's training, they were no longer ignorant and uncultured. They had become like Him in mind and character, and men took knowledge of them that they had been with Jesus.

It is not the highest work of education to communicate knowledge merely, but to impart that vitalizing energy which is received through the contact of mind with mind, and soul with soul. It is only life that can beget life. What privilege, then, was theirs who for three years were in daily contact with that divine life from which has flowed every life-giving impulse that has blessed the world! Above all his companions, John the beloved disciple yielded himself to the power of that wondrous life. He says, "The life was manifested, and we have seen it, and bear witness, and show unto you that eternal life, which was with the Father, and was manifested unto us." "Of His fullness have all we received, and grace for grace." 1 John 1:2; John 1:16.

In the apostles of our Lord there was nothing to bring glory to themselves. It was evident that the success of their labors was due only to God. The lives of these men, the characters they developed, and the mighty work that God wrought through them, are a testimony to what He will do for all who are teachable and obedient.

He who loves Christ the most will do the greatest amount of good. There is no limit to the usefulness of one who, by putting self aside, makes room for the working of the Holy Spirit upon his heart, and lives a life wholly consecrated to God. If men will endure the necessary discipline, without complaining or fainting by the way, God will teach them hour by hour, and day by day. He longs to reveal His grace. If His people will remove the obstructions, He will pour forth the waters of salvation in abundant streams through the human channels. If men in humble life were encouraged to do all the good they could do, if restraining hands were not laid upon them to repress their zeal, there would be a hundred workers for Christ where now there is one.

God takes men as they are, and educates them for His service, if they will yield themselves to Him. The Spirit of God, received into the soul, will quicken all its faculties. Under the guidance of the Holy Spirit, the mind that is devoted unreservedly to God develops harmoniously, and is strengthened to comprehend and fulfill the requirements of God. The weak, vacillating character becomes changed to one of strength and steadfastness. Continual devotion establishes so close a relation between Jesus and His disciple that the Christian becomes like Him in mind and character. Through a connection with Christ he will have clearer and broader views. His discernment will be more penetrative, his judgment better balanced. He who longs to be of service to Christ is so quickened by the life-giving power of the Sun of Righteousness that he is enabled to bear much fruit to the glory of God.

Men of the highest education in the arts and sciences have learned precious lessons from Christians in humble life who were designated by the world as unlearned. But these obscure disciples had obtained an education in the highest of all schools. They had sat at the feet of Him who spoke as "never man spake."

26

At Capernaum

At Capernaum Jesus dwelt in the intervals of His journeys to and fro, and it came to be known as "His own city." It was on the shores of the Sea of Galilee, and near the borders of the beautiful plain of Gennesaret, if not actually upon it.

The deep depression of the lake gives to the plain that skirts its shores the genial climate of the south. Here in the days of Christ flourished the palm tree and the olive, here were orchards and vineyards, green fields, and brightly blooming flowers in rich luxuriance, all watered by living streams bursting from the cliffs. The shores of the lake, and the hills that at a little distance encircle it, were dotted with towns and villages. The lake was covered with fishing boats. Everywhere was the stir of busy, active life.

Capernaum itself was well adapted to be the center of the Saviour's work. Being on the high-

way from Damascus to Jerusalem and Egypt, and to the Mediterranean Sea, it was a great thoroughfare of travel. People from many lands passed through the city, or tarried for rest in their journeyings to and fro. Here Jesus could meet all nations and all ranks, the rich and great as well as the poor and lowly, and His lessons would be carried to other countries and into many households. Investigation of the prophecies would thus be excited, attention would be directed to the Saviour, and His mission would be brought before the world.

Notwithstanding the action of the Sanhedrin against Jesus, the people eagerly awaited the development of His mission. All heaven was astir with interest. Angels were preparing the way for His ministry, moving upon men's hearts, and drawing them to the Saviour.

In Capernaum the nobleman's son whom Christ had healed was a witness to His power. And the court official and his household joyfully testified of their faith. When it was known that the Teacher Himself was among them, the whole city was aroused. Multitudes flocked to His presence. On the Sabbath the people crowded the synagogue until great numbers had to turn away, unable to find entrance.

All who heard the Saviour "were astonished at His doctrine: for His word was with power." "He taught them as one having authority, and not as the scribes." Luke 4:32; Matt. 7:29. The teaching of the scribes and elders was cold and formal, like a lesson learned by rote. To them the word of God possessed no vital power. Their own ideas and traditions were substituted for its teaching. In the accustomed round of service they professed to explain the law, but no inspiration from God stirred their own hearts or the hearts of their hearers.

Jesus had nothing to do with the various subjects of dissension among the Jews. It was His work to present the truth. His words shed a flood of light upon the teachings of patriarchs and prophets, and the Scriptures came to men as a new revelation. Never before had His hearers perceived such a depth of meaning in the word of God.

Jesus met the people on their own ground, as one who was acquainted with their perplexities. He made truth beautiful by presenting it in the most direct and simple way. His language was pure, refined, and clear as a running stream. His voice was as music to those who had listened to the monotonous tones of the rabbis. But while His teaching was simple, He spoke as one having authority. This characteristic set His teaching in contrast with that of all others. The rabbis spoke with doubt and hesitancy, as if the Scriptures might be interpreted to mean one thing or exactly the opposite. The hearers were daily involved in greater uncertainty. But Jesus taught the Scriptures as of unquestionable authority.

Whatever His subject, it was presented with power, as if His words could not be controverted.

254 Yet He was earnest, rather than vehement. He spoke as one who had a definite purpose to fulfill. He was bringing to view the realities of the eternal world. In every theme God was revealed. Jesus sought to break the spell of infatuation which keeps men absorbed in earthly things. He placed the things of this life in their true relation, as subordinate to those of eternal interest; but He did not ignore their importance. He taught that heaven and earth are linked together, and that a knowledge of divine truth prepares men better to perform the duties of everyday life. He spoke as one familiar with heaven, conscious of His relationship to God, yet recognizing His unity with every member of the human family.

His messages of mercy were varied to suit His audience. He knew "how to speak a word in season to him that is weary" (Isa. 50:4); for grace was poured upon His lips, that He might convey to men in the most attractive way the treasures of truth. He had tact to meet the prejudiced minds, and surprise them with illustrations that won their attention. Through the imagination He reached the heart. His illustrations were taken from the things of daily life, and although they were simple, they had in them a wonderful depth of meaning. The birds of the air, the lilies of the field, the seed, the shepherd and the sheep,—with these objects Christ illustrated immortal truth; and ever afterward, when His hearers chanced to see these things of nature, they recalled His words. Christ's illustrations constantly repeated His lessons.

Christ never flattered men. He never spoke that which would exalt their fancies and imaginations, nor did He praise them for their clever inventions; but deep, unprejudiced thinkers received His teaching, and found that it tested their wisdom. They marveled at the spiritual truth expressed in the simplest language. The most highly educated were charmed with His words, and the uneducated were always profited. He had a message for the illiterate; and He made even the heathen to understand that He had a message for them.

His tender compassion fell with a touch of healing upon weary and troubled hearts. Even amid the turbulence of angry enemies He was surrounded with an atmosphere of peace. The beauty of His countenance, the loveliness of His character, above all, the love expressed in look and tone, drew to Him all who were not hardened in unbelief. Had it not been for the sweet, sympathetic spirit that shone out in every look and word, He would not have attracted the large 255 congregations that He did. The afflicted ones who came to Him felt that He linked His interest with theirs as a faithful and tender friend, and they desired to know more of the truths He taught. Heaven was brought near. They longed to abide in His presence, that the comfort of His love might be with them continually.

Jesus watched with deep earnestness the changing countenances of His hearers. The faces that expressed interest and pleasure gave Him great satisfaction. As the arrows of truth pierced to the soul, breaking through the barriers of selfishness, and working contrition, and finally gratitude, the Saviour was made glad. When His eye swept over the throng of listeners, and He recognized among them the faces He had before seen, His countenance lighted up with joy. He saw in them hopeful subjects for His kingdom. When the truth, plainly spoken, touched some cherished idol, He marked the change of countenance, the cold, forbidding look, which told that the light was unwelcome. When He saw men refuse the message of peace, His heart was pierced to the very depths.

Jesus in the synagogue spoke of the kingdom He had come to establish, and of His mission to set free the captives of Satan. He was interrupted by a shriek of terror. A madman rushed forward from among the people, crying out, "Let us alone; what have we to do with Thee, Thou Jesus of Nazareth? art Thou come to destroy us? I know Thee who Thou art; the Holy One of God."

All was now confusion and alarm. The attention of the people was diverted from Christ, and His words were unheeded. This was Satan's purpose in leading his victim to the synagogue. But Jesus rebuked the demon, saying, "Hold thy peace, and come out of him. And when the devil had thrown him in the midst, he came out of him, and hurt him not."

The mind of this wretched sufferer had been darkened by Satan, but in the Saviour's presence a ray of light had pierced the gloom. He was roused to long for freedom from Satan's control; but the demon resisted the power of Christ. When the man tried to appeal to Jesus for help, the evil spirit put words into his mouth, and he cried out in an agony of fear. The demoniac partially comprehended that he was in the presence of One who could set him free; but when he tried to come within reach of that mighty hand, another's will held him, another's words found utterance through him. The conflict between the power of Satan and his own desire for freedom was terrible.

He who had conquered Satan in the wilderness of temptation was again brought face to 256 face with His enemy. The demon exerted all his power to retain control of his victim. To lose ground here would be to give Jesus a victory. It seemed that the tortured man must lose his life in the struggle with the foe that had been the ruin of his manhood. But the Saviour spoke with authority, and set the captive free. The man who had been possessed stood before the wondering people happy in the freedom of self-possession. Even the demon had testified to the divine power of the Saviour.

The man praised God for his deliverance. The eye that had so lately glared with the fire of insanity, now beamed with intelligence, and overflowed with grateful tears. The people were dumb with amazement. As soon as they recovered speech they exclaimed, one to another, "What is this? a new teaching! with authority He commandeth even the unclean spirits, and they obey Him." Mark 1:27, R. V.

The secret cause of the affliction that had made this man a fearful spectacle to his friends and a burden to himself was in his own life. He had been fascinated by the pleasures of sin, and had thought to make life a grand carnival. He did not dream of becoming a terror to the world and the reproach of his family. He thought his time could be spent in innocent folly. But once in the downward path, his feet rapidly descended. Intemperance and frivolity perverted the noble attributes of his nature, and Satan took absolute control of him.

Remorse came too late. When he would have sacrificed wealth and pleasure to regain his lost manhood, he had become helpless in the grasp of the evil one. He had placed himself on the enemy's ground, and Satan had taken possession of all his faculties. The tempter had allured him with many charming presentations; but when once the wretched man was in his power, the fiend became relentless in his cruelty, and terrible in his angry visitations. So it will be with all who yield to evil; the fascinating pleasure of their early career ends in the darkness of despair or the madness of a ruined soul.

The same evil spirit that tempted Christ in the wilderness, and that possessed the maniac of Capernaum, controlled the unbelieving Jews. But with them he assumed an air of piety, seeking to deceive them as to their motives in rejecting the Saviour. Their condition was more hopeless than that of the demoniac, for they felt no need of Christ and were therefore held fast under the power of Satan.

257 The period of Christ's personal ministry among men was the time of greatest activity for the forces of the kingdom of darkness. For ages Satan with his evil angels had been seeking to control the bodies and the souls of men, to bring upon them sin and suffering; then he had charged all this misery upon God. Jesus was revealing to men the character of God. He was breaking Satan's power, and setting his captives free. New life and love and power from heaven were moving upon the hearts of men, and the prince of evil was aroused to contend for the supremacy of his kingdom. Satan summoned all his forces, and at every step contested the work of Christ.

So it will be in the great final conflict of the controversy between righteousness and sin. While new life and light and power are descending from on high upon the disciples of Christ, a new life is springing up from beneath, and energizing the agencies of Satan. Intensity is taking possession of every earthly element. With a subtlety gained through centuries of conflict, the prince of evil works under a disguise. He appears clothed as an angel of light, and multitudes are "giving heed to seducing spirits, and doctrines of devils." 1 Tim. 4:1.

In the days of Christ the leaders and teachers of Israel were powerless to resist the work of Satan. They were neglecting the only means by which they could have withstood evil spirits. It was by the word of God that Christ overcame the wicked one. The leaders of Israel professed to be the expositors of God's word, but they had studied it only to sustain their traditions, and enforce their man-made observances. By their interpretation they made it express sentiments that God had never given. Their mystical construction made indistinct that which He had made plain. They disputed over insignificant technicalities, and practically denied the most essential truths. Thus infidelity was sown broadcast. God's word was robbed of its power, and evil spirits worked their will.

History is repeating. With the open Bible 258 before them, and professing to reverence its teachings, many of the religious leaders of our time are destroying faith in it as the word of God. They busy themselves with dissecting the word, and set their own opinions above its plainest statements. In their hands God's word loses its regenerating power. This is why infidelity runs riot, and iniquity is rife.

When Satan has undermined faith in the Bible, he directs men to other sources for light and power. Thus he insinuates himself. Those who turn from the plain teaching of Scripture and the convicting power of God's Holy Spirit are inviting the control of demons. Criticism and speculation concerning the Scriptures have opened the way for spiritism and theosophy—those modernized forms of ancient heathenism—to gain a foothold even in the professed churches of our Lord Jesus Christ.

Side by side with the preaching of the gospel, agencies are at work which are but the medium of lying spirits. Many a man tampers with these merely from curiosity, but seeing evidence of the working of a more than human power, he is lured on and on, until he is controlled by a will stronger than his own. He cannot escape from its mysterious power.

The defenses of the soul are broken down. He has no barrier against sin. When once the restraints of God's word and His Spirit are rejected, no man knows to what depths of degradation he may sink. Secret sin or master passion may hold him a captive as helpless as was the demoniac of Capernaum. Yet his condition is not hopeless.

The means by which we can overcome the wicked one is that by which Christ overcame,— the power of the word. God does not control our minds without our consent; but if we desire to know and to do His will, His promises are ours: "Ye shall know the truth, and the truth shall make you free." "If any man willeth to do His will, he shall know of the teaching." John 8:32; 7:17, R. V. Through faith in these promises, every man may be delivered from the snares of error and the control of sin.

Every man is free to choose what power he will have to rule over him. None have fallen so low, none are so vile, but that they can find deliverance in Christ. The demoniac, in place of prayer, could utter only the words of Satan; yet the heart's unspoken appeal was heard. No cry from a soul in need, though it fail of utterance in words, will be unheeded. Those who will consent to enter into covenant relation with the God of heaven are not left to the power of Satan or to the infirmity of their own nature. They are invited by the Saviour, "Let him take hold of My strength, that he may make peace with Me; and he shall make peace with Me." Isa. 27:5. The spirits of darkness will battle for the soul once under their dominion, but angels of God will contend for that soul with prevailing power. The Lord says, "Shall the prey be taken from the mighty, or the lawful captive delivered? . . . Thus saith the Lord, Even the captives of the mighty shall be taken away, and the prey of the terrible shall be delivered: for I will contend with him that contendeth with thee, and I will save thy children." Isa. 49:24, 25.

While the congregation in the synagogue were still spellbound with awe, Jesus withdrew to the home of Peter for a little rest. But here also a shadow had fallen. The mother of Peter's wife lay sick, stricken with a "great fever." Jesus rebuked the disease, and the sufferer arose, and ministered to the wants of the Master and His disciples.

Tidings of the work of Christ spread rapidly throughout Capernaum. For fear of the rabbis, the people dared not come for healing upon the Sabbath; but no sooner had the sun disappeared below the horizon than there was a great commotion. From the homes, the shops, the market places, the inhabitants of the city pressed toward the humble dwelling that sheltered Jesus. The sick were brought upon couches, they came leaning upon staffs, or, supported by friends, they tottered feebly into the Saviour's presence.

Hour after hour they came and went; for none could know whether tomorrow would find the Healer still among them. Never before had Capernaum witnessed a day like this. The air was filled with the voice of triumph and shouts of deliverance. The Saviour was joyful in the joy He had awakened. As He witnessed the sufferings of those who had come to Him, His heart was stirred with sympathy, and He rejoiced in His power to restore them to health and happiness.

Not until the last sufferer had been relieved did Jesus cease His work. It was far into the night when the multitude departed, and silence settled down upon the home of Simon. The long, exciting day was past, and Jesus sought rest. But while the city was still wrapped in slumber, the Saviour, "rising up a great while before day, . . . went out, and departed into a solitary place, and there prayed."

Thus were spent the days in the earthly life of Jesus. He often dismissed His disciples to visit their homes and rest; but He gently resisted their efforts to draw Him away from His labors. All day He toiled, teaching the ignorant, healing the sick, giving sight to the blind, feeding the multitude; and at the eventide or in the early morning, He went away to the sanctuary of the mountains for communion with His Father. Often He passed the entire night in prayer and meditation, returning at daybreak to His work among the people.

Early in the morning, Peter and his companions came to Jesus, saying that already the people of Capernaum were seeking Him. The disciples had been bitterly disappointed at the reception which Christ had met hitherto. The authorities at Jerusalem were seeking to murder Him; even His own townsmen had tried to take His life; but at Capernaum He was welcomed with joyful enthusiasm, and the hopes of the disciples kindled anew. It might be that among the liberty-loving Galileans were to be found the supporters of the new kingdom. But with surprise they heard Christ's words, "I must preach the kingdom of God to other cities also: for therefore am I sent."

In the excitement which then pervaded Capernaum, there was danger that the object of His mission would be lost sight of. Jesus was not satisfied to attract attention to Himself merely as a wonder worker or a healer of physical diseases. He was seeking to draw men to Him as their Saviour. While the people were eager to believe that He had come as a king, to establish an earthly reign, He desired to turn their minds away from the earthly to the spiritual. Mere worldly success would interfere with His work.

And the wonder of the careless crowd jarred upon His spirit. In His life no self-assertion mingled. The homage which the world gives to position, or wealth, or talent, was foreign to the Son of man. None of the means that men employ to win allegiance or command homage did Jesus use. Centuries before His birth, it had been prophesied of Him, "He shall not cry, nor lift up, nor cause His voice to be heard in the street. A bruised reed shall He not break, and the dimly burning flax shall He not quench: He shall bring forth judgment unto truth. He shall not fail nor be discouraged, till He have set judgment in the earth." Isa. 42:2-4, margin.

The Pharisees sought distinction by their scrupulous ceremonialism, and the ostentation of their worship and charities. They proved their zeal for religion by making it the theme of discussion. Disputes between opposing sects were loud and long, and it was not unusual to hear on the streets the voice of angry controversy from learned doctors of the law.

In marked contrast to all this was the life of Jesus. In that life no noisy disputation, no ostentatious worship, no act to gain applause, was ever witnessed. Christ was hid in God, and God was revealed in the character of His Son. To this revelation Jesus desired the minds of the people to be directed, and their homage to be given.

The Sun of Righteousness did not burst upon the world in splendor, to dazzle the senses with His glory. It is written of Christ, "His going forth is prepared as the morning." Hosea 6:3. Quietly and gently the daylight breaks upon the earth, dispelling the shadow of darkness, and waking the world to life. So did the Sun of Righteousness arise, "with healing in His wings." Mal. 4:2.

27

"Thou Canst Make Me Clean"

Of all diseases known in the East the leprosy was most dreaded. Its incurable and contagious character, and its horrible effect upon its victims, filled the bravest with fear. Among the Jews it was regarded as a judgment on account of sin, and hence was called "the stroke," "the finger of God." Deep-rooted, ineradicable, deadly, it was looked upon as a symbol of sin. By the ritual law, the leper was pronounced unclean. Like one already dead, he was shut out from the habitations of men. Whatever he touched was unclean. The air was polluted by his breath. One who was suspected of having the disease must present himself to the priests, who were to examine and decide his case. If pronounced a leper, he was isolated from his family, cut off from the congregation of Israel, and was doomed to associate with those only who were similarly afflicted. The law was inflexible in its requirement. Even kings and rulers were not exempt. A monarch who was attacked by this terrible disease must yield up the scepter, and flee from society.

Away from his friends and his kindred, the leper must bear the curse of his malady. He was obliged to publish his own calamity, to rend his garments, and sound the alarm, warning all to flee from his contaminating presence. The cry, "Unclean! unclean!" coming in mournful tones from the lonely exile, was a signal heard with fear and abhorrence.

In the region of Christ's ministry, there were many of these sufferers, and the news of His work reached them, kindling a gleam of hope. But since the days of Elisha the prophet, such a thing had never been known as the cleansing of one upon whom this disease had fastened. They dared not expect Jesus to do for them what He had never done for any man. There was one, however, in whose heart faith began to spring up. Yet the man knew not how to reach Jesus. Debarred as he was from contact with his fellow men, how could he present himself to the Healer? And he questioned if Christ would heal *him*. Would He stoop to notice one believed to be suffering under the judgment of God? Would He not, like the Pharisees, and even the physicians, pronounce a curse upon him, and warn him to flee from the haunts of men? He thought of all that had been told him of Jesus. Not one who had sought His help had been turned away. The wretched man determined to find the Saviour. Though shut out from the cities, it might be that he could cross His path in some byway along the mountain roads, or find Him as He was teaching outside the towns. The difficulties were great, but this was his only hope.

The leper is guided to the Saviour. Jesus is teaching beside the lake, and the people are gathered about Him. Standing afar off, the leper catches a few words from the Saviour's lips. He sees Him laying His hands upon the sick. He sees the lame, the blind, the paralytic, and those dying of various maladies rise up in health, praising God for their deliverance. Faith strengthens in his heart. He draws nearer and yet nearer to the gathered throng. The restrictions laid upon him, the safety of the people, and the fear with which all men regard him are forgotten. He thinks only of the blessed hope of healing.

He is a loathsome spectacle. The disease has made frightful inroads, and his decaying body is horrible to look upon. At sight of him the people fall back in terror. They crowd upon one another in their eagerness to escape from contact with him. Some try to prevent him from approaching Jesus, but in vain. He neither sees nor hears them. Their expressions of loathing are lost upon him. He sees only the Son of God. He hears only the voice that speaks life to the dying. Pressing to Jesus, he casts himself at His feet with the cry, "Lord, if Thou wilt, Thou canst make *me* clean."

Jesus replied, "I will; be thou made clean," and laid His hand upon him. Matt. 8:3, R. V.

Immediately a change passed over the leper. His flesh became healthy, the nerves sensitive,

This chapter is based on Matthew 8:2-4; 9:1-8, 32-34; Mark 1:40-45; 2:1-12; Luke 5:12-28.

the muscles firm. The rough, scaly surface peculiar to leprosy disappeared, and a soft glow, like that upon the skin of a healthy child, took its place.

264   Jesus charged the man not to make known the work that had been wrought, but straightway to present himself with an offering at the temple. Such an offering could not be accepted until the priests had made examination and pronounced the man wholly free from the disease. However unwilling they might be to perform this service, they could not evade an examination and decision of the case.

The words of Scripture show with what urgency Christ enjoined upon the man the necessity of silence and prompt action. "He straitly charged him, and forthwith sent him away; and saith unto him, See thou say nothing to any man: but go thy way, show thyself to the priest, and offer for thy cleansing those things which Moses commanded, for a testimony unto them." Had the priests known the facts concerning the healing of the leper, their hatred of Christ might have led them to render a dishonest sentence. Jesus desired the man to present himself at the temple before any rumors concerning the miracle had reached them. Thus an impartial decision could be secured, and the restored leper would be permitted to unite once more with his family and friends.

There were other objects which Christ had in view in enjoining silence on the man. The Saviour knew that His enemies were ever seeking to limit His work, and to turn the people from Him. He knew that if the healing of the leper were noised abroad, other sufferers from this terrible disease would crowd about Him, and the cry would be raised that the people would be contaminated by contact with them. Many of the lepers would not so use the gift of health as to make it a blessing to themselves or to others. And by drawing the lepers about Him, He would give occasion for the charge that He was breaking down the restrictions of the ritual law. Thus His work in preaching the gospel would be hindered.

The event justified Christ's warning. A multitude of people had witnessed the healing of the leper, and they were eager to learn of the priests' decision. When the man returned to his 265 friends, there was great excitement. Notwithstanding the caution of Jesus, the man made no further effort to conceal the fact of his cure. It would indeed have been impossible to conceal it, but the leper published the matter abroad. Conceiving that it was only the modesty of Jesus which laid this restriction upon him, he went about proclaiming the power of this Great Healer. He did not understand that every such manifestation made the priests and elders more determined to destroy Jesus. The restored man felt that the boon of health was very precious.

He rejoiced in the vigor of manhood, and in his restoration to his family and society, and felt it impossible to refrain from giving glory to the Physician who had made him whole. But his act in blazing abroad the matter resulted in hindering the Saviour's work. It caused the people to flock to Him in such multitudes that He was forced for a time to cease His labors.

Every act of Christ's ministry was far-reaching in its purpose. It comprehended more than appeared in the act itself. So in the case of the leper. While Jesus ministered to all who came unto Him, He yearned to bless those who came not. While He drew the publicans, the heathen, and the Samaritans, He longed to reach the priests and teachers who were shut in by prejudice and tradition. He left untried no means by which they might be reached. In sending the healed leper to the priests, He gave them a testimony calculated to disarm their prejudices.

The Pharisees had asserted that Christ's teaching was opposed to the law which God had given through Moses; but His direction to the cleansed leper to present an offering according to the law disproved this charge. It was sufficient testimony for all who were willing to be convinced.

The leaders at Jerusalem had sent out spies to find some pretext for putting Christ to death. He responded by giving them an evidence of His love for humanity, His respect for the law, and His power to deliver from sin and death. Thus He bore witness of them: "They have rewarded Me evil for good, and hatred for My love." Ps. 109:5. He who on the mount gave the precept, "Love your enemies," Himself exemplified the principle, not rendering "evil for evil, or railing for railing: but contrariwise blessing." Matt. 5:44; 1 Peter 3:9.

The same priests who condemned the leper to banishment certified his cure. This sentence, publicly pronounced and registered, was a standing testimony for Christ. And as the healed man was reinstated in the congregation of Israel, upon the priests' own assurance that there was 266 not a taint of the disease upon him, he himself was a living witness for his Benefactor. Joyfully he presented his offering, and magnified the name of Jesus. The priests were convinced of the divine power of the Saviour. Opportunity was granted them to know the truth and to be profited by the light. Rejected, it would pass away, never to return. By many the light was rejected; yet it was not given in vain. Many hearts were moved that for a time made no sign. During the Saviour's life, His mission seemed to call forth little response of love from the priests and teachers; but after His ascension "a great company of the priests were obedient to the faith." Acts 6:7.

The work of Christ in cleansing the leper from his terrible disease is an illustration of His work in cleansing the soul from sin. The man who came to Jesus was "full of leprosy." Its deadly poison permeated his whole body. The disciples sought to prevent their Master from touching him; for he who touched a leper became himself unclean. But in laying His hand upon the leper, Jesus received no defilement. His touch imparted life-giving power. The leprosy was cleansed. Thus it is with the leprosy of sin,—deep-rooted, deadly, and impossible to be cleansed by human power. "The whole head is sick, and the whole heart faint. From the sole of the foot even unto the head there is no soundness in it; but wounds, and bruises, and putrefying sores." Isa. 1:5, 6. But Jesus, coming to dwell in humanity, receives no pollution. His presence has healing virtue for the sinner. Whoever will fall at His feet, saying in faith, "Lord, if Thou wilt, Thou canst make me clean," shall hear the answer, "I will; be thou made clean." Matt. 8:2, 3, R. V.

In some instances of healing, Jesus did not at once grant the blessing sought. But in the case of leprosy, no sooner was the appeal made than it was granted. When we pray for earthly blessings, the answer to our prayer may be delayed, or God may give us something other than we ask, but not so when we ask for deliverance from sin. It is His will to cleanse us from sin, to make us His children, and to enable us to live a holy life. Christ "gave Himself for our sins, that He might deliver us from this present evil world, according to the will of God and our Father." Gal. 1:4. And "this is the confidence that we have in Him, that, if we ask anything according to His will, He heareth us: and if we know that He hear us, whatsoever we ask, we know that we have the petitions that we desired of Him." 1 John 5:14, 15. "If we confess our sins, He is faithful and just to forgive us our sins, and to cleanse us from all unrighteousness." 1 John 1:9.

267 In the healing of the paralytic at Capernaum, Christ again taught the same truth. It was to manifest His power to forgive sins that the miracle was performed. And the healing of the paralytic also illustrates other precious truths. It is full of hope and encouragement, and from its connection with the caviling Pharisees it has a lesson of warning as well.

Like the leper, this paralytic had lost all hope of recovery. His disease was the result of a life of sin, and his sufferings were embittered by remorse. He had long before appealed to the Pharisees and doctors, hoping for relief from mental suffering and physical pain. But they coldly pronounced him incurable, and abandoned him to the wrath of God. The Pharisees regarded affliction as an evidence of divine displeasure, and they held themselves aloof from the sick and the needy. Yet often these very ones who exalted themselves as holy were more guilty than the sufferers they condemned.

The palsied man was entirely helpless, and, seeing no prospect of aid from any quarter, he had sunk into despair. Then he heard of the wonderful works of Jesus. He was told that others as sinful and helpless as he had been healed; even lepers had been cleansed. And the friends who reported these things encouraged him to believe that he too might be cured if he could be carried to Jesus. But his hope fell when he remembered how the disease had been brought upon him. He feared that the pure Physician would not tolerate him in His presence.

Yet it was not physical restoration he desired so much as relief from the burden of sin. If he could see Jesus, and receive the assurance of forgiveness and peace with Heaven, he would be content to live or die, according to God's will. The cry of the dying man was, Oh that I might come into His presence! There was no time to lose; already his wasted flesh was showing signs of decay. He besought his friends to carry him on his bed to Jesus, and this they gladly undertook to do. But so dense was the crowd that had assembled in and about the house where the Saviour was, that it was impossible for the sick man and his friends to reach Him, or even to come within hearing of His voice.

Jesus was teaching in the house of Peter. According to their custom, His disciples sat close about Him, and "there were Pharisees and doctors of the law sitting by, which were come out of every town of Galilee, and Judea, and Jerusalem." These had come as spies, seeking an accusation against Jesus. Outside of these officials thronged the promiscuous multitude, the eager, the reverent, the curious, and the unbelieving. Different nationalities and all 268 grades of society were represented. "And the power of the Lord was present to heal." The Spirit of life brooded over the assembly, but Pharisees and doctors did not discern its presence. They felt no sense of need, and the healing was not for them. "He hath filled the hungry with good things; and the rich He hath sent empty away." Luke 1:53.

Again and again the bearers of the paralytic tried to push their way through the crowd, but in vain. The sick man looked about him in unutterable anguish. When the longed-for help was so near, how could he relinquish hope? At his suggestion his friends bore him to the top of the house and, breaking up the roof, let him down at the feet of Jesus. The discourse was interrupted. The Saviour looked upon the mournful countenance, and saw the pleading eyes fixed upon Him. He understood the case; He had drawn to Himself that perplexed and doubting spirit. While the paralytic was yet at home, the Saviour had brought conviction to his conscience. When he repented of his sins, and believed in the power of Jesus to make him whole, the life-giving mercies of the Saviour had first blessed his spirit, and Jesus had watched the first glimmer of faith grow into a belief that He was the sinner's only helper, and had seen it grow stronger with every effort to come into His presence.

Now, in words that fell like music on the sufferer's ear, the Saviour said, "Son, be of good cheer; thy sins be forgiven thee."

The burden of despair rolls from the sick man's soul; the peace of forgiveness rests upon his spirit, and shines out upon his countenance. His physical pain is gone, and his whole being is transformed. The helpless paralytic is healed! the guilty sinner is pardoned!

In simple faith he accepted the words of Jesus as the boon of new life. He urged no further request, but lay in blissful silence, too happy for words. The light of heaven irradiated his countenance, and the people looked with awe upon the scene.

The rabbis had waited anxiously to see what disposition Christ would make of this case. They recollected how the man had appealed to them for help, and they had refused him hope or sympathy. Not satisfied with this, they had declared that he was suffering the curse of God for his sins. These things came fresh to their minds when they saw the sick man before them. They marked the interest with which all were watching the scene, and they felt a terrible fear of losing their own influence over the people.

269 These dignitaries did not exchange words together, but looking into one another's faces they read the same thought in each, that something must be done to arrest the tide of feeling. Jesus had declared that the sins of the paralytic were forgiven. The Pharisees caught at these words as blasphemy, and conceived that they could present this as a sin worthy of death. They said in their hearts, "He blasphemeth: who can forgive sins but One, even God?" Mark 2:7, R. V.

Fixing His glance upon them, beneath which they cowered, and drew back, Jesus said, "Wherefore think ye evil in your hearts? For whether is easier, to say, Thy sins be forgiven thee; or to say, Arise, and walk? But that ye may know that the Son of man hath power on earth to forgive sins," He said, turning to the paralytic, "Arise, take up thy bed, and go unto thine house."

Then he who had been borne on a litter to Jesus rises to his feet with the elasticity and strength of youth. The life-giving blood bounds through his veins. Every organ of his body springs into sudden activity. The glow of health succeeds the pallor of approaching death. "And immediately he arose, took up the bed, and went forth before them all; insomuch that they were all amazed, and glorified God, saying, We never saw it on this fashion."

Oh, wondrous love of Christ, stooping to heal the guilty and the afflicted! Divinity sorrowing over and soothing the ills of suffering humanity! Oh, marvelous power thus displayed to the children of men! Who can doubt the message of salvation? Who can slight the mercies of a compassionate Redeemer?

It required nothing less than creative power to restore health to that decaying body. The same voice that spoke life to man created from the 270 dust of the earth had spoken life to the dying paralytic. And the same power that gave life to the body had renewed the heart. He who at the creation "spake, and it was," who "commanded, and it stood fast" (Ps. 33:9), had spoken life to the soul dead in trespasses and sins. The healing of the body was an evidence of the power that had renewed the heart. Christ bade the paralytic arise and walk, "that ye may know," He said, "that the Son of man hath power on earth to forgive sins."

The paralytic found in Christ healing for both the soul and the body. The spiritual healing was followed by physical restoration. This lesson should not be overlooked. There are today thousands suffering from physical disease, who, like the paralytic, are longing for the message, "Thy sins are forgiven." The burden of sin, with its unrest and unsatisfied desires, is the foundation of their maladies. They can find no relief until they come to the Healer of the soul. The peace which He alone can give would impart vigor to the mind, and health to the body.

Jesus came to "destroy the works of the devil." "In Him was life," and He says, "I am come that they might have life, and that they might have it more abundantly." He is "a quickening spirit." 1 John 3:8; John 1:4; 10:10; 1 Cor. 15:45. And He still has the same life-giving power as when on earth He healed the sick, and spoke forgiveness to the sinner. He "forgiveth all thine iniquities," He "healeth all thy diseases." Ps. 103:3.

The effect produced upon the people by the healing of the paralytic was as if heaven had opened, and revealed the glories of the better world. As the man who had been cured passed through the multitude, blessing God at every step, and bearing his burden as if it were a feather's weight, the people fell back to give him room, and with awe-stricken faces gazed upon him, whispering softly among themselves, "We have seen strange things today."

The Pharisees were dumb with amazement and overwhelmed with defeat. They saw that here was no opportunity for their jealousy to inflame the multitude. The wonderful work wrought upon the man whom they had given over to the wrath of God had so impressed the people that the rabbis were for the time forgotten. They saw that Christ possessed a power which they had ascribed to God alone; yet the gentle dignity of His manner was in marked contrast to their own haughty bearing. They were disconcerted and abashed, recognizing, but not confessing, the presence of a superior being. The stronger the evidence that Jesus had power on earth to forgive sins, the more firmly they entrenched themselves in unbelief. From the home of Peter, where they had seen the paralytic restored by His word, they went away to invent new schemes for silencing the Son of God.

Physical disease, however malignant and deep-seated, was healed by the power of Christ; but the disease of the soul took a firmer hold upon those who closed their eyes against the light. Leprosy and palsy were not so terrible as bigotry and unbelief.

In the home of the healed paralytic there was great rejoicing when he returned to his family, carrying with ease the couch upon which he had been slowly borne from their presence but a short time before. They gathered round with tears of joy, scarcely daring to believe their eyes. He stood before them in the full vigor of manhood. Those arms that they had seen lifeless were quick to obey his will. The flesh that had been shrunken and leaden-hued was now fresh and ruddy. He walked with a firm, free step. Joy and hope were written in every lineament of his countenance; and an expression of purity and peace had taken the place of the marks of sin and suffering. Glad thanksgiving went up from that home, and God was glorified through His Son, who had restored hope to the hopeless, and strength to the stricken one. This man and his family were ready to lay down their lives for Jesus. No doubt dimmed their faith, no unbelief marred their fealty to Him who had brought light into their darkened home.

28

Levi-Matthew

Of the Roman officials in Palestine, none were more hated than the publicans. The fact that the taxes were imposed by a foreign power was a continual irritation to the Jews, being a reminder that their independence had departed. And the taxgatherers were not merely the instruments of Roman oppression; they were extortioners on their own account, enriching themselves at the expense of the people. A Jew who accepted this office at the hands of the Romans was looked upon as betraying the honor of his nation. He was despised as an apostate, and was classed with the vilest of society.

To this class belonged Levi-Matthew, who, after the four disciples at Gennesaret, was the next to be called to Christ's service. The Pharisees had judged Matthew according to his employment, but Jesus saw in this man a heart open for the reception of truth. Matthew had listened to the Saviour's teaching. As the convicting Spirit of God revealed his sinfulness, he longed to seek help from Christ; but he was accustomed to the exclusiveness of the rabbis, and had no thought that this Great Teacher would notice him.

Sitting at his toll booth one day, the publican saw Jesus approaching. Great was his astonishment to hear the words addressed to himself, "Follow Me."

Matthew "left all, rose up, and followed Him." There was no hesitation, no questioning, no thought of the lucrative business to be exchanged for poverty and hardship. It was enough for him that he was to be with Jesus, that he might listen to His words, and unite with Him in His work.

So it was with the disciples previously called. When Jesus bade Peter and his companions follow Him, immediately they left their boats and nets. Some of these disciples had friends dependent on them for support; but when they received the Saviour's invitation, they did not hesitate, and inquire, How shall I live, and sustain my family? They were obedient to the call; and when afterward Jesus asked them, "When I sent you without purse, and scrip, and shoes, lacked ye anything?" they could answer, "Nothing." Luke 22:35.

To Matthew in his wealth, and to Andrew and Peter in their poverty, the same test was brought; the same consecration was made by each. At the moment of success, when the nets were filled with fish, and the impulses of the old life were strongest, Jesus asked the disciples at the sea to leave all for the work of the gospel. So every soul is tested as to whether the desire for temporal good or for fellowship with Christ is strongest.

Principle is always exacting. No man can succeed in the service of God unless his whole heart is in the work and he counts all things but loss for the excellency of the knowledge of Christ. No man who makes any reserve can be the disciple of Christ, much less can he be His colaborer. When men appreciate the great salvation, the self-sacrifice seen in Christ's life will be seen in theirs. Wherever He leads the way, they will rejoice to follow.

The calling of Matthew to be one of Christ's disciples excited great indignation. For a religious teacher to choose a publican as one of his immediate attendants was an offense against the religious, social, and national customs. By appealing to the prejudices of the people the Pharisees hoped to turn the current of popular feeling against Jesus.

Among the publicans a widespread interest

This chapter is based on Matthew 9:9-17; Mark 2:14-22; Luke 5:27-39.

was created. Their hearts were drawn toward the divine Teacher. In the joy of his new discipleship, Matthew longed to bring his former associates to Jesus. Accordingly he made a feast at his own house, and called together his relatives and friends. Not only were publicans included, but many others who were of doubtful reputation, and were proscribed by their more scrupulous neighbors.

The entertainment was given in honor of Jesus, and He did not hesitate to accept the courtesy. He well knew that this would give offense to the Pharisaic party, and would also compromise Him in the eyes of the people. But no question of policy could influence His movements. With Him external distinctions weighed nothing. That which appealed to His heart was a soul thirsting for the water of life.

Jesus sat as an honored guest at the table of the publicans, by His sympathy and social kindliness showing that He recognized the dignity of humanity; and men longed to become worthy of His confidence. Upon their thirsty hearts His words fell with blessed, life-giving power. New impulses were awakened, and the possibility of a new life opened to these outcasts of society.

At such gatherings as this, not a few were impressed by the Saviour's teaching who did not acknowledge Him until after His ascension. When the Holy Spirit was poured out, and three thousand were converted in a day, there were among them many who first heard the truth at the table of the publicans, and some of these became messengers of the gospel. To Matthew himself the example of Jesus at the feast was a constant lesson. The despised publican became one of the most devoted evangelists, in his own ministry following closely in his Master's steps.

When the rabbis learned of the presence of Jesus at Matthew's feast, they seized the opportunity of accusing Him. But they chose to work through the disciples. By arousing their prejudices they hoped to alienate them from their Master. It was their policy to accuse Christ to the disciples, and the disciples to Christ, aiming their arrows where they would be most likely to wound. This is the way in which Satan has worked ever since the disaffection in heaven; and all who try to cause discord and alienation are actuated by his spirit.

"Why eateth your Master with publicans and sinners?" questioned the envious rabbis.

Jesus did not wait for His disciples to answer the charge, but Himself replied: "They that be whole need not a physician, but they that are sick. But go ye and learn what that meaneth, I will have mercy, and not sacrifice: for I am not come to call the righteous, but sinners to repentance." The Pharisees claimed to be spiritually whole, and therefore in no need of a physician, while they regarded the publicans and Gentiles as perishing from diseases of the soul. Then was it not His work, as a physician, to go to the very class that needed His help?

But although the Pharisees thought so highly of themselves, they were really in a worse condition than the ones they despised. The publicans were less bigoted and self-sufficient, and thus were more open to the influence of truth. Jesus said to the rabbis, "Go ye and learn what that meaneth, I will have mercy, and not sacrifice." Thus He showed that while they claimed to expound the word of God, they were wholly ignorant of its spirit.

The Pharisees were silenced for the time, but only became more determined in their enmity. They next sought out the disciples of John the Baptist, and tried to set them against the Saviour. These Pharisees had not accepted the mission of the Baptist. They had pointed in scorn to his abstemious life, his simple habits, his coarse garments, and had declared him a fanatic. Because he denounced their hypocrisy, they had resisted his words, and had tried to stir up the people against him. The Spirit of God had moved upon the hearts of these scorners, convicting them of sin; but they had rejected the counsel of God, and had declared that John was possessed of a devil.

Now when Jesus came mingling with the people, eating and drinking at their tables, they accused Him of being a glutton and a winebibber. The very ones who made this charge were themselves guilty. As God is misrepresented, and clothed by Satan with his own attributes, so the Lord's messengers were falsified by these wicked men.

The Pharisees would not consider that Jesus was eating with publicans and sinners in order to bring the light of heaven to those who sat in darkness. They would not see that every word dropped by the divine Teacher was a living seed that would germinate and bear fruit to the glory of God. They had determined not to accept the light; and although they had opposed the mission of the Baptist, they were now ready to court the friendship of his disciples, hoping to secure their co-operation against Jesus. They represented that Jesus was setting at nought the ancient traditions; and they contrasted the austere piety of the Baptist with the course of Jesus in feasting with publicans and sinners.

The disciples of John were at this time in great sorrow. It was before their visit to Jesus with John's message. Their beloved teacher was in prison, and they passed their days in mourning. And Jesus was making no effort to release John, and even appeared to cast discredit on his teaching. If John had been sent by God, why did Jesus and His disciples pursue a course so widely different?

The disciples of John had not a clear understanding of Christ's work; they thought there might be some foundation for the charges of the

Pharisees. They observed many of the rules prescribed by the rabbis, and even hoped to be justified by the works of the law. Fasting was practiced by the Jews as an act of merit, and the most rigid among them fasted two days in every week. The Pharisees and John's disciples were fasting when the latter came to Jesus with the inquiry, "Why do we and the Pharisees fast oft, but Thy disciples fast not?"

Very tenderly Jesus answered them. He did not try to correct their erroneous conception of fasting, but only to set them right in regard to His own mission. And He did this by employing the same figure that the Baptist himself had used in his testimony to Jesus. John had said, "He that hath the bride is the bridegroom: but the friend of the bridegroom, which standeth 277 and heareth him, rejoiceth greatly because of the bridegroom's voice: this my joy therefore is fulfilled." John 3:29. The disciples of John could not fail to recall these words of their teacher, as, taking the illustration, Jesus said, "Can ye make the children of the bridechamber fast, while the bridegroom is with them?"

The Prince of heaven was among His people. The greatest gift of God had been given to the world. Joy to the poor; for Christ had come to make them heirs of His kingdom. Joy to the rich; for He would teach them how to secure eternal riches. Joy to the ignorant; He would make them wise unto salvation. Joy to the learned; He would open to them deeper mysteries than they had ever fathomed; truths that had been hidden from the foundation of the world would be opened to men by the Saviour's mission.

John the Baptist had rejoiced to behold the Saviour. What occasion for rejoicing had the disciples who were privileged to walk and talk with the Majesty of heaven! This was not a time for them to mourn and fast. They must open their hearts to receive the light of His glory, that they might shed light upon those who sat in darkness and in the shadow of death.

It was a bright picture which the words of Christ had called up, but across it lay a heavy shadow, which His eye alone discerned. "The days will come," He said, "when the bridegroom shall be taken away from them, and then shall they fast in those days." When they should see their Lord betrayed and crucified, the disciples would mourn and fast. In His last words to them in the upper chamber, He said, "A little while, and ye shall not see Me: and again, a little while, and ye shall see Me. Verily, verily, I say unto you, That ye shall weep and lament, but the world shall rejoice: and ye shall be sorrowful, but your sorrow shall be turned into joy." John 16:19, 20.

When He should come forth from the tomb, their sorrow would be turned to joy. After His ascension He was to be absent in person; but

through the Comforter He would still be with them, and they were not to spend their time in mourning. This was what Satan wanted. He desired them to give the world the impression that they had been deceived and disappointed; but by faith they were to look to the sanctuary above, where Jesus was ministering for them; they were to open their hearts to the Holy Spirit, His representative, and to rejoice in the light of His presence. Yet days of temptation and trial would come, when they would be brought into conflict with the rulers of this world, and the leaders of the kingdom of darkness; when Christ was not personally with them, and they failed to 278 discern the Comforter, then it would be more fitting for them to fast.

The Pharisees sought to exalt themselves by their rigorous observance of forms, while their hearts were filled with envy and strife. "Behold," says the Scripture, "ye fast for strife and debate, and to smite with the fist of wickedness: ye shall not fast as ye do this day, to make your voice to be heard on high. Is it such a fast that I have chosen? a day for a man to afflict his soul? is it to bow down his head as a bulrush, and to spread sackcloth and ashes under him? wilt thou call this a fast, and an acceptable day to the Lord?" Isa. 58:4, 5.

The true fast is no mere formal service. The Scripture describes the fast that God has chosen,—"to loose the bands of wickedness, to undo the heavy burdens, and to let the oppressed go free, and that ye break every yoke;" to "draw out thy soul to the hungry, and satisfy the afflicted soul." Isa. 58:6, 10. Here is set forth the very spirit and character of the work of Christ. His whole life was a sacrifice of Himself for the saving of the world. Whether fasting in the wilderness of temptation or eating with the publicans at Matthew's feast, He was giving His life for the redemption of the lost. Not in idle mourning, in mere bodily humiliation and multitudinous sacrifices, is the true spirit of devotion manifested, but it is shown in the surrender of self in willing service to God and man.

Continuing His answer to the disciples of John, Jesus spoke a parable, saying, "No man putteth a piece of a new garment upon an old; if otherwise, then both the new maketh a rent, and the piece that was taken out of the new agreeth not with the old." The message of John the Baptist was not to be interwoven with tradition and superstition. An attempt to blend the pretense of the Pharisees with the devotion of John would only make more evident the breach between them.

Nor could the principles of Christ's teaching be united with the forms of Pharisaism. Christ was not to close up the breach that had been made by the teachings of John. He would make more distinct the separation between the old and the new. Jesus further illustrated this fact, saying, "No man putteth new wine into old bottles; else the new wine will burst the bottles, and be spilled, and the bottles shall perish." The skin bottles which were used as vessels to contain the new wine, after a time became dry and brittle, and were then worthless to serve the same purpose again. In this familiar illustration Jesus presented the condition of the Jewish leaders. Priests and scribes and rulers were fixed in a rut of ceremonies and traditions. Their hearts had become contracted, like the dried-up wine skins to which He had compared them. While they remained satisfied with a legal religion, it was impossible for them to become the depositaries of the living truth of heaven. They thought their own righteousness all-sufficient, and did not desire that a new element should be brought into their religion. The good will of God to men they did not accept as something apart from themselves. They connected it with their own merit because of their good works. The faith that works by love and purifies the soul could find no place for union with the religion of the Pharisees, made up of ceremonies and the injunctions of men. The effort to unite the teachings of Jesus with the established religion would be vain. The vital truth of God, like fermenting wine, would burst the old, decaying bottles of the Pharisaical tradition.

The Pharisees thought themselves too wise to need instruction, too righteous to need salvation, too highly honored to need the honor that comes from Christ. The Saviour turned away from them to find others who would receive the message of heaven. In the untutored fishermen, in the publican at the market place, in the woman of Samaria, in the common people who heard Him gladly, He found His new bottles for the new wine. The instrumentalities to be used in the gospel work are those souls who gladly receive the light which God sends them. These are His agencies for imparting the knowledge of truth to the world. If through the grace of Christ His people will become new bottles, He will fill them with new wine.

The teaching of Christ, though it was represented by the new wine, was not a new doctrine, but the revelation of that which had been taught from the beginning. But to the Pharisees the truth of God had lost its original significance and beauty. To them Christ's teaching was new in almost every respect, and it was unrecognized and unacknowledged.

Jesus pointed out the power of false teaching to destroy the appreciation and desire for truth. "No man," He said, "having drunk old wine straightway desireth new: for he saith, The old is better." All the truth that has been given to the world through patriarchs and prophets shone out in new beauty in the words of Christ. But the scribes and Pharisees had no desire for the precious new wine. Until emptied of the old traditions, customs, and practices, they had no place in mind or heart for the teachings of Christ. They clung to the dead forms, and turned away from the living truth and the power of God.

It was this that proved the ruin of the Jews, and it will prove the ruin of many souls in our own day. Thousands are making the same mistake as did the Pharisees whom Christ reproved at Matthew's feast. Rather than give up some cherished idea, or discard some idol of opinion, many refuse the truth which comes down from the Father of light. They trust in self, and depend upon their own wisdom, and do not realize their spiritual poverty. They insist on being saved in some way by which they may perform some important work. When they see that there is no way of weaving self into the work, they reject the salvation provided.

A legal religion can never lead souls to Christ; for it is a loveless, Christless religion. Fasting or prayer that is actuated by a self-justifying spirit is an abomination in the sight of God. The solemn assembly for worship, the round of religious ceremonies, the external humiliation, the imposing sacrifice, proclaim that the doer of these things regards himself as righteous, and as entitled to heaven; but it is all a deception. Our own works can never purchase salvation.

As it was in the days of Christ, so it is now; the Pharisees do not know their spiritual destitution. To them comes the message, "Because thou sayest, I am rich, and increased with goods, and have need of nothing; and knowest not that thou art wretched, and miserable, and poor, and blind, and naked: I counsel thee to buy of Me gold tried in the fire, that thou mayest be rich; and white raiment, that thou mayest be clothed, and that the shame of thy nakedness do not appear." Rev. 3:17, 18. Faith and love are the gold tried in the fire. But with many the gold has become dim, and the rich treasure has been lost. The righteousness of Christ is to them as a robe unworn, a fountain untouched. To them it is said, "I have somewhat against thee, because thou hast left thy first love. Remember therefore from whence thou art fallen, and repent, and do the first works; or else I will come unto thee quickly, and will remove thy candlestick out of his place, except thou repent." Rev. 2:4, 5.

"The sacrifices of God are a broken spirit: a broken and a contrite heart, O God, Thou wilt not despise." Ps. 51:17. Man must be emptied of self before he can be, in the fullest sense, a believer in Jesus. When self is renounced, then the Lord can make man a new creature. New bottles can contain the new wine. The love of Christ will animate the believer with new life. In him who looks unto the Author and Finisher of our faith the character of Christ will be manifest.

281

29

The Sabbath

The Sabbath was hallowed at the creation. As ordained for man, it had its origin when "the morning stars sang together, and all the sons of God shouted for joy." Job 38:7. Peace brooded over the world; for earth was in harmony with heaven. "God saw everything that He had made, and, behold, it was very good;" and He rested in the joy of His completed work. Gen. 1:31.

Because He had rested upon the Sabbath, "God blessed the seventh day, and sanctified it,"—set it apart to a holy use. He gave it to Adam as a day of rest. It was a memorial of the work of creation, and thus a sign of God's power and His love. The Scripture says, "He hath made His wonderful works to be remembered." "The things that are made," declare "the invisible things of Him since the creation of the world," "even His everlasting power and divinity." Gen. 2:3; Ps. 111:4; Rom. 1:20, R. V.

All things were created by the Son of God. "In the beginning was the Word, and the Word was with God. . . . All things were made by Him; and without Him was not anything made that was made." John 1:1-3. And since the Sabbath is a memorial of the work of creation, it is a token of the love and power of Christ.

The Sabbath calls our thoughts to nature, and brings us into communion with the Creator. In the song of the bird, the sighing of the trees, and the music of the sea, we still may hear His voice
282
who talked with Adam in Eden in the cool of the day. And as we behold His power in nature we find comfort, for the word that created all things is that which speaks life to the soul. He "who commanded the light to shine out of darkness, hath shined in our hearts, to give the light of the knowledge of the glory of God in the face of Jesus Christ." 2 Cor. 4:6.

It was this thought that awoke the song,—

"Thou, Lord, hast made me glad through Thy work;
I will triumph in the works of Thy hands.
O Lord, how great are Thy works!
And Thy thoughts are very deep."
Ps. 92:4, 5.

And the Holy Spirit through the prophet Isaiah declares: "To whom then will ye liken God? or what likeness will ye compare unto Him? . . . Have ye not known? have ye not heard? hath it not been told you from the beginning? have ye not understood from the foundations of the earth? It is He that sitteth upon the circle of the earth, and the inhabitants thereof are as grasshoppers; that stretcheth out the heavens as a curtain, and spreadeth them out as a tent to dwell in. . . . To whom then will ye liken Me, or shall I be equal? saith the Holy One. Lift up your eyes on high, and behold who hath created these things, that bringeth out their host by number: He calleth them all by names by the greatness of His might, for that He is strong in power; not one faileth. Why sayest thou, O Jacob, and speakest, O Israel, My way is hid from the Lord, and my judgment is passed over from my God? Hast thou not known? hast thou not heard, that the everlasting God, the Lord, the Creator of the ends of the earth, fainteth not, neither is weary? . . . He giveth power to the
283
faint; and to them that have no might He increaseth strength." "Fear thou not; for I am with thee: be not dismayed; for I am thy God: I will strengthen thee; yea, I will help thee; yea, I will uphold thee with the right hand of My righteousness." "Look unto Me, and be ye saved, all the ends of the earth: for I am God, and there is none else." This is the message written in nature, which the Sabbath is appointed to keep in memory. When the Lord bade Israel hallow His Sabbaths, He said, "They shall be a sign between Me and you, that ye may know that I am Jehovah your God." Isa. 40:18-29; 41:10; 45:22; Ezek. 20:20, R. V.

The Sabbath was embodied in the law given from Sinai; but it was not then first made known as a day of rest. The people of Israel had a knowledge of it before they came to Sinai. On the way thither the Sabbath was kept. When some profaned it, the Lord reproved them, saying, "How long refuse ye to keep My commandments and My laws?" Ex. 16:28.

The Sabbath was not for Israel merely, but for the world. It had been made known to man in Eden, and, like the other precepts of the Decalogue, it is of imperishable obligation. Of that law of which the fourth commandment forms a part, Christ declares, "Till heaven and earth pass, one jot or one tittle shall in nowise pass from the law." So long as the heavens and the earth endure, the Sabbath will continue as a sign of the Creator's power. And when Eden shall bloom on earth again, God's holy rest day will be honored by all beneath the sun. "From one Sabbath to another" the inhabitants of the glorified new earth shall go up "to worship before Me, saith the Lord." Matt. 5:18; Isa. 66:23.

No other institution which was committed to the Jews tended so fully to distinguish them from surrounding nations as did the Sabbath. God designed that its observance should designate them as His worshipers. It was to be a token of their separation from idolatry, and their connection with the true God. But in order to keep the Sabbath holy, men must themselves be holy. Through faith they must become partakers of the righteousness of Christ. When the command was given to Israel, "Remember the Sabbath day, to keep it holy," the Lord said also to them, "Ye shall be holy men unto Me." Ex. 20:8; 22:31. Only thus could the Sabbath distinguish Israel as the worshipers of God.

As the Jews departed from God, and failed to make the righteousness of Christ their own by faith, the Sabbath lost its significance to them. Satan was seeking to exalt himself and to draw men away from Christ, and he worked to pervert 284 the Sabbath, because it is the sign of the power of Christ. The Jewish leaders accomplished the will of Satan by surrounding God's rest day with burdensome requirements. In the days of Christ the Sabbath had become so perverted that its observance reflected the character of selfish and arbitrary men rather than the character of the loving heavenly Father. The rabbis virtually represented God as giving laws which it was impossible for men to obey. They led the people to look upon God as a tyrant, and to think that the observance of the Sabbath, as He required it, made men hardhearted and cruel. It was the work of Christ to clear away these misconceptions. Although the rabbis followed Him with merciless hostility, He did not even appear to conform to their requirements, but went straight forward, keeping the Sabbath according to the law of God.

Upon one Sabbath day, as the Saviour and His disciples returned from the place of worship, they passed through a field of ripening grain. Jesus had continued His work to a late hour, and while passing through the fields, the disciples began to gather the heads of grain, and to eat the kernels after rubbing them in their hands. On any other day this act would have excited no comment, for one passing through a field of grain, an orchard, or a vineyard, was at liberty to gather what he desired to eat. See Deut. 23:24, 25. But to do this on the Sabbath was held to be an act of desecration. Not only was the gathering of the grain a kind of reaping, but the rubbing of it in the hands was a kind of threshing. Thus, in the opinion of the rabbis, there was a double offense.

The spies at once complained to Jesus, saying, "Behold, Thy disciples do that which is not lawful to do upon the Sabbath day."

When accused of Sabbathbreaking at Bethesda, Jesus defended Himself by affirming His Sonship to God, and declaring that He worked in harmony with the Father. Now that the disci-285 ples are attacked, He cites His accusers to examples from the Old Testament, acts performed on the Sabbath by those who were in the service of God.

The Jewish teachers prided themselves on their knowledge of the Scriptures, and in the Saviour's answer there was an implied rebuke for their ignorance of the Sacred Writings. "Have ye not read so much as this," He said, "what David did, when himself was an hun-

gered, and they which were with him; how he went into the house of God, and did take and eat the shewbread, . . . which it is not lawful to eat but for the priests alone?" "And He said unto them, The Sabbath was made for man, and not man for the Sabbath." "Have ye not read in the law, how that on the Sabbath days the priests in the temple profane the Sabbath, and are blameless? But I say unto you, That in this place is one greater than the temple." "The Son of man is Lord also of the Sabbath." Luke 6:3, 4; Mark 2:27, 28; Matt. 12:5, 6.

If it was right for David to satisfy his hunger by eating of the bread that had been set apart to a holy use, then it was right for the disciples to supply their need by plucking the grain upon the sacred hours of the Sabbath. Again, the priests in the temple performed greater labor on the Sabbath than upon other days. The same labor in secular business would be sinful; but the work of the priests was in the service of God. They were performing those rites that pointed to the redeeming power of Christ, and their labor was in harmony with the object of the Sabbath. But now Christ Himself had come. The disciples, in doing the work of Christ, were engaged in God's service, and that which was necessary for the accomplishment of this work it was right to do on the Sabbath day.

Christ would teach His disciples and His enemies that the service of God is first of all. The object of God's work in this world is the redemption of man; therefore that which is necessary to be done on the Sabbath in the accomplishment of this work is in accord with the Sabbath law. Jesus then crowned His argument by declaring Himself the "Lord of the Sabbath,"—One above all question and above all law. This infinite Judge acquits the disciples of blame, appealing to the very statutes they are accused of violating.

Jesus did not let the matter pass with administering a rebuke to His enemies. He declared that in their blindness they had mistaken the object of the Sabbath. He said, "If ye had known what this meaneth, I will have mercy, and not sacrifice, ye would not have condemned the guiltless." Matt. 12:7. Their many heartless rites could not supply the lack of that truthful integri-286 ty and tender love which will ever characterize the true worshiper of God.

Again Christ reiterated the truth that the sacrifices were in themselves of no value. They were a means, and not an end. Their object was to direct men to the Saviour, and thus to bring them into harmony with God. It is the service of love that God values. When this is lacking, the mere round of ceremony is an offense to Him. So with the Sabbath. It was designed to bring men into communion with God; but when the mind was absorbed with wearisome rites, the object of the Sabbath was thwarted. Its mere outward observance was a mockery.

Upon another Sabbath, as Jesus entered a synagogue, He saw there a man who had a withered hand. The Pharisees watched Him, eager to see what He would do. The Saviour well knew that in healing on the Sabbath He would be regarded as a transgressor, but He did not hesitate to break down the wall of traditional requirements that barricaded the Sabbath. Jesus bade the afflicted man stand forth, and then asked, "Is it lawful to do good on the Sabbath days, or to do evil? to save life, or to kill?" It was a maxim among the Jews that a failure to do good, when one had opportunity, was to do evil; to neglect to save life was to kill. Thus Jesus met the rabbis on their own ground. "But they held their peace. And when He had looked round about on them with anger, being grieved for the hardness of their hearts, He saith unto the man, Stretch forth thine hand. And he stretched it out: and his hand was restored whole as the other." Mark 3:4, 5.

When questioned, "Is it lawful to heal on the Sabbath days?" Jesus answered, "What man shall there be among *you*, that shall have one sheep, and if it fall into a pit on the Sabbath day, will he not lay hold on it, and lift it out? How much then is a man better than a sheep? Wherefore it is lawful to do well on the Sabbath days." Matt. 12:10-12.

The spies dared not answer Christ in the presence of the multitude, for fear of involving themselves in difficulty. They knew that He had spoken the truth. Rather than violate their traditions, they would leave a man to suffer, while they would relieve a brute because of the loss to the owner if it were neglected. Thus greater care was shown for a dumb animal than for man, who is made in the image of God. This illustrates the working of all false religions. They originate in man's desire to exalt himself above God, but 287 they result in degrading man below the brute. Every religion that wars against the sovereignty of God defrauds man of the glory which was his at the creation, and which is to be restored to him in Christ. Every false religion teaches its adherents to be careless of human needs, sufferings, and rights. The gospel places a high value upon humanity as the purchase of the blood of Christ, and it teaches a tender regard for the wants and woes of man. The Lord says, "I will make a man more precious than fine gold; even a man than the golden wedge of Ophir." Isa. 13:12.

When Jesus turned upon the Pharisees with the question whether it was lawful on the Sabbath day to do good or to do evil, to save life or to kill, He confronted them with their own wicked purposes. They were hunting His life with bitter hatred, while He was saving life and bringing happiness to multitudes. Was it better to slay upon the Sabbath, as they were planning to do, than to heal the afflicted, as He had done?

Was it more righteous to have murder in the heart upon God's holy day than love to all men, which finds expression in deeds of mercy?

In the healing of the withered hand, Jesus condemned the custom of the Jews, and left the fourth commandment standing as God had given it. "It is lawful to do well on the Sabbath days," He declared. By sweeping away the senseless restrictions of the Jews, Christ honored the Sabbath, while those who complained of Him were dishonoring God's holy day.

Those who hold that Christ abolished the law teach that He broke the Sabbath and justified His disciples in doing the same. Thus they are really taking the same ground as did the caviling Jews. In this they contradict the testimony of Christ Himself, who declared, "I have kept My Father's commandments, and abide in His love." John 15:10. Neither the Saviour nor His followers broke the law of the Sabbath. Christ was a living representative of the law. No violation of its holy precepts was found in His life. Looking upon a nation of witnesses who were seeking occasion to condemn Him, He could say unchallenged, "Which of you convicteth Me of sin?" John 8:46, R. V.

The Saviour had not come to set aside what patriarchs and prophets had spoken; for He Himself had spoken through these representative men. All the truths of God's word came from Him. But these priceless gems had been placed in false settings. Their precious light had been made to minister to error. God desired them to be removed from their settings of error 288 and replaced in the framework of truth. This work could only a divine hand could accomplish. By its connection with error, the truth had been serving the cause of the enemy of God and man. Christ had come to place it where it would glorify God, and work the salvation of humanity.

"The Sabbath was made for man, and not man for the Sabbath," Jesus said. The institutions that God has established are for the benefit of mankind. "All things are for your sakes." "Whether Paul, or Apollos, or Cephas, or the world, or life, or death, or things present, or things to come; all are yours; and ye are Christ's; and Christ is God's." 2 Cor. 4:15; 1 Cor. 3:22, 23. The law of Ten Commandments, of which the Sabbath forms a part, God gave to His people as a blessing. "The Lord commanded us," said Moses, "to do all these statutes, to fear the Lord our God, for our good always, that He might preserve us alive." Deut. 6:24. And through the psalmist the message was given to Israel, "Serve the Lord with gladness: come before His presence with singing. Know ye that the Lord He is God: it is He that hath made us, and not we ourselves; we are His people, and the sheep of His pasture. Enter into His gates with thanksgiving, and into His courts with praise." Ps. 100:2-4. And of all who keep "the

Sabbath from polluting it," the Lord declares, "Even them will I bring to My holy mountain, and make them joyful in My house of prayer." Isa. 56:6, 7.

"Wherefore the Son of man is Lord also of the Sabbath." These words are full of instruction and comfort. Because the Sabbath was made for man, it is the Lord's day. It belongs to Christ. For "all things were made by Him; and without Him was not anything made that was made." John 1:3. Since He made all things, He made the Sabbath. By Him it was set apart as a memorial of the work of creation. It points to Him as both the Creator and the Sanctifier. It declares that He who created all things in heaven and in earth, and by whom all things hold together, is the head of the church, and that by His power we are reconciled to God. For, speaking of Israel, He said, "I gave them My Sabbaths, to be a sign between Me and them, that they might know that I am the Lord that sanctify them,"—make them holy. Ezek. 20:12. Then the Sabbath is a sign of Christ's power to make us holy. And it is given to all whom Christ makes holy. As a sign of His sanctifying power, the Sabbath is given to all who through Christ become a part of the Israel of God.

289 And the Lord says, "If thou turn away thy foot from the Sabbath, from doing thy pleasure on My holy day; and call the Sabbath a delight, the holy of the Lord, honorable; . . . then shalt thou delight thyself in the Lord." Isa. 58:13, 14. To all who receive the Sabbath as a sign of Christ's creative and redeeming power, it will be a delight. Seeing Christ in it, they delight themselves in Him. The Sabbath points them to the works of creation as an evidence of His mighty power in redemption. While it calls to mind the lost peace of Eden, it tells of peace restored through the Saviour. And every object in nature repeats His invitation, "Come unto Me, all ye that labor and are heavy-laden, and I will give you rest." Matt. 11:28.

290

30

"He Ordained Twelve"

"And He goeth up into a mountain, and calleth unto Him whom He would: and they came unto Him. And He ordained twelve, that they should be with Him, and that He might send them forth to preach."

It was beneath the sheltering trees of the mountainside, but a little distance from the Sea of Galilee, that the twelve were called to the apostolate, and the Sermon on the Mount was given. The fields and hills were the favorite resorts of Jesus, and much of His teaching was given under the open sky, rather than in the temple or the synagogues. No synagogue could have received the throngs that followed Him; but not for this reason only did He choose to teach in the fields and groves. Jesus loved the scenes of nature. To Him each quiet retreat was a sacred temple.

It was under the trees of Eden that the first dwellers on earth had chosen their sanctuary. There Christ had communed with the father of mankind. When banished from Paradise, our first parents still worshiped in the fields and groves, and there Christ met them with the gospel of His grace. It was Christ who spoke with Abraham under the oaks at Mamre; with 291 Isaac as he went out to pray in the fields at the eventide; with Jacob on the hillside at Bethel; with Moses among the mountains of Midian; and with the boy David as he watched his flocks. It was at Christ's direction that for fifteen centuries the Hebrew people had left their homes for one week every year, and had dwelt in booths formed from the green branches "of goodly trees, branches of palm trees, and boughs of thick trees, and willows of the brook." Lev. 23:40.

In training His disciples, Jesus chose to withdraw from the confusion of the city to the quiet of the fields and hills, as more in harmony with the lessons of self-abnegation He desired to teach them. And during His ministry He loved to gather the people about Him under the blue heavens, on some grassy hillside, or on the beach beside the lake. Here, surrounded by the works of His own creation, He could turn the thoughts of His hearers from the artificial to the natural. In the growth and development of nature were revealed the principles of His kingdom. As men should lift up their eyes to the hills of God, and behold the wonderful works of His hands, they could learn precious lessons of divine truth. Christ's teaching would be repeated to them in the things of nature. So it is with all who go into the fields with Christ in their hearts. They will feel themselves surrounded with a holy influence. The things of nature take up the parables of our Lord, and repeat His counsels. By communion with God in nature, the mind is uplifted, and the heart finds rest.

The first step was now to be taken in the organization of the church that after Christ's departure was to be His representative on earth. No costly sanctuary was at their command, but the Saviour led His disciples to the retreat He loved, and in their minds the sacred experiences of that day were forever linked with the beauty of mountain and vale and sea.

Jesus had called His disciples that He might send them forth as His witnesses, to declare to the world what they had seen and heard of Him. Their office was the most important to which human beings had ever been called, and was second only to that of Christ Himself. They

This chapter is based on Mark 3:13-19; Luke 6:12-16.

600

were to be workers together with God for the saving of the world. As in the Old Testament the twelve patriarchs stand as representatives of Israel, so the twelve apostles were to stand as representatives of the gospel church.

The Saviour knew the character of the men whom He had chosen; all their weaknesses and errors were open before Him; He knew the perils through which they must pass, the responsibility that would rest upon them; and His heart yearned over these chosen ones. Alone upon a mountain near the Sea of Galilee He spent the entire night in prayer for them, while they were sleeping at the foot of the mountain. With the first light of dawn He summoned them to meet Him; for He had something of importance to communicate to them.

These disciples had been for some time associated with Jesus in active labor. John and James, Andrew and Peter, with Philip, Nathanael, and Matthew, had been more closely connected with Him than the others, and had witnessed more of His miracles. Peter, James, and John stood in still nearer relationship to Him. They were almost constantly with Him, witnessing His miracles, and hearing His words. John pressed into still closer intimacy with Jesus, so that he is distinguished as the one whom Jesus loved. The Saviour loved them all, but John's was the most receptive spirit. He was younger than the others, and with more of the child's confiding trust he opened his heart to Jesus. Thus he came more into sympathy with Christ, and through him the Saviour's deepest spiritual teaching was communicated to His people.

At the head of one of the groups into which the apostles are divided stands the name of Philip. He was the first disciple to whom Jesus addressed the distinct command, "Follow Me." Philip was of Bethsaida, the city of Andrew and Peter. He had listened to the teaching of John the Baptist, and had heard his announcement of Christ as the Lamb of God. Philip was a sincere seeker for truth, but he was slow of heart to believe. Although he had joined himself to Christ, yet his announcement of Him to Nathanael shows that he was not fully convinced of the divinity of Jesus. Though Christ had been proclaimed by the voice from heaven as the Son of God, to Philip He was "Jesus of Nazareth, the son of Joseph." John 1:45. Again, when the five thousand were fed, Philip's lack of faith was shown. It was to test him that Jesus questioned, "Whence shall we buy bread, that these may eat?" Philip's answer was on the side of unbelief: "Two hundred pennyworth of bread is not sufficient for them, that every one of them may take a little." John 6:5, 7. Jesus was grieved. Although Philip had seen His works and felt His power, yet he had not faith. When the Greeks inquired of Philip concerning Jesus, he

did not seize upon the opportunity of introducing them to the Saviour, but he went to tell Andrew. Again, in those last hours before the crucifixion, the words of Philip were such as to discourage faith. When Thomas said to Jesus, "Lord, we know not whither Thou goest; and how can we know the way?" the Saviour answered, "I am the Way, the Truth, and the Life. . . . If ye had known Me, ye should have known My Father also." From Philip came the response of unbelief: "Lord, show us the Father, and it sufficeth us." John 14:5-8. So slow of heart, so weak in faith, was that disciple who for three years had been with Jesus.

In happy contrast to Philip's unbelief was the childlike trust of Nathanael. He was a man of intensely earnest nature, one whose faith took hold upon unseen realities. Yet Philip was a student in the school of Christ, and the divine Teacher bore patiently with his unbelief and dullness. When the Holy Spirit was poured out upon the disciples, Philip became a teacher after the divine order. He knew whereof he spoke, and he taught with an assurance that carried conviction to the hearers.

While Jesus was preparing the disciples for their ordination, one who had not been summoned urged his presence among them. It was Judas Iscariot, a man who professed to be a follower of Christ. He now came forward, soliciting a place in this inner circle of disciples. With great earnestness and apparent sincerity he declared, "Master, I will follow Thee whithersoever Thou goest." Jesus neither repulsed nor welcomed him, but uttered only the mournful words: "The foxes have holes, and the birds of the air have nests; but the Son of man hath not where to lay His head." Matt. 8:19, 20. Judas believed Jesus to be the Messiah; and by joining the apostles, he hoped to secure a high position in the new kingdom. This hope Jesus designed to cut off by the statement of His poverty.

The disciples were anxious that Judas should become one of their number. He was of commanding appearance, a man of keen discernment and executive ability, and they commended him to Jesus as one who would greatly assist Him in His work. They were surprised that Jesus received him so coolly.

The disciples had been much disappointed that Jesus had not tried to secure the co-operation of the leaders in Israel. They felt that it was a mistake not to strengthen His cause by securing the support of these influential men. If He had repulsed Judas, they would, in their own minds, have questioned the wisdom of their Master. The after history of Judas would show them the danger of allowing any worldly consideration to have weight in deciding the fitness of men for the work of God. The co-operation of such men as the disciples were anxious to secure would have betrayed the work into the hands of its worst enemies.

Yet when Judas joined the disciples, he was not insensible to the beauty of the character of Christ. He felt the influence of that divine power which was drawing souls to the Saviour. He who came not to break the bruised reed nor quench the smoking flax would not repulse this soul while even one desire was reaching toward the light. The Saviour read the heart of Judas; He knew the depths of iniquity to which, unless delivered by the grace of God, Judas would sink. In connecting this man with Himself, He placed him where he might, day by day, be brought in contact with the outflowing of His own unselfish love. If he would open his heart to Christ, divine grace would banish the demon of selfishness, and even Judas might become a subject of the kingdom of God.

God takes men as they are, with the human elements in their character, and trains them for His service, if they will be disciplined and learn of Him. They are not chosen because they are perfect, but notwithstanding their imperfections, that through the knowledge and practice of the truth, through the grace of Christ, they may become transformed into His image.

Judas had the same opportunities as had the other disciples. He listened to the same precious lessons. But the practice of the truth, which Christ required, was at variance with the desires and purposes of Judas, and he would not yield his ideas in order to receive wisdom from Heaven.

How tenderly the Saviour dealt with him who was to be His betrayer! In His teaching, Jesus dwelt upon principles of benevolence that struck at the very root of covetousness. He presented before Judas the heinous character of greed, and many a time the disciple realized that his character had been portrayed, and his sin pointed out; but he would not confess and forsake his unrighteousness. He was self-sufficient, and instead of resisting temptation, he continued to follow his fraudulent practices. Christ was before him, a living example of what he must become if he reaped the benefit of the divine mediation and ministry; but lesson after lesson fell unheeded on the ears of Judas.

Jesus dealt him no sharp rebuke for his covetousness, but with divine patience bore with this erring man, even while giving him evidence that He read his heart as an open book. He presented before him the highest incentives for right doing; and in rejecting the light of Heaven, Judas would be without excuse.

Instead of walking in the light, Judas chose to retain his defects. Evil desires, revengeful passions, dark and sullen thoughts, were cherished, until Satan had full control of the man. Judas became a representative of the enemy of Christ.

When he came into association with Jesus, he had some precious traits of character that might

have been made a blessing to the church. If he had been willing to wear the yoke of Christ, he might have been among the chief of the apostles; but he hardened his heart when his defects were pointed out, and in pride and rebellion chose his own selfish ambitions, and thus unfitted himself for the work that God would have given him to do.

All the disciples had serious faults when Jesus called them to His service. Even John, who came into closest association with the meek and lowly One, was not himself naturally meek and yielding. He and his brother were called "the sons of thunder." While they were with Jesus, any slight shown to Him aroused their indignation and combativeness. Evil temper, revenge, the spirit of criticism, were all in the beloved disciple. He was proud, and ambitious to be first in the kingdom of God. But day by day, in contrast with his own violent spirit, he beheld the tenderness and forbearance of Jesus, and heard His lessons of humility and patience. He opened his heart to the divine influence, and became not only a hearer but a doer of the Saviour's words. Self was hid in Christ. He learned to wear the yoke of Christ and to bear His burden.

Jesus reproved His disciples, He warned and cautioned them; but John and his brethren did not leave Him; they chose Jesus, notwithstanding the reproofs. The Saviour did not withdraw from them because of their weakness and errors. They continued to the end to share His trials and to learn the lessons of His life. By beholding Christ, they became transformed in character.

The apostles differed widely in habits and disposition. There were the publican, Levi-Matthew, and the fiery zealot Simon, the uncompromising hater of the authority of Rome; the generous, impulsive Peter, and the mean-spirited Judas; Thomas, truehearted, yet timid and fearful, Philip, slow of heart, and inclined to doubt, and the ambitious, outspoken sons of Zebedee, with their brethren. These were brought together, with their different faults, all with inherited and cultivated tendencies to evil; but in and through Christ they were to dwell in the family of God, learning to become one in faith, in doctrine, in spirit. They would have their tests, their grievances, their differences of opinion; but while Christ was abiding in the heart, there could be no dissension. His love would lead to love for one another; the lessons of the Master would lead to the harmonizing of all differences, bringing the disciples into unity, till they would be of one mind and one judgment. Christ is the great center, and they would approach one another just in proportion as they approached the center.

When Jesus had ended His instruction to the disciples, He gathered the little band close about Him, and kneeling in the midst of them, and laying His hands upon their heads, He offered a prayer dedicating them to His sacred work. Thus the Lord's disciples were ordained to the gospel ministry.

As His representatives among men, Christ does not choose angels who have never fallen, but human beings, men of like passions with those they seek to save. Christ took upon Himself humanity, that He might reach humanity. Divinity needed humanity; for it required both the divine and the human to bring salvation to the world. Divinity needed humanity, that humanity might afford a channel of communication between God and man. So with the servants and messengers of Christ. Man needs a power outside of and beyond himself, to restore him to the likeness of God, and enable him to do the work of God; but this does not make the human agency unessential. Humanity lays hold upon divine power, Christ dwells in the heart by faith; and through co-operation with the divine, the power of man becomes efficient for good.

He who called the fishermen of Galilee is still calling men to His service. And He is just as willing to manifest His power through us as through the first disciples. However imperfect and sinful we may be, the Lord holds out to us the offer of partnership with Himself, of apprenticeship to Christ. He invites us to come under the divine instruction, that, uniting with Christ, we may work the works of God.

"We have this treasure in earthen vessels, that the exceeding greatness of the power may be of God, and not from ourselves." 2 Cor. 4:7, R. V. This is why the preaching of the gospel was committed to erring men rather than to the angels. It is manifest that the power which works through the weakness of humanity is the power of God; and thus we are encouraged to believe that the power which can help others as weak as ourselves can help us. And those who are themselves "compassed with infirmity" should be able to "have compassion on the ignorant, and on them that are out of the way." Heb. 5:2. Having been in peril themselves, they are acquainted with the dangers and difficulties of the way, and for this reason are called to reach out for others in like peril. There are souls perplexed with doubt, burdened with infirmities, weak in faith, and unable to grasp the Unseen; but a friend whom they can see, coming to them in Christ's stead, can be a connecting link to fasten their trembling faith upon Christ.

We are to be laborers together with the heavenly angels in presenting Jesus to the world. With almost impatient eagerness the angels wait for our co-operation; for man must be the channel to communicate with man. And when we give ourselves to Christ in wholehearted devotion, angels rejoice that they may speak through our voices to reveal God's love.

31

The Sermon on the Mount

Christ seldom gathered His disciples alone to receive His words. He did not choose for His audience those only who knew the way of life. It was His work to reach the multitudes who were in ignorance and error. He gave His lessons of truth where they could reach the darkened understanding. He Himself was the Truth, standing with girded loins and hands ever outstretched to bless, and in words of warning, entreaty, and encouragement, seeking to uplift all who would come unto Him.

The Sermon on the Mount, though given especially to the disciples, was spoken in the hearing of the multitude. After the ordination of the apostles, Jesus went with them to the seaside. Here in the early morning the people had begun to assemble. Besides the usual crowds from the Galilean towns, there were people from Judea, and even from Jerusalem itself; from Perea, from Decapolis, from Idumea, away to the south of Judea; and from Tyre and Sidon, the Phoenician cities on the shore of the Mediterranean. "When they had heard what great things He did," they "came to hear Him, and to be healed of their diseases: . . . there went virtue out of Him, and healed them all." Mark 3:8; Luke 6:17-19.

The narrow beach did not afford even standing room within reach of His voice for all who desired to hear Him, and Jesus led the way back to the mountainside. Reaching a level space that offered a pleasant gathering place for the vast assembly, He seated Himself on the grass, and the disciples and the multitude followed His example.

The disciples' place was always next to Jesus. The people constantly pressed upon Him, yet the disciples understood that they were not to be crowded away from His presence. They sat close beside Him, that they might not lose a word of His instruction. They were attentive listeners, eager to understand the truths they were to make known to all lands and all ages.

With a feeling that something more than usual might be expected, they now pressed about their Master. They believed that the kingdom was soon to be established, and from the events of the morning they gathered assurance that some announcement concerning it was about to be made. A feeling of expectancy pervaded the multitude also, and eager faces gave evidence of the deep interest. As the people sat upon the green hillside, awaiting the words of the divine Teacher, their hearts were filled with thoughts of future glory. There were scribes and

This chapter is based on Matthew 5; 6; 7.

Pharisees who looked forward to the day when they should have dominion over the hated Romans, and possess the riches and splendor of the world's great empire. The poor peasants and fishermen hoped to hear the assurance that their wretched hovels, the scanty food, the life of toil, and fear of want were to be exchanged for mansions of plenty and days of ease. In place of the one coarse garment which was their covering by day, and their blanket at night, they hoped that Christ would give them the rich and costly robes of their conquerors. All hearts thrilled with the proud hope that Israel was soon to be honored before the nations as the chosen of the Lord, and Jerusalem exalted as the head of a universal kingdom.

Christ disappointed the hope of worldly greatness. In the Sermon on the Mount He sought to undo the work that had been wrought by false education, and to give His hearers a right conception of His kingdom and of His own character. Yet He did not make a direct attack on the errors of the people. He saw the misery of the world on account of sin, yet He did not present before them a vivid delineation of their wretchedness. He taught them of something infinitely better than they had known. Without combating their ideas of the kingdom of God, He told them the conditions of entrance therein, leaving them to draw their own conclusions as to its nature. The truths He taught are no less important to us than to the multitude that followed Him. We no less than they need to learn the foundation principles of the kingdom of God.

Christ's first words to the people on the mount were words of blessing. Happy are they, He said, who recognize their spiritual poverty, and feel their need of redemption. The gospel is to be preached to the poor. Not to the spiritually proud, those who claim to be rich and in need of nothing, is it revealed, but to those who are humble and contrite. One fountain only has been opened for sin, a fountain for the poor in spirit.

The proud heart strives to earn salvation; but both our title to heaven and our fitness for it are found in the righteousness of Christ. The Lord can do nothing toward the recovery of man until, convinced of his own weakness, and stripped of all self-sufficiency, he yields himself to the control of God. Then he can receive the gift that God is waiting to bestow. From the soul that feels his need, nothing is withheld. He has unrestricted access to Him in whom all fullness dwells. "For thus saith the high and lofty One that inhabiteth eternity, whose name is Holy; I dwell in the high and holy place, with him also that is of a contrite and humble spirit, to revive the spirit of the humble, and to revive the heart of the contrite ones." Isa. 57:15.

"Blessed are they that mourn: for they shall be comforted." By these words Christ does not teach that mourning in itself has power to remove the guilt of sin. He gives no sanction to pretense or to voluntary humility. The mourning of which He speaks does not consist in melancholy and lamentation. While we sorrow on account of sin, we are to rejoice in the precious privilege of being children of God.

We often sorrow because our evil deeds bring unpleasant consequences to ourselves; but this is not repentance. Real sorrow for sin is the result of the working of the Holy Spirit. The Spirit reveals the ingratitude of the heart that has slighted and grieved the Saviour, and brings us in contrition to the foot of the cross. By every sin Jesus is wounded afresh; and as we look upon Him whom we have pierced, we mourn for the sins that have brought anguish upon Him. Such mourning will lead to the renunciation of sin.

The worldling may pronounce this sorrow a weakness; but it is the strength which binds the penitent to the Infinite One with links that cannot be broken. It shows that the angels of God are bringing back to the soul the graces that were lost through hardness of heart and transgression. The tears of the penitent are only the raindrops that precede the sunshine of holiness. This sorrow heralds a joy which will be a living fountain in the soul. "Only acknowledge thine iniquity, that thou hast transgressed against the Lord thy God;" "and I will not cause Mine anger to fall upon you: for I am merciful, saith the Lord." Jer. 3:13, 12. "Unto them that mourn in Zion," He has appointed to give "beauty for ashes, the oil of joy for mourning, the garment of praise for the spirit of heaviness." Isa. 61:3.

And for those also who mourn in trial and sorrow there is comfort. The bitterness of grief and humiliation is better than the indulgences of sin. Through affliction God reveals to us the plague spots in our characters, that by His grace we may overcome our faults. Unknown chapters in regard to ourselves are opened to us, and the test comes, whether we will accept the reproof and the counsel of God. When brought into trial, we are not to fret and complain. We should not rebel, or worry ourselves out of the hand of Christ. We are to humble the soul before God. The ways of the Lord are obscure to him who desires to see things in a light pleasing to himself. They appear dark and joyless to our human nature. But God's ways are ways of mercy and the end is salvation. Elijah knew not what he was doing when in the desert he said that he had had enough of life, and prayed that he might die. The Lord in His mercy did not take him at his word. There was yet a great work for Elijah to do; and when his work was done, he was not to perish in discouragement and solitude in the wilderness. Not for him the descent into the dust of death, but the ascent in

604

glory, with the convoy of celestial chariots, to the throne on high.

God's word for the sorrowing is, "I have seen his ways, and will heal him: I will lead him also, and restore comforts unto him and to his mourners." "I will turn their mourning into joy, and will comfort them, and make them rejoice from their sorrow." Isa. 57:18; Jer. 31:13.

"Blessed are the meek." The difficulties we have to encounter may be very much lessened by that meekness which hides itself in Christ. If we possess the humility of our Master, we shall rise above the slights, the rebuffs, the annoyances, to which we are daily exposed, and they will cease to cast a gloom over the spirit. The highest evidence of nobility in a Christian is self-control. He who under abuse or cruelty fails to maintain a calm and trustful spirit robs God of His right to reveal in him His own perfection of character. Lowliness of heart is the strength that gives victory to the followers of Christ; it is the token of their connection with the courts above.

"Though the Lord be high, yet hath He respect unto the lowly." Ps. 138:6. Those who reveal the meek and lowly spirit of Christ are tenderly regarded by God. They may be looked upon with scorn by the world, but they are of great value in His sight. Not only the wise, the great, the beneficent, will gain a passport to the 302 heavenly courts; not only the busy worker, full of zeal and restless activity. No; the poor in spirit, who crave the presence of an abiding Christ, the humble in heart, whose highest ambition is to do God's will,—these will gain an abundant entrance. They will be among that number who have washed their robes and made them white in the blood of the Lamb. "Therefore are they before the throne of God, and serve Him day and night in His temple: and He that sitteth on the throne shall dwell among them." Rev. 7:15.

"Blessed are they which do hunger and thirst after righteousness." The sense of unworthiness will lead the heart to hunger and thirst for righteousness, and this desire will not be disappointed. Those who make room in their hearts for Jesus will realize His love. All who long to bear the likeness of the character of God shall be satisfied. The Holy Spirit never leaves unassisted the soul who is looking unto Jesus. He takes of the things of Christ and shows them unto him. If the eye is kept fixed on Christ, the work of the Spirit ceases not until the soul is conformed to His image. The pure element of love will expand the soul, giving it a capacity for higher attainments, for increased knowledge of heavenly things, so that it will not rest short of the fullness. "Blessed are they which do hunger and thirst after righteousness; for they shall be filled."

The merciful shall find mercy, and the pure in heart shall see God. Every impure thought defiles the soul, impairs the moral sense, and tends to obliterate the impressions of the Holy Spirit. It dims the spiritual vision, so that men cannot behold God. The Lord may and does forgive the repenting sinner; but though forgiven, the soul is marred. All impurity of speech or of thought must be shunned by him who would have clear discernment of spiritual truth.

But the words of Christ cover more than freedom from sensual impurity, more than freedom from that ceremonial defilement which the Jews so rigorously shunned. Selfishness prevents us from beholding God. The self-seeking spirit judges of God as altogether such a one as itself. Until we have renounced this, we cannot understand Him who is love. Only the unselfish heart, the humble and trustful spirit, shall see God as "merciful and gracious, long-suffering, and abundant in goodness and truth." Ex. 34:6.

"Blessed are the peacemakers." The peace of Christ is born of truth. It is harmony with God. The world is at enmity with the law of God; sin- 305 ners are at enmity with their Maker; and as a result they are at enmity with one another. But the psalmist declares, "Great peace have they which love Thy law: and nothing shall offend them." Ps. 119:165. Men cannot manufacture peace. Human plans for the purification and uplifting of individuals or of society will fail of producing peace, because they do not reach the heart. The only power that can create or perpetuate true peace is the grace of Christ. When this is implanted in the heart, it will cast out the evil passions that cause strife and dissension. "Instead of the thorn shall come up the fir tree, and instead of the brier shall come up the myrtle tree;" and life's desert "shall rejoice, and blossom as the rose." Isa. 55:13; 35:1.

The multitudes were amazed at this teaching, which was so at variance with the precepts and example of the Pharisees. The people had come to think that happiness consisted in the possession of the things of this world, and that fame and the honor of men were much to be coveted. It was very pleasing to be called "Rabbi," and to be extolled as wise and religious, having their virtues paraded before the public. This was regarded as the crown of happiness. But in the presence of that vast throng, Jesus declared that earthly gain and honor were all the reward such persons would ever receive. He spoke with certainty, and a convincing power attended His words. The people were silenced, and a feeling of fear crept over them. They looked at one another doubtfully. Who of them would be saved if this Man's teachings were true? Many were convicted that this remarkable Teacher was actuated by the Spirit of God, and that the sentiments He uttered were divine.

After explaining what constitutes true happiness, and how it may be obtained, Jesus more definitely pointed out the duty of His disciples, as teachers chosen of God to lead others into the path of righteousness and eternal life. He knew that they would often suffer from disappointment and discouragement, that they would meet with decided opposition, that they would be insulted, and their testimony rejected. Well He knew that in the fulfillment of their mission, the humble men who listened so attentively to His words were to bear calumny, torture, imprisonment, and death, and He continued:

306 "Blessed are they which are persecuted for righteousness' sake: for theirs is the kingdom of heaven. Blessed are ye, when men shall revile you, and persecute you, and shall say all manner of evil against you falsely, for My sake. Rejoice, and be exceeding glad: for great is your reward in heaven: for so persecuted they the prophets which were before you."

The world loves sin, and hates righteousness, and this was the cause of its hostility to Jesus. All who refuse His infinite love will find Christianity a disturbing element. The light of Christ sweeps away the darkness that covers their sins, and the need of reform is made manifest. While those who yield to the influence of the Holy Spirit begin war with themselves, those who cling to sin war against the truth and its representatives.

Thus strife is created, and Christ's followers are accused as troublers of the people. But it is fellowship with God that brings them the world's enmity. They are bearing the reproach of Christ. They are treading the path that has been trodden by the noblest of the earth. Not with sorrow, but with rejoicing, should they meet persecution. Each fiery trial is God's agent for their refining. Each is fitting them for their work as colaborers with Him. Each conflict has its place in the great battle for righteousness, and each will add to the joy of their final triumph. Having this in view, the test of their faith and patience will be cheerfully accepted rather than dreaded and avoided. Anxious to fulfill their obligation to the world, fixing their desire upon the approval of God, His servants are to fulfill every duty, irrespective of the fear or the favor of men.

"Ye are the salt of the earth," Jesus said. Do not withdraw yourselves from the world in order to escape persecution. You are to abide among men, that the savor of the divine love may be as salt to preserve the world from corruption.

Hearts that respond to the influence of the Holy Spirit are the channels through which God's blessing flows. Were those who serve God removed from the earth, and His Spirit withdrawn from among men, this world would be left to desolation and destruction, the fruit of Satan's dominion. Though the wicked know it not, they owe even the blessings of this life to the presence, in the world, of God's people whom they despise and oppress. But if Christians are such in name only, they are like the salt that has lost its savor. They have no influence for good in the world. Through their misrepresentation of God they are worse than unbelievers.

"Ye are the light of the world." The Jews thought to confine the benefits of salvation to their own nation; but Christ showed them that salvation is like the sunshine. It belongs to the 307 whole world. The religion of the Bible is not to be confined between the covers of a book, nor within the walls of a church. It is not to be brought out occasionally for our own benefit, and then to be carefully laid aside again. It is to sanctify the daily life, to manifest itself in every business transaction and in all our social relations.

True character is not shaped from without, and put on; it radiates from within. If we wish to direct others in the path of righteousness, the principles of righteousness must be enshrined in our own hearts. Our profession of faith may proclaim the theory of religion, but it is our practical piety that holds forth the word of truth. The consistent life, the holy conversation, the unswerving integrity, the active, benevolent spirit, the godly example,—these are the mediums through which light is conveyed to the world.

Jesus had not dwelt on the specifications of the law, but He did not leave His hearers to conclude that He had come to set aside its requirements. He knew that spies stood ready to seize upon every word that might be wrested to serve their purpose. He knew the prejudice that existed in the minds of many of His hearers, and He said nothing to unsettle their faith in the religion and institutions that had been committed to them through Moses. Christ Himself had given both the moral and the ceremonial law. He did not come to destroy confidence in His own instruction. It was because of His great reverence for the law and the prophets that He sought to break through the wall of traditional requirements that hemmed in the Jews. While He set aside their false interpretations of the law, He carefully guarded His disciples against yielding up the vital truths committed to the Hebrews.

The Pharisees prided themselves on their obedience to the law; yet they knew so little of its principles through everyday practice that to them the Saviour's words sounded like heresy. As He swept away the rubbish under which the truth had been buried, they thought He was sweeping away the truth itself. They whispered to one another that He was making light of the law. He read their thoughts, and answered them, saying,—

"Think not that I am come to destroy the law, or the prophets: I am not come to destroy, but to fulfill." Here Jesus refutes the charge of the Pharisees. His mission to the world is to vindicate the sacred claims of that law which they charge Him with breaking. If the law of God could have been changed or abrogated, then Christ need not have suffered the consequences of our transgression. He came to explain the relation of the law to man, and to illustrate its precepts by His own life of obedience.

God has given us His holy precepts, because He loves mankind. To shield us from the results of transgression, He reveals the principles of righteousness. The law is an expression of the thought of God; when received in Christ, it becomes our thought. It lifts us above the power of natural desires and tendencies, above temptations that lead to sin. God desires us to be happy, and He gave us the precepts of the law that in obeying them we might have joy. When at Jesus' birth the angels sang,—

"Glory to God in the highest,
And on earth peace, good will toward men"
            (Luke 2:14),

they were declaring the principles of the law which He had come to magnify and make honorable.

When the law was proclaimed from Sinai, God made known to men the holiness of His character, that by contrast they might see the sinfulness of their own. The law was given to convict them of sin, and reveal their need of a Saviour. It would do this as its principles were applied to the heart by the Holy Spirit. This work it is still to do. In the life of Christ the principles of the law are made plain; and as the Holy Spirit of God touches the heart, as the light of Christ reveals to men their need of His cleansing blood and His justifying righteousness, the law is still an agent in bringing us to Christ, that we may be justified by faith. "The law of the Lord is perfect, converting the soul." Ps. 19:7.

"Till heaven and earth pass," said Jesus, "one jot or one tittle shall in nowise pass from the law, till all be fulfilled." The sun shining in the heavens, the solid earth upon which you dwell, are God's witnesses that His law is changeless and eternal. Though they may pass away, the divine precepts shall endure. "It is easier for heaven and earth to pass, than one tittle of the law to fail." Luke 16:17. The system of types that pointed to Jesus as the Lamb of God was to be abolished at His death; but the precepts of the Decalogue are as immutable as the throne of God.

Since "the law of the Lord is perfect," every variation from it must be evil. Those who disobey the commandments of God, and teach others to do so, are condemned by Christ. The Saviour's life of obedience maintained the claims of the law; it proved that the law could be kept in humanity, and showed the excellence of character that obedience would develop. All who obey as He did are likewise declaring that the law is "holy, and just, and good." Rom. 7:12. On the other hand, all who break God's commandments are sustaining Satan's claim that the law is unjust, and cannot be obeyed. Thus they second the deceptions of the great adversary, and cast dishonor upon God. They are the children of the wicked one, who was the first rebel against God's law. To admit them into heaven would again bring in the elements of discord and rebellion, and imperil the well-being of the universe. No man who willfully disregards one principle of the law shall enter the kingdom of heaven.

The rabbis counted their righteousness a passport to heaven; but Jesus declared it to be insufficient and unworthy. External ceremonies and a theoretical knowledge of truth constituted Pharisaical righteousness. The rabbis claimed to be holy through their own efforts in keeping the law; but their works had divorced righteousness from religion. While they were punctilious in ritual observances, their lives were immoral and debased. Their so-called righteousness could never enter the kingdom of heaven.

The greatest deception of the human mind in Christ's day was that a mere assent to the truth constitutes righteousness. In all human experience a theoretical knowledge of the truth has been proved to be insufficient for the saving of the soul. It does not bring forth the fruits of righteousness. A jealous regard for what is termed theological truth often accompanies a hatred of genuine truth as made manifest in life. The darkest chapters of history are burdened with the record of crimes committed by bigoted religionists. The Pharisees claimed to be children of Abraham, and boasted of their possession of the oracles of God; yet these advantages did not preserve them from selfishness, malignity, greed for gain, and the basest hypocrisy. They thought themselves the greatest religionists of the world, but their so-called orthodoxy led them to crucify the Lord of glory.

The same danger still exists. Many take it for granted that they are Christians, simply because they subscribe to certain theological tenets. But they have not brought the truth into practical life. They have not believed and loved it, therefore they have not received the power and grace that come through sanctification of the truth. Men may profess faith in the truth; but if it does not make them sincere, kind, patient, forbearing, heavenly-minded, it is a curse to its possessors, and through their influence it is a curse to the world.

The righteousness which Christ taught is conformity of heart and life to the revealed will of God. Sinful men can become righteous only as they have faith in God and maintain a vital connection with Him. Then true godliness will elevate the thoughts and ennoble the life. Then the external forms of religion accord with the Christian's internal purity. Then the ceremonies required in the service of God are not meaningless rites, like those of the hypocritical Pharisees.

Jesus takes up the commandments separately, and explains the depth and breadth of their requirement. Instead of removing one jot of their force, He shows how far-reaching their principles are, and exposes the fatal mistake of the Jews in their outward show of obedience. He declares that by the evil thought or the lustful look the law of God is transgressed. One who becomes a party to the least injustice is breaking the law and degrading his own moral nature. Murder first exists in the mind. He who gives hatred a place in his heart is setting his feet in the path of the murderer, and his offerings are abhorrent to God.

The Jews cultivated a spirit of retaliation. In their hatred of the Romans they gave utterance to hard denunciations, and pleased the wicked one by manifesting his attributes. Thus they were training themselves to do the terrible deeds to which he led them on. In the religious life of the Pharisees there was nothing to recommend piety to the Gentiles. Jesus bade them not to deceive themselves with the thought that they could in heart rise up against their oppressors, and cherish the longing to avenge their wrongs.

It is true there is an indignation that is justifiable, even in the followers of Christ. When they see that God is dishonored, and His service brought into disrepute, when they see the innocent oppressed, a righteous indignation stirs the soul. Such anger, born of sensitive morals, is not a sin. But those who at any supposed provocation feel at liberty to indulge anger or resentment are opening the heart to Satan. Bitterness and animosity must be banished from the soul if we would be in harmony with heaven.

The Saviour goes farther than this. He says, "If thou bring thy gift to the altar, and there rememberest that thy brother hath aught against thee; leave there thy gift before the altar, and go 311 thy way; first be reconciled to thy brother, and then come and offer thy gift." Many are zealous in religious services, while between them and their brethren are unhappy differences which they might reconcile. God requires them to do all in their power to restore harmony. Until they do this, He cannot accept their services. The Christian's duty in this matter is clearly pointed out.

God pours His blessings upon all. "He maketh His sun to rise on the evil and on the good, and sendeth rain on the just and on the unjust." He is "kind unto the unthankful and to the evil." Luke 6:35. He bids us to be like Him.

"Bless them that curse you," said Jesus; "do good to them that hate you, . . . that ye may be the children of your Father which is in heaven." These are the principles of the law, and they are the wellsprings of life.

God's ideal for His children is higher than the highest human thought can reach. "Be ye therefore perfect, even as your Father which is in heaven is perfect." This command is a promise. The plan of redemption contemplates our complete recovery from the power of Satan. Christ always separates the contrite soul from sin. He came to destroy the works of the devil, and He has made provision that the Holy Spirit shall be imparted to every repentant soul, to keep him from sinning.

The tempter's agency is not to be accounted an excuse for one wrong act. Satan is jubilant when he hears the professed followers of Christ making excuses for their deformity of character. It is these excuses that lead to sin. There is no excuse for sinning. A holy temper, a Christlike life, is accessible to every repenting, believing child of God.

The ideal of Christian character is Christlikeness. As the Son of man was perfect in His life, so His followers are to be perfect in their life. Jesus was in all things made like unto His brethren. He became flesh, even as we are. He was hungry and thirsty and weary. He was sustained by food and refreshed by sleep. He shared the lot of man; yet He was the blameless Son of God. He was God in the flesh. His character is to be ours. The Lord says of those who believe in Him, "I will dwell in them, and walk in them; and I will be their God, and they shall be My people." 2 Cor. 6:16.

Christ is the ladder that Jacob saw, the base resting on the earth, and the topmost round reaching to the gate of heaven, to the very threshold of glory. If that ladder had failed by a single step of reaching the earth, we should have been lost. But Christ reaches us where we are. He took our nature and overcame, that we through taking His nature might overcome. 312 Made "in the likeness of sinful flesh" (Rom. 8:3), He lived a sinless life. Now by His divinity He lays hold upon the throne of heaven, while by His humanity He reaches us. He bids us by faith in Him attain to the glory of the character of God. Therefore are we to be perfect, even as our "Father which is in heaven is perfect."

Jesus had shown in what righteousness consists, and had pointed to God as its source. Now He turned to practical duties. In almsgiving, in prayer, in fasting, He said, let nothing be done to attract attention or win praise to self. Give in sincerity, for the benefit of the suffering poor. In prayer, let the soul commune with God. In fasting, go not with the head bowed down, and heart filled with thoughts of self. The heart of the Pharisee is a barren and profitless soil, in which no seeds of divine life can flourish. It is he who yields himself most unreservedly to God that will render Him the most acceptable service. For through fellowship with God men become workers together with Him in presenting His character in humanity.

The service rendered in sincerity of heart has great recompense. "Thy Father which seeth in secret Himself shall reward thee openly." By the life we live through the grace of Christ the character is formed. The original loveliness begins to be restored to the soul. The attributes of the character of Christ are imparted, and the image of the Divine begins to shine forth. The faces of men and women who walk and work with God express the peace of heaven. They are surrounded with the atmosphere of heaven. For these souls the kingdom of God has begun. They have Christ's joy, the joy of being a blessing to humanity. They have the honor of being accepted for the Master's use; they are trusted to do His work in His name.

"No man can serve two masters." We cannot serve God with a divided heart. Bible religion is not one influence among many others; its influence is to be supreme, pervading and controlling every other. It is not to be like a dash of color brushed here and there upon the canvas, but it is to pervade the whole life, as if the canvas were dipped into the color, until every thread of the fabric were dyed a deep, unfading hue.

"If therefore thine eye be single, thy whole body shall be full of light. But if thine eye be evil, thy whole body shall be full of darkness." Purity and steadfastness of purpose are the conditions of receiving light from God. He who desires to know the truth must be willing to accept all that it reveals. He can make no compromise with error. To be wavering and half-hearted in allegiance to truth is to choose the darkness of error and satanic delusion.

313

Worldly policy and the undeviating principles of righteousness do not blend into each other imperceptibly, like the colors of the rainbow. Between the two a broad, clear line is drawn by the eternal God. The likeness of Christ stands out as distinct from that of Satan as midday in contrast with midnight. And only those who live the life of Christ are His co-workers. If one sin is cherished in the soul, or one wrong practice retained in the life, the whole being is contaminated. The man becomes an instrument of unrighteousness.

All who have chosen God's service are to rest in His care. Christ pointed to the birds flying in the heavens, to the flowers of the field, and bade His hearers consider these objects of God's creation. "Are not ye of much more value than they?" He said. Matt. 6:26, R. V. The measure of divine attention bestowed on any object is proportionate to its rank in the scale of being. The little brown sparrow is watched over by Providence. The flowers of the field, the grass that carpets the earth, share the notice and care of our heavenly Father. The great Master Artist has taken thought for the lilies, making them so beautiful that they outshine the glory of Solomon. How much more does He care for man, who is the image and glory of God. He longs to see His children reveal a character after His similitude. As the sunbeam imparts to the flowers their varied and delicate tints, so does God impart to the soul the beauty of His own character.

All who choose Christ's kingdom of love and righteousness and peace, making its interest paramount to all other, are linked to the world above, and every blessing needed for this life is theirs. In the book of God's providence, the volume of life, we are each given a page. That page contains every particular of our history; even the hairs of the head are numbered. God's children are never absent from His mind.

"Be not therefore anxious for the morrow." Matt. 6:34, R. V. We are to follow Christ day by day. God does not bestow help for tomorrow. He does not give His children all the directions for their life journey at once, lest they should become confused. He tells them just as much as they can remember and perform. The strength and wisdom imparted are for the present emergency. "If any of you lack wisdom,"—for today,—"let him ask of God, that giveth to all men liberally, and upbraideth not; and it shall be given him." James 1:5.

"Judge not, that ye be not judged." Do not 314 think yourself better than other men, and set yourself up as their judge. Since you cannot discern motive, you are incapable of judging another. In criticizing him, you are passing sentence upon yourself; for you show that you are a participant with Satan, the accuser of the brethren. The Lord says, "Examine yourselves, whether ye be in the faith; prove your own selves." This is our work. "If we would judge ourselves, we should not be judged." 2 Cor. 13:5; 1 Cor. 11:31.

The good tree will produce good fruit. If the fruit is unpalatable and worthless, the tree is evil. So the fruit borne in the life testifies as to the condition of the heart and the excellence of the character. Good works can never purchase salvation, but they are an evidence of the faith that acts by love and purifies the soul. And though the eternal reward is not bestowed because of our merit, yet it will be in proportion to the work that has been done through the grace of Christ.

Thus Christ set forth the principles of His kingdom, and showed them to be the great rule of life. To impress the lesson He adds an illustration. It is not enough, He says, for you to hear My words. By obedience you must make them the foundation of your character. Self is but shifting sand. If you build upon human theories and inventions, your house will fall. By the winds of temptation, the tempests of trial, it will be swept away. But these principles that I have given will endure. Receive Me; build on My words.

"Everyone therefore which heareth these words of Mine, and doeth them, shall be likened unto a wise man, which built his house upon the rock: and the rain descended, and the floods came, and the winds blew, and beat upon that house; and it fell not: for it was founded upon the rock." Matt. 7:24, 25, R. V.

32

The Centurion

Christ had said to the nobleman whose son He healed, "Except ye see signs and wonders, ye will not believe." John 4:48. He was grieved that His own nation should require these outward signs of His Messiahship. Again and again He had marveled at their unbelief. But He marveled at the faith of the centurion who came to Him. The centurion did not question the Saviour's power. He did not even ask Him to come in person to perform the miracle. "Speak the word only," he said, "and my servant shall be healed."

The centurion's servant had been stricken with palsy, and lay at the point of death. Among the Romans the servants were slaves, bought and sold in the market places, and treated with abuse and cruelty; but the centurion was tenderly attached to his servant, and greatly desired his recovery. He believed that Jesus could heal him. He had not seen the Saviour, but the reports he heard had inspired him with faith. Notwithstanding the formalism of the Jews, this Roman was convinced that their religion was superior to his own. Already he had broken through the barriers of national prejudice and hatred that separated the conquerors from the conquered people. He had manifested respect for the service of God, and had shown kindness to the Jews as His worshipers. In the teaching of Christ, as it had been reported to him, he found that which met the need of the soul. All that was spiritual within him responded to the Saviour's words. But he felt unworthy to come into the presence of Jesus, and he appealed to the Jewish elders to make request for the healing of his servant. They were acquainted with the Great Teacher, and would, he thought, know how to approach Him so as to win His favor.

As Jesus entered Capernaum, He was met by a delegation of the elders, who told Him of the centurion's desire. They urged "that he was worthy for whom He should do this: for he loveth

our nation, and he hath built us a synagogue."

Jesus immediately set out for the officer's home; but, pressed by the multitude, He advanced slowly. The news of His coming preceded Him, and the centurion, in his self-distrust, sent Him the message, "Lord, trouble not Thyself: for I am not worthy that Thou shouldest enter under my roof." But the Saviour kept on His way, and the centurion, venturing at last to approach Him, completed the message, saying, "Neither thought I myself worthy to come unto Thee;" "but speak the word only, and my servant shall be healed. For I am a man under authority, having soldiers under me: and I say to this man, Go, and he goeth; and to another, Come, and he cometh; and to my servant, Do this, and he doeth it." As I represent the power of Rome, and my soldiers recognize my authority as supreme, so dost Thou represent the power of the Infinite God, and all created things obey Thy word. Thou canst command the disease to depart, and it shall obey Thee. Thou canst summon Thy heavenly messengers, and they shall impart healing virtue. Speak but the word, and my servant shall be healed.

"When Jesus heard these things, He marveled at him, and turned Him about, and said unto the people that followed Him, I say unto you, I have not found so great faith, no, not in Israel." And to the centurion He said, "As thou hast believed, so be it done unto thee. And his servant was healed in the selfsame hour."

The Jewish elders who recommended the centurion to Christ had shown how far they were from possessing the spirit of the gospel. They did not recognize that our great need is our only claim on God's mercy. In their self-righteousness they commended the centurion because of the favor he had shown to "our nation." But the centurion said of himself, "I am not worthy." His heart had been touched by the grace of Christ. He saw his own unworthiness; yet he feared not to ask help. He trusted not to his own goodness; his argument was his great need. His faith took hold upon Christ in His true character. He did not believe in Him merely as a worker of miracles, but as the friend and Saviour of mankind.

It is thus that every sinner may come to Christ. "Not by works of righteousness which we have done, but according to His mercy He saved us." Titus 3:5. When Satan tells you that you are a sinner, and cannot hope to receive blessing from God, tell him that Christ came into the world to save sinners. We have nothing to recommend us to God; but the plea that we may urge now and ever is our utterly helpless condition that makes His redeeming power a necessity. Renouncing all self-dependence, we may look to the cross of Calvary and say,—

"In my hand no price I bring;

Simply to Thy cross I cling."

The Jews had been instructed from childhood concerning the work of the Messiah. The inspired utterances of patriarchs and prophets and the symbolic teaching of the sacrificial service had been theirs. But they had disregarded the light; and now they saw in Jesus nothing to be desired. But the centurion, born in heathenism, educated in the idolatry of imperial Rome, trained as a soldier, seemingly cut off from spiritual life by his education and surroundings, and still further shut out by the bigotry of the Jews, and by the contempt of his own countrymen for the people of Israel,—this man perceived the truth to which the children of Abraham were blinded. He did not wait to see whether the Jews themselves would receive the One who claimed to be their Messiah. As the "light, which lighteth every man that cometh into the world" (John 1:9) had shone upon him, he had, though afar off, discerned the glory of the Son of God.

To Jesus this was an earnest of the work which the gospel was to accomplish among the Gentiles. With joy He looked forward to the gathering of souls from all nations to His kingdom. With deep sadness He pictured to the Jews the result of their rejection of His grace: "I say unto you, That many shall come from the east and west, and shall sit down with Abraham, and Isaac, and Jacob, in the kingdom of heaven. But the children of the kingdom shall be cast out into outer darkness: there shall be weeping and gnashing of teeth." Alas, how many are still preparing for the same fatal disappointment! While souls in heathen darkness accept His grace, how many there are in Christian lands upon whom the light shines only to be disregarded.

More than twenty miles from Capernaum, on a tableland overlooking the wide, beautiful plain of Esdraelon, lay the village of Nain, and thither Jesus next bent His steps. Many of His disciples and others were with Him, and all along the way the people came, longing for His words of love and pity, bringing their sick for His healing, and ever with the hope that He who wielded such wondrous power would make Himself known as the King of Israel. A multitude thronged His steps, and it was a glad, expectant company that followed Him up the rocky path toward the gate of the mountain village.

As they draw near, a funeral train is seen coming from the gates. With slow, sad steps it is proceeding to the place of burial. On an open bier carried in front is the body of the dead, and about it are the mourners, filling the air with their wailing cries. All the people of the town seem to have gathered to show their respect for the dead and their sympathy with the bereaved.

It was a sight to awaken sympathy. The deceased was the only son of his mother, and she a widow. The lonely mourner was following to the grave her sole earthly support and comfort. "When the Lord saw her, He had compassion on her." As she moved on blindly, weeping, noting not His presence, He came close beside her, and gently said, "Weep not." Jesus was about to change her grief to joy, yet He could not forbear this expression of tender sympathy.

"He came and touched the bier;" to Him even contact with death could impart no defilement. The bearers stood still, and the lamentations of the mourners ceased. The two companies gathered about the bier, hoping against hope. One was present who had banished disease and vanquished demons; was death also subject to His power?

In clear, authoritative voice the words are spoken, "Young man, I say unto thee, Arise." That voice pierces the ears of the dead. The young man opens his eyes. Jesus takes him by the hand, and lifts him up. His gaze falls upon her who has been weeping beside him, and mother and son unite in a long, clinging, joyous embrace. The multitude look on in silence, as if spellbound. "There came a fear on all." Hushed and reverent they stood for a little time, as if in the very presence of God. Then they "glorified God, saying, That a great prophet is risen up among us; and, That God hath visited His people." The funeral train returned to Nain as a triumphal procession. "And this rumor of Him went forth throughout all Judea, and throughout all the region round about."

He who stood beside the sorrowing mother at the gate of Nain, watches with every mourning one beside the bier. He is touched with sympathy for our grief. His heart, that loved and pitied, is a heart of unchangeable tenderness. His word, that called the dead to life, is no less efficacious now than when spoken to the young man of Nain. He says, "All power is given unto Me in heaven and in earth." Matt. 28:18. That power is not diminished by the lapse of years, nor exhausted by the ceaseless activity of His overflowing grace. To all who believe on Him He is still a living Saviour.

Jesus changed the mother's grief to joy when He gave back her son; yet the youth was but called forth to this earthly life, to endure its sorrows, its toils, and its perils, and to pass again under the power of death. But Jesus comforts our sorrow for the dead with a message of infinite hope: "I am He that liveth, and was dead; and, behold, I am alive forevermore, . . . and have the keys of hell and of death." "Forasmuch then as the children are partakers of flesh and blood, He also Himself likewise took part of the same; that through death He might destroy him that had the power of death, that is, the devil; and deliver them who through fear of death were all their lifetime subject to bondage." Rev. 1:18; Heb. 2:14, 15.

Satan cannot hold the dead in his grasp when the Son of God bids them live. He cannot hold in spiritual death one soul who in faith receives Christ's word of power. God is saying to all who are dead in sin, "Awake thou that sleepest, and arise from the dead." Eph. 5:14. That word is eternal life. As the word of God which bade the first man live, still gives us life; as Christ's word, "Young man, I say unto thee, Arise," gave life to the youth of Nain, so that word, "Arise from the dead," is life to the soul that receives it. God "hath delivered us from the power of darkness, and hath translated us into the kingdom of His dear Son." Col. 1:13. It is all offered us in His word. If we receive the word, we have the deliverance.

And "if the Spirit of Him that raised up Jesus from the dead dwell in you, He that raised up Christ from the dead shall also quicken your mortal bodies by His Spirit that dwelleth in you." "For the Lord Himself shall descend from heaven with a shout, with the voice of the Archangel, and with the trump of God: and the dead in Christ shall rise first: then we which are alive and remain shall be caught up together with them in the clouds, to meet the Lord in the air: and so shall we ever be with the Lord." Rom. 8:11; 1 Thess. 4:16, 17. This is the word of comfort wherewith He bids us comfort one another.

321

33

Who Are My Brethren?

The sons of Joseph were far from being in sympathy with Jesus in His work. The reports that reached them in regard to His life and labors filled them with astonishment and dismay. They heard that He devoted entire nights to prayer, that through the day He was thronged by great companies of people, and did not give Himself time so much as to eat. His friends felt that He was wearing Himself out by His incessant labor; they were unable to account for His attitude toward the Pharisees, and there were some who feared that His reason was becoming unsettled.

His brothers heard of this, and also of the charge brought by the Pharisees that He cast out devils through the power of Satan. They felt keenly the reproach that came upon them through their relation to Jesus. They knew what a tumult His words and works created, and were not only alarmed at His bold statements, but indignant at His denunciation of the scribes and Pharisees. They decided that He must be persuaded or constrained to cease this manner of

labor, and they induced Mary to unite with them, thinking that through His love for her they might prevail upon Him to be more prudent.

It was just before this that Jesus had a second time performed the miracle of healing a man possessed, blind and dumb, and the Pharisees had reiterated the charge, "He casteth out devils through the prince of the devils." Matt. 9:34. Christ told them plainly that in attributing the work of the Holy Spirit to Satan, they were cutting themselves off from the fountain of blessing. Those who had spoken against Jesus Himself, not discerning His divine character, might receive forgiveness; for through the Holy Spirit they might be brought to see their error and repent. Whatever the sin, if the soul repents and believes, the guilt is washed away in the blood of Christ; but he who rejects the work of the Holy Spirit is placing himself where repentance and faith cannot come to him. It is by the Spirit that God works upon the heart; when men willfully reject the Spirit, and declare It to be from Satan, they cut off the channel by which God can communicate with them. When the Spirit is finally rejected, there is no more that God can do for the soul.

The Pharisees to whom Jesus spoke this warning did not themselves believe the charge they brought against Him. There was not one of those dignitaries but had felt drawn toward the Saviour. They had heard the Spirit's voice in their own hearts declaring Him to be the Anointed of Israel, and urging them to confess themselves His disciples. In the light of His presence they had realized their unholiness, and had longed for a righteousness which they could not create. But after their rejection of Him it would be too humiliating to receive Him as the Messiah. Having set their feet in the path of unbelief, they were too proud to confess their error. And in order to avoid acknowledging the truth, they tried with desperate violence to dispute the Saviour's teaching. The evidence of His power and mercy exasperated them. They could not prevent the Saviour from working miracles, they could not silence His teaching; but they did everything in their power to misrepresent Him and to falsify His words. Still the convicting Spirit of God followed them, and they had to build up many barriers in order to withstand its power. The mightiest agency that can be brought to bear upon the human heart was striving with them, but they would not yield.

It is not God that blinds the eyes of men or hardens their hearts. He sends them light to correct their errors, and to lead them in safe paths; it is by the rejection of this light that the eyes are blinded and the heart hardened. Often the process is gradual, and almost imperceptible. Light comes to the soul through God's word,

322

through His servants, or by the direct agency of His Spirit; but when one ray of light is disregarded, there is a partial benumbing of the spiritual perceptions, and the second revealing of light is less clearly discerned. So the darkness increases, until it is night in the soul. Thus it had been with these Jewish leaders. They were convinced that a divine power attended Christ, but in order to resist the truth, they attributed the work of the Holy Spirit to Satan. In doing this they deliberately chose deception; they yielded themselves to Satan, and henceforth they were controlled by his power.

Closely connected with Christ's warning in regard to the sin against the Holy Spirit is a warning against idle and evil words. The words are an indication of that which is in the heart. "Out of the abundance of the heart the mouth speaketh." But the words are more than an indication of character; they have power to react on the character. Men are influenced by their own words. Often under a momentary impulse, prompted by Satan, they give utterance to jealousy or evil surmising, expressing that which they do not really believe; but the expression reacts on the thoughts. They are deceived by their words, and come to believe that true which was spoken at Satan's instigation. Having once expressed an opinion or decision, they are often too proud to retract it, and try to prove themselves in the right, until they come to believe that they are. It is dangerous to utter a word of doubt, dangerous to question and criticize divine light. The habit of careless and irreverent criticism reacts upon the character, in fostering irreverence and unbelief. Many a man indulging this habit has gone on unconscious of danger, until he was ready to criticize and reject the work of the Holy Spirit. Jesus said, "Every idle word that men shall speak, they shall give account thereof in the day of judgment. For by thy words thou shalt be justified, and by thy words thou shalt be condemned."

Then He added a warning to those who had been impressed by His words, who had heard Him gladly, but who had not surrendered themselves for the indwelling of the Holy Spirit. It is not only by resistance but by neglect that the soul is destroyed. "When the unclean spirit is gone out of a man," said Jesus, "he walketh through dry places, seeking rest, and findeth none. Then he saith, I will return into my house from whence I came out; and when he is come, he findeth it empty, swept, and garnished. Then goeth he, and taketh with himself seven other spirits more wicked than himself, and they enter in and dwell there."

There were many in Christ's day, as there are today, over whom the control of Satan for the time seemed broken; through the grace of God they were set free from the evil spirits that had held dominion over the soul. They rejoiced in the love of God; but, like the stony-ground hearers of the parable, they did not abide in His love. They did not surrender themselves to God daily, that Christ might dwell in the heart; and when the evil spirit returned, with "seven other spirits more wicked than himself," they were wholly dominated by the power of evil.

When the soul surrenders itself to Christ, a new power takes possession of the new heart. A change is wrought which man can never accomplish for himself. It is a supernatural work, bringing a supernatural element into human nature. The soul that is yielded to Christ becomes His own fortress, which He holds in a revolted world, and He intends that no authority shall be known in it but His own. A soul thus kept in possession by the heavenly agencies is impregnable to the assaults of Satan. But unless we do yield ourselves to the control of Christ, we shall be dominated by the wicked one. We must inevitably be under the control of the one or the other of the two great powers that are contending for the supremacy of the world. It is not necessary for us deliberately to choose the service of the kingdom of darkness in order to come under its dominion. We have only to neglect to ally ourselves with the kingdom of light. If we do not co-operate with the heavenly agencies, Satan will take possession of the heart, and will make it his abiding place. The only defense against evil is the indwelling of Christ in the heart through faith in His righteousness. Unless we become vitally connected with God, we can never resist the unhallowed effects of self-love, self-indulgence, and temptation to sin. We may leave off many bad habits, for the time we may part company with Satan; but without a vital connection with God, through the surrender of ourselves to Him moment by moment, we shall be overcome. Without a personal acquaintance with Christ, and a continual communion, we are at the mercy of the enemy, and shall do his bidding in the end.

"The last state of that man is worse than the first. Even so," said Jesus, "shall it be also unto this wicked generation." There are none so hardened as those who have slighted the invitation of mercy, and done despite to the Spirit of grace. The most common manifestation of the sin against the Holy Spirit is in persistently slighting Heaven's invitation to repent. Every step in the rejection of Christ is a step toward the rejection of salvation, and toward the sin against the Holy Spirit.

In rejecting Christ the Jewish people committed the unpardonable sin; and by refusing the invitation of mercy, we may commit the same error. We offer insult to the Prince of life, and put Him to shame before the synagogue of Satan and before the heavenly universe when we refuse to listen to His delegated messengers, and instead listen to the agents of Satan, who would draw the soul away from Christ. So long as one does this, he can find no hope or pardon, and he will finally lose all desire to be reconciled to God.

While Jesus was still teaching the people, His disciples brought the message that His mother and His brothers were without, and desired to see Him. He knew what was in their hearts, and "He answered and said unto him that told Him, Who is My mother? and who are My brethren? And He stretched forth His hand toward His disciples, and said, Behold My mother and My brethren! For whosoever shall do the will of My Father which is in heaven, the same is My brother, and sister, and mother."

All who would receive Christ by faith were united to Him by a tie closer than that of human kinship. They would become one with Him, as He was one with the Father. As a believer and doer of His words, His mother was more nearly and savingly related to Him than through her natural relationship. His brothers would receive no benefit from their connection with Him unless they accepted Him as their personal Saviour.

What a support Christ would have found in His earthly relatives if they had believed in Him as one from heaven, and had co-operated with Him in doing the work of God! Their unbelief cast a shadow over the earthly life of Jesus. It was a part of the bitterness of that cup of woe which He drained for us.

326   The enmity kindled in the human heart against the gospel was keenly felt by the Son of God, and it was most painful to Him in His home; for His own heart was full of kindness and love, and He appreciated tender regard in the family relation. His brothers desired that He should concede to their ideas, when such a course would have been utterly out of harmony with His divine mission. They looked upon Him as in need of their counsel. They judged Him from their human point of view, and thought that if He would speak only such things as would be acceptable to the scribes and Pharisees, He would avoid the disagreeable controversy that His words aroused. They thought that He was beside Himself in claiming divine authority, and in placing Himself before the rabbis as a reprover of their sins. They knew that the Pharisees were seeking occasion to accuse Him, and they felt that He had given them sufficient occasion.

With their short measuring line they could not fathom the mission which He came to fulfill, and therefore could not sympathize with Him in His trials. Their coarse, unappreciative words showed that they had no true perception of His character, and did not discern that the divine blended with the human. They often saw Him full of grief; but instead of comforting Him, their spirit and words only wounded His heart.

His sensitive nature was tortured, His motives were misunderstood, His work was uncomprehended.

His brothers often brought forward the philosophy of the Pharisees, which was threadbare and hoary with age, and presumed to think that they could teach Him who understood all truth, and comprehended all mysteries. They freely condemned that which they could not understand. Their reproaches probed Him to the quick, and His soul was wearied and distressed. They avowed faith in God, and thought they were vindicating God, when God was with them in the flesh, and they knew Him not.

These things made His path a thorny one to travel. So pained was Christ by the misapprehension in His own home that it was a relief to Him to go where it did not exist. There was one home that He loved to visit,—the home of Lazarus, and Mary, and Martha; for in the atmosphere of faith and love His spirit had rest. Yet there were none on earth who could comprehend His divine mission, or know the burden which He bore in behalf of humanity. Often He could find relief only in being alone, and communing with His heavenly Father.

Those who are called to suffer for Christ's 327 sake, who have to endure misapprehension and distrust, even in their own home, may find comfort in the thought that Jesus has endured the same. He is moved with compassion for them. He bids them find companionship in Him, and relief where He found it, in communion with the Father.

Those who accept Christ as their personal Saviour are not left as orphans, to bear the trials of life alone. He receives them as members of the heavenly family; He bids them call His Father their Father. They are His "little ones," dear to the heart of God, bound to Him by the most tender and abiding ties. He has toward them an exceeding tenderness, as far surpassing what our father or mother has felt toward us in our helplessness as the divine is above the human.

Of Christ's relation to His people, there is a beautiful illustration in the laws given to Israel. When through poverty a Hebrew had been forced to part with his patrimony, and to sell himself as a bondservant, the duty of redeeming him and his inheritance fell to the one who was nearest of kin. See Lev. 25:25, 47-49; Ruth 2:20. So the work of redeeming us and our inheritance, lost through sin, fell upon Him who is "near of kin" unto us. It was to redeem us that He became our kinsman. Closer than father, mother, brother, friend, or lover is the Lord our Saviour. "Fear not," He says, "for I have redeemed thee, I have called thee by thy name; thou art Mine." "Since thou wast precious in My sight, thou hast been honorable, and I have loved thee: therefore will I give men for thee, and people for thy life." Isa. 43:1, 4.

Christ loves the heavenly beings that surround His throne; but what shall account for the great love wherewith He has loved us? We cannot understand it, but we can know it true in our own experience. And if we do hold the relation of kinship to Him, with what tenderness should we regard those who are brethren and sisters of our Lord! Should we not be quick to recognize the claims of our divine relationship? Adopted into the family of God, should we not honor our Father and our kindred?

328

34

The Invitation

"Come unto Me, all ye that labor and are heavy-laden, and I will give you rest."

These words of comfort were spoken to the multitude that followed Jesus. The Saviour had said that only through Himself could men receive a knowledge of God. He had spoken of His disciples as the ones to whom a knowledge of heavenly things had been given. But He left none to feel themselves shut out from His care and love. All who labor and are heavy-laden may come unto Him.

Scribes and rabbis, with their punctilious attention to religious forms, had a sense of want that rites of penance could never satisfy. Publicans and sinners might pretend to be content with the sensual and earthly, but in their hearts were distrust and fear. Jesus looked upon the distressed and heart burdened, those whose hopes were blighted, and who with earthly joys were seeking to quiet the longing of the soul, and He invited all to find rest in Him.

Tenderly He bade the toiling people, "Take My yoke upon you, and learn of Me; for I am meek and lowly in heart: and ye shall find rest unto your souls."

In these words Christ is speaking to every human being. Whether they know it or not, all are weary and heavy-laden. All are weighed down with burdens that only Christ can remove. The heaviest burden that we bear is the burden of sin. If we were left to bear this burden, it

329 would crush us. But the Sinless One has taken our place. "The Lord hath laid on Him the iniquity of us all." Isa. 53:6. He has borne the burden of our guilt. He will take the load from our weary shoulders. He will give us rest. The burden of care and sorrow also He will bear. He invites us to cast all our care upon Him; for He carries us upon His heart.

The Elder Brother of our race is by the eternal throne. He looks upon every soul who is turning his face toward Him as the Saviour. He knows by experience what are the weaknesses of

humanity, what are our wants, and where lies the strength of our temptations; for He was in all points tempted like as we are, yet without sin. He is watching over you, trembling child of God. Are you tempted? He will deliver. Are you weak? He will strengthen. Are you ignorant? He will enlighten. Are you wounded? He will heal. The Lord "telleth the number of the stars;" and yet "He healeth the broken in heart, and bindeth up their wounds." Ps. 147:4, 3. "Come unto Me," is His invitation. Whatever your anxieties and trials, spread out your case before the Lord. Your spirit will be braced for endurance. The way will be opened for you to disentangle yourself from embarrassment and difficulty. The weaker and more helpless you know yourself to be, the stronger will you become in His strength. The heavier your burdens, the more blessed the rest in casting them upon the Burden Bearer. The rest that Christ offers depends upon conditions, but these conditions are plainly specified. They are those with which all can comply. He tells us just how His rest is to be found.

"Take My yoke upon you," Jesus says. The yoke is an instrument of service. Cattle are yoked for labor, and the yoke is essential that they may labor effectually. By this illustration Christ teaches us that we are called to service as long as life shall last. We are to take upon us His yoke, that we may be co-workers with Him.

The yoke that binds to service is the law of God. The great law of love revealed in Eden, proclaimed upon Sinai, and in the new covenant written in the heart, is that which binds the human worker to the will of God. If we were left to follow our own inclinations, to go just where our will would lead us, we should fall into Satan's ranks and become possessors of his attributes. Therefore God confines us to His will, which is high, and noble, and elevating. He desires that we shall patiently and wisely take up the duties of service. The yoke of service Christ Himself has borne in humanity. He said, "I delight to do Thy will, O My God: yea, Thy law is within My heart." Ps. 40:8. "I came down from heaven, not to do Mine own will, but the 330 will of Him that sent Me." John 6:38. Love for God, zeal for His glory, and love for fallen humanity, brought Jesus to earth to suffer and to die. This was the controlling power of His life. This principle He bids us adopt.

There are many whose hearts are aching under a load of care because they seek to reach the world's standard. They have chosen its service, accepted its perplexities, adopted its customs. Thus their character is marred, and their life made a weariness. In order to gratify ambition and worldly desires, they wound the conscience, and bring upon themselves an additional burden of remorse. The continual worry is wearing out the life forces. Our Lord desires them to lay aside this yoke of bondage. He

This chapter is based on Matthew 11:28-30.

invites them to accept His yoke; He says, "My yoke is easy, and My burden is light." He bids them seek first the kingdom of God and His righteousness, and His promise is that all things needful to them for this life shall be added. Worry is blind, and cannot discern the future; but Jesus sees the end from the beginning. In every difficulty He has His way prepared to bring relief. Our heavenly Father has a thousand ways to provide for us, of which we know nothing. Those who accept the one principle of making the service and honor of God supreme will find perplexities vanish, and a plain path before their feet.

"Learn of Me," says Jesus; "for I am meek and lowly in heart: and ye shall find rest." We are to enter the school of Christ, to learn from Him meekness and lowliness. Redemption is that process by which the soul is trained for heaven. This training means a knowledge of Christ. It means emancipation from ideas, habits, and practices that have been gained in the school of the prince of darkness. The soul must be delivered from all that is opposed to loyalty to God.

In the heart of Christ, where reigned perfect harmony with God, there was perfect peace. He was never elated by applause, nor dejected by censure or disappointment. Amid the greatest opposition and the most cruel treatment, He was still of good courage. But many who profess to be His followers have an anxious, troubled heart, because they are afraid to trust themselves with God. They do not make a complete surrender to Him; for they shrink from the consequences that such a surrender may involve. Unless they do make this surrender, they cannot find peace.

It is the love of self that brings unrest. When we are born from above, the same mind will be [331] in us that was in Jesus, the mind that led Him to humble Himself that we might be saved. Then we shall not be seeking the highest place. We shall desire to sit at the feet of Jesus, and learn of Him. We shall understand that the value of our work does not consist in making a show and noise in the world, and in being active and zealous in our own strength. The value of our work is in proportion to the impartation of the Holy Spirit. Trust in God brings holier qualities of mind, so that in patience we may possess our souls.

The yoke is placed upon the oxen to aid them in drawing the load, to lighten the burden. So with the yoke of Christ. When our will is swallowed up in the will of God, and we use His gifts to bless others, we shall find life's burden light. He who walks in the way of God's commandments is walking in company with Christ, and in His love the heart is at rest. When Moses prayed, "Show me now Thy way, that I may know Thee," the Lord answered him, "My pres-

ence shall go with thee, and I will give thee rest." And through the prophets the message was given, "Thus saith the Lord, Stand ye in the ways, and see, and ask for the old paths, where is the good way, and walk therein, and ye shall find rest for your souls." Ex. 33:13, 14; Jer. 6:16. And He says, "O that thou hadst hearkened to My commandments! then had thy peace been as a river, and thy righteousness as the waves of the sea." Isa. 48:18.

Those who take Christ at His word, and surrender their souls to His keeping, their lives to His ordering, will find peace and quietude. Nothing of the world can make them sad when Jesus makes them glad by His presence. In perfect acquiescence there is perfect rest. The Lord says, "Thou wilt keep him in perfect peace, whose mind is stayed on Thee: because he trusteth in Thee." Isa. 26:3. Our lives may seem a tangle; but as we commit ourselves to the wise Master Worker, He will bring out the pattern of life and character that will be to His own glory. And that character which expresses the glory—character—of Christ will be received into the Paradise of God. A renovated race shall walk with Him in white, for they are worthy.

As through Jesus we enter into rest, heaven begins here. We respond to His invitation, Come, learn of Me, and in thus coming we begin the life eternal. Heaven is a ceaseless approaching to God through Christ. The longer we are in the heaven of bliss, the more and still more of glory will be opened to us; and the more we know of God, the more intense will be our happiness. As we walk with Jesus in this life, we may be filled with His love, satisfied with His presence. All that human nature can [332] bear, we may receive here. But what is this compared with the hereafter? There "are they before the throne of God, and serve Him day and night in His temple: and He that sitteth on the throne shall dwell among them. They shall hunger no more, neither thirst any more; neither shall the sun light on them, nor any heat. For the Lamb which is in the midst of the throne shall feed them, and shall lead them unto living fountains of waters: and God shall wipe away all tears from their eyes." Rev. 7:15-17.

35

[333]

"Peace, Be Still"

It had been an eventful day in the life of Jesus. Beside the Sea of Galilee He had spoken His first parables, by familiar illustrations again explaining to the people the nature of His kingdom and the manner in which it was to be established. He had likened His own work to that of the sower; the development of His kingdom to

This chapter is based on Matthew 8:23-34; Mark 4:35-41; 5:1-20; Luke 8:22-39.

616

the growth of the mustard seed and the effect of leaven in the measure of meal. The great final separation of the righteous and the wicked He had pictured in the parables of the wheat and tares and the fishing net. The exceeding preciousness of the truths He taught had been illustrated by the hidden treasure and the pearl of great price, while in the parable of the householder He taught His disciples how they were to labor as His representatives.

All day He had been teaching and healing; and as evening came on the crowds still pressed upon Him. Day after day He had ministered to them, scarcely pausing for food or rest. The malicious criticism and misrepresentation with which the Pharisees constantly pursued Him made His labors much more severe and harassing; and now the close of the day found Him so utterly wearied that He determined to seek retirement in some solitary place across the lake.

334 The eastern shore of Gennesaret was not uninhabited, for there were towns here and there beside the lake; yet it was a desolate region when compared with the western side. It contained a population more heathen than Jewish, and had little communication with Galilee. Thus it offered Jesus the seclusion He sought, and He now bade His disciples accompany Him thither.

After He had dismissed the multitude, they took Him, even "as He was," into the boat, and hastily set off. But they were not to depart alone. There were other fishing boats lying near the shore, and these were quickly crowded with people who followed Jesus, eager still to see and hear Him.

The Saviour was at last relieved from the pressure of the multitude, and, overcome with weariness and hunger, He lay down in the stern of the boat, and soon fell asleep. The evening had been calm and pleasant, and quiet rested upon the lake; but suddenly darkness overspread the sky, the wind swept wildly down the mountain gorges along the eastern shore, and a fierce tempest burst upon the lake.

The sun had set, and the blackness of night settled down upon the stormy sea. The waves, lashed into fury by the howling winds, dashed fiercely over the disciples' boat, and threatened to engulf it. Those hardy fishermen had spent their lives upon the lake, and had guided their craft safely through many a storm; but now their strength and skill availed nothing. They were helpless in the grasp of the tempest, and hope failed them as they saw that their boat was filling.

Absorbed in their efforts to save themselves, they had forgotten that Jesus was on board. Now, seeing their labor vain and only death before them, they remembered at whose command they had set out to cross the sea. In Jesus was their only hope. In their helplessness and despair they cried, "Master, Master!" But the dense darkness hid Him from their sight. Their voices were drowned by the roaring of the tempest, and there was no reply. Doubt and fear assailed them. Had Jesus forsaken them? Was He who had conquered disease and demons, and even death, powerless to help His disciples now? Was He unmindful of them in their distress?

Again they call, but there is no answer except the shrieking of the angry blast. Already their boat is sinking. A moment, and apparently they will be swallowed up by the hungry waters.

Suddenly a flash of lightning pierces the darkness, and they see Jesus lying asleep, undisturbed by the tumult. In amazement and despair they exclaim, "Master, carest Thou not that we perish?" How can He rest so peacefully while they are in danger and battling with death?

Their cry arouses Jesus. As the lightning's 335 glare reveals Him, they see the peace of heaven in His face; they read in His glance self-forgetful, tender love, and, their hearts turning to Him, cry, "Lord, save us: we perish."

Never did a soul utter that cry unheeded. As the disciples grasp their oars to make a last effort, Jesus rises. He stands in the midst of His disciples, while the tempest rages, the waves break over them, and the lightning illuminates His countenance. He lifts His hand, so often employed in deeds of mercy, and says to the angry sea, "Peace, be still."

The storm ceases. The billows sink to rest. The clouds roll away, and the stars shine forth. The boat rests upon a quiet sea. Then turning to His disciples, Jesus asks sorrowfully, "Why are ye fearful? have ye not yet faith?" Mark 4:40, R.V.

A hush fell upon the disciples. Even Peter did not attempt to express the awe that filled his heart. The boats that had set out to accompany Jesus had been in the same peril with that of the disciples. Terror and despair had seized their occupants; but the command of Jesus brought quiet to the scene of tumult. The fury of the storm had driven the boats into close proximity, and all on board beheld the miracle. In the calm that followed, fear was forgotten. The people whispered among themselves, "What manner of man is this, that even the winds and the sea obey Him?"

When Jesus was awakened to meet the storm, 336 He was in perfect peace. There was no trace of fear in word or look, for no fear was in His heart. But He rested not in the possession of almighty power. It was not as the "Master of earth and sea and sky" that He reposed in quiet. That power He had laid down, and He says, "I can of Mine own self do nothing." John 5:30. He trusted in the Father's might. It was in faith—faith in God's love and care—that Jesus rested, and the power of that word which stilled the storm was the power of God.

As Jesus rested by faith in the Father's care, so we are to rest in the care of our Saviour. If the disciples had trusted in Him, they would have been kept in peace. Their fear in the time of danger revealed their unbelief. In their efforts to save themselves, they forgot Jesus; and it was only when, in despair of self-dependence, they turned to Him that He could give them help.

How often the disciples' experience is ours! When the tempests of temptation gather, and the fierce lightnings flash, and the waves sweep over us, we battle with the storm alone, forgetting that there is One who can help us. We trust to our own strength till our hope is lost, and we are ready to perish. Then we remember Jesus, and if we call upon Him to save us, we shall not cry in vain. Though He sorrowfully reproves our unbelief and self-confidence, He never fails to give us the help we need. Whether on the land or on the sea, if we have the Saviour in our hearts, there is no need of fear. Living faith in the Redeemer will smooth the sea of life, and will deliver us from danger in the way that He knows to be best.

There is another spiritual lesson in this miracle of the stilling of the tempest. Every man's experience testifies to the truth of the words of Scripture, "The wicked are like the troubled sea, when it cannot rest. . . . There is no peace, saith my God, to the wicked." Isa. 57:20, 21. Sin has destroyed our peace. While self is unsubdued, we can find no rest. The masterful passions of the heart no human power can control. We are as helpless here as were the disciples to quiet the raging storm. But He who spoke peace to the billows of Galilee has spoken the word of peace for every soul. However fierce the tempest, those who turn to Jesus with the cry, "Lord, save us," will find deliverance. His grace, that reconciles the soul to God, quiets the strife of human passion, and in His love the heart is at rest. "He maketh the storm a calm, so that the waves thereof are still. Then are they glad because they be quiet; so He bringeth them unto their desired haven." Ps. 107:29, 30. "Being justified by faith, we have peace with God through our Lord Jesus Christ." "The work of righteousness shall be peace; and the effect of righteousness quietness and assurance forever." Rom. 5:1; Isa. 32:17.

In the early morning the Saviour and His companions came to shore, and the light of the rising sun touched sea and land as with the benediction of peace. But no sooner had they stepped upon the beach than their eyes were greeted by a sight more terrible than the fury of the tempest. From some hiding place among the tombs, two madmen rushed upon them as if to tear them in pieces. Hanging about these men were parts of chains which they had broken in escaping from confinement. Their flesh was torn and bleeding where they had cut themselves with sharp stones. Their eyes glared out from their long and matted hair, the very likeness of humanity seemed to have been blotted out by the demons that possessed them, and they looked more like wild beasts than like men.

The disciples and their companions fled in terror; but presently they noticed that Jesus was not with them, and they turned to look for Him. He was standing where they had left Him. He who had stilled the tempest, who had before met Satan and conquered him, did not flee before these demons. When the men, gnashing their teeth, and foaming at the mouth, approached Him, Jesus raised that hand which had beckoned the waves to rest, and the men could come no nearer. They stood raging but helpless before Him.

With authority He bade the unclean spirits come out of them. His words penetrated the darkened minds of the unfortunate men. They realized dimly that One was near who could save them from the tormenting demons. They fell at the Saviour's feet to worship Him; but when their lips were opened to entreat His mercy, the demons spoke through them, crying vehemently, "What have I to do with Thee, Jesus, Thou Son of God most high? I beseech Thee, torment me not."

Jesus asked, "What is thy name?" And the answer was, "My name is Legion: for we are many." Using the afflicted men as mediums of communication, they besought Jesus not to send them out of the country. Upon a mountainside not far distant a great herd of swine was feeding. Into these the demons asked to be allowed to enter, and Jesus suffered them. Immediately a panic seized the herd. They rushed madly down the cliff, and, unable to check themselves upon the shore, plunged into the lake, and perished.

Meanwhile a marvelous change had come over the demoniacs. Light had shone into their minds. Their eyes beamed with intelligence. The countenances, so long deformed into the image of Satan, became suddenly mild, the bloodstained hands were quiet, and with glad voices the men praised God for their deliverance.

From the cliff the keepers of the swine had seen all that had occurred, and they hurried away to publish the news to their employers and to all the people. In fear and amazement the whole population flocked to meet Jesus. The two demoniacs had been the terror of the country. No one had been safe to pass the place where they were; for they would rush upon every traveler with the fury of demons. Now these men were clothed and in their right mind, sitting at the feet of Jesus, listening to His words, and glorifying the name of Him who had made them whole. But the people who beheld this wonderful scene did not rejoice. The loss of the swine seemed to them of greater moment than the deliverance of these captives of Satan.

It was in mercy to the owners of the swine that this loss had been permitted to come upon them. They were absorbed in earthly things, and cared not for the great interests of spiritual life. Jesus desired to break the spell of selfish indifference, that they might accept His grace. But regret and indignation for their temporal loss blinded their eyes to the Saviour's mercy.

The manifestation of supernatural power aroused the superstitions of the people, and excited their fears. Further calamities might follow from having this Stranger among them. They apprehended financial ruin, and determined to be freed from His presence. Those who had crossed the lake with Jesus told of all that had happened on the preceding night, of their peril in the tempest, and how the wind and the sea had been stilled. But their words were without effect. In terror the people thronged about Jesus, beseeching Him to depart from them, and He complied, taking ship at once for the opposite shore.

The people of Gergesa had before them the living evidence of Christ's power and mercy. They saw the men who had been restored to reason; but they were so fearful of endangering their earthly interests that He who had vanquished the prince of darkness before their eyes was treated as an intruder, and the Gift of heaven was turned from their doors. We have not the opportunity of turning from the person of Christ as had the Gergesenes; but still there are many who refuse to obey His word, because obedience would involve the sacrifice of some worldly interest. Lest His presence shall cause them pecuniary loss, many reject His grace, and drive His Spirit from them.

But far different was the feeling of the restored demoniacs. They desired the company of their deliverer. In His presence they felt secure from the demons that had tormented their lives and wasted their manhood. As Jesus was about to enter the boat, they kept close to His side, knelt at His feet, and begged Him to keep them near Him, where they might ever listen to His words. But Jesus bade them go home and tell what great things the Lord had done for them.

Here was a work for them to do,—to go to a heathen home, and tell of the blessing they had received from Jesus. It was hard for them to be separated from the Saviour. Great difficulties were sure to beset them in association with their heathen countrymen. And their long isolation from society seemed to have disqualified them for the work He had indicated. But as soon as Jesus pointed out their duty they were ready to obey. Not only did they tell their own households and neighbors about Jesus, but they went throughout Decapolis, everywhere declaring His

power to save, and describing how He had freed them from the demons. In doing this work they could receive a greater blessing than if, merely for benefit to themselves, they had remained in His presence. It is in working to spread the good news of salvation that we are brought near to the Saviour.

The two restored demoniacs were the first missionaries whom Christ sent to preach the gospel in the region of Decapolis. For a few moments only these men had been privileged to hear the teachings of Christ. Not one sermon from His lips had ever fallen upon their ears. They could not instruct the people as the disciples who had been daily with Christ were able to do. But they bore in their own persons the evidence that Jesus was the Messiah. They could tell what they knew; what they themselves had seen, and heard, and felt of the power of Christ. This is what everyone can do whose heart has been touched by the grace of God. John, the beloved disciple, wrote: "That which was from the beginning, which we have heard, which we have seen with our eyes, which we have looked upon, and our hands have handled, of the Word of life; . . . that which we have seen and heard declare we unto you." 1 John 1:1-3. As witnesses for Christ, we are to tell what we know, what we ourselves have seen and heard and felt. If we have been following Jesus step by step, we shall have something right to the point to tell concerning the way in which He has led us. We can tell how we have tested His promise, and found the promise true. We can bear witness to what we have known of the grace of Christ. This is the witness for which our Lord calls, and for want of which the world is perishing.

Though the people of Gergesa had not received Jesus, He did not leave them to the darkness they had chosen. When they bade Him depart from them, they had not heard His words. They were ignorant of that which they were rejecting. Therefore He again sent the light to them, and by those to whom they would not refuse to listen.

In causing the destruction of the swine, it was Satan's purpose to turn the people away from the Saviour, and prevent the preaching of the gospel in that region. But this very occurrence roused the whole country as nothing else could have done, and directed attention to Christ. Though the Saviour Himself departed, the men whom He had healed remained as witnesses to His power. Those who had been mediums of the prince of darkness became channels of light, messengers of the Son of God. Men marveled as they listened to the wondrous news. A door was opened to the gospel throughout that region. When Jesus returned to Decapolis, the people flocked about Him, and for three days, not merely the inhabitants of one town, but thousands from all the surrounding region, heard the message of salvation. Even the power of demons is under the control of our Saviour, and the working of evil is overruled for good.

The encounter with the demoniacs of Gergesa had a lesson for the disciples. It showed the depths of degradation to which Satan is seeking to drag the whole human race, and the mission of Christ to set men free from his power. Those wretched beings, dwelling in the place of graves, possessed by demons, in bondage to uncontrolled passions and loathsome lusts, represent what humanity would become if given up to satanic jurisdiction. Satan's influence is constantly exerted upon men to distract the senses, control the mind for evil, and incite to violence and crime. He weakens the body, darkens the intellect, and debases the soul. Whenever men reject the Saviour's invitation, they are yielding themselves to Satan. Multitudes in every department in life, in the home, in business, and even in the church, are doing this today. It is because of this that violence and crime have overspread the earth, and moral darkness, like the pall of death, enshrouds the habitations of men. Through his specious temptations Satan leads men to worse and worse evils, till utter depravity and ruin are the result. The only safeguard against his power is found in the presence of Jesus. Before men and angels Satan has been revealed as man's enemy and destroyer; Christ, as man's friend and deliverer. His Spirit will develop in man all that will ennoble the character and dignify the nature. It will build man up for the glory of God in body and soul and spirit. "For God hath not given us the spirit of fear; but of power, and of love, and of a sound mind." 2 Tim. 1:7. He has called us "to the obtaining of the glory"—character—"of our Lord Jesus Christ;" has called us to be "conformed to the image of His Son." 2 Thess. 2:14; Rom. 8:29.

And souls that have been degraded into instruments of Satan are still through the power of Christ transformed into messengers of righteousness, and sent forth by the Son of God to tell what "great things the Lord hath done for thee, and hath had compassion on thee."

36

The Touch of Faith

Returning from Gergesa to the western shore, Jesus found a multitude gathered to receive Him, and they greeted Him with joy. He remained by the seaside for a time, teaching and healing, and then repaired to the house of Levi-Matthew to meet the publicans at the feast. Here Jairus, the ruler of the synagogue, found Him.

This elder of the Jews came to Jesus in great distress, and cast himself at His feet, exclaiming, "My little daughter lieth at the point of death: I pray Thee, come and lay Thy hands on her, that she may be healed; and she shall live."

Jesus set out at once with the ruler for his home. Though the disciples had seen so many of His works of mercy, they were surprised at His compliance with the entreaty of the haughty rabbi; yet they accompanied their Master, and the people followed, eager and expectant.

The ruler's house was not far distant, but Jesus and His companions advanced slowly, for the crowd pressed Him on every side. The anxious father was impatient of delay; but Jesus, pitying the people, stopped now and then to relieve some suffering one, or to comfort a troubled heart.

While they were still on the way, a messenger pressed through the crowd, bearing to Jairus the news that his daughter was dead, and it was useless to trouble the Master further. The word caught the ear of Jesus. "Fear not," He said; "believe only, and she shall be made whole." 343

Jairus pressed closer to the Saviour, and together they hurried to the ruler's home. Already the hired mourners and flute players were there, filling the air with their clamor. The presence of the crowd and the tumult jarred upon the spirit of Jesus. He tried to silence them, saying, "Why make ye this ado, and weep? the damsel is not dead, but sleepeth." They were indignant at the words of the Stranger. They had seen the child in the embrace of death, and they laughed Him to scorn. Requiring them all to leave the house, Jesus took with Him the father and mother of the maiden, and the three disciples, Peter, James, and John, and together they entered the chamber of death.

Jesus approached the bedside, and, taking the child's hand in His own, He pronounced softly, in the familiar language of her home, the words, "Damsel, I say unto thee, arise."

Instantly a tremor passed through the unconscious form. The pulses of life beat again. The lips unclosed with a smile. The eyes opened widely as if from sleep, and the maiden gazed with wonder on the group beside her. She arose, and her parents clasped her in their arms, and wept for joy.

On the way to the ruler's house, Jesus had met, in the crowd, a poor woman who for twelve years had suffered from a disease that made her life a burden. She had spent all her means upon physicians and remedies, only to be pronounced incurable. But her hopes revived when she heard of the cures that Christ performed. She felt assured that if she could only go to Him she would be healed. In weakness and suffering she came to the seaside where He was teaching, and tried to press through the crowd, but in vain. Again she followed Him

This chapter is based on Matthew 9:18-26; Mark 5:21-43; Luke 8:40-56.

from the house of Levi-Matthew, but was still unable to reach Him. She had begun to despair, when, in making His way through the multitude, He came near where she was.

The golden opportunity had come. She was in the presence of the Great Physician! But amid the confusion she could not speak to Him, nor catch more than a passing glimpse of His figure. Fearful of losing her one chance of relief, she pressed forward, saying to herself, "If I may but touch His garment, I shall be whole." As He was passing, she reached forward, and succeeded in barely touching the border of His garment. But in that moment she knew that she was healed. In that one touch was concentrated the faith of her life, and instantly her pain and feebleness gave place to the vigor of perfect health.

344   With a grateful heart she then tried to withdraw from the crowd; but suddenly Jesus stopped, and the people halted with Him. He turned, and looking about asked in a voice distinctly heard above the confusion of the multitude, "Who touched Me?" The people answered this query with a look of amazement. Jostled upon all sides, and rudely pressed hither and thither, as He was, it seemed a strange inquiry.

Peter, ever ready to speak, said, "Master, the multitude throng Thee and press Thee, and sayest Thou, Who touched Me?" Jesus answered, "Somebody hath touched Me: for I perceive that virtue is gone out of Me." The Saviour could distinguish the touch of faith from the casual contact of the careless throng. Such trust should not be passed without comment. He would speak to the humble woman words of comfort that would be to her a wellspring of joy,—words that would be a blessing to His followers to the close of time.

Looking toward the woman, Jesus insisted on knowing who had touched Him. Finding concealment vain, she came forward tremblingly,
347   and cast herself at His feet. With grateful tears she told the story of her suffering, and how she had found relief. Jesus gently said, "Daughter, be of good comfort: thy faith hath made thee whole; go in peace." He gave no opportunity for superstition to claim healing virtue for the mere act of touching His garments. It was not through the outward contact with Him, but through the faith which took hold on His divine power, that the cure was wrought.

The wondering crowd that pressed close about Christ realized no accession of vital power. But when the suffering woman put forth her hand to touch Him, believing that she would be made whole, she felt the healing virtue. So in spiritual things. To talk of religion in a casual way, to pray without soul hunger and living faith, avails nothing. A nominal faith in Christ, which accepts Him merely as the Saviour of the world, can never bring healing to the soul. The

faith that is unto salvation is not a mere intellectual assent to the truth. He who waits for entire knowledge before he will exercise faith cannot receive blessing from God. It is not enough to believe *about* Christ; we must believe *in* Him. The only faith that will benefit us is that which embraces Him as a personal Saviour; which appropriates His merits to ourselves. Many hold faith as an opinion. Saving faith is a transaction by which those who receive Christ join themselves in covenant relation with God. Genuine faith is life. A living faith means an increase of vigor, a confiding trust, by which the soul becomes a conquering power.

After healing the woman, Jesus desired her to acknowledge the blessing she had received. The gifts which the gospel offers are not to be secured by stealth or enjoyed in secret. So the Lord calls upon us for confession of His goodness. "Ye are My witnesses, saith the Lord, that I am God." Isa. 43:12.

Our confession of His faithfulness is Heaven's chosen agency for revealing Christ to the world. We are to acknowledge His grace as made known through the holy men of old; but that which will be most effectual is the testimony of our own experience. We are witnesses for God as we reveal in ourselves the working of a power that is divine. Every individual has a life distinct from all others, and an experience differing essentially from theirs. God desires that our praise shall ascend to Him, marked by our own individuality. These precious acknowledgments to the praise of the glory of His grace, when supported by a Christ-like life, have an irresistible power that works for the salvation of souls.

When the ten lepers came to Jesus for heal- 348 ing, He bade them go and show themselves to the priest. On the way they were cleansed, but only one of them returned to give Him glory. The others went their way, forgetting Him who had made them whole. How many are still doing the same thing! The Lord works continually to benefit mankind. He is ever imparting His bounties. He raises up the sick from beds of languishing, He delivers men from peril which they do not see, He commissions heavenly angels to save them from calamity, to guard them from "the pestilence that walketh in darkness" and "the destruction that wasteth at noonday" (Ps. 91:6); but their hearts are unimpressed. He has given all the riches of heaven to redeem them, and yet they are unmindful of His great love. By their ingratitude they close their hearts against the grace of God. Like the heath in the desert they know not when good cometh, and their souls inhabit the parched places of the wilderness.

It is for our own benefit to keep every gift of God fresh in our memory. Thus faith is strengthened to claim and to receive more and more. There is greater encouragement for us in the least blessing we ourselves receive from God than in all the accounts we can read of the faith and experience of others. The soul that responds to the grace of God shall be like a watered garden. His health shall spring forth speedily; his light shall rise in obscurity, and the glory of the Lord shall be seen upon him. Let us then remember the loving-kindness of the Lord, and the multitude of His tender mercies. Like the people of Israel, let us set up our stones of witness, and inscribe upon them the precious story of what God has wrought for us. And as we review His dealings with us in our pilgrimage, let us, out of hearts melted with gratitude, declare, "What shall I render unto the Lord for all His benefits toward me? I will take the cup of salvation, and call upon the name of the Lord. I will pay my vows unto the Lord now in the presence of all His people." Ps. 116:12-14.

37

The First Evangelists

The apostles were members of the family of Jesus, and they had accompanied Him as He traveled on foot through Galilee. They had shared with Him the toils and hardships that overtook them. They had listened to His discourses, they had walked and talked with the Son of God, and from His daily instruction they had learned how to work for the elevation of humanity. As Jesus ministered to the vast multitudes that gathered about Him, His disciples were in attendance, eager to do His bidding and to lighten His labor. They assisted in arranging the people, bringing the afflicted ones to the Saviour, and promoting the comfort of all. They watched for interested hearers, explained the Scriptures to them, and in various ways worked for their spiritual benefit. They taught what they had learned of Jesus, and were every day obtaining a rich experience. But they needed also an experience in laboring alone. They were still in need of much instruction, great patience and tenderness. Now, while He was personally with them, to point out their errors, and counsel and correct them, the Saviour sent them forth as His representatives.

While they had been with Him, the disciples had often been perplexed by the teaching of the priests and Pharisees, but they had brought their perplexities to Jesus. He had set before them the truths of Scripture in contrast with tradition. Thus He had strengthened their confidence in God's word, and in a great measure had set them free from their fear of the rabbis and their bondage to tradition. In the training of the disciples the example of the Saviour's life was far

more effective than any mere doctrinal instruction. When they were separated from Him, every look and tone and word came back to them. Often when in conflict with the enemies of the gospel, they repeated His words, and as they saw their effect upon the people, they rejoiced greatly.

Calling the twelve about Him, Jesus bade them go out two and two through the towns and villages. None were sent forth alone, but brother was associated with brother, friend with friend. Thus they could help and encourage each other, counseling and praying together, each one's strength supplementing the other's weakness. In the same manner He afterward sent forth the seventy. It was the Saviour's purpose that the messengers of the gospel should be associated in this way. In our own time evangelistic work would be far more successful if this example were more closely followed.

The disciples' message was the same as that of John the Baptist and of Christ Himself: "The kingdom of heaven is at hand." They were to enter into no controversy with the people as to whether Jesus of Nazareth was the Messiah; but in His name they were to do the same works of mercy as He had done. He bade them, "Heal the sick, cleanse the lepers, raise the dead, cast out devils: freely ye have received, freely give."

During His ministry Jesus devoted more time to healing the sick than to preaching. His miracles testified to the truth of His words, that He came not to destroy but to save. His righteousness went before Him, and the glory of the Lord was His rearward. Wherever He went, the tidings of His mercy preceded Him. Where He had passed, the objects of His compassion were rejoicing in health, and making trial of their new-found powers. Crowds were collecting around them to hear from their lips the works that the Lord had wrought. His voice was the first sound that many had ever heard, His name the first word they had ever spoken, His face the first they had ever looked upon. Why should they not love Jesus, and sound His praise? As He passed through the towns and cities He was like a vital current, diffusing life and joy wherever He went.

The followers of Christ are to labor as He did. We are to feed the hungry, clothe the naked, and comfort the suffering and afflicted. We are to minister to the despairing, and inspire hope in the hopeless. And to us also the promise will be fulfilled, "Thy righteousness shall go before thee; the glory of the Lord shall be thy rearward." Isa. 58:8. The love of Christ, manifested in unselfish ministry, will be more effective in reforming the evildoer than will the sword or the court of justice. These are necessary to strike terror to the lawbreaker, but the loving missionary can do more than this. Often the heart will harden under reproof; but it will melt under the

This chapter is based on Matthew 10; Mark 6:7-11; Luke 9:1-6.

love of Christ. The missionary cannot only relieve physical maladies, but he can lead the sinner to the Great Physician, who can cleanse the soul from the leprosy of sin. Through His servants, God designs that the sick, the unfortunate, those possessed of evil spirits, shall hear His voice. Through His human agencies He desires to be a Comforter such as the world knows not.

The disciples on their first missionary tour were to go only to "the lost sheep of the house of Israel." If they had now preached the gospel to the Gentiles or the Samaritans, they would have lost their influence with the Jews. By exciting the prejudice of the Pharisees they would have involved themselves in controversy which would have discouraged them at the outset of their labors. Even the apostles were slow to understand that the gospel was to be carried to all nations. Until they themselves could grasp this truth they were not prepared to labor for the Gentiles. If the Jews would receive the gospel, God purposed to make them His messengers to the Gentiles. Therefore they were first to hear the message.

All over the field of Christ's labor there were souls awakened to their need, and hungering and thirsting for the truth. The time had come to send the tidings of His love to these longing hearts. To all these the disciples were to go as His representatives. The believers would thus be led to look upon them as divinely appointed teachers, and when the Saviour should be taken from them they would not be left without instructors.

On this first tour the disciples were to go only where Jesus had been before them, and had made friends. Their preparation for the journey was to be of the simplest kind. Nothing must be allowed to divert their minds from their great work, or in any way excite opposition and close the door for further labor. They were not to adopt the dress of the religious teachers, nor use any guise in apparel to distinguish them from the humble peasants. They were not to enter into the synagogues and call the people together for public service; their efforts were to be put forth in house-to-house labor. They were not to waste time in needless salutations, or in going from house to house for entertainment. But in every place they were to accept the hospitality of those who were worthy, those who would welcome them heartily as if entertaining Christ Himself. They were to enter the dwelling with the beautiful salutation, "Peace be to this house." Luke 10:5. That home would be blessed by their prayers, their songs of praise, and the opening of the Scriptures in the family circle.

These disciples were to be heralds of the truth, to prepare the way for the coming of their Master. The message they had to bear was the word of eternal life, and the destiny of men depended upon their reception or rejection of it. To impress the people with its solemnity, Jesus bade His disciples, "Whosoever shall not receive you, nor hear your words, when ye depart out of that house or city, shake off the dust of your feet. Verily I say unto you, It shall be more tolerable for the land of Sodom and Gomorrah in the day of judgment, than for that city."

Now the Saviour's eye penetrates the future; He beholds the broader fields in which, after His death, the disciples are to be witnesses for Him. His prophetic glance takes in the experience of His servants through all the ages till He shall come the second time. He shows His followers the conflicts they must meet; He reveals the character and plan of the battle. He lays open before them the perils they must encounter, the self-denial that will be required. He desires them to count the cost, that they may not be taken unawares by the enemy. Their warfare is not to be waged against flesh and blood, but "against the principalities, against the powers, against the world rulers of this darkness, against the spiritual hosts of wickedness in the heavenly places." Eph. 6:12, R. V. They are to contend with supernatural forces, but they are assured of supernatural help. All the intelligences of heaven are in this army. And more than angels are in the ranks. The Holy Spirit, the representative of the Captain of the Lord's host, comes down to direct the battle. Our infirmities may be many, our sins and mistakes grievous; but the grace of God is for all who seek it with contrition. The power of Omnipotence is enlisted in behalf of those who trust in God.

"Behold," said Jesus, "I send you forth as sheep in the midst of wolves: be ye therefore wise as serpents, and harmless as doves." Christ Himself did not suppress one word of truth, but He spoke it always in love. He exercised the greatest tact, and thoughtful, kind attention in His intercourse with the people. He was never rude, never needlessly spoke a severe word, never gave needless pain to a sensitive soul. He did not censure human weakness. He fearlessly denounced hypocrisy, unbelief, and iniquity, but tears were in His voice as He uttered His scathing rebukes. He wept over Jerusalem, the city He loved, that refused to receive Him, the Way, the Truth, and the Life. They rejected Him, the Saviour, but He regarded them with pitying tenderness, and sorrow so deep that it broke His heart. Every soul was precious in His eyes. While He always bore Himself with divine dignity, He bowed with tenderest regard to every member of the family of God. In all men He saw fallen souls whom it was His mission to save.

The servants of Christ are not to act out the dictates of the natural heart. They need to have close communion with God, lest, under provocation, self rise up, and they pour forth a torrent of words that are unbefitting, that are not as dew or the still showers that refresh the withering plants. This is what Satan wants them to do; for these are his methods. It is the dragon that is wroth; it is the spirit of Satan that is revealed in anger and accusing. But God's servants are to be representatives of Him. He desires them to deal only in the currency of heaven, the truth that bears His own image and superscription. The power by which they are to overcome evil is the power of Christ. The glory of Christ is their strength. They are to fix their eyes upon His loveliness. Then they can present the gospel with divine tact and gentleness. And the spirit that is kept gentle under provocation will speak more effectively in favor of the truth than will any argument, however forcible.

Those who are brought in controversy with the enemies of truth have to meet, not only men, but Satan and his agents. Let them remember the Saviour's words, "Behold, I send you forth as lambs among wolves." Luke 10:3. Let them rest in the love of God, and the spirit will be kept calm, even under personal abuse. The Lord will clothe them with a divine panoply. His Holy Spirit will influence the mind and heart, so that their voices shall not catch the notes of the baying of the wolves.

354   Continuing His instruction to His disciples, Jesus said, "Beware of men." They were not to put implicit confidence in those who knew not God, and open to them their counsels; for this would give Satan's agents an advantage. Man's inventions often counterwork God's plans. Those who build the temple of the Lord are to build according to the pattern shown in the mount,—the divine similitude. God is dishonored and the gospel is betrayed when His servants depend on the counsel of men who are not under the guidance of the Holy Spirit. Worldly wisdom is foolishness with God. Those who rely upon it will surely err.

"They will deliver you up to councils, . . . yea and before governors and kings shall ye be brought for My sake, for a testimony to them and to the Gentiles." Matt. 10:17, 18, R. V. Persecution will spread the light. The servants of Christ will be brought before the great men of the world, who, but for this, might never hear the gospel. The truth has been misrepresented to these men. They have listened to false charges concerning the faith of Christ's disciples. Often their only means of learning its real character is the testimony of those who are brought to trial for their faith. Under examination these are required to answer, and their judges to listen to the testimony borne. God's grace will be dispensed to His servants to meet the emergency. "It shall be given you," says Jesus, "in that same hour what ye shall speak. For it is not ye that speak, but the Spirit of your Father which

speaketh in you." As the Spirit of God illuminates the minds of His servants, the truth will be presented in its divine power and preciousness. Those who reject the truth will stand to accuse and oppress the disciples. But under loss and suffering, even unto death, the Lord's children are to reveal the meekness of their divine Example. Thus will be seen the contrast between Satan's agents and the representatives of Christ. The Saviour will be lifted up before the rulers and the people.

The disciples were not endowed with the courage and fortitude of the martyrs until such grace was needed. Then the Saviour's promise was fulfilled. When Peter and John testified before the Sanhedrin council, men "marveled; and they took knowledge of them, that they had been with Jesus." Acts 4:13. Of Stephen it is written that "all that sat in the council, looking steadfastly on him, saw his face as it had been the face of an angel." Men "were not able to resist the wisdom and the spirit by which he spake." Acts 6:15, 10. And Paul, writing of his own trial at the court of the Caesars, says, "At my first defense no one took my part, but all 355 forsook me. . . . But the Lord stood by me, and strengthened me; that through me the message might be fully proclaimed, and that all the Gentiles might hear: and I was delivered out of the mouth of the lion." 2 Tim. 4:16, 17, R. V.

The servants of Christ were to prepare no set speech to present when brought to trial. Their preparation was to be made day by day in treasuring up the precious truths of God's word, and through prayer strengthening their faith. When they were brought into trial, the Holy Spirit would bring to their remembrance the very truths that would be needed.

A daily, earnest striving to know God, and Jesus Christ whom He has sent, would bring power and efficiency to the soul. The knowledge obtained by diligent searching of the Scriptures would be flashed into the memory at the right time. But if any had neglected to acquaint themselves with the words of Christ, if they had never tested the power of His grace in trial, they could not expect that the Holy Spirit would bring His words to their remembrance. They were to serve God daily with undivided affection, and then trust Him.

So bitter would be the enmity to the gospel that even the tenderest earthly ties would be disregarded. The disciples of Christ would be betrayed to death by the members of their own households. "Ye shall be hated of all men for My name's sake," He added; "but he that shall endure unto the end, the same shall be saved." Mark 13:13. But He bade them not to expose themselves unnecessarily to persecution. He Himself often left one field of labor for another, in order to escape from those who were seeking His life. When He was rejected at Nazareth, and

His own townsmen tried to kill Him, He went down to Capernaum, and there the people were astonished at His teaching; "for His word was with power." Luke 4:32. So His servants were not to be discouraged by persecution, but to seek a place where they could still labor for the salvation of souls.

The servant is not above his master. The Prince of heaven was called Beelzebub, and His disciples will be misrepresented in like manner. But whatever the danger, Christ's followers must avow their principles. They should scorn concealment. They cannot remain uncommitted until assured of safety in confessing the truth. They are set as watchmen, to warn men of their peril. The truth received from Christ must be imparted to all, freely and openly. Jesus said, "What I tell you in darkness, that speak ye in light: and what ye hear in the ear, that preach ye upon the housetops."

356   Jesus Himself never purchased peace by compromise. His heart overflowed with love for the whole human race, but He was never indulgent to their sins. He was too much their friend to remain silent while they were pursuing a course that would ruin their souls,—the souls He had purchased with His own blood. He labored that man should be true to himself, true to his higher and eternal interest. The servants of Christ are called to the same work, and they should beware lest, in seeking to prevent discord, they surrender the truth. They are to "follow after the things which make for peace" (Rom. 14:19); but real peace can never be secured by compromising principle. And no man can be true to principle without exciting opposition. A Christianity that is spiritual will be opposed by the children of disobedience. But Jesus bade His disciples, "Fear not them which kill the body, but are not able to kill the soul." Those who are true to God need not fear the power of men nor the enmity of Satan. In Christ their eternal life is secure. Their only fear should be lest they surrender the truth, and thus betray the trust with which God has honored them.

It is Satan's work to fill men's hearts with doubt. He leads them to look upon God as a stern judge. He tempts them to sin, and then to regard themselves as too vile to approach their heavenly Father or to excite His pity. The Lord understands all this. Jesus assures His disciples of God's sympathy for them in their needs and weaknesses. Not a sigh is breathed, not a pain felt, not a grief pierces the soul, but the throb vibrates to the Father's heart.

The Bible shows us God in His high and holy place, not in a state of inactivity, not in silence and solitude, but surrounded by ten thousand times ten thousand and thousands of thousands of holy intelligences, all waiting to do His will. Through channels which we cannot discern He is in active communication with every part of His dominion. But it is in this speck of a world, in the souls that He gave His only-begotten Son to save, that His interest and the interest of all heaven is centered. God is bending from His throne to hear the cry of the oppressed. To every sincere prayer He answers, "Here am I." He uplifts the distressed and downtrodden. In all our afflictions He is afflicted. In every temptation and every trial the angel of His presence is near to deliver.

Not even a sparrow falls to the ground without the Father's notice. Satan's hatred against God leads him to hate every object of the Saviour's care. He seeks to mar the handiwork of God, and he delights in destroying even the 357 dumb creatures. It is only through God's protecting care that the birds are preserved to gladden us with their songs of joy. But He does not forget even the sparrows. "Fear ye not therefore, ye are of more value than many sparrows."

Jesus continues: As you confess Me before men, so I will confess you before God and the holy angels. You are to be My witnesses upon earth, channels through which My grace can flow for the healing of the world. So I will be your representative in heaven. The Father beholds not your faulty character, but He sees you as clothed in My perfection. I am the medium through which Heaven's blessings shall come to you. And everyone who confesses Me by sharing My sacrifice for the lost shall be confessed as a sharer in the glory and joy of the redeemed.

He who would confess Christ must have Christ abiding in him. He cannot communicate that which he has not received. The disciples might speak fluently on doctrines, they might repeat the words of Christ Himself; but unless they possessed Christlike meekness and love, they were not confessing Him. A spirit contrary to the spirit of Christ would deny Him, whatever the profession. Men may deny Christ by evil-speaking, by foolish talking, by words that are untruthful or unkind. They may deny Him by shunning life's burdens, by the pursuit of sinful pleasure. They may deny Him by conforming to the world, by uncourteous behavior, by the love of their own opinions, by justifying self, by cherishing doubt, borrowing trouble, and dwelling in darkness. In all these ways they declare that Christ is not in them. And "whosoever shall deny Me before men," He says, "him will I also deny before My Father which is in heaven."

The Saviour bade His disciples not to hope that the world's enmity to the gospel would be overcome, and that after a time its opposition would cease. He said, "I came not to send peace, but a sword." This creating of strife is not the effect of the gospel, but the result of opposition to it. Of all persecution the hardest to bear is variance in the home, the estrangement of dearest earthly friends. But Jesus declares, "He that loveth father or mother more than Me is not worthy of Me: and he that loveth son or daughter more than Me is not worthy of Me. And he that taketh not his cross, and followeth after Me, is not worthy of Me."

The mission of Christ's servants is a high honor, and a sacred trust. "He that receiveth you," He says, "receiveth Me, and he that receiveth Me receiveth Him that sent Me." No act of kindness shown to them in His name will fail to be recognized and rewarded. And in the same tender recognition He includes the feeblest and lowliest of the family of God: "Whosoever shall give to drink unto one of these little ones"—those who are as children in their faith and their knowledge of Christ—"a cup of cold water only in the name of a disciple, verily I say unto you, he shall in nowise lose his reward."

Thus the Saviour ended His instruction. In the name of Christ the chosen twelve went out, as He had gone, "to preach the gospel to the poor, . . . to heal the brokenhearted, to preach deliverance to the captives, and recovering of sight to the blind, to set at liberty them that are bruised, to preach the acceptable year of the Lord." Luke 4:18, 19.

38

Come Rest Awhile

On returning from their missionary tour, "the apostles gathered themselves together unto Jesus, and told Him all things, both what they had done, and what they had taught. And He said unto them, Come ye yourselves apart into a desert place, and rest awhile: for there were many coming and going, and they had no leisure so much as to eat."

The disciples came to Jesus and told Him all things. Their intimate relationship with Him encouraged them to lay before Him their favorable and unfavorable experiences, their joy at seeing results from their labors, and their sorrow at their failures, their faults, and their weaknesses. They had committed errors in their first work as evangelists, and as they frankly told Christ of their experiences, He saw that they needed much instruction. He saw, too, that they had become weary in their labors, and that they needed to rest.

But where they then were they could not obtain the needed privacy; "for there were many coming and going, and they had no leisure so much as to eat." The people were thronging after Christ, anxious to be healed, and eager to listen to His words. Many felt drawn to Him; for He seemed to them to be the fountain of all blessings. Many of those who then thronged about Christ to receive the precious boon of health accepted Him as their Saviour. Many others, afraid then to confess Him, because of the Pharisees, were converted at the descent of the Holy Spirit, and, before the angry priests and rulers, acknowledged Him as the Son of God.

But now Christ longed for retirement, that He might be with His disciples; for He had much to say to them. In their work they had passed through the test of conflict, and had encountered opposition in various forms. Hitherto they had consulted Christ in everything; but for some time they had been alone, and at times they had been much troubled to know what to do. They had found much encouragement in their work; for Christ did not send them away without His Spirit, and by faith in Him they worked many miracles; but they needed now to feed on the Bread of Life. They needed to go to a place of retirement, where they could hold communion with Jesus and receive instruction for future work.

"And He said unto them, Come ye yourselves apart into a desert place, and rest awhile." Christ is full of tenderness and compassion for all in His service. He would show His disciples that God does not require sacrifice, but mercy. They had been putting their whole souls into labor for the people, and this was exhausting their physical and mental strength. It was their duty to rest.

As the disciples had seen the success of their labors, they were in danger of taking credit to themselves, in danger of cherishing spiritual pride, and thus falling under Satan's temptations. A great work was before them, and first of all they must learn that their strength was not in self, but in God. Like Moses in the wilderness of Sinai, like David among the hills of Judea, or Elijah by the brook Cherith, the disciples needed to come apart from the scenes of their busy activity, to commune with Christ, with nature, and with their own hearts.

While the disciples had been absent on their missionary tour, Jesus had visited other towns and villages, preaching the gospel of the kingdom. It was about this time that He received tidings of the Baptist's death. This event brought vividly before Him the end to which His own steps were tending. The shadows were gathering thickly about His path. Priests and rabbis were watching to compass His death, spies hung upon His steps, and on every hand plots for His ruin were multiplying. News of the preaching of the apostles throughout Galilee reached Herod, calling his attention to Jesus and His work. "This is John the Baptist," he said; "he is risen from the dead;" and he expressed a desire to see Jesus. Herod was in constant fear lest a revolution might be secretly carried forward, with the object of unseating him from the throne, and breaking the Roman yoke from the Jewish

This chapter is based on Matthew 14:1, 2, 12, 13; Mark 6:30-32; Luke 9:7-10.

nation. Among the people the spirit of discontent and insurrection was rife. It was evident that Christ's public labors in Galilee could not be long continued. The scenes of His suffering were drawing near, and He longed to be apart for a season from the confusion of the multitude.

With saddened hearts the disciples of John had borne his mutilated body to its burial. Then they "went and told Jesus." These disciples had been envious of Christ when He seemed to be drawing the people away from John. They had sided with the Pharisees in accusing Him when He sat with the publicans at Matthew's feast. They had doubted His divine mission because He did not set the Baptist at liberty. But now that their teacher was dead, and they longed for consolation in their great sorrow, and for guidance as to their future work, they came to Jesus, and united their interest with His. They too needed a season of quiet for communion with the Saviour.

Near Bethsaida, at the northern end of the lake, was a lonely region, now beautiful with the fresh green of spring, that offered a welcome retreat to Jesus and His disciples. For this place they set out, going in their boat across the water. Here they would be away from the thoroughfares of travel, and the bustle and agitation of the city. The scenes of nature were in themselves a rest, a change grateful to the senses. Here they could listen to the words of Christ without hearing the angry interruptions, the retorts and accusations of the scribes and Pharisees. Here they could enjoy a short season of precious fellowship in the society of their Lord.

The rest which Christ and His disciples took was not self-indulgent rest. The time they spent in retirement was not devoted to pleasure seeking. They talked together regarding the work of God, and the possibility of bringing greater efficiency to the work. The disciples had been with Christ, and could understand Him; to them He need not talk in parables. He corrected their errors, and made plain to them the right way of approaching the people. He opened more fully to them the precious treasures of divine truth. They were vitalized by divine power, and inspired with hope and courage.

Though Jesus could work miracles, and had empowered His disciples to work miracles, He directed His worn servants to go apart into the country and rest. When He said that the harvest was great, and the laborers were few, He did not urge upon His disciples the necessity of ceaseless toil, but said, "Pray ye therefore the Lord of the harvest, that He will send forth laborers into His harvest." Matt. 9:38. God has appointed to every man his work, according to his ability (Eph. 4:11-13), and He would not have a few weighted with responsibilities while others have no burden, no travail of soul.

Christ's words of compassion are spoken to His workers today just as surely as they were spoken to His disciples. "Come ye yourselves apart, . . . and rest awhile," He says to those who are worn and weary. It is not wise to be always under the strain of work and excitement, even in ministering to men's spiritual needs; for in this way personal piety is neglected, and the powers of mind and soul and body are overtaxed. Self-denial is required of the disciples of Christ, and sacrifices must be made; but care must also be exercised lest through their overzeal Satan take advantage of the weakness of humanity, and the work of God be marred.

In the estimation of the rabbis it was the sum of religion to be always in a bustle of activity. They depended upon some outward performance to show their superior piety. Thus they separated their souls from God, and built themselves up in self-sufficiency. The same dangers still exist. As activity increases and men become successful in doing any work for God, there is danger of trusting to human plans and methods. There is a tendency to pray less, and to have less faith. Like the disciples, we are in danger of losing sight of our dependence on God, and seeking to make a savior of our activity. We need to look constantly to Jesus, realizing that it is His power which does the work. While we are to labor earnestly for the salvation of the lost, we must also take time for meditation, for prayer, and for the study of the word of God. Only the work accomplished with much prayer, and sanctified by the merit of Christ, will in the end prove to have been efficient for good.

No other life was ever so crowded with labor and responsibility as was that of Jesus; yet how often He was found in prayer! How constant was His communion with God! Again and again in the history of His earthly life are found records such as these: "Rising up a great while before day, He went out, and departed into a solitary place, and there prayed." "Great multitudes came together to hear, and to be healed by Him of their infirmities. And He withdrew Himself into the wilderness, and prayed." "And it came to pass in those days, that He went out into a mountain to pray, and continued all night in prayer to God." Mark 1:35; Luke 5:15, 16; 6:12.

In a life wholly devoted to the good of others, the Saviour found it necessary to withdraw from the thoroughfares of travel and from the throng that followed Him day after day. He must turn aside from a life of ceaseless activity and contact with human needs, to seek retirement and unbroken communion with His Father. As one with us, a sharer in our needs and weaknesses, He was wholly dependent upon God, and in the secret place of prayer He sought divine strength, that He might go forth braced for duty and trial.

In a world of sin Jesus endured struggles and torture of soul. In communion with God He could unburden the sorrows that were crushing Him. Here He found comfort and joy.

In Christ the cry of humanity reached the Father of infinite pity. As a man He supplicated the throne of God till His humanity was charged with a heavenly current that should connect humanity with divinity. Through continual communion He received life from God, that He might impart life to the world. His experience is to be ours.

"Come ye yourselves apart," He bids us. If we would give heed to His word, we should be stronger and more useful. The disciples sought Jesus, and told Him all things; and He encouraged and instructed them. If today we would take time to go to Jesus and tell Him our needs, we should not be disappointed; He would be at our right hand to help us. We need more simplicity, more trust and confidence in our Saviour. He whose name is called "The mighty God, The everlasting Father, The Prince of Peace;" He of whom it is written, "The government shall be upon His shoulder," is the Wonderful Counselor. We are invited to ask wisdom of Him. He "giveth to all men liberally, and upbraideth not." Isa. 9:6; James 1:5.

In all who are under the training of God is to be revealed a life that is not in harmony with the world, its customs, or its practices; and everyone needs to have a personal experience in obtaining a knowledge of the will of God. We must individually hear Him speaking to the heart. When every other voice is hushed, and in quietness we wait before Him, the silence of the soul makes more distinct the voice of God. He bids us, "Be still, and know that I am God." Ps. 46:10. Here alone can true rest be found. And this is the effectual preparation for all who labor for God. Amid the hurrying throng, and the strain of life's intense activities, the soul that is thus refreshed will be surrounded with an atmosphere of light and peace. The life will breathe out fragrance, and will reveal a divine power that will reach men's hearts.

39

"Give Ye Them to Eat"

Christ had retired to a secluded place with His disciples, but this rare season of peaceful quietude was soon broken. The disciples thought they had retired where they would not be disturbed; but as soon as the multitude missed the divine Teacher, they inquired, "Where is He?" Some among them had noticed the direction in which Christ and His disciples had gone. Many went by land to meet them,

while others followed in their boats across the water. The Passover was at hand, and, from far and near, bands of pilgrims on their way to Jerusalem gathered to see Jesus. Additions were made to their number, until there were assembled five thousand men besides women and children. Before Christ reached the shore, a multitude were waiting for Him. But He landed unobserved by them, and spent a little time apart with the disciples.

From the hillside He looked upon the moving multitude, and His heart was stirred with sympathy. Interrupted as He was, and robbed of His rest, He was not impatient. He saw a greater necessity demanding His attention as He watched the people coming and still coming. He "was moved with compassion toward them, because they were as sheep not having a shepherd." Leaving His retreat, He found a convenient place where He could minister to them. They received no help from the priests and rulers; but the healing waters of life flowed from Christ as He taught the multitude the way of salvation.

The people listened to the words of mercy flowing so freely from the lips of the Son of God. They heard the gracious words, so simple and so plain that they were as the balm of Gilead to their souls. The healing of His divine hand brought gladness and life to the dying, and ease and health to those suffering with disease. The day seemed to them like heaven upon earth, and they were utterly unconscious of how long it had been since they had eaten anything.

At length the day was far spent. The sun was sinking in the west, and yet the people lingered. Jesus had labored all day without food or rest. He was pale from weariness and hunger, and the disciples besought Him to cease from His toil. But He could not withdraw Himself from the multitude that pressed upon Him.

The disciples finally came to Him, urging that for their own sake the people should be sent away. Many had come from far, and had eaten nothing since morning. In the surrounding towns and villages they might be able to buy food. But Jesus said, "Give them to eat," and then, turning to Philip, questioned, "Whence shall we buy bread, that these may eat?" This He said to test the faith of the disciple. Philip looked over the sea of heads, and thought how impossible it would be to provide food to satisfy the wants of such a crowd. He answered that two hundred pennyworth of bread would not be nearly enough to divide among them, so that each might have a little. Jesus inquired how much food could be found among the company. "There is a lad here," said Andrew, "which hath five barley loaves, and two small fishes: but what are they among so many?" Jesus directed that these be brought to Him. Then He bade the disciples seat the people on the grass in parties

This chapter is based on Matthew 14:13-21; Mark 6:32-44; Luke 9:10-17; John 6:1-13.

of fifty or a hundred, to preserve order, and that all might witness what He was about to do. When this was accomplished, Jesus took the food, "and looking up to heaven, He blessed, and brake, and gave the loaves to His disciples, and the disciples to the multitude." "And they did all eat, and were filled. And they took up twelve baskets full of the fragments, and of the fishes."

He who taught the people the way to secure peace and happiness was just as thoughtful of their temporal necessities as of their spiritual need. The people were weary and faint. There were mothers with babes in their arms, and little children clinging to their skirts. Many had been standing for hours. They had been so intensely interested in Christ's words that they had not once thought of sitting down, and the crowd was so great that there was danger of their trampling on one another. Jesus would give them a chance to rest, and He bade them sit down. There was much grass in the place, and all could rest in comfort.

Christ never worked a miracle except to supply a genuine necessity, and every miracle was of a character to lead the people to the tree of life, whose leaves are for the healing of the nations. The simple food passed round by the hands of the disciples contained a whole treasure of lessons. It was humble fare that had been provided; the fishes and barley loaves were the daily food of the fisher folk about the Sea of Galilee. Christ could have spread before the people a rich repast, but food prepared merely for the gratification of appetite would have conveyed no lesson for their good. Christ taught them in this lesson that the natural provisions of God for man had been perverted. And never did people enjoy the luxurious feasts prepared for the gratification of perverted taste as this people enjoyed the rest and the simple food which Christ provided so far from human habitations.

If men today were simple in their habits, living in harmony with nature's laws, as did Adam and Eve in the beginning, there would be an abundant supply for the needs of the human family. There would be fewer imaginary wants, and more opportunities to work in God's ways. But selfishness and the indulgence of unnatural taste have brought sin and misery into the world, from excess on the one hand, and from want on the other.

Jesus did not seek to attract the people to Him by gratifying the desire for luxury. To that great throng, weary and hungry after the long, exciting day, the simple fare was an assurance not only of His power, but of His tender care for them in the common needs of life. The Saviour has not promised His followers the luxuries of the world; their fare may be plain, and even scanty; their lot may be shut in by poverty; but His word is pledged that their need shall be sup-

plied, and He has promised that which is far better than worldly good,—the abiding comfort of His own presence.

In feeding the five thousand, Jesus lifts the veil from the world of nature, and reveals the power that is constantly exercised for our good. In the production of earth's harvests God is working a miracle every day. Through natural agencies the same work is accomplished that was wrought in the feeding of the multitude. Men prepare the soil and sow the seed, but it is the life from God that causes the seed to germinate. It is God's rain and air and sunshine that cause it to put forth, "first the blade, then the ear, after that the full corn in the ear." Mark 4:28. It is God who is every day feeding millions from earth's harvest fields. Men are called upon to co-operate with God in the care of the grain and the preparation of the loaf, and because of this they lose sight of the divine agency. They do not give God the glory due unto His holy name. The working of His power is ascribed to natural causes or to human instrumentality. Man is glorified in place of God, and His gracious gifts are perverted to selfish uses, and made a curse instead of a blessing. God is seeking to change all this. He desires that our dull senses shall be quickened to discern His merciful kindness and to glorify Him for the working of His power. He desires us to recognize Him in His gifts, that they may be, as He intended, a blessing to us. It was to accomplish this purpose that the miracles of Christ were performed.

After the multitude had been fed, there was an abundance of food left. But He who had all the resources of infinite power at His command said, "Gather up the fragments that remain, that nothing be lost." These words meant more than putting the bread into the baskets. The lesson was twofold. Nothing is to be wasted. We are to let slip no temporal advantage. We should neglect nothing that will tend to benefit a human being. Let everything be gathered up that will relieve the necessity of earth's hungry ones. And there should be the same carefulness in spiritual things. When the baskets of fragments were collected, the people thought of their friends at home. They wanted them to share in the bread that Christ had blessed. The contents of the baskets were distributed among the eager throng, and were carried away into all the region round about. So those who were at the feast were to give to others the bread that comes down from heaven, to satisfy the hunger of the soul. They were to repeat what they had learned of the wonderful things of Christ. Nothing was to be lost. Not one word that concerned their eternal salvation was to fall useless to the ground.

The miracle of the loaves teaches a lesson of dependence upon God. When Christ fed the five thousand, the food was not nigh at hand.

Apparently He had no means at His command. Here He was, with five thousand men, besides women and children, in the wilderness. He had not invited the large multitude to follow Him; they came without invitation or command; but He knew that after they had listened so long to His instruction, they would feel hungry and faint; for He was one with them in their need of food. They were far from home, and the night was close at hand. Many of them were without means to purchase food. He who for their sake had fasted forty days in the wilderness would not suffer them to return fasting to their homes. The providence of God had placed Jesus where He was; and He depended on His heavenly Father for the means to relieve the necessity.

369 And when we are brought into strait places, we are to depend on God. We are to exercise wisdom and judgment in every action of life, that we may not, by reckless movements, place ourselves in trial. We are not to plunge into difficulties, neglecting the means God has provided, and misusing the faculties He has given us. Christ's workers are to obey His instructions implicitly. The work is God's, and if we would bless others His plans must be followed. Self cannot be made a center; self can receive no honor. If we plan according to our own ideas, the Lord will leave us to our own mistakes. But when, after following His directions, we are brought into strait places, He will deliver us. We are not to give up in discouragement, but in every emergency we are to seek help from Him who has infinite resources at His command. Often we shall be surrounded with trying circumstances, and then, in the fullest confidence, we must depend upon God. He will keep every soul that is brought into perplexity through trying to keep the way of the Lord.

Christ has bidden us, through the prophet, "Deal thy bread to the hungry," and "satisfy the afflicted soul;" "when thou seest the naked, that thou cover him," and "bring the poor that are cast out to thy house." Isa. 58:7-10. He has bidden us, "Go ye into all the world, and preach the gospel to every creature." Mark 16:15. But how often our hearts sink, and faith fails us, as we see how great is the need, and how small the means in our hands. Like Andrew looking upon the five barley loaves and the two little fishes, we exclaim, "What are they among so many?" Often we hesitate, unwilling to give all that we have, fearing to spend and to be spent for others. But Jesus has bidden us, "Give ye them to eat." His command is a promise; and behind it is the same power that fed the multitude beside the sea.

In Christ's act of supplying the temporal necessities of a hungry multitude is wrapped up a deep spiritual lesson for all His workers. Christ received from the Father; He imparted to the disciples; they imparted to the multitude; and the people to one another. So all who are united to Christ will receive from Him the bread of life, the heavenly food, and impart it to others.

In full reliance upon God, Jesus took the small store of loaves; and although there was but a small portion for His own family of disciples, He did not invite them to eat, but began to distribute to them, bidding them serve the people. The food multiplied in His hands; and the hands of the disciples, reaching out to Christ Himself the Bread of Life, were never empty. 370 The little store was sufficient for all. After the wants of the people had been supplied, the fragments were gathered up, and Christ and His disciples ate together of the precious, Heaven-supplied food.

The disciples were the channel of communication between Christ and the people. This should be a great encouragement to His disciples today. Christ is the great center, the source of all strength. His disciples are to receive their supplies from Him. The most intelligent, the most spiritually minded, can bestow only as they receive. Of themselves they can supply nothing for the needs of the soul. We can impart only that which we receive from Christ; and we can receive only as we impart to others. As we continue imparting, we continue to receive; and the more we impart, the more we shall receive. Thus we may be constantly believing, trusting, receiving, and imparting.

The work of building up the kingdom of Christ will go forward, though to all appearance it moves slowly and impossibilities seem to testify against advance. The work is of God, and He will furnish means, and will send helpers, true, earnest disciples, whose hands also will be filled with food for the starving multitude. God is not unmindful of those who labor in love to give the word of life to perishing souls, who in their turn reach forth their hands for food for other hungry souls.

In our work for God there is danger of relying too largely upon what man with his talents and ability can do. Thus we lose sight of the one Master Worker. Too often the worker for Christ fails to realize his personal responsibility. He is in danger of shifting his burden upon organizations, instead of relying upon Him who is the source of all strength. It is a great mistake to trust in human wisdom or numbers in the work of God. Successful work for Christ depends not so much on numbers or talent as upon pureness of purpose, the true simplicity of earnest, dependent faith. Personal responsibilities must be borne, personal duties must be taken up, personal efforts must be made for those who do not know Christ. In the place of shifting your responsibility upon someone whom you think more richly endowed than you are, work according to your ability.

When the question comes home to your heart, "Whence shall we buy bread, that these may eat?" let not your answer be the response of unbelief. When the disciples heard the Saviour's direction, "Give ye them to eat," all the difficulties arose in their minds. They questioned, Shall we go away into the villages to buy food? So now, when the people are destitute of the bread of life, the Lord's children question, Shall we send for someone from afar, to come and feed them? But what said Christ? "Make the men sit down," and He fed them there. So when you are surrounded by souls in which, know that Christ is there. Commune with Him. Bring your barley loaves to Jesus.

The means in our possession may not seem to be sufficient for the work; but if we will move forward in faith, believing in the all-sufficient power of God, abundant resources will open before us. If the work be of God, He Himself will provide the means for its accomplishment. He will reward honest, simple reliance upon Him. The little that is wisely and economically used in the service of the Lord of heaven will increase in the very act of imparting. In the hand of Christ the small supply of food remained undiminished until the famished multitude were satisfied. If we go to the Source of all strength, with our hands of faith outstretched to receive, we shall be sustained in our work, even under the most forbidding circumstances, and shall be enabled to give to others the bread of life.

The Lord says, "Give, and it shall be given unto you." "He that soweth sparingly shall reap also sparingly; and he that soweth with blessings shall reap also with blessings. . . . And God is able to make all grace abound unto you; that ye, having always all sufficiency in everything, may abound unto every good work: as it is written,—

"He hath scattered abroad, he hath given to the poor:

His righteousness abideth forever.

"And He that supplieth seed to the sower and bread for food, shall supply and multiply your seed for sowing, and increase the fruits of your righteousness: ye being enriched in everything unto all liberality, which worketh through us to thanksgiving to God." Luke 6:38; 2 Cor. 9:6-11, R. V., margin.

40

A Night on the Lake

Seated upon the grassy plain, in the twilight of the spring evening, the people ate of the food that Christ had provided. The words they had heard that day had come to them as the voice of God. The works of healing they had witnessed were such as only divine power could perform. But the miracle of the loaves appealed to everyone in that vast multitude. All were sharers in its benefit. In the days of Moses, God had fed Israel with manna in the desert; and who was this that had fed them that day but He whom Moses had foretold? No human power could create from five barley loaves and two small fishes food sufficient to feed thousands of hungry people. And they said one to another, "This is of a truth that Prophet that should come into the world."

All day the conviction has strengthened. That crowning act is assurance that the long-looked-for Deliverer is among them. The hopes of the people rise higher and higher. This is He who will make Judea an earthly paradise, a land flowing with milk and honey. He can satisfy every desire. He can break the power of the hated Romans. He can deliver Judah and Jerusalem. He can heal the soldiers who are wounded in battle. He can supply whole armies with food. He can conquer the nations, and give to Israel the long-sought dominion.

In their enthusiasm the people are ready at once to crown Him king. They see that He makes no effort to attract attention or secure honor to Himself. In this He is essentially different from the priests and rulers, and they fear that He will never urge His claim to David's throne. Consulting together, they agree to take Him by force, and proclaim Him the king of Israel. The disciples unite with the multitude in declaring the throne of David the rightful inheritance of their Master. It is the modesty of Christ, they say, that causes Him to refuse such honor. Let the people exalt their Deliverer. Let the arrogant priests and rulers be forced to honor Him who comes clothed with the authority of God.

They eagerly arrange to carry out their purpose; but Jesus sees what is on foot, and understands, as they cannot, what would be the result of such a movement. Even now the priests and rulers are hunting His life. They accuse Him of drawing the people away from them. Violence and insurrection would follow an effort to place Him on the throne, and the work of the spiritual kingdom would be hindered. Without delay the movement must be checked. Calling His disciples, Jesus bids them take the boat and return at

This chapter is based on Matthew 14:22-33; Mark 6:45-52; John 6:14-21.

once to Capernaum, leaving Him to dismiss the people.

Never before had a command from Christ seemed so impossible of fulfillment. The disciples had long hoped for a popular movement to place Jesus on the throne; they could not endure the thought that all this enthusiasm should come to nothing. The multitudes that were assembling to keep the Passover were anxious to see the new prophet. To His followers this seemed the golden opportunity to establish their beloved Master on the throne of Israel. In the glow of this new ambition it was hard for them to go away by themselves, and leave Jesus alone upon that desolate shore. They protested against the arrangement; but Jesus now spoke with an authority He had never before assumed toward them. They knew that further opposition on their part would be useless, and in silence they turned toward the sea.

Jesus now commands the multitude to disperse; and His manner is so decisive that they dare not disobey. The words of praise and exaltation die on their lips. In the very act of advancing to seize Him their steps are stayed, and the glad, eager look fades from their countenances. In that throng are men of strong mind and firm determination; but the kingly bearing of Jesus, and His few quiet words of command, quell the tumult, and frustrate their designs. 379 They recognize in Him a power above all earthly authority, and without a question they submit.

When left alone, Jesus "went up into a mountain apart to pray." For hours He continued pleading with God. Not for Himself but for men were those prayers. He prayed for power to reveal to men the divine character of His mission, that Satan might not blind their understanding and pervert their judgment. The Saviour knew that His days of personal ministry on earth were nearly ended, and that few would receive Him as their Redeemer. In travail and conflict of soul He prayed for His disciples. They were to be grievously tried. Their long-cherished hopes, based on a popular delusion, were to be disappointed in a most painful and humiliating manner. In the place of His exaltation to the throne of David they were to witness His crucifixion. This was to be indeed His true coronation. But they did not discern this, and in consequence strong temptations would come to them, which it would be difficult for them to recognize as temptations. Without the Holy Spirit to enlighten the mind and enlarge the comprehension the faith of the disciples would fail. It was painful to Jesus that their conceptions of His kingdom were, to so great a degree, limited to worldly aggrandizement and honor. For them the burden was heavy upon His heart, and He poured out His supplications with bitter agony and tears.

The disciples had not put off immediately from the land, as Jesus directed them. They waited for a time, hoping that He would come to them. But as they saw that darkness was fast 380 gathering, they "entered into a ship, and went over the sea toward Capernaum." They had left Jesus with dissatisfied hearts, more impatient with Him than ever before since acknowledging Him as their Lord. They murmured because they had not been permitted to proclaim Him king. They blamed themselves for yielding so readily to His command. They reasoned that if they had been more persistent they might have accomplished their purpose.

Unbelief was taking possession of their minds and hearts. Love of honor had blinded them. They knew that Jesus was hated by the Pharisees, and they were eager to see Him exalted as they thought He should be. To be united with a teacher who could work mighty miracles, and yet to be reviled as deceivers, was a trial they could ill endure. Were they always to be accounted followers of a false prophet? Would Christ never assert His authority as king? Why did not He who possessed such power reveal Himself in His true character, and make their way less painful? Why had He not saved John the Baptist from a violent death? Thus the disciples reasoned until they brought upon themselves great spiritual darkness. They questioned, Could Jesus be an impostor, as the Pharisees asserted?

The disciples had that day witnessed the wonderful works of Christ. It had seemed that heaven had come down to the earth. The memory of that precious, glorious day should have filled them with faith and hope. Had they, out of the abundance of their hearts, been conversing together in regard to these things, they would not have entered into temptation. But their disappointment had absorbed their thoughts. The words of Christ, "Gather up the fragments, . . . that nothing be lost," were unheeded. Those were hours of large blessing to the disciples, but they had forgotten it all. They were in the midst of troubled waters. Their thoughts were stormy and unreasonable, and the Lord gave them something else to afflict their souls and occupy their minds. God often does this when men create burdens and troubles for themselves. The disciples had no need to make trouble. Already danger was fast approaching.

A violent tempest had been stealing upon them, and they were unprepared for it. It was a sudden contrast, for the day had been perfect; and when the gale struck them, they were afraid. They forgot their disaffection, their unbelief, their impatience. Everyone worked to keep the boat from sinking. It was but a short distance by sea from Bethsaida to the point where they expected to meet Jesus, and in ordinary weather the journey required but a few hours; but now they were driven farther and farther from the 381

632

point they sought. Until the fourth watch of the night they toiled at the oars. Then the weary men gave themselves up for lost. In storm and darkness the sea had taught them their own helplessness, and they longed for the presence of their Master.

Jesus had not forgotten them. The Watcher on the shore saw those fear-stricken men battling with the tempest. Not for a moment did He lose sight of His disciples. With deepest solicitude His eyes followed the storm-tossed boat with its precious burden; for these men were to be the light of the world. As a mother in tender love watches her child, so the compassionate Master watched His disciples. When their hearts were subdued, their unholy ambition quelled, and in humility they prayed for help, it was given them.

At the moment when they believe themselves lost, a gleam of light reveals a mysterious figure approaching them upon the water. But they know not that it is Jesus. The One who has come for their help they count as an enemy. Terror overpowers them. The hands that have grasped the oars with muscles like iron let go their hold. The boat rocks at the will of the waves; all eyes are riveted on this vision of a man walking upon the white-capped billows of the foaming sea.

They think it a phantom that omens their destruction, and they cry out for fear. Jesus advances as if He would pass them; but they recognize Him, and cry out, entreating His help. Their beloved Master turns, His voice silences their fear, "Be of good cheer: it is I; be not afraid."

As soon as they could credit the wondrous fact, Peter was almost beside himself with joy. As if he could scarcely yet believe, he cried out, "Lord, if it be Thou, bid me come unto Thee on the water. And He said, Come."

Looking unto Jesus, Peter walks securely; but as in self-satisfaction he glances back toward his companions in the boat, his eyes are turned from the Saviour. The wind is boisterous. The waves roll high, and come directly between him and the Master; and he is afraid. For a moment Christ is hidden from his view, and his faith gives way. He begins to sink. But while the billows talk with death, Peter lifts his eyes from the angry waters, and fixing them upon Jesus, cries, "Lord, save me." Immediately Jesus grasps the outstretched hand, saying, "O thou of little faith, wherefore didst thou doubt?"

Walking side by side, Peter's hand in that of his Master, they stepped into the boat together. But Peter was now subdued and silent. He had no reason to boast over his fellows, for through unbelief and self-exaltation he had very nearly lost his life. When he turned his eyes from Jesus, his footing was lost, and he sank amid the waves.

When trouble comes upon us, how often we are like Peter! We look upon the waves, instead of keeping our eyes fixed upon the Saviour. Our footsteps slide, and the proud waters go over our souls. Jesus did not bid Peter come to Him that he should perish; He does not call us to follow Him, and then forsake us. "Fear not," He says; "for I have redeemed thee, I have called thee by thy name; thou art Mine. When thou passest through the waters, I will be with thee; and through the rivers, they shall not overflow thee: when thou walkest through the fire, thou shalt not be burned; neither shall the flame kindle upon thee. For I am the Lord thy God, the Holy One of Israel, thy Saviour." Isa. 43:1-3.

Jesus read the character of His disciples. He knew how sorely their faith was to be tried. In this incident on the sea He desired to reveal to Peter his own weakness,—to show that his safety was in constant dependence upon divine power. Amid the storms of temptation he could walk safely only as in utter self-distrust he should rely upon the Saviour. It was on the point where he thought himself strong that Peter was weak; and not until he discerned his weakness could he realize his need of dependence upon Christ. Had he learned the lesson that Jesus sought to teach him in that experience on the sea, he would not have failed when the great test came upon him.

Day by day God instructs His children. By the circumstances of the daily life He is preparing them to act their part upon that wider stage to which His providence has appointed them. It is the issue of the daily test that determines their victory or defeat in life's great crisis.

Those who fail to realize their constant dependence upon God will be overcome by temptation. We may now suppose that our feet stand secure, and that we shall never be moved. We may say with confidence, "I know in whom I have believed; nothing can shake my faith in God and in His word." But Satan is planning to take advantage of our hereditary and cultivated traits of character, and to blind our eyes to our own necessities and defects. Only through realizing our own weakness and looking steadfastly unto Jesus can we walk securely.

No sooner had Jesus taken His place in the boat than the wind ceased, "and immediately the ship was at the land whither they went." The night of horror was succeeded by the light of dawn. The disciples, and others who also were on board, bowed at the feet of Jesus with thankful hearts, saying, "Of a truth Thou art the Son of God!"

41

The Crisis in Galilee

When Christ forbade the people to declare Him king, He knew that a turning point in His history was reached. Multitudes who desired to exalt Him to the throne today would turn from Him tomorrow. The disappointment of their selfish ambition would turn their love to hatred, and their praise to curses. Yet knowing this, He took no measures to avert the crisis. From the first He had held out to His followers no hope of earthly rewards. To one who came desiring to become His disciple He had said, "The foxes have holes, and the birds of the air have nests; but the Son of man hath not where to lay His head." Matt. 8:20. If men could have had the world with Christ, multitudes would have proffered Him their allegiance; but such service He could not accept. Of those now connected with Him there were many who had been attracted by the hope of a worldly kingdom. These must be undeceived. The deep spiritual teaching in the miracle of the loaves had not been comprehended. This was to be made plain. And this new revelation would bring with it a closer test.

The miracle of the loaves was reported far and near, and very early next morning the people flocked to Bethsaida to see Jesus. They came in great numbers, by land and sea. Those who had left Him the preceding night returned, expecting to find Him still there; for there had been no boat by which He could pass to the other side. But their search was fruitless, and many repaired to Capernaum, still seeking Him.

Meanwhile He had arrived at Gennesaret, after an absence of but one day. As soon as it was known that He had landed, the people "ran through that whole region round about, and began to carry about in beds those that were sick, where they heard He was." Mark 6:55.

After a time He went to the synagogue, and there those who had come from Bethsaida found Him. They learned from His disciples how He had crossed the sea. The fury of the storm, and the many hours of fruitless rowing against adverse winds, the appearance of Christ walking upon the water, the fears thus aroused, His reassuring words, the adventure of Peter and its result, with the sudden stilling of the tempest and landing of the boat, were all faithfully recounted to the wondering crowd. Not content with this, however, many gathered about Jesus, questioning, "Rabbi, when camest Thou hither?" They hoped to receive from His own lips a further account of the miracle.

Jesus did not gratify their curiosity. He sadly said, "Ye seek Me, not because ye saw the miracles, but because ye did eat of the loaves, and were filled." They did not seek Him from any worthy motive; but as they had been fed with the loaves, they hoped still to receive temporal benefit by attaching themselves to Him. The Saviour bade them, "Labor not for the meat which perisheth, but for that meat which endureth unto everlasting life." Seek not merely for material benefit. Let it not be the chief effort to provide for the life that now is, but seek for spiritual food, even that wisdom which will endure unto everlasting life. This the Son of God alone can give; "for Him hath God the Father sealed."

For the moment the interest of the hearers was awakened. They exclaimed, "What shall we do, that we might work the works of God?" They had been performing many and burdensome works in order to recommend themselves to God; and they were ready to hear of any new observance by which they could secure greater merit. Their question meant, What shall we do that we may deserve heaven? What is the price we are required to pay in order to obtain the life to come?

"Jesus answered and said unto them, This is the work of God, that ye believe on Him whom He hath sent." The price of heaven is Jesus. The way to heaven is through faith in "the Lamb of God, which taketh away the sin of the world." John 1:29.

But the people did not choose to receive this statement of divine truth. Jesus had done the very work which prophecy had foretold that the Messiah would do; but they had not witnessed what their selfish hopes had pictured as His work. Christ had indeed once fed the multitude with barley loaves; but in the days of Moses Israel had been fed with manna forty years, and far greater blessings were expected from the Messiah. Their dissatisfied hearts queried why, if Jesus could perform so many wondrous works as they had witnessed, could He not give health, strength, and riches to all His people, free them from their oppressors, and exalt them to power and honor? The fact that He claimed to be the Sent of God, and yet refused to be Israel's king, was a mystery which they could not fathom. His refusal was misinterpreted. Many concluded that He dared not assert His claims because He Himself doubted as to the divine character of His mission. Thus they opened their hearts to unbelief, and the seed which Satan had sown bore fruit of its kind, in misunderstanding and defection.

Now, half mockingly, a rabbi questioned, "What sign showest Thou then, that we may see, and believe Thee? what dost Thou work? Our fathers did eat manna in the desert; as it is written, He gave them bread from heaven to eat."

The Jews honored Moses as the giver of the

This chapter is based on John 6:22-71.

manna, ascribing praise to the instrument, and losing sight of Him by whom the work had been accomplished. Their fathers had murmured against Moses, and had doubted and denied his divine mission. Now in the same spirit the children rejected the One who bore the message of God to themselves. "Then said Jesus unto them, Verily, verily, I say unto you, Moses gave you not that bread from heaven." The giver of the manna was standing among them. It was Christ Himself who had led the Hebrews through the wilderness, and had daily fed them with the bread from heaven. That food was a type of the real bread from heaven. The life-giving Spirit, flowing from the infinite fullness of God, is the true manna. Jesus said, "The bread of God is that which cometh down out of heaven, and giveth life unto the world." John 6:33, R. V.

Still thinking that it was temporal food to which Jesus referred, some of His hearers exclaimed, "Lord, evermore give us this bread." Jesus then spoke plainly: "I am the bread of life."

The figure which Christ used was a familiar one to the Jews. Moses, by the inspiration of the Holy Spirit, had said, "Man doth not live by bread only, but by every word that proceedeth out of the mouth of the Lord." And the prophet Jeremiah had written, "Thy words were found, and I did eat them; and Thy word was unto me the joy and rejoicing of mine heart." Deut. 8:3; Jer. 15:16. The rabbis themselves had a saying, that the eating of bread, in its spiritual significance, was the study of the law and the practice of good works; and it was often said that at the Messiah's coming all Israel would be fed. The teaching of the prophets made plain the deep spiritual lesson in the miracle of the loaves. This lesson Christ was seeking to open to His hearers in the synagogue. Had they understood the Scriptures, they would have understood His words when He said, "I am the bread of life." Only the day before, the great multitude, when faint and weary, had been fed by the bread which He had given. As from that bread they had received physical strength and refreshment, so from Christ they might receive spiritual strength unto eternal life. "He that cometh to Me," He said, "shall never hunger; and he that believeth on Me shall never thirst." But He added, "Ye also have seen Me, and believe not."

They had seen Christ by the witness of the Holy Spirit, by the revelation of God to their souls. The living evidences of His power had been before them day after day, yet they asked for still another sign. Had this been given, they would have remained as unbelieving as before. If they were not convinced by what they had seen and heard, it was useless to show them more marvelous works. Unbelief will ever find excuse for doubt, and will reason away the most positive proof.

Again Christ appealed to those stubborn hearts. "Him that cometh to Me I will in nowise cast out." All who received Him in faith, He said, should have eternal life. Not one could be lost. No need for Pharisees and Sadducees to dispute concerning the future life. No longer need men mourn in hopeless grief over their dead. "This is the will of Him that sent Me, that everyone which seeth the Son, and believeth on Him, may have everlasting life: and I will raise him up at the last day."

But the leaders of the people were offended, "and they said, Is not this Jesus, the son of Joseph, whose father and mother we know? how is it then that He saith, I came down from heaven?" They tried to arouse prejudice by referring scornfully to the lowly origin of Jesus. They contemptuously alluded to His life as a Galilean laborer, and to His family as being poor and lowly. The claims of this uneducated carpenter, they said, were unworthy of their attention. And on account of His mysterious birth they insinuated that He was of doubtful parentage, thus representing the human circumstances of His birth as a blot upon His history.

Jesus did not attempt to explain the mystery of His birth. He made no answer to the questionings in regard to His having come down from heaven, as He had made none to the questions concerning His crossing the sea. He did not call attention to the miracles that marked His life. Voluntarily He had made Himself of no reputation, and taken upon Him the form of a servant. But His words and works revealed His character. All whose hearts were open to divine illumination would recognize in Him "the Only-begotten of the Father, full of grace and truth." John 1:14.

The prejudice of the Pharisees lay deeper than their questions would indicate; it had its root in the perversity of their hearts. Every word and act of Jesus aroused antagonism in them; for the spirit which they cherished could find in Him no answering chord.

"No man can come to Me, except the Father which hath sent Me draw him: and I will raise him up at the last day. It is written in the prophets, And they shall be all taught of God. Every man therefore that hath heard, and hath learned of the Father, cometh unto Me." None will ever come to Christ, save those who respond to the drawing of the Father's love. But God is drawing all hearts unto Him, and only those who resist His drawing will refuse to come to Christ.

In the words, "They shall be all taught of God," Jesus referred to the prophecy of Isaiah: "All thy children shall be taught of the Lord; and great shall be the peace of thy children." Isa. 54:13. This scripture the Jews appropriated to themselves. It was their boast that God was their teacher. But Jesus showed how vain is this claim; for He said, "Every man therefore that hath heard, and hath learned of the Father, cometh unto Me." Only through Christ could they receive a knowledge of the Father. Humanity could not endure the vision of His glory. Those who had learned of God had been listening to the voice of His Son, and in Jesus of Nazareth they would recognize Him who through nature and revelation has declared the Father.

"Verily, verily, I say unto you, He that believeth on Me hath everlasting life." Through the beloved John, who listened to these words, the Holy Spirit declared to the churches, "This is the record, that God hath given to us eternal life, and this life is in His Son. He that hath the Son hath life." 1 John 5:11, 12. And Jesus said, "I will raise him up at the last day." Christ became one flesh with us, in order that we might become one spirit with Him. It is by virtue of this union that we are to come forth from the grave,—not merely as a manifestation of the power of Christ, but because, through faith, His life has become ours. Those who see Christ in His true character, and receive Him into the heart, have everlasting life. It is through the Spirit that Christ dwells in us; and the Spirit of God, received into the heart by faith, is the beginning of the life eternal.

The people had referred Christ to the manna which their fathers ate in the wilderness, as if the furnishing of that food was a greater miracle than Jesus had performed; but He shows how meager was that gift when compared with the blessings He had come to bestow. The manna could sustain only this earthly existence; it did not prevent the approach of death, nor insure immortality; but the bread of heaven would nourish the soul unto everlasting life. The Saviour said, "I am that bread of life. Your fathers did eat manna in the wilderness, and are dead. This is the bread which cometh down from heaven, that a man may eat thereof, and not die. I am the living bread which came down from heaven: if any man eat of this bread, he shall live forever." To this figure Christ now adds another. Only through dying could He impart life to men, and in the words that follow He points to His death as the means of salvation. He says, "The bread that I will give is My flesh, which I will give for the life of the world."

The Jews were about to celebrate the Passover at Jerusalem, in commemoration of the night of Israel's deliverance, when the destroying angel smote the homes of Egypt. In the

389

paschal lamb God desired them to behold the Lamb of God, and through the symbol receive Him who gave Himself for the life of the world. But the Jews had come to make the symbol all-important, while its significance was unnoticed. They discerned not the Lord's body. The same truth that was symbolized in the paschal service

was taught in the words of Christ. But it was still undiscerned.

Now the rabbis exclaimed angrily, "How can this Man give us His flesh to eat?" They affected to understand His words in the same literal sense as did Nicodemus when he asked, "How can a man be born when he is old?" John 3:4. To some extent they comprehended the meaning of Jesus, but they were not willing to acknowledge it. By misconstruing His words, they hoped to prejudice the people against Him.

Christ did not soften down His symbolical representation. He reiterated the truth in yet stronger language: "Verily, verily, I say unto you, Except ye eat the flesh of the Son of man, and drink His blood, ye have no life in you. Whoso eateth My flesh, and drinketh My blood, hath eternal life; and I will raise him up at the last day. For My flesh is meat indeed, and My blood is drink indeed. He that eateth My flesh, and drinketh My blood, dwelleth in Me, and I in him."

To eat the flesh and drink the blood of Christ is to receive Him as a personal Saviour, believing that He forgives our sins, and that we are complete in Him. It is by beholding His love, by dwelling upon it, by drinking it in, that we are to become partakers of His nature. What food is to the body, Christ must be to the soul. Food cannot benefit us unless we eat it, unless it becomes a part of our being. So Christ is of no value to us if we do not know Him as a personal Saviour. A theoretical knowledge will do us no good. We must feed upon Him, receive Him into the heart, so that His life becomes our life. His love, His grace, must be assimilated.

But even these figures fail to present the privilege of the believer's relation to Christ. Jesus said, "As the living Father hath sent Me, and I live by the Father: so he that eateth Me, even he shall live by Me." As the Son of God lived by faith in the Father, so are we to live by faith in Christ. So fully was Jesus surrendered to the will of God that the Father alone appeared in His life. Although tempted in all points like as we are, He stood before the world untainted by the evil that surrounded Him. Thus we also are to overcome as Christ overcame.

Are you a follower of Christ? Then all that is written concerning the spiritual life is written for you, and may be attained through uniting yourself to Jesus. Is your zeal languishing? has 390 your first love grown cold? Accept again of the proffered love of Christ. Eat of His flesh, drink of His blood, and you will become one with the Father and with the Son.

The unbelieving Jews refused to see any except the most literal meaning in the Saviour's words. By the ritual law they were forbidden to taste blood, and they now construed Christ's language into a sacrilegious speech, and disputed over it among themselves. Many even of the disciples said, "This is an hard saying; who can hear it?"

The Saviour answered them: "Doth *this* offend you? What and if ye shall see the Son of man ascend up where He was before? It is the spirit that quickeneth; the flesh profiteth nothing: the words that I speak unto you, they are spirit, and they are life."

The life of Christ that gives life to the world is in His word. It was by His word that Jesus healed disease and cast out demons; by His word He stilled the sea, and raised the dead; and the people bore witness that His word was with power. He spoke the word of God, as He had spoken through all the prophets and teachers of the Old Testament. The whole Bible is a manifestation of Christ, and the Saviour desired to fix the faith of His followers on the word. When His visible presence should be withdrawn, the word must be their source of power. Like their Master, they were to live "by every word that proceedeth out of the mouth of God." Matt. 4:4.

As our physical life is sustained by food, so our spiritual life is sustained by the word of God. And every soul is to receive life from God's word for himself. As we must eat for ourselves in order to receive nourishment, so we must receive the word for ourselves. We are not to obtain it merely through the medium of another's mind. We should carefully study the Bible, asking God for the aid of the Holy Spirit, that we may understand His word. We should take one verse, and concentrate the mind on the task of ascertaining the thought which God has put in that verse for us. We should dwell upon the thought until it becomes our own, and we know "what saith the Lord."

In His promises and warnings, Jesus means me. God so loved the world, that He gave His only-begotten Son, that *I* by believing in Him, might not perish, but have everlasting life. The experiences related in God's word are to be *my* experiences. Prayer and promise, precept and warning, are mine. "I am crucified with Christ: nevertheless I live; yet not I, but Christ liveth in me: and the life which I now live in the flesh I live by the faith of the Son of God, who loved 391 *me*, and gave Himself for *me*." Gal. 2:20. As faith thus receives and assimilates the principles of truth, they become a part of the being and the motive power of the life. The word of God, received into the soul, molds the thoughts, and enters into the development of character.

By looking constantly to Jesus with the eye of faith, we shall be strengthened. God will make the most precious revelations to His hungering, thirsting people. They will find that Christ is a personal Saviour. As they feed upon His word, they find that it is spirit and life. The word destroys the natural, earthly nature, and imparts a new life in Christ Jesus. The Holy Spirit comes to the soul as a Comforter. By the transforming agency of His grace, the image of God is reproduced in the disciple; he becomes a new creature. Love takes the place of hatred, and the heart receives the divine similitude. This is what it means to live "by every word that proceedeth out of the mouth of God." This is eating the Bread that comes down from heaven.

Christ had spoken a sacred, eternal truth regarding the relation between Himself and His followers. He knew the character of those who claimed to be His disciples, and His words tested their faith. He declared that they were to believe and act upon His teaching. All who received Him would partake of His nature, and be conformed to His character. This involved the relinquishment of their cherished ambitions. It required the complete surrender of themselves to Jesus. They were called to become self-sacrificing, meek and lowly in heart. They must walk in the narrow path traveled by the Man of Calvary, if they would share in the gift of life and the glory of heaven.

The test was too great. The enthusiasm of those who had sought to take Him by force and make Him king grew cold. This discourse in the synagogue, they declared, had opened their eyes. Now they were undeceived. In their minds His words were a direct confession that He was not the Messiah, and that no earthly rewards were to be realized from connection with Him. They had welcomed His miracle-working power; they were eager to be freed from disease and suffering; but they would not come into sympathy with His self-sacrificing life. They cared not for the mysterious spiritual kingdom of which He spoke. The insincere, the selfish, who had sought Him, no longer desired Him. If He would not devote His power and influence to obtaining their freedom from the Romans, they would have nothing to do with Him.

Jesus told them plainly, "There are some of you that believe not;" adding, "Therefore said I unto you, that no man can come unto Me, except it were given unto him of My Father." 392 He wished them to understand that if they were not drawn to Him it was because their hearts were not open to the Holy Spirit. "The natural man receiveth not the things of the Spirit of God: for they are foolishness unto him: neither can he know them, because they are spiritually discerned." 1 Cor. 2:14. It is by faith that the soul beholds the glory of Jesus. This glory is hidden, until, through the Holy Spirit, faith is kindled in the soul.

By the public rebuke of their unbelief these disciples were still further alienated from Jesus. They were greatly displeased, and wishing to wound the Saviour and gratify the malice of the Pharisees, they turned their backs upon Him, and left Him with disdain. They had made their choice,—had taken the form without the spirit, the husk without the kernel. Their decision was never afterward reversed; for they walked no more with Jesus.

"Whose fan is in His hand, and He will throughly purge His floor, and gather His wheat into the garner." Matt. 3:12. This was one of the times of purging. By the words of truth, the chaff was being separated from the wheat. Because they were too vain and self-righteous to receive reproof, too world-loving to accept a life of humility, many turned away from Jesus. Many are still doing the same thing. Souls are tested today as were those disciples in the synagogue at Capernaum. When truth is brought home to the heart, they see that their lives are not in accordance with the will of God. They see the need of an entire change in themselves; but they are not willing to take up the self-denying work. Therefore they are angry when their sins are discovered. They go away offended, even as the disciples left Jesus, murmuring, "This is an hard saying; who can hear it?"

Praise and flattery would be pleasing to their ears; but the truth is unwelcome; they cannot hear it. When the crowds follow, and the multitudes are fed, and the shouts of triumph are heard, their voices are loud in praise; but when the searching of God's Spirit reveals their sin, and bids them leave it, they turn their backs upon the truth, and walk no more with Jesus.

As those disaffected disciples turned away from Christ, a different spirit took control of them. They could see nothing attractive in Him whom they had once found so interesting. They sought out His enemies, for they were in harmony with their spirit and work. They misinterpreted His words, falsified His statements, and impugned His motives. They sustained their course by gathering up every item that could be 393 turned against Him; and such indignation was stirred up by these false reports that His life was in danger.

The news spread swiftly that by His own confession Jesus of Nazareth was not the Messiah. And thus in Galilee the current of popular feeling was turned against Him, as, the year before, it had been in Judea. Alas for Israel! They rejected their Saviour, because they longed for a conqueror who would give them temporal power. They wanted the meat which perishes, and not that which endures unto everlasting life.

With a yearning heart, Jesus saw those who had been His disciples departing from Him, the Life and the Light of men. The consciousness that His compassion was unappreciated, His love unrequited, His mercy slighted, His salvation rejected, filled Him with sorrow that was inexpressible. It was such developments as these that made Him a man of sorrows, and acquainted with grief.

Without attempting to hinder those who were leaving Him, Jesus turned to the twelve and said, "Will ye also go away?"

Peter replied by asking, "Lord, to whom shall we go?" "Thou hast the words of eternal life," he added. "And we believe and are sure that Thou art that Christ, the Son of the living God."

"To whom shall we go?" The teachers of Israel were slaves to formalism. The Pharisees and Sadducees were in constant contention. To leave Jesus was to fall among sticklers for rites and ceremonies, and ambitious men who sought their own glory. The disciples had found more peace and joy since they had accepted Christ than in all their previous lives. How could they go back to those who had scorned and persecuted the Friend of sinners? They had long been looking for the Messiah; now He had come, and they could not turn from His presence to those who were hunting His life, and had persecuted them for becoming His followers.

"To whom shall we go?" Not from the teaching of Christ, His lessons of love and mercy, to the darkness of unbelief, the wickedness of the world. While the Saviour was forsaken by many who had witnessed His wonderful works, Peter expressed the faith of the disciples,—"Thou art that Christ." The very thought of losing this anchor of their souls filled them with fear and pain. To be destitute of a Saviour was to be adrift on a dark and stormy sea.

Many of the words and acts of Jesus appear mysterious to finite minds, but every word and act had its definite purpose in the work for our redemption; each was calculated to produce its own result. If we were capable of understanding 394 His purposes, all would appear important, complete, and in harmony with His mission.

While we cannot now comprehend the works and ways of God, we can discern His great love, which underlies all His dealings with men. He who lives near to Jesus will understand much of the mystery of godliness. He will recognize the mercy that administers reproof, that tests the character, and brings to light the purpose of the heart.

When Jesus presented the testing truth that caused so many of His disciples to turn back, He knew what would be the result of His words; but He had a purpose of mercy to fulfill. He foresaw that in the hour of temptation every one of His beloved disciples would be severely tested. His agony in Gethsemane, His betrayal and crucifixion, would be to them a most trying ordeal. Had no previous test been given, many who were actuated by merely selfish motives would have been connected with them. When their Lord was condemned in the judgment hall; when the multitude who had hailed Him as their king hissed at Him and reviled Him; when the jeering crowd cried, "Crucify Him!"—when their worldly ambitions were disappointed, these self-seeking ones would, by renouncing their allegiance to Jesus, have brought upon the disciples a bitter, heart-burdening sorrow, in addition to their grief and disappointment in the ruin of their fondest hopes. In that hour of darkness, the example of those who turned from Him might have carried others with them. But Jesus brought about this crisis while by His personal presence He could still strengthen the faith of His true followers.

Compassionate Redeemer, who in the full knowledge of the doom that awaited Him, tenderly smoothed the way for the disciples, prepared them for their crowning trial, and strengthened them for the final test!

395

42

Tradition

The scribes and Pharisees, expecting to see Jesus at the Passover, had laid a trap for Him. But Jesus, knowing their purpose, had absented Himself from this gathering. "Then came together unto Him the Pharisees, and certain of the scribes." As He did not go to them, they came to Him. For a time it had seemed that the people of Galilee would receive Jesus as the Messiah, and that the power of the hierarchy in that region would be broken. The mission of the twelve, indicating the extension of Christ's work, and bringing the disciples more directly into conflict with the rabbis, had excited anew the jealousy of the leaders at Jerusalem. The spies they sent to Capernaum in the early part of His ministry, who had tried to fix on Him the charge of Sabbathbreaking, had been put to confusion; but the rabbis were bent on carrying out their purpose. Now another deputation was sent to watch His movements, and find some accusation against Him.

As before, the ground of complaint was His disregard of the traditional precepts that encumbered the law of God. These were professedly designed to guard the observance of the law, but they were regarded as more sacred than the law itself. When they came in collision with the commandments given from Sinai, preference was given to the rabbinical precepts.

Among the observances most strenuously enforced was that of ceremonial purification. A neglect of the forms to be observed before eating was accounted a heinous sin, to be punished both in this world and in the next; and it was regarded as a virtue to destroy the transgressor.

396

The rules in regard to purification were numberless. The period of a lifetime was scarcely sufficient for one to learn them all. The life of those who tried to observe the rabbinical requirements was one long struggle against ceremonial defilement, an endless round of washings and purifications. While the people were occupied with trifling distinctions, and observances which God had not required, their attention was turned away from the great principles of His law.

Christ and His disciples did not observe these ceremonial washings, and the spies made this neglect the ground of their accusation. They did not, however, make a direct attack on Christ, but came to Him with criticism of His disciples. In the presence of the multitude they said, "Why do Thy disciples transgress the tradition of the elders? for they wash not their hands when they eat bread."

Whenever the message of truth comes home to souls with special power, Satan stirs up his agents to start a dispute over some minor question. Thus he seeks to attract attention from the real issue. Whenever a good work is begun, there are cavilers ready to enter into dispute over forms or technicalities, to draw minds away from the living realities. When it appears that God is about to work in a special manner for His people, let there not be enticed into a controversy that will work only ruin of souls. The questions that most concern us are, Do I believe with saving faith on the Son of God? Is my life in harmony with the divine law? "He that believeth on the Son hath everlasting life: and he that believeth not the Son shall not see life." "And hereby we do know that we know Him, if we keep His commandments." John 3:36; 1 John 2:3.

Jesus made no attempt to defend Himself or His disciples. He made no reference to the charges against Him, but proceeded to show the spirit that actuated these sticklers for human rites. He gave them an example of what they were repeatedly doing, and had done just before coming in search of Him. "Full well ye reject the commandment of God," He said, "that ye may keep your own tradition. For Moses said, Honor thy father and thy mother; and, Whoso curseth father or mother, let him die the death: but ye say, If a man shall say to his father or mother, It is Corban, that is to say, a gift, by whatsoever thou mightest be profited by me; he shall be free. And ye suffer him no more to do aught for his father or his mother." They set aside the fifth commandment as of no conse- 397 quence, but were very exact in carrying out the traditions of the elders. They taught the people that the devotion of their property to the temple was a duty more sacred than even the support of their parents; and that, however great the necessity, it was sacrilege to impart to father or mother any part of what had been thus consecrated. An undutiful child had only to pronounce the word "Corban" over his property, thus devoting it to God, and he could retain it for his own use during his lifetime, and after his death it was to be appropriated to the temple service. Thus he was at liberty, both in life and in death, to dishonor and defraud his parents, under cover of a

This chapter is based on Matthew 15:1-20; Mark 7:1-23.

pretended devotion to God.

Never, by word or deed, did Jesus lessen man's obligation to present gifts and offerings to God. It was Christ who gave all the directions of the law in regard to tithes and offerings. When on earth He commended the poor woman who gave her all to the temple treasury. But the apparent zeal for God on the part of the priests and rabbis was a pretense to cover their desire for self-aggrandizement. The people were deceived by them. They were bearing heavy burdens which God had not imposed. Even the disciples of Christ were not wholly free from the yoke that had been bound upon them by inherited prejudice and rabbinical authority. Now, by revealing the true spirit of the rabbis, Jesus sought to free from the bondage of tradition all who were really desirous of serving God.

"Ye hypocrites," He said, addressing the wily spies, "well did Esaias prophesy of you, saying, This people draweth nigh unto Me with their mouth, and honoreth Me with their lips; but their heart is far from Me. But in vain they do worship Me, teaching for doctrines the commandments of men." The words of Christ were an arraignment of the whole system of Pharisaism. He declared that by placing their requirements above the divine precepts the rabbis were setting themselves above God.

The deputies from Jerusalem were filled with rage. They could not accuse Christ as a violator of the law given from Sinai, for He spoke as its defender against their traditions. The great precepts of the law, which He had presented, appeared in striking contrast to the petty rules that men had devised.

To the multitude, and afterward more fully to His disciples, Jesus explained that defilement comes not from without, but from within. Purity and impurity pertain to the soul. It is the evil deed, the evil word, the evil thought, the transgression of the law of God, not the neglect of external, man-made ceremonies, that defiles a man.

398   The disciples noted the rage of the spies as their false teaching was exposed. They saw the angry looks, and heard the half-muttered words of dissatisfaction and revenge. Forgetting how often Christ had given evidence that He read the heart as an open book, they told Him of the effect of His words. Hoping that He might conciliate the enraged officials, they said to Jesus, "Knowest Thou that the Pharisees were offended, after they heard this saying?"

He answered, "Every plant, which My heavenly Father hath not planted, shall be rooted up." The customs and traditions so highly valued by the rabbis were of this world, not from heaven. However great their authority with the people, they could not endure the testing of God. Every human invention that has been sub-

stituted for the commandments of God will be found worthless in that day when "God shall bring every work into judgment, with every secret thing, whether it be good, or whether it be evil." Eccl. 12:14.

The substitution of the precepts of men for the commandments of God has not ceased. Even among Christians are found institutions and usages that have no better foundation than the traditions of the fathers. Such institutions, resting upon mere human authority, have supplanted those of divine appointment. Men cling to their traditions, and revere their customs, and cherish hatred against those who seek to show them their error. In this day, when we are bidden to call attention to the commandments of God and the faith of Jesus, we see the same enmity as was manifested in the days of Christ. Of the remnant people of God it is written, "The dragon was wroth with the woman, and went to make war with the remnant of her seed, which keep the commandments of God, and have the testimony of Jesus Christ." Rev. 12:17.

But "every plant, which My heavenly Father hath not planted, shall be rooted up." In place of the authority of the so-called fathers of the church, God bids us accept the word of the eternal Father, the Lord of heaven and earth. Here alone is truth unmixed with error. David said, "I have more understanding than all my teachers: for Thy testimonies are my meditation. I understand more than the ancients, because I keep Thy precepts." Ps. 119:99, 100. Let all who accept human authority, the customs of the church, or the traditions of the fathers, take heed to the warning conveyed in the words of Christ, "In vain they do worship Me, teaching for doctrines the commandments of men."

43

399

Barriers Broken Down

After the encounter with the Pharisees, Jesus withdrew from Capernaum, and crossing Galilee, repaired to the hill country on the borders of Phoenicia. Looking westward, He could see, spread out upon the plain below, the ancient cities of Tyre and Sidon, with their heathen temples, their magnificent palaces and marts of trade, and the harbors filled with shipping. Beyond was the blue expanse of the Mediterranean, over which the messengers of the gospel were to bear its glad tidings to the centers of the world's great empire. But the time was not yet. The work before Him now was to prepare His disciples for their mission. In coming to this region He hoped to find the retirement He had

This chapter is based on Matthew 15:21-28; Mark 7:24-30.

failed to secure at Bethsaida. Yet this was not His only purpose in taking this journey.

"Behold, a Canaanitish woman came out from those borders, and cried, saying, Have mercy on me, O Lord, Thou Son of David; my daughter is grievously vexed with a devil." Matt. 15:22, R. V. The people of this district were of the old Canaanite race. They were idolaters, and were despised and hated by the Jews. To this class belonged the woman who now came to Jesus. She was a heathen, and was therefore excluded from the advantages which the Jews daily enjoyed. There were many Jews living among the Phoenicians, and the tidings of Christ's work had penetrated to this region. Some of the people had listened to His words and had witnessed His wonderful works. This woman had heard of the prophet, who, it was reported, healed all manner of diseases. As she heard of His power, hope sprang up in her heart. Inspired by a mother's love, she determined to present her daughter's case to Him. It was her resolute purpose to bring her affliction to Jesus. He must heal her child. She had sought help from the heathen gods, but had obtained no relief. And at times she was tempted to think, What can this Jewish teacher do for me? But the word had come, He heals all manner of diseases, whether those who come to Him for help are rich or poor. She determined not to lose her only hope.

Christ knew this woman's situation. He knew that she was longing to see Him, and He placed Himself in her path. By ministering to her sorrow, He could give a living representation of the lesson He designed to teach. For this He had brought His disciples into this region. He desired them to see the ignorance existing in cities and villages close to the land of Israel. The people who had been given every opportunity to understand the truth were without a knowledge of the needs of those around them. No effort was made to help souls in darkness. The partition wall which Jewish pride had erected, shut even the disciples from sympathy with the heathen world. But these barriers were to be broken down.

Christ did not immediately reply to the woman's request. He received this representative of a despised race as the Jews would have done. In this He designed that His disciples should be impressed with the cold and heartless manner in which the Jews would treat such a case, as evinced by His reception of the woman, and the compassionate manner in which He would have them deal with such distress, as manifested by His subsequent granting of her petition.

But although Jesus did not reply, the woman did not lose faith. As He passed on, as if not hearing her, she followed Him, continuing her supplications. Annoyed by her importunities,

the disciples asked Jesus to send her away. They saw that their Master treated her with indifference, and they therefore supposed that the prejudice of the Jews against the Canaanites was pleasing to Him. But it was a pitying Saviour to whom the woman made her plea, and in answer to the request of the disciples, Jesus said, "I am not sent but unto the lost sheep of the house of Israel." Although this answer appeared to be in accordance with the prejudice of the Jews, it was an implied rebuke to the disciples, which they afterward understood as reminding them of what He had often told them,—that He came to the world to save all who would accept Him.

The woman urged her case with increased earnestness, bowing at Christ's feet, and crying, "Lord, help me." Jesus, still apparently rejecting her entreaties, according to the unfeeling prejudice of the Jews, answered, "It is not meet to take the children's bread, and to cast it to dogs." This was virtually asserting that it was not just to lavish the blessings brought to the favored people of God upon strangers and aliens from Israel. This answer would have utterly discouraged a less earnest seeker. But the woman saw that her opportunity had come. Beneath the apparent refusal of Jesus, she saw a compassion that He could not hide. "Truth, Lord," she answered, "yet the dogs eat of the crumbs which fall from their masters' table." While the children of the household eat at the father's table, even the dogs are not left unfed. They have a right to the crumbs that fall from the table abundantly supplied. So while there were many blessings given to Israel, was there not also a blessing for her? She was looked upon as a dog, and had she not then a dog's claim to a crumb from His bounty?

Jesus had just departed from His field of labor because the scribes and Pharisees were seeking to take His life. They murmured and complained. They manifested unbelief and bitterness, and refused the salvation so freely offered them. Here Christ meets one of an unfortunate and despised race, that has not been favored with the light of God's word; yet she yields at once to the divine influence of Christ, and has implicit faith in His ability to grant the favor she asks. She begs for the crumbs that fall from the Master's table. If she may have the privilege of a dog, she is willing to be regarded as a dog. She has no national or religious prejudice or pride to influence her course, and she immediately acknowledges Jesus as the Redeemer, and as being able to do all that she asks of Him.

The Saviour is satisfied. He has tested her faith in Him. By His dealings with her, He has shown that she who has been regarded as an outcast from Israel is no longer an alien, but a child in God's household. As a child it is her privilege to share in the Father's gifts. Christ now grants her request, and finishes the lesson to the disciples. Turning to her with a look of pity and love, He says, "O woman, great is thy faith: be it unto thee even as thou wilt." From that hour her daughter became whole. The demon troubled her no more. The woman departed, acknowledging her Saviour, and happy in the granting of her prayer.

This was the only miracle that Jesus wrought while on this journey. It was for the performance of this act that He went to the borders of Tyre and Sidon. He wished to relieve the afflicted woman, and at the same time to leave an example in His work of mercy toward one of a despised people for the benefit of His disciples when He should no longer be with them. He wished to lead them from their Jewish exclusiveness to be interested in working for others besides their own people.

Jesus longed to unfold the deep mysteries of the truth which had been hid for ages, that the Gentiles should be fellow heirs with the Jews, and "partakers of His promise in Christ by the gospel." Eph. 3:6. This truth the disciples were slow to learn, and the divine Teacher gave them lesson upon lesson. In rewarding the faith of the centurion at Capernaum, and preaching the gospel to the inhabitants of Sychar, He had already given evidence that He did not share the intolerance of the Jews. But the Samaritans had some knowledge of God; and the centurion had shown kindness to Israel. Now Jesus brought the disciples in contact with a heathen, whom they regarded as having no reason above any of her people, to expect favor from Him. He would give an example of how such a one should be treated. The disciples had thought that He dispensed too freely the gifts of His grace. He would show that His love was not to be circumscribed to race or nation.

When He said, "I am not sent but unto the lost sheep of the house of Israel," He stated the truth, and in His work for the Canaanite woman He was fulfilling His commission. This woman was one of the lost sheep that Israel should have rescued. It was their appointed work, the work which they had neglected, that Christ was doing.

This act opened the minds of the disciples more fully to the labor that lay before them among the Gentiles. They saw a wide field of usefulness outside of Judea. They saw souls bearing sorrows unknown to those more highly favored. Among those whom they had been taught to despise were souls longing for help from the mighty Healer, hungering for the light of truth, which had been so abundantly given to the Jews.

Afterward, when the Jews turned still more persistently from the disciples, because they declared Jesus to be the Saviour of the world, and when the partition wall between Jew and Gentile was broken down by the death of Christ, this lesson, and similar ones which pointed to the gospel work unrestricted by custom or nationality, had a powerful influence upon the representatives of Christ, in directing their labors.

The Saviour's visit to Phoenicia and the miracle there performed had a yet wider purpose. Not alone for the afflicted woman, nor even for His disciples and those who received their labors, was the work accomplished; but also "that ye might believe that Jesus is the Christ, the Son of God; and that believing ye might have life through His name." John 20:31. The same agencies that barred men away from Christ eighteen hundred years ago are at work today. The spirit which built up the partition wall between Jew and Gentile is still active. Pride and prejudice have built strong walls of separation between different classes of men. Christ and His mission have been misrepresented, and multitudes feel that they are virtually shut away from the ministry of the gospel. But let them not feel that they are shut away from Christ. There are no barriers which man or Satan can erect but that faith can penetrate.

In faith the woman of Phoenicia flung herself against the barriers that had been piled up between Jew and Gentile. Against discouragement, regardless of appearances that might have led her to doubt, she trusted the Saviour's love. It is thus that Christ desires us to trust in Him. The blessings of salvation are for every soul. Nothing but his own choice can prevent any man from becoming a partaker of the promise in Christ by the gospel.

Caste is hateful to God. He ignores everything of this character. In His sight the souls of all men are of equal value. He "hath made of one blood all nations of men for to dwell on all the face of the earth, and hath determined the times before appointed, and the bounds of their habitation; that they should seek the Lord, if haply they might feel after Him, and find Him, though He be not far from every one of us." Without distinction of age, or rank, or nationality, or religious privilege, all are invited to come unto Him and live. "Whosoever believeth on Him shall not be ashamed. For there is no difference." "There is neither Jew nor Greek, there is neither bond nor free." "The rich and poor meet together: the Lord is the Maker of them all." "The same Lord over all is rich unto all that call upon Him. For whosoever shall call upon the name of the Lord shall be saved." Acts 17:26, 27; Gal. 3:28; Prov. 22:2; Rom. 10:11-13.

404

44

The True Sign

"Again He went out from the borders of Tyre, and came through Sidon unto the Sea of Galilee, through the midst of the borders of Decapolis." Mark 7:31, R. V.

It was in the region of Decapolis that the demoniacs of Gergesa had been healed. Here the people, alarmed at the destruction of the swine, had constrained Jesus to depart from among them. But they had listened to the messengers He left behind, and a desire was aroused to see Him. As He came again into that region, a crowd gathered about Him, and a deaf, stammering man was brought to Him. Jesus did not, according to His custom, restore the man by a word only. Taking him apart from the multitude, He put His fingers in his ears, and touched his tongue; looking up to heaven, He sighed at thought of the ears that would not be open to the truth, the tongues that refused to acknowledge the Redeemer. At the word, "Be opened," the man's speech was restored, and, disregarding the command to tell no man, he published abroad the story of his cure.

Jesus went up into a mountain, and there the multitude flocked to Him, bringing their sick and lame, and laying them at His feet. He healed them all; and the people, heathen as they were, glorified the God of Israel. For three days they continued to throng about the Saviour, sleeping at night in the open air, and through the day pressing eagerly to hear the words of Christ, 405 and to see His works. At the end of three days their food was spent. Jesus would not send them away hungry, and He called upon His disciples to give them food. Again the disciples revealed their unbelief. At Bethsaida they had seen how, with Christ's blessing, their little store availed for the feeding of the multitude; yet they did not now bring forward their all, trusting His power to multiply it for the hungry crowds. Moreover, those whom He fed at Bethsaida were Jews; these were Gentiles and heathen. Jewish prejudice was still strong in the hearts of the disciples, and they answered Jesus, "Whence can a man satisfy these men with bread here in the wilderness?" But obedient to His word they brought Him what they had,—seven loaves and two fishes. The multitude were fed, seven large baskets of fragments remaining. Four thousand men, besides women and children, were thus refreshed, and Jesus sent them away with glad and grateful hearts.

Then taking a boat with His disciples, He crossed the lake to Magdala, at the southern end of the plain of Gennesaret. In the border of Tyre

and Sidon His spirit had been refreshed by the confiding trust of the Syrophoenician woman. The heathen people of Decapolis had received Him with gladness. Now as He landed once more in Galilee, where His power had been most strikingly manifested, where most of His works of mercy had been performed, and His teaching given, He was met with contemptuous unbelief.

A deputation of Pharisees had been joined by representatives from the rich and lordly Sadducees, the party of the priests, the skeptics and aristocracy of the nation. The two sects had been at bitter enmity. The Sadducees courted the favor of the ruling power in order to maintain their own position and authority. The Pharisees, on the other hand, fostered the popular hatred against the Romans, longing for the time when they could throw off the yoke of the conqueror. But Pharisee and Sadducee now united against Christ. Like seeks like; and evil, wherever it exists, leagues with evil for the destruction of the good.

Now the Pharisees and Sadducees came to 406 Christ, asking for a sign from heaven. When in the days of Joshua Israel went out to battle with the Canaanites at Bethhoron, the sun had stood still at the leader's command until victory was gained; and many similar wonders had been manifest in their history. Some such sign was demanded of Jesus. But these signs were not what the Jews needed. No mere external evidence could benefit them. What they needed was not intellectual enlightenment, but spiritual renovation.

"O ye hypocrites," said Jesus, "ye can discern the face of the sky,"—by studying the sky they could foretell the weather,—"but can ye not discern the signs of the times?" Christ's own words, spoken with the power of the Holy Spirit that convicted them of sin, were the sign that God had given for their salvation. And signs direct from heaven had been given to attest the mission of Christ. The song of the angels to the shepherds, the star that guided the wise men, the dove and the voice from heaven at His baptism, were witnesses for Him.

"And He sighed deeply in His spirit, and saith, Why doth this generation seek after a sign?" "There shall no sign be given unto it, but the sign of the prophet Jonas." As Jonah was three days and three nights in the belly of the whale, Christ was to be the same time "in the heart of the earth." And as the preaching of Jonah was a sign to the Ninevites, so Christ's preaching was a sign to His generation. But what a contrast in the reception of the word! The people of the great heathen city trembled as they heard the warning from God. Kings and nobles humbled themselves; the high and the lowly together cried to the God of heaven, and His mercy was granted unto them. "The men of

This chapter is based on Matthew 15:29-39; 16:1-12; Mark 7:31-37; 8:1-21.

Nineveh shall rise in judgment with this generation," Christ had said, "and shall condemn it: because they repented at the preaching of Jonas; and, behold, a greater than Jonas is here." Matt. 12:40, 41.

Every miracle that Christ performed was a sign of His divinity. He was doing the very work that had been foretold of the Messiah; but to the Pharisees these works of mercy were a positive offense. The Jewish leaders looked with heartless indifference on human suffering. In many cases their selfishness and oppression had caused the affliction that Christ relieved. Thus His miracles were to them a reproach.

That which led the Jews to reject the Saviour's work was the highest evidence of His divine character. The greatest significance of His miracles is seen in the fact that they were 407 for the blessing of humanity. The highest evidence that He came from God is that His life revealed the character of God. He did the works and spoke the words of God. Such a life is the greatest of all miracles.

When the message of truth is presented in our day, there are many who, like the Jews, cry, Show us a sign. Work us a miracle. Christ wrought no miracle at the demand of the Pharisees. He wrought no miracle in the wilderness in answer to Satan's insinuations. He does not impart to us power to vindicate ourselves or to satisfy the demands of unbelief and pride. But the gospel is not without a sign of its divine origin. Is it not a miracle that we can break from the bondage of Satan? Enmity against Satan is not natural to the human heart; it is implanted by the grace of God. When one who has been controlled by a stubborn, wayward will is set free, and yields himself wholeheartedly to the drawing of God's heavenly agencies, a miracle is wrought; so also when a man who has been under strong delusion comes to understand moral truth. Every time a soul is converted, and learns to love God and keep His commandments, the promise of God is fulfilled, "A new heart also will I give you, and a new spirit will I put within you." Ezek. 36:26. The change in human hearts, the transformation of human characters, is a miracle that reveals an ever-living Saviour, working to rescue souls. A consistent life in Christ is a great miracle. In the preaching of the word of God, the sign that should be manifest now and always is the presence of the Holy Spirit, to make the word a regenerating power to those that hear. This is God's witness before the world to the divine mission of His Son.

Those who desired a sign from Jesus had so hardened their hearts in unbelief that they did not discern in His character the likeness of God. They would not see that His mission was in fulfillment of the Scriptures. In the parable of the rich man and Lazarus, Jesus said to the Pharisees, "If they hear not Moses and the prophets, neither will they be persuaded, though one rose from the dead." Luke 16:31. No sign that could be given in heaven or earth would benefit them.

Jesus "sighed deeply in His spirit," and, turning from the group of cavilers, re-entered the boat with His disciples. In sorrowful silence they again crossed the lake. They did not, however, return to the place they had left, but directed their course toward Bethsaida, near where the five thousand had been fed. Upon reaching the farther side, Jesus said, "Take heed and beware of the leaven of the Pharisees and of the Sadducees." The Jews had been accustomed 408 since the days of Moses to put away leaven from their houses at the Passover season, and they had thus been taught to regard it as a type of sin. Yet the disciples failed to understand Jesus. In their sudden departure from Magdala they had forgotten to take bread, and they had with them only one loaf. To this circumstance they understood Christ to refer, warning them not to buy bread of a Pharisee or a Sadducee. Their lack of faith and spiritual insight had often led them to similar misconception of His words. Now Jesus reproved them for thinking that He who had fed thousands with a few fishes and barley loaves could in that solemn warning have referred merely to temporal food. There was danger that the crafty reasoning of the Pharisees and the Sadducees would leaven His disciples with unbelief, causing them to think lightly of the works of Christ.

The disciples were inclined to think that their Master should have granted the demand for a sign in the heavens. They believed that He was fully able to do this, and that such a sign would put His enemies to silence. They did not discern the hypocrisy of these cavilers.

Months afterward, "when there were gathered together an innumerable multitude of people, insomuch that they trode one upon another," Jesus repeated the same teaching. "He began to say unto His disciples first of all, Beware ye of the leaven of the Pharisees, which is hypocrisy." Luke 12:1.

The leaven placed in the meal works imperceptibly, changing the whole mass to its own nature. So if hypocrisy is allowed to exist in the heart, it permeates the character and the life. A striking example of the hypocrisy of the Pharisees, Christ had already rebuked in denouncing the practice of "Corban," by which a neglect of filial duty was concealed under a pretense of liberality to the temple. The scribes and Pharisees were insinuating deceptive principles. They concealed the real tendency of their doctrines, and improved every occasion to instill them artfully into the minds of their hearers. These false principles, when once accepted, worked like leaven in the meal, permeating and transforming the character. It was this deceptive teaching that made it so hard for the people to receive the words of Christ.

The same influences are working today through those who try to explain the law of God in such a way as to make it conform to their practices. This class do not attack the law openly, but put forward speculative theories that undermine its principles. They explain it so as to destroy its force.

The hypocrisy of the Pharisees was the product of self-seeking. The glorification of themselves was the object of their lives. It was this that led them to pervert and misapply the Scriptures, and blinded them to the purpose of Christ's mission. This subtle evil even the disciples of Christ were in danger of cherishing. Those who classed themselves with the followers of Jesus, but who had not left all in order to become His disciples, were influenced in a great degree by the reasoning of the Pharisees. They were often vacillating between faith and unbelief, and they did not discern the treasures of wisdom hidden in Christ. Even the disciples, though outwardly they had left all for Jesus' sake, had not in heart ceased to seek great things for themselves. It was this spirit that prompted the strife as to who should be greatest. It was this that came between them and Christ, making them so little in sympathy with His mission of self-sacrifice, so slow to comprehend the mystery of redemption. As leaven, if left to complete its work, will cause corruption and decay, so does the self-seeking spirit, cherished, work the defilement and ruin of the soul.

Among the followers of our Lord today, as of old, how widespread is this subtle, deceptive sin! How often our service to Christ, our communion with one another, is marred by the secret desire to exalt self! How ready the thought of self-gratulation, and the longing for human approval! It is the love of self, the desire for an easier way than God has appointed that leads to the substitution of human theories and traditions for the divine precepts. To His own disciples the warning words of Christ are spoken, "Take heed and beware of the leaven of the Pharisees."

The religion of Christ is sincerity itself. Zeal for God's glory is the motive implanted by the Holy Spirit; and only the effectual working of the Spirit can implant this motive. Only the power of God can banish self-seeking and hypocrisy. This change is the sign of His working. When the faith we accept destroys selfishness and pretense, when it leads us to seek God's glory and not our own, we may know that it is of the right order. "Father, glorify Thy name" (John 12:28), was the keynote of Christ's life, and if we follow Him, this will be the keynote of our life. He commands us to "walk, even as He walked;" and "hereby we do know that we know Him, if we keep His commandments." 1 John 2:6, 3.

45

The Foreshadowing of the Cross

The work of Christ on earth was hastening to a close. Before Him, in vivid outline, lay the scenes whither His feet were tending. Even before He took humanity upon Him, He saw the whole length of the path He must travel in order to save that which was lost. Every pang that rent His heart, every insult that was heaped upon His head, every privation that He was called to endure, was open to His view before He laid aside His crown and royal robe, and stepped down from the throne, to clothe His divinity with humanity. The path from the manger to Calvary was all before His eyes. He knew the anguish that would come upon Him. He knew it all, and yet He said, "Lo, I come: in the volume of the Book it is written of Me, I delight to do Thy will, O My God: yea, Thy law is within My heart." Ps. 40:7, 8.

Ever before Him He saw the result of His mission. His earthly life, so full of toil and self-sacrifice, was cheered by the prospect that He would not have all this travail for nought. By giving His life for the life of men, He would win back the world to its loyalty to God. Although the baptism of blood must first be received; although the sins of the world were to weigh upon His innocent soul; although the shadow of an unspeakable woe was upon Him; yet for the joy that was set before Him, He chose to endure the cross, and despised the shame.

From the chosen companions of His ministry the scenes that lay before Him were as yet hidden; but the time was near when they must behold His agony. They must see Him whom they had loved and trusted, delivered into the hands of His enemies, and hung upon the cross of Calvary. Soon He must leave them to face the world without the comfort of His visible presence. He knew how bitter hate and unbelief would persecute them, and He desired to prepare them for their trials.

Jesus and His disciples had now come into one of the towns about Caesarea Philippi. They were beyond the limits of Galilee, in a region where idolatry prevailed. Here the disciples were withdrawn from the controlling influence of Judaism, and brought into closer contact with the heathen worship. Around them were represented forms of superstition that existed in all parts of the world. Jesus desired that a view of

This chapter is based on Matthew 16:13-28; Mark 8:27-38; Luke 9:18-27.

these things might lead them to feel their responsibility to the heathen. During His stay in this region, He endeavored to withdraw from teaching the people, and to devote Himself more fully to His disciples.

He was about to tell them of the suffering that awaited Him. But first He went away alone, and prayed that their hearts might be prepared to receive His words. Upon joining them, He did not at once communicate that which He desired to impart. Before doing this, He gave them an opportunity of confessing their faith in Him that they might be strengthened for the coming trial. He asked, "Whom do men say that I the Son of man am?"

Sadly the disciples were forced to acknowledge that Israel had failed to recognize their Messiah. Some indeed, when they saw His miracles, had declared Him to be the Son of David. The multitudes that had been fed at Bethsaida had desired to proclaim Him king of Israel. Many were ready to accept Him as a prophet; but they did not believe Him to be the Messiah.

Jesus now put a second question, relating to the disciples themselves: "But whom say ye that I am?" Peter answered, "Thou art the Christ, the Son of the living God."

From the first, Peter had believed Jesus to be the Messiah. Many others who had been convicted by the preaching of John the Baptist, and had accepted Christ, began to doubt as to John's mission when he was imprisoned and put to death; and they now doubted that Jesus was the Messiah, for whom they had looked so long. Many of the disciples who had ardently expected Jesus to take His place on David's throne left Him when they perceived that He had no such 412 intention. But Peter and his companions turned not from their allegiance. The vacillating course of those who praised yesterday and condemned today did not destroy the faith of the true follower of the Saviour. Peter declared, "Thou art the Christ, the Son of the living God." He waited not for kingly honors to crown his Lord, but accepted Him in His humiliation.

Peter had expressed the faith of the twelve. Yet the disciples were still far from understanding Christ's mission. The opposition and misrepresentation of the priests and rulers, while it could not turn them away from Christ, still caused them great perplexity. They did not see their way clearly. The influence of their early training, the teaching of the rabbis, the power of tradition, still intercepted their view of truth. From time to time precious rays of light from Jesus shone upon them, yet often they were like men groping among shadows. But on this day, before they were brought face to face with the great trial of their faith, the Holy Spirit rested upon them in power. For a little time their eyes were turned away from "the things which are seen," to behold "the things which are not seen." 2 Cor. 4:18. Beneath the guise of humanity they discerned the glory of the Son of God.

Jesus answered Peter, saying, "Blessed art thou, Simon Bar-jona: for flesh and blood hath not revealed it unto thee, but My Father which is in heaven."

The truth which Peter had confessed is the foundation of the believer's faith. It is that which Christ Himself has declared to be eternal life. But the possession of this knowledge was no ground for self-glorification. Through no wisdom or goodness of his own had it been revealed to Peter. Never can humanity, of itself, attain to a knowledge of the divine. "It is as high as heaven; what canst thou do? deeper than hell; what canst thou know?" Job 11:8. Only the spirit of adoption can reveal to us the deep things of God, which "eye hath not seen, nor ear heard, neither have entered into the heart of man." "God hath revealed them unto us by His Spirit: for the Spirit searcheth all things, yea, the deep things of God." 1 Cor. 2:9, 10. "The secret of the Lord is with them that fear Him;" and the fact that Peter discerned the glory of Christ was an evidence that he had been "taught of God." Ps. 25:14; John 6:45. Ah, indeed, "blessed art thou, Simon Bar-jona: for flesh and blood hath not revealed it unto thee."

Jesus continued: "I say also unto thee, That thou art Peter, and upon this rock I will build My church; and the gates of hell shall not prevail against it." The word Peter signifies a 413 stone,—a rolling stone. Peter was not the rock upon which the church was founded. The gates of hell did prevail against him when he denied his Lord with cursing and swearing. The church was built upon One against whom the gates of hell could not prevail.

Centuries before the Saviour's advent Moses had pointed to the Rock of Israel's salvation. The psalmist had sung of "the Rock of my strength." Isaiah had written, "Thus saith the Lord God, Behold, I lay in Zion for a foundation a stone, a tried stone, a precious cornerstone, a sure foundation." Deut. 32:4; Ps. 62:7; Isa. 28:16. Peter himself, writing by inspiration, applies this prophecy to Jesus. He says, "If ye have tasted that the Lord is gracious: unto whom coming, a living stone, rejected indeed of men, but with God elect, precious, ye also, as living stones, are built up a spiritual house." 1 Peter 2:3-5, R. V.

"Other foundation can no man lay than that is laid, which is Jesus Christ." 1 Cor. 3:11. "Upon this rock," said Jesus, "I will build My church." In the presence of God, and all the heavenly intelligences, in the presence of the unseen army of hell, Christ founded His church upon the living Rock. That Rock is Himself,—His own body, for us broken and bruised. Against the church built upon this foundation, the gates of hell shall not prevail.

How feeble the church appeared when Christ spoke these words! There was only a handful of believers, against whom all the power of demons and evil men would be directed; yet the followers of Christ were not to fear. Built upon the Rock of their strength, they could not be overthrown.

For six thousand years, faith has builded upon Christ. For six thousand years the floods and tempests of satanic wrath have beaten upon the Rock of our salvation; but it stands unmoved.

Peter had expressed the truth which is the foundation of the church's faith, and Jesus now honored him as the representative of the whole body of believers. He said, "I will give unto thee the keys of the kingdom of heaven: and whatsoever thou shalt bind on earth shall be bound in heaven: and whatsoever thou shalt loose on earth shall be loosed in heaven."

"The keys of the kingdom of heaven" are the words of Christ. All the words of Holy Scripture are His, and are here included. These words have power to open and to shut heaven. They
414 declare the conditions upon which men are received or rejected. Thus the work of those who preach God's word is a savor of life unto life or of death unto death. Theirs is a mission weighted with eternal results.

The Saviour did not commit the work of the gospel to Peter individually. At a later time, repeating the words that were spoken to Peter, He applied them directly to the church. And the same in substance was spoken also to the twelve as representatives of the body of believers. If Jesus had delegated any special authority to one of the disciples above the others, we should not find them so often contending as to who should be the greatest. They would have submitted to the wish of their Master, and honored the one whom He had chosen.

Instead of appointing one to be their head, Christ said to the disciples, "Be not ye called Rabbi;" "neither be ye called masters: for one is your Master, even Christ." Matt. 23:8, 10.

"The head of every man is Christ." God, who put all things under the Saviour's feet, "gave Him to be the head over all things to the church, which is His body, the fullness of Him that filleth all in all." 1 Cor. 11:3; Eph. 1:22, 23. The church is built upon Christ as its foundation; it is to obey Christ as its head. It is not to depend upon man, or be controlled by man. Many claim that a position of trust in the church gives them authority to dictate what other men shall believe and what they shall do. This claim God does not sanction. The Saviour declares, "All ye are brethren." All are exposed to temptation, and are liable to error. Upon no finite being can we depend for guidance. The Rock of faith is the living presence of Christ in the church. Upon this the weakest may depend, and those who

think themselves the strongest will prove to be the weakest, unless they make Christ their efficiency. "Cursed be the man that trusteth in man, and maketh flesh his arm." The Lord "is the Rock, His work is perfect." "Blessed are all they that put their trust in Him." Jer. 17:5; Deut. 32:4; Ps. 2:12.

After Peter's confession, Jesus charged the disciples to tell no man that He was the Christ. This charge was given because of the determined opposition of the scribes and Pharisees. More than this, the people, and even the disciples, had so false a conception of the Messiah that a public announcement of Him would give them no true idea of His character or His work. But day by day He was revealing Himself to them as the Saviour, and thus He desired to give them a true conception of Him as the Messiah.

The disciples still expected Christ to reign as 415 a temporal prince. Although He had so long concealed His design, they believed that He would not always remain in poverty and obscurity; the time was near when He would establish His kingdom. That the hatred of the priests and rabbis would never be overcome, that Christ would be rejected by His own nation, condemned as a deceiver, and crucified as a malefactor,—such a thought the disciples had never entertained. But the hour of the power of darkness was drawing on, and Jesus must open to His disciples the conflict before them. He was sad as He anticipated the trial.

Hitherto He had refrained from making known to them anything relative to His sufferings and death. In His conversation with Nicodemus He had said, "As Moses lifted up the serpent in the wilderness, even so must the Son of man be lifted up: that whosoever believeth in Him should not perish, but have eternal life." John 3:14, 15. But the disciples did not hear this, and had they heard, would not have understood. But now they have been with Jesus, listening to His words, beholding His works, until, notwithstanding the humility of His surroundings, and the opposition of priests and people, they can join in the testimony of Peter, "Thou art the Christ, the Son of the living God." Now the time has come for the veil that hides the future to be withdrawn. "From that time forth began Jesus to show unto His disciples, how that He must go unto Jerusalem, and suffer many things of the elders and chief priests and scribes, and be killed, and be raised again the third day."

Speechless with grief and amazement, the disciples listened. Christ had accepted Peter's acknowledgment of Him as the Son of God; and now His words pointing to His suffering and death seemed incomprehensible. Peter could not keep silent. He laid hold upon his Master, as if to draw Him back from His impending doom, exclaiming, "Be it far from Thee, Lord: this shall not be unto Thee."

Peter loved his Lord; but Jesus did not commend him for thus manifesting the desire to shield Him from suffering. Peter's words were not such as would be a help and solace to Jesus in the great trial before Him. They were not in harmony with God's purpose of grace toward a lost world, nor with the lesson of self-sacrifice that Jesus had come to teach by His own example. Peter did not desire to see the cross in the work of Christ. The impression which his words would make was directly opposed to that which Christ desired to make on the minds of His followers, and the Saviour was moved to utter one of the sternest rebukes that ever fell from His lips: "Get thee behind Me, Satan: thou art an offense unto Me: for thou savorest not the things that be of God, but those that be of men."

Satan was trying to discourage Jesus, and turn Him from His mission; and Peter, in his blind love, was giving voice to the temptation. The prince of evil was the author of the thought. His instigation was behind that impulsive appeal. In the wilderness, Satan had offered Christ the dominion of the world on condition of forsaking the path of humiliation and sacrifice. Now he was presenting the same temptation to the disciple of Christ. He was seeking to fix Peter's gaze upon the earthly glory, that he might not behold the cross to which Jesus desired to turn his eyes. And through Peter, Satan was again pressing the temptation upon Jesus. But the Saviour heeded it not; His thought was for His disciple. Satan had interposed between Peter and his Master, that the heart of the disciple might not be touched at the vision of Christ's humiliation for him. The words of Christ were spoken, not to Peter, but to the one who was trying to separate him from his Redeemer. "Get thee behind Me, Satan." No longer interpose between Me and My erring servant. Let Me come face to face with Peter, that I may reveal to him the mystery of My love.

It was to Peter a bitter lesson, and one which he learned but slowly, that the path of Christ on earth lay through agony and humiliation. The disciple shrank from fellowship with his Lord in suffering. But in the heat of the furnace fire he was to learn its blessing. Long afterward, when his active form was bowed with the burden of years and labors, he wrote, "Beloved, think it not strange concerning the fiery trial which is to try you, as though some strange thing happened unto you: but rejoice, inasmuch as ye are partakers of Christ's sufferings; that, when His glory shall be revealed, ye may be glad also with exceeding joy." 1 Peter 4:12, 13.

Jesus now explained to His disciples that His own life of self-abnegation was an example of what theirs should be. Calling about Him, with the disciples, the people who had been lingering near, He said, "If any man will come after Me,

let him deny himself, and take up his cross daily, and follow Me." The cross was associated with the power of Rome. It was the instrument of the most cruel and humiliating form of death. The lowest criminals were required to bear the cross to the place of execution; and often as it was about to be laid upon their shoulders, they resisted with desperate violence, until they were overpowered, and the instrument of torture was bound upon them. But Jesus bade His followers take up the cross and bear it after Him. To the disciples His words, though dimly comprehended, pointed to their submission to the most bitter humiliation,—submission even unto death for the sake of Christ. No more complete self-surrender could the Saviour's words have pictured. But all this He had accepted for them. Jesus did not count heaven a place to be desired while we were lost. He left the heavenly courts for a life of reproach and insult, and a death of shame. He who was rich in heaven's priceless treasure, became poor, that through His poverty we might be rich. We are to follow in the path He trod.

Love for souls for whom Christ died means crucifixion of self. He who is a child of God should henceforth look upon himself as a link in the chain let down to save the world, one with Christ in His plan of mercy, going forth with Him to seek and save the lost. The Christian is ever to realize that he has consecrated himself to God, and that in character he is to reveal Christ to the world. The self-sacrifice, the sympathy, the love, manifested in the life of Christ are to reappear in the life of the worker for God.

"Whosoever will save his life shall lose it; but whosoever shall lose his life for My sake and the gospel's, the same shall save it." Selfishness is death. No organ of the body could live should it confine its service to itself. The heart, failing to send its lifeblood to the hand and the head, would quickly lose its power. As our lifeblood, so is the love of Christ diffused through every part of His mystical body. We are members one of another, and the soul that refuses to impart will perish. And "what is a man profited," said Jesus, "if he shall gain the whole world, and lose his own soul? or what shall a man give in exchange for his soul?"

Beyond the poverty and humiliation of the present, He pointed the disciples to His coming in glory, not in the splendor of an earthly throne, but with the glory of God and the hosts of heaven. And then, He said, "He shall reward every man according to his works." Then for their encouragement He gave the promise, "Verily I say unto you, There be some standing here, which shall not taste of death, till they see the Son of man coming in His kingdom." But the disciples did not comprehend His words. The glory seemed far away. Their eyes were fixed upon the nearer view, the earthly life of poverty, humiliation, and suffering. Must their glowing expectations of the Messiah's kingdom be relinquished? Were they not to see their Lord exalted to the throne of David? Could it be that Christ was to live a humble, homeless wanderer, to be despised, rejected, and put to death? Sadness oppressed their hearts, for they loved their Master. Doubt also harassed their minds, for it seemed incomprehensible that the Son of God should be subjected to such cruel humiliation. They questioned why He should voluntarily go to Jerusalem to meet the treatment which He had told them He was there to receive. How could He resign Himself to such a fate, and leave them in greater darkness than that in which they were groping before He revealed Himself to them?

In the region of Caesarea Philippi, Christ was out of the reach of Herod and Caiaphas, the disciples reasoned. He had nothing to fear from the hatred of the Jews or from the power of the Romans. Why not work there, at a distance from the Pharisees? Why need He give Himself up to death? If He was to die, how was it that His kingdom was to be established so firmly that the gates of hell should not prevail against it? To the disciples this was indeed a mystery.

They were even now journeying along the shores of the Sea of Galilee toward the city where all their hopes were to be crushed. They dared not remonstrate with Christ, but they talked together in low, sorrowful tones in regard to what the future would be. Even amid their questionings they clung to the thought that some unforeseen circumstance might avert the doom which seemed to await their Lord. Thus they sorrowed and doubted, hoped and feared, for six long, gloomy days.

46

He Was Transfigured

Evening is drawing on as Jesus calls to His side three of His disciples, Peter, James, and John, and leads them across the fields, and far up a rugged path, to a lonely mountainside. The Saviour and His disciples have spent the day in traveling and teaching, and the mountain climb adds to their weariness. Christ has lifted burdens from mind and body of many sufferers; He has sent the thrill of life through their enfeebled frames; but He also is compassed with humanity, and with His disciples He is wearied with the ascent.

The light of the setting sun still lingers on the mountain top, and gilds with its fading glory the path they are traveling. But soon the light dies out from hill as well as valley, the sun disappears behind the western horizon, and the solitary travelers are wrapped in the darkness of night. The gloom of their surroundings seems in harmony with their sorrowful lives, around which the clouds are gathering and thickening.

The disciples do not venture to ask Christ whither He is going, or for what purpose. He has often spent entire nights in the mountains in prayer. He whose hand formed mountain and valley is at home with nature, and enjoys its quietude. The disciples follow where Christ leads the way; yet they wonder why their Master should lead them up this toilsome ascent when they are weary, and when He too is in need of rest.

Presently Christ tells them that they are now to go no farther. Stepping a little aside from them, the Man of Sorrows pours out His supplications with strong crying and tears. He prays for strength to endure the test in behalf of humanity. He must Himself gain a fresh hold on Omnipotence, for only thus can He contemplate the future. And He pours out His heart longings for His disciples, that in the hour of the power of darkness their faith may not fail. The dew is heavy upon His bowed form, but He heeds it not. The shadows of night gather thickly about Him, but He regards not their gloom. So the hours pass slowly by. At first the disciples unite their prayers with His in sincere devotion; but after a time they are overcome with weariness, and, even while trying to retain their interest in the scene, they fall asleep. Jesus has told them of His sufferings; He has taken them with Him that they might unite with Him in prayer; even now He is praying for them. The Saviour has seen the gloom of His disciples, and has longed to lighten their grief by an assurance that their faith has not been in vain. Not all, even of the twelve, can receive the revelation He desires to give. Only the three who are to witness His anguish in Gethsemane have been chosen to be with Him on the mount. Now the burden of His prayer is that they may be given a manifestation of the glory He had with the Father before the world was, that His kingdom may be revealed to human eyes, and that His disciples may be strengthened to behold it. He pleads that they may witness a manifestation of His divinity that will comfort them in the hour of His supreme agony with the knowledge that He is of a surety the Son of God and that His shameful death is a part of the plan of redemption.

His prayer is heard. While He is bowed in lowliness upon the stony ground, suddenly the heavens open, the golden gates of the city of God are thrown wide, and holy radiance descends upon the mount, enshrouding the Saviour's form. Divinity from within flashes through humanity, and meets the glory coming from above. Arising from His prostrate position,

This chapter is based on Matthew 17:1-8; Mark 9:2-8; Luke 9:28-36.

Christ stands in godlike majesty. The soul agony is gone. His countenance now shines "as the sun," and His garments are "white as the light."

The disciples, awaking, behold the flood of glory that illuminates the mount. In fear and amazement they gaze upon the radiant form of their Master. As they become able to endure the wondrous light, they see that Jesus is not alone. Beside Him are two heavenly beings, in close converse with Him. They are Moses, who upon Sinai had talked with God; and Elijah, to whom the high privilege was given—granted to but one other of the sons of Adam—never to come under the power of death.

Upon Mount Pisgah fifteen centuries before, Moses had stood gazing upon the Land of Promise. But because of his sin at Meribah, it was not for him to enter there. Not for him was the joy of leading the host of Israel into the inheritance of their fathers. His agonized entreaty, "I pray Thee, let me go over, and see the good land that is beyond Jordan, that goodly mountain, and Lebanon" (Deut. 3:25), was refused. The hope that for forty years had lighted up the darkness of the desert wanderings must be denied. A wilderness grave was the goal of those years of toil and heart-burdening care. But He who is "able to do exceeding abundantly above all that we ask or think" (Eph. 3:20), had in this measure answered His servant's prayer. Moses passed under the dominion of death, but he was not to remain in the tomb. Christ Himself called him forth to life. Satan the tempter had claimed the body of Moses because of his sin; but Christ the Saviour brought him forth from the grave. Jude 9.

Moses upon the mount of transfiguration was a witness to Christ's victory over sin and death. He represented those who shall come forth from the grave at the resurrection of the just. Elijah, who had been translated to heaven without seeing death, represented those who will be living upon the earth at Christ's second coming, and who will be "changed, in a moment, in the twinkling of an eye, at the last trump;" when "this mortal must put on immortality," and "this corruptible must put on incorruption." 1 Cor. 15:51-53. Jesus was clothed with the light of heaven, as He will appear when He shall come "the second time without sin unto salvation." For He will come "in the glory of His Father with the holy angels." Heb. 9:28; Mark 8:38. The Saviour's promise to the disciples was now fulfilled. Upon the mount the future kingdom of glory was represented in miniature,—Christ the King, Moses a representative of the risen saints, and Elijah of the translated ones.

The disciples do not yet comprehend the scene; but they rejoice that the patient Teacher, the meek and lowly One, who has wandered to and fro a helpless stranger, is honored by the favored ones of heaven. They believe that Elijah has come to announce the Messiah's reign, and that the kingdom of Christ is about to be set up on the earth. The memory of their fear and disappointment they would banish forever. Here, where the glory of God is revealed, they long to tarry. Peter exclaims, "Master, it is good for us to be here: and let us make three tabernacles; one for Thee, and one for Moses, and one for Elias." The disciples are confident that Moses and Elijah have been sent to protect their Master, and to establish His authority as king.

But before the crown must come the cross. Not the inauguration of Christ as king, but the decease to be accomplished at Jerusalem, is the subject of their conference with Jesus. Bearing the weakness of humanity, and burdened with its sorrow and sin, Jesus walked alone in the midst of men. As the darkness of the coming trial pressed upon Him, He was in loneliness of spirit, in a world that knew Him not. Even His loved disciples, absorbed in their own doubt and sorrow and ambitious hopes, had not comprehended the mystery of His mission. He had dwelt amid the love and fellowship of heaven; but in the world that He had created, He was in solitude. Now heaven had sent its messengers to Jesus; not angels, but men who had endured suffering and sorrow, and who could sympathize with the Saviour in the trial of His earthly life. Moses and Elijah had been colaborers with Christ. They had shared His longing for the salvation of men. Moses had pleaded for Israel: "Yet now, if Thou wilt forgive their sin—; and if not, blot me, I pray Thee, out of Thy book which Thou hast written." Ex. 32:32. Elijah had known loneliness of spirit, as for three years and a half of famine he had borne the burden of the nation's hatred and its woe. Alone he had stood for God upon Mount Carmel. Alone he had fled to the desert in anguish and despair. These men, chosen above every angel around the throne, had come to commune with Jesus concerning the scenes of His suffering, and to comfort Him with the assurance of the sympathy of heaven. The hope of the world, the salvation of every human being, was the burden of their interview.

Through being overcome with sleep, the disciples heard little of what passed between Christ and the heavenly messengers. Failing to watch and pray, they had not received that which God desired to give them,—a knowledge of the sufferings of Christ, and the glory that should follow. They lost the blessing that might have been theirs through sharing His self-sacrifice. Slow of heart to believe were these disciples, little appreciative of the treasure with which Heaven sought to enrich them.

Yet they received great light. They were assured that all heaven knew of the sin of the Jewish nation in rejecting Christ. They were given a clearer insight into the work of the

Redeemer. They saw with their eyes and heard with their ears things that were beyond the comprehension of man. They were "eyewitnesses of His majesty" (2 Peter 1:16), and they realized that Jesus was indeed the Messiah, to whom patriarchs and prophets had witnessed, and that He was recognized as such by the heavenly universe.

While they were still gazing on the scene upon the mount, "a bright cloud overshadowed them: and behold a voice out of the cloud, which said, This is My beloved Son, in whom I am well pleased; hear ye Him." As they beheld the cloud of glory, brighter than that which went before the tribes of Israel in the wilderness; as they heard the voice of God speak in awful majesty that caused the mountain to tremble, the disciples fell smitten to the earth. They remained prostrate, their faces hidden, till Jesus came near, and touched them, dispelling their fears with His well-known voice, "Arise, and be not afraid." Venturing to lift up their eyes, they saw that the heavenly glory had passed away, the forms of Moses and Elijah had disappeared. They were upon the mount, alone with Jesus.

426

47

Ministry

The entire night had been passed in the mountain; and as the sun arose, Jesus and His disciples descended to the plain. Absorbed in thought, the disciples were awed and silent. Even Peter had not a word to say. Gladly would they have lingered in that holy place which had been touched with the light of heaven, and where the Son of God had manifested His glory; but there was work to be done for the people, who were already searching far and near for Jesus.

At the foot of the mountain a large company had gathered, led hither by the disciples who had remained behind, but who knew whither Jesus had resorted. As the Saviour drew near, He charged His three companions to keep silence concerning what they had witnessed, saying, "Tell the vision to no man, until the Son of man be risen again from the dead." The revelation made to the disciples was to be pondered in their own hearts, not to be published abroad. To relate it to the multitudes would excite only ridicule or idle wonder. And even the nine apostles would not understand the scene until after Christ had risen from the dead. How slow of comprehension even the three favored disciples were, is seen in the fact that notwithstanding all that Christ had said of what was before Him, they queried among themselves what the rising

427 from the dead should mean. Yet they asked no

explanation from Jesus. His words in regard to the future had filled them with sorrow; they sought no further revelation concerning that which they were fain to believe might never come to pass.

As the people on the plain caught sight of Jesus, they ran to meet Him, greeting Him with expressions of reverence and joy. Yet His quick eye discerned that they were in great perplexity. The disciples appeared troubled. A circumstance had just occurred that had caused them bitter disappointment and humiliation.

While they were waiting at the foot of the mountain, a father had brought to them his son, to be delivered from a dumb spirit that tormented him. Authority over unclean spirits, to cast them out, had been conferred on the disciples when Jesus sent out the twelve to preach through Galilee. As they went forth strong in faith, the evil spirits had obeyed their word. Now in the name of Christ they commanded the torturing spirit to leave his victim; but the demon only mocked them by a fresh display of his power. The disciples, unable to account for their defeat, felt that they were bringing dishonor upon themselves and their Master. And in the crowd there were scribes who made the most of this opportunity to humiliate them. Pressing around the disciples, they plied them with questions, seeking to prove that they and their Master were deceivers. Here, the rabbis triumphantly declared, was an evil spirit that neither the disciples nor Christ Himself could conquer. The people were inclined to side with the scribes, and a feeling of contempt and scorn pervaded the crowd.

But suddenly the accusations ceased. Jesus and the three disciples were seen approaching, and with a quick revulsion of feeling the people turned to meet them. The night of communion with the heavenly glory had left its trace upon the Saviour and His companions. Upon their countenances was a light that awed the beholders. The scribes drew back in fear, while the people welcomed Jesus.

As if He had been a witness of all that had occurred, the Saviour came to the scene of conflict, and fixing His gaze upon the scribes inquired, "What question ye with them?"

But the voices so bold and defiant before were now silent. A hush had fallen upon the entire company. Now the afflicted father made his way through the crowd, and falling at the feet of Jesus, poured out the story of his trouble and disappointment.

"Master," he said, "I have brought unto Thee 428 my son, which hath a dumb spirit; and wheresoever he taketh him, he teareth him: . . . and I spake to Thy disciples that they should cast him out; and they could not."

Jesus looked about Him upon the awe-stricken multitude, the caviling scribes, the perplexed disciples. He read the unbelief in every heart; and in a voice filled with sorrow He exclaimed, "O faithless generation, how long shall I be with you? how long shall I suffer you?" Then He bade the distressed father, "Bring thy son hither."

The boy was brought, and as the Saviour's eyes fell upon him, the evil spirit cast him to the ground in convulsions of agony. He lay wallowing and foaming, rending the air with unearthly shrieks.

Again the Prince of life and the prince of the powers of darkness had met on the field of battle,—Christ in fulfillment of His mission to "preach deliverance to the captives, . . . to set at liberty them that are bruised" (Luke 4:18), Satan seeking to hold his victim under his control. Angels of light and the hosts of evil angels, unseen, were pressing near to behold the conflict. For a moment, Jesus permitted the evil spirit to display his power, that the beholders might comprehend the deliverance about to be wrought.

The multitude looked on with bated breath, the father in an agony of hope and fear. Jesus asked, "How long is it ago since this came unto him?" The father told the story of long years of suffering, and then, as if he could endure no more, exclaimed, "If Thou canst do anything, have compassion on us, and help us." "If Thou canst!" Even now the father questioned the power of Christ.

Jesus answers, "If thou canst believe, all things are possible to him that believeth." There is no lack of power on the part of Christ; the healing of the son depends upon the father's faith. With a burst of tears, realizing his own weakness, the father casts himself upon Christ's mercy, with the cry, "Lord, I believe; help Thou mine unbelief."

Jesus turns to the suffering one, and says, "Thou dumb and deaf spirit, I charge thee, come out of him, and enter no more into him." There is a cry, an agonized struggle. The demon, in passing, seems about to rend the life from his victim. Then the boy lies motionless, and apparently lifeless. The multitude whisper, "He is dead." But Jesus takes him by the hand, and lifting him up, presents him, in perfect soundness of mind and body, to his father. Father and son 429 praise the name of their Deliverer. The multitude are "amazed at the mighty power of God," while the scribes, defeated and crestfallen, turn sullenly away.

"If Thou canst do anything, have compassion on us, and help us." How many a sin-burdened soul has echoed that prayer. And to all, the pitying Saviour's answer is, "If thou canst believe, all things are possible to him that believeth." It is faith that connects us with heaven, and brings us strength for coping with the powers of darkness. In Christ, God has provided means for subduing every sinful trait, and resisting every temptation, however strong. But many feel that they lack faith, and therefore they remain away from Christ. Let these souls, in their helpless unworthiness, cast themselves upon the mercy of their compassionate Saviour. Look not to self, but to Christ. He who healed the sick and cast out demons when He walked among men is the same mighty Redeemer today. Faith comes by the word of God. Then grasp His promise, "Him that cometh to Me I will in no wise cast out." John 6:37. Cast yourself at His feet with the cry, "Lord, I believe; help *Thou* mine unbelief." You can never perish while you do this—never.

In a brief space of time the favored disciples have beheld the extreme of glory and of humiliation. They have seen humanity as transfigured into the image of God, and as debased into the likeness of Satan. From the mountain where He has talked with the heavenly messengers, and has been proclaimed the Son of God by the voice from the radiant glory, they have seen Jesus descend to meet that most distressing and revolting spectacle, the maniac boy, with distorted countenance, gnashing his teeth in spasms of agony that no human power could relieve. And this mighty Redeemer, who but a few hours before stood glorified before His wondering disciples, stoops to lift the victim of Satan from the earth where he is wallowing, and in health of mind and body restores him to his father and his home.

It was an object lesson of redemption,—the Divine One from the Father's glory stooping to save the lost. It represented also the disciples' mission. Not alone upon the mountaintop with Jesus, in hours of spiritual illumination, is the life of Christ's servants to be spent. There is work for them down in the plain. Souls whom Satan has enslaved are waiting for the word of faith and prayer to set them free.

The nine disciples were yet pondering upon the bitter fact of their own failure; and when Jesus was once more alone with them, they questioned, "Why could not we cast him out?" Jesus answered them, "Because of your unbe- 430 lief: for verily I say unto you, If ye have faith as a grain of mustard seed, ye shall say unto this mountain, Remove hence to yonder place; and it shall remove; and nothing shall be impossible unto you. Howbeit this kind goeth not out but by prayer and fasting." Their unbelief, that shut them out from deeper sympathy with Christ, and the 431 carelessness with which they regarded the sacred work committed to them, had caused their failure in the conflict with the powers of darkness.

The words of Christ pointing to His death had brought sadness and doubt. And the selection of the three disciples to accompany Jesus to the mountain had excited the jealousy of the nine. Instead of strengthening their faith by prayer and meditation on the words of Christ, they had been dwelling on their discouragements and personal grievances. In this state of darkness they had undertaken the conflict with Satan.

In order to succeed in such a conflict they must come to the work in a different spirit. Their faith must be strengthened by fervent prayer and fasting, and humiliation of heart. They must be emptied of self, and be filled with the Spirit and power of God. Earnest, persevering supplication to God in faith—faith that leads to entire dependence upon God, and unreserved consecration to His work—can alone avail to bring men the Holy Spirit's aid in the battle against principalities and powers, the rulers of the darkness of this world, and wicked spirits in high places.

"If ye have faith as a grain of mustard seed," said Jesus, "ye shall say unto this mountain, Remove hence to yonder place; and it shall remove." Though the grain of mustard seed is so small, it contains that same mysterious life principle which produces growth in the loftiest tree. When the mustard seed is cast into the ground, the tiny germ lays hold of every element that God has provided for its nutriment, and it speedily develops a sturdy growth. If you have faith like this, you will lay hold upon God's word, and upon all the helpful agencies He has appointed. Thus your faith will strengthen, and will bring to your aid the power of heaven. The obstacles that are piled by Satan across your path, though apparently as insurmountable as the eternal hills, shall disappear before the demand of faith. "Nothing shall be impossible unto you."

48

Who Is the Greatest?

On returning to Capernaum, Jesus did not repair to the well-known resorts where He had taught the people, but with His disciples quietly sought the house that was to be His temporary home. During the remainder of His stay in Galilee it was His object to instruct the disciples rather than to labor for the multitudes.

On the journey through Galilee, Christ had again tried to prepare the minds of His disciples for the scenes before Him. He told them that He was to go up to Jerusalem to be put to death and to rise again. And He added the strange and solemn announcement that He was to be betrayed into the hands of His enemies. The disciples did not even now comprehend His words. Although the shadow of a great sorrow fell upon them, a spirit of rivalry found a place in their hearts. They disputed among themselves which should be accounted greatest in the kingdom. This strife they thought to conceal from Jesus, and they did not, as usual, press close to His side, but loitered behind, so that He was in advance of them as they entered Capernaum. Jesus read their thoughts, and He longed to

counsel and instruct them. But for this He awaited a quiet hour, when their hearts should be open to receive His words.

Soon after they reached the town, the collector of the temple revenue came to Peter with the question, "Doth not your Master pay tribute?" This tribute was not a civil tax, but a religious contribution, which every Jew was required to pay annually for the support of the temple. A refusal to pay the tribute would be regarded as disloyalty to the temple,—in the estimation of the rabbis a most grievous sin. The Saviour's attitude toward the rabbinical laws, and His plain reproofs to the defenders of tradition, afforded a pretext for the charge that He was seeking to overthrow the temple service. Now His enemies saw an opportunity of casting discredit upon Him. In the collector of the tribute they found a ready ally.

Peter saw in the collector's question an insinuation touching Christ's loyalty to the temple. Zealous for his Master's honor, he hastily answered, without consulting Him, that Jesus would pay the tribute.

But Peter only partially comprehended the purpose of his questioner. There were some classes who were held to be exempt from the payment of the tribute. In the time of Moses, when the Levites were set apart for the service of the sanctuary, they were given no inheritance among the people. The Lord said, "Levi hath no part nor inheritance with his brethren; the Lord is his inheritance." Deut. 10:9. In the days of Christ the priests and Levites were still regarded as especially devoted to the temple, and were not required to make the annual contribution for its support. Prophets also were exempted from this payment. In requiring the tribute from Jesus, the rabbis were setting aside His claim as a prophet or teacher, and were dealing with Him as with any commonplace person. A refusal on His part to pay the tribute would be represented as disloyalty to the temple; while, on the other hand, the payment of it would be taken as justifying their rejection of Him as a prophet.

Only a little before, Peter had acknowledged Jesus as the Son of God; but he now missed an opportunity of setting forth the character of his Master. By his answer to the collector, that Jesus would pay the tribute, he had virtually sanctioned the false conception of Him to which the priests and rulers were trying to give currency.

When Peter entered the house, the Saviour made no reference to what had taken place, but inquired, "What thinkest thou, Simon? of whom do the kings of the earth take custom or tribute? of their own children, or of strangers?" Peter answered, "Of strangers." And Jesus said, "Then are the children free." While the people of a country are taxed for the maintenance of their king, the monarch's own children are

This chapter is based on Matthew 17:22-27; 18:1-20; Mark 9:30-50; Luke 9:46-48.

exempt. So Israel, the professed people of God, were required to maintain His service; but Jesus, the Son of God, was under no such obligation. If priests and Levites were exempt because of their connection with the temple, how much more He to whom the temple was His Father's house.

If Jesus had paid the tribute without a protest, He would virtually have acknowledged the justice of the claim, and would thus have denied His divinity. But while He saw good to meet the demand, He denied the claim upon which it was based. In providing for the payment of the tribute He gave evidence of His divine character. It was made manifest that He was one with God, and therefore was not under tribute as a mere subject of the kingdom.

"Go thou to the sea," He directed Peter, "and cast an hook, and take up the fish that first cometh up; and when thou hast opened his mouth, thou shalt find a piece of money: that take, and give unto them for Me and thee."

Though He had clothed His divinity with humanity, in this miracle He revealed His glory. It was evident that this was He who through David had declared, "Every beast of the forest is Mine, and the cattle upon a thousand hills. I know all the fowls of the mountains: and the wild beasts of the field are Mine. If I were hungry, I would not tell thee: for the world is Mine, and the fullness thereof." Ps. 50:10-12.

While Jesus made it plain that He was under no obligation to pay the tribute, He entered into no controversy with the Jews in regard to the matter; for they would have misinterpreted His words, and turned them against Him. Lest He should give offense by withholding the tribute, He did that which He could not justly be required to do. This lesson would be of great value to His disciples. Marked changes were soon to take place in their relation to the temple service, and Christ taught them not to place themselves needlessly in antagonism to established order. So far as possible, they were to avoid giving occasion for misinterpretation of their faith. While Christians are not to sacrifice one principle of truth, they should avoid controversy whenever it is possible to do so.

When Christ and the disciples were alone in the house, while Peter was gone to the sea, Jesus called the others to Him, and asked, "What was it that ye disputed among yourselves by the way?" The presence of Jesus, and His question, put the matter in an entirely different light from that in which it had appeared to them while they were contending by the way. Shame and self-condemnation kept them silent. Jesus had told them that He was to die for their sake, and their selfish ambition was in painful contrast to His unselfish love.

When Jesus told them that He was to be put to death and to rise again, He was trying to draw them into conversation in regard to the great test of their faith. Had they been ready to receive what He desired to make known to them, they would have been saved bitter anguish and despair. His words would have brought consolation in the hour of bereavement and disappointment. But although He had spoken so plainly of what awaited Him, His mention of the fact that He was soon to go to Jerusalem again kindled their hope that the kingdom was about to be set up. This had led to questioning as to who should fill the highest offices. On Peter's return from the sea, the disciples told him of the Saviour's question, and at last one ventured to ask Jesus, "Who is the greatest in the kingdom of heaven?"

The Saviour gathered His disciples about Him, and said to them, "If any man desire to be first, the same shall be last of all, and servant of all." There was in these words a solemnity and impressiveness which the disciples were far from comprehending. That which Christ discerned they could not see. They did not understand the nature of Christ's kingdom, and this ignorance was the apparent cause of their contention. But the real cause lay deeper. By explaining the nature of the kingdom, Christ might for the time have quelled their strife; but this would not have touched the underlying cause. Even after they had received the fullest knowledge, any question of precedence might have renewed the trouble. Thus disaster would have been brought to the church after Christ's departure. The strife for the highest place was the outworking of that same spirit which was the beginning of the great controversy in the worlds above, and which had brought Christ from heaven to die. There rose up before Him a vision of Lucifer, the "son of the morning," in glory surpassing all the angels that surround the throne, and united in closest ties to the Son of God. Lucifer had said, "I will be like the Most High" (Isa. 14:12, 14); and the desire for self-exaltation had brought strife into the heavenly courts, and had banished a multitude of the hosts of God. Had Lucifer really desired to be like the Most High, he would never have deserted his appointed place in heaven; for the spirit of the Most High is manifested in unselfish ministry. Lucifer desired God's power, but not His character. He sought for himself the highest place, and every being who is actuated by his spirit will do the same. Thus alienation, discord, and strife will be inevitable. Dominion becomes the prize of the strongest. The kingdom of Satan is a kingdom of force; every individual regards every other as an obstacle in the way of his own advancement, or a steppingstone on which he himself may climb to a higher place.

While Lucifer counted it a thing to be grasped to be equal with God, Christ, the Exalted One, "made Himself of no reputation, and took upon

Him the form of a servant, and was made in the likeness of men: and being found in fashion as a man, He humbled Himself, and became obedient unto death, even the death of the cross." Phil. 2:7, 8. Now the cross was just before Him; and His own disciples were so filled with self-seeking—the very principle of Satan's kingdom—that they could not enter into sympathy with their Lord, or even understand Him as He spoke of His humiliation for them.

Very tenderly, yet with solemn emphasis, Jesus tried to correct the evil. He showed what is the principle that bears sway in the kingdom of heaven, and in what true greatness consists, as estimated by the standard of the courts above. Those who were actuated by pride and love of distinction were thinking of themselves, and of the rewards they were to have, rather than how they were to render back to God the gifts they had received. They would have no place in the kingdom of heaven, for they were identified with the ranks of Satan.

Before honor is humility. To fill a high place before men, Heaven chooses the worker who, like John the Baptist, takes a lowly place before God. The most childlike disciple is the most efficient in labor for God. The heavenly intelligences can co-operate with him who is seeking, not to exalt self, but to save souls. He who feels most deeply his need of divine aid will plead for it; and the Holy Spirit will give unto him glimpses of Jesus that will strengthen and uplift the soul. From communion with Christ he will go forth to work for those who are perishing in their sins. He is anointed for his mission; and he succeeds where many of the learned and intellectually wise would fail.

But when men exalt themselves, feeling that they are a necessity for the success of God's great plan, the Lord causes them to be set aside. It is made evident that the Lord is not dependent upon them. The work does not stop because of their removal from it, but goes forward with greater power.

437 It was not enough for the disciples of Jesus to be instructed as to the nature of His kingdom. What they needed was a change of heart that would bring them into harmony with its principles. Calling a little child to Him, Jesus set him in the midst of them; then tenderly folding the little one in His arms He said, "Except ye be converted, and become as little children, ye shall not enter into the kingdom of heaven." The simplicity, the self-forgetfulness, and the confiding love of a little child are the attributes that Heaven values. These are the characteristics of real greatness.

Again Jesus explained to the disciples that His kingdom is not characterized by earthly dignity and display. At the feet of Jesus all these distinctions are forgotten. The rich and the poor, the learned and the ignorant, meet together, with no thought of caste or worldly preeminence. All meet as blood-bought souls, alike dependent upon One who has redeemed them to God.

The sincere, contrite soul is precious in the sight of God. He places His own signet upon men, not by their rank, not by their wealth, not by their intellectual greatness, but by their oneness with Christ. The Lord of glory is satisfied with those who are meek and lowly in heart. "Thou hast also given me," said David, "the shield of Thy salvation: . . . and Thy gentleness"—as an element in the human character—"hath made me great." Ps. 18:35.

"Whosoever shall receive one of such children in My name," said Jesus, "receiveth Me: and whosoever shall receive Me, receiveth not Me, but Him that sent Me." "Thus saith the Lord, The heaven is My throne, and the earth is My footstool: . . . but to this man will I look, even to him that is poor and of a contrite spirit, and trembleth at My word." Isa. 66:1, 2.

The Saviour's words awakened in the disciples a feeling of self-distrust. No one had been specially pointed out in the reply; but John was led to question whether in one case his action had been right. With the spirit of a child he laid the matter before Jesus. "Master," he said, "we saw one casting out devils in Thy name, and he followeth not us: and we forbade him, because he followeth not us."

James and John had thought that in checking this man they had had in view their Lord's honor; they began to see that they were jealous for their own. They acknowledged their error, and accepted the reproof of Jesus, "Forbid him not: for there is no man which shall do a miracle in My name, that can lightly speak evil of Me." None who showed themselves in any way 438 friendly to Christ were to be repulsed. There were many who had been deeply moved by the character and the work of Christ, and whose hearts were opening to Him in faith; and the disciples, who could not read motives, must be careful not to discourage these souls. When Jesus was no longer personally among them, and the work was left in their hands, they must not indulge a narrow, exclusive spirit, but manifest the same far-reaching sympathy which they had seen in their Master.

The fact that one does not in all things conform to our personal ideas or opinions will not justify us in forbidding him to labor for God. Christ is the Great Teacher; we are not to judge or to command, but in humility each is to sit at the feet of Jesus, and learn of Him. Every soul whom God has made willing is a channel through which Christ will reveal His pardoning love. How careful we should be lest we discourage one of God's light bearers, and thus intercept the rays that He would have shine to the world!

Harshness or coldness shown by a disciple

toward one whom Christ was drawing—such an act as that of John in forbidding one to work miracles in Christ's name—might result in turning the feet into the path of the enemy, and causing the loss of a soul. Rather than for one to do this, said Jesus, "it is better for him that a millstone were hanged about his neck, and he were cast into the sea." And He added, "If thy hand cause thee to stumble, cut it off: it is good for thee to enter into life maimed, rather than having thy two hands to go into hell, into the unquenchable fire. And if thy foot cause thee to stumble, cut it off: it is good for thee to enter into life halt, rather than having thy two feet to be cast into hell." Mark 9:43-45, R. V.

Why does this earnest language, than which none can be stronger? Because "the Son of man is come to save that which was lost." Shall His disciples show less regard for the souls of their fellow men than the Majesty of heaven has shown? Every soul has cost an infinite price, and how terrible is the sin of turning one soul away from Christ, so that for him the Saviour's love and humiliation and agony shall have been in vain.

"Woe unto the world because of occasions of stumbling! for it must needs be that the occasions come." Matt. 18:7, R. V. The world, inspired by Satan, will surely oppose the followers of Christ, and seek to destroy their faith; but 439 woe to him who has taken Christ's name, and yet is found doing this work. Our Lord is put to shame by those who claim to serve Him, but who misrepresent His character; and multitudes are deceived, and led into false paths.

Any habit or practice that would lead into sin, and bring dishonor upon Christ, would better be put away, whatever the sacrifice. That which dishonors God cannot benefit the soul. The blessing of heaven cannot attend any man in violating the eternal principles of right. And one sin cherished is sufficient to work the degradation of the character, and to mislead others. If the foot or the hand would be cut off, or even the eye would be plucked out, to save the body from death, how much more earnest should we be to put away sin, that brings death to the soul!

In the ritual service, salt was added to every sacrifice. This, like the offering of incense, signified that only the righteousness of Christ could make the service acceptable to God. Referring to this practice, Jesus said, "Every sacrifice shall be salted with salt." "Have salt in yourselves, and have peace one with another." All who would present themselves "a living sacrifice, holy, acceptable unto God" (Rom. 12:1), must receive the saving salt, the righteousness of our Saviour. Then they become "the salt of the earth," restraining evil among men, as salt preserves from corruption. Matt. 5:13. But if the salt has lost its savor; if there is only a profession of godliness, without the love of Christ,

there is no power for good. The life can exert no saving influence upon the world. Your energy and efficiency in the upbuilding of My kingdom, Jesus says, depend upon your receiving of My Spirit. You must be partakers of My grace, in order to be a savor of life unto life. Then there will be no rivalry, no self-seeking, no desire for the highest place. You will have that love which seeks not her own, but another's wealth.

Let the repenting sinner fix his eyes upon "the Lamb of God, which taketh away the sin of the world" (John 1:29); and by beholding, he becomes changed. His fear is turned to joy, his doubts to hope. Gratitude springs up. The stony heart is broken. A tide of love sweeps into the soul. Christ is in him a well of water springing up unto everlasting life. When we see Jesus, a Man of Sorrows and acquainted with grief, working to save the lost, slighted, scorned, derided, driven from city to city till His mission was accomplished; when we behold Him in Gethsemane, sweating great drops of blood, and on the cross dying in agony,—when we see this, self will no longer clamor to be recognized. Looking unto Jesus, we shall be ashamed of our coldness, our lethargy, our self-seeking. We shall be willing to be anything or nothing, so that we may do heart service for the Master. We 440 shall rejoice to bear the cross after Jesus, to endure trial, shame, or persecution for His dear sake.

"We then that are strong ought to bear the infirmities of the weak, and not to please ourselves." Rom. 15:1. No soul who believes in Christ, though his faith may be weak, and his steps wavering as those of a little child, is to be lightly esteemed. By all that has given us advantage over another,—be it education and refinement, nobility of character, Christian training, religious experience,—we are in debt to those less favored; and, so far as lies in our power, we are to minister unto them. If we are strong, we are to stay up the hands of the weak. Angels of glory, that do always behold the face of the Father in heaven, joy in ministering to His little ones. Trembling souls, who have many objectionable traits of character, are their special charge. Angels are ever present where they are most needed, with those who have the hardest battle with self to fight, and whose surroundings are the most discouraging. And in this ministry Christ's true followers will co-operate.

If one of these little ones shall be overcome, and commit a wrong against you, then it is your work to seek his restoration. Do not wait for him to make the first effort for reconciliation. "How think ye?" said Jesus; "if a man have an hundred sheep, and one of them be gone astray, doth he not leave the ninety and nine, and goeth into the mountains, and seeketh that which is gone astray? And if so be that he find it, verily I say unto you, he rejoiceth more of that sheep, than of the ninety and nine which went not astray. Even so it is not the will of your Father which is in heaven, that one of these little ones should perish."

In the spirit of meekness, "considering thyself, lest thou also be tempted" (Gal. 6:1), go to the erring one, and "tell him his fault between thee and him alone." Do not put him to shame by exposing his fault to others, nor bring dishonor upon Christ by making public the sin or error of one who bears His name. Often the truth must be plainly spoken to the erring; he must be led to see his error, that he may reform. But you are not to judge or to condemn. Make no attempt at self-justification. Let all your effort be for his recovery. In treating the wounds of the soul, there is need of the most delicate touch, the finest sensibility. Only the love that flows from the Suffering One of Calvary can avail here. With pitying tenderness, let brother deal with brother, knowing that if you succeed, you will "save a soul from death," and "hide a multitude of sins." James 5:20.

441 But even this effort may be unavailing. Then, said Jesus, "take with thee one or two more." It may be that their united influence will prevail where that of the first was unsuccessful. Not being parties to the trouble, they will be more likely to act impartially, and this fact will give their counsel greater weight with the erring one.

If he will not hear them, then, and not till then, the matter is to be brought before the whole body of believers. Let the members of the church, as the representatives of Christ, unite in prayer and loving entreaty that the offender may be restored. The Holy Spirit will speak through His servants, pleading with the wanderer to return to God. Paul the apostle, speaking by inspiration, says, "As though God did beseech you by us: we pray you in Christ's stead, be ye reconciled to God." 2 Cor. 5:20. He who rejects this united overture has broken the tie that binds him to Christ, and thus has severed himself from the fellowship of the church. Henceforth, said Jesus, "let him be unto thee as an heathen man and a publican." But he is not to be regarded as cut off from the mercy of God. Let him not be despised or neglected by his former brethren, but be treated with tenderness and compassion, as one of the lost sheep that Christ is still seeking to bring to His fold.

Christ's instruction as to the treatment of the erring repeats in more specific form the teaching given to Israel through Moses: "Thou shalt not hate thy brother in thine heart: thou shalt in anywise rebuke thy neighbor, that thou bear not sin for him." Lev. 19:17, margin. That is, if one neglects the duty Christ has enjoined, of trying to restore those who are in error and sin, he becomes a partaker in the sin. For evils that we might have checked, we are just as responsible as if we were guilty of the acts ourselves.

But it is to the wrongdoer himself that we are to present the wrong. We are not to make it a matter of comment and criticism among ourselves; nor even after it is told to the church, are we at liberty to repeat it to others. A knowledge of the faults of Christians will be only a cause of stumbling to the unbelieving world; and by dwelling upon these things, we ourselves can receive only harm; for it is by beholding that we become changed. While we seek to correct the errors of a brother, the Spirit of Christ will lead us to shield him, as far as possible, from the criticism of even his own brethren, and how much more from the censure of the unbelieving world. We ourselves are erring, and need Christ's pity and forgiveness, and just as we wish Him to deal with us, He bids us deal with one another.

"Whatsoever ye shall bind on earth shall be 442 bound in heaven: and whatsoever ye shall loose on earth shall be loosed in heaven." You are acting as the ambassadors of heaven, and the issues of your work are for eternity.

But we are not to bear this great responsibility alone. Wherever His word is obeyed with a sincere heart, there Christ abides. Not only is He present in the assemblies of the church, but wherever disciples, however few, meet in His name, there also He will be. And He says, "If two of you shall agree on earth as touching anything that they shall ask, it shall be done for them of My Father which is in heaven."

Jesus says, "*My* Father which is in heaven," as reminding His disciples that while by His humanity He is linked with them, a sharer in their trials, and sympathizing with them in their sufferings, by His divinity He is connected with the throne of the Infinite. Wonderful assurance! The heavenly intelligences unite with men in sympathy and labor for the saving of that which was lost. And all the power of heaven is brought to combine with human ability in drawing souls to Christ.

49

447

At the Feast of Tabernacles

Three times a year the Jews were required to assemble at Jerusalem for religious purposes. Enshrouded in the pillar of cloud, Israel's invisible Leader had given the directions in regard to these gatherings. During the captivity of the Jews, they could not be observed; but when the people were restored to their own land, the observance of these memorials was once more begun. It was God's design that these anniversaries should call Him to the minds of the people. But with few exceptions, the priests and leaders of the nation had lost sight of this purpose. He who had ordained these national

This chapter is based on John 7:1-15, 37-39.

assemblies and understood their significance witnessed their perversion.

The Feast of Tabernacles was the closing gathering of the year. It was God's design that at this time the people should reflect on His goodness and mercy. The whole land had been under His guidance, receiving His blessing. Day and night His watchcare had continued. The sun and rain had caused the earth to produce her fruits. From the valleys and plains of Palestine the harvest had been gathered. The olive berries had been picked, and the precious oil stored in bottles. The palm had yielded her store. The purple clusters of the vine had been trodden in the wine press.

448   The feast continued for seven days, and for its celebration the inhabitants of Palestine, with many from other lands, left their homes, and came to Jerusalem. From far and near the people came, bringing in their hands a token of rejoicing. Old and young, rich and poor, all brought some gift as a tribute of thanksgiving to Him who had crowned the year with His goodness, and made His paths drop fatness. Everything that could please the eye, and give expression to the universal joy, was brought from the woods; the city bore the appearance of a beautiful forest.

This feast was not only the harvest thanksgiving, but the memorial of God's protecting care over Israel in the wilderness. In commemoration of their tent life, the Israelites during the feast dwelt in booths or tabernacles of green boughs. These were erected in the streets, in the courts of the temple, or on the housetops. The hills and valleys surrounding Jerusalem were also dotted with these leafy dwellings, and seemed to be alive with people.

With sacred song and thanksgiving the worshipers celebrated this occasion. A little before the feast was the Day of Atonement, when, after confession of their sins, the people were declared to be at peace with Heaven. Thus the way was prepared for the rejoicing of the feast. "O give thanks unto the Lord; for He is good: for His mercy endureth forever" (Ps. 106:1) rose triumphantly, while all kinds of music, mingled with shouts of hosanna, accompanied the united singing. The temple was the center of the universal joy. Here was the pomp of the sacrificial ceremonies. Here, ranged on either side of the white marble steps of the sacred building, the choir of Levites led the service of song. The multitude of worshipers, waving their branches of palm and myrtle, took up the strain, and echoed the chorus; and again the melody was caught up by voices near and afar off, till the encircling hills were vocal with praise.

At night the temple and its court blazed with artificial light. The music, the waving of palm branches, the glad hosannas, the great concourse of people, over whom the light streamed from the hanging lamps, the array of the priests, and the majesty of the ceremonies, combined to make a scene that deeply impressed the beholders. But the most impressive ceremony of the feast, one that called forth greatest rejoicing, was one commemorating an event in the wilderness sojourn.

At the first dawn of day, the priests sounded a long, shrill blast upon their silver trumpets, and the answering trumpets, and the glad shouts of the people from their booths, echoing over hill and valley, welcomed the festal day. Then the 449 priest dipped from the flowing waters of the Kedron a flagon of water, and, lifting it on high, while the trumpets were sounding, he ascended the broad steps of the temple, keeping time with the music with slow and measured tread, chanting meanwhile, "Our feet shall stand within thy gates, O Jerusalem." Ps. 122:2.

He bore the flagon to the altar, which occupied a central position in the court of the priests. Here were two silver basins, with a priest standing at each one. The flagon of water was poured into one, and a flagon of wine into the other; and the contents of both flowed into a pipe which communicated with the Kedron, and was conducted to the Dead Sea. This display of the consecrated water represented the fountain that at the command of God had gushed from the rock to quench the thirst of the children of Israel. Then the jubilant strains rang forth, "The Lord Jehovah is my strength and my song;" "therefore with joy shall ye draw water out of the wells of salvation." Isa. 12:2, 3.

As the sons of Joseph made preparation to 450 attend the Feast of Tabernacles, they saw that Christ made no movement signifying His intention of attending. They watched Him with anxiety. Since the healing at Bethesda He had not attended the national gatherings. To avoid useless conflict with the leaders at Jerusalem, He had restricted His labors to Galilee. His apparent neglect of the great religious assemblies, and the enmity manifested toward Him by the priests and rabbis, were a cause of perplexity to the people about Him, and even to His own disciples and His kindred. In His teachings He had dwelt upon the blessings of obedience to the law of God, and yet He Himself seemed to be indifferent to the service which had been divinely established. His mingling with publicans and others of ill repute, His disregard of the rabbinical observances, and the freedom with which He set aside the traditional requirements concerning the Sabbath, all seeming to place Him in antagonism to the religious authorities, excited much questioning. His brothers thought it a mistake for Him to alienate the great and learned men of the nation. They felt that these men must be in the right, and that Jesus was at fault in placing Himself in antagonism to them. But they had witnessed His blameless life, and though they did not rank themselves with His disciples, they had been deeply impressed by His works. His popularity in Galilee was gratifying to their ambition; they still hoped that He would give an evidence of His power which would lead the Pharisees to see that He was what He claimed to be. What if He were the Messiah, the Prince of Israel! They cherished this thought with proud satisfaction.

So anxious were they about this that they urged Christ to go to Jerusalem. "Depart hence," they said, "and go into Judea, that Thy disciples also may see the works that Thou doest. For there is no man that doeth anything in secret, and he himself seeketh to be known openly. If Thou do these things, show Thyself to the world." The "if" expressed doubt and unbelief. They attributed cowardice and weakness to Him. If He knew that He was the Messiah, why this strange reserve and inaction? If He really possessed such power, why not go boldly to Jerusalem, and assert His claims? Why not perform in Jerusalem the wonderful works reported of Him in Galilee? Do not hide in secluded provinces, they said, and perform your mighty works for the benefit of ignorant peasants and fishermen. Present yourself at the capital, win the support of the priests and rulers, and unite the nation in establishing the new kingdom.

451 These brothers of Jesus reasoned from the selfish motive so often found in the hearts of those ambitious for display. This spirit was the ruling spirit of the world. They were offended because, instead of seeking a temporal throne, Christ had declared Himself to be the bread of life. They were greatly disappointed when so many of His disciples forsook Him. They themselves turned from Him to escape the cross of acknowledging what His works revealed—that He was the Sent of God.

"Then Jesus said unto them, My time is not yet come: but your time is alway ready. The world cannot hate you; but Me it hateth, because I testify of it, that the works thereof are evil. Go ye up unto this feast: I go not up yet unto this feast; for My time is not yet full come. When He had said these words unto them, He abode still in Galilee." His brothers had spoken to Him in a tone of authority, prescribing the course He should pursue. He cast their rebuke back to them, classing them not with His self-denying disciples, but with the world. "The world cannot hate you," He said, "but Me it hateth, because I testify of it, that the works thereof are evil." The world does not hate those who are like it in spirit; it loves them as its own.

The world for Christ was not a place of ease and self-aggrandizement. He was not watching for an opportunity to seize its power and its glory. It held out no such prize for Him. It was the place into which His Father had sent Him. He had been given for the life of the world, to work out the great plan of redemption. He was accomplishing His work for the fallen race. But He was not to be presumptuous, not to rush into danger, not to hasten a crisis. Each event in His work had its appointed hour. He must wait patiently. He knew that He was to receive the world's hatred; He knew that His work would result in His death; but to prematurely expose Himself would not be the will of His Father.

From Jerusalem the report of Christ's miracles had spread wherever the Jews were dispersed; and although for many months He had been absent from the feasts, the interest in Him had not abated. Many from all parts of the world had come up to the Feast of Tabernacles in the hope of seeing Him. At the beginning of the feast many inquiries were made for Him. The Pharisees and rulers looked for Him to come, hoping for an opportunity to condemn Him. They anxiously inquired, "Where is He?" but no one knew. The thought of Him was uppermost in all minds. Through fear of the priests and rulers, none dared acknowledge Him as the 452 Messiah, but everywhere there was quiet yet earnest discussion concerning Him. Many defended Him as one sent from God, while others denounced Him as a deceiver of the people.

Meanwhile Jesus had quietly arrived at Jerusalem. He had chosen an unfrequented route by which to go, in order to avoid the travelers who were making their way to the city from all quarters. Had He joined any of the caravans that went up to the feast, public attention would have been attracted to Him on His entrance into the city, and a popular demonstration in His favor would have aroused the authorities against Him. It was to avoid this that He chose to make the journey alone.

In the midst of the feast, when the excitement concerning Him was at its height, He entered the court of the temple in the presence of the multitude. Because of His absence from the feast, it had been urged that He dared not place Himself in the power of the priests and rulers. All were surprised at His presence. Every voice was hushed. All wondered at the dignity and courage of His bearing in the midst of powerful enemies who were thirsting for His life.

Standing thus, the center of attraction to that vast throng, Jesus addressed them as no man had ever done. His words showed a knowledge 453 of the laws and institutions of Israel, of the sacrificial service and the teachings of the prophets, far exceeding that of the priests and rabbis. He broke through the barriers of formalism and tradition. The scenes of the future life seemed outspread before Him. As one who beheld the Unseen, He spoke of the earthly and the heavenly, the human and the divine, with positive authority. His words were most clear and convincing; and again, as at Capernaum, the people were astonished at His teaching; "for His word was with power." Luke 4:32. Under a variety of representations He warned His hearers of the calamity that would follow all who rejected the blessings He came to bring them. He had given them every possible proof that He came forth from God, and made every possible effort to bring them to repentance. He would not be rejected and murdered by His own nation if He could save them from the guilt of such a deed.

All wondered at His knowledge of the law and the prophecies; and the question passed from one to another, "How knoweth this Man letters, having never learned?" No one was regarded as qualified to be a religious teacher unless he had studied in the rabbinical schools, and both Jesus and John the Baptist had been represented as ignorant because they had not received this training. Those who heard them were astonished at their knowledge of the Scriptures, "having never learned." Of men they had not, truly; but the God of heaven was their teacher, and from Him they had received the highest kind of wisdom.

As Jesus spoke in the temple court, the people were held spellbound. The very men who were the most violent against Him felt themselves powerless to do Him harm. For the time, all other interests were forgotten.

Day after day He taught the people, until the last, "that great day of the feast." The morning of this day found the people wearied from the long season of festivity. Suddenly Jesus lifted up His voice, in tones that rang through the courts of the temple:

"If any man thirst, let him come unto Me, and drink. He that believeth on Me, as the scripture hath said, out of his belly shall flow rivers of living water." The condition of the people made this appeal very forcible. They had been engaged in a continued scene of pomp and festivity, their eyes had been dazzled with light and color, and their ears regaled with the richest music; but there had been nothing in all this round of ceremonies to meet the wants of the 454 spirit, nothing to satisfy the thirst of the soul for that which perishes not. Jesus invited them to come and drink of the fountain of life, of that which would be in them a well of water, springing up unto everlasting life.

The priest had that morning performed the ceremony which commemorated the smiting of the rock in the wilderness. That rock was a symbol of Him who by His death would cause living streams of salvation to flow to all who are athirst. Christ's words were the water of life. There in the presence of the assembled multitude He set Himself apart to be smitten, that the water of life might flow to the world. In smiting Christ, Satan thought to destroy the Prince of life; but from the smitten rock there flowed living water. As Jesus thus spoke to the people, their hearts thrilled with a strange awe, and many were ready to exclaim, with the woman of Samaria,

"Give me this water, that I thirst not." John 4:15.

Jesus knew the wants of the soul. Pomp, riches, and honor cannot satisfy the heart. "If any man thirst, let him come unto Me." The rich, the poor, the high, the low, are alike welcome. He promises to relieve the burdened mind, to comfort the sorrowing, and to give hope to the despondent. Many of those who heard Jesus were mourners over disappointed hopes, many were nourishing a secret grief, many were seeking to satisfy their restless longing with the things of the world and the praise of men; but when all was gained, they found that they had toiled only to reach a broken cistern, from which they could not quench their thirst. Amid the glitter of the joyous scene they stood, dissatisfied and sad. That sudden cry, "If any man thirst," startled them from their sorrowful meditation, and as they listened to the words that followed, their minds kindled with a new hope. The Holy Spirit presented the symbol before them until they saw in it the offer of the priceless gift of salvation.

The cry of Christ to the thirsty soul is still going forth, and it appeals to us with even greater power than to those who heard it in the temple on that last day of the feast. The fountain is open for all. The weary and exhausted ones are offered the refreshing draught of eternal life. Jesus is still crying, "If any man thirst, let him come unto Me, and drink." "Let him that is athirst come. And whosoever will, let him take the water of life freely." "Whosoever drinketh of the water that I shall give him shall never thirst; but the water that I shall give him shall be in him a well of water springing up into everlasting life." Rev. 22:17; John 4:14.

50

Among Snares

All the while Jesus was at Jerusalem during the feast He was shadowed by spies. Day after day new schemes to silence Him were tried. The priests and rulers were watching to entrap Him. They were planning to stop Him by violence. But this was not all. They wanted to humble this Galilean rabbi before the people.

On the first day of His presence at the feast, the rulers had come to Him, demanding by what authority He taught. They wished to divert attention from Him to the question of His right to teach, and thus to their own importance and authority.

"My teaching is not Mine," said Jesus, "but His that sent Me. If any man willeth to do His will, he shall know of the teaching, whether it be of God, or whether I speak from Myself." John 7:16, 17, R. V. The question of these cavil-

This chapter is based on John 7:16-36, 40-53; 8:1-11.

ers Jesus met, not by answering the cavil, but by opening up truth vital to the salvation of the soul. The perception and appreciation of truth, He said, depends less upon the mind than upon the heart. Truth must be received into the soul; it claims the homage of the will. If truth could be submitted to the reason alone, pride would be no hindrance in the way of its reception. But it is to be received through the work of grace in the heart; and its reception depends upon the renunciation of every sin that the Spirit of God reveals. Man's advantages for obtaining a knowledge of the truth, however great these may be, will prove of no benefit to him unless 456 the heart is open to receive the truth, and there is a conscientious surrender of every habit and practice that is opposed to its principles. To those who thus yield themselves to God, having an honest desire to know and to do His will, the truth is revealed as the power of God for their salvation. These will be able to distinguish between him who speaks for God, and him who speaks merely from himself. The Pharisees had not put their will on the side of God's will. They were not seeking to know the truth, but to find some excuse for evading it; Christ showed that this was why they did not understand His teaching.

He now gave a test by which the true teacher might be distinguished from the deceiver: "He that speaketh from himself seeketh his own glory: but he that seeketh the glory of Him that sent him, the same is true, and no unrighteousness is in him." John 7:18, R. V. He that seeketh his own glory is speaking only from himself. The spirit of self-seeking betrays its origin. But Christ was seeking the glory of God. He spoke the words of God. This was the evidence of His authority as a teacher of the truth.

Jesus gave the rabbis an evidence of His divinity by showing that He read their hearts. Ever since the healing at Bethesda they had been plotting His death. Thus they were themselves breaking the law which they professed to be defending. "Did not Moses give you the law," He said, "and yet none of you keepeth the law? Why go ye about to kill Me?"

Like a swift flash of light these words revealed to the rabbis the pit of ruin into which they were about to plunge. For an instant they were filled with terror. They saw that they were in conflict with Infinite Power. But they would not be warned. In order to maintain their influence with the people, their murderous designs must be concealed. Evading the question of Jesus, they exclaimed, "Thou hast a devil: who goeth about to kill Thee?" They insinuated that the wonderful works of Jesus were instigated by an evil spirit.

To this insinuation Christ gave no heed. He went on to show that His work of healing at Bethesda was in harmony with the Sabbath law, and that it was justified by the interpretation which the Jews themselves put upon the law. He said, "Moses therefore gave unto you circumcision; . . . and ye on the Sabbath day circumcise a man." According to the law, every child must be circumcised on the eighth day. Should the appointed time fall upon the Sabbath, the rite must then be performed. How much more must it be in harmony with the spirit of the law to 457 make a man "every whit whole on the Sabbath day." And He warned them to "judge not according to the appearance, but judge righteous judgment."

The rulers were silenced; and many of the people exclaimed, "Is not this He, whom they seek to kill? But, lo, He speaketh boldly, and they say nothing unto Him. Do the rulers know indeed that this is the very Christ?"

Many among Christ's hearers who were dwellers at Jerusalem, and who were not ignorant of the plots of the rulers against Him, felt themselves drawn to Him by an irresistible power. The conviction pressed upon them that He was the Son of God. But Satan was ready to suggest doubt; and for this the way was prepared by their own erroneous ideas of the Messiah and His coming. It was generally believed that Christ would be born at Bethlehem, but that after a time He would disappear, and at His second appearance none would know whence He came. There were not a few who held that the Messiah would have no natural relationship to humanity. And because the popular conception of the glory of the Messiah was not met by Jesus of Nazareth, many gave heed to the suggestion, "Howbeit we know this Man whence He is: but when Christ cometh, no man knoweth whence He is."

While they were thus wavering between doubt and faith, Jesus took up their thoughts and answered them: "Ye both know Me, and ye know whence I am: and I am not come of Myself, but He that sent Me is true, whom ye know not." They claimed a knowledge of what the origin of Christ should be, but they were in utter ignorance of it. If they had lived in accordance with the will of God, they would have known His Son when He was manifested to them.

The hearers could not but understand Christ's words. Clearly they were a repetition of the claim He had made in the presence of the Sanhedrin many months before, when He declared Himself the Son of God. As the rulers then tried to compass His death, so now they sought to take Him; but they were prevented by an unseen power, which put a limit to their rage, saying to them, Thus far shalt thou go, and no farther.

Among the people many believed on Him, and they said, "When Christ cometh, will He do more miracles than these which this Man hath done?" The leaders of the Pharisees, who were anxiously watching the course of events, caught the expressions of sympathy among the throng. Hurrying away to the chief priests, they laid 458 their plans to arrest Him. They arranged, however, to take Him when He was alone; for they dared not seize Him in the presence of the people. Again Jesus made it manifest that He read their purpose. "Yet a little while am I with you," He said, "and then I go unto Him that sent Me. Ye shall seek Me, and shall not find Me: and where I am, thither ye cannot come." Soon He would find a refuge beyond the reach of their scorn and hate. He would ascend to the Father, to be again the Adored of the angels; and thither His murderers could never come.

Sneeringly the rabbis said, "Whither will He go, that we shall not find Him? will He go unto the dispersed among the Gentiles, and teach the Gentiles?" Little did these cavilers dream that in their mocking words they were picturing the mission of the Christ! All day long He had stretched forth His hands unto a disobedient and gainsaying people; yet He would be found of them that sought Him not; among a people that had not called upon His name He would be manifest. Rom. 10:20, 21.

Many who were convinced that Jesus was the Son of God were misled by the false reasoning of the priests and rabbis. These teachers had repeated with great effect the prophecies concerning the Messiah, that He would "reign in Mount Zion, and in Jerusalem, and before His ancients gloriously;" that He would "have dominion also from sea to sea, and from the river unto the ends of the earth." Isa. 24:23; Ps. 72:8. Then they made contemptuous comparisons between the glory here pictured and the humble appearance of Jesus. The very words of prophecy were so perverted as to sanction error. Had the people in sincerity studied the word for themselves, they would not have been misled. The sixty-first chapter of Isaiah testifies that Christ was to do the very work He did. Chapter fifty-three sets forth His rejection and sufferings in the world, and chapter fifty-nine describes the character of the priests and rabbis.

God does not compel men to give up their unbelief. Before them are light and darkness, truth and error. It is for them to decide which they will accept. The human mind is endowed with power to discriminate between right and wrong. God designs that men shall not decide from impulse, but from weight of evidence, carefully comparing scripture with scripture. Had the Jews laid by their prejudice and compared written prophecy with the facts characterizing the life of Jesus, they would have perceived a beautiful harmony between the prophecies and their fulfillment in the life and ministry of the lowly Galilean.

459   Many are deceived today in the same way as were the Jews. Religious teachers read the Bible in the light of their own understanding and traditions; and the people do not search the Scriptures for themselves, and judge for themselves as to what is truth; but they yield up their judgment, and commit their souls to their leaders. The preaching and teaching of His word is one of the means that God has ordained for diffusing light; but we must bring every man's teaching to the test of Scripture. Whoever will prayerfully study the Bible, desiring to know the truth, that he may obey it, will receive divine enlightenment. He will understand the Scriptures. "If any man willeth to do His will, he shall know of the teaching." John 7:17, R. V.

On the last day of the feast, the officers sent out by the priests and rulers to arrest Jesus, returned without Him. They were angrily questioned, "Why have ye not brought Him?" With solemn countenance they answered, "Never man spake like this Man."

Hardened as were their hearts, they were melted by His words. While He was speaking in the temple court, they had lingered near, to catch something that might be turned against Him. But as they listened, the purpose for which they had been sent was forgotten. They stood as men entranced. Christ revealed Himself to their souls. They saw that which priests and rulers would not see,—humanity flooded with the glory of divinity. They returned, so filled with this thought, so impressed by His words, that to the inquiry, "Why have ye not brought Him?" they could only reply, "Never man spake like this Man."

The priests and rulers, on first coming into the presence of Christ, had felt the same conviction. Their hearts were deeply moved, and the thought was forced upon them, "Never man spake like this Man." But they had stifled the conviction of the Holy Spirit. Now, enraged that even the instruments of the law should be influenced by the hated Galilean, they cried, "Are ye also deceived? Have any of the rulers or of the Pharisees believed on Him? But this people who knoweth not the law are cursed."

Those to whom the message of truth is spoken seldom ask, "Is it true?" but, "By whom is it advocated?" Multitudes estimate it by the numbers who accept it; and the question is still asked, "Have any of the learned men or religious leaders believed?" Men are no more favorable to real godliness now than in the days of Christ. They are just as intently seeking earthly good, to the neglect of eternal riches; and it is not an argument against the truth, that 460 large numbers are not ready to accept it, or that it is not received by the world's great men, or even by the religious leaders.

Again the priests and rulers proceeded to lay plans for arresting Jesus. It was urged that if He were longer left at liberty, He would draw the people away from the established leaders, and the only safe course was to silence Him without delay. In the full tide of their discussion, they were suddenly checked. Nicodemus questioned, "Doth our law judge any man, before it hear him, and know what he doeth?" Silence fell on the assembly. The words of Nicodemus came home to their consciences. They could not condemn a man unheard. But it was not for this reason alone that the haughty rulers remained silent, gazing at him who had dared to speak in favor of justice. They were startled and chagrined that one of their own number had been so far impressed by the character of Jesus as to speak a word in His defense. Recovering from their astonishment, they addressed Nicodemus with cutting sarcasm, "Art thou also of Galilee? Search and look: for out of Galilee ariseth no prophet."

Yet the protest resulted in staying the proceedings of the council. The rulers were unable to carry out their purpose and condemn Jesus without a hearing. Defeated for the time, "every man went unto his own house. Jesus went unto the Mount of Olives."

From the excitement and confusion of the city, from the eager crowds and the treacherous rabbis, Jesus turned away to the quiet of the olive groves, where He could be alone with God. But in the early morning He returned to the temple, and as the people gathered about Him, He sat down and taught them.

He was soon interrupted. A group of Pharisees and scribes approached Him, dragging with them a terror-stricken woman, whom with hard, eager voices they accused of having violated the seventh commandment. Having pushed her into the presence of Jesus, they said to Him, with a hypocritical show of respect, "Moses in the law commanded us, that such should be stoned: but what sayest Thou?"

Their pretended reverence veiled a deep-laid plot for His ruin. They had seized upon this opportunity to secure His condemnation, thinking that whatever decision He might make, they would find occasion to accuse Him. Should He acquit the woman, He might be charged with despising the law of Moses. Should He declare 461 her worthy of death, He could be accused of assuming authority that belonged only to them.

Jesus looked for a moment upon the scene,—the trembling victim in her shame, the hard-faced dignitaries, devoid of even human pity. His spirit of stainless purity shrank from the spectacle. Well He knew for what purpose this case had been brought to Him. He read the heart, and knew the character and life history of everyone in His presence. These would-be guardians of justice had themselves led their victim into sin, that they might lay a snare for Jesus. Giving no sign that He had heard their question, He stooped, and fixing His eyes upon the ground, began to write in the dust.

Impatient at His delay and apparent indifference, the accusers drew nearer, urging the matter upon His attention. But as their eyes, following those of Jesus, fell upon the pavement at His feet, their countenances changed. There, traced before them, were the guilty secrets of their own lives. The people, looking on, saw the sudden change of expression, and pressed forward to discover what it was that they were regarding with such astonishment and shame.

With all their professions of reverence for the law, these rabbis, in bringing the charge against the woman, were disregarding its provisions. It was the husband's duty to take action against her, and the guilty parties were to be punished equally. The action of the accusers was wholly unauthorized. Jesus, however, met them on their own ground. The law specified that in punishment by stoning, the witnesses in the case should be the first to cast a stone. Now rising, and fixing His eyes upon the plotting elders, Jesus said, "He that is without sin among you, let him first cast a stone at her." And stooping down, He continued writing on the ground.

He had not set aside the law given through Moses, nor infringed upon the authority of Rome. The accusers had been defeated. Now, their robe of pretended holiness torn from them, they stood, guilty and condemned, in the presence of Infinite Purity. They trembled lest the hidden iniquity of their lives should be laid open to the multitude; and one by one, with bowed heads and downcast eyes, they stole away, leaving their victim with the pitying Saviour.

Jesus arose, and looking at the woman said, "Woman, where are those thine accusers? hath no man condemned thee? She said, No man, Lord. And Jesus said unto her, Neither do I condemn thee: go, and sin no more."

The woman had stood before Jesus, cowering 462 with fear. His words, "He that is without sin among you, let him first cast a stone," had come to her as a death sentence. She dared not lift her eyes to the Saviour's face, but silently awaited her doom. In astonishment she saw her accusers depart speechless and confounded; then those words of hope fell upon her ear, "Neither do I condemn thee: go, and sin no more." Her heart was melted, and she cast herself at the feet of Jesus, sobbing out her grateful love, and with bitter tears confessing her sins.

This was to her the beginning of a new life, a life of purity and peace, devoted to the service of God. In the uplifting of this fallen soul, Jesus performed a greater miracle than in healing the most grievous physical disease; He cured the spiritual malady which is unto death everlasting. This penitent woman became one of His most steadfast followers. With self-sacrificing love and devotion she repaid His forgiving mercy.

In His act of pardoning this woman and

encouraging her to live a better life, the character of Jesus shines forth in the beauty of perfect righteousness. While He does not palliate sin, nor lessen the sense of guilt, He seeks not to condemn, but to save. The world had for this erring woman only contempt and scorn; but Jesus speaks words of comfort and hope. The Sinless One pities the weakness of the sinner, and reaches to her a helping hand. While the hypocritical Pharisees denounce, Jesus bids her, "Go, and sin no more."

It is not Christ's follower that, with averted eyes, turns from the erring, leaving them unhindered to pursue their downward course. Those who are forward in accusing others, and zealous in bringing them to justice, are often in their own lives more guilty than they. Men hate the sinner, while they love the sin. Christ hates the sin, but loves the sinner. This will be the spirit of all who follow Him. Christian love is slow to censure, quick to discern penitence, ready to forgive, to encourage, to set the wanderer in the path of holiness, and to stay his feet therein.

463

51

"The Light of Life"

"Then spake Jesus again unto them, saying, I am the light of the world: he that followeth Me shall not walk in darkness, but shall have the light of life."

When He spoke these words, Jesus was in the court of the temple specially connected with the services of the Feast of Tabernacles. In the center of this court rose two lofty standards, supporting lampstands of great size. After the evening sacrifice, all the lamps were kindled, shedding their light over Jerusalem. This ceremony was in commemoration of the pillar of light that guided Israel in the desert, and was also regarded as pointing to the coming of the Messiah. At evening when the lamps were lighted, the court was a scene of great rejoicing. Gray-haired men, the priests of the temple and the rulers of the people, united in the festive dances to the sound of instrumental music and the chants of the Levites.

In the illumination of Jerusalem, the people expressed their hope of the Messiah's coming to shed His light upon Israel. But to Jesus the scene had a wider meaning. As the radiant lamps of the temple lighted up all about them, so Christ, the source of spiritual light, illumines the darkness of the world. Yet the symbol was imperfect. That great light which His own hand had set in the heavens was a truer representation of the glory of His mission.

It was morning; the sun had just risen above the Mount of Olives, and its rays fell with dazzling brightness on the marble palaces, and lighted up the gold of the temple walls, when 464 Jesus, pointing to it, said, "I am the light of the world."

By one who listened to these words, they were long afterward reechoed in that sublime passage, "In Him was life; and the life was the light of men. And the light shineth in the darkness; and the darkness apprehended it not." "That was the true light, which lighteth every man that cometh into the world." John 1:4, 5, R. V., 9. And long after Jesus had ascended to heaven, Peter also, writing under the illumination of the divine Spirit, recalled the symbol Christ had used: "We have also a more sure word of prophecy; whereunto ye do well that ye take heed, as unto a light that shineth in a dark place, until the day dawn, and the daystar arise in your hearts." 2 Peter 1:19.

In the manifestation of God to His people, light had ever been a symbol of His presence. At the creative word in the beginning, light had shone out of darkness. Light had been enshrouded in the pillar of cloud by day and the pillar of fire by night, leading the vast armies of Israel. Light blazed with awful grandeur about the Lord on Mount Sinai. Light rested over the mercy seat in the tabernacle. Light filled the temple of Solomon at its dedication. Light shone on the hills of Bethlehem when the angels brought the message of redemption to the watching shepherds.

God is light; and in the words, "I am the light of the world," Christ declared His oneness with God, and His relation to the whole human family. It was He who at the beginning had caused "the light to shine out of darkness." 2 Cor. 4:6. He is the light of sun and moon and star. He was the spiritual light that in symbol and type and prophecy had shone upon Israel. But not to the Jewish nation alone was the light given. As the sunbeams penetrate to the remotest corners of the earth, so does the light of the Sun of Righteousness shine upon every soul.

"That was the true light, which lighteth every man that cometh into the world." The world has had its great teachers, men of giant intellect and wonderful research, men whose utterances have stimulated thought, and opened to view vast fields of knowledge; and these men have been honored as guides and benefactors of their race. But there is One who stands higher than they. "As many as received Him, to them gave He power to become the sons of God." "No man hath seen God at any time; the only-begotten Son, which is in the bosom of the Father, He hath declared Him." John 1:12, 18. We can trace the life of the world's great teachers as far back as human records extend; but the Light 465 was before them. As the moon and the stars of the solar system shine by the reflected light of the sun, so, as far as their teaching is true, do the world's great thinkers reflect the rays of the Sun of Righteousness. Every gem of thought, every flash of the intellect, is from the Light of the world. In these days we hear much about "higher education." The true "higher education" is that imparted by Him "in whom are hid all the treasures of wisdom and knowledge." "In Him was life; and the life was the light of men." Col. 2:3; John 1:4. "He that followeth Me," said Jesus, "shall not walk in darkness, but shall have the light of life."

In the words, "I am the light of the world," Jesus declared Himself the Messiah. The aged Simeon, in the temple where Christ was now teaching, had spoken of Him as "a light to lighten the Gentiles, and the glory of Thy people Israel." Luke 2:32. In these words he was applying to Him a prophecy familiar to all Israel. By the prophet Isaiah, the Holy Spirit had declared, "It is too light a thing that Thou shouldest be My servant to raise up the tribes of Jacob, and to restore the preserved of Israel: I will also give Thee for a light to the Gentiles, that Thou mayest be My salvation unto the end of the earth." Isa. 49:6, R. V. This prophecy was generally understood as spoken of the Messiah, and when Jesus said, "I am the light of the world," the people could not fail to recognize His claim to be the Promised One.

To the Pharisees and rulers this claim seemed an arrogant assumption. That a man like themselves should make such pretensions they could not tolerate. Seeming to ignore His words, they demanded, "Who art Thou?" They were bent upon forcing Him to declare Himself the Christ. His appearance and His work were so at variance with the expectations of the people, that, as His wily enemies believed, a direct announcement of Himself as the Messiah would cause Him to be rejected as an impostor.

But to their question, "Who art Thou?" Jesus replied, "Even that which I have also spoken unto you from the beginning." John 8:25, R. V. That which had been revealed in His words was revealed also in His character. He was the embodiment of the truths He taught. "I do nothing of Myself," He continued; "but as My Father hath taught Me, I speak these things. And He that sent Me is with Me: the Father hath not left Me alone; for I do always those things that please Him." He did not attempt to prove His Messianic claim, but showed His unity with God. If their minds had been open to God's love, they would have received Jesus.

Among His hearers many were drawn to Him in faith, and to them He said, "If ye continue in My word, then are ye My disciples indeed; and ye shall know the truth, and the truth shall make you free."

These words offended the Pharisees. The nation's long subjection to a foreign yoke, they disregarded, and angrily exclaimed, "We be Abraham's seed, and were never in bondage to any man: how sayest Thou, Ye shall be made free?" Jesus looked upon these men, the slaves of malice, whose thoughts were bent upon revenge, and sadly answered, "Verily, verily, I say unto you, Whosoever committeth sin is the servant of sin." They were in the worst kind of bondage,—ruled by the spirit of evil.

Every soul that refuses to give himself to God is under the control of another power. He is not his own. He may talk of freedom, but he is in the most abject slavery. He is not allowed to see the beauty of truth, for his mind is under the control of Satan. While he flatters himself that he is following the dictates of his own judgment, he obeys the will of the prince of darkness. Christ came to break the shackles of sin-slavery from the soul. "If the Son therefore shall make you free, ye shall be free indeed." "The law of the Spirit of life in Christ Jesus" sets us "free from the law of sin and death." Rom. 8:2.

In the work of redemption there is no compulsion. No external force is employed. Under the influence of the Spirit of God, man is left free to choose whom he will serve. In the change that takes place when the soul surrenders to Christ, there is the highest sense of freedom. The expulsion of sin is the act of the soul itself. True, we have no power to free ourselves from Satan's control; but when we desire to be set free from sin, and in our great need cry out for a power out of and above ourselves, the powers of the soul are imbued with the divine energy of the Holy Spirit, and they obey the dictates of the will in fulfilling the will of God.

The only condition upon which the freedom of man is possible is that of becoming one with Christ. "The truth shall make you free;" and Christ is the truth. Sin can triumph only by enfeebling the mind, and destroying the liberty of the soul. Subjection to God is restoration to one's self,—to the true glory and dignity of man. The divine law, to which we are brought into subjection, is "the law of liberty." James 2:12.

The Pharisees had declared themselves the children of Abraham. Jesus told them that this claim could be established only by doing the works of Abraham. The true children of Abraham would live, as he did, a life of obedience to God. They would not try to kill One who was speaking the truth that was given Him from God. In plotting against Christ, the rabbis were not doing the works of Abraham. A mere lineal descent from Abraham was of no value. Without a spiritual connection with him, which would be manifested in possessing the same spirit, and doing the same works, they were not his children.

This principle bears with equal weight upon a question which has long agitated the Christian world,—the question of apostolic succession.

Descent from Abraham was proved, not by name and lineage, but by likeness of character. So the apostolic succession rests not upon the transmission of ecclesiastical authority, but upon spiritual relationship. A life actuated by the apostles' spirit, the belief and teaching of the truth they taught, this is the true evidence of apostolic succession. This is what constitutes men the successors of the first teachers of the gospel.

Jesus denied that the Jews were children of Abraham. He said, "Ye do the deeds of your father." In mockery they answered, "*We* be not born of fornication; we have one Father, even God." These words, in allusion to the circumstances of His birth, were intended as a thrust against Christ in the presence of those who were beginning to believe on Him. Jesus gave no heed to the base insinuation, but said, "If God were your Father, ye would love Me: for I proceeded forth and came from God."

Their works testified of their relationship to him who was a liar and a murderer. "Ye are of your father the devil," said Jesus, "and the lusts of your father it is your will to do. He was a murderer from the beginning, and stood not in the truth, because there is no truth in him. . . . Because I say the truth, ye believe Me not." John 8:44, 45, R. V. The fact that Jesus spoke the truth, and that with certainty, was why He was not received by the Jewish leaders. It was the truth that offended these self-righteous men. The truth exposed the fallacy of error; it condemned their teaching and practice, and it was unwelcome. They would rather close their eyes to the truth than humble themselves to confess that they had been in error. They did not love the truth. They did not desire it, even though it was truth.

"Which of you convicteth [Revised Version] Me of sin? And if I say the truth, why do ye not believe Me?" Day by day for three years His enemies had been following Christ, trying to find some stain in His character. Satan and all the confederacy of evil had been seeking to overcome Him; but they had found nothing in Him by which to gain an advantage. Even the devils were forced to confess, "Thou art the Holy One of God." Mark 1:24. Jesus lived the 468 law in the sight of heaven, in the sight of unfallen worlds, and in the sight of sinful men. Before angels, men, and demons, He had spoken, unchallenged, words that from any other lips would have been blasphemy: "I do always those things that please Him."

The fact that although they could find no sin in Christ the Jews would not receive Him proved that they themselves had no connection with God. They did not recognize His voice in the message of His Son. They thought themselves passing judgment on Christ; but in rejecting Him they were pronouncing sentence upon themselves. "He that is of God," said Jesus, "heareth God's words: ye therefore hear them not, because ye are not of God."

The lesson is true for all time. Many a man who delights to quibble, to criticize, seeking for something to question in the word of God, thinks that he is thereby giving evidence of independence of thought, and mental acuteness. He supposes that he is sitting in judgment on the Bible, when in truth he is judging himself. He makes it manifest that he is incapable of appreciating truths that originate in heaven, and that compass eternity. In presence of the great mountain of God's righteousness, his spirit is not awed. He busies himself with hunting for sticks and straws, and in this betrays a narrow and earthly nature, a heart that is fast losing its capacity to appreciate God. He whose heart has responded to the divine touch will be seeking for that which will increase his knowledge of God, and will refine and elevate the character. As a flower turns to the sun, that the bright rays may touch it with tints of beauty, so will the soul turn to the Sun of Righteousness, that heaven's light may beautify the character with the graces of the character of Christ.

Jesus continued, drawing a sharp contrast between the position of the Jews and that of Abraham: "Your father Abraham rejoiced to see My day: and he saw it, and was glad."

Abraham had greatly desired to see the promised Saviour. He offered up the most earnest prayer that before his death he might behold the Messiah. And he saw Christ. A supernatural light was given him, and he acknowledged Christ's divine character. He saw His day, and was glad. He was given a view of the divine sacrifice for sin. Of this sacrifice he had an illustration in his own experience. The command came to him, "Take now thy son, thine only son Isaac, whom thou lovest, . . . and offer him . . . for a burnt offering." Gen. 22:2. Upon the altar of sacrifice he laid the son of 469 promise, the son in whom his hopes were centered. Then as he waited beside the altar with knife upraised to obey God, he heard a voice from heaven saying, "Lay not thine hand upon the lad, neither do thou anything unto him: for now I know that thou fearest God, seeing thou hast not withheld thy son, thine only son from Me." Gen. 22:12. This terrible ordeal was imposed upon Abraham that he might see the day of Christ, and realize the great love of God for the world, so great that to raise it from its degradation, He gave His only-begotten Son to a most shameful death.

Abraham learned of God the greatest lesson ever given to mortal. His prayer that he might see Christ before he should die was answered. He saw Christ; he saw all that mortal can see, and live. By making an entire surrender, he was able to understand the vision of Christ, which had been given him. He was shown that in giving His only-begotten Son to save sinners from eternal ruin, God was making a greater and more wonderful sacrifice than ever man could make.

Abraham's experience answered the question: "Wherewith shall I come before the Lord, and bow myself before the high God? Shall I come before Him with burnt offerings, with calves of a year old? Will the Lord be pleased with thousands of rams, or with ten thousands of rivers of oil? shall I give my first-born for my transgression, the fruit of my body for the sin of my soul?" Micah 6:6, 7. In the words of Abraham, "My son, God will provide Himself a lamb for a burnt offering" (Gen. 22:8), and in God's provision of a sacrifice instead of Isaac, it was declared that no man could make expiation for himself. The pagan system of sacrifice was wholly unacceptable to God. No father was to offer up his son or his daughter for a sin offering. The Son of God alone can bear the guilt of the world.

Through his own suffering, Abraham was enabled to behold the Saviour's mission of sacrifice. But Israel would not understand that which was so unwelcome to their proud hearts. Christ's words concerning Abraham conveyed to His hearers no deep significance. The Pharisees saw in them only fresh ground for caviling. They retorted with a sneer, as if they would prove Jesus to be a madman, "Thou art not yet fifty years old, and hast Thou seen Abraham?"

With solemn dignity Jesus answered, "Verily, verily, I say unto you, Before Abraham was, I AM."

Silence fell upon the vast assembly. The name of God, given to Moses to express the idea of the eternal presence, had been claimed as His own by this Galilean Rabbi. He had announced Himself to be the self-existent One, He who had been promised to Israel, "whose goings forth have been from of old, from the days of eternity." Micah 5:2, margin.

Again the priests and rabbis cried out against Jesus as a blasphemer. His claim to be one with God had before stirred them to take His life, and a few months later they plainly declared, "For a good work we stone Thee not; but for blasphemy; and because that Thou, being a man, makest Thyself God." John 10:33. Because He was, and avowed Himself to be, the Son of God, they were bent on destroying Him. Now many of the people, siding with the priests and rabbis, took up stones to cast at Him. "But Jesus hid Himself, and went out of the temple, going through the midst of them, and so passed by."

The Light was shining in darkness; but "the darkness apprehended it not." John 1:5, R. V.

"As Jesus passed by, He saw a man which was blind from his birth. And His disciples asked Him, saying, Master, who did sin, this man, or his parents, that he was born blind? Jesus answered, Neither hath this man sinned, nor his parents: but that the works of God should be made manifest in him. . . . When He had thus spoken, He spat on the ground, and made clay of the spittle, and He anointed the eyes of the blind man with the clay, and said unto him, Go, wash in the pool of Siloam, (which is by interpretation, Sent). He went his way therefore, and washed, and came seeing."

It was generally believed by the Jews that sin is punished in this life. Every affliction was regarded as the penalty of some wrongdoing, either of the sufferer himself or of his parents. It is true that all suffering results from the transgression of God's law, but this truth had become perverted. Satan, the author of sin and all its results, had led men to look upon disease and death as proceeding from God,—as punishment arbitrarily inflicted on account of sin. Hence one upon whom some great affliction or calamity had fallen had the additional burden of being regarded as a great sinner.

Thus the way was prepared for the Jews to reject Jesus. He who "hath borne our griefs, and carried our sorrows" was looked upon by the Jews as "stricken, smitten of God, and afflicted;" and they hid their faces from Him. Isa. 53:4, 3.

God had given a lesson designed to prevent this. The history of Job had shown that suffering is inflicted by Satan, and is overruled by God for purposes of mercy. But Israel did not understand the lesson. The same error for which God had reproved the friends of Job was repeated by the Jews in their rejection of Christ.

The belief of the Jews in regard to the relation of sin and suffering was held by Christ's disciples. While Jesus corrected their error, He did not explain the cause of the man's affliction, but told them what would be the result. Because of it the works of God would be made manifest. "As long as I am in the world," He said, "I am the light of the world." Then having anointed the eyes of the blind man, He sent him to wash in the pool of Siloam, and the man's sight was restored. Thus Jesus answered the question of the disciples in a practical way, as He usually answered questions put to Him from curiosity. The disciples were not called upon to discuss the question as to who had sinned or had not sinned, but to understand the power and mercy of God in giving sight to the blind. It was evident that there was no healing virtue in the clay, or in the pool wherein the blind man was sent to wash, but that the virtue was in Christ.

The Pharisees could not but be astonished at the cure. Yet they were more than ever filled with hatred; for the miracle had been performed on the Sabbath day.

The neighbors of the young man, and those who knew him before in his blindness, said, "Is not this he that sat and begged?" They looked upon him with doubt; for when his eyes were opened, his countenance was changed and brightened, and he appeared like another man. 472 From one to another the question passed. Some said, "This is he;" others, "He is like him." But he who had received the great blessing settled the question by saying, "I am he." He then told them of Jesus, and by what means he had been healed, and they inquired, "Where is He? He said, I know not."

Then they brought him before a council of the Pharisees. Again the man was asked how he had received his sight. "He said unto them, He put clay upon mine eyes, and I washed, and do see. Therefore said some of the Pharisees, This man is not of God, because He keepeth not the Sabbath day." The Pharisees hoped to make Jesus out to be a sinner, and therefore not the Messiah. They knew not that it was He who had made the Sabbath and knew all its obligation, who had healed the blind man. They appeared wonderfully zealous for the observance of the Sabbath, yet were planning murder on that very day. But many were greatly moved at hearing of this miracle, and were convicted that He who had opened the eyes of the blind was more than a common man. In answer to the charge that Jesus was a sinner because He kept not the Sabbath day, they said, "How can a man that is a sinner do such miracles?"

Again the rabbis appealed to the blind man, "What sayest thou of Him, that He hath opened thine eyes? He said, He is a prophet." The Pharisees then asserted that he had not been born blind and received his sight. They called for his parents, and asked them, saying, "Is this your son, who ye say was born blind?"

There was the man himself, declaring that he had been blind, and had had his sight restored; but the Pharisees would rather deny the evidence of their own senses than admit that they were in error. So powerful is prejudice, so distorting is Pharisaical righteousness.

The Pharisees had one hope left, and that was to intimidate the man's parents. With apparent sincerity they asked, "How then doth he now see?" The parents feared to compromise themselves; for it had been declared that whoever should acknowledge Jesus as the Christ should be "put out of the synagogue;" that is, should be excluded from the synagogue for thirty days. During this time no child could be circumcised nor dead be lamented in the offender's home. The sentence was regarded as a great calamity; and if it failed to produce repentance, a far heavier penalty followed. The great work wrought for their son had brought conviction to the parents, yet they answered, "We know that this is our son, and that he was born blind: but 473 by what means he now seeth, we know not; or who hath opened his eyes, we know not: he is of

age; ask him: he shall speak for himself." Thus they shifted all responsibility from themselves to their son; for they dared not confess Christ.

The dilemma in which the Pharisees were placed, their questioning and prejudice, their unbelief in the facts of the case, were opening the eyes of the multitude, especially of the common people. Jesus had frequently wrought His miracles in the open street, and His work was always of a character to relieve suffering. The question in many minds was, Would God do such mighty works through an impostor, as the Pharisees insisted that Jesus was? The controversy was becoming very earnest on both sides.

The Pharisees saw that they were giving publicity to the work done by Jesus. They could not deny the miracle. The blind man was filled with joy and gratitude; he beheld the wondrous things of nature, and was filled with delight at the beauty of earth and sky. He freely related his experience, and again they tried to silence him, saying, "Give God the praise: we know that this Man is a sinner." That is, Do not say again that this Man gave you sight; it is God who has done this.

The blind man answered, "Whether He be a sinner or no, I know not: one thing I know, that, whereas I was blind, now I see."

Then they questioned again, "What did He to thee? how opened He thine eyes?" With many words they tried to confuse him, so that he might think himself deluded. Satan and his evil angels were on the side of the Pharisees, and united their energies and subtlety with man's reasoning in order to counteract the influence of Christ. They blunted the convictions that were deepening in many minds. Angels of God were also on the ground to strengthen the man who had had his sight restored.

The Pharisees did not realize that they had to 474 deal with any other than the uneducated man who had been born blind; they knew not Him with whom they were in controversy. Divine light shone into the chambers of the blind man's soul. As these hypocrites tried to make him disbelieve, God helped him to show, by the vigor and pointedness of his replies, that he was not to be ensnared. He answered, "I have told you already, and ye did not hear: wherefore would ye hear it again? will ye also be His disciples? Then they reviled him, and said, Thou art His disciple; but we are Moses' disciples. We know that God spake unto Moses: as for this fellow, we know not from whence He is."

The Lord Jesus knew the ordeal through which the man was passing, and He gave him grace and utterance, so that he became a witness for Christ. He answered the Pharisees in words that were a cutting rebuke to his questioners. They claimed to be the expositors of Scripture, the religious guides of the nation; and yet here was One performing miracles, and they were confessedly ignorant as to the source of His power, and as to His character and claims. "Why herein is a marvelous thing," said the man, "that ye know not from whence He is, and yet He hath opened mine eyes. Now we know that God heareth not sinners: but if any man be a worshiper of God, and doeth His will, him He heareth. Since the world began was it not heard that any man opened the eyes of one that was born blind. If this Man were not of God, He could do nothing."

The man had met his inquisitors on their own ground. His reasoning was unanswerable. The Pharisees were astonished, and they held their peace,—spellbound before his pointed, determined words. For a few moments there was silence. Then the frowning priests and rabbis gathered about them their robes, as though they feared contamination from contact with him; they shook off the dust from their feet, and hurled denunciations against him,—"Thou wast altogether born in sins, and dost thou teach *us*?" And they excommunicated him.

Jesus heard what had been done; and finding him soon after, He said, "Dost thou believe on the Son of God?"

For the first time the blind man looked upon the face of his Restorer. Before the council he had seen his parents troubled and perplexed; he had looked upon the frowning faces of the rabbis; now his eyes rested upon the loving, peaceful countenance of Jesus. Already, at great cost to himself, he had acknowledged Him as a delegate of divine power; now a higher revelation was granted him.

475   To the Saviour's question, "Dost thou believe on the Son of God?" the blind man replied by asking, "Who is He, Lord, that I might believe on Him?" And Jesus said, "Thou hast both seen Him, and it is He that talketh with thee." The man cast himself at the Saviour's feet in worship. Not only had his natural sight been restored, but the eyes of his understanding had been opened. Christ had been revealed to his soul, and he received Him as the Sent of God.

A group of Pharisees had gathered near, and the sight of them brought to the mind of Jesus the contrast ever manifest in the effect of His words and works. He said, "For judgment I am come into this world, that they which see not might see; and that they which see might be made blind." Christ had come to open the blind eyes, to give light to them that sit in darkness. He had declared Himself to be the light of the world, and the miracle just performed was in attestation of His mission. The people who beheld the Saviour at His advent were favored with a fuller manifestation of the divine presence than the world had ever enjoyed before. The knowledge of God was revealed more perfectly. But in this very revelation, judgment was passing upon men. Their character was tested, their destiny determined.

The manifestation of divine power that had given to the blind man both natural and spiritual sight had left the Pharisees in yet deeper darkness. Some of His hearers, feeling that Christ's words applied to them, inquired, "Are we blind also?" Jesus answered, "If ye were blind, ye should have no sin." If God had made it impossible for you to see the truth, your ignorance would involve no guilt. "But now ye say, We see." You believe yourselves able to see, and reject the means through which alone you could receive sight. To all who realized their need, Christ came with infinite help. But the Pharisees would confess no need; they refused to come to Christ, and hence they were left in blindness,—a blindness for which they were themselves guilty. Jesus said, "Your sin remaineth."

52   476

The Divine Shepherd

"I am the Good Shepherd: the good shepherd giveth his life for the sheep." "I am the Good Shepherd, and know My sheep, and am known of Mine. As the Father knoweth Me, even so know I the Father: and I lay down My life for the sheep."

Again Jesus found access to the minds of His hearers by the pathway of their familiar associations. He had likened the Spirit's influence to the cool, refreshing water. He had represented Himself as the light, the source of life and gladness to nature and to man. Now in a beautiful pastoral picture He represents His relation to those that believe on Him. No picture was more familiar to His hearers than this, and Christ's words linked it forever with Himself. Never could the disciples look on the shepherds tending their flocks without recalling the Saviour's lesson. They would see Christ in each faithful shepherd. They would see themselves in each helpless and dependent flock.

This figure the prophet Isaiah had applied to the Messiah's mission, in the comforting words, "O Zion, that bringest good tidings, get thee up into the high mountain; O Jerusalem, that bringest good tidings, lift up thy voice with strength; lift it up, be not afraid; say unto the cities of Judah, Behold your God! . . . He shall feed His flock like a shepherd: He shall gather the lambs with His arm, and carry them in His bosom." Isa. 40:9-11. David had sung, "The Lord is my shepherd; I shall not want." Ps. 23:1.   477 And the Holy Spirit through Ezekiel had declared: "I will set up one Shepherd over them, and He shall feed them." "I will seek that which was lost, and bring again that which was driven away, and will bind up that which was broken,

This chapter is based on John 10:1-30.

and will strengthen that which was sick." "And I will make with them a covenant of peace." "And they shall no more be a prey to the heathen; . . . but they shall dwell safely, and none shall make them afraid." Ezek. 34:23, 16, 25, 28.

Christ applied these prophecies to Himself, and He showed the contrast between His own character and that of the leaders in Israel. The Pharisees had just driven one from the fold, because he dared to bear witness to the power of Christ. They had cut off a soul whom the True Shepherd was drawing to Himself. In this they had shown themselves ignorant of the work committed to them, and unworthy of their trust as shepherds of the flock. Jesus now set before them the contrast between them and the Good Shepherd, and He pointed to Himself as the real keeper of the Lord's flock. Before doing this, however, He speaks of Himself under another figure.

He said, "He that entereth not by the door into the sheepfold, but climbeth up some other way, the same is a thief and a robber. But he that entereth in by the door is the shepherd of the sheep." The Pharisees did not discern that these words were spoken against them. When they reasoned in their hearts as to the meaning, Jesus told them plainly, "I am the door: by Me if any man enter in, he shall be saved, and shall go in and out, and find pasture. The thief cometh not, but for to steal, and to kill, and to destroy: I am come that they might have life, and that they might have it more abundantly."

Christ is the door to the fold of God. Through this door all His children, from the earliest times, have found entrance. In Jesus, as shown in types, as shadowed in symbols, as manifested in the revelation of the prophets, as unveiled in the lessons given to His disciples, and in the miracles wrought for the sons of men, they have beheld "the Lamb of God, which taketh away the sin of the world" (John 1:29), and through Him they are brought within the fold of His grace. Many have come presenting other objects for the faith of the world; ceremonies and systems have been devised by which men hope to receive justification and peace with God, and thus find entrance to His fold. But the only door is Christ, and all who have interposed something to take the place of Christ, all who have tried to enter the fold in some other way, are thieves and robbers.

478

The Pharisees had not entered by the door. They had climbed into the fold by another way than Christ, and they were not fulfilling the work of the true shepherd. The priests and rulers, the scribes and Pharisees, destroyed the living pastures, and defiled the wellsprings of the water of life. Faithfully do the words of inspiration describe those false shepherds: "The diseased have ye not strengthened, neither have ye healed that which was sick, neither have ye bound up that which was broken, neither have ye brought again that which was driven away; . . . but with force and with cruelty have ye ruled them." Ezek. 34:4.

In all ages, philosophers and teachers have been presenting to the world theories by which to satisfy the soul's need. Every heathen nation has had its great teachers and religious systems offering some other means of redemption than Christ, turning the eyes of men away from the Father's face, and filling their hearts with fear of Him who has given them only blessing. The trend of their work is to rob God of that which is His own, both by creation and by redemption. And these false teachers rob man as well. Millions of human beings are bound down under false religions, in the bondage of slavish fear, of stolid indifference, toiling like beasts of burden, bereft of hope or joy or aspiration here, and with only a dull fear of the hereafter. It is the gospel of the grace of God alone that can uplift the soul. The contemplation of the love of God manifested in His Son will stir the heart and arouse the powers of the soul as nothing else can. Christ came that He might re-create the image of God in man; and whoever turns men away from Christ is turning them away from the source of true development; he is defrauding them of the hope and purpose and glory of life. He is a thief and a robber.

"He that entereth in by the door is the shepherd of the sheep." Christ is both the door and the shepherd. He enters in by Himself. It is through His own sacrifice that He becomes the shepherd of the sheep. "To Him the porter openeth; and the sheep hear His voice: and He calleth His own sheep by name, and leadeth them out. And when He putteth forth His own sheep, He goeth before them, and the sheep follow Him: for they know His voice."

Of all creatures the sheep is one of the most timid and helpless, and in the East the shepherd's care for his flock is untiring and incessant. Anciently as now there was little security outside of the walled towns. Marauders from the roving border tribes, or beasts of prey from their hiding places in the rocks, lay in wait to plunder the flocks. The shepherd watched his charge, knowing that it was at the peril of his own life. Jacob, who kept the flocks of Laban in the pasture grounds of Haran, describing his own unwearied labor, said, "In the day the drought consumed me, and the frost by night; and my sleep departed from mine eyes." Gen. 31:40. And it was while guarding his father's sheep that the boy David, single-handed, encountered the lion and the bear, and rescued from their teeth the stolen lamb.

479

As the shepherd leads his flock over the rocky hills, through forest and wild ravines, to grassy nooks by the riverside; as he watches them on the mountains through the lonely night, shielding from robbers, caring tenderly for the sickly and feeble, his life comes to be one with theirs. A strong and tender attachment unites him to the objects of his care. However large the flock, the shepherd knows every sheep. Every one has its name, and responds to the name at the shepherd's call.

As an earthly shepherd knows his sheep, so does the divine Shepherd know His flock that are scattered throughout the world. "Ye My flock, the flock of My pasture, are men, and I am your God, saith the Lord God." Jesus says, "I have called thee by thy name; thou art Mine." "I have graven thee upon the palms of My hands." Ezek. 34:31; Isa. 43:1; 49:16.

Jesus knows us individually, and is touched with the feeling of our infirmities. He knows us all by name. He knows the very house in which we live, the name of each occupant. He has at times given directions to His servants to go to a certain street in a certain city, to such a house, to find one of His sheep.

480 Every soul is as fully known to Jesus as if he were the only one for whom the Saviour died. The distress of every one touches His heart. The cry for aid reaches His ear. He came to draw all men unto Himself. He bids them, "Follow Me," and His Spirit moves upon their hearts to draw them to come to Him. Many refuse to be drawn. Jesus knows who they are. He also knows who gladly hear His call, and are ready to come under His pastoral care. He says, "My sheep hear My voice, and I know them, and they follow Me." He cares for each one as if there were not another on the face of the earth.

"He calleth His own sheep by name, and leadeth them out. . . . And the sheep follow Him: for they know His voice." The Eastern shepherd does not drive his sheep. He depends not upon force or fear; but going before, he calls them. They know his voice, and obey the call. So does the Saviour-Shepherd with His sheep. The Scripture says, "Thou leddest Thy people like a flock by the hand of Moses and Aaron." Through the prophet, Jesus declares, "I have loved thee with an everlasting love: therefore with loving-kindness have I drawn thee." He compels none to follow Him. "I drew them," He says, "with cords of a man, with bands of love." Ps. 77:20; Jer. 31:3; Hosea 11:4.

It is not the fear of punishment, or the hope of everlasting reward, that leads the disciples of Christ to follow Him. They behold the Saviour's matchless love, revealed throughout His pilgrimage on earth, from the manger of Bethlehem to Calvary's cross, and the sight of Him attracts, it softens and subdues the soul. Love awakens in the heart of the beholders. They hear His voice, and they follow Him.

As the shepherd goes before his sheep, himself first encountering the perils of the way, so does Jesus with His people. "When He putteth forth His own sheep, He goeth before them." The way to heaven is consecrated by the Saviour's footprints. The path may be steep and rugged, but Jesus has traveled that way; His feet have pressed down the cruel thorns, to make the pathway easier for us. Every burden that we are called to bear He Himself has borne.

Though now He has ascended to the presence of God, and shares the throne of the universe, Jesus has lost none of His compassionate nature. Today the same tender, sympathizing heart is open to all the woes of humanity. Today the hand that was pierced is reached forth to bless more abundantly His people that are in the world. "And they shall never perish, neither shall any man pluck them out of My hand." The 483 soul that has given himself to Christ is more precious in His sight than the whole world. The Saviour would have passed through the agony of Calvary that one might be saved in His kingdom. He will never abandon one for whom He has died. Unless His followers choose to leave Him, He will hold them fast.

Through all our trials we have a never-failing Helper. He does not leave us alone to struggle with temptation, to battle with evil, and be finally crushed with burdens and sorrow. Though now He is hidden from mortal sight, the ear of faith can hear His voice saying, Fear not; I am with you. "I am He that liveth, and was dead; and, behold, I am alive forevermore." Rev. 1:18. I have endured your sorrows, experienced your struggles, encountered your temptations. I know your tears; I also have wept. The griefs that lie too deep to be breathed into any human ear, I know. Think not that you are desolate and forsaken. Though your pain touch no responsive chord in any heart on earth, look unto Me, and live. "The mountains shall depart, and the hills be removed; but My kindness shall not depart from thee, neither shall the covenant of My peace be removed, saith the Lord that hath mercy on thee." Isa. 54:10.

However much a shepherd may love his sheep, he loves his sons and daughters more. Jesus is not only our shepherd; He is our "everlasting Father." And He says, "I know Mine own, and Mine own know Me, even as the Father knoweth Me, and I know the Father." John 10:14, 15, R. V. What a statement is this!—the only-begotten Son, He who is in the bosom of the Father, He whom God has declared to be "the Man that is My fellow" (Zech. 13:7),—the communion between Him and the eternal God is taken to represent the communion between Christ and His children on the earth!

Because we are the gift of His Father, and the reward of His work, Jesus loves us. He loves us as His children. Reader, He loves you. Heaven itself can bestow nothing greater, nothing better. Therefore trust.

Jesus thought upon the souls all over the earth who were misled by false shepherds. Those whom He longed to gather as the sheep of His pasture were scattered among wolves, and He said, "Other sheep I have, which are not of this fold: them also I must bring, and they shall hear My voice; and they shall become one flock, one shepherd." John 10:16, R. V.

"Therefore doth My Father love Me, because I lay down My life, that I might take it again." That is, My Father has so loved you, that He even loves Me more for giving My life to redeem you. In becoming your substitute and surety, by surrendering My life, by taking your liabilities, your transgressions, I am endeared to My Father.

"I lay down My life, that I might take it again. No man taketh it from Me, but I lay it down of Myself. I have power to lay it down, and I have power to take it again." While as a member of the human family He was mortal, as God He was the fountain of life for the world. He could have withstood the advances of death, and refused to come under its dominion; but voluntarily He laid down His life, that He might bring life and immortality to light. He bore the sin of the world, endured its curse, yielded up His life as a sacrifice, that men might not eternally die. "Surely He hath borne our griefs, and carried our sorrows. . . . He was wounded for our transgressions, He was bruised for our iniquities: the chastisement of our peace was upon Him; and with His stripes we are healed. All we like sheep have gone astray; we have turned every one to his own way; and the Lord hath laid on Him the iniquity of us all." Isa. 53:4-6.

53

The Last Journey From Galilee

As the close of His ministry drew near, there was a change in Christ's manner of labor. Heretofore He had sought to shun excitement and publicity. He had refused the homage of the people, and had passed quickly from place to place when the popular enthusiasm in His favor seemed kindling beyond control. Again and again He had commanded that none should declare Him to be the Christ.

At the time of the Feast of Tabernacles His journey to Jerusalem was made swiftly and secretly. When urged by His brothers to present Himself publicly as the Messiah, His answer was, "My time is not yet come." John 7:6. He made His way to Jerusalem unob-

served, and entered the city unannounced, and unhonored by the multitude. But not so with His last journey. He had left Jerusalem for a season because of the malice of the priests and rabbis. But He now set out to return, traveling in the most public manner, by a circuitous route, and preceded by such an announcement of His coming as He had never made before. He was going forward to the scene of His great sacrifice, and to this the attention of the people must be directed.

"As Moses lifted up the serpent in the wilderness, even so must the Son of man be lifted up." John 3:14. As the eyes of all Israel had been directed to the uplifted serpent, the symbol appointed for their healing, so all eyes must be drawn to Christ, the sacrifice that brought salvation to the lost world.

It was a false conception of the Messiah's work, and a lack of faith in the divine character of Jesus, that had led His brothers to urge Him to present Himself publicly to the people at the Feast of Tabernacles. Now, in a spirit akin to this, the disciples would have prevented Him from making the journey to Jerusalem. They remembered His words concerning what was to befall Him there, they knew the deadly hostility of the religious leaders, and they would fain have dissuaded their Master from going thither.

To the heart of Christ it was a bitter task to press His way against the fears, disappointment, and unbelief of His beloved disciples. It was hard to lead them forward to the anguish and despair that awaited them at Jerusalem. And Satan was at hand to press his temptations upon the Son of man. Why should He now go to Jerusalem, to certain death? All around Him were souls hungering for the bread of life. On every hand were suffering ones waiting for His word of healing. The work to be wrought by the gospel of His grace was but just begun. And He was full of the vigor of manhood's prime. Why not go forward to the vast fields of the world with the words of His grace, the touch of His healing power? Why not take to Himself the joy of giving light and gladness to those darkened and sorrowing millions? Why leave the harvest gathering to His disciples, so weak in faith, so dull of understanding, so slow to act? Why face death now, and leave the work in its infancy? The foe who in the wilderness had confronted Christ assailed Him now with fierce and subtle temptations. Had Jesus yielded for a moment, had He changed His course in the least particular to save Himself, Satan's agencies would have triumphed, and the world would have been lost.

But Jesus had "steadfastly set His face to go to Jerusalem." The one law of His life was the Father's will. In the visit to the temple in His boyhood, He had said to Mary, "Wist ye not

This chapter is based on Luke 9:51-56; 10:1-24.

that I must be about My Father's business?" Luke 2:49. At Cana, when Mary desired Him to reveal His miraculous power, His answer was, "Mine hour is not yet come." John 2:4. With the same words He replied to His brothers when they urged Him to go to the feast. But in God's great plan the hour had been appointed for the offering of Himself for the sins of men, and that hour was soon to strike. He would not fail nor falter. His steps are turned toward Jerusalem, where His foes have long plotted to take His life; now He will lay it down. He set His face steadfastly to go to persecution, denial, rejection, condemnation, and death.

And He "sent messengers before His face: and they went, and entered into a village of the Samaritans, to make ready for Him." But the people refused to receive Him, because He was on His way to Jerusalem. This they interpreted as meaning that Christ showed a preference for the Jews, whom they hated with intense bitterness. Had He come to restore the temple and worship upon Mount Gerizim, they would gladly have received Him; but He was going to Jerusalem, and they would show Him no hospitality. Little did they realize that they were turning from their doors the best gift of heaven. Jesus invited men to receive Him, He asked favors at their hands, that He might come near to them, to bestow the richest blessings. For every favor manifested toward Him, He requited a more precious grace. But all was lost to the Samaritans because of their prejudice and bigotry.

James and John, Christ's messengers, were greatly annoyed at the insult shown to their Lord. They were filled with indignation because He had been so rudely treated by the Samaritans whom He was honoring by His presence. They had recently been with Him on the mount of transfiguration, and had seen Him glorified by God, and honored by Moses and Elijah. This manifest dishonor on the part of the Samaritans, should not, they thought, be passed over without marked punishment.

Coming to Christ, they reported to Him the words of the people, telling Him that they had even refused to give Him a night's lodging. They thought that a grievous wrong had been done Him, and seeing Mount Carmel in the distance, where Elijah had slain the false prophets, they said, "Wilt Thou that we command fire to come down from heaven, and consume them, even as Elias did?" They were surprised to see that Jesus was pained by their words, and still more surprised as His rebuke fell upon their ears, "Ye know not what manner of spirit ye are of. For the Son of man is not come to destroy men's lives, but to save them." And He went to another village.

It is no part of Christ's mission to compel men to receive Him. It is Satan, and men actuated by his spirit, that seek to compel the conscience. Under a pretense of zeal for righteousness, men who are confederate with evil angels bring suffering upon their fellow men, in order to convert them to their ideas of religion; but Christ is ever showing mercy, ever seeking to win by the revealing of His love. He can admit no rival in the soul, nor accept of partial service; but He desires only voluntary service, the willing surrender of the heart under the constraint of love. There can be no more conclusive evidence that we possess the spirit of Satan than the disposition to hurt and destroy those who do not appreciate our work, or who act contrary to our ideas.

Every human being, in body, soul, and spirit, is the property of God. Christ died to redeem all. Nothing can be more offensive to God than for men, through religious bigotry, to bring suffering upon those who are the purchase of the Saviour's blood.

"And He arose from thence, and cometh into the coasts of Judea by the farther side of Jordan: and the people resort unto Him again; and, as He was wont, He taught them again." Mark 10:1.

A considerable part of the closing months of Christ's ministry was spent in Perea, the province on "the farther side of Jordan" from Judea. Here the multitude thronged His steps, as in His early ministry in Galilee, and much of His former teaching was repeated.

As He had sent out the twelve, so He "appointed seventy others, and sent them two and two before His face into every city and place, whither He Himself was about to come." Luke 10:1, R. V. These disciples had been for some time with Him, in training for their work. When the twelve were sent out on their first separate mission, other disciples accompanied Jesus in His journey through Galilee. Thus they had the privilege of intimate association with Him, and direct personal instruction. Now this larger number also were to go forth on a separate mission.

The directions to the seventy were similar to those that had been given to the twelve; but the command to the twelve, not to enter into any city of the Gentiles or of the Samaritans, was not given to the seventy. Though Christ had just been repulsed by the Samaritans, His love toward them was unchanged. When the seventy went forth in His name, they visited, first of all, the cities of Samaria.

The Saviour's own visit to Samaria, and later, the commendation of the good Samaritan, and the grateful joy of that leper, a Samaritan, who alone of the ten returned to give thanks to Christ, were full of significance to the disciples. The lesson sank deep into their hearts. In His commission to them, just before His ascension,

Jesus mentioned Samaria with Jerusalem and Judea as the places where they were first to preach the gospel. This commission His teaching had prepared them to fulfill. When in their Master's name they went to Samaria, they found the people ready to receive them. The Samaritans had heard of Christ's words of commendation and His works of mercy for men of their nation. They saw that, notwithstanding their rude treatment of Him, He had only thoughts of love toward them, and their hearts were won. After His ascension they welcomed the Saviour's messengers, and the disciples gathered a precious harvest from among those who had once been their bitterest enemies. "A bruised reed shall He not break, and the dimly burning flax shall He not quench: He shall bring forth judgment unto truth." "And in His name shall the Gentiles trust." Isa. 42:3, margin; Matt. 12:21.

489

In sending out the seventy, Jesus bade them, as He had bidden the twelve, not to urge their presence where they were unwelcome. "Into whatsoever city ye enter, and they receive you not," He said, "go your ways out into the streets of the same, and say, Even the very dust of your city, which cleaveth on us, we do wipe off against you: notwithstanding be ye sure of this, that the kingdom of God is come nigh unto you." They were not to do this from motives of resentment or through wounded dignity, but to show how grievous a thing it is to refuse the Lord's message or His messengers. To reject the Lord's servants is to reject Christ Himself.

"I say unto you," Jesus added, "that it shall be more tolerable in that day for Sodom, than for that city." Then His mind reverted to the Galilean towns where so much of His ministry had been spent. In deeply sorrowful accents He exclaimed, "Woe unto thee, Chorazin! woe unto thee, Bethsaida! for if the mighty works had been done in Tyre and Sidon, which have been done in you, they had a great while ago repented, sitting in sackcloth and ashes. But it shall be more tolerable for Tyre and Sidon at the judgment, than for you. And thou, Capernaum, which art exalted to heaven, shalt be thrust down to hell."

To those busy towns about the Sea of Galilee, heaven's richest blessings had been freely offered. Day after day the Prince of life had gone in and out among them. The glory of God, which prophets and kings had longed to see, had shone upon the multitudes that thronged the Saviour's steps. Yet they had refused the heavenly Gift.

With a great show of prudence the rabbis had warned the people against receiving the new doctrines taught by this new teacher; for His theories and practices were contrary to the teachings of the fathers. The people gave credence to what the priests and Pharisees taught, in place of seeking to understand the word of God for themselves. They honored the priests and rulers instead of honoring God, and rejected the truth that they might keep their own traditions. Many had been impressed and almost persuaded; but they did not act upon their convictions, and were not reckoned on the side of Christ. Satan presented his temptations, until the light appeared as darkness. Thus many rejected the truth that would have proved the saving of the soul.

The True Witness says, "Behold, I stand at the door, and knock." Rev. 3:20. Every warning, reproof, and entreaty in the word of God or through His messengers is a knock at the door of the heart. It is the voice of Jesus asking for entrance. With every knock unheeded, the disposition to open becomes weaker. The impressions of the Holy Spirit if disregarded today, will not be as strong tomorrow. The heart becomes less impressible, and lapses into a perilous unconsciousness of the shortness of life, and of the great eternity beyond. Our condemnation in the judgment will not result from the fact that we have been in error, but from the fact that we have neglected heaven-sent opportunities for learning what is truth.

490

Like the apostles, the seventy had received supernatural endowments as a seal of their mission. When their work was completed, they returned with joy, saying, "Lord, even the devils are subject unto us through Thy name." Jesus answered, "I beheld Satan as lightning fall from heaven."

The scenes of the past and the future were presented to the mind of Jesus. He beheld Lucifer as he was first cast out from the heavenly places. He looked forward to the scenes of His own agony, when before all the worlds the character of the deceiver should be unveiled. He heard the cry, "It is finished" (John 19:30), announcing that the redemption of the lost race was forever made certain, that heaven was made eternally secure against the accusations, the deceptions, the pretensions, that Satan would instigate.

Beyond the cross of Calvary, with its agony and shame, Jesus looked forward to the great final day, when the prince of the power of the air will meet his destruction in the earth so long marred by his rebellion. Jesus beheld the work of evil forever ended, and the peace of God filling heaven and earth.

Henceforward Christ's followers were to look upon Satan as a conquered foe. Upon the cross, Jesus was to gain the victory for them; that victory He desired them to accept as their own. "Behold," He said, "I give unto you power to tread on serpents and scorpions, and over all the power of the enemy: and nothing shall by any means hurt you."

The omnipotent power of the Holy Spirit is

the defense of every contrite soul. Not one that in penitence and faith has claimed His protection will Christ permit to pass under the enemy's power. The Saviour is by the side of His tempted and tried ones. With Him there can be no such thing as failure, loss, impossibility, or defeat; we can do all things through Him who strengthens us. When temptations and trials come, do not wait to adjust all the difficulties, but look to Jesus, your helper.

There are Christians who think and speak altogether too much about the power of Satan. They think of their adversary, they pray about him, they talk about him, and he looms up greater and greater in their imagination. It is true that Satan is a powerful being; but, thank God, we have a mighty Saviour, who cast out the evil one from heaven. Satan is pleased when we magnify his power. Why not talk of Jesus? Why not magnify His power and His love?

The rainbow of promise encircling the throne on high is an everlasting testimony that "God so loved the world, that He gave His only-begotten Son, that whosoever believeth in Him should not perish, but have everlasting life." John 3:16. It testifies to the universe that God will never forsake His people in their struggle with evil. It is an assurance to us of strength and protection as long as the throne itself shall endure.

Jesus added, "Notwithstanding in this rejoice not, that the spirits are subject unto you; but rather rejoice, because your names are written in heaven." Rejoice not in the possession of power, lest you lose sight of your dependence upon God. Be careful lest self-sufficiency come in, and you work in your own strength, rather than in the spirit and strength of your Master. Self is ever ready to take the credit if any measure of success attends the work. Self is flattered and exalted, and the impression is not made upon other minds that God is all and in all. The apostle Paul says, "When I am weak, then am I strong." 2 Cor. 12:10. When we have a realization of our weakness, we learn to depend upon a power not inherent. Nothing can take so strong a hold on the heart as the abiding sense of our responsibility to God. Nothing reaches so fully down to the deepest motives of conduct as a sense of the pardoning love of Christ. We are to come in touch with God, then we shall be imbued with His Holy Spirit, that enables us to come in touch with our fellow men. Then rejoice that through Christ you have become connected with God, members of the heavenly family. While you look higher than yourself, you will have a continual sense of the weakness of humanity. The less you cherish self, the more distinct and full will be your comprehension of the excellence of your Saviour. The more closely you connect yourself with the source of light and power, the greater light will be shed upon you, and the greater power will be yours to

work for God. Rejoice that you are one with God, one with Christ, and with the whole family of heaven.

As the seventy listened to the words of Christ, the Holy Spirit was impressing their minds with living realities, and writing truth upon the tablets of the soul. Though multitudes surrounded them, they were as though shut in with God.

Knowing that they had caught the inspiration of the hour, Jesus "rejoiced in spirit, and said, I thank Thee, O Father, Lord of heaven and earth, that Thou hast hid these things from the wise and prudent, and hast revealed them unto babes: even so, Father; for so it seemed good in Thy sight. All things are delivered to Me of My Father: and no man knoweth who the Son is, but the Father, and who the Father is, but the Son, and he to whom the Son will reveal Him."

The honored men of the world, the so-called great and wise men, with all their boasted wisdom, could not comprehend the character of Christ. They judged Him from outward appearance, from the humiliation that came upon Him as a human being. But to fishermen and publicans it had been given to see the Invisible. Even the disciples failed of understanding all that Jesus desired to reveal to them; but from time to time, as they surrendered themselves to the Holy Spirit's power, their minds were illuminated. They realized that the mighty God, clad in the garb of humanity, was among them. Jesus rejoiced that though this knowledge was not possessed by the wise and prudent, it had been revealed to these humble men. Often as He had presented the Old Testament Scriptures, and showed their application to Himself and His work of atonement, they had been awakened by His Spirit, and lifted into a heavenly atmosphere. Of the spiritual truths spoken by the prophets they had a clearer understanding than had the original writers themselves. Hereafter they would read the Old Testament Scriptures, not as the doctrines of the scribes and Pharisees, not as the utterances of wise men who were dead, but as a new revelation from God. They beheld Him "whom the world cannot receive, because it seeth Him not, neither knoweth Him: but ye know Him; for He dwelleth with you, and shall be in you." John 14:17.

The only way in which we can gain a more perfect apprehension of truth is by keeping the heart tender and subdued by the Spirit of Christ. The soul must be cleansed from vanity and pride, and vacated of all that has held it in possession, and Christ must be enthroned within. Human science is too limited to comprehend the atonement. The plan of redemption is so far-reaching that philosophy cannot explain it. It will ever remain a mystery that the most profound reasoning cannot fathom. The science of salvation cannot be explained; but it can be known by experience. Only he who sees his own sinfulness can discern the preciousness of the Saviour.

Full of instruction were the lessons which Christ taught as He slowly made His way from Galilee toward Jerusalem. Eagerly the people listened to His words. In Perea as in Galilee the people were less under the control of Jewish bigotry than in Judea, and His teaching found a response in their hearts.

During these last months of His ministry, many of Christ's parables were spoken. The priests and rabbis pursued Him with ever-increasing bitterness, and His warnings to them He veiled in symbols. They could not mistake His meaning, yet they could find in His words nothing on which to ground an accusation against Him. In the parable of the Pharisee and the publican, the self-sufficient prayer, "God, I thank Thee that I am not as the rest of men," stood out in sharp contrast to the penitent's plea, "Be merciful to me the sinner." Luke 18:11, 13, R. V., margin. Thus Christ rebuked the hypocrisy of the Jews. And under the figures of the barren fig tree and the great supper He foretold the doom about to fall upon the impenitent nation. Those who had scornfully rejected the invitation to the gospel feast heard His warning words: "I say unto you, That none of those men which were bidden shall taste of My supper." Luke 14:24.

Very precious was the instruction given to the disciples. The parable of the importunate widow and the friend asking for bread at midnight gave new force to His words, "Ask, and it shall be given you; seek, and ye shall find; knock, and it shall be opened unto you." Luke 11:9. And often their wavering faith was strengthened by the memory that Christ had said, "Shall not God do justice for His elect, which cry to Him day and night, and He is long-suffering over them? I say unto you, that He will do them justice speedily." Luke 18:7, 8, R. V., margin.

The beautiful parable of the lost sheep Christ repeated. And He carried its lesson still farther, as He told of the lost piece of silver and the prodigal son. The force of these lessons the disciples could not then fully appreciate; but after the outpouring of the Holy Spirit, as they saw the ingathering of the Gentiles and the envious anger of the Jews, they better understood the lesson of the prodigal son, and could enter into the joy of Christ's words, "It was meet that we should make merry, and be glad;" "for this my son was dead, and is alive again; he was lost, and is found." Luke 15:32, 24. And as they went out in their Master's name, facing reproach and poverty and persecution, they often strengthened their hearts by repeating His injunction, spoken on this last journey, "Fear not, little flock; for it is your Father's good pleasure to give you the kingdom. Sell that ye have, and give alms; provide yourselves bags which

wax not old, a treasure in the heavens that faileth not, where no thief approacheth, neither moth corrupteth. For where your treasure is, there will your heart be also." Luke 12:32-34.

54

The Good Samaritan

In the story of the good Samaritan, Christ illustrates the nature of true religion. He shows that it consists not in systems, creeds, or rites, but in the performance of loving deeds, in bringing the greatest good to others, in genuine goodness.

As Christ was teaching the people, "a certain lawyer stood up, and tempted Him, saying, Master, what shall I do to inherit eternal life?" With breathless attention the large congregation awaited the answer. The priests and rabbis had thought to entangle Christ by having the lawyer ask this question. But the Saviour entered into no controversy. He required the answer from the questioner himself. "What is written in the law?" He said; "how readest thou?" The Jews still accused Jesus of lightly regarding the law given from Sinai; but He turned the question of salvation upon the keeping of God's commandments.

The lawyer said, "Thou shalt love the Lord thy God with all thy heart, and with all thy soul, and with all thy strength, and with all thy mind; and thy neighbor as thyself." Jesus said, "Thou hast answered right: this do, and thou shalt live."

The lawyer was not satisfied with the position and works of the Pharisees. He had been studying the Scriptures with a desire to learn their real meaning. He had a vital interest in the matter, and had asked in sincerity, "What shall I do?" In his answer as to the requirements of the law, he passed by all the mass of ceremonial and ritualistic precepts. For these he claimed no value, but presented the two great principles on which hang all the law and the prophets. This answer, being commended by Christ, placed the Saviour on vantage ground with the rabbis. They could not condemn Him for sanctioning that which had been advanced by an expositor of the law.

"This do, and thou shalt live," Jesus said. He presented the law as a divine unity, and in this lesson taught that it is not possible to keep one precept, and break another; for the same principle runs through them all. Man's destiny will be determined by his obedience to the whole law. Supreme love to God and impartial love to man are the principles to be wrought out in the life.

The lawyer found himself a lawbreaker. He was convicted under Christ's searching words. The righteousness of the law, which he claimed

This chapter is based on Luke 10:25-37.

to understand, he had not practiced. He had not manifested love toward his fellow man. Repentance was demanded; but instead of repenting, he tried to justify himself. Rather than acknowledge the truth, he sought to show how difficult of fulfillment the commandment is. Thus he hoped both to parry conviction and to vindicate himself in the eyes of the people. The Saviour's words had shown that his question was needless, since he had been able to answer it himself. Yet he put another question, saying, "Who is my neighbor?"

Among the Jews this question caused endless dispute. They had no doubt as to the heathen and the Samaritans; these were strangers and enemies. But where should the distinction be made among the people of their own nation, and among the different classes of society? Whom should the priest, the rabbi, the elder, regard as neighbor? They spent their lives in a round of ceremonies to make themselves pure. Contact with the ignorant and careless multitude, they taught, would cause defilement that would require wearisome effort to remove. Were they to regard the "unclean" as neighbors?

Again Jesus refused to be drawn into controversy. He did not denounce the bigotry of those who were watching to condemn Him. But by a simple story He held up before His hearers such a picture of the outflowing of heaven-born love as touched all hearts, and drew from the lawyer a confession of the truth.

The way to dispel darkness is to admit light. The best way to deal with error is to present truth. It is the revelation of God's love that makes manifest the deformity and sin of the heart centered in self.

499 "A certain man," said Jesus, "was going down from Jerusalem to Jericho; and he fell among robbers, which both stripped him and beat him, and departed, leaving him half dead. And by chance a certain priest was going down that way: and when he saw him, he passed by on the other side. And in like manner a Levite also, when he came to the place, and saw him, passed by on the other side." Luke 10:30-32, R. V. This was no imaginary scene, but an actual occurrence, which was known to be exactly as represented. The priest and the Levite who had passed by on the other side were in the company that listened to Christ's words.

In journeying from Jerusalem to Jericho, the traveler had to pass through a portion of the wilderness of Judea. The road led down a wild, rocky ravine, which was infested by robbers, and was often the scene of violence. It was here that the traveler was attacked, stripped of all that was valuable, wounded and bruised, and left half dead by the wayside. As he lay thus, the priest came that way; but he merely glanced toward the wounded man. Then the Levite appeared. Curious to know what had happened,

he stopped and looked at the sufferer. He was convicted of what he ought to do; but it was not an agreeable duty. He wished that he had not come that way, so that he need not have seen the wounded man. He persuaded himself that the case was no concern of his.

Both these men were in sacred office, and professed to expound the Scriptures. They were of the class specially chosen to be representatives of God to the people. They were to "have compassion on the ignorant, and on them that are out of the way" (Heb. 5:2), that they might 500 lead men to understand God's great love toward humanity. The work they were called to do was the same that Jesus had described as His own when He said, "The Spirit of the Lord is upon Me, because He hath anointed Me to preach the gospel to the poor; He hath sent Me to heal the brokenhearted, to preach deliverance to the captives, and recovering of sight to the blind, to set at liberty them that are bruised." Luke 4:18.

The angels of heaven look upon the distress of God's family upon the earth, and they are prepared to co-operate with men in relieving oppression and suffering. God in His providence had brought the priest and the Levite along the road where the wounded sufferer lay, that they might see his need of mercy and help. All heaven watched to see if the hearts of these men would be touched with pity for human woe. The Saviour was the One who had instructed the Hebrews in the wilderness; from the pillar of cloud and of fire He had taught a very different lesson from that which the people were now receiving from their priests and teachers. The merciful provisions of the law extended even to the lower animals, which cannot express in words their want and suffering. Directions had been given to Moses for the children of Israel to this effect: "If thou meet thine enemy's ox or his ass going astray, thou shalt surely bring it back to him again. If thou see the ass of him that hateth thee lying under his burden, and wouldest forbear to help him, thou shalt surely help with him." Ex. 23:4, 5. But in the man wounded by robbers, Jesus presented the case of a brother in suffering. How much more should their hearts have been moved with pity for him than for a beast of burden! The message had been given them through Moses that the Lord their God, "a great God, a mighty, and a terrible," "doth execute the judgment of the fatherless and widow, and loveth the stranger." Wherefore He commanded, "Love ye therefore the stranger." "Thou shalt love him as thyself." Deut. 10:17-19; Lev. 19:34.

Job had said, "The stranger did not lodge in the street: but I opened my doors to the traveler." And when the two angels in the guise of men came to Sodom, Lot bowed himself with his face toward the ground, and said, "Behold now, my lords, turn in, I pray you, into your servant's house, and tarry all night." Job 31:32; Gen. 19:2. With all these lessons the priest and the Levite were familiar, but they had not brought them into practical life. Trained in the school of national bigotry, they had become selfish, narrow, and exclusive. When they looked upon the wounded man, they could not tell whether he was of their nation or not. They thought he might be of the Samaritans, and they turned away.

503   In their action, as Christ had described it, the lawyer saw nothing contrary to what he had been taught concerning the requirements of the law. But now another scene was presented:

A certain Samaritan, in his journey, came where the sufferer was, and when he saw him, he had compassion on him. He did not question whether the stranger was a Jew or a Gentile. If a Jew, the Samaritan well knew that, were their condition reversed, the man would spit in his face, and pass him by with contempt. But he did not hesitate on account of this. He did not consider that he himself might be in danger of violence by tarrying in the place. It was enough that there was before him a human being in need and suffering. He took off his own garment with which to cover him. The oil and wine provided for his own journey he used to heal and refresh the wounded man. He lifted him on his own beast, and moved slowly along with even pace, so that the stranger might not be jarred, and made to suffer increased pain. He brought him to an inn, and cared for him through the night, watching him tenderly. In the morning, as the sick man had improved, the Samaritan ventured to go on his way. But before doing this, he placed him in the care of the innkeeper, paid the charges, and left a deposit for his benefit; and not satisfied even with this, he made provision for any further need, saying to the host, "Take care of him; and whatsoever thou spendest more, when I come again, I will repay thee."

The story ended, Jesus fixed His eyes upon the lawyer, in a glance that seemed to read his soul, and said, "Which of these three, thinkest *thou*, proved neighbor unto him that fell among the robbers?" Luke 10:36, R. V.

The lawyer would not, even now, take the name Samaritan upon his lips, and he made answer, "He that showed mercy on him." Jesus said, "Go, and do *thou* likewise."

Thus the question, "Who is my neighbor?" is forever answered. Christ has shown that our neighbor does not mean merely one of the church or faith to which we belong. It has no reference to race, color, or class distinction. Our neighbor is every person who needs our help. Our neighbor is every soul who is wounded and bruised by the adversary. Our neighbor is everyone who is the property of God.

In the story of the good Samaritan, Jesus gave a picture of Himself and His mission. Man had been deceived, bruised, robbed, and ruined by Satan, and left to perish; but the Saviour had compassion on our helpless condition. He left 504 His glory, to come to our rescue. He found us ready to die, and He undertook our case. He healed our wounds. He covered us with His robe of righteousness. He opened to us a refuge of safety, and made complete provision for us at His own charges. He died to redeem us. Pointing to His own example, He says to His followers, "These things I command you, that ye love one another." "As I have loved you, that ye also love one another." John 15:17; 13:34.

The lawyer's question to Jesus had been, "What shall I do?" And Jesus, recognizing love to God and man as the sum of righteousness, had said, "This do, and thou shalt live." The Samaritan had obeyed the dictates of a kind and loving heart, and in this had proved himself a doer of the law. Christ bade the lawyer, "Go, and do thou likewise." Doing, and not saying merely, is expected of the children of God. "He that saith he abideth in Him ought himself also so to walk, even as He walked." 1 John 2:6.

The lesson is no less needed in the world today than when it fell from the lips of Jesus. Selfishness and cold formality have well-nigh extinguished the fire of love, and dispelled the graces that should make fragrant the character. Many who profess His name have lost sight of the fact that Christians are to represent Christ. Unless there is practical self-sacrifice for the good of others, in the family circle, in the neighborhood, in the church, and wherever we may be, then whatever our profession, we are not Christians.

Christ has linked His interest with that of humanity, and He asks us to become one with Him for the saving of humanity. "Freely ye have received," He says, "freely give." Matt. 10:8. Sin is the greatest of all evils, and it is ours to pity and help the sinner. There are many who err, and who feel their shame and their folly. They are hungry for words of encouragement. They look upon their mistakes and errors, until they are driven almost to desperation. These souls we are not to neglect. If we are Christians, we shall not pass by on the other side, keeping as far as possible from the very ones who most need our help. When we see human beings in distress, whether through affliction or through sin, we shall never say, This does not concern me.

"Ye which are spiritual, restore such an one in the spirit of meekness." Gal. 6:1. By faith and prayer press back the power of the enemy. Speak words of faith and courage that will be as a healing balsam to the bruised and wounded one. Many, many, have fainted and become discouraged in the great struggle of life, when one 505 word of kindly cheer would have strengthened them to overcome. Never should we pass by one suffering soul without seeking to impart to him of the comfort wherewith we are comforted of God.

All this is but a fulfillment of the principle of the law,—the principle that is illustrated in the story of the good Samaritan, and made manifest in the life of Jesus. His character reveals the true significance of the law, and shows what is meant by loving our neighbor as ourselves. And when the children of God manifest mercy, kindness, and love toward all men, they also are witnessing to the character of the statutes of heaven. They are bearing testimony to the fact that "the law of the Lord is perfect, converting the soul." Ps. 19:7. And whoever fails to manifest this love is breaking the law which he professes to revere. For the spirit we manifest toward our brethren declares what is our spirit toward God. The love of God in the heart is the only spring of love toward our neighbor. "If a man say, I love God, and hateth his brother, he is a liar: for he that loveth not his brother whom he hath seen, how can he love God whom he hath not seen?" Beloved, "if we love one another, God dwelleth in us, and His love is perfected in us." 1 John 4:20, 12.

506

55

Not With Outward Show

Some of the Pharisees had come to Jesus demanding "when the kingdom of God should come." More than three years had passed since John the Baptist gave the message that like a trumpet call had sounded through the land, "The kingdom of heaven is at hand." Matt. 3:2. And as yet these Pharisees saw no indication of the establishment of the kingdom. Many of those who rejected John, and at every step had opposed Jesus, were insinuating that His mission had failed.

Jesus answered, "The kingdom of God cometh not with outward show [margin]: neither shall they say, Lo here! or, lo there! for, behold, the kingdom of God is within you." The kingdom of God begins in the heart. Look not here or there for manifestations of earthly power to mark its coming.

"The days will come," He said, turning to His disciples, "when ye shall desire to see one of the days of the Son of man, and ye shall not see it." Because it is not attended by worldly pomp, you are in danger of failing to discern the glory of My mission. You do not realize how great is your present privilege in having among you, though veiled in humanity, Him who is the life and the light of men. The days will come when you will look back with longing upon the opportunities you now enjoy to walk and talk with the Son of God.

Because of their selfishness and earthliness, even the disciples of Jesus could not comprehend the spiritual glory which He sought to reveal unto them. It was not until after Christ's ascension to His Father, and the outpouring of the Holy Spirit upon the believers, that the disciples fully appreciated the Saviour's character and mission. After they had received the baptism of the Spirit, they began to realize that they had been in the very presence of the Lord of glory. As the sayings of Christ were brought to their remembrance, their minds were opened to comprehend the prophecies, and to understand the miracles which He had wrought. The wonders of His life passed before them, and they were as men awakened from a dream. They realized that "the Word was made flesh, and dwelt among us, (and we beheld His glory, the glory as of the Only-begotten of the Father,) full of grace and truth." John 1:14. Christ had actually come from God to a sinful world to save the fallen sons and daughters of Adam. The disciples now seemed, to themselves, of much less importance than before they realized this. They never wearied of rehearsing His words and works. His lessons, which they had but dimly understood, now came to them as a fresh revelation. The Scriptures became to them a new book.

As the disciples searched the prophecies that testified of Christ, they were brought into fellowship with the Deity, and learned of Him who had ascended to heaven to complete the work He had begun on earth. They recognized the fact that in Him dwelt knowledge which no human being, unaided by divine agency, could comprehend. They needed the help of Him whom kings, prophets, and righteous men had foretold. With amazement they read and reread the prophetic delineations of His character and work. How dimly had they comprehended the prophetic scriptures! how slow they had been in taking in the great truths which testified of Christ! Looking upon Him in His humiliation, as He walked a man among men, they had not understood the mystery of His incarnation, the dual character of His nature. Their eyes were holden, so that they did not fully recognize divinity in humanity. But after they were illuminated by the Holy Spirit, how they longed to see Him again, and to place themselves at His feet! How they wished that they might come to Him, and have Him explain the scriptures which they could not comprehend! How attentively would they listen to His words! What had Christ meant when He said, "I have yet many things to say unto you, but ye cannot bear them now"? John 16:12. How eager they were to know it all! They grieved that their faith had been so feeble, that their ideas had been so wide of the mark,

507

508

This chapter is based on Luke 17:20-22.

that they had so failed of comprehending the reality.

A herald had been sent from God to proclaim the coming of Christ, and to call the attention of the Jewish nation and of the world to His mission, that men might prepare for His reception. The wonderful personage whom John had announced had been among them for more than thirty years, and they had not really known Him as the One sent from God. Remorse took hold of the disciples because they had allowed the prevailing unbelief to leaven their opinions and becloud their understanding. The Light of this dark world had been shining amid its gloom, and they had failed to comprehend whence were its beams. They asked themselves why they had pursued a course that made it necessary for Christ to reprove them. They often repeated His conversations, and said, Why did we allow earthly considerations and the opposition of priests and rabbis to confuse our senses, so that we did not comprehend that a greater than Moses was among us, that One wiser than Solomon was instructing us? How dull were our ears! how feeble was our understanding!

Thomas would not believe until he had thrust his finger into the wound made by the Roman soldiers. Peter had denied Him in His humiliation and rejection. These painful remembrances came before them in distinct lines. They had been with Him, but they had not known or appreciated Him. But how these things now stirred their hearts as they recognized their unbelief!

As priests and rulers combined against them, and they were brought before councils and thrust into prison, the followers of Christ rejoiced "that they were counted worthy to suffer shame for His name." Acts 5:41. They rejoiced to prove, before men and angels, that they recognized the glory of Christ, and chose to follow Him at the loss of all things.

It is as true now as in apostolic days, that without the illumination of the divine Spirit, humanity cannot discern the glory of Christ. The truth and the work of God are unappreciated by a world-loving and compromising Christianity. Not in the ways of ease, of earthly honor or worldly conformity, are the followers of the Master found. They are far in advance, in the paths of toil, and humiliation, and reproach, in the front of the battle "against the principalities, against the powers, against the world rulers of this darkness, against the spiritual hosts of wickedness in the heavenly places." Eph. 6:12, 509 R. V. And now, as in Christ's day, they are misunderstood and reproached and oppressed by the priests and Pharisees of their time.

The kingdom of God comes not with outward show. The gospel of the grace of God, with its spirit of self-abnegation, can never be in harmony with the spirit of the world. The two principles are antagonistic. "The natural man receiveth not the things of the Spirit of God: for they are foolishness unto him: neither can he know them, because they are spiritually discerned." 1 Cor. 2:14.

But today in the religious world there are multitudes who, as they believe, are working for the establishment of the kingdom of Christ as an earthly and temporal dominion. They desire to make our Lord the ruler of the kingdoms of this world, the ruler in its courts and camps, its legislative halls, its palaces and market places. They expect Him to rule through legal enactments, enforced by human authority. Since Christ is not now here in person, they themselves will undertake to act in His stead, to execute the laws of His kingdom. The establishment of such a kingdom is what the Jews desired in the days of Christ. They would have received Jesus, had He been willing to establish a temporal dominion, to enforce what they regarded as the laws of God, and to make them the expositors of His will and the agents of His authority. But He said, "My kingdom is not of this world." John 18:36. He would not accept the earthly throne.

The government under which Jesus lived was corrupt and oppressive; on every hand were crying abuses,—extortion, intolerance, and grinding cruelty. Yet the Saviour attempted no civil reforms. He attacked no national abuses, nor condemned the national enemies. He did not interfere with the authority or administration of those in power. He who was our example kept aloof from earthly governments. Not because He was indifferent to the woes of men, but because the remedy did not lie in merely human and external measures. To be efficient, the cure must reach men individually, and must regenerate the heart.

Not by the decisions of courts or councils or legislative assemblies, not by the patronage of worldly great men, is the kingdom of Christ established, but by the implanting of Christ's nature in humanity through the work of the Holy Spirit. "As many as received Him, to them gave He power to become the sons of God, even to them that believe on His name: which were born, not of blood, nor of the will of the flesh, nor of the will of man, but of God." John 1:12, 13. Here is the only power that can work the 510 uplifting of mankind. And the human agency for the accomplishment of this work is the teaching and practicing of the word of God.

When the apostle Paul began his ministry in Corinth, that populous, wealthy, and wicked city, polluted by the nameless vices of heathenism, he said, "I determined not to know anything among you, save Jesus Christ, and Him crucified." 1 Cor. 2:2. Writing afterward to some of those who had been corrupted by the foulest sins, he could say, "But ye are washed, but ye are sanctified, but ye are justified in the name of the Lord Jesus, and by the Spirit of our God." "I thank my God always on your behalf, for the grace of God which is given you by Jesus Christ." 1 Cor. 6:11; 1:4.

Now, as in Christ's day, the work of God's kingdom lies not with those who are clamoring for recognition and support by earthly rulers and human laws, but with those who are declaring to the people in His name those spiritual truths that will work in the receivers the experience of Paul: "I am crucified with Christ: nevertheless I live; yet not I, but Christ liveth in me." Gal. 2:20. Then they will labor as did Paul for the benefit of men. He said, "Now then we are ambassadors for Christ, as though God did beseech you by us: we pray you in Christ's stead, be ye reconciled to God." 2 Cor. 5:20.

56

Blessing the Children

Jesus was ever a lover of children. He accepted their childish sympathy and their open, unaffected love. The grateful praise from their pure lips was music in His ears, and refreshed His spirit when oppressed by contact with crafty and hypocritical men. Wherever the Saviour went, the benignity of His countenance, and His gentle, kindly manner won the love and confidence of children.

Among the Jews it was customary for children to be brought to some rabbi, that he might lay his hands upon them in blessing; but the Saviour's disciples thought His work too important to be interrupted in this way. When the mothers came to Him with their little ones, the disciples looked on them with disfavor. They thought these children too young to be benefited by a visit to Jesus, and concluded that He would be displeased at their presence. But it was the disciples with whom He was displeased. The Saviour understood the care and burden of the mothers who were seeking to train their children according to the word of God. He had heard their prayers. He Himself had drawn them into His presence.

One mother with her child had left her home to find Jesus. On the way she told a neighbor her errand, and the neighbor wanted to have Jesus bless her children. Thus several mothers came together, with their little ones. Some of the children had passed beyond the years of infancy to childhood and youth. When the mothers made known their desire, Jesus heard with sympathy the timid, tearful request. But He waited to see how the disciples would treat them. When He saw them send the mothers away, thinking to do Him a favor, He showed

them their error, saying, "Suffer the little children to come unto Me, and forbid them not: for of such is the kingdom of God." He took the children in His arms, He laid His hands upon them, and gave them the blessing for which they came.

The mothers were comforted. They returned to their homes strengthened and blessed by the words of Christ. They were encouraged to take up their burden with new cheerfulness, and to work hopefully for their children. The mothers of today are to receive His words with the same faith. Christ is as verily a personal Saviour today as when He lived a man among men. He is as verily the helper of mothers today as when He gathered the little ones to His arms in Judea. The children of our hearths are as much the purchase of His blood as were the children of long ago.

Jesus knows the burden of every mother's heart. He who had a mother that struggled with poverty and privation sympathizes with every mother in her labors. He who made a long journey in order to relieve the anxious heart of a Canaanite woman will do as much for the mothers of today. He who gave back to the widow of Nain her only son, and who in His agony upon the cross remembered His own mother, is touched today by the mother's sorrow. In every grief and every need He will give comfort and help.

Let mothers come to Jesus with their perplexities. They will find grace sufficient to aid them in the management of their children. The gates are open for every mother who would lay her burdens at the Saviour's feet. He who said, "Suffer the little children to come unto Me, and forbid them not," still invites the mothers to lead up their little ones to be blessed by Him. Even the babe in its mother's arms may dwell as under the shadow of the Almighty through the faith of the praying mother. John the Baptist was filled with the Holy Spirit from his birth. If we will live in communion with God, we too may expect the divine Spirit to mold our little ones, even from their earliest moments.

In the children who were brought in contact with Him, Jesus saw the men and women who should be heirs of His grace and subjects of His kingdom, and some of whom would become martyrs for His sake. He knew that these children would listen to Him and accept Him as their Redeemer far more readily than would grown-up people, many of whom were the worldly-wise and hardhearted. In His teaching He came down to their level. He, the Majesty of heaven, did not disdain to answer their questions, and simplify His important lessons to meet their childish understanding. He planted in their minds the seeds of truth, which in after years would spring up, and bear fruit unto eternal life.

This chapter is based on Matthew 19:13-15; Mark 10:13-16; Luke 18:15-17.

It is still true that children are the most susceptible to the teachings of the gospel; their hearts are open to divine influences, and strong to retain the lessons received. The little children may be Christians, having an experience in accordance with their years. They need to be educated in spiritual things, and parents should give them every advantage, that they may form characters after the similitude of the character of Christ.

Fathers and mothers should look upon their children as younger members of the Lord's family, committed to them to educate for heaven. The lessons that we ourselves learn from Christ we should give to our children, as the young minds can receive them, little by little opening to them the beauty of the principles of heaven. Thus the Christian home becomes a school, where the parents serve as underteachers, while Christ Himself is the chief instructor.

In working for the conversion of our children, we should not look for violent emotion as the essential evidence of conviction of sin. Nor is it necessary to know the exact time when they are converted. We should teach them to bring their sins to Jesus, asking His forgiveness, and believing that He pardons and receives them as He received the children when He was personally on earth.

As the mother teaches her children to obey her because they love her, she is teaching them the first lessons in the Christian life. The mother's love represents to the child the love of Christ, and the little ones who trust and obey their mother are learning to trust and obey the Saviour.

Jesus was the pattern for children, and He was also the father's example. He spoke as one having authority, and His word was with power; yet in all His intercourse with rude and violent men He did not use one unkind or discourteous expression. The grace of Christ in the heart will impart a heaven-born dignity and sense of propriety. It will soften whatever is harsh, and subdue all that is coarse and unkind. It will lead fathers and mothers to treat their children as intelligent beings, as they themselves would like to be treated.

516 Parents, in the training of your children, study the lessons that God has given in nature. If you would train a pink, or rose, or lily, how would you do it? Ask the gardener by what process he makes every branch and leaf to flourish so beautifully, and to develop in symmetry and loveliness. He will tell you that it was by no rude touch, no violent effort; for this would only break the delicate stems. It was by little attentions, often repeated. He moistened the soil, and protected the growing plants from the fierce blasts and from the scorching sun, and God caused them to flourish and to blossom into loveliness. In dealing with your children, follow the method of the gardener. By gentle touches, by loving ministrations, seek to fashion their characters after the pattern of the character of Christ.

Encourage the expression of love toward God and toward one another. The reason why there are so many hardhearted men and women in the world is that true affection has been regarded as weakness, and has been discouraged and repressed. The better nature of these persons was stifled in childhood; and unless the light of divine love shall melt away their cold selfishness, their happiness will be forever ruined. If we wish our children to possess the tender spirit of Jesus, and the sympathy that angels manifest for us, we must encourage the generous, loving impulses of childhood.

Teach the children to see Christ in nature. Take them out into the open air, under the noble trees, into the garden; and in all the wonderful works of creation teach them to see an expression of His love. Teach them that He made the laws which govern all living things, that He has made laws for us, and that these laws are for our happiness and joy. Do not weary them with long 517 prayers and tedious exhortations, but through nature's object lessons teach them obedience to the law of God.

As you win their confidence in you as followers of Christ, it will be easy to teach them of the great love wherewith He has loved us. As you try to make plain the truths of salvation, and point the children to Christ as a personal Saviour, angels will be by your side. The Lord will give to fathers and mothers grace to interest their little ones in the precious story of the Babe of Bethlehem, who is indeed the hope of the world.

When Jesus told the disciples not to forbid the children to come to Him, He was speaking to His followers in all ages,—to officers of the church, to ministers, helpers, and all Christians. Jesus is drawing the children, and He bids us, Suffer them to come; as if He would say, They will come if you do not hinder them.

Let not your un-Christlike character misrepresent Jesus. Do not keep the little ones away from Him by your coldness and harshness. Never give them cause to feel that heaven will not be a pleasant place to them if you are there. Do not speak of religion as something that children cannot understand, or act as if they were not expected to accept Christ in their childhood. Do not give them the false impression that the religion of Christ is a religion of gloom, and that in coming to the Saviour they must give up all that makes life joyful.

As the Holy Spirit moves upon the hearts of the children, co-operate with His work. Teach them that the Saviour is calling them, that nothing can give Him greater joy than for them to give themselves to Him in the bloom and freshness of their years.

The Saviour regards with infinite tenderness the souls whom He has purchased with His own blood. They are the claim of His love. He looks upon them with unutterable longing. His heart is drawn out, not only to the best-behaved children, but to those who have by inheritance objectionable traits of character. Many parents do not understand how much they are responsible for these traits in their children. They have not the tenderness and wisdom to deal with the erring ones whom they have made what they are. But Jesus looks upon these children with pity. He traces from cause to effect.

The Christian worker may be Christ's agent in drawing these children to the Saviour. By wisdom and tact he may bind them to his heart, he may give them courage and hope, and through the grace of Christ may see them transformed in character, so that of them it may be said, "Of such is the kingdom of God."

57

"One Thing Thou Lackest"

"And when He was gone forth into the way, there came one running, and kneeled to Him, and asked Him, Good Master, what shall I do that I may inherit eternal life?"

The young man who asked this question was a ruler. He had great possessions, and occupied a position of responsibility. He saw the love that Christ manifested toward the children brought to Him; he saw how tenderly He received them, and took them up in His arms, and his heart kindled with love for the Saviour. He felt a desire to be His disciple. He was so deeply moved that as Christ was going on His way, he ran after Him, and kneeling at His feet, asked with sincerity and earnestness the question so important to his soul and to the soul of every human being, "Good Master, what shall I do that I may inherit eternal life?"

"Why callest thou Me good?" said Christ, "there is none good but One, that is, God." Jesus desired to test the ruler's sincerity, and to draw from him the way in which he regarded Him as good. Did he realize that the One to whom he was speaking was the Son of God? What was the true sentiment of his heart?

This ruler had a high estimate of his own righteousness. He did not really suppose that he was defective in anything, yet he was not altogether satisfied. He felt the want of something that he did not possess. Could not Jesus bless him as He blessed the little children, and satisfy his soul want?

In reply to this question Jesus told him that obedience to the commandments of God was necessary if he would obtain eternal life; and He quoted several of the commandments which show man's duty to his fellow men. The ruler's answer was positive: "All these things have I kept from my youth up: what lack I yet?"

Christ looked into the face of the young man, as if reading his life and searching his character. He loved him, and He hungered to give him that peace and grace and joy which would materially change his character. "One thing thou lackest," He said; "go thy way, sell whatsoever thou hast, and give to the poor, and thou shalt have treasure in heaven: and come, take up the cross, and follow Me."

Christ was drawn to this young man. He knew him to be sincere in his assertion, "All these things have I kept from my youth." The Redeemer longed to create in him that discernment which would enable him to see the necessity of heart devotion and Christian goodness. He longed to see in him a humble and contrite heart, conscious of the supreme love to be given to God, and hiding its lack in the perfection of Christ.

Jesus saw in this ruler just the help He needed if the young man would become a colaborer with Him in the work of salvation. If he would place himself under Christ's guidance, he would be a power for good. In a marked degree the ruler could have represented Christ; for he possessed qualifications, which, if he were united with the Saviour, would enable him to become a divine force among men. Christ, seeing into his character, loved him. Love for Christ was awakening in the ruler's heart; for love begets love. Jesus longed to see him a co-worker with Him. He longed to make him like Himself, a mirror in which the likeness of God would be reflected. He longed to develop the excellence of his character, and sanctify it to the Master's use. If the ruler had then given himself to Christ, he would have grown in the atmosphere of His presence. If he had made this choice, how different would have been his future!

"One thing thou lackest," Jesus said. "If thou wilt be perfect, go and sell that thou hast, and give to the poor, and thou shalt have treasure in heaven: and come and follow Me." Christ read the ruler's heart. Only one thing he lacked, but that was a vital principle. He needed the love of God in the soul. This lack, unless supplied, would prove fatal to him; his whole nature would become corrupted. By indulgence, selfishness would strengthen. That he might receive the love of God, his supreme love of self must be surrendered.

Christ gave this man a test. He called upon him to choose between the heavenly treasure and worldly greatness. The heavenly treasure was assured him if he would follow Christ. But self must yield; his will must be given into Christ's control. The very holiness of God was

---

This chapter is based on Matthew 19:16-22; Mark 10:17-22; Luke 18:18-23.

offered to the young ruler. He had the privilege of becoming a son of God, and a coheir with Christ to the heavenly treasure. But he must take up the cross, and follow the Saviour in the path of self-denial.

Christ's words were verily to the ruler the invitation, "Choose you this day whom ye will serve." Joshua 24:15. The choice was left with him. Jesus was yearning for his conversion. He had shown him the plague spot in his character, and with what deep interest He watched the issue as the young man weighed the question! If he decided to follow Christ, he must obey His words in everything. He must turn from his ambitious projects. With what earnest, anxious longing, what soul hunger, did the Saviour look at the young man, hoping that he would yield to the invitation of the Spirit of God!

Christ made the only terms which could place the ruler where he would perfect a Christian character. His words were words of wisdom, though they appeared severe and exacting. In accepting and obeying them was the ruler's only hope of salvation. His exalted position and his possessions were exerting a subtle influence for evil upon his character. If cherished, they would supplant God in his affections. To keep back little or much from God was to retain that which would lessen his moral strength and efficiency; for if the things of this world are cherished, however uncertain and unworthy they may be, they will become all-absorbing.

The ruler was quick to discern all that Christ's words involved, and he became sad. If he had realized the value of the offered gift, quickly would he have enrolled himself as one of Christ's followers. He was a member of the honored council of the Jews, and Satan was tempting him with flattering prospects of the future. He wanted the heavenly treasure, but he wanted also the temporal advantages his riches would bring him. He was sorry that such conditions existed; he desired eternal life, but he was not willing to make the sacrifice. The cost of eternal life seemed too great, and he went away sorrowful; "for he had great possessions."

His claim that he had kept the law of God was a deception. He showed that riches were his idol. He could not keep the commandments of God while the world was first in his affections. He loved the gifts of God more than he loved the Giver. Christ had offered the young man fellowship with Himself. "Follow Me," He said. But the Saviour was not so much to him as his own name among men or his possessions. To give up his earthly treasure, that was seen, for the heavenly treasure, that was unseen, was too great a risk. He refused the offer of eternal life, and went away, and ever after the world was to receive his worship. Thousands are passing through this ordeal, weighing Christ against the world; and many choose the world. Like the young ruler, they turn from the Saviour, saying in their hearts, I will not have this Man as my leader.

Christ's dealing with the young man is presented as an object lesson. God has given us the rule of conduct which every one of His servants must follow. It is obedience to His law, not merely a legal obedience, but an obedience which enters into the life, and is exemplified in the character. God has set His own standard of character for all who would become subjects of His kingdom. Only those who will become co-workers with Christ, only those who will say, Lord, all I have and all I am is Thine, will be acknowledged as sons and daughters of God. All should consider what it means to desire heaven, and yet to turn away because of the conditions laid down. Think of what it means to say "No" to Christ. The ruler said, No, I cannot give You all. Do we say the same? The Saviour offers to share with us the work God has given us to do. He offers to use the means God has given us, to carry forward His work in the world. Only in this way can He save us.

The ruler's possessions were entrusted to him that he might prove himself a faithful steward; he was to dispense these goods for the blessing of those in need. So God now entrusts men with means, with talents and opportunities, that they may be His agents in helping the poor and the suffering. He who uses his entrusted gifts as God designs becomes a co-worker with the Saviour. He wins souls to Christ, because he is a representative of His character.

To those who, like the young ruler, are in high positions of trust and have great possessions, it may seem too great a sacrifice to give up all in order to follow Christ. But this is the rule of conduct for all who would become His disciples. Nothing short of obedience can be accepted. Self-surrender is the substance of the teachings of Christ. Often it is presented and enjoined in language that seems authoritative, because there is no other way to save man than to cut away those things which, if entertained, will demoralize the whole being.

When Christ's followers give back to the Lord His own, they are accumulating treasure which will be given to them when they shall hear the words, "Well done, good and faithful servant; . . . enter thou into the joy of thy Lord." "Who for the joy that was set before Him endured the cross, despising the shame, and is set down at the right hand of the throne of God." Matt. 25:23; Heb. 12:2. The joy of seeing souls redeemed, souls eternally saved, is the reward of all that put their feet in the footprints of Him who said, "Follow Me."

58

"Lazarus, Come Forth"

Among the most steadfast of Christ's disciples was Lazarus of Bethany. From their first meeting his faith in Christ had been strong; his love for Him was deep, and he was greatly beloved by the Saviour. It was for Lazarus that the greatest of Christ's miracles was performed. The Saviour blessed all who sought His help; He loves all the human family, but to some He is bound by peculiarly tender associations. His heart was knit by a strong bond of affection to the family at Bethany, and for one of them His most wonderful work was wrought.

At the home of Lazarus, Jesus had often found rest. The Saviour had no home of His own; He was dependent on the hospitality of His friends and disciples, and often, when weary, thirsting for human fellowship, He had been glad to escape to this peaceful household, away from the suspicion and jealousy of the angry Pharisees. Here He found a sincere welcome, and pure, holy friendship. Here He could speak with simplicity and perfect freedom, knowing that His words would be understood and treasured.

Our Saviour appreciated a quiet home and interested listeners. He longed for human tenderness, courtesy, and affection. Those who received the heavenly instruction He was always ready to impart were greatly blessed. As the multitudes followed Christ through the open fields, He unfolded to them the beauties of the natural world. He sought to open the eyes of their understanding, that they might see how the hand of God upholds the world. In order to call out an appreciation of God's goodness and benevolence, He called the attention of His hearers to the gently falling dew, to the soft showers of rain and the bright sunshine, given alike to good and evil. He desired men to realize more fully the regard that God bestows on the human instrumentalities He has created. But the multitudes were slow of hearing, and in the home at Bethany Christ found rest from the weary conflict of public life. Here He opened to an appreciative audience the volume of Providence. In these private interviews He unfolded to His hearers that which He did not attempt to tell to the mixed multitude. He needed not to speak to His friends in parables.

As Christ gave His wonderful lessons, Mary sat at His feet, a reverent and devoted listener. On one occasion, Martha, perplexed with the care of preparing the meal, went to Christ, saying, "Lord, dost Thou not care that my sister hath left me to serve alone? bid her therefore that she help me." This was the time of Christ's first visit to Bethany. The Saviour and His disciples had just made the toilsome journey on foot from Jericho. Martha was anxious to provide for their comfort, and in her anxiety she forgot the courtesy due to her Guest. Jesus answered her with mild and patient words, "Martha, Martha, thou art careful and troubled about many things: but one thing is needful: and Mary hath chosen that good part, which shall not be taken away from her." Mary was storing her mind with the precious words falling from the Saviour's lips, words that were more precious to her than earth's most costly jewels.

The "one thing" that Martha needed was a calm, devotional spirit, a deeper anxiety for knowledge concerning the future, immortal life, and the graces necessary for spiritual advancement. She needed less anxiety for the things which pass away, and more for those things which endure forever. Jesus would teach His children to seize every opportunity of gaining that knowledge which will make them wise unto salvation. The cause of Christ needs careful, energetic workers. There is a wide field for the Marthas, with their zeal in active religious work. But let them first sit with Mary at the feet of Jesus. Let diligence, promptness, and energy be sanctified by the grace of Christ; then the life will be an unconquerable power for good.

Sorrow entered the peaceful home where Jesus had rested. Lazarus was stricken with sudden illness, and his sisters sent to the Saviour, saying, "Lord, behold, he whom Thou lovest is sick." They saw the violence of the disease that had seized their brother, but they knew that Christ had shown Himself able to heal all manner of diseases. They believed that He would sympathize with them in their distress; therefore they made no urgent demand for His immediate presence, but sent only the confiding message, "He whom Thou lovest is sick." They thought that He would immediately respond to their message, and be with them as soon as He could reach Bethany.

Anxiously they waited for a word from Jesus. As long as the spark of life was yet alive in their brother, they prayed and watched for Jesus to come. But the messenger returned without Him. Yet he brought the message, "This sickness is not unto death," and they clung to the hope that Lazarus would live. Tenderly they tried to speak words of hope and encouragement to the almost unconscious sufferer. When Lazarus died, they were bitterly disappointed; but they felt the sustaining grace of Christ, and this kept them from reflecting any blame on the Saviour.

When Christ heard the message, the disciples thought He received it coldly. He did not manifest the sorrow they expected Him to show. Looking up to them, He said, "This sickness is not unto death, but for the glory of God, that the

Son of God might be glorified thereby." For two days He remained in the place where He was. This delay was a mystery to the disciples. What a comfort His presence would be to the afflicted household! they thought. His strong affection for the family at Bethany was well known to the disciples, and they were surprised that He did not respond to the sad message, "He whom Thou lovest is sick."

During the two days Christ seemed to have dismissed the message from His mind; for He did not speak of Lazarus. The disciples thought of John the Baptist, the forerunner of Jesus. They had wondered why Jesus, with the power to perform wonderful miracles, had permitted John to languish in prison, and to die a violent death. Possessing such power, why did not Christ save John's life? This question had often been asked by the Pharisees, who presented it as an unanswerable argument against Christ's claim to be the Son of God. The Saviour had warned His disciples of trials, losses, and persecution. Would He forsake them in trial? Some questioned if they had mistaken His mission. All were deeply troubled.

After waiting for two days, Jesus said to the disciples, "Let us go into Judea again." The disciples questioned why, if Jesus were going to Judea, He had waited two days. But anxiety for Christ and for themselves was now uppermost in their minds. They could see nothing but danger in the course He was about to pursue. "Master," they said, "the Jews of late sought to stone Thee; and goest Thou thither again? Jesus answered, Are there not twelve hours in the day?" I am under the guidance of My Father; as long as I do His will, My life is safe. My twelve hours of day are not yet ended. I have entered upon the last remnant of My day; but while any of this remains, I am safe.

"If any man walk in the day," He continued, "he stumbleth not, because he seeth the light of this world." He who does the will of God, who walks in the path that God has marked out, cannot stumble and fall. The light of God's guiding Spirit gives him a clear perception of his duty, and leads him aright till the close of his work. "But if a man walk in the night, he stumbleth, because there is no light in him." He who walks in a path of his own choosing, where God has not called him, will stumble. For him day is turned into night, and wherever he may be, he is not secure.

"These things said He: and after that He saith unto them, Our friend Lazarus sleepeth; but I go, that I may awake him out of sleep." "Our friend Lazarus sleepeth." How touching the words! how full of sympathy! In the thought of the peril their Master was about to incur by going to Jerusalem, the disciples had almost forgotten the bereaved family at Bethany. But not so Christ. The disciples felt rebuked. They had

been disappointed because Christ did not respond more promptly to the message. They had been tempted to think that He had not the tender love for Lazarus and his sisters that they had thought He had, or He would have hastened back with the messenger. But the words, "Our friend Lazarus sleepeth," awakened right feelings in their minds. They were convinced that Christ had not forgotten His suffering friends.

"Then said His disciples, Lord, if he sleep, he shall do well. Howbeit Jesus spake of his death: but they thought that He had spoken of taking of rest in sleep." Christ represents death as a sleep to His believing children. Their life is hid with Christ in God, and until the last trump shall sound those who die will sleep in Him.

"Then said Jesus unto them plainly, Lazarus is dead. And I am glad for your sakes that I was not there, to the intent ye may believe; nevertheless let us go unto him." Thomas could see nothing but death in store for his Master if he went to Judea; but he girded up his spirit, and said to the other disciples, "Let us also go, that we may die with Him." He knew the hatred of the Jews toward Christ. It was their purpose to compass His death, but this purpose had not succeeded, because some of His allotted time still remained. During this time Jesus had the guardianship of heavenly angels; and even in the regions of Judea, where the rabbis were plotting how they might take Him and put Him to death, no harm could come to Him.

The disciples marveled at Christ's words when He said, "Lazarus is dead. And I am glad . . . that I was not there." Did the Saviour by His own choice avoid the home of His suffering friends? Apparently Mary and Martha and the dying Lazarus were left alone. But they were not alone. Christ beheld the whole scene, and after the death of Lazarus the bereaved sisters were upheld by His grace. Jesus witnessed the sorrow of their rent hearts, as their brother wrestled with his strong foe, death. He felt every pang of anguish, as He said to His disciples, "Lazarus is dead." But Christ had not only the loved ones at Bethany to think of; He had the training of His disciples to consider. They were to be His representatives to the world, that the Father's blessing might embrace all. For their sake He permitted Lazarus to die. Had He restored him from illness to health, the miracle that is the most positive evidence of His divine character would not have been performed.

Had Christ been in the sickroom, Lazarus would not have died; for Satan would have had no power over him. Death could not have aimed his dart at Lazarus in the presence of the Lifegiver. Therefore Christ remained away. He suffered the enemy to exercise his power, that He might drive him back, a conquered foe. He permitted Lazarus to pass under the dominion of death; and the suffering sisters saw their brother laid in the grave. Christ knew that as they looked on the dead face of their brother their faith in their Redeemer would be severely tried. But He knew that because of the struggle through which they were now passing their faith would shine forth with far greater power. He suffered every pang of sorrow that they endured. He loved them no less because He tarried; but He knew that for them, for Lazarus, for Himself, and for His disciples, a victory was to be gained.

"For your sakes," "to the intent ye may believe." To all who are reaching out to feel the guiding hand of God, the moment of greatest discouragement is the time when divine help is nearest. They will look back with thankfulness upon the darkest part of their way. "The Lord knoweth how to deliver the godly." 2 Peter 2:9. From every temptation and every trial He will bring them forth with firmer faith and a richer experience.

529   In delaying to come to Lazarus, Christ had a purpose of mercy toward those who had not received Him. He tarried, that by raising Lazarus from the dead He might give to His stubborn, unbelieving people another evidence that He was indeed "the resurrection, and the life." He was loath to give up all hope of the people, the poor, wandering sheep of the house of Israel. His heart was breaking because of their impenitence. In His mercy He purposed to give them one more evidence that He was the Restorer, the One who alone could bring life and immortality to light. This was to be an evidence that the priests could not misinterpret. This was the reason of His delay in going to Bethany. This crowning miracle, the raising of Lazarus, was to set the seal of God on His work and on His claim to divinity.

On His journey to Bethany, Jesus, according to His custom, ministered to the sick and the needy. Upon reaching the town He sent a messenger to the sisters with the tidings of His arrival. Christ did not at once enter the house, but remained in a quiet place by the wayside. The great outward display observed by the Jews at the death of friends or relatives was not in harmony with the spirit of Christ. He heard the sound of wailing from the hired mourners, and He did not wish to meet the sisters in the scene of confusion. Among the mourning friends were relatives of the family, some of whom held high positions of responsibility in Jerusalem. Among these were some of Christ's bitterest enemies. Christ knew their purposes, and therefore He did not at once make Himself known.

The message was given to Martha so quietly that others in the room did not hear. Absorbed in her grief, Mary did not hear the words. Rising at once, Martha went out to meet her Lord, but thinking that she had gone to the place where Lazarus was buried, Mary sat still in her sorrow, making no outcry.

Martha hastened to meet Jesus, her heart agitated by conflicting emotions. In His expressive face she read the same tenderness and love that had always been there. Her confidence in Him was unbroken, but she thought of her dearly loved brother, whom Jesus also had loved. With grief surging in her heart because Christ had not come before, yet with hope that even now He would do something to comfort them, she said, "Lord, if Thou hadst been here, my brother had not died." Over and over again, amid the tumult made by the mourners, the sisters had repeated these words.

With human and divine pity Jesus looked into her sorrowful, careworn face. Martha had no 530 inclination to recount the past; all was expressed by the pathetic words, "Lord, if Thou hadst been here, my brother had not died." But looking into that face of love, she added, "I know, that even now, whatsoever Thou wilt ask of God, God will give it Thee."

Jesus encouraged her faith, saying, "Thy brother shall rise again." His answer was not intended to inspire hope of an immediate change. He carried Martha's thoughts beyond the present restoration of her brother, and fixed them upon the resurrection of the just. This He did that she might see in the resurrection of Lazarus a pledge of the resurrection of all the righteous dead, and an assurance that it would be accomplished by the Saviour's power.

Martha answered, "I know that he shall rise again in the resurrection at the last day."

Still seeking to give a true direction to her faith, Jesus declared, "I am the resurrection, and the life." In Christ is life, original, unborrowed, underived. "He that hath the Son hath life." 1 John 5:12. The divinity of Christ is the believer's assurance of eternal life. "He that believeth in Me," said Jesus, "though he were dead, yet shall he live: and whosoever liveth and believeth in Me shall never die. Believest thou this?" Christ here looks forward to the time of His second coming. Then the righteous dead shall be raised incorruptible, and the living righteous shall be translated to heaven without seeing death. The miracle which Christ was about to perform, in raising Lazarus from the dead, would represent the resurrection of all the righteous dead. By His word and His works He declared Himself the Author of the resurrection. He who Himself was soon to die upon the cross stood with the keys of death, a conqueror of the grave, and asserted His right and power to give eternal life.

To the Saviour's words, "Believest thou?" Martha responded, "Yea, Lord: I believe that Thou art the Christ, the Son of God, which should come into the world." She did not comprehend in all their significance the words spoken by Christ, but she confessed her faith in His divinity, and her confidence that He was able to perform whatever it pleased Him to do.

"And when she had so said, she went her way, and called Mary her sister secretly, saying, The Master is come, and calleth for thee." She delivered her message as quietly as possible; for the priests and rulers were prepared to arrest Jesus when opportunity offered. The cries of the mourners prevented her words from being heard.

533 On hearing the message, Mary rose hastily, and with an eager look on her face left the room. Thinking that she had gone to the grave to weep, the mourners followed her. When she reached the place where Jesus was waiting, she knelt at His feet, and said with quivering lips, "Lord, if Thou hadst been here, my brother had not died." The cries of the mourners were painful to her; for she longed for a few quiet words alone with Jesus. But she knew of the envy and jealousy cherished in the hearts of some present against Christ, and she was restrained from fully expressing her grief.

"When Jesus therefore saw her weeping, and the Jews also weeping which came with her, He groaned in the spirit, and was troubled." He read the hearts of all assembled. He saw that with many, what passed as a demonstration of grief was only pretense. He knew that some in the company, now manifesting hypocritical sorrow, would erelong be planning the death, not only of the mighty miracle worker, but of the one to be raised from the dead. Christ could have stripped from them their robe of pretended sorrow. But He restrained His righteous indignation. The words He could in all truth have spoken, He did not speak, because of the loved one kneeling at His feet in sorrow, who truly believed in Him.

"Where have ye laid him?" He asked. "They said unto Him, Lord, come and see." Together they proceeded to the grave. It was a mournful scene. Lazarus had been much beloved, and his sisters wept for him with breaking hearts, while those who had been his friends mingled their tears with those of the bereaved sisters. In view of this human distress, and of the fact that the afflicted friends could mourn over the dead while the Saviour of the world stood by,— "Jesus wept." Though He was the Son of God, yet He had taken human nature upon Him, and He was moved by human sorrow. His tender, pitying heart is ever awakened to sympathy by suffering. He weeps with those that weep, and rejoices with those that rejoice.

But it was not only because of His human sympathy with Mary and Martha that Jesus wept. In His tears there was a sorrow as high above human sorrow as the heavens are higher than the earth. Christ did not weep for Lazarus; for He was about to call him from the grave. He wept because many of those now mourning for

Lazarus would soon plan the death of Him who was the resurrection and the life. But how unable were the unbelieving Jews rightly to interpret His tears! Some, who could see noth- 534 ing more than the outward circumstances of the scene before Him as a cause for His grief, said softly, "Behold how He loved him!" Others, seeking to drop the seed of unbelief into the hearts of those present, said derisively, "Could not this Man, which opened the eyes of the blind, have caused that even this man should not have died?" If it were in Christ's power to save Lazarus, why then did He suffer him to die?

With prophetic eye Christ saw the enmity of the Pharisees and the Sadducees. He knew that they were premeditating His death. He knew that some of those now apparently so sympathetic would soon close against themselves the door of hope and the gates of the city of God. A scene was about to take place, in His humiliation and crucifixion, that would result in the destruction of Jerusalem, and at that time none would make lamentation for the dead. The retribution that was coming upon Jerusalem was plainly portrayed before Him. He saw Jerusalem compassed by the Roman legions. He knew that many now weeping for Lazarus would die in the siege of the city, and in their death there would be no hope.

It was not only because of the scene before Him that Christ wept. The weight of the grief of ages was upon Him. He saw the terrible effects of the transgression of God's law. He saw that in the history of the world, beginning with the death of Abel, the conflict between good and evil had been unceasing. Looking down the years to come, He saw the suffering and sorrow, tears and death, that were to be the lot of men. His heart was pierced with the pain of the human family of all ages and in all lands. The woes of the sinful race were heavy upon His soul, and the fountain of His tears was broken up as He longed to relieve all their distress.

"Jesus therefore again groaning in Himself cometh to the grave." Lazarus had been laid in a cave in a rock, and a massive stone had been placed before the entrance. "Take ye away the stone," Christ said. Thinking that He only wished to look upon the dead, Martha objected, saying that the body had been buried four days, and corruption had already begun its work. This statement, made before the raising of Lazarus, left no room for Christ's enemies to say that a deception had been practiced. In the past the Pharisees had circulated false statements regarding the most wonderful manifestations of the power of God. When Christ raised to life the daughter of Jairus, He had said, "The damsel is not dead, but sleepeth." Mark 5:39. As she had been sick only a short time, and was raised 535 immediately after death, the Pharisees declared that the child had not been dead; that Christ

Himself had said she was only asleep. They had tried to make it appear that Christ could not cure disease, that there was foul play about His miracles. But in this case, none could deny that Lazarus was dead.

When the Lord is about to do a work, Satan moves upon someone to object. "Take ye away the stone," Christ said. As far as possible, prepare the way for My work. But Martha's positive and ambitious nature asserted itself. She was unwilling that the decomposing body should be brought to view. The human heart is slow to understand Christ's words, and Martha's faith had not grasped the true meaning of His promise.

Christ reproved Martha, but His words were spoken with the utmost gentleness. "Said I not unto thee, that, if thou wouldest believe, thou shouldest see the glory of God?" Why should you doubt in regard to My power? Why reason in opposition to My requirements? You have My word. If you will believe, you shall see the glory of God. Natural impossibilities cannot prevent the work of the Omnipotent One. Skepticism and unbelief are not humility. Implicit belief in Christ's word is true humility, true self-surrender.

"Take ye away the stone." Christ could have commanded the stone to remove, and it would have obeyed His voice. He could have bidden the angels who were close by His side to do this. At His bidding, invisible hands would have removed the stone. But it was to be taken away by human hands. Thus Christ would show that humanity is to co-operate with divinity. What human power can do divine power is not summoned to do. God does not dispense with man's aid. He strengthens him, co-operating with him as he uses the powers and capabilities given him.

The command is obeyed. The stone is rolled away. Everything is done openly and deliberately. All are given a chance to see that no deception is practiced. There lies the body of Lazarus in its rocky grave, cold and silent in death. The cries of the mourners are hushed. Surprised and expectant, the company stand around the sepulcher, waiting to see what is to follow.

Calmly Christ stands before the tomb. A sacred solemnity rests upon all present. Christ steps closer to the sepulcher. Lifting His eyes to heaven, He says, "Father, I thank Thee that Thou hast heard Me." Not long before this, Christ's enemies had accused Him of blasphemy, and had taken up stones to cast at Him because He claimed to be the Son of God. They accused Him of performing miracles by the power of Satan. But here Christ claims God as His Father, and with perfect confidence declares that He is the Son of God.

In all that He did, Christ was co-operating with His Father. Ever He had been careful to make it evident that He did not work independently; it was by faith and prayer that He wrought His miracles. Christ desired all to know His relationship with His Father. "Father," He said, "I thank Thee that Thou hast heard Me. And I knew that Thou hearest Me always: but because of the people which stand by I said it, that they may believe that Thou hast sent Me." Here the disciples and the people were to be given the most convincing evidence in regard to the relationship existing between Christ and God. They were to be shown that Christ's claim was not a deception.

"And when He thus had spoken, He cried with a loud voice, Lazarus, come forth." His voice, clear and penetrating, pierces the ear of the dead. As He speaks, divinity flashes through humanity. In His face, which is lighted up by the glory of God, the people see the assurance of His power. Every eye is fastened on the entrance to the cave. Every ear is bent to catch the slightest sound. With intense and painful interest all wait for the test of Christ's divinity, the evidence that is to substantiate His claim to be the Son of God, or to extinguish the hope forever.

There is a stir in the silent tomb, and he who was dead stands at the door of the sepulcher. His movements are impeded by the grave-clothes in which he was laid away, and Christ says to the astonished spectators, "Loose him, and let him go." Again they are shown that the human worker is to co-operate with God. Humanity is to work for humanity. Lazarus is set free, and stands before the company, not as one emaciated from disease, and with feeble, tottering limbs, but as a man in the prime of life, and in the vigor of a noble manhood. His eyes beam with intelligence and with love for his Saviour. He casts himself in adoration at the feet of Jesus.

The beholders are at first speechless with amazement. Then there follows an inexpressible scene of rejoicing and thanksgiving. The sisters receive their brother back to life as the gift of God, and with joyful tears they brokenly express their thanks to the Saviour. But while brother, sisters, and friends are rejoicing in this reunion, Jesus withdraws from the scene. When they look for the Life-giver, He is not to be found.

59

Priestly Plottings

Bethany was so near Jerusalem that the news of the raising of Lazarus was soon carried to the city. Through spies who had witnessed the miracle the Jewish rulers were speedily in possession of the facts. A meeting of the Sanhedrin

This chapter is based on John 11:47-54.

was at once called to decide as to what should be done. Christ had now fully made manifest His control of death and the grave. That mighty miracle was the crowning evidence offered by God to men that He had sent His Son into the world for their salvation. It was a demonstration of divine power sufficient to convince every mind that was under the control of reason and enlightened conscience. Many who witnessed the resurrection of Lazarus were led to believe on Jesus. But the hatred of the priests against Him was intensified. They had rejected all lesser evidence of His divinity, and they were only enraged at this new miracle. The dead had been raised in the full light of day, and before a crowd of witnesses. No artifice could explain away such evidence. For this very reason the enmity of the priests grew deadlier. They were more than ever determined to put a stop to Christ's work.

The Sadducees, though not favorable to Christ, had not been so full of malignity toward Him as were the Pharisees. Their hatred had not been so bitter. But they were now thoroughly 538 alarmed. They did not believe in a resurrection of the dead. Producing so-called science, they had reasoned that it would be an impossibility for a dead body to be brought to life. But by a few words from Christ their theory had been overthrown. They were shown to be ignorant both of the Scriptures and of the power of God. They could see no possibility of removing the impression made on the people by the miracle. How could men be turned away from Him who had prevailed to rob the grave of its dead? Lying reports were put in circulation, but the miracle could not be denied, and how to counteract its effect they knew not. Thus far the Sadducees had not encouraged the plan of putting Christ to death. But after the resurrection of Lazarus they decided that only by His death could His fearless denunciations against them be stopped.

The Pharisees believed in the resurrection, and they could not but see that this miracle was an evidence that the Messiah was among them. But they had ever opposed Christ's work. From the first they had hated Him because He had exposed their hypocritical pretensions. He had torn aside the cloak of rigorous rites under which their moral deformity was hidden. The pure religion that He taught had condemned their hollow professions of piety. They thirsted to be revenged upon Him for His pointed rebukes. They had tried to provoke Him to say or do something that would give them occasion to condemn Him. Several times they had attempted to stone Him, but He had quietly withdrawn, and they had lost sight of Him.

The miracles He performed on the Sabbath were all for the relief of the afflicted, but the Pharisees had sought to condemn Him as a Sabbathbreaker. They had tried to arouse the Herodians against Him. They represented that He was seeking to set up a rival kingdom, and consulted with them how to destroy Him. To excite the Romans against Him, they had represented Him as trying to subvert their authority. They had tried every pretext to cut Him off from influencing the people. But so far their attempts had been foiled. The multitudes who witnessed His works of mercy and heard His pure and holy teachings knew that these were not the deeds and words of a Sabbathbreaker or blasphemer. Even the officers sent by the Pharisees had been so influenced by His words that they could not lay hands on Him. In desperation the Jews had finally passed an edict that any man who professed faith in Jesus should be cast out of the synagogue.

So, as the priests, the rulers, and the elders gathered for consultation, it was their fixed determination to silence Him who did such marvelous works that all men wondered. Pharisees 539 and Sadducees were more nearly united than ever before. Divided hitherto, they became one in their opposition to Christ. Nicodemus and Joseph had, in former councils, prevented the condemnation of Jesus, and for this reason they were not now summoned. There were present at the council other influential men who believed on Jesus, but their influence prevailed nothing against that of the malignant Pharisees.

Yet the members of the council were not all agreed. The Sanhedrin was not at this time a legal assembly. It existed only by tolerance. Some of its number questioned the wisdom of putting Christ to death. They feared that this would excite an insurrection among the people, causing the Romans to withhold further favors from the priesthood, and to take from them the power they still held. The Sadducees were united in their hatred of Christ, yet they were inclined to be cautious in their movements, fearing that the Romans would deprive them of their high standing.

In this council, assembled to plan the death of Christ, the Witness was present who heard the boastful words of Nebuchadnezzar, who witnessed the idolatrous feast of Belshazzar, who was present when Christ in Nazareth announced Himself the Anointed One. This Witness was now impressing the rulers with the work they were doing. Events in the life of Christ rose up before them with a distinctness that alarmed them. They remembered the scene in the temple, when Jesus, then a child of twelve, stood before the learned doctors of the law, asking them questions at which they wondered. The miracle just performed bore witness that Jesus was none other than the Son of God. In their true significance, the Old Testament Scriptures regarding Christ flashed before their minds. Perplexed and troubled, the rulers asked, "What do we?" There was a division in the council. Under the impression of the Holy Spirit, the priests and rulers could not banish the conviction that they were fighting against God.

While the council was at the height of its perplexity, Caiaphas the high priest arose. Caiaphas was a proud and cruel man, overbearing and intolerant. Among his family connections were Sadducees, proud, bold, reckless, full of ambition and cruelty, which they hid under a cloak of pretended righteousness. Caiaphas had studied the prophecies, and although ignorant of their true meaning, he spoke with great authority and assurance: "Ye know nothing at all, nor consider that it is expedient for us, that one man should die for the people, and that the whole nation perish not." Even if Jesus were innocent, urged the high priest, He must be put out of the way. He was troublesome, drawing the people to Himself, and lessening the authority of the rulers. He was only one; it was better that He should die than that the authority of the rulers should be weakened. If the people were to lose confidence in their rulers, the national power would be destroyed. Caiaphas urged that after this miracle the followers of Jesus would likely rise in revolt. The Romans will then come, he said, and will close our temple, and abolish our laws, destroying us as a nation. What is the life of this Galilean worth in comparison with the life of the nation? If He stands in the way of Israel's well-being, is it not doing God a service to remove Him? Better that one man perish than that the whole nation be destroyed.

In declaring that one man should die for the nation, Caiaphas indicated that he had some knowledge of the prophecies, although it was very limited. But John, in his account of this scene, takes up the prophecy, and shows its broad and deep significance. He says, "And not for that nation only, but that also He should gather together in one the children of God that were scattered abroad." How blindly did the haughty Caiaphas acknowledge the Saviour's mission!

On the lips of Caiaphas this most precious truth was turned into a lie. The policy he advocated was based on a principle borrowed from heathenism. Among the heathen, the dim consciousness that one was to die for the human race had led to the offering of human sacrifices. So Caiaphas proposed by the sacrifice of Jesus to save the guilty nation, not from transgression, but in transgression, that they might continue in sin. And by his reasoning he thought to silence the remonstrances of those who might dare to say that as yet nothing worthy of death had been found in Jesus.

At this council Christ's enemies had been deeply convicted. The Holy Spirit had impressed their minds. But Satan strove to gain control of them. He urged upon their notice the grievances they had suffered on account of Christ. How little He had honored their righteousness. He presented a righteousness far greater, which all who would be children of God must possess. Taking no notice of their forms and ceremonies, He had encouraged sinners to go directly to God as a merciful Father, and make known their wants. Thus, in their opinion, He had set aside the priesthood. He had refused to acknowledge the theology of the rabbinical schools. He had exposed the evil practices of the priests, and had irreparably hurt their influence. He had injured the effect of their maxims and traditions, declaring that though they strictly enforced the ritual law, they made void the law of God. All this Satan now brought to their minds.

Satan told them that in order to maintain their authority, they must put Jesus to death. This counsel they followed. The fact that they might lose the power they then exercised, was, they thought, sufficient reason for coming to some decision. With the exception of a few who dared not speak their minds, the Sanhedrin received the words of Caiaphas as the words of God. Relief came to the council; the discord ceased. They resolved to put Christ to death at the first favorable opportunity. In rejecting the proof of the divinity of Jesus, these priests and rulers had locked themselves in impenetrable darkness. They had come wholly under the sway of Satan, to be hurried by him over the brink of eternal ruin. Yet such was their deception that they were well pleased with themselves. They regarded themselves as patriots, who were seeking the nation's salvation.

The Sanhedrin feared, however, to take rash measures against Jesus, lest the people should become incensed, and the violence meditated toward Him should fall upon themselves. On this account the council delayed to execute the sentence they had pronounced. The Saviour understood the plotting of the priests. He knew that they longed to remove Him, and that their purpose would soon be accomplished. But it was not His place to hasten the crisis, and He withdrew from that region, taking the disciples with Him. Thus by His own example Jesus again enforced the instruction He had given to the disciples, "When they persecute you in this city, flee ye into another." Matt. 10:23. There was a wide field in which to work for the salvation of souls; and unless loyalty to Him required it, the Lord's servants were not to imperil their lives.

Jesus had now given three years of public labor to the world. His example of self-denial and disinterested benevolence was before them. His life of purity, of suffering and devotion, was known to all. Yet this short period of three years was as long as the world could endure the presence of its Redeemer.

His life had been one of persecution and insult. Driven from Bethlehem by a jealous king, rejected by His own people at Nazareth, condemned to death without a cause at Jerusalem, Jesus, with His few faithful followers, found a temporary asylum in a strange city. He who was ever touched by human woe, who healed the sick, restored sight to the blind, hearing to the deaf, and speech to the dumb, who fed the hungry and comforted the sorrowful, was driven from the people He had labored to save. He who walked upon the heaving billows, and by a word silenced their angry roaring, who cast out devils that in departing acknowledged Him to be the Son of God, who broke the slumbers of the dead, who held thousands entranced by His words of wisdom, was unable to reach the hearts of those who were blinded by prejudice and hatred, and who stubbornly rejected the light.

60

The Law of the New Kingdom

The time of the Passover was drawing near, and again Jesus turned toward Jerusalem. In His heart was the peace of perfect oneness with the Father's will, and with eager steps He pressed on toward the place of sacrifice. But a sense of mystery, of doubt and fear, fell upon the disciples. The Saviour "went before them: and they were amazed; and as they followed, they were afraid."

Again Christ called the twelve about Him, and with greater definiteness than ever before, He opened to them His betrayal and sufferings. "Behold," He said, "we go up to Jerusalem, and all things that are written by the prophets concerning the Son of man shall be accomplished. For He shall be delivered unto the Gentiles, and shall be mocked, and spitefully entreated, and spitted on: and they shall scourge Him, and put Him to death: and the third day He shall rise again. And they understood none of these things: and this saying was hid from them, neither knew they the things which were spoken."

Had they not just before proclaimed everywhere, "The kingdom of heaven is at hand"? Had not Christ Himself promised that many should sit down with Abraham and Isaac and Jacob in the kingdom of God? Had He not promised to all who had left aught for His sake a hundredfold in this life, and a part in His kingdom? And had He not given to the twelve special promise of positions of high honor in His kingdom,—to sit on thrones judging the twelve tribes of Israel? Even now He had said that all things written in the prophets concerning Him should be fulfilled. And had not the

prophets foretold the glory of the Messiah's reign? In the light of these thoughts, His words in regard to betrayal, persecution, and death seemed vague and shadowy. Whatever difficulties might intervene, they believed that the kingdom was soon to be established.

John, the son of Zebedee, had been one of the first two disciples who had followed Jesus. He and his brother James had been among the first group who had left all for His service. Gladly they had forsaken home and friends that they might be with Him; they had walked and talked with Him; they had been with Him in the privacy of the home, and in the public assemblies. He had quieted their fears, delivered them from danger, relieved their sufferings, comforted their grief, and with patience and tenderness had taught them, till their hearts seemed linked with His, and in the ardor of their love they longed to be nearest to Him in His kingdom. At every possible opportunity, John took his place next the Saviour, and James longed to be honored with as close connection with Him.

Their mother was a follower of Christ, and had ministered to Him freely of her substance. With a mother's love and ambition for her sons, she coveted for them the most honored place in the new kingdom. For this she encouraged them to make request.

Together the mother and her sons came to Jesus, asking that He would grant a petition on which their hearts were set.

"What would ye that I should do for you?" He questioned.

The mother answered, "Grant that these my two sons may sit, the one on Thy right hand, and the other on the left, in Thy kingdom."

Jesus bears tenderly with them, not rebuking their selfishness in seeking preference above their brethren. He reads their hearts, He knows the depth of their attachment to Him. Their love is not a mere human affection; though defiled by the earthliness of its human channel, it is an outflowing from the fountain of His own redeeming love. He will not rebuke, but deepen and purify. He said, "Are ye able to drink of the cup that I shall drink of, and to be baptized with the baptism that I am baptized with?" They recall His mysterious words, pointing to trial and suffering, yet answer confidently, "We are able." They would count it highest honor to prove their loyalty by sharing all that is to befall their Lord.

"Ye shall drink indeed of My cup, and be baptized with the baptism that I am baptized with," He said; before Him a cross instead of a throne, two malefactors His companions at His right hand and His left. John and James were to share with their Master in suffering; the one, first of the brethren to perish with the sword; the other, longest of all to endure toil, and reproach, and persecution.

This chapter is based on Matthew 20:20-28; Mark 10:32-45; Luke 18:31-34.

"But to sit on My right hand, and on My left," He continued, "is not Mine to give, but it shall be given to them for whom it is prepared of My Father." In the kingdom of God, position is not gained through favoritism. It is not earned, nor is it received through an arbitrary bestowal. It is the result of character. The crown and the throne are the tokens of a condition attained; they are the tokens of self-conquest through our Lord Jesus Christ.

Long afterward, when the disciple had been brought into sympathy with Christ through the fellowship of His sufferings, the Lord revealed to John what is the condition of nearness in His kingdom. "To him that overcometh," Christ said, "will I grant to sit with Me in My throne, even as I also overcame, and am set down with My Father in His throne." "Him that overcometh will I make a pillar in the temple of My God, and he shall go no more out: and I will write upon him the name of My God, . . . and I will write upon him My new name." Rev. 3:21, 12. So Paul the apostle wrote, "I am now ready to be offered, and the time of my departure is at hand. I have fought a good fight, I have finished my course, I have kept the faith: henceforth there is laid up for me a crown of righteousness, which the Lord, the righteous Judge, shall give me at that day." 2 Tim. 4:6-8.

The one who stands nearest to Christ will be he who on earth has drunk most deeply of the spirit of His self-sacrificing love,—love that "vaunteth not itself, is not puffed up, . . . seeketh not her own, is not easily provoked, thinketh no evil" (1 Cor. 13:4, 5),—love that moves the disciple, as it moved our Lord, to give all, to live and labor and sacrifice, even unto death, for the saving of humanity. This spirit was made manifest in the life of Paul. He said, "For to me to live is Christ;" for his life revealed Christ to men; "and to die is gain,"—gain to Christ; death itself would make manifest the power of His grace, and gather souls to Him. "Christ shall be magnified in my body," he said, "whether it be by life or by death." Phil. 1:21, 20.

When the ten heard of the request of James and John, they were much displeased. The highest place in the kingdom was just what every one of them was seeking for himself, and they were angry that the two disciples had gained a seeming advantage over them.

550 Again the strife as to which should be greatest seemed about to be renewed, when Jesus, calling them to Him, said to the indignant disciples, "Ye know that they which are accounted to rule over the Gentiles exercise lordship over them; and their great ones exercise authority upon them. But so shall it not be among you."

In the kingdoms of the world, position meant self-aggrandizement. The people were supposed to exist for the benefit of the ruling classes. Influence, wealth, education, were so many means of gaining control of the masses for the use of the leaders. The higher classes were to think, decide, enjoy, and rule; the lower were to obey and serve. Religion, like all things else, was a matter of authority. The people were expected to believe and practice as their superiors directed. The right of man as man, to think and act for himself, was wholly unrecognized.

Christ was establishing a kingdom on different principles. He called men, not to authority, but to service, the strong to bear the infirmities of the weak. Power, position, talent, education, placed their possessor under the greater obligation to serve his fellows. To even the lowliest of Christ's disciples it is said, "All things are for your sakes." 2 Cor. 4:15.

"The Son of man came not to be ministered unto, but to minister, and to give His life a ransom for many." Among His disciples Christ was in every sense a caretaker, a burden bearer. He shared their poverty, He practiced self-denial on their account, He went before them to smooth the more difficult places, and soon He would consummate His work on earth by laying down His life. The principle on which Christ acted is to actuate the members of the church which is His body. The plan and ground of salvation is love. In the kingdom of Christ those are greatest who follow the example He has given, and act as shepherds of His flock.

The words of Paul reveal the true dignity and honor of the Christian life: "Though I be free from all men, yet have I made myself servant unto all," "not seeking mine own profit, but the profit of many, that they may be saved." 1 Cor. 9:19; 10:33.

In matters of conscience the soul must be left untrammeled. No one is to control another's mind, to judge for another, or to prescribe his duty. God gives to every soul freedom to think, and to follow his own convictions. "Every one of us shall give account of himself to God." No one has a right to merge his own individuality in that of another. In all matters where principle is involved, "let every man be fully persuaded in his own mind." Rom. 14:12, 5. In Christ's kingdom there is no lordly oppression, no compulsion of manner. The angels of heaven do not come to the earth to rule, and to exact homage, but as messengers of mercy, to co-operate with men in uplifting humanity.

551

The principles and the very words of the Saviour's teaching, in their divine beauty, dwelt in the memory of the beloved disciple. To his latest days the burden of John's testimony to the churches was, "This is the message that ye heard from the beginning, that we should love one another." "Hereby perceive we the love of God, because He laid down His life for us: and we ought to lay down our lives for the brethren." 1 John 3:11, 16.

This was the spirit that pervaded the early

church. After the outpouring of the Holy Spirit, "the multitude of them that believed were of one heart and of one soul: neither said any of them that aught of the things which he possessed was his own." "Neither was there any among them that lacked." "And with great power gave the apostles witness of the resurrection of the Lord Jesus: and great grace was upon them all." Acts 4:32, 34, 33.

61

Zacchaeus

On the way to Jerusalem "Jesus entered and passed through Jericho." A few miles from the Jordan, on the western edge of the valley that here spread out into a plain, the city lay in the midst of tropic verdure and luxuriance of beauty. With its palm trees and rich gardens watered by living springs, it gleamed like an emerald in the setting of limestone hills and desolate ravines that interposed between Jerusalem and the city of Jericho.

Many caravans on their way to the feast passed through Jericho. Their arrival was always a festive season, but now a deeper interest stirred the people. It was known that the Galilean Rabbi who had so lately brought Lazarus to life was in the throng; and though whispers were rife as to the plottings of the priests, the multitudes were eager to do Him homage.

Jericho was one of the cities anciently set apart for the priests, and at this time large numbers of priests had their residence there. But the city had also a population of a widely different character. It was a great center of traffic, and Roman officials and soldiers, with strangers from different quarters, were found there, while the collection of customs made it the home of many publicans.

"The chief among the publicans," Zacchaeus, was a Jew, and detested by his countrymen. His rank and wealth were the reward of a calling they abhorred, and which was regarded as another name for injustice and extortion. Yet the wealthy customs officer was not altogether the hardened man of the world that he seemed. Beneath the appearance of worldliness and pride was a heart susceptible to divine influences. Zacchaeus had heard of Jesus. The report of One who had borne Himself with kindness and courtesy toward the proscribed classes had spread far and wide. In this chief of the publicans was awakened a longing for a better life. Only a few miles from Jericho, John the Baptist had preached at the Jordan, and Zacchaeus had heard of the call to repentance. The instruction to the publicans, "Exact no more than that which is appointed you" (Luke 3:13), though

outwardly disregarded, had impressed his mind. He knew the Scriptures, and was convicted that his practice was wrong. Now, hearing the words reported to have come from the Great Teacher, he felt that he was a sinner in the sight of God. Yet what he had heard of Jesus kindled hope in his heart. Repentance, reformation of life, was possible, even to him; was not one of the new Teacher's most trusted disciples a publican? Zacchaeus began at once to follow the conviction that had taken hold upon him, and to make restitution to those whom he had wronged.

Already he had begun thus to retrace his steps, when the news sounded through Jericho that Jesus was entering the town. Zacchaeus determined to see Him. He was beginning to realize how bitter are the fruits of sin, and how difficult the path of him who tries to return from a course of wrong. To be misunderstood, to be met with suspicion and distrust in the effort to correct his errors, was hard to bear. The chief publican longed to look upon the face of Him whose words had brought hope to his heart.

The streets were crowded, and Zacchaeus, who was small of stature, could see nothing over the heads of the people. None would give way for him; so, running a little in advance of the multitude, to where a wide-branching fig tree hung over the way, the rich tax collector climbed to a seat among the boughs, whence he could survey the procession as it passed below. The crowd comes near, it is going by, and Zacchaeus scans with eager eyes to discern the one figure he longs to see.

Above the clamor of priests and rabbis and the shouts of welcome from the multitude, that unuttered desire of the chief publican spoke to the heart of Jesus. Suddenly, just beneath the fig tree, a group halts, the company before and behind come to a standstill, and One looks upward whose glance seems to read the soul. Almost doubting his senses, the man in the tree hears the words, "Zacchaeus, make haste, and come down; for today I must abide at thy house."

The multitude give way, and Zacchaeus, walking as in a dream, leads the way toward his own home. But the rabbis look on with scowling faces, and murmur in discontent and scorn, "that He was gone to be guest with a man that is a sinner."

Zacchaeus had been overwhelmed, amazed, and silenced at the love and condescension of Christ in stooping to him, so unworthy. Now love and loyalty to his new-found Master unseal his lips. He will make public his confession and his repentance.

In the presence of the multitude, "Zacchaeus stood, and said unto the Lord; Behold, Lord, the half of my goods I give to the poor; and if I have taken anything from any man by false accusation, I restore him fourfold.

This chapter is based on Luke 19:1-10.

"And Jesus said unto him, This day is salvation come to this house, forsomuch as he also is a son of Abraham."

When the rich young ruler had turned away from Jesus, the disciples had marveled at their Master's saying, "How hard is it for them that trust in riches to enter into the kingdom of God!" They had exclaimed one to another, "Who then can be saved?" Now they had a demonstration of the truth of Christ's words, "The things which are impossible with men are possible with God." Mark 10:24, 26; Luke 18:27. They saw how, through the grace of God, a rich man could enter into the kingdom.

Before Zacchaeus had looked upon the face of Christ, he had begun the work that made him manifest as a true penitent. Before being accused by man, he had confessed his sin. He had yielded to the conviction of the Holy Spirit, and had begun to carry out the teaching of the words written for ancient Israel as well as for ourselves. The Lord had said long before, "If thy brother be waxen poor, and fallen in decay with thee; then thou shalt relieve him: yea, though he be a stranger, or a sojourner; that he may live with thee. Take thou no usury of him, or increase: but fear thy God; that thy brother may live with thee. Thou shalt not give him thy money upon usury, nor lend him thy victuals for increase." "Ye shall not therefore oppress one another; but thou shalt fear thy God." Lev. 25:35-37, 17. These words had been spoken by Christ Himself when He was enshrouded in the pillar of cloud, and the very first response of Zacchaeus to the love of Christ was in manifesting compassion toward the poor and suffering.

Among the publicans there was a confederacy, so that they could oppress the people, and sustain one another in their fraudulent practices. In their extortion they were but carrying out what had become an almost universal custom. Even the priests and rabbis who despised them were guilty of enriching themselves by dishonest practices under cover of their sacred calling. But no sooner did Zacchaeus yield to the influence of the Holy Spirit than he cast aside every practice contrary to integrity.

No repentance is genuine that does not work reformation. The righteousness of Christ is not a cloak to cover unconfessed and unforsaken sin; it is a principle of life that transforms the character and controls the conduct. Holiness is wholeness for God; it is the entire surrender of heart and life to the indwelling of the principles of heaven.

The Christian in his business life is to represent to the world the manner in which our Lord would conduct business enterprises. In every transaction he is to make it manifest that God is his teacher. "Holiness unto the Lord" is to be written upon daybooks and ledgers, on deeds, receipts, and bills of exchange. Those who profess to be followers of Christ, and who deal in an unrighteous manner, are bearing false witness against the character of a holy, just, and merciful God. Every converted soul will, like Zacchaeus, signalize the entrance of Christ into his heart by an abandonment of the unrighteous practices that have marked his life. Like the chief publican, he will give proof of his sincerity by making restitution. The Lord says, "If the wicked restore the pledge, give again that he had robbed, walk in the statutes of life, without committing iniquity; . . . none of his sins that he hath committed shall be mentioned unto him: . . . He shall surely live." Ezek. 33:15, 16.

If we have injured others through any unjust business transaction, if we have overreached in trade, or defrauded any man, even though it be within the pale of the law, we should confess our wrong, and make restitution as far as lies in our power. It is right for us to restore not only that which we have taken, but all that it would have accumulated if put to a right and wise use during the time it has been in our possession.

To Zacchaeus the Saviour said, "This day is salvation come to this house." Not only was Zacchaeus himself blessed, but all his household with him. Christ went to his home to give him lessons of truth, and to instruct his household in the things of the kingdom. They had been shut out from the synagogues by the contempt of rabbis and worshipers; but now, the most favored household in all Jericho, they gathered in their own home about the divine Teacher, and heard for themselves the words of life.

It is when Christ is received as a personal Saviour that salvation comes to the soul. Zacchaeus had received Jesus, not merely as a passing guest in his home, but as One to abide in the soul temple. The scribes and Pharisees accused him as a sinner, they murmured against Christ for becoming his guest, but the Lord recognized him as a son of Abraham. For "they which are of faith, the same are the children of Abraham." Gal. 3:7.

The Feast at Simon's House

Simon of Bethany was accounted a disciple of Jesus. He was one of the few Pharisees who had openly joined Christ's followers. He acknowledged Jesus as a teacher, and hoped that He might be the Messiah, but he had not accepted Him as a Saviour. His character was not transformed; his principles were unchanged.

Simon had been healed of the leprosy, and it was this that had drawn him to Jesus. He desired to show his gratitude, and at Christ's last visit to

This chapter is based on Matthew 26:6-13; Mark 14:3-11; Luke 7:36-50; John 11:55-57; 12:1-11.

Bethany he made a feast for the Saviour and His disciples. This feast brought together many of the Jews. There was at this time much excitement at Jerusalem. Christ and His mission were attracting greater attention than ever before. Those who had come to the feast closely watched His movements, and some of them with unfriendly eyes.

The Saviour had reached Bethany only six days before the Passover, and according to His custom had sought rest at the home of Lazarus. The crowds of travelers who passed on to the city spread the tidings that He was on His way to Jerusalem, and that He would rest over the Sabbath at Bethany. Among the people there was great enthusiasm. Many flocked to Bethany, some out of sympathy with Jesus, and others from curiosity to see one who had been raised from the dead.

Many expected to hear from Lazarus a wonderful account of scenes witnessed after death. They were surprised that he told them nothing. 558 He had nothing of this kind to tell. Inspiration declares, "The dead know not anything. . . . Their love, and their hatred, and their envy, is now perished." Eccl. 9:5, 6. But Lazarus did have a wonderful testimony to bear in regard to the work of Christ. He had been raised from the dead for this purpose. With assurance and power he declared that Jesus was the Son of God.

The reports carried back to Jerusalem by the visitors to Bethany increased the excitement. The people were eager to see and hear Jesus. There was a general inquiry as to whether Lazarus would accompany Him to Jerusalem, and if the prophet would be crowned king at the Passover. The priests and rulers saw that their hold upon the people was still weakening, and their rage against Jesus grew more bitter. They could hardly wait for the opportunity of removing Him forever from their way. As time passed, they began to fear that after all He might not come to Jerusalem. They remembered how often He had baffled their murderous designs, and they were fearful that He had now read their purposes against Him, and would remain away. They could ill conceal their anxiety, and questioned among themselves, "What think ye, that He will not come to the feast?"

A council of the priests and Pharisees was called. Since the raising of Lazarus the sympathies of the people were so fully with Christ that it would be dangerous to seize upon Him openly. So the authorities determined to take Him secretly, and carry on the trial as quietly as possible. They hoped that when His condemnation became known, the fickle tide of public opinion would set in their favor.

Thus they proposed to destroy Jesus. But so long as Lazarus lived, the priests and rabbis knew that they were not secure. The very existence of a man who had been four days in the grave, and who had been restored by a word from Jesus, would sooner or later cause a reaction. The people would be avenged on their leaders for taking the life of One who could perform such a miracle. The Sanhedrin therefore decided that Lazarus also must die. To such lengths do envy and prejudice lead their slaves. The hatred and unbelief of the Jewish leaders had increased until they would even take the life of one whom infinite power had rescued from the grave.

While this plotting was going on at Jerusalem, Jesus and His friends were invited to Simon's feast. At the table the Saviour sat with Simon, whom He had cured of a loathsome disease, on one side, and Lazarus, whom He had raised from the dead, on the other. Martha served at the table, but Mary was earnestly listening to every word from the lips of Jesus. In 559 His mercy, Jesus had pardoned her sins, He had called forth her beloved brother from the grave, and Mary's heart was filled with gratitude. She had heard Jesus speak of His approaching death, and in her deep love and sorrow she had longed to show Him honor. At great personal sacrifice she had purchased an alabaster box of "ointment of spikenard, very costly," with which to anoint His body. But now many were declaring that He was about to be crowned king. Her grief was turned to joy, and she was eager to be first in honoring her Lord. Breaking her box of ointment, she poured its contents upon the head and feet of Jesus; then, as she knelt weeping, moistening them with her tears, she wiped His feet with her long, flowing hair.

She had sought to avoid observation, and her movements might have passed unnoticed, but the ointment filled the room with its fragrance, and published her act to all present. Judas looked upon this act with great displeasure. Instead of waiting to hear what Christ would say of the matter, he began to whisper his complaints to those near him, throwing reproach upon Christ for suffering such waste. Craftily he made suggestions that would be likely to cause disaffection.

Judas was treasurer for the disciples, and from their little store he had secretly drawn for his own use, thus narrowing down their resources to a meager pittance. He was eager to put into the bag all that he could obtain. The treasure in the bag was often drawn upon to relieve the poor; and when something that Judas did not think essential was bought, he would say, Why is this waste? why was not the cost of this put into the bag that I carry for the poor? Now the act of Mary was in such marked contrast to his selfishness that he was put to shame; and according to his custom, he sought to assign a worthy motive for his objection to her gift. Turning to the disciples, he asked, "Why was not this ointment sold for three hundred pence, and given to the poor? This he said, not that he cared for the poor; but because he was a thief, and had the bag, and bare what was put therein." Judas had no heart for the poor. Had Mary's ointment been sold, and the proceeds fallen into his possession, the poor would have received no benefit.

Judas had a high opinion of his own executive ability. As a financier he thought himself greatly superior to his fellow disciples, and he had led them to regard him in the same light. He had gained their confidence, and had a strong influence over them. His professed sympathy for the poor deceived them, and his artful insinuation caused them to look distrustfully upon Mary's devotion. The murmur passed round the table, "To what purpose is this waste? For this ointment might have been sold for much, and given to the poor."

Mary heard the words of criticism. Her heart trembled within her. She feared that her sister would reproach her for extravagance. The Master, too, might think her improvident. Without apology or excuse she was about to shrink away, when the voice of her Lord was heard, "Let her alone; why trouble ye her?" He saw that she was embarrassed and distressed. He knew that in this act of service she had expressed her gratitude for the forgiveness of her sins, and He brought relief to her mind. Lifting His voice above the murmur of criticism, He said, "She hath wrought a good work on Me. For ye have the poor with you always, and whensoever ye will ye may do them good: but Me ye have not always. She hath done what she could: she is come aforehand to anoint My body to the burying."

The fragrant gift which Mary had thought to lavish upon the dead body of the Saviour she poured upon His living form. At the burial its sweetness could only have pervaded the tomb; now it gladdened His heart with the assurance of her faith and love. Joseph of Arimathaea and Nicodemus offered not their gift of love to Jesus in His life. With bitter tears they brought their costly spices for His cold, unconscious form. The women who bore spices to the tomb found their errand in vain, for He had risen. But Mary, pouring out her love upon the Saviour while He was conscious of her devotion, was anointing Him for the burial. And as He went down into the darkness of His great trial, He carried with Him the memory of that deed, an earnest of the love that would be His from His redeemed ones forever.

Many there are who bring their precious gifts for the dead. As they stand about the cold, silent form, words of love are freely spoken. Tenderness, appreciation, devotion, all are lavished upon one who sees not nor hears. Had these words been spoken when the weary spirit needed them so much, when the ear could hear and the heart could feel, how precious would have been their fragrance!

Mary knew not the full significance of her deed of love. She could not answer her accusers. She could not explain why she had chosen that occasion for anointing Jesus. The Holy Spirit had planned for her, and she had obeyed His promptings. Inspiration stoops to give no reason. An unseen presence, it speaks to mind and soul, and moves the heart to action. It is its own justification.

Christ told Mary the meaning of her act, and in this He gave her more than He had received. "In that she hath poured this ointment on My body," He said, "she did it for My burial." As the alabaster box was broken, and filled the whole house with its fragrance, so Christ was to die, His body was to be broken; but He was to rise from the tomb, and the fragrance of His life was to fill the earth. Christ "hath loved us, and hath given Himself for us an offering and a sacrifice to God for a sweet-smelling savor." Eph. 5:2.

"Verily I say unto you," Christ declared, "Wheresoever this gospel shall be preached throughout the whole world, this also that she hath done shall be spoken of for a memorial of her." Looking into the future, the Saviour spoke with certainty concerning His gospel. It was to be preached throughout the world. And as far as the gospel extended, Mary's gift would shed its fragrance, and hearts would be blessed through her unstudied act. Kingdoms would rise and fall; the names of monarchs and conquerors would be forgotten; but this woman's deed would be immortalized upon the pages of sacred history. Until time should be no more, that broken alabaster box would tell the story of the abundant love of God for a fallen race.

Mary's act was in marked contrast with that which Judas was about to do. What a sharp lesson Christ might have given him who had dropped the seed of criticism and evil thinking into the minds of the disciples! How justly the accuser might have been accused! He who reads the motives of every heart, and understands every action, might have opened before those at the feast dark chapters in the experience of Judas. The hollow pretense on which the traitor based his words might have been laid bare; for, instead of sympathizing with the poor, he was robbing them of the money intended for their relief. Indignation might have been excited against him for his oppression of the widow, the orphan, and the hireling. But had Christ unmasked Judas, this would have been urged as a reason for the betrayal. And though charged with being a thief, Judas would have gained sympathy, even among the disciples. The Saviour reproached him not, and thus avoided giving him an excuse for his treachery.

But the look which Jesus cast upon Judas convinced him that the Saviour penetrated his hypocrisy, and read his base, contemptible character. And in commending Mary's action, which had been so severely condemned, Christ had rebuked Judas. Prior to this, the Saviour had never given him a direct rebuke. Now the reproof rankled in his heart. He determined to be revenged. From the supper he went directly to the palace of the high priest, where he found the council assembled, and he offered to betray Jesus into their hands.

The priests were greatly rejoiced. These leaders of Israel had been given the privilege of receiving Christ as their Saviour, without money and without price. But they refused the precious gift offered them in the most tender spirit of constraining love. They refused to accept that salvation which is of more value than gold, and bought their Lord for thirty pieces of silver.

Judas had indulged avarice until it overpowered every good trait of his character. His heart burned with envy that the Saviour should be the recipient of a gift suitable for the monarchs of the earth. For a sum far less than the box of ointment cost, he betrayed his Lord.

The disciples were not like Judas. They loved the Saviour. But they did not rightly appreciate His exalted character. Had they realized what He had done for them, they would have felt that nothing bestowed upon Him was wasted. The wise men from the East, who knew so little of Jesus, had shown a truer appreciation of the honor due Him. They brought precious gifts to the Saviour, and bowed in homage before Him when He was but a babe, and cradled in a manger.

Christ values acts of heartfelt courtesy. When anyone did Him a favor, with heavenly politeness He blessed the actor. He did not refuse the simplest flower plucked by the hand of a child, and offered to Him in love. He accepted the offerings of children, and blessed the givers, inscribing their names in the book of life. In the Scriptures, Mary's anointing of Jesus is mentioned as distinguishing her from the other Marys. Acts of love and reverence for Jesus are an evidence of faith in Him as the Son of God. And the Holy Spirit mentions, as evidences of woman's loyalty to Christ: "If she have washed the saints' feet, if she have relieved the afflicted, if she have diligently followed every good work." 1 Tim. 5:10.

Christ delighted in the earnest desire of Mary to do the will of her Lord. He accepted the wealth of pure affection which His disciples did not, would not, understand. The desire that Mary had to do this service for her Lord was of more value to Christ than all the precious ointment in the world, because it expressed her

appreciation of the world's Redeemer. It was the love of Christ that constrained her. The matchless excellence of the character of Christ filled her soul. That ointment was a symbol of the heart of the giver. It was the outward demonstration of a love fed by heavenly streams until it overflowed.

The work of Mary was just the lesson the disciples needed to show them that the expression of their love for Him would be pleasing to Christ. He had been everything to them, and they did not realize that soon they would be deprived of His presence, that soon they could offer Him no token of their gratitude for His great love. The loneliness of Christ, separated from the heavenly courts, living the life of humanity, was never understood or appreciated by the disciples as it should have been. He was often grieved because His disciples did not give Him that which He should have received from them. He knew that if they were under the influence of the heavenly angels that accompanied Him, they too would think no offering of sufficient value to declare the heart's spiritual affection.

Their afterknowledge gave them a true sense of the many things they might have done for Jesus expressive of the love and gratitude of their hearts, while they were near Him. When Jesus was no longer with them, and they felt indeed as sheep without a shepherd, they began to see how they might have shown Him attentions that would have brought gladness to His heart. They no longer cast blame upon Mary, but upon themselves. Oh, if they could have taken back their censuring, their presenting the poor as more worthy of the gift than was Christ! They felt the reproof keenly as they took from the cross the bruised body of their Lord.

The same want is evident in our world today. But few appreciate all that Christ is to them. If they did, the great love of Mary would be expressed, the anointing would be freely bestowed. The expensive ointment would not be called a waste. Nothing would be thought too costly to give for Christ, no self-denial or self-sacrifice too great to be endured for His sake.

The words spoken in indignation, "To what purpose is this waste?" brought vividly before Christ the greatest sacrifice ever made,—the gift of Himself as the propitiation for a lost world. The Lord would be so bountiful to His human family that it could not be said of Him that He could do more. In the gift of Jesus, God gave all heaven. From a human point of view, such a sacrifice was a wanton waste. To human reasoning the whole plan of salvation is a waste of mercies and resources. Self-denial and wholehearted sacrifice meet us everywhere. Well may the heavenly host look with amazement upon the human family who refuse to be uplifted and enriched with the boundless love expressed in

Christ. Well may they exclaim, Why this great waste?

566 But the atonement for a lost world was to be full, abundant, and complete. Christ's offering was exceedingly abundant to reach every soul that God had created. It could not be restricted so as not to exceed the number who would accept the great Gift. All men are not saved; yet the plan of redemption is not a waste because it does not accomplish all that its liberality has provided for. There must be enough and to spare.

Simon the host had been influenced by the criticism of Judas upon Mary's gift, and he was surprised at the conduct of Jesus. His Pharisaic pride was offended. He knew that many of his guests were looking upon Christ with distrust and displeasure. Simon said in his heart, "This Man, if He were a prophet, would have known who and what manner of woman this is that toucheth Him: for she is a sinner."

By curing Simon of leprosy, Christ had saved him from a living death. But now Simon questioned whether the Saviour were a prophet. Because Christ allowed this woman to approach Him, because He did not indignantly spurn her as one whose sins were too great to be forgiven, because He did not show that He realized she had fallen, Simon was tempted to think that He was not a prophet. Jesus knows nothing of this woman who is so free in her demonstrations, he thought, or He would not allow her to touch Him.

But it was Simon's ignorance of God and of Christ that led him to think as he did. He did not realize that God's Son must act in God's way, with compassion, tenderness, and mercy. Simon's way was to take no notice of Mary's penitent service. Her act of kissing Christ's feet and anointing them with ointment was exasperating to his hardheartedness. He thought that if Christ were a prophet, He would recognize sinners and rebuke them.

To this unspoken thought the Saviour answered: "Simon, I have somewhat to say unto thee. . . . There was a certain creditor which had two debtors: the one owed five hundred pence, and the other fifty. And when they had nothing to pay, he frankly forgave them both. Tell Me therefore, which of them will love him most? Simon answered and said, I suppose that he, to whom he forgave most. And He said unto him, Thou hast rightly judged."

As did Nathan with David, Christ concealed His home thrust under the veil of a parable. He threw upon His host the burden of pronouncing sentence upon himself. Simon had led into sin the woman he now despised. She had been deeply wronged by him. By the two debtors of the parable, Simon and the woman were represented. Jesus did not design to teach that different degrees of obligation should be felt by the

two persons, for each owed a debt of gratitude 567 that never could be repaid. But Simon felt himself more righteous than Mary, and Jesus desired him to see how great his guilt really was. He would show him that his sin was greater than hers, as much greater as a debt of five hundred pence exceeds a debt of fifty pence.

Simon now began to see himself in a new light. He saw how Mary was regarded by One who was more than a prophet. He saw that with keen prophetic eye Christ read her heart of love and devotion. Shame seized upon him, and he realized that he was in the presence of One superior to himself.

"I entered into thine house," Christ continued, "thou gavest Me no water for My feet;" but with tears of repentance, prompted by love, Mary hath washed My feet, and wiped them with the hair of her head. "Thou gavest Me no kiss: but this woman," whom you despise, "since the time I came in hath not ceased to kiss My feet." Christ recounted the opportunities Simon had had to show his love for his Lord, and his appreciation of what had been done for him. Plainly, yet with delicate politeness, the Saviour assured His disciples that His heart is grieved when His children neglect to show their gratitude to Him by words and deeds of love.

The Heart Searcher read the motive that led to Mary's action, and He saw also the spirit that prompted Simon's words. "Seest thou this woman?" He said to him. She is a sinner. "I say unto thee, Her sins, which are many, are forgiven; for she loved much: but to whom little is forgiven, the same loveth little."

Simon's coldness and neglect toward the Saviour showed how little he appreciated the mercy he had received. He had thought he honored Jesus by inviting Him to his house. But he now saw himself as he really was. While he thought himself reading his Guest, his Guest had been reading him. He saw how true Christ's judgment of him was. His religion had been a robe of Pharisaism. He had despised the compassion of Jesus. He had not recognized Him as the representative of God. While Mary was a sinner pardoned, he was a sinner unpardoned. The rigid rule of justice he had desired to enforce against her condemned him.

Simon was touched by the kindness of Jesus in not openly rebuking him before the guests. He had not been treated as he desired Mary to be treated. He saw that Jesus did not wish to expose his guilt to others, but sought by a true statement of the case to convince his mind, and by pitying kindness to subdue his heart. Stern denunciation would have hardened Simon against repentance, but patient admonition convinced him of his error. He saw the magnitude 568 of the debt which he owed his Lord. His pride was humbled, he repented, and the proud Pharisee became a lowly, self-sacrificing disciple.

Mary had been looked upon as a great sinner, but Christ knew the circumstances that had shaped her life. He might have extinguished every spark of hope in her soul, but He did not. It was He who had lifted her from despair and ruin. Seven times she had heard His rebuke of the demons that controlled her heart and mind. She had heard His strong cries to the Father in her behalf. She knew how offensive is sin to His unsullied purity, and in His strength she had overcome.

When to human eyes her case appeared hopeless, Christ saw in Mary capabilities for good. He saw the better traits of her character. The plan of redemption has invested humanity with great possibilities, and in Mary these possibilities were to be realized. Through His grace she became a partaker of the divine nature. The one who had fallen, and whose mind had been a habitation of demons, was brought very near to the Saviour in fellowship and ministry. It was Mary who sat at His feet and learned of Him. It was Mary who poured upon His head the precious anointing oil, and bathed His feet with her tears. Mary stood beside the cross, and followed Him to the sepulcher. Mary was first at the tomb after His resurrection. It was Mary who first proclaimed a risen Saviour.

Jesus knows the circumstances of every soul. You may say, I am sinful, very sinful. You may be; but the worse you are, the more you need Jesus. He turns no weeping, contrite one away. He does not tell to any all that He might reveal, but He bids every trembling soul take courage. Freely will He pardon all who come to Him for forgiveness and restoration.

Christ might commission the angels of heaven to pour out the vials of His wrath on our world, to destroy those who are filled with hatred of God. He might wipe this dark spot from His universe. But He does not do this. He is today standing at the altar of incense, presenting before God the prayers of those who desire His help.

The souls that turn to Him for refuge, Jesus lifts above the accusing and the strife of tongues. No man or evil angel can impeach these souls. Christ unites them to His own divine-human nature. They stand beside the great Sin Bearer, in the light proceeding from the throne of God. "Who shall lay anything to the charge of God's elect? It is God that justifieth. Who is he that condemneth? It is Christ that died, yea rather, that is risen again, who is even at the right hand of God, who also maketh intercession for us." Rom. 8:33, 34.

63

"Thy King Cometh"

"Rejoice greatly, O daughter of Zion; shout, O daughter of Jerusalem: behold, thy King cometh unto thee: He is just, and having salvation; lowly, and riding upon an ass, and upon a colt the foal of an ass." Zech. 9:9.

Five hundred years before the birth of Christ, the prophet Zechariah thus foretold the coming of the King to Israel. This prophecy is now to be fulfilled. He who has so long refused royal honors now comes to Jerusalem as the promised heir to David's throne.

It was on the first day of the week that Christ made His triumphal entry into Jerusalem. Multitudes who had flocked to see Him at Bethany now accompanied Him, eager to witness His reception. Many people were on their way to the city to keep the Passover, and these joined the multitude attending Jesus. All nature seemed to rejoice. The trees were clothed with verdure, and their blossoms shed a delicate fragrance on the air. A new life and joy animated the people. The hope of the new kingdom was again springing up.

Purposing to ride into Jerusalem, Jesus had sent two of His disciples to bring to Him an ass and its colt. At His birth the Saviour was dependent upon the hospitality of strangers. The manger in which He lay was a borrowed resting place. Now, although the cattle on a thousand hills are His, He is dependent on a stranger's kindness for an animal on which to enter Jerusalem as its King. But again His divinity is revealed, even in the minute directions given His disciples for this errand. As He foretold, the plea, "The Lord hath need of them," was readily granted. Jesus chose for His use the colt on which never man had sat. The disciples, with glad enthusiasm, spread their garments on the beast, and seated their Master upon it. Heretofore Jesus had always traveled on foot, and the disciples had at first wondered that He should now choose to ride. But hope brightened in their hearts with the joyous thought that He was about to enter the capital, proclaim Himself King, and assert His royal power. While on their errand they communicated their glowing expectations to the friends of Jesus, and the excitement spread far and near, raising the expectations of the people to the highest pitch.

Christ was following the Jewish custom for a royal entry. The animal on which He rode was that ridden by the kings of Israel, and prophecy had foretold that thus the Messiah should come to His kingdom. No sooner was He seated upon the colt than a loud shout of triumph rent the air.

This chapter is based on Matthew 21:1-11; Mark 11:1-10; Luke 19:29-44; John 12:12-19.

The multitude hailed Him as Messiah, their King. Jesus now accepted the homage which He had never before permitted, and the disciples received this as proof that their glad hopes were to be realized by seeing Him established on the throne. The multitude were convinced that the hour of their emancipation was at hand. In imagination they saw the Roman armies driven from Jerusalem, and Israel once more an independent nation. All were happy and excited; the people vied with one another in paying Him homage. They could not display outward pomp and splendor, but they gave Him the worship of happy hearts. They were unable to present Him with costly gifts, but they spread their outer garments as a carpet in His path, and they also strewed the leafy branches of the olive and the palm in the way. They could lead the triumphal procession with no royal standards, but they cut down the spreading palm boughs, Nature's emblem of victory, and waved them aloft with loud acclamations and hosannas.

As they proceeded, the multitude was continually increased by those who had heard of the coming of Jesus and hastened to join the procession. Spectators were constantly mingling with the throng, and asking, Who is this? What does all this commotion signify? They had all heard of Jesus, and expected Him to go to Jerusalem; but they knew that He had heretofore discouraged all effort to place Him on the throne, and they were greatly astonished to learn that this was He. They wondered what could have wrought this change in Him who had declared that His kingdom was not of this world.

Their questionings are silenced by a shout of triumph. Again and again it is repeated by the eager throng; it is taken up by the people afar off, and echoed from the surrounding hills and valleys. And now the procession is joined by crowds from Jerusalem. From the multitudes gathered to attend the Passover, thousands go forth to welcome Jesus. They greet Him with the waving of palm branches and a burst of sacred song. The priests at the temple sound the trumpet for evening service, but there are few to respond, and the rulers say to one another in alarm, "The world is gone after Him."

Never before in His earthly life had Jesus permitted such a demonstration. He clearly foresaw the result. It would bring Him to the cross. But it was His purpose thus publicly to present Himself as the Redeemer. He desired to call attention to the sacrifice that was to crown His mission to a fallen world. While the people were assembling at Jerusalem to celebrate the Passover, He, the antitypical Lamb, by a voluntary act set Himself apart as an oblation. It would be needful for His church in all succeeding ages to make His death for the sins of the world a subject of deep thought and study. Every fact connected with it should be verified beyond a doubt. It was necessary, then, that the eyes of all people should now be directed to Him; the events which preceded His great sacrifice must be such as to call attention to the sacrifice itself. After such a demonstration as that attending His entry into Jerusalem, all eyes would follow His rapid progress to the final scene.

The events connected with this triumphal ride would be the talk of every tongue, and would bring Jesus before every mind. After His crucifixion, many would recall these events in their connection with His trial and death. They would be led to search the prophecies, and would be convinced that Jesus was the Messiah; and in all lands converts to the faith would be multiplied.

In this one triumphant scene of His earthly life, the Saviour might have appeared escorted by heavenly angels, and heralded by the trump of God; but such a demonstration would have been contrary to the purpose of His mission, contrary to the law which had governed His life. He remained true to the humble lot He had accepted. The burden of humanity He must bear until His life was given for the life of the world.

This day, which seemed to the disciples the crowning day of their lives, would have been shadowed with gloomy clouds had they known that this scene of rejoicing was but a prelude to the suffering and death of their Master. Although He had repeatedly told them of His certain sacrifice, yet in the glad triumph of the present they forgot His sorrowful words, and looked forward to His prosperous reign on David's throne.

New accessions were made continually to the procession, and, with few exceptions, all who joined it caught the inspiration of the hour, and helped to swell the hosannas that echoed and reechoed from hill to hill and from valley to valley. The shouts went up continually, "Hosanna to the Son of David; Blessed is He that cometh in the name of the Lord; Hosanna in the highest."

Never before had the world seen such a triumphal procession. It was not like that of the earth's famous conquerors. No train of mourning captives, as trophies of kingly valor, made a feature of that scene. But about the Saviour were the glorious trophies of His labors of love for sinful man. There were the captives whom He had rescued from Satan's power, praising God for their deliverance. The blind whom He had restored to sight were leading the way. The dumb whose tongues He had loosed shouted the loudest hosannas. The cripples whom He had healed bounded with joy, and were the most active in breaking the palm branches and waving them before the Saviour. Widows and orphans were exalting the name of Jesus for His works of mercy to them. The lepers whom He had cleansed spread their untainted garments in

His path, and hailed Him as the King of glory. Those whom His voice had awakened from the sleep of death were in that throng. Lazarus, whose body had seen corruption in the grave, but who now rejoiced in the strength of glorious manhood, led the beast on which the Saviour rode.

Many Pharisees witnessed the scene, and, burning with envy and malice, sought to turn the current of popular feeling. With all their authority they tried to silence the people; but their appeals and threats only increased the enthusiasm. They feared that this multitude, in the strength of their numbers, would make Jesus king. As a last resort they pressed through the crowd to where the Saviour was, and accosted Him with reproving and threatening words: "Master, rebuke Thy disciples." They declared that such noisy demonstrations were unlawful, and would not be permitted by the authorities. But they were silenced by the reply of Jesus, "I tell you that, if these should hold their peace, the stones would immediately cry out." That scene of triumph was of God's own appointing. It had been foretold by the prophet, and man was powerless to turn aside God's purpose. Had men failed to carry out His plan, He would have given a voice to the inanimate stones, and they would have hailed His Son with acclamations of praise. As the silenced Pharisees drew back, the words of Zechariah were taken up by hundreds of voices: "Rejoice greatly, O daughter of Zion; shout, O daughter of Jerusalem: behold, thy King cometh unto thee: He is just, and having salvation; lowly, and riding upon an ass, and upon a colt the foal of an ass."

When the procession reached the brow of the hill, and was about to descend into the city, Jesus halted, and all the multitude with Him. Before them lay Jerusalem in its glory, now bathed in the light of the declining sun. The temple attracted all eyes. In stately grandeur it towered above all else, seeming to point toward heaven as if directing the people to the only true and living God. The temple had long been the pride and glory of the Jewish nation. The Romans also prided themselves in its magnificence. A king appointed by the Romans had united with the Jews to rebuild and embellish it, and the emperor of Rome had enriched it with his gifts. Its strength, richness, and magnificence had made it one of the wonders of the world.

While the westering sun was tinting and gilding the heavens, its resplendent glory lighted up the pure white marble of the temple walls, and sparkled on its gold-capped pillars. From the crest of the hill where Jesus and His followers stood, it had the appearance of a massive structure of snow, set with golden pinnacles. At the entrance to the temple was a vine of gold and silver, with green leaves and massive clusters of grapes executed by the most skillful artists. This design represented Israel as a prosperous vine. The gold, silver, and living green were combined with rare taste and exquisite workmanship; as it twined gracefully about the white and glistening pillars, clinging with shining tendrils to their golden ornaments, it caught the splendor of the setting sun, shining as if with a glory borrowed from heaven.

Jesus gazes upon the scene, and the vast multitude hush their shouts, spellbound by the sudden vision of beauty. All eyes turn upon the Saviour, expecting to see in His countenance the admiration they themselves feel. But instead of this they behold a cloud of sorrow. They are surprised and disappointed to see His eyes fill with tears, and His body rock to and fro like a tree before the tempest, while a wail of anguish bursts from His quivering lips, as if from the depths of a broken heart. What a sight was this for angels to behold! their loved Commander in an agony of tears! What a sight was this for the glad throng that with shouts of triumph and the waving of palm branches were escorting Him to the glorious city, where they fondly hoped He was about to reign! Jesus had wept at the grave of Lazarus, but it was in a godlike grief in sympathy with human woe. But this sudden sorrow was like a note of wailing in a grand triumphal chorus. In the midst of a scene of rejoicing, where all were paying Him homage, Israel's King was in tears; not silent tears of gladness, but tears and groans of insuppressible agony. The multitude were struck with a sudden gloom. Their acclamations were silenced. Many wept in sympathy with a grief they could not comprehend.

The tears of Jesus were not in anticipation of His own suffering. Just before Him was Gethsemane, where soon the horror of a great darkness would overshadow Him. The sheepgate also was in sight, through which for centuries the beasts for sacrificial offerings had been led. This gate was soon to open for Him, the great Antitype, toward whose sacrifice for the sins of the world all these offerings had pointed. Near by was Calvary, the scene of His approaching agony. Yet it was not because of these reminders of His cruel death that the Redeemer wept and groaned in anguish of spirit. His was no selfish sorrow. The thought of His own agony did not intimidate that noble, self-sacrificing soul. It was the sight of Jerusalem that pierced the heart of Jesus—Jerusalem that had rejected the Son of God and scorned His love, that refused to be convinced by His mighty miracles, and was about to take His life. He saw what she was in her guilt of rejecting her Redeemer, and what she might have been had she accepted Him who alone could heal her wound. He had come to save her; how could He give her up?

Israel had been a favored people; God had made their temple His habitation; it was "beautiful for situation, the joy of the whole earth." Ps. 48:2. The record of more than a thousand years of Christ's guardian care and tender love, such as a father bears his only child, was there. In that temple the prophets had uttered their solemn warnings. There had the burning censers waved, while incense, mingled with the prayers of the worshipers, had ascended to God. There the blood of beasts had flowed, typical of the blood of Christ. There Jehovah had manifested His glory above the mercy seat. There the priests had officiated, and the pomp of symbol and ceremony had gone on for ages. But all this must have an end.

Jesus raised His hand,—that had so often blessed the sick and suffering,—and waving it toward the doomed city, in broken utterances of grief exclaimed: "If thou hadst known, even thou, at least in this thy day, the things which belong unto thy peace!—" Here the Saviour paused, and left unsaid what might have been 577 the condition of Jerusalem had she accepted the help that God desired to give her,—the gift of His beloved Son. If Jerusalem had known what it was her privilege to know, and had heeded the light which Heaven had sent her, she might have stood forth in the pride of prosperity, the queen of kingdoms, free in the strength of her God-given power. There would have been no armed soldiers standing at her gates, no Roman banners waving from her walls. The glorious destiny that might have blessed Jerusalem had she accepted her Redeemer rose before the Son of God. He saw that she might through Him have been healed of her grievous malady, liberated from bondage, and established as the mighty metropolis of the earth. From her walls the dove of peace would have gone forth to all nations. She would have been the world's diadem of glory.

But the bright picture of what Jerusalem might have been fades from the Saviour's sight. He realizes what she now is under the Roman yoke, bearing the frown of God, doomed to His retributive judgment. He takes up the broken thread of His lamentation: "But now they are hid from thine eyes. For the days shall come upon thee, that thine enemies shall cast a trench about thee, and compass thee round, and keep thee in on every side, and shall lay thee even with the ground, and thy children within thee; and they shall not leave in thee one stone upon another; because thou knewest not the time of thy visitation."

Christ came to save Jerusalem with her children; but Pharisaical pride, hypocrisy, jealousy, and malice had prevented Him from accomplishing His purpose. Jesus knew the terrible retribution which would be visited upon the doomed city. He saw Jerusalem encompassed with armies, the besieged inhabitants driven to starvation and death, mothers feeding upon the dead bodies of their own children, and both parents and children snatching the last morsel of food from one another, natural affection being destroyed by the gnawing pangs of hunger. He saw that the stubbornness of the Jews, as evinced in their rejection of His salvation, would also lead them to refuse submission to the invading armies. He beheld Calvary, on which He was to be lifted up, set with crosses as thickly as forest trees. He saw the wretched inhabitants suffering torture on the rack and by crucifixion, the beautiful palaces destroyed, the temple in ruins, and of its massive walls not one stone left upon another, while the city was plowed like a field. Well might the Saviour weep in agony in view of that fearful scene.

Jerusalem had been the child of His care, and as a tender father mourns over a wayward son, so Jesus wept over the beloved city. How can I 578 give thee up? How can I see thee devoted to destruction? Must I let thee go to fill up the cup of thine iniquity? One soul is of such value that, in comparison with it, worlds sink into insignificance; but here was a whole nation to be lost. When the fast westering sun should pass from sight in the heavens, Jerusalem's day of grace would be ended. While the procession was halting on the brow of Olivet, it was not yet too late for Jerusalem to repent. The angel of mercy was then folding her wings to step down from the golden throne to give place to justice and swift-coming judgment. But Christ's great heart of love still pleaded for Jerusalem, that had scorned His mercies, despised His warnings, and was about to imbrue her hands in His blood. If Jerusalem would but repent, it was not yet too late. While the last rays of the setting sun were lingering on temple, tower, and pinnacle, would not some good angel lead her to the Saviour's love, and avert her doom? Beautiful and unholy city, that had stoned the prophets, that had rejected the Son of God, that was locking herself by her impenitence in fetters of bondage,—her day of mercy was almost spent!

Yet again the Spirit of God speaks to Jerusalem. Before the day is done, another testimony is borne to Christ. The voice of witness is lifted up, responding to the call from a prophetic past. If Jerusalem will hear the call, if she will receive the Saviour who is entering her gates, she may yet be saved.

Reports have reached the rulers in Jerusalem that Jesus is approaching the city with a great concourse of people. But they have no welcome for the Son of God. In fear they go out to meet Him, hoping to disperse the throng. As the procession is about to descend the Mount of Olives, it is intercepted by the rulers. They inquire the cause of the tumultuous rejoicing. As they question, "Who is this?" the disciples, filled with the spirit of inspiration, answer this question. In eloquent strains they repeat the prophecies concerning Christ:

Adam will tell you, It is the seed of the woman that shall bruise the serpent's head.

Ask Abraham, he will tell you, It is "Melchizedek King of Salem," King of Peace. Gen. 14:18.

Jacob will tell you, He is Shiloh of the tribe of Judah.

Isaiah will tell you, "Immanuel," "Wonderful, Counselor, The mighty God, The everlasting Father, The Prince of Peace." Isa. 7:14; 9:6.

Jeremiah will tell you, The Branch of David, "the Lord our Righteousness." Jer. 23:6.

579 Daniel will tell you, He is the Messiah.

Hosea will tell you, He is "the Lord God of hosts; the Lord is His memorial." Hosea 12:5.

John the Baptist will tell you, He is "the Lamb of God, which taketh away the sin of the world." John 1:29.

The great Jehovah has proclaimed from His throne, "This is My beloved Son." Matt. 3:17.

We, His disciples, declare, This is Jesus, the Messiah, the Prince of life, the Redeemer of the world.

And the prince of the powers of darkness acknowledges Him, saying, "I know Thee who Thou art, the Holy One of God." Mark 1:24.

580

64

A Doomed People

The triumphal ride of Christ into Jerusalem was the dim foreshadowing of His coming in the clouds of heaven with power and glory, amid the triumph of angels and the rejoicing of the saints. Then will be fulfilled the words of Christ to the priests and Pharisees: "Ye shall not see Me henceforth, till ye shall say, Blessed is He that cometh in the name of the Lord." Matt. 23:39. In prophetic vision Zechariah was shown that day of final triumph; and he beheld also the doom of those who at the first advent had rejected Christ: "They shall look upon Me whom they have pierced, and they shall mourn for Him, as one mourneth for his only son, and shall be in bitterness for Him, as one that is in bitterness for his first-born." Zech. 12:10. This scene Christ foresaw when He beheld the city and wept over it. In the temporal ruin of Jerusalem He saw the final destruction of that people who were guilty of the blood of the Son of God.

The disciples saw the hatred of the Jews to Christ, but they did not yet see to what it would lead. They did not yet understand the true condition of Israel, nor comprehend the retribution that was to fall upon Jerusalem. This Christ opened to them by a significant object lesson.

The last appeal to Jerusalem had been in vain. The priests and rulers had heard the prophetic voice of the past echoed by the multitude, in answer to the question, "Who is this?" but they did not accept it as the voice of Inspiration. In 581 anger and amazement they tried to silence the people. There were Roman officers in the throng, and to them His enemies denounced Jesus as the leader of a rebellion. They represented that He was about to take possession of the temple, and reign as king in Jerusalem.

But the calm voice of Jesus hushed for a moment the clamorous throng as He again declared that He had not come to establish a temporal rule; He should soon ascend to His Father, and His accusers would see Him no more until He should come again in glory. Then, too late for their salvation, they would acknowledge Him. These words Jesus spoke with sadness and with singular power. The Roman officers were silenced and subdued. Their hearts, though strangers to divine influence, were moved as they had never been moved before. In the calm, solemn face of Jesus they read love, benevolence, and quiet dignity. They were stirred by a sympathy they could not understand. Instead of arresting Jesus, they were more inclined to pay Him homage. Turning upon the priests and rulers, they charged them with creating the disturbance. These leaders, chagrined and defeated, turned to the people with their complaints, and disputed angrily among themselves.

Meanwhile Jesus passed unnoticed to the temple. All was quiet there, for the scene upon Olivet had called away the people. For a short time Jesus remained at the temple, looking upon it with sorrowful eyes. Then He withdrew with His disciples, and returned to Bethany. When the people sought for Him to place Him on the throne, He was not to be found.

The entire night Jesus spent in prayer, and in the morning He came again to the temple. On the way He passed a fig orchard. He was hungry, "and seeing a fig tree afar off having leaves, He came, if haply He might find anything thereon: and when He came to it, He found nothing but leaves; for the time of figs was not yet."

It was not the season for ripe figs, except in certain localities; and on the highlands about Jerusalem it might truly be said, "The time of figs was not yet." But in the orchard to which Jesus came, one tree appeared to be in advance of all the others. It was already covered with leaves. It is the nature of the fig tree that before the leaves open, the growing fruit appears. Therefore this tree in full leaf gave promise of well-developed fruit. But its appearance was deceptive. Upon searching its branches, from the lowest bough to the topmost twig, Jesus found "nothing but leaves." It was a mass of

This chapter is based on Mark 11:11-14, 20, 21; Matthew 21:17-19.

pretentious foliage, nothing more.

Christ uttered against it a withering curse. "No man eat fruit of thee hereafter forever," He said. The next morning, as the Saviour and His disciples were again on their way to the city, the blasted branches and drooping leaves attracted their attention. "Master," said Peter, "behold, the fig tree which Thou cursedst is withered away."

Christ's act in cursing the fig tree had astonished the disciples. It seemed to them unlike His ways and works. Often they had heard Him declare that He came not to condemn the world, but that the world through Him might be saved. They remembered His words, "The Son of man is not come to destroy men's lives, but to save them." Luke 9:56. His wonderful works had been done to restore, never to destroy. The disciples had known Him only as the Restorer, the Healer. This act stood alone. What was its purpose? they questioned.

God "delighteth in mercy." "As I live, saith the Lord God, I have no pleasure in the death of the wicked." Micah 7:18; Ezek. 33:11. To Him the work of destruction and the denunciation of judgment is a "strange work." Isa. 28:21. But it is in mercy and love that He lifts the veil from the future, and reveals to men the results of a course of sin.

The cursing of the fig tree was an acted parable. That barren tree, flaunting its pretentious foliage in the very face of Christ, was a symbol of the Jewish nation. The Saviour desired to make plain to His disciples the cause and the certainty of Israel's doom. For this purpose He invested the tree with moral qualities, and made it the expositor of divine truth. The Jews stood forth distinct from all other nations, professing allegiance to God. They had been specially favored by Him, and they laid claim to righteousness above every other people. But they were corrupted by the love of the world and the greed of gain. They boasted of their knowledge, but they were ignorant of the requirements of God, and were full of hypocrisy. Like the barren tree, they spread their pretentious branches aloft, luxuriant in appearance, and beautiful to the eye, but they yielded "nothing but leaves." The Jewish religion, with its magnificent temple, its sacred altars, its mitered priests and impressive ceremonies, was indeed fair in outward appearance, but humility, love, and benevolence were lacking.

All the trees in the fig orchard were destitute of fruit; but the leafless trees raised no expectation, and caused no disappointment. By these trees the Gentiles were represented. They were as destitute as were the Jews of godliness; but they had not professed to serve God. They made no boastful pretensions to goodness. They were blind to the works and ways of God. With them the time of figs was not yet. They were still waiting for a day which would bring them light and hope. The Jews, who had received greater blessings from God, were held accountable for their abuse of these gifts. The privileges of which they boasted only increased their guilt.

Jesus had come to the fig tree hungry, to find food. So He had come to Israel, hungering to find in them the fruits of righteousness. He had lavished on them His gifts, that they might bear fruit for the blessing of the world. Every opportunity and privilege had been granted them, and in return He sought their sympathy and co-operation in His work of grace. He longed to see in them self-sacrifice and compassion, zeal for God, and a deep yearning of soul for the salvation of their fellow men. Had they kept the law of God, they would have done the same unselfish work that Christ did. But love to God and man was eclipsed by pride and self-sufficiency. They brought ruin upon themselves by refusing to minister to others. The treasures of truth which God had committed to them, they did not give to the world. In the barren tree they might read both their sin and its punishment. Withered beneath the Saviour's curse, standing forth sere and blasted, dried up by the roots, the fig tree showed what the Jewish people would be when the grace of God was removed from them. Refusing to impart blessing, they would no longer receive it. "O Israel," the Lord says, "thou hast destroyed thyself." Hosea 13:9.

The warning is for all time. Christ's act in cursing the tree which His own power had created stands as a warning to all churches and to all Christians. No one can live the law of God without ministering to others. But there are many who do not live out Christ's merciful, unselfish life. Some who think themselves excellent Christians do not understand what constitutes service for God. They plan and study to please themselves. They act only in reference to self. Time is of value to them only as they can gather for themselves. In all the affairs of life this is their object. Not for others but for themselves do they minister. God created them to live in a world where unselfish service must be performed. He designed them to help their fellow men in every possible way. But self is so large that they cannot see anything else. They are not in touch with humanity. Those who thus live for self are like the fig tree, which made every pretension but was fruitless. They observe the forms of worship, but without repentance or faith. In profession they honor the law of God, but obedience is lacking. They say, but do not. In the sentence pronounced on the fig tree Christ demonstrates how hateful in His eyes is this vain pretense. He declares that the open sinner is less guilty than is he who professes to serve God, but who bears no fruit to His glory.

The parable of the fig tree, spoken before Christ's visit to Jerusalem, had a direct connection with the lesson He taught in cursing the fruitless tree. For the barren tree of the parable the gardener pleaded, Let it alone this year, until I shall dig about it and dress it; and if it bear fruit, well; but if not, then after that thou shalt cut it down. Increased care was to be given the unfruitful tree. It was to have every advantage. But if it remained fruitless, nothing could save it from destruction. In the parable the result of the gardener's work was not foretold. It depended upon that people to whom Christ's words were spoken. They were represented by the fruitless tree, and it rested with them to decide their own destiny. Every advantage that Heaven could bestow was given them, but they did not profit by their increased blessings. By Christ's act in cursing the barren fig tree, the result was shown. They had determined their own destruction.

For more than a thousand years the Jewish nation had abused God's mercy and invited His judgments. They had rejected His warnings and slain His prophets. For these sins the people of Christ's day made themselves responsible by 587 following the same course. In the rejection of their present mercies and warnings lay the guilt of that generation. The fetters which the nation had for centuries been forging, the people of Christ's day were fastening upon themselves.

In every age there is given to men their day of light and privilege, a probationary time in which they may become reconciled to God. But there is a limit to this grace. Mercy may plead for years and be slighted and rejected; but there comes a time when mercy makes her last plea. The heart becomes so hardened that it ceases to respond to the Spirit of God. Then the sweet, winning voice entreats the sinner no longer, and reproofs and warnings cease.

That day had come to Jerusalem. Jesus wept in anguish over the doomed city, but He could not deliver her. He had exhausted every resource. In rejecting the warnings of God's Spirit, Israel had rejected the only means by which they could be delivered.

The Jewish nation was a symbol of the people of all ages who scorn the pleadings of Infinite Love. The tears of Christ when He wept over Jerusalem were for the sins of all time. In the judgments pronounced upon Israel, those who reject the reproofs and warnings of God's Holy Spirit may read their own condemnation.

In this generation there are many who are treading on the same ground as were the unbelieving Jews. They have witnessed the manifestation of the power of God; the Holy Spirit has spoken to their hearts; but they cling to their unbelief and resistance. God sends them warnings and reproof, but they are not willing to confess their errors, and they reject His message and His messenger. The very means He uses for their recovery becomes to them a stone of stum-

bling.

The prophets of God were hated by apostate Israel because through them their hidden sins were brought to light. Ahab regarded Elijah as his enemy because the prophet was faithful to rebuke the king's secret iniquities. So today the servant of Christ, the reprover of sin, meets with scorn and rebuffs. Bible truth, the religion of Christ, struggles against a strong current of moral impurity. Prejudice is even stronger in the hearts of men now than in Christ's day. Christ did not fulfill men's expectations; His life was a rebuke to their sins, and they rejected Him. So now the truth of God's word does not harmonize with men's practices and their natural inclination, and thousands reject its light. Men prompted by Satan cast doubt upon God's word, and choose to exercise their independent judgment. They choose darkness rather than light, but they do it at the peril of their souls. Those who caviled at the words of Christ found ever-increased cause for cavil, until they turned from the Truth and the Life. So it is now. God does not propose to remove every objection which the carnal heart may bring against His truth. To those who refuse the precious rays of light which would illuminate the darkness, the mysteries of God's word remain such forever. From them the truth is hidden. They walk blindly, and know not the ruin before them. 588

Christ overlooked the world and all ages from the height of Olivet; and His words are applicable to every soul who slights the pleadings of divine mercy. Scorner of His love, He addresses you today. It is "thou, even thou," who shouldest know the things that belong to thy peace. Christ is shedding bitter tears for you, who have no tears to shed for yourself. Already that fatal hardness of heart which destroyed the Pharisees is manifest in you. And every evidence of the grace of God, every ray of divine light, is either melting and subduing the soul, or confirming it in hopeless impenitence.

Christ foresaw that Jerusalem would remain obdurate and impenitent; yet all the guilt, all the consequences of rejected mercy, lay at her own door. Thus it will be with every soul who is following the same course. The Lord declares, "O Israel, thou hast destroyed thyself." "Hear, O earth: behold, I will bring evil upon this people, even the fruit of their thoughts, because they have not hearkened unto My words, nor to My law, but rejected it." Hosea 13:9; Jer. 6:19.

65

589

The Temple Cleansed Again

At the beginning of His ministry, Christ had driven from the temple those who defiled it by

This chapter is based on Matthew 21:12-16, 23-46; Mark 11:15-19, 27-33; 12:1-12; Luke 19:45-48; 20:1-19.

their unholy traffic; and His stern and godlike demeanor had struck terror to the hearts of the scheming traders. At the close of His mission He came again to the temple, and found it still desecrated as before. The condition of things was even worse than before. The outer court of the temple was like a vast cattle yard. With the cries of the animals and the sharp chinking of coin was mingled the sound of angry altercation between traffickers, and among them were heard the voices of men in sacred office. The dignitaries of the temple were themselves engaged in buying and selling and the exchange of money. So completely were they controlled by their greed of gain that in the sight of God they were no better than thieves.

Little did the priests and rulers realize the solemnity of the work which it was theirs to perform. At every Passover and Feast of Tabernacles, thousands of animals were slain, and their blood was caught by the priests and poured upon the altar. The Jews had become familiar with the offering of blood, and had almost lost sight of the fact that it was sin which made necessary all this shedding of the blood of beasts. They did not discern that it prefigured the blood of God's dear Son, which was to be shed for the life of the world, and that by the offering of sacrifices men were to be directed to a crucified Redeemer.

Jesus looked upon the innocent victims of sacrifice, and saw how the Jews had made these great convocations scenes of bloodshed and cruelty. In place of humble repentance of sin, they had multiplied the sacrifice of beasts, as if God could be honored by a heartless service. The priests and rulers had hardened their hearts through selfishness and avarice. The very symbols pointing to the Lamb of God they had made a means of getting gain. Thus in the eyes of the people the sacredness of the sacrificial service had been in a great measure destroyed. The indignation of Jesus was stirred; He knew that His blood, so soon to be shed for the sins of the world, would be as little appreciated by the priests and elders as was the blood of beasts which they kept incessantly flowing.

Against these practices Christ had spoken through the prophets. Samuel had said, "Hath the Lord as great delight in burnt offerings and sacrifices, as in obeying the voice of the Lord? Behold, to obey is better than sacrifice, and to hearken than the fat of rams." And Isaiah, seeing in prophetic vision the apostasy of the Jews, addressed them as rulers of Sodom and Gomorrah: "Hear the word of the Lord, ye rulers of Sodom; give ear unto the law of our God, ye people of Gomorrah. To what purpose is the multitude of your sacrifices unto Me? saith the Lord: I am full of the burnt offerings of rams, and the fat of fed beasts; and I delight not in the blood of bullocks, or of lambs, or of he-goats.

When ye come to appear before Me, who hath required this at your hand, to tread My courts?" "Wash you, make you clean; put away the evil of your doings from before Mine eyes; cease to do evil; learn to do well; seek judgment, relieve the oppressed, judge the fatherless, plead for the widow." 1 Sam. 15:22; Isa. 1:10-12, 16, 17.

He who had Himself given these prophecies now for the last time repeated the warning. In fulfillment of prophecy the people had proclaimed Jesus king of Israel. He had received their homage, and accepted the office of king. In this character He must act. He knew that His efforts to reform a corrupt priesthood would be in vain; nevertheless His work must be done; to an unbelieving people the evidence of His divine mission must be given.

Again the piercing look of Jesus swept over the desecrated court of the temple. All eyes were turned toward Him. Priest and ruler, Pharisee and Gentile, looked with astonishment and awe upon Him who stood before them with the majesty of heaven's King. Divinity flashed through humanity, investing Christ with a dignity and glory He had never manifested before. Those standing nearest Him drew as far away as the crowd would permit. Except for a few of His disciples, the Saviour stood alone. Every sound was hushed. The deep silence seemed unbearable. Christ spoke with a power that swayed the people like a mighty tempest: "It is written, My house shall be called the house of prayer; but ye have made it a den of thieves." His voice sounded like a trumpet through the temple. The displeasure of His countenance seemed like consuming fire. With authority He commanded, "Take these things hence." John 2:16.

Three years before, the rulers of the temple had been ashamed of their flight before the command of Jesus. They had since wondered at their own fears, and their unquestioning obedience to a single humble Man. They had felt that it was impossible for their undignified surrender to be repeated. Yet they were now more terrified than before, and in greater haste to obey His command. There were none who dared question His authority. Priests and traders fled from His presence, driving their cattle before them.

On the way from the temple they were met by a throng who came with their sick inquiring for the Great Healer. The report given by the fleeing people caused some of these to turn back. They feared to meet One so powerful, whose very look had driven the priests and rulers from His presence. But a large number pressed through the hurrying crowd, eager to reach Him who was their only hope. When the multitude fled from the temple, many had remained behind. These were now joined by the newcomers. Again the temple court was filled by the sick and the dying, and once more Jesus ministered to them.

After a season the priests and rulers ventured back to the temple. When the panic had abated, they were seized with anxiety to know what would be the next movement of Jesus. They expected Him to take the throne of David. Quietly returning to the temple, they heard the voices of men, women, and children praising God. Upon entering, they stood transfixed before the wonderful scene. They saw the sick healed, the blind restored to sight, the deaf receive their hearing, and the crippled leap for joy. The children were foremost in the rejoicing. Jesus had healed their maladies; He had clasped them in His arms, received their kisses of grateful affection, and some of them had fallen asleep upon His breast as He was teaching the people. Now with glad voices the children sounded His praise. They repeated the hosannas of the day before, and waved palm branches triumphantly before the Saviour. The temple echoed and re-echoed with their acclamations, "Blessed be He that cometh in the name of the Lord!" "Behold, thy King cometh unto thee: He is just, and having salvation!" Ps. 118:26; Zech. 9:9. "Hosanna to the Son of David!"

The sound of these happy, unrestrained voices was an offense to the rulers of the temple. They set about putting a stop to such demonstrations. They represented to the people that the house of God was desecrated by the feet of the children and the shouts of rejoicing. Finding that their words made no impression on the people, the rulers appealed to Christ: "Hearest Thou what these say? And Jesus saith unto them, Yea; have ye never read, Out of the mouth of babes and sucklings Thou hast perfected praise?" Prophecy had foretold that Christ should be proclaimed as king, and that word must be fulfilled. The priests and rulers of Israel refused to herald His glory, and God moved upon the children to be His witnesses. Had the voices of the children been silent, the very pillars of the temple would have sounded the Saviour's praise.

The Pharisees were utterly perplexed and disconcerted. One whom they could not intimidate was in command. Jesus had taken His position as guardian of the temple. Never before had He assumed such kingly authority. Never before had His words and works possessed so great power. He had done marvelous works throughout Jerusalem, but never before in a manner so solemn and impressive. In presence of the people who had witnessed His wonderful works, the priests and rulers dared not show Him open hostility. Though enraged and confounded by His answer, they were unable to accomplish anything further that day.

The next morning the Sanhedrin again considered what course to pursue toward Jesus. Three years before, they had demanded a sign of His Messiahship. Since that time He had wrought mighty works throughout the land. He had healed the sick, miraculously fed thousands of people, walked upon the waves, and spoken peace to the troubled sea. He had repeatedly read the hearts of men as an open book; He had cast out demons, and raised the dead. The rulers had before them the evidences of His Messiahship. They now decided to demand no sign of His authority, but to draw out some admission or declaration by which He might be condemned.

Repairing to the temple where He was teaching, they proceeded to question Him: "By what authority doest Thou these things? and who gave Thee this authority?" They expected Him to claim that His authority was from God. Such an assertion they intended to deny. But Jesus met them with a question apparently pertaining to another subject, and He made His reply to them conditional on their answering this question. "The baptism of John," He said, "whence was it? from heaven, or of men?"

The priests saw that they were in a dilemma from which no sophistry could extricate them. If they said that John's baptism was from heaven, their inconsistency would be made apparent. Christ would say, Why have ye not then believed on him? John had testified of Christ, "Behold the Lamb of God, which taketh away the sin of the world." John 1:29. If the priests believed John's testimony, how could they deny the Messiahship of Christ? If they declared their real belief, that John's ministry was of men, they would bring upon themselves a storm of indignation; for the people believed John to be a prophet.

With intense interest the multitude awaited the decision. They knew that the priests had professed to accept the ministry of John, and they expected them to acknowledge without a question that he was sent from God. But after conferring secretly together, the priests decided not to commit themselves. Hypocritically professing ignorance, they said, "We cannot tell." "Neither tell I you," said Christ, "by what authority I do these things."

Scribes, priests, and rulers were all silenced. Baffled and disappointed, they stood with lowering brows, not daring to press further questions upon Christ. By their cowardice and indecision they had in a great measure forfeited the respect of the people, who now stood by, amused to see these proud, self-righteous men defeated.

All these sayings and doings of Christ were important, and their influence was to be felt in an ever-increasing degree after His crucifixion and ascension. Many of those who had anxiously awaited the result of the questioning of Jesus were finally to become His disciples, first drawn toward Him by His words on that eventful day.

The scene in the temple court was never to fade from their minds. The contrast between Jesus and the high priest as they talked together was marked. The proud dignitary of the temple was clothed in rich and costly garments. Upon his head was a glittering tiara. His bearing was majestic, his hair and his long flowing beard were silvered by age. His appearance awed the beholders. Before this august personage stood the Majesty of heaven, without adornment or display. His garments were travel stained; His face was pale, and expressed a patient sadness; yet written there were dignity and benevolence that contrasted strangely with the proud, self-confident, and angry air of the high priest. Many of those who witnessed the words and deeds of Jesus in the temple from that time enshrined Him in their hearts as a prophet of God. But as the popular feeling turned in His favor, the hatred of the priests toward Jesus increased. The wisdom by which He escaped the snares set for His feet, being a new evidence of His divinity, added fuel to their wrath.

595 In His contest with the rabbis, it was not Christ's purpose to humiliate His opponents. He was not glad to see them in a hard place. He had an important lesson to teach. He had mortified His enemies by allowing them to be entangled in the net they had spread for Him. Their acknowledged ignorance in regard to the character of John's baptism gave Him an opportunity to speak, and He improved the opportunity by presenting before them their real position, adding another warning to the many already given.

"What think ye?" He said. "A certain man had two sons; and he came to the first, and said, Son, go work today in my vineyard. He answered and said, I will not: but afterward he repented, and went. And he came to the second, and said likewise. And he answered and said, I go, sir: and went not. Whether of them twain did the will of his father?"

This abrupt question threw His hearers off their guard. They had followed the parable closely, and now immediately answered, "The first." Fixing His steady eye upon them, Jesus responded in stern and solemn tones: "Verily I say unto you, That the publicans and the harlots go into the kingdom of God before you. For John came unto you in the way of righteousness, and ye believed him not: but the publicans and the harlots believed him: and ye, when ye had seen it, repented not afterward, that ye might believe him."

The priests and rulers could not but give a correct answer to Christ's question, and thus He obtained their opinion in favor of the first son. This son represented the publicans, those who were despised and hated by the Pharisees. The publicans had been grossly immoral. They had indeed been transgressors of the law of God,

showing in their lives an absolute resistance to His requirements. They had been unthankful and unholy; when told to go and work in the Lord's vineyard, they had given a contemptuous refusal. But when John came, preaching repentance and baptism, the publicans received his message and were baptized.

The second son represented the leading men of the Jewish nation. Some of the Pharisees had repented and received the baptism of John; but the leaders would not acknowledge that he came from God. His warnings and denunciations did not lead them to reformation. They "rejected the counsel of God against themselves, being not baptized of him." Luke 7:30. They treated his message with disdain. Like the second son, who, when called, said, "I go, sir," but went not, the priests and rulers professed obedience, but acted disobedience. They made great professions of piety, they claimed to be obeying the law of God, but they rendered only a false obedience. The publicans were denounced and cursed by the Pharisees as infidels; but they showed by their faith and works that they were 596 going into the kingdom of heaven before those self-righteous men who had been given great light, but whose works did not correspond to their profession of godliness.

The priests and rulers were unwilling to bear these searching truths; they remained silent, however, hoping that Jesus would say something which they could turn against Him; but they had still more to bear.

"Hear another parable," Christ said: "There was a certain householder, which planted a vineyard, and hedged it round about, and digged a wine press in it, and built a tower, and let it out to husbandmen, and went into a far country: and when the time of the fruit drew near, he sent his servants to the husbandmen, that they might receive the fruits of it. And the husbandmen took his servants, and beat one, and killed another, and stoned another. Again, he sent other servants more than the first: and they did unto them likewise. But last of all he sent unto them his son, saying, They will reverence my son. But when the husbandmen saw the son, they said among themselves, This is the heir; come, let us kill him, and let us seize on his inheritance. And they caught him, and cast him out of the vineyard, and slew him. When the lord therefore of the vineyard cometh, what will he do unto those husbandmen?"

Jesus addressed all the people present; but the priests and rulers answered. "He will miserably destroy those wicked men," they said, "and will let out his vineyard unto other husbandmen, which shall render him the fruits in their seasons." The speakers had not at first perceived the application of the parable, but they now saw that they had pronounced their own condemnation. In the parable the householder represented

God, the vineyard the Jewish nation, and the hedge the divine law which was their protection. The tower was a symbol of the temple. The lord of the vineyard had done everything needful for its prosperity. "What could have been done more to my vineyard," he says, "that I have not done in it?" Isa. 5:4. Thus was represented God's unwearied care for Israel. And as the husbandmen were to return to the lord a due proportion of the fruits of the vineyard, so God's people were to honor Him by a life corresponding to their sacred privileges. But as the husbandmen had killed the servants whom the master sent to them for fruit, so the Jews had put to death the prophets whom God sent to call them to repentance. Messenger after messenger had been slain. Thus far the application of the parable could not be questioned, and in what followed it was not less evident. In the beloved son whom the lord of the vineyard finally sent to his disobedient servants, and whom they seized and slew, the priests and rulers saw a distinct picture of Jesus and His impending fate. Already they were planning to slay Him whom the Father had sent to them as a last appeal. In the retribution inflicted upon the ungrateful husbandmen was portrayed the doom of those who should put Christ to death.

Looking with pity upon them, the Saviour continued, "Did ye never read in the Scriptures, The stone which the builders rejected, the same is become the head of the corner: this is the Lord's doing, and it is marvelous in our eyes? Therefore say I unto you, The kingdom of God shall be taken from you, and given to a nation bringing forth the fruits thereof. And whosoever shall fall on this stone shall be broken: but on whomsoever it shall fall, it will grind him to powder."

This prophecy the Jews had often repeated in the synagogues, applying it to the coming Messiah. Christ was the cornerstone of the Jewish economy, and of the whole plan of salvation. This foundation stone the Jewish builders, the priests and rulers of Israel, were now rejecting. The Saviour called their attention to the prophecies that would show them their danger. By every means in His power He sought to make plain to them the nature of the deed they were about to do.

And His words had another purpose. In asking the question, "When the lord therefore of the vineyard cometh, what will he do unto those husbandmen?" Christ designed that the Pharisees should answer as they did. He designed that they should condemn themselves. His warnings, failing to arouse them to repentance, would seal their doom, and He wished them to see that they had brought ruin on themselves. He designed to show them the justice of God in the withdrawal of their national privileges, which had already begun, and which would end,

not only in the destruction of their temple and their city, but in the dispersion of the nation.

The hearers recognized the warning. But notwithstanding the sentence they themselves had pronounced, the priests and rulers were ready to fill out the picture by saying, "This is the heir; come, let us kill him." "But when they sought to lay hands on Him, they feared the multitude," for the public sentiment was in Christ's favor.

In quoting the prophecy of the rejected stone, Christ referred to an actual occurrence in the history of Israel. The incident was connected with the building of the first temple. While it had a special application at the time of Christ's first advent, and should have appealed with special force to the Jews, it has also a lesson for us. When the temple of Solomon was erected, the immense stones for the walls and the foundation were entirely prepared at the quarry; after they were brought to the place of building, not an instrument was to be used upon them; the workmen had only to place them in position. For use in the foundation, one stone of unusual size and peculiar shape had been brought; but the workmen could find no place for it, and would not accept it. It was an annoyance to them as it lay unused in their way. Long it remained a rejected stone. But when the builders came to the laying of the corner, they searched for a long time to find a stone of sufficient size and strength, and of the proper shape, to take that particular place, and bear the great weight which would rest upon it. Should they make an unwise choice for this important place, the safety of the entire building would be endangered. They must find a stone capable of resisting the influence of the sun, of frost, and of tempest. Several stones had at different times been chosen, but under the pressure of immense weights they had crumbled to pieces. Others could not bear the test of the sudden atmospheric changes. But at last attention was called to the stone so long rejected. It had been exposed to the air, to sun and storm, without revealing the slightest crack. The builders examined this stone. It had borne every test but one. If it could bear the test of severe pressure, they decided to accept it for the cornerstone. The trial was made. The stone was accepted, brought to its assigned position, and found to be an exact fit. In prophetic vision, Isaiah was shown that this stone was a symbol of Christ. He says:

"Sanctify the Lord of hosts Himself; and let Him be your fear, and let Him be your dread. And He shall be for a sanctuary; but for a stone of stumbling and for a rock of offense to both the houses of Israel, for a gin and for a snare to the inhabitants of Jerusalem. And many among them shall stumble, and fall, and be broken, and be snared, and be taken." Carried down in prophetic vision to the first advent, the prophet is shown that Christ is to bear trials and tests of which the treatment of the chief cornerstone in the temple of Solomon was symbolic. "Therefore thus saith the Lord God, Behold, I lay in Zion for a foundation a stone, a tried stone, a precious cornerstone, a sure foundation: he that believeth shall not make haste." Isa. 8:13-15; 28:16.

In infinite wisdom, God chose the foundation stone, and laid it Himself. He called it "a sure foundation." The entire world may lay upon it their burdens and griefs; it can endure them all. With perfect safety they may build upon it. Christ is a "tried stone." Those who trust in Him, He never disappoints. He has borne every test. He has endured the pressure of Adam's guilt, and the guilt of his posterity, and has come off more than conqueror of the powers of evil. He has borne the burdens cast upon Him by every repenting sinner. In Christ the guilty heart has found relief. He is the sure foundation. All who make Him their dependence rest in perfect security.

In Isaiah's prophecy, Christ is declared to be both a sure foundation and a stone of stumbling. The apostle Peter, writing by inspiration of the Holy Spirit, clearly shows to whom Christ is a foundation stone, and to whom a rock of offense:

"If so be ye have tasted that the Lord is gracious. To whom coming, as unto a living stone, disallowed indeed of men, but chosen of God, and precious, ye also, as lively stones, are built up a spiritual house, an holy priesthood, to offer up spiritual sacrifices, acceptable to God by Jesus Christ. Wherefore also it is contained in the Scripture, Behold, I lay in Sion a chief cornerstone, elect, precious: and he that believeth on Him shall not be confounded. Unto you therefore which believe He is precious: but unto them which be disobedient, the stone which the builders disallowed, the same is made the head of the corner, and a stone of stumbling, and a rock of offense, even to them which stumble at the word, being disobedient." 1 Peter 2:3-8.

To those who believe, Christ is the sure foundation. These are they who fall upon the Rock and are broken. Submission to Christ and faith in Him are here represented. To fall upon the Rock and be broken is to give up our self-righteousness and to go to Christ with the humility of a child, repenting of our transgressions, and believing in His forgiving love. And so also it is by faith and obedience that we build on Christ as our foundation.

Upon this living stone, Jews and Gentiles alike may build. This is the only foundation upon which we may securely build. It is broad enough for all, and strong enough to sustain the weight and burden of the whole world. And by connection with Christ, the living stone, all who build upon this foundation become living

stones. Many persons are by their own endeavors hewn, polished, and beautified; but they cannot become "living stones," because they are not connected with Christ. Without this connection, no man can be saved. Without the life of Christ in us, we cannot withstand the storms of temptation. Our eternal safety depends upon our building upon the sure foundation. Multitudes are today building upon foundations that have not been tested. When the rain falls, and the tempest rages, and the floods come, their house will fall, because it is not founded upon the eternal Rock, the chief cornerstone Christ Jesus.

"To them which stumble at the word, being disobedient," Christ is a rock of offense. But "the stone which the builders disallowed, the same is made the head of the corner." Like the rejected stone, Christ in His earthly mission had borne neglect and abuse. He was "despised and rejected of men; a man of sorrows, and acquainted with grief: . . . He was despised, and we esteemed Him not." Isa. 53:3. But the time was near when He would be glorified. By the resurrection from the dead He would be declared "the Son of God with power." Rom. 1:4. At His second coming He would be revealed as Lord of heaven and earth. Those who were now about to crucify Him would recognize His greatness. Before the universe the rejected stone would become the head of the corner.

And on "whomsoever it shall fall, it will grind him to powder." The people who rejected Christ were soon to see their city and their nation destroyed. Their glory would be broken, and scattered as the dust before the wind. And what was it that destroyed the Jews? It was the rock which, had they built upon it, would have been their security. It was the goodness of God despised, the righteousness spurned, the mercy slighted. Men set themselves in opposition to God, and all that would have been their salvation was turned to their destruction. All that God ordained unto life they found to be unto death. In the Jews' crucifixion of Christ was involved the destruction of Jerusalem. The blood shed upon Calvary was the weight that sank them to ruin for this world and for the world to come. So it will be in the great final day, when judgment shall fall upon the rejecters of God's grace. Christ, their rock of offense, will then appear to them as an avenging mountain. The glory of His countenance, which to the righteous was life, will be to the wicked a consuming fire. Because of love rejected, grace despised, the sinner will be destroyed.

By many illustrations and repeated warnings, Jesus showed what would be the result to the Jews of rejecting the Son of God. In these words He was addressing all in every age who refuse to receive Him as their Redeemer. Every warning is for them. The desecrated temple, the disobedient son, the false husbandmen, the contemptuous builders, have their counterpart in the experience of every sinner. Unless he repent, the doom which they foreshadowed will be his.

601

66

Controversy

The priests and rulers had listened in silence to Christ's pointed rebukes. They could not refute His charges. But they were only the more determined to entrap Him, and with this object they sent to Him spies, "which should feign themselves just men, that they might take hold of His words, that so they might deliver Him unto the power and authority of the governor." They did not send the old Pharisees whom Jesus had often met, but young men, who were ardent and zealous, and whom, they thought, Christ did not know. These were accompanied by certain of the Herodians, who were to hear Christ's words, that they might testify against Him at His trial. The Pharisees and Herodians had been bitter enemies, but they were now one in enmity to Christ.

The Pharisees had ever chafed under the exaction of tribute by the Romans. The payment of tribute they held to be contrary to the law of God. Now they saw opportunity to lay a snare for Jesus. The spies came to Him, and with apparent sincerity, as though desiring to know their duty, said, "Master, we know that Thou sayest and teachest rightly, neither acceptest Thou the person of any, but teachest the way of God truly: is it lawful for us to give tribute unto Caesar, or no?"

602
The words, "We know that Thou sayest and teachest rightly," had they been sincere, would have been a wonderful admission. But they were spoken to deceive; nevertheless their testimony was true. The Pharisees did know that Christ said and taught rightly, and by their own testimony will they be judged.

Those who put the question to Jesus thought that they had sufficiently disguised their purpose; but Jesus read their hearts as an open book, and sounded their hypocrisy. "Why tempt ye Me?" He said; thus giving them a sign they had not asked, by showing that He read their hidden purpose. They were still more confused when He added, "Show Me a penny." They brought it, and He asked them, "Whose image and superscription hath it? They answered and said, Caesar's." Pointing to the inscription on the coin, Jesus said, "Render therefore unto Caesar the things which are Caesar's; and unto God the things that are God's."

The spies had expected Jesus to answer their question directly, in one way or the other. If He should say, It is unlawful to give tribute to Cae-

sar, He would be reported to the Roman authorities and arrested for inciting rebellion. But in case He should pronounce it lawful to pay the tribute, they designed to accuse Him to the people as opposing the law of God. Now they felt themselves baffled and defeated. Their plans were disarranged. The summary manner in which their question had been settled left them nothing further to say.

Christ's reply was no evasion, but a candid answer to the question. Holding in His hand the Roman coin, upon which were stamped the name and image of Caesar, He declared that since they were living under the protection of the Roman power, they should render to that power the support it claimed, so long as this did not conflict with a higher duty. But while peaceably subject to the laws of the land, they should at all times give their first allegiance to God.

The Saviour's words, "Render . . . unto God the things that are God's," were a severe rebuke to the intriguing Jews. Had they faithfully fulfilled their obligations to God, they would not have become a broken nation, subject to a foreign power. No Roman ensign would have waved over Jerusalem, no Roman sentinel would have stood at her gates, no Roman governor would have ruled within her walls. The Jewish nation was then paying the penalty of its apostasy from God.

When the Pharisees heard Christ's answer, "they marveled, and left Him, and went their way." He had rebuked their hypocrisy and presumption, and in doing this He had stated a 603 great principle, a principle that clearly defines the limits of man's duty to the civil government and his duty to God. In many minds a vexed question had been settled. Ever after they held to the right principle. And although many went away dissatisfied, they saw that the principle underlying the question had been clearly set forth, and they marveled at Christ's far-seeing discernment.

No sooner were the Pharisees silenced than the Sadducees came forward with their artful questions. The two parties stood in bitter opposition to each other. The Pharisees were rigid adherents to tradition. They were exact in outward ceremonies, diligent in washings, fastings, and long prayers, and ostentatious in almsgiving. But Christ declared that they made void the law of God by teaching for doctrines the commandments of men. As a class they were bigoted and hypocritical; yet among them were persons of genuine piety, who accepted Christ's teachings and became His disciples. The Sadducees rejected the traditions of the Pharisees. They professed to believe the greater portion of the Scriptures, and to regard them as the rule of action; but practically they were skeptics and materialists.

The Sadducees denied the existence of

This chapter is based on Matthew 22:15-46; Mark 12:13-40; Luke 20:20-47.

angels, the resurrection of the dead, and the doctrine of a future life, with its rewards and punishments. On all these points they differed with the Pharisees. Between the two parties the resurrection was especially a subject of controversy. The Pharisees had been firm believers in the resurrection, but in these discussions their views in regard to the future state became confused. Death became to them an inexplicable mystery. Their inability to meet the arguments of the Sadducees gave rise to continual irritation. The discussions between the two parties usually resulted in angry disputes, leaving them farther apart than before.

In numbers the Sadducees fell far below their opponents, and they had not so strong a hold upon the common people; but many of them were wealthy, and they had the influence which wealth imparts. In their ranks were included most of the priests, and from among them the high priest was usually chosen. This was, however, with the express stipulation that their skeptical opinions should not be made prominent. On account of the numbers and popularity of the Pharisees, it was necessary for the Sadducees to concede outwardly to their doctrines when holding any priestly office; but the very fact that they were eligible to such office gave influence to their errors.

The Sadducees rejected the teaching of Jesus; He was animated by a spirit which they would not acknowledge as manifesting itself thus; and His teaching in regard to God and the future life contradicted their theories. They believed in God as the only being superior to man; but they argued that an overruling providence and a divine foresight would deprive man of free moral agency, and degrade him to the position of a slave. It was their belief, that, having created man, God had left him to himself, independent of a higher influence. They held that man was free to control his own life and to shape the events of the world; that his destiny was in his own hands. They denied that the Spirit of God works through human efforts or natural means. Yet they still held that, through the proper employment of his natural powers, man could become elevated and enlightened; that by rigorous and austere exactions his life could be purified.

Their ideas of God molded their own character. As in their view He had no interest in man, so they had little regard for one another; there was little union among them. Refusing to acknowledge the influence of the Holy Spirit upon human action, they lacked His power in their lives. Like the rest of the Jews, they boasted much of their birthright as children of Abraham, and of their strict adherence to the requirements of the law; but of the true spirit of the law and the faith and benevolence of Abraham, they were destitute. Their natural sympathies were brought within a narrow compass. They believed it possible for all men to secure the comforts and blessings of life; and their hearts were not touched by the wants and sufferings of others. They lived for themselves.

By His words and His works, Christ testified to a divine power that produces supernatural results, to a future life beyond the present, to God as a Father of the children of men, ever watchful of their true interests. He revealed the working of divine power in benevolence and compassion that rebuked the selfish exclusiveness of the Sadducees. He taught that both for man's temporal and for his eternal good, God moves upon the heart by the Holy Spirit. He showed the error of trusting to human power for that transformation of character which can be wrought only by the Spirit of God.

This teaching the Sadducees were determined to discredit. In seeking a controversy with Jesus, they felt confident of bringing Him into disrepute, even if they could not secure His condemnation. The resurrection was the subject on which they chose to question Him. Should He agree with them, He would give still further offense to the Pharisees. Should He differ with them, they designed to hold His teaching up to ridicule.

The Sadducees reasoned that if the body is to be composed of the same particles of matter in its immortal as in its mortal state, then when raised from the dead it must have flesh and blood, and must resume in the eternal world the life interrupted on earth. In that case they concluded that earthly relationships would be resumed, husband and wife would be reunited, marriages consummated, and all things go on the same as before death, the frailties and passions of this life being perpetuated in the life beyond.

In answer to their questions, Jesus lifted the veil from the future life. "In the resurrection," He said, "they neither marry, nor are given in marriage, but are as the angels of God in heaven." He showed that the Sadducees were wrong in their belief. Their premises were false. "Ye do err," He added, "not knowing the Scriptures, nor the power of God." He did not charge them, as He had charged the Pharisees, with hypocrisy, but with error of belief.

The Sadducees had flattered themselves that they of all men adhered most strictly to the Scriptures. But Jesus showed that they had not known their true meaning. That knowledge must be brought home to the heart by the enlightenment of the Holy Spirit. Their ignorance of the Scriptures and the power of God He declared to be the cause of their confusion of faith and darkness of mind. They were seeking to bring the mysteries of God within the compass of their finite reasoning. Christ called upon them to open their minds to those sacred truths that would broaden and strengthen the understanding. Thousands become infidels because their finite minds cannot comprehend the mysteries of God. They cannot explain the wonderful exhibition of divine power in His providences, therefore they reject the evidences of such power, attributing them to natural agencies which they can comprehend still less. The only key to the mysteries that surround us is to acknowledge in them all the presence and power of God. Men need to recognize God as the Creator of the universe, One who commands and executes all things. They need a broader view of His character, and of the mystery of His agencies.

Christ declared to His hearers that if there were no resurrection of the dead, the Scriptures which they professed to believe would be of no avail. He said, "But as touching the resurrection of the dead, have ye not read that which was spoken unto you by God, saying, I am the God of Abraham, and the God of Isaac, and the God of Jacob? God is not the God of the dead, but of the living." God counts the things that are not as though they were. He sees the end from the beginning, and beholds the result of His work as though it were now accomplished. The precious dead, from Adam down to the last saint who dies, will hear the voice of the Son of God, and will come forth from the grave to immortal life. God will be their God, and they shall be His people. There will be a close and tender relationship between God and the risen saints. This condition, which is anticipated in His purpose, He beholds as if it were already existing. The dead live unto Him.

By the words of Christ the Sadducees were put to silence. They could not answer Him. Not a word had been spoken of which the least advantage could be taken for His condemnation. His adversaries had gained nothing but the contempt of the people.

The Pharisees, however, did not yet despair of driving Him to speak that which they could use against Him. They prevailed upon a certain learned scribe to question Jesus as to which of the ten precepts of the law was of the greatest importance.

The Pharisees had exalted the first four commandments, which point out the duty of man to his Maker, as of far greater consequence than the other six, which define man's duty to his fellow man. As the result, Jesus had shown the people their great deficiency, and had taught the necessity of good works, declaring that the tree is known by its fruits. For this reason He had been charged with exalting the last six commandments above the first four.

The lawyer approached Jesus with a direct question, "Which is the first commandment of all?" The answer of Christ is direct and forcible:

"The first of all the commandments is, Hear, O Israel; The Lord our God is one Lord: and thou shalt love the Lord thy God with all thy heart, and with all thy soul, and with all thy mind, and with all thy strength: this is the first commandment." The second is like the first, said Christ; for it flows out of it, "Thou shalt love thy neighbor as thyself. There is none other commandment greater than these." "On these two commandments hang all the law and the prophets."

The first four of the Ten Commandments are summed up in the one great precept, "Thou shalt love the Lord thy God with all thy heart." The last six are included in the other, "Thou shalt love thy neighbor as thyself." Both these commandments are an expression of the principle of love. The first cannot be kept and the second broken, nor can the second be kept while the first is broken. When God has His rightful place on the throne of the heart, the right place will be given to our neighbor. We shall love him as ourselves. And only as we love God supremely is it possible to love our neighbor impartially.

And since all the commandments are summed up in love to God and man, it follows that not one precept can be broken without violating this principle. Thus Christ taught His hearers that the law of God is not so many separate precepts, some of which are of great importance, while others are of small importance and may with impunity be ignored. Our Lord presents the first four and the last six commandments as a divine whole, and teaches that love to God will be shown by obedience to all His commandments.

The scribe who had questioned Jesus was well read in the law, and he was astonished at His words. He did not expect Him to manifest so deep and thorough a knowledge of the Scriptures. He had gained a broader view of the principles underlying the sacred precepts. Before the assembled priests and rulers he honestly acknowledged that Christ had given the right interpretation to the law, saying:

"Well, Master, Thou hast said the truth: for there is one God; and there is none other but He: and to love Him with all the heart, and with all the understanding, and with all the soul, and with all the strength, and to love his neighbor as himself, is more than all whole burnt offerings and sacrifices."

The wisdom of Christ's answer had convicted the scribe. He knew that the Jewish religion consisted in outward ceremonies rather than inward piety. He had some sense of the worthlessness of mere ceremonial offerings, and the faithless shedding of blood for expiation of sin. Love and obedience to God, and unselfish regard for man, appeared to him of more value than all these rites. The readiness of this man to acknowledge the correctness of Christ's reasoning, and his decided and prompt response before the people, manifested a spirit entirely different from that of the priests and rulers. The heart of Jesus went out in pity to the honest scribe who had dared to face the frowns of the priests and the threats of the rulers to speak the convictions of his heart. "And when Jesus saw that he answered discreetly, He said unto him, Thou art not far from the kingdom of God."

The scribe was near to the kingdom of God, in that he recognized deeds of righteousness as more acceptable to God than burnt offerings and sacrifices. But he needed to recognize the divine character of Christ, and through faith in Him receive power to do the works of righteousness. The ritual service was of no value, unless connected with Christ by living faith. Even the moral law fails of its purpose, unless it is understood in its relation to the Saviour. Christ had repeatedly shown that His Father's law contained something deeper than mere authoritative commands. In the law is embodied the same principle that is revealed in the gospel. The law points out man's duty and shows him his guilt. To Christ he must look for pardon and for power to do what the law enjoins.

The Pharisees had gathered close about Jesus as He answered the question of the scribe. Now turning He put a question to them: "What think ye of Christ? whose son is He?" This question was designed to test their belief concerning the Messiah,—to show whether they regarded Him simply as a man or as the Son of God. A chorus of voices answered, "The Son of David." This was the title which prophecy had given to the Messiah. When Jesus revealed His divinity by His mighty miracles, when He healed the sick and raised the dead, the people had inquired among themselves, "Is not this the Son of David?" The Syrophoenician woman, blind Bartimaeus, and many others had cried to Him for help, "Have mercy on me, O Lord, Thou Son of David." Matt. 15:22. While riding into 609 Jerusalem He had been hailed with the joyful shout, "Hosanna to the Son of David: Blessed is He that cometh in the name of the Lord." Matt. 21:9. And the little children in the temple had that day echoed the glad ascription. But many who called Jesus the Son of David did not recognize His divinity. They did not understand that the Son of David was also the Son of God.

In reply to the statement that Christ was the Son of David, Jesus said, "How then doth David in Spirit [the Spirit of Inspiration from God] call Him Lord, saying, The Lord said unto my Lord, Sit Thou on My right hand, till I make Thine enemies Thy footstool? If David then call Him Lord, how is He his son? And no man was able to answer Him a word, neither durst any man from that day forth ask Him any more questions."

67

Woes on the Pharisees

It was the last day of Christ's teaching in the temple. Of the vast throngs that were gathered at Jerusalem, the attention of all had been attracted to Him; the people had crowded the temple courts, watching the contest that had been in progress, and they eagerly caught every word that fell from His lips. Never before had such a scene been witnessed. There stood the young Galilean, bearing no earthly honor or royal badge. Surrounding Him were priests in their rich apparel, rulers with robes and badges significant of their exalted station, and scribes with scrolls in their hands, to which they made frequent reference. Jesus stood calmly before them, with the dignity of a king. As one invested with the authority of heaven, He looked unflinchingly upon His adversaries, who had rejected and despised His teachings, and who thirsted for His life. They had assailed Him in great numbers, but their schemes to ensnare and condemn Him had been in vain. Challenge after challenge He had met, presenting the pure, bright truth in contrast to the darkness and errors of the priests and Pharisees. He had set before these leaders their real condition, and the retribution sure to follow persistence in their evil deeds. The warning had been faithfully given. Yet another work remained for Christ to 611 do. Another purpose was still to be accomplished.

The interest of the people in Christ and His work had steadily increased. They were charmed with His teaching, but they were also greatly perplexed. They had respected the priests and rabbis for their intelligence and apparent piety. In all religious matters they had ever yielded implicit obedience to their authority. Yet they now saw these men trying to cast discredit upon Jesus, a teacher whose virtue and knowledge shone forth the brighter from every assault. They looked upon the lowering countenances of the priests and elders, and there saw discomfiture and confusion. They marveled that the rulers would not believe on Jesus, when His teachings were so plain and simple. They themselves knew not what course to take. With eager anxiety they watched the movements of those whose counsel they had always followed.

In the parables which Christ had spoken, it was His purpose both to warn the rulers and to instruct the people who were willing to be taught. But there was need to speak yet more plainly. Through their reverence for tradition and their blind faith in a corrupt priesthood, the people were enslaved. These chains Christ must 612

This chapter is based on Matthew 23; Mark 12:41-44; Luke 20:45-47; 21:1-4.

break. The character of the priests, rulers, and Pharisees must be more fully exposed.

"The scribes and the Pharisees," He said, "sit in Moses' seat: all therefore whatsoever they bid you observe, that observe and do; but do not ye after their works: for they say, and do not." The scribes and Pharisees claimed to be invested with divine authority similar to that of Moses. They assumed to take his place as expounders of the law and judges of the people. As such they claimed from the people the utmost deference and obedience. Jesus bade His hearers do that which the rabbis taught according to the law, but not to follow their example. They themselves did not practice their own teaching.

And they taught much that was contrary to the Scriptures. Jesus said, "They bind heavy burdens and grievous to be borne, and lay them on men's shoulders; but they themselves will not move them with one of their fingers." The Pharisees enjoined a multitude of regulations, having their foundation in tradition, and unreasonably restricting personal liberty. And certain portions of the law they so explained as to impose upon the people observances which they themselves secretly ignored, and from which, when it served their purpose, they actually claimed exemption.

To make a show of their piety was their constant aim. Nothing was held too sacred to serve this end. To Moses God had said concerning His commandments, "Thou shalt bind them for a sign upon thine hand, and they shall be as frontlets between thine eyes." Deut. 6:8. These words have a deep meaning. As the word of God is meditated upon and practiced, the whole man will be ennobled. In righteous and merciful dealing, the hands will reveal, as a signet, the principles of God's law. They will be kept clean from bribes, and from all that is corrupt and deceptive. They will be active in works of love and compassion. The eyes, directed toward a noble purpose, will be clear and true. The expressive countenance, the speaking eye, will testify to the blameless character of him who loves and honors the word of God. But by the Jews of Christ's day all this was undiscerned. The command given to Moses was construed into a direction that the precepts of Scripture should be worn upon the person. They were accordingly written upon strips of parchment, and bound in a conspicuous manner about the head and wrists. But this did not cause the law of God to take a firmer hold of the mind and heart. These parchments were worn merely as 613 badges, to attract attention. They were thought to give the wearers an air of devotion which would command the reverence of the people. Jesus struck a blow at this vain pretense:

"But all their works they do for to be seen of men: they make broad their phylacteries, and enlarge the borders of their garments, and love the uppermost rooms at feasts, and the chief seats in the synagogues, and greetings in the markets, and to be called of men, Rabbi, Rabbi. But be not ye called Rabbi: for one is your Master, even Christ; and all ye are brethren. And call no man your father upon the earth: for One is your Father, which is in heaven. Neither be ye called master: for One is your Master, even Christ." In such plain words the Saviour revealed the selfish ambition that was ever reaching for place and power, displaying a mock humility, while the heart was filled with avarice and envy. When persons were invited to a feast, the guests were seated according to their rank, and those who were given the most honorable place received the first attention and special favors. The Pharisees were ever scheming to secure these honors. This practice Jesus rebuked.

He also reproved the vanity shown in coveting the title of rabbi, or master. Such a title, He declared, belonged not to men, but to Christ. Priests, scribes, and rulers, expounders and administrators of the law, were all brethren, children of one Father. Jesus impressed upon the people that they were to give no man a title of honor indicating his control of their conscience or their faith.

If Christ were on earth today, surrounded by those who bear the title of "Reverend" or "Right Reverend," would He not repeat His saying, "Neither be ye called masters: for One is your Master, even Christ"? The Scripture declares of God, "Holy and reverend is His name." Ps. 111:9. To what human being is such a title befitting? How little does man reveal of the wisdom and righteousness it indicates! How many of those who assume this title are misrepresenting the name and character of God! Alas, how often have worldly ambition, despotism, and the basest sins been hidden under the broidered garments of a high and holy office! The Saviour continued:

"But he that is greatest among you shall be your servant. And whosoever shall exalt himself shall be abased; and he that shall humble himself shall be exalted." Again and again Christ had taught that true greatness is measured by moral worth. In the estimation of heaven, greatness of character consists in living for the welfare of our fellow men, in doing works of love 614 and mercy. Christ the King of glory was a servant to fallen man.

"Woe unto you, scribes and Pharisees, hypocrites," said Jesus; "for ye shut up the kingdom of heaven against men: for ye neither go in yourselves, neither suffer ye them that are entering to go in." By perverting the Scriptures, the priests and lawyers blinded the minds of those who would otherwise have received a knowledge of Christ's kingdom, and that inward, divine life which is essential to true holiness.

"Woe unto you, scribes and Pharisees, hypocrites! for ye devour widows' houses, and for a pretense make long prayer: therefore ye shall receive the greater damnation." The Pharisees had great influence with the people, and of this they took advantage to serve their own interests. They gained the confidence of pious widows, and then represented it as a duty for them to devote their property to religious purposes. Having secured control of their money, the wily schemers used it for their own benefit. To cover their dishonesty, they offered long prayers in public, and made a great show of piety. This hypocrisy Christ declared would bring them the greater damnation. The same rebuke falls upon many in our day who make a high profession of piety. Their lives are stained by selfishness and avarice, yet they throw over it all a garment of seeming purity, and thus for a time deceive their fellow men. But they cannot deceive God. He reads every purpose of the heart, and will judge every man according to his deeds.

Christ unsparingly condemned abuses, but He was careful not to lessen obligation. He rebuked the selfishness that extorted and misapplied the widow's gifts. At the same time He commended the widow who brought her offering for God's treasury. Man's abuse of the gift could not turn God's blessing from the giver.

Jesus was in the court where were the treasure chests, and He watched those who came to deposit their gifts. Many of the rich brought large sums, which they presented with great ostentation. Jesus looked upon them sadly, but made no comment on their liberal offerings. Presently His countenance lighted as He saw a poor widow approach hesitatingly, as though fearful of being observed. As the rich and haughty swept by, to deposit their offerings, she shrank back as if hardly daring to venture farther. And yet she longed to do something, little though it might be, for the cause she loved. She looked at the gift in her hand. It was very small in comparison with the gifts of those around her, yet it was her all. Watching her opportunity, she hurriedly threw in her two mites, and turned to hasten away. But in doing this she caught the eye of Jesus, which was fastened earnestly upon her.

The Saviour called His disciples to Him, and bade them mark the widow's poverty. Then His words of commendation fell upon her ear: "Of a truth I say unto you, that this poor widow hath cast in more than they all." Tears of joy filled her eyes as she felt that her act was understood and appreciated. Many would have advised her to keep her pittance for her own use; given into the hands of the well-fed priests, it would be lost sight of among the many costly gifts brought to the treasury. But Jesus understood her motive. She believed the service of the temple to be of God's appointment, and she was anxious to do her utmost to sustain it. She did what she could, and her act was to be a monument to her memory through all time, and her joy in eternity. Her heart went with her gift; its value was estimated, not by the worth of the coin, but by the love to God and the interest in His work that had prompted the deed.

Jesus said of the poor widow, She "hath cast in more than they all." The rich had bestowed from their abundance, many of them to be seen and honored by men. Their large donations had deprived them of no comfort, or even luxury; they had required no sacrifice, and could not be compared in value with the widow's mite.

It is the motive that gives character to our acts, stamping them with ignominy or with high moral worth. Not the great things which every eye sees and every tongue praises does God account most precious. The little duties cheerfully done, the little gifts which make no show, and which to human eyes may appear worthless, often stand highest in His sight. A heart of faith and love is dearer to God than the most costly gift. The poor widow gave her living to do the little that she did. She deprived herself of food in order to give those two mites to the cause she loved. And she did it in faith, believing that her heavenly Father would not overlook her great need. It was this unselfish spirit and childlike faith that won the Saviour's commendation.

Among the poor there are many who long to show their gratitude to God for His grace and truth. They greatly desire to share with their more prosperous brethren in sustaining His service. These souls should not be repulsed. Let them lay up their mites in the bank of heaven. If given from a heart filled with love for God, these seeming trifles become consecrated gifts, priceless offerings, which God smiles upon and blesses.

When Jesus said of the widow, She "hath cast in more than they all," His words were true, not only of the motive, but of the results of her gift. The "two mites which make a farthing" have brought to God's treasury an amount of money far greater than the contributions of those rich Jews. The influence of that little gift has been like a stream, small in its beginning, but widening and deepening as it flowed down through the ages. In a thousand ways it has contributed to the relief of the poor and the spread of the gospel. Her example of self-sacrifice has acted and reacted upon thousands of hearts in every land and in every age. It has appealed to both the rich and the poor, and her offerings have swelled the value of her gift. God's blessing upon the widow's mite has made it the source of great results. So with every gift bestowed and every act performed with a sincere desire for God's glory. It is linked with the purposes of Omnipotence. Its results for good no man can measure.

The Saviour continued His denunciations of the scribes and Pharisees: "Woe unto you, ye blind guides, which say, Whosoever shall swear by the temple, it is nothing; but whosoever shall swear by the gold of the temple, he is a debtor! Ye fools and blind: for whether is greater, the gold, or the temple that sanctifieth the gold? and, Whosoever shall swear by the altar, it is nothing; but whosoever sweareth by the gift that is upon it, he is guilty. Ye fools and blind: for whether is greater, the gift, or the altar that sanctifieth the gift?" The priests interpreted God's requirements according to their own false and narrow standard. They presumed to make nice distinctions as to the comparative guilt of various sins, passing over some lightly, and treating others of perhaps less consequence as unpardonable. For a money consideration they excused persons from their vows. And for large sums of money they sometimes passed over aggravated crimes. At the same time these priests and rulers would in other cases pronounce severe judgment for trivial offenses.

"Woe unto you, scribes and Pharisees, hypocrites! for ye pay tithe of mint and anise and cummin, and have omitted the weightier matters of the law, judgment, mercy, and faith: these ought ye to have done, and not to leave the other undone." In these words Christ again condemns the abuse of sacred obligation. The obligation itself He does not set aside. The tithing system was ordained by God, and it had been observed from the earliest times. Abraham, the father of the faithful, paid tithes of all that he possessed. The Jewish rulers recognized the obligation of tithing, and this was right; but they did not leave the people to carry out their own convictions of duty. Arbitrary rules were laid down for every case. The requirements had become so complicated that it was impossible for them to be fulfilled. None knew when their obligations were met. As God gave it, the system was just and reasonable; but the priests and rabbis had made it a wearisome burden.

All that God commands is of consequence. Christ recognized the payment of tithes as a duty; but He showed that this could not excuse the neglect of other duties. The Pharisees were very exact in tithing garden herbs, such as mint, anise, and rue; this cost them little, and it gave them a reputation for exactness and sanctity. At the same time their useless restrictions oppressed the people and destroyed respect for the sacred system of God's own appointing. They occupied men's minds with trifling distinctions, and turned their attention from essential truths. The weightier matters of the law, justice, mercy, and truth, were neglected. "These," Christ said, "ought ye to have done, and not to leave the other undone."

Other laws had been perverted by the rabbis in like manner. In the directions given through Moses it was forbidden to eat any unclean thing. The use of swine's flesh, and the flesh of certain other animals, was prohibited, as likely to fill the blood with impurities, and to shorten life. But the Pharisees did not leave these restrictions as God had given them. They went to unwarranted extremes. Among other things the people were required to strain all the water used, lest it should contain the smallest insect, which might be classed with the unclean animals. Jesus, contrasting these trivial exactions with the magnitude of their actual sins, said to the Pharisees, "Ye blind guides, which strain at a gnat, and swallow a camel."

"Woe unto you, scribes and Pharisees, hypocrites! for ye are like unto whited sepulchers, which indeed appear beautiful outward, but are within full of dead men's bones, and of all uncleanness." As the whited and beautifully decorated tomb concealed the putrefying remains within, so the outward holiness of the priests and rulers concealed iniquity. Jesus continued:

"Woe unto you, scribes and Pharisees, hypocrites! because ye build the tombs of the prophets, and garnish the sepulchers of the righteous, and say, If we had been in the days of our fathers, we would not have been partakers with them in the blood of the prophets. Wherefore ye be witnesses unto yourselves, that ye are the children of them which killed the prophets." To show their esteem for the dead prophets, the Jews were very zealous in beautifying their tombs; but they did not profit by their teachings, nor give heed to their reproofs.

In the days of Christ a superstitious regard was cherished for the resting places of the dead, and vast sums of money were lavished upon their decoration. In the sight of God this was idolatry. In their undue regard for the dead, men showed that they did not love God supremely, nor their neighbor as themselves. The same idolatry is carried to great lengths today. Many are guilty of neglecting the widow and the fatherless, the sick and the poor, in order to build expensive monuments for the dead. Time, money, and labor are freely spent for this purpose, while duties to the living—duties which Christ has plainly enjoined—are left undone.

The Pharisees built the tombs of the prophets, and adorned their sepulchers, and said one to another, If we had lived in the days of our fathers, we would not have united with them in shedding the blood of God's servants. At the same time they were planning to take the life of His Son. This should be a lesson to us. It should open our eyes to the power of Satan to deceive the mind that turns from the light of truth. Many follow in the track of the Pharisees. They revere those who have died for their faith. They wonder at the blindness of the Jews in rejecting

Christ. Had we lived in His day, they declare, we would gladly have received His teaching; we would never have been partakers in the guilt of those who rejected the Saviour. But when obedience to God requires self-denial and humiliation, these very persons stifle their convictions, and refuse obedience. Thus they manifest the same spirit as did the Pharisees whom Christ condemned.

Little did the Jews realize the terrible responsibility involved in rejecting Christ. From the time when the first innocent blood was shed, when righteous Abel fell by the hand of Cain, the same history had been repeated, with increasing guilt. In every age prophets had lifted up their voices against the sins of kings, rulers, and people, speaking the words which God gave them, and obeying His will at the peril of their lives. From generation to generation there had been heaping up a terrible punishment for the rejecters of light and truth. This the enemies of Christ were now drawing down upon their own heads. The sin of the priests and rulers was greater than that of any preceding generation. By their rejection of the Saviour, they were making themselves responsible for the blood of all the righteous men slain from Abel to Christ. They were about to fill to overflowing their cup of iniquity. And soon it was to be poured upon their heads in retributive justice. Of this, Jesus warned them:

"That upon you may come all the righteous blood shed upon the earth, from the blood of righteous Abel unto the blood of Zacharias son of Barachias, whom ye slew between the temple and the altar. Verily I say unto you, All these things shall come upon this generation."

The scribes and Pharisees who listened to Jesus knew that His words were true. They knew how the prophet Zacharias had been slain. While the words of warning from God were upon his lips, a satanic fury seized the apostate king, and at his command the prophet was put to death. His blood had imprinted itself upon the very stones of the temple court, and could not be erased; it remained to bear testimony against apostate Israel. As long as the temple should stand, there would be the stain of that righteous blood, crying to God to be avenged. As Jesus referred to these fearful sins, a thrill of horror ran through the multitude.

Looking forward, Jesus declared that the impenitence of the Jews and their intolerance of God's servants would be the same in the future as it had been in the past:

"Wherefore, behold, I send unto you prophets, and wise men, and scribes: and some of them ye shall kill and crucify; and some of them shall ye scourge in your synagogues, and persecute them from city to city." Prophets and wise men, full of faith and the Holy Ghost,— Stephen, James, and many others,—would be condemned and slain. With hand uplifted to heaven, and a divine light enshrouding His person, Christ spoke as a judge to those before Him. His voice, that had so often been heard in gentleness and entreaty, was now heard in rebuke and condemnation. The listeners shuddered. Never was the impression made by His words and His look to be effaced.

Christ's indignation was directed against the hypocrisy, the gross sins, by which men were destroying their own souls, deceiving the people and dishonoring God. In the specious deceptive reasoning of the priests and rulers He discerned the working of satanic agencies. Keen and searching had been His denunciation of sin; but He spoke no words of retaliation. He had a holy wrath against the prince of darkness; but He manifested no irritated temper. So the Christian who lives in harmony with God, possessing the sweet attributes of love and mercy, will feel a righteous indignation against sin; but he will not be roused by passion to revile those who revile him. Even in meeting those who are moved by a power from beneath to maintain falsehood, in Christ he will still preserve calmness and self-possession.

Divine pity marked the countenance of the Son of God as He cast one lingering look upon the temple and then upon His hearers. In a voice choked by deep anguish of heart and bitter tears He exclaimed, "O Jerusalem, Jerusalem, thou that killest the prophets, and stonest them which are sent unto thee, how often would I have gathered thy children together, even as a hen gathereth her chickens under her wings, and ye would not!" This is the separation struggle. In the lamentation of Christ the very heart of God is pouring itself forth. It is the mysterious farewell of the long-suffering love of the Deity.

Pharisees and Sadducees were alike silenced. Jesus summoned His disciples, and prepared to leave the temple, not as one defeated and forced from the presence of his adversaries, but as one whose work was accomplished. He retired a victor from the contest.

The gems of truth that fell from Christ's lips on that eventful day were treasured in many hearts. For them new thoughts started into life, new aspirations were awakened, and a new history began. After the crucifixion and resurrection of Christ, these persons came to the front, and fulfilled their divine commission with a wisdom and zeal corresponding to the greatness of the work. They bore a message that appealed to the hearts of men, weakening the old superstitions that had long dwarfed the lives of thousands. Before their testimony human theories and philosophies became as idle fables. Mighty were the results flowing from the words of the Saviour to that wondering, awestruck crowd in the temple at Jerusalem.

But Israel as a nation had divorced herself

from God. The natural branches of the olive tree were broken off. Looking for the last time upon the interior of the temple, Jesus said with mournful pathos, "Behold, your house is left unto you desolate. For I say unto you, Ye shall not see Me henceforth, till ye shall say, Blessed is He that cometh in the name of the Lord." Hitherto He had called the temple His Father's house; but now, as the Son of God should pass out from those walls, God's presence would be withdrawn forever from the temple built to His glory. Henceforth its ceremonies would be meaningless, its services a mockery.

68

In the Outer Court

"And there were certain Greeks among them that came up to worship at the feast: the same came therefore to Philip, which was of Bethsaida of Galilee, and desired him, saying, Sir, we would see Jesus. Philip cometh and telleth Andrew: and again Andrew and Philip tell Jesus."

At this time Christ's work bore the appearance of cruel defeat. He had been victor in the controversy with the priests and Pharisees, but it was evident that He would never be received by them as the Messiah. The final separation had come. To His disciples the case seemed hopeless. But Christ was approaching the consummation of His work. The great event which concerned not only the Jewish nation, but the whole world, was about to take place. When Christ heard the eager request, "We would see Jesus," echoing the hungering cry of the world, His countenance lighted up, and He said, "The hour is come, that the Son of man should be glorified." In the request of the Greeks He saw an earnest of the results of His great sacrifice.

These men came from the West to find the Saviour at the close of His life, as the wise men had come from the East at the beginning. At the time of Christ's birth the Jewish people were so engrossed with their own ambitious plans that they knew not of His advent. The magi from a heathen land came to the manger with their gifts, to worship the Saviour. So these Greeks, representing the nations, tribes, and peoples of the world, came to see Jesus. So the people of all lands and all ages would be drawn by the Saviour's cross. So shall many "come from the east and west, and shall sit down with Abraham, and Isaac, and Jacob, in the kingdom of heaven." Matt. 8:11.

The Greeks had heard of Christ's triumphal entry into Jerusalem. Some supposed, and had circulated the report, that He had driven the priests and rulers from the temple, and that He

was to take possession of David's throne, and reign as king of Israel. The Greeks longed to know the truth in regard to His mission. "We would see Jesus," they said. Their desire was granted. When the request was brought to Jesus, He was in that part of the temple from which all except Jews were excluded, but He went out to the Greeks in the outer court, and had a personal interview with them.

The hour of Christ's glorification had come. He was standing in the shadow of the cross, and the inquiry of the Greeks showed Him that the sacrifice He was about to make would bring many sons and daughters to God. He knew that the Greeks would soon see Him in a position they did not then dream of. They would see Him placed beside Barabbas, a robber and murderer, who would be chosen for release before the Son of God. They would hear the people, inspired by the priests and rulers, making their choice. And to the question, "What shall I do then with Jesus which is called Christ?" the answer would be given, "Let Him be crucified." Matt. 27:22. By making this propitiation for the sins of men, Christ knew that His kingdom would be perfected, and would extend throughout the world. He would work as the Restorer, and His Spirit would prevail. For a moment He looked into futurity, and heard the voices proclaiming in all parts of the earth, "Behold the Lamb of God, which taketh away the sin of the world." John 1:29. In these strangers He saw the pledge of a great harvest, when the partition wall between Jew and Gentile should be broken down, and all nations, tongues, and peoples should hear the message of salvation. The anticipation of this, the consummation of His hopes, is expressed in the words, "The hour is come, that the Son of man should be glorified." But the way in which this glorification must take place was never absent from Christ's mind. The gathering in of the Gentiles was to follow His approaching death. Only by His death could the world be saved. Like a grain of wheat, the Son of man must be cast into the ground and die, and be buried out of sight; but He was to live again.

Christ presented His future, illustrating it by the things of nature, that the disciples might understand. The true result of His mission was to be reached by His death. "Verily, verily, I say unto you," He said, "Except a corn of wheat fall into the ground and die, it abideth alone: but if it die, it bringeth forth much fruit." When the grain of wheat falls into the ground and dies, it springs up, and bears fruit. So the death of Christ would result in fruit for the kingdom of God. In accordance with the law of the vegetable kingdom, life was to be the result of His death.

Those who till the soil have the illustration ever before them. Year by year man preserves his supply of grain by apparently throwing away

720

the choicest part. For a time it must be hidden under the furrow, to be watched over by the Lord. Then appears the blade, then the ear, and then the corn in the ear. But this development cannot take place unless the grain is buried out of sight, hidden, and to all appearance, lost.

The seed buried in the ground produces fruit, and in turn this is planted. Thus the harvest is multiplied. So the death of Christ on the cross of Calvary will bear fruit unto eternal life. The contemplation of this sacrifice will be the glory of those who, as the fruit of it, will live through the eternal ages.

The grain of wheat that preserves its own life can produce no fruit. It abides alone. Christ could, if He chose, save Himself from death. But should He do this, He must abide alone. He could bring no sons and daughters to God. Only by yielding up His life could He impart life to humanity. Only by falling into the ground to die could He become the seed of that vast harvest,—the great multitude that out of every nation, and kindred, and tongue, and people, are redeemed to God.

With this truth Christ connects the lesson of self-sacrifice that all should learn: "He that loveth his life shall lose it; and he that hateth his life in this world shall keep it unto life eternal." All who would bring forth fruit as workers together with Christ must first fall into the ground and die. The life must be cast into the furrow of the world's need. Self-love, self-interest, must perish. And the law of self-sacrifice is the law of self-preservation. The husbandman preserves his grain by casting it away. So in human life. To give is to live. The life that will be preserved is the life that is freely given in 624 service to God and man. Those who for Christ's sake sacrifice their life in this world will keep it unto life eternal.

The life spent on self is like the grain that is eaten. It disappears, but there is no increase. A man may gather all he can for self; he may live and think and plan for self; but his life passes away, and he has nothing. The law of self-serving is the law of self-destruction.

"If any man serve Me," said Jesus, "let him follow Me; and where I am, there shall also My servant be: if any man serve Me, him will My Father honor." All who have borne with Jesus the cross of sacrifice will be sharers with Him of His glory. It was the joy of Christ in His humiliation and pain that His disciples should be glorified with Him. They are the fruit of His self-sacrifice. The outworking in them of His own character and spirit is His reward, and will be His joy throughout eternity. This joy they share with Him as the fruit of their labor and sacrifice is seen in other hearts and lives. They are workers together with Christ, and the Father will honor them as He honors His Son.

The message of the Greeks, foreshadowing as

it did the gathering in of the Gentiles, brought to the mind of Jesus His entire mission. The work of redemption passed before Him, from the time when in heaven the plan was laid, to the death that was now so near at hand. A mysterious cloud seemed to enshroud the Son of God. Its gloom was felt by those near Him. He sat rapt in thought. At last the silence was broken by His mournful voice, "Now is My soul troubled; and what shall I say? Father, save Me from this hour." In anticipation Christ was already drinking the cup of bitterness. His humanity shrank from the hour of abandonment, when to all appearance He would be deserted even by God, when all would see Him stricken, smitten of God, and afflicted. He shrank from public exposure, from being treated as the worst of criminals, from a shameful and dishonored death. A foreboding of His conflict with the powers of darkness, a sense of the awful burden of human transgression, and the Father's wrath because of sin caused the spirit of Jesus to faint, and the pallor of death to overspread His countenance.

Then came divine submission to His Father's will. "For this cause," He said, "came I unto this hour. Father, glorify Thy name." Only through the death of Christ could Satan's kingdom be overthrown. Only thus could man be redeemed, and God be glorified. Jesus consented to the agony, He accepted the sacrifice. The Majesty of heaven consented to suffer as the Sin Bearer. "Father, glorify Thy name," He said. As Christ 625 spoke these words, a response came from the cloud which hovered above His head: "I have both glorified it, and will glorify it again." Christ's whole life, from the manger to the time when these words were spoken, had glorified God; and in the coming trial His divine-human sufferings would indeed glorify His Father's name.

As the voice was heard, a light darted from the cloud, and encircled Christ, as if the arms of Infinite Power were thrown about Him like a wall of fire. The people beheld this scene with terror and amazement. No one dared to speak. With silent lips and bated breath all stood with eyes fixed upon Jesus. The testimony of the Father having been given, the cloud lifted, and scattered in the heavens. For the time the visible communion between the Father and the Son was ended.

"The people therefore, that stood by, and heard it, said that it thundered: others said, An angel spake to Him." But the inquiring Greeks saw the cloud, heard the voice, comprehended its meaning, and discerned Christ indeed; to them He was revealed as the Sent of God.

The voice of God had been heard at the baptism of Jesus at the beginning of His ministry, and again at His transfiguration on the mount. Now at the close of His ministry it was heard for the third time, by a larger number of persons, and under peculiar circumstances. Jesus had just spoken the most solemn truth regarding the condition of the Jews. He had made His last appeal, and pronounced their doom. Now God again set His seal to the mission of His Son. He recognized the One whom Israel had rejected. "This voice came not because of Me," said Jesus, "but for your sakes." It was the crowning evidence of His Messiahship, the signal from the Father that Jesus had spoken the truth, and was the Son of God.

"Now is the judgment of this world," Christ continued; "now shall the prince of this world be cast out. And I, if I be lifted up from the earth, will draw all men unto Me. This He said, signifying what death He should die." This is the crisis of the world. If I become the propitiation for the sins of men, the world will be lighted up. Satan's hold upon the souls of men will be broken. The defaced image of God will be restored in humanity, and a family of believing saints will finally inherit the heavenly home. This is the result of Christ's death. The Saviour is lost in contemplation of the scene of triumph called up before Him. He sees the cross, the cruel, ignominious cross, with all its attending horrors, blazing with glory.

626 But the work of human redemption is not all that is accomplished by the cross. The love of God is manifested to the universe. The prince of this world is cast out. The accusations which Satan has brought against God are refuted. The reproach which he has cast upon heaven is forever removed. Angels as well as men are drawn to the Redeemer. "I, if I be lifted up from the earth," He said, "will draw all men unto Me."

Many people were round about Christ as He spoke these words, and one said, "We have heard out of the law that Christ abideth forever: and how sayest Thou, The Son of man must be lifted up? who is this Son of man? Then Jesus said unto them, Yet a little while is the light with you. Walk while ye have the light, lest darkness come upon you: for he that walketh in darkness knoweth not whither he goeth. While ye have light, believe in the light, that ye may be the children of light."

"But though He had done so many miracles before them, yet they believed not on Him." They had once asked the Saviour, "What sign showest Thou then, that we may see, and believe Thee?" John 6:30. Innumerable signs had been given; but they had closed their eyes and hardened their hearts. Now that the Father Himself had spoken, and they could ask for no further sign, they still refused to believe.

"Nevertheless among the chief rulers also many believed on Him; but because of the Pharisees they did not confess Him, lest they should be put out of the synagogue." They loved the praise of men rather than the approval of God. To save themselves from reproach and shame,

they denied Christ, and rejected the offer of eternal life. And how many through all the centuries since have been doing the same thing! To them all the Saviour's warning words apply: "He that loveth his life shall lose it." "He that rejecteth Me," said Jesus, "and receiveth not My words, hath one that judgeth him: the word that I have spoken, the same shall judge him in the last day." John 12:48.

Alas for those who knew not the time of their visitation! Slowly and regretfully Christ left forever the precincts of the temple.

69   627

On the Mount of Olives

Christ's words to the priests and rulers, "Behold, your house is left unto you desolate" (Matt. 23:38), had struck terror to their hearts. They affected indifference, but the question kept rising in their minds as to the import of these words. An unseen danger seemed to threaten them. Could it be that the magnificent temple, which was the nation's glory, was soon to be a heap of ruins? The foreboding of evil was shared by the disciples, and they anxiously waited for some more definite statement from Jesus. As they passed with Him out of the temple, they called His attention to its strength and beauty. The stones of the temple were of the purest marble, of perfect whiteness, and some of them of almost fabulous size. A portion of the wall had withstood the siege by Nebuchadnezzar's army. In its perfect masonry it appeared like one solid stone dug entire from the quarry. How those mighty walls could be overthrown the disciples could not comprehend.

As Christ's attention was attracted to the magnificence of the temple, what must have been the unuttered thoughts of that Rejected One! The view before Him was indeed beautiful, but He said with sadness, I see it all. The buildings are indeed wonderful. You point to these walls as apparently indestructible; but listen to My words: The day will come when "there shall not be left one stone upon another, that shall not be thrown down."

Christ's words had been spoken in the hearing of a large number of people; but when He was alone, Peter, John, James, and Andrew came to Him as He sat upon the Mount of Olives. "Tell us," they said, "when shall these things be? and what shall be the sign of Thy coming, and of the end of the world?" Jesus did not answer His disciples by taking up separately the destruction of Jerusalem and the great day of His coming. He mingled the description of these two events. Had He opened to His disciples future events as He beheld them, they would 628

This chapter is based on Matthew 24; Mark 13; Luke 21:5-38.

have been unable to endure the sight. In mercy to them He blended the description of the two great crises, leaving the disciples to study out the meaning for themselves. When He referred to the destruction of Jerusalem, His prophetic words reached beyond that event to the final conflagration in that day when the Lord shall rise out of His place to punish the world for their iniquity, when the earth shall disclose her blood, and shall no more cover her slain. This entire discourse was given, not for the disciples only, but for those who should live in the last scenes of this earth's history.

Turning to the disciples, Christ said, "Take heed that no man deceive you. For many shall come in My name, saying, I am Christ; and shall deceive many." Many false messiahs will appear, claiming to work miracles, and declaring that the time of the deliverance of the Jewish nation has come. These will mislead many. Christ's words were fulfilled. Between His death and the siege of Jerusalem many false messiahs appeared. But this warning was given also to those who live in this age of the world. The same deceptions practiced prior to the destruction of Jerusalem have been practiced through the ages, and will be practiced again.

"And ye shall hear of wars and rumors of wars: see that ye be not troubled: for all these things must come to pass, but the end is not yet." Prior to the destruction of Jerusalem, men wrestled for the supremacy. Emperors were murdered. Those supposed to be standing next the throne were slain. There were wars and rumors of wars. "All these things must come to pass," said Christ, "but the end [of the Jewish nation as a nation] is not yet. For nation shall rise against nation, and kingdom against kingdom: and there shall be famines, and pestilences, and earthquakes, in divers places. All these are the beginning of sorrows." Christ said, As the rabbis see these signs, they will declare them to be God's judgments upon the nations for holding in bondage His chosen people. They will declare that these signs are the token of the 629 advent of the Messiah. Be not deceived; they are the beginning of His judgments. The people have looked to themselves. They have not repented and been converted that I should heal them. The signs that they represent as tokens of their release from bondage are signs of their destruction.

"Then shall they deliver you up to be afflicted, and shall kill you: and ye shall be hated of all nations for My name's sake. And then shall many be offended, and shall betray one another, and shall hate one another." All this the Christians suffered. Fathers and mothers betrayed their children. Children betrayed their parents. Friends delivered their friends up to the Sanhedrin. The persecutors wrought out their purpose by killing Stephen, James, and other Christians.

Through His servants, God gave the Jewish 630 people a last opportunity to repent. He manifested Himself through His witnesses in their arrest, in their trial, and in their imprisonment. Yet their judges pronounced on them the death sentence. They were men of whom the world was not worthy, and by killing them the Jews crucified afresh the Son of God. So it will be again. The authorities will make laws to restrict religious liberty. They will assume the right that is God's alone. They will think they can force the conscience, which God alone should control. Even now they are making a beginning; this work they will continue to carry forward till they reach a boundary over which they cannot step. God will interpose in behalf of His loyal, commandment-keeping people.

On every occasion when persecution takes place, those who witness it make decisions either for Christ or against Him. Those who manifest sympathy for the ones wrongly condemned show their attachment for Christ. Others are offended because the principles of truth cut directly across their practice. Many stumble and fall, apostatizing from the faith they once advocated. Those who apostatize in time of trial will, to secure their own safety, bear false witness, and betray their brethren. Christ has warned us of this, that we may not be surprised at the unnatural, cruel course of those who reject the light.

Christ gave His disciples a sign of the ruin to come on Jerusalem, and He told them how to escape: "When ye shall see Jerusalem compassed with armies, then know that the desolation thereof is nigh. Then let them which are in Judea flee to the mountains; and let them which are in the midst of it depart out; and let not them that are in the countries enter thereinto. For these be the days of vengeance, that all things which are written may be fulfilled." This warning was given to be heeded forty years after, at the destruction of Jerusalem. The Christians obeyed the warning, and not a Christian perished in the fall of the city.

"Pray ye that your flight be not in the winter, neither on the Sabbath day," Christ said. He who made the Sabbath did not abolish it, nailing it to His cross. The Sabbath was not rendered null and void by His death. Forty years after His crucifixion it was still to be held sacred. For forty years the disciples were to pray that their flight might not be on the Sabbath day.

From the destruction of Jerusalem, Christ passed on rapidly to the greater event, the last link in the chain of this earth's history,—the coming of the Son of God in majesty and glory. Between these two events, there lay open to Christ's view long centuries of darkness, centuries for His church marked with blood and 631 tears and agony. Upon these scenes His disciples could not then endure to look, and Jesus passed them by with a brief mention. "Then shall be great tribulation," He said, "such as was not since the beginning of the world to this time, no, nor ever shall be. And except those days should be shortened, there should no flesh be saved: but for the elect's sake those days shall be shortened." For more than a thousand years such persecution as the world had never before known was to come upon Christ's followers. Millions upon millions of His faithful witnesses were to be slain. Had not God's hand been stretched out to preserve His people, all would have perished. "But for the elect's sake," He said, "those days shall be shortened."

Now, in unmistakable language, our Lord speaks of His second coming, and He gives warning of dangers to precede His advent to the world. "If any man shall say unto you, Lo, here is Christ, or there; believe it not. For there shall arise false christs, and false prophets, and shall show great signs and wonders; insomuch that, if it were possible, they shall deceive the very elect. Behold, I have told you before. Wherefore if they shall say unto you, Behold, He is in the desert; go not forth: behold, He is in the secret chambers; believe it not. For as the lightning cometh out of the east, and shineth even unto the west; so shall also the coming of the Son of man be." As one of the signs of Jerusalem's destruction, Christ had said, "Many false prophets shall rise, and shall deceive many." False prophets did rise, deceiving the people, and leading great numbers into the desert. Magicians and sorcerers, claiming miraculous power, drew the people after them into the mountain solitudes. But this prophecy was spoken also for the last days. This sign is given as a sign of the second advent. Even now false christs and false prophets are showing signs and wonders to seduce His disciples. Do we not hear the cry, "Behold, He is in the desert"? Have not thousands gone forth into the desert, hoping to find Christ? And from thousands of gatherings where men profess to hold communion with departed spirits is not the call now heard, "Behold, He is in the secret chambers"? This is the very claim that spiritism puts forth. But what says Christ? "Believe it not. For as the lightning cometh out of the east, and shineth even unto the west; so shall also the coming of the Son of man be."

The Saviour gives signs of His coming, and more than this, He fixes the time when the first of these signs shall appear: "Immediately after the tribulation of those days shall the sun be darkened, and the moon shall not give her light, and the stars shall fall from heaven, and the powers of the heavens shall be shaken: and then shall appear the sign of the Son of man in heaven: and then shall all the tribes of the earth mourn, and they shall see the Son of man com-

ing in the clouds of heaven with power and great glory. And He shall send His angels with a great sound of a trumpet, and they shall gather together His elect from the four winds, from one end of heaven to the other."

At the close of the great papal persecution, Christ declared, the sun should be darkened, and the moon should not give her light. Next, the stars should fall from heaven. And He says, "Learn a parable of the fig tree; When his branch is yet tender, and putteth forth leaves, ye know that summer is nigh: so likewise ye, when ye shall see all these things, know that He is near, even at the doors." Matt. 24:32, 33, margin.

Christ has given signs of His coming. He declares that we may know when He is near, even at the doors. He says of those who see these signs, "This generation shall not pass, till all these things be fulfilled." These signs have appeared. Now we know of a surety that the Lord's coming is at hand. "Heaven and earth shall pass away," He says, "but My words shall not pass away."

Christ is coming with clouds and with great glory. A multitude of shining angels will attend Him. He will come to raise the dead, and to change the living saints from glory to glory. He will come to honor those who have loved Him, and kept His commandments, and to take them to Himself. He has not forgotten them nor His promise. There will be a relinking of the family chain. When we look upon our dead, we may think of the morning when the trump of God shall sound, when "the dead shall be raised incorruptible, and we shall be changed." 1 Cor. 15:52. A little longer, and we shall see the King in His beauty. A little longer, and He will wipe all tears from our eyes. A little longer, and He will present us "faultless before the presence of His glory with exceeding joy." Jude 24. Wherefore, when He gave the signs of His coming He said, "When these things begin to come to pass, then look up, and lift up your heads; for your redemption draweth nigh."

But the day and the hour of His coming Christ has not revealed. He stated plainly to His disciples that He Himself could not make known the day or the hour of His second appearing. Had He been at liberty to reveal this, why need He have exhorted them to maintain an attitude of constant expectancy? There are those who claim to know the very day and hour of our Lord's appearing. Very earnest are they in mapping out the future. But the Lord has warned them off the ground they occupy. The exact time of the second coming of the Son of man is God's mystery.

Christ continues, pointing out the condition of the world at His coming: "As the days of Noah were, so shall also the coming of the Son of man be. For as in the days that were before the

632

633

Flood they were eating and drinking, marrying and giving in marriage, until the day that Noah entered into the ark, and knew not until the Flood came, and took them all away; so shall also the coming of the Son of man be." Christ does not here bring to view a temporal millennium, a thousand years in which all are to prepare for eternity. He tells us that as it was in Noah's day, so will it be when the Son of man comes again.

How was it in Noah's day? "God saw that the wickedness of man was great in the earth, and that every imagination of the thoughts of his heart was only evil continually." Gen. 6:5. The inhabitants of the antediluvian world turned from Jehovah, refusing to do His holy will. They followed their own unholy imagination and perverted ideas. It was because of their wickedness that they were destroyed; and today the world is following the same way. It presents no flattering signs of millennial glory. The transgressors of God's law are filling the earth with wickedness. Their betting, their horse racing, their gambling, their dissipation, their lustful practices, their untamable passions, are fast filling the world with violence.

In the prophecy of Jerusalem's destruction Christ said, "Because iniquity shall abound, the love of many shall wax cold. But he that shall endure unto the end, the same shall be saved. And this gospel of the kingdom shall be preached in all the world for a witness unto all nations; and then shall the end come." This prophecy will again be fulfilled. The abounding iniquity of that day finds its counterpart in this generation. So with the prediction in regard to the preaching of the gospel. Before the fall of Jerusalem, Paul, writing by the Holy Spirit, declared that the gospel was preached to "every creature which is under heaven." Col. 1:23. So now, before the coming of the Son of man, the everlasting gospel is to be preached "to every nation, and kindred, and tongue, and people." Rev. 14:6, 14. God "hath appointed a day, in the which He will judge the world." Acts 17:31. Christ tells us when that day shall be ushered in. He does not say that all the world will be converted, but that "this gospel of the kingdom shall be preached in all the world for a witness unto all nations; and then shall the end come." By giving the gospel to the world it is in our power to hasten our Lord's return. We are not only to look for but to hasten the coming of the day of God. 2 Peter 3:12, margin. Had the church of Christ done her appointed work as the Lord ordained, the whole world would before this have been warned, and the Lord Jesus would have come to our earth in power and great glory.

After He had given the signs of His coming, Christ said, "When ye see these things come to pass, know ye that the kingdom of God is nigh at hand." "Take ye heed, watch and pray." God has always given men warning of coming judgments. Those who had faith in His message for their time, and who acted out their faith, in obedience to His commandments, escaped the judgments that fell upon the disobedient and unbelieving. The word came to Noah, "Come thou and all thy house into the ark; for thee have I seen righteous before Me." Noah obeyed and was saved. The message came to Lot, "Up, get you out of this place; for the Lord will destroy this city." Gen. 7:1; 19:14. Lot placed himself under the guardianship of the heavenly messengers, and was saved. So Christ's disciples were given warning of the destruction of Jerusalem. Those who watched for the sign of the coming ruin, and fled from the city, escaped the destruction. So now we are given warning of Christ's second coming and of the destruction to fall upon the world. Those who heed the warning will be saved.

Because we know not the exact time of His coming, we are commanded to watch. "Blessed are those servants, whom the Lord when He cometh shall find watching." Luke 12:37. Those who watch for the Lord's coming are not waiting in idle expectancy. The expectation of Christ's coming is to make men fear the Lord, and fear His judgments upon transgression. It is to awaken them to the great sin of rejecting His offers of mercy. Those who are watching for the Lord are purifying their souls by obedience to the truth. With vigilant watching they combine earnest working. Because they know that the Lord is at the door, their zeal is quickened to cooperate with the divine intelligences in working for the salvation of souls. These are the faithful and wise servants who give to the Lord's household "their portion of meat in due season." Luke 12:42. They are declaring the truth that is now specially applicable. As Enoch, Noah, Abraham, and Moses each declared the truth for his time, so will Christ's servants now give the special warning for their generation.

But Christ brings to view another class: "If that evil servant shall say in his heart, My lord delayeth his coming; and shall begin to smite his fellow servants, and to eat and drink with the drunken; the lord of that servant shall come in a day when he looketh not for him."

The evil servant says in his heart, "My lord delayeth his coming." He does not say that Christ will not come. He does not scoff at the idea of His second coming. But in his heart and by his actions and words he declares that the Lord's coming is delayed. He banishes from the minds of others the conviction that the Lord is coming quickly. His influence leads men to presumptuous, careless delay. They are confirmed in their worldliness and stupor. Earthly passions, corrupt thoughts, take possession of the mind. The evil servant eats and drinks with the drunken, unites with the world in pleasure seeking. He smites his fellow servants, accusing and condemning those who are faithful to their Master. He mingles with the world. Like grows with like in transgression. It is a fearful assimilation. With the world he is taken in the snare. "The lord of that servant shall come . . . in an hour that he is not aware of, and shall cut him asunder, and appoint him his portion with the hypocrites."

"If therefore thou shalt not watch, I will come on thee as a thief, and thou shalt not know what hour I will come upon thee." Rev. 3:3. The advent of Christ will surprise the false teachers. They are saying, "Peace and safety." Like the priests and teachers before the fall of Jerusalem, they look for the church to enjoy earthly prosperity and glory. The signs of the times they interpret as foreshadowing this. But what saith the word of Inspiration? "Sudden destruction cometh upon them." 1 Thess. 5:3. Upon all who dwell on the face of the whole earth, upon all who make this world their home, the day of God will come as a snare. It comes to them as a prowling thief.

The world, full of rioting, full of godless pleasure, is asleep, asleep in carnal security. Men are putting afar off the coming of the Lord. They laugh at warnings. The proud boast is made, "All things continue as they were from the beginning." "Tomorrow shall be as this day, and much more abundant." 2 Peter 3:4; Isa. 56:12. We will go deeper into pleasure loving. But Christ says, "Behold, I come as a thief." Rev. 16:15. At the very time when the world is asking in scorn, "Where is the promise of His coming?" the signs are fulfilling. While they cry, "Peace and safety," sudden destruction is coming. When the scorner, the rejecter of truth, has become presumptuous; when the routine of work in the various money-making lines is carried on without regard to principle; when the student is eagerly seeking knowledge of everything but his Bible, Christ comes as a thief.

Everything in the world is in agitation. The signs of the times are ominous. Coming events cast their shadows before. The Spirit of God is withdrawing from the earth, and calamity follows calamity by sea and by land. There are tempests, earthquakes, fires, floods, murders of every grade. Who can read the future? Where is security? There is assurance in nothing that is human or earthly. Rapidly are men ranging themselves under the banner they have chosen. Restlessly are they waiting and watching the movements of their leaders. There are those who are waiting and watching and working for our Lord's appearing. Another class are falling into line under the generalship of the first great apostate. Few believe with heart and soul that we have a hell to shun and a heaven to win.

The crisis is stealing gradually upon us. The sun shines in the heavens, passing over its usual round, and the heavens still declare the glory of God. Men are still eating and drinking, planting and building, marrying, and giving in marriage. Merchants are still buying and selling. Men are jostling one against another, contending for the highest place. Pleasure lovers are still crowding to theaters, horse races, gambling hells. The highest excitement prevails, yet probation's hour is fast closing, and every case is about to be eternally decided. Satan sees that his time is short. He has set all his agencies at work that men may be deceived, deluded, occupied and entranced, until the day of probation shall be ended, and the door of mercy be forever shut.

Solemnly there come to us down through the centuries the warning words of our Lord from the Mount of Olives: "Take heed to yourselves, lest at any time your hearts be overcharged with surfeiting, and drunkenness, and cares of this life, and so that day come upon you unawares." "Watch ye therefore, and pray always, that ye may be accounted worthy to escape all these things that shall come to pass, and to stand before the Son of man."

70

"The Least of These My Brethren"

"When the Son of man shall come in His glory, and all the holy angels with Him, then shall He sit upon the throne of His glory: and before Him shall be gathered all nations: and He shall separate them one from another." Thus Christ on the Mount of Olives pictured to His disciples the scene of the great judgment day. And He represented its decision as turning upon one point. When the nations are gathered before Him, there will be but two classes, and their eternal destiny will be determined by what they have done or have neglected to do for Him in the person of the poor and the suffering.

In that day Christ does not present before men the great work He has done for them in giving His life for their redemption. He presents the faithful work they have done for Him. To those whom He sets upon His right hand He will say, "Come, ye blessed of My Father, inherit the kingdom prepared for you from the foundation of the world: for I was an hungered, and ye gave Me meat: I was thirsty, and ye gave Me drink: I was a stranger, and ye took Me in: naked, and ye clothed Me: I was sick, and ye visited Me: I was in prison, and ye came unto Me." But those whom Christ commends know not that they have been ministering unto Him. To their perplexed inquiries He answers, "Inas-

This chapter is based on Matthew 25:31-46.

much as ye have done it unto one of the least of these My brethren, ye have done it unto Me."

Jesus had told His disciples that they were to be hated of all men, to be persecuted and afflicted. Many would be driven from their homes, and brought to poverty. Many would be in distress through disease and privation. Many would be cast into prison. To all who forsook friends or home for His sake He had promised in this life a hundredfold. Now He assured a special blessing to all who should minister to their brethren. In all who suffer for My name, said Jesus, you are to recognize Me. As you would minister to Me, so you are to minister to them. This is the evidence that you are My disciples.

All who have been born into the heavenly family are in a special sense the brethren of our Lord. The love of Christ binds together the members of His family, and wherever that love is made manifest there the divine relationship is revealed. "Everyone that loveth is born of God, and knoweth God." 1 John 4:7.

Those whom Christ commends in the judgment may have known little of theology, but they have cherished His principles. Through the influence of the divine Spirit they have been a blessing to those about them. Even among the heathen are those who have cherished the spirit of kindness; before the words of life had fallen upon their ears, they have befriended the missionaries, even ministering to them at the peril of their own lives. Among the heathen are those who worship God ignorantly, those to whom the light is never brought by human instrumentality, yet they will not perish. Though ignorant of the written law of God, they have heard His voice speaking to them in nature, and have done the things that the law required. Their works are evidence that the Holy Spirit has touched their hearts, and they are recognized as the children of God.

How surprised and gladdened will be the lowly among the nations, and among the heathen, to hear from the lips of the Saviour, "Inasmuch as ye have done it unto one of the least of these My brethren, ye have done it unto Me"! How glad will be the heart of Infinite Love as His followers look up with surprise and joy at His words of approval!

But not to any class is Christ's love restricted. He identifies Himself with every child of humanity. That we might become members of the heavenly family, He became a member of the earthly family. He is the Son of man, and thus a brother to every son and daughter of Adam. His followers are not to feel themselves detached from the perishing world around them. They are a part of the great web of humanity; and Heaven looks upon them as brothers to sinners as well as to saints. The fallen, the erring, and the sinful, Christ's love embraces; and every deed of kindness done to uplift a fallen soul, every act of mercy, is accepted as done to Him.

The angels of heaven are sent forth to minister to those who shall be heirs of salvation. We know not now who they are; it is not yet made manifest who shall overcome, and share the inheritance of the saints in light; but angels of heaven are passing throughout the length and breadth of the earth, seeking to comfort the sorrowing, to protect the imperiled, to win the hearts of men to Christ. Not one is neglected or passed by. God is no respecter of persons, and He has an equal care for all the souls He has created.

As you open your door to Christ's needy and suffering ones, you are welcoming unseen angels. You invite the companionship of heavenly beings. They bring a sacred atmosphere of joy and peace. They come with praises upon their lips, and an answering strain is heard in heaven. Every deed of mercy makes music there. The Father from His throne numbers the unselfish workers among His most precious treasures.

Those on the left hand of Christ, those who had neglected Him in the person of the poor and the suffering, were unconscious of their guilt. Satan had blinded them; they had not perceived what they owed to their brethren. They had been self-absorbed, and cared not for others' needs.

To the rich, God has given wealth that they may relieve and comfort His suffering children; but too often they are indifferent to the wants of others. They feel themselves superior to their poor brethren. They do not put themselves in the poor man's place. They do not understand the temptations and struggles of the poor, and mercy dies out of their hearts. In costly dwellings and splendid churches, the rich shut themselves away from the poor; the means that God has given to bless the needy is spent in pampering pride and selfishness. The poor are robbed daily of the education they should have concerning the tender mercies of God; for He has made ample provision that they should be comforted with the necessities of life. They are compelled to feel the poverty that narrows life, and are often tempted to become envious, jealous, and full of evil surmisings. Those who themselves have not endured the pressure of want too often treat the poor in a contemptuous way, and make them feel that they are looked upon as paupers.

But Christ beholds it all, and He says, It was I who was hungry and thirsty. It was I who was a stranger. It was I who was sick. It was I who was in prison. While you were feasting at your bountifully spread table, I was famishing in the hovel or the empty street. While you were at ease in your luxurious home, I had not where to lay My head. While you crowded your wardrobe with rich apparel, I was destitute.

While you pursued your pleasures, I languished in prison.

When you doled out the pittance of bread to the starving poor, when you gave those flimsy garments to shield them from the biting frost, did you remember that you were giving to the Lord of glory? All the days of your life I was near you in the person of these afflicted ones, but you did not seek Me. You would not enter into fellowship with Me. I know you not.

Many feel that it would be a great privilege to visit the scenes of Christ's life on earth, to walk where He trod, to look upon the lake beside which He loved to teach, and the hills and valleys on which His eyes so often rested. But we need not go to Nazareth, to Capernaum, or to Bethany, in order to walk in the steps of Jesus. We shall find His footprints beside the sickbed, in the hovels of poverty, in the crowded alleys of the great city, and in every place where there are human hearts in need of consolation. In doing as Jesus did when on earth, we shall walk in His steps.

All may find something to do. "The poor always ye have with you" (John 12:8), Jesus said, and none need feel that there is no place where they can labor for Him. Millions upon millions of human souls ready to perish, bound in chains of ignorance and sin, have never so much as heard of Christ's love for them. Were our condition and theirs to be reversed, what would we desire them to do for us? All this, so far as lies in our power, we are under the most solemn obligation to do for them. Christ's rule of life, by which every one of us must stand or fall in the judgment, is, "Whatsoever ye would that men should do to you, do ye even so to them." Matt. 7:12.

The Saviour has given His precious life in order to establish a church capable of caring for sorrowful, tempted souls. A company of believers may be poor, uneducated, and unknown; yet in Christ they may do a work in the home, the neighborhood, the church, and even in "the regions beyond," whose results shall be as far-reaching as eternity.

It is because this work is neglected that so many young disciples never advance beyond the mere alphabet of Christian experience. The light which was glowing in their own hearts when Jesus spoke to them, "Thy sins are forgiven thee," they might have kept alive by helping those in need. The restless energy that is so often a source of danger to the young might be directed into channels through which it would flow out in streams of blessing. Self would be forgotten in earnest work to do others good.

Those who minister to others will be ministered unto by the Chief Shepherd. They themselves will drink of the living water, and will be satisfied. They will not be longing for exciting amusements, or for some change in their lives. The great topic of interest will be, how to save the souls that are ready to perish. Social intercourse will be profitable. The love of the Redeemer will draw hearts together in unity.

When we realize that we are workers together with God, His promises will not be spoken with indifference. They will burn in our hearts, and kindle upon our lips. To Moses, when called to minister to an ignorant, undisciplined, and rebellious people, God gave the promise, "My presence shall go with thee, and I will give thee rest." And He said, "Certainly I will be with thee." Ex. 33:14; 3:12. This promise is to all who labor in Christ's stead for His afflicted and suffering ones.

Love to man is the earthward manifestation of the love of God. It was to implant this love, to make us children of one family, that the King of glory became one with us. And when His parting words are fulfilled, "Love one another, as I have loved you" (John 15:12); when we love the world as He has loved it, then for us His mission is accomplished. We are fitted for heaven; for we have heaven in our hearts.

But "if thou forbear to deliver them that are drawn unto death, and those that are ready to be slain; if thou sayest, Behold, we knew it not; doth not He that pondereth the heart consider it? and He that keepeth thy soul, doth not He know it? and shall not He render to every man according to his works?" Prov. 24:11, 12. In the great judgment day, those who have not worked for Christ, who have drifted along thinking of themselves, caring for themselves, will be placed by the Judge of the whole earth with those who did evil. They receive the same condemnation.

To every soul a trust is given. Of everyone the Chief Shepherd will demand, "Where is the flock that was given thee, thy beautiful flock?" And "what wilt thou say when He shall punish thee?" Jer. 13:20, 21.

71

642

A Servant of Servants

In the upper chamber of a dwelling at Jerusalem, Christ was sitting at table with His disciples. They had gathered to celebrate the Passover. The Saviour desired to keep this feast alone with the twelve. He knew that His hour was come; He Himself was the true paschal lamb, and on the day the Passover was eaten He was to be sacrificed. He was about to drink the cup of wrath; He must soon receive the final baptism of suffering. But a few quiet hours yet remained to Him, and these were to be spent for the benefit of His beloved disciples.

The whole life of Christ had been a life of unselfish service. "Not to be ministered unto, but to minister" (Matt. 20:28), had been the les-

641

This chapter is based on Luke 22:7-18, 24; John 13:1-17.

728

son of His every act. But not yet had the disciples learned the lesson. At this last Passover supper, Jesus repeated His teaching by an illustration that impressed it forever on their minds and hearts.

The interviews between Jesus and His disciples were usually seasons of calm joy, highly prized by them all. The Passover suppers had been scenes of special interest; but upon this occasion Jesus was troubled. His heart was burdened, and a shadow rested upon His countenance. As He met the disciples in the upper chamber, they perceived that something weighed heavily upon His mind, and although they knew not its cause, they sympathized with His grief.

As they were gathered about the table, He said in tones of touching sadness, "With desire I have desired to eat this Passover with you before I suffer: for I say unto you, I will not any more eat thereof, until it be fulfilled in the kingdom of God. And He took the cup, and gave thanks, and said, Take this, and divide it among yourselves: for I say unto you, I will not drink of the fruit of the vine, until the kingdom of God shall come."

Christ knew that the time had come for Him to depart out of the world, and go to His Father. And having loved His own that were in the world, He loved them unto the end. He was now in the shadow of the cross, and the pain was torturing His heart. He knew that He would be deserted in the hour of His betrayal. He knew that by the most humiliating process to which criminals were subjected He would be put to death. He knew the ingratitude and cruelty of those He had come to save. He knew how great the sacrifice that He must make, and for how many it would be in vain. Knowing all that was before Him, He might naturally have been overwhelmed with the thought of His own humiliation and suffering. But He looked upon the twelve, who had been with Him as His own, and who, after His shame and sorrow and painful usage were over, would be left to struggle in the world. His thoughts of what He Himself must suffer were ever connected with His disciples. He did not think of Himself. His care for them was uppermost in His mind.

On this last evening with His disciples, Jesus had much to tell them. If they had been prepared to receive what He longed to impart, they would have been saved from heartbreaking anguish, from disappointment and unbelief. But Jesus saw that they could not bear what He had to say. As He looked into their faces, the words of warning and comfort were stayed upon His lips. Moments passed in silence. Jesus appeared to be waiting. The disciples were ill at ease. The sympathy and tenderness awakened by Christ's grief seemed to have passed away. His sorrowful words, pointing to His own suffering, had made little impression. The glances they cast upon each other told of jealousy and contention.

There was "a strife among them, which of them should be accounted the greatest." This contention, carried on in the presence of Christ, grieved and wounded Him. The disciples clung to their favorite idea that Christ would assert His power, and take His position on the throne of David. And in heart each still longed for the highest place in the kingdom. They had placed their own estimate upon themselves and upon one another, and, instead of regarding their brethren as more worthy, they had placed themselves first. The request of James and John to sit on the right and left of Christ's throne had excited the indignation of the others. That the two brothers should presume to ask for the highest position so stirred the ten that alienation threatened. They felt that they were misjudged, that their fidelity and talents were not appreciated. Judas was the most severe upon James and John.

When the disciples entered the supper room, their hearts were full of resentful feelings. Judas pressed next to Christ on the left side; John was on the right. If there was a highest place, Judas was determined to have it, and that place was thought to be next to Christ. And Judas was a traitor.

Another cause of dissension had arisen. At a feast it was customary for a servant to wash the feet of the guests, and on this occasion preparation had been made for the service. The pitcher, the basin, and the towel were there, in readiness for the feet washing; but no servant was present, and it was the disciples' part to perform it. But each of the disciples, yielding to wounded pride, determined not to act the part of a servant. All manifested a stoical unconcern, seeming unconscious that there was anything for them to do. By their silence they refused to humble themselves.

How was Christ to bring these poor souls where Satan would not gain over them a decided victory? How could He show that a mere profession of discipleship did not make them disciples, or insure them a place in His kingdom? How could He show that it is loving service, true humility, which constitutes real greatness? How was He to kindle love in their hearts, and enable them to comprehend what He longed to tell them?

The disciples made no move toward serving one another. Jesus waited for a time to see what they would do. Then He, the divine Teacher, rose from the table. Laying aside the outer garment that would have impeded His movements, He took a towel, and girded Himself. With surprised interest the disciples looked on, and in silence waited to see what was to follow. "After that He poureth water into a basin, and began to wash the disciples' feet, and to wipe them with the towel wherewith He was girded." This action opened the eyes of the disciples. Bitter shame and humiliation filled their hearts. They understood the unspoken rebuke, and saw themselves in altogether a new light.

So Christ expressed His love for His disciples. Their selfish spirit filled Him with sorrow, but He entered into no controversy with them regarding their difficulty. Instead He gave them an example they would never forget. His love for them was not easily disturbed or quenched. He knew that the Father had given all things into His hands, and that He came from God, and went to God. He had a full consciousness of His divinity; but He had laid aside His royal crown and kingly robes, and had taken the form of a servant. One of the last acts of His life on earth was to gird Himself as a servant, and perform a servant's part.

Before the Passover Judas had met a second time with the priests and scribes, and had closed the contract to deliver Jesus into their hands. Yet he afterward mingled with the disciples as though innocent of any wrong, and interested in the work of preparing for the feast. The disciples knew nothing of the purpose of Judas. Jesus alone could read his secret. Yet He did not expose him. Jesus hungered for his soul. He felt for him such a burden as for Jerusalem when He wept over the doomed city. His heart was crying, How can I give thee up? The constraining power of that love was felt by Judas. When the Saviour's hands were bathing those soiled feet, and wiping them with the towel, the heart of Judas thrilled through and through with the impulse then and there to confess his sin. But he would not humble himself. He hardened his heart against repentance; and the old impulses, for the moment put aside, again controlled him. Judas was now offended at Christ's act in washing the feet of His disciples. If Jesus could so humble Himself, he thought, He could not be Israel's king. All hope of worldly honor in a temporal kingdom was destroyed. Judas was satisfied that there was nothing to be gained by following Christ. After seeing Him degrade Himself, as he thought, he was confirmed in his purpose to disown Him, and confess himself deceived. He was possessed by a demon, and he resolved to complete the work he had agreed to do in betraying his Lord.

Judas, in choosing his position at table, had tried to place himself first, and Christ as a servant served him first. John, toward whom Judas had felt so much bitterness, was left till the last. But John did not take this as a rebuke or slight. As the disciples watched Christ's action, they were greatly moved. When Peter's turn came, he exclaimed with astonishment, "Lord, dost Thou wash my feet?" Christ's condescension broke his heart. He was filled with shame to think that one of the disciples was not perform-

ing this service. "What I do," Christ said, "thou knowest not now; but thou shalt know hereafter." Peter could not bear to see his Lord, whom he believed to be the Son of God, acting the part of a servant. His whole soul rose up against this humiliation. He did not realize that for this Christ came into the world. With great emphasis he exclaimed, "Thou shalt never wash my feet."

Solemnly Christ said to Peter, "If I wash thee not, thou hast no part with Me." The service which Peter refused was the type of a higher cleansing. Christ had come to wash the heart from the stain of sin. In refusing to allow Christ to wash his feet, Peter was refusing the higher cleansing included in the lower. He was really rejecting his Lord. It is not humiliating to the Master to allow Him to work for our purification. The truest humility is to receive with thankful heart any provision made in our behalf, and with earnestness do service for Christ.

At the words, "If I wash thee not, thou hast no part with Me," Peter surrendered his pride and self-will. He could not endure the thought of separation from Christ; that would have been death to him. "Not my feet only," he said, "but also my hands and my head. Jesus saith to him, He that is washed needeth not save to wash his feet, but is clean every whit."

These words mean more than bodily cleanliness. Christ is still speaking of the higher cleansing as illustrated by the lower. He who came from the bath was clean, but the sandaled feet soon became dusty, and again needed to be washed. So Peter and his brethren were washed in the great fountain opened for sin and uncleanness. Christ acknowledged them as His. But temptation had led them into evil, and they still needed His cleansing grace. When Jesus girded Himself with a towel to wash the dust from their feet, He desired by that very act to wash the alienation, jealousy, and pride from their hearts. This was of far more consequence than the washing of their dusty feet. With the spirit they then had, not one of them was prepared for communion with Christ. Until brought into a state of humility and love, they were not prepared to partake of the paschal supper, or to share in the memorial service which Christ was about to institute. Their hearts must be cleansed. Pride and self-seeking create dissension and hatred, but all this Jesus washed away in washing their feet. A change of feeling was brought about. Looking upon them, Jesus could say, "Ye are clean." Now there was union of heart, love for one another. They had become humble and teachable. Except Judas, each was ready to concede to another the highest place. Now with subdued and grateful hearts they could receive Christ's words.

Like Peter and his brethren, we too have been washed in the blood of Christ, yet often through contact with evil the heart's purity is soiled. We must come to Christ for His cleansing grace. Peter shrank from bringing his soiled feet in contact with the hands of his Lord and Master; but how often we bring our sinful, polluted hearts in contact with the heart of Christ! How grievous to Him is our evil temper, our vanity and pride! Yet all our infirmity and defilement we must bring to Him. He alone can wash us clean. We are not prepared for communion with Him unless cleansed by His efficacy.

Jesus said to the disciples, "Ye are clean, but not all." He had washed the feet of Judas, but the heart had not been yielded to Him. It was not purified. Judas had not submitted himself to Christ.

After Christ had washed the disciples' feet, and had taken His garments and sat down again, He said to them, "Know ye what I have done to you? Ye call Me Master and Lord: and ye say well; for so I am. If I then, your Lord and Master, have washed your feet; ye also ought to wash one another's feet. For I have given you an example, that ye should do as I have done to you. Verily, verily, I say unto you, The servant is not greater than his lord; neither he that is sent greater than he that sent him."

Christ would have His disciples understand that although He had washed their feet, this did not in the least detract from His dignity. "Ye call Me Master and Lord: and ye say well; for so I am." And being so infinitely superior, He imparted grace and significance to the service. No one was so exalted as Christ, and yet He stooped to the humblest duty. That His people might not be misled by the selfishness which dwells in the natural heart, and which strengthens by self-serving, Christ Himself set the example of humility. He would not leave this great subject in man's charge. Of so much consequence did He regard it, that He Himself, One equal with God, acted as servant to His disciples. While they were contending for the highest place, He to whom every knee shall bow, He whom the angels of glory count it honor to serve, bowed down to wash the feet of those who called Him Lord. He washed the feet of His betrayer.

In His life and lessons, Christ has given a perfect exemplification of the unselfish ministry which has its origin in God. God does not live for Himself. By creating the world, and by upholding all things, He is constantly ministering for others. "He maketh His sun to rise on the evil and on the good, and sendeth rain on the just and on the unjust." Matt. 5:45. This ideal of ministry God has committed to His Son. Jesus was given to stand at the head of humanity, that by His example He might teach what it means to minister. His whole life was under a law of service. He served all, ministered to all. Thus He lived the law of God, and by His example

showed how we are to obey it.

Again and again Jesus had tried to establish this principle among His disciples. When James and John made their request for pre-eminence, He had said, "Whosoever will be great among you, let him be your minister." Matt. 20:26. In My kingdom the principle of preference and supremacy has no place. The only greatness is the greatness of humility. The only distinction is found in devotion to the service of others.

Now, having washed the disciples' feet, He said, "I have given you an example, that ye should do as I have done to you." In these words Christ was not merely enjoining the practice of hospitality. More was meant than the washing of the feet of guests to remove the dust of travel. Christ was here instituting a religious service. By the act of our Lord this humiliating ceremony was made a consecrated ordinance. It was to be observed by the disciples, that they might ever keep in mind His lessons of humility and service.

This ordinance is Christ's appointed preparation for the sacramental service. While pride, variance, and strife for supremacy are cherished, the heart cannot enter into fellowship with Christ. We are not prepared to receive the communion of His body and His blood. Therefore it was that Jesus appointed the memorial of His humiliation to be first observed.

As they come to this ordinance, the children of God should bring to remembrance the words of the Lord of life and glory: "Know ye what I have done to you? Ye call Me Master and Lord: and ye say well; for so I am. If I then, your Lord and Master, have washed your feet; ye also ought to wash one another's feet. For I have given you an example, that ye should do as I have done to you. Verily, verily, I say unto you, The servant is not greater than his lord; neither he that is sent greater than he that sent him. If ye know these things, happy are ye if ye do them." There is in man a disposition to esteem himself more highly than his brother, to work for self, to seek the highest place; and often this results in evil surmisings and bitterness of spirit. The ordinance preceding the Lord's Supper is to clear away these misunderstandings, to bring man out of his selfishness, down from his stilts of self-exaltation, to the humility of heart that will lead him to serve his brother.

The holy Watcher from heaven is present at this season to make it one of soul searching, of conviction of sin, and of the blessed assurance of sins forgiven. Christ in the fullness of His grace is there to change the current of the thoughts that have been running in selfish channels. The Holy Spirit quickens the sensibilities of those who follow the example of their Lord. As the Saviour's humiliation for us is remembered, thought links with thought; a chain of memories is called up, memories of God's great goodness and of the favor and tenderness of earthly friends. Blessings forgotten, mercies abused, kindnesses slighted, are called to mind. Roots of bitterness that have crowded out the precious plant of love are made manifest. Defects of character, neglect of duties, ingratitude to God, coldness toward our brethren, are called to remembrance. Sin is seen in the light in which God views it. Our thoughts are not thoughts of self-complacency, but of severe self-censure and humiliation. The mind is energized to break down every barrier that has caused alienation. Evil thinking and evilspeaking are put away. Sins are confessed, they are forgiven. The subduing grace of Christ comes into the soul, and the love of Christ draws hearts together in a blessed unity.

As the lesson of the preparatory service is thus learned, the desire is kindled for a higher spiritual life. To this desire the divine Witness will respond. The soul will be uplifted. We can partake of the Communion with a consciousness of sins forgiven. The sunshine of Christ's righteousness will fill the chambers of the mind and the soul temple. We "behold the Lamb of God, which taketh away the sin of the world." John 1:29.

To those who receive the spirit of this service, it can never become a mere ceremonial. Its constant lesson will be, "By love serve one another." Gal. 5:13. In washing the feet of His disciples, Christ gave evidence that He would do any service, however humble, that would make them heirs with Him of the eternal wealth of heaven's treasure. His disciples, in performing the same rite, pledge themselves in like manner to serve their brethren. Whenever this ordinance is rightly celebrated, the children of God are brought into a holy relationship, to help and bless each other. They covenant that the life shall be given to unselfish ministry. And this, not only for one another. Their field of labor is as wide as their Master's was. The world is full of those who need our ministry. The poor, the helpless, the ignorant, are on every hand. Those who have communed with Christ in the upper chamber will go forth to minister as He did.

Jesus, the served of all, came to be the servant of all. And because He ministered to all, He will again be served and honored by all. And those who would partake of His divine attributes, and share with Him the joy of seeing souls redeemed, must follow His example of unselfish ministry.

All this was comprehended in the words of Jesus, "I have given you an example, that ye should do as I have done to you." This was the intent of the service He established. And He says, "If ye know these things," if you know the purpose of His lessons, "happy are ye if ye do them."

72

"In Remembrance of Me"

"The Lord Jesus the same night in which He was betrayed took bread: and when He had given thanks, He brake it, and said, Take, eat: this is My body, which is broken for you: this do in remembrance of Me. After the same manner also He took the cup, when He had supped, saying, This cup is the new testament in My blood: this do ye, as oft as ye drink it, in remembrance of Me. For as often as ye eat this bread, and drink this cup, ye do show the Lord's death till He come." 1 Cor. 11:23-26.

Christ was standing at the point of transition between two economies and their two great festivals. He, the spotless Lamb of God, was about to present Himself as a sin offering, that He would thus bring to an end the system of types and ceremonies that for four thousand years had pointed to His death. As He ate the Passover with His disciples, He instituted in its place the service that was to be the memorial of His great sacrifice. The national festival of the Jews was to pass away forever. The service which Christ established was to be observed by His followers in all lands and through all ages.

The Passover was ordained as a commemoration of the deliverance of Israel from Egyptian bondage. God had directed that, year by year, as the children should ask the meaning of this ordinance, the history should be repeated. Thus the wonderful deliverance was to be kept fresh in the minds of all. The ordinance of the Lord's Supper was given to commemorate the great deliverance wrought out as the result of the death of Christ. Till He shall come the second time in power and glory, this ordinance is to be celebrated. It is the means by which His great work for us is to be kept fresh in our minds.

At the time of their deliverance from Egypt, the children of Israel ate the Passover supper standing, with their loins girded, and with their staves in their hands, ready for their journey. The manner in which they celebrated this ordinance harmonized with their condition; for they were about to be thrust out of the land of Egypt, and were to begin a painful and difficult journey through the wilderness. But in Christ's time the condition of things had changed. They were not now about to be thrust out of a strange country, but were dwellers in their own land. In harmony with the rest that had been given them, the people then partook of the Passover supper in a reclining position. Couches were placed about the table, and the guests lay upon them, resting upon the left arm, and having the right hand free for use in eating. In this position a guest could

This chapter is based on Matthew 26:20-29; Mark 14:17-25; Luke 22:14-23; John 13:18-30.

lay his head upon the breast of the one who sat next above him. And the feet, being at the outer edge of the couch, could be washed by one passing around the outside of the circle.

Christ is still at the table on which the paschal supper has been spread. The unleavened cakes used at the Passover season are before Him. The Passover wine, untouched by fermentation, is on the table. These emblems Christ employs to represent His own unblemished sacrifice. Nothing corrupted by fermentation, the symbol of sin and death, could represent the "Lamb without blemish and without spot." 1 Peter 1:19.

"And as they were eating, Jesus took bread, and blessed it, and brake it, and gave it to the disciples, and said, Take, eat; this is My body. And He took the cup, and gave thanks, and gave it to them, saying, Drink ye all of it; for this is My blood of the new testament, which is shed for many for the remission of sins. But I say unto you, I will not drink henceforth of this fruit of the vine, until that day when I drink it new with you in My Father's kingdom."

Judas the betrayer was present at the sacramental service. He received from Jesus the emblems of His broken body and His spilled blood. He heard the words, "This do in remembrance of Me." And sitting there in the very presence of the Lamb of God, the betrayer brooded upon his own dark purposes, and cherished his sullen, revengeful thoughts.

At the feet washing, Christ had given convincing proof that He understood the character of Judas. "Ye are not all clean" (John 13:11), He said. These words convinced the false disciple that Christ read his secret purpose. Now Christ spoke out more plainly. As they were seated at the table He said, looking upon His disciples, "I speak not of you all: I know whom I have chosen: but that the scripture may be fulfilled, He that eateth bread with Me hath lifted up his heel against Me."

Even now the disciples did not suspect Judas. But they saw that Christ appeared greatly troubled. A cloud settled over them all, a premonition of some dreadful calamity, the nature of which they did not understand. As they ate in silence, Jesus said, "Verily I say unto you, that one of you shall betray Me." At these words amazement and consternation seized them. They could not comprehend how any one of them could deal treacherously with their divine Teacher. For what cause could they betray Him? and to whom? Whose heart could give birth to such a design? Surely not one of the favored twelve, who had been privileged above all others to hear His teachings, who had shared His wonderful love, and for whom He had shown such great regard by bringing them into close communion with Himself!

As they realized the import of His words, and remembered how true His sayings were, fear and self-distrust seized them. They began to search their own hearts to see if one thought against their Master were harbored there. With the most painful emotion, one after another inquired, "Lord, is it I?" But Judas sat silent. John in deep distress at last inquired, "Lord, who is it?" And Jesus answered, "He that dippeth his hand with Me in the dish, the same shall betray Me. The Son of man goeth as it is written of Him: but woe unto that man by whom the Son of man is betrayed! it had been good for that man if he had not been born." The disciples had searched one another's faces closely as they asked, "Lord, is it I?" And now the silence of Judas drew all eyes to him. Amid the confusion of questions and expressions of astonishment, Judas had not heard the words of Jesus in answer to John's question. But now, to escape the scrutiny of the disciples, he asked as they had done, "Master, is it I?" Jesus solemnly replied, "Thou hast said."

In surprise and confusion at the exposure of his purpose, Judas rose hastily to leave the room. "Then said Jesus unto him, That thou doest, do quickly. . . . He then having received the sop went immediately out: and it was night." Night it was to the traitor as he turned away from Christ into the outer darkness.

Until this step was taken, Judas had not passed beyond the possibility of repentance. But when he left the presence of his Lord and his fellow disciples, the final decision had been made. He had passed the boundary line.

Wonderful had been the long-suffering of Jesus in His dealing with this tempted soul. Nothing that could be done to save Judas had been left undone. After he had twice covenanted to betray his Lord, Jesus still gave him opportunity for repentance. By reading the secret purpose of the traitor's heart, Christ gave to Judas the final, convincing evidence of His divinity. This was to the false disciple the last call to repentance. No appeal that the divine-human heart of Christ could make had been spared. The waves of mercy, beaten back by stubborn pride, returned in a stronger tide of subduing love. But although surprised and alarmed at the discovery of his guilt, Judas became only the more determined. From the sacramental supper he went out to complete the work of betrayal.

In pronouncing the woe upon Judas, Christ also had a purpose of mercy toward His disciples. He thus gave them the crowning evidence of His Messiahship. "I tell you before it come," He said, "that, when it is come to pass, ye may believe that I AM." Had Jesus remained silent, in apparent ignorance of what was to come upon Him, the disciples might have thought that their Master had not divine foresight, and had been surprised and betrayed into the hands of the murderous mob. A year before, Jesus had told the disciples that He had chosen twelve, and that one was a devil. Now His words to Judas, showing that his treachery was fully known to his Master, would strengthen the faith of Christ's true followers during His humiliation. And when Judas should have come to his dreadful end, they would remember the woe that Jesus had pronounced upon the betrayer.

And the Saviour had still another purpose. He had not withheld His ministry from him whom He knew to be a traitor. The disciples did not understand His words when He said at the feet washing, "Ye are not all clean," nor yet when at the table He declared, "He that eateth bread with Me hath lifted up his heel against Me." John 13:11, 18. But afterward, when His meaning was made plain, they had something to consider as to the patience and mercy of God toward the most grievously erring.

Though Jesus knew Judas from the beginning, He washed his feet. And the betrayer was privileged to unite with Christ in partaking of the sacrament. A long-suffering Saviour held out every inducement for the sinner to receive Him, to repent, and to be cleansed from the defilement of sin. This example is for us. When we suppose one to be in error and sin, we are not to divorce ourselves from him. By no careless separation are we to leave him a prey to temptation, or drive him upon Satan's battleground. This is not Christ's method. It was because the disciples were erring and faulty that He washed their feet, and all but one of the twelve were thus brought to repentance.

Christ's example forbids exclusiveness at the Lord's Supper. It is true that open sin excludes the guilty. This the Holy Spirit plainly teaches. 1 Cor. 5:11. But beyond this none are to pass judgment. God has not left it with men to say who shall present themselves on these occasions. For who can read the heart? Who can distinguish the tares from the wheat? "Let a man examine himself, and so let him eat of that bread, and drink of that cup." For "whosoever shall eat this bread, and drink this cup of the Lord, unworthily, shall be guilty of the body and blood of the Lord." "He that eateth and drinketh unworthily, eateth and drinketh damnation to himself, not discerning the Lord's body." 1 Cor. 11:28, 27, 29.

When believers assemble to celebrate the ordinances, there are present messengers unseen by human eyes. There may be a Judas in the company, and if so, messengers from the prince of darkness are there, for they attend all who refuse to be controlled by the Holy Spirit. Heavenly angels also are present. These unseen visitants are present on every such occasion. There may come into the company persons who are not in heart servants of truth and holiness, but who may wish to take part in the service. They should not be forbidden. There are witnesses present who were present when Jesus washed the feet of the disciples and of Judas. More than human eyes beheld the scene.

Christ by the Holy Spirit is there to set the seal to His own ordinance. He is there to convict and soften the heart. Not a look, not a thought of contrition, escapes His notice. For the repentant, brokenhearted one He is waiting. All things are ready for that soul's reception. He who would wash the feet of Judas longs to wash every heart from the stain of sin.

None should exclude themselves from the Communion because some who are unworthy may be present. Every disciple is called upon to participate publicly, and thus bear witness that he accepts Christ as a personal Saviour. It is at these, His own appointments, that Christ meets His people, and energizes them by His presence. Hearts and hands that are unworthy may even administer the ordinance, yet Christ is there to minister to His children. All who come with their faith fixed upon Him will be greatly blessed. All who neglect these seasons of divine privilege will suffer loss. Of them it may appropriately be said, "Ye are not all clean."

In partaking with His disciples of the bread and wine, Christ pledged Himself to them as their Redeemer. He committed to them the new covenant, by which all who receive Him become children of God, and joint heirs with Christ. By this covenant every blessing that heaven could bestow for this life and the life to come was theirs. This covenant deed was to be ratified with the blood of Christ. And the administration of the Sacrament was to keep before the disciples the infinite sacrifice made for each of them individually as a part of the great whole of fallen humanity.

But the Communion service was not to be a season of sorrowing. This was not its purpose. As the Lord's disciples gather about His table, they are not to remember and lament their shortcomings. They are not to dwell upon their past religious experience, whether that experience has been elevating or depressing. They are not to recall the differences between them and their brethren. The preparatory service has embraced all this. The self-examination, the confession of sin, the reconciling of differences, has all been done. Now they come to meet with Christ. They are not to stand in the shadow of the cross, but in its saving light. They are to open the soul to the bright beams of the Sun of Righteousness. With hearts cleansed by Christ's most precious blood, in full consciousness of His presence, although unseen, they are to hear His words, "Peace I leave with you, My peace I give unto you: not as the world giveth, give I unto you." John 14:27.

Our Lord says, Under conviction of sin, remember that I died for you. When oppressed and persecuted and afflicted for My sake and the gospel's, remember My love, so great that for you I gave My life. When your duties appear stern and severe, and your burdens too heavy to bear, remember that for your sake I endured the cross, despising the shame. When your heart shrinks from the trying ordeal, remember that your Redeemer liveth to make intercession for you.

The Communion service points to Christ's second coming. It was designed to keep this hope vivid in the minds of the disciples. Whenever they met together to commemorate His death, they recounted how "He took the cup, and gave thanks, and gave it to them, saying, Drink ye all of it; for this is My blood of the new testament, which is shed for many for the remission of sins. But I say unto you, I will not drink henceforth of this fruit of the vine, until that day when I drink it new with you in My Father's kingdom." In their tribulation they found comfort in the hope of their Lord's return. Unspeakably precious to them was the thought, "As often as ye eat this bread, and drink this cup, ye do show the Lord's death till He come." 1 Cor. 11:26.

660   These are the things we are never to forget. The love of Jesus, with its constraining power, is to be kept fresh in our memory. Christ has instituted this service that it may speak to our senses of the love of God that has been expressed in our behalf. There can be no union between our souls and God except through Christ. The union and love between brother and brother must be cemented and rendered eternal by the love of Jesus. And nothing less than the death of Christ could make His love efficacious for us. It is only because of His death that we can look with joy to His second coming. His sacrifice is the center of our hope. Upon this we must fix our faith.

The ordinances that point to our Lord's humiliation and suffering are regarded too much as a form. They were instituted for a purpose. Our senses need to be quickened to lay hold of the mystery of godliness. It is the privilege of all to comprehend, far more than we do, the expiatory sufferings of Christ. "As Moses lifted up the serpent in the wilderness," even so has the Son of man been lifted up, "that whosoever believeth in Him should not perish, but have eternal life." John 3:14, 15. To the cross of Calvary, bearing a dying Saviour, we must look. Our eternal interests demand that we show faith in Christ.

Our Lord has said, "Except ye eat the flesh of the Son of man, and drink His blood, ye have no life in you. . . . For My flesh is meat indeed, and My blood is drink indeed." John 6:53-55. This is true of our physical nature. To the death of Christ we owe even this earthly life. The bread we eat is the purchase of His broken body. The water we drink is bought by His spilled blood. Never one, saint or sinner, eats his daily food,

but he is nourished by the body and the blood of Christ. The cross of Calvary is stamped on every loaf. It is reflected in every water spring. All this Christ has taught in appointing the emblems of His great sacrifice. The light shining from that Communion service in the upper chamber makes sacred the provisions for our daily life. The family board becomes as the table of the Lord, and every meal a sacrament.

And how much more are Christ's words true of our spiritual nature. He declares, "Whoso eateth My flesh, and drinketh My blood, hath eternal life." It is by receiving the life for us poured out on Calvary's cross, that we can live the life of holiness. And this life we receive by receiving His word, by doing those things which He has commanded. Thus we become one with Him. "He that eateth My flesh," He says, "and drinketh My blood, dwelleth in Me, and I in him. As the living Father hath sent Me, 661 and I live by the Father: so he that eateth Me, even he shall live by Me." John 6:54, 56, 57. To the holy Communion this scripture in a special sense applies. As faith contemplates our Lord's great sacrifice, the soul assimilates the spiritual life of Christ. That soul will receive spiritual strength from every Communion. The service forms a living connection by which the believer is bound up with Christ, and thus bound up with the Father. In a special sense it forms a connection between dependent human beings and God.

As we receive the bread and wine symbolizing Christ's broken body and spilled blood, we in imagination join in the scene of Communion in the upper chamber. We seem to be passing through the garden consecrated by the agony of Him who bore the sins of the world. We witness the struggle by which our reconciliation with God was obtained. Christ is set forth crucified among us.

Looking upon the crucified Redeemer, we more fully comprehend the magnitude and meaning of the sacrifice made by the Majesty of heaven. The plan of salvation is glorified before us, and the thought of Calvary awakens living and sacred emotions in our hearts. Praise to God and the Lamb will be in our hearts and on our lips; for pride and self-worship cannot flourish in the soul that keeps fresh in memory the scenes of Calvary.

He who beholds the Saviour's matchless love will be elevated in thought, purified in heart, transformed in character. He will go forth to be a light to the world, to reflect in some degree this mysterious love. The more we contemplate the cross of Christ, the more fully shall we adopt the language of the apostle when he said, "God forbid that I should glory, save in the cross of our Lord Jesus Christ, by whom the world is crucified unto me, and I unto the world." Gal. 6:14.

73

"Let Not Your Heart Be Troubled"

Looking upon His disciples with divine love and with the tenderest sympathy, Christ said, "Now is the Son of man glorified, and God is glorified in Him." Judas had left the upper chamber, and Christ was alone with the eleven. He was about to speak of His approaching separation from them; but before doing this He pointed to the great object of His mission. It was this that He kept ever before Him. It was His joy that all His humiliation and suffering would glorify the Father's name. To this He first directs the thoughts of His disciples.

Then addressing them by the endearing term, "Little children," He said, "yet a little while I am with you. Ye shall seek Me: and as I said unto the Jews, Whither I go, ye cannot come; so now I say to you."

The disciples could not rejoice when they heard this. Fear fell upon them. They pressed close about the Saviour. Their Master and Lord, their beloved Teacher and Friend, He was dearer to them than life. To Him they had looked for help in all their difficulties, for comfort in their sorrows and disappointments. Now He was to leave them, a lonely, dependent company. Dark were the forebodings that filled their hearts.

But the Saviour's words to them were full of hope. He knew that they were to be assailed by the enemy, and that Satan's craft is most successful against those who are depressed by difficulties. Therefore He pointed them away from "the things which are seen," to "the things which are not seen." 2 Cor. 4:18. From earthly exile He turned their thoughts to the heavenly home.

"Let not your heart be troubled," He said; "ye believe in God, believe also in Me. In My Father's house are many mansions: if it were not so, I would have told you. I go to prepare a place for you. And if I go and prepare a place for you, I will come again, and receive you unto Myself; that where I am, there ye may be also. And whither I go ye know, and the way ye know." For your sake I came into the world. I am working in your behalf. When I go away, I shall still work earnestly for you. I came into the world to reveal Myself to you, that you might believe. I go to the Father to co-operate with Him in your behalf. The object of Christ's departure was the opposite of what the disciples feared. It did not mean a final separation. He was going to prepare a place for them, that He

might come again, and receive them unto Himself. While He was building mansions for them, they were to build characters after the divine similitude.

Still the disciples were perplexed. Thomas, always troubled by doubts, said, "Lord, we know not whither Thou goest; and how can we know the way? Jesus saith unto him, I am the way, the truth, and the life: no man cometh unto the Father, but by Me. If ye had known Me, ye should have known My Father also: and from henceforth ye know Him, and have seen Him."

There are not many ways to heaven. Each one may not choose his own way. Christ says, "I am the way: . . . no man cometh unto the Father, but by Me." Since the first gospel sermon was preached, when in Eden it was declared that the seed of the woman should bruise the serpent's head, Christ had been uplifted as the way, the truth, and the life. He was the way when Adam lived, when Abel presented to God the blood of the slain lamb, representing the blood of the Redeemer. Christ was the way by which patriarchs and prophets were saved. He is the way by which alone we can have access to God.

"If ye had known Me," Christ said, "ye should have known My Father also: and from henceforth ye know Him, and have seen Him." But not yet did the disciples understand. "Lord, show us the Father," exclaimed Philip, "and it sufficeth us."

Amazed at his dullness of comprehension, Christ asked with pained surprise, "Have I been so long time with you, and yet hast thou not known Me, Philip?" Is it possible that you do not see the Father in the works He does through Me? Do you not believe that I came to testify of the Father? "How sayest thou then, Show us the Father?" "He that hath seen Me hath seen the Father." Christ had not ceased to be God when He became man. Though He had humbled Himself to humanity, the Godhead was still His own. Christ alone could represent the Father to humanity, and this representation the disciples had been privileged to behold for over three years.

"Believe Me that I am in the Father, and the Father in Me: or else believe Me for the very works' sake." Their faith might safely rest on the evidence given in Christ's works, works that no man, of himself, ever had done, or ever could do. Christ's work testified to His divinity. Through Him the Father had been revealed.

If the disciples believed this vital connection between the Father and the Son, their faith would not forsake them when they saw Christ's suffering and death to save a perishing world. Christ was seeking to lead them from their low condition of faith to the experience they might receive if they truly realized what He was—God in human flesh. He desired them to see that their faith must lead up to God, and be anchored

This chapter is based on John 13:31-38; 14-17.

there. How earnestly and perseveringly our compassionate Saviour sought to prepare His disciples for the storm of temptation that was soon to beat upon them. He would have them hid with Him in God.

As Christ was speaking these words, the glory of God was shining from His countenance, and all present felt a sacred awe as they listened with rapt attention to His words. Their hearts were more decidedly drawn to Him; and as they were drawn to Christ in greater love, they were drawn to one another. They felt that heaven was very near, and that the words to which they listened were a message to them from their heavenly Father.

"Verily, verily, I say unto you," Christ continued, "He that believeth on Me, the works that I do shall he do also." The Saviour was deeply anxious for His disciples to understand for what purpose His divinity was united to humanity. He came to the world to display the glory of God, that man might be uplifted by its restoring power. God was manifested in Him that He might be manifested in them. Jesus revealed no qualities, and exercised no powers, that men may not have through faith in Him. His perfect humanity is that which all His followers may possess, if they will be in subjection to God as He was.

"And greater works than these shall he do; because I go unto My Father." By this Christ did not mean that the disciples' work would be of a more exalted character than His, but that it would have greater extent. He did not refer merely to miracle working, but to all that would take place under the working of the Holy Spirit.

667
After the Lord's ascension, the disciples realized the fulfillment of His promise. The scenes of the crucifixion, resurrection, and ascension of Christ were a living reality to them. They saw that the prophecies had been literally fulfilled. They searched the Scriptures, and accepted their teaching with a faith and assurance unknown before. They knew that the divine Teacher was all that He had claimed to be. As they told their experience, and exalted the love of God, men's hearts were melted and subdued, and multitudes believed on Jesus.

The Saviour's promise to His disciples is a promise to His church to the end of time. God did not design that His wonderful plan to redeem men should achieve only insignificant results. All who will go to work, trusting not in what they themselves can do, but in what God can do for and through them, will certainly realize the fulfillment of His promise. "Greater works than these shall he do," He declares; "because I go unto My Father."

As yet the disciples were unacquainted with the Saviour's unlimited resources and power. He said to them, "Hitherto have ye asked nothing in My name." John 16:24. He explained that

the secret of their success would be in asking for strength and grace in His name. He would be present before the Father to make request for them. The prayer of the humble suppliant He presents as His own desire in that soul's behalf. Every sincere prayer is heard in heaven. It may not be fluently expressed; but if the heart is in it, it will ascend to the sanctuary where Jesus ministers, and He will present it to the Father without one awkward, stammering word, beautiful and fragrant with the incense of His own perfection.

The path of sincerity and integrity is not a path free from obstruction, but in every difficulty we are to see a call to prayer. There is no one living who has any power that he has not received from God, and the source whence it comes is open to the weakest human being. "Whatsoever ye shall ask in My name," said Jesus, "that will I do, that the Father may be glorified in the Son. If ye shall ask anything in My name, I will do it."

"In My name," Christ bade His disciples pray. In Christ's name His followers are to stand before God. Through the value of the sacrifice made for them, they are of value in the Lord's sight. Because of the imputed righteousness of Christ they are accounted precious. For Christ's sake the Lord pardons those that fear Him. He does not see in them the vileness of the sinner. He recognizes in them the likeness of His Son, in whom they believe.

The Lord is disappointed when His people 668 place a low estimate upon themselves. He desires His chosen heritage to value themselves according to the price He has placed upon them. God wanted them, else He would not have sent His Son on such an expensive errand to redeem them. He has a use for them, and He is well pleased when they make the very highest demands upon Him, that they may glorify His name. They may expect large things if they have faith in His promises.

But to pray in Christ's name means much. It means that we are to accept His character, manifest His spirit, and work His works. The Saviour's promise is given on condition. "If ye love Me," He says, "keep My commandments." He saves men, not in sin, but from sin; and those who love Him will show their love by obedience.

All true obedience comes from the heart. It was heart work with Christ. And if we consent, He will so identify Himself with our thoughts and aims, so blend our hearts and minds into conformity to His will, that when obeying Him we shall be but carrying out our own impulses. The will, refined and sanctified, will find its highest delight in doing His service. When we know God as it is our privilege to know Him, our life will be a life of continual obedience. Through an appreciation of the character of

Christ, through communion with God, sin will become hateful to us.

As Christ lived the law in humanity, so we may do if we will take hold of the Strong for strength. But we are not to place the responsibility of our duty upon others, and wait for them to tell us what to do. We cannot depend for counsel upon humanity. The Lord will teach us our duty just as willingly as He will teach somebody else. If we come to Him in faith, He will speak His mysteries to us personally. Our hearts will often burn within us as One draws nigh to commune with us as He did with Enoch. Those who decide to do nothing in any line that will displease God, will know, after presenting their case before Him, just what course to pursue. And they will receive not only wisdom, but strength. Power for obedience, for service, will be imparted to them, as Christ has promised. Whatever was given to Christ—the "all things" to supply the need of fallen men—was given to Him as the head and representative of humanity. And "whatsoever we ask, we receive of Him, because we keep His commandments, and do those things that are pleasing in His sight." 1 John 3:22.

669 Before offering Himself as the sacrificial victim, Christ sought for the most essential and complete gift to bestow upon His followers, a gift that would bring within their reach the boundless resources of grace. "I will pray the Father," He said, "and He shall give you another Comforter, that He may abide with you forever; even the Spirit of truth; whom the world cannot receive, because it seeth Him not, neither knoweth Him: but ye know Him; for He dwelleth with you, and shall be in you. I will not leave you orphans: I will come to you." John 14:16-18, margin.

Before this the Spirit had been in the world; from the very beginning of the work of redemption He had been moving upon men's hearts. But while Christ was on earth, the disciples had desired no other helper. Not until they were deprived of His presence would they feel their need of the Spirit, and then He would come.

The Holy Spirit is Christ's representative, but divested of the personality of humanity, and independent thereof. Cumbered with humanity, Christ could not be in every place personally. Therefore it was for their interest that He should go to the Father, and send the Spirit to be His successor on earth. No one could then have any advantage because of his location or his personal contact with Christ. By the Spirit the Saviour would be accessible to all. In this sense He would be nearer to them than if He had not ascended on high.

"He that loveth Me shall be loved of My Father, and I will love him, and will manifest Myself to him." Jesus read the future of His disciples. He saw one brought to the scaffold, one to the cross, one to exile among the lonely rocks of the sea, others to persecution and death. He encouraged them with the promise that in every trial He would be with them. That promise has lost none of its force. The Lord knows all about His faithful servants who for His sake are lying in prison or who are banished to lonely islands. He comforts them with His own presence. When for the truth's sake the believer stands at the bar of unrighteous tribunals, Christ stands by his side. All the reproaches that fall upon him, fall upon Christ. Christ is condemned over again in the person of His disciple. When one is incarcerated in prison walls, Christ ravishes the heart with His love. When one suffers death for His sake, Christ says, "I am He that liveth, and was dead; and, behold, I am alive forevermore, . . . and have the keys of hell and of death." Rev. 1:18. The life that is sacrificed for Me is preserved unto eternal glory.

At all times and in all places, in all sorrows and in all afflictions, when the outlook seems dark and the future perplexing, and we feel helpless and alone, the Comforter will be sent in answer to the prayer of faith. Circumstances 670 may separate us from every earthly friend; but no circumstance, no distance, can separate us from the heavenly Comforter. Wherever we are, wherever we may go, He is always at our right hand to support, sustain, uphold, and cheer.

The disciples still failed to understand Christ's words in their spiritual sense, and again He explained His meaning. By the Spirit, He said, He would manifest Himself to them. "The Comforter, which is the Holy Ghost, whom the Father will send in My name, He shall teach you all things." No more will you say, I cannot comprehend. No longer will you see through a glass, darkly. You shall "be able to comprehend with all saints what is the breadth, and length, and depth, and height; and to know the love of Christ, which passeth knowledge." Eph. 3:18, 19.

The disciples were to bear witness to the life and work of Christ. Through their word He was to speak to all the people on the face of the earth. But in the humiliation and death of Christ they were to suffer great trial and disappointment. That after this experience their word might be accurate, Jesus promised that the Comforter should "bring all things to your remembrance, whatsoever I have said unto you."

"I have yet many things to say unto you," He continued, "but ye cannot bear them now. Howbeit when He, the Spirit of truth, is come, He will guide you into all truth: for He shall not speak of Himself; but whatsoever He shall hear, that shall He speak: and He will show you things to come. He shall glorify Me: for He shall receive of Mine, and shall show it unto you." Jesus had opened before His disciples a vast tract of truth. But it was most difficult for them to keep His lessons distinct from the traditions and maxims of the scribes and Pharisees. They had been educated to accept the teaching of the rabbis as the voice of God, and it still held a power over their minds, and molded their sentiments. Earthly ideas, temporal things, still had a large place in their thoughts. They did not understand the spiritual nature of Christ's kingdom, though He had so often explained it to them. Their minds had become confused. They did not comprehend the value of the scriptures Christ presented. Many of His lessons seemed almost lost upon them. Jesus saw that they did not lay hold of the real meaning of His words. He compassionately promised that the Holy Spirit should recall these sayings to their minds. And He had left unsaid many things that could not be comprehended by the disciples. These also would be opened to them by the Spirit. The Spirit was to quicken their understanding, that they might have an appreciation of heavenly things. "When He, the Spirit of truth, is come," said Jesus, "He will guide you into all truth."

671

The Comforter is called "the Spirit of truth." His work is to define and maintain the truth. He first dwells in the heart as the Spirit of truth, and thus He becomes the Comforter. There is comfort and peace in the truth, but no real peace or comfort can be found in falsehood. It is through false theories and traditions that Satan gains his power over the mind. By directing men to false standards, he misshapes the character. Through the Scriptures the Holy Spirit speaks to the mind, and impresses truth upon the heart. Thus He exposes error, and expels it from the soul. It is by the Spirit of truth, working through the word of God, that Christ subdues His chosen people to Himself.

In describing to His disciples the office work of the Holy Spirit, Jesus sought to inspire them with the joy and hope that inspired His own heart. He rejoiced because of the abundant help He had provided for His church. The Holy Spirit was the highest of all gifts that He could solicit from His Father for the exaltation of His people. The Spirit was to be given as a regenerating agent, and without this the sacrifice of Christ would have been of no avail. The power of evil had been strengthening for centuries, and the submission of men to this satanic captivity was amazing. Sin could be resisted and overcome only through the mighty agency of the Third Person of the Godhead, who would come with no modified energy, but in the fullness of divine power. It is the Spirit that makes effectual what has been wrought out by the world's Redeemer. It is by the Spirit that the heart is made pure. Through the Spirit the believer becomes a partaker of the divine nature. Christ has given His Spirit as a divine power to overcome all hereditary and cultivated tendencies to evil, and to impress His own character upon His church.

Of the Spirit Jesus said, "He shall glorify Me." The Saviour came to glorify the Father by the demonstration of His love; so the Spirit was to glorify Christ by revealing His grace to the world. The very image of God is to be reproduced in humanity. The honor of God, the honor of Christ, is involved in the perfection of the character of His people.

"When He [the Spirit of truth] is come, He will reprove the world of sin, and of righteousness, and of judgment." The preaching of the word will be of no avail without the continual presence and aid of the Holy Spirit. This is the only effectual teacher of divine truth. Only when the truth is accompanied to the heart by the Spirit will it quicken the conscience or transform the life. One might be able to present the letter of the word of God, he might be familiar with all its commands and promises; but unless the Holy Spirit sets home the truth, no souls will fall on the Rock and be broken. No amount of education, no advantages, however great, can make one a channel of light without the cooperation of the Spirit of God. The sowing of the gospel seed will not be a success unless the seed is quickened into life by the dew of heaven. Before one book of the New Testament was written, before one gospel sermon had been preached after Christ's ascension, the Holy Spirit came upon the praying apostles. Then the testimony of their enemies was, "Ye have filled Jerusalem with your doctrine." Acts 5:28.

672

Christ has promised the gift of the Holy Spirit to His church, and the promise belongs to us as much as to the first disciples. But like every other promise, it is given on conditions. There are many who believe and profess to claim the Lord's promise; they talk *about* Christ and *about* the Holy Spirit, yet receive no benefit. They do not surrender the soul to be guided and controlled by the divine agencies. We cannot use the Holy Spirit. The Spirit is to use us. Through the Spirit God works in His people "to will and to do of His good pleasure." Phil. 2:13. But many will not submit to this. They want to manage themselves. This is why they do not receive the heavenly gift. Only to those who wait humbly upon God, who watch for His guidance and grace, is the Spirit given. The power of God awaits their demand and reception. This promised blessing, claimed by faith, brings all other blessings in its train. It is given according to the riches of the grace of Christ, and He is ready to supply every soul according to the capacity to receive.

In His discourse to the disciples, Jesus made no mournful allusion to His own sufferings and death. His last legacy to them was a legacy of peace. He said, "Peace I leave with you: not as the world giveth, give I unto you. Let not your heart be troubled, neither let it be afraid."

Before leaving the upper chamber, the Saviour led His disciples in a song of praise. His voice was heard, not in the strains of some mournful lament, but in the joyful notes of the Passover hallel:

"O praise the Lord, all ye nations:
Praise Him, all ye people.
For His merciful kindness is great toward us:
And the truth of the Lord endureth forever.
Praise ye the Lord."

Psalm 117.

673 After the hymn, they went out. Through the crowded streets they made their way, passing out of the city gate toward the Mount of Olives. Slowly they proceeded, each busy with his own thoughts. As they began to descend toward the mount, Jesus said, in a tone of deepest sadness, "All ye shall be offended because of Me this night: for it is written, I will smite the shepherd, and the sheep of the flock shall be scattered abroad." Matt. 26:31. The disciples listened in sorrow and amazement. They remembered how in the synagogue at Capernaum, when Christ spoke of Himself as the bread of life, many had been offended, and had turned away from Him. But the twelve had not shown themselves unfaithful. Peter, speaking for his brethren, had then declared his loyalty to Christ. Then the Saviour had said, "Have not I chosen you twelve, and one of you is a devil?" John 6:70. In the upper chamber Jesus said that one of the twelve would betray Him, and that Peter would deny Him. But now His words include them all.

Now Peter's voice is heard vehemently protesting, "Although all shall be offended, yet will not I." In the upper chamber he had declared, "I will lay down my life for Thy sake." Jesus had warned him that he would that very night deny his Saviour. Now Christ repeats the warning: "Verily I say unto thee, That this day, even in this night, before the cock crow twice, thou shalt deny Me thrice." But Peter only "spake the more vehemently, If I should die with Thee, I will not deny Thee in anywise. Likewise also said they all." Mark 14:29, 30, 31. In their self-confidence they denied the repeated statement of Him who knew. They were unprepared for the test; when temptation should overtake them, they would understand their own weakness.

When Peter said he would follow his Lord to prison and to death, he meant it, every word of it; but he did not know himself. Hidden in his heart were elements of evil that circumstances would fan into life. Unless he was made conscious of his danger, these would prove his eternal ruin. The Saviour saw in him a self-love and assurance that would overbear even his love for Christ. Much of infirmity, of unmortified sin, carelessness of spirit, unsanctified temper, heedlessness in entering into temptation, had been revealed in his experience. Christ's solemn warning was a call to heart searching. Peter needed to distrust himself, and to have a deeper faith in Christ. Had he in humility received the warning, he would have appealed to the Shepherd of the flock to keep His sheep. When on the Sea of Galilee he was about to sink, he cried, "Lord, save me." Matt. 14:30. Then the hand of Christ was outstretched to grasp his 674 hand. So now if he had cried to Jesus, Save me from myself, he would have been kept. But Peter felt that he was distrusted, and he thought it cruel. He was already offended, and he became more persistent in his self-confidence.

Jesus looks with compassion on His disciples. He cannot save them from the trial, but He does not leave them comfortless. He assures them that He is to break the fetters of the tomb, and that His love for them will not fail. "After I am risen again," He says, "I will go before you into Galilee." Matt. 26:32. Before the denial, they have the assurance of forgiveness. After His death and resurrection, they knew that they were forgiven, and were dear to the heart of Christ.

Jesus and the disciples were on the way to Gethsemane, at the foot of Mount Olivet, a retired spot which He had often visited for meditation and prayer. The Saviour had been explaining to His disciples His mission to the world, and the spiritual relation to Him which they were to sustain. Now He illustrates the lesson. The moon is shining bright, and reveals to Him a flourishing grapevine. Drawing the attention of the disciples to it, He employs it as a symbol.

"I am the true Vine," He says. Instead of choosing the graceful palm, the lofty cedar, or the strong oak, Jesus takes the vine with its clinging tendrils to represent Himself. The palm tree, the cedar, and the oak stand alone. They require no support. But the vine entwines about the trellis, and thus climbs heavenward. So Christ in His humanity was dependent upon 675 divine power. "I can of Mine own self do nothing," He declared. John 5:30.

"I am the true Vine." The Jews had always regarded the vine as the most noble of plants, and a type of all that was powerful, excellent, and fruitful. Israel had been represented as a vine which God had planted in the Promised Land. The Jews based their hope of salvation on the fact of their connection with Israel. But Jesus says, I am the real Vine. Think not that through a connection with Israel you may become partakers of the life of God, and inheritors of His promise. Through Me alone is spiritual life received.

"I am the true Vine, and My Father is the husbandman." On the hills of Palestine our heavenly Father had planted this goodly Vine, and He Himself was the husbandman. Many were attracted by the beauty of this Vine, and declared its heavenly origin. But to the leaders in Israel it appeared as a root out of a dry ground. They took the plant, and bruised it, and trampled it under their unholy feet. Their thought was to destroy it forever. But the heavenly Husbandman never lost sight of His plant. After men thought they had killed it, He took it, and replanted it on the other side of the wall. The vine stock was to be no longer visible. It was hidden from the rude assaults of men. But the branches of the Vine hung over the wall. They were to represent the Vine. Through them grafts might still be united to the Vine. From them fruit has been obtained. There has been a harvest which the passers-by have plucked.

"I am the Vine, ye are the branches," Christ said to His disciples. Though He was about to be removed from them, their spiritual union with Him was to be unchanged. The connection of the branch with the vine, He said, represents the relation you are to sustain to Me. The scion is engrafted into the living vine, and fiber by fiber, vein by vein, it grows into the vine stock. The life of the vine becomes the life of the branch. So the soul dead in trespasses and sins receives life through connection with Christ. By faith in Him as a personal Saviour the union is formed. The sinner unites his weakness to Christ's strength, his emptiness to Christ's fullness, his frailty to Christ's enduring might. Then he has the mind of Christ. The humanity of Christ has touched our humanity, and our humanity has touched divinity. Thus through the agency of the Holy Spirit man becomes a partaker of the divine nature. He is accepted in the Beloved.

676   This union with Christ, once formed, must be maintained. Christ said, "Abide in Me, and I in you. As the branch cannot bear fruit of itself, except it abide in the vine; no more can ye, except ye abide in Me." This is no casual touch, no off-and-on connection. The branch becomes a part of the living vine. The communication of life, strength, and fruitfulness from the root to the branches is unobstructed and constant. Separated from the vine, the branch cannot live. No more, said Jesus, can you live apart from Me. The life you have received from Me can be preserved only by continual communion. Without Me you cannot overcome one sin, or resist one temptation.

"Abide in Me, and I in you." Abiding in Christ means a constant receiving of His Spirit, a life of unreserved surrender to His service. The channel of communication must be open continually between man and his God. As the vine branch constantly draws the sap from the living vine, so are we to cling to Jesus, and receive from Him by faith the strength and perfection of His own character.

The root sends its nourishment through the branch to the outermost twig. So Christ communicates the current of spiritual strength to every believer. So long as the soul is united to Christ, there is no danger that it will wither or decay.

The life of the vine will be manifest in fragrant fruit on the branches. "He that abideth in Me," said Jesus, "and I in him, the same bringeth forth much fruit: for without Me ye can do nothing." When we live by faith on the Son of God, the fruits of the Spirit will be seen in our lives; not one will be missing.

"My Father is the husbandman. Every branch in Me that beareth not fruit He taketh away." While the graft is outwardly united with the vine, there may be no vital connection. Then there will be no growth or fruitfulness. So there may be an apparent connection with Christ without a real union with Him by faith. A profession of religion places men in the church, but the character and conduct show whether they are in connection with Christ. If they bear no fruit, they are false branches. Their separation from Christ involves a ruin as complete as that represented by the dead branch. "If a man abide not in Me," said Christ, "he is cast forth as a branch, and is withered; and men gather them, and cast them into the fire, and they are burned."

"And every branch that beareth fruit, He purgeth [pruneth] it, that it may bring forth more fruit." From the chosen twelve who had followed Jesus, one as a withered branch was 677 about to be taken away; the rest were to pass under the pruning knife of bitter trial. Jesus with solemn tenderness explained the purpose of the husbandman. The pruning will cause pain, but it is the Father who applies the knife. He works with no wanton hand or indifferent heart. There are branches trailing upon the ground; these must be cut loose from the earthly supports to which their tendrils are fastening. They are to reach heavenward, and find their support in God. The excessive foliage that draws away the life current from the fruit must be pruned off. The overgrowth must be cut out, to give room for the healing beams of the Sun of Righteousness. The husbandman prunes away the harmful growth, that the fruit may be richer and more abundant.

"Herein is My Father glorified," said Jesus, "that ye bear much fruit." God desires to manifest through you the holiness, the benevolence, the compassion, of His own character. Yet the Saviour does not bid the disciples labor to bear fruit. He tells them to abide in Him. "If ye abide in Me," He says, "and My words abide in you, ye shall ask what ye will, and it shall be done unto you." It is through the word that Christ abides in His followers. This is the same vital union that is represented by eating His flesh and drinking His blood. The words of Christ are spirit and life. Receiving them, you receive the life of the Vine. You live "by every word that proceedeth out of the mouth of God." Matt. 4:4. The life of Christ in you produces the same fruits as in Him. Living in Christ, adhering to Christ, supported by Christ, drawing nourishment from Christ, you bear fruit after the similitude of Christ.

In this last meeting with His disciples, the great desire which Christ expressed for them was that they might love one another as He had loved them. Again and again He spoke of this. "These things I command you," He said repeatedly, "that ye love one another." His very first injunction when alone with them in the upper chamber was, "A new commandment I give unto you, That ye love one another; as I have loved you, that ye also love one another." To the disciples this commandment was new; for they had not loved one another as Christ had loved them. He saw that new ideas and impulses must control them; that new principles must be practiced by them; through His life and death they were to receive a new conception of love. The command to love one another had a new meaning in the light of His self-sacrifice. The 678 whole work of grace is one continual service of love, of self-denying, self-sacrificing effort. During every hour of Christ's sojourn upon the earth, the love of God was flowing from Him in irrepressible streams. All who are imbued with His Spirit will love as He loved. The very principle that actuated Christ will actuate them in all their dealing one with another.

This love is the evidence of their discipleship. "By this shall all men know that ye are My disciples," said Jesus, "if ye have love one to another." When men are bound together, not by force or self-interest, but by love, they show the working of an influence that is above every human influence. Where this oneness exists, it is evidence that the image of God is being restored in humanity, that a new principle of life has been implanted. It shows that there is power in the divine nature to withstand the supernatural agencies of evil, and that the grace of God subdues the selfishness inherent in the natural heart.

This love, manifested in the church, will surely stir the wrath of Satan. Christ did not mark out for His disciples an easy path. "If the world hate you," He said, "ye know that it hated Me before it hated you. If ye were of the world, the world would love his own: but because ye are not of the world, but I have chosen you out of the world, therefore the world hateth you. Remember the word that I said unto you, The servant is not greater than his lord. If they have persecuted Me, they will also persecute you; if they have kept My saying, they will keep yours also. But all these things will they do unto you for My name's sake, because they know not Him that sent Me." The gospel is to be carried forward by aggressive warfare, in the midst of opposition, peril, loss, and suffering. But those who do this work are only following in their Master's steps.

As the world's Redeemer, Christ was constantly confronted with apparent failure. He, the messenger of mercy to our world, seemed to do little of the work He longed to do in uplifting and saving. Satanic influences were constantly working to oppose His way. But He would not be discouraged. Through the prophecy of Isaiah He declares, "I have labored in vain, I have spent My strength for nought, and in vain: yet surely My judgment is with the Lord, and My work with My God. . . . Though Israel be not gathered, yet shall I be glorious in the eyes of the Lord, and My God shall be My strength." It is to Christ that the promise is given, "Thus saith the Lord, the Redeemer of Israel, and His Holy One, to Him whom man despiseth, to Him whom the nation abhorreth; . . . thus saith the 679 Lord: . . . I will preserve Thee, and give Thee for a covenant of the people, to establish the earth, to cause to inherit the desolate heritages; that Thou mayest say to the prisoners, Go forth; to them that are in darkness, Show yourselves. . . . They shall not hunger nor thirst; neither shall the heat nor sun smite them: for He that hath mercy on them shall lead them, even by the springs of water shall He guide them." Isa. 49:4, 5, 7-10.

Upon this word Jesus rested, and He gave Satan no advantage. When the last steps of Christ's humiliation were to be taken, when the deepest sorrow was closing about His soul, He said to His disciples, "The prince of this world cometh, and hath nothing in Me." "The prince of this world is judged." Now shall he be cast out. John 14:30; 16:11; 12:31. With prophetic eye Christ traced the scenes to take place in His last great conflict. He knew that when He should exclaim, "It is finished," all heaven would triumph. His ear caught the distant music and the shouts of victory in the heavenly courts. He knew that the knell of Satan's empire would then be sounded, and the name of Christ would be heralded from world to world throughout the universe.

Christ rejoiced that He could do more for His followers than they could ask or think. He spoke with assurance, knowing that an almighty decree had been given before the world was made. He knew that truth, armed with the omnipotence of the Holy Spirit, would conquer in the contest with evil; and that the blood-stained banner would wave triumphantly over His followers. He knew that the life of His trusting disciples would be like His, a series of uninterrupted victories, not seen to be such here, but recognized as such in the great hereafter.

"These things I have spoken unto you," He said, "that in Me ye might have peace. In the world ye shall have tribulation: but be of good cheer; I have overcome the world." Christ did not fail, neither was He discouraged, and His followers are to manifest a faith of the same enduring nature. They are to live as He lived, and work as He worked, because they depend on Him as the great Master Worker. Courage, energy, and perseverance they must possess. Though apparent impossibilities obstruct their way, by His grace they are to go forward. Instead of deploring difficulties, they are called upon to surmount them. They are to despair of nothing, and to hope for everything. With the golden chain of His matchless love Christ has bound them to the throne of God. It is His purpose that the highest influence in the universe, emanating from the source of all power, shall be theirs. They are to have power to resist evil, power that neither earth, nor death, nor hell can master, power that will enable them to overcome as Christ overcame.

Christ designs that heaven's order, heaven's plan of government, heaven's divine harmony, shall be represented in His church on earth. Thus in His people He is glorified. Through them the Sun of Righteousness will shine in undimmed luster to the world. Christ has given to His church ample facilities, that He may receive a large revenue of glory from His redeemed, purchased possession. He has bestowed upon His people capabilities and blessings that they may represent His own sufficiency. The church, endowed with the righteousness of Christ, is His depositary, in which the riches of His mercy, His grace, and His love, are to appear in full and final display. Christ looks upon His people in their purity and perfection, as the reward of His humiliation, and the supplement of His glory,—Christ, the great Center, from whom radiates all glory.

With strong, hopeful words the Saviour ended His instruction. Then He poured out the burden of His soul in prayer for His disciples. Lifting His eyes to heaven, He said, "Father, the hour is come; glorify Thy Son, that Thy Son also may glorify Thee: as Thou hast given Him power over all flesh, that He should give eternal life to as many as Thou hast given Him. And this is life eternal, that they might know Thee the only true God, and Jesus Christ, whom Thou hast sent."

Christ had finished the work that was given Him to do. He had glorified God on the earth. He had manifested the Father's name. He had gathered out those who were to continue His work among men. And He said, "I am glorified in them. And now I am no more in the world, but these are in the world, and I come to Thee. Holy Father, keep through Thine own name those whom Thou hast given Me, that they may be one, as We are." "Neither pray I for these alone, but for them also which shall believe on Me through their word; that they all may be

one; . . . I in them, and Thou in Me, that they may be made perfect in one; and that the world may know that Thou hast sent Me, and hast loved them, as Thou hast loved Me."

Thus in the language of one who has divine authority, Christ gives His elect church into the Father's arms. As a consecrated high priest He intercedes for His people. As a faithful shepherd He gathers His flock under the shadow of the Almighty, in the strong and sure refuge. For Him there waits the last battle with Satan, and He goes forth to meet it.

74

Gethsemane

In company with His disciples, the Saviour slowly made His way to the garden of Gethsemane. The Passover moon, broad and full, shone from a cloudless sky. The city of pilgrims' tents was hushed into silence.

Jesus had been earnestly conversing with His disciples and instructing them; but as He neared Gethsemane, He became strangely silent. He had often visited this spot for meditation and prayer; but never with a heart so full of sorrow as upon this night of His last agony. Throughout His life on earth He had walked in the light of God's presence. When in conflict with men who were inspired by the very spirit of Satan, He could say, "He that sent Me is with Me: the Father hath not left Me alone; for I do always those things that please Him." John 8:29. But now He seemed to be shut out from the light of God's sustaining presence. Now He was numbered with the transgressors. The guilt of fallen humanity He must bear. Upon Him who knew no sin must be laid the iniquity of us all. So dreadful does sin appear to Him, so great is the weight of guilt which He must bear, that He is tempted to fear it will shut Him out forever from His Father's love. Feeling how terrible is the wrath of God against transgression, He exclaims, "My soul is exceeding sorrowful, even unto death."

As they approached the garden, the disciples had marked the change that came over their Master. Never before had they seen Him so utterly sad and silent. As He proceeded, this strange sadness deepened; yet they dared not question Him as to the cause. His form swayed as if He were about to fall. Upon reaching the garden, the disciples looked anxiously for His usual place of retirement, that their Master might rest. Every step that He now took was with labored effort. He groaned aloud, as if suffering under the pressure of a terrible burden. Twice His companions supported Him, or He would have fallen to the earth.

Near the entrance to the garden, Jesus left all

This chapter is based on Matthew 26:36-56; Mark 14:32-50; Luke 22:39-53; John 18:1-12.

but three of the disciples, bidding them pray for themselves and for Him. With Peter, James, and John, He entered its secluded recesses. These three disciples were Christ's closest companions. They had beheld His glory on the mount of transfiguration; they had seen Moses and Elijah talking with Him; they had heard the voice from heaven; now in His great struggle, Christ desired their presence near Him. Often they had passed the night with Him in this retreat. On these occasions, after a season of watching and prayer, they would sleep undisturbed at a little distance from their Master, until He awoke them in the morning to go forth anew to labor. But now He desired them to spend the night with Him in prayer. Yet He could not bear that even they should witness the agony He was to endure.

"Tarry ye here," He said, "and watch with Me."

He went a little distance from them—not so far but that they could both see and hear Him—and fell prostrate upon the ground. He felt that by sin He was being separated from His Father. The gulf was so broad, so black, so deep, that His spirit shuddered before it. This agony He must not exert His divine power to escape. As man He must suffer the consequences of man's sin. As man He must endure the wrath of God against transgression.

Christ was now standing in a different attitude from that in which He had ever stood before. His suffering can best be described in the words of the prophet, "Awake, O sword, against My shepherd, and against the man that is My fellow, saith the Lord of hosts." Zech. 13:7. As the substitute and surety for sinful man, Christ was suffering under divine justice. He saw what justice meant. Hitherto He had been as an intercessor for others; now He longed to have an intercessor for Himself.

As Christ felt His unity with the Father broken up, He feared that in His human nature He would be unable to endure the coming conflict with the powers of darkness. In the wilderness of temptation the destiny of the human race had been at stake. Christ was then conqueror. Now 687 the tempter had come for the last fearful struggle. For this he had been preparing during the three years of Christ's ministry. Everything was at stake with him. If he failed here, his hope of mastery was lost; the kingdoms of the world would finally become Christ's; he himself would be overthrown and cast out. But if Christ could be overcome, the earth would become Satan's kingdom, and the human race would be forever in his power. With the issues of the conflict before Him, Christ's soul was filled with dread of separation from God. Satan told Him that if He became the surety for a sinful world, the separation would be eternal. He would be identified with Satan's kingdom, and would

nevermore be one with God.

And what was to be gained by this sacrifice? How hopeless appeared the guilt and ingratitude of men! In its hardest features Satan pressed the situation upon the Redeemer: The people who claim to be above all others in temporal and spiritual advantages have rejected You. They are seeking to destroy You, the foundation, the center and seal of the promises made to them as a peculiar people. One of Your own disciples, who has listened to Your instruction, and has been among the foremost in church activities, will betray You. One of Your most zealous followers will deny You. All will forsake You. Christ's whole being abhorred the thought. That those whom He had undertaken to save, those whom He loved so much, should unite in the plots of Satan, this pierced His soul. The conflict was terrible. Its measure was the guilt of His nation, of His accusers and betrayer, the guilt of a world lying in wickedness. The sins of men weighed heavily upon Christ, and the sense of God's wrath against sin was crushing out His life.

Behold Him contemplating the price to be paid for the human soul. In His agony He clings to the cold ground, as if to prevent Himself from being drawn farther from God. The chilling dew of night falls upon His prostrate form, but He heeds it not. From His pale lips comes the bitter cry, "O My Father, if it be possible, let this cup pass from Me." Yet even now He adds, "Nevertheless not as I will, but as Thou wilt."

The human heart longs for sympathy in suffering. This longing Christ felt to the very depths of His being. In the supreme agony of His soul He came to His disciples with a yearning desire to hear some words of comfort from those whom He had so often blessed and comforted, and shielded in sorrow and distress. The One who had always had words of sympathy for them was now suffering superhuman agony, and He longed to know that they were praying for Him and for themselves. How dark seemed 688 the malignity of sin! Terrible was the temptation to let the human race bear the consequences of its own guilt, while He stood innocent before God. If He could only know that His disciples understood and appreciated this, He would be strengthened.

Rising with painful effort, He staggered to the place where He had left His companions. But He "findeth them asleep." Had He found them praying, He would have been relieved. Had they been seeking refuge in God, that satanic agencies might not prevail over them, He would have been comforted by their steadfast faith. But they had not heeded the repeated warning, "Watch and pray." At first they had been much troubled to see their Master, usually so calm and dignified, wrestling with a sorrow that was beyond comprehension. They had prayed as they heard the strong cries of the sufferer. They did not intend to forsake their Lord, but they seemed paralyzed by a stupor which they might have shaken off if they had continued pleading with God. They did not realize the necessity of watchfulness and earnest prayer in order to withstand temptation.

Just before He bent His footsteps to the garden, Jesus had said to the disciples, "All ye shall be offended because of Me this night." They had given Him the strongest assurance that they would go with Him to prison and to death. And poor, self-sufficient Peter had added, "Although all shall be offended, yet will not I." Mark 14:27, 29. But the disciples trusted to themselves. They did not look to the mighty Helper as Christ had counseled them to do. Thus when the Saviour was most in need of their sympathy and prayers, they were found asleep. Even Peter was sleeping.

And John, the loving disciple who had leaned upon the breast of Jesus, was asleep. Surely, the love of John for his Master should have kept him awake. His earnest prayers should have mingled with those of his loved Saviour in the time of His supreme sorrow. The Redeemer had spent entire nights praying for His disciples, that their faith might not fail. Should Jesus now put to James and John the question He had once asked them, "Are ye able to drink of the cup that I shall drink of, and to be baptized with the baptism that I am baptized with?" they would not have ventured to answer, "We are able." Matt. 20:22.

The disciples awakened at the voice of Jesus, but they hardly knew Him, His face was so changed by anguish. Addressing Peter, Jesus said, "Simon, sleepest thou? couldest not thou watch one hour? Watch ye and pray, lest ye enter into temptation. The spirit truly is ready, but the flesh is weak." The weakness of His disciples awakened the sympathy of Jesus. He feared that they would not be able to endure the test which would come upon them in His betrayal and death. He did not reprove them, but said, "Watch ye and pray, lest ye enter into temptation." Even in His great agony, He was seeking to excuse their weakness. "The spirit truly is ready," He said, "but the flesh is weak."

Again the Son of God was seized with superhuman agony, and fainting and exhausted, He staggered back to the place of His former struggle. His suffering was even greater than before. As the agony of soul came upon Him, "His sweat was as it were great drops of blood falling down to the ground." The cypress and palm trees were the silent witnesses of His anguish. From their leafy branches dropped heavy dew upon His stricken form, as if nature wept over its Author wrestling alone with the powers of darkness.

A short time before, Jesus had stood like a mighty cedar, withstanding the storm of opposition that spent its fury upon Him. Stubborn wills, and hearts filled with malice and subtlety, had striven in vain to confuse and overpower Him. He stood forth in divine majesty as the Son of God. Now He was like a reed beaten and bent by the angry storm. He had approached the consummation of His work a conqueror, having at each step gained the victory over the powers of darkness. As one already glorified, He had claimed oneness with God. In unfaltering accents He had poured out His songs of praise. He had spoken to His disciples in words of courage and tenderness. Now had come the hour of the power of darkness. Now His voice was heard on the still evening air, not in tones of triumph, but full of human anguish. The words of the Saviour were borne to the ears of the drowsy disciples, "O My Father, if this cup may not pass away from Me, except I drink it, Thy will be done."

The first impulse of the disciples was to go to Him; but He had bidden them tarry there, watching unto prayer. When Jesus came to them, He found them still sleeping. Again He had felt a longing for companionship, for some words from His disciples which would bring relief, and break the spell of darkness that wellnigh overpowered Him. But their eyes were heavy; "neither wist they what to answer Him." His presence aroused them. They saw His face marked with the bloody sweat of agony, and they were filled with fear. His anguish of mind they could not understand. "His visage was so marred more than any man, and His form more than the sons of men." Isa. 52:14.

Turning away, Jesus sought again His retreat, and fell prostrate, overcome by the horror of a great darkness. The humanity of the Son of God trembled in that trying hour. He prayed not now for His disciples that their faith might not fail, but for His own tempted, agonized soul. The awful moment had come—that moment which was to decide the destiny of the world. The fate of humanity trembled in the balance. Christ might even now refuse to drink the cup apportioned to guilty man. It was not yet too late. He might wipe the bloody sweat from His brow, and leave man to perish in his iniquity. He might say, Let the transgressor receive the penalty of his sin, and I will go back to My Father. Will the Son of God drink the bitter cup of humiliation and agony? Will the innocent suffer the consequences of the curse of sin, to save the guilty? The words fall tremblingly from the pale lips of Jesus, "O My Father, if this cup may not pass away from Me, except I drink it, Thy will be done."

Three times has He uttered that prayer. Three times has humanity shrunk from the last, crowning sacrifice. But now the history of the human race comes up before the world's Redeemer. He sees that the transgressors of the law, if left to themselves, must perish. He sees the helplessness of man. He sees the power of sin. The woes and lamentations of a doomed world rise before Him. He beholds its impending fate, and His decision is made. He will save man at any cost to Himself. He accepts His baptism of blood, that through Him perishing millions may gain everlasting life. He has left the courts of heaven, where all is purity, happiness, and glory, to save the one lost sheep, the one world that has fallen by transgression. And He will not turn from His mission. He will become the propitiation of a race that has willed to sin. His prayer now breathes only submission: "If this cup may not pass away from Me, except I drink it, Thy will be done."

Having made the decision, He fell dying to the ground from which He had partially risen. Where now were His disciples, to place their hands tenderly beneath the head of their fainting Master, and bathe that brow, marred indeed more than the sons of men? The Saviour trod the wine press alone, and of the people there was none with Him.

But God suffered with His Son. Angels beheld the Saviour's agony. They saw their Lord enclosed by legions of satanic forces, His nature weighed down with a shuddering, mysterious dread. There was silence in heaven. No harp was touched. Could mortals have viewed the amazement of the angelic host as in silent grief they watched the Father separating His beams of light, love, and glory from His beloved Son, they would better understand how offensive in His sight is sin.

The worlds unfallen and the heavenly angels had watched with intense interest as the conflict drew to its close. Satan and his confederacy of evil, the legions of apostasy, watched intently this great crisis in the work of redemption. The powers of good and evil waited to see what answer would come to Christ's thrice-repeated prayer. Angels had longed to bring relief to the divine sufferer, but this might not be. No way of escape was found for the Son of God. In this awful crisis, when everything was at stake, when the mysterious cup trembled in the hand of the sufferer, the heavens opened, a light shone forth amid the stormy darkness of the crisis hour, and the mighty angel who stands in God's presence, occupying the position from which Satan fell, came to the side of Christ. The angel came not to take the cup from Christ's hand, but to strengthen Him to drink it, with the assurance of the Father's love. He came to give power to the divine-human suppliant. He pointed Him to the open heavens, telling Him of the souls that would be saved as the result of His sufferings. He assured Him that His Father is greater and more powerful than Satan, that His death would result in the utter discomfiture of

Satan, and that the kingdom of this world would be given to the saints of the Most High. He told Him that He would see of the travail of His soul, and be satisfied, for He would see a multitude of the human race saved, eternally saved.

Christ's agony did not cease, but His depression and discouragement left Him. The storm had in nowise abated, but He who was its object was strengthened to meet its fury. He came forth calm and serene. A heavenly peace rested upon His bloodstained face. He had borne that which no human being could ever bear; for He had tasted the sufferings of death for every man.

The sleeping disciples had been suddenly awakened by the light surrounding the Saviour. They saw the angel bending over their prostrate Master. They saw him lift the Saviour's head upon his bosom, and point toward heaven. They heard his voice, like sweetest music, speaking words of comfort and hope. The disciples recalled the scene upon the mount of transfiguration. They remembered the glory that in the temple had encircled Jesus, and the voice of God that spoke from the cloud. Now that same glory was again revealed, and they had no further fear for their Master. He was under the care of God; a mighty angel had been sent to protect Him. Again the disciples in their weariness yield to the strange stupor that overpowers them. Again Jesus finds them sleeping.

Looking sorrowfully upon them He says, "Sleep on now, and take your rest: behold, the hour is at hand, and the Son of man is betrayed into the hands of sinners."

Even as He spoke these words, He heard the footsteps of the mob in search of Him, and said, "Rise, let us be going: behold, he is at hand that doth betray Me."

No traces of His recent agony were visible as Jesus stepped forth to meet His betrayer. Standing in advance of His disciples He said, "Whom seek ye?" They answered, "Jesus of Nazareth." Jesus replied, "I am He." As these words were spoken, the angel who had lately ministered to Jesus moved between Him and the mob. A divine light illuminated the Saviour's face, and a dovelike form overshadowed Him. In the presence of this divine glory, the murderous throng could not stand for a moment. They staggered back. Priests, elders, soldiers, and even Judas, fell as dead men to the ground.

The angel withdrew, and the light faded away. Jesus had opportunity to escape, but He remained, calm and self-possessed. As one glorified He stood in the midst of that hardened band, now prostrate and helpless at His feet. The disciples looked on, silent with wonder and awe.

But quickly the scene changed. The mob started up. The Roman soldiers, the priests and Judas, gathered about Christ. They seemed ashamed of their weakness, and fearful that He would yet escape. Again the question was asked by the Redeemer, "Whom seek ye?" They had had evidence that He who stood before them was the Son of God, but they would not be convinced. To the question, "Whom seek ye?" again they answered, "Jesus of Nazareth." The Saviour then said, "I have told you that I am He: if therefore ye seek Me, let these go their way"—pointing to the disciples. He knew how weak was their faith, and He sought to shield them from temptation and trial. For them He was ready to sacrifice Himself.

Judas the betrayer did not forget the part he was to act. When the mob entered the garden, he had led the way, closely followed by the high priest. To the pursuers of Jesus he had given a sign, saying, "Whomsoever I shall kiss, that same is He: hold Him fast." Matt. 26:48. Now he pretends to have no part with them. Coming 696 close to Jesus, he takes His hand as a familiar friend. With the words, "Hail, Master," he kisses Him repeatedly, and appears to weep as if in sympathy with Him in His peril.

Jesus said to him, "Friend, wherefore art thou come?" His voice trembled with sorrow as He added, "Judas, betrayest thou the Son of man with a kiss?" This appeal should have aroused the conscience of the betrayer, and touched his stubborn heart; but honor, fidelity, and human tenderness had forsaken him. He stood bold and defiant, showing no disposition to relent. He had given himself up to Satan, and he had no power to resist him. Jesus did not refuse the traitor's kiss.

The mob grew bold as they saw Judas touch the person of Him who had so recently been glorified before their eyes. They now laid hold of Jesus, and proceeded to bind those precious hands that had ever been employed in doing good.

The disciples had thought that their Master would not suffer Himself to be taken. For the same power that had caused the mob to fall as dead men could keep them helpless, until Jesus and His companions should escape. They were disappointed and indignant as they saw the cords brought forward to bind the hands of Him whom they loved. Peter in his anger rashly drew his sword and tried to defend his Master, but he only cut off an ear of the high priest's servant. When Jesus saw what was done, He released His hands, though held firmly by the Roman soldiers, and saying, "Suffer ye thus far," He touched the wounded ear, and it was instantly made whole. He then said to Peter, "Put up again thy sword into his place: for all they that take the sword shall perish with the sword. Thinkest thou that I cannot now pray to My Father, and He shall presently give Me more than twelve legions of angels?"—a legion in place of each one of the disciples. Oh, why, the disciples thought, does He not save Himself and

us? Answering their unspoken thought, He added, "But how then shall the scriptures be fulfilled, that thus it must be?" "The cup which My Father hath given Me, shall I not drink it?"

The official dignity of the Jewish leaders had not prevented them from joining in the pursuit of Jesus. His arrest was too important a matter to be trusted to subordinates; the wily priests and elders had joined the temple police and the rabble in following Judas to Gethsemane. What a company for those dignitaries to unite with—a mob that was eager for excitement, and armed with all kinds of implements, as if in pursuit of a wild beast!

Turning to the priests and elders, Christ fixed 697 upon them His searching glance. The words He spoke they would never forget as long as life should last. They were as the sharp arrows of the Almighty. With dignity He said: You come out against Me with swords and staves as you would against a thief or a robber. Day by day I sat teaching in the temple. You had every opportunity of laying hands upon Me, and you did nothing. The night is better suited to your work. "This is your hour, and the power of darkness."

The disciples were terrified as they saw Jesus permit Himself to be taken and bound. They were offended that He should suffer this humiliation to Himself and them. They could not understand His conduct, and they blamed Him for submitting to the mob. In their indignation and fear, Peter proposed that they save themselves. Following this suggestion, "they all forsook Him, and fled." But Christ had foretold this desertion. "Behold," He had said, "the hour cometh, yea, is now come, that ye shall be scattered, every man to his own, and shall leave Me alone: and yet I am not alone, because the Father is with Me." John 16:32.

75   698

Before Annas and
the Court of Caiaphas

Over the brook Kedron, past gardens and olive groves, and through the hushed streets of the sleeping city, they hurried Jesus. It was past midnight, and the cries of the hooting mob that followed Him broke sharply upon the still air. The Saviour was bound and closely guarded, and He moved painfully. But in eager haste His captors made their way with Him to the palace of Annas, the ex-high priest.

Annas was the head of the officiating priestly family, and in deference to his age he was recognized by the people as high priest. His counsel was sought and carried out as the voice of

This chapter is based on Matthew 26:57-75; 27:1; Mark 14:53-72; 15:1; Luke 22:54-71; John 18:13-27.

God. He must first see Jesus a captive to priestly power. He must be present at the examination of the prisoner, for fear that the less-experienced Caiaphas might fail of securing the object for which they were working. His artifice, cunning, and subtlety must be used on this occasion; for, at all events, Christ's condemnation must be secured.

Christ was to be tried formally before the Sanhedrin; but before Annas He was subjected to a preliminary trial. Under the Roman rule the Sanhedrin could not execute the sentence of death. They could only examine a prisoner, and pass judgment, to be ratified by the Roman authorities. It was therefore necessary to bring against Christ charges that would be regarded as criminal by the Romans. An accusation must also be found which would condemn Him in the eyes of the Jews. Not a few among the priests and rulers had been convicted by Christ's teaching, and only fear of excommunication prevented them from confessing Him. The priests well remembered the question of Nicodemus, "Doth our law judge any man, before it hear him, and know what he doeth?" John 7:51. This question had for the time broken up the council, and thwarted their plans. Joseph of Arimathaea and Nicodemus were not now to be summoned, but there were others who might dare to speak in favor of justice. The trial must be so conducted as to unite the members of the Sanhedrin against Christ. There were two charges which the priests desired to maintain. If Jesus could be proved a blasphemer, He would be condemned by the Jews. If convicted of sedition, it would secure His condemnation by the Romans. The second charge Annas tried first to establish. He questioned Jesus concerning His disciples and His doctrines, hoping the prisoner would say something that would give him material upon which to work. He thought to draw out some statement to prove that He was seeking to establish a secret society, with the purpose of setting up a new kingdom. Then the priests could deliver Him to the Romans as a disturber of the peace and a creator of insurrection.

Christ read the priest's purpose as an open book. As if reading the inmost soul of His questioner, He denied that there was between Him and His followers any secret bond of union, or that He gathered them secretly and in the darkness to conceal His designs. He had no secrets in regard to His purposes or doctrines. "I spake openly to the world," He answered; "I ever taught in the synagogue, and in the temple, whither the Jews always resort; and in secret have I said nothing."

The Saviour contrasted His own manner of work with the methods of His accusers. For months they had hunted Him, striving to entrap Him and bring Him before a secret tribunal, where they might obtain by perjury what it was impossible to gain by fair means. Now they were carrying out their purpose. The midnight seizure by a mob, the mockery and abuse before He was condemned, or even accused, was their manner of work, not His. Their action was in violation of the law. Their own rules declared that every man should be treated as innocent until proved guilty. By their own rules the priests stood condemned.

Turning upon His questioner, Jesus said, "Why askest thou Me?" Had not the priests and rulers sent spies to watch His movements, and report His every word? Had not these been present at every gathering of the people, and carried to the priests information of all His sayings and doings? "Ask them which heard Me, what I have said unto them," replied Jesus; "behold, they know what I said."

Annas was silenced by the decision of the answer. Fearing that Christ would say something regarding his course of action that he would prefer to keep covered up, he said nothing more to Him at this time. One of his officers, filled with wrath as he saw Annas silenced, struck Jesus on the face, saying, "Answerest Thou the high priest so?"

Christ calmly replied, "If I have spoken evil, bear witness of the evil: but if well, why smitest thou Me?" He spoke no burning words of retaliation. His calm answer came from a heart sinless, patient, and gentle, that would not be provoked.

Christ suffered keenly under abuse and insult. At the hands of the beings whom He had created, and for whom He was making an infinite sacrifice, He received every indignity. And He suffered in proportion to the perfection of His holiness and His hatred of sin. His trial by men who acted as fiends was to Him a perpetual sacrifice. To be surrounded by human beings under the control of Satan was revolting to Him. And He knew that in a moment, by the flashing forth of His divine power, He could lay His cruel tormentors in the dust. This made the trial the harder to bear.

The Jews were looking for a Messiah to be revealed in outward show. They expected Him, by one flash of overmastering will, to change the current of men's thoughts, and force from them an acknowledgment of His supremacy. Thus, they believed, He was to secure His own exaltation, and gratify their ambitious hopes. Thus when Christ was treated with contempt, there came to Him a strong temptation to manifest His divine character. By a word, by a look, He could compel His persecutors to confess that He was Lord above kings and rulers, priests and temple. But it was His difficult task to keep to the position He had chosen as one with humanity.

The angels of heaven witnessed every movement made against their loved Commander.

They longed to deliver Christ. Under God the angels are all-powerful. On one occasion, in obedience to the command of Christ, they slew of the Assyrian army in one night one hundred and eighty-five thousand men. How easily could the angels, beholding the shameful scene of the trial of Christ, have testified their indignation by consuming the adversaries of God! But they were not commanded to do this. He who could have doomed His enemies to death bore with their cruelty. His love for His Father, and His pledge, made from the foundation of the world, to become the Sin Bearer, led Him to endure uncomplainingly the coarse treatment of those He came to save. It was a part of His mission to bear, in His humanity, all the taunts and abuse that men could heap upon Him. The only hope of humanity was in this submission of Christ to all that He could endure from the hands and hearts of men.

Christ had said nothing that could give His accusers an advantage; yet He was bound, to signify that He was condemned. There must, however, be a pretense of justice. It was necessary that there should be the form of a legal trial. This the authorities were determined to hasten. They knew the regard in which Jesus was held by the people, and feared that if the arrest were noised abroad, a rescue would be attempted. Again, if the trial and execution were not brought about at once, there would be a week's delay on account of the celebration of the Passover. This might defeat their plans. In securing the condemnation of Jesus they depended largely upon the clamor of the mob, many of them the rabble of Jerusalem. Should there be a week's delay, the excitement would abate, and a reaction would be likely to set in. The better part of the people would be aroused in Christ's favor; many would come forward with testimony in His vindication, bringing to light the mighty works He had done. This would excite popular indignation against the Sanhedrin. Their proceedings would be condemned, and Jesus would be set free, to receive new homage from the multitudes. The priests and rulers therefore determined that before their purpose could become known, Jesus should be delivered into the hands of the Romans.

But first of all, an accusation was to be found. They had gained nothing as yet. Annas ordered Jesus to be taken to Caiaphas. Caiaphas belonged to the Sadducees, some of whom were now the most desperate enemies of Jesus. He himself, though wanting in force of character, was fully as severe, heartless, and unscrupulous as was Annas. He would leave no means untried to destroy Jesus. It was now early morning, and very dark; by the light of torches and lanterns the armed band with their prisoner proceeded to the high priest's palace. Here, while the members of the Sanhedrin were coming together,

Annas and Caiaphas again questioned Jesus, but without success.

When the council had assembled in the judgment hall, Caiaphas took his seat as presiding officer. On either side were the judges, and those specially interested in the trial. The Roman soldiers were stationed on the platform below the throne. At the foot of the throne stood Jesus. Upon Him the gaze of the whole multitude was fixed. The excitement was intense. Of all the throng He alone was calm and serene. The very atmosphere surrounding Him seemed pervaded by a holy influence.

Caiaphas had regarded Jesus as his rival. The eagerness of the people to hear the Saviour, and their apparent readiness to accept His teachings, had aroused the bitter jealousy of the high priest. But as Caiaphas now looked upon the prisoner, he was struck with admiration for His noble and dignified bearing. A conviction came over him that this Man was akin to God. The next instant he scornfully banished the thought. Immediately his voice was heard in sneering, haughty tones demanding that Jesus work one of His mighty miracles before them. But his words fell upon the Saviour's ears as though He heard them not. The people compared the excited and malignant deportment of Annas and Caiaphas with the calm, majestic bearing of Jesus. Even in the minds of that hardened multitude arose the question, Is this man of godlike presence to be condemned as a criminal?

Caiaphas, perceiving the influence that was obtaining, hastened the trial. The enemies of Jesus were in great perplexity. They were bent on securing His condemnation, but how to accomplish this they knew not. The members of the council were divided between the Pharisees and the Sadducees. There was bitter animosity and controversy between them; certain disputed points they dared not approach for fear of a quarrel. With a few words Jesus could have excited their prejudices against each other, and thus have averted their wrath from Himself. Caiaphas knew this, and he wished to avoid stirring up a contention. There were plenty of witnesses to prove that Christ had denounced the priests and scribes, that He had called them hypocrites and murderers; but their testimony it was not expedient to bring forward. The Sadducees in their sharp contentions with the Pharisees had used to them similar language. And such testimony would have no weight with the Romans, who were themselves disgusted with the pretensions of the Pharisees. There was abundant evidence that Jesus had disregarded the traditions of the Jews, and had spoken irreverently of many of their ordinances; but in regard to tradition the Pharisees and Sadducees were at swords' points; and this evidence also would have no weight with the Romans. Christ's enemies dared not accuse Him of Sabbathbreaking, lest an examination should reveal the character of His work. If His miracles of healing were brought to light, the very object of the priests would be defeated.

False witnesses had been bribed to accuse Jesus of inciting rebellion and seeking to establish a separate government. But their testimony proved to be vague and contradictory. Under examination they falsified their own statements.

Early in His ministry Christ had said, "Destroy this temple, and in three days I will raise it up." In the figurative language of prophecy, He had thus foretold His own death and resurrection. "He spake of the temple of His body." John 2:19, 21. These words the Jews had understood in a literal sense, as referring to the temple at Jerusalem. Of all that Christ had said, the priests could find nothing to use against Him 706 save this. By misstating these words they hoped to gain an advantage. The Romans had engaged in rebuilding and embellishing the temple, and they took great pride in it; any contempt shown to it would be sure to excite their indignation. Here Romans and Jews, Pharisees and Sadducees, could meet; for all held the temple in great veneration. On this point two witnesses were found whose testimony was not so contradictory as that of the others had been. One of them, who had been bribed to accuse Jesus, declared, "This fellow said, I am able to destroy the temple of God, and to build it in three days." Thus Christ's words were misstated. If they had been reported exactly as He spoke them, they would not have secured His condemnation even by the Sanhedrin. Had Jesus been a mere man, as the Jews claimed, His declaration would only have indicated an unreasonable, boastful spirit, but could not have been construed into blasphemy. Even as misrepresented by the false witnesses, His words contained nothing which would be regarded by the Romans as a crime worthy of death.

Patiently Jesus listened to the conflicting testimonies. No word did He utter in self-defense. At last His accusers were entangled, confused, and maddened. The trial was making no headway; it seemed that their plottings were to fail. Caiaphas was desperate. One last resort remained; Christ must be forced to condemn Himself. The high priest started from the judgment seat, his face contorted with passion, his voice and demeanor plainly indicating that were it in his power he would strike down the prisoner before him. "Answerest Thou nothing?" he exclaimed; "what is it which these witness against Thee?"

Jesus held His peace. "He was oppressed, and He was afflicted, yet He opened not His mouth: He is brought as a lamb to the slaughter, and as a sheep before her shearers is dumb, so He openeth not His mouth." Isaiah 53:7.

At last, Caiaphas, raising his right hand toward heaven, addressed Jesus in the form of a solemn oath: "I adjure Thee by the living God, that Thou tell us whether Thou be the Christ, the Son of God."

To this appeal Christ could not remain silent. There was a time to be silent, and a time to speak. He had not spoken until directly questioned. He knew that to answer now would make His death certain. But the appeal was made by the highest acknowledged authority of the nation, and in the name of the Most High. Christ would not fail to show proper respect for the law. More than this, His own relation to the Father was called in question. He must plainly declare His character and mission. Jesus had 707 said to His disciples, "Whosoever therefore shall confess Me before men, him will I confess also before My Father which is in heaven." Matt. 10:32. Now by His own example He repeated the lesson.

Every ear was bent to listen, and every eye was fixed on His face as He answered, "Thou hast said." A heavenly light seemed to illuminate His pale countenance as He added, "Nevertheless I say unto you, Hereafter shall ye see the Son of man sitting on the right hand of power, and coming in the clouds of heaven."

For a moment the divinity of Christ flashed through His guise of humanity. The high priest quailed before the penetrating eyes of the Saviour. That look seemed to read his hidden thoughts, and burn into his heart. Never in after-life did he forget that searching glance of the persecuted Son of God.

"Hereafter," said Jesus, "shall ye see the Son of man sitting on the right hand of power, and 708 coming in the clouds of heaven." In these words Christ presented the reverse of the scene then taking place. He, the Lord of life and glory, would be seated at God's right hand. He would be the judge of all the earth, and from His decision there could be no appeal. Then every secret thing would be set in the light of God's countenance, and judgment be passed upon every man according to his deeds.

The words of Christ startled the high priest. The thought that there was to be a resurrection of the dead, when all would stand at the bar of God, to be rewarded according to their works, was a thought of terror to Caiaphas. He did not wish to believe that in future he would receive sentence according to his works. There rushed before his mind a panorama of the scenes of the final judgment. For a moment he saw the fearful spectacle of the graves giving up their dead, with the secrets he had hoped were forever hidden. For a moment he felt as if standing before the eternal Judge, whose eye, which sees all things, was reading his soul, bringing to light mysteries supposed to be hidden with the dead.

The scene passed from the priest's vision. Christ's words cut him, the Sadducee, to the quick. Caiaphas had denied the doctrine of the resurrection, the judgment, and a future life. Now he was maddened by satanic fury. Was this man, a prisoner before him, to assail his most cherished theories? Rending his robe, that the people might see his pretended horror, he demanded that without further preliminaries the prisoner be condemned for blasphemy. "What further need have we of witnesses?" he said; "behold, now ye have heard His blasphemy. What think ye?" And they all condemned Him.

Conviction mingled with passion led Caiaphas to do as he did. He was furious with himself for believing Christ's words, and instead of rending his heart under a deep sense of truth, and confessing that Jesus was the Messiah, he rent his priestly robes in determined resistance. This act was deeply significant. Little did Caiaphas realize its meaning. In this act, done to influence the judges and secure Christ's condemnation, the high priest had condemned himself. By the law of God he was disqualified for the priesthood. He had pronounced upon himself the death sentence.

A high priest was not to rend his garments. By the Levitical law, this was prohibited under sentence of death. Under no circumstances, on no occasion, was the priest to rend his robe. It was the custom among the Jews for the garments to be rent at the death of friends, but this

709 custom the priests were not to observe. Express command had been given by Christ to Moses concerning this. Lev. 10:6.

Everything worn by the priest was to be whole and without blemish. By those beautiful official garments was represented the character of the great antitype, Jesus Christ. Nothing but perfection, in dress and attitude, in word and spirit, could be acceptable to God. He is holy, and His glory and perfection must be represented by the earthly service. Nothing but perfection could properly represent the sacredness of the heavenly service. Finite man might rend his own heart by showing a contrite and humble spirit. This God would discern. But no rent must be made in the priestly robes, for this would mar the representation of heavenly things. The high priest who dared to appear in holy office, and engage in the service of the sanctuary, with a rent robe, was looked upon as having severed himself from God. By rending his garment he cut himself off from being a representative character. He was no longer accepted by God as an officiating priest. This course of action, as exhibited by Caiaphas, showed human passion, human imperfection.

By rending his garments, Caiaphas made of no effect the law of God, to follow the tradition of men. A man-made law provided that in case of blasphemy a priest might rend his garments in horror at the sin, and be guiltless. Thus the law of God was made void by the laws of men.

Each action of the high priest was watched with interest by the people; and Caiaphas thought for effect to display his piety. But in this act, designed as an accusation against Christ, he was reviling the One of whom God had said, "My name is in Him." Ex. 23:21. He himself was committing blasphemy. Standing under the condemnation of God, he pronounced sentence upon Christ as a blasphemer.

When Caiaphas rent his garment, his act was significant of the place that the Jewish nation as a nation would thereafter occupy toward God. The once favored people of God were separating themselves from Him, and were fast becoming a people disowned by Jehovah. When Christ upon the cross cried out, "It is finished" (John 19:30), and the veil of the temple was rent in twain, the Holy Watcher declared that the Jewish people had rejected Him who was the antitype of all their types, the substance of all their shadows. Israel was divorced from God. Well might Caiaphas then rend his official robes, which signified that he claimed to be a representative of the great High Priest; for no longer had they any meaning for him or for the people. Well might the high priest rend his robes in horror for himself and for the nation.

The Sanhedrin had pronounced Jesus worthy 710 of death; but it was contrary to the Jewish law to try a prisoner by night. In legal condemnation nothing could be done except in the light of day and before a full session of the council. Notwithstanding this, the Saviour was now treated as a condemned criminal, and given up to be abused by the lowest and vilest of humankind. The palace of the high priest surrounded an open court in which the soldiers and the multitude had gathered. Through this court, Jesus was taken to the guardroom, on every side meeting with mockery of His claim to be the Son of God. His own words, "sitting on the right hand of power," and, "coming in the clouds of heaven," were jeeringly repeated. While in the guardroom, awaiting His legal trial, He was not protected. The ignorant rabble had seen the cruelty with which He was treated before the council, and from this they took license to manifest all the satanic elements of their nature. Christ's very nobility and godlike bearing goaded them to madness. His meekness, His innocence, His majestic patience, filled them with hatred born of Satan. Mercy and justice were trampled upon. Never was criminal treated in so inhuman a manner as was the Son of God.

But a keener anguish rent the heart of Jesus; the blow that inflicted the deepest pain no enemy's hand could have dealt. While He was undergoing the mockery of an examination before Caiaphas, Christ had been denied by one of His own disciples.

After deserting their Master in the garden,

two of the disciples had ventured to follow, at a distance, the mob that had Jesus in charge. These disciples were Peter and John. The priests recognized John as a well-known disciple of Jesus, and admitted him to the hall, hoping that as he witnessed the humiliation of his Leader, he would scorn the idea of such a one being the Son of God. John spoke in favor of Peter, and gained an entrance for him also.

In the court a fire had been kindled; for it was the coldest hour of the night, being just before the dawn. A company drew about the fire, and Peter presumptuously took his place with them. He did not wish to be recognized as a disciple of Jesus. By mingling carelessly with the crowd, he hoped to be taken for one of those who had brought Jesus to the hall.

But as the light flashed upon Peter's face, the woman who kept the door cast a searching glance upon him. She had noticed that he came in with John, she marked the look of dejection 711 on his face, and thought that he might be a disciple of Jesus. She was one of the servants of Caiaphas' household, and was curious to know. She said to Peter, "Art not thou also one of this Man's disciples?" Peter was startled and confused; the eyes of the company instantly fastened upon him. He pretended not to understand her; but she was persistent, and said to those around her that this man was with Jesus. Peter felt compelled to answer, and said angrily, "Woman, I know Him not." This was the first denial, and immediately the cock crew. O Peter, so soon ashamed of thy Master! so soon to deny thy Lord!

The disciple John, upon entering the judgment hall, did not try to conceal the fact that he was a follower of Jesus. He did not mingle with the rough company who were reviling his Master. He was not questioned, for he did not assume a false character, and thus lay himself liable to suspicion. He sought a retired corner 712 secure from the notice of the mob, but as near Jesus as it was possible for him to be. Here he could see and hear all that took place at the trial of his Lord.

Peter had not designed that his real character should be known. In assuming an air of indifference he had placed himself on the enemy's ground, and he became an easy prey to temptation. If he had been called to fight for his Master, he would have been a courageous soldier; but when the finger of scorn was pointed at him, he proved himself a coward. Many who do not shrink from active warfare for their Lord are driven by ridicule to deny their faith. By associating with those whom they should avoid, they place themselves in the way of temptation. They invite the enemy to tempt them, and are led to say and do that of which under other circumstances they would never have been guilty. The disciple of Christ who in our day disguises his

faith through dread of suffering or reproach denies his Lord as really as did Peter in the judgment hall.

Peter tried to show no interest in the trial of his Master, but his heart was wrung with sorrow as he heard the cruel taunts, and saw the abuse He was suffering. More than this, he was surprised and angry that Jesus should humiliate Himself and His followers by submitting to such treatment. In order to conceal his true feelings, he endeavored to join with the persecutors of Jesus in their untimely jests. But his appearance was unnatural. He was acting a lie, and while seeking to talk unconcernedly he could not restrain expressions of indignation at the abuse heaped upon his Master.

Attention was called to him the second time, and he was again charged with being a follower of Jesus. He now declared with an oath, "I do not know the Man." Still another opportunity was given him. An hour had passed, when one of the servants of the high priest, being a near kinsman of the man whose ear Peter had cut off, asked him, "Did not I see thee in the garden with Him?" "Surely thou art one of them: for thou art a Galilean, and thy speech agreeth thereto." At this Peter flew into a rage. The disciples of Jesus were noted for the purity of their language, and in order fully to deceive his questioners, and justify his assumed character, Peter now denied his Master with cursing and swearing. Again the cock crew. Peter heard it then, and he remembered the words of Jesus, "Before the cock crow twice, thou shalt deny Me thrice." Mark 14:30.

While the degrading oaths were fresh upon Peter's lips, and the shrill crowing of the cock 713 was still ringing in his ears, the Saviour turned from the frowning judges, and looked full upon His poor disciple. At the same time Peter's eyes were drawn to his Master. In that gentle countenance he read deep pity and sorrow, but there was no anger there.

The sight of that pale, suffering face, those quivering lips, that look of compassion and forgiveness, pierced his heart like an arrow. Conscience was aroused. Memory was active. Peter called to mind his promise of a few short hours before that he would go with his Lord to prison and to death. He remembered his grief when the Saviour told him in the upper chamber that he would deny his Lord thrice that same night. Peter had just declared that he knew not Jesus, but he now realized with bitter grief how well his Lord knew him, and how accurately He had read his heart, the falseness of which was unknown even to himself.

A tide of memories rushed over him. The Saviour's tender mercy, His kindness and longsuffering, His gentleness and patience toward His erring disciples,—all was remembered. He recalled the caution, "Simon, behold, Satan hath desired to have you, that he may sift you as wheat: but I have prayed for thee, that thy faith fail not." Luke 22:31, 32. He reflected with horror upon his own ingratitude, his falsehood, his perjury. Once more he looked at his Master, and saw a sacrilegious hand raised to smite Him in the face. Unable longer to endure the scene, he rushed, heartbroken, from the hall.

He pressed on in solitude and darkness, he knew not and cared not whither. At last he found himself in Gethsemane. The scene of a few hours before came vividly to his mind. The suffering face of his Lord, stained with bloody sweat and convulsed with anguish, rose before him. He remembered with bitter remorse that Jesus had wept and agonized in prayer alone, while those who should have united with Him in that trying hour were sleeping. He remembered His solemn charge, "Watch and pray, that ye enter not into temptation." Matt. 26:41. He witnessed again the scene in the judgment hall. It was torture to his bleeding heart to know that he had added the heaviest burden to the Saviour's humiliation and grief. On the very spot where Jesus had poured out His soul in agony to His Father, Peter fell upon his face, and wished that he might die.

It was in sleeping when Jesus bade him watch and pray that Peter had prepared the way for his 714 great sin. All the disciples, by sleeping in that critical hour, sustained a great loss. Christ knew the fiery ordeal through which they were to pass. He knew how Satan would work to paralyze their senses that they might be unready for the trial. Therefore it was that He gave them warning. Had those hours in the garden been spent in watching and prayer, Peter would not have been left to depend upon his own feeble strength. He would not have denied his Lord. Had the disciples watched with Christ in His agony, they would have been prepared to behold His suffering upon the cross. They would have understood in some degree the nature of His overpowering anguish. They would have been able to recall His words that foretold His sufferings, His death, and His resurrection. Amid the gloom of the most trying hour, some rays of hope would have lighted up the darkness and sustained their faith.

As soon as it was day, the Sanhedrin again assembled, and again Jesus was brought into the council room. He had declared Himself the Son of God, and they had construed His words into a charge against Him. But they could not condemn Him on this, for many of them had not been present at the night session, and they had not heard His words. And they knew that the Roman tribunal would find in them nothing worthy of death. But if from His own lips they could all hear those words repeated, their object might be gained. His claim to the Messiahship they might construe into a seditious political claim.

"Art Thou the Christ?" they said, "tell us." But Christ remained silent. They continued to ply Him with questions. At last in tones of mournful pathos He answered, "If I tell you, ye will not believe: and if I also ask you, ye will not answer Me, nor let Me go." But that they might be left without excuse He added the solemn warning, "Hereafter shall the Son of man sit on the right hand of the power of God."

"Art Thou then the Son of God?" they asked with one voice. He said unto them, "Ye say that I am." They cried out, "What need we any further witness? for we ourselves have heard of His own mouth."

And so by the third condemnation of the Jewish authorities, Jesus was to die. All that was now necessary, they thought, was for the Romans to ratify this condemnation, and deliver Him into their hands.

Then came the third scene of abuse and mockery, worse even than that received from the ignorant rabble. In the very presence of the priests and rulers, and with their sanction, this took place. Every feeling of sympathy or humanity had gone out of their hearts. If their arguments were weak, and failed to silence His 715 voice, they had other weapons, such as in all ages have been used to silence heretics,—suffering, and violence, and death.

When the condemnation of Jesus was pronounced by the judges, a satanic fury took possession of the people. The roar of voices was like that of wild beasts. The crowd made a rush toward Jesus, crying, He is guilty, put Him to death! Had it not been for the Roman soldiers, Jesus would not have lived to be nailed to the cross of Calvary. He would have been torn in pieces before His judges, had not Roman authority interfered, and by force of arms restrained the violence of the mob.

Heathen men were angry at the brutal treatment of one against whom nothing had been proved. The Roman officers declared that the Jews in pronouncing condemnation upon Jesus were infringing upon the Roman power, and that it was even against the Jewish law to condemn a man to death upon his own testimony. This intervention brought a momentary lull in the proceedings; but the Jewish leaders were dead alike to pity and to shame.

Priests and rulers forgot the dignity of their office, and abused the Son of God with foul epithets. They taunted Him with His parentage. They declared that His presumption in proclaiming Himself the Messiah made Him deserving of the most ignominious death. The most dissolute men engaged in infamous abuse of the Saviour. An old garment was thrown over His head, and His persecutors struck Him in the face, saying, "Prophesy unto us, Thou Christ, Who is he that smote Thee?" When the garment was removed, one poor wretch spat in His face.

The angels of God faithfully recorded every insulting look, word, and act against their beloved Commander. One day the base men who scorned and spat upon the calm, pale face of Christ will look upon it in its glory, shining brighter than the sun.

76

Judas

The history of Judas presents the sad ending of a life that might have been honored of God. Had Judas died before his last journey to Jerusalem he would have been regarded as a man worthy of a place among the twelve, and one who would be greatly missed. The abhorrence which has followed him through the centuries would not have existed but for the attributes revealed at the close of his history. But it was for a purpose that his character was laid open to the world. It was to be a warning to all who, like him, should betray sacred trusts.

A little before the Passover, Judas had renewed his contract with the priests to deliver Jesus into their hands. Then it was arranged that the Saviour should be taken at one of His resorts for meditation and prayer. Since the feast at the house of Simon, Judas had had opportunity to reflect upon the deed which he had covenanted to perform, but his purpose was unchanged. For thirty pieces of silver—the price of a slave—he sold the Lord of glory to ignominy and death.

Judas had naturally a strong love for money; but he had not always been corrupt enough to do such a deed as this. He had fostered the evil spirit of avarice until it had become the ruling motive of his life. The love of mammon overbalanced his love for Christ. Through becoming the slave of one vice he gave himself to Satan, to be driven to any lengths in sin.

Judas had joined the disciples when multitudes were following Christ. The Saviour's teaching moved their hearts as they hung entranced upon His words, spoken in the synagogue, by the seaside, upon the mount. Judas saw the sick, the lame, the blind, flock to Jesus from the towns and cities. He saw the dying laid at His feet. He witnessed the Saviour's mighty works in healing the sick, casting out devils, and raising the dead. He felt in his own person the evidence of Christ's power. He recognized the teaching of Christ as superior to all that he had ever heard. He loved the Great Teacher, and desired to be with Him. He felt a desire to be changed in character and life, and he hoped to experience this through connecting himself with Jesus. The Saviour did not repulse Judas. He gave him a place among the twelve. He trusted him to do the work of an evangelist. He endowed him with power to heal the sick and to cast out devils. But Judas did not come to the point of surrendering himself fully to Christ. He did not give up his worldly ambition or his love of money. While he accepted the position of a minister of Christ, he did not bring himself under the divine molding. He felt that he could retain his own judgment and opinions, and he cultivated a disposition to criticize and accuse.

Judas was highly regarded by the disciples, and had great influence over them. He himself had a high opinion of his own qualifications, and looked upon his brethren as greatly inferior to him in judgment and ability. They did not see their opportunities, he thought, and take advantage of circumstances. The church would never prosper with such shortsighted men as leaders. Peter was impetuous; he would move without consideration. John, who was treasuring up the truths that fell from Christ's lips, was looked upon by Judas as a poor financier. Matthew, whose training had taught him accuracy in all things, was very particular in regard to honesty, and he was ever contemplating the words of Christ, and became so absorbed in them that, as Judas thought, he could not be trusted to do sharp, far-seeing business. Thus Judas summed up all the disciples, and flattered himself that the church would often be brought into perplexity and embarrassment if it were not for his ability as a manager. Judas regarded himself as the capable one, who could not be overreached. In his own estimation he was an honor to the cause, and as such he always represented himself.

Judas was blinded to his own weakness of character, and Christ placed him where he would have an opportunity to see and correct this. As treasurer for the disciples, he was called upon to provide for the needs of the little company, and to relieve the necessities of the poor. When in the Passover chamber Jesus said to him, "That thou doest, do quickly" (John 13:27), the disciples thought He had bidden him buy what was needed for the feast, or give something to the poor. In ministering to others, Judas might have developed an unselfish spirit. But while listening daily to the lessons of Christ and witnessing His unselfish life, Judas indulged his covetous disposition. The small sums that came into his hands were a continual temptation. Often when he did a little service for Christ, or devoted time to religious purposes, he paid himself out of this meager fund. In his own eyes these pretexts served to excuse his action; but in God's sight he was a thief.

Christ's oft-repeated statement that His kingdom was not of this world offended Judas. He had marked out a line upon which he expected Christ to work. He had planned that John the Baptist should be delivered from prison. But lo, John was left to be beheaded. And Jesus, instead of asserting His royal right and avenging the death of John, retired with His disciples into a country place. Judas wanted more aggressive warfare. He thought that if Jesus would not prevent the disciples from carrying out their schemes, the work would be more successful. He marked the increasing enmity of the Jewish leaders, and saw their challenge unheeded when they demanded from Christ a sign from heaven. His heart was open to unbelief, and the enemy supplied thoughts of questioning and rebellion. Why did Jesus dwell so much upon that which was discouraging? Why did He predict trial and persecution for Himself and for His disciples? The prospect of having a high place in the new kingdom had led Judas to espouse the cause of Christ. Were his hopes to be disappointed? Judas had not decided that Jesus was not the Son of God; but he was questioning, and seeking to find some explanation of His mighty works.

Notwithstanding the Saviour's own teaching, Judas was continually advancing the idea that Christ would reign as king in Jerusalem. At the feeding of the five thousand he tried to bring this about. On this occasion Judas assisted in distributing the food to the hungry multitude. He had an opportunity to see the benefit which it was in his power to impart to others. He felt the satisfaction that always comes in service to God. He helped to bring the sick and suffering from among the multitude to Christ. He saw what relief, what joy and gladness, come to human hearts through the healing power of the Restorer. He might have comprehended the methods of Christ. But he was blinded by his own selfish desires. Judas was first to take advantage of the enthusiasm excited by the miracle of the loaves. It was he who set on foot the 719 project to take Christ by force and make Him king. His hopes were high. His disappointment was bitter.

Christ's discourse in the synagogue concerning the bread of life was the turning point in the history of Judas. He heard the words, "Except ye eat the flesh of the Son of man, and drink His blood, ye have no life in you." John 6:53. He saw that Christ was offering spiritual rather than worldly good. He regarded himself as farsighted, and thought he could see that Jesus would have no honor, and that He could bestow no high position upon His followers. He determined not to unite himself so closely to Christ but that he could draw away. He would watch. And he did watch.

From that time he expressed doubts that confused the disciples. He introduced controversies and misleading sentiments, repeating the arguments urged by the scribes and Pharisees against the claims of Christ. All the little and large troubles and crosses, the difficulties and the apparent hindrances to the advancement of the gospel, Judas interpreted as evidences against its truthfulness. He would introduce texts of Scripture that had no connection with the truths Christ was presenting. These texts, separated from their connection, perplexed the disciples, and increased the discouragement that was constantly pressing upon them. Yet all this was done by Judas in such a way as to make it appear that he was conscientious. And while the disciples were searching for evidence to confirm the words of the Great Teacher, Judas would lead them almost imperceptibly on another track. Thus in a very religious, and apparently wise, way he was presenting matters in a different light from that in which Jesus had given them, and attaching to His words a meaning that He had not conveyed. His suggestions were constantly exciting an ambitious desire for temporal preferment, and thus turning the disciples from the important things they should have considered. The dissension as to which of them should be greatest was generally excited by Judas.

When Jesus presented to the rich young ruler the condition of discipleship, Judas was displeased. He thought that a mistake had been made. If such men as this ruler could be connected with the believers, they would help sustain Christ's cause. If Judas were only received as a counselor, he thought, he could suggest many plans for the advantage of the little church. His principles and methods would differ somewhat from Christ's, but in these things he thought himself wiser than Christ.

In all that Christ said to His disciples, there 720 was something with which, in heart, Judas disagreed. Under his influence the leaven of disaffection was fast doing its work. The disciples did not see the real agency in all this; but Jesus saw that Satan was communicating his attributes to Judas, and thus opening up a channel through which to influence the other disciples. This, a year before the betrayal, Christ declared. "Have not I chosen you twelve," He said, "and one of you is a devil?" John 6:70.

Yet Judas made no open opposition, nor seemed to question the Saviour's lessons. He made no outward murmur until the time of the feast in Simon's house. When Mary anointed the Saviour's feet, Judas manifested his covetous disposition. At the reproof from Jesus his very spirit seemed turned to gall. Wounded pride and desire for revenge broke down the barriers, and the greed so long indulged held him in control. This will be the experience of everyone who persists in tampering with sin. The elements of depravity that are not resisted and overcome respond to Satan's temptation, and the soul is led captive at his will.

But Judas was not yet wholly hardened. Even after he had twice pledged himself to betray the Saviour, there was opportunity for repentance. At the Passover supper Jesus proved His divinity by revealing the traitor's purpose. He tenderly included Judas in the ministry to the disciples. But the last appeal of love was unheeded. Then the case of Judas was decided, and the feet that Jesus had washed went forth to the betrayer's work.

Judas reasoned that if Jesus was to be crucified, the event must come to pass. His own act in betraying the Saviour would not change the result. If Jesus was not to die, it would only force Him to deliver Himself. At all events, Judas would gain something by his treachery. He counted that he had made a sharp bargain in betraying his Lord.

Judas did not, however, believe that Christ would permit Himself to be arrested. In betraying Him, it was his purpose to teach Him a lesson. He intended to play a part that would make the Saviour careful thenceforth to treat him with due respect. But Judas knew not that he was giving Christ up to death. How often, as the Saviour taught in parables, the scribes and Pharisees had been carried away with His striking illustrations! How often they had pronounced judgment against themselves! Often when the truth was brought home to their hearts, they had been filled with rage, and had taken up stones to 721 cast at Him; but again and again He had made His escape. Since He had escaped so many snares, thought Judas, He certainly would not now allow Himself to be taken.

Judas decided to put the matter to the test. If Jesus really was the Messiah, the people, for whom He had done so much, would rally about Him, and would proclaim Him king. This would forever settle many minds that were now in uncertainty. Judas would have the credit of having placed the king on David's throne. And this act would secure to him the first position, next to Christ, in the new kingdom.

The false disciple acted his part in betraying Jesus. In the garden, when he said to the leaders of the mob, "Whomsoever I shall kiss, that same is He: hold Him fast" (Matt. 26:48), he fully believed that Christ would escape out of their hands. Then if they should blame him, he could say, Did I not tell you to hold Him fast?

Judas beheld the captors of Christ, acting upon his words, bind Him firmly. In amazement he saw that the Saviour suffered Himself to be led away. Anxiously he followed Him from the garden to the trial before the Jewish rulers. At every movement he looked for Him to surprise His enemies, by appearing before them as the Son of God, and setting at nought all their plots and power. But as hour after hour went by, and Jesus submitted to all the abuse heaped upon Him, a terrible fear came to the traitor that he had sold his Master to His death.

As the trial drew to a close, Judas could endure the torture of his guilty conscience no longer. Suddenly a hoarse voice rang through the hall, sending a thrill of terror to all hearts: He is innocent; spare Him, O Caiaphas!

The tall form of Judas was now seen pressing through the startled throng. His face was pale and haggard, and great drops of sweat stood on his forehead. Rushing to the throne of judgment, he threw down before the high priest the pieces 722 of silver that had been the price of his Lord's betrayal. Eagerly grasping the robe of Caiaphas, he implored him to release Jesus, declaring that He had done nothing worthy of death. Caiaphas angrily shook him off, but was confused, and knew not what to say. The perfidy of the priests was revealed. It was evident that they had bribed the disciple to betray his Master.

"I have sinned," again cried Judas, "in that I have betrayed the innocent blood." But the high priest, regaining his self-possession, answered with scorn, "What is that to us? see thou to that." Matt. 27:4. The priests had been willing to make Judas their tool; but they despised his baseness. When he turned to them with confession, they spurned him.

Judas now cast himself at the feet of Jesus, acknowledging Him to be the Son of God, and entreating Him to deliver Himself. The Saviour did not reproach His betrayer. He knew that Judas did not repent; his confession was forced from his guilty soul by an awful sense of condemnation and a looking for of judgment, but he felt no deep, heartbreaking grief that he had betrayed the spotless Son of God, and denied the Holy One of Israel. Yet Jesus spoke no word of condemnation. He looked pityingly upon Judas, and said, For this hour came I into the world.

A murmur of surprise ran through the assembly. With amazement they beheld the forbearance of Christ toward His betrayer. Again there swept over them the conviction that this Man was more than mortal. But if He was the Son of God, they questioned, why did He not free Himself from His bonds and triumph over His accusers?

Judas saw that his entreaties were in vain, and he rushed from the hall exclaiming, It is too late! It is too late! He felt that he could not live to see Jesus crucified, and in despair went out and hanged himself.

Later that same day, on the road from Pilate's hall to Calvary, there came an interruption to the shouts and jeers of the wicked throng who were leading Jesus to the place of crucifixion. As they passed a retired spot, they saw at the foot of a lifeless tree, the body of Judas. It was a most revolting sight. His weight had broken the cord by which he had hanged himself to the tree. In falling, his body had been horribly mangled, and dogs were now devouring it. His remains were immediately buried out of sight; but there was less mockery among the throng, and many a pale face revealed the thoughts within. Retribution seemed already visiting those who were guilty of the blood of Jesus.

77

In Pilate's Judgment Hall

In the judgment hall of Pilate, the Roman governor, Christ stands bound as a prisoner. About Him are the guard of soldiers, and the hall is fast filling with spectators. Just outside the entrance are the judges of the Sanhedrin, priests, rulers, elders, and the mob.

After condemning Jesus, the council of the Sanhedrin had come to Pilate to have the sentence confirmed and executed. But these Jewish officials would not enter the Roman judgment hall. According to their ceremonial law they would be defiled thereby, and thus prevented from taking part in the feast of the Passover. In their blindness they did not see that murderous hatred had defiled their hearts. They did not see that Christ was the real Passover lamb, and that, since they had rejected Him, the great feast had for them lost its significance.

When the Saviour was brought into the judgment hall, Pilate looked upon Him with no friendly eyes. The Roman governor had been called from his bedchamber in haste, and he determined to do his work as quickly as possible. He was prepared to deal with the prisoner with magisterial severity. Assuming his severest expression, he turned to see what kind of man he had to examine, that he had been called from his repose at so early an hour. He knew that it must be someone whom the Jewish authorities were anxious to have tried and punished with haste.

Pilate looked at the men who had Jesus in charge, and then his gaze rested searchingly on Jesus. He had had to deal with all kinds of criminals; but never before had a man bearing marks of such goodness and nobility been brought before him. On His face he saw no sign of guilt, no expression of fear, no boldness or defiance. He saw a man of calm and dignified bearing, whose countenance bore not the marks of a criminal, but the signature of heaven.

Christ's appearance made a favorable impression upon Pilate. His better nature was roused. He had heard of Jesus and His works. His wife had told him something of the wonderful deeds performed by the Galilean prophet, who cured the sick and raised the dead. Now this revived as a dream in Pilate's mind. He recalled rumors that he had heard from several sources. He resolved to demand of the Jews their charges against the prisoner.

Who is this Man, and wherefore have ye brought Him? he said. What accusation bring ye against Him? The Jews were disconcerted. Knowing that they could not substantiate their charges against Christ, they did not desire a public examination. They answered that He was a deceiver called Jesus of Nazareth.

Again Pilate asked, "What accusation bring ye against this Man?" The priests did not answer his question, but in words that showed their irritation, they said, "If He were not a malefactor, we would not have delivered Him up unto thee." When those composing the Sanhedrin, the first men of the nation, bring to you a man they deem worthy of death, is there need to ask for an accusation against him? They hoped to impress Pilate with a sense of their importance, and thus lead him to accede to their request without going through many preliminaries. They were eager to have their sentence ratified; for they knew that the people who had witnessed Christ's marvelous works could tell a story very different from the fabrication they themselves were now rehearsing.

The priests thought that with the weak and vacillating Pilate they could carry through their plans without trouble. Before this he had signed the death warrant hastily, condemning to death men they knew were not worthy of death. In his estimation the life of a prisoner was of little account; whether he were innocent or guilty was of no special consequence. The priests hoped that Pilate would now inflict the death penalty on Jesus without giving Him a hearing. This they besought as a favor on the occasion of their great national festival.

But there was something in the prisoner that held Pilate back from this. He dared not do it. He read the purposes of the priests. He remembered how, not long before, Jesus had raised Lazarus, a man that had been dead four days; and he determined to know, before signing the sentence of condemnation, what were the charges against Him, and whether they could be proved.

If your judgment is sufficient, he said, why bring the prisoner to me? "Take ye Him, and judge Him according to your law." Thus pressed, the priests said that they had already passed sentence upon Him, but that they must have Pilate's sentence to render their condemnation valid. What is your sentence? Pilate asked. The death sentence, they answered; but it is not lawful for us to put any man to death. They asked Pilate to take their word as to Christ's guilt, and enforce their sentence. They would take the responsibility of the result.

Pilate was not a just or a conscientious judge; but weak though he was in moral power, he refused to grant this request. He would not condemn Jesus until a charge had been brought against Him.

The priests were in a dilemma. They saw that they must cloak their hypocrisy under the thickest concealment. They must not allow it to appear that Christ had been arrested on religious

This chapter is based on Matthew 27:2, 11-31; Mark 15:1-20; Luke 23:1-25; John 18:28-40; 19:1-16.

grounds. Were this put forward as a reason, their proceedings would have no weight with Pilate. They must make it appear that Jesus was working against the common law; then He could be punished as a political offender. Tumults and insurrection against the Roman government were constantly arising among the Jews. With these revolts the Romans had dealt very rigorously, and they were constantly on the watch to repress everything that could lead to an outbreak.

Only a few days before this the Pharisees had tried to entrap Christ with the question, "Is it lawful for us to give tribute unto Caesar?" But Christ had unveiled their hypocrisy. The Romans who were present had seen the utter failure of the plotters, and their discomfiture at His answer, "Render therefore unto Caesar the things which be Caesar's." Luke 20:22-25.

726 Now the priests thought to make it appear that on this occasion Christ had taught what they hoped He would teach. In their extremity they called false witnesses to their aid, "and they began to accuse Him, saying, We found this fellow perverting the nation, and forbidding to give tribute to Caesar, saying that He Himself is Christ a King." Three charges, each without foundation. The priests knew this, but they were willing to commit perjury could they but secure their end.

Pilate saw through their purpose. He did not believe that the prisoner had plotted against the government. His meek and humble appearance was altogether out of harmony with the charge. Pilate was convinced that a deep plot had been laid to destroy an innocent man who stood in the way of the Jewish dignitaries. Turning to Jesus he asked, "Art Thou the King of the Jews?" The Saviour answered, "Thou sayest it." And as He spoke, His countenance lighted up as if a sunbeam were shining upon it.

When they heard His answer, Caiaphas and those that were with him called Pilate to witness that Jesus had admitted the crime with which He was charged. With noisy cries, priests, scribes, and rulers demanded that He be sentenced to death. The cries were taken up by the mob, and the uproar was deafening. Pilate was confused. Seeing that Jesus made no answer to His accusers, Pilate said to Him, "Answerest Thou nothing? behold how many things they witness against Thee. But Jesus yet answered nothing."

Standing behind Pilate, in view of all in the court, Christ heard the abuse; but to all the false charges against Him He answered not a word. His whole bearing gave evidence of conscious innocence. He stood unmoved by the fury of the waves that beat about Him. It was as if the heavy surges of wrath, rising higher and higher, like the waves of the boisterous ocean, broke about Him, but did not touch Him. He stood silent, but His silence was eloquence. It was as a light shining from the inner to the outer man.

Pilate was astonished at His bearing. Does this Man disregard the proceedings because He does not care to save His life? he asked himself. As he looked at Jesus, bearing insult and mockery without retaliation, he felt that He could not be as unrighteous and unjust as were the clamoring priests. Hoping to gain the truth from Him and to escape the tumult of the crowd, Pilate took Jesus aside with him, and again questioned, "Art Thou the King of the Jews?"

Jesus did not directly answer this question. He knew that the Holy Spirit was striving with 727 Pilate, and He gave him opportunity to acknowledge his conviction. "Sayest thou this thing of thyself," He asked, "or did others tell it thee of Me?" That is, was it the accusations of the priests, or a desire to receive light from Christ, that prompted Pilate's question? Pilate understood Christ's meaning; but pride arose in his heart. He would not acknowledge the conviction that pressed upon him. "Am I a Jew?" he said. "Thine own nation and the chief priests have delivered Thee unto me: what hast Thou done?"

Pilate's golden opportunity had passed. Yet Jesus did not leave him without further light. While He did not directly answer Pilate's question, He plainly stated His own mission. He gave Pilate to understand that He was not seeking an earthly throne.

"My kingdom is not of this world," He said; "if My kingdom were of this world, then would My servants fight, that I should not be delivered to the Jews: but now is My kingdom not from hence. Pilate therefore said unto Him, Art Thou a king then? Jesus answered, Thou sayest that I am a king. To this end was I born, and for this cause came I into the world, that I should bear witness unto the truth. Everyone that is of the truth heareth My voice."

Christ affirmed that His word was in itself a key which would unlock the mystery to those who were prepared to receive it. It had a self-commending power, and this was the secret of the spread of His kingdom of truth. He desired Pilate to understand that only by receiving and appropriating truth could his ruined nature be reconstructed.

Pilate had a desire to know the truth. His mind was confused. He eagerly grasped the words of the Saviour, and his heart was stirred with a great longing to know what it really was, and how he could obtain it. "What is truth?" he inquired. But he did not wait for an answer. The tumult outside recalled him to the interests of the hour; for the priests were clamorous for immediate action. Going out to the Jews, he declared emphatically, "I find in Him no fault at all."

These words from a heathen judge were a

scathing rebuke to the perfidy and falsehood of the rulers of Israel who were accusing the Saviour. As the priests and elders heard this from Pilate, their disappointment and rage knew no bounds. They had long plotted and waited for this opportunity. As they saw the prospect of the release of Jesus, they seemed ready to tear Him in pieces. They loudly denounced Pilate, and threatened him with the censure of the Roman

728 government. They accused him of refusing to condemn Jesus, who, they affirmed, had set Himself up against Caesar.

Angry voices were now heard, declaring that the seditious influence of Jesus was well known throughout the country. The priests said, "He stirreth up the people, teaching throughout all Jewry, beginning from Galilee to this place."

Pilate at this time had no thought of condemning Jesus. He knew that the Jews had accused Him through hatred and prejudice. He knew what his duty was. Justice demanded that Christ should be immediately released. But Pilate dreaded the ill will of the people. Should he refuse to give Jesus into their hands, a tumult would be raised, and this he feared to meet. When he heard that Christ was from Galilee, he decided to send Him to Herod, the ruler of that province, who was then in Jerusalem. By this course, Pilate thought to shift the responsibility of the trial from himself to Herod. He also thought this a good opportunity to heal an old quarrel between himself and Herod. And so it proved. The two magistrates made friends over the trial of the Saviour.

Pilate delivered Jesus again to the soldiers, and amid the jeers and insults of the mob He was hurried to the judgment hall of Herod. "When Herod saw Jesus, he was exceeding glad." He had never before met the Saviour, but "he was desirous to see Him of a long season, because he had heard many things of Him; and he hoped to have seen some miracle done by Him." This Herod was he whose hands were stained with the blood of John the Baptist. When Herod first heard of Jesus, he was terror-stricken, and said, "It is John, whom I behead-

729 ed: he is risen from the dead;" "therefore mighty works do show forth themselves in him." Mark 6:16; Matt. 14:2. Yet Herod desired to see Jesus. Now there was opportunity to save the life of this prophet, and the king hoped to banish forever from his mind the memory of that bloody head brought to him in a charger. He also desired to have his curiosity gratified, and thought that if Christ were given any prospect of release, He would do anything that was asked of Him.

A large company of the priests and elders had accompanied Christ to Herod. And when the Saviour was brought in, these dignitaries, all speaking excitedly, urged their accusations against Him. But Herod paid little regard to their charges. He commanded silence, desiring an opportunity to question Christ. He ordered that the fetters of Christ should be unloosed, at the same time charging His enemies with roughly treating Him. Looking with compassion into the serene face of the world's Redeemer, he read in it only wisdom and purity. He as well as Pilate was satisfied that Christ had been accused through malice and envy.

Herod questioned Christ in many words, but throughout the Saviour maintained a profound silence. At the command of the king, the decrepit and maimed were then called in, and Christ was ordered to prove His claims by working a miracle. Men say that Thou canst heal the sick, said Herod. I am anxious to see that Thy widespread fame has not been belied. Jesus did not respond, and Herod still continued to urge: If Thou canst work miracles for others, work them now for Thine own good, and it will serve Thee a good purpose. Again he commanded, Show us a sign that Thou hast the power with which rumor hath accredited Thee. But Christ was as one who heard and saw not. The Son of God had taken upon Himself man's nature. He must do as man must do in like circumstances. Therefore He would not work a miracle to save Himself the pain and humiliation that man must endure when placed in a similar position.

Herod promised that if Christ would perform some miracle in his presence, He should be released. Christ's accusers had seen with their own eyes the mighty works wrought by His power. They had heard Him command the grave to give up its dead. They had seen the dead come forth obedient to His voice. Fear seized them lest He should now work a miracle. Of all things they most dreaded an exhibition of His power. Such a manifestation would prove a deathblow to their plans, and would perhaps 730 cost them their lives. Again the priests and rulers, in great anxiety, urged their accusations against Him. Raising their voices, they declared, He is a traitor, a blasphemer. He works His miracles through the power given Him by Beelzebub, the prince of the devils. The hall became a scene of confusion, some crying one thing and some another.

Herod's conscience was now far less sensitive than when he had trembled with horror at the request of Herodias for the head of John the Baptist. For a time he had felt the keen stings of remorse for his terrible act; but his moral perceptions had become more and more degraded by his licentious life. Now his heart had become so hardened that he could even boast of the punishment he had inflicted upon John for daring to reprove him. And he now threatened Jesus, declaring repeatedly that he had power to release or to condemn Him. But no sign from Jesus gave evidence that He heard a word.

Herod was irritated by this silence. It seemed to indicate utter indifference to his authority. To the vain and pompous king, open rebuke would have been less offensive than to be thus ignored. Again he angrily threatened Jesus, who still remained unmoved and silent.

The mission of Christ in this world was not to gratify idle curiosity. He came to heal the brokenhearted. Could He have spoken any word to heal the bruises of sin-sick souls, He would not have kept silent. But He had no words for those who would but trample the truth under their unholy feet.

Christ might have spoken words to Herod that would have pierced the ears of the hardened king. He might have stricken him with fear and trembling by laying before him the full iniquity of his life, and the horror of his approaching doom. But Christ's silence was the severest rebuke that He could have given. Herod had rejected the truth spoken to him by the greatest of the prophets, and no other message was he to receive. Not a word had the Majesty of heaven for him. That ear that had ever been open to human woe, had no room for Herod's commands. Those eyes that had ever rested upon the penitent sinner in pitying, forgiving love had no look to bestow upon Herod. Those lips that had uttered the most impressive truth, that in tones of tenderest entreaty had pleaded with the most sinful and the most degraded, were closed to the haughty king who felt no need of a Saviour.

Herod's face grew dark with passion. Turning 731 to the multitude, he angrily denounced Jesus as an impostor. Then to Christ he said, If You will give no evidence of Your claim, I will deliver You up to the soldiers and the people. They may succeed in making You speak. If You are an impostor, death at their hands is only what You merit; if You are the Son of God, save Yourself by working a miracle.

No sooner were these words spoken than a rush was made for Christ. Like wild beasts, the crowd darted upon their prey. Jesus was dragged this way and that, Herod joining the mob in seeking to humiliate the Son of God. Had not the Roman soldiers interposed, and forced back the maddened throng, the Saviour would have been torn in pieces.

"Herod with his men of war set Him at nought, and mocked Him, and arrayed Him in a gorgeous robe." The Roman soldiers joined in this abuse. All that these wicked, corrupt soldiers, helped on by Herod and the Jewish dignitaries, could instigate was heaped upon the Saviour. Yet His divine patience failed not.

Christ's persecutors had tried to measure His character by their own; they had represented Him as vile as themselves. But back of all the present appearance another scene intruded itself,—a scene which they will one day see in all its glory. There were some who trembled in Christ's presence. While the rude throng were bowing in mockery before Him, some who came forward for that purpose turned back, afraid and silenced. Herod was convicted. The last rays of merciful light were shining upon his sin-hardened heart. He felt that this was no common man; for divinity had flashed through humanity. At the very time when Christ was encompassed by mockers, adulterers, and murderers, Herod felt that he was beholding a God upon His throne.

Hardened as he was, Herod dared not ratify the condemnation of Christ. He wished to relieve himself of the terrible responsibility, and he sent Jesus back to the Roman judgment hall.

Pilate was disappointed and much displeased. When the Jews returned with their prisoner, he asked impatiently what they would have him do. He reminded them that he had already examined Jesus, and found no fault in Him; he told them that they had brought complaints against Him, but they had not been able to prove a single charge. He had sent Jesus to Herod, the tetrarch of Galilee, and one of their own nation, but he also had found in Him nothing worthy of death. "I will therefore chastise Him," Pilate said, "and release Him."

Here Pilate showed his weakness. He had declared that Jesus was innocent, yet he was 732 willing for Him to be scourged to pacify His accusers. He would sacrifice justice and principle in order to compromise with the mob. This placed him at a disadvantage. The crowd presumed upon his indecision, and clamored the more for the life of the prisoner. If at the first Pilate had stood firm, refusing to condemn a man whom he found guiltless, he would have broken the fatal chain that was to bind him in remorse and guilt as long as he lived. Had he carried out his convictions of right, the Jews would not have presumed to dictate to him. Christ would have been put to death, but the guilt would not have rested upon Pilate. But Pilate had taken step after step in the violation of his conscience. He had excused himself from judging with justice and equity, and he now found himself almost helpless in the hands of the priests and rulers. His wavering and indecision proved his ruin.

Even now Pilate was not left to act blindly. A message from God warned him from the deed he was about to commit. In answer to Christ's prayer, the wife of Pilate had been visited by an angel from heaven, and in a dream she had beheld the Saviour and conversed with Him. Pilate's wife was not a Jew, but as she looked upon Jesus in her dream, she had no doubt of His character or mission. She knew Him to be the Prince of God. She saw Him on trial in the judgment hall. She saw the hands tightly bound as the hands of a criminal. She saw Herod and his soldiers doing their dreadful work. She heard the priests and rulers, filled with envy and malice, madly accusing. She heard the words, "We have a law, and by our law He ought to die." She saw Pilate give Jesus to the scourging, after he had declared, "I find no fault in Him." She heard the condemnation pronounced by Pilate, and saw him give Christ up to His murderers. She saw the cross uplifted on Calvary. She saw the earth wrapped in darkness, and heard the mysterious cry, "It is finished." Still another scene met her gaze. She saw Christ seated upon the great white cloud, while the earth reeled in space, and His murderers fled from the presence of His glory. With a cry of horror she awoke, and at once wrote to Pilate words of warning.

While Pilate was hesitating as to what he should do, a messenger pressed through the crowd, and handed him the letter from his wife, which read:

"Have thou nothing to do with that just Man: for I have suffered many things this day in a dream because of Him."

733   Pilate's face grew pale. He was confused by his own conflicting emotions. But while he had been delaying to act, the priests and rulers were still further inflaming the minds of the people. Pilate was forced to action. He now bethought himself of a custom which might serve to secure Christ's release. It was customary at this feast to release some one prisoner whom the people might choose. This custom was of pagan invention; there was not a shadow of justice in it, but it was greatly prized by the Jews. The Roman authorities at this time held a prisoner named Barabbas, who was under sentence of death. This man had claimed to be the Messiah. He claimed authority to establish a different order of things, to set the world right. Under satanic delusion he claimed that whatever he could obtain by theft and robbery was his own. He had done wonderful things through satanic agencies, he had gained a following among the people, and had excited sedition against the Roman government. Under cover of religious enthusiasm he was a hardened and desperate villain, bent on rebellion and cruelty. By giving the people a choice between this man and the innocent Saviour, Pilate thought to arouse them to a sense of justice. He hoped to gain their sympathy for Jesus in opposition to the priests and rulers. So, turning to the crowd, he said with great earnestness, "Whom will ye that I release unto you? Barabbas, or Jesus which is called Christ?"

Like the bellowing of wild beasts came the answer of the mob, "Release unto us Barabbas!" Louder and louder swelled the cry, Barabbas! Barabbas! Thinking that the people had not understood his question, Pilate asked, "Will ye that I release unto you the King of the Jews?" But they cried out again, "Away with this Man,

and release unto us Barabbas"! "What shall I do then with Jesus which is called Christ?" Pilate asked. Again the surging multitude roared like demons. Demons themselves, in human form, were in the crowd, and what could be expected but the answer, "Let Him be crucified"?

Pilate was troubled. He had not thought it would come to that. He shrank from delivering an innocent man to the most ignominious and cruel death that could be inflicted. After the roar of voices had ceased, he turned to the people, saying, "Why, what evil hath He done?" But the case had gone too far for argument. It was not evidence of Christ's innocence that they wanted, but His condemnation.

Still Pilate endeavored to save Him. "He said unto them the third time, Why, what evil hath 734 He done? I have found no cause of death in Him: I will therefore chastise Him, and let Him go." But the very mention of His release stirred the people to a tenfold frenzy. "Crucify Him, crucify Him," they cried. Louder and louder swelled the storm that Pilate's indecision had called forth.

Jesus was taken, faint with weariness and covered with wounds, and scourged in the sight of the multitude. "And the soldiers led Him away into the hall, called Praetorium; and they call together the whole band. And they clothed Him with purple, and platted a crown of thorns, and put it about His head, and began to salute Him, Hail, King of the Jews! And they . . . . did spit upon Him, and bowing their knees worshiped Him." Occasionally some wicked hand snatched the reed that had been placed in His hand, and struck the crown upon His brow, forcing the thorns into His temples, and sending the blood trickling down His face and beard.

Wonder, O heavens! and be astonished, O earth! Behold the oppressor and the oppressed. A maddened throng enclose the Saviour of the world. Mocking and jeering are mingled with the coarse oaths of blasphemy. His lowly birth and humble life are commented upon by the unfeeling mob. His claim to be the Son of God is ridiculed, and the vulgar jest and insulting sneer are passed from lip to lip.

Satan led the cruel mob in its abuse of the Saviour. It was his purpose to provoke Him to retaliation if possible, or to drive Him to perform a miracle to release Himself, and thus break up the plan of salvation. One stain upon His human life, one failure of His humanity to endure the terrible test, and the Lamb of God would have been an imperfect offering, and the redemption of man a failure. But He who by a command could bring the heavenly host to His aid—He who could have driven that mob in terror from His sight by the flashing forth of His divine majesty—submitted with perfect calmness to the coarsest insult and outrage.

Christ's enemies had demanded a miracle as

evidence of His divinity. They had evidence far greater than any they had sought. As their cruelty degraded His torturers below humanity into the likeness of Satan, so did His meekness and patience exalt Jesus above humanity, and prove His kinship to God. His abasement was the pledge of His exaltation. The blood drops of agony that from His wounded temples flowed down His face and beard were the pledge of His anointing with "the oil of gladness" (Heb. 1:9) as our great high priest.

35   Satan's rage was great as he saw that all the abuse inflicted upon the Saviour had not forced the least murmur from His lips. Although He had taken upon Him the nature of man, He was sustained by a godlike fortitude, and departed in no particular from the will of His Father.

When Pilate gave Jesus up to be scourged and mocked, he thought to excite the pity of the multitude. He hoped they would decide that this was sufficient punishment. Even the malice of the priests, he thought, would now be satisfied. But with keen perception the Jews saw the weakness of thus punishing a man who had been declared innocent. They knew that Pilate was trying to save the life of the prisoner, and they were determined that Jesus should not be released. To please and satisfy us, Pilate has scourged Him, they thought, and if we press the matter to a decided issue, we shall surely gain our end.

Pilate now sent for Barabbas to be brought into the court. He then presented the two prisoners side by side, and pointing to the Saviour he said in a voice of solemn entreaty, "Behold the Man!" "I bring Him forth to you, that ye may know that I find no fault in Him."

There stood the Son of God, wearing the robe of mockery and the crown of thorns. Stripped to the waist, His back showed the long, cruel stripes, from which the blood flowed freely. His face was stained with blood, and bore the marks of exhaustion and pain; but never had it appeared more beautiful than now. The Saviour's visage was not marred before His enemies. Every feature expressed gentleness and resignation and the tenderest pity for His cruel foes. In His manner there was no cowardly weakness, but the strength and dignity of long-suffering. In striking contrast was the prisoner at His side. Every line of the countenance of Barabbas proclaimed him the hardened ruffian that he was. The contrast spoke to every beholder. Some of the spectators were weeping. As they looked upon Jesus, their hearts were full of sympathy. Even the priests and rulers were convicted that He was all that He claimed to be.

The Roman soldiers that surrounded Christ were not all hardened; some were looking earnestly into His face for one evidence that He was a criminal or dangerous character. From time to time they would turn and cast a look of contempt upon Barabbas. It needed no deep insight to read him through and through. Again they would turn to the One upon trial. They looked at the divine sufferer with feelings of deep pity. The silent submission of Christ stamped upon their minds the scene, never to be 736 effaced until they either acknowledged Him as the Christ, or by rejecting Him decided their own destiny.

Pilate was filled with amazement at the uncomplaining patience of the Saviour. He did not doubt that the sight of this Man, in contrast with Barabbas, would move the Jews to sympathy. But he did not understand the fanatical hatred of the priests for Him, who, as the Light of the world, had made manifest their darkness and error. They had moved the mob to a mad fury, and again priests, rulers, and people raised that awful cry, "Crucify Him, crucify Him." At last, losing all patience with their unreasoning cruelty, Pilate cried out despairingly, "Take ye Him, and crucify Him: for I find no fault in Him."

The Roman governor, though familiar with cruel scenes, was moved with sympathy for the suffering prisoner, who, condemned and scourged, with bleeding brow and lacerated back, still had the bearing of a king upon his throne. But the priests declared, "We have a law, and by our law He ought to die, because He made Himself the Son of God."

Pilate was startled. He had no correct idea of Christ and His mission; but he had an indistinct faith in God and in beings superior to humanity. A thought that had once before passed through his mind now took more definite shape. He questioned whether it might not be a divine being that stood before him, clad in the purple robe of mockery, and crowned with thorns.

Again he went into the judgment hall, and said to Jesus, "Whence art Thou?" But Jesus gave him no answer. The Saviour had spoken freely to Pilate, explaining His own mission as a witness to the truth. Pilate had disregarded the light. He had abused the high office of judge by yielding his principles and authority to the demands of the mob. Jesus had no further light for him. Vexed at His silence, Pilate said haughtily:

"Speakest Thou not unto me? knowest Thou not that I have power to crucify Thee, and have power to release Thee?"

Jesus answered, "Thou couldest have no power at all against Me, except it were given thee from above: therefore he that delivered Me unto thee hath the greater sin."

Thus the pitying Saviour, in the midst of His intense suffering and grief, excused as far as possible the act of the Roman governor who gave Him up to be crucified. What a scene was this to hand down to the world for all time! What a light it sheds upon the character of Him who is the Judge of all the earth!

737 "He that delivered Me unto thee," said Jesus, "hath the greater sin." By this Christ meant Caiaphas, who, as high priest, represented the Jewish nation. They knew the principles that controlled the Roman authorities. They had light in the prophecies that testified of Christ, and in His own teachings and miracles. The Jewish judges had received unmistakable evidence of the divinity of Him whom they condemned to death. And according to their light would they be judged.

The greatest guilt and heaviest responsibility belonged to those who stood in the highest places in the nation, the depositaries of sacred trusts that they were basely betraying. Pilate, Herod, and the Roman soldiers were comparatively ignorant of Jesus. They thought to please the priests and rulers by abusing Him. They had not the light which the Jewish nation had so abundantly received. Had the light been given to the soldiers, they would not have treated Christ as cruelly as they did.

Again Pilate proposed to release the Saviour. "But the Jews cried out, saying, If thou let this man go, thou art not Caesar's friend." Thus these hypocrites pretended to be jealous for the authority of Caesar. Of all the opponents of the Roman rule, the Jews were most bitter. When it was safe for them to do so, they were most tyrannical in enforcing their own national and religious requirements; but when they desired to bring about some purpose of cruelty, they exalted the power of Caesar. To accomplish the destruction of Christ, they would profess loyalty to the foreign rule which they hated.

"Whosoever maketh himself a king," they continued, "speaketh against Caesar." This was touching Pilate in a weak point. He was under suspicion by the Roman government, and he knew that such a report would be ruin to him. He knew that if the Jews were thwarted, their rage would be turned against him. They would leave nothing undone to accomplish their revenge. He had before him an example of the persistence with which they sought the life of One whom they hated without reason.

Pilate then took his place on the judgment seat, and again presented Jesus to the people, saying, "Behold your King!" Again the mad cry was heard, "Away with Him, crucify Him." In a voice that was heard far and near, Pilate asked, "Shall I crucify your King?" But from profane, blasphemous lips went forth the words, "We have no king but Caesar."

738 Thus by choosing a heathen ruler, the Jewish nation had withdrawn from the theocracy. They had rejected God as their king. Henceforth they had no deliverer. They had no king but Caesar. To this the priests and teachers had led the people. For this, with the fearful results that followed, they were responsible. A nation's sin and a nation's ruin were due to the religious leaders.

"When Pilate saw that he could prevail nothing, but that rather a tumult was made, he took water, and washed his hands before the multitude, saying, I am innocent of the blood of this just Person: see ye to it." In fear and self-condemnation Pilate looked upon the Saviour. In the vast sea of upturned faces, His alone was peaceful. About His head a soft light seemed to shine. Pilate said in his heart, He is a God. Turning to the multitude he declared, I am clear of His blood. Take ye Him, and crucify Him. But mark ye, priests and rulers, I pronounce Him a just man. May He whom He claims as His Father judge you and not me for this day's work. Then to Jesus he said, Forgive me for this act; I cannot save You. And when he had again scourged Jesus, he delivered Him to be crucified.

Pilate longed to deliver Jesus. But he saw that he could not do this, and yet retain his own position and honor. Rather than lose his worldly power, he chose to sacrifice an innocent life. How many, to escape loss or suffering, in like manner sacrifice principle. Conscience and duty point one way, and self-interest points another. The current sets strongly in the wrong direction, and he who compromises with evil is swept away into the thick darkness of guilt.

Pilate yielded to the demands of the mob. Rather than risk losing his position, he delivered Jesus up to be crucified. But in spite of his precautions, the very thing he dreaded afterward came upon him. His honors were stripped from him, he was cast down from his high office, and, stung by remorse and wounded pride, not long after the crucifixion he ended his own life. So all who compromise with sin will gain only sorrow and ruin. "There is a way which seemeth right unto a man, but the end thereof are the ways of death." Prov. 14:12.

When Pilate declared himself innocent of the blood of Christ, Caiaphas answered defiantly, "His blood be on us, and on our children." The awful words were taken up by the priests and rulers, and echoed by the crowd in an inhuman roar of voices. The whole multitude answered and said, "His blood be on us, and on our children."

The people of Israel had made their choice. 739 Pointing to Jesus they had said, "Not this man, but Barabbas." Barabbas, the robber and murderer, was the representative of Satan. Christ was the representative of God. Christ had been rejected; Barabbas had been chosen. Barabbas they were to have. In making this choice they accepted him who from the beginning was a liar and a murderer. Satan was their leader. As a nation they would act out his dictation. His works they would do. His rule they must endure. That people who chose Barabbas in the place of Christ were to feel the cruelty of Barabbas as long as time should last.

Looking upon the smitten Lamb of God, the Jews had cried, "His blood be on us, and on our children." That awful cry ascended to the throne of God. That sentence, pronounced upon themselves, was written in heaven. That prayer was heard. The blood of the Son of God was upon their children and their children's children, a perpetual curse.

Terribly was it realized in the destruction of Jerusalem. Terribly has it been manifested in the condition of the Jewish nation for eighteen hundred years,—a branch severed from the vine, a dead, fruitless branch, to be gathered up and burned. From land to land throughout the world, from century to century, dead, dead in trespasses and sins!

Terribly will that prayer be fulfilled in the great judgment day. When Christ shall come to the earth again, not as a prisoner surrounded by a rabble will men see Him. They will see Him then as heaven's King. Christ will come in His own glory, in the glory of His Father, and the glory of the holy angels. Ten thousand times ten thousand, and thousands of thousands of angels, the beautiful and triumphant sons of God, possessing surpassing loveliness and glory, will escort Him on His way. Then shall He sit upon the throne of His glory, and before Him shall be gathered all nations. Then every eye shall see Him, and they also that pierced Him. In the place of a crown of thorns, He will wear a crown of glory,—a crown within a crown. In place of that old purple kingly robe, He will be clothed in raiment of whitest white, "so as no fuller on earth can white them." Mark 9:3. And on His vesture and on His thigh a name will be written, "King of kings, and Lord of lords." Rev. 19:16. Those who mocked and smote Him will be there. The priests and rulers will behold again the scene in the judgment hall. Every circumstance will appear before them, as if written in letters of fire. Then those who prayed, "His blood be on us, and on our children," will receive the answer to their prayer. Then the whole world will know and understand. They will realize who and what they, poor, feeble, finite beings, have been warring against. In awful agony and horror they will cry to the mountains and rocks, "Fall on us, and hide us from the face of Him that sitteth on the throne, and from the wrath of the Lamb: for the great day of His wrath is come; and who shall be able to stand?" Rev. 6:16, 17.

78

Calvary

"And when they were come to the place, which is called Calvary, there they crucified Him."

"That He might sanctify the people with His own blood," Christ "suffered without the gate." Heb. 13:12. For transgression of the law of God, Adam and Eve were banished from Eden. Christ, our substitute, was to suffer without the boundaries of Jerusalem. He died outside the gate, where felons and murderers were executed. Full of significance are the words, "Christ hath redeemed us from the curse of the law, being made a curse for us." Gal. 3:13.

A vast multitude followed Jesus from the judgment hall to Calvary. The news of His condemnation had spread throughout Jerusalem, and people of all classes and all ranks flocked toward the place of crucifixion. The priests and rulers had been bound by a promise not to molest Christ's followers if He Himself were delivered to them, and the disciples and believers from the city and the surrounding region joined the throng that followed the Saviour.

As Jesus passed the gate of Pilate's court, the cross which had been prepared for Barabbas was laid upon His bruised and bleeding shoulders. Two companions of Barabbas were to suffer death at the same time with Jesus, and upon them also crosses were placed. The Saviour's burden was too heavy for Him in His weak and suffering condition. Since the Passover supper with His disciples, He had taken neither food nor drink. He had agonized in the garden of Gethsemane in conflict with satanic agencies. He had endured the anguish of the betrayal, and had seen His disciples forsake Him and flee. He had been taken to Annas, then to Caiaphas, and then to Pilate. From Pilate He had been sent to Herod, then sent again to Pilate. From insult to renewed insult, from mockery to mockery, twice tortured by the scourge,—all that night there had been scene after scene of a character to try the soul of man to the uttermost. Christ had not failed. He had spoken no word but that tended to glorify God. All through the disgraceful farce of a trial He had borne Himself with firmness and dignity. But when after the second scourging the cross was laid upon Him, human nature could bear no more. He fell fainting beneath the burden.

The crowd that followed the Saviour saw His weak and staggering steps, but they manifested no compassion. They taunted and reviled Him because He could not carry the heavy cross.

This chapter is based on Matthew 27:31-53; Mark 15:20-38; Luke 23:26-46; John 19:16-30.

Again the burden was laid upon Him, and again He fell fainting to the ground. His persecutors saw that it was impossible for Him to carry His burden farther. They were puzzled to find anyone who would bear the humiliating load. The Jews themselves could not do this, because the defilement would prevent them from keeping the Passover. None even of the mob that followed Him would stoop to bear the cross.

At this time a stranger, Simon a Cyrenian, coming in from the country, meets the throng. He hears the taunts and ribaldry of the crowd; he hears the words contemptuously repeated, Make way for the King of the Jews! He stops in astonishment at the scene; and as he expresses his compassion, they seize him and place the cross upon his shoulders.

Simon had heard of Jesus. His sons were believers in the Saviour, but he himself was not a disciple. The bearing of the cross to Calvary was a blessing to Simon, and he was ever after grateful for this providence. It led him to take upon himself the cross of Christ from choice, and ever cheerfully stand beneath its burden.

Not a few women are in the crowd that follow the Uncondemned to His cruel death. Their attention is fixed upon Jesus. Some of them have seen Him before. Some have carried to Him their sick and suffering ones. Some have themselves been healed. The story of the scenes that have taken place is related. They wonder at the hatred of the crowd toward Him for whom their own hearts are melting and ready to break. 743 And notwithstanding the action of the maddened throng, and the angry words of the priests and rulers, these women give expression to their sympathy. As Jesus falls fainting beneath the cross, they break forth into mournful wailing.

This was the only thing that attracted Christ's attention. Although full of suffering, while bearing the sins of the world, He was not indifferent to the expression of grief. He looked upon these women with tender compassion. They were not believers in Him; He knew that they were not lamenting Him as one sent from God, but were moved by feelings of human pity. He did not despise their sympathy, but it awakened in His heart a deeper sympathy for them. "Daughters of Jerusalem," He said, "weep not for Me, but weep for yourselves, and for your children." From the scene before Him, Christ looked forward to the time of Jerusalem's destruction. In that terrible scene, many of those who were now weeping for Him were to perish with their children.

From the fall of Jerusalem the thoughts of Jesus passed to a wider judgment. In the destruction of the impenitent city He saw a symbol of the final destruction to come upon the world. He said, "Then shall they begin to say to the mountains, Fall on us; and to the hills, Cover us. For if they do these things in a green tree, what shall be done in the dry?" By the green tree, Jesus represented Himself, the innocent Redeemer. God suffered His wrath against transgression to fall on His beloved Son. Jesus was to be crucified for the sins of men. What suffering, then, would the sinner bear who continued in sin? All the impenitent and unbelieving would know a sorrow and misery that language would fail to express.

Of the multitude that followed the Saviour to Calvary, many had attended Him with joyful hosannas and the waving of palm branches as He rode triumphantly into Jerusalem. But not a few who had then shouted His praise, because it was popular to do so, now swelled the cry of "Crucify Him, crucify Him." When Christ rode into Jerusalem, the hopes of the disciples had been raised to the highest pitch. They had pressed close about their Master, feeling that it was a high honor to be connected with Him. Now in His humiliation they followed Him at a distance. They were filled with grief, and bowed down with disappointed hopes. How were the words of Jesus verified: "All ye shall be offended because of Me this night: for it is written, I will smite the shepherd, and the sheep of the flock shall be scattered abroad." Matt. 26:31.

Arriving at the place of execution, the prisoners were bound to the instruments of torture. 744 The two thieves wrestled in the hands of those who placed them on the cross; but Jesus made no resistance. The mother of Jesus, supported by John the beloved disciple, had followed the steps of her Son to Calvary. She had seen Him fainting under the burden of the cross, and had longed to place a supporting hand beneath His wounded head, and to bathe that brow which had once been pillowed upon her bosom. But she was not permitted this mournful privilege. With the disciples she still cherished the hope that Jesus would manifest His power, and deliver Himself from His enemies. Again her heart would sink as she recalled the words in which He had foretold the very scenes that were then taking place. As the thieves were bound to the cross, she looked on with agonizing suspense. Would He who had given life to the dead suffer Himself to be crucified? Would the Son of God suffer Himself to be thus cruelly slain? Must she give up her faith that Jesus was the Messiah? Must she witness His shame and sorrow, without even the privilege of ministering to Him in His distress? She saw His hands stretched upon the cross; the hammer and the nails were brought, and as the spikes were driven through the tender flesh, the heart-stricken disciples bore away from the cruel scene the fainting form of the mother of Jesus.

The Saviour made no murmur of complaint. His face remained calm and serene, but great drops of sweat stood upon His brow. There was no pitying hand to wipe the death dew from His face, nor words of sympathy and unchanging fidelity to stay His human heart. While the soldiers were doing their fearful work, Jesus prayed for His enemies, "Father, forgive them; for they know not what they do." His mind passed from His own suffering to the sin of His persecutors, and the terrible retribution that would be theirs. No curses were called down upon the soldiers who were handling Him so roughly. No vengeance was invoked upon the priests and rulers, who were gloating over the accomplishment of their purpose. Christ pitied them in their ignorance and guilt. He breathed only a plea for their forgiveness,—"for they know not what they do."

Had they known that they were putting to torture One who had come to save the sinful race from eternal ruin, they would have been seized with remorse and horror. But their ignorance did not remove their guilt; for it was their privilege to know and accept Jesus as their Saviour. Some of them would yet see their sin, and repent, and be converted. Some by their impenitence would make it an impossibility for the prayer of Christ to be answered for them. Yet, just the same, God's purpose was reaching its fulfillment. Jesus was earning the right to become the advocate of men in the Father's presence.

That prayer of Christ for His enemies embraced the world. It took in every sinner that had lived or should live, from the beginning of the world to the end of time. Upon all rests the guilt of crucifying the Son of God. To all, forgiveness is freely offered. "Whosoever will" may have peace with God, and inherit eternal life.

As soon as Jesus was nailed to the cross, it was lifted by strong men, and with great violence thrust into the place prepared for it. This caused the most intense agony to the Son of God. Pilate then wrote an inscription in Hebrew, Greek, and Latin, and placed it upon the cross, above the head of Jesus. It read, "Jesus of Nazareth the King of the Jews." This inscription irritated the Jews. In Pilate's court they had cried, "Crucify Him." "We have no king but Caesar." John 19:15. They had declared that whoever should acknowledge any other king was a traitor. Pilate wrote out the sentiment they had expressed. No offense was mentioned, except that Jesus was the King of the Jews. The inscription was a virtual acknowledgment of the allegiance of the Jews to the Roman power. It declared that whoever might claim to be the King of Israel would be judged by them worthy of death. The priests had overreached themselves. When they were plotting the death of Christ, Caiaphas had declared it expedient that one man should die to save the nation. Now their hypocrisy was revealed. In order to destroy Christ, they had been ready to sacrifice even their national existence.

The priests saw what they had done, and asked Pilate to change the inscription. They said, "Write not, The King of the Jews; but that He said, I am King of the Jews." But Pilate was angry with himself because of his former weakness, and he thoroughly despised the jealous and artful priests and rulers. He replied coldly, "What I have written I have written."

A higher power than Pilate or the Jews had directed the placing of that inscription above the head of Jesus. In the providence of God it was to awaken thought, and investigation of the Scriptures. The place where Christ was crucified was near to the city. Thousands of people from all lands were then at Jerusalem, and the inscription declaring Jesus of Nazareth the Messiah would come to their notice. It was a living truth, transcribed by a hand that God had guided.

In the sufferings of Christ upon the cross prophecy was fulfilled. Centuries before the crucifixion, the Saviour had foretold the treatment He was to receive. He said, "Dogs have compassed Me: the assembly of the wicked have enclosed Me: they pierced My hands and My feet. I may tell all My bones: they look and stare upon Me. They part My garments among them, and cast lots upon My vesture." Ps. 22:16-18. The prophecy concerning His garments was carried out without counsel or interference from the friends or the enemies of the Crucified One. To the soldiers who had placed Him upon the cross, His clothing was given. Christ heard the men's contention as they parted the garments among them. His tunic was woven throughout without seam, and they said, "Let us not rend it, but cast lots for it, whose it shall be."

In another prophecy the Saviour declared, "Reproach hath broken My heart; and I am full of heaviness: and I looked for some to take pity, but there was none; and for comforters, but I found none. They gave Me also gall for My meat; and in My thirst they gave Me vinegar to drink." Ps. 69:20, 21. To those who suffered death by the cross, it was permitted to give a stupefying potion, to deaden the sense of pain. This was offered to Jesus; but when He had tasted it, He refused it. He would receive nothing that could becloud His mind. His faith must keep fast hold upon God. This was His only strength. To becloud His senses would give Satan an advantage.

The enemies of Jesus vented their rage upon Him as He hung upon the cross. Priests, rulers, and scribes joined with the mob in mocking the dying Saviour. At the baptism and at the transfiguration the voice of God had been heard proclaiming Christ as His Son. Again, just before Christ's betrayal, the Father had spoken, witnessing to His divinity. But now the voice from heaven was silent. No testimony in Christ's favor was heard. Alone He suffered abuse and mockery from wicked men.

"If Thou be the Son of God," they said, "come down from the cross." "Let Him save Himself, if He be Christ, the chosen of God." In the wilderness of temptation Satan had declared, "If Thou be the Son of God, command that these stones be made bread." "If Thou be the Son of God, cast Thyself down" from the pinnacle of the temple. Matt. 4:3, 6. And Satan with his angels, in human form, was present at the cross. The archfiend and his hosts were co-operating with the priests and rulers. The teachers of the people had stimulated the ignorant mob to pronounce judgment against One upon whom many of them had never looked, until urged to bear testimony against Him. Priests, rulers, Pharisees, and the hardened rabble were confederated together in a satanic frenzy. Religious rulers united with Satan and his angels. They were doing his bidding.

Jesus, suffering and dying, heard every word as the priests declared, "He saved others; Himself He cannot save. Let Christ the King of Israel descend now from the cross, that we may see and believe." Christ could have come down from the cross. But it is because He would not save Himself that the sinner has hope of pardon and favor with God.

In their mockery of the Saviour, the men who professed to be the expounders of prophecy were repeating the very words which Inspiration had foretold they would utter upon this occasion. Yet in their blindness they did not see that they were fulfilling the prophecy. Those who in derision uttered the words, "He trusted in God; let Him deliver Him now, if He will have Him: for He said, I am the Son of God," little thought that their testimony would sound down the ages. But although spoken in mockery, these words led men to search the Scriptures as they had never done before. Wise men heard, searched, pondered, and prayed. There were those who never rested until, by comparing scripture with scripture, they saw the meaning of Christ's mission. Never before was there such a general knowledge of Jesus as when He hung upon the cross. Into the hearts of many who beheld the crucifixion scene, and who heard Christ's words, the light of truth was shining.

To Jesus in His agony on the cross there came one gleam of comfort. It was the prayer of the penitent thief. Both the men who were crucified with Jesus had at first railed upon Him; and one under his suffering only became more desperate and defiant. But not so with his companion. This man was not a hardened criminal; he had been led astray by evil associations, but he was less guilty than many of those who stood beside the cross reviling the Saviour. He had seen and heard Jesus, and had been convicted by His teaching, but he had been turned away from Him by the priests and rulers. Seeking to stifle conviction, he had plunged deeper and deeper into sin, until he was arrested, tried as a criminal, and condemned to die on the cross. In the judgment hall and on the way to Calvary he had been in company with Jesus. He had heard Pilate declare, "I find no fault in Him." John 19:4. He had marked His godlike bearing, and His pitying forgiveness of His tormentors. On the cross he sees the many great religionists shoot out the tongue with scorn, and ridicule the Lord Jesus. He sees the wagging heads. He hears the upbraiding speeches taken up by his companion in guilt: "If Thou be Christ, save Thyself and us." Among the passers-by he hears many defending Jesus. He hears them repeat His words, and tell of His works. The conviction comes back to him that this is the Christ. Turning to his fellow criminal he says, "Dost not thou fear God, seeing thou art in the same condemnation?" The dying thieves have no longer anything to fear from man. But upon one of them presses the conviction that there is a God to fear, a future to cause him to tremble. And now, all sin-polluted as it is, his life history is about to close. "And we indeed justly," he moans; "for we receive the due reward of our deeds: but this Man hath done nothing amiss."

There is no question now. There are no doubts, no reproaches. When condemned for his crime, the thief had become hopeless and despairing; but strange, tender thoughts now spring up. He calls to mind all he has heard of Jesus, how He has healed the sick and pardoned sin. He has heard the words of those who believed in Jesus and followed Him weeping. He has seen and read the title above the Saviour's head. He has heard the passers-by repeat it, some with grieved, quivering lips, others with jesting and mockery. The Holy Spirit illuminates his mind, and little by little the chain of evidence is joined together. In Jesus, bruised, mocked, and hanging upon the cross, he sees the Lamb of God, that taketh away the sin of the world. Hope is mingled with anguish in his voice as the helpless, dying soul casts himself upon a dying Saviour. "Lord, remember me," he cries, "when Thou comest into Thy kingdom."

Quickly the answer came. Soft and melodious the tone, full of love, compassion, and power the words: Verily I say unto thee today, Thou shalt be with Me in paradise.

For long hours of agony, reviling and mockery have fallen upon the ears of Jesus. As He hangs upon the cross, there floats up to Him still the sound of jeers and curses. With longing heart He has listened for some expression of faith from His disciples. He has heard only the mournful words, "We trusted that it had been He which should have redeemed Israel." How grateful then to the Saviour was the utterance of faith and love from the dying thief! While the leading Jews deny Him, and even the disciples doubt His divinity, the poor thief, upon the brink of eternity, calls Jesus Lord. Many were ready to call Him Lord when He wrought miracles, and after He had risen from the grave; but none acknowledged Him as He hung dying upon the cross save the penitent thief who was saved at the eleventh hour.

The bystanders caught the words as the thief called Jesus Lord. The tone of the repentant man arrested their attention. Those who at the foot of the cross had been quarreling over Christ's garments, and casting lots upon His vesture, stopped to listen. Their angry tones were hushed. With bated breath they looked upon Christ, and waited for the response from those dying lips.

As He spoke the words of promise, the dark cloud that seemed to enshroud the cross was pierced by a bright and living light. To the penitent thief came the perfect peace of acceptance with God. Christ in His humiliation was glorified. He who in all other eyes appeared to be conquered was a Conqueror. He was acknowledged as the Sin Bearer. Men may exercise power over His human body. They may pierce the holy temples with the crown of thorns. They may strip from Him His raiment, and quarrel over its division. But they cannot rob Him of His power to forgive sins. In dying He bears testimony to His own divinity and to the glory of the Father. His ear is not heavy that it cannot hear, neither His arm shortened that it cannot save. It is His royal right to save unto the uttermost all who come unto God by Him.

I say unto thee today, Thou shalt be with Me in Paradise. Christ did not promise that the thief should be with Him in Paradise that day. He Himself did not go that day to Paradise. He slept in the tomb, and on the morning of the resurrection He said, "I am not yet ascended to My Father." John 20:17. But on the day of the crucifixion, the day of apparent defeat and darkness, the promise was given. "Today" while dying upon the cross as a malefactor, Christ assures the poor sinner, Thou shalt be with Me in Paradise.

The thieves crucified with Jesus were placed "on either side one, and Jesus in the midst." This was done by the direction of the priests and rulers. Christ's position between the thieves was to indicate that He was the greatest criminal of the three. Thus was fulfilled the scripture, "He was numbered with the transgressors." Isa. 53:12. But the full meaning of their act the priests did not see. As Jesus, crucified with the thieves, was placed "in the midst," so His cross was placed in the midst of a world lying in sin. And the words of pardon spoken to the penitent thief kindled a light that will shine to the earth's remotest bounds.

With amazement the angels beheld the infinite love of Jesus, who, suffering the most intense agony of mind and body, thought only of others, and encouraged the penitent soul to believe. In His humiliation He as a prophet had addressed the daughters of Jerusalem; as priest and advocate He had pleaded with the Father to forgive His murderers; as a loving Saviour He had forgiven the sins of the penitent thief.

As the eyes of Jesus wandered over the multitude about Him, one figure arrested His attention. At the foot of the cross stood His mother, supported by the disciple John. She could not endure to remain away from her Son; and John, knowing that the end was near, had brought her again to the cross. In His dying hour, Christ remembered His mother. Looking into her grief-stricken face and then upon John, He said to her, "Woman, behold thy son!" then to John, "Behold thy mother!" John understood Christ's words, and accepted the trust. He at once took Mary to his home, and from that hour cared for her tenderly. O pitiful, loving Saviour; amid all His physical pain and mental anguish, He had a thoughtful care for His mother! He had no money with which to provide for her comfort; but He was enshrined in the heart of John, and He gave His mother to him as a precious legacy. Thus He provided for her that which she most needed,—the tender sympathy of one who loved her because she loved Jesus. And in receiving her as a sacred trust, John was receiving a great blessing. She was a constant reminder of his beloved Master.

The perfect example of Christ's filial love shines forth with undimmed luster from the mist of ages. For nearly thirty years Jesus by His daily toil had helped bear the burdens of the home. And now, even in His last agony, He remembers to provide for His sorrowing, widowed mother. The same spirit will be seen in every disciple of our Lord. Those who follow Christ will feel that it is a part of their religion to respect and provide for their parents. From the heart where His love is cherished, father and mother will never fail of receiving thoughtful care and tender sympathy.

And now the Lord of glory was dying, a ransom for the race. In yielding up His precious life, Christ was not upheld by triumphant joy. All was oppressive gloom. It was not the dread of death that weighed upon Him. It was not the pain and ignominy of the cross that caused His inexpressible agony. Christ was the prince of sufferers; but His suffering was from a sense of the malignity of sin, a knowledge that through familiarity with evil, man had become blinded to its enormity. Christ saw how deep is the hold of sin upon the human heart, how few would be willing to break from its power. He knew that without help from God, humanity must perish, and He saw multitudes perishing within reach of abundant help.

Upon Christ as our substitute and surety was

laid the iniquity of us all. He was counted a transgressor, that He might redeem us from the condemnation of the law. The guilt of every descendant of Adam was pressing upon His heart. The wrath of God against sin, the terrible manifestation of His displeasure because of iniquity, filled the soul of His Son with consternation. All His life Christ had been publishing to a fallen world the good news of the Father's mercy and pardoning love. Salvation for the chief of sinners was His theme. But now with the terrible weight of guilt He bears, He cannot see the Father's reconciling face. The withdrawal of the divine countenance from the Saviour in this hour of supreme anguish pierced His heart with a sorrow that can never be fully understood by man. So great was this agony that His physical pain was hardly felt.

Satan with his fierce temptations wrung the heart of Jesus. The Saviour could not see through the portals of the tomb. Hope did not present to Him His coming forth from the grave a conqueror, or tell Him of the Father's acceptance of the sacrifice. He feared that sin was so offensive to God that Their separation was to be eternal. Christ felt the anguish which the sinner will feel when mercy shall no longer plead for the guilty race. It was the sense of sin, bringing the Father's wrath upon Him as man's substitute, that made the cup He drank so bitter, and broke the heart of the Son of God.

With amazement angels witnessed the Saviour's despairing agony. The hosts of heaven veiled their faces from the fearful sight. Inanimate nature expressed sympathy with its insulted and dying Author. The sun refused to look upon the awful scene. Its full, bright rays were illuminating the earth at midday, when suddenly it seemed to be blotted out. Complete darkness, like a funeral pall, enveloped the cross. "There was darkness over all the land unto the ninth hour." There was no eclipse or other natural cause for this darkness, which was as deep as midnight without moon or stars. It was a miraculous testimony given by God that the faith of after generations might be confirmed.

In that thick darkness God's presence was hidden. He makes darkness His pavilion, and conceals His glory from human eyes. God and 754 His holy angels were beside the cross. The Father was with His Son. Yet His presence was not revealed. Had His glory flashed forth from the cloud, every human beholder would have been destroyed. And in that dreadful hour Christ was not to be comforted with the Father's presence. He trod the wine press alone, and of the people there was none with Him.

In the thick darkness, God veiled the last human agony of His Son. All who had seen Christ in His suffering had been convicted of His divinity. That face, once beheld by humanity, was never forgotten. As the face of Cain expressed his guilt as a murderer, so the face of Christ revealed innocence, serenity, benevolence,—the image of God. But His accusers would not give heed to the signet of heaven. Through long hours of agony Christ had been gazed upon by the jeering multitude. Now He was mercifully hidden by the mantle of God.

The silence of the grave seemed to have fallen upon Calvary. A nameless terror held the throng that was gathered about the cross. The cursing and reviling ceased in the midst of half-uttered sentences. Men, women, and children fell prostrate upon the earth. Vivid lightnings occasionally flashed forth from the cloud, and revealed the cross and the crucified Redeemer. Priests, rulers, scribes, executioners, and the mob, all thought that their time of retribution had come. After a while some whispered that Jesus would now come down from the cross. Some attempted to grope their way back to the city, beating their breasts and wailing in fear.

At the ninth hour the darkness lifted from the people, but still enveloped the Saviour. It was a symbol of the agony and horror that weighed upon His heart. No eye could pierce the gloom that surrounded the cross, and none could penetrate the deeper gloom that enshrouded the suffering soul of Christ. The angry lightnings seemed to be hurled at Him as He hung upon the cross. Then "Jesus cried with a loud voice, saying, Eloi, Eloi, lama sabachthani?" "My God, My God, why hast Thou forsaken Me?" As the outer gloom settled about the Saviour, many voices exclaimed: The vengeance of heaven is upon Him. The bolts of God's wrath are hurled at Him, because He claimed to be the Son of God. Many who believed on Him heard His despairing cry. Hope left them. If God had forsaken Jesus, in what could His followers trust?

When the darkness lifted from the oppressed spirit of Christ, He revived to a sense of physical suffering, and said, "I thirst." One of the Roman soldiers, touched with pity as he looked 755 at the parched lips, took a sponge on a stalk of hyssop, and dipping it in a vessel of vinegar, offered it to Jesus. But the priests mocked at His agony. When darkness covered the earth, they had been filled with fear; as their terror abated, the dread returned that Jesus would yet escape them. His words, "Eloi, Eloi, lama sabachthani?" they had misinterpreted. With bitter contempt and scorn they said, "This man calleth for Elias." The last opportunity to relieve His sufferings they refused. "Let be," they said, "let us see whether Elias will come to save Him."

The spotless Son of God hung upon the cross, His flesh lacerated with stripes; those hands so often reached out in blessing, nailed to the wooden bars; those feet so tireless on ministries of love, spiked to the tree; that royal head pierced by the crown of thorns; those quivering lips shaped to the cry of woe. And all that He endured—the blood drops that flowed from His head, His hands, His feet, the agony that racked His frame, and the unutterable anguish that filled His soul at the hiding of His Father's face—speaks to each child of humanity, declaring, It is for thee that the Son of God consents to bear this burden of guilt; for thee He spoils the domain of death, and opens the gates of Paradise. He who stilled the angry waves and walked the foam-capped billows, who made devils tremble and disease flee, who opened blind eyes and called forth the dead to life,— offers Himself upon the cross as a sacrifice, and this from love to thee. He, the Sin Bearer, endures the wrath of divine justice, and for thy sake becomes sin itself.

In silence the beholders watched for the end of the fearful scene. The sun shone forth; but the cross was still enveloped in darkness. Priests and rulers looked toward Jerusalem; and lo, the dense cloud had settled over the city and the plains of Judea. The Sun of Righteousness, the Light of the world, was withdrawing His beams from the once favored city of Jerusalem. The fierce lightnings of God's wrath were directed against the fated city.

Suddenly the gloom lifted from the cross, and in clear, trumpetlike tones, that seemed to resound throughout creation, Jesus cried, "It is finished." "Father, into Thy hands I commend My spirit." A light encircled the cross, and the face of the Saviour shone with a glory like the sun. He then bowed His head upon His breast, and died.

Amid the awful darkness, apparently forsaken of God, Christ had drained the last dregs in the cup of human woe. In those dreadful hours He had relied upon the evidence of His Father's acceptance heretofore given Him. He was acquainted with the character of His Father; He understood His justice, His mercy, and His great love. By faith He rested in Him whom it had ever been His joy to obey. And as in submission He committed Himself to God, the sense of the loss of His Father's favor was withdrawn. By faith, Christ was victor.

Never before had the earth witnessed such a scene. The multitude stood paralyzed, and with bated breath gazed upon the Saviour. Again darkness settled upon the earth, and a hoarse rumbling, like heavy thunder, was heard. There was a violent earthquake. The people were shaken together in heaps. The wildest confusion and consternation ensued. In the surrounding mountains, rocks were rent asunder, and went crashing down into the plains. Sepulchers were broken open, and the dead were cast out of their tombs. Creation seemed to be shivering to atoms. Priests, rulers, soldiers, executioners, and people, mute with terror, lay prostrate upon the ground.

When the loud cry, "It is finished," came from the lips of Christ, the priests were officiating in the temple. It was the hour of the evening sacrifice. The lamb representing Christ had been brought to be slain. Clothed in his significant and beautiful dress, the priest stood with lifted knife, as did Abraham when he was about to slay his son. With intense interest the people were looking on. But the earth trembles and quakes; for the Lord Himself draws near. With a rending noise the inner veil of the temple is torn from top to bottom by an unseen hand, throwing open to the gaze of the multitude a place once filled with the presence of God. In this place the Shekinah had dwelt. Here God had manifested His glory above the mercy seat. No one but the high priest ever lifted the veil separating this apartment from the rest of the temple. He entered in once a year to make an atonement for the sins of the people. But lo, this veil is rent in twain. The most holy place of the earthly sanctuary is no longer sacred.

All is terror and confusion. The priest is about to slay the victim; but the knife drops from his nerveless hand, and the lamb escapes. Type has met antitype in the death of God's Son. The great sacrifice has been made. The way into the holiest is laid open. A new and living way is prepared for all. No longer need sinful, sorrowing humanity await the coming of the high priest. Henceforth the Saviour was to officiate as priest and advocate in the heaven of heavens. It was as if a living voice had spoken to the worshipers: There is now an end to all sacrifices and offerings for sin. The Son of God is come according to His word, "Lo, I come (in the volume (in the volume of the Book it is written of Me,) to do Thy will, O God." "By His own blood" He entereth "in once into the holy place, having obtained eternal redemption for us." Heb. 10:7; 9:12.

79

"It is Finished"

Christ did not yield up His life till He had accomplished the work which He came to do, and with His parting breath He exclaimed, "It is finished." John 19:30. The battle had been won. His right hand and His holy arm had gotten Him the victory. As a Conqueror He planted His banner on the eternal heights. Was there not joy among the angels? All heaven triumphed in the Saviour's victory. Satan was defeated, and knew that his kingdom was lost.

To the angels and the unfallen worlds the cry, "It is finished," had a deep significance. It was for them as well as for us that the great work of redemption had been accomplished. They with us share the fruits of Christ's victory.

Not until the death of Christ was the character of Satan clearly revealed to the angels or to the unfallen worlds. The archapostate had so clothed himself with deception that even holy beings had not understood his principles. They had not clearly seen the nature of his rebellion.

It was a being of wonderful power and glory that had set himself against God. Of Lucifer the Lord says, "Thou sealest up the sum, full of wisdom, and perfect in beauty." Ezek. 28:12. Lucifer had been the covering cherub. He had stood in the light of God's presence. He had been the highest of all created beings, and had been foremost in revealing God's purposes to the universe. After he had sinned, his power to deceive was the more deceptive, and the unveiling of his character was the more difficult, because of the exalted position he had held with the Father.

759

God could have destroyed Satan and his sympathizers as easily as one can cast a pebble to the earth; but He did not do this. Rebellion was not to be overcome by force. Compelling power is found only under Satan's government. The Lord's principles are not of this order. His authority rests upon goodness, mercy, and love; and the presentation of these principles is the means to be used. God's government is moral, and truth and love are to be the prevailing power.

It was God's purpose to place things on an eternal basis of security, and in the councils of heaven it was decided that time must be given for Satan to develop the principles which were the foundation of his system of government. He had claimed that these were superior to God's principles. Time was given for the working of Satan's principles, that they might be seen by the heavenly universe.

Satan led men into sin, and the plan of redemption was put in operation. For four thousand years, Christ was working for man's uplifting, and Satan for his ruin and degradation. And the heavenly universe beheld it all.

When Jesus came into the world, Satan's power was turned against Him. From the time when He appeared as a babe in Bethlehem, the usurper worked to bring about His destruction. In every possible way he sought to prevent Jesus from developing a perfect childhood, a faultless manhood, a holy ministry, and an unblemished sacrifice. But he was defeated. He could not lead Jesus into sin. He could not discourage Him, or drive Him from a work He had come on earth to do. From the desert to Calvary, the storm of Satan's wrath beat upon Him, but the more mercilessly it fell, the more firmly did the Son of God cling to the hand of His Father, and press on in the bloodstained path. All the efforts of Satan to oppress and overcome Him only brought out in a purer light His spotless character.

All heaven and the unfallen worlds had been witnesses to the controversy. With what intense interest did they follow the closing scenes of the conflict. They beheld the Saviour enter the garden of Gethsemane, His soul bowed down with the horror of a great darkness. They heard His bitter cry, "Father, if it be possible, let this cup pass from Me." Matt. 26:39. As the Father's presence was withdrawn, they saw Him sorrowful with a bitterness of sorrow exceeding that of the last great struggle with death. The bloody sweat was forced from His pores, and fell in drops upon the ground. Thrice the prayer for deliverance was wrung from His lips. Heaven could no longer endure the sight, and a messenger of comfort was sent to the Son of God.

760

Heaven beheld the Victim betrayed into the hands of the murderous mob, and with mockery and violence hurried from one tribunal to another. It heard the sneers of His persecutors because of His lowly birth. It heard the denial with cursing and swearing by one of His best-loved disciples. It saw the frenzied work of Satan, and his power over the hearts of men. Oh, fearful scene! the Saviour seized at midnight in Gethsemane, dragged to and fro from palace to judgment hall, arraigned twice before the priests, twice before the Sanhedrin, twice before Pilate, and once before Herod, mocked, scourged, condemned, and led out to be crucified, bearing the heavy burden of the cross, amid the wailing of the daughters of Jerusalem and the jeering of the rabble.

Heaven viewed with grief and amazement Christ hanging upon the cross, blood flowing from His wounded temples, and sweat tinged with blood standing upon His brow. From His hands and feet the blood fell, drop by drop, upon the rock drilled for the foot of the cross. The wounds made by the nails gaped as the weight of His body dragged upon His hands. His labored breath grew quick and deep, as His soul panted under the burden of the sins of the world. All heaven was filled with wonder when the prayer of Christ was offered in the midst of His terrible suffering,—"Father, forgive them; for they know not what they do." Luke 23:34. Yet there stood men, formed in the image of God, joining to crush out the life of His only-begotten Son. What a sight for the heavenly universe!

The principalities and powers of darkness were assembled around the cross, casting the hellish shadow of unbelief into the hearts of men. When the Lord created these beings to stand before His throne, they were beautiful and glorious. Their loveliness and holiness were in accordance with their exalted station. They were enriched with the wisdom of God, and girded with the panoply of heaven. They were Jehovah's ministers. But who could recognize in the fallen angels the glorious seraphim that once ministered in the heavenly courts?

Satanic agencies confederated with evil men in leading the people to believe Christ the chief of sinners, and to make Him the object of detestation. Those who mocked Christ as He hung upon the cross were imbued with the spirit of the first great rebel. He filled them with vile and loathsome speeches. He inspired their taunts. But by all this he gained nothing.

Could one sin have been found in Christ, had He in one particular yielded to Satan to escape the terrible torture, the enemy of God and man would have triumphed. Christ bowed His head and died, but He held fast His faith and His submission to God. "And I heard a loud voice saying in heaven, Now is come salvation, and strength, and the kingdom of our God, and the power of His Christ: for the accuser of our brethren is cast down, which accused them before our God day and night." Rev. 12:10.

Satan saw that his disguise was torn away. His administration was laid open before the unfallen angels and before the heavenly universe. He had revealed himself as a murderer. By shedding the blood of the Son of God, he had uprooted himself from the sympathies of the heavenly beings. Henceforth his work was restricted. Whatever attitude he might assume, he could no longer await the angels as they came from the heavenly courts, and before them accuse Christ's brethren of being clothed with the garments of blackness and the defilement of sin. The last link of sympathy between Satan and the heavenly world was broken.

Yet Satan was not then destroyed. The angels did not even then understand all that was involved in the great controversy. The principles at stake were to be more fully revealed. And for the sake of man, Satan's existence must be continued. Man as well as angels must see the contrast between the Prince of light and the prince of darkness. He must choose whom he will serve.

In the opening of the great controversy, Satan had declared that the law of God could not be obeyed, that justice was inconsistent with mercy, and that, should the law be broken, it would be impossible for the sinner to be pardoned. Every sin must meet its punishment, urged Satan; and if God should remit the punishment of sin, He would not be a God of truth and justice. When men broke the law of God, and defied His will, Satan exulted. It was proved, he declared, that the law could not be obeyed; man could not be forgiven. Because he, after his rebellion, had been banished from heaven, Satan claimed that the human race must be forever shut out from God's favor. God could not be just, he urged, and yet show mercy to the sinner.

But even as a sinner, man was in a different position from that of Satan. Lucifer in heaven had sinned in the light of God's glory. To him as to no other created being was given a revelation of God's love. Understanding the character of God, knowing His goodness, Satan chose to follow his own selfish, independent will. This choice was final. There was no more that God could do to save him. But man was deceived; his mind was darkened by Satan's sophistry. The height and depth of the love of God he did not know. For him there was hope in a knowledge of God's love. By beholding His character he might be drawn back to God.

Through Jesus, God's mercy was manifested to men; but mercy does not set aside justice. The law reveals the attributes of God's character, and not a jot or tittle of it could be changed to meet man in his fallen condition. God did not change His law, but He sacrificed Himself, in Christ, for man's redemption. "God was in Christ, reconciling the world unto Himself." 2 Cor. 5:19.

The law requires righteousness,—a righteous life, a perfect character; and this man has not to give. He cannot meet the claims of God's holy law. But Christ, coming to the earth as man, lived a holy life, and developed a perfect character. These He offers as a free gift to all who will receive them. His life stands for the life of men. Thus they have remission of sins that are past, through the forbearance of God. More than this, Christ imbues men with the attributes of God. He builds up the human character after the similitude of the divine character, a goodly fabric of spiritual strength and beauty. Thus the very righteousness of the law is fulfilled in the believer in Christ. God can "be just, and the justifier of him which believeth in Jesus." Rom. 3:26.

God's love has been expressed in His justice no less than in His mercy. Justice is the foundation of His throne, and the fruit of His love. It had been Satan's purpose to divorce mercy from truth and justice. He sought to prove that the righteousness of God's law is an enemy to peace. But Christ shows that in God's plan they are indissolubly joined together; the one cannot exist without the other. "Mercy and truth are met together; righteousness and peace have kissed each other." Ps. 85:10.

By His life and His death, Christ proved that God's justice did not destroy His mercy, but that sin could be forgiven, and that the law is righteous, and can be perfectly obeyed. Satan's charges were refuted. God had given man unmistakable evidence of His love.

Another deception was now to be brought forward. Satan declared that mercy destroyed justice, that the death of Christ abrogated the Father's law. Had it been possible for the law to be changed or abrogated, then Christ need not have died. But to abrogate the law would be to immortalize transgression, and place the world under Satan's control. It was because the law was changeless, because man could be saved only through obedience to its precepts, that Jesus was lifted up on the cross. Yet the very means by which Christ established the law Satan represented as destroying it. Here will come the last conflict of the great controversy between Christ and Satan.

That the law which was spoken by God's own voice is faulty, that some specification has been set aside, is the claim which Satan now puts forward. It is the last great deception that he will bring upon the world. He needs not to assail the whole law; if he can lead men to disregard one precept, his purpose is gained. For "whosoever shall keep the whole law, and yet offend in one point, he is guilty of all." James 2:10. By consenting to break one precept, men are brought under Satan's power. By substituting human law for God's law, Satan will seek to control the world. This work is foretold in prophecy. Of the great apostate power which is the representative of Satan, it is declared, "He shall speak great words against the Most High, and shall wear out the saints of the Most High, and think to change times and laws: and they shall be given into his hand." Dan. 7:25.

Men will surely set up their laws to counterwork the laws of God. They will seek to compel the consciences of others, and in their zeal to enforce these laws they will oppress their fellow men.

The warfare against God's law, which was begun in heaven, will be continued until the end of time. Every man will be tested. Obedience or disobedience is the question to be decided by the whole world. All will be called to choose between the law of God and the laws of men. Here the dividing line will be drawn. There will be but two classes. Every character will be fully developed; and all will show whether they have chosen the side of loyalty or that of rebellion.

Then the end will come. God will vindicate His law and deliver His people. Satan and all who have joined him in rebellion will be cut off. Sin and sinners will perish, root and branch (Mal. 4:1),—Satan the root, and his followers the branches. The word will be fulfilled to the prince of evil, "Because thou hast set thine heart as the heart of God; . . . I will destroy thee, O covering cherub, from the midst of the stones of fire. . . . Thou shalt be a terror, and never shalt thou be any more." Then "the wicked shall not be: yea, thou shalt diligently consider his place, and it shall not be;" "they shall be as though they had not been." Ezek. 28:6-19; Ps. 37:10; Obadiah 16.

764   This is not an act of arbitrary power on the part of God. The rejecters of His mercy reap that which they have sown. God is the fountain of life; and when one chooses the service of sin,

he separates from God, and thus cuts himself off from life. He is "alienated from the life of God." Christ says, "All they that hate Me love death." Eph. 4:18; Prov. 8:36. God gives them existence for a time that they may develop their character and reveal their principles. This accomplished, they receive the results of their own choice. By a life of rebellion, Satan and all who unite with him place themselves so out of harmony with God that His very presence is to them a consuming fire. The glory of Him who is love will destroy them.

At the beginning of the great controversy, the angels did not understand this. Had Satan and his host then been left to reap the full result of their sin, they would have perished; but it would not have been apparent to heavenly beings that this was the inevitable result of sin. A doubt of God's goodness would have remained in their minds as evil seed, to produce its deadly fruit of sin and woe.

But not so when the great controversy shall be ended. Then, the plan of redemption having been completed, the character of God is revealed to all created intelligences. The precepts of His law are seen to be perfect and immutable. Then sin has made manifest its nature, Satan his character. Then the extermination of sin will vindicate God's love and establish His honor before a universe of beings who delight to do His will, and in whose heart is His law.

Well, then, might the angels rejoice as they looked upon the Saviour's cross; for though they did not then understand all, they knew that the destruction of sin and Satan was forever made certain, that the redemption of man was assured, and that the universe was made eternally secure. Christ Himself fully comprehended the results of the sacrifice made upon Calvary. To all these He looked forward when upon the cross He cried out, "It is finished."

80

769

In Joseph's Tomb

At last Jesus was at rest. The long day of shame and torture was ended. As the last rays of the setting sun ushered in the Sabbath, the Son of God lay in quietude in Joseph's tomb. His work completed, His hands folded in peace, He rested through the sacred hours of the Sabbath day.

In the beginning the Father and the Son had rested upon the Sabbath after Their work of creation. When "the heavens and the earth were finished, and all the host of them" (Gen. 2:1), the Creator and all heavenly beings rejoiced in contemplation of the glorious scene. "The morning stars sang together, and all the sons of God shouted for joy." Job 38:7. Now Jesus rested from the work of redemption; and though there was grief among those who loved Him on earth, yet there was joy in heaven. Glorious to the eyes of heavenly beings was the promise of the future. A restored creation, a redeemed race, that having conquered sin could never fall,— this, the result to flow from Christ's completed work, God and angels saw. With this scene the day upon which Jesus rested is forever linked. For "His work is perfect;" and "whatsoever God doeth, it shall be forever." Deut. 32:4; Eccl. 3:14. When there shall be a "restitution of all things, which God hath spoken by the mouth of all His holy prophets since the world began" (Acts 3:21), the creation Sabbath, the day on which Jesus lay at rest in Joseph's tomb, will still be a day of rest and rejoicing. Heaven and earth will unite in praise, as "from one Sabbath to another" (Isa. 66:23) the nations of the saved shall bow in joyful worship to God and the Lamb.

In the closing events of the crucifixion day, fresh evidence was given of the fulfillment of prophecy, and new witness borne to Christ's divinity. When the darkness had lifted from the cross, and the Saviour's dying cry had been uttered, immediately another voice was heard, saying, "Truly this was the Son of God." Matt. 27:54.

These words were said in no whispered tones. All eyes were turned to see whence they came. Who had spoken? It was the centurion, the Roman soldier. The divine patience of the Saviour, and His sudden death, with the cry of victory upon His lips, had impressed this heathen. In the bruised, broken body hanging upon the cross, the centurion recognized the form of the Son of God. He could not refrain from confessing his faith. Thus again evidence was given that our Redeemer was to see of the travail of His soul. Upon the very day of His death, three men, differing widely from one another, had declared their faith,—he who commanded the Roman guard, he who bore the cross of the Saviour, and he who died upon the cross at His side.

As evening drew on, an unearthly stillness hung over Calvary. The crowd dispersed, and many returned to Jerusalem greatly changed in spirit from what they had been in the morning. Many had flocked to the crucifixion from curiosity, and not from hatred toward Christ. Still they believed the accusations of the priests, and looked upon Christ as a malefactor. Under an unnatural excitement they had united with the mob in railing against Him. But when the earth was wrapped in blackness, and they stood accused by their own consciences, they felt guilty of a great wrong. No jest or mocking laughter was heard in the midst of that fearful gloom; and when it was lifted, they made their way to their homes in solemn silence. They were convinced that the charges of the priests were false, that Jesus was no pretender; and a few weeks later, when Peter preached upon the day of Pentecost, they were among the thousands who became converts to Christ.

But the Jewish leaders were unchanged by the events they had witnessed. Their hatred of Jesus had not abated. The darkness that had mantled the earth at the crucifixion was not more dense than that which still enveloped the minds of the priests and rulers. At His birth the star had known Christ, and had guided the wise men to the manger where He lay. The heavenly hosts had known Him, and had sung His praise over the plains of Bethlehem. The sea had known His voice, and had obeyed His command. Disease and death had recognized His authority, and had yielded to Him their prey. The sun had known Him, and at the sight of His dying anguish, had hidden its face of light. The rocks had known Him, and had shivered into fragments at His cry. Inanimate nature had known Christ, and had borne witness to His divinity. But the priests and rulers of Israel knew not the Son of God.

Yet the priests and rulers were not at rest. They had carried out their purpose in putting Christ to death; but they did not feel the sense of victory they had expected. Even in the hour of their apparent triumph, they were harassed with doubts as to what would next take place. They had heard the cry, "It is finished." "Father, into Thy hands I commend My spirit." John 19:30; Luke 23:46. They had seen the rocks rent, and had felt the mighty earthquake, and they were restless and uneasy.

They had been jealous of Christ's influence with the people when living; they were jealous of Him even in death. They dreaded the dead Christ more, far more, than they had ever feared the living Christ. They dreaded to have the attention of the people directed any further to the events attending His crucifixion. They feared the results of that day's work. Not on any account would they have had His body remain on the cross during the Sabbath. The Sabbath was now drawing on, and it would be a violation of its sanctity for the bodies to hang upon the cross. So, using this as a pretext, the leading Jews requested Pilate that the death of the victims might be hastened, and their bodies removed before the setting of the sun.

Pilate was as unwilling as they for the body of Jesus to remain upon the cross. His consent having been obtained, the legs of the two thieves were broken to hasten their death; but Jesus was found to be already dead. The rude soldiers had been softened by what they had heard and seen of Christ, and they were restrained from breaking His limbs. Thus in the offering of the Lamb of God was fulfilled the law of the Passover, "They shall leave none of it unto the morning, nor break any bone of it: according to all the ordinances of the Passover they shall keep it." Num. 9:12.

The priests and rulers were amazed to find that Christ was dead. Death by the cross was a lingering process; it was difficult to determine when life had ceased. It was an unheard-of thing for one to die within six hours of crucifixion. The priests wished to make sure of the death of Jesus, and at their suggestion a soldier thrust a spear into the Saviour's side. From the wound thus made, there flowed two copious and distinct streams, one of blood, the other of water. This was noted by all the beholders, and John states the occurrence very definitely. He says, "One of the soldiers with a spear pierced His side, and forthwith came there out blood and water. And he that saw it bare record, and his record is true: and he knoweth that he saith true, that ye might believe. For these things were done, that the scripture should be fulfilled, A bone of Him shall not be broken. And again another scripture saith, They shall look on Him whom they pierced." John 19:34-37.

After the resurrection the priests and rulers circulated the report that Christ did not die upon the cross, that He merely fainted, and was afterward revived. Another report affirmed that it was not a real body of flesh and bone, but the likeness of a body, that was laid in the tomb. The action of the Roman soldiers disproves these falsehoods. They broke not His legs, because He was already dead. To satisfy the priests, they pierced His side. Had not life been already extinct, this wound would have caused instant death.

But it was not the spear thrust, it was not the pain of the cross, that caused the death of Jesus. That cry, uttered "with a loud voice" (Matt. 27:50; Luke 23:46), at the moment of death, the stream of blood and water that flowed from His side, declared that He died of a broken heart. His heart was broken by mental anguish. He was slain by the sin of the world.

With the death of Christ the hopes of His disciples perished. They looked upon His closed eyelids and drooping head, His hair matted with blood, His pierced hands and feet, and their anguish was indescribable. Until the last they had not believed that He would die; they could hardly believe that He was really dead. Overwhelmed with sorrow, they did not recall His words foretelling this very scene. Nothing that He had said now gave them comfort. They saw only the cross and its bleeding Victim. The future seemed dark with despair. Their faith in Jesus had perished; but never had they loved their Lord as now. Never before had they so felt His worth, and their need of His presence.

Even in death, Christ's body was very precious to His disciples. They longed to give Him an honored burial, but knew not how to accomplish this. Treason against the Roman government was the crime for which Jesus was condemned, and persons put to death for this offense were consigned to a burial ground especially provided for such criminals. The disciple John with the women from Galilee had remained at the cross. They could not leave the body of their Lord to be handled by the unfeeling soldiers, and buried in a dishonored grave. Yet they could not prevent it. They could obtain no favors from the Jewish authorities, and they had no influence with Pilate.

In this emergency, Joseph of Arimathaea and Nicodemus came to the help of the disciples. Both these men were members of the Sanhedrin, and were acquainted with Pilate. Both were men of wealth and influence. They were determined that the body of Jesus should have an honorable burial.

Joseph went boldly to Pilate, and begged from him the body of Jesus. For the first time, Pilate learned that Jesus was really dead. Conflicting reports had reached him in regard to the events attending the crucifixion, but the knowledge of Christ's death had been purposely kept from him. Pilate had been warned by the priests and rulers against deception by Christ's disciples in regard to His body. Upon hearing Joseph's request, he therefore sent for the centurion who had charge at the cross, and learned for a certainty of the death of Jesus. He also drew from him an account of the scenes of Calvary, confirming the testimony of Joseph.

The request of Joseph was granted. While John was troubled about the burial of his Master, Joseph returned with Pilate's order for the body of Christ; and Nicodemus came bringing a costly mixture of myrrh and aloes, of about a hundred pounds' weight, for His embalming. The most honored in all Jerusalem could not have been shown more respect in death. The disciples were astonished to see these wealthy rulers as much interested as they themselves in the burial of their Lord.

Neither Joseph nor Nicodemus had openly accepted the Saviour while He was living. They knew that such a step would exclude them from the Sanhedrin, and they hoped to protect Him by their influence in its councils. For a time they had seemed to succeed; but the wily priests, seeing their favor to Christ, had thwarted their plans. In their absence Jesus had been condemned and delivered to be crucified. Now that He was dead, they no longer concealed their attachment to Him. While the disciples feared to show themselves openly as His followers, Joseph and Nicodemus came boldly to their aid. The help of these rich and honored men was greatly needed at this time. They could do for their dead Master what it was impossible for the poor disciples to do; and their wealth and influence protected them, in a great measure, from the malice of the priests and rulers.

Gently and reverently they removed with their own hands the body of Jesus from the cross. Their tears of sympathy fell fast as they looked upon His bruised and lacerated form. Joseph owned a new tomb, hewn in a rock. This he was reserving for himself; but it was near Calvary, and he now prepared it for Jesus. The body, together with the spices brought by Nicodemus, was carefully wrapped in a linen sheet, and the Redeemer was borne to the tomb. There the three disciples straightened the mangled limbs, and folded the bruised hands upon the pulseless breast. The Galilean women came to see that all had been done that could be done for the lifeless form of their beloved Teacher. Then they saw the heavy stone rolled against the entrance of the tomb, and the Saviour was left at rest. The women were last at the cross, and last at the tomb of Christ. While the evening shades were gathering, Mary Magdalene and the other Marys lingered about the resting place of their Lord, shedding tears of sorrow over the fate of Him whom they loved. "And they returned, . . . and rested the Sabbath day according to the commandment." Luke 23:56.

That was a never-to-be-forgotten Sabbath to the sorrowing disciples, and also to the priests, rulers, scribes, and people. At the setting of the sun on the evening of the preparation day the trumpets sounded, signifying that the Sabbath had begun. The Passover was observed as it had been for centuries, while He to whom it pointed had been slain by wicked hands, and lay in Joseph's tomb. On the Sabbath the courts of the temple were filled with worshipers. The high priest from Golgotha was there, splendidly robed in his sacerdotal garments. White-turbaned priests, full of activity, performed their duties. But some present were not at rest as the blood of bulls and goats was offered for sin. They were not conscious that type had met antitype, that an infinite sacrifice had been made for the sins of the world. They knew not that there was no further value in the performance of the ritual service. But never before had that service been witnessed with such conflicting feelings. The trumpets and musical instruments and the voices of the singers were as loud and clear as usual. But a sense of 775 strangeness pervaded everything. One after another inquired about a strange event that had taken place. Hitherto the most holy place had been sacredly guarded from intrusion. But now it was open to all eyes. The heavy veil of tapestry, made of pure linen, and beautifully wrought with gold, scarlet, and purple, was rent from top to bottom. The place where Jehovah had met with the high priest, to communicate His glory, the place that had been God's sacred audience chamber, lay open to every eye,—a place no longer recognized by the Lord. With gloomy presentiments the priests ministered before the altar. The uncovering of the sacred mystery of the most holy place filled them with dread of coming calamity.

Many minds were busy with thoughts started by the scenes of Calvary. From the crucifixion to the resurrection many sleepless eyes were constantly searching the prophecies, some to learn the full meaning of the feast they were then celebrating, some to find evidence that Jesus was not what He claimed to be; and others with sorrowful hearts were searching for proofs that He was the true Messiah. Though searching with different objects in view, all were convicted of the same truth,—that prophecy had been fulfilled in the events of the past few days, and that the Crucified One was the world's Redeemer. Many who at that time united in the service never again took part in the paschal rites. Many even of the priests were convicted of the true character of Jesus. Their searching of the prophecies had not been in vain, and after His resurrection they acknowledged Him as the Son of God.

Nicodemus, when he saw Jesus lifted up on the cross, remembered His words spoken by night in the Mount of Olives: "As Moses lifted up the serpent in the wilderness, even so must the Son of man be lifted up: that whosoever believeth in Him should not perish, but have eternal life." John 3:14, 15. On that Sabbath, when Christ lay in the grave, Nicodemus had opportunity for reflection. A clearer light now illuminated his mind, and the words which Jesus had spoken to him were no longer mysterious. He felt that he had lost much by not connecting himself with the Saviour during His life. Now he recalled the events of Calvary. The prayer of Christ for His murderers and His answer to the petition of the dying thief spoke to the heart of the learned councilor. Again he looked upon the Saviour in His agony; again he heard that last cry, "It is finished," spoken like the words of a conqueror. Again he beheld the reeling earth, the darkened heavens, the rent veil, the shivered rocks, and his faith was forever established. The very event that destroyed the 776 hopes of the disciples convinced Joseph and Nicodemus of the divinity of Jesus. Their fears were overcome by the courage of a firm and unwavering faith.

Never had Christ attracted the attention of the multitude as now that He was laid in the tomb. According to their practice, the people brought their sick and suffering ones to the temple courts, inquiring, Who can tell us of Jesus of Nazareth? Many had come from far to find Him who had healed the sick and raised the dead. On every side was heard the cry, We want Christ the Healer! Upon this occasion those who were thought to show indications of the leprosy were examined by the priests. Many were forced to hear their husbands, wives, or children pronounced leprous, and doomed to go forth from the shelter of their homes and the care of their friends, to warn off the stranger with the mournful cry, "Unclean, unclean!" The friendly hands of Jesus of Nazareth, that never refused to touch with healing the loathsome leper, were folded on His breast. The lips that had answered his petition with the comforting words, "I will; be thou clean" (Matt. 8:3), were now silent. Many appealed to the chief priests and rulers for sympathy and relief, but in vain. Apparently they were determined to have the living Christ among them again. With persistent earnestness they asked for Him. They would not be turned away. But they were driven from the temple courts, and soldiers were stationed at the gates to keep back the multitude that came with their sick and dying, demanding entrance.

The sufferers who had come to be healed by the Saviour sank under their disappointment. The streets were filled with mourning. The sick were dying for want of the healing touch of Jesus. Physicians were consulted in vain; there was no skill like that of Him who lay in Joseph's tomb.

The mourning cries of the suffering ones brought home to thousands of minds the conviction that a great light had gone out of the world. Without Christ, the earth was blackness and darkness. Many whose voices had swelled the cry of "Crucify Him, crucify Him," now realized the calamity that had fallen upon them, and would as eagerly have cried, Give us Jesus! had He still been alive.

When the people learned that Jesus had been put to death by the priests, inquiries were made regarding His death. The particulars of His trial were kept as private as possible; but during the time when He was in the grave, His name was on thousands of lips, and reports of His mock trial, and of the inhumanity of the priests and rulers, were circulated everywhere. By men of intellect these priests and rulers were called upon to explain the prophecies of the Old Testament concerning the Messiah, and while trying to frame some falsehood in reply, they became like men insane. The prophecies that pointed to Christ's sufferings and death they could not explain, and many inquirers were convinced that the Scriptures had been fulfilled.

The revenge which the priests had thought would be so sweet was already bitterness to them. They knew that they were meeting the severe censure of the people; they knew that the very ones whom they had influenced against Jesus were now horrified by their own shameful work. These priests had tried to believe Jesus a deceiver; but it was in vain. Some of them had stood by the grave of Lazarus, and had seen the dead brought back to life. They trembled for fear that Christ would Himself rise from the dead, and again appear before them. They had heard Him declare that He had power to lay down His life and to take it again. They remembered that He had said, "Destroy this temple, and in three days I will raise it up." John 2:19. Judas had told them the words spoken by Jesus to the disciples while on the last journey to Jerusalem: "Behold, we go up to Jerusalem; and the Son of man shall be betrayed unto the chief priests and unto the scribes, and they shall condemn Him to death, and shall deliver Him to the Gentiles to mock, and to scourge, and to crucify Him: and the third day He shall rise again." Matt. 20:18, 19. When they heard these words, they had mocked and ridiculed. But now they remembered that Christ's predictions had so far been fulfilled. He had said that He would rise again the third day, and who could say that this also would not come to pass? They longed to shut out these thoughts, but they could not. Like their father, the devil, they believed and trembled.

Now that the frenzy of excitement was past, the image of Christ would intrude upon their minds. They beheld Him as He stood serene and uncomplaining before His enemies, suffering without a murmur their taunts and abuse. All the events of His trial and crucifixion came back to them with an overpowering conviction that He was the Son of God. They felt that He might at any time stand before them, the accused to become the accuser, the condemned to condemn, the slain to demand justice in the death of His murderers.

They could rest little upon the Sabbath. Though they would not step over a Gentile's threshold for fear of defilement, yet they held a council concerning the body of Christ. Death and the grave must hold Him whom they had crucified. "The chief priests and Pharisees came together unto Pilate, saying, Sir, we remember that that deceiver said, while He was yet alive, After three days I will rise again. Command therefore that the sepulcher be made sure until the third day, lest His disciples come by night, and steal Him away, and say unto the people, He is risen from the dead: so the last error shall be worse than the first. Pilate said unto them, Ye have a watch: go your way, make it as sure as ye can." Matt. 27:62-65.

The priests gave directions for securing the sepulcher. A great stone had been placed before the opening. Across this stone they placed cords, securing the ends to the solid rock, and sealing them with the Roman seal. The stone could not be moved without breaking the seal. A guard of one hundred soldiers was then stationed around the sepulcher to prevent it from being tampered with. The priests did all they could to keep Christ's body where it had been laid. He was sealed as securely in His tomb as if He were to remain there through all time.

So weak men counseled and planned. Little did these murderers realize the uselessness of their efforts. But by their action God was glorified. The very efforts made to prevent Christ's resurrection are the most convincing arguments in its proof. The greater the number of soldiers placed around the tomb, the stronger would be the testimony that He had risen. Hundreds of years before the death of Christ, the Holy Spirit had declared through the psalmist, "Why do the heathen rage, and the people imagine a vain thing? The kings of the earth set themselves, and the rulers take counsel together, against the Lord, and against His anointed. . . . He that sitteth in the heavens shall laugh: the Lord shall have them in derision." Ps. 2:1-4. Roman guards and Roman arms were powerless to confine the Lord of life within the tomb. The hour of His release was near.

81

"The Lord Is Risen"

The night of the first day of the week had worn slowly away. The darkest hour, just before daybreak, had come. Christ was still a prisoner in His narrow tomb. The great stone was in its place; the Roman seal was unbroken; the Roman guards were keeping their watch. And there were unseen watchers. Hosts of evil angels were gathered about the place. Had it been possible, the prince of darkness with his apostate army would have kept forever sealed the tomb that held the Son of God. But a heavenly host surrounded the sepulcher. Angels that excel in strength were guarding the tomb, and waiting to welcome the Prince of life.

"And, behold, there was a great earthquake: for the angel of the Lord descended from heaven." Clothed with the panoply of God, this angel left the heavenly courts. The bright beams of God's glory went before him, and illuminated his pathway. "His countenance was like lightning, and his raiment white as snow: and for fear of him the keepers did shake, and became as dead men."

Now, priests and rulers, where is the power of your guard? Brave soldiers that have never been afraid of human power are now as captives taken without sword or spear. The face they look upon is not the face of mortal warrior; it is the face of the mightiest of the Lord's host. This messenger is he who fills the position from which Satan fell. It is he who on the hills of Bethlehem proclaimed Christ's birth. The earth trembles at his approach, the hosts of darkness flee, and as he rolls away the stone, heaven seems to come down to the earth. The soldiers see him removing the stone as he would a pebble, and hear him cry, Son of God, come forth; Thy Father calls Thee. They see Jesus come

forth from the grave, and hear Him proclaim over the rent sepulcher, "I am the resurrection, and the life." As He comes forth in majesty and glory, the angel host bow low in adoration before the Redeemer, and welcome Him with songs of praise.

An earthquake marked the hour when Christ laid down His life, and another earthquake witnessed the moment when He took it up in triumph. He who had vanquished death and the grave came forth from the tomb with the tread of a conqueror, amid the reeling of the earth, the flashing of lightning, and the roaring of thunder. When He shall come to the earth again, He will shake "not the earth only, but also heaven." "The earth shall reel to and fro like a drunkard, and shall be removed like a cottage." "The heavens shall be rolled together as a scroll;" "the elements shall melt with fervent heat, the earth also and the works that are therein shall be burned up." But "the Lord will be the hope of His people, and the strength of the children of Israel." Heb. 12:26; Isa. 24:20; 34:4; 2 Peter 3:10; Joel 3:16.

At the death of Jesus the soldiers had beheld the earth wrapped in darkness at midday; but at the resurrection they saw the brightness of the angels illuminate the night, and heard the inhabitants of heaven singing with great joy and triumph: Thou hast vanquished Satan and the powers of darkness; Thou hast swallowed up death in victory!

Christ came forth from the tomb glorified, and the Roman guard beheld Him. Their eyes were riveted upon the face of Him whom they had so recently mocked and derided. In this glorified Being they beheld the prisoner whom they had seen in the judgment hall, the one for whom they had plaited a crown of thorns. This was the One who had stood unresisting before Pilate and Herod, His form lacerated by the cruel scourge. This was He who had been nailed to the cross, at whom the priests and rulers, full of self-satisfaction, had wagged their heads, saying, "He saved others; Himself He cannot save." Matt. 27:42. This was He who had been laid in Joseph's new tomb. The decree of heaven had loosed the captive. Mountains piled upon mountains over His sepulcher could not have prevented Him from coming forth.

At sight of the angels and the glorified Saviour the Roman guard had fainted and become as dead men. When the heavenly train was hidden from their view, they arose to their feet, and as quickly as their trembling limbs could carry them, made their way to the gate of the garden. Staggering like drunken men, they hurried on to the city, telling those whom they met the wonderful news. They were making their way to Pilate, but their report had been carried to the Jewish authorities, and the chief priests and rulers sent for them to be brought first into their presence. A strange appearance those soldiers

This chapter is based on Matthew 28:2-4, 11-15.

presented. Trembling with fear, their faces colorless, they bore testimony to the resurrection of Christ. The soldiers told all, just as they had seen it; they had not had time to think or speak anything but the truth. With painful utterance they said, It was the Son of God who was crucified; we have heard an angel proclaiming Him as the Majesty of heaven, the King of glory.

The faces of the priests were as those of the dead. Caiaphas tried to speak. His lips moved, but they uttered no sound. The soldiers were about to leave the council room, when a voice stayed them. Caiaphas had at last found speech. Wait, wait, he said. Tell no one the things you have seen.

A lying report was then given to the soldiers. "Say ye," said the priests, "His disciples came by night, and stole Him away while we slept." Here the priests overreached themselves. How could the soldiers say that the disciples had stolen the body while they slept? If they were asleep, how could they know? And if the disciples had been proved guilty of stealing Christ's body, would not the priests have been first to condemn them? Or if the sentinels had slept at the tomb, would not the priests have been foremost in accusing them to Pilate?

The soldiers were horrified at the thought of bringing upon themselves the charge of sleeping at their post. This was an offense punishable with death. Should they bear false witness, deceiving the people, and placing their own lives in peril? Had they not kept their weary watch with sleepless vigilance? How could they stand the trial, even for the sake of money, if they perjured themselves?

In order to silence the testimony they feared, the priests promised to secure the safety of the guard, saying that Pilate would not desire to have such a report circulated any more than they did. The Roman soldiers sold their integrity to the Jews for money. They came in before the priests burdened with a most startling message of truth; they went out with a burden of money, and on their tongues a lying report which had been framed for them by the priests.

Meanwhile the report of Christ's resurrection had been carried to Pilate. Though Pilate was responsible for having given Christ up to die, he had been comparatively unconcerned. While he had condemned the Saviour unwillingly, and with a feeling of pity, he had felt no real compunction until now. In terror he now shut himself within his house, determined to see no one. But the priests made their way into his presence, told the story which they had invented, and urged him to overlook the sentinels' neglect of duty. Before consenting to this, he himself privately questioned the guard. They, fearing for their own safety, dared not conceal anything, and Pilate drew from them an account of all that had taken place. He did not prosecute the matter further, but from that time there was no peace for him.

When Jesus was laid in the grave, Satan triumphed. He dared to hope that the Saviour would not take up His life again. He claimed the Lord's body, and set his guard about the tomb, seeking to hold Christ a prisoner. He was bitterly angry when his angels fled at the approach of the heavenly messenger. When he saw Christ come forth in triumph, he knew that his kingdom would have an end, and that he must finally die.

The priests, in putting Christ to death, had made themselves the tools of Satan. Now they were entirely in his power. They were entangled in a snare from which they saw no escape but in continuing their warfare against Christ. When they heard the report of His resurrection, they feared the wrath of the people. They felt that their own lives were in danger. The only hope for them was to prove Christ an impostor by denying that He had risen. They bribed the soldiers, and secured Pilate's silence. They spread their lying reports far and near. But there were witnesses whom they could not silence. Many had heard of the soldiers' testimony to Christ's resurrection. And certain of the dead who came forth with Christ appeared to many, and declared that He had risen. Reports were brought to the priests of persons who had seen these risen ones, and heard their testimony. The priests and rulers were in continual dread, lest in walking the streets, or within the privacy of their own homes, they should come face to face with Christ. They felt that there was no safety for them. Bolts and bars were but poor protection against the Son of God. By day and by night that awful scene in the judgment hall, when they had cried, "His blood be on us, and on our children," was before them. Matt. 27:25. Nevermore would the memory of that scene fade from their minds. Nevermore would peaceful sleep come to their pillows.

When the voice of the mighty angel was heard at Christ's tomb, saying, Thy Father calls Thee, the Saviour came forth from the grave by the life that was in Himself. Now was proved the truth of His words, "I lay down My life, that I might take it again. . . . I have power to lay it down, and I have power to take it again." Now was fulfilled the prophecy He had spoken to the priests and rulers, "Destroy this temple, and in three days I will raise it up." John 10:17, 18; 2:19.

Over the rent sepulcher of Joseph, Christ had proclaimed in triumph, "I am the resurrection, and the life." These words could be spoken only by the Deity. All created beings live by the will and power of God. They are dependent recipients of the life of God. From the highest seraph to the humblest animate being, all are replenished from the Source of life. Only He who is one with God could say, I have power to lay down My life, and I have power to take it again.

In His divinity, Christ possessed the power to break the bonds of death.

Christ arose from the dead as the first fruits of those that slept. He was the antitype of the wave sheaf, and His resurrection took place on the very day when the wave sheaf was to be presented before the Lord. For more than a thousand years this symbolic ceremony had been performed. From the harvest fields the first heads of ripened grain were gathered, and when the people went up to Jerusalem to the Passover, the sheaf of first fruits was waved as a thank offering before the Lord. Not until this was presented could the sickle be put to the grain, and it be gathered into sheaves. The sheaf dedicated to God represented the harvest. So Christ the first fruits represented the great spiritual harvest to be gathered for the kingdom of God. His resurrection is the type and pledge of the resurrection of all the righteous dead. "For if we believe that Jesus died and rose again, even so them also which sleep in Jesus will God bring with Him." 1 Thess. 4:14.

As Christ arose, He brought from the grave a multitude of captives. The earthquake at His death had rent open their graves, and when He arose, they came forth with Him. They were those who had been co-laborers with God, and who at the cost of their lives had borne testimony to the truth. Now they were to be witnesses for Him who had raised them from the dead.

During His ministry, Jesus had raised the dead to life. He had raised the son of the widow of Nain, and the ruler's daughter and Lazarus. But these were not clothed with immortality. After they were raised, they were still subject to death. But those who came forth from the grave at Christ's resurrection were raised to everlasting life. They ascended with Him as trophies of His victory over death and the grave. These, said Christ, are no longer the captives of Satan; I have redeemed them. I have brought them from the grave as the first fruits of My power, to be with Me where I am, nevermore to see death or experience sorrow.

These went into the city, and appeared unto many, declaring, Christ has risen from the dead, and we be risen with Him. Thus was immortalized the sacred truth of the resurrection. The risen saints bore witness to the truth of the words, "Thy dead men shall live, together with My dead body shall they arise." Their resurrection was an illustration of the fulfillment of the prophecy, "Awake and sing, ye that dwell in dust: for thy dew is as the dew of herbs, and the earth shall cast out the dead." Isa. 26:19.

To the believer, Christ is the resurrection and the life. In our Saviour the life that was lost through sin is restored; for He has life in Himself to quicken whom He will. He is invested with the right to give immortality. The life that He laid down in humanity, He takes up again,

and gives to humanity. "I am come," He said, "that they might have life, and that they might have it more abundantly." "Whosoever drinketh of the water that I shall give him shall never thirst; but the water that I shall give him shall be in him a well of water springing up into everlasting life." "Whoso eateth My flesh, and drinketh My blood, hath eternal life; and I will raise him up at the last day." John 10:10; 4:14; 6:54.

To the believer, death is but a small matter. Christ speaks of it as if it were of little moment. "If a man keep My saying, he shall never see death," "he shall never taste of death." To the Christian, death is but a sleep, a moment of silence and darkness. The life is hid with Christ in God, and "when Christ, who is our life, shall appear, then shall ye also appear with Him in glory." John 8:51, 52; Col. 3:4.

The voice that cried from the cross, "It is finished," was heard among the dead. It pierced the walls of sepulchers, and summoned the sleepers to arise. Thus will it be when the voice of Christ shall be heard from heaven. That voice will penetrate the graves and unbar the tombs, and the dead in Christ shall arise. At the Saviour's resurrection a few graves were opened, but at His second coming all the precious dead shall hear His voice, and shall come forth to glorious, immortal life. The same power that raised Christ from the dead will raise His church, and glorify it with Him, above all principalities, above all powers, above every name that is named, not only in this world, but also in the world to come.

82

"Why Weepest Thou?"

The women who had stood by the cross of Christ waited and watched for the hours of the Sabbath to pass. On the first day of the week, very early, they made their way to the tomb, taking with them precious spices to anoint the Saviour's body. They did not think about His rising from the dead. The sun of their hope had set, and night had settled down on their hearts. As they walked, they recounted Christ's works of mercy and His words of comfort. But they remembered not His words, "I will see you again." John 16:22.

Ignorant of what was even then taking place, they drew near the garden, saying as they went, "Who shall roll us away the stone from the door of the sepulcher?" They knew that they could not remove the stone, yet they kept on their way. And lo, the heavens were suddenly alight with glory that came not from the rising sun. The earth trembled. They saw that the great stone was rolled away. The grave was empty.

The women had not all come to the tomb

This chapter is based on Matthew 28:1, 5-8; Mark 16:1-8; Luke 24:1-12; John 20:1-18.

from the same direction. Mary Magdalene was the first to reach the place; and upon seeing that the stone was removed, she hurried away to tell the disciples. Meanwhile the other women came up. A light was shining about the tomb, but the body of Jesus was not there. As they lingered about the place, suddenly they saw that they were not alone. A young man clothed in shining garments was sitting by the tomb. It was the angel who had rolled away the stone. He had 789 taken the guise of humanity that he might not alarm these friends of Jesus. Yet about him the light of the heavenly glory was still shining, and the women were afraid. They turned to flee, but the angel's words stayed their steps. "Fear not ye," he said; "for I know that ye seek Jesus, which was crucified. He is not here: for He is risen, as He said. Come, see the place where the Lord lay. And go quickly, and tell His disciples that He is risen from the dead." Again they look into the tomb, and again they hear the wonderful news. Another angel in human form is there, and he says, "Why seek ye the living among the dead? He is not here, but is risen: remember how He spake unto you when He was yet in Galilee, saying, The Son of man must be delivered into the hands of sinful men, and be crucified, and the third day rise again."

He is risen, He is risen! The women repeat the words again and again. No need now for the anointing spices. The Saviour is living, and not dead. They remember now that when speaking of His death He said that He would rise again. What a day is this to the world! Quickly the women departed from the sepulcher "with fear and great joy; and did run to bring His disciples word."

Mary had not heard the good news. She went to Peter and John with the sorrowful message, "They have taken away the Lord out of the sepulcher, and we know not where they have laid Him." The disciples hurried to the tomb, and found it as Mary had said. They saw the shroud and the napkin, but they did not find their Lord. Yet even here was testimony that He had risen. The graveclothes were not thrown heedlessly aside, but carefully folded, each in a place by itself. John "saw, and believed." He did not yet understand the scripture that Christ must rise from the dead; but he now remembered the Saviour's words foretelling His resurrection.

It was Christ Himself who had placed those graveclothes with such care. When the mighty angel came down to the tomb, he was joined by another, who with his company had been keeping guard over the Lord's body. As the angel from heaven rolled away the stone, the other entered the tomb, and unbound the wrappings from the body of Jesus. But it was the Saviour's hand that folded each, and laid it in its place. In His sight who guides alike the star and the atom, there is nothing unimportant. Order and perfection are seen in all His work.

Mary had followed John and Peter to the tomb; when they returned to Jerusalem, she remained. As she looked into the empty tomb, grief filled her heart. Looking in, she saw the two angels, one at the head and the other at the 790 foot where Jesus had lain. "Woman, why weepest thou?" they asked her. "Because they have taken away my Lord," she answered, "and I know not where they have laid Him."

Then she turned away, even from the angels, thinking that she must find someone who could tell her what had been done with the body of Jesus. Another voice addressed her, "Woman, why weepest thou? whom seekest thou?" Through her tear-dimmed eyes, Mary saw the form of a man, and thinking that it was the gardener, she said, "Sir, if thou have borne Him hence, tell me where thou hast laid Him, and I will take Him away." If this rich man's tomb was thought too honorable a burial place for Jesus, she herself would provide a place for Him. There was a grave that Christ's own voice had made vacant, the grave where Lazarus had lain. Might she not there find a burial place for her Lord? She felt that to care for His precious crucified body would be a great consolation to her in her grief.

But now in His own familiar voice Jesus said to her, "Mary." Now she knew that it was not a stranger who was addressing her, and turning she saw before her the living Christ. In her joy she forgot that He had been crucified. Springing toward Him, as if to embrace His feet, she said, "Rabboni." But Christ raised His hand, saying, Detain Me not; "for I am not yet ascended to My Father: but go to My brethren, and say unto them, I ascend unto My Father, and your Father; and to My God, and your God." And Mary went her way to the disciples with the joyful message.

Jesus refused to receive the homage of His people until He had the assurance that His sacrifice was accepted by the Father. He ascended to the heavenly courts, and from God Himself heard the assurance that His atonement for the sins of men had been ample, that through His blood all might gain eternal life. The Father ratified the covenant made with Christ, that He would receive repentant and obedient men, and would love them even as He loves His Son. Christ was to complete His work, and fulfill His pledge to "make a man more precious than fine gold; even a man than the golden wedge of Ophir." Isa. 13:12. All power in heaven and on earth was given to the Prince of life, and He returned to His followers in a world of sin, that He might impart to them of His power and glory.

While the Saviour was in God's presence, receiving gifts for His church, the disciples thought upon His empty tomb, and mourned and wept. The day that was a day of rejoicing to all heaven was to the disciples a day of uncertainty, confusion, and perplexity. Their unbelief in the testimony of the women gives evidence of how low their faith had sunk. The news of Christ's resurrection was so different from what they had anticipated that they could not believe it. It was too good to be true, they thought. They had heard so much of the doctrines and the so-called scientific theories of the Sadducees that the impression made on their minds in regard to the resurrection was vague. They scarcely knew what the resurrection from the dead could mean. They were unable to take in the great subject.

"Go your way," the angels had said to the women, "tell His disciples and Peter that He goeth before you into Galilee: there shall ye see Him, as He said unto you." These angels had been with Christ as guardian angels throughout His life on earth. They had witnessed His trial and crucifixion. They had heard His words to His disciples. This was shown by their message to the disciples, and should have convinced them of its truth. Such words could have come only from the messengers of their risen Lord.

"Tell His disciples and Peter," the angels said. Since the death of Christ, Peter had been bowed down with remorse. His shameful denial of the Lord, and the Saviour's look of love and anguish, were ever before him. Of all the disciples he had suffered most bitterly. To him the assurance is given that his repentance is accepted and his sin forgiven. He is mentioned by name.

"Tell His disciples and Peter that He goeth before you into Galilee: there shall ye see Him." All the disciples had forsaken Jesus, and the call to meet Him again includes them all. He has not cast them off. When Mary Magdalene told them she had seen the Lord, she repeated the call to the meeting in Galilee. And a third time the message was sent to them. After He had ascended to the Father, Jesus appeared to the other women, saying, "All hail. And they came and held Him by the feet, and worshiped Him. Then said Jesus unto them, Be not afraid: go tell My brethren that they go into Galilee, and there shall they see Me."

Christ's first work on earth after His resurrection was to convince His disciples of His undiminished love and tender regard for them. To give them proof that He was their living Saviour, that He had broken the fetters of the tomb, and could no longer be held by the enemy death; to reveal that He had the same heart of love as when He was with them as their beloved Teacher, He appeared to them again and again. He would draw the bonds of love still closer around them. Go tell My brethren, He said, that they meet Me in Galilee.

As they heard this appointment, so definitely given, the disciples began to think of Christ's words to them foretelling His resurrection. But even now they did not rejoice. They could not cast off their doubt and perplexity. Even when the women declared that they had seen the Lord, the disciples would not believe. They thought them under an illusion.

Trouble seemed crowding upon trouble. On the sixth day of the week they had seen their Master die; on the first day of the next week they found themselves deprived of His body, and they were accused of having stolen it away for the sake of deceiving the people. They despaired of ever correcting the false impressions that were gaining ground against them. They feared the enmity of the priests and the wrath of the people. They longed for the presence of Jesus, who had helped them in every perplexity.

Often they repeated the words, "We trusted that it had been He which should have redeemed Israel." Lonely and sick at heart they remembered His words, "If they do these things in a green tree, what shall be done in the dry?" Luke 24:21; 23:31. They met together in the upper chamber, and closed and fastened the doors, knowing that the fate of their beloved Teacher might at any time be theirs.

And all the time they might have been rejoicing in the knowledge of a risen Saviour. In the garden, Mary had stood weeping, when Jesus was close beside her. Her eyes were so blinded by tears that she did not discern Him. And the hearts of the disciples were so full of grief that they did not believe the angels' message or the words of Christ Himself.

How many are still doing what these disciples did! How many echo Mary's despairing cry, "They have taken away the Lord, . . . and we know not where they have laid Him"! To how many might the Saviour's words be spoken, "Why weepest thou? whom seekest thou?" He is close beside them, but their tear-blinded eyes do not discern Him. He speaks to them, but they do not understand.

Oh that the bowed head might be lifted, that the eyes might be opened to behold Him, that the ears might listen to His voice! "Go quickly, and tell His disciples that He is risen." Bid them look not to Joseph's new tomb, that was closed with a great stone, and sealed with the Roman seal. Christ is not there. Look not to the empty sepulcher. Mourn not as those who are hopeless and helpless. Jesus lives, and because He lives, we shall live also. From grateful hearts, from lips touched with holy fire, let the glad song ring out, Christ is risen! He lives to make intercession for us. Grasp this hope, and it will hold the soul like a sure, tried anchor. Believe, and thou shalt see the glory of God.

The Walk to Emmaus

tn

The Desire of Ages — 782

83

The Walk to Emmaus

Late in the afternoon of the day of the resurrection, two of the disciples were on their way to Emmaus, a little town eight miles from Jerusalem. These disciples had had no prominent place in Christ's work, but they were earnest believers in Him. They had come to the city to keep the Passover, and were greatly perplexed by the events that had recently taken place. They had heard the news of the morning in regard to the removal of Christ's body from the tomb, and also the report of the women who had seen the angels and had met Jesus. They were now returning to their homes to meditate and pray. Sadly they pursued their evening walk, talking over the scenes of the trial and the crucifixion. Never before had they been so utterly disheartened. Hopeless and faithless, they were walking in the shadow of the cross.

They had not advanced far on their journey when they were joined by a stranger, but they were so absorbed in their gloom and disappointment that they did not observe him closely. They continued their conversation, expressing the thoughts of their hearts. They were reasoning in regard to the lessons that Christ had given, which they seemed unable to comprehend. As they talked of the events that had taken place, Jesus longed to comfort them. He had seen their grief; He understood the conflicting, perplexing ideas that brought to their minds the thought, Can this Man, who suffered Himself to be so humiliated, be the Christ? Their grief could not be restrained, and they wept. Jesus knew that their hearts were bound up with Him in love, and He longed to wipe away their tears, and fill them with joy and gladness. But He must first give them lessons they would never forget.

"He said unto them, What manner of communications are these that ye have one to another, as ye walk, and are sad? And the one of them, whose name was Cleopas, answering said unto Him, Art Thou only a stranger in Jerusalem, and hast not known the things which are come to pass there in these days?" They told Him of their disappointment in regard to their Master, "which was a prophet mighty in deed and word before God and all the people;" but "the chief priests and our rulers," they said, "delivered Him to be condemned to death, and have crucified Him." With hearts sore with disappointment, and with quivering lips, they added, "We trusted that it had been He which should have redeemed Israel: and beside all this, today is the third day since these things were done."

Strange that the disciples did not remember Christ's words, and realize that He had foretold the events which had come to pass! They did not realize that the last part of His disclosure would be just as verily fulfilled as the first part, that the third day He would rise again. This was the part they should have remembered. The priests and rulers did not forget this. On the day "that followed the day of the preparation, the chief priests and Pharisees came together unto Pilate, saying, Sir, we remember that that deceiver said, while He was yet alive, After three days I will rise again." Matt. 27:62, 63. But the disciples did not remember these words.

"Then He said unto them, O fools, and slow of heart to believe all that the prophets have spoken: ought not Christ to have suffered these things, and to enter into His glory?" The disciples wondered who this stranger could be, that He should penetrate to their very souls, and speak with such earnestness, tenderness, and sympathy, and with such hopefulness. For the first time since Christ's betrayal, they began to feel hopeful. Often they looked earnestly at their companion, and thought that His words were just the words that Christ would have spoken. They were filled with amazement, and their hearts began to throb with joyful expectation.

Beginning at Moses, the very Alpha of Bible history, Christ expounded in all the Scriptures the things concerning Himself. Had He first made Himself known to them, their hearts would have been satisfied. In the fullness of their joy they would have hungered for nothing more. But it was necessary for them to understand the witness borne to Him by the types and prophecies of the Old Testament. Upon these their faith must be established. Christ performed no miracle to convince them, but it was His first work to explain the Scriptures. They had looked upon His death as the destruction of all their hopes. Now He showed from the prophets that this was the very strongest evidence for their faith.

In teaching these disciples, Jesus showed the importance of the Old Testament as a witness to His mission. Many professed Christians now discard the Old Testament, claiming that it is no longer of any use. But such is not Christ's teaching. So highly did He value it that at one time He said, "If they hear not Moses and the prophets, neither will they be persuaded, though one rose from the dead." Luke 16:31.

It is the voice of Christ that speaks through patriarchs and prophets, from the days of Adam even to the closing scenes of time. The Saviour is revealed in the Old Testament as clearly as in the New. It is the light from the prophetic past that brings out the life of Christ and the teachings of the New Testament with clearness and beauty. The miracles of Christ are a proof of His divinity; but a stronger proof that He is the

This chapter is based on Luke 24:13-33.

world's Redeemer is found in comparing the prophecies of the Old Testament with the history of the New.

Reasoning from prophecy, Christ gave His disciples a correct idea of what He was to be in humanity. Their expectation of a Messiah who was to take His throne and kingly power in accordance with the desires of men had been misleading. It would interfere with a correct apprehension of His descent from the highest to the lowest position that could be occupied. Christ desired that the ideas of His disciples might be pure and true in every specification. They must understand as far as possible in regard to the cup of suffering that had been apportioned to Him. He showed them that the awful conflict which they could not yet comprehend was the fulfillment of the covenant made before the foundation of the world was laid. Christ must die, as every transgressor of the law must die if he continues in sin. All this was to be, but it was not to end in defeat, but in glorious, eternal victory. Jesus told them that every effort must be made to save the world from sin. His followers must live as He lived, and work as He worked, with intense, persevering effort.

800   Thus Christ discoursed to His disciples, opening their minds that they might understand the Scriptures. The disciples were weary, but the conversation did not flag. Words of life and assurance fell from the Saviour's lips. But still their eyes were holden. As He told them of the overthrow of Jerusalem, they looked upon the doomed city with weeping. But little did they yet suspect who their traveling companion was. They did not think that the subject of their conversation was walking by their side; for Christ referred to Himself as though He were another person. They thought that He was one of those who had been in attendance at the great feast, and who was now returning to his home. He walked as carefully as they over the rough stones, now and then halting with them for a little rest. Thus they proceeded along the mountainous road, while the One who was soon to take His position at God's right hand, and who could say, "All power is given unto Me in heaven and in earth," walked beside them. Matt. 28:18.

During the journey the sun had gone down, and before the travelers reached their place of rest, the laborers in the fields had left their work. As the disciples were about to enter their home, the stranger appeared as though He would continue His journey. But the disciples felt drawn to Him. Their souls hungered to hear more from Him. "Abide with us," they said. He did not seem to accept the invitation, but they pressed it upon Him, urging, "It is toward evening, and the day is far spent." Christ yielded to this entreaty and "went in to tarry with them."

Had the disciples failed to press their invitation, they would not have known that their traveling companion was the risen Lord. Christ never forces His company upon anyone. He interests Himself in those who need Him. Gladly will He enter the humblest home, and cheer the lowliest heart. But if men are too indifferent to think of the heavenly Guest, or ask Him to abide with them, He passes on. Thus many meet with great loss. They do not know Christ any more than did the disciples as He walked with them by the way.

The simple evening meal of bread is soon prepared. It is placed before the guest, who has taken His seat at the head of the table. Now He puts forth His hands to bless the food. The disciples start back in astonishment. Their companion spreads forth His hands in exactly the same way as their Master used to do. They look again, and lo, they see in His hands the print of nails. Both exclaim at once, It is the Lord Jesus! He has risen from the dead!

They rise to cast themselves at His feet and   801 worship Him, but He has vanished out of their sight. They look at the place which had been occupied by One whose body had lately lain in the grave, and say to each other, "Did not our heart burn within us, while He talked with us by the way, and while He opened to us the Scriptures?"

But with this great news to communicate they cannot sit and talk. Their weariness and hunger are gone. They leave their meal untasted, and full of joy immediately set out again on the same path by which they came, hurrying to tell the tidings to the disciples in the city. In some parts the road is not safe, but they climb over the steep places, slipping on the smooth rocks. They do not see, they do not know, that they have the protection of Him who has traveled the road with them. With their pilgrim staff in hand, they press on, desiring to go faster than they dare. They lose their track, but find it again. Sometimes running, sometimes stumbling, they press forward, their unseen Companion close beside them all the way.

The night is dark, but the Sun of Righteousness is shining upon them. Their hearts leap for joy. They seem to be in a new world. Christ is a living Saviour. They no longer mourn over Him as dead. Christ is risen—over and over again they repeat it. This is the message they are carrying to the sorrowing ones. They must tell them the wonderful story of the walk to Emmaus. They must tell who joined them by the way. They carry the greatest message ever given to the world, a message of glad tidings upon which the hopes of the human family for time and for eternity depend.

84

"Peace Be Unto You"

On reaching Jerusalem the two disciples enter at the eastern gate, which is open at night on festal occasions. The houses are dark and silent, but the travelers make their way through the narrow streets by the light of the rising moon. They go to the upper chamber where Jesus spent the hours of the last evening before His death. Here they know that their brethren are to be found. Late as it is, they know that the disciples will not sleep till they learn for a certainty what has become of the body of their Lord. They find the door of the chamber securely barred. They knock for admission, but no answer comes. All is still. Then they give their names. The door is carefully unbarred, they enter, and Another, unseen, enters with them. Then the door is again fastened, to keep out spies.

The travelers find all in surprised excitement. The voices of those in the room break out into thanksgiving and praise, saying, "The Lord is risen indeed, and hath appeared to Simon." Then the two travelers, panting with the haste with which they have made their journey, tell the wondrous story of how Jesus has appeared to them. They have just ended, and some are saying that they cannot believe it, for it is too good to be true, when behold, another Person stands before them. Every eye is fastened upon the Stranger. No one has knocked for entrance.

No footstep has been heard. The disciples are startled, and wonder what it means. Then they hear a voice which is no other than the voice of their Master. Clear and distinct the words fall from His lips, "Peace be unto you."

"But they were terrified and affrighted, and supposed that they had seen a spirit. And He said unto them, Why are ye troubled? and why do thoughts arise in your hearts? Behold My hands and My feet, that it is I Myself: handle Me, and see; for a spirit hath not flesh and bones, as ye see Me have. And when He had thus spoken, He showed them His hands and His feet."

They beheld the hands and feet marred by the cruel nails. They recognized His voice, like no other they had ever heard. "And while they yet believed not for joy, and wondered, He said unto them, Have ye here any meat? And they gave Him a piece of a broiled fish, and of an honeycomb. And He took it, and did eat before them." "Then were the disciples glad, when they saw the Lord." Faith and joy took the place of unbelief, and with feelings which no words could express they acknowledged their risen

Saviour.

At the birth of Jesus the angel announced, Peace on earth, and good will to men. And now at His first appearance to the disciples after His resurrection, the Saviour addressed them with the blessed words, "Peace be unto you." Jesus is ever ready to speak peace to souls that are burdened with doubts and fears. He waits for us to open the door of the heart to Him, and say, Abide with us. He says, "Behold, I stand at the door, and knock: if any man hear My voice, and open the door, I will come in to him, and will sup with him, and he with Me." Rev. 3:20.

The resurrection of Jesus was a type of the final resurrection of all who sleep in Him. The countenance of the risen Saviour, His manner, His speech, were all familiar to His disciples. As Jesus arose from the dead, so those who sleep in Him are to rise again. We shall know our friends, even as the disciples knew Jesus. They may have been deformed, diseased, or disfigured, in this mortal life, and they rise in perfect health and symmetry; yet in the glorified body their identity will be perfectly preserved. Then shall we know even as also we are known. 1 Cor. 13:12. In the face radiant with the light shining from the face of Jesus, we shall recognize the lineaments of those we love.

When Jesus met with His disciples, He reminded them of the words He had spoken to them before His death, that all things must be fulfilled which were written in the law of Moses, and in the prophets, and in the Psalms concerning Him. "Then opened He their understanding, that they might understand the Scriptures, and said unto them, Thus it is written, and thus it behooved Christ to suffer, and to rise from the dead the third day; and that repentance and remission of sins should be preached in His name among all nations, beginning at Jerusalem. And ye are witnesses of these things."

The disciples began to realize the nature and extent of their work. They were to proclaim to the world the wonderful truths which Christ had entrusted to them. The events of His life, His death and resurrection, the prophecies that pointed to these events, the sacredness of the law of God, the mysteries of the plan of salvation, the power of Jesus for the remission of sins,—to all these things they were witnesses, and they were to make them known to the world. They were to proclaim the gospel of peace and salvation through repentance and the power of the Saviour.

"And when He had said this, He breathed on them, and saith unto them, Receive ye the Holy Ghost: Whosesoever sins ye remit, they are remitted unto them; and whosesoever sins ye retain, they are retained." The Holy Spirit was not yet fully manifested; for Christ had not yet been glorified. The more abundant impartation

This chapter is based on Luke 24:33-48; John 20:19-29.

of the Spirit did not take place till after Christ's ascension. Not until this was received could the disciples fulfill the commission to preach the gospel to the world. But the Spirit was now given for a special purpose. Before the disciples could fulfill their official duties in connection with the church, Christ breathed His Spirit upon them. He was committing to them a most sacred trust, and He desired to impress them with the fact that without the Holy Spirit this work could not be accomplished.

The Holy Spirit is the breath of spiritual life in the soul. The impartation of the Spirit is the impartation of the life of Christ. It imbues the receiver with the attributes of Christ. Only those who are thus taught of God, those who possess the inward working of the Spirit, and in whose life the Christ-life is manifested, are to stand as representative men, to minister in behalf of the church.

"Whosoever sins ye remit," said Christ, "they are remitted; . . . and whosoever sins ye retain, they are retained." Christ here gives no liberty for any man to pass judgment upon others. In the Sermon on the Mount He forbade this. It is the prerogative of God. But on the church in its organized capacity He places a responsibility for the individual members. Toward those who fall into sin, the church has a duty, to warn, to instruct, and if possible to restore. "Reprove, rebuke, exhort," the Lord says, "with all long-suffering and doctrine." 2 Tim. 4:2. Deal faithfully with wrongdoing. Warn every soul that is in danger. Leave none to deceive themselves. Call sin by its right name. Declare what God has said in regard to lying, Sabbathbreaking, stealing, idolatry, and every other evil. "They which do such things shall not inherit the kingdom of God." Gal. 5:21. If they persist in sin, the judgment you have declared from God's word is pronounced upon them in heaven. In choosing to sin, they disown Christ; the church must show that she does not sanction their deeds, or she herself dishonors her Lord. She must say about sin what God says about it. She must deal with it as God directs, and her action is ratified in heaven. He who despises the authority of the church despises the authority of Christ Himself.

But there is a brighter side to the picture. "Whosoever sins ye remit, they are remitted." Let this thought be kept uppermost. In labor for the erring, let every eye be directed to Christ. Let the shepherds have a tender care for the flock of the Lord's pasture. Let them speak to the erring of the forgiving mercy of the Saviour. Let them encourage the sinner to repent, and believe in Him who can pardon. Let them declare, on the authority of God's word, "If we confess our sins, He is faithful and just to forgive us our sins, and to cleanse us from all unrighteousness." 1 John 1:9. All who repent have the assurance, "He will have compassion upon us; He will subdue our iniquities; and Thou wilt cast all their sins into the depths of the sea." Micah 7:19.

Let the repentance of the sinner be accepted by the church with grateful hearts. Let the repenting one be led out from the darkness of unbelief into the light of faith and righteousness. Let his trembling hand be placed in the loving hand of Jesus. Such a remission is ratified in heaven.

Only in this sense has the church power to absolve the sinner. Remission of sins can be obtained only through the merits of Christ. To no man, to no body of men, is given power to free the soul from guilt. Christ charged His disciples to preach the remission of sins in His name among all nations; but they themselves were not empowered to remove one stain of sin. The name of Jesus is the only "name under heaven given among men, whereby we must be saved." Acts 4:12.

When Jesus first met the disciples in the upper chamber, Thomas was not with them. He heard the reports of the others, and received abundant proof that Jesus had risen; but gloom and unbelief filled his heart. As he heard the disciples tell of the wonderful manifestations of the risen Saviour, it only plunged him in deeper despair. If Jesus had really risen from the dead, there could be no further hope of a literal earthly kingdom. And it wounded his vanity to think that his Master should reveal Himself to all the disciples except him. He was determined not to believe, and for a whole week he brooded over his wretchedness, which seemed all the darker in contrast with the hope and faith of his brethren.

During this time he repeatedly declared, "Except I shall see in His hands the print of the nails, and put my finger into the print of the nails, and thrust my hand into His side, I will not believe." He would not see through the eyes of his brethren, or exercise faith which was dependent upon their testimony. He ardently loved his Lord, but he had allowed jealousy and unbelief to take possession of his mind and heart.

A number of the disciples now made the familiar upper chamber their temporary home, and at evening all except Thomas gathered here. One evening Thomas determined to meet with the others. Notwithstanding his unbelief, he had a faint hope that the good news was true. While the disciples were taking their evening meal, they talked of the evidences which Christ had given them in the prophecies. "Then came Jesus, the doors being shut, and stood in the midst, and said, Peace be unto you."

Turning to Thomas He said, "Reach hither thy finger, and behold My hands; and reach hither thy hand, and thrust it into My side: and

806

807

be not faithless, but believing." These words showed that He was acquainted with the thoughts and words of Thomas. The doubting disciple knew that none of his companions had seen Jesus for a week. They could not have told the Master of his unbelief. He recognized the One before him as his Lord. He had no desire for further proof. His heart leaped for joy, and he cast himself at the feet of Jesus crying, "My Lord and my God."

Jesus accepted his acknowledgment, but gently reproved his unbelief: "Thomas, because thou hast seen Me, thou hast believed: blessed are they that have not seen, and yet have believed." The faith of Thomas would have been more pleasing to Christ if he had been willing to believe upon the testimony of his brethren. Should the world now follow the example of Thomas, no one would believe unto salvation; for all who receive Christ must do so through the testimony of others.

Many who are given to doubt excuse themselves by saying that if they had the evidence which Thomas had from his companions, they would believe. They do not realize that they have not only that evidence, but much more. Many who, like Thomas, wait for all cause of doubt to be removed, will never realize their desire. They gradually become confirmed in unbelief. Those who educate themselves to look on the dark side, and murmur and complain, know not what they do. They are sowing the seeds of doubt, and they will have a harvest of doubt to reap. At a time when faith and confidence are most essential, many will thus find themselves powerless to hope and believe.

In His treatment of Thomas, Jesus gave a lesson for His followers. His example shows how we should treat those whose faith is weak, and who make their doubts prominent. Jesus did not overwhelm Thomas with reproach, nor did He enter into controversy with him. He revealed Himself to the doubting one. Thomas had been most unreasonable in dictating the conditions of his faith, but Jesus, by His generous love and consideration, broke down all the barriers. Unbelief is seldom overcome by controversy. It is rather put upon self-defense, and finds new support and excuse. But let Jesus, in His love and mercy, be revealed as the crucified Saviour, and from many once unwilling lips will be heard the acknowledgment of Thomas, "My Lord and my God."

808

809

85

By the Sea Once More

Jesus had appointed to meet His disciples in Galilee; and soon after the Passover week was

This chapter is based on John 21:1-22.

ended, they bent their steps thither. Their absence from Jerusalem during the feast would have been interpreted as disaffection and heresy, therefore they remained till its close; but this over, they gladly turned homeward to meet the Saviour as He had directed.

Seven of the disciples were in company. They were clad in the humble garb of fishermen; they were poor in worldly goods, but rich in the knowledge and practice of the truth, which in the sight of Heaven gave them the highest rank as teachers. They had not been students in the schools of the prophets, but for three years they had been taught by the greatest Educator the world has ever known. Under His instruction they had become elevated, intelligent, and refined, agents through whom men might be led to a knowledge of the truth.

Much of the time of Christ's ministry had been passed near the Sea of Galilee. As the disciples gathered in a place where they were not likely to be disturbed, they found themselves surrounded by reminders of Jesus and His mighty works. On this sea, when their hearts were filled with terror, and the fierce storm was hurrying them to destruction, Jesus had walked upon the billows to their rescue. Here the tempest had been hushed by His word. Within sight was the beach where above ten thousand persons had been fed from a few small loaves and fishes. Not far distant was Capernaum, the scene of so many miracles. As the disciples looked upon the scene, their minds were full of the words and deeds of their Saviour. 810

The evening was pleasant, and Peter, who still had much of his old love for boats and fishing, proposed that they should go out upon the sea and cast their nets. In this plan all were ready to join; they were in need of food and clothing, which the proceeds of a successful night's fishing would supply. So they went out in their boat, but they caught nothing. All night they toiled, without success. Through the weary hours they talked of their absent Lord, and recalled the wonderful events they had witnessed in His ministry beside the sea. They questioned as to their own future, and grew sad at the prospect before them.

All the while a lone watcher upon the shore followed them with His eye, while He Himself was unseen. At length the morning dawned. The boat was but a little way from the shore, and the disciples saw a stranger standing upon the beach, who accosted them with the question, "Children, have ye any meat?" When they answered, "No," "He said unto them, Cast the net on the right side of the ship, and ye shall find. They cast therefore, and now they were not able to draw it for the multitude of fishes."

John recognized the stranger, and exclaimed to Peter, "It is the Lord." Peter was so elated and so glad that in his eagerness he cast himself into the water and was soon standing by the side of his Master. The other disciples came in their boat, dragging the net with fishes. "As soon then as they were come to land, they saw a fire of coals there, and fish laid thereon, and bread."

They were too much amazed to question whence came the fire and the food. "Jesus saith unto them, Bring of the fish which ye have now caught." Peter rushed for the net, which he had dropped, and helped his brethren drag it to the shore. After the work was done, and the preparation made, Jesus bade the disciples come and dine. He broke the food, and divided it among them, and was known and acknowledged by all the seven. The miracle of feeding the five thousand on the mountainside was now brought to their minds; but a mysterious awe was upon them, and in silence they gazed upon the risen Saviour.

Vividly they recalled the scene beside the sea when Jesus had bidden them follow Him. They remembered how, at His command, they had launched out into the deep, and had let down their net, and the catch had been so abundant as to fill the net, even to breaking. Then Jesus had called them to leave their fishing boats, and had promised to make them fishers of men. It was to bring this scene to their minds, and to deepen its impression, that He had again performed the miracle. His act was a renewal of the commission to the disciples. It showed them that the death of their Master had not lessened their obligation to do the work He had assigned them. Though they were to be deprived of His personal companionship, and of the means of support by their former employment, the risen Saviour would still have a care for them. While they were doing His work, He would provide for their needs. And Jesus had a purpose in bidding them cast their net on the right side of the ship. On that side He stood upon the shore. That was the side of faith. If they labored in connection with Him,—His divine power combining with their human effort,—they could not fail of success.

Another lesson Christ had to give, relating especially to Peter. Peter's denial of his Lord had been in shameful contrast to his former professions of loyalty. He had dishonored Christ, and had incurred the distrust of his brethren. They thought he would not be allowed to take his former position among them, and he himself felt that he had forfeited his trust. Before being called to take up again his apostolic work, he must before them all give evidence of his repentance. Without this, his sin, though repented of, might have destroyed his influence as a minister of Christ. The Saviour gave him opportunity to regain the confidence of his brethren, and, so far as possible, to remove the reproach he had brought upon the gospel.

Here is given a lesson for all Christ's followers. The gospel makes no compromise with evil. It cannot excuse sin. Secret sins are to be confessed in secret to God; but, for open sin, open confession is required. The reproach of the disciple's sin is cast upon Christ. It causes Satan to triumph, and wavering souls to stumble. By giving proof of repentance, the disciple, so far as lies in his power, is to remove this reproach.

While Christ and the disciples were eating together by the seaside, the Saviour said to Peter, "Simon, son of Jonas, lovest thou Me more than these?" referring to his brethren. Peter had once declared, "Though all men shall be offended because of Thee, yet will I never be offended." Matt. 26:33. But he now put a truer estimate upon himself. "Yea, Lord," he said, "Thou knowest that I love Thee." There is no vehement assurance that his love is greater than that of his brethren. He does not express his own opinion of his devotion. To Him who can read all the motives of the heart he appeals to judge as to his sincerity,—"Thou knowest that I love Thee." And Jesus bids him, "Feed My lambs."

Again Jesus applied the test to Peter, repeating His former words: "Simon, son of Jonas, lovest thou Me?" This time He did not ask Peter whether he loved Him better than did his brethren. The second response was like the first, free from extravagant assurance: "Yea, Lord; Thou knowest that I love Thee." Jesus said to him, "Feed My sheep." Once more the Saviour put the trying question: "Simon, son of Jonas, lovest thou Me?" Peter was grieved; he thought that Jesus doubted his love. He knew that his Lord had cause to distrust him, and with an aching heart he answered, "Lord, Thou knowest all things; Thou knowest that I love Thee." Again Jesus said to him, "Feed My sheep."

Three times Peter had openly denied his Lord, and three times Jesus drew from him the assurance of his love and loyalty, pressing home that pointed question, like a barbed arrow to his wounded heart. Before the assembled disciples Jesus revealed the depth of Peter's repentance, and showed how thoroughly humbled was the once boasting disciple.

Peter was naturally forward and impulsive, and Satan had taken advantage of these characteristics to overthrow him. Just before the fall of Peter, Jesus had said to him, "Satan hath desired to have you, that he may sift you as wheat: but I have prayed for thee, that thy faith fail not: and when thou art converted, strengthen thy brethren." Luke 22:31, 32. That time had now come, and the transformation in Peter was evident. The close, testing questions of the Lord had not called out one forward, self-sufficient reply; and because of his humiliation and repentance, Peter was better prepared than ever before to act as shepherd to the flock.

The first work that Christ entrusted to Peter

on restoring him to the ministry was to feed the lambs. This was a work in which Peter had little experience. It would require great care and tenderness, much patience and perseverance. It called him to minister to those who were young in the faith, to teach the ignorant, to open the Scriptures to them, and to educate them for usefulness in Christ's service. Heretofore Peter had not been fitted to do this, or even to understand its importance. But this was the work which Jesus now called upon him to do. For this work his own experience of suffering and repentance had prepared him.

Before his fall, Peter was always speaking unadvisedly, from the impulse of the moment. He was always ready to correct others, and to express his mind, before he had a clear comprehension of himself or of what he had to say. But the converted Peter was very different. He retained his former fervor, but the grace of Christ regulated his zeal. He was no longer impetuous, self-confident, and self-exalted, but 815 calm, self-possessed, and teachable. He could then feed the lambs as well as the sheep of Christ's flock.

The Saviour's manner of dealing with Peter had a lesson for him and for his brethren. It taught them to meet the transgressor with patience, sympathy, and forgiving love. Although Peter had denied his Lord, the love which Jesus bore him never faltered. Just such love should the undershepherd feel for the sheep and lambs committed to his care. Remembering his own weakness and failure, Peter was to deal with his flock as tenderly as Christ had dealt with him.

The question that Christ had put to Peter was significant. He mentioned only one condition of discipleship and service. "Lovest thou Me?" He said. This is the essential qualification. Though Peter might possess every other, yet without the love of Christ he could not be a faithful shepherd over the Lord's flock. Knowledge, benevolence, eloquence, gratitude, and zeal are all aids in the good work; but without the love of Jesus in the heart, the work of the Christian minister is a failure.

Jesus walked alone with Peter, for there was something which He wished to communicate to him only. Before His death, Jesus had said to him, "Whither I go, thou canst not follow Me now; but thou shalt follow Me afterwards." To this Peter had replied, "Lord, why cannot I follow Thee now? I will lay down my life for Thy sake." John 13:36, 37. When he said this, he little knew to what heights and depths Christ's feet would lead the way. Peter had failed when the test came, but again he was to have opportunity to prove his love for Christ. That he might be strengthened for the final test of his faith, the Saviour opened to him his future. He told him that after living a life of usefulness, when age

was telling upon his strength, he would indeed follow his Lord. Jesus said, "When thou wast young, thou girdedst thyself, and walkedst whither thou wouldest: but when thou shalt be old, thou shalt stretch forth thy hands, and another shall gird thee, and carry thee whither thou wouldest not. This spake He, signifying by what death he should glorify God."

Jesus thus made known to Peter the very manner of his death; He even foretold the stretching forth of his hands upon the cross. Again He bade His disciple, "Follow Me." Peter was not disheartened by the revelation. He felt willing to suffer any death for his Lord.

Heretofore Peter had known Christ after the flesh, as many know Him now; but he was no more to be thus limited. He knew Him no more as he had known Him in his association with Him in humanity. He had loved Him as a man, 816 as a heaven-sent teacher; he now loved Him as God. He had been learning the lesson that to him Christ was all in all. Now he was prepared to share in his Lord's mission of sacrifice. When at last brought to the cross, he was, at his own request, crucified with his head downward. He thought it too great an honor to suffer in the same way as his Master did.

To Peter the words "Follow Me" were full of instruction. Not only for his death, but for every step of his life, was the lesson given. Hitherto Peter had been inclined to act independently. He had tried to plan for the work of God, instead of waiting to follow out God's plan. But he could gain nothing by rushing on before the Lord. Jesus bids him, "Follow Me." Do not run ahead of Me. Then you will not have the hosts of Satan to meet alone. Let Me go before you, and you will not be overcome by the enemy.

As Peter walked beside Jesus, he saw that John was following. A desire came over him to know *his* future, and he "saith to Jesus, Lord, and what shall this man do? Jesus saith unto him, If I will that he tarry till I come, what is that to thee? follow thou Me." Peter should have considered that his Lord would reveal to him all that it was best for him to know. It is the duty of everyone to follow Christ, without undue anxiety as to the work assigned to others. In saying of John, "If I will that he tarry till I come," Jesus gave no assurance that this disciple should live until the Lord's second coming. He merely asserted His own supreme power, and that even if He should will this to be so, it would in no way affect Peter's work. The future of both John and Peter was in the hands of their Lord. Obedience in following Him was the duty required of each.

How many today are like Peter! They are interested in the affairs of others, and anxious to know their duty, while they are in danger of neglecting their own. It is our work to look to Christ and follow Him. We shall see mistakes in the lives of others, and defects in their character. Humanity is encompassed with infirmity. But in Christ we shall find perfection. Beholding Him, we shall become transformed.

John lived to be very aged. He witnessed the destruction of Jerusalem, and the ruin of the stately temple,—a symbol of the final ruin of the world. To his latest days John closely followed his Lord. The burden of his testimony to the churches was, "Beloved, let us love one another;" "he that dwelleth in love dwelleth in God, and God in him." 1 John 4:7, 16.

817   Peter had been restored to his apostleship, but the honor and authority he received from Christ had not given him supremacy over his brethren. This Christ had made plain when in answer to Peter's question, "What shall this man do?" He had said, "What is that to thee? follow thou Me." Peter was not honored as the head of the church. The favor which Christ had shown him in forgiving his apostasy, and entrusting him with the feeding of the flock, and Peter's own faithfulness in following Christ, won for him the confidence of his brethren. He had much influence in the church. But the lesson which Christ had taught him by the Sea of Galilee Peter carried with him throughout his life. Writing by the Holy Spirit to the churches, he said:

"The elders which are among you I exhort, who am also an elder, and a witness of the sufferings of Christ, and also a partaker of the glory that shall be revealed: Feed the flock of God which is among you, taking the oversight thereof, not by constraint, but willingly; not for filthy lucre, but of a ready mind; neither as being lords over God's heritage, but being ensamples to the flock. And when the Chief Shepherd shall appear, ye shall receive a crown of glory that fadeth not away." 1 Peter 5:1-4.

86

Go Teach All Nations

818   Standing but a step from His heavenly throne, Christ gave the commission to His disciples. "All power is given unto Me in heaven and in earth," He said. "Go ye therefore, and teach all nations." "Go ye into all the world, and preach the gospel to every creature." Mark 16:15. Again and again the words were repeated, that the disciples might grasp their significance. Upon all the inhabitants of the earth, high and low, rich and poor, was the light of heaven to shine in clear, strong rays. The disciples were to be colaborers with their Redeemer in the work of saving the world.

The commission had been given to the twelve when Christ met with them in the upper chamber; but it was now to be given to a larger number. At the meeting on a mountain in Galilee, all the believers who could be called together were assembled. Of this meeting Christ Himself, before His death, had designated the time and place. The angel at the tomb reminded the disciples of His promise to meet them in Galilee. The promise was repeated to the believers who were gathered at Jerusalem during the Passover week, and through them it reached many lonely ones who were mourning the death of their Lord. With intense interest all looked forward to the interview. They made their way to the place of meeting by circuitous routes, coming in from every direction, to avoid exciting the suspicion of the jealous Jews. With wondering hearts they came, talking earnestly together of the news that had reached them concerning Christ.

At the time appointed, about five hundred believers were collected in little knots on the mountainside, eager to learn all that could be learned from those who had seen Christ since 819 His resurrection. From group to group the disciples passed, telling all they had seen and heard of Jesus, and reasoning from the Scriptures as He had done with them. Thomas recounted the story of his unbelief, and told how his doubts had been swept away. Suddenly Jesus stood among them. No one could tell whence or how He came. Many who were present had never before seen Him; but in His hands and feet they beheld the marks of the crucifixion; His countenance was as the face of God, and when they saw Him, they worshiped Him.

But some doubted. So it will always be. There are those who find it hard to exercise faith, and they place themselves on the doubting side. These lose much because of their unbelief.

This was the only interview that Jesus had with many of the believers after His resurrection. He came and spoke to them saying, "All power is given unto Me in heaven and in earth." The disciples had worshiped Him before He spoke, but His words, falling from lips that had been closed in death, thrilled them with peculiar power. He was now the risen Saviour. Many of them had seen Him exercise His power in healing the sick and controlling satanic agencies. They believed that He possessed power to set up His kingdom at Jerusalem, power to quell all opposition, power over the elements of nature. He had stilled the angry waters; He had walked upon the white-crested billows; He had raised the dead to life. Now He declared that "all power" was given to Him. His words carried the minds of His hearers above earthly and temporal things to the heavenly and eternal. They were lifted to the highest conception of His dignity and glory.

Christ's words on the mountainside were the announcement that His sacrifice in behalf of man was full and complete. The conditions of the atonement had been fulfilled; the work for

This chapter is based on Matthew 28:16-20.

which He came to this world had been accomplished. He was on His way to the throne of God, to be honored by angels, principalities, and powers. He had entered upon His mediatorial work. Clothed with boundless authority, He gave His commission to the disciples: "Go ye therefore, and teach all nations," "baptizing them into the name of the Father and of the Son and of the Holy Spirit: teaching them to observe all things whatsoever I commanded you: and lo, I am with you always, even unto the end of the world." Matt. 28:19, 20, R. V.

The Jewish people had been made the depositaries of sacred truth; but Pharisaism had made 820 them the most exclusive, the most bigoted, of all the human race. Everything about the priests and rulers—their dress, customs, ceremonies, traditions—made them unfit to be the light of the world. They looked upon themselves, the Jewish nation, as the world. But Christ commissioned His disciples to proclaim a faith and worship that would have in it nothing of caste or country, a faith that would be adapted to all peoples, all nations, all classes of men.

Before leaving His disciples, Christ plainly stated the nature of His kingdom. He called to their minds what He had previously told them concerning it. He declared that it was not His purpose to establish in this world a temporal, but a spiritual kingdom. He was not to reign as an earthly king on David's throne. Again He opened to them the Scriptures, showing that all He had passed through had been ordained in heaven, in the councils between the Father and Himself. All had been foretold by men inspired by the Holy Spirit. He said, You see that all I have revealed to you concerning My rejection as the Messiah has come to pass. All I have said in regard to the humiliation I should endure and the death I should die, has been verified. On the third day I rose again. Search the Scriptures more diligently, and you will see that in all these things the specifications of prophecy concerning Me have been fulfilled.

Christ commissioned His disciples to do the work He had left in their hands, beginning at Jerusalem. Jerusalem had been the scene of His amazing condescension for the human race. There He had suffered, been rejected and condemned. The land of Judea was His birthplace. There, clad in the garb of humanity, He had walked with men, and few had discerned how near heaven came to the earth when Jesus was among them. At Jerusalem the work of the disciples must begin.

In view of all that Christ had suffered there, and the unappreciated labor He had put forth, the disciples might have pleaded for a more promising field; but they made no such plea. The very ground where He had scattered the seed of truth was to be cultivated by the disciples, and the seed would spring up and yield an abundant harvest. In their work the disciples would have to meet persecution through the jealousy and hatred of the Jews; but this had been endured by their Master, and they were not to flee from it. The first offers of mercy must be made to the murderers of the Saviour.

And there were in Jerusalem many who had secretly believed on Jesus, and many who had been deceived by the priests and rulers. To these also the gospel was to be presented. They were to be called to repentance. The wonderful truth 821 that through Christ alone could remission of sins be obtained was to be made plain. While all Jerusalem was stirred by the thrilling events of the past few weeks, the preaching of the gospel would make the deepest impression.

But the work was not to stop here. It was to be extended to the earth's remotest bounds. To His disciples Christ said, You have been witnesses of My life of self-sacrifice in behalf of the world. You have witnessed My labors for Israel. Although they would not come unto Me that they might have life, although priests and rulers have done to Me as they listed, although they have rejected Me as the Scriptures foretold, they shall have still another opportunity of accepting the Son of God. You have seen that all who come to Me, confessing their sins, I freely receive. Him that cometh to Me I will in nowise cast out. All who will, may be reconciled to God, and receive everlasting life. To you, My disciples, I commit this message of mercy. It is to be given to Israel first, and then to all nations, tongues, and peoples. It is to be given to Jews and Gentiles. All who believe are to be gathered into one church.

Through the gift of the Holy Spirit the disciples were to receive a marvelous power. Their testimony was to be confirmed by signs and wonders. Miracles would be wrought, not only by the apostles, but by those who received their message. Jesus said, "In My name shall they cast out devils; they shall speak with new tongues; they shall take up serpents; and if they drink any deadly thing, it shall not hurt them; they shall lay hands on the sick, and they shall recover." Mark 16:17, 18.

At that time poisoning was often practiced. Unscrupulous men did not hesitate to remove by this means those who stood in the way of their ambition. Jesus knew that the life of His disciples would thus be imperiled. Many would think it doing God service to put His witnesses to death. He therefore promised them protection from this danger.

The disciples were to have the same power which Jesus had to heal "all manner of sickness and all manner of disease among the people." By healing in His name the diseases of the body, they would testify to His power for the healing of the soul. Matt. 4:23; 9:6. And a new endowment was now promised. The disciples were to preach among other nations, and they would receive power to speak other tongues. The apostles and their associates were unlettered men, yet through the outpouring of the Spirit on the day of Pentecost, their speech, whether in their own or a foreign language, became pure, simple, and accurate, both in word and in accent.

Thus Christ gave His disciples their commission. He made full provision for the prosecution of the work, and took upon Himself the responsibility for its success. So long as they obeyed His word, and worked in connection with Him, they could not fail. Go to all nations, He bade them. Go to the farthest part of the habitable globe, but know that My presence will be there. Labor in faith and confidence, for the time will never come when I will forsake you.

The Saviour's commission to the disciples included all the believers. It includes all believers in Christ to the end of time. It is a fatal mistake to suppose that the work of saving souls depends alone on the ordained minister. All to whom the heavenly inspiration has come are put in trust with the gospel. All who receive the life of Christ are ordained to work for the salvation of their fellow men. For this work the church was established, and all who take upon themselves its sacred vows are thereby pledged to be co-workers with Christ.

"The Spirit and the bride say, Come. And let him that heareth say, Come." Rev. 22:17. Everyone who hears is to repeat the invitation. Whatever one's calling in life, his first interest should be to win souls for Christ. He may not be able to speak to congregations, but he can work for individuals. To them he can communicate the instruction received from his Lord. Ministry does not consist alone in preaching. Those minister who relieve the sick and suffering, helping the needy, speaking words of comfort to the desponding and those of little faith. Nigh and afar off are souls weighed down by a sense of guilt. It is not hardship, toil, or poverty that degrades humanity. It is guilt, wrongdoing. This brings unrest and dissatisfaction. Christ would have His servants minister to sin-sick souls.

The disciples were to begin their work where they were. The hardest and most unpromising field was not to be passed by. So every one of Christ's workers is to begin where he is. In our own families may be souls hungry for sympathy, starving for the bread of life. There may be children to be trained for Christ. There are heathen at our very doors. Let us do faithfully the work that is nearest. Then let our efforts be extended as far as God's hand may lead the way. The work of many may appear to be restricted by circumstances; but, wherever it is, if performed with faith and diligence it will be felt to the uttermost parts of the earth. Christ's work when upon earth appeared to be confined to a narrow field, but multitudes from all lands heard His message. God often uses the simplest means to accomplish the greatest results. It is His plan that every part of His work shall depend on every other part, as a wheel within a wheel, all acting in harmony. The humblest worker, moved by the Holy Spirit, will touch invisible chords, whose vibrations will ring to the ends of the earth, and make melody through eternal ages.

But the command, "Go ye into all the world," is not to be lost sight of. We are called upon to lift our eyes to the "regions beyond." Christ tears away the wall of partition, the dividing prejudice of nationality, and teaches a love for all the human family. He lifts men from the narrow circle which their selfishness prescribes; He abolishes all territorial lines and artificial distinctions of society. He makes no difference between neighbors and strangers, friends and enemies. He teaches us to look upon every needy soul as our brother, and the world as our field.

When the Saviour said, "Go, . . . teach all nations," He said also, "These signs shall follow them that believe; In My name shall they cast out devils; they shall speak with new tongues; they shall take up serpents; and if they drink any deadly thing, it shall not hurt them; they shall lay hands on the sick, and they shall recover." The promise is as far-reaching as the commission. Not that all the gifts are imparted to each believer. The Spirit divides "to every man severally as He will." 1 Cor. 12:11. But the gifts of the Spirit are promised to every believer according to his need for the Lord's work. The promise is just as strong and trustworthy now as in the days of the apostles. "These signs shall follow them that believe." This is the privilege of God's children, and faith should lay hold on all that it is possible to have as an indorsement of faith.

"They shall lay hands on the sick, and they shall recover." This world is a vast lazar house, but Christ came to heal the sick, to proclaim deliverance to the captives of Satan. He was in Himself health and strength. He imparted His life to the sick, the afflicted, those possessed of demons. He turned away none who came to receive His healing power. He knew that those who petitioned Him for help had brought disease upon themselves; yet He did not refuse to heal them. And when virtue from Christ entered into these poor souls, they were convicted of sin, and many were healed of their spiritual disease, as well as of their physical maladies. The gospel still possesses the same power, and why should we not today witness the same results?

Christ feels the woes of every sufferer. When evil spirits rend a human frame, Christ feels the curse. When fever is burning up the life current, He feels the agony. And He is just as willing to heal the sick now as when He was personally on earth. Christ's servants are His representatives, the channels for His working. He desires through them to exercise His healing power.

In the Saviour's manner of healing there were lessons for His disciples. On one occasion He anointed the eyes of a blind man with clay, and bade him, "Go, wash in the pool of Siloam. . . . He went his way therefore, and washed, and came seeing." John 9:7. The cure could be wrought only by the power of the Great Healer, yet Christ made use of the simple agencies of nature. While He did not give countenance to drug medication, He sanctioned the use of simple and natural remedies.

To many of the afflicted ones who received healing, Christ said, "Sin no more, lest a worse thing come unto thee." John 5:14. Thus He taught that disease is the result of violating God's laws, both natural and spiritual. The great misery in the world would not exist did men but live in harmony with the Creator's plan.

Christ had been the guide and teacher of ancient Israel, and He taught them that health is the reward of obedience to the laws of God. The Great Physician who healed the sick in Palestine had spoken to His people from the pillar of cloud, telling them what they must do, and what God would do for them. "If thou wilt diligently hearken to the voice of the Lord thy God," He said, "and wilt do that which is right in His sight, and wilt give ear to His commandments, and keep all His statutes, I will put none of these diseases upon thee, which I have brought upon the Egyptians: for I am the Lord that healeth thee." Ex. 15:26. Christ gave to Israel definite instruction in regard to their habits of life, and He assured them, "The Lord will take away from thee all sickness." Deut. 7:15. When they fulfilled the conditions, the promise was verified to them. "There was not one feeble person among their tribes." Ps. 105:37.

These lessons are for us. There are conditions to be observed by all who would preserve health. All should learn what these conditions are. The Lord is not pleased with ignorance in regard to His laws, either natural or spiritual. We are to be workers together with God for the restoration of health to the body as well as to the soul.

And we should teach others how to preserve and to recover health. For the sick we should use the remedies which God has provided in nature, and we should point them to Him who alone can restore. It is our work to present the sick and suffering to Christ in the arms of our faith. We should teach them to believe in the Great Healer. We should lay hold on His promise, and pray for the manifestation of His power. The very essence of the gospel is restoration, and the Saviour would have us bid the sick, the hopeless, and the afflicted take hold upon His strength.

The power of love was in all Christ's healing, and only by partaking of that love, through faith, can we be instruments for His work. If we neglect to link ourselves in divine connection with Christ, the current of life-giving energy cannot flow in rich streams from us to the people. There were places where the Saviour Himself could not do many mighty works because of their unbelief. So now unbelief separates the church from her divine Helper. Her hold upon eternal realities is weak. By her lack of faith, God is disappointed, and robbed of His glory.

It is in doing Christ's work that the church has the promise of His presence. Go teach all nations, He said; "and, lo, I am with you alway, even unto the end of the world." To take His yoke is one of the first conditions of receiving His power. The very life of the church depends upon her faithfulness in fulfilling the Lord's commission. To neglect this work is surely to invite spiritual feebleness and decay. Where there is no active labor for others, love wanes, and faith grows dim.

Christ intends that His ministers shall be educators of the church in gospel work. They are to teach the people how to seek and save the lost. But is this the work they are doing? Alas, how many are toiling to fan the spark of life in a church that is ready to die! How many churches are tended like sick lambs by those who ought to be seeking for the lost sheep! And all the time millions upon millions without Christ are perishing.

Divine love has been stirred to its unfathomable depths for the sake of men, and angels marvel to behold in the recipients of so great love a mere surface gratitude. Angels marvel at man's shallow appreciation of the love of God. Heaven stands indignant at the neglect shown to the souls of men. Would we know how Christ regards it? How would a father and mother feel, did they know that their child, lost in the cold and the snow, had been passed by, and left to perish, by those who might have saved it? Would they not be terribly grieved, wildly indignant? Would they not denounce those murderers with wrath hot as their tears, intense as their love? The sufferings of every man are the sufferings of God's child, and those who reach out no helping hand to their perishing fellow beings provoke His righteous anger. This is the wrath of the Lamb. To those who claim fellowship with Christ, yet have been indifferent to the needs of their fellow men, He will declare in the great judgment day, "I know you not whence ye are; depart from Me, all ye workers of iniquity." Luke 13:27.

In the commission to His disciples, Christ not only outlined their work, but gave them their message. Teach the people, He said, "to observe all things whatsoever I have commanded you."

The disciples were to teach what Christ had taught. That which He had spoken, not only in person, but through all the prophets and teachers of the Old Testament, is here included. Human teaching is shut out. There is no place for tradition, for man's theories and conclusions, or for church legislation. No laws ordained by ecclesiastical authority are included in the commission. None of these are Christ's servants to teach. "The law and the prophets," with the record of His own words and deeds, are the treasure committed to the disciples to be given to the world. Christ's name is their watchword, their badge of distinction, their bond of union, the authority for their course of action, and the source of their success. Nothing that does not bear His superscription is to be recognized in His kingdom.

The gospel is to be presented, not as a lifeless theory, but as a living force to change the life. God desires that the receivers of His grace shall be witnesses to its power. Those whose course has been most offensive to Him He freely accepts; when they repent, He imparts to them His divine Spirit, places them in the highest positions of trust, and sends them forth into the camp of the disloyal to proclaim His boundless mercy. He would have His servants bear testimony to the fact that through His grace men may possess Christlikeness of character, and may rejoice in the assurance of His great love. He would have us bear testimony to the fact that He cannot be satisfied until the human race are reclaimed and reinstated in their holy privileges as His sons and daughters.

In Christ is the tenderness of the shepherd, the affection of the parent, and the matchless grace of the compassionate Saviour. His blessings He presents in the most alluring terms. He is not content merely to announce these blessings; He presents them in the most attractive way, to excite a desire to possess them. So His servants are to present the riches of the glory of the unspeakable Gift. The wonderful love of Christ will melt and subdue hearts, when the mere reiteration of doctrines would accomplish nothing. "Comfort ye, comfort ye My people, saith your God." "O Zion, that bringest good tidings, get thee up into the high mountain; O Jerusalem, that bringest good tidings, lift up thy voice with strength; lift it up, be not afraid; say unto the cities of Judah, Behold your God! . . . He shall feed His flock like a shepherd: He shall gather the lambs with His arm, and carry them in His bosom." Isa. 40:1, 9-11. Tell the people of Him who is "the Chiefest among ten thousand," and the One "altogether lovely." The Song of Solomon 5:10, 16. Words alone cannot tell it. Let it be reflected in the character and manifested in the life. Christ is sitting for His portrait in every disciple. Every one God has predestinated to be "conformed to the image of His Son." Rom. 8:29. In every one Christ's long-suffering love, His holiness, meekness, mercy, and truth are to be manifested to the world.

The first disciples went forth preaching the word. They revealed Christ in their lives. And the Lord worked with them, "confirming the word with signs following." Mark 16:20. These disciples prepared themselves for their work. Before the day of Pentecost they met together, and put away all differences. They were of one accord. They believed Christ's promise that the blessing would be given, and they prayed in faith. They did not ask for a blessing for themselves merely; they were weighted with the burden for the salvation of souls. The gospel was to be carried to the uttermost parts of the earth, and they claimed the endowment of power that Christ had promised. Then it was that the Holy Spirit was poured out, and thousands were converted in a day.

So it may be now. Instead of man's speculations, let the word of God be preached. Let Christians put away their dissensions, and give themselves to God for the saving of the lost. Let them in faith ask for the blessing, and it will come. The outpouring of the Spirit in apostolic days was the "former rain," and glorious was the result. But the "latter rain" will be more abundant. Joel 2:23.

All who consecrate soul, body, and spirit to God will be constantly receiving a new endowment of physical and mental power. The inexhaustible supplies of heaven are at their command. Christ gives them the breath of His own spirit, the life of His own life. The Holy Spirit puts forth its highest energies to work in heart and mind. The grace of God enlarges and multiplies their faculties, and every perfection of the divine nature comes to their assistance in the work of saving souls. Through co-operation with Christ they are complete in Him, and in their human weakness they are enabled to do the deeds of Omnipotence.

The Saviour longs to manifest His grace and stamp His character on the whole world. It is His purchased possession, and He desires to make men free, and pure, and holy. Though Satan works to hinder this purpose, yet through the blood shed for the world there are triumphs to be achieved that will bring glory to God and the Lamb. Christ will not be satisfied till the victory is complete, and "He shall see of the travail of His soul, and shall be satisfied." Isa. 53:11. All the nations of the earth shall hear the gospel of His grace. Not all will receive His grace; but "a seed shall serve Him; it shall be accounted to the Lord for a generation." Ps. 22:30. "The kingdom and dominion, and the greatness of the kingdom under the whole heaven, shall be given to the people of the saints of the Most High," and "the earth shall be full of the knowledge of the Lord, as the waters cover the sea." "So shall they fear the name of the Lord from the west, and His glory from the rising of the sun." Dan. 7:27; Isa. 11:9; 59:19.

"How beautiful upon the mountains are the feet of him that bringeth good tidings, that publisheth peace; that bringeth good tidings of good, that publisheth salvation; that saith unto Zion, Thy God reigneth! . . . Break forth into joy, sing together, ye waste places; . . . for the Lord hath comforted His people. . . . The Lord hath made bare His holy arm in the eyes of all the nations; and all the ends of the earth shall see the salvation of our God." Isa. 52:7-10.

829

87

"To My Father, and
Your Father"

The time had come for Christ to ascend to His Father's throne. As a divine conqueror He was about to return with the trophies of victory to the heavenly courts. Before His death He had declared to His Father, "I have finished the work which Thou gavest Me to do." John 17:4. After His resurrection He tarried on earth for a season, that His disciples might become familiar with Him in His risen and glorified body. Now He was ready for the leave-taking. He had authenticated the fact that He was a living Saviour. His disciples need no longer associate Him with the tomb. They could think of Him as glorified before the heavenly universe.

As the place of His ascension, Jesus chose the spot so often hallowed by His presence while He dwelt among men. Not Mount Zion, the place of David's city, not Mount Moriah, the temple site, was to be thus honored. There Christ had been mocked and rejected. There the waves of mercy, still returning in a stronger tide of love, had been beaten back by hearts as hard as rock. Thence Jesus, weary and heart-burdened, had gone forth to find rest in the Mount of Olives. The holy Shekinah, in departing from the first temple, had stood upon the eastern mountain, as if loath to forsake the chosen city; so Christ stood upon Olivet, with yearning heart overlooking Jerusalem. The groves and glens of 830 the mountain had been consecrated by His prayers and tears. Its steeps had echoed the triumphant shouts of the multitude that proclaimed Him king. On its sloping descent He had found a home with Lazarus at Bethany. In the garden of Gethsemane at its foot He had prayed and agonized alone. From this mountain He was to ascend to heaven. Upon its summit His feet will rest when He shall come again. Not as a man of sorrows, but as a glorious and triumphant king He will stand upon Olivet, while

Hebrew hallelujahs mingle with Gentile hosannas, and the voices of the redeemed as a mighty host shall swell the acclamation, Crown Him Lord of all!

Now with the eleven disciples Jesus made His way toward the mountain. As they passed through the gate of Jerusalem, many wondering eyes looked upon the little company, led by One whom a few weeks before the rulers had condemned and crucified. The disciples knew not that this was to be their last interview with their Master. Jesus spent the time in conversation with them, repeating His former instruction. As they approached Gethsemane, He paused, that they might call to mind the lessons He had given them on the night of His great agony. Again He looked upon the vine by which He had then represented the union of His church with Himself and His Father; again He repeated the truths He had then unfolded. All around Him were reminders of His unrequited love. Even the disciples who were so dear to His heart, had, in the hour of His humiliation, reproached and forsaken Him.

Christ had sojourned in the world for thirty-three years; He had endured its scorn, insult, and mockery; He had been rejected and crucified. Now, when about to ascend to His throne of glory,—as He reviews the ingratitude of the people He came to save,—will He not withdraw from them His sympathy and love? Will not His affections be centered upon that realm where He is appreciated, and where sinless angels wait to do His bidding? No; His promise to those loved ones whom He leaves on earth is, "I am with you alway, even unto the end of the world." Matt. 28:20.

Upon reaching the Mount of Olives, Jesus led the way across the summit, to the vicinity of Bethany. Here He paused, and the disciples gathered about Him. Beams of light seemed to radiate from His countenance as He looked lovingly upon them. He upbraided them not for their faults and failures; words of the deepest tenderness were the last that fell upon their ears from the lips of their Lord. With hands outstretched in blessing, and as if in assurance of 831 His protecting care, He slowly ascended from among them, drawn heavenward by a power stronger than any earthly attraction. As He passed upward, the awestricken disciples looked with straining eyes for the last glimpse of their ascending Lord. A cloud of glory hid Him from their sight; and the words came back to them as the cloudy chariot of angels received Him, "Lo, I am with you alway, even unto the end of the world." At the same time there floated down to them the sweetest and most joyous music from the angel choir.

While the disciples were still gazing upward, voices addressed them which sounded like richest music. They turned, and saw two angels in

This chapter is based on Luke 24:50-53; Acts 1:9-12.

the form of men, who spoke to them, saying, "Ye men of Galilee, why stand ye gazing up into heaven? this same Jesus, which is taken up from you into heaven, shall so come in like manner as ye have seen Him go into heaven."

These angels were of the company that had been waiting in a shining cloud to escort Jesus to His heavenly home. The most exalted of the angel throng, they were the two who had come to the tomb at Christ's resurrection, and they had been with Him throughout His life on earth. With eager desire all heaven had waited for the end of His tarrying in a world marred by the curse of sin. The time had now come for the heavenly universe to receive their King. Did not the two angels long to join the throng that welcomed Jesus? But in sympathy and love for those whom He had left, they waited to give them comfort. "Are they not all ministering spirits, sent forth to minister for them who shall be heirs of salvation?" Heb. 1:14.

Christ had ascended to heaven in the form of humanity. The disciples had beheld the cloud receive Him. The same Jesus who had walked and talked and prayed with them; who had broken bread with them; who had been with them in their boats on the lake; and who had that very day toiled with them up the ascent of Olivet,— the same Jesus had now gone to share His Father's throne. And the angels had assured them that the very One whom they had seen go up into heaven, would come again even as He had ascended. He will come "with clouds; and every eye shall see Him." "The Lord Himself shall descend from heaven with a shout, with the voice of the Archangel, and with the trump of God: and the dead in Christ shall rise." "The Son of man shall come in His glory, and all the holy angels with Him, then shall He sit upon the throne of His glory." Rev. 1:7; 1 Thess. 4:16; Matt. 25:31. Thus will be fulfilled the Lord's own promise to His disciples: "If I go and prepare a place for you, I will come again, and receive you unto Myself; that where I am, there ye may be also." John 14:3. Well might the disciples rejoice in the hope of their Lord's return.

When the disciples went back to Jerusalem, the people looked upon them with amazement. After the trial and crucifixion of Christ, it had been thought that they would appear downcast and ashamed. Their enemies expected to see upon their faces an expression of sorrow and defeat. Instead of this there was only gladness and triumph. Their faces were aglow with a happiness not born of earth. They did not mourn over disappointed hopes, but were full of praise and thanksgiving to God. With rejoicing they told the wonderful story of Christ's resurrection and His ascension to heaven, and their testimony was received by many.

The disciples no longer had any distrust of the future. They knew that Jesus was in heaven, and that His sympathies were with them still. They knew that they had a friend at the throne of God, and they were eager to present their requests to the Father in the name of Jesus. In solemn awe they bowed in prayer, repeating the assurance, "Whatsoever ye shall ask the Father in My name, He will give it you. Hitherto have ye asked nothing in My name: ask, and ye shall receive, that your joy may be full." John 16:23, 24. They extended the hand of faith higher and higher, with the mighty argument, "It is Christ that died, yea rather, that is risen again, who is even at the right hand of God, who also maketh intercession for us." Rom. 8:34. And Pentecost brought them fullness of joy in the presence of the Comforter, even as Christ had promised.

All heaven was waiting to welcome the Saviour to the celestial courts. As He ascended, He led the way, and the multitude of captives set free at His resurrection followed. The heavenly host, with shouts and acclamations of praise and celestial song, attended the joyous train.

As they drew near to the city of God, the challenge is given by the escorting angels,—

"Lift up your heads, O ye gates;
And be ye lift up, ye everlasting doors;
And the King of glory shall come in."

Joyfully the waiting sentinels respond,—

"Who is this King of glory?"

This they say, not because they know not who He is, but because they would hear the answer of exalted praise,—

"The Lord strong and mighty,
The Lord mighty in battle!
Lift up your heads, O ye gates;
Even lift them up, ye everlasting doors;
And the King of glory shall come in."

Again is heard the challenge, "Who is this King of glory?" for the angels never weary of hearing His name exalted. The escorting angels make reply,—

"The Lord of hosts;
He is the King of glory."

Ps. 24:7-10.

Then the portals of the city of God are opened wide, and the angelic throng sweep through the gates amid a burst of rapturous music.

There is the throne, and around it the rainbow of promise. There are cherubim and seraphim. The commanders of the angel hosts, the sons of God, the representatives of the unfallen worlds, are assembled. The heavenly council before which Lucifer had accused God and His Son, the representatives of those sinless realms over which Satan had thought to establish his dominion,—all are there to welcome the Redeemer. They are eager to celebrate His triumph and to glorify their King.

But He waves them back. Not yet; He cannot now receive the coronet of glory and the royal robe. He enters into the presence of His Father. He points to His wounded head, the pierced side, the marred feet; He lifts His hands, bearing the print of nails. He points to the tokens of His triumph; He presents to God the wave sheaf, those raised with Him as representatives of that great multitude who shall come forth from the grave at His second coming. He approaches the Father, with whom there is joy over one sinner that repents; who rejoices over one with singing. Before the foundations of the earth were laid, the Father and the Son had united in a covenant to redeem man if he should be overcome by Satan. They had clasped Their hands in a solemn pledge that Christ should become the surety for the human race. This pledge Christ has fulfilled. When upon the cross He cried out, "It is finished," He addressed the Father. The compact had been fully carried out. Now He declares: Father, it is finished. I have done Thy will, O My God. I have completed the work of redemption. If Thy justice is satisfied, "I will that they also, whom Thou hast given Me, be with Me where I am." John 19:30; 17:24.

The voice of God is heard proclaiming that justice is satisfied. Satan is vanquished. Christ's toiling, struggling ones on earth are "accepted in the Beloved." Eph. 1:6. Before the heavenly angels and the representatives of unfallen worlds, they are declared justified. Where He is, there His church shall be. "Mercy and truth are met together; righteousness and peace have kissed each other." Ps. 85:10. The Father's arms encircle His Son, and the word is given, "Let all the angels of God worship Him." Heb. 1:6.

With joy unutterable, rulers and principalities and powers acknowledge the supremacy of the Prince of life. The angel host prostrate themselves before Him, while the glad shout fills all the courts of heaven, "Worthy is the Lamb that was slain to receive power, and riches, and wisdom, and strength, and honor, and glory, and blessing." Rev. 5:12.

Songs of triumph mingle with the music from angel harps, till heaven seems to overflow with joy and praise. Love has conquered. The lost is found. Heaven rings with voices in lofty strains proclaiming, "Blessing, and honor, and glory, and power, be unto Him that sitteth upon the throne, and unto the Lamb forever and ever." Rev. 5:13.

From that scene of heavenly joy, there comes back to us on earth the echo of Christ's own wonderful words, "I ascend unto My Father, and your Father; and to My God, and your God." John 20:17. The family of heaven and the family of earth are one. For us our Lord ascended, and for us He lives. "Wherefore He is able also to save them to the uttermost that come unto God by Him, seeing He ever liveth to make intercession for them." Heb. 7:25.

4

THOUGHTS FROM

THE MOUNT OF BLESSING

INDEX

SUMMARY	PAGE	SUMMARY	PAGE

MB

INDEX

PAGE	SUMMARY	PAGE	SUMMARY

PREFACE

The Sermon on the Mount is Heaven's benediction to the world—a voice from the throne of God.

It was given to mankind to be to them the law of duty and the light of heaven, their hope and consolation in despondency, their joy and comfort in all the vicissitudes and walks of life. Here the Prince of preachers, the Master Teacher, utters the words that the Father gave Him to speak.

The Beatitudes are Christ's greeting, not only to those who believe, but to the whole human family. He seems to have forgotten for a moment that He is in the world, not in heaven; and He uses the familiar salutation of the world of light. Blessings flow from His lips as the gushing forth of a long-sealed current of rich life.

Christ leaves us in no doubt as to the traits of character that He will always recognize and bless. From the ambitious favorites of the world, He turns to those whom they disown, pronouncing all blessed who receive His light and life. To the poor in spirit, the meek, the lowly, the sorrowful, the despised, the persecuted, He opens His arms of refuge, saying, "Come unto Me, . . . and I will give you rest."

Christ can look upon the misery of the world without a shade of sorrow for having created man. In the human heart He sees more than sin, more than misery. In His infinite wisdom and love He sees man's possibilities, the height to which he may attain. He knows that, even though human beings have abused their mercies and destroyed their God-given dignity, yet the Creator is to be glorified in their redemption.

Throughout all time the words that Christ spoke from the mount of Beatitudes will retain their power. Every sentence is a jewel from the treasure house of truth. The principles enunciated in this discourse are for all ages and for all classes of men. With divine energy, Christ expressed His faith and hope as He pointed out class after class as blessed because of having formed righteous characters. Living the life of the Life-giver, through faith in Him, everyone can reach the standard held up in His words.

E. G. white

CONTENTS

1. On the Mountainside   803

2. The Beatitudes   804

3. The Spirituality of the Law 815

4. The True Motive in Service   825

5. The Lord's Prayer   831

6. Not Judging, but Doing   837

1

On the Mountainside

More than fourteen centuries before Jesus was born in Bethlehem, the children of Israel gathered in the fair vale of Shechem, and from the mountains on either side the voices of the priests were heard proclaiming the blessings and the curses—"a blessing, if ye obey the commandments of the Lord your God: . . . and a curse, if ye will not obey." Deuteronomy 11:27, 28. And thus the mountain from which the words of benediction were spoken came to be known as the mount of blessing. But it was not upon Gerizim that the words were spoken which have come as a benediction to a sinning and sorrowing world. Israel fell short of the high ideal which had been set before her. Another than Joshua must guide His people to the true rest of faith. No longer is Gerizim known as the mount of the Beatitudes, but that unnamed mountain beside the Lake of Gennesaret, where Jesus spoke the words of blessing to His disciples and the multitude.

Let us in imagination go back to that scene, and, as we sit with the disciples on the mountainside, enter into the thoughts and feelings that filled their hearts. Understanding what the words of Jesus meant to those who heard them, we may discern in them a new vividness and beauty, and may also gather for ourselves their deeper lessons.

When the Saviour began His ministry, the popular conception of the Messiah and His work was such as wholly unfitted the people to receive Him. The spirit of true devotion had been lost in tradition and ceremonialism, and the prophecies were interpreted at the dictate of proud, world-loving hearts. The Jews looked for the coming One, not as a Saviour from sin, but as a great prince who should bring all nations under the supremacy of the Lion of the tribe of Judah. In vain had John the Baptist, with the heart-searching power of the ancient prophets, called them to repentance. In vain had he, beside the Jordan, pointed to Jesus as the Lamb of God, that taketh away the sin of the world. God was seeking to direct their minds to Isaiah's prophecy of the suffering Saviour, but they would not hear.

Had the teachers and leaders in Israel yielded to His transforming grace, Jesus would have made them His ambassadors among men. In Judea first the coming of the kingdom had been proclaimed, and the call to repentance had been given. In the act of driving out the desecrators

from the temple at Jerusalem, Jesus had announced Himself as the Messiah—the One who should cleanse the soul from the defilement of sin and make His people a holy temple unto the Lord. But the Jewish leaders would not humble themselves to receive the lowly Teacher from Nazareth. At His second visit to Jerusalem He was arraigned before the Sanhedrin, and fear of the people alone prevented these dignitaries from trying to take His life. Then it was that, leaving Judea, He entered upon His ministry in Galilee.

His work there had continued some months before the Sermon on the Mount was given. The message He had proclaimed throughout the land, "The kingdom of heaven is at hand" (Matthew 4:17), had arrested the attention of all classes, and had still further fanned the flame of their ambitious hopes. The fame of the new Teacher had spread beyond the limits of Palestine, and, notwithstanding the attitude of the hierarchy, the feeling was widespread that this might be the hoped-for Deliverer. Great multitudes thronged the steps of Jesus, and the popular enthusiasm ran high.

The time had come for the disciples who had been most closely associated with Christ to unite more directly in His work, that these vast throngs might not be left uncared for, as sheep without a shepherd. Some of these disciples had joined themselves to Him at the beginning of His ministry, and nearly all the twelve had been associated together as members of the family of Jesus. Yet they also, misled by the teaching of the rabbis, shared the popular expectation of an earthly kingdom. They could not comprehend the movements of Jesus. Already they had been perplexed and troubled that He made no effort to strengthen His cause by securing the support of the priests and rabbis, that He did nothing to establish His authority as an earthly king. A great work was yet to be accomplished for these disciples before they would be prepared for the sacred trust that would be theirs when Jesus should ascend to heaven. Yet they had responded to the love of Christ, and, though slow of heart to believe, Jesus saw in them those whom He could train and discipline for His great work. And now that they had been long enough with Him to establish, in a measure, their faith in the divine character of His mission, and the people also had received evidence of His power which they could not question, the way was prepared for an avowal of the principles of His kingdom that would help them to comprehend its true nature.

Alone upon a mountain near the Sea of Galilee, Jesus had spent all night in prayer for these chosen ones. At the dawn He called them to Him, and, with words of prayer and instruction, laid His hands upon their heads in benediction, setting them apart to the gospel work. Then He repaired with them to the seaside, where in the early morning a great multitude had already begun to assemble.

Besides the usual crowd from the Galilean towns, there were great numbers from Judea, and from Jerusalem itself; from Perea, and from the half-heathen population of Decapolis; from Idumea, away to the south of Judea, and from Tyre and Sidon, the Phoenician cities on the shore of the Mediterranean. "Hearing what great things He did," they "came to hear Him, and to be healed of their diseases; and . . . power came forth from Him, and healed them all." Mark 3:8, R.V.; Luke 6:17-19, R.V.

Then, as the narrow beach did not afford even standing room within reach of His voice for all who desired to hear Him, Jesus led the way back to the mountainside. Reaching a level space that afforded a pleasant gathering place for the vast assembly, He seated Himself upon the grass, and His disciples and the multitude followed His example.

With a feeling that something more than usual might be expected, the disciples had pressed about their Master. From the events of the morning they gathered assurance that some announcement was about to be made in regard to the kingdom which, as they fondly hoped, He was soon to establish. A feeling of expectancy pervaded the multitude also, and eager faces gave evidence of the deep interest.

As they sat upon the green hillside, awaiting the words of the divine Teacher, their hearts were filled with thoughts of future glory. There were scribes and Pharisees who looked forward to the day when they should have dominion over the hated Romans and possess the riches and splendor of the world's great empire. The poor peasants and fishermen hoped to hear the assurance that their wretched hovels, the scanty food, the life of toil, and fear of want, were to be exchanged for mansions of plenty and days of ease. In place of the one coarse garment which was their covering by day and their blanket at night, they hoped that Christ would give them the rich and costly robes of their conquerors.

All hearts thrilled with the proud hope that Israel was soon to be honored before the nations as the chosen of the Lord, and Jerusalem exalted as the head of a universal kingdom.

2

The Beatitudes

"He opened His mouth, and taught them, saying, Blessed are the poor in spirit:

for theirs is the kingdom of heaven."
Matthew 5:2, 3.

As something strange and new, these words fall upon the ears of the wondering multitude. Such teaching is contrary to all they have ever heard from priest or rabbi. They see in it nothing to flatter their pride or to feed their ambitious hopes. But there is about this new Teacher a power that holds them spellbound. The sweetness of divine love flows from His very presence as the fragrance from a flower. His words fall like "rain upon the mown grass: as showers that water the earth." Psalm 72:6. All feel instinctively that here is One who reads the secrets of the soul, yet who comes near to them with tender compassion. Their hearts open to Him, and, as they listen, the Holy Spirit unfolds to them something of the meaning of that lesson which humanity in all ages so needs to learn.

In the days of Christ the religious leaders of the people felt that they were rich in spiritual treasure. The prayer of the Pharisee, "God, I thank Thee, that I am not as the rest of men" (Luke 18:11, R.V.), expressed the feeling of his class and, to a great degree, of the whole nation. But in the throng that surrounded Jesus there were some who had a sense of their spiritual poverty. When in the miraculous draft of fishes the divine power of Christ was revealed, Peter fell at the Saviour's feet, exclaiming, "Depart from me; for I am a sinful man, O Lord" (Luke 5:8); so in the multitude gathered upon the mount there were souls who, in the presence of His purity, felt that they were "wretched, and miserable, and poor, and blind, and naked" (Revelation 3:17); and they longed for "the grace of God that bringeth salvation" (Titus 2:11). In these souls, Christ's words of greeting awakened hope; they saw that their lives were under the benediction of God.

Jesus had presented the cup of blessing to those who felt that they were "rich, and increased with goods" (Revelation 3:17), and had need of nothing, and they had turned with scorn from the gracious gift. He who feels whole, who thinks that he is reasonably good, and is contented with his condition, does not seek to become a partaker of the grace and righteousness of Christ. Pride feels no need, and so it closes the heart against Christ and the infinite blessings He came to give. There is no room for Jesus in the heart of such a person. Those who are rich and honorable in their own eyes do not ask in faith, and receive the blessing of God. They feel that they are full, therefore they go away empty. Those who know that they cannot possibly save themselves, or of themselves do any righteous action, are the ones who appreciate the help that Christ can bestow. They are the poor in spirit, whom He declares to be blessed.

Whom Christ pardons, He first makes penitent, and it is the office of the Holy Spirit to convince of sin. Those whose hearts have been 8 moved by the convicting Spirit of God see that there is nothing good in themselves. They see that all they have ever done is mingled with self and sin. Like the poor publican, they stand afar off, not daring to lift up so much as their eyes to heaven, and cry, "God, be merciful to me the sinner." Luke 18:13, R.V., margin. And they are blessed. There is forgiveness for the penitent; for Christ is "the Lamb of God, which taketh away the sin of the world." John 1:29. God's promise is: "Though your sins be as scarlet, they shall be as white as snow; though they be red like crimson, they shall be as wool." "A new heart also will I give you. . . . And I will put My Spirit within you." Isaiah 1:18; Ezekiel 36:26, 27.

Of the poor in spirit Jesus says, "Theirs is the kingdom of heaven." This kingdom is not, as Christ's hearers had hoped, a temporal and earthly dominion. Christ was opening to men the spiritual kingdom of His love, His grace, His righteousness. The ensign of the Messiah's reign is distinguished by the likeness of the Son of man. His subjects are the poor in spirit, the meek, the persecuted for righteousness' sake. The kingdom of heaven is theirs. Though not yet fully accomplished, the work is begun in them which will make them "meet to be partakers of the inheritance of the saints in light." Colossians 1:12.

All who have a sense of their deep soul poverty, who feel that they have nothing good in themselves, may find righteousness and strength by looking unto Jesus. He says, "Come unto Me, all ye that labor and are heavy-laden." Matthew 11:28. He bids you exchange your 9 poverty for the riches of His grace. We are not worthy of God's love, but Christ, our surety, is worthy, and is abundantly able to save all who shall come unto Him. Whatever may have been your past experience, however discouraging your present circumstances, if you will come to Jesus just as you are, weak, helpless, and despairing, our compassionate Saviour will meet you a great way off, and will throw about you His arms of love and His robe of righteousness. He presents us to the Father clothed in the white raiment of His own character. He pleads before God in our behalf, saying: I have taken the sinner's place. Look not upon this wayward child, but look on Me. Does Satan plead loudly against our souls, accusing of sin, and claiming us as his prey, the blood of Christ pleads with greater power.

"Surely, shall one say, in the Lord have I righteousness and strength. . . . In the Lord shall all the seed of Israel be justified, and shall glory." Isaiah 45:24, 25.

"Blessed are they that mourn: for they shall be comforted." Matthew 5:4.

The mourning here brought to view is true heart sorrow for sin. Jesus says, "I, if I be lifted up from the earth, will draw all men unto Me." John 12:32. And as one is drawn to behold Jesus uplifted on the cross, he discerns the sinfulness of humanity. He sees that it is sin which scourged and crucified the Lord of glory. He sees that, while he has been loved with unspeakable tenderness, his life has been a continual scene of ingratitude and rebellion. He has forsaken his best Friend and abused heaven's most precious gift. He has crucified to himself the 10 Son of God afresh and pierced anew that bleeding and stricken heart. He is separated from God by a gulf of sin that is broad and black and deep, and he mourns in brokenness of heart.

Such mourning "shall be comforted." God reveals to us our guilt that we may flee to Christ, and through Him be set free from the bondage of sin, and rejoice in the liberty of the sons of God. In true contrition we may come to the foot of the cross, and there leave our burdens.

The Saviour's words have a message of comfort to those also who are suffering affliction or bereavement. Our sorrows do not spring out of the ground. God "doth not afflict willingly nor grieve the children of men." Lamentations 3:33. When He permits trials and afflictions, it is "for our profit, that we might be partakers of His holiness." Hebrews 12:10. If received in faith, the trial that seems so bitter and hard to bear will prove a blessing. The cruel blow that blights the joys of earth will be the means of turning our eyes to heaven. How many there are who would never have known Jesus had not sorrow led them to seek comfort in Him!

The trials of life are God's workmen, to remove the impurities and roughness from our character. Their hewing, squaring, and chiseling, their burnishing and polishing, is a painful process; it is hard to be pressed down to the grinding wheel. But the stone is brought forth prepared to fill its place in the heavenly temple. Upon no useless material does the Master bestow such careful, thorough work. Only His precious stones are polished after the similitude of a palace.

The Lord will work for all who put their trust 11 in Him. Precious victories will be gained by the faithful. Precious lessons will be learned. Precious experiences will be realized.

Our heavenly Father is never unmindful of those whom sorrow has touched. When David went up the Mount Olivet, "and wept as he went up, and had his head covered, and he went barefoot" (2 Samuel 15:30), the Lord was looking pityingly upon him. David was clothed in sackcloth, and his conscience was scourging him. The outward signs of humiliation testified of his contrition. In tearful, heartbroken utterances he presented his case to God, and the Lord did not forsake His servant. Never was David dearer to the heart of Infinite Love than when, conscience-smitten, he fled for his life from his enemies, who had been stirred to rebellion by his own son. The Lord says, "As many as I love, I rebuke and chasten: be zealous therefore, and repent." Revelation 3:19. Christ lifts up the contrite heart and refines the mourning soul until it becomes His abode.

But when tribulation comes upon us, how many of us are like Jacob! We think it the hand of an enemy; and in the darkness we wrestle blindly until our strength is spent, and we find no comfort or deliverance. To Jacob the divine touch at break of day revealed the One with whom he had been contending—the Angel of the covenant; and, weeping and helpless, he fell upon the breast of Infinite Love, to receive the blessing for which his soul longed. We also need to learn that trials mean benefit, and not to despise the chastening of the Lord nor faint when we are rebuked of Him.

12 "Happy is the man whom God correcteth: . . . He maketh sore, and bindeth up: He woundeth, and His hands make whole. He shall deliver thee in six troubles: yea, in seven there shall no evil touch thee." Job 5:17-19. To every stricken one, Jesus comes with the ministry of healing. The life of bereavement, pain, and suffering may be brightened by precious revealings of His presence.

God would not have us remain pressed down by dumb sorrow, with sore and breaking hearts. He would have us look up and behold His dear face of love. The blessed Saviour stands by many whose eyes are so blinded by tears that they do not discern Him. He longs to clasp our hands, to have us look to Him in simple faith, permitting Him to guide us. His heart is open to our griefs, our sorrows, and our trials. He has loved us with an everlasting love and with loving-kindness compassed us about. We may keep the heart stayed upon Him and meditate upon His loving-kindness all the day. He will lift the soul above the daily sorrow and perplexity, into a realm of peace.

Think of this, children of suffering and sorrow, and rejoice in hope. "This is the victory that overcometh the world, even our faith." 1 John 5:4.

Blessed are they also who weep with Jesus in sympathy with the world's sorrow and in sorrow for its sin. In such mourning there is intermingled no thought of self. Jesus was the Man of Sorrows, enduring heart anguish such as no language can portray. His spirit was torn and bruised by the transgressions of men. He toiled with self-consuming zeal to relieve the wants

and woes of humanity, and His heart was heavy with sorrow as He saw multitudes refuse to 13 come to Him that they might have life. All who are followers of Christ will share in this experience. As they partake of His love they will enter into His travail for the saving of the lost. They share in the sufferings of Christ, and they will share also in the glory that shall be revealed. One with Him in His work, drinking with Him the cup of sorrow, they are partakers also of His joy.

It was through suffering that Jesus obtained the ministry of consolation. In all the affliction of humanity He is afflicted; and "in that He Himself hath suffered being tempted, He is able to succor them that are tempted." Isaiah 63:9; Hebrews 2:18. In this ministry every soul that has entered into the fellowship of His sufferings is privileged to share. "As the sufferings of Christ abound in us, so our consolation also aboundeth by Christ." 2 Corinthians 1:5. The Lord has special grace for the mourner, and its power is to melt hearts, to win souls. His love opens a channel into the wounded and bruised soul, and becomes a healing balsam to those who sorrow. "The Father of mercies, and the God of all comfort . . . comforteth us in all our tribulation, that we may be able to comfort them which are in any trouble, by the comfort wherewith we ourselves are comforted of God." 2 Corinthians 1:3, 4.

"Blessed are the meek." Matthew 5:5.

Throughout the Beatitudes there is an advancing line of Christian experience. Those who have felt their need of Christ, those who have mourned because of sin and have sat with Christ 14 in the school of affliction, will learn meekness from the divine Teacher.

Patience and gentleness under wrong were not characteristics prized by the heathen or by the Jews. The statement made by Moses under the inspiration of the Holy Spirit, that he was the meekest man upon the earth, would not have been regarded by the people of his time as a commendation; it would rather have excited pity or contempt. But Jesus places meekness among the first qualifications for His kingdom. In His own life and character the divine beauty of this precious grace is revealed.

Jesus, the brightness of the Father's glory, thought "it not a thing to be grasped to be on an equality with God, but emptied Himself, taking the form of a servant." Philippians 2:6, 7, R.V., margin. Through all the lowly experiences of life He consented to pass, walking among the children of men, not as a king, to demand homage, but as one whose mission it was to serve others. There was in His manner no taint of bigotry, no cold austerity. The world's

Redeemer had a greater than angelic nature, yet united with His divine majesty were meekness and humility that attracted all to Himself.

Jesus emptied Himself, and in all that He did, self did not appear. He subordinated all things to the will of His Father. When His mission on earth was about to close, He could say, "I have glorified Thee on the earth: I have finished the work which Thou gavest Me to do." John 17:4. And He bids us, "Learn of Me; for I am meek and lowly in heart." "If any man will come after Me, let him deny himself" (Matthew 11:29; 15 16:24); let self be dethroned and no longer hold the supremacy of the soul.

He who beholds Christ in His self-denial, His lowliness of heart, will be constrained to say, as did Daniel, when he beheld One like the sons of men, "My comeliness was turned in me into corruption." Daniel 10:8. The independence and self-supremacy in which we glory are seen in their true vileness as tokens of servitude to Satan. Human nature is ever struggling for expression, ready for contest; but he who learns of Christ is emptied of self, of pride, of love of supremacy, and there is silence in the soul. Self is yielded to the disposal of the Holy Spirit. Then we are not anxious to have the highest place. We have no ambition to crowd and elbow ourselves into notice; but we feel that our highest place is at the feet of our Saviour. We look to Jesus, waiting for His hand to lead, listening for His voice to guide. The apostle Paul had this experience, and he said, "I am crucified with Christ: nevertheless I live; yet not I, but Christ liveth in me: and the life which I now live in the flesh I live by the faith of the Son of God, who loved me, and gave Himself for me." Galatians 2:20.

When we receive Christ as an abiding guest in the soul, the peace of God, which passeth all understanding, will keep our hearts and minds through Christ Jesus. The Saviour's life on earth, though lived in the midst of conflict, was a life of peace. While angry enemies were constantly pursuing Him, He said, "He that sent Me is with Me: the Father hath not left Me alone; for I do always those things that please Him." John 8:29. No storm of human or satanic wrath 16 could disturb the calm of that perfect communion with God. And He says to us, "Peace I leave with you, My peace I give unto you." "Take My yoke upon you, and learn of Me; for I am meek and lowly in heart: and ye shall find rest." John 14:27; Matthew 11:29. Bear with Me the yoke of service for the glory of God and the uplifting of humanity, and you will find the yoke easy and the burden light.

It is the love of self that destroys our peace. While self is all alive, we stand ready continually to guard it from mortification and insult; but when we are dead, and our life is hid with Christ in God, we shall not take neglects or slights to heart. We shall be deaf to reproach and blind to scorn and insult. "Love suffereth long, and is kind; love envieth not; love vaunteth not itself, is not puffed up, doth not behave itself unseemly, seeketh not its own, is not provoked, taketh not account of evil; rejoiceth not in unrighteousness, but rejoiceth with the truth; beareth all things, believeth all things, hopeth all things, endureth all things. Love never faileth." 1 Corinthians 13:4-8, R.V.

Happiness drawn from earthly sources is as changeable as varying circumstances can make it; but the peace of Christ is a constant and abiding peace. It does not depend upon any circumstances in life, on the amount of worldly goods or the number of earthly friends. Christ is the fountain of living water, and happiness drawn from Him can never fail.

The meekness of Christ, manifested in the home, will make the inmates happy; it provokes no quarrel, gives back no angry answer, but soothes the irritated temper and diffuses a gentleness that is felt by all within its charmed circle. Wherever cherished, it makes the families 17 of earth a part of the one great family above.

Far better would it be for us to suffer under false accusation than to inflict upon ourselves the torture of retaliation upon our enemies. The spirit of hatred and revenge originated with Satan, and can bring only evil to him who cherishes it. Lowliness of heart, that meekness which is the fruit of abiding in Christ, is the true secret of blessing. "He will beautify the meek with salvation." Psalm 149:4.

The meek "shall inherit the earth." It was through the desire for self-exaltation that sin entered into the world, and our first parents lost the dominion over this fair earth, their kingdom. It is through self-abnegation that Christ redeems what was lost. And He says we are to overcome as He did. Revelation 3:21. Through humility and self-surrender we may become heirs with Him when "the meek shall inherit the earth." Psalm 37:11.

The earth promised to the meek will not be like this, darkened with the shadow of death and the curse. "We, according to His promise, look for new heavens and a new earth, wherein dwelleth righteousness." "There shall be no more curse: but the throne of God and of the Lamb shall be in it; and His servants shall serve Him." 2 Peter 3:13; Revelation 22:3.

There is no disappointment, no sorrow, no sin, no one who shall say, I am sick; there are no burial trains, no mourning, no death, no partings, no broken hearts; but Jesus is there, peace is there. There "they shall not hunger nor thirst; neither shall the heat nor sun smite them: for He 18 that hath mercy on them shall lead them, even by the springs of water shall He guide them." Isaiah 49:10.

"Blessed are they which do hunger and thirst after righteousness: for they shall be filled." Matthew 5:6.

Righteousness is holiness, likeness to God, and "God is love." 1 John 4:16. It is conformity to the law of God, for "all Thy commandments are righteousness" (Psalm 119:172), and "love is the fulfilling of the law" (Romans 13:10). Righteousness is love, and love is the light and the life of God. The righteousness of God is embodied in Christ. We receive righteousness by receiving Him.

Not by painful struggles or wearisome toil, not by gift or sacrifice, is righteousness obtained; but it is freely given to every soul who hungers and thirsts to receive it. "Ho, every one that thirsteth, come ye to the waters, and he that hath no money; come ye, buy, and eat, . . . without money and without price." "Their righteousness is of Me, saith the Lord," and, "This is His name whereby He shall be called, THE LORD OUR RIGHTEOUSNESS." Isaiah 55:1; 54:17; Jeremiah 23:6.

No human agent can supply that which will satisfy the hunger and thirst of the soul. But Jesus says, "Behold, I stand at the door, and knock: if any man hear My voice, and open the door, I will come in to him, and will sup with him, and he with Me." "I am the bread of life: he that cometh to Me shall never hunger; and he that believeth on Me shall never thirst." Revelation 3:20; John 6:35.

As we need food to sustain our physical strength, so do we need Christ, the Bread from heaven, to sustain spiritual life and impart strength to work the works of God. As the body is continually receiving the nourishment that sustains life and vigor, so the soul must be constantly communing with Christ, submitting to Him and depending wholly upon Him.

As the weary traveler seeks the spring in the desert and, finding it, quenches his burning thirst so and, will the Christian thirst for and obtain the pure water of life, of which Christ is the fountain.

As we discern the perfection of our Saviour's character we shall desire to become wholly transformed and renewed in the image of His purity. The more we know of God, the higher will be our ideal of character and the more earnest our longing to reflect His likeness. A divine element combines with the human when the soul reaches out after God and the longing heart can say, "My soul, wait thou only upon God; for my expectation is from Him." Psalm 62:5.

If you have a sense of need in your soul, if you hunger and thirst after righteousness, this is an evidence that Christ has wrought upon your heart, in order that He may be sought unto to do for you, through the endowment of the Holy Spirit, those things which it is impossible for you to do for yourself. We need not seek to quench our thirst at shallow streams; for the great fountain is just above us, of whose abundant waters we may freely drink, if we will rise a little higher in the pathway of faith.

The words of God are the wellsprings of life. As you seek unto those living springs you will, through the Holy Spirit, be brought into communion with Christ. Familiar truths will present themselves to your mind in a new aspect, texts of Scripture will burst upon you with a new meaning as a flash of light, you will see the relation of other truths to the work of redemption, and you will know that Christ is leading you, a divine Teacher is at your side.

Jesus said, "The water that I shall give him shall be in him a well of water springing up into everlasting life." John 4:14. As the Holy Spirit opens to you the truth you will treasure up the most precious experiences and will long to speak to others of the comforting things that have been revealed to you. When brought into association with them you will communicate some fresh thought in regard to the character or the work of Christ. You will have some fresh revelation of His pitying love to impart to those who love Him and to those who love Him not.

"Give, and it shall be given unto you" (Luke 6:38); for the word of God is "a fountain of gardens, a well of living waters, and streams of Lebanon" (Song of Solomon 4:15). The heart that has once tasted the love of Christ, cries out continually for a deeper draft, and as you impart you will receive in richer and more abundant measure. Every revelation of God to the soul increases the capacity to know and to love. The continual cry of the heart is, "More of Thee," and ever the Spirit's answer is, "Much more." Romans 5:9, 10. For our God delights to do "exceeding abundantly above all that we ask or think." Ephesians 3:20. To Jesus, who emptied Himself for the salvation of lost humanity, the Holy Spirit was given without measure. So it will be given to every follower of Christ when the whole heart is surrendered for His indwelling. Our Lord Himself has given the command, "Be filled with the Spirit" (Ephesians 5:18), and this command is also a promise of its fulfillment. It was the good pleasure of the Father that in Christ should "all the fullness dwell," and "in Him ye are made full." Colossians 1:19, R.V.; 2:10, R.V.

God has poured out His love unstintedly, as the showers that refresh the earth. He says, "Let the skies pour down righteousness: let the earth open, and let them bring forth salvation, and let righteousness spring up together." "When the poor and needy seek water, and there is none, and their tongue faileth for thirst, I the Lord will hear them, I the God of Israel will not forsake them. I will open rivers in high places, and fountains in the midst of the valleys: I will make the wilderness a pool of water, and the dry land springs of water." Isaiah 45:8; 41:17, 18.

"Of His fullness have all we received, and grace for grace." John 1:16.

"Blessed are the merciful: for they shall obtain mercy." Matthew 5:7.

The heart of man is by nature cold and dark and unloving; whenever one manifests a spirit of mercy and forgiveness, he does it not of him-

22 self, but through the influence of the divine Spirit moving upon his heart. "We love, because He first loved us." 1 John 4:19, R.V.

God is Himself the source of all mercy. His name is "merciful and gracious." Exodus 34:6. He does not treat us according to our desert. He does not ask if we are worthy of His love, but He pours upon us the riches of His love, to make us worthy. He is not vindictive. He seeks not to punish, but to redeem. Even the severity which He manifests through His providences is manifested for the salvation of the wayward. He yearns with intense desire to relieve the woes of men and to apply His balsam to their wounds. It is true that God "will by no means clear the guilty" (Exodus 34:7), but He would take away the guilt.

The merciful are "partakers of the divine nature," and in them the compassionate love of God finds expression. All whose hearts are in sympathy with the heart of Infinite Love will seek to reclaim and not to condemn. Christ dwelling in the soul is a spring that never runs dry. Where He abides, there will be an overflowing of beneficence.

To the appeal of the erring, the tempted, the wretched victims of want and sin, the Christian does not ask, Are they worthy? but, How can I benefit them? In the most wretched, the most debased, he sees souls whom Christ died to save and for whom God has given to His children the ministry of reconciliation.

The merciful are those who manifest compassion to the poor, the suffering, and the

23 oppressed. Job declares, "I delivered the poor that cried, and the fatherless, and him that had none to help him. The blessing of him that was ready to perish came upon me: and I caused the widow's heart to sing for joy. I put on righteousness, and it clothed me: my judgment was as a robe and a diadem. I was eyes to the blind, and feet was I to the lame. I was a father to the poor: and the cause which I knew not I searched out." Job 29:12-16.

There are many to whom life is a painful struggle; they feel their deficiencies and are miserable and unbelieving; they think they have nothing for which to be grateful. Kind words, looks of sympathy, expressions of appreciation,

would be to many a struggling and lonely one as the cup of cold water to a thirsty soul. A word of sympathy, an act of kindness, would lift burdens that rest heavily upon weary shoulders. And every word or deed of unselfish kindness is an expression of the love of Christ for lost humanity.

The merciful "shall obtain mercy." "The soul of blessing shall be made fat: and he that watereth shall be watered also himself." Proverbs 11:25, margin. There is sweet peace for the compassionate spirit, a blessed satisfaction in the life of self-forgetful service for the good of others. The Holy Spirit that abides in the soul and is manifest in the life will soften hard hearts and awaken sympathy and tenderness. You will reap that which you sow. "Blessed is he that considereth the poor. . . . The Lord will preserve him, and keep him alive; and he shall be blessed upon the earth: and Thou wilt not deliver him unto the will of his ene-

24 mies. The Lord will strengthen him upon the bed of languishing: Thou wilt make all his bed in his sickness." Psalm 41:1-3.

He who has given his life to God in ministry to His children is linked with Him who has all the resources of the universe at His command. His life is bound up by the golden chain of the immutable promises with the life of God. The Lord will not fail him in the hour of suffering and need. "My God shall supply all your need according to His riches in glory by Christ Jesus." Philippians 4:19. And in the hour of final need the merciful shall find refuge in the mercy of the compassionate Saviour and shall be received into everlasting habitations.

"Blessed are the pure in heart: for they shall see God." Matthew 5:8.

The Jews were so exacting in regard to ceremonial purity that their regulations were extremely burdensome. Their minds were occupied with rules and restrictions and the fear of outward defilement, and they did not perceive the stain that selfishness and malice impart to the soul.

Jesus does not mention this ceremonial purity as one of the conditions of entering into His kingdom, but points out the need of purity of heart. The wisdom that is from above "is first pure." James 3:17. Into the city of God there will enter nothing that defiles. All who are to be dwellers there will here have become pure in heart. In one who is learning of Jesus, there will be manifest a growing distaste for careless man-

25 ners, unseemly language, and coarse thought. When Christ abides in the heart, there will be purity and refinement of thought and manner.

But the words of Jesus, "Blessed are the pure in heart," have a deeper meaning—not merely pure in the sense in which the world understands purity, free from that which is sensual, pure from lust, but true in the hidden purposes and motives of the soul, free from pride and self-seeking, humble, unselfish, childlike.

Only like can appreciate like. Unless you accept in your own life the principle of self-sacrificing love, which is the principle of His character, you cannot know God. The heart that is deceived by Satan, looks upon God as a tyrannical, relentless being; the selfish characteristics of humanity, even of Satan himself, are attributed to the loving Creator. "Thou thoughtest," He says, "that I was altogether such an one as thyself." Psalm 50:21. His providences are interpreted as the expression of an arbitrary, vindictive nature. So with the Bible, the treasure house of the riches of His grace. The glory of its truths, that are as high as heaven and compass eternity, is undiscerned. To the great mass of mankind, Christ Himself is "as a root out of a dry ground," and they see in Him "no beauty that" they "should desire Him." Isaiah 53:2. When Jesus was among men, the revelation of God in humanity, the scribes and Pharisees declared to Him, "Thou art a Samaritan, and hast a devil." John 8:48. Even His disciples were so blinded by the selfishness of their hearts that they were slow to understand Him who had come to manifest to them the Father's love. This was why Jesus walked in solitude in the midst of men. He was understood fully in heaven alone.

When Christ shall come in His glory, the wicked cannot endure to behold Him. The light of His presence, which is life to those who love Him, is death to the ungodly. The expectation of His coming is to them a "fearful looking for of judgment and fiery indignation." Hebrews 10:27. When He shall appear, they will pray to be hidden from the face of Him who died to redeem them.

But to hearts that have become purified through the indwelling of the Holy Spirit, all is changed. These can know God. Moses was hid in the cleft of the rock when the glory of the Lord was revealed to him; and it is when we are hid in Christ that we behold the love of God.

"He that loveth pureness of heart, for the grace of his lips the King shall be his friend." Proverbs 22:11. By faith we behold Him here and now. In our daily experience we discern His goodness and compassion in the manifestation of His providence. We recognize Him in the character of His Son. The Holy Spirit takes the truth concerning God and Him whom He hath sent, and opens it to the understanding and to the heart. The pure in heart see God in a new and endearing relation, as their Redeemer; and while they discern the purity and loveliness of His character, they long to reflect His image.

They see Him as a Father longing to embrace a repenting son, and their hearts are filled with joy unspeakable and full of glory.

The pure in heart discern the Creator in the works of His mighty hand, in the things of beauty that comprise the universe. In His written word they read in clearer lines the revelation of His mercy, His goodness, and His grace. The truths that are hidden from the wise and prudent are revealed to babes. The beauty and preciousness of truth, which are undiscerned by the worldly-wise, are constantly unfolding to those who have a trusting, childlike desire to know and to do the will of God. We discern the truth by becoming, ourselves, partakers of the divine nature.

The pure in heart live as in the visible presence of God during the time He apportions them in this world. And they will also see Him face to face in the future, immortal state, as did Adam when he walked and talked with God in Eden. "Now we see through a glass, darkly; but then face to face." 1 Corinthians 13:12.

"Blessed are the peacemakers: for they shall be called the children of God."
Matthew 5:9.

Christ is "the Prince of Peace" (Isaiah 9:6), and it is His mission to restore to earth and heaven the peace that sin has broken. "Being justified by faith, we have peace with God through our Lord Jesus Christ." Romans 5:1. Whoever consents to renounce sin and open his heart to the love of Christ, becomes a partaker of this heavenly peace.

There is no other ground of peace than this. The grace of Christ received into the heart, subdues enmity; it allays strife and fills the soul with love. He who is at peace with God and his fellow men cannot be made miserable. Envy will not be in his heart; evil surmisings will find no room there; hatred cannot exist. The heart that is in harmony with God is a partaker of the peace of heaven and will diffuse its blessed influence on all around. The spirit of peace will rest like dew upon hearts weary and troubled with worldly strife.

Christ's followers are sent to the world with the message of peace. Whoever, by the quiet, unconscious influence of a holy life, shall reveal the love of Christ; whoever, by word or deed, shall lead another to renounce sin and yield his heart to God, is a peacemaker.

And "blessed are the peacemakers: for they shall be called the children of God." The spirit of peace is evidence of their connection with heaven. The sweet savor of Christ surrounds them. The fragrance of the life, the loveliness of the character, reveal to the world the fact that they are children of God. Men take knowledge of them that they have been with Jesus. "Everyone that loveth is born of God." "If any man have not the Spirit of Christ, he is none of His;" but "as many as are led by the Spirit of God, they are the sons of God." 1 John 4:7; Romans 8:9, 14.

"And the remnant of Jacob shall be in the midst of many people as a dew from the Lord, as the showers upon the grass, that tarrieth not for man, nor waiteth for the sons of men." Micah 5:7.

29   *"Blessed are they which are persecuted for righteousness' sake: for theirs is the kingdom of heaven." Matthew 5:10.*

Jesus does not present to His followers the hope of attaining earthly glory and riches, and of having a life free from trial, but He presents to them the privilege of walking with their Master in the paths of self-denial and reproach, because the world knows them not.

He who came to redeem the lost world was opposed by the united forces of the adversaries of God and man. In an unpitying confederacy, evil men and evil angels arrayed themselves against the Prince of Peace. Though His every word and act breathed of divine compassion, His unlikeness to the world provoked the bitterest hostility. Because He would give no license for the exercise of the evil passions of our nature, He aroused the fiercest opposition and enmity. So it is with all who will live godly in Christ Jesus. Between righteousness and sin, love and hatred, truth and falsehood, there is an irrepressible conflict. When one presents the love of Christ and the beauty of holiness, he is drawing away the subjects of Satan's kingdom, and the prince of evil is aroused to resist it. Persecution and reproach await all who are imbued with the Spirit of Christ. The character of the persecution changes with the times, but the principle-the spirit that underlies it—is the same that has slain the chosen of the Lord ever since the days of Abel.

30 As men seek to come into harmony with God, they will find that the offense of the cross has not ceased. Principalities and powers and wicked spirits in high places are arrayed against all who yield obedience to the law of heaven. Therefore, so far from causing grief, persecution should bring joy to the disciples of Christ, for it is an evidence that they are following in the steps of their Master.

While the Lord has not promised His people exemption from trials, He has promised that which is far better. He has said, "As thy days, so shall thy strength be." "My grace is sufficient for thee: for My strength is made perfect in weakness." Deuteronomy 33:25; 2 Corinthians 12:9. If you are called to go through the fiery furnace for His sake, Jesus will be by your side even as He was with the faithful three in Baby-

lon. Those who love their Redeemer will rejoice at every opportunity of sharing with Him humiliation and reproach. The love they bear their Lord makes suffering for His sake sweet.

In all ages Satan has persecuted the people of God. He has tortured them and put them to death, but in dying they became conquerors. They revealed in their steadfast faith a mightier One than Satan. Satan could torture and kill the body, but he could not touch the life that was hid with Christ in God. He could incarcerate in prison walls, but he could not bind the spirit. They could look beyond the gloom to the glory, saying, "I reckon that the sufferings of this present time are not worthy to be compared with the glory which shall be revealed in us." "Our light affliction, which is but for a moment, worketh for us a far more exceeding and eternal weight of glory." Romans 8:18; 2 Corinthians 4:17.

Through trials and persecution, the glory— **31** character—of God is revealed in His chosen ones. The church of God, hated and persecuted by the world, are educated and disciplined in the school of Christ. They walk in narrow paths on earth; they are purified in the furnace of affliction. They follow Christ through sore conflicts; they endure self-denial and experience bitter disappointments; but their painful experience teaches them the guilt and woe of sin, and they look upon it with abhorrence. Being partakers of Christ's sufferings, they are destined to be partakers of His glory. In holy vision the prophet saw the triumph of the people of God. He says, "I saw as it were a sea of glass mingled with fire: and them that had gotten the victory, . . . stand on the sea of glass, having the harps of God. And they sing the song of Moses the servant of God, and the song of the Lamb, saying, Great and marvelous are Thy works, Lord God Almighty; just and true are Thy ways, Thou King of saints." "These are they which came out of great tribulation, and have washed their robes, and made them white in the blood of the Lamb. Therefore are they before the throne of God, and serve Him day and night in His temple: and He that sitteth on the throne shall dwell among them." Revelation 15:2, 3; 7:14, 15.

"Blessed are ye, when men shall revile you." Matthew 5:11.

Ever since his fall, Satan has worked by means of deception. As he has misrepresented God, so, through his agents, he misrepresents the children of God. The Saviour says, "The reproaches of them that reproached Thee are **32** fallen upon Me." Psalm 69:9. In like manner they fall upon His disciples.

There was never one who walked among men more cruelly slandered than the Son of man. He was derided and mocked because of His unswerving obedience to the principles of God's holy law. They hated Him without a cause. Yet He stood calmly before His enemies, declaring that reproach is a part of the Christian's legacy, counseling His followers how to meet the arrows of malice, bidding them not to faint under persecution.

While slander may blacken the reputation, it cannot stain the character. That is in God's keeping. So long as we do not consent to sin, there is no power, whether human or satanic, that can bring a stain upon the soul. A man whose heart is stayed upon God is just the same in the hour of his most afflicting trials and most discouraging surroundings as when he was in prosperity, when the light and favor of God seemed to be upon him. His words, his motives, his actions, may be misrepresented and falsified, but he does not mind it, because he has greater interests at stake. Like Moses, he endures as "seeing Him who is invisible" (Hebrews 11:27); looking "not at the things which are seen, but at the things which are not seen" (2 Corinthians 4:18).

Christ is acquainted with all that is misunderstood and misrepresented by men. His children can afford to wait in calm patience and trust, no matter how much maligned and despised; for nothing is secret that shall not be made manifest, and those who honor God shall be honored by Him in the presence of men and angels.

33 "When men shall revile you, and persecute you," said Jesus, "rejoice, and be exceeding glad." And He pointed His hearers to the prophets who had spoken in the name of the Lord, as "an example of suffering affliction, and of patience." James 5:10. Abel, the very first Christian of Adam's children, died a martyr. Enoch walked with God, and the world knew him not. Noah was mocked as a fanatic and an alarmist. "Others had trial of cruel mockings and scourgings, yea, moreover of bonds and imprisonment." "Others were tortured, not accepting deliverance; that they might obtain a better resurrection." Hebrews 11:36, 35.

In every age God's chosen messengers have been reviled and persecuted, yet through their affliction the knowledge of God has been spread abroad. Every disciple of Christ is to step into the ranks and carry forward the same work, knowing that its foes can do nothing against the truth, but for the truth. God means that truth shall be brought to the front and become the subject of examination and discussion, even through the contempt placed upon it. The minds of the people must be agitated; every controversy, every reproach, every effort to restrict liberty of conscience, is God's means of awakening minds that otherwise might slumber.

How often this result has been seen in the history of God's messengers! When the noble and eloquent Stephen was stoned to death at the instigation of the Sanhedrin council, there was no loss to the cause of the gospel. The light of heaven that glorified his face, the divine compassion breathed in his dying prayer, were as a sharp arrow of conviction to the bigoted Sanhedrist who stood by, and Saul, the persecuting Pharisee, became a chosen vessel to bear the name of Christ before Gentiles and kings and the children of Israel. And long afterward Paul the aged wrote from his prison house at Rome: "Some indeed preach Christ even of envy and strife: . . . not sincerely, supposing to add affliction to my bonds. . . . Notwithstanding, every way, whether in pretense, or in truth, Christ is preached." Philippians 1:15-18. Through Paul's imprisonment the gospel was spread abroad, and souls were won for Christ in the very palace of the Caesars. By the efforts of Satan to destroy it, the "incorruptible" seed of the word of God, "which liveth and abideth forever" (1 Peter 1:23), is sown in the hearts of men; through the reproach and persecution of His children the name of Christ is magnified and souls are saved.

Great is the reward in heaven of those who are witnesses for Christ through persecution and reproach. While the people are looking for earthly good, Jesus points them to a heavenly reward. But He does not place it all in the future life; it begins here. The Lord appeared of old time to Abraham and said, "*I* am thy shield, and thy exceeding great reward." Genesis 15:1. This is the reward of all who follow Christ. Jehovah Immanuel—He "in whom are hid all the treasures of wisdom and knowledge," in whom dwells "all the fullness of the Godhead bodily" (Colossians 2:3, 9)—to be brought into sympathy with Him, to know Him, to possess Him, as the heart opens more and more to receive His attributes; to know His love and power, to possess the unsearchable riches of Christ, to comprehend more and more "what is the breadth, and length, and depth, and height; and to know the love of Christ, which passeth knowledge, that ye might be filled with all the fullness of God" (Ephesians 3:18, 19)—"this is the heritage of the servants of the Lord, and their righteousness is of Me, saith the Lord." Isaiah 54:17.

It was this joy that filled the hearts of Paul and Silas when they prayed and sang praises to God at midnight in the Philippian dungeon. Christ was beside them there, and the light of His presence irradiated the gloom with the glory of the courts above. From Rome, Paul wrote, unmindful of his fetters as he saw the spread of the gospel, "I therein do rejoice, yea, and will rejoice." Philippians 1:18. And the very words of Christ upon the mount are re-echoed in Paul's message to the Philippian church, in the midst of their persecutions, "Rejoice in the Lord alway: and again I say, Rejoice." Philippians 4:4.

"Ye are the salt of the earth." Matthew 5:13.

Salt is valued for its preservative properties; and when God calls His children salt, He would teach them that His purpose in making them the subjects of His grace is that they may become agents in saving others. The object of God in choosing a people before all the world was not only that He might adopt them as His sons and daughters, but that through them the world might receive the grace that bringeth salvation. Titus 2:11. When the Lord chose Abraham, it was not simply to be the special friend of God, but to be a medium of the peculiar privileges the Lord desired to bestow upon the nations. Jesus, in that last prayer with His disciples before His crucifixion, said, "For their sakes I sanctify Myself, that they also might be sanctified through the truth." John 17:19. In like manner Christians who are purified through the truth will possess saving qualities that preserve the world from utter moral corruption.

Salt must be mingled with the substance to which it is added; it must penetrate and infuse in order to preserve. So it is through personal contact and association that men are reached by the saving power of the gospel. They are not saved in masses, but as individuals. Personal influence is a power. We must come close to those whom we desire to benefit.

The savor of the salt represents the vital power of the Christian—the love of Jesus in the heart, the righteousness of Christ pervading the life. The love of Christ is diffusive and aggressive. If it is dwelling in us, it will flow out to others. We shall come close to them till their hearts are warmed by our unselfish interest and love. The sincere believers diffuse vital energy, which is penetrating and imparts new moral power to the souls for whom they labor. It is not the power of the man himself, but the power of the Holy Spirit that does the transforming work.

Jesus added the solemn warning: "If the salt have lost his savor, wherewith shall it be salted? It is thenceforth good for nothing, but to be cast out, and to be trodden underfoot of men."

As they listened to the words of Christ, the people could see the white salt glistening in the pathways where it had been cast out because it had lost its savor and was therefore useless. It well represented the condition of the Pharisees and the effect of their religion upon society. It represents the life of every soul from whom the power of the grace of God has departed and who has become cold and Christless. Whatever may be his profession, such a one is looked upon by men and angels as insipid and disagreeable. It is to such that Christ says: "I would thou wert cold or hot. So then because thou art lukewarm, and neither cold nor hot, I will spue thee out of My mouth." Revelation 3:15, 16.

Without a living faith in Christ as a personal Saviour it is impossible to make our influence felt in a skeptical world. We cannot give to others that which we do not ourselves possess. It is in proportion to our own devotion and consecration to Christ that we exert an influence for the blessing and uplifting of mankind. If there is no actual service, no genuine love, no reality of experience, there is no power to help, no connection with heaven, no savor of Christ in the life. Unless the Holy Spirit can use us as agents through whom to communicate to the world the truth as it is in Jesus, we are as salt that has lost its savor and is entirely worthless. By our lack of the grace of Christ we testify to the world that the truth which we claim to believe has no sanctifying power; and thus, so far as our influence goes, we make of no effect the word of God. "If I speak with the tongues of men and of angels, but have not love, I am become sounding brass, or a clanging cymbal. And if I have the gift of prophecy, and know all mysteries and all knowledge; and if I have all faith, so as to remove mountains, but have not love, I am nothing. And if I bestow all my goods to feed the poor, and if I give my body to be burned, but have not love, it profiteth me nothing." 1 Corinthians 13:1-3, A.R.V.

When love fills the heart, it will flow out to others, not because of favors received from them, but because love is the principle of action. Love modifies the character, governs the impulses, subdues enmity, and ennobles the affections. This love is as broad as the universe, and is in harmony with that of the angel workers. Cherished in the heart, it sweetens the entire life and sheds its blessing upon all around. It is this, and this only, that can make us the salt of the earth.

"Ye are the light of the world." Matthew 5:14.

As Jesus taught the people, He made His lessons interesting and held the attention of His hearers by frequent illustrations from the scenes of nature about them. The people had come together while it was yet morning. The glorious sun, climbing higher and higher in the blue sky, was chasing away the shadows that lurked in the valleys and among the narrow defiles of the mountains. The glory of the eastern heavens had not yet faded out. The sunlight flooded the land with its splendor; the placid surface of the lake reflected the golden light and mirrored the rosy clouds of morning. Every bud and flower and leafy spray glistened with dewdrops. Nature smiled under the benediction of a new day, and the birds sang sweetly among the trees. The Saviour looked upon the company before Him, and then to the rising sun, and said to His disciples, "Ye are the light of the world." As the sun goes forth on its errand of love, dispelling the shades of night and awakening the world to life, so the followers of Christ are to go forth on their mission, diffusing the light of heaven upon those who are in the darkness of error and sin.

In the brilliant light of the morning, the towns and villages upon the surrounding hills stood forth clearly, making an attractive feature of the scene. Pointing to them, Jesus said, "A city set on a hill cannot be hid." And he added, "Neither do men light a lamp, and put it under the bushel, but on the stand; and it shineth unto all that are in the house." R.V. Most of those who listened to the words of Jesus were peasants and fishermen whose lowly dwellings contained but one room, in which the single lamp on its stand shone to all in the house. Even so, said Jesus, "Let your light so shine before men, that they may see your good works, and glorify your Father which is in heaven."

No other light ever has shone or ever will shine upon fallen man save that which emanates from Christ. Jesus, the Saviour, is the only light that can illuminate the darkness of a world lying in sin. Of Christ it is written, "In Him was life; and the life was the light of men." John 1:4. It was by receiving of His life that His disciples could become light bearers. The life of Christ in 40 the soul, His love revealed in the character, would make them the light of the world.

Humanity has in itself no light. Apart from Christ we are like an unkindled taper, like the moon when her face is turned away from the sun; we have not a single ray of brightness to shed into the darkness of the world. But when we turn toward the Sun of Righteousness, when we come in touch with Christ, the whole soul is aglow with the brightness of the divine presence.

Christ's followers are to be more than a light in the midst of men. They are *the* light of the world. Jesus says to all who have named His name, You have given yourselves to Me, and I have given you to the world as My representatives. As the Father had sent Him into the world, so, He declares, "have I also sent them into the world." John 17:18. As Christ is the channel for the revelation of the Father, so we are to be the channel for the revelation of Christ. While our Saviour is the great source of illumination, forget not, O Christian, that He is revealed through humanity. God's blessings are bestowed through human instrumentality. Christ Himself came to the world as the Son of man. Humanity, united to the divine nature, must touch humanity. The church of Christ, every individual disciple of the Master, is heaven's appointed channel for the revelation of God to men. Angels of glory wait to communicate through you heaven's light and power to souls that are ready to perish. Shall the human agent fail of accomplishing his appointed work? Oh,

then to that degree is the world robbed of the promised influence of the Holy Spirit!

But Jesus did not bid the disciples, "Strive to 41 *make* your light shine;" He said, "*Let* it shine." If Christ is dwelling in the heart, it is impossible to conceal the light of His presence. If those who profess to be followers of Christ are not the light of the world, it is because the vital power has left them; if they have no light to give, it is because they have no connection with the Source of light.

In all ages the "Spirit of Christ which was in them" (1 Peter 1:11) has made God's true children the light of the people of their generation. Joseph was a light bearer in Egypt. In his purity and benevolence and filial love he represented Christ in the midst of a nation of idolaters. While the Israelites were on their way from Egypt to the Promised Land, the true-hearted among them were a light to the surrounding nations. Through them God was revealed to the world. From Daniel and his companions in Babylon, and from Mordecai in Persia, bright beams of light shone out amid the darkness of the kingly courts. In like manner the disciples of Christ are set as light bearers on the way to heaven; through them the Father's mercy and goodness are made manifest to a world enshrouded in the darkness of misapprehension of God. By seeing their good works, others are led to glorify the Father who is above; for it is made manifest that there is a God on the throne of the universe whose character is worthy of praise and imitation. The divine love glowing in the heart, the Christlike harmony manifested in the life, are as a glimpse of heaven granted to men of the world, that they may appreciate its excellence.

It is thus that men are led to believe "the love 42 that God hath to us." 1 John 4:16. Thus hearts once sinful and corrupt are purified and transformed, to be presented "faultless before the presence of His glory with exceeding joy." Jude 24.

The Saviour's words, "Ye are the light of the world," point to the fact that He has committed to His followers a world-wide mission. In the days of Christ, selfishness and pride and prejudice had built strong and high the wall of partition between the appointed guardians of the sacred oracles and every other nation on the globe. But the Saviour had come to change all this. The words which the people were hearing from His lips were unlike anything to which they had ever listened from priest or rabbi. Christ tears away the wall of partition, the self-love, the dividing prejudice of nationality, and teaches a love for all the human family. He lifts men from the narrow circle that their selfishness prescribes; He abolishes all territorial lines and artificial distinctions of society. He makes no difference between neighbors and strangers, friends and enemies. He teaches us to look upon every needy soul as our neighbor and the world as our field.

As the rays of the sun penetrate to the remotest corners of the globe, so God designs that the light of the gospel shall extend to every soul upon the earth. If the church of Christ were fulfilling the purpose of our Lord, light would be shed upon all that sit in darkness and in the region and shadow of death. Instead of congregating together and shunning responsibility and cross bearing, the members of the church would scatter into all lands, letting the light of Christ shine out from them, working as He did for the salvation of souls, and this "gospel of the kingdom" would speedily be carried to all the world.

It is thus that God's purpose in calling His people, from Abraham on the plains of Mesopotamia to us in this age, is to reach its fulfillment. He says, "I will bless thee, . . . and thou shalt be a blessing." Genesis 12:2. The words of Christ through the gospel prophet, which are but re-echoed in the Sermon on the Mount, are for us in this last generation: "Arise, shine; for thy light is come, and the glory of the Lord is risen upon thee." Isaiah 60:1. If upon your spirit the glory of the Lord is risen, if you have beheld His beauty who is "the chiefest among ten thousand" and the One "altogether lovely," if your soul has become radiant in the presence of His glory, to you is this word from the Master sent. Have you stood with Christ on the mount of transfiguration? Down in the plain there are souls enslaved by Satan; they are waiting for the word of faith and prayer to set them free.

We are not only to contemplate the glory of Christ, but also to speak of His excellences. Isaiah not only beheld the glory of Christ, but he also spoke of Him. While David mused, the fire burned; then spoke he with his tongue. While he mused upon the wondrous love of God he could not but speak of that which he saw and felt. Who can by faith behold the wonderful plan of redemption, the glory of the only-begotten Son of God, and not speak of it? Who can contemplate the unfathomable love that was manifested upon the cross of Calvary in the death of Christ, that we might not perish, but have everlasting life—who can behold this and have no words with which to extol the Saviour's glory?

"In His temple doth everyone speak of His glory." Psalm 29:9. The sweet singer of Israel praised Him upon the harp, saying, "I will speak of the glorious honor of Thy majesty, and of Thy wondrous works. And men shall speak of the might of Thy terrible acts: and I will declare Thy greatness." Psalm 145:5, 6.

The cross of Calvary is to be lifted high above the people, absorbing their minds and concentrating their thoughts. Then all the spiritual faculties will be charged with divine power direct from God. Then there will be a concentration of the energies in genuine work for the Master. The workers will send forth to the world beams of light, as living agencies to enlighten the earth.

Christ accepts, oh, so gladly, every human agency that is surrendered to Him. He brings the human into union with the divine, that He may communicate to the world the mysteries of incarnate love. Talk it, pray it, sing it; proclaim abroad the message of His glory, and keep pressing onward to the regions beyond.

Trials patiently borne, blessings gratefully received, temptations manfully resisted, meekness, kindness, mercy, and love habitually revealed, are the lights that shine forth in the character in contrast with the darkness of the selfish heart, into which the light of life has never shone.

3

The Spirituality of the Law

"I am not come to destroy, but to fulfill."
Matthew 5:17.

It was Christ who, amid thunder and flame, had proclaimed the law upon Mount Sinai. The glory of God, like devouring fire, rested upon its summit, and the mountain quaked at the presence of the Lord. The hosts of Israel, lying prostrate upon the earth, had listened in awe to the sacred precepts of the law. What a contrast to the scene upon the mount of the Beatitudes! Under the summer sky, with no sound to break the stillness but the song of birds, Jesus unfolded the principles of His kingdom. Yet He who spoke to the people that day in accents of love, was opening to them the principles of the law proclaimed upon Sinai.

When the law was given, Israel, degraded by the long bondage in Egypt, had need to be impressed with the power and majesty of God; yet He revealed Himself to them no less as a God of love.

"The Lord came from Sinai,
And rose from Seir unto them;
He shined forth from Mount Paran,
And He came from the ten thousands of holy
    ones:
At His right hand was a fiery law unto them.
Yea, He loveth the tribes;
All their holy ones are in Thy hand:
And they sat down at Thy feet;
Everyone received of Thy words."
    Deuteronomy 33:2, 3, R.V., margin.

It was to Moses that God revealed His glory in those wonderful words that have been the treasured heritage of the ages: "The Lord, The Lord God, merciful and gracious, long-suffering, and abundant in goodness and truth, keeping mercy for thousands, forgiving iniquity and transgression and sin." Exodus 34:6, 7.

The law given upon Sinai was the enunciation of the principle of love, a revelation to earth of the law of heaven. It was ordained in the hand of a Mediator—spoken by Him through whose power the hearts of men could be brought into harmony with its principles. God had revealed the purpose of the law when He declared to Israel, "Ye shall be holy men unto Me." Exodus 22:31.

But Israel had not perceived the spiritual nature of the law, and too often their professed obedience was but an observance of forms and ceremonies, rather than a surrender of the heart to the sovereignty of love. As Jesus in His character and work represented to men the holy, benevolent, and paternal attributes of God, and presented the worthlessness of mere ceremonial obedience, the Jewish leaders did not receive or understand His words. They thought that He dwelt too lightly upon the requirements of the law; and when He set before them the very truths that were the soul of their divinely appointed service, they, looking only at the external, accused Him of seeking to overthrow it.

The words of Christ, though calmly spoken, were uttered with an earnestness and power that stirred the hearts of the people. They listened for a repetition of the lifeless traditions and exactions of the rabbis, but in vain. They "were astonished at His teaching: for He taught them as one having authority, and not as their scribes." Matthew 7:29, R.V. The Pharisees noted the vast difference between their manner of instruction and that of Christ. They saw that the majesty and purity and beauty of the truth, with its deep and gentle influence, was taking firm hold upon many minds. The Saviour's divine love and tenderness drew the hearts of men to Him. The rabbis saw that by His teaching the whole tenor of the instruction they had given to the people was set at nought. He was tearing down the partition wall that had been so flattering to their pride and exclusiveness; and they feared that, if permitted, He would draw the people entirely away from them. Therefore they followed Him with determined hostility, hoping to find some occasion for bringing Him into disfavor with the multitudes and thus enabling the Sanhedrin to secure His condemnation and death.

On the mount, Jesus was closely watched by spies; and as He unfolded the principles of righteousness, the Pharisees caused it to be whispered about that His teaching was in opposition to the precepts that God had given from Sinai. The Saviour said nothing to unsettle faith in the religion and institutions that had been given through Moses; for every ray of divine light that Israel's great leader communicated to his people was received from Christ. While many are saying in their hearts that He has come to do away with the law, Jesus in unmistakable language reveals His attitude toward the divine statutes. "Think not," He said, "that I am come to destroy the law, or the prophets."

It is the Creator of men, the Giver of the law, who declares that it is not His purpose to set aside its precepts. Everything in nature, from the mote in the sunbeam to the worlds on high, is under law. And upon obedience to these laws the order and harmony of the natural world depend. So there are great principles of righteousness to control the life of all intelligent beings, and upon conformity to these principles the well-being of the universe depends. Before this earth was called into being, God's law existed. Angels are governed by its principles, and in order for earth to be in harmony with heaven, man also must obey the divine statutes. To man in Eden Christ made known the precepts of the law "when the morning stars sang together, and all the sons of God shouted for joy." Job 38:7. The mission of Christ on earth was not to destroy the law, but by His grace to bring man back to obedience to its precepts.

The beloved disciple, who listened to the words of Jesus on the mount, writing long afterward under the inspiration of the Holy Spirit, speaks of the law as of perpetual obligation. He says that "sin is the transgression of the law" and that "whosoever committeth sin transgresseth also the law." 1 John 3:4. He makes it plain that the law to which he refers is "an old commandment which ye had from the beginning." 1 John 2:7. He is speaking of the law that existed at the creation and was reiterated upon Mount Sinai.

Speaking of the law, Jesus said, "I am not come to destroy, but to fulfill." He here used the word "fulfill" in the same sense as when He declared to John the Baptist His purpose to "fulfill all righteousness" (Matthew 3:15); that is, to fill up the measure of the law's requirement, to give an example of perfect conformity to the will of God.

His mission was to "magnify the law, and make it honorable." Isaiah 42:21. He was to show the spiritual nature of the law, to present its far-reaching principles, and to make plain its eternal obligation.

The divine beauty of the character of Christ, of whom the noblest and most gentle among men are but a faint reflection; of whom Solomon by the Spirit of inspiration wrote, He is "the chiefest among ten thousand, . . . yea, He is altogether lovely" (Song of Solomon 5:10-16); of whom David, seeing Him in prophetic vision, said, "Thou art fairer than the children of men" (Psalm 45:2); Jesus, the express image of the Father's person, the effulgence of His glory; the self-denying Redeemer, throughout His pilgrimage of love on earth, was a living representation of the character of the law of God. In His life it is made manifest that heaven-born love, Christlike principles, underlie the laws of eternal rectitude.

"Till heaven and earth pass," said Jesus, "one jot or one tittle shall in nowise pass from the law, till all be fulfilled." By His own obedience to the law, Christ testified to its immutable character and proved that through His grace it could be perfectly obeyed by every son and daughter of Adam. On the mount He declared that not the smallest iota should pass from the law till all things should be accomplished—all things that concern the human race, all that 50 relates to the plan of redemption. He does not teach that the law is ever to be abrogated, but He fixes the eye upon the utmost verge of man's horizon and assures us that until this point is reached the law will retain its authority so that none may suppose it was His mission to abolish the precepts of the law. So long as heaven and earth continue, the holy principles of God's law will remain. His righteousness, "like the great mountains" (Psalm 36:6), will continue, a source of blessing, sending forth streams to refresh the earth.

Because the law of the Lord is perfect, and therefore changeless, it is impossible for sinful men, in themselves, to meet the standard of its requirement. This was why Jesus came as our Redeemer. It was His mission, by making men partakers of the divine nature, to bring them into harmony with the principles of the law of heaven. When we forsake our sins and receive Christ as our Saviour, the law is exalted. The apostle Paul asks, "Do we then make void the law through faith? God forbid: yea, we establish the law." Romans 3:31.

The new-covenant promise is, "I will put My laws into their hearts, and in their minds will I write them." Hebrews 10:16. While the system of types which pointed to Christ as the Lamb of God that should take away the sin of the world was to pass away at His death, the principles of righteousness embodied in the Decalogue are as immutable as the eternal throne. Not one command has been annulled, not a jot or tittle has been changed. Those principles that were made known to man in Paradise as the great law of 51 life will exist unchanged in Paradise restored. When Eden shall bloom on earth again, God's law of love will be obeyed by all beneath the sun.

"Forever, O Lord, Thy word is settled in heaven." "All His commandments are sure. They stand fast for ever and ever, and are done in truth and uprightness." "Concerning Thy testimonies, I have known of old that Thou hast founded them forever." Psalms 119:89; 111:7, 8; 119:152.

> *"Whosoever . . . shall break one of these least commandments, and shall teach men so, he shall be called the least in the kingdom of heaven." Matthew 5:19.*

That is, he shall have no place therein. For he who willfully breaks one commandment, does not, in spirit and truth, keep any of them. "Whosoever shall keep the whole law, and yet offend in one point, he is guilty of all." James 2:10.

It is not the greatness of the act of disobedience that constitutes sin, but the fact of variance from God's expressed will in the least particular; for this shows that there is yet communion between the soul and sin. The heart is divided in its service. There is a virtual denial of God, a rebellion against the laws of His government.

Were men free to depart from the Lord's requirements and to set up a standard of duty for themselves, there would be a variety of standards to suit different minds and the government would be taken out of the Lord's hands. 52 The will of man would be made supreme, and the high and holy will of God—His purpose of love toward His creatures—would be dishonored, disrespected.

Whenever men choose their own way, they place themselves in controversy with God. They will have no place in the kingdom of heaven, for they are at war with the very principles of heaven. In disregarding the will of God, they are placing themselves on the side of Satan, the enemy of God and man. Not by one word, not by many words, but by every word that God has spoken, shall man live. We cannot disregard one word, however trifling it may seem to us, and be safe. There is not a commandment of the law that is not for the good and happiness of man, both in this life and in the life to come. In obedience to God's law, man is surrounded as with a hedge and kept from the evil. He who breaks down this divinely erected barrier at one point has destroyed its power to protect him; for he has opened a way by which the enemy can enter to waste and ruin.

By venturing to disregard the will of God upon one point, our first parents opened the floodgates of woe upon the world. And every individual who follows their example will reap a similar result. The love of God underlies every precept of His law, and he who departs from the commandment is working his own unhappiness and ruin.

53

"Except your righteousness shall exceed the righteousness of the scribes and Pharisees, ye shall in no case enter into the kingdom of heaven." Matthew 5:20.

The scribes and Pharisees had accused not only Christ but His disciples as sinners because of their disregard of the rabbinical rites and observances. Often the disciples had been perplexed and troubled by censure and accusation from those whom they had been accustomed to revere as religious teachers. Jesus unveiled the deception. He declared that the righteousness upon which the Pharisees set so great value was worthless. The Jewish nation had claimed to be the special, loyal people who were favored of God; but Christ represented their religion as devoid of saving faith. All their pretensions of piety, their human inventions and ceremonies, and even their boasted performance of the outward requirements of the law, could not avail to make them holy. They were not pure in heart or noble and Christlike in character.

A legal religion is insufficient to bring the soul into harmony with God. The hard, rigid orthodoxy of the Pharisees, destitute of contrition, tenderness, or love, was only a stumbling block to sinners. They were like the salt that had lost its savor; for their influence had no power to preserve the world from corruption. The only true faith is that which "worketh by love" (Galatians 5:6) to purify the soul. It is as leaven that transforms the character.

All this the Jews should have learned from 54 the teachings of the prophets. Centuries before, the cry of the soul for justification with God had found voice and answer in the words of the prophet Micah: "Wherewith shall I come before the Lord, and bow myself before the high God? shall I come before Him with burnt offerings, with calves of a year old? Will the Lord be pleased with thousands of rams, or with ten thousands of rivers of oil? . . . He hath showed thee, O man, what is good; and what doth the Lord require of thee, but to do justly, and to love mercy, and to walk humbly with thy God?" Micah 6:6-8.

The prophet Hosea had pointed out what constitutes the very essence of Pharisaism, in the words, "Israel is an empty vine, he bringeth forth fruit unto himself." Hosea 10:1. In their professed service to God, the Jews were really working for self. Their righteousness was the fruit of their own efforts to keep the law according to their own ideas and for their own selfish benefit. Hence it could be no better than they were. In their endeavor to make themselves holy, they were trying to bring a clean thing out of an unclean. The law of God is as holy as He is holy, as perfect as He is perfect. It presents to men the righteousness of God. It is impossible

for man, of himself, to keep this law; for the nature of man is depraved, deformed, and wholly unlike the character of God. The works of the selfish heart are "as an unclean thing;" and "all our righteousnesses are as filthy rags." Isaiah 64:6.

While the law is holy, the Jews could not attain righteousness by their own efforts to keep the law. The disciples of Christ must obtain righteousness of a different character 55 from that of the Pharisees, if they would enter the kingdom of heaven. God offered them, in His Son, the perfect righteousness of the law. If they would open their hearts fully to receive Christ, then the very life of God, His love, would dwell in them, transforming them into His own likeness; and thus through God's free gift they would possess the righteousness which the law requires. But the Pharisees rejected Christ; "being ignorant of God's righteousness, and going about to establish their own righteousness" (Romans 10:3), they would not submit themselves unto the righteousness of God.

Jesus proceeded to show His hearers what it means to keep the commandments of God—that it is a reproduction in themselves of the character of Christ. For in Him, God was daily made manifest before them.

"Everyone who is angry with his brother shall be in danger of the judgment." Matthew 5:22, R.V.

Through Moses the Lord had said, "Thou shalt not hate thy brother in thine heart. . . . Thou shalt not avenge, nor bear any grudge against the children of thy people, but thou shalt love thy neighbor as thyself." Leviticus 19:17, 18. The truths which Christ presented were the same that had been taught by the prophets, but they had become obscured through hardness of heart and love of sin.

The Saviour's words revealed to His hearers the fact that, while they were condemning others as transgressors, they were themselves 56 equally guilty; for they were cherishing malice and hatred.

Across the sea from the place where they were assembled was the country of Bashan, a lonely region, whose wild gorges and wooded hills had long been a favorite lurking ground for criminals of all descriptions. Reports of robbery and murder committed there were fresh in the minds of the people, and many were zealous in denouncing these evildoers. At the same time they were themselves passionate and contentious; they cherished the most bitter hatred of their Roman oppressors and felt themselves at liberty to hate and despise all other peoples, and even their own countrymen who did not in all things conform to their ideas. In all this they were violating the law which declares, "Thou shalt not kill."

The spirit of hatred and revenge originated with Satan, and it led him to put to death the Son of God. Whoever cherishes malice or unkindness is cherishing the same spirit, and its fruit will be unto death. In the revengeful thought the evil deed lies enfolded, as the plant in the seed. "Whosoever hateth his brother is a murderer: and ye know that no murderer hath eternal life abiding in him." 1 John 3:15.

"Whosoever shall say to his brother, Raca [vain fellow], shall be in danger of the council." In the gift of His Son for our redemption, God has shown how high a value He places upon every human soul, and He gives to no man liberty to speak contemptuously of another. We shall see faults and weaknesses in those about us, but God claims every soul as His property— His by creation, and doubly His as purchased by the precious blood of Christ. All were created in His image, and even the most degraded are to be treated with respect and tenderness. God will hold us accountable for even a word spoken in contempt of one soul for whom Christ laid down His life.

"Who maketh thee to differ from another? and what hast thou that thou didst not receive? now if thou didst receive it, why dost thou glory, as if thou hadst not received it?" "Who art thou that judgest another man's servant? to his own master he standeth or falleth." 1 Corinthians 4:7; Romans 14:4.

"Whosoever shall say, Thou fool, shall be in danger of the hell of fire." R.V. In the Old Testament the word "fool" is used to designate an apostate, or one who has abandoned himself to wickedness. Jesus says that whoever shall condemn his brother as an apostate or a despiser of God shows that he himself is worthy of the same condemnation.

Christ Himself, when contending with Satan about the body of Moses, "durst not bring against him a railing accusation." Jude 9. Had He done this, He would have placed Himself on Satan's ground, for accusation is the weapon of the evil one. He is called in Scripture, "the accuser of our brethren." Revelation 12:10. Jesus would employ none of Satan's weapons. He met him with the words, "The Lord rebuke thee." Jude 9.

His example is for us. When we are brought in conflict with the enemies of Christ, we should say nothing in a spirit of retaliation or that would bear even the appearance of a railing accusation. He who stands as a mouthpiece for God should not utter words which even the Majesty of heaven would not use when contending with Satan. We are to leave with God the work of judging and condemning.

"Be reconciled to thy brother." Matthew 5:24.

The love of God is something more than a mere negation; it is a positive and active principle, a living spring, ever flowing to bless others. If the love of Christ dwells in us, we shall not only cherish no hatred toward our fellows, but we shall seek in every way to manifest love toward them.

Jesus said, "If thou bring thy gift to the altar, and there rememberest that thy brother hath aught against thee; leave there thy gift before the altar, and go thy way; first be reconciled to thy brother, and then come and offer thy gift." The sacrificial offerings expressed faith that through Christ the offerer had become a partaker of the mercy and love of God. But for one to express faith in God's pardoning love, while he himself indulged an unloving spirit, would be a mere farce.

When one who professes to serve God wrongs or injures a brother, he misrepresents the character of God to that brother, and the wrong must be confessed, he must acknowledge it to be sin, in order to be in harmony with God. Our brother may have done us a greater wrong than we have done him, but this does not lessen our responsibility. If when we come before God we remember that another has aught against us, we are to leave our gift of prayer, of thanksgiving, of freewill offering, and go to the brother with whom we are at variance, and in humility confess our own sin and ask to be forgiven.

If we have in any manner defrauded or injured our brother, we should make restitution. If we have unwittingly borne false witness, if we have misstated his words, if we have injured his influence in any way, we should go to the ones with whom we have conversed about him, and take back all our injurious misstatements.

If matters of difficulty between brethren were not laid open before others, but frankly spoken of between themselves in the spirit of Christian love, how much evil might be prevented! How many roots of bitterness whereby many are defiled would be destroyed, and how closely and tenderly might the followers of Christ be united in His love!

"Whosoever looketh on a woman to lust after her hath committed adultery with her already in his heart." Matthew 5:28.

The Jews prided themselves on their morality and looked with horror upon the sensual practices of the heathen. The presence of the Roman officers whom the imperial rule had brought into Palestine was a continual offense to the people, for with these foreigners had come in a flood of heathen customs, lust, and dissipation.

In Capernaum, Roman officials with their gay paramours haunted the parades and promenades, and often the sound of revelry broke upon the stillness of the lake as their pleasure boats glided over the quiet waters. The people expected to hear from Jesus a stern denunciation of this class, but what was their astonishment as they listened to words that laid bare the evil of their own hearts!

When the thought of evil is loved and cherished, however secretly, said Jesus, it shows that sin still reigns in the heart. The soul is still in the gall of bitterness and in the bond of iniquity. He who finds pleasure in dwelling upon scenes of impurity, who indulges the evil thought, the lustful look, may behold in the open sin, with its burden of shame and heartbreaking grief, the true nature of the evil which he has hidden in the chambers of the soul. The season of temptation, under which, it may be, one falls into grievous sin, does not create the evil that is revealed, but only develops or makes manifest that which was hidden and latent in the heart. As a man "thinketh in his heart, so is he;" for out of the heart "are the issues of life." Proverbs 23:7; 4:23.

"If thy right hand causeth thee to stumble, cut it off, and cast it from thee." Matthew 5:30, R.V.

To prevent disease from spreading to the body and destroying life, a man would submit to part even with his right hand. Much more should he be willing to surrender that which imperils the life of the soul.

Through the gospel, souls that are degraded and enslaved by Satan are to be redeemed to share the glorious liberty of the sons of God. God's purpose is not merely to deliver from the suffering that is the inevitable result of sin, but to save from sin itself. The soul, corrupted and deformed, is to be purified, transformed, that it may be clothed in "the beauty of the Lord our God," "conformed to the image of His Son." "Eye hath not seen, nor ear heard, neither have entered into the heart of man, the things which God hath prepared for them that love Him." Psalm 90:17; Romans 8:29; 1 Corinthians 2:9. Eternity alone can reveal the glorious destiny to which man, restored to God's image, may attain.

In order for us to reach this high ideal, that which causes the soul to stumble must be sacrificed. It is through the will that sin retains its hold upon us. The surrender of the will is represented as plucking out the eye or cutting off the hand. Often it seems to us that to surrender the will to God is to consent to go through life maimed or crippled. But it is better, says Christ, for self to be maimed, wounded, crippled, if thus you may enter into life. That which you

look upon as disaster is the door to highest benefit.

God is the fountain of life, and we can have life only as we are in communion with Him. Separated from God, existence may be ours for a little time, but we do not possess life. "She that liveth in pleasure is dead while she liveth." 1 Timothy 5:6. Only through the surrender of our will to God is it possible for Him to impart life to us. Only by receiving His life through self-surrender is it possible, said Jesus, for these hidden sins, which I have pointed out, to be overcome. It is possible that you may bury them in your hearts and conceal them from human eyes, but how will you stand in God's presence?

If you cling to self, refusing to yield your will to God, you are choosing death. To sin, wherever found, God is a consuming fire. If you choose sin, and refuse to separate from it, the presence of God, which consumes sin, must consume you.

It will require a sacrifice to give yourself to God; but it is a sacrifice of the lower for the higher, the earthly for the spiritual, the perishable for the eternal. God does not design that our will should be destroyed, for it is only through its exercise that we can accomplish what He would have us do. Our will is to be yielded to Him, that we may receive it again, purified and refined, and so linked in sympathy with the Divine that He can pour through us the tides of His love and power. However bitter and painful this surrender may appear to the willful, wayward heart, yet "it is profitable for thee."

Not until he fell crippled and helpless upon the breast of the covenant angel did Jacob know the victory of conquering faith and receive the title of a prince with God. It was when he "halted upon his thigh" (Genesis 32:31) that the armed bands of Esau were stilled before him, and the Pharaoh, proud heir of a kingly line, stooped to crave his blessing. So the Captain of our salvation was made "perfect through sufferings" (Hebrews 2:10), and the children of faith "out of weakness were made strong," and "turned to flight the armies of the aliens" (Hebrews 11:34). So do "the lame take the prey" (Isaiah 33:23), and the weak become "as David," and "the house of David . . . as the angel of the Lord" (Zechariah 12:8).

"Is it lawful for a man to put away his wife?" Matthew 19:3.

Among the Jews a man was permitted to put away his wife for the most trivial offenses, and the woman was then at liberty to marry again. This practice led to great wretchedness and sin. In the Sermon on the Mount Jesus declared plainly that there could be no dissolution of the marriage tie, except for unfaithfulness to the marriage vow. "Everyone," He said, "that putteth away his wife, saving for the cause of fornication, maketh her an adulteress: and whosoever shall marry her when she is put away committeth adultery." R.V.

When the Pharisees afterward questioned Him concerning the lawfulness of divorce, Jesus pointed His hearers back to the marriage institution as ordained at creation. "Because of the hardness of your hearts," He said, Moses "suffered you to put away your wives: but from the beginning it was not so." Matthew 19:8. He referred them to the blessed days of Eden, when God pronounced all things "very good." Then marriage and the Sabbath had their origin, twin institutions for the glory of God in the benefit of humanity. Then, as the Creator joined the hands of the holy pair in wedlock, saying, "A man shall "leave his father and his mother, and shall cleave unto his wife: and they shall be one" (Genesis 2:24), He enunciated the law of marriage for all the children of Adam to the close of time. That which the Eternal Father Himself had pronounced good was the law of highest blessing and development for man.

Like every other one of God's good gifts entrusted to the keeping of humanity, marriage has been perverted by sin; but it is the purpose of the gospel to restore its purity and beauty. In both the Old and the New Testament the marriage relation is employed to represent the tender and sacred union that exists between Christ and His people, the redeemed ones whom He has purchased at the cost of Calvary. "Fear not," He says; "thy Maker is thine husband; the Lord of hosts is His name; and thy Redeemer, the Holy One of Israel." "Turn, O backsliding children, saith the Lord; for I am married unto you." Isaiah 54:4, 5; Jeremiah 3:14. In the "Song of Songs" we hear the bride's voice saying, "My Beloved is mine, and I am His." And He who is to her "the chiefest among ten thousand," speaks to His chosen one, "Thou art all fair, My love; there is no spot in thee." Song of Solomon 2:16; 5:10; 4:7.

In later times Paul the apostle, writing to the Ephesian Christians, declares that the Lord has constituted the husband the head of the wife, to be her protector, the house-band, binding the members of the family together, even as Christ is the head of the church and the Saviour of the mystical body. Therefore he says, "As the church is subject unto Christ, so let the wives be to their own husbands in everything. Husbands, love your wives, even as Christ also loved the church, and gave Himself for it; that He might sanctify and cleanse it with the washing of water by the word, that He might present it to Himself a glorious church, not having spot, or wrinkle, or any such thing; but that it should be holy and without blemish. So ought men to love

their wives." Ephesians 5:24-28.

The grace of Christ, and this alone, can make this institution what God designed it should be—an agent for the blessing and uplifting of humanity. And thus the families of earth, in their unity and peace and love, may represent the family of heaven.

Now, as in Christ's day, the condition of society presents a sad comment upon heaven's ideal of this sacred relation. Yet even for those who have found bitterness and disappointment where they had hoped for companionship and joy, the gospel of Christ offers a solace. The patience and gentleness which His Spirit can impart will sweeten the bitter lot. The heart in which Christ dwells will be so filled, so satisfied, with His love that it will not be consumed with longing to attract sympathy and attention to itself. And through the surrender of the soul to God, His wisdom can accomplish what human wisdom fails to do. Through the revelation of His grace, hearts that were once indifferent or estranged may be united in bonds that are firmer and more enduring than those of earth—the golden bonds of a love that will bear the test of trial.

"Swear not at all." Matthew 5:34.

The reason for this command is given: We are not to swear "by the heaven, for it is the throne of God; nor by the earth, for it is the footstool of His feet; nor by Jerusalem, for it is the city of the great King. Neither shalt thou swear by thy head, for thou canst not make one hair white or black." R.V.

All things come of God. We have nothing that we have not received; and, more than this, we have nothing that has not been purchased for us by the blood of Christ. Everything we possess comes to us stamped with the cross, bought with the blood that is precious above all estimate, because it is the life of God. Hence there is nothing that we have a right to pledge, as if it were our own, for the fulfillment of our word.

The Jews understood the third commandment as prohibiting the profane use of the name of God; but they thought themselves at liberty to employ other oaths. Oath taking was common among them. Through Moses they had been forbidden to swear falsely, but they had many devices for freeing themselves from the obligation imposed by an oath. They did not fear to indulge in what was really profanity, nor did they shrink from perjury so long as it was veiled by some technical evasion of the law.

Jesus condemned their practices, declaring that their custom in oath taking was a transgression of the commandment of God. Our Saviour did not, however, forbid the use of the judicial oath, in which God is solemnly called to witness that what is said is truth and nothing but the truth. Jesus Himself, at His trial before the Sanhedrin, did not refuse to testify under oath. The high priest said unto Him, "I adjure Thee by the living God, that Thou tell us whether Thou be the Christ, the Son of God." Jesus answered, "Thou hast said." Matthew 26:63, 64. Had Christ in the Sermon on the Mount condemned the judicial oath, He would at His trial have reproved the high priest and thus, for the benefit of His followers, have enforced His own teaching.

There are very many who do not fear to deceive their fellow men, but they have been taught, and have been impressed by the Spirit of God, that it is a fearful thing to lie to their Maker. When put under oath they are made to feel that they are not testifying merely before men, but before God; that if they bear false witness, it is to Him who reads the heart and who knows the exact truth. The knowledge of the fearful judgments that have followed this sin has a restraining influence upon them.

But if there is anyone who can consistently testify under oath, it is the Christian. He lives constantly as in the presence of God, knowing that every thought is open to the eyes of Him with whom we have to do; and when required to do so in a lawful manner, it is right for him to appeal to God as a witness that what he says is the truth, and nothing but the truth.

Jesus proceeded to lay down a principle that would make oath taking needless. He teaches that the exact truth should be the law of speech. "Let your speech be, Yea, yea; Nay, nay: and whatsoever is more than these is of the evil one." R.V.

68 These words condemn all those meaningless phrases and expletives that border on profanity. They condemn the deceptive compliments, the evasion of truth, the flattering phrases, the exaggerations, the misrepresentations in trade, that are current in society and in the business world. They teach that no one who tries to appear what he is not, or whose words do not convey the real sentiment of his heart, can be called truthful.

If these words of Christ were heeded, they would check the utterance of evil surmising and unkind criticism; for in commenting upon the actions and motives of another, who can be certain of speaking the exact truth? How often pride, passion, personal resentment, color the impression given! A glance, a word, even an intonation of the voice, may be vital with falsehood. Even facts may be so stated as to convey a false impression. And "whatsoever is more than" truth, "is of the evil one."

Everything that Christians do should be as transparent as the sunlight. Truth is of God; deception, in every one of its myriad forms, is of Satan; and whoever in any way departs from the straight line of truth is betraying himself into the power of the wicked one. Yet it is not a light or an easy thing to speak the exact truth. We cannot speak the truth unless we know the truth; and how often preconceived opinions, mental bias, imperfect knowledge, errors of judgment, prevent a right understanding of matters with which we have to do! We cannot speak the truth unless our minds are continually guided by Him who is truth.

Through the apostle Paul, Christ bids us, "Let your speech be alway with grace." "Let no 69 corrupt communication proceed out of your mouth, but that which is good to the use of edifying, that it may minister grace unto the hearers." Colossians 4:6; Ephesians 4:29. In the light of these scriptures the words of Christ upon the mount are seen to condemn jesting, trifling, and unchaste conversation. They require that our words should be not only truthful, but pure.

Those who have learned of Christ will "have no fellowship with the unfruitful works of darkness." Ephesians 5:11. In speech, as in life, they will be simple, straightforward, and true; for they are preparing for the fellowship of those holy ones in whose mouth "was found no guile." Revelation 14:5.

"Resist not him that is evil: but whosoever smiteth thee on thy right cheek, turn to him the other also." Matthew 5:39, R.V.

Occasions of irritation to the Jews were constantly arising from their contact with the Roman soldiery. Detachments of troops were stationed at different points throughout Judea and Galilee, and their presence reminded the people of their own degradation as a nation. With bitterness of soul they heard the loud blast of the trumpet and saw the troops forming around the standard of Rome and bowing in homage to this symbol of her power. Collisions between the people and the soldiers were frequent, and these inflamed the popular hatred. Often as some Roman official with his guard of soldiers hastened from point to point, he would 70 seize upon the Jewish peasants who were laboring in the field and compel them to carry burdens up the mountainside or render any other service that might be needed. This was in accordance with the Roman law and custom, and resistance to such demands only called forth taunts and cruelty. Every day deepened in the hearts of the people the longing to cast off the Roman yoke. Especially among the bold, roughhanded Galileans the spirit of insurrection was rife. Capernaum, being a border town, was the seat of a Roman garrison, and even while Jesus was teaching, the sight of a company of soldiers recalled to His hearers the bitter thought of Israel's humiliation. The people looked eagerly to Christ, hoping that He was the One who was to humble the pride of Rome.

With sadness Jesus looks into the upturned faces before Him. He notes the spirit of revenge that has stamped its evil imprint upon them, and knows how bitterly the people long for power to crush their oppressors. Mournfully He bids them, "Resist not him that is evil: but whosoever smiteth thee on thy right cheek, turn to him the other also."

These words were but a reiteration of the teaching of the Old Testament. It is true that the rule, "Eye for eye, tooth for tooth" (Leviticus 24:20), was a provision in the laws given through Moses; but it was a civil statute. None were justified in avenging themselves, for they had the words of the Lord: "Say not thou, I will recompense evil." "Say not, I will do so to him as he hath done to me." "Rejoice not when thine 71 enemy falleth." "If he that hateth thee be hungry, give him bread to eat; and if he be thirsty, give him water to drink." Proverbs 20:22; 24:29, 17; 25:21, 22, R.V., margin.

The whole earthly life of Jesus was a manifestation of this principle. It was to bring the bread of life to His enemies that our Saviour left His home in heaven. Though calumny and persecution were heaped upon Him from the cradle to the grave, they called forth from Him only the expression of forgiving love. Through the prophet Isaiah He says, "I gave My back to the smiters, and My cheeks to them that plucked off the hair: I hid not My face from shame and spitting." "He was oppressed, and He was afflicted, yet He opened not His mouth: He is brought as a lamb to the slaughter, and as a sheep before her shearers is dumb, so He openeth not His mouth." Isaiah 50:6; 53:7. And from the cross of Calvary there come down through the ages His prayer for His murderers and the message of hope to the dying thief.

The Father's presence encircled Christ, and nothing befell Him but that which infinite love permitted for the blessing of the world. Here was His source of comfort, and it is for us. He who is imbued with the Spirit of Christ abides in Christ. The blow that is aimed at him falls upon the Saviour, who surrounds him with His presence. Whatever comes to him comes from Christ. He has no need to resist evil, for Christ is his defense. Nothing can touch him except by our Lord's permission, and "all things" that are permitted "work together for good to them that love God." Romans 8:28.

"If any man would go to law with thee, and 72 take away thy coat [tunic], let him have thy cloak [mantle] also. And whosoever shall impress thee to go one mile, go with him twain." R.V., margin.

Jesus bade His disciples, instead of resisting the demands of those in authority, to do even more than was required of them. And, so far as possible, they should discharge every obligation, even if it were beyond what the law of the

land required. The law, as given through Moses, enjoined a very tender regard for the poor. When a poor man gave his garment as a pledge, or as security for a debt, the creditor was not permitted to enter the dwelling to obtain it; he must wait in the street for the pledge to be brought to him. And whatever the circumstances the pledge must be returned to its owner at nightfall. Deuteronomy 24:10-13. In the days of Christ these merciful provisions were little regarded; but Jesus taught His disciples to submit to the decision of the court, even though this should demand more than the law of Moses authorized. Though it should demand a part of their raiment, they were to yield. More than this, they were to give to the creditor his due, if necessary surrendering even more than the court gave him authority to seize. "If any man would go to law with thee," He said, "and take away thy coat, let him have thy cloak also." R.V. And if the couriers require you to go a mile with them, go two miles.

Jesus added, "Give to him that asketh thee, and from him that would borrow of thee turn not thou away." The same lesson had been taught through Moses: "Thou shalt not harden thine heart, nor shut thine hand from thy poor 73 brother: but thou shalt open thine hand wide unto him, and shalt surely lend him sufficient for his need, in that which he wanteth." Deuteronomy 15:7, 8. This scripture makes plain the meaning of the Saviour's words. Christ does not teach us to give indiscriminately to all who ask for charity; but He says, "Thou shalt surely lend him sufficient for his need;" and this is to be a gift, rather than a loan; for we are to "lend, hoping for nothing again." Luke 6:35.

"Who gives himself with his alms feeds three, Himself, his hungering neighbor, and Me."

"Love your enemies." Matthew 5:44.

The Saviour's lesson, "Resist not him that is evil," was a hard saying for the revengeful Jews, and they murmured against it among themselves. But Jesus now made a still stronger declaration:

"Ye have heard that it hath been said, Thou shalt love thy neighbor, and hate thine enemy. But I say unto you, Love your enemies, bless them that curse you, do good to them that hate you, and pray for them which despitefully use you and persecute you; that ye may be the children of your Father which is in heaven."

Such was the spirit of the law which the rabbis had misinterpreted as a cold and rigid code of exactions. They regarded themselves as better than other men, and as entitled to the special favor of God by virtue of their birth as Israelites; but Jesus pointed to the spirit of for-

74 giving love as that which would give evidence that they were actuated by any higher motives than even the publicans and sinners, whom they despised.

He pointed His hearers to the Ruler of the universe, under the new name, "Our Father." He would have them understand how tenderly the heart of God yearned over them. He teaches that God cares for every lost soul; that "like as a father pitieth his children, so the Lord pitieth them that fear Him." Psalm 103:13. Such a conception of God was never given to the world by any religion but that of the Bible. Heathenism teaches men to look upon the Supreme Being as an object of fear rather than of love—a malign deity to be appeased by sacrifices, rather than a Father pouring upon His children the gift of His love. Even the people of Israel had become so blinded to the precious teaching of the prophets concerning God that this revelation of His paternal love was an original subject, a new gift to the world.

The Jews held that God loved those who served Him,—according to their view, those who fulfilled the requirements of the rabbis,—and that all the rest of the world lay under His frown and curse. Not so, said Jesus; the whole world, the evil and the good, lies in the sunshine of His love. This truth you should have learned from nature itself; for God "maketh His sun to rise on the evil and on the good, and sendeth rain on the just and on the unjust."

It is not because of inherent power that year by year the earth produces her bounties and continues her motion round the sun. The hand of God guides the planets and keeps them in posi-

75 tion in their orderly march through the heavens. It is through His power that summer and winter, seedtime and harvest, day and night follow each other in their regular succession. It is by His word that vegetation flourishes, that the leaves appear and the flowers bloom. Every good thing we have, each ray of sunshine and shower of rain, every morsel of food, every moment of life, is a gift of love.

While we were yet unloving and unlovely in character, "hateful, and hating one another," our heavenly Father had mercy on us. "After that the kindness and love of God our Saviour toward man appeared, not by works of righteousness which we have done, but according to His mercy He saved us." Titus 3:3-5. His love received, will make us, in like manner, kind and tender, not merely toward those who please us, but to the most faulty and erring and sinful.

The children of God are those who are partakers of His nature. It is not earthly rank, nor birth, nor nationality, nor religious privilege, which proves that we are members of the family of God; it is love, a love that embraces all humanity. Even sinners whose hearts are not utterly closed to God's Spirit, will respond to kindness; while they may give hate for hate, they will also give love for love. But it is only the Spirit of God that gives love for hatred. To be kind to the unthankful and to the evil, to do good hoping for nothing again, is the insignia of the royalty of heaven, the sure token by which the children of the Highest reveal their high estate.

76 *"Be ye therefore perfect, even as your Father which is in heaven is perfect." Matthew 5:48.*

The word "therefore" implies a conclusion, an inference from what has gone before. Jesus has been describing to His hearers the unfailing mercy and love of God, and He bids them therefore to be perfect. Because your heavenly Father "is kind unto the unthankful and to the evil" (Luke 6:35), because He has stooped to lift you up, therefore, said Jesus, you may become like Him in character, and stand without fault in the presence of men and angels.

The conditions of eternal life, under grace, are just what they were in Eden—perfect righteousness, harmony with God, perfect conformity to the principles of His law. The standard of character presented in the Old Testament is the same that is presented in the New Testament. This standard is not one to which we cannot attain. In every command or injunction that God gives there is a promise, the most positive, underlying the command. God has made provision that we may become like unto Him, and He will accomplish this for all who do not interpose a perverse will and thus frustrate His grace.

With untold love our God has loved us, and our love awakens toward Him as we comprehend something of the length and breadth and depth and height of this love that passeth knowledge. By the revelation of the attractive loveliness of Christ, by the knowledge of His love expressed to us while we were yet sinners, the stubborn heart is melted and subdued, and the 77 sinner is transformed and becomes a child of heaven. God does not employ compulsory measures; love is the agent which He uses to expel sin from the heart. By it He changes pride into humility, and enmity and unbelief into love and faith.

The Jews had been wearily toiling to reach perfection by their own efforts, and they had failed. Christ had already told them that their righteousness could never enter the kingdom of heaven. Now He points out to them the character of the righteousness that all who enter heaven will possess. Throughout the Sermon on the Mount He describes its fruits, and now in one sentence He points out its source and its nature: Be perfect as God is perfect. The law is but a transcript of the character of God. Behold in your heavenly Father a perfect manifestation of the principles which are the foundation of His government.

God is love. Like rays of light from the sun, love and light and joy flow out from Him to all His creatures. It is His nature to give. His very life is the outflow of unselfish love.

"His glory is His children's good;
His joy, His tender Fatherhood."

He tells us to be perfect as He is, in the same manner. We are to be centers of light and blessing to our little circle, even as He is to the universe. We have nothing of ourselves, but the light of His love shines upon us, and we are to reflect its brightness. "In His borrowed goodness good," we may be perfect in our sphere, even as God is perfect in His.

Jesus said, Be perfect as *your Father* is perfect. If you are the children of God you are partakers of His nature, and you cannot but be like Him. Every child lives by the life of his father. If you are God's children, begotten by His Spirit, you live by the life of God. In Christ dwells "all the fullness of the Godhead bodily" (Colossians 2:9); and the life of Jesus is made manifest "in our mortal flesh" (2 Corinthians 4:11). That life in you will produce the same character and manifest the same works as it did in Him. Thus you will be in harmony with every precept of His law; for "the law of the Lord is perfect, restoring the soul." Psalm 19:7, margin. Through love "the righteousness of the law" will be "fulfilled in us, who walk not after the flesh, but after the Spirit." Romans 8:4.

4

The True Motive in Service

"Take heed that ye do not your righteousness before men, to be seen of them."
Matthew 6:1, margin.

The words of Christ on the mount were an expression of that which had been the unspoken teaching of His life, but which the people had failed to comprehend. They could not understand how, having such great power, He neglected to use it in securing what they regarded as the chief good. Their spirit and motives and methods were the opposite of His. While they claimed to be very jealous for the honor of the law, self-glory was the real object which they sought; and Christ would make it manifest to them that the lover of self is a transgressor of the law.

But the principles cherished by the Pharisees are such as are characteristic of humanity in all ages. The spirit of Pharisaism is the spirit of human nature; and as the Saviour showed the contrast between His own spirit and methods and those of the rabbis, His teaching is equally applicable to the people of all time.

In the days of Christ the Pharisees were continually trying to earn the favor of Heaven in order to secure the worldly honor and prosperity which they regarded as the reward of virtue. At the same time they paraded their acts of charity before the people in order to attract their attention and gain a reputation for sanctity.

Jesus rebuked their ostentation, declaring that God does not recognize such service and that the flattery and admiration of the people, which they so eagerly sought, was the only reward they would ever receive.

"When thou doest alms," He said, "let not thy left hand know what thy right hand doeth: that thine alms may be in secret: and thy Father which seeth in secret Himself shall reward thee openly."

In these words Jesus did not teach that acts of kindness should always be kept secret. Paul the apostle, writing by the Holy Spirit, did not conceal the generous self-sacrifice of the Macedonian Christians, but told of the grace that Christ had wrought in them, and thus others were imbued with the same spirit. He also wrote to the church at Corinth and said, "Your zeal hath stirred up very many." 2 Corinthians 9:2, R.V.

Christ's own words make His meaning plain, that in acts of charity the aim should not be to secure praise and honor from men. Real godliness never prompts an effort at display. Those who desire words of praise and flattery, and feed upon them as a sweet morsel, are Christians in name only.

By their good works, Christ's followers are to bring glory, not to themselves, but to Him through whose grace and power they have wrought. It is through the Holy Spirit that every good work is accomplished, and the Spirit is given to glorify, not the receiver, but the Giver. When the light of Christ is shining in the soul, the lips will be filled with praise and thanksgiving to God. Your prayers, your performance of duty, your benevolence, your self-denial, will not be the theme of your thought or conversation. Jesus will be magnified, self will be hidden, and Christ will appear as all in all.

We are to give in sincerity, not to make a show of our good deeds, but from pity and love to the suffering ones. Sincerity of purpose, real kindness of heart, is the motive that Heaven values. The soul that is sincere in its love, wholehearted in its devotion, God regards as more precious than the golden wedge of Ophir.

We are not to think of reward, but of service; yet kindness shown in this spirit will not fail of its recompense. "Thy Father which seeth in secret Himself shall reward thee openly." While it is true that God Himself is the great Reward, that embraces every other, the soul receives and enjoys Him only as it becomes assimilated to Him in character. Only like can appreciate like. It is as we give ourselves to God for the service of humanity that He gives Himself to us.

No one can give place in his own heart and life for the stream of God's blessing to flow to others, without receiving in himself a rich reward. The hillsides and plains that furnish a channel for the mountain streams to reach the sea suffer no loss thereby. That which they give is repaid a hundredfold. For the stream that goes singing on its way leaves behind its gift of verdure and fruitfulness. The grass on its banks is a fresher green, the trees have a richer verdure, the flowers are more abundant. When the earth lies bare and brown under the summer's parching heat, a line of verdure marks the river's course; and the plain that opened her bosom to bear the mountain's treasure to the sea is clothed with freshness and beauty, a witness to the recompense that God's grace imparts to all who give themselves as a channel for its outflow to the world.

This is the blessing of those who show mercy to the poor. The prophet Isaiah says, "Is it not to deal thy bread to the hungry, and that thou bring the poor that are cast out to thy house? when thou seest the naked, that thou cover him; and that thou hide not thyself from thine own flesh? Then shall thy light break forth as the morning, and thine health shall spring forth speedily. . . . And the Lord shall guide thee continually, and satisfy thy soul in drought: . . . and thou shalt be like a watered garden, and like a spring of water, whose waters fail not." Isaiah 58:7-11.

The work of beneficence is twice blessed. While he that gives to the needy blesses others, he himself is blessed in a still greater degree. The grace of Christ in the soul is developing traits of character that are the opposite of selfishness,-traits that will refine, ennoble, and enrich the life. Acts of kindness performed in secret will bind hearts together, and will draw them closer to the heart of Him from whom every generous impulse springs. The little attentions, the small acts of love and self-sacrifice, that flow out from the life as quietly as the fragrance from a flower—these constitute no small share of the blessings and happiness of life. And it will be found at last that the denial of self for the good and happiness of others, however humble and uncommended here, is recognized in heaven as the token of our union with Him, the King of glory, who was rich, yet for our sake became poor.

The deeds of kindness may have been done in secret, but the result upon the character of the doer cannot be hidden. If we work with whole-hearted interest as a follower of Christ, the heart will be in close sympathy with God, and the Spirit of God, moving upon our spirit, will call forth the sacred harmonies of the soul in answer to the divine touch.

He who gives increased talents to those who have made a wise improvement of the gifts entrusted to them is pleased to acknowledge the service of His believing people in the Beloved, through whose grace and strength they have wrought. Those who have sought for the development and perfection of Christian character by exercising their faculties in good works, will, in the world to come, reap that which they have sown. The work begun upon earth will reach its consummation in that higher and holier life to endure throughout eternity.

"When thou prayest, thou shalt not be as the hypocrites are." Matthew 6:5.

The Pharisees had stated hours for prayer; and when, as often came to pass, they would be abroad at the appointed time, they would pause wherever they might be—perhaps in the street or the market place, amid the hurrying throngs of men—and there in a loud voice rehearse their formal prayers. Such worship, offered merely for self-glorification, called forth unsparing rebuke from Jesus. He did not, however, discountenance public prayer, for He Himself prayed with His disciples and in the presence of the multitude. But He teaches that private prayer is not to be made public. In secret devotion our prayers are to reach the ears of none but the prayer-hearing God. No curious ear is to receive the burden of such petitions.

"When thou prayest, enter into thy closet." Have a place for secret prayer. Jesus had select places for communion with God, and so should we. We need often to retire to some spot, however humble, where we can be alone with God.

"Pray to thy Father which is in secret." In the name of Jesus we may come into God's presence with the confidence of a child. No man is needed to act as a mediator. Through Jesus we may open our hearts to God as to one who knows and loves us.

In the secret place of prayer, where no eye but God's can see, no ear but His can hear, we may pour out our most hidden desires and longings to the Father of infinite pity, and in the hush and silence of the soul that voice which never fails to answer the cry of human need will speak to our hearts.

"The Lord is very pitiful, and of tender mercy." James 5:11. He waits with unwearied love to hear the confessions of the wayward and to accept their penitence. He watches for some return of gratitude from us, as the mother watches for the smile of recognition from her beloved child. He would have us understand how earnestly and tenderly His heart yearns over us. He invites us to take our trials to His sympathy, our sorrows to His love, our wounds to His healing, our weakness to His strength, our emptiness to His fullness. Never has one been disappointed who came unto Him. "They looked unto Him, and were lightened: and their faces were not ashamed." Psalm 34:5.

Those who seek God in secret telling the Lord their needs and pleading for help, will not plead in vain. "Thy Father which seeth in secret Himself shall reward thee openly." As we make Christ our daily companion we shall feel that the powers of an unseen world are all around us; and by looking unto Jesus we shall become assimilated to His image. By beholding we become changed. The character is softened, refined, and ennobled for the heavenly kingdom. The sure result of our intercourse and fellowship with our Lord will be to increase piety, purity, and fervor. There will be a growing intelligence in prayer. We are receiving a divine education, and this is illustrated in a life of diligence and zeal.

The soul that turns to God for its help, its support, its power, by daily, earnest prayer, will have noble aspirations, clear perceptions of truth and duty, lofty purposes of action, and a continual hungering and thirsting after righteousness. By maintaining a connection with God, we shall be enabled to diffuse to others, through our association with them, the light, the peace, the serenity, that rule in our hearts. The strength acquired in prayer to God, united with persevering effort in training the mind in thoughtfulness and care-taking, prepares one for daily duties and keeps the spirit in peace under all circumstances.

If we draw near to God, He will put a word in our mouth to speak for Him, even praise unto His name. He will teach us a strain from the song of the angels, even thanksgiving to our heavenly Father. In every act of life, the light and love of an indwelling Saviour will be revealed. Outward troubles cannot reach the life that is lived by faith in the Son of God.

"When ye pray, use not vain repetitions, as the heathen do." Matthew 6:7.

The heathen looked upon their prayers as having in themselves merit to atone for sin. Hence the longer the prayer the greater the merit. If they could become holy by their own efforts they would have something in themselves in which to rejoice, some ground for boasting. This idea of prayer is an outworking of the principle of self-expiation which lies at the foundation of all systems of false religion. The Pharisees had adopted this pagan idea of prayer, and it is by no means extinct in our day,

even among those who profess to be Christians. The repetition of set, customary phrases, when the heart feels no need of God, is of the same character as the "vain repetitions" of the heathen.

Prayer is not an expiation for sin; it has no virtue or merit of itself. All the flowery words at our command are not equivalent to one holy desire. The most eloquent prayers are but idle words if they do not express the true sentiments of the heart. But the prayer that comes from an earnest heart, when the simple wants of the soul are expressed, as we would ask an earthly friend for a favor, expecting it to be granted—this is the prayer of faith. God does not desire our ceremonial compliments, but the unspoken cry of the heart broken and subdued with a sense of its sin and utter weakness finds its way to the Father of all mercy.

"When ye fast, be not, as the hypocrites." Matthew 6:16.

The fasting which the word of God enjoins is something more than a form. It does not consist merely in refusing food, in wearing sackcloth, in sprinkling ashes upon the head. He who fasts in real sorrow for sin will never court display.

The object of the fast which God calls upon us to keep is not to afflict the body for the sin of the soul, but to aid us in perceiving the grievous character of sin, in humbling the heart before God and receiving His pardoning grace. His command to Israel was, "Rend your heart, and not your garments, and turn unto the Lord your God." Joel 2:13.

It will avail nothing for us to do penance or to flatter ourselves that by our own works we shall merit or purchase an inheritance among the saints. When the question was asked Christ, "What shall we do, that we might work the works of God?" He answered, "This is the work of God, that ye believe on Him whom He hath sent." John 6:28, 29. Repentance is turning from self to Christ; and when we receive Christ so that through faith He can live His life in us, good works will be manifest.

Jesus said, "When thou fastest, anoint thine head, and wash thy face; that thou appear not unto men to fast, but unto thy Father which is in secret." Matthew 6:17, 18. Whatever is done to the glory of God is to be done with cheerfulness, not with sadness and gloom. There is nothing gloomy in the religion of Jesus. If Christians give the impression by a mournful attitude that they have been disappointed in their Lord, they misrepresent His character and put arguments into the mouth of His enemies. Though in words they may claim God as their Father, yet in gloom and sorrow they present to the world the aspect of orphans.

Christ desires us to make His service appear

attractive, as it really is. Let the self-denials and the secret heart trials be revealed to the compassionate Saviour. Let the burdens be left at the foot of the cross, and go on your way rejoicing in His love who first loved you. Men may never know of the work going on secretly between the soul and God, but the result of the Spirit's work upon the heart will be manifest to all, for He "which seeth in secret, shall reward thee openly."

"Lay not up for yourselves treasures upon earth." Matthew 6:19.

Treasure laid up on earth will not endure; thieves break through and steal; moth and rust corrupt; fire and storm sweep away your possessions. And "where your treasure is, there will your heart be also." Treasure laid up on the earth will engross the mind to the exclusion of heavenly things.

The love of money was the ruling passion in the Jewish age. Worldliness usurped the place of God and religion in the soul. So it is now. Avaricious greed for wealth exerts such a fascinating, bewitching influence over the life that it results in perverting the nobility and corrupting the humanity of men until they are drowned in perdition. The service of Satan is full of care, perplexity, and wearing labor, and the treasure men toil to accumulate on earth is only for a season.

Jesus said, "Lay up for yourselves treasures in heaven, where neither moth nor rust doth corrupt, and where thieves do not break through nor steal: for where your treasure is, there will your heart be also."

The instruction is to "lay up for *yourselves* treasures in heaven." It is for your own interest to secure heavenly riches. These alone, of all that you possess, are really yours. The treasure laid up in heaven is imperishable. No fire or flood can destroy it, no thief despoil it, no moth or rust corrupt it; for it is in the keeping of God.

This treasure, which Christ esteems as precious above all estimate, is "the riches of the glory of His inheritance in the saints." Ephesians 1:18. The disciples of Christ are called His jewels, His precious and peculiar treasure. He says, "They shall be as the stones of a crown." "I will make a man more precious than fine gold; even a man than the golden wedge of Ophir." Zechariah 9:16; Isaiah 13:12. Christ looks upon His people in their purity and perfection as the reward of all His sufferings, His humiliation, and His love, and the supplement of His glory—Christ, the great Center, from whom radiates all glory.

And we are permitted to unite with Him in the great work of redemption and to be sharers with Him in the riches which His death and suffering have won. The apostle Paul wrote to the Thessalonian Christians: "What is our hope, or joy, or crown of rejoicing? Are not even ye in the presence of our Lord Jesus Christ at His coming? for ye are our glory and joy." 1 Thessalonians 2:19, 20. This is the treasure for which Christ bids us labor. Character is the great harvest of life. And every word or deed that through the grace of Christ shall kindle in one soul an impulse that reaches heavenward, every effort that tends to the formation of a Christlike character, is laying up treasure in heaven.

Where the treasure is, there the heart will be. In every effort to benefit others, we benefit ourselves. He who gives money or time for spreading the gospel enlists his own interest and prayers for the work, and for the souls to be reached through it; his affections go out to others, and he is stimulated to greater devotion to God, that he may be enabled to do them the greatest good.

And at the final day, when the wealth of earth shall perish, he who has laid up treasure in heaven will behold that which his life has gained. If we have given heed to the words of Christ, then, as we gather around the great white throne, we shall see souls who have been saved through our agency, and shall know that one has saved others, and these still others—a large company brought into the haven of rest as the result of our labors, there to lay their crowns at Jesus' feet, and praise Him through the ceaseless ages of eternity. With what joy will the worker for Christ behold these redeemed ones, who share the glory of the Redeemer! How precious will heaven be to those who have been faithful in the work of saving souls!

"If ye then be risen with Christ, seek those things which are above, where Christ sitteth on the right hand of God." Colossians 3:1.

"If . . . thine eye be single, thy whole body shall be full of light." Matthew 6:22.

Singleness of purpose, wholehearted devotion to God, is the condition pointed out by the Saviour's words. Let the purpose be sincere and unwavering to discern the truth and to obey it at whatever cost, and you will receive divine enlightenment. Real piety begins when all compromise with sin is at an end. Then the language of the heart will be that of the apostle Paul: "This one thing I do, forgetting those things which are behind, and reaching forth unto those things which are before, I press toward the mark for the prize of the high calling of God in Christ Jesus." "I count all things but loss for the excellency of the knowledge of Christ Jesus my Lord: for whom I have suffered the loss of all things, and do count them but dung, that I may win Christ." Philippians 3:13, 14, 8.

But when the eye is blinded by the love of self, there is only darkness. "If thine eye be evil, thy whole body shall be full of darkness." It was this fearful darkness that wrapped the 92 Jews in stubborn unbelief, making it impossible for them to appreciate the character and mission of Him who came to save them from their sins.

Yielding to temptation begins in permitting the mind to waver, to be inconstant in your trust in God. If we do not choose to give ourselves fully to God then we are in darkness. When we make any reserve we are leaving open a door through which Satan can enter to lead us astray by his temptations. He knows that if he can obscure our vision, so that the eye of faith cannot see God, there will be no barrier against sin.

The prevalence of a sinful desire shows the delusion of the soul. Every indulgence of that desire strengthens the soul's aversion to God. In following the path of Satan's choosing, we are encompassed by the shadows of evil, and every step leads into deeper darkness and increases the blindness of the heart.

The same law obtains in the spiritual as in the natural world. He who abides in darkness will at last lose the power of vision. He is shut in by a deeper than midnight blackness; and to him the brightest noontide can bring no light. He "walketh in darkness, and knoweth not whither he goeth, because that darkness hath blinded his eyes." 1 John 2:11. Through persistently cherishing evil, willfully disregarding the pleadings of divine love, the sinner loses the love for good, the desire for God, the very capacity to receive the light of heaven. The invitation of mercy is still full of love, the light is shining as brightly as when it first dawned upon his soul; but the voice falls on deaf ears, the light on blinded eyes.

93 No soul is ever finally deserted of God, given up to his own ways, so long as there is any hope of his salvation. "Man turns from God, not God from him." Our heavenly Father follows us with appeals and warnings and assurances of compassion, until further opportunities and privileges would be wholly in vain. The responsibility rests with the sinner. By resisting the Spirit of God today, he prepares the way for a second resistance of light when it comes with mightier power. Thus he passes on from one stage of resistance to another, until at last the light will fail to impress, and he will cease to respond in any measure to the Spirit of God. Then even "the light that is in thee" has become darkness. The very truth we do know has become so perverted as to increase the blindness of the soul.

"No man can serve two masters."
Matthew 6:24.

Christ does not say that man will not or shall not serve two masters, but that he *cannot*. The interests of God and the interests of mammon have no union or sympathy. Just where the conscience of the Christian warns him to forbear, to deny himself, to stop, just there the worldling steps over the line, to indulge his selfish propensities. On one side of the line is the self-denying follower of Christ; on the other side is the self-indulgent world lover, pandering to fashion, engaging in frivolity, and pampering himself in forbidden pleasure. On that side of the line the Christian cannot go.

No one can occupy a neutral position; there is 94 no middle class, who neither love God nor serve the enemy of righteousness. Christ is to live in His human agents and work through their faculties and act through their capabilities. Their will must be submitted to His will; they must act with His Spirit. Then it is no more they that live, but Christ that lives in them. He who does not give himself wholly to God is under the control of another power, listening to another voice, whose suggestions are of an entirely different character. Half-and-half service places the human agent on the side of the enemy as a successful ally of the hosts of darkness. When men who claim to be soldiers of Christ engage with the confederacy of Satan, and help along his side, they prove themselves enemies of Christ. They betray sacred trusts. They form a link between Satan and the true soldiers, so that through these agencies the enemy is constantly working to steal away the hearts of Christ's soldiers.

The strongest bulwark of vice in our world is not the iniquitous life of the abandoned sinner or the degraded outcast; it is that life which otherwise appears virtuous, honorable, and noble, but in which one sin is fostered, one vice indulged. To the soul that is struggling in secret against some giant temptation, trembling upon the very verge of the precipice, such an example is one of the most powerful enticements to sin. He who, endowed with high conceptions of life and truth and honor, does yet willfully transgress one precept of God's holy law, has perverted His noble gifts into a lure to sin. Genius, talent, sympathy, even generous and kindly deeds, may become decoys of Satan to entice 95 other souls over the precipice of ruin for this life and the life to come.

"Love not the world, neither the things that are in the world. If any man love the world, the love of the Father is not in him. For all that is in the world, the lust of the flesh, and the lust of the eyes, and the pride of life, is not of the Father, but is of the world." 1 John 2:15, 16.

"Be not anxious." Matthew 6:25, R.V.

He who has given you life knows your need of food to sustain it. He who created the body is not unmindful of your need of raiment. Will not He who has bestowed the greater gift bestow also what is needed to make it complete?

Jesus pointed His hearers to the birds as they warbled their carols of praise, unencumbered with thoughts of care, for "they sow not, neither do they reap;" and yet the great Father provides for their needs. And He asks, "Are not ye of much more value than they?" R.V.

"No sparrow falls without His care,
No soul bows low but Jesus knows;
For He is with us everywhere,
And marks each bitter tear that flows.
And He will never, never, never
Forsake the soul that trusts Him ever."

96   The hillsides and the fields were bright with flowers, and, pointing to them in the dewy freshness of the morning, Jesus said, "Consider the lilies of the field, how they grow." The graceful forms and delicate hues of the plants and flowers may be copied by human skill, but what touch can impart life to even one flower or blade of grass? Every wayside blossom owes its being to the same power that set the starry worlds on high. Through all created things thrills one pulse of life from the great heart of God. The flowers of the field are clothed by His hand in richer robes than have ever graced the forms of earthly kings. And "if God so clothe the grass of the field, which today is, and tomorrow is cast into the oven, shall He not much more clothe you, O ye of little faith?"

It is He who made the flowers and who gave to the sparrow its song who says, "Consider the lilies," "Behold the birds." R.V. In the loveliness of the things of nature you may learn more of the wisdom of God than the schoolmen know. On the lily's petals, God has written a message for you, written in language that your heart can read only as it unlearns the lessons of distrust and selfishness and corroding care. Why has He given you the singing birds and the gentle blossoms, but from the overflowing love of a Father's heart, that would brighten and gladden your path of life? All that was needed for existence would have been yours without the flowers and birds, but God was not content to provide what would suffice for mere existence. He has filled earth and air and sky with glimpses of beauty to tell you of His loving thought for you. The beauty of all created things is but a gleam from the shining of His glory. If He has lavished

97   such infinite skill upon the things of nature, for your happiness and joy, can you doubt that He

will give you every needed blessing?

"Consider the lilies." Every flower that opens its petals to the sunshine obeys the same great laws that guide the stars, and how simple and beautiful and how sweet its life! Through the flowers, God would call our attention to the loveliness of Christlike character. He who has given such beauty to the blossoms desires far more that the soul should be clothed with the beauty of the character of Christ.

Consider, says Jesus, how the lilies grow; how, springing from the cold, dark earth, or from the mud of the river bed, the plants unfold in loveliness and fragrance. Who would dream of the possibilities of beauty in the rough brown bulb of the lily? But when the life of God, hidden therein, unfolds at His call in the rain and the sunshine, men marvel at the vision of grace and loveliness. Even so will the life of God unfold in every human soul that will yield itself to the ministry of His grace, which, free as the rain and the sunshine, comes with its benediction to all. It is the word of God that creates the flowers, and the same word will produce in you the graces of His Spirit.

God's law is the law of love. He has surrounded you with beauty to teach you that you are not placed on earth merely to delve for self, to dig and build, to toil and spin, but to make life bright and joyous and beautiful with the love of Christ—like the flowers, to gladden other lives by the ministry of love.

Fathers and mothers, let your children learn from the flowers. Take them with you into garden and field and under the leafy trees, and 98 teach them to read in nature the message of God's love. Let the thoughts of Him be linked with bird and flower and tree. Lead the children to see in every pleasant and beautiful thing an expression of God's love for them. Recommend your religion to them by its pleasantness. Let the law of kindness be in your lips.

Teach the children that because of God's great love their natures may be changed and brought into harmony with His. Teach them that He would have their lives beautiful with the graces of the flowers. Teach them, as they gather the sweet blossoms, that He who made the flowers is more beautiful than they. Thus the tendrils of their hearts will be entwined about Him. He who is "altogether lovely" will become to them as a daily companion and familiar friend, and their lives will be transformed into the image of His purity.

"Seek ye first the kingdom of God." Matthew 6:33.

The people who listened to the words of Christ were still anxiously watching for some announcement of the earthly kingdom. While

Jesus was opening to them the treasures of heaven, the question uppermost in many minds was, How will a connection with Him advance our prospects in the world? Jesus shows that in making the things of the world their supreme anxiety they were like the heathen nations about them, living as if there were no God, whose tender care is over His creatures.

"All these things," said Jesus, "do the nations of the world seek after." "Your heavenly Father knoweth that ye have need of all these things. But seek ye first the kingdom of God, and His righteousness; and all these things shall be added unto you." Luke 12:30; Matt. 6:32, 33. I have come to open to you the kingdom of love and righteousness and peace. Open your hearts to receive this kingdom, and make its service your highest interest. Though it is a spiritual kingdom, fear not that your needs for this life will be uncared-for. If you give yourself to God's service, He who has all power in heaven and earth will provide for your needs.

Jesus does not release us from the necessity of effort, but He teaches that we are to make Him first and last and best in everything. We are to engage in no business, follow no pursuit, seek no pleasure, that would hinder the outworking of His righteousness in our character and life. Whatever we do is to be done heartily, as unto the Lord.

Jesus, while He dwelt on earth, dignified life in all its details by keeping before men the glory of God, and by subordinating everything to the will of His Father. If we follow His example, His assurance to us is that all things needful in this life "shall be added." Poverty or wealth, sickness or health, simplicity or wisdom-all are provided for in the promise of His grace.

God's everlasting arm encircles the soul that turns to Him for aid, however feeble that soul may be. The precious things of the hills shall perish, but the soul that lives for God shall abide with Him. "The world passeth away, and the lust thereof; but he that doeth the will of God abideth forever." 1 John 2:17. The city of God will open its golden gates to receive him who learned while on earth to lean on God for guidance and wisdom, for comfort and hope, amid loss and affliction. The songs of the angels will welcome him there, and for him the tree of life shall yield its fruit. "The mountains shall depart, and the hills be removed; but My kindness shall not depart from thee, neither shall the covenant of My peace be removed, saith the Lord that hath mercy on thee." Isaiah 54:10.

"Be not therefore anxious for the morrow. . . . Sufficient unto the day is the evil thereof." Matthew 6:34, R.V.

If you have given yourself to God, to do His work, you have no need to be anxious for tomorrow. He whose servant you are, knows the end from the beginning. The events of tomorrow, which are hidden from your view, are open to the eyes of Him who is omnipotent.

When we take into our hands the management of things with which we have to do, and depend upon our own wisdom for success, we are taking a burden which God has not given us, and are trying to bear it without His aid. We are taking upon ourselves the responsibility that belongs to God, and thus are really putting ourselves in His place. We may well have anxiety and anticipate danger and loss, for it is certain to befall us. But when we really believe that God loves us and means to do us good we shall cease to worry about the future. We shall trust God as a child trusts a loving parent. Then our troubles and torments will disappear, for our will is swallowed up in the will of God.

Christ has given us no promise of help in bearing today the burdens of tomorrow. He has said, "My grace is sufficient for thee" (2 Corinthians 12:9); but, like the manna given in the wilderness, His grace is bestowed daily, for the day's need. Like the hosts of Israel in their pilgrim life, we may find morning by morning the bread of heaven for the day's supply.

One day alone is ours, and during this day we are to live for God. For this one day we are to place in the hand of Christ, in solemn service, all our purposes and plans, casting all our care upon Him, for He careth for us. "I know the thoughts that I think toward you, saith the Lord, thoughts of peace, and not of evil, to give you an expected end." "In returning and rest shall ye be saved; in quietness and in confidence shall be your strength." Jeremiah 29:11; Isaiah 30:15.

If you will seek the Lord and be converted every day; if you will of your own spiritual choice be free and joyous in God; if with gladsome consent of heart to His gracious call you come wearing the yoke of Christ,—the yoke of obedience and service,—all your murmurings will be stilled, all your difficulties will be removed, all the perplexing problems that now confront you will be solved.

5

The Lord's Prayer

"After this manner therefore pray ye." Matthew 6:9.

The Lord's Prayer was twice given by our Saviour, first to the multitude in the Sermon on the Mount, and again, some months later, to the disciples alone. The disciples had been for a short time absent from their Lord, when on their return they found Him absorbed in communion with God. Seeming unconscious of their presence, He continued praying aloud. The Saviour's face was irradiated with a celestial brightness. He seemed to be in the very presence of the Unseen, and there was a living power in His words as of one who spoke with God.

The hearts of the listening disciples were deeply moved. They had marked how often He spent long hours in solitude in communion with His Father. His days were passed in ministry to the crowds that pressed upon Him, and in unveiling the treacherous sophistry of the rabbis, and this incessant labor often left Him so utterly wearied that His mother and brothers, and even His disciples, had feared that His life would be sacrificed. But as He returned from the hours of prayer that closed the toilsome day, they marked the look of peace upon His face, the sense of refreshment that seemed to pervade His presence. It was from hours spent with God that He came forth, morning by morning, to bring the light of heaven to men. The disciples had come to connect His hours of prayer with the power of His words and works. Now, as they listened to His supplication, their hearts were awed and humbled. As He ceased praying, it was with a conviction of their own deep need that they exclaimed, "Lord, teach us to pray." Luke 11:1.

Jesus gives them no new form of prayer. That which He has before taught them He repeats, as if He would say, You need to understand what I have already given. It has a depth of meaning you have not yet fathomed.

The Saviour does not, however, restrict us to the use of these exact words. As one with humanity, He presents His own ideal of prayer, words so simple that they may be adopted by the little child, yet so comprehensive that their significance can never be fully grasped by the greatest minds. We are taught to come to God with our tribute of thanksgiving, to make known our wants, to confess our sins, and to claim His mercy in accordance with His promise.

"When ye pray, say Our Father." Luke 11:2.

Jesus teaches us to call *His* Father our Father. He is not ashamed to call us brethren. Hebrews 2:11. So ready, so eager, is the Saviour's heart to welcome us as members of the family of God, that in the very first words we are to use in approaching God He places the assurance of our divine relationship, "Our Father."

Here is the announcement of that wonderful truth, so full of encouragement and comfort, that God loves us as He loves His Son. This is what Jesus said in His last prayer for His disciples, Thou "hast loved them, as Thou hast loved Me." John 17:23.

The world that Satan has claimed and has ruled over with cruel tyranny, the Son of God has, by one vast achievement, encircled in His love and connected again with the throne of Jehovah. Cherubim and seraphim, and the unnumbered hosts of all the unfallen worlds, sang anthems of praise to God and the Lamb when this triumph was assured. They rejoiced that the way of salvation had been opened to the fallen race and that the earth would be redeemed from the curse of sin. How much more should those rejoice who are the objects of such amazing love!

How can we ever be in doubt and uncertainty, and feel that we are orphans? It was in behalf of those who had transgressed the law that Jesus took upon Him human nature; He became like unto us, that we might have everlasting peace and assurance. We have an Advocate in the heavens, and whoever accepts Him as a personal Saviour is not left an orphan to bear the burden of his own sins.

"Beloved, now are we the sons of God." "And if children, then heirs; heirs of God, and joint heirs with Christ; if so be that we suffer with Him, that we may be also glorified together." "It doth not yet appear what we shall be: but we know that, when He shall appear, we shall be like Him; for we shall see Him as He is." 1 John 3:2; Romans 8:17.

The very first step in approaching God is to know and believe the love that He has to us (1 John 4:16); for it is through the drawing of His love that we are led to come to Him.

The perception of God's love works the renunciation of selfishness. In calling God our Father, we recognize all His children as our brethren. We are all a part of the great web of humanity, all members of one family. In our petitions we are to include our neighbors as well as ourselves. No one prays aright who seeks a blessing for himself alone.

The infinite God, said Jesus, makes it your privilege to approach Him by the name of Father. Understand all that this implies. No earthly parent ever pleaded so earnestly with an erring child as He who made you pleads with the transgressor. No human, loving interest ever followed the impenitent with such tender invitations. God dwells in every abode; He hears every word that is spoken, listens to every prayer that is offered, tastes the sorrows and disappointments of every soul, regards the treatment that is given to father, mother, sister, friend, and neighbor. He cares for our necessities, and His love and mercy and grace are continually flowing to satisfy our need.

But if you call God your Father you acknowledge yourselves His children, to be guided by

His wisdom and to be obedient in all things, knowing that His love is changeless. You will accept His plan for your life. As children of God, you will hold His honor, His character, His family, His work, as the objects of your highest interest. It will be your joy to recognize and honor your relation to your Father and to every member of His family. You will rejoice to do any act, however humble, that will tend to His glory or to the well-being of your kindred.

"Which art in heaven." He to whom Christ bids us look as "our Father" "is in the heavens: He hath done whatsoever He hath pleased." In His care we may safely rest, saying, "What time I am afraid, I will trust in Thee." Psalms 115:3; 56:3.

"Hallowed be Thy name." Matthew 6:9.

To hallow the name of the Lord requires that the words in which we speak of the Supreme Being be uttered with reverence. "Holy and reverend is His name." Psalm 111:9. We are never in any manner to treat lightly the titles or appellations of the Deity. In prayer we enter the audience chamber of the Most High; and we should come before Him with holy awe. The angels veil their faces in His presence. The cherubim and the bright and holy seraphim approach His throne with solemn reverence. How much more should we, finite, sinful beings, come in a reverent manner before the Lord, our Maker!

But to hallow the name of the Lord means much more than this. We may, like the Jews in Christ's day, manifest the greatest outward reverence for God, and yet profane His name continually. "The name of the Lord" is "merciful and gracious, long-suffering, and abundant in goodness and truth, . . . forgiving iniquity and transgression and sin." Exodus 34:5-7. Of the church of Christ it is written, "This is the name wherewith she shall be called, The Lord our Righteousness." Jeremiah 33:16. This name is put upon every follower of Christ. It is the heritage of the child of God. The family are called after the Father. The prophet Jeremiah, in the time of Israel's sore distress and tribulation, prayed, "We are called by Thy name; leave us not." Jeremiah 14:9.

This name is hallowed by the angels of heaven, by the inhabitants of unfallen worlds. When you pray, "Hallowed be Thy name," you ask that it may be hallowed in this world, hallowed in you. God has acknowledged you before men and angels as His child; pray that you may do no dishonor to the "worthy name by which ye are called." James 2:7. God sends you into the world as His representative. In every act of life you are to make manifest the name of God. This petition calls upon you to possess His character. You cannot hallow His name, you cannot represent Him to the world, unless in life and charac-

ter you represent the very life and character of God. This you can do only through the acceptance of the grace and righteousness of Christ.

"Thy kingdom come." Matthew 6:10.

God is our Father, who loves and cares for us as His children; He is also the great King of the universe. The interests of His kingdom are our interests, and we are to work for its upbuilding.

The disciples of Christ were looking for the immediate coming of the kingdom of His glory, but in giving them this prayer Jesus taught that the kingdom was not then to be established. They were to pray for its coming as an event yet future. But this petition was also an assurance to them. While they were not to behold the coming of the kingdom in their day, the fact that Jesus bade them pray for it is evidence that in God's own time it will surely come.

The kingdom of God's grace is now being established, as day by day hearts that have been full of sin and rebellion yield to the sovereignty of His love. But the full establishment of the kingdom of His glory will not take place until the second coming of Christ to this world. "The kingdom and dominion, and the greatness of the kingdom under the whole heaven," is to be given to "the people of the saints of the Most High." Daniel 7:27. They shall inherit the kingdom prepared for them "from the foundation of the world." Matthew 25:34. And Christ will take to Himself His great power and will reign.

The heavenly gates are again to be lifted up, and with ten thousand times ten thousand and thousands of thousands of holy ones, our Saviour will come forth as King of kings and Lord of lords. Jehovah Immanuel "shall be king over all the earth: in that day shall there be one Lord, and His name one." "The tabernacle of God" shall be with men, "and He will dwell with them, and they shall be His people, and God Himself shall be with them, and be their God." Zechariah 14:9; Revelation 21:3.

But before that coming, Jesus said, "This gospel of the kingdom shall be preached in all the world for a witness unto all nations." Matthew 24:14. His kingdom will not come until the good tidings of His grace have been carried to all the earth. Hence, as we give ourselves to God, and win other souls to Him, we hasten the coming of His kingdom. Only those who devote themselves to His service, saying, "Here am I; send me" (Isaiah 6:8), to open blind eyes, to turn men "from darkness to light and from the power of Satan unto God, that they may receive forgiveness of sins and inheritance among them which are sanctified" (Acts 26:18)—they alone pray in sincerity, "Thy kingdom come."

"Thy will be done in earth, as it is in heaven." Matthew 6:10.

The will of God is expressed in the precepts of His holy law, and the principles of this law are the principles of heaven. The angels of heaven attain unto no higher knowledge than to know the will of God, and to do His will is the highest service that can engage their powers.

But in heaven, service is not rendered in the spirit of legality. When Satan rebelled against the law of Jehovah, the thought that there was a law came to the angels almost as an awakening to something unthought of. In their ministry the angels are not as servants, but as sons. There is perfect unity between them and their Creator. Obedience is to them no drudgery. Love for God makes their service a joy. So in every soul wherein Christ, the hope of glory, dwells, His words are re-echoed, "I delight to do Thy will, O My God: yea, Thy law is within My heart." Psalm 40:8.

110 The petition, "Thy will be done in earth, as it is in heaven," is a prayer that the reign of evil on this earth may be ended, that sin may be forever destroyed, and the kingdom of righteousness be established. Then in earth as in heaven will be fulfilled "all the good pleasure of His goodness." 2 Thessalonians 1:11.

"Give us this day our daily bread." Matthew 6:11.

The first half of the prayer Jesus has taught us is in regard to the name and kingdom and will of God—that His name may be honored, His kingdom established, His will performed. When you have thus made God's service your first interest, you may ask with confidence that your own needs may be supplied. If you have renounced self and given yourself to Christ you are a member of the family of God, and everything in the Father's house is for you. All the treasures of God are opened to you, both the world that now is and that which is to come. The ministry of angels, the gift of His Spirit, the labors of His servants—all are for you. The world, with everything in it, is yours so far as it can do you good. Even the enmity of the wicked will prove a blessing by disciplining you for heaven. If "ye are Christ's," "all things are yours." 1 Corinthians 3:23, 21.

But you are as a child who is not yet placed in control of his inheritance. God does not entrust to you your precious possession, lest Satan by his wily arts should beguile you, as he did the first pair in Eden. Christ holds it for you, safe beyond the spoiler's reach. Like the child, you shall receive day by day what is required for the day's need. Every day you are to pray, "Give us this day our daily bread." Be not dismayed if you have not sufficient for tomorrow. You have the assurance of His promise, "So shalt thou dwell in the land, and verily thou shalt be fed." David says, "I have been young, and now am old; yet have I not seen the righteous forsaken, nor his seed begging bread." Psalm 37:3, 25. That God who sent the ravens to feed Elijah by the brook Cherith will not pass by one of His faithful, self-sacrificing children. Of him that walketh righteously it is written: "Bread shall be given him; his waters shall be sure." "They shall not be ashamed in the evil time: and in the days of famine they shall be satisfied." "He that spared not His own Son, but delivered Him up for us all, how shall He not with Him also freely give us all things?" Isaiah 33:16; Psalm 37:19; Romans 8:32. He who lightened the cares and anxieties of His widowed mother and helped her to provide for the household at Nazareth, sympathizes with every mother in her struggle to provide her children food. He who had compassion on the multitude because they "fainted, and were scattered abroad" (Matthew 9:36), still has compassion on the suffering poor. His hand is stretched out toward them in blessing; and in the very prayer which He gave His disciples, He teaches us to remember the poor.

When we pray, "Give us this day our daily bread," we ask for others as well as ourselves. And we acknowledge that what God gives us is not for ourselves alone. God gives to us in trust, 112 that we may feed the hungry. Of His goodness He has prepared for the poor. Psalm 68:10. And He says, "When thou makest a dinner or a supper, call not thy friends, nor thy brethren, neither thy kinsmen, nor thy rich neighbors. . . . But when thou makest a feast, call the poor, the maimed, the lame, the blind: and thou shalt be blessed; for they cannot recompense thee: for thou shalt be recompensed at the resurrection of the just." Luke 14:12-14.

"God is able to make all grace abound toward you; that ye, always having all sufficiency in all things, may abound to every good work." "He which soweth sparingly shall reap also sparingly; and he which soweth bountifully shall reap also bountifully." 2 Corinthians 9:8, 6.

The prayer for daily bread includes not only food to sustain the body, but that spiritual bread which will nourish the soul unto life everlasting. Jesus bids us, "Labor not for the meat which perisheth, but for that meat which endureth unto everlasting life." John 6:27. He says, "I am the living bread which came down from heaven: if any man eat of this bread, he shall live forever." Verse 51. Our Saviour is the bread of life, and it is by beholding His love, by receiving it into the soul, that we feed upon the bread which came down from heaven.

We receive Christ through His word, and the Holy Spirit is given to open the word of God to our understanding, and bring home its truths to our hearts. We are to pray day by day that as we read His word, God will send His Spirit to 113 reveal to us the truth that will strengthen our souls for the day's need.

In teaching us to ask every day for what we need—both temporal and spiritual blessings—God has a purpose to accomplish for our good. He would have us realize our dependence upon His constant care, for He is seeking to draw us into communion with Himself. In this communion with Christ, through prayer and the study of the great and precious truths of His word, we shall as hungry souls be fed; as those that thirst, we shall be refreshed at the fountain of life.

"Forgive us our sins; for we also forgive everyone that is indebted to us." Luke 11:4.

Jesus teaches that we can receive forgiveness from God only as we forgive others. It is the love of God that draws us unto Him, and that love cannot touch our hearts without creating love for our brethren.

After completing the Lord's Prayer, Jesus added: "If ye forgive men their trespasses, your heavenly Father will also forgive you: but if ye forgive not men their trespasses, neither will your Father forgive your trespasses." He who is unforgiving cuts off the very channel through which alone he can receive mercy from God. We should not think that unless those who have injured us confess the wrong we are justified in withholding from them our forgiveness. It is their part, no doubt, to humble their hearts by repentance and confession; but we are to have a 14 spirit of compassion toward those who have trespassed against us, whether or not they confess their faults. However sorely they may have wounded us, we are not to cherish our grievances and sympathize with ourselves over our injuries; but as we hope to be pardoned for our offenses against God we are to pardon all who have done evil to us.

But forgiveness has a broader meaning than many suppose. When God gives the promise that He "will abundantly pardon," He adds, as if the meaning of that promise exceeded all that we could comprehend: "My thoughts are not your thoughts, neither are your ways My ways, saith the Lord. For as the heavens are higher than the earth, so are My ways higher than your ways, and My thoughts than your thoughts." Isaiah 55:7-9. God's forgiveness is not merely a judicial act by which He sets us free from condemnation. It is not only forgiveness *for* sin, but reclaiming *from* sin. It is the outflow of redeeming love that transforms the heart. David had the true conception of forgiveness when he prayed, "Create in me a clean heart, O God; and renew a right spirit within me." Psalm 51:10. And again he says, "As far as the east is from the west, so

far hath He removed our transgressions from us." Psalm 103:12.

God in Christ gave Himself for our sins. He suffered the cruel death of the cross, bore for us the burden of guilt, "the just for the unjust," that He might reveal to us His love and draw us to Himself. And He says, "Be ye kind one to another, tenderhearted, forgiving each other, even as God also in Christ forgave you." Ephesians 4:32, R.V. Let Christ, the divine Life, 115 dwell in you and through you reveal the heavenborn love that will inspire hope in the hopeless and bring heaven's peace to the sin-stricken heart. As we come to God, this is the condition which meets us at the threshold, that, receiving mercy from Him, we yield ourselves to reveal His grace to others.

The one thing essential for us in order that we may receive and impart the forgiving love of God is to know and believe the love that He has to us. 1 John 4:16. Satan is working by every deception he can command, in order that we may not discern that love. He will lead us to think that our mistakes and transgressions have been so grievous that the Lord will not have respect unto our prayers and will not bless and save us. In ourselves we can see nothing but weakness, nothing to recommend us to God, and Satan tells us that it is of no use; we cannot remedy our defects of character. When we try to come to God, the enemy will whisper, It is of no use for you to pray; did not you do that evil thing? Have you not sinned against God and violated your own conscience? But we may tell the enemy that "the blood of Jesus Christ His Son cleanseth us from all sin." 1 John 1:7. When we feel that we have sinned and cannot pray, it is then the time to pray. Ashamed we may be and deeply humbled, but we must pray and believe. "This is a faithful saying, and worthy of all acceptation, that Christ Jesus came into the world to save sinners; of whom I am chief." 1 Timothy 1:15. Forgiveness, reconciliation with God, comes to us, not as a reward for our works, it is not bestowed because of the 116 merit of sinful men, but it is a gift unto us, having in the spotless righteousness of Christ its foundation for bestowal.

We should not try to lessen our guilt by excusing sin. We must accept God's estimate of sin, and that is heavy indeed. Calvary alone can reveal the terrible enormity of sin. If we had to bear our own guilt, it would crush us. But the sinless One has taken our place; though undeserving, He has borne our iniquity. "If we confess our sins," God "is faithful and just to forgive us our sins, and to cleanse us from all unrighteousness." 1 John 1:9. Glorious truth!—just to His own law, and yet the Justifier of all that believe in Jesus. "Who is a God like unto Thee, that pardoneth iniquity, and passeth by the transgression of the remnant of His heritage? He retaineth not His anger forever, because He delighteth in mercy." Micah 7:18.

"Bring us not into temptation, but deliver us from the evil one." Matthew 6:13, R.V.

Temptation is enticement to sin, and this does not proceed from God, but from Satan and from the evil of our own hearts. "God cannot be tempted with evil, and He Himself tempteth no man." James 1:13, R.V.

Satan seeks to bring us into temptation, that the evil of our characters may be revealed before men and angels, that he may claim us as his own. In the symbolic prophecy of Zechariah, Satan is seen standing at the right hand of the Angel of the Lord, accusing Joshua, the high priest, who is clothed in filthy garments, and resisting the work that the Angel desires to do for him. This represents the attitude of Satan toward every soul whom Christ is seeking to draw unto Himself. The enemy leads us into sin, and then he accuses us before the heavenly universe as unworthy of the love of God. But "the Lord said unto Satan, The Lord rebuke thee, O Satan; even the Lord that hath chosen Jerusalem rebuke thee: is not this a brand plucked out of the fire?" And unto Joshua He said, "Behold, I have caused thine iniquity to pass from thee, and I will clothe thee with change of raiment." Zechariah 3:1-4.

God in His great love is seeking to develop in us the precious graces of His Spirit. He permits us to encounter obstacles, persecution, and hardships, not as a curse, but as the greatest blessing of our lives. Every temptation resisted, every trial bravely borne, gives us a new experience and advances us in the work of character building. The soul that through divine power resists temptation reveals to the world and to the heavenly universe the efficiency of the grace of Christ.

But while we are not to be dismayed by trial, bitter though it be, we should pray that God will not permit us to be brought where we shall be drawn away by the desires of our own evil hearts. In offering the prayer that Christ has given, we surrender ourselves to the guidance of God, asking Him to lead us in safe paths. We cannot offer this prayer in sincerity, and yet decide to walk in any way of our own choosing. We shall wait for His hand to lead us; we shall listen to His voice, saying, "This is the way, walk ye in it." Isaiah 30:21.

It is not safe for us to linger to contemplate the advantages to be reaped through yielding to Satan's suggestions. Sin means dishonor and disaster to every soul that indulges in it; but it is blinding and deceiving in its nature, and it will entice us with flattering presentations. If we venture on Satan's ground we have no assurance of protection from his power. So far as in us lies, we should close every avenue by which the tempter may find access to us.

The prayer, "Bring us not into temptation," is itself a promise. If we commit ourselves to God we have the assurance, He "will not suffer you to be tempted above that ye are able; but will with the temptation also make a way to escape, that ye may be able to bear it." 1 Corinthians 10:13.

The only safeguard against evil is the indwelling of Christ in the heart through faith in His righteousness. It is because selfishness exists in our hearts that temptation has power over us. But when we behold the great love of God, selfishness appears to us in its hideous and repulsive character, and we desire to have it expelled from the soul. As the Holy Spirit glorifies Christ, our hearts are softened and subdued, the temptation loses its power, and the grace of Christ transforms the character.

Christ will never abandon the soul for whom He has died. The soul may leave Him and be overwhelmed with temptation, but Christ can never turn from one for whom He has paid the ransom of His own life. Could our spiritual vision be quickened, we should see souls bowed under oppression and burdened with grief, pressed as a cart beneath sheaves and ready to die in discouragement. We should see angels flying swiftly to aid these tempted ones, who are standing as on the brink of a precipice. The angels from heaven force back the hosts of evil that encompass these souls, and guide them to plant their feet on the sure foundation. The battles waging between the two armies are as real as those fought by the armies of this world, and on the issue of the spiritual conflict eternal destinies depend.

To us, as to Peter, the word is spoken, "Satan hath desired to have you, that he may sift you as wheat: but I have prayed for thee, that thy faith fail not." Luke 22:31, 32. Thank God, we are not left alone. He who "so loved the world, that He gave His only-begotten Son, that whosoever believeth in Him should not perish, but have everlasting life" (John 3:16), will not desert us in the battle with the adversary of God and man. "Behold," He says, "I give unto you power to tread on serpents and scorpions, and over all the power of the enemy: and nothing shall by any means hurt you." Luke 10:19.

Live in contact with the living Christ, and He will hold you firmly by a hand that will never let go. Know and believe the love that God has to us, and you are secure; that love is a fortress impregnable to all the delusions and assaults of Satan. "The name of the Lord is a strong tower: the righteous runneth into it, and is safe." Proverbs 18:10.

¹²⁰

"Thine is the kingdom, and the power, and the glory." Matthew 6:13.

The last like the first sentence of the Lord's Prayer, points to our Father as above all power and authority and every name that is named. The Saviour beheld the years that stretched out before His disciples, not, as they had dreamed, lying in the sunshine of worldly prosperity and honor, but dark with the tempests of human hatred and satanic wrath. Amid national strife and ruin, the steps of the disciples would be beset with perils, and often their hearts would be oppressed by fear. They were to see Jerusalem a desolation, the temple swept away, its worship forever ended, and Israel scattered to all lands, like wrecks on a desert shore. Jesus said, "Ye shall hear of wars and rumors of wars." "Nation shall rise against nation, and kingdom against kingdom: and there shall be famines, and pestilences, and earthquakes, in divers places. All these are the beginning of sorrows." Matthew 24:6-8. Yet Christ's followers were not to fear that their hope was lost or that God had forsaken the earth. The power and the glory belong unto Him whose great purposes would still move on unthwarted toward their consummation. In the prayer that breathes their daily wants, the disciples of Christ were directed to look above all the power and dominion of evil, unto the Lord their God, whose kingdom ruleth over all and who is their Father and everlasting Friend.

The ruin of Jerusalem was a symbol of the final ruin that shall overwhelm the world. The prophecies that received a partial fulfillment in ¹²¹ the overthrow of Jerusalem have a more direct application to the last days. We are now standing on the threshold of great and solemn events. A crisis is before us, such as the world has never witnessed. And sweetly to us, as to the first disciples, comes the assurance that God's kingdom ruleth over all. The program of coming events is in the hands of our Maker. The Majesty of heaven has the destiny of nations, as well as the concerns of His church, in His own charge. The divine Instructor is saying to every agent in the accomplishment of His plans, as He said to Cyrus, "I girded thee, though thou hast not known Me." Isaiah 45:5.

In the vision of the prophet Ezekiel there was the appearance of a hand beneath the wings of the cherubim. This is to teach His servants that it is divine power which gives them success. Those whom God employs as His messengers are not to feel that His work is dependent upon them. Finite beings are not left to carry this burden of responsibility. He who slumbers not, who is continually at work for the accomplishment of His designs, will carry forward His own work. He will thwart the purposes of wicked men, and will bring to confusion the counsels of those who plot mischief against His people. He who is the King, the Lord of hosts, sitteth between the cherubim, and amid the strife and tumult of nations He guards His children still. He who ruleth in the heavens is our Saviour. He measures every trial, He watches the furnace fire that must test every soul. When the strongholds of kings shall be overthrown, when the arrows of wrath shall strike through the hearts of His enemies, His people will be safe in His hands.

"Thine, O Lord, is the greatness, and the ¹²² power, and the glory, and the victory, and the majesty: for all that is in the heaven and in the earth is Thine. . . . In Thine hand is power and might; and in Thine hand it is to make great, and to give strength unto all." 1 Chronicles 29:11, 12.

6

¹²³

Not Judging, but Doing

"Judge not, that ye be not judged." Matthew 7:1.

The effort to earn salvation by one's own works inevitably leads men to pile up human exactions as a barrier against sin. For, seeing that they fail to keep the law, they will devise rules and regulations of their own to force themselves to obey. All this turns the mind away from God to self. His love dies out of the heart, and with it perishes love for his fellow men. A system of human invention, with its multitudinous exactions, will lead its advocates to judge all who come short of the prescribed human standard. The atmosphere of selfish and narrow criticism stifles the noble and generous emotions, and causes men to become self-centered judges and petty spies.

The Pharisees were of this class. They came forth from their religious services, not humbled with a sense of their own weakness, not grateful for the great privileges that God had given them. They came forth filled with spiritual pride, and their theme was, "Myself, my feelings, my knowledge, my ways." Their own attainments became the standard by which they judged others. Putting on the robes of self-dignity, they mounted the judgment seat to criticize and condemn.

The people partook largely of the same spirit, intruding upon the province of conscience and judging one another in matters that lay between ¹²⁴ the soul and God. It was in reference to this spirit and practice that Jesus said, "Judge not, that ye be not judged." That is, do not set yourself up as a standard. Do not make your opinions, your views of duty, your interpretations of Scripture, a criterion for others and in your heart condemn them if they do not come up to your ideal. Do not criticize others, conjecturing as to their motives and passing judgment upon them.

"Judge nothing before the time, until the Lord come, who both will bring to light the hidden things of darkness, and will make manifest the counsels of the hearts." 1 Corinthians 4:5. We cannot read the heart. Ourselves faulty, we are not qualified to sit in judgment upon others. Finite men can judge only from outward appearance. To Him alone who knows the secret springs of action, and who deals tenderly and compassionately, is it given to decide the case of every soul.

"Thou art inexcusable, O man, whosoever thou art that judgest: for wherein thou judgest another, thou condemnest thyself; for thou that judgest doest the same things." Romans 2:1. Thus those who condemn or criticize others, proclaim themselves guilty, for they do the same things. In condemning others, they are passing sentence upon themselves, and God declares that this sentence is just. He accepts their own verdict against themselves.

> "These clumsy feet, still in the mire,
> Go crushing blossoms without end;
> These hard, well-meaning hands we thrust
> Among the heartstrings of a friend."

125   *"Why beholdest thou the mote that is in thy brother's eye?" Matthew 7:3.*

Even the sentence, "Thou that judgest doest the same things," does not reach the magnitude of his sin who presumes to criticize and condemn his brother. Jesus said, "Why beholdest thou the mote that is in thy brother's eye, but considerest not the beam that is in thine own eye?"

His words describe one who is swift to discern a defect in others. When he thinks he has detected a flaw in the character or the life he is exceedingly zealous in trying to point it out; but Jesus declares that the very trait of character developed in doing this un-Christlike work, is, in comparison with the fault criticized, as a beam in proportion to a mote. It is one's own lack of the spirit of forbearance and love that leads him to make a world of an atom. Those who have never experienced the contrition of an entire surrender to Christ do not in their life make manifest the softening influence of the Saviour's love. They misrepresent the gentle, courteous spirit of the gospel and wound precious souls, for whom Christ died. According to the figure that our Saviour uses, he who indulges a censorious spirit is guilty of greater

sin than is the one he accuses, for he not only commits the same sin, but adds to it conceit and censoriousness.

Christ is the only true standard of character, and he who sets himself up as a standard for others is putting himself in the place of Christ. And since the Father "hath committed all judgment unto the Son" (John 5:22), whoever presumes to judge the motives of others is again 126 usurping the prerogative of the Son of God. These would-be judges and critics are placing themselves on the side of antichrist, "who opposeth and exalteth himself above all that is called God, or that is worshiped; so that he as God sitteth in the temple of God, showing himself that he is God." 2 Thessalonians 2:4.

The sin that leads to the most unhappy results is the cold, critical, unforgiving spirit that characterizes Pharisaism. When the religious experience is devoid of love, Jesus is not there; the sunshine of His presence is not there. No busy activity or Christless zeal can supply the lack. There may be a wonderful keenness of perception to discover the defects of others; but to everyone who indulges this spirit, Jesus says, "Thou hypocrite, first cast out the beam out of thine own eye; and then shalt thou see clearly to cast out the mote out of thy brother's eye." He who is guilty of wrong is the first to suspect wrong. By condemning another he is trying to conceal or excuse the evil of his own heart. It was through sin that men gained the knowledge of evil; no sooner had the first pair sinned than they began to accuse each other; and this is what human nature will inevitably do when uncontrolled by the grace of Christ.

When men indulge this accusing spirit, they are not satisfied with pointing out what they suppose to be a defect in their brother. If milder means fail of making him do what they think ought to be done, they will resort to compulsion. Just as far as lies in their power they will force men to comply with their ideas of what is right. This is what the Jews did in the days of Christ 127 and what the church has done ever since whenever she has lost the grace of Christ. Finding herself destitute of the power of love, she has reached out for the strong arm of the state to enforce her dogmas and execute her decrees. Here is the secret of all religious laws that have ever been enacted, and the secret of all persecution from the days of Abel to our own time.

Christ does not drive but draws men unto Him. The only compulsion which He employs is the constraint of love. When the church begins to seek for the support of secular power, it is evident that she is devoid of the power of Christ—the constraint of divine love.

But the difficulty lies with the individual members of the church, and it is here that the cure must be wrought. Jesus bids the accuser first cast the beam out of his own eye, renounce his censorious spirit, confess and forsake his own sin, before trying to correct others. For "a good tree bringeth not forth corrupt fruit; neither doth a corrupt tree bring forth good fruit." Luke 6:43. This accusing spirit which you indulge is evil fruit, and shows that the tree is evil. It is useless for you to build yourselves up in self-righteousness. What you need is a change of heart. You must have this experience before you are fitted to correct others; for "out of the abundance of the heart the mouth speaketh." Matthew 12:34.

128   When a crisis comes in the life of any soul, and you attempt to give counsel or admonition, your words will have only the weight of influence for good that your own example and spirit have gained for you. You must *be* good before you can *do* good. You cannot exert an influence that will transform others until your own heart has been humbled and refined and made tender by the grace of Christ. When this change has been wrought in you, it will be as natural for you to live to bless others as it is for the rose-bush to yield its fragrant bloom or the vine its purple clusters.

If Christ is in you "the hope of glory," you will have no disposition to watch others, to expose their errors. Instead of seeking to accuse and condemn, it will be your object to help, to bless, and to save. In dealing with those who are in error, you will heed the injunction, Consider "thyself, lest thou also be tempted." Galatians 6:1. You will call to mind the many times you have erred and how hard it was to find the right way when you had once left it. You will not push your brother into greater darkness, but with a heart full of pity will tell him of his danger.

He who looks often upon the cross of Calvary, remembering that his sins placed the Saviour there, will never try to estimate the degree of his guilt in comparison with that of others. He will not climb upon the judgment seat to bring accusation against another. There can be no spirit of criticism or self-exaltation on the part of those who walk in the shadow of Calvary's cross.

Not until you feel that you could sacrifice your own self-dignity, and even lay down your life in order to save an erring brother, have you cast the beam out of your own eye so that you are prepared to help your brother. Then you can
129   approach him and touch his heart. No one has ever been reclaimed from a wrong position by censure and reproach; but many have thus been driven from Christ and led to seal their hearts against conviction. A tender spirit, a gentle, winning deportment, may save the erring and hide a multitude of sins. The revelation of Christ in your own character will have a transforming power upon all with whom you come in contact. Let Christ be daily made manifest in

you, and He will reveal through you the creative energy of His word—a gentle, persuasive, yet mighty influence to re-create other souls in the beauty of the Lord our God.

"Give not that which is holy unto the dogs." Matthew 7:6.

Jesus here refers to a class who have no desire to escape from the slavery of sin. By indulgence in the corrupt and vile their natures have become so degraded that they cling to the evil and will not be separated from it. The servants of Christ should not allow themselves to be hindered by those who would make the gospel only a matter of contention and ridicule.

But the Saviour never passed by one soul, however sunken in sin, who was willing to receive the precious truths of heaven. To publicans and harlots His words were the beginning of a new life. Mary Magdalene, out of whom He cast seven devils, was the last at the Saviour's tomb and the first whom He greeted in the morning of His resurrection. It was Saul of Tarsus, one of the most determined enemies of the   130 gospel, who became Paul the devoted minister of Christ. Beneath an appearance of hatred and contempt, even beneath crime and degradation, may be hidden a soul that the grace of Christ will rescue to shine as a jewel in the Redeemer's crown.

"Ask, and it shall be given you; seek, and ye shall find; knock, and it shall be opened unto you." Matthew 7:7.

To leave no chance for unbelief, misunderstanding, or misinterpretation of His words, the Lord repeats the thrice-given promise. He longs to have those who would seek after God believe in Him who is able to do all things. Therefore He adds, "For everyone that asketh receiveth; and he that seeketh findeth; and to him that knocketh it shall be opened."

The Lord specifies no conditions except that you hunger for His mercy, desire His counsel, and long for His love. "Ask." The asking, makes it manifest that you realize your necessity; and if you ask in faith you will receive. The Lord has pledged His word, and it cannot fail. If you come with true contrition you need not feel that you are presumptuous in asking for what the Lord has promised. When you ask for the blessings you need, that you may perfect a character after Christ's likeness, the Lord assures you that you are asking according to a promise that will be verified. That you feel and know you are a sinner is sufficient ground for asking for His mercy and compassion. The condition   131 upon which you may come to God is not that you shall be holy, but that you desire Him to cleanse you from all sin and purify you from all iniquity. The argument that we may plead now and ever is our great need, our utterly helpless state, that makes Him and His redeeming power a necessity.

"Seek." Desire not merely His blessing, but Himself. "Acquaint now thyself with Him, and be at peace." Job 22:21. Seek, and you shall find. God is seeking you, and the very desire you feel to come to Him is but the drawing of His Spirit. Yield to that drawing. Christ is pleading the cause of the tempted, the erring, and the faithless. He is seeking to lift them into companionship with Himself. "If thou seek Him, He will be found of thee." 1 Chronicles 28:9.

"Knock." We come to God by special invitation, and He waits to welcome us to His audience chamber. The first disciples who followed Jesus were not satisfied with a hurried conversation with Him by the way; they said, "Rabbi, . . . where dwellest Thou? . . . They came and saw where He dwelt, and abode with Him that day." John 1:38, 39. So we may be admitted into closest intimacy and communion with God. "He that dwelleth in the secret place of the Most High shall abide under the shadow of the Almighty." Psalm 91:1. Let those who desire the blessing of God knock and wait at the door of mercy with firm assurance, saying, For Thou, O Lord, hast said, "Everyone that asketh receiveth; and he that seeketh findeth; and to him that knocketh it shall be opened."

132 Jesus looked upon those who were assembled to hear His words, and earnestly desired that the great multitude might appreciate the mercy and loving-kindness of God. As an illustration of their need, and of God's willingness to give, He presents before them a hungry child asking his earthly parent for bread. "What man is there of *you*," He said, "whom if his son ask bread, will he give him a stone?" He appeals to the tender, natural affection of a parent for his child and then says, "If ye then, being evil, know how to give good gifts unto your children, how much more shall your Father which is in heaven give good things to them that ask Him?" No man with a father's heart would turn from his son who is hungry and is asking for bread. Would they think him capable of trifling with his child, of tantalizing him by raising his expectations only to disappoint him? Would he promise to give him good and nourishing food, and then give him a stone? And should anyone dishonor God by imagining that He would not respond to the appeals of His children?

If ye, then, being human and evil, "know how to give good gifts unto your children: how much more shall your heavenly Father give the Holy Spirit to them that ask Him?" Luke 11:13. The Holy Spirit, the representative of Himself, is the greatest of all gifts. All "good things" are comprised in this. The Creator Himself can give us nothing greater, nothing better. When we beseech the Lord to pity us in our distress, and to guide us by His Holy Spirit, He will never turn away our prayer. It is possible even for a parent to turn away from his hungry child, but God can never reject the cry of the needy and longing heart. With what wonderful tenderness He has described His love! To those who in 133 days of darkness feel that God is unmindful of them, this is the message from the Father's heart: "Zion said, The Lord hath forsaken me, and my Lord hath forgotten me. Can a woman forget her sucking child, that she should not have compassion on the son of her womb? Yea, they may forget, yet will I not forget thee. Behold, I have graven thee upon the palms of My hands." Isaiah 49:14-16.

Every promise in the word of God furnishes us with subject matter for prayer, presenting the pledged word of Jehovah as our assurance. Whatever spiritual blessing we need, it is our privilege to claim through Jesus. We may tell the Lord, with the simplicity of a child, exactly what we need. We may state to Him our temporal matters, asking Him for bread and raiment as well as for the bread of life and the robe of Christ's righteousness. Your heavenly Father knows that you have need of all these things, and you are invited to ask Him concerning them. It is through the name of Jesus that every favor is received. God will honor that name, and will supply your necessities from the riches of His liberality.

But do not forget that in coming to God as a father you acknowledge your relation to Him as a child. You not only trust His goodness, but in all things yield to His will, knowing that His love is changeless. You give yourself to do His work. It was to those whom He had bidden to seek first the kingdom of God and His righteousness that Jesus gave the promise, "Ask, and ye shall receive." John 16:24.

The gifts of Him who has all power in heaven and earth are in store for the children of God. Gifts so precious that they come to us through the costly sacrifice of the Redeemer's blood; 134 gifts that will satisfy the deepest craving of the heart, gifts lasting as eternity, will be received and enjoyed by all who will come to God as little children. Take God's promises as your own, plead them before Him as His own words, and you will receive fullness of joy.

"Therefore all things whatsoever ye would that men should do to you, do ye even so to them." Matthew 7:12.

On the assurance of the love of God toward us, Jesus enjoins love to one another, in one comprehensive principle covering all the relations of human fellowship.

The Jews had been concerned about what they should receive; the burden of their anxiety was to secure what they thought their due of power and respect and service. But Christ teaches that our anxiety should not be, How much are we to receive? but, How much can we give? The standard of our obligation to others is found in what we ourselves would regard as their obligation to us.

In your association with others, put yourself in their place. Enter into their feelings, their difficulties, their disappointments, their joys, and their sorrows. Identify yourself with them, and then do to them as, were you to exchange places with them, you would wish them to deal with you. This is the true rule of honesty. It is another expression of the law, "Thou shalt love thy neighbor as thyself." Matthew 22:39. And it is the substance of the teaching of the prophets. It is a principle of heaven, and will be developed in all who are fitted for its holy companionship.

The golden rule is the principle of true courtesy, and its truest illustration is seen in the life and character of Jesus. Oh, what rays of softness and beauty shone forth in the daily life of our Saviour! What sweetness flowed from His very presence! The same spirit will be revealed in His children. Those with whom Christ dwells will be surrounded with a divine atmosphere. Their white robes of purity will be fragrant with perfume from the garden of the Lord. Their faces will reflect light from His, brightening the path for stumbling and weary feet.

No man who has the true ideal of what constitutes a perfect character will fail to manifest the sympathy and tenderness of Christ. The influence of grace is to soften the heart, to refine and purify the feelings, giving a heaven-born delicacy and sense of propriety.

But there is a yet deeper significance to the golden rule. Everyone who has been made a steward of the manifold grace of God is called upon to impart to souls in ignorance and darkness, even as, were he in their place, he would desire them to impart to him. The apostle Paul said, "I am debtor both to the Greeks, and to the barbarians; both to the wise, and to the unwise." Romans 1:14. By all that you have known of the love of God, by all that you have received of the rich gifts of His grace above the most benighted and degraded soul upon the earth are you in debt to that soul to impart these gifts unto him.

So also with the gifts and blessings of this life: whatever you may possess above your fellows places you in debt, to that degree, to all who are less favored. Have we wealth, or even the comforts of life, then we are under the most solemn obligation to care for the suffering sick, the widow, and the fatherless exactly as we would desire them to care for us were our condition and theirs to be reversed.

The golden rule teaches, by implication, the same truth which is taught elsewhere in the Sermon on the Mount, that "with what measure ye mete, it shall be measured to you again." That which we do to others, whether it be good or evil, will surely react upon ourselves, in blessing or in cursing. Whatever we give, we shall receive again. The earthly blessings which we impart to others may be, and often are, repaid in kind. What we give does, in time of need, often come back to us in fourfold measure in the coin of the realm. But, besides this, all gifts are repaid, even in this life, in the fuller inflowing of His love, which is the sum of all heaven's glory and its treasure. And evil imparted also returns again. Everyone who has been free to condemn or discourage, will in his own experience be brought over the ground where he has caused others to pass; he will feel what they have suffered because of his want of sympathy and tenderness.

It is the love of God toward us that has decreed this. He would lead us to abhor our own hardness of heart and to open our hearts to let Jesus abide in them. And thus, out of evil, good is brought, and what appeared a curse becomes a blessing.

The standard of the golden rule is the true standard of Christianity; anything short of it is a deception. A religion that leads men to place a low estimate upon human beings, whom Christ has esteemed of such value as to give Himself for them; a religion that would lead us to be careless of human needs, sufferings, or rights, is a spurious religion. In slighting the claims of the poor, the suffering, and the sinful, we are proving ourselves traitors to Christ. It is because men take upon themselves the name of Christ, while in life they deny His character, that Christianity has so little power in the world. The name of the Lord is blasphemed because of these things.

Of the apostolic church, in those bright days when the glory of the risen Christ shone upon them, it is written that no man said "that aught of the things which he possessed was his own." "Neither was there any among them that lacked." "And with great power gave the apostles witness of the resurrection of the Lord Jesus: and great grace was upon them all." "And they, continuing daily with one accord in the temple, and breaking bread from house to house, did eat their meat with gladness and singleness of heart, praising God, and having favor with all the people. And the Lord added to the church daily such as should be saved." Acts 4:32, 34, 33; 2:46, 47.

Search heaven and earth, and there is no truth revealed more powerful than that which is made manifest in works of mercy to those who need our sympathy and aid. This is the truth as it is in Jesus. When those who profess the name of

842

Christ shall practice the principles of the golden rule, the same power will attend the gospel as in apostolic times.

138 *"Strait is the gate, and narrow is the way, which leadeth unto life."*
Matthew 7:14.

In the time of Christ the people of Palestine lived in walled towns, which were mostly situated upon hills or mountains. The gates, which were closed at sunset, were approached by steep, rocky roads, and the traveler journeying homeward at the close of the day often had to press his way in eager haste up the difficult ascent in order to reach the gate before nightfall. The loiterer was left without.

The narrow, upward road leading to home and rest furnished Jesus with an impressive figure of the Christian way. The path which I have set before you, He said, is narrow; the gate is difficult of entrance; for the golden rule excludes all pride and self-seeking. There is, indeed, a wider road; but its end is destruction. If you would climb the path of spiritual life, you must constantly ascend; for it is an upward way. You must go with the few; for the multitude will choose the downward path.

In the road to death the whole race may go, with all their worldliness, all their selfishness, all their pride, dishonesty, and moral debasement. There is room for every man's opinions and doctrines, space to follow his inclinations, to do whatever his self-love may dictate. In order to go in the path that leads to destruction, there is no need of searching for the way; for the gate is wide, and the way is broad, and the feet naturally turn into the path that ends in death.

But the way to life is narrow and the entrance
139 strait. If you cling to any besetting sin you will find the way too narrow for you to enter. Your own ways, your own will, your evil habits and practices, must be given up if you would keep the way of the Lord. He who would serve Christ cannot follow the world's opinions or meet the world's standard. Heaven's path is too narrow for rank and riches to ride in state, too narrow for the play of self-centered ambition, too steep and rugged for lovers of ease to climb. Toil, patience, self-sacrifice, reproach, poverty, the contradiction of sinners against Himself, was the portion of Christ, and it must be our portion, if we ever enter the Paradise of God.

Yet do not therefore conclude that the upward path is the hard and the downward road the easy way. All along the road that leads to death there are pains and penalties, there are sorrows and disappointments, there are warnings not to go on. God's love has made it hard for the heedless and headstrong to destroy themselves. It is true that Satan's path is made to appear attractive, but it is all a deception; in the way of evil there are bitter remorse and cankering care. We may think it pleasant to follow pride and worldly ambition, but the end is pain and sorrow. Selfish plans may present flattering promises and hold out the hope of enjoyment, but we shall find that our happiness is poisoned and our life embittered by hopes that center in self. In the downward road the gateway may be bright with flowers, but thorns are in the path. The light of hope which shines from its entrance fades into the darkness of despair, and the soul who follows that path descends into the shadows of unending night.

"The way of transgressors is hard," but wis- 140 dom's "ways are ways of pleasantness and all her paths are peace." Proverbs 13:15; 3:17. Every act of obedience to Christ, every act of self-denial for His sake, every trial well endured, every victory gained over temptation, is a step in the march to the glory of final victory. If we take Christ for our guide, He will lead us safely. The veriest sinner need not miss his way. Not one trembling seeker need fail of walking in pure and holy light. Though the path is so narrow, so holy that sin cannot be tolerated therein, yet access has been secured for all, and not one doubting, trembling soul need say, "God cares nought for me."

The road may be rough and the ascent steep; there may be pitfalls upon the right hand and upon the left; we may have to endure toil in our journey; when weary, when longing for rest, we may have to toil on; when faint, we may have to fight; when discouraged, we must still hope; but with Christ as our guide we shall not fail of reaching the desired haven at last. Christ Himself has trodden the rough way before us and has smoothed the path for our feet.

And all the way up the steep road leading to eternal life are well-springs of joy to refresh the weary. Those who walk in wisdom's ways are, even in tribulation, exceeding joyful; for He whom their soul loveth, walks, invisible, beside them. At each upward step they discern more distinctly the touch of His hand; at every step brighter gleamings of glory from the Unseen fall upon their path; and their songs of praise, reaching ever a higher note, ascend to join the songs of angels before the throne. "The path of the righteous is as the light of dawn, that shineth 141 more and more unto the perfect day." Proverbs 4:18, R.V., margin.

"Strive to enter in at the strait gate."
Luke 13:24.

The belated traveler, hurrying to reach the city gate by the going down of the sun, could not turn aside for any attractions by the way. His whole mind was bent on the one purpose of entering the gate. The same intensity of purpose, said Jesus, is required in the Christian life. I have opened to you the glory of character, which is the true glory of My kingdom. It offers you no promise of earthly dominion; yet it is worthy of your supreme desire and effort. I do not call you to battle for the supremacy of the world's great empire, but do not therefore conclude that there is no battle to be fought nor victories to be won. I bid you strive, agonize, to enter into My spiritual kingdom.

The Christian life is a battle and a march. But the victory to be gained is not won by human power. The field of conflict is the domain of the heart. The battle which we have to fight—the greatest battle that was ever fought by man—is the surrender of self to the will of God, the yielding of the heart to the sovereignty of love. The old nature, born of blood and of the will of the flesh, cannot inherit the kingdom of God. The hereditary tendencies, the former habits, must be given up.

142 He who determines to enter the spiritual kingdom will find that all the powers and passions of an unregenerate nature, backed by the forces of the kingdom of darkness, are arrayed against him. Selfishness and pride will make a stand against anything that would show them to be sinful. We cannot, of ourselves, conquer the evil desires and habits that strive for the mastery. We cannot overcome the mighty foe who holds us in his thrall. God alone can give us the victory. He desires us to have the mastery over ourselves, our own will and ways. But He cannot work in us without our consent and co-operation. The divine Spirit works through the faculties and powers given to man. Our energies are required to co-operate with God.

The victory is not won without much earnest prayer, without the humbling of self at every step. Our will is not to be forced into co-operation with divine agencies, but it must be voluntarily submitted. Were it possible to force upon you with a hundredfold greater intensity the influence of the Spirit of God, it would not make you a Christian, a fit subject for heaven. The stronghold of Satan would not be broken. The will must be placed on the side of God's will. You are not able, of yourself, to bring your purposes and desires and inclinations into submission to the will of God; but if you are "willing to be made willing," God will accomplish the work for you, even "casting down imaginations, and every high thing that exalteth itself against the knowledge of God, and bringing into captivity every thought to the obedience of Christ." 2 Corinthians 10:5. Then you will "work out your own salvation with fear and 143 trembling. For it is God which worketh in you both to will and to do of His good pleasure." Philippians 2:12, 13.

But many are attracted by the beauty of Christ and the glory of heaven, who yet shrink from the conditions by which alone these can become their own. There are many in the broad way who are not fully satisfied with the path in which they walk. They long to break from the slavery of sin, and in their own strength they seek to make a stand against their sinful practices. They look toward the narrow way and the strait gate; but selfish pleasure, love of the world, pride, unsanctified ambition, place a barrier between them and the Saviour. To renounce their own will, their chosen objects of affection or pursuit, requires a sacrifice at which they hesitate and falter and turn back. Many "will seek to enter in, and shall not be able." Luke 13:24. They desire the good, they make some effort to obtain it; but they do not choose it; they have not a settled purpose to secure it at the cost of all things.

The only hope for us if we would overcome is to unite our will to God's will and work in co-operation with Him, hour by hour and day by day. We cannot retain self and yet enter the kingdom of God. If we ever attain unto holiness, it will be through the renunciation of self and the reception of the mind of Christ. Pride and self-sufficiency must be crucified. Are we willing to pay the price required of us? Are we willing to have our will brought into perfect conformity to the will of God? Until we are willing, the transforming grace of God cannot be manifest upon us.

The warfare which we are to wage is the "good fight of faith." "I also labor," said the 144 apostle Paul, "striving according to His working, which worketh in me mightily." Colossians 1:29.

Jacob, in the great crisis of his life, turned aside to pray. He was filled with one overmastering purpose—to seek for transformation of character. But while he was pleading with God, an enemy, as he supposed, placed his hand upon him, and all night he wrestled for his life. But the purpose of his soul was not changed by peril of life itself. When his strength was nearly spent, the Angel put forth His divine power, and at His touch Jacob knew Him with whom he had been contending. Wounded and helpless, he fell upon the Saviour's breast, pleading for a blessing. He would not be turned aside nor cease his intercession, and Christ granted the petition of this helpless, penitent soul, according to His promise, "Let him take hold of My strength, that he may make peace with Me; and he shall make peace with Me." Isaiah 27:5. Jacob pleaded with determined spirit, "I will not let Thee go, except Thou bless me." Genesis 32:26. This spirit of persistence was inspired by Him who wrestled with the patriarch. It was He who gave him the victory, and He changed his name from Jacob to Israel, saying, "As a prince hast thou power with God and with men, and hast prevailed." Genesis 32:28. That for which

Jacob had vainly wrestled in his own strength was won through self-surrender and steadfast faith. "This is the victory that overcometh the world, even our faith." 1 John 5:4.

145   *"Beware of false prophets." Matthew 7:15.*

Teachers of falsehood will arise to draw you away from the narrow path and the strait gate. Beware of them; though concealed in sheep's clothing, inwardly they are ravening wolves. Jesus gives a test by which false teachers may be distinguished from the true. "Ye shall know them by their fruits," He says. "Do men gather grapes of thorns, or figs of thistles?"

We are not bidden to prove them by their fair speeches and exalted professions. They are to be judged by the word of God. "To the law and to the testimony: if they speak not according to this word it is because there is no light in them." "Cease, my son, to hear the instruction that causeth to err from the words of knowledge." Isaiah 8:20; Proverbs 19:27. What message do these teachers bring? Does it lead you to reverence and fear God? Does it lead you to manifest your love for Him by loyalty to His commandments? If men do not feel the weight of the moral law; if they make light of God's precepts; if they break one of the least of His commandments, and teach men so, they shall be of no esteem in the sight of heaven. We may know that their claims are without foundation. They are doing the very work that originated with the prince of darkness, the enemy of God.

Not all who profess His name and wear His badge are Christ's. Many who have taught in My name, said Jesus, will be found wanting at last. "Many will say to Me in that day, Lord, Lord, have we not prophesied in Thy name? and in Thy name have we not cast out devils? and in Thy

146   name done many wonderful works? And then will I profess unto them, I never knew you: depart from Me, ye that work iniquity."

There are persons who believe that they are right, when they are wrong. While claiming Christ as their Lord, and professedly doing great works in His name, they are workers of iniquity. "With their mouth they show much love, but their heart goeth after their covetousness." He who declares God's word is to them "as a very lovely song of one that hath a pleasant voice, and can play well on an instrument: for they hear Thy words, but they do them not." Ezekiel 33:31, 32.

A mere profession of discipleship is of no value. The faith in Christ which saves the soul is not what it is represented to be by many. "Believe, believe," they say, "and you need not keep the law." But a belief that does not lead to obedience is presumption. The apostle John says, "He that saith, I know Him, and keepeth

not His commandments, is a liar, and the truth is not in him." 1 John 2:4. Let none cherish the idea that special providences or miraculous manifestations are to be the proof of the genuineness of their work or of the ideas they advocate. When persons will speak lightly of the word of God, and set their impressions, feelings, and exercises above the divine standard, we may know that they have no light in them.

Obedience is the test of discipleship. It is the keeping of the commandments that proves the sincerity of our professions of love. When the doctrine we accept kills sin in the heart, purifies the soul from defilement, bears fruit unto holiness, we may know that it is the truth of God. When benevolence, kindness, tenderheartedness, sympathy, are manifest in our lives; when   147 the joy of right doing is in our hearts; when we exalt Christ, and not self, we may know that our faith is of the right order. "Hereby we do know that we know Him, if we keep His commandments." 1 John 2:3.

"It fell not: for it was founded upon the rock." Matthew 7:25, R.V.

The people had been deeply moved by the words of Christ. The divine beauty of the principles of truth attracted them; and Christ's solemn warnings had come to them as the voice of the heart-searching God. His words had struck at the very root of their former ideas and opinions; to obey His teaching would require a change in all their habits of thought and action. It would bring them into collision with their religious teachers; for it would involve the overthrow of the whole structure which for generations the rabbis had been rearing. Therefore, while the hearts of the people responded to His words, few were ready to accept them as the guide of life.

Jesus ended His teaching on the mount with an illustration that presented with startling vividness the importance of putting in practice the words He had spoken. Among the crowds that thronged about the Saviour were many who had spent their lives about the Sea of Galilee. As they sat upon the hillside, listening to the words of Christ, they could see valleys and ravines through which the mountain streams found their way to the sea. In summer these streams often wholly disappeared, leaving only   148 a dry and dusty channel. But when the wintry storms burst upon the hills, the rivers became fierce, raging torrents, at times overspreading the valleys and bearing everything away on their resistless flood. Often, then, the hovels reared by the peasants on the grassy plain, apparently beyond the reach of danger, were swept away. But high upon the hills were houses built upon the rock. In some parts of the land were dwellings built wholly of rock, and many of them had withstood the tempests of a thousand years. These houses were reared with toil and difficulty. They were not easy of access, and their location appeared less inviting than the grassy plain. But they were founded upon the rock, and wind and flood and tempest beat upon them in vain.

Like the builders of these houses on the rock, said Jesus, is he who shall receive the words that I have spoken to you, and make them the foundation of his character and life. Centuries before, the prophet Isaiah had written, "The word of our God shall stand forever" (Isaiah 40:8); and Peter, long after the Sermon on the Mount was given, quoting these words of Isaiah added, "This is the word which by the gospel is preached unto you" (1 Peter 1:25). The word of God is the only steadfast thing our world knows. It is the sure foundation. "Heaven and earth shall pass away," said Jesus, "but My words shall not pass away." Matthew 24:35.

The great principles of the law, of the very nature of God, are embodied in the words of Christ on the mount. Whoever builds upon them is building upon Christ, the Rock of Ages. In receiving the word, we receive Christ. And only those who thus receive His words are building upon Him. "Other foundation can no man lay than that is laid, which is Jesus Christ." 1 Corinthians 3:11. "There is none other name under heaven, given among men, whereby we must be saved." Acts 4:12. Christ, the Word, the revelation of God,—the manifestation of His character, His law, His love, His life,—is the only foundation upon which we can build a character that will endure.

We build on Christ by obeying His word. It is not he who merely enjoys righteousness, that is righteous, but he who does righteousness. Holiness is not rapture; it is the result of surrendering all to God; it is doing the will of our heavenly Father. When the children of Israel were encamped on the borders of the Promised Land, it was not enough for them to have a knowledge of Canaan, or to sing the songs of Canaan. This alone would not bring them into possession of the vineyards and olive groves of the goodly land. They could make it theirs in truth only by occupation, by complying with the conditions, by exercising living faith in God, by appropriating His promises to themselves, while they obeyed His instruction.

Religion consists in doing the words of Christ; not doing to earn God's favor, but because, all undeserving, we have received the gift of His love. Christ places the salvation of man, not upon profession merely, but upon faith that is made manifest in works of righteousness. Doing, not saying merely, is expected of the followers of Christ. It is through action that character is built. "As many as are *led* by the Spirit of God, they are the sons of God." Romans 8:14. Not those whose hearts are touched by the Spirit, not those who now and then yield to its power, but they that are led by the Spirit, are the sons of God.

Do you desire to become a follower of Christ, yet know not how to begin? Are you in darkness and know not how to find the light? Follow the light you have. Set your heart to obey what you do know of the word of God. His power, His very life, dwells in His word. As you receive the word in faith, it will give you power to obey. As you give heed to the light you have, greater light will come. You are building on God's word, and your character will be builded after the similitude of the character of Christ.

Christ, the true foundation, is a living stone; His life is imparted to all that are built upon Him. "Ye also, as living stones, are built up a spiritual house." "Each several building, fitly framed together, groweth into a holy temple in the Lord." 1 Peter 2:5, R.V.; Ephesians 2:21, R.V. The stones became one with the foundation; for a common life dwells in all. That building no tempest can overthrow; for—

"That which shares the life of God,
With Him surviveth all."

But every building erected on other foundation than God's word will fall. He who, like the Jews in Christ's day, builds on the foundation of human ideas and opinions, of forms and ceremonies of man's invention, or on any works that he can do independently of the grace of Christ, is erecting his structure of character upon the shifting sand. The fierce tempests of temptation will sweep away the sandy foundation and leave his house a wreck on the shores of time.

"Therefore thus saith the Lord God, . . . Judgment also will I lay to the line, and righteousness to the plummet: and the hail shall sweep away the refuge of lies, and the waters shall overflow the hiding place." Isaiah 28:16, 17.

But today mercy pleads with the sinner. "As I live, saith the Lord God, I have no pleasure in the death of the wicked; but that the wicked turn from his way and live: turn ye, turn ye from your evil ways; for why will ye die?" Ezekiel 33:11. The voice that speaks to the impenitent today is the voice of Him who in heart anguish exclaimed as He beheld the city of His love: "O Jerusalem, Jerusalem, which killeth the prophets, and stoneth them that are sent unto her! how often would I have gathered thy children together, even as a hen gathereth her own brood under her wings, and ye would not! Behold, your house is left unto you desolate." Luke 13:34, 35, R.V. In Jerusalem, Jesus beheld a symbol of the world that had rejected and despised His grace. He was weeping, O stubborn heart, for you! Even when Jesus' tears were shed upon the mount, Jerusalem might yet have repented, and escaped her doom. For a little space the Gift of heaven still waited her acceptance. So, O heart, to you Christ is still speaking in accents of love: "Behold, I stand at the door, and knock: if any man hear My voice, and open the door, I will come in to him, and will sup with him, and he with Me." "Now is the accepted time; behold, now is the day of salvation." Revelation 3:20; 2 Corinthians 6:2.

152   You who are resting your hope on self are building on the sand. But it is not yet too late to escape the impending ruin. Before the tempest breaks, flee to the sure foundation. "Thus saith the Lord God, Behold, I lay in Zion for a foundation a stone, a tried stone, a precious cornerstone, of sure foundation: he that believeth shall not make haste." "Look unto Me, and be ye saved, all the ends of the earth: for I am God, and there is none else." "Fear thou not; for I am with thee: be not dismayed; for I am thy God: I will strengthen thee; yea, I will help thee; yea, I will uphold thee with the right hand of My righteousness." "Ye shall not be ashamed nor confounded world without end." Isaiah 28:16, R.V.; 45:22; 41:10; 45:17.

5

CHRIST'S OBJECT LESSONS

INDEX

SUMMARY	PAGE	SUMMARY	PAGE

COL

DATE	SUMMARY	PAGE NO.	DATE	SUMMARY	PAGE NO.

CONTENTS

1. Teaching in Parables ... 855
2. The Sower Went Forth to Sow ... 858
3. First the Blade, Then the Ear ... 861
4. Tares ... 865
5. Like a Grain of Mustard Seed ... 867
6. Other Lessons from Seed-Sowing ... 868
7. Like unto Leaven ... 871
8. Hidden Treasure ... 873
9. The Pearl ... 877
10. The Net ... 879
11. Things New and Old ... 872
12. Asking to Give ... 881
13. Two Worshipers ... 886
14. "Shall Not God Avenge His Own?" ... 890
15. The Man Regardeth Himself ... 896

16. "Lost and Is Found" ... 869
17. "Spare It This Year Also" ...
19. ... Highways and Hedges ... 900
13. The Measure of Forgiveness ... 910
20. Gain that Is Loss ... 913
21. A Great Gulf Fixed ... 916
22. Confessing in Doing ...
23. The Lord's Vineyard ... 922
24. Without a Wedding Garment ... 930
25. Talents ... 938
26. ... (Unconscious ...) ...
27. "Who Is My Neighbor?" ...
28. The Reward of Grace ... 965
29. "To Meet the Bridegroom" ...

CONTENTS

1. Teaching in Parables — 853

2. "The Sower Went Forth to Sow" — 855

3. "First the Blade, then the Ear" — 864

4. Tares — 865

5. "Like a Grain of Mustard Seed" — 867

6. Other Lessons from Seed-Sowing — 868

7. "Like unto Leaven" — 871

8. Hidden Treasure — 873

9. The Pearl — 877

10. The Net — 879

11. "Things New and Old" — 879

12. Asking to Give — 882

13. Two Worshipers — 886

14. "Shall Not God Avenge His Own?" — 890

15. "This Man Receiveth Sinners" — 895

16. "Lost and Is Found" — 899

17. "Spare It This Year Also" — 903

18. "Go into the Highways and Hedges" — 905

19. The Measure of Forgiveness — 910

20. Gain That Is Loss — 913

21. "A Great Gulf Fixed" — 915

22. Saying and Doing — 919

23. The Lord's Vineyard — 922

24. Without a Wedding Garment — 930

25. Talents — 933

26. "Friends by the Mammon of Unrighteousness" — 946

27. "Who Is My Neighbor?" — 949

28. The Reward of Grace — 953

29. "To Meet the Bridegroom" — 957

1

Teaching in Parables

In Christ's parable teaching the same principle is seen as in His own mission to the world. That we might become acquainted with His divine character and life, Christ took our nature and dwelt among us. Divinity was revealed in humanity; the invisible glory in the visible human form. Men could learn of the unknown through the known; heavenly things were revealed through the earthly; God was made manifest in the likeness of men. So it was in Christ's teaching: the unknown was illustrated by the known; divine truths by earthly things with which the people were most familiar.

The Scripture says, "All these things spake Jesus unto the multitude in parables; . . . that it might be fulfilled which was spoken by the prophet, saying, I will open My mouth in parables; I will utter things which have been kept secret from the foundation of the world." Matt. 13:34, 35. Natural things were the medium for the spiritual; the things of nature and the life-experience of His hearers were connected with the truths of the written word. Leading thus from the natural to the spiritual kingdom, Christ's parables are links in the chain of truth that unites man with God, and earth with heaven.

In His teaching from nature, Christ was speaking of the things which His own hands had made, and which had qualities and powers that He Himself had imparted. In their original perfection all created things were an expression of the thought of God. To Adam and Eve in their Eden home nature was full of the knowledge of God, teeming with divine instruction. Wisdom spoke to the eye and was received into the heart; for they communed with God in His created works. As soon as the holy pair transgressed the law of the Most High, the brightness from the face of God departed from the face of nature. The earth is now marred and defiled by sin. Yet even in its blighted state much that is beautiful remains. God's object lessons are not obliterated; rightly understood, nature speaks of her Creator.

In the days of Christ these lessons had been lost sight of. Men had well-nigh ceased to discern God in His works. The sinfulness of humanity had cast a pall over the fair face of creation; and instead of manifesting God, His works became a barrier that concealed Him. Men "worshiped and served the creature more than the Creator." Thus the heathen "became vain in their imaginations, and their foolish heart was darkened." Rom. 1:25, 21. So in Israel, man's

teaching had been put in the place of God's. Not only the things of nature, but the sacrificial service and the Scriptures themselves—all given to reveal God—were so perverted that they became the means of concealing Him.

Christ sought to remove that which obscured the truth. The veil that sin has cast over the face of nature, He came to draw aside, bringing to view the spiritual glory that all things were created to reflect. His words placed the teachings of nature as well as of the Bible in a new aspect, and made them a new revelation.

Jesus plucked the beautiful lily, and placed it in the hands of children and youth; and as they looked into His own youthful face, fresh with the sunlight of His Father's countenance, He gave the lesson, "Consider the lilies of the field, how they grow [in the simplicity of natural beauty]; they toil not, neither do they spin; and yet I say unto you, that even Solomon in all his glory was not arrayed like one of these." Then followed the sweet assurance and the important lesson, "Wherefore, if God so clothe the grass of the field, which today is, and tomorrow is cast into the oven, shall He not much more clothe you, O ye of little faith?"

In the sermon on the mount these words were spoken to others besides children and youth. They were spoken to the multitude, among whom were men and women full of worries and perplexities, and sore with disappointment and sorrow. Jesus continued: "Therefore take no thought, saying, What shall we eat? or, What shall we drink? or, Wherewithal shall we be clothed? (for after all these things do the Gentiles seek:) for your Heavenly Father knoweth that ye have need of all these things." Then spreading out His hands to the surrounding multitude, He said, "But seek ye first the kingdom of God, and His righteousness; and all these things shall be added unto you." Matt. 6:28-33.

Thus Christ interpreted the message which He Himself had given to the lilies and the grass of the field. He desires us to read it in every lily and every spire of grass. His words are full of assurance, and tend to confirm trust in God.

So wide was Christ's view of truth, so extended His teaching, that every phase of nature was employed in illustrating truth. The scenes upon which the eye daily rests were all connected with some spiritual truth, so that nature is clothed with the parables of the Master.

In the earlier part of His ministry, Christ had spoken to the people in words so plain that all His hearers might have grasped truths which would make them wise unto salvation. But in many hearts the truth had taken no root, and it had been quickly caught away. "Therefore speak I to them in parables," He said; "because they seeing see not; and hearing they hear not, neither do they understand. . . . For this people's heart is waxed gross, and their ears are dull of hearing, and their eyes they have closed." Matt. 13:13-15.

21   Jesus desired to awaken inquiry. He sought to arouse the careless, and impress truth upon the heart. Parable teaching was popular, and commanded the respect and attention, not only of the Jews, but of the people of other nations. No more effective method of instruction could He have employed. If His hearers had desired a knowledge of divine things, they might have understood His words; for He was always willing to explain them to the honest inquirer.

Again, Christ had truths to present which the people were unprepared to accept or even to understand. For this reason also He taught them in parables. By connecting His teaching with the scenes of life, experience, or nature, He secured their attention and impressed their hearts. Afterward, as they looked upon the objects that illustrated His lessons, they recalled the words of the divine Teacher. To minds that were open to the Holy Spirit, the significance of the Saviour's teaching unfolded more and more. Mysteries grew clear, and that which had been hard to grasp became evident.

Jesus sought an avenue to every heart. By using a variety of illustrations, He not only presented truth in its different phases, but appealed to the different hearers. Their interest was aroused by figures drawn from the surroundings
22   of their daily life. None who listened to the Saviour could feel that they were neglected or forgotten. The humblest, the most sinful, heard in His teaching a voice that spoke to them in sympathy and tenderness.

And He had another reason for teaching in parables. Among the multitudes that gathered about Him, there were priests and rabbis, scribes and elders, Herodians and rulers, worldloving, bigoted, ambitious men, who desired above all things to find some accusation against Him. Their spies followed His steps day after day, to catch from His lips something that would cause His condemnation, and forever silence the One who seemed to draw the world after Him. The Saviour understood the character of these men, and He presented truth in such a way that they could find nothing by which to bring His case before the Sanhedrin. In parables He rebuked the hypocrisy and wicked works of those who occupied high positions, and in figurative language clothed truth of so cutting a character that had it been spoken in direct denunciation, they would not have listened to His words, and would speedily have put an end

to His ministry. But while He evaded the spies, He made truth so clear that error was manifested, and the honest in heart were profited by His lessons. Divine wisdom, infinite grace, were made plain by the things of God's creation. Through nature and the experiences of life, men were taught of God. "The invisible things of Him since the creation of the world," were "perceived through the things that are made, even His everlasting power and divinity." Rom. 1:20, R. V.

In the Saviour's parable teaching is an indication of what constitutes the true "higher education." Christ might have opened to men the deepest truths of science. He might have unlocked mysteries which have required many centuries of toil and study to penetrate. He might have made suggestions in scientific lines that would have afforded food for thought and 23 stimulus for invention to the close of time. But He did not do this. He said nothing to gratify curiosity, or to satisfy man's ambition by opening doors to worldly greatness. In all His teaching, Christ brought the mind of man in contact with the Infinite Mind. He did not direct the people to study men's theories about God, His word, or His works. He taught them to behold Him as manifested in His works, in His word, and by His providences.

Christ did not deal in abstract theories, but in that which is essential to the development of character, that which will enlarge man's capacity for knowing God, and increase his efficiency to do good. He spoke to men of those truths that relate to the conduct of life, and that take hold upon eternity.

It was Christ who directed the education of Israel. Concerning the commandments and ordinances of the Lord He said, "Thou shalt teach them diligently unto thy children, and shalt talk of them when thou sittest in thine house, and when thou walkest by the way, and when thou liest down, and when thou risest up. And thou 24 shalt bind them for a sign upon thine hand, and they shall be as frontlets between thine eyes. And thou shalt write them upon the posts of thy house, and on thy gates." Deut. 6:7-9. In His own teaching, Jesus showed how this command is to be fulfilled—how the laws and principles of God's kingdom can be so presented as to reveal their beauty and preciousness. When the Lord was training Israel to be the special representatives of Himself, He gave them homes among the hills and valleys. In their home life and their religious service they were brought in constant contact with nature and with the word of God. So Christ taught His disciples by the lake, on the mountainside, in the fields and groves, where

"Therefore speak I to them in parables: because they seeing see not; and hearing they hear not, neither do they understand. And in them is fulfilled the prophecy of Esaias. . . . For this people's heart is waxed gross, and their ears are dull of hearing, and their eyes they have closed." Matt. 13: 13-15.

they could look upon the things of nature by which He illustrated His teachings. And as they learned of Christ, they put their knowledge to use by co-operating with Him in His work.

So through the creation we are to become acquainted with the Creator. The book of nature is a great lesson book, which in connection with the Scriptures we are to use in teaching others of His character, and guiding lost sheep back to the fold of God. As the works of God are studied, the Holy Spirit flashes conviction into the mind. It is not the conviction that logical reasoning produces; but unless the mind has become too dark to know God, the eye too dim to see Him, the ear too dull to hear His voice, a deeper meaning is grasped, and the sublime, spiritual truths of the written word are impressed on the heart.

In these lessons direct from nature, there is a simplicity and purity that makes them of the highest value. All need the teaching to be derived from this source. In itself the beauty of nature leads the soul away from sin and worldly attractions, and toward purity, peace, and God. Too often the minds of students are occupied with men's theories and speculations, falsely 25 called science and philosophy. They need to be brought into close contact with nature. Let them learn that creation and Christianity have one God. Let them be taught to see the harmony of the natural with the spiritual. Let everything which their eyes see or their hands handle be made a lesson in character building. Thus the mental powers will be strengthened, the character developed, the whole life ennobled.

Christ's purpose in parable teaching was in direct line with the purpose of the Sabbath. God gave to men the memorial of His creative power, that they might discern Him in the works of His hand. The Sabbath bids us behold in His 26 created works the glory of the Creator. And it was because He desired us to do this that Jesus bound up His precious lessons with the beauty of natural things. On the holy rest day, above all other days, we should study the messages that God has written for us in nature. We should study the Saviour's parables where He spoke them, in the fields and groves, under the open sky, among the grass and flowers. As we come close to the heart of nature, Christ makes His presence real to us, and speaks to our hearts of His peace and love.

And Christ has linked His teaching, not only with the day of rest, but with the week of toil. He has wisdom for him who drives the plow and sows the seed. In the plowing and sowing, the tilling and reaping, He teaches us to see an illustration of His work of grace in the heart. So in every line of useful labor and every association of life, He desires us to find a lesson of divine truth. Then our daily toil will no longer 27 absorb our attention and lead us to forget God; it will continually remind us of our Creator and

Redeemer. The thought of God will run like a thread of gold through all our homely cares and occupations. For us the glory of His face will again rest upon the face of nature. We shall ever be learning new lessons of heavenly truth, and growing into the image of His purity. Thus shall we "be taught of the Lord"; and in the lot wherein we are called, we shall "abide with God." Isa. 54:13; 1 Cor. 7:24.

2

"The Sower Went Forth to Sow"

The Sower and the Seed

By the parable of the sower, Christ illustrates the things of the kingdom of heaven, and the work of the great Husbandman for His people. Like a sower in the field, He came to scatter the heavenly grain of truth. And His parable teaching itself was the seed with which the most precious truths of His grace were sown. Because of its simplicity the parable of the sower has not been valued as it should be. From the natural seed cast into the soil, Christ desires to lead our minds to the gospel seed, the sowing of which results in bringing man back to his loyalty to God. He who gave the parable of the tiny seed is the Sovereign of heaven, and the same laws that govern earthly seed sowing govern the sowing of the seeds of truth.

By the Sea of Galilee a company had gathered to see and hear Jesus—an eager, expectant throng. The sick were there, lying on their mats, waiting to present their cases before Him. It was 34 Christ's God-given right to heal the woes of a sinful race, and He now rebuked disease, and diffused around Him life and health and peace.

As the crowd continued to increase, the people pressed close about Christ until there was no room to receive them. Then, speaking a word to the men in their fishing boats, He stepped into the boat that was waiting to take Him across the lake, and bidding His disciples push off a little from the land, He spoke to the multitude upon the shore.

Beside the sea lay the beautiful plain of Gennesaret, beyond rose the hills, and upon hillside and plain both sowers and reapers were busy, the one casting seed and the other harvesting the early grain. Looking upon the scene, Christ said—

"Behold, the sower went forth to sow; and as he sowed, some seeds fell by the wayside, and the birds came and devoured them" (R.V.); "some fell upon stony places, where they had not much earth; and forthwith they sprung up, because they had no deepness of earth: and when the sun was up, they were scorched; and because they had no root, they withered away.

This chapter is based on Matthew 13:1-9, 18-23; Mark 4:1-20; Luke 8:4-15.

And some fell among thorns; and the thorns sprung up, and choked them: but other fell into good ground, and brought forth fruit, some an hundredfold, some sixtyfold, some thirtyfold."

Christ's mission was not understood by the people of His time. The manner of His coming was not in accordance with their expectations. The Lord Jesus was the foundation of the whole Jewish economy. Its imposing services were of divine appointment. They were designed to teach the people that at the time appointed One would come to whom those ceremonies pointed. But the Jews had exalted the forms and ceremonies and had lost sight of their object. The traditions, maxims, and enactments of men hid from them the lessons which God intended to convey. These maxims and traditions became an obstacle to their understanding and practice of true religion. And when the Reality came, in the person of Christ, they did not recognize in Him the fulfillment of all their types, the substance of all their shadows. They rejected the antitype, and clung to their types and useless ceremonies. The Son of God had come, but they continued to ask for a sign. The message, "Repent ye; for the kingdom of heaven is at hand," they answered by demands for a miracle. Matt. 3:2. The gospel of Christ was a stumbling block to them because they demanded signs instead of a Saviour. They expected the Messiah to prove His claims by mighty deeds of conquest, to establish His empire on the ruins of earthly kingdoms. This expectation Christ answered in the parable of the sower. Not by force of arms, not by violent interpositions, was the kingdom of God to prevail, but by the implanting of a new principle in the hearts of men.

"He that soweth the good seed is the Son of man." Matt. 13:37. Christ had come, not as a king, but as a sower; not for the overthrow of kingdoms, but for the scattering of seed; not to point His followers to earthly triumphs and national greatness, but to a harvest to be gathered after patient toil and through losses and disappointments.

The Pharisees perceived the meaning of Christ's parable, but to them its lesson was unwelcome. They affected not to understand it. To the multitude it involved in still greater mystery the purpose of the new teacher, whose words had so strangely moved their hearts and so bitterly disappointed their ambitions. The disciples themselves had not understood the parable, but their interest was awakened. They came to Jesus privately and asked for an explanation.

This was the desire which Christ wished to arouse, that He might give them more definite instruction. He explained the parable to them, as He will make plain His word to all who seek Him in sincerity of heart. Those who study the word of God with hearts open to the enlightenment of the Holy Spirit, will not remain in darkness as to the meaning of the word. "If any man willeth to do His will," Christ said, "he shall know of the teaching whether it be of God, or whether I speak from Myself." John 7:17, R.V. All who come to Christ for a clearer knowledge of the truth will receive it. He will unfold to them the mysteries of the kingdom of heaven, and these mysteries will be understood by the heart that longs to know the truth. A heavenly light will shine into the soul temple, and will be revealed to others as the bright shining of a lamp on a dark path.

"The sower went forth to sow" (R.V.). In the East the state of affairs was so unsettled, and there was so great danger from violence that the people dwelt chiefly in walled towns, and the husbandmen went forth daily to their labor outside the walls. So Christ, the heavenly Sower, went forth to sow. He left His home of security and peace, left the glory that He had with the Father before the world was, left His position upon the throne of the universe. He went forth, a suffering, tempted man; went forth in solitude, to sow in tears, to water with His blood, the seed of life for a world lost.

His servants in like manner must go forth to sow. When called to become a sower of the seed of truth, Abraham was bidden, "Get thee out of thy country, and from thy kindred, and from thy father's house, unto a land that I will show thee." Gen. 12:1. "And he went out, not knowing whither he went." Heb. 11:8. So to the apostle Paul, praying in the temple at Jerusalem, came the message from God, "Depart; for I will send thee far hence unto the Gentiles." Acts 22:21. So those who are called to unite with Christ must leave all, in order to follow Him. Old associations must be broken up, plans of life relinquished, earthly hopes surrendered. In toil and tears, in solitude, and through sacrifice, must the seed be sown.

"The sower soweth the word." Christ came to sow the world with truth. Ever since the fall of man, Satan has been sowing the seeds of error. It was by a lie that he first gained control over men, and thus he still works to overthrow God's kingdom in the earth and to bring men under his power. A sower from a higher world, Christ came to sow the seeds of truth. He who had stood in the councils of God, who had dwelt in the innermost sanctuary of the Eternal, could bring to men the pure principles of truth. Ever since the fall of man, Christ had been the Revealer of truth to the world. By Him the incorruptible seed, "the word of God, which liveth and abideth forever," is communicated to men. 1 Peter 1:23. In that first promise spoken to our fallen race in Eden, Christ was sowing the gospel seed. But it is to His personal ministry among men and to the work which He thus established that the parable of the sower especially applies.

The word of God is the seed. Every seed has in itself a germinating principle. In it the life of the plant is enfolded. So there is life in God's word. Christ says, "The words that I speak unto you, they are Spirit, and they are life." John 6:63. "He that heareth My word, and believeth on Him that sent Me, hath everlasting life." John 5:24. In every command and in every promise of the word of God is the power, the very life of God, by which the command may be fulfilled and the promise realized. He who by faith receives the word is receiving the very life and character of God.

Every seed brings forth fruit after its kind. Sow the seed under right conditions, and it will develop its own life in the plant. Receive into the soul by faith the incorruptible seed of the word, and it will bring forth a character and a life after the similitude of the character and the life of God.

The teachers of Israel were not sowing the seed of the word of God. Christ's work as a teacher of truth was in marked contrast to that of the rabbis of His time. They dwelt upon traditions, upon human theories and speculations. Often that which man had taught and written about the word, they put in place of the word itself. Their teaching had no power to quicken the soul. The subject of Christ's teaching and preaching was the word of God. He met questioners with a plain, "It is written." "What saith the Scriptures?" "How readest thou?" At every opportunity, when an interest was awakened by either friend or foe, He sowed the seed of the word. He who is the Way, the Truth, and the Life, Himself the living Word, points to the Scriptures, saying, "They are they which testify of Me." And "beginning at Moses and all the prophets," He opened to His disciples "in all the Scriptures the things concerning Himself." John 5:39; Luke 24:27.

Christ's servants are to do the same work. In our day, as of old, the vital truths of God's word are set aside for human theories and speculations. Many professed ministers of the gospel do not accept the whole Bible as the inspired word. One wise man rejects one portion; another questions another part. They set up their judgment as superior to the word; and the Scripture which they do teach rests upon their own authority. Its divine authenticity is destroyed. Thus the seeds of infidelity are sown broadcast; for the people become confused and know not what to believe. There are many beliefs that the mind has no right to entertain. In the days of Christ the rabbis put a forced, mystical construction upon many portions of Scripture. Because the plain teaching of God's word condemned their practices, they tried to destroy its force. The same thing is done today. The word of God is made to appear mysterious and obscure in order to excuse transgression of His law. Christ rebuked these practices in His day. He taught that the word of God was to be understood by all. He pointed to the Scriptures as of unquestionable authority, and we should do the same. The Bible is to be presented as the word of the infinite God, as the end of all controversy and the foundation of all faith.

The Bible has been robbed of its power, and the results are seen in a lowering of the tone of spiritual life. In the sermons from many pulpits of today there is not that divine manifestation which awakens the conscience and brings life to the soul. The hearers can not say, "Did not our heart burn within us, while He talked with us by the way, and while He opened to us the Scriptures?" Luke 24:32. There are many who are crying out for the living God, longing for the divine presence. Philosophical theories or literary essays, however brilliant, cannot satisfy the heart. The assertions and inventions of men are of no value. Let the word of God speak to the people. Let those who have heard only traditions and human theories and maxims hear the voice of Him whose word can renew the soul unto everlasting life.

Christ's favorite theme was the paternal tenderness and abundant grace of God; He dwelt much upon the holiness of His character and His law; He presented Himself to the people as the Way, the Truth, and the Life. Let these be the themes of Christ's ministers. Present the truth as it is in Jesus. Make plain the requirements of the law and the gospel. Tell the people of Christ's life of self-denial and sacrifice; of His humiliation and death; of His resurrection and ascension; of His intercession for them in the courts of God; of His promise, "I will come again, and receive you unto Myself." John 14:3.

Instead of discussing erroneous theories, or seeking to combat the opponents of the gospel, follow the example of Christ. Let fresh truths from God's treasure house flash into life. "Preach the word." "Sow beside all waters." "Be instant in season, out of season." "He that hath My word, let him speak My word faithfully. What is the chaff to the wheat? saith the Lord." "Every word of God is pure. . . . Add thou not unto His words, lest He reprove thee, and thou be found a liar." 2 Tim. 4:2; Isa. 32:20; Jer. 23:28; Prov. 30:5, 6.

"The sower soweth the word." Here is presented the great principle which should underlie all educational work. "The seed is the word of God." But in too many schools of our day God's word is set aside. Other subjects occupy the mind. The study of infidel authors holds a large place in the educational system. Skeptical sentiments are interwoven in the matter placed in school books. Scientific research becomes misleading, because its discoveries are misinterpreted and perverted. The word of God is compared with the supposed teachings of science, and is made to appear uncertain and untrustworthy. Thus the seeds of doubt are planted in the minds of the youth, and in time of temptation they spring up. When faith in God's word is lost, the soul has no guide, no safeguard. The youth are drawn into paths which lead away from God and from everlasting life.

To this cause may in great degree be attributed the widespread iniquity in our world today. When the word of God is set aside, its power to restrain the evil passions of the natural heart is rejected. Men sow to the flesh, and of the flesh they reap corruption.

And here, too, is the great cause of mental weakness and inefficiency. In turning from God's word to feed on the writings of uninspired men, the mind becomes dwarfed and cheapened. It is not brought in contact with deep, broad principles of eternal truth. The understanding adapts itself to the comprehension of the things with which it is familiar, and in this devotion to finite things it is weakened, its power is contracted, and after a time it becomes unable to expand.

All this is false education. The work of every [42] teacher should be to fasten the mind of the youth upon the grand truths of the word of Inspiration. This is the education essential for this life and for the life to come.

And let it not be thought that this will prevent the study of the sciences, or cause a lower standard in education. The knowledge of God is as high as heaven and as broad as the universe. There is nothing so ennobling and invigorating as a study of the great themes which concern our eternal life. Let the youth seek to grasp these God-given truths, and their minds will expand and grow strong in the effort. It will bring every student who is a doer of the word into a broader field of thought, and secure for him a wealth of knowledge that is imperishable.

The education to be secured by searching the Scriptures is an experimental knowledge of the [43] plan of salvation. Such an education will restore the image of God in the soul. It will strengthen and fortify the mind against temptation, and fit the learner to become a co-worker with Christ in His mission of mercy to the world. It will make him a member of the heavenly family, and prepare him to share the inheritance of the saints in light.

But the teacher of sacred truth can impart only that which he himself knows by experience. "The sower sowed *his* seed." Christ taught the truth because He was the truth. His own thought, His character, His life-experience, were embodied in His teaching. So with His servants: those who would teach the word are to make it their own by a personal experience. They must know what it is to have Christ made unto them wisdom and righteousness and sanctification and redemption. In presenting

the word of God to others, they are not to make it a suppose-so or a may-be. They should declare with the apostle Peter, "We have not followed cunningly devised fables when we made known unto you the power and coming of our Lord Jesus Christ, but were eye-witnesses of His majesty." 2 Peter 1:16. Every minister of Christ and every teacher should be able to say with the beloved John, "The life was manifested, and we have seen it, and bear witness, and show unto you that eternal life which was with the Father, and was manifested unto us." 1 John 1:2.

The Soil—by the Wayside

That with which the parable of the sower chiefly deals is the effect produced on the growth of the seed by the soil into which it is cast. By this parable Christ was virtually saying to His hearers, It is not safe for you to stand as critics of My work, or to indulge disappointment because it does not meet your ideas. The question of greatest importance to you is, How [44] do you treat My message? Upon your reception or rejection of it your eternal destiny depends.

Explaining the seed that fell by the wayside, He said, "When any one heareth the word of the kingdom, and understandeth it not, then cometh the wicked one, and catcheth away that which was sown in his heart. This is he which received seed by the wayside."

The seed sown by the wayside represents the word of God as it falls upon the heart of an inattentive hearer. Like the hard-beaten path, trodden down by the feet of men and beasts, is the heart that becomes a highway for the world's traffic, its pleasures and sins. Absorbed in selfish aims and sinful indulgences, the soul is "hardened through the deceitfulness of sin." Heb. 3:13. The spiritual faculties are paralyzed. Men hear the word, but understand it not. They do not discern that it applies to themselves. They do not realize their need or their danger. They do not perceive the love of Christ, and they pass by the message of His grace as something that does not concern them.

As the birds are ready to catch up the seed from the wayside, so Satan is ready to catch away the seeds of divine truth from the soul. He fears that the word of God may awaken the careless, and take effect upon the hardened heart. Satan and his angels are in the assemblies where the gospel is preached. While angels of heaven endeavor to impress hearts with the word of God, the enemy is on the alert to make the word of no effect. With an earnestness equaled only by his malice, he tries to thwart the work of the Spirit of God. While Christ is drawing the soul by His love, Satan tries to turn away the attention of the one who is moved to seek the Saviour. He engages the mind with worldly schemes. He excites criticism, or insin- [45]

uates doubt and unbelief. The speaker's choice of language or his manner may not please the hearers, and they dwell upon these defects. Thus the truth they need, and which God has graciously sent them, makes no lasting impression.

Satan has many helpers. Many who profess to be Christians are aiding the tempter to catch away the seeds of truth from other hearts. Many who listen to the preaching of the word of God make it the subject of criticism at home. They sit in judgment on the sermon as they would on the words of a lecturer or a political speaker. The message that should be regarded as the word of the Lord to them is dwelt upon with trifling or sarcastic comment. The minister's character, motives, and actions, and the conduct of fellow members of the church, are freely discussed. Severe judgment is pronounced, gossip or slander repeated, and this in the hearing of the unconverted. Often these things are spoken by parents in the hearing of their own children. Thus are destroyed respect for God's messengers, and reverence for their message. And many are taught to regard lightly God's word itself.

Thus in the homes of professed Christians many youth are educated to be infidels. And the parents question why their children are so little interested in the gospel, and so ready to doubt the truth of the Bible. They wonder that it is so difficult to reach them with moral and religious influences. They do not see that their own example has hardened the hearts of their children. The good seed finds no place to take root, and Satan catches it away.

In Stony Places

"He that receiveth the seed into stony places, the same is he that heareth the word, and anon with joy receiveth it; yet hath he not root in himself, but dureth for a while; for when tribulation or persecution ariseth because of the word, by and by he is offended."

The seed sown upon stony ground finds little depth of soil. The plant springs up quickly, but the root cannot penetrate the rock to find nutriment to sustain its growth, and it soon perishes. Many who make a profession of religion are stony-ground hearers. Like the rock underlying the layer of earth, the selfishness of the natural heart underlies the soil of their good desires and aspirations. The love of self is not subdued. They have not seen the exceeding sinfulness of sin, and the heart has not been humbled under a sense of its guilt. This class may be easily convinced, and appear to be bright converts, but they have only a superficial religion.

It is not because men receive the word immediately, nor because they rejoice in it, that they fall away. As soon as Matthew heard the Saviour's call, immediately he rose up, left all, and followed Him. As soon as the divine word

comes to our hearts, God desires us to receive it; and it is right to accept it with joy. "Joy shall be in heaven over one sinner that repenteth." Luke 15:7. And there is joy in the soul that believes on Christ. But those who in the parable are said to receive the word immediately, do not count the cost. They do not consider what the word of God requires of them. They do not bring it face to face with all their habits of life, and yield themselves fully to its control.

The roots of the plant strike down deep into the soil, and hidden from sight nourish the life of the plant. So with the Christian; it is by the invisible union of the soul with Christ, through faith, that the spiritual life is nourished. But the stony-ground hearers depend upon self instead of Christ. They trust in their good works and good impulses, and are strong in their own righteousness. They are not strong in the Lord, and in the power of His might. Such a one "hath not root in himself"; for he is not connected with Christ.

The hot summer sun, that strengthens and ripens the hardy grain, destroys that which has no depth of root. So he who "hath not root in himself," "dureth for a while"; but "when tribulation or persecution ariseth because of the word, by and by he is offended." Many receive the gospel as a way of escape from suffering, rather than as a deliverance from sin. They rejoice for a season, for they think that religion will free them from difficulty and trial. While life moves smoothly with them, they may appear to be consistent Christians. But they faint beneath the fiery test of temptation. They cannot bear reproach for Christ's sake. When the word of God points out some cherished sin, or requires self-denial or sacrifice, they are offended. It would cost them too much effort to make a radical change in their life. They look at the present inconvenience and trial, and forget the eternal realities. Like the disciples who left Jesus, they are ready to say, "This is an hard saying; who can hear it?" John 6:60.

There are very many who claim to serve God, but who have no experimental knowledge of Him. Their desire to do His will is based upon their own inclination, not upon the deep conviction of the Holy Spirit. Their conduct is not brought into harmony with the law of God. They profess to accept Christ as their Saviour, but they do not believe that He will give them power to overcome their sins. They have not a personal relation with a living Saviour, and their characters reveal defects both hereditary and cultivated.

It is one thing to assent in a general way to the agency of the Holy Spirit, and another thing to accept His work as a reprover calling to repentance. Many feel a sense of estrangement from God, a realization of their bondage to self and sin; they make efforts for reform; but they do not crucify self. They do not give themselves entirely into the hands of Christ, seeking for divine power to do His will. They are not willing to be molded after the divine similitude. In a general way they acknowledge their imperfections, but they do not give up their particular sins. With each wrong act the old selfish nature is gaining strength.

The only hope for these souls is to realize in themselves the truth of Christ's words to Nicodemus, "Ye must be born again." "Except a man be born from above, he can not see the kingdom of God." John 3:7, 3, margin.

True holiness is wholeness in the service of God. This is the condition of true Christian living. Christ asks for an unreserved consecration, for undivided service. He demands the heart, the mind, the soul, the strength. Self is not to be cherished. He who lives to himself is not a Christian.

Love must be the principle of action. Love is the underlying principle of God's government in heaven and earth, and it must be the foundation of the Christian's character. This alone can make and keep him steadfast. This alone can enable him to withstand trial and temptation.

And love will be revealed in sacrifice. The plan of redemption was laid in sacrifice—a sacrifice so broad and deep and high that it is immeasurable. Christ gave all for us, and those who receive Christ will be ready to sacrifice all for the sake of their Redeemer. The thought of His honor and glory will come before anything else.

If we love Jesus, we shall love to live for Him, to present our thank offerings to Him, to labor for Him. The very labor will be light. For His sake we shall covet pain and toil and sacrifice. We shall sympathize with His longing for the salvation of men. We shall feel the same tender craving for souls that He has felt.

This is the religion of Christ. Anything short of it is a deception. No mere theory of truth or profession of discipleship will save any soul. We do not belong to Christ unless we are His wholly. It is by halfheartedness in the Christian life that men become feeble in purpose and changeable in desire. The effort to serve both self and Christ makes one a stony-ground hearer, and he will not endure when the test comes upon him.

Among Thorns

"He also that received seed among the thorns is he that heareth the word; and the care of this world, and the deceitfulness of riches, choke the word, and he becometh unfruitful."

The gospel seed often falls among thorns and noxious weeds; and if there is not a moral transformation in the human heart, if old habits and practices and the former life of sin are not left behind, if the attributes of Satan are not expelled from the soul, the wheat crop will be choked. The thorns will come to be the crop, and will kill out the wheat.

Grace can thrive only in the heart that is being constantly prepared for the precious seeds of truth. The thorns of sin will grow in any soil; they need no cultivation; but grace must be carefully cultivated. The briers and thorns are always ready to spring up, and the work of purification must advance continually. If the heart is not kept under the control of God, if the Holy Spirit does not work unceasingly to refine and ennoble the character, the old habits will reveal themselves in the life. Men may profess to believe the gospel; but unless they are sanctified by the gospel their profession is of no avail. If they do not gain the victory over sin, then sin is gaining the victory over them. The thorns that have been cut off but not uprooted grow apace, until the soul is overspread with them.

Christ specified the things that are dangerous to the soul. As recorded by Mark He mentions the cares of this world, the deceitfulness of riches, and the lusts of other things. Luke specifies the cares, riches, and pleasures of this life. These are what choke the word, the growing spiritual seed. The soul ceases to draw nourishment from Christ, and spirituality dies out of the heart.

"The cares of this world." No class is free from the temptation to worldly care. To the poor, toil and deprivation and the fear of want bring perplexities and burdens. To the rich come fear of loss and a multitude of anxious cares. Many of Christ's followers forget the lesson He has bidden us learn from the flowers of the field. They do not trust to His constant care. Christ cannot carry their burden, because they do not cast it upon Him. Therefore the cares of life, which should drive them to the Saviour for help and comfort, separate them from Him.

Many who might be fruitful in God's service become bent on acquiring wealth. Their whole energy is absorbed in business enterprises, and they feel obliged to neglect things of a spiritual nature. Thus they separate themselves from God. We are enjoined in the Scriptures to be "not slothful in business." Rom. 12:11. We are to labor that we may impart to him who needs. Christians must work, they must engage in business, and they can do this without committing sin. But many become so absorbed in business that they have no time for prayer, no time for the study of the Bible, no time to seek and serve God. At times the longings of the soul go out for holiness and heaven; but there is no time to turn aside from the din of the world to listen to the majestic and authoritative utterances of the Spirit of God. The things of eternity are made subordinate, the things of the world supreme. It is impossible for the seed of the word to bring forth fruit; for the life of the soul is given to nourish the thorns of worldliness.

And many who are working with a very different purpose, fall into a like error. They are working for others' good; their duties are pressing, their responsibilities are many, and they allow their labor to crowd out devotion. Communion with God through prayer and a study of His word is neglected. They forget that Christ has said, "Without Me ye can do nothing." John 15:5. They walk apart from Christ, their life is not pervaded by His grace, and the characteristics of self are revealed. Their service is marred by desire for supremacy, and the harsh, unlovely traits of the unsubdued heart. Here is one of the chief secrets of failure in Christian work. This is why its results are often so meager.

"The deceitfulness of riches." The love of riches has an infatuating, deceptive power. Too often those who possess worldly treasure forget that it is God who gives them power to get wealth. They say, "My power and the might of mine hand hath gotten me this wealth." Deut. 8:17. Their riches, instead of awakening gratitude to God, lead to the exaltation of self. They lose the sense of their dependence upon God and their obligation to their fellow men. Instead of regarding wealth as a talent to be employed for the glory of God and the uplifting of humanity, they look upon it as a means of serving themselves. Instead of developing in man the attributes of God, riches thus used are developing in him the attributes of Satan. The seed of the word is choked with thorns.

53 "And pleasures of this life." There is danger in amusement that is sought merely for self-gratification. All habits of indulgence that weaken the physical powers, that becloud the mind, or that benumb the spiritual perceptions, are "fleshly lusts, which war against the soul." 1 Peter 2:11.

"And the lusts of other things." These are not necessarily things sinful in themselves, but something that is made first instead of the kingdom of God. Whatever attracts the mind from God, whatever draws the affections away from Christ, is an enemy to the soul.

When the mind is youthful and vigorous and susceptible of rapid development, there is great temptation to be ambitious for self, to serve self. If worldly schemes are successful, there is an inclination to continue in a line that deadens conscience, and prevents a correct estimate as to what constitutes real excellence of character. When circumstances favor this development, growth will be seen in a direction prohibited by the word of God.

In this formative period of their children's life, the responsibility of parents is very great. It should be their study to surround the youth with right influences, influences that will give them

correct views of life and its true success. Instead of this, how many parents make it their first object to secure for their children worldly prosperity. All their associations are chosen with reference to this object. Many parents make their home in some large city, and introduce their children into fashionable society. They surround them with influences that encourage worldliness and pride. In this atmosphere the mind and soul are dwarfed. The high and noble aims of life are lost sight of. The privilege of being sons of God, heirs of eternity, is bartered for worldly gain.

Many parents seek to promote the happiness 54 of their children by gratifying their love of amusement. They allow them to engage in sports, and to attend parties of pleasure, and provide them with money to use freely in display and self-gratification. The more the desire for pleasure is indulged, the stronger it becomes. The interest of these youth is more and more absorbed in amusement, until they come to look upon it as the great object of life. They form habits of idleness and self-indulgence that make it almost impossible for them ever to become steadfast Christians.

Even the church, which should be the pillar and ground of the truth, is found encouraging the selfish love of pleasure. When money is to be raised for religious purposes, to what means do many churches resort? To bazaars, suppers, fancy fairs, even to lotteries, and like devices. Often the place set apart for God's worship is desecrated by feasting and drinking, buying, selling, and merrymaking. Respect for the house of God and reverence for His worship are lessened in the minds of the youth. The barriers of self-restraint are weakened. Selfishness, appetite, the love of display, are appealed to, and they strengthen as they are indulged.

The pursuit of pleasure and amusement centers in the cities. Many parents who choose a city home for their children, thinking to give them greater advantages, meet with disappointment, and too late repent their terrible mistake. The cities of today are fast becoming like Sodom and Gomorrah. The many holidays encourage idleness. The exciting sports—theatergoing, horse racing, gambling, liquor-drinking, and reveling—stimulate every passion to intense activity. The youth are swept away by the popular current. Those who learn to love amusement for its own sake open the door to a 55 flood of temptations. They give themselves up to social gaiety and thoughtless mirth, and their intercourse with pleasure lovers has an intoxicating effect upon the mind. They are led on from one form of dissipation to another, until they lose both the desire and the capacity for a life of usefulness. Their religious aspirations are chilled; their spiritual life is darkened. All the nobler faculties of the soul, all that link man with the spiritual world, are debased.

It is true that some may see their folly and repent. God may pardon them. But they have wounded their own souls, and brought upon themselves a lifelong peril. The power of discernment, which ought ever to be kept keen and sensitive to distinguish between right and wrong, is in a great measure destroyed. They are not quick to recognize the guiding voice of the Holy Spirit, or to discern the devices of Satan. Too often in time of danger they fall under temptation, and are led away from God. The end of their pleasure-loving life is ruin for this world and for the world to come.

Cares, riches, pleasures, all are used by Satan in playing the game of life for the human soul. The warning is given, "Love not the world, neither the things that are in the world. If any man love the world, the love of the Father is not in him. For all that is in the world, the lust of the flesh, and the lust of the eyes, and the pride of life, is not of the Father, but is of the world." 1 John 2:15, 16. He who reads the hearts of men as an open book says, "Take heed to yourselves, lest at any time your hearts be overcharged with surfeiting and drunkenness and cares of this life." Luke 21:34. And the apostle Paul by the Holy Spirit writes, "They that will be rich fall into temptation and 56 a snare, and into many foolish and hurtful lusts, which drown men in destruction and perdition. For the love of money is the root of all evil; which, while some coveted after, they have erred from the faith, and pierced themselves through with many sorrows." 1 Tim. 6:9, 10.

Preparation of the Soil

Throughout the parable of the sower, Christ represents the different results of the sowing as depending upon the soil. In every case the sower and the seed are the same. Thus He teaches that if the word of God fails of accomplishing its work in our hearts and lives, the reason is to be found in ourselves. But the result is not beyond our control. True, we cannot change ourselves; but the power of choice is ours, and it rests with us to determine what we will become. The wayside, the stony-ground, the thorny-ground hearers need not remain such. The Spirit of God is ever seeking to break the spell of infatuation that holds men absorbed in worldly things, and to awaken a desire for the imperishable treasure. It is by resisting the Spirit that men become inattentive to or neglectful of God's word. They are themselves responsible for the hardness of heart that prevents the good seed from taking root, and for the evil growths that check its development.

The garden of the heart must be cultivated. The soil must be broken up by deep repentance for sin. Poisonous, Satanic plants must be uprooted. The soil once overgrown by thorns can be reclaimed only by diligent labor. So the evil tendencies of the natural heart can be overcome only by earnest effort in the name and strength of Jesus. The Lord bids us by His prophet, "Break up your fallow ground, and sow not among thorns." "Sow to yourselves in righteousness; reap in mercy." Jer. 4:3; Hosea 10:12. This work He desires to accomplish for us, and He asks us to co-operate with Him.

The sowers of the seed have a work to do in 57 preparing hearts to receive the gospel. In the ministry of the word there is too much sermonizing, and too little of real heart-to-heart work. There is need of personal labor for the souls of the lost. In Christlike sympathy we should come close to men individually, and seek to awaken their interest in the great things of eternal life. Their hearts may be as hard as the beaten highway, and apparently it may be a useless effort to present the Saviour to them; but while logic may fail to move, and argument be powerless to convince, the love of Christ, revealed in personal ministry, may soften the stony heart, so that the seed of truth can take root.

So the sowers have something to do that the seed may not be choked with thorns or perish because of shallowness of soil. At the very outset of the Christian life every believer should be 58 taught its foundation principles. He should be taught that he is not merely to be saved by Christ's sacrifice, but that he is to make the life of Christ his life and the character of Christ his character. Let all be taught that they are to bear burdens and to deny natural inclination. Let them learn the blessedness of working for Christ, following Him in self-denial, and enduring hardness as good soldiers. Let them learn to trust His love and to cast on Him their cares. Let them taste the joy of winning souls for Him. In their love and interest for the lost, they will lose sight of self. The pleasures of the world will lose their power to attract and its burdens to dishearten. The plowshare of truth will do its work. It will break up the fallow ground. It will not merely cut off the tops of the thorns, but will take them out by the roots.

In Good Ground

The sower is not always to meet with disappointment. Of the seed that fell into good ground the Saviour said, This "is he that heareth the word, and understandeth it; which also beareth fruit, and bringeth forth, some an hundredfold, some sixty, some thirty." "That on the good ground are they, which, in an honest and good heart, having heard the word, keep it, and bring forth fruit with patience."

The "honest and good heart" of which the parable speaks, is not a heart without sin; for the gospel is to be preached to the lost. Christ said,

"I came not to call the righteous, but sinners to repentance." Mark 2:17. He has an honest heart who yields to the conviction of the Holy Spirit. He confesses his guilt, and feels his need of the mercy and love of God. He has a sincere desire to know the truth, that he may obey it. The good heart is a believing heart, one that has faith in the word of God. Without faith it is impossible to receive the word. "He that cometh to God must believe that He is, and that He is a rewarder of them that diligently seek Him." Heb. 11:6.

This "is he that heareth the word, and understandeth it." The Pharisees of Christ's day closed their eyes lest they should see, and their ears lest they should hear; therefore the truth could not reach their hearts. They were to suffer retribution for their willful ignorance and self-imposed blindness. But Christ taught His disciples that they were to open their minds to instruction, and be ready to believe. He pronounced a blessing upon them because they saw and heard with eyes and ears that believed.

The good-ground hearer receives the word "not as the word of men, but as it is in truth, the word of God." 1 Thess. 2:13. Only he who receives the Scriptures as the voice of God speaking to himself is a true learner. He trembles at the word; for to him it is a living reality. He opens his understanding and his heart to receive it. Such hearers were Cornelius and his friends, who said to the apostle Peter, "Now therefore are we all here present before God, to hear all things that are commanded thee of God." Acts 10:33.

A knowledge of the truth depends not so much upon strength of intellect as upon pureness of purpose, the simplicity of an earnest, dependent faith. To those who in humility of heart seek for divine guidance, angels of God draw near. The Holy Spirit is given to open to them the rich treasures of the truth.

The good-ground hearers, having heard the word, keep it. Satan with all his agencies of evil is not able to catch it away.

Merely to hear or to read the word is not enough. He who desires to be profited by the Scriptures must meditate upon the truth that has been presented to him. By earnest attention and prayerful thought he must learn the meaning of the words of truth, and drink deep of the spirit of the holy oracles.

God bids us fill the mind with great thoughts, pure thoughts. He desires us to meditate upon His love and mercy, to study His wonderful work in the great plan of redemption. Then clearer and still clearer will be our perception of truth, higher, holier, our desire for purity of heart and clearness of thought. The soul dwelling in the pure atmosphere of holy thought will be transformed by communion with God through the study of the Scriptures.

"And bring forth fruit." Those who, having heard the word, keep it, will bring forth fruit in obedience. The word of God, received into the soul, will be manifest in good works. Its results will be seen in a Christlike character and life. Christ said of Himself, "I delight to do Thy will, O My God; yea, Thy law is within My heart." Ps. 40:8. "I seek not Mine own will, but the will of the Father which hath sent Me." John 5:30. And the Scripture says, "He that saith he abideth in Him ought himself also so to walk, even as He walked." 1 John 2:6.

The word of God often comes in collision with man's hereditary and cultivated traits of character and his habits of life. But the good-ground hearer, in receiving the word, accepts all its conditions and requirements. His habits, customs, and practices are brought into submission to God's word. In his view the commands of finite, erring man sink into insignificance beside the word of the infinite God. With the whole heart, with undivided purpose, he is seeking the life eternal, and at the cost of loss, persecution, or death itself, he will obey the truth.

And he brings forth fruit "with patience." None who receive God's word are exempt from difficulty and trial; but when affliction comes, the true Christian does not become restless, distrustful, or despondent. Though we can not see the definite outcome of affairs, or discern the purpose of God's providences, we are not to cast away our confidence. Remembering the tender mercies of the Lord, we should cast our care upon Him, and with patience wait for His salvation.

Through conflict the spiritual life is strengthened. Trials well borne will develop steadfastness of character and precious spiritual graces. The perfect fruit of faith, meekness, and love often matures best amid storm clouds and darkness.

"The husbandman waiteth for the precious fruit of the earth, and hath long patience for it, until he receive the early and latter rain." James 5:7. So the Christian is to wait with patience for the fruition in his life of the word of God. Often when we pray for the graces of the Spirit, God works to answer our prayers by placing us in circumstances to develop these fruits; but we do not understand His purpose, and wonder, and are dismayed. Yet none can develop these graces except through the process of growth and fruit bearing. Our part is to receive God's word and to hold it fast, yielding ourselves fully to its control, and its purpose in us will be accomplished.

"If a man love Me," Christ said, "he will keep My words; and My Father will love him, and we will come unto him, and make our abode with him." John 14:23. The spell of a stronger, a perfect mind will be over us; for we have a living connection with the source of all-enduring strength. In our divine life we shall be brought into captivity to Jesus Christ. We shall no longer live the common life of selfishness, but Christ will live in us. His character will be reproduced in our nature. Thus shall we bring forth the fruits of the Holy Spirit—"some thirty, and some sixty, and some an hundred."

3

"First the Blade, Then the Ear"

The parable of the sower excited much questioning. Some of the hearers gathered from it that Christ was not to establish an earthly kingdom, and many were curious and perplexed. Seeing their perplexity, Christ used other illustrations, still seeking to turn their thoughts from the hope of a worldly kingdom to the work of God's grace in the soul.

"And He said, So is the kingdom of God, as if a man should cast seed into the ground; and should sleep, and rise night and day, and the seed should spring and grow up, he knoweth not how. For the earth bringeth forth fruit of herself; first the blade, then the ear, after that the full corn in the ear. But when the fruit is brought forth, immediately he putteth in the sickle, because the harvest is come."

The husbandman who "putteth in the sickle, because the harvest is come," can be no other than Christ. It is He who at the last great day will reap the harvest of the earth. But the sower of the seed represents those who labor in Christ's stead. The seed is said to "spring and grow up, he knoweth not how," and this is not true of the Son of God. Christ does not sleep over His charge, but watches it day and night. He is not ignorant of how the seed grows.

The parable of the seed reveals that God is at work in nature. The seed has in itself a germinating principle, a principle that God Himself has implanted; yet if left to itself the seed would have no power to spring up. Man has his part to act in promoting the growth of the grain. He must prepare and enrich the soil and cast in the seed. He must till the fields. But there is a point beyond which he can accomplish nothing. No strength or wisdom of man can bring forth from the seed the living plant. Let man put forth his efforts to the utmost limit, he must still depend upon One who has connected the sowing and the reaping by wonderful links of His own omnipotent power.

There is life in the seed, there is power in the soil; but unless an infinite power is exercised day and night, the seed will yield no returns. The showers of rain must be sent to give moisture to the thirsty fields, the sun must impart heat, electricity must be conveyed to the buried

seed. The life which the Creator has implanted, He alone can call forth. Every seed grows, every plant develops, by the power of God.

"As the earth bringeth forth her bud, and as the garden causeth the things that are sown in it to spring forth, so the Lord God will cause righteousness and praise to spring forth." Isa. 61:11. As in the natural, so in the spiritual sowing; the teacher of truth must seek to prepare the soil of the heart; he must sow the seed; but the power that alone can produce life is from God. There is a point beyond which human effort is in vain. While we are to preach the word, we can not impart the power that will quicken the soul, and cause righteousness and praise to spring forth. In the preaching of the word there must be the working of an agency beyond any human power. Only through the divine Spirit will the word be living and powerful to renew the soul unto eternal life. This is what Christ tried to impress upon His disciples. He taught that it was nothing they possessed in themselves which would give success to their labors, but that it is the miracle-working power of God which gives efficiency to His own word.

The work of the sower is a work of faith. The mystery of the germination and growth of the seed he cannot understand. But he has confidence in the agencies by which God causes vegetation to flourish. In casting his seed into the ground, he is apparently throwing away the precious grain that might furnish bread for his family. But he is only giving up a present good for a larger return. He casts the seed away, expecting to gather it manyfold in an abundant harvest. So Christ's servants are to labor, expecting a harvest from the seed they sow.

The good seed may for a time lie unnoticed in a cold, selfish, worldly heart, giving no evidence that it has taken root; but afterward, as the Spirit of God breathes on the soul, the hidden seed springs up, and at last bears fruit to the glory of God. In our lifework we know not which shall prosper, this or that. This is not a question for us to settle. We are to do our work, and leave the results with God. "In the morning sow thy seed, and in the evening withhold not thine hand." Eccl. 11:6. God's great covenant declares that "while the earth remaineth, seedtime and harvest . . . shall not cease." Gen. 8:22. In the confidence of this promise the husbandman tills and sows. Not less confidently are we in the spiritual sowing to labor, trusting His assurance, "So shall My word be that goeth forth out of My mouth; it shall not return unto Me void, but it shall accomplish that which I please, and it shall prosper in the thing whereto I sent it." Isa. 55:11. "He that goeth forth and weepeth, bearing precious seed, shall doubtless come again with rejoicing, bringing his sheaves with him." Ps. 126:6.

The germination of the seed represents the

beginning of spiritual life, and the development of the plant is a beautiful figure of Christian growth. As in nature, so in grace; there can be no life without growth. The plant must either grow or die. As its growth is silent and imperceptible, but continuous, so is the development of the Christian life. At every stage of development our life may be perfect; yet if God's purpose for us is fulfilled, there will be continual advancement. Sanctification is the work of a lifetime. As our opportunities multiply, our experience will enlarge, and our knowledge increase. We shall become strong to bear responsibility, and our maturity will be in proportion to our privileges.

The plant grows by receiving that which God has provided to sustain its life. It sends down its roots into the earth. It drinks in the sunshine, the dew, and the rain. It receives the life-giving properties from the air. So the Christian is to grow by co-operating with the divine agencies. Feeling our helplessness, we are to improve all the opportunities granted us to gain a fuller experience. As the plant takes root in the soil, so we are to take deep root in Christ. As the plant receives the sunshine, the dew, and the rain, we are to open our hearts to the Holy Spirit. The work is to be done "not by might, nor by power, but by My Spirit, saith the Lord of hosts." Zech. 4:6. If we keep our minds stayed upon Christ, He will come unto us "as the rain, as the latter and former rain unto the earth." Hosea 6:3. As the Sun of Righteousness, He will arise upon us "with healing in His wings." Mal. 4:2. We shall "grow as the lily." We shall "revive as the corn, and grow as the vine." Hosea 14:5, 7. By constantly relying upon Christ as our personal Saviour, we shall grow up into Him in all things who is our head.

The wheat develops "first the blade, then the ear, after that the full corn in the ear." The object of the husbandman in the sowing of the seed and the culture of the growing plant is the production of grain. He desires bread for the hungry, and seed for future harvests. So the divine Husbandman looks for a harvest as the reward of His labor and sacrifice. Christ is seeking to reproduce Himself in the hearts of men; and He does this through those who believe in Him. The object of the Christian life is fruit bearing—the reproduction of Christ's character in the believer, that it may be reproduced in others.

The plant does not germinate, grow, or bring forth fruit for itself, but to "give seed to the sower, and bread to the eater." Isa. 55:10. So no man is to live unto himself. The Christian is in the world as a representative of Christ, for the salvation of other souls.

There can be no growth or fruitfulness in the life that is centered in self. If you have accepted Christ as a personal Saviour, you are to forget yourself, and try to help others. Talk of the love of Christ, tell of His goodness. Do every duty that presents itself. Carry the burden of souls upon your heart, and by every means in your power seek to save the lost. As you receive the Spirit of Christ—the Spirit of unselfish love and labor for others—you will grow and bring forth fruit. The graces of the Spirit will ripen in your character. Your faith will increase, your convictions deepen, your love be made perfect. More and more you will reflect the likeness of Christ in all that is pure, noble, and lovely.

"The fruit of the Spirit is love, joy, peace, longsuffering, gentleness, goodness, faith, meekness, temperance." Gal. 5:22, 23. This fruit can never perish, but will produce after its kind a harvest unto eternal life.

"When the fruit is brought forth, immediately he putteth in the sickle, because the harvest is come." Christ is waiting with longing desire for the manifestation of Himself in His church. When the character of Christ shall be perfectly reproduced in His people, then He will come to claim them as His own.

It is the privilege of every Christian not only to look for but to hasten the coming of our Lord Jesus Christ, (2 Peter 3:12, margin). Were all who profess His name bearing fruit to His glory, how quickly the whole world would be sown with the seed of the gospel. Quickly the last great harvest would be ripened, and Christ would come to gather the precious grain.

4
Tares

"Another parable put He forth unto them, saying, The kingdom of heaven is likened unto a man which sowed good seed in his field; but while men slept, his enemy came and sowed tares among the wheat, and went his way. But when the blade was sprung up, and brought forth fruit, then appeared the tares also."

"The field," Christ said, "is the world." But we must understand this as signifying the church of Christ in the world. The parable is a description of that which pertains to the kingdom of God, His work of salvation of men; and this work is accomplished through the church. True, the Holy Spirit has gone out into all the world; everywhere it is moving upon the hearts of men; but it is in church that we are to grow and ripen for the garner of God.

"He that sowed the good seed is the Son of man. . . . The good seed are the children of the kingdom; but the tares are the children of the wicked one." The good seed represents those who are born of the word of God, the truth. The tares represent a class who are the fruit or embodiment of error, of false principles. "The

This chapter is based on Matthew 13:24-30, 37-43.

enemy that sowed them is the devil." Neither God nor His angels ever sowed a seed that would produce a tare. The tares are always sown by Satan, the enemy of God and man.

In the East, men sometimes took revenge upon an enemy by strewing his newly sown fields with the seeds of some noxious weed that, while growing, closely resembled wheat. Springing up with the wheat, it injured the crop and brought trouble and loss to the owner of the field. So it is from enmity to Christ that Satan scatters his evil seed among the good grain of the kingdom. The fruit of his sowing he attributes to the Son of God. By bringing into the church those who bear Christ's name while they deny His character, the wicked one causes that God shall be dishonored, the work of salvation misrepresented, and souls imperiled.

Christ's servants are grieved as they see true and false believers mingled in the church. They long to do something to cleanse the church. Like the servants of the householder, they are ready to uproot the tares. But Christ says to them, "Nay; lest while ye gather up the tares, ye root up also the wheat with them. Let both grow together until the harvest."

Christ has plainly taught that those who persist in open sin must be separated from the church, but He has not committed to us the work of judging character and motive. He knows our nature too well to entrust this work to us. Should we try to uproot from the church those whom we suppose to be spurious Christians, we should be sure to make mistakes. Often we regard as hopeless subjects the very ones whom Christ is drawing to Himself. Were we to deal with these souls according to our imperfect judgment, it would perhaps extinguish their last hope. Many who think themselves Christians will at last be found wanting. Many will be in heaven who their neighbors supposed would never enter there. Man judges from appearance, but God judges the heart. The tares and the wheat are to grow together until the harvest; and the harvest is the end of probationary time.

There is in the Saviour's words another lesson of wonderful forbearance and tender love. As the tares have their roots closely intertwined with those of the good grain, so false brethren in the church may be closely linked with true disciples. The real character of these pretended believers is not fully manifested. Were they to be separated from the church, others might be caused to stumble, who but for this would have remained steadfast.

The teaching of this parable is illustrated in God's own dealing with men and angels. Satan is a deceiver. When he sinned in heaven, even the loyal angels did not fully discern his character. This was why God did not at once destroy Satan. Had He done so, the holy angels would

not have perceived the justice and love of God. A doubt of God's goodness would have been as evil seed that would yield the bitter fruit of sin and woe. Therefore the author of evil was spared, fully to develop his character. Through long ages God has borne the anguish of beholding the work of evil, He has given the infinite Gift of Calvary, rather than leave any to be deceived by the misrepresentations of the wicked one; for the tares could not be plucked up without danger of uprooting the precious grain. And shall we not be as forbearing toward our fellow men as the Lord of heaven and earth is toward Satan?

The world has no right to doubt the truth of Christianity because there are unworthy members in the church, nor should Christians become disheartened because of these false brethren. How was it with the early church? Ananias and Sapphira joined themselves to the disciples. Simon Magus was baptized. Demas, who forsook Paul, had been counted a believer. Judas Iscariot was numbered with the apostles. The Redeemer does not want to lose one soul; His experience with Judas is recorded to show His long patience with perverse human nature; and He bids us bear with it as He has borne. He has said that false brethren will be found in the church till the close of time.

Notwithstanding Christ's warning, men have sought to uproot the tares. To punish those who were supposed to be evildoers, the church has had recourse to the civil power. Those who differed from the established doctrines have been imprisoned, put to torture and to death, at the instigation of men who claimed to be acting under the sanction of Christ. But it is the spirit of Satan, not the Spirit of Christ, that inspires such acts. This is Satan's own method of bringing the world under his dominion. God has been misrepresented through the church by this way of dealing with those supposed to be heretics.

Not judgment and condemnation of others, but humility and distrust of self, is the teaching of Christ's parable. Not all that is sown in the field is good grain. The fact that men are in the church does not prove them Christians.

The tares closely resembled the wheat while the blades were green; but when the field was white for the harvest, the worthless weeds bore no likeness to the wheat that bowed under the weight of its full, ripe heads. Sinners who make a pretension of piety mingle for a time with the true followers of Christ, and the semblance of Christianity is calculated to deceive many; but in the harvest of the world there will be no likeness between good and evil. Then those who have joined the church, but who have not joined Christ, will be manifest.

The tares are permitted to grow among the wheat, to have all the advantage of sun and shower; but in the time of harvest ye shall "return, and discern between the righteous and the wicked, between him that serveth God and him that serveth Him not." Mal. 3:18. Christ Himself will decide who are worthy to dwell with the family of heaven. He will judge every man according to his words and his works. Profession is as nothing in the scale. It is character that decides destiny.

75   The Saviour does not point forward to a time when all the tares become wheat. The wheat and tares grow together until the harvest, the end of the world. Then the tares are bound in bundles to be burned, and the wheat is gathered into the garner of God. "Then shall the righteous shine forth as the sun in the kingdom of their Father." Then "the Son of man shall send forth His angels, and they shall gather out of His kingdom all things that offend, and them which do iniquity; and shall cast them into a furnace of fire; there shall be wailing and gnashing of teeth."

76

5

"Like a Grain of Mustard Seed"

In the multitude that listened to Christ's teaching there were many Pharisees. These noted contemptuously how few of His hearers acknowledged Him as the Messiah. And they questioned with themselves how this unpretending teacher could exalt Israel to universal dominion. Without riches, power, or honor, how was He to establish the new kingdom? Christ read their thoughts and answered them:

"Whereunto shall we liken the kingdom of God? or with what comparison shall we compare it?" In earthly governments there was nothing that could serve for a similitude. No civil society could afford Him a symbol. "It is like a grain of mustard seed," He said, "which, when it is sown upon the earth, though it be less than all the seeds that are upon the earth, yet when it is sown, groweth up, and becometh greater than all the herbs, and putteth out great branches; so that the birds of the heaven can lodge under the shadow thereof." (R.V.)

77   The germ in the seed grows by the unfolding of the life-principle which God has implanted. Its development depends upon no human power. So it is with the kingdom of Christ. It is a new creation. Its principles of development are the opposite of those that rule the kingdoms of this world. Earthly governments prevail by physical force; they maintain their dominion by war; but the founder of the new kingdom is the Prince of Peace. The Holy Spirit represents worldly kingdoms under the symbol of fierce beasts of prey; but Christ is "the Lamb of God, which taketh away the sin of the world." John 1:29. In His plan of government there is no

employment of brute force to compel the conscience. The Jews looked for the kingdom of God to be established in the same way as the kingdoms of the world. To promote righteousness they resorted to external measures. They devised methods and plans. But Christ implants a principle. By implanting truth and righteousness, He counterworks error and sin.

As Jesus spoke this parable, the mustard plant could be seen far and near, lifting itself above the grass and grain, and waving its branches lightly in the air. Birds flitted from twig to twig, and sang amid the leafy foliage. Yet the seed from which sprang this giant plant was among the least of all seeds. At first it sent up a tender shoot, but it was of strong vitality, and grew and flourished until it reached its present great size. So the kingdom of Christ in its beginning seemed humble and insignificant. Compared with earthly kingdoms it appeared to be the least of all. By the rulers of this world Christ's claim to be a king was ridiculed. Yet in the mighty truths committed to His followers the kingdom of the gospel possessed a divine life. And how rapid was its growth, how widespread its influence! When Christ spoke this parable, there were only a few Galilean peasants to represent the new kingdom. Their poverty, the fewness of   78 their numbers, were urged over and over again as a reason why men should not connect themselves with these simple-minded fishermen who followed Jesus. But the mustard seed was to grow and spread forth its branches throughout the world. When the earthly kingdoms whose glory then filled the hearts of men should perish, the kingdom of Christ would remain, a mighty and far-reaching power.

So the work of grace in the heart is small in its beginning. A word is spoken, a ray of light is shed into the soul, an influence is exerted that is the beginning of the new life; and who can measure its results?

Not only is the growth of Christ's kingdom illustrated by the parable of the mustard seed, but in every stage of its growth the experience represented in the parable is repeated. For His church in every generation God has a special truth and a special work. The truth that is hid from the worldly wise and prudent is revealed to the child-like and humble. It calls for self-sacrifice. It has battles to fight and victories to win. At the outset its advocates are few. By the great men of the world and by a world-conforming church, they are opposed and despised. See John the Baptist, the forerunner of Christ, standing alone to rebuke the pride and formalism of the Jewish nation. See the first bearers of the gospel into Europe. How obscure, how hopeless, seemed the mission of Paul and Silas, the two tentmakers, as they with their companions took ship at Troas for Philippi. See "Paul the aged," in chains, preaching Christ in the strong-

This chapter is based on Matthew 13:31, 32; Mark 4:30-32; Luke 13:18, 19.

hold of the Caesars. See the little communities of slaves and peasants in conflict with the heathenism of imperial Rome. See Martin Luther withstanding that mighty church which is the masterpiece of the world's wisdom. See him holding fast God's word against emperor and pope, declaring, "Here I take my stand; I can not do otherwise. God be my help." See John Wesley preaching Christ and His righteousness in the midst of formalism, sensualism, and infidelity. See one burdened with the woes of the heathen world, pleading for the privilege of carrying to them Christ's message of love. Hear the response of ecclesiasticism: "Sit down, young man. When God wants to convert the heathen, He will do it without your help or mine."

The great leaders of religious thought in this generation sound the praises and build the monuments of those who planted the seed of truth centuries ago. Do not many turn from this work to trample down the growth springing from the same seed today? The old cry is repeated, "We *know* that God spake unto Moses; as for this fellow [Christ in the messenger He sends], we know not from whence he is." John 9:29. As in earlier ages, the special truths for this time are found, not with the ecclesiastical authorities, but with men and women who are not too learned or too wise to believe the word of God.

"For ye see your calling, brethren, how that not many wise men after the flesh, not many mighty, not many noble, are called; but God hath chosen the foolish things of the world to confound the wise; and God hath chosen the weak things of the world to confound the things which are mighty. And base things of the world, and things which are despised, hath God chosen, yea, and things which are not, to bring to naught things that are" (1 Cor. 1:26-28); "that your faith should not stand in the wisdom of men, but in the power of God" (1 Cor. 2:5).

And in this last generation the parable of the mustard seed is to reach a signal and triumphant fulfillment. The little seed will become a tree. The last message of warning and mercy is to go to "every nation and kindred and tongue" (Rev. 14:6-14), "to take out of them a people for His name" (Acts 15:14; Rev. 18:1). And the earth shall be lightened with His glory.

6

Other Lessons From Seed-sowing

From the work of seed sowing and the growth of the plant from the seed, precious lessons may be taught in the family and the school. Let the children and youth learn to recognize in natural things the working of divine agencies, and they will be enabled to grasp by faith unseen benefits. As they come to understand the wonderful work of God in supplying the wants of His great family, and how we are to co-operate with Him, they will have more faith in God, and will realize more of His power in their own daily life.

God created the seed, as He created the earth, by His word. By His word He gave it power to grow and multiply. He said, "Let the earth bring forth grass, the herb yielding seed, and the fruit tree yielding fruit after his kind, whose seed is in itself, upon the earth; and it was so. . . : And God saw that it was good." Gen. 1:11, 12. It is that word which still causes the seed to grow. Every seed that sends up its green blade to the sunlight declares the wonder-working power of that word uttered by Him who "spake, and it was"; who "commanded, and it stood fast." Ps. 33:9.

Christ taught His disciples to pray "Give us this day our daily bread." And pointing to the flowers He gave them the assurance, "If God so clothe the grass of the field, . . . shall He not much more clothe you?" Matt. 6:11, 30. Christ is constantly working to answer this prayer, and to make good this assurance. There is an invisible power constantly at work as man's servant to feed and to clothe him. Many agencies our Lord employs to make the seed, apparently thrown away, a living plant. And He supplies in due proportion all that is required to perfect the harvest. In the beautiful words of the psalmist:

"Thou visitest the earth, and waterest it;
Thou greatly enrichest it;
The river of God is full of water;
Thou providest them corn when Thou hast so prepared the earth.
Thou waterest her furrows abundantly;
Thou settlest the ridges thereof;
Thou makest it soft with showers;
Thou blessest the springing thereof.
Thou crownest the year with Thy goodness;
And Thy paths drop fatness."
Ps. 65:9-11, R.V.

The material world is under God's control. The laws of nature are obeyed by nature. Everything speaks and acts the will of the Creator. Cloud and sunshine, dew and rain, wind and storm, all are under the supervision of God, and yield implicit obedience to His command. It is in obedience to the law of God that the spire of grain bursts through the ground, "first the blade, then the ear, after that the full corn in the ear." Mark 4:28. These the Lord develops in their proper season because they do not resist His working. And can it be that man, made in the image of God, endowed with reason and speech, shall alone be unappreciative of His gifts and disobedient to His will? Shall rational beings alone cause confusion in our world?

In everything that tends to the sustenance of man is seen the concurrence of divine and human effort. There can be no reaping unless the human hand acts its part in the sowing of the seed. But without the agencies which God provides in giving sunshine and showers, dew and clouds, there would be no increase. Thus it is in every business pursuit, in every department of study and science. Thus it is in spiritual things, in the formation of the character, and in every line of Christian work. We have a part to act, but we must have the power of divinity to unite with us, or our efforts will be in vain.

Whenever man accomplishes anything, whether in spiritual or in temporal lines, he should bear in mind that he does it through co-operation with his Maker. There is great necessity for us to realize our dependence on God. Too much confidence is placed in man, too much reliance on human inventions. There is too little confidence in the power which God stands ready to give. "We are laborers together with God." 1 Cor. 3:9. Immeasurably inferior is the part which the human agent sustains; but if he is linked with the divinity of Christ, he can do all things through the strength that Christ imparts.

83 The gradual development of the plant from the seed is an object lesson in child training. There is "first the blade, then the ear, after that the full corn in the ear." He who gave this parable created the tiny seed, gave it its vital properties, and ordained the laws that govern its growth. And the truths which the parable teaches were made a living reality in His own life. In both His physical and His spiritual nature He followed the divine order of growth illustrated by the plant, as He wishes all youth to do. Although He was the Majesty of heaven, the King of glory, He became a babe in Bethlehem, and for a time represented the helpless infant in its mother's care. In childhood He did the works of an obedient child. He spoke and acted with the wisdom of a child and not of a man, honoring His parents and carrying out their wishes in helpful ways, according to the ability of a child. But at each stage of His development He was perfect, with the simple, natural grace of a sinless life. The sacred record says of His childhood, "The child grew, and waxed strong in spirit, filled with wisdom; and the grace of God was upon Him." And of His youth it is recorded, "Jesus increased in wisdom and stature, and in favor with God and man." Luke 2:40, 52.

The work of parents and teachers is here suggested. They should aim so to cultivate the tendencies of the youth that at each stage of their life they may represent the natural beauty appropriate to that period, unfolding naturally, as do the plants in the garden.

Those children are most attractive who are natural, unaffected. It is not wise to give them special notice, and repeat their clever sayings before them. Vanity should not be encouraged by praising their looks, their words, or their actions. Nor should they be dressed in an expensive or showy manner. This encourages pride in them, and awakens envy in the hearts of their companions.

The little ones should be educated in childlike 84 simplicity. They should be trained to be content with the small, helpful duties and the pleasures and experiences natural to their years. Childhood answers to the blade in the parable, and the blade has a beauty peculiarly its own. The children should not be forced into a precocious maturity but should retain as long as possible the freshness and grace of their early years.

The little children may be Christians, having an experience in accordance with their years. This is all that God expects of them. They need to be educated in spiritual things; and parents should give them every advantage that they may form characters after the similitude of the character of Christ.

In the laws of God in nature, effect follows cause with unerring certainty. The reaping will testify as to what the sowing has been. The slothful worker is condemned by his work. The harvest bears witness against him. So in spiritual things: the faithfulness of every worker is measured by the results of his work. The character of his work, whether diligent or slothful, is revealed by the harvest. It is thus that his destiny for eternity is decided.

Every seed sown produces a harvest of its kind. So it is in human life. We all need to sow the seeds of compassion, sympathy, and love; for we shall reap what we sow. Every characteristic of selfishness, self-love, self-esteem, every act of self-indulgence, will bring forth a like harvest. He who lives for self is sowing to the flesh, and of the flesh he will reap corruption.

God destroys no man. Everyone who is destroyed will have destroyed himself. Everyone who stifles the admonitions of conscience is sowing the seeds of unbelief, and these will produce a sure harvest. By rejecting the first warning from God, Pharaoh of old sowed the seeds 85 of obstinacy, and he reaped obstinacy. God did not compel him to disbelieve. The seed of unbelief which he sowed produced a harvest of its kind. Thus his resistance continued, until he looked upon his devastated land, upon the cold, dead form of his first-born, and the first-born of all in his house and of all the families in his kingdom, until the waters of the sea closed over his horses and his chariots and his men of war. His history is a fearful illustration of the truth of the words that "whatsoever a man soweth, that shall he also reap." Gal. 6:7. Did men but realize this, they would be careful what seed they sow.

As the seed sown produces a harvest, and this in turn is sown, the harvest is multiplied. In our relation to others, this law holds true. Every act, every word, is a seed that will bear fruit. Every deed of thoughtful kindness, of obedience, or of self-denial, will reproduce itself in others, and through them in still others. So every act of envy, malice, or dissension is a seed that will spring up in a "root of bitterness" (Heb. 12:15), whereby many shall be defiled. And how much larger number will the "many" poison. Thus the sowing of good and evil goes on for time and for eternity.

Liberality both in spiritual and in temporal things is taught in the lesson of seed sowing. The Lord says, "Blessed are ye that sow beside all waters." Isa. 32:20. "This I say, He which soweth sparingly shall reap also sparingly; and he which soweth bountifully shall reap also bountifully." 2 Cor. 9:6. To sow beside all waters means a continual imparting of God's gifts. It means giving wherever the cause of God or the needs of humanity demand our aid. This will not tend to poverty. "He which soweth bountifully shall reap also bountifully." The sower multiplies his seed by casting it away. So it is with those who are faithful in distributing God's gifts. By imparting they increase their blessings. God has promised them a sufficiency that they may continue to give. "Give, and it shall be given unto you; good measure, pressed down, and shaken together, and running over, shall men give into your bosom." Luke 6:38.

And more than this is wrapped up in the sowing and the reaping. As we distribute God's temporal blessings, the evidence of our love and sympathy awakens in the receiver gratitude and thanksgiving to God. The soil of the heart is prepared to receive the seeds of spiritual truth. And He who ministers seed to the sower will cause the seed to germinate and bear fruit unto eternal life.

By the casting of the grain into the soil, Christ represents the sacrifice of Himself for our redemption. "Except a corn of wheat fall into the ground and die," He says, "it abideth alone; but if it die, it bringeth forth much fruit." John 12:24. So the death of Christ will result in fruit for the kingdom of God. In accordance with the law of the vegetable kingdom, life will be the result of His death.

And all who would bring forth fruit as workers together with Christ must first fall into the ground and die. The life must be cast into the furrow of the world's need. Self-love, self-interest, must perish. But the law of self-sacrifice is the law of self-preservation. The seed buried in the ground produces fruit, and in turn this is planted. Thus the harvest is multiplied. The husbandman preserves his grain by casting it away. So in human life, to give is to live. The life that will be preserved is the life that is freely given in service to God and man. Those who for Christ's sake sacrifice their life in this world, will keep it unto life eternal.

The seed dies to spring forth into new life, and in this we are taught the lesson of the resurrection. All who love God will live again in the Eden above. Of the human body laid away to molder in the grave God has said, "It is sown in corruption; it is raised in incorruption: it is sown in dishonor; it is raised in glory: it is sown in weakness; it is raised in power." 1 Cor. 15:42, 43.

Such are a few of the many lessons taught by nature's living parable of the sower and the seed. As parents and teachers try to teach these lessons, the work should be made practical. Let the children themselves prepare the soil and sow the seed. As they work, the parent or teacher can explain the garden of the heart with the good or bad seed sown there, and that as the garden must be prepared for the natural seed, so the heart must be prepared for the seed of truth. As the seed is cast into the ground, they can teach the lesson of Christ's death; and as the blade springs up, they can teach the lesson of the truth of the resurrection. As the plants grow, the correspondence between the natural and the spiritual sowing may be continued.

The youth should be instructed in a similar way. They should be taught to till the soil. It would be well if there were, connected with every school, lands for cultivation. Such lands should be regarded as God's own schoolroom. The things of nature should be looked upon as a lesson book which His children are to study, and from which they may obtain knowledge as to the culture of the soul.

In tilling the soil, in disciplining and subduing the land, lessons may constantly be learned. No one would think of settling upon a raw piece of land, expecting it at once to yield a harvest. Earnestness, diligence, and persevering labor are to be put forth in treating the soil preparatory to sowing the seed. So it is in the spiritual work in the human heart. Those who would be benefited by the tilling of the soil must go forth with the word of God in their hearts. They will then find the fallow ground of the heart broken by the softening, subduing influence of the Holy Spirit. Unless hard work is bestowed on the soil, it will not yield a harvest. So with the soil of the heart: the Spirit of God must work upon it to refine and discipline it before it can bring forth fruit to the glory of God.

The soil will not produce its riches when worked by impulse. It needs thoughtful, daily attention. It must be plowed often and deep, with a view to keeping out the weeds that take nourishment from the good seed planted. Thus those who plow and sow prepare for the harvest. None need stand in the field amid the sad wreck of their hopes.

The blessing of the Lord will rest upon those who thus work the land, learning spiritual lessons from nature. In cultivating the soil the worker knows little what treasures will open up before him. While he is not to despise the instruction he may gather from minds that have had an experience, and from the information that intelligent men may impart, he should gather lessons for himself. This is a part of his training. The cultivation of the soil will prove an education to the soul.

89 He who causes the seed to spring up, who tends it day and night, who gives it power to develop, is the Author of our being, the King of heaven, and He exercises still greater care and interest in behalf of His children. While the human sower is planting the seed to sustain our earthly life, the Divine Sower will plant in the soul the seed that will bring forth fruit unto life everlasting.

95

7

Like Unto Leaven

Many educated and influential men had come to hear the Prophet of Galilee. Some of these looked with curious interest upon the multitude that had gathered about Christ as He taught by the sea. In this great throng all classes of society were represented. There were the poor, the illiterate, the ragged beggar, the robber with the seal of guilt upon his face, the maimed, the dissipated, the merchant and the man of leisure, high and low, rich and poor, all crowding upon one another for a place to stand and hear the words of Christ. As these cultured men gazed upon the strange assembly, they asked themselves, Is the kingdom of God composed of such material as this? Again the Saviour replied by a parable:

"The kingdom of heaven is like unto leaven, which a woman took, and hid in three measures of meal, till the whole was leavened."

Among the Jews leaven was sometimes used as an emblem of sin. At the time of the Passover 96 the people were directed to remove all the leaven from their houses as they were to put away sin from their hearts. Christ warned His disciples, "Beware ye of the leaven of the Pharisees, which is hypocrisy." Luke 12:1. And the apostle Paul speaks of the "leaven of malice and wickedness." 1 Cor. 5:8. But in the Saviour's parable, leaven is used to represent the kingdom

of heaven. It illustrates the quickening, assimilating power of the grace of God.

None are so vile, none have fallen so low, as to be beyond the working of this power. In all who will submit themselves to the Holy Spirit a new principle of life is to be implanted; the lost image of God is to be restored in humanity.

But man cannot transform himself by the exercise of his will. He possesses no power by which this change can be effected. The leaven—something wholly from without—must be put into the meal before the desired change can be wrought in it. So the grace of God must be received by the sinner before he can be fitted for the kingdom of glory. All the culture and education which the world can give will fail of making a degraded child of sin a child of heaven. The renewing energy must come from God. The change can be made only by the Holy Spirit. All 97 who would be saved, high or low, rich or poor, must submit to the working of this power.

As the leaven, when mingled with the meal, works from within outward, so it is by the renewing of the heart that the grace of God works to transform the life. No mere external change is sufficient to bring us into harmony with God. There are many who try to reform by correcting this or that bad habit, and they hope in this way to become Christians, but they are beginning in the wrong place. Our first work is with the heart.

A profession of faith and the possession of truth in the soul are two different things. The mere knowledge of truth is not enough. We may possess this, but the tenor of our thoughts may not be changed. The heart must be converted and sanctified.

The man who attempts to keep the commandments of God from a sense of obligation merely—because he is required to do so—will never enter into the joy of obedience. He does not obey. When the requirements of God are accounted a burden because they cut across human inclination, we may know that the life is not a Christian life. True obedience is the outworking of a principle within. It springs from the love of righteousness, the love of the law of God. The essence of all righteousness is loyalty 98 to our Redeemer. This will lead us to do right because it is right—because right doing is pleasing to God.

The great truth of the conversion of the heart by the Holy Spirit is presented in Christ's words

---

"Blessed are the undefiled in the way, who walk in the law of the Lord. Blessed are they that keep His testimonies, and that seek Him with the whole heart. They also do no iniquity: they walk in His ways. Thou hast commanded us to keep Thy precepts diligently. O that my ways were directed to keep Thy statutes!" Ps. 119: 1-5.

"For ever, O Lord, Thy word is settled in heaven. Thy faithfulness is unto all generations: Thou hast established the earth, and it abideth. . . . I will never forget Thy precepts: for with them Thou hast quickened me. . . . I have seen an end of all perfection: but Thy commandment is exceeding broad." Ps. 119: 89-96.

This chapter is based on Matthew 13:33; Luke 13:20, 21.

to Nicodemus: "Verily, verily, I say unto thee, Except a man be born from above, he can not see the kingdom of God. . . . That which is born of the flesh is flesh, and that which is born of the Spirit is spirit. Marvel not that I said unto thee, Ye must be born again. The wind bloweth where it listeth, and thou hearest the sound thereof, but canst not tell whence it cometh and whither it goeth. So is every one that is born of the Spirit." John 3:3-8, margin.

The apostle Paul, writing by the Holy Spirit, says, "God, who is rich in mercy, for His great love wherewith He loved us, even when we were dead in sins, hath quickened us together with Christ, (by grace ye are saved;) and hath raised us up together, and made us sit together in heavenly places in Christ Jesus: that in the ages to come He might show the exceeding riches of His grace in His kindness toward us through Christ Jesus. For by grace are ye saved through faith; and that not of yourselves; it is the gift of God." Eph. 2:4-8.

The leaven hidden in the flour works invisibly to bring the whole mass under its leavening process; so the leaven of truth works secretly, silently, steadily, to transform the soul. The natural inclinations are softened and subdued. New thoughts, new feelings, new motives, are implanted. A new standard of character is set up—the life of Christ. The mind is changed; the faculties are roused to action in new lines. Man is not endowed with new faculties, but the faculties he has are sanctified. The conscience is awakened. We are endowed with traits of character that enable us to do service for God.

Often the question arises, Why, then, are there so many, claiming to believe God's word, in whom there is not seen a reformation in words, in spirit, and in character? Why are there so many who cannot bear opposition to their purposes and plans, who manifest an unholy temper, and whose words are harsh, overbearing, and passionate? There is seen in their lives the same love of self, the same selfish indulgence, the same temper and hasty speech, that is seen in the life of the worldling. There is the same sensitive pride, the same yielding to natural inclination, the same perversity of character, as if the truth were wholly unknown to them.

The reason is that they are not converted. They have not hidden the leaven of truth in the heart. It has not had opportunity to do its work. Their natural and cultivated tendencies to evil have not been submitted to its transforming power. Their lives reveal the absence of the grace of Christ, an unbelief in His power to transform the character.

"Faith cometh by hearing, and hearing by the word of God." Rom. 10:17. The Scriptures are the great agency in the transformation of character. Christ prayed, "Sanctify them through Thy truth; Thy word is truth." John 17:17. If studied and obeyed, the word of God works in the heart, subduing every unholy attribute. The Holy Spirit comes to convict of sin, and the faith that springs up in the heart works by love to Christ, conforming us in body, soul, and spirit to His own image. Then God can use us to do His will. The power given us works from within outwardly, leading us to communicate to others the truth that has been communicated to us.

The truths of the word of God meet man's great practical necessity—the conversion of the soul through faith. These grand principles are not to be thought too pure and holy to be brought into the daily life. They are truths which reach to heaven and compass eternity, yet their vital influence is to be woven into human experience. They are to permeate all the great things and all the little things of life.

Received into the heart, the leaven of truth will regulate the desires, purify the thoughts, and sweeten the disposition. It quickens the faculties of the mind and the energies of the soul. It enlarges the capacity for feeling, for loving.

The world regards as a mystery the man who is imbued with this principle. The selfish, money-loving man lives only to secure for himself the riches, honors, and pleasures of this world. He loses the eternal world from his reckoning. But with the follower of Christ these things will not be all-absorbing. For Christ's sake he will labor and deny self, that he may aid in the great work of saving souls who are without Christ and without hope in the world. Such a man the world cannot understand; for he is keeping in view eternal realities. The love of

"I will praise Thee with uprightness of heart, when I shall have learned Thy righteous judgments. I will keep Thy statutes." Ps. 119:7, 8.

"Wherewithal shall a young man cleanse his way? by taking heed thereto according to Thy Work. With my whole heart have I sought Thee: O let me not wander from Thy commandments. Thy word have I hid in mine heart that I might not sin agaist Thee. . . . I will meditate in Thy precepts, and have respect unto Thy ways. I will delight myself in Thy statutes: I will not forget Thy Word." Ps. 119: 9-16.

"Teach me, O Lord, the way of Thy stautes; and I shall keep it unto the end. Give me understanding, and I shall keep Thy law; yea, I shall observe it with my whole heart. Make me go in the path of Thy commandments; for therein do I delight. . . . Stablish Thy word unto Thy servant, who is devoted to Thy fear. Turn away my reproach which I fear: for Thy judgments are good." Ps. 119: 33-39.

Christ with its redeeming power has come into the heart. This love masters every other motive, and raises its possessor above the corrupting influence of the world.

The word of God is to have a sanctifying effect on our association with every member of the human family. The leaven of truth will not produce the spirit of rivalry, the love of ambition, the desire to be first. True, heaven-born love is not selfish and changeable. It is not dependent on human praise. The heart of him who receives the grace of God overflows with love for God and for those for whom Christ died. Self is not struggling for recognition. He does not love others because they love and please him, because they appreciate his merits, but because they are Christ's purchased possession. If his motives, words, or actions are misunderstood or misrepresented, he takes no offense, but pursues the even tenor of his way. He is kind and thoughtful, humble in his opinion of himself, yet full of hope, always trusting in the mercy and love of God.

The apostle exhorts us, "As He which hath called you is holy, so be ye holy in all manner of conversation; because it is written, Be ye holy; for I am holy." 1 Peter 1:15, 16. The grace of Christ is to control the temper and the voice. Its working will be seen in politeness and tender regard shown by brother for brother, in kind, encouraging words. An angel presence is in the home. The life breathes a sweet perfume, which ascends to God as holy incense. Love is manifested in kindness, gentleness, forbearance, and long-suffering.

The countenance is changed. Christ abiding in the heart shines out in the faces of those who love Him and keep His commandments. Truth is written there. The sweet peace of heaven is revealed. There is expressed a habitual gentleness, a more than human love.

The leaven of truth works a change in the whole man, making the coarse refined, the rough gentle, the selfish generous. By it the impure are cleansed, washed in the blood of the Lamb. Through its life-giving power it brings all there is of mind and soul and strength into harmony with the divine life. Man with his human nature becomes a partaker of divinity. Christ is honored in excellence and perfection of character. As these changes are effected, angels break forth in rapturous song, and God and Christ rejoice over souls fashioned after the divine similitude.

8

Hidden Treasure

"Again, the kingdom of heaven is like unto treasure hid in a field; the which when a man hath found, he hideth, and for joy thereof goeth and selleth all that he hath, and buyeth that field."

In ancient times it was customary for men to hide their treasures in the earth. Thefts and robberies were frequent. And whenever there was a change in the ruling power, those who had large possessions were liable to be put under heavy tribute. Moreover the country was in constant danger of invasion by marauding armies. As a consequence, the rich endeavored to preserve their wealth by concealing it, and the earth was looked upon as a safe hiding place. But often the place of concealment was forgotten; death might claim the owner, imprisonment or exile might separate him from his treasure, and the wealth he had taken such pains to preserve was left for the fortunate finder. In Christ's day it was not uncommon to discover in neglected land old coins and ornaments of gold and silver.

A man hires land to cultivate, and as the oxen plow the soil, buried treasure is unearthed. As the man discovers this treasure, he sees that a fortune is within his reach. Restoring the gold to its hiding place, he returns to his home and sells all that he has, in order to purchase the field containing the treasure. His family and his neighbors think that he is acting like a madman. Looking on the field, they see no value in the neglected soil. But the man knows what he is doing; and when he has a title to the field, he searches every part of it to find the treasure that he has secured.

This parable illustrates the value of the heavenly treasure, and the effort that should be made to secure it. The finder of the treasure in the field was ready to part with all that he had, ready to put forth untiring labor, in order to secure the hidden riches. So the finder of heavenly treasure will count no labor too great and no sacrifice too dear, in order to gain the treasures of truth.

In the parable the field containing the treasure represents the Holy Scriptures. And the gospel is the treasure. The earth itself is not so interlaced with golden veins and filled with precious things as is the word of God.

"Thy word is a lamp unto my feet, and a light unto my path. I have sworn, and I will perform it, that I will keep Thy righteous judgments. . . . Thy testimonies have I taken as an heritage forever: for they are the rejoicing of my heart. I have inclined mine heart to perform Thy statutes." Ps. 119:105-112.

This chapter is based on Matthew 13:44.

How Hidden

The treasures of the gospel are said to be hidden. By those who are wise in their own estimation, who are puffed up by the teaching of vain philosophy, the beauty and power and mystery of the plan of redemption are not perceived. Many have eyes, but they see not; they have ears, but they hear not; they have intellect, but they discern not the hidden treasure.

A man might pass over the place where treasure had been concealed. In dire necessity he might sit down to rest at the foot of a tree, not knowing of the riches hidden at its roots. So it was with the Jews. As a golden treasure, truth had been intrusted to the Hebrew people. The Jewish economy, bearing the signature of Heaven, had been instituted by Christ Himself. In types and symbols the great truths of redemption were veiled. Yet when Christ came, the Jews did not recognize Him to whom all these symbols pointed. They had the word of God in their hands; but the traditions which had been handed down from generation to generation, and the human interpretation of the Scriptures, hid from them the truth as it is in Jesus. The spiritual import of the sacred writings was lost. The treasure house of all knowledge was open to them, but they knew it not.

God does not conceal His truth from men. By their own course of action they make it obscure to themselves. Christ gave the Jewish people abundant evidence that He was the Messiah; but His teaching called for a decided change in their lives. They saw that if they received Christ, they must give up their cherished maxims and traditions, their selfish, ungodly practices. It required a sacrifice to receive changeless, eternal truth. Therefore they would not admit the most conclusive evidence that God could give to establish faith in Christ. They professed to believe the Old Testament Scriptures, yet they refused to accept the testimony contained therein concerning Christ's life and character. They were afraid of being convinced lest they should be converted and be compelled to give up their preconceived opinions. The treasure of the gospel, the Way, the Truth, and the Life, was among them, but they rejected the greatest gift that Heaven could bestow.

"Among the chief rulers also many believed on Him," we read; "but because of the Pharisees they did not confess Him, lest they should be put out of the synagogue." John 12:42. They were convinced; they believed Jesus to be the Son of God; but it was not in harmony with their ambitious desires to confess Him. They had not the faith that would have secured for them the heavenly treasure. They were seeking worldly treasure.

And today men are eagerly seeking for earthly treasure. Their minds are filled with selfish, ambitious thoughts. For the sake of gaining worldly riches, honor, or power, they place the maxims, traditions, and requirements of men above the requirements of God. From them the treasures of His word are hidden.

"The natural man receiveth not the things of the Spirit of God; for they are foolishness unto him; neither can he know them, because they are spiritually discerned." 1 Cor. 2:14.

"If our gospel be hid, it is hid to them that are lost; in whom the god of this world hath blinded the minds of them which believe not, lest the light of the glorious gospel of Christ, who is the image of God, should shine unto them." 2 Cor. 4:3, 4.

Value of the Treasure

The Saviour saw that men were absorbed in getting gain, and were losing sight of eternal realities. He undertook to correct this evil. He sought to break the infatuating spell that was paralyzing the soul. Lifting up His voice He cried, "What is a man profited, if he shall gain the whole world, and lose his own soul? or what shall a man give in exchange for his soul?" Matt. 16:26. He presents before fallen humanity the nobler world they have lost sight of, that they may behold eternal realities. He takes them to the threshold of the Infinite, flushed with the indescribable glory of God, and shows them the treasure there.

The value of this treasure is above gold or silver. The riches of earth's mines cannot compare with it.

"The depth saith, It is not in me;
And the sea saith, It is not with me.
It can not be gotten for gold,
Neither shall silver be weighed for the price thereof.
It can not be valued with the gold of Ophir,
With the precious onyx, or the sapphire.
The gold and the crystal can not equal it;
And the exchange of it shall not be for jewels of fine gold.
No mention shall be made of coral or of pearls,
For the price of wisdom is above rubies."
Job 28:14-18.

This is the treasure that is found in the Scriptures. The Bible is God's great lesson book, His great educator. The foundation of all true science is contained in the Bible. Every branch of knowledge may be found by searching the word of God. And above all else it contains the science of all sciences, the science of salvation. The Bible is the mine of the unsearchable riches of Christ.

The true higher education is gained by studying and obeying the word of God. But when

God's word is laid aside for books that do not lead to God and the kingdom of heaven, the education acquired is a perversion of the name.

There are wonderful truths in nature. The earth, the sea, and the sky are full of truth. They are our teachers. Nature utters her voice in lessons of heavenly wisdom and eternal truth. But fallen man will not understand. Sin has obscured his vision, and he cannot of himself interpret nature without placing it above God. Correct lessons cannot impress the minds of those who reject the word of God. The teaching of nature is by them so perverted that it turns the mind away from the Creator.

By many, man's wisdom is thought to be higher than the wisdom of the divine Teacher, and God's lesson book is looked upon as old-fashioned, stale, and uninteresting. But by those who have been vivified by the Holy Spirit it is not so regarded. They see the priceless treasure, and would sell all to buy the field that contains it. Instead of books containing the suppositions of reputedly great authors, they choose the word of Him who is the greatest author and the greatest teacher the world has ever known, who gave His life for us, that through Him we might have everlasting life.

Results of Neglecting the Treasure

Satan works on human minds, leading them to think that there is wonderful knowledge to be gained apart from God. By deceptive reasoning he led Adam and Eve to doubt God's word, and to supply its place with a theory that led to disobedience. And his sophistry is doing today what it did in Eden. Teachers who mingle the sentiments of infidel authors with the education they are giving, plant in the minds of youth thoughts that will lead to distrust of God and transgression of His law. Little do they know what they are doing. Little do they realize what will be the result of their work.

A student may go through all the grades of the schools and colleges of today. He may devote all his powers to acquiring knowledge. But unless he has a knowledge of God, unless he obeys the laws that govern his being, he will destroy himself. By wrong habits he loses his power of self-apprecia-tion. He loses self-control. He cannot reason correctly about matters that concern him most closely. He is reckless and irrational in his treatment of mind and body. By wrong habits he makes of himself a wreck. Happi-ness he cannot have; for his neglect to culti-vate pure, healthful principles places him under the control of habits that ruin his peace. His years of taxing study are lost, for he has destroyed himself. He has misused his physical and mental powers, and the temple of the body is in ruins. He is ruined for this life and for the life to come. By acquiring

earthly knowledge he thought to gain a trea-sure, but by laying his Bible aside he sacri-ficed a treasure worth everything else.

Search for the Treasure

The word of God is to be our study. We are to educate our children in the truths found therein. It is an inexhaustible treasure; but men fail to find this treasure because they do not search until it is within their possession. Very many are content with a supposition in regard to the truth. They are content with a surface work, taking for granted that they have all that is essential. They take the sayings of others for truth, being too indolent to put themselves to diligent, earnest labor, represented in the word as digging for hidden treasure. But man's inventions are not only unreliable, they are dangerous; for they place man where God should be. They place the sayings of men where a "Thus saith the Lord" should be.

Christ is the truth. His words are truth, and they have a deeper significance than appears on the surface. All the sayings of Christ have a value beyond their unpretending appearance. Minds that are quickened by the Holy Spirit will discern the value of these sayings. They will discern the precious gems of truth, though these may be buried treasures.

Human theories and speculations will never lead to an understanding of God's word. Those who suppose that they understand philosophy think that their explanations are necessary to unlock the treasures of knowledge and to pre-vent heresies from coming into the church. But it is these explanations that have brought in false theories and heresies. Men have made des-perate efforts to explain what they thought to be intricate scriptures; but too often their efforts have only darkened that which they tried to make clear.

The priests and Pharisees thought they were doing great things as teachers by putting their own interpretation upon the word of God, but Christ said of them, "Ye know not the scrip-tures, neither the power of God." Mark 12:24. He charged them with the guilt of "teaching for doctrines the commandments of men." Mark 7:7. Though they were the teachers of the ora-cles of God, though they were supposed to understand His word, they were not doers of the word. Satan had blinded their eyes that they should not see its true import.

This is the work of many in our day. Many churches are guilty of this sin. There is danger, great danger, that the supposed wise men of today will repeat the experience of the Jewish teachers. They falsely interpret the divine ora-cles, and souls are brought into perplexity and shrouded in darkness because of their misconc-eption of divine truth.

The Scriptures need not be read by the dim

light of tradition or human speculation. As well might we try to give light to the sun with a torch as to explain the Scriptures by human tradition or imagination. God's holy word needs not the torchlight glimmer of earth to make its glories distinguishable. It is light in itself—the glory of God revealed, and beside it every other light is dim.

But there must be earnest study and close investigation. Sharp, clear perceptions of truth will never be the reward of indolence. No earthly blessing can be obtained without earnest, patient, persevering effort. If men attain success in business, they must have a will to do and a faith to look for results. And we cannot expect to gain spiritual knowledge without earnest toil. Those who desire to find the treasures of truth must dig for them as the miner digs for the treasure hidden in the earth. No halfhearted, indifferent work will avail. It is essential for old and young, not only to read God's word, but to study it with wholehearted earnestness, praying and searching for truth as for hidden treasure. Those who do this will be rewarded, for Christ will quicken the understanding.

Our salvation depends on a knowledge of the truth contained in the Scriptures. It is God's will that we should possess this. Search, O search the precious Bible with hungry hearts. Explore God's word as the miner explores the earth to find veins of gold. Never give up the search until you have ascertained your relation to God and His will in regard to you. Christ declared, "Whatsoever ye shall ask in My name, that will I do, that the Father may be glorified in the Son. If ye shall ask anything in My name, I will do it." John 14:13, 14.

112   Men of piety and talent catch views of eternal realities, but often they fail of understanding, because the things that are seen eclipse the glory of the unseen. He who would seek successfully for the hidden treasure must rise to higher pursuits than the things of this world. His affections and all His capabilities must be consecrated to the search.

Disobedience has closed the door to a vast amount of knowledge that might have been gained from the Scriptures. Understanding means obedience to God's commandments. The Scriptures are not to be adapted to meet the prejudice and jealousy of men. They can be understood only by those who are humbly seeking for a knowledge of the truth that they may obey it.

Do you ask, What shall I do to be saved? You must lay your preconceived opinions, your hereditary and cultivated ideas, at the door of investigation. If you search the Scriptures to vindicate your own opinions, you will never reach the truth. Search in order to learn what the Lord says. If conviction comes as you search, if

you see that your cherished opinions are not in harmony with the truth, do not misinterpret the truth in order to suit your own belief, but accept the light given. Open mind and heart that you may behold wondrous things out of God's word.

Faith in Christ as the world's Redeemer calls for an acknowledgment of the enlightened intellect controlled by a heart that can discern and appreciate the heavenly treasure. This faith is inseparable from repentance and transformation of character. To have faith means to find and accept the gospel treasure, with all the obligations which it imposes.

"Except a man be born again, he cannot see the kingdom of God." John 3:3. He may conjecture and imagine, but without the eye of faith he cannot see the treasure. Christ gave His life to secure for us this inestimable treasure; but without regeneration through faith in His blood, there is no remission of sins, no treasure for any perishing soul.

We need the enlightenment of the Holy Spirit in order to discern the truths in God's word. The lovely things of the natural world are not seen until the sun, dispelling the darkness, floods them with its light. So the treasures in the word of God are not appreciated until they are revealed by the bright beams of the Sun of Righteousness.

The Holy Spirit, sent from heaven by the benevolence of infinite love, takes the things of God and reveals them to every soul that has an implicit faith in Christ. By His power the vital truths upon which the salvation of the soul depends are impressed upon the mind, and the way of life is made so plain that none need err therein. As we study the Scriptures, we should pray for the light of God's Holy Spirit to shine upon the word, that we may see and appreciate its treasures.

Reward of Searching

Let none think that there is no more knowledge for them to gain. The depth of human intellect may be measured; the works of human authors may be mastered; but the highest, deepest, broadest flight of the imagination cannot find out God. There is infinity beyond all that we can comprehend. We have seen only the glimmering of divine glory and of the infinitude of knowledge and wisdom; we have, as it were, been working on the surface of the mine, when rich golden ore is beneath the surface, to reward the one who will dig for it. The shaft must be sunk deeper and yet deeper in the mine, and the result will be glorious treasure. Through a correct faith, divine knowledge will become human knowledge.

No one can search the Scriptures in the spirit of Christ without being rewarded. When man is willing to be instructed as a little child, when he submits wholly to God, he will find the truth in His word. If men would be obedient, they would understand the plan of God's government. The heavenly world would open its chambers of grace and glory for exploration. Human beings would be altogether different from what they now are, for by exploring the mines of truth men would be ennobled. The mystery of redemption, the incarnation of Christ, His atoning sacrifice, would not be as they are now, vague in our minds. They would be not only better understood, but altogether more highly appreciated.

In His prayer to the Father, Christ gave to the world a lesson which should be graven on mind and soul. "This is life eternal," He said, "that they might know Thee the only true God, and Jesus Christ, whom Thou hast sent." John 17:3. This is true education. It imparts power. The experimental knowledge of God and of Jesus Christ whom He has sent, transforms man into the image of God. It gives to man the mastery of himself, bringing every impulse and passion of the lower nature under the control of the higher powers of the mind. It makes its possessor a son of God and an heir of heaven. It brings him into communion with the mind of the Infinite, and opens to him the rich treasures of the universe.

This is the knowledge which is obtained by searching the word of God. And this treasure may be found by every soul who will give all to obtain it.

"If thou criest after knowledge, and liftest up thy voice for understanding; if thou seekest her as silver, and searchest for her as for hid treasures; then shalt thou understand the fear of the Lord, and find the knowledge of God." Prov. 2:3-5.

9

The Pearl

The blessings of redeeming love our Saviour compared to a precious pearl. He illustrated His lesson by the parable of the merchantman seeking goodly pearls "who, when he had found one pearl of great price, went and sold all that he had, and bought it." Christ Himself is the pearl of great price. In Him is gathered all the glory of the Father, the fullness of the Godhead. He is the brightness of the Father's glory and the express image of His person. The glory of the attributes of God is expressed in His character. Every page of the Holy Scriptures shines with His light. The righteousness of Christ, as a pure, white pearl, has no defect, no stain. No work of man can improve the great and precious gift of God. It is without a flaw. In Christ are "hid all

This chapter is based on Matthew 13:45, 46.

the treasures of wisdom and knowledge." Col. 2:3. He is "made unto us wisdom, and righteousness, and sanctification, and redemption." 1 Cor. 1:30. All that can satisfy the needs and longings of the human soul, for this world and for the world to come, is found in Christ. Our Redeemer is the pearl so precious that in comparison all things else may be accounted loss.

Christ "came unto His own, and His own received Him not." John 1:11. The light of God shone into the darkness of the world, and "the darkness comprehended it not." John 1:5. But not all were found indifferent to the gift of heaven. The merchantman in the parable represents a class who were sincerely desiring truth. In different nations there were earnest and thoughtful men who had sought in literature and science and the religions of the heathen world for that which they could receive as the soul's treasure. Among the Jews there were those who were seeking for that which they had not. Dissatisfied with a formal religion, they longed for that which was spiritual and uplifting. Christ's chosen disciples belonged to the latter class, Cornelius and the Ethiopian eunuch to the former. They had been longing and praying for light from heaven; and when Christ was revealed to them, they received Him with gladness.

In the parable the pearl is not represented as a gift. The merchantman bought it at the price of all that he had. Many question the meaning of this, since Christ is represented in the Scriptures as a gift. He is a gift, but only to those who give themselves, soul, body, and spirit, to Him without reserve. We are to give ourselves to Christ, to live a life of willing obedience to all His requirements. All that we are, all the talents and capabilities we possess, are the Lord's, to be consecrated to His service. When we thus give ourselves wholly to Him, Christ, with all the treasures of heaven, gives Himself to us. We obtain the pearl of great price.

Salvation is a free gift, and yet it is to be bought and sold. In the market of which divine mercy has the management, the precious pearl is represented as being bought without money and without price. In this market all may obtain the goods of heaven. The treasury of the jewels of truth is open to all. "Behold, I have set before thee an open door," the Lord declares, "and no man can shut it." No sword guards the way through this door. Voices from within and at the door say, Come. The Saviour's voice earnestly and lovingly invites us: "I counsel thee to buy of Me gold tried in the fire, that thou mayest be rich." Rev. 3:8, 18.

The gospel of Christ is a blessing that all may possess. The poorest are as well able as the richest to purchase salvation; for no amount of worldly wealth can secure it. It is obtained by willing obedience, by giving ourselves to Christ as His own purchased possession. Education, even of the highest class, cannot of itself bring a man nearer to God. The Pharisees were favored with every temporal and every spiritual advantage, and they said with boastful pride, We are "rich, and increased with goods, and have need of nothing"; yet they were "wretched, and miserable, and poor, and blind, and naked." Rev. 3:17. Christ offered them the pearl of great price; but they disdained to accept it, and He said to them, "The publicans and the harlots go into the kingdom of God before you." Matt. 21:31.

We cannot earn salvation, but we are to seek for it with as much interest and perseverance as though we would abandon everything in the world for it.

We are to seek for the pearl of great price, but not in worldly marts or in worldly ways. The price we are required to pay is not gold or silver, for this belongs to God. Abandon the idea that temporal or spiritual advantages will win for you salvation. God calls for your willing obedience. He asks you to give up your sins. "To him that overcometh," Christ declares, "will I grant to sit with Me in My throne, even as I also overcame, and am set down with My Father in His throne." Rev. 3:21.

118   There are some who seem to be always seeking for the heavenly pearl. But they do not make an entire surrender of their wrong habits. They do not die to self that Christ may live in them. Therefore they do not find the precious pearl. They have not overcome unholy ambition and their love for worldly attractions. They do not take up the cross and follow Christ in the path of self-denial and sacrifice. Almost Christians, yet not fully Christians, they seem near the kingdom of heaven, but they cannot enter there. Almost but not wholly saved, means to be not almost but wholly lost.

The parable of the merchantman seeking goodly pearls has a double significance: it applies not only to men as seeking the kingdom of heaven, but to Christ as seeking His lost inheritance. Christ, the heavenly merchantman seeking goodly pearls, saw in lost humanity the pearl of price. In man, defiled and ruined by sin, He saw the possibilities of redemption. Hearts that have been the battleground of the conflict with Satan, and that have been rescued by the power of love, are more precious to the Redeemer than are those who have never fallen. God looked upon humanity, not as vile and worthless; He looked upon it in Christ, saw it as it might become through redeeming love. He collected all the riches of the universe, and laid them down in order to buy the pearl. And Jesus, having found it, resets it in His own diadem. "For they shall be as the stones of a crown, lifted up as an ensign upon His land." Zech. 9:16. "They shall be Mine, saith the Lord of hosts, in that day when I make up My jewels." Mal. 3:17.

But Christ as the precious pearl, and our privilege of possessing this heavenly treasure, is the theme on which we most need to dwell. It is the Holy Spirit that reveals to men the preciousness of the goodly pearl. The time of the Holy Spirit's power is the time when in a special sense the heavenly gift is sought and found. In Christ's day many heard the gospel, but their minds were darkened by false teaching, and they did not recognize in the humble Teacher of Galilee the Sent of God. But after Christ's ascension His enthronement in His mediatorial kingdom was signalized by the outpouring of the Holy Spirit. On the day of Pentecost the Spirit was given. Christ's witnesses proclaimed the power of the risen Saviour. The light of heaven penetrated the darkened minds of those who had been deceived by the enemies of Christ. They now saw Him exalted to be "a Prince and a Saviour, for to give repentance to Israel, and forgiveness of sins." Acts 5:31. They saw Him encircled with the glory of heaven, with infinite treasures in His hands to bestow upon all who would turn from their rebellion. As the apostles set forth the glory of the Only-Begotten of the Father, three thousand souls were convicted. They were made to see themselves as they were, sinful and polluted, and Christ as their friend and Redeemer. Christ was lifted up, Christ was glorified, through the power of the Holy Spirit resting upon men. By faith these believers saw Him as the One who had borne humiliation, suffering, and death that they might not perish but have everlasting life. The revelation of Christ by the Spirit brought to them a realizing sense of His power and majesty, and they stretched forth their hands to Him by faith, saying, "I believe."

Then the glad tidings of a risen Saviour were carried to the uttermost bounds of the inhabited world. The church beheld converts flocking to her from all directions. Believers were reconverted. Sinners united with Christians in seeking the pearl of great price. The prophecy was fulfilled, The weak shall be "as David," and the house of David "as the angel of the Lord." Zech. 12:8. Every Christian saw in his brother the divine similitude of benevolence and love. One interest prevailed. One object swallowed up all others. All hearts beat in harmony. The only ambition of the believers was to reveal the likeness of Christ's character, and to labor for the enlargement of His kingdom. "The multitude of them that believed were of one heart and of one soul. . . . With great power gave the apostles witness of the resurrection of the Lord Jesus; and great grace was upon them all." Acts 4:32, 33. "And the Lord added to the church daily such as should be saved." Acts 2:47. The Spirit of Christ animated the whole congregation; for they had found the pearl of great price.

These scenes are to be repeated, and with

greater power. The outpouring of the Holy Spirit on the day of Pentecost was the former rain, but the latter rain will be more abundant. The Spirit awaits our demand and reception. Christ is again to be revealed in His fulness by the Holy Spirit's power. Men will discern the value of the precious pearl, and with the apostle Paul they will say, "What things were gain to me, those I counted loss for Christ. Yea doubtless, and I count all things but loss for the excellency of the knowledge of Christ Jesus my Lord." Phil. 3:7, 8.

10
The Net

"The kingdom of heaven is like unto a net, that was cast into the sea, and gathered of every kind; which, when it was full, they drew to shore, and sat down, and gathered the good into vessels, but cast the bad away. So shall it be at the end of the world: the angels shall come forth, and sever the wicked from among the just, and shall cast them into the furnace of fire: there shall be wailing and gnashing of teeth."

The casting of the net is the preaching of the gospel. This gathers both good and evil into the church. When the mission of the gospel is completed, the judgment will accomplish the work of separation. Christ saw how the existence of false brethren in the church would cause the way of truth to be evil spoken of. The world would revile the gospel because of the inconsistent lives of false professors. Even Christians would be caused to stumble as they saw that many who bore Christ's name were not controlled by His Spirit. Because these sinners were in the church, men would be in danger of thinking that God excused their sins. Therefore Christ lifts the veil from the future and bids all to behold that it is character, not position, which decides man's destiny.

Both the parable of the tares and that of the net plainly teach that there is no time when all the wicked will turn to God. The wheat and the tares grow together until the harvest. The good and the bad fish are together drawn ashore for a final separation.

Again, these parables teach that there is to be no probation after the judgment. When the work of the gospel is completed, there immediately follows the separation between the good and the evil, and the destiny of each class is forever fixed.

God does not desire the destruction of any. "As I live, saith the Lord God, I have no pleasure in the death of the wicked; but that the wicked turn from his way and live. Turn ye, turn ye from your evil ways; for why will ye

die?" Eze. 33:11. Throughout the period of probationary time His Spirit is entreating men to accept the gift of life. It is only those who reject His pleading that will be left to perish. God has declared that sin must be destroyed as an evil ruinous to the universe. Those who cling to sin will perish in its destruction.

11
Things New and Old

While Christ was teaching the people, He was also educating His disciples for their future work. In all His instruction there were lessons for them. After giving the parable of the net, He asked them, "Have ye understood all these things?" They said unto Him, "Yea, Lord." Then in another parable He set before them their responsibility in regard to the truths they had received. "Therefore," He said, "every scribe which is instructed unto the kingdom of heaven is like unto a man that is an householder, which bringeth forth out of his treasure things new and old."

The treasure gained by the householder he does not hoard. He brings it forth to communicate to others. And by use the treasure increases. The householder has precious things both new and old. So Christ teaches that the truth committed to His disciples is to be communicated to the world. And as the knowledge of truth is imparted, it will increase.

All who receive the gospel message into the heart will long to proclaim it. The heaven-born love of Christ must find expression. Those who have put on Christ will relate their experience, tracing step by step the leadings of the Holy Spirit—their hungering and thirsting for the knowledge of God and of Jesus Christ whom He has sent, the results of their searching of the Scriptures, their prayers, their soul agony, and the words of Christ to them, "Thy sins be forgiven thee." It is unnatural for any to keep these things secret, and those who are filled with the love of Christ will not do so. In proportion as the Lord has made them the depositaries of sacred truth will be their desire that others shall receive the same blessing. And as they make known the rich treasures of God's grace, more and still more of the grace of Christ will be imparted to them. They will have the heart of a little child in its simplicity and unreserved obedience. Their souls will pant after holiness, and more and more of the treasures of truth and grace will be revealed to them to be given to the world.

The great storehouse of truth is the word of God—the written word, the book of nature, and the book of experience in God's dealing with

This chapter is based on Matthew 13:47-50.

This chapter is based on Matthew 13:51, 52.

human life. Here are the treasures from which Christ's workers are to draw. In the search after truth they are to depend upon God, not upon human intelligences, the great men whose wisdom is foolishness with God. Through His own appointed channels the Lord will impart a knowledge of Himself to every seeker.

If the follower of Christ will believe His word and practice it, there is no science in the natural world that he will not be able to grasp and appreciate. There is nothing but that will furnish him means for imparting the truth to others. Natural science is a treasure house of knowledge from which every student in the school of 126 Christ may draw. As we contemplate the beauty of nature, as we study its lessons in the cultivation of the soil, in the growth of the trees, in all the wonders of earth and sea and sky, there will come to us a new perception of truth. And the mysteries connected with God's dealings with men, the depths of His wisdom and judgment as seen in human life—these are found to be a storehouse rich in treasure.

But it is in the written word that a knowledge of God is most clearly revealed to fallen man. This is the treasure house of the unsearchable riches of Christ.

The word of God includes the Scriptures of the Old Testament as well as of the New. One is not complete without the other. Christ declared that the truths of the Old Testament are as valuable as those of the New. Christ was as much man's Redeemer in the beginning of the world as He is today. Before He clothed His divinity with humanity and came to our world, the gospel message was given by Adam, Seth, Enoch, Methuselah, and Noah. Abraham in Canaan and Lot in Sodom bore the message, and from generation to generation faithful messengers proclaimed the Coming One. The rites of the Jewish economy were instituted by Christ Himself. He was the foundation of their system of sacrificial offerings, the great antitype of all their religious service. The blood shed as the sacrifices were offered pointed to the sacrifice of the Lamb of God. All the typical offerings were fulfilled in Him.

Christ as manifested to the patriarchs, as symbolized in the sacrificial service, as portrayed in the law, and as revealed by the prophets, is the riches of the Old Testament. Christ in His life, His death, and His resurrection, Christ as He is manifested by the Holy Spirit, is the treasure of the New Testament. Our Saviour, the outshining of the Father's glory, is both the Old and the New.

Of Christ's life and death and intercession, 127 which prophets had foretold, the apostles were to go forth as witnesses. Christ in His humiliation, in His purity and holiness, in His matchless love, was to be their theme. And in order to preach the gospel in its fullness, they must present the Saviour not only as revealed in His life and teachings, but as foretold by the prophets of the Old Testament and as symbolized by the sacrificial service.

Christ in His teaching presented old truths of which He Himself was the originator, truths which He had spoken through patriarchs and prophets; but He now shed upon them a new light. How different appeared their meaning! A flood of light and spirituality was brought in by His explanation. And He promised that the Holy Spirit should enlighten the disciples, that the word of God should be ever unfolding to them. They would be able to present its truths in new beauty.

Ever since the first promise of redemption was spoken in Eden, the life, the character, and the mediatorial work of Christ have been the study of human minds. Yet every mind through whom the Holy Spirit has worked has presented these themes in a light that is fresh and new. The truths of redemption are capable of constant development and expansion. Though old, they are ever new, constantly revealing to the seeker for truth a greater glory and a mightier power.

In every age there is a new development of truth, a message of God to the people of that generation. The old truths are all essential; new truth is not independent of the old, but an unfolding of it. It is only as the old truths are understood that we can comprehend the new. When Christ desired to open to His disciples the truth of His resurrection, He began "at Moses and all the prophets" and "expounded unto them 128 in all the scriptures the things concerning Himself." Luke 24:27. But it is the light which shines in the fresh unfolding of truth that glorifies the old. He who rejects or neglects the new does not really possess the old. For him it loses its vital power and becomes but a lifeless form.

There are those who profess to believe and to teach the truths of the Old Testament, while they reject the New. But in refusing to receive the teachings of Christ, they show that they do not believe that which patriarchs and prophets have spoken. "Had ye believed Moses," Christ said, "ye would have believed Me; for he wrote of Me." John 5:46. Hence there is no real power in their teaching of even the Old Testament.

Many who claim to believe and to teach the gospel are in a similar error. They set aside the Old Testament Scriptures, of which Christ declared, "They are they which testify of Me." John 5:39. In rejecting the Old, they virtually reject the New; for both are parts of an inseparable whole. No man can rightly present the law of God without the gospel, or the gospel without the law. The law is the gospel embodied, and the gospel is the law unfolded. The law is the root, the gospel is the fragrant blossom and fruit which it bears.

The Old Testament sheds light upon the New,

and the New upon the Old. Each is a revelation of the glory of God in Christ. Both present truths that will continually reveal new depths of meaning to the earnest seeker.

Truth in Christ and through Christ is measureless. The student of Scripture looks, as it were, into a fountain that deepens and broadens as he gazes into its depths. Not in this life shall we comprehend the mystery of God's love in giving His Son to be the propitiation for our sins. The work of our Redeemer on this earth is 129 and ever will be a subject that will put to the stretch our highest imagination. Man may tax every mental power in the endeavor to fathom this mystery, but his mind will become faint and weary. The most diligent searcher will see before him a boundless, shoreless sea.

The truth as it is in Jesus can be experienced, but never explained. Its height and breadth and depth pass our knowledge. We may task our imagination to the utmost, and then we shall see only dimly the outlines of a love that is unexplainable, that is as high as heaven, but that stooped to the earth to stamp the image of God on all mankind.

Yet it is possible for us to see all that we can bear of the divine compassion. This is unfolded to the humble, contrite soul. We shall understand God's compassion just in proportion as we appreciate His sacrifice for us. As we search the word of God in humility of heart, the grand theme of redemption will open to our research. It will increase in brightness as we behold it, and as we aspire to grasp it, its height and depth will ever increase.

Our life is to be bound up with the life of Christ; we are to draw constantly from Him, partaking of Him, the living Bread that came down from heaven, drawing from a fountain ever fresh, ever giving forth its abundant treasures. If we keep the Lord ever before us, allowing our hearts to go out in thanksgiving and praise to Him, we shall have a continual freshness in our religious life. Our prayers will take the form of a conversation with God as we would talk with a friend. He will speak His mysteries to us personally. Often there will come to us a sweet joyful sense of the presence of Jesus. Often our hearts will burn within us as 130 He draws nigh to commune with us as He did with Enoch. When this is in truth the experience of the Christian, there is seen in his life a simplicity, a humility, meekness, and lowliness of heart, that show to all with whom he associates that he has been with Jesus and learned of Him.

In those who possess it, the religion of Christ will reveal itself as a vitalizing, pervading principle, a living, working, spiritual energy. There will be manifest the freshness and power and joyousness of perpetual youth. The heart that receives the word of God is not as a pool that evaporates, not like a broken cistern that loses its treasure. It is like the mountain stream fed by unfailing springs, whose cool, sparkling waters leap from rock to rock, refreshing the weary, the thirsty, the heavy laden.

This experience gives every teacher of truth the very qualifications that will make him a representative of Christ. The spirit of Christ's teaching will give a force and directness to his communications and to his prayers. His witness to Christ will not be a narrow, lifeless testimony. The minister will not preach over and over the same set discourses. His mind will be open to the constant illumination of the Holy Spirit.

Christ said, "Whoso eateth My flesh, and drinketh My blood, hath eternal life. . . . As the living Father hath sent Me, and I live by the Father; so he that eateth Me, even he shall live by Me. . . . It is the Spirit that quickeneth; . . . the words that I speak unto you, they are spirit, and they are life." John 6:54-63.

When we eat Christ's flesh and drink His blood, the element of eternal life will be found in the ministry. There will not be a fund of stale, oft-repeated ideas. The tame, dull sermonizing will cease. The old truths will be presented, but they will be seen in a new light. There will be a new perception of truth, a clearness and a power that all will discern. Those who have the privi- 131 lege of sitting under such a ministry will, if susceptible to the Holy Spirit's influence, feel the energizing power of a new life. The fire of God's love will be kindled within them. Their perceptive faculties will be quickened to discern the beauty and majesty of truth.

The faithful householder represents what every teacher of the children and youth should be. If he makes the word of God his treasure, he will continually bring forth new beauty and new truth. When the teacher will rely upon God in prayer, the Spirit of Christ will come upon him, and God will work through him by the Holy Spirit upon the minds of others. The Spirit fills the mind and heart with sweet hope and courage 132 and Bible imagery, and all this will be communicated to the youth under his instruction.

The springs of heavenly peace and joy, unsealed in the soul of the teacher by the words of Inspiration, will become a mighty river of influence to bless all who connect with him. The Bible will not become a tiresome book to the student. Under a wise instructor the word will become more and more desirable. It will be as the bread of life, and will never grow old. Its freshness and beauty will attract and charm the children and youth. It is like the sun shining upon the earth, perpetually imparting brightness and warmth, yet never exhausted.

God's holy, educating Spirit is in His word. A light, a new and precious light, shines forth from every page. Truth is there revealed, and words and sentences are made bright and appropriate for the occasion, as the voice of God speaking to the soul.

The Holy Spirit loves to address the youth, and to discover to them the treasures and beauties of God's word. The promises spoken by the great Teacher will captivate the senses and animate the soul with a spiritual power that is divine. There will grow in the fruitful mind a familiarity with divine things that will be as a barricade against temptation.

The words of truth will grow in importance, and assume a breadth and fullness of meaning of which we have never dreamed. The beauty and riches of the word have a transforming influence on mind and character. The light of heavenly love will fall upon the heart as an inspiration.

The appreciation of the Bible grows with its study. Whichever way the student may turn, he will find displayed the infinite wisdom and love of God.

133   The significance of the Jewish economy is not yet fully comprehended. Truths vast and profound are shadowed forth in its rites and symbols. The gospel is the key that unlocks its mysteries. Through a knowledge of the plan of redemption, its truths are opened to the understanding. Far more than we do, it is our privilege to understand these wonderful themes. We are to comprehend the deep things of God. Angels desire to look into the truths that are revealed to the people who with contrite hearts are searching the word of God, and praying for greater lengths and breadths and depths and heights of the knowledge which He alone can give.

As we near the close of this world's history, the prophecies relating to the last days especially demand our study. The last book of the New Testament scriptures is full of truth that we need to understand. Satan has blinded the minds of many, so that they have been glad of any excuse for not making the Revelation their study. But Christ through His servant John has here declared what shall be in the last days, and He says, "Blessed is he that readeth, and they that hear the words of this prophecy, and keep those things which are written therein." Rev. 1:3.

"This is life eternal," Christ said, "that they might know Thee the only true God, and Jesus Christ, whom Thou hast sent." John 17:3. Why is it that we do not realize the value of this knowledge? Why are not these glorious truths glowing in our hearts, trembling upon our lips, and pervading our whole being?

In giving us His word, God has put us in possession of every truth essential for our salvation. Thousands have drawn water from these wells of life, yet there is no diminishing of the supply. Thousands have set the Lord before them, and

134   by beholding have been changed into the same image. Their spirit burns within them as they speak of His character, telling what Christ is to

them, and what they are to Christ. But these searchers have not exhausted these grand and holy themes. Thousands more may engage in the work of searching out the mysteries of salvation. As the life of Christ and the character of His mission are dwelt upon, rays of light will shine forth more distinctly at every attempt to discover truth. Each fresh search will reveal something more deeply interesting than has yet been unfolded. The subject is inexhaustible. The study of the incarnation of Christ, His atoning sacrifice and mediatorial work, will employ the mind of the diligent student as long as time shall last; and looking to heaven with its unnumbered years he will exclaim, "Great is the mystery of godliness."

In eternity we shall learn that which, had we received the enlightenment it was possible to obtain here, would have opened our understanding. The themes of redemption will employ the hearts and minds and tongues of the redeemed through the everlasting ages. They will understand the truths which Christ longed to open to His disciples, but which they did not have faith to grasp. Forever and forever new views of the perfection and glory of Christ will appear. Through endless ages will the faithful Householder bring forth from His treasure things new and old.

12   139

Asking to Give

Christ was continually receiving from the Father that He might communicate to us. "The word which ye hear," He said, "is not Mine, but the Father's which sent Me." John 14:24. "The Son of man came not to be ministered unto, but to minister." Matt. 20:28. Not for Himself, but for others, He lived and thought and prayed. From hours spent with God He came forth morning by morning, to bring the light of heaven to men. Daily He received a fresh baptism of the Holy Spirit. In the early hours of the new day the Lord awakened Him from His slumbers, and His soul and His lips were anointed with grace, that He might impart to others. His words were given Him fresh from the heavenly courts, words that He might speak in season to the weary and oppressed. "The Lord God hath given Me," He said, "the tongue of the learned, that I should know how to speak a word in season to him that is weary: He wakeneth morning by morning, He wakeneth Mine ear to hear as the learned." Isa. 50:4.

Christ's disciples were much impressed by   14
His prayers and by His habit of communion with God. One day after a short absence from their Lord, they found Him absorbed in suppli-

cation. Seeming unconscious of their presence, He continued praying aloud. The hearts of the disciples were deeply moved. As He ceased praying, they exclaimed, "Lord, teach us to pray."

In answer, Christ repeated the Lord's prayer, as He had given it in the sermon on the mount. Then in a parable He illustrated the lesson He desired to teach them.

"Which of you," He said, "shall have a friend, and shall go unto him at midnight, and say unto him, Friend, lend me three loaves; for a friend of mine in his journey is come to me, and I have nothing to set before him? And he from within shall answer and say, Trouble me not; the door is now shut, and my children are with me in bed: I cannot rise and give thee. I say unto you, Though he will not rise and give him because he is his friend, yet because of his importunity he will rise and give him as many as he needeth."

Here Christ represents the petitioner as asking that he may obtain again. He must obtain the bread, else he cannot supply the necessities of a weary, belated wayfarer. Though his neighbor is unwilling to be troubled, he will not desist his pleading; his friend must be relieved; and at last his importunity is rewarded, his wants are supplied.

In like manner the disciples were to seek blessings from God. In the feeding of the multitude and in the sermon on the bread from heaven, Christ had opened to them their work as His representatives. They were to give the bread of life to the people. He who had appointed their work, saw how often their faith would be tried. 141 Often they would be thrown into unexpected positions, and would realize their human insufficiency. Souls that were hungering for the bread of life would come to them, and they would feel themselves to be destitute and helpless. They must receive spiritual food, or they would have nothing to impart. But they were not to turn one soul away unfed. Christ directs them to the source of supply. The man whose friend came to him for entertainment, even at the unseasonable hour of midnight, did not turn him away. He had nothing to set before him, but he went to one who had food and pressed his request until the neighbor supplied his need. And would not God, who had sent His servants to feed the hungry, supply their need for His own work?

But the selfish neighbor in the parable does not represent the character of God. The lesson is drawn, not by comparison, but by contrast. A selfish man will grant an urgent request, in order to rid himself of one who disturbs his rest. But God delights to give. He is full of compassion, and He longs to grant the requests of those who come unto Him in faith. He gives to us that we may minister to others and thus become like Himself.

Christ declares, "Ask, and it shall be given you; seek, and ye shall find; knock, and it shall be opened unto you. For every one that asketh receiveth; and he that seeketh findeth; and to him that knocketh it shall be opened."

The Saviour continues: "If a son shall ask bread of any of you that is a father, will he give him a stone? or if he ask a fish, will he for a fish give him a serpent? or if he shall ask an egg, will he offer him a scorpion? If ye then, being evil, know how to give good gifts unto your children, how much more shall your heavenly Father give the Holy Spirit to them that ask Him?"

In order to strengthen our confidence in God, Christ teaches us to address Him by a new name, a name entwined with the dearest associ- 142 ations of the human heart. He gives us the privilege of calling the infinite God our Father. This name, spoken to Him and of Him, is a sign of our love and trust toward Him, and a pledge of His regard and relationship to us. Spoken when asking His favor or blessing, it is as music in His ears. That we might not think it presumption to call Him by this name, He has repeated it again and again. He desires us to become familiar with the appellation.

God regards us as His children. He has redeemed us out of the careless world and has chosen us to become members of the royal family, sons and daughters of the heavenly King. He invites us to trust in Him with a trust deeper and stronger than that of a child in his earthly father. Parents love their children, but the love of God is larger, broader, deeper, than human love can possibly be. It is immeasurable. Then if earthly parents know how to give good gifts to their children, how much more shall our Father in heaven give the Holy Spirit to those who ask Him?

Christ's lessons in regard to prayer should be carefully considered. There is a divine science in prayer, and His illustration brings to view principles that all need to understand. He shows what is the true spirit of prayer, He teaches the necessity of perseverance in presenting our requests to God, and assures us of His willingness to hear and answer prayer.

Our prayers are not to be a selfish asking, merely for our own benefit. We are to ask that we may give. The principle of Christ's life must be the principle of our lives. "For their sakes," He said, speaking of His disciples, "I sanctify Myself, that they also might be sanctified." John 17:19. The same devotion, the same self-sacrifice, the same subjection to the claims of the word of God, that were manifest in Christ, must be seen in His servants. Our mission to the world is not to serve or please ourselves; we are 143 to glorify God by co-operating with Him to save sinners. We are to ask blessings from God that we may communicate to others. The capacity for receiving is preserved only by imparting. We cannot continue to receive heavenly treasure without communicating to those around us.

In the parable the petitioner was again and again repulsed, but he did not relinquish his purpose. So our prayers do not always seem to receive an immediate answer; but Christ teaches that we should not cease to pray. Prayer is not to work any change in God; it is to bring us into harmony with God. When we make request of Him, He may see that it is necessary for us to search our hearts and repent of sin. Therefore He takes us through test and trial, He brings us through humiliation, that we may see what hinders the working of His Holy Spirit through us.

There are conditions to the fulfillment of God's promises, and prayer can never take the place of duty. "If ye love Me," Christ says, "Keep My commandments." "He that hath My commandments, and keepeth them, he it is that loveth Me; and he that loveth Me shall be loved of My Father, and I will love him, and will manifest Myself to him." John 14:15, 21. Those who bring their petitions to God, claiming His promise while they do not comply with the conditions, insult Jehovah. They bring the name of Christ as their authority for the fulfillment of the promise, but they do not those things that would show faith in Christ and love for Him.

Many are forfeiting the condition of acceptance with the Father. We need to examine closely the deed of trust wherewith we approach God. If we are disobedient, we bring to the Lord a note to be cashed when we have not fulfilled the conditions that would make it payable to us. We present to God His promises, and ask Him to fulfill them, when by so doing He would dishonor His own name.

144   The promise is "If ye abide in Me, and My words abide in you, ye shall ask what ye will, and it shall be done unto you." John 15:7. And John declares: "Hereby do we know that we know Him, if we keep His commandments. He that saith, I know Him, and keepeth not His commandments, is a liar, and the truth is not in him. But whoso keepeth His word, in him verily is the love of God perfected." 1 John 2:3-5.

One of Christ's last commands to His disciples was "Love one another as I have loved you." John 13:34. Do we obey this command, or are we indulging sharp, unchristlike traits of character? If we have in any way grieved or wounded others, it is our duty to confess our fault and seek for reconciliation. This is an essential preparation that we may come before God in faith, to ask His blessing.

There is another matter too often neglected by those who seek the Lord in prayer. Have you been honest with God? By the prophet Malachi the Lord declares, "Even from the days of your fathers ye are gone away from Mine ordinances, and have not kept them. Return unto Me, and I will return unto you, saith the Lord of hosts. But ye said, Wherein shall we return? Will a man rob God? Yet ye have robbed Me. But ye say, Wherein have we robbed Thee? In tithes and offerings." Mal. 3:7, 8.

As the Giver of every blessing, God claims a certain portion of all we possess. This is His provision to sustain the preaching of the gospel. And by making this return to God, we are to show our appreciation of His gifts. But if we withhold from Him that which is His own, how can we claim His blessing? If we are unfaithful stewards of earthly things, how can we expect Him to entrust us with the things of heaven? It may be that here is the secret of unanswered prayer.

But the Lord in His great mercy is ready to forgive, and He says, "Bring ye all the tithes into the storehouse, that there may be meat in 145 Mine house, and prove Me now herewith, . . . if I will not open you the windows of heaven, and pour you out a blessing, that there shall not be room enough to receive it. And I will rebuke the devourer for your sakes, and he shall not destroy the fruits of your ground; neither shall your vine cast her fruit before the time in the field. . . . And all nations shall call you blessed; for ye shall be a delightsome land, saith the Lord of hosts." Mal. 3:10-12.

So it is with every other one of God's requirements. All His gifts are promised on condition of obedience. God has a heaven full of blessings for those who will co-operate with Him. All who obey Him may with confidence claim the fulfillment of His promises.

But we must show a firm, undeviating trust in God. Often He delays to answer us in order to try our faith or test the genuineness of our desire. Having asked according to His word, we should believe His promise and press our petitions with a determination that will not be denied.

God does not say, Ask once, and you shall receive. He bids us ask. Unwearyingly persist in prayer. The persistent asking brings the petitioner into a more earnest attitude, and gives him an increased desire to receive the things for which he asks. Christ said to Martha at the grave of Lazarus, "If thou wouldest believe, thou shouldest see the glory of God." John 11:40.

But many have not a living faith. This is why they do not see more of the power of God. Their weakness is the result of their unbelief. They have more faith in their own working than in the working of God for them. They take themselves into their own keeping. They plan and devise, but pray little, and have little real trust in God. They think they have faith, but it is only the impulse of the moment. Failing to realize their own need, or God's willingness to give, they do 146 not persevere in keeping their requests before the Lord.

Our prayers are to be as earnest and persistent as was the petition of the needy friend who asked for the loaves at midnight. The more earnestly and steadfastly we ask, the closer will be our spiritual union with Christ. We shall receive increased blessings because we have increased faith.

Our part is to pray and believe. Watch unto prayer. Watch, and co-operate with the prayer-hearing God. Bear in mind that "we are labourers together with God." 1 Cor. 3:9. Speak and act in harmony with your prayers. It will make an infinite difference with you whether trial shall prove your faith to be genuine, or show that your prayers are only a form.

When perplexities arise, and difficulties confront you, look not for help to humanity. Trust all with God. The practice of telling our difficulties to others only makes us weak, and brings no strength to them. It lays upon them the burden of our spiritual infirmities, which they cannot relieve. We seek the strength of erring, finite man, when we might have the strength of the unerring, infinite God.

You need not go to the ends of the earth for wisdom, for God is near. It is not the capabilities you now possess or ever will have that will give you success. It is that which the Lord can do for you. We need to have far less confidence in what man can do and far more confidence in what God can do for every believing soul. He longs to have you reach after Him by faith. He longs to have you expect great things from Him. He longs to give you understanding in temporal as well as in spiritual matters. He can sharpen the intellect. He can give tact and skill. Put your talents into the work, ask God for wisdom, and it will be given you.

147   Take the word of Christ as your assurance. Has He not invited you to come unto Him? Never allow yourself to talk in a hopeless, discouraged way. If you do you will lose much. By looking at appearances and complaining when difficulties and pressure come, you give evidence of a sickly, enfeebled faith. Talk and act as if your faith was invincible. The Lord is rich in resources; He owns the world. Look heavenward in faith. Look to Him who has light and power and efficiency.

There is in genuine faith a buoyancy, a steadfastness of principle, and a fixedness of purpose that neither time nor toil can weaken. "Even the youths shall faint and be weary, and the young men shall utterly fall: but they that wait upon the Lord shall renew their strength; they shall mount up with wings as eagles; they shall run, and not be weary; and they shall walk, and not faint." Isa. 40:30, 31.

There are many who long to help others, but they feel that they have no spiritual strength or light to impart. Let them present their petitions at the throne of grace. Plead for the Holy Spirit.

God stands back of every promise He has made. With your Bible in your hands say, I have done as Thou hast said. I present Thy promise, "Ask, and it shall be given you; seek, and ye shall find; knock, and it shall be opened unto you."

We must not only pray in Christ's name, but by the inspiration of the Holy Spirit. This explains what is meant when it is said that the Spirit "maketh intercession for us, with groanings which cannot be uttered." Rom. 8:26. Such prayer God delights to answer. When with earnestness and intensity we breathe a prayer in the name of Christ, there is in that very intensity a pledge from God that He is about to answer our prayer "exceeding abundantly above all that we ask or think." Eph. 3:20.

Christ has said, "What things soever ye desire, when ye pray, believe that ye receive them, and ye shall have them." Mark 11:24. 148 "Whatsoever ye shall ask in My name, that will I do, that the Father may be glorified in the Son." John 14:13. And the beloved John, under the inspiration of the Holy Spirit, speaks with great plainness and assurance: "If we ask anything according to His will, He heareth us: and if we know that He hear us, whatsoever we ask, we know that we have the petitions that we desired of Him." 1 John 5:14, 15. Then press your petition to the Father in the name of Jesus. God will honor that name.

The rainbow round about the throne is an assurance that God is true, that in Him is no variableness, neither shadow of turning. We have sinned against Him, and are undeserving of His favor; yet He Himself has put into our lips that most wonderful of pleas, "Do not abhor us, for Thy name's sake; do not disgrace the throne of Thy glory; remember, break not Thy covenant with us." Jer. 14:21. When we come to Him confessing our unworthiness and sin, He has pledged Himself to give heed to our cry. The honor of His throne is staked for the fulfillment of His word unto us.

Like Aaron, who symbolized Christ, our Saviour bears the names of all His people on His heart in the holy place. Our great High Priest remembers all the words by which He has encouraged us to trust. He is ever mindful of His covenant.

All who seek of Him shall find. All who knock will have the door opened to them. The excuse will not be made, Trouble Me not; the door is closed; I do not wish to open it. Never will one be told, I cannot help you. Those who beg at midnight for loaves to feed the hungry souls will be successful.

In the parable, he who asks bread for the stranger, receives "as many as he needeth." And in what measure will God impart to us that we may impart to others? "According to the mea- 149 sure of the gift of Christ." Eph. 4:7. Angels are watching with intense interest to see how man is dealing with his fellow men. When they see one manifest Christlike sympathy for the erring, they press to his side and bring to his remembrance words to speak that will be as the bread of life to the soul. So "God shall supply all your need according to His riches in glory by Christ Jesus." Phil. 4:19. Your testimony in its genuineness and reality He will make powerful in the power of the life to come. The word of the Lord will be in your mouth as truth and righteousness.

Personal effort for others should be preceded by much secret prayer; for it requires great wisdom to understand the science of saving souls. Before communicating with men, commune with Christ. At the throne of heavenly grace obtain a preparation for ministering to the people.

Let your heart break for the longing it has for God, for the living God. The life of Christ has shown what humanity can do by being partaker of the divine nature. All that Christ received from God we too may have. Then ask and receive. With the persevering faith of Jacob, with the unyielding persistence of Elijah, claim for yourself all that God has promised.

Let the glorious conceptions of God possess your mind. Let your life be knit by hidden links to the life of Jesus. He who commanded the light to shine out of darkness is willing to shine in your heart, to give the light of the knowledge of the glory of God in the face of Jesus Christ. The Holy Spirit will take the things of God and show them unto you, conveying them as a living power into the obedient heart. Christ will lead you to the threshold of the Infinite. You may behold the glory beyond the veil, and reveal to men the sufficiency of Him who ever liveth to make intercession for us.

150

13

Two Worshipers

"Unto certain which trusted in themselves that they were righteous, and despised others," Christ spoke the parable of the Pharisee and the publican. The Pharisee goes up to the temple to worship, not because he feels that he is a sinner in need of pardon, but because he thinks himself righteous and hopes to win commendation. His worship he regards as an act of merit that will recommend him to God. At the same time it will give the people a high opinion of his piety. He hopes to secure favor with both God and man. His worship is prompted by self-interest.

And he is full of self-praise. He looks it, he walks it, he prays it. Drawing apart from others as if to say, "Come not near to me; for I am holier than thou" (Isa. 65:5), he stands and prays

This chapter is based on Luke 18:9-14.

"with himself." Wholly self-satisfied, he thinks that God and men regard him with the same complacency.

"God, I thank thee," he says, "that I am not as other men are, extortioners, unjust, adulterers, or even as this publican." He judges his character, not by the holy character of God, but by the character of other men. His mind is turned away from God to humanity. This is the secret of his self-satisfaction.   151

He proceeds to recount his good deeds: "I fast twice in the week, I give tithes of all that I possess." The religion of the Pharisee does not touch the soul. He is not seeking Godlikeness of character, a heart filled with love and mercy. He is satisfied with a religion that has to do only with the outward life. His righteousness is his own—the fruit of his own works—and judged by a human standard.

Whoever trusts in himself that he is righteous, will despise others. As the Pharisee judges himself by other men, so he judges other men by himself. His righteousness is estimated by theirs, and the worse they are the more righteous by contrast he appears. His self-righteousness leads to accusing. "Other men" he condemns as transgressors of God's law. Thus he is making manifest the very spirit of Satan, the accuser of the brethren. With this spirit it is impossible for him to enter into communion with God. He goes down to his house destitute of the divine blessing.

The publican had gone to the temple with other worshipers, but he soon drew apart from them as unworthy to unite in their devotions. Standing afar off, he "would not lift up so much as his eyes unto heaven, but smote upon his breast," in bitter anguish and self-abhorrence. He felt that he had transgressed against God, that he was sinful and polluted. He could not expect even pity from those around him, for they looked upon him with contempt. He knew that he had no merit to commend him to God, and in utter self-despair he cried, "God be merciful to me, a sinner." He did not compare himself with others. Overwhelmed with a sense of   152 guilt, he stood as if alone in God's presence. His only desire was for pardon and peace, his only plea was the mercy of God. And he was blessed. "I tell you," Christ said, "this man went down to his house justified rather than the other."

The Pharisee and the publican represent two great classes into which those who come to worship God are divided. Their first two representatives are found in the first two children that were born into the world. Cain thought himself righteous, and he came to God with a thank offering only. He made no confession of sin, and acknowledged no need of mercy. But Abel came with the blood that pointed to the Lamb of God. He came as a sinner, confessing himself lost; his only hope was the unmerited love of

God. The Lord had respect to his offering, but to Cain and his offering He had not respect. The sense of need, the recognition of our poverty and sin, is the very first condition of acceptance with God. "Blessed are the poor in spirit; for theirs is the kingdom of heaven." Matt. 5:3.

For each of the classes represented by the Pharisee and the publican there is a lesson in the history of the apostle Peter. In his early discipleship Peter thought himself strong. Like the Pharisee, in his own estimation he was "not as other men are." When Christ on the eve of His betrayal forewarned His disciples, "All ye shall be offended because of Me this night," Peter confidently declared, "Although all shall be offended, yet will not I." Mark 14:27, 29. Peter did not know his own danger. Self-confidence misled him. He thought himself able to withstand temptation; but in a few short hours the test came, and with cursing and swearing he denied his Lord.

154 When the crowing of the cock reminded him of the words of Christ, surprised and shocked at what he had just done he turned and looked at his Master. At that moment Christ looked at Peter, and beneath that grieved look, in which compassion and love for him were blended, Peter understood himself. He went out and wept bitterly. That look of Christ's broke his heart. Peter had come to the turning point, and bitterly did he repent his sin. He was like the publican in his contrition and repentance, and like the publican he found mercy. The look of Christ assured him of pardon.

Now his self-confidence was gone. Never again were the old boastful assertions repeated.

Christ after His resurrection thrice tested Peter. "Simon, son of Jonas," He said, "lovest thou Me more than these?" Peter did not now exalt himself above his brethren. He appealed to the One who could read His heart. "Lord," he said, "Thou knowest all things; Thou knowest that I love Thee." John 21:15, 17.

Then he received his commission. A work broader and more delicate than had heretofore been his was appointed him. Christ bade him feed the sheep and the lambs. In thus committing to his stewardship the souls for whom the Saviour had laid down his own life, Christ gave to Peter the strongest proof of confidence in his restoration. The once restless, boastful, self-confident disciple had become subdued and contrite. Henceforth he followed his Lord in self-denial and self-sacrifice. He was a partaker of Christ's sufferings; and when Christ shall sit upon the throne of His glory, Peter will be a partaker in His glory.

The evil that led to Peter's fall and that shut out the Pharisee from communion with God is proving the ruin of thousands today. There is nothing so offensive to God or so dangerous to the human soul as pride and self-sufficiency. Of

all sins it is the most hopeless, the most incurable.

Peter's fall was not instantaneous, but gradual. Self-confidence led him to the belief that he 155 was saved, and step after step was taken in the downward path, until he could deny his Master. Never can we safely put confidence in self or feel, this side of heaven, that we are secure against temptation. Those who accept the Saviour, however sincere their conversion, should never be taught to say or to feel that they are saved. This is misleading. Every one should be taught to cherish hope and faith; but even when we give ourselves to Christ and know that He accepts us, we are not beyond the reach of temptation. God's word declares, "Many shall be purified, and made white, and tried." Dan. 12:10. Only he who endures the trial will receive the crown of life. (James 1:12.)

Those who accept Christ, and in their first confidence say, I am saved, are in danger of trusting to themselves. They lose sight of their own weakness and their constant need of divine strength. They are unprepared for Satan's devices, and under temptation many, like Peter, fall into the very depths of sin. We are admonished, "Let him that thinketh he standeth, take heed lest he fall." 1 Cor. 10:12. Our only safety is in constant distrust of self, and dependence on Christ.

It was necessary for Peter to learn his own defects of character, and his need of the power and grace of Christ. The Lord could not save him from trial, but He could have saved him from defeat. Had Peter been willing to receive Christ's warning, he would have been watching unto prayer. He would have walked with fear and trembling lest his feet should stumble. And he would have received divine help so that Satan could not have gained the victory.

It was through self-sufficiency that Peter fell; and it was through repentance and humiliation that his feet were again established. In the record of his experience every repenting sinner may find encouragement. Though Peter had 156 grievously sinned, he was not forsaken. The words of Christ were written upon his soul, "I have prayed for thee, that thy faith fail not." Luke 22:32. In his bitter agony of remorse, this prayer, and the memory of Christ's look of love and pity, gave him hope. Christ after His resurrection remembered Peter, and gave the angel the message for the women, "Go your way, tell His disciples and Peter that He goeth before you into Galilee; there shall ye see Him." Mark 16:7. Peter's repentance was accepted by the sin-pardoning Saviour.

And the same compassion that reached out to rescue Peter is extended to every soul who has fallen under temptation. It is Satan's special device to lead man into sin, and then leave him, helpless and trembling, fearing to seek for pardon. But why should we fear, when God has said, "Let him take hold of My strength, that he may make peace with Me; and he shall make peace with Me"? Isa. 27:5. Every provision has been made for our infirmities, every encouragement offered us to come to Christ.

Christ offered up His broken body to purchase back God's heritage, to give man another trial. "Wherefore He is able also to save them to the uttermost that come unto God by Him, seeing He ever liveth to make intercession for them." Heb. 7:25. By His spotless life, His obedience, His death on the cross of Calvary, Christ interceded for the lost race. And now, not as a mere petitioner does the Captain of our salvation intercede for us, but as a Conqueror claiming His victory. His offering is complete, and as our Intercessor He executes His self-appointed work, holding before God the censer containing His own spotless merits and the prayers, confessions, and thanksgiving of His people. Perfumed with the fragrance of His righteousness, these ascend to God as a sweet savor. The offering is wholly acceptable, and pardon covers all transgression.

157 Christ has pledged Himself to be our substitute and surety, and He neglects no one. He who could not see human beings exposed to eternal ruin without pouring out His soul unto death in their behalf, will look with pity and compassion upon every soul who realizes that he cannot save himself.

He will look upon no trembling suppliant without raising him up. He who through His own atonement provided for man an infinite fund of moral power, will not fail to employ this power in our behalf. We may take our sins and sorrows to His feet; for He loves us. His every look and word invites our confidence. He will shape and mold our characters according to His own will.

In the whole Satanic force there is not power to overcome one soul who in simple trust casts himself on Christ. "He giveth power to the faint; and to them that have no might He increaseth strength." Isa. 40:29.

158 "If we confess our sins, He is faithful and just to forgive us our sins, and to cleanse us from all unrighteousness." The Lord says, "Only acknowledge thine iniquity, that thou hast transgressed against the Lord thy God." "Then will I sprinkle clean water upon you, and ye shall be clean; from all your filthiness and from all your idols will I cleanse you." 1 John 1:9; Jer. 3:13; Eze. 36:25.

But we must have a knowledge of ourselves, a knowledge that will result in contrition, before we can find pardon and peace. The Pharisee felt no conviction of sin. The Holy Spirit could not work with him. His soul was encased in a self-righteous armor which the arrows of God, barbed and true-aimed by angel hands, failed to

penetrate. It is only he who knows himself to be a sinner that Christ can save. He came "to heal the brokenhearted, to preach deliverance to the captives, and recovering of sight to the blind, to set at liberty them that are bruised." Luke 4:18. But "they that are whole need not a physician." Luke 5:31. We must know our real condition, or we shall not feel our need of Christ's help. We must understand our danger, or we shall not flee to the refuge. We must feel the pain of our wounds, or we should not desire healing.

The Lord says, "Because thou sayest, I am rich, and increased with goods, and have need of nothing; and knowest not that thou art wretched, and miserable, and poor, and blind, and naked: I counsel thee to buy of Me gold tried in the fire, that thou mayest be rich; and white raiment, that thou mayest be clothed, and that the shame of thy nakedness do not appear; and anoint thine eyes with eyesalve, that thou mayest see." Rev. 3:17, 18. The gold tried in the fire is faith that works by love. Only this can bring us into harmony with God. We may be active, we may do much work; but without love, such love as dwelt in the heart of Christ, we can never be numbered with the family of heaven.

No man can of himself understand his errors. 159 "The heart is deceitful above all things, and desperately wicked; who can know it?" Jer. 17:9. The lips may express a poverty of soul that the heart does not acknowledge. While speaking to God of poverty of spirit, the heart may be swelling with the conceit of its own superior humility and exalted righteousness. In one way only can a true knowledge of self be obtained. We must behold Christ. It is ignorance of Him that makes men so uplifted in their own righteousness. When we contemplate His purity and excellence, we shall see our own weakness and poverty and defects as they really are. We shall see ourselves lost and hopeless, clad in garments of self-righteousness, like every other sinner. We shall see that if we are ever saved, it will not be through our own goodness, but through God's infinite grace.

The prayer of the publican was heard because it showed dependence reaching forth to lay hold upon Omnipotence. Self to the publican appeared nothing but shame. Thus it must be seen by all who seek God. By faith—faith that renounces all self-trust—the needy suppliant is to lay hold upon infinite power.

No outward observances can take the place of simple faith and entire renunciation of self. But no man can empty himself of self. We can only consent for Christ to accomplish the work. Then the language of the soul will be, Lord, take my heart; for I cannot give it. It is Thy property. Keep it pure, for I cannot keep it for Thee. Save me in spite of myself, my weak, unchristlike self. Mold me, fashion me, raise me into a pure and holy atmosphere, where the rich current of

Thy love can flow through my soul.

It is not only at the beginning of the Christian life that this renunciation of self is to be made. At every advance step heavenward it is to be renewed. All our good works are dependent on a power outside of ourselves. Therefore there needs to be a continual reaching out of the heart after God, a continual, earnest, heartbreaking confession of sin and humbling of the soul before Him. Only by constant renunciation of self and dependence on Christ can we walk safely.

The nearer we come to Jesus and the more clearly we discern the purity of His character, the more clearly we shall discern the exceeding sinfulness of sin and the less we shall feel like exalting ourselves. Those whom heaven recognizes as holy ones are the last to parade their own goodness. The apostle Peter became a faithful minister of Christ, and he was greatly honored with divine light and power; he had an active part in the upbuilding of Christ's church; but Peter never forgot the fearful experience of his humiliation; his sin was forgiven; yet well he knew that for the weakness of character which had caused his fall only the grace of Christ could avail. He found in himself nothing in which to glory.

None of the apostles or prophets ever claimed to be without sin. Men who have lived nearest to God, men who would sacrifice life itself rather than knowingly commit a wrong act, men whom God had honored with divine light and power, have confessed the sinfulness of their own nature. They have put no confidence in the flesh, have claimed no righteousness of their own, but have trusted wholly in the righteousness of Christ. So will it be with all who behold Christ.

At every advance step in Christian experience our repentance will deepen. It is to those whom the Lord has forgiven, to those whom He acknowledges as His people, that He says, "Then shall ye remember your own evil ways, and your doings that were not good, and shall loathe yourselves in your own sight." Eze. 36:31. Again He says, "I will establish My covenant with thee, and thou shalt know that I am the Lord; that thou mayest remember, and be confounded, and never open thy mouth any more because of thy shame, when I am pacified toward thee for all that thou hast done, saith the Lord God." Eze. 16:62, 63. Then our lips will not be opened in self-glorification. We shall know that our sufficiency is in Christ alone. We shall make the apostle's confession our own. "I know that in me (that is, in my flesh) dwelleth no good thing." Rom. 7:18. "God forbid that I should glory, save in the cross of our Lord Jesus Christ, by whom the world is crucified unto me, and I unto the world." Gal. 6:14.

In harmony with this experience is the command, "Work out your own salvation with fear and trembling. For it is God which worketh in you both to will and to do of His good pleasure." Phil. 2:12, 13. God does not bid you fear that He will fail to fulfill His promises, that His patience will weary, or His compassion be found wanting. Fear lest your will shall not be held in subjection to Christ's will, lest your hereditary and cultivated traits of character shall control your life. "It is God which worketh in you both to will and to do of His good pleasure." Fear lest self shall interpose between your soul and the great Master Worker. Fear lest self-will shall mar the high purpose that through you God desires to accomplish. Fear to trust to your own strength, fear to withdraw your hand from the hand of Christ and attempt to walk life's pathway without His abiding presence.

We need to shun everything that would encourage pride and self-sufficiency; therefore we should beware of giving or receiving flattery or praise. It is Satan's work to flatter. He deals in flattery as well as in accusing and condemnation. Thus he seeks to work the ruin of the soul. Those who give praise to men are used by Satan as his agents. Let the workers for Christ direct every word of praise away from themselves. Let self be put out of sight. Christ alone is to be exalted. "Unto Him that loved us, and washed us from our sins in His own blood," let every eye be directed, and praise from every heart ascend. (Rev. 1:5.)

The life in which the fear of the Lord is cherished will not be a life of sadness and gloom. It is the absence of Christ that makes the countenance sad, and the life a pilgrimage of sighs. Those who are filled with self-esteem and self-love do not feel the need of a living, personal union with Christ. The heart that has not fallen on the Rock is proud of its wholeness. Men want a dignified religion. They desire to walk in a path wide enough to take in their own attributes. Their self-love, their love of popularity and love of praise, exclude the Saviour from their hearts, and without Him there is gloom and sadness. But Christ dwelling in the soul is a wellspring of joy. For all who receive Him, the very keynote of the word of God is rejoicing.

"For thus saith the high and lofty One that inhabiteth eternity, whose name is Holy: I dwell in the high and holy place, with him also that is of a contrite and humble spirit, to revive the spirit of the humble, and to revive the heart of the contrite ones." Isa. 57:15.

It was when Moses was hidden in the cleft of the rock that he beheld the glory of God. It is when we hide in the riven Rock that Christ will cover us with His own pierced hand, and we shall hear what the Lord saith unto His servants. To us as to Moses, God will reveal Himself as "merciful and gracious, long-suffering, and abundant in goodness and truth, keeping mercy for thousands, forgiving iniquity and transgression and sin." Ex. 34:6, 7.

163 The work of redemption involves consequences of which it is difficult for man to have any conception. "Eye hath not seen, nor ear heard, neither have entered into the heart of man, the things which God hath prepared for them that love Him." 1 Cor. 2:9. As the sinner, drawn by the power of Christ, approaches the uplifted cross, and prostrates himself before it, there is a new creation. A new heart is given him. He becomes a new creature in Christ Jesus. Holiness finds that it has nothing more to require. God Himself is "the justifier of him which believeth in Jesus." Rom. 3:26. And "whom He justified, them He also glorified." Rom. 8:30. Great as is the shame and degradation through sin, even greater will be the honor and exaltation through redeeming love. To human beings striving for conformity to the divine image there is imparted an outlay of heaven's treasure, an excellency of power, that will place them higher than even the angels who have never fallen.

"Thus saith the Lord, the Redeemer of Israel, and His Holy One, to him whom man despiseth, to him whom the nation abhorreth, . . . Kings shall see and arise, princes also shall worship, because of the Lord that is faithful, and the Holy One of Israel, and He shall choose thee." Isa. 49:7.

"For every one that exalteth himself shall be abased; and he that humbleth himself shall be exalted."

164

14

"Shall Not God Avenge His Own?"

Christ had been speaking of the period just before His second coming, and of the perils through which His followers must pass. With special reference to that time He related the parable "to this end, that men ought always to pray, and not to faint."

"There was in a city," He said, "a judge, which feared not God, neither regarded man; and there was a widow in that city; and she came unto him, saying, Avenge me of mine adversary. And he would not for a while; but afterward he said within himself, Though I fear not God, nor regard man; yet because this widow troubleth me, I will avenge her, lest by her continual coming she weary me. And the Lord said, Hear what the unjust judge saith. And shall not God avenge His own elect, which cry day and night unto Him, though He bear long with them? I tell you that He will avenge them speedily."

The judge who is here pictured had no regard

This chapter is based on Luke 18:1-8.

for right, nor pity for suffering. The widow who 165 pressed her case before him was persistently repulsed. Again and again she came to him, only to be treated with contempt, and to be driven from the judgment seat. The judge knew that her cause was righteous, and he could have relieved her at once, but he would not. He wanted to show his arbitrary power, and it gratified him to let her ask and plead and entreat in vain. But he would not fail nor become discouraged. Notwithstanding his indifference and hardheartedness, she pressed her petition until the judge consented to attend to her case. "Though I fear not God, nor regard man," he said, "yet because this widow troubleth me, I will avenge her, lest by her continual coming she weary me." To save his reputation, to avoid giving publicity to his partial, one-sided judgment, he avenged the persevering woman.

"And the Lord said, Hear what the unjust judge saith. And shall not God avenge His own elect, which cry day and night unto him, though He bear long with them? I tell you that He will avenge them speedily." Christ here draws a sharp contrast between the unjust judge and God. The judge yielded to the widow's request merely through selfishness, that he might be relieved of her importunity. He felt for her no pity or compassion; her misery was nothing to him. How different is the attitude of God toward those who seek Him. The appeals of the needy and distressed are considered by Him with infinite compassion.

The woman who entreated the judge for justice had lost her husband by death. Poor and friendless, she had no means of retrieving her ruined fortunes. So by sin, man lost his connection with God. Of himself he has no means of salvation. But in Christ we are brought nigh unto the Father. The elect of God are dear to His heart. They are those whom He has called out of darkness into His marvelous light, to show forth His praise, to shine as lights amid the darkness 166 of the world. The unjust judge had no special interest in the widow who importuned him for deliverance; yet in order to rid himself of her pitiful appeals, he heard her plea, and delivered her from her adversary. But God loves His children with infinite love. To Him the dearest object on earth is His church.

"For the Lord's portion is His people; Jacob is the lot of His inheritance. He found him in a desert land, and in the waste, howling wilderness; He led him about, He instructed him, He kept him as the apple of His eye." Deut. 32:9, 10. "For thus saith the Lord of hosts: After the glory hath He sent Me unto the nations which spoiled you; for he that toucheth you toucheth the apple of His eye." Zech. 2:8.

The widow's prayer, "Avenge me"—"do me justice" (R.V.)—"of mine adversary," represents the prayer of God's children. Satan is their great adversary. He is the "accuser of our brethren," who accuses them before God day and night. (Rev. 12:10.) He is continually working to misrepresent and accuse, to deceive and destroy the people of God. And it is for deliverance from the power of Satan and his agents that in this parable Christ teaches His disciples to pray.

In the prophecy of Zechariah is brought to view Satan's accusing work, and the work of Christ in resisting the adversary of His people. The prophet says, "He showed me Joshua the high priest standing before the angel of the Lord, and Satan standing at his right hand to resist him. And the Lord said unto Satan, The Lord rebuke thee, O Satan; even the Lord that hath chosen Jerusalem rebuke thee: is not this a brand plucked out of the fire? Now Joshua was clothed with filthy garments, and stood before the angel." Zech. 3:1-3.

167 The people of God are here represented as a criminal on trial. Joshua, as high priest, is seeking for a blessing for his people, who are in great affliction. While he is pleading before God, Satan is standing at his right hand as his adversary. He is accusing the children of God, and making their case appear as desperate as possible. He presents before the Lord their evil doings and their defects. He shows their faults and failures, hoping they will appear of such a character in the eyes of Christ that He will render them no help in their great need. Joshua, as the representative of God's people, stands under condemnation, clothed with filthy garments. Aware of the sins of his people, he is weighed down with discouragement. Satan is pressing upon his soul a sense of guiltiness that makes him feel almost hopeless. Yet there he stands as a suppliant, with Satan arrayed against him.

168 The work of Satan as an accuser began in heaven. This has been his work on earth ever since man's fall, and it will be his work in a special sense as we approach nearer to the close of this world's history. As he sees that his time is short, he will work with greater earnestness to deceive and destroy. He is angry when he sees a people on the earth who, even in their weakness and sinfulness, have respect to the law of Jehovah. He is determined that they shall not obey God. He delights in their unworthiness, and has devices prepared for every soul, that all may be ensnared and separated from God. He seeks to accuse and condemn God and all who strive to carry out His purposes in this world in mercy and love, in compassion and forgiveness.

Every manifestation of God's power for His people arouses the enmity of Satan. Every time God works in their behalf, Satan with his angels works with renewed vigor to compass their ruin. He is jealous of all who make Christ their strength. His object is to instigate evil, and when he has succeeded, throw all the blame upon the tempted ones. He points to their filthy garments, their defective characters. He presents their weakness and folly, their sins of ingratitude, their unlikeness to Christ, which have dishonored their Redeemer. All this he urges as an argument proving his right to work his will in their destruction. He endeavors to affright their souls with the thought that their case is hopeless, that the stain of their defilement can never be washed away. He hopes so to destroy their faith that they will yield fully to his temptations, and turn from their allegiance to God.

The Lord's people cannot of themselves answer the charges of Satan. As they look to themselves they are ready to despair. But they appeal to the divine Advocate. They plead the merits of the Redeemer. God can be "just, and the justifier of him which believeth in Jesus." Rom. 3:26. With confidence the Lord's children cry unto Him to silence the accusations of 169 Satan, and bring to naught his devices. "Do me justice of mine adversary," they pray; and with the mighty argument of the cross, Christ silences the bold accuser.

"The Lord said unto Satan, The Lord rebuke thee, O Satan, even the Lord that hath chosen Jerusalem rebuke thee: is not this a brand plucked out of the fire?" When Satan seeks to cover the people of God with blackness, and ruin them, Christ interposes. Although they have sinned, Christ has taken the guilt of their sins upon His own soul. He has snatched the race as a brand from the fire. By His human nature He is linked with man, while through His divine nature He is one with the infinite God. Help is brought within the reach of perishing souls. The adversary is rebuked.

"Now Joshua was clothed with filthy garments, and stood before the angel: and he answered and spake unto those that stood before him, saying, Take away the filthy garments from him. And unto him he said, Behold, I have caused thine iniquity to pass from thee, and I will clothe thee with change of raiment. And I said, Let them set a fair miter upon his head. So they set a fair miter upon his head, and clothed him with garments." Then with the authority of the Lord of hosts the angel made a solemn pledge to Joshua, the representative of God's people: "If thou wilt walk in My ways, and if thou wilt keep My charge, then thou shalt also judge My house, and shalt also keep My courts, and I will give thee places to walk among these that stand by"—even among the angels that surround the throne of God. (Zech. 3:3-7.)

Notwithstanding the defects of the people of God, Christ does not turn away from the objects of His care. He has the power to change their raiment. He removes the filthy garments, He 170 places upon the repenting, believing ones His own robe of righteousness, and writes pardon against their names on the records of heaven. He confesses them as His before the heavenly universe. Satan their adversary is shown to be an accuser and deceiver. God will do justice for His own elect.

The prayer, "Do me justice of mine adversary," applies not only to Satan, but to the agencies whom he instigates to misrepresent, to tempt, and to destroy the people of God. Those who have decided to obey the commandments of God will understand by experience that they have adversaries who are controlled by a power from beneath. Such adversaries beset Christ at every step, how constantly and determinedly no human being can ever know. Christ's disciples, like their Master, are followed by continual temptation.

The Scriptures describe the condition of the world just before Christ's second coming. James the apostle pictures the greed and oppression that will prevail. He says, "Go to now, ye rich men, ... ye have heaped treasure together for the last days. Behold, the hire of the labourers who have reaped down your fields, which is of you kept back by fraud, crieth: and the cries of them which have reaped are entered into the ears of the Lord of sabaoth. Ye have lived in pleasure on the earth, and been wanton. Ye have nourished your hearts, as in a day of slaughter. Ye have condemned and killed the just; and he doth not resist you." James 5:1-6. This is a picture of what exists today. By every species of oppression and extortion, men are piling up colossal fortunes, while the cries of starving humanity are coming up before God.

171 "Judgment is turned away backward, and justice standeth afar off; for truth is fallen in the street, and equity cannot enter. Yea, truth faileth; and he that departeth from evil maketh himself a prey." Isa. 59:14, 15. This was fulfilled in the life of Christ on earth. He was loyal to God's commandments, setting aside the human traditions and requirements which had been exalted in their place. Because of this He was hated and persecuted. This history is repeated. The laws and traditions of men are exalted above the law of God, and those who are true to God's commandments suffer reproach and persecution. Christ, because of His faithfulness to God, was accused as a Sabbathbreaker and blasphemer. He was declared to be possessed of a devil, and was denounced as Beelzebub. In like manner His followers are accused and misrepresented. Thus Satan hopes to lead them to sin, and cast dishonor upon God.

The character of the judge in the parable, who feared not God nor regarded man, was presented by Christ to show the kind of judgment that was then being executed, and that would soon be witnessed at His trial. He desires His people in all time to realize how little dependence can be placed on earthly rulers or judges in the day of adversity. Often the elect people of God have to stand before men in official positions who do not make the word of God their guide and counselor, but who follow their own unconsecrated, undisciplined impulses.

In the parable of the unjust judge, Christ has shown what we should do. "Shall not God avenge His own elect, which cry day and night unto Him?" Christ, our example, did nothing to vindicate or deliver Himself. He committed His case to God. So His followers are not to accuse or condemn, or to resort to force in order to deliver themselves.

When trials arise that seem unexplainable, we should not allow our peace to be spoiled. However unjustly we may be treated, let not passion arise. By indulging a spirit of retaliation we 172 injure ourselves. We destroy our own confidence in God, and grieve the Holy Spirit. There is by our side a witness, a heavenly messenger, who will lift up for us a standard against the enemy. He will shut us in with the bright beams of the Sun of Righteousness. Beyond this Satan cannot penetrate. He cannot pass this shield of holy light.

While the world is progressing in wickedness, none of us need flatter ourselves that we shall have no difficulties. But it is these very difficulties that bring us into the audience chamber of the Most High. We may seek counsel of One who is infinite in wisdom.

The Lord says, "Call upon Me in the day of trouble." Ps. 50:15. He invites us to present to Him our perplexities and necessities, and our need of divine help. He bids us be instant in prayer. As soon as difficulties arise, we are to offer to Him our sincere, earnest petitions. By our importunate prayers we give evidence of our strong confidence in God. The sense of our need leads us to pray earnestly, and our heavenly Father is moved by our supplications.

Often those who suffer reproach or persecution for their faith are tempted to think themselves forsaken by God. In the eyes of men they are in the minority. To all appearance their enemies triumph over them. But let them not violate their conscience. He who has suffered in their behalf, and has borne their sorrows and afflictions, has not forsaken them.

The children of God are not left alone and defenseless. Prayer moves the arm of Omnipotence. Prayer has "subdued kingdoms, wrought righteousness, obtained promises, stopped the mouths of lions, quenched the violence of fire"—we shall know what it means when we hear the reports of the martyrs who died for their faith—"turneth to flight the armies of the aliens." Heb. 11:33, 34.

If we surrender our lives to His service, we 173 can never be placed in a position for which God has not made provision. Whatever may be our situation, we have a Guide to direct our way; whatever our perplexities, we have a sure Counselor; whatever our sorrow, bereavement, or loneliness, we have a sympathizing Friend. If in our ignorance we make missteps, Christ does not leave us. His voice, clear and distinct, is heard saying, "I am the Way, the Truth, and the Life." John 14:6. "He shall deliver the needy when he crieth; the poor also, and him that hath no helper." Ps. 72:12.

The Lord declares that He will be honored by those who draw nigh to Him, who faithfully do His service. "Thou wilt keep him in perfect peace whose mind is stayed on Thee, because he trusteth in Thee." Isa. 26:3. The arm of Omnipotence is outstretched to lead us onward and still onward. Go forward, the Lord says; I will send you help. It is for My name's glory that you ask, and you shall receive. I will be honored before those who are watching for your failure. They shall see My word triumph gloriously. "All things, whatsoever ye shall ask in prayer, believing, ye shall receive." Matt. 21:22.

Let all who are afflicted or unjustly used, cry to God. Turn away from those whose hearts are as steel, and make your requests known to your Maker. Never is one repulsed who comes to Him with a contrite heart. Not one sincere prayer is lost. Amid the anthems of the celestial choir, God hears the cries of the weakest human being. We pour out our heart's desire in our closets, we breathe a prayer as we walk by the way, and our words reach the throne of the Monarch of the universe. They may be inaudible to any human ear, but they cannot die away into silence, nor can they be lost through the activities of business that are going on. Nothing can drown the soul's desire. It rises above the din of the street, above the confusion of the multitude, to the heavenly courts. It is God to whom we are speaking, and our prayer is heard.

You who feel the most unworthy, fear not to commit your case to God. When He gave Himself in Christ for the sin of the world, He undertook the case of every soul. "He that spared not His own Son, but delivered Him up for us all, how shall He not with Him also freely give us all things?" Rom. 8:32. Will He not fulfill the gracious word given for our encouragement and strength?

Christ desires nothing so much as to redeem His heritage from the dominion of Satan. But before we are delivered from Satan's power without, we must be delivered from his power within. The Lord permits trials in order that we may be cleansed from earthliness, from selfishness, from harsh, unchristlike traits of character. He suffers the deep waters of affliction to go over our souls in order that we may know Him and Jesus Christ whom He has sent, in order that we may have deep heart longings to be cleansed from defilement, and may come forth from the trial purer, holier, happier. Often we enter the furnace of trial with our souls darkened with selfishness; but if patient under the crucial test, we shall come forth reflecting the divine character. When His purpose in the affliction is accomplished, "He shall bring forth thy righteousness as the light, and thy judgment as the noonday." Ps. 37:6.

There is no danger that the Lord will neglect the prayers of His people. The danger is that in temptation and trial they will become discouraged, and fail to persevere in prayer.

The Saviour manifested divine compassion toward the Syrophenician woman. His heart was touched as He saw her grief. He longed to give her an immediate assurance that her prayer was heard; but He desired to teach His disciples a lesson, and for a time He seemed to neglect the cry of her tortured heart. When her faith had been made manifest, He spoke to her words of commendation and sent her away with the precious boon she had asked. The disciples never forgot this lesson, and it is placed on record to show the result of persevering prayer.

It was Christ Himself who put into that mother's heart the persistence which would not be repulsed. It was Christ who gave the pleading widow courage and determination before the judge. It was Christ who, centuries before, in the mysterious conflict by the Jabbok, had inspired Jacob with the same persevering faith. And the confidence which He Himself had implanted, He did not fail to reward.

He who dwells in the heavenly sanctuary judges righteously. His pleasure is more in His people, struggling with temptation in a world of sin, than in the host of angels that surround His throne.

In this speck of a world the whole heavenly universe manifests the greatest interest, for Christ has paid an infinite price for the souls of its inhabitants. The world's Redeemer has bound earth to heaven by ties of intelligence, for the redeemed of the Lord are here. Heavenly beings still visit the earth as in the days when they walked and talked with Abraham and with Moses. Amid the busy activity of our great cities, amid the multitudes that crowd the thoroughfares and fill the marts of trade where from morning till evening the people act as if business and sport and pleasure were all there is to life, where there are so few to contemplate unseen realities—even here heaven has still its watchers and its holy ones. There are invisible agencies observing every word and deed of human beings. In every assembly for business or pleasure, in every gathering for worship, there are more listeners than can be seen with the natural sight. Sometimes the heavenly intelligences draw aside the curtain which hides the unseen world that our thoughts may be withdrawn from the hurry and rush of life to consider that there are unseen witnesses to all we do or say.

We need to understand better than we do the

mission of the angel visitants. It would be well to consider that in all our work we have the co-operation and care of heavenly beings. Invisible armies of light and power attend the meek and lowly ones who believe and claim the promises of God. Cherubim and seraphim and angels that excel in strength—ten thousand times ten thousand and thousands of thousands—stand at His right hand, "all ministering spirits, sent forth to minister for them who shall be heirs of salvation." Heb. 1:14.

177   By these angel messengers a faithful record is kept of the words and deeds of the children of men. Every act of cruelty or injustice toward God's people, all they are caused to suffer through the power of evil workers, is registered in heaven.

"Shall not God avenge His own elect, which cry day and night unto Him, though He bear long with them? I tell you that He will avenge them speedily."

"Cast not away therefore your confidence, which hath great recompense of reward. For ye have need of patience, that, after ye have done the will of God, ye might receive the promise. For yet a little while, and He that shall come will come, and will not tarry." Heb. 10:35-37. "Behold, the husbandman waiteth for the precious fruit of the earth, and hath long patience for it, until he receive the early and latter rain. Be ye also patient; stablish your hearts; for the coming of the Lord draweth nigh." James 5:7, 8.

The long-suffering of God is wonderful. Long does justice wait while mercy pleads with the sinner. But "righteousness and judgment are the establishment of His throne." Ps. 97:2, margin. "The Lord is slow to anger;" but He is "great in power, and will not at all acquit the wicked: the Lord hath His way in the whirlwind and in the storm, and the clouds are the dust of His feet." Nahum 1:3.

The world has become bold in transgression of God's law. Because of His long forbearance, men have trampled upon His authority. They have strengthened one another in oppression and cruelty toward His heritage, saying, "How doth God know? and is there knowledge in the Most High?" Ps. 73:11. But there is a line beyond which they cannot pass. The time is near when they will have reached the prescribed limit. Even now they have almost exceeded the bounds of the long-suffering of God, the limits 178   of His grace, the limits of His mercy. The Lord will interpose to vindicate His own honor, to deliver His people, and to repress the swellings of unrighteousness.

In Noah's day, men had disregarded the law of God until almost all remembrance of the Creator had passed away from the earth. Their iniquity reached so great a height that the Lord brought a flood of waters upon the earth, and swept away its wicked inhabitants.

From age to age the Lord has made known the manner of His working. When a crisis has come, He has revealed Himself, and has interposed to hinder the working out of Satan's plans. With nations, with families, and with individuals, He has often permitted matters to come to a crisis, that His interference might become marked. Then He has made manifest that there is a God in Israel who will maintain His law and vindicate His people.

In this time of prevailing iniquity we may know that the last great crisis is at hand. When the defiance of God's law is almost universal, when His people are oppressed and afflicted by their fellow men, the Lord will interpose.

The time is near when He will say, "Come, My people, enter thou into thy chambers, and shut thy doors about thee: hide thyself as it were for a little moment, until the indignation be overpast. For, behold, the Lord cometh out of His place to punish the inhabitants of the earth for their iniquity; the earth also shall disclose her blood, and shall no more cover her slain." Isa. 26:20, 21. Men who claim to be Christians may now defraud and oppress the poor; they may rob the widow and fatherless; they may indulge their Satanic hatred because they cannot control the consciences of God's people; but for all this God will bring them into judgment. They "shall have judgment without mercy" that have "showed no mercy." (James 2:13.) Not long hence they will stand before the Judge of all the earth, to render an account for the pain 179 they have caused to the bodies and souls of His heritage. They may now indulge in false accusations, they may deride those whom God has appointed to do His work, they may consign His believing ones to prison, to the chain gang, to banishment, to death; but for every pang of anguish, every tear shed, they must answer. God will reward them double for their sins. Concerning Babylon, the symbol of the apostate church, He says to His ministers of judgment, "Her sins have reached unto heaven, and God hath remembered her iniquities. Reward her even as she rewarded you, and double unto her double according to her works: in the cup which she hath filled fill to her double." Rev. 18:5, 6.

From India, from Africa, from China, from the islands of the sea, from the downtrodden millions of so-called Christian lands, the cry of human woe is ascending to God. That cry will not long be unanswered. God will cleanse the earth from its moral corruption, not by a sea of water as in Noah's day, but by a sea of fire that cannot be quenched by any human devising.

"There shall be a time of trouble, such as never was since there was a nation even to that same time; and at that time Thy people shall be delivered, every one that shall be found written in the book." Dan. 12:1.

From garrets, from hovels, from dungeons,

from scaffolds, from mountains and deserts, from the caves of the earth and the caverns of the sea, Christ will gather His children to Himself. On earth they have been destitute, afflicted, and tormented. Millions have gone down to the grave loaded with infamy because they refused to yield to the deceptive claims of Satan. By human tribunals the children of God have been adjudged the vilest criminals. But the day is near when "God is judge Himself." (Ps. 50:6). Then the decisions of earth shall be reversed. "The rebuke of His people shall He take away." Isa. 25:8. White robes will be given to every one of them. (Rev. 6:11.) And "they shall call them the holy people, the redeemed of the Lord." Isa. 62:12.

Whatever crosses they have been called to bear, whatever losses they have sustained, whatever persecution they have suffered, even to the loss of their temporal life, the children of God are amply recompensed. "They shall see His face; and His name shall be in their foreheads." Rev. 22:4.

15

"This Man Receiveth Sinners"

As the "publicans and sinners" gathered about Christ, the rabbis expressed their displeasure. "This man receiveth sinners," they said, "and eateth with them."

By this accusation they insinuated that Christ liked to associate with the sinful and vile, and was insensible to their wickedness. The rabbis had been disappointed in Jesus. Why was it that one who claimed so lofty a character did not mingle with them and follow their methods of teaching? Why did He go about so unpretendingly, working among all classes? If He were a true prophet, they said, He would harmonize with them, and would treat the publicans and sinners with the indifference they deserved. It angered these guardians of society that He with whom they were continually in controversy, yet whose purity of life awed and condemned them, should meet, in such apparent sympathy, with social outcasts. They did not approve of His methods. They regarded themselves as educated, refined, and pre-eminently religious; but Christ's example laid bare their selfishness.

It angered them also that those who showed only contempt for the rabbis and who were never seen in the synagogues should flock about Jesus and listen with rapt attention to His words. The scribes and Pharisees felt only condemnation in that pure presence; how was it, then, that publicans and sinners were drawn to Jesus?

They knew not that the explanation lay in the very words they had uttered as a scornful

charge, "This man receiveth sinners." The souls who came to Jesus felt in His presence that even for them there was escape from the pit of sin. The Pharisees had only scorn and condemnation for them; but Christ greeted them as children of God, estranged indeed from the Father's house, but not forgotten by the Father's heart. And their very misery and sin made them only the more the objects of His compassion. The farther they had wandered from Him, the more earnest the longing and the greater the sacrifice for their rescue.

All this the teachers of Israel might have learned from the sacred scrolls of which it was their pride to be the keepers and expounders. Had not David written—David, who had fallen into deadly sin—"I have gone astray like a lost sheep; seek Thy servant"? Ps. 119:176. Had not Micah revealed God's love to the sinner, saying, "Who is a God like unto Thee, that pardoneth iniquity, and passeth by the transgression of the remnant of His heritage? He retaineth not His anger forever, because He delighteth in mercy"? Micah 7:18.

The Lost Sheep

Christ did not at this time remind His hearers of the words of Scripture. He appealed to the witness of their own experience. The widespreading tablelands on the east of Jordan afforded abundant pasturage for flocks, and through the gorges and over the wooded hills had wandered many a lost sheep, to be searched for and brought back by the shepherd's care. In the company about Jesus there were shepherds, and also men who had money invested in flocks and herds, and all could appreciate His illustration: "What man of you, having an hundred sheep, if he lose one of them, doth not leave the ninety and nine in the wilderness, and go after that which is lost, until he find it?"

These souls whom you despise, said Jesus, are the property of God. By creation and by redemption they are His, and they are of value in His sight. As the shepherd loves his sheep, and cannot rest if even one be missing, so, in an infinitely higher degree, does God love every outcast soul. Men may deny the claim of His love, they may wander from Him, they may choose another master; yet they are God's, and He longs to recover His own. He says, "As a shepherd seeketh out his flock in the day that he is among his sheep that are scattered; so will I seek out My sheep, and will deliver them out of all places where they have been scattered in the cloudy and dark day." Eze. 34:12.

In the parable the shepherd goes out to search for one sheep—the very least that can be numbered. So if there had been but one lost soul, Christ would have died for that one.

The sheep that has strayed from the fold is the most helpless of all creatures. It must be sought

This chapter is based on Luke 15:1-10.

for by the shepherd, for it cannot find its way back. So with the soul that has wandered away from God; he is as helpless as the lost sheep, and unless divine love had come to his rescue he could never find his way to God.

The shepherd who discovers that one of his sheep is missing does not look carelessly upon the flock that is safely housed, and say, "I have ninety and nine, and it will cost me too much trouble to go in search of the straying one. Let him come back, and I will open the door of the sheepfold, and let him in." No; no sooner does the sheep go astray than the shepherd is filled with grief and anxiety. He counts and recounts the flock. When he is sure that one sheep is lost, he slumbers not. He leaves the ninety and nine within the fold, and goes in search of the straying sheep. The darker and more tempestuous the night and the more perilous the way, the greater is the shepherd's anxiety and the more earnest his search. He makes every effort to find that one lost sheep.

With what relief he hears in the distance its first faint cry. Following the sound, he climbs the steepest heights, he goes to the very edge of the precipice, at the risk of his own life. Thus he searches, while the cry, growing fainter, tells him that his sheep is ready to die. At last his effort is rewarded; the lost is found. Then he does not scold it because it has caused him so much trouble. He does not drive it with a whip. He does not even try to lead it home. In his joy he takes the trembling creature upon his shoulders; if it is bruised and wounded, he gathers it in his arms, pressing it close to his bosom, that the warmth of his own heart may give it life. With gratitude that his search has not been in vain, he bears it back to the fold.

Thank God, He has presented to our imagination no picture of a sorrowful shepherd returning without the sheep. The parable does not speak of failure but of success and joy in the recovery. Here is the divine guarantee that not even one of the straying sheep of God's fold is overlooked, not one is left unsuccored. Every one that will submit to be ransomed, Christ will rescue from the pit of corruption and from the briers of sin.

Desponding soul, take courage, even though you have done wickedly. Do not think that *perhaps* God will pardon your transgressions and permit you to come into His presence. God has made the first advance. While you were in rebellion against Him, He went forth to seek you. With the tender heart of the shepherd He left the ninety and nine and went out into the wilderness to find that which was lost. The soul, bruised and wounded and ready to perish, He encircles in His arms of love and joyfully bears it to the fold of safety.

It was taught by the Jews that before God's love is extended to the sinner, he must first repent. In their view, repentance is a work by which men earn the favor of Heaven. And it was this thought that led the Pharisees to exclaim in astonishment and anger, "This man receiveth sinners." According to their ideas He should permit none to approach Him but those who had repented. But in the parable of the lost sheep, Christ teaches that salvation does not come through our seeking after God but through God's seeking after us. "There is none that understandeth, there is none that seeketh after God. They are all gone out of the way." Rom. 3:11, 12. We do not repent in order that God may love us, but He reveals to us His love in order that we may repent.

When the straying sheep is at last brought home, the shepherd's gratitude finds expression in melodious songs of rejoicing. He calls upon his friends and neighbors, saying unto them, "Rejoice with me; for I have found my sheep which was lost." So when a wanderer is found by the great Shepherd of the sheep, heaven and earth unite in thanksgiving and rejoicing.

"Joy shall be in heaven over one sinner that repenteth, more than over ninety and nine just persons, which need no repentance." You Pharisees, said Christ, regard yourselves as the favorites of heaven. You think yourselves secure in your own righteousness. Know, then, that if you need no repentance, My mission is not to you. These poor souls who feel their poverty and sinfulness, are the very ones whom I have come to rescue. Angels of heaven are interested in these lost ones whom you despise. You complain and sneer when one of these souls joins himself to Me; but know that angels rejoice, and the song of triumph rings through the courts above.

The rabbis had a saying that there is rejoicing in heaven when one who has sinned against God is destroyed; but Jesus taught that to God the work of destruction is a strange work. That in which all heaven delights is the restoration of God's own image in the souls whom He has made.

When one who has wandered far in sin seeks to return to God, he will encounter criticism and distrust. There are those who will doubt whether his repentance is genuine, or will whisper, "He has no stability; I do not believe that he will hold out." These persons are doing not the work of God but the work of Satan, who is the accuser of the brethren. Through their criticisms the wicked one hopes to discourage that soul, and to drive him still farther from hope and from God. Let the repenting sinner contemplate the rejoicing in heaven over the return of the one that was lost. Let him rest in the love of God and in no case be disheartened by the scorn and suspicion of the Pharisees.

The rabbis understood Christ's parable as applying to the publicans and sinners; but it has also a wider meaning. By the lost sheep Christ represents not only the individual sinner but the one world that has apostatized and has been ruined by sin. This world is but an atom in the vast dominions over which God presides, yet this little fallen world—the one lost sheep—is more precious in His sight than are the ninety and nine that went not astray from the fold. Christ, the loved Commander in the heavenly courts, stooped from His high estate, laid aside the glory that He had with the Father, in order to save the one lost world. For this He left the sinless worlds on high, the ninety and nine that loved Him, and came to this earth, to be "wounded for our transgressions" and "bruised for our iniquities." (Isa. 53:5.) God gave Himself in His Son that He might have the joy of receiving back the sheep that was lost.

"Behold, what manner of love the Father hath bestowed upon us, that we should be called the sons of God." 1 John 3:1. And Christ says, "As Thou hast sent Me into the world, even so have I also sent them into the world" (John 17:18)—to "fill up that which is behind of the afflictions of Christ, . . . for His body's sake, which is the church." Col. 1:24. Every soul whom Christ has rescued is called to work in His name for the saving of the lost. This work had been neglected in Israel. Is it not neglected today by those who profess to be Christ's followers?

How many of the wandering ones have you, reader, sought for and brought back to the fold? When you turn from those who seem unpromising and unattractive, do you realize that you are neglecting the souls for whom Christ is seeking? At the very time when you turn from them, they may be in the greatest need of your compassion. In every assembly for worship, there are souls longing for rest and peace. They may appear to be living careless lives, but they are not insensible to the influence of the Holy Spirit. Many among them might be won for Christ.

If the lost sheep is not brought back to the fold, it wanders until it perishes. And many souls go down to ruin for want of a hand stretched out to save. These erring ones may appear hard and reckless; but if they had received the same advantages that others have had, they might have revealed far more nobility of soul, and greater talent for usefulness. Angels pity these wandering ones. Angels weep, while human eyes are dry and hearts are closed to pity.

O the lack of deep, soul-touching sympathy for the tempted and the erring! O for more of Christ's spirit, and for less, far less, of self!

The Pharisees understood Christ's parable as a rebuke to them. Instead of accepting their criticism of His work, He had reproved their neglect of the publicans and sinners. He had not done this openly, lest it should close their hearts

against Him; but His illustration set before them the very work which God required of them, and which they had failed to do. Had they been true shepherds, these leaders in Israel would have done the work of a shepherd. They would have manifested the mercy and love of Christ, and would have united with Him in His mission. Their refusal to do this had proved their claims of piety to be false. Now many rejected Christ's reproof; yet to some His words brought conviction. Upon these, after Christ's ascension to heaven, the Holy Spirit came, and they united with His disciples in the very work outlined in the parable of the lost sheep.

The Lost Piece of Silver

After giving the parable of the lost sheep Christ spoke another, saying, "What woman having ten pieces of silver, if she lose one piece, doth not light a candle, and sweep the house, and seek diligently till she find it?"

In the East the houses of the poor usually consisted of but one room, often windowless and dark. The room was rarely swept, and a piece of money falling on the floor would be speedily covered by the dust and rubbish. In order that it might be found, even in the daytime, a candle must be lighted, and the house must be swept diligently.

The wife's marriage portion usually consisted of pieces of money, which she carefully preserved as her most cherished possession, to be transmitted to her own daughters. The loss of one of these pieces would be regarded as a serious calamity, and its recovery would cause great rejoicing, in which the neighboring women would readily share.

"When she hath found it," Christ said, "she calleth her friends and her neighbors together, saying, Rejoice with me; for I have found the piece which I had lost. Likewise, I say unto you, there is joy in the presence of the angels of God over one sinner that repenteth."

This parable, like the preceding, sets forth the loss of something which with proper search may be recovered, and that with great joy. But the two parables represent different classes. The lost sheep knows that it is lost. It has left the shepherd and the flock, and it cannot recover itself. It represents those who realize that they are separated from God and who are in a cloud of perplexity, in humiliation, and sorely tempted. The lost coin represents those who are lost in trespasses and sins, but who have no sense of their condition. They are estranged from God, but they know it not. Their souls are in peril, but they are unconscious and unconcerned. In this parable Christ teaches that even those who are indifferent to the claims of God are the objects of His pitying love. They are to be sought for that they may be brought back to God.

The sheep wandered away from the fold; it

was lost in the wilderness or upon the mountains. The piece of silver was lost in the house. It was close at hand, yet it could be recovered only by diligent search.

This parable has a lesson to families. In the household there is often great carelessness concerning the souls of its members. Among their number may be one who is estranged from God; but how little anxiety is felt lest in the family relationship there be lost one of God's entrusted gifts.

The coin, though lying among dust and rubbish, is a piece of silver still. Its owner seeks it because it is of value. So every soul, however degraded by sin, is in God's sight accounted precious. As the coin bears the image and superscription of the reigning power, so man at his creation bore the image and superscription of God; and though now marred and dim through the influence of sin, the traces of this inscription remain upon every soul. God desires to recover that soul and to retrace upon it His own image in righteousness and holiness.

The woman in the parable searches diligently for her lost coin. She lights the candle and sweeps the house. She removes everything that might obstruct her search. Though only one piece is lost, she will not cease her efforts until that piece is found. So in the family if one member is lost to God every means should be used for his recovery. On the part of all the others let there be diligent, careful self-examination. Let the life-practice be investigated. See if there is not some mistake, some error in management, by which that soul is confirmed in impenitence.

195   If there is in the family one child who is unconscious of his sinful state, parents should not rest. Let the candle be lighted. Search the word of God, and by its light let everything in the home be diligently examined, to see why this child is lost. Let parents search their own hearts, examine their habits and practices. Children are the heritage of the Lord, and we are answerable to Him for our management of His property.

There are fathers and mothers who long to labor in some foreign mission field; there are many who are active in Christian work outside the home, while their own children are strangers to the Saviour and His love. The work of winning their children for Christ many parents trust to the minister or the Sabbath school teacher, but in doing this they are neglecting their own God-given responsibility. The education and training of their children to be Christians is the highest service that parents can render to God. It is a work that demands patient labor, a lifelong diligent and persevering effort. By a neglect of

this trust we prove ourselves unfaithful stewards. No excuse for such neglect will be accepted by God.

But those who have been guilty of neglect are not to despair. The woman whose coin was lost searched until she found it. So in love, faith, and prayer let parents work for their households, until with joy they can come to God saying, 196 "Behold, I and the children whom the Lord hath given me." Isa. 8:18.

This is true home missionary work, and it is as helpful to those who do it as to those for whom it is done. By our faithful interest for the home circle we are fitting ourselves to work for the members of the Lord's family, with whom, if loyal to Christ, we shall live through eternal ages. For our brethren and sisters in Christ we are to show the same interest that as members of one family we have for one another.

And God designs that all this shall fit us to labor for still others. As our sympathies shall broaden and our love increase, we shall find everywhere a work to do. God's great human household embraces the world, and none of its members are to be passed by with neglect.

Wherever we may be, there the lost piece of silver awaits our search. Are we seeking for it? Day by day we meet with those who take no interest in religious things; we talk with them, we visit among them; do we show an interest in their spiritual welfare? Do we present Christ to them as the sin-pardoning Saviour? With our own hearts warm with the love of Christ, do we tell them about that love? If we do not, how shall we meet these souls—lost, eternally lost— when with them we stand before the throne of God?

The value of a soul, who can estimate? Would you know its worth, go to Gethsemane, and there watch with Christ through those hours of anguish, when He sweat as it were great drops of blood. Look upon the Saviour uplifted on the cross. Hear that despairing cry, "My God, My God, why hast Thou forsaken Me?" Mark 15:34. Look upon the wounded head, the pierced side, the marred feet. Remember that Christ risked all. For our redemption, heaven itself was imperiled. At the foot of the cross, remembering that for one sinner Christ would have laid down His life, you may estimate the value of a soul.

If you are in communion with Christ, you will 197 place His estimate upon every human being. You will feel for others the same deep love that Christ has felt for you. Then you will be able to win, not drive, to attract, not repulse, those for whom He died. None would ever have been brought back to God if Christ had not made a

---

"My people have been lost sheep: their shepherds have caused them to go astray, they have turned them away on the mountains: they have gone from mountain to hill, they have forgotten their restingplace." Jer. 50:6. "I have gone astray like a lost sheep; seek Thy servant; for I do not forget Thy commandments." Ps. 119: 176.

personal effort for them; and it is by this personal work that we can rescue souls. When you see those who are going down to death, you will not rest in quiet indifference and ease. The greater their sin and the deeper their misery, the more earnest and tender will be your efforts for their recovery. You will discern the need of those who are suffering, who have been sinning against God, and who are oppressed with a burden of guilt. Your heart will go out in sympathy for them, and you will reach out to them a helping hand. In the arms of your faith and love you will bring them to Christ. You will watch over and encourage them, and your sympathy and confidence will make it hard for them to fall from their steadfastness.

In this work all the angels of heaven are ready to co-operate. All the resources of heaven are at the command of those who are seeking to save the lost. Angels will help you to reach the most careless and the most hardened. And when one is brought back to God, all heaven is made glad; seraphs and cherubs touch their golden harps, and sing praises to God and the Lamb for their mercy and loving-kindness to the children of men.

16

"Lost, and Is Found"

The parables of the lost sheep, the lost coin, and the prodigal son, bring out in distinct lines God's pitying love for those who are straying from Him. Although they have turned away from God, He does not leave them in their misery. He is full of kindness and tender pity toward all who are exposed to the temptations of the artful foe.

In the parable of the prodigal son is presented the Lord's dealing with those who have once known the Father's love, but who have allowed the tempter to lead them captive at his will.

"A certain man had two sons; and the younger of them said to his father, Father, give me the portion of goods that falleth to me. And he divided unto them his living. And not many days after the younger son gathered all together, and took his journey into a far country."

This younger son had become weary of the restraint of his father's house. He thought that his liberty was restricted. His father's love and care for him were misinterpreted, and he determined to follow the dictates of his own inclination.

The youth acknowledges no obligation to his

father, and expresses no gratitude; yet he claims the privilege of a child in sharing his father's goods. The inheritance that would fall to him at his father's death he desires to receive now. He is bent on present enjoyment, and cares not for the future.

Having obtained his patrimony, he goes into "a far country," away from his father's home. With money in plenty, and liberty to do as he likes, he flatters himself that the desire of his heart is reached. There is no one to say, Do not do this, for it will be an injury to yourself; or, Do this, because it is right. Evil companions help him to plunge ever deeper into sin, and he wastes his "substance with riotous living."

The Bible tells of men who "professing themselves to be wise" "became fools" (Rom. 1:22); and this is the history of the young man of the parable. The wealth which he has selfishly claimed from his father he squanders upon harlots. The treasure of his young manhood is wasted. The precious years of life, the strength of intellect, the bright visions of youth, the spiritual aspirations—all are consumed in the fires of lust.

A great famine arises, he begins to be in want, and he joins himself to a citizen of the country, who sends him into the field to feed swine. To a Jew this was the most menial and degrading of employments. The youth who had boasted of his liberty, now finds himself a slave. He is in the worst of bondage—"holden with the cords of his sins." (Prov. 5:22.) The glitter and tinsel that enticed him have disappeared, and he feels the burden of his chain. Sitting upon the ground in that desolate and famine-stricken land, with no companions but the swine, he is fain to fill himself with the husks on which the beasts are fed. Of the gay companions who flocked about him in his prosperous days and ate and drank at his expense, there is not one left to befriend him. Where now is his riotous joy? Stilling his conscience, benumbing his sensibilities, he thought himself happy; but now, with money spent, with hunger unsatisfied, with pride humbled, with his moral nature dwarfed, with his will weak and untrustworthy, with his finer feelings seemingly dead, he is the most wretched of mortals.

What a picture here of the sinner's state! Although surrounded with the blessings of His love, there is nothing that the sinner, bent on self-indulgence and sinful pleasure, desires so much as separation from God. Like the ungrateful son, he claims the good things of God as his by right. He takes them as a matter of course, and makes no return of gratitude, renders no service of love. As Cain went out

"Jesus called them unto Him, and said, Suffer little children to come unto Me, and forbid them not: for of such is the kingdom of God. Verily I say unto you, Whosoever shall not receive the kingdom of God as a little child shall in no wise enter therein." Luke 18: 16, 17

This chapter is based on Luke 15:11-32.

from the presence of the Lord to seek his home; as the prodigal wandered into the "far country," so do sinners seek happiness in forgetfulness of God. (Rom. 1:28.)

201 Whatever the appearance may be, every life centered in self is squandered. Whoever attempts to live apart from God is wasting his substance. He is squandering the precious years, squandering the powers of mind and heart and soul, and working to make himself bankrupt for eternity. The man who separates from God that he may serve himself, is the slave of mammon. The mind that God created for the companionship of angels has become degraded to the service of that which is earthly and bestial. This is the end to which self-serving tends.

If you have chosen such a life, you know that you are spending money for that which is not bread, and labor for that which satisfieth not. There come to you hours when you realize your degradation. Alone in the far country you feel your misery, and in despair you cry, "O wretched man that I am! who shall deliver me from the body of this death?" Rom. 7:24. It is the statement of a universal truth which is contained in the prophet's words, "Cursed be the man that trusteth in man, and maketh flesh his arm, and whose heart departeth from the Lord. For he shall be like the heath in the desert, and shall not see when good cometh; but shall inhabit the parched places in the wilderness, in a salt land and not inhabited." Jer. 17:5, 6. God

202 "maketh His sun to rise on the evil and on the good, and sendeth rain on the just and on the unjust" (Matt. 5:45); but men have the power to shut themselves away from sunshine and shower. So while the Sun of Righteousness shines, and the showers of grace fall freely for all, we may by separating ourselves from God still "inhabit the parched places in the wilderness."

The love of God still yearns over the one who has chosen to separate from Him, and He sets in operation influences to bring him back to the Father's house. The prodigal son in his wretchedness "came to himself." The deceptive power that Satan had exercised over him was broken. He saw that his suffering was the result of his own folly, and he said, "How many hired servants of my father's have bread enough and to spare, and I perish with hunger! I will arise and go to my father." Miserable as he was, the prodigal found hope in the conviction of his father's love. It was that love which was drawing him toward home. So it is the assurance of God's love that constrains the sinner to return to God. "The goodness of God leadeth thee to repentance." Rom. 2:4. A golden chain, the mercy and compassion of divine love, is passed around every imperiled soul. The Lord declares, "I have loved thee with an everlasting love; therefore with loving-kindness have I drawn thee." Jer. 31:3.

The son determines to confess his guilt. He will go to his father, saying, "I have sinned against heaven, and before thee, and am no more worthy to be called thy son." But he adds, showing how stinted is his conception of his father's love, "Make me as one of thy hired servants."

The young man turns from the swine herds and the husks, and sets his face toward home. Trembling with weakness and faint from hunger, he presses eagerly on his way. He has no covering to conceal his rags; but his misery 203 has conquered pride, and he hurries on to beg a servant's place where he was once a child.

Little did the gay, thoughtless youth, as he went out from his father's gate, dream of the ache and longing left in that father's heart. When he danced and feasted with his wild companions, little did he think of the shadow that had fallen on his home. And now as with weary and painful steps he pursues the homeward way, he knows not that one is watching for his return. But while he is yet "a great way off" the father discerns his form. Love is of quick sight. Not even the degradation of the years of sin can conceal the son from the father's eyes. He "had compassion, and ran, and fell on his neck" in a long, clinging, tender embrace.

The father will permit no contemptuous eye to mock at his son's misery and tatters. He takes from his own shoulders the broad, rich mantle, and wraps it around the son's wasted form, and 204 the youth sobs out his repentance, saying, "Father, I have sinned against heaven, and in thy sight, and am no more worthy to be called thy son." The father holds him close to his side, and brings him home. No opportunity is given him to ask a servant's place. He is a son, who shall be honored with the best the house affords, and whom the waiting men and women shall respect and serve.

The father said to his servants, "Bring forth the best robe, and put it on him; and put a ring on his hand, and shoes on his feet; and bring hither the fatted calf, and kill it; and let us eat and be merry; for this my son was dead, and is alive again; he was lost, and is found. And they began to be merry."

In his restless youth the prodigal looked upon his father as stern and severe. How different his conception of him now! So those who are deceived by Satan look upon God as hard and exacting. They regard Him as watching to denounce and condemn, as unwilling to receive the sinner so long as there is a legal excuse for not helping him. His law they regard as a restriction upon men's happiness, a burdensome yoke from which they are glad to escape. But he whose eyes have been opened by the love of Christ will behold God as full of compassion. He does not appear as a tyrannical, relentless being, but as a father longing to embrace his repenting son. The sinner will exclaim with the Psalmist, "Like as a father pitieth his children, so the Lord pitieth them that fear Him." Ps. 103:13.

In the parable there is no taunting, no casting up to the prodigal of his evil course. The son feels that the past is forgiven and forgotten, blotted out forever. And so God says to the sinner, "I have blotted out, as a thick cloud, thy transgressions, and, as a cloud, thy sins." Isa. 44:22. "I will forgive their iniquity, and I will 205 remember their sin no more." Jer. 31:34. "Let the wicked forsake his way, and the unrighteous man his thoughts; and let him return unto the Lord, and He will have mercy upon him; and to our God, for He will abundantly pardon." Isa. 55:7. "In those days, and in that time, saith the Lord, the iniquity of Israel shall be sought for, and there shall be none; and the sins of Judah, and they shall not be found." Jer. 50:20.

What assurance here, of God's willingness to receive the repenting sinner! Have you, reader, chosen your own way? Have you wandered far from God? Have you sought to feast upon the fruits of transgression, only to find them turn to ashes upon your lips? And now, your substance spent, your life-plans thwarted, and your hopes dead, do you sit alone and desolate? Now that voice which has long been speaking to your heart but to which you would not listen comes to you distinct and clear, "Arise ye, and depart; for this is not your rest; because it is polluted, it shall destroy you, even with a sore destruction." Micah 2:10. Return to your Father's house. He invites you, saying, "Return unto Me; for I have redeemed thee." Isa. 44:22.

Do not listen to the enemy's suggestion to stay away from Christ until you have made yourself better; until you are good enough to 206 come to God. If you wait until then, you will never come. When Satan points to your filthy garments, repeat the promise of Jesus, "Him that cometh to Me I will in no wise cast out." John 6:37. Tell the enemy that the blood of Jesus Christ cleanses from all sin. Make the prayer of David your own, "Purge me with hyssop, and I shall be clean; wash me, and I shall be whiter than snow." Ps. 51:7.

Arise and go to your Father. He will meet you a great way off. If you take even one step toward Him in repentance, He will hasten to enfold you in His arms of infinite love. His ear is open to the cry of the contrite soul. The very first reaching out of the heart after God is known to Him. Never a prayer is offered, however faltering, never a tear is shed, however secret, never a sincere desire after God is cherished, however feeble, but the Spirit of God

goes forth to meet it. Even before the prayer is uttered or the yearning of the heart made known, grace from Christ goes forth to meet the grace that is working upon the human soul.

Your heavenly Father will take from you the garments defiled by sin. In the beautiful parabolic prophecy of Zechariah, the high priest Joshua, standing clothed in filthy garments before the angel of the Lord, represents the sinner. And the word is spoken by the Lord, "Take away the filthy garments from him. And unto him He said, Behold, I have caused thine iniquity to pass from thee, and I will clothe thee with change of raiment. . . . So they set a fair miter upon his head, and clothed him with garments." Zech. 3:4, 5. Even so God will clothe you with "the garments of salvation," and cover you with "the robe of righteousness." Isa. 61:10. "Though ye have lien among the pots, yet shall ye be as the wings of a dove covered with silver, and her feathers with yellow gold." Ps. 68:13.

He will bring you into His banqueting house, and His banner over you shall be love. (Cant. 207 2:4.) "If thou wilt walk in My ways," He declares, "I will give thee places to walk among these that stand by"—even among the holy angels that surround His throne. (Zech. 3:7.)

"As the bridegroom rejoiceth over the bride, so shall thy God rejoice over thee." Isa. 62:5. "He will save, He will rejoice over thee with joy; He will rest in His love; He will joy over thee with singing." Zeph. 3:17. And heaven and earth shall unite in the Father's song of rejoicing: "For this My son was dead, and is alive again; he was lost, and is found."

Thus far in the Saviour's parable there is no discordant note to jar the harmony of the scene of joy; but now Christ introduces another element. When the prodigal came home, the elder son "was in the field; and as he came and drew nigh to the house, he heard music and dancing. And he called one of the servants, and asked what these things meant. And he said unto him, Thy brother is come; and thy father hath killed the fatted calf, because he hath received him safe and sound. And he was angry, and would not go in." This elder brother has not been sharing in his father's anxiety and watching for the one that was lost. He shares not, therefore, in the father's joy at the wanderer's return. The sounds of rejoicing kindle no gladness in his heart. He inquires of a servant the reason of the festivity, and the answer excites his jealousy. He will not go in to welcome his lost brother. The favor shown the prodigal he regards as an insult to himself.

When the father comes out to remonstrate with him, the pride and malignity of his nature

---

"Seek ye the Lord while He may be found, call ye upon Him while He is near: let the wicked forsake his way, and the unrighteous man his thoughts: and let him return unto the Lord, and He will have mercy upon him; and to our God, for He will abundantly pardon." Isa. 55:6, 7.

are revealed. He dwells upon his own life in his father's house as a round of unrequited service, and then places in mean contrast the favor shown to the son just returned. He makes it plain that his own service has been that of a servant rather than a son. When he should have found an abiding joy in his father's presence, his mind has rested upon the profit to accrue from his circumspect life. His words show that it is for this he has foregone the pleasures of sin. Now if this brother is to share in the father's gifts, the elder son counts that he himself has been wronged. He grudges his brother the favor shown him. He plainly shows that had he been in the father's place, he would not have received the prodigal. He does not even acknowledge him as a brother, but coldly speaks of him as "thy son."

Yet the father deals tenderly with him. "Son," he says, "thou art ever with me, and all that I have is thine." Through all these years of your brother's outcast life, have you not had the privilege of companionship with me?

Everything that could minister to the happiness of his children was freely theirs. The son need have no question of gift or reward. "All that I have is thine." You have only to believe my love, and take the gift that is freely bestowed.

One son had for a time cut himself off from the household, not discerning the father's love. But now he has returned, and the tide of joy sweeps away every disturbing thought. "This thy brother was dead, and is alive again; and was lost, and is found."

Was the elder brother brought to see his own mean, ungrateful spirit? Did he come to see that though his brother had done wickedly, he was his brother still? Did the elder brother repent of his jealousy and hardheartedness? Concerning this, Christ was silent. For the parable was still enacting, and it rested with His hearers to determine what the outcome should be.

By the elder son were represented the unrepenting Jews of Christ's day, and also the Pharisees in every age, who look with contempt upon those whom they regard as publicans and sinners. Because they themselves have not gone to great excesses in vice, they are filled with self-righteousness. Christ met these cavilers on their own ground. Like the elder son in the parable, they had enjoyed special privileges from God. They claimed to be sons in God's house, but they had the spirit of the hireling. They were working, not from love, but from hope of reward. In their eyes, God was an exacting taskmaster. They saw Christ inviting publicans and sinners to receive freely the gift of His grace—the gift which the rabbis hoped to secure only by toil and penance—and they were offended. The prodigal's return, which filled the Father's heart with joy, only stirred them to jealousy.

In the parable the father's remonstrance with the elder son was Heaven's tender appeal to the Pharisees. "All that I have is thine"—not as wages, but as a gift. Like the prodigal, you can receive it only as the unmerited bestowal of the Father's love.

Self-righteousness not only leads men to misrepresent God, but makes them coldhearted and critical toward their brethren. The elder son, in his selfishness and jealousy, stood ready to watch his brother, to criticize every action, and to accuse him for the least deficiency. He would detect every mistake, and make the most of every wrong act. Thus he would seek to justify his own unforgiving spirit. Many today are doing the same thing. While the soul is making its very first struggles against a flood of temptations, they stand by, stubborn, self-willed, complaining, accusing. They may claim to be children of God, but they are acting out the spirit of Satan. By their attitude toward their brethren, these accusers place themselves where God cannot give them the light of His countenance.

Many are constantly questioning, "Wherewith shall I come before the Lord, and bow myself before the high God? Shall I come before Him with burnt-offerings, with calves of a year old? Will the Lord be pleased with thousands of rams, or with ten thousands of rivers of oil?" But "He hath showed thee, O man, what is good; and what doth the Lord require of thee, but to do justly, and to love mercy, and to walk humbly with thy God?" Micah 6:6-8.

This is the service that God has chosen—"to loose the bands of wickedness, to undo the heavy burdens, and to let the oppressed go free, and that ye break every yoke, . . . and that thou hide not thyself from thine own flesh." Isa. 58:6, 7. When you see yourselves as sinners saved only by the love of your heavenly Father, you will have tender pity for others who are suffering in sin. You will no longer meet misery and repentance with jealousy and censure. When the ice of selfishness is melted from your hearts, you will be in sympathy with God, and will share His joy in the saving of the lost.

It is true that you claim to be a child of God; but if this claim be true, it is "thy brother" that was "dead, and is alive again; and was lost, and is found." He is bound to you by the closest ties; for God recognizes him as a son. Deny your relationship to him, and you show that you are but a hireling in the household, not a child in the family of God.

Though you will not join in the greeting to the lost, the joy will go on, the restored one will have his place by the Father's side and in the Father's work. He that is forgiven much, the same loves much. But you will be in the darkness without. For "he that loveth not knoweth not God; for God is love." 1 John 4:8.

212

17

"Spare It This Year Also"

Christ in His teaching linked with the warning of judgment the invitation of mercy. "The Son of man is not come," He said, "to destroy men's lives, but to save them." Luke 9:56. "God sent not His Son into the world to condemn the world; but that the world through Him might be saved." John 3:17. His mission of mercy in its relation to God's justice and judgment is illustrated in the parable of the barren fig tree.

Christ had been warning the people of the coming of the kingdom of God, and He had sharply rebuked their ignorance and indifference. The signs in the sky, which foretold the weather, they were quick to read; but the signs of the times, which so clearly pointed to His mission, were not discerned.

But men were as ready then as men are now to conclude that they themselves are the favorites of heaven, and that the message of reproof is meant for another. The hearers told Jesus of an event which had just caused great excitement. Some of the measures of Pontius Pilate, the governor of Judea, had given offense 213 to the people. There had been a popular tumult in Jerusalem, and Pilate had attempted to quell this by violence. On one occasion his soldiers had even invaded the precincts of the temple, and had cut down some Galilean pilgrims in the very act of slaying their sacrifices. The Jews regarded calamity as a judgment on account of the sufferer's sin, and those who told of this act of violence did so with secret satisfaction. In their view their own good fortune proved them to be much better, and therefore more favored by God, than were these Galileans. They expected to hear from Jesus words of condemnation for these men, who, they doubted not, richly deserved their punishment.

The disciples of Christ did not venture to express their ideas until they had heard the opinion of their Master. He had given them pointed lessons in reference to judging other men's characters, and measuring retribution according to their finite judgment. Yet they looked for Christ to denounce these men as sinners above others. Great was their surprise at His answer.

Turning to the multitude, the Saviour said, "Suppose ye that these Galileans were sinners above all the Galileans, because they suffered such things? I tell you, Nay; but, except ye repent, ye shall all likewise perish." These startling calamities were designed to lead them to humble their hearts, and to repent of their sins. The storm of vengeance was gathering, which was soon to burst upon all who had not found a

refuge in Christ.

As Jesus talked with the disciples and the multitude, He looked forward with prophetic glance and saw Jerusalem besieged with armies. He heard the tramp of the aliens marching against the chosen city and saw the thousands upon thousands perishing in the siege. Many of the Jews were, like those Galileans, slain in the temple courts, in the very act of offering sacrifice. The calamities that had fallen upon indi- 214 viduals were warnings from God to a nation equally guilty. "Except ye repent," said Jesus, "ye shall all likewise perish." For a little time the day of probation lingered for them. There was still time for them to know the things that belonged to their peace.

"A certain man," He continued, "had a fig-tree planted in his vineyard; and he came and sought fruit thereon, and found none. Then said he unto the dresser of his vineyard, Behold, these three years I come seeking fruit on this fig-tree, and find none: cut it down; why cumbereth it the ground?"

Christ's hearers could not misunderstand the application of His words. David had sung of Israel as the vine brought out of Egypt. Isaiah had written, "The vineyard of the Lord of hosts is the house of Israel, and the men of Judah His pleasant plant." Isa. 5:7. The generation to whom the Saviour had come were represented by the fig tree in the Lord's vineyard—within the circle of His special care and blessing.

God's purpose toward His people, and the glorious possibilities before them, had been set forth in the beautiful words, "That they might be called trees of righteousness, the planting of the Lord, that He might be glorified." Isa. 61:3. The dying Jacob, under the Spirit of inspiration, had said of his best-loved son, "Joseph is a fruitful bough, even a fruitful bough by a well; whose branches run over the wall." And he said, "The God of thy Father" "shall help thee," the Almighty "shall bless thee with blessings of heaven above, blessings of the deep that lieth under." Gen. 49:22, 25. So God had planted Israel as a goodly vine by the wells of life. He had made His vineyard "in a very fruitful hill." He had "fenced it, and gathered out the stones thereof, and planted it with the choicest vine." Isa. 5:1, 2.

"And He looked that it should bring forth 215 grapes, and it brought forth wild grapes." Isa. 5:2. The people of Christ's day made a greater show of piety than did the Jews of earlier ages, but they were even more destitute of the sweet graces of the Spirit of God. The precious fruits of character that made the life of Joseph so fragrant and beautiful, were not manifest in the Jewish nation.

God in His Son had been seeking fruit, and had found none. Israel was a cumberer of the ground. Its very existence was a curse; for it filled the place in the vineyard that a fruitful tree might fill. It robbed the world of the blessings that God designed to give. The Israelites had misrepresented God among the nations. They were not merely useless, but a decided hindrance. To a great degree their religion was misleading, and wrought ruin instead of salvation.

In the parable the dresser of the vineyard does not question the sentence that the tree, if it remained fruitless, should be cut down; but he knows and shares the owner's interest in that barren tree. Nothing could give him greater joy than to see its growth and fruitfulness. He responds to the desire of the owner, saying, "Let it alone this year also, till I shall dig about it and dung it; and if it bear fruit, well."

The gardener does not refuse to minister to so unpromising a plant. He stands ready to give it still greater care. He will make its surroundings most favorable, and will lavish upon it every attention.

The owner and the dresser of the vineyard are one in their interest in the fig tree. So the Father and the Son were one in their love for the chosen people. Christ was saying to His hearers that increased opportunities would be given them. Every means that the love of God could devise would be put in operation that they might become trees of righteousness, bringing forth fruit for the blessing of the world.

Jesus did not in the parable tell the result of the gardener's work. At that point His story was cut short. Its conclusion rested with the generation that heard His words. To them the solemn warning was given, "If not, then after that thou shalt cut it down." Upon them it depended whether the irrevocable words should be spoken. The day of wrath was near. In the calamities that had already befallen Israel, the owner of the vineyard was mercifully forewarning them of the destruction of the unfruitful tree.

The warning sounds down along the line to us in this generation. Are you, O careless heart, a fruitless tree in the Lord's vineyard? Shall the words of doom erelong be spoken of you? How long have you received His gifts? How long has He watched and waited for a return of love? Planted in His vineyard, under the watchful care of the gardener, what privileges are yours! How often has the tender gospel message thrilled your heart! You have taken the name of Christ, you are outwardly a member of the church which is His body, and yet you are conscious of no living connection with the great heart of love. The tide of His life does not flow through you. The sweet graces of His character,

"the fruits of the Spirit," are not seen in your life.

The barren tree receives the rain and the sunshine and the gardener's care. It draws nourishment from the soil. But its unproductive boughs only darken the ground, so that fruit-bearing plants cannot flourish in its shadow. So God's gifts, lavished on you, convey no blessing to the world. You are robbing others of privileges that, but for you, might be theirs.

You realize, though it may be but dimly, that you are a cumberer of the ground. Yet in His great mercy God has not cut you down. He does not look coldly upon you. He does not turn away with indifference, or leave you to destruction. Looking upon you He cries, as He cried so many centuries ago concerning Israel, "How shall I give thee up, Ephraim? How shall I deliver thee, Israel? . . . I will not execute the fierceness of Mine anger. I will not return to destroy Ephraim; for I am God, and not man." Hosea 11:8, 9. The pitying Saviour is saying concerning you, Spare it this year also, till I shall dig about it and dress it.

With what unwearied love did Christ minister to Israel during the period of added probation. Upon the cross He prayed, "Father, forgive them; for they know not what they do." Luke 23:24. After His ascension the gospel was preached first at Jerusalem. There the Holy Spirit was poured out. There the first gospel church revealed the power of the risen Saviour. There Stephen—"his face as it had been the face of an angel" (Acts 6:15)—bore his testimony and laid down his life. All that heaven itself could give was bestowed. "What could have been done more to My vineyard," Christ said, "that I have not done in it?" Isa. 5:4. So His care and labor for you are not lessened, but increased. Still He says, "I the Lord do keep it; I will water it every moment; lest any hurt it, I will keep it night and day." Isa. 27:3.

"If it bear fruit, well; and if not, then after that"—

The heart that does not respond to divine agencies becomes hardened until it is no longer susceptible to the influence of the Holy Spirit. Then it is that the word is spoken, "Cut it down; why cumbereth it the ground?"

Today He invites you: "O Israel, return unto the Lord thy God. . . . I will heal their backsliding, I will love them freely. . . . I will be as the dew unto Israel; he shall grow as the lily, and cast forth his roots as Lebanon. . . . They that dwell under his shadow shall return; they shall revive as the corn, and grow as the vine. . . . From Me is thy fruit found." Hosea 14:1-8.

18

"Go Into the Highways and Hedges"

The Saviour was a guest at the feast of a Pharisee. He accepted invitations from the rich as well as the poor, and according to His custom He linked the scene before Him with His lessons of truth. Among the Jews the sacred feast was connected with all their seasons of national and religious rejoicing. It was to them a type of the blessings of eternal life. The great feast at which they were to sit down with Abraham, Isaac, and Jacob, while the Gentiles stood without, and looked on with longing eyes, was a theme on which they delighted to dwell. The lesson of warning and instruction which Christ desired to give, He now illustrated by the parable of a great supper. The blessings of God, both for the present and for the future life, the Jews thought to shut up to themselves. They denied God's mercy to the Gentiles. By the parable Christ showed that they were themselves at that very time rejecting the invitation of mercy, the call to God's kingdom. He showed that the invitation which they had slighted was to be sent to those whom they despised, those from whom they had drawn away their garments as if they were lepers to be shunned.

In choosing the guests for his feast, the Pharisee had consulted his own selfish interest. Christ said to him, "When thou makest a dinner or a supper, call not thy friends, nor thy brethren, neither thy kinsmen, nor thy rich neighbors, lest they also bid thee again, and a recompense be made thee. But when thou makest a feast, call the poor, the maimed, the lame, the blind: and thou shalt be blessed; for they cannot recompense thee: for thou shalt be recompensed at the resurrection of the just."

Christ was here repeating the instruction He had given to Israel through Moses. At their sacred feasts the Lord had directed that "the stranger, and the fatherless, and the widow, which are within thy gates, shall come, and shall eat, and be satisfied." Deut. 14:29. These gatherings were to be as object lessons to Israel. Being thus taught the joy of true hospitality, the people were throughout the year to care for the bereaved and the poor. And these feasts had a wider lesson. The spiritual blessings given to Israel were not for themselves alone. God had given the bread of life to them, that they might break it to the world.

This work they had not fulfilled. Christ's words were a rebuke to their selfishness. To the Pharisees His words were distasteful. Hoping to turn the conversation into another channel, one of them, with a sanctimonious air, exclaimed, "Blessed is he that shall eat bread in the kingdom of God." This man spoke with great assurance, as if he himself were certain of a place in the kingdom. His attitude was similar to the attitude of those who rejoice that they are saved by Christ, when they do not comply with the conditions upon which salvation is promised. His spirit was like that of Balaam when he prayed, "Let me die the death of the righteous, and let my last end be like his." Num. 23:10. The Pharisee was not thinking of his own fitness for heaven but of what he hoped to enjoy in heaven. His remark was designed to turn away the minds of the guests at the feast from the subject of their practical duty. He thought to carry them past the present life to the remote time of the resurrection of the just.

Christ read the heart of the pretender, and fastening His eyes upon him He opened before the company the character and value of their present privileges. He showed them that they had a part to act at that very time, in order to share in the blessedness of the future.

"A certain man," He said, "made a great supper, and bade many." When the time of the feast arrived, the host sent his servant to the expected guests with a second message, "Come; for all things are now ready." But a strange indifference was shown. "All with one consent began to make excuse. The first said unto him, I have bought a piece of ground, and I must needs go and see it; I pray thee have me excused. And another said, I have bought five yoke of oxen, and I go to prove them; I pray thee have me excused. And another said, I have married a wife, and therefore I cannot come."

None of the excuses were founded on a real necessity. The man who "must needs go and see" his piece of ground, had already purchased it. His haste to go and see it was due to the fact that his interest was absorbed in his purchase. The oxen, too, had been bought. The proving of them was only to satisfy the interest of the buyer. The third excuse had no more semblance of reason. The fact that the intended guest had married a wife need not have prevented his presence at the feast. His wife also would have been made welcome. But he had his own plans for enjoyment, and these seemed to him more desirable than the feast he had

---

"Ho, every one that thirsteth, come ye to the waters, and he that hath no money; come ye, buy, and eat; yea, come, buy wine and milk without money and without price. Wherefore do ye spend money for that which is not bread? and your labour for that which satisfieth not? hearken diligently unto me, and eat ye that which is good, and let your soul delight itself in fatness."   Isa 55: 1, 2

This chapter is based on Luke 14:1, 12-24.

promised to attend. He had learned to find pleasure in other society than that of the host. He did not ask to be excused, made not even a pretense of courtesy in his refusal. The "I cannot" was only a veil for the truth—"I do not care to come."

All the excuses betray a preoccupied mind. To these intended guests other interests had become all-absorbing. The invitation they had pledged themselves to accept was put aside, and the generous friend was insulted by their indifference.

By the great supper, Christ represents the blessings offered through the gospel. The provision is nothing less than Christ Himself. He is the bread that comes down from heaven; and from Him the streams of salvation flow. The Lord's messengers had proclaimed to the Jews the advent of the Saviour; they had pointed to Christ as "the Lamb of God, which taketh away the sin of the world." John 1:29. In the feast He had pro-
223 vided, God offered to them the greatest gift that Heaven can bestow—a gift that is beyond computation. The love of God had furnished the costly banquet, and had provided inexhaustible resources. "If any man eat of this bread," Christ said, "he shall live for ever." John 6:51.

But in order to accept the invitation to the gospel feast, they must make their worldly interests subordinate to the one purpose of receiving Christ and His righteousness. God gave all for man, and He asks him to place His service above every earthly and selfish consideration. He cannot accept a divided heart. The heart that is absorbed in earthly affections cannot be given up to God.

The lesson is for all time. We are to follow the Lamb of God whithersoever He goeth. His guidance is to be chosen, His companionship valued above the companionship of earthly friends. Christ says, "He that loveth father or mother more than Me is not worthy of Me, and he that loveth son or daughter more than Me is not worthy of Me." Matt. 10:37.

Around the family board, when breaking their daily bread, many in Christ's day repeated the words, "Blessed is he that shall eat bread in the kingdom of God." But Christ showed how difficult it was to find guests for the table provided at infinite cost. Those who listened to His words knew that they had slighted the invitation of mercy. To them worldly possessions, riches, and pleasures
224 were all-absorbing. With one consent they had made excuse.

So it is now. The excuses urged for refusing the invitation to the feast cover the whole ground of excuses for refusing the gospel invitation. Men declare that they cannot imperil their worldly prospects by giving attention to the claims of the gospel. They count their temporal interests as of more value than the things of eternity. The very blessings they have received from God become a barrier to separate their souls from their Creator and Redeemer. They will not be interrupted in their worldly pursuits, and they say to the messenger of mercy, "Go thy way for this time; when I have a convenient season, I will call for thee." Acts 24:25. Others urge the difficulties that would arise in their social relations should they obey the call of God. They say they cannot afford to be out of harmony with their relatives and acquaintances. Thus they prove themselves to be the very actors described in the parable. The Master of the feast regards their flimsy excuses as showing contempt for His invitation.

The man who said, "I have married a wife, and therefore I cannot come," represents a large class. Many there are who allow their wives or their husbands to prevent them from heeding the call of God. The husband says, "I cannot obey my convictions of duty while my wife is opposed to it. Her influence would make it exceedingly hard for me to do so." The wife hears the gracious call, "Come; for all things are now ready," and she says, " 'I pray thee have me excused.' My husband refuses the invitation of mercy. He says that his business stands in the way. I must go with my husband, and therefore I cannot come." The children's hearts are impressed. They desire to come. But they love their father and mother, and since these do not heed the gospel call, the
225 children think that they cannot be expected to come. They too say, "Have me excused."

All these refuse the Saviour's call because they fear division in the family circle. They suppose that in refusing to obey God they are insuring the peace and prosperity of the home; but this is a delusion. Those who sow selfishness will reap selfishness. In rejecting the love of Christ they reject that which alone can impart purity and steadfastness to human love. They will not only lose heaven, but will fail of the true enjoyment of that for which heaven was sacrificed.

In the parable, the giver of the feast learned how his invitation had been treated, and "being angry, said to his servant, Go out quickly into the streets and lanes of the city, and bring in hither the poor, and the maimed, and the halt, and the blind."

The host turned from those who despised his bounty, and invited a class who were not full, who were not in possession of houses and lands.

"I am that bread of life. Your fathers did eat manna in the wilderness, and are dead. This is the bread which cometh down from heaven, that a man may eat thereof, and not die. I am the living bread which came down from heaven." John 6: 48-51.

226 He invited those who were poor and hungry, and who would appreciate the bounties provided. "The publicans and the harlots," Christ said, "go into the kingdom of God before you." Matt. 21:31. However wretched may be the specimens of humanity that men spurn and turn aside from, they are not too low, too wretched, for the notice and love of God. Christ longs to have care-worn, weary, oppressed human beings come to Him. He longs to give them the light and joy and peace that are to be found nowhere else. The veriest sinners are the objects of His deep, earnest pity and love. He sends His Holy Spirit to yearn over them with tenderness, seeking to draw them to Himself.

The servant who brought in the poor and the blind reported to his master, "It is done as thou hast commanded, and yet there is room. And the Lord said unto the servant, Go out into the highways and hedges, and compel them to come in, that my house may be filled." Here Christ pointed to the work of the gospel outside the pale of Judaism, in the highways and byways of the world.

In obedience to this command, Paul and Barnabas declared to the Jews, "It was necessary that the word of God should first have been spoken to you; but seeing ye put it from you, and judge yourselves unworthy of everlasting life, lo, we turn to the Gentiles. For so hath the Lord commanded us, saying, I have set Thee to be a light of the Gentiles, that Thou shouldest be for salvation unto the ends of the earth. And when the Gentiles heard this, they were glad, and glorified the word of the Lord; and as many as were ordained to eternal life believed." Acts 13:46-48.

The gospel message proclaimed by Christ's disciples was the announcement of His first advent to the world. It bore to men the good tidings of salvation through faith in Him. It pointed forward to His second coming in glory 227 to redeem His people, and it set before men the hope, through faith and obedience, of sharing the inheritance of the saints in light. This message is given to men today, and at this time there is coupled with it the announcement of Christ's second coming as at hand. The signs which He Himself gave of His coming have been fulfilled, and by the teaching of God's word we may know that the Lord is at the door.

John in the Revelation foretells the proclamation of the gospel message just before Christ's second coming. He beholds an angel flying "in the midst of heaven, having the everlasting gospel to preach unto them that dwell on the earth, and to every nation, and kindred, and tongue, and people, saying with a loud voice, Fear God, and give glory to Him; for the hour of His judgment is come." Rev. 14:6, 7.

In the prophecy this warning of the judgment, with its connected messages, is followed by the coming of the Son of man in the clouds of heaven. The proclamation of the judgment is an announcement of Christ's second coming as at hand. And this proclamation is called the everlasting gospel. Thus the preaching of Christ's second coming, the announcement of 228 its nearness, is shown to be an essential part of the gospel message.

The Bible declares that in the last days men will be absorbed in worldly pursuits, in pleasure and money-getting. They will be blind to eternal realities. Christ says, "As the days of Noah were, so shall also the coming of the Son of man be. For as in the days that were before the flood they were eating and drinking, marrying and giving in marriage, until the day that Noah entered into the ark, and knew not until the flood came, and took them all away; so shall also the coming of the Son of man be." Matt. 24:37-39.

So it is today. Men are rushing on in the chase for gain and selfish indulgence as if there were no God, no heaven, and no hereafter. In Noah's day the warning of the flood was sent to startle men in their wickedness and call them to repentance. So the message of Christ's soon coming is designed to arouse men from their absorption in worldly things. It is intended to awaken them to a sense of eternal realities, that they may give heed to the invitation to the Lord's table.

The gospel invitation is to be given to all the world—"to every nation, and kindred, and tongue, and people." Rev. 14:6. The last message of warning and mercy is to lighten the whole earth with its glory. It is to reach all classes of men, rich and poor, high and low. "Go out into the highways and hedges," Christ says, "and compel them to come in, that My house may be filled."

The world is perishing for want of the gospel. There is a famine for the word of God. There are few who preach the word unmixed with human tradition. Though men have the Bible in their hands, they do not receive the blessing that God has placed in it for them. The

---

"They said therefore unto Him, . . . Our fathers did eat manna in the desert; as it is written, He gave them bread from heaven to eat. Then Jesus said unto them, Verily, verily, I say unto you, Moses gave you not that bread from heaven; but My Father giveth you the true bread from heaven. For the bread of God is He which cometh down from heaven, and giveth life unto the world. . . . I am the bread of life: he that cometh to Me shall never hunger; and he that believeth on Me shall never thirst." John 6: 30-35.

229 Lord calls upon His servants to carry His message to the people. The word of everlasting life must be given to those who are perishing in their sins.

In the command to go into the highways and hedges, Christ sets forth the work of all whom He calls to minister in His name. The whole world is the field for Christ's ministers. The whole human family is comprised in their congregation. The Lord desires that His word of grace shall be brought home to every soul.

To a great degree this must be accomplished by personal labor. This was Christ's method. His work was largely made up of personal interviews. He had a faithful regard for the one-soul audience. Through that one soul the message was often extended to thousands.

We are not to wait for souls to come to us; we must seek them out where they are. When the word has been preached in the pulpit, the work has but just begun. There are multitudes who will never be reached by the gospel unless it is carried to them.

The invitation to the feast was first given to the Jewish people, the people who had been called to stand as teachers and leaders among men, the people in whose hands were the prophetic scrolls foretelling Christ's advent, and to whom was committed the symbolic service foreshadowing His mission. Had priests and people heeded the call, they would have united with Christ's messengers in giving the gospel invitation to the world. The truth was sent to them that they might impart it. When they refused the call, it was sent to the poor, the maimed, the halt, and the blind. Publicans and sinners received the invitation. When the gospel call is sent to the Gentiles, there is the same plan of working. The message is first to be given "in the highways"—to men who have an active part in the world's work, to the teachers and leaders of the people.

230 Let the Lord's messengers bear this in mind. To the shepherds of the flock, the teachers divinely appointed, it should come as a word to be heeded. Those who belong to the higher ranks of society are to be sought out with tender affection and brotherly regard. Men in business life, in high positions of trust, men with large inventive faculties and scientific insight, men of genius, teachers of the gospel whose minds have not been called to the special truths for this time—these should be the first to hear the call. To them the invitation must be given.

There is a work to be done for the wealthy.

They need to be awakened to their responsibility as those entrusted with the gifts of heaven. They need to be reminded that they must give an account to Him who shall judge the living and the dead. The wealthy man needs your labor in the love and fear of God. Too often he trusts in his riches, and feels not his danger. The eyes of his mind need to be attracted to things of enduring value. He needs to recognize the authority of true goodness, which says, "Come unto Me, all ye that labour and are heavy laden, and I will give you rest. Take My yoke upon you, and learn of Me; for I am meek and lowly in heart, and ye shall find rest unto your souls; for My yoke is easy, and My burden is light." Matt. 11:28-30.

Those who stand high in the world for their education, wealth, or calling, are seldom addressed personally in regard to the interests of the soul. Many Christian workers hesitate to approach these classes. But this should not be. If a man were drowning, we would not stand by and see him perish because he was a lawyer, a merchant, or a judge. If we saw persons rushing over a precipice, we would not hesitate to urge them back, whatever might be their position or calling. Neither should we hesitate to warn men of the peril of the soul.

None should be neglected because of their 231 apparent devotion to worldly things. Many in high social positions are heartsore, and sick of vanity. They are longing for a peace which they have not. In the very highest ranks of society are those who are hungering and thirsting for salvation. Many would receive help if the Lord's workers would approach them personally, with a kind manner, a heart made tender by the love of Christ.

The success of the gospel message does not depend upon learned speeches, eloquent testimonies, or deep arguments. It depends upon the simplicity of the message and its adaptation to the souls that are hungering for the bread of life. "What shall I do to be saved?"—this is the want of the soul.

Thousands can be reached in the most simple 232 and humble way. The most intellectual, those who are looked upon as the world's most gifted men and women, are often refreshed by the simple words of one who loves God, and who can speak of that love as naturally as the worldling speaks of the things that interest him most deeply.

Often the words well prepared and studied have but little influence. But the true, honest expression of a son or daughter of God, spoken

---

"I beheld till the thrones were cast down, and the Ancient of days did sit, whose garment was white as snow, and the hair of His head like the pure wool: His throne was like the burning fiery flame, and His wheels as burning fire. A fiery stream issued and came forth from before Him: thousand thousands ministered unto Him . . . : the judgment was set, and the books were opened." Dan 7: 9, 10.

in natural simplicity, has power to unbolt the door to hearts that have long been closed against Christ and His love.

Let the worker for Christ remember that he is not to labor in his own strength. Let him lay hold of the throne of God with faith in His power to save. Let him wrestle with God in prayer, and then work with all the facilities God has given him. The Holy Spirit is provided as his efficiency. Ministering angels will be by his side to impress hearts.

If the leaders and teachers at Jerusalem had received the truth Christ brought, what a missionary center their city would have been! Backslidden Israel would have been converted. A vast army would have been gathered for the Lord. And how rapidly they could have carried the gospel to all parts of the world. So now, if men of influence and large capacity for usefulness could be won for Christ, then through them what a work could be accomplished in lifting up the fallen, gathering in the outcasts, and spreading far and wide the tidings of salvation. Rapidly the invitation might be given, and the guests be gathered for the Lord's table.

But we are not to think only of great and gifted men, to the neglect of the poorer classes. Christ instructs His messengers to go also to those in the byways and hedges, to the poor and lowly of the earth. In the courts and lanes of the 233 great cities, in the lonely byways of the country, are families and individuals—perhaps strangers in a strange land—who are without church relations, and who, in their loneliness, come to feel that God has forgotten them. They do not understand what they must do to be saved. Many are sunken in sin. Many are in distress. They are pressed with suffering, want, unbelief, despondency. Disease of every type afflicts them, both in body and in soul. They long to find a solace for their troubles, and Satan tempts them to seek it in lusts and pleasures that lead to ruin and death. He is offering them the apples of Sodom, that will turn to ashes upon their lips. They are spending their money for that which is not bread and their labor for that which satisfieth not.

In these suffering ones we are to see those whom Christ came to save. His invitation to them is "Ho, every one that thirsteth, come ye to the waters, and he that hath no money; come ye, buy and eat; yea, come, buy wine and milk without money and without price. . . . Hearken diligently unto Me, and eat ye that which is good, and let your soul delight itself in fatness. Incline your ear, and come unto Me: hear, and your soul shall live." Isa. 55:1-3.

God has given a special command that we should regard the stranger, the outcast, and the poor souls who are weak in moral power. Many who appear wholly indifferent to religious things are in heart longing for rest and peace. Although they may have sunken to the very depths of sin, there is a possibility of saving them.

Christ's servants are to follow His example. As He went from place to place, He comforted the suffering and healed the sick. Then He placed before them the great truths in regard to His kingdom. This is the work of His followers. As you relieve the sufferings of the body, you will find ways for ministering to the wants of the soul. You can point to the uplifted Saviour, and tell of the love of the great Physician, who 234 alone has power to restore.

Tell the poor desponding ones who have gone astray that they need not despair. Though they have erred, and have not been building a right character, God has joy to restore them, even the joy of His salvation. He delights to take apparently hopeless material, those through whom Satan has worked, and make them the subjects of His grace. He rejoices to deliver them from the wrath which is to fall upon the disobedient. Tell them there is healing, cleansing for every soul. There is a place for them at the Lord's table. He is waiting to bid them welcome.

Those who go into the byways and hedges will find others of a widely different character, who need their ministry. There are those who are living up to all the light they have, and are serving God the best they know how. But they realize that there is a great work to be done for themselves and for those about them. They are longing for an increased knowledge of God, but they have only begun to see the glimmering of greater light. They are praying with tears that God will send them the blessing which by faith they discern afar off. In the midst of the wickedness of the great cities many of these souls are to be found. Many of them are in very humble circumstances, and because of this they are unnoticed by the world. There are many of whom ministers and churches know nothing. But in lowly, miserable places they are the Lord's witnesses. They may have had little light and few opportunities for Christian training, but in the midst of nakedness, hunger, and cold they are seeking to minister to others. Let the stewards of the manifold grace of God seek out these souls, visit their homes, and through the power of the Holy Spirit minister to their needs. Study the Bible with them and pray with them with that simplicity which the Holy Spirit inspires. Christ will give His servants a message that will be as the bread of heaven to the soul. The pre- 235 cious blessing will be carried from heart to heart, from family to family.

The command given in the parable, to "compel them to come in," has often been misinterpreted. It has been regarded as teaching that we should force men to receive the gospel. But it denotes rather the urgency of the invitation, and the effectiveness of the inducements presented. The gospel never employs force in bringing men to Christ. Its message is "Ho, every one that thirsteth, come ye to the waters." Isa. 55:1. "The Spirit and the bride say, Come. . . . And whosoever will, let him take the water of life freely." Rev. 22:17. The power of God's love and grace constrains us to come.

The Saviour says, "Behold, I stand at the door, and knock; if any man hear My voice, and open the door, I will come in to him, and will sup with him, and he with Me." Rev. 3:20. He is not repulsed by scorn or turned aside by threatening, but continually seeks the lost ones, saying, "How shall I give thee up?" Hosea 11:8. Although His love is driven back by the stubborn heart, He returns to plead with greater force, "Behold, I stand at the door, and knock." The winning power of His love compels souls to come in. And to Christ they say, "Thy gentleness hath made me great." Ps. 18:35.

Christ will impart to His messengers the same yearning love that He Himself has in seeking for the lost. We are not merely to say, "Come." There are those who hear the call, but their ears are too dull to take in its meaning. Their eyes are too blind to see anything good in store for them. Many realize their great degradation. They say, I am not fit to be helped; leave me alone. But the workers must not desist. In tender, pitying love, lay hold of the discouraged and helpless ones. Give them your courage, your hope, your strength. By kindness compel them to come. "Of some have compassion, making a difference; and others save with fear, pulling them out of the fire." Jude 22, 23.

If the servants of God will walk with Him in faith, He will give power to their message. They will be enabled so to present His love and the danger of rejecting the grace of God that men will be constrained to accept the gospel. Christ will perform wonderful miracles if men will but do their God-given part. In human hearts today as great a transformation may be wrought as has ever been wrought in generations past. John Bunyan was redeemed from profanity and reveling, John Newton from slave dealing, to proclaim an uplifted Saviour. A Bunyan and a Newton may be redeemed from among men today. Through human agents who co-operate with the divine, many a poor outcast will be reclaimed, and in his turn will seek to restore the image of God in man. There are those who have had very meager opportunities, who have walked in ways of error because they knew no better way, to whom beams of light will come. As the word of Christ came to Zacchaeus, "Today I must abide at thy house" (Luke 19:5), so the word will come to them; and those who were supposed to be hardened sinners will be found to have hearts as tender as a child's because Christ has deigned to notice them. Many will come from the grossest error and sin, and will take the place of others who have had

opportunities and privileges but have not prized them. They will be accounted the chosen of God, elect, precious; and when Christ shall come into His kingdom, they will stand next His throne.

But "see that ye refuse not Him that speaketh." Heb. 12:25. Jesus said, "None of those men which were bidden shall taste of My supper." They had rejected the invitation, and none of them were to be invited again. In rejecting Christ, the Jews were hardening their hearts, and giving themselves into the power of Satan so that it would be impossible for them to accept His grace. So it is now. If the love of God is not appreciated and does not become an abiding principle to soften and subdue the soul, we are utterly lost. The Lord can give no greater manifestation of His love than He has given. If the love of Jesus does not subdue the heart, there are no means by which we can be reached.

Every time you refuse to listen to the message of mercy, you strengthen yourself in unbelief. Every time you fail to open the door of your heart to Christ, you become more and more unwilling to listen to the voice of Him that speaketh. You diminish your chance of responding to the last appeal of mercy. Let it not be written of you, as of ancient Israel, "Ephraim is joined to idols; let him alone." Hosea 4:17. Let not Christ weep over you as He wept over Jerusalem, saying, "How often would I have gathered thy children together, as a hen doth gather her brood under her wings, and ye would not! Behold, your house is left unto you desolate." Luke 13:34, 35.

We are living in a time when the last message of mercy, the last invitation, is sounding to the children of men. The command, "Go out into the highways and hedges," is reaching its final fulfillment. To every soul Christ's invitation will be given. The messengers are saying, "Come; for all things are now ready." Heavenly angels are still working in co-operation with human agencies. The Holy Spirit is presenting every inducement to constrain you to come. Christ is watching for some sign that will betoken the removing of the bolts and the opening of the door of your heart for His entrance. Angels are waiting to bear the tidings to heaven that another lost sinner has been found. The hosts of heaven are waiting, ready to strike their harps and to sing a song of rejoicing that another soul has accepted the invitation to the gospel feast.

19

The Measure of Forgiveness

Peter had come to Christ with the question, "How oft shall my brother sin against me, and I

This chapter is based on Matthew 18:21-35.

forgive him? till seven times?" The rabbis limited the exercise of forgiveness to three offenses. Peter, carrying out, as he supposed, the teaching of Christ, thought to extend it to seven, the number signifying perfection. But Christ taught that we are never to become weary of forgiving. Not "Until seven times," He said, "but, Until seventy times seven."

Then He showed the true ground upon which forgiveness is to be granted and the danger of cherishing an unforgiving spirit. In a parable He told of a king's dealing with the officers who administered the affairs of his government. Some of these officers were in receipt of vast sums of money belonging to the state. As the king investigated their administration of this trust, there was brought before him one man whose account showed a debt to his lord for the immense sum of ten thousand talents. He had

245 nothing to pay, and according to the custom, the king ordered him to be sold, with all that he had, that payment might be made. But the terrified man fell at his feet and besought him, saying, "Have patience with me, and I will pay thee all. Then the lord of that servant was moved with compassion, and loosed him, and forgave him the debt.

"But the same servant went out, and found one of his fellowservants, which owed him an hundred pence; and he laid hands on him, and took him by the throat, saying, Pay me that thou owest. And his fellowservant fell down at his feet, and besought him, saying, Have patience with me, and I will pay thee all. And he would not; but went and cast him into prison, till he should pay the debt. So when his fellowservants saw what was done, they were very sorry, and came and told unto their lord all that was done. Then his lord, after that he had called him, said unto him, O thou wicked servant, I forgave thee all that debt, because thou desiredst me: shouldest not thou also have had compassion on thy fellowservant, even as I had pity on thee? And his lord was wroth, and delivered him to the tormentors, till he should pay all that was due unto him."

This parable presents details which are needed for the filling out of the picture but which have no counterpart in its spiritual significance. The attention should not be diverted to them. Certain great truths are illustrated, and to these our thought should be given.

The pardon granted by this king represents a divine forgiveness of all sin. Christ is represented by the king, who, moved with compassion, forgave the debt of his servant. Man was under the condemnation of the broken law. He could not save himself, and for this reason Christ came to this world, clothed His divinity with humanity, and gave His life, the just for the

245 unjust. He gave Himself for our sins, and to every soul He freely offers the blood-bought

pardon. "With the Lord there is mercy, and with Him is plenteous redemption." Ps. 130:7.

Here is the ground upon which we should exercise compassion toward our fellow sinners. "If God so loved us, we ought also to love one another." John 4:11. "Freely ye have received," Christ says, "freely give." Matt. 10:8.

In the parable, when the debtor pleaded for delay, with the promise, "Have patience with me, and I will pay thee all," the sentence was revoked. The whole debt was canceled. And he was soon given an opportunity to follow the example of the master who had forgiven him. Going out, he met a fellow servant who owed him a small sum. He had been forgiven ten thousand talents; the debtor owed him a hundred pence. But he who had been so mercifully treated, dealt with his fellow laborer in an altogether different manner. His debtor made an appeal similar to that which he himself had made to the king, but without a similar result. He who had so recently been forgiven was not tenderhearted and pitiful. The mercy shown him he did not exercise in dealing with his fellowservant. He heeded not the request to be patient. The small sum owed to him was all that the ungrateful servant would keep in mind. He demanded all that he thought his due, and carried into effect a sentence similar to that which had been so graciously revoked for him.

How many are today manifesting the same spirit. When the debtor pleaded with his lord for mercy, he had no true sense of the greatness of his debt. He did not realize his helplessness. He hoped to deliver himself. "Have patience with me," he said, "and I will pay thee all." So there are many who hope by their own works to merit God's favor. They do not realize their helpless-

246 ness. They do not accept the grace of God as a free gift, but are trying to build themselves up in self-righteousness. Their own hearts are not broken and humbled on account of sin, and they are exacting and unforgiving toward others. Their

247 own sins against God, compared with their brother's sins against them, are as ten thousand talents to one hundred pence—nearly one million to one; yet they dare to be unforgiving.

In the parable the lord summoned the unmerciful debtor, and "said unto him, O thou wicked servant, I forgave thee all that debt, because thou desiredst me; shouldest not thou also have had compassion on thy fellowservant, even as I had pity on thee? And his lord was wroth, and delivered him to the tormentors, till he should pay all that was due unto him." "So likewise," said Jesus, "shall My Heavenly Father do also unto you, if ye from your hearts forgive not every one his brother their trespasses." He who refuses to forgive is thereby casting away his own hope of pardon.

But the teaching of this parable should not be

misapplied. God's forgiveness toward us lessens in no wise our duty to obey Him. So the spirit of forgiveness toward our fellow men does not lessen the claim of just obligation. In the prayer which Christ taught His disciples He said, "Forgive us our debts, as we forgive our debtors." Matt. 6:12. By this He did not mean that in order to be forgiven our sins we must not require our just dues from our debtors. If they cannot pay, even though this may be the result of unwise management, they are not to be cast into prison, oppressed, or even treated harshly; but the parable does not teach us to encourage indolence. The word of God declares that if a man will not work, neither shall he eat. (2 Thess. 3:10.) The Lord does not require the hard-working man to support others in idleness. With many there is a waste of time, a lack of effort, which brings to poverty and want. If these faults are not corrected by those who indulge them, all that might be done in their behalf would be like putting treasure into a bag with holes. Yet there is an unavoidable poverty, and we are to manifest tenderness and compassion toward those who are unfortunate. We should treat others just as we ourselves, in like circumstances, would wish to be treated.

248 The Holy Spirit through the apostle Paul charges us: "If there be therefore any consolation in Christ, if any comfort of love, if any fellowship of the Spirit, if any bowels and mercies, fulfil ye my joy, that ye be like-minded, having the same love, being of one accord, of one mind. Let nothing be done through strife or vainglory; but in lowliness of mind let each esteem other better than themselves. Look not every man on his own things, but every man also on the things of others. Let this mind be in you, which was also in Christ Jesus." Phil. 2:1-5.

But sin is not to be lightly regarded. The Lord has commanded us not to suffer wrong upon our brother. He says, "If thy brother trespass against thee, rebuke him." Luke 17:3. Sin is to be called by its right name, and is to be plainly laid out before the wrongdoer.

In his charge to Timothy, Paul, writing by the Holy Spirit, says, "Be instant in season, out of season; reprove, rebuke, exhort with all longsuffering and doctrine." 2 Tim. 4:2. And to Titus he writes, "There are many unruly and vain talkers and deceivers. . . . Wherefore rebuke them sharply, that they may be sound in the faith." Titus 1:10-13.

"If thy brother shall trespass against thee," Christ said, "go and tell him his fault between thee and him alone: if he shall hear thee, thou hast gained thy brother. But if he will not hear thee, then take with thee one or two more, that in the mouth of two or three witnesses every word may be established. And if he shall neglect to hear them, tell it unto the church: but

if he neglect to hear the church, let him be unto thee as an heathen man and a publican." Matt. 18:15-17.

Our Lord teaches that matters of difficulty between Christians are to be settled within the church. They should not be opened before those 249 who do not fear God. If a Christian is wronged by his brother, let him not appeal to unbelievers in a court of justice. Let him follow out the instruction Christ has given. Instead of trying to avenge himself, let him seek to save his brother. God will guard the interests of those who love and fear Him, and with confidence we may commit our case to Him who judges righteously.

Too often when wrongs are committed again and again, and the wrongdoer confesses his fault, the injured one becomes weary, and thinks he has forgiven quite enough. But the Saviour has plainly told us how to deal with the erring: "If thy brother trespass against thee, rebuke him; and if he repent, forgive him." Luke 17:3. Do not hold him off as unworthy of your confidence. Consider "thyself, lest thou also be tempted." Gal. 6:1.

If your brethren err, you are to forgive them. When they come to you with confession, you should not say, I do not think they are humble enough. I do not think they feel their confession. 250 What right have you to judge them, as if you could read the heart? The word of God says, "If he repent, forgive him. And if he trespasses against thee seven times in a day, and seven times in a day turn again to thee, saying, I repent; thou shalt forgive him." Luke 17:3, 4. And not only seven times, but seventy times seven—just as often as God forgives you.

We ourselves owe everything to God's free grace. Grace in the covenant ordained our adoption. Grace in the Saviour effected our redemption, our regeneration, and our exaltation to heirship with Christ. Let this grace be revealed to others.

Give the erring one no occasion for discouragement. Suffer not a Pharisaical hardness to come in and hurt your brother. Let no bitter sneer rise in mind or heart. Let no tinge of scorn be manifest in the voice. If you speak a word of your own, if you take an attitude of indifference, or show suspicion or distrust, it may prove the ruin of a soul. He needs a brother with the Elder Brother's heart of sympathy to touch his heart of humanity. Let him feel the strong clasp of a sympathizing hand, and hear the whisper, Let us pray. God will give a rich experience to you both. Prayer unites us with one another and with God. Prayer brings Jesus to our side, and gives to the fainting, perplexed soul new strength to overcome the world, the flesh, and the devil. Prayer turns aside the attacks of Satan.

When one turns away from human imperfections to behold Jesus, a divine transformation takes place in the character. The Spirit of Christ working upon the heart conforms it to His image. Then let it be your effort to lift up Jesus. Let the mind's eye be directed to "the Lamb of God, which taketh away the sin of the world." John 1:29. And as you engage in this work, remember that "he which converteth the sinner from the error of his way, shall save a soul from death, and shall hide a multitude of sins." James 5:20.

"But if ye forgive not men their trespasses, neither will your Father forgive your trespasses." Matt. 6:15. Nothing can justify an unforgiving spirit. He who is unmerciful toward others shows that he himself is not a partaker of God's pardoning grace. In God's forgiveness the heart of the erring one is drawn close to the great heart of Infinite Love. The tide of divine compassion flows into the sinner's soul, and from him to the souls of others. The tenderness and mercy that Christ has revealed in His own precious life will be seen in those who become sharers of His grace. But "if any man have not the Spirit of Christ, he is none of His." Rom. 8:9. He is alienated from God, fitted only for eternal separation from Him.

It is true that he may once have received forgiveness; but his unmerciful spirit shows that he now rejects God's pardoning love. He has separated himself from God, and is in the same condition as before he was forgiven. He has denied his repentance, and his sins are upon him as if he had not repented.

But the great lesson of the parable lies in the contrast between God's compassion and man's hardheartedness; in the fact that God's forgiving mercy is to be the measure of our own. "Shouldest not thou also have had compassion on thy fellowservant, even as I had pity on thee?"

We are not forgiven *because* we forgive, but *as* we forgive. The ground of all forgiveness is found in the unmerited love of God, but by our attitude toward others we show whether we have made that love our own. Wherefore Christ says, "With what judgment ye judge, ye shall be judged; and with what measure ye mete, it shall be measured to you again." Matt. 7:2.

20

Gain That Is Loss

Christ was teaching, and, as usual, others besides His disciples had gathered about Him. He had been speaking to the disciples of the scenes in which they were soon to act a part. They were to publish abroad the truths He had committed to them, and they would be brought in conflict with the rulers of this world. For His sake they would be called into courts, and before magistrates and kings. He had assured them of wisdom which none could gainsay. His own words, that moved the hearts of the multitude, and brought to confusion His wily adversaries, witnessed to the power of that indwelling Spirit which He had promised to His followers.

But there were many who desired the grace of heaven only to serve their selfish purposes. They recognized the marvelous power of Christ in setting forth the truth in a clear light. They heard the promise to His followers of wisdom to speak before rulers and magistrates. Would He not lend His power for their worldly benefit?

"And one of the company said unto Him, Master, speak to my brother, that he divide the inheritance with me." Through Moses, God had given directions concerning the transmission of property. The eldest son received a double portion of the father's estate (Deut. 21:17), while the younger brothers were to share alike. This man thinks that his brother has defrauded him of his inheritance. His own efforts have failed to secure what he regards as his due, but if Christ will interpose the end will surely be gained. He has heard Christ's stirring appeals, and His solemn denunciations of the scribes and Pharisees. If words of such command could be spoken to this brother, he would not dare to refuse the aggrieved man his portion.

In the midst of the solemn instruction that Christ had given, this man had revealed his selfish disposition. He could appreciate that ability of the Lord which might work for the advancement of his own temporal affairs; but spiritual truths had taken no hold on his mind and heart. The gaining of the inheritance was his absorbing theme. Jesus, the King of glory, who was rich, yet for our sake became poor, was opening to him the treasures of divine love. The Holy Spirit was pleading with him to become an heir of the inheritance that is "incorruptible, and undefiled, and that fadeth not away." 1 Peter 1:4. He had seen evidence of the power of Christ. Now the opportunity was his to speak to the great Teacher, to express the desire uppermost in his heart. But like the man with the muck rake in Bunyan's allegory, his eyes were fixed on the earth. He saw not the crown above his head. Like Simon Magus, he valued the gift of God as a means of worldly gain.

The Saviour's mission on earth was fast drawing to a close. Only a few months remained for Him to complete what He had come to do, in establishing the kingdom of His grace. Yet human greed would have turned Him from His work to take up the dispute over a piece of land. But Jesus was not to be diverted from His mission. His answer was, "Man, who made Me a judge or a divider over you?"

Jesus could have told this man just what was right. He knew the right in the case; but the brothers were in a quarrel because both were covetous. Christ virtually said, It is not My work to settle controversies of this kind. He came for another purpose, to preach the gospel, and thus to arouse men to a sense of eternal realities.

In Christ's treatment of this case is a lesson for all who minister in His name. When He sent forth the twelve, He said, "As ye go, preach, saying, The kingdom of heaven is at hand. Heal the sick, cleanse the lepers, raise the dead, cast out devils: freely ye have received, freely give." Matt. 10:7, 8. They were not to settle the temporal affairs of the people. Their work was to persuade men to be reconciled to God. In this work lay their power to bless humanity. The only remedy for the sins and sorrows of men is Christ. The gospel of His grace alone can cure the evils that curse society. The injustice of the rich toward the poor, the hatred of the poor toward the rich, alike have their root in selfishness, and this can be eradicated only through submission to Christ. He alone, for the selfish heart of sin, gives the new heart of love. Let the servants of Christ preach the gospel with the Spirit sent down from heaven, and work as He did for the benefit of men. Then such results will be manifest in the blessing and uplifting of mankind as are wholly impossible of accomplishment by human power.

Our Lord struck at the root of the affair that troubled this questioner, and of all similar disputes, saying, "Take heed, and beware of cov- 255 etousness; for a man's life consisteth not in the abundance of the things which he possesseth.

"And He spake a parable unto them, saying, The ground of a certain rich man brought forth plentifully; and he thought within himself, saying, What shall I do, because I have no room where to bestow my fruits? And he said, This will I do: I will pull down my barns, and build greater; and there will I bestow all my fruits and my goods. And I will say to my soul, Soul, thou 256 hast much goods laid up for many years; take thine ease, eat, drink, be merry. But God said unto him, Thou fool, this night thy soul shall be required of thee: then whose shall these things be, which thou hast provided? So is he that layeth up treasure for himself, and is not rich toward God."

By the parable of the foolish rich man, Christ showed the folly of those who make the world their all. This man had received everything from God. The sun had been permitted to shine upon his land; for its rays fall on the just and on the unjust. The showers of heaven descend on the evil and on the good. The Lord had caused vegetation to flourish, and the fields to bring forth abundantly. The rich man was in perplexity as to what he should do with his produce. His barns were full to overflowing, and he had no place to put the surplus of his harvest. He did

not think of God, from whom all his mercies had come. He did not realize that God had made him a steward of His goods that he might help the needy. He had a blessed opportunity of being God's almoner, but he thought only of ministering to his own comfort.

The situation of the poor, the orphan, the widow, the suffering, the afflicted, was brought to this rich man's attention; there were many places in which to bestow his goods. He could easily have relieved himself of a portion of his abundance, and many homes would have been freed from want, many who were hungry would have been fed, many naked clothed, many hearts made glad, many prayers for bread and clothing answered, and a melody of praise would have ascended to heaven. The Lord had heard the prayers of the needy, and of His goodness He had prepared for the poor. (Ps. 68:10.) Abundant provision for the wants of many had been made in the blessings bestowed upon the rich man. But he closed his heart to the cry of the needy, and said to his servants, "This will I do: I will pull down my barns, and build greater; 257 and there will I bestow all my fruits and my goods. And I will say to my soul, Soul, thou hast much goods laid up for many years; take thine ease, eat, drink, and be merry."

This man's aims were no higher than those of the beasts that perish. He lived as if there were no God, no heaven, no future life; as if every- 258 thing he possessed were his own, and he owed nothing to God or man. The psalmist described this rich man when he wrote, "The fool hath said in his heart, There is no God." Ps. 14:1.

This man has lived and planned for self. He sees that the future is abundantly provided for; there is nothing for him now but to treasure and enjoy the fruits of his labors. He regards himself as favored above other men, and takes credit to himself for his wise management. He is honored by his fellow townsmen as a man of good judgment and a prosperous citizen. For "men will praise thee, when thou doest well to thyself." Ps. 49:18.

But "the wisdom of this world is foolishness with God." 1 Cor. 3:19. While the rich man is looking forward to years of enjoyment, the Lord is making far different plans. The message comes to this unfaithful steward, "Thou fool, this night thy soul shall be required of thee." Here is a demand that money cannot supply. The wealth he has treasured can purchase no reprieve. In one moment that which he has toiled through his whole life to secure becomes worthless to him. "Then whose shall those things be which thou hast provided?" His broad fields and well-filled granaries pass from under his control. "He heapeth up riches, and knoweth not who shall gather them." Ps. 39:6.

The only thing that would be of value to him now he has not secured. In living for self he has rejected that divine love which would have flowed out in mercy to his fellow men. Thus he has rejected life. For God is love, and love is life. This man has chosen the earthly rather than the spiritual, and with the earthly he must pass away. "Man that is in honour, and understandeth not, is like the beasts that perish." Ps. 49:20.

259 "So is he that layeth up treasure for himself, and is not rich toward God." The picture is true for all time. You may plan for merely selfish good, you may gather together treasure, you may build mansions great and high, as did the builders of ancient Babylon; but you cannot build wall so high or gate so strong as to shut out the messengers of doom. Belshazzar the king "feasted in his palace," and "praised the gods of gold, and of silver, of brass, of iron, of wood, and of stone." But the hand of One invisible wrote upon his walls the words of doom, and the tread of hostile armies was heard at his palace gates. "In that night was Belshazzar the king of the Chaldeans slain," and an alien monarch sat upon the throne. (Dan. 5:30.)

To live for self is to perish. Covetousness, the desire of benefit for self's sake, cuts the soul off from life. It is the spirit of Satan to get, to draw to self. It is the spirit of Christ to give, to sacrifice self for the good of others. "And this is the record, that God hath given to us eternal life, and this life is in His Son. He that hath the Son hath life; and he that hath not the Son of God hath not life." 1 John 5:11, 12.

Wherefore He says, "Take heed, and beware of covetousness; for a man's life consisteth not in the abundance of the things which he possesseth."

260

21

"A Great Gulf Fixed"

In the parable of the rich man and Lazarus, Christ shows that in this life men decide their eternal destiny. During probationary time the grace of God is offered to every soul. But if men waste their opportunities in self-pleasing, they cut themselves off from everlasting life. No afterprobation will be granted them. By their own choice they have fixed an impassable gulf between them and their God.

This parable draws a contrast between the rich who have not made God their dependence, and the poor who have made God their dependence. Christ shows that the time is coming when the position of the two classes will be reversed. Those who are poor in this world's goods, yet who trust in God and are patient in suffering, will one day be exalted above those who now hold the highest positions the world

This chapter is based on Luke 16:19-31.

can give but who have not surrendered their life to God.

"There was a certain rich man," Christ said, "which was clothed in purple and fine linen, and fared sumptuously every day. And there was a certain beggar named Lazarus, which was laid 261 at his gate, full of sores, and desiring to be fed with the crumbs which fell from the rich man's table."

The rich man did not belong to the class represented by the unjust judge, who openly declared his disregard for God and man. He claimed to be a son of Abraham. He did not treat the beggar with violence or require him to go away because the sight of him was disagreeable. If the poor, loathsome specimen of humanity could be comforted by beholding him as he entered his gates, the rich man was willing that he should remain. But he was selfishly indifferent to the needs of his suffering brother.

There were then no hospitals in which the sick might be cared for. The suffering and needy were brought to the notice of those to whom the Lord had entrusted wealth, that they might receive help and sympathy. Thus it was with the beggar and the rich man. Lazarus was in great need of help; for he was without friends, home, money, or food. Yet he was allowed to remain in this condition day after day, while the wealthy nobleman had every want supplied. The one who was abundantly able to relieve the sufferings of his fellow creature, lived to himself, as many live today.

There are today close beside us many who are hungry, naked, and homeless. A neglect to impart of our means to these needy, suffering ones places upon us a burden of guilt which we shall one day fear to meet. All covetousness is condemned as idolatry. All selfish indulgence is an offense in God's sight.

God had made the rich man a steward of His means, and it was his duty to attend to just such cases as that of the beggar. The command had been given, "Thou shalt love the Lord thy God with all thine heart, and with all thy soul, and with all thy might" (Deut. 6:5); and "thou shalt love thy neighbor as thyself" (Lev. 19:18). The rich man was a Jew, and he was acquainted with 262 the command of God. But he forgot that he was accountable for the use of his entrusted means and capabilities. The Lord's blessings rested upon him abundantly, but he employed them selfishly, to honor himself, not his Maker. In proportion to his abundance was his obligation to use his gifts for the uplifting of humanity. This was the Lord's command, but the rich man had no thought of his obligation to God. He lent money, and took interest for what he loaned; but he returned no interest for what God had lent him. He had knowledge and talents, but did not improve them. Forgetful of his accountability to God, he devoted all his powers to pleasure.

Everything with which he was surrounded, his round of amusements, the praise and flattery of his friends, ministered to his selfish enjoyment. So engrossed was he in the society of his friends that he lost all sense of his responsibility to co-operate with God in His ministry of mercy. He had opportunity to understand the word of God, and to practice its teachings; but the pleasure-loving society he chose so occupied his time that he forgot the God of eternity.

The time came when a change took place in the condition of the two men. The poor man had suffered day by day, but he had patiently and quietly endured. In the course of time he died and was buried. There was no one to mourn for him; but by his patience in suffering he had witnessed for Christ, he had endured the test of his faith, and at his death he is represented as being carried by the angels into Abraham's bosom.

Lazarus represents the suffering poor who believe in Christ. When the trumpet sounds and all that are in the graves hear Christ's voice and come forth, they will receive their reward; for their faith in God was not a mere theory, but a reality.

263 "The rich man also died, and was buried; and in hell he lift up his eyes, being in torments, and seeth Abraham afar off, and Lazarus in his bosom. And he cried and said, Father Abraham, have mercy on me, and send Lazarus, that he may dip the tip of his finger in water, and cool my tongue; for I am tormented in this flame."

In this parable Christ was meeting the people on their own ground. The doctrine of a conscious state of existence between death and the resurrection was held by many of those who were listening to Christ's words. The Saviour knew of their ideas, and He framed His parable so as to inculcate important truths through these preconceived opinions. He held up before His hearers a mirror wherein they might see themselves in their true relation to God. He used the prevailing opinion to convey the idea He wished to make prominent to all—that no man is valued for his possessions; for all he has belongs to him only as lent by the Lord. A misuse of these gifts will place him below the poorest and most afflicted man who loves God and trusts in Him.

Christ desires His hearers to understand that it is impossible for men to secure the salvation of the soul after death. "Son," Abraham is represented as answering, "remember that thou in thy lifetime receivedst thy good things, and likewise Lazarus evil things; but now he is comforted, and thou art tormented. And beside all this, between us and you there is a great gulf fixed; so that they which would pass from hence to you can not; neither can they pass to us, that would come from thence." Thus Christ represented the hopelessness of looking for a second probation. This life is the only time given to man in which to prepare for eternity.

The rich man had not abandoned the idea that he was a child of Abraham, and in his distress he is represented as calling upon him for aid. 264 "Father Abraham," he prayed, "have mercy on me." He did not pray to God, but to Abraham. Thus he showed that he placed Abraham above God, and that he relied on his relationship to Abraham for salvation. The thief on the cross offered his prayer to Christ. "Remember me when Thou comest into Thy kingdom," he said. (Luke 23:42.) And at once the response came, Verily I say unto thee today (as I hang on the cross in humiliation and suffering), thou shalt be with Me in Paradise. But the rich man prayed to Abraham, and his petition was not granted. Christ alone is exalted to be "a Prince and a Saviour, for to give repentance to Israel, and forgiveness of sins." Acts 5:31. "Neither is there salvation in any other." Acts 4:12.

The rich man had spent his life in self-pleasing, and too late he saw that he had made no provision for eternity. He realized his folly, and thought of his brothers, who would go on as he had gone, living to please themselves. Then he made the request, "I pray thee therefore, father, that thou wouldest send him [Lazarus] to my father's house; for I have five brethren; that he may testify unto them, lest they also come into this place of torment." But "Abraham saith unto him, They have Moses and the prophets; let them hear them. And he said, Nay, father Abraham; but if one went unto them from the dead, they will repent. And he said unto him, If they hear not Moses and the prophets, neither will they be persuaded though one rose from the dead."

When the rich man solicited additional evidence for his brothers, he was plainly told that should this evidence be given, they would not be persuaded. His request cast a reflection on God. It was as if the rich man had said, If you had more thoroughly warned me, I should not now be here. Abraham in his answer to this request is represented as saying, Your brothers 265 have been sufficiently warned. Light has been given them, but they would not see; truth has been presented to them, but they would not hear.

"If they hear not Moses and the prophets, neither will they be persuaded, though one rose from the dead." These words were proved true in the history of the Jewish nation. Christ's last and crowning miracle was the raising of Lazarus of Bethany, after he had been dead four days. The Jews were given this wonderful evidence of the Saviour's divinity, but they rejected it. Lazarus rose from the dead and bore his testimony before them, but they hardened their hearts against all evidence, and even sought to take his life. (John 12:9-11.)

The law and the prophets are God's appointed agencies for the salvation of men. Christ said, Let them give heed to these evidences. If they do not listen to the voice of God in His word, the testimony of a witness raised from the dead would not be heeded.

Those who heed Moses and the prophets will require no greater light than God has given; but if men reject the light, and fail to appreciate the opportunities granted them, they would not hear if one from the dead should come to them with a message. They would not be convinced even by this evidence; for those who reject the law and the prophets so harden their hearts that they will reject all light.

The conversation between Abraham and the once-rich man is figurative. The lesson to be gathered from it is that every man is given sufficient light for the discharge of the duties required of him. Man's responsibilities are proportionate to his opportunities and privileges. God gives to every one sufficient light and grace to do the work He has given him to do. If man fails to do that which a little light shows to be his duty, greater light would only reveal unfaithfulness, neglect to improve the blessings 266 given. "He that is faithful in that which is least is faithful also in much; and he that is unjust in the least is unjust also in much." Luke 16:10. Those who refuse to be enlightened by Moses and the prophets and ask for some wonderful miracle to be performed would not be convinced if their wish were granted.

The parable of the rich man and Lazarus shows how the two classes represented by these men are estimated in the unseen world. There is no sin in being rich if riches are not acquired by injustice. A rich man is not condemned for having riches, but condemnation rests upon him if the means entrusted to him is spent in selfishness. Far better might he lay up his money beside the throne of God, by using it to do good. Death cannot make any man poor who thus devotes himself to seeking eternal riches. But the man who hoards his treasure for self can not take any of it to heaven. He has proved himself to be an unfaithful steward. During his lifetime he had his good things, but he was forgetful of his obligation to God. He failed of securing the heavenly treasure.

The rich man who had so many privileges is represented to us as one who should have cultivated his gifts, so that his works should reach to the great beyond, carrying with them improved spiritual advantages. It is the purpose of redemption, not only to blot out sin, but to give back to man those spiritual gifts lost because of sin's dwarfing power. Money cannot be carried into the next life; it is not needed there; but the good deeds done in winning souls to Christ are carried to the heavenly courts. But those who selfishly spend the Lord's gifts on themselves, leaving their needy fellow creatures without aid and doing nothing to advance God's work in the world, dishonor their Maker. Robbery of God is written opposite their names in the books of heaven.

The rich man had all that money could pro- 267 cure, but he did not possess the riches that would have kept his account right with God. He had lived as if all that he possessed were his own. He had neglected the call of God and the claims of the suffering poor. But at length there comes a call which he cannot neglect. By a power which he cannot question or resist he is commanded to quit the premises of which he is no longer steward. The once-rich man is reduced to hopeless poverty. The robe of Christ's righteousness, woven in the loom of heaven, can never cover him. He who once wore the richest purple, the finest linen, is reduced to nakedness. His probation is ended. He brought nothing into the world, and he can take nothing out of it.

Christ lifted the curtain and presented this picture before priests and rulers, scribes and Pharisees. Look at it, you who are rich in this world's goods and are not rich toward God. Will you not contemplate this scene? That which is highly esteemed among men is abhorrent in the sight of God. Christ asks, "What shall it profit a man, if he shall gain the whole world, and lose his own soul? or what shall a man give in exchange for his soul?" Mark 8:36, 37.

Application to the Jewish Nation

When Christ gave the parable of the rich man and Lazarus, there were many in the Jewish nation in the pitiable condition of the rich man, using the Lord's goods for selfish gratification, preparing themselves to hear the sentence, "Thou art weighed in the balances, and art found wanting." Dan. 5:27. The rich man was favored with every temporal and spiritual blessing, but he refused to cooperate with God in the use of these blessings. Thus it was with the Jewish nation. The Lord had made the Jews the depositaries of sacred truth. He had appointed them stewards of His grace. He had given them 268 every spiritual and temporal advantage, and He called upon them to impart these blessings. Special instruction had been given them in regard to their treatment of their brethren who had fallen into decay, of the stranger within their gates, and of the poor among them. They were not to seek to gain everything for their own advantage, but were to remember those in need and share with them. And God promised to bless them in accordance with their deeds of love and mercy. But like the rich man, they put forth no helping hand to relieve the temporal or spiritual necessities of suffering humanity. Filled with pride, they regarded themselves as the chosen and favored people of God; yet they did not serve or worship God. They put their dependence in the fact that they were children of Abraham. "We be Abraham's seed," they said proudly. (John 8:33.) When the crisis came, it was revealed that they had divorced themselves from God, and had placed their trust in Abraham, as if he were God.

Christ longed to let light shine into the darkened minds of the Jewish people. He said to them, "If ye were Abraham's children, ye would do the works of Abraham. But now ye seek to kill Me, a man that hath told you the truth, which I have heard of God. This did not Abraham." John 8:39, 40.

Christ recognized no virtue in lineage. He taught that spiritual connection supersedes all natural connection. The Jews claimed to have descended from Abraham; but by failing to do the works of Abraham, they proved that they were not his true children. Only those who prove themselves to be spiritually in harmony with Abraham by obeying the voice of God, are reckoned as of true descent. Although the beggar belonged to the class looked upon by men as inferior, Christ recognized him as one whom Abraham would take into the very closest friendship.

269 The rich man though surrounded with all the luxuries of life was so ignorant that he put Abraham where God should have been. If he had appreciated his exalted privileges and had allowed God's Spirit to mold his mind and heart, he would have had an altogether different position. So with the nation he represented. If they had responded to the divine call, their future would have been wholly different. They would have shown true spiritual discernment. They had means which God would have increased, making it sufficient to bless and enlighten the whole world. But they had so far separated from the Lord's arrangement that their whole life was perverted. They failed to use their gifts as God's stewards in accordance with truth and righteousness. Eternity was not brought into their reckoning, and the result of their unfaithfulness was ruin to the whole nation.

Christ knew that at the destruction of Jerusalem the Jews would remember His warning. And it was so. When calamity came upon Jerusalem, when starvation and suffering of every kind came upon the people, they remembered these words of Christ and understood the parable. They had brought their suffering upon themselves by their neglect to let their God-given light shine forth to the world.

In the Last Days

The closing scenes of this earth's history are portrayed in the closing of the rich man's history. The rich man claimed to be a son of Abraham, but he was separated from Abraham by an impassable gulf—a character wrongly developed. Abraham served God, following His word in faith and obedience. But the rich man was unmindful of God and of the needs of suffering humanity. The great gulf fixed between him and Abraham was the gulf of disobedience. There 270 are many today who are following the same course. Though church members, they are unconverted. They may take part in the church service, they may chant the psalm, "As the hart panteth after the water brooks, so panteth my soul after Thee, O God" (Ps. 42:1); but they testify to a falsehood. They are no more righteous in God's sight than is the veriest sinner. The soul that longs after the excitement of worldly pleasure, the mind that is full of love for display, cannot serve God. Like the rich man in the parable, such a one has no inclination to war against the lust of the flesh. He longs to indulge appetite. He chooses the atmosphere of sin. He is suddenly snatched away by death, and he goes down to the grave with the character formed during his lifetime in copartnership with Satanic agencies. In the grave he has no power to choose anything, be it good or evil; for in the day when a man dies, his thoughts perish. (Ps. 146:4; Eccl. 9:5, 6.)

When the voice of God awakes the dead, he will come from the grave with the same appetites and passions, the same likes and dislikes, that he cherished when living. God works no miracle to re-create a man who would not be re-created when he was granted every opportunity and provided with every facility. During his lifetime he took no delight in God, nor found pleasure in His service. His character is not in harmony with God, and he could not be happy in the heavenly family.

Today there is a class in our world who are self-righteous. They are not gluttons, they are not drunkards, they are not infidels; but they desire to live for themselves, not for God. He is not in their thoughts; therefore they are classed with unbelievers. Were it possible for them to enter the gates of the city of God, they could have no right to the tree of life, for when God's commandments were laid before them with all their binding claims they said, No. They have 271 not served God here; therefore they would not serve Him hereafter. They could not live in His presence, and they would feel that any place was preferable to heaven.

To learn of Christ means to receive His grace, which is His character. But those who do not appreciate and utilize the precious opportunities and sacred influences granted them on earth, are not fitted to take part in the pure devotion of heaven. Their characters are not molded according to the divine similitude. By their own neglect they have formed a chasm which nothing can bridge. Between them and the righteous there is a great gulf fixed.

272

22

Saying and Doing

"A certain man had two sons; and he came to the first, and said, Son, go work today in my vineyard. He answered and said, I will not; but afterward he repented, and went. And he came to the second, and said likewise. And he answered and said, I go, sir; and went not. Whether of them twain did the will of his father? They say unto him, The first."

In the sermon on the mount Christ said, "Not every one that saith unto Me, Lord, Lord, shall enter into the kingdom of heaven; but he that doeth the will of My Father which is in heaven." Matt. 7:21. The test of sincerity is not in words, but in deeds. Christ does not say to any man, What say ye more than others? but, "What do ye more than others?" Matt. 5:47. Full of meaning are His words, "If ye know these things, happy are ye if ye do them." John 13:17. Words are of no value unless they are accompanied with appropriate deeds. This is the lesson taught in the parable of the two sons.

273 This parable was spoken at Christ's last visit to Jerusalem before His death. He had driven out the buyers and sellers from the temple. His voice had spoken to their hearts with the power of God. Amazed and terrified, they had obeyed His command without excuse or resistance.

When their terror was abated, the priests and elders, returning to the temple, had found Christ healing the sick and the dying. They had heard the voice of rejoicing and the song of praise. In the temple itself the children who had been restored to health were waving palm branches and singing hosannas to the Son of David. Baby voices were lisping the praises of the mighty Healer. Yet with the priests and elders all this did not suffice to overcome their prejudice and jealousy.

The next day, as Christ was teaching in the temple, the chief priests and elders of the people came to Him and said, "By what authority doest Thou these things? and who gave Thee this authority?"

The priests and elders had had unmistakable evidence of Christ's power. In His cleansing of the temple they had seen Heaven's authority flashing from His face. They could not resist the power by which He spoke. Again in His wonderful deeds of healing He had answered their question. He had given evidence of His authority which could not be controverted. But it was not evidence that was wanted. The priests and elders were anxious for Jesus to proclaim Himself the Messiah that they might misapply His words and stir up the people against Him. They

This chapter is based on Matthew 21:23-32.

wished to destroy His influence and to put Him to death.

Jesus knew that if they could not recognize God in Him or see in His works the evidence of His divine character, they would not believe His own testimony that He was the Christ. In His answer He evades the issue they hope to bring about and turns the condemnation upon themselves.

"I also will ask you one thing," He said, 274 "which if ye tell Me, I in like wise will tell you by what authority I do these things. The baptism of John, whence was it? from heaven, or of men?"

The priests and rulers were perplexed. "They reasoned with themselves, saying, If we shall say, From heaven, He will say unto us, Why did ye not then believe him? But if we shall say, Of men, we fear the people; for all hold John as a prophet. And they answered Jesus, and said, We can not tell. And He said unto them, Neither tell I you by what authority I do these things."

"We can not tell." This answer was a falsehood. But the priests saw the position they were in, and falsified in order to screen themselves. John the Baptist had come bearing witness of the One whose authority they were now questioning. He had pointed Him out, saying, "Behold the Lamb of God, which taketh away the sin of the world." John 1:29. He had baptized Him, and after the baptism, as Christ was praying, the heavens were opened, and the Spirit of God like a dove rested upon Him, while a voice from heaven was heard saying, "This is My beloved Son, in whom I am well pleased." Matt. 3:17.

Remembering how John had repeated the prophecies concerning the Messiah, remembering the scene at the baptism of Jesus, the priests and rulers dared not say that John's baptism was from heaven. If they acknowledged John to be a prophet, as they believed him to be, how could they deny his testimony that Jesus of Nazareth was the Son of God? And they could not say that John's baptism was of men, because of the people, who believed John to be a prophet. So they said, "We can not tell."

Then Christ gave the parable of the father and the two sons. When the father went to the first son, saying, "Go work today in my vineyard," 275 the son promptly answered, "I will not." He refused to obey, and gave himself up to wicked ways and associations. But afterward he repented, and obeyed the call.

The father went to the second son with the same command, "Go work today in my vineyard." This son made reply, "I go, sir," but he went not.

In this parable the father represents God, the vineyard the church. By the two sons are represented two classes of people. The son who 276 refused to obey the command, saying, "I will not," represented those who were living in open transgression, who made no profession of piety, who openly refused to come under the yoke of restraint and obedience which the law of God imposes. But many of these afterward repented and obeyed the call of God. When the gospel came to them in the message of John the Baptist, "Repent ye; for the kingdom of heaven is at hand," they repented, and confessed their sins. (Matt. 3:2.)

In the son who said, "I go, sir," and went not, the character of the Pharisees was revealed. Like this son, the Jewish leaders were impenitent and self-sufficient. The religious life of the Jewish nation had become a pretense. When the law was proclaimed on Mount Sinai by the voice of God, all the people pledged themselves to obey. They said, "I go, sir," but they went not. When Christ came in person to set before them the principles of the law, they rejected Him. Christ had given the Jewish leaders of His day abundant evidence of His authority and divine power, but although they were convinced, they would not accept the evidence. Christ had shown them that they continued to disbelieve because they had not the spirit which leads to obedience. He had declared to them, "Ye made the commandment of God of none effect by your tradition. . . . In vain they do worship Me, teaching for doctrines the commandments of men." Matt. 15:6, 9.

In the company before Christ there were scribes and Pharisees, priests and rulers, and after giving the parable of the two sons, Christ addressed to His hearers the question, "Whether of them twain did the will of his father?" Forgetting themselves, the Pharisees answered, "The first." This they said without realizing that they were pronouncing sentence against themselves. Then there fell from Christ's lips the denunciation, "Verily I say unto you, That 277 publicans and the harlots go into the kingdom of God before you. For John came unto you in the way of righteousness, and ye believed him not; but the publicans and the harlots believed him: and ye, when ye had seen it, repented not afterward, that ye might believe him."

John the Baptist came preaching truth, and by his preaching sinners were convicted and converted. These would go into the kingdom of heaven before the ones who in self-righteousness resisted the solemn warning. The publicans and harlots were ignorant, but these learned men knew the way of truth. Yet they refused to walk in the path which leads to the Paradise of God. The truth that should have been to them a savor of life unto life became a savor of death unto death. Open sinners who loathed themselves had received baptism at the hands of John; but these teachers were hypocrites. Their own stubborn hearts were the obstacle to their receiving the truth. They resisted the conviction of the

Spirit of God. They refused obedience to God's commandments.

Christ did not say to them, Ye cannot enter the kingdom of heaven; but He showed that the obstacle which prevented them from entering was of their own creating. The door was still open to these Jewish leaders; the invitation was still held out. Christ longed to see them convict- 278 ed and converted.

The priests and elders of Israel spent their lives in religious ceremonies, which they regarded as too sacred to be connected with secular business. Therefore their lives were supposed to be wholly religious. But they performed their ceremonies to be seen by men that they might be thought by the world to be pious and devoted. While professing to obey they refused to render obedience to God. They were not doers of the truth which they professed to teach.

Christ declared John the Baptist to be one of the greatest of the prophets, and He showed His hearers that they had had sufficient evidence that John was a messenger from God. The words of the preacher in the wilderness were with power. He bore his message unflinchingly, rebuking the sins of priests and rulers, and enjoining upon them the works of the kingdom of heaven. He pointed out to them their sinful disregard of their Father's authority in refusing to do the work appointed them. He made no compromise with sin, and many were turned from their unrighteousness.

Had the profession of the Jewish leaders been genuine, they would have received John's testimony and accepted Jesus as the Messiah. But they did not show the fruits of repentance and righteousness. The very ones whom they despised were pressing into the kingdom of God before them.

In the parable the son who said, "I go, sir," represented himself as faithful and obedient; but time proved that his profession was not real. He had no true love for his father. So the Pharisees prided themselves on their holiness, but when tested, it was found wanting. When it was for their interest to do so, they made the requirements of the law very exacting; but when obedience was required from themselves, by cunning sophistries they reasoned away the force of God's precepts. Of them Christ declared, "Do not ye after their works; for they say, and do 279 not." Matt. 23:3. They had no true love for God or man. God called them to be co-workers with Him in blessing the world; but while in profession they accepted the call, in action they refused obedience. They trusted to self, and prided themselves on their goodness; but they set the commands of God at defiance. They refused to do the work which God had appointed them, and because of their transgression the Lord was about to divorce Himself from the disobedient nation.

Self-righteousness is not true righteousness, and those who cling to it will be left to take the consequences of holding a fatal deception. Many today claim to obey the commandments of God, but they have not the love of God in their hearts to flow forth to others. Christ calls them to unite with Him in His work for the saving of the world, but they content themselves with saying, "I go, sir." They do not go. They do not co-operate with those who are doing God's service. They are idlers. Like the unfaithful son, they make false promises to God. In taking upon themselves the solemn covenant of the church they have pledged themselves to receive and obey the word of God, to give themselves to God's service, but they do not do this. In profession they claim to be sons of God, but in life and character they deny the relationship. They do not surrender the will to God. They are living a lie.

The promise of obedience they appear to fulfill when this involves no sacrifice; but when self-denial and self-sacrifice are required, when they see the cross to be lifted, they draw back. Thus the conviction of duty wears away, and known transgression of God's commandments becomes habit. The ear may hear God's word, but the spiritual perceptive powers have departed. The heart is hardened, the conscience seared.

280 Do not think that because you do not manifest decided hostility to Christ you are doing Him service. We thus deceive our own souls. By withholding that which God has given us to use in His service, be it time or means or any other of His entrusted gifts, we work against Him.

Satan uses the listless, sleepy indolence of professed Christians to strengthen his forces and win souls to his side. Many, who think that though they are doing no actual work for Christ, they are yet on His side, are enabling the enemy to pre-occupy ground and gain advantages. By their failure to be diligent workers for the Master, by leaving duties undone and words unspoken, they have allowed Satan to gain control of souls who might have been won for Christ.

We can never be saved in indolence and inactivity. There is no such thing as a truly converted person living a helpless, useless life. It is not possible for us to drift into heaven. No sluggard can enter there. If we do not strive to gain an entrance into the kingdom, if we do not seek earnestly to learn what constitutes its laws, we are not fitted for a part in it. Those who refuse to co-operate with God on earth would not co-operate with Him in heaven. It would not be safe to take them to heaven.

There is more hope for publicans and sinners than for those who know the word of God but refuse to obey it. He who sees himself a sinner with no cloak for his sin, who knows that he is corrupting soul, body, and spirit before God, becomes alarmed lest he be eternally separated from the kingdom of heaven. He realizes his diseased condition, and seeks healing from the great Physician who has said, "Him that cometh to Me, I will in no wise cast out." John 6:37. These souls the Lord can use as workers in His vineyard.

The son who for a time refused obedience to his father's command was not condemned by Christ; and neither was he commended. The class who act the part of the first son in refusing 281 obedience deserve no credit for holding this position. Their frankness is not to be regarded as a virtue. Sanctified by truth and holiness, it would make men bold witnesses for Christ; but used as it is by the sinner, it is insulting and defiant, and approaches to blasphemy. The fact that a man is not a hypocrite does not make him any the less really a sinner. When the appeals of the Holy Spirit come to the heart, our only safety lies in responding to them without delay. When the call comes, "Go work today in My vineyard," do not refuse the invitation. "Today if ye will hear His voice, harden not your hearts." Heb. 4:7. It is unsafe to delay obedience. You may never hear the invitation again.

And let none flatter themselves that sins cherished for a time can easily be given up by and by. This is not so. Every sin cherished weakens the character and strengthens habit; and physical, mental, and moral depravity is the result. You may repent of the wrong you have done, and set your feet in right paths; but the mold of your mind and your familiarity with evil will make it difficult for you to distinguish between right and wrong. Through the wrong habits formed, Satan will assail you again and again.

In the command, "Go work today in My vineyard," the test of sincerity is brought to every soul. Will there be deeds as well as words? Will the one called put to use all the knowledge he has, working faithfully, disinterestedly, for the Owner of the vineyard?

The apostle Peter instructs us as to the plan on which we must work. "Grace and peace be multiplied unto you," he says, "through the knowledge of God, and of Jesus our Lord, according as His divine power hath given unto us all things that pertain unto life and godliness, through the knowledge of Him that hath called us to glory and virtue: whereby are given unto us exceeding great and precious promises; that 282 by these ye might be partakers of the divine

---

"Thus shalt thou say to the house of Jacob, . . . If ye will obey My voice indeed, and keep My covenant, then ye shall be a peculiar treasure unto Me above all people: for all the earth is Mine: and ye shall be unto Me a kingdom of priests, and an holy nation." Ex. 19: 3-6.

nature, having escaped the corruption that is in the world through lust.

"And beside this, giving all diligence, add to your faith virtue; and to virtue knowledge; and to knowledge temperance; and to temperance patience; and to patience godliness; and to godliness brotherly kindness; and to brotherly kindness charity." 2 Peter 1:2-7.

If you cultivate faithfully the vineyard of your soul, God is making you a laborer together with Himself. And you will have a work to do not only for yourself, but for others. In representing the church as the vineyard, Christ does not teach that we are to restrict our sympathies and labors to our own numbers. The Lord's vineyard is to be enlarged. In all parts of the earth He desires it to be extended. As we receive the instruction and grace of God, we should impart to others a knowledge of how to care for the precious plants. Thus we may extend the vineyard of the Lord. God is watching for evidence of our faith, love, and patience. He looks to see if we are using every spiritual advantage to become skillful workers in His vineyard on earth, that we may enter the Paradise of God, that Eden home from which Adam and Eve were excluded by transgression.

God stands toward His people in the relation of a father, and He has a father's claim to our faithful service. Consider the life of Christ. Standing at the head of humanity, serving His Father, He is an example of what every son should and may be. The obedience that Christ rendered God requires from human beings today. He served His Father with love, in willingness and freedom. "I delight to do Thy will, O My God," He declared; "yea, Thy law is within My heart." Ps. 40:8. Christ counted no sacrifice too great, no toil too hard, in order to accomplish the work which He came to do. At 283 the age of twelve He said, "Wist ye not that I must be about My Father's business?" Luke 2:49. He had heard the call, and had taken up the work. "My meat," He said, "is to do the will of Him that sent Me, and to finish His work." John 4:34.

Thus we are to serve God. He only serves who acts up to the highest standard of obedience. All who would be sons and daughters of God must prove themselves co-workers with God and Christ and the heavenly angels. This is the test for every soul. Of those who faithfully serve Him the Lord says, "They shall be Mine, . . . in that day when I make up My jewels; and I will spare them, as a man spareth his own son that serveth him." Mal. 3:17.

God's great object in the working out of His providences is to try men, to give them opportunity to develop character. Thus He proves whether they are obedient or disobedient to His commands. Good works do not purchase the love of God, but they reveal that we possess that

love. If we surrender the will to God, we shall not work in order to earn God's love. His love as a free gift will be received into the soul, and from love to Him we shall delight to obey His commandments.

There are only two classes in the world today, and only two classes will be recognized in the judgment—those who violate God's law and those who obey it. Christ gives the test by which to prove our loyalty or disloyalty. "If ye love Me," He says, "keep My commandments. . . . He that hath My commandments, and keepeth them, he it is that loveth Me. And he that loveth Me shall be loved of My Father, and I will love him, and will manifest Myself to him. . . . He that loveth Me not keepeth not My sayings; and the word which ye hear is not Mine, but the Father's which sent Me." "If ye keep My commandments, ye shall abide in My love; even as I have kept My Father's commandments, and abide in His love." John 14:15-24; 15:10.

23 284

The Lord's Vineyard

The Jewish Nation

The parable of the two sons was followed by the parable of the vineyard. In the one, Christ had set before the Jewish teachers the importance of obedience. In the other, He pointed to the rich blessings bestowed upon Israel, and in these showed God's claim to their obedience. He set before them the glory of God's purpose, which through obedience they might have fulfilled. Withdrawing the veil from the future, He showed how, by failure to fulfill His purpose, the whole nation was forfeiting His blessing, and bringing ruin upon itself.

"There was a certain householder," Christ said, "which planted a vineyard, and hedged it round about, and digged a winepress in it, and built a tower, and let it out to husbandmen, and went into a far country."

A description of this vineyard is given by the prophet Isaiah: "Now will I sing to my wellbeloved a song of my beloved touching His vineyard. My wellbeloved hath a vineyard in a 285 very fruitful hill; and He fenced it, and gathered out the stones thereof, and planted it with the choicest vine, and built a tower in the midst of it, and also made a winepress therein; and He looked that it should bring forth grapes." Isa. 5:1, 2.

The husbandman chooses a piece of land from the wilderness; he fences, clears, and tills it, and plants it with choice vines, expecting a rich harvest. This plot of ground, in its superiority to the uncultivated waste, he expects to do

This chapter is based on Matthew 21:33-44.

him honor by showing the results of his care and toil in its cultivation. So God had chosen a people from the world to be trained and educated by Christ. The prophet says, "The vineyard of the Lord of hosts is the house of Israel, and the men of Judah His pleasant plant." Isa. 5:7. Upon this people God had bestowed great privileges, blessing them richly from His abundant goodness. He looked for them to honor Him by yielding fruit. They were to reveal the principles of His kingdom. In the midst of a fallen, wicked world they were to represent the character of God.

As the Lord's vineyard they were to produce fruit altogether different from that of the heathen nations. These idolatrous peoples had given themselves up to work wickedness. Violence and crime, greed, oppression, and the most corrupt practices, were indulged without restraint. Iniquity, degradation, and misery were the fruits of the corrupt tree. In marked contrast was to be the fruit borne on the vine of God's planting.

It was the privilege of the Jewish nation to represent the character of God as it had been revealed to Moses. In answer to the prayer of Moses, "Show me Thy glory," the Lord promised, "I will make all My goodness pass before thee." Ex. 33:18, 19. "And the Lord passed by before him, and proclaimed, The Lord, the Lord God, merciful and gracious, longsuffering, and abundant in goodness and truth, keeping mercy for thousands, forgiving iniquity and transgression and sin." Ex. 34:6, 7. This was the fruit that God desired from His people. In the purity of their characters, in the holiness of their lives, in their mercy and loving-kindness and compassion, they were to show that "the law of the Lord is perfect, converting the soul." Ps. 19:7.

Through the Jewish nation it was God's purpose to impart rich blessings to all peoples. Through Israel the way was to be prepared for the diffusion of His light to the whole world. The nations of the world, through following corrupt practices, had lost the knowledge of God. Yet in His mercy God did not blot them out of existence. He purposed to give them opportunity for becoming acquainted with Him through His church. He designed that the principles revealed through His people should be the means of restoring the moral image of God in man.

It was for the accomplishment of this purpose that God called Abraham out from his idolatrous kindred and bade him dwell in the land of Canaan. "I will make of thee a great nation," He said, "and I will bless thee, and make thy name great; and thou shalt be a blessing." Gen. 12:2.

The descendants of Abraham, Jacob and his posterity, were brought down to Egypt that in the midst of that great and wicked nation they might reveal the principles of God's kingdom. The integrity of Joseph and his wonderful work in preserving the lives of the whole Egyptian people were a representation of the life of Christ. Moses and many others were witnesses for God.

In bringing forth Israel from Egypt, the Lord again manifested His power and His mercy. His wonderful works in their deliverance from bondage and His dealings with them in their travels through the wilderness were not for their benefit alone. These were to be as an object lesson to the surrounding nations. The Lord revealed Himself as a God above all human authority and greatness. The signs and wonders He wrought in behalf of His people showed His power over nature and over the greatest of those who worshiped nature. God went through the proud land of Egypt as He will go through the earth in the last days. With fire and tempest, earthquake and death, the great I AM redeemed His people. He took them out of the land of bondage. He led them through the "great and terrible wilderness, wherein were fiery serpents, and scorpions, and drought." Deut. 8:15. He brought them forth water out of "the rock of flint," and fed them with "the corn of heaven." Ps. 78:24. "For," said Moses, "the Lord's portion is His people; Jacob is the lot of His inheritance. He found him in a desert land, and in the waste howling wilderness; He led him about, He instructed him, He kept him as the apple of His eye. As an eagle stirreth up her nest, fluttereth over her young, spreadeth abroad her wings, taketh them, beareth them on her wings: so the Lord alone did lead him, and there was no strange god with him." Deut. 32:9-12. Thus He brought them unto Himself, that they might dwell as under the shadow of the Most High.

Christ was the leader of the children of Israel in their wilderness wanderings. Enshrouded in the pillar of cloud by day and the pillar of fire by night, He led and guided them. He preserved them from the perils of the wilderness, He brought them into the land of promise, and in the sight of all the nations that acknowledged not God He established Israel as His own chosen possession, the Lord's vineyard.

To this people were committed the oracles of God. They were hedged about by the precepts of His law, the everlasting principles of truth, justice, and purity. Obedience to these principles was to be their protection, for it would save them from destroying themselves by sinful practices. And as the tower in the vineyard, God placed in the midst of the land His holy temple.

Christ was their instructor. As He had been with them in the wilderness, so He was still to be their teacher and guide. In the tabernacle and the temple His glory dwelt in the holy shekinah above the mercy seat. In their behalf He constantly manifested the riches of His love and patience.

God desired to make of His people Israel a praise and a glory. Every spiritual advantage was given them. God withheld from them nothing favorable to the formation of character that would make them representatives of Himself.

Their obedience to the law of God would make them marvels of prosperity before the nations of the world. He who could give them wisdom and skill in all cunning work would continue to be their teacher, and would ennoble and elevate them through obedience to His laws. If obedient, they would be preserved from the diseases that afflicted other nations, and would be blessed with vigor of intellect. The glory of God, His majesty and power, were to be revealed in all their prosperity. They were to be a kingdom of priests and princes. God furnished them with every facility for becoming the greatest nation on the earth.

In the most definite manner Christ through Moses had set before them God's purpose, and had made plain the terms of their prosperity. "Thou art an holy people unto the Lord thy God," He said; "the Lord thy God hath chosen thee to be a special people unto Himself, above all people that are upon the face of the earth. . . . Know therefore that the Lord thy God, He is God, the faithful God, which keepeth covenant and mercy with them that love Him and keep His commandments to a thousand generations. . . . Thou shalt therefore keep the commandments, and the statutes, and the judgments, which I command thee this day, to do them. Wherefore it shall come to pass, if ye hearken to these judgments, and keep, and do them, that the Lord thy God shall keep unto thee the covenant and the mercy which He sware unto thy fathers; and He will love thee, and bless thee, and multiply thee: He will also bless the fruit of thy womb, and the fruit of thy land, thy corn, and thy wine, and thine oil, the increase of thy kine, and the flocks of thy sheep, in the land which He sware unto thy fathers to give thee. Thou shalt be blessed above all people. . . . And the Lord will take away from thee all sickness, and will put none of the evil diseases of Egypt, which thou knowest, upon thee." Deut. 7:6, 9, 11-15.

If they would keep His commandments, God promised to give them the finest of the wheat, and bring them honey out of the rock. With long life would He satisfy them, and show them His salvation.

Through disobedience to God, Adam and Eve had lost Eden, and because of sin the whole earth was cursed. But if God's people followed His instruction, their land would be restored to fertility and beauty. God Himself gave them directions in regard to the culture of the soil, and they were to co-operate with Him in its restoration. Thus the whole land, under God's control, would become an object lesson of spiritual truth. As in obedience to His natural laws the earth should produce its treasures, so in obedience to His moral law the hearts of the people were to reflect the attributes of His character. Even the heathen would recognize the superiority of those who served and worshiped the living God.

"Behold," said Moses, "I have taught you statutes and judgments, even as the Lord my God commanded me, that ye should do so in the land whither ye go to possess it. Keep therefore and do them; for this is your wisdom and your understanding in the sight of the nations, which shall hear all these statutes, and say, Surely this great nation is a wise and understanding people. For what nation is there so great, who hath God so nigh unto them, as the Lord our God is in all things that we call upon Him for? And what nation is there so great, that hath statutes and judgments so righteous as all this law, which I set before you this day?" Deut. 4:5-8.

The children of Israel were to occupy all the territory which God appointed them. Those nations that rejected the worship and service of the true God were to be dispossessed. But it was God's purpose that by the revelation of His character through Israel men should be drawn unto Him. To all the world the gospel invitation was to be given. Through the teaching of the sacrificial service Christ was to be uplifted before the nations, and all who would look unto Him should live. All who, like Rahab the Canaanite, and Ruth the Moabitess, turned from idolatry to the worship of the true God, were to unite themselves with His chosen people. As the numbers of Israel increased they were to enlarge their borders, until their kingdom should embrace the world.

God desired to bring all peoples under His merciful rule. He desired that the earth should be filled with joy and peace. He created man for happiness, and He longs to fill human hearts with the peace of heaven. He desires that the families below shall be a symbol of the great family above.

But Israel did not fulfill God's purpose. The Lord declared, "I had planted thee a noble vine, wholly a right seed: how then art thou turned into the degenerate plant of a strange vine unto Me?" Jer. 2:21. "Israel is an empty vine, he bringeth forth fruit unto himself." Hosea 10:1. "And now, O inhabitants of Jerusalem, and men of Judah, judge, I pray you, betwixt Me and My vineyard. What could have been done more to My vineyard, that I have not done in it? Wherefore when I looked that it should bring forth grapes, brought it forth wild grapes? And now go to; I will tell you what I will do to My vineyard: I will take away the hedge thereof, and it shall be eaten up; and break down the wall thereof, and it shall be trodden down: and I will lay it waste; it shall not be pruned nor digged; but there shall come up briers and thorns: I will also command the clouds that they rain no rain upon it. For . . . He looked for judgment, but behold oppression; for righteousness, but behold a cry." Isa. 5:3-7.

The Lord had through Moses set before His people the result of unfaithfulness. By refusing to keep His covenant, they would cut themselves off from the life of God, and His blessing could not come upon them. "Beware," said Moses, "that thou forget not the Lord thy God, in not keeping His commandments, and His judgments, and His statutes, which I command thee this day: lest when thou hast eaten and art full, and hast built goodly houses, and dwelt therein; and when thy herds and thy flocks multiply, and thy silver and thy gold is multiplied, and all that thou hast is multiplied; then thine heart be lifted up, and thou forget the Lord thy God. . . . And thou say in thine heart, My power and the might of mine hand hath gotten me this wealth. . . . And it shall be, if thou do at all forget the Lord thy God, and walk after other gods, and serve them, and worship them, I testify against you this day that ye shall surely perish. As the nations which the Lord destroyeth before your face, so shall ye perish; because ye would not be obedient unto the voice of the Lord your God." Deut. 8:11-14, 17, 19, 20.

The warning was not heeded by the Jewish people. They forgot God, and lost sight of their high privilege as His representatives. The blessings they had received brought no blessing to the world. All their advantages were appropriated for their own glorification. They robbed God of the service He required of them, and they robbed their fellow men of religious guidance and a holy example. Like the inhabitants of the antediluvian world, they followed out every imagination of their evil hearts. Thus they made sacred things appear a farce, saying, "The temple of the Lord, the temple of the Lord, are these" (Jer. 7:4), while at the same time they were misrepresenting God's character, dishonoring His name, and polluting His sanctuary.

The husbandmen who had been placed in charge of the Lord's vineyard were untrue to their trust. The priests and teachers were not faithful instructors of the people. They did not keep before them the goodness and mercy of God and His claim to their love and service. These husbandmen sought their own glory. They desired to appropriate the fruits of the vineyard. It was their study to attract attention and homage to themselves.

The guilt of these leaders in Israel was not like the guilt of the ordinary sinner. These men stood under the most solemn obligation to God. They had pledged themselves to teach a "Thus saith the Lord" and to bring strict obedience into their practical life. Instead of doing this they

were perverting the Scriptures. They laid heavy burdens upon men, enforcing ceremonies that reached to every step in life. The people lived in continual unrest, for they could not fulfill the requirements laid down by the rabbis. As they saw the impossibility of keeping man-made commandments, they became careless in regard to the commandments of God.

The Lord had instructed His people that He was the owner of the vineyard, and that all their possessions were given them in trust to be used for Him. But the priests and teachers did not perform the work of their sacred office as if they were handling the property of God. They were systematically robbing Him of the means and facilities entrusted to them for the advancement of His work. Their covetousness and greed caused them to be despised even by the heathen. Thus the Gentile world was given occasion to misinterpret the character of God and the laws of His kingdom.

With a father's heart, God bore with His people. He pleaded with them by mercies given and mercies withdrawn. Patiently He set their sins before them, and in forbearance waited for their acknowledgment. Prophets and messengers were sent to urge God's claim upon the husbandmen; but instead of being welcomed, they were treated as enemies. The husbandmen persecuted and killed them. God sent still other messengers, but they received the same treatment as the first, only that the husbandmen showed still more determined hatred.

As a last resource, God sent His Son, saying, "They will reverence My Son." But their resistance had made them vindictive, and they said among themselves, "This is the heir; come, let us kill Him, and let us seize on His inheritance." We shall then be left to enjoy the vineyard, and to do as we please with the fruit.

The Jewish rulers did not love God; therefore they cut themselves away from Him, and rejected all His overtures for a just settlement. Christ, the Beloved of God, came to assert the claims of the Owner of the vineyard; but the husbandmen treated Him with marked contempt, saying, We will not have this man to rule over us. They envied Christ's beauty of character. His manner of teaching was far superior to theirs, and they dreaded His success. He remonstrated with them, unveiling their hypocrisy, and showing them the sure results of their course of action. This stirred them to madness. They smarted under the rebukes they could not silence. They hated the high standard of righteousness which Christ continually presented. They saw that His teaching was placing them where their selfishness would be uncloaked, and they determined to kill Him. They hated His example of truthfulness and piety and the elevated spirituality revealed in all He did. His whole life was a reproof to their selfishness, and when the final test came, the test which meant obedience unto eternal life or disobedience unto eternal death, they rejected the Holy One of Israel. When they were asked to choose between Christ and Barabbas, they cried out, "Release unto us Barabbas!" Luke 23:18. And when Pilate asked, "What shall I do then with Jesus?" they cried fiercely, "Let Him be crucified." Matt. 27:22. "Shall I crucify your King?" Pilate asked, and from the priests and rulers came the answer, "We have no king but Caesar." John 19:15. When Pilate washed his hands, saying, "I am innocent of the blood of this just person," the priests joined with the ignorant mob in declaring passionately, "His blood be on us, and on our children." Matt. 27:24, 25.

Thus the Jewish leaders made their choice. Their decision was registered in the book which John saw in the hand of Him that sat upon the throne, the book which no man could open. In all its vindictiveness this decision will appear before them in the day when this book is unsealed by the Lion of the tribe of Judah.

The Jewish people cherished the idea that they were the favorites of heaven, and that they were always to be exalted as the church of God. They were the children of Abraham, they declared, and so firm did the foundation of their prosperity seem to them that they defied earth and heaven to dispossess them of their rights. But by lives of unfaithfulness they were preparing for the condemnation of heaven and for separation from God.

295 In the parable of the vineyard, after Christ had portrayed before the priests their crowning act of wickedness, He put to them the question, "When the Lord therefore of the vineyard cometh, what will he do unto those husbandmen?" The priests had been following the narrative with deep interest, and without considering the relation of the subject to themselves they joined with the people in answering, "He will miserably destroy those wicked men, and will let out His vineyard unto other husbandmen, which shall render Him the fruits in their seasons."

Unwittingly they had pronounced their own doom. Jesus looked upon them, and under His searching gaze they knew that He read the secrets of their hearts. His divinity flashed out before them with unmistakable power. They saw in the husbandmen a picture of themselves, and they involuntarily exclaimed, "God forbid!"

Solemnly and regretfully Christ asked, "Did ye never read in the scriptures, The stone which the builders rejected, the same is become the head of the corner; this is the Lord's doing, and it is marvelous in our eyes? Therefore say I unto you, The kingdom of God shall be taken from you, and given to a nation bringing forth the fruits thereof. And whosoever shall fall on this stone shall be broken; but on whomsoever it shall fall, it will grind him to powder."

Christ would have averted the doom of the Jewish nation if the people had received Him. But envy and jealousy made them implacable. They determined that they would not receive Jesus of Nazareth as the Messiah. They rejected the Light of the world, and thenceforth their lives were surrounded with darkness as the darkness of midnight. The doom foretold came upon the Jewish nation. Their own fierce passions, uncontrolled, wrought their ruin. In their blind rage they destroyed one another. Their rebellious, stubborn pride brought upon them 296 the wrath of their Roman conquerors. Jerusalem was destroyed, the temple laid in ruins, and its site plowed like a field. The children of Judah perished by the most horrible forms of death. Millions were sold, to serve as bondmen in heathen lands.

As a people the Jews had failed of fulfilling God's purpose, and the vineyard was taken from them. The privileges they had abused, the work they had slighted, was entrusted to others.

The Church of Today

The parable of the vineyard applies not alone to the Jewish nation. It has a lesson for us. The church in this generation has been endowed by God with great privileges and blessings, and He expects corresponding returns.

We have been redeemed by a costly ransom. Only by the greatness of this ransom can we conceive of its results. On this earth, the earth whose soil has been moistened by the tears and blood of the Son of God, are to be brought forth the precious fruits of Paradise. In the lives of God's people the truths of His word are to reveal their glory and excellence. Through His people Christ is to manifest His character and the principles of His kingdom.

Satan seeks to counterwork the work of God, and he is constantly urging men to accept his principles. He represents the chosen people of God as a deluded people. He is an accuser of the brethren, and his accusing power is employed against those who work righteousness. The Lord desires through His people to answer Satan's charges by showing the results of obedience to right principles.

These principles are to be manifest in the individual Christian, in the family, in the church, and in every institution established for God's service. All are to be symbols of what 297 can be done for the world. They are to be types of the saving power of the truths of the gospel. All are agencies in the fulfillment of God's great purpose for the human race.

The Jewish leaders looked with pride upon their magnificent temple, and the imposing rites of their religious service; but justice, mercy, and the love of God were lacking. The glory of the temple, the splendor of their service, could not recommend them to God; for that which alone is of value in His sight they did not offer. They did not bring Him the sacrifice of a humble and contrite spirit. It is when the vital principles of the kingdom of God are lost that ceremonies become multitudinous and extravagant. It is when the character building is neglected, when the adornment of the soul is lacking, when the simplicity of godliness is lost sight of, that pride and love of display demand magnificent church edifices, splendid adornings, and imposing ceremonials. In all this God is not honored. A fashionable religion that consists of ceremonies, pretense, and display, is not acceptable to Him. Its services call forth no response from the heavenly messengers.

The church is very precious in God's sight. He values it, not for its external advantages, but for the sincere piety which distinguishes it from the world. He estimates it according to the growth of the members in the knowledge of Christ, according to their progress in spiritual experience.

Christ hungers to receive from His vineyard the fruit of holiness and unselfishness. He looks for the principles of love and goodness. Not all the beauty of art can bear comparison with the beauty of temper and character to be revealed in those who are Christ's representatives. It is the atmosphere of grace which surrounds the soul of the believer, the Holy Spirit working upon mind and heart, that makes him a savor of life unto life, and enables God to bless his work.

A congregation may be the poorest in the land. It may be without the attraction of any outward show; but if the members possess the principles of the character of Christ, they will have His joy in their souls. Angels will unite with them in their worship. The praise and thanksgiving from grateful hearts will ascend to God as a sweet oblation.

The Lord desires us to make mention of His goodness and tell of His power. He is honored by the expression of praise and thanksgiving. He says, "Whoso offereth praise glorifieth Me." Ps. 50:23. The people of Israel, as they journeyed through the wilderness, praised God in sacred song. The commandments and promises of the Lord were set to music, and all along the journey these were sung by the pilgrim travelers. And in Canaan as they met at their sacred feasts God's wonderful works were to be recounted, and grateful thanksgiving was to be offered to His name. God desired that the whole life of His people should be a life of praise. Thus His way was to be made "known upon earth," His "saving health among all nations." Ps. 67:2.

So it should be now. The people of the world are worshiping false gods. They are to be turned from their false worship, not by hearing denunciation of their idols, but by beholding something better. God's goodness is to be made known. "Ye are My witnesses, saith the Lord, that I am God." Isa. 43:12.

The Lord desires us to appreciate the great plan of redemption, to realize our high privilege as the children of God, and to walk before Him in obedience, with grateful thanksgiving. He desires us to serve Him in newness of life, with gladness every day. He longs to see gratitude welling up in our hearts because our names are written in the Lamb's book of life, because we may cast all our care upon Him who cares for us. He bids us rejoice because we are the heritage of the Lord, because the righteousness of Christ is the white robe of His saints, because we have the blessed hope of the soon coming of our Saviour.

To praise God in fullness and sincerity of heart is as much a duty as is prayer. We are to show to the world and to all the heavenly intelligences that we appreciate the wonderful love of God for fallen humanity and that we are expecting larger and yet larger blessings from His infinite fullness. Far more than we do, we need to speak of the precious chapters in our experience. After a special outpouring of the Holy Spirit, our joy in the Lord and our efficiency in His service would be greatly increased by recounting His goodness and His wonderful works in behalf of His children.

These exercises drive back the power of Satan. They expel the spirit of murmuring and complaint, and the tempter loses ground. They cultivate those attributes of character which will fit the dwellers on earth for the heavenly mansions.

Such a testimony will have an influence upon others. No more effective means can be employed for winning souls to Christ.

We are to praise God by tangible service, by doing all in our power to advance the glory of His name. God imparts His gifts to us that we also may give, and thus make known His character to the world. Under the Jewish economy, gifts and offerings formed an essential part of God's worship. The Israelites were taught to devote a tithe of all their income to the service of the sanctuary. Besides this they were to bring sin offerings, free-will gifts, and offerings of gratitude. These were the means for supporting the ministry of the gospel for that time. God expects no less from us than He expected from His people anciently. The great work for the salvation of souls must be carried forward. In the tithe, with gifts and offerings, He has made provision for this work. Thus He intends that the ministry of the gospel shall be sustained. He claims the tithe as His own, and it should ever be regarded as a sacred reserve, to be placed in His treasury for the benefit of His cause. He asks also for our free-will gifts and offerings of gratitude. All are to be devoted to the sending of the gospel unto the uttermost parts of the earth.

Service to God includes personal ministry. By personal effort we are to co-operate with Him for the saving of the world. Christ's commission, "Go ye into all the world, and preach the gospel to every creature," is spoken to every one of His followers. (Mark 16:15.) All who are ordained unto the life of Christ are ordained to work for the salvation of their fellow men. Their hearts will throb in unison with the heart of Christ. The same longing for souls that He has felt will be manifest in them. Not all can fill the same place in the work, but there is a place and a work for all.

In ancient times, Abraham, Isaac, Jacob, Moses with his meekness and wisdom, and Joshua with his varied capabilities, were all enlisted in God's service. The music of Miriam, the courage and piety of Deborah, the filial affection of Ruth, the obedience and faithfulness of Samuel, the stern fidelity of Elijah, the softening, subduing influence of Elisha—all were needed. So now all upon whom God's blessing has been bestowed are to respond by actual service; every gift is to be employed for the advancement of His kingdom and the glory of His name.

All who receive Christ as a personal Saviour are to demonstrate the truth of the gospel and its saving power upon the life. God makes no requirement without making provision for its fulfillment. Through the grace of Christ we may accomplish everything that God requires. All the riches of heaven are to be revealed through God's people. "Herein is My Father glorified," Christ says, "that ye bear much fruit; so shall ye be My disciples." John 15:8.

God claims the whole earth as His vineyard. Though now in the hands of the usurper, it belongs to God. By redemption no less than by creation it is His. For the world Christ's sacrifice was made. "God so loved the world, that He gave His only begotten Son." John 3:16. It is through that one gift that every other is imparted to men. Daily the whole world receives blessing from God. Every drop of rain, every ray of light shed on our unthankful race, every leaf and flower and fruit, testifies to God's long forbearance and His great love.

And what returns are made to the great Giver? How are men treating the claims of God? To whom are the masses of mankind giving the service of their lives? They are serving mammon. Wealth, position, pleasure in the world, is their aim. Wealth is gained by robbery, not of man only, but of God. Men are using His gifts to gratify their selfishness. Everything they can grasp is made to minister to their greed and their love of selfish pleasure.

The sin of the world today is the sin that brought destruction upon Israel. Ingratitude to God, the neglect of opportunities and blessings, the selfish appropriation of God's gifts—these were comprised in the sin that brought wrath upon Israel. They are bringing ruin upon the world today.

The tears which Christ shed upon Olivet as He stood overlooking the chosen city were not for Jerusalem alone. In the fate of Jerusalem He beheld the destruction of the world.

"If thou hadst known, even thou, at least in this thy day, the things which belong unto thy peace! but now they are hid from thine eyes." Luke 19:42.

"In this thy day." The day is nearing its close. The period of mercy and privilege is well-nigh ended. The clouds of vengeance are gathering. The rejecters of God's grace are about to be involved in swift and irretrievable ruin.

Yet the world is asleep. The people know not the time of their visitation.

In this crisis, where is the church to be found? Are its members meeting the claims of God? Are they fulfilling His commission, and representing His character to the world? Are they urging upon the attention of their fellow men the last merciful message of warning?

Men are in peril. Multitudes are perishing. But how few of the professed followers of Christ are burdened for these souls. The destiny of a world hangs in the balance; but this hardly moves even those who claim to believe the most far-reaching truth ever given to mortals. There is a lack of that love which led Christ to leave His heavenly home and take man's nature that humanity might touch humanity and draw humanity to divinity. There is a stupor, a paralysis, upon the people of God, which prevents them from understanding the duty of the hour.

When the Israelites entered Canaan, they did not fulfill God's purpose by taking possession of the whole land. After making a partial conquest, they settled down to enjoy the fruit of their victories. In their unbelief and love of ease, they congregated in the portions already conquered instead of pushing forward to occupy new territory. Thus they began to depart from God. By their failure to carry out His purpose, they made it impossible for Him to fulfill to them His promise of blessing. Is not the church of today doing the same thing? With the whole world before them in need of the gospel, professed Christians congregate where they themselves can enjoy gospel privileges. They do not feel the necessity of occupying new territory, carrying the message of salvation into regions beyond. They refuse to fulfill Christ's commission, "Go ye into all the world, and preach the gospel to every creature." Mark 16:15. Are they less guilty than was the Jewish church?

The professed followers of Christ are on trial before the heavenly universe; but the coldness of their zeal and the feebleness of their efforts in

God's service mark them as unfaithful. If what they are doing were the best they could do, condemnation would not rest upon them; but were their hearts enlisted in the work, they could do much more. They know and the world knows that they have to a great degree lost the spirit of self-denial and cross bearing. Many there are against whose names will be found written in the books of heaven, Not producers, but consumers. By many who bear Christ's name, His glory is obscured, His beauty veiled, His honor withheld.

There are many whose names are on the church books, but who are not under Christ's rule. They are not heeding His instruction or doing His work. Therefore they are under the control of the enemy. They are doing no positive good; therefore they are doing incalculable harm. Because their influence is not a savor of life unto life, it is a savor of death unto death.

The Lord says, "Shall I not visit for these things?" Jer. 5:9. Because they failed of fulfilling God's purpose, the children of Israel were set aside, and God's call was extended to other peoples. If these too prove unfaithful, will they not in like manner be rejected?

In the parable of the vineyard it was the husbandmen whom Christ pronounced guilty. It was they who had refused to return to their lord the fruit of his ground. In the Jewish nation it was the priests and teachers who, by misleading the people, had robbed God of the service which He claimed. It was they who turned the nation away from Christ.

The law of God unmixed with human tradition was presented by Christ as the great standard of obedience. This aroused the enmity of the rabbis. They had set human teaching above God's word, and had turned the people away from His precepts. They would not give up their man-made commandments in order to obey the requirements of the word of God. They would not, for the truth's sake, sacrifice the pride of reason and the praise of men. When Christ came, presenting to the nation the claims of God, the priests and elders denied His right to interpose between them and the people. They would not accept His rebukes and warnings, and they set themselves to turn the people against Him and to compass His destruction.

For the rejection of Christ, with the results that followed, they were responsible. A nation's sin and a nation's ruin were due to the religious leaders.

In our day are not the same influences at work? Of the husbandmen of the Lord's vineyard are not many following in the steps of the Jewish leaders? Are not religious teachers turning men away from the plain requirements of the word of God? Instead of educating them in obedience to God's law, are they not educating them in transgression? From many of the pulpits of the churches the people are taught that the law of God is not binding upon them. Human traditions, ordinances, and customs are exalted. Pride and self-satisfaction because of the gifts of God are fostered, while the claims of God are ignored.

In setting aside the law of God, men know not what they are doing. God's law is the transcript of His character. It embodies the principles of His kingdom. He who refuses to accept these principles is placing himself outside the channel where God's blessings flow.

The glorious possibilities set before Israel could be realized only through obedience to God's commandments. The same elevation of character, the same fulness of blessing—blessing on mind and soul and body, blessing on house and field, blessing for this life and for the life to come—is possible for us only through obedience.

In the spiritual as in the natural world, obedience to the laws of God is the condition of fruit bearing. And when men teach the people to disregard God's commandments, they are preventing them from bearing fruit to His glory. They are guilty of withholding from the Lord the fruits of His vineyard.

To us God's messengers come at the bidding of the Master. They come demanding, as did Christ, obedience to the word of God. They present His claim to the fruits of the vineyard, the fruits of love, and humility, and self-sacrificing service. Like the Jewish leaders, are not many of the husbandmen of the vineyard stirred to anger? When the claim of God's law is set before the people, do not these teachers use their influence in leading men to reject it? Such teachers God calls unfaithful servants.

The words of God to ancient Israel have a solemn warning to the church and its leaders today. Of Israel the Lord said, "I have written to him the great things of My law; but they were counted as a strange thing." Hosea 8:12. And to the priests and teachers He declared, "My people are destroyed for lack of knowledge; because thou hast rejected knowledge, I will also reject thee; . . . seeing thou hast forgotten the law of thy God, I will also forget thy children." Hosea 4:6.

Shall the warnings from God be passed by unheeded? Shall the opportunities for service be unimproved? Shall the world's scorn, the pride of reason, conformity to human customs and traditions, hold the professed followers of Christ from service to Him? Will they reject God's word as the Jewish leaders rejected Christ? The result of Israel's sin is before us. Will the church of today take warning?

"If some of the branches be broken off, and thou, being a wild olive tree, wert graffed in among them, and with them partakest of the root and fatness of the olive tree; boast not. . . .

Because of unbelief they were broken off, and thou standest by faith. Be not highminded, but fear; for if God spared not the natural branches, take heed lest He also spare not thee." Rom. 11:17-21.

307

24

Without a Wedding Garment

The parable of the wedding garment opens before us a lesson of the highest consequence. By the marriage is represented the union of humanity with divinity; the wedding garment represents the character which all must possess who shall be accounted fit guests for the wedding.

In this parable, as in that of the great supper, are illustrated the gospel invitation, its rejection by the Jewish people, and the call of mercy to the Gentiles. But on the part of those who reject the invitation, this parable brings to view a deeper insult and a more dreadful punishment. The call to the feast is a king's invitation. It proceeds from one who is vested with power to command. It confers high honor. Yet the honor is unappreciated. The king's authority is despised. While the householder's invitation was regarded with indifference, the king's is met with insult and murder. They treated his servants with scorn, despitefully using them and slaying them.

The householder, on seeing his invitation slighted, declared that none of the men who were bidden should taste of his supper. But for
308   those who had done despite to the king, more than exclusion from his presence and his table is decreed. "He sent forth his armies, and destroyed those murderers, and burned up their city."

In both parables the feast is provided with guests, but the second shows that there is a preparation to be made by all who attend the feast. Those who neglect this preparation are cast out. "The king came in to see the guests," and "saw there a man which had not on a wedding garment; and he saith unto him, Friend, how camest thou in hither not having a wedding garment? And he was speechless. Then said the king to the servants, Bind him hand and foot, and take him away, and cast him into outer darkness; there shall be weeping and gnashing of teeth."

The call to the feast had been given by Christ's disciples. Our Lord had sent out the twelve and afterward the seventy, proclaiming that the kingdom of God was at hand, and calling upon men to repent and believe the gospel. But the call was not heeded. Those who were bidden to the feast did not come. The servants were sent out later to say, "Behold, I have pre-

pared my dinner; my oxen and my fatlings are killed, and all things are ready: come unto the marriage." This was the message borne to the Jewish nation after the crucifixion of Christ; but the nation that claimed to be God's peculiar people rejected the gospel brought to them in the power of the Holy Spirit. Many did this in the most scornful manner. Others were so exasperated by the offer of salvation, the offer of pardon for rejecting the Lord of glory, that they turned upon the bearers of the message. There was "a great persecution." Acts 8:1. Many both of men and women were thrust into prison, and some of the Lord's messengers, as Stephen and James, were put to death.

Thus the Jewish people sealed their rejection of God's mercy. The result was foretold by 309 Christ in the parable. The king "sent forth his armies, and destroyed those murderers, and burned up their city." The judgment pronounced came upon the Jews in the destruction of Jerusalem and the scattering of the nation.

The third call to the feast represents the giving of the gospel to the Gentiles. The king said, "The wedding is ready, but they which were bidden were not worthy. Go ye therefore into the highways, and as many as ye shall find, bid to the marriage."

The king's servants who went out into the highways "gathered together all as many as they found, both bad and good." It was a mixed company. Some of them had no more real regard for the giver of the feast than had the ones who rejected the call. The class first bidden could not afford, they thought, to sacrifice any worldly advantage for the sake of attending the king's banquet. And of those who accepted the invitation, there were some who thought only of benefiting themselves. They came to share the provisions of the feast, but had no desire to honor the king.

When the king came in to view the guests, the real character of all was revealed. For every guest at the feast there had been provided a wedding garment. This garment was a gift from the king. By wearing it the guests showed their respect for the giver of the feast. But one man was clothed in his common citizen dress. He had refused to make the preparation required by the king. The garment provided for him at great cost he disdained to wear. Thus he insulted his lord. To the king's demand, "How camest thou in hither not having a wedding garment?" he could answer nothing. He was self-condemned. Then the king said, "Bind him hand and foot, and take him away, and cast him into outer darkness."

By the king's examination of the guests at the 310 feast is represented a work of judgment. The guests at the gospel feast are those who profess to serve God, those whose names are written in the book of life. But not all who profess to be

This chapter is based on Matthew 22:1-14.

Christians are true disciples. Before the final reward is given, it must be decided who are fitted to share the inheritance of the righteous. This decision must be made prior to the second coming of Christ in the clouds of heaven; for when He comes, His reward is with Him, "to give every man according as his work shall be." Rev. 22:12. Before His coming, then, the character of every man's work will have been determined, and to every one of Christ's followers the reward will have been apportioned according to his deeds.

It is while men are still dwelling upon the earth that the work of investigative judgment takes place in the courts of heaven. The lives of all His professed followers pass in review before God. All are examined according to the record of the books of heaven, and according to his deeds the destiny of each is forever fixed.

By the wedding garment in the parable is represented the pure, spotless character which Christ's true followers will possess. To the church it is given "that she should be arrayed in fine linen, clean and white," "not having spot, or wrinkle, or any such thing." Eph. 5:27. The fine linen, says the Scripture, "is the righteousness of saints." Rev. 19:8. It is the righteousness of Christ, His own unblemished character, that through faith is imparted to all who receive Him as their personal Saviour.

The white robe of innocence was worn by our first parents when they were placed by God in holy Eden. They lived in perfect conformity to the will of God. All the strength of their affections was given to their heavenly Father. A beautiful soft light, the light of God, enshrouded 311 the holy pair. This robe of light was a symbol of their spiritual garments of heavenly innocence. Had they remained true to God it would ever have continued to enshroud them. But when sin entered, they severed their connection with God, and the light that had encircled them departed. Naked and ashamed, they tried to supply the place of the heavenly garments by sewing together fig leaves for a covering.

This is what the transgressors of God's law have done ever since the day of Adam and Eve's disobedience. They have sewed together fig leaves to cover the nakedness caused by transgression. They have worn the garments of their own devising, by works of their own they have tried to cover their sins, and make themselves acceptable with God.

But this they can never do. Nothing can man devise to supply the place of his lost robe of innocence. No fig-leaf garment, no worldly citizen dress, can be worn by those who sit down with Christ and angels at the marriage supper of the Lamb.

Only the covering which Christ Himself has provided can make us meet to appear in God's presence. This covering, the robe of His own righteousness, Christ will put upon every repenting, believing soul. "I counsel thee," He says, "to buy of Me . . . white raiment, that thou mayest be clothed, and that the shame of thy nakedness do not appear." Rev. 3:18.

This robe, woven in the loom of heaven, has in it not one thread of human devising. Christ in His humanity wrought out a perfect character, and this character He offers to impart to us. "All our righteousnesses are as filthy rags." Isa. 64:6. Everything that we of ourselves can do is defiled by sin. But the Son of God "was manifested to take away our sins; and in Him is no sin." Sin is defined to be "the transgression of the law." 1 John 3:5, 4. But Christ was obedient 312 to every requirement of the law. He said of Himself, "I delight to do Thy will, O My God; yea, Thy law is within My heart." Ps. 40:8. When on earth, He said to His disciples, "I have kept My Father's commandments." John 15:10. By His perfect obedience He has made it possible for every human being to obey God's commandments. When we submit ourselves to Christ, the heart is united with His heart, the will is merged in His will, the mind becomes one with His mind, the thoughts are brought into captivity to Him; we live His life. This is what it means to be clothed with the garment of His righteousness. Then as the Lord looks upon us He sees, not the fig-leaf garment, not the nakedness and deformity of sin, but His own robe of righteousness, which is perfect obedience to the law of Jehovah.

The guests at the marriage feast were inspected by the king. Only those were accepted who had obeyed his requirements and put on the wedding garment. So it is with the guests at the gospel feast. All must pass the scrutiny of the great King, and only those are received who have put on the robe of Christ's righteousness.

Righteousness is right doing, and it is by their deeds that all will be judged. Our characters are revealed by what we do. The works show whether the faith is genuine.

It is not enough for us to believe that Jesus is not an impostor, and that the religion of the Bible is no cunningly devised fable. We may believe that the name of Jesus is the only name under heaven whereby man may be saved, and yet we may not through faith make Him our personal Saviour. It is not enough to believe the theory of truth. It is not enough to make a profession of faith in Christ and have our names registered on the church roll. "He that keepeth His commandments dwelleth in Him, and He in him. And hereby we know that He abideth in us, by the Spirit which He hath given us." "Hereby we do know that we know Him if we keep His 313 commandments." 1 John 3:24; 2:3. This is the genuine evidence of conversion. Whatever our profession, it amounts to nothing unless Christ is revealed in works of righteousness.

314   The truth is to be planted in the heart. It is to control the mind and regulate the affections. The whole character must be stamped with the divine utterances. Every jot and tittle of the word of God is to be brought into the daily practice.

He who becomes a partaker of the divine nature will be in harmony with God's great standard of righteousness, His holy law. This is the rule by which God measures the actions of men. This will be the test of character in the judgment.

There are many who claim that by the death of Christ the law was abrogated; but in this they contradict Christ's own words, "Think not that I am come to destroy the law, or the prophets. . . . Till heaven and earth pass, one jot or one tittle shall in no wise pass from the law." Matt. 5:17, 18. It was to atone for man's transgression of the law that Christ laid down His life. Could the law have been changed or set aside, then Christ need not have died. By His life on earth He honored the law of God. By His death He established it. He gave His life as a sacrifice, not to destroy God's law, not to create a lower standard, but that justice might be maintained, that the law might be shown to be immutable, that it might stand fast forever.

Satan had claimed that it was impossible for man to obey God's commandments; and in our own strength it is true that we cannot obey them. But Christ came in the form of humanity, and by His perfect obedience He proved that humanity and divinity combined can obey every one of God's precepts.

"As many as received Him, to them gave He power to become the sons of God, even to them that believe on His name." John 1:12. This power is not in the human agent. It is the power of God. When a soul receives Christ, he receives power to live the life of Christ.

315   God requires perfection of His children. His law is a transcript of His own character, and it is the standard of all character. This infinite standard is presented to all that there may be no mistake in regard to the kind of people whom God will have to compose His kingdom. The life of Christ on earth was a perfect expression of God's law, and when those who claim to be children of God become Christlike in character, they will be obedient to God's commandments. Then the Lord can trust them to be of the number who shall compose the family of heaven. Clothed in the glorious apparel of Christ's righteousness, they have a place at the King's feast. They have a right to join the blood-washed throng.

The man who came to the feast without a wedding garment represents the condition of many in our world today. They profess to be Christians, and lay claim to the blessings and privileges of the gospel; yet they feel no need of a transformation of character. They have never felt true repentance for sin. They do not realize their need of Christ or exercise faith in Him. They have not overcome their hereditary or cultivated tendencies to wrongdoing. Yet they think that they are good enough in themselves, and they rest upon their own merits instead of trusting in Christ. Hearers of the word, they come to the banquet, but they have not put on the robe of Christ's righteousness.

Many who call themselves Christians are mere human moralists. They have refused the gift which alone could enable them to honor Christ by representing Him to the world. The work of the Holy Spirit is to them a strange work. They are not doers of the word. The heavenly principles that distinguish those who are one with Christ from those who are one with the world have become almost indistinguishable. The professed followers of Christ are no longer 316 a separate and peculiar people. The line of demarcation is indistinct. The people are subordinating themselves to the world, to its practices, its customs, its selfishness. The church has gone over to the world in transgression of the law, when the world should have come over to the church in obedience to the law. Daily the church is being converted to the world.

All these expect to be saved by Christ's death, while they refuse to live His self-sacrificing life. They extol the riches of free grace, and attempt to cover themselves with an appearance of righteousness, hoping to screen their defects of character; but their efforts will be of no avail in the day of God.

The righteousness of Christ will not cover one cherished sin. A man may be a law-breaker in heart; yet if he commits no outward act of transgression, he may be regarded by the world as possessing great integrity. But God's law looks into the secrets of the heart. Every act is judged by the motives that prompt it. Only that which is in accord with the principles of God's law will stand in the judgment.

God is love. He has shown that love in the gift of Christ. When "He gave His only begotten Son, that whosoever believeth in Him should not perish, but have everlasting life," He withheld nothing from His purchased possession. (John 3:16.) He gave all heaven, from which we may draw strength and efficiency, that we be not repulsed or overcome by our great adversary. But the love of God does not lead Him to excuse sin. He did not excuse it in Satan; He did not excuse it in Adam or in Cain; nor will He excuse it in any other of the children of men. He will not connive at our sins or overlook our defects of character. He expects us to overcome in His name.

Those who reject the gift of Christ's righteousness are rejecting the attributes of character 31 which would constitute them the sons and daughters of God. They are rejecting that which alone could give them a fitness for a place at the marriage feast.

In the parable, when the king inquired, "How camest thou in hither not having a wedding garment?" the man was speechless. So it will be in the great judgment day. Men may now excuse their defects of character, but in that day they will offer no excuse.

The professed churches of Christ in this generation are exalted to the highest privileges. The Lord has been revealed to us in ever-increasing light. Our privileges are far greater than were the privileges of God's ancient people. We have not only the great light committed to Israel, but we have the increased evidence of the great salvation brought to us through Christ. That which was type and symbol to the Jews is reality to us. They had the Old Testament history; we have that and the New Testament also. We have the assurance of a Saviour who has come, a Saviour who has been crucified, who has risen, and over the rent sepulcher of Joseph has proclaimed, "I am the resurrection and the life." In our knowledge of Christ and His love the kingdom of God is placed in the midst of us. Christ is revealed to us in sermons and chanted to us in songs. The spiritual banquet is set before us in rich abundance. The wedding garment, provided at infinite cost, is freely offered to every soul. By the messengers of God are presented to us the righteousness of Christ, justification by faith, the exceeding great and precious promises of God's word, free access to the Father by Christ, the comfort of the Spirit, the well-grounded assurance of eternal life in the kingdom of God. What could God do for us that He has not done in providing the great supper, the heavenly banquet?

318 In heaven it is said by the ministering angels: The ministry which we have been commissioned to perform we have done. We pressed back the army of evil angels. We sent brightness and light into the souls of men, quickening their memory of the love of God expressed in Jesus. We attracted their eyes to the cross of Christ. Their hearts were deeply moved by a sense of the sin that crucified the Son of God. They were convicted. They saw the steps to be taken in conversion; they felt the power of the gospel; their hearts were made tender as they saw the sweetness of the love of God. They beheld the beauty of the character of Christ. But with the many it was all in vain. They would not surrender their own habits and character. They would not put off the garments of earth in order to be clothed with the robe of heaven. Their hearts were given to covetousness. They loved the associations of the world more than they loved their God.

Solemn will be the day of final decision. In prophetic vision the apostle John describes it: "I saw a great white throne, and Him that sat on it, from whose face the earth and the heaven fled away; and there was found no place for them. And I saw the dead, small and great, stand before God; and the books were opened; and another book was opened, which is the book of life; and the dead were judged out of those things which were written in the books, according to their works." Rev. 20:11, 12.

Sad will be the retrospect in that day when men stand face to face with eternity. The whole life will present itself just as it has been. The world's pleasures, riches, and honors will not then seem so important. Men will then see that the righteousness they despised is alone of value. They will see that they have fashioned their characters under the deceptive allurements of Satan. The garments they have chosen are the badge of their allegiance to the first great apostate. Then they will see the results of their choice. They will have a knowledge of what it means to transgress the commandments of God. 319

There will be no future probation in which to prepare for eternity. It is in this life that we are to put on the robe of Christ's righteousness. This is our only opportunity to form characters for the home which Christ has made ready for those who obey His commandments.

The days of our probation are fast closing. The end is near. To us the warning is given, "Take heed to yourselves, lest at any time your hearts be overcharged with surfeiting, and drunkenness, and cares of this life, and so that day come upon you unawares." Luke 21:34. Beware lest it find you unready. Take heed lest you be found at the King's feast without a wedding garment.

"In such an hour as ye think not the Son of man cometh." "Blessed is he that watcheth, and keepeth his garments, lest he walk naked, and they see his shame." Matt. 24:44; Rev. 16:15.

25   325

Talents

Christ on the Mount of Olives had spoken to His disciples of His second advent to the world. He had specified certain signs that were to show when His coming was near, and had bidden His disciples watch and be ready. Again He repeated the warning, "Watch therefore; for ye know neither the day nor the hour wherein the Son of man cometh." Then He showed what it means to watch for His coming. The time is to be spent, not in idle waiting, but in diligent working. This lesson He taught in the parable of the talents.

"The kingdom of heaven," He said, "is as a man traveling into a far country, who called his own servants, and delivered unto them his goods. And unto one he gave five talents, to another two, and to another one; to every man according to his several ability; and straightway took his journey."

326 The man traveling into a far country represents Christ, who, when speaking this parable, was soon to depart from this earth to heaven. The "bondservants" (R.V.), or slaves, of the parable, represent the followers of Christ. We are not our own. We have been "bought with a price" (1 Cor. 6:20), not "with corruptible things, as silver and gold, . . . but with the precious blood of Christ" (1 Peter 1:18, 19); "that they which live should not henceforth live unto themselves, but unto Him which died for them, and rose again" (2 Cor. 5:15).

All men have been bought with this infinite price. By pouring the whole treasury of heaven into this world, by giving us in Christ all heaven, God has purchased the will, the affections, the mind, the soul, of every human being. Whether believers or unbelievers, all men are the Lord's property. All are called to do service for Him, and for the manner in which they have met this claim, all will be required to render an account at the great judgment day.

But the claims of God are not recognized by all. It is those who profess to have accepted Christ's service who in the parable are represented as His own servants.

Christ's followers have been redeemed for service. Our Lord teaches that the true object of life is ministry. Christ Himself was a worker, and to all His followers He gives the law of service—service to God and to their fellow men. Here Christ has presented to the world a higher conception of life than they had ever known. By living to minister for others, man is brought into connection with Christ. The law of service becomes the connecting link which binds us to God and to our fellow men.

To His servants Christ commits "His goods"—something to be put to use for Him. He gives "to every man his work." Each has his place in the eternal plan of heaven. Each is to 327 work in co-operation with Christ for the salvation of souls. Not more surely is the place prepared for us in the heavenly mansions than is the special place designated on earth where we are to work for God.

Gifts of the Holy Spirit

The talents that Christ entrusts to His church represent especially the gifts and blessings imparted by the Holy Spirit. "To one is given by the Spirit the word of wisdom; to another the word of knowledge by the same Spirit; to another faith by the same Spirit; to another the gifts of healing by the same Spirit; to another the working of miracles; to another prophecy; to another discerning of spirits; to another

divers kinds of tongues; to another the interpretation of tongues: but all these worketh that one and the selfsame Spirit, dividing to every man severally as He will." 1 Cor. 12:8-11. All men do not receive the same gifts, but to every servant of the Master some gift of the Spirit is promised.

Before He left His disciples, Christ "breathed on them, and saith unto them, Receive ye the Holy Ghost." John 20:22. Again He said, "Behold, I send the promise of My Father upon you." Luke 24:49. But not until after the ascension was the gift received in its fullness. Not until through faith and prayer the disciples had surrendered themselves fully for His working was the outpouring of the Spirit received. Then in a special sense the goods of heaven were committed to the followers of Christ. "When He ascended up on high, He led captivity captive, and gave gifts unto men." Eph. 4:8. "Unto every one of us is given grace, according to the measure of the gift of Christ," the Spirit "dividing to every man severally as He will." Eph. 4:7; 1 Cor. 12:11. The gifts are already ours in Christ, but their actual possession depends upon our reception of the Spirit of God.

The promise of the Spirit is not appreciated as 328 it should be. Its fulfillment is not realized as it might be. It is the absence of the Spirit that makes the gospel ministry so powerless. Learning, talents, eloquence, every natural or acquired endowment, may be possessed; but without the presence of the Spirit of God, no heart will be touched, no sinner be won to Christ. On the other hand, if they are connected with Christ, if the gifts of the Spirit are theirs, the poorest and most ignorant of His disciples will have a power that will tell upon hearts. God makes them the channel for the outworking of the highest influence in the universe.

Other Talents

The special gifts of the Spirit are not the only talents represented in the parable. It includes all gifts and endowments, whether original or acquired, natural or spiritual. All are to be employed in Christ's service. In becoming His disciples, we surrender ourselves to Him with all that we are and have. These gifts He returns to us purified and ennobled, to be used for His glory in blessing our fellow men.

To every man God has given "according to his several ability." The talents are not apportioned capriciously. He who has ability to use five talents receives five. He who can improve but two, receives two. He who can wisely use only one, receives one. None need lament that they have not received larger gifts; for He who has apportioned to every man is equally honored by the improvement of each trust, whether it be great or small. The one to whom five talents have been committed is to render the improvement of five; he who has but one, the improvement of one. God expects returns "according to that a man hath, and not according to that he hath not." 2 Cor. 8:12.

329 In the parable he that had "received the five talents went and traded with the same, and made them other five talents; and likewise he that had received two, he also gained other two."

The talents, however few, are to be put to use. The question that most concerns us is not, How much have I received? but, What am I doing with that which I have? The development of all our powers is the first duty we owe to God and to our fellow men. No one who is not growing daily in capability and usefulness is fulfilling 330 the purpose of life. In making a profession of faith in Christ we pledge ourselves to become all that it is possible for us to be as workers for the Master, and we should cultivate every faculty to the highest degree of perfection, that we may do the greatest amount of good of which we are capable.

The Lord has a great work to be done, and He will bequeath the most in the future life to those who do the most faithful, willing service in the present life. The Lord chooses His own agents, and each day under different circumstances He gives them a trial in His plan of operation. In each true-hearted endeavor to work out His plan, He chooses His agents not because they are perfect but because, through a connection with Him, they may gain perfection.

God will accept only those who are determined to aim high. He places every human agent under obligation to do his best. Moral perfection is required of all. Never should we lower the standard of righteousness in order to accommodate inherited or cultivated tendencies to wrongdoing. We need to understand that imperfection of character is sin. All righteous attributes of character dwell in God as a perfect, harmonious whole, and every one who receives Christ as a personal Saviour is privileged to possess these attributes.

And those who would be workers together with God must strive for perfection of every organ of the body and quality of the mind. True education is the preparation of the physical, mental, and moral powers for the performance of every duty; it is the training of body, mind, and soul for divine service. This is the education that will endure unto eternal life.

Of every Christian the Lord requires growth in efficiency and capability in every line. Christ has paid us our wages, even His own blood and 331 suffering, to secure our willing service. He came to our world to give us an example of how we should work, and what spirit we should bring into our labor. He desires us to study how we can best advance His work and glorify His name in the world, crowning with honor, with the greatest love and devotion, the Father who

"so loved the world, that He gave His only begotten Son, that whosoever believeth in Him should not perish, but have everlasting life." John 3:16.

But Christ has given us no assurance that to attain perfection of character is an easy matter. A noble, all-round character is not inherited. It does not come to us by accident. A noble character is earned by individual effort through the merits and grace of Christ. God gives the talents, the powers of the mind; we form the character. It is formed by hard, stern battles with self. Conflict after conflict must be waged against hereditary tendencies. We shall have to criticize ourselves closely, and allow not one unfavorable trait to remain uncorrected.

Let no one say, I cannot remedy my defects of character. If you come to this decision, you will certainly fail of obtaining everlasting life. The impossibility lies in your own will. If you will not, then you can not overcome. The real difficulty arises from the corruption of an unsanctified heart, and an unwillingness to submit to the control of God.

Many whom God has qualified to do excellent work accomplish very little, because they attempt little. Thousands pass through life as if they had no definite object for which to live, no standard to reach. Such will obtain a reward proportionate to their works.

Remember that you will never reach a higher standard than you yourself set. Then set your mark high, and step by step, even though it be by painful effort, by self-denial and sacrifice, ascend the whole length of the ladder of 332 progress. Let nothing hinder you. Fate has not woven its meshes about any human being so firmly that he need remain helpless and in uncertainty. Opposing circumstances should create a firm determination to overcome them. The breaking down of one barrier will give greater ability and courage to go forward. Press with determination in the right direction, and circumstances will be your helpers, not your hindrances.

Be ambitious, for the Master's glory, to cultivate every grace of character. In every phase of your character building you are to please God. This you may do; for Enoch pleased Him though living in a degenerate age. And there are Enochs in this our day.

Stand like Daniel, that faithful statesman, a man whom no temptation could corrupt. Do not disappoint Him who so loved you that He gave His own life to cancel your sins. He says, "Without Me ye can do nothing." John 15:5. Remember this. If you have made mistakes, you certainly gain a victory if you see these mistakes and regard them as beacons of warning. Thus you turn defeat into victory, disappointing the enemy and honoring your Redeemer.

A character formed according to the divine likeness is the only treasure that we can take from this world to the next. Those who are under the instruction of Christ in this world will take every divine attainment with them to the heavenly mansions. And in heaven we are continually to improve. How important, then, is the development of character in this life.

The heavenly intelligences will work with the human agent who seeks with determined faith that perfection of character which will reach out to perfection in action. To everyone engaged in this work Christ says, I am at your right hand to help you.

333   As the will of man co-operates with the will of God, it becomes omnipotent. Whatever is to be done at His command may be accomplished in His strength. All His biddings are enablings.

Mental Faculties

God requires the training of the mental faculties. He designs that His servants shall possess more intelligence and clearer discernment than the worldling, and He is displeased with those who are too careless or too indolent to become efficient, well-informed workers. The Lord bids us love Him with all the heart, and with all the soul, and with all the strength, and with all the mind. This lays upon us the obligation of developing the intellect to its fullest capacity, that with all the mind we may know and love our Creator.

If placed under the control of His Spirit, the more thoroughly the intellect is cultivated, the more effectively it can be used in the service of God. The uneducated man who is consecrated to God and who longs to bless others can be, and is, used by the Lord in His service. But those who, with the same spirit of consecration, have had the benefit of a thorough education, can do a much more extensive work for Christ. They stand on vantage ground.

The Lord desires us to obtain all the education possible, with the object in view of imparting our knowledge to others. None can know where or how they may be called to labor or to speak for God. Our heavenly Father alone sees what He can make of men. There are before us possibilities which our feeble faith does not discern. Our minds should be so trained that if necessary we can present the 334   truths of His word before the highest earthly authorities in such a way as to glorify His name. We should not let slip even one opportunity of qualifying ourselves intellectually to work for God.

Let the youth who need an education set to work with a determination to obtain it. Do not wait for an opening; make one for yourselves. Take hold in any small way that presents itself. Practice economy. Do not spend your means for the gratification of appetite, or in pleasure seek-

ing. Be determined to become as useful and efficient as God calls you to be. Be thorough and faithful in whatever you undertake. Procure every advantage within your reach for strengthening the intellect. Let the study of books be combined with useful manual labor, and by faithful endeavor, watchfulness, and prayer secure the wisdom that is from above. This will give you an all-round education. Thus you may rise in character, and gain an influence over other minds, enabling you to lead them in the path of uprightness and holiness.

Far more might be accomplished in the work of self-education if we were awake to our own opportunities and privileges. True education means more than the colleges can give. While the study of the sciences is not to be neglected, there is a higher training to be obtained through a vital connection with God. Let every student take his Bible and place himself in communion with the great Teacher. Let the mind be trained and disciplined to wrestle with hard problems in the search for divine truth.

Those who hunger for knowledge that they may bless their fellow men will themselves receive blessing from God. Through the study of His word their mental powers will be aroused to earnest activity. There will be an expansion and development of the faculties, and the mind will acquire power and efficiency.

Self-discipline must be practiced by everyone 335 who would be a worker for God. This will accomplish more than eloquence or the most brilliant talents. An ordinary mind, well disciplined, will accomplish more and higher work than will the most highly educated mind and the greatest talents without self-control.

Speech

The power of speech is a talent that should be diligently cultivated. Of all the gifts we have received from God, none is capable of being a greater blessing than this. With the voice we convince and persuade, with it we offer prayer and praise to God, and with it we tell others of the Redeemer's love. How important, then, that it be so trained as to be most effective for good.

The culture and right use of the voice are greatly neglected, even by persons of intelligence and Christian activity. There are many who read or speak in so low or so rapid a manner that they cannot be readily understood. Some have a thick, indistinct utterance; others speak in a high key, in sharp, shrill tones, that are painful to the hearers. Texts, hymns, and the reports and other papers presented before public assemblies are sometimes read in such a way that they are not understood and often so that their force and impressiveness are destroyed.

This is an evil that can and should be corrected. On this point the Bible gives instruction. Of the Levites who read the Scriptures to the people in the days of Ezra, it is said, "They read in the book in the law of God distinctly, and gave the sense, and caused them to understand the reading." Neh. 8:8.

By diligent effort all may acquire the power to read intelligibly, and to speak in a full, clear, round tone, in a distinct and impressive manner. By doing this we may greatly increase our efficiency as workers for Christ.

Every Christian is called to make known to others the unsearchable riches of Christ; therefore he should seek for perfection in speech. He should present the word of God in a way that will commend it to the hearers. God does not design that His human channels shall be uncouth. It is not His will that man shall belittle or degrade the heavenly current that flows through him to the world.

We should look to Jesus, the perfect pattern; we should pray for the aid of the Holy Spirit, and in His strength we should seek to train every organ for perfect work.

Especially is this true of those who are called to public service. Every minister and every teacher should bear in mind that he is giving to the people a message that involves eternal interests. The truth spoken will judge them in the great day of final reckoning. And with some souls the manner of the one delivering the message will determine its reception or rejection. Then let the word be so spoken that it will appeal to the understanding and impress the heart. Slowly, distinctly, and solemnly should it be spoken, yet with all the earnestness which its importance demands.

The right culture and use of the power of speech has to do with every line of Christian work; it enters into the home life, and into all our intercourse with one another. We should accustom ourselves to speak in pleasant tones, to use pure and correct language, and words that are kind and courteous. Sweet, kind words are as dew and gentle showers to the soul. The Scripture says of Christ that grace was poured into His lips that He might "know how to speak a word in season to him that is weary." Ps. 45:2; Isa. 50:4. And the Lord bids us, "Let your speech be alway with grace" (Col. 4:6) "that it may minister grace unto the hearers" (Eph. 4:29).

In seeking to correct or reform others we should be careful of our words. They will be a savor of life unto life or of death unto death. In giving reproof or counsel, many indulge in sharp, severe speech, words not adapted to heal the wounded soul. By these ill-advised expressions the spirit is chafed, and often the erring ones are stirred to rebellion. All who would advocate the principles of truth need to receive the heavenly oil of love. Under all circumstances reproof should be spoken in love. Then our words will reform but not exasperate. Christ by His Holy Spirit will supply the force and the power. This is His work.

Not one word is to be spoken unadvisedly. No evil speaking, no frivolous talk, no fretful repining or impure suggestion, will escape the lips of him who is following Christ. The apostle Paul, writing by the Holy Spirit, says, "Let no corrupt communication proceed out of your mouth." Eph. 4:29. A corrupt communication does not mean only words that are vile. It means any expression contrary to holy principles and pure and undefiled religion. It includes impure hints and covert insinuations of evil. Unless instantly resisted, these lead to great sin.

Upon every family, upon every individual Christian, is laid the duty of barring the way against corrupt speech. When in the company of those who indulge in foolish talk, it is our duty to change the subject of conversation if possible. By the help of the grace of God we should quietly drop words or introduce a subject that will turn the conversation into a profitable channel.

It is the work of parents to train their children to proper habits of speech. The very best school for this culture is the home life. From the earliest years the children should be taught to speak respectfully and lovingly to their parents and to one another. They should be taught that only words of gentleness, truth, and purity must pass their lips. Let the parents themselves be daily learners in the school of Christ. Then by precept and example they can teach their children the use of "sound speech, that cannot be condemned." Titus 2:8. This is one of the greatest and most responsible of their duties.

As followers of Christ we should make our words such as to be a help and an encouragement to one another in the Christian life. Far more than we do, we need to speak of the precious chapters in our experience. We should speak of the mercy and loving-kindness of God, of the matchless depths of the Saviour's love. Our words should be words of praise and thanksgiving. If the mind and heart are full of the love of God, this will be revealed in the conversation. It will not be a difficult matter to impart that which enters into our spiritual life. Great thoughts, noble aspirations, clear perceptions of truth, unselfish purposes, yearnings for piety and holiness, will bear fruit in words that reveal the character of the heart treasure. When Christ is thus revealed in our speech, it will have power in winning souls to Him.

We should speak of Christ to those who know Him not. We should do as Christ did. Wherever He was, in the synagogue, by the wayside, in the boat thrust out a little from the land, at the Pharisee's feast or the table of the publican, He spoke to men of the things pertaining to the higher life. The things of nature, the events of daily life, were bound up by Him with the words of truth. The hearts of His hearers were drawn to Him; for He had healed their sick, had comforted their sorrowing ones, and had taken their children in His arms and blessed them. When He opened His lips to speak, their attention was riveted upon Him, and every word was to some soul a savor of life unto life.

339   So it should be with us. Wherever we are, we should watch for opportunities of speaking to others of the Saviour. If we follow Christ's example in doing good, hearts will open to us as they did to Him. Not abruptly, but with tact born of divine love, we can tell them of Him who is the "Chiefest among ten thousand" and the One "altogether lovely." Cant. 5:10, 16. This is the very highest work in which we can employ the talent of speech. It was given to us that we might present Christ as the sin-pardoning Saviour.

Influence

The life of Christ was an ever-widening, shoreless influence, an influence that bound Him to God and to the whole human family. Through Christ, God has invested man with an influence that makes it impossible for him to live to himself. Individually we are connected with our fellow men, a part of God's great whole, and we stand under mutual obligations. No man can be independent of his fellow men; for the well-being of each affects others. It is God's purpose that each shall feel himself necessary to others' welfare, and seek to promote their happiness.

Every soul is surrounded by an atmosphere of its own—an atmosphere, it may be, charged with the life-giving power of faith, courage, and hope, and sweet with the fragrance of love. Or it may be heavy and chill with the gloom of discontent and selfishness, or poisonous with the deadly taint of cherished sin. By the atmosphere surrounding us, every person with whom we come in contact is consciously or unconsciously affected.

This is a responsibility from which we cannot free ourselves. Our words, our acts, our dress, our deportment, even the expression of our 340   countenance, has an influence. Upon the impression thus made there hang results for good or evil which no man can measure. Every impulse thus imparted is seed sown which will produce its harvest. It is a link in the long chain of human events, extending we know not whither. If by our example we aid others in the development of good principles, we give them power to do good. In their turn they exert the same influence upon others, and they upon still others. Thus by our unconscious influence thousands may be blessed.

Throw a pebble into the lake, and a wave is formed, and another and another; and as they increase, the circle widens, until it reaches the very shore. So with our influence. Beyond our knowledge or control it tells upon others in blessing or in cursing.

Character is power. The silent witness of a true, unselfish, godly life carries an almost irresistible influence. By revealing in our own life the character of Christ we co-operate with Him in the work of saving souls. It is only by revealing in our life His character that we can co-operate with Him. And the wider the sphere of our influence, the more good we may do. When those who profess to serve God follow Christ's example, practicing the principles of the law in their daily life; when every act bears witness that they love God supremely and their neighbor as themselves, then will the church have power to move the world.

But never should it be forgotten that influence is no less a power for evil. To lose one's own soul is a terrible thing; but to cause the loss of other souls is still more terrible. That our influence should be a savor of death unto death is a fearful thought; yet this is possible. Many who profess to gather with Christ are scattering from Him. This is why the church is so weak. Many indulge freely in criticism and 341 accusing. By giving expression to suspicion, jealousy, and discontent, they yield themselves as instruments to Satan. Before they realize what they are doing, the adversary has through them accomplished his purpose. The impression of evil has been made, the shadow has been cast, the arrows of Satan have found their mark. Distrust, unbelief, and downright infidelity have fastened upon those who otherwise might have accepted Christ. Meanwhile the workers for Satan look complacently upon those whom they have driven to skepticism, and who are now hardened against reproof and entreaty. They flatter themselves that in comparison with these souls they are virtuous and righteous. They do not realize that these sad wrecks of character are the work of their own unbridled tongues and rebellious hearts. It is through their influence that these tempted ones have fallen.

So frivolity, selfish indulgence, and careless indifference on the part of professed Christians are turning away many souls from the path of life. Many there are who will fear to meet at the bar of God the results of their influence.

It is only through the grace of God that we can make a right use of this endowment. There is nothing in us of ourselves by which we can influence others for good. If we realize our helplessness and our need of divine power, we shall not trust to ourselves. We know not what results a day, an hour, or a moment may determine, and never should we begin the day without committing our ways to our heavenly Father. His angels are appointed to watch over us, and if we put ourselves under their guardianship, then in every time of danger they will be at our right hand. When unconsciously we are in danger of exerting a wrong influence, the angels will be

342 by our side, prompting us to a better course, choosing our words for us, and influencing our actions. Thus our influence may be a silent, unconscious, but mighty power in drawing others to Christ and the heavenly world.

Time

Our time belongs to God. Every moment is His, and we are under the most solemn obligation to improve it to His glory. Of no talent He has given will He require a more strict account than of our time.

The value of time is beyond computation. Christ regarded every moment as precious, and it is thus that we should regard it. Life is too short to be trifled away. We have but a few days of probation in which to prepare for eternity. We have no time to waste, no time to devote to selfish pleasure, no time for the indulgence of sin. It is now that we are to form characters for the future, immortal life. It is now that we are to prepare for the searching judgment.

The human family have scarcely begun to live when they begin to die, and the world's incessant labor ends in nothingness unless a true knowledge in regard to eternal life is gained. The man who appreciates time as his working day will fit himself for a mansion and for a life that is immortal. It is well that he was born.

We are admonished to redeem the time. But time squandered can never be recovered. We cannot call back even one moment. The only way in which we can redeem our time is by making the most of that which remains, by being co-workers with God in His great plan of redemption.

In him who does this, a transformation of character takes place. He becomes a son of God, a member of the royal family, a child of the heavenly King. He is fitted to be the companion of the angels.

343 Now is our time to labor for the salvation of our fellow men. There are some who think that if they give money to the cause of Christ, this is all they are required to do; the precious time in which they might do personal service for Him passes unimproved. But it is the privilege and duty of all who have health and strength to render to God active service. All are to labor in winning souls to Christ. Donations of money cannot take the place of this.

Every moment is freighted with eternal consequences. We are to stand as minute men, ready for service at a moment's notice. The opportunity that is now ours to speak to some needy soul the word of life may never offer

again. God may say to that one, "This night thy soul shall be required of thee," and through our neglect he may not be ready. (Luke 12:20.) In the great judgment day, how shall we render our account to God?

Life is too solemn to be absorbed in temporal and earthly matters, in a treadmill of care and anxiety for the things that are but an atom in comparison with the things of eternal interest. Yet God has called us to serve Him in the temporal affairs of life. Diligence in this work is as much a part of true religion as is devotion. The Bible gives no indorsement to idleness. It is the greatest curse that afflicts our world. Every man and woman who is truly converted will be a diligent worker.

Upon the right improvement of our time depends our success in acquiring knowledge and mental culture. The cultivation of the intellect need not be prevented by poverty, humble origin, or unfavorable surroundings. Only let the moments be treasured. A few moments here and a few there, that might be frittered away in aimless talk; the morning hours so often wasted in bed; the time spent in traveling on trams or rail-

344 way cars, or waiting at the station; the moments of waiting for meals, waiting for those who are tardy in keeping an appointment—if a book were kept at hand, and these fragments of time were improved in study, reading, or careful thought, what might not be accomplished. A resolute purpose, persistent industry, and careful economy of time, will enable men to acquire knowledge and mental discipline which will qualify them for almost any position of influence and usefulness.

It is the duty of every Christian to acquire habits of order, thoroughness, and dispatch. There is no excuse for slow bungling at work of any character. When one is always at work and the work is never done, it is because mind and heart are not put into the labor. The one who is slow and who works at a disadvantage should realize that these are faults to be corrected. He needs to exercise his mind in planning how to use the time so as to secure the best results. By tact and method, some will accomplish as much in five hours as others do in ten. Some who are engaged in domestic labor are always at work not because they have so much to do but because they do not plan so as to save time. By their slow, dilatory ways they make much work out of very little. But all who will, may overcome these fussy, lingering habits. In their work let them have a definite aim. Decide how long a time is required for a given task, and then bend every effort toward accomplishing the work in the given time. The exercise of the will power will make the hands move deftly.

Through lack of determination to take themselves in hand and reform, persons can become stereotyped in a wrong course of action; or by cultivating their powers they may acquire ability to do the very best of service. Then they will find themselves in demand anywhere and everywhere. They will be appreciated for all that they are worth.

345   By many children and youth, time is wasted that might be spent in carrying home burdens, and thus showing a loving interest in father and mother. The youth might take upon their strong young shoulders many responsibilities which someone must bear.

The life of Christ from His earliest years was a life of earnest activity. He lived not to please Himself. He was the Son of the infinite God, yet He worked at the carpenter's trade with His father Joseph. His trade was significant. He had come into the world as the character builder, and as such all His work was perfect. Into all His secular labor He brought the same perfection as into the characters He was transforming by His divine power. He is our pattern.

Parents should teach their children the value and right use of time. Teach them that to do something which will honor God and bless humanity is worth striving for. Even in their early years they can be missionaries for God.

Parents cannot commit a greater sin than to allow their children to have nothing to do. The children soon learn to love idleness, and they grow up shiftless, useless men and women. When they are old enough to earn their living, and find employment, they work in a lazy, droning way, yet expect to be paid as much as if they were faithful. There is a world-wide difference between this class of workers and those who realize that they must be faithful stewards.

Indolent, careless habits indulged in secular work will be brought into the religious life and will unfit one to do any efficient service for God. Many who through diligent labor might have been a blessing to the world, have been ruined through idleness. Lack of employment and of steadfast purpose opens the door to a thousand temptations. Evil companions and vicious habits deprave mind and soul, and the result is ruin for this life and for the life to come.

346   Whatever the line of work in which we engage, the word of God teaches us to be "not slothful in business; fervent in spirit; serving the Lord." "Whatsoever thy hand findeth to do, do it with thy might," "knowing that of the Lord ye shall receive the reward of the inheritance; for ye serve the Lord Christ." Rom. 12:11; Eccl. 9:10; Col. 3:24.

Health

Health is a blessing of which few appreciate the value; yet upon it the efficiency of our mental and physical powers largely depends. Our impulses and passions have their seat in the body, and it must be kept in the best condition

physically and under the most spiritual influences in order that our talents may be put to the highest use.

Anything that lessens physical strength enfeebles the mind and makes it less capable of discriminating between right and wrong. We become less capable of choosing the good and have less strength of will to do that which we know to be right.

The misuse of our physical powers shortens the period of time in which our lives can be used for the glory of God. And it unfits us to accomplish the work God has given us to do. By allowing ourselves to form wrong habits, by keeping late hours, by gratifying appetite at the expense of health, we lay the foundation for feebleness. By neglecting physical exercise, by overworking mind or body, we unbalance the nervous system. Those who thus shorten their lives and unfit themselves for service by disregarding nature's laws, are guilty of robbery toward God. And they are robbing their fellow men also. The opportunity of blessing others, the very work for which God sent them into the world, has by their own course of action been cut short. And they have unfitted themselves to do even that which in a   347 briefer period of time they might have accomplished. The Lord holds us guilty when by our injurious habits we thus deprive the world of good.

Transgression of physical law is transgression of the moral law; for God is as truly the author of physical laws as He is the author of the moral law. His law is written with His own finger   348 upon every nerve, every muscle, every faculty, which has been entrusted to man. And every misuse of any part of our organism is a violation of that law.

All should have an intelligent knowledge of the human frame that they may keep their bodies in the condition necessary to do the work of the Lord. The physical life is to be carefully preserved and developed that through humanity the divine nature may be revealed in its fullness. The relation of the physical organism to the spiritual life is one of the most important branches of education. It should receive careful attention in the home and in the school. All need to become acquainted with their physical structure and the laws that control natural life. He who remains in willing ignorance of the laws of his physical being and who violates them through ignorance is sinning against God. All should place themselves in the best possible relation to life and health. Our habits should be brought under the control of a mind that is itself under the control of God.

"Know ye not," says the apostle Paul, "that your body is the temple of the Holy Ghost which is in you, which ye have of God, and ye are not your own? For ye are bought with a price; therefore glorify God in your body, and in your spirit, which are God's." 1 Cor. 6:19, 20.

Strength

We are to love God, not only with all the heart, mind, and soul, but with all the strength. This covers the full, intelligent use of the physical powers.

Christ was a true worker in temporal as well as in spiritual things, and into all His work He brought a determination to do His Father's will. The things of heaven and earth are more closely connected and are more directly under the supervision of Christ than many realize. It was Christ who planned the arrangement for the first earthly tabernacle. He gave every specification in regard to the building of Solomon's temple. The One who in His earthly life worked as a carpenter in the village of Nazareth was the heavenly architect who marked out the plan for the sacred building where His name was to be honored.

It was Christ who gave to the builders of the tabernacle wisdom to execute the most skillful and beautiful workmanship. He said, "See, I have called by name Bezaleel the son of Uri, the son of Hur, of the tribe of Judah; and I have filled him with the Spirit of God, in wisdom, and in understanding, and in knowledge, and in all manner of workmanship. . . . And I, behold, I have given with him Aholiab, the son of Ahisamach, of the tribe of Dan; and in the hearts of all that are wise hearted I have put wisdom, that they may make all that I have commanded thee." Ex. 31:2-6.

God desires that His workers in every line shall look to Him as the Giver of all they possess. All right inventions and improvements have their source in Him who is wonderful in counsel and excellent in working. The skillful touch of the physician's hand, his power over nerve and muscle, his knowledge of the delicate organism of the body, is the wisdom of divine power, to be used in behalf of the suffering. The skill with which the carpenter uses the hammer, the strength with which the blacksmith makes the anvil ring, comes from God. He has entrusted men with talents, and He expects them to look to Him for counsel. Whatever we do, in whatever department of the work we are placed, He desires to control our minds that we may do perfect work.

Religion and business are not two separate things; they are one. Bible religion is to be interwoven with all we do or say. Divine and human agencies are to combine in temporal as well as in spiritual achievements. They are to be united in all human pursuits, in mechanical and agricultural labors, in mercantile and scientific enterprises. There must be co-operation in everything embraced in Christian activity. God has proclaimed the principles on which

alone this co-operation is possible. His glory must be the motive of all who are laborers together with Him. All our work is to be done from love of God and in accordance with His will.

It is just as essential to do the will of God when erecting a building as when taking part in a religious service. And if the workers have brought the right principles into their own character making, then in the erection of every building they will grow in grace and knowledge.

But God will not accept the greatest talents or the most splendid service unless self is laid upon the altar, a living, consuming sacrifice. The root must be holy, else there can be no fruit acceptable to God.

The Lord made Daniel and Joseph shrewd managers. He could work through them because they did not live to please their own inclination but to please God.

The case of Daniel has a lesson for us. It reveals the fact that a businessman is not necessarily a sharp, policy man. He can be instructed by God at every step. Daniel, while prime minister of the kingdom of Babylon, was a prophet of God, receiving the light of heavenly inspiration. Worldly, ambitious statesmen are represented in the word of God as the grass that groweth up and as the flower of the grass that fadeth. Yet the Lord desires to have in His service intelligent men, men qualified for various lines of work. There is need of businessmen who will weave the grand principles of truth into all their transactions. And their talents should be perfected by most thorough study and training. If men in any line of work need to improve their opportunities to become wise and efficient, it is those who are using their ability in building up the kingdom of God in our world. Of Daniel we learn that in all his business transactions, when subjected to the closest scrutiny, not one fault or error could be found. He was a sample of what every businessman may be. His history shows what may be accomplished by one who consecrates the strength of brain and bone and muscle, of heart and life, to the service of God.

Money

God also entrusts men with means. He gives them power to get wealth. He waters the earth with the dews of heaven and with the showers of refreshing rain. He gives the sunlight, which warms the earth, awakening to life the things of nature and causing them to flourish and bear fruit. And He asks for a return of His own.

Our money has not been given us that we might honor and glorify ourselves. As faithful stewards we are to use it for the honor and glory of God. Some think that only a portion of their means is the Lord's. When they have set apart a portion for religious and charitable purposes, they regard the remainder as their own, to be used as they see fit. But in this they mistake. All we possess is the Lord's, and we are accountable to Him for the use we make of it. In the use of every penny, it will be seen whether we love God supremely and our neighbor as ourselves.

Money has great value, because it can do great good. In the hands of God's children it is food for the hungry, drink for the thirsty, and clothing for the naked. It is a defense for the oppressed, and a means of help to the sick. But money is of no more value than sand, only as it is put to use in providing for the necessities of life, in blessing others, and advancing the cause of Christ.

352 Hoarded wealth is not merely useless, it is a curse. In this life it is a snare to the soul, drawing the affections away from the heavenly treasure. In the great day of God its witness to unused talents and neglected opportunities will condemn its possessor. The Scripture says, "Go to now, ye rich men, weep and howl for your miseries that shall come upon you. Your riches are corrupted, and your garments are motheaten. Your gold and silver is cankered; and the rust of them shall bear witness against you, and shall eat your flesh as it were fire. Ye have heaped treasure together for the last days. Behold, the hire of the labourers who have reaped down your fields, which is of you kept back by fraud, crieth; and the cries of them which have reaped are entered into the ears of the Lord of sabaoth." James 5:1-4.

But Christ sanctions no lavish or careless use of means. His lesson in economy, "Gather up the fragments that remain, that nothing be lost," is for all His followers. (John 6:12.) He who realizes that his money is a talent from God will use it economically, and will feel it a duty to save that he may give.

The more means we expend in display and self-indulgence, the less we can have to feed the hungry and clothe the naked. Every penny used unnecessarily deprives the spender of a precious opportunity of doing good. It is robbing God of the honor and glory which should flow back to Him through the improvement of His entrusted talents.

Kindly Impulses and Affections

Kindly affections, generous impulses, and a quick apprehension of spiritual things are precious talents, and lay their possessor under a weighty responsibility. All are to be used in God's service. But here many err. Satisfied with the possession of these qualities, they fail to 353 bring them into active service for others. They flatter themselves that if they had opportunity, if circumstances were favorable, they would do a

great and good work. But they are awaiting the opportunity. They despise the narrowness of the poor niggard who grudges even a pittance to the needy. They see that he is living for self, and that he is responsible for his misused talents. With much complacency they draw the contrast between themselves and such narrow-minded ones, feeling that their own condition is much more favorable than that of their mean-souled neighbors. But they are deceiving themselves. The mere possession of unused qualities only increases their responsibility. Those who possess large affections are under obligation to God to bestow them, not merely on their friends, but on all who need their help. Social advantages are talents, and are to be used for the benefit of all within reach of our influence. The love that gives kindness to only a few is not love, but selfishness. It will not in any way work for the good of souls or the glory of God. Those who thus leave their Master's talents unimproved are even more guilty than are the ones for whom they feel such contempt. To them it will be said, Ye knew your Master's will, but did it not.

Talents Multiplied by Use

Talents used are talents multiplied. Success is not the result of chance or of destiny; it is the outworking of God's own providence, the reward of faith and discretion, of virtue and persevering effort. The Lord desires us to use every gift we have; and if we do this, we shall have greater gifts to use. He does not supernaturally endow us with the qualifications we lack; but while we use that which we have, He will work with us to increase and strengthen every faculty. By every wholehearted, earnest 35 sacrifice for the Master's service our powers will increase. While we yield ourselves as instruments for the Holy Spirit's working, the grace of God works in us to deny old inclinations, to overcome powerful propensities, and to form new habits. As we cherish and obey the promptings of the Spirit, our hearts are enlarged to receive more and more of His power, and to do more and better work. Dormant energies are aroused, and palsied faculties receive new life.

The humble worker who obediently responds to the call of God may be sure of receiving divine assistance. To accept so great and holy a responsibility is itself elevating to the character. It calls into action the highest mental and spiritual powers, and strengthens and purifies the mind and heart. Through faith in the power of God, it is wonderful how strong a weak man may become, how decided his efforts, how prolific of great results. He who begins with a little knowledge, in a humble way, and tells what he knows, while seeking diligently for further knowledge, will find the whole heavenly treasure awaiting his demand. The more he seeks to impart light, the more light he will receive. The more one tries to explain the word of God to others, with a love for souls, the plainer it becomes to himself. The more we use our knowledge and exercise our powers, the more knowledge and power we shall have.

Every effort made for Christ will react in blessing upon ourselves. If we use our means for His glory, He will give us more. As we seek to win others to Christ, bearing the burden of souls in our prayers, our own hearts will throb with the quickening influence of God's grace; our own affections will glow with more divine fervor; our whole Christian life will be more of a reality, more earnest, more prayerful.

The value of man is estimated in heaven 355 according to the capacity of the heart to know God. This knowledge is the spring from which flows all power. God created man that every faculty might be the faculty of the divine mind; and He is ever seeking to bring the human mind into association with the divine. He offers us the privilege of co-operation with Christ in revealing His grace to the world, that we may receive increased knowledge of heavenly things.

Looking unto Jesus we obtain brighter and more distinct views of God, and by beholding we become changed. Goodness, love for our fellow men, becomes our natural instinct. We develop a character which is the counterpart of the divine character. Growing into His likeness, we enlarge our capacity for knowing God. More and more we enter into fellowship with the heavenly world, and we have continually increasing power to receive the riches of the knowledge and wisdom of eternity.

The One Talent

The man who received the one talent "went and digged in the earth, and hid his lord's money."

It was the one with the smallest gift who left his talent unimproved. In this is given a warning to all who feel that the smallness of their endowments excuses them from service for Christ. If they could do some great thing, how gladly would they undertake it; but because they can serve only in little things, they think themselves justified in doing nothing. In this they err. The Lord in His distribution of gifts is testing character. The man who neglected to improve his talent proved himself an unfaithful servant. Had he received five talents, he would have buried them as he buried the one. His misuse of the one talent showed that he despised the gifts of heaven.

356 "He that is faithful in that which is least is faithful also in much." Luke 16:10. The importance of the little things is often underrated because they are small; but they supply much of the actual discipline of life. There are really no nonessentials in the Christian's life. Our character building will be full of peril while we underrate the importance of the little things.

"He that is unjust in the least is unjust also in much." By unfaithfulness in even the smallest duties, man robs his Maker of the service which is His due. This unfaithfulness reacts upon himself. He fails of gaining the grace, the power, the force of character, which may be received through an unreserved surrender to God. Living apart from Christ he is subject to Satan's temptations, and he makes mistakes in his work for the Master. Because he is not guided by right principles in little things, he fails to obey God in the great matters which he regards as his special work. The defects cherished in dealing with life's minor details pass into more important affairs. He acts on the principles to which he has accustomed himself. Thus actions repeated form habits, habits form character, and by the character our destiny for time and for eternity is decided.

Only by faithfulness in the little things can the soul be trained to act with fidelity under larger responsibilities. God brought Daniel and his fellows into connection with the great men of Babylon, that these heathen men might become acquainted with the principles of true religion. In the midst of a nation of idolaters, Daniel was to represent the character of God. How did he become fitted for a position of so great trust and honor? It was his faithfulness in the little things that gave complexion to his whole life. He honored God in the smallest duties, and the Lord co-operated with him. To Daniel and his companions God gave "knowl- 357 edge and skill in all learning and wisdom; and Daniel had understanding in all visions and dreams." Dan. 1:17.

As God called Daniel to witness for Him in Babylon, so He calls us to be His witnesses in the world today. In the smallest as well as the largest affairs of life He desires us to reveal to men the principles of His kingdom.

Christ in His life on earth taught the lesson of careful attention to the little things. The great work of redemption weighed continually upon His soul. As He was teaching and healing, all the energies of mind and body were taxed to the utmost; yet He noticed the most simple things in life and in nature. His most instructive lessons were those in which by the simple things of nature He illustrated the great truths of the king- 358 dom of God. He did not overlook the necessities of the humblest of His servants. His ear heard every cry of need. He was awake to the touch of the afflicted woman in the crowd; the very slightest touch of faith brought a response. When He raised from the dead the daughter of Jairus, He reminded her parents that she must have something to eat. When by His own mighty power He rose from the tomb, He did not disdain to fold and put carefully in the proper place the graveclothes in which He had been laid away.

The work to which as Christians we are called is to co-operate with Christ for the salvation of souls. This work we have entered into covenant with Him to do. To neglect the work is to prove disloyal to Christ. But in order to accomplish this work we must follow His example of faithful, conscientious attention to the little things. This is the secret of success in every line of Christian effort and influence.

The Lord desires His people to reach the highest round of the ladder that they may glorify Him by possessing the ability He is willing to bestow. Through the grace of God every provision has been made for us to reveal that we act upon better plans than those upon which the world acts. We are to show a superiority in intellect, in understanding, in skill and knowledge, because we believe in God and in His power to work upon human hearts.

But those who have not a large endowment of gifts need not become discouraged. Let them use what they have, faithfully guarding every weak point in their characters, seeking by divine grace to make it strong. Into every action of life we are to weave faithfulness and loyalty, cultivating the attributes that will enable us to accomplish the work.

359 Habits of negligence should be resolutely overcome. Many think it a sufficient excuse for the grossest errors to plead forgetfulness. But do they not, as well as others, possess intellectual faculties? Then they should discipline their minds to be retentive. It is a sin to forget, a sin to be negligent. If you form a habit of negligence, you may neglect your own soul's salvation and at last find that you are unready for the kingdom of God.

Great truths must be brought into little things. Practical religion is to be carried into the lowly duties of daily life. The greatest qualification for any man is to obey implicitly the word of the Lord.

Because they are not connected with some directly religious work, many feel that their lives are useless; that they are doing nothing for the advancement of God's kingdom. But this is a mistake. If their work is that which someone must do, they should not accuse themselves of uselessness in the great household of God. The humblest duties are not to be ignored. Any honest work is a blessing, and faithfulness in it may prove a training for higher trusts.

However lowly, any work done for God with a full surrender of self is as acceptable to Him as the highest service. No offering is small that is given with trueheartedness and gladness of soul.

Wherever we may be, Christ bids us take up the duty that presents itself. If this is in the home, take hold willingly and earnestly to make home a pleasant place. If you are a mother, train your children for Christ. This is as verily a work for God as is that of the minister in the pulpit. If your duty is in the kitchen, seek to be a perfect cook. Prepare food that will be healthful, nourishing, and appetizing. And as you employ the best ingredients in preparing food remember that you are to give your mind the best thoughts. If it is your work to till the soil or to engage in any other trade or occupation, make a success of 360 the present duty. Put your mind on what you are doing. In all your work represent Christ. Do as He would do in your place.

However small your talent, God has a place for it. That one talent, wisely used, will accomplish its appointed work. By faithfulness in little duties, we are to work on the plan of addition, and God will work for us on the plan of multiplication. These littles will become the most precious influences in His work.

Let a living faith run like threads of gold through the performance of even the smallest duties. Then all the daily work will promote Christian growth. There will be a continual looking unto Jesus. Love for Him will give vital force to everything that is undertaken. Thus through the right use of our talents, we may link ourselves by a golden chain to the higher world. This is true sanctification; for sanctification consists in the cheerful performance of daily duties in perfect obedience to the will of God.

But many Christians are waiting for some great work to be brought to them. Because they cannot find a place large enough to satisfy their ambition, they fail to perform faithfully the common duties of life. These seem to them uninteresting. Day by day they let slip opportunities for showing their faithfulness to God. While they are waiting for some great work, life passes away, its purposes unfulfilled, its work unaccomplished.

The Talents Returned

"After a long time the lord of those servants cometh, and reckoneth with them." When the Lord takes account of His servants, the return from every talent will be scrutinized. The work done reveals the character of the worker.

Those who have received the five and the two talents return to the Lord the entrusted gifts with their increase. In doing this they claim no merit 361 for themselves. Their talents are those that have been delivered to them; they have gained other talents, but there could have been no gain without the deposit. They see that they have done only their duty. The capital was the Lord's; the improvement is His. Had not the Saviour bestowed upon them His love and grace, they would have been bankrupt for eternity.

But when the Master receives the talents, He approves and rewards the workers as though the merit were all their own. His countenance is full of joy and satisfaction. He is filled with delight that He can bestow blessings upon them. For every service and every sacrifice He requites them, not because it is a debt He owes, but because His heart is overflowing with love and tenderness.

"Well done, thou good and faithful servant," He says; "thou hast been faithful over a few things, I will make thee ruler over many things; enter thou into the joy of thy Lord."

It is the faithfulness, the loyalty to God, the loving service, that wins the divine approval. Every impulse of the Holy Spirit leading men to goodness and to God, is noted in the books of heaven, and in the day of God the workers through whom He has wrought will be commended.

They will enter into the joy of the Lord as they see in His kingdom those who have been redeemed through their instrumentality. And they are privileged to participate in His work there, because they have gained a fitness for it by participation in His work here. What we shall be in heaven is the reflection of what we are now in character and holy service. Christ said of Himself, "The Son of man came not to be ministered unto, but to minister." Matt. 20:28. This, His work on earth, is His work in heaven. And our reward for working with Christ in this world is the greater power and wider privilege of working with Him in the world to come.

362 "Then he which had received the one talent came and said, Lord, I knew thee that thou art an hard man, reaping where thou hast not sown, and gathering where thou hast not strewed; and I was afraid, and went and hid thy talent in the earth; lo, there thou hast that is thine."

Thus men excuse their neglect of God's gifts. They look upon God as severe and tyrannical, as watching to spy out their mistakes and visit them with judgments. They charge Him with demanding what He has never given, with reaping where He has not sown.

There are many who in their hearts charge God with being a hard master because He claims their possessions and their service. But we can bring to God nothing that is not already His. "All things come of Thee," said King David; "and of Thine own have we given Thee." 1 Chron. 29:14. All things are God's, not only by creation, but by redemption. All the blessings of this life and of the life to come are delivered to us stamped with the cross of Calvary. Therefore the charge that God is a hard master, reaping where He has not sown, is false.

The master does not deny the charge of the wicked servant, unjust as it is; but taking him on his own ground he shows that his conduct is without excuse. Ways and means had been provided whereby the talent might have been improved to the owner's profit. "Thou oughtest," he said, "to have put my money to the exchangers, and then at my coming I should have received mine own with usury."

Our heavenly Father requires no more nor less than He has given us ability to do. He lays upon His servants no burdens that they are not able to bear. "He knoweth our frame; He remembereth that we are dust." Ps. 103:14. All that He claims from us we through divine grace can render.

"Unto whomsoever much is given, of him shall be much required." Luke 12:48. We shall 363 individually be held responsible for doing one jot less than we have ability to do. The Lord measures with exactness every possibility for service. The unused capabilities are as much brought into account as are those that are improved. For all that we might become through the right use of our talents God holds us responsible. We shall be judged according to what we ought to have done, but did not accomplish because we did not use our powers to glorify God. Even if we do not lose our souls, we shall realize in eternity the result of our unused talents. For all the knowledge and ability that we might have gained and did not, there will be an eternal loss.

But when we give ourselves wholly to God and in our work follow His directions, He makes Himself responsible for its accomplishment. He would not have us conjecture as to the success of our honest endeavors. Not once should we even think of failure. We are to co-operate with One who knows no failure.

We should not talk of our own weakness and inability. This is a manifest distrust of God, a denial of His word. When we murmur because of our burdens, or refuse the responsibilities He calls upon us to bear, we are virtually saying that He is a hard master, that He requires what He has not given us power to do.

The spirit of the slothful servant we are often fain to call humility. But true humility is widely different. To be clothed with humility does not mean that we are to be dwarfs in intellect, deficient in aspiration, and cowardly in our lives, shunning burdens lest we fail to carry them successfully. Real humility fulfills God's purposes by depending upon His strength.

God works by whom He will. He sometimes selects the humblest instrument to do the greatest work, for His power is revealed through the 364 weakness of men. We have our standard, and by it we pronounce one thing great and another small; but God does not estimate according to our rule. We are not to suppose that what is great to us must be great to God, or that what is small to us must be small to Him. It does not rest with us to pass judgment on our talents or to choose our work. We are to take up the burdens that God appoints, bearing them for His sake, and ever going to Him for rest. Whatever our work, God is honored by wholehearted, cheerful service. He is pleased when we take up our duties with gratitude, rejoicing that we are accounted worthy to be co-laborers with Him.

The Talent Removed

Upon the slothful servant the sentence was, "Take therefore the talent from him, and give it unto him which hath ten talents." Here, as in the reward of the faithful worker, is indicated not merely the reward at the final judgment but the gradual process of retribution in this life. As in the natural, so in the spiritual world: every power unused will weaken and decay. Activity is the law of life; idleness is death. "The manifestation of the Spirit is given to every man to profit withal." 1 Cor. 12:7. Employed to bless others, his gifts increase. Shut up to self-serving they diminish, and are finally withdrawn. He who refuses to impart that which he has received will at last find that he has nothing to give. He is consenting to a process that surely dwarfs and finally destroys the faculties of the soul.

Let none suppose that they can live a life of selfishness, and then, having served their own interests, enter into the joy of their Lord. In the joy of unselfish love they could not participate. They would not be fitted for the heavenly courts. They could not appreciate the pure atmosphere of love that pervades heaven. The voices of the angels and the music of their harps would not satisfy them. To their minds the science of heaven would be as an enigma.

In the great judgment day those who have not worked for Christ, those who have drifted along, carrying no responsibility, thinking of themselves, pleasing themselves, will be placed by the Judge of all the earth with those who did evil. They receive the same condemnation.

Many who profess to be Christians neglect the claims of God, and yet they do not feel that in this there is any wrong. They know that the blasphemer, the murderer, the adulterer, deserves punishment; but as for them, they enjoy the services of religion. They love to hear the gospel preached, and therefore they think themselves Christians. Though they have spent their lives in caring for themselves, they will be as much surprised as was the unfaithful servant in the parable to hear the sentence, "Take the talent from him." Like the Jews, they mistake the enjoyment of their blessings for the use they should make of them.

Many who excuse themselves from Christian effort plead their inability for the work. But did God make them so incapable? No, never. This inability has been produced by their own inactivity and perpetuated by their deliberate choice.

Already, in their own characters, they are realizing the result of the sentence, "Take the talent from him." The continual misuse of their talents will effectually quench for them the Holy Spirit, which is the only light. The sentence, "Cast ye the unprofitable servant into outer darkness," sets Heaven's seal to the choice which they themselves have made for eternity.

26

"Friends by the Mammon of Unrighteousness"

Christ's coming was at a time of intense worldliness. Men were subordinating the eternal to the temporal, the claims of the future to the affairs of the present. They were mistaking phantoms for realities, and realities for phantoms. They did not by faith behold the unseen world. Satan presented before them the things of this life as all-attractive and all-absorbing, and they gave heed to his temptations.

Christ came to change this order of things. He sought to break the spell by which men were infatuated and ensnared. In His teaching He sought to adjust the claims of heaven and earth, to turn men's thoughts from the present to the future. From their pursuit of the things of time, He called them to make provision for eternity.

"There was a certain rich man," He said, "which had a steward; and the same was accused unto him that he had wasted his goods." The rich man had left all his possessions in the hands of this servant; but the servant was unfaithful, and the master was convinced that he was being systematically robbed. He determined to retain him no longer in his service, and he called for an investigation of his accounts. "How is it," he said, "that I hear this of thee? Give an account of thy stewardship; for thou mayest be no longer steward."

With the prospect of discharge before him, the steward saw three paths open to his choice. He must labor, beg, or starve. And he said within himself, "What shall I do? for my lord taketh away from me the stewardship: I cannot dig; to beg I am ashamed. I am resolved what to do, that, when I am put out of the stewardship, they may receive me into their houses. So he called every one of his lord's debtors unto him, and said unto the first, How much owest thou unto my lord? And he said, An hundred measures of oil. And he said unto him, Take thy bill, and sit down quickly, and write fifty. Then said he to another, And how much owest thou? And he said, An hundred measures of wheat. And he said unto him, Take thy bill, and write fourscore."

This chapter is based on Luke 16:1-9.

This unfaithful servant made others sharers with him in his dishonesty. He defrauded his master to advantage them, and by accepting this advantage they placed themselves under obligation to receive him as a friend into their homes.

"And the lord commended the unjust steward, because he had done wisely." The worldly man praised the sharpness of the man who had defrauded him. But the rich man's commendation was not the commendation of God.

Christ did not commend the unjust steward, but He made use of a well-known occurrence to illustrate the lesson He desired to teach. "Make to yourselves friends by means of the mammon of unrighteousness," He said, "that when it shall fail, they may receive you into the eternal tabernacles." R.V.

368 The Saviour had been censured by the Pharisees for mingling with publicans and sinners. But His interest in them was not lessened, nor did His efforts for them cease. He saw that their employment brought them into temptation. They were surrounded with enticements to evil. The first wrong step was easy, and the descent was rapid to greater dishonesty and increased crimes. Christ was seeking by every means to win them to higher aims and nobler principles. This purpose He had in mind in the story of the unfaithful steward. There had been among the publicans just such a case as that represented in the parable, and in Christ's description they recognized their own practices. Their attention was arrested, and from the picture of their own dishonest practices many of them learned a lesson of spiritual truth.

The parable was, however, spoken directly to the disciples. To them first the leaven of truth was imparted, and through them it was to reach others. Much of Christ's teaching the disciples did not at first understand, and often His lessons seemed to be almost forgotten. But under the influence of the Holy Spirit these truths were 369 afterward revived with distinctness, and through the disciples they were brought vividly before the new converts who were added to the church.

And the Saviour was speaking also to the Pharisees. He did not relinquish the hope that they would perceive the force of His words. Many had been deeply convicted, and as they should hear the truth under the dictation of the Holy Spirit, not a few would become believers in Christ.

The Pharisees had tried to bring Christ into disrepute by accusing Him of mingling with publicans and sinners. Now He turns the rebuke on these accusers. The scene known to have taken place among the publicans He holds up before the Pharisees both as representing their course of action and as showing the only way in which they can redeem their errors.

To the unfaithful steward his lord's goods had been entrusted for benevolent purposes; but he had used them for himself. So with Israel. God had chosen the seed of Abraham. With a high arm He had delivered them from bondage in Egypt. He had made them the depositaries of sacred truth for the blessing of the world. He had entrusted to them the living oracles that they might communicate the light to others. But His stewards had used these gifts to enrich and exalt themselves.

The Pharisees, filled with self-importance and self-righteousness, were misapplying the goods lent them by God to use for His glory.

The servant in the parable had made no provision for the future. The goods entrusted to him for the benefit of others he had used for himself; but he had thought only of the present. When the stewardship should be taken from him, he would have nothing to call his own. But his master's goods were still in his hands, and he determined to use them so as to secure himself 370 against future want. To accomplish this he must work on a new plan. Instead of gathering for himself, he must impart to others. Thus he might secure friends, who, when he should be cast out, would receive him. So with the Pharisees. The stewardship was soon to be taken from them, and they were called upon to provide for the future. Only by seeking the good of others could they benefit themselves. Only by imparting God's gifts in the present life could they provide for eternity.

After relating the parable, Christ said, "The children of this world are in their generation wiser than the children of light." That is, worldly-wise men display more wisdom and earnestness in serving themselves than do the professed children of God in their service to Him. So it was in Christ's day. So it is now. Look at the life of many who claim to be Christians. The Lord has endowed them with capabilities, and power, and influence; He has entrusted them with money, that they may be co-workers with Him in the great redemption. All His gifts are to be used in blessing humanity, in relieving the suffering and the needy. We are to feed the hungry, to clothe the naked, to care for the widow and the fatherless, to minister to the distressed and downtrodden. God never meant that the widespread misery in the world should exist. He never meant that one man should have an abun-

"If riches increase, set not your your upon them." Ps. 62:10. "Wilt thou set thine eyes upon that which is not? for riches certainly make themselves wings; they fly away as an eagle toward heaven." Prov. 23:5. "They that trust in their wealth, and boast themselves in the multitude of their riches; none of them can by any means redeem his brother, nor give to God a ransom for him." Ps. 49: 6, 7.

dance of the luxuries of life, while the children of others should cry for bread. The means over and above the actual necessities of life are entrusted to man to do good, to bless humanity. The Lord says, "Sell that ye have, and give alms." Luke 12:33. Be "ready to distribute, willing to communicate." 1 Tim. 6:18. "When thou makest a feast, call the poor, the maimed, the lame, the blind." Luke 14:13. "Loose the bands of wickedness," "undo the heavy burdens," "let 371 the oppressed go free," "break every yoke." "Deal thy bread to the hungry," "bring the poor that are cast out to thy house." "When thou seest the naked, . . . cover him." "Satisfy the afflicted soul." Isa. 58:6, 7, 10. "Go ye into all the world, and preach the gospel to every creature." Mark 16:15. These are the Lord's commands. Are the great body of professed Christians doing this work?

Alas, how many are appropriating to themselves the gifts of God! How many are adding house to house and land to land. How many are spending their money for pleasure, for the gratification of appetite, for extravagant houses, furniture, and dress. Their fellow beings are left to misery and crime, to disease and death. Multitudes are perishing without one pitying look, one word or deed of sympathy.

Men are guilty of robbery toward God. Their selfish use of means robs the Lord of the glory that should be reflected back to Him in the relief of suffering humanity and the salvation of souls. 372 They are embezzling His entrusted goods. The Lord declares, "I will come near to you to judgment; and I will be a swift witness against . . . those that oppress the hireling in his wages, the widow, and the fatherless, and that turn aside the stranger from his right." "Will a man rob God? Yet ye have robbed Me. But ye say, Wherein have we robbed Thee? In tithes and offerings. Ye are cursed with a curse; for ye have robbed Me, even this whole nation." Mal. 3:5, 8, 9. "Go to now, ye rich men, . . . your riches are corrupted, and your garments are motheaten. Your gold and silver is cankered, and the rust of them shall be a witness against you. . . . Ye have heaped treasure together for the last days." "Ye have lived in pleasure on the earth, and been wanton." "Behold, the hire of the laborers who have reaped down your fields, which is of you kept back by fraud, crieth: and the cries of them which have reaped are entered into the ears of the Lord of sabaoth." James 5:1-3, 5, 4.

Everyone will be required to render up his entrusted gifts. In the day of final judgment men's hoarded wealth will be worthless to them. They have nothing they can call their own.

Those who spend their lives in laying up worldly treasure show less wisdom, less thought and care for their eternal well-being, than did the unjust steward for his earthly support. Less wise than the children of this world in their gen-eration are these professed children of the light. These are they of whom the prophet declared, in his vision of the great judgment day, "A man shall cast the idols of his silver, and the idols of his gold [margin]; which they made each one for himself to worship, to the moles and to the bats; to go into the clefts of the rocks, and into the tops of the ragged rocks, for fear of the Lord, and for the glory of His majesty, when He ariseth to shake terribly the earth." Isa. 2:20, 21.

"Make to yourselves friends by means of the 373 mammon of unrighteousness," Christ says, "that when it shall fail, they may receive you into the eternal tabernacles." R.V. God and Christ and angels are all ministering to the afflicted, the suffering, and the sinful. Give yourself to God for this work, use His gifts for this purpose, and you enter into partnership with heavenly beings. Your heart will throb in sympathy with theirs. You will be assimilated to them in character. To you these dwellers in the eternal tabernacles will not be strangers. When earthly things shall have passed away, the watchers at heaven's gates will bid you welcome.

And the means used to bless others will bring returns. Riches rightly employed will accomplish great good. Souls will be won to Christ. He who follows Christ's plan of life will see in the courts of God those for whom he has labored and sacrificed on earth. Gratefully will the ransomed ones remember those who have been instrumental in their salvation. Precious will heaven be to those who have been faithful in the work of saving souls.

The lesson of this parable is for all. Everyone will be held responsible for the grace given him through Christ. Life is too solemn to be absorbed in temporal or earthly matters. The Lord desires that we shall communicate to others that which the eternal and unseen communicates to us.

Every year millions upon millions of human souls are passing into eternity unwarned and unsaved. From hour to hour in our varied life opportunities to reach and save souls are opened to us. These opportunities are continually coming and going. God desires us to make the most of them. Days, weeks, and months are passing; we have one day, one week, one month less in which to do our work. A few more years at the longest, and the voice which we cannot refuse 374 to answer will be heard saying, "Give an account of thy stewardship."

Christ calls upon every one to consider. Make an honest reckoning. Put into one scale Jesus, which means eternal treasure, life, truth, heaven, and the joy of Christ in souls redeemed; put into the other every attraction the world can offer. Into one scale put the loss of your own soul, and the souls of those whom you might have been instrumental in saving; into the other, for yourself and for them, a life that measures with the life of God. Weigh for time and for eternity. While you are thus engaged, Christ speaks: "What shall it profit a man, if he shall gain the whole world, and lose his own soul?" Mark 8:36.

God desires us to choose the heavenly in place of the earthly. He opens before us the possibilities of a heavenly investment. He would give encouragement to our loftiest aims, security to our choicest treasure. He declares, "I will make a man more precious than fine gold; even a man than the golden wedge of Ophir." Isa. 13:12. When the riches that moth devours and rust corrupts shall be swept away, Christ's followers can rejoice in their heavenly treasure, the riches that are imperishable.

Better than all the friendship of the world is the friendship of Christ's redeemed. Better than a title to the noblest palace on earth is a title to the mansions our Lord has gone to prepare. And better than all the words of earthly praise will be the Saviour's words to His faithful servants, "Come, ye blessed of My Father, inherit the kingdom prepared for you from the foundation of the world." Matt. 25:34.

To those who have squandered His goods, Christ still gives opportunity to secure lasting riches. He says, "Give, and it shall be given unto you." "Provide yourselves bags which wax 375 not old, a treasure in the heavens that faileth not, where no thief approacheth, neither moth corrupteth." Luke 6:38; 12:33. "Charge them that are rich in this world, . . . that they do good, that they be rich in good works, ready to distribute, willing to communicate; laying up in store for themselves a good foundation against the time to come, that they may lay hold on eternal life." 1 Tim. 6:17-19.

Then let your property go beforehand to heaven. Lay up your treasures beside the throne of God. Make sure your title to the unsearchable riches of Christ. "Make to yourselves friends by means of the mammon of unrighteousness, that when it shall fail, they may receive you into the eternal tabernacles." R.V.

376

27

"Who Is My Neighbour?"

Among the Jews the question, "Who is my neighbour?" caused endless dispute. They had no doubt as to the heathen and the Samaritans. These were strangers and enemies. But where should the distinction be made among the people of their own nation and among the different classes of society? Whom should the priest, the rabbi, the elder, regard as neighbor? They spent their lives in a round of ceremonies to make themselves pure. Contact with the ignorant and

This chapter is based on Luke 10:25-37.

careless multitude, they taught, would cause defilement that would require wearisome effort to remove. Were they to regard the "unclean" as neighbors?

This question Christ answered in the parable of the good Samaritan. He showed that our neighbor does not mean merely one of the church or faith to which we belong. It has no reference to race, color, or class distinction. Our neighbor is every person who needs our help. Our neighbor is every soul who is wounded and bruised by the adversary. Our neighbor is every one who is the property of God.

The parable of the good Samaritan was called 377 forth by a question put to Christ by a doctor of the law. As the Saviour was teaching, "a certain lawyer stood up, and tempted Him, saying, Master, what shall I do to inherit eternal life?" The Pharisees had suggested this question to the lawyer in the hope that they might entrap Christ in His words, and they listened eagerly for His answer. But the Saviour entered into no controversy. He required the answer from the questioner himself. "What is written in the law?" He asked, "How readest thou?" The Jews still accused Jesus of lightly regarding the law given from Sinai, but He turned the question of salvation upon the keeping of God's commandments.

The lawyer said, "Thou shalt love the Lord thy God with all thy heart, and with all thy soul, and with all thy strength, and with all thy mind; and thy neighbour as thyself." "Thou hast answered right," Christ said; "this do, and thou shalt live."

The lawyer was not satisfied with the position and works of the Pharisees. He had been studying the scriptures with a desire to learn their real meaning. He had a vital interest in the matter, and he asked in sincerity, "What shall I do?" In his answer as to the requirements of the law, he passed by all the mass of ceremonial and ritualistic precepts. For these he claimed no value, but presented the two great principles on which hang all the law and the prophets. The Saviour's commendation of this answer placed Him on vantage ground with the rabbis. They could not condemn Him for sanctioning that which had been advanced by an expositor of the law.

"This do, and thou shalt live," Christ said. In His teaching He ever presented the law as a divine unity, showing that it is impossible to keep one precept and break another; for the same principle runs through all. Man's destiny 378 will be determined by his obedience to the whole law.

Christ knew that no one could obey the law in his own strength. He desired to lead the lawyer to clearer and more critical research that he might find the truth. Only by accepting the virtue and grace of Christ can we keep the law. Belief in the propitiation for sin enables fallen man to love God with his whole heart and his neighbor as himself.

The lawyer knew that he had kept neither the first four nor the last six commandments. He was convicted under Christ's searching words, but instead of confessing his sin he tried to excuse it. Rather than acknowledge the truth, he endeavored to show how difficult of fulfillment the commandment is. Thus he hoped both to parry conviction and to vindicate himself in the eyes of the people. The Saviour's words had shown that his question was needless, since he was able to answer it himself. Yet he put another question, saying, "Who is my neighbour?"

Again Christ refused to be drawn into controversy. He answered the question by relating an incident, the memory of which was fresh in the minds of His hearers. He said, "went down from Jerusalem to Jericho, and fell among thieves, which stripped him of his raiment, and wounded him, and departed, leaving him half dead."

In journeying from Jerusalem to Jericho, the traveler had to pass through a portion of the wilderness of Judea. The road led down a wild, rocky ravine, which was infested with robbers, and was often the scene of violence. It was here that the traveler was attacked, stripped of all that was valuable, and left half dead by the wayside. As he lay thus, a priest came that way; he saw the man lying wounded and bruised, weltering in his own blood; but he left him without rendering any assistance. He "passed by on the other side." Then a Levite appeared. Curious to know what had happened, he stopped and looked at the sufferer. He was convicted of what he ought to do, but it was not an agreeable duty. He wished that he had not come that way so that he would not have seen the wounded man. He persuaded himself that the case was no concern of his, and he too "passed by on the other side."

But a Samaritan, traveling the same road, saw the sufferer, and he did the work that the others had refused to do. With gentleness and kindness he ministered to the wounded man. "When he saw him, he had compassion on him, and went to him, and bound up his wounds, pouring in oil and wine, and set him on his own beast, and brought him to an inn, and took care of him. And on the morrow when he departed, he took out two pence, and gave them to the host, and said unto him, Take care of him; and whatsoever thou spendest more, when I come again, I will repay thee." The priest and the Levite both professed piety, but the Samaritan showed that he was truly converted. It was no more agreeable for him to do the work than for the priest and the Levite, but in spirit and works he proved himself to be in harmony with God.

In giving this lesson, Christ presented the principles of the law in a direct, forcible way, showing His hearers that they had neglected to carry out these principles. His words were so definite and pointed that the listeners could find no opportunity to cavil. The lawyer found in the lesson nothing that he could criticize. His prejudice in regard to Christ was removed. But he had not overcome his national dislike sufficiently to give credit to the Samaritan by name. When Christ asked, "Which now of these three, thinkest thou, was neighbour unto him that fell among the thieves?" he answered, "He that showed mercy on him."

"Then said Jesus unto him, Go, and do thou likewise." Show the same tender kindness to those in need. Thus you will give evidence that you keep the whole law.

The great difference between the Jews and the Samaritans was a difference in religious belief, a question as to what constitutes true worship. The Pharisees would say nothing good of the Samaritans, but poured their bitterest curses upon them. So strong was the antipathy between the Jews and the Samaritans that to the Samaritan woman it seemed a strange thing for Christ to ask her for a drink. "How is it," she said, "that Thou, being a Jew, askest drink of me, which am a woman of Samaria?" "For," adds the evangelist, "the Jews have no dealings with the Samaritans." John 4:9. And when the Jews were so filled with murderous hatred against Christ that they rose up in the temple to stone Him, they could find no better words by which to express their hatred than, "Say we not well that Thou art a Samaritan, and hast a devil?" John 8:48. Yet the priest and Levite neglected the very work the Lord had enjoined on them, leaving a hated and despised Samaritan to minister to one of their own countrymen.

The Samaritan had fulfilled the command, "Thou shalt love thy neighbour as thyself," thus showing that he was more righteous than those by whom he was denounced. Risking his own life, he had treated the wounded man as his brother. This Samaritan represents Christ. Our Saviour manifested for us a love that the love of man can never equal. When we were bruised and dying, He had pity upon us. He did not pass us by on the other side, and leave us, helpless and hopeless, to perish. He did not remain in His holy, happy home, where He was beloved by all the heavenly host. He beheld our sore need, He undertook our case, and identified His interests with those of humanity. He died to save His enemies. He prayed for His murderers. Pointing to His own example, He says to His followers, "These things I command you, that ye love one another"; "as I have loved you, that ye also love one another." John 15:17; 13:34.

The priest and the Levite had been for worship to the temple whose service was appointed by God Himself. To participate in that service was a great and exalted privilege, and the priest and Levite felt that having been thus honored, it was beneath them to minister to an unknown sufferer by the wayside. Thus they neglected the special opportunity which God had offered them as His agents to bless a fellow being.

Many today are making a similar mistake. They separate their duties into two distinct classes. The one class is made up of great things, to be regulated by the law of God; the other class is made up of so-called little things, in which the command, "Thou shalt love thy neighbour as thyself," is ignored. This sphere of work is left to caprice, subject to inclination or impulse. Thus the character is marred, and the religion of Christ misrepresented.

There are those who would think it lowering to their dignity to minister to suffering humanity. Many look with indifference and contempt upon those who have laid the temple of the soul in ruins. Others neglect the poor from a different motive. They are working, as they believe, in the cause of Christ, seeking to build up some 383 worthy enterprise. They feel that they are doing a great work, and they cannot stop to notice the wants of the needy and distressed. In advancing their supposedly great work they may even oppress the poor. They may place them in hard and trying circumstances, deprive them of their rights, or neglect their needs. Yet they feel that all this is justifiable because they are, as they think, advancing the cause of Christ.

Many will allow a brother or a neighbor to struggle unaided under adverse circumstances. Because they profess to be Christians he may be led to think that in their cold selfishness they are representing Christ. Because the Lord's professed servants are not in co-operation with Him, the love of God, which should flow forth from them, is in great degree cut off from their fellow men. And a large revenue of praise and thanksgiving from human hearts and human lips is prevented from flowing back to God. He is robbed of the glory due to His holy name. He is robbed of the souls for whom Christ died, souls whom He longs to bring into His kingdom to dwell in His presence through endless ages.

Divine truth exerts little influence upon the world, when it should exert much influence through our practice. The mere profession of religion abounds, but it has little weight. We may claim to be followers of Christ, we may claim to believe every truth in the word of God; but this will do our neighbor no good unless our belief is carried into our daily life. Our profession may be as high as heaven, but it will save neither ourselves nor our fellow men unless we are Christians. A right example will do more to benefit the world than all our profession.

By no selfish practices can the cause of Christ be served. His cause is the cause of the 384 oppressed and the poor. In the hearts of His professed followers there is need of the tender sympathy of Christ—a deeper love for those whom He has so valued as to give His own life for

their salvation. These souls are precious, infinitely more precious than any other offering we can bring to God. To bend every energy toward some apparently great work, while we neglect the needy or turn the stranger from his right, is not a service that will meet His approval.

The sanctification of the soul by the working of the Holy Spirit is the implanting of Christ's nature in humanity. Gospel religion is Christ in the life—a living, active principle. It is the grace of Christ revealed in character and wrought out in good works. The principles of the gospel cannot be disconnected from any department of practical life. Every line of Christian experience and labor is to be a representation of the life of Christ.

Love is the basis of godliness. Whatever the profession, no man has pure love to God unless he has unselfish love for his brother. But we can never come into possession of this spirit by *trying* to love others. What is needed is the love of Christ in the heart. When self is merged in Christ, love springs forth spontaneously. The completeness of Christian character is attained when the impulse to help and bless others springs constantly from within—when the sunshine of heaven fills the heart and is revealed in the countenance.

It is not possible for the heart in which Christ abides to be destitute of love. If we love God because He first loved us, we shall love all for whom Christ died. We cannot come in touch with divinity without coming in touch with humanity; for in Him who sits upon the throne of the universe, divinity and humanity are combined. Connected with Christ, we are connected with our fellow men by the golden links of the 385 chain of love. Then the pity and compassion of Christ will be manifest in our life. We shall not wait to have the needy and unfortunate brought to us. We shall not need to be entreated to feel for the woes of others. It will be as natural for us to minister to the needy and suffering as it was for Christ to go about doing good.

Wherever there is an impulse of love and sympathy, wherever the heart reaches out to bless and uplift others, there is revealed the working of God's Holy Spirit. In the depths of heathenism, men who have had no knowledge of the written law of God, who have never even heard the name of Christ, have been kind to His servants, protecting them at the risk of their own lives. Their acts show the working of a divine power. The Holy Spirit has implanted the grace of Christ in the heart of the savage, quickening his sympathies contrary to his nature, contrary to his education. The "Light which lighteth every man that cometh into the world" (John 1:9), is shining in his soul; and this light, if heeded, will guide his feet to the kingdom of God.

The glory of heaven is in lifting up the fallen, 386

comforting the distressed. And wherever Christ abides in human hearts, He will be revealed in the same way. Wherever it acts, the religion of Christ will bless. Wherever it works, there is brightness.

No distinction on account of nationality, race, or caste, is recognized by God. He is the Maker of all mankind. All men are of one family by creation, and all are one through redemption. Christ came to demolish every wall of partition, to throw open every compartment of the temple, that every soul may have free access to God. His love is so broad, so deep, so full, that it penetrates everywhere. It lifts out of Satan's circle the poor souls who have been deluded by his deceptions. It places them within reach of the throne of God, the throne encircled by the rainbow of promise.

In Christ there is neither Jew nor Greek, bond nor free. All are brought nigh by His precious blood. (Gal. 3:28; Eph. 2:13.)

Whatever the difference in religious belief, a call from suffering humanity must be heard and answered. Where bitterness of feeling exists because of difference in religion, much good may be done by personal service. Loving ministry will break down prejudice, and win souls to God.

We should anticipate the sorrows, the difficulties, the troubles of others. We should enter into the joys and cares of both high and low, rich and poor. "Freely ye have received," Christ says, "freely give." Matt. 10:8. All around us are poor, tried souls that need sympathizing words and helpful deeds. There are widows who need sympathy and assistance. There are orphans whom Christ has bidden His followers receive as a trust from God. Too often these are passed by with neglect. They may be ragged, uncouth, and seemingly in every way unattractive; yet they are God's property. They have 387 been bought with a price, and they are as precious in His sight as we are. They are members of God's great household, and Christians as His stewards are responsible for them. "Their souls," He says, "will I require at thine hand."

Sin is the greatest of all evils, and it is ours to pity and help the sinner. But not all can be reached in the same way. There are many who hide their soul hunger. These would be greatly helped by a tender word or a kind remembrance. There are others who are in the greatest need, yet they know it not. They do not realize the terrible destitution of the soul. Multitudes are so sunken in sin that they have lost the sense of eternal realities, lost the similitude of God, and they hardly know whether they have souls to be saved or not. They have neither faith in God nor confidence in man. Many of these can be reached only through acts of disinterested kindness. Their physical wants must first be cared for. They must be fed, cleansed, and decently clothed. As they see the evidence of your unselfish love, it will be easier for them to believe in the love of Christ.

There are many who err, and who feel their shame and their folly. They look upon their mistakes and errors until they are driven almost to desperation. These souls we are not to neglect. When one has to swim against the stream, there is all the force of the current driving him back. Let a helping hand then be held out to him as was the Elder Brother's hand to the sinking Peter. Speak to him hopeful words, words that will establish confidence and awaken love.

Thy brother, sick in spirit, needs thee, as thou thyself hast needed a brother's love. He needs the experience of one who has been as weak as he, one who can sympathize with him and help him. The knowledge of our own weakness should help us to help another in his bitter need. Never should we pass by one suffering soul 388 without seeking to impart to him the comfort wherewith we are comforted of God.

It is fellowship with Christ, personal contact with a living Saviour, that enables the mind and heart and soul to triumph over the lower nature. Tell the wanderer of an almighty hand that will hold him up, of an infinite humanity in Christ that pities him. It is not enough for him to believe in law and force, things that have no pity, and never hear the cry for help. He needs to clasp a hand that is warm, to trust in a heart full of tenderness. Keep his mind stayed upon the thought of a divine presence ever beside him, ever looking upon him with pitying love. Bid him think of a Father's heart that ever grieves over sin, of a Father's hand stretched out still, of a Father's voice saying, "Let him take hold of My strength, that he may make peace with Me; and he shall make peace." Isa. 27:5.

As you engage in this work, you have companions unseen by human eyes. Angels of heaven were beside the Samaritan who cared for the wounded stranger. Angels from the heavenly courts stand by all who do God's service in ministering to their fellow men. And you have the co-operation of Christ Himself. He is the Restorer, and as you work under His supervision, you will see great results.

Upon your faithfulness in this work not only the well-being of others but your own eternal destiny depends. Christ is seeking to uplift all who will be lifted to companionship with

---

"God that made the world and all things therein, . . . hath made of one blood all nations of men for to dwell on all the face of the earth, . . . that they should seek the Lord, if haply they might feel after Him, and find Him." Acts 17: 24-27. "I beheld, and lo, a great multitude . . . of all nations, and kindreds, and people, and tongues, stood before the throne, and before the Lamb, clothed with white robes, and palms in their hands." Rev. 7: 9.

Himself, that we may be one with Him as He is one with the Father. He permits us to come in contact with suffering and calamity in order to call us out of our selfishness; He seeks to develop in us the attributes of His character—compassion, tenderness, and love. By accepting this work of ministry we place ourselves in His school, to be fitted for the courts of God. By rejecting it, we reject His instruction, and choose eternal separation from His presence.

"If thou wilt keep My charge," the Lord declares, "I will give thee places to walk among these that stand by"—even among the angels that surround His throne. (Zech. 3:7.) By co-operating with heavenly beings in their work on earth, we are preparing for their companionship in heaven. "Ministering spirits, sent forth to minister for them who shall be heirs of salvation" (Heb. 1:14), angels in heaven will welcome those who on earth have lived "not to be ministered unto, but to minister" (Matt. 20:28). In this blessed companionship we shall learn, to our eternal joy, all that is wrapped up in the question, "Who is my neighbour?"

28

The Reward of Grace

The truth of God's free grace had been almost lost sight of by the Jews. The rabbis taught that God's favor must be earned. The reward of the righteous they hoped to gain by their own works. Thus their worship was prompted by a grasping, mercenary spirit. From this spirit even the disciples of Christ were not wholly free, and the Saviour sought every opportunity of showing them their error. Just before He gave the parable of the laborers, an event occurred that opened the way for Him to present the right principles.

As He was walking by the way, a young ruler came running to Him, and kneeling, reverently saluted Him. "Good Master," he said, "what good thing shall I do, that I may have eternal life?"

The ruler had addressed Christ merely as an honored rabbi, not discerning in Him the Son of God. The Saviour said, "Why callest thou Me good? There is none good but one, that is, God." On what ground do you call *Me* good? God is the one good. If you recognize Me as such, you must receive Me as His Son and representative.

"If thou wilt enter into life," He added, "keep the commandments." The character of God is expressed in His law; and in order for you to be in harmony with God, the principles of His law must be the spring of your every action.

Christ does not lessen the claims of the law. In unmistakable language He presents obedi-

ence to it as the condition of eternal life—the same condition that was required of Adam before his fall. The Lord expects no less of the soul now than He expected of man in Paradise, perfect obedience, unblemished righteousness. The requirement under the covenant of grace is just as broad as the requirement made in Eden—harmony with God's law, which is holy, just, and good.

To the words, "Keep the commandments," the young man answered, "Which?" He supposed that some ceremonial precept was meant, but Christ was speaking of the law given from Sinai. He mentioned several commandments from the second table of the Decalogue, then summed them all up in the precept, "Thou shalt love thy neighbour as thyself."

The young man answered without hesitation, "All these things have I kept from my youth up; what lack I yet?" His conception of the law was external and superficial. Judged by a human standard, he had preserved an unblemished character. To a great degree his outward life had been free from guilt; he verily thought that his obedience had been without a flaw. Yet he had a secret fear that all was not right between his soul and God. This prompted the question, "What lack I yet?"

"If thou wilt be perfect," Christ said, "go and sell that thou hast, and give to the poor, and thou shalt have treasure in heaven, and come and follow Me. But when the young man heard that saying, he went away sorrowful; for he had great possessions."

The lover of self is a transgressor of the law. This Jesus desired to reveal to the young man, and He gave him a test that would make manifest the selfishness of his heart. He showed him the plague spot in his character. The young man desired no further enlightenment. He had cherished an idol in the soul; the world was his god. He professed to have kept the commandments, but he was destitute of the principle which is the very spirit and life of them all. He did not possess true love for God or man. This want was the want of everything that would qualify him to enter the kingdom of heaven. In his love of self and worldly gain he was out of harmony with the principles of heaven.

When this young ruler came to Jesus, his sincerity and earnestness won the Saviour's heart. He "beholding him loved him." In this young man He saw one who might do service as a preacher of righteousness. He would have received this talented and noble youth as readily as He received the poor fishermen who followed Him. Had the young man devoted his ability to the work of saving souls, he might have become a diligent and successful laborer for Christ.

But first he must accept the conditions of discipleship. He must give himself unreservedly to

God. At the Saviour's call, John, Peter, Matthew, and their companions "left all, rose up, and followed Him." Luke 5:28. The same consecration was required of the young ruler. And in this Christ did not ask a greater sacrifice than He Himself had made. "He was rich, yet for your sakes He became poor, that ye through His poverty might be rich." 2 Cor. 8:9. The young man had only to follow where Christ led the way.

Christ looked upon the young man and longed after his soul. He longed to send him forth as a messenger of blessing to men. In the place of that which He called upon him to surrender, Christ offered him the privilege of companionship with Himself. "Follow Me," He said. This privilege had been counted a joy by Peter, James, and John. The young man himself looked upon Christ with admiration. His heart was drawn toward the Saviour. But he was not ready to accept the Saviour's principle of self-sacrifice. He chose his riches before Jesus. He wanted eternal life, but would not receive into the soul that unselfish love which alone is life, and with a sorrowful heart he turned away from Christ.

As the young man turned away, Jesus said to His disciples, "How hardly shall they that have riches enter into the kingdom of God." These words astonished the disciples. They had been taught to look upon the rich as the favorites of heaven; worldly power and riches they themselves hoped to receive in the Messiah's kingdom; if the rich were to fail of entering the kingdom, what hope could there be for the rest of men?

"Jesus answereth again, and saith unto them, Children, how hard is it for them that trust in riches to enter into the kingdom of God! It is easier for a camel to go through the eye of a needle, than for a rich man to enter into the kingdom of God. And they were astonished out of measure." Now they realized that they themselves were included in the solemn warning. In the light of the Saviour's words, their own secret longing for power and riches was revealed. With misgivings for themselves they exclaimed, "Who then can be saved?"

"Jesus looking upon them saith, With men it is impossible, but not with God; for with God all things are possible."

A rich man, as such, cannot enter heaven. His wealth gives him no title to the inheritance of the saints in light. It is only through the unmerited grace of Christ that any man can find entrance into the city of God.

To the rich no less than to the poor are the words of the Holy Spirit spoken, "Ye are not

your own; for ye are bought with a price." 1 Cor. 6:19, 20. When men believe this, their possessions will be held as a trust, to be used as God shall direct, for the saving of the lost, and the comfort of the suffering and the poor. With man this is impossible, for the heart clings to its earthly treasure. The soul that is bound in service to mammon is deaf to the cry of human need. But with God all things are possible. By beholding the matchless love of Christ, the selfish heart will be melted and subdued. The rich man will be led, as was Saul the Pharisee, to say, "What things were gain to me, those I counted loss for Christ. Yea doubtless, and I count all things but loss for the excellency of the knowledge of Christ Jesus my Lord." Phil. 3:7, 8. Then they will not count anything their own. They will joy to regard themselves as stewards of the manifold grace of God, and for His sake servants of all men.

Peter was the first to rally from the secret conviction wrought by the Saviour's words. He thought with satisfaction of what he and his brethren had given up for Christ. "Behold," he said, "we have forsaken all, and followed Thee." Remembering the conditional promise to the young ruler, "Thou shalt have treasure in heaven," he now asked what he and his companions were to receive as a reward for their sacrifices.

The Saviour's answer thrilled the hearts of those Galilean fishermen. It pictured honors that fulfilled their highest dreams: "Verily I say unto you, That ye which have followed Me, in the regeneration when the Son of man shall sit in the throne of His glory, ye also shall sit upon twelve thrones, judging the twelve tribes of Israel." And He added, "There is no man that hath left house, or brethren, or sisters, or father, or mother, or wife, or children, or lands, for My sake, and the gospel's, but he shall receive an hundredfold now in this time, houses, and brethren, and sisters, and mothers, and children, and lands, with persecutions; and in the world to come eternal life."

But Peter's question, "What shall we have therefore?" had revealed a spirit that uncorrected would unfit the disciples to be messengers for Christ; for it was the spirit of a hireling. While they had been attracted by the love of Jesus, the disciples were not wholly free from Pharisaism. They still worked with the thought of meriting a reward in proportion to their labor. They cherished a spirit of self-exaltation and self-complacency, and made comparisons among themselves. When one of them failed in any particular, the others indulged feelings of superiority.

"Whatsoever ye do, do it heartily, as to the Lord, and not unto men; knowing that of the Lord ye shall receive the reward of the inheritance." Col. 3: 23, 24.

"Behold, I come quickly; and My reward is with Me, to give every man according as his work shall be." Rev. 22: 12.

Lest the disciples should lose sight of the principles of the gospel, Christ related to them a parable illustrating the manner in which God deals with His servants, and the spirit in which He desires them to labor for Him.

"The kingdom of heaven," He said, "is like unto a man that is an householder, which went out early in the morning to hire labourers into his vineyard." It was the custom for men seeking employment to wait in the market places, and thither the employers went to find servants. The man in the parable is represented as going out at different hours to engage workmen. Those who are hired at the earliest hours agree to work for a stated sum; those hired later leave their wages to the discretion of the householder.

"So when even was come, the lord of the vineyard saith unto his steward, Call the labourers, and give them their hire, beginning from the last unto the first. And when they came that were hired about the eleventh hour, they received every man a penny. But when the first came, they supposed that they should have received more; and they likewise received every man a penny."

The householder's dealing with the workers in his vineyard represents God's dealing with the human family. It is contrary to the customs that prevail among men. In worldly business, compensation is given according to the work accomplished. The laborer expects to be paid only that which he earns. But in the parable, Christ was illustrating the principles of His kingdom—a kingdom not of this world. He is not controlled by any human standard. The Lord says, "My thoughts are not your thoughts, neither are your ways My ways. . . . For as the heavens are higher than the earth, so are My ways higher than your ways, and My thoughts than your thoughts." Isa. 55:8, 9.

In the parable the first laborers agreed to work for a stipulated sum, and they received the amount specified, nothing more. Those later hired believed the master's promise, "Whatsoever is right, that shall ye receive." They showed their confidence in him by asking no question in regard to wages. They trusted to his justice and equity. They were rewarded, not according to the amount of their labor, but according to the generosity of his purpose.

So God desires us to trust in Him who justifieth the ungodly. His reward is given not according to our merit but according to His own purpose, "which He purposed in Christ Jesus our Lord." Eph. 3:11. "Not by works of righteousness which we have done, but according to His mercy He saved us." Titus 3:5. And for those who trust in Him He will do "exceeding abundantly above all that we ask or think." Eph. 3:20.

Not the amount of labor performed or its visible results but the spirit in which the work is done makes it of value with God. Those who came into the vineyard at the eleventh hour were thankful for an opportunity to work. Their hearts were full of gratitude to the one who had accepted them; and when at the close of the day the householder paid them for a full day's work, they were greatly surprised. They knew they had not earned such wages. And the kindness expressed in the countenance of their employer filled them with joy. They never forgot the goodness of the householder or the generous compensation they had received. Thus it is with the sinner who, knowing his unworthiness, has entered the Master's vineyard at the eleventh hour. His time of service seems so short, he feels that he is undeserving of reward; but he is filled with joy that God has accepted him at all. He works with a humble, trusting spirit, thankful for the privilege of being a co-worker with Christ. This spirit God delights to honor.

The Lord desires us to rest in Him without a question as to our measure of reward. When Christ abides in the soul, the thought of reward is not uppermost. This is not the motive that actuates our service. It is true that in a subordinate sense we should have respect to the recompense of reward. God desires us to appreciate His promised blessings. But He would not have us eager for rewards nor feel that for every duty we must receive compensation. We should not be so anxious to gain the reward as to do what is right, irrespective of all gain. Love to God and to our fellow men should be our motive.

This parable does not excuse those who hear the first call to labor but who neglect to enter the Lord's vineyard. When the householder went to the market place at the eleventh hour and found men unemployed he said, "Why stand ye here all the day idle?" The answer was, "Because no man hath hired us." None of those called later in the day were there in the morning. They had not refused the call. Those who refuse and afterward repent, do well to repent; but it is not safe to trifle with the first call of mercy.

When the laborers in the vineyard received "every man a penny," those who had begun work early in the day were offended. Had they not worked for twelve hours? they reasoned, and was it not right that they should receive more than those who had worked for only one hour in the cooler part of the day? "These last have wrought but one hour," they said, "and thou hast made them equal unto us, which have borne the burden and heat of the day."

"Friend," the householder replied to one of them, "I do thee no wrong; didst not thou agree with me for a penny? Take that thine is, and go thy way; I will give unto this last, even as unto thee. Is it not lawful for me to do what I will with mine own? Is thine eye evil, because I am good?

"So the last shall be first, and the first last; for

many be called, but few chosen."

The first laborers of the parable represent those who, because of their services, claim preference above others. They take up their work in a self-gratulatory spirit, and do not bring into it self-denial and sacrifice. They may have professed to serve God all their lives; they may have been foremost in enduring hardship, privation, and trial, and they therefore think themselves entitled to a large reward. They think more of the reward than of the privilege of being servants of Christ. In their view their labors and sacrifices entitle them to receive honor above others, and because this claim is not recognized, they are offended. Did they bring into their work a loving, trusting spirit, they would continue to be first; but their querulous, complaining disposition is un-Christlike, and proves them to be untrustworthy. It reveals their desire for self-advancement, their distrust of God, and their jealous, grudging spirit toward their brethren. The Lord's goodness and liberality is to them only an occasion for murmuring. Thus they show that there is no connection between their souls and God. They do not know the joy of co-operation with the Master Worker.

There is nothing more offensive to God than this narrow, self-caring spirit. He cannot work with any who manifest these attributes. They are insensible to the working of His Spirit.

The Jews had been first called into the Lord's vineyard, and because of this they were proud and self-righteous. Their long years of service they regarded as entitling them to receive a larger reward than others. Nothing was more exasperating to them than an intimation that the Gentiles were to be admitted to equal privileges with themselves in the things of God.

Christ warned the disciples who had been first called to follow Him, lest the same evil should be cherished among them. He saw that the weakness, the curse of the church, would be a spirit of self-righteousness. Men would think they could do something toward earning a place in the kingdom of heaven. They would imagine that when they had made certain advancement, the Lord would come in to help them. Thus there would be an abundance of self and little of Jesus. Many who had made a little advancement would be puffed up and think themselves superior to others. They would be eager for flattery, jealous if not thought most important. Against this danger Christ seeks to guard His disciples.

All boasting of merit in ourselves is out of place. "Let not the wise man glory in his wisdom, neither let the mighty man glory in his might, let not the rich man glory in his riches; but let him that glorieth, glory in this, that he understandeth and knoweth Me, that I am the Lord which exercise loving kindness, judgment, and righteousness in the earth; for in these things I delight, saith the Lord." Jer. 9:23, 24.

The reward is not of works, lest any man should boast; but it is all of grace. "What shall we say then that Abraham our father, as pertaining to the flesh, hath found? For if Abraham were justified by works, he hath whereof to glory; but not before God. For what saith the scripture? Abraham believed God, and it was counted unto him for righteousness. Now to him that worketh is the reward not reckoned of grace, but of debt. But to him that worketh not, but believeth on Him that justifieth the ungodly, his faith is counted for righteousness." Rom. 4:1-5. Therefore there is no occasion for one to glory over another or to grudge against another. No one is privileged above another, nor can anyone claim the reward as a right.

The first and the last are to be sharers in the great, eternal reward, and the first should gladly welcome the last. He who grudges the reward to another forgets that he himself is saved by grace alone. The parable of the laborers rebukes all jealousy and suspicion. Love rejoices in the truth and institutes no envious comparisons. He who possesses love compares only the loveliness of Christ and his own imperfect character.

This parable is a warning to all laborers, however long their service, however abundant their labors, that without love to their brethren, without humility before God, they are nothing. There is no religion in the enthronement of self. He who makes self-glorification his aim will find himself destitute of that grace which alone can make him efficient in Christ's service. Whenever pride and self-complacency are indulged, the work is marred.

It is not the length of time we labor but our willingness and fidelity in the work that makes it acceptable to God. In all our service a full surrender of self is demanded. The smallest duty done in sincerity and self-forgetfulness is more pleasing to God than the greatest work when marred with self-seeking. He looks to see how

---

"Neither is he that planteth any thing, neither he that watereth; but God that giveth the increase. Now he that planteth and he that watereth are one: and every man shall receive his own reward according to his own labour. For we are labourers together with God: . . . other foundation can no man lay than that is laid, which is Jesus Christ. . . . Every man's work shall be made manifest: . . . If any man's work abide which he hath built thereupon, he shall receive a reward." 1 Cor. 3: 7-14.

"The Lord recompense thy work, and a full reward be given thee of the Lord God of Israel." Ruth 2: 12.
"Verily there is a reward for the righteous." Ps. 58: 11.
"To him that soweth righteousness shall be a sure reward." Prov. 11: 18.

much of the spirit of Christ we cherish, and how much of the likeness of Christ our work reveals. He regards more the love and faithfulness with which we work than the amount we do.

Only when selfishness is dead, when strife for supremacy is banished, when gratitude fills the heart, and love makes fragrant the life—it is only then that Christ is abiding in the soul, and we are recognized as laborers together with God.

403 However trying their labor, the true workers do not regard it as drudgery. They are ready to spend and to be spent; but it is a cheerful work, done with a glad heart. Joy in God is expressed through Jesus Christ. Their joy is the joy set before Christ—"to do the will of Him that sent Me, and to finish His work." John 4:34. They are in co-operation with the Lord of glory. This thought sweetens all toil, it braces the will, it nerves the spirit for whatever may befall. Working with unselfish heart, ennobled by being partakers of Christ's sufferings, sharing His sympathies, and co-operating with Him in His labor, they help to swell the tide of His joy and bring honor and praise to His exalted name.

This is the spirit of all true service for God. Through a lack of this spirit, many who appear to be first will become last, while those who possess it, though accounted last, will become first.

There are many who have given themselves to Christ, yet who see no opportunity of doing a large work or making great sacrifices in His service. These may find comfort in the thought that it is not necessarily the martyr's self-surrender which is most acceptable to God; it may not be the missionary who has daily faced danger and death that stands highest in heaven's records. The Christian who is such in his private life, in the daily surrender of self, in sincerity of purpose and purity of thought, in meekness under provocation, in faith and piety, in fidelity in that which is least, the one who in the home life represents the character of Christ—such a one may in the sight of God be more precious than even the world-renowned missionary or martyr.

Oh, how different are the standards by which God and men measure character. God sees many temptations resisted of which the world and even near friends never know—temptations in the home, in the heart. He sees the soul's 404 humility in view of its own weakness; the sincere repentance over even a thought that is evil. He sees the wholehearted devotion to His service. He has noted the hours of hard battle with self—battle that won the victory. All this God and angels know. A book of remembrance is written before Him for them that fear the Lord and that think upon His name.

Not in our learning, not in our position, not in our numbers or entrusted talents, not in the will

of man, is to be found the secret of success. Feeling our inefficiency we are to contemplate Christ, and through Him who is the strength of all strength, the thought of all thought, the willing and obedient will gain victory after victory.

And however short our service or humble our work, if in simple faith we follow Christ, we shall not be disappointed of the reward. That which even the greatest and wisest cannot earn, the weakest and most humble may receive. Heaven's golden gate opens not to the self-exalted. It is not lifted up to the proud in spirit. But the everlasting portals will open wide to the trembling touch of a little child. Blessed will be the recompense of grace to those who have wrought for God in the simplicity of faith and love.

29
"To Meet the Bridegroom"

405

Christ with His disciples is seated upon the Mount of Olives. The sun has set behind the mountains, and the heavens are curtained with the shades of evening. In full view is a dwelling house lighted up brilliantly as if for some festive scene. The light streams from the openings, and an expectant company wait around, indicating that a marriage procession is soon to appear. In many parts of the East, wedding festivities are held in the evening. The bridegroom goes forth to meet his bride and bring her to his home. By torchlight the bridal party proceed from her father's house to his own, where a feast is provided for the invited guests. In the scene upon which Christ looks, a company are awaiting the appearance of the bridal party, intending to join the procession.

Lingering near the bride's house are ten young women robed in white. Each carries a lighted lamp and a small flagon for oil. All are 406 anxiously watching for the appearance of the bridegroom. But there is a delay. Hour after hour passes; the watchers become weary and fall asleep. At midnight the cry is heard, "Behold, the bridegroom cometh; go ye out to meet him." The sleepers, suddenly awaking, spring to their feet. They see the procession moving on, bright with torches and glad with music. They hear the voice of the bridegroom and the voice of the bride. The ten maidens seize their lamps and begin to trim them, in haste to go forth. But five have neglected to fill their flasks with oil. They did not anticipate so long a delay, and they have not prepared for the emergency. In distress they appeal to their wiser companions saying, "Give us of your oil; for our lamps are going out." (Margin.) But the waiting five, with their freshly trimmed lamps,

This chapter is based on Matthew 25:1-13.

have emptied their flagons. They have no oil to spare, and they answer, "Not so; lest there be not enough for us and you: but go ye rather to them that sell, and buy for yourselves."

While they went to buy, the procession moved on, and left them behind. The five with lighted lamps joined the throng and entered the house with the bridal train, and the door was shut. When the foolish virgins reached the banqueting hall, they received an unexpected denial. The master of the feast declared, "I know you not." They were left standing without, in the empty street, in the blackness of the night.

As Christ sat looking upon the party that waited for the bridegroom, He told His disciples the story of the ten virgins, by their experience illustrating the experience of the church that shall live just before His second coming.

The two classes of watchers represent the two classes who profess to be waiting for their Lord. They are called virgins because they profess a pure faith. By the lamps is represented the word 407 of God. The psalmist says, "Thy word is a lamp unto my feet, and a light unto my path." Ps. 119:105. The oil is a symbol of the Holy Spirit. Thus the Spirit is represented in the prophecy of Zechariah. "The angel that talked with me came again," he says, "and waked me, as a man that is wakened out of his sleep, and said unto me, What seest thou? And I said, I have looked, and behold a candlestick all of gold, with a bowl upon the top of it, and his seven lamps thereon, and seven pipes to the seven lamps, which are upon the top thereof; and two olive trees by it, one upon the right side of the bowl, and the other upon the left side thereof. So I answered and spake to the angel that talked with me, saying, What are these, my lord? . . . Then he answered and spake unto me, saying, This is the word of the Lord unto Zerubbabel, saying, Not by might, nor by power, but by My Spirit, saith the Lord of hosts. . . . And I answered again, 408 and said unto him, What be these two olive branches which through the two golden pipes empty the golden oil out of themselves? . . . Then said he, These are the two anointed ones, that stand by the Lord of the whole earth." Zech. 4:1-14.

From the two olive trees the golden oil was emptied through the golden pipes into the bowl of the candlestick, and thence into the golden lamps that gave light to the sanctuary. So from the holy ones that stand in God's presence His Spirit is imparted to the human instrumentalities who are consecrated to His service. The mission of the two anointed ones is to communicate to God's people that heavenly grace which alone can make His word a lamp to the feet and a light to the path. "Not by might, nor by power, but by My Spirit, saith the Lord of hosts." Zech. 4:6.

In the parable, all the ten virgins went out to meet the bridegroom. All had lamps and vessels for oil. For a time there was seen no difference between them. So with the church that lives just before Christ's second coming. All have a knowledge of the Scriptures. All have heard the message of Christ's near approach, and confidently expect His appearing. But as in the parable, so it is now. A time of waiting intervenes, faith is tried; and when the cry is heard, "Behold, the Bridegroom cometh; go ye out to meet Him," many are unready. They have no oil in their vessels with their lamps. They are destitute of the Holy Spirit.

Without the Spirit of God a knowledge of His word is of no avail. The theory of truth, unaccompanied by the Holy Spirit, cannot quicken the soul or sanctify the heart. One may be familiar with the commands and promises of the Bible; but unless the Spirit of God sets the truth home, the character will not be transformed. Without the enlightenment of the Spirit, men 411 will not be able to distinguish truth from error, and they will fall under the masterful temptations of Satan.

The class represented by the foolish virgins are not hypocrites. They have a regard for the truth, they have advocated the truth, they are attracted to those who believe the truth; but they have not yielded themselves to the Holy Spirit's working. They have not fallen upon the Rock, Christ Jesus, and permitted their old nature to be broken up. This class are represented also by the stony-ground hearers. They receive the word with readiness, but they fail of assimilating its principles. Its influence is not abiding. The Spirit works upon man's heart, according to his desire and consent implanting in him a new nature; but the class represented by the foolish virgins have been content with a superficial work. They do not know God. They have not studied His character; they have not held communion with Him; therefore they do not know how to trust, how to look and live. Their service to God degenerates into a form. "They come unto thee as the people cometh, and they sit before thee as My people, and they hear thy words, but they will not do them; for with their mouth they show much love, but their heart goeth after their covetousness." Eze. 33:31. The apostle Paul points out that this will be the special characteristic of those who live just before Christ's second coming. He says, "In the last days perilous times shall come: for men shall be lovers of their own selves; . . . lovers of pleasures more than lovers of God; having a form of godliness, but denying the power thereof." 2 Tim. 3:1-5.

This is the class that in time of peril are found crying, Peace and safety. They lull their hearts into security, and dream not of danger. When startled from their lethargy, they discern their destitution, and entreat others to supply their

412 lack; but in spiritual things no man can make up another's deficiency. The grace of God has been freely offered to every soul. The message of the gospel has been heralded, "Let him that is athirst come. And whosoever will, let him take the water of life freely." Rev. 22:17. But character is not transferable. No man can believe for another. No man can receive the Spirit for another. No man can impart to another the character which is the fruit of the Spirit's working. "Though Noah, Daniel, and Job were in it [the land], as I live, saith the Lord God, they shall deliver neither son nor daughter; they shall but deliver their own souls by their righteousness." Eze. 14:20.

It is in a crisis that character is revealed. When the earnest voice proclaimed at midnight, "Behold, the bridegroom cometh; go ye out to meet him," and the sleeping virgins were roused from their slumbers, it was seen who had made preparation for the event. Both parties were taken unawares; but one was prepared for the emergency, and the other was found without preparation. So now, a sudden and unlooked-for calamity, something that brings the soul face to face with death, will show whether there is any real faith in the promises of God. It will show whether the soul is sustained by grace. The great final test comes at the close of human probation, when it will be too late for the soul's need to be supplied.

The ten virgins are watching in the evening of this earth's history. All claim to be Christians. All have a call, a name, a lamp, and all profess to be doing God's service. All apparently wait for Christ's appearing. But five are unready. Five will be found surprised, dismayed, outside the banquet hall.

At the final day, many will claim admission to Christ's kingdom, saying, "We have eaten 413 and drunk in Thy presence, and Thou hast taught in our streets." "Lord, Lord, have we not prophesied in Thy name? and in Thy name have cast out devils? and in Thy name done many wonderful works?" But the answer is, "I tell you, I know you not whence ye are; depart from Me." Luke 13:26; Matt. 7:22; Luke 13:27. In this life they have not entered into fellowship with Christ; therefore they know not the language of heaven, they are strangers to its joy. "What man knoweth the things of a man, save the spirit of man which is in him? even so the things of God knoweth no man, but the Spirit of God." 1 Cor. 2:11.

Saddest of all words that ever fell on mortal ear are those words of doom, "I know you not." The fellowship of the Spirit, which you have slighted, could alone make you one with the joyous throng at the marriage feast. In that scene you cannot participate. Its light would fall on blinded eyes, its melody upon deaf ears. Its love and joy could awake no chord of gladness in the world-benumbed heart. You are shut out from heaven by your own unfitness for its companionship. 414

We cannot be ready to meet the Lord by waking when the cry is heard, "Behold, the Bridegroom!" and then gathering up our empty lamps to have them replenished. We cannot keep Christ apart from our lives here, and yet be fitted for His companionship in heaven.

In the parable the wise virgins had oil in their vessels with their lamps. Their light burned with undimmed flame through the night of watching. It helped to swell the illumination for the bridegroom's honor. Shining out in the darkness, it helped to illuminate the way to the home of the bridegroom, to the marriage feast.

So the followers of Christ are to shed light into the darkness of the world. Through the Holy Spirit, God's word is a light as it becomes a transforming power in the life of the receiver. By implanting in their hearts the principles of His word, the Holy Spirit develops in men the attributes of God. The light of His glory—His character—is to shine forth in His followers. Thus they are to glorify God, to lighten the path to the Bridegroom's home, to the city of God, to the marriage supper of the Lamb.

The coming of the bridegroom was at midnight—the darkest hour. So the coming of Christ will take place in the darkest period of this earth's history. The days of Noah and Lot pictured the condition of the world just before the coming of the Son of man. The Scriptures pointing forward to this time declare that Satan will work with all power and "with all deceivableness of unrighteousness." 2 Thess. 2:9, 10. His working is plainly revealed by the rapidly increasing darkness, the multitudinous errors, heresies, and delusions of these last days. Not only is Satan leading the world captive, but his deceptions are leavening the professed churches of our Lord Jesus Christ. The great apostasy will develop into darkness deep as midnight, impenetrable as sackcloth of hair. To God's 415 people it will be a night of trial, a night of weeping, a night of persecution for the truth's sake. But out of that night of darkness God's light will shine.

He causes "the light to shine out of darkness." 2 Cor. 4:6. When "the earth was without form, and void, and darkness was upon the face of the deep," "the Spirit of God moved upon the face of the waters. And God said, Let there be light; and there was light." Gen. 1:2, 3. So in the night of spiritual darkness, God's word goes forth, "Let there be light." To His people He says, "Arise, shine; for thy light is come, and the glory of the Lord is risen upon thee." Isa. 60:1.

"Behold," says the Scripture, "the darkness shall cover the earth, and gross darkness the people; but the Lord shall arise upon thee, and His glory shall be seen upon thee." Isa. 60:2.

It is the darkness of misapprehension of God that is enshrouding the world. Men are losing their knowledge of His character. It has been misunderstood and misinterpreted. At this time a message from God is to be proclaimed, a message illuminating in its influence and saving in its power. His character is to be made known. Into the darkness of the world is to be shed the light of His glory, the light of His goodness, mercy, and truth.

This is the work outlined by the prophet Isaiah in the words, "O Jerusalem, that bringest good tidings, lift up thy voice with strength; lift it up, be not afraid; say unto the cities of Judah, Behold your God! Behold, the Lord God will come with strong hand, and His arm shall rule for Him; behold, His reward is with Him, and His work before Him." Isa. 40:9, 10.

Those who wait for the Bridegroom's coming are to say to the people, "Behold your God." The last rays of merciful light, the last message of mercy to be given to the world, is a revelation of His character of love. The children of God are to manifest His glory. In their own life and character they are to reveal what the grace of God has done for them.

The light of the Sun of Righteousness is to shine forth in good works—in words of truth and deeds of holiness.

Christ, the outshining of the Father's glory, came to the world as its light. He came to represent God to men, and of Him it is written that He was anointed "with the Holy Ghost and with power," and "went about doing good." Acts 10:38. In the synagogue at Nazareth He said, "The Spirit of the Lord is upon Me, because He hath anointed Me to preach the gospel to the poor; He hath sent Me to heal the brokenhearted, to preach deliverance to the captives, and recovering of sight to the blind, to set at liberty them that are bruised, to preach the acceptable year of the Lord." Luke 4:18, 19. This was the work He commissioned His disciples to do. "Ye are the light of the world," He said. "Let your light so shine before men, that they may see your good works, and glorify your Father which is in heaven." Matt. 5:14, 16.

This is the work which the prophet Isaiah describes when he says, "Is it not to deal thy bread to the hungry, and that thou bring the poor that are cast out to thy house? when thou seest the naked, that thou cover him; and that thou hide not thyself from thine own flesh? Then shall thy light break forth as the morning, and thine health shall spring forth speedily; and thy righteousness shall go before thee; the glory of the Lord shall be thy rereward." Isa. 58:7, 8.

Thus in the night of spiritual darkness God's glory is to shine forth through His church in lifting up the bowed down and comforting those that mourn.

All around us are heard the wails of a world's

sorrow. On every hand are the needy and distressed. It is ours to aid in relieving and softening life's hardships and misery.

Practical work will have far more effect than mere sermonizing. We are to give food to the hungry, clothing to the naked, and shelter to the homeless. And we are called to do more than this. The wants of the soul, only the love of Christ can satisfy. If Christ is abiding in us, our hearts will be full of divine sympathy. The sealed fountains of earnest, Christlike love will be unsealed.

God calls not only for our gifts for the needy, but for our cheerful countenance, our hopeful words, our kindly handclasp. When Christ healed the sick, He laid His hands upon them. So should we come in close touch with those whom we seek to benefit.

There are many from whom hope has departed. Bring back the sunshine to them. Many have lost their courage. Speak to them words of cheer. Pray for them. There are those who need the bread of life. Read to them from the word of God. Upon many is a soul sickness which no earthly balm can reach nor physician heal. Pray for these souls, bring them to Jesus. Tell them that there is a balm in Gilead and a Physician there.

Light is a blessing, a universal blessing, pouring forth its treasures on a world unthankful, unholy, demoralized. So it is with the light of the Sun of Righteousness. The whole earth, wrapped as it is in the darkness of sin, and sorrow, and pain, is to be lighted with the knowledge of God's love. From no sect, rank, or class of people is the light shining from heaven's throne to be excluded.

The message of hope and mercy is to be carried to the ends of the earth. Whosoever will, may reach forth and take hold of God's strength and make peace with Him, and he shall make peace. No longer are the heathen to be wrapped in midnight darkness. The gloom is to disappear before the bright beams of the Sun of Righteousness. The power of hell has been overcome.

But no man can impart that which he himself has not received. In the work of God, humanity can originate nothing. No man can by his own effort make himself a light bearer for God. It was the golden oil emptied by the heavenly messengers into the golden tubes, to be conducted from the golden bowl into the lamps of the sanctuary, that produced a continuous bright and shining light. It is the love of God continually transferred to man that enables him to impart light. Into the hearts of all who are united to God by faith the golden oil of love flows freely, to shine out again in good works, in real, heartfelt service for God.

In the great and measureless gift of the Holy Spirit are contained all of heaven's resources. It is not because of any restriction on the part of

God that the riches of His grace do not flow earthward to men. If all were willing to receive, all would become filled with His Spirit.

It is the privilege of every soul to be a living channel through which God can communicate to the world the treasures of His grace, the unsearchable riches of Christ. There is nothing that Christ desires so much as agents who will represent to the world His Spirit and character. There is nothing that the world needs so much as the manifestation through humanity of the Saviour's love. All heaven is waiting for channels through which can be poured the holy oil to be a joy and blessing to human hearts.

Christ has made every provision that His church shall be a transformed body, illumined with the Light of the world, possessing the glory of Emmanuel. It is His purpose that every Christian shall be surrounded with a spiritual atmosphere of light and peace. He desires that we shall reveal His own joy in our lives.

The indwelling of the Spirit will be shown by the outflowing of heavenly love. The divine fullness will flow through the consecrated human agent, to be given forth to others.

The Sun of Righteousness has "healing in His wings." Mal. 4:2. So from every true disciple is to be diffused an influence for life, courage, helpfulness, and true healing.

The religion of Christ means more than the forgiveness of sin; it means taking away our sins, and filling the vacuum with the graces of the Holy Spirit. It means divine illumination, rejoicing in God. It means a heart emptied of self, and blessed with the abiding presence of Christ. When Christ reigns in the soul, there is purity, freedom from sin. The glory, the fullness, the completeness of the gospel plan is fulfilled in the life. The acceptance of the Saviour brings a glow of perfect peace, perfect love, perfect assurance. The beauty and fragrance of the character of Christ revealed in the life testifies that God has indeed sent His Son into the world to be its Saviour.

Christ does not bid His followers strive to shine. He says, *Let* your light shine. If you have received the grace of God, the light is in you. Remove the obstructions, and the Lord's glory will be revealed. The light will shine forth to penetrate and dispel the darkness. You cannot help shining within the range of your influence.

The revelation of His own glory in the form of humanity will bring heaven so near to men

that the beauty adorning the inner temple will be seen in every soul in whom the Saviour dwells. Men will be captivated by the glory of an abiding Christ. And in currents of praise and thanksgiving from the many souls thus won to God, glory will flow back to the great Giver.

"Arise, shine; for thy light is come, and the glory of the Lord is risen upon thee." Isa. 60:1. To those who go out to meet the Bridegroom is this message given. Christ is coming with power and great glory. He is coming with His own glory and with the glory of the Father. He is coming with all the holy angels with Him. While all the world is plunged in darkness, there will be light in every dwelling of the saints. They will catch the first light of His second appearing. The unsullied light will shine from His splendor, and Christ the Redeemer will be admired by all who have served Him. While the wicked flee from His presence, Christ's followers will rejoice. The patriarch Job, looking down to the time of Christ's second advent, said, "Whom I shall see for myself, and mine eyes shall behold, and not a stranger." Job 19:27, margin. To His faithful followers Christ has been a daily companion and familiar friend. They have lived in close contact, in constant communion with God. Upon them the glory of the Lord has risen. In them the light of the knowledge of the glory of God in the face of Jesus Christ has been reflected. Now they rejoice in the undimmed rays of the brightness and glory of the King in His majesty. They are prepared for the communion of heaven; for they have heaven in their hearts.

With uplifted heads, with the bright beams of the Sun of Righteousness shining upon them, with rejoicing that their redemption draweth nigh, they go forth to meet the Bridegroom, saying, "Lo, this is our God; we have waited for Him, and He will save us." Isa. 25:9.

"And I heard as it were the voice of a great multitude, and as the voice of many waters, and as the voice of mighty thunderings, saying, Alleluia; for the Lord God omnipotent reigneth. Let us be glad and rejoice, and give honour to Him; for the marriage of the Lamb is come, and His wife hath made herself ready. . . . And he saith unto me, Write, Blessed are they which are called unto the marriage supper of the Lamb." "He is Lord of lords, and King of kings; and they that are with Him are called, and chosen, and faithful." Rev. 19:6-9; 17:14.

6

THE ACTS OF THE APOSTLES

INDEX

SUMMARY	PAGE	SUMMARY	PAGE

AA

INDEX

CONTENTS

1. God's Purpose for the Church	969
2. The Training of the Twelve	971
3. The Great Commission	97?
4. Pentecost	976
5. The Gift of the Spirit	979
6. At the Temple Gate	987
7. A Warning Against Hypocrisy	28?
8. Before the Sanhedrin	287
9. The Seven Deacons	990
10. (The First Christian Martyr)	
11. The Gospel in Samaria	994
12. From Persecution to Disciple...	998
13. Days of Preparation	100?
14. A Seeker for Truth	
15. Delivered from Prison	1005
16. The Gospel Message in Antioch	100?
17. Heralds of the Gospel	101?
18. Preaching Among the Heathen	101?
19. Jew and Gentile	101?
20. Exalting the Cross	102?
21. In the Regions Beyond	102?
22. Thessalonica	102?
23. Berea and Athens	1029
24. Corinth	1037
25. The Thessalonian Letters	125?
26. Apollos at Corinth	1039
27. Ephesus	1058
28. Days of Toil and Trial	1049
29. A Message of Warning and Entreaty	1047

30. Called to Reach a Higher Standard	1030
34. A Consecrated Ministry	1063
40. Paul Appeals to Caesar	108?

CONTENTS

1. God's Purpose for His Church	969	
2. The Training of the Twelve	971	
3. The Great Commission	973	
4. Pentecost	975	
5. The Gift of the Spirit	979	
6. At the Temple Gate	981	
7. A Warning Against Hypocrisy	985	
8. Before the Sanhedrin	987	
9. The Seven Deacons	990	
10. The First Christian Martyr	992	
11. The Gospel in Samaria	994	
12. From Persecutor to Disciple	996	
13. Days of Preparation	1000	
14. A Seeker for Truth	1002	
15. Delivered From Prison	1005	
16. The Gospel Message in Antioch	1008	
17. Heralds of the Gospel	1011	
18. Preaching Among the Heathen	1014	
19. Jew and Gentile	1017	
20. Exalting the Cross	1021	
21. In the Regions Beyond	1024	
22. Thessalonica	1026	
23. Berea and Athens	1029	
24. Corinth	1032	
25. The Thessalonian Letters	1036	
26. Apollos at Corinth	1039	
27. Ephesus	1043	
28. Days of Toil and Trial	1045	
29. A Message of Warning and Entreaty	1047	

30. Called to Reach a Higher Standard	1050	
31. The Message Heeded	1054	
32. A Liberal Church	1057	
33. Laboring Under Difficulties	1060	
34. A Consecrated Ministry	1063	
35. Salvation to the Jews	1067	
36. Apostasy in Galatia	1070	
37. Paul's Last Journey to Jerusalem	1071	
38. Paul a Prisoner	1074	
39. The Trial at Caesarea	1080	
40. Paul Appeals to Caesar	1082	
41. "Almost Thou Persuadest Me"	1083	
42. The Voyage and Shipwreck	1085	
43. In Rome	1087	
44. Caesar's Household	1091	
45. Written From Rome	1093	
46. At Liberty	1098	
47. The Final Arrest	1099	
48. Paul Before Nero	1099	
49. Paul's Last Letter	1101	
50. Condemned to Die	1104	
51. A Faithful Undershepherd	1105	
52. Steadfast Unto the End	1109	
53. John the Beloved	1112	
54. A Faithful Witness	1114	
55. Transformed by Grace	1117	
56. Patmos	1119	
57. The Revelation	1122	
58. The Church Triumphant	1126	

1

God's Purpose for His Church

The church is God's appointed agency for the salvation of men. It was organized for service, and its mission is to carry the gospel to the world. From the beginning it has been God's plan that through His church shall be reflected to the world His fullness and His sufficiency. The members of the church, those whom He has called out of darkness into His marvelous light, are to show forth His glory. The church is the repository of the riches of the grace of Christ; and through the church will eventually be made manifest, even to "the principalities and powers in heavenly places," the final and full display of the love of God. Ephesians 3:10.

Many and wonderful are the promises recorded in the Scriptures regarding the church. "Mine house shall be called an house of prayer for all people." Isaiah 56:7. "I will make them and the places round about My hill a blessing; and I will cause the shower to come down in his season; there shall be showers of blessing." "And I will raise up for them a plant of renown, and they shall be no more consumed with hunger in the land, neither bear the shame of the heathen any more. Thus shall they know that I the Lord their God am with them, and that they, even the house of Israel, are My people, saith the Lord God. And ye My flock, the flock of My pasture, are men, and I am your God, saith the Lord God." Ezekiel 34:26, 29-31.

"Ye are My witnesses, saith the Lord, and My servant whom I have chosen: that ye may know and believe Me, and understand that I am He: before Me there was no God formed, neither shall there be after Me. I, even I, am the Lord; and beside Me there is no Saviour. I have declared, and have saved, and I have showed, when there was no strange god among you: therefore ye are My witnesses." "I the Lord have called thee in righteousness, and will hold thine hand, and will keep thee, and give thee for a covenant of the people, for a light of the Gentiles; to open the blind eyes, to bring out the prisoners from the prison, and them that sit in darkness out of the prison house." Isaiah 43:10-12; 42:6, 7.

"In an acceptable time have I heard thee, and in a day of salvation have I helped thee: and I will preserve thee, and give thee for a covenant of the people, to establish the earth, to cause to inherit the desolate heritages; that thou mayest say to the prisoners, Go forth; to them that are in darkness, Show yourselves. They shall feed in the ways, and their pastures shall be in all high places. They shall not hunger nor thirst; neither shall the heat nor sun smite them: for He that hath mercy on them shall lead them, even by the springs of water shall He guide them. And I will make all My mountains a way, and My highways shall be exalted. . . .

"Sing, O heavens; and be joyful, O earth; and break forth into singing, O mountains: for the Lord hath comforted His people, and will have mercy upon His afflicted. But Zion said, The Lord hath forsaken me, and my Lord hath forgotten me. Can a woman forget her sucking child, that she should not have compassion on the son of her womb? yea, they may forget, yet will I not forget thee. Behold, I have graven thee upon the palms of My hands; thy walls are continually before Me." Isaiah 49:8-16.

The church is God's fortress, His city of refuge, which He holds in a revolted world. Any betrayal of the church is treachery to Him who has bought mankind with the blood of His only-begotten Son. From the beginning, faithful souls have constituted the church on earth. In every age the Lord has had His watchmen, who have borne a faithful testimony to the generation in which they lived. These sentinels gave the message of warning; and when they were called to lay off their armor, others took up the work. God brought these witnesses into covenant relation with Himself, uniting the church on earth with the church in heaven. He has sent forth His angels to minister to His church, and the gates of hell have not been able to prevail against His people.

Through centuries of persecution, conflict, and darkness, God has sustained His church. Not one cloud has fallen upon it that He has not prepared for; not one opposing force has risen to counterwork His work, that He has not foreseen. All has taken place as He predicted. He has not left His church forsaken, but has traced in prophetic declarations what would occur, and that which His Spirit inspired the prophets to foretell has been brought about. All His purposes will be fulfilled. His law is linked with His throne, and no power of evil can destroy it. Truth is inspired and guarded by God; and it will triumph over all opposition.

During ages of spiritual darkness the church of God has been as a city set on a hill. From age to age, through successive generations, the pure doctrines of heaven have been unfolding within its borders. Enfeebled and defective as it may appear, the church is the one object upon which God bestows in a special sense His supreme regard. It is the theater of His grace, in which He delights to reveal His power to transform hearts.

"Whereunto," asked Christ, "shall we liken the kingdom of God? or with what comparison shall we compare it?" Mark 4:30. He could not employ the kingdoms of the world as a similitude. In society He found nothing with which to compare it. Earthly kingdoms rule by the ascendancy of physical power; but from Christ's kingdom every carnal weapon, every instrument of coercion, is banished. This kingdom is to uplift and ennoble humanity. God's church is the court of holy life, filled with varied gifts and endowed with the Holy Spirit. The members are to find their happiness in the happiness of those whom they help and bless.

13   Wonderful is the work which the Lord designs to accomplish through His church, that His name may be glorified. A picture of this work is given in Ezekiel's vision of the river of healing: "These waters issue out toward the east country, and go down into the desert, and go into the sea: which being brought forth into the sea, the waters shall be healed. And it shall come to pass, that everything that liveth, which moveth, whithersoever the rivers shall come, shall live: . . . and by the river upon the bank thereof, on this side and on that side, shall grow all trees for meat, whose leaf shall not fade, neither shall the fruit thereof be consumed: it shall bring forth new fruit according to his months, because their waters they issued out of the sanctuary: and the fruit thereof shall be for meat, and the leaf thereof for medicine." Ezekiel 47:8-12.

From the beginning God has wrought through His people to bring blessing to the world. To the ancient Egyptian nation God made Joseph a fountain of life. Through the integrity of Joseph the life of that whole people was preserved. Through Daniel God saved the life of all the wise men of Babylon. And these deliverances are as object lessons; they illustrate the spiritual blessings offered to the world through connection with the God whom Joseph and Daniel worshiped. Everyone in whose heart Christ abides, everyone who will show forth His love to the world, is a worker together with God for the blessing of humanity. As he receives from the Saviour grace to impart to others, from his whole being flows forth the tide of spiritual life.

14   God chose Israel to reveal His character to men. He desired them to be as wells of salvation in the world. To them were committed the oracles of heaven, the revelation of God's will. In the early days of Israel the nations of the world, through corrupt practices, had lost the knowledge of God. They had once known Him; but because "they glorified Him not as God, neither were thankful; but became vain in their imaginations, . . . their foolish heart was darkened." Romans 1:21. Yet in His mercy God did not blot them out of existence. He purposed to give them an opportunity of again becoming acquainted with Him through His chosen people. Through the teachings of the sacrificial service, Christ was to be uplifted before all nations, and all who would look to Him should live. Christ was the foundation of the Jewish economy. The whole system of types and symbols was a compacted prophecy of the gospel, a presentation in which were bound up the promises of redemption.

But the people of Israel lost sight of their high privileges as God's representatives. They forgot God and failed to fulfill their holy mission. The blessings they received brought no blessing to the world. All their advantages they appropriated for their own glorification. They shut themselves away from the world in order to escape temptation. The restrictions that God had placed upon their association with idolaters as a means of preventing them from conforming to the practices of the heathen, they used to build up a wall of separation between themselves and all other nations. They robbed God of the service 15 He required of them, and they robbed their fellow men of religious guidance and a holy example.

Priests and rulers became fixed in a rut of ceremonialism. They were satisfied with a legal religion, and it was impossible for them to give to others the living truths of heaven. They thought their own righteousness all-sufficient, and did not desire that a new element should be brought into their religion. The good will of God to men they did not accept as something apart from themselves, but connected it with their own merit because of their good works. The faith that works by love and purifies the soul could find no place for union with the religion of the Pharisees, made up of ceremonies and the injunctions of men.

Of Israel God declared: "I had planted thee a noble vine, wholly a right seed: how then art thou turned into the degenerate plant of a strange vine unto Me?" Jeremiah 2:21. "Israel is an empty vine, he bringeth forth fruit unto himself." Hosea 10:1. "And now, O inhabitants of Jerusalem, and men of Judah, judge, I pray you, betwixt Me and My vineyard. What could have been done more to My vineyard, that I have not done in it? wherefore, when I looked that it should bring forth grapes, brought it forth wild grapes?

"And now go to; I will tell you what I will do to My vineyard: I will take away the hedge thereof, and it shall be eaten up; and break down the wall thereof, and it shall be trodden down: and I will lay it waste: it shall not be pruned, nor digged; but there shall come up briers and thorns: I will also command the clouds that they 16 rain no rain upon it. For the vineyard of the Lord of hosts is the house of Israel, and the men of Judah His pleasant plant: and He looked for judgment, but behold oppression; for righteousness, but behold a cry." Isaiah 5:3-7. "The diseased have ye not strengthened, neither have ye healed that which was sick, neither have ye bound up that which was broken, neither have ye brought again that which was driven away, neither have ye sought that which was lost; but with force and with cruelty have ye ruled them." Ezekiel 34:4.

The Jewish leaders thought themselves too wise to need instruction, too righteous to need salvation, too highly honored to need the honor that comes from Christ. The Saviour turned from them to entrust to others the privileges they had abused and the work they had slighted. God's glory must be revealed, His word established. Christ's kingdom must be set up in the world. The salvation of God must be made known in the cities of the wilderness; and the disciples were called to do the work that the Jewish leaders had failed to do.

2

The Training of the Twelve

For the carrying on of His work, Christ did not choose the learning or eloquence of the Jewish Sanhedrin or the power of Rome. Passing by the self-righteous Jewish teachers, the Master Worker chose humble, unlearned men to proclaim the truths that were to move the world. These men He purposed to train and educate as the leaders of His church. They in turn were to educate others and send them out with the gospel message. That they might have success in their work they were to be given the power of the Holy Spirit. Not by human might or human wisdom was the gospel to be proclaimed, but by the power of God.

For three years and a half the disciples were under the instruction of the greatest Teacher the world has ever known. By personal contact and association, Christ trained them for His service. Day by day they walked and talked with Him, hearing His words of cheer to the weary and heavy-laden, and seeing the manifestation of His power in behalf of the sick and the afflicted. Sometimes He taught them, sitting among them on the mountainside; sometimes beside the sea or walking by the way, He revealed the mysteries of the kingdom of God. Wherever hearts were open to receive the divine message, He unfolded the truths of the way of salvation. He did not command the disciples to do this or that, but said, "Follow Me." On His journeys through country and cities, He took them with Him, that they might see how He taught the people. They traveled with Him from place to place. They shared His frugal fare, and like Him were sometimes hungry and often weary. On the crowded streets, by the lakeside, in the lonely desert, they were with Him. They saw Him in every phase of life.

It was at the ordination of the Twelve that the first step was taken in the organization of the church that after Christ's departure was to carry on His work on the earth. Of this ordination the record says, "He goeth up into a mountain, and calleth unto Him whom He would: and they came unto Him. And He ordained twelve, that they should be with Him, and that He might send them forth to preach." Mark 3:13, 14.

Look upon the touching scene. Behold the Majesty of heaven surrounded by the Twelve whom He has chosen. He is about to set them apart for their work. By these feeble agencies, through His word and Spirit, He designs to place salvation within the reach of all.

With gladness and rejoicing, God and the angels beheld this scene. The Father knew that from these men the light of heaven would shine forth; that the words spoken by them as they witnessed for His Son, would echo from generation to generation till the close of time.

The disciples were to go forth as Christ's witnesses, to declare to the world what they had seen and heard of Him. Their office was the most important to which human beings had ever been called, second only to that of Christ Himself. They were to be workers together with God for the saving of men. As in the Old Testament the twelve patriarchs stood as representatives of Israel, so the twelve apostles stand as representatives of the gospel church.

During His earthly ministry Christ began to break down the partition wall between Jew and Gentile, and to preach salvation to all mankind. Though He was a Jew, He mingled freely with the Samaritans, setting at nought the Pharisaic customs of the Jews with regard to this despised people. He slept under their roofs, ate at their tables, and taught in their streets.

The Saviour longed to unfold to His disciples the truth regarding the breaking down of the "middle wall of partition" between Israel and the other nations—the truth that "the Gentiles should be fellow heirs" with the Jews and "partakers of His promise in Christ by the gospel." Ephesians 2:14; 3:6. This truth was revealed in part at the time when He rewarded the faith of the centurion at Capernaum, and also when He preached the gospel to the inhabitants of Sychar. Still more plainly was it revealed on the occasion of His visit to Phoenicia, when He healed the daughter of the Canaanite woman. These experiences helped the disciples to understand that among those whom many regarded as unworthy of salvation, there were souls hungering for the light of truth.

Thus Christ sought to teach the disciples the truth that in God's kingdom there are no territorial lines, no caste, no aristocracy; that they must go to all nations, bearing to them the message of a Saviour's love. But not until later did they realize in all its fullness that God "hath made of one blood all nations of men for to dwell on all the face of the earth, and hath determined the times before appointed, and the bounds of their habitation; that they should seek the Lord, if haply they might feel after Him, and find Him, though He be not far from every one of us." Acts 17:26, 27.

In these first disciples was presented marked diversity. They were to be the world's teachers, and they represented widely varied types of character. In order successfully to carry forward the work to which they had been called, these men, differing in natural characteristics and in habits of life, needed to come into unity of feeling, thought, and action. This unity it was Christ's object to secure. To this end He sought to bring them into unity with Himself. The burden of His labor for them is expressed in His prayer to His Father, "That they all may be one; as Thou, Father, art in Me, and I in Thee, that they also may be one in Us;" "that the world may know that Thou hast sent Me, and hast loved them, as Thou hast loved Me." John 17:21, 23. His constant prayer for them was that they might be sanctified through the truth; and He prayed with assurance, knowing that an Almighty decree had been given before the world was made. He knew that the gospel of the kingdom would be preached to all nations for a witness; He knew that truth armed with the omnipotence of the Holy Spirit, would conquer in the battle with evil, and that the bloodstained banner would one day wave triumphantly over His followers.

As Christ's earthly ministry drew to a close, and He realized that He must soon leave His disciples to carry on the work without His personal supervision, He sought to encourage them and to prepare them for the future. He did not deceive them with false hopes. As an open book He read what was to be. He knew He was about to be separated from them, to leave them as sheep among wolves. He knew that they would suffer persecution, that they would be cast out of the synagogues, and would be thrown into prison. He knew that for witnessing to Him as the Messiah, some of them would suffer death. And something of this He told them. In speaking of their future, He was plain and definite, that in their coming trial they might remember His words and be strengthened to believe in Him as the Redeemer.

He spoke to them also words of hope and courage. "Let not your heart be troubled," He said; "ye believe in God, believe also in Me. In My Father's house are many mansions: if it were not so, I would have told you. I go to prepare a place for you. And if I go and prepare a place for you, I will come again, and receive you unto Myself; that where I am, there ye may be also. And whither I go ye know, and the way ye know." John 14:1-4. For your sake I came into the world; for you I have been working. When I go away I shall still work earnestly for you. I came to the world to reveal Myself to you, that you might believe. I go to My Father and yours to co-operate with Him in your behalf.

"Verily, verily, I say unto you, He that believeth on Me, the works that I do shall he do also; and greater works than these shall he do; because I go unto My Father." John 14:12. By this, Christ did not mean that the disciples would make more exalted exertions than He had made, but that their work would have greater magnitude. He did not refer merely to miracle working, but to all that would take place under the agency of the Holy Spirit. "When the Comforter is come," He said, "whom I will send unto you from the Father, even the Spirit of truth, which proceedeth from the Father, He shall testify of Me: and ye also shall bear witness, because ye have been with Me from the beginning." John 15:26, 27.

Wonderfully were these words fulfilled. After the descent of the Holy Spirit, the disciples were so filled with love for Him and for those for whom He died, that hearts were melted by the words they spoke and the prayers they offered. They spoke in the power of the Spirit; and under the influence of that power, thousands were converted.

As Christ's representatives the apostles were to make a decided impression on the world. The fact that they were humble men would not diminish their influence, but increase it; for the minds of their hearers would be carried from them to the Saviour, who, though unseen, was still working with them. The wonderful teaching of the apostles, their words of courage and trust, would assure all that it was not in their own power that they worked, but in the power of Christ. Humbling themselves, they would declare that He whom the Jews had crucified was the Prince of life, the Son of the living God, and that in His name they did the works that He had done.

In His parting conversation with His disciples on the night before the crucifixion the Saviour made no reference to the suffering that He had endured and must yet endure. He did not speak of the humiliation that was before Him, but sought to bring to their minds that which would strengthen their faith, leading them to look forward to the joys that await the overcomer. He rejoiced in the consciousness that He could and would do more for His followers than He had promised; that from Him would flow forth love and compassion, cleansing the soul temple, and making men like Him in character; that His truth, armed with the power of the Spirit, would go forth conquering and to conquer.

"These things I have spoken unto you," He said, "that in Me ye might have peace. In the world ye shall have tribulation: but be of good cheer; I have overcome the world." John 16:33. Christ did not fail, neither was He discouraged; and the disciples were to show a faith of the same enduring nature. They were to work as He had worked, depending on Him for strength. Though their way would be obstructed by apparent impossibilities, yet by His grace they were to go forward, despairing of nothing and hoping for everything.

24   Christ had finished the work that was given Him to do. He had gathered out those who were to continue His work among men. And He said: "I am glorified in them. And now I am no more in the world, but these are in the world, and I come to Thee. Holy Father, keep through Thine own name those whom Thou hast given Me, that they may be one, as We are." "Neither pray I for these alone, but for them also which shall believe on Me through their word; that they all may be one; . . . I in them and Thou in Me, that they may be made perfect in one; and that the world may know that Thou hast sent Me, and hast loved them, as Thou hast loved Me." John 17:10, 11, 20-23.

25

3

The Great Commission

After the death of Christ the disciples were well-nigh overcome by discouragement. Their Master had been rejected, condemned, and crucified. The priests and rulers had declared scornfully, "He saved others; Himself He cannot save. If He be the King of Israel, let Him now come down from the cross, and we will believe Him." Matthew 27:42. The sun of the disciples' hope had set, and night settled down upon their hearts. Often they repeated the words, "We trusted that it had been He which should have redeemed Israel." Luke 24:21. Lonely and sick at heart, they remembered His words, "If they do these things in a green tree, what shall be done in the dry?" Luke 23:31.

Jesus had several times attempted to open the future to His disciples, but they had not cared to think about what He said. Because of this His death had come to them as a surprise; and afterward, as they reviewed the past and saw the result of their unbelief, they were filled with 26   sorrow. When Christ was crucified, they did not believe that He would rise. He had stated plainly that He was to rise on the third day, but they were perplexed to know what He meant. This lack of comprehension left them at the time of His death in utter hopelessness. They were bitterly disappointed. Their faith did not penetrate beyond the shadow that Satan had cast athwart their horizon. All seemed vague and mysterious to them. If they had believed the Saviour's words, how much sorrow they might have been spared!

Crushed by despondency, grief, and despair, the disciples met together in the upper chamber, and closed and fastened the doors, fearing that the fate of their beloved Teacher might be theirs. It was here that the Saviour, after His resurrection, appeared to them.

For forty days Christ remained on the earth, preparing the disciples for the work before them and explaining that which heretofore they had been unable to comprehend. He spoke of the prophecies concerning His advent, His rejection by the Jews, and His death, showing that every specification of these prophecies had been fulfilled. He told them that they were to regard this fulfillment of prophecy as an assurance of the power that would attend them in their future labors. "Then opened He their understanding," we read, "that they might understand the Scriptures, and said unto them, Thus it is written, and thus it behooved Christ to suffer, and to rise from the dead the third day: and that repentance and remission of sins should be preached in His name among all nations, beginning at Jerusalem." And He added, "Ye are witnesses 27 of these things." Luke 24:45-48.

During these days that Christ spent with His disciples, they gained a new experience. As they heard their beloved Master explaining the Scriptures in the light of all that had happened, their faith in Him was fully established. They reached the place where they could say, "I know whom I have believed." 2 Timothy 1:12. They began to realize the nature and extent of their work, to see that they were to proclaim to the world the truths entrusted to them. The events of Christ's life, His death and resurrection, the prophecies pointing to these events, the mysteries of the plan of salvation, the power of Jesus for the remission of sins—to all these things they had been witnesses, and they were to make them known to the world. They were to proclaim the gospel of peace and salvation through repentance and the power of the Saviour.

Before ascending to heaven, Christ gave His disciples their commission. He told them that they were to be the executors of the will in which He bequeathed to the world the treasures of eternal life. You have been witnesses of My life of sacrifice in behalf of the world, He said to them. You have seen My labors for Israel. And although My people would not come to Me that they might have life, although priests and rulers have done unto Me as they listed, although they have rejected Me, they shall have still another opportunity of accepting the Son of God. You have seen that all who come to Me confessing their sins, I freely receive. Him that 28 cometh to Me I will in no wise cast out. To you, My disciples, I commit this message of mercy. It is to be given to both Jews and Gentiles—to Israel, first, and then to all nations, tongues, and peoples. All who believe are to be gathered into one church.

The gospel commission is the great missionary charter of Christ's kingdom. The disciples were to work earnestly for souls, giving to all the invitation of mercy. They were not to wait for the people to come to them; they were to go to the people with their message.

The disciples were to carry their work forward in Christ's name. Their every word and act was to fasten attention on His name, as possessing that vital power by which sinners may be saved. Their faith was to center in Him who is the source of mercy and power. In His name they were to present their petitions to the Father, and they would receive answer. They were to baptize in the name of the Father, the Son, and the Holy Spirit. Christ's name was to be their watchword, their badge of distinction, their bond of union, the authority for their course of action, and the source of their success. Nothing was to be recognized in His kingdom that did not bear His name and superscription.

When Christ said to the disciples, Go forth in My name to gather into the church all who believe, He plainly set before them the necessity of maintaining simplicity. The less ostentation and show, the greater would be their influence for good. The disciples were to speak with the same simplicity with which Christ had spoken. They were to impress upon their hearers the lessons He had taught them.

Christ did not tell His disciples that their work would be easy. He showed them the vast confederacy of evil arrayed against them. They would have to fight "against principalities, against powers, against the rulers of the darkness of this world, against spiritual wickedness in high places." Ephesians 6:12. But they would not be left to fight alone. He assured them that He would be with them; and that if they would go forth in faith, they should move under the shield of Omnipotence. He bade them be brave and strong; for One mightier than angels would be in their ranks—the General of the armies of heaven. He made full provision for the prosecution of their work and took upon Himself the responsibility of its success. So long as they obeyed His word, and worked in connection with Him, they could not fail. Go to all nations, He bade them. Go to the farthest part of the habitable globe and be assured that My presence will be with you even there. Labor in faith and confidence; for the time will never come when I will forsake you. I will be with you always, helping you to perform your duty, guiding, comforting, sanctifying, sustaining you, giving you success in speaking words that shall draw the attention of others to heaven.

Christ's sacrifice in behalf of man was full and complete. The condition of the atonement had been fulfilled. The work for which He had come to this world had been accomplished. He had won the kingdom. He had wrested it from Satan and had become heir of all things. He was on His way to the throne of God, to be honored by the heavenly host. Clothed with boundless authority, He gave His disciples their commission, "Go ye therefore, and teach all nations, baptizing them in the name of the Father, and of the Son, and of the Holy Ghost: teaching them to observe all things whatsoever I have commanded you: and, lo, I am with you alway, even unto the end." Matthew 28:19, 20.

Just before leaving His disciples, Christ once more plainly stated the nature of His kingdom. He recalled to their remembrance things He had previously told them regarding it. He declared that it was not His purpose to establish in this world a temporal kingdom. He was not appointed to reign as an earthly monarch on David's throne. When the disciples asked Him, "Lord, wilt Thou at this time restore again the kingdom to Israel?" He answered, "It is not for you to know the times or the seasons, which the Father hath put in His own power." Acts 1:6, 7. It was not necessary for them to see farther into the future than the revelations He had made enabled them to see. Their work was to proclaim the gospel message.

Christ's visible presence was about to be withdrawn from the disciples, but a new endowment of power was to be theirs. The Holy Spirit was to be given them in its fullness, sealing them for their work. "Behold," the Saviour said, "I send the promise of My Father upon you: but tarry ye in the city of Jerusalem, until ye be endued with power from on high." Luke 24:49. "For John truly baptized with water; but ye shall be baptized with the Holy Ghost not many days hence." "Ye shall receive power, after that the Holy Ghost is come upon you: and ye shall be witnesses unto Me both in Jerusalem, and in all Judea, and in Samaria, and unto the uttermost part of the earth." Acts 1:5, 8.

The Saviour knew that no argument, however logical, would melt hard hearts or break through the crust of worldliness and selfishness. He knew that His disciples must receive the heavenly endowment; that the gospel would be effective only as it was proclaimed by hearts made warm and lips made eloquent by a living knowledge of Him who is the way, the truth, and the life. The work committed to the disciples would require great efficiency; for the tide of evil ran deep and strong against them. A vigilant, determined leader was in command of the forces of darkness, and the followers of Christ could battle for the right only through the help that God, by His Spirit, would give them.

Christ told His disciples that they were to

begin their work at Jerusalem. That city had been the scene of His amazing sacrifice for the human race. There, clad in the garb of humanity, He had walked and talked with men, and few had discerned how near heaven came to earth. There He had been condemned and crucified. In Jerusalem were many who secretly believed Jesus of Nazareth to be the Messiah, and many who had been deceived by priests and rulers. To these the gospel must be proclaimed. They were to be called to repentance. The wonderful truth that through Christ alone could remission of sins be obtained, was to be made plain. And it was while all Jerusalem was stirred by the thrilling events of the past few weeks, that the preaching of the disciples would make the deepest impression.

During His ministry, Jesus had kept constantly before the disciples the fact that they were to be one with Him in His work for the recovery of the world from the slavery of sin. When He sent forth the Twelve and afterward the Seventy, to proclaim the kingdom of God, He was teaching them their duty to impart to others what He had made known to them. In all His work He was training them for individual labor, to be extended as their numbers increased, and eventually to reach to the uttermost parts of the earth. The last lesson He gave His followers was that they held in trust for the world the glad tidings of salvation.

When the time came for Christ to ascend to His Father, He led the disciples out as far as Bethany. Here He paused, and they gathered about Him. With hands outstretched in blessing, as if in assurance of His protecting care, He slowly ascended from among them. "It came to pass, while He blessed them, He was parted from them, and carried up into heaven." Luke 24:51.

While the disciples were gazing upward to catch the last glimpse of their ascending Lord, He was received into the rejoicing ranks of heavenly angels. As these angels escorted Him to the courts above, they sang in triumph, "Sing unto God, ye kingdoms of the earth; O sing praises unto the Lord, to Him that rideth upon the heavens of heavens. . . . Ascribe ye strength unto God: His excellency is over Israel, and His strength is in the heavens." Psalm 68:32-34, margin.

The disciples were still looking earnestly toward heaven when, "behold, two men stood by them in white apparel; which also said, Ye men of Galilee, why stand ye gazing up into heaven? this same Jesus, which is taken up from you into heaven, shall so come in like manner as ye have seen Him go into heaven." Acts 1:10, 11.

The promise of Christ's second coming was ever to be kept fresh in the minds of His disciples. The same Jesus whom they had seen ascending into heaven, would come again, to take to Himself those who here below give

themselves to His service. The same voice that had said to them, "Lo, I am with you alway, even unto the end," would bid them welcome to His presence in the heavenly kingdom.

As in the typical service the high priest laid aside his pontifical robes and officiated in the white linen dress of an ordinary priest; so Christ laid aside His royal robes and garbed Himself with humanity and offered sacrifice, Himself the priest, Himself the victim. As the high priest, after performing his service in the holy of holies, came forth to the waiting congregation in his pontifical robes; so Christ will come the second time, clothed in garments of whitest white, "so as no fuller on earth can white them." Mark 9:3. He will come in His own glory, and in the glory of His Father, and all the angelic host will escort Him on His way.

Thus will be fulfilled Christ's promise to His disciples, "I will come again, and receive you unto Myself." John 14:3. Those who have loved Him and waited for Him, He will crown with glory and honor and immortality. The righteous dead will come forth from their graves, and those who are alive will be caught up with them to meet the Lord in the air. They will hear the voice of Jesus, sweeter than any music that ever fell on mortal ear, saying to them, Your warfare is accomplished. "Come, ye blessed of My Father, inherit the kingdom prepared for you from the foundation of the world." Matthew 25:34.

Well might the disciples rejoice in the hope of their Lord's return.

4

Pentecost

As the disciples returned from Olivet to Jerusalem, the people looked on them, expecting to see on their faces expressions of sorrow, confusion, and defeat; but they saw there gladness and triumph. The disciples did not now mourn over disappointed hopes. They had seen the risen Saviour, and the words of His parting promise echoed constantly in their ears.

In obedience to Christ's command, they waited in Jerusalem for the promise of the Father—the outpouring of the Spirit. They did not wait in idleness. The record says that they were "continually in the temple, praising and blessing God." Luke 24:53. They also met together to present their requests to the Father in the name of Jesus. They knew that they had a Representative in heaven, an Advocate at the throne of God. In solemn awe they bowed in prayer, repeating the assurance, "Whatsoever ye shall ask the Father in My name, He will give it you. Hitherto have ye asked nothing in My name:

This chapter is based on Acts 2:1-39.

ask, and ye shall receive, that your joy may be full." John 16:23, 24. Higher and still higher they extended the hand of faith, with the mighty argument, "It is Christ that died, yea rather, that is risen again, who is even at the right hand of God, who also maketh intercession for us." Romans 8:34.

As the disciples waited for the fulfillment of the promise, they humbled their hearts in true repentance and confessed their unbelief. As they called to remembrance the words that Christ had spoken to them before His death they understood more fully their meaning. Truths which had passed from their memory were again brought to their minds, and these they repeated to one another. They reproached themselves for their misapprehension of the Saviour. Like a procession, scene after scene of His wonderful life passed before them. As they meditated upon His pure, holy life they felt that no toil would be too hard, no sacrifice too great, if only they could bear witness in their lives to the loveliness of Christ's character. Oh, if they could but have the past three years to live over, they thought, how differently they would act! If they could only see the Master again, how earnestly they would strive to show Him how deeply they loved Him, and how sincerely they sorrowed for having ever grieved Him by a word or an act of unbelief! But they were comforted by the thought that they were forgiven. And they determined that, so far as possible, they would atone for their unbelief by bravely confessing Him before the world.

37 The disciples prayed with intense earnestness for a fitness to meet men and in their daily intercourse to speak words that would lead sinners to Christ. Putting away all differences, all desire for the supremacy, they came close together in Christian fellowship. They drew nearer and nearer to God, and as they did this they realized what a privilege had been theirs in being permitted to associate so closely with Christ. Sadness filled their hearts as they thought of how many times they had grieved Him by their slowness of comprehension, their failure to understand the lessons that, for their good, He was trying to teach them.

These days of preparation were days of deep heart searching. The disciples felt their spiritual need and cried to the Lord for the holy unction that was to fit them for the work of soul saving. They did not ask for a blessing for themselves merely. They were weighted with the burden of the salvation of souls. They realized that the gospel was to be carried to the world, and they claimed the power that Christ had promised.

During the patriarchal age the influence of the Holy Spirit had often been revealed in a marked manner, but never in its fullness. Now, in obedience to the word of the Saviour, the disciples offered their supplications for this gift, and in

heaven Christ added His intercession. He claimed the gift of the Spirit, that He might pour it upon His people.

"And when the Day of Pentecost was fully come, they were all with one accord in one place. And suddenly there came a sound from heaven as of a rushing mighty wind, and it filled all the house where they were sitting."

The Spirit came upon the waiting, praying 38 disciples with a fullness that reached every heart. The Infinite One revealed Himself in power to His church. It was as if for ages this influence had been held in restraint, and now Heaven rejoiced in being able to pour out upon the church the riches of the Spirit's grace. And under the influence of the Spirit, words of penitence and confession mingled with songs of praise for sins forgiven. Words of thanksgiving and of prophecy were heard. All heaven bent low to behold and to adore the wisdom of matchless, incomprehensible love. Lost in wonder, the apostles exclaimed, "Herein is love." They grasped the imparted gift. And what followed? The sword of the Spirit, newly edged with power and bathed in the lightnings of heaven, cut its way through unbelief. Thousands were converted in a day.

"It is expedient for you that I go away," Christ had said to His disciples; "for if I go not away, the Comforter will not come unto you; but if I depart, I will send Him unto you." "When He, the Spirit of truth, is come, He will guide you into all truth: for He shall not speak of Himself; but whatsoever He shall hear, that shall He speak: and He will show you things to come." John 16:7, 13.

Christ's ascension to heaven was the signal that His followers were to receive the promised blessing. For this they were to wait before they entered upon their work. When Christ passed within the heavenly gates, He was enthroned amidst the adoration of the angels. As soon as this ceremony was completed, the Holy Spirit descended upon the disciples in rich currents, and Christ was indeed glorified, even with the 39 glory which He had with the Father from all eternity. The Pentecostal outpouring was Heaven's communication that the Redeemer's inauguration was accomplished. According to His promise He had sent the Holy Spirit from heaven to His followers as a token that He had, as priest and king, received all authority in heaven and on earth, and was the Anointed One over His people.

"And there appeared unto them cloven tongues like as of fire, and it sat upon each of them. And they were all filled with the Holy Ghost, and began to speak with other tongues, as the Spirit gave them utterance." The Holy Spirit, assuming the form of tongues of fire, rested upon those assembled. This was an emblem of the gift then bestowed on the disciples, which enabled them to speak with fluency languages with which they had heretofore been unacquainted. The appearance of fire signified the fervent zeal with which the apostles would labor and the power that would attend their work.

"There were dwelling at Jerusalem Jews, devout men, out of every nation under heaven." During the dispersion the Jews had been scattered to almost every part of the inhabited world, and in their exile they had learned to speak various languages. Many of these Jews were on this occasion in Jerusalem, attending the religious festivals then in progress. Every known tongue was represented by those assembled. This diversity of languages would have been a great hindrance to the proclamation of the gospel; God therefore in a miraculous manner supplied the deficiency of the apostles. The

40 Holy Spirit did for them that which they could not have accomplished for themselves in a lifetime. They could now proclaim the truths of the gospel abroad, speaking with accuracy the languages of those for whom they were laboring. This miraculous gift was a strong evidence to the world that their commission bore the signet of Heaven. From this time forth the language of the disciples was pure, simple, and accurate, whether they spoke in their native tongue or in a foreign language.

"Now when this was noised abroad, the multitude came together, and were confounded, because that every man heard them speak in his own language. And they were all amazed and marveled, saying one to another, Behold, are not all these which speak Galileans? and how hear we every man in our own tongue, wherein we were born?"

The priests and rulers were greatly enraged at this wonderful manifestation, but they dared not give way to their malice, for fear of exposing themselves to the violence of the people. They had put the Nazarene to death; but here were His servants, unlettered men of Galilee, telling in all the languages then spoken, the story of His life and ministry. The priests, determined to account for the miraculous power of the disciples in some natural way, declared that they were drunken from partaking largely of the new wine prepared for the feast. Some of the most ignorant of the people present seized upon this suggestion as the truth, but the more intelligent knew it to be false; and those who understood the different languages testified to the accuracy with which these languages were used by the disciples.

41 In answer to the accusation of the priests Peter showed that this demonstration was in direct fulfillment of the prophecy of Joel, wherein he foretold that such power would come upon men to fit them for a special work. "Ye men of Judea, and all ye that dwell at Jerusalem," he said, "be this known unto you, and hearken to my words: for these are not drunken, as ye suppose, seeing it is but the third hour of the day. But this is that which was spoken by the prophet Joel: And it shall come to pass in the last days, saith God, I will pour out of My Spirit upon all flesh: and your sons and your daughters shall prophesy, and your young men shall see visions, and your old men shall dream dreams: and on My servants and on My handmaidens I will pour out in those days of My Spirit; and they shall prophesy."

With clearness and power Peter bore witness of the death and resurrection of Christ: "Ye men of Israel, hear these words: Jesus of Nazareth, a man approved of God among you by miracles and wonders and signs, which God did by Him in the midst of you, as ye yourselves also know: Him . . . ye have taken, and by wicked hands have crucified and slain: whom God hath raised up, having loosed the pains of death: because it was not possible that He should be holden of it."

Peter did not refer to the teachings of Christ to prove his position, because he knew that the prejudice of his hearers was so great that his words on this subject would be of no effect. Instead, he spoke to them of David, who was regarded by the Jews as one of the patriarchs of their nation. "David speaketh concerning Him," he declared: "I foresaw the Lord always before 42 My face, for He is on My right hand, that I should not be moved: therefore did My heart rejoice, and My tongue was glad; moreover also My flesh shall rest in hope: because Thou wilt not leave My soul in hell, neither wilt Thou suffer Thine Holy One to see corruption. . . .

"Men and brethren, let me freely speak unto you of the patriarch David, that he is both dead and buried, and his sepulcher is with us unto this day." "He . . . spake of the resurrection of Christ, that His soul was not left in hell, neither His flesh did see corruption. This Jesus hath God raised up, whereof we all are witnesses."

The scene is one full of interest. Behold the people coming from all directions to hear the disciples witness to the truth as it is in Jesus. They press in, crowding the temple. Priests and rulers are there, the dark scowl of malignity still on their faces, their hearts still filled with abiding hatred against Christ, their hands uncleansed from the blood shed when they crucified the world's Redeemer. They had thought to find the apostles cowed with fear under the strong hand of oppression and murder, but they find them lifted above all fear and filled with the Spirit, proclaiming with power the divinity of Jesus of Nazareth. They hear them declaring with boldness that the One so recently humiliated, derided, smitten by cruel hands, and crucified, is the Prince of life, now exalted to the right hand of God.

Some of those who listened to the apostles

had taken an active part in the condemnation and death of Christ. Their voices had mingled with the rabble in calling for His crucifixion. When Jesus and Barabbas stood before them in the judgment hall and Pilate asked, "Whom will ye that I release unto you?" they had shouted, "Not this Man, but Barabbas!" Matthew 27:17; John 18:40. When Pilate delivered Christ to them, saying, "Take ye Him, and crucify Him: for I find no fault in Him;" "I am innocent of the blood of this just Person," they had cried, "His blood be on us, and on our children." John 19:6; Matthew 27:24, 25.

Now they heard the disciples declaring that it was the Son of God who had been crucified. Priests and rulers trembled. Conviction and anguish seized the people. "They were pricked in their heart, and said unto Peter and to the rest of the apostles, Men and brethren, what shall we do?" Among those who listened to the disciples were devout Jews, who were sincere in their belief. The power that accompanied the words of the speaker convinced them that Jesus was indeed the Messiah.

"Then Peter said unto them, Repent, and be baptized every one of you in the name of Jesus Christ for the remission of sins, and ye shall receive the gift of the Holy Ghost. For the promise is unto you, and to your children, and to all that are afar off, even as many as the Lord our God shall call."

Peter urged home upon the convicted people the fact that they had rejected Christ because they had been deceived by priests and rulers; and that if they continued to look to these men for counsel, and waited for them to acknowledge Christ before they dared to do so, they would never accept Him. These powerful men, though making a profession of godliness, were ambitious for earthly riches and glory. They were not willing to come to Christ to receive light.

Under the influence of this heavenly illumination the scriptures that Christ had explained to the disciples stood out before them with the luster of perfect truth. The veil that had prevented them from seeing to the end of that which had been abolished, was now removed, and they comprehended with perfect clearness the object of Christ's mission and the nature of His kingdom. They could speak with power of the Saviour; and as they unfolded to their hearers the plan of salvation, many were convicted and convinced. The traditions and superstitions inculcated by the priests were swept away from their minds, and the teachings of the Saviour were accepted.

"Then they that gladly received his word were baptized: and the same day there were added unto them about three thousand souls."

The Jewish leaders had supposed that the work of Christ would end with His death; but,

instead of this, they witnessed the marvelous scenes of the Day of Pentecost. They heard the disciples, endowed with a power and energy hitherto unknown, preaching Christ, their words confirmed by signs and wonders. In Jerusalem, the stronghold of Judaism, thousands openly declared their faith in Jesus of Nazareth as the Messiah.

The disciples were astonished and overjoyed at the greatness of the harvest of souls. They did not regard this wonderful ingathering as the result of their own efforts; they realized that they were entering into other men's labors. Ever since the fall of Adam, Christ had been committing to chosen servants the seed of His word, to be sown in human hearts. During His life on this earth He had sown the seed of truth and had watered it with His blood. The conversions that took place on the Day of Pentecost were the result of this sowing, the harvest of Christ's work, revealing the power of His teaching.

The arguments of the apostles alone, though clear and convincing, would not have removed the prejudice that had withstood so much evidence. But the Holy Spirit sent the arguments home to hearts with divine power. The words of the apostles were as sharp arrows of the Almighty, convicting men of their terrible guilt in rejecting and crucifying the Lord of glory.

Under the training of Christ the disciples had been led to feel their need of the Spirit. Under the Spirit's teaching they received the final qualification, and went forth to their lifework. No longer were they ignorant and uncultured. No longer were they a collection of independent units or discordant, conflicting elements. No longer were their hopes set on worldly greatness. They were of "one accord," "of one heart and of one soul." Acts 2:46; 4:32. Christ filled their thoughts; the advancement of His kingdom was their aim. In mind and character they had become like their Master, and men "took knowledge of them, that they had been with Jesus." Acts 4:13.

Pentecost brought them the heavenly illumination. The truths they could not understand while Christ was with them were now unfolded. With a faith and assurance that they had never before known, they accepted the teachings of the Sacred Word. No longer was it a matter of faith with them that Christ was the Son of God. They knew that, although clothed with humanity, He was indeed the Messiah, and they told their experience to the world with a confidence which carried with it the conviction that God was with them.

They could speak the name of Jesus with assurance; for was He not their Friend and Elder Brother? Brought into close communion with Christ, they sat with Him in heavenly places. With what burning language they clothed their ideas as they bore witness for Him! Their hearts were surcharged with a benevolence so full, so deep, so far-reaching, that it impelled them to go to the ends of the earth, testifying to the power of Christ. They were filled with an intense longing to carry forward the work He had begun. They realized the greatness of their debt to heaven and the responsibility of their work. Strengthened by the endowment of the Holy Spirit, they went forth filled with zeal to extend the triumphs of the cross. The Spirit animated them and spoke through them. The peace of Christ shone from their faces. They had consecrated their lives to Him for service, and their very features bore evidence to the surrender they had made.

47

5

The Gift of the Spirit

When Christ gave His disciples the promise of the Spirit, He was nearing the close of His earthly ministry. He was standing in the shadow of the cross, with a full realization of the load of guilt that was to rest upon Him as the Sin Bearer. Before offering Himself as the sacrificial victim, He instructed His disciples regarding a most essential and complete gift which He was to bestow upon His followers—the gift that would bring within their reach the boundless resources of His grace. "I will pray the Father," He said, "and He shall give you another Comforter, that He may abide with you forever; even the Spirit of truth; whom the world cannot receive, because it seeth Him not, neither knoweth Him: but ye know Him; for He dwelleth with you, and shall be in you." John 14:16, 17. The Saviour was pointing forward to the time when the Holy Spirit should come to do a mighty work as His representative. The evil that had been accumulating for centuries was to be resisted by the divine power of the Holy Spirit.

48

What was the result of the outpouring of the Spirit on the Day of Pentecost? The glad tidings of a risen Saviour were carried to the uttermost parts of the inhabited world. As the disciples proclaimed the message of redeeming grace, hearts yielded to the power of this message. The church beheld converts flocking to her from all directions. Backsliders were reconverted. Sinners united with believers in seeking the pearl of great price. Some who had been the bitterest opponents of the gospel became its champions. The prophecy was fulfilled, "He that is feeble. . . shall be as David; and the house of David . . . as the angel of the Lord." Zechariah 12:8. Every Christian saw in his brother a revelation of divine love and benevolence. One interest prevailed; one subject of emulation swallowed up all others. The ambition of the believers was to reveal the likeness of Christ's character and to labor for the enlargement of His kingdom.

"With great power gave the apostles witness of the resurrection of the Lord Jesus: and great grace was upon them all." Acts 4:33. Under their labors were added to the church chosen men, who, receiving the word of truth, consecrated their lives to the work of giving to others the hope that filled their hearts with peace and joy. They could not be restrained or intimidated by threatenings. The Lord spoke through them, and as they went from place to place, the poor had the gospel preached to them, and miracles of divine grace were wrought.

So mightily can God work when men give themselves up to the control of His Spirit.

49

The promise of the Holy Spirit is not limited to any age or to any race. Christ declared that the divine influence of His Spirit was to be with His followers unto the end. From the Day of Pentecost to the present time, the Comforter has been sent to all who have yielded themselves fully to the Lord and to His service. To all who have accepted Christ as a personal Saviour, the Holy Spirit has come as a counselor, sanctifier, guide, and witness. The more closely believers have walked with God, the more clearly and powerfully have they testified of their Redeemer's love and of His saving grace. The men and women who through the long centuries of persecution and trial enjoyed a large measure of the presence of the Spirit in their lives, have stood as signs and wonders in the world. Before angels and men they have revealed the transforming power of redeeming love.

Those who at Pentecost were endued with power from on high, were not thereby freed from further temptation and trial. As they witnessed for truth and righteousness they were repeatedly assailed by the enemy of all truth, who sought to rob them of their Christian experience. They were compelled to strive with all their God-given powers to reach the measure of the stature of men and women in Christ Jesus. Daily they prayed for fresh supplies of grace, that they might reach higher and still higher toward perfection. Under the Holy Spirit's working even the weakest, by exercising faith in God, learned to improve their entrusted powers and to become sanctified, refined, and ennobled. As in humility they submitted to the molding influence of the Holy Spirit, they received of the fullness of the Godhead and were fashioned in the likeness of the divine.

50

The lapse of time has wrought no change in Christ's parting promise to send the Holy Spirit as His representative. It is not because of any restriction on the part of God that the riches of His grace do not flow earthward to men. If the fulfillment of the promise is not seen as it might be, it is because the promise is not appreciated as it should be. If all were willing, all would be filled with the Spirit. Wherever the need of the Holy Spirit is a matter little thought of, there is seen spiritual drought, spiritual darkness, spiritual declension and death. Whenever minor matters occupy the attention, the divine power which is necessary for the growth and prosperity of the church, and which would bring all other blessings in its train, is lacking, though offered in infinite plenitude.

Since this is the means by which we are to receive power, why do we not hunger and thirst for the gift of the Spirit? Why do we not talk of it, pray for it, and preach concerning it? The Lord is more willing to give the Holy Spirit to those who serve Him than parents are to give good gifts to their children. For the daily baptism of the Spirit every worker should offer his petition to God. Companies of Christian workers should gather to ask for special help, for heavenly wisdom, that they may know how to plan and execute wisely. Especially should they pray that God will baptize His chosen ambassadors in mission fields with a rich measure of His Spirit. The presence of the Spirit with God's workers will give the proclamation of truth a power that not all the honor or glory of the world could give.

With the consecrated worker for God, in whatever place he may be, the Holy Spirit abides. The words spoken to the disciples are spoken also to us. The Comforter is ours as well as theirs. The Spirit furnishes the strength that sustains striving, wrestling souls in every emergency, amidst the hatred of the world, and the realization of their own failures and mistakes. In sorrow and affliction, when the outlook seems dark and the future perplexing, and we feel helpless and alone,—these are the times when, in answer to the prayer of faith, the Holy Spirit brings comfort to the heart.

It is not a conclusive evidence that a man is a Christian because he manifests spiritual ecstasy under extraordinary circumstances. Holiness is not rapture: it is an entire surrender of the will to God; it is living by every word that proceeds from the mouth of God; it is doing the will of our heavenly Father; it is trusting God in trial, in darkness as well as in the light; it is walking by faith and not by sight; it is relying on God with unquestioning confidence, and resting in His love.

It is not essential for us to be able to define just what the Holy Spirit is. Christ tells us that the Spirit is the Comforter, "the Spirit of truth, which proceedeth from the Father." It is plainly declared regarding the Holy Spirit that, in His work of guiding men into all truth, "He shall not speak of Himself." John 15:26; 16:13.

The nature of the Holy Spirit is a mystery. Men cannot explain it, because the Lord has not revealed it to them. Men having fanciful views may bring together passages of Scripture and put a human construction on them, but the acceptance of these views will not strengthen the church. Regarding such mysteries, which are too deep for human understanding, silence is golden.

The office of the Holy Spirit is distinctly specified in the words of Christ: "When He is come, He will reprove the world of sin, and of righteousness, and of judgment." John 16:8. It is the Holy Spirit that convicts of sin. If the sinner responds to the quickening influence of the Spirit, he will be brought to repentance and aroused to the importance of obeying the divine requirements.

To the repentant sinner, hungering and thirsting for righteousness, the Holy Spirit reveals the Lamb of God that taketh away the sin of the world. "He shall receive of Mine, and shall show it unto you," Christ said. "He shall teach you all things, and bring all things to your remembrance, whatsoever I have said unto you." John 16:14; 14:26.

The Spirit is given as a regenerating agency, to make effectual the salvation wrought by the death of our Redeemer. The Spirit is constantly seeking to draw the attention of men to the great offering that was made on the cross of Calvary, to unfold to the world the love of God, and to open to the convicted soul the precious things of the Scriptures.

Having brought conviction of sin, and presented before the mind the standard of righteousness, the Holy Spirit withdraws the affections from the things of this earth and fills the soul with a desire for holiness. "He will guide you into all truth" (John 16:13), the Saviour declared. If men are willing to be molded, there will be brought about a sanctification of the whole being. The Spirit will take the things of God and stamp them on the soul. By His power the way of life will be made so plain that none need err therein.

From the beginning, God has been working by His Holy Spirit through human instrumentalities for the accomplishment of His purpose in behalf of the fallen race. This was manifest in the lives of the patriarchs. To the church in the wilderness also, in the time of Moses, God gave His "good Spirit to instruct them." Nehemiah 9:20. And in the days of the apostles He wrought mightily for His church through the agency of the Holy Spirit. The same power that sustained the patriarchs, that gave Caleb and Joshua faith and courage, and that made the work of the apostolic church effective, has upheld God's faithful children in every succeeding age. It was through the power of the Holy Spirit that during the Dark Ages the Waldensian Christians helped to prepare the way for the Reformation. It was the same power that made successful the efforts of the noble men and women who pioneered the way for the establishment of modern missions and for the translation of the Bible into the languages and dialects of all nations and peoples.

And today God is still using His church to make known His purpose in the earth. Today the heralds of the cross are going from city to 54 city, and from land to land, preparing the way for the second advent of Christ. The standard of God's law is being exalted. The Spirit of the Almighty is moving upon men's hearts, and those who respond to its influence become witnesses for God and His truth. In many places consecrated men and women may be seen communicating to others the light that has made plain to them the way of salvation through Christ. And as they continue to let their light shine, as did those who were baptized with the Spirit on the Day of Pentecost, they receive more and still more of the Spirit's power. Thus the earth is to be lightened with the glory of God.

On the other hand, there are some who, instead of wisely improving present opportunities, are idly waiting for some special season of spiritual refreshing by which their ability to enlighten others will be greatly increased. They neglect present duties and privileges, and allow their light to burn dim, while they look forward to a time when, without any effort on their part, they will be made the recipients of special blessing, by which they will be transformed and fitted for service.

It is true that in the time of the end, when God's work in the earth is closing, the earnest efforts put forth by consecrated believers under the guidance of the Holy Spirit are to be accompanied by special tokens of divine favor. Under the figure of the early and the latter rain, that falls in Eastern lands at seedtime and harvest, the Hebrew prophets foretold the bestowal of spiritual grace in extraordinary measure upon God's church. The outpouring of the Spirit in the days of the apostles was the beginning of the early, or former, rain, and glorious was the result. To the end of time the presence of the Spirit is to abide with the true church.

But near the close of earth's harvest, a special bestowal of spiritual grace is promised to prepare the church for the coming of the Son of man. This outpouring of the Spirit is likened to the falling of the latter rain; and it is for this added power that Christians are to send their petitions to the Lord of the harvest "in the time of the latter rain." In response, "the Lord shall make bright clouds, and give them showers of rain." "He will cause to come down . . . the rain, 55 the former rain, and the latter rain." Zechariah 10:1; Joel 2:23.

But unless the members of God's church today have a living connection with the Source of all spiritual growth, they will not be ready for the time of reaping. Unless they keep their lamps trimmed and burning, they will fail of receiving added grace in times of special need.

Those only who are constantly receiving fresh supplies of grace, will have power proportionate to their daily need and their ability to use that power. Instead of looking forward to some future time when, through a special endowment of spiritual power, they will receive a miraculous fitting up for soul winning, they are yielding themselves daily to God, that He may make them vessels meet for His use. Daily they are improving the opportunities for service that lie within their reach. Daily they are witnessing for the Master wherever they may be, whether in some humble sphere of labor in the home, or in a public field of usefulness.

To the consecrated worker there is wonderful 56 consolation in the knowledge that even Christ during His life on earth sought His Father daily for fresh supplies of needed grace; and from this communion with God He went forth to strengthen and bless others. Behold the Son of God bowed in prayer to His Father! Though He is the Son of God, He strengthens His faith by prayer, and by communion with heaven gathers to Himself power to resist evil and to minister to the needs of men. As the Elder Brother of our race He knows the necessities of those who, compassed with infirmity and living in a world of sin and temptation, still desire to serve Him. He knows that the messengers whom He sees fit to send are weak, erring men; but to all who give themselves wholly to His service He promises divine aid. His own example is an assurance that earnest, persevering supplication to God in faith—faith that leads to entire dependence upon God, and unreserved consecration to His work—will avail to bring to men the Holy Spirit's aid in the battle against sin.

Every worker who follows the example of Christ will be prepared to receive and use the power that God has promised to His church for the ripening of earth's harvest. Morning by morning, as the heralds of the gospel kneel before the Lord and renew their vows of consecration to Him, He will grant them the presence of His Spirit, with its reviving, sanctifying power. As they go forth to the day's duties, they have the assurance that the unseen agency of Holy Spirit enables them to be "laborers together with God."

6
57

At the Temple Gate

The disciples of Christ had a deep sense of their own inefficiency, and with humiliation and prayer they joined their weakness to His strength, their ignorance to His wisdom, their

This chapter is based on Acts 3; 4:1-31.

unworthiness to His righteousness, their poverty to His exhaustless wealth. Thus strengthened and equipped, they hesitated not to press forward in the service of the Master.

A short time after the descent of the Holy Spirit, and immediately after a season of earnest prayer, Peter and John, going up to the temple to worship, saw at the gate Beautiful a cripple, forty years of age, whose life, from his birth, had been one of pain and infirmity. This unfortunate man had long desired to see Jesus, that he might be healed; but he was almost helpless, and was far removed from the scene of the great Physician's labors. His pleadings at last induced some friends to bear him to the gate of the temple, but upon arriving there, he found that the One upon whom his hopes were centered, had been put to a cruel death.

His disappointment excited the sympathy of those who knew for how long he had eagerly hoped to be healed by Jesus, and daily they brought him to the temple, in order that passersby might be induced by pity to give him a trifle to relieve his wants. As Peter and John passed, he asked an alms from them. The disciples regarded him compassionately, and Peter said, "Look on us. And he gave heed unto them, expecting to receive something of them. Then Peter said, Silver and gold have I none." As Peter thus declared his poverty, the countenance of the cripple fell; but it grew bright with hope as the apostle continued, "But such as I have give I thee: In the name of Jesus Christ of Nazareth rise up and walk.

"And he took him by the right hand, and lifted him up: and immediately his feet and anklebones received strength. And he leaping up stood, and walked, and entered with them into the temple, walking, and leaping, and praising God. And all the people saw him walking and praising God: and they knew that it was he which sat for alms at the Beautiful Gate of the temple: and they were filled with wonder and amazement at that which had happened."

"And as the lame man which was healed held Peter and John, all the people ran together unto them in the porch that is called Solomon's, greatly wondering." They were astonished that the disciples could perform miracles similar to those performed by Jesus. Yet here was this man, for forty years a helpless cripple, now rejoicing in the full use of his limbs, free from pain, and happy in believing in Jesus.

When the disciples saw the amazement of the people, Peter asked, "Why marvel ye at this? or why look ye so earnestly on us, as though by our own power or holiness we had made this man to walk?" He assured them that the cure had been wrought in the name and through the merits of Jesus of Nazareth, whom God had raised from the dead. "His name through faith in His name," the apostle declared, "hath made

this man strong, whom ye see and know: yea, the faith which is by Him hath given him this perfect soundness in the presence of you all."

The apostles spoke plainly of the great sin of the Jews in rejecting and putting to death the Prince of life; but they were careful not to drive their hearers to despair. "Ye denied the Holy One and the Just," Peter said, "and desired a murderer to be granted unto you; and killed the Prince of life, whom God hath raised from the dead; whereof we are witnesses." "And now, brethren, I wot that through ignorance ye did it, as did also your rulers. But those things, which God before had showed by the mouth of all His prophets, that Christ should suffer, He hath so fulfilled." He declared that the Holy Spirit was calling upon them to repent and be converted, and assured them that there was no hope of salvation except through the mercy of the One whom they had crucified. Only through faith in Him could their sins be forgiven.

"Repent ye therefore, and be converted," he cried, "that your sins may be blotted out, when the times of refreshing shall come from the presence of the Lord."

"Ye are the children of the prophets, and of the covenant which God made with our fathers, saying unto Abraham, And in thy seed shall all the kindreds of the earth be blessed. Unto you first God, having raised up His Son Jesus, sent Him to bless you, in turning away every one of you from his iniquities."

Thus the disciples preached the resurrection of Christ. Many among those who listened were waiting for this testimony, and when they heard it they believed. It brought to their minds the words that Christ had spoken, and they took their stand in the ranks of those who accepted the gospel. The seed that the Saviour had sown sprang up and bore fruit.

While the disciples were speaking to the people, "the priests, and the captain of the temple, and the Sadducees, came upon them, being grieved that they taught the people, and preached through Jesus the resurrection from the dead."

After Christ's resurrection the priests had spread far and near the lying report that His body had been stolen by the disciples while the Roman guard slept. It is not surprising that they were displeased when they heard Peter and John preaching the resurrection of the One they had murdered. The Sadducees especially were greatly aroused. They felt that their most cherished doctrine was in danger, and their reputation at stake.

Converts to the new faith were rapidly increasing, and both Pharisees and Sadducees agreed that if these new teachers were suffered to go unchecked, their own influence would be in greater danger than when Jesus was upon the earth. Accordingly, the captain of the temple, with the help of a number of Sadducees, arrested Peter and John, and put them in prison, as it was too late that day for them to be examined.

The enemies of the disciples could not but be convinced that Christ had risen from the dead. The evidence was too clear to be doubted. Nevertheless, they hardened their hearts, refusing to repent of the terrible deed they had committed in putting Jesus to death. Abundant evidence that the apostles were speaking and acting under divine inspiration had been given the Jewish rulers, but they firmly resisted the message of truth. Christ had not come in the manner that they expected, and though at times they had been convinced that He was the Son of God, yet they had stifled conviction, and crucified Him. In mercy God gave them still further evidence, and now another opportunity was granted them to turn to Him. He sent the disciples to tell them that they had killed the Prince of life, and in this terrible charge He gave them another call to repentance. But feeling secure in their own righteousness, the Jewish teachers refused to admit that the men charging them with crucifying Christ were speaking by the direction of the Holy Spirit.

Having committed themselves to a course of opposition to Christ, every act of resistance became to the priests an additional incentive to pursue the same course. Their obstinacy became more and more determined. It was not that they could not yield; they could, but would not. It was not alone because they were guilty and deserving of death, not alone because they had put to death the Son of God, that they were cut off from salvation; it was because they armed themselves with opposition to God. They persistently rejected light and stifled the convictions of the Spirit. The influence that controls the children of disobedience worked in them, leading them to abuse the men through whom God was working. The malignity of their rebellion was intensified by each successive act of resistance against God and the message He had given His servants to declare. Every day, in their refusal to repent, the Jewish leaders took up their rebellion afresh, preparing to reap that which they had sown.

The wrath of God is not declared against unrepentant sinners merely because of the sins they have committed, but because, when called to repent, they choose to continue in resistance, repeating the sins of the past in defiance of the light given them. If the Jewish leaders had submitted to the convicting power of the Holy Spirit, they would have been pardoned; but they were determined not to yield. In the same way, the sinner, by continued resistance, places himself where the Holy Spirit cannot influence him.

On the day following the healing of the cripple, Annas and Caiaphas, with the other dignitaries of the temple, met together for the trial, and the prisoners were brought before them. In that very room and before some of those very men, Peter had shamefully denied his Lord. This came distinctly to his mind as he appeared for his own trial. He now had an opportunity of redeeming his cowardice.

Those present who remembered the part that Peter had acted at the trial of his Master, flattered themselves that he could now be intimidated by the threat of imprisonment and death. But the Peter who denied Christ in the hour of His greatest need was impulsive and self-confident, differing widely from the Peter who was brought before the Sanhedrin for examination. Since his fall he had been converted. He was no longer proud and boastful, but modest and self-distrustful. He was filled with the Holy Spirit, and by the help of this power he was resolved to remove the stain of his apostasy by honoring the name he had once disowned.

Hitherto the priests had avoided mentioning the crucifixion or the resurrection of Jesus. But now, in fulfillment of their purpose, they were forced to inquire of the accused how the cure of the impotent man had been accomplished. "By what power, or by what name, have ye done this?" they asked.

With holy boldness and in the power of the Spirit Peter fearlessly declared: "Be it known unto you all, and to all the people of Israel, that by the name of Jesus Christ of Nazareth, whom ye crucified, whom God raised from the dead, even by Him doth this man stand here before you whole. This is the stone which was set at nought of you builders, which is become the head of the corner. Neither is there salvation in any other: for there is none other name under heaven given among men, whereby we must be saved."

This courageous defense appalled the Jewish leaders. They had supposed that the disciples would be overcome with fear and confusion when brought before the Sanhedrin. But, instead, these witnesses spoke as Christ had spoken, with a convincing power that silenced their adversaries. There was no trace of fear in Peter's voice as he declared of Christ, "This is the stone which was set at nought of you builders, which is become the head of the corner."

Peter here used a figure of speech familiar to the priests. The prophets had spoken of the rejected stone; and Christ Himself, speaking on one occasion to the priests and elders, said: "Did ye never read in the Scriptures, The stone which the builders rejected, the same is become the head of the corner: this is the Lord's doing, and it is marvelous in our eyes? Therefore say I unto you, The kingdom of God shall be taken from you, and given to a nation bringing forth the fruits thereof. And whosoever shall fall on this stone shall be broken: but on whomsoever it shall fall, it will grind him to powder." Matthew 21:42-44.

As the priests listened to the apostles' fearless words, "they took knowledge of them, that they had been with Jesus."

Of the disciples after the transfiguration of Christ it is written that at the close of that wonderful scene "they saw no man, save Jesus only." Matthew 17:8. "Jesus only"—in these words is contained the secret of the life and power that marked the history of the early church. When the disciples first heard the words of Christ, they felt their need of Him. They sought, they found, they followed Him. They were with Him in the temple, at the table, on the mountainside, in the field. They were as pupils with a teacher, daily receiving from Him lessons of eternal truth.

65   After the Saviour's ascension, the sense of the divine presence, full of love and light, was still with them. It was a personal presence. Jesus, the Saviour, who had walked and talked and prayed with them, who had spoken hope and comfort to their hearts, had, while the message of peace was upon His lips, been taken from them into heaven. As the chariot of angels received Him, His words had come to them, "Lo, I am with you alway, even unto the end." Matthew 28:20. He had ascended to heaven in the form of humanity. They knew that He was before the throne of God, their Friend and Saviour still; that His sympathies were unchanged; that He would forever be identified with suffering humanity. They knew that He was presenting before God the merit of His blood, showing His wounded hands and feet as a remembrance of the price He had paid for His redeemed ones; and this thought strengthened them to endure reproach for His sake. Their union with Him was stronger now than when He was with them in person. The light and love and power of an indwelling Christ shone out through them, so that men, beholding, marveled.

Christ placed His seal on the words that Peter spoke in His defense. Close beside the disciple, as a convincing witness, stood the man who had been so miraculously healed. The appearance of this man, a few hours before a helpless cripple, but now restored to soundness of health, added a weight of testimony to Peter's words. Priests and rulers were silent. They were unable to refute Peter's statement, but they were nonetheless determined to put a stop to the teaching of the disciples.

66   Christ's crowning miracle—the raising of Lazarus—had sealed the determination of the priests to rid the world of Jesus and His wonderful works, which were fast destroying their influence over the people. They had crucified Him; but here was a convincing proof that they had not put a stop to the working of miracles in His name, nor to the proclamation of the truth

He taught. Already the healing of the cripple and the preaching of the apostles had filled Jerusalem with excitement.

In order to conceal their perplexity, the priests and rulers ordered the apostles to be taken away, that they might counsel among themselves. They all agreed that it would be useless to deny that the man had been healed. Gladly would they have covered up the miracle by falsehoods; but this was impossible, for it had been wrought in the full light of day, before a multitude of people, and had already come to the knowledge of thousands. They felt that the work of the disciples must be stopped or Jesus would gain many followers. Their own disgrace would follow, for they would be held guilty of the murder of the Son of God.

But notwithstanding their desire to destroy the disciples, the priests dared not do more than threaten them with the severest punishment if they continued to speak or to work in the name of Jesus. Calling them again before the Sanhedrin, they commanded them not to speak or teach in the name of Jesus. But Peter and John answered: "Whether it be right in the sight of God to hearken unto you more than unto God, judge ye. For we cannot but speak the things which we have seen and heard."

Gladly would the priests have punished these men for their unswerving fidelity to their sacred calling, but they feared the people; "for all men glorified God for that which was done." So, with repeated threats and injunctions, the apostles were set at liberty.   67

While Peter and John were prisoners, the other disciples, knowing the malignity of the Jews, had prayed unceasingly for their brethren, fearing that the cruelty shown to Christ might be repeated. As soon as the apostles were released, they sought the rest of the disciples and reported to them the result of the examination. Great was the joy of the believers. "They lifted up their voice to God with one accord, and said, Lord, Thou art God, which hast made heaven, and earth, and the sea, and all that in them is: who by the mouth of Thy servant David hast said, Why did the heathen rage, and the people imagine vain things? The kings of the earth stood up, and the rulers were gathered together against the Lord, and against His Christ. For of a truth against Thy Holy Child Jesus, whom Thou hast anointed, both Herod, and Pontius Pilate, with the Gentiles, and the people of Israel, were gathered together, for to do whatsoever Thy hand and Thy counsel determined before to be done.

"And now, Lord, behold their threatenings: and grant unto Thy servants, that with all boldness they may speak Thy word, by stretching forth Thine hand to heal; and that signs and wonders may be done by the name of Thy Holy Child Jesus."

The disciples prayed that greater strength

might be imparted to them in the work of the ministry; for they saw that they would meet the same determined opposition that Christ had encountered when upon the earth. While their united prayers were ascending in faith to heaven, the answer came. The place where they were assembled was shaken, and they were endowed anew with the Holy Spirit. Their hearts filled with courage, they again went forth to proclaim the word of God in Jerusalem. "With great power gave the apostles witness of the resurrection of the Lord Jesus," and God marvelously blessed their efforts.

The principle for which the disciples stood so fearlessly when, in answer to the command not to speak any more in the name of Jesus, they declared, "Whether it be right in the sight of God to hearken unto you more than unto God, judge ye," is the same that the adherents of the gospel struggled to maintain in the days of the Reformation. When in 1529 the German princes assembled at the Diet of Spires, there was presented the emperor's decree restricting religious liberty, and prohibiting all further dissemination of the reformed doctrines. It seemed that the hope of the world was about to be crushed out. Would the princes accept the decree? Should the light of the gospel be shut out from the multitudes still in darkness? Mighty issues for the world were at stake. Those who had accepted the reformed faith met together, and their unanimous decision was, "Let us reject this decree. In matters of conscience the majority has no power."—Merle D'Aubigné, *History of the Reformation,* b. 13, ch. 5.

This principle in our day are firmly to maintain. The banner of truth and religious liberty held aloft by the founders of the gospel church and by God's witnesses during the centuries that have passed since then, has, in this last conflict, been committed to our hands. The responsibility for this great gift rests with those whom God has blessed with a knowledge of His word. We are to receive this word as supreme authority. We are to recognize human government as an ordinance of divine appointment, and teach obedience to it as a sacred duty, within its legitimate sphere. But when its claims conflict with the claims of God, we must obey God rather than men. God's word must be recognized as above all human legislation. A "Thus saith the Lord" is not to be set aside for a "Thus saith the church" or a "Thus saith the state." The crown of Christ is to be lifted above the diadems of earthly potentates.

We are not required to defy authorities. Our words, whether spoken or written, should be carefully considered, lest we place ourselves on record as uttering that which would make us appear antagonistic to law and order. We are not to say or do anything that would unnecessarily close up our way. We are to go forward in

Christ's name, advocating the truths committed to us. If we are forbidden by men to do this work, then we may say, as did the apostles, "Whether it be right in the sight of God to hearken unto you more than unto God, judge ye. For we cannot but speak the things which we have seen and heard."

7

A Warning Against Hypocrisy

As the disciples proclaimed the truths of the gospel in Jerusalem, God bore witness to their word, and a multitude believed. Many of these early believers were immediately cut off from family and friends by the zealous bigotry of the Jews, and it was necessary to provide them with food and shelter.

The record declares, "Neither was there any among them that lacked," and it tells how the need was filled. Those among the believers who had money and possessions cheerfully sacrificed them to meet the emergency. Selling their houses or their lands, they brought the money and laid it at the apostles' feet, "and distribution was made unto every man according as he had need."

This liberality on the part of the believers was the result of the outpouring of the Spirit. The converts to the gospel were "of one heart and of one soul." One common interest controlled them—the success of the mission entrusted to them; and covetousness had no place in their lives. Their love for their brethren and the cause they had espoused, was greater than their love of money and possessions. Their works testified that they accounted the souls of men of higher value than earthly wealth.

Thus it will ever be when the Spirit of God takes possession of the life. Those whose hearts are filled with the love of Christ, will follow the example of Him who for our sake became poor, that through His poverty we might be made rich. Money, time, influence—all the gifts they have received from God's hand, they will value only as a means of advancing the work of the gospel. Thus it was in the early church; and when in the church of today it is seen that by the power of the Spirit the members have taken their affections from the things of the world, and that they are willing to make sacrifices in order that their fellow men may hear the gospel, the truths proclaimed will have a powerful influence upon the hearers.

In sharp contrast to the example of benevolence shown by the believers, was the conduct of Ananias and Sapphira, whose experience, traced by the pen of Inspiration, has left a dark stain upon the history of the early church. With others, these professed disciples had shared the

This chapter is based on Acts 4:32 to 5:11.

privilege of hearing the gospel preached by the apostles. They had been present with other believers when, after the apostles had prayed, "the place was shaken where they were assembled together; and they were all filled with the Holy Ghost." Acts 4:31. Deep conviction had rested upon all present, and under the direct influence of the Spirit of God, Ananias and Sapphira had made a pledge to give to the Lord the proceeds from the sale of certain property.

Afterward, Ananias and Sapphira grieved the Holy Spirit by yielding to feelings of covetousness. They began to regret their promise and soon lost the sweet influence of the blessing that had warmed their hearts with a desire to do large things in behalf of the cause of Christ. They thought they had been too hasty, that they ought to reconsider their decision. They talked the matter over, and decided not to fulfill their pledge. They saw, however, that those who parted with their possessions to supply the needs of their poorer brethren, were held in high esteem among the believers; and ashamed to have their brethren know that their selfish souls grudged that which they had solemnly dedicated to God, they deliberately decided to sell their property and pretend to give all the proceeds into the general fund, but really to keep a large share for themselves. Thus they would secure their living from the common store and at the same time gain the high esteem of their brethren.

But God hates hypocrisy and falsehood. Ananias and Sapphira practiced fraud in their dealing with God; they lied to the Holy Spirit, and their sin was visited with swift and terrible judgment. When Ananias came with his offering, Peter said: "Ananias, why hath Satan filled thine heart to lie to the Holy Ghost, and to keep back part of the price of the land? Whiles it remained, was it not thine own? and after it was sold, was it not in thine own power? why hast thou conceived this thing in thine heart? thou hast not lied unto men, but unto God."

"Ananias hearing these words fell down, and gave up the ghost: and great fear came upon all them that heard these things."

"Whiles it remained, was it not thine own?" Peter asked. No undue influence had been brought to bear upon Ananias to compel him to sacrifice his possessions to the general good. He had acted from choice. But in attempting to deceive the disciples, he had lied to the Almighty.

"It was about the space of three hours after, when his wife, not knowing what was done, came in. And Peter answered unto her, Tell me whether ye sold the land for so much? And she said, Yea, for so much. Then Peter said unto her, How is it that ye have agreed together to tempt the Spirit of the Lord? behold, the feet of them which have buried thy husband are at the door, and shall carry thee out. Then fell she down straightway at his feet, and yielded up the ghost: and the young men came in, and found her dead, and, carrying her forth, buried her by her husband. And great fear came upon all the church, and upon as many as heard these things."

Infinite Wisdom saw that this signal manifestation of the wrath of God was necessary to guard the young church from becoming demoralized. Their numbers were rapidly increasing. The church would have been endangered if, in the rapid increase of converts, men and women had been added who, while professing to serve God, were worshiping mammon. This judgment testified that men cannot deceive God, that He detects the hidden sin of the heart, and that He will not be mocked. It was designed as a warning to the church, to lead them to avoid pretense and hypocrisy, and to beware of robbing God.

Not to the early church only, but to all future generations, this example of God's hatred of covetousness, fraud, and hypocrisy, was given as a danger-signal. It was covetousness that Ananias and Sapphira had first cherished. The desire to retain for themselves a part of that which they had promised to the Lord, led them into fraud and hypocrisy.

God has made the proclamation of the gospel dependent upon the labors and the gifts of His people. Voluntary offerings and the tithe constitute the revenue of the Lord's work. Of the means entrusted to man, God claims a certain portion,—the tenth. He leaves all free to say whether or not they will give more than this. But when the heart is stirred by the influence of the Holy Spirit, and a vow is made to give a certain amount, the one who vows has no longer any right to the consecrated portion. Promises of this kind made to men would be looked upon as binding; are those not more binding that are made to God? Are promises tried in the court of conscience less binding than written agreements of men?

When divine light is shining into the heart with unusual clearness and power, habitual selfishness relaxes its grasp and there is a disposition to give to the cause of God. But none need think that they will be allowed to fulfill the promises then made, without a protest on the part of Satan. He is not pleased to see the Redeemer's kingdom on earth built up. He suggests that the pledge made was too much, that it may cripple them in their efforts to acquire property or gratify the desires of their families.

It is God who blesses men with property, and He does this that they may be able to give toward the advancement of His cause. He sends the sunshine and the rain. He causes vegetation to flourish. He gives health and the ability to acquire means. All our blessings come from His bountiful hand. In turn, He would have men and women show their gratitude by returning Him a portion in tithes and offerings—in thank offerings, in freewill offerings, in trespass offerings. Should means flow into the treasury in accordance with this divinely appointed plan,—a tenth of all the increase, and liberal offerings,—there would be an abundance for the advancement of the Lord's work.

But the hearts of men become hardened through selfishness, and, like Ananias and Sapphira, they are tempted to withhold part of the price, while pretending to fulfill God's requirements. Many spend money lavishly in self-gratification. Men and women consult their pleasure and gratify their taste, while they bring to God, almost unwillingly, a stinted offering. They forget that God will one day demand a strict account of how His goods have been used, and that He will no more accept the pittance they hand into the treasury than He accepted the offering of Ananias and Sapphira.

From the stern punishment meted out to those perjurers, God would have us learn also how deep is His hatred and contempt for all hypocrisy and deception. In pretending that they had given all, Ananias and Sapphira lied to the Holy Spirit, and, as a result, they lost this life and the life that is to come. The same God who punished them, today condemns all falsehood. Lying lips are an abomination to Him. He declares that into the Holy City "there shall in no wise enter . . . anything that defileth, neither whatsoever worketh abomination, or maketh a lie." Revelation 21:27. Let truth telling be held with no loose hand or uncertain grasp. Let it become a part of the life. Playing fast and loose with truth, and dissembling to suit one's own selfish plans, means shipwreck of faith. "Stand therefore, having your loins girt about with truth." Ephesians 6:14. He who utters untruths sells his soul in a cheap market. His falsehoods may seem to serve in emergencies; he may thus seem to make business advancement that he could not gain by fair dealing; but he finally reaches the place where he can trust no one. Himself a falsifier, he has no confidence in the word of others.

In the case of Ananias and Sapphira, the sin of fraud against God was speedily punished. The same sin was often repeated in the after history of the church and is committed by many in our time. But though it may not be attended by the visible manifestation of God's displeasure, it is no less heinous in His sight now than in the apostles' time. The warning has been given; God has clearly manifested His abhorrence of this sin; and all who give themselves up to hypocrisy and covetousness may be sure that they are destroying their own souls.

8

Before the Sanhedrin

It was the cross, that instrument of shame and torture, which brought hope and salvation to the world. The disciples were but humble men, without wealth, and with no weapon but the word of God; yet in Christ's strength they went forth to tell the wonderful story of the manger and the cross, and to triumph over all opposition. Without earthly honor or recognition, they were heroes of faith. From their lips came words of divine eloquence that shook the world.

In Jerusalem, where the deepest prejudice existed, and where the most confused ideas prevailed in regard to Him who had been crucified as a malefactor, the disciples continued to speak with boldness the words of life, setting before the Jews the work and mission of Christ, His crucifixion, resurrection, and ascension. Priests and rulers heard with amazement the clear, bold testimony of the apostles. The power of the risen Saviour had indeed fallen on the disciples, and their work was accompanied by signs and miracles that daily increased the number of believers. Along the streets where the disciples were to pass, the people laid their sick "on beds and couches, that at the least the shadow of Peter passing by might overshadow some of them." Here also were brought those vexed with unclean spirits. The crowds gathered round them, and those who were healed shouted the praises of God and glorified the name of the Redeemer.

The priests and rulers saw that Christ was extolled above them. As the Sadducees, who did not believe in a resurrection, heard the apostles declaring that Christ had risen from the dead, they were enraged, realizing that if the apostles were allowed to preach a risen Saviour, and to work miracles in His name, the doctrine that there would be no resurrection would be rejected by all, and the sect of the Sadducees would soon become extinct. The Pharisees were angry as they perceived that the tendency of the disciples' teaching was to undermine the Jewish ceremonies, and make the sacrificial offerings of no effect.

Hitherto all the efforts made to suppress this new teaching had been in vain; but now both Sadducees and Pharisees determined that the work of the disciples should be stopped, for it was proving them guilty of the death of Jesus. Filled with indignation, the priests laid violent hands on Peter and John, and put them in the common prison.

The leaders in the Jewish nation had signally failed of fulfilling God's purpose for His chosen

This chapter is based on Acts 5:12-42.

79 people. Those whom the Lord had made the depositaries of truth had proved unfaithful to their trust, and God chose others to do His work. In their blindness these leaders now gave full sway to what they called righteous indignation against the ones who were setting aside their cherished doctrines. They would not admit even the possibility that they themselves did not rightly understand the word, or that they had misinterpreted or misapplied the Scriptures. They acted like men who had lost their reason. What right have these teachers, they said, some of them mere fishermen, to present ideas contrary to the doctrines that we have taught the people? Being determined to suppress the teaching of these ideas, they imprisoned those who were presenting them.

The disciples were not intimidated or cast down by this treatment. The Holy Spirit brought to their minds the words spoken by Christ: "The servant is not greater than his lord. If they have persecuted Me, they will also persecute you; if they have kept My saying, they will keep yours also. But all these things will they do unto you for My name's sake, because they know not Him that sent Me." "They shall put you out of the synagogues: yea, the time cometh, that whosoever killeth you will think that he doeth God service." "These things have I told you, that when the time shall come, ye may remember that I told you of them." John 15:20, 21; 16:2, 4.

The God of heaven, the mighty Ruler of the universe, took the matter of the imprisonment of the disciples into His own hands, for men were 80 warring against His work. By night the angel of the Lord opened the prison doors and said to the disciples, "Go, stand and speak in the temple to the people all the words of this life." This command was directly contrary to the order given by the Jewish rulers; but did the apostles say, We cannot do this until we have consulted the magistrates and received permission from them? No; God had said, "Go," and they obeyed. "They entered into the temple early in the morning, and taught."

When Peter and John appeared among the believers and recounted how the angel had led them directly through the band of soldiers guarding the prison, bidding them resume the work that had been interrupted, the brethren were filled with amazement and joy.

In the meantime the high priest and those with him had "called the council together, and all the senate of the children of Israel." The priests and rulers had decided to fix upon the disciples the charge of insurrection, to accuse them of murdering Ananias and Sapphira, and of conspiring to deprive the priests of their authority. They hoped so to excite the mob that it would take the matter in hand and deal with the disciples as it had dealt with Jesus. They were aware that many who did not accept the teachings of Christ were weary of the arbitrary rule of the Jewish authorities and anxious for some change. The priests feared that if these dissatisfied ones were to accept the truths proclaimed by the apostles, and were to acknowledge Jesus as the Messiah, the anger of the entire people would be raised against the religious leaders, who would then be made to answer for the murder of Christ. They decided 81 to take strong measures to prevent this.

When they sent for the prisoners to be brought before them, great was their amazement at the word brought back that the prison doors were found to be securely bolted and the guard stationed before them, but that the prisoners were nowhere to be found.

Soon the astonishing report came, "Behold, the men whom ye put in prison are standing in the temple, and teaching the people. Then went the captain with the officers, and brought them without violence: for they feared the people, lest they should have been stoned."

Although the apostles were miraculously delivered from prison, they were not safe from examination and punishment. Christ had said when He was with them, "Take heed to yourselves: for they shall deliver you up to councils." Mark 13:9. By sending an angel to deliver them, God had given them a token of His love and an assurance of His presence. It was now their part to suffer for the sake of the One whose gospel they were preaching.

In the history of prophets and apostles, are many noble examples of loyalty to God. Christ's witnesses have endured imprisonment, torture, and death itself, rather than break God's commands. The record left by Peter and John is as heroic as any in the gospel dispensation. As they stood for the second time before the men who seemed bent on their destruction, no fear or hesitation could be discerned in their words or attitude. And when the high priest said, "Did we not straitly command you that ye should not teach in this name? and, behold, ye have filled 82 Jerusalem with your doctrine, and intend to bring this Man's blood upon us," Peter answered, "We ought to obey God rather than men." It was an angel from heaven who delivered them from prison and bade them teach in the temple. In following his directions they were obeying the divine command, and this they must continue to do at whatever cost to themselves.

Then the Spirit of Inspiration came upon the disciples; the accused became the accusers, charging the murder of Christ upon those who composed the council. "The God of our fathers raised up Jesus," Peter declared, "whom ye slew and hanged on a tree. Him hath God exalted with His right hand to be a Prince and a Saviour, for to give repentance to Israel, and forgiveness of sins. And we are His witnesses of these things; and so is also the Holy Ghost, whom God hath given to them that obey Him."

So enraged were the Jews at these words that they decided to take the law into their own hands and without further trial, or without authority from the Roman officers, to put the prisoners to death. Already guilty of the blood of Christ, they were now eager to stain their hands with the blood of His disciples.

But in the council there was one man who recognized the voice of God in the words spoken by the disciples. This was Gamaliel, a Pharisee of good reputation and a man of learning and high position. His clear intellect saw that the violent step contemplated by the priests would lead to terrible consequences. Before 83 addressing those present, he requested that the prisoners be removed. He well knew the elements he had to deal with; he knew that the murderers of Christ would hesitate at nothing in order to carry out their purpose.

He then spoke with great deliberation and calmness, saying: "Ye men of Israel, take heed to yourselves what ye intend to do as touching these men. For before these days rose up Theudas, boasting himself to be somebody; to whom a number of men, about four hundred, joined themselves: who was slain; and all, as many as obeyed him, were scattered, and brought to nought. After this man rose up Judas of Galilee in the days of the taxing, and drew away much people after him: he also perished; and all, even as many as obeyed him, were dispersed. And now I say unto you, Refrain from these men, and let them alone: for if this counsel or this work be of men, it will come to nought: but if it be of God, ye cannot overthrow it; lest haply ye be found even to fight against God."

The priests saw the reasonableness of these views, and were obliged to agree with Gamaliel. Yet their prejudice and hatred could hardly be restrained. Very reluctantly, after beating the disciples and charging them again at the peril of their lives to preach no more in the name of Jesus, they released them. "And they departed from the presence of the council, rejoicing that they were counted worthy to suffer shame for His name. And daily in the temple, and in every house, they ceased not to teach and preach Jesus Christ."

84 Shortly before His crucifixion Christ had bequeathed to His disciples a legacy of peace. "Peace I leave with you," He said, "My peace I give unto you: not as the world giveth, give I unto you. Let not your heart be troubled, neither let it be afraid." John 14:27. This peace is not the peace that comes through conformity to the world. Christ never purchased peace by compromise with evil. The peace that Christ left His disciples is internal rather than external and was ever to remain with His witnesses through strife and contention.

Christ said of Himself, "Think not that I am come to send peace on earth: I came not to send peace, but a sword." Matthew 10:34. The Prince of Peace, He was yet the cause of division. He who came to proclaim glad tidings and to create hope and joy in the hearts of the children of men, opened a controversy that burns deep and arouses intense passion in the human heart. And He warns His followers, "In the world ye shall have tribulation." "They shall lay their hands on you, and persecute you, delivering you up to the synagogues, and into prisons, being brought before kings and rulers for My name's sake." "Ye shall be betrayed both by parents, and brethren, and kinsfolks, and friends; and some of you shall they cause to be put to death." John 16:33; Luke 21:12, 16.

This prophecy has been fulfilled in a marked manner. Every indignity, reproach, and cruelty that Satan could instigate human hearts to devise, has been visited upon the followers of Jesus. And it will be again fulfilled in a marked manner; for the carnal heart is still at enmity with the law of God, and will not be subject to 85 its commands. The world is no more in harmony with the principles of Christ today than it was in the days of the apostles. The same hatred that prompted the cry, "Crucify Him! crucify Him!" the same hatred that led to the persecution of the disciples, still works in the children of disobedience. The same spirit which in the Dark Ages consigned men and women to prison, to exile, and to death, which conceived the exquisite torture of the Inquisition, which planned and executed the Massacre of St. Bartholomew, and which kindled the fires of Smithfield, is still at work with malignant energy in unregenerate hearts. The history of truth has ever been the record of a struggle between right and wrong. The proclamation of the gospel has ever been carried forward in this world in the face of opposition, peril, loss, and suffering.

What was the strength of those who in the past have suffered persecution for Christ's sake? It was union with God, union with the Holy Spirit, union with Christ. Reproach and persecution have separated many from earthly friends, but never from the love of Christ. Never is the tempesttried soul more dearly loved by His Saviour than when he is suffering reproach for the truth's sake. "I will love him," Christ said, "and will manifest Myself to him." John 14:21. When for the truth's sake the believer stands at the bar of earthly tribunals, Christ stands by his side. When he is confined within prison walls, Christ manifests Himself to him and cheers his heart with His love. When he suffers death for Christ's sake, the Saviour says to him, They may kill the body, but they cannot hurt the soul. "Be of good cheer; I have overcome the world." 86 "Fear thou not; for I am with thee: be not dismayed; for I am thy God: I will strengthen thee; yea, I will help thee; yea, I will uphold thee with the right hand of My righteousness." John 16:33; Isaiah 41:10.

"They that trust in the Lord shall be as Mount Zion, which cannot be removed, but abideth forever. As the mountains are round about Jerusalem, so the Lord is round about His people from henceforth even forever." "He shall redeem their soul from deceit and violence: and precious shall their blood be in His sight." Psalms 125:1-3; 72:14.

"The Lord of hosts shall defend them; . . . the Lord their God shall save them in that day as the flock of His people: for they shall be as the stones of a crown, lifted up as an ensign upon His land." Zechariah 9:15, 16.

9
The Seven Deacons

"In those days, when the number of the disciples was multiplied, there arose a murmuring of the Grecians against the Hebrews, because their widows were neglected in the daily ministration."

The early church was made up of many classes of people, of various nationalities. At the time of the outpouring of the Holy Spirit at Pentecost, "there were dwelling at Jerusalem Jews, devout men, out of every nation under heaven." Acts 2:5. Among those of the Hebrew faith who were gathered at Jerusalem were some commonly known as Grecians, between whom and the Jews of Palestine there had long existed distrust and even antagonism.

The hearts of those who had been converted under the labors of the apostles, were softened and united by Christian love. Despite former prejudices, all were in harmony with one another. Satan knew that so long as this union continued to exist, he would be powerless to check the progress of gospel truth; and he sought to take advantage of former habits of thought, in the hope that thereby he might be able to introduce into the church elements of disunion.

Thus it came to pass that as disciples were multiplied, the enemy succeeded in arousing the suspicions of some who had formerly been in the habit of looking with jealousy on their brethren in the faith and of finding fault with their spiritual leaders, and so "there arose a murmuring of the Grecians against the Hebrews." The cause of complaint was an alleged neglect of the Greek widows in the daily distribution of assistance. Any inequality would have been contrary to the spirit of the gospel, yet Satan had succeeded in arousing suspicion. Prompt measures must now be taken to remove all occasion

for dissatisfaction, lest the enemy triumph in his effort to bring about a division among the believers.

The disciples of Jesus had reached a crisis in their experience. Under the wise leadership of the apostles, who labored unitedly in the power of the Holy Spirit, the work committed to the gospel messengers was developing rapidly. The church was continually enlarging, and this growth in membership brought increasingly heavy burdens upon those in charge. No one man, or even one set of men, could continue to bear these burdens alone, without imperiling the future prosperity of the church. There was necessity for a further distribution of the responsibilities which had been borne so faithfully by a few during the earlier days of the church. The apostles must now take an important step in the perfecting of gospel order in the church by laying upon others some of the burdens thus far borne by themselves.

Summoning a meeting of the believers, the apostles were led by the Holy Spirit to outline a plan for the better organization of all the working forces of the church. The time had come, the apostles stated, when the spiritual leaders having the oversight of the church should be relieved from the task of distributing to the poor and from similar burdens, so that they might be free to carry forward the work of preaching the gospel. "Wherefore, brethren," they said, "look ye out among you seven men of honest report, full of the Holy Ghost and wisdom, whom we may appoint over this business. But we will give ourselves continually to prayer, and to the ministry of the word." This advice was followed, and by prayer and the laying on of hands, seven chosen men were solemnly set apart for their duties as deacons.

The appointment of the seven to take the oversight of special lines of work, proved a great blessing to the church. These officers gave careful consideration to individual needs as well as to the general financial interests of the church, and by their prudent management and their godly example they were an important aid to their fellow officers in binding together the various interests of the church into a united whole.

That this step was in the order of God, is revealed in the immediate results for good that were seen. "The word of God increased; and the number of the disciples multiplied in Jerusalem greatly; and a great company of the priests were obedient to the faith." This ingathering of souls was due both to the greater freedom secured by the apostles and to the zeal and power shown by the seven deacons. The fact that these brethren had been ordained for the special work of looking after the needs of the poor, did not exclude them from teaching the faith. On the contrary, they were fully qualified to instruct others in the truth, and they engaged in the work with great earnestness and success.

To the early church had been entrusted a constantly enlarging work—that of establishing centers of light and blessing wherever there were honest souls willing to give themselves to the service of Christ. The proclamation of the gospel was to be world-wide in its extent, and the messengers of the cross could not hope to fulfill their important mission unless they should remain united in the bonds of Christian unity, and thus reveal to the world that they were one with Christ in God. Had not their divine Leader prayed to the Father, "Keep through Thine own name those whom Thou hast given Me, that they may be one, as We are"? And had He not declared of His disciples, "The world hath hated them, because they are not of the world"? Had He not pleaded with the Father that they might be "made perfect in one," "that the world may believe that Thou hast sent Me"? John 17:11, 14, 23, 21. Their spiritual life and power was dependent on a close connection with the One by whom they had been commissioned to preach the gospel.

Only as they were united with Christ could the disciples hope to have the accompanying power of the Holy Spirit and the co-operation of angels of heaven. With the help of these divine agencies they would present before the world a united front and would be victorious in the conflict they were compelled to wage unceasingly against the powers of darkness. As they should continue to labor unitedly, heavenly messengers would go before them, opening the way; hearts would be prepared for the reception of truth, and many would be won to Christ. So long as they remained united, the church would go forth "fair as the moon, clear as the sun, and terrible as an army with banners." Song of Solomon 6:10. Nothing could withstand her onward progress. The church would advance from victory to victory, gloriously fulfilling her divine mission of proclaiming the gospel to the world.

The organization of the church at Jerusalem was to serve as a model for the organization of churches in every other place where messengers of truth should win converts to the gospel. Those to whom was given the responsibility of the general oversight of the church were not to lord it over God's heritage, but, as wise shepherds, were to "feed the flock of God, . . . being ensamples to the flock" (1 Peter 5:2, 3); and the deacons were to be "men of honest report, full of the Holy Ghost and wisdom." These men were to take their position unitedly on the side of right and to maintain it with firmness and decision. Thus they would have a uniting influence upon the entire flock.

Later in the history of the early church, when in various parts of the world many groups of believers had been formed into churches, the organization of the church was further perfected, so that order and harmonious action might be maintained. Every member was exhorted to act well his part. Each was to make a wise use of the talents entrusted to him. Some were endowed by the Holy Spirit with special gifts—"first apostles, secondarily prophets, thirdly teachers, after that miracles, then gifts of healings, helps, governments, diversities of tongues." 1 Corinthians 12:28. But all these classes of workers were to labor in harmony.

"There are diversities of gifts, but the same Spirit. And there are differences of administrations, but the same Lord. And there are diversities of operations, but it is the same God which worketh all in all. But the manifestation of the Spirit is given to every man to profit withal. For to one is given by the Spirit the word of wisdom; to another the word of knowledge by the same Spirit; to another faith by the same Spirit; to another the gifts of healing by the same Spirit; to another the working of miracles; to another prophecy; to another discerning of spirits; to another divers kinds of tongues; to another the interpretation of tongues: but all these worketh that one and the selfsame Spirit, dividing to every man severally as He will. For as the body is one, and hath many members, and all the members of that one body, being many, are one body: so also is Christ." 1 Corinthians 12:4-12.

Solemn are the responsibilities resting upon those who are called to act as leaders in the church of God on earth. In the days of the theocracy, when Moses was endeavoring to carry alone burdens so heavy that he would soon have worn away under them, he was counseled by Jethro to plan for a wise distribution of responsibilities. "Be thou for the people to Godward," Jethro advised, "that thou mayest bring the causes unto God: and thou shalt teach them ordinances and laws, and shalt show them the way wherein they must walk, and the work that they must do." Jethro further advised that men be appointed to act as "rulers of thousands, and rulers of hundreds, rulers of fifties, and rulers of tens." These were to be "able men, such as fear God, men of truth, hating covetousness." They were to "judge the people at all seasons," thus relieving Moses of the wearing responsibility of giving consideration to many minor matters that could be dealt with wisely by consecrated helpers.

The time and strength of those who in the providence of God have been placed in leading positions of responsibility in the church, should be spent in dealing with the weightier matters demanding special wisdom and largeness of heart. It is not in the order of God that such men should be appealed to for the adjustment of minor matters that others are well qualified to handle. "Every great matter they shall bring unto thee," Jethro proposed to Moses, "but every small matter they shall judge: so shall it be easier for thyself, and they shall bear the burden with thee. If thou shalt do this thing, and God command thee so, then thou shalt be able to endure, and all this people shall also go to their place in peace."

In harmony with this plan, "Moses chose able men out of all Israel, and made them heads over the people, rulers of thousands, rulers of hundreds, rulers of fifties, and rulers of tens: and they judged the people at all seasons: the hard causes they brought unto Moses, but every small matter they judged themselves." Exodus 18:19-26.

Later, when choosing seventy elders to share with him the responsibilities of leadership, Moses was careful to select, as his helpers, men possessing dignity, sound judgment, and experience. In his charge to these elders at the time of their ordination, he outlined some of the qualifications that fit a man to be a wise ruler in the church. "Hear the causes between your brethren," said Moses, "and judge righteously between every man and his brother, and the stranger that is with him. Ye shall not respect persons in judgment; but ye shall hear the small as well as the great; ye shall not be afraid of the face of man; for the judgment is God's." Deuteronomy 1:16, 17.

King David, toward the close of his reign, delivered a solemn charge to those bearing the burden of the work of God in his day. Summoning to Jerusalem "all the princes of Israel, the princes of the tribes, and the captains of the companies that ministered to the king by course, and the captains over the thousands, and captains over the hundreds, and the stewards over all the substance and possession of the king, and of his sons, with the officers, and with the mighty men, and with all the valiant men," the aged king solemnly charged them, "in the sight of all Israel the congregation of the Lord, and in the audience of our God," to "keep and seek for all the commandments of the Lord your God." 1 Chronicles 28:1, 8.

To Solomon, as one called to occupy a position of leading responsibility, David gave a special charge: "Thou, Solomon my son, know thou the God of thy father, and serve Him with a perfect heart and with a willing mind: for the Lord searcheth all hearts, and understandeth all the imaginations of the thoughts: if thou seek Him, He will be found of thee; but if thou forsake Him, He will cast thee off forever. Take heed now; for the Lord hath chosen thee: . . . be strong." 1 Chronicles 28:9, 10.

The same principles of piety and justice that were to guide the rulers among God's people in the time of Moses and of David, were also to be followed by those given the oversight of the newly organized church of God in the gospel dispensation. In the work of setting things in order in all the churches, and ordaining suitable men to act as officers, the apostles held to the high standards of leadership outlined in the Old Testament Scriptures. They maintained that he who is called to stand in a position of leading responsibility in the church "must be blameless, as the steward of God; not self-willed, not soon angry, not given to wine, no striker, not given to filthy lucre; but a lover of hospitality, a lover of good men, sober, just, holy, temperate; holding fast the faithful word as he hath been taught, that he may be able by sound doctrine both to exhort and to convince the gainsayers." Titus 1:7-9.

The order that was maintained in the early Christian church made it possible for them to move forward solidly as a well-disciplined army clad with the armor of God. The companies of believers, though scattered over a large territory, were all members of one body; all moved in concert and in harmony with one another. When dissension arose in a local church, as later it did arise in Antioch and elsewhere, and the believers were unable to come to an agreement among themselves, such matters were not permitted to create a division in the church, but were referred to a general council of the entire body of believers, made up of appointed delegates from the various local churches, with the apostles and elders in positions of leading responsibility. Thus the efforts of Satan to attack the church in isolated places were met by concerted action on the part of all, and the plans of the enemy to disrupt and destroy were thwarted.

"God is not the author of confusion, but of peace, as in all churches of the saints." 1 Corinthians 14:33. He requires that order and system be observed in the conduct of church affairs today no less than in the days of old. He desires His work to be carried forward with thoroughness and exactness so that He may place upon it the seal of His approval. Christian is to be united with Christian, church with church, the human instrumentality co-operating with the divine, every agency subordinate to the Holy Spirit, and all combined in giving to the world the good tidings of the grace of God.

10

The First Christian Martyr

Stephen, the foremost of the seven deacons, was a man of deep piety and broad faith. Though a Jew by birth, he spoke the Greek language and was familiar with the customs and manners of the Greeks. He therefore found opportunity to preach the gospel in the synagogues of the Greek Jews. He was very active in the cause of Christ and boldly proclaimed his

This chapter is based on Acts 6:5-15; 7.

faith. Learned rabbis and doctors of the law engaged in public discussion with him, confidently expecting an easy victory. But "they were not able to resist the wisdom and the spirit by which he spake." Not only did he speak in the power of the Holy Spirit, but it was plain that he was a student of the prophecies and learned in all matters of the law. He ably defended the truths that he advocated and utterly defeated his opponents. To him was the promise fulfilled, "Settle it therefore in your hearts, not to meditate before what ye shall answer: for I will give you a mouth and wisdom, which all your adversaries shall not be able to gainsay nor resist." Luke 21:14, 15.

As the priests and rulers saw the power that attended the preaching of Stephen, they were filled with bitter hatred. Instead of yielding to the evidence that he presented, they determined to silence his voice by putting him to death. On several occasions they had bribed the Roman authorities to pass over without comment instances where the Jews had taken the law into their own hands and had tried, condemned, and executed prisoners in accordance with their national custom. The enemies of Stephen did not doubt that they could again pursue such a course without danger to themselves. They determined to risk the consequences and therefore seized Stephen and brought him before the Sanhedrin council for trial.

Learned Jews from the surrounding countries were summoned for the purpose of refuting the arguments of the prisoner. Saul of Tarsus was present and took a leading part against Stephen. He brought the weight of eloquence and the logic of the rabbis to bear upon the case, to convince the people that Stephen was preaching delusive and dangerous doctrines; but in Stephen he met one who had a full understanding of the purpose of God in the spreading of the gospel to other nations.

Because the priests and rulers could not prevail against the clear, calm wisdom of Stephen, they determined to make an example of him; and while thus satisfying their revengeful hatred, they would prevent others, through fear, from adopting his belief. Witnesses were hired to bear false testimony that they had heard him speak blasphemous words against the temple and the law. "We have heard him say," these witnesses declared, "that this Jesus of Nazareth shall destroy this place, and shall change the customs which Moses delivered us."

As Stephen stood face to face with his judges to answer to the charge of blasphemy, a holy radiance shone upon his countenance, and "all that sat in the council, looking steadfastly on him, saw his face as it had been the face of an angel." Many who beheld this light trembled and veiled their faces, but the stubborn unbelief and prejudice of the rulers did not waver.

When Stephen was questioned as to the truth of the charges against him, he began his defense in a clear, thrilling voice, which rang through the council hall. In words that held the assembly spellbound, he proceeded to rehearse the history of the chosen people of God. He showed a thorough knowledge of the Jewish economy and the spiritual interpretation of it now made manifest through Christ. He repeated the words of Moses that foretold of the Messiah: "A Prophet shall the Lord your God raise up unto you of your brethren, like unto me; Him shall ye hear." He made plain his own loyalty to God and to the Jewish faith, while he showed that the law in which the Jews trusted for salvation had not been able to save Israel from idolatry. He connected Jesus Christ with all the Jewish history. He referred to the building of the temple by Solomon, and to the words of both Solomon and Isaiah: "Howbeit the Most High dwelleth not in temples made with hands; as saith the prophet, Heaven is My throne, and earth is My footstool: what house will ye build Me? saith the Lord: or what is the place of My rest? Hath not My hand made all these things?"

When Stephen reached this point, there was a tumult among the people. When he connected Christ with the prophecies and spoke as he did of the temple, the priest, pretending to be horror-stricken, rent his robe. To Stephen this act was a signal that his voice would soon be silenced forever. He saw the resistance that met his words and knew that he was giving his last testimony. Although in the midst of his sermon, he abruptly concluded it.

Suddenly breaking away from the train of history that he was following, and turning upon his infuriated judges, he cried: "Ye stiff-necked and uncircumcised in heart and ears, ye do always resist the Holy Ghost: as your fathers did, so do ye. Which of the prophets have not your fathers persecuted? and they have slain them which showed before of the coming of the Just One; of whom ye have been now the betrayers and murderers: who have received the law by the disposition of angels, and have not kept it."

At this, priests and rulers were beside themselves with anger. Acting more like beasts of prey than human beings, they rushed upon Stephen, gnashing their teeth. In the cruel faces about him the prisoner read his fate; but he did not waver. For him the fear of death was gone. For him the enraged priests and the excited mob had no terror. The scene before him faded from his vision. To him the gates of heaven were ajar, and, looking in, he saw the glory of the courts of God, and Christ, as if just risen from His throne, standing ready to sustain His servant. In words of triumph Stephen exclaimed, "Behold, I see the heavens opened, and the Son of man standing on the right hand of God."

As he described the glorious scene upon

which his eyes were gazing, it was more than his persecutors could endure. Stopping their ears, that they might not hear his words, and uttering loud cries, they ran furiously upon him with one accord "and cast him out of the city." "And they stoned Stephen, calling upon God, and saying, Lord Jesus, receive my spirit. And he kneeled down, and cried with a loud voice, Lord, lay not this sin to their charge. And when he had said this, he fell asleep."

No legal sentence had been passed upon Stephen, but the Roman authorities were bribed by large sums of money to make no investigation into the case.

The martyrdom of Stephen made a deep impression upon all who witnessed it. The memory of the signet of God upon his face; his words, which touched the very souls of those who heard them, remained in the minds of the beholders, and testified to the truth of that which he had proclaimed. His death was a sore trial to the church, but it resulted in the conviction of Saul, who could not efface from his memory the faith and constancy of the martyr, and the glory that had rested on his countenance.

At the scene of Stephen's trial and death, Saul had seemed to be imbued with a frenzied zeal. Afterward he was angered by his own secret conviction that Stephen had been honored by God at the very time when he was dishonored 102 by men. Saul continued to persecute the church of God, hunting them down, seizing them in their houses, and delivering them up to the priests and rulers for imprisonment and death. His zeal in carrying forward this persecution brought terror to the Christians at Jerusalem. The Roman authorities made no special effort to stay the cruel work and secretly aided the Jews in order to conciliate them and to secure their favor.

After the death of Stephen, Saul was elected a member of the Sanhedrin council in consideration of the part he had acted on that occasion. For a time he was a mighty instrument in the hands of Satan to carry out his rebellion against the Son of God. But soon this relentless persecutor was to be employed in building up the church that he was now tearing down. A Mightier than Satan had chosen Saul to take the place of the martyred Stephen, to preach and suffer for His name, and to spread far and wide the tidings of salvation through His blood.

103

11

The Gospel in Samaria

After the death of Stephen there arose against the believers in Jerusalem a persecution so relentless that "they were all scattered abroad

This chapter is based on Acts 8.

throughout the regions of Judea and Samaria." Saul "made havoc of the church, entering into every house, and haling men and women committed them to prison." Of his zeal in this cruel work he said at a later date: "I verily thought with myself, that I ought to do many things contrary to the name of Jesus of Nazareth. Which thing I also did in Jerusalem: and many of the saints did I shut up in prison. . . . And I punished them oft in every synagogue, and compelled them to blaspheme; and being exceedingly mad against them, I persecuted them even unto strange cities." That Stephen was not the only one who suffered death may be seen from Saul's own words, "And when they were put to death, I gave my voice against them." Acts 26:9-11.

At this time of peril Nicodemus came forward in fearless avowal of his faith in the crucified Saviour. Nicodemus was a member of the Sanhedrin and with others had been stirred by the teaching of Jesus. As he had witnessed Christ's wonderful works, the conviction had fastened itself upon his mind that this was the Sent of God. Too proud openly to acknowledge himself in sympathy with the Galilean Teacher, he had sought a secret interview. In this interview Jesus had unfolded to him the plan of salvation and His mission to the world, yet still Nicodemus had hesitated. He hid the truth in his heart, and for three years there was little apparent fruit. But while Nicodemus had not publicly acknowledged Christ, he had in the Sanhedrin council repeatedly thwarted the schemes of the priests to destroy Him. When at last Christ had been lifted up on the cross, Nicodemus remembered the words that He had spoken to him in the night interview on the Mount of Olives, "As Moses lifted up the serpent in the wilderness, even so must the Son of man be lifted up" (John 3:14); and he saw in Jesus the world's Redeemer.

With Joseph of Arimathea, Nicodemus had borne the expense of the burial of Jesus. The disciples had been afraid to show themselves openly as Christ's followers, but Nicodemus and Joseph had come boldly to their aid. The help of these rich and honored men was greatly needed in that hour of darkness. They had been able to do for their dead Master what it would have been impossible for the poor disciples to do; and their wealth and influence had protected them, in a great measure, from the malice of the priests and rulers.

Now, when the Jews were trying to destroy the infant church, Nicodemus came forward in its defense. No longer cautious and questioning, he encouraged the faith of the disciples and used his wealth in helping to sustain the church at Jerusalem and in advancing the work of the gospel. Those who in other days had paid him reverence, now scorned and persecuted him,

104

105

and he became poor in this world's goods; yet he faltered not in the defense of his faith.

The persecution that came upon the church in Jerusalem resulted in giving a great impetus to the work of the gospel. Success had attended the ministry of the word in that place, and there was danger that the disciples would linger there too long, unmindful of the Saviour's commission to go to all the world. Forgetting that strength to resist evil is best gained by aggressive service, they began to think that they had no work so important as that of shielding the church in Jerusalem from the attacks of the enemy. Instead of educating the new converts to carry the gospel to those who had not heard it, they were in danger of taking a course that would lead all to be satisfied with what had been accomplished. To scatter His representatives abroad, where they could work for others, God permitted persecution to come upon them. Driven from Jerusalem, the believers "went everywhere preaching the word."

Among those to whom the Saviour had given the commission, "Go ye therefore, and teach all nations" (Matthew 28:19), were many from the humbler walks of life—men and women who had learned to love their Lord and who had determined to follow His example of unselfish service. To these lowly ones, as well as to the disciples who had been with the Saviour during His earthly ministry, had been given a precious trust. They were to carry to the world the glad tidings of salvation through Christ.

When they were scattered by persecution they went forth filled with missionary zeal. They realized the responsibility of their mission. They knew that they held in their hands the bread of life for a famishing world; and they were constrained by the love of Christ to break this bread to all who were in need. The Lord wrought through them. Wherever they went, the sick were healed and the poor had the gospel preached unto them.

Philip, one of the seven deacons, was among those driven from Jerusalem. He "went down to the city of Samaria, and preached Christ unto them. And the people with one accord gave heed unto those things which Philip spake, hearing and seeing the miracles which he did. For unclean spirits . . . came out of many that were possessed with them: and many taken with palsies, and that were lame, were healed. And there was great joy in that city."

Christ's message to the Samaritan woman with whom He had talked at Jacob's well had borne fruit. After listening to His words, the woman had gone to the men of the city, saying, "Come, see a man, which told me all things that ever I did: is not this the Christ?" They went with her, heard Jesus, and believed on Him. Anxious to hear more, they begged Him to remain. For two days He stayed with them, "and many more believed because of His own word." John 4:29, 41.

And when His disciples were driven from Jerusalem, some found in Samaria a safe asylum. The Samaritans welcomed these messengers of the gospel, and the Jewish converts gathered a precious harvest from among those who had once been their bitterest enemies.

Philip's work in Samaria was marked with great success, and, thus encouraged, he sent to Jerusalem for help. The apostles now perceived more fully the meaning of the words of Christ, "Ye shall be witnesses unto Me both in Jerusalem, and in all Judea, and in Samaria, and unto the uttermost part of the earth." Acts 1:8.

While Philip was still in Samaria, he was directed by a heavenly messenger to "go toward the south unto the way that goeth down from Jerusalem unto Gaza. . . . And he arose and went." He did not question the call, nor did he hesitate to obey; for he had learned the lesson of conformity to God's will.

"And, behold, a man of Ethiopia, a eunuch of great authority under Candace queen of the Ethiopians, who had the charge of all her treasure, and had come to Jerusalem for to worship, was returning, and sitting in his chariot read Esaias the prophet." This Ethiopian was a man of good standing and of wide influence. God saw that when converted he would give others the light he had received and would exert a strong influence in favor of the gospel. Angels of God were attending this seeker for light, and he was being drawn to the Saviour. By the ministration of the Holy Spirit the Lord brought him into touch with one who could lead him to the light.

Philip was directed to go to the Ethiopian and explain to him the prophecy that he was reading. "Go near," the Spirit said, "and join thyself to this chariot." As Philip drew near, he asked the eunuch, "Understandest thou what thou readest? And he said, How can I, except some man should guide me? And he desired Philip that he would come up and sit with him." The scripture that he was reading was the prophecy of Isaiah relating to Christ: "He was led as a sheep to the slaughter; and like a lamb dumb before his shearer, so opened He not His mouth: in His humiliation His judgment was taken away: and who shall declare His generation? for His life is taken from the earth."

"Of whom speaketh the prophet this?" the eunuch asked, "of himself, or of some other man?" Then Philip opened to him the great truth of redemption. Beginning at the same scripture, he "preached unto him Jesus."

The man's heart thrilled with interest as the Scriptures were explained to him; and when the disciple had finished, he was ready to accept the light given. He did not make his high worldly position an excuse for refusing the gospel. "As they went on their way, they came unto a certain water: and the eunuch said, See, here is water; what doth hinder me to be baptized? And Philip said, If thou believest with all thine heart, thou mayest. And he answered and said, I believe that Jesus Christ is the Son of God. And he commanded the chariot to stand still: and they went down both into the water, both Philip and the eunuch; and he baptized him.

"And when they were come up out of the water, the Spirit of the Lord caught away Philip, that the eunuch saw him no more: and he went on his way rejoicing. But Philip was found at Azotus: and passing through he preached in all the cities, till he came to Caesarea."

This Ethiopian represented a large class who need to be taught by such missionaries as Philip—men who will hear the voice of God and go where He sends them. There are many who are reading the Scriptures who cannot understand their true import. All over the world men and women are looking wistfully to heaven. Prayers and tears and inquiries go up from souls longing for light, for grace, for the Holy Spirit. Many are on the verge of the kingdom, waiting only to be gathered in.

An angel guided Philip to the one who was seeking for light and who was ready to receive the gospel, and today angels will guide the footsteps of those workers who will allow the Holy Spirit to sanctify their tongues and refine and ennoble their hearts. The angel sent to Philip could himself have done the work for the Ethiopian, but this is not God's way of working. It is His plan that men are to work for their fellow men.

In the trust given to the first disciples, believers in every age have shared. Everyone who has received the gospel has been given sacred truth to impart to the world. God's faithful people have always been aggressive missionaries, consecrating their resources to the honor of His name and wisely using their talents in His service.

The unselfish labor of Christians in the past should be to us an object lesson and an inspiration. The members of God's church are to be zealous of good works, separating from worldly ambition and walking in the footsteps of Him who went about doing good. With hearts filled with sympathy and compassion, they are to minister to those in need of help, bringing to sinners a knowledge of the Saviour's love. Such work calls for laborious effort, but it brings a rich reward. Those who engage in it with sincerity of purpose will see souls won to the Saviour, for the influence that attends the practical carrying out of the divine commission is irresistible.

Not upon the ordained minister only rests the responsibility of going forth to fulfill this commission. Everyone who has received Christ is called to work for the salvation of his fellow men. "The Spirit and the bride say, Come. And let him that heareth say, Come." Revelation 22:17. The charge to give this invitation includes the entire church. Everyone who has heard the invitation is to echo the message from hill and valley, saying, "Come."

It is a fatal mistake to suppose that the work of soul-saving depends alone upon the ministry. The humble, consecrated believer upon whom the Master of the vineyard places a burden for souls is to be given encouragement by the men upon whom the Lord has laid larger responsibilities. Those who stand as leaders in the church of God are to realize that the Saviour's commission is given to all who believe in His name. God will send forth into His vineyard many who have not been dedicated to the ministry by the laying on of hands.

Hundreds, yea, thousands, who have heard the message of salvation are still idlers in the market place, when they might be engaged in some line of active service. To these Christ is saying, "Why stand ye here all the day idle?" and He adds, "Go ye also into the vineyard." Matthew 20:6, 7. Why is it that many more do not respond to the call? Is it because they think themselves excused in that they do not stand in the pulpit? Let them understand that there is a large work to be done outside the pulpit by thousands of consecrated lay members.

Long has God waited for the spirit of service to take possession of the whole church so that everyone shall be working for Him according to his ability. When the members of the church of God do their appointed work in the needy fields at home and abroad, in fulfillment of the gospel commission, the whole world will soon be warned and the Lord Jesus will return to this earth with power and great glory. "This gospel of the kingdom shall be preached in all the world for a witness unto all nations; and then shall the end come." Matthew 24:14.

12

From Persecutor to Disciple

Prominent among the Jewish leaders who became thoroughly aroused by the success attending the proclamation of the gospel, was Saul of Tarsus. A Roman citizen by birth, Saul was nevertheless a Jew by descent and had been educated in Jerusalem by the most eminent of the rabbis. "Of the stock of Israel, of the tribe of Benjamin," Saul was "a Hebrew of the Hebrews; as touching the law, a Pharisee; concerning zeal, persecuting the church; touching the righteousness which is in the law, blameless." Philippians 3:5, 6. He was regarded by the rabbis as a young man of great promise, and

This chapter is based on Acts 9:1-18.

high hopes were cherished concerning him as an able and zealous defender of the ancient faith. His elevation to membership in the Sanhedrin council placed him in a position of power.

Saul had taken a prominent part in the trial and conviction of Stephen, and the striking evidences of God's presence with the martyr had led Saul to doubt the righteousness of the cause he had espoused against the followers of Jesus. His mind was deeply stirred. In his perplexity he appealed to those in whose wisdom and judgment he had full confidence. The arguments of the priests and rulers finally convinced him that Stephen was a blasphemer, that the Christ whom the martyred disciple had preached was an impostor, and that those ministering in holy office must be right.

Not without severe trial did Saul come to this conclusion. But in the end his education and prejudices, his respect for his former teachers, and his pride of popularity braced him to rebel against the voice of conscience and the grace of God. And having fully decided that the priests and scribes were right, Saul became very bitter in his opposition to the doctrines taught by the disciples of Jesus. His activity in causing holy men and women to be dragged before tribunals, where some were condemned to imprisonment and some even to death, solely because of their faith in Jesus, brought sadness and gloom to the newly organized church, and caused many to seek safety in flight.

Those who were driven from Jerusalem by this persecution "went everywhere preaching the word." Acts 8:4. Among the cities to which they went was Damascus, where the new faith gained many converts.

The priests and rulers had hoped that by vigilant effort and stern persecution the heresy might be suppressed. Now they felt that they must carry forward in other places the decided measures taken in Jerusalem against the new teaching. For the special work that they desired to have done at Damascus, Saul offered his services. "Breathing out threatenings and slaughter against the disciples of the Lord," he "went unto the high priest, and desired of him letters to Damascus to the synagogues, that if he found any of this way, whether they were men or women, he might bring them bound unto Jerusalem." Thus "with authority and commission from the chief priests" (Acts 26:12), Saul of Tarsus, in the strength and vigor of manhood, and fired with mistaken zeal, set out on that memorable journey, the strange occurrences of which were to change the whole current of his life.

On the last day of the journey, "at midday," as the weary travelers neared Damascus, they came within full view of broad stretches of fertile lands, beautiful gardens, and fruitful orchards, watered by cool streams from the sur-rounding mountains. After the long journey over desolate wastes such scenes were refreshing indeed. While Saul, with his companions, gazed with admiration on the fruitful plain and the fair city below, "suddenly," as he afterward declared, there shone "round about me and them which journeyed with me" "a light from heaven, above the brightness of the sun" (Acts 26:13), too glorious for mortal eyes to bear. Blinded and bewildered, Saul fell prostrate to the ground.

While the light continued to shine round about them, Saul heard "a voice speaking . . . in the Hebrew tongue" (Acts 26:14), "saying unto him, Saul, Saul, why persecutest thou Me? And he said, Who art Thou, Lord? And the Lord said, I am Jesus whom thou persecutest: it is hard for thee to kick against the pricks."

Filled with fear, and almost blinded by the intensity of the light, the companions of Saul heard a voice, but saw no man. But Saul understood the words that were spoken, and to him was clearly revealed the One who spoke—even the Son of God. In the glorious Being who stood before him he saw the Crucified One. Upon the soul of the stricken Jew the image of the Saviour's countenance was imprinted forever. The words spoken struck home to his heart with appalling force. Into the darkened chambers of his mind there poured a flood of light, revealing the ignorance and error of his former life and his present need of the enlightenment of the Holy Spirit.

Saul now saw that in persecuting the followers of Jesus he had in reality been doing the work of Satan. He saw that his convictions of right and of his own duty had been based largely on his implicit confidence in the priests and rulers. He had believed them when they told him that the story of the resurrection was an artful fabrication of the disciples. Now that Jesus Himself stood revealed, Saul was convinced of the truthfulness of the claims made by the disciples.

In that hour of heavenly illumination Saul's mind acted with remarkable rapidity. The prophetic records of Holy Writ were opened to his understanding. He saw that the rejection of Jesus by the Jews, His crucifixion, resurrection, and ascension, had been foretold by the prophets and proved Him to be the promised Messiah. Stephen's sermon at the time of his martyrdom was brought forcibly to Saul's mind, and he realized that the martyr had indeed beheld "the glory of God" when he said, "Behold, I see the heavens opened, and the Son of man standing on the right hand of God." Acts 7:55, 56. The priests had pronounced these words blasphemy, but Saul now knew them to be truth.

What a revelation was all this to the persecutor! Now Saul knew for a certainty that the promised Messiah had come to this earth as Jesus of Nazareth and that He had been rejected and crucified by those whom He came to save. He knew also that the Saviour had risen in triumph from the tomb and had ascended into the heavens. In that moment of divine revelation Saul remembered with terror that Stephen, who had borne witness of a crucified and risen Saviour, had been sacrificed by his consent, and that later, through his instrumentality, many other worthy followers of Jesus had met their death by cruel persecution.

The Saviour had spoken to Saul through Stephen, whose clear reasoning could not be controverted. The learned Jew had seen the face of the martyr reflecting the light of Christ's glory—appearing as if "it had been the face of an angel." Acts 6:15. He had witnessed Stephen's forbearance toward his enemies and his forgiveness of them. He had also witnessed the fortitude and cheerful resignation of many whom he had caused to be tormented and afflicted. He had seen some yield up even their lives with rejoicing for the sake of their faith.

All these things had appealed loudly to Saul and at times had thrust upon his mind an almost overwhelming conviction that Jesus was the promised Messiah. At such times he had struggled for entire nights against this conviction, and always he had ended the matter by avowing 117 his belief that Jesus was not the Messiah and that His followers were deluded fanatics.

Now Christ had spoken to Saul with His own voice, saying, "Saul, Saul, why persecutest thou Me?" And the question, "Who art Thou, Lord?" was answered by the same voice, "I am Jesus whom thou persecutest." Christ here identifies Himself with His people. In persecuting the followers of Jesus, Saul had struck directly against the Lord of heaven. In falsely accusing and testifying against them, he had falsely accused and testified against the Saviour of the world.

No doubt entered the mind of Saul that the One who spoke to him was Jesus of Nazareth, the long-looked-for Messiah, the Consolation and Redeemer of Israel. "Trembling and astonished," he inquired, "Lord, what wilt Thou have me to do? And the Lord said unto him, Arise, and go into the city, and it shall be told thee what thou must do."

When the glory was withdrawn, and Saul arose from the ground, he found himself totally deprived of sight. The brightness of Christ's glory had been too intense for his mortal eyes; and when it was removed, the blackness of night settled upon his vision. He believed that this blindness was a punishment from God for his cruel persecution of the followers of Jesus. In terrible darkness he groped about, and his companions, in fear and amazement, "led him by the hand, and brought him into Damascus."

On the morning of that eventful day, Saul had neared Damascus with feelings of self-satisfaction because of the confidence that had been placed in him by the chief priest. To him had been entrusted grave responsibilities. He was commissioned to further the interests of the Jewish religion by checking, if possible, the spread of the new faith in Damascus. He had determined that his mission should be crowned with success and had looked forward with eager anticipation to the experiences that he expected were before him. 118

But how unlike his anticipations was his entrance into the city? Stricken with blindness, helpless, tortured by remorse, knowing not what further judgment might be in store for him, he sought out the home of the disciple Judas, where, in solitude, he had ample opportunity for reflection and prayer.

For three days Saul was "without sight, and neither did eat nor drink." These days of soul agony were to him as years. Again and again he recalled, with anguish of spirit, the part he had taken in the martyrdom of Stephen. With horror he thought of his guilt in allowing himself to be controlled by the malice and prejudice of the priests and rulers, even when the face of Stephen had been lighted up with the radiance of heaven. In sadness and brokenness of spirit he recounted the many times he had closed his eyes and ears against the most striking evidences and had relentlessly urged on the persecution of the believers in Jesus of Nazareth.

These days of close self-examination and of heart humiliation were spent in lonely seclusion. The believers, having been given warning of the purpose of Saul in coming to Damascus, feared that he might be acting a part, in order the more readily to deceive them; and they held themselves aloof, refusing him their sympathy. He 119 had no desire to appeal to the unconverted Jews, with whom he had planned to unite in persecuting the believers; for he knew that they would not even listen to his story. Thus he seemed to be shut away from all human sympathy. His only hope of help was in a merciful God, and to Him he appealed in brokenness of heart.

During the long hours when Saul was shut in with God alone, he recalled many of the passages of Scripture referring to the first advent of Christ. Carefully he traced down the prophecies, with a memory sharpened by the conviction that had taken possession of his mind. As he reflected on the meaning of these prophecies he was astonished at his former blindness of understanding and at the blindness of the Jews in general, which had led to the rejection of Jesus as the promised Messiah. To his enlightened vision all now seemed plain. He knew that his former prejudice and unbelief had clouded his spiritual perception and had prevented him from discerning in Jesus of Nazareth the Messiah of prophecy.

As Saul yielded himself fully to the convicting power of the Holy Spirit, he saw the mistakes of his life and recognized the far-reaching claims of the law of God. He who had been a proud Pharisee, confident that he was justified by his good works, now bowed before God with the humility and simplicity of a little child, confessing his own unworthiness and pleading the merits of a crucified and risen Saviour. Saul longed to come into full harmony and communion with the Father and the Son; and in the intensity of his desire for pardon and acceptance he offered up fervent supplications to the throne of grace.

The prayers of the penitent Pharisee were not in vain. The inmost thoughts and emotions of his heart were transformed by divine grace; and his nobler faculties were brought into harmony with the eternal purposes of God. Christ and His righteousness became to Saul more than the whole world.

The conversion of Saul is a striking evidence of the miraculous power of the Holy Spirit to convict men of sin. He had verily believed that Jesus of Nazareth had disregarded the law of God and had taught His disciples that it was of no effect. But after his conversion, Saul recognized Jesus as the one who had come into the world for the express purpose of vindicating His Father's law. He was convinced that Jesus was the originator of the entire Jewish system of sacrifices. He saw that at the crucifixion type had met antitype, that Jesus had fulfilled the Old Testament prophecies concerning the Redeemer of Israel.

In the record of the conversion of Saul important principles are given us, which we should ever bear in mind. Saul was brought directly into the presence of Christ. He was one whom Christ intended for a most important work, one who was to be a "chosen vessel" unto Him; yet the Lord did not at once tell him of the work that had been assigned him. He arrested him in his course and convicted him of sin; but when Saul asked, "What wilt Thou have me to do?" the Saviour placed the inquiring Jew in connection with His church, there to obtain a knowledge of God's will concerning him.

The marvelous light that illumined the darkness of Saul was the work of the Lord; but there was also a work that was to be done for him by the disciples. Christ had performed the work of revelation and conviction; and now the penitent was in a condition to learn from those whom God had ordained to teach His truth.

While Saul in solitude at the house of Judas continued in prayer and supplication, the Lord appeared in vision to "a certain disciple at Damascus, named Ananias," telling him that Saul of Tarsus was praying and in need of help. "Arise, and go into the street which is called Straight," the heavenly messenger said, "and inquire in the house of Judas for one called Saul, of Tarsus: for, behold, he prayeth, and hath seen in a vision a man named Ananias coming in, and putting his hand on him, that he might receive his sight."

Ananias could scarcely credit the words of the angel; for the reports of Saul's bitter persecution of the saints at Jerusalem had spread far and wide. He presumed to expostulate: "Lord, I have heard by many of this man, how much evil he hath done to Thy saints at Jerusalem: and here he hath authority from the chief priests to bind all that call on Thy name." But the command was imperative: "Go thy way: for he is a chosen vessel unto Me, to bear My name before the Gentiles, and kings, and the children of Israel."

Obedient to the direction of the angel, Ananias sought out the man who had but recently breathed out threatenings against all who believed on the name of Jesus; and putting his hands on the head of the penitent sufferer, he said, "Brother Saul, the Lord, even Jesus, that appeared unto thee in the way as thou camest, hath sent me, that thou mightest receive thy sight, and be filled with the Holy Ghost.

"And immediately there fell from his eyes as it had been scales: and he received sight forthwith, and arose, and was baptized."

Thus Jesus gave sanction to the authority of His organized church and placed Saul in connection with His appointed agencies on earth. Christ had now a church as His representative on earth, and to it belonged the work of directing the repentant sinner in the way of life.

Many have an idea that they are responsible to Christ alone for their light and experience, independent of His recognized followers on earth. Jesus is the friend of sinners, and His heart is touched with their woe. He has all power, both in heaven and on earth; but He respects the means that He has ordained for the enlightenment and salvation of men; He directs sinners to the church, which He has made a channel of light to the world.

When, in the midst of his blind error and prejudice, Saul was given a revelation of the Christ whom he was persecuting, he was placed in direct communication with the church, which is the light of the world. In this case Ananias represents Christ, and also represents Christ's ministers upon the earth, who are appointed to act in His stead. In Christ's stead Ananias touches the eyes of Saul, that they may receive sight. In Christ's stead he places his hands upon him, and, as he prays in Christ's name, Saul receives the Holy Ghost. All is done in the name and by the authority of Christ. Christ is the fountain; the church is the channel of communication.

123

13

Days of Preparation

After his baptism, Paul broke his fast and remained "certain days with the disciples which were at Damascus. And straightway he preached Christ in the synagogues, that He is the Son of God." Boldly he declared Jesus of Nazareth to be the long-looked-for Messiah, who "died for our sins according to the Scriptures; . . . was buried, and . . . rose again the third day," after which He was seen by the Twelve and by others. "And last of all," Paul added, "He was seen of me also, as of one born out of due time." 1 Corinthians 15:3, 4, 8. His arguments from prophecy were so conclusive, and his efforts were so manifestly attended by the power of God, that the Jews were confounded and unable to answer him.

The news of Paul's conversion had come to the Jews as a great surprise. He who had journeyed to Damascus "with authority and commission from the chief priests" (Acts 26:12) to apprehend and persecute the believers was now 124 preaching the gospel of a crucified and risen Saviour, strengthening the hands of those who were already its disciples, and continually bringing in new converts to the faith he had once so bitterly opposed.

Paul had formerly been known as a zealous defender of the Jewish religion and an untiring persecutor of the followers of Jesus. Courageous, independent, persevering, his talents and training would have enabled him to serve in almost any capacity. He could reason with extraordinary clearness, and by his withering sarcasm could place an opponent in no enviable light. And now the Jews saw this young man of unusual promise united with those whom he formerly persecuted, and fearlessly preaching in the name of Jesus.

A general slain in battle is lost to his army, but his death gives no additional strength to the enemy. But when a man of prominence joins the opposing force, not only are his services lost, but those to whom he joins himself gain a decided advantage. Saul of Tarsus, on his way to Damascus, might easily have been struck dead by the Lord, and much strength would have been withdrawn from the persecuting power. But God in His providence not only spared Saul's life, but converted him, thus transferring a champion from the side of the enemy to the side of Christ. An eloquent speaker and a severe critic, Paul, with his stern purpose and undaunted courage, possessed the very qualifications needed in the early church.

As Paul preached Christ in Damascus, all

who heard him were amazed and said, "Is not 125 this he that destroyed them which called on this name in Jerusalem, and came hither for that intent, that he might bring them bound unto the chief priests?" Paul declared that his change of faith had not been prompted by impulse or fanaticism, but had been brought about by overwhelming evidence. In his presentation of the gospel he sought to make plain the prophecies relating to the first advent of Christ. He showed conclusively that these prophecies had been literally fulfilled in Jesus of Nazareth. The foundation of his faith was the sure word of prophecy.

As Paul continued to appeal to his astonished hearers to "repent and turn to God, and do works meet for repentance" (Acts 26:20), he "increased the more in strength, and confounded the Jews which dwelt at Damascus, proving that this is very Christ." But many hardened their hearts, refusing to respond to his message, and soon their astonishment at his conversion was changed into intense hatred like that which they had shown toward Jesus.

The opposition grew so fierce that Paul was not allowed to continue his labors at Damascus. A messenger from heaven bade him leave for a time, and he "went into Arabia" (Galatians 1:17), where he found a safe retreat.

Here, in the solitude of the desert, Paul had ample opportunity for quiet study and meditation. He calmly reviewed his past experience and made sure work of repentance. He sought God with all his heart, resting not until he knew for a certainty that his repentance was accepted and his sin pardoned. He longed for the assurance that Jesus would be with him in his coming ministry. He emptied his soul of the prejudices 126 and traditions that had hitherto shaped his life, and received instruction from the Source of truth. Jesus communed with him and established him in the faith, bestowing upon him a rich measure of wisdom and grace.

When the mind of man is brought into communion with the mind of God, the finite with the Infinite, the effect on body and mind and soul is beyond estimate. In such communion is found the highest education. It is God's own method of development. "Acquaint now thyself with Him" (Job 22:21), is His message to mankind.

The solemn charge that had been given Paul on the occasion of his interview with Ananias, rested with increasing weight upon his heart. When, in response to the word, "Brother Saul, receive thy sight," Paul had for the first time looked upon the face of this devout man, Ananias under the inspiration of the Holy Spirit said to him: "The God of our fathers hath chosen thee, that thou shouldest know His will, and see that Just One, and shouldest hear the voice of His mouth. For thou shalt be His witness unto

This chapter is based on Acts 9:19-30.

all men of what thou hast seen and heard. And now why tarriest thou? arise, and be baptized, and wash away thy sins, calling on the name of the Lord." Acts 22:13-16.

These words were in harmony with the words of Jesus Himself, who, when He arrested Saul on the journey to Damascus, declared: "I have appeared unto thee for this purpose, to make thee a minister and a witness both of these things which thou hast seen, and of those things in the which I will appear unto thee; delivering

127 thee from the people, and from the Gentiles, unto whom now I send thee, to open their eyes, and to turn them from darkness to light, and from the power of Satan unto God, that they may receive forgiveness of sins, and inheritance among them which are sanctified by faith that is in Me." Acts 26:16-18.

As he pondered these things in his heart, Paul understood more and more clearly the meaning of his call "to be an apostle of Jesus Christ through the will of God." 1 Corinthians 1:1. His call had come, "not of men, neither by man, but by Jesus Christ, and God the Father." Galatians 1:1. The greatness of the work before him led him to give much study to the Holy Scriptures, in order that he might preach the gospel "not with wisdom of words, lest the cross of Christ should be made of none effect," "but in demonstration of the Spirit and of power," that the faith of all who heard "should not stand in the wisdom of men, but in the power of God." 1 Corinthians 1:17; 2:4, 5.

As Paul searched the Scriptures, he learned that throughout the ages "not many wise men after the flesh, not many mighty, not many noble, are called: but God hath chosen the foolish things of the world to confound the wise; and God hath chosen the weak things of the world to confound the things which are mighty; and base things of the world, and things which are despised, hath God chosen, yea, and things which are not, to bring to nought things that are: that no flesh should glory in His presence." 1 Corinthians 1:26-29. And so, viewing the wisdom of the world in the light of the cross, Paul

128 "determined not to know anything, . . . save Jesus Christ, and Him crucified." 1 Corinthians 2:2.

Throughout his later ministry, Paul never lost sight of the Source of his wisdom and strength. Hear him, years afterward, still declaring, "For to me to live is Christ." Philippians 1:21. And again: "I count all things but loss for the excellency of the knowledge of Christ Jesus my Lord: for whom I have suffered the loss of all things, . . . that I may win Christ, and be found in Him, not having mine own righteousness, which is of the law, but that which is through the faith of Christ, the righteousness which is of God by faith: that I may know Him, and the power of His resurrection, and the fellowship of

His sufferings." Philippians 3:8-10.

From Arabia Paul "returned again unto Damascus" (Galatians 1:17), and "preached boldly . . . in the name of Jesus." Unable to withstand the wisdom of his arguments, "the Jews took counsel to kill him." The gates of the city were diligently guarded day and night to cut off his escape. This crisis led the disciples to seek God earnestly, and finally they "took him by night, and let him down through the wall, lowering him in a basket." Acts 9:25, R.V.

After his escape from Damascus, Paul went to Jerusalem, about three years having passed since his conversion. His chief object in making this visit, as he himself declared afterward, was "to see Peter." Galatians 1:18. Upon arriving in the city where he had once been well known as "Saul the persecutor," "he assayed to join himself to the disciples: but they were all afraid of him, and believed not that he was a disciple." It 129 was difficult for them to believe that so bigoted a Pharisee, and one who had done so much to destroy the church, could become a sincere follower of Jesus. "But Barnabas took him, and brought him to the apostles, and declared unto them how he had seen the Lord in the way, and that He had spoken to him, and how he had preached boldly at Damascus in the name of Jesus."

Upon hearing this, the disciples received him as one of their number. Soon they had abundant evidence as to the genuineness of his Christian experience. The future apostle to the Gentiles was now in the city where many of his former associates lived, and to these Jewish leaders he longed to make plain the prophecies concerning the Messiah, which had been fulfilled by the advent of the Saviour. Paul felt sure that these teachers in Israel, with whom he had once been so well acquainted, were as sincere and honest as he had been. But he had miscalculated the spirit of his Jewish brethren, and in the hope of their speedy conversion he was doomed to bitter disappointment. Although "he spake boldly in the name of the Lord Jesus, and disputed against the Grecians," those who stood at the head of the Jewish church refused to believe, but "went about to slay him." Sorrow filled his heart. He would willingly have yielded up his life if by that means he might bring some to a knowledge of the truth. With shame he thought of the active part he had taken in the martyrdom of Stephen, and now in his anxiety to wipe out the stain resting upon one so falsely accused, he sought to vindicate the truth for which Stephen had given his life.

Burdened in behalf of those who refused to 130 believe, Paul was praying in the temple, as he himself afterward testified, when he fell into a trance; whereupon a heavenly messenger appeared before him and said, "Make haste, and get thee quickly out of Jerusalem: for they will not receive thy testimony concerning Me." Acts 22:18.

Paul was inclined to remain at Jerusalem, where he could face the opposition. To him it seemed an act of cowardice to flee, if by remaining he might be able to convince some of the obstinate Jews of the truth of the gospel message, even if to remain should cost him his life. And so he answered, "Lord, they know that I imprisoned and beat in every synagogue them that believed on Thee: and when the blood of Thy martyr Stephen was shed, I also was standing by, and consenting unto his death, and kept the raiment of them that slew him." But it was not in harmony with the purpose of God that His servant should needlessly expose his life; and the heavenly messenger replied, "Depart: for I will send thee far hence unto the Gentiles." Acts 22:19-21.

Upon learning of this vision, the brethren hastened Paul's secret escape from Jerusalem, for fear of his assassination. "They brought him down to Caesarea, and sent him forth to Tarsus." The departure of Paul suspended for a time the violent opposition of the Jews, and the church had a period of rest, in which many were added to the number of believers.

131

14

A Seeker for Truth

In the course of his ministry the apostle Peter visited the believers at Lydda. Here he healed Aeneas, who for eight years had been confined to his bed with palsy. "Aeneas, Jesus Christ maketh thee whole," the apostle said; "arise, and make thy bed." "He arose immediately. And all that dwelt at Lydda and Saron saw him, and turned to the Lord."

At Joppa, which was near Lydda, there lived a woman named Dorcas, whose good deeds had made her greatly beloved. She was a worthy disciple of Jesus, and her life was filled with acts of kindness. She knew who needed comfortable clothing and who needed sympathy, and she freely ministered to the poor and the sorrowful. Her skillful fingers were more active than her tongue.

"And it came to pass in those days, that she was sick, and died." The church in Joppa realized their loss, and hearing that Peter was at
132   Lydda, the believers sent messengers to him, "desiring him that he would not delay to come to them. Then Peter arose and went with them. When he was come, they brought him into the upper chamber: and all the widows stood by him weeping, and showing the coats and garments which Dorcas made, while she was with them." In view of the life of service that Dorcas had lived, it is little wonder that they mourned,

This chapter is based on Acts 9:32 to 11:18.

that warm teardrops fell upon the inanimate clay.

The apostle's heart was touched with sympathy as he beheld their sorrow. Then, directing that the weeping friends be sent from the room, he kneeled down and prayed fervently to God to restore Dorcas to life and health. Turning to the body, he said, "Tabitha, arise. And she opened her eyes: and when she saw Peter, she sat up." Dorcas had been of great service to the church, and God saw fit to bring her back from the land of the enemy, that her skill and energy might still be a blessing to others, and also that by this manifestation of His power the cause of Christ might be strengthened.

It was while Peter was still at Joppa that he was called by God to take the gospel to Cornelius, in Caesarea.

Cornelius was a Roman centurion. He was a man of wealth and noble birth, and his position was one of trust and honor. A heathen by birth, training, and education, through contact with the Jews he had gained a knowledge of God, and he worshiped Him with a true heart, showing the sincerity of his faith by compassion to the poor. He was known far and near for his beneficence, and his righteous life made him of good repute among both Jews and Gentiles. His influence 133 was a blessing to all with whom he came in contact. The inspired record describes him as "a devout man, and one that feared God with all his house, which gave much alms to the people, and prayed to God alway."

Believing in God as the Creator of heaven and earth, Cornelius revered Him, acknowledged His authority, and sought His counsel in all the affairs of life. He was faithful to Jehovah in his home life and in his official duties. He had erected the altar of God in his home, for he dared not attempt to carry out his plans or to bear his responsibilities without the help of God.

Though Cornelius believed the prophecies and was looking for the Messiah to come, he had not a knowledge of the gospel as revealed in the life and death of Christ. He was not a member of the Jewish church and would have been looked upon by the rabbis as a heathen and unclean. But the same Holy Watcher who said of Abraham, "I know him," knew Cornelius also, and sent a message direct from heaven to him.

The angel appeared to Cornelius while he was at prayer. As the centurion heard himself addressed by name, he was afraid, yet he knew that the messenger had come from God, and he said, "What is it, Lord?" The angel answered, "Thy prayers and thine alms are come up for a memorial before God. And now send men to Joppa, and call for one Simon, whose surname is Peter: he lodgeth with one Simon a tanner, whose house is by the seaside."

The explicitness of these directions, in which was named even the occupation of the man with whom Peter was staying, shows that Heaven is acquainted with the history and business of men in every station of life. God is familiar with the experience and work of the humble laborer, as well as with that of the king upon his throne.

"Send men to Joppa, and call for one Simon." Thus God gave evidence of His regard for the gospel ministry and for His organized church. The angel was not commissioned to tell Cornelius the story of the cross. A man subject, even as the centurion himself, to human frailties and temptations, was to be the one to tell him of the crucified and risen Saviour.

As His representatives among men, God does not choose angels who have never fallen, but human beings, men of like passions with those they seek to save. Christ took humanity that He might reach humanity. A divine-human Saviour was needed to bring salvation to the world. And to men and women has been committed the sacred trust of making known "the unsearchable riches of Christ." Ephesians 3:8.

In His wisdom the Lord brings those who are seeking for truth into touch with fellow beings who know the truth. It is the plan of Heaven that those who have received light shall impart it to those in darkness. Humanity, drawing its efficiency from the great Source of wisdom, is made the instrumentality, the working agency, through which the gospel exercises its transforming power on mind and heart.

Cornelius was gladly obedient to the vision. When the angel had gone, the centurion "called two of his household servants, and a devout soldier of them that waited on him continually; and when he had declared all these things unto them, he sent them to Joppa."

The angel, after his interview with Cornelius, went to Peter, in Joppa. At the time, Peter was praying upon the housetop of his lodging, and we read that he "became very hungry, and would have eaten: but while they made ready, he fell into a trance." It was not for physical food alone that Peter hungered. As from the housetop he viewed the city of Joppa and the surrounding country he hungered for the salvation of his countrymen. He had an intense desire to point out to them from the Scriptures the prophecies relating to the sufferings and death of Christ.

In the vision Peter "saw heaven opened, and a certain vessel descending unto them, as it had been a great sheet knit at the four corners, and let down to the earth: wherein were all manner of four-footed beasts of the earth, and wild beasts, and creeping things, and fowls of the air. And there came a voice to him, Rise, Peter; kill, and eat. But Peter said, Not so, Lord; for I have never eaten anything that is common or unclean. And the voice spake unto him again the second time, What God hath cleansed, that call not thou common. This was done thrice: and the vessel was received up again into heaven."

This vision conveyed to Peter both reproof and instruction. It revealed to him the purpose of God—that by the death of Christ the Gentiles should be made fellow heirs with the Jews to the blessings of salvation. As yet none of the disciples had preached the gospel to the Gentiles. In their minds the middle wall of partition, broken down by the death of Christ, still existed, and their labors had been confined to the Jews, for they had looked upon the Gentiles as excluded from the blessings of the gospel. Now the Lord was seeking to teach Peter the worldwide extent of the divine plan.

Many of the Gentiles had been interested listeners to the preaching of Peter and the other apostles, and many of the Greek Jews had become believers in Christ, but the conversion of Cornelius was to be the first of importance among the Gentiles.

The time had come for an entirely new phase of work to be entered upon by the church of Christ. The door that many of the Jewish converts had closed against the Gentiles was now to be thrown open. And the Gentiles who accepted the gospel were to be regarded as on an equality with the Jewish disciples, without the necessity of observing the rite of circumcision.

How carefully the Lord worked to overcome the prejudice against the Gentiles that had been so firmly fixed in Peter's mind by his Jewish training! By the vision of the sheet and its contents He sought to divest the apostle's mind of this prejudice and to teach the important truth that in heaven there is no respect of persons; that Jew and Gentile are alike precious in God's sight; that through Christ the heathen may be made partakers of the blessings and privileges of the gospel.

While Peter was meditating on the meaning of the vision, the men sent from Cornelius arrived in Joppa and stood before the gate of his lodginghouse. Then the Spirit said to him, "Behold, three men seek thee. Arise therefore, and get thee down, and go with them, doubting nothing: for I have sent them."

To Peter this was a trying command, and it was with reluctance at every step that he undertook the duty laid upon him; but he dared not disobey. He "went down to the men which were sent unto him from Cornelius; and said, Behold, I am he whom ye seek: what is the cause wherefore ye are come?" They told him of their singular errand, saying, "Cornelius the centurion, a just man, and one that feareth God, and of good report among all the nation of the Jews, was warned from God by a holy angel to send for thee into his house, and to hear words of thee."

In obedience to the directions just received

from God, the apostle promised to go with them. On the following morning he set out for Caesarea, accompanied by six of his brethren. These were to be witnesses of all that he should say or do while visiting the Gentiles, for Peter knew that he would be called to account for so direct a violation of the Jewish teachings.

As Peter entered the house of the Gentile, Cornelius did not salute him as an ordinary visitor, but as one honored of Heaven and sent to him by God. It is an Eastern custom to bow before a prince or other high dignitary and for children to bow before their parents; but Cornelius, overwhelmed with reverence for the one sent by God to teach him, fell at the apostle's feet and worshiped him. Peter was horror-stricken, and he lifted the centurion up, saying, "Stand up; I myself also am a man."

138   While the messengers of Cornelius had been gone upon their errand, the centurion "had called together his kinsmen and near friends," that they as well as he might hear the preaching of the gospel. When Peter arrived, he found a large company eagerly waiting to listen to his words.

To those assembled, Peter spoke first of the custom of the Jews, saying that it was looked upon as unlawful for Jews to mingle socially with the Gentiles, that to do this involved ceremonial defilement. "Ye know," he said, "how that it is an unlawful thing for a man that is a Jew to keep company, or come unto one of another nation; but God hath showed me that I should not call any man common or unclean. Therefore came I unto you without gainsaying, as soon as I was sent for: I ask therefore for what intent ye have sent for me?"

Cornelius then related his experience and the words of the angel, saying in conclusion, "Immediately therefore I sent to thee; and thou hast well done that thou art come. Now therefore are we all here present before God, to hear all things that are commanded thee of God."

Peter said, "Of a truth I perceive that God is no respecter of persons: but in every nation he that feareth Him, and worketh righteousness, is accepted with Him."

Then to that company of attentive hearers the apostle preached Christ—His life, His miracles, His betrayal and crucifixion, His resurrection and ascension, and His work in heaven as man's representative and advocate. As Peter pointed those present to Jesus as the sinner's only hope,

139   he himself understood more fully the meaning of the vision he had seen, and his heart glowed with the spirit of the truth that he was presenting.

Suddenly the discourse was interrupted by the descent of the Holy Spirit. "While Peter yet spake these words, the Holy Ghost fell on all them which heard the word. And they of the circumcision which believed were astonished, as many as came with Peter, because that on the Gentiles also was poured out the gift of the Holy Ghost. For they heard them speak with tongues, and magnify God.

"Then answered Peter, Can any man forbid water, that these should not be baptized, which have received the Holy Ghost as well as we? And he commanded them to be baptized in the name of the Lord."

Thus was the gospel brought to those who had been strangers and foreigners, making them fellow citizens with the saints, and members of the household of God. The conversion of Cornelius and his household was but the first fruits of a harvest to be gathered in. From this household a wide-spread work of grace was carried on in that heathen city.

Today God is seeking for souls among the high as well as the lowly. There are many like Cornelius, men whom the Lord desires to connect with His work in the world. Their sympathies are with the Lord's people, but the ties that bind them to the world hold them firmly. It requires moral courage for them to take their position for Christ. Special efforts should be made for these souls, who are in so great danger, because of their responsibilities and associations.

140

God calls for earnest, humble workers, who will carry the gospel to the higher class. There are miracles to be wrought in genuine conversions,—miracles that are not now discerned. The greatest men of this earth are not beyond the power of a wonder-working God. If those who are workers together with Him will be men of opportunity, doing their duty bravely and faithfully, God will convert men who occupy responsible positions, men of intellect and influence. Through the power of the Holy Spirit many will accept the divine principles. Converted to the truth, they will become agencies in the hand of God to communicate the light. They will have a special burden for other souls of this neglected class. Time and money will be consecrated to the work of the Lord, and new efficiency and power will be added to the church.

Because Cornelius was living in obedience to all the instruction he had received, God so ordered events that he was given more truth. A messenger from the courts of heaven was sent to the Roman officer and to Peter in order that Cornelius might be brought into touch with one who could lead him into greater light.

There are in our world many who are nearer the kingdom of God than we suppose. In this dark world of sin the Lord has many precious jewels, to whom He will guide His messengers. Everywhere there are those who will take their stand for Christ. Many will prize the wisdom of God above any earthly advantage, and will become faithful light bearers. Constrained by the love of Christ, they will constrain others to

141

come to Him.

When the brethren in Judea heard that Peter had gone to the house of a Gentile and preached to those assembled, they were surprised and offended. They feared that such a course, which looked to them presumptuous, would have the effect of counteracting his own teaching. When they next saw Peter they met him with severe censure, saying, "Thou wentest in to men uncircumcised, and didst eat with them."

Peter laid the whole matter before them. He related his experience in regard to the vision and pleaded that it admonished him to observe no longer the ceremonial distinction of circumcision and uncircumcision, nor to look upon the Gentiles as unclean. He told them of the command given him to go to the Gentiles, of the coming of the messengers, of his journey to Caesarea, and of the meeting with Cornelius. He recounted the substance of his interview with the centurion, in which the latter had told him of the vision by which he had been directed to send for Peter.

"As I began to speak," he said, in relating his experience, "the Holy Ghost fell on them, as on us at the beginning. Then remembered I the word of the Lord, how that He said, John indeed baptized with water; but ye shall be baptized with the Holy Ghost. Forasmuch then as God gave them the like gift as He did unto us, who believed on the Lord Jesus Christ; what was I, that I could withstand God?"

142   On hearing this account, the brethren were silenced. Convinced that Peter's course was in direct fulfillment of the plan of God, and that their prejudices and exclusiveness were utterly contrary to the spirit of the gospel, they glorified God, saying, "Then hath God also to the Gentiles granted repentance unto life."

Thus, without controversy, prejudice was broken down, the exclusiveness established by the custom of ages was abandoned, and the way was opened for the gospel to be proclaimed to the Gentiles.

143

15

Delivered From Prison

"Now about that time Herod the king stretched forth his hands to vex certain of the church." The government of Judea was then in the hands of Herod Agrippa, subject to Claudius, the Roman emperor. Herod also held the position of tetrarch of Galilee. He was professedly a proselyte to the Jewish faith, and apparently very zealous in carrying out the ceremonies of the Jewish law. Desirous of obtaining the favor of the Jews, hoping thus to make secure his offices and honors, he proceeded to carry out their desires by persecuting the church of Christ, spoiling the houses and goods of the believers, and imprisoning the leading members of the church. He cast James, the brother of John, into prison, and sent an executioner to kill him with the sword, as another Herod had caused the prophet John to be beheaded. Seeing that the Jews were well pleased with these efforts, he imprisoned Peter also.

It was during the Passover that these cruelties 144 were practiced. While the Jews were celebrating their deliverance from Egypt and pretending great zeal for the law of God, they were at the same time transgressing every principle of that law by persecuting and murdering the believers in Christ.

The death of James caused great grief and consternation among the believers. When Peter also was imprisoned, the entire church engaged in fasting and prayer.

Herod's act in putting James to death was applauded by the Jews, though some complained of the private manner in which it was accomplished, maintaining that a public execution would have more thoroughly intimidated the believers and those sympathizing with them. Herod therefore held Peter in custody, meaning still further to gratify the Jews by the public spectacle of his death. But it was suggested that it would not be safe to bring the veteran apostle out for execution before all the people then assembled in Jerusalem. It was feared that the sight of him being led out to die might excite the pity of the multitude.

The priests and elders also feared lest Peter might make one of those powerful appeals which had frequently aroused the people to study the life and character of Jesus—appeals which they, with all their arguments, had been unable to controvert. Peter's zeal in advocating the cause of Christ had led many to take their stand for the gospel, and the rulers feared that should he be given an opportunity to defend his faith in the presence of the multitude who had come to the city to worship, his release would 145 be demanded at the hands of the king.

While, upon various pretexts, the execution of Peter was being delayed until after the Passover, the members of the church had time for deep searching of heart and earnest prayer. They prayed without ceasing for Peter, for they felt that he could not be spared from the cause. They realized that they had reached a place where, without the special help of God, the church of Christ would be destroyed.

Meanwhile worshipers from every nation sought the temple which had been dedicated to the worship of God. Glittering with gold and precious stones, it was a vision of beauty and grandeur. But Jehovah was no longer to be found in that palace of loveliness. Israel as a nation had divorced herself from God. When

This chapter is based on Acts 12:1-23.

Christ, near the close of His earthly ministry, looked for the last time upon the interior of the temple, He said, "Behold, your house is left unto you desolate." Matthew 23:38. Hitherto He had called the temple His Father's house; but as the Son of God passed out from those walls, God's presence was withdrawn forever from the temple built to His glory.

The day of Peter's execution was at last appointed, but still the prayers of the believers ascended to heaven; and while all their energies and sympathies were called out in fervent appeals for help, angels of God were watching over the imprisoned apostle.

Remembering the former escape of the apostles from prison, Herod on this occasion had taken double precautions. To prevent all possi-146 bility of release, Peter had been put under the charge of sixteen soldiers, who, in different watches, guarded him day and night. In his cell he was placed between two soldiers and was bound by two chains, each chain being fastened to the wrist of one of the soldiers. He was unable to move without their knowledge. With the prison doors securely fastened, and a strong guard before them, all chance of rescue or escape through human means was cut off. But man's extremity is God's opportunity.

Peter was confined in a rock-hewn cell, the doors of which were strongly bolted and barred; and the soldiers on guard were made answerable for the safekeeping of the prisoner. But the bolts and bars and the Roman guard, which effectually cut off all possibility of human aid, were but to make more complete the triumph of God in the deliverance of Peter. Herod was lifting his hand against Omnipotence, and he was to be utterly defeated. By the putting forth of His might, God was about to save the precious life that the Jews were plotting to destroy.

It is the last night before the proposed execution. A mighty angel is sent from heaven to rescue Peter. The strong gates that shut in the saint of God open without the aid of human hands. The angel of the Most High passes through, and the gates close noiselessly behind him. He enters the cell, and there lies Peter, sleeping the peaceful sleep of perfect trust.

The light that surrounds the angel fills the cell, but does not rouse the apostle. Not until he feels the touch of the angel's hand and hears a voice saying, "Arise up quickly," does he awak-147 en sufficiently to see his cell illuminated by the light of heaven, and an angel of great glory standing before him. Mechanically he obeys the word spoken to him, and as in rising he lifts his hands he is dimly conscious that the chains have fallen from his wrists.

Again the voice of the heavenly messenger bids him, "Gird thyself, and bind on thy sandals," and again Peter mechanically obeys, keeping his wondering gaze riveted upon his visitor and believing himself to be dreaming or in a vision. Once more the angel commands, "Cast thy garment about thee, and follow me." He moves toward the door, followed by the usually talkative Peter, now dumb from amazement. They step over the guard and reach the heavily bolted door, which of its own accord swings open and closes again immediately, while the guards within and without are motionless at their post.

The second door, also guarded within and without, is reached. It opens as did the first, with no creaking of hinges or rattling of iron bolts. They pass through, and it closes again as noiselessly. In the same way they pass through the third gateway and find themselves in the open street. No word is spoken; there is no sound of footsteps. The angel glides on in front, encircled by a light of dazzling brightness, and Peter, bewildered, and still believing himself to be in a dream, follows his deliverer. Thus they pass on through one street, and then, the mission of the angel being accomplished, he suddenly disappears.

The heavenly light faded away, and Peter felt himself to be in profound darkness; but as his eyes became accustomed to the darkness, it gradually seemed to lessen, and he found him- 148 self alone in the silent street, with the cool night air blowing upon his brow. He now realized that he was free, in a familiar part of the city; he recognized the place as one that he had often frequented and had expected to pass on the morrow for the last time.

He tried to recall the events of the past few moments. He remembered falling asleep, bound between two soldiers, with his sandals and outer garments removed. He examined his person and found himself fully dressed and girded. His wrists, swollen from wearing the cruel irons, were free from the manacles. He realized that his freedom was no delusion, no dream or vision, but a blessed reality. On the morrow he was to have been led forth to die; but, lo, an angel had delivered him from prison and from death. "And when Peter was come to himself, he said, Now I know of a surety, that the Lord hath sent His angel, and hath delivered me out of the hand of Herod, and from all the expectation of the people of the Jews."

The apostle made his way at once to the house where his brethren were assembled and where they were at that moment engaged in earnest prayer for him. "As Peter knocked at the door of the gate, a damsel came to hearken, named Rhoda. And when she knew Peter's voice, she opened not the gate for gladness, but ran in, and told how Peter stood before the gate. And they said unto her, Thou art mad. But she constantly affirmed that it was even so. Then said they, It is his angel."

"But Peter continued knocking: and when
149 they had opened the door, and saw him, they
were astonished. But he, beckoning unto them
with the hand to hold their peace, declared unto
them how the Lord had brought him out of the
prison." And Peter "departed, and went into
another place." Joy and praise filled the hearts
of the believers, because God had heard and
answered their prayers and had delivered Peter
from the hands of Herod.

In the morning a large concourse of people
gathered to witness the execution of the apostle.
Herod sent officers to the prison for Peter, who
was to be brought with a great display of arms
and guards in order not only to ensure against
his escape, but to intimidate all sympathizers
and to show the power of the king.

When the keepers before the door found that
Peter had escaped, they were seized with terror.
It had been expressly stated that their lives
would be required for the life of their charge,
and because of this they had been especially
vigilant. When the officers came for Peter, the
soldiers were still at the door of the prison, the
bolts and bars were still fast, the chains were
still secured to the wrists of the two soldiers; but
the prisoner was gone.

When the report of Peter's escape was
brought to Herod, he was exasperated and
enraged. Charging the prison guard with
unfaithfulness, he ordered them to be put to
death. Herod knew that no human power had
rescued Peter, but he was determined not to
acknowledge that a divine power had frustrated
his design, and he set himself in bold defiance
against God.

Not long after Peter's deliverance from
150 prison, Herod went to Caesarea. While there he
made a great festival designed to excite the
admiration and gain the applause of the people.
This festival was attended by pleasure lovers
from all quarters, and there was much feasting
and wine drinking. With great pomp and ceremony Herod appeared before the people and
addressed them in an eloquent oration. Clad in a
robe sparkling with silver and gold, which
caught the rays of the sun in its glittering folds
and dazzled the eyes of the beholders, he was a
gorgeous figure. The majesty of his appearance
and the force of his well-chosen language
swayed the assembly with a mighty power.
Their senses already perverted by feasting and
wine drinking, they were dazzled by Herod's
decorations and charmed by his deportment and
oratory; and wild with enthusiasm they show-
ered adulation upon him, declaring that no mortal could present such an appearance or command such startling eloquence. They further
declared that while they had ever respected him
as a ruler, henceforth they should worship him
as a god.

Some of those whose voices were now heard

glorifying a vile sinner had but a few years
before raised the frenzied cry, Away with Jesus!
Crucify Him, crucify Him! The Jews had
refused to receive Christ, whose garments,
coarse and often travel-stained, covered a heart
of divine love. Their eyes could not discern,
under the humble exterior, the Lord of life and
glory, even though Christ's power was revealed
before them in works that no mere man could
do. But they were ready to worship as a god the
haughty king whose splendid garments of silver
and gold covered a corrupt, cruel heart.

Herod knew that he deserved none of the 151
praise and homage offered him, yet he accepted
the idolatry of the people as his due. His heart
bounded with triumph, and a glow of gratified
pride overspread his countenance as he heard
the shout ascend, "It is the voice of a god, and
not of a man."

But suddenly a terrible change came over
him. His face became pallid as death and distorted with agony. Great drops of sweat started
from his pores. He stood for a moment as if
transfixed with pain and terror; then turning his
blanched and livid face to his horror-stricken
friends, he cried in hollow, despairing tones, He
whom you have exalted as a god is stricken with
death.

Suffering the most excruciating anguish, he
was borne from the scene of revelry and display. A moment before he had been the proud
recipient of the praise and worship of that vast
throng; now he realized that he was in the hands
of a Ruler mightier than himself. Remorse
seized him; he remembered his relentless persecution of the followers of Christ; he remembered his cruel command to slay the innocent
James, and his design to put to death the apostle
Peter; he remembered how in his mortification
and disappointed rage he had wreaked an unreasoning vengeance upon the prison guards. He
felt that God was now dealing with him, the
relentless persecutor. He found no relief from
pain of body or anguish of mind, and he expected none.

Herod was acquainted with the law of God,
which says, "Thou shalt have no other gods
before Me" (Exodus 20:3); and he knew that in
accepting the worship of the people he had 152
filled up the measure of his iniquity and brought
upon himself the just wrath of Jehovah.

The same angel who had come from the royal
courts to rescue Peter, had been the messenger
of wrath and judgment to Herod. The angel
smote Peter to arouse him from slumber; it was
with a different stroke that he smote the wicked
king, laying low his pride and bringing upon
him the punishment of the Almighty. Herod
died in great agony of mind and body, under the
retributive judgment of God.

This demonstration of divine justice had a
powerful influence upon the people. The tidings

that the apostle of Christ had been miraculously delivered from prison and death, while his persecutor had been stricken down by the curse of God, were borne to all lands and became the means of leading many to a belief in Christ.

The experience of Philip, directed by an angel from heaven to go to the place where he met one seeking for truth; of Cornelius, visited by an angel with a message from God; of Peter, in prison and condemned to death, led by an angel forth to safety—all show the closeness of the connection between heaven and earth.

To the worker for God the record of these angel visits should bring strength and courage. Today, as verily as in the days of the apostles, heavenly messengers are passing through the length and breadth of the land, seeking to comfort the sorrowing, to protect the impenitent, to win the hearts of men to Christ. We cannot see 153 them personally; nevertheless they are with us, guiding, directing, protecting.

Heaven is brought near to earth by that mystic ladder, the base of which is firmly planted on the earth, while the topmost round reaches the throne of the Infinite. Angels are constantly ascending and descending this ladder of shining brightness, bearing the prayers of the needy and distressed to the Father above, and bringing blessing and hope, courage and help, to the children of men. These angels of light create a heavenly atmosphere about the soul, lifting us toward the unseen and the eternal. We cannot behold their forms with our natural sight; only by spiritual vision can we discern heavenly things. The spiritual ear alone can hear the harmony of heavenly voices.

"The angel of the Lord encampeth round about them that fear Him, and delivereth them." Psalm 34:7. God commissions His angels to save His chosen ones from calamity, to guard them from "the pestilence that walketh in darkness" and "the destruction that wasteth at noonday." Psalm 91:6. Again and again have angels talked with men as a man speaketh with a friend, and led them to places of security. Again and again have the encouraging words of angels renewed the drooping spirits of the faithful and, carrying their minds above the things of earth, caused them to behold by faith the white robes, the crowns, the palm branches of victory, which overcomers will receive when they surround the great white throne.

It is the work of the angels to come close to the tried, the suffering, the tempted. They labor 154 untiringly in behalf of those for whom Christ died. When sinners are led to give themselves to the Saviour, angels bear the tidings heavenward, and there is great rejoicing among the heavenly host. "Joy shall be in heaven over one sinner that repenteth, more than over ninety and nine just persons, which need no repentance." Luke 15:7. A report is borne to heaven of every successful effort on our part to dispel the darkness and to spread abroad the knowledge of Christ. As the deed is recounted before the Father, joy thrills through all the heavenly host.

The principalities and powers of heaven are watching the warfare which, under apparently discouraging circumstances, God's servants are carrying on. New conquests are being achieved, new honors won, as the Christians, rallying round the banner of their Redeemer, go forth to fight the good fight of faith. All the heavenly angels are at the service of the humble, believing people of God; and as the Lord's army of workers here below sing their songs of praise, the choir above join with them in ascribing praise to God and to His Son.

We need to understand better than we do the mission of the angels. It would be well to remember that every true child of God has the co-operation of heavenly beings. Invisible armies of light and power attend the meek and lowly ones who believe and claim the promises of God. Cherubim and seraphim, and angels that excel in strength, stand at God's right hand, "all ministering spirits, sent forth to minister for them who shall be heirs of salvation." Hebrews 1:14.

16 155

The Gospel Message in Antioch

After the disciples had been driven from Jerusalem by persecution, the gospel message spread rapidly through the regions lying beyond the limits of Palestine; and many small companies of believers were formed in important centers. Some of the disciples "traveled as far as Phenice, and Cyprus, and Antioch, preaching the word." Their labors were usually confined to the Hebrew and Greek Jews, large colonies of whom were at this time to be found in nearly all the cities of the world.

Among the places mentioned where the gospel was gladly received is Antioch, at that time the metropolis of Syria. The extensive commerce carried on from that populous center brought to the city many people of various nationalities. Besides, Antioch was favorably known as a resort for lovers of ease and pleasure, because of its healthful situation, its beautiful surroundings, and the wealth, culture, and refinement to be found there. In the days of the 156 apostles it had become a city of luxury and vice.

The gospel was publicly taught in Antioch by certain disciples from Cyprus and Cyrene, who came "preaching the Lord Jesus." "The hand of the Lord was with them," and their earnest labors were productive of fruit. "A great number believed, and turned unto the Lord."

This chapter is based on Acts 11:19-26; 13:1-3.

"Tidings of these things came unto the ears of the church which was in Jerusalem: and they sent forth Barnabas, that he should go as far as Antioch." Upon arrival in his new field of labor, Barnabas saw the work that had already been accomplished by divine grace, and he "was glad, and exhorted them all, that with purpose of heart they would cleave unto the Lord."

The labors of Barnabas in Antioch were richly blessed, and many were added to the number of believers there. As the work developed, Barnabas felt the need of suitable help in order to advance in the opening providences of God, and he went to Tarsus to seek for Paul, who, after his departure from Jerusalem some time before, had been laboring in "the regions of Syria and Cilicia," proclaiming "the faith which once he destroyed." Galatians 1:21, 23. Barnabas was successful in finding Paul and in persuading him to return with him as a companion in ministry.

In the populous city of Antioch, Paul found an excellent field of labor. His learning, wisdom, and zeal exerted a powerful influence over the inhabitants and frequenters of that city of culture; and he proved just the help that Barnabas needed. For a year the two disciples labored unitedly in faithful ministry, bringing to many a saving knowledge of Jesus of Nazareth, the world's Redeemer.

It was in Antioch that the disciples were first called Christians. The name was given them because Christ was the main theme of their preaching, their teaching, and their conversation. Continually they were recounting the incidents that had occurred during the days of His earthly ministry, when His disciples were blessed with His personal presence. Untiringly they dwelt upon His teachings and His miracles of healing. With quivering lips and tearful eyes they spoke of His agony in the garden, His betrayal, trial, and execution, the forbearance and humility with which He had endured the contumely and torture imposed upon Him by His enemies, and the Godlike pity with which He had prayed for those who persecuted Him. His resurrection and ascension, and His work in heaven as the Mediator for fallen man, were topics on which they rejoiced to dwell. Well might the heathen call them Christians, since they preached Christ and addressed their prayers to God through Him.

It was God who gave to them the name of Christian. This is a royal name, given to all who join themselves to Christ. It was of this name that James wrote later, "Do not rich men oppress you, and draw you before the judgment seats? Do not they blaspheme that worthy name by the which ye are called?" James 2:6, 7. And Peter declared, "If any man suffer as a Christian, let him not be ashamed; but let him glorify God on this behalf." "If ye be reproached for the name of Christ, happy are ye; for the spirit of glory and of God resteth upon you." 1 Peter 4:16, 14.

The believers at Antioch realized that God was willing to work in their lives "both to will and to do of His good pleasure." Philippians 2:13. Living, as they were, in the midst of a people who seemed to care but little for the things of eternal value, they sought to arrest the attention of the honest in heart, and to bear positive testimony concerning Him whom they loved and served. In their humble ministry they learned to depend upon the power of the Holy Spirit to make effective the word of life. And so, in the various walks of life, they daily bore testimony of their faith in Christ.

The example of the followers of Christ at Antioch should be an inspiration to every believer living in the great cities of the world today. While it is in the order of God that chosen workers of consecration and talent should be stationed in important centers of population to lead out in public efforts, it is also His purpose that the church members living in these cities shall use their God-given talents in working for souls. There are rich blessings in store for those who surrender fully to the call of God. As such workers endeavor to win souls to Jesus, they will find that many who never could have been reached in any other way are ready to respond to intelligent personal effort.

The cause of God in the earth today is in need of living representatives of Bible truth. The ordained ministers alone are not equal to the task of warning the great cities. God is calling not only upon ministers, but also upon physicians, nurses, colporteurs, Bible workers, and other consecrated laymen of varied talent who have a knowledge of the word of God and who know the power of His grace, to consider the needs of the unwarned cities. Time is rapidly passing, and there is much to be done. Every agency must be set in operation, that present opportunities may be wisely improved.

Paul's labors at Antioch, in association with Barnabas, strengthened him in his conviction that the Lord had called him to do a special work for the Gentile world. At the time of Paul's conversion, the Lord had declared that he was to be made a minister to the Gentiles, "to open their eyes, and to turn them from darkness to light, and from the power of Satan unto God, that they may receive forgiveness of sins, and inheritance among them which are sanctified by faith that is in Me." Acts 26:18. The angel that appeared to Ananias had said of Paul, "He is a chosen vessel unto Me, to bear My name before the Gentiles, and kings, and the children of Israel." Acts 9:15. And Paul himself, later in his Christian experience, while praying in the temple at Jerusalem, had been visited by an angel from heaven, who bade him, "Depart: for I will send thee far hence unto the Gentiles." Acts 22:21.

Thus the Lord had given Paul his commission to enter the broad missionary field of the Gentile world. To prepare him for this extensive and difficult work, God had brought him into close connection with Himself and had opened before his enraptured vision views of the beauty and glory of heaven. To him had been given the ministry of making known "the mystery" which had been "kept secret since the world began" 160 (Romans 16:25),—"the mystery of His will" (Ephesians 1:9), "which in other ages was not made known unto the sons of men, as it is now revealed unto His holy apostles and prophets by the Spirit; that the Gentiles should be fellow heirs, and of the same body, and partakers of His promise in Christ by the gospel: whereof," declares Paul, "I was made a minister. . . . Unto me, who am less than the least of all saints, is this grace given, that I should preach among the Gentiles the unsearchable riches of Christ; and to make all men see what is the fellowship of the mystery, which from the beginning of the world hath been hid in God, who created all things by Jesus Christ: to the intent that now unto the principalities and powers in heavenly places might be known by the church the manifold wisdom of God, according to the eternal purpose which He purposed in Christ Jesus our Lord." Ephesians 3:5-11.

God had abundantly blessed the labors of Paul and Barnabas during the year they remained with the believers in Antioch. But neither of them had as yet been formally ordained to the gospel ministry. They had now reached a point in their Christian experience when God was about to entrust them with the carrying forward of a difficult missionary enterprise, in the prosecution of which they would need every advantage that could be obtained through the agency of the church.

"There were in the church that was at Antioch certain prophets and teachers; as Barnabas, and Simeon that was called Niger, and Lucius of Cyrene, and Manaen, . . . and Saul. As they 161 ministered to the Lord, and fasted, the Holy Ghost said, Separate Me Barnabas and Saul for the work whereunto I have called them." Before being sent forth as missionaries to the heathen world, these apostles were solemnly dedicated to God by fasting and prayer and the laying on of hands. Thus they were authorized by the church, not only to teach the truth, but to perform the rite of baptism and to organize churches, being invested with full ecclesiastical authority.

The Christian church was at this time entering upon an important era. The work of proclaiming the gospel message among the Gentiles was now to be prosecuted with vigor; and as a result the church was to be strengthened by a great ingath-

ering of souls. The apostles who had been appointed to lead out in this work would be exposed to suspicion, prejudice, and jealousy. Their teachings concerning the breaking down of "the middle wall of partition" (Ephesians 2:14) that had so long separated the Jewish and the Gentile world, would naturally subject them to the charge of heresy, and their authority as ministers of the gospel would be questioned by many zealous, believing Jews. God foresaw the difficulties that His servants would be called to meet, and, in order that their work should be above challenge, He instructed the church by revelation to set them apart publicly to the work of the ministry. Their ordination was a public recognition of their divine appointment to bear to the Gentiles the glad tidings of the gospel.

Both Paul and Barnabas had already received their commission from God Himself, and the ceremony of the laying on of hands added no 162 new grace or virtual qualification. It was an acknowledged form of designation to an appointed office and a recognition of one's authority in that office. By it the seal of the church was set upon the work of God.

To the Jew this form was a significant one. When a Jewish father blessed his children, he laid his hands reverently upon their heads. When an animal was devoted to sacrifice, the hand of the one invested with priestly authority was laid upon the head of the victim. And when the ministers of the church of believers in Antioch laid their hands upon Paul and Barnabas, they, by that action, asked God to bestow His blessing upon the chosen apostles in their devotion to the specific work to which they had been appointed.

At a later date the rite of ordination by the laying on of hands was greatly abused; unwarrantable importance was attached to the act, as if a power came at once upon those who received such ordination, which immediately qualified them for any and all ministerial work. But in the setting apart of these two apostles, there is no record indicating that any virtue was imparted by the mere act of laying on of hands. There is only the simple record of their ordination and of the bearing that it had on their future work.

The circumstances connected with the separation of Paul and Barnabas by the Holy Spirit to a definite line of service show clearly that the Lord works through appointed agencies in His organized church. Years before, when the divine purpose concerning Paul was first revealed to him by the Saviour Himself, Paul was immediately afterward brought into contact with members of the newly organized church at Damas- 163 cus. Furthermore, the church at that place was not long left in darkness as to the personal experience of the converted Pharisee. And now, when the divine commission given at that time was to be more fully carried out, the Holy Spirit, again bearing witness concerning Paul as a chosen vessel to bear the gospel to the Gentiles, laid upon the church the work of ordaining him and his fellow laborer. As the leaders of the church in Antioch "ministered to the Lord, and fasted, the Holy Ghost said, Separate Me Barnabas and Saul for the work whereunto I have called them."

God has made His church on the earth a channel of light, and through it He communicates His purposes and His will. He does not give to one of His servants an experience independent of and contrary to the experience of the church itself. Neither does He give one man a knowledge of His will for the entire church while the church—Christ's body—is left in darkness. In His providence He places His servants in close connection with His church in order that they may have less confidence in themselves and greater confidence in others whom He is leading out to advance His work.

There have ever been in the church those who are constantly inclined toward individual independence. They seem unable to realize that independence of spirit is liable to lead the human agent to have too much confidence in himself and to trust in his own judgment rather than to respect the counsel and highly esteem the judgment of his brethren, especially of those in the offices that God has appointed for the leadership of His people. God has invested His church with special authority and power which no one can be justified in disregarding and despising, for he who does this despises the voice of God.

Those who are inclined to regard their individual judgment as supreme are in grave peril. It is Satan's studied effort to separate such ones from those who are channels of light, through whom God has wrought to build up and extend His work in the earth. To neglect or despise those whom He has appointed to bear the responsibilities of leadership in connection with the advancement of the truth, is to reject the means that He has ordained for the help, encouragement, and strength of His people. For any worker in the Lord's cause to pass these by, and to think that his light must come through no other channel than directly from God, is to place himself in a position where he is liable to be deceived by the enemy and overthrown. The Lord in His wisdom has arranged that by means of the close relationship that should be maintained by all believers, Christian shall be united to Christian and church to church. Thus the human instrumentality will be enabled to cooperate with the divine. Every agency will be subordinate to the Holy Spirit, and all the believers will be united in an organized and well-directed effort to give to the world the glad tidings of the grace of God.

Paul regarded the occasion of his formal ordination as marking the beginning of a new and important epoch in his lifework. It was from this time that he afterward dated the beginning of his apostleship in the Christian church.

While the light of the gospel was shining brightly at Antioch, an important work was continued by the apostles who had remained in Jerusalem. Every year, at the time of the festivals, many Jews from all lands came to Jerusalem to worship at the temple. Some of these pilgrims were men of fervent piety and earnest students of the prophecies. They were looking and longing for the advent of the promised Messiah, the hope of Israel. While Jerusalem was filled with these strangers, the apostles preached Christ with unflinching courage, though they knew that in so doing they were placing their lives in constant jeopardy. The Spirit of God set its seal upon their labors; many converts to the faith were made; and these, returning to their homes in different parts of the world, scattered the seeds of truth through all nations and among all classes of society.

Prominent among the apostles who engaged in this work were Peter, James, and John, who felt confident that God had appointed them to preach Christ among their countrymen at home. Faithfully and wisely they labored, testifying of the things they had seen and heard, and appealing to "a more sure word of prophecy" (2 Peter 1:19), in an effort to persuade "the house of Israel . . . that God hath made that same Jesus, whom" the Jews "crucified, both Lord and Christ" (Acts 2:36).

17

Heralds of the Gospel

"Sent forth by the Holy Ghost," Paul and Barnabas, after their ordination by the brethren in Antioch, "departed unto Seleucia; and from thence they sailed to Cyprus." Thus the apostles began their first missionary journey.

Cyprus was one of the places to which the believers had fled from Jerusalem because of the persecution following the death of Stephen. It was from Cyprus that certain men had journeyed to Antioch, "preaching the Lord Jesus." Acts 11:20. Barnabas himself was "of the country of Cyprus" (Acts 4:36); and now he and Paul, accompanied by John Mark, a kinsman of Barnabas, visited this island field.

Mark's mother was a convert to the Christian religion, and her home at Jerusalem was an asylum for the disciples. There they were always sure of a welcome and a season of rest. It was during one of these visits of the apostles to his mother's home, that Mark proposed to Paul and Barnabas that he should accompany them on

This chapter is based on Acts 13:4-52.

their missionary tour. He felt the favor of God in his heart and longed to devote himself entirely to the work of the gospel ministry.

Arriving at Salamis, the apostles "preached the word of God in the synagogues of the Jews. . . . And when they had gone through the isle unto Paphos, they found a certain sorcerer, a false prophet, a Jew, whose name was Bar-Jesus: which was with the deputy of the country, Sergius Paulus, a prudent man; who called for Barnabas and Saul, and desired to hear the word of God. But Elymas the sorcerer (for so is his name by interpretation) withstood them, seeking to turn away the deputy from the faith."

Not without a struggle does Satan allow the kingdom of God to be built up in the earth. The forces of evil are engaged in unceasing warfare against the agencies appointed for the spread of the gospel, and these powers of darkness are especially active when the truth is proclaimed before men of repute and sterling integrity. Thus it was when Sergius Paulus, the deputy of Cyprus, was listening to the gospel message. The deputy had sent for the apostles, that he might be instructed in the message they had come to bear, and now the forces of evil, working through the sorcerer Elymas, sought with their baleful suggestions to turn him from the faith and so thwart the purpose of God.

Thus the fallen foe ever works to keep in his ranks men of influence who, if converted, might render effective service in God's cause. But the 168 faithful gospel worker need not fear defeat at the hand of the enemy; for it is his privilege to be endued with power from above to withstand every satanic influence.

Although sorely beset by Satan, Paul had the courage to rebuke the one through whom the enemy was working. "Filled with the Holy Ghost," the apostle "set his eyes on him, and said, O full of all subtlety and all mischief, thou child of the devil, thou enemy of all righteousness, wilt thou not cease to pervert the right ways of the Lord? And now, behold, the hand of the Lord is upon thee, and thou shalt be blind, not seeing the sun for a season. And immediately there fell on him a mist and a darkness; and he went about seeking some to lead him by the hand. Then the deputy, when he saw what was done, believed, being astonished at the doctrine of the Lord."

The sorcerer had closed his eyes to the evidences of gospel truth, and the Lord, in righteous anger, caused his natural eyes to be closed, shutting out from him the light of day. This blindness was not permanent, but only for a season, that he might be warned to repent and seek pardon of the God whom he had so grievously offended. The confusion into which he was thus brought made of no effect his subtle arts against the doctrine of Christ. The fact that he was obliged to grope about in blindness proved to all

that the miracles which the apostles had performed, and which Elymas had denounced as sleight of hand, were wrought by the power of God. The deputy, convinced of the truth of the doctrine taught by the apostles, accepted the gospel.

Elymas was not a man of education, yet he 169 was peculiarly fitted to do the work of Satan. Those who preach the truth of God will meet the wily foe in many different forms. Sometimes it will be in the person of learned, but more often of ignorant, men, whom Satan has trained to be successful instruments to deceive souls. It is the duty of the minister of Christ to stand faithful at his post, in the fear of God and in the power of His might. Thus he may put to confusion the hosts of Satan and may triumph in the name of the Lord.

Paul and his company continued their journey, going to Perga, in Pamphylia. Their way was toilsome; they encountered hardships and privations, and were beset with dangers on every side. In the towns and cities through which they passed, and along the lonely highways, they were surrounded by dangers seen and unseen. But Paul and Barnabas had learned to trust God's power to deliver. Their hearts were filled with fervent love for perishing souls. As faithful shepherds in search of the lost sheep, they gave no thought to their own ease and convenience. Forgetful of self, they faltered not when weary, hungry, and cold. They had in view but one object—the salvation of those who had wandered far from the fold.

It was here that Mark, overwhelmed with fear and discouragement, wavered for a time in his purpose, going to give himself wholeheartedly to the Lord's work. Unused to hardships, he was disheartened by the perils and privations of the way. He had labored with success under favorable circumstances; but now, amidst the opposition and perils that so often beset the pioneer 170 worker, he failed to endure hardness as a good soldier of the cross. He had yet to learn to face danger and persecution and adversity with a brave heart. As the apostles advanced, and still greater difficulties were apprehended, Mark was intimidated and, losing all courage, refused to go farther and returned to Jerusalem.

This desertion caused Paul to judge Mark unfavorably, and even severely, for a time. Barnabas, on the other hand, was inclined to excuse him because of his inexperience. He felt anxious that Mark should not abandon the ministry, for he saw in him qualifications that would fit him to be a useful worker for Christ. In after years his solicitude in Mark's behalf was richly rewarded, for the young man gave himself unreservedly to the Lord and to the work of proclaiming the gospel message in difficult fields. Under the blessing of God, and the wise training of Barnabas, he developed into a valuable worker.

Paul was afterward reconciled to Mark and received him as a fellow laborer. He also recommended him to the Colossians as one who was a fellow worker "unto the kingdom of God," and "a comfort unto me." Colossians 4:11. Again, not long before his own death, he spoke of Mark as "profitable" to him "for the ministry." 2 Timothy 4:11.

After the departure of Mark, Paul and Barnabas visited Antioch in Pisidia and on the Sabbath day went into the Jewish synagogue and sat down. "After the reading of the law and the prophets the rulers of the synagogue sent unto 171 them, saying, Ye men and brethren, if ye have any word of exhortation for the people, say on." Being thus invited to speak, "Paul stood up, and beckoning with his hand said, Men of Israel, and ye that fear God, give audience." Then followed a wonderful discourse. He proceeded to give a history of the manner in which the Lord had dealt with the Jews from the time of their deliverance from Egyptian bondage, and how a Saviour had been promised, of the seed of David, and he boldly declared that "of this man's seed hath God according to His promise raised unto Israel a Saviour, Jesus: when John had first preached before His coming the baptism of repentance to all the people of Israel. And as John fulfilled his course, he said, Whom think ye that I am? I am not He. But, behold, there cometh One after me, whose shoes of His feet I am not worthy to loose." Thus with power he preached Jesus as the Saviour of men, the Messiah of prophecy.

Having made this declaration, Paul said, "Men and brethren, children of the stock of Abraham, and whosoever among you feareth God, to you is the word of this salvation sent. For they that dwell at Jerusalem, and their rulers, because they knew Him not, nor yet the voices of the prophets which are read every Sabbath day, they have fulfilled them in condemning Him."

Paul did not hesitate to speak the plain truth concerning the rejection of the Saviour by the Jewish leaders. "Though they found no cause of death in Him," the apostle declared, "yet desired they Pilate that He should be slain. And when 172 they had fulfilled all that was written of Him, they took Him down from the tree, and laid Him in a sepulcher. But God raised Him from the dead: and He was seen many days of them which came up with Him from Galilee to Jerusalem, who are His witnesses unto the people."

"We declare unto you glad tidings," the apostle continued, "how that the promise which was made unto the fathers, God hath fulfilled the same unto us their children, in that He hath raised up Jesus again; as it is also written in the second psalm, Thou art My Son, this day have I begotten Thee. And as concerning that He raised Him up from the dead, now no more to return to corruption, He said on this wise, I will give you the sure mercies of David. Wherefore He saith also in another psalm, Thou shalt not suffer Thine Holy One to see corruption. For David, after he had served his own generation by the will of God, fell on sleep, and was laid unto his fathers, and saw corruption: but He, whom God raised again, saw no corruption."

And now, having spoken plainly of the fulfillment of familiar prophecies concerning the Messiah, Paul preached unto them repentance and the remission of sin through the merits of Jesus their Saviour. "Be it known unto you," he said, "that through this Man is preached unto you the forgiveness of sins: and by Him all that believe are justified from all things, from which ye could not be justified by the law of Moses."

The Spirit of God accompanied the words that were spoken, and hearts were touched. The apostle's appeal to Old Testament prophecies, and his declaration that these had been fulfilled in the ministry of Jesus of Nazareth, carried 17: conviction to many a soul longing for the advent of the promised Messiah. And the speaker's words of assurance that the "glad tidings" of salvation were for Jew and Gentile alike, brought hope and joy to those who had not been numbered among the children of Abraham according to the flesh.

"When the Jews were gone out of the synagogue, the Gentiles besought that these words might be preached to them the next Sabbath." The congregation having finally broken up, "many of the Jews and religious proselytes," who had accepted the glad tidings borne to them that day, "followed Paul and Barnabas: who, speaking to them, persuaded them to continue in the grace of God."

The interest aroused in Antioch of Pisidia by Paul's discourse brought together on the next Sabbath day "almost the whole city . . . to hear the word of God. But when the Jews saw the multitudes, they were filled with envy, and spake against those things which were spoken by Paul, contradicting and blaspheming.

"Then Paul and Barnabas waxed bold, and said, It was necessary that the word of God should first have been spoken to you: but seeing ye put it from you, and judge yourselves unworthy of everlasting life, lo, we turn to the Gentiles. For so hath the Lord commanded us, saying, I have set thee to be a light of the Gentiles, that thou shouldest be for salvation unto the ends of the earth."

"When the Gentiles heard this, they were glad, and glorified the word of the Lord: and as many as were ordained to eternal life believed." They rejoiced exceedingly that Christ recog- 17: nized them as the children of God, and with grateful hearts they listened to the word preached. Those who believed were zealous in communicating the gospel message to others, and thus "the word of the Lord was published throughout all the region."

Centuries before, the pen of inspiration had traced this ingathering of the Gentiles; but those prophetic utterances had been but dimly understood. Hosea had said: "Yet the number of the children of Israel shall be as the sand of the sea, which cannot be measured nor numbered; and it shall come to pass, that in the place where it was said unto them, Ye are not My people, there it shall be said unto them, Ye are the sons of the living God." And again: "I will sow her unto Me in the earth; and I will have mercy upon her that had not obtained mercy; and I will say to them which were not My people, Thou art My people; and they shall say, Thou art my God." Hosea 1:10; 2:23.

The Saviour Himself, during His earthly ministry, foretold the spread of the gospel among the Gentiles. In the parable of the vineyard He declared to the impenitent Jews, "The kingdom of God shall be taken from you, and given to a nation bringing forth the fruits thereof." Matthew 21:43. And after His resurrection He commissioned His disciples to go "into all the world" and "teach all nations." They were to leave none unwarned, but were to "preach the gospel to every creature." Matthew 28:19; Mark 16:15.

In turning to the Gentiles in Antioch of Pisidia, Paul and Barnabas did not cease laboring for the Jews elsewhere, wherever there was 175 a favorable opportunity to gain a hearing. Later, in Thessalonica, in Corinth, in Ephesus, and in other important centers, Paul and his companions in labor preached the gospel to both Jews and Gentiles. But their chief energies were henceforth directed toward the building up of the kingdom of God in heathen territory, among peoples who had but little or no knowledge of the true God and of His Son.

The hearts of Paul and his associate workers were drawn out in behalf of those who were "without Christ, being aliens from the commonwealth of Israel, and strangers from the covenants of promise, having no hope, and without God in the world." Through the untiring ministrations of the apostles to the Gentiles, the "strangers and foreigners," who "sometimes were far off," learned that they had been "made nigh by the blood of Christ," and that through faith in His atoning sacrifice they might become "fellow citizens with the saints, and of the household of God." Ephesians 2:12, 13, 19.

Advancing in faith, Paul labored unceasingly for the upbuilding of God's kingdom among those who had been neglected by the teachers in Israel. Constantly he exalted Christ Jesus as "the King of kings, and Lord of lords" (1 Timothy 6:15), and exhorted the believers to be "rooted and built up in Him, and stablished in the faith." Colossians 2:7.

To those who believe, Christ is a sure foundation. Upon this living stone, Jews and Gentiles alike may build. It is broad enough for all and strong enough to sustain the weight and burden of the whole world. This is a fact plainly recog- 176 nized by Paul himself. In the closing days of his ministry, when addressing a group of Gentile believers who had remained steadfast in their love of the gospel truth, the apostle wrote, "Ye . . . are built upon the foundation of the apostles and prophets, Jesus Christ Himself being the chief cornerstone." Ephesians 2:19, 20.

As the gospel message spread in Pisidia, the unbelieving Jews of Antioch in their blind prejudice "stirred up the devout and honorable women, and the chief men of the city, and raised persecution against Paul and Barnabas, and expelled them" from that district.

The apostles were not discouraged by this treatment; they remembered the words of their Master: "Blessed are ye, when men shall revile you, and persecute you, and shall say all manner of evil against you falsely, for My sake. Rejoice, and be exceeding glad: for great is your reward in heaven: for so persecuted they the prophets which were before you." Matthew 5:11, 12.

The gospel message was advancing, and the apostles had every reason for feeling encouraged. Their labors had been richly blessed among the Pisidians at Antioch, and the believers whom they left to carry forward the work alone for a time, "were filled with joy, and with the Holy Ghost."

18

Preaching Among the Heathen

From Antioch in Pisidia, Paul and Barnabas went to Iconium. In this place, as at Antioch, they began their labors in the synagogue of their own people. They met with marked success; "a great multitude both of the Jews and also of the Greeks believed." But in Iconium, as in other places where the apostles labored, "the unbelieving Jews stirred up the Gentiles, and made their minds evil affected against the brethren."

The apostles, however, were not turned aside from their mission, for many were accepting the gospel of Christ. In the face of opposition, envy, and prejudice they went on with their work, "speaking boldly in the Lord," and God "gave testimony unto the word of His grace, and granted signs and wonders to be done by their hands." These evidences of divine approval had a powerful influence on those whose minds were open to conviction, and converts to the gospel multiplied.

This chapter is based on Acts 14:1-26.

178   The increasing popularity of the message borne by the apostles, filled the unbelieving Jews with envy and hatred, and they determined to stop the labors of Paul and Barnabas at once. By means of false and exaggerated reports they led the authorities to fear that the entire city was in danger of being incited to insurrection. They declared that large numbers were attaching themselves to the apostles and suggested that it was for secret and dangerous designs.

In consequence of these charges the disciples were repeatedly brought before the authorities; but their defense was so clear and sensible, and their statement of what they were teaching so calm and comprehensive, that a strong influence was exerted in their favor. Although the magistrates were prejudiced against them by the false statements they had heard, they dared not condemn them. They could but acknowledge that the teachings of Paul and Barnabas tended to make men virtuous, law-abiding citizens, and that the morals and order of the city would improve if the truths taught by the apostles were accepted.

Through the opposition that the disciples met, the message of truth gained great publicity; the Jews saw that their efforts to thwart the work of the new teachers resulted only in adding greater numbers to the new faith. "The multitude of the city was divided: and part held with the Jews, and part with the apostles."

So enraged were the leaders among the Jews by the turn that matters were taking, that they determined to gain their ends by violence.
179 Arousing the worst passions of the ignorant, noisy mob, they succeeded in creating a tumult, which they attributed to the teaching of the disciples. By this false charge they hoped to gain the help of the magistrates in carrying out their purpose. They determined that the apostles should have no opportunity to vindicate themselves and that the mob should interfere by stoning Paul and Barnabas, thus putting an end to their labors.

Friends of the apostles, though unbelievers, warned them of the malicious designs of the Jews and urged them not to expose themselves needlessly to the fury of the mob, but to escape for their lives. Paul and Barnabas accordingly departed in secret from Iconium, leaving the believers to carry on the work alone for a time. But they by no means took final leave; they purposed to return after the excitement had abated, and complete the work begun.

In every age and in every land, God's messengers have been called upon to meet bitter opposition from those who deliberately choose to reject the light of heaven. Often, by misrepresentation and falsehood, the enemies of the gospel have seemingly triumphed, closing the doors by which God's messengers might gain access to the people. But these doors cannot remain forever closed, and often, as God's servants have returned after a time to resume their labors, the Lord has wrought mightily in their behalf, enabling them to establish memorials to the glory of His name.

Driven by persecution from Iconium, the apostles went to Lystra and Derbe, in Lycaonia. These towns were inhabited largely by a heathen, superstitious people, but among them were 180 some who were willing to hear and accept the gospel message. In these places and in the surrounding country the apostles decided to labor, hoping to avoid Jewish prejudice and persecution.

In Lystra there was no Jewish synagogue, though a few Jews were living in the town. Many of the inhabitants of Lystra worshiped at a temple dedicated to Jupiter. When Paul and Barnabas appeared in the town and, gathering the Lystrians about them, explained the simple truths of the gospel, many sought to connect these doctrines with their own superstitious belief in the worship of Jupiter.

The apostles endeavored to impart to these idolaters a knowledge of God the Creator and of His Son, the Saviour of the human race. They first directed attention to the wonderful works of God—the sun, the moon, and the stars, the beautiful order of the recurring seasons, the mighty snow-capped mountains, the lofty trees, and other varied wonders of nature, which showed a skill beyond human comprehension. Through these works of the Almighty, the apostles led the minds of the heathen to a contemplation of the great Ruler of the universe.

Having made plain these fundamental truths concerning the Creator, the apostles told the Lystrians of the Son of God, who came from heaven to our world because He loved the children of men. They spoke of His life and ministry, His rejection by those He came to save, His trial and crucifixion, His resurrection, and His ascension to heaven, there to act as man's advocate. Thus, in the Spirit and power of God, 181 Paul and Barnabas preached the gospel in Lystra.

At one time, while Paul was telling the people of Christ's work as a healer of the sick and afflicted, he saw among his hearers a cripple whose eyes were fastened on him and who received and believed his words. Paul's heart went out in sympathy toward the afflicted man, in whom he discerned one who "had faith to be healed." In the presence of the idolatrous assembly Paul commanded the cripple to stand upright on his feet. Heretofore the sufferer had been able to take a sitting posture only, but now he instantly obeyed Paul's command and for the first time in his life stood on his feet. Strength came with this effort of faith, and he who had been a cripple "leaped and walked."

"When the people saw what Paul had done,

they lifted up their voices, saying in the speech of Lycaonia, The gods are come down to us in the likeness of men." This statement was in harmony with a tradition of theirs that the gods occasionally visited the earth. Barnabas they called Jupiter, the father of gods, because of his venerable appearance, his dignified bearing, and the mildness and benevolence expressed in his countenance. Paul they believe to be Mercury, "because he was the chief speaker," earnest and active, and eloquent with words of warning and exhortation.

The Lystrians, eager to show their gratitude, prevailed upon the priest of Jupiter to do the apostles honor, and he "brought oxen and garlands unto the gates, and would have done sacrifice with the people." Paul and Barnabas, who had sought retirement and rest, were not aware 182 of these preparations. Soon, however, their attention was attracted by the sound of music and the enthusiastic shouting of a large crowd who had come to the house where they were staying.

When the apostles ascertained the cause of this visit and its attendant excitement, "they rent their clothes, and ran in among the people" in the hope of preventing further proceedings. In a loud, ringing voice, which rose above the shouting of the people, Paul demanded their attention; and as the tumult suddenly ceased, he said: "Sirs, why do ye these things? We also are men of like passions with you, and preach unto you that ye should turn from these vanities unto the living God, which made heaven, and earth, and the sea, and all things that are therein: who in times past suffered all nations to walk in their own ways. Nevertheless He left not Himself without witness, in that He did good, and gave us rain from heaven, and fruitful seasons, filling our hearts with food and gladness."

Notwithstanding the positive denial of the apostles that they were divine, and notwithstanding Paul's endeavors to direct the minds of the people to the true God as the only object worthy of adoration, it was almost impossible to turn the heathen from their intention to offer sacrifice. So firm had been their belief that these men were indeed gods, and so great their enthusiasm, that they were loath to acknowledge their error. The record says that they were "scarce restrained."

The Lystrians reasoned that they had beheld with their own eyes the miraculous power exer- 183 cised by the apostles. They had seen a cripple who had never before been able to walk, made to rejoice in perfect health and strength. It was only after much persuasion on the part of Paul, and careful explanation regarding the mission of himself and Barnabas as representatives of the God of heaven and of His Son, the great Healer, that the people were persuaded to give up their purpose.

The labors of Paul and Barnabas at Lystra were suddenly checked by the malice of "certain Jews from Antioch and Iconium," who, upon learning of the success of the apostles' work among the Lycaonians, had determined to follow them and persecute them. On arriving at Lystra, these Jews soon succeeded in inspiring the people with the same bitterness of spirit that actuated their own minds. By words of misrepresentation and calumny those who had recently regarded Paul and Barnabas as divine beings were persuaded that in reality the apostles were worse than murderers and were deserving of death.

The disappointment that the Lystrians had suffered in being refused the privilege of offering sacrifice to the apostles, prepared them to turn against Paul and Barnabas with an enthusiasm approaching that with which they had hailed them as gods. Incited by the Jews, they planned to attack the apostles by force. The Jews charged them not to allow Paul an opportunity to speak, alleging that if they were to grant him this privilege, he would bewitch the people.

Soon the murderous designs of the enemies of the gospel were carried out. Yielding to the influence of evil, the Lystrians became possessed with a satanic fury and, seizing Paul, mercilessly stoned him. The apostle thought that 184 his end had come. The martyrdom of Stephen, and the cruel part that he himself had acted upon that occasion, came vividly to his mind. Covered with bruises and faint with pain, he fell to the ground, and the infuriated mob "drew him out of the city, supposing he had been dead."

In this dark and trying hour the company of Lystrian believers, who through the ministry of Paul and Barnabas had been converted to the faith of Jesus, remained loyal and true. The unreasoning opposition and cruel persecution by their enemies served only to confirm the faith of these devoted brethren; and now, in the face of danger and scorn, they showed their loyalty by gathering sorrowfully about the form of him whom they believed to be dead.

What was their surprise when in the midst of their lamentations the apostle suddenly lifted up his head and rose to his feet with the praise of God upon his lips. To the believers this unexpected restoration of God's servant was regarded as a miracle of divine power and seemed to set the signet of Heaven upon their change of belief. They rejoiced with inexpressible gladness and praised God with renewed faith.

Among those who had been converted at Lystra, and who were eyewitnesses of the sufferings of Paul, was one who was afterward to become a prominent worker for Christ and who was to share with the apostle the trials and the joys of pioneer service in difficult fields. This was a young man named Timothy. When Paul was dragged out of the city, this youthful disciple was among the number who took their stand beside his apparently lifeless body and who saw him arise, bruised and covered with blood, but with praises upon his lips because he had been permitted to suffer for the sake of Christ.

The day following the stoning of Paul, the apostles departed for Derbe, where their labors were blessed, and many souls were led to receive Christ as the Saviour. But "when they had preached the gospel to that city, and had taught many," neither Paul nor Barnabas was content to take up work elsewhere without confirming the faith of the converts whom they had been compelled to leave alone for a time in the places where they had recently labored. And so, undaunted by danger, "they returned again to Lystra, and to Iconium, and Antioch, confirming the souls of the disciples, and exhorting them to continue in the faith." Many had accepted the glad tidings of the gospel and had thus exposed themselves to reproach and opposition. These apostles sought to establish in the faith in order that the work done might abide.

As an important factor in the spiritual growth of the new converts the apostles were careful to surround them with the safeguards of gospel order. Churches were duly organized in all places in Lycaonia and Pisidia where there were believers. Officers were appointed in each church, and proper order and system were established for the conduct of all the affairs pertaining to the spiritual welfare of the believers.

This was in harmony with the gospel plan of uniting in one body all believers in Christ, and this plan Paul was careful to follow throughout his ministry. Those who in any place were by his labor led to accept Christ as the Saviour were at the proper time organized into a church. Even when the believers were but few in number, this was done. The Christians were thus taught to help one another, remembering the promise, "Where two or three are gathered together in My name, there am I in the midst of them." Matthew 18:20.

And Paul did not forget the churches thus established. The care of these churches rested on his mind as an ever-increasing burden. However small a company might be, it was nevertheless the object of his constant solicitude. He watched over the smaller churches tenderly, realizing that they were in need of special care in order that the members might be thoroughly established in the truth and taught to put forth earnest, unselfish efforts for those around them.

In all their missionary endeavors Paul and Barnabas sought to follow Christ's example of willing sacrifice and faithful, earnest labor for souls. Wide-awake, zealous, untiring, they did not consult inclination or personal ease, but with prayerful anxiety and unceasing activity they sowed the seed of truth. And with the sowing of the seed, the apostles were careful to give to all who took their stand for the gospel, practical instruction that was of untold value. This spirit of earnestness and godly fear made upon the minds of the new disciples a lasting impression regarding the importance of the gospel message.

When men of promise and ability were converted, as in the case of Timothy, Paul and Barnabas sought earnestly to show them the necessity of laboring in the vineyard. And when the apostles left for another place, the faith of these men did not fail, but rather increased. They had been faithfully instructed in the way of the Lord, and had been taught how to labor unselfishly, earnestly, perseveringly, for the salvation of their fellow men. This careful training of new converts was an important factor in the remarkable success that attended Paul and Barnabas as they preached the gospel in heathen lands.

The first missionary journey was fast drawing to a close. Commending the newly organized churches to the Lord, the apostles went to Pamphylia, "and when they had preached the word in Perga, they went down into Attalia, and thence sailed to Antioch."

19

Jew and Gentile

On reaching Antioch in Syria, from which place they had been sent forth on their mission, Paul and Barnabas took advantage of an early opportunity to assemble the believers and rehearse "all that God had done with them, and how He had opened the door of faith unto the Gentiles." Acts 14:27. The church at Antioch was a large and growing one. A center of missionary activity, it was one of the most important of the groups of Christian believers. Its membership was made up of many classes of people from among both Jews and Gentiles.

While the apostles united with the ministers and lay members at Antioch in an earnest effort to win many souls to Christ, certain Jewish believers from Judea "of the sect of the Pharisees" succeeded in introducing a question that soon led to wide-spread controversy in the church and brought consternation to the believing Gentiles. With great assurance these Judaizing teachers asserted that in order to be saved, one must be circumcised and must keep the entire ceremonial law.

Paul and Barnabas met this false doctrine with promptness and opposed the introduction of the subject to the Gentiles. On the other hand, many of the believing Jews of Antioch favored the position of the brethren recently come from Judea.

This chapter is based on Acts 15:1-35.

The Jewish converts generally were not inclined to move as rapidly as the providence of God opened the way. From the result of the apostles' labors among the Gentiles it was evident that the converts among the latter people would far exceed the Jewish converts in number. The Jews feared that if the restrictions and ceremonies of their law were not made obligatory upon the Gentiles as a condition of church fellowship, the national peculiarities of the Jews, which had hitherto kept them distinct from all other people, would finally disappear from among those who received the gospel message.

The Jews had always prided themselves upon their divinely appointed services, and many of those who had been converted to the faith of Christ still felt that since God had once clearly outlined the Hebrew manner of worship, it was improbable that He would ever authorize a change in any of its specifications. They insisted that the Jewish laws and ceremonies should be incorporated into the rites of the Christian religion. They were slow to discern that all the sacrificial offerings had but prefigured the death of the Son of God, in which type met antitype, and after which the rites and ceremonies of the Mosaic dispensation were no longer binding.

190   Before his conversion Paul had regarded himself as blameless "touching the righteousness which is in the law." Philippians 3:6. But since his change of heart he had gained a clear conception of the mission of the Saviour as the Redeemer of the entire race, Gentile as well as Jew, and had learned the difference between a living faith and a dead formalism. In the light of the gospel the ancient rites and ceremonies committed to Israel had gained a new and deeper significance. That which they shadowed forth had come to pass, and those who were living under the gospel dispensation had been freed from their observance. God's unchangeable law of Ten Commandments, however, Paul still kept in spirit as well as in letter.

In the church at Antioch the consideration of the question of circumcision resulted in much discussion and contention. Finally, the members of the church, fearing that a division among them would be the outcome of continued discussion, decided to send Paul and Barnabas, with some responsible men from the church, to Jerusalem to lay the matter before the apostles and elders. There they were to meet delegates from the different churches and those who had come to Jerusalem to attend the approaching festivals. Meanwhile all controversy was to cease until a final decision should be given in general council. This decision was then to be universally accepted by the different churches throughout the country.

On the way to Jerusalem the apostles visited the believers in the cities through which they passed, and encouraged them by relating their experience in the work of God and the conversion of the Gentiles.

At Jerusalem the delegates from Antioch met the brethren of the various churches, who had 191 gathered for a general meeting, and to them they related the success that had attended their ministry among the Gentiles. They then gave a clear outline of the confusion that had resulted because certain converted Pharisees had gone to Antioch declaring that, in order to be saved, the Gentile converts must be circumcised and keep the law of Moses.

This question was warmly discussed in the assembly. Intimately connected with the question of circumcision were several others demanding careful study. One was the problem as to what attitude should be taken toward the use of meats offered to idols. Many of the Gentile converts were living among ignorant and superstitious people who made frequent sacrifices and offerings to idols. The priests of this heathen worship carried on an extensive merchandise with the offerings brought to them, and the Jews feared that the Gentile converts would bring Christianity into disrepute by purchasing that which had been offered to idols, thereby sanctioning, in some measure, idolatrous customs.

Again, the Gentiles were accustomed to eat the flesh of animals that had been strangled, while the Jews had been divinely instructed that when beasts were killed for food, particular care was to be taken that the blood should flow from the body; otherwise the meat would not be regarded as wholesome. God had given these injunctions to the Jews for the purpose of preserving their health. The Jews regarded it as sinful to use blood as an article of diet. They held that the blood was the life, and that the shedding of blood was in consequence of sin.

The Gentiles, on the contrary, practiced 192 catching the blood that flowed from the sacrificial victim and using it in the preparation of food. The Jews could not believe that they ought to change the customs they had adopted under the special direction of God. Therefore, as things then stood, if Jew and Gentile should attempt to eat at the same table, the former would be shocked and outraged by the latter.

The Gentiles, and especially the Greeks, were extremely licentious, and there was danger that some, unconverted in heart, would make a profession of faith without renouncing their evil practices. The Jewish Christians could not tolerate the immorality that was not even regarded as criminal by the heathen. The Jews therefore held it as highly proper that circumcision and the observance of the ceremonial law should be enjoined on the Gentile converts as a test of their sincerity and devotion. This, they believed, would prevent the addition to the church of those who, adopting the faith without true conversion of heart, might afterward bring reproach upon the cause by immorality and excess.

The various points involved in the settlement of the main question at issue seemed to present before the council insurmountable difficulties. But the Holy Spirit had, in reality, already settled this question, upon the decision of which seemed to depend the prosperity, if not the very existence, of the Christian church.

"When there had been much disputing, Peter rose up, and said unto them, Men and brethren, ye know how that a good while ago God made choice among us, that the Gentiles by my mouth should hear the word of the gospel, and 193 believe." He reasoned that the Holy Spirit had decided the matter under dispute by descending with equal power upon the uncircumcised Gentiles and the circumcised Jews. He recounted his vision, in which God had presented before him a sheet filled with all manner of four-footed beasts and had bidden him kill and eat. When he refused, affirming that he had never eaten that which was common or unclean, the answer had been, "What God hath cleansed, that call not thou common." Acts 10:15.

Peter related the plain interpretation of these words, which was given him almost immediately in his summons to go to the centurion and instruct him in the faith of Christ. This message showed that God was no respecter of persons, but accepted and acknowledged all who feared Him. Peter told of his astonishment when, in speaking the words of truth to those assembled at the home of Cornelius, he witnessed the Holy Spirit taking possession of his hearers, Gentiles as well as Jews. The same light and glory that was reflected upon the circumcised Jews shone also upon the faces of the uncircumcised Gentiles. This was God's warning that Peter was not to regard one as inferior to the other, for the blood of Christ could cleanse from all uncleanness.

Once before, Peter had reasoned with his brethren concerning the conversion of Cornelius and his friends, and his fellowship with them. As he on that occasion related how the Holy Spirit fell on the Gentiles he declared, "Forasmuch then as God gave them the like gift as He did unto us, who believed on the Lord Jesus Christ; what was I, that I could withstand God?" Acts 11:17. Now, with equal fervor and force, 194 he said: "God, which knoweth the hearts, bare them witness, giving them the Holy Ghost, even as He did unto us; and put no difference between us and them, purifying their hearts by faith. Now therefore why tempt ye God, to put a yoke upon the neck of the disciples, which neither our fathers nor we were able to bear?" This yoke was not the law of Ten Commandments, as some who oppose the binding claims of the law assert; Peter here referred to the law of cere-

monies, which was made null and void by the crucifixion of Christ.

Peter's address brought the assembly to a point where they could listen with patience to Paul and Barnabas, who related their experience in working for the Gentiles. "All the multitude kept silence, and gave audience to Barnabas and Paul, declaring what miracles and wonders God had wrought among the Gentiles by them."

James also bore his testimony with decision, declaring that it was God's purpose to bestow upon the Gentiles the same privileges and blessings that had been granted to the Jews.

The Holy Spirit saw good not to impose the ceremonial law on the Gentile converts, and the mind of the apostles regarding this matter was as the mind of the Spirit of God. James presided at the council, and his final decision was, "Wherefore my sentence is, that we trouble not them, which from among the Gentiles are turned to God."

This ended the discussion. In this instance we have a refutation of the doctrine held by the Roman Catholic Church that Peter was the head of the church. Those who, as popes, have claimed to be his successors, have no Scriptural foundation for their pretensions. Nothing in the 195 life of Peter gives sanction to the claim that he was elevated above his brethren as the vicegerent of the Most High. If those who are declared to be the successors of Peter had followed his example, they would always have been content to remain on an equality with their brethren.

In this instance James seems to have been chosen as the one to announce the decision arrived at by the council. It was his sentence that the ceremonial law, and especially the ordinance of circumcision, should not be urged upon the Gentiles, or even recommended to them. James sought to impress the minds of his brethren with the fact that, in turning to God, the Gentiles had made a great change in their lives and that much caution should be used not to trouble them with perplexing and doubtful questions of minor importance, lest they be discouraged in following Christ.

The Gentile converts, however, were to give up the customs that were inconsistent with the principles of Christianity. The apostles and elders therefore agreed to instruct the Gentiles by letter to abstain from meats offered to idols, from fornication, from things strangled, and from blood. They were to be urged to keep the commandments and to lead holy lives. They were also to be assured that the men who had declared circumcision to be binding were not authorized to do so by the apostles.

Paul and Barnabas were recommended to them as men who had hazarded their lives for the Lord. Judas and Silas were sent with these apostles to declare to the Gentiles by word of mouth the decision of the council: "It seemed good to the Holy Ghost, and to us, to lay upon you no greater burden than these necessary things; that ye abstain from meats offered to idols, and from blood, and from things strangled, and from fornication: from which if ye keep yourselves, ye shall do well." The four servants of God were sent to Antioch with the epistle and message that was to put an end to all controversy; for it was the voice of the highest authority upon the earth.

The council which decided this case was composed of apostles and teachers who had been prominent in raising up the Jewish and Gentile Christian churches, with chosen delegates from various places. Elders from Jerusalem and deputies from Antioch were present, and the most influential churches were represented. The council moved in accordance with the dictates of enlightened judgment, and with the dignity of a church established by the divine will. As a result of their deliberations they all saw that God Himself had answered the question at issue by bestowing upon the Gentiles the Holy Ghost; and they realized that it was their part to follow the guidance of the Spirit.

The entire body of Christians was not called to vote upon the question. The "apostles and elders," men of influence and judgment, framed and issued the decree, which was thereupon generally accepted by the Christian churches. Not all, however, were pleased with the decision; there was a faction of ambitious and self-confident brethren who disagreed with it. These men assumed to engage in the work on their own responsibility. They indulged in much murmuring and faultfinding, proposing new plans and seeking to pull down the work of the men whom God had ordained to teach the gospel message. From the first the church has had such obstacles to meet and ever will have till the close of time.

Jerusalem was the metropolis of the Jews, and it was there that the greatest exclusiveness and bigotry were found. The Jewish Christians living within sight of the temple naturally allowed their minds to revert to the peculiar privileges of the Jews as a nation. When they saw the Christian church departing from the ceremonies and traditions of Judaism, and perceived that the peculiar sacredness with which the Jewish customs had been invested would soon be lost sight of in the light of the new faith, many grew indignant with Paul as the one who had, in a large measure, caused this change. Even the disciples were not all prepared to accept willingly the decision of the council. Some were zealous for the ceremonial law, and they regarded Paul with disfavor because they thought that his principles in regard to the obligations of the Jewish law were lax.

The broad and far-reaching decisions of the general council brought confidence into the ranks of the Gentile believers, and the cause of God prospered. In Antioch the church was favored with the presence of Judas and Silas, the special messengers who had returned with the apostles from the meeting in Jerusalem. "Being prophets also themselves," Judas and Silas "exhorted the brethren with many words, and confirmed them." These godly men tarried in Antioch for a time. "Paul also and Barnabas continued in Antioch, teaching and preaching the word of the Lord, with many others also."

When Peter, at a later date, visited Antioch, he won the confidence of many by his prudent conduct toward the Gentile converts. For a time he acted in accordance with the light given from heaven. He so far overcame his natural prejudice as to sit at table with the Gentile converts. But when certain Jews who were zealous for the ceremonial law, came from Jerusalem, Peter injudiciously changed his deportment toward the converts from paganism. A number of the Jews "dissembled likewise with him; insomuch that Barnabas also was carried away with their dissimulation." This revelation of weakness on the part of those who had been respected and loved as leaders, left a most painful impression on the minds of the Gentile believers. The church was threatened with division. But Paul, who saw the subverting influence of the wrong done to the church through the double part acted by Peter, openly rebuked him for thus disguising his true sentiments. In the presence of the church, Paul inquired of Peter, "If thou, being a Jew, livest after the manner of Gentiles, and not as do the Jews, why compellest thou the Gentiles to live as do the Jews?" Galatians 2:13, 14.

Peter saw the error into which he had fallen, and immediately set about repairing the evil that had been wrought, so far as was in his power. God, who knows the end from the beginning, permitted Peter to reveal this weakness of character in order that the tried apostle might see that there was nothing in himself whereof he might boast. Even the best of men, if left to themselves, will err in judgment. God also saw that in time to come some would be so deluded as to claim for Peter and his pretended successors the exalted prerogatives that belong to God alone. And this record of the apostle's weakness was to remain as a proof of his fallibility and of the fact that he stood in no way above the level of the other apostles.

The history of this departure from right principles stands as a solemn warning to men in positions of trust in the cause of God, that they may not fail in integrity, but firmly adhere to principle. The greater the responsibilities placed upon the human agent, and the larger his opportunities to dictate and control, the more harm he is sure to do if he does not carefully follow the way of the Lord and labor in harmony with the decisions arrived at by the general body of believers in united council.

After all Peter's failures; after his fall and restoration, his long course of service, his intimate acquaintance with Christ, his knowledge of the Saviour's straightforward practice of right principles; after all the instruction he had received, all the gifts and knowledge and influence he had gained by preaching and teaching the word—is it not strange that he should dissemble and evade the principles of the gospel through fear of man, or in order to gain esteem? Is it not strange that he should waver in his adherence to right? May God give every man a realization of his helplessness, his inability to steer his own vessel straight and safe into the harbor.

In his ministry, Paul was often compelled to stand alone. He was specially taught of God and dared make no concessions that would involve principle. At times the burden was heavy, but Paul stood firm for the right. He realized that the church must never be brought under the control of human power. The traditions and maxims of men must not take the place of revealed truth. The advance of the gospel message must not be hindered by the prejudices and preferences of men, whatever might be their position in the church.

Paul had dedicated himself and all his powers to the service of God. He had received the truths of the gospel direct from heaven, and throughout his ministry he maintained a vital connection with heavenly agencies. He had been taught by God regarding the binding of unnecessary burdens upon the Gentile Christians; thus when the Judaizing believers introduced into the Antioch church the question of circumcision, Paul knew the mind of the Spirit of God concerning such teaching and took a firm and unyielding position which brought to the churches freedom from Jewish rites and ceremonies.

Notwithstanding the fact that Paul was personally taught by God, he had no strained ideas of individual responsibility. While looking to God for direct guidance, he was ever ready to recognize the authority vested in the body of believers united in church fellowship. He felt the need of counsel, and when matters of importance arose, he was glad to lay these before the church and to unite with his brethren in seeking God for wisdom to make right decisions. Even "the spirits of the prophets," he declared, "are subject to the prophets. For God is not the author of confusion, but of peace, as in all churches of the saints." 1 Corinthians 14:32, 33. With Peter, he taught that all united in church capacity should be "subject one to another." 1 Peter 5:5.

20

Exalting the Cross

After spending some time in ministry at Antioch, Paul proposed to his fellow worker that they set forth on another missionary journey. "Let us go again," he said to Barnabas, "and visit our brethren in every city where we have preached the word of the Lord, and see how they do."

Both Paul and Barnabas had a tender regard for those who had recently accepted the gospel message under their ministry, and they longed to see them once more. This solicitude Paul never lost. Even when in distant mission fields, far from the scene of his earlier labors, he continued to bear upon his heart the burden of urging these converts to remain faithful, "perfecting holiness in the fear of God." 2 Corinthians 7:1. Constantly he tried to help them to become self-reliant, growing Christians, strong in faith, ardent in zeal, and wholehearted in their consecration to God and to the work of advancing His kingdom.

Barnabas was ready to go with Paul, but wished to take with them Mark, who had again decided to devote himself to the ministry. To this Paul objected. He "thought not good to take . . . with them" one who during their first missionary journey had left them in a time of need. He was not inclined to excuse Mark's weakness in deserting the work for the safety and comforts of home. He urged that one with so little stamina was unfitted for a work requiring patience, self-denial, bravery, devotion, faith, and a willingness to sacrifice, if need be, even life itself. So sharp was the contention that Paul and Barnabas separated, the latter following out his convictions and taking Mark with him. "So Barnabas took Mark, and sailed unto Cyprus; and Paul chose Silas, and departed, being recommended by the brethren unto the grace of God."

Journeying through Syria and Cilicia, where they strengthened the church, Paul and Silas at length reached Derbe and Lystra in the province of Lycaonia. It was at Lystra that Paul had been stoned, yet we find him again on the scene of his former danger. He was anxious to see how those who through his labors had accepted the gospel were enduring the test of trial. He was not disappointed, for he found that the Lystrian believers had remained firm in the face of violent opposition.

Here Paul again met Timothy, who had witnessed his sufferings at the close of his first visit to Lystra and upon whose mind the impression then made had deepened with the passing of

This chapter is based on Acts 15:36-41; 16:1-6.

time until he was convinced that it was his duty to give himself fully to the work of the ministry. His heart was knit with the heart of Paul, and he longed to share the apostle's labors by assisting as the way might open.

Silas, Paul's companion in labor, was a tried worker, gifted with the spirit of prophecy; but the work to be done was so great that there was need of training more laborers for active service. In Timothy Paul saw one who appreciated the sacredness of the work of a minister; who was not appalled at the prospect of suffering and persecution; and who was willing to be taught. Yet the apostle did not venture to take the responsibility of giving Timothy, an untried youth, a training in the gospel ministry, without first fully satisfying himself in regard to his character and his past life.

Timothy's father was a Greek and his mother a Jewess. From a child he had known the Scriptures. The piety that he saw in his home life was sound and sensible. The faith of his mother and his grandmother in the sacred oracles was to him a constant reminder of the blessing in doing God's will. The word of God was the rule by which these two godly women had guided Timothy. The spiritual power of the lessons that he had received from them kept him pure in speech and unsullied by the evil influences with which he was surrounded. Thus his home instructors had co-operated with God in preparing him to bear burdens.

Paul saw that Timothy was faithful, steadfast, and true, and he chose him as a companion in labor and travel. Those who had taught Timothy in his childhood were rewarded by seeing the son of their care linked in close fellowship with the great apostle. Timothy was a mere youth when he was chosen by God to be a teacher, but his principles had been so established by his early education that he was fitted to take his place as Paul's helper. And though young, he bore his responsibilities with Christian meekness.

As a precautionary measure, Paul wisely advised Timothy to be circumcised—not that God required it, but in order to remove from the minds of the Jews that which might be an objection to Timothy's ministration. In his work Paul was to journey from city to city, in many lands, and often he would have opportunity to preach Christ in Jewish synagogues, as well as in other places of assembly. If it should be known that one of his companions in labor was uncircumcised, his work might be greatly hindered by the prejudice and bigotry of the Jews. Everywhere the apostle met determined opposition and severe persecution. He desired to bring to his Jewish brethren, as well as to the Gentiles, a knowledge of the gospel, and therefore he sought, so far as was consistent with the faith, to remove every pretext for opposition. Yet while he conceded this much to Jewish prejudice, he believed and taught circumcision or uncircumcision to be nothing and the gospel of Christ everything.

Paul loved Timothy, his "own son in the faith." 1 Timothy 1:2. The great apostle often drew the younger disciple out, questioning him in regard to Scripture history, and as they traveled from place to place, he carefully taught him how to do successful work. Both Paul and Silas, in all their association with Timothy, sought to deepen the impression that had already been made upon his mind, of the sacred, serious nature of the work of the gospel minister.

In his work, Timothy constantly sought Paul's advice and instruction. He did not move from impulse, but exercised consideration and calm thought, inquiring at every step, Is this the way of the Lord? The Holy Spirit found in him one who could be molded and fashioned as a temple for the indwelling of the divine Presence.

As the lessons of the Bible are wrought into the daily life, they have a deep and lasting influence upon the character. These lessons Timothy learned and practiced. He had no specially brilliant talents, but his work was valuable because he used his God-given abilities in the Master's service. His knowledge of experimental piety distinguished him from other believers and gave him influence.

Those who labor for souls must attain to a deeper, fuller, clearer knowledge of God than can be gained by ordinary effort. They must throw all their energies into the work of the Master. They are engaged in a high and holy calling, and if they gain souls for their hire they must lay firm hold upon God, daily receiving grace and power from the Source of all blessing. "For the grace of God that bringeth salvation hath appeared to all men, teaching us that, denying ungodliness and worldly lusts, we should live soberly, righteously, and godly, in this present world; looking for that blessed hope, and the glorious appearing of the great God and our Saviour Jesus Christ; who gave Himself for us, that He might redeem us from all iniquity, and purify unto Himself a peculiar people, zealous of good works." Titus 2:11-14.

Before pressing forward into new territory, Paul and his companions visited the churches that had been established in Pisidia and the regions round about. "As they went through the cities, they delivered them the decrees for to keep, that were ordained of the apostles and elders which were at Jerusalem. And so were the churches established in the faith, and increased in number daily."

The apostle Paul felt a deep responsibility for those converted under his labors. Above all things, he longed that they should be faithful, "that I may rejoice in the day of Christ," he said, "that I have not run in vain, neither labored in vain." Philippians 2:16. He trembled for the result of his ministry. He felt that even his own salvation might be imperiled if he should fail of fulfilling his duty and the church should fail of co-operating with him in the work of saving souls. He knew that preaching alone would not suffice to educate the believers to hold forth the word of life. He knew that line upon line, precept upon precept, here a little and there a little, they must be taught to advance in the work of Christ.

It is a universal principle that whenever one refuses to use his God-given powers, these powers decay and perish. Truth that is not lived, that is not imparted, loses its life-giving power, its healing virtue. Hence the apostle's fear that he might fail of presenting every man perfect in Christ. Paul's hope of heaven grew dim when he contemplated any failure on his part that would result in giving the church the mold of the human instead of the divine. His knowledge, his eloquence, his miracles, his view of eternal scenes when caught up to the third heaven—all would be unavailing if through unfaithfulness in 207 his work those for whom he labored should fail of the grace of God. And so, by word of mouth and by letter, he pleaded with those who had accepted Christ, to pursue a course that would enable them to be "blameless and harmless, the sons of God, without rebuke, in the midst of a crooked and perverse nation, . . . as lights in the world, holding forth the word of life." Philippians 2:15, 16.

Every true minister feels a heavy responsibility for the spiritual advancement of the believers entrusted to his care, a longing desire that they shall be laborers together with God. He realizes that upon the faithful performance of his God-given work depends in a large degree the well-being of the church. Earnestly and untiringly he seeks to inspire the believers with a desire to win souls for Christ, remembering that every addition to the church should be one more agency for the carrying out of the plan of redemption.

Having visited the churches in Pisidia and the neighboring region, Paul and Silas, with Timothy, pressed on into "Phrygia and the region of Galatia," where with mighty power they proclaimed the glad tidings of salvation. The Galatians were given up to the worship of idols; but, as the apostles preached to them, they rejoiced in the message that promised freedom from the thralldom of sin. Paul and his fellow workers proclaimed the doctrine of righteousness by faith in the atoning sacrifice of Christ. They presented Christ as the one who, seeing the helpless condition of the fallen race, came to redeem men and women by living a life of obedience to God's law and by paying the penalty of disobedience. And in the light of the cross many who

had never before known of the true God, began 208 to comprehend the greatness of the Father's love.

Thus the Galatians were taught the fundamental truths concerning "God the Father" and "our Lord Jesus Christ, who gave Himself for our sins, that He might deliver us from this present evil world, according to the will of God and our Father." "By the hearing of faith" they received the Spirit of God and became "the children of God by faith in Christ." Galatians 1:3, 4; 3:2, 26.

Paul's manner of life while among the Galatians was such that he could afterward say, "I beseech you, be as I am." Galatians 4:12. His lips had been touched with a live coal from off the altar, and he was enabled to rise above bodily infirmities and to present Jesus as the sinner's only hope. Those who heard him knew that he had been with Jesus. Endued with power from on high, he was able to compare spiritual things with spiritual and to tear down the strongholds of Satan. Hearts were broken by his presentation of the love of God, as revealed in the sacrifice of His only-begotten Son, and many were led to inquire, What must I do to be saved?

This method of presenting the gospel characterized the labors of the apostle throughout his ministry among the Gentiles. Always he kept before them the cross of Calvary. "We preach not ourselves," he declared in the later years of his experience, "but Christ Jesus the Lord; and ourselves your servants for Jesus' sake. For God, who commanded the light to shine out of 209 darkness, hath shined in our hearts, to give the light of the knowledge of the glory of God in the face of Jesus Christ." 2 Corinthians 4:5, 6.

The consecrated messengers who in the early days of Christianity carried to a perishing world the glad tidings of salvation, allowed no thought of self-exaltation to mar their presentation of Christ and Him crucified. They coveted neither authority nor pre-eminence. Hiding self in the Saviour, they exalted the great plan of salvation, and the life of Christ, the Author and Finisher of this plan. Christ, the same yesterday, today, and forever, was the burden of their teaching.

If those who today are teaching the word of God, would uplift the cross of Christ higher and still higher, their ministry would be far more successful. If sinners can be led to give one earnest look at the cross, if they can obtain a full view of the crucified Saviour, they will realize the depth of God's compassion and the sinfulness of sin.

Christ's death proves God's great love for man. It is our pledge of salvation. To remove the cross from the Christian would be like blotting the sun from the sky. The cross brings us near to God, reconciling us to Him. With the relenting compassion of a father's love, Jehovah looks upon the suffering that His Son endured in order to save the race from eternal death, and accepts us in the Beloved.

Without the cross, man could have no union with the Father. On it depends our every hope. From it shines the light of the Saviour's love, and when at the foot of the cross the sinner looks up to the One who died to save him, he 210 may rejoice with fullness of joy, for his sins are pardoned. Kneeling in faith at the cross, he has reached the highest place to which man can attain.

Through the cross we learn that the heavenly Father loves us with a love that is infinite. Can we wonder that Paul exclaimed, "God forbid that I should glory, save in the cross of our Lord Jesus Christ"? Galatians 6:14. It is our privilege also to glory in the cross, our privilege to give ourselves wholly to Him who gave Himself for us. Then, with the light that streams from Calvary shining in our faces, we may go forth to reveal this light to those in darkness.

211

21

In the Regions Beyond

The time had come for the gospel to be proclaimed beyond the confines of Asia Minor. The way was preparing for Paul and his fellow workers to cross over into Europe. At Troas, on the borders of the Mediterranean Sea, "a vision appeared to Paul in the night: There stood a man of Macedonia, and prayed him, saying, Come over into Macedonia, and help us."

The call was imperative, admitting of no delay. "After he had seen the vision," declares Luke, who accompanied Paul and Silas and Timothy on the journey across to Europe, "immediately we endeavored to go into Macedonia, assuredly gathering that the Lord had called us for to preach the gospel unto them. Therefore loosing from Troas, we came with a straight course to Samothracia, and the next day to Neapolis; and from thence to Philippi, which is the chief city of that part of Macedonia, and a colony."

212 "On the Sabbath," Luke continues, "we went out of the city by a riverside, where prayer was wont to be made; and we sat down, and spake unto the women which resorted thither. And a certain woman named Lydia, a seller of purple, of the city of Thyatira, which worshiped God, heard us: whose heart the Lord opened." Lydia received the truth gladly. She and her household were converted and baptized, and she entreated the apostles to make her house their home.

As the messengers of the cross went about their work of teaching, a woman possessed of a spirit of divination followed them, crying, "These men are the servants of the most high

God, which show unto us the way of salvation." And this did she many days."

This woman was a special agent of Satan and had brought to her masters much gain by soothsaying. Her influence had helped to strengthen idolatry. Satan knew that his kingdom was being invaded, and he resorted to this means of opposing the work of God, hoping to mingle his sophistry with the truths taught by those who were proclaiming the gospel message. The words of recommendation uttered by this woman were an injury to the cause of truth, distracting the minds of the people from the teachings of the apostles and bringing disrepute upon the gospel, and by them many were led to believe that the men who spoke with the Spirit and power of God were actuated by the same spirit as this emissary of Satan.

For some time the apostles endured this opposition; then under the inspiration of the Holy Ghost Paul commanded the evil spirit to leave the woman. Her immediate silence testified that 213 the apostles were the servants of God and that the demon had acknowledged them to be such and had obeyed their command.

Dispossessed of the evil spirit and restored to her right mind, the woman chose to become a follower of Christ. Then her masters were alarmed for their craft. They saw that all hope of receiving money from her divinations and soothsayings was at an end and that their source of income would soon be entirely cut off if the apostles were allowed to continue the work of the gospel.

Many others in the city were interested in gaining money through satanic delusions, and these, fearing the influence of a power that could so effectually stop their work, raised a mighty cry against the servants of God. They brought the apostles before the magistrates with the charge: "These men, being Jews, do exceedingly trouble our city, and teach customs, which are not lawful for us to receive, neither to observe, being Romans."

Stirred by a frenzy of excitement, the multitude rose against the disciples. A mob spirit prevailed and was sanctioned by the authorities, who tore the outer garments from the apostles and commanded that they should be scourged. "And when they had laid many stripes upon them, they cast them into prison, charging the jailer to keep them safely: who, having received such a charge, thrust them into the inner prison, and made their feet fast in the stocks."

The apostles suffered extreme torture because of the painful position in which they were left, but they did not murmur. Instead, in the utter darkness and desolation of the dungeon, they 214 encouraged each other by words of prayer and sang praises to God because they were found worthy to suffer shame for His sake. Their hearts were cheered by a deep and earnest love

This chapter is based on Acts 16:7-40.

for the cause of their Redeemer. Paul thought of the persecution he had been instrumental in bringing upon the disciples of Christ, and he rejoiced that his eyes had been opened to see, and his heart to feel, the power of the glorious truths which once he despised.

With astonishment the other prisoners heard the sound of prayer and singing issuing from the inner prison. They had been accustomed to hear shrieks and moans, cursing and swearing, breaking the silence of the night; but never before had they heard words of prayer and praise ascending from that gloomy cell. Guards and prisoners marveled and asked themselves who these men could be, who, cold, hungry, and tortured, could yet rejoice.

Meanwhile the magistrates returned to their homes, congratulating themselves that by prompt and decisive measures they had quelled a tumult. But on the way they heard further particulars concerning the character and work of the men they had sentenced to scourging and imprisonment. They saw the woman who had been freed from satanic influence and were struck by the change in her countenance and demeanor. In the past she had caused the city much trouble; now she was quiet and peaceable. As they realized that in all probability they had visited upon two innocent men the rigorous penalty of the Roman law they were indignant with themselves and decided that in the morning they would command that the apostles be pri- 215 vately released and escorted from the city, beyond the danger of violence from the mob.

But while men were cruel and vindictive, or criminally negligent of the solemn responsibilities devolving upon them, God had not forgotten to be gracious to His servants. All heaven was interested in the men who were suffering for Christ's sake, and angels were sent to visit the prison. At their tread the earth trembled. The heavily bolted prison doors were thrown open; the chains and fetters fell from the hands and feet of the prisoners; and a bright light flooded the prison.

The keeper of the jail had heard with amazement the prayers and songs of the imprisoned apostles. When they were led in, he had seen their swollen and bleeding wounds, and had himself caused their feet to be fastened in the stocks. He had expected to hear from them bitter groans and imprecations, but he heard instead songs of joy and praise. With these sounds in his ears the jailer had fallen into a sleep from which he was awakened by the earthquake and the shaking of the prison walls.

Starting up in alarm, he saw with dismay that all the prison doors were open, and the fear flashed upon him that the prisoners had escaped. He remembered with what explicit charge Paul and Silas had been entrusted to his care the night before, and he was certain that death would be the penalty of his apparent unfaithfulness. In the bitterness of his spirit he felt that it was better for him to die by his own hand than to submit to a disgraceful execution. Drawing his sword, he was about to kill himself, when Paul's voice was heard in the words of cheer, "Do thyself no harm: for we are all here." Every 216 man was in his place, restrained by the power of God exerted through one fellow prisoner.

The severity with which the jailer had treated the apostles had not aroused their resentment. Paul and Silas had the spirit of Christ, not the spirit of revenge. Their hearts, filled with the love of the Saviour, had no room for malice against their persecutors.

The jailer dropped his sword and, calling for lights, hastened into the inner dungeon. He would see what manner of men these were who repaid with kindness the cruelty with which they had been treated. Reaching the place where the apostles were, and casting himself before them, he asked their forgiveness. Then, bringing them out into the open court, he inquired, "Sirs, what must I do to be saved?"

The jailer had trembled as he beheld the wrath of God manifested in the earthquake; when he thought that the prisoners had escaped he had been ready to die by his own hand; but now all these things seemed of little consequence compared with the new, strange dread that agitated his mind, and his desire to possess the tranquillity and cheerfulness shown by the apostles under suffering and abuse. He saw in their countenances the light of heaven; he knew that God had interposed in a miraculous manner to save their lives; and with peculiar force the words of the spirit-possessed woman came to his mind: "These men are the servants of the most high God, which show unto us the way of salvation.

With deep humility he asked the apostles to 217 show him the way of life. "Believe on the Lord Jesus Christ, and thou shalt be saved, and thy house," they answered; and "they spake unto him the word of the Lord, and to all that were in his house." The jailer then washed the wounds of the apostles and ministered to them, after which he was baptized by them, with all his household. A sanctifying influence diffused itself among the inmates of the prison, and the minds of all were opened to listen to the truths spoken by the apostles. They were convinced that the God whom these men served had miraculously released them from bondage.

The citizens of Philippi had been greatly terrified by the earthquake, and when in the morning the officers of the prison told the magistrates of what had occurred during the night, they were alarmed and sent the sergeants to liberate the apostles. But Paul declared, "They have beaten us openly uncondemned, being Romans, and have cast us into prison; and now do they thrust us out privily? nay verily; but let them come themselves and fetch us out."

The apostles were Roman citizens, and it was unlawful to scourge a Roman, save for the most flagrant crime, or to deprive him of his liberty without a fair trial. Paul and Silas had been publicly imprisoned, and they now refused to be privately released without the proper explanation on the part of the magistrates.

When this word was brought to the authorities, they were alarmed for fear that the apostles would complain to the emperor, and going at 218 once to the prison, they apologized to Paul and Silas for the injustice and cruelty done them and personally conducted them out of the prison, entreating them to depart from the city. The magistrates feared the apostles' influence over the people, and they also feared the Power that had interposed in behalf of these innocent men.

Acting upon the instruction given by Christ, the apostles would not urge their presence where it was not desired. "They went out of the prison, and entered into the house of Lydia: and when they had seen the brethren, they comforted them, and departed."

The apostles did not regard as in vain their labors in Philippi. They had met much opposition and persecution; but the intervention of Providence in their behalf, and the conversion of the jailer and his household, more than atoned for the disgrace and suffering they had endured. The news of their unjust imprisonment and miraculous deliverance became known through all that region, and this brought the work of the apostles to the notice of a large number who otherwise would not have been reached.

Paul's labors at Philippi resulted in the establishment of a church whose membership steadily increased. His zeal and devotion, and, above all, his willingness to suffer for Christ's sake, exerted a deep and lasting influence upon the converts. They prized the precious truths for which the apostles had sacrificed so much, and gave themselves with wholehearted devotion to the cause of their Redeemer.

That this church did not escape persecution is shown by an expression in Paul's letter to them. 219 He says, "Unto you it is given in the behalf of Christ, not only to believe on Him, but also to suffer for His sake; having the same conflict which ye saw in me." Yet such was their steadfastness in the faith that he declares, "I thank my God upon every remembrance of you, always in every prayer of mine for you all making request with joy, for your fellowship in the gospel from the first day until now." Philippians 1:29, 30, 3-5.

Terrible is the struggle that takes place between the forces of good and of evil in important centers where the messengers of truth are called upon to labor. "We wrestle not against

flesh and blood," declares Paul, "but against principalities, against powers, against the rulers of the darkness of this world." Ephesians 6:12. Till the close of time there will be a conflict between the church of God and those who are under the control of evil angels.

The early Christians were often called to meet the powers of darkness face to face. By sophistry and by persecution the enemy endeavored to turn them from the true faith. At the present time, when the end of all things earthly is rapidly approaching, Satan is putting forth desperate efforts to ensnare the world. He is devising many plans to occupy minds and to divert attention from the truths essential to salvation. In every city his agencies are busily organizing into parties those who are opposed to the law of God. The archdeceiver is at work to introduce elements of confusion and rebellion, and men are being fired with a zeal that is not according to knowledge.

Wickedness is reaching a height never before 220 attained, and yet many ministers of the gospel are crying, "Peace and safety." But God's faithful messengers are to go steadily forward with their work. Clothed with the panoply of heaven, they are to advance fearlessly and victoriously, never ceasing their warfare until every soul within their reach shall have received the message of truth for this time.

22
221

Thessalonica

After leaving Philippi, Paul and Silas made their way to Thessalonica. Here they were given the privilege of addressing large congregations in the Jewish synagogue. Their appearance bore evidence of the shameful treatment they had recently received, and necessitated an explanation of what had taken place. This they made without exalting themselves, but magnified the One who had wrought their deliverance.

In preaching to the Thessalonians, Paul appealed to the Old Testament prophecies concerning the Messiah. Christ in His ministry had opened the minds of His disciples to these prophecies; "beginning at Moses and all the prophets, He expounded unto them in all the Scriptures the things concerning Himself." Luke 24:27. Peter in preaching Christ had produced his evidence from the Old Testament. Stephen had pursued the same course. And Paul also in his ministry appealed to the scriptures foretelling the birth, sufferings, death, resurrection, 222 and ascension of Christ. By the inspired testimony of Moses and the prophets he clearly proved the identity of Jesus of Nazareth with the Messiah and showed that from the days of

This chapter is based on Acts 17:1-10.

Adam it was the voice of Christ which had been speaking through patriarchs and prophets.

Plain and specific prophecies had been given regarding the appearance of the Promised One. To Adam was given an assurance of the coming of the Redeemer. The sentence pronounced on Satan, "I will put enmity between thee and the woman, and between thy seed and her seed; it shall bruise thy head, and thou shalt bruise his heel" (Genesis 3:15), was to our first parents a promise of the redemption to be wrought out through Christ.

To Abraham was given the promise that of his line the Saviour of the world should come: "In thy seed shall all the nations of the earth be blessed." "He saith not, And to seeds, as of many; but as of one, And to thy seed, which is Christ." Genesis 22:18; Galatians 3:16.

Moses, near the close of his work as a leader and teacher of Israel, plainly prophesied of the Messiah to come. "The Lord thy God," he declared to the assembled hosts of Israel, "will raise up unto thee a Prophet from the midst of thee, of thy brethren, like unto me; unto Him ye shall hearken." And Moses assured the Israelites that God Himself had revealed this to him while in Mount Horeb, saying, "I will raise them up a Prophet from among their brethren, like unto thee, and will put My words in His mouth; and He shall speak unto them all that I shall command Him." Deuteronomy 18:15, 18.

223 The Messiah was to be of the royal line, for in the prophecy uttered by Jacob the Lord said, "The scepter shall not depart from Judah, nor a lawgiver from between his feet, until Shiloh come; and unto Him shall the gathering of the people be." Genesis 49:10.

Isaiah prophesied: "There shall come forth a rod out of the stem of Jesse, and a Branch shall grow out of his roots." "Incline your ear, and come unto Me: hear, and your soul shall live; and I will make an everlasting covenant with you, even the sure mercies of David. Behold, I have given Him for a witness to the people, a leader and commander to the people. Behold, thou shalt call a nation that thou knowest not, and nations that knew not thee shall run unto thee because of the Lord thy God, and for the Holy One of Israel; for He hath glorified thee." Isaiah 11:1; 55:3-5.

Jeremiah also bore witness of the coming Redeemer as a Prince of the house of David: "Behold, the days come, saith the Lord, that I will raise unto David a righteous Branch, and a King shall reign and prosper, and shall execute judgment and justice in the earth. In His days Judah shall be saved, and Israel shall dwell safely: and this is His name whereby He shall be called, The Lord Our Righteousness." And again: "Thus saith the Lord: David shall never want a man to sit upon the throne of the house of Israel; neither shall the priests the Levites

want a man before Me to offer burnt offerings, and to kindle meat offerings, and to do sacrifice continually." Jeremiah 23:5, 6; 33:17, 18.

Even the birthplace of the Messiah was fore-told: "Thou, Bethlehem Ephratah, though thou be little among the thousands of Judah, yet out 224 of thee shall He come forth unto Me that is to be Ruler in Israel; whose goings forth have been from of old, from everlasting." Micah 5:2.

The work that the Saviour was to do on the earth had been fully outlined: "The Spirit of the Lord shall rest upon Him, the spirit of wisdom and understanding, the spirit of counsel and might, the spirit of knowledge and of the fear of the Lord; and shall make Him of quick understanding in the fear of the Lord." The One thus anointed was "to preach good tidings unto the meek; . . . to bind up the brokenhearted, to proclaim liberty to the captives, and the opening of the prison to them that are bound; to proclaim the acceptable year of the Lord, and the day of vengeance of our God; to comfort all that mourn; to appoint unto them that mourn in Zion, to give unto them beauty for ashes, the oil of joy for mourning, the garment of praise for the spirit of heaviness; that they might be called trees of righteousness, the planting of the Lord, that He might be glorified." Isaiah 11:2, 3; 61:1-3.

"Behold My servant, whom I uphold; Mine elect, in whom My soul delighteth; I have put My Spirit upon Him: He shall bring forth judgment to the Gentiles. He shall not cry, nor lift up, nor cause His voice to be heard in the street. A bruised reed shall He not break, and the smoking flax shall He not quench: He shall bring forth judgment unto truth. He shall not fail nor be discouraged, till He have set judgment in the earth: and the isles shall wait for His law." Isaiah 42:1-4.

With convincing power Paul reasoned from 225 the Old Testament Scriptures that "Christ must needs have suffered, and risen again from the dead." Had not Micah prophesied, "They shall smite the Judge of Israel with a rod upon the cheek"? Micah 5:1. And had not the Promised One, through Isaiah, prophesied of Himself, "I gave My back to the smiters, and My cheeks to them that plucked off the hair: I hid not My face from shame and spitting"? Isaiah 50:6. Through the psalmist Christ had foretold the treatment that He should receive from men: "I am . . . a reproach of men, and despised of the people. All they that see Me laugh Me to scorn: they shoot out the lip, they shake the head, saying, He trusted on the Lord that He would deliver Him: let Him deliver Him, seeing He delighted in Him." "I may tell all My bones: they look and stare upon Me. They part My garments among them, and cast lots upon My vesture." "I am become a stranger unto My brethren, and an alien unto My mother's children. For the zeal of

Thine house hath eaten Me up; and the reproaches of them that reproached Thee are fallen upon Me." "Reproach hath broken My heart; and I am full of heaviness: and I looked for some to take pity, but there was none; and for comforters, but I found none." Psalms 22:6-8, 17, 18; 69:8, 9, 20.

How unmistakably plain were Isaiah's prophecies of Christ's sufferings and death! "Who hath believed our report?" the prophet inquires, "and to whom is the arm of the Lord revealed? For He shall grow up before Him as a
226 tender plant, and as a root out of a dry ground: He hath no form nor comeliness; and when we shall see Him, there is no beauty that we should desire Him. He is despised and rejected of men; a man of sorrows, and acquainted with grief: and we hid as it were our faces from Him; He was despised, and we esteemed Him not.

"Surely He hath borne our griefs, and carried our sorrows: yet we did esteem Him stricken, smitten of God, and afflicted. But He was wounded for our transgressions, He was bruised for our iniquities: the chastisement of our peace was upon Him; and with His stripes we are healed.

"All we like sheep have gone astray; we have turned everyone to his own way; and the Lord hath laid on Him the iniquity of us all. He was oppressed, and He was afflicted, yet He opened not His mouth: He is brought as a lamb to the slaughter, and as a sheep before her shearers is dumb, so He openeth not His mouth. He was taken from prison and from judgment: and who shall declare His generation? for He was cut off out of the land of the living: for the transgression of my people was He stricken." Isaiah 53:1-8.

Even the manner of His death had been shadowed forth. As the brazen serpent had been uplifted in the wilderness, so was the coming Redeemer to be lifted up, "that whosoever believeth in Him should not perish, but have everlasting life." John 3:16.

"One shall say unto Him, What are these wounds in Thine hands? Then He shall answer, Those with which I was wounded in the house of My friends." Zechariah 13:6.

"He made His grave with the wicked, and
227 with the rich in His death; because He had done no violence, neither was any deceit in His mouth. Yet it pleased the Lord to bruise Him; He hath put Him to grief." Isaiah 53:9, 10.

But He who was to suffer death at the hands of evil men was to rise again as a conqueror over sin and the grave. Under the inspiration of the Almighty the Sweet Singer of Israel had testified of the glories of the resurrection morn. "My flesh also," he joyously proclaimed, "shall rest in hope. For Thou wilt not leave My soul in hell [the grave]; neither wilt Thou suffer Thine Holy One to see corruption." Psalm 16:9, 10.

Paul showed how closely God had linked the sacrificial service with the prophecies relating to the One who was to be "brought as a lamb to the slaughter." The Messiah was to give His life as "an offering for sin." Looking down through the centuries to the scenes of the Saviour's atonement, the prophet Isaiah had testified that the Lamb of God "poured out His soul unto death: and He was numbered with the transgressors; and He bare the sin of many, and made intercession for the transgressors." Isaiah 53:7, 10, 12.

The Saviour of prophecy was to come, not as a temporal king, to deliver the Jewish nation from earthly oppressors, but as a man among men, to live a life of poverty and humility, and at last to be despised, rejected, and slain. The Saviour foretold in the Old Testament Scriptures was to offer Himself as a sacrifice in behalf of the fallen race, thus fulfilling every requirement of the broken law. In Him the sacri-
228 ficial types were to meet their antitype, and His death on the cross was to lend significance to the entire Jewish economy.

Paul told the Thessalonian Jews of his former zeal for the ceremonial law and of his wonderful experience at the gate of Damascus. Before his conversion he had been confident in a hereditary piety, a false hope. His faith had not been anchored in Christ; he had trusted instead in forms and ceremonies. His zeal for the law had been disconnected from faith in Christ and was of no avail. While boasting that he was blameless in the performance of the deeds of the law, he had refused the One who made the law of value.

But at the time of his conversion all had been changed. Jesus of Nazareth, whom he had been persecuting in the person of His saints, appeared before him as the promised Messiah. The persecutor saw Him as the Son of God, the one who had come to the earth in fulfillment of the prophecies and who in His life had met every specification of the Sacred Writings.

As with holy boldness Paul proclaimed the gospel in the synagogue at Thessalonica, a flood of light was thrown upon the true meaning of the rites and ceremonies connected with the tabernacle service. He carried the minds of his hearers beyond the earthly service and the ministry of Christ in the heavenly sanctuary, to the time when, having completed His mediatorial work, Christ would come again in power and great glory, and establish His kingdom on the earth. Paul was a believer in the second coming of Christ; so clearly and forcibly did he present the truths concerning this event, that upon the minds of many who heard there was made an
229 impression which never wore away.

For three successive Sabbaths Paul preached to the Thessalonians, reasoning with them from the Scriptures regarding the life, death, resurrection, office work, and future glory of Christ, the "Lamb slain from the foundation of the world." Revelation 13:8. He exalted Christ, the proper understanding of whose ministry is the key that unlocks the Old Testament Scriptures, giving access to their rich treasures.

As the truths of the gospel were thus proclaimed in Thessalonica with mighty power, the attention of large congregations was arrested. "Some of them believed, and consorted with Paul and Silas; and of the devout Greeks a great multitude, and of the chief women not a few."

As in the places formerly entered, the apostles met with determined opposition. "The Jews which believed not" were "moved with envy." These Jews were not then in favor with the Roman power, because, not long before, they had raised an insurrection in Rome. They were looked upon with suspicion, and their liberty was in a measure restricted. They now saw an opportunity to take advantage of circumstances to re-establish themselves in favor and at the same time to throw reproach upon the apostles and the converts to Christianity.

This they set about doing by uniting with "certain lewd fellows of the baser sort," by which means they succeeded in setting "all the city on an uproar." In the hope of finding the apostles, they "assaulted the house of Jason;" 230 but they could find neither Paul nor Silas. And "when they found them not," the mob in their mad disappointment "drew Jason and certain brethren unto the rulers of the city, crying, These that have turned the world upside down are come hither also; whom Jason hath received: and these all do contrary to the decrees of Caesar, saying that there is another king, one Jesus."

As Paul and Silas were not to be found, the magistrates put the accused believers under bonds to keep the peace. Fearing further violence, "the brethren immediately sent away Paul and Silas by night unto Berea."

Those who today teach unpopular truths need not be discouraged if at times they meet with no more favorable reception, even from those who claim to be Christians, than did Paul and his fellow workers from the people among whom they labored. The messengers of the cross must arm themselves with watchfulness and prayer, and move forward with faith and courage, working always in the name of Jesus. They must exalt Christ as man's mediator in the heavenly sanctuary, the One in whom all the sacrifices of the Old Testament dispensation centered, and through whose atoning sacrifice the transgressors of God's law may find peace and pardon.

23

Berea and Athens

231

At Berea Paul found Jews who were willing to investigate the truths he taught. Luke's record declares of them: "These were more noble than those in Thessalonica, in that they received the word with all readiness of mind, and searched the Scriptures daily, whether those things were so. Therefore many of them believed; also of honorable women which were Greeks, and of men, not a few."

The minds of the Bereans were not narrowed by prejudice. They were willing to investigate the truthfulness of the doctrines preached by the apostles. They studied the Bible, not from curiosity, but in order that they might learn what had been written concerning the promised Messiah. Daily they searched the inspired records, and as they compared scripture with scripture, heavenly angels were beside them, enlightening their minds and impressing their hearts.

Wherever the truths of the gospel are pro- 232 claimed, those who honestly desire to do right are led to a diligent searching of the Scriptures. If, in the closing scenes of this earth's history, those to whom testing truths are proclaimed would follow the example of the Bereans, searching the Scriptures daily, and comparing with God's word the messages brought them, there would today be a large number loyal to the precepts of God's law, where now there are comparatively few. But when unpopular Bible truths are presented, many refuse to make this investigation. Though unable to controvert the plain teachings of Scripture, they yet manifest the utmost reluctance to study the evidences offered. Some assume that even if these doctrines are indeed true, it matters little whether or not they accept the new light, and they cling to pleasing fables which the enemy uses to lead souls astray. Thus their minds are blinded by error, and they become separated from heaven.

All will be judged according to the light that has been given. The Lord sends forth His ambassadors with a message of salvation, and those who hear He will hold responsible for the way in which they treat the words of His servants. Those who are sincerely seeking for truth will make a careful investigation, in the light of God's word, of the doctrines presented to them.

The unbelieving Jews of Thessalonica, filled with jealousy and hatred of the apostles, and not content with having driven them from their own city, followed them to Berea and aroused against them the excitable passions of the lower class. Fearing that violence would be done to Paul if he remained there, the brethren sent him 233

This chapter is based on Acts 17:11-34.

to Athens, accompanied by some of the Bereans who had newly accepted the faith.

Thus persecution followed the teachers of truth from city to city. The enemies of Christ could not prevent the advancement of the gospel, but they succeeded in making the work of the apostles exceedingly hard. Yet in the face of opposition and conflict, Paul pressed steadily forward, determined to carry out the purpose of God as revealed to him in the vision at Jerusalem: "I will send thee far hence unto the Gentiles." Acts 22:21.

Paul's hasty departure from Berea deprived him of the opportunity he had anticipated of visiting the brethren at Thessalonica.

On arriving at Athens, the apostle sent the Berean brethren back with a message to Silas and Timothy to join him immediately. Timothy had come to Berea prior to Paul's departure, and with Silas had remained to carry on the work so well begun there, and to instruct the new converts in the principles of the faith.

The city of Athens was the metropolis of heathendom. Here Paul did not meet with an ignorant, credulous populace, as at Lystra, but with a people famous for their intelligence and culture. Everywhere statues of their gods and of the deified heroes of history and poetry met the eye, while magnificent architecture and paintings represented the national glory and the popular worship of heathen deities. The senses of the people were entranced by the beauty and splendor of art. On every hand sanctuaries and tem- 234 ples, involving untold expense, reared their massive forms. Victories of arms and deeds of celebrated men were commemorated by sculpture, shrines, and tablets. All these made Athens a vast gallery of art.

As Paul looked upon the beauty and grandeur surrounding him, and saw the city wholly given to idolatry, his spirit was stirred with jealousy for God, whom he saw dishonored on every side, and his heart was drawn out in pity for the people of Athens, who, notwithstanding their intellectual culture, were ignorant of the true God.

The apostle was not deceived by that which he saw in this center of learning. His spiritual nature was so alive to the attraction of heavenly things that the joy and glory of the riches which will never perish made valueless in his eyes the pomp and splendor with which he was surrounded. As he saw the magnificence of Athens he realized its seductive power over lovers of art and science, and his mind was deeply impressed with the importance of the work before him.

In this great city, where God was not worshiped, Paul was oppressed by a feeling of solitude, and he longed for the sympathy and aid of his fellow laborers. So far as human friendship was concerned, he felt himself to be utterly alone. In his epistle to the Thessalonians he expresses his feelings in the words, "Left at Athens alone." 1 Thessalonians 3:1. Obstacles that were apparently insurmountable presented themselves before him, making it seem almost hopeless for him to attempt to reach the hearts of the people.

While waiting for Silas and Timothy, Paul was not idle. He "disputed . . . in the synagogue 235 with the Jews, and with the devout persons, and in the market daily with them that met with him." But his principal work in Athens was to bear the tidings of salvation to those who had no intelligent conception of God and of His purpose in behalf of the fallen race. The apostle was soon to meet paganism in its most subtle, alluring form.

The great men of Athens were not long in learning of the presence in their city of a singular teacher who was setting before the people doctrines new and strange. Some of these men sought Paul out and entered into conversation with him. Soon a crowd of listeners gathered about them. Some were prepared to ridicule the apostle as one who was far beneath them both socially and intellectually, and these said jeeringly among themselves, "What will this babbler say?" Others, "because he preached unto them Jesus, and the resurrection," said, "He seemeth to be a setter forth of strange gods."

Among those who encountered Paul in the market place were "certain philosophers of the Epicureans, and of the Stoics;" but they, and all others who came in contact with him, soon saw that he had a store of knowledge even greater than their own. His intellectual power commanded the respect of the learned; while his earnest, logical reasoning and the power of his oratory held the attention of all in the audience. His hearers recognized the fact that he was no novice, but was able to meet all classes with convincing arguments in support of the doctrines he taught. Thus the apostle stood undaunted, meeting his opposers on their own ground, 236 matching logic with logic, philosophy with philosophy, eloquence with eloquence.

His heathen opponents called his attention to the fate of Socrates, who, because he was a setter forth of strange gods, had been condemned to death, and they counseled Paul not to endanger his life in the same way. But the apostle's discourses riveted the attention of the people, and his unaffected wisdom commanded their respect and admiration. He was not silenced by the science or the irony of the philosophers, and satisfying themselves that he was determined to accomplish his errand among them, and, at all hazards, to tell his story, they decided to give him a fair hearing.

They accordingly conducted him to Mars' Hill. This was one of the most sacred spots in all Athens, and its recollections and associations were such as to cause it to be regarded with a superstitious reverence that in the minds of some amounted to dread. It was in this place that matters connected with religion were often carefully considered by men who acted as final judges on all the more important moral as well as civil questions.

Here, away from the noise and bustle of crowded thoroughfares, and the tumult of promiscuous discussion, the apostle could be heard without interruption. Around him gathered poets, artists, and philosophers—the scholars and sages of Athens, who thus addressed him: "May we know what this new doctrine, whereof thou speakest, is? for thou bringest certain strange things to our ears: we would know therefore what these things mean."

237   In that hour of solemn responsibility, the apostle was calm and self-possessed. His heart was burdened with an important message, and the words that fell from his lips convinced his hearers that he was no idle babbler. "Ye men of Athens," he said, "I perceive that in all things ye are too superstitious. For as I passed by, and beheld your devotions, I found an altar with this inscription, To the Unknown God. Whom therefore ye ignorantly worship, Him declare I unto you." With all their intelligence and general knowledge, they were ignorant of the God who created the universe. Yet there were some who were longing for greater light. They were reaching out toward the Infinite.

With hand outstretched toward the temple crowded with idols, Paul poured out the burden of his soul, and exposed the fallacies of the religion of the Athenians. The wisest of his hearers were astonished as they listened to his reasoning. He showed himself familiar with their works of art, their literature, and their religion. Pointing to their statuary and idols, he declared that God could not be likened to forms of man's devising. These graven images could not, in the faintest sense, represent the glory of Jehovah. He reminded them that these images had no life, but were controlled by human power, moving only when the hands of men moved them; and therefore those who worshiped them were in every way superior to that which they worshiped.

Paul drew the minds of his idolatrous hearers beyond the limits of their false religion to a true view of the Deity, whom they had styled the "Unknown God." This Being, whom he now 238 declared unto them, was independent of man, needing nothing from human hands to add to His power and glory.

The people were carried away with admiration for Paul's earnest and logical presentation of the attributes of the true God—of His creative power and the existence of His overruling providence. With earnest and fervid eloquence the apostle declared, "God that made the world and all things therein, seeing that He is Lord of heaven and earth, dwelleth not in temples made with hands; neither is worshiped with men's hands, as though He needed anything, seeing He giveth to all life, and breath, and all things." The heavens were not large enough to contain God, how much less were the temples made by human hands!

In that age of caste, when the rights of men were often unrecognized, Paul set forth the great truth of human brotherhood, declaring that God "hath made of one blood all nations of men for to dwell on all the face of the earth." In the sight of God all are on an equality, and to the Creator every human being owes supreme allegiance. Then the apostle showed how, through all God's dealings with man, His purpose of grace and mercy runs like a thread of gold. He "hath determined the times before appointed, and the bounds of their habitation; that they should seek the Lord, if haply they might feel after Him, and find Him, though He be not far from every one of us."

Pointing to the noble specimens of manhood about him, with words borrowed from a poet of their own he pictured the infinite God as a Father, whose children they were. "In Him we live, and move, and have our being," he declared; "as certain also of your own poets 239 have said, For we are also His offspring. Forasmuch then as we are the offspring of God, we ought not to think that the Godhead is like unto gold, or silver, or stone, graven by art and man's device.

"And the times of this ignorance God winked at; but now commandeth all men everywhere to repent." In the ages of darkness that had preceded the advent of Christ, the divine Ruler had passed lightly over the idolatry of the heathen; but now, through His Son, He had sent men the light of truth; and He expected from all repentance unto salvation, not only from the poor and humble, but from the proud philosopher and the princes of the earth. "Because He hath appointed a day, in the which He will judge the world in righteousness by that Man whom He hath ordained; whereof He hath given assurance unto all men, in that He hath raised Him from the dead." As Paul spoke of the resurrection from the dead, "some mocked: and others said, We will hear thee again of this matter."

Thus closed the labors of the apostle at Athens, the center of heathen learning, for the Athenians, clinging persistently to their idolatry, turned from the light of the true religion. When a people are wholly satisfied with their own attainments, little more need be expected of them. Though boasting of learning and refinement, the Athenians were constantly becoming more corrupt and more content with the vague mysteries of idolatry.

Among those who listened to the words of Paul were some to whose minds the truths pre-

240 sented brought conviction, but they would not humble themselves to acknowledge God and to accept the plan of salvation. No eloquence of words, no force of argument, can convert the sinner. The power of God alone can apply the truth to the heart. He who persistently turns from this power cannot be reached. The Greeks sought after wisdom, yet the message of the cross was to them foolishness because they valued their own wisdom more highly than the wisdom that comes from above.

In their pride of intellect and human wisdom may be found the reason why the gospel message met with comparatively little success among the Athenians. The worldly-wise men who come to Christ as poor lost sinners, will become wise unto salvation; but those who come as distinguished men, extolling their own wisdom, will fail of receiving the light and knowledge that He alone can give.

Thus Paul met the paganism of his day. His labors in Athens were not wholly in vain. Dionysius, one of the most prominent citizens, and some others, accepted the gospel message and united themselves fully with the believers.

Inspiration has given us this glance into the life of the Athenians, who, with all their knowledge, refinement, and art, were yet sunken in vice, that it might be seen how God, through His servant, rebuked idolatry and the sins of a proud, self-sufficient people. The words of the apostle, and the description of his attitude and surroundings, as traced by the pen of inspiration, were to be handed down to all coming generations, bearing witness of his unshaken confidence, his courage in loneliness and adversity,

241 and the victory he gained for Christianity in the very heart of paganism.

Paul's words contain a treasure of knowledge for the church. He was in a position where he might easily have said that which would have irritated his proud listeners and brought himself into difficulty. Had his oration been a direct attack upon their gods and the great men of the city, he would have been in danger of meeting the fate of Socrates. But with a tact born of divine love, he carefully drew their minds away from heathen deities, by revealing to them the true God, who was to them unknown.

Today the truths of Scripture are to be brought before the great men of the world in order that they may choose between obedience to God's law and allegiance to the prince of evil. God sets everlasting truth before them—truth that will make them wise unto salvation, but He does not force them to accept it. If they turn from it, He leaves them to themselves, to be filled with the fruit of their own doings.

"The preaching of the cross is to them that perish foolishness; but unto us which are saved it is the power of God. For it is written, I will destroy the wisdom of the wise, and will bring

to nothing the understanding of the prudent." "God hath chosen the foolish things of the world to confound the wise; and God hath chosen the weak things of the world to confound the things which are mighty; and base things of the world, and things which are despised, hath God chosen, yea, and things which are not, to bring to nought things that are." 1 Corinthians 1:18, 19, 27, 28. Many of the greatest scholars and statesmen, the world's most eminent men, will in these last days turn from the light because the world by wisdom knows not God. Yet God's servants are to improve every opportunity to communicate the truth to these men. 242 Some will acknowledge their ignorance of the things of God and will take their place as humble learners at the feet of Jesus, the Master Teacher.

In every effort to reach the higher classes, the worker for God needs strong faith. Appearances may seem forbidding, but in the darkest hour there is light above. The strength of those who love and serve God will be renewed day by day. The understanding of the Infinite is placed at their service, that in carrying out His purposes they may not err. Let these workers hold the beginning of their confidence firm unto the end, remembering that the light of God's truth is to shine amid the darkness that enshrouds our world. There is to be no despondency in connection with God's service. The faith of the consecrated worker is to stand every test brought to bear upon it. God is able and willing to bestow upon His servants all the strength they need and to give them the wisdom that their varied necessities demand. He will more than fulfill the highest expectations of those who put their trust in Him.

24 243

Corinth

During the first century of the Christian Era, Corinth was one of the leading cities, not only of Greece, but of the world. Greeks, Jews, and Romans, with travelers from every land, thronged its streets, eagerly intent on business and pleasure. A great commercial center, situated within easy access of all parts of the Roman Empire, it was an important place in which to establish memorials for God and His truth.

Among the Jews who had taken up their residence in Corinth were Aquila and Priscilla, who afterward became distinguished as earnest workers for Christ. Becoming acquainted with the character of these persons, Paul "abode with them."

At the very beginning of his labors in this thoroughfare of travel, Paul saw on every hand

This chapter is based on Acts 18:1-18.

serious obstacles to the progress of his work. The city was almost wholly given up to idolatry. Venus was the favorite goddess, and with the 244 worship of Venus were connected many demoralizing rites and ceremonies. The Corinthians had become conspicuous, even among the heathen, for their gross immorality. They seemed to have little thought or care beyond the pleasures and gaieties of the hour.

In preaching the gospel in Corinth, the apostle followed a course different from that which had marked his labors at Athens. While in the latter place, he had sought to adapt his style to the character of his audience; he had met logic with logic, science with science, philosophy with philosophy. As he thought of the time thus spent, and realized that his teaching in Athens had been productive of but little fruit, he decided to follow another plan of labor in Corinth in his efforts to arrest the attention of the careless and the indifferent. He determined to avoid elaborate arguments and discussions, and "not to know anything" among the Corinthians "save Jesus Christ, and Him crucified." He would preach to them "not with enticing words of man's wisdom, but in demonstration of the Spirit and of power." 1 Corinthians 2:2, 4.

Jesus, whom Paul was about to present before the Greeks in Corinth as the Christ, was a Jew of lowly origin, reared in a town proverbial for its wickedness. He had been rejected by His own nation and at last crucified as a malefactor. The Greeks believed that there was need of elevating the human race, but they regarded the study of philosophy and science as the only means of attaining to true elevation and honor. Could Paul lead them to believe that faith in the power of this obscure Jew would uplift and ennoble every power of the being?

245 To the minds of multitudes living at the present time, the cross of Calvary is surrounded by sacred memories. Hallowed associations are connected with the scenes of the crucifixion. But in Paul's day the cross was regarded with feelings of repulsion and horror. To uphold as the Saviour of mankind one who had met death on the cross, would naturally call forth ridicule and opposition.

Paul well knew how his message would be regarded by both the Jews and the Greeks of Corinth. "We preach Christ crucified," he admitted, "unto the Jews a stumbling block, and unto the Greeks foolishness." 1 Corinthians 1:23. Among his Jewish hearers there were many who would be angered by the message he was about to proclaim. In the estimation of the Greeks his words would be absurd folly. He would be looked upon as weak-minded for attempting to show how the cross could have any connection with the elevation of the race or the salvation of mankind.

But to Paul the cross was the one object of supreme interest. Ever since he had been arrested in his career of persecution against the followers of the crucified Nazarene he had never ceased to glory in the cross. At that time there had been given him a revelation of the infinite love of God, as revealed in the death of Christ; and a marvelous transformation had been wrought in his life, bringing all his plans and purposes into harmony with heaven. From that hour he had been a new man in Christ. He knew by personal experience that when a sinner once beholds the love of the Father, as seen in the sacrifice of His Son, and yields to the divine influence, a change of heart takes place, and henceforth Christ is all and in all.

At the time of his conversion, Paul was 246 inspired with a longing desire to help his fellow men to behold Jesus of Nazareth as the Son of the living God, mighty to transform and to save. Henceforth his life was wholly devoted to an effort to portray the love and power of the Crucified One. His great heart of sympathy took in all classes. "I am debtor," he declared, "both to the Greeks, and to the barbarians; both to the wise, and to the unwise." Romans 1:14. Love for the Lord of glory, whom he had so relentlessly persecuted in the person of His saints, was the actuating principle of his conduct, his motive power. If ever his ardor in the path of duty flagged, one glance at the cross and the amazing love there revealed, was enough to cause him to gird up the loins of his mind and press forward in the path of self-denial.

Behold the apostle preaching in the synagogue at Corinth, reasoning from the writings of Moses and the prophets, and bringing his hearers down to the advent of the promised Messiah. Listen as he makes plain the work of the Redeemer as the great high priest of mankind—the One who through the sacrifice of His own life was to make atonement for sin once for all, and was then to take up His ministry in the heavenly sanctuary. Paul's hearers were made to understand that the Messiah for whose advent they had been longing, had already come; that His death was the antitype of all the sacrificial offerings, and that His ministry in the sanctuary in heaven was the great object that cast its shadow backward and made clear the ministry of the Jewish priesthood.

Paul "testified to the Jews that Jesus was 247 Christ." From the Old Testament Scriptures he showed that according to the prophecies and the universal expectation of the Jews, the Messiah would be of the lineage of Abraham and of David; then he traced the descent of Jesus from the patriarch Abraham through the royal psalmist. He read the testimony of the prophets regarding the character and work of the promised Messiah, and His reception and treatment on the earth; then he showed that all these predictions had been fulfilled in the life, ministry, and death of Jesus of Nazareth.

Paul showed that Christ had come to offer salvation first of all to the nation that was looking for the Messiah's coming as the consummation and glory of their national existence. But that nation had rejected Him who would have given them life, and had chosen another leader, whose reign would end in death. He endeavored to bring home to his hearers the fact that repentance alone could save the Jewish nation from impending ruin. He revealed their ignorance concerning the meaning of those Scriptures which it was their chief boast and glory that they fully understood. He rebuked their worldliness, their love of station, titles, and display, and their inordinate selfishness.

In the power of the Spirit, Paul related the story of his own miraculous conversion and of his confidence in the Old Testament Scriptures, which had been so completely fulfilled in Jesus of Nazareth. His words were spoken with solemn earnestness, and his hearers could not 248 but discern that he loved with all his heart the crucified and risen Saviour. They saw that his mind was centered in Christ, that his whole life was bound up with his Lord. So impressive were his words, that only those who were filled with the bitterest hatred against the Christian religion could stand unmoved by them.

But the Jews of Corinth closed their eyes to the evidence so clearly presented by the apostle, and refused to listen to his appeals. The same spirit that had led them to reject Christ, filled them with wrath and fury against His servant; and had not God especially protected him, that he might continue to bear the gospel message to the Gentiles, they would have put an end to his life.

"And when they opposed themselves, and blasphemed, he shook his raiment, and said unto them, Your blood be upon your own heads; I am clean: from henceforth I will go unto the Gentiles. And he departed thence, and entered into a certain man's house, named Justus, one that worshiped God, whose house joined hard to the synagogue."

Silas and Timothy had "come from Macedonia" to help Paul, and together they labored for the Gentiles. To the heathen, as well as to the Jews, Paul and his companions preached Christ as the Saviour of the fallen race. Avoiding complicated, far-fetched reasoning, the messengers of the cross dwelt upon the attributes of the Creator of the world, the Supreme Ruler of the universe. Their hearts aglow with the love of God and of His Son, they appealed to the heathen to behold the infinite sacrifice made in man's behalf. They knew that if those who had long 249 been groping in the darkness of heathenism could but see the light streaming from Calvary's cross, they would be drawn to the Redeemer. "I, if I be lifted up," the Saviour had declared, "will draw all men unto Me." John 12:32.

The gospel workers in Corinth realized the terrible dangers threatening the souls of those for whom they were laboring; and it was with a sense of the responsibility resting on them that they presented the truth as it is in Jesus. Clear, plain, and decided was their message—a savor of life unto life, or of death unto death. And not only in their words, but in the daily life, was the gospel revealed. Angels co-operated with them, and the grace and power of God was shown in the conversion of many. "Crispus, the chief ruler of the synagogue, believed on the Lord with all his house; and many of the Corinthians hearing believed, and were baptized."

The hatred with which the Jews had always regarded the apostles was now intensified. The conversion and baptism of Crispus had the effect of exasperating instead of convincing these stubborn opposers. They could not bring arguments to disprove Paul's preaching, and for lack of such evidence they resorted to deception and malignant attack. They blasphemed the gospel and the name of Jesus. In their blind anger no words were too bitter, no device too low, for them to use. They could not deny that Christ had worked miracles; but they declared that He had performed them through the power of Satan; and they boldly affirmed that the wonderful works wrought by Paul were accomplished through the same agency.

Though Paul had a measure of success in 250 Corinth, yet the wickedness that he saw and heard in that corrupt city almost disheartened him. The depravity that he witnessed among the Gentiles, and the contempt and insult that he received from the Jews, caused him great anguish of spirit. He doubted the wisdom of trying to build up a church from the material that he found there.

As he was planning to leave the city for a more promising field, and seeking earnestly to understand his duty, the Lord appeared to him in a vision and said, "Be not afraid, but speak, and hold not thy peace: for I am with thee, and no man shall set on thee to hurt thee: for I have much people in this city." Paul understood this to be a command to remain in Corinth and a guarantee that the Lord would give increase to the seed sown. Strengthened and encouraged, he continued to labor there with zeal and perseverance.

The apostle's efforts were not confined to public speaking; there were many who could not have been reached in that way. He spent much time in house-to-house labor, thus availing himself of the familiar intercourse of the home circle. He visited the sick and the sorrowing, comforted the afflicted, and lifted up the oppressed. And in all that he said and did he magnified the name of Jesus. Thus he labored, "in weakness, and in fear, and in much trembling." 1 Corinthians 2:3. He trembled lest his teaching should reveal the impress of the human rather than the divine.

"We speak wisdom among them that are perfect," Paul afterward declared; "yet not the wisdom of this world, nor of the princes of this world, that come to nought: but we speak the wisdom of God in a mystery, even the hidden wisdom, which God ordained before the world unto our glory: which none of the princes of this world knew: for had they known it, they would not have crucified the Lord of glory. But as it is written, Eye hath not seen, nor ear heard, neither have entered into the heart of man, the things which God hath prepared for them that love Him. But God hath revealed them unto us by His Spirit: for the Spirit searcheth all things, yea, the deep things of God. For what man knoweth the things of a man, save the spirit of man which is in him? even so the things of God knoweth no man, but the Spirit of God.

"Now we have received, not the spirit of the world, but the spirit which is of God; that we might know the things that are freely given to us of God. Which things also we speak, not in the words which man's wisdom teacheth, but which the Holy Ghost teacheth; comparing spiritual things with spiritual." 1 Corinthians 2:6-13.

Paul realized that his sufficiency was not in himself, but in the presence of the Holy Spirit, whose gracious influence filled his heart, bringing every thought into subjection to Christ. He spoke of himself as "always bearing about in the body the dying of the Lord Jesus, that the life also of Jesus might be made manifest in our body." 2 Corinthians 4:10. In the apostle's teachings Christ was the central figure. "I live," he declared, "yet not I, but Christ liveth in me." Galatians 2:20. Self was hidden; Christ was revealed and exalted.

Paul was an eloquent speaker. Before his conversion he had often sought to impress his hearers by flights of oratory. But now he set all this aside. Instead of indulging in poetic descriptions and fanciful representations, which might please the senses and feed the imagination, but which would not touch the daily experience, Paul sought by the use of simple language to bring home to the heart the truths that are of vital importance. Fanciful representations of truth may cause an ecstasy of feeling, but all too often truths presented in this way do not supply the food necessary to strengthen and fortify the believer for the battles of life. The immediate needs, the present trials, of struggling souls—these must be met with sound, practical instruction in the fundamental principles of Christianity.

Paul's efforts in Corinth were not without fruit. Many turned from the worship of idols to serve the living God, and a large church was enrolled under the banner of Christ. Some were rescued from among the most dissipated of the Gentiles and became monuments of the mercy of God and the efficacy of the blood of Christ to cleanse from sin.

The increased success that Paul had in presenting Christ, roused the unbelieving Jews to more determined opposition. They rose in a body and "made insurrection with one accord against Paul, and brought him to the judgment seat" of Gallio, who was then proconsul of Achaia. They expected that the authorities, as on former occasions, would side with them; and with loud, angry voices they uttered their complaints against the apostle, saying, "This fellow persuadeth men to worship God contrary to the law."

The Jewish religion was under the protection of the Roman power, and the accusers of Paul thought that if they could fasten upon him the charge of violating the laws of their religion, he would probably be delivered to them for trial and sentence. They hoped thus to compass his death. But Gallio was a man of integrity, and refused to become the dupe of the jealous, intriguing Jews. Disgusted with their bigotry and self-righteousness, he would take no notice of the charge. As Paul prepared to speak in self-defense, Gallio told him that it was not necessary. Then turning to the angry accusers, he said, "If it were a matter of wrong or wicked lewdness, O ye Jews, reason would that I should bear with you: but if it be a question of words and names, and of your law, look ye to it; for I will be no judge of such matters. And he drave them from the judgment seat."

Both Jews and Greeks had waited eagerly for Gallio's decision; and his immediate dismissal of the case, as one that had no bearing upon the public interest, was the signal for the Jews to retire, baffled and angry. The proconsul's decided course opened the eyes of the clamorous crowd who had been abetting the Jews. For the first time during Paul's labors in Europe, the mob turned to his side; under the very eye of the proconsul, and without interference from him, they violently beset the most prominent accusers of the apostle. "All the Greeks took Sosthenes, the chief ruler of the synagogue, and beat him before the judgment seat. And Gallio cared for none of those things." Thus Christianity obtained a signal victory.

"Paul after this tarried there yet a good while." If the apostle had at this time been compelled to leave Corinth, the converts to the faith of Jesus would have been placed in a perilous position. The Jews would have endeavored to follow up the advantage gained, even to the extermination of Christianity in that region.

255

25

The Thessalonian Letters

The arrival of Silas and Timothy from Macedonia, during Paul's sojourn in Corinth, had greatly cheered the apostle. They brought him "good tidings" of the "faith and charity" of those who had accepted the truth during the first visit of the gospel messengers to Thessalonica. Paul's heart went out in tender sympathy toward these believers, who, in the midst of trial and adversity, had remained true to God. He longed to visit them in person, but as this was not then possible, he wrote to them.

In this letter to the church at Thessalonica the apostle expresses his gratitude to God for the joyful news of their increase of faith. "Brethren," he wrote, "we were comforted over you in all our affliction and distress by your faith: for now we live, if ye stand fast in the Lord. For what thanks can we render to God again for you, for all the joy wherewith we joy for your sakes before our God; night and day praying exceedingly that we might see your face, and might perfect that which is lacking in your faith?"

256 "We give thanks to God always for you all, making mention of you in our prayers; remembering without ceasing your work of faith, and labor of love, and patience of hope in our Lord Jesus Christ, in the sight of God and our Father."

Many of the believers in Thessalonica had "turned . . . from idols to serve the living and true God." They had "received the word in much affliction;" and their hearts were filled with "joy of the Holy Ghost." The apostle declared that in their faithfulness in following the Lord they were "ensamples to all that believe in Macedonia and Achaia." These words of commendation were not unmerited; "for from you," he wrote, "sounded out the word of the Lord not only in Macedonia and Achaia, but also in every place your faith to Godward is spread abroad."

The Thessalonian believers were true missionaries. Their hearts burned with zeal for their Saviour, who had delivered them from fear of "the wrath to come." Through the grace of Christ a marvelous transformation had taken place in their lives, and the word of the Lord, as spoken through them, was accompanied with power. Hearts were won by the truths presented, and souls were added to the number of believers.

In this first epistle, Paul referred to his manner of labor among the Thessalonians. He declared that he had not sought to win converts

through deception or guile. "As we were allowed of God to be put in trust with the gospel, even so we speak; not as pleasing men, but God, which trieth our hearts. For neither at 257 any time used we flattering words, as ye know, nor a cloak of covetousness; God is witness: nor of men sought we glory, neither of you, nor yet of others, when we might have been burdensome, as the apostles of Christ. But we were gentle among you, even as a nurse cherisheth her children: so being affectionately desirous of you, we were willing to have imparted unto you, not the gospel of God only, but also our own souls, because ye were dear unto us."

"Ye are witnesses, and God also," the apostle continued, "how holily and justly and unblamably we behaved ourselves among you that believe: as ye know how we exhorted and comforted and charged every one of you, as a father doth his children, that ye would walk worthy of God, who hath called you unto His kingdom and glory.

"For this cause also thank we God without ceasing, because, when ye receive the word of God which ye heard of us, ye received it not as the word of men, but as it is in truth, the word of God, which effectually worketh also in you that believe." "What is our hope, or joy, or crown of rejoicing? Are not even ye in the presence of our Lord Jesus Christ at His coming? For ye are our glory and joy."

In his first epistle to the Thessalonian believers, Paul endeavored to instruct them regarding the true state of the dead. He spoke of those who die as being asleep—in a state of unconsciousness: "I would not have you to be ignorant, brethren, concerning them which are asleep, that ye sorrow not, even as others which have no hope. For if we believe that Jesus died 258 and rose again, even so them also which sleep in Jesus will God bring with Him. . . . For the Lord Himself shall descend from heaven with a shout, with the voice of the Archangel, and with the trump of God: and the dead in Christ shall rise first: then we which are alive and remain shall be caught up together with them in the clouds, to meet the Lord in the air: and so shall we ever be with the Lord."

The Thessalonians had eagerly grasped the idea that Christ was coming to change the faithful who were alive, and to take them to Himself. They had carefully guarded the lives of their friends, lest they should die and lose the blessing which they looked forward to receiving at the coming of their Lord. But one after another their loved ones had been taken from them, and with anguish the Thessalonians had looked for the last time upon the faces of their dead, hardly daring to hope to meet them in a future life.

As Paul's epistle was opened and read, great joy and consolation was brought to the church by the words revealing the true state of the dead.

This chapter is based on Epistles to the Thessalonians.

Paul showed that those living when Christ should come would not go to meet their Lord in advance of those who had fallen asleep in Jesus. The voice of the Archangel and the trump of God would reach the sleeping ones, and the dead in Christ should rise first, before the touch of immortality should be given to the living. "Then we which are alive and remain shall be caught up together with them in the clouds, to meet the Lord in the air: and so shall we ever be with the Lord. Wherefore comfort one another with these words."

259 The hope and joy that this assurance brought to the young church at Thessalonica can scarcely be appreciated by us. They believed and cherished the letter sent to them by their father in the gospel, and their hearts went out in love to him. He had told them these things before; but at that time their minds were striving to grasp doctrines that seemed new and strange, and it is not surprising that the force of some points had not been vividly impressed on their minds. But they were hungering for truth, and Paul's epistle gave them new hope and strength, and a firmer faith in, and a deeper affection for, the One who through His death had brought life and immortality to light.

Now they rejoiced in the knowledge that their believing friends would be raised from the grave to live forever in the kingdom of God. The darkness that had enshrouded the resting place of the dead was dispelled. A new splendor crowned the Christian faith, and they saw a new glory in the life, death, and resurrection of Christ.

"Even so them also which sleep in Jesus will God bring with Him," Paul wrote. Many interpret this passage to mean that the sleeping ones will be brought with Christ from heaven; but Paul meant that as Christ was raised from the dead, so God will call the sleeping saints from their graves and take them with Him to heaven. Precious consolation! glorious hope! not only to the church of Thessalonica, but to all Christians wherever they may be.

While laboring at Thessalonica, Paul had so fully covered the subject of the signs of the times, showing what events would occur prior 260 to the revelation of the Son of man in the clouds of heaven, that he did not think it necessary to write at length regarding this subject. He, however, pointedly referred to his former teachings. "Of the times and the seasons," he said, "ye have no need that I write unto you. For yourselves know perfectly that the day of the Lord so cometh as a thief in the night. For when they shall say, Peace and safety; then sudden destruction cometh upon them."

There are in the world today many who close their eyes to the evidences that Christ has given to warn men of His coming. They seek to quiet all apprehension, while at the same time the

signs of the end are rapidly fulfilling, and the world is hastening to the time when the Son of man shall be revealed in the clouds of heaven. Paul teaches that it is sinful to be indifferent to the signs which are to precede the second coming of Christ. Those guilty of this neglect he calls children of the night and of darkness. He encourages the vigilant and watchful with these words: "But ye, brethren, are not in darkness, that that day should overtake you as a thief. Ye are all the children of light, and the children of the day: we are not of the night, nor of darkness. Therefore let us not sleep, as do others; but let us watch and be sober."

Especially important to the church in our time are the teachings of the apostle upon this point. To those living so near the great consummation, the words of Paul should come with telling force: "Let us, who are of the day, be sober, 261 putting on the breastplate of faith and love; and for a helmet, the hope of salvation. For God hath not appointed us to wrath, but to obtain salvation by our Lord Jesus Christ, who died for us, that, whether we wake or sleep, we should live together with Him."

The watchful Christian is a working Christian, seeking zealously to do all in his power for the advancement of the gospel. As love for his Redeemer increases, so also does love for his fellow men. He has severe trials, as had his Master; but he does not allow affliction to sour his temper or destroy his peace of mind. He knows that trial, if well borne, will refine and purify him, and bring him into closer fellowship with Christ. Those who are partakers of Christ's sufferings will also be partakers of His consolation and at last sharers of His glory.

"We beseech you, brethren," Paul continued in his letter to the Thessalonians, "to know them which labor among you, and are over you in the Lord, and admonish you; and to esteem them very highly in love for their work's sake. And be at peace among yourselves."

The Thessalonian believers were greatly annoyed by men coming among them with fanatical ideas and doctrines. Some were "disorderly, working not at all, but . . . busybodies." The church had been properly organized, and officers had been appointed to act as ministers and deacons. But there were some, self-willed and impetuous, who refused to be subordinate to those who held positions of authority in the church. They claimed not only the right of private judgment, but that of publicly urging their views upon the church. In view of this, Paul called the attention of the Thessalonians to the respect and deference due to those who had 262 been chosen to occupy positions of authority in the church.

In his anxiety that the believers at Thessalonica should walk in the fear of God, the apostle pleaded with them to reveal practical godliness in the daily life. "We beseech you, brethren," he wrote, "and exhort you by the Lord Jesus, that as ye have received of us how ye ought to walk and to please God, so ye would abound more and more. For ye know what commandments we gave you by the Lord Jesus. For this is the will of God, even your sanctification, that ye should abstain from fornication." "For God hath not called us unto uncleanness, but unto holiness."

The apostle felt that he was to a large extent responsible for the spiritual welfare of those converted under his labors. His desire for them was that they might increase in a knowledge of the only true God, and Jesus Christ, whom He had sent. Often in his ministry he would meet with little companies of men and women who loved Jesus, and bow with them in prayer, asking God to teach them how to maintain a living connection with Him. Often he took counsel with them as to the best methods of giving to others the light of gospel truth. And often, when separated from those for whom he had thus labored, he pleaded with God to keep them from evil and help them to be earnest, active missionaries.

One of the strongest evidences of true conversion is love to God and man. Those who accept Jesus as their Redeemer have a deep, sincere love for others of like precious faith. Thus it was with the believers at Thessalonica. "As 263 touching brotherly love," the apostle wrote, "ye need not that I write unto you: for ye yourselves are taught of God to love one another. And indeed ye do it toward all the brethren which are in all Macedonia: but we beseech you, brethren, that ye increase more and more; and that ye study to be quiet, and to do your own business, and to work with your own hands, as we commanded you; that ye may walk honestly toward them that are without, and that ye may have lack of nothing."

"The Lord make you to increase and abound in love one toward another, and toward all men, even as we do toward you: to the end He may stablish your hearts unblamable in holiness before God, even our Father, at the coming of our Lord Jesus Christ with all His saints."

"Now we exhort you, brethren, warn them that are unruly, comfort the feeble-minded, support the weak, be patient toward all men. See that none render evil for evil unto any man; but ever follow that which is good, both among yourselves, and to all men. Rejoice evermore. Pray without ceasing. In everything give thanks: for this is the will of God in Christ Jesus concerning you."

The apostle cautioned the Thessalonians not to despise the gift of prophecy, and in the words, "Quench not the Spirit; despise not prophesyings; prove all things; hold fast that which is good," he enjoined a careful discrimi-

nation in distinguishing the false from the true. He besought them to "abstain from all appearance of evil;" and closed his letter with the prayer that God would sanctify them wholly, that in "Spirit and soul and body" they might 264 "be preserved blameless unto the coming of our Lord Jesus Christ. Faithful is He that calleth you," he added, "who also will do it."

The instruction that Paul sent the Thessalonians in his first epistle regarding the second coming of Christ, was in perfect harmony with his former teaching. Yet his words were misapprehended by some of the Thessalonian brethren. They understood him to express the hope that he himself would live to witness the Saviour's advent. This belief served to increase their enthusiasm and excitement. Those who had previously neglected their responsibilities and duties, now became more persistent in urging their erroneous views.

In his second letter Paul sought to correct their misunderstanding of his teaching and to set before them his true position. He again expressed his confidence in their integrity, and his gratitude that their faith was strong, and that their love abounded for one another and for the cause of their Master. He told them that he presented them to other churches as an example of the patient, persevering faith that bravely withstands persecution and tribulation, and he carried their minds forward to the time of the second coming of Christ, when the people of God shall rest from all their cares and perplexities.

"We ourselves," he wrote, "glory in you in the churches of God for your patience and faith in all your persecutions and tribulations that ye endure: . . . and to you who are troubled rest with us, when the Lord Jesus shall be revealed from heaven with His mighty angels, in flaming 265 fire taking vengeance on them that know not God, and that obey not the gospel of our Lord Jesus Christ: who shall be punished with everlasting destruction from the presence of the Lord, and from the glory of His power. . . . Wherefore also we pray always for you, that our God would count you worthy of this calling, and fulfill all the good pleasure of His goodness, and the work of faith with power: that the name of our Lord Jesus Christ may be glorified in you, and ye in Him, according to the grace of our God and the Lord Jesus Christ."

But before the coming of Christ, important developments in the religious world, foretold in prophecy, were to take place. The apostle declared: "Be not soon shaken in mind, or be troubled, neither by spirit, nor by word, nor by letter as from us, as that the day of Christ is at hand. Let no man deceive you by any means: for that day shall not come, except there come a falling away first, and that man of sin be revealed, the son of perdition; who opposeth and exalteth himself above all that is called

God, or that is worshiped; so that he as God sitteth in the temple of God, showing himself that he is God."

Paul's words were not to be misinterpreted. It was not to be taught that he, by special revelation, had warned the Thessalonians of the immediate coming of Christ. Such a position would cause confusion of faith; for disappointment often leads to unbelief. The apostle therefore cautioned the brethren to receive no such 266 message as coming from him, and he proceeded to emphasize the fact that the papal power, so clearly described by the prophet Daniel, was yet to rise and wage war against God's people. Until this power should have performed its deadly and blasphemous work, it would be in vain for the church to look for the coming of their Lord. "Remember ye not," Paul inquired, "that, when I was yet with you, I told you these things?"

Terrible were the trials that were to beset the true church. Even at the time when the apostle was writing, the "mystery of iniquity" had already begun to work. The developments that were to take place in the future were to be "after the working of Satan with all power and signs and lying wonders, and with all deceivableness of unrighteousness in them that perish."

Especially solemn is the apostle's statement regarding those who should refuse to receive "the love of the truth." "For this cause," he declared of all who should deliberately reject the messages of truth, "God shall send them strong delusion, that they should believe a lie: that they all might be damned who believed not the truth, but had pleasure in unrighteousness." Men cannot with impunity reject the warnings that God in mercy sends them. From those who persist in turning from these warnings, God withdraws His Spirit, leaving them to the deceptions that they love.

Thus Paul outlined the baleful work of that power of evil which was to continue through long centuries of darkness and persecution before the second coming of Christ. The Thessalonian believers had hoped for immediate 267 deliverance; now they were admonished to take up bravely and in the fear of God the work before them. The apostle charged them not to neglect their duties or resign themselves to idle waiting. After their glowing anticipations of immediate deliverance the round of daily life and the opposition that they must meet would appear doubly forbidding. He therefore exhorted them to steadfastness in the faith:

"Stand fast, and hold the traditions which ye have been taught, whether by word, or our epistle. Now our Lord Jesus Christ Himself, and God, even our Father, which hath loved us, and hath given us everlasting consolation and good hope through grace, comfort your hearts, and stablish you in every good word and work."

"The Lord is faithful, who shall stablish you, and keep you from evil. And we have confidence in the Lord touching you, that ye both do and will do the things which we command you. And the Lord direct your hearts into the love of God, and into the patient waiting for Christ."

The work of the believers had been given them by God. By their faithful adherence to the truth they were to give to others the light which they had received. The apostle bade them not to become weary in well-doing, and pointed them to his own example of diligence in temporal matters while laboring with untiring zeal in the cause of Christ. He reproved those who had given themselves up to sloth and aimless excitement, and directed that "with quietness they work, and eat their own bread." He also enjoined upon the church to separate from their 268 fellowship anyone who should persist in disregarding the instruction given by God's ministers. "Yet," he added, "count him not as an enemy, but admonish him as a brother."

This epistle also Paul concluded with a prayer that amidst life's toils and trials the peace of God and the grace of the Lord Jesus Christ might be their consolation and support.

26
269

Apollos at Corinth

After leaving Corinth, Paul's next scene of labor was Ephesus. He was on his way to Jerusalem to attend an approaching festival, and his stay at Ephesus was necessarily brief. He reasoned with the Jews in the synagogue, and so favorable was the impression made upon them that they entreated him to continue his labors among them. His plan to visit Jerusalem prevented him from tarrying then, but he promised to return to them, "if God will." Aquila and Priscilla had accompanied him to Ephesus, and he left them there to carry on the work that he had begun.

It was at this time that "a certain Jew named Apollos, born at Alexandria, an eloquent man, and mighty in the Scriptures, came to Ephesus." He had heard the preaching of John the Baptist, had received the baptism of repentance, and was a living witness that the work of the prophet had not been in vain. The Scripture record of Apollos is that he "was instructed in the way of the 270 Lord; and being fervent in the spirit, he spake and taught diligently the things of the Lord, knowing only the baptism of John."

While in Ephesus, Apollos "began to speak boldly in the synagogue." Among his hearers were Aquila and Priscilla, who, perceiving that he had not yet received the full light of the gospel, "took him unto them, and expounded

This chapter is based on Acts 18:18-28.

unto him the way of God more perfectly." Through their teaching he obtained a clearer understanding of the Scriptures and became one of the ablest advocates of the Christian faith.

Apollos was desirous of going on into Achaia, and the brethren at Ephesus "wrote, exhorting the disciples to receive him" as a teacher in full harmony with the church of Christ. He went to Corinth, where, in public labor and from house to house, "he mightily convinced the Jews, . . . showing by the Scriptures that Jesus was Christ." Paul had planted the seed of truth; Apollos now watered it. The success that attended Apollos in preaching the gospel led some of the believers to exalt his labors above those of Paul. This comparison of man with man brought into the church a party spirit that threatened to hinder greatly the progress of the gospel.

During the year and a half that Paul had spent in Corinth, he had purposely presented the gospel in its simplicity. "Not with excellency of speech or of wisdom" had he come to the Corinthians; but with fear and trembling, and "in demonstration of the Spirit and of power," had he declared "the testimony of God," that their "faith should not stand in the wisdom of men, but in the power of God." 1 Corinthians 2:1, 4, 5.

271 Paul had necessarily adapted his manner of teaching to the condition of the church. "I, brethren, could not speak unto you as unto spiritual," he afterward explained to them, "but as unto carnal, even as unto babes in Christ. I have fed you with milk, and not with meat: for hitherto ye were not able to bear it, neither yet now are ye able." 1 Corinthians 3:1, 2. Many of the Corinthian believers had been slow to learn the lessons that he was endeavoring to teach them. Their advancement in spiritual knowledge had not been proportionate to their privileges and opportunities. When they should have been far advanced in Christian experience, and able to comprehend and to practice the deeper truths of the word, they were standing where the disciples stood when Christ said to them, "I have yet many things to say unto you, but ye cannot bear them now." John 16:12. Jealousy, evil surmising, and accusation had closed the hearts of many of the Corinthian believers against the full working of the Holy Spirit, which "searcheth all things, yea, the deep things of God." 1 Corinthians 2:10. However wise they might be in worldly knowledge, they were but babes in the knowledge of Christ.

It had been Paul's work to instruct the Corinthian converts in the rudiments, the very alphabet, of the Christian faith. He had been obliged to instruct them as those who were ignorant of the operations of divine power upon the heart. At that time they were unable to comprehend the mysteries of salvation; for "the natural man receiveth not the things of the Spirit of God: for they are foolishness unto him: neither can he know them, because they are spiritually 272 discerned." Verse 14. Paul had endeavored to sow the seed, which others must water. Those who followed him must carry forward the work from the point where he had left it, giving spiritual light and knowledge in due season, as the church was able to bear it.

When the apostle took up his work in Corinth, he realized that he must introduce most carefully the great truths he wished to teach. He knew that among his hearers would be proud believers in human theories, and exponents of false systems of worship, who were groping with blind eyes, hoping to find in the book of nature theories that would contradict the reality of the spiritual and immortal life as revealed in the Scriptures. He also knew that critics would endeavor to controvert the Christian interpretation of the revealed word, and that skeptics would treat the gospel of Christ with scoffing and derision.

As he endeavored to lead souls to the foot of the cross, Paul did not venture to rebuke, directly, those who were licentious, or to show how heinous was their sin in the sight of a holy God. Rather he set before them the true object of life and tried to impress upon their minds the lessons of the divine Teacher, which, if received, would lift them from worldliness and sin to purity and righteousness. He dwelt especially upon practical godliness and the holiness to which those must attain who shall be accounted worthy of a place in God's kingdom. He longed to see the light of the gospel of Christ piercing the darkness of their minds, that they might see how offensive in the sight of God were their immoral practices. Therefore the burden of his teaching among them was Christ and Him crucified. He sought to show them that 273 their most earnest study and their greatest joy must be the wonderful truth of salvation through repentance toward God and faith in the Lord Jesus Christ.

The philosopher turns aside from the light of salvation, because it puts his proud theories to shame; the worldling refuses to receive it, because it would separate him from his earthly idols. Paul saw that the character of Christ must be understood before men could love Him or view the cross with the eye of faith. Here must begin that study which shall be the science and the song of the redeemed through all eternity. In the light of the cross alone can the true value of the human soul be estimated.

The refining influence of the grace of God changes the natural disposition of man. Heaven would not be desirable to the carnal-minded; their natural, unsanctified hearts would feel no attraction toward that pure and holy place, and if it were possible for them to enter, they would find there nothing congenial. The propensities that control the natural heart must be subdued by the grace of Christ before fallen man is fitted to enter heaven and enjoy the society of the pure, holy angels. When man dies to sin and is quickened to new life in Christ, divine love fills his heart; his understanding is sanctified; he drinks from an inexhaustible fountain of joy and knowledge, and the light of an eternal day shines upon his path, for with him continually is the Light of life.

Paul had sought to impress upon the minds of his Corinthian brethren the fact that he and the ministers associated with him were but men 274 commissioned by God to teach the truth, that they were all engaged in the same work, and that they were alike dependent upon God for success in their labors. The discussion that had arisen in the church regarding the relative merits of different ministers was not in the order of God, but was the result of cherishing the attributes of the natural heart. "While one saith, I am of Paul; and another, I am of Apollos; are ye not carnal? Who then is Paul, and who is Apollos, but ministers by whom ye believed, even as the Lord gave to every man? I have planted, Apollos watered; but God gave the increase. So then neither is he that planteth anything, neither he that watereth; but God that giveth the increase." 1 Corinthians 3:4-7.

It was Paul who had first preached the gospel in Corinth, and who had organized the church there. This was the work that the Lord had assigned him. Later, by God's direction, other workers were brought in, to stand in their lot and place. The seed sown must be watered, and this Apollos was to do. He followed Paul in his work, to give further instruction, and to help the seed sown to develop. He won his way to the hearts of the people, but it was God who gave the increase. It is not human, but divine power, that works transformation of character. Those who plant and those who water do not cause the growth of the seed; they work under God, as His appointed agencies, co-operating with Him in His work. To the Master Worker belongs the honor and glory that comes with success.

God's servants do not all possess the same gifts, but they are all His workmen. Each is to 275 learn of the Great Teacher, and is then to communicate what he has learned. God has given to each of His messengers an individual work. There is a diversity of gifts, but all the workers are to blend in harmony, controlled by the sanctifying influence of the Holy Spirit. As they make known the gospel of salvation, many will be convicted and converted by the power of God. The human instrumentality is hid with Christ in God, and Christ appears as the chiefest among ten thousand, the One altogether lovely.

"Now he that planteth and he that watereth are one: and every man shall receive his own reward according to his own labor. For we are laborers together with God: ye are God's husbandry, ye are God's building." Verses 8, 9. In this scripture the apostle compares the church to a cultivated field, in which the husbandmen labor, caring for the vines of the Lord's planting; and also to a building, which is to grow into a holy temple for the Lord. God is the Master Worker, and He has appointed to each man his work. All are to labor under His supervision, letting Him work for and through His workmen. He gives them tact and skill, and if they heed His instruction, crowns their efforts with success.

God's servants are to work together, blending in kindly, courteous order, "in honor preferring one another." Romans 12:10. There is to be no unkind criticism, no pulling to pieces of another's work; and there are to be no separate parties. Every man to whom the Lord has entrusted a message has his specific work. Each one has an individuality of his own, which he is not to sink in that of any other man. Yet each is to 276 work in harmony with his brethren. In their service God's workers are to be essentially one. No one is to set himself up as a criterion, speaking disrespectfully of his fellow workers or treating them as inferior. Under God each is to do his appointed work, respected, loved, and encouraged by the other laborers. Together they are to carry the work forward to completion.

These principles are dwelt upon at length in Paul's first letter to the Corinthian church. The apostle refers to "the ministers of Christ" as "stewards of the mysteries of God," and of their work he declares: "It is required in stewards, that a man be found faithful. But with me it is a very small thing that I should be judged of you, or of man's judgment: yea, I judge not mine own self. For I know nothing by myself; yet am I not hereby justified: but He that judgeth me is the Lord. Therefore judge nothing before the time, until the Lord come, who both will bring to light the hidden things of darkness, and will make manifest the counsels of the hearts: and then shall every man have praise of God." 1 Corinthians 4:1-5.

It is not given to any human being to judge between the different servants of God. The Lord alone is the judge of man's work, and He will give to each his just reward.

The apostle, continuing, referred directly to the comparisons that had been made between his labors and those of Apollos: "These things, brethren, I have in a figure transferred to myself and to Apollos for your sakes; that ye might learn in us not to think of men above that which is written, that no one of you be puffed up for 277 one against another. For who maketh thee to differ from another? and what hast thou that thou didst not receive? now if thou didst receive it, why dost thou glory, as if thou hadst not received it?" Verses 6, 7.

Paul plainly set before the church the perils and the hardships that he and his associates had patiently endured in their service for Christ. "Even unto this present hour," he declared, "we both hunger, and thirst, and are naked, and are buffeted, and have no certain dwelling place; and labor, working with our own hands: being reviled, we bless; being persecuted, we suffer it: being defamed, we entreat: we are made as the filth of the world, and are the offscouring of all things unto this day. I write not these things to shame you, but as my beloved sons I warn you. For though ye have ten thousand instructors in Christ, yet have ye not many fathers: for in Christ Jesus I have begotten you through the gospel." Verses 11-15.

He who sends forth gospel workers as His ambassadors is dishonored when there is manifested among the hearers so strong an attachment to some favorite minister that there is an unwillingness to accept the labors of some other teacher. The Lord sends help to His people, not always as they may choose, but as they need; for men are shortsighted and cannot discern what is for their highest good. It is seldom that one minister has all the qualifications necessary to perfect a church in all the requirements of Christianity; therefore God often sends to them 278 other ministers, each possessing some qualifications in which the others were deficient.

The church should gratefully accept these servants of Christ, even as they would accept the Master Himself. They should seek to derive all the benefit possible from the instruction which each minister may give them from the word of God. The truths that the servants of God bring are to be accepted and appreciated in the meekness of humility, but no minister is to be idolized.

Through the grace of Christ, God's ministers are made messengers of light and blessing. As by earnest, persevering prayer they obtain the endowment of the Holy Spirit and go forth weighted with the burden of soulsaving, their hearts filled with zeal to extend the triumphs of the cross, they will see fruit of their labors. Resolutely refusing to display human wisdom or to exalt self, they will accomplish a work that will withstand the assaults of Satan. Many souls will be turned from darkness to light, and many churches will be established. Men will be converted, not to the human instrumentality, but to Christ. Self will be kept in the background; Jesus only, the Man of Calvary, will appear.

Those who are working for Christ today may reveal the same distinguishing excellencies revealed by those who in the apostolic age proclaimed the gospel. God is just as ready to give power to His servants today as He was to give power to Paul and Apollos, to Silas and Timothy, to Peter, James, and John.

In the apostles' day there were some misguided souls who claimed to believe in Christ, yet refused to show respect to His ambassadors. They declared that they followed no human 279 teacher, but were taught directly by Christ without the aid of the ministers of the gospel. They were independent in spirit and unwilling to submit to the voice of the church. Such men were in grave danger of being deceived.

God has placed in the church, as His appointed helpers, men of varied talents, that through the combined wisdom of many the mind of the Spirit may be met. Men who move in accordance with their own strong traits of character, refusing to yoke up with others who have had a long experience in the work of God, will become blinded by self-confidence, unable to discern between the false and the true. It is not safe for such ones to be chosen as leaders in the church; for they would follow their own judgment and plans, regardless of the judgment of their brethren. It is easy for the enemy to work through those who, themselves needing counsel at every step, undertake the guardianship of souls in their own strength, without having learned the lowliness of Christ.

Impressions alone are not a safe guide to duty. The enemy often persuades men to believe that it is God who is guiding them, when in reality they are following only human impulse. But if we watch carefully, and take counsel with our brethren, we shall be given an understanding of the Lord's will; for the promise is, "The meek will He guide in judgment: and the meek will He teach His way." Psalm 25:9.

In the early Christian church there were some who refused to recognize either Paul or Apollos, but held that Peter was their leader. They affirmed that Peter had been most intimate with 280 Christ when the Master was upon the earth, while Paul had been a persecutor of the believers. Their views and feelings were bound about by prejudice. They did not show the liberality, the generosity, the tenderness, which reveals that Christ is abiding in the heart.

There was danger that this party spirit would result in great evil to the Christian church, and Paul was instructed by the Lord to utter words of earnest admonition and solemn protest. Of those who were saying, "I am of Paul; and I of Apollos; and I of Cephas; and I of Christ," the apostle inquired, "Is Christ divided? was Paul crucified for you? or were ye baptized in the name of Paul?" "Let no man glory in men," he pleaded. "For all things are yours; whether Paul, or Apollos, or Cephas, or the world, or life, or death, or things present, or things to come; all are yours; and ye are Christ's; and Christ is God's." 1 Corinthians 1:12, 13; 3:21-23.

Paul and Apollos were in perfect harmony. The latter was disappointed and grieved because of the dissension in the church at Corinth; he took no advantage of the preference shown to himself, nor did he encourage it, but hastily left the field of strife. When Paul afterward urged him to revisit Corinth, he declined and did not again labor there until long afterward when the church had reached a better spiritual state.

281

27

Ephesus

While Apollos was preaching at Corinth, Paul fulfilled his promise to return to Ephesus. He had made a brief visit to Jerusalem and had spent some time at Antioch, the scene of his early labors. Thence he traveled through Asia Minor, "over all the country of Galatia and Phrygia" (Acts 18:23), visiting the churches which he himself had established, and strengthening the faith of the believers.

In the time of the apostles the western portion of Asia Minor was known as the Roman province of Asia. Ephesus, the capital, was a great commercial center. Its harbor was crowded with shipping, and its streets were thronged with people from every country. Like Corinth, it presented a promising field for missionary effort.

The Jews, now widely dispersed in all civilized lands, were generally expecting the advent 282 of the Messiah. When John the Baptist was preaching, many, in their visits to Jerusalem at the annual feasts, had gone out to the banks of the Jordan to listen to him. There they had heard Jesus proclaimed as the Promised One, and they had carried the tidings to all parts of the world. Thus had Providence prepared the way for the labors of the apostles.

On his arrival at Ephesus, Paul found twelve brethren, who, like Apollos, had been disciples of John the Baptist, and like him had gained some knowledge of the mission of Christ. They had not the ability of Apollos, but with the same sincerity and faith they were seeking to spread abroad the knowledge they had received.

These brethren knew nothing of the mission of the Holy Spirit. When asked by Paul if they had received the Holy Ghost, they answered, "We have not so much as heard whether there be any Holy Ghost." "Unto what then were ye baptized?" Paul inquired, and they said, "Unto John's baptism."

Then the apostle set before them the great truths that are the foundation of the Christian's hope. He told them of Christ's life on this earth and of His cruel death of shame. He told them how the Lord of life had broken the barriers of the tomb and risen triumphant over death. He repeated the Saviour's commission to His disciples: "All power is given unto Me in heaven and in earth. Go ye therefore, and teach all nations, baptizing them in the name of the Father, and of

the Son, and of the Holy Ghost." Matthew 28:18, 19. He told them also of Christ's promise to send the Comforter, through whose power mighty signs and wonders would be wrought, 283 and he described how gloriously this promise had been fulfilled on the Day of Pentecost.

With deep interest and grateful, wondering joy the brethren listened to Paul's words. By faith they grasped the wonderful truth of Christ's atoning sacrifice and received Him as their Redeemer. They were then baptized in the name of Jesus, and as Paul "laid his hands upon them," they received also the baptism of the Holy Spirit, by which they were enabled to speak the languages of other nations and to prophesy. Thus they were qualified to labor as missionaries in Ephesus and its vicinity and also to go forth to proclaim the gospel in Asia Minor.

It was by cherishing a humble, teachable spirit that these men gained the experience that enabled them to go out as workers into the harvest field. Their example presents to Christians a lesson of great value. There are many who make but little progress in the divine life because they are too self-sufficient to occupy the position of learners. They are content with a superficial knowledge of God's word. They do not wish to change their faith or practice and hence make no effort to obtain greater light.

If the followers of Christ were but earnest seekers after wisdom, they would be led into rich fields of truth as yet wholly unknown to them. He who will give himself fully to God will be guided by the divine hand. He may be lowly and apparently ungifted; yet if with a loving, trusting heart he obeys every intimation of God's will, his powers will be purified, ennobled, energized, and his capabilities will be increased. As he treasures the lessons of divine wisdom, a sacred commission will be entrusted 284 to him; he will be enabled to make his life an honor to God and a blessing to the world. "The entrance of Thy words giveth light; it giveth understanding unto the simple." Psalm 119:130.

There are today many as ignorant of the Holy Spirit's work upon the heart as were those believers in Ephesus; yet no truth is more clearly taught in the word of God. Prophets and apostles have dwelt upon this theme. Christ Himself calls our attention to the growth of the vegetable world as an illustration of the agency of His Spirit in sustaining spiritual life. The sap of the vine, ascending from the root, is diffused to the branches, sustaining growth and producing blossoms and fruit. So the life-giving power of the Holy Spirit, proceeding from the Saviour, pervades the soul, renews the motives and affections, and brings even the thoughts into obedience to the will of God, enabling the receiver to bear the precious fruit of holy deeds.

The Author of this spiritual life is unseen, and

This chapter is based on Acts 19:1-20.

the exact method by which that life is imparted and sustained, it is beyond the power of human philosophy to explain. Yet the operations of the Spirit are always in harmony with the written word. As in the natural, so in the spiritual world. The natural life is preserved moment by moment by divine power; yet it is not sustained by a direct miracle, but through the use of blessings placed within our reach. So the spiritual life is sustained by the use of those means that Providence has supplied. If the follower of Christ would grow up "unto a perfect man, unto the 285 measure of the stature of the fullness of Christ" (Ephesians 4:13), he must eat of the bread of life and drink of the water of salvation. He must watch and pray and work, in all things giving heed to the instructions of God in His word.

There is still another lesson for us in the experience of those Jewish converts. When they received baptism at the hand of John they did not fully comprehend the mission of Jesus as the Sin Bearer. They were holding serious errors. But with clearer light, they gladly accepted Christ as their Redeemer, and with this step of advance came a change in their obligations. As they received a purer faith, there was a corresponding change in their life. In token of this change, and as an acknowledgment of their faith in Christ, they were rebaptized in the name of Jesus.

As was his custom, Paul had begun his work at Ephesus by preaching in the synagogue of the Jews. He continued to labor there for three months, "disputing and persuading the things concerning the kingdom of God." At first he met with a favorable reception; but as in other fields, he was soon violently opposed. "Divers were hardened, and believed not, but spake evil of that way before the multitude." As they persisted in their rejection of the gospel, the apostle ceased to preach in the synagogue.

The Spirit of God had wrought with and through Paul in his labors for his countrymen. Sufficient evidence had been presented to convince all who honestly desired to know the truth. But many permitted themselves to be controlled by prejudice and unbelief, and refused to 286 yield to the most conclusive evidence. Fearing that the faith of the believers would be endangered by continued association with these opposers of the truth, Paul separated from them and gathered the disciples into a distinct body, continuing his public instructions in the school of Tyrannus, a teacher of some note.

Paul saw that "a great door and effectual" was opening before him, although there were "many adversaries." 1 Corinthians 16:9. Ephesus was not only the most magnificent, but the most corrupt, of the cities of Asia. Superstition and sensual pleasure held sway over her teeming population. Under the shadow of her temples, criminals of every grade found shelter, and the most degrading vices flourished.

Ephesus was a popular center for the worship of Diana. The fame of the magnificent temple of "Diana of the Ephesians" extended throughout all Asia and the world. Its surpassing splendor made it the pride, not only of the city, but of the nation. The idol within the temple was declared by tradition to have fallen from the sky. Upon it were inscribed symbolic characters, which were believed to possess great power. Books had been written by the Ephesians to explain the meaning and use of these symbols.

Among those who gave close study to these costly books were many magicians, who wielded a powerful influence over the minds of the superstitious worshipers of the image within the temple.

The apostle Paul, in his labors at Ephesus, was given special tokens of divine favor. The power of God accompanied his efforts, and many were healed of physical maladies. "God 287 wrought special miracles by the hands of Paul: so that from his body were brought unto the sick handkerchiefs or aprons, and the diseases departed from them, and the evil spirits went out of them." These manifestations of supernatural power were far more potent than had ever before been witnessed in Ephesus, and were of such a character that they could not be imitated by the skill of the juggler or the enchantments of the sorcerer. As these miracles were wrought in the name of Jesus of Nazareth, the people had opportunity to see that the God of heaven was more powerful than the magicians who were worshipers of the goddess Diana. Thus the Lord exalted His servant, even before the idolaters themselves, immeasurably above the most powerful and favored of the magicians.

But the One to whom all the spirits of evil are subject and who had given His servants authority over them, was about to bring still greater shame and defeat upon those who despised and profaned His holy name. Sorcery had been prohibited by the Mosaic law, on pain of death, yet from time to time it had been secretly practiced by apostate Jews. At the time of Paul's visit to Ephesus there were in the city "certain of the vagabond Jews, exorcists," who, seeing the wonders wrought by him, "took upon them to call over them which had evil spirits the name of the Lord Jesus." An attempt was made by "seven sons of one Sceva, a Jew, and chief of the priests." Finding a man possessed with a demon, they addressed him, "We adjure you by Jesus whom Paul preacheth." But "the evil spirit answered and said, Jesus I know, and Paul I 288 know; but who are ye? And the man in whom the evil spirit was leaped on them, and overcame them, and prevailed against them, so that they fled out of that house naked and wounded."

Thus unmistakable proof was given of the sacredness of the name of Christ, and the peril which they incurred who should invoke it without faith in the divinity of the Saviour's mission. "Fear fell on them all, and the name of the Lord Jesus was magnified."

Facts which had previously been concealed were now brought to light. In accepting Christianity, some of the believers had not fully renounced their superstitions. To some extent they still continued the practice of magic. Now, convinced of their error, "many that believed came, and confessed, and showed their deeds." Even to some of the sorcerers themselves the good work extended; and "many of them also which used curious arts brought their books together, and burned them before all men: and they counted the price of them, and found it fifty thousand pieces of silver. So mightily grew the word of God and prevailed."

By burning their books on magic, the Ephesian converts showed that the things in which they had once delighted they now abhorred. It was by and through magic that they had especially offended God and imperiled their souls; and it was against magic that they showed such indignation. Thus they gave evidence of true conversion.

These treatises on divination contained rules and forms of communication with evil spirits. They were the regulations of the worship of Satan—directions for soliciting his help and obtaining information from him. By retaining these books the disciples would have exposed themselves to temptation; by selling them they would have placed temptation in the way of others. They had renounced the kingdom of darkness, and to destroy its power they did not hesitate at any sacrifice. Thus truth triumphed over men's prejudices and their love of money.

By this manifestation of the power of Christ, a mighty victory for Christianity was gained in the very stronghold of superstition. The influence of what had taken place was more widespread than even Paul realized. From Ephesus the news was widely circulated, and a strong impetus was given to the cause of Christ. Long after the apostle himself had finished his course, these scenes lived in the memory of men and were the means of winning converts to the gospel.

It is fondly supposed that heathen superstitions have disappeared before the civilization of the twentieth century. But the word of God and the stern testimony of facts declare that sorcery is practiced in this age as verily as in the days of the old-time magicians. The ancient system of magic is, in reality, the same as what is now known as modern spiritualism. Satan is finding access to thousands of minds by presenting himself under the guise of departed friends. The Scriptures declare that "the dead know not anything." Ecclesiastes 9:5. Their thoughts, their love, their hatred, have perished. The dead do not hold communion with the living. But true to his early cunning, Satan employs this device in order to gain control of minds.

Through spiritualism many of the sick, the bereaved, the curious, are communicating with evil spirits. All who venture to do this are on dangerous ground. The word of truth declares how God regards them. In ancient times He pronounced a stern judgment on a king who had sent for counsel to a heathen oracle: "Is it not because there is not a God in Israel, that ye go to inquire of Baal-zebub the god of Ekron? Now therefore thus saith the Lord, Thou shalt not come down from that bed on which thou art gone up, but shalt surely die." 2 Kings 1:3, 4.

The magicians of heathen times have their counterpart in the spiritualistic mediums, the clairvoyants, and the fortune-tellers of today. The mystic voices that spoke at Endor and at Ephesus are still by their lying words misleading the children of men. Could the veil be lifted from before our eyes, we should see evil angels employing all their arts to deceive and to destroy. Wherever an influence is exerted to cause men to forget God, there Satan is exercising his bewitching power. When men yield to his influence, ere they are aware the mind is bewildered and the soul polluted. The apostle's admonition to the Ephesian church should be heeded by the people of God today: "Have no fellowship with the unfruitful works of darkness, but rather reprove them." Ephesians 5:11.

28

Days of Toil and Trial

For over three years Ephesus was the center of Paul's work. A flourishing church was raised up here, and from this city the gospel spread throughout the province of Asia, among both Jews and Gentiles.

The apostle had now for some time been contemplating another missionary journey. He "purposed in the spirit, when he had passed through Macedonia and Achaia, to go to Jerusalem, saying, After I have been there, I must also see Rome." In harmony with this plan "he sent into Macedonia two of them that ministered unto him, Timotheus and Erastus;" but feeling that the cause in Ephesus still demanded his presence, he decided to remain until after Pentecost. An event soon occurred, however, which hastened his departure.

Once a year, special ceremonies were held at Ephesus in honor of the goddess Diana. These attracted great numbers of people from all parts of the province. Throughout this period, festivities were conducted with the utmost pomp and splendor.

This chapter is based on Acts 19:21-41; 20:1.

This gala season was a trying time for those who had newly come to the faith. The company of believers who met in the school of Tyrannus were an inharmonious note in the festive chorus, and ridicule, reproach, and insult were freely heaped upon them. Paul's labors had given the heathen worship a telling blow, in consequence of which there was a perceptible falling off in the attendance at the national festival and in the enthusiasm of the worshipers. The influence of his teachings extended far beyond the actual converts to the faith. Many who had not openly accepted the new doctrines became so far enlightened as to lose all confidence in their heathen gods.

There existed also another cause of dissatisfaction. An extensive and profitable business had grown up at Ephesus from the manufacture and sale of small shrines and images, modeled after the temple and the image of Diana. Those interested in this industry found their gains diminishing, and all united in attributing the unwelcome change to Paul's labors.

Demetrius, a manufacturer of silver shrines, calling together the workmen of his craft, said: "Sirs, ye know that by this craft we have our wealth. Moreover ye see and hear, that not alone at Ephesus, but almost throughout all Asia, this Paul hath persuaded and turned away much people, saying that they be no gods, which are made with hands: so that not only this our craft is in danger to be set at nought; but also that the temple of the great goddess Diana should be despised, and her magnificence should be destroyed, whom all Asia and the world worshipeth." These words roused the excitable passions of the people. "They were full of wrath, and cried out, saying, Great is Diana of the Ephesians."

A report of this speech was rapidly circulated. "The whole city was filled with confusion." Search was made for Paul, but the apostle was not to be found. His brethren, receiving an intimation of the danger, had hurried him from the place. Angels of God had been sent to guard the apostle; his time to die a martyr's death had not yet come.

Failing to find the object of their wrath, the mob seized "Gaius and Aristarchus, men of Macedonia, Paul's companions in travel," and with these "they rushed with one accord into the theater."

Paul's place of concealment was not far distant, and he soon learned of the peril of his beloved brethren. Forgetful of his own safety, he desired to go at once to the theater to address the rioters. But "the disciples suffered him not." Gaius and Aristarchus were not the prey the people sought; no serious harm to them was apprehended. But should the apostle's pale, care-worn face be seen, it would arouse at once the worst passions of the mob and there would

not be the least human possibility of saving his life.

Paul was still eager to defend the truth before the multitude, but he was at last deterred by a message of warning from the theater. "Certain of the chief of Asia, which were his friends, sent unto him, desiring him that he would not adventure himself into the theater."

The tumult in the theater was continually [294] increasing. "Some . . . cried one thing, and some another: for the assembly was confused; and the more part knew not wherefore they were come together." The fact that Paul and some of his companions were of Hebrew extraction made the Jews anxious to show plainly that they were not sympathizers with him and his work. They therefore brought forward one of their own number to set the matter before the people. The speaker chosen was Alexander, one of the craftsmen, a coppersmith, to whom Paul afterward referred as having done him much evil. 2 Timothy 4:14. Alexander was a man of considerable ability, and he bent all his energies to direct the wrath of the people exclusively against Paul and his companions. But the crowd, seeing that Alexander was a Jew, thrust him aside, and "all with one voice about the space of two hours cried out, Great is Diana of the Ephesians."

At last, from sheer exhaustion, they ceased, and there was a momentary silence. Then the recorder of the city arrested the attention of the crowd, and by virtue of his office obtained a hearing. He met the people on their own ground and showed that there was no cause for the present tumult. He appealed to their reason. "Ye men of Ephesus," he said, "what man is there that knoweth not how that the city of the Ephesians is a worshiper of the great goddess Diana, and of the image which fell down from Jupiter? Seeing then that these things cannot be spoken against, ye ought to be quiet, and to do nothing rashly. For ye have brought hither these men, which are neither robbers of churches, nor [295] yet blasphemers of your goddess. Wherefore if Demetrius, and the craftsmen which are with him, have a matter against any man, the law is open, and there are deputies: let them implead one another. But if ye inquire anything concerning other matters, it shall be determined in a lawful assembly. For we are in danger to be called in question for this day's uproar, there being no cause whereby we may give an account of this concourse. And when he had thus spoken, he dismissed the assembly."

In his speech Demetrius had said, "This our craft is in danger." These words reveal the real cause of the tumult at Ephesus, and also the cause of much of the persecution which followed the apostles in their work. Demetrius and his fellow craftsmen saw that by the teaching and spread of the gospel the business of image making was endangered. The income of pagan priests and artisans was at stake, and for this reason they aroused against Paul the most bitter opposition.

The decision of the recorder and of others holding honorable offices in the city had set Paul before the people as one innocent of any unlawful act. This was another triumph of Christianity over error and superstition. God had raised up a great magistrate to vindicate His apostle and hold the tumultuous mob in check. Paul's heart was filled with gratitude to God that his life had been preserved and that Christianity had not been brought into disrepute by the tumult at Ephesus.

296 "After the uproar was ceased, Paul called unto him the disciples, and embraced them, and departed for to go into Macedonia." On this journey he was accompanied by two faithful Ephesian brethren, Tychicus and Trophimus.

Paul's labors in Ephesus were concluded. His ministry there had been a season of incessant labor, of many trials, and of deep anguish. He had taught the people in public and from house to house, with many tears instructing and warning them. Continually he had been opposed by the Jews, who lost no opportunity to stir up the popular feeling against him.

And while thus battling against opposition, pushing forward with untiring zeal the gospel work, and guarding the interests of a church yet young in the faith, Paul was bearing upon his soul a heavy burden for all the churches.

News of apostasy in some of the churches of his planting caused him deep sorrow. He feared that his efforts in their behalf might prove to be in vain. Many a sleepless night was spent in prayer and earnest thought as he learned of the methods employed to counteract his work. As he had opportunity and as their condition demanded, he wrote to the churches, giving reproof, counsel, admonition, and encouragement. In these letters the apostle does not dwell on his own trials, yet there are occasional glimpses of his labors and sufferings in the cause of Christ. Stripes and imprisonment, cold and hunger and thirst, perils by land and by sea, in the city and in the wilderness, from his own countrymen, from the heathen, and from false brethren—all this he endured for the sake of the gospel. He was "defamed," "reviled," made "the 297 offscouring of all things," "perplexed," "persecuted," "troubled on every side," "in jeopardy every hour," "alway delivered unto death for Jesus' sake."

Amidst the constant storm of opposition, the clamor of enemies, and the desertion of friends the intrepid apostle almost lost heart. But he looked back to Calvary and with new ardor pressed on to spread the knowledge of the Crucified. He was but treading the blood-stained path that Christ had trodden before him. He sought no discharge from the warfare till he should lay off his armor at the feet of his Redeemer.

29

A Message of Warning and Entreaty

The first epistle to the Corinthian church was written by the apostle Paul during the latter part of his stay at Ephesus. For no others had he felt a deeper interest or put forth more untiring effort than for the believers in Corinth. For a year and a half he had labored among them, pointing them to a crucified and risen Saviour as the only means of salvation, and urging them to rely implicitly on the transforming power of His grace. Before accepting into church fellowship those who made a profession of Christianity, he had been careful to give them special instruction as to the privileges and duties of the Christian believer, and he had earnestly endeavored to help them to be faithful to their baptismal vows.

Paul had a keen sense of the conflict which every soul must wage with the agencies of evil that are continually seeking to deceive and ensnare, and he had worked untiringly to 299 strengthen and confirm those who were young in the faith. He had entreated them to make an entire surrender to God; for he knew that when the soul fails to make this surrender, then sin is not forsaken, the appetites and passions still strive for the mastery, and temptations confuse the conscience.

The surrender must be complete. Every weak, doubting, struggling soul who yields fully to the Lord is placed in direct touch with agencies that enable him to overcome. Heaven is near to him, and he has the support and help of angels of mercy in every time of trial and need.

The members of the church at Corinth were surrounded by idolatry and sensuality of the most alluring form. While the apostle was with them, these influences had but little power over them. Paul's firm faith, his fervent prayers and earnest words of instruction, and, above all, his godly life had helped them to deny self for Christ's sake rather than to enjoy the pleasures of sin.

After the departure of Paul, however, unfavorable conditions arose; tares that had been sown by the enemy appeared among the wheat, and erelong these began to bring forth their evil fruit. This was a time of severe trial to the Corinthian church. The apostle was no longer with them to quicken their zeal and aid them in their endeavors to live in harmony with God,

This chapter is based on the First Epistle to the Corinthians.

and little by little many became careless and indifferent, and allowed natural tastes and inclinations to control them. He who had so often urged them to high ideals of purity and uprightness was no longer with them, and not a few 300 who, at the time of their conversion, had put away their evil habits, returned to the debasing sins of heathenism.

Paul had written briefly to the church, admonishing them "not to company" with members who should persist in profligacy; but many of the believers perverted the apostle's meaning, quibbled over his words, and excused themselves for disregarding his instruction.

A letter was sent to Paul by the church, asking for counsel concerning various matters, but saying nothing of the grievous sins existing among them. The apostle was, however, forcibly impressed by the Holy Spirit that the true state of the church had been concealed and that this letter was an attempt to draw from him statements which the writers could construe to serve their own purposes.

About this time there came to Ephesus members of the household of Chloe, a Christian family of high repute in Corinth. Paul asked them regarding the condition of things, and they told him that the church was rent by divisions. The dissensions that had prevailed at the time of Apollos's visit had greatly increased. False teachers were leading the members to despise the instructions of Paul. The doctrines and ordinances of the gospel had been perverted. Pride, idolatry, and sensualism were steadily increasing among those who had once been zealous in the Christian life.

As this picture was presented before him, Paul saw that his worst fears were more than realized. But he did not because of this give way to the thought that his work had been a failure. 301 With "anguish of heart" and with "many tears" he sought counsel from God. Gladly would he have visited Corinth at once, had this been the wisest course to pursue. But he knew that in their present condition the believers would not profit by his labors, and therefore he sent Titus to prepare the way for a visit from himself later on. Then, putting aside all personal feelings over the course of those whose conduct revealed such strange perverseness, and keeping his soul stayed upon God, the apostle wrote to the church at Corinth one of the richest, most instructive, most powerful of all his letters.

With remarkable clearness he proceeded to answer the various questions brought forward by the church, and to lay down general principles, which, if heeded, would lead them to a higher spiritual plane. They were in peril, and he could not bear the thought of failing at this critical time to reach their hearts. Faithfully he warned them of their dangers and reproved them for their sins. He pointed them again to

Christ and sought to kindle anew the fervor of their early devotion.

The apostle's great love for the Corinthian believers was revealed in his tender greeting to the church. He referred to their experience in turning from idolatry to the worship and service of the true God. He reminded them of the gifts of the Holy Spirit which they had received, and showed that it was their privilege to make continual advancement in the Christian life until they should attain to the purity and holiness of Christ. "In everything ye are enriched by Him," he wrote, "in all utterance, and in all knowledge; even as the testimony of Christ was con- 302 firmed in you: so that ye come behind in no gift; waiting for the coming of our Lord Jesus Christ: who shall also confirm you unto the end, that ye may be blameless in the day of our Lord Jesus Christ."

Paul spoke plainly of the dissensions that had arisen in the Corinthian church, and exhorted the members to cease from strife. "I beseech you, brethren," he wrote, "by the name of our Lord Jesus Christ, that ye all speak the same thing, and that there be no divisions among you; but that ye be perfectly joined together in the same mind and in the same judgment."

The apostle felt at liberty to mention how and by whom he had been informed of the divisions in the church. "It hath been declared unto me of you, my brethren, by them which are of the house of Chloe, that there are contentions among you."

Paul was an inspired apostle. The truths he taught to others he had received "by revelation;" yet the Lord did not directly reveal to him at all times just the condition of His people. In this instance those who were interested in the prosperity of the church at Corinth, and who had seen evils creeping in, had presented the matter before the apostle, and from divine revelations which he had formerly received he was prepared to judge of the character of these developments. Notwithstanding the fact that the Lord did not give him a new revelation for that special time, those who were really seeking for light accepted his message as expressing the 303 mind of Christ. The Lord had shown him the difficulties and dangers which would arise in the churches, and, as these evils developed, the apostle recognized their significance. He had been set for the defense of the church. He was to watch for souls as one who must render account to God, and was it not consistent and right for him to take notice of the reports concerning the anarchy and divisions among them? Most assuredly; and the reproof he sent them was as certainly written under the inspiration of the Spirit of God as were any of his other epistles.

The apostle made no mention of the false teachers who were seeking to destroy the fruit of his labor. Because of the darkness and division in the church, he wisely forbore to irritate them by such references, for fear of turning some entirely from the truth. He called attention to his own work among them as that of "a wise master builder," who had laid the foundation upon which others had built. But he did not thereby exalt himself; for he declared, "We are laborers together with God." He claimed no wisdom of his own, but acknowledged that divine power alone had enabled him to present the truth in a manner pleasing to God. United with Christ, the greatest of all teachers, Paul had been enabled to communicate lessons of divine wisdom, which met the necessities of all classes, and which were to apply at all times, in all places, and under all conditions.

304 Among the more serious of the evils that had developed among the Corinthian believers, was that of a return to many of the debasing customs of heathenism. One former convert had so far backslidden that his licentious course was a violation of even the low standard of morality held by the Gentile world. The apostle pleaded with the church to put away from among them "that wicked person." "Know ye not," he admonished them, "that a little leaven leaveneth the whole lump? Purge out therefore the old leaven, that ye may be a new lump, as ye are unleavened."

Another grave evil that had arisen in the church was that of brethren going to law against one another. Abundant provision had been made for the settlement of difficulties among believers. Christ Himself had given plain instruction as to how such matters were to be adjusted. "If thy brother shall trespass against thee," the Saviour had counseled, "go and tell him his fault between thee and him alone: if he shall hear thee, thou hast gained thy brother. But if he will not hear thee, then take with thee one or two more, that in the mouth of two or three witnesses every word may be established. And if he shall neglect to hear them, tell it unto the church: but if he neglect to hear the church, let him be unto thee as a heathen man and a publican. Verily I say unto you, Whatsoever ye shall bind on earth shall be bound in heaven: and whatsoever ye shall loose on earth shall be loosed in heaven." Matthew 18:15-18.

To the Corinthian believers who had lost sight of this plain counsel, Paul wrote in no uncertain terms of admonition and rebuke. "Dare any of you," he asked, "having a matter against another, go to law before the unjust, and not before the saints? Do ye not know that the saints shall judge the world? and if the world 305 shall be judged by you, are ye unworthy to judge the smallest matters? Know ye not that we shall judge angels? how much more things that pertain to this life? If then ye have judgments of things pertaining to this life, set them

to judge who are least esteemed in the church. I speak to your shame. Is it so, that there is not a wise man among you? no, not one that shall be able to judge between his brethren? But brother goeth to law with brother, and that before the unbelievers. Now therefore there is utterly a fault among you, because ye go to law one with another. Why do ye not rather take wrong? . . . Nay, ye do wrong, and defraud, and that your brethren. Know ye not that the unrighteous shall not inherit the kingdom of God?"

Satan is constantly seeking to introduce distrust, alienation, and malice among God's people. We shall often be tempted to feel that our rights are invaded, even when there is no real cause for such feelings. Those whose love for self is stronger than their love for Christ and His cause will place their own interests first and will resort to almost any expedient to guard and maintain them. Even many who appear to be conscientious Christians are hindered by pride and self-esteem from going privately to those whom they think in error, that they may talk with them in the spirit of Christ and pray together for one another. When they think themselves injured by their brethren, some will even go to law instead of following the Saviour's rule.

Christians should not appeal to civil tribunals to settle differences that may arise among church members. Such differences should be settled among themselves, or by the church, in 306 harmony with Christ's instruction. Even though injustice may have been done, the follower of the meek and lowly Jesus will suffer himself "to be defrauded" rather than open before the world the sins of his brethren in the church.

Lawsuits between brethren are a reproach to the cause of truth. Christians who go to law with one another expose the church to the ridicule of her enemies and cause the powers of darkness to triumph. They are wounding Christ afresh and putting Him to open shame. By ignoring the authority of the church, they show contempt for God, who gave to the church its authority.

In this letter to the Corinthians Paul endeavored to show them Christ's power to keep them from evil. He knew that if they would comply with the conditions laid down, they would be strong in the strength of the Mighty One. As a means of helping them to break away from the thralldom of sin and to perfect holiness in the fear of the Lord, Paul urged upon them the claims of Him to whom they had dedicated their lives at the time of their conversion. "Ye are Christ's," he declared. "Ye are not your own. . . . Ye are bought with a price: therefore glorify God in your body, and in your spirit, which are God's."

The apostle plainly outlined the result of turning from a life of purity and holiness to the corrupt practices of heathenism. "Be not deceived," he wrote; "neither fornicators, nor idolaters, nor adulterers, . . . nor thieves, nor covetous, nor drunkards, nor revilers, nor extortioners, shall inherit the kingdom of God." He begged them 307 to control the lower passions and appetites. "Know ye not," he asked, "that your body is the temple of the Holy Ghost which is in you, which ye have of God?"

While Paul possessed high intellectual endowments, his life revealed the power of a rarer wisdom, which gave him quickness of insight and sympathy of heart, and brought him into close touch with others, enabling him to arouse their better nature and inspire them to strive for a higher life. His heart was filled with an earnest love for the Corinthian believers. He longed to see them revealing an inward piety that would fortify them against temptation. He knew that at every step in the Christian pathway they would be opposed by the synagogue of Satan and that they would have to engage in conflicts daily. They would have to guard against the stealthy approach of the enemy, forcing back old habits and natural inclinations, and ever watching unto prayer. Paul knew that the higher Christian attainments can be reached only through much prayer and constant watchfulness, and this he tried to instill into their minds. But he knew also that in Christ crucified they were offered power sufficient to convert the soul and divinely adapted to enable them to resist all temptations to evil. With faith in God as their armor, and with His word as their weapon of warfare, they would be supplied with an inner power that would enable them to turn aside the attacks of the enemy.

The Corinthian believers needed a deeper experience in the things of God. They did not know fully what it meant to behold His glory 308 and to be changed from character to character. They had seen but the first rays of the early dawn of that glory. Paul's desire for them was that they might be filled with all the fullness of God, following on to know Him whose going forth is prepared as the morning, and continuing to learn of Him until they should come into the full noontide of a perfect gospel faith.

309

30

Called to Reach a
Higher Standard

In the hope of impressing vividly upon the minds of the Corinthian believers the importance of firm self-control, strict temperance, and unflagging zeal in the service of Christ, Paul in his letter to them made a striking comparison

This chapter is based on the First Epistle to the Corinthians.

between the Christian warfare and the celebrated foot races held at stated intervals near Corinth. Of all the games instituted among the Greeks and the Romans, the foot races were the most ancient and the most highly esteemed. They were witnessed by kings, nobles, and statesmen. Young men of rank and wealth took part in them and shrank from no effort or discipline necessary to obtain the prize.

The contests were governed by strict regulations, from which there was no appeal. Those who desired their names entered as competitors for the prize had first to undergo a severe preparatory training. Harmful indulgence of appetite, or any other gratification that would lower mental or physical vigor, was strictly forbidden. For one to have any hope of success in 310 these trials of strength and speed, the muscles must be strong and supple, and the nerves well under control. Every movement must be certain, every step swift and unswerving; the physical powers must reach the highest mark.

As the contestants in the race made their appearance before the waiting multitude, their names were heralded, and the rules of the race were distinctly stated. Then they all started together, the fixed attention of the spectators inspiring them with a determination to win. The judges were seated near the goal, that they might watch the race from its beginning to its close and give the prize to the true victor. If a man reached the goal first by taking an unlawful advantage, he was not awarded the prize.

In these contests great risks were run. Some never recovered from the terrible physical strain. It was not unusual for men to fall on the course, bleeding at the mouth and nose, and sometimes a contestant would drop dead when about to seize the prize. But the possibility of lifelong injury or of death was not looked upon as too great a risk to run for the sake of the honor awarded the successful contestant.

As the winner reached the goal, the applause of the vast multitude of onlookers rent the air and awoke the echoes of the surrounding hills and mountains. In full view of the spectators, the judge presented him with the emblems of victory—a laurel crown and a palm branch to carry in his right hand. His praise was sung throughout the land; his parents received their share of honor; and even the city in which he 311 lived was held in high esteem for having produced so great an athlete.

In referring to these races as a figure of the Christian warfare, Paul emphasized the preparation necessary to the success of the contestants in the race—the preliminary discipline, the abstemious diet, the necessity for temperance. "Every man that striveth for the mastery," he declared, "is temperate in all things." The runners put aside every indulgence that would tend to weaken the physical powers, and by severe and continuous discipline trained their muscles to strength and endurance, that when the day of the contest should arrive, they might put the heaviest tax upon their powers. How much more important that the Christian, whose eternal interests are at stake, bring appetite and passion under subjection to reason and the will of God! Never must he allow his attention to be diverted by amusements, luxuries, or ease. All his habits and passions must be brought under the strictest discipline. Reason, enlightened by the teachings of God's word, and guided by His Spirit, must hold the reins of control.

And after this has been done, the Christian must put forth the utmost exertion in order to gain the victory. In the Corinthian games, the last few strides of the contestants in the race were made with agonizing effort to keep up undiminished speed. So the Christian, as he nears the goal, will press onward with even more zeal and determination than at the first of his course.

Paul presents the contrast between the chaplet of fading laurel received by the victor in the foot 312 races, and the crown of immortal glory that will be given to him who runs with triumph the Christian race. "They do it," he declares, "to obtain a corruptible crown; but we an incorruptible." To win a perishable prize, the Grecian runners spared themselves no toil or discipline. We are striving for a prize infinitely more valuable, even the crown of everlasting life. How much more careful should be our striving, how much more willing our sacrifice and self-denial!

In the epistle to the Hebrews is pointed out the single-hearted purpose that should characterize the Christian's race for eternal life: "Let us lay aside every weight, and the sin which doth so easily beset us, and let us run with patience the race that is set before us, looking unto Jesus the author and finisher of our faith." Hebrews 12:1, 2. Envy, malice, evil thinking, evilspeaking, covetousness—these are weights that the Christian must lay aside if he would run successfully the race for immortality. Every habit or practice that leads into sin and brings dishonor upon Christ must be put away, whatever the sacrifice. The blessing of heaven cannot attend any man in violating the eternal principles of right. One sin cherished is sufficient to work degradation of character and to mislead others.

"If thy hand cause thee to stumble," the Saviour said, "cut it off: it is good for thee to enter into life maimed, rather than having thy two hands to go into hell, into the unquenchable fire. And if thy foot cause thee to stumble, cut it off: it is good for thee to enter into life halt, rather than having thy two feet to be cast into hell." 313 Mark 9:43-45, R.V. If to save the body from death, the foot or the hand should be cut off, or even the eye plucked out, how much more

earnest should the Christian be to put away sin, which brings death to the soul!

The competitors in the ancient games, after they had submitted to self-denial and rigid discipline, were not even then sure of the victory. "Know ye not," Paul asked, "that they which run in a race run all, but one receiveth the prize?" However eagerly and earnestly the runners might strive, the prize could be awarded to but one. One hand only could grasp the coveted garland. Some might put forth the utmost effort to obtain the prize, but as they reached forth the hand to secure it, another, an instant before them, might grasp the coveted treasure.

Such is not the case in the Christian warfare. Not one who complies with the conditions will be disappointed at the end of the race. Not one who is earnest and persevering will fail of success. The race is not to the swift, nor the battle to the strong. The weakest saint, as well as the strongest, may wear the crown of immortal glory. All may win who, through the power of divine grace, bring their lives into conformity to the will of Christ. The practice, in the details of life, of the principles laid down in God's word, is too often looked upon as unimportant—a matter too trivial to demand attention. But in view of the issue at stake, nothing is small that will help or hinder. Every act casts its weight into the scale that determines life's victory or defeat. And the reward given to those who win will be in proportion to the energy and earnest- 314 ness with which they have striven.

The apostle compared himself to a man running in a race, straining every nerve to win the prize. "I therefore so run," he says, "not as uncertainly; so fight I, not as one that beateth the air: but I keep under my body, and bring it into subjection: lest that by any means, when I have preached to others, I myself should be a castaway." That he might not run uncertainly or at random in the Christian race, Paul subjected himself to severe training. The words, "I keep under my body," literally mean to beat back by severe discipline the desires, impulses, and passions.

Paul feared lest, having preached to others, he himself should be a castaway. He realized that if he did not carry out in his life the principles he believed and preached, his labors in behalf of others would avail him nothing. His conversation, his influence, his refusal to yield to self-gratification, must show that his religion was not a profession merely, but a daily, living connection with God. One goal he kept ever before him, and strove earnestly to reach—"the righteousness which is of God by faith." Philippians 3:9.

Paul knew that his warfare against evil would not end so long as life should last. Ever he realized the need of putting a strict guard upon himself, that earthly desires might not overcome spiritual zeal. With all his power he continued to strive against natural inclinations. Ever he kept before him the ideal to be attained, and this ideal he strove to reach by willing obedience to 315 the law of God. His words, his practices, his passions—all were brought under the control of the Spirit of God.

It was this singlehearted purpose to win the race for eternal life that Paul longed to see revealed in the lives of the Corinthian believers. He knew that in order to reach Christ's ideal for them, they had before them a life struggle from which there would be no release. He entreated them to strive lawfully, day by day seeking for piety and moral excellence. He pleaded with them to lay aside every weight and to press forward to the goal of perfection in Christ.

Paul pointed the Corinthians to the experiences of ancient Israel, to the blessings that rewarded their obedience, and to the judgments that followed their transgressions. He reminded them of the miraculous way in which the Hebrews were led from Egypt under the protection of the cloud by day and the pillar of fire by night. Thus they were safely conducted through the Red Sea, while the Egyptians, essaying to cross in like manner, were all drowned. By these acts God had acknowledged Israel as His church. They "did all eat the same spiritual meat; and did all drink the same spiritual drink: for they drank of that spiritual Rock that followed them: and that Rock was Christ." The Hebrews, in all their travels, had Christ as a leader. The smitten rock typified Christ, who was to be wounded for men's transgressions, that the stream of salvation might flow to all.

Notwithstanding the favor that God showed to the Hebrews, yet because of their lust for the luxuries left behind in Egypt, and because of 316 their sin and rebellion, the judgments of God came upon them. The apostle enjoined the Corinthian believers to heed the lesson contained in Israel's experience. "Now these things were our examples," he declared, "to the intent we should not lust after evil things, as they also lusted." He showed how love of ease and pleasure had prepared the way for sins that called forth the signal vengeance of God. It was when the children of Israel sat down to eat and drink, and rose up to play, that they threw off the fear of God, which they had felt as they listened to the giving of the law; and, making a golden calf to represent God, they worshiped it. And it was after enjoying a luxurious feast connected with the worship of Baalpeor, that many of the Hebrews fell through licentiousness. The anger of God was aroused, and at His command "three and twenty thousand" were slain by the plague in one day.

The apostle adjured the Corinthians, "Let him that thinketh he standeth take heed lest he fall." Should they become boastful and self-confident, neglecting to watch and pray, they would fall into grievous sin, calling down upon themselves the wrath of God. Yet Paul would not have them yield to despondency or discouragement. He gave them the assurance: "God is faithful, who will not suffer you to be tempted above that ye are able; but will with the temptation also make a way of escape, that ye may be able to bear it."

Paul urged his brethren to ask themselves what influence their words and deeds would have upon others and to do nothing, however innocent in itself, that would seem to sanction 317 idolatry or offend the scruples of those who might be weak in the faith. "Whether therefore ye eat, or drink, or whatsoever ye do, do all to the glory of God. Give none offense, neither to the Jews, nor to the Gentiles, nor to the church of God."

The apostle's words of warning to the Corinthian church are applicable to all time and are especially adapted to our day. By idolatry he meant not only the worship of idols, but self-serving, love of ease, the gratification of appetite and passion. A mere profession of faith in Christ, a boastful knowledge of the truth, does not make a man a Christian. A religion that seeks only to gratify the eye, the ear, and the taste, or that sanctions self-indulgence, is not the religion of Christ.

By a comparison of the church with the human body, the apostle aptly illustrated the close and harmonious relationship that should exist among all members of the church of Christ. "By one Spirit," he wrote, "are we all baptized into one body, whether we be Jews or Gentiles, whether we be bond or free; and have been all made to drink into one Spirit. For the body is not one member, but many. If the foot shall say, Because I am not the hand, I am not of the body; is it therefore not of the body? And if the ear shall say, Because I am not the eye, I am not of the body; is it therefore not of the body? If the whole body were an eye, where were the hearing? If the whole were hearing, where were the smelling? But now hath God set the members every one of them in the body, as it hath pleased Him. And if they were all one member, where were the body? But now are 318 they many members, yet but one body. And the eye cannot say unto the hand, I have no need of thee: nor again the head to the feet, I have no need of you. . . . God hath tempered the body together, having given more abundant honor to that part which lacked: that there should be no schism in the body; but that the members should have the same care one for another. And whether one member suffer, all the members suffer with it; or one member be honored, all the members rejoice with it. Now ye are the body of Christ, and members in particular."

And then, in words which from that day to

this have been to men and women a source of inspiration and encouragement, Paul set forth the importance of that love which should be cherished by the followers of Christ: "Though I speak with the tongues of men and of angels, and have not charity, I am become as sounding brass, or a tinkling cymbal. And though I have the gift of prophecy, and understand all mysteries, and all knowledge; and though I have all faith, so that I could remove mountains, and have not charity, I am nothing. And though I bestow all my goods to feed the poor, and though I give my body to be burned, and have not charity, it profiteth me nothing."

No matter how high the profession, he whose heart is not filled with love for God and his fellow men is not a true disciple of Christ. Though he should possess great faith and have power even to work miracles, yet without love his faith would be worthless. He might display great liberality; but should he, from some other motive 319 than genuine love, bestow all his goods to feed the poor, the act would not commend him to the favor of God. In his zeal he might even meet a martyr's death, yet if not actuated by love, he would be regarded by God as a deluded enthusiast or an ambitious hypocrite.

"Charity suffereth long, and is kind; charity envieth not; charity vaunteth not itself, is not puffed up." The purest joy springs from the deepest humiliation. The strongest and noblest characters are built on the foundation of patience, love, and submission to God's will.

Charity "doth not behave itself unseemly, seeketh not her own, is not easily provoked, thinketh no evil." Christlike love places the most favorable construction on the motives and acts of others. It does not needlessly expose their faults; it does not listen eagerly to unfavorable reports, but seeks rather to bring to mind the good qualities of others.

Love "rejoiceth not in iniquity, but rejoiceth in the truth; beareth all things, believeth all things, hopeth all things, endureth all things." This love "never faileth." It can never lose its value; it is a heavenly attribute. As a precious treasure, it will be carried by its possessor through the portals of the city of God.

"And now abideth faith, hope, charity, these three; but the greatest of these is charity."

In the lowering of the moral standard among the Corinthian believers, there were those who had given up some of the fundamental features of their faith. Some had gone so far as to deny the doctrine of the resurrection. Paul met this heresy with a very plain testimony regarding the 320 unmistakable evidence of the resurrection of Christ. He declared that Christ, after His death, "rose again the third day according to the Scriptures," after which "He was seen of Cephas, then of the Twelve: after that, He was seen of above five hundred brethren at once; of whom

the greater part remain unto this present, but some are fallen asleep. After that, He was seen of James; then of all the apostles. And last of all He was seen of me also."

With convincing power the apostle set forth the great truth of the resurrection. "If there be no resurrection of the dead," he argued, "then is Christ not risen: and if Christ be not risen, then is our preaching vain, and your faith is also vain. Yea, and we are found false witnesses of God; because we have testified of God that He raised up Christ: whom He raised not up, if so be that the dead rise not. For if the dead rise not, then is not Christ raised: and if Christ be not raised, your faith is vain; ye are yet in your sins. Then they also which are fallen asleep in Christ are perished. If in this life only we have hope in Christ, we are of all men most miserable. But now is Christ risen from the dead, and become the first fruits of them that slept."

The apostle carried the minds of the Corinthian brethren forward to the triumphs of the resurrection morn, when all the sleeping saints are to be raised, henceforth to live forever with their Lord. "Behold," the apostle declared, "I show you a mystery: We shall not all sleep, but we shall all be changed, in a moment, in the twinkling of an eye, at the last trump: for the trumpet shall sound, and the dead shall be raised incorruptible, and we shall be changed. For this corruptible must put on incorruption, and this mortal must put on immortality. So when this cor- 321 ruptible shall have put on incorruption, and this mortal shall have put on immortality, then shall be brought to pass the saying that is written, Death is swallowed up in victory. O death, where is thy sting? O grave, where is thy victory? . . . Thanks be to God, which giveth us the victory through our Lord Jesus Christ."

Glorious is the triumph awaiting the faithful. The apostle, realizing the possibilities before the Corinthian believers, sought to set before them that which uplifts from the selfish and the sensual, and glorifies life with the hope of immortality. Earnestly he exhorted them to be true to their high calling in Christ. "My beloved brethren," he pleaded, "be ye steadfast, unmovable, always abounding in the work of the Lord, forasmuch as ye know that your labor is not in vain in the Lord."

Thus the apostle, in the most decided and impressive manner, endeavored to correct the false and dangerous ideas and practices that were prevailing in the Corinthian church. He spoke plainly, yet in love for their souls. In his warnings and reproofs, light from the throne of God was shining upon them, to reveal the hidden sins that were defiling their lives. How would it be received?

After the letter had been dispatched, Paul feared lest that which he had written might wound too deeply those whom he desired to benefit. He keenly dreaded a further alienation and sometimes longed to recall his words. Those who, like the apostle, have felt a responsibility for beloved churches or institutions, can best appreciate his depression of spirit and self-accusing. The servants of God who bear the burden of His work for this time know something of the same experience of labor, conflict, and anxious care that fell to the lot of the great apostle. Burdened by divisions in the church, meeting with ingratitude and betrayal from some to whom he looked for sympathy and support, realizing the peril of the churches that harbored iniquity, compelled to bear a close, searching testimony in reproof of sin, he was at the same time weighed down with fear that he might have dealt with too great severity. With trembling anxiety he waited to receive some tidings as to the reception of his message.

31

The Message Heeded

From Ephesus Paul set forth on another missionary tour, during which he hoped to visit once more the scenes of his former labors in Europe. Tarrying for a time at Troas, "to preach Christ's gospel," he found some who were ready to listen to his message. "A door was opened unto me of the Lord," he afterward declared of his labors in this place. But successful as were his efforts at Troas, he could not remain there long. "The care of all the churches," and particularly of the church at Corinth, rested heavily on his heart. He had hoped to meet Titus at Troas and to learn from him how the words of counsel and reproof sent to the Corinthian brethren had been received, but in this he was disappointed. "I had no rest in my spirit," he wrote concerning this experience, "because I found not Titus my brother." He therefore left Troas and crossed over to Macedonia, where, at Philippi he met Timothy.

During this time of anxiety concerning the church at Corinth, Paul hoped for the best; yet at times feelings of deep sadness would sweep over his soul, lest his counsels and admonitions might be misunderstood. "Our flesh had no rest," he afterward wrote, "but we were troubled on every side; without were fightings, within were fears. Nevertheless God, that comforteth those that are cast down, comforted us by the coming of Titus."

This faithful messenger brought the cheering news that a wonderful change had taken place among the Corinthian believers. Many had accepted the instruction contained in Paul's letter and had repented of their sins. Their lives were no longer a reproach to Christianity, but

exerted a powerful influence in favor of practical godliness.

Filled with joy, the apostle sent another letter to the Corinthian believers, expressing his gladness of heart because of the good work wrought in them: "Though I made you sorry with a letter, I do not repent, though I did repent." When tortured by the fear that his words would be despised, he had sometimes regretted that he had written so decidedly and severely. "Now I rejoice," he continued, "not that ye were made sorry, but that ye sorrowed to repentance: for ye were made sorry after a godly manner, that ye might receive damage by us in nothing. For godly sorrow worketh repentance to salvation not to be repented of." That repentance which is produced by the influence of divine grace upon the heart will lead to confession and forsaking of sin. Such were the fruits which the apostle declared had been seen in the lives of the Corinthian believers. "What carefulness it wrought in you, yea, what clearing of yourselves, yea, what indignation, yea, what fear, yea, what vehement desire, yea, what zeal."

For some time Paul had been carrying a burden of soul for the churches—a burden so heavy that he could scarcely endure it. False teachers had sought to destroy his influence among the believers and to urge their own doctrines in the place of gospel truth. The perplexities and discouragements with which Paul was surrounded are revealed in the words, "We were pressed out of measure, above strength, insomuch that we despaired even of life."

But now one cause of anxiety was removed. At the tidings of the acceptance of his letter to the Corinthians, Paul broke forth into words of rejoicing: "Blessed be God, even the Father of our Lord Jesus Christ, the Father of mercies, and the God of all comfort; who comforteth us in all our tribulation, that we may be able to comfort them which are in any trouble, by the comfort wherewith we ourselves are comforted of God. For as the sufferings of Christ abound in us, so our consolation also aboundeth by Christ. And whether we be afflicted, it is for your consolation and salvation, which is effectual in the enduring of the same sufferings which we also suffer: or whether we be comforted, it is for your consolation and salvation. And our hope of you is steadfast, knowing, that as ye are partakers of the sufferings, so shall ye be also of the consolation."

In expressing his joy over their reconversion and their growth in grace, Paul ascribed to God all the praise for this transformation of heart and life. "Thanks be unto God," he exclaimed, "which always causeth us to triumph in Christ, and maketh manifest the savor of His knowledge by us in every place. For we are unto God a sweet savor of Christ, in them that are saved, and in them that perish." It was the custom of the day for a general victorious in warfare to bring with him on his return a train of captives. On such occasions incense bearers were appointed, and as the army marched triumphantly home, the fragrant odor was to the captives appointed to die, a savor of death, showing that they were nearing the time of their execution; but to those of the prisoners who had found favor with their captors, and whose lives were to be spared, it was a savor of life, in that it showed them that their freedom was near.

Paul was now full of faith and hope. He felt that Satan was not to triumph over the work of God in Corinth, and in words of praise he poured forth the gratitude of his heart. He and his fellow laborers would celebrate their victory over the enemies of Christ and the truth, by going forth with new zeal to extend the knowledge of the Saviour. Like incense the fragrance of the gospel was to be diffused throughout the world. To those who should accept Christ, the message would be a savor of life unto life; but to those who should persist in unbelief, a savor of death unto death.

Realizing the overwhelming magnitude of the work, Paul exclaimed, "Who is sufficient for these things?" Who is able to preach Christ in such a way that His enemies shall have no just cause to despise the messenger or the message ³²⁷ that he bears? Paul desired to impress upon believers the solemn responsibility of the gospel ministry. Faithfulness in preaching the word, united with a pure, consistent life, can alone make the efforts of ministers acceptable to God and profitable to souls. Ministers of our day, burdened with a sense of the greatness of the work, may well exclaim with the apostle, "Who is sufficient for these things?"

There were those who had charged Paul with self-commendation in writing his former letter. The apostle now referred to this by asking the members of the church if they thus judged his motives. "Do we begin again to commend ourselves?" he inquired; "or need we, as some others, epistles of commendation to you, or letters of commendation from you?" Believers moving to a new place often carried with them letters of commendation from the church with which they had formerly been united; but the leading workers, the founders of these churches, had no need of such commendation. The Corinthian believers, who had been led from the worship of idols to the faith of the gospel, were themselves all the recommendation that Paul needed. Their reception of the truth, and the reformation wrought in their lives, bore eloquent testimony to the faithfulness of his labors and to his authority to counsel, reprove, and exhort as a minister of Christ.

Paul regarded the Corinthian brethren as his testimonial. "Ye are our epistle," he said, "written in our hearts, known and read of all men:

forasmuch as ye are manifestly declared to be the epistle of Christ ministered by us, written not with ink, but with the Spirit of the living ³²⁸ God; not in tables of stone, but in fleshy tables of the heart."

The conversion of sinners and their sanctification through the truth is the strongest proof a minister can have that God has called him to the ministry. The evidence of his apostleship is written upon the hearts of those converted, and is witnessed to by their renewed lives. Christ is formed within, the hope of glory. A minister is greatly strengthened by these seals of his ministry.

Today the ministers of Christ should have the same witness as that which the Corinthian church bore to Paul's labors. But though in this age there are many preachers, there is a great scarcity of able, holy ministers—men filled with the love that dwelt in the heart of Christ. Pride, self-confidence, love of the world, faultfinding, bitterness, envy, are the fruit borne by many who profess the religion of Christ. Their lives, in sharp contrast to the life of the Saviour, often bear sad testimony to the character of the ministerial labor under which they were converted.

A man can have no greater honor than to be accepted by God as an able minister of the gospel. But those whom the Lord blesses with power and success in His work do not boast. They acknowledge their entire dependence on Him, realizing that of themselves they have no power. With Paul they say, "Not that we are sufficient of ourselves to think anything as of ourselves; but our sufficiency is of God; who also hath made us able ministers of the new testament."

A true minister does the work of the Master. He feels the importance of his work, realizing ³²⁹ that he sustains to the church and to the world a relation similar to that which Christ sustained. He works untiringly to lead sinners to a nobler, higher life, that they may obtain the reward of the overcomer. His lips are touched with a live coal from the altar, and he uplifts Jesus as the sinner's only hope. Those who hear him know that he has drawn near to God in fervent, effectual prayer. The Holy Spirit has rested upon him, his soul has felt the vital, heavenly fire, and he is able to compare spiritual things with spiritual. Power is given him to tear down the strongholds of Satan. Hearts are broken by his presentation of the love of God, and many are led to inquire, "What must I do to be saved?"

"Therefore seeing we have this ministry, as we have received mercy, we faint not; but have renounced the hidden things of dishonesty, not walking in craftiness, nor handling the word of God deceitfully; but by manifestation of the truth commending ourselves to every man's conscience in the sight of God. But if our gospel be hid, it is hid to them that are lost: in whom the god of this world hath blinded the minds of them which believe not, lest the light of the glorious gospel of Christ, who is the image of God, should shine unto them. For we preach not ourselves, but Christ Jesus the Lord; and ourselves your servants for Jesus' sake. For God, who commanded the light to shine out of darkness, hath shined in our hearts, to give the light of the knowledge of the glory of God in the face of Jesus Christ."

330 Thus the apostle magnified the grace and mercy of God, shown in the sacred trust committed to him as a minister of Christ. By God's abundant mercy he and his brethren had been sustained in difficulty, affliction, and danger. They had not modeled their faith and teaching to suit the desires of their hearers, nor kept back truths essential to salvation in order to make their teaching more attractive. They had presented the truth with simplicity and clearness, praying for the conviction and conversion of souls. And they had endeavored to bring their conduct into harmony with their teaching, that the truth presented might commend itself to every man's conscience.

"We have this treasure," the apostle continued, "in earthen vessels, that the excellency of the power may be of God, and not of us." God could have proclaimed His truth through sinless angels, but this is not His plan. He chooses human beings, men compassed with infirmity, as instruments in the working out of His designs. The priceless treasure is placed in earthen vessels. Through men His blessings are to be conveyed to the world. Through them His glory is to shine forth into the darkness of sin. In loving ministry they are to meet the sinful and the needy, and lead them to the cross. And in all their work they are to ascribe glory, honor, and praise to Him who is above all and over all.

Referring to his own experience, Paul showed that in choosing the service of Christ he had not been prompted by selfish motives, for his pathway had been beset by trial and temptation. "We are troubled on every side," he wrote, "yet not distressed; we are perplexed, but not in 331 despair; persecuted, but not forsaken; cast down, but not destroyed; always bearing about in the body the dying of the Lord Jesus, that the life also of Jesus might be made manifest in our body."

Paul reminded his brethren that as Christ's messengers he and his fellow laborers were continually in peril. The hardships they endured were wearing away their strength. "We which live," he wrote, "are alway delivered unto death for Jesus' sake, that the life also of Jesus might be made manifest in our mortal flesh. So then death worketh in us, but life in you." Suffering physically through privation and toil, these ministers of Christ were conforming to His death. But that which was working death in them was

bringing spiritual life and health to the Corinthians, who by a belief in the truth were being made partakers of life eternal. In view of this, the followers of Jesus were to be careful not to increase, by neglect and disaffection, the burdens and trials of the laborers.

"We having the same spirit of faith," Paul continued, "according as it is written, I believed, and therefore have I spoken; we also believe, and therefore speak." Fully convinced of the reality of the truth entrusted to him, nothing could induce Paul to handle the word of God deceitfully or to conceal the convictions of his soul. He would not purchase wealth, honor, or pleasure by conformity to the opinions of the world. Though in constant danger of martyrdom for the faith that he had preached to the Corinthians, he was not intimidated, for he knew that He who had died and risen again would raise him from the grave and present him to the Father.

"All things are for your sakes," he said, "that 332 the abundant grace might through the thanksgiving of many redound to the glory of God." Not for self-aggrandizement did the apostles preach the gospel. It was the hope of saving souls that led them to devote their lives to this work. And it was this hope that kept them from ceasing their efforts because of threatened danger or actual suffering.

"For which cause," Paul declared, "we faint not; but though our outward man perish, yet the inward man is renewed day by day." Paul felt the power of the enemy; but though his physical strength was declining, yet faithfully and unflinchingly he declared the gospel of Christ. Clad in the whole armor of God, this hero of the cross pressed forward in the conflict. His voice of cheer proclaimed him triumphant in the combat. Fixing his gaze on the reward of the faithful, he exclaimed in tones of victory, "Our light affliction, which is but for a moment, worketh for us a far more exceeding and eternal weight of glory; while we look not at the things which are seen, but at the things which are not seen: for the things which are seen are temporal; but the things which are not seen are eternal."

Very earnest and touching is the apostle's appeal that his Corinthian brethren consider anew the matchless love of their Redeemer. "Ye know the grace of our Lord Jesus Christ," he wrote, "that, though He was rich, yet for your sakes He became poor, that ye through His poverty might be rich." You know the height from which He stooped, the depth of humiliation to which He descended. Having once entered upon the path of self-denial and sacrifice, he turned not aside until He had given His 333 life. There was no rest for Him between the throne and the cross.

Point after point Paul lingered over, in order that those who should read his epistle might fully comprehend the wonderful condescension of the Saviour in their behalf. Presenting Christ as He was when equal with God and with Him receiving the homage of the angels, the apostle traced His course until He had reached the lowest depths of humiliation. Paul was convinced that if they could be brought to comprehend the amazing sacrifice made by the Majesty of heaven, all selfishness would be banished from their lives. He showed how the Son of God had laid aside His glory, voluntarily subjecting Himself to the conditions of human nature, and then had humbled Himself as a servant, becoming obedient unto death, "even the death of the cross" (Philippians 2:8), that He might lift fallen man from degradation to hope and joy and heaven.

When we study the divine character in the light of the cross we see mercy, tenderness, and forgiveness blended with equity and justice. We see in the midst of the throne One bearing in hands and feet and side the marks of the suffering endured to reconcile man to God. We see a Father, infinite, dwelling in light unapproachable, yet receiving us to Himself through the merits of His Son. The cloud of vengeance that threatened only misery and despair, in the light reflected from the cross reveals the writing of God: Live, sinner, live! ye penitent, believing souls, live! I have paid a ransom.

334 In the contemplation of Christ we linger on the shore of a love that is measureless. We endeavor to tell of this love, and language fails us. We consider His life on earth, His sacrifice for us, His work in heaven as our advocate, and the mansions He is preparing for those who love Him, and we can only exclaim, O the height and depth of the love of Christ! "Herein is love, not that we loved God, but that He loved us, and sent His Son to be the propitiation for our sins." "Behold, what manner of love the Father hath bestowed upon us, that we should be called the sons of God." 1 John 4:10; 3:1.

In every true disciple this love, like sacred fire, burns on the altar of the heart. It was on the earth that the love of God was revealed through Christ. It is on the earth that His children are to reflect this love through blameless lives. Thus sinners will be led to the cross to behold the Lamb of God.

335

32

A Liberal Church

In his first letter to the church at Corinth, Paul gave the believers instruction regarding the general principles underlying the support of God's work in the earth. Writing of his apostolic labors in their behalf, he inquired:

"Who goeth a warfare any time at his own charges? who planteth a vineyard, and eateth not of the fruit thereof? or who feedeth a flock, and eateth not of the milk of the flock? Say I these things as a man? or saith not the law the same also? For it is written in the law of Moses, Thou shalt not muzzle the mouth of the ox that treadeth out the corn. Doth God take care for oxen? or saith He it altogether for our sakes? For our sakes, no doubt, this is written: that he that ploweth should plow in hope; and that he that thresheth in hope should be partaker of his hope.

"If we have sown unto you spiritual things," the apostle further inquired, "is it a great thing if we shall reap your carnal things? If others be 336 partakers of this power over you, are not we rather? Nevertheless we have not used this power; but suffer all things, lest we should hinder the gospel of Christ. Do ye not know that they which minister about holy things live of the things of the temple? and they which wait at the altar are partakers with the altar? Even so hath the Lord ordained that they which preach the gospel should live of the gospel." 1 Corinthians 9:7-14.

The apostle here referred to the Lord's plan for the maintenance of the priests who ministered in the temple. Those who were set apart to this holy office were supported by their brethren, to whom they ministered spiritual blessings. "Verily they that are of the sons of Levi, who receive the office of the priesthood, have a commandment to take tithes of the people according to the law." Hebrews 7:5. The tribe of Levi was chosen by the Lord for the sacred offices pertaining to the temple and the priesthood. Of the priest it was said, "The Lord thy God hath chosen him . . . to stand to minister in the name of the Lord." (Deuteronomy 18:5.) One tenth of all the increase was claimed by the Lord as His own, and to withhold the tithe was regarded by Him as robbery.

It was to this plan for the support of the ministry that Paul referred when he said, "Even so hath the Lord ordained that they which preach the gospel should live of the gospel." And later, in writing to Timothy, the apostle said, "The laborer is worthy of his reward." 1 Timothy 5:18.

The payment of the tithe was but a part of God's plan for the support of His service. 337 Numerous gifts and offerings were divinely specified. Under the Jewish system the people were taught to cherish a spirit of liberality both in sustaining the cause of God and in supplying the wants of the needy. For special occasions there were freewill offerings. At the harvest and the vintage, the first fruits of the field—corn, wine, and oil—were consecrated as an offering to the Lord. The gleanings and the corners of the field were reserved for the poor. The first fruits of the wool when the sheep were shorn, of the grain when the wheat was threshed, were set apart for God. So also were the first-born of all animals, and a redemption price was paid for the first-born son. The first fruits were to be presented before the Lord at the sanctuary and were then devoted to the use of the priests.

By this system of benevolence the Lord sought to teach Israel that in everything He must be first. Thus they were reminded that God was the proprietor of their fields, their flocks, and their herds; that it was He who sent them the sunshine and the rain that developed and ripened the harvest. Everything that they possessed was His; they were but the stewards of His goods.

It is not God's purpose that Christians, whose privileges far exceed those of the Jewish nation, shall give less freely than they gave. "Unto whomsoever much is given," the Saviour declared, "of him shall be much required." Luke 12:48. The liberality required of the Hebrews was largely to benefit their own nation; today 338 the work of God extends over all the earth. In the hands of His followers, Christ has placed the treasures of the gospel, and upon them He has laid the responsibility of giving the glad tidings of salvation to the world. Surely our obligations are much greater than were those of ancient Israel.

As God's work extends, calls for help will come more and more frequently. That these calls may be answered, Christians should heed the command, "Bring ye all the tithes into the storehouse, that there may be meat in Mine house." Malachi 3:10. If professing Christians would faithfully bring to God their tithes and offerings, His treasury would be full. There would then be no occasion to resort to fairs, lotteries, or parties of pleasure to secure funds for the support of the gospel.

Men are tempted to use their means in self-indulgence, in the gratification of appetite, in personal adornment, or in the embellishment of their homes. For these objects many church members do not hesitate to spend freely and even extravagantly. But when asked to give to the Lord's treasury, to carry forward His work in the earth, they demur. Perhaps, feeling that they cannot well do otherwise, they dole out a sum far smaller than they often spend for needless indulgence. They manifest no real love for Christ's service, no earnest interest in the salvation of souls. What marvel that the Christian life of such ones is but a dwarfed, sickly existence!

He whose heart is aglow with the love of Christ will regard it as not only a duty, but a 339 pleasure, to aid in the advancement of the highest, holiest work committed to man—the work of presenting to the world the riches of goodness, mercy, and truth.

It is the spirit of covetousness which leads men to keep for gratification of self means that rightfully belong to God, and this spirit is as abhorrent to Him now as when through His prophet He sternly rebuked His people, saying, "Will a man rob God? Yet ye have robbed Me. But ye say, Wherein have we robbed Thee? In tithes and offerings. Ye are cursed with a curse: for ye have robbed Me, even this whole nation." Malachi 3:8, 9.

The spirit of liberality is the spirit of heaven. This spirit finds its highest manifestation in Christ's sacrifice on the cross. In our behalf the Father gave His only-begotten Son; and Christ, having given up all that He had, then gave Himself, that man might be saved. The cross of Calvary should appeal to the benevolence of every follower of the Saviour. The principle there illustrated is to give, give. "He that saith he abideth in Him ought himself also so to walk, even as He walked." 1 John 2:6.

On the other hand, the spirit of selfishness is the spirit of Satan. The principle illustrated in the lives of worldlings is to get, get. Thus they hope to secure happiness and ease, but the fruit of their sowing is misery and death.

Not until God ceases to bless His children will they cease to be under bonds to return to Him the portion that He claims. Not only should they render the Lord the portion that belongs to Him, but they should bring also to His treasury, 340 as a gratitude offering, a liberal tribute. With joyful hearts they should dedicate to the Creator the first fruits of their bounties—their choicest possessions, their best and holiest service. Thus they will gain rich blessings. God Himself will make their souls like a watered garden whose waters fail not. And when the last great harvest is gathered in, the sheaves that they are enabled to bring to the Master will be the recompense of their unselfish use of the talents lent them.

God's chosen messengers, who are engaged in aggressive labor, should never be compelled to go a warfare at their own charges, unaided by the sympathetic and hearty support of their brethren. It is the part of church members to deal liberally with those who lay aside their secular employment that they may give themselves to the ministry. When God's ministers are encouraged, His cause is greatly advanced. But when, through the selfishness of men, their rightful support is withheld, their hands are weakened, and often their usefulness is seriously crippled.

The displeasure of God is kindled against those who claim to be His followers, yet allow consecrated workers to suffer for the necessities of life while engaged in active ministry. These selfish ones will be called to render an account, not only for the misuse of their Lord's money, but for the depression and heartache which their course has brought upon His faithful servants. Those who are called to the work of the ministry, and at the call of duty give up all to engage in God's service, should receive for their self-sacrificing efforts wages sufficient to support themselves and their families.

In the various departments of secular labor, mental and physical, faithful workmen can earn good wages. Is not the work of disseminating truth, and leading souls to Christ, of more importance than any ordinary business? And are not those who faithfully engage in this work justly entitled to ample remuneration? By our estimate of the relative value of labor for moral and for physical good, we show our appreciation of the heavenly in contrast with the earthly.

That there may be funds in the treasury for the support of the ministry, and to meet the calls for assistance in missionary enterprises, it is necessary that the people of God give cheerfully and liberally. A solemn responsibility rests upon ministers to keep before the churches the needs of the cause of God and to educate them to be liberal. When this is neglected, and the churches fail to give for the necessities of others, not only does the work of the Lord suffer, but the blessing that should come to believers is withheld.

Even the very poor should bring their offerings to God. They are to be sharers of the grace of Christ by denying self to help those whose need is more pressing than their own. The poor man's gift, the fruit of self-denial, comes up before God as fragrant incense. And every act of self-sacrifice strengthens the spirit of beneficence in the giver's heart, allying him more closely to the One who was rich, yet for our sakes became poor, that we through His poverty might be rich.

The act of the widow who cast two mites—all that she had—into the treasury, is placed on record for the encouragement of those who, struggling with poverty, still desire by their gifts to aid the cause of God. Christ called the attention of the disciples to this woman, who had given "all her living." Mark 12:44. He esteemed her gift of more value than the large offerings of those whose alms did not call for self-denial. From their abundance they had given a small portion. To make her offering, the widow had deprived herself of even the necessities of life, trusting God to supply her needs for the morrow. Of her the Saviour declared, "Verily I say unto you, That this poor widow hath cast more in, than all they which have cast into the treasury." Verse 43. Thus He taught that the value of the gift is estimated not by the amount, but by the proportion that is given and the motive that actuates the giver.

The apostle Paul in his ministry among the churches was untiring in his efforts to inspire in the hearts of the new converts a desire to do large things for the cause of God. Often he exhorted them to the exercise of liberality. In speaking to the elders of Ephesus of his former labors among them, he said, "I have showed you all things, how that so laboring ye ought to support the weak, and to remember the words of the Lord Jesus, how He said, It is more blessed to give than to receive." "He which soweth sparingly," he wrote to the Corinthians, "shall reap also sparingly; and he which soweth bountifully shall reap also bountifully. Every man according as he purposeth in his heart, so let him give; not grudgingly, or of necessity: for God loveth a cheerful giver." Acts 20:35; 2 Corinthians 9:6, 7.

Nearly all the Macedonian believers were poor in this world's goods, but their hearts were overflowing with love for God and His truth, and they gladly gave for the support of the gospel. When general collections were taken up in the Gentile churches for the relief of the Jewish believers, the liberality of the converts in Macedonia was held up as an example to other churches. Writing to the Corinthian believers, the apostle called their attention to "the grace of God bestowed on the churches of Macedonia; how that in a great trial of affliction the abundance of their joy and their deep poverty abounded unto the riches of their liberality. For to their power, . . . yea, and beyond their power they were willing of themselves; praying us with much entreaty that we would receive the gift, and take upon us the fellowship of the ministering to the saints." 2 Corinthians 8:1-4.

The willingness to sacrifice on the part of the Macedonian believers came as a result of wholehearted consecration. Moved by the Spirit of God, they "first gave their own selves to the Lord" (2 Corinthians 8:5), then they were willing to give freely of their means for the support of the gospel. It was not necessary to urge them to give; rather, they rejoiced in the privilege of denying themselves even of necessary things in order to supply the needs of others. When the apostle would have restrained them, they importuned him to accept their offering. In their simplicity and integrity, and in their love for the brethren, they gladly denied self, and thus abounded in the fruit of benevolence.

When Paul sent Titus to Corinth to strengthen the believers there, he instructed him to build up that church in the grace of giving, and in a personal letter to the believers he also added his own appeal. "As ye abound in everything," he pleaded, "in faith, and utterance, and knowledge, and in all diligence, and in your love to us, see that ye abound in this grace also." "Now therefore perform the doing of it; that as there was a readiness to will, so there may be a performance also out of that which ye have. For if there be first a willing mind, it is accepted according to that a man hath, and not according to that he hath not." "And God is able to make all grace abound toward you; that ye, always having all sufficiency in all things, may abound to every good work: . . . . being enriched in everything to all bountifulness, which causeth through us thanksgiving to God." 2 Corinthians 8:7, 11, 12; 9:8-11.

Unselfish liberality threw the early church into a transport of joy; for the believers knew that their efforts were helping to send the gospel message to those in darkness. Their benevolence testified that they had not received the grace of God in vain. What could produce such liberality but the sanctification of the Spirit? In the eyes of believers and unbelievers it was a miracle of grace.

Spiritual prosperity is closely bound up with Christian liberality. The followers of Christ should rejoice in the privilege of revealing in their lives the beneficence of their Redeemer. As they give to the Lord they have the assurance that their treasure is going before them to the heavenly courts. Would men make their property secure? Let them place it in the hands that bear the marks of the crucifixion. Would they enjoy their substance? Let them use it to bless the needy and suffering. Would they increase their possessions? Let them heed the divine injunction, "Honor the Lord with thy substance, and with the first fruits of all thine increase: so shall thy barns be filled with plenty, and thy presses shall burst out with new wine." Proverbs 3:9, 10. Let them seek to retain their possessions for selfish purposes, and it will be to their eternal loss. But let their treasure be given to God, and from that moment it bears His inscription. It is sealed with His immutability.

God declares, "Blessed are ye that sow beside all waters." Isaiah 32:20. A continual imparting of God's gifts wherever the cause of God or the needs of humanity demand our aid, does not tend to poverty. "There is that scattereth, and yet increaseth; and there is that withholdeth more than is meet, but it tendeth to poverty." Proverbs 11:24. The sower multiplies his seed by casting it away. So it is with those who are faithful in distributing God's gifts. By imparting they increase their blessings. "Give, and it shall be given unto you," God has promised; "good measure, pressed down, and shaken together, and running over, shall men give into your bosom." Luke 6:38.

33

Laboring Under Difficulties

While Paul was careful to set before his converts the plain teaching of Scripture regarding the proper support of the work of God, and while he claimed for himself as a minister of the gospel the "power to forbear working" (1

Corinthians 9:6) at secular employment as a means of self-support, yet at various times during his ministry in the great centers of civilization he wrought at a handicraft for his own maintenance.

Among the Jews physical toil was not thought strange or degrading. Through Moses the Hebrews had been instructed to train their children to industrious habits, and it was regarded as a sin to allow the youth to grow up in ignorance of physical labor. Even though a child was to be educated for holy office, a knowledge of practical life was thought essential. Every youth, whether his parents were rich or poor, was taught some trade. Those parents who neglected to provide such a training for their children were looked upon as departing from the instruction of the Lord. In accordance with this custom, Paul had early learned the trade of tentmaking.

Before he became a disciple of Christ, Paul had occupied a high position and was not dependent upon manual labor for support. But afterward, when he had used all his means in furthering the cause of Christ, he resorted at times to his trade to gain a livelihood. Especially was this the case when he labored in places where his motives might have been misunderstood.

It is at Thessalonica that we first read of Paul's working with his hands in self-supporting labor while preaching the word. Writing to the church of believers there, he reminded them that he "might have been burdensome" to them, and added: "Ye remember, brethren, our labor and travail: for laboring night and day, because we would not be chargeable unto any of you, we preached unto you the gospel of God." 1 Thessalonians 2:6, 9. And again, in his second epistle to them, he declared that he and his fellow laborer while with them had not eaten "any man's bread for nought." Night and day we worked, he wrote, "that we might not be chargeable to any of you: not because we have not power, but to make ourselves an ensample unto you to follow us." 2 Thessalonians 3:8, 9.

At Thessalonica Paul had met those who refused to work with their hands. It was of this class that he afterward wrote: "There are some which walk among you disorderly, working not at all, but are busybodies. Now them that are such we command and exhort by our Lord Jesus Christ, that with quietness they work, and eat their own bread." While laboring in Thessalonica, Paul had been careful to set before such ones a right example. "Even when we were with you," he wrote, "this we commanded you, that if any would not work, neither should he eat." Verses 11, 12, 10.

In every age Satan has sought to impair the efforts of God's servants by introducing into the church a spirit of fanaticism. Thus it was in

345

346

347

348

Paul's day, and thus it was in later centuries during the time of the Reformation. Wycliffe, Luther, and many others who blessed the world by their influence and their faith, encountered the wiles by which the enemy seeks to lead into fanaticism overzealous, unbalanced, and unsanctified minds. Misguided souls have taught that the attainment of true holiness carries the mind above all earthly thoughts and leads men to refrain wholly from labor. Others, taking extreme views of certain texts of Scripture, have taught that it is a sin to work—that Christians should take no thought concerning the temporal welfare of themselves or their families, but should devote their lives wholly to spiritual things. The teaching and example of the apostle Paul are a rebuke to such extreme views.

Paul was not wholly dependent upon the labor of his hands for support while at Thessalonica. Referring later to his experiences in that city, he wrote to the Philippian believers in acknowledgment of the gifts he had received from them while there, saying, "Even in Thessalonica ye sent once and again unto my necessity." Philippians 4:16. Notwithstanding the fact 349 that he received this help he was careful to set before the Thessalonians an example of diligence, so that none could rightfully accuse him of covetousness, and also that those who held fanatical views regarding manual labor might be given a practical rebuke.

When Paul first visited Corinth, he found himself among a people who were suspicious of the motives of strangers. The Greeks on the seacoast were keen traders. So long had they trained themselves in sharp business practices, that they had come to believe that gain was godliness, and that to make money, whether by fair means or foul, was commendable. Paul was acquainted with their characteristics, and he would give them no occasion for saying that he preached the gospel in order to enrich himself. He might justly have claimed support from his Corinthian hearers; but this right he was willing to forgo, lest his usefulness and success as a minister should be injured by the unjust suspicion that he was preaching the gospel for gain. He would seek to remove all occasion for misrepresentation, that the force of his message might not be lost.

Soon after his arrival at Corinth, Paul found "a certain Jew named Aquila, born in Pontus, lately come from Italy, with his wife Priscilla." These were "of the same craft" with himself. Banished by the decree of Claudius, which commanded all Jews to leave Rome, Aquila and Priscilla had come to Corinth, where they established a business as manufacturers of tents. Paul made inquiry concerning them, and learning that they feared God and were seeking to avoid the contaminating influences with which they

were surrounded, "he abode with them, and 350 wrought. . . . And he reasoned in the synagogue every Sabbath, and persuaded the Jews and the Greeks." Acts 18:2-4.

Later, Silas and Timothy joined Paul at Corinth. These brethren brought with them funds from the churches in Macedonia, for the support of the work.

In his second letter to the believers in Corinth, written after he had raised up a strong church there, Paul reviewed his manner of life among them. "Have I committed an offense," he asked, "in abasing myself that ye might be exalted, because I have preached to you the gospel of God freely? I robbed other churches, taking wages of them, to do you service. And when I was present with you, and wanted, I was chargeable to no man: for that which was lacking to me the brethren which came from Macedonia supplied: and in all things I have kept myself from being burdensome unto you, and so will I keep myself. As the truth of Christ is in me, no man shall stop me of this boasting in the regions of Achaia." 2 Corinthians 11:7-10.

Paul tells why he had followed this course in Corinth. It was that he might give no cause for reproach to "them which desire occasion." 2 Corinthians 11:12. While he had worked at tentmaking he had also labored faithfully in the proclamation of the gospel. He himself declares of his labors, "Truly the signs of an apostle were wrought among you in all patience, in signs, and wonders, and mighty deeds." And he adds, "For what is it wherein ye were inferior to other churches, except it be that I myself was not burdensome to you? Forgive me this wrong. Behold, the third time I am ready to come to 351 you; and I will not be burdensome to you: for I seek not yours, but you. . . . And I will very gladly spend and be spent for you." 2 Corinthians 12:12-15.

During the long period of his ministry in Ephesus, where for three years he carried forward an aggressive evangelistic effort throughout that region, Paul again worked at his trade. In Ephesus, as in Corinth, the apostle was cheered by the presence of Aquila and Priscilla, who had accompanied him on his return to Asia at the close of his second missionary journey.

There were some who objected to Paul's toiling with his hands, declaring that it was inconsistent with the work of a gospel minister. Why should Paul, a minister of the highest rank, thus connect mechanical work with the preaching of the word? Was not the laborer worthy of his hire? Why should he spend in making tents time that to all appearance could be put to better account?

But Paul did not regard as lost the time thus spent. As he worked with Aquila he kept in touch with the Great Teacher, losing no opportunity of witnessing for the Saviour, and of helping those who needed help. His mind was ever reaching out for spiritual knowledge. He gave his fellow workers instruction in spiritual things, and he also set an example of industry and thoroughness. He was a quick, skillful worker, diligent in business, "fervent in spirit, serving the Lord." Romans 12:11. As he worked at his trade, the apostle had access to a class of people that he could not otherwise have 352 reached. He showed his associates that skill in the common arts is a gift from God, who provides both the gift and the wisdom to use it aright. He taught that even in everyday toil God is to be honored. His toil-hardened hands detracted nothing from the force of his pathetic appeals as a Christian minister.

Paul sometimes worked night and day, not only for his own support, but that he might assist his fellow laborers. He shared his earnings with Luke, and he helped Timothy. He even suffered hunger at times, that he might relieve the necessities of others. His was an unselfish life. Toward the close of his ministry, on the occasion of his farewell talk to the elders of Ephesus, at Miletus, he could lift up before them his toilworn hands, and say, "I have coveted no man's silver, or gold, or apparel. Yea, ye yourselves know, that these hands have ministered unto my necessities, and to them that were with me. I have showed you all things, how that so laboring ye ought to support the weak, and to remember the words of the Lord Jesus, how He said, It is more blessed to give than to receive." Acts 20:33-35.

If ministers feel that they are suffering hardship and privation in the cause of Christ, let them in imagination visit the workshop where Paul labored. Let them bear in mind that while this chosen man of God is fashioning the canvas, he is working for bread which he has justly earned by his labors as an apostle.

Work is a blessing, not a curse. A spirit of indolence destroys godliness and grieves the 353 Spirit of God. A stagnant pool is offensive, but a pure, flowing stream spreads health and gladness over the land. Paul knew that those who neglect physical work soon become enfeebled. He desired to teach young ministers that by working with their hands, by bringing into exercise their muscles and sinews, they would become strong to endure the toils and privations that awaited them in the gospel field. And he realized that his own teachings would lack vitality and force if he did not keep all parts of the system properly exercised.

The indolent forfeit the invaluable experience gained by a faithful performance of the common duties of life. Not a few, but thousands of human beings exist only to consume the benefits which God in His mercy bestows upon them. They forget to bring to the Lord gratitude offerings for the riches He has entrusted to them. They forget that by trading wisely on the talents lent them they are to be producers as well as consumers. If they comprehended the work that the Lord desires them to do as His helping hand they would not shun responsibility.

The usefulness of young men who feel that they are called by God to preach, depends much upon the manner in which they enter upon their labors. Those who are chosen of God for the work of the ministry will give proof of their high calling and by every possible means will seek to develop into able workmen. They will endeavor to gain an experience that will fit them to plan, organize, and execute. Appreciating the sacredness of their calling, they will, by self-discipline, become more and still more like their Master, revealing His goodness, love, and truth. 354 And as they manifest earnestness in improving the talents entrusted to them, the church should help them judiciously.

Not all who feel that they have been called to preach, should be encouraged to throw themselves and their families at once upon the church for continuous financial support. There is danger that some of limited experience may be spoiled by flattery, and by unwise encouragement to expect full support independent of any serious effort on their part. The means dedicated to the extension of the work of God should not be consumed by men who desire to preach only that they may receive support and thus gratify a selfish ambition for an easy life.

Young men who desire to exercise their gifts in the work of the ministry, will find a helpful lesson in the example of Paul at Thessalonica, Corinth, Ephesus, and other places. Although an eloquent speaker, and chosen by God to do a special work, he was never above labor, nor did he ever weary of sacrificing for the cause he loved. "Even unto this present hour," he wrote to the Corinthians, "we both hunger, and thirst, and are naked, and are buffeted, and have no certain dwelling place; and labor, working with our own hands: being reviled, we bless; being persecuted, we suffer it." 1 Corinthians 4:11, 12.

One of the greatest of human teachers, Paul cheerfully performed the lowliest as well as the highest duties. When in his service for the Master circumstances seemed to require it, he willingly labored at his trade. Nevertheless, he ever held himself ready to lay aside his secular work, in order to meet the opposition of the enemies of the gospel, or to improve a special 355 opportunity to win souls to Jesus. His zeal and industry are a rebuke to indolence and desire for ease.

Paul set an example against the sentiment, then gaining influence in the church, that the gospel could be proclaimed successfully only by those who were wholly freed from the necessity of physical toil. He illustrated in a practical way what might be done by consecrated laymen in many places where the people were unacquainted with the truths of the gospel. His course inspired many humble toilers with a desire to do what they could to advance the cause of God, while at the same time they supported themselves in daily labor. Aquila and Priscilla were not called to give their whole time to the ministry of the gospel, yet these humble laborers were used by God to show Apollos the way of truth more perfectly. The Lord employs various instrumentalities for the accomplishment of His purpose, and while some with special talents are chosen to devote all their energies to the work of teaching and preaching the gospel, many others, upon whom human hands have never been laid in ordination, are called to act an important part in soul-saving.

There is a large field open before the self-supporting gospel worker. Many may gain valuable experiences in ministry while toiling a portion of the time at some form of manual labor, and by this method strong workers may be developed for important service in needy fields.

The self-sacrificing servant of God who labors untiringly in word and doctrine, carries on his heart a heavy burden. He does not mea356 sure his work by hours. His wages do not influence him in his labor, nor is he turned from his duty because of unfavorable conditions. From heaven he received his commission, and to heaven he looks for his recompense when the work entrusted to him is done.

It is God's design that such workers shall be freed from unnecessary anxiety, that they may have full opportunity to obey the injunction of Paul to Timothy, "Meditate upon these things; give thyself wholly to them." 1 Timothy 4:15. While they should be careful to exercise sufficiently to keep mind and body vigorous, yet it is not God's plan that they should be compelled to spend a large part of their time at secular employment.

These faithful workers, though willing to spend and be spent for the gospel, are not exempt from temptation. When hampered and burdened with anxiety because of a failure on the part of the church to give them proper financial support, some are fiercely beset by the tempter. When they see their labors so lightly prized, they become depressed. True, they look forward to the time of the judgment for their just award, and this buoys them up; but meanwhile their families must have food and clothing. If they could feel that they were released from their divine commission they would willingly labor with their hands. But they realize that their time belongs to God, notwithstanding the short-sightedness of those who should provide them with sufficient funds. They rise above the temptation to enter into pursuits by which they could

soon place themselves beyond the reach of want, and they continue to labor for the advancement of the cause that is dearer to them than life itself. In order to do this, they may, 357 however, be forced to follow the example of Paul and engage for a time in manual labor while continuing to carry forward their ministerial work. This they do to advance not their own interests, but the interests of God's cause in the earth.

There are times when it seems to the servant of God impossible to do the work necessary to be done, because of the lack of means to carry on a strong, solid work. Some are fearful that with the facilities at their command they cannot do all that they feel it their duty to do. But if they advance in faith, the salvation of God will be revealed, and prosperity will attend their efforts. He who has bidden His followers go into all parts of the world will sustain every laborer who in obedience to His command seeks to proclaim His message.

In the upbuilding of His work the Lord does not always make everything plain before His servants. He sometimes tries the confidence of His people by bringing about circumstances which compel them to move forward in faith. Often He brings them into strait and trying places, and bids them advance when their feet seem to be touching the waters of Jordan. It is at such times, when the prayers of His servants ascend to Him in earnest faith, that God opens the way before them and brings them out into a large place.

When God's messengers recognize their responsibilities toward the needy portions of the Lord's vineyard, and in the spirit of the Master Worker labor untiringly for the conversion of souls, the angels of God will prepare the way before them, and the means necessary for the carrying forward of the work will be provided. 358 Those who are enlightened will give freely to support the work done in their behalf. They will respond liberally to every call for help, and the Spirit of God will move upon their hearts to sustain the Lord's cause not only in the home fields, but in the regions beyond. Thus strength will come to the working forces in other places, and the work of the Lord will advance in His own appointed way.

34

A Consecrated Ministry

In His life and lessons Christ has given a perfect exemplification of the unselfish ministry which has its origin in God. God does not live for Himself. By creating the world, and by upholding all things, He is constantly minister-

359

ing to others. "He maketh His sun to rise on the evil and on the good, and sendeth rain on the just and on the unjust." Matthew 5:45. This ideal of ministry the Father committed to His Son. Jesus was given to stand at the head of humanity, by His example to teach what it means to minister. His whole life was under a law of service. He served all, ministered to all.

Again and again Jesus tried to establish this principle among His disciples. When James and John made their request for pre-eminence, He said, "Whosoever will be great among you, let him be your minister; and whosoever will be chief among you, let him be your servant: even as the Son of man came not to be ministered unto, but to minister, and to give His life a ransom for many." Matthew 20:26-28.

360 Since His ascension Christ has carried forward His work on the earth by chosen ambassadors, through whom He speaks to the children of men and ministers to their needs. The great Head of the church superintends His work through the instrumentality of men ordained by God to act as His representatives.

The position of those who have been called of God to labor in word and doctrine for the upbuilding of His church, is one of grave responsibility. In Christ's stead they are to beseech men and women to be reconciled to God, and they can fulfill their mission only as they receive wisdom and power from above.

Christ's ministers are the spiritual guardians of the people entrusted to their care. Their work has been likened to that of watchmen. In ancient times sentinels were often stationed on the walls of cities, where, from points of vantage, they could overlook important posts to be guarded, and give warning of the approach of an enemy. Upon their faithfulness depended the safety of all within. At stated intervals they were required to call to one another, to make sure that all were awake and that no harm had befallen any. The cry of good cheer or of warning was borne from one to another, each repeating the call till it echoed round the city.

To every minister the Lord declares: "O son of man, I have set thee a watchman unto the house of Israel; therefore thou shalt hear the word at My mouth, and warn them from Me. When I say unto the wicked, O wicked man, thou shalt surely die; if thou dost not speak to 361 warn the wicked from his way, that wicked man shall die in his iniquity; but his blood will I require at thine hand. Nevertheless, if thou warn the wicked of his way to turn from it, . . . thou hast delivered thy soul." Ezekiel 33:7-9.

The words of the prophet declare the solemn responsibility of those who are appointed as guardians of the church of God, stewards of the mysteries of God. They are to stand as watchmen on the walls of Zion, to sound the note of alarm at the approach of the enemy. Souls are in

danger of falling under temptation, and they will perish unless God's ministers are faithful to their trust. If for any reason their spiritual senses become so benumbed that they are unable to discern danger, and through their failure to give warning the people perish, God will require at their hands the blood of those who are lost.

It is the privilege of the watchmen on the walls of Zion to live so near to God, and to be so susceptible to the impressions of His Spirit, that He can work through them to tell men and women of their peril and point them to the place of safety. Faithfully are they to warn them of the sure result of transgression, and faithfully are they to safeguard the interests of the church. At no time may they relax their vigilance. Theirs is a work requiring the exercise of every faculty of the being. In trumpet tones their voices are to be lifted, and never are they to sound one wavering, uncertain note. Not for wages are they to labor, but because they cannot do otherwise, because they realize that there is a woe upon them if they fail to preach the gospel. Chosen of 362 God, sealed with the blood of consecration, they are to rescue men and women from impending destruction.

The minister who is a co-worker with Christ will have a deep sense of the sacredness of his work and of the toil and sacrifice required to perform it successfully. He does not study his own ease or convenience. He is forgetful of self. In his search for the lost sheep he does not realize that he himself is weary, cold, and hungry. He has but one object in view—the saving of the lost.

He who serves under the bloodstained banner of Immanuel will have that to do which will call for heroic effort and patient endurance. But the soldier of the cross stands unshrinkingly in the forefront of the battle. As the enemy presses the attack against him, he turns to the stronghold for aid, and as he brings to the Lord the promises of the word, he is strengthened for the duties of the hour. He realizes his need of strength from above. The victories that he gains do not lead to self exaltation, but cause him to lean more and more heavily on the Mighty One. Relying upon that Power, he is enabled to present the message of salvation so forcibly that it vibrates in other minds.

He who teaches the word must himself live in conscious, hourly communion with God through prayer and a study of His word, for here is the source of strength. Communion with God will impart to the minister's efforts a power greater than the influence of his preaching. Of this power he must not allow himself to be deprived. With an earnestness that cannot be denied, he must plead with God to strengthen and fortify him for duty and trial, and to touch his lips with living fire. All too slight is the hold 363 that Christ's ambassadors often have upon eternal realities. If men will walk with God, He will hide them in the cleft of the Rock. Thus hidden, they can see God, even as Moses saw Him. By the power and light that He imparts they can comprehend more and accomplish more than their finite judgment had seemed possible.

Satan's craft is most successfully used against those who are depressed. When discouragement threatens to overwhelm the minister, let him spread out before God his necessities. It was when the heavens were as brass over Paul that he trusted most fully in God. More than most men, he knew the meaning of affliction; but listen to his triumphant cry as, beset by temptation and conflict, his feet press heavenward: "Our light affliction, which is but for a moment, worketh for us a far more exceeding and eternal weight of glory; while we look not at the things which are seen, but at the things which are not seen." 2 Corinthians 4:17, 18. Paul's eyes were ever fastened on the unseen and eternal. Realizing that he was fighting against supernatural powers, he placed his dependence on God, and in this lay his strength. It is by seeing Him who is invisible that strength and vigor of soul are gained and the power of earth over mind and character is broken.

A pastor should mingle freely with the people for whom he labors, that by becoming acquainted with them he may know how to adapt his teaching to their needs. When a minister has preached a sermon, his work has but just begun. There is personal work for him to do. He should
364 visit the people in their homes, talking and praying with them in earnestness and humility. There are families who will never be reached by the truths of God's word unless the stewards of His grace enter their homes and point them to the higher way. But the hearts of those who do this work must throb in unison with the heart of Christ.

Much is comprehended in the command, "Go out into the highways and hedges, and compel them to come in, that My house may be filled." Luke 14:23. Let ministers teach the truth in families, drawing close to those for whom they labor, and as they thus co-operate with God, He will clothe them with spiritual power. Christ will guide them in their work, giving them words to speak that will sink deep into the hearts of the listeners. It is the privilege of every minister to be able to say with Paul, "I have not shunned to declare unto you all the counsel of God." "I kept back nothing that was profitable unto you, but have showed you, and have taught you publicly, and from house to house, . . . repentance toward God, and faith toward our Lord Jesus Christ." Acts 20:27, 20, 21.

The Saviour went from house to house, healing the sick, comforting the mourners, soothing the afflicted, speaking peace to the disconsolate. He took the little children in His arms and blessed them, and spoke words of hope and comfort to the weary mothers. With unfailing tenderness and gentleness He met every form of human woe and affliction. Not for Himself but for others did He labor. He was the servant of all. It was His meat and drink to bring hope and strength to all with whom He came in contact. And as men and women listened to the truths 365 that fell from His lips, so different from the traditions and dogmas taught by the rabbis, hope sprang up in their hearts. In His teaching there was an earnestness that sent His words home with convicting power.

God's ministers are to learn Christ's method of laboring, that they may bring from the storehouse of His word that which will supply the spiritual needs of those for whom they labor. Thus only can they fulfill their trust. The same Spirit that dwelt in Christ as He imparted the instruction He was constantly receiving, is to be the source of their knowledge and the secret of their power in carrying on the Saviour's work in the world.

Some who have labored in the ministry have failed of attaining success because they have not given their undivided interest to the Lord's work. Ministers should have no engrossing interests aside from the great work of leading souls to the Saviour. The fishermen whom Christ called, straightway left their nets and followed Him. Ministers cannot do acceptable work for God and at the same time carry the burden of large personal business enterprises. Such a division of interest dims their spiritual perception. The mind and heart are occupied with earthly things, and the service of Christ takes a second place. They seek to shape their work for God by their circumstances, instead of shaping circumstances to meet the demands of God.

The energies of the minister are all needed for his high calling. His best powers belong to God. He should not engage in speculation or in any other business that would turn him aside from 366 his great work. "No man that warreth," Paul declared, "entangleth himself with the affairs of this life; that he may please him who hath chosen him to be a soldier." 2 Timothy 2:4. Thus the apostle emphasized the minister's need of unreserved consecration to the Master's service. The minister who is wholly consecrated to God refuses to engage in business that would hinder him from giving himself fully to his sacred calling. He is not striving for earthly honor or riches; his one purpose is to tell others of the Saviour, who gave Himself to bring to human beings the riches of eternal life. His highest desire is not to lay up treasure in this world, but to bring to the attention of the indifferent and the disloyal the realities of eternity. He may be asked to engage in enterprises which promise large worldly gain, but to such temptations he returns the answer, "What shall it profit a man, if he shall gain the whole world, and lose his own soul?" Mark 8:36.

Satan presented this inducement to Christ, knowing that if He accepted it, the world would never be ransomed. And under different guises he presents the same temptation to God's ministers today, knowing that those who are beguiled by it will be false to their trust.

It is not God's will that His ministers should seek to be rich. Regarding this, Paul wrote to Timothy: "The love of money is the root of all evil: which while some coveted after, they have erred from the faith, and pierced themselves through with many sorrows. But thou, O man of God, flee these things; and follow after right- 367 eousness, godliness, faith, love, patience, meekness." By example as well as by precept, the ambassador for Christ is to "charge them that are rich in this world, that they be not highminded, nor trust in uncertain riches, but in the living God, who giveth us richly all things to enjoy; that they do good, that they be rich in good works, ready to distribute, willing to communicate; laying up in store for themselves a good foundation against the time to come, that they may lay hold on eternal life." 1 Timothy 6:10, 11, 17-19.

The experiences of the apostle Paul and his instruction regarding the sacredness of the minister's work are a source of help and inspiration to those engaged in the gospel ministry. Paul's heart burned with a love for sinners, and he put all his energies into the work of soul winning. There never lived a more self-denying, persevering worker. The blessings he received he prized as so many advantages to be used in blessing others. He lost no opportunity of speaking of the Saviour or of helping those in trouble. From place to place he went, preaching the gospel of Christ and establishing churches. Wherever he could find a hearing, he sought to counteract wrong, and to turn the feet of men and women into the path of righteousness.

Paul did not forget the churches that he had established. After making a missionary tour, he and Barnabas retraced their steps and visited the churches they had raised up, choosing from them men whom they could train to unite in proclaiming the gospel.

This feature of Paul's work contains an 368 important lesson for ministers today. The apostle made it a part of his work to educate young men for the office of the ministry. He took them with him on his missionary journeys, and thus they gained an experience that later enabled them to fill positions of responsibility. When separated from them, he still kept in touch with their work, and his letters to Timothy and to Titus are evidences of how deep was his desire for their success.

Experienced workers today do a noble work

when, instead of trying to carry all the burdens themselves, they train younger workers and place burdens on their shoulders.

Paul never forgot the responsibility resting on him as a minister of Christ, or that if souls were lost through unfaithfulness on his part, God would hold him accountable. "Whereof I am made a minister," he declared of the gospel, "according to the dispensation of God which is given to me for you, to fulfill the word of God; even the mystery which hath been hid from ages and from generations, but now is made manifest to His saints: to whom God would make known what is the riches of the glory of this mystery among the Gentiles; which is Christ in you, the hope of glory: whom we preach, warning every man, and teaching every man in all wisdom; that we may present every man perfect in Christ Jesus: whereunto I also labor, striving according to His working, which worketh in me mightily." Colossians 1:25-29.

These words present before the worker for Christ a high attainment, yet this attainment all can reach who, putting themselves under the control of the Great Teacher, learn daily in the 369 school of Christ. The power at God's command is limitless, and the minister who in his great need shuts himself in with the Lord may be assured that he will receive that which will be to his hearers a savor of life unto life.

Paul's writings show that the gospel minister should be an example of the truths that he teaches, "giving no offense in anything, that the ministry be not blamed." Of his own work he has left us a picture in his letter to the Corinthian believers: "In all things approving ourselves as the ministers of God, in much patience, in afflictions, in necessities, in distresses, in stripes, in imprisonments, in tumults, in labors, in watchings, in fastings; by pureness, by knowledge, by long suffering, by kindness, by the Holy Ghost, by love unfeigned, by the word of truth, by the power of God, by the armor of righteousness on the right hand and on the left, by honor and dishonor, by evil report and good report: as deceivers, and yet true; as unknown, and yet well known; as dying, and, behold, we live; as chastened, and not killed; as sorrowful, yet alway rejoicing; as poor, yet making many rich." 2 Corinthians 6:3, 4-10.

To Titus he wrote: "Young men likewise exhort to be sober-minded. In all things showing thyself a pattern of good works: in doctrine showing uncorruptness, gravity, sincerity, sound speech, that cannot be condemned; that he that is of the contrary part may be ashamed, having no evil thing to say of you." Titus 2:6-8.

There is nothing more precious in the sight of God than His ministers, who go forth into the waste places of the earth to sow the seeds of truth, looking forward to the harvest. None but 370 Christ can measure the solicitude of His servants as they seek for the lost. He imparts His Spirit to them, and by their efforts souls are led to turn from sin to righteousness.

God is calling for men who are willing to leave their farms, their business, if need be their families, to become missionaries for Him. And the call will be answered. In the past there have been men who, stirred by the love of Christ and the needs of the lost, have left the comforts of home and the society of friends, even that of wife and children, to go into foreign lands, among idolaters and savages, to proclaim the message of mercy. Many in the attempt have lost their lives, but others have been raised up to carry on the work. Thus step by step the cause of Christ has progressed, and the seed sown in sorrow has yielded a bountiful harvest. The knowledge of God has been widely extended and the banner of the cross planted in heathen lands.

For the conversion of one sinner the minister should tax his resources to the utmost. The soul that God has created and Christ has redeemed is of great value because of the possibilities before it, the spiritual advantages that have been granted it, the capabilities that it may possess if vitalized by the word of God, and the immortality it may gain through the hope presented in the gospel. And if Christ left the ninety and nine that He might seek and save one lost sheep, can we be justified in doing less? Is not a neglect to work as Christ worked, to sacrifice as He sacrificed, a betrayal of sacred trusts, an insult to God?

371   The heart of the true minister is filled with an intense longing to save souls. Time and strength are spent, toilsome effort is not shunned; for others must hear the truths that brought to his own soul such gladness and peace and joy. The Spirit of Christ rests upon him. He watches for souls as one that must give an account. With his eyes fixed on the cross of Calvary, beholding the uplifted Saviour, relying on His grace, believing that He will be with him until the end, as his shield, his strength, his efficiency, he works for God. With invitations and pleadings, mingled with the assurances of God's love, he seeks to win souls to Jesus, and in heaven he is numbered among those who are "called, and chosen, and faithful." Revelation 17:14.

372

35

Salvation to the Jews

After many unavoidable delays, Paul at last reached Corinth, the scene of so much anxious labor in the past, and for a time the object of deep solicitude. He found that many of the early believers still regarded him with affection as the

This chapter is based on the Epistle to the Romans.

one who had first borne to them the light of the gospel. As he greeted these disciples and saw the evidences of their fidelity and zeal he rejoiced that his work in Corinth had not been in vain.

The Corinthian believers, once so prone to lose sight of their high calling in Christ, had developed strength of Christian character. Their words and acts revealed the transforming power of the grace of God, and they were now a strong force for good in that center of heathenism and superstition. In the society of his beloved companions and these faithful converts the apostle's worn and troubled spirit found rest.

During his sojourn at Corinth, Paul found 373 time to look forward to new and wider fields of service. His contemplated journey to Rome especially occupied his thoughts. To see the Christian faith firmly established at the great center of the known world was one of his dearest hopes and most cherished plans. A church had already been established in Rome, and the apostle desired to secure the co-operation of the believers there in the work to be accomplished in Italy and in other countries. To prepare the way for his labors among these brethren, many of whom were as yet strangers to him, he sent them a letter announcing his purpose of visiting Rome and his hope of planting the standard of the cross in Spain.

In his epistle to the Romans, Paul set forth the great principles of the gospel. He stated his position on the questions which were agitating the Jewish and the Gentile churches, and showed that the hopes and promises which had once belonged especially to the Jews were now offered to the Gentiles also.

With great clearness and power the apostle presented the doctrine of justification by faith in Christ. He hoped that other churches also might be helped by the instruction sent to the Christians at Rome; but how dimly could he foresee the far-reaching influence of his words! Through all the ages the great truth of justification by faith has stood as a mighty beacon to guide repentant sinners into the way of life. It was this light that scattered the darkness which enveloped Luther's mind and revealed to him the power of the blood of Christ to cleanse from 374 sin. The same light has guided thousands of sin-burdened souls to the true Source of pardon and peace. For the epistle to the church at Rome, every Christian has reason to thank God.

In this letter Paul gave free expression to his burden in behalf of the Jews. Ever since his conversion, he had longed to help his Jewish brethren to gain a clear understanding of the gospel message. "My heart's desire and prayer to God for Israel is," he declared, "that they might be saved."

It was no ordinary desire that the apostle felt. Constantly he was petitioning God to work in behalf of the Israelites who had failed to recognize Jesus of Nazareth as the promised Messiah. "I say the truth in Christ," he assured the believers at Rome, "my conscience also bearing me witness in the Holy Ghost, that I have great heaviness and continual sorrow in my heart. For I could wish that myself were accursed from Christ for my brethren, my kinsmen according to the flesh: who are Israelites; to whom pertaineth the adoption, and the glory, and the covenants, and the giving of the law, and the service of God, and the promises; whose are the fathers, and of whom as concerning the flesh Christ came, who is over all, God blessed forever."

The Jews were God's chosen people, through whom He had purposed to bless the entire race. From among them God had raised up many prophets. These had foretold the advent of a Redeemer who was to be rejected and slain by those who should have been the first to recognize Him as the Promised One.

375 The prophet Isaiah, looking down through the centuries and witnessing the rejection of prophet after prophet and finally of the Son of God, was inspired to write concerning the acceptance of the Redeemer by those who had never before been numbered among the children of Israel. Referring to this prophecy, Paul declares: "Esaias is very bold, and saith, I was found of them that sought Me not; I was made manifest unto them that asked not after Me. But to Israel He saith, All day long I have stretched forth My hands unto a disobedient and gainsaying people."

Even though Israel rejected His Son, God did not reject them. Listen to Paul as he continues the argument: "I say then, Hath God cast away His people? God forbid. For I also am an Israelite, of the seed of Abraham, of the tribe of Benjamin. God hath not cast away His people which He foreknew. Wot ye not what the Scripture saith of Elias? how he maketh intercession to God against Israel, saying, Lord, they have killed Thy prophets, and digged down Thine altars; and I am left alone, and they seek my life. But what saith the answer of God unto him? I have reserved to Myself seven thousand men, who have not bowed the knee to the image of Baal. Even so then at this present time also there is a remnant according to the election of grace."

Israel had stumbled and fallen, but this did not make it impossible for them to rise again. In answer to the question, "Have they stumbled that they should fall?" the apostle replies: "God forbid: but rather through their fall salvation is 376 come unto the Gentiles, for to provoke them to jealousy. Now if the fall of them be the riches of the world, and the diminishing of them the riches of the Gentiles; how much more their fullness? For I speak to you Gentiles, inasmuch as I am the apostle of the Gentiles, I magnify mine office: if by any means I may provoke to emulation them which are my flesh, and might save some of them. For if the casting away of them be the reconciling of the world, what shall the receiving of them be, but life from the dead?"

It was God's purpose that His grace should be revealed among the Gentiles as well as among the Israelites. This had been plainly outlined in Old Testament prophecies. The apostle uses some of these prophecies in his argument. "Hath not the potter power over the clay," he inquires, "of the same lump to make one vessel unto honor, and another unto dishonor? What if God, willing to show His wrath, and to make His power known, endured with much long-suffering the vessels of wrath fitted to destruction: and that He might make known the riches of His glory on the vessels of mercy, which He had afore prepared unto glory, even us, whom He hath called, not of the Jews only, but also of the Gentiles? As He saith also in Osee, I will call them My people, which were not My people; and her beloved, which was not beloved. And it shall come to pass, that in the place where it was said unto them, Ye are not My people; there shall they be called the children of the living God." See Hosea 1:10.

Notwithstanding Israel's failure as a nation, there remained among them a goodly remnant of such as should be saved. At the time of the 377 Saviour's advent there were faithful men and women who had received with gladness the message of John the Baptist, and had thus been led to study anew the prophecies concerning the Messiah. When the early Christian church was founded, it was composed of these faithful Jews who recognized Jesus of Nazareth as the one for whose advent they had been longing. It is to this remnant that Paul refers when he writes, "If the first fruit be holy, the lump is also holy: and if the root be holy, so are the branches."

Paul likens the remnant in Israel to a noble olive tree, some of whose branches have been broken off. He compares the Gentiles to branches from a wild olive tree, grafted into the parent stock. "If some of the branches be broken off," he writes to the Gentile believers, "and thou, being a wild olive tree, wert grafted in among them, and with them partakest of the root and fatness of the olive tree; boast not against the branches. But if thou boast, thou barest not the root, but the root thee. Thou wilt say then, The branches were broken off, that I might be grafted in. Well; because of unbelief they were broken off, and thou standest by faith. Be not highminded, but fear: for if God spared not the natural branches, take heed lest He also spare not thee. Behold therefore the goodness and severity of God: on them which fell, severity; but toward thee, goodness, if thou continue in His goodness: otherwise thou also shalt be cut off."

Through unbelief and the rejection of Heaven's purpose for her, Israel as a nation had lost her connection with God. But the branches that had been separated from the parent stock God was able to reunite with the true stock of Israel—the remnant who had remained true to the God of their fathers. "They also," the apostle declares of these broken branches, "if they abide not still in unbelief, shall be grafted in: for God is able to graft them in again." "If thou," he writes to the Gentiles, "wert cut out of the olive tree which is wild by nature, and wert grafted contrary to nature into a good olive tree: how much more shall these, which be the natural branches, be grafted into their own olive tree? For I would not, brethren, that ye should be ignorant of this mystery, lest ye should be wise in your own conceits; that blindness in part is happened to Israel, until the fullness of the Gentiles be come in.

"And so all Israel shall be saved: as it is written, There shall come out of Sion the Deliverer, and shall turn away ungodliness from Jacob: for this is My covenant unto them, when I shall take away their sins. As concerning the gospel, they are enemies for your sakes: but as touching the election, they are beloved for the fathers' sakes. For the gifts and calling of God are without repentance. For as ye in times past have not believed God, yet have now obtained mercy through their unbelief: even so have these also now not believed, that through your mercy they also may obtain mercy. For God had concluded them all in unbelief, that He might have mercy upon all.

"O the depth of the riches both of the wisdom and knowledge of God! how unsearchable are His judgments, and His ways past finding out! For who hath known the mind of the Lord? or who hath been His counselor? or who hath first given to Him, and it shall be recompensed unto him again? For of Him, and through Him, and to Him, are all things: to whom be glory forever."

Thus Paul shows that God is abundantly able to transform the hearts of Jew and Gentile alike, and to grant to every believer in Christ the blessings promised to Israel. He repeats Isaiah's declaration concerning God's people: "Though the number of the children of Israel be as the sand of the sea, a remnant shall be saved: for He will finish the work, and cut it short in righteousness: because a short work will the Lord make upon the earth. And as Esaias said before, Except the Lord of Sabaoth had left us a seed, we had been as Sodoma, and been made like unto Gomorrah."

At the time when Jerusalem was destroyed and the temple laid in ruins, many thousands of the Jews were sold to serve as bondmen in heathen lands. Like wrecks on a desert shore they were scattered among the nations. For eighteen hundred years the Jews have wandered from land to land throughout the world, and in no place have they been given the privilege of regaining their ancient prestige as a nation. Maligned, hated, persecuted, from century to century theirs has been a heritage of suffering.

Notwithstanding the awful doom pronounced upon the Jews as a nation at the time of their rejection of Jesus of Nazareth, there have lived from age to age many noble, God-fearing Jewish men and women who have suffered in silence. God has comforted their hearts in affliction and has beheld with pity their terrible situation. He has heard the agonizing prayers of those who have sought Him with all the heart for a right understanding of His word. Some have learned to see in the lowly Nazarene whom their forefathers rejected and crucified, the true Messiah of Israel. As their minds have grasped the significance of the familiar prophecies so long obscured by tradition and misinterpretation, their hearts have been filled with gratitude to God for the unspeakable gift He bestows upon every human being who chooses to accept Christ as a personal Saviour.

It is to this class that Isaiah referred in his prophecy, "A remnant shall be saved." From Paul's day to the present time, God by His Holy Spirit has been calling after the Jew as well as the Gentile. "There is no respect of persons with God," declared Paul. The apostle regarded himself as "debtor both to the Greeks, and to the barbarians," as well as to the Jews; but he never lost sight of the decided advantages possessed by the Jews over others, "chiefly, because that unto them were committed the oracles of God." "The gospel," he declared, "is the power of God unto salvation to everyone that believeth; to the Jew first, and also to the Greek. For therein is the righteousness of God revealed from faith to faith: as it is written, The just shall live by faith." It is of this gospel of Christ, equally efficacious for Jew and Gentile, that Paul in his epistle to the Romans declared he was not ashamed.

When this gospel shall be presented in its fullness to the Jews, many will accept Christ as the Messiah. Among Christian ministers there are only a few who feel called upon to labor for the Jewish people; but to those who have been often passed by, as well as to all others, the message of mercy and hope in Christ is to come.

In the closing proclamation of the gospel, when special work is to be done for classes of people hitherto neglected, God expects His messengers to take particular interest in the Jewish people whom they find in all parts of the earth. As the Old Testament Scriptures are blended with the New in an explanation of Jehovah's eternal purpose, this will be to many of the Jews as the dawn of a new creation, the resurrection of the soul. As they see the Christ of the gospel dispensation portrayed in the pages of the Old Testament Scriptures, and perceive how clearly the New Testament explains the Old, their slumbering faculties will be aroused, and they will recognize Christ as the Saviour of the world. Many will by faith receive Christ as their Redeemer. To them will be fulfilled the words, "As many as received Him, to them gave He power to become the sons of God, even to them that believe on His name." John 1:12.

Among the Jews are some who, like Saul of Tarsus, are mighty in the Scriptures, and these will proclaim with wonderful power the immutability of the law of God. The God of Israel will bring this to pass in our day. His arm is not shortened that it cannot save. As His servants labor in faith for those who have long been neglected and despised, His salvation will be revealed.

"Thus saith the Lord, who redeemed Abraham, concerning the house of Jacob, Jacob shall not now be ashamed, neither shall his face now wax pale. But when he seeth his children, the work of Mine hands, in the midst of him, they shall sanctify My name, and sanctify the Holy One of Jacob, and shall fear the God of Israel. They also that erred in spirit shall come to understanding, and they that murmured shall learn doctrine." Isaiah 29:22-24.

36

Apostasy in Galatia

While tarrying at Corinth, Paul had cause for serious apprehension concerning some of the churches already established. Through the influence of false teachers who had arisen among the believers in Jerusalem, division, heresy, and sensualism were rapidly gaining ground among the believers in Galatia. These false teachers were mingling Jewish traditions with the truths of the gospel. Ignoring the decision of the general council at Jerusalem, they urged upon the Gentile converts the observance of the ceremonial law.

The situation was critical. The evils that had been introduced threatened speedily to destroy the Galatian churches.

Paul was cut to the heart, and his soul was stirred by this open apostasy on the part of those to whom he had faithfully taught the principles of the gospel. He immediately wrote to the deluded believers, exposing the false theories that they had accepted and with great severity rebuking those who were departing from the faith. After saluting the Galatians in the words, "Grace be to you and peace from God the Father, and from our Lord Jesus Christ," he

addressed to them these words of sharp reproof:

"I marvel that ye are so soon removed from Him that called you into the grace of Christ unto another gospel: which is not another; but there be some that trouble you, and would pervert the gospel of Christ. But though we, or an angel from heaven, preach any other gospel unto you than that which we have preached unto you, let him be accursed." Paul's teachings had been in harmony with the Scriptures, and the Holy Spirit had witnessed to his labors; therefore he warned his brethren not to listen to anything that contradicted the truths he had taught them.

The apostle bade the Galatian believers consider carefully their first experience in the Christian life. "O foolish Galatians," he exclaimed, "who hath bewitched you, that ye should not obey the truth, before whose eyes Jesus Christ hath been evidently set forth, crucified among you? This only would I learn of you, Received ye the Spirit by the works of the law, or by the hearing of faith? Are ye so foolish? having begun in the Spirit, are ye now made perfect by the flesh? Have ye suffered so many things in vain? if it be yet in vain. He therefore that ministereth to you the Spirit, and worketh miracles among you, doeth he it by the works of the law, or by the hearing of faith?"

Thus Paul arraigned the believers in Galatia before the tribunal of their own conscience and sought to arrest them in their course. Relying on the power of God to save, and refusing to recognize the doctrines of the apostate teachers, the apostle endeavored to lead the converts to see that they had been grossly deceived, but that by returning to their former faith in the gospel they might yet defeat the purpose of Satan. He took his position firmly on the side of truth and righteousness; and his supreme faith and confidence in the message he bore, helped many whose faith had failed, to return to their allegiance to the Saviour.

How different from Paul's manner of writing to the Corinthian church was the course he pursued toward the Galatians! The former he rebuked with caution and tenderness, the latter with words of unsparing reproof. The Corinthians had been overcome by temptation. Deceived by the ingenious sophistry of teachers who presented errors under the guise of truth, they had become confused and bewildered. To teach them to distinguish the false from the true, called for caution and patience. Harshness or injudicious haste on Paul's part would have destroyed his influence over many of those whom he longed to help.

In the Galatian churches, open, unmasked error was supplanting the gospel message. Christ, the true foundation of the faith, was virtually renounced for the obsolete ceremonies of Judaism. The apostle saw that if the believers in Galatia were saved from the dangerous influ-

This chapter is based on the Epistle to the Galatians.

ences which threatened them, the most decisive measures must be taken, the sharpest warnings given.

An important lesson for every minister of Christ to learn is that of adapting his labors to the condition of those whom he seeks to benefit. Tenderness, patience, decision, and firmness are alike needful; but these are to be exercised with proper discrimination. To deal wisely with different classes of minds, under varied circumstances and conditions, is a work requiring wisdom and judgment enlightened and sanctified by the Spirit of God.

In his letter to the Galatian believers Paul briefly reviewed the leading incidents connected with his own conversion and early Christian experience. By this means he sought to show that it was through a special manifestation of divine power that he had been led to see and grasp the great truths of the gospel. It was through instruction received from God Himself that Paul was led to warn and admonish the Galatians in so solemn and positive a manner. He wrote, not in hesitancy and doubt, but with the assurance of settled conviction and absolute knowledge. He clearly outlined the difference between being taught by man and receiving instruction direct from Christ.

The apostle urged the Galatians to leave the false guides by whom they had been misled, and to return to the faith that had been accompanied by unmistakable evidences of divine approval. The men who had attempted to lead them from their belief in the gospel were hypocrites, unholy in heart and corrupt in life. Their religion was made up of a round of ceremonies, through the performance of which they expected to gain the favor of God. They had no desire for a gospel that called for obedience to the word, "Except a man be born again, he cannot see the kingdom of God." John 3:3. They felt that a religion based on such a doctrine, required too great a sacrifice, and they clung to their errors, deceiving themselves and others.

To substitute external forms of religion for holiness of heart and life is still as pleasing to the unrenewed nature as it was in the days of these Jewish teachers. Today, as then, there are false spiritual guides, to whose doctrines many listen eagerly. It is Satan's studied effort to divert minds from the hope of salvation through faith in Christ and obedience to the law of God. In every age the archenemy adapts his temptations to the prejudices or inclinations of those whom he is seeking to deceive. In apostolic times he led the Jews to exalt the ceremonial law and reject Christ; at the present time he induces many professing Christians, under pretense of honoring Christ, to cast contempt on the moral law and to teach that its precepts may be transgressed with impunity. It is the duty of every servant of God to withstand firmly and

decidedly these perverters of the faith and by the word of truth fearlessly to expose their errors.

In his effort to regain the confidence of his brethren in Galatia, Paul ably vindicated his position as an apostle of Christ. He declared himself to be an apostle, "not of men, neither by man, but by Jesus Christ, and God the Father, who raised Him from the dead." Not from men, but from the highest Authority in heaven, had he received his commission. And his position had been acknowledged by a general council at Jerusalem, with the decisions of which Paul had complied in all his labors among the Gentiles.

It was not to exalt self, but to magnify the grace of God, that Paul thus presented to those who were denying his apostleship, proof that he was "not a whit behind the very chiefest apostles." 2 Corinthians 11:5. Those who sought to belittle his calling and his work were fighting against Christ, whose grace and power were manifested through Paul. The apostle was forced, by the opposition of his enemies, to take a decided stand in maintaining his position and authority.

Paul pleaded with those who had once known in their lives the power of God, to return to their first love of gospel truth. With unanswerable arguments he set before them their privilege of becoming free men and women in Christ, through whose atoning grace all who make full surrender are clothed with the robe of His righteousness. He took the position that every soul who would be saved must have a genuine, personal experience in the things of God.

The apostle's earnest words of entreaty were not fruitless. The Holy Spirit wrought with mighty power, and many whose feet had wandered into strange paths, returned to their former faith in the gospel. Henceforth they were steadfast in the liberty wherewith Christ had made them free. In their lives were revealed the fruits of the Spirit—"love, joy, peace, long-suffering, gentleness, goodness, faith, meekness, temperance." The name of God was glorified, and many were added to the number of believers throughout that region.

37

Paul's Last Journey to Jerusalem

Paul greatly desired to reach Jerusalem before the Passover as he would thus have an opportunity to meet those who should come from all parts of the world to attend the feast. Ever he cherished the hope that in some way he might be instrumental in removing the prejudice of his

This chapter is based on Acts 20:4 to 21:16.

unbelieving countrymen, so that they might be led to accept the precious light of the gospel. He also desired to meet the church at Jerusalem and bear to them the gifts sent by the Gentile churches to the poor brethren in Judea. And by this visit he hoped to bring about a firmer union between the Jewish and the Gentile converts to the faith.

Having completed his work at Corinth, he determined to sail directly for one of the ports on the coast of Palestine. All the arrangements had been made, and he was about to step on board the ship, when he was told of a plot laid by the Jews to take his life. In the past these [390] opposers of the faith had been foiled in all their efforts to put an end to the apostle's work.

The success attending the preaching of the gospel aroused the anger of the Jews anew. From every quarter were coming accounts of the spread of the new doctrine by which Jews were released from the observance of the rites of the ceremonial law and Gentiles were admitted to equal privileges with the Jews as children of Abraham. Paul, in his preaching at Corinth, presented the same arguments which he urged so forcibly in his epistles. His emphatic statement, "There is neither Greek nor Jew, circumcision nor uncircumcision" (Colossians 3:11), was regarded by his enemies as daring blasphemy, and they determined that his voice should be silenced.

Upon receiving warning of the plot, Paul decided to go around by way of Macedonia. His plan to reach Jerusalem in time for the Passover services had to be given up, but he hoped to be there at Pentecost.

Accompanying Paul and Luke were "Sopater of Berea; and of the Thessalonians, Aristarchus and Secundus; and Gaius of Derbe, and Timotheus; and of Asia, Tychicus and Trophimus." Paul had with him a large sum of money from the Gentile churches, which he purposed to place in the hands of the brethren in charge of the work in Judea; and because of this he made arrangements for these representative brethren from various contributing churches, to accompany him to Jerusalem.

At Philippi Paul tarried to keep the Passover. Only Luke remained with him, the other mem- [391] bers of the company passing on to Troas to await him there. The Philippians were the most loving and truehearted of the apostle's converts, and during the eight days of the feast he enjoyed peaceful and happy communion with them.

Sailing from Philippi, Paul and Luke reached their companions at Troas five days later, and remained for seven days with the believers in that place.

Upon the last evening of his stay the brethren "came together to break bread." The fact that their beloved teacher was about to depart, had called together a larger company than usual.

They assembled in an "upper chamber" on the third story. There, in the fervency of his love and solicitude for them, the apostle preached until midnight.

In one of the open windows sat a youth named Eutychus. In this perilous position he went to sleep and fell to the court below. At once all was alarm and confusion. The youth was taken up dead, and many gathered about him with cries and mourning. But Paul, passing through the frightened company, embraced him and offered up an earnest prayer that God would restore the dead to life. His petition was granted. Above the sound of mourning and lamentation the apostle's voice was heard, saying, "Trouble not yourselves; for his life is in him." With rejoicing the believers again assembled in the upper chamber. They partook of the Communion, and then Paul "talked a long while, even till break of day."

The ship on which Paul and his companions were to continue their journey, was about to sail, and the brethren hastened on board. The apostle himself, however, chose to take the nearer route by land between Troas and Assos, meeting his companions at the latter city. This [392] gave him a short season for meditation and prayer. The difficulties and dangers connected with his coming visit to Jerusalem, the attitude of the church there toward him and his work, as well as the condition of the churches and the interests of the gospel work in other fields, were subjects of earnest, anxious thought, and he took advantage of this special opportunity to seek God for strength and guidance.

As the travelers sailed southward from Assos, they passed the city of Ephesus, so long the scene of the apostle's labors. Paul had greatly desired to visit the church there, for he had important instruction and counsel to give them. But upon consideration he determined to hasten on, for he desired, "if it were possible for him, to be at Jerusalem the Day of Pentecost." On arriving at Miletus, however, about thirty miles from Ephesus, he learned that it might be possible to communicate with the church before the ship should sail. He therefore immediately sent a message to the elders, urging them to hasten to Miletus, that he might see them before continuing his journey.

In answer to his call they came, and he spoke to them strong, touching words of admonition and farewell. "Ye know," he said, "from the first day that I came into Asia, after what manner I have been with you at all seasons, serving the Lord with all humility of mind, and with many tears, and temptations, which befell me by the lying in wait of the Jews: and how I kept [393] back nothing that was profitable unto you, but have showed you, and have taught you publicly, and from house to house, testifying both to the Jews, and also to the Greeks, repentance toward

God, and faith toward our Lord Jesus Christ."

Paul had ever exalted the divine law. He had shown that in the law there is no power to save men from the penalty of disobedience. Wrongdoers must repent of their sins and humble themselves before God, whose just wrath they have incurred by breaking His law, and they must also exercise faith in the blood of Christ as their only means of pardon. The Son of God had died as their sacrifice and had ascended to heaven to stand before the Father as their advocate. By repentance and faith they might be freed from the condemnation of sin and through the grace of Christ be enabled henceforth to render obedience to the law of God.

"And now, behold," Paul continued, "I go bound in the spirit unto Jerusalem, not knowing the things that shall befall me there: save that the Holy Ghost witnesseth in every city, saying that bonds and afflictions abide me. But none of these things move me, neither count I my life dear unto myself, so that I might finish my course with joy, and the ministry, which I have received of the Lord Jesus, to testify the gospel of the grace of God. And now, behold, I know that ye all, among whom I have gone preaching the kingdom of God, shall see my face no more."

Paul had not designed to bear this testimony; but, while he was speaking, the Spirit of Inspiration came upon him, confirming his fears that this would be his last meeting with his Ephesian brethren.

374 "Wherefore I take you to record this day, that I am pure from the blood of all men. For I have not shunned to declare unto you all the counsel of God." No fear of giving offense, no desire for friendship or applause, could lead Paul to withhold the words that God had given him for their instruction, warning, or correction. From His servants today God requires fearlessness in preaching the word and in carrying out its precepts. The minister of Christ is not to present to the people only those truths that are the most pleasing, while he withholds others that might cause them pain. He should watch with deep solicitude the development of character. If he sees that any of his flock are cherishing sin he must as a faithful shepherd give them from God's word the instruction that is applicable to their case. Should he permit them in their self-confidence to go on unwarned, he would be held responsible for their souls. The pastor who fulfills his high commission must give his people faithful instruction on every point of the Christian faith, showing them what they must be and do in order to stand perfect in the day of God. He only who is a faithful teacher of the truth will at the close of his work be able to say with Paul, "I am pure from the blood of all men."

"Take heed therefore unto yourselves," the apostle admonished his brethren, "and to all the flock, over the which the Holy Ghost hath made you overseers, to feed the church of God, which He hath purchased with His own blood." If ministers of the gospel were to bear constantly in mind the fact that they are dealing with the purchase of the blood of Christ, they would have a deeper sense of the importance of their work. They are to take heed to themselves and to their flock. Their own example is to illustrate and 395 enforce their instructions. As teachers of the way of life they should give no occasion for the truth to be evil spoken of. As representatives of Christ they are to maintain the honor of His name. By their devotion, their purity of life, their godly conversation, they are to prove themselves worthy of their high calling.

The dangers that would assail the church at Ephesus were revealed to the apostle. "I know this," he said, "that after my departing shall grievous wolves enter in among you, not sparing the flock. Also of your own selves shall men arise, speaking perverse things, to draw away disciples after them." Paul trembled for the church as, looking into the future, he saw the attacks which she must suffer from both external and internal foes. With solemn earnestness he bade his brethren guard vigilantly their sacred trust. For an example he pointed them to his own unwearied labors among them: "Therefore watch, and remember, that by the space of three years I ceased not to warn everyone night and day with tears.

"And now, brethren," he continued, "I commend you to God, and to the word of His grace, which is able to build you up, and to give you an inheritance among all them which are sanctified. I have coveted no man's silver, or gold, or apparel." Some of the Ephesian brethren were wealthy, but Paul had never sought personal benefit from them. It was no part of his message to call attention to his own wants. "These hands," he declared, "have ministered unto my necessities, and to them that were with me." Amidst his arduous labors and extensive journeys for the cause of Christ, he was able, not 396 only to supply his own wants, but to spare something for the support of his fellow laborers and the relief of the worthy poor. This he accomplished only by unremitting diligence and the closest economy. Well might he point to his own example as he said, "I have showed you all things, how that so laboring ye ought to support the weak, and to remember the words of the Lord Jesus, how He said, It is more blessed to give than to receive."

"And when he had thus spoken, he kneeled down, and prayed with them all. And they all wept sore, and fell on Paul's neck, and kissed him, sorrowing most of all for the words which he spake, that they should see his face no more. And they accompanied him unto the ship."

From Miletus the travelers sailed in "a straight course unto Coos, and the day following unto Rhodes, and from thence unto Patara," on the southwest shore of Asia Minor, where, "finding a ship sailing over unto Phoenicia," they "went aboard, and set forth." At Tyre, where the ship was unloaded, they found a few disciples, with whom they were permitted to tarry seven days. Through the Holy Spirit these disciples were warned of the perils awaiting Paul at Jerusalem, and they urged him "that he should not go up to Jerusalem." But the apostle allowed not the fear of affliction and imprisonment to turn him from his purpose.

At the close of the week spent in Tyre, all the brethren, with their wives and children, went with Paul to the ship, and before he stepped on board, they knelt upon the shore and prayed, he for them, and they for him.

397   Pursuing their journey southward, the travelers arrived at Caesarea and "entered into the house of Philip the evangelist, which was one of the seven; and abode with him." Here Paul spent a few peaceful, happy days—the last of perfect freedom that he was to enjoy for a long time.

While Paul tarried at Caesarea, "there came down from Judea a certain prophet, named Agabus. And when he was come unto us," Luke says, "he took Paul's girdle, and bound his own hands and feet, and said, Thus saith the Holy Ghost, So shall the Jews at Jerusalem bind the man that owneth this girdle, and shall deliver him into the hands of the Gentiles."

"When we heard these things," Luke continues, "both we, and they of that place, besought him not to go up to Jerusalem." But Paul would not swerve from the path of duty. He would follow Christ if need be to prison and to death. "What mean ye to weep and to break mine heart?" he exclaimed; "for I am ready not to be bound only, but also to die at Jerusalem for the name of the Lord Jesus." Seeing that they caused him pain without changing his purpose, the brethren ceased their importunity, saying only, "The will of the Lord be done."

The time soon came for the brief stay at Caesarea to end, and, accompanied by some of the brethren, Paul and his company set out for Jerusalem, their hearts deeply shadowed by the presentiment of coming evil.

Never before had the apostle approached Jerusalem with so sad a heart. He knew that he
398 would find few friends and many enemies. He was nearing the city which had rejected and slain the Son of God and over which now hung the threatenings of divine wrath. Remembering how bitter had been his own prejudice against the followers of Christ, he felt the deepest pity for his deluded countrymen. And yet how little could he hope that he would be able to help them! The same blind wrath which had once

burned in his own heart, was now with untold power kindling the hearts of a whole nation against him.

And he could not count upon the sympathy and support of even his own brethren in the faith. The unconverted Jews who had followed so closely upon his track, had not been slow to circulate the most unfavorable reports at Jerusalem, both personally and by letter, concerning him and his work; and some, even of the apostles and elders, had received these reports as truth, making no attempt to contradict them, and manifesting no desire to harmonize with him.

Yet in the midst of discouragements the apostle was not in despair. He trusted that the Voice which had spoken to his own heart would yet speak to the hearts of his countrymen, and that the Master whom his fellow disciples loved and served would yet unite their hearts with his in the work of the gospel.

38

399

Paul a Prisoner

"When we were come to Jerusalem, the brethren received us gladly. And the day following Paul went in with us unto James; and all the elders were present."

On this occasion, Paul and his companions formally presented to the leaders of the work at Jerusalem the contributions forwarded by the Gentile churches for the support of the poor among their Jewish brethren. The gathering of these contributions had cost the apostle and his fellow workers much time, anxious thought, and wearisome labor. The sum, which far exceeded the expectations of the elders at Jerusalem, represented many sacrifices and even severe privations on the part of the Gentile believers.

These freewill offerings betokened the loyalty of the Gentile converts to the organized work of God throughout the world and should have been received by all with grateful acknowledgment, 400 yet it was apparent to Paul and his companions that even among those before whom they now stood were some who were unable to appreciate the spirit of brotherly love that had prompted the gifts.

In the earlier years of the gospel work among the Gentiles some of the leading brethren at Jerusalem, clinging to former prejudices and habits of thought, had not co-operated heartily with Paul and his associates. In their anxiety to preserve a few meaningless forms and ceremonies, they had lost sight of the blessing that would come to them and to the cause they loved, through an effort to unite in one all parts of the Lord's work. Although desirous of safe-

This chapter is based on Acts 21:17 to 23:35.

guarding the best interests of the Christian church, they had failed to keep step with the advancing providences of God, and in their human wisdom attempted to throw about workers many unnecessary restrictions. Thus there arose a group of men who were unacquainted personally with the changing circumstances and peculiar needs met by laborers in distant fields, yet who insisted that they had the authority to direct their brethren in these fields to follow certain specified methods of labor. They felt as if the work of preaching the gospel should be carried forward in harmony with their opinions.

Several years had passed since the brethren in Jerusalem, with representatives from other leading churches, gave careful consideration to the perplexing questions that had arisen over methods followed by those who were laboring for the Gentiles. As a result of this council, the brethren had united in making definite recommendations to the churches concerning certain rites and customs, including circumcision. It was at this general council that the brethren had also united in commending to the Christian churches Barnabas and Paul as laborers worthy of the full confidence of every believer.

Among those present at this meeting, were some who had severely criticized the methods of labor followed by the apostles upon whom rested the chief burden of carrying the gospel to the Gentile world. But during the council their views of God's purpose had broadened, and they had united with their brethren in making wise decisions which made possible the unification of the entire body of believers.

Afterward, when it became apparent that the converts among the Gentiles were increasing rapidly, there were a few of the leading brethren at Jerusalem who began to cherish anew their former prejudices against the methods of Paul and his associates. These prejudices strengthened with the passing of the years, until some of the leaders determined that the work of preaching the gospel must henceforth be conducted in accordance with their own ideas. If Paul would conform his methods to certain policies which they advocated they would acknowledge and sustain his work; otherwise they could no longer look upon it with favor or grant it their support.

These men had lost sight of the fact that God is the teacher of His people; that every worker in His cause is to obtain an individual experience in following the divine Leader, not looking to man for direct guidance; that His workers are to be molded and fashioned, not after man's ideas, but after the similitude of the divine.

In his ministry the apostle Paul had taught the people "not with enticing words of man's wisdom, but in demonstration of the Spirit and of power." The truths that he proclaimed had been revealed to him by the Holy Spirit, "for the

Spirit searcheth all things, yea, the deep things of God. For what man knoweth the things of a man, save the spirit of man which is in him? even so the things of God knoweth no man, but the Spirit of God. . . . Which things," declared Paul, "we speak, not in the words which man's wisdom teacheth, but which the Holy Ghost teacheth; comparing spiritual things with spiritual." 1 Corinthians 2:4, 10-13.

Throughout his ministry, Paul had looked to God for direct guidance. At the same time, he had been very careful to labor in harmony with the decisions of the general council at Jerusalem, and as a result the churches were "established in the faith, and increased in number daily." Acts 16:5. And now, notwithstanding the lack of sympathy shown him by some, he found comfort in the consciousness that he had done his duty in encouraging in his converts a spirit of loyalty, generosity, and brotherly love, as revealed on this occasion in the liberal contributions which he was enabled to place before the Jewish elders.

After the presentation of the gifts, Paul "declared particularly what things God had wrought among the Gentiles by his ministry." This recital of facts brought to the hearts of all, even of those who had been doubting, the conviction that the blessing of heaven had accompanied his labors. "When they heard it, they glorified the Lord." They felt that the methods of labor pursued by the apostle bore the signet of Heaven. The liberal contributions lying before them added weight to the testimony of the apostle concerning the faithfulness of the new churches established among the Gentiles. The men who, while numbered among those who were in charge of the work at Jerusalem, had urged that arbitrary measures of control be adopted, saw Paul's ministry in a new light and were convinced that their own course had been wrong, that they had been held in bondage by Jewish customs and traditions, and that the work of the gospel had been greatly hindered by their failure to recognize that the wall of partition between Jew and Gentile had been broken down by the death of Christ.

This was the golden opportunity for all the leading brethren to confess frankly that God had wrought through Paul, and that at times they had erred in permitting the reports of his enemies to arouse their jealousy and prejudice. But instead of uniting in an effort to do justice to the one who had been injured, they gave him counsel which showed that they still cherished a feeling that Paul should be held largely responsible for the existing prejudice. They did not stand nobly in his defense, endeavoring to show the disaffected ones where they were wrong, but sought to effect a compromise by counseling him to pursue a course which in their opinion would remove all cause for misapprehension.

"Thou seest, brother," they said, in response to his testimony, "how many thousands of Jews there are which believe; and they are all zealous of the law: and they are informed of thee, that thou teachest all the Jews which are among the Gentiles to forsake Moses, saying that they ought not to circumcise their children, neither to walk after the customs. What is it therefore? the multitude must needs come together: for they will hear that thou art come. Do therefore this that we say to thee: We have four men which have a vow on them; them take, and purify thyself with them, and be at charges with them, that they may shave their heads: and all may know that those things, whereof they were informed concerning thee, are nothing; but that thou thyself also walkest orderly, and keepest the law. As touching the Gentiles which believe, we have written and concluded that they observe no such thing, save only that they keep themselves from things offered to idols, and from blood, and from strangled, and from fornication."

The brethren hoped that Paul, by following the course suggested, might give a decisive contradiction to the false reports concerning him. They assured him that the decision of the former council concerning the Gentile converts and the ceremonial law, still held good. But the advice now given was not consistent with that decision. The Spirit of God did not prompt this instruction; it was the fruit of cowardice. The leaders of the church in Jerusalem knew that by nonconformity to the ceremonial law, Christians would bring upon themselves the hatred of the Jews and expose themselves to persecution. The Sanhedrin was doing its utmost to hinder the progress of the gospel. Men were chosen by this body to follow up the apostles, especially Paul, and in every possible way to oppose their work. Should the believers in Christ be condemned before the Sanhedrin as breakers of the law, they would suffer swift and severe punishment as apostates from the Jewish faith.

Many of the Jews who had accepted the gospel still cherished a regard for the ceremonial law and were only too willing to make unwise concessions, hoping thus to gain the confidence of their countrymen, to remove their prejudice, and to win them to faith in Christ as the world's Redeemer. Paul realized that so long as many of the leading members of the church at Jerusalem should continue to cherish prejudice against him, they would work constantly to counteract his influence. He felt that if by any reasonable concession he could win them to the truth he would remove a great obstacle to the success of the gospel in other places. But he was not authorized of God to concede as much as they asked.

When we think of Paul's great desire to be in harmony with his brethren, his tenderness toward the weak in the faith, his reverence for the apostles who had been with Christ, and for James, the brother of the Lord, and his purpose to become all things to all men so far as he could without sacrificing principle—when we think of all this, it is less surprising that he was constrained to deviate from the firm, decided course that he had hitherto followed. But instead of accomplishing the desired object, his efforts for conciliation only precipitated the crisis, hastened his predicted sufferings, and resulted in separating him from his brethren, depriving the church of one of its strongest pillars, and bringing sorrow to Christian hearts in every land.

On the following day Paul began to carry out the counsel of the elders. The four men who were under the Nazarite vow (Numbers 6), the term of which had nearly expired, were taken by Paul into the temple, "to signify the accomplishment of the days of purification, until that an offering should be offered for every one of them." Certain costly sacrifices for purification were yet to be offered.

Those who advised Paul to take this step had not fully considered the great peril to which he would thus be exposed. At this season, Jerusalem was filled with worshipers from many lands. As, in fulfillment of the commission given him by God, Paul had borne the gospel to the Gentiles, he had visited many of the world's largest cities, and he was well known to thousands who from foreign parts had come to Jerusalem to attend the feast. Among these were men whose hearts were filled with bitter hatred for Paul, and for him to enter the temple on a public occasion was to risk his life. For several days he passed in and out among the worshipers, apparently unnoticed; but before the close of the specified period, as he was talking with a priest concerning the sacrifices to be offered, he was recognized by some of the Jews from Asia.

With the fury of demons they rushed upon him, crying, "Men of Israel, help: This is the man, that teacheth all men everywhere against the people, and the law, and this place." And as the people responded to the call for help, another accusation was added—"and further brought Greeks also into the temple, and hath polluted this holy place."

By the Jewish law it was a crime punishable with death for an uncircumcised person to enter the inner courts of the sacred edifice. Paul had been seen in the city in company with Trophimus, an Ephesian, and it was conjectured that he had brought him into the temple. This he had not done; and being himself a Jew, his act in entering the temple was no violation of the law. But though the charge was wholly false, it served to arouse the popular prejudice. As the cry was taken up and borne through the temple courts, the throngs gathered there were thrown into wild excitement. The news quickly spread through Jerusalem, "and all the city was moved, and the people ran together."

That an apostate from Israel should presume to profane the temple at the very time when thousands had come there from all parts of the world to worship, excited the fiercest passions of the mob. "They took Paul, and drew him out of the temple: and forthwith the doors were shut."

"As they went about to kill him, tidings came unto the chief captain of the band, that all Jerusalem was in an uproar." Claudius Lysias well knew the turbulent elements with which he had to deal, and he "immediately took soldiers and centurions, and ran down unto them: and when they saw the chief captain and the soldiers, they left beating of Paul." Ignorant of the cause of the tumult, but seeing that the rage of the multitude was directed against Paul, the Roman captain concluded that he must be a cer-
408 tain Egyptian rebel of whom he had heard, who had thus far escaped capture. He therefore "took him, and commanded him to be bound with two chains; and demanded who he was, and what he had done." At once many voices were raised in loud and angry accusation; "some cried one thing, some another, among the multitude: and when he could not know the certainty for the tumult, he commanded him to be carried into the castle. And when he came upon the stairs, so it was, that he was borne of the soldiers for the violence of the people. For the multitude of the people followed after, crying, Away with him."

In the midst of the tumult the apostle was calm and self-possessed. His mind was stayed upon God, and he knew that angels of heaven were about him. He felt unwilling to leave the temple without making an effort to set the truth before his countrymen. As he was about to be led into the castle he said to the chief captain, "May I speak unto thee?" Lysias responded, "Canst thou speak Greek? Art not thou that Egyptian, which before these days madest an uproar, and leddest out into the wilderness four thousand men that were murderers?" In reply Paul said, "I am a man which am a Jew of Tarsus, a city in Cilicia, a citizen of no mean city: and, I beseech thee, suffer me to speak unto the people."

The request was granted, and "Paul stood on the stairs, and beckoned with the hand unto the people." The gesture attracted their attention, while his bearing commanded respect. "And when there was made a great silence, he spake unto them in the Hebrew tongue, saying, Men,
409 brethren, and fathers, hear ye my defense which I make now unto you." At the sound of the familiar Hebrew words, "they kept the more silence," and in the universal hush he continued:

"I am verily a man which am a Jew, born in Tarsus, a city in Cilicia, yet brought up in this city at the feet of Gamaliel, and taught accord-

ing to the perfect manner of the law of the fathers, and was zealous toward God, as ye all are this day." None could deny the apostle's statements, as the facts that he referred to were well known to many who were still living in Jerusalem. He then spoke of his former zeal in persecuting the disciples of Christ, even unto death; and he narrated the circumstances of his conversion, telling his hearers how his own proud heart had been led to bow to the crucified Nazarene. Had he attempted to enter into argument with his opponents, they would have stubbornly refused to listen to his words; but the relation of his experience was attended with a convincing power that for the time seemed to soften and subdue their hearts.

He then endeavored to show that his work among the Gentiles had not been entered upon from choice. He had desired to labor for his own nation; but in that very temple the voice of God had spoken to him in holy vision, directing his course "far hence unto the Gentiles."

Hitherto the people had listened with close attention, but when Paul reached the point in his history where he was appointed Christ's ambassador to the Gentiles, their fury broke forth anew. Accustomed to look upon themselves as the only people favored by God, they were unwilling to permit the despised Gentiles to 410
share the privileges which had hitherto been regarded as exclusively their own. Lifting their voices above the voice of the speaker, they cried, "Away with such a fellow from the earth: for it is not fit that he should live."

"As they cried out, and cast off their clothes, and threw dust into the air, the chief captain commanded him to be brought into the castle, and bade that he should be examined by scourging; that he might know wherefore they cried so against him.

"And as they bound him with thongs, Paul said unto the centurion that stood by, Is it lawful for you to scourge a man that is a Roman, and uncondemned? When the centurion heard that, he went and told the chief captain, saying, Take heed what thou doest: for this man is a Roman. Then the chief captain came, and said unto him, Tell me, art thou a Roman? He said, Yea. And the chief captain answered, With a great sum obtained I this freedom. And Paul said, But I was freeborn. Then straightway they departed from him which should have examined him: and the chief captain also was afraid, after he knew that he was a Roman, and because he had bound him.

"On the morrow, because he would have known the certainty wherefore he was accused of the Jews, he loosed him from his bands, and commanded the chief priests and all their council to appear, and brought Paul down, and set him before them."

The apostle was now to be tried by the same

411 tribunal of which he himself had been a member before his conversion. As he stood before the Jewish rulers, his bearing was calm, and his countenance revealed the peace of Christ. "Earnestly beholding the council," he said, "Men and brethren, I have lived in all good conscience before God until this day." Upon hearing these words, their hatred was kindled afresh; "and the high priest Ananias commanded them that stood by him to smite him on the mouth." At this inhuman command, Paul exclaimed, "God shall smite thee, thou whited wall: for sittest thou to judge me after the law, and commandest me to be smitten contrary to the law?" "They that stood by said, Revilest thou God's high priest?" With his usual courtesy Paul answered, "I wist not, brethren, that he was the high priest: for it is written, Thou shalt not speak evil of the ruler of thy people.

"But when Paul perceived that the one part were Sadducees, and the other Pharisees, he cried out in the council, Men and brethren, I am a Pharisee, the son of a Pharisee: of the hope and resurrection of the dead I am called in question.

"And when he had so said, there arose a dissension between the Pharisees and the Sadducees: and the multitude was divided. For the Sadducees say that there is no resurrection, neither angel, nor spirit: but the Pharisees confess both." The two parties began to dispute between themselves, and thus the strength of their opposition against Paul was broken. "The scribes that were of the Pharisees' part arose, and strove, saying, We find no evil in this man: but if a spirit or an angel hath spoken to him, let us not fight against God."

412 In the confusion that followed, the Sadducees were eagerly striving to gain possession of the apostle, that they might put him to death; and the Pharisees were as eager in striving to protect him. "The chief captain, fearing lest Paul should have been pulled in pieces of them, commanded the soldiers to go down, and to take him by force from among them, and to bring him into the castle."

Later, while reflecting on the trying experiences of the day, Paul began to fear that his course might not have been pleasing to God. Could it be that he had made a mistake after all in visiting Jerusalem? Had his great desire to be in union with his brethren led to this disastrous result?

The position which the Jews as God's professed people occupied before an unbelieving world, caused the apostle intense anguish of spirit. How would those heathen officers look upon them?—claiming to be worshipers of Jehovah, and assuming sacred office, yet giving themselves up to the control of blind, unreasoning anger, seeking to destroy even their brethren who dared to differ with them in religious faith,

and turning their most solemn deliberative council into a scene of strife and wild confusion. Paul felt that the name of his God had suffered reproach in the eyes of the heathen.

And now he was in prison, and he knew that his enemies, in their desperate malice, would resort to any means to put him to death. Could it be that his work for the churches was ended and that ravening wolves were to enter in now? The cause of Christ was very near to Paul's heart, and with deep anxiety he thought of the perils of the scattered churches, exposed as they were to 413 the persecutions of just such men as he had encountered in the Sanhedrin council. In distress and discouragement he wept and prayed.

In this dark hour the Lord was not unmindful of His servant. He had guarded him from the murderous throng in the temple courts; He had been with him before the Sanhedrin council; He was with him in the fortress; and He revealed Himself to His faithful witness in response to the earnest prayers of the apostle for guidance. "The night following the Lord stood by him, and said, Be of good cheer, Paul: for as thou hast testified of Me in Jerusalem, so must thou bear witness also at Rome."

Paul had long looked forward to visiting Rome; he greatly desired to witness for Christ there, but had felt that his purposes were frustrated by the enmity of the Jews. He little thought, even now, that it would be as a prisoner that he would go.

While the Lord encouraged His servant, Paul's enemies were eagerly plotting his destruction. "And when it was day, certain of the Jews banded together, and bound themselves under a curse, saying that they would neither eat nor drink till they had killed Paul. And they were more than forty which had made this conspiracy." Here was a fast such as the Lord through Isaiah had condemned—a fast "for strife and debate, and to smite with the fist of wickedness." Isaiah 58:4.

The conspirators "came to the chief priests and elders, and said, We have bound ourselves under a great curse, that we will eat nothing until we have slain Paul. Now therefore ye with 414 the council signify to the chief captain that he bring him down unto you tomorrow, as though ye would inquire something more perfectly concerning him: and we, or ever he come near, are ready to kill him."

Instead of rebuking this cruel scheme, the priests and rulers eagerly agreed to it. Paul had spoken the truth when he compared Ananias to a whited sepulcher.

But God interposed to save the life of His servant. Paul's sister's son, hearing of the "lying in wait" of the assassins, "went and entered into the castle, and told Paul. Then Paul called one of the centurions unto him, and said, Bring this young man unto the chief captain: for he hath a certain thing to tell him. So he took him, and brought him to the chief captain, and said, Paul the prisoner called me unto him, and prayed me to bring this young man unto thee, who hath something to say unto thee."

Claudius Lysias received the youth kindly, and taking him aside, asked, "What is that thou hast to tell me?" The youth replied: "The Jews have agreed to desire thee that thou wouldest bring down Paul tomorrow into the council, as though they would inquire somewhat of him more perfectly. But do not thou yield unto them: for there lie in wait for him of them more than forty men, which have bound themselves with an oath, that they will neither eat nor drink till they have killed him: and now are they ready, looking for a promise from thee."

"The chief captain then let the young man depart, and charged him, See thou tell no man that thou hast showed these things to me."

415   Lysias at once decided to transfer Paul from his jurisdiction to that of Felix the procurator. As a people, the Jews were in a state of excitement and irritation, and tumults were of frequent occurrence. The continued presence of the apostle in Jerusalem might lead to consequences dangerous to the city and even to the commandant himself. He therefore "called unto him two centurions, saying, Make ready two hundred soldiers to go to Caesarea, and horsemen threescore and ten, and spearmen two hundred, at the third hour of the night; and provide them beasts, that they may set Paul on, and bring him safe unto Felix the governor."

No time was to be lost in sending Paul away. "The soldiers, as it was commanded them, took Paul, and brought him by night to Antipatris." From that place the horsemen went on with the prisoner to Caesarea, while the four hundred soldiers returned to Jerusalem.

The officer in charge of the detachment delivered his prisoner to Felix, also presenting a letter with which he had been entrusted by the chief captain:

"Claudius Lysias unto the most excellent governor Felix sendeth greeting. This man was taken of the Jews, and should have been killed of them: then came I with an army, and rescued him, having understood that he was a Roman. And when I would have known the cause wherefore they accused him, I brought him forth into their council: whom I perceived to be accused of questions of their law, but to have nothing laid to his charge worthy of death or of bonds. And when it was told me how that the Jews laid wait for the man, I sent straightway to 416 thee, and gave commandment to his accusers also to say before thee what they had against him. Farewell."

After reading the communication, Felix inquired to what province the prisoner belonged, and being informed that he was of

Cilicia, said: "I will hear thee . . . when thine accusers are also come. And he commanded him to be kept in Herod's judgment hall."

The case of Paul was not the first in which a servant of God had found among the heathen an asylum from the malice of the professed people of Jehovah. In their rage against Paul the Jews had added another crime to the dark catalogue which marked the history of that people. They had still further hardened their hearts against the truth and had rendered their doom more certain.

Few realize the full meaning of the words that Christ spoke when, in the synagogue at Nazareth, He announced Himself as the Anointed One. He declared His mission to comfort, bless, and save the sorrowing and the sinful; and then, seeing that pride and unbelief controlled the hearts of His hearers, He reminded them that in time past God had turned away from His chosen people because of their unbelief and rebellion, and had manifested Himself to those in heathen lands who had not rejected the light of heaven. The widow of Sarepta and Naaman the Syrian had lived up to all the light they had; hence they were accounted more righteous than God's chosen people who had backslidden from Him and had sacrificed principle to convenience and worldly honor.

Christ told the Jews at Nazareth a fearful truth 417 when He declared that with backsliding Israel there was no safety for the faithful messenger of God. They would not know his worth or appreciate his labors. While the Jewish leaders professed to have great zeal for the honor of God and the good of Israel, they were enemies of both. By precept and example they were leading the people farther and farther from obedience to God—leading them where He could not be their defense in the day of trouble.

The Saviour's words of reproof to the men of Nazareth applied, in the case of Paul, not only to the unbelieving Jews, but to his own brethren in the faith. Had the leaders in the church fully surrendered their feeling of bitterness toward the apostle, and accepted him as one specially called of God to bear the gospel to the Gentiles, the Lord would have spared him to them. God had not ordained that Paul's labors should so soon end, but He did not work a miracle to counteract the train of circumstances to which the course of the leaders in the church at Jerusalem had given rise.

The same spirit is still leading to the same results. A neglect to appreciate and improve the provisions of divine grace has deprived the church of many a blessing. How often would the Lord have prolonged the work of some faithful minister, had his labors been appreciated! But if the church permits the enemy of souls to pervert the understanding, so that they misrepresent and misinterpret the words and acts of the servant of Christ; if they allow themselves to

418 stand in his way and hinder his usefulness, the Lord sometimes removes from them the blessing which He gave.

Satan is constantly working through his agents to dishearten and destroy those whom God has chosen to accomplish a great and good work. They may be ready to sacrifice even life itself for the advancement of the cause of Christ, yet the great deceiver will suggest to their brethren doubts concerning them which, if entertained, would undermine confidence in their integrity of character, and thus cripple their usefulness. Too often he succeeds in bringing upon them, through their own brethren, such sorrow of heart that God graciously interposes to give His persecuted servants rest. After the hands are folded upon the pulseless breast, when the voice of warning and encouragement is silent, then the obdurate may be aroused to see and prize the blessings they have cast from them. Their death may accomplish that which their life has failed to do.

419

39

The Trial at Caesarea

Five days after Paul's arrival at Caesarea his accusers came from Jerusalem, accompanied by Tertullus, an orator whom they had engaged as their counsel. The case was granted a speedy hearing. Paul was brought before the assembly, and Tertullus "began to accuse him." Judging that flattery would have more influence upon the Roman governor than the simple statements of truth and justice, the wily orator began his speech by praising Felix: "Seeing that by thee we enjoy great quietness, and that very worthy deeds are done unto this nation by thy providence, we accept it always, and in all places, most noble Felix, with all thankfulness."

Tertullus here descended to barefaced falsehood; for the character of Felix was base and contemptible. It was said of him, that "in the practice of all kinds of lust and cruelty, he exercised the power of a king with the temper of a slave."—Tacitus, *History*, ch. 5, par. 9. Those who heard Tertullus knew that his flattering words were untrue, but their desire to secure the condemnation of Paul was stronger than their love of truth.

420 In his speech, Tertullus charged Paul with crimes which, if proved, would have resulted in his conviction for high treason against the government. "We have found this man a pestilent fellow," declared the orator, "and a mover of sedition among all the Jews throughout the world, and a ringleader of the sect of the Nazarenes: who also hath gone about to profane the temple." Tertullus then stated that Lysias,

the commandant of the garrison at Jerusalem, had violently taken Paul from the Jews when they were about to judge him by their ecclesiastical law, and had thus forced them to bring the matter before Felix. These statements were made with the design of inducing the procurator to deliver Paul over to the Jewish court. All the charges were vehemently supported by the Jews present, who made no effort to conceal their hatred of the prisoner.

Felix had sufficient penetration to read the disposition and character of Paul's accusers. He knew from what motive they had flattered him, and he saw also that they had failed to substantiate their charges against Paul. Turning to the accused, he beckoned to him to answer for himself. Paul wasted no words in compliments, but simply stated that he could the more cheerfully defend himself before Felix, since the latter had been so long a procurator, and therefore had so good an understanding of the laws and customs of the Jews. Referring to the charges brought 421 against him, he plainly showed that not one of them was true. He declared that he had caused no disturbance in any part of Jerusalem, nor had he profaned the sanctuary. "They neither found me in the temple disputing with any man," he said, "neither raising up the people, neither in the synagogues, nor in the city: neither can they prove the things whereof they now accuse me."

While confessing that "after the way which they call heresy" he had worshiped the God of his fathers, he asserted that he had always believed "all things which are written in the law and in the prophets;" and that in harmony with the plain teaching of the Scriptures, he held the faith of the resurrection of the dead. And he further declared that the ruling purpose of his life was to "have always a conscience void of offense toward God, and toward men."

In a candid, straightforward manner he stated the object of his visit to Jerusalem, and the circumstances of his arrest and trial: "Now after many years I came to bring alms to my nation, and offerings. Whereupon certain Jews from Asia found me purified in the temple, neither with multitude, nor with tumult. Who ought to have been here before thee, and object, if they had aught against me. Or else let these same here say, if they have found any evil doing in me, while I stood before the council, except it be for this one voice, that I cried standing among them, Touching the resurrection of the dead I am called in question by you this day."

The apostle spoke with earnestness and evident sincerity, and his words carried with them a weight of conviction. Claudius Lysias, in his letter to Felix, had borne a similar testimony in 422 regard to Paul's conduct. Moreover, Felix himself had a better knowledge of the Jewish religion than many supposed. Paul's plain statement of the facts in the case enabled Felix to understand still more clearly the motives by which the Jews were governed in attempting to convict the apostle of sedition and treasonable conduct. The governor would not gratify them by unjustly condemning a Roman citizen, neither would he give him up to them to be put to death without a fair trial. Yet Felix knew no higher motive than self-interest, and he was controlled by love of praise and a desire for promotion. Fear of offending the Jews held him back from doing full justice to a man whom he knew to be innocent. He therefore decided to suspend the trial until Lysias should be present, saying, "When Lysias the chief captain shall come down, I will know the uttermost of your matter."

The apostle remained a prisoner, but Felix commanded the centurion who had been appointed to keep Paul, "to let him have liberty," and to "forbid none of his acquaintance to minister or come unto him."

It was not long after this that Felix and his wife, Drusilla, sent for Paul in order that in a private interview they might hear from him "concerning the faith in Christ." They were willing and even eager to listen to these new truths—truths which they might never hear again and which, if rejected, would prove a swift witness against them in the day of God.

Paul regarded this as a God-given opportunity, and faithfully he improved it. He knew that he stood in the presence of one who had power to put him to death or to set him free; yet he did not address Felix and Drusilla with praise or flattery. He knew that his words would be to them a savor of life or of death, and, forgetting all selfish considerations, he sought to arouse them to a sense of their peril. [423]

The apostle realized that the gospel had a claim upon whoever might listen to his words; that one day they would stand either among the pure and holy around the great white throne, or with those to whom Christ would say, "Depart from Me, ye that work iniquity." Matthew 7: 23. He knew that he must meet every one of his hearers before the tribunal of heaven and must there render an account, not only for all that he had said and done, but for the motive and spirit of his words and deeds.

So violent and cruel had been the course of Felix that few had ever before dared even to intimate to him that his character and conduct were not faultless. But Paul had no fear of man. He plainly declared his faith in Christ, and the reasons for that faith, and was thus led to speak particularly of those virtues essential to Christian character, but of which the haughty pair before him were so strikingly destitute.

He held up before Felix and Drusilla the character of God—His righteousness, justice, and equity, and the nature of His law. He clearly showed that it is man's duty to live a life of sobriety and temperance, keeping the passions under the control of reason, in conformity to God's law, and preserving the physical and mental powers in a healthy condition. He declared that there would surely come a day of judgment when all would be rewarded according to the deeds done in the body, and when it would be plainly revealed that wealth, position, or titles are powerless to gain for man the favor of God or to deliver him from the results of sin. He showed that this life is man's time of preparation for the future life. Should he neglect present privileges and opportunities he would suffer an eternal loss; no new probation would be given him. [424]

Paul dwelt especially upon the far-reaching claims of God's law. He showed how it extends to the deep secrets of man's moral nature and throws a flood of light upon that which has been concealed from the sight and knowledge of men. What the hands may do or the tongue may utter—what the outer life reveals—but imperfectly shows man's moral character. The law searches his thoughts, motives, and purposes. The dark passions that lie hidden from the sight of men, the jealousy, hatred, lust, and ambition, the evil deeds meditated upon in the dark recesses of the soul, yet never executed for want of opportunity—all these God's law condemns.

Paul endeavored to direct the minds of his hearers to the one great Sacrifice for sin. He pointed to the sacrifices that were shadows of good things to come, and then presented Christ as the antitype of all those ceremonies—the object to which they pointed as the only source of life and hope for fallen man. Holy men of old were saved by faith in the blood of Christ. As they saw the dying agonies of the sacrificial victims they looked across the gulf of ages to the Lamb of God that was to take away the sin of the world. [425]

God justly claims the love and obedience of all His creatures. He has given them in His law a perfect standard of right. But many forget their Maker and choose to follow their own way in opposition to His will. They return enmity for love that is as high as heaven and as broad as the universe. God cannot lower the requirements of His law to meet the standard of wicked men; neither can man in his own power meet the demands of the law. Only by faith in Christ can the sinner be cleansed from guilt and be enabled to render obedience to the law of his Maker.

Thus Paul, the prisoner, urged the claims of the divine law upon Jew and Gentile, and presented Jesus, the despised Nazarene, as the Son of God, the world's Redeemer.

The Jewish princess well understood the sacred character of that law which she had so shamelessly transgressed, but her prejudice against the Man of Calvary steeled her heart against the word of life. But Felix had never before listened to the truth, and as the Spirit of God sent conviction to his soul, he became deeply agitated. Conscience, now aroused, made her voice heard, and Felix felt that Paul's words were true. Memory went back over the guilty past. With terrible distinctness there came up before him the secrets of his early life of profligacy and bloodshed, and the black record of his later years. He saw himself licentious, cruel, rapacious. Never before had the truth been thus brought home to his heart. Never before had his soul been so filled with terror. The thought that all the secrets of his career of crime were open before the eye of God, and that he must be judged according to his deeds, caused him to tremble with dread.

But instead of permitting his convictions to lead him to repentance, he sought to dismiss these unwelcome reflections. The interview with Paul was cut short. "Go thy way for this time," he said; "when I have a convenient season, I will call for thee."

How wide the contrast between the course of Felix and that of the jailer of Philippi! The servants of the Lord were brought in bonds to the jailer, as was Paul to Felix. The evidence they gave of being sustained by a divine power, their rejoicing under suffering and disgrace, their fearlessness when the earth was reeling with the earthquake shock, and their spirit of Christlike forgiveness, sent conviction to the jailer's heart, and with trembling he confessed his sins and found pardon. Felix trembled, but he did not repent. The jailer joyfully welcomed the Spirit of God to his heart and to his home; Felix bade the divine Messenger depart. The one chose to become a child of God and an heir of heaven; the other cast his lot with the workers of iniquity.

For two years no further action was taken against Paul, yet he remained a prisoner. Felix visited him several times and listened attentively to his words. But the real motive for this apparent friendliness was a desire for gain, and he intimated that by the payment of a large sum of money Paul might secure his release. The apostle, however, was of too noble a nature to free himself by a bribe. He was not guilty of any crime, and he would not stoop to commit a wrong in order to gain freedom. Furthermore, he was himself too poor to pay such a ransom, had he been disposed to do so, and he would not, in his own behalf, appeal to the sympathy and generosity of his converts. He also felt that he was in the hands of God, and he would not interfere with the divine purposes respecting himself.

Felix was finally summoned to Rome because of gross wrongs committed against the Jews. Before leaving Caesarea in answer to this summons, he thought to "show the Jews a pleasure" by allowing Paul to remain in prison. But Felix was not successful in his attempt to regain the confidence of the Jews. He was removed from office in disgrace, and Porcius Festus was appointed to succeed him, with headquarters at Caesarea.

A ray of light from heaven had been permitted to shine upon Felix, when Paul reasoned with him concerning righteousness, temperance, and a judgment to come. That was his heaven-sent opportunity to see and to forsake his sins. But he said to the messenger of God, "Go thy way for this time; when I have a convenient season, I will call for thee." He had slighted his last offer of mercy. Never was he to receive another call from God.

40

Paul Appeals to Caesar

"When Festus was come into the province, after three days he ascended from Caesarea to Jerusalem. Then the high priest and the chief of the Jews informed him against Paul, and besought him, and desired favor against him, that he would send for him to Jerusalem." In making this request they purposed to waylay Paul along the road to Jerusalem and murder him. But Festus had a high sense of the responsibility of his position, and courteously declined to send for Paul. "It is not the manner of the Romans," he declared, "to deliver any man to die, before that he which is accused have the accusers face to face, and have license to answer for himself concerning the crime laid against him." He stated that "he himself would depart shortly" for Caesarea. "Let them therefore . . . . which among you are able, go down with me, and accuse this man, if there be any wickedness in him."

This was not what the Jews wanted. They had not forgotten their former defeat at Caesarea. In contrast with the calm bearing and forcible arguments of the apostle, their own malignant spirit and baseless accusations would appear in the worst possible light. Again they urged that Paul be brought to Jerusalem for trial, but Festus held firmly to his purpose of giving Paul a fair trial at Caesarea. God in His providence controlled the decision of Festus, that the life of the apostle might be lengthened.

Their purposes defeated, the Jewish leaders at once prepared to witness against Paul at the court of the procurator. Upon returning to Caesarea, after a few days' sojourn at Jerusalem, Festus "the next day sitting on the judgment seat commanded Paul to be brought." "The Jews which came down from Jerusalem stood round about, and laid many and grievous complaints against Paul, which they could not prove." Being on this occasion without a lawyer, the Jews preferred their charges themselves. As the trial proceeded, the accused with calmness and candor clearly showed the falsity of their statements.

Festus discerned that the question in dispute related wholly to Jewish doctrines, and that, rightly understood, there was nothing in the charges against Paul, could they be proved, that would render him subject to sentence of death, or even to imprisonment. Yet he saw clearly the storm of rage that would be created if Paul were not condemned or delivered into their hands. And so, "willing to do the Jews a pleasure," 430 Festus turned to Paul, and asked if he was willing to go to Jerusalem under his protection, to be tried by the Sanhedrin.

The apostle knew that he could not look for justice from the people who by their crimes were bringing down upon themselves the wrath of God. He knew that, like the prophet Elijah, he would be safer among the heathen than with those who had rejected light from heaven and hardened their hearts against the gospel. Weary of strife, his active spirit could ill endure the repeated delays and wearing suspense of his trial and imprisonment. He therefore decided to exercise his privilege, as a Roman citizen, of appealing to Caesar.

In answer to the governor's question, Paul said: "I stand at Caesar's judgment seat, where I ought to be judged: to the Jews have I done no wrong, as thou very well knowest. For if I be an offender, or have committed anything worthy of death, I refuse not to die: but if there be none of these things whereof they accuse me, no man may deliver me unto them. I appeal unto Caesar."

Festus knew nothing of the conspiracies of the Jews to murder Paul, and he was surprised at this appeal to Caesar. However, the words of the apostle put a stop to the proceedings of the court. "Festus, when he had conferred with the council, answered, Hast thou appealed unto Caesar? unto Caesar shalt thou go."

Thus it was that once more, because of hatred born of bigotry and self-righteousness, a servant of God was driven to turn for protection to the heathen. It was this same hatred that forced the 431 prophet Elijah to flee for succor to the widow of Sarepta; and that forced the heralds of the gospel to turn from the Jews to proclaim their message to the Gentiles. And this hatred the people of God living in this age have yet to meet. Among many of the professing followers of Christ there is the same pride, formalism, and selfishness, the same spirit of oppression, that held so large a place in the Jewish heart. In the future, men claiming to be Christ's representatives will take a course similar to that followed by the priests and rulers in their treatment of

Christ and the apostles. In the great crisis through which they are soon to pass, the faithful servants of God will encounter the same hardness of heart, the same cruel determination, the same unyielding hatred.

All who in that evil day would fearlessly serve God according to the dictates of conscience, will need courage, firmness, and a knowledge of God and His word; for those who are true to God will be persecuted; their motives will be impugned, their best efforts misinterpreted, and their names cast out as evil. Satan will work with all his deceptive power to influence the heart and becloud the understanding, to make evil appear good, and good evil. The stronger and purer the faith of God's people, and the firmer their determination to obey Him, the more fiercely will Satan strive to stir up against them the rage of those who, while claiming to be righteous, trample upon the law of God. It will require the firmest trust, the most heroic purpose, to hold fast the faith once delivered to the saints.

God desires His people to prepare for the soon-coming crisis. Prepared or unprepared, 432 they must all meet it; and those only who have brought their lives into conformity to the divine standard, will stand firm at that time of test and trial. When secular rulers unite with ministers of religion to dictate in matters of conscience, then it will be seen who really fear and serve God. When the darkness is deepest, the light of a godlike character will shine the brightest. When every other trust fails, then it will be seen who have an abiding trust in Jehovah. And while the enemies of truth are on every side, watching the Lord's servants for evil, God will watch over them for good. He will be to them as the shadow of a great rock in a weary land.

41   433

"Almost Thou Persuadest Me"

Paul had appealed to Caesar, and Festus could not do otherwise than send him to Rome. But some time passed before a suitable ship could be found; and as other prisoners were to be sent with Paul, the consideration of their cases also occasioned delay. This gave Paul opportunity to present the reasons of his faith before the principal men of Caesarea, and also before King Agrippa II, the last of the Herods.

"After certain days King Agrippa and Bernice came unto Caesarea to salute Festus. And when they had been there many days, Festus declared Paul's cause unto the king, saying, There is a certain man left in bonds by Felix: about whom, when I was at Jerusalem, the chief priests and the elders of the Jews informed me, desiring to

This chapter is based on Acts 25:13-27; 26.

have judgment against him." He outlined the circumstances that led to the prisoner's appeal to Caesar, telling of Paul's recent trial before him, and saying that the Jews had brought against Paul no accusation such as he had supposed they would bring, but "certain questions . . . of their own superstition, and of one Jesus, which was dead, whom Paul affirmed to be alive."

As Festus told his story, Agrippa became interested and said, "I would also hear the man myself." In harmony with his wish, a meeting was arranged for the following day. "And on the morrow, when Agrippa was come, and Bernice, with great pomp, and was entered into the place of hearing, with the chief captains, and principal men of the city, at Festus' commandment Paul was brought forth."

In honor of his visitors, Festus had sought to make this an occasion of imposing display. The rich robes of the procurator and his guests, the swords of the soldiers, and the gleaming armor of their commanders, lent brilliancy to the scene.

And now Paul, still manacled, stood before the assembled company. What a contrast was here presented! Agrippa and Bernice possessed power and position, and because of this they were favored by the world. But they were destitute of the traits of character that God esteems. They were transgressors of His law, corrupt in heart and life. Their course of action was abhorred by heaven.

The aged prisoner, chained to his soldier guard, had in his appearance nothing that would lead the world to pay him homage. Yet in this man, apparently without friends or wealth or position, and held a prisoner for his faith in the Son of God, all heaven was interested. Angels were his attendants. Had the glory of one of those shining messengers flashed forth, the pomp and pride of royalty would have paled; king and courtiers would have been stricken to the earth, as were the Roman guards at the sepulcher of Christ.

Festus himself presented Paul to the assembly with the words: "King Agrippa, and all men which are here present with us, ye see this man, about whom all the multitude of the Jews have dealt with me, both at Jerusalem, and also here, crying that he ought not to live any longer. But when I found that he had committed nothing worthy of death, and that he himself hath appealed to Augustus, I have determined to send him. Of whom I have no certain thing to write unto my lord. Wherefore I have brought him forth before you, and specially before thee, O King Agrippa, that, after examination had, I might have somewhat to write. For it seemeth to me unreasonable to send a prisoner, and not withal to signify the crimes laid against him."

King Agrippa now gave Paul liberty to speak for himself. The apostle was not disconcerted by the brilliant display or the high rank of his audience; for he knew of how little worth were worldly wealth and position. Earthly pomp and power could not for a moment daunt his courage or rob him of his self-control.

"I think myself happy, King Agrippa," he declared, "because I shall answer for myself this day before thee touching all the things whereof I am accused of the Jews: especially because I know thee to be expert in all customs and questions which are among the Jews: wherefore I beseech thee to hear me patiently."

Paul related the story of his conversion from stubborn unbelief to faith in Jesus of Nazareth as the world's Redeemer. He described the heavenly vision that at first had filled him with unspeakable terror, but afterward proved to be a source of the greatest consolation—a revelation of divine glory, in the midst of which sat enthroned He whom he had despised and hated, whose followers he was even then seeking to destroy. From that hour Paul had been a new man, a sincere and fervent believer in Jesus, made such by transforming mercy.

With clearness and power Paul outlined before Agrippa the leading events connected with the life of Christ on earth. He testified that the Messiah of prophecy had already appeared in the person of Jesus of Nazareth. He showed how the Old Testament Scriptures had declared that the Messiah was to appear as a man among men, and how in the life of Jesus had been fulfilled every specification outlined by Moses and the prophets. For the purpose of redeeming a lost world, the divine Son of God had endured the cross, despising the shame, and had ascended to heaven triumphant over death and the grave.

Why, Paul reasoned, should it seem incredible that Christ should rise from the dead? Once it had thus seemed to him, but how could he disbelieve that which he himself had seen and heard? At the gate of Damascus he had verily looked upon the crucified and risen Christ, the same who had walked the streets of Jerusalem, died on Calvary, broken the bands of death, and ascended to heaven. As verily as had Cephas, James, John, or any others of the disciples, he had seen and talked with Him. The Voice had bidden him proclaim the gospel of a risen Saviour, and how could he disobey? In Damascus, in Jerusalem, throughout all Judea, and in the regions afar off, he had borne witness of Jesus the Crucified, showing all classes "that they should repent and turn to God, and do works meet for repentance."

"For these causes," the apostle declared, "the Jews caught me in the temple, and went about to kill me. Having therefore obtained help of God, I continue unto this day, witnessing both to small and great, saying none other things than those which the prophets and Moses did say should come: that Christ should suffer, and that He should be the first that should rise from the dead, and should show light unto the people, and to the Gentiles."

The whole company had listened spellbound to Paul's account of his wonderful experiences. The apostle was dwelling upon his favorite theme. None who heard him could doubt his sincerity. But in the full tide of his persuasive eloquence he was interrupted by Festus, who cried out, "Paul, thou art beside thyself; much learning doth make thee mad."

The apostle replied, "I am not mad, most noble Festus; but speak forth the words of truth and soberness. For the king knoweth of these things, before whom also I speak freely: for I am persuaded that none of these things are hidden from him; for this thing was not done in a corner." Then, turning to Agrippa, he addressed him directly, "King Agrippa, believest thou the prophets? I know that thou believest."

438   Deeply affected, Agrippa for the moment lost sight of his surroundings and the dignity of his position. Conscious only of the truths which he had heard, seeing only the humble prisoner standing before him as God's ambassador, he answered involuntarily, "Almost thou persuadest me to be a Christian."

Earnestly the apostle made answer, "I would to God, that not only thou, but also all that hear me this day, were both almost, and altogether such as I am," adding, as he raised his fettered hands, "except these bonds."

Festus, Agrippa, and Bernice might in justice have worn the fetters that bound the apostle. All were guilty of grievous crimes. These offenders had that day heard the offer of salvation through the name of Christ. One, at least, had been almost persuaded to accept the grace and pardon offered. But Agrippa put aside the proffered mercy, refusing to accept the cross of a crucified Redeemer.

The king's curiosity was satisfied, and, rising from his seat, he signified that the interview was at an end. As the assembly dispersed, they talked among themselves, saying, "This man doeth nothing worthy of death or of bonds."

Though Agrippa was a Jew, he did not share the bigoted zeal and blind prejudice of the Pharisees. "This man," he said to Festus, "might have been set at liberty, if he had not appealed unto Caesar." But the case had been referred to that higher tribunal, and it was now beyond the jurisdiction of either Festus or Agrippa.

42

The Voyage and Shipwreck

At last Paul was on his way to Rome. "When it was determined," Luke writes, "that we should sail into Italy, they delivered Paul and certain other prisoners unto one named Julius, a centurion of Augustus' band. And entering into a ship of Adramyttium, we launched, meaning to sail by the coasts of Asia; one Aristarchus, a Macedonian of Thessalonica, being with us."

In the first century of the Christian Era traveling by sea was attended with peculiar hardship and peril. Mariners directed their course largely by the position of the sun and stars; and when these did not appear, and there were indications of storm, the owners of vessels were fearful of venturing into the open sea. During a portion of the year, safe navigation was almost impossible.

The apostle Paul was now called upon to endure the trying experiences that would fall to his lot as a prisoner in chains during the long and tedious voyage to Italy. One circumstance greatly lightened the hardship of his lot—he was permitted the companionship of Luke and Aristarchus. In his letter to the Colossians he afterward referred to the latter as his "fellow prisoner" (Colossians 4:10); but it was from choice that Aristarchus shared Paul's bondage, that he might minister to him in his afflictions.

The voyage began prosperously. The following day they cast anchor in the harbor of Sidon. Here Julius, the centurion, "courteously entreated Paul," and being informed that there were Christians in the place, "gave him liberty to go unto his friends to refresh himself." This permission was greatly appreciated by the apostle, who was in feeble health.

Upon leaving Sidon, the ship encountered contrary winds; and being driven from a direct course, its progress was slow. At Myra, in the province of Lycia, the centurion found a large Alexandrian ship, bound for the coast of Italy, and to this he immediately transferred his prisoners. But the winds were still contrary, and the ship's progress was difficult. Luke writes, "When we had sailed slowly many days, and scarce were come over against Cnidus, the wind not suffering us, we sailed under Crete, over against Salmone; and, hardly passing it, came unto a place which is called the Fair Havens."

At Fair Havens they were compelled to remain for some time, waiting for favoring winds. Winter was approaching rapidly; "sailing was now dangerous;" and those in charge of the vessel had to give up hope of reaching their destination before the season for travel by sea should be closed for the year. The only question 441

439

440

This chapter is based on Acts 27; 28:1-10.

now to be decided was, whether to remain at Fair Havens, or attempt to reach a more favorable place in which to winter.

This question was earnestly discussed, and was finally referred by the centurion to Paul, who had won the respect of both sailors and soldiers. The apostle unhesitatingly advised remaining where they were. "I perceive," he said, "that this voyage will be with hurt and much damage, not only of the lading and ship, but also of our lives." But "the master and the owner of the ship," and the majority of passengers and crew, were unwilling to accept this counsel. Because the haven in which they had anchored "was not commodious to winter in, the more part advised to depart thence also, if by any means they might attain to Phenice, and there to winter; which is an haven of Crete, and lieth toward the southwest and northwest."

The centurion decided to follow the judgment of the majority. Accordingly, "when the south wind blew softly," they set sail from Fair Havens, in the hope that they would soon reach the desired harbor. "But not long after there arose . . . a tempestuous wind;" "the ship was caught, and could not bear up into the wind."

Driven by the tempest, the vessel neared the small island of Clauda, and while under its shelter the sailors made ready for the worst. The lifeboat, their only means of escape in case the ship should founder, was in tow and liable to be dashed in pieces any moment. Their first work was to hoist this boat on board. All possible precautions were then taken to strengthen the ship and prepare it to withstand the tempest. The scant protection afforded by the little island did not avail them long, and soon they were again exposed to the full violence of the storm.

All night the tempest raged, and notwithstanding the precautions that had been taken, the vessel leaked. "The next day they lightened the ship." Night came again, but the wind did not abate. The storm-beaten ship, with its shattered mast and rent sails, was tossed hither and thither by the fury of the gale. Every moment it seemed that the groaning timbers must give way as the vessel reeled and quivered under the tempest's shock. The leak increased rapidly, and passengers and crew worked continually at the pumps. There was not a moment's rest for any on board. "The third day," writes Luke, "we cast out with our own hands the tackling of the ship. And when neither sun nor stars in many days appeared, and no small tempest lay on us, all hope that we should be saved was then taken away."

For fourteen days they drifted under a sunless and starless heaven. The apostle, though himself suffering physically, had words of hope for the darkest hour, a helping hand in every emergency. He grasped by faith the arm of Infinite Power, and his heart was stayed upon God. He had no fears for himself; he knew that God would preserve him to witness at Rome for the truth of Christ. But his heart yearned with pity for the poor souls around him, sinful, degraded, and unprepared to die. As he earnestly pleaded with God to spare their lives, it was revealed to him that his prayer was granted.

Taking advantage of a lull in the tempest, Paul stood forth on the deck and, lifting up his voice, said: "Sirs, ye should have hearkened unto me, and not have loosed from Crete, and to have gained this harm and loss. And now I exhort you to be of good cheer: for there shall be no loss of any man's life among you, but of the ship. For there stood by me this night the angel of God, whose I am, and whom I serve, saying, Fear not, Paul; thou must be brought before Caesar: and, lo, God hath given thee all them that sail with thee. Wherefore, sirs, be of good cheer: for I believe God, that it shall be even as it was told me. Howbeit we must be cast upon a certain island."

At these words, hope revived. Passengers and crew roused from their apathy. There was much yet to be done, and every effort within their power must be put forth to avert destruction.

It was on the fourteenth night of tossing on the black, heaving billows, that "about midnight" the sailors, hearing the sound of breakers, "deemed that they drew near to some country; and sounded, and found it twenty fathoms: and when they had gone a little further, they sounded again, and found it fifteen fathoms. Then fearing," Luke writes, "lest we should have fallen upon rocks, they cast four anchors out of the stern, and wished for the day."

At break of day the outlines of the stormy coast were dimly visible, but no familiar landmarks could be seen. So gloomy was the outlook that the heathen sailors, losing all courage, "were about to flee out of the ship," and feigning to make preparations for casting "anchors out of the foreship," they had already let down the lifeboat, when Paul, perceiving their base design, said to the centurion and the soldiers, "Except these abide in the ship, ye cannot be saved." The soldiers immediately "cut off the ropes of the boat, and let her fall off" into the sea.

The most critical hour was still before them. Again the apostle spoke words of encouragement, and entreated all, both sailors and passengers, to take some food, saying, "This day is the fourteenth day that ye have tarried and continued fasting, having taken nothing. Wherefore I pray you to take some meat: for this is for your health: for there shall not a hair fall from the head of any of you."

"When he had thus spoken, he took bread, and gave thanks to God in presence of them all: and when he had broken it, he began to eat." Then that worn and discouraged company of two hundred and seventy-five souls, who but for Paul would have become desperate, joined with the apostle in partaking of food. "And when they had eaten enough, they lightened the ship, and cast out the wheat into the sea."

Daylight had now fully come, but they could see nothing by which to determine their whereabouts. However, "they discovered a certain creek with a shore, into the which they were minded, if it were possible, to thrust in the ship. And when they had taken up the anchors, they committed themselves unto the sea, and loosed the rudder bands, and hoisted up the mainsail to the wind, and made toward shore. And falling into a place where two seas met, they ran the ship aground; and the fore part stuck fast, and 445 remained unmovable, but the hinder part was broken with the violence of the waves."

Paul and the other prisoners were now threatened by a fate more terrible than shipwreck. The soldiers saw that while endeavoring to reach land it would be impossible for them to keep their prisoners in charge. Every man would have all he could do to save himself. Yet if any of the prisoners were missing, the lives of those who were responsible for them would be forfeited. Hence the soldiers desired to put all the prisoners to death. The Roman law sanctioned this cruel policy, and the plan would have been executed at once, but for him to whom all alike were under deep obligation. Julius the centurion knew that Paul had been instrumental in saving the lives of all on board, and, moreover, convinced that the Lord was with him, he feared to do him harm. He therefore "commanded that they which could swim should cast themselves first into the sea, and get to land: and the rest, some on boards, and some on broken pieces of the ship. And so it came to pass, that they escaped all safe to land." When the roll was called, not one was missing.

The shipwrecked crew were now kindly received by the barbarous people of Melita. "They kindled a fire," Luke writes, "and received us everyone, because of the present rain, and because of the cold." Paul was among those who were active in ministering to the comfort of others. Having gathered "a bundle of sticks," he "laid them on the fire," when a viper came forth "out of the heat, and fastened on his hand." The 446 bystanders were horror-stricken; and seeing by his chain that Paul was a prisoner, they said to one another, "No doubt this man is a murderer, whom, though he hath escaped the sea, yet vengeance suffereth not to live." But Paul shook off the creature into the fire and felt no harm. Knowing its venomous nature, the people looked for him to fall down at any moment in terrible agony. "But after they had looked a great while, and saw no harm come to him, they changed their minds, and said that he was a god."

During the three months that the ship's company remained at Melita, Paul and his fellow laborers improved many opportunities to preach the gospel. In a remarkable manner the Lord wrought through them. For Paul's sake the entire shipwrecked company were treated with great kindness; all their wants were supplied, and upon leaving Melita they were liberally provided with everything needful for their voyage. The chief incidents of their stay are thus briefly related by Luke:

"In the same quarters were possessions of the chief man of the island, whose name was Publius; who received us, and lodged us three days courteously. And it came to pass, that the father of Publius lay sick of a fever and of a bloody flux: to whom Paul entered in, and prayed, and laid his hands on him, and healed him. So when this was done, others also, which had diseases in the island, came, and were healed: who also honored us with many honors; and when we departed, they laded us with such things as were necessary."

<h1 style="text-align:center">43</h1>

447

<h1 style="text-align:center">In Rome</h1>

With the opening of navigation, the centurion and his prisoners set out on their journey to Rome. An Alexandrian ship, the "Castor and Pollux," had wintered at Melita on her way westward, and in this the travelers embarked. Though somewhat delayed by contrary winds, the voyage was safely accomplished, and the ship cast anchor in the beautiful harbor of Puteoli, on the coast of Italy.

In this place there were a few Christians, and they entreated the apostle to remain with them for seven days, a privilege kindly granted by the centurion. Since receiving Paul's epistle to the Romans, the Christians of Italy had eagerly looked forward to a visit from the apostle. They had not thought to see him come as a prisoner, but his sufferings only endeared him to them the more. The distance from Puteoli to Rome being but a hundred and forty miles, and the seaport being in constant communication with the metropolis, the Roman Christians were informed of Paul's approach, and some of them 448 started to meet and welcome him.

On the eighth day after landing, the centurion and his prisoners set out for Rome. Julius willingly granted the apostle every favor which it was in his power to bestow; but he could not change his condition as a prisoner, or release him from the chain that bound him to his soldier guard. It was with a heavy heart that Paul went forward to his long-expected visit to the world's metropolis. How different the circumstances

This chapter is based on Acts 28:11-31 and the Epistle to Philemon.

from those he had anticipated! How was he, fettered and stigmatized, to proclaim the gospel? His hopes of winning many souls to the truth in Rome, seemed destined to disappointment.

At last the travelers reach Appii Forum, forty miles from Rome. As they make their way through the crowds that throng the great thoroughfare, the gray-haired old man, chained with a group of hardened-looking criminals, receives many a glance of scorn and is made the subject of many a rude, mocking jest.

Suddenly a cry of joy is heard, and a man springs from the passing throng and falls upon the prisoner's neck, embracing him with tears and rejoicing, as a son would welcome a long-absent father. Again and again is the scene repeated as, with eyes made keen by loving expectation, many discern in the chained captive the one who at Corinth, at Philippi, at Ephesus, had spoken to them the words of life.

As the warmhearted disciples eagerly flock around their father in the gospel, the whole 449 company is brought to a standstill. The soldiers are impatient of delay, yet they have not the heart to interrupt this happy meeting; for they, too, have learned to respect and esteem their prisoner. In that worn, pain-stricken face, the disciples see reflected the image of Christ. They assure Paul that they have not forgotten him nor ceased to love him; that they are indebted to him for the joyful hope which animates their lives and gives them peace toward God. In the ardor of their love they would bear him upon their shoulders the whole way to the city, could they but have the privilege.

Few realize the significance of those words of Luke, that when Paul saw his brethren, "he thanked God, and took courage." In the midst of the weeping, sympathizing company of believers, who were not ashamed of his bonds, the apostle praised God aloud. The cloud of sadness that had rested upon his spirit was swept away. His Christian life had been a succession of trials, sufferings, and disappointments, but in that hour he felt abundantly repaid. With firmer step and joyful heart he continued on his way. He would not complain of the past, nor fear for the future. Bonds and afflictions awaited him, he knew; but he knew also that it had been his to deliver souls from a bondage infinitely more terrible, and he rejoiced in his sufferings for Christ's sake.

At Rome the centurion Julius delivered up his prisoners to the captain of the emperor's guard. The good account which he gave of Paul, together with the letter from Festus, caused the apostle to be favorably regarded by the chief 450 captain, and, instead of being thrown into prison, he was permitted to live in his own hired house. Although still constantly chained to a soldier, he was at liberty to receive his friends and to labor for the advancement of the cause of Christ.

Many of the Jews who had been banished from Rome some years previously, had been allowed to return, so that large numbers were now to be found there. To these, first of all, Paul determined to present the facts concerning himself and his work, before his enemies should have opportunity to embitter them against him. Three days after his arrival in Rome, therefore, he called together their leading men and in a simple, direct manner stated why he had come to Rome as a prisoner.

"Men and brethren," he said, "though I have committed nothing against the people, or customs of our fathers, yet was I delivered prisoner from Jerusalem into the hands of the Romans. Who, when they had examined me, would have let me go, because there was no cause of death in me. But when the Jews spake against it, I was constrained to appeal unto Caesar; not that I had aught to accuse my nation of. For this cause therefore have I called for you, to see you, and to speak with you: because that for the hope of Israel I am bound with this chain."

He said nothing of the abuse which he had suffered at the hands of the Jews, or of their repeated plots to assassinate him. His words were marked with caution and kindness. He was not seeking to win personal attention or sympathy, but to defend the truth and to maintain the honor of the gospel.

In reply, his hearers stated that they had 451 received no charges against him by letters public or private, and that none of the Jews who had come to Rome had accused him of any crime. They also expressed a strong desire to hear for themselves the reasons of his faith in Christ. "As concerning this sect," they said, "we know that everywhere it is spoken against."

Since they themselves desired it, Paul bade them set a day when he could present to them the truths of the gospel. At the time appointed, many came together, "to whom he expounded and testified the kingdom of God, persuading them concerning Jesus, both out of the law of Moses, and out of the prophets, from morning till evening." He related his own experience, and presented arguments from the Old Testament Scriptures with simplicity, sincerity, and power.

The apostle showed that religion does not consist in rites and ceremonies, creeds and theories. If it did, the natural man could understand it by investigation, as he understands worldly things. Paul taught that religion is a practical, saving energy, a principle wholly from God, a personal experience of God's renewing power upon the soul.

He showed how Moses had pointed Israel forward to Christ as that Prophet whom they were to hear; how all the prophets had testified of Him as God's great remedy for sin, the guiltless One who was to bear the sins of the guilty. He did not find fault with their observance of forms and ceremonies, but showed that while 452 they maintained the ritual service with great exactness, they were rejecting Him who was the antitype of all that system.

Paul declared that in his unconverted state he had known Christ, not by personal acquaintance, but merely by the conception which he, in common with others, cherished concerning the character and work of the Messiah to come. He had rejected Jesus of Nazareth as an impostor because He did not fulfill this conception. But now Paul's views of Christ and His mission were far more spiritual and exalted, for he had been converted. The apostle asserted that he did not present to them Christ after the flesh. Herod had seen Christ in the days of His humanity; Annas had seen Him; Pilate and the priests and rulers had seen Him; the Roman soldiers had seen Him. But they had not seen Him with the eye of faith; they had not seen Him as the glorified Redeemer. To apprehend Christ by faith, to have a spiritual knowledge of Him, was more to be desired than a personal acquaintance with Him as He appeared on the earth. The communion with Christ which Paul now enjoyed was more intimate, more enduring, than a mere earthly and human companionship.

As Paul spoke of what he knew, and testified of what he had seen, concerning Jesus of Nazareth as the hope of Israel, those who were honestly seeking for truth were convinced. Upon some minds, at least, his words made an impression that was never effaced. But others stubbornly refused to accept the plain testimony of the Scriptures, even when presented to them by one who had the special illumination of the 453 Holy Spirit. They could not refute his arguments, but they refused to accept his conclusions.

Many months passed by after Paul's arrival in Rome, before the Jews of Jerusalem appeared in person to present their accusations against the prisoner. They had been repeatedly thwarted in their designs; and now that Paul was to be tried before the highest tribunal of the Roman Empire, they had no desire to risk another defeat. Lysias, Felix, Festus, and Agrippa had all declared their belief in his innocence. His enemies could hope for success only in seeking by intrigue to influence the emperor in their favor. Delay would further their object, as it would afford them time to perfect and execute their plans, and so they waited for a while before preferring their charges in person against the apostle.

In the providence of God this delay resulted in the furtherance of the gospel. Through the favor of those who had Paul in charge, he was permitted to dwell in a commodious house, where he could meet freely with his friends and also present the truth daily to those who came to hear. Thus for two years he continued his labors, "preaching the kingdom of God, and teaching those things which concern the Lord Jesus Christ, with all confidence, no man forbidding him."

During this time the churches that he had established in many lands were not forgotten. Realizing the dangers that threatened the converts to the new faith, the apostle sought so far as possible to meet their needs by letters of warning and practical instruction. And from Rome he sent out consecrated workers to labor 454 not only for these churches, but in fields that he himself had not visited. These workers, as wise shepherds, strengthened the work so well begun by Paul; and the apostle, kept informed of the condition and dangers of the churches by constant communication with them, was enabled to exercise a wise supervision over all.

Thus, while apparently cut off from active labor, Paul exerted a wider and more lasting influence than if he had been free to travel among the churches as in former years. As a prisoner of the Lord, he had a firmer hold upon the affections of his brethren; and his words, written by one under bonds for the sake of Christ, commanded greater attention and respect than they did when he was personally with them. Not until Paul was removed from them, did the believers realize how heavy were the burdens he had borne in their behalf. Heretofore they had largely excused themselves from responsibility and burden bearing because they lacked his wisdom, tact, and indomitable energy; but now, left in their inexperience to learn the lessons they had shunned, they prized his warnings, counsels, and instructions as they had not prized his personal work. And as they learned of his courage and faith during his long imprisonment they were stimulated to greater fidelity and zeal in the cause of Christ.

Among Paul's assistants at Rome were many of his former companions and fellow workers. Luke, "the beloved physician," who had attended him on the journey to Jerusalem, through the two years' imprisonment at Caesarea, and upon his perilous voyage to Rome, was with him still. Timothy also ministered to his comfort. Tychi- 455 cus, "a beloved brother, and a faithful minister and fellow servant in the Lord," stood nobly by the apostle. Demas and Mark were also with him. Aristarchus and Epaphras were his "fellow prisoners." Colossians 4:7-14.

Since the earlier years of his profession of faith, Mark's Christian experience had deepened. As he had studied more closely the life and death of Christ he had obtained clearer views of the Saviour's mission, its toils and conflicts. Reading in the scars in Christ's hands and feet the marks of His service for humanity, and the length to which self-abnegation leads to save the lost and perishing, Mark had become willing to follow the Master in the path of self-sacrifice. Now, sharing the lot of Paul the prisoner, he understood better than ever before that it is infinite gain to win Christ, infinite loss to win the world and lose the soul for whose redemption the blood of Christ was shed. In the face of severe trial and adversity, Mark continued steadfast, a wise and beloved helper of the apostle.

Demas, steadfast for a time, afterward forsook the cause of Christ. In referring to this, Paul wrote, "Demas hath forsaken me, having loved this present world." 2 Timothy 4:10. For worldly gain, Demas bartered every high and noble consideration. How shortsighted the exchange! Possessing only worldly wealth or honor, Demas was poor indeed, however much he might proudly call his own; while Mark, choosing to suffer for Christ's sake, possessed eternal riches, being accounted in heaven an heir of God and a joint heir with His Son.

456 Among those who gave their hearts to God through the labors of Paul in Rome was Onesimus, a pagan slave who had wronged his master, Philemon, a Christian believer in Colosse, and had escaped to Rome. In the kindness of his heart, Paul sought to relieve the poverty and distress of the wretched fugitive and then endeavored to shed the light of truth into his darkened mind. Onesimus listened to the words of life, confessed his sins, and was converted to the faith of Christ.

Onesimus endeared himself to Paul by his piety and sincerity, no less than by his tender care for the apostle's comfort, and his zeal in promoting the work of the gospel. Paul saw in him traits of character that would render him a useful helper in missionary labor, and he counseled him to return without delay to Philemon, beg his forgiveness, and plan for the future. The apostle promised to hold himself responsible for the sum of which Philemon had been robbed. Being about to dispatch Tychicus with letters to various churches in Asia Minor, he sent Onesimus with him. It was a severe test for this servant thus to deliver himself up to the master he had wronged; but he had been truly converted, and he did not turn aside from this duty.

Paul made Onesimus the bearer of a letter to Philemon, in which, with his usual tact and kindness, the apostle pleaded the cause of the repentant slave and expressed a desire to retain his services in the future. The letter began with an affectionate greeting to Philemon as a friend and fellow laborer:

457 "Grace to you, and peace, from God our Father and the Lord Jesus Christ. I thank my God, making mention of thee always in my prayers, hearing of thy love and faith, which thou hast toward the Lord Jesus, and toward all saints; that the communication of thy faith may become effectual by the acknowledging of every good thing which is in you in Christ Jesus." The apostle reminded Philemon that every good purpose and trait of character which he possessed was due to the grace of Christ; this alone made him different from the perverse and the sinful. The same grace could make the debased criminal a child of God and a useful laborer in the gospel.

Paul might have urged upon Philemon his duty as a Christian; but he chose rather the language of entreaty: "As Paul the aged, and now also a prisoner of Jesus Christ, I beseech thee for my son Onesimus, whom I have begotten in my bonds; which in time past was to thee unprofitable, but now profitable to thee and to me."

The apostle asked Philemon, in view of the conversion of Onesimus, to receive the repentant slave as his own child, showing him such affection that he would choose to dwell with his former master, "not now as a servant, but above a servant, a brother beloved." He expressed his desire to retain Onesimus as one who could minister to him in his bonds as Philemon himself would have done, though he did not desire his services unless Philemon should of his own accord set the slave free.

The apostle well knew the severity which masters exercised toward their slaves, and he knew also that Philemon was greatly incensed 458 because of the conduct of his servant. He tried to write to him in a way that would arouse his deepest and tenderest feelings as a Christian. The conversion of Onesimus had made him a brother in the faith, and any punishment inflicted on this new convert would be regarded by Paul as inflicted on himself.

Paul voluntarily proposed to assume the debt of Onesimus in order that the guilty one might be spared the disgrace of punishment, and might again enjoy the privileges he had forfeited. "If thou count me therefore a partner," he wrote to Philemon, "receive him as myself. If he hath wronged thee, or oweth thee aught, put that on mine account; I Paul have written it with mine own hand, I will repay it."

How fitting an illustration of the love of Christ for the repentant sinner! The servant who had defrauded his master had nothing with which to make restitution. The sinner who has robbed God of years of service has no means of canceling the debt. Jesus interposes between the sinner and God, saying, I will pay the debt. Let the sinner be spared; I will suffer in his stead.

After offering to assume the debt of Onesimus, Paul reminded Philemon how greatly he himself was indebted to the apostle. He owed him his own self, since God had made Paul the instrument of his conversion. Then, in a tender, earnest appeal, he besought Philemon that as he had by his liberalities refreshed the saints, so he

would refresh the spirit of the apostle by grant-
459 ing him this cause of rejoicing. "Having confidence in thy obedience," he added, "I wrote
unto thee, knowing that thou wilt also do more
than I say."

Paul's letter to Philemon shows the influence
of the gospel upon the relation between master
and servant. Slaveholding was an established
institution throughout the Roman Empire, and
both masters and slaves were found in most of
the churches for which Paul labored. In the
cities, where slaves often greatly outnumbered
the free population, laws of terrible severity
were regarded as necessary to keep them in subjection. A wealthy Roman often owned hundreds of slaves, of every rank, of every nation,
and of every accomplishment. With full control
over the souls and bodies of these helpless
beings, he could inflict upon them any suffering
he chose. If one of them in retaliation or self-
defense ventured to raise a hand against his
owner, the whole family of the offender might
be inhumanly sacrificed. The slightest mistake,
accident, or carelessness was often punished
without mercy.

Some masters, more humane than others,
were more indulgent toward their servants; but
the vast majority of the wealthy and noble,
given up without restraint to the indulgence of
lust, passion, and appetite, made their slaves the
wretched victims of caprice and tyranny. The
tendency of the whole system was hopelessly
degrading.

It was not the apostle's work to overturn arbitrarily or suddenly the established order of society. To attempt this would be to prevent the success of the gospel. But he taught principles
which struck at the very foundation of slavery
and which, if carried into effect, would surely
460 undermine the whole system. "Where the Spirit
of the Lord is, there is liberty," he declared. 2
Corinthians 3:17. When converted, the slave
became a member of the body of Christ, and as
such was to be loved and treated as a brother, a
fellow heir with his master to the blessings of
God and the privileges of the gospel. On the
other hand, servants were to perform their
duties, "not with eyeservice, as men pleasers;
but as the servants of Christ, doing the will of
God from the heart." Ephesians 6:6.

Christianity makes a strong bond of union
between master and slave, king and subject, the
gospel minister and the degraded sinner who
has found in Christ cleansing from sin. They
have been washed in the same blood, quickened
by the same Spirit; and they are made one in
Christ Jesus.

44
Caesar's Household

The gospel has ever achieved its greatest success among the humbler classes. "Not many
wise men after the flesh, not many mighty, not
many noble, are called." 1 Corinthians 1:26. It
could not be expected that Paul, a poor and
friendless prisoner, would be able to gain the
attention of the wealthy and titled classes of
Roman citizens. To them vice presented all its
glittering allurements and held them willing
captives. But from among the toilworn, want-
stricken victims of their oppression, even from
among the poor slaves, many gladly listened to
the words of Paul and in the faith of Christ
found a hope and peace that cheered them under
the hardships of their lot.

Yet while the apostle's work began with the
humble and the lowly, its influence extended
until it reached the very palace of the emperor.

Rome was at this time the metropolis of the
world. The haughty Caesars were giving laws to
nearly every nation upon the earth. King and
courtier were either ignorant of the humble
Nazarene or regarded Him with hatred and derision. And yet in less than two years the gospel
found its way from the prisoner's lowly home
into the imperial halls. Paul is in bonds as an evildoer; but "the word of God is not bound." 2 Timothy 2:9.

In former years the apostle had publicly proclaimed the faith of Christ with winning power,
and by signs and miracles he had given unmistakable evidence of its divine character. With
noble firmness he had risen up before the sages
of Greece and by his knowledge and eloquence
had put to silence the arguments of proud philosophy. With undaunted courage he had stood
before kings and governors, and reasoned of
righteousness, temperance, and judgment to
come, until the haughty rulers trembled as if
already beholding the terrors of the day of God.

No such opportunities were now granted the
apostle, confined as he was to his own dwelling,
and able to proclaim the truth to those only who
sought him there. He had not, like Moses and
Aaron, a divine command to go before the profligate king and in the name of the great I AM
rebuke his cruelty and oppression. Yet it was at
this very time, when its chief advocate was
apparently cut off from public labor, that a great
victory was won for the gospel; for from the
very household of the king, members were
added to the church.

Nowhere could there exist an atmosphere
more uncongenial to Christianity than in the
Roman court. Nero seemed to have obliterated

from his soul the last trace of the divine, and even of the human, and to bear the impress of Satan. His attendants and courtiers were in general of the same character as himself—fierce, debased, and corrupt. To all appearance it would be impossible for Christianity to gain a foothold in the court and palace of Nero.

Yet in this case, as in so many others, was proved the truth of Paul's assertion that the weapons of his warfare were "mighty through God to the pulling down of strongholds." 2 Corinthians 10:4. Even in Nero's household, trophies of the cross were won. From the vile attendants of a viler king were gained converts who became sons of God. These were not Christians secretly, but openly. They were not ashamed of their faith.

And by what means was an entrance achieved and a firm footing gained for Christianity where even its admission seemed impossible? In his epistle to the Philippians, Paul ascribed to his own imprisonment his success in winning converts to the faith from Nero's household. Fearful lest it might be thought that his afflictions had impeded the progress of the gospel, he assured them: "I would ye should understand, brethren, that the things which happened unto me have fallen out rather unto the furtherance of the gospel." Philippians 1:12.

When the Christian churches first learned that Paul was to visit Rome, they looked forward to a signal triumph of the gospel in that city. Paul had borne the truth to many lands; he had proclaimed it in great cities. Might not this champion of the faith succeed in winning souls to Christ even in the metropolis of the world? But their hopes were crushed by the tidings that Paul had gone to Rome as a prisoner. They had confidently hoped to see the gospel, once established at this great center, extend rapidly to all nations and become a prevailing power in the earth. How great their disappointment! Human expectations had failed, but not the purpose of God.

Not by Paul's sermons, but by his bonds, was the attention of the court attracted to Christianity. It was as a captive that he broke from so many souls the bonds that held them in the slavery of sin. Nor was this all. He declared: "Many of the brethren in the Lord, waxing confident by my bonds, are much more bold to speak the word without fear." Philippians 1:14.

Paul's patience and cheerfulness during his long and unjust imprisonment, his courage and faith, were a continual sermon. His spirit, so unlike the spirit of the world, bore witness that a power higher than that of earth was abiding with him. And by his example, Christians were impelled to greater energy as advocates of the cause from the public labors of which Paul had been withdrawn. In these ways were the apostle's bonds influential, so that when his power and usefulness seemed cut off, and to all

appearance he could do the least, then it was that he gathered sheaves for Christ in fields from which he seemed wholly excluded.

Before the close of that two years' imprisonment, Paul was able to say, "My bonds in Christ are manifest in all the palace, and in all other places," and among those who sent greetings to the Philippians he mentions chiefly them "that are of Caesar's household." Verse 13; 4:22.

Patience as well as courage has its victories. By meekness under trial, no less than by boldness in enterprise, souls may be won to Christ. The Christian who manifests patience and cheerfulness under bereavement and suffering, who meets even death itself with the peace and calmness of an unwavering faith, may accomplish for the gospel more than he could have effected by a long life of faithful labor. Often when the servant of God is withdrawn from active duty, the mysterious providence which our shortsighted vision would lament is designed by God to accomplish a work that otherwise would never have been done.

Let not the follower of Christ think, when he is no longer able to labor openly and actively for God and His truth, that he has no service to render, no reward to secure. Christ's true witnesses are never laid aside. In health and sickness, in life and death, God uses them still. When through Satan's malice the servants of Christ have been persecuted, their active labors hindered, when they have been cast into prison, or dragged to the scaffold or to the stake, it was that truth might gain a greater triumph. As these faithful ones sealed their testimony with their blood, souls hitherto in doubt and uncertainty were convinced of the faith of Christ and took their stand courageously for Him. From the ashes of the martyrs has sprung an abundant harvest for God.

The zeal and fidelity of Paul and his fellow workers, no less than the faith and obedience of these converts to Christianity, under circumstances so forbidding, rebuke slothfulness and lack of faith in the minister of Christ. The apostle and his associate workers might have argued that it would be vain to call to repentance and faith in Christ the servants of Nero, subjected, as they were, to fierce temptations, surrounded by formidable hindrances, and exposed to bitter opposition. Even should they be convinced of the truth, how could they render obedience? But Paul did not reason thus; in faith he presented the gospel to these souls, and among those who heard were some who decided to obey at any cost. Notwithstanding obstacles and dangers, they would accept the light, and trust God to help them let their light shine forth to others.

Not only were converts won to the truth in Caesar's household, but after their conversion they remained in that household. They did not feel at liberty to abandon their post of duty because their surroundings were no longer congenial. The truth had found them there, and there they remained, by their changed life and character testifying to the transforming power of the new faith.

Are any tempted to make their circumstances an excuse for failing to witness for Christ? Let them consider the situation of the disciples in Caesar's household—the depravity of the emperor, the profligacy of the court. We can hardly imagine circumstances more unfavorable to a religious life, and entailing greater sacrifice or opposition, than those in which these converts found themselves. Yet amidst difficulties and dangers they maintained their fidelity. Because of obstacles that seem insurmountable, the Christian may seek to excuse himself from obeying the truth as it is in Jesus; but he can offer no excuse that will bear investigation. Could he do this he would prove God unjust in that He had made for His children conditions of salvation with which they could not comply.

He whose heart is fixed to serve God will find opportunity to witness for Him. Difficulties will be powerless to hinder him who is determined to seek first the kingdom of God and His righteousness. In the strength gained by prayer and a study of the word, he will seek virtue and forsake vice. Looking to Jesus, the Author and Finisher of the faith, who endured the contradiction of sinners against Himself, the believer will willingly brave contempt and derision. And help and grace sufficient for every circumstance are promised by Him whose word is truth. His everlasting arms encircle the soul that turns to Him for aid. In His care we may rest safely, saying, "What time I am afraid, I will trust in Thee." Psalm 56:3. To all who put their trust in Him, God will fulfill His promise.

By His own example the Saviour has shown that His followers can be in the world and yet not of the world. He came not to partake of its delusive pleasures, to be swayed by its customs, and to follow its practices, but to do His Father's will, to seek and save the lost. With this object before him the Christian may stand uncontaminated in any surroundings. Whatever his station or circumstances, exalted or humble, he will manifest the power of true religion in the faithful performance of duty.

Not in freedom from trial, but in the midst of it, is Christian character developed. Exposure to rebuffs and opposition leads the follower of Christ to greater watchfulness and more earnest prayer to the mighty Helper. Severe trial endured by the grace of God develops patience, vigilance, fortitude, and a deep and abiding trust in God. It is the triumph of the Christian faith that it enables its follower to suffer and be strong; to submit, and thus to conquer; to be killed all the day long, and yet to live; to bear the cross, and thus to win the crown of glory.

45

Written From Rome

The apostle Paul early in his Christian experience was given special opportunities to learn the will of God concerning the followers of Jesus. He was "caught up to the third heaven," "into paradise, and heard unspeakable words, which it is not lawful for a man to utter." He himself acknowledged that many "visions and revelations" had been given him "of the Lord." His understanding of the principles of gospel truth was equal to that of "the very chiefest apostles." 2 Corinthians 12:2, 4, 1, 11. He had a clear, full comprehension of "the breadth, and length, and depth, and height" of "the love of Christ, which passeth knowledge." Ephesians 3:18, 19.

Paul could not tell all that he had seen in vision; for among his hearers were some who would have misapplied his words. But that which was revealed to him enabled him to labor as a leader and a wise teacher, and also molded the messages that he in later years sent to the churches. The impression that he received when in vision was ever with him, enabling him to give a correct representation of Christian character. By word of mouth and by letter he bore a message that ever since has brought help and strength to the church of God. To believers today this message speaks plainly of the dangers that will threaten the church, and the false doctrines that they will have to meet.

The apostle's desire for those to whom he addressed his letters of counsel and admonition was that they should "be no more children, tossed to and fro, and carried about with every wind of doctrine;" but that they should all come into "the unity of the faith, and of the knowledge of the Son of God, unto a perfect man, unto the measure of the stature of the fullness of Christ." He entreated those who were followers of Jesus in heathen communities not to walk "as other Gentiles walk, in the vanity of their mind, having the understanding darkened, being alienated from the life of God . . . because of the blindness of their heart," but "circumspectly, not as fools, but as wise, redeeming the time." Ephesians 4:14, 13, 17, 18; 5:15, 16. He encouraged the believers to look forward to the time when Christ, who "loved the church, and gave Himself for it," would "present it to Himself a glorious church, not having spot, or wrinkle, or any such thing"—a church "holy and without blemish." Ephesians 5:25, 27.

These messages, written with a power not of man but of God, contain lessons which should be studied by all and which may with profit be often repeated. In them practical godliness is

This chapter is based on the Epistle to the Colossians and the Philippians.

outlined, principles are laid down that should be followed in every church, and the way that leads to life eternal is made plain.

In his letter to "the saints and faithful brethren in Christ which are at Colosse," written while he was a prisoner in Rome, Paul makes mention of his joy over their steadfastness in the faith, tidings of which had been brought him by Epaphras, who, the apostle wrote, "declared unto us your love in the Spirit. For this cause," he continued, "we also, since the day we heard it, do not cease to pray for you, and to desire that ye might be filled with the knowledge of His will in all wisdom and spiritual understanding; that ye might walk worthy of the Lord unto all pleasing, being fruitful in every good work, and increasing in the knowledge of God; strengthened with all might, according to His glorious power, unto all patience and long-suffering with joyfulness."

Thus Paul put into words his desire for the Colossian believers. How high the ideal that these words hold before the follower of Christ! They show the wonderful possibilities of the Christian life and make it plain that there is no limit to the blessings that the children of God may receive. Constantly increasing in a knowledge of God, they may go on from strength to strength, from height to height in Christian experience, until by "His glorious power" they are made "meet to be partakers of the inheritance of the saints in light."

472 The apostle exalted Christ before his brethren as the One by whom God had created all things and by whom He had wrought out their redemption. He declared that the hand that sustains the worlds in space, and holds in their orderly arrangements and tireless activity all things throughout the universe of God, is the hand that was nailed to the cross for them. "By Him were all things created," Paul wrote, "that are in heaven, and that are in earth, visible and invisible, whether they be thrones, or dominions, or principalities, or powers: all things were created by Him, and for Him: and He is before all things, and by Him all things consist." "And you, that were sometime alienated and enemies in your mind by wicked works, yet now hath He reconciled in the body of His flesh through death, to present you holy and unblamable and unreprovable in His sight."

The Son of God stooped to uplift the fallen. For this He left the sinless worlds on high, the ninety and nine that loved Him, and came to this earth to be "wounded for our transgressions" and "bruised for our iniquities." Isaiah 53:5. He was in all things made like unto His brethren. He became flesh, even as we are. He knew what it meant to be hungry and thirsty and weary. He was sustained by food and refreshed by sleep. He was a stranger and a sojourner on the earth—in the world, but not of

the world; tempted and tried as men and women of today are tempted and tried, yet living a life free from sin. Tender, compassionate, sympathetic, ever considerate of others, He represented the character of God. "The Word was made flesh, and dwelt among us, . . . full of grace and truth." John 1:14.

Surrounded by the practices and influences of 473 heathenism, the Colossian believers were in danger of being drawn away from the simplicity of the gospel, and Paul, in warning them against this, pointed them to Christ as the only safe guide. "I would that ye knew," he wrote, "what great conflict I have for you, and for them at Laodicea, and for as many as have not seen my face in the flesh; that their hearts might be comforted, being knit together in love, and unto all riches of the full assurance of understanding, to the acknowledgment of the mystery of God, and of the Father, and of Christ; in whom are hid all the treasures of wisdom and knowledge.

"And this I say, lest any man should beguile you with enticing words. . . . As ye have therefore received Christ Jesus the Lord, so walk ye in Him: rooted and built up in Him, and stablished in the faith, as ye have been taught, abounding therein with thanksgiving. Beware lest any man spoil you through philosophy and vain deceit, after the tradition of men, after the rudiments of the world, and not after Christ. For in Him dwelleth all the fullness of the Godhead bodily. And ye are complete in Him, which is the head of all principality and power."

Christ had foretold that deceivers would arise, through whose influence "iniquity" should "abound," and "the love of many" should "wax cold." Matthew 24:12. He had warned the disciples that the church would be in more danger from this evil than from the persecution of her enemies. Again and again Paul warned the believers against these false teachers. This peril, above all others, they must guard against; for by 474 receiving false teachers, they would open the door to errors by which the enemy would dim the spiritual perceptions and shake the confidence of those newly come to the faith of the gospel. Christ was the standard by which they were to test the doctrines presented. All that was not in harmony with His teachings they were to reject. Christ crucified for sin, Christ risen from the dead, Christ ascended on high—this was the science of salvation that they were to learn and teach.

The warnings of the word of God regarding the perils surrounding the Christian church belong to us today. As in the days of the apostles men tried by tradition and philosophy to destroy faith in the Scriptures, so today, by the pleasing sentiments of higher criticism, evolution, spiritualism, theosophy, and pantheism, the enemy of righteousness is seeking to lead souls into forbidden paths. To many the Bible is as a lamp without oil, because they have turned their minds into channels of speculative belief that bring misunderstanding and confusion. The work of higher criticism, in dissecting, conjecturing, reconstructing, is destroying faith in the Bible as a divine revelation. It is robbing God's word of power to control, uplift, and inspire human lives. By spiritualism, multitudes are taught to believe that desire is the highest law, that license is liberty, and that man is accountable only to himself.

The follower of Christ will meet with the "enticing words" against which the apostle warned the Colossian believers. He will meet 475 with spiritualistic interpretations of the Scriptures, but he is not to accept them. His voice is to be heard in clear affirmation of the eternal truths of the Scriptures. Keeping his eyes fixed on Christ, he is to move steadily forward in the path marked out, discarding all ideas that are not in harmony with His teaching. The truth of God is to be the subject for his contemplation and meditation. He is to regard the Bible as the voice of God speaking directly to him. Thus he will find the wisdom which is divine.

The knowledge of God as revealed in Christ is the knowledge that all who are saved must have. This is the knowledge that works transformation of character. Received into the life, it will re-create the soul in the image of Christ. This is the knowledge that God invites His children to receive, beside which all else is vanity and nothingness.

In every generation and in every land the true foundation for character building has been the same—the principles contained in the word of God. The only safe and sure rule is to do what God says. "The statutes of the Lord are right," and "he that doeth these things shall never be moved." Psalms 19:8; 15:5. It was with the word of God that the apostles met the false theories of their day, saying, "Other foundation can no man lay than that is laid." 1 Corinthians 3:11.

At the time of their conversion and baptism the Colossian believers pledged themselves to put away beliefs and practices that had hitherto been a part of their lives, and to be true to their allegiance to Christ. In his letter, Paul reminded them of this, and entreated them not to forget 476 that in order to keep their pledge they must put forth constant effort against the evils that would seek for mastery over them. "If ye then be risen with Christ," he said, "seek those things which are above, where Christ sitteth on the right hand of God. Set your affection on things above, not on things on the earth. For ye are dead, and your life is hid with Christ in God."

"If any man be in Christ, he is a new creature: old things are passed away; behold, all things are become new." 2 Corinthians 5:17. Through the power of Christ, men and women have broken the chains of sinful habit. They have renounced selfishness. The profane have become reverent, the drunken sober, the profligate pure. Souls that have borne the likeness of Satan have become transformed into the image of God. This change is in itself the miracle of miracles. A change wrought by the Word, it is one of the deepest mysteries of the Word. We cannot understand it; we can only believe, as declared by the Scriptures, it is "Christ in you, the hope of glory."

When the Spirit of God controls mind and heart, the converted soul breaks forth into a new song; for he realizes that in his experience the promise of God has been fulfilled, that his transgression has been forgiven, his sin covered. He has exercised repentance toward God for the violation of the divine law, and faith toward Christ, who died for man's justification. "Being justified by faith," he has "peace with God through our Lord Jesus Christ." Romans 5:1.

But because this experience is his, the Christian is not therefore to fold his hands, content 477 with that which has been accomplished for him. He who has determined to enter the spiritual kingdom will find that all the powers and passions of unregenerate nature, backed by the forces of the kingdom of darkness, are arrayed against him. Each day he must renew his consecration, each day do battle with evil. Old habits, hereditary tendencies to wrong, will strive for the mastery, and against these he is to be ever on guard, striving in Christ's strength for victory.

"Mortify therefore your members which are upon the earth," Paul wrote to the Colossians; "in the which ye also walked sometime, when ye lived in them. But now ye also put off all these: anger, wrath, malice, blasphemy, filthy communication out of your mouth. . . . Put on therefore, as the elect of God, holy and beloved, bowels of mercies, kindness, humbleness of mind, meekness, long-suffering; forbearing one another, and forgiving one another, if any man have a quarrel against any: even as Christ forgave you, so also do ye. And above all these things put on charity, which is the bond of perfectness. And let the peace of God rule in your hearts, to the which also ye are called in one body; and be ye thankful."

The letter to the Colossians is filled with lessons of highest value to all who are engaged in the service of Christ, lessons that show the singleness of purpose and the loftiness of aim which will be seen in the life of him who rightly represents the Saviour. Renouncing all that would hinder him from making progress in the upward way or that would turn the feet of 478 another from the narrow path, the believer will reveal in his daily life mercy, kindness, humility, meekness, forbearance, and the love of Christ.

The power of a higher, purer, nobler life is our great need. The world has too much of our thought, and the kingdom of heaven too little.

In his efforts to reach God's ideal for him, the Christian is to despair of nothing. Moral and spiritual perfection, through the grace and power of Christ, is promised to all. Jesus is the source of power, the fountain of life. He brings us to His word, and from the tree of life presents to us leaves for the healing of sin-sick souls. He leads us to the throne of God, and puts into our mouth a prayer through which we are brought into close contact with Himself. In our behalf He sets in operation the all-powerful agencies of heaven. At every step we touch His living power.

God fixes no limit to the advancement of those who desire to be "filled with the knowledge of His will in all wisdom and spiritual understanding." Through prayer, through watchfulness, through growth in knowledge and understanding, they are to be "strengthened with all might, according to His glorious power." Thus they are prepared to work for others. It is the Saviour's purpose that human beings, purified and sanctified, shall be His helping hand. For this great privilege let us give thanks to Him who "hath made us meet to be partakers of the inheritance of the saints in light: who hath delivered us from the power of darkness, and hath translated us into the kingdom of His dear Son."

479 Paul's letter to the Philippians, like the one to the Colossians, was written while he was a prisoner at Rome. The church at Philippi had sent gifts to Paul by the hand of Epaphroditus, whom Paul calls "my brother, and companion in labor, and fellow soldier, but your messenger, and he that ministered to my wants." While in Rome, Epaphroditus was sick, "nigh unto death: but God had mercy on him," Paul wrote, "and not on him only, but on me also, lest I should have sorrow upon sorrow." Hearing of the sickness of Epaphroditus, the believers at Philippi were filled with anxiety regarding him, and he decided to return to them. "He longed after you all," Paul wrote, "and was full of heaviness, because that ye had heard that he had been sick. . . . I sent him therefore the more carefully, that, when ye see him again, ye may rejoice, and that I may be the less sorrowful. Receive him therefore in the Lord with all gladness; and hold such in reputation: because for the work of Christ he was nigh unto death, not regarding his life, to supply your lack of service toward me."

By Epaphroditus, Paul sent the Philippian believers a letter, in which he thanked them for their gifts to him. Of all the churches, that of Philippi had been the most liberal in supplying Paul's wants. "Now ye Philippians know also," the apostle said in his letter, "that in the beginning of the gospel, when I departed from Macedonia, no church communicated with me as concerning giving and receiving, but ye only. For even in Thessalonica ye sent once and again unto my necessity. Not because I desire a gift: but I desire fruit that may abound to your account. But I have all, and abound: I am full, having received of Epaphroditus the things which were sent from you, an odor of a sweet 480 smell, a sacrifice acceptable, well-pleasing to God."

"Grace be unto you, and peace, from God our Father, and from the Lord Jesus Christ. I thank my God upon every remembrance of you, always in every prayer of mine for you all making request with joy, for your fellowship in the gospel from the first day until now; being confident of this very thing, that He which hath begun a good work in you will perform it until the day of Jesus Christ: even as it is meet for me to think this of you all, because I have you in my heart; inasmuch as both in my bonds, and in the defense and confirmation of the gospel, ye all are partakers of my grace. For God is my record, how greatly I long after you all. . . . And this I pray, that your love may abound yet more and more in knowledge and in all judgment; that ye may approve things that are excellent; that ye may be sincere and without offense till the day of Christ; being filled with the fruits of righteousness, which are by Jesus Christ, unto the glory and praise of God."

The grace of God sustained Paul in his imprisonment, enabling him to rejoice in tribulation. With faith and assurance he wrote to his Philippian brethren that his imprisonment had resulted in the furtherance of the gospel. "I would ye should understand, brethren," he declared, "that the things which happened unto me have fallen out rather unto the furtherance of the gospel; so that my bonds in Christ are manifest in all the palace, and in all other places; and many of the brethren in the Lord, waxing confident by my bonds, are much more bold to speak 481 the word without fear."

There is a lesson for us in this experience of Paul's, for it reveals God's way of working. The Lord can bring victory out of that which may seem to us discomfiture and defeat. We are in danger of forgetting God, of looking at the things which are seen, instead of beholding by the eye of faith the things which are unseen. When misfortune or calamity comes, we are ready to charge God with neglect or cruelty. If He sees fit to cut off our usefulness in some line, we mourn, not stopping to think that thus God may be working for our good. We need to learn that chastisement is a part of His great plan and that under the rod of affliction the Christian may sometimes do more for the Master than when engaged in active service.

As their example in the Christian life, Paul pointed the Philippians to Christ, who, "being in the form of God, thought it not robbery to be equal with God: but made Himself of no reputation, and took upon Him the form of a servant, and was made in the likeness of men: and being found in fashion as a man, He humbled Himself, and became obedient unto death, even the death of the cross."

"Wherefore, my beloved," he continued, "as ye have always obeyed, not as in my presence only, but now much more in my absence, work out your own salvation with fear and trembling. For it is God which worketh in you both to will and to do of His good pleasure. Do all things without murmurings and disputings: that ye may be blameless and harmless, the sons of 482 God, without rebuke, in the midst of a crooked and perverse nation, among whom ye shine as lights in the world; holding forth the word of life; that I may rejoice in the day of Christ, that I have not run in vain, neither labored in vain."

These words were recorded for the help of every striving soul. Paul holds up the standard of perfection and shows how it may be reached. "Work out your own salvation," he says, "for it is God which worketh in you."

The work of gaining salvation is one of copartnership, a joint operation. There is to be co-operation between God and the repentant sinner. This is necessary for the formation of right principles in the character. Man is to make earnest efforts to overcome that which hinders him from attaining to perfection. But he is wholly dependent upon God for success. Human effort of itself is not sufficient. Without the aid of divine power it avails nothing. God works and man works. Resistance of temptation must come from man, who must draw his power from God. On the one side there is infinite wisdom, compassion, and power; on the other, weakness, sinfulness, absolute helplessness.

God wishes us to have the mastery over ourselves. But He cannot help us without our consent and co-operation. The divine Spirit works through the powers and faculties given to man. Of ourselves, we are not able to bring the purposes and desires and inclinations into harmony with the will of God; but if we are "willing to be made willing," the Saviour will accomplish this for us, "Casting down imaginations, and every 483 high thing that exalteth itself against the knowledge of God, and bringing into captivity every thought to the obedience of Christ." 2 Corinthians 10:5.

He who would build up a strong, symmetrical character, he who would be a well-balanced Christian, must give all and do all for Christ; for the Redeemer will not accept divided service. Daily he must learn the meaning of self-surrender. He must study the word of God, learning its meaning and obeying its precepts. Thus he may reach the standard of Christian excellence. Day by day God works with him, perfecting the character that is to stand in the time of final test.

And day by day the believer is working out before men and angels a sublime experiment, showing what the gospel can do for fallen human beings.

"I count not myself to have apprehended," Paul wrote; "but this one thing I do, forgetting those things which are behind, and reaching forth unto those things which are before, I press toward the mark for the prize of the high calling of God in Christ Jesus."

Paul did many things. From the time that he gave his allegiance to Christ, his life was filled with untiring service. From city to city, from country to country, he journeyed, telling the story of the cross, winning converts to the gospel, and establishing churches. For these churches he had a constant care, and he wrote many letters of instruction to them. At times he worked at his trade to earn his daily bread. But in all the busy activities of his life, Paul never lost sight of one great purpose—to press toward 484 the prize of his high calling. One aim he kept steadfastly before him—to be faithful to the One who at the gate of Damascus had revealed Himself to him. From this aim nothing had power to turn him aside. To exalt the cross of Calvary—this was the all-absorbing motive that inspired his words and acts.

The great purpose that constrained Paul to press forward in the face of hardship and difficulty should lead every Christian worker to consecrate himself wholly to God's service. Worldly attractions will be presented to draw his attention from the Saviour, but he is to press on toward the goal, showing to the world, to angels, and to men that the hope of seeing the face of God is worth all the effort and sacrifice that the attainment of this hope demands.

Though he was a prisoner, Paul was not discouraged. Instead, a note of triumph rings through the letters that he wrote from Rome to the churches. "Rejoice in the Lord alway," he wrote to the Philippians, "and again I say, Rejoice. . . . Be careful for nothing; but in everything by prayer and supplication with thanksgiving let your requests be made known unto God. And the peace of God, which passeth all understanding, shall keep your hearts and minds through Christ Jesus. Finally, brethren, whatsoever things are true, whatsoever things are honest, whatsoever things are just, whatsoever things are pure, whatsoever things are lovely, whatsoever things are of good report; if there be any virtue, and if there be any praise, think on these things."

"My God shall supply all your need according to His riches in glory by Christ Jesus. . . . The grace of our Lord Jesus Christ be with you all."

485

46

At Liberty

While Paul's labors in Rome were being blessed to the conversion of many souls and the strengthening and encouragement of the believers, clouds were gathering that threatened not only his own safety, but also the prosperity of the church. On his arrival in Rome he had been placed in charge of the captain of the imperial guards, a man of justice and integrity, by whose clemency he was left comparatively free to pursue the work of the gospel. But before the close of the two years' imprisonment, this man was replaced by an official from whom the apostle could expect no special favor.

The Jews were now more active than ever in their efforts against Paul, and they found an able helper in the profligate woman whom Nero had made his second wife, and who, being a Jewish proselyte, lent all her influence to aid their murderous designs against the champion of Christianity.

Paul could hope for little justice from the Caesar to whom he had appealed. Nero was
486 more debased in morals, more frivolous in character, and at the same time capable of more atrocious cruelty, than any ruler who had preceded him. The reins of government could not have been entrusted to a more despotic ruler. The first year of his reign had been marked by the poisoning of his young stepbrother, the rightful heir to the throne. From one depth of vice and crime to another, Nero had descended, until he had murdered his own mother, and then his wife. There was no atrocity which he would not perpetrate, no vile act to which he would not stoop. In every noble mind he inspired only abhorrence and contempt.

The details of the iniquity practiced in his court are too degrading, too horrible, for description. His abandoned wickedness created disgust and loathing, even in many who were forced to share his crimes. They were in constant fear as to what enormities he would suggest next. Yet even such crimes as Nero's did not shake the allegiance of his subjects. He was acknowledged as the absolute ruler of the whole civilized world. More than this, he was made the recipient of divine honors and was worshiped as a god.

From the viewpoint of human judgment, Paul's condemnation before such a judge was certain. But the apostle felt that so long as he was loyal to God, he had nothing to fear. The One who in the past had been his protector could shield him still from the malice of the Jews and from the power of Caesar.

And God did shield His servant. At Paul's examination the charges against him were not sustained, and, contrary to the general expectation, and with a regard for justice wholly at variance with his character, Nero declared the prisoner guiltless. Paul's bonds were removed; he was again a free man.

Had his trial been longer deferred, or had he from any cause been detained in Rome until the following year, he would doubtless have perished in the persecution which then took place. During Paul's imprisonment the converts to Christianity had become so numerous as to attract the attention and arouse the enmity of the authorities. The anger of the emperor was especially excited by the conversion of members of his own household, and he soon found a pretext to make the Christians the objects of his merciless cruelty.

About this time a terrible fire occurred in Rome by which nearly one half of the city was burned. Nero himself, it was rumored, had caused the flames to be kindled, but to avert suspicion he made a pretense of great generosity by assisting the homeless and destitute. He was, however, accused of the crime. The people were excited and enraged, and in order to clear himself, and also to rid the city of a class whom he feared and hated, Nero turned the accusation upon the Christians. His device succeeded, and thousands of the followers of Christ—men, women, and children—were cruelly put to death.

From this terrible persecution Paul was spared, for soon after his release he had left Rome. This last interval of freedom he diligently improved in laboring among the churches. He sought to establish a firmer union between the Greek and the Eastern churches and to fortify the minds of the believers against the false doctrines that were creeping in to corrupt the faith.

The trials and anxieties that Paul had endured had preyed upon his physical powers. The infirmities of age were upon him. He felt that he was now doing his last work, and, as the time of his labor grew shorter, his efforts became more intense. There seemed to be no limit to his zeal. Resolute in purpose, prompt in action, strong in faith, he journeyed from church to church, in many lands, and sought by every means within his power to strengthen the hands of the believers, that they might do faithful work in winning souls to Jesus, and that in the trying times upon which they were even then entering, they might remain steadfast to the gospel, bearing faithful witness for Christ.

487

488

bearable.

In the last letter that the apostle ever wrote, he speaks thus of this faithful disciple: "The Lord give mercy unto the house of Onesiphorus; for he oft refreshed me, and was not ashamed of my chain: but, when he was in Rome, he sought me out very diligently, and found me. The Lord grant unto him that he may find mercy of the Lord in that day." 2 Timothy 1:16-18.

The desire for love and sympathy is implanted in the heart by God Himself. Christ, in His hour of agony in Gethsemane, longed for the sympathy of His disciples. And Paul, though apparently indifferent to hardship and suffering, yearned for sympathy and companionship. The visit of Onesiphorus, testifying to his fidelity at a time of loneliness and desertion, brought gladness and cheer to one who had spent his life in service for others.

489

47
The Final Arrest

Paul's work among the churches after his acquittal at Rome, could not escape the observation of his enemies. Since the beginning of the persecution under Nero the Christians had everywhere been a proscribed sect. After a time the unbelieving Jews conceived the idea of fastening upon Paul the crime of instigating the burning of Rome. Not one of them thought for a moment that he was guilty; but they knew that such a charge, made with the faintest show of plausibility, would seal his doom. Through their efforts, Paul was again arrested, and hurried away to his final imprisonment.

On his second voyage to Rome, Paul was accompanied by several of his former companions; others earnestly desired to share his lot, but he refused to permit them thus to imperil their lives. The prospect before him was far less favorable than at the time of his former imprisonment. The persecution under Nero had greatly lessened the number of Christians in Rome. Thousands had been martyred for their faith, many had left the city, and those who remained were greatly depressed and intimidated.

Upon his arrival at Rome, Paul was placed in a gloomy dungeon, there to remain until his course should be finished. Accused of instigating one of the basest and most terrible of crimes against the city and the nation, he was the object of universal execration.

The few friends who had shared the burdens of the apostle, now began to leave him, some by desertion, and others on missions to the various churches. Phygellus and Hermogenes were the first to go. Then Demas, dismayed by the thickening clouds of difficulty and danger, forsook the persecuted apostle. Crescens was sent by Paul to the churches of Galatia, Titus to Dalmatia, Tychicus to Ephesus. Writing to Timothy of this experience, Paul said, "Only Luke is with me." 2 Timothy 4:11. Never had the apostle needed the ministrations of his brethren as now, enfeebled as he was by age, toil, and infirmities, and confined in the damp, dark vaults of a Roman prison. The services of Luke, the beloved disciple and faithful friend, were a great comfort to Paul and enabled him to communicate with his brethren and the world without.

In this trying time Paul's heart was cheered by frequent visits from Onesiphorus. This warmhearted Ephesian did all in his power to lighten the burden of the apostle's imprisonment. His beloved teacher was in bonds for the truth's sake, while he himself went free, and he spared himself no effort to make Paul's lot more

490

491

48
Paul Before Nero

When Paul was summoned to appear before the emperor Nero for trial, it was with the near prospect of certain death. The serious nature of the crime charged against him, and the prevailing animosity toward Christians, left little ground for hope of a favorable issue.

Among the Greeks and Romans it was customary to allow an accused person the privilege of employing an advocate to plead in his behalf before courts of justice. By force of argument, by impassioned eloquence, or by entreaties, prayers, and tears, such an advocate often secured a decision in favor of the prisoner or, failing in this, succeeded in mitigating the severity of the sentence. But when Paul was summoned before Nero, no man ventured to act as his counsel or advocate; no friend was at hand even to preserve a record of the charges brought against him, or of the arguments that he urged in his own defense. Among the Christians at Rome there was not one who came forward to stand by him in that trying hour.

The only reliable record of the occasion is given by Paul himself, in his second letter to Timothy. "At my first answer," the apostle wrote, "no man stood with me, but all men forsook me: I pray God that it may not be laid to their charge. Notwithstanding the Lord stood with me, and strengthened me; that by me the preaching might be fully known, and that all the Gentiles might hear: and I was delivered out of the mouth of the lion." 2 Timothy 4:16, 17.

Paul before Nero—how striking the contrast! The haughty monarch before whom the man of God was to answer for his faith, had reached the height of earthly power, authority, and wealth,

492

493

as well as the lowest depths of crime and iniquity. In power and greatness he stood unrivaled. There were none to question his authority, none to resist his will. Kings laid their crowns at his feet. Powerful armies marched at his command, and the ensigns of his navies betokened victory. His statue was set up in the halls of justice, and the decrees of senators and the decisions of judges were but the echo of his will. Millions bowed in obedience to his mandates. The name of Nero made the world tremble. To incur his displeasure was to lose property, liberty, life; and his frown was more to be dreaded than a pestilence.

494 Without money, without friends, without counsel, the aged prisoner stood before Nero— the countenance of the emperor bearing the shameful record of the passions that raged within; the face of the accused telling of a heart at peace with God. Paul's experience had been one of poverty, self-denial, and suffering. Notwithstanding constant misrepresentation, reproach, and abuse, by which his enemies had endeavored to intimidate him, he had fearlessly held aloft the standard of the cross. Like his Master, he had been a homeless wanderer, and like Him, he had lived to bless humanity. How could Nero, a capricious, passionate, licentious tyrant, understand or appreciate the character and motives of this son of God?

The vast hall was thronged by an eager, restless crowd that surged and pressed to the front to see and hear all that should take place. The high and the low were there, the rich and the poor, the learned and the ignorant, the proud and the humble, all alike destitute of a true knowledge of the way of life and salvation.

The Jews brought against Paul the old charges of sedition and heresy, and both Jews and Romans accused him of instigating the burning of the city. While these accusations were urged against him, Paul preserved an unbroken serenity. The people and the judges looked at him in surprise. They had been present at many trials and had looked upon many a criminal, but never had they seen a man wear a look of such holy calmness as did the prisoner before them. The keen eyes of the judges, accustomed to read the countenances of prisoners, searched Paul's face in vain for some evidence of guilt. When he was permitted to speak in his own behalf, all listened with eager interest.

495 Once more Paul has an opportunity to uplift before a wondering multitude the banner of the cross. As he gazes upon the throng before him,—Jews, Greeks, Romans, with strangers from many lands,—his soul is stirred with an intense desire for their salvation. He loses sight of the occasion, of the perils surrounding him, of the terrible fate that seems so near. He sees only Jesus, the Intercessor, pleading before God in behalf of sinful men. With more than human eloquence and power, Paul presents the truths of the gospel. He points his hearers to the sacrifice made for the fallen race. He declares that an infinite price has been paid for man's redemption. Provision has been made for him to share the throne of God. By angel messengers, earth is connected with heaven, and all the deeds of men, whether good or evil, are open to the eye of Infinite Justice.

Thus pleads the advocate of truth. Faithful among the faithless, loyal among the disloyal, he stands as God's representative, and his voice is as a voice from heaven. There is no fear, no sadness, no discouragement in word or look. Strong in a consciousness of innocence, clothed in the panoply of truth, he rejoices that he is a son of God. His words are as a shout of victory above the roar of battle. He declares the cause to which he has devoted his life, to be the only cause that can never fail. Though he may perish, the gospel will not perish. God lives, and His truth will triumph.

Many who that day looked upon him "saw his face as it had been the face of an angel." Acts 6:15.

Never before had that company listened to words like these. They struck a cord that vibrated in the hearts of even the most hardened. 496 Truth, clear and convincing, overthrew error. Light shone into the minds of many who afterward gladly followed its rays. The truths spoken on that day were destined to shake nations and to live through all time, influencing the hearts of men when the lips that had uttered them should be silent in a martyr's grave.

Never before had Nero heard the truth as he heard it on this occasion. Never before had the enormous guilt of his own life been so revealed to him. The light of heaven pierced the sin-polluted chambers of his soul, and he trembled with terror at the thought of a tribunal before which he, the ruler of the world, would finally be arraigned, and his deeds receive their just award. He feared the apostle's God, and he dared not pass sentence upon Paul, against whom no accusation had been sustained. A sense of awe restrained for a time his bloodthirsty spirit.

For a moment, heaven was opened to the guilty and hardened Nero, and its peace and purity seemed desirable. That moment the invitation of mercy was extended even to him. But only for a moment was the thought of pardon welcomed. Then the command was issued that Paul be taken back to his dungeon; and as the door closed upon the messenger of God, the door of repentance closed forever against the emperor of Rome. No ray of light from heaven was ever again to penetrate the darkness that enveloped him. Soon he was to suffer the retributive judgments of God.

Not long after this, Nero sailed on his infamous expedition to Greece, where he disgraced himself and his kingdom by contemptible and debasing frivolity. Returning to Rome with great pomp, he surrounded himself with his courtiers and engaged in scenes of revolting debauchery. In the midst of this revelry a voice of tumult in the streets was heard. A messenger dispatched to learn the cause, returned with the appalling news that Galba, at the head of an army, was marching rapidly upon Rome, that insurrection had already broken out in the city, and that the streets were filled with an enraged mob, which, threatening death to the emperor and all his supporters, was rapidly approaching the palace.

In this time of peril, Nero had not, like the faithful Paul, a powerful and compassionate God on whom to rely. Fearful of the suffering and possible torture he might be compelled to endure at the hands of the mob, the wretched tyrant thought to end his life by his own hand, but at the critical moment his courage failed. Completely unmanned, he fled ignominiously from the city and sought shelter at a countryseat a few miles distant, but to no avail. His hiding place was soon discovered, and as the pursuing horsemen drew near, he summoned a slave to his aid and inflicted on himself a mortal wound. Thus perished the tyrant Nero, at the early age of thirty-two.

49

Paul's Last Letter

From the judgment hall of Caesar, Paul returned to his cell, realizing that he had gained for himself only a brief respite. He knew that his enemies would not rest until they had compassed his death. But he knew also that for a time truth had triumphed. To have proclaimed a crucified and risen Saviour before the vast crowd who had listened to him, was in itself a victory. That day a work had begun which would grow and strengthen, and which Nero and all other enemies of Christ would seek in vain to hinder or destroy.

Sitting day after day in his gloomy cell, knowing that at a word or a nod from Nero his life might be sacrificed, Paul thought of Timothy and determined to send for him. To Timothy had been committed the care of the church at Ephesus, and he had therefore been left behind when Paul made his last journey to Rome. Paul and Timothy were bound together by an affection unusually deep and strong. Since his conversion, Timothy had shared Paul's labors and sufferings, and the friendship between the two had grown stronger, deeper, and more sacred,

until all that a son could be to a loved and honored father, Timothy was to the aged, toilworn apostle. It is little wonder that in his loneliness and solitude, Paul longed to see him.

Under the most favorable circumstances several months must pass before Timothy could reach Rome from Asia Minor. Paul knew that his life was uncertain, and he feared that Timothy might arrive too late to see him. He had important counsel and instruction for the young man, to whom so great responsibility had been entrusted; and while urging him to come without delay, he dictated the dying testimony that he might not be spared to utter. His soul filled with loving solicitude for his son in the gospel and for the church under his care, Paul sought to impress Timothy with the importance of fidelity to his sacred trust.

Paul began his letter with the salutation: "To Timothy, my dearly beloved son: Grace, mercy, and peace, from God the Father and Christ Jesus our Lord. I thank God, whom I serve from my forefathers with pure conscience, that without ceasing I have remembrance of thee in my prayers night and day."

The apostle then urged upon Timothy the necessity of steadfastness in the faith. "I put thee in remembrance," he wrote, "that thou stir up the gift of God, which is in thee by the putting on of my hands. For God hath not given us the spirit of fear; but of power, and of love, and of a sound mind. Be not thou therefore ashamed of the testimony of our Lord, nor of me His prisoner: but be thou partaker of the afflictions of the gospel according to the power of God." Paul entreated Timothy to remember that he had been called "with a holy calling" to proclaim the power of Him who had "brought life and immortality to light through the gospel: whereunto," he declared, "I am appointed a preacher, and an apostle, and a teacher of the Gentiles. For the which cause I also suffer these things: nevertheless I am not ashamed: for I know whom I have believed, and am persuaded that He is able to keep that which I have committed unto Him against that day."

Through his long term of service, Paul had never faltered in his allegiance to his Saviour. Wherever he was—whether before scowling Pharisees, or Roman authorities; before the furious mob at Lystra, or the convicted sinners in the Macedonian dungeon; whether reasoning with the panic-stricken sailors on the shipwrecked vessel, or standing alone before Nero to plead for his life—he had never been ashamed of the cause he was advocating. The one great purpose of his Christian life had been to serve Him whose name had once filled him with contempt; and from this purpose no opposition or persecution had been able to turn him aside. His faith, made strong by effort and pure by sacrifice, upheld and strengthened him.

This chapter is based on the Second Epistle to Timothy.

"Thou therefore, my son," Paul continued, "be strong in the grace that is in Christ Jesus. And the things that thou hast heard of me among many witnesses, the same commit thou to faithful men, who shall be able to teach others also. Thou therefore endure hardness, as a good soldier of Jesus Christ."

501

The true minister of God will not shun hardship or responsibility. From the Source that never fails those who sincerely seek for divine power, he draws strength that enables him to meet and overcome temptation, and to perform the duties that God places upon him. The nature of the grace that he receives, enlarges his capacity to know God and His Son. His soul goes out in longing desire to do acceptable service for the Master. And as he advances in the Christian pathway he becomes "strong in the grace that is in Christ Jesus." This grace enables him to be a faithful witness of the things that he has heard. He does not despise or neglect the knowledge that he has received from God, but commits this knowledge to faithful men, who in their turn teach others.

In this his last letter to Timothy, Paul held up before the younger worker a high ideal, pointing out the duties devolving on him as a minister of Christ. "Study to show thyself approved unto God," the apostle wrote, "a workman that needeth not to be ashamed, rightly dividing the word of truth." "Flee also youthful lusts: but follow righteousness, faith, charity, peace, with them that call on the Lord out of a pure heart. But foolish and unlearned questions avoid, knowing that they do gender strifes. And the servant of the Lord must not strive; but be gentle unto all men, apt to teach, patient, in meekness instructing those that oppose themselves; if God peradventure will give them repentance to the acknowledging of the truth."

502

The apostle warned Timothy against the false teachers who would seek to gain entrance into the church. "This know also," he declared, "that in the last days perilous times shall come. For men shall be lovers of their own selves, covetous, boasters, proud, blasphemers, disobedient to parents, unthankful, unholy; . . . having a form of godliness, but denying the power thereof: from such turn away."

"Evil men and seducers shall wax worse and worse," he continued, "deceiving, and being deceived. But continue thou in the things which thou hast learned and hast been assured of, knowing of whom thou hast learned them; and that from a child thou hast known the Holy Scriptures, which are able to make thee wise unto salvation. . . . All Scripture is given by inspiration of God, and is profitable for doctrine, for reproof, for correction, for instruction in righteousness: that the man of God may be perfect, throughly furnished unto all good works." God has provided abundant means for successful warfare against the evil that is in the world. The Bible is the armory where we may equip for the struggle. Our loins must be girt about with truth. Our breastplate must be righteousness. The shield of faith must be in our hand, the helmet of salvation on our brow; and with the sword of the Spirit, which is the word of God, we are to cut our way through the obstructions and entanglements of sin.

Paul knew that there was before the church a time of great peril. He knew that faithful, earnest work would have to be done by those left in charge of the churches; and he wrote to Timothy, "I charge thee therefore before God, and the Lord Jesus Christ, who shall judge the quick and the dead at His appearing and His kingdom; Preach the word; be instant in season, out of season; reprove, rebuke, exhort with all long-suffering and doctrine."

503

This solemn charge to one so zealous and faithful as was Timothy is a strong testimony to the importance and responsibility of the work of the gospel minister. Summoning Timothy before the bar of God, Paul bids him preach the word, not the sayings and customs of men; to be ready to witness for God whenever opportunity should present itself—before large congregations and private circles, by the way and at the fireside, to friends and to enemies, whether in safety or exposed to hardship and peril, reproach and loss.

Fearing that Timothy's mild, yielding disposition might lead him to shun an essential part of his work, Paul exhorted him to be faithful in reproving sin and even to rebuke with sharpness those who were guilty of gross evils. Yet he was to do this "with all long-suffering and doctrine." He was to reveal the patience and love of Christ, explaining and enforcing his reproofs by the truths of the word.

To hate and reprove sin, and at the same time to show pity and tenderness for the sinner, is a difficult attainment. The more earnest our own efforts to attain to holiness of heart and life, the more acute will be our perception of sin and the more decided our disapproval of any deviation from the right. We must guard against undue severity toward the wrongdoer, but we must also be careful not to lose sight of the exceeding sinfulness of sin. There is need of showing Christlike patience and love for the erring one, but there is also danger of showing so great toleration for his error that he will look upon himself as undeserving of reproof, and will reject it as uncalled for and unjust.

504

Ministers of the gospel sometimes do great harm by allowing their forbearance toward the erring to degenerate into toleration of sins and even participation in them. Thus they are led to excuse and palliate that which God condemns, and after a time they become so blinded as to commend the very ones whom God commands them to reprove. He who has blunted his spiritual perceptions by sinful leniency toward those whom God condemns, will erelong commit a greater sin by severity and harshness toward those whom God approves.

By the pride of human wisdom, by contempt for the influence of the Holy Spirit, and by disrelish for the truths of God's word, many who profess to be Christians, and who feel competent to teach others, will be led to turn away from the requirements of God. Paul declared to Timothy, "The time will come when they will not endure sound doctrine; but after their own lusts shall they heap to themselves teachers, having itching ears; and they shall turn away their ears from the truth, and shall be turned unto fables."

The apostle does not here refer to the openly irreligious, but to the professing Christians who make inclination their guide, and thus become enslaved by self. Such are willing to listen to those doctrines only that do not rebuke their sins 505 or condemn their pleasure-loving course. They are offended by the plain words of the faithful servants of Christ and choose teachers who praise and flatter them. And among professing ministers there are those who preach the opinions of men instead of the word of God. Unfaithful to their trust, they lead astray those who look to them for spiritual guidance.

In the precepts of His holy law, God has given a perfect rule of life; and He has declared that until the close of time this law, unchanged in a single jot or tittle, is to maintain its claim upon human beings. Christ came to magnify the law and make it honorable. He showed that it is based upon the broad foundation of love to God and love to man, and that obedience to its precepts comprises the whole duty of man. In His own life He gave an example of obedience to the law of God. In the Sermon on the Mount He showed how its requirements extend beyond the outward acts and take cognizance of the thoughts and intents of the heart.

The law, obeyed, leads men to deny "ungodliness and worldly lusts," and to "live soberly, righteously, and godly, in this present world." Titus 2:12. But the enemy of all righteousness has taken the world captive and has led men and women to disobey the law. As Paul foresaw, multitudes have turned from the plain, searching truths of God's word and have chosen teachers who present to them the fables they desire. Many among both ministers and people are trampling under their feet the commandments of God. Thus the Creator of the world is insulted, and Satan laughs in triumph at the success of his devices.

506   With the growing contempt for God's law there is an increasing distaste for religion, an increase of pride, love of pleasure, disobedience to parents, and self-indulgence; and thoughtful minds everywhere are anxiously inquiring, What can be done to correct these alarming evils? The answer is found in Paul's exhortation to Timothy, "Preach the word." In the Bible are found the only safe principles of action. It is a transcript of the will of God, an expression of divine wisdom. It opens to man's understanding the great problems of life, and to all who heed its precepts it will prove an unerring guide, keeping them from wasting their lives in misdirected effort.

God has made known His will, and it is folly for man to question that which has gone out of His lips. After Infinite Wisdom has spoken, there can be no doubtful questions for man to settle, no wavering possibilities for him to adjust. All that is required of him is a frank, earnest concurrence in the expressed will of God. Obedience is the highest dictate of reason as well as of conscience.

Paul continued his charge: "Watch thou in all things, endure afflictions, do the work of an evangelist, make full proof of thy ministry." Paul was about to finish his course, and he desired Timothy to take his place, guarding the church from the fables and heresies by which the enemy, in various ways, would endeavor to lead them from the simplicity of the gospel. He admonished him to shun all temporal pursuits and entanglements that would prevent him from giving himself wholly to his work for God; to endure with cheerfulness the opposition, reproach, and persecution to which his faithful- 507 ness would expose him; to make full proof of his ministry by employing every means within his reach of doing good to those for whom Christ died.

Paul's life was an exemplification of the truths he taught, and herein lay his power. His heart was filled with a deep, abiding sense of his responsibility, and he labored in close communion with Him who is the fountain of justice, mercy, and truth. He clung to the cross of Christ as his only guarantee of success. The love of the Saviour was the undying motive that upheld him in his conflicts with self and in his struggles against evil as in the service of Christ he pressed forward against the unfriendliness of the world and the opposition of his enemies.

What the church needs in these days of peril is an army of workers who, like Paul, have educated themselves for usefulness, who have a deep experience in the things of God, and who are filled with earnestness and zeal. Sanctified, self-sacrificing men are needed; men who will not shun trial and responsibility; men who are brave and true; men in whose hearts Christ is formed "the hope of glory," and who with lips touched with holy fire will "preach the word." For want of such workers the cause of God languishes, and fatal errors, like a deadly poison, taint the morals and blight the hopes of a large part of the human race.

As the faithful, toilworn standard-bearers are offering up their lives for the truth's sake, who will come forward to take their place? Will our young men accept the holy trust at the hands of their fathers? Are they preparing to fill the vacancies made by the death of the faithful? 508 Will the apostle's charge be heeded, the call to duty be heard, amidst the incitements to selfishness and ambition that allure the youth?

Paul concluded his letter with personal messages to different ones and again repeated the urgent request that Timothy come to him soon, if possible before the winter. He spoke of his loneliness, caused by the desertion of some of his friends and the necessary absence of others; and lest Timothy should hesitate, fearing that the church at Ephesus might need his labors, Paul stated that he had already dispatched Tychicus to fill the vacancy.

After speaking of the scene of his trial before Nero, the desertion of his brethren, and the sustaining grace of a covenant-keeping God, Paul closed his letter by commending his beloved Timothy to the guardianship of the Chief Shepherd, who, though the undershepherds might be stricken down, would still care for His flock.

509 ## 50
Condemned to Die

During Paul's final trial before Nero, the emperor had been so strongly impressed with the force of the apostle's words that he deferred the decision of the case, neither acquitting nor condemning the accused servant of God. But the emperor's malice against Paul soon returned. Exasperated by his inability to check the spread of the Christian religion, even in the imperial household, he determined that as soon as a plausible pretext could be found, the apostle should be put to death. Not long afterward Nero pronounced the decision that condemned Paul to a martyr's death. Inasmuch as a Roman citizen could not be subjected to torture, he was sentenced to be beheaded.

Paul was taken in a private manner to the place of execution. Few spectators were allowed to be present; for his persecutors, alarmed at the extent of his influence, feared that converts might be won to Christianity by the scenes of his death. But even the hardened soldiers who 510 attended him listened to his words and with amazement saw him cheerful and even joyous in the prospect of death. To some who witnessed his martyrdom, his spirit of forgiveness toward his murderers and his unwavering confidence in Christ till the last, proved a savor of life unto life. More than one accepted the Sav-

iour whom Paul preached, and erelong fearlessly sealed their faith with their blood.

Until his latest hour the life of Paul testified to the truth of his words to the Corinthians: "God, who commanded the light to shine out of darkness, hath shined in our hearts, to give the light of the knowledge of the glory of God in the face of Jesus Christ. But we have this treasure in earthen vessels, that the excellency of the power may be of God, and not of us. We are troubled on every side, yet not distressed; we are perplexed, but not in despair; persecuted, but not forsaken; cast down, but not destroyed; always bearing about in the body the dying of the Lord Jesus, that the life also of Jesus might be made manifest in our body." 2 Corinthians 4:6-10. His sufficiency was not in himself, but in the presence and agency of the divine Spirit that filled his soul and brought every thought into subjection to the will of Christ. The prophet declares, "Thou wilt keep him in perfect peace, whose mind is stayed on Thee: because he trusteth in Thee." Isaiah 26:3. The heaven-born peace expressed on Paul's countenance won many a soul to the gospel.

Paul carried with him the atmosphere of heaven. All who associated with him felt the influence of his union with Christ. The fact that 511 his own life exemplified the truth he proclaimed, gave convincing power to his preaching. Here lies the power of truth. The unstudied, unconscious influence of a holy life is the most convincing sermon that can be given in favor of Christianity. Argument, even when unanswerable, may provoke only opposition; but a godly example has a power that it is impossible wholly to resist.

The apostle lost sight of his own approaching sufferings in his solicitude for those whom he was about to leave to cope with prejudice, hatred, and persecution. The few Christians who accompanied him to the place of execution he endeavored to strengthen and encourage by repeating the promises given for those who are persecuted for righteousness' sake. He assured them that nothing would fail of all that the Lord had spoken concerning His tried and faithful children. For a little season they might be in heaviness through manifold temptations; they might be destitute of earthly comforts; but they could encourage their hearts with the assurance of God's faithfulness, saying, "I know whom I have believed, and am persuaded that He is able to keep that which I have committed unto Him." 2 Timothy 1:12. Soon the night of trial and suffering would end, and then would dawn the glad morning of peace and perfect day.

The apostle was looking into the great beyond, not with uncertainty or dread, but with joyous hope and longing expectation. As he stands at the place of martyrdom he sees not the sword of the executioner or the earth so soon to

512 receive his blood; he looks up through the calm blue heaven of that summer day to the throne of the Eternal.

This man of faith beholds the ladder of Jacob's vision, representing Christ, who has connected earth with heaven, and finite man with the infinite God. His faith is strengthened as he calls to mind how patriarchs and prophets have relied upon the One who is his support and consolation, and for whom he is giving his life. From these holy men who from century to century have borne testimony for their faith, he hears the assurance that God is true. His fellow apostles, who, to preach the gospel of Christ, went forth to meet religious bigotry and heathen superstition, persecution, and contempt, who counted not their lives dear unto themselves that they might bear aloft the light of the cross amidst the dark mazes of infidelity—these he hears witnessing to Jesus as the Son of God, the Saviour of the world. From the rack, the stake, the dungeon, from dens and caves of the earth, there falls upon his ear the martyr's shout of triumph. He hears the witness of steadfast souls, who, though destitute, afflicted, tormented, yet bear fearless, solemn testimony for the faith, declaring, "I know whom I have believed." These, yielding up their lives for the faith, declare to the world that He in whom they have trusted is able to save to the uttermost.

Ransomed by the sacrifice of Christ, washed from sin in His blood, and clothed in His righteousness, Paul has the witness in himself that his soul is precious in the sight of his Redeemer. His life is hid with Christ in God, and he is per-
513 suaded that He who has conquered death is able to keep that which is committed to His trust. His mind grasps the Saviour's promise, "I will raise him up at the last day." John 6:40. His thoughts and hopes are centered on the second coming of his Lord. And as the sword of the executioner descends and the shadows of death gather about the martyr, his latest thought springs forward, as will his earliest in the great awakening, to meet the Life-giver, who shall welcome him to the joy of the blest.

Well-nigh a score of centuries have passed since Paul the aged poured out his blood as a witness for the word of God and the testimony of Jesus Christ. No faithful hand recorded for the generations to come the last scenes in the life of this holy man, but Inspiration has preserved for us his dying testimony. Like a trumpet peal his voice has rung out through all the ages since, nerving with his own courage thousands of witnesses for Christ and wakening in thousands of sorrow-stricken hearts the echo of his own triumphant joy: "I am now ready to be offered, and the time of my departure is at hand. I have fought a good fight, I have finished my course, I have kept the faith: hence-

forth there is laid up for me a crown of righteousness, which the Lord, the righteous Judge, shall give me at that day: and not to me only, but unto all them also that love His appearing." 2 Timothy 4:6-8.

51

A Faithful Undershepherd

514

Little mention is made in the book of Acts of the later work of the apostle Peter. During the busy years of ministry that followed the outpouring of the Spirit on the Day of Pentecost, he was among those who put forth untiring efforts to reach the Jews who came to Jerusalem to worship at the time of the annual festivals.

As the number of believers multiplied in Jerusalem and in other places visited by the messengers of the cross, the talents possessed by Peter proved of untold value to the early Christian church. The influence of his testimony concerning Jesus of Nazareth extended far and wide. Upon him had been laid a double responsibility. He bore positive witness concerning the Messiah before unbelievers, laboring earnestly for their conversion; and at the same time he did a special work for believers, strengthening them in the faith of Christ.

It was after Peter had been led to self-renunci-
515 ation and entire reliance upon divine power, that he received his call to act as an undershepherd. Christ had said to Peter, before his denial of Him, "When thou art converted, strengthen thy brethren." Luke 22:32. These words were significant of the wide and effectual work which this apostle was to do in the future for those who should come to the faith. For this work, Peter's own experience of sin and suffering and repentance had prepared him. Not until he had learned his weakness, could he know the believer's need of dependence on Christ. Amid the storm of temptation he had come to understand that man can walk safely only as in utter self-distrust he relies upon the Saviour.

At the last meeting of Christ with His disciples by the sea, Peter, tested by the thrice-repeated question, "Lovest thou Me?" (John 21:15-17), had been restored to his place among the Twelve. His work had been appointed him; he was to feed the Lord's flock. Now, converted and accepted, he was not only to seek to save those without the fold, but was to be a shepherd of the sheep.

Christ mentioned to Peter only one condition of service—"Lovest thou Me?" This is the essential qualification. Though Peter might possess every other, yet without the love of Christ he could not be a faithful shepherd over the flock of God. Knowledge, benevolence, elo-

This chapter is based on the First Epistle of Peter.

quence, zeal—all are essential in the good work; but without the love of Christ in the heart, the work of the Christian minister is a failure.

516   The love of Christ is not a fitful feeling, but a living principle, which is to be made manifest as an abiding power in the heart. If the character and deportment of the shepherd is an exemplification of the truth he advocates, the Lord will set the seal of His approval to the work. The shepherd and the flock will become one, united by their common hope in Christ.

The Saviour's manner of dealing with Peter had a lesson for him and his brethren. Although Peter had denied his Lord, the love which Jesus bore him had never faltered. And as the apostle should take up the work of ministering the word to others, he was to meet the transgressor with patience, sympathy, and forgiving love. Remembering his own weakness and failure, he was to deal with the sheep and lambs committed to his care as tenderly as Christ had dealt with him.

Human beings, themselves given to evil, are prone to deal untenderly with the tempted and the erring. They cannot read the heart; they know not its struggle and its pain. Of the rebuke that is love, of the blow that wounds to heal, of the warning that speaks hope, they have need to learn.

Throughout his ministry, Peter faithfully watched over the flock entrusted to his care, and thus proved himself worthy of the charge and responsibility given him by the Saviour. Ever he exalted Jesus of Nazareth as the Hope of Israel, the Saviour of mankind. He brought his own life under the discipline of the Master Worker. By every means within his power he sought to educate the believers for active service. His godly 517 example and untiring activity inspired many young men of promise to give themselves wholly to the work of the ministry. As time went on, the apostle's influence as an educator and leader increased; and while he never lost his burden to labor especially for the Jews, yet he bore his testimony in many lands and strengthened the faith of multitudes in the gospel.

In the later years of his ministry, Peter was inspired to write to the believers "scattered throughout Pontus, Galatia, Cappadocia, Asia, and Bithynia." His letters were the means of reviving the courage and strengthening the faith of those who were enduring trial and affliction, and of renewing to good works those who through manifold temptations were in danger of losing their hold upon God. These letters bear the impress of having been written by one in whom the sufferings of Christ and also His consolation had been made to abound; one whose entire being had been transformed by grace, and whose hope of eternal life was sure and steadfast.

At the very beginning of his first letter the aged servant of God ascribed to his Lord a tribute of praise and thanksgiving. "Blessed be the God and Father of our Lord Jesus Christ," he exclaimed, "which according to His abundant mercy hath begotten us again unto a lively hope by the resurrection of Jesus Christ from the dead, to an inheritance incorruptible, and undefiled, and that fadeth not away, reserved in heaven for you, who are kept by the power of God through faith unto salvation ready to be revealed in the last time."

In this hope of a sure inheritance in the earth made new, the early Christians rejoiced, even in 518 times of severe trial and affliction. "Ye greatly rejoice," Peter wrote, "though now for a season, if need be, ye are in heaviness through manifold temptations: that the trial of your faith, being much more precious than of gold that perisheth, though it be tried with fire, might be found unto praise and honor and glory at the appearing of Jesus Christ: whom having not seen, ye love; in whom, though now ye see Him not, . . . ye rejoice with joy unspeakable and full of glory: receiving the end of your faith, even the salvation of your souls."

The apostle's words were written for the instruction of believers in every age, and they have a special significance for those who live at the time when "the end of all things is at hand." His exhortations and warnings, and his words of faith and courage, are needed by every soul who would maintain his faith "steadfast unto the end." Hebrews 3:14.

The apostle sought to teach the believers how important it is to keep the mind from wandering to forbidden themes or from spending its energies on trifling subjects. Those who would not fall a prey to Satan's devices, must guard well the avenues of the soul; they must avoid reading, seeing, or hearing that which will suggest impure thoughts. The mind must not be left to dwell at random upon every subject that the enemy of souls may suggest. The heart must be faithfully sentineled, or evils without will awaken evils within, and the soul will wander in darkness. "Gird up the loins of your mind," Peter wrote, "be sober, and hope to the end for the grace that is to be brought unto you at the revelation of Jesus Christ; . . . not fashioning 519 yourselves according to the former lusts in your ignorance: but as He which hath called you is holy, so be ye holy in all manner of conversation; because it is written, Be ye holy; for I am holy."

"Pass the time of your sojourning here in fear: forasmuch as ye know that ye were not redeemed with corruptible things, as silver and gold, from your vain conversation received by tradition from your fathers; but with the precious blood of Christ, as of a Lamb without blemish and without spot: who verily was foreordained before the foundation of the world, but was manifest in these last times for you, who by Him do believe in God, that raised Him up from the dead, and gave Him glory; that your faith and hope might be in God."

Had silver and gold been sufficient to purchase the salvation of men, how easily might it have been accomplished by Him who says, "The silver is Mine, and the gold is Mine." Haggai 2:8. But only by the precious blood of the Son of God could the transgressor be redeemed. The plan of salvation was laid in sacrifice. The apostle Paul wrote, "Ye know the grace of our Lord Jesus Christ, that, though He was rich, yet for your sakes He became poor, that ye through His poverty might be rich." 2 Corinthians 8:9. Christ gave Himself for us that He might redeem us from all iniquity. And as the crowning blessing of salvation, "the gift of God is eternal life through Jesus Christ our Lord." Romans 6:23.

"Seeing ye have purified your souls in obeying the truth through the Spirit unto unfeigned
520 love of the brethren," Peter continued, "see that ye love one another with a pure heart fervently." The word of God—the truth—is the channel through which the Lord manifests His Spirit and power. Obedience to the word produces fruit of the required quality—"unfeigned love of the brethren." This love is heaven-born and leads to high motives and unselfish actions.

When truth becomes an abiding principle in the life, the soul is "born again, not of corruptible seed, but of incorruptible, by the word of God, which liveth and abideth forever." This new birth is the result of receiving Christ as the Word of God. When by the Holy Spirit divine truths are impressed upon the heart, new conceptions are awakened, and the energies hitherto dormant are aroused to co-operate with God.

Thus it had been with Peter and his fellow disciples. Christ was the revealer of truth to the world. By Him the incorruptible seed—the word of God—was sown in the hearts of men. But many of the most precious lessons of the Great Teacher were spoken to those who did not then understand them. When, after His ascension, the Holy Spirit brought His teachings to the remembrance of the disciples, their slumbering senses awoke. The meaning of these truths flashed upon their minds as a new revelation, and truth, pure and unadulterated, made a place for itself. Then the wonderful experience of His life became theirs. The Word bore testimony through them, the men of His appointment, and they proclaimed the mighty truth, "The Word was made flesh, and dwelt among us, . . . full of
521 grace and truth." "And of His fullness have all we received, and grace for grace." John 1:14, 16.

The apostle exhorted the believers to study the Scriptures, through a proper understanding of which they might make sure work for eterni-

ty. Peter realized that in the experience of every soul who is finally victorious there would be scenes of perplexity and trial; but he knew also that an understanding of the Scriptures would enable the tempted one to bring to mind promises that would comfort the heart and strengthen faith in the Mighty One.

"All flesh is as grass," he declared, "and all the glory of man as the flower of grass. The grass withereth, and the flower thereof falleth away: but the word of the Lord endureth forever. And this is the word which by the gospel is preached unto you. Wherefore laying aside all malice, and all guile, and hypocrisies, and envies, and all evilspeakings, as newborn babes, desire the sincere milk of the word, that ye may grow thereby: if so be ye have tasted that the Lord is gracious."

Many of the believers to whom Peter addressed his letters, were living in the midst of heathen, and much depended on their remaining true to the high calling of their profession. The apostle urged upon them their privileges as followers of Christ Jesus. "Ye are a chosen generation," he wrote, "a royal priesthood, an holy nation, a peculiar people; that ye should show forth the praises of Him who hath called you out of darkness into His marvelous light: which in time past were not a people, but are now the people of God: which had not obtained mercy, but now have obtained mercy.

"Dearly beloved, I beseech you as strangers 522 and pilgrims, abstain from fleshly lusts, which war against the soul; having your conversation honest among the Gentiles: that, whereas they speak against you as evildoers, they may by your good works, which they shall behold, glorify God in the day of visitation."

The apostle plainly outlined the attitude that believers should sustain toward the civil authorities: "Submit yourselves to every ordinance of man for the Lord's sake: whether it be to the king, as supreme; or unto governors, as unto them that are sent by him for the punishment of evildoers, and for the praise of them that do well. For so is the will of God, that with well-doing ye may put to silence the ignorance of foolish men: as free, and not using your liberty for a cloak of maliciousness, but as the servants of God. Honor all men. Love the brotherhood. Fear God. Honor the king."

Those who were servants were advised to remain subject to their masters "with all fear; not only to the good and gentle, but also to the froward. For this is thankworthy," the apostle explained, "if a man for conscience toward God endure grief, suffering wrongfully. For what glory is it, if, when ye be buffeted for your faults, ye shall take it patiently? but if, when ye do well, and suffer for it, ye take it patiently, this is acceptable with God. For even hereunto were ye called: because Christ also suffered for us, leaving us an example, that ye should follow His steps: who did no sin, neither was guile 523 found in His mouth: who, when He was reviled, reviled not again; when He suffered, He threatened not; but committed Himself to Him that judgeth righteously: who His own self bare our sins in His own body on the tree, that we, being dead to sins, should live unto righteousness: by whose stripes ye were healed. For ye were as sheep going astray; but are now returned unto the Shepherd and Bishop of your souls."

The apostle exhorted the women in the faith to be chaste in conversation and modest in dress and deportment. "Whose adorning," he counseled, "let it not be that outward adorning of plaiting the hair, and of wearing of gold, or of putting on of apparel; but let it be the hidden man of the heart, in that which is not corruptible, even the ornament of a meek and quiet spirit, which is in the sight of God of great price."

The lesson applies to believers in every age. "By their fruits ye shall know them." Matthew 7:20. The inward adorning of a meek and quiet spirit is priceless. In the life of the true Christian the outward adorning is always in harmony with the inward peace and holiness. "If any man will come after Me," Christ said, "let him deny himself, and take up his cross, and follow Me." Matthew 16:24. Self-denial and sacrifice will mark the Christian's life. Evidence that the taste is converted will be seen in the dress of all who walk in the path cast up for the ransomed of the Lord.

It is right to love beauty and to desire it; but God desires us to love and seek first the highest beauty, that which is imperishable. No outward adorning can compare in value or loveliness with that "meek and quiet spirit," the "fine 524 linen, white and clean" (Revelation 19:14), which all the holy ones of earth will wear. This apparel will make them beautiful and beloved here, and will hereafter be their badge of admission to the palace of the King. His promise is, "They shall walk with Me in white: for they are worthy." Revelation 3:4.

Looking forward with prophetic vision to the perilous times into which the church of Christ was to enter, the apostle exhorted the believers to steadfastness in the face of trial and suffering. "Beloved," he wrote, "think it not strange concerning the fiery trial which is to try you."

Trial is part of the education given in the school of Christ, to purify God's children from the dross of earthliness. It is because God is leading His children that trying experiences come to them. Trials and obstacles are His chosen methods of discipline, and His appointed conditions of success. He who reads the hearts of men knows their weaknesses better than they themselves can know them. He sees that some have qualifications which, if rightly directed, could be used in the advancement of His work. In His providence He brings these souls into different positions and varied circumstances, that they may discover the defects that are concealed from their own knowledge. He gives them opportunity to overcome these defects and to fit themselves for service. Often He permits the fires of affliction to burn, that they may be purified.

God's care for His heritage is unceasing. He suffers no affliction to come upon His children but such as is essential for their present and eter- 525 nal good. He will purify His church, even as Christ purified the temple during His ministry on earth. All that He brings upon His people in test and trial comes that they may gain deeper piety and greater strength to carry forward the triumphs of the cross.

There had been a time in Peter's experience when he was unwilling to see the cross in the work of Christ. When the Saviour made known to the disciples His impending sufferings and death, Peter exclaimed, "Be it far from Thee, Lord: this shall not be unto Thee." Matthew 16:22. Self-pity, which shrank from fellowship with Christ in suffering, prompted Peter's remonstrance. It was to the disciple a bitter lesson, and one which he learned but slowly, that the path of Christ on earth lay through agony and humiliation. But in the heat of the furnace fire he was to learn its lesson. Now, when his once active form was bowed with the burden of years and labors, he could write, "Beloved, think it not strange concerning the fiery trial which is to try you, as though some strange thing happened unto you: but rejoice, inasmuch as ye are partakers of Christ's sufferings; that, when His glory shall be revealed, ye may be glad also with exceeding joy."

Addressing the church elders regarding their responsibilities as undershepherds of Christ's flock, the apostle wrote: "Feed the flock of God which is among you, taking the oversight thereof, not by constraint, but willingly; not for filthy lucre, but of a ready mind; neither as being lords over God's heritage, but being ensamples to the flock. And when the Chief Shepherd shall 526 appear, ye shall receive a crown of glory that fadeth not away."

Those who occupy the position of undershepherds are to exercise a watchful diligence over the Lord's flock. This is not to be a dictatorial vigilance, but one that tends to encourage and strengthen and uplift. Ministry means more than sermonizing; it means earnest, personal labor. The church on earth is composed of erring men and women, who need patient, painstaking effort that they may be trained and disciplined to work with acceptance in this life, and in the future life to be crowned with glory and immortality. Pastors are needed—faithful shepherds— who will not flatter God's people, nor treat them harshly, but who will feed them with the bread of life—men who in their lives feel daily the converting power of the Holy Spirit and who cherish a strong, unselfish love toward those for whom they labor.

There is tactful work for the undershepherd to do as he is called to meet alienation, bitterness, envy, and jealousy in the church, and he will need to labor in the spirit of Christ to set things in order. Faithful warnings are to be given, sins rebuked, wrongs made right, not only by the minister's work in the pulpit, but by personal labor. The wayward heart may take exception to the message, and the servant of God may be misjudged and criticized. Let him then remember that "the wisdom that is from above is first pure, then peaceable, gentle, and easy to be entreated, full of mercy and good fruits, without 527 partiality, and without hypocrisy. And the fruit of righteousness is sown in peace of them that make peace." James 3:17, 18.

The work of the gospel minister is "to make all men see what is the fellowship of the mystery, which from the beginning of the world hath been hid in God." Ephesians 3:9. If one entering upon this work chooses the least self-sacrificing part, contenting himself with preaching, and leaving the work of personal ministry for someone else, his labors will not be acceptable to God. Souls for whom Christ died are perishing for want of well-directed, personal labor; and he has mistaken his calling who, entering upon the ministry, is unwilling to do the personal work that the care of the flock demands.

The spirit of the true shepherd is one of self-forgetfulness. He loses sight of self in order that he may work the works of God. By the preaching of the word and by personal ministry in the homes of the people, he learns their needs, their sorrows, their trials; and, co-operating with the great Burden Bearer, he shares their afflictions, comforts their distresses, relieves their soul hunger, and wins their hearts to God. In this work the minister is attended by the angels of heaven, and he himself is instructed and enlightened in the truth that maketh wise unto salvation.

In connection with his instruction to those in positions of trust in the church, the apostle outlined some general principles that were to be followed by all who were associated in church fellowship. The younger members of the flock were urged to follow the example of their elders in the practice of Christlike humility: "Likewise, ye younger, submit yourselves unto the elder. Yea, all of you be subject one to another, 528 and be clothed with humility: for God resisteth the proud, and giveth grace to the humble. Humble yourselves therefore under the mighty hand of God, that He may exalt you in due time: casting all your care upon Him; for He careth

for you. Be sober, be vigilant; because your adversary the devil, as a roaring lion, walketh about, seeking whom he may devour: whom resist steadfast in the faith."

Thus Peter wrote to the believers at a time of peculiar trial to the church. Many had already become partakers of Christ's sufferings, and soon the church was to undergo a period of terrible persecution. Within a few brief years many of those who had stood as teachers and leaders in the church were to lay down their lives for the gospel. Soon grievous wolves were to enter in, not sparing the flock. But none of these things were to bring discouragement to those whose hopes were centered in Christ. With words of encouragement and good cheer Peter directed the minds of the believers from present trials and future scenes of suffering "to an inheritance incorruptible, and undefiled, and that fadeth not away." "The God of all grace," he fervently prayed, "who hath called us unto His eternal glory by Christ Jesus, after that ye have suffered awhile, make you perfect, stablish, strengthen, settle you. To Him be glory and dominion for ever and ever. Amen."

52

529

Steadfast Unto the End

In the second letter addressed by Peter to those who had obtained "like precious faith" with himself, the apostle sets forth the divine plan for the development of Christian character. He writes:

"Grace and peace be multiplied unto you through the knowledge of God, and of Jesus our Lord, according as His divine power hath given unto us all things that pertain unto life and godliness, through the knowledge of Him that hath called us to glory and virtue: whereby are given unto us exceeding great and precious promises: that by these ye might be partakers of the divine nature, having escaped the corruption that is in the world through lust.

"And beside this, giving all diligence, add to your faith virtue; and to virtue knowledge; and to knowledge temperance; and to temperance patience; and to patience godliness; and to godliness brotherly kindness; and to brotherly kindness charity. For if these things be in you, and abound, they make you that ye shall neither be 530 barren nor unfruitful in the knowledge of our Lord Jesus Christ."

These words are full of instruction, and strike the keynote of victory. The apostle presents before the believers the ladder of Christian progress, every step of which represents advancement in the knowledge of God, and in the climbing of which there is to be no stand-

This chapter is based on the Second Epistle of Peter.

still. Faith, virtue, knowledge, temperance, patience, godliness, brotherly kindness, and charity are the rounds of the ladder. We are saved by climbing round after round, mounting step after step, to the height of Christ's ideal for us. Thus He is made unto us wisdom, and righteousness, and sanctification, and redemption.

God has called His people to glory and virtue, and these will be manifest in the lives of all who are truly connected with Him. Having become partakers of the heavenly gift, they are to go on unto perfection, being "kept by the power of God through faith." 1 Peter 1:5. It is the glory of God to give His virtue to His children. He desires to see men and women reaching the highest standard; and when by faith they lay hold of the power of Christ, when they plead His unfailing promises, and claim them as their own, when with an importunity that will not be denied they seek for the power of the Holy Spirit, they will be made complete in Him.

Having received the faith of the gospel, the next work of the believer is to add to his character virtue, and thus cleanse the heart and prepare the mind for the reception of the knowledge of God. This knowledge is the foundation of all 531 true education and of all true service. It is the only real safeguard against temptation; and it is this alone that can make one like God in character. Through the knowledge of God and of His Son Jesus Christ, are given to the believer "all things that pertain unto life and godliness." No good gift is withheld from him who sincerely desires to obtain the righteousness of God.

"This is life eternal," Christ said, "that they might know Thee the only true God, and Jesus Christ, whom Thou hast sent." John 17:3. And the prophet Jeremiah declared: "Let not the wise man glory in his wisdom, neither let the mighty man glory in his might, let not the rich man glory in his riches: but let him that glorieth glory in this, that he understandeth and knoweth Me, that I am the Lord which exercise lovingkindness, judgment, and righteousness, in the earth: for in these things I delight, saith the Lord." Jeremiah 9:23, 24. Scarcely can the human mind comprehend the breadth and depth and height of the spiritual attainments of him who gains this knowledge.

None need fail of attaining, in his sphere, to perfection of Christian character. By the sacrifice of Christ, provision has been made for the believer to receive all things that pertain to life and godliness. God calls upon us to reach the standard of perfection and places before us the example of Christ's character. In His humanity, perfected by a life of constant resistance of evil, the Saviour showed that through co-operation with Divinity, human beings may in this life attain to perfection of character. This is God's assurance to us that we, too, may obtain complete victory.

Before the believer is held out the wonderful 532 possibility of being like Christ, obedient to all the principles of the law. But of himself man is utterly unable to reach this condition. The holiness that God's word declares he must have before he can be saved is the result of the working of divine grace as he bows in submission to the discipline and restraining influences of the Spirit of truth. Man's obedience can be made perfect only by the incense of Christ's righteousness, which fills with divine fragrance every act of obedience. The part of the Christian is to persevere in overcoming every fault. Constantly he is to pray to the Saviour to heal the disorders of his sin-sick soul. He has not the wisdom or the strength to overcome; these belong to the Lord, and He bestows them on those who in humiliation and contrition seek Him for help.

The work of transformation from unholiness to holiness is a continuous one. Day by day God labors for man's sanctification, and man is to co-operate with Him, putting forth persevering efforts in the cultivation of right habits. He is to add grace to grace; and as he thus works on the plan of addition, God works for him on the plan of multiplication. Our Saviour is always ready to hear and answer the prayer of the contrite heart, and grace and peace are multiplied to His faithful ones. Gladly He grants them the blessings they need in their struggle against the evils that beset them.

There are those who attempt to ascend the ladder of Christian progress; but as they advance they begin to put their trust in the power of man, and soon lose sight of Jesus, the 533 Author and Finisher of their faith. The result is failure—the loss of all that has been gained. Sad indeed is the condition of those who, becoming weary of the way, allow the enemy of souls to rob them of the Christian graces that have been developing in their hearts and lives. "He that lacketh these things," declares the apostle, "is blind, and cannot see afar off, and hath forgotten that he was purged from his old sins."

The apostle Peter had had a long experience in the things of God. His faith in God's power to save had strengthened with the years, until he had proved beyond question that there is no possibility of failure before the one who, advancing by faith, ascends round by round, ever upward and onward, to the topmost round of the ladder that reaches even to the portals of heaven.

For many years Peter had been urging upon the believers the necessity of a constant growth in grace and in a knowledge of the truth; and now, knowing that soon he would be called to suffer martyrdom for his faith, he once more drew attention to the precious privileges within the reach of every believer. In the full assurance of his faith the aged disciple exhorted his brethren to steadfastness of purpose in the

Christian life. "Give diligence," he pleaded, "to make your calling and election sure: for if ye do these things, ye shall never fall: for so an entrance shall be ministered unto you abundantly into the everlasting kingdom of our Lord and Saviour Jesus Christ." Precious assurance! Glorious is the hope before the believer as he advances by faith toward the heights of Christian perfection!

534 "I will not be negligent," the apostle continued, "to put you always in remembrance of these things, though ye know them, and be established in the present truth. Yea, I think it meet, as long as I am in this tabernacle, to stir you up by putting you in remembrance; knowing that shortly I must put off this my tabernacle, even as our Lord Jesus Christ hath showed me. Moreover I will endeavor that ye may be able after my decease to have these things always in remembrance."

The apostle was well qualified to speak of the purposes of God concerning the human race; for during the earthly ministry of Christ he had seen and heard much that pertained to the kingdom of God. "We have not followed cunningly devised fables," he reminded the believers, "when we made known unto you the power and coming of our Lord Jesus Christ, but were eyewitnesses of His majesty. For He received from God the Father honor and glory, when there came such a voice to Him from the excellent glory, This is My beloved Son, in whom I am well pleased. And this voice which came from heaven we heard, when we were with Him in the holy mount."

Yet convincing as was this evidence of the certainty of the believers' hope, there was another still more convincing in the witness of prophecy, through which the faith of all might be confirmed and securely anchored. "We have also," Peter declared, "a more sure word of prophecy; whereunto ye do well that ye take heed, as unto a light that shineth in a dark place,

535 until the day dawn, and the daystar arise in your hearts: knowing this first, that no prophecy of the Scripture is of any private interpretation. For the prophecy came not in old time by the will of man: but holy men of God spake as they were moved by the Holy Ghost."

While exalting the "sure word of prophecy" as a safe guide in times of peril, the apostle solemnly warned the church against the torch of false prophecy, which would be uplifted by "false teachers," who would privily bring in "damnable heresies, even denying the Lord." These false teachers, arising in the church and accounted true by many of their brethren in the faith, the apostle compared to "wells without water, clouds that are carried with a tempest; to whom the mist of darkness is reserved forever." "The latter end is worse with them," he declared, "than the beginning. For it had been

better for them not to have known the way of righteousness, than, after they have known it, to turn from the holy commandment delivered unto them."

Looking down through the ages to the close of time, Peter was inspired to outline conditions that would exist in the world just prior to the second coming of Christ. "There shall come in the last days scoffers," he wrote, "walking after their own lusts, and saying, Where is the promise of His coming? for since the fathers fell asleep, all things continue as they were from the beginning of the creation." But "when they shall say, Peace and safety; then sudden destruction cometh upon them." 1 Thessalonians 5:3. Not all, however, would be ensnared by the enemy's devices. As the end of all things earthly should approach, there would be faithful ones able to 536 discern the signs of the times. While a large number of professing believers would deny their faith by their works, there would be a remnant who would endure to the end.

Peter kept alive in his heart the hope of Christ's return, and he assured the church of the certain fulfillment of the Saviour's promise, "If I go and prepare a place for you, I will come again, and receive you unto Myself." John 14:3. To the tried and faithful ones the coming might seem long delayed, but the apostle assured them: "The Lord is not slack concerning His promise, as some men count slackness; but is long-suffering to usward, not willing that any should perish, but that all should come to repentance. But the day of the Lord will come as a thief in the night; in the which the heavens shall pass away with a great noise, and the elements shall melt with fervent heat, the earth also and the works that are therein shall be burned up.

"Seeing then that all these things shall be dissolved, what manner of persons ought ye to be in all holy conversation and godliness, looking for and hasting unto the coming of the day of God, wherein the heavens being on fire shall be dissolved, and the elements shall melt with fervent heat? Nevertheless we, according to His promise, look for new heavens and a new earth, wherein dwelleth righteousness.

"Wherefore, beloved, seeing that ye look for such things, be diligent that ye may be found of Him in peace, without spot, and blameless. And account that the long-suffering of our Lord is salvation; even as our beloved brother Paul also according to the wisdom given unto him hath written unto you. . . . Ye therefore, beloved, see- 537 ing ye know these things before, beware lest ye also, being led away with the error of the wicked, fall from your own steadfastness. But grow in grace, and in the knowledge of our Lord and Saviour Jesus Christ."

In the providence of God, Peter was permitted to close his ministry in Rome, where his imprisonment was ordered by the emperor Nero about the time of Paul's final arrest. Thus the two veteran apostles, who for many years had been widely separated in their labors, were to bear their last witness for Christ in the world's metropolis, and upon its soil to shed their blood as the seed of a vast harvest of saints and martyrs.

Since his reinstatement after his denial of Christ, Peter had unflinchingly braved danger and had shown a noble courage in preaching a crucified, risen, and ascended Saviour. As he lay in his cell he called to mind the words that Christ had spoken to him: "Verily, verily, I say unto thee, When thou wast young, thou girdedst thyself, and walkedst whither thou wouldest: but when thou shalt be old, thou shalt stretch forth thy hands, and another shall gird thee, and carry thee whither thou wouldest not." John 21:18. Thus Jesus had made known to the disciple the very manner of his death, and even foretold the stretching of his hands upon the cross.

Peter, as a Jew and a foreigner, was condemned to be scourged and crucified. In prospect of this fearful death, the apostle remembered his great sin in denying Jesus in the 538 hour of His trial. Once so unready to acknowledge the cross, he now counted it a joy to yield up his life for the gospel, feeling only that, for him who had denied his Lord, to die in the same manner as his Master died was too great an honor. Peter had sincerely repented of that sin and had been forgiven by Christ, as is shown by the high commission given him to feed the sheep and lambs of the flock. But he could never forgive himself. Not even the thought of the agonies of the last terrible scene could lessen the bitterness of his sorrow and repentance. As a last favor he entreated his executioners that he might be nailed to the cross with his head downward. The request was granted, and in this manner died the great apostle Peter.

539

53

John the Beloved

John is distinguished above the other apostles as "the disciple whom Jesus loved." John 21:20. He seems to have enjoyed to a pre-eminent degree the friendship of Christ, and he received many tokens of the Saviour's confidence and love. He was one of the three permitted to witness Christ's glory upon the mount of transfiguration and His agony in Gethsemane, and it was to his care that our Lord confided His mother in those last hours of anguish upon the cross.

The Saviour's affection for the beloved disciple was returned with all the strength of ardent devotion. John clung to Christ as the vine clings to the stately pillar. For his Master's sake he braved the dangers of the judgment hall and lingered about the cross, and at the tidings that Christ had risen, he hastened to the sepulcher, in his zeal outstripping even the impetuous Peter.

The confiding love and unselfish devotion manifested in the life and character of John pre- 540 sent lessons of untold value to the Christian church. John did not naturally possess the loveliness of character that his later experience revealed. By nature he had serious defects. He was not only proud, self-assertive, and ambitious for honor, but impetuous, and resentful under injury. He and his brother were called "sons of thunder." Evil temper, the desire for revenge, the spirit of criticism, were all in the beloved disciple. But beneath all this the divine Teacher discerned the ardent, sincere, loving heart. Jesus rebuked his self-seeking, disappointed his ambitions, tested his faith. But He revealed to him that for which his soul longed—the beauty of holiness, the transforming power of love.

The defects in John's character came strongly to the front on several occasions during his personal association with the Saviour. At one time Christ sent messengers before Him into a village of the Samaritans, requesting the people to prepare refreshments for Him and His disciples. But when the Saviour approached the town, He appeared to be desirous of passing on toward Jerusalem. This aroused the envy of the Samaritans, and instead of inviting Him to tarry with them, they withheld the courtesies which they would have given to a common wayfarer. Jesus never urges His presence upon any, and the Samaritans lost the blessing which would have been granted them had they solicited Him to be their guest.

The disciples knew that it was the purpose of Christ to bless the Samaritans by His presence; and the coldness, jealousy, and disrespect shown to their Master filled them with surprise and indignation. James and John especially were aroused. That He whom they so highly 541 reverenced should be thus treated, seemed to them a wrong too great to be passed over without immediate punishment. In their zeal they said, "Lord, wilt Thou that we command fire to come down from heaven, and consume them, even as Elias did?" referring to the destruction of the Samaritan captains and their companies sent out to take the prophet Elijah. They were surprised to see that Jesus was pained by their words, and still more surprised as His rebuke fell upon their ears: "Ye know not what manner of spirit ye are of. For the Son of man is not come to destroy men's lives, but to save them." Luke 9:54-56.

It is no part of Christ's mission to compel men to receive Him. It is Satan, and men actuated by his spirit, who seek to compel the conscience. Under a pretense of zeal for righteousness, men who are confederated with evil angels sometimes bring suffering upon their fellow men in order to convert them to their ideas of religion; but Christ is ever showing mercy, ever seeking to win by the revealing of His love. He can admit no rival in the soul, nor accept of partial service; but He desires only voluntary service, the willing surrender of the heart under the constraint of love.

On another occasion James and John presented through their mother a petition requesting that they might be permitted to occupy the highest positions of honor in Christ's kingdom. Notwithstanding Christ's repeated instruction concerning the nature of His kingdom, these young disciples still cherished the hope for a Messiah who would take His throne and kingly 542 power in accordance with the desires of men. The mother, coveting with them the place of honor in this kingdom for her sons, asked, "Grant that these my two sons may sit, the one on Thy right hand, and the other on the left, in Thy kingdom."

But the Saviour answered, "Ye know not what ye ask. Are ye able to drink of the cup that I shall drink of, and to be baptized with the baptism that I am baptized with?" They recalled His mysterious words pointing to trial and suffering, yet answered confidently, "We are able." They would count it highest honor to prove their loyalty by sharing all that was to befall their Lord.

"Ye shall drink indeed of My cup, and be baptized with the baptism that I am baptized with," Christ declared—before Him a cross instead of a throne, two malefactors His companions at His right hand and at His left. James and John were to be sharers with their Master in suffering—the one, destined to swift-coming death by the sword; the other, longest of all the disciples to follow his Master in labor and reproach and persecution. "But to sit on My right hand, and on My left," He continued, "is not Mine to give, but it shall be given to them for whom it is prepared of My Father." Matthew 20:21-23.

Jesus understood the motive that prompted the request and thus reproved the pride and ambition of the two disciples: "The princes of the Gentiles exercise dominion over them, and they that are great exercise authority upon them. But it shall not be so among you: but whosoever will be great among you, let him be your minister; and whosoever will be chief among you, let 543 him be your servant: even as the Son of man came not to be ministered unto, but to minister, and to give His life a ransom for many." Matthew 20:25-28.

In the kingdom of God, position is not gained through favoritism. It is not earned, nor is it received through an arbitrary bestowal. It is the result of character. The crown and the throne are the tokens of a condition attained—tokens of self-conquest through the grace of our Lord Jesus Christ.

Long afterward, when John had been brought into sympathy with Christ through the fellowship of His sufferings, the Lord Jesus revealed to him what is the condition of nearness to His kingdom. "To him that overcometh," Christ said, "will I grant to sit with Me in My throne, even as I also overcame, and am set down with My Father in His throne." Revelation 3:21. The one who stands nearest to Christ will be he who has drunk most deeply of His spirit of self-sacrificing love,—love that "vaunteth not itself, is not puffed up, . . . seeketh not her own, is not easily provoked, thinketh no evil" (1 Corinthians 13:4, 5),—love that moves the disciple, as it moved our Lord, to give all, to live and labor and sacrifice even unto death, for the saving of humanity.

At another time during their early evangelistic labors, James and John met one who, while not an acknowledged follower of Christ, was casting out devils in His name. The disciples forbade the man to work and thought they were right in doing this. But when they laid the matter before Christ, He reproved them, saying, "Forbid him not: for there is no man which shall do a miracle in My name, that can lightly speak evil of Me." Mark 9:39. None who showed 544 themselves in any way friendly to Christ were to be repulsed. The disciples must not indulge a narrow, exclusive spirit, but must manifest the same far-reaching sympathy which they had seen in their Master. James and John thought that in checking this man they had in view the Lord's honor; but they began to see that they were jealous for their own. They acknowledged their error and accepted the reproof.

The lessons of Christ, setting forth meekness and humility and love as essential to growth in grace and a fitness for His work, were of the highest value to John. He treasured every lesson and constantly sought to bring his life into harmony with the divine pattern. John had begun to discern the glory of Christ—not the worldly pomp and power for which he had been taught to hope, but "the glory as of the Only Begotten of the Father, full of grace and truth." John 1:14.

The depth and fervor of John's affection for his Master was not the cause of Christ's love for him, but the effect of that love. John desired to become like Jesus, and under the transforming influence of the love of Christ he did become meek and lowly. Self was hid in Jesus. Above all his companions, John yielded himself to the power of that wondrous life. He says, "The life was manifested, and we have seen it." "And of His fullness have all we received, and grace for grace." 1 John 1:2; John 1:16. John knew the Saviour by an experimental knowledge. His Master's lessons were graven on his soul. When 545 he testified of the Saviour's grace, his simple language was eloquent with the love that pervaded his whole being.

It was John's deep love for Christ which led him always to desire to be close by His side. The Saviour loved all the Twelve, but John's was the most receptive spirit. He was younger than the others, and with more of the child's confiding trust he opened his heart to Jesus. Thus he came more into sympathy with Christ, and through him the Saviour's deepest spiritual teaching was communicated to the people.

Jesus loves those who represent the Father, and John could talk of the Father's love as no other of the disciples could. He revealed to his fellow men that which he felt in his own soul, representing in his character the attributes of God. The glory of the Lord was expressed in his face. The beauty of holiness which had transformed him shone with a Christlike radiance from his countenance. In adoration and love he beheld the Saviour until likeness to Christ and fellowship with Him became his one desire, and in his character was reflected the character of his Master.

"Behold," he said, "what manner of love the Father hath bestowed upon us, that we should be called the sons of God. . . . Beloved, now are we the sons of God, and it doth not yet appear what we shall be: but we know that, when He shall appear, we shall be like Him; for we shall see Him as He is." 1 John 3:1, 2.

546

54

A Faithful Witness

After the ascension of Christ, John stands forth as a faithful, earnest laborer for the Master. With the other disciples he enjoyed the outpouring of the Spirit on the Day of Pentecost, and with fresh zeal and power he continued to speak to the people the words of life, seeking to lead their thoughts to the Unseen. He was a powerful preacher, fervent, and deeply in earnest. In beautiful language and with a musical voice he told of the words and works of Christ, speaking in a way that impressed the hearts of those who heard him. The simplicity of his words, the sublime power of the truths he uttered, and the fervor that characterized his teachings, gave him access to all classes.

The apostle's life was in harmony with his teachings. The love for Christ which glowed in his heart led him to put forth earnest, untiring labor for his fellow men, especially for his brethren in the Christian church.

547   Christ had bidden the first disciples love one another as He had loved them. Thus they were to bear testimony to the world that Christ was formed within, the hope of glory. "A new com-

mandment I give unto you," He had said, "That ye love one another; as I have loved you, that ye also love one another." John 13:34. At the time when these words were spoken, the disciples could not understand them; but after they had witnessed the sufferings of Christ, after His crucifixion and resurrection, and ascension to heaven, and after the Holy Spirit had rested on them at Pentecost, they had a clearer conception of the love of God and of the nature of that love which they must have for one another. Then John could say to his fellow disciples:

"Hereby perceive we the love of God, because He laid down His life for us: and we ought to lay down our lives for the brethren."

After the descent of the Holy Spirit, when the disciples went forth to proclaim a living Saviour, their one desire was the salvation of souls. They rejoiced in the sweetness of communion with saints. They were tender, thoughtful, self-denying, willing to make any sacrifice for the truth's sake. In their daily association with one another, they revealed the love that Christ had enjoined upon them. By unselfish words and deeds they strove to kindle this love in other hearts.

Such a love the believers were ever to cherish. They were to go forward in willing obedience to the new commandment. So closely were they to be united with Christ that they would be 548 enabled to fulfill all His requirements. Their lives were to magnify the power of a Saviour who could justify them by His righteousness.

But gradually a change came. The believers began to look for defects in others. Dwelling upon mistakes, giving place to unkind criticism, they lost sight of the Saviour and His love. They became more strict in regard to outward ceremonies, more particular about the theory than the practice of the faith. In their zeal to condemn others, they overlooked their own errors. They lost the brotherly love that Christ had enjoined, and, saddest of all, they were unconscious of their loss. They did not realize that happiness and joy were going out of their lives and that, having shut the love of God out of their hearts, they would soon walk in darkness.

John, realizing that brotherly love was waning in the church, urged upon believers the constant need of this love. His letters to the church are full of this thought. "Beloved, let us love one another," he writes; "for love is of God; and everyone that loveth is born of God, and knoweth God. He that loveth not knoweth not God; for God is love. In this was manifested the love of God toward us, because that God sent His only-begotten Son into the world, that we might live through Him. Herein is love, not that we loved God, but that He loved us, and sent His Son to be the propitiation for our sins. Beloved, if God so loved us, we ought also to love one another."

This chapter is based on the Epistle of John.

Of the special sense in which this love should be manifested by believers, the apostle writes: "A new commandment I write unto you, which thing is true in Him and in you: because the darkness is past, and the true light now shineth. He that saith he is in the light, and hateth his brother, is in darkness even until now. He that loveth his brother abideth in the light, and there is none occasion of stumbling in him. But he that hateth his brother is in darkness, and walketh in darkness, and knoweth not whither he goeth, because that darkness hath blinded his eyes." "This is the message that ye heard from the beginning, that we should love one another." "He that loveth not his brother abideth in death. Whosoever hateth his brother is a murderer: and ye know that no murderer hath eternal life abiding in him. Hereby perceive we the love of God, because He laid down His life for us: and we ought to lay down our lives for the brethren."

It is not the opposition of the world that most endangers the church of Christ. It is the evil cherished in the hearts of believers that works their most grievous disaster and most surely retards the progress of God's cause. There is no surer way of weakening spirituality than by cherishing envy, suspicion, faultfinding, and evil surmising. On the other hand, the strongest witness that God has sent His Son into the world is the existence of harmony and union among men of varied dispositions who form His church. This witness it is the privilege of the followers of Christ to bear. But in order to do this, they must place themselves under Christ's command. Their characters must be conformed to His character and their wills to His will.

"A new commandment I give unto you," Christ said, "That ye love one another; as I have loved you, that ye also love one another." John 13:34. What a wonderful statement; but, oh, how poorly practiced! In the church of God today brotherly love is sadly lacking. Many who profess to love the Saviour do not love one another. Unbelievers are watching to see if the faith of professed Christians is exerting a sanctifying influence upon their lives; and they are quick to discern the defects in character, the inconsistencies in action. Let Christians not make it possible for the enemy to point to them and say, Behold how these people, standing under the banner of Christ, hate one another. Christians are all members of one family, all children of the same heavenly Father, with the same blessed hope of immortality. Very close and tender should be the tie that binds them together.

Divine love makes its most touching appeals to the heart when it calls upon us to manifest the same tender compassion that Christ manifested. That man only who has unselfish love for his brother has true love for God. The true Christian will not willingly permit the soul in peril and need to go unwarned, uncared for. He will not hold himself aloof from the erring, leaving them to plunge farther into unhappiness and discouragement or to fall on Satan's battleground.

Those who have never experienced the tender, winning love of Christ cannot lead others to the fountain of life. His love in the heart is a constraining power, which leads men to reveal Him in the conversation, in the tender, pitiful spirit, in the uplifting of the lives of those with whom they associate. Christian workers who succeed in their efforts must know Christ; and in order to know Him, they must know His love. In heaven their fitness as workers is measured by their ability to love as Christ loved and to work as He worked.

"Let us not love in word," the apostle writes, "but in deed and in truth." The completeness of Christian character is attained when the impulse to help and bless others springs constantly from within. It is the atmosphere of this love surrounding the soul of the believer that makes him a savor of life unto life and enables God to bless his work.

Supreme love for God and unselfish love for one another—this is the best gift that our heavenly Father can bestow. This love is not an impulse, but a divine principle, a permanent power. The unconsecrated heart cannot originate or produce it. Only in the heart where Jesus reigns is it found. "We love Him, because He first loved us." In the heart renewed by divine grace, love is the ruling principle of action. It modifies the character, governs the impulses, controls the passions, and ennobles the affections. This love, cherished in the soul, sweetens the life and sheds a refining influence on all around.

John strove to lead the believers to understand the exalted privileges that would come to them through the exercise of the spirit of love. This redeeming power, filling the heart, would control every other motive and raise its possessors above the corrupting influences of the world. And as this love was allowed full sway and became the motive power in the life, their trust and confidence in God and His dealing with them would be complete. They could then come to Him in full confidence of faith, knowing that they would receive from Him everything needful for their present and eternal good. "Herein is our love made perfect," he wrote, "that we may have boldness in the day of judgment: because as He is, so are we in this world. There is no fear in love; but perfect love casteth out fear." "And this is the confidence that we have in Him, that, if we ask anything according to His will, He heareth us: and if we know that He hear us, . . . we know that we have the petitions that we desired of Him."

"And if any man sin, we have an advocate with the Father, Jesus Christ the righteous: and

He is the propitiation for our sins: and not for ours only, but also for the sins of the whole world." "If we confess our sins, He is faithful and just to forgive us our sins, and to cleanse us from all unrighteousness." The conditions of obtaining mercy from God are simple and reasonable. The Lord does not require us to do some grievous thing in order to gain forgiveness. We need not make long and wearisome pilgrimages, or perform painful penances, to commend our souls to the God of heaven or to expiate our transgression. He that "confesseth and forsaketh" his sin "shall have mercy." Proverbs 28:13.

553 In the courts above, Christ is pleading for His church—pleading for those for whom He has paid the redemption price of His blood. Centuries, ages, can never lessen the efficacy of His atoning sacrifice. Neither life nor death, height nor depth, can separate us from the love of God which is in Christ Jesus; not because we hold Him so firmly, but because He holds us so fast. If our salvation depended on our own efforts, we could not be saved; but it depends on the One who is behind all the promises. Our grasp on Him may seem feeble, but His love is that of an elder brother; so long as we maintain our union with Him, no one can pluck us out of His hand.

As the years went by and the number of believers grew, John labored with increasing fidelity and earnestness for his brethren. The times were full of peril for the church. Satanic delusions existed everywhere. By misrepresentation and falsehood the emissaries of Satan sought to arouse opposition against the doctrines of Christ, and in consequence dissensions and heresies were imperiling the church. Some who professed Christ claimed that His love released them from obedience to the law of God. On the other hand, many taught that it was necessary to observe the Jewish customs and ceremonies; that a mere observance of the law, without faith in the blood of Christ, was sufficient for salvation. Some held that Christ was a good man, but denied His divinity. Some who pretended to be true to the cause of God were deceivers, and in practice they denied Christ and His gospel. Living themselves in transgression, they were bringing heresies into the church. Thus many were being led into the mazes of skepticism and delusion.

554 John was filled with sadness as he saw these poisonous errors creeping into the church. He saw the dangers to which the church was exposed, and he met the emergency with promptness and decision. The epistles of John breathe the spirit of love. It seems as if he wrote with a pen dipped in love. But when he came in contact with those who were breaking the law of God, yet claiming that they were living without sin, he did not hesitate to warn them of their fearful deception.

Writing to a helper in the gospel work, a woman of good repute and wide influence, he said: "Many deceivers are entered into the world, who confess not that Jesus Christ is come in the flesh. This is a deceiver and an antichrist. Look to yourselves, that we lose not those things which we have wrought, but that we receive a full reward. Whosoever transgresseth, and abideth not in the doctrine of Christ, hath not God. He that abideth in the doctrine of Christ, he hath both the Father and the Son. If there come any unto you, and bring not this doctrine, receive him not into your house, neither bid him Godspeed: for he that biddeth him Godspeed is partaker of his evil deeds."

We are authorized to hold in the same estimation as did the beloved disciple those who claim to abide in Christ while living in transgression of God's law. There exist in these last days evils similar to those that threatened the prosperity of the early church; and the teachings of the apostle John on these points should be carefully heeded. "You must have charity," is the cry heard everywhere, especially from those who 555 profess sanctification. But true charity is too pure to cover an unconfessed sin. While we are to love the souls for whom Christ died, we are to make no compromise with evil. We are not to unite with the rebellious and call this charity. God requires His people in this age of the world to stand for the right as unflinchingly as did John in opposition to soul-destroying errors.

The apostle teaches that while we should manifest Christian courtesy we are authorized to deal in plain terms with sin and sinners; that this is not inconsistent with true charity. "Whosoever committeth sin," he writes, "transgresseth also the law: for sin is the transgression of the law. And ye know that He was manifested to take away our sins; and in Him is no sin. Whosoever abideth in Him sinneth not: whosoever sinneth hath not seen Him, neither known Him."

As a witness for Christ, John entered into no controversy, no wearisome contention. He declared what he knew, what he had seen and heard. He had been intimately associated with Christ, had listened to His teachings, had witnessed His mighty miracles. Few could see the beauties of Christ's character as John saw them. For him the darkness had passed away; on him the true light was shining. His testimony in regard to the Saviour's life and death was clear and forcible. Out of the abundance of a heart overflowing with love for the Saviour he spoke; and no power could stay his words.

"That which was from the beginning," he declared, "which we have heard, which we have seen with our eyes, which we have looked upon, and our hands have handled, of the Word of life; . . . that which we have seen and heard declare 556 we unto you, that ye also may have fellowship with us; and truly our fellowship is with the Father, and with His Son Jesus Christ."

So may every true believer be able, through his own experience, to "set to his seal that God is true." John 3:33. He can bear witness to that which he has seen and heard and felt of the power of Christ.

55

Transformed by Grace

In the life of the disciple John true sanctification is exemplified. During the years of his close association with Christ, he was often warned and cautioned by the Saviour; and these reproofs he accepted. As the character of the Divine One was manifested to him, John saw his own deficiencies, and was humbled by the revelation. Day by day, in contrast with his own violent spirit, he beheld the tenderness and forbearance of Jesus, and heard His lessons of humility and patience. Day by day his heart was drawn out to Christ, until he lost sight of self in love for his Master. The power and tenderness, the majesty and meekness, the strength and patience, that he saw in the daily life of the Son of God, filled his soul with admiration. He yielded his resentful, ambitious temper to the molding power of Christ, and divine love wrought in him a transformation of character.

In striking contrast to the sanctification worked out in the life of John is the experience of his fellow disciple, Judas. Like his associate, Judas professed to be a disciple of Christ, but he possessed only a form of godliness. He was not insensible to the beauty of the character of Christ; and often, as he listened to the Saviour's words, conviction came to him, but he would not humble his heart or confess his sins. By resisting the divine influence he dishonored the Master whom he professed to love. John warred earnestly against his faults; but Judas violated his conscience and yielded to temptation, fastening upon himself more securely his habits of evil. The practice of the truths that Christ taught was at variance with his desires and purposes, and he could not bring himself to yield his ideas in order to receive wisdom from heaven. Instead of walking in the light, he chose to walk in darkness. Evil desires, covetousness, revengeful passions, dark and sullen thoughts, were cherished until Satan gained full control of him.

John and Judas are representatives of those who profess to be Christ's followers. Both these disciples had the same opportunities to study and follow the divine Pattern. Both were closely associated with Jesus and were privileged to listen to His teaching. Each possessed serious defects of character; and each had access to the divine grace that transforms character. But while one in humility was learning of Jesus, the other revealed that he was not a doer of the word, but a hearer only. One, daily dying to self and overcoming sin, was sanctified through the truth; the other, resisting the transforming power of grace and indulging selfish desires, was brought into bondage to Satan.

Such transformation of character as is seen in the life of John is ever the result of communion with Christ. There may be marked defects in the character of an individual, yet when he becomes a true disciple of Christ, the power of divine grace transforms and sanctifies him. Beholding as in a glass the glory of the Lord, he is changed from glory to glory, until he is like Him whom he adores.

John was a teacher of holiness, and in his letters to the church he laid down unerring rules for the conduct of Christians. "Every man that hath this hope in him," he wrote, "purifieth himself, even as He is pure." "He that saith he abideth in Him ought himself also so to walk, even as He walked." 1 John 3:3; 2:6. He taught that the Christian must be pure in heart and life. Never should he be satisfied with an empty profession. As God is holy in His sphere, so fallen man, through faith in Christ, is to be holy in his sphere.

"This is the will of God," the apostle Paul wrote, "even your sanctification." 1 Thessalonians 4:3. The sanctification of the church is God's object in all His dealings with His people. He has chosen them from eternity, that they might be holy. He gave His Son to die for them, that they might be sanctified through obedience to the truth, divested of all the littleness of self. From them He requires a personal work, a personal surrender. God can be honored by those who profess to believe in Him, only as they are conformed to His image and controlled by His Spirit. Then, as witnesses for the Saviour, they may make known what divine grace has done for them.

True sanctification comes through the working out of the principle of love. "God is love; and he that dwelleth in love dwelleth in God, and God in him." 1 John 4:16. The life of him in whose heart Christ abides, will reveal practical godliness. The character will be purified, elevated, ennobled, and glorified. Pure doctrine will blend with works of righteousness; heavenly precepts will mingle with holy practices.

Those who would gain the blessing of sanctification must first learn the meaning of self-sacrifice. The cross of Christ is the central pillar on which hangs the "far more exceeding and eternal weight of glory." "If any man will come after Me," Christ says, "let him deny himself, and take up his cross, and follow Me." 2 Corinthians 4:17; Matthew 16:24. It is the fragrance of our love for our fellow men that reveals our love for God. It is patience in service that brings rest to the soul. It is through humble, diligent, faithful toil that the welfare of Israel is promoted. God upholds and strengthens the one who is willing to follow in Christ's way.

Sanctification is not the work of a moment, an hour, a day, but of a lifetime. It is not gained by a happy flight of feeling, but is the result of constantly dying to sin, and constantly living for Christ. Wrongs cannot be righted nor reformations wrought in the character by feeble, intermittent efforts. It is only by long, persevering effort, sore discipline, and stern conflict, that we shall overcome. We know not one day how strong will be our conflict the next. So long as Satan reigns, we shall have self to subdue, besetting sins to overcome; so long as life shall last, there will be no stopping place, no point which we can reach and say, I have fully attained. Sanctification is the result of lifelong obedience.

None of the apostles and prophets ever claimed to be without sin. Men who have lived the nearest to God, men who would sacrifice life itself rather than knowingly commit a wrong act, men whom God has honored with divine light and power, have confessed the sinfulness of their nature. They have put no confidence in the flesh, have claimed no righteousness of their own, but have trusted wholly in the righteousness of Christ.

So will it be with all who behold Christ. The nearer we come to Jesus, and the more clearly we discern the purity of His character, the more clearly shall we see the exceeding sinfulness of sin, and the less shall we feel like exalting ourselves. There will be a continual reaching out of the soul after God, a continual, earnest, heart-breaking confession of sin and humbling of the heart before Him. At every advance step in our Christian experience our repentance will deepen. We shall know that our sufficiency is in Christ alone and shall make the apostle's confession our own: "I know that in me (that is, in my flesh,) dwelleth no good thing." "God forbid that I should glory, save in the cross of our Lord Jesus Christ, by whom the world is crucified unto me, and I unto the world." Romans 7:18; Galatians 6:14.

Let the recording angels write the history of the holy struggles and conflicts of the people of God; let them record their prayers and tears; but let not God be dishonored by the declaration from human lips, "I am sinless; I am holy." Sanctified lips will never give utterance to such presumptuous words.

The apostle Paul had been caught up to the third heaven and had seen and heard things that could not be uttered, and yet his unassuming statement is: "Not as though I had already attained, either were already perfect: but I follow after." Philippians 3:12. Let the angels of heaven write of Paul's victories in fighting the good fight of faith. Let heaven rejoice in his steadfast tread heavenward, and that, keeping the prize in view, he counts every other consideration dross. Angels rejoice to tell his triumphs, but Paul makes no boast of his attainments. The attitude of Paul is the attitude that every follower of Christ should take as he urges his way onward in the strife for the immortal crown.

Let those who feel inclined to make a high profession of holiness look into the mirror of God's law. As they see its far-reaching claims, and understand its work as a discerner of the thoughts and intents of the heart, they will not boast of sinlessness. "If we," says John, not separating himself from his brethren, "say that we have no sin, we deceive ourselves, and the truth is not in us." "If we say that we have not sinned, we make Him a liar, and His word is not in us." "If we confess our sins, He is faithful and just to forgive us our sins, and to cleanse us from all unrighteousness." 1 John 1:8, 10, 9.

There are those who profess holiness, who declare that they are wholly the Lord's, who claim a right to the promises of God, while refusing to render obedience to His commandments. These transgressors of the law claim everything that is promised to the children of God; but this is presumption on their part, for John tells us that true love for God will be revealed in obedience to all His commandments. It is not enough to believe the theory of truth, to make a profession of faith in Christ, to believe that Jesus is no impostor, and that the religion of the Bible is no cunningly devised fable. "He that saith, I know Him, and keepeth not His commandments," John wrote, "is a liar, and the truth is not in him. But whoso keepeth His word, in him verily is the love of God perfected: hereby know we that we are in Him." "He that keepeth His commandments dwelleth in Him, and He in him." 1 John 2:4, 5; 3:24.

John did not teach that salvation was to be earned by obedience; but that obedience was the fruit of faith and love. "Ye know that He was manifested to take away our sins," he said, "and in Him is no sin. Whosoever abideth in Him sinneth not: whosoever sinneth hath not seen Him, neither known Him." 1 John 3:5, 6. If we abide in Christ, if the love of God dwells in the heart, our feelings, our thoughts, our actions, will be in harmony with the will of God. The sanctified heart is in harmony with the precepts of God's law.

There are many who, though striving to obey God's commandments, have little peace or joy. This lack in their experience is the result of a failure to exercise faith. They walk as it were in a salt land, a parched wilderness. They claim little, when they might claim much; for there is no limit to the promises of God. Such ones do not correctly represent the sanctification that comes through obedience to the truth. The Lord would have all His sons and daughters happy, peaceful, and obedient. Through the exercise of faith the believer comes into possession of these blessings. Through faith, every deficiency of character may be supplied, every defilement cleansed, every fault corrected, every excellence developed.

Prayer is heaven's ordained means of success in the conflict with sin and the development of Christian character. The divine influences that come in answer to the prayer of faith will accomplish in the soul of the suppliant all for which he pleads. For the pardon of sin, for the Holy Spirit, for a Christlike temper, for wisdom and strength to do His work, for any gift He has promised, we may ask; and the promise is, "Ye shall receive."

It was in the mount with God that Moses beheld the pattern of that wonderful building that was to be the abiding place of His glory. It is in the mount with God—in the secret place of communion—that we are to contemplate His glorious ideal for humanity. In all ages, through the medium of communion with heaven, God has worked out His purpose for His children, by unfolding gradually to their minds the doctrines of grace. His manner of imparting truth is illustrated in the words, "His going forth is prepared as the morning." Hosea 6:3. He who places himself where God can enlighten him, advances, as it were, from the partial obscurity of dawn to the full radiance of noonday.

565   True sanctification means perfect love, perfect obedience, perfect conformity to the will of God. We are to be sanctified to God through obedience to the truth. Our conscience must be purged from dead works to serve the living God. We are not yet perfect; but it is our privilege to cut away from the entanglements of self and sin, and advance to perfection. Great possibilities, high and holy attainments, are placed within the reach of all.

The reason many in this age of the world make no greater advancement in the divine life is because they interpret the will of God to be just what they will to do. While following their own desires, they flatter themselves that they are conforming to God's will. These have no conflicts with self. There are others who for a time are successful in the struggle against their selfish desire for pleasure and ease. They are sincere and earnest, but grow weary of protracted effort, of daily death, of ceaseless turmoil. Indolence seems inviting, death to self repulsive; and they close their drowsy eyes and fall under the power of temptation instead of resisting it.

The directions laid down in the word of God leave no room for compromise with evil. The Son of God was manifested that He might draw all men unto Himself. He came not to lull the world to sleep, but to point out the narrow path in which all must travel who reach at last the gates of the City of God. His children must follow where He has led the way; at whatever sacrifice of ease or selfish indulgence, at whatever cost of labor or suffering, they must maintain a constant battle with self.

The greatest praise that men can bring to God 566 is to become consecrated channels through whom He can work. Time is rapidly passing into eternity. Let us not keep back from God that which is His own. Let us not refuse Him that which, though it cannot be given with merit, cannot be denied without ruin. He asks for a whole heart; give it to Him; it is His, both by creation and by redemption. He asks for your intellect; give it to Him; it is His. He asks for your money; give it to Him; it is His. "Ye are not your own, for ye are bought with a price." 1 Corinthians 6:19, 20. God requires the homage of a sanctified soul, which has prepared itself, by the exercise of the faith that works by love, to serve Him. He holds up before us the highest ideal, even perfection. He asks us to be absolutely and completely for Him in this world as He is for us in the presence of God.

"This is the will of God" concerning you, "even your sanctification." 1 Thessalonians 4:3. Is it your will also? Your sins may be as mountains before you; but if you humble your heart and confess your sins, trusting in the merits of a crucified and risen Saviour, He will forgive and will cleanse you from all unrighteousness. God demands of you entire conformity to His law. This law is the echo of His voice saying to you, Holier, yes, holier still. Desire the fullness of the grace of Christ. Let your heart be filled with an intense longing for His righteousness, the work of which God's word declares is peace, and its effect quietness and assurance forever.

As your soul yearns after God, you will find 567 more and still more of the unsearchable riches of His grace. As you contemplate these riches you will come into possession of them and will reveal the merits of the Saviour's sacrifice, the protection of His righteousness, the fullness of His wisdom, and His power to present you before the Father "without spot, and blameless." 2 Peter 3:14.

56

568

Patmos

More than half a century had passed since the organization of the Christian church. During that time the gospel message had been constantly opposed. Its enemies had never relaxed their efforts, and had at last succeeded in enlisting the power of the Roman emperor against the Christians.

In the terrible persecution that followed, the apostle John did much to confirm and strengthen the faith of the believers. He bore a testimony which his adversaries could not controvert and which helped his brethren to meet with courage and loyalty the trials that came upon them. When the faith of the Christians would seem to waver under the fierce opposition they were forced to meet, the old, tried servant of Jesus would repeat with power and eloquence the story of the crucified and risen Saviour. He steadfastly maintained his faith, and from his lips came ever the same glad message: "That which was from the beginning, which we have heard, which we have seen with our eyes, which 569 we have looked upon, and our hands have handled, of the Word of life; . . . that which we have seen and heard declare we unto you." 1 John 1:1-3.

John lived to be very old. He witnessed the destruction of Jerusalem and the ruin of the stately temple. The last survivor of the disciples who had been intimately connected with the Saviour, his message had great influence in setting forth the fact that Jesus was the Messiah, the Redeemer of the world. No one could doubt his sincerity, and through his teachings many were led to turn from unbelief.

The rulers of the Jews were filled with bitter hatred against John for his unwavering fidelity to the cause of Christ. They declared that their efforts against the Christians would avail nothing so long as John's testimony kept ringing in the ears of the people. In order that the miracles and teachings of Jesus might be forgotten, the voice of the bold witness must be silenced.

John was accordingly summoned to Rome to be tried for his faith. Here before the authorities the apostle's doctrines were misstated. False witnesses accused him of teaching seditious heresies. By these accusations his enemies hoped to bring about the disciple's death.

John answered for himself in a clear and convincing manner, and with such simplicity and candor that his words had a powerful effect. His hearers were astonished at his wisdom and eloquence. But the more convincing his testimony, the deeper was the hatred of his opposers. The emperor Domitian was filled with rage. He 570 could neither dispute the reasoning of Christ's faithful advocate, nor match the power that attended his utterance of truth; yet he determined that he would silence his voice.

John was cast into a caldron of boiling oil; but the Lord preserved the life of His faithful servant, even as He preserved the three Hebrews in the fiery furnace. As the words were spoken, Thus perish all who believe in that deceiver, Jesus Christ of Nazareth, John declared, My Master patiently submitted to all that Satan and his angels could devise to humiliate and torture Him. He gave His life to save the world. I am honored in being permitted to suffer for His sake. I am a weak, sinful man. Christ was holy, harmless, undefiled. He did no sin, neither was guile found in His mouth.

These words had their influence, and John was removed from the caldron by the very men who had cast him in.

Again the hand of persecution fell heavily upon the apostle. By the emperor's decree John was banished to the Isle of Patmos, condemned "for the word of God, and for the testimony of Jesus Christ." Revelation 1:9. Here, his enemies thought, his influence would no longer be felt, and he must finally die of hardship and distress.

Patmos, a barren, rocky island in the Aegean Sea, had been chosen by the Roman government as a place of banishment for criminals; but to the servant of God this gloomy abode became the gate of heaven. Here, shut away from the busy scenes of life, and from the active labors of former years, he had the companionship of God and Christ and the heavenly angels, and from them he received instruction for the church for 571 all future time. The events that would take place in the closing scenes of this earth's history were outlined before him; and there he wrote out the visions he received from God. When his voice could no longer testify to the One whom he loved and served, the messages given him on that barren coast were to go forth as a lamp that burneth, declaring the sure purpose of the Lord concerning every nation on the earth.

Among the cliffs and rocks of Patmos, John held communion with his Maker. He reviewed his past life, and at thought of the blessings he had received, peace filled his heart. He had lived the life of a Christian, and he could say in faith, "We know that we have passed from death unto life." 1 John 3:14. Not so the emperor who had banished him. He could look back only on fields of warfare and carnage, on desolated homes, on weeping widows and orphans, the fruit of his ambitious desire for pre-eminence.

In his isolated home John was able to study more closely than ever before the manifestations of divine power as recorded in the book of nature and in the pages of inspiration. To him it was a delight to meditate on the work of creation and to adore the divine Architect. In former years his eyes had been greeted by the sight of forest-covered hills, green valleys, and fruitful plains; and in the beauties of nature it had ever been his delight to trace the wisdom and skill of the Creator. He was now surrounded by scenes that to many would appear gloomy and uninteresting; but to John it was otherwise. While his surroundings might be desolate and 572 barren, the blue heavens that bent above him were as bright and beautiful as the skies above his loved Jerusalem. In the wild, rugged rocks, in the mysteries of the deep, in the glories of the firmament, he read important lessons. All bore the message of God's power and glory.

All around him the apostle beheld witnesses to the Flood that had deluged the earth because the inhabitants ventured to transgress the law of God. The rocks thrown up from the great deep and from the earth by the breaking forth of the waters, brought vividly to his mind the terrors of that awful outpouring of God's wrath. In the voice of many waters—deep calling unto deep—the prophet heard the voice of the Creator. The sea, lashed to fury by the merciless winds, represented to him the wrath of an offended God. The mighty waves, in their terrible commotion, restrained within limits appointed by an invisible hand, spoke of the control of an infinite Power. And in contrast he realized the weakness and folly of mortals, who, though but worms of the dust, glory in their supposed wisdom and strength, and set their hearts against the Ruler of the universe, as if God were altogether such a one as themselves. By the rocks he was reminded of Christ, the Rock of his strength, in whose shelter he could hide without fear. From the exiled apostle on rocky Patmos there went up the most ardent longing of soul after God, the most fervent prayers.

573 The history of John affords a striking illustration of the way in which God can use aged workers. When John was exiled to the Isle of Patmos, there were many who thought him to be past service, an old and broken reed, ready to fall at any time. But the Lord saw fit to use him still. Though banished from the scenes of his former labor, he did not cease to bear witness to the truth. Even in Patmos he made friends and converts. His was a message of joy, proclaiming a risen Saviour who on high was interceding for His people until He should return to take them to Himself. And it was after John had grown old in the service of his Lord that he received more communications from heaven than he had received during all the former years of his life.

The most tender regard should be cherished for those whose life interest has been bound up with the work of God. These aged workers have stood faithful amid storm and trial. They may have infirmities, but they still possess talents that qualify them to stand in their place in God's cause. Though worn, and unable to bear the heavier burdens that younger men can and should carry, the counsel they can give is of the highest value.

They may have made mistakes, but from their failures they have learned to avoid errors and dangers, and are they not therefore competent to give wise counsel? They have borne test and trial, and though they have lost some of their vigor, the Lord does not lay them aside. He gives them special grace and wisdom.

Those who have served their Master when the work went hard, who endured poverty and remained faithful when there were few to stand for truth, are to be honored and respected. The 574 Lord desires the younger laborers to gain wisdom, strength, and maturity by association with these faithful men. Let the younger men realize that in having such workers among them they are highly favored. Let them give them an honored place in their councils.

As those who have spent their lives in the service of Christ draw near to the close of their earthly ministry, they will be impressed by the Holy Spirit to recount the experiences they have had in connection with the work of God. The record of His wonderful dealings with His people, of His great goodness in delivering them from trial, should be repeated to those newly come to the faith. God desires the old and tried laborers to stand in their place, doing their part to save men and women from being swept downward by the mighty current of evil, He desires them to keep the armor on till He bids them lay it down.

In the experience of the apostle John under persecution, there is a lesson of wonderful strength and comfort for the Christian. God does not prevent the plottings of wicked men, but He causes their devices to work for good to those who in trial and conflict maintain their faith and loyalty. Often the gospel laborer carries on his work amid storms of persecution, bitter opposition, and unjust reproach. At such times let him remember that the experience to be gained in the furnace of trial and affliction is worth all the pain it costs. Thus God brings His children near to Him, that He may show them their weakness and His strength. He teaches them to lean on Him. Thus He prepares them to meet emergen- 575 cies, to fill positions of trust, and to accomplish the great purpose for which their powers were given them.

In all ages God's appointed witnesses have exposed themselves to reproach and persecution for the truth's sake. Joseph was maligned and persecuted because he preserved his virtue and integrity. David, the chosen messenger of God, was hunted like a beast of prey by his enemies. Daniel was cast into a den of lions because he was true to his allegiance to heaven. Job was deprived of his worldly possessions, and so afflicted in body that he was abhorred by his relatives and friends; yet he maintained his integrity. Jeremiah could not be deterred from speaking the words that God had given him to speak; and his testimony so enraged the king and princes that he was cast into a loathsome pit. Stephen was stoned because he preached Christ and Him crucified. Paul was imprisoned, beaten with rods, stoned, and finally put to death because he was a faithful messenger for God to the Gentiles. And John was banished to the Isle of Patmos "for the word of God, and for the testimony of Jesus Christ."

These examples of human steadfastness bear witness to the faithfulness of God's promises—of His abiding presence and sustaining grace. They testify to the power of faith to withstand the powers of the world. It is the work of faith to rest in God in the darkest hour, to feel, however sorely tried and tempest-tossed, that our Father is at the helm. The eye of faith alone can ⁵⁷⁶ look beyond the things of time to estimate aright the worth of the eternal riches.

Jesus does not present to His followers the hope of attaining earthly glory and riches, of living a life free from trial. Instead He calls upon them to follow Him in the path of self-denial and reproach. He who came to redeem the world was opposed by the united forces of evil. In an unpitying confederacy, evil men and evil angels arrayed themselves against the Prince of Peace. His every word and act revealed divine compassion, and His unlikeness to the world provoked the bitterest hostility.

So it will be with all who will live godly in Christ Jesus. Persecution and reproach await all who are imbued with the Spirit of Christ. The character of the persecution changes with the times, but the principle—the spirit that underlies it—is the same that has slain the chosen of the Lord ever since the days of Abel.

In all ages Satan has persecuted the people of God. He has tortured them and put them to death, but in dying they became conquerors. They bore witness to the power of One mightier than Satan. Wicked men may torture and kill the body, but they cannot touch the life that is hid with Christ in God. They can incarcerate men and women in prison walls, but they cannot bind the spirit.

Through trial and persecution the glory—the character—of God is revealed in His chosen ones. The believers in Christ, hated and persecuted by the world, are educated and disciplined in the school of Christ. On earth they walk in narrow paths; they are purified in the furnace of ⁵⁷⁷ affliction. They follow Christ through sore conflicts; they endure self-denial and experience bitter disappointments; but thus they learn the guilt and woe of sin, and they look upon it with abhorrence. Being partakers of Christ's sufferings, they can look beyond the gloom to the glory, saying, "I reckon that the sufferings of this present time are not worthy to be compared with the glory which shall be revealed in us." Romans 8:18.

57

The Revelation

⁵⁷⁸

In the days of the apostles the Christian believers were filled with earnestness and enthusiasm. So untiringly did they labor for their Master that in a comparatively short time, notwithstanding fierce opposition, the gospel of the kingdom was sounded to all the inhabited parts of the earth. The zeal manifested at this time by the followers of Jesus has been recorded by the pen of inspiration for the encouragement of believers in every age. Of the church at Ephesus, which the Lord Jesus used as a symbol of the entire Christian church in the apostolic age, the faithful and true Witness declared:

"I know thy works, and thy labor, and thy patience, and how thou canst not bear them which are evil: and thou hast tried them which say they are apostles, and are not, and hast found them liars: and hast borne, and hast patience, and for My name's sake hast labored, and hast not fainted." Revelation 2:2, 3.

At the first the experience of the church at Ephesus was marked with childlike simplicity ⁵⁷⁹ and fervor. The believers sought earnestly to obey every word of God, and their lives revealed an earnest, sincere love for Christ. They rejoiced to do the will of God because the Saviour was in their hearts as an abiding presence. Filled with love for their Redeemer, their highest aim was to win souls to Him. They did not think of hoarding the precious treasure of the grace of Christ. They felt the importance of their calling; and, weighted with the message, "On earth peace, good will toward men," they burned with desire to carry the glad tidings of salvation to earth's remotest bounds. And the world took knowledge of them that they had been with Jesus. Sinful men, repentant, pardoned, cleansed, and sanctified, were brought into partnership with God through His Son.

The members of the church were united in sentiment and action. Love for Christ was the golden chain that bound them together. They followed on to know the Lord more and still more perfectly, and in their lives were revealed the joy and peace of Christ. They visited the fatherless and widows in their affliction, and kept themselves unspotted from the world, realizing that a failure to do this would be a contradiction of their profession and a denial of their Redeemer.

In every city the work was carried forward. Souls were converted, who in their turn felt that they must tell of the inestimable treasure they had received. They could not rest till the light which had illumined their minds was shining

upon others. Multitudes of unbelievers were
580 made acquainted with the reasons of the Christian's hope. Warm, inspired personal appeals were made to the erring, to the outcast, and to those who, while professing to know the truth, were lovers of pleasure more than lovers of God.

But after a time the zeal of the believers began to wane, and their love for God and for one another grew less. Coldness crept into the church. Some forgot the wonderful manner in which they had received the truth. One by one the old standard-bearers fell at their post. Some of the younger workers, who might have shared the burdens of these pioneers, and thus have been prepared for wise leadership, had become weary of oft-repeated truths. In their desire for something novel and startling they attempted to introduce new phases of doctrine, more pleasing to many minds, but not in harmony with the fundamental principles of the gospel. In their self-confidence and spiritual blindness they failed to discern that these sophistries would cause many to question the experiences of the past, and would thus lead to confusion and unbelief.

As these false doctrines were urged, differences sprang up, and the eyes of many were turned from beholding Jesus as the Author and Finisher of their faith. The discussion of unimportant points of doctrine, and the contemplation of pleasing fables of man's invention, occupied time that should have been spent in proclaiming the gospel. The masses that might have been convicted and converted by a faithful presentation of the truth were left unwarned. Piety was rapidly waning, and Satan seemed
581 about to gain the ascendancy over those who claimed to be followers of Christ.

It was at this critical time in the history of the church that John was sentenced to banishment. Never had his voice been needed by the church as now. Nearly all his former associates in the ministry had suffered martyrdom. The remnant of believers was facing fierce opposition. To all outward appearance the day was not far distant when the enemies of the church of Christ would triumph.

But the Lord's hand was moving unseen in the darkness. In the providence of God, John was placed where Christ could give him a wonderful revelation of Himself and of divine truth for the enlightenment of the churches.

In exiling John, the enemies of truth had hoped to silence forever the voice of God's faithful witness; but on Patmos the disciple received a message, the influence of which was to continue to strengthen the church till the end of time. Though not released from the responsibility of their wrong act, those who banished John became instruments in the hands of God to carry out Heaven's purpose; and the very effort

to extinguish the light placed the truth in bold relief.

It was on the Sabbath that the Lord of glory appeared to the exiled apostle. The Sabbath was as sacredly observed by John on Patmos as when he was preaching to the people in the towns and cities of Judea. He claimed as his own the precious promises that had been given regarding that day. "I was in the Spirit on the Lord's day," John writes, "and heard behind me a great voice, as of a trumpet, saying, I am 582 Alpha and Omega, the first and the last. . . . And I turned to see the voice that spake with me. And being turned, I saw seven golden candlesticks; and in the midst of the seven candlesticks One like unto the Son of man." Revelation 1:10-13.

Richly favored was this beloved disciple. He had seen his Master in Gethsemane, His face marked with the blood drops of agony, His "visage . . . marred more than any man, and His form more than the sons of men." Isaiah 52:14. He had seen Him in the hands of the Roman soldiers, clothed with an old purple robe and crowned with thorns. He had seen Him hanging on the cross of Calvary, the object of cruel mockery and abuse. Now John is once more permitted to behold his Lord. But how changed is His appearance! He is no longer a Man of Sorrows, despised and humiliated by men. He is clothed in a garment of heavenly brightness. "His head and His hairs" are "white like wool, as white as snow; and His eyes . . . as a flame of fire; and His feet like unto fine brass, as if they burned in a furnace." Revelation 1:14, 15, 17. His voice is like the music of many waters. His countenance shines as the sun. In His hand are seven stars, and out of His mouth issues a sharp two-edged sword, an emblem of the power of His word. Patmos is made resplendent with the glory of the risen Lord.

"And when I saw Him," John writes, "I fell at His feet as dead. And He laid His right hand upon me, saying unto me, Fear not." Verse 17.

John was strengthened to live in the presence of his glorified Lord. Then before his wondering vision were opened the glories of heaven. He 583 was permitted to see the throne of God and, looking beyond the conflicts of earth, to behold the white-robed throng of the redeemed. He heard the music of the heavenly angels and the triumphant songs of those who had overcome by the blood of the Lamb and the word of their testimony. In the revelation given to him there was unfolded scene after scene of thrilling interest in the experience of the people of God, and the history of the church foretold to the very close of time. In figures and symbols, subjects of vast importance were presented to John, which he was to record, that the people of God living in his age and in future ages might have an intelligent understanding of the perils and conflicts before them.

This revelation was given for the guidance and comfort of the church throughout the Christian dispensation. Yet religious teachers have declared that it is a sealed book and its secrets cannot be explained. Therefore many have turned from the prophetic record, refusing to devote time and study to its mysteries. But God does not wish His people to regard the book thus. It is "the revelation of Jesus Christ, which God gave unto Him, to show unto His servants things which must shortly come to pass." "Blessed is he that readeth," the Lord declares, "and they that hear the words of this prophecy, and keep those things which are written therein: for the time is at hand." Verses 1, 3. "I testify unto every man that heareth the words of the prophecy of this book, If any man shall add unto these things, God shall add unto him the plagues that are written in this book: and if any man shall take away from the words of the book of this prophecy, God shall take away his part out of the book of life, and out of the Holy City, and from the things which are written in this book. He which testifieth these things saith, Surely I come quickly." Revelation 22:18-20.

In the Revelation are portrayed the deep things of God. The very name given to its inspired pages, "the Revelation," contradicts the statement that this is a sealed book. A revelation is something revealed. The Lord Himself revealed to His servant the mysteries contained in this book, and He designs that they shall be open to the study of all. Its truths are addressed to those living in the last days of this earth's history, as well as to those living in the days of John. Some of the scenes depicted in this prophecy are in the past, some are now taking place; some bring to view the close of the great conflict between the powers of darkness and the Prince of heaven, and some reveal the triumphs and joys of the redeemed in the earth made new.

Let none think, because they cannot explain the meaning of every symbol in the Revelation, that it is useless for them to search this book in an effort to know the meaning of the truth it contains. The One who revealed these mysteries to John will give to the diligent searcher for truth a foretaste of heavenly things. Those whose hearts are open to the reception of truth will be enabled to understand its teachings, and will be granted the blessing promised to those who "hear the words of this prophecy, and keep those things which are written therein."

In the Revelation all the books of the Bible meet and end. Here is the complement of the book of Daniel. One is a prophecy; the other a revelation. The book that was sealed is not the Revelation, but that portion of the prophecy of Daniel relating to the last days. The angel commanded, "But thou, O Daniel, shut up the words, and seal the book, even to the time of the end." Daniel 12:4.

It was Christ who bade the apostle record that which was to be opened before him. "What thou seest, write in a book," He commanded, "and send it unto the seven churches which are in Asia; unto Ephesus, and unto Smyrna, and unto Pergamos, and unto Thyatira, and unto Sardis, and unto Philadelphia, and unto Laodicea." "I am He that liveth, and was dead; and, behold, I am alive for evermore. . . . Write the things which thou hast seen, and the things which are, and the things which shall be hereafter; the mystery of the seven stars which thou sawest in My right hand, and the seven golden candlesticks. The seven stars are the angels of the seven churches: and the seven candlesticks which thou sawest are the seven churches." Revelation 1:11, 18-20.

The names of the seven churches are symbolic of the church in different periods of the Christian Era. The number 7 indicates completeness, and is symbolic of the fact that the messages extend to the end of time, while the symbols used reveal the condition of the church at different periods in the history of the world.

Christ is spoken of as walking in the midst of the golden candlesticks. Thus is symbolized His relation to the churches. He is in constant communication with His people. He knows their true state. He observes their order, their piety, their devotion. Although He is high priest and mediator in the sanctuary above, yet He is represented as walking up and down in the midst of His churches on the earth. With untiring wakefulness and unremitting vigilance, He watches to see whether the light of any of His sentinels is burning dim or going out. If the candlesticks were left to mere human care, the flickering flame would languish and die; but He is the true watchman in the Lord's house, the true warden of the temple courts. His continued care and sustaining grace are the source of life and light.

Christ is represented as holding the seven stars in His right hand. This assures us that no church faithful to its trust need fear coming to nought, for not a star that has the protection of Omnipotence can be plucked out of the hand of Christ.

"These things saith He that holdeth the seven stars in His right hand." Revelation 2:1. These words are spoken to the teachers in the church—those entrusted by God with weighty responsibilities. The sweet influences that are to be abundant in the church are bound up with God's ministers, who are to reveal the love of Christ. The stars of heaven are under His control. He fills them with light. He guides and directs their movements. If He did not do this, they would become fallen stars. So with His ministers. They are but instruments in His hands, and all the good they accomplish is done through His power. Through them His light is to shine forth. The Saviour is to be their efficiency. If they will look to Him as He looked to the Father they will be enabled to do His work. As they make God their dependence, He will give them His brightness to reflect to the world.

Early in the history of the church the mystery of iniquity foretold by the apostle Paul began its baleful work; and as the false teachers concerning whom Peter had warned the believers, urged their heresies, many were ensnared by false doctrines. Some faltered under trial and were tempted to give up the faith. At the time when John was given this revelation, many had lost their first love of gospel truth. But in His mercy God did not leave the church to continue in a backslidden state. In a message of infinite tenderness He revealed His love for them and His desire that they should make sure work for eternity. "Remember," He pleaded, "from whence thou art fallen, and repent, and do the first works." Verse 5.

The church was defective and in need of stern reproof and chastisement, and John was inspired to record messages of warning and reproof and entreaty to those who, losing sight of the fundamental principles of the gospel, should imperil their hope of salvation. But always the words of rebuke that God finds it necessary to send are spoken in tender love and with the promise of peace to every penitent believer. "Behold, I stand at the door, and knock," the Lord declares; "if any man hear My voice, and open the door, I will come in to him, and will sup with him, and he with Me." Revelation 3:20.

And for those who in the midst of conflict [588] should maintain their faith in God, the prophet was given the words of commendation and promise: "I know thy works: behold, I have set before thee an open door, and no man can shut it: for thou hast a little strength, and hast kept My word, and hast not denied My name." "Because thou hast kept the word of My patience, I also will keep thee from the hour of temptation, which shall come upon all the world, to try them that dwell upon the earth." The believers were admonished: "Be watchful, and strengthen the things which remain, that are ready to die." "Behold, I come quickly: hold that fast which thou hast, that no man take thy crown." Verses 8, 10, 2, 11.

It was through one who declared himself to be a "brother, and companion in tribulation" (Revelation 1:9), that Christ revealed to His church the things that they must suffer for His sake. Looking down through long centuries of darkness and superstition, the aged exile saw multitudes suffering martyrdom because of their love for the truth. But he saw also that He who sustained His early witnesses would not forsake His faithful followers during the centuries of persecution that they must pass through before the close of time. "Fear none of those things which thou shalt suffer," the Lord declared; "behold, the devil shall cast some of you into prison, that ye may be tried; and ye shall have tribulation: . . . be thou faithful unto death, and I will give thee a crown of life." Revelation 2:10.

And to all the faithful ones who were striving against evil, John heard the promises made: "To him that overcometh will I give to eat of the tree [589] of life, which is in the midst of the Paradise of God." "He that overcometh, the same shall be clothed in white raiment; and I will not blot out his name out of the book of life, but I will confess his name before My Father, and before His angels." "To him that overcometh will I grant to sit with Me in My throne, even as I also overcame, and am set down with My Father in His throne." Verse 7; 3:5, 21.

John saw the mercy, the tenderness, and the love of God blending with His holiness, justice, and power. He saw sinners finding a Father in Him of whom their sins had made them afraid. And looking beyond the culmination of the great conflict, he beheld upon Zion "them that had gotten the victory . . . stand on the sea of glass, having the harps of God," and singing "the song of Moses" and the Lamb. Revelation 15:2, 3.

The Saviour is presented before John under the symbols of "the Lion of the tribe of Judah" and of "a Lamb as it had been slain." Revelation 5:5, 6. These symbols represent the union of omnipotent power and self-sacrificing love. The Lion of Judah, so terrible to the rejectors of His grace, will be the Lamb of God to the obedient and faithful. The pillar of fire that speaks terror and wrath to the transgressor of God's law is a token of light and mercy and deliverance to those who have kept His commandments. The arm strong to smite the rebellious will be strong to deliver the loyal. Everyone who is faithful will be saved. "He shall send His angels with a great sound of a trumpet, and they shall gather together His elect from the [590] four winds, from one end of heaven to the other." Matthew 24:31.

In comparison with the millions of the world, God's people will be, as they have ever been, a little flock; but if they stand for the truth as revealed in His word, God will be their refuge. They stand under the broad shield of Omnipotence. God is always a majority. When the sound of the last trump shall penetrate the prison house of the dead, and the righteous shall come forth with triumph, exclaiming, "O death, where is thy sting? O grave, where is thy victory?" (1 Corinthians 15:55)—standing then with God, with Christ, with the angels, and with the loyal and true of all ages, the children of God will be far in the majority.

Christ's true disciples follow Him through sore conflicts, enduring self-denial and experiencing bitter disappointment; but this teaches them the guilt and woe of sin, and they are led to look upon it with abhorrence. Partakers of Christ's sufferings, they are destined to be partakers of His glory. In holy vision the prophet saw the ultimate triumph of God's remnant church. He writes:

"I saw as it were a sea of glass mingled with fire: and them that had gotten the victory . . . stand on the sea of glass, having the harps of God. And they sing the song of Moses the servant of God, and the song of the Lamb, saying, Great and marvelous are Thy works, Lord God Almighty; just and true are Thy ways, Thou King of saints." Revelation 15:2, 3.

591 "And I looked, and, lo, a Lamb stood on the Mount Sion, and with Him a hundred forty and four thousand, having His Father's name written in their foreheads." Revelation 14:1. In this world their minds were consecrated to God; they served Him with the intellect and with the heart; and now He can place His name "in their foreheads." "And they shall reign for ever and ever." Revelation 22:5. They do not go in and out as those who beg a place. They are of that number to whom Christ says, "Come, ye blessed of My Father, inherit the kingdom prepared for you from the foundation of the world." He welcomes them as His children, saying, "Enter thou into the joy of thy Lord." Matthew 25:34, 21.

"These are they which follow the Lamb whithersoever He goeth. These were redeemed from among men, being the first fruits unto God and to the Lamb." Revelation 14:4. The vision of the prophet pictures them as standing on Mount Zion, girt for holy service, clothed in white linen, which is the righteousness of the saints. But all who follow the Lamb in heaven must first have followed Him on earth, not fretfully or capriciously, but in trustful, loving, willing obedience, as the flock follows the shepherd.

"I heard the voice of harpers harping with their harps: and they sung as it were a new song before the throne: . . . and no man could learn that song but the hundred and forty and four thousand, which were redeemed from the earth. . . . In their mouth was found no guile: for they are without fault before the throne of God." Verses 2-5.

"And I John saw the Holy City, New Jerusalem, coming down from God out of heaven, prepared as a bride adorned for her husband." "Her light was like unto a stone most 592 precious, even like a jasper stone, clear as crystal; and had a wall great and high, and had twelve gates, and at the gates twelve angels, and names written thereon, which are the names of the twelve tribes of the children of Israel." "The twelve gates were twelve pearls; every several gate was of one pearl: and the street of the city was pure gold, as it were transparent glass. And I saw no temple therein: for the Lord God

Almighty and the Lamb are the temple of it." Revelation 21:2, 11, 12, 21, 22.

"And there shall be no more curse: but the throne of God and of the Lamb shall be in it; and His servants shall serve Him: and they shall see His face; and His name shall be in their foreheads. And there shall be no night there; and they need no candle, neither light of the sun; for the Lord God giveth them light." Revelation 22:3-5.

"He showed me a pure river of water of life, clear as crystal, proceeding out of the throne of God and of the Lamb. In the midst of the street of it, and on either side of the river, was there the tree of life, which bare twelve manner of fruits, and yielded her fruit every month: and the leaves of the tree were for the healing of the nations." "Blessed are they that do His commandments, that they may have right to the tree of life, and may enter in through the gates into the city." Verses 1, 2, 14.

"And I heard a great voice out of heaven saying,

"Behold, the tabernacle of God is with men,
And He will dwell with them,
And they shall be His people,
And God Himself shall be with them,
And be their God." Revelation 21:3.

58

The Church Triumphant

More than eighteen centuries have passed since the apostles rested from their labors, but the history of their toils and sacrifices for Christ's sake is still among the most precious treasures of the church. This history, written under the direction of the Holy Spirit, was recorded in order that by it the followers of Christ in every age might be impelled to greater zeal and earnestness in the cause of the Saviour.

The commission that Christ gave to the disciples, they fulfilled. As these messengers of the cross went forth to proclaim the gospel, there was such a revelation of the glory of God as had never before been witnessed by mortal man. By the co-operation of the divine Spirit, the apostles did a work that shook the world. To every nation was the gospel carried in a single generation.

Glorious were the results that attended the ministry of the chosen apostles of Christ. At the beginning of their ministry some of them were unlearned men, but their consecration to the 594 cause of their Master was unreserved, and under His instruction they gained a preparation for the great work committed to them. Grace and truth reigned in their hearts, inspiring their motives and controlling their actions. Their lives were hid with Christ in God, and self was lost sight of, submerged in the depths of infinite love.

The disciples were men who knew how to speak and pray sincerely, men who could take hold of the might of the Strength of Israel. How closely they stood by the side of God, and bound their personal honor to His throne! Jehovah was their God. His honor was their honor. His truth was their truth. Any attack made upon the gospel was as if cutting deep into their souls, and with every power of their being they battled for the cause of Christ. They could hold forth the word of life because they had received the heavenly anointing. They expected much, and therefore they attempted much. Christ had revealed Himself to them, and to Him they looked for guidance. Their understanding of truth and their power to withstand opposition were proportionate to their conformity to God's will. Jesus Christ, the wisdom and power of God, was the theme of every discourse. His name—the only name given under heaven whereby men can be saved—was by them exalted. As they proclaimed the completeness of Christ, the risen Saviour, their words moved hearts, and men and women were won to the gospel. Multitudes who had reviled the Saviour's name and despised His power now confessed themselves disciples of the Crucified.

595   Not in their own power did the apostles accomplish their mission, but in the power of the living God. Their work was not easy. The opening labors of the Christian church were attended by hardship and bitter grief. In their work the disciples constantly encountered privation, calumny, and persecution; but they counted not their lives dear unto themselves and rejoiced that they were called to suffer for Christ. Irresolution, indecision, weakness of purpose, found no place in their efforts. They were willing to spend and be spent. The consciousness of the responsibility resting on them purified and enriched their experience, and the grace of heaven was revealed in the conquests they achieved for Christ. With the might of omnipotence God worked through them to make the gospel triumphant.

Upon the foundation that Christ Himself had laid, the apostles built the church of God. In the Scriptures the figure of the erection of a temple is frequently used to illustrate the building of the church. Zechariah refers to Christ as the Branch that should build the temple of the Lord. He speaks of the Gentiles as helping in the work: "They that are far off shall come and build in the temple of the Lord;" and Isaiah declares, "The sons of strangers shall build up thy walls." Zechariah 6:12, 15; Isaiah 60:10.

Writing of the building of this temple, Peter says, "To whom coming, as unto a living stone, disallowed indeed of men, but chosen of God,

and precious, ye also, as lively stones, are built up a spiritual house, an holy priesthood, to offer up spiritual sacrifices, acceptable to God by Jesus Christ." 1 Peter 2:4, 5.

In the quarry of the Jewish and the Gentile 596 world the apostles labored, bringing out stones to lay upon the foundation. In his letter to the believers at Ephesus, Paul said, "Now therefore ye are no more strangers and foreigners, but fellow citizens with the saints, and of the household of God; and are built upon the foundation of the apostles and prophets, Jesus Christ Himself being the Chief Cornerstone; in whom all the building fitly framed together groweth unto an holy temple in the Lord: in whom ye also are builded together for an habitation of God through the Spirit." Ephesians 2:19-22.

And to the Corinthians he wrote: "According to the grace of God which is given unto me, as a wise master builder, I have laid the foundation, and another buildeth thereon. But let every man take heed how he buildeth thereupon. For other foundation can no man lay than that is laid, which is Jesus Christ. Now if any man build upon this foundation gold, silver, precious stones, wood, hay, stubble; every man's work shall be made manifest: for the day shall declare it, because it shall be revealed by fire; and the fire shall try every man's work of what sort it is." 1 Corinthians 3:10-13.

The apostles built upon a sure foundation, even the Rock of Ages. To this foundation they brought the stones that they quarried from the world. Not without hindrance did the builders labor. Their work was made exceedingly difficult by the opposition of the enemies of Christ. They had to contend against the bigotry, prejudice, and hatred of those who were building upon a false foundation. Many who wrought as 597 builders of the church could be likened to the builders of the wall in Nehemiah's day, of whom it is written: "They which builded on the wall, and they that bare burdens, with those that laded, everyone with one of his hands wrought in the work, and with the other hand held a weapon." Nehemiah 4:17.

Kings and governors, priests and rulers, sought to destroy the temple of God. But in the face of imprisonment, torture, and death, faithful men carried the work forward; and the structure grew, beautiful and symmetrical. At times the workmen were almost blinded by the mists of superstition that settled around them. At times they were almost overpowered by the violence of their opponents. But with unfaltering faith and unfailing courage they pressed on with the work.

One after another the foremost of the builders fell by the hand of the enemy. Stephen was stoned; James was slain by the sword; Paul was beheaded; Peter was crucified; John was exiled. Yet the church grew. New workers took the place of those who fell, and stone after stone was added to the building. Thus slowly ascended the temple of the church of God.

Centuries of fierce persecution followed the establishment of the Christian church, but there were never wanting men who counted the work of building God's temple dearer than life itself. Of such it is written: "Others had trial of cruel mockings and scourgings, yea, moreover of bonds and imprisonment: they were stoned, they were sawn asunder, were tempted, were slain 598 with the sword: they wandered about in sheepskins and goatskins; being destitute, afflicted, tormented; (of whom the world was not worthy:) they wandered in deserts, and in mountains, and in dens and caves of the earth." Hebrews 11:36-38.

The enemy of righteousness left nothing undone in his effort to stop the work committed to the Lord's builders. But God "left not Himself without witness." Acts 14:17. Workers were raised up who ably defended the faith once delivered to the saints. History bears record to the fortitude and heroism of these men. Like the apostles, many of them fell at their post, but the building of the temple went steadily forward. The workmen were slain, but the work advanced. The Waldenses, John Wycliffe, Huss and Jerome, Martin Luther and Zwingli, Cranmer, Latimer, and Knox, the Huguenots, John and Charles Wesley, and a host of others brought to the foundation material that will endure throughout eternity. And in later years those who have so nobly endeavored to promote the circulation of God's word, and those who by their service in heathen lands have prepared the way for the proclamation of the last great message—these also have helped to rear the structure.

Through the ages that have passed since the days of the apostles, the building of God's temple has never ceased. We may look back through the centuries and see the living stones of which it is composed gleaming like jets of light through the darkness of error and superstition. Throughout eternity these precious jewels will shine with increasing luster, testifying to the power of the truth of God. The flashing light 599 of these polished stones reveals the strong contrast between light and darkness, between the gold of truth and the dross of error.

Paul and the other apostles, and all the righteous who have lived since then, have acted their part in the building of the temple. But the structure is not yet complete. We who are living in this age have a work to do, a part to act. We are to bring to the foundation material that will stand the test of fire—gold, silver, and precious stones, "polished after the similitude of a palace." Psalm 144:12. To those who thus build for God, Paul speaks words of encouragement and warning: "If any man's work abide which

he hath built thereupon, he shall receive a reward. If any man's work shall be burned, he shall suffer loss: but he himself shall be saved; yet so as by fire." 1 Corinthians 3:14, 15. The Christian who faithfully presents the word of life, leading men and women into the way of holiness and peace, is bringing to the foundation material that will endure, and in the kingdom of God he will be honored as a wise builder.

Of the apostles it is written, "They went forth, and preached everywhere, the Lord working with them, and confirming the word with signs following." Mark 16:20. As Christ sent forth His disciples, so today He sends forth the members of His church. The same power that the apostles had is for them. If they will make God their strength, He will work with them, and they shall not labor in vain. Let them realize that the work in which they are engaged is one upon which the Lord has placed His signet. God said to Jeremiah, "Say not, I am a child: for thou 600 shalt go to all that I shall send thee, and whatsoever I command thee thou shalt speak. Be not afraid of their faces: for I am with thee to deliver thee." Then the Lord put forth His hand and touched His servant's mouth, saying, "Behold, I have put My words in thy mouth." Jeremiah 1:7-9. And He bids us go forth to speak the words He gives us, feeling His holy touch upon our lips.

Christ has given to the church a sacred charge. Every member should be a channel through which God can communicate to the world the treasures of His grace, the unsearchable riches of Christ. There is nothing that the Saviour desires so much as agents who will represent to the world His Spirit and His character. There is nothing that the world needs so much as the manifestation through humanity of the Saviour's love. All heaven is waiting for men and women through whom God can reveal the power of Christianity.

The church is God's agency for the proclamation of truth, empowered by Him to do a special work; and if she is loyal to Him, obedient to all His commandments, there will dwell within her the excellency of divine grace. If she will be true to her allegiance, if she will honor the Lord God of Israel, there is no power that can stand against her.

Zeal for God and His cause moved the disciples to bear witness to the gospel with mighty power. Should not a like zeal fire our hearts with a determination to tell the story of redeeming love, of Christ and Him crucified? It is the privilege of every Christian, not only to look for, but to hasten the coming of the Saviour.

If the church will put on the robe of Christ's 601 righteousness, withdrawing from all allegiance with the world, there is before her the dawn of a bright and glorious day. God's promise to her will stand fast forever. He will make her an eternal excellency, a joy of many generations. Truth, passing by those who despise and reject it, will triumph. Although at times apparently retarded, its progress has never been checked. When the message of God meets with opposition, He gives it additional force, that it may exert greater influence. Endowed with divine energy, it will cut its way through the strongest barriers and triumph over every obstacle.

What sustained the Son of God during His life of toil and sacrifice? He saw the results of the travail of His soul and was satisfied. Looking into eternity, He beheld the happiness of those who through His humiliation had received pardon and everlasting life. His ear caught the shout of the redeemed. He heard the ransomed ones singing the song of Moses and the Lamb.

We may have a vision of the future, the blessedness of heaven. In the Bible are revealed visions of the future glory, scenes pictured by the hand of God, and these are dear to His church. By faith we may stand on the threshold of the eternal city, and hear the gracious welcome given to those who in this life co-operate with Christ, regarding it as an honor to suffer for His sake. As the words are spoken, "Come, ye blessed of My Father," they cast their crowns at the feet of the Redeemer, exclaiming, "Worthy is the Lamb that was slain to receive power, and riches, and wisdom, and strength, and honor, and glory, and blessing. . . . Honor, and glory, and power, be unto Him that sitteth upon the throne, and unto the Lamb for ever and ever." Matthew 25:34; Revelation 5:12, 13.

There the redeemed greet those who led them to the Saviour, and all unite in praising Him who died that human beings might have the life that measures with the life of God. The conflict is over. Tribulation and strife are at an end. Songs of victory fill all heaven as the ransomed ones take up the joyful strain, Worthy, worthy is the Lamb that was slain, and lives again, a triumphant conqueror.

"I beheld, and, lo, a great multitude, which no man could number, of all nations, and kindreds, and people, and tongues, stood before the throne, and before the Lamb, clothed with white robes, and palms in their hands; and cried with a loud voice, saying, Salvation to our God which sitteth upon the throne, and unto the Lamb." Revelation 7:9, 10.

"These are they which came out of great tribulation, and have washed their robes, and made them white in the blood of the Lamb. Therefore are they before the throne of God, and serve Him day and night in His temple: and He that sitteth on the throne shall dwell among them. They shall hunger no more, neither thirst any more; neither shall the sun light on them, nor any heat. For the Lamb which is in the midst of the throne shall feed them, and shall lead them unto living fountains of waters: and God shall wipe away all tears from their eyes." "And there shall be no more death, neither sorrow, nor crying, neither shall there be any more pain: for the former things are passed away." Revelation 7:14-17; 21:4.

7

INDEX

SUMMARY	PAGE	SUMMARY	PAGE

GC

INTRODUCTION

Before the entrance of sin, Adam enjoyed open communion with his Maker; but since man separated himself from God by transgression, the human race has been cut off from this high privilege. By the plan of redemption, however, a way has been opened whereby the inhabitants of the earth may still have connection with heaven. God has communicated with men by His Spirit, and divine light has been imparted to the world by revelations to His chosen servants. "Holy men of God spake as they were moved by the Holy Ghost." 2 Peter 1:21.

During the first twenty-five hundred years of human history, there was no written revelation. Those who had been taught of God, communicated their knowledge to others, and it was handed down from father to son, through successive generations. The preparation of the written word began in the time of Moses. Inspired revelations were then embodied in an inspired book. This work continued during the long period of sixteen hundred years—from Moses, the historian of creation and the law, to John, the recorder of the most sublime truths of the gospel.

The Bible points to God as its author; yet it was written by human hands; and in the varied style of its different books it presents the characteristics of the several writers. The truths revealed are all "given by inspiration of God" (2 Timothy 3:16); yet they are expressed in the words of men. The Infinite One by His Holy Spirit has shed light into the minds and hearts of His servants. He has given dreams and visions, symbols and figures; and those to whom the truth was thus revealed have themselves embodied the thought in human language.

The Ten Commandments were spoken by God Himself, and were written by His own hand. They are of divine, and not of human composition. But the Bible, with its God-given truths expressed in the language of men, presents a union of the divine and the human. Such a union existed in the nature of Christ, who was the Son of God and the Son of man. Thus it is true of the Bible, as it was of Christ, that "the Word was made flesh, and dwelt among us." John 1:14.

Written in different ages, by men who differed widely in rank and occupation, and in mental and spiritual endowments, the books of the Bible present a wide contrast in style, as well as a diversity in the nature of the subjects unfolded. Different forms of expression are employed by different writers; often the same truth is more strikingly presented by one than by another. And as several writers present a subject under varied aspects and relations, there may appear, to the superficial, careless, or prejudiced reader, to be discrepancy or contradiction, where the thoughtful, reverent student, with clearer insight, discerns the underlying harmony.

As presented through different individuals, the truth is brought out in its varied aspects. One writer is more strongly impressed with one phase of the subject; he grasps those points that harmonize with his experience or with his power of perception and appreciation; another seizes upon a different phase; and each, under the guidance of the Holy Spirit, presents what is most forcibly impressed upon his own mind—a different aspect of the truth in each, but a perfect harmony through all. And the truths thus revealed unite to form a perfect whole, adapted to meet the wants of men in all the circumstances and experiences of life.

God has been pleased to communicate His truth to the world by human agencies, and He Himself, by His Holy Spirit, qualified men and enabled them to do this work. He guided the mind in the selection of what to speak and what to write. The treasure was entrusted to earthen vessels, yet it is, nonetheless, from Heaven. The testimony is conveyed through the imperfect expression of human language, yet it is the testimony of God; and the obedient, believing child of God beholds in it the glory of a divine power, full of grace and truth.

In His word, God has committed to men the knowledge necessary for salvation. The Holy Scriptures are to be accepted as an authoritative, infallible revelation of His will. They are the standard of character, the revealer of doctrines, and the test of experience. "Every scripture inspired of God is also profitable for teaching, for reproof, for correction, for instruction which is in righteousness; that the man of God may be complete, furnished completely unto every good work." 2 Timothy 3:16, 17, R.V.

Yet the fact that God has revealed His will to men through His word, has not rendered needless the continued presence and guiding of the Holy Spirit. On the contrary, the Spirit was promised by our Saviour, to open the word to His servants, to illuminate and apply its teachings. And since it was the Spirit of God that inspired the Bible, it is impossible that the teaching of the Spirit should ever be contrary to that of the word.

The Spirit was not given—nor can it ever be bestowed—to supersede the Bible; for the Scriptures explicitly state that the word of God is the standard by which all teaching and experience must be tested. Says the apostle John,

"Believe not every spirit, but try the spirits whether they are of God: because many false prophets are gone out into the world." 1 John 4:1. And Isaiah declares, "To the law and to the testimony: if they speak not according to this word, it is because there is no light in them." Isaiah 8:20.

Great reproach has been cast upon the work of the Holy Spirit by the errors of a class that, claiming its enlightenment, profess to have no further need of guidance from the word of God. They are governed by impressions which they regard as the voice of God in the soul. But the spirit that controls them is not the Spirit of God. This following of impressions, to the neglect of the Scriptures, can lead only to confusion, to deception and ruin. It serves only to further the designs of the evil one. Since the ministry of the Holy Spirit is of vital importance to the church of Christ, it is one of the devices of Satan, through the errors of extremists and fanatics, to cast contempt upon the work of the Spirit and cause the people of God to neglect this source of strength which our Lord Himself has provided.

In harmony with the word of God, His Spirit was to continue its work throughout the period of the gospel dispensation. During the ages while the Scriptures of both the Old and the New Testament were being given, the Holy Spirit did not cease to communicate light to individual minds, apart from the revelations to be embodied in the Sacred Canon. The Bible itself relates how, through the Holy Spirit, men received warning, reproof, counsel, and instruction, in matters in no way relating to the giving of the Scriptures. And mention is made of prophets in different ages, of whose utterances nothing is recorded. In like manner, after the close of the canon of the Scripture, the Holy Spirit was still to continue its work, to enlighten, warn, and comfort the children of God.

Jesus promised His disciples, "The Comforter which is the Holy Ghost, whom the Father will send in My name, He shall teach you all things, and bring all things to your remembrance, whatsoever I have said unto you." "When He, the Spirit of truth, is come, He will guide you into all truth: . . . and He will show you things to come." John 14:26; 16:13. Scripture plainly teaches that these promises, so far from being limited to apostolic days, extend to the church of Christ in all ages. The Saviour assures His followers, "I am with you alway, even unto the end of the world." Matthew 28:20. And Paul declares that the gifts and manifestations of the Spirit were set in the church "for the perfecting of the saints, for the work of the ministry, for the edifying of the body of Christ: till we all come in the unity of the faith, and of the knowledge of the Son of God, unto a perfect man, unto the measure of the stature of the fullness of Christ." Ephesians 4:12, 13.

For the believers at Ephesus the apostle prayed, "That the God of our Lord

Jesus Christ, the Father of glory, may give unto you the *Spirit of wisdom and revelation* in the knowledge of Him: *the eyes of your understanding being enlightened*; that ye may know what is the hope of His calling, and . . . what is the *exceeding greatness* of His power to usward who believe." Ephesians 1:17-19. The ministry of the divine Spirit in enlightening the understanding and opening to the mind the deep things of God's holy word, was the blessing which Paul thus besought for the Ephesian church.

After the wonderful manifestation of the Holy Spirit on the Day of Pentecost, Peter exhorted the people to repentance and baptism in the name of Christ, for the remission of their sins; and he said: "Ye shall receive the gift of the Holy Ghost. For the promise is unto you, and to your children, and to all that are afar off, even as many as the Lord our God shall call." Acts 2:38, 39.

In immediate connection with the scenes of the great day of God, the Lord by the prophet Joel has promised a special manifestation of His Spirit. Joel 2:28. This prophecy received a partial fulfillment in the outpouring of the Spirit on the Day of Pentecost; but it will reach its full accomplishment in the manifestation of divine grace which will attend the closing work of the gospel.

The great controversy between good and evil will increase in intensity to the very close of time. In all ages the wrath of Satan has been manifested against the church of Christ; and God has bestowed His grace and Spirit upon His people to strengthen them to stand against the power of the evil one. When the apostles of Christ were to bear His gospel to the world and to record it for all future ages, they were especially endowed with the enlightenment of the Spirit. But as the church approaches her final deliverance, Satan is to work with greater power. He comes down "having great wrath, because he knoweth that he hath but a short time." Revelation 12:12. He will work "with all power and signs and lying wonders." 2 Thessalonians 2:9. For six thousand years that mastermind that once was highest among the angels of God has been wholly bent to the work of deception and ruin. And all the depths of satanic skill and subtlety acquired, all the cruelty developed, during these struggles of the ages, will be brought to bear against God's people in the final conflict. And in this time of peril the followers of Christ are to bear to the world the warning of the Lord's second advent; and a people are to be prepared to stand before Him at His coming, "without spot, and blameless." 2 Peter 3:14. At this time the special endowment of divine grace and power is not less needful to the church than in apostolic days.

Through the illumination of the Holy Spirit, the scenes of the long-continued conflict between good and evil have been opened to the writer of these pages. From time to time I have been permitted to behold the working, in different ages, of the great controversy between Christ, the Prince of life, the Author of our salvation, and Satan, the prince of evil, the author of sin, the first transgressor of God's holy law. Satan's enmity against Christ has been manifested against His followers. The same hatred of the principles of God's law, the same policy of deception, by which error is made to appear as truth, by which human laws are substituted for the law of God, and men are led to worship the creature rather than the Creator, may be traced in all the history of the past. Satan's efforts to misrepresent the character of God, to cause men to cherish a false conception of the Creator, and thus to regard Him with fear and hate rather than with love; his endeavors to set aside the divine law, leading the people to think themselves free from its requirements; and his persecution of those who dare to resist his deceptions, have been steadfastly pursued in all ages. They may be traced in the history of patriarchs, prophets, and apostles, of martyrs and reformers.

In the great final conflict, Satan will employ the same policy, manifest the same spirit, and work for the same end as in all preceding ages. That which has been, will be, except that the coming struggle will be marked with a terrible intensity such as the world has never witnessed. Satan's deceptions will be more subtle, his assaults more determined. If it were possible, he would lead astray the elect. Mark 13:22, R.V.

As the Spirit of God has opened to my mind the great truths of His word, and the scenes of the past and the future, I have been bidden to make known to others that which has thus been revealed—to trace the history of the controversy in past ages, and especially so to present it as to shed a light on the fast-approaching struggle of the future. In pursuance of this purpose, I have endeavored to select and group together events in the history of the church in such a manner as to trace the unfolding of the great testing truths that at different periods have been given to the world, that have excited the wrath of Satan, and the enmity of a world-loving church, and that have been maintained by the witness of those who "loved not their lives unto the death."

In these records we may see a foreshadowing of the conflict before us. Regarding them in the light of God's word, and by the illumination of His Spirit, we may see unveiled the devices of the wicked one, and the dangers which they must shun who would be found "without fault" before the Lord at His coming.

The great events which have marked the progress of reform in past ages are matters of history, well known and universally acknowledged by the Protestant world; they are facts which none can gainsay. This history I have presented briefly, in accordance with the scope of the book, and the brevity which must necessarily be observed, the facts having been condensed into as little space as seemed consistent with a proper understanding of their application. In some cases where a historian has so grouped together events as to afford, in brief, a comprehensive view of the subject, or has summarized details in a convenient manner, his words have been quoted; but in some instances no specific credit has been given, since the quotations are not given for the purpose of citing that writer as authority, but because his statement affords a ready and forcible presentation of the subject. In narrating the experience and views of those carrying forward the work of reform in our own time, similar use has been made of their published works.

It is not so much the object of this book to present new truths concerning the struggles of former times, as to bring out facts and principles which have a bearing on coming events. Yet viewed as a part of the controversy between the forces of light and darkness, all these records of the past are seen to have a new significance; and through them a light is cast upon the future, illumining the pathway of those who, like the reformers of past ages, will be called, even at the peril of all earthly good, to witness "for the word of God, and for the testimony of Jesus Christ."

To unfold the scenes of the great controversy between truth and error; to reveal the wiles of Satan, and the means by which he may be successfully resisted; to present a satisfactory solution of the great problem of evil, shedding such a light upon the origin and the final disposition of sin as to make fully manifest the justice and benevolence of God in all His dealings with His creatures; and to show the holy, unchanging nature of His law, is the object of this book. That through its influence souls may be delivered from the power of darkness, and become "partakers of the inheritance of the saints in light," to the praise of Him who loved us, and gave Himself for us, is the earnest prayer of the writer.

E. G. White

CONTENTS

1. The Destruction of Jerusalem 1143

2. Persecution in the First Centuries 1150

3. An Era of Spiritual Darkness 1154
   (The Apostasy)

4. The Waldenses 1158

5. John Wycliffe 1164

6. Huss and Jerome 1171

7. Luther's Separation From Rome 1179

8. Luther Before the Diet 1188

9. The Swiss Reformer 1198

10. Progress of Reform in Germany 1202

11. Protest of the Princes 1207

12. The French Reformation 1212

13. The Netherlands and Scandinavia 1222

14. Later English Reformers 1224

15. The Bible and the French Revolution 1232

16. The Pilgrim Fathers 1240

17. Heralds of the Morning 1244

18. An American Reformer 1251

19. Light Through Darkness 1260

20. A Great Religious Awakening 1264

21. A Warning Rejected 1271

22. Prophecies Fulfilled 1277

23. What Is the Sanctuary? 1284

24. In the Holy of Holies 1289

25. God's Law Immutable 1292

26. A Work of Reform 1298

27. Modern Revivals 1302

28. Facing Life's Record 1308
    (The Investigative Judgment)

29. The Origin of Evil 1313

30. Enmity Between Man and Satan 1318

31. Agency of Evil Spirits 1320

32. Snares of Satan 1322

33. The First Great Deception 1327

34. Can Our Dead Speak to Us? 1334
    (Spiritualism)

35. Liberty of Conscience Threatened 1338
    (Aims of the Papacy)

36. The Impending Conflict 1345

37. The Scriptures a Safeguard 1349

38. The Final Warning 1352

39. The Time of Trouble 1355

40. God's People Delivered 1363

41. Desolation of the Earth 1370

42. The Controversy Ended 1373

Appendix 1380

1

The Destruction of Jerusalem

"If thou hadst known, even thou, at least in this thy day, the things which belong unto thy peace! but now they are hid from thine eyes. For the days shall come upon thee, that thine enemies shall cast a trench about thee, and compass thee round, and keep thee in on every side, and shall lay thee even with the ground, and thy children within thee; and they shall not leave in thee one stone upon another; because thou knewest not the time of thy visitation." Luke 19:42-44.

From the crest of Olivet, Jesus looked upon Jerusalem. Fair and peaceful was the scene spread out before Him. It was the season of the Passover, and from all lands the children of Jacob had gathered there to celebrate the great national festival. In the midst of gardens and vineyards, and green slopes studded with pilgrims' tents, rose the terraced hills, the stately palaces, and massive bulwarks of Israel's capital. The daughter of Zion seemed in her pride to say, I sit a queen and shall see no sorrow; as lovely then, and deeming herself as secure in Heaven's favor, as when, ages before, the royal minstrel sang: "Beautiful for situation, the joy of the whole earth, is Mount Zion, . . . the city of the great King." Psalm 48:2. In full view were the magnificent buildings of the temple. The rays of the setting sun lighted up the snowy whiteness of its marble walls and gleamed from golden gate and tower and pinnacle. "The perfection of beauty" it stood, the pride of the Jewish nation. What child of Israel could gaze upon the scene without a thrill of joy and admiration! But far other thoughts occupied the mind of Jesus. "When He was come near, He beheld the city, and wept over it." Luke 19:41. Amid the universal rejoicing of the triumphal entry, while palm branches waved, while glad hosannas awoke the echoes of the hills, and thousands of voices declared Him king, the world's Redeemer was overwhelmed with a sudden and mysterious sorrow. He, the Son of God, the Promised One of Israel, whose power had conquered death and called its captives from the grave, was in tears, not of ordinary grief, but of intense, irrepressible agony.

His tears were not for Himself, though He well knew whither His feet were tending. Before Him lay Gethsemane, the scene of His approaching agony. The sheepgate also was in sight, through which for centuries the victims for sacrifice had been led, and which was to open for Him when He should be "brought as a lamb to the slaughter." Isaiah 53:7. Not far distant was Calvary, the place of crucifixion. Upon the path which Christ was soon to tread must fall the horror of great darkness as He should make His soul an offering for sin. Yet it was not the contemplation of these scenes that cast the shadow upon Him in this hour of gladness. No foreboding of His own superhuman anguish clouded that unselfish spirit. He wept for the doomed thousands of Jerusalem—because of the blindness and impenitence of those whom He came to bless and to save.

The history of more than a thousand years of God's special favor and guardian care, manifested to the chosen people, was open to the eye of Jesus. There was Mount Moriah, where the son of promise, an unresisting victim, had been bound to the altar—emblem of the offering of the Son of God. There the covenant of blessing, the glorious Messianic promise, had been confirmed to the father of the faithful. Genesis 22:9, 16-18. There the flames of the sacrifice ascending to heaven from the threshing floor of Ornan had turned aside the sword of the destroying angel (1 Chronicles 21)—fitting symbol of the Saviour's sacrifice and mediation for guilty men. Jerusalem had been honored of God above all the earth. The Lord had "chosen Zion," He had "desired it for His habitation." Psalm 132:13. There, for ages, holy prophets had uttered their messages of warning. There priests had waved their censers, and the cloud of incense, with the prayers of the worshipers, had ascended before God. There daily the blood of slain lambs had been offered, pointing forward to the Lamb of God. There Jehovah had revealed His presence in the cloud of glory above the mercy seat. There rested the base of that mystic ladder connecting earth with heaven (Genesis 28:12; John 1:51)—that ladder upon which angels of God descended and ascended, and which opened to the world the way into the holiest of all. Had Israel as a nation preserved her allegiance to Heaven, Jerusalem would have stood forever, the elect of God. Jeremiah 17:21-25. But the history of that favored people was a record of backsliding and rebellion. They had resisted Heaven's grace, abused their privileges, and slighted their opportunities.

Although Israel had "mocked the messengers of God, and despised His words, and misused His prophets" (2 Chronicles 36:16), He had still manifested Himself to them, as "the Lord God, merciful and gracious, long-suffering, and abundant in goodness and truth" (Exodus 34:6); notwithstanding repeated rejections, His mercy had continued its pleadings. With more than a father's pitying love for the son of His care, God had "sent to them by His messengers, rising up betimes, and sending; because He had compassion on His people, and on His dwelling place." 2 Chronicles 36:15. When remonstrance, entreaty, and rebuke had failed, He sent to them the best gift of heaven; nay, He poured out all heaven in that one Gift.

The Son of God Himself was sent to plead with the impenitent city. It was Christ that had brought Israel as a goodly vine out of Egypt.

20 Psalm 80:8. His own hand had cast out the heathen before it. He had planted it "in a very fruitful hill." His guardian care had hedged it about. His servants had been sent to nurture it. "What could have been done more to My vineyard," He exclaims, "that I have not done in it?" Isaiah 5:1-4. Though when He looked that it should bring forth grapes, it brought forth wild grapes, yet with a still yearning hope of fruitfulness He came in person to His vineyard, if haply it might be saved from destruction. He digged about His vine; He pruned and cherished it. He was unwearied in His efforts to save this vine of His own planting.

For three years the Lord of light and glory had gone in and out among His people. He "went about doing good, and healing all that were oppressed of the devil," binding up the brokenhearted, setting at liberty them that were bound, restoring sight to the blind, causing the lame to walk and the deaf to hear, cleansing the lepers, raising the dead, and preaching the gospel to the poor. Acts 10:38; Luke 4:18; Matthew 11:5. To all classes alike was addressed the gracious call: "Come unto Me, all ye that labor and are heavy-laden, and I will give you rest." Matthew 11:28.

Though rewarded with evil for good, and hatred for His love (Psalm 109:5), He had steadfastly pursued His mission of mercy. Never were those repelled that sought His grace. A homeless wanderer, reproach and penury His daily lot, He lived to minister to the needs and lighten the woes of men, to plead with them to accept the gift of life. The waves of mercy, beaten back by those stubborn hearts, returned in a stronger tide of pitying, inexpressible love. But Israel had turned from her best Friend and only Helper. The pleadings of His love had been despised, His counsels spurned, His warnings ridiculed.

The hour of hope and pardon was fast passing; the cup of God's long-deferred wrath was almost full. The cloud that had been gathering through ages of apostasy and rebellion, now black with woe, was about to burst upon a guilty 21 people; and He who alone could save them from their impending fate had been slighted, abused, rejected, and was soon to be crucified. When Christ should hang upon the cross of Calvary, Israel's day as a nation favored and blessed of God would be ended. The loss of even one soul is a calamity infinitely outweighing the gains and treasures of a world; but as Christ looked upon Jerusalem, the doom of a whole city, a whole nation, was before Him—that city, that nation, which had once been the chosen of God,

His peculiar treasure.

Prophets had wept over the apostasy of Israel and the terrible desolations by which their sins were visited. Jeremiah wished that his eyes were a fountain of tears, that he might weep day and night for the slain of the daughter of his people, for the Lord's flock that was carried away captive. Jeremiah 9:1; 13:17. What, then, was the grief of Him whose prophetic glance took in, not years, but ages! He beheld the destroying angel with sword uplifted against the city which had so long been Jehovah's dwelling place. From the ridge of Olivet, the very spot afterward occupied by Titus and his army, He looked across the valley upon the sacred courts and porticoes, and with tear-dimmed eyes He saw, in awful perspective, the walls surrounded by alien hosts. He heard the tread of armies marshaling for war. He heard the voice of mothers and children crying for bread in the besieged city. He saw her holy and beautiful house, her palaces and towers, given to the flames, and where once they stood, only a heap of smoldering ruins.

Looking down the ages, He saw the covenant people scattered in every land, "like wrecks on a desert shore." In the temporal retribution about to fall upon her children, He saw but the first draft from that cup of wrath which at the final judgment she must drain to its dregs. Divine pity, yearning love, found utterance in the mournful words: "O Jerusalem, Jerusalem, thou that killest the prophets, and stonest them which are sent unto thee, how often would I have gathered thy children together, even as a hen gathereth her chickens under her wings, and ye would not!" O that thou, a nation favored above every other, hadst known the time of thy visitation, and the things that belong unto thy peace! I have stayed the angel of justice, I have called thee to repentance, but in vain. It is not merely servants, delegates, and prophets, whom thou hast refused and rejected, but the Holy One of Israel, thy Redeemer. If thou art destroyed, thou alone art responsible. "Ye will not come to Me, that ye might have life." Matthew 23:37; John 5:40.

22

Christ saw in Jerusalem a symbol of the world hardened in unbelief and rebellion, and hastening on to meet the retributive judgments of God. The woes of a fallen race, pressing upon His soul, forced from His lips that exceeding bitter cry. He saw the record of sin traced in human misery, tears, and blood; His heart was moved with infinite pity for the afflicted and suffering ones of earth; He yearned to relieve them all. But even His hand might not turn back the tide of human woe; few would seek their only Source of help. He was willing to pour out His soul unto death, to bring salvation within their reach; but few would come to Him that they might have life.

The Majesty of heaven in tears! the Son of the infinite God troubled in spirit, bowed down with anguish! The scene filled all heaven with wonder. That scene reveals to us the exceeding sinfulness of sin; it shows how hard a task it is, even for Infinite Power, to save the guilty from the consequences of transgressing the law of God. Jesus, looking down to the last generation, saw the world involved in a deception similar to that which caused the destruction of Jerusalem. The great sin of the Jews was their rejection of Christ; the great sin of the Christian world would be their rejection of the law of God, the foundation of His government in heaven and earth. The precepts of Jehovah would be despised and set at nought. Millions in bondage to sin, slaves of Satan, doomed to suffer the sec- ²³ ond death, would refuse to listen to the words of truth in their day of visitation. Terrible blindness! strange infatuation!

Two days before the Passover, when Christ had for the last time departed from the temple, after denouncing the hypocrisy of the Jewish rulers, He again went out with His disciples to the Mount of Olives and seated Himself with them upon the grassy slope overlooking the city. Once more He gazed upon its walls, its towers, and its palaces. Once more He beheld the temple in its dazzling splendor, a diadem of beauty crowning the sacred mount.

A thousand years before, the psalmist had magnified God's favor to Israel in making her holy house His dwelling place: "In Salem also is His tabernacle, and His dwelling place in Zion." He "chose the tribe of Judah, the Mount Zion which He loved. And He built His sanctuary like high palaces." Psalms 76:2; 78:68, 69. The first temple had been erected during the most prosperous period of Israel's history. Vast stores of treasure for this purpose had been collected by King David, and the plans for its construction were made by divine inspiration. 1 Chronicles 28:12, 19. Solomon, the wisest of Israel's monarchs, had completed the work. This temple was the most magnificent building which the world ever saw. Yet the Lord had declared by the prophet Haggai, concerning the second temple: "The glory of this latter house shall be greater than of the former." "I will shake all nations, and the Desire of all nations shall come: and I will fill this house with glory, saith the Lord of hosts." Haggai 2:9, 7.

After the destruction of the temple by Nebuchadnezzar it was rebuilt about five hundred years before the birth of Christ by a people who from a lifelong captivity had returned to a wasted and almost deserted country. There were then among them aged men who had seen the glory of Solomon's temple, and who wept at the foundation of the new building, that it must be so inferior to the former. The feeling that prevailed is forcibly described by the prophet: "Who is left among you that saw this house in her first ²⁴ glory? and how do ye see it now? is it not in your eyes in comparison of it as nothing?" Haggai 2:3; Ezra 3:12. Then was given the promise that the glory of this latter house should be greater than that of the former.

But the second temple had not equaled the first in magnificence; nor was it hallowed by those visible tokens of the divine presence which pertained to the first temple. There was no manifestation of supernatural power to mark its dedication. No cloud of glory was seen to fill the newly erected sanctuary. No fire from heaven descended to consume the sacrifice upon its altar. The Shekinah no longer abode between the cherubim in the most holy place; the ark, the mercy seat, and the tables of the testimony were not to be found therein. No voice sounded from heaven to make known to the inquiring priest the will of Jehovah.

For centuries the Jews had vainly endeavored to show wherein the promise of God given by Haggai had been fulfilled; yet pride and unbelief blinded their minds to the true meaning of the prophet's words. The second temple was not honored with the cloud of Jehovah's glory, but with the living presence of One in whom dwelt the fullness of the Godhead bodily—who was God Himself manifest in the flesh. The "Desire of all nations" had indeed come to His temple when the Man of Nazareth taught and healed in the sacred courts. In the presence of Christ, and in this only, did the second temple exceed the first in glory. But Israel had put from her the proffered Gift of heaven. With the humble Teacher who had that day passed out from its golden gate, the glory had forever departed from the temple. Already were the Saviour's words fulfilled: "Your house is left unto you desolate." Matthew 23:38.

The disciples had been filled with awe and wonder at Christ's prediction of the overthrow of the temple, and they desired to understand more fully the meaning of His words. Wealth, labor, and architectural skill had for more than forty years been freely expended to enhance its splendors. Herod the Great had lavished upon it ²⁵ both Roman wealth and Jewish treasure, and even the emperor of the world had enriched it with his gifts. Massive blocks of white marble, of almost fabulous size, forwarded from Rome for this purpose, formed a part of its structure; and to these the disciples had called the attention of their Master, saying: "See what manner of stones and what buildings are here!" Mark 13:1.

To these words, Jesus made the solemn and startling reply: "Verily I say unto you, There shall not be left here one stone upon another, that shall not be thrown down." Matthew 24:2.

With the overthrow of Jerusalem the disciples associated the events of Christ's personal coming in temporal glory to take the throne of universal empire, to punish the impenitent Jews, and to break from off the nation the Roman yoke. The Lord had told them that He would come the second time. Hence at the mention of judgments upon Jerusalem, their minds reverted to that coming; and as they were gathered about the Saviour upon the Mount of Olives, they asked: "When shall these things be? and what shall be the sign of Thy coming, and of the end of the world?" Verse 3.

The future was mercifully veiled from the disciples. Had they at that time fully comprehended the two awful facts—the Redeemer's sufferings and death, and the destruction of their city and temple—they would have been overwhelmed with horror. Christ presented before them an outline of the prominent events to take place before the close of time. His words were not then fully understood; but their meaning was to be unfolded as His people should need the instruction therein given. The prophecy which He uttered was twofold in its meaning; while foreshadowing the destruction of Jerusalem, it prefigured also the terrors of the last great day.

Jesus declared to the listening disciples the judgments that were to fall upon apostate Israel, and especially the retributive vengeance that would come upon them for their rejection and crucifixion of the Messiah. Unmistakable signs would precede the awful climax. The dreaded hour would come suddenly and swiftly. And the Saviour warned His followers: "When ye therefore shall see the abomination of desolation, spoken of by Daniel the prophet, stand in the holy place, (whoso readeth, let him understand:) then let them which be in Judea flee into the mountains." Matthew 24:15, 16; Luke 21:20, 21. When the idolatrous standards of the Romans should be set up in the holy ground, which extended some furlongs outside the city walls, then the followers of Christ were to find safety in flight. When the warning sign should be seen, those who would escape must make no delay. Throughout the land of Judea, as well as in Jerusalem itself, the signal for flight must be immediately obeyed. He who chanced to be upon the housetop must not go down into his house, even to save his most valued treasures. Those who were working in the fields or vineyards must not take time to return for the outer garment laid aside while they should be toiling in the heat of the day. They must not hesitate a moment, lest they be involved in the general destruction.

In the reign of Herod, Jerusalem had not only been greatly beautified, but by the erection of towers, walls, and fortresses, adding to the natural strength of its situation, it had been rendered apparently impregnable. He who would at this time have foretold publicly its destruction,

would, like Noah in his day, have been called a crazed alarmist. But Christ had said: "Heaven and earth shall pass away, but My words shall not pass away." Matthew 24:35. Because of her sins, wrath had been denounced against Jerusalem, and her stubborn unbelief rendered her doom certain.

The Lord had declared by the prophet Micah: "Hear this, I pray you, ye heads of the house of Jacob, and princes of the house of Israel, that abhor judgment, and pervert all equity. They build up Zion with blood, and Jerusalem with iniquity. The heads thereof judge for reward, and the priests thereof teach for hire, and the prophets thereof divine for money: yet will they lean upon the Lord, and say, Is not the Lord among us? none evil can come upon us." Micah 3:9-11.

These words faithfully described the corrupt and self-righteous inhabitants of Jerusalem. While claiming to observe rigidly the precepts of God's law, they were transgressing all its principles. They hated Christ because His purity and holiness revealed their iniquity; and they accused Him of being the cause of all the troubles which had come upon them in consequence of their sins. Though they knew Him to be sinless, they had declared that His death was necessary to their safety as a nation. "If we let Him thus alone," said the Jewish leaders, "all men will believe on Him: and the Romans shall come and take away both our place and nation." John 11:48. If Christ were sacrificed, they might once more become a strong, united people. Thus they reasoned, and they concurred in the decision of their high priest, that it would be better for one man to die than for the whole nation to perish.

Thus the Jewish leaders had built up "Zion with blood, and Jerusalem with iniquity." Micah 3:10. And yet, while they slew their Saviour because He reproved their sins, such was their self-righteousness that they regarded themselves as God's favored people and expected the Lord to deliver them from their enemies. "Therefore," continued the prophet, "shall Zion for your sake be plowed as a field, and Jerusalem shall become heaps, and the mountain of the house as the high places of the forest." Verse 12.

For nearly forty years after the doom of Jerusalem had been pronounced by Christ Himself, the Lord delayed His judgments upon the city and the nation. Wonderful was the long-suffering of God toward the rejectors of His gospel and the murderers of His Son. The parable of the unfruitful tree represented God's dealings with the Jewish nation. The command had gone forth, "Cut it down; why cumbereth it the ground?" (Luke 13:7) but divine mercy had spared it yet a little longer. There were still many among the Jews who were ignorant of the character and the work of Christ. And the chil-

28 dren had not enjoyed the opportunities or received the light which their parents had spurned. Through the preaching of the apostles and their associates, God would cause light to shine upon them; they would be permitted to see how prophecy had been fulfilled, not only in the birth and life of Christ, but in His death and resurrection. The children were not condemned for the sins of the parents; but when, with a knowledge of all the light given to their parents, the children rejected the additional light granted to themselves, they became partakers of the parents' sins, and filled up the measure of their iniquity.

The long-suffering of God toward Jerusalem only confirmed the Jews in their stubborn impenitence. In their hatred and cruelty toward the disciples of Jesus they rejected the last offer of mercy. Then God withdrew His protection from them and removed His restraining power from Satan and his angels, and the nation was left to the control of the leader she had chosen. Her children had spurned the grace of Christ, which would have enabled them to subdue their evil impulses, and now these became the conquerors. Satan aroused the fiercest and most debased passions of the soul. Men did not reason; they were beyond reason—controlled by impulse and blind rage. They became satanic in their cruelty. In the family and in the nation, among the highest and the lowest classes alike, there was suspicion, envy, hatred, strife, rebellion, murder. There was no safety anywhere. Friends and kindred betrayed one another. Parents slew their children, and children their parents. The rulers of the people had no power to rule themselves. Uncontrolled passions made them tyrants. The Jews had accepted false testimony to condemn the innocent Son of God. Now false accusations made their own lives uncertain. By their actions they had long been saying: "Cause the Holy One of Israel to cease from before us." Isaiah 30:11. Now their desire was granted. The fear of God no longer dis-

29 turbed them. Satan was at the head of the nation, and the highest civil and religious authorities were under his sway.

The leaders of the opposing factions at times united to plunder and torture their wretched victims, and again they fell upon each other's forces and slaughtered without mercy. Even the sanctity of the temple could not restrain their horrible ferocity. The worshipers were stricken down before the altar, and the sanctuary was polluted with the bodies of the slain. Yet in their blind and blasphemous presumption the instigators of this hellish work publicly declared that they had no fear that Jerusalem would be destroyed, for it was God's own city. To establish their power more firmly, they bribed false prophets to proclaim, even while Roman legions were besieging the temple, that the people were

to wait for deliverance from God. To the last, multitudes held fast to the belief that the Most High would interpose for the defeat of their adversaries. But Israel had spurned the divine protection, and now she had no defense. Unhappy Jerusalem! rent by internal dissensions, the blood of her children slain by one another's hands crimsoning her streets, while alien armies beat down her fortifications and slew her men of war!

All the predictions given by Christ concerning the destruction of Jerusalem were fulfilled to the letter. The Jews experienced the truth of His words of warning: "With what measure ye mete, it shall be measured to you again." Matthew 7:2.

Signs and wonders appeared, foreboding disaster and doom. In the midst of the night an unnatural light shone over the temple and the altar. Upon the clouds at sunset were pictured chariots and men of war gathering for battle. The priests ministering by night in the sanctuary were terrified by mysterious sounds; the earth trembled, and a multitude of voices were heard crying: "Let us depart hence." The great eastern gate, which was so heavy that it could hardly be shut by a score of men, and which was secured by immense bars of iron fastened deep in the 30 pavement of solid stone, opened at midnight, without visible agency.—Milman, *The History of the Jews, book* 13.

For seven years a man continued to go up and down the streets of Jerusalem, declaring the woes that were to come upon the city. By day and by night he chanted the wild dirge: "A voice from the east! a voice from the west! a voice from the four winds! a voice against Jerusalem and against the temple! a voice against the bridegrooms and the brides! a voice against the whole people!"—*Ibid.* This strange being was imprisoned and scourged, but no complaint escaped his lips. To insult and abuse he answered only: "Woe, woe to Jerusalem!" "woe, woe to the inhabitants thereof!" His warning cry ceased not until he was slain in the siege he had foretold.

Not one Christian perished in the destruction of Jerusalem. Christ had given His disciples warning, and all who believed His words watched for the promised sign. "When ye shall see Jerusalem compassed with armies," said Jesus, "then know that the desolation thereof is nigh. Then let them which are in Judea flee to the mountains; and let them which are in the midst of it depart out." Luke 21:20, 21. After the Romans under Cestius had surrounded the city, they unexpectedly abandoned the siege when everything seemed favorable for an immediate attack. The besieged, despairing of successful resistance, were on the point of surrender, when the Roman general withdrew his forces without the least apparent reason. But

God's merciful providence was directing events for the good of His own people. The promised sign had been given to the waiting Christians, and now an opportunity was offered for all who would, to obey the Saviour's warning. Events were so overruled that neither Jews nor Romans should hinder the flight of the Christians. Upon the retreat of Cestius, the Jews, sallying from Jerusalem, pursued after his retiring army; and while both forces were thus fully engaged, the Christians had an opportunity to leave the city. At this time the country also had been cleared of enemies who might have endeavored to intercept them. At the time of the siege, the Jews were assembled at Jerusalem to keep the Feast of Tabernacles, and thus the Christians throughout the land were able to make their escape unmolested. Without delay they fled to a place of safety—the city of Pella, in the land of Perea, beyond Jordan.

The Jewish forces, pursuing after Cestius and his army, fell upon their rear with such fierceness as to threaten them with total destruction. It was with great difficulty that the Romans succeeded in making their retreat. The Jews escaped almost without loss, and with their spoils returned in triumph to Jerusalem. Yet this apparent success brought them only evil. It inspired them with that spirit of stubborn resistance to the Romans which speedily brought unutterable woe upon the doomed city.

Terrible were the calamities that fell upon Jerusalem when the siege was resumed by Titus. The city was invested at the time of the Passover, when millions of Jews were assembled within its walls. Their stores of provision, which if carefully preserved would have supplied the inhabitants for years, had previously been destroyed through the jealousy and revenge of the contending factions, and now all the horrors of starvation were experienced. A measure of wheat was sold for a talent. So fierce were the pangs of hunger that men would gnaw the leather of their belts and sandals and the covering of their shields. Great numbers of the people would steal out at night to gather wild plants growing outside the city walls, though many were seized and put to death with cruel torture, and often those who returned in safety were robbed of what they had gleaned at so great peril. The most inhuman tortures were inflicted by those in power, to force from the want-stricken people the last scanty supplies which they might have concealed. And these cruelties were not infrequently practiced by men who were themselves well fed, and who were merely desirous of laying up a store of provision for the future.

Thousands perished from famine and pestilence. Natural affection seemed to have been destroyed. Husbands robbed their wives, and wives their husbands. Children would be seen snatching the food from the mouths of their aged parents. The question of the prophet, "Can a woman forget her sucking child?" received the answer within the walls of that doomed city: "The hands of the pitiful women have sodden their own children: they were their meat in the destruction of the daughter of my people." Isaiah 49:15; Lamentations 4:10. Again was fulfilled the warning prophecy given fourteen centuries before: "The tender and delicate woman among you, which would not adventure to set the sole of her foot upon the ground for delicateness and tenderness, her eye shall be evil toward the husband of her bosom, and toward her son, and toward her daughter, . . . and toward her children which she shall bear: for she shall eat them for want of all things secretly in the siege and straitness, wherewith thine enemy shall distress thee in thy gates." Deuteronomy 28:56, 57.

The Roman leaders endeavored to strike terror to the Jews and thus cause them to surrender. Those prisoners who resisted when taken, were scourged, tortured, and crucified before the wall of the city. Hundreds were daily put to death in this manner, and the dreadful work continued until, along the Valley of Jehoshaphat and at Calvary, crosses were erected in so great numbers that there was scarcely room to move among them. So terribly was visited that awful imprecation uttered before the judgment seat of Pilate: "His blood be on us, and on our children." Matthew 27:25.

Titus would willingly have put an end to the fearful scene, and thus have spared Jerusalem the full measure of her doom. He was filled with horror as he saw the bodies of the dead lying in heaps in the valleys. Like one entranced, he looked from the crest of Olivet upon the magnificent temple and gave command that not one stone of it be touched. Before attempting to gain possession of this stronghold, he made an earnest appeal to the Jewish leaders not to force him to defile the sacred place with blood. If they would come forth and fight in any other place, no Roman should violate the sanctity of the temple. Josephus himself, in a most eloquent appeal, entreated them to surrender, to save themselves, their city, and their place of worship. But his words were answered with bitter curses. Darts were hurled at him, their last human mediator, as he stood pleading with them. The Jews had rejected the entreaties of the Son of God, and now expostulation and entreaty only made them more determined to resist to the last. In vain were the efforts of Titus to save the temple; One greater than he had declared that not one stone was to be left upon another.

The blind obstinacy of the Jewish leaders, and the detestable crimes perpetrated within the besieged city, excited the horror and indignation of the Romans, and Titus at last decided to take the temple by storm. He determined, however, that if possible it should be saved from destruction. But his commands were disregarded. After he had retired to his tent at night, the Jews, sallying from the temple, attacked the soldiers without. In the struggle, a firebrand was flung by a soldier through an opening in the porch, and immediately the cedar-lined chambers about the holy house were in a blaze. Titus rushed to the place, followed by his generals and legionaries, and commanded the soldiers to quench the flames. His words were unheeded. In their fury the soldiers hurled blazing brands into the chambers adjoining the temple, and then with their swords they slaughtered in great numbers those who had found shelter there. Blood flowed down the temple steps like water. Thousands upon thousands of Jews perished. Above the sound of battle, voices were heard shouting: "Ichabod!"—the glory is departed.

"Titus found it impossible to check the rage of the soldiery; he entered with his officers, and surveyed the interior of the sacred edifice. The splendor filled them with wonder; and as the flames had not yet penetrated to the holy place, 34 he made a last effort to save it, and springing forth, again exhorted the soldiers to stay the progress of the conflagration. The centurion Liberalis endeavored to force obedience with his staff of office; but even respect for the emperor gave way to the furious animosity against the Jews, to the fierce excitement of battle, and to the insatiable hope of plunder. The soldiers saw everything around them radiant with gold, which shone dazzlingly in the wild light of the flames; they supposed that incalculable treasures were laid up in the sanctuary. A soldier, unperceived, thrust a lighted torch between the hinges of the door: the whole building was in flames in an instant. The blinding smoke and fire forced the officers to retreat, and the noble edifice was left to its fate.

"It was an appalling spectacle to the Roman—what was it to the Jew? The whole summit of the hill which commanded the city, blazed like a volcano. One after another the buildings fell in, with a tremendous crash, and were swallowed up in the fiery abyss. The roofs of cedar were like sheets of flame; the gilded pinnacles shone like spikes of red light; the gate towers sent up tall columns of flame and smoke. The neighboring hills were lighted up; and dark groups of people were seen watching in horrible anxiety the progress of the destruction: the walls and heights of the upper city were crowded with faces, some pale with the agony of despair, others scowling unavailing vengeance. The shouts of the Roman soldiery as they ran to and fro, and the howlings of the insurgents who were perishing in the flames, mingled with the roaring of the conflagration and the thundering sound of falling timbers. The echoes of the mountains replied or brought back the shrieks of the people on the heights; all along the walls resounded screams and wailings; men who were expiring with famine rallied their remaining strength to utter a cry of anguish and desolation.

"The slaughter within was even more dreadful than the spectacle from without. Men and women, old and young, insurgents and priests, those who fought and those who entreated mercy, were hewn down in indiscriminate carnage. The number of the slain exceeded that of the slayers. The legionaries had to clamber over heaps of dead to carry on the work of extermination."—Milman, *The History of the Jews*, book 16.

After the destruction of the temple, the whole city soon fell into the hands of the Romans. The leaders of the Jews forsook their impregnable towers, and Titus found them solitary. He gazed upon them with amazement, and declared that God had given them into his hands; for no engines, however powerful, could have prevailed against those stupendous battlements. Both the city and the temple were razed to their foundations, and the ground upon which the holy house had stood was "plowed like a field." Jeremiah 26:18. In the siege and the slaughter that followed, more than a million of the people perished; the survivors were carried away as captives, sold as slaves, dragged to Rome to grace the conqueror's triumph, thrown to wild beasts in the amphitheaters, or scattered as homeless wanderers throughout the earth.

The Jews had forged their own fetters; they had filled for themselves the cup of vengeance. In the utter destruction that befell them as a nation, and in all the woes that followed them in their dispersion, they were but reaping the harvest which their own hands had sown. Says the prophet: "O Israel, thou hast destroyed thyself;" "for thou hast fallen by thine iniquity." Hosea 13:9; 14:1. Their sufferings are often represented as a punishment visited upon them by the direct decree of God. It is thus that the great deceiver seeks to conceal his own work. By stubborn rejection of divine love and mercy, the Jews had caused the protection of God to be withdrawn from them, and Satan was permitted to rule them according to his will. The horrible cruelties enacted in the destruction of Jerusalem 36 are a demonstration of Satan's vindictive power over those who yield to his control.

We cannot know how much we owe to Christ for the peace and protection which we enjoy. It is the restraining power of God that prevents mankind from passing fully under the control of Satan. The disobedient and unthankful have great reason for gratitude for God's mercy and long-suffering in holding in check the cruel, malignant power of the evil one. But when men pass the limits of divine forbearance, that restraint is removed. God does not stand toward the sinner as an executioner of the sentence against transgression; but He leaves the rejectors of His mercy to themselves, to reap that which they have sown. Every ray of light rejected, every warning despised or unheeded, every passion indulged, every transgression of the law of God, is a seed sown which yields its unfailing harvest. The Spirit of God, persistently resisted, is at last withdrawn from the sinner, and then there is left no power to control the evil passions of the soul, and no protection from the malice and enmity of Satan. The destruction of Jerusalem is a fearful and solemn warning to all who are trifling with the offers of divine grace and resisting the pleadings of divine mercy. Never was there given a more decisive testimony to God's hatred of sin and to the certain punishment that will fall upon the guilty.

The Saviour's prophecy concerning the visitation of judgments upon Jerusalem is to have another fulfillment, of which that terrible desolation was but a faint shadow. In the fate of the chosen city we may behold the doom of a world that has rejected God's mercy and trampled upon His law. Dark are the records of human misery that earth has witnessed during its long centuries of crime. The heart sickens, and the mind grows faint in contemplation. Terrible have been the results of rejecting the authority of Heaven. But a scene yet darker is presented in the revelations of the future. The records of 37 the past,—the long procession of tumults, conflicts, and revolutions, the "battle of the warrior . . . with confused noise, and garments rolled in blood" (Isaiah 9:5),—what are these, in contrast with the terrors of that day when the restraining Spirit of God shall be wholly withdrawn from the wicked, no longer to hold in check the outburst of human passion and satanic wrath! The world will then behold, as never before, the results of Satan's rule.

But in that day, as in the time of Jerusalem's destruction, God's people will be delivered, everyone that shall be found written among the living. Isaiah 4:3. Christ has declared that He will come the second time to gather His faithful ones to Himself: "Then shall all the tribes of the earth mourn, and they shall see the Son of man coming in the clouds of heaven with power and great glory. And He shall send His angels with a great sound of a trumpet, and they shall gather together His elect from the four winds, from one end of heaven to the other." Matthew 24:30, 31. Then shall they that obey not the gospel be consumed with the spirit of His mouth and be destroyed with the brightness of His coming. 2 Thessalonians 2:8. Like Israel of old the wicked destroy themselves; they fall by their iniquity. By a life of sin, they have placed themselves so out of harmony with God, their natures have become so debased with evil, that the manifestation of His glory is to them a consuming fire.

Let men beware lest they neglect the lesson conveyed to them in the words of Christ. As He warned His disciples of Jerusalem's destruction, giving them a sign of the approaching ruin, that they might make their escape; so He has warned the world of the day of final destruction and has given them tokens of its approach, that all who will may flee from the wrath to come. Jesus declares: "There shall be signs in the sun, and in the moon, and in the stars; and upon the earth distress of nations." Luke 21:25; Matthew 24:29; Mark 13:24-26; Revelation 6:12-17. Those who behold these harbingers of His coming are to "know that it is near, even at the 38 doors." Matthew 24:33. "Watch ye therefore," are His words of admonition. Mark 13:35. They that heed the warning shall not be left in darkness, that that day should overtake them unawares. But to them that will not watch, "the day of the Lord so cometh as a thief in the night." 1 Thessalonians 5:2-5.

The world is no more ready to credit the message for this time than were the Jews to receive the Saviour's warning concerning Jerusalem. Come when it may, the day of God will come unawares to the ungodly. When life is going on in its unvarying round; when men are absorbed in pleasure, in business, in traffic, in money-making; when religious leaders are magnifying the world's progress and enlightenment, and the people are lulled in a false security—then, as the midnight thief steals within the unguarded dwelling, so shall sudden destruction come upon the careless and ungodly, "and they shall not escape." Verse 3.

2

Persecution in the First Centuries

When Jesus revealed to His disciples the fate of Jerusalem and the scenes of the second advent, He foretold also the experience of His people from the time when He should be taken from them, to His return in power and glory for their deliverance. From Olivet the Saviour beheld the storms about to fall upon the apostolic church; and penetrating deeper into the future, His eye discerned the fierce, wasting tempest that were to beat upon His followers in the coming ages of darkness and persecution. In a few brief utterances of awful significance He foretold the portion which the rulers of this world would mete out to the church of God. Matthew 24:9, 21, 22. The followers of Christ must tread the same path of humiliation, reproach, and suffering which their Master trod. The enmity that burst forth against the world's Redeemer would be manifested against all who

39

should believe on His name.

The history of the early church testified to the fulfillment of the Saviour's words. The powers of earth and hell arrayed themselves against Christ in the person of His followers. Paganism foresaw that should the gospel triumph, her temples and altars would be swept away; therefore she summoned her forces to destroy Christianity. The fires of persecution were kindled. Christians were stripped of their possessions and driven from their homes. They "endured a great fight of afflictions." Hebrews 10:32. They "had trial of cruel mockings and scourgings, yea, moreover of bonds and imprisonment." Hebrews 11:36. Great numbers sealed their testimony with their blood. Noble and slave, rich and poor, learned and ignorant, were alike slain without mercy.

These persecutions, beginning under Nero about the time of the martyrdom of Paul, continued with greater or less fury for centuries. Christians were falsely accused of the most dreadful crimes and declared to be the cause of great calamities—famine, pestilence, and earthquake. As they became the objects of popular hatred and suspicion, informers stood ready, for the sake of gain, to betray the innocent. They were condemned as rebels against the empire, as foes of religion, and pests to society. Great numbers were thrown to wild beasts or burned alive in the amphitheaters. Some were crucified; others were covered with the skins of wild animals and thrust into the arena to be torn by dogs. Their punishment was often made the chief entertainment at public fetes. Vast multitudes assembled to enjoy the sight and greeted their dying agonies with laughter and applause.

Wherever they sought refuge, the followers of Christ were hunted like beasts of prey. They were forced to seek concealment in desolate and solitary places. "Destitute, afflicted, tormented; (of whom the world was not worthy:) they wandered in deserts, and in mountains, and in dens and caves of the earth." Verses 37, 38. The catacombs afforded shelter for thousands. Beneath the hills outside the city of Rome, long galleries had been tunneled through earth and rock; the dark and intricate network of passages extended for miles beyond the city walls. In these underground retreats the followers of Christ buried their dead; and here also, when suspected and proscribed, they found a home. When the Life-giver shall awaken those who have fought the good fight, many a martyr for Christ's sake will come forth from those gloomy caverns.

41 Under the fiercest persecution these witnesses for Jesus kept their faith unsullied. Though deprived of every comfort, shut away from the light of the sun, making their home in the dark but friendly bosom of the earth, they uttered no complaint. With words of faith, patience, and hope they encouraged one another to endure privation and distress. The loss of every earthly blessing could not force them to renounce their belief in Christ. Trials and persecution were but steps bringing them nearer their rest and their reward.

Like God's servants of old, many were "tortured, not accepting deliverance; that they might obtain a better resurrection." Verse 35. These called to mind the words of their Master, that when persecuted for Christ's sake, they were to be exceeding glad, for great would be their reward in heaven; for so the prophets had been persecuted before them. They rejoiced that they were accounted worthy to suffer for the truth, and songs of triumph ascended from the midst of crackling flames. Looking upward by faith, they saw Christ and angels leaning over the battlements of heaven, gazing upon them with the deepest interest and regarding their steadfastness with approval. A voice came down to them from the throne of God: "Be thou faithful unto death, and I will give thee a crown of life." Revelation 2:10.

In vain were Satan's efforts to destroy the church of Christ by violence. The great controversy in which the disciples of Jesus yielded up their lives did not cease when these faithful standard-bearers fell at their post. By defeat they conquered. God's workmen were slain, but His work went steadily forward. The gospel continued to spread and the number of its adherents to increase. It penetrated into regions that were inaccessible even to the eagles of Rome. Said a Christian, expostulating with the heathen rulers who were urging forward the persecution: You may "kill us, torture us, condemn us. . . . Your injustice is the proof that we are innocent .   42 . . . Nor does your cruelty . . . avail you." It was but a stronger invitation to bring others to their persuasion. "The oftener we are mown down by you, the more in number we grow; the blood of Christians is seed."—Tertullian, Apology, paragraph 50.

Thousands were imprisoned and slain, but others sprang up to fill their places. And those who were martyred for their faith were secured to Christ and accounted Him as conquerors. They had fought the good fight, and they were to receive the crown of glory when Christ should come. The sufferings which they endured brought Christians nearer to one another and to their Redeemer. Their living example and dying testimony were a constant witness for the truth; and where least expected, the subjects of Satan were leaving his service and enlisting under the banner of Christ.

Satan therefore laid his plans to war more successfully against the government of God by planting his banner in the Christian church. If the followers of Christ could be deceived and led to displease God, then their strength, fortitude, and firmness would fail, and they would fall an easy prey.

The great adversary now endeavored to gain by artifice what he had failed to secure by force. Persecution ceased, and in its stead were substituted the dangerous allurements of temporal prosperity and worldly honor. Idolaters were led to receive a part of the Christian faith, while they rejected other essential truths. They professed to accept Jesus as the Son of God and to believe in His death and resurrection, but they had no conviction of sin and felt no need of repentance or of a change of heart. With some concessions on their part they proposed that Christians should make concessions, that all might unite on the platform of belief in Christ.

Now the church was in fearful peril. Prison, torture, fire, and sword were blessings in comparison with this. Some of the Christians stood firm, declaring that they could make no compromise. Others were in favor of yielding or modifying some features of their faith and uniting with those who had accepted a part of Christianity, urging that this might be the means of their full conversion. That was a time of deep anguish to the faithful followers of Christ. Under a cloak of pretended Christianity, Satan was insinuating himself into the church, to corrupt their faith and turn their minds from the word of truth.

Most of the Christians at last consented to lower their standard, and a union was formed between Christianity and paganism. Although the worshipers of idols professed to be converted, and united with the church, they still clung to their idolatry, only changing the objects of their worship to images of Jesus, and even of Mary and the saints. The foul leaven of idolatry, thus brought into the church, continued its baleful work. Unsound doctrines, superstitious rites, and idolatrous ceremonies were incorporated into her faith and worship. As the followers of Christ united with idolaters, the Christian religion became corrupted, and the church lost her purity and power. There were some, however, who were not misled by these delusions. They still maintained their fidelity to the Author of truth and worshiped God alone.

There have ever been two classes among those who profess to be followers of Christ. While one class study the Saviour's life and earnestly seek to correct their defects and conform to the Pattern, the other class shun the plain, practical truths which expose their errors. Even in her best estate the church was not composed wholly of the true, pure, and sincere. Our Saviour taught that those who willfully indulge in sin are not to be received into the church; yet He connected with Himself men who were faulty in character, and granted them the benefits of His teachings and example, that they might have an opportunity to see their errors and correct them. Among the twelve apostles

was a traitor. Judas was accepted, not because of his defects of character, but notwithstanding them. He was connected with the disciples, that, through the instruction and example of Christ, he might learn what constitutes Christian character, and thus be led to see his errors, to repent, and, by the aid of divine grace, to purify his soul "in obeying the truth." But Judas did not walk in the light so graciously permitted to shine upon him. By indulgence in sin he invited the temptations of Satan. His evil traits of character became predominant. He yielded his mind to the control of the powers of darkness, he became angry when his faults were reproved, and thus he was led to commit the fearful crime of betraying his Master. So do all who cherish evil under a profession of godliness hate those who disturb their peace by condemning their course of sin. When a favorable opportunity is presented, they will, like Judas, betray those who for their good have sought to reprove them.

The apostles encountered those in the church who professed godliness while they were secretly cherishing iniquity. Ananias and Sapphira acted the part of deceivers, pretending to make an entire sacrifice for God, when they were covetously withholding a portion for themselves. The Spirit of truth revealed to the apostles the real character of these pretenders, and the judgments of God rid the church of this foul blot upon its purity. This signal evidence of the discerning Spirit of Christ in the church was a terror to hypocrites and evildoers. They could not long remain in connection with those who were, in habit and disposition, constant representatives of Christ; and as trials and persecution came upon His followers, those only who were willing to forsake all for the truth's sake desired to become His disciples. Thus, as long as persecution continued, the church remained comparatively pure. But as it ceased, converts were added who were less sincere and devoted, and the way was open for Satan to obtain a foothold.

But there is no union between the Prince of light and the prince of darkness, and there can be no union between their followers. When Christians consented to unite with those who were but half converted from paganism, they entered upon a path which led further and further from the truth. Satan exulted that he had succeeded in deceiving so large a number of the followers of Christ. He then brought his power to bear more fully upon these, and inspired them to persecute those who remained true to God. None understood so well how to oppose the true Christian faith as did those who had once been its defenders; and these apostate Christians, uniting with their half-pagan companions, directed their warfare against the most essential features of the doctrines of Christ.

It required a desperate struggle for those who would be faithful to stand firm against the deceptions and abominations which were disguised in sacerdotal garments and introduced into the church. The Bible was not accepted as the standard of faith. The doctrine of religious freedom was termed heresy, and its upholders were hated and proscribed.

After a long and severe conflict, the faithful few decided to dissolve all union with the apostate church if she still refused to free herself from falsehood and idolatry. They saw that separation was an absolute necessity if they would obey the word of God. They dared not tolerate errors fatal to their own souls, and set an example which would imperil the faith of their children and children's children. To secure peace and unity they were ready to make any concession consistent with fidelity to God; but they felt that even peace would be too dearly purchased at the sacrifice of principle. If unity could be secured only by the compromise of truth and righteousness, then let there be difference, and even war.

46   Well would it be for the church and the world if the principles that actuated those steadfast souls were revived in the hearts of God's professed people. There is an alarming indifference in regard to the doctrines which are the pillars of the Christian faith. The opinion is gaining ground, that, after all, these are not of vital importance. This degeneracy is strengthening the hands of the agents of Satan, so that false theories and fatal delusions which the faithful in ages past imperiled their lives to resist and expose, are now regarded with favor by thousands who claim to be followers of Christ.

The early Christians were indeed a peculiar people. Their blameless deportment and unswerving faith were a continual reproof that disturbed the sinner's peace. Though few in numbers, without wealth, position, or honorary titles, they were a terror to evildoers wherever their character and doctrines were known. Therefore they were hated by the wicked, even as Abel was hated by the ungodly Cain. For the same reason that Cain slew Abel, did those who sought to throw off the restraint of the Holy Spirit, put to death God's people. It was for the same reason that the Jews rejected and crucified the Saviour—because the purity and holiness of His character was a constant rebuke to their selfishness and corruption. From the days of Christ until now His faithful disciples have excited the hatred and opposition of those who love and follow the ways of sin.

How, then, can the gospel be called a message of peace? When Isaiah foretold the birth of the Messiah, he ascribed to Him the title, "Prince of Peace." When angels announced to the shepherds that Christ was born, they sang above the plains of Bethlehem: "Glory to God in the highest, and on earth peace, good will toward men." Luke 2:14. There is a seeming contradiction between these prophetic declarations and the words of Christ: "I came not to send peace, but a sword." Matthew 10:34. But, rightly understood, the two are in perfect harmony. The gospel is a message of peace. Christianity is a system which, received and obeyed, would spread peace, harmony, and happiness throughout the earth. The religion of Christ will unite in close brotherhood all who accept its teachings. It was the mission of Jesus to reconcile men to God, and thus to one another. But the world at large are under the control of Satan, Christ's bitterest foe. The gospel presents to them principles of life which are wholly at variance with their habits and desires, and they rise in rebellion against it. They hate the purity which reveals and condemns their sins, and they persecute and destroy those who would urge upon them its just and holy claims. It is in this sense—because the exalted truths it brings occasion hatred and strife—that the gospel is called a sword.

47

The mysterious providence which permits the righteous to suffer persecution at the hand of the wicked has been a cause of great perplexity to many who are weak in faith. Some are even ready to cast away their confidence in God because He suffers the basest of men to prosper, while the best and purest are afflicted and tormented by their cruel power. How, it is asked, can One who is just and merciful, and who is also infinite in power, tolerate such injustice and oppression? This is a question with which we have nothing to do. God has given us sufficient evidence of His love, and we are not to doubt His goodness because we cannot understand the workings of His providence. Said the Saviour to His disciples, foreseeing the doubts that would press upon their souls in days of trial and darkness: "Remember the word that I said unto you, The servant is not greater than his lord. If they have persecuted Me, they will also persecute you." John 15:20. Jesus suffered for us more than any of His followers can be made to suffer through the cruelty of wicked men. Those who are called to endure torture and martyrdom are but following in the steps of God's dear Son.

"The Lord is not slack concerning His promise." 2 Peter 3:9. He does not forget or neglect His children; but He permits the wicked to reveal their true character, that none who desire to do His will may be deceived concerning them. Again, the righteous are placed in the furnace of affliction, that they themselves may be purified; that their example may convince others of the reality of faith and godliness; and also that their consistent course may condemn the ungodly and unbelieving.

48

God permits the wicked to prosper and to reveal their enmity against Him, that when they shall have filled up the measure of their iniquity all may see His justice and mercy in their utter destruction. The day of His vengeance hastens, when all who have transgressed His law and oppressed His people will meet the just recompense of their deeds; when every act of cruelty or injustice toward God's faithful ones will be punished as though done to Christ Himself.

There is another and more important question that should engage the attention of the churches of today. The apostle Paul declares that "all that will live godly in Christ Jesus shall suffer persecution." 2 Timothy 3:12. Why is it, then, that persecution seems in a great degree to slumber? The only reason is that the church has conformed to the world's standard and therefore awakens no opposition. The religion which is current in our day is not of the pure and holy character that marked the Christian faith in the days of Christ and His apostles. It is only because of the spirit of compromise with sin, because the great truths of the word of God are so indifferently regarded, because there is so little vital godliness in the church, that Christianity is apparently so popular with the world. Let there be a revival of the faith and power of the early church, and the spirit of persecution will be revived, and the fires of persecution will be rekindled.

49

3

An Era of Spiritual Darkness

The apostle Paul, in his second letter to the Thessalonians, foretold the great apostasy which would result in the establishment of the papal power. He declared that the day of Christ should not come, "except there come a falling away first, and that man of sin be revealed, the son of perdition; who opposeth and exalteth himself above all that is called God, or that is worshiped; so that he as God sitteth in the temple of God, showing himself that he is God." And furthermore, the apostle warns his brethren that "the mystery of iniquity doth already work." 2 Thessalonians 2:3, 4, 7. Even at that early date he saw, creeping into the church, errors that would prepare the way for the development of the papacy.

Little by little, at first in stealth and silence, and then more openly as it increased in strength and gained control of the minds of men, "the mystery of iniquity" carried forward its deceptive and blasphemous work. Almost imperceptibly the customs of heathenism found their way into the Christian church. The spirit of compromise and conformity was restrained for a time by the fierce persecutions which the church endured under paganism. But as persecution ceased, and Christianity entered the courts and palaces of kings, she laid aside the humble simplicity of Christ and His apostles for the pomp and pride of pagan priests and rulers; and in place of the requirements of God, she substituted human theories and traditions. The nominal conversion of Constantine, in the early part of the fourth century, caused great rejoicing; and the world, cloaked with a form of righteousness, walked into the church. Now the work of corruption rapidly progressed. Paganism, while appearing to be vanquished, became the conqueror. Her spirit controlled the church. Her doctrines, ceremonies, and superstitions were incorporated into the faith and worship of the professed followers of Christ.

This compromise between paganism and Christianity resulted in the development of "the man of sin" foretold in prophecy as opposing and exalting himself above God. That gigantic system of false religion is a masterpiece of Satan's power—a monument of his efforts to seat himself upon the throne to rule the earth according to his will.

Satan once endeavored to form a compromise with Christ. He came to the Son of God in the wilderness of temptation, and showing Him all the kingdoms of the world and the glory of them, offered to give all into His hands if He would but acknowledge the supremacy of the prince of darkness. Christ rebuked the presumptuous tempter and forced him to depart. But Satan meets with greater success in presenting the same temptations to man. To secure worldly gains and honors, the church was led to seek the favor and support of the great men of earth; and having thus rejected Christ, she was induced to yield allegiance to the representative of Satan—the bishop of Rome.

It is one of the leading doctrines of Romanism that the pope is the visible head of the universal church of Christ, invested with supreme authority over bishops and pastors in all parts of the world. More than this, the pope has been given the very titles of Deity. He has been styled "Lord God the Pope" (see Appendix), and has been declared infallible. He demands the homage of all men. The same claim urged by Satan in the wilderness of temptation is still urged by him through the Church of Rome, and vast numbers are ready to yield him homage.

But those who fear and reverence God meet this heaven-daring assumption as Christ met the solicitations of the wily foe: "Thou shalt worship the Lord thy God, and Him only shalt thou serve." Luke 4:8. God has never given a hint in His word that He has appointed any man to be the head of the church. The doctrine of papal supremacy is directly opposed to the teachings of the Scriptures. The pope can have no power over Christ's church except by usurpation.

Romanists have persisted in bringing against Protestants the charge of heresy and willful separation from the true church. But these accusa-

50

51

49

tions apply rather to themselves. They are the ones who laid down the banner of Christ and departed from "the faith which was once delivered unto the saints." Jude 3.

Satan well knew that the Holy Scriptures would enable men to discern his deceptions and withstand his power. It was by the word that even the Saviour of the world had resisted his attacks. At every assault, Christ presented the shield of eternal truth, saying, "It is written." To every suggestion of the adversary, He opposed the wisdom and power of the word. In order for Satan to maintain his sway over men, and establish the authority of the papal usurper, he must keep them in ignorance of the Scriptures. The Bible would exalt God and place finite men in their true position; therefore its sacred truths must be concealed and suppressed. This logic was adopted by the Roman Church. For hundreds of years the circulation of the Bible was prohibited. The people were forbidden to read it or to have it in their houses, and unprincipled priests and prelates interpreted its teachings to sustain their pretensions. Thus the pope came to be almost universally acknowledged as the vicegerent of God on earth, endowed with authority over church and state.

The detector of error having been removed, Satan worked according to his will. Prophecy had declared that the papacy was to "think to 52 change times and laws." Daniel 7:25. This work it was not slow to attempt. To afford converts from heathenism a substitute for the worship of idols, and thus to promote their nominal acceptance of Christianity, the adoration of images and relics was gradually introduced into the Christian worship. The decree of a general council (see Appendix) finally established this system of idolatry. To complete the sacrilegious work, Rome presumed to expunge from the law of God the second commandment, forbidding image worship, and to divide the tenth commandment, in order to preserve the number.

The spirit of concession to paganism opened the way for a still further disregard of Heaven's authority. Satan, working through unconsecrated leaders of the church, tampered with the fourth commandment also, and essayed to set aside the ancient Sabbath, the day which God had blessed and sanctified (Genesis 2:2, 3), and in its stead to exalt the festival observed by the heathen as "the venerable day of the sun." This change was not at first attempted openly. In the first centuries the true Sabbath had been kept by all Christians. They were jealous for the honor of God, and, believing that His law is immutable, they zealously guarded the sacredness of its precepts. But with great subtlety Satan worked through his agents to bring about his object. That the attention of the people might be called to the Sunday, it was made a festival in honor of the resurrection of Christ.

Religious services were held upon it; yet it was regarded as a day of recreation, the Sabbath being still sacredly observed.

To prepare the way for the work which he designed to accomplish, Satan had led the Jews, before the advent of Christ, to load down the Sabbath with the most rigorous exactions, making its observance a burden. Now, taking advantage of the false light in which he had thus caused it to be regarded, he cast contempt upon it as a Jewish institution. While Christians generally continued to observe the Sunday as a joyous festival, he led them, in order to show their 53 hatred of Judaism, to make the Sabbath a fast, a day of sadness and gloom.

In the early part of the fourth century the emperor Constantine issued a decree making Sunday a public festival throughout the Roman Empire. (See Appendix.) The day of the sun was reverenced by his pagan subjects and was honored by Christians; it was the emperor's policy to unite the conflicting interests of heathenism and Christianity. He was urged to do this by the bishops of the church, who, inspired by ambition and thirst for power, perceived that if the same day was observed by both Christians and heathen, it would promote the nominal acceptance of Christianity by pagans and thus advance the power and glory of the church. But while many God-fearing Christians were gradually led to regard Sunday as possessing a degree of sacredness, they still held the true Sabbath as the holy of the Lord and observed it in obedience to the fourth commandment.

The archdeceiver had not completed his work. He was resolved to gather the Christian world under his banner and to exercise his power through his vicegerent, the proud pontiff who claimed to be the representative of Christ. Through half-converted pagans, ambitious prelates, and world-loving churchmen he accomplished his purpose. Vast councils were held from time to time, in which the dignitaries of the church were convened from all the world. In nearly every council the Sabbath which God had instituted was pressed down a little lower, while the Sunday was correspondingly exalted. Thus the pagan festival came finally to be honored as a divine institution, while the Bible Sabbath was pronounced a relic of Judaism, and its observers were declared to be accursed.

The great apostate had succeeded in exalting himself "above all that is called God, or that is worshiped." 2 Thessalonians 2:4. He had dared to change the only precept of the divine law that unmistakably points all mankind to the true and living God. In the fourth commandment, God is revealed as the Creator of the heavens and the 54 earth, and is thereby distinguished from all false gods. It was as a memorial of the work of creation that the seventh day was sanctified as a rest day for man. It was designed to keep the living God ever before the minds of men as the source of being and the object of reverence and worship. Satan strives to turn men from their allegiance to God, and from rendering obedience to His law; therefore he directs his efforts especially against that commandment which points to God as the Creator.

Protestants now urge that the resurrection of Christ on Sunday made it the Christian Sabbath. But Scripture evidence is lacking. No such honor was given to the day by Christ or His apostles. The observance of Sunday as a Christian institution had its origin in that "mystery of lawlessness" (2 Thessalonians 2:7, R.V.) which, even in Paul's day, had begun its work. Where and when did the Lord adopt this child of the papacy? What valid reason can be given for a change which the Scriptures do not sanction?

In the sixth century the papacy had become firmly established. Its seat of power was fixed in the imperial city, and the bishop of Rome was declared to be the head over the entire church. Paganism had given place to the papacy. The dragon had given to the beast "his power, and his seat, and great authority." Revelation 13:2. And now began the 1260 years of papal oppression foretold in the prophecies of Daniel and the Revelation. Daniel 7:25; Revelation 13:5-7. (See Appendix.) Christians were forced to choose either to yield their integrity and accept the papal ceremonies and worship, or to wear away their lives in dungeons or suffer death by the rack, the fagot, or the headsman's ax. Now were fulfilled the words of Jesus: "Ye shall be betrayed both by parents, and brethren, and kinsfolks, and friends; and some of you shall they cause to be put to death. And ye shall be hated of all men for My name's sake." Luke 21:16, 17. Persecution opened upon the faithful with greater fury than ever before, and the world became a vast battlefield. For hundreds of years the church of Christ found refuge in seclusion and obscurity. Thus says the prophet: "The woman fled into the wilderness, where she hath a place prepared of God, that they should feed her there a thousand two hundred and threescore days." Revelation 12:6.

The accession of the Roman Church to power marked the beginning of the Dark Ages. As her power increased, the darkness deepened. Faith was transferred from Christ, the true foundation, to the pope of Rome. Instead of trusting in the Son of God for forgiveness of sins and for eternal salvation, the people looked to the pope, and to the priests and prelates to whom he delegated authority. They were taught that the pope was their earthly mediator and that none could approach God except through him; and, further, that he stood in the place of God to them and was therefore to be implicitly obeyed. A deviation from his requirements was sufficient cause for the severest punishment to be visited upon the bodies and souls of the offenders. Thus the minds of the people were turned away from God to fallible, erring, and cruel men, nay, more, to the prince of darkness himself, who exercised his power through them. Sin was disguised in a garb of sanctity. When the Scriptures are suppressed, and man comes to regard himself as supreme, we need look only for fraud, deception, and debasing iniquity. With the elevation of human laws and traditions was manifest the corruption that ever results from setting aside the law of God.

Those were days of peril for the church of Christ. The faithful standard-bearers were few indeed. Though the truth was not left without witnesses, yet at times it seemed that error and superstition would wholly prevail, and true religion would be banished from the earth. The gospel was lost sight of, but the forms of religion were multiplied, and the people were burdened with rigorous exactions.

They were taught not only to look to the pope as their mediator, but to trust to works of their own to atone for sin. Long pilgrimages, acts of penance, the worship of relics, the erection of churches, shrines, and altars, the payment of large sums to the church—these and many similar acts were enjoined to appease the wrath of God or to secure His favor; as if God were like men, to be angered at trifles, or pacified by gifts or acts of penance!

Notwithstanding that vice prevailed, even among the leaders of the Roman Church, her influence seemed steadily to increase. About the close of the eighth century, papists put forth the claim that in the first ages of the church the bishops of Rome had possessed the same spiritual power which they now assumed. To establish this claim, some means must be employed to give it a show of authority; and this was readily suggested by the father of lies. Ancient writings were forged by monks. Decrees of councils before unheard of were discovered, establishing the universal supremacy of the pope from the earliest times. And a church that had rejected the truth greedily accepted these deceptions. (See Appendix.)

The few faithful builders upon the true foundation (1 Corinthians 3:10, 11) were perplexed and hindered as the rubbish of false doctrine obstructed the work. Like the builders upon the wall of Jerusalem in Nehemiah's day, some were ready to say: "The strength of the bearers of burdens is decayed, and there is much rubbish; so that we are not able to build." Nehemiah 4:10. Wearied with the constant struggle against persecution, fraud, iniquity, and every other obstacle that Satan could devise to hinder their progress, some who had been faithful builders became disheartened; and for the sake of peace and security for their property and their lives, they turned away from the true foundation. Others, undaunted by the opposition of their enemies, fearlessly declared: "Be not ye afraid of them: remember the Lord, which is great and terrible" (verse 14); and they proceeded with the work, everyone with his sword girded by his side. Ephesians 6:17.

57 The same spirit of hatred and opposition to the truth has inspired the enemies of God in every age, and the same vigilance and fidelity have been required in His servants. The words of Christ to the first disciples are applicable to His followers to the close of time: "What I say unto you I say unto all, Watch." Mark 13:37.

The darkness seemed to grow more dense. Image worship became more general. Candles were burned before images, and prayers were offered to them. The most absurd and superstitious customs prevailed. The minds of men were so completely controlled by superstition that reason itself seemed to have lost its sway. While priests and bishops were themselves pleasure-loving, sensual, and corrupt, it could only be expected that the people who looked to them for guidance would be sunken in ignorance and vice.

Another step in papal assumption was taken, when, in the eleventh century, Pope Gregory VII proclaimed the perfection of the Roman Church. Among the propositions which he put forth was one declaring that the church had never erred, nor would it ever err, according to the Scriptures. But the Scripture proofs did not accompany the assertion. The proud pontiff also claimed the power to depose emperors, and declared that no sentence which he pronounced could be reversed by anyone, but that it was his prerogative to reverse the decisions of all others. (See Appendix.)

A striking illustration of the tyrannical character of this advocate of infallibility was given in his treatment of the German emperor, Henry IV. For presuming to disregard the pope's authority, this monarch was declared to be excommunicated and dethroned. Terrified by the desertion and threats of his own princes, who were encouraged in rebellion against him by the papal mandate, Henry felt the necessity of making his peace with Rome. In company with his wife and a faithful servant he crossed the Alps in midwinter, that he might humble himself before the pope. Upon reaching the castle whither Gregory had withdrawn, he was conducted, without his guards, into an outer court, and there, in the severe cold of winter, with
58 uncovered head and naked feet, and in a miserable dress, he awaited the pope's permission to come into his presence. Not until he had continued three days fasting and making confession, did the pontiff condescend to grant him pardon. Even then it was only upon condition that the emperor should await the sanction of the pope before resuming the insignia or exercising the

power of royalty. And Gregory, elated with his triumph, boasted that it was his duty to pull down the pride of kings.

How striking the contrast between the overbearing pride of this haughty pontiff and the meekness and gentleness of Christ, who represents Himself as pleading at the door of the heart for admittance, that He may come in to bring pardon and peace, and who taught His disciples: "Whosoever will be chief among you, let him be your servant." Matthew 20:27.

The advancing centuries witnessed a constant increase of error in the doctrines put forth from Rome. Even before the establishment of the papacy the teachings of heathen philosophers had received attention and exerted an influence in the church. Many who professed conversion still clung to the tenets of their pagan philosophy, and not only continued its study themselves, but urged it upon others as a means of extending their influence among the heathen. Serious errors were thus introduced into the Christian faith. Prominent among these was the belief in man's natural immortality and his consciousness in death. This doctrine laid the foundation upon which Rome established the invocation of saints and the adoration of the Virgin Mary. From this sprang also the heresy of eternal torment for the finally impenitent, which was early incorporated into the papal faith.

Then the way was prepared for the introduction of still another invention of paganism, which Rome named purgatory, and employed to terrify the credulous and superstitious multitudes. By this heresy is affirmed the existence of a place of torment, in which the souls of such as have not merited eternal damnation are to suffer punishment for their sins, and from which, 59 when freed from impurity, they are admitted to heaven. (See Appendix.)

Still another fabrication was needed to enable Rome to profit by the fears and the vices of her adherents. This was supplied by the doctrine of indulgences. Full remission of sins, past, present, and future, and release from all the pains and penalties incurred, were promised to all who would enlist in the pontiff's wars to extend his temporal dominion, to punish his enemies, or to exterminate those who dared deny his spiritual supremacy. The people were also taught that by the payment of money to the church they might free themselves from sin, and also release the souls of their deceased friends who were confined in the tormenting flames. By such means did Rome fill her coffers and sustain the magnificence, luxury, and vice of the pretended representatives of Him who had not where to lay His head. (See Appendix.)

The Scriptural ordinance of the Lord's Supper had been supplanted by the idolatrous sacrifice of the mass. Papal priests pretended, by their senseless mummery, to convert the simple bread and wine into the actual "body and blood of Christ."—Cardinal Wiseman, The Real Presence of the Body and Blood of Our Lord Jesus Christ in the Blessed Eucharist, Proved From Scripture, lecture 8, sec. 3, par. 26. With blasphemous presumption, they openly claimed the power of creating God, the Creator of all things. Christians were required, on pain of death, to avow their faith in this horrible, Heaven-insulting heresy. Multitudes who refused were given to the flames. (See Appendix.)

In the thirteenth century was established that most terrible of all the engines of the papacy—the Inquisition. The prince of darkness wrought with the leaders of the papal hierarchy. In their secret councils Satan and his angels controlled the minds of evil men, while unseen in the midst stood an angel of God, taking the fearful record of their iniquitous decrees and writing the history of deeds too horrible to appear to human eyes. "Babylon the great" was "drunken with the blood of the saints." The mangled forms of millions of martyrs cried to God for vengeance upon that apostate power.

Popery had become the world's despot. Kings and emperors bowed to the decrees of the Roman pontiff. The destinies of men, both for time and for eternity, seemed under his control. For hundreds of years the doctrines of Rome had been extensively and implicitly received, its rites reverently performed, its festivals generally observed. Its clergy were honored and liberally sustained. Never since has the Roman Church attained to greater dignity, magnificence, or power.

But "the noon of the papacy was the midnight of the world."—J. A. Wylie, The History of Protestantism, b. 1, ch. 4. The Holy Scriptures were almost unknown, not only to the people, but to the priests. Like the Pharisees of old, the papal leaders hated the light which would reveal their sins. God's law, the standard of righteousness, having been removed, they exercised power without limit, and practiced vice without restraint. Fraud, avarice, and profligacy prevailed. Men shrank from no crime by which they could gain wealth or position. The palaces of popes and prelates were scenes of the vilest debauchery. Some of the reigning pontiffs were guilty of crimes so revolting that secular rulers endeavored to depose these dignitaries of the church as monsters too vile to be tolerated. For centuries Europe had made no progress in learning, arts, or civilization. A moral and intellectual paralysis had fallen upon Christendom.

The condition of the world under the Romish power presented a fearful and striking fulfillment of the words of the prophet Hosea: "My people are destroyed for lack of knowledge: because thou hast rejected knowledge, I will also reject thee: . . . seeing thou hast forgotten the law of thy God, I will also forget thy chil-

dren." "There is no truth, nor mercy, nor knowledge of God in the land. By swearing, and lying, and killing, and stealing, and committing adultery, they break out, and blood toucheth blood." Hosea 4:6, 1, 2. Such were the results of banishing the word of God.

4

The Waldenses

Amid the gloom that settled upon the earth during the long period of papal supremacy, the light of truth could not be wholly extinguished. In every age there were witnesses for God—men who cherished faith in Christ as the only mediator between God and man, who held the Bible as the only rule of life, and who hallowed the true Sabbath. How much the world owes to these men, posterity will never know. They were branded as heretics, their motives impugned, their characters maligned, their writings suppressed, misrepresented, or mutilated. Yet they stood firm, and from age to age maintained their faith in its purity, as a sacred heritage for the generations to come.

The history of God's people during the ages of darkness that followed upon Rome's supremacy is written in heaven, but they have little place in human records. Few traces of their existence can be found, except in the accusations of their persecutors. It was the policy of Rome to obliterate every trace of dissent from her doctrines or decrees. Everything heretical, whether persons or writings, she sought to destroy. Expressions of doubt, or questions as to the authority of papal dogmas, were enough to forfeit the life of rich or poor, high or low. Rome endeavored also to destroy every record of her cruelty toward dissenters. Papal councils decreed that books and writings containing such records should be committed to the flames. Before the invention of printing, books were few in number, and in a form not favorable for preservation; therefore there was little to prevent the Romanists from carrying out their purpose.

No church within the limits of Romish jurisdiction was long left undisturbed in the enjoyment of freedom of conscience. No sooner had the papacy obtained power than she stretched out her arms to crush all that refused to acknowledge her sway, and one after another the churches submitted to her dominion.

In Great Britain primitive Christianity had very early taken root. The gospel received by the Britons in the first centuries was then uncorrupted by Romish apostasy. Persecution from pagan emperors, which extended even to these far-off shores, was the only gift that the first churches of Britain received from Rome. Many of the Christians, fleeing from persecution in England, found refuge in Scotland; thence the truth was carried to Ireland, and in all these countries it was received with gladness.

When the Saxons invaded Britain, heathenism gained control. The conquerors disdained to be instructed by their slaves, and the Christians were forced to retreat to the mountains and the wild moors. Yet the light, hidden for a time, continued to burn. In Scotland, a century later, it shone out with a brightness that extended to far-distant lands. From Ireland came the pious Columba and his colaborers, who, gathering about them the scattered believers on the lonely island of Iona, made this the center of their missionary labors. Among these evangelists was an observer of the Bible Sabbath, and thus this truth was introduced among the people. A school was established at Iona, from which missionaries went out, not only to Scotland and England, but to Germany, Switzerland, and even Italy.

But Rome had fixed her eyes on Britain, and resolved to bring it under her supremacy. In the sixth century her missionaries undertook the
63 conversion of the heathen Saxons. They were received with favor by the proud barbarians, and they induced many thousands to profess the Romish faith. As the work progressed, the papal leaders and their converts encountered the primitive Christians. A striking contrast was presented. The latter were simple, humble, and Scriptural in character, doctrine, and manners, while the former manifested the superstition, pomp, and arrogance of popery. The emissary of Rome demanded that these Christian churches acknowledge the supremacy of the sovereign pontiff. The Britons meekly replied that they desired to love all men, but that the pope was not entitled to supremacy in the church, and they could render to him only that submission which was due to every follower of Christ. Repeated attempts were made to secure their allegiance to Rome; but these humble Christians, amazed at the pride displayed by her emissaries, steadfastly replied that they knew no other master than Christ. Now the true spirit of the papacy was revealed. Said the Romish leader: "If you will not receive brethren who bring you peace, you shall receive enemies who will bring you war. If you will not unite with us in showing the Saxons the way of life, you shall receive from them the stroke of death."—J. H. Merle D'Aubigné, History of the Reformation of the Sixteenth Century, b. 17, ch. 2. These were no idle threats. War, intrigue, and deception were employed against these witnesses for a Bible faith, until the churches of Britain were destroyed, or forced to submit to the authority of the pope.

In lands beyond the jurisdiction of Rome there existed for many centuries bodies of Christians who remained almost wholly free from papal corruption. They were surrounded by heathenism and in the lapse of ages were affected by its errors; but they continued to regard the Bible as the only rule of faith and adhered to many of its truths. These Christians believed in the perpetuity of the law of God and observed the Sabbath of the fourth commandment. Churches that held to this faith and practice existed in Central Africa and among the Armenians of Asia.

But of those who resisted the encroachments 64 of the papal power, the Waldenses stood foremost. In the very land where popery had fixed its seat, there its falsehood and corruption were most steadfastly resisted. For centuries the churches of Piedmont maintained their independence; but the time came at last when Rome insisted upon their submission. After ineffectual struggles against her tyranny, the leaders of these churches reluctantly acknowledged the supremacy of the power to which the whole world seemed to pay homage. There were some, however, who refused to yield to the authority of pope or prelate. They were determined to maintain their allegiance to God and to preserve the purity and simplicity of their faith. A separation took place. Those who adhered to the ancient faith now withdrew; some, forsaking their native Alps, raised the banner of truth in foreign lands; others retreated to the secluded glens and rocky fastnesses of the mountains, and there preserved their freedom to worship God.

The faith which for centuries was held and taught by the Waldensian Christians was in marked contrast to the false doctrines put forth from Rome. Their religious belief was founded upon the written word of God, the true system of Christianity. But those humble peasants, in their obscure retreats, shut away from the world, and bound to daily toil among their flocks and their vineyards, had not by themselves arrived at the truth in opposition to the dogmas and heresies of the apostate church. Theirs was not a faith newly received. Their religious belief was their inheritance from their fathers. They contended for the faith of the apostolic church,— "the faith which was once delivered unto the saints." Jude 3. "The church in the wilderness," and not the proud hierarchy enthroned in the world's great capital, was the true church of Christ, the guardian of the treasures of truth which God has committed to His people to be given to the world.

Among the leading causes that had led to the 65 separation of the true church from Rome was the hatred of the latter toward the Bible Sabbath. As foretold by prophecy, the papal power cast down the truth to the ground. The law of God was trampled in the dust, while the traditions and customs of men were exalted. The churches that were under the rule of the papacy were early compelled to honor the Sunday as a holy day. Amid the prevailing error and superstition, many, even of the true people of God, became so bewildered that while they observed the Sabbath, they refrained from labor also on the Sunday. But this did not satisfy the papal leaders. They demanded not only that Sunday be hallowed, but that the Sabbath be profaned; and they denounced in the strongest language those who dared to show it honor. It was only by fleeing from the power of Rome that any could obey God's law in peace. (See Appendix.)

The Waldenses were among the first of the peoples of Europe to obtain a translation of the Holy Scriptures. (See Appendix.) Hundreds of years before the Reformation they possessed the Bible in manuscript in their native tongue. They had the truth unadulterated, and this rendered them the special objects of hatred and persecution. They declared the Church of Rome to be the apostate Babylon of the Apocalypse, and at the peril of their lives they stood up to resist her corruptions. While, under the pressure of long-continued persecution, some compromised their faith, little by little yielding its distinctive principles, others held fast the truth. Through ages of darkness and apostasy there were Waldenses who denied the supremacy of Rome, who rejected image worship as idolatry, and who kept the true Sabbath. Under the fiercest tempests of opposition they maintained their faith. Though gashed by the Savoyard spear, and scorched by the Romish fagot, they stood unflinchingly for God's word and His honor.

Behind the lofty bulwarks of the mountains— in all ages the refuge of the persecuted and 66 oppressed—the Waldenses found a hiding place. Here the light of truth was kept burning amid the darkness of the Middle Ages. Here, for a thousand years, witnesses for the truth maintained the ancient faith.

God had provided for His people a sanctuary of awful grandeur, befitting the mighty truths committed to their trust. To those faithful exiles the mountains were an emblem of the immutable righteousness of Jehovah. They pointed their children to the heights towering above them in unchanging majesty, and spoke to them of Him with whom there is no variableness nor shadow of turning, whose word is as enduring as the everlasting hills. God had set fast the mountains and girded them with strength; no arm but that of Infinite Power could move them out of their place. In like manner He had established His law, the foundation of His government in heaven and upon earth. The arm of man might reach his fellow men and destroy their lives; but that arm could as readily uproot the mountains from their foundations, and hurl them into the sea, as it could change one precept of the law of Jehovah, or blot out one of His promises to those who do His will. In their fidelity to His law, God's servants should be as firm as the unchanging hills.

The mountains that girded their lowly valleys were a constant witness to God's creative power, and a never-failing assurance of His protecting care. Those pilgrims learned to love the silent symbols of Jehovah's presence. They indulged no repining because of the hardships of their lot; they were never lonely amid the mountain solitudes. They thanked God that He had provided for them an asylum from the wrath and cruelty of men. They rejoiced in their freedom to worship before Him. Often when pursued by their enemies, the strength of the hills proved a sure defense. From many a lofty cliff they chanted the praise of God, and the armies of Rome could not silence their songs of thanksgiving.

Pure, simple, and fervent was the piety of 67 these followers of Christ. The principles of truth they valued above houses and lands, friends, kindred, even life itself. These principles they earnestly sought to impress upon the hearts of the young. From earliest childhood the youth were instructed in the Scriptures and taught to regard sacredly the claims of the law of God. Copies of the Bible were rare; therefore its precious words were committed to memory. Many were able to repeat large portions of both the Old and the New Testament. Thoughts of God were associated alike with the sublime scenery of nature and with the humble blessings of daily life. Little children learned to look with gratitude to God as the giver of every favor and every comfort.

Parents, tender and affectionate as they were, loved their children too wisely to accustom them to self-indulgence. Before them was a life of trial and hardship, perhaps a martyr's death. They were educated from childhood to endure hardness, to submit to control, and yet to think and act for themselves. Very early they were taught to bear responsibilities, to be guarded in speech, and to understand the wisdom of silence. One indiscreet word let fall in the hearing of their enemies might imperil not only the life of the speaker, but the lives of hundreds of his brethren; for as wolves hunting their prey did the enemies of truth pursue those who dared to claim freedom of religious faith.

The Waldenses had sacrificed their worldly prosperity for the truth's sake, and with persevering patience they toiled for their bread. Every spot of tillable land among the mountains was carefully improved; the valleys and the less fertile hillsides were made to yield their increase. Economy and severe self-denial formed a part of the education which the children received as their only legacy. They were taught that God designs life to be a discipline, and that their wants could be supplied only by personal labor, by forethought, care, and faith. The process was laborious and wearisome, but it was wholesome, just what man needs in his fallen state, the school which God has provided for his training and development. While the youth were inured to toil and hardship, the culture of the intellect was not neglected. They were taught that all their powers belonged to God, and that all were to be improved and developed for His service.

The Vaudois churches, in their purity and simplicity, resembled the church of apostolic times. Rejecting the supremacy of the pope and prelate, they held the Bible as the only supreme, infallible authority. Their pastors, unlike the lordly priests of Rome, followed the example of their Master, who "came not to be ministered unto, but to minister." They fed the flock of God, leading them to the green pastures and living fountains of His holy word. Far from the monuments of human pomp and pride the people assembled, not in magnificent churches or grand cathedrals, but beneath the shadow of the mountains, in the Alpine valleys, or, in time of danger, in some rocky stronghold, to listen to the words of truth from the servants of Christ. The pastors not only preached the gospel, but they visited the sick, catechized the children, admonished the erring, and labored to settle disputes and promote harmony and brotherly love. In times of peace they were sustained by the freewill offerings of the people; but, like Paul the tentmaker, each learned some trade or profession by which, if necessary, to provide for his own support.

From their pastors the youth received instruction. While attention was given to branches of general learning, the Bible was made the chief study. The Gospels of Matthew and John were committed to memory, with many of the Epistles. They were employed also in copying the Scriptures. Some manuscripts contained the whole Bible, others only brief selections, to which some simple explanations of the text were added by those who were able to expound the Scriptures. Thus were brought forth the treasures of truth so long concealed by those who sought to exalt themselves above God.

By patient, untiring labor, sometimes in the deep, dark caverns of the earth, by the light of torches, the Sacred Scriptures were written out, verse by verse, chapter by chapter. Thus the work went on, the revealed will of God shining out like pure gold; how much brighter, clearer, and more powerful because of the trials undergone for its sake only those could realize who were engaged in the work. Angels from heaven surrounded these faithful workers.

Satan had urged on the papal priests and prelates to bury the word of truth beneath the rubbish of error, heresy, and superstition; but in a most wonderful manner it was preserved uncorrupted through all the ages of darkness. It bore not the stamp of man, but the impress of God. Men have been unwearied in their efforts to obscure the plain, simple meaning of the Scriptures, and to make them contradict their own testimony; but like the ark upon the billowy deep, the word of God outrides the storms that threaten it with destruction. As the mine has rich veins of gold and silver hidden beneath the surface, so that all must dig who would discover its precious stores, so the Holy Scriptures have treasures of truth that are revealed only to the earnest, humble, prayerful seeker. God designed the Bible to be a lessonbook to all mankind, in childhood, youth, and manhood, and to be studied through all time. He gave His word to men as a revelation of Himself. Every new truth discerned is a fresh disclosure of the character of its Author. The study of the Scriptures is the means divinely ordained to bring men into closer connection with their Creator and to give them a clearer knowledge of His will. It is the medium of communication between God and man.

While the Waldenses regarded the fear of the Lord as the beginning of wisdom, they were not blind to the importance of a contact with the world, a knowledge of men and of active life, in expanding the mind and quickening the perceptions. From their schools in the mountains some of the youth were sent to institutions of learning in the cities of France or Italy, where was a more extended field for study, thought, and observation than in their native Alps. The youth thus sent forth were exposed to temptation, they witnessed vice, they encountered Satan's wily agents, who urged upon them the most subtle heresies and the most dangerous deceptions. But their education from childhood had been of a character to prepare them for all this.

In the schools whither they went, they were not to make confidants of any. Their garments were so prepared as to conceal their greatest treasure—the precious manuscripts of the Scriptures. These, the fruit of months and years of toil, they carried with them, and whenever they could do so without exciting suspicion, they cautiously placed some portion in the way of those whose hearts seemed open to receive the truth. From their mother's knee the Waldensian youth had been trained with this purpose in view; they understood their work and faithfully performed it. Converts to the true faith were won in these institutions of learning, and frequently its principles were found to be permeating the entire school; yet the papal leaders could not, by the closest inquiry, trace the so-called corrupting heresy to its source.

The spirit of Christ is a missionary spirit. The very first impulse of the renewed heart is to bring others also to the Saviour. Such was the spirit of the Vaudois Christians. They felt that

God required more of them than merely to preserve the truth in its purity in their own churches; that a solemn responsibility rested upon them to let their light shine forth to those who were in darkness; by the mighty power of God's word they sought to break the bondage which Rome had imposed. The Vaudois ministers were trained as missionaries, everyone who expected to enter the ministry being required first to gain an experience as an evangelist. Each was to serve three years in some mission field before taking charge of a church at home. This service, requiring at the outset self-denial and sacrifice, was a fitting introduction to the pastor's life in those times that tried men's souls. The youth who received ordination to the sacred office saw before them, not the prospect of earthly wealth and glory, but a life of toil and danger, and possibly a martyr's fate. The missionaries went out two and two, as Jesus sent forth His disciples. With each young man was usually associated a man of age and experience, the youth being under the guidance of his companion, who was held responsible for his training, and whose instruction he was required to heed. These colaborers were not always together, but often met for prayer and counsel, thus strengthening each other in the faith.

To have made known the object of their mission would have ensured its defeat; therefore they carefully concealed their real character. Every minister possessed a knowledge of some trade or profession, and the missionaries prosecuted their work under cover of a secular calling. Usually they chose that of merchant or peddler. "They carried silks, jewelry, and other articles, at that time not easily purchasable save at distant marts; and they were welcomed as merchants where they would have been spurned as missionaries."—Wylie, b. 1, ch. 7. All the while their hearts were uplifted to God for wisdom to present a treasure more precious than gold or gems. They secretly carried about with them copies of the Bible, in whole or in part; and whenever an opportunity was presented, they called the attention of their customers to these manuscripts. Often an interest to read God's word was thus awakened, and some portion was gladly left with those who desired to receive it.

The work of these missionaries began in the plains and valleys at the foot of their own mountains, but it extended far beyond these limits. With naked feet and in garments coarse and travel-stained as were those of their Master, they passed through great cities and penetrated to distant lands. Everywhere they scattered the precious seed. Churches sprang up in their path, and the blood of martyrs witnessed for the truth. The day of God will reveal a rich harvest of souls garnered by the labors of these faithful men. Veiled and silent, the word of God was making its way through Christendom and meeting a glad reception in the homes and hearts of men.

To the Waldenses the Scriptures were not merely a record of God's dealings with men in the past, and a revelation of the responsibilities and duties of the present, but an unfolding of the perils and glories of the future. They believed that the end of all things was not far distant, and as they studied the Bible with prayer and tears they were the more deeply impressed with its precious utterances and with their duty to make known to others its saving truths. They saw the plan of salvation clearly revealed in the sacred pages, and they found comfort, hope, and peace in believing in Jesus. As the light illuminated their understanding and made glad their hearts, they longed to shed its beams upon those who were in the darkness of papal error.

They saw that under the guidance of pope and priest, multitudes were vainly endeavoring to obtain pardon by afflicting their bodies for the sin of their souls. Taught to trust to their good works to save them, they were ever looking to themselves, their minds dwelling upon their sinful condition, seeing themselves exposed to the wrath of God, afflicting soul and body, yet finding no relief. Thus conscientious souls were bound by the doctrines of Rome. Thousands abandoned friends and kindred, and spent their lives in convent cells. By oft-repeated fasts and cruel scourgings, by midnight vigils, by prostration for weary hours upon the cold, damp stones of their dreary abode, by long pilgrimages, by humiliating penance and fearful torture, thousands vainly sought to obtain peace of conscience. Oppressed with a sense of sin, and haunted with the fear of God's avenging wrath, many suffered on, until exhausted nature gave way, and without one ray of light or hope they sank into the tomb.

The Waldenses longed to break to these starving souls the bread of life, to open to them the messages of peace in the promises of God, and to point them to Christ as their only hope of salvation. The doctrine that good works can atone for the transgression of God's law they held to be based upon falsehood. Reliance upon human merit intercepts the view of Christ's infinite love. Jesus died as a sacrifice for man because the fallen race can do nothing to recommend themselves to God. The merits of a crucified and risen Saviour are the foundation of the Christian's faith. The dependence of the soul upon Christ is as real, and its connection with Him must be as close, as that of a limb to the body, or of a branch to the vine.

The teachings of popes and priests had led men to look upon the character of God, and even of Christ, as stern, gloomy, and forbidding. The Saviour was represented as so far devoid of sympathy with man in his fallen state that the mediation of priests and saints must be invoked.

Those whose minds had been enlightened by the word of God longed to point these souls to Jesus as their compassionate, loving Saviour, standing with outstretched arms, inviting all to come to Him with their burden of sin, their care and weariness. They longed to clear away the obstructions which Satan had piled up that men might not see the promises, and come directly to God, confessing their sins, and obtaining pardon and peace.

Eagerly did the Vaudois missionary unfold to the inquiring mind the precious truths of the gospel. Cautiously he produced the carefully written portions of the Holy Scriptures. It was his greatest joy to give hope to the conscientious, sin-stricken soul, who could see only a God of vengeance, waiting to execute justice. With quivering lip and tearful eye did he, often on bended knees, open to his brethren the precious promises that reveal the sinner's only hope. Thus the light of truth penetrated many a darkened mind, rolling back the cloud of gloom, until the Sun of Righteousness shone into the heart with healing in His beams. It was often the case that some portion of Scripture was read again and again, the hearer desiring it to be repeated, as if he would assure himself that he had heard aright. Especially was the repetition of these words eagerly desired: "The blood of Jesus Christ His Son cleanseth us from all sin." 1 John 1:7. "As Moses lifted up the serpent in the wilderness, even so must the Son of man be lifted up: that whosoever believeth in Him should not perish, but have eternal life." John 3:14, 15.

Many were undeceived in regard to the claims of Rome. They saw how vain is the mediation of men or angels in behalf of the sinner. As the true light dawned upon their minds they exclaimed with rejoicing: "Christ is my priest; His blood is my sacrifice; His altar is my confessional." They cast themselves wholly upon the merits of Jesus, repeating the words, "Without faith it is impossible to please Him." Hebrews 11:6. "There is none other name under heaven given among men, whereby we must be saved." Acts 4:12.

The assurance of a Saviour's love seemed too much for some of these poor tempest-tossed souls to realize. So great was the relief which it brought, such a flood of light was shed upon them, that they seemed transported to heaven. Their hands were laid confidingly in the hand of Christ; their feet were planted upon the Rock of Ages. All fear of death was banished. They could now covet the prison and the fagot if they might thereby honor the name of their Redeemer.

In secret places the word of God was thus brought forth and read, sometimes to a single soul, sometimes to a little company who were longing for light and truth. Often the entire night was spent in this manner. So great would be the wonder and admiration of the listeners that the messenger of mercy was not infrequently compelled to cease his reading until the understanding could grasp the tidings of salvation. Often would words like these be uttered: "Will God indeed accept *my* offering? Will He smile upon *me*? Will He pardon *me*?" The answer was read: "Come unto Me, all ye that labor and are heavy-laden, and I will give you rest." Matthew 11:28.

Faith grasped the promise, and the glad response was heard: "No more long pilgrimages to make; no more painful journeys to holy shrines. I may come to Jesus just as I am, sinful and unholy, and He will not spurn the penitential prayer. 'Thy sins be forgiven thee.' Mine, even mine, may be forgiven!"

A tide of sacred joy would fill the heart, and the name of Jesus would be magnified by praise and thanksgiving. Those happy souls returned to their homes to diffuse light, to repeat to others, as well as they could, their new experience; that they had found the true and living Way. There was a strange and solemn power in the words of Scripture that spoke directly to the hearts of those who were longing for the truth. It was the voice of God, and it carried conviction to those who heard.

The messenger of truth went on his way; but his appearance of humility, his sincerity, his earnestness and deep fervor, were subjects of frequent remark. In many instances his hearers had not asked him whence he came or whither he went. They had been so overwhelmed, at first with surprise, and afterward with gratitude and joy, that they had not thought to question him. When they had urged him to accompany them to their homes, he had replied that he must visit the lost sheep of the flock. Could he have been an angel from heaven? they queried.

In many cases the messenger of truth was seen no more. He had made his way to other lands, or he was wearing out his life in some unknown dungeon, or perhaps his bones were whitening on the spot where he had witnessed for the truth. But the words he had left behind could not be destroyed. They were doing their work in the hearts of men; the blessed results will be fully known only in the judgment.

The Waldensian missionaries were invading the kingdom of Satan, and the powers of darkness aroused to greater vigilance. Every effort to advance the truth was watched by the prince of evil, and he excited the fears of his agents. The papal leaders saw a portent of danger to their cause from the labors of these humble itinerants. If the light of truth were allowed to shine unobstructed, it would sweep away the heavy clouds of error that enveloped the people. It would direct the minds of men to God alone and would eventually destroy the supremacy of Rome.

The very existence of this people, holding the faith of the ancient church, was a constant testimony to Rome's apostasy, and therefore excited the most bitter hatred and persecution. Their refusal to surrender the Scriptures was also an offense that Rome could not tolerate. She determined to blot them from the earth. Now began the most terrible crusades against God's people in their mountain homes. Inquisitors were put upon their track, and the scene of innocent Abel falling before the murderous Cain was often repeated.

Again and again were their fertile lands laid waste, their dwellings and chapels swept away, so that where once were flourishing fields and the homes of an innocent, industrious people, there remained only a desert. As the ravenous beast is rendered more furious by the taste of blood, so the rage of the papists was kindled to greater intensity by the sufferings of their victims. Many of these witnesses for a pure faith were pursued across the mountains and hunted down in the valleys where they were hidden, shut in by mighty forests and pinnacles of rock.

No charge could be brought against the moral character of this proscribed class. Even their enemies declared them to be a peaceable, quiet, pious people. Their grand offense was that they 77 would not worship God according to the will of the pope. For this crime every humiliation, insult, and torture that men or devils could invent was heaped upon them.

When Rome at one time determined to exterminate the hated sect, a bull was issued by the pope, condemning them as heretics, and delivering them to slaughter. (See Appendix.) They were not accused as idlers, or dishonest, or disorderly; but it was declared that they had an appearance of piety and sanctity that seduced "the sheep of the true fold." Therefore the pope ordered "that malicious and abominable sect of malignants," if they "refuse to abjure, to be crushed like venomous snakes."—Wylie, b. 16, ch. 1. Did this haughty potentate expect to meet those words again? Did he know that they were registered in the books of heaven, to confront him at the judgment? "Inasmuch as ye have done it unto one of the least of these My brethren," said Jesus, "ye have done it unto Me." Matthew 25:40.

This bull called upon all members of the church to join in the crusade against the heretics. As an incentive to engage in this cruel work, it "absolved from all ecclesiastical pains and penalties, general and particular; it released all who joined the crusade from any oaths they might have taken; it legitimatized their title to any property they might have illegally acquired; and promised remission of all their sins to such as should kill any heretic. It annulled all contracts made in favor of Vaudois, ordered their domestics to abandon them, forbade all persons to give them any aid whatever, and empowered all persons to take possession of their property."—Wylie, b. 16, ch. 1. This document clearly reveals the master spirit behind the scenes. It is the roar of the dragon, and not the voice of Christ, that is heard therein.

The papal leaders would not conform their characters to the great standard of God's law, but erected a standard to suit themselves, and determined to compel all to conform to this because Rome willed it. The most horrible tragedies were enacted. Corrupt and blasphemous priests and popes were doing the work which Satan appointed them. Mercy had no 78 place in their natures. The same spirit that crucified Christ and slew the apostles, the same that moved the bloodthirsty Nero against the faithful in his day, was at work to rid the earth of those who were beloved of God.

The persecutions visited for many centuries upon this God-fearing people were endured by them with a patience and constancy that honored their Redeemer. Notwithstanding the crusades against them, and the inhuman butchery to which they were subjected, they continued to send out their missionaries to scatter the precious truth. They were hunted to death; yet their blood watered the seed sown, and it failed not of yielding fruit. Thus the Waldenses witnessed for God centuries before the birth of Luther. Scattered over many lands, they planted the seeds of the Reformation that began in the time of Wycliffe, grew broad and deep in the days of Luther, and is to be carried forward to the close of time by those who also are willing to suffer all things for "the word of God, and for the testimony of Jesus Christ." Revelation 1:9.

5

79

John Wycliffe

Before the Reformation there were at times but very few copies of the Bible in existence, but God had not suffered His word to be wholly destroyed. Its truths were not to be forever hidden. He could as easily unchain the words of life as He could open prison doors and unbolt iron gates to set His servants free. In the different countries of Europe men were moved by the Spirit of God to search for the truth as for hid treasures. Providentially guided to the Holy Scriptures, they studied the sacred pages with intense interest. They were willing to accept the light at any cost to themselves. Though they did not see all things clearly, they were enabled to perceive many long-buried truths. As Heaven-sent messengers they went forth, rending asunder the chains of error and superstition, and calling upon those who had been so long enslaved, to arise and assert their liberty.

Except among the Waldenses, the word of God had for ages been locked up in languages known only to the learned; but the time had come for the Scriptures to be translated and given to the people of different lands in their native tongue. The world had passed its midnight. The hours of darkness were wearing away, and in many lands appeared tokens of the coming dawn.

80　　In the fourteenth century arose in England the "morning star of the Reformation." John Wycliffe was the herald of reform, not for England alone, but for all Christendom. The great protest against Rome which it was permitted him to utter was never to be silenced. That protest opened the struggle which was to result in the emancipation of individuals, of churches, and of nations.

Wycliffe received a liberal education, and with him the fear of the Lord was the beginning of wisdom. He was noted at college for his fervent piety as well as for his remarkable talents and sound scholarship. In his thirst for knowledge he sought to become acquainted with every branch of learning. He was educated in the scholastic philosophy, in the canons of the church, and in the civil law, especially that of his own country. In his after labors the value of this early training was apparent. A thorough acquaintance with the speculative philosophy of his time enabled him to expose its errors; and by his study of national and ecclesiastical law he was prepared to engage in the great struggle for civil and religious liberty. While he could wield the weapons drawn from the word of God, he had acquired the intellectual discipline of the schools, and he understood the tactics of the schoolmen. The power of his genius and the extent and thoroughness of his knowledge commanded the respect of both friends and foes. His adherents saw with satisfaction that their champion stood foremost among the leading minds of the nation; and his enemies were prevented from casting contempt upon the cause of reform by exposing the ignorance or weakness of its supporter.

While Wycliffe was still at college, he entered upon the study of the Scriptures. In those early times, when the Bible existed only in the ancient languages, scholars were enabled to find their way to the fountain of truth, which was closed to the uneducated classes. Thus already the way had been prepared for

81　　Wycliffe's future work as a Reformer. Men of learning had studied the word of God and had found the great truth of His free grace there revealed. In their teachings they had spread a knowledge of this truth, and had led others to turn to the living oracles.

When Wycliffe's attention was directed to the Scriptures, he entered upon their investigation with the same thoroughness which had enabled him to master the learning of the schools. Heretofore he had felt a great want, which neither his scholastic studies nor the teaching of the church could satisfy. In the word of God he found that which he had before sought in vain. Here he saw the plan of salvation revealed and Christ set forth as the only advocate for man. He gave himself to the service of Christ and determined to proclaim the truths he had discovered.

Like after Reformers, Wycliffe did not, at the opening of his work, foresee whither it would lead him. He did not set himself deliberately in opposition to Rome. But devotion to truth could not but bring him in conflict with falsehood. The more clearly he discerned the errors of the papacy, the more earnestly he presented the teaching of the Bible. He saw that Rome had forsaken the word of God for human tradition; he fearlessly accused the priesthood of having banished the Scriptures, and demanded that the Bible be restored to the people and that its authority be again established in the church. He was an able and earnest teacher and an eloquent preacher, and his daily life was a demonstration of the truths he preached. His knowledge of the Scriptures, the force of his reasoning, the purity of his life, and his unbending courage and integrity won for him general esteem and confidence. Many of the people had become dissatisfied with their former faith as they saw the iniquity that prevailed in the Roman Church, and they hailed with unconcealed joy the truths brought to view by Wycliffe; but the papal leaders were filled with rage when they perceived that this Reformer was gaining an influence greater than their own.

Wycliffe was a keen detector of error, and he 82 struck fearlessly against many of the abuses sanctioned by the authority of Rome. While acting as chaplain for the king, he took a bold stand against the payment of tribute claimed by the pope from the English monarch and showed that the papal assumption of authority over secular rulers was contrary to both reason and revelation. The demands of the pope had excited great indignation, and Wycliffe's teachings exerted an influence upon the leading minds of the nation. The king and the nobles united in denying the pontiff's claim to temporal authority and in refusing the payment of the tribute. Thus an effectual blow was struck against the papal supremacy in England.

Another evil against which the Reformer waged long and resolute battle was the institution of the orders of mendicant friars. These friars swarmed in England, casting a blight upon the greatness and prosperity of the nation. Industry, education, morals, all felt the withering influence. The monk's life of idleness and beggary was not only a heavy drain upon the resources of the people, but it brought useful labor into contempt. The youth were demoralized and corrupted. By the influence of the friars many were induced to enter a cloister and devote themselves to a monastic life, and this not only without the consent of their parents, but even without their knowledge and contrary to their commands. One of the early Fathers of the Roman Church, urging the claims of monasticism above the obligations of filial love and duty, had declared: "Though thy father should lie before thy door weeping and lamenting, and thy mother should show the body that bore thee and the breasts that nursed thee, see that thou trample them underfoot, and go onward straightway to Christ." By this "monstrous inhumanity," as Luther afterward styled it, "savoring more of the wolf and the tyrant than of the Christian and the man," were the hearts of children steeled against their parents.—Barnas Sears, The Life of Luther, pages 70, 69. Thus did the papal leaders, like the Pharisees of old, make the commandment of God of none effect by their tradition. Thus homes were made desolate and parents were deprived of the society of their sons and daughters.

Even the students in the universities were deceived by the false representations of the monks and induced to join their orders. Many afterward repented this step, seeing that they had blighted their own lives and had brought sorrow upon their parents; but once fast in the snare it was impossible for them to obtain their freedom. Many parents, fearing the influence of the monks, refused to send their sons to the universities. There was a marked falling off in the number of students in attendance at the great centers of learning. The schools languished, and ignorance prevailed.

The pope had bestowed on these monks the power to hear confessions and to grant pardon. This became a source of great evil. Bent on enhancing their gains, the friars were so ready to grant absolution that criminals of all descriptions resorted to them, and, as a result, the worst vices rapidly increased. The sick and the poor were left to suffer, while the gifts that should have relieved their wants went to the monks, who with threats demanded the alms of the people, denouncing the impiety of those who should withhold gifts from their orders. Notwithstanding their profession of poverty, the wealth of the friars was constantly increasing, and their magnificent edifices and luxurious tables made more apparent the growing poverty of the nation. And while spending their time in luxury and pleasure, they sent out in their stead ignorant men, who could only recount marvelous tales, legends, and jests to amuse the people and make them still more completely the dupes of the monks. Yet the friars continued to maintain their hold on the superstitious multitudes and led them to believe that all religious duty was comprised in acknowledging the supremacy of the pope, adoring the saints, and making gifts to the monks, and that this was sufficient to secure them a place in heaven.

Men of learning and piety had labored in vain to bring about a reform in these monastic orders; but Wycliffe, with clearer insight, struck at the root of the evil, declaring that the system itself was false and that it should be abolished. Discussion and inquiry were awakening. As the monks traversed the country, vending the pope's pardons, many were led to doubt the possibility of purchasing forgiveness with money, and they questioned whether they should not seek pardon from God rather than from the pontiff of Rome. (See Appendix note for page 59.) Not a few were alarmed at the rapacity of the friars, whose greed seemed never to be satisfied. "The monks and priests of Rome," said they, "are eating us away like a cancer. God must deliver us, or the people will perish."—D'Aubigné, b. 17, ch. 7. To cover their avarice, these begging monks claimed that they were following the Saviour's example, declaring that Jesus and His disciples had been supported by the charities of the people. This claim resulted in injury to their cause, for it led many to the Bible to learn the truth for themselves—a result which of all others was least desired by Rome. The minds of men were directed to the Source of truth, which it was her object to conceal.

Wycliffe began to write and publish tracts against the friars, not, however, seeking so much to enter into dispute with them as to call the minds of the people to the teachings of the Bible and its Author. He declared that the power of pardon or of excommunication is possessed by the pope in no greater degree than by common priests, and that no man can be truly excommunicated unless he has first brought upon himself the condemnation of God. In no more effectual way could he have undertaken the overthrow of that mammoth fabric of spiritual and temporal dominion which the pope had erected and in which the souls and bodies of millions were held captive.

Again Wycliffe was called to defend the rights of the English crown against the encroachments of Rome; and being appointed a royal ambassador, he spent two years in the Netherlands, in conference with the commissioners of the pope. Here he was brought into communication with ecclesiastics from France, Italy, and Spain, and he had an opportunity to look behind the scenes and gain a knowledge of many things which would have remained hidden from him in England. He learned much that was to give point to his after labors. In these representatives from the papal court he read the true character and aims of the hierarchy. He returned to England to repeat his former teachings more openly and with greater zeal, declaring that covetousness, pride, and deception were the gods of Rome.

In one of his tracts he said, speaking of the pope and his collectors: "They draw out of our land poor men's livelihood, and many thousand marks, by the year, of the king's money, for sacraments and spiritual things, that is cursed heresy of simony, and maketh all Christendom assent and maintain this heresy. And certes though our realm had a huge hill of gold, and never other man took thereof but only this proud worldly priest's collector, by process of time this hill must be spended; for he taketh ever money out of our land, and sendeth nought again but God's curse for his simony."—John Lewis, History of the Life and Sufferings of J. Wiclif, page 37.

Soon after his return to England, Wycliffe received from the king the appointment to the rectory of Lutterworth. This was an assurance that the monarch at least had not been displeased by his plain speaking. Wycliffe's influence was felt in shaping the action of the court, as well as in molding the belief of the nation.

The papal thunders were soon hurled against him. Three bulls were dispatched to England,— to the university, to the king, and to the prelates,—all commanding immediate and decisive measures to silence the teacher of heresy. (Augustus Neander, General History of the Christian Religion and Church, period 6, sec. 2, pt. 1, par. 8. See also Appendix.) Before the arrival of the bulls, however, the bishops, in their zeal, had summoned Wycliffe before them for trial. But two of the most powerful princes in the kingdom accompanied him to the tribunal; and the people, surrounding the building and rushing in, so intimidated the judges that the proceedings were for the time suspended, and he was allowed to go his way in peace. A little later, Edward III, whom in his old age the prelates were seeking to influence against the Reformer, died, and Wycliffe's former protector became regent of the kingdom.

But the arrival of the papal bulls laid upon all England a peremptory command for the arrest and imprisonment of the heretic. These measures pointed directly to the stake. It appeared certain that Wycliffe must soon fall a prey to the vengeance of Rome. But He who declared to one of old, "Fear not: . . . I am thy shield" (Genesis 15:1), again stretched out His hand to protect His servant. Death came, not to the Reformer, but to the pontiff who had decreed his destruction. Gregory XI died, and the ecclesiastics who had assembled for Wycliffe's trial, dispersed.

God's providence still further overruled events to give opportunity for the growth of the Reformation. The death of Gregory was followed by the election of two rival popes. Two conflicting powers, each professedly infallible, now claimed obedience. (See Appendix notes for pages 50 and 86.) Each called upon the faithful to assist him in making war upon the other, enforcing his demands by terrible anathemas against his adversaries, and promises of rewards in heaven to his supporters. This occurrence greatly weakened the power of the papacy. The rival factions had all they could do to attack each other, and Wycliffe for a time had rest. Anathemas and recriminations were flying from pope to pope, and torrents of blood were poured out to support their conflicting claims. Crimes and scandals flooded the church. Meanwhile the Reformer, in the quiet retirement of his parish of Lutterworth, was laboring diligently to point men from the contending popes to Jesus, the Prince of Peace.

The schism, with all the strife and corruption which it caused, prepared the way for the Reformation by enabling the people to see what the papacy really was. In a tract which he published, On the Schism of the Popes, Wycliffe called upon the people to consider whether these two priests were not speaking the truth in condemning each other as the antichrist. "God," said he, "would no longer suffer the fiend to reign in only one such priest, but . . . made division among two, so that men, in Christ's name, may the more easily overcome them both."—R. Vaughan, Life and Opinions of John de Wycliffe, vol. 2, p. 6.

Wycliffe, like his Master, preached the gospel to the poor. Not content with spreading the light in their humble homes in his own parish of Lutterworth, he determined that it should be carried to every part of England. To accomplish this he organized a body of preachers, simple, devout men, who loved the truth and desired nothing so much as to extend it. These men went everywhere, teaching in the market places, in the streets of the great cities, and in the country lanes. They sought out the aged, the sick, and the poor, and opened to them the glad tidings of the grace of God.

As a professor of theology at Oxford, Wycliffe preached the word of God in the halls of the university. So faithfully did he present the truth to the students under his instruction, that he received the title of "the gospel doctor." But the greatest work of his life was to be the translation of the Scriptures into the English language. In a work, On the Truth and Meaning of Scripture, he expressed his intention to translate the Bible, so that every man in England might read, in the language in which he was born, the wonderful works of God.

But suddenly his labors were stopped. Though not yet sixty years of age, unceasing toil, study, and the assaults of his enemies had told upon his strength and made him prematurely old. He was attacked by a dangerous illness.

The tidings brought great joy to the friars. Now they thought he would bitterly repent the evil he had done the church, and they hurried to his chamber to listen to his confession. Representatives from the four religious orders, with four civil officers, gathered about the supposed dying man. "You have death on your lips," they said; "be touched by your faults, and retract in our presence all that you have said to our injury." The Reformer listened in silence; then he bade his attendant raise him in his bed, and, gazing steadily upon them as they stood waiting for his recantation, he said, in the firm, strong voice which had so often caused them to tremble: "I shall not die, but live; and again declare the evil deeds of the friars."—D'Aubigné, b. 17, ch. 7. Astonished and abashed, the monks hurried from the room.

Wycliffe's words were fulfilled. He lived to place in the hands of his countrymen the most powerful of all weapons against Rome—to give them the Bible, the Heaven-appointed agent to liberate, enlighten, and evangelize the people. There were many and great obstacles to surmount in the accomplishment of this work. Wycliffe was weighed down with infirmities; he knew that only a few years for labor remained for him; he saw the opposition which he must meet; but, encouraged by the promises of God's word, he went forward nothing daunted. In the full vigor of his intellectual powers, rich in experience, he had been preserved and prepared by God's special providence for this, the greatest of his labors. While all Christendom was filled with tumult, the Reformer in his rectory at Lutterworth, unheeding the storm that raged without, applied himself to his chosen task.

At last the work was completed—the first English translation of the Bible ever made. The word of God was opened to England. The Reformer feared not now the prison or the stake. He had placed in the hands of the English people a light which should never be extinguished. In giving the Bible to his countrymen, he had done more to break the fetters of ignorance and vice, more to liberate and elevate his country, than was ever achieved by the most brilliant victories on fields of battle.

The art of printing being still unknown, it was only by slow and wearisome labor that copies of the Bible could be multiplied. So great was the interest to obtain the book, that many willingly engaged in the work of transcribing it, but it was with difficulty that the copyists could supply the demand. Some of the more wealthy purchasers desired the whole Bible. Others bought only a portion. In many cases, several families united to purchase a copy. Thus Wycliffe's Bible soon found its way to the homes of the people.

The appeal to men's reason aroused them from their passive submission to papal dogmas. Wycliffe now taught the distinctive doctrines of Protestantism—salvation through faith in Christ, and the sole infallibility of the Scriptures. The preachers whom he had sent out circulated the Bible, together with the Reformer's writings, and with such success that the new faith was accepted by nearly one half of the people of England.

The appearance of the Scriptures brought dismay to the authorities of the church. They had now to meet an agency more powerful than Wycliffe—an agency against which their weapons would avail little. There was at this time no law in England prohibiting the Bible, for it had never before been published in the language of the people. Such laws were afterward enacted and rigorously enforced. Meanwhile, notwithstanding the efforts of the priests, there was for a season opportunity for the circulation of the word of God.

Again the papal leaders plotted to silence the Reformer's voice. Before three tribunals he was successively summoned for trial, but without avail. First a synod of bishops declared his writings heretical, and, winning the young king, Richard II, to their side, they obtained a royal decree consigning to prison all who should hold the condemned doctrines.

Wycliffe appealed from the synod to Parliament; he fearlessly arraigned the hierarchy before the national council and demanded a reform of the enormous abuses sanctioned by the church. With convincing power he portrayed the usurpation and corruptions of the papal see. His enemies were brought to confusion. The friends and supporters of Wycliffe had been forced to yield, and it had been confidently expected that the Reformer himself, in his old age, alone and friendless, would bow to the combined authority of the crown and the miter. But instead of this the papists saw themselves defeated. Parliament, roused by the stirring appeals of Wycliffe, repealed the persecuting edict, and the Reformer was again at liberty.

A third time he was brought to trial, and now before the highest ecclesiastical tribunal in the kingdom. Here no favor would be shown to heresy. Here at last Rome would triumph, and the Reformer's work would be stopped. So thought the papists. If they could but accomplish their purpose, Wycliffe would be forced to abjure his doctrines, or would leave the court only for the flames.

But Wycliffe did not retract; he would not dissemble. He fearlessly maintained his teachings and repelled the accusations of his persecutors. Losing sight of himself, of his position, of the occasion, he summoned his hearers before the divine tribunal, and weighed their sophistries and deceptions in the balances of eternal truth. The power of the Holy Spirit was felt in the council room. A spell from God was upon the hearers. They seemed to have no power to leave the place. As arrows from the Lord's quiver, the Reformer's words pierced their hearts. The charge of heresy, which they had brought against him, he with convincing power threw back upon themselves. Why, he demanded, did they dare to spread their errors? For the sake of gain, to make merchandise of the grace of God?

"With whom, think you," he finally said, "are ye contending? with an old man on the brink of the grave? No! with Truth—Truth which is stronger than you, and will overcome you."—Wylie, b. 2, ch. 13. So saying, he withdrew from the assembly, and not one of his adversaries attempted to prevent him.

Wycliffe's work was almost done; the banner of truth which he had so long borne was soon to fall from his hand; but once more he was to bear witness for the gospel. The truth was to be proclaimed from the very stronghold of the kingdom of error. Wycliffe was summoned for trial before the papal tribunal at Rome, which had so often shed the blood of the saints. He was not blind to the danger that threatened him, yet he would have obeyed the summons had not a shock of palsy made it impossible for him to perform the journey. But though his voice was not to be heard at Rome, he could speak by letter, and this he determined to do. From his rectory the Reformer wrote to the pope a letter, which, while respectful in tone and Christian in spirit, was a keen rebuke to the pomp and pride of the papal see.

"Verily I do rejoice," he said, "to open and declare unto every man the faith which I do hold, and especially unto the bishop of Rome: which, forasmuch as I do suppose to be sound and true, he will most willingly confirm my said faith, or if it be erroneous, amend the same.

"First, I suppose that the gospel of Christ is the whole body of God's law. . . . I do give and hold the bishop of Rome, forasmuch as he is the vicar of Christ here on earth, to be most bound, of all other men, unto that law of the gospel. For the greatness among Christ's disciples did not consist in worldly dignity or honors, but in the near and exact following of Christ in His life and manners. . . . Christ, for the time of His pilgrimage here, was a most poor man, abjecting and casting off all worldly rule and honor. . . .

"No faithful man ought to follow either the pope himself or any of the holy men, but in such points as he hath followed the Lord Jesus Christ; for Peter and the sons of Zebedee, by desiring worldly honor, contrary to the following of Christ's steps, did offend, and therefore in those errors they are not to be followed. . . .

"The pope ought to leave unto the secular power all temporal dominion and rule, and thereunto effectually to move and exhort his whole clergy; for so did Christ, and especially by His apostles. Wherefore, if I have erred in

any of these points, I will most humbly submit myself unto correction, even by death, if necessity so require; and if I could labor according to my will or desire in mine own person, I would surely present myself before the bishop of Rome; but the Lord hath otherwise visited me to the contrary, and hath taught me rather to obey God than men."

In closing he said: "Let us pray unto our God, that He will so stir up our Pope Urban VI, as he began, that he with his clergy may follow the Lord Jesus Christ in life and manners; and that they may teach the people effectually, and that they, likewise, may faithfully follow them in the same."—John Foxe, *Acts and Monuments*, vol. 3, pp. 49, 50.

Thus Wycliffe presented to the pope and his cardinals the meekness and humility of Christ, exhibiting not only to themselves but to all Christendom the contrast between them and the Master whose representatives they professed to be.

Wycliffe fully expected that his life would be the price of his fidelity. The king, the pope, and the bishops were united to accomplish his ruin, and it seemed certain that a few months at most would bring him to the stake. But his courage was unshaken. "Why do you talk of seeking the crown of martyrdom afar?" he said. "Preach the gospel of Christ to haughty prelates, and martyrdom will not fail you. What! I should live and be silent? . . . Never! Let the blow fall, I await its coming."—D'Aubigné, b. 17, ch. 8.

But God's providence still shielded His servant. The man who for a whole lifetime had stood boldly in defense of the truth, in daily peril of his life, was not to fall a victim of the hatred of its foes. Wycliffe had never sought to shield himself, but the Lord had been his protector; and now, when his enemies felt sure of their prey, God's hand removed him beyond their reach. In his church at Lutterworth, as he was about to dispense the communion, he fell, stricken with palsy, and in a short time yielded up his life.

God had appointed to Wycliffe his work. He had put the word of truth in his mouth, and He set a guard about him that this word might come to the people. His life was protected, and his labors were prolonged, until a foundation was laid for the great work of the Reformation.

Wycliffe came from the obscurity of the Dark Ages. There were none who went before him from whose work he could shape his system of reform. Raised up like John the Baptist to accomplish a special mission, he was the herald of a new era. Yet in the system of truth which he presented there was a unity and completeness which Reformers who followed him did not exceed, and which some did not reach, even a hundred years later. So broad and deep was laid the foundation, so firm and true was the framework, that it needed not to be reconstructed by those who came after him.

The great movement that Wycliffe inaugurated, which was to liberate the conscience and the intellect, and set free the nations so long bound to the triumphal car of Rome, had its spring in the Bible. Here was the source of that stream of blessing, which, like the water of life, has flowed down the ages since the fourteenth century. Wycliffe accepted the Holy Scriptures with implicit faith as the inspired revelation of God's will, a sufficient rule of faith and practice. He had been educated to regard the Church of Rome as the divine, infallible authority, and to accept with unquestioning reverence the established teachings and customs of a thousand years; but he turned away from all these to listen to God's holy word. This was the authority which he urged the people to acknowledge. Instead of the church speaking through the pope, he declared the only true authority to be the voice of God speaking through His word. And he taught not only that the Bible is a perfect revelation of God's will, but that the Holy Spirit is its only interpreter, and that every man is, by the study of its teachings, to learn his duty for himself. Thus he turned the minds of men from the pope and the Church of Rome to the word of God.

94   Wycliffe was one of the greatest of the Reformers. In breadth of intellect, in clearness of thought, in firmness to maintain the truth, and in boldness to defend it, he was equaled by few who came after him. Purity of life, unwearying diligence in study and in labor, incorruptible integrity, and Christlike love and faithfulness in his ministry, characterized the first of the Reformers. And this notwithstanding the intellectual darkness and moral corruption of the age from which he emerged.

The character of Wycliffe is a testimony to the educating, transforming power of the Holy Scriptures. It was the Bible that made him what he was. The effort to grasp the great truths of revelation imparts freshness and vigor to all the faculties. It expands the mind, sharpens the perceptions, and ripens the judgment. The study of the Bible will ennoble every thought, feeling, and aspiration as no other study can. It gives stability of purpose, patience, courage, and fortitude; it refines the character and sanctifies the soul. An earnest, reverent study of the Scriptures, bringing the mind of the student in direct contact with the infinite mind, would give to the world men of stronger and more active intellect, as well as of nobler principle, than has ever resulted from the ablest training that human philosophy affords. "The entrance of Thy words," says the psalmist, "giveth light; it giveth understanding." Psalm 119:130.

The doctrines which had been taught by Wycliffe continued for a time to spread; his followers, known as Wycliffites and Lollards, not only traversed England, but scattered to other lands, carrying the knowledge of the gospel. Now that their leader was removed, the preachers labored with even greater zeal than before, and multitudes flocked to listen to their teachings. Some of the nobility, and even the wife of the king, were among the converts. In many places there was a marked reform in the manners of the people, and the idolatrous symbols of Romanism were removed from the churches. But soon the pitiless storm of persecution burst upon those who had dared to accept the Bible as their guide. The English monarchs, eager to   95 strengthen their power by securing the support of Rome, did not hesitate to sacrifice the Reformers. For the first time in the history of England the stake was decreed against the disciples of the gospel. Martyrdom succeeded martyrdom. The advocates of truth, proscribed and tortured, could only pour their cries into the ear of the Lord of Sabaoth. Hunted as foes of the church and traitors to the realm, they continued to preach in secret places, finding shelter as best they could in the humble homes of the poor, and often hiding away even in dens and caves.

Notwithstanding the rage of persecution, a calm, devout, earnest, patient protest against the prevailing corruption of religious faith continued for centuries to be uttered. The Christians of that early time had only a partial knowledge of the truth, but they had learned to love and obey God's word, and they patiently suffered for its sake. Like the disciples in apostolic days, many sacrificed their worldly possessions for the cause of Christ. Those who were permitted to dwell in their homes gladly sheltered their banished brethren, and when they too were driven forth they cheerfully accepted the lot of the outcast. Thousands, it is true, terrified by the fury of their persecutors, purchased their freedom at the sacrifice of their faith, and went out of their prisons, clothed in penitents' robes, to publish their recantation. But the number was not small—and among them were men of noble birth as well as the humble and lowly—who bore fearless testimony to the truth in dungeon cells, in "Lollard towers," and in the midst of torture and flame, rejoicing that they were counted worthy to know "the fellowship of His sufferings."

The papists had failed to work their will with Wycliffe during his life, and their hatred could not be satisfied while his body rested quietly in the grave. By the decree of the Council of Constance, more than forty years after his death his bones were exhumed and publicly burned, and the ashes were thrown into a neighboring brook. "This brook," says an old writer, "hath con-   96 veyed his ashes into Avon, Avon into Severn, Severn into the narrow seas, they into the main ocean. And thus the ashes of Wycliffe are the emblem of his doctrine, which now is dispersed all the world over."—T. Fuller, *Church History of Britain*, b. 4, sec. 2, par. 54. Little did his enemies realize the significance of their malicious act.

It was through the writings of Wycliffe that John Huss, of Bohemia, was led to renounce many of the errors of Romanism and to enter upon the work of reform. Thus in these two countries, so widely separated, the seed of truth was sown. From Bohemia the work extended to other lands. The minds of men were directed to the long-forgotten word of God. A divine hand was preparing the way for the Great Reformation.

6

Huss and Jerome

The gospel had been planted in Bohemia as early as the ninth century. The Bible was translated, and public worship was conducted, in the language of the people. But as the power of the pope increased, so the word of God was obscured. Gregory VII, who had taken it upon himself to humble the pride of kings, was no less intent upon enslaving the people, and accordingly a bull was issued forbidding public worship to be conducted in the Bohemian tongue. The pope declared that "it was pleasing to the Omnipotent that His worship should be celebrated in an unknown language, and that many evils and heresies had arisen from not observing this rule."—Wylie, b. 3, ch. 1. Thus Rome decreed that the light of God's word should be extinguished and the people should be shut up in darkness. But Heaven had provided other agencies for the preservation of the church. Many of the Waldenses and Albigenses, driven by persecution from their homes in France and Italy, came to Bohemia. Though they dared not teach openly, they labored zealously in secret. Thus the true faith was preserved from century to century.

Before the days of Huss there were men in Bohemia who rose up to condemn openly the corruption in the church and the profligacy of the people. Their labors excited widespread interest. The fears of the hierarchy were roused, and persecution was opened against the disciples of the gospel. Driven to worship in the forests and the mountains, they were hunted by soldiers, and many were put to death. After a time it was decreed that all who departed from the Romish worship should be burned. But while the Christians yielded up their lives, they looked forward to the triumph of their cause. One of those who "taught that salvation was only to be found by faith in the crucified Saviour," declared when dying: "The rage of the enemies of the truth now prevails against us, but it will not be forever; there shall arise one from among the common people, without sword or authority, and against him they shall not be able to prevail."—*Ibid.*, b. 3, ch. 1. Luther's time was yet far distant; but already one was rising, whose testimony against Rome would stir the nations.

John Huss was of humble birth, and was early left an orphan by the death of his father. His pious mother, regarding education and the fear of God as the most valuable of possessions, sought to secure this heritage for her son. Huss studied at the provincial school, and then repaired to the university at Prague, receiving admission as a charity scholar. He was accompanied on the journey to Prague by his mother; widowed and poor, she had no gifts of worldly wealth to bestow upon her son, but as they drew near to the great city, she kneeled down beside the fatherless youth and invoked for him the blessing of their Father in heaven. Little did that mother realize how her prayer was to be answered.

At the university, Huss soon distinguished himself by his untiring application and rapid progress, while his blameless life and gentle, winning deportment gained him universal esteem. He was a sincere adherent of the Roman Church and an earnest seeker for the spiritual blessings which it professes to bestow. On the occasion of a jubilee he went to confession, paid the last few coins in his scanty store, and joined in the processions, that he might share in the absolution promised. After completing his college course, he entered the priesthood, and rapidly attaining to eminence, he soon became attached to the court of the king. He was also made professor and afterward rector of the university where he had received his education. In a few years the humble charity scholar had become the pride of his country, and his name was renowned throughout Europe.

But it was in another field that Huss began the work of reform. Several years after taking priest's orders he was appointed preacher of the chapel of Bethlehem. The founder of this chapel had advocated, as a matter of great importance, the preaching of the Scriptures in the language of the people. Notwithstanding Rome's opposition to this practice, it had not been wholly discontinued in Bohemia. But there was great ignorance of the Bible, and the worst vices prevailed among the people of all ranks. These evils Huss unsparingly denounced, appealing to the word of God to enforce the principles of truth and purity which he inculcated.

A citizen of Prague, Jerome, who afterward became so closely associated with Huss, had, on returning from England, brought with him the writings of Wycliffe. The queen of England, who had been a convert to Wycliffe's teachings, was a Bohemian princess, and through her influence also the Reformer's works were widely circulated in her native country. These works Huss read with interest; he believed their author to be a sincere Christian and was inclined to regard with favor the reforms which he advocated. Already, though he knew it not, Huss had entered upon a path which was to lead him far away from Rome.

About this time there arrived in Prague two strangers from England, men of learning, who had received the light and had come to spread it in this distant land. Beginning with an open attack on the pope's supremacy, they were soon silenced by the authorities; but being unwilling to relinquish their purpose, they had recourse to other measures. Being artists as well as preachers, they proceeded to exercise their skill. In a place open to the public they drew two pictures. One represented the entrance of Christ into 100 Jerusalem, "meek, and sitting upon an ass" (Matthew 21:5), and followed by His disciples in travel-worn garments and with naked feet. The other picture portrayed a pontifical procession—the pope arrayed in his rich robes and triple crown, mounted upon a horse magnificently adorned, preceded by trumpeters and followed by cardinals and prelates in dazzling array.

Here was a sermon which arrested the attention of all classes. Crowds came to gaze upon the drawings. None could fail to read the moral, and many were deeply impressed by the contrast between the meekness and humility of Christ the Master and the pride and arrogance of the pope, His professed servant. There was great commotion in Prague, and the strangers after a time found it necessary, for their own safety, to depart. But the lesson they had taught was not forgotten. The pictures made a deep impression on the mind of Huss and led him to a closer study of the Bible and of Wycliffe's writings. Though he was not prepared, even yet, to accept all the reforms advocated by Wycliffe, he saw more clearly the true character of the papacy, and with greater zeal denounced the pride, the ambition, and the corruption of the hierarchy.

From Bohemia the light extended to Germany, for disturbances in the University of Prague caused the withdrawal of hundreds of German students. Many of them had received from Huss their first knowledge of the Bible, and on their return they spread the gospel in their fatherland.

Tidings of the work at Prague were carried to Rome, and Huss was soon summoned to appear before the pope. To obey would be to expose himself to certain death. The king and queen of Bohemia, the university, members of the nobility, and officers of the government united in an appeal to the pontiff that Huss be permitted to remain at Prague and to answer at Rome by deputy. Instead of granting this request, the pope proceeded to the trial and condemnation of Huss, and then declared the city of Prague to be under interdict.

In that age this sentence, whenever pro- 101 nounced, created widespread alarm. The ceremonies by which it was accompanied were well adapted to strike terror to a people who looked upon the pope as the representative of God Himself, holding the keys of heaven and hell, and possessing power to invoke temporal as well as spiritual judgments. It was believed that the gates of heaven were closed against the region smitten with interdict; that until it should please the pope to remove the ban, the dead were shut out from the abodes of bliss. In token of this terrible calamity, all the services of religion were suspended. The churches were closed. Marriages were solemnized in the churchyard. The dead, denied burial in consecrated ground, were interred, without the rites of sepulture, in the ditches or the fields. Thus by measures which appealed to the imagination, Rome essayed to control the consciences of men.

The city of Prague was filled with tumult. A large class denounced Huss as the cause of all their calamities and demanded that he be given up to the vengeance of Rome. To quiet the storm, the Reformer withdrew for a time to his native village. Writing to the friends whom he had left at Prague, he said: "If I have withdrawn from the midst of you, it is to follow the precept and example of Jesus Christ, in order not to give room to the ill-minded to draw on themselves eternal condemnation, and in order not to be to the pious a cause of affliction and persecution. I have retired also through an apprehension that impious priests might continue for a longer time to prohibit the preaching of the word of God amongst you; but I have not quitted you to deny the divine truth, for which, with God's assistance, I am willing to die."—Bonnechose, *The Reformers Before the Reformation*, vol. 1, p. 87. Huss did not cease his labors, but traveled through the surrounding country, preaching to eager crowds. Thus the measures to which the pope resorted to suppress the gospel were causing it to be the more widely extended. "We can do nothing against the truth, but for the truth." 2 Corinthians 13:8. 102

"The mind of Huss, at this stage of his career, would seem to have been the scene of a painful conflict. Although the church was seeking to overwhelm him by her thunderbolts, he had not renounced her authority. The Roman Church was still to him the spouse of Christ, and the pope was the representative and vicar of God. What Huss was warring against was the abuse of authority, not the principle itself. This brought on a terrible conflict between the convictions of his understanding and the claims of his conscience. If the authority was just and infallible, as he believed it to be, how came it that he felt compelled to disobey it? To obey, he saw, was to sin; but why should obedience to an infallible church lead to such an issue? This was the problem he could not solve; this was the doubt that tortured him hour by hour. The nearest approximation to a solution which he was able to make was that it had happened again, as once before in the days of the Saviour, that the priests of the church had become wicked persons and were using their lawful authority for unlawful ends. This led him to adopt for his own guidance, and to preach to others for theirs, the maxim that the precepts of Scripture, conveyed through the understanding, are to rule the conscience; in other words, that God speaking in the Bible, and not the church speaking through the priesthood, is the one infallible guide."—Wylie, b. 3, ch. 2.

When after a time the excitement in Prague subsided, Huss returned to his chapel of Bethlehem, to continue with greater zeal and courage the preaching of the word of God. His enemies were active and powerful, but the queen and many of the nobles were his friends, and the people in great numbers sided with him. Comparing his pure and elevating teachings and holy life with the degrading dogmas which the Romanists preached, and the avarice and debauchery which they practiced, many regarded it an honor to be on his side.

Hitherto Huss had stood alone in his labors; but now Jerome, who while in England had 103 accepted the teachings of Wycliffe, joined in the work of reform. The two were hereafter united in their lives, and in death they were not to be divided. Brilliancy of genius, eloquence and learning—gifts that win popular favor—were possessed in a pre-eminent degree by Jerome; but in those qualities which constitute real strength of character, Huss was the greater. His calm judgment served as a restraint upon the impulsive spirit of Jerome, who, with true humility, perceived his worth, and yielded to his counsels. Under their united labors the reform was more rapidly extended.

God permitted great light to shine upon the minds of these chosen men, revealing to them many of the errors of Rome; but they did not receive all the light that was to be given to the world. Through these, His servants, God was leading the people out of the darkness of Romanism; but there were many and great obstacles for them to meet, and He led them on, step by step, as they could bear it. They were not prepared to receive all the light at once. Like the full glory of the noontide sun to those who have long dwelt in darkness, it would, if presented, have caused them to turn away. Therefore He revealed it to the leaders little by little, as it could be received by the people. From cen-

tury to century, other faithful workers were to follow, to lead the people on still further in the path of reform.

The schism in the church still continued. Three popes were now contending for the supremacy, and their strife filled Christendom with crime and tumult. Not content with hurling anathemas, they resorted to temporal weapons. Each cast about him to purchase arms and to obtain soldiers. Of course money must be had; and to procure this, the gifts, offices, and blessings of the church were offered for sale. (See Appendix note for page 59.) The priests also, imitating their superiors, resorted to simony and war to humble their rivals and strengthen their own power. With daily increasing boldness Huss thundered against the abominations which were tolerated in the name of religion; and the people openly accused the Romish leaders as the cause of the miseries that overwhelmed Christendom. 104

Again the city of Prague seemed on the verge of a bloody conflict. As in former ages, God's servant was accused as "he that troubleth Israel." 1 Kings 18:17. The city was again placed under interdict, and Huss withdrew to his native village. The testimony so faithfully borne from his loved chapel of Bethlehem was ended. He was to speak from a wider stage, to all Christendom, before laying down his life as a witness for the truth.

To cure the evils that were distracting Europe, a general council was summoned to meet at Constance. The council was called at the desire of the emperor Sigismund, by one of the three rival popes, John XXIII. The demand for a council had been far from welcome to Pope John, whose character and policy could ill bear investigation, even by prelates as lax in morals as were the churchmen of those times. He dared not, however, oppose the will of Sigismund. (See Appendix.)

The chief objects to be accomplished by the council were to heal the schism in the church and to root out heresy. Hence the two antipopes were summoned to appear before it, as well as the leading propagator of the new opinions, John Huss. The former, having regard to their own safety, did not attend in person, but were represented by their delegates. Pope John, while ostensibly the convoker of the council, came to it with many misgivings, suspecting the emperor's secret purpose to depose him, and fearing to be brought to account for the vices which had disgraced the tiara, as well as for the crimes which had secured it. Yet he made his entry into the city of Constance with great pomp, attended by ecclesiastics of the highest rank and followed by a train of courtiers. All the clergy and dignitaries of the city, with an immense crowd of citizens, went out to welcome him. Above his head was a golden canopy, borne by four of the chief magistrates. The host was carried before him, and the rich dresses of the cardinals and nobles made an imposing display.

Meanwhile another traveler was approaching Constance. Huss was conscious of the dangers which threatened him. He parted from his friends as if he were never to meet them again, and went on his journey feeling that it was leading him to the stake. Notwithstanding he had obtained a safe-conduct from the king of Bohemia, and received one also from the emperor Sigismund while on his journey, he made all his arrangements in view of the probability of his death.

In a letter addressed to his friends at Prague he said: "My brethren, . . . I am departing with a safe-conduct from the king to meet my numerous and mortal enemies. . . . I confide altogether in the all-powerful God, in my Saviour; I trust that He will listen to your ardent prayers, that He will infuse His prudence and His wisdom into my mouth, in order that I may resist them; and that He will accord me His Holy Spirit to fortify me in His truth, so that I may face with courage, temptations, prison, and, if necessary, a cruel death. Jesus Christ suffered for His well-beloved; and therefore ought we to be astonished that He has left us His example, in order that we may ourselves endure with patience all things for our own salvation? He is God, and we are His creatures; He is the Lord, and we are His servants; He is Master of the world, and we are contemptible mortals—yet He suffered! Why, then, should we not suffer also, particularly when suffering is for us a purification? Therefore, beloved, if my death ought to contribute to His glory, pray that it may come quickly, and that He may enable me to support all my calamities with constancy. But if it be better that I return amongst you, let us pray to God that I may return without stain—that is, that I may not suppress one tittle of the truth of the gospel, in order to leave my brethren an excellent example to follow. Probably, therefore, you will nevermore behold my face at Prague; but should the will of the all-powerful God deign to restore me to you, let us then advance with a firmer heart in the knowledge and the love of His law."—Bonnechose, vol. 1, pp. 147, 148.

In another letter, to a priest who had become a disciple of the gospel, Huss spoke with deep humility of his own errors, accusing himself "of having felt pleasure in wearing rich apparel and of having wasted hours in frivolous occupations." He then added these touching admonitions: "May the glory of God and the salvation of souls occupy thy mind, and not the possession of benefices and estates. Beware of adorning thy house more than thy soul; and, above all, give thy care to the spiritual edifice. Be pious and humble with the poor, and consume not thy substance in feasting. Shouldst thou not amend thy life and refrain from superfluities, I fear that thou wilt be severely chastened, as I am myself. . . . Thou knowest my doctrine, for thou hast received my instructions from thy childhood; it is therefore useless for me to write to thee any further. But I conjure thee, by the mercy of our Lord, not to imitate me in any of the vanities into which thou hast seen me fall." On the cover of the letter he added: "I conjure thee, my friend, not to break this seal until thou shalt have acquired the certitude that I am dead."—*Ibid.*, vol. 1, pp. 148, 149.

On his journey, Huss everywhere beheld indications of the spread of his doctrines and the favor with which his cause was regarded. The people thronged to meet him, and in some towns the magistrates attended him through their streets.

Upon arriving at Constance, Huss was granted full liberty. To the emperor's safe-conduct was added a personal assurance of protection by the pope. But, in violation of these solemn and repeated declarations, the Reformer was in a short time arrested, by order of the pope and cardinals, and thrust into a loathsome dungeon. Later he was transferred to a strong castle across the Rhine and there kept a prisoner. The pope, profiting little by his perfidy, was soon after committed to the same prison. *Ibid.*, vol. 1, p. 247. He had been proved before the council to be guilty of the basest crimes, besides murder, simony, and adultery, "sins not fit to be named." So the council itself declared, and he was finally deprived of the tiara and thrown into prison. The antipopes also were deposed, and a new pontiff was chosen.

Though the pope himself had been guilty of greater crimes than Huss had ever charged upon the priests, and for which he had demanded a reformation, yet the same council which degraded the pontiff proceeded to crush the Reformer. The imprisonment of Huss excited great indignation in Bohemia. Powerful noblemen addressed to the council earnest protests against this outrage. The emperor, who was loath to permit the violation of a safe-conduct, opposed the proceedings against him. But the enemies of the Reformer were malignant and determined. They appealed to the emperor's prejudices, to his fears, to his zeal for the church. They brought forward arguments of great length to prove that "faith ought not to be kept with heretics, nor persons suspected of heresy, though they are furnished with safe-conducts from the emperor and kings."—Jacques Lenfant, *History of the Council of Constance*, vol. 1, p. 516. Thus they prevailed.

Enfeebled by illness and imprisonment,—for the damp, foul air of his dungeon had brought on a fever which nearly ended his life,—Huss was at last brought before the council. Loaded with chains he stood in the presence of the emperor, whose honor and good faith had been pledged to protect him. During his long trial he firmly maintained the truth, and in the presence of the assembled dignitaries of church and state he uttered a solemn and faithful protest against the corruptions of the hierarchy. When required to choose whether he would recant his doctrines or suffer death, he accepted the martyr's fate.

The grace of God sustained him. During the weeks of suffering that passed before his final sentence, heaven's peace filled his soul. "I write this letter," he said to a friend, "in my prison, and with my fettered hand, expecting my sentence of death tomorrow. . . . When, with the assistance of Jesus Christ, we shall again meet in the delicious peace of the future life, you will learn how merciful God has shown Himself toward me, how effectually He has supported me in the midst of my temptations and trials."—

108 Bonnechose, vol. 2, p. 67.

In the gloom of his dungeon he foresaw the triumph of the true faith. Returning in his dreams to the chapel at Prague where he had preached the gospel, he saw the pope and his bishops effacing the pictures of Christ which he had painted on its walls. "This vision distressed him: but on the next day he saw many painters occupied in restoring these figures in greater number and in brighter colors. As soon as their task was ended, the painters, who were surrounded by an immense crowd, exclaimed, 'Now let the popes and bishops come; they shall never efface them more!'" Said the Reformer, as he related his dream: "I maintain this for certain, that the image of Christ will never be effaced. They have wished to destroy it, but it shall be painted afresh in all hearts by much better preachers than myself."—D'Aubigné, b. 1, ch. 6.

For the last time, Huss was brought before the council. It was a vast and brilliant assembly—the emperor, the princes of the empire, the royal deputies, the cardinals, bishops, and priests, and an immense crowd who had come as spectators of the events of the day. From all parts of Christendom had been gathered the witnesses of this first great sacrifice in the long struggle by which liberty of conscience was to be secured.

Being called upon for his final decision, Huss declared his refusal to abjure, and, fixing his penetrating glance upon the monarch whose plighted word had been so shamelessly violated, he declared: "I determined, of my own free will, to appear before this council, under the public protection and faith of the emperor here present."—Bonnechose, vol. 2, p. 84. A deep flush crimsoned the face of Sigismund as the eyes of all in the assembly turned upon him.

Sentence having been pronounced, the ceremony of degradation began. The bishops clothed their prisoner in the sacerdotal habit,

and as he took the priestly robe, he said: "Our Lord Jesus Christ was covered with a white 109 robe, by way of insult, when Herod had Him conducted before Pilate."—*Ibid.*, vol. 2, p. 86. Being again exhorted to retract, he replied, turning toward the people: "With what face, then, should I behold the heavens? How should I look on those multitudes of men to whom I have preached the pure gospel? No; I esteem their salvation more than this poor body, now appointed unto death." The vestments were removed one by one, each bishop pronouncing a curse as he performed his part of the ceremony. Finally "they put on his head a cap or pyramidal-shaped miter of paper, on which were painted frightful figures of demons, with the word 'Archheretic' conspicuous in front. 'Most joyfully,' said Huss, 'will I wear this crown of shame for Thy sake, O Jesus, who for me didst wear a crown of thorns.'"

When he was thus arrayed, "the prelates said, 'Now we devote thy soul to the devil.' 'And I,' said John Huss, lifting up his eyes toward heaven, 'do commit my spirit into Thy hands, O Lord Jesus, for Thou hast redeemed me.'"—Wylie, b. 3, ch. 7.

He was now delivered up to the secular authorities and led away to the place of execution. An immense procession followed, hundreds of men at arms, priests and bishops in their costly robes, and the inhabitants of Constance. When he had been fastened to the stake, and all was ready for the fire to be lighted, the martyr was once more exhorted to save himself by renouncing his errors. "What errors," said Huss, "shall I renounce? I know myself guilty of none. I call God to witness that all that I have written and preached has been with the view of rescuing souls from sin and perdition; and, therefore, most joyfully will I confirm with my blood that truth which I have written and preached."—*Ibid.*, b. 3, ch. 7. When the flames kindled about him, he began to sing, "Jesus, Thou Son of David, have mercy on me," and so continued till his voice was silenced forever.

Even his enemies were struck with his heroic bearing. A zealous papist, describing the mar-110 tyrdom of Huss, and of Jerome, who died soon after, said: "Both bore themselves with constant mind when their last hour approached. They prepared for the fire as if they were going to a marriage feast. They uttered no cry of pain. When the flames rose, they began to sing hymns; and scarce could the vehemency of the fire stop their singing."—*Ibid.*, b. 3, ch. 7.

When the body of Huss had been wholly consumed, his ashes, with the soil upon which they rested, were gathered up and cast into the Rhine, and thus borne onward to the ocean. His persecutors vainly imagined that they had rooted out the truths he preached. Little did they dream that the ashes that day borne away to the sea were to be as seed scattered in all the countries of the earth; that in lands yet unknown it would yield abundant fruit in witnesses for the truth. The voice which had spoken in the council hall of Constance had wakened echoes that would be heard through all coming ages. Huss was no more, but the truths for which he died could never perish. His example of faith and constancy would encourage multitudes to stand firm for the truth, in the face of torture and death. His execution had exhibited to the whole world the perfidious cruelty of Rome. The enemies of truth, though they knew it not, had been furthering the cause which they vainly sought to destroy.

Yet another stake was to be set up at Constance. The blood of another witness must testify for the truth. Jerome, upon bidding farewell to Huss on his departure for the council, had exhorted him to courage and firmness, declaring that if he should fall into any peril, he himself would fly to his assistance. Upon hearing of the Reformer's imprisonment, the faithful disciple immediately prepared to fulfill his promise. Without a safe-conduct he set out, with a single companion, for Constance. On arriving there he was convinced that he had only exposed himself to peril, without the possibility of doing anything for the deliverance of Huss. He fled from the city, but was arrested on the homeward journey and brought back loaded with fetters and under the custody of a band of soldiers. At his first appearance before the council his attempts to reply to the accusations brought against him were met with shouts, "To the flames with him! to the flames!"—Bonnechose, vol. 1, p. 234. He was thrown into a dungeon, chained in a position which caused him great suffering, and fed on bread and water. After some months the cruelties of his imprisonment brought upon Jerome an illness that threatened his life, and his enemies, fearing that he might escape them, treated him with less severity, though he remained in prison for one year.

The death of Huss had not resulted as the papists had hoped. The violation of his safe-conduct had roused a storm of indignation, and as the safer course, the council determined, instead of burning Jerome, to force him, if possible, to retract. He was brought before the assembly, and offered the alternative to recant, or to die at the stake. Death at the beginning of his imprisonment would have been a mercy in comparison with the terrible sufferings which he had undergone; but now, weakened by illness, by the rigors of his prison house, and the torture of anxiety and suspense, separated from his friends, and disheartened by the death of Huss, Jerome's fortitude gave way, and he consented to submit to the council. He pledged himself to adhere to the Catholic faith, and accepted the action of the council in condemning the doctrines of Wycliffe and Huss, excepting, however, the "holy truths" which they had taught.—*Ibid*, vol. 2, p. 141.

By this expedient Jerome endeavored to silence the voice of conscience and escape his doom. But in the solitude of his dungeon he saw more clearly what he had done. He thought of the courage and fidelity of Huss, and in contrast pondered upon his own denial of the truth. He thought of the divine Master whom he had pledged himself to serve, and who for his sake endured the death of the cross. Before his retraction he had found comfort, amid all his sufferings, in the assurance of God's favor; but now remorse and doubts tortured his soul. He knew that still other retractions must be made before he could be at peace with Rome. The path upon which he was entering could end only in complete apostasy. His resolution was taken: To escape a brief period of suffering he would not deny his Lord.

Soon he was again brought before the council. His submission had not satisfied his judges. Their thirst for blood, whetted by the death of Huss, clamored for fresh victims. Only by an unreserved surrender of the truth could Jerome preserve his life. But he had determined to avow his faith and follow his brother martyr to the flames.

He renounced his former recantation and, as a dying man, solemnly required an opportunity to make his defense. Fearing the effect of his words, the prelates insisted that he should merely affirm or deny the truth of the charges brought against him. Jerome protested against such cruelty and injustice. "You have held me shut up three hundred and forty days in a frightful prison," he said, "in the midst of filth, noisomeness, stench, and the utmost want of everything; you then bring me out before you, and lending an ear to my mortal enemies, you refuse to hear me. . . . If you be really wise men, and the lights of the world, take care not to sin against justice. As to me, I am only a feeble mortal; my life is but of little importance; and when I exhort you not to deliver an unjust sentence, I speak less for myself than for you."—*Ibid.*, vol. 2, pp. 146, 147.

His request was finally granted. In the presence of his judges, Jerome kneeled down and prayed that the divine Spirit might control his thoughts and words, that he might speak nothing contrary to the truth or unworthy of his Master. To him that day was fulfilled the promise of God to the first disciples: "Ye shall be brought before governors and kings for My sake. . . . But when they deliver you up, take no thought how or what ye shall speak: for it shall be given you in that same hour what ye shall speak. For it is not ye that speak, but the Spirit of your Father which speaketh in you." Matthew 10:18-20.

The words of Jerome excited astonishment
113 and admiration, even in his enemies. For a
whole year he had been immured in a dungeon,
unable to read or even to see, in great physical
suffering and mental anxiety. Yet his arguments
were presented with as much clearness and
power as if he had had undisturbed opportunity
for study. He pointed his hearers to the long line
of holy men who had been condemned by
unjust judges. In almost every generation have
been those who, while seeking to elevate the
people of their time, have been reproached and
cast out, but who in later times have been shown
to be deserving of honor. Christ Himself was
condemned as a malefactor at an unrighteous
tribunal.

At his retraction, Jerome had assented to the
justice of the sentence condemning Huss; he
now declared his repentance and bore witness to
the innocence and holiness of the martyr. "I
knew him from his childhood," he said. "He
was a most excellent man, just and holy; he was
condemned, notwithstanding his innocence. . . .
I also—I am ready to die: I will not recoil
before the torments that are prepared for me by
my enemies and false witnesses, who will one
day have to render an account of their impostures before the great God, whom nothing can
deceive."—Bonnechose, vol. 2, p. 151.

In self-reproach for his own denial of the
truth, Jerome continued: "Of all the sins that I
have committed since my youth, none weigh so
heavily on my mind, and cause me such
poignant remorse, as that which I committed in
this fatal place, when I approved of the iniquitous sentence rendered against Wycliffe, and
against the holy martyr, John Huss, my master
and my friend. Yes! I confess it from my heart,
and declare with horror that I disgracefully
quailed when, through a dread of death, I condemned their doctrines. I therefore supplicate . .
. Almighty God to deign to pardon me my sins,
and this one in particular, the most heinous of
all." Pointing to his judges, he said firmly: "You
condemned Wycliffe and John Huss, not for
having shaken the doctrine of the church, but
simply because they branded with reprobation
the scandals proceeding from the clergy—their
114 pomp, their pride, and all the vices of the
prelates and priests. The things which they have
affirmed, and which are irrefutable, I also think
and declare, like them."

His words were interrupted. The prelates,
trembling with rage, cried out: "What need is
there of further proof? We behold with our own
eyes the most obstinate of heretics!"

Unmoved by the tempest, Jerome exclaimed:
"What! do you suppose that I fear to die? You
have held me for a whole year in a frightful
dungeon, more horrible than death itself. You
have treated me more cruelly than a Turk, Jew,
or pagan, and my flesh has literally rotted off

my bones alive; and yet I make no complaint,
for lamentation ill becomes a man of heart and
spirit; but I cannot but express my astonishment
at such great barbarity toward a Christian."—
Ibid., vol. 2, pp. 151-153.

Again the storm of rage burst out, and Jerome
was hurried away to prison. Yet there were
some in the assembly upon whom his words had
made a deep impression and who desired to
save his life. He was visited by dignitaries of the
church and urged to submit himself to the council. The most brilliant prospects were presented
before him as the reward of renouncing his
opposition to Rome. But like his Master when
offered the glory of the world, Jerome remained
steadfast.

"Prove to me from the Holy Writings that I
am in error," he said, "and I will abjure it."

"The Holy Writings!" exclaimed one of his
tempters, "is everything then to be judged by
them? Who can understand them till the church
has interpreted them?"

"Are the traditions of men more worthy of
faith than the gospel of our Saviour?" replied
Jerome. "Paul did not exhort those to whom he
wrote to listen to the traditions of men, but said,
'Search the Scriptures.'"

"Heretic!" was the response, "I repent having
pleaded so long with you. I see that you are
urged on by the devil."—Wylie, b. 3, ch. 10.

Erelong sentence of condemnation was
passed upon him. He was led out to the same   115
spot upon which Huss had yielded up his life.
He went singing on his way, his countenance
lighted up with joy and peace. His gaze was
fixed upon Christ, and to him death had lost its
terrors. When the executioner, about to kindle
the pile, stepped behind him, the martyr
exclaimed: "Come forward boldly; apply the
fire before my face. Had I been afraid, I should
not be here."

His last words, uttered as the flames rose
about him, were a prayer. "Lord, Almighty
Father," he cried, "have pity on me, and pardon
me my sins; for Thou knowest that I have
always loved Thy truth."—Bonnechose, vol. 2,
p. 168. His voice ceased, but his lips continued
to move in prayer. When the fire had done its
work, the ashes of the martyr, with the earth
upon which they rested, were gathered up, and
like those of Huss, were thrown into the Rhine.

So perished God's faithful light bearers. But
the light of the truths which they proclaimed—
the light of their heroic example—could not be
extinguished. As well might men attempt to turn
back the sun in its course as to prevent the
dawning of that day which was even then breaking upon the world.

The execution of Huss had kindled a flame of
indignation and horror in Bohemia. It was felt
by the whole nation that he had fallen a prey to
the malice of the priests and the treachery of the

emperor. He was declared to have been a faithful teacher of the truth, and the council that decreed his death was charged with the guilt of murder. His doctrines now attracted greater attention than ever before. By the papal edicts the writings of Wycliffe had been condemned to the flames. But those that had escaped destruction were now brought out from their hiding places and studied in connection with the Bible, or such parts of it as the people could obtain, and many were thus led to accept the reformed faith.

The murderers of Huss did not stand quietly by and witness the triumph of his cause. The pope and the emperor united to crush out the movement, and the armies of Sigismund were [116] hurled upon Bohemia.

But a deliverer was raised up. Ziska, who soon after the opening of the war became totally blind, yet who was one of the ablest generals of his age, was the leader of the Bohemians. Trusting in the help of God and the righteousness of their cause, that people withstood the mightiest armies that could be brought against them. Again and again the emperor, raising fresh armies, invaded Bohemia, only to be ignominiously repulsed. The Hussites were raised above the fear of death, and nothing could stand against them. A few years after the opening of the war, the brave Ziska died; but his place was filled by Procopius, who was an equally brave and skillful general, and in some respects a more able leader.

The enemies of the Bohemians, knowing that the blind warrior was dead, deemed the opportunity favorable for recovering all that they had lost. The pope now proclaimed a crusade against the Hussites, and again an immense force was precipitated upon Bohemia, but only to suffer terrible defeat. Another crusade was proclaimed. In all the papal countries of Europe, men, money, and munitions of war were raised. Multitudes flocked to the papal standard, assured that at last an end would be made of the Hussite heretics. Confident of victory, the vast force entered Bohemia. The people rallied to repel them. The two armies approached each other until only a river lay between them. "The crusaders were in greatly superior force, but instead of dashing across the stream, and closing in battle with the Hussites whom they had come so far to meet, they stood gazing in silence at those warriors."—Wylie, b. 3, ch. 17. Then suddenly a mysterious terror fell upon the host. Without striking a blow, that mighty force broke and scattered as if dispelled by an unseen power. Great numbers were slaughtered by the Hussite army, which pursued the fugitives, and an immense booty fell into the hands of the victors, so that the war, instead of impoverishing, enriched the Bohemians.

A few years later, under a new pope, still another crusade was set on foot. As before, men [117] and means were drawn from all the papal countries of Europe. Great were the inducements held out to those who should engage in this perilous enterprise. Full forgiveness of the most heinous crimes was ensured to every crusader. All who died in the war were promised a rich reward in heaven, and those who survived were to reap honor and riches on the field of battle. Again a vast army was collected, and, crossing the frontier they entered Bohemia. The Hussite forces fell back before them, thus drawing the invaders farther and farther into the country, and leading them to count the victory already won. At last the army of Procopius made a stand, and turning upon the foe, advanced to give them battle. The crusaders, now discovering their mistake, lay in their encampment awaiting the onset. As the sound of the approaching force was heard, even before the Hussites were in sight, a panic again fell upon the crusaders. Princes, generals, and common soldiers, casting away their armor, fled in all directions. In vain the papal legate, who was the leader of the invasion, endeavored to rally his terrified and disorganized forces. Despite his utmost endeavors, he himself was swept along in the tide of fugitives. The rout was complete, and again an immense booty fell into the hands of the victors.

Thus the second time a vast army, sent forth by the most powerful nations of Europe, a host of brave, warlike men, trained and equipped for battle, fled without a blow before the defenders of a small and hitherto feeble nation. Here was a manifestation of divine power. The invaders were smitten with a supernatural terror. He who overthrew the hosts of Pharaoh in the Red Sea, who put to flight the armies of Midian before Gideon and his three hundred, who in one night laid low the forces of the proud Assyrian, had again stretched out His hand to wither the power of the oppressor. "There were they in great fear, where no fear was: for God hath scattered the bones of him that encampeth against thee: thou hast put them to shame, because God hath despised them." Psalm 53:5. [118]

The papal leaders, despairing of conquering by force, at last resorted to diplomacy. A compromise was entered into, that while professing to grant to the Bohemians freedom of conscience, really betrayed them into the power of Rome. The Bohemians had specified four points as the condition of peace with Rome: the free preaching of the Bible; the right of the whole church to both the bread and the wine in the communion, and the use of the mother tongue in divine worship; the exclusion of the clergy from all secular offices and authority; and, in cases of crime, the jurisdiction of the civil courts over clergy and laity alike. The papal authorities at last "agreed that the four articles of the Hussites should be accepted, but that the right of explaining them, that is, of determining their precise import, should belong to the council—in other words, to the pope and the emperor."—Wylie, b. 3, ch. 18. On this basis a treaty was entered into, and Rome gained by dissimulation and fraud what she had failed to gain by conflict; for, placing her own interpretation upon the Hussite articles, as upon the Bible, she could pervert their meaning to suit her own purposes.

A large class in Bohemia, seeing that it betrayed their liberties, could not consent to the compact. Dissensions and divisions arose, leading to strife and bloodshed among themselves. In this strife the noble Procopius fell, and the liberties of Bohemia perished.

Sigismund, the betrayer of Huss and Jerome, now became king of Bohemia, and regardless of his oath to support the rights of the Bohemians, he proceeded to establish popery. But he had gained little by his subservience to Rome. For twenty years his life had been filled with labors and perils. His armies had been wasted and his treasuries drained by a long and fruitless struggle; and now, after reigning one year, he died, leaving his kingdom on the brink of civil war, and bequeathing to posterity a name branded with infamy.

Tumults, strife, and bloodshed were protract-
119 ed. Again foreign armies invaded Bohemia, and internal dissension continued to distract the nation. Those who remained faithful to the gospel were subjected to a bloody persecution.

As their former brethren, entering into compact with Rome, imbibed her errors, those who adhered to the ancient faith had formed themselves into a distinct church, taking the name of "United Brethren." This act drew upon them maledictions from all classes. Yet their firmness was unshaken. Forced to find refuge in the woods and caves, they still assembled to read God's word and unite in His worship.

Through messengers secretly sent out into different countries, they learned that here and there were "isolated confessors of the truth, a few in this city and a few in that, the object, like themselves, of persecution; and that amid the mountains of the Alps was an ancient church, resting on the foundations of Scripture, and protesting against the idolatrous corruptions of Rome."—Wylie, b. 3, ch. 19. This intelligence was received with great joy, and a correspondence was opened with the Waldensian Christians.

Steadfast to the gospel, the Bohemians waited through the night of their persecution, in the darkest hour still turning their eyes toward the horizon like men who watch for the morning. "Their lot was cast in evil days, but . . . they remembered the words first uttered by Huss, and repeated by Jerome, that a century must revolve before the day should break. These were to the Taborites [Hussites] what the words of

Joseph were to the tribes in the house of bondage: 'I die, and God will surely visit you, and bring you out.'"—*Ibid.*, b. 3, ch. 19. "The closing period of the fifteenth century witnessed the slow but sure increase of the churches of the Brethren. Although far from being unmolested, they yet enjoyed comparative rest. At the commencement of the sixteenth century their churches numbered two hundred in Bohemia and Moravia."—Ezra Hall Gillett, *Life and Times of John Huss*, vol. 2, p. 570. "So goodly was the remnant which, escaping the destructive fury of fire and sword, was permitted to see the dawning of that day which Huss had foretold."—Wylie, b. 3, ch. 19.

7

120

Luther's Separation
From Rome

Foremost among those who were called to lead the church from the darkness of popery into the light of a purer faith, stood Martin Luther. Zealous, ardent, and devoted, knowing no fear but the fear of God, and acknowledging no foundation for religious faith but the Holy Scriptures, Luther was the man for his time; through him God accomplished a great work for the reformation of the church and the enlightenment of the world.

Like the first heralds of the gospel, Luther sprang from the ranks of poverty. His early years were spent in the humble home of a German peasant. By daily toil as a miner his father earned the means for his education. He intended him for a lawyer; but God purposed to make him a builder in the great temple that was rising so slowly through the centuries. Hardship, privation, and severe discipline were the school in which Infinite Wisdom prepared Luther for the important mission of his life.

Luther's father was a man of strong and active mind and great force of character, honest, resolute, and straightforward. He was true to his convictions of duty, let the consequences be what they might. His sterling good sense led him to regard the monastic system with distrust. He was highly displeased when Luther, without his consent, entered a monastery; and it was two years before the father was reconciled to his son, and even then his opinions remained the same.

Luther's parents bestowed great care upon the education and training of their children. They endeavored to instruct them in the knowledge of God and the practice of Christian virtues. The father's prayer often ascended in the hearing of his son that the child might remember the name

121

of the Lord and one day aid in the advancement of His truth. Every advantage for moral or intellectual culture which their life of toil permitted them to enjoy was eagerly improved by these parents. Their efforts were earnest and persevering to prepare their children for a life of piety and usefulness. With their firmness and strength of character they sometimes exercised too great severity; but the Reformer himself, though conscious that in some respects they had erred, found in their discipline more to approve than to condemn.

At school, where he was sent at an early age, Luther was treated with harshness and even violence. So great was the poverty of his parents that upon going from home to school in another town he was for a time obliged to obtain his food by singing from door to door, and he often suffered from hunger. The gloomy, superstitious ideas of religion then prevailing filled him with fear. He would lie down at night with a sorrowful heart, looking forward with trembling to the dark future and in constant terror at the thought of God as a stern, unrelenting judge, a cruel tyrant, rather than a kind heavenly Father.

Yet under so many and so great discouragements Luther pressed resolutely forward toward the high standard of moral and intellectual excellence which attracted his soul. He thirsted for knowledge, and the earnest and practical character of his mind led him to desire the solid and useful rather than the showy and superficial.

When, at the age of eighteen, he entered the University of Erfurt, his situation was more favorable and his prospects were brighter than in his earlier years. His parents having by thrift and industry acquired a competence, they were 122 able to render him all needed assistance. And the influence of judicious friends had somewhat lessened the gloomy effects of his former training. He applied himself to the study of the best authors, diligently treasuring their most weighty thoughts and making the wisdom of the wise his own. Even under the harsh discipline of his former instructors he had early given promise of distinction, and with favorable influences his mind rapidly developed. A retentive memory, a lively imagination, strong reasoning powers, and untiring application soon placed him in the foremost rank among his associates. Intellectual discipline ripened his understanding and aroused an activity of mind and a keenness of perception that were preparing him for the conflicts of his life.

The fear of the Lord dwelt in the heart of Luther, enabling him to maintain his steadfastness of purpose and leading him to deep humility before God. He had an abiding sense of his dependence upon divine aid, and he did not fail to begin each day with prayer, while his heart was continually breathing a petition for guidance and support. "To pray well," he often said,

"is the better half of study."—D'Aubigné, b. 2, ch. 2.

While one day examining the books in the library of the university, Luther discovered a Latin Bible. Such a book he had never before seen. He was ignorant even of its existence. He had heard portions of the Gospels and Epistles, which were read to the people at public worship, and he supposed that these were the entire Bible. Now, for the first time, he looked upon the whole of God's word. With mingled awe and wonder he turned the sacred pages; with quickened pulse and throbbing heart he read for himself the words of life, pausing now and then to exclaim: "O that God would give me such a book for myself!"—*Ibid.*, b. 2, ch. 2. Angels of heaven were by his side, and rays of light from the throne of God revealed the treasures of truth to his understanding. He had ever feared to offend God, but now the deep conviction of his condition as a sinner took hold upon him as never before. 123

An earnest desire to be free from sin and to find peace with God led him at last to enter a cloister and devote himself to a monastic life. Here he was required to perform the lowest drudgery and to beg from house to house. He was at an age when respect and appreciation are most eagerly craved, and these menial offices were deeply mortifying to his natural feelings; but he patiently endured this humiliation, believing that it was necessary because of his sins.

Every moment that could be spared from his daily duties he employed in study, robbing himself of sleep and grudging even the time spent at his scanty meals. Above everything else he delighted in the study of God's word. He had found a Bible chained to the convent wall, and to this he often repaired. As his convictions of sin deepened, he sought by his own works to obtain pardon and peace. He led a most rigorous life, endeavoring by fasting, vigils, and scourgings to subdue the evils of his nature, from which the monastic life had brought no release. He shrank from no sacrifice by which he might attain to that purity of heart which would enable him to stand approved before God. "I was indeed a pious monk," he afterward said, "and followed the rules of my order more strictly than I can express. If ever monk could obtain heaven by his monkish works, I should certainly have been entitled to it. . . . If it had continued much longer, I should have carried my mortifications even to death."—*Ibid.*, b. 2, ch. 3. As the result of this painful discipline he lost strength and suffered from fainting spasms, from the effects of which he never fully recovered. But with all his efforts his burdened soul found no relief. He was at last driven to the verge of despair.

When it appeared to Luther that all was lost,

God raised up a friend and helper for him. The pious Staupitz opened the word of God to Luther's mind and bade him look away from himself, cease the contemplation of infinite punishment for the violation of God's law, and look 124 to Jesus, his sin-pardoning Saviour. "Instead of torturing yourself on account of your sins, throw yourself into the Redeemer's arms. Trust in Him, in the righteousness of His life, in the atonement of His death. . . . Listen to the Son of God. He became man to give you the assurance of divine favor." "Love Him who first loved you."—*Ibid*., b. 2, ch. 4. Thus spoke this messenger of mercy. His words made a deep impression upon Luther's mind. After many a struggle with long-cherished errors, he was enabled to grasp the truth, and peace came to his troubled soul.

Luther was ordained a priest and was called from the cloister to a professorship in the University of Wittenberg. Here he applied himself to the study of the Scriptures in the original tongues. He began to lecture upon the Bible; and the book of Psalms, the Gospels, and the Epistles were opened to the understanding of crowds of delighted listeners. Staupitz, his friend and superior, urged him to ascend the pulpit and preach the word of God. Luther hesitated, feeling himself unworthy to speak to the people in Christ's stead. It was only after a long struggle that he yielded to the solicitations of his friends. Already he was mighty in the Scriptures, and the grace of God rested upon him. His eloquence captivated his hearers, the clearness and power with which he presented the truth convinced their understanding, and his fervor touched their hearts.

Luther was still a true son of the papal church and had no thought that he would ever be anything else. In the providence of God he was led to visit Rome. He pursued his journey on foot, lodging at the monasteries on the way. At a convent in Italy he was filled with wonder at the wealth, magnificence, and luxury that he witnessed. Endowed with a princely revenue, the monks dwelt in splendid apartments, attired themselves in the richest and most costly robes, and feasted at a sumptuous table. With painful misgivings Luther contrasted this scene with the self-denial and hardship of his own life. His mind was becoming perplexed.

125 At last he beheld in the distance the seven-hilled city. With deep emotion he prostrated himself upon the earth, exclaiming: "Holy Rome, I salute thee!"—*Ibid*., b. 2, ch. 6. He entered the city, visited the churches, listened to the marvelous tales repeated by priests and monks, and performed all the ceremonies required. Everywhere he looked upon scenes that filled him with astonishment and horror. He saw that iniquity existed among all classes of the clergy. He heard indecent jokes from prelates, and was filled with horror at their awful profanity, even during mass. As he mingled with the monks and citizens he met dissipation, debauchery. Turn where he would, in the place of sanctity he found profanation. "No one can imagine," he wrote, "what sins and infamous actions are committed in Rome; they must be seen and heard to be believed. Thus they are in the habit of saying, 'If there is a hell, Rome is built over it: it is an abyss whence issues every kind of sin.'"—*Ibid*., b. 2, ch. 6.

By a recent decretal an indulgence had been promised by the pope to all who should ascend upon their knees "Pilate's staircase," said to have been descended by our Saviour on leaving the Roman judgment hall and to have been miraculously conveyed from Jerusalem to Rome. Luther was one day devoutly climbing these steps, when suddenly a voice like thunder seemed to say to him: "The just shall live by faith." Romans 1:17. He sprang to his feet and hastened from the place in shame and horror. That text never lost its power upon his soul. From that time he saw more clearly than ever before the fallacy of trusting to human works for salvation, and the necessity of constant faith in the merits of Christ. His eyes had been opened, and were never again to be closed, to the delusions of the papacy. When he turned his face from Rome he had turned away also in heart, and from that time the separation grew wider, until he severed all connection with the papal church.

After his return from Rome, Luther received at the University of Wittenberg the degree of doctor of divinity. Now he was at liberty to 126 devote himself, as never before, to the Scriptures that he loved. He had taken a solemn vow to study carefully and to preach with fidelity the word of God, not the sayings and doctrines of the popes, all the days of his life. He was no longer the mere monk or professor, but the authorized herald of the Bible. He had been called as a shepherd to feed the flock of God, that were hungering and thirsting for the truth. He firmly declared that Christians should receive no other doctrines than those which rest on the authority of the Sacred Scriptures. These words struck at the very foundation of papal supremacy. They contained the vital principle of the Reformation.

Luther saw the danger of exalting human theories above the word of God. He fearlessly attacked the speculative infidelity of the schoolmen and opposed the philosophy and theology which had so long held a controlling influence upon the people. He denounced such studies as not only worthless but pernicious, and sought to turn the minds of his hearers from the sophistries of philosophers and theologians to the eternal truths set forth by prophets and apostles.

Precious was the message which he bore to the eager crowds that hung upon his words. Never before had such teachings fallen upon their ears. The glad tidings of a Saviour's love, the assurance of pardon and peace through His atoning blood, rejoiced their hearts and inspired within them an immortal hope. At Wittenberg a light was kindled whose rays should extend to the uttermost parts of the earth, and which was to increase in brightness to the close of time.

But light and darkness cannot harmonize. Between truth and error there is an irrepressible conflict. To uphold and defend the one is to attack and overthrow the other. Our Saviour Himself declared: "I came not to send peace, but a sword." Matthew 10:34. Said Luther, a few years after the opening of the Reformation: "God does not guide me, He pushes me forward. He carries me away. I am not master of myself. I desire to live in repose; but I am thrown into the midst of tumults and revolutions."—D'Aubigné, b. 5, ch. 2. He was now about to be urged into the contest.

The Roman Church had made merchandise of the grace of God. The tables of the money-changers (Matthew 21:12) were set up beside her altars, and the air resounded with the shouts of buyers and sellers. Under the plea of raising funds for the erection of St. Peter's Church at Rome, indulgences for sin were publicly offered for sale by the authority of the pope. By the price of crime a temple was to be built up for God's worship—the cornerstone laid with the wages of iniquity! But the very means adopted for Rome's aggrandizement provoked the deadliest blow to her power and greatness. It was this that aroused the most determined and successful of the enemies of popery, and led to the battle which shook the papal throne and jostled the triple crown upon the pontiff's head.

The official appointed to conduct the sale of indulgences in Germany—Tetzel by name—had been convicted of the basest offenses against society and against the law of God; but having escaped the punishment due for his crimes, he was employed to further the mercenary and unscrupulous projects of the pope. With great effrontery he repeated the most glaring falsehoods and related marvelous tales to deceive an ignorant, credulous, and superstitious people. Had they possessed the word of God they would not have been thus deceived. It was to keep them under the control of the papacy, in order to swell the power and wealth of her ambitious leaders, that the Bible had been withheld from them. (See John C. L. Gieseler, A Compendium of Ecclesiastical History, per. 4, sec. 1, par. 5.)

As Tetzel entered a town, a messenger went before him, announcing: "The grace of God and of the holy father is at your gates."—D'Aubigné, b. 3, ch. 1. And the people welcomed the blasphemous pretender as if he were God Himself come down from heaven to them. The infamous traffic was set up in the church, and Tetzel, [128] ascending the pulpit, extolled the indulgences as the most precious gift of God. He declared that by virtue of his certificates of pardon all the sins which the purchaser should afterward desire to commit would be forgiven him, and that "not even repentance is necessary."—*Ibid.*, b. 3, ch. 1. More than this, he assured his hearers that the indulgences had power to save not only the living but the dead; that the very moment the money should clink against the bottom of his chest, the soul in whose behalf it had been paid would escape from purgatory and make its way to heaven. (See K. R. Hagenbach, *History of the Reformation*, vol. 1, p. 96.)

When Simon Magus offered to purchase of the apostles the power to work miracles, Peter answered him: "Thy money perish with thee, because thou hast thought that the gift of God may be purchased with money." Acts 8:20. But Tetzel's offer was grasped by eager thousands. Gold and silver flowed into his treasury. A salvation that could be bought with money was more easily obtained than that which requires repentance, faith, and diligent effort to resist and overcome sin. (See Appendix note for page 59.)

The doctrine of indulgences had been opposed by men of learning and piety in the Roman Church, and there were many who had no faith in pretensions so contrary to both reason and revelation. No prelate dared lift his voice against this iniquitous traffic; but the minds of men were becoming disturbed and uneasy, and many eagerly inquired if God would not work through some instrumentality for the purification of His church.

Luther, though still a papist of the straitest sort, was filled with horror at the blasphemous assumptions of the indulgence mongers. Many of his own congregation had purchased certificates of pardon, and they soon began to come to their pastor, confessing their various sins, and expecting absolution, not because they were penitent and wished to reform, but on the ground of the indulgence. Luther refused them absolution, and warned [129] them that unless they should repent and reform their lives, they must perish in their sins. In great perplexity they repaired to Tetzel with the complaint that their confessor had refused his certificates; and some boldly demanded that their money be returned to them. The friar was filled with rage. He uttered the most terrible curses, caused fires to be lighted in the public squares, and declared that he "had received an order from the pope to burn all heretics who presumed to oppose his most holy indulgences."— D'Aubigné, b. 3, ch. 4.

Luther now entered boldly upon his work as a

champion of the truth. His voice was heard from the pulpit in earnest, solemn warning. He set before the people the offensive character of sin, and taught them that it is impossible for man, by his own works, to lessen its guilt or evade its punishment. Nothing but repentance toward God and faith in Christ can save the sinner. The grace of Christ cannot be purchased; it is a free gift. He counseled the people not to buy indulgences, but to look in faith to a crucified Redeemer. He related his own painful experience in vainly seeking by humiliation and penance to secure salvation, and assured his hearers that it was by looking away from himself and believing in Christ that he found peace and joy.

As Tetzel continued his traffic and his impious pretensions, Luther determined upon a more effectual protest against these crying abuses. An occasion soon offered. The castle church of Wittenberg possessed many relics, which on certain holy days were exhibited to the people, and full remission of sins was granted to all who then visited the church and made confession. Accordingly on these days the people in great numbers resorted thither. One of the most important of these occasions, the festival of All Saints, was approaching. On the preceding day, Luther, joining the crowds that were already making their way to the church, posted on its door a paper containing ninety-five propositions 130 against the doctrine of indulgences. He declared his willingness to defend these theses next day at the university, against all who should see fit to attack them.

His propositions attracted universal attention. They were read and reread, and repeated in every direction. Great excitement was created in the university and in the whole city. By these theses it was shown that the power to grant the pardon of sin, and to remit its penalty, had never been committed to the pope or to any other man. The whole scheme was a farce,—an artifice to extort money by playing upon the superstitions of the people,—a device of Satan to destroy the souls of all who should trust to its lying pretensions. It was also clearly shown that the gospel of Christ is the most valuable treasure of the church, and that the grace of God, therein revealed, is freely bestowed upon all who seek it by repentance and faith.

Luther's theses challenged discussion; but no one dared accept the challenge. The questions which he proposed had in a few days spread through all Germany, and in a few weeks they had sounded throughout Christendom. Many devoted Romanists, who had seen and lamented the terrible iniquity prevailing in the church, but had not known how to arrest its progress, read the propositions with great joy, recognizing in them the voice of God. They felt that the Lord had graciously set His hand to arrest the rapidly

swelling tide of corruption that was issuing from the see of Rome. Princes and magistrates secretly rejoiced that a check was to be put upon the arrogant power which denied the right of appeal from its decisions.

But the sin-loving and superstitious multitudes were terrified as the sophistries that had soothed their fears were swept away. Crafty ecclesiastics, interrupted in their work of sanctioning crime, and seeing their gains endangered, were enraged, and rallied to uphold their pretensions. The Reformer had bitter accusers to meet. Some charged him with acting hastily and from impulse. Others accused him of presumption, declaring that he was not directed of God, but was acting from pride and forwardness. 131 "Who does not know," he responded, "that a man rarely puts forth any new idea without having some appearance of pride, and without being accused of exciting quarrels? . . . Why were Christ and all the martyrs put to death? Because they seemed to be proud contemners of the wisdom of the time, and because they advanced novelties without having first humbly taken counsel of the oracles of the ancient opinions."

Again he declared: "Whatever I do will be done, not by the prudence of men, but by the counsel of God. If the work be of God, who shall stop it? if it be not, who can forward it? Not my will, nor theirs, nor ours; but Thy will, O holy Father, which art in heaven."—*Ibid.*, b. 3, ch. 6.

Though Luther had been moved by the Spirit of God to begin his work, he was not to carry it forward without severe conflicts. The reproaches of his enemies, their misrepresentation of his purposes, and their unjust and malicious reflections upon his character and motives, came in upon him like an overwhelming flood; and they were not without effect. He had felt confident that the leaders of the people, both in the church and in the schools, would gladly unite with him in efforts for reform. Words of encouragement from those in high position had inspired him with joy and hope. Already in anticipation he had seen a brighter day dawning for the church. But encouragement had changed to reproach and condemnation. Many dignitaries, of both church and state, were convicted of the truthfulness of his theses; but they soon saw that the acceptance of these truths would involve great changes. To enlighten and reform the people would be virtually to undermine the authority of Rome, to stop thousands of streams now flowing into her treasury, and thus greatly to curtail the extravagance and luxury of the papal leaders. Furthermore, to teach the people to think and act as responsible beings, looking to Christ alone for salvation, would overthrow the pontiff's throne and eventually destroy their own authority. For this reason they refused the

132 knowledge tendered them of God and arrayed themselves against Christ and the truth by their opposition to the man whom He had sent to enlighten them.

Luther trembled as he looked upon himself— one man opposed to the mightiest powers of earth. He sometimes doubted whether he had indeed been led of God to set himself against the authority of the church. "Who was I," he writes, "to oppose the majesty of the pope, before whom . . . the kings of the earth and the whole world trembled? . . . No one can know what my heart suffered during these first two years, and into what despondency, I may say into what despair, I was sunk."—*Ibid.*, b. 3, ch. 6. But he was not left to become utterly disheartened. When human support failed, he looked to God alone and learned that he could lean in perfect safety upon that all-powerful arm.

To a friend of the Reformation Luther wrote: "We cannot attain to the understanding of Scripture either by study or by the intellect. Your first duty is to begin by prayer. Entreat the Lord to grant you, of His great mercy, the true understanding of His word. There is no other interpreter of the word of God than the Author of this word, as He Himself has said, 'They shall be all taught of God.' Hope for nothing from your own labors, from your own understanding: trust solely in God, and in the influence of His Spirit. Believe this on the word of a man who has had experience."—*Ibid.*, b. 3, ch. 7. Here is a lesson of vital importance to those who feel that God has called them to present to others the solemn truths for this time. These truths will stir the enmity of Satan and of men who love the fables that he has devised. In the conflict with the powers of evil there is need of something more than strength of intellect and human wisdom.

When enemies appealed to custom and tradition, or to the assertions and authority of the pope, Luther met them with the Bible and the Bible only. Here were arguments which they could not answer; therefore the slaves of formalism and superstition clamored for his blood, 133 as the Jews had clamored for the blood of Christ. "He is a heretic," cried the Roman zealots. "It is high treason against the church to allow so horrible a heretic to live one hour longer. Let the scaffold be instantly erected for him!"—*Ibid.*, b. 3, ch. 9. But Luther did not fall a prey to their fury. God had a work for him to do, and angels of heaven were sent to protect him. Many, however, who had received from Luther the precious light were made the objects of Satan's wrath and for the truth's sake fearlessly suffered torture and death.

Luther's teachings attracted the attention of thoughtful minds throughout all Germany. From his sermons and writings issued beams of light which awakened and illuminated thousands. A living faith was taking the place of the dead formalism in which the church had so long been held. The people were daily losing confidence in the superstitions of Romanism. The barriers of prejudice were giving way. The word of God, by which Luther tested every doctrine and every claim, was like a two-edged sword, cutting its way to the hearts of the people. Everywhere there was awakening a desire for spiritual progress. Everywhere was such a hungering and thirsting after righteousness as had not been known for ages. The eyes of the people, so long directed to human rites and earthly mediators, were now turning in penitence and faith to Christ and Him crucified.

This widespread interest aroused still further the fears of the papal authorities. Luther received a summons to appear at Rome to answer to the charge of heresy. The command filled his friends with terror. They knew full well the danger that threatened him in that corrupt city, already drunk with the blood of the martyrs of Jesus. They protested against his going to Rome and requested that he receive his examination in Germany.

This arrangement was finally effected, and the pope's legate was appointed to hear the case. In the instructions communicated by the pontiff to this official, it was stated that Luther had already been declared a heretic. The legate was therefore charged "to prosecute and con- 134 strain without any delay." If he should remain steadfast, and the legate should fail to gain possession of his person, he was empowered "to proscribe him in every part of Germany; to banish, curse, and excommunicate all those who are attached to him."—*Ibid.*, b. 4, ch. 2. And, further, the pope directed his legate, in order entirely to root out the pestilent heresy, to excommunicate all, of whatever dignity in church or state, except the emperor, who should neglect to seize Luther and his adherents, and deliver them up to the vengeance of Rome.

Here is displayed the true spirit of popery. Not a trace of Christian principle, or even of common justice, is to be seen in the whole document. Luther was at a great distance from Rome; he had had no opportunity to explain or defend his position; yet before his case had been investigated, he was summarily pronounced a heretic, and in the same day, exhorted, accused, judged, and condemned; and all this by the self-styled holy father, the only supreme, infallible authority in church or state!

At this time, when Luther so much needed the sympathy and counsel of a true friend, God's providence sent Melanchthon to Wittenberg. Young in years, modest and diffident in his manners, Melanchthon's sound judgment, extensive knowledge, and winning eloquence, combined with the purity and uprightness of his character, won universal admiration and esteem. The brilliancy of his talents was not more marked than his gentleness of disposition. He soon became an earnest disciple of the gospel, and Luther's most trusted friend and valued supporter; his gentleness, caution, and exactness serving as a complement to Luther's courage and energy. Their union in the work added strength to the Reformation and was a source of great encouragement to Luther.

Augsburg had been fixed upon as the place of trial, and the Reformer set out on foot to perform the journey thither. Serious fears were entertained in his behalf. Threats had been made openly that he would be seized and murdered on 135 the way, and his friends begged him not to venture. They even entreated him to leave Wittenberg for a time and find safety with those who would gladly protect him. But he would not leave the position where God had placed him. He must continue faithfully to maintain the truth, notwithstanding the storms that were beating upon him. His language was: "I am like Jeremiah, a man of strife and contention; but the more their threats increase, the more my joy is multiplied. . . . They have already destroyed my honor and my reputation. One single thing remains; it is my wretched body: let them take it; they will thus shorten my life by a few hours. But as for my soul, they cannot take that. He who desires to proclaim the word of Christ to the world, must expect death at every moment."—*Ibid.*, b. 4, ch. 4.

The tidings of Luther's arrival at Augsburg gave great satisfaction to the papal legate. The troublesome heretic who was exciting the attention of the whole world seemed now in the power of Rome, and the legate determined that he should not escape. The Reformer had failed to provide himself with a safe-conduct. His friends urged him not to appear before the legate without one, and they themselves undertook to procure it from the emperor. The legate intended to force Luther, if possible, to retract, or, failing in this, to cause him to be conveyed to Rome, to share the fate of Huss and Jerome. Therefore through his agents he endeavored to induce Luther to appear without a safe-conduct, trusting himself to his mercy. This the Reformer firmly declined to do. Not until he had received the document pledging him the emperor's protection, did he appear in the presence of the papal ambassador.

As a matter of policy, the Romanists had decided to attempt to win Luther by an appearance of gentleness. The legate, in his interviews with him, professed great friendliness; but he demanded that Luther submit implicitly to the authority of the church, and yield every point without argument or question. He had not rightly estimated the character of the man with whom he had to deal. Luther, in reply,

expressed his regard for the church, his desire 136 for the truth, his readiness to answer all objections to what he had taught, and to submit his doctrines to the decision of certain leading universities. But at the same time he protested against the cardinal's course in requiring him to retract without having proved him in error.

The only response was: "Retract, retract!" The Reformer showed that his position was sustained by the Scriptures and firmly declared that he could not renounce the truth. The legate, unable to reply to Luther's arguments, overwhelmed him with a storm of reproaches, gibes, and flattery, interspersed with quotations from tradition and the sayings of the Fathers, granting the Reformer no opportunity to speak. Seeing that the conference, thus continued, would be utterly futile, Luther finally obtained a reluctant permission to present his answer in writing.

"In so doing," said he, writing to a friend, "the oppressed find double gain; first, what is written may be submitted to the judgment of others; and second, one has a better chance of working on the fears, if not on the conscience, of an arrogant and babbling despot, who would otherwise overpower by his imperious language."—Martyn, *The Life and Times of Luther*, pages 271, 272.

At the next interview, Luther presented a clear, concise, and forcible exposition of his views, fully supported by many quotations from Scripture. This paper, after reading aloud, he handed to the cardinal, who, however, cast it contemptuously aside, declaring it to be a mass of idle words and irrelevant quotations. Luther, fully aroused, now met the haughty prelate on his own ground—the traditions and teachings of the church—and utterly overthrew his assumptions.

When the prelate saw that Luther's reasoning was unanswerable, he lost all self-control, and in a rage cried out: "Retract! or I will send you to Rome, there to appear before the judges commissioned to take cognizance of your cause. I will excommunicate you and all your partisans, 137 and all who shall at any time countenance you, and will cast them out of the church." And he finally declared, in a haughty and angry tone: "Retract, or return no more."—D'Aubigné, London ed., b. 4, ch. 8.

The Reformer promptly withdrew with his friends, thus declaring plainly that no retraction was to be expected from him. This was not what the cardinal had purposed. He had flattered himself that by violence he could awe Luther to submission. Now, left alone with his supporters, he looked from one to another in utter chagrin at the unexpected failure of his schemes.

Luther's efforts on this occasion were not without good results. The large assembly present had opportunity to compare the two men, and to judge for themselves of the spirit manifested by them, as well as of the strength and truthfulness of their positions. How marked the contrast! The Reformer, simple, humble, firm, stood up in the strength of God, having truth on his side; the pope's representative, self-important, overbearing, haughty, and unreasonable, was without a single argument from the Scriptures, yet vehemently crying: "Retract, or be sent to Rome for punishment."

Notwithstanding Luther had secured a safe-conduct, the Romanists were plotting to seize and imprison him. His friends urged that as it was useless for him to prolong his stay, he should return to Wittenberg without delay, and that the utmost caution should be observed in order to conceal his intentions. He accordingly left Augsburg before daybreak, on horseback, accompanied only by a guide furnished him by the magistrate. With many forebodings he secretly made his way through the dark and silent streets of the city. Enemies, vigilant and cruel, were plotting his destruction. Would he escape the snares prepared for him? Those were moments of anxiety and earnest prayer. He reached a small gate in the wall of the city. It was opened for him, and with his guide he passed through without hindrance. Once safely outside, the fugitives hastened their flight, and before the legate learned of Luther's departure, he was beyond the reach of his persecutors. Satan and his emissaries were defeated. The man whom they had thought in their power was gone, escaped as a bird from the snare of the fowler.

At the news of Luther's escape the legate was overwhelmed with surprise and anger. He had expected to receive great honor for his wisdom and firmness in dealing with this disturber of the church; but his hope was disappointed. He gave expression to his wrath in a letter to Frederick, the elector of Saxony, bitterly denouncing Luther and demanding that Frederick send the Reformer to Rome or banish him from Saxony.

In defense, Luther urged that the legate or the pope show him his errors from the Scriptures, and pledged himself in the most solemn manner to renounce his doctrines if they could be shown to contradict the word of God. And he expressed his gratitude to God that he had been counted worthy to suffer in so holy a cause.

The elector had, as yet, little knowledge of the reformed doctrines, but he was deeply impressed by the candor, force, and clearness of Luther's words; and until the Reformer should be proved to be in error, Frederick resolved to stand as his protector. In reply to the legate's demand he wrote: "'Since Dr. Martin has appeared before you at Augsburg, you should be satisfied. We did not expect that you would endeavor to make him retract without having convinced him of his errors. None of the learned men in our principality have informed me that

Martin's doctrine is impious, antichristian, or heretical.' The prince refused, moreover, to send Luther to Rome, or to expel him from his states."—D'Aubigné, b. 4, ch. 10.

The elector saw that there was a general breaking down of the moral restraints of society. A great work of reform was needed. The complicated and expensive arrangements to restrain and punish crime would be unnecessary if men but acknowledged and obeyed the requirements of God and the dictates of an enlightened conscience. He saw that Luther was laboring to secure this object, and he secretly rejoiced that a better influence was making itself felt in the church.

He saw also that as a professor in the university Luther was eminently successful. Only a year had passed since the Reformer posted his theses on the castle church, yet there was already a great falling off in the number of pilgrims that visited the church at the festival of All Saints. Rome had been deprived of worshipers and offerings, but their place was filled by another class, who now came to Wittenberg, not pilgrims to adore her relics, but students to fill her halls of learning. The writings of Luther had kindled everywhere a new interest in the Holy Scriptures, and not only from all parts of Germany, but from other lands, students flocked to the university. Young men, coming in sight of Wittenberg for the first time, "raised their hands to heaven, and praised God for having caused the light of truth to shine forth from this city, as from Zion in times of old, and whence it spread even to the most distant countries."— *Ibid.*, b. 4, ch. 10.

Luther was as yet but partially converted from the errors of Romanism. But as he compared the Holy Oracles with the papal decrees and constitutions, he was filled with wonder. "I am reading," he wrote, "the decrees of the pontiffs, and . . . I do not know whether the pope is antichrist himself, or his apostle, so greatly is Christ misrepresented and crucified in them."— *Ibid.*, b. 5, ch. 1. Yet at this time Luther was still a supporter of the Roman Church, and had no thought that he would ever separate from her communion.

The Reformer's writings and his doctrine were extending to every nation in Christendom. The work spread to Switzerland and Holland. Copies of his writings found their way to France and Spain. In England his teachings were received as the word of life. To Belgium and Italy also the truth had extended. Thousands were awakening from their deathlike stupor to the joy and hope of a life of faith.

Rome became more and more exasperated by the attacks of Luther, and it was declared by some of his fanatical opponents, even by doctors in Catholic universities, that he who should kill the rebellious monk would be without sin.

One day a stranger, with a pistol hidden under his cloak, approached the Reformer and inquired why he went thus alone. "I am in God's hands," answered Luther. "He is my strength and my shield. What can man do unto me?"—*Ibid.*, b. 6, ch. 2. Upon hearing these words, the stranger turned pale and fled away as from the presence of the angels of heaven.

Rome was bent upon the destruction of Luther; but God was his defense. His doctrines were heard everywhere—"in cottages and convents, . . . in the castles of the nobles, in the universities, and in the palaces of kings;" and noble men were rising on every hand to sustain his efforts.—*Ibid.*, b. 6, ch. 2.

It was about this time that Luther, reading the works of Huss, found that the great truth of justification by faith, which he himself was seeking to uphold and teach, had been held by the Bohemian Reformer. "We have all," said Luther, "Paul, Augustine, and myself, been Hussites without knowing it!" "God will surely visit it upon the world," he continued, "that the truth was preached to it a century ago, and burned!"—Wylie, b. 6. ch. 1

In an appeal to the emperor and nobility of Germany in behalf of the reformation of Christianity, Luther wrote concerning the pope: "It is a horrible thing to behold the man who styles himself Christ's vicegerent, displaying a magnificence that no emperor can equal. Is this being like the poor Jesus, or the humble Peter? He is, say they, the lord of the world! But Christ, whose vicar he boasts of being, has said, 'My kingdom is not of this world.' Can the dominions of a vicar extend beyond those of his superior?"—D'Aubigné, b. 6, ch. 3.

He wrote thus of the universities: "I am much 141 afraid that the universities will prove to be the great gates of hell, unless they diligently labor in explaining the Holy Scriptures, and engraving them in the hearts of youth. I advise no one to place his child where the Scriptures do not reign paramount. Every institution in which men are not unceasingly occupied with the word of God must become corrupt."—*Ibid.*, b. 6, ch. 3.

This appeal was rapidly circulated throughout Germany and exerted a powerful influence upon the people. The whole nation was stirred, and multitudes were roused to rally around the standard of reform. Luther's opponents, burning with a desire for revenge, urged the pope to take decisive measures against him. It was decreed that his doctrines should be immediately condemned. Sixty days were granted the Reformer and his adherents, after which, if they did not recant, they were all to be excommunicated.

That was a terrible crisis for the Reformation. For centuries Rome's sentence of excommunication had struck terror to powerful monarchs; it had filled mighty empires with woe and desolation. Those upon whom its condemnation fell were universally regarded with dread and horror; they were cut off from intercourse with their fellows and treated as outlaws, to be hunted to extermination. Luther was not blind to the tempest about to burst upon him; but he stood firm, trusting in Christ to be his support and shield. With a martyr's faith and courage he wrote: "What is about to happen I know not, nor do I care to know. . . . Let the blow light where it may, I am without fear. Not so much as a leaf falls, without the will of our Father. How much rather will He care for us! It is a light thing to die for the Word, since the Word which was made flesh hath Himself died. If we die with Him, we shall live with Him; and passing through that which He has passed through before us, we shall be where He is and dwell with Him forever."—*Ibid.*, 3d London ed., Walther, 1840, b. 6, ch. 9.

When the papal bull reached Luther, he said: "I despise and attack it, as impious, false. . . . It 142 is *Christ* Himself who is condemned therein. . . . I rejoice in having to bear such ills for the best of causes. Already I feel greater liberty in my heart; for at last I know that the pope is antichrist, and that his throne is that of Satan himself."—D'Aubigné, b. 6, ch. 9.

Yet the mandate of Rome was not without effect. Prison, torture, and sword were weapons potent to enforce obedience. The weak and superstitious trembled before the decree of the pope; and while there was general sympathy for Luther, many felt that life was too dear to be risked in the cause of reform. Everything seemed to indicate that the Reformer's work was about to close.

But Luther was fearless still. Rome had hurled her anathemas against him, and the world looked on, nothing doubting that he would perish or be forced to yield. But with terrible power he flung back upon herself the sentence of condemnation and publicly declared his determination to abandon her forever. In the presence of a crowd of students, doctors, and citizens of all ranks Luther burned the pope's bull, with the canon laws, the decretals, and certain writings sustaining the papal power. "My enemies have been able, by burning my books," he said, "to injure the cause of truth in the minds of the common people, and destroy their souls; for this reason I consumed their books in return. A serious struggle has just begun. Hitherto I have been only playing with the pope. I began this work in God's name; it will be ended without me, and by His might."—*Ibid.*, b. 6, ch. 10.

To the reproaches of his enemies who taunted him with the weakness of his cause, Luther answered: "Who knows if God has not chosen and called me, and if they ought not to fear that, by despising me, they despise God Himself? Moses was alone at the departure from Egypt; Elijah was alone in the reign of King Ahab; Isaiah alone in Jerusalem; Ezekiel alone in Babylon. . . . God never selected as a prophet either the high priest or any other great personage; but ordinarily He chose low and despised men, once even the shepherd Amos. In every age, the saints have had to reprove the great, kings, princes, priests, and wise men, at the peril of their lives. . . . I do not say that I am a prophet; but I say that they ought to fear precisely because I am alone and that they are many. I am sure of this, that the word of God is with me, and that it is not with them."—*Ibid.*, b. 6, ch. 10.

Yet it was not without a terrible struggle with himself that Luther decided upon a final separation from the church. It was about this time that he wrote: "I feel more and more every day how difficult it is to lay aside the scruples which one has imbibed in childhood. Oh, how much pain it has caused me, though I had the Scriptures on my side, to justify it to myself that I should dare to make a stand alone against the pope, and hold him forth as antichrist! What have the tribulations of my heart not been! How many times have I not asked myself with bitterness that question which was so frequent on the lips of the papists: 'Art thou alone wise? Can everyone else be mistaken? How will it be, if, after all, it is thyself who art wrong, and who art involving in thy error so many souls, who will then be eternally damned?' 'Twas so I fought with myself and with Satan, till Christ, by His own infallible word, fortified my heart against these doubts."—Martyn, pages 372, 373.

The pope had threatened Luther with excommunication if he did not recant, and the threat was now fulfilled. A new bull appeared, declaring the Reformer's final separation from the Roman Church, denouncing him as accursed of Heaven, and including in the same condemnation all who should receive his doctrines. The great contest had been fully entered upon.

Opposition is the lot of all whom God employs to present truths specially applicable to their time. There was a present truth in the days of Luther,—a truth at that time of special importance; there is a present truth for the church today. He who does all things according to the counsel of His will has been pleased to place men under various circumstances and to enjoin upon them duties peculiar to the times in which they live and the conditions under which they are placed. If they would prize the light given them, broader views of truth would be opened before them. But truth is no more desired by the majority today than it was by the papists who opposed Luther. There is the same disposition to accept the theories and traditions of men instead of the word of God as in former ages. Those who present the truth for this time should not expect to be received with greater favor than were earlier reformers. The great controversy between truth and error, between Christ and

Satan, is to increase in intensity to the close of this world's history.

Said Jesus to His disciples: "If ye were of the world, the world would love his own: but because ye are not of the world, but I have chosen you out of the world, therefore the world hateth you. Remember the word that I said unto you, The servant is not greater than his Lord. If they have persecuted Me, they will also persecute you; if they have kept My saying, they will keep yours also." John 15:19, 20. And on the other hand our Lord declared plainly: "Woe unto you, when all men shall speak well of you! for so did their fathers to the false prophets." Luke 6:26. The spirit of the world is no more in harmony with the spirit of Christ today than in earlier times, and those who preach the word of God in its purity will be received with no greater favor now than then. The forms of opposition to the truth may change, the enmity may be less open because it is more subtle; but the same antagonism still exists and will be manifested to the end of time.

8

Luther Before the Diet

A new emperor, Charles V, had ascended the throne of Germany, and the emissaries of Rome hastened to present their congratulations and induce the monarch to employ his power against the Reformation. On the other hand, the elector of Saxony, to whom Charles was in great degree indebted for his crown, entreated him to take no step against Luther until he should have granted him a hearing. The emperor was thus placed in a position of great perplexity and embarrassment. The papists would be satisfied with nothing short of an imperial edict sentencing Luther to death. The elector had declared firmly that "neither his imperial majesty nor any other person had shown that Luther's writings had been refuted;" therefore he requested "that Dr. Luther should be furnished with a safe-conduct, so that he might appear before a tribunal of learned, pious, and impartial judges."—D'Aubigné, b. 6, ch. 11.

The attention of all parties was now directed to the assembly of the German states which convened at Worms soon after the accession of Charles to the empire. There were important political questions and interests to be considered by this national council; for the first time the princes of Germany were to meet their youthful monarch in deliberative assembly. From all parts of the fatherland had come the dignitaries of church and state. Secular lords, highborn, powerful, and jealous of their hereditary rights; princely ecclesiastics, flushed with their conscious superiority in rank and power; courtly knights and their armed retainers; and ambassadors from foreign and distant lands,—all gathered at Worms. Yet in that vast assembly the subject that excited the deepest interest was the cause of the Saxon Reformer.

Charles had previously directed the elector to bring Luther with him to the Diet, assuring him of protection, and promising a free discussion, with competent persons, of the questions in dispute. Luther was anxious to appear before the emperor. His health was at this time much impaired; yet he wrote to the elector: "If I cannot go to Worms in good health, I will be carried there, sick as I am. For if the emperor calls me, I cannot doubt that it is the call of God Himself. If they desire to use violence against me, and that is very probable (for it is not for their instruction that they order me to appear), I place the matter in the Lord's hands. He still lives and reigns who preserved the three young men in the burning fiery furnace. If He will not save me, my life is of little consequence. Let us only prevent the gospel from being exposed to the scorn of the wicked, and let us shed our blood for it, for fear they should triumph. It is not for me to decide whether my life or my death will contribute most to the salvation of all. . . . You may expect everything from me . . . except flight and recantation. Fly I cannot, and still less retract."—*Ibid.*, b. 7, ch. 1.

As the news was circulated at Worms that Luther was to appear before the Diet, a general excitement was created. Aleander, the papal legate to whom the case had been specially entrusted, was alarmed and enraged. He saw that the result would be disastrous to the papal cause. To institute inquiry into a case in which the pope had already pronounced sentence of condemnation would be to cast contempt upon the authority of the sovereign pontiff. Furthermore, he was apprehensive that the eloquent and powerful arguments of this man might turn away many of the princes from the cause of the pope. He therefore, in the most urgent manner, remonstrated with Charles against Luther's appearance at Worms. About this time the bull declaring Luther's excommunication was published; and this, coupled with the representations of the legate, induced the emperor to yield. He wrote to the elector that if Luther would not retract, he must remain at Wittenberg.

Not content with this victory, Aleander labored with all the power and cunning at his command to secure Luther's condemnation. With a persistence worthy of a better cause, he urged the matter upon the attention of princes, prelates, and other members of the assembly, accusing the Reformer of "sedition, rebellion, impiety, and blasphemy." But the vehemence and passion manifested by the legate revealed too plainly the spirit by which he was actuated.

"He is moved by hatred and vengeance," was the general remark, "much more than by zeal and piety."—*Ibid.*, b. 7, ch. 1. The majority of the Diet were more than ever inclined to regard Luther's cause with favor.

With redoubled zeal Aleander urged upon the emperor the duty of executing the papal edicts. But under the laws of Germany this could not be done without the concurrence of the princes; and, overcome at last by the legate's importunity, Charles bade him present his case to the Diet. "It was a proud day for the nuncio. The assembly was a great one: the cause was even greater. Aleander was to plead for Rome, . . . the mother and mistress of all churches." He was to vindicate the princedom of Peter before the assembled principalities of Christendom. "He had the gift of eloquence, and he rose to the greatness of the occasion. Providence ordered it that Rome should appear and plead by the ablest of her orators in the presence of the most august of tribunals, before she was condemned."— Wylie, b. 6, ch. 4. With some misgivings those who favored the Reformer looked forward to the effect of Aleander's speech. The elector of Saxony was not present, but by his direction some of his councilors attended to take notes of the nuncio's address.

With all the power of learning and eloquence, Aleander set himself to overthrow the truth. Charge after charge he hurled against Luther as an enemy of the church and the state, the living and the dead, clergy and laity, councils and private Christians. "In Luther's errors there is enough," he declared, to warrant the burning of "a hundred thousand heretics."

In conclusion he endeavored to cast contempt upon the adherents of the reformed faith: "What are all these Lutherans? A crew of insolent pedagogues, corrupt priests, dissolute monks, ignorant lawyers, and degraded nobles, with the common people whom they have misled and perverted. How far superior to them is the Catholic party in number, ability, and power! A unanimous decree from this illustrious assembly will enlighten the simple, warn the imprudent, decide the waverers, and give strength to the weak."—D'Aubigné, b. 7, ch. 3.

With such weapons the advocates of truth in every age have been attacked. The same arguments are still urged against all who dare to present, in opposition to established errors, the plain and direct teachings of God's word. "Who are these preachers of new doctrines?" exclaim those who desire a popular religion. "They are unlearned, few in numbers, and of the poorer class. Yet they claim to have the truth, and to be the chosen people of God. They are ignorant and deceived. How greatly superior in numbers and influence is our church! How many great and learned men are among us! How much more power is on our side!" These are the arguments that have a telling influence upon the world; but they are no more conclusive now than in the days of the Reformer.

The Reformation did not, as many suppose, end with Luther. It is to be continued to the close of this world's history. Luther had a great work to do in reflecting to others the light which God had permitted to shine upon him; yet he did not receive all the light which was to be given to the world. From that time to this, new light has been continually shining upon the Scriptures, and new truths have been constantly unfolding.

The legate's address made a deep impression upon the Diet. There was no Luther present, with the clear and convincing truths of God's word, to vanquish the papal champion. No attempt was made to defend the Reformer. There was manifest a general disposition not only to condemn him and the doctrines which he taught, but if possible to uproot the heresy. Rome had enjoyed the most favorable opportunity to defend her cause. All that she could say in her own vindication had been said. But the apparent victory was the signal of defeat. Henceforth the contrast between truth and error would be more clearly seen, as they should take the field in open warfare. Never from that day would Rome stand as secure as she had stood.

While most of the members of the Diet would not have hesitated to yield up Luther to the vengeance of Rome, many of them saw and deplored the existing depravity in the church, and desired a suppression of the abuses suffered by the German people in consequence of the corruption and greed of the hierarchy. The legate had presented the papal rule in the most favorable light. Now the Lord moved upon a member of the Diet to give a true delineation of the effects of papal tyranny. With noble firmness, Duke George of Saxony stood up in that princely assembly and specified with terrible exactness the deceptions and abominations of popery, and their dire results. In closing he said: "These are some of the abuses that cry out against Rome. All shame has been put aside, and their only object is . . . money, money, money, . . . so that the preachers who should teach the truth, utter nothing but falsehoods, and are not only tolerated, but rewarded, because the greater their lies, the greater their gain. It is from this foul spring that such tainted waters flow. Debauchery stretches out the hand to avarice. . . . Alas, it is the scandal caused by the clergy that hurls so many poor souls into eternal condemnation. A general reform must be effected."—*Ibid.*, b. 7, ch. 4.

A more able and forcible denunciation of the papal abuses could not have been presented by Luther himself; and the fact that the speaker was a determined enemy of the Reformer's gave greater influence to his words.

Had the eyes of the assembly been opened, they would have beheld angels of God in the midst of them, shedding beams of light athwart the darkness of error and opening minds and hearts to the reception of truth. It was the power of the God of truth and wisdom that controlled even the adversaries of the reformation, and thus prepared the way for the great work about to be accomplished. Martin Luther was not present; but the voice of One greater than Luther had been heard in that assembly.

A committee was at once appointed by the Diet to prepare an enumeration of the papal oppressions that weighed so heavily on the German people. This list, containing a hundred and one specifications, was presented to the emperor, with a request that he would take immediate measures for the correction of these abuses. "What a loss of Christian souls," said the petitioners, "what depredations, what extortions, on account of the scandals by which the spiritual head of Christendom is surrounded! It is our duty to prevent the ruin and dishonor of our people. For this reason we most humbly but most urgently entreat you to order a general reformation, and to undertake its accomplishment."—*Ibid.*, b. 7, ch. 4.

The council now demanded the Reformer's appearance before them. Notwithstanding the entreaties, protests, and threats of Aleander, the emperor at last consented, and Luther was summoned to appear before the Diet. With the summons was issued a safe-conduct, ensuring his return to a place of security. These were borne to Wittenberg by a herald, who was commissioned to conduct him to Worms.

The friends of Luther were terrified and distressed. Knowing the prejudice and enmity against him, they feared that even his safe-conduct would not be respected, and they entreated him not to imperil his life. He replied: "The papists do not desire my coming to Worms, but my condemnation and my death. It matters not. Pray not for me, but for the word of God. . . . Christ will give me His Spirit to overcome these ministers of error. I despise them during my life; I shall triumph over them by my death. They are busy at Worms about compelling me to retract; and this shall be my retraction: I said formerly that the pope was Christ's vicar; now I assert that he is our Lord's adversary, and the devil's apostle."—*Ibid.*, b. 7, ch. 6.

Luther was not to make his perilous journey alone. Besides the imperial messenger, three of his firmest friends determined to accompany him. Melanchthon earnestly desired to join them. His heart was knit to Luther's, and he yearned to follow him, if need be, to prison or to death. But his entreaties were denied. Should Luther perish, the hopes of the Reformation must center upon his youthful colaborer. Said the Reformer as he parted from Melanchthon: "If I do not return, and my enemies put me to death, continue to teach, and stand fast in the truth. Labor in my stead. . . . If you survive, my death will be of little consequence."—*Ibid.*, b. 7, ch. 7. Students and citizens who had gathered to witness Luther's departure were deeply moved. A multitude whose hearts had been touched by the gospel, bade him farewell with weeping. Thus the Reformer and his companions set out from Wittenberg.

On the journey they saw that the minds of the people were oppressed by gloomy forebodings. At some towns no honors were proffered them. As they stopped for the night, a friendly priest expressed his fears by holding up before Luther the portrait of an Italian reformer who had suffered martyrdom. The next day they learned that Luther's writings had been condemned at Worms. Imperial messengers were proclaiming the emperor's decree and calling upon the people to bring the proscribed works to the magistrates. The herald, fearing for Luther's safety at the council, and thinking that already his resolution might be shaken, asked if he still wished to go forward. He answered: "Although interdicted 152 in every city, I shall go on."—*Ibid.*, b. 7, ch. 7.

At Erfurt, Luther was received with honor. Surrounded by admiring crowds, he passed through the streets that he had often traversed with his beggar's wallet. He visited his convent cell, and thought upon the struggles through which the light now flooding Germany had been shed upon his soul. He was urged to preach. This he had been forbidden to do, but the herald granted him permission, and the friar who had once been made the drudge of the convent, now entered the pulpit.

To a crowded assembly he spoke from the words of Christ, "Peace be unto you." "Philosophers, doctors, and writers," he said, "have endeavored to teach men the way to obtain everlasting life, and they have not succeeded. I will now tell it to you: . . . God has raised one Man from the dead, the Lord Jesus Christ, that He might destroy death, extirpate sin, and shut the gates of hell. This is the work of salvation. . . . Christ has vanquished! this is the joyful news; and we are saved by His work, and not by our own. . . . Our Lord Jesus Christ said, 'Peace be unto you; behold My hands;' that is to say, Behold, O man! it is I, I alone, who have taken away thy sin, and ransomed thee; and now thou hast peace, saith the Lord."

He continued, showing that true faith will be manifested by a holy life. "Since God has saved us, let us so order our works that they may be acceptable to Him. Art thou rich? let thy goods administer to the necessities of the poor. Art thou poor? let thy services be acceptable to the rich. If thy labor is useful to thyself alone, the service that thou pretendest to render unto God is a lie."—*Ibid.*, b. 7, ch. 7.

The people listened as if spellbound. The bread of life was broken to those starving souls. Christ was lifted up before them as above popes, legates, emperors, and kings. Luther made no reference to his own perilous position. He did not seek to make himself the object of thought or sympathy. In the contemplation of Christ he had lost sight of self. He hid behind the Man of Calvary, seeking only to present Jesus as the sinner's Redeemer.   153

As the Reformer proceeded on his journey, he was everywhere regarded with great interest. An eager multitude thronged about him, and friendly voices warned him of the purpose of the Romanists. "They will burn you," said some, "and reduce your body to ashes, as they did with John Huss." Luther answered, "Though they should kindle a fire all the way from Worms to Wittenberg, the flames of which reached to heaven, I would walk through it in the name of the Lord; I would appear before them; I would enter the jaws of this behemoth, and break his teeth, confessing the Lord Jesus Christ."—*Ibid.*, b. 7, ch. 7.

The news of his approach to Worms created great commotion. His friends trembled for his safety; his enemies feared for the success of their cause. Strenuous efforts were made to dissuade him from entering the city. At the instigation of the papists he was urged to repair to the castle of a friendly knight, where, it was declared, all difficulties could be amicably adjusted. Friends endeavored to excite his fears by describing the dangers that threatened him. All their efforts failed. Luther, still unshaken, declared: "Even should there be as many devils in Worms as tiles on the housetops, still I would enter it."—*Ibid.*, b. 7, ch. 7.

Upon his arrival at Worms, a vast crowd flocked to the gates to welcome him. So great a concourse had not assembled to greet the emperor himself. The excitement was intense, and from the midst of the throng a shrill and plaintive voice chanted a funeral dirge as a warning to Luther of the fate that awaited him. "God will be my defense," said he, as he alighted from his carriage.

The papists had not believed that Luther would really venture to appear at Worms, and his arrival filled them with consternation. The emperor immediately summoned his councilors to consider what course should be pursued. One of the bishops, a rigid papist, declared: "We have long consulted on this matter. Let your imperial majesty get rid of this man at once. Did not Sigismund cause John Huss to be burnt? We 154 are not bound either to give or to observe the safe-conduct of a heretic." "No," said the emperor, "we must keep our promise."—*Ibid.*, b. 7, ch. 8. It was therefore decided that the Reformer should be heard.

All the city were eager to see this remarkable man, and a throng of visitors soon filled his lodgings. Luther had scarcely recovered from his recent illness; he was wearied from the journey, which had occupied two full weeks; he must prepare to meet the momentous events of the morrow, and he needed quiet and repose. But so great was the desire to see him that he had enjoyed only a few hours' rest when noblemen, knights, priests, and citizens gathered eagerly about him. Among these were many of the nobles who had so boldly demanded of the emperor a reform of ecclesiastical abuses and who, says Luther, "had all been freed by my gospel."—Martyn, page 393. Enemies, as well as friends, came to look upon the dauntless monk; but he received them with unshaken calmness, replying to all with dignity and wisdom. His bearing was firm and courageous. His pale, thin face, marked with the traces of toil and illness, wore a kindly and even joyous expression. The solemnity and deep earnestness of his words gave him a power that even his enemies could not wholly withstand. Both friends and foes were filled with wonder. Some were convinced that a divine influence attended him; others declared, as had the Pharisees concerning Christ: "He hath a devil."

On the following day Luther was summoned to attend the Diet. An imperial officer was appointed to conduct him to the hall of audience; yet it was with difficulty that he reached the place. Every avenue was crowded with spectators eager to look upon the monk who had dared resist the authority of the pope.

As he was about to enter the presence of his judges, an old general, the hero of many battles, said to him kindly: "Poor monk, poor monk, thou art now going to make a nobler stand than I or any other captains have ever made in the bloodiest of our battles. But if thy cause is just, 155 and thou art sure of it, go forward in God's name, and fear nothing. God will not forsake thee."—D'Aubigné, b. 7, ch. 8.

At length Luther stood before the council. The emperor occupied the throne. He was surrounded by the most illustrious personages in the empire. Never had any man appeared in the presence of a more imposing assembly than that before which Martin Luther was to answer for his faith. "This appearance was of itself a signal victory over the papacy. The pope had condemned the man, and he was now standing before a tribunal which, by this very act, set itself above the pope. The pope had laid him under an interdict, and cut him off from all human society; and yet he was summoned in respectful language, and received before the most august assembly in the world. The pope had condemned him to perpetual silence, and he was now about to speak before thousands of attentive hearers drawn together from the farthest parts of Christendom. An immense revolution had thus been effected by Luther's instrumentality. Rome was already descending from her throne, and it was the voice of a monk that caused this humiliation."—Ibid., b. 7, ch. 8.

In the presence of that powerful and titled assembly the lowly born Reformer seemed awed and embarrassed. Several of the princes, observing his emotion, approached him, and one of them whispered: "Fear not them which kill the body, but are not able to kill the soul." Another said: "When ye shall be brought before governors and kings for My sake, it shall be given you, by the Spirit of your Father, what ye shall say." Thus the words of Christ were brought by the world's great men to strengthen His servant in the hour of trial.

Luther was conducted to a position directly in front of the emperor's throne. A deep silence fell upon the crowded assembly. Then an imperial officer arose and, pointing to a collection of Luther's writings, demanded that the Reformer answer two questions—whether he acknowledged them as his, and whether he proposed to retract the opinions which he had therein 156 advanced. The titles of the books having been read, Luther replied that as to the first question, he acknowledged the books to be his. "As to the second," he said, "seeing that it is a question which concerns faith and the salvation of souls, and in which the word of God, the greatest and most precious treasure either in heaven or earth, is involved, I should act imprudently were I to reply without reflection. I might affirm less than the circumstance demands, or more than truth requires, and so sin against this saying of Christ: 'Whosoever shall deny Me before men, him will I also deny My Father which is in heaven.' [Matthew 10:33.] For this reason I entreat your imperial majesty, with all humility, to allow me time, that I may answer without offending against the word of God."—D'Aubigné, b. 7, ch. 8.

In making this request, Luther moved wisely. His course convinced the assembly that he did not act from passion or impulse. Such calmness and self-command, unexpected in one who had shown himself bold and uncompromising, added to his power, and enabled him afterward to answer with a prudence, decision, wisdom, and dignity that surprised and disappointed his adversaries, and rebuked their insolence and pride.

The next day he was to appear to render his final answer. For a time his heart sank within him as he contemplated the forces that were combined against the truth. His faith faltered; fearfulness and trembling came upon him, and horror overwhelmed him. Dangers multiplied before him; his enemies seemed about to triumph, and the powers of darkness to prevail. Clouds gathered about him and seemed to separate him from God. He longed for the assurance that the Lord of hosts would be with him. In anguish of spirit he threw himself with his face upon the earth and poured out those broken, heart-rending cries, which none but God can fully understand.

"O almighty and everlasting God," he pleaded, "how terrible is this world! Behold, it 157 openeth its mouth to swallow me up, and I have so little trust in Thee. . . . If it is only in the strength of this world that I must put my trust, all is over. . . . My last hour is come, my condemnation has been pronounced. . . . O God, do Thou help me against all the wisdom of the world. Do this, . . . Thou alone; . . . for this is not my work, but Thine. I have nothing to do here, nothing to contend for with these great ones of the world. . . . But the cause is Thine, . . . and it is a righteous and eternal cause. O Lord, help me! Faithful and unchangeable God, in no man do I place my trust. . . . All that is of man is uncertain; all that cometh of man fails. . . . Thou hast chosen me for this work. . . . Stand at my side, for the sake of Thy well-beloved Jesus Christ, who is my defense, my shield, and my strong tower."—*Ibid.*, b. 7, ch. 8.

An all-wise Providence had permitted Luther to realize his peril, that he might not trust to his own strength and rush presumptuously into danger. Yet it was not the fear of personal suffering, a dread of torture or death, which seemed immediately impending, that overwhelmed him with its terror. He had come to the crisis, and he felt his insufficiency to meet it. Through his weakness the cause of truth might suffer loss. Not for his own safety, but for the triumph of the gospel did he wrestle with God. Like Israel's, in that night struggle beside the lonely stream, was the anguish and conflict of his soul. Like Israel, he prevailed with God. In his utter helplessness his faith fastened upon Christ, the mighty Deliverer. He was strengthened with the assurance that he would not appear alone before the council. Peace returned to his soul, and he rejoiced that he was permitted to uplift the word of God before the rulers of the nations.

With his mind stayed upon God, Luther prepared for the struggle before him. He thought upon the plan of his answer, examined passages in his own writings, and drew from the Holy Scriptures suitable proofs to sustain his positions. Then, laying his left hand on the Sacred Volume, which was open before him, he lifted 158 his right hand to heaven and vowed "to remain faithful to the gospel, and freely to confess his faith, even should he seal his testimony with his blood."—*Ibid.*, b. 7, ch. 8.

When he was again ushered into the presence of the Diet, his countenance bore no trace of fear or embarrassment. Calm and peaceful, yet grandly brave and noble, he stood as God's witness among the great ones of the earth. The imperial officer now demanded his decision as to whether he desired to retract his doctrines.

Luther made his answer in a subdued and humble tone, without violence or passion. His demeanor was diffident and respectful; yet he manifested a confidence and joy that surprised the assembly.

"Most serene emperor, illustrious princes, gracious lords," said Luther, "I appear before you this day, in conformity with the order given me yesterday, and by God's mercies I conjure your majesty and your august highnesses to listen graciously to the defense of a cause which I am assured is just and true. If, through ignorance, I should transgress the usages and proprieties of courts, I entreat you to pardon me; for I was not brought up in the palaces of kings, but in the seclusion of a convent."—*Ibid.*, b. 7, ch. 8.

Then, proceeding to the question, he stated that his published works were not all of the same character. In some he had treated of faith and good works, and even his enemies declared them not only harmless but profitable. To retract these would be to condemn truths which all parties confessed. The second class consisted of writings exposing the corruptions and abuses of the papacy. To revoke these works would strengthen the tyranny of Rome and open a wider door to many and great impieties. In the third class of his books he had attacked individuals who had defended existing evils. Concerning these he freely confessed that he had been more violent than was becoming. He did not claim to be free from fault; but even these books he could not revoke, for such a course would embolden the enemies of truth, and they would then take occasion to crush God's people with still greater cruelty.   159

"Yet I am but a mere man, and not God," he continued; "I shall therefore defend myself as Christ did: 'If I have spoken evil, bear witness of the evil.' . . . By the mercy of God, I conjure you, most serene emperor, and you, most illustrious princes, and all men of every degree, to prove from the writings of the prophets and apostles that I have erred. As soon as I am convinced of this, I will retract every error, and be the first to lay hold of my books and throw them into the fire.

"What I have just said plainly shows, I hope, that I have carefully weighed and considered the dangers to which I expose myself; but far from being dismayed, I rejoice to see that the gospel is now, as in former times, a cause of trouble and dissension. This is the character, this is the destiny, of the word of God. 'I came not to send peace on earth, but a sword,' said Jesus Christ. God is wonderful and terrible in His counsels; beware lest, by presuming to quench dissensions, you should persecute the holy word of God, and draw down upon yourselves a frightful deluge of insurmountable dangers, of present disasters, and eternal desolation. . . . I might quote many examples from the oracles of God. I might speak of the Pharaohs, the kings of Babylon, and those of Israel, whose labors never more effectually contributed to their own destruction than when they sought by counsels, to all appearance most wise, to strengthen their dominion. 'God removeth mountains, and they know it not.'"—*Ibid.*, b. 7, ch. 8.

Luther had spoken in German; he was now requested to repeat the same words in Latin. Though exhausted by the previous effort, he complied, and again delivered his speech, with the same clearness and energy as at the first. God's providence directed in this matter. The minds of many of the princes were so blinded by error and superstition that at the first delivery they did not see the force of Luther's reasoning; but the repetition enabled them to perceive clearly the points presented.

160   Those who stubbornly closed their eyes to the light, and determined not to be convinced of the truth, were enraged at the power of Luther's words. As he ceased speaking, the spokesman of the Diet said angrily: "You have not answered the question put to you. . . . You are required to give a clear and precise answer. . . . Will you, or will you not, retract?"

The Reformer answered: "Since your most serene majesty and your high mightinesses require from me a clear, simple, and precise answer, I will give you one, and it is this: I cannot submit my faith either to the pope or to the councils, because it is clear as the day that they have frequently erred and contradicted each other. Unless therefore I am convinced by the testimony of Scripture or by the clearest reasoning, unless I am persuaded by means of the passages I have quoted, and unless they thus render my conscience bound by the word of God, *I cannot and I will not retract*, for it is unsafe for a Christian to speak against his conscience. Here I stand, I can do no other; may God help me. Amen."—*Ibid.*, b. 7, ch. 8.

Thus stood this righteous man upon the sure foundation of the word of God. The light of heaven illuminated his countenance. His greatness and purity of character, his peace and joy of heart, were manifest to all as he testified against the power of error and witnessed to the superiority of that faith that overcomes the world.

The whole assembly were for a time speechless with amazement. At his first answer Luther had spoken in a low tone, with a respectful, almost submissive bearing. The Romanists had interpreted this as evidence that his courage was beginning to fail. They regarded the request for delay as merely the prelude to his recantation. Charles himself, noting, half contemptuously, the monk's worn frame, his plain attire, and the simplicity of his address, had declared: "This monk will never make a heretic of me." The

courage and firmness which he now displayed, as well as the power and clearness of his reasoning, filled all parties with surprise. The emperor, moved to admiration, exclaimed: "This monk speaks with an intrepid heart and unshaken courage." Many of the German princes looked with pride and joy upon this representative of their nation.   161

The partisans of Rome had been worsted; their cause appeared in a most unfavorable light. They sought to maintain their power, not by appealing to the Scriptures, but by a resort to threats, Rome's unfailing argument. Said the spokesman of the Diet: "If you do not retract, the emperor and the states of the empire will consult what course to adopt against an incorrigible heretic."

Luther's friend, who had with great joy listened to his noble defense, trembled at these words; but the doctor himself said calmly: "May God be my helper, for I can retract nothing."—*Ibid.*, b. 7, ch. 8.

He was directed to withdraw from the Diet while the princes consulted together. It was felt that a great crisis had come. Luther's persistent refusal to submit might affect the history of the church for ages. It was decided to give him one more opportunity to retract. For the last time he was brought into the assembly. Again the question was put, whether he would renounce his doctrines. "I have no other reply to make," he said, "than that which I have already made." It was evident that he could not be induced, either by promises or threats, to yield to the mandate of Rome.

The papal leaders were chagrined that their power, which had caused kings and nobles to tremble, should be thus despised by a humble monk; they longed to make him feel their wrath by torturing his life away. But Luther, understanding his danger, had spoken to all with Christian dignity and calmness. His words had been free from pride, passion, and misrepresentation. He had lost sight of himself, and the great men surrounding him, and felt only that he was in the presence of One infinitely superior to popes, prelates, kings, and emperors. Christ had spoken through Luther's testimony with a power and grandeur that for the time inspired both friends and foes with awe and wonder. The Spirit of God had been present in that council, impressing the hearts of the chiefs of the empire. Several of the princes boldly acknowledged the justice of Luther's cause. Many were convinced of the truth; but with some the impressions received were not lasting. There was another class who did not at the time express their convictions, but who, having searched the Scriptures for themselves, at a future time became fearless supporters of the Reformation.   162

The elector Frederick had looked forward

anxiously to Luther's appearance before the Diet, and with deep emotion he listened to his speech. With joy and pride he witnessed the doctor's courage, firmness, and self-possession, and determined to stand more firmly in his defense. He contrasted the parties in contest, and saw that the wisdom of popes, kings, and prelates had been brought to nought by the power of truth. The papacy had sustained a defeat which would be felt among all nations and in all ages.

As the legate perceived the effect produced by Luther's speech, he feared, as never before, for the security of the Romish power, and resolved to employ every means at his command to effect the Reformer's overthrow. With all the eloquence and diplomatic skill for which he was so eminently distinguished, he represented to the youthful emperor the folly and danger of sacrificing, in the cause of an insignificant monk, the friendship and support of the powerful see of Rome.

His words were not without effect. On the day following Luther's answer, Charles caused a message to be presented to the Diet, announcing his determination to carry out the policy of his predecessors to maintain and protect the Catholic religion. Since Luther had refused to renounce his errors, the most vigorous measures should be employed against him and the heresies he taught. "A single monk, misled by his own folly, has risen against the faith of Chris-

163 tendom. To stay such impiety, I will sacrifice my kingdoms, my treasures, my friends, my body, my blood, my soul, and my life. I am about to dismiss the Augustine Luther, forbidding him to cause the least disorder among the people; I shall then proceed against him and his adherents as contumacious heretics, by excommunication, by interdict, and by every means calculated to destroy them. I call on the members of the states to behave like faithful Christians."—*Ibid.*, b. 7, ch. 9. Nevertheless the emperor declared that Luther's safe-conduct must be respected, and that before proceedings against him could be instituted, he must be allowed to reach his home in safety.

Two conflicting opinions were now urged by the members of the Diet. The emissaries and representatives of the pope again demanded that the Reformer's safe-conduct should be disregarded. "The Rhine," they said, "should receive his ashes, as it had received those of John Huss a century ago."—*Ibid.*, b. 7, ch. 9. But princes of Germany, though themselves papists and avowed enemies to Luther, protested against such a breach of public faith, as a stain upon the honor of the nation. They pointed to the calamities which had followed the death of Huss, and declared that they dared not call down upon Germany, and upon the head of their youthful emperor, a repetition of those terrible evils.

Charles himself, in answer to the base proposal, said: "Though honor and faith should be banished from all the world, they ought to find a refuge in the hearts of princes."—*Ibid.*, b. 7, ch. 9. He was still further urged by the most bitter of Luther's papal enemies to deal with the Reformer as Sigismund had dealt with Huss—abandon him to the mercies of the church; but recalling the scene when Huss in public assembly had pointed to his chains and reminded the monarch of his plighted faith, Charles V declared: "I should not like to blush like Sigismund."—Lenfant, vol. 1, p. 422.

Yet Charles had deliberately rejected the truths presented by Luther. "I am firmly resolved to imitate the example of my ancestors," wrote the monarch.—D'Aubigné, b. 7, ch. 164
9. He had decided that he would not step out of the path of custom, even to walk in the ways of truth and righteousness. Because his fathers did, he would uphold the papacy, with all its cruelty and corruption. Thus he took his position, refusing to accept any light in advance of what his fathers had received, or to perform any duty that they had not performed.

There are many at the present day thus clinging to the customs and traditions of their fathers. When the Lord sends them additional light, they refuse to accept it, because, not having been granted to their fathers, it was not received by them. We are not placed where our fathers were; consequently our duties and responsibilities are not the same as theirs. We shall not be approved of God in looking to the example of our fathers to determine our duty instead of searching the word of truth for ourselves. Our responsibility is greater than was that of our ancestors. We are accountable for the light which they received, and which was handed down as an inheritance for us, and we are accountable also for the additional light which is now shining upon us from the word of God.

Said Christ of the unbelieving Jews: "If I had not come and spoken unto them, they had not had sin: but now they have no cloak for their sin." John 15:22. The same divine power had spoken through Luther to the emperor and princes of Germany. And as the light shone forth from God's word, His Spirit pleaded for the last time with many in that assembly. As Pilate, centuries before, permitted pride and popularity to close his heart against the world's Redeemer; as the trembling Felix bade the messenger of truth, "Go thy way for this time; when I have a convenient season, I will call for thee;" as the proud Agrippa confessed, "Almost thou persuadest me to be a Christian" (Acts 24:25; 26:28), yet turned away from the Heaven-sent message—so had Charles V, yielding to the dictates of worldly pride and policy, decided to reject the light of truth.

Rumors of the designs against Luther were

165 widely circulated, causing great excitement throughout the city. The Reformer had made many friends, who, knowing the treacherous cruelty of Rome toward all who dared expose her corruptions, resolved that he should not be sacrificed. Hundreds of nobles pledged themselves to protect him. Not a few openly denounced the royal message as evincing a weak submission to the controlling power of Rome. On the gates of houses and in public places, placards were posted, some condemning and others sustaining Luther. On one of these were written merely the significant words of the wise man: "Woe to thee, O land, when thy king is a child." Ecclesiastes 10:16. The popular enthusiasm in Luther's favor throughout all Germany convinced both the emperor and the Diet that any injustice shown him would endanger the peace of the empire and even the stability of the throne.

Frederick of Saxony maintained a studied reserve, carefully concealing his real feelings toward the Reformer, while at the same time he guarded him with tireless vigilance, watching all his movements and all those of his enemies. But there were many who made no attempt to conceal their sympathy with Luther. He was visited by princes, counts, barons, and other persons of distinction, both lay and ecclesiastical. "The doctor's little room," wrote Spalatin, "could not contain all the visitors who presented themselves."—Martyn, vol. 1, p. 404. The people gazed upon him as if he were more than human. Even those who had no faith in his doctrines could not but admire that lofty integrity which led him to brave death rather than violate his conscience.

Earnest efforts were made to obtain Luther's consent to a compromise with Rome. Nobles and princes represented to him that if he persisted in setting up his own judgment against that of the church and the councils he would soon be banished from the empire and would have no defense. To this appeal Luther answered: "The gospel of Christ cannot be preached without offense. . . . Why then should the fear or apprehension of danger separate me from the Lord, 166 and from that divine word which alone is truth? No; I would rather give up my body, my blood, and my life."—D'Aubigné, b. 7, ch. 10.

Again he was urged to submit to the judgment of the emperor, and then he would have nothing to fear. "I consent," said he in reply, "with all my heart, that the emperor, the princes, and even the meanest Christian, should examine and judge my works; but on one condition, that they take the word of God for their standard. Men have nothing to do but to obey it. Do not offer violence to my conscience, which is bound and chained up with the Holy Scriptures."—*Ibid.*, b. 7, ch. 10.

To another appeal he said: "I consent to renounce my safe-conduct. I place my person and my life in the emperor's hands, but the word of God—never!"—*Ibid.*, b. 7, ch. 10. He stated his willingness to submit to the decision of a general council, but only on condition that the council be required to decide according to the Scriptures. "In what concerns the word of God and the faith," he added, "every Christian is as good a judge as the pope, though supported by a million councils, can be for him."—Martyn, vol. 1, p. 410. Both friends and foes were at last convinced that further effort for reconciliation would be useless.

Had the Reformer yielded a single point, Satan and his hosts would have gained the victory. But his unwavering firmness was the means of emancipating the church, and beginning a new and better era. The influence of this one man, who dared to think and act for himself in religious matters, was to affect the church and the world, not only in his own time, but in all future generations. His firmness and fidelity would strengthen all, to the close of time, who should pass through a similar experience. The power and majesty of God stood forth above the counsel of men, above the mighty power of Satan.

Luther was soon commanded by the authority of the emperor to return home, and he knew that this notice would be speedily followed by his condemnation. Threatening clouds overhung his 167 path; but as he departed from Worms, his heart was filled with joy and praise. "The devil himself," said he, "guarded the pope's citadel; but Christ has made a wide breach in it, and Satan was constrained to confess that the Lord is mightier than he."—D'Aubigné, b. 7, ch. 11.

After his departure, still desirous that his firmness should not be mistaken for rebellion, Luther wrote to the emperor. "God, who is the searcher of hearts, is my witness," he said, "that I am ready most earnestly to obey your majesty, in honor or in dishonor, in life or in death, and with no exception save the word of God, by which man lives. In all the affairs of this present life, my fidelity shall be unshaken, for here to lose or to gain is of no consequence to salvation. But when eternal interests are concerned, God wills not that man should submit unto man. For such submission in spiritual matters is a real worship, and ought to be rendered solely to the Creator."—*Ibid.*, b. 7, ch. 11.

On the journey from Worms, Luther's reception was even more flattering than during his progress thither. Princely ecclesiastics welcomed the excommunicated monk, and civil rulers honored the man whom the emperor had denounced. He was urged to preach, and, notwithstanding the imperial prohibition, he again entered the pulpit. "I never pledged myself to chain up the word of God," he said, "nor will I."—Martyn, vol. 1, p. 420.

He had not been long absent from Worms, when the papists prevailed upon the emperor to issue an edict against him. In this decree Luther was denounced as "Satan himself under the form of a man and dressed in a monk's frock."— D'Aubigné, b. 7, ch. 11. It was commanded that as soon as his safe-conduct should expire, measures be taken to stop his work. All persons were forbidden to harbor him, to give him food or drink, or by word or act, in public or private, to aid or abet him. He was to be seized wherever he might be, and delivered to the authorities. His adherents also were to be imprisoned and their property confiscated. His writings were to be destroyed, and, finally, all who should dare to 168 act contrary to this decree were included in its condemnation. The elector of Saxony and the princes most friendly to Luther had left Worms soon after his departure, and the emperor's decree received the sanction of the Diet. Now the Romanists were jubilant. They considered the fate of the Reformation sealed.

God had provided a way of escape for His servant in this hour of peril. A vigilant eye had followed Luther's movements, and a true and noble heart had resolved upon his rescue. It was plain that Rome would be satisfied with nothing short of his death; only by concealment could he be preserved from the jaws of the lion. God gave wisdom to Frederick of Saxony to devise a plan for the Reformer's preservation. With the co-operation of true friends the elector's purpose was carried out, and Luther was effectually hidden from friends and foes. Upon his homeward journey he was seized, separated from his attendants, and hurriedly conveyed through the forest to the castle of Wartburg, an isolated mountain fortress. Both his seizure and his concealment were so involved in mystery that even Frederick himself for a long time knew not whither he had been conducted. This ignorance was not without design; so long as the elector knew nothing of Luther's whereabouts, he could reveal nothing. He satisfied himself that the Reformer was safe, and with this knowledge he was content.

Spring, summer, and autumn passed, and winter came, and Luther still remained a prisoner. Aleander and his partisans exulted as the light of the gospel seemed about to be extinguished. But instead of this, the Reformer was filling his lamp from the storehouse of truth; and its light was to shine forth with brighter radiance.

In the friendly security of the Wartburg, Luther for a time rejoiced in his release from the heat and turmoil of battle. But he could not long find satisfaction in quiet and repose. Accustomed to a life of activity and stern conflict, he could ill endure to remain inactive. In those soli-169 tary days the condition of the church rose up before him, and he cried in despair: "Alas! there is no one in this latter day of His anger, to stand like a wall before the Lord, and save Israel!"— *Ibid.*, b. 9, ch. 2. Again, his thoughts returned to himself, and he feared being charged with cowardice in withdrawing from the contest. Then he reproached himself for his indolence and self-indulgence. Yet at the same time he was daily accomplishing more than it seemed possible for one man to do. His pen was never idle. While his enemies flattered themselves that he was silenced, they were astonished and confused by tangible proof that he was still active. A host of tracts, issuing from his pen, circulated throughout Germany. He also performed a most important service for his countrymen by translating the New Testament into the German tongue. From his rocky Patmos he continued for nearly a whole year to proclaim the gospel and rebuke the sins and errors of the times.

But it was not merely to preserve Luther from the wrath of his enemies, nor even to afford him a season of quiet for these important labors, that God had withdrawn His servant from the stage of public life. There were results more precious than these to be secured. In the solitude and obscurity of his mountain retreat, Luther was removed from earthly supports and shut out from human praise. He was thus saved from the pride and self-confidence that are so often caused by success. By suffering and humiliation he was prepared again to walk safely upon the dizzy heights to which he had been so suddenly exalted.

As men rejoice in the freedom which the truth brings them, they are inclined to extol those whom God has employed to break the chains of error and superstition. Satan seeks to divert men's thoughts and affections from God, and to fix them upon human agencies; he leads them to honor the mere instrument and to ignore the Hand that directs all the events of providence. Too often religious leaders who are thus praised and reverenced lose sight of their dependence upon God and are led to trust in themselves. As 170 a result they seek to control the minds and consciences of the people, who are disposed to look to them for guidance instead of looking to the word of God. The work of reform is often retarded because of this spirit indulged by its supporters. From this danger, God would guard the cause of the Reformation. He desired that work to receive, not the impress of man, but that of God. The eyes of men had been turned to Luther as the expounder of the truth; he was removed that all eyes might be directed to the eternal Author of truth.

171

9

The Swiss Reformer

In the choice of instrumentalities for the reforming of the church, the same divine plan is seen as in that for the planting of the church. The heavenly Teacher passed by the great men of the earth, the titled and wealthy, who were accustomed to receive praise and homage as leaders of the people. They were so proud and self-confident in their boasted superiority that they could not be molded to sympathize with their fellow men and to become colaborers with the humble Man of Nazareth. To the unlearned, toiling fishermen of Galilee was the call addressed: "Follow Me, and I will make you fishers of men." Matthew 4:19. These disciples were humble and teachable. The less they had been influenced by the false teaching of their time, the more successfully could Christ instruct and train them for His service. So in the days of the Great Reformation. The leading Reformers were men from humble life—men who were most free of any of their time from pride of rank and from the influence of bigotry and priest-craft. It is God's plan to employ humble instruments to accomplish great results. Then the glory will not be given to men, but to Him who works through them to will and to do of His own good pleasure.

A few weeks after the birth of Luther in a miner's cabin in Saxony, Ulric Zwingli was born in a herdsman's cottage among the Alps.
172 Zwingli's surroundings in childhood, and his early training, were such as to prepare him for his future mission. Reared amid scenes of natural grandeur, beauty, and awful sublimity, his mind was early impressed with a sense of the greatness, the power, and the majesty of God. The history of the brave deeds achieved upon his native mountains kindled his youthful aspirations. And at the side of his pious grandmother he listened to the few precious Bible stories which she had gleaned from amid the legends and traditions of the church. With eager interest he heard of the grand deeds of patriarchs and prophets, of the shepherds who watched their flocks on the hills of Palestine where angels talked with them, of the Babe of Bethlehem and the Man of Calvary.

Like John Luther, Zwingli's father desired an education for his son, and the boy was early sent from his native valley. His mind rapidly developed, and it soon became a question where to find teachers competent to instruct him. At the age of thirteen he went to Bern, which then possessed the most distinguished school in Switzerland. Here, however, a danger arose which

threatened to blight the promise of his life. Determined efforts were put forth by the friars to allure him into a monastery. The Dominican and Franciscan monks were in rivalry for popular favor. This they endeavored to secure by the showy adornments of their churches, the pomp of their ceremonials, and the attractions of famous relics and miracle-working images.

The Dominicans of Bern saw that if they could win this talented young scholar, they would secure both gain and honor. His extreme youth, his natural ability as a speaker and writer, and his genius for music and poetry, would be more effective than all their pomp and display, in attracting the people to their services and increasing the revenues of their order. By deceit and flattery they endeavored to induce Zwingli to enter their convent. Luther, while a student at school, had buried himself in a convent cell, and he would have been lost to the world had not God's providence released him. Zwingli was not permitted to encounter the same peril. Provi- 173 dentially his father received information of the designs of the friars. He had no intention of allowing his son to follow the idle and worthless life of the monks. He saw that his future usefulness was at stake, and directed him to return home without delay.

The command was obeyed; but the youth could not be long content in his native valley, and he soon resumed his studies, repairing, after a time, to Basel. It was here that Zwingli first heard the gospel of God's free grace. Wittembach, a teacher of the ancient languages, had, while studying Greek and Hebrew, been led to the Holy Scriptures, and thus rays of divine light were shed into the minds of the students under his instruction. He declared that there was a truth more ancient, and of infinitely greater worth, than the theories taught by schoolmen and philosophers. This ancient truth was that the death of Christ is the sinner's only ransom. To Zwingli these words were as the first ray of light that precedes the dawn.

Zwingli was soon called from Basel to enter upon his lifework. His first field of labor was in an Alpine parish, not far distant from his native valley. Having received ordination as a priest, he "devoted himself with his whole soul to the search after divine truth; for he was well aware," says a fellow Reformer, "how much he must know to whom the flock of Christ is entrusted."—Wylie, b. 8, ch. 5. The more he searched the Scriptures, the clearer appeared the contrast between their truths and the heresies of Rome. He submitted himself to the Bible as the word of God, the only sufficient, infallible rule. He saw that it must be its own interpreter. He dared not attempt to explain Scripture to sustain a preconceived theory or doctrine, but held it his duty to learn what is its direct and obvious teaching. He sought to avail himself of every help to obtain a full and correct understanding of its meaning, and he invoked the aid of the Holy Spirit, which would, he declared, reveal it to all who sought it in sincerity and with prayer. "The Scriptures," said Zwingli, "come from God, not from man, and even that God who enlightens will give thee to understand that the speech comes from God. The word of God . . . cannot fail; it is bright, it teaches itself, it discloses itself, it illumines the soul with all salvation and grace, comforts it in God, humbles it, so that it loses and even forfeits itself, and embraces God." The truth of these words Zwingli himself had proved. Speaking of his experience at this time, he afterward wrote: "When . . . I began to give myself wholly up to the Holy Scriptures, philosophy and theology (scholastic) would always keep suggesting quarrels to me. At last I came to this, that I thought, 'Thou must let all that lie, and learn the meaning of God purely out of His own simple word.' Then I began to ask God for His light, and the Scriptures began to be much easier to me."— *Ibid.*, b. 8, ch. 6.

The doctrine preached by Zwingli was not received from Luther. It was the doctrine of Christ. "If Luther preaches Christ," said the Swiss Reformer, "he does what I am doing. Those whom he has brought to Christ are more numerous than those whom I have led. But this matters not. I will bear no other name than that of Christ, whose soldier I am, and who alone is my Chief. Never has one single word been written by me to Luther, nor by Luther to me. And why? . . . That it might be shown how much the Spirit of God is in unison with itself, since both of us, without any collusion, teach the doctrine of Christ with such uniformity."—D'Aubigné, b. 8, ch. 9.

In 1516 Zwingli was invited to become a preacher in the convent at Einsiedeln. Here he was to have a closer view of the corruptions of Rome and was to exert an influence as a Reformer that would be felt far beyond his native Alps. Among the chief attractions of Einsiedeln was an image of the Virgin which was said to have the power of working miracles. Above the gateway of the convent was the inscription, "Here a plenary remission of sins may be obtained."—*Ibid.*, b. 8, ch. 5. Pilgrims at all seasons resorted to the shrine of the Virgin; but at the great yearly festival of its consecration multitudes came from all parts of Switzerland, and even from France and Germany. Zwingli, greatly afflicted at the sight, seized the opportunity to proclaim liberty through the gospel to these bondslaves of superstition.

"Do not imagine," he said, "that God is in this temple more than in any other part of creation. Whatever be the country in which you dwell, God is around you, and hears you. . . . Can unprofitable works, long pilgrimages, offerings, images, the invocation of the Virgin or of the saints, secure for you the grace of God? . . . What avails the multitude of words with which we embody our prayers? What efficacy has a glossy cowl, a smooth-shorn head, a long and flowing robe, or gold-embroidered slippers? . . . God looks at the heart, and our hearts are far from Him." "Christ," he said, "who was once offered upon the cross, is the sacrifice and victim, that had made satisfaction for the sins of believers to all eternity."—*Ibid.*, b. 8, ch. 5.

To many listeners these teachings were unwelcome. It was a bitter disappointment to them to be told that their toilsome journey had been made in vain. The pardon freely offered to them through Christ they could not comprehend. They were satisfied with the old way to heaven which Rome had marked out for them. They shrank from the perplexity of searching for anything better. It was easier to trust their salvation to the priests and the pope than to seek for purity of heart.

But another class received with gladness the tidings of redemption through Christ. The observances enjoined by Rome had failed to bring peace of soul, and in faith they accepted the Saviour's blood as their propitiation. These returned to their homes to reveal to others the precious light which they had received. The truth was thus carried from hamlet to hamlet, from town to town, and the number of pilgrims to the Virgin's shrine greatly lessened. There was a falling off in the offerings, and consequently in the salary of Zwingli, which was drawn from them. But this caused him only joy as he saw that the power of fanaticism and superstition was being broken.

The authorities of the church were not blind to the work which Zwingli was accomplishing; but for the present they forbore to interfere. Hoping yet to secure him to their cause, they endeavored to win him by flatteries; and meanwhile the truth was gaining a hold upon the hearts of the people.

Zwingli's labors at Einsiedeln had prepared him for a wider field, and this he was soon to enter. After three years here he was called to the office of preacher in the cathedral at Zurich. This was then the most important town of the Swiss confederacy, and the influence exerted here would be widely felt. The ecclesiastics by whose invitation he came to Zurich were, however, desirous of preventing any innovations, and they accordingly proceeded to instruct him as to his duties.

"You will make every exertion," they said, "to collect the revenues of the chapter, without overlooking the least. You will exhort the faithful, both from the pulpit and in the confessional, to pay all tithes and dues, and to show by their offerings their affection to the church. You will be diligent in increasing the income arising from the sick, from masses, and in general from every ecclesiastical ordinance." "As for the administration of the sacraments, the preaching, and the care of the flock," added his instructors, "these are also the duties of the chaplain. But for these you may employ a substitute, and particularly in preaching. You should administer the sacraments to none but persons of note, and only when called upon; you are forbidden to do so without distinction of persons."—*Ibid.*, b. 8, ch. 6.

177 Zwingli listened in silence to this charge, and in reply, after expressing his gratitude for the honor of a call to this important station, he proceeded to explain the course which he proposed to adopt. "The life of Christ," he said, "has been too long hidden from the people. I shall preach upon the whole of the Gospel of St. Matthew, . . . drawing solely from the fountains of Scripture, sounding its depths, comparing one passage with another, and seeking for understanding by constant and earnest prayer. It is to God's glory, to the praise of His only Son, to the real salvation of souls, and to their edification in the true faith, that I shall consecrate my ministry."—*Ibid.*, b. 8, ch. 6. Though some of the ecclesiastics disapproved his plan, and endeavored to dissuade him from it, Zwingli remained steadfast. He declared that he was about to introduce no new method, but the old method employed by the church in earlier and purer times.

Already an interest had been awakened in the truths he taught; and the people flocked in great numbers to listen to his preaching. Many who had long since ceased to attend service were among his hearers. He began his ministry by opening the Gospels and reading and explaining to his hearers the inspired narrative of the life, teachings, and death of Christ. Here, as at Einsiedeln, he presented the word of God as the only infallible authority and the death of Christ as the only complete sacrifice. "It is to Christ," he said, "that I desire to lead you—to Christ, the true source of salvation."—*Ibid.*, b. 8, ch. 6. Around the preacher crowded the people of all classes, from statesmen and scholars to the artisan and the peasant. With deep interest they listened to his words. He not only proclaimed the offer of a free salvation, but fearlessly rebuked the evils and corruptions of the times. Many returned from the cathedral praising God. "This man," they said, "is a preacher of the truth. He will be our Moses, to lead us forth from this Egyptian darkness."—*Ibid.*, b. 8, ch. 6.

But though at first his labors were received with great enthusiasm, after a time opposition arose. The monks set themselves to hinder his 178 work and condemn his teachings. Many assailed him with gibes and sneers; others resorted to insolence and threats. But Zwingli bore all with patience, saying: "If we desire to gain over the wicked to Jesus Christ, we must shut our eyes against many things."—*Ibid.*, b. 8, ch. 6.

About this time a new agency came in to advance the work of reform. One Lucian was sent to Zurich with some of Luther's writings, by a friend of the reformed faith at Basel, who suggested that the sale of these books might be a powerful means of scattering the light. "Ascertain," he wrote to Zwingli, "whether this man possesses sufficient prudence and skill; if so, let him carry from city to city, from town to town, from village to village, and even from house to house, among the Swiss, the works of Luther, and especially his exposition of the Lord's Prayer written for the laity. The more they are known, the more purchasers they will find."—*Ibid.*, b. 8, ch. 6. Thus the light found entrance.

At the time when God is preparing to break the shackles of ignorance and superstition, then it is that Satan works with greatest power to enshroud men in darkness and to bind their fetters still more firmly. As men were rising up in different lands to present to the people forgiveness and justification through the blood of Christ, Rome proceeded with renewed energy to open her market throughout Christendom, offering pardon for money.

Every sin had its price, and men were granted free license for crime if the treasury of the church was kept well filled. Thus the two movements advanced,—one offering forgiveness of sin for money, the other forgiveness through Christ,—Rome licensing sin and making it her source of revenue; the Reformers condemning sin and pointing to Christ as the propitiation and deliverer.

In Germany the sale of indulgences had been committed to the Dominican friars and was conducted by the infamous Tetzel. In Switzerland the traffic was put into the hands of the Franciscans, under the control of Samson, an Italian monk. Samson had already done good service to 179 the church, having secured immense sums from Germany and Switzerland to fill the papal treasury. Now he traversed Switzerland, attracting great crowds, despoiling the poor peasants of their scanty earnings, and exacting rich gifts from the wealthy classes. But the influence of the reform already made itself felt in curtailing, though it could not stop, the traffic. Zwingli was still at Einsiedeln when Samson, soon after entering Switzerland, arrived with his wares at a neighboring town. Being apprised of his mission, the Reformer immediately set out to oppose him. The two did not meet, but such was Zwingli's success in exposing the friar's pretensions that he was obliged to leave for other quarters.

At Zurich, Zwingli preached zealously against the pardonmongers; and when Samson approached the place, he was met by a messenger from the council with an intimation that he was expected to pass on. He finally secured an entrance by stratagem, but was sent away without the sale of a single pardon, and he soon after left Switzerland.

A strong impetus was given to the reform by the appearance of the plague, or Great Death, which swept over Switzerland in the year 1519. As men were thus brought face to face with the destroyer, many were led to feel how vain and worthless were the pardons which they had so lately purchased; and they longed for a surer foundation for their faith. Zwingli at Zurich was smitten down; he was brought so low that all hope of his recovery was relinquished, and the report was widely circulated that he was dead. In that trying hour his hope and courage were unshaken. He looked in faith to the cross of Calvary, trusting in the all-sufficient propitiation for sin. When he came back from the gates of death, it was to preach the gospel with greater fervor than ever before; and his words exerted an unwonted power. The people welcomed with joy their beloved pastor, returned to them from the brink of the grave. They themselves had come from attending upon the sick and the dying, and they felt, as never before, the value of the gospel.

Zwingli had arrived at a clearer understanding of its truths, and had more fully experienced in himself its renewing power. The fall of man and the plan of redemption were the subjects upon which he dwelt. "In Adam," he said, "we are all dead, sunk in corruption and condemnation."—Wylie, b. 8, ch. 9. "Christ . . . has purchased for us a never-ending redemption. . . . His passion is . . . an eternal sacrifice, and everlastingly effectual to heal; it satisfies the divine justice forever in behalf of all those who rely upon it with firm and unshaken faith." Yet he clearly taught that men are not, because of the grace of Christ, free to continue in sin. "Wherever there is faith in God, there God is; and wherever God abideth, there a zeal exists urging and impelling men to good works."—D'Aubigné, b. 8, ch. 9.

Such was the interest in Zwingli's preaching that the cathedral was filled to overflowing with the crowds that came to listen to him. Little by little, as they could bear it, he opened the truth to his hearers. He was careful not to introduce, at first, points which would startle them and create prejudice. His work was to win their hearts to the teachings of Christ, to soften them by His love, and keep before them His example; and as they should receive the principles of the gospel, their superstitious beliefs and practices would inevitably be overthrown.

Step by step the Reformation advanced in Zurich. In alarm its enemies aroused to active opposition. One year before, the monk of Wittenberg had uttered his No to the pope and the emperor at Worms, and now everything seemed to indicate a similar withstanding of the papal claims at Zurich. Repeated attacks were made upon Zwingli. In the papal cantons, from time to time, disciples of the gospel were brought to the stake, but this was not enough; the teacher of heresy must be silenced. Accordingly the bishop of Constance dispatched three deputies to the Council of Zurich, accusing Zwingli of teaching the people to transgress the laws of the church, thus endangering the peace and good order of society. If the authority of the church were to be set aside, he urged, universal anarchy would result. Zwingli replied that he had been for four years teaching the gospel in Zurich, "which was more quiet and peaceful than any other town in the confederacy." "Is not, then," he said, "Christianity the best safeguard of the general security?"—Wylie, b. 8, ch. 11.

The deputies had admonished the councilors to continue in the church, out of which, they declared, there was no salvation. Zwingli responded: "Let not this accusation move you. The foundation of the church is the same Rock, the same Christ, that gave Peter his name because he confessed Him faithfully. In every nation whosoever believes with all his heart in the Lord Jesus is accepted of God. Here, truly, is the church, out of which no one can be saved."—D'Aubigné, London ed., b. 8, ch. 11. As a result of the conference, one of the bishop's deputies accepted the reformed faith.

The council declined to take action against Zwingli, and Rome prepared for a fresh attack. The Reformer, when apprised of the plots of his enemies, exclaimed: "Let them come on; I fear them as the beetling cliff fears the waves that thunder at its feet."—Wylie, b. 8, ch. 11. The efforts of the ecclesiastics only furthered the cause which they sought to overthrow. The truth continued to spread. In Germany its adherents, cast down by Luther's disappearance, took heart again, as they saw the progress of the gospel in Switzerland.

As the Reformation became established in Zurich, its fruits were more fully seen in the suppression of vice and the promotion of order and harmony. "Peace has her habitation in our town," wrote Zwingli; "no quarrel, no hypocrisy, no envy, no strife. Whence can such union come but from the Lord, and our doctrine, which fills us with the fruits of peace and piety?"—*Ibid.*, b. 8, ch. 15.

The victories gained by the Reformation stirred the Romanists to still more determined efforts for its overthrow. Seeing how little had been accomplished by persecution in suppressing Luther's work in Germany, they decided to meet the reform with its own weapons. They would hold a disputation with Zwingli, and having the arrangement of matters, they would make sure of victory by choosing, themselves, not only the place of the combat, but the judges that should decide between the disputants. And if they could once get Zwingli into their power, they would take care that he did not escape them. The leader silenced, the movement could speedily be crushed. This purpose, however, was carefully concealed.

The disputation was appointed to be held at Baden; but Zwingli was not present. The Council of Zurich, suspecting the designs of the papists, and warned by the burning piles kindled in the papal cantons for confessors of the gospel, forbade their pastor to expose himself to this peril. At Zurich he was ready to meet all the partisans that Rome might send; but to go to Baden, where the blood of martyrs for the truth had just been shed, was to go to certain death. Oecolampadius and Haller were chosen to represent the Reformers, while the famous Dr. Eck, supported by a host of learned doctors and prelates, was the champion of Rome.

Though Zwingli was not present at the conference, his influence was felt. The secretaries were all chosen by the papists, and others were forbidden to take notes, on pain of death. Notwithstanding this, Zwingli received daily a faithful account of what was said at Baden. A student in attendance at the disputation made a record each evening of the arguments that day presented. These papers two other students undertook to deliver, with the daily letters of Oecolampadius, to Zwingli at Zurich. The Reformer answered, giving counsel and suggestions. His letters were written by night, and the students returned with them to Baden in the morning. To elude the vigilance of the guard stationed at the city gates, these messengers brought baskets of poultry on their heads, and they were permitted to pass without hindrance.

183 Thus Zwingli maintained the battle with his wily antagonists. He "has labored more," said Myconius, "by his meditations, his sleepless nights, and the advice which he transmitted to Baden, than he would have done by discussing in person in the midst of his enemies."—D'Aubigné, b. 11, ch. 13.

The Romanists, flushed with anticipated triumph, had come to Baden attired in their richest robes and glittering with jewels. They fared luxuriously, their tables spread with the most costly delicacies and the choicest wines. The burden of their ecclesiastical duties was lightened by gaiety and reveling. In marked contrast appeared the Reformers, who were looked upon by the people as little better than a company of beggars, and whose frugal fare kept them but short time at table. Oecolampadius's landlord, taking occasion to watch him in his room, found him always engaged in study or at prayer, and greatly wondering, reported that the heretic was at least "very pious."

At the conference, "Eck haughtily ascended a pulpit splendidly decorated, while the humble Oecolampadius, meanly clothed, was forced to take his seat in front of his opponent on a rudely carved stool."—Ibid., b. 11, ch. 13. Eck's stentorian voice and unbounded assurance never failed him. His zeal was stimulated by the hope of gold as well as fame; for the defender of the faith was to be rewarded by a handsome fee. When better arguments failed, he had resort to insults, and even to oaths.

Oecolampadius, modest and self-distrustful, had shrunk from the combat, and he entered upon it with the solemn avowal: "I acknowledge no other standard of judgment than the word of God."—Ibid., b. 11, ch. 13. Though gentle and courteous in demeanor, he proved himself able and unflinching. While the Romanists, according to their wont, appealed for authority to the customs of the church, the Reformer adhered steadfastly to the Holy Scriptures. "Custom," he said, "has no force in our Switzerland, unless it be according to the constitution; now, in matters of faith, the Bible is our constitution."—Ibid., b. 11, ch. 13.

The contrast between the two disputants was 184 not without effect. The calm, clear reasoning of the Reformer, so gently and modestly presented, appealed to minds that turned in disgust from Eck's boastful and boisterous assumptions.

The discussion continued eighteen days. At its close the papists with great confidence claimed the victory. Most of the deputies sided with Rome, and the Diet pronounced the Reformers vanquished and declared that they, together with Zwingli, their leader, were cut off from the church. But the fruits of the conference revealed on which side the advantage lay. The contest resulted in a strong impetus to the Protestant cause, and it was not long afterward that the important cities of Bern and Basel declared for the Reformation.

10 185

Progress of Reform
in Germany

Luther's mysterious disappearance excited consternation throughout all Germany. Inquiries concerning him were heard everywhere. The wildest rumors were circulated, and many believed that he had been murdered. There was great lamentation, not only by his avowed friends, but by thousands who had not openly taken their stand with the Reformation. Many bound themselves by a solemn oath to avenge his death.

The Romish leaders saw with terror to what a pitch had risen the feeling against them. Though at first exultant at the supposed death of Luther, they soon desired to hide from the wrath of the people. His enemies had not been so troubled by his most daring acts while among them as they were at his removal. Those who in their rage had sought to destroy the bold Reformer were filled with fear now that he had become a helpless captive. "The only remaining way of saving ourselves," said one, "is to light torches, and hunt for Luther through the whole world, to restore him to the nation that is calling for him."—D'Aubigné, b. 9, ch. 1. The edict of the emperor seemed to fall powerless. The papal legates were filled with indignation as they saw that it commanded far less attention than did the fate of Luther.

The tidings that he was safe, though a prisoner, calmed the fears of the people, while it still further aroused their enthusiasm in his favor. 186 His writings were read with greater eagerness than ever before. Increasing numbers joined the cause of the heroic man who had, at such fearful odds, defended the word of God. The Reformation was constantly gaining in strength. The seed which Luther had sown sprang up everywhere. His absence accomplished a work which his presence would have failed to do. Other laborers felt a new responsibility, now that their great leader was removed. With new faith and earnestness they pressed forward to do all in their power, that the work so nobly begun might not be hindered.

But Satan was not idle. He now attempted what he has attempted in every other reformatory movement—to deceive and destroy the people by palming off upon them a counterfeit in place of the true work. As there were false christs in the first century of the Christian church, so there arose false prophets in the sixteenth century.

A few men, deeply affected by the excitement in the religious world, imagined themselves to have received special revelations from Heaven, and claimed to have been divinely commissioned to carry forward to its completion the Reformation which, they declared, had been but feebly begun by Luther. In truth, they were undoing the very work which he had accomplished. They rejected the great principle which was the very foundation of the Reformation— that the word of God is the all-sufficient rule of faith and practice; and for that unerring guide they substituted the changeable, uncertain standard of their own feelings and impressions. By this act of setting aside the great detector of error and falsehood the way was opened for Satan to control minds as best pleased himself.

One of these prophets claimed to have been instructed by the angel Gabriel. A student who united with him forsook his studies, declaring that he had been endowed by God Himself with wisdom to expound His word. Others who were naturally inclined to fanaticism united with them. The proceedings of these enthusiasts created no little excitement. 187 The preaching of Luther had aroused the people everywhere to feel the necessity of reform, and now some really honest persons were misled by the pretensions of the new prophets.

The leaders of the movement proceeded to Wittenberg and urged their claims upon Melanchthon and his colaborers. Said they: "We are sent by God to instruct the people. We have held familiar conversations with the Lord; we know what will happen; in a word, we are apostles and prophets, and appeal to Dr. Luther."— Ibid., b. 9, ch. 7.

The Reformers were astonished and perplexed. This was such an element as they had never before encountered, and they knew not what course to pursue. Said Melanchthon: "There are indeed extraordinary spirits in these men; but what spirits? . . . On the one hand, let us beware of quenching the Spirit of God, and on the other, of being led astray by the spirit of Satan."—Ibid., b. 9, ch. 7.

The fruit of the new teaching soon became apparent. The people were led to neglect the Bible or to cast it wholly aside. The schools were thrown into confusion. Students, spurning all restraint, abandoned their studies and withdrew from the university. The men who thought themselves competent to revive and control the work of the Reformation succeeded only in bringing it to the verge of ruin. The Romanists now regained their confidence and exclaimed exultingly: "One last struggle, and all will be ours."—Ibid., b. 9, ch. 7.

Luther at the Wartburg, hearing of what had occurred, said with deep concern: "I always expected that Satan would send us this plague."—Ibid., b. 9, ch. 7. He perceived the true character of those pretended prophets and saw the danger that threatened the cause of truth. The opposition of the pope and the emperor had not caused him so great perplexity and distress as he now experienced. From the professed friends of the Reformation had risen its worst enemies. The very truths which had brought him so great joy and consolation were 188 being employed to stir up strife and create confusion in the church.

In the work of reform, Luther had been urged forward by the Spirit of God, and had been carried beyond himself. He had not purposed to take such positions as he did, or to make so radical changes. He had been but the instrument in the hand of Infinite Power. Yet he often trembled for the result of his work. He had once said: "If I knew that my doctrine injured one man, one single man, however lowly and obscure,—which it cannot, for it is the gospel itself,—I would rather die ten times than not retract it."—Ibid., b. 9, ch. 7.

And now Wittenberg itself, the very center of the Reformation, was fast falling under the power of fanaticism and lawlessness. This terrible condition had not resulted from the teachings of Luther; but throughout Germany his enemies were charging it upon him. In bitterness of soul he sometimes asked: "Can such, then, be the end of this great work of the Reformation?"—*Ibid.*, b. 9, ch. 7. Again, as he wrestled with God in prayer, peace flowed into his heart. He was under the ban of the empire. "The work is not mine, but Thine own," he said; "Thou wilt not suffer it to be corrupted by superstition or fanaticism." But the thought of remaining longer from the conflict in such a crisis, became insupportable. He determined to return to Wittenberg.

Without delay he set out on his perilous journey. He was under the ban of the empire. Enemies were at liberty to take his life; friends were forbidden to aid or shelter him. The imperial government was adopting the most stringent measures against his adherents. But he saw that the work of the gospel was imperiled, and in the name of the Lord he went out fearlessly to battle for the truth.

In a letter to the elector, after stating his purpose to leave the Wartburg, Luther said: "Be it known to your highness that I am going to Wittenberg under a protection far higher than that of princes and electors. I think not of soliciting your highness's support, and far from desiring your protection, I would rather protect you myself. If I knew that your highness could or would protect me, I would not go to Wittenberg at all. There is no sword that can further this cause. God alone must do everything, without the help or concurrence of man. He who has the greatest faith is he who is most able to protect."—*Ibid.*, b. 9, ch. 8.

In a second letter, written on the way to Wittenberg, Luther added: "I am ready to incur the displeasure of your highness and the anger of the whole world. Are not the Wittenbergers my sheep? Has not God entrusted them to me? And ought I not, if necessary, to expose myself to death for their sakes? Besides, I fear to see a terrible outbreak in Germany, by which God will punish our nation."—*Ibid.*, b. 9, ch. 7.

With great caution and humility, yet with decision and firmness, he entered upon his work. "By the word," said he, "must we overthrow and destroy what has been set up by violence. I will not make use of force against the superstitious and unbelieving. . . . No one must be constrained. Liberty is the very essence of faith."—*Ibid.*, b. 9, ch. 8.

It was soon noised through Wittenberg that Luther had returned and that he was to preach. The people flocked from all directions, and the church was filled to overflowing. Ascending the pulpit, he with great wisdom and gentleness instructed, exhorted, and reproved. Touching

the course of some who had resorted to violent measures in abolishing the mass, he said:

"The mass is a bad thing; God is opposed to it; it ought to be abolished; and I would that throughout the whole world it were replaced by the supper of the gospel. But let no one be torn from it by force. We must leave the matter in God's hands. His word must act, and not we. And why so? you will ask. Because I do not hold men's hearts in my hand, as the potter holds the clay. We have a right to speak: we have not the right to act. Let us preach; the rest belongs unto God. Were I to employ force, what should I gain? Grimace, formality, apings, human ordinances, and hypocrisy. . . . But there would be no sincerity of heart, nor faith, nor charity. Where these three are wanting, all is wanting, and I would not give a pear stalk for such a result. . . . God does more by His word alone than you and I and all the world by our united strength. God lays hold upon the heart; and when the heart is taken, all is won. . . .

"I will preach, discuss, and write; but I will constrain none, for faith is a voluntary act. See what I have done. I stood up against the pope, indulgences, and papists, but without violence or tumult. I put forward God's word; I preached and wrote—this was all I did. And yet while I was asleep, . . . the word that I had preached overthrew popery, so that neither prince nor emperor has done it so much harm. And yet I did nothing; the word alone did all. If I had wished to appeal to force, the whole of Germany would perhaps have been deluged with blood. But what would have been the result? Ruin and desolation both to body and soul. I therefore kept quiet, and left the word to run through the world alone."—*Ibid.*, b. 9, ch. 8.

Day after day, for a whole week, Luther continued to preach to eager crowds. The word of God broke the spell of fanatical excitement. The power of the gospel brought back the misguided people into the way of truth.

Luther had no desire to encounter the fanatics whose course had been productive of so great evil. He knew them to be men of unsound judgment and undisciplined passions, who, while claiming to be specially illuminated from heaven, would not endure the slightest contradiction or even the kindest reproof or counsel. Arrogating to themselves supreme authority, they required everyone, without a question, to acknowledge their claims. But, as they demanded an interview with him, he consented to meet them; and so successfully did he expose their pretensions that the impostors at once departed from Wittenberg.

The fanaticism was checked for a time; but several years later it broke out with greater violence and more terrible results. Said Luther, concerning the leaders in this movement: "To them the Holy Scriptures were but a dead letter, and they all began to cry, 'The Spirit! the Spirit!' But most assuredly I will not follow where their spirit leads them. May God of His mercy preserve me from a church in which there are none but saints. I desire to dwell with the humble, the feeble, the sick, who know and feel their sins, and who groan and cry continually to God from the bottom of their hearts to obtain His consolation and support."—*Ibid.*, b. 10, ch. 10.

Thomas Munzer, the most active of the fanatics, was a man of considerable ability, which, rightly directed, would have enabled him to do good; but he had not learned the first principles of true religion. "He was possessed with a desire of reforming the world, and forgot, as all enthusiasts do, that the reformation should begin with himself."—*Ibid.*, b. 9, ch. 8. He was ambitious to obtain position and influence, and was unwilling to be second, even to Luther. He declared that the Reformers, in substituting the authority of Scripture for that of the pope, were only establishing a different form of popery. He himself, he claimed, had been divinely commissioned to introduce the true reform. "He who possesses this spirit," said Munzer, "possesses the true faith, although he should never see the Scriptures in his life."—*Ibid.*, b. 10, ch. 10.

The fanatical teachers gave themselves up to be governed by impressions, regarding every thought and impulse as the voice of God; consequently they went to great extremes. Some even burned their Bibles, exclaiming: "The letter killeth, but the Spirit giveth life." Munzer's teaching appealed to men's desire for the marvelous, while it gratified their pride by virtually placing human ideas and opinions above the word of God. His doctrines were received by thousands. He soon denounced all order in public worship, and declared that to obey princes was to attempt to serve both God and Belial.

The minds of the people, already beginning to throw off the yoke of the papacy, were also becoming impatient under the restraints of civil authority. Munzer's revolutionary teachings, claiming divine sanction, led them to break away from all control and give the rein to their prejudices and passions. The most terrible scenes of sedition and strife followed, and the fields of Germany were drenched with blood.

The agony of soul which Luther had so long before experienced at Erfurt now pressed upon him with redoubled power as he saw the results of fanaticism charged upon the Reformation. The papist princes declared—and many were ready to credit the statement—that the rebellion was the legitimate fruit of Luther's doctrines. Although this charge was without the slightest foundation, it could not but cause the Reformer great distress. That the cause of truth should be thus disgraced by being ranked with the basest fanaticism, seemed more than he could endure. On the other hand, the leaders in the revolt

hated Luther because he had not only opposed their doctrines and denied their claims to divine inspiration, but had pronounced them rebels against the civil authority. In retaliation they denounced him as a base pretender. He seemed to have brought upon himself the enmity of both princes and people.

The Romanists exulted, expecting to witness the speedy downfall of the Reformation; and they blamed Luther, even for the errors which he had been most earnestly endeavoring to correct. The fanatical party, by falsely claiming to have been treated with great injustice, succeeded in gaining the sympathies of a large class of the people, and, as is often the case with those who take the wrong side, they came to be regarded as martyrs. Thus the ones who were exerting every energy in opposition to the Reformation were pitied and lauded as the victims of cruelty and oppression. This was the work of Satan, prompted by the same spirit of rebellion which was first manifested in heaven.

Satan is constantly seeking to deceive men and lead them to call sin righteousness, and righteousness sin. How successful has been his work! How often censure and reproach are cast upon God's faithful servants because they will stand fearlessly in defense of the truth! Men who are but agents of Satan are praised and flattered, and even looked upon as martyrs, while those who should be respected and sustained for their fidelity to God, are left to stand alone, under suspicion and distrust.

Counterfeit holiness, spurious sanctification, is still doing its work of deception. Under various forms it exhibits the same spirit as in the days of Luther, diverting minds from the Scriptures and leading men to follow their own feelings and impressions rather than to yield obedience to the law of God. This is one of Satan's most successful devices to cast reproach upon purity and truth.

Fearlessly did Luther defend the gospel from the attacks which came from every quarter. The word of God proved itself a weapon mighty in every conflict. With that word he warred against the usurped authority of the pope, and the rationalistic philosophy of the schoolmen, while he stood firm as a rock against the fanaticism that sought to ally itself with the Reformation.

Each of these opposing elements was in its own way setting aside the Holy Scriptures and exalting human wisdom as the source of religious truth and knowledge. Rationalism idolizes reason and makes this the criterion for religion. Romanism, claiming for her sovereign pontiff an inspiration descended in unbroken line from the apostles, and unchangeable through all time, gives ample opportunity for every species of extravagance and corruption to be concealed under the sanctity of the apostolic commission. The inspiration claimed by Munzer and his associates proceeded from no higher source than the vagaries of the imagination, and its influence was subversive of all authority, human or divine. True Christianity receives the word of God as the great treasure house of inspired truth and the test of all inspiration.

194 Upon his return from the Wartburg, Luther completed his translation of the New Testament, and the gospel was soon after given to the people of Germany in their own language. This translation was received with great joy by all who loved the truth; but it was scornfully rejected by those who chose human traditions and the commandments of men.

The priests were alarmed at the thought that the common people would now be able to discuss with them the precepts of God's word, and that their own ignorance would thus be exposed. The weapons of their carnal reasoning were powerless against the sword of the Spirit. Rome summoned all her authority to prevent the circulation of the Scriptures; but decrees, anathemas, and tortures were alike in vain. The more she condemned and prohibited the Bible, the greater was the anxiety of the people to know what it really taught. All who could read were eager to study the word of God for themselves. They carried it about with them, and read and reread, and could not be satisfied until they had committed large portions to memory. Seeing the favor with which the New Testament was received, Luther immediately began the translation of the Old, and published it in parts as fast as completed.

Luther's writings were welcomed alike in city and in hamlet. "What Luther and his friends composed, others circulated. Monks, convinced of the unlawfulness of monastic obligations, desirous of exchanging a long life of slothfulness for one of active exertion, but too ignorant to proclaim the word of God, traveled through the provinces, visiting hamlets and cottages, where they sold the books of Luther and his friends. Germany soon swarmed with these bold colporteurs."—*Ibid.*, b. 9, ch. 11.

These writings were studied with deep interest by rich and poor, the learned and the ignorant. At night the teachers of the village schools read them aloud to little groups gathered at the fireside. With every effort some souls would be convicted of the truth and, receiving the word with gladness, would in their turn tell the good news to others.

195 The words of Inspiration were verified: "The entrance of Thy words giveth light; it giveth understanding unto the simple." Psalm 119:130. The study of the Scriptures was working a mighty change in the minds and hearts of the people. The papal rule had placed upon its subjects an iron yoke which held them in ignorance and degradation. A superstitious observance of forms had been scrupulously maintained; but in

all their service the heart and intellect had had little part. The preaching of Luther, setting forth the plain truths of God's word, and then the word itself, placed in the hands of the common people, had aroused their dormant powers, not only purifying and ennobling the spiritual nature, but imparting new strength and vigor to the intellect.

Persons of all ranks were to be seen with the Bible in their hands, defending the doctrines of the Reformation. The papists who had left the study of the Scriptures to the priests and monks now called upon them to come forward and refute the new teachings. But, ignorant alike of the Scriptures and of the power of God, priests and friars were totally defeated by those whom they denounced as unlearned and heretical. "Unhappily," said a Catholic writer, "Luther had persuaded his followers to put no faith in any other oracle than the Holy Scriptures."— D'Aubigné, b. 9, ch. 11. Crowds would gather to hear the truth advocated by men of little education, and even discussed by them with learned and eloquent theologians. The shameful ignorance of these great men was made apparent as their arguments were met by the simple teachings of God's word. Laborers, soldiers, women, and even children, were better acquainted with the Bible teachings than were the priests and learned doctors.

The contrast between the disciples of the gospel and the upholders of popish superstition was no less manifest in the ranks of scholars than among the common people. "Opposed to the old champions of the hierarchy, who had neglected the study of languages and the cultivation of literature, . . . were generous-minded youth, devoted to study, investigating Scripture, and familiarizing themselves with the masterpieces of antiquity. Possessing an active mind, an elevated soul, and intrepid heart, these young men soon acquired such knowledge that for a long period none could compete with them. . . . Accordingly, when these youthful defenders of the Reformation met the Romish doctors in any assembly, they attacked them with such ease and confidence that these ignorant men hesitated, became embarrassed, and fell into a contempt merited in the eyes of all."—*Ibid.*, b. 9, ch. 11.

As the Romish clergy saw their congregations diminishing, they invoked the aid of the magistrates, and by every means in their power endeavored to bring back their hearers. But the people had found in the new teachings that which supplied the wants of their souls, and they turned away from those who had so long fed them with the worthless husks of superstitious rites and human traditions.

When persecution was kindled against the teachers of the truth, they gave heed to the words of Christ: "When they persecute you in this city, flee ye into another." Matthew 10:23. The light penetrated everywhere. The fugitives would find somewhere a hospitable door opened to them, and there abiding, they would preach Christ, sometimes in the church, or, if denied that privilege, in private houses or in the open air. Wherever they could obtain a hearing was a consecrated temple. The truth, proclaimed with such energy and assurance, spread with irresistible power.

In vain both ecclesiastical and civil authorities were invoked to crush the heresy. In vain they resorted to imprisonment, torture, fire, and sword. Thousands of believers sealed their faith with their blood, and yet the work went on. Persecution served only to extend the truth, and the fanaticism which Satan endeavored to unite with it resulted in making more clear the contrast between the work of Satan and the work of God.

11

Protest of the Princes

One of the noblest testimonies ever uttered for the Reformation was the Protest offered by the Christian princes of Germany at the Diet of Spires in 1529. The courage, faith, and firmness of those men of God gained for succeeding ages liberty of thought and of conscience. Their Protest gave to the reformed church the name of Protestant; its principles are "the very essence of Protestantism."—D'Aubigné, b. 13, ch. 6.

A dark and threatening day had come for the Reformation. Notwithstanding the Edict of Worms, declaring Luther to be an outlaw and forbidding the teaching or belief of his doctrines, religious toleration had thus far prevailed in the empire. God's providence had held in check the forces that opposed the truth. Charles V was bent on crushing the Reformation, but often as he raised his hand to strike he had been forced to turn aside the blow. Again and again the immediate destruction of all who dared to oppose themselves to Rome appeared inevitable; but at the critical moment the armies of the Turk appeared on the eastern frontier, or the king of France, or even the pope himself, jealous of the increasing greatness of the emperor, made war upon him; and thus, amid the strife and tumult of nations, the Reformation had been left to strengthen and extend.

At last, however, the papal sovereigns had stifled their feuds, that they might make common cause against the Reformers. The Diet of Spires in 1526 had given each state full liberty in matters of religion until the meeting of a general council; but no sooner had the dangers passed which secured this concession, than the emperor summoned a second Diet to convene at Spires in 1529 for the purpose of crushing heresy. The princes were to be induced, by peaceable means if possible, to side against the Reformation; but if these failed, Charles was prepared to resort to the sword.

The papists were exultant. They appeared at Spires in great numbers, and openly manifested their hostility toward the Reformers and all who favored them. Said Melanchthon: "We are the execration and the sweepings of the world; but Christ will look down on His poor people, and will preserve them."—*Ibid.*, b. 13, ch. 5. The evangelical princes in attendance at the Diet were forbidden even to have the gospel preached in their dwellings. But the people of Spires thirsted for the word of God, and, notwithstanding the prohibition, thousands flocked to the services held in the chapel of the elector of Saxony.

This hastened the crisis. An imperial message announced to the Diet that as the resolution granting liberty of conscience had given rise to great disorders, the emperor required that it be annulled. This arbitrary act excited the indignation and alarm of the evangelical Christians. Said one: "Christ has again fallen into the hands of Caiaphas and Pilate." The Romanists became more violent. A bigoted papist declared: "The Turks are better than the Lutherans; for the Turks observe fast days, and the Lutherans violate them. If we must choose between the Holy Scriptures of God and the old errors of the church, we should reject the former." Said Melanchthon: "Every day, in full assembly, Faber casts some new stone at us gospelers."—*Ibid.*, b. 13, ch. 5.

Religious toleration had been legally established, and the evangelical states were resolved to oppose the infringement of their rights. Luther, being still under the ban imposed by the Edict of Worms, was not permitted to be present at Spires; but his place was supplied by his colaborers and the princes whom God had raised up to defend His cause in this emergency. The noble Frederick of Saxony, Luther's former protector, had been removed by death; but Duke John, his brother and successor, had joyfully welcomed the Reformation, and while a friend of peace, he displayed great energy and courage in all matters relating to the interests of the faith.

The priests demanded that the states which had accepted the Reformation submit implicitly to Romish jurisdiction. The Reformers, on the other hand, claimed the liberty which had previously been granted. They could not consent that Rome should again bring under her control those states that had with so great joy received the word of God.

As a compromise it was finally proposed that where the Reformation had not become established, the Edict of Worms should be rigorously enforced; and that "in those where the people had deviated from it, and where they could not conform to it without danger of revolt, they should at least effect no new reform, they should touch upon no controverted point, they should not oppose the celebration of the mass, they should permit no Roman Catholic to embrace Lutheranism."—*Ibid.*, b. 13, ch. 5. This measure passed the Diet, to the great satisfaction of the popish priests and prelates.

If this edict were enforced, "the Reformation could neither be extended . . . where as yet it was unknown, nor be established on solid foundations . . . where it already existed."—*Ibid.*, b. 13, ch. 5. Liberty of speech would be prohibited. No conversions would be allowed. And to these restrictions and prohibitions the friends of the Reformation were required at once to submit. The hopes of the world seemed about to be extinguished. "The re-establishment of the Romish hierarchy . . . would infallibly bring back the ancient abuses;" and an occasion would readily be found for "completing the destruction of a work already so violently shaken" by fanaticism and dissension.—*Ibid.*, b. 13, ch. 5.

As the evangelical party met for consultation, one looked to another in blank dismay. From one to another passed the inquiry: "What is to be done?" Mighty issues for the world were at 200 stake. "Shall the chiefs of the Reformation submit, and accept the edict? How easily might the Reformers at this crisis, which was truly a tremendous one, have argued themselves into a wrong course! How many plausible pretexts and fair reasons might they have found for submission! The Lutheran princes were guaranteed the free exercise of their religion. The same boon was extended to all those of their subjects who, prior to the passing of the measure, had embraced the reformed views. Ought not this to content them? How many perils would submission avoid! On what unknown hazards and conflicts would opposition launch them! Who knows what opportunities the future may bring? Let us embrace peace; let us seize the olive branch Rome holds out, and close the wounds of Germany. With arguments like these might the Reformers have justified their adoption of a course which would have assuredly issued in no long time in the overthrow of their cause.

"Happily they looked at the principle on which this arrangement was based, and they acted in faith. What was that principle? It was the right of Rome to coerce conscience and forbid free inquiry. But were not themselves and their Protestant subjects to enjoy religious freedom? Yes, as a favor specially stipulated for in the arrangement, but not as a right. As to all outside that arrangement, the great principle of authority was to rule; conscience was out of court; Rome was infallible judge, and must be

obeyed. The acceptance of the proposed arrangement would have been a virtual admission that religious liberty ought to be confined to reformed Saxony; and as to all the rest of Christendom, free inquiry and the profession of the reformed faith were crimes, and must be visited with the dungeon and the stake. Could they consent to localize religious liberty? to have it proclaimed that the Reformation had made its last convert? had subjugated its last acre? and that wherever Rome bore sway at this hour, there her dominion was to be perpetuated? Could the Reformers have pleaded that they were innocent of the blood of those hundreds and thousands who, in pursuance of this arrangement, would have to yield up their lives 201 in popish lands? This would have been to betray, at that supreme hour, the cause of the gospel and the liberties of Christendom."—Wylie, b. 9, ch. 15. Rather would they "sacrifice everything, even their states, their crowns, and their lives."—D'Aubigné, b. 13, ch. 5.

"Let us reject this decree," said the princes. "In matters of conscience the majority has no power." The deputies declared: "It is to the decree of 1526 that we are indebted for the peace that the empire enjoys: its abolition would fill Germany with troubles and divisions. The Diet is incompetent to do more than preserve religious liberty until the council meets."—*Ibid.*, b. 13, ch. 5. To protect liberty of conscience is the duty of the state, and this is the limit of its authority in matters of religion. Every secular government that attempts to regulate or enforce religious observances by civil authority is sacrificing the very principle for which the evangelical Christians so nobly struggled.

The papists determined to put down what they termed "daring obstinacy." They began by endeavoring to cause divisions among the supporters of the Reformation and to intimidate all who had not openly declared in its favor. The representatives of the free cities were at last summoned before the Diet and required to declare whether they would accede to the terms of the proposition. They pleaded for delay, but in vain. When brought to the test, nearly one half their number sided with the Reformers. Those who thus refused to sacrifice liberty of conscience and the right of individual judgment well knew that their position marked them for future criticism, condemnation, and persecution. Said one of the delegates: "We must either deny the word of God, or—be burnt."—*Ibid.*, b. 13, ch. 5.

King Ferdinand, the emperor's representative at the Diet, saw that the decree would cause serious divisions unless the princes could be induced to accept and sustain it. He therefore tried the art of persuasion, well knowing that to employ force with such men would only render them the more determined.

He "begged the princes to accept the decree, assuring them that the emperor would be exceedingly pleased with them." But these faithful men acknowledged an authority above that of earthly rulers, and they answered calmly: "We will obey the emperor in everything that may contribute to maintain peace and the honor of God."—*Ibid.*, b. 13, ch. 5.

In the presence of the Diet the king at last announced to the elector and his friends that the edict "was about to be drawn up in the form of an imperial decree," and that "their only remaining course was to submit to the majority." Having thus spoken, he withdrew from the assembly, giving the Reformers no opportunity for deliberation or reply. "To no purpose they sent a deputation entreating the king to return." To their remonstrances he answered only: "It is a settled affair; submission is all that remains."—*Ibid.*, b. 13, ch. 5.

The imperial party were convinced that the Christian princes would adhere to the Holy Scriptures as superior to human doctrines and requirements; and they knew that wherever this principle was accepted, the papacy would eventually be overthrown. But, like thousands since their time, looking only "at the things which are seen," they flattered themselves that the cause of the emperor and the pope was strong, and that of the Reformers weak. Had the Reformers depended upon human aid alone, they would have been as powerless as the papists supposed. But though weak in numbers, and at variance with Rome, they had their strength. They appealed "from the report of the Diet to the word of God, and from the emperor Charles to Jesus Christ, the King of kings and Lord of lords."—*Ibid.*, b. 13, ch. 6.

As Ferdinand had refused to regard their conscientious convictions, the princes decided not to heed his absence, but to bring their Protest before the national council without delay. A solemn declaration was therefore drawn up and presented to the Diet:

"We protest by these presents, before God, our only Creator, Preserver, Redeemer, and Saviour, and who will one day be our Judge, as well as before all men and all creatures, that we, for us and for our people, neither consent nor adhere in any manner whatsoever to the proposed decree, in anything that is contrary to God, to His holy word, to our right conscience, to the salvation of our souls."

"What! we ratify this edict! We assert that when Almighty God calls a man to His knowledge, this man nevertheless cannot receive the knowledge of God!" "There is no sure doctrine but such as is conformable to the word of God. . . . The Lord forbids the teaching of any other doctrine. . . . The Holy Scriptures ought to be explained by other and clearer texts; . . . this Holy Book is, in all things necessary for the

Christian, easy of understanding, and calculated to scatter the darkness. We are resolved, with the grace of God, to maintain the pure and exclusive preaching of His only word, such as it is contained in the biblical books of the Old and New Testaments, without adding anything thereto that may be contrary to it. This word is the only truth; it is the sure rule of all doctrine and of all life, and can never fail or deceive us. He who builds on this foundation shall stand against all the powers of hell, while all the human vanities that are set up against it shall fall before the face of God."

"For this reason we reject the yoke that is imposed on us." "At the same time we are in expectation that his imperial majesty will behave toward us like a Christian prince who loves God above all things; and we declare ourselves ready to pay unto him, as well as unto you, gracious lords, all the affection and obedience that are our just and legitimate duty."—*Ibid.*, b. 13, ch. 6.

A deep impression was made upon the Diet. The majority were filled with amazement and alarm at the boldness of the protesters. The future appeared to them stormy and uncertain. Dissension, strife, and bloodshed seemed inevitable. But the Reformers, assured of the justice of their cause, and relying upon the arm of Omnipotence, were "full of courage and firmness."

"The principles contained in this celebrated Protest . . . constitute the very essence of Protestantism. Now this Protest opposes two abuses of man in matters of faith: the first is the intrusion of the civil magistrate, and the second the arbitrary authority of the church. Instead of these abuses, Protestantism sets the power of conscience above the magistrate, and the authority of the word of God above the visible church. In the first place, it rejects the civil power in divine things, and says with the prophets and apostles, '*We must obey God rather than man.*' In presence of the crown of Charles the Fifth, it uplifts the crown of Jesus Christ. But it goes farther: it lays down the principle that all human teaching should be subordinate to the oracles of God."—*Ibid.*, b. 13, ch. 6. The protesters had moreover affirmed their right to utter freely their convictions of truth. They would not only believe and obey, but teach what the word of God presents, and they denied the right of priest or magistrate to interfere. The Protest of Spires was a solemn witness against religious intolerance, and an assertion of the right of all men to worship God according to the dictates of their own consciences.

The declaration had been made. It was written in the memory of thousands and registered in the books of heaven, where no effort of man could erase it. All evangelical Germany adopted the Protest as the expression of its faith. Everywhere men beheld in this declaration the promise of a new and better era. Said one of the princes to the Protestants of Spires: "May the Almighty, who has given you grace to confess energetically, freely, and fearlessly, preserve you in that Christian firmness until the day of eternity."—*Ibid.*, b. 13, ch. 6.

Had the Reformation, after attaining a degree of success, consented to temporize to secure favor with the world, it would have been untrue to God and to itself, and would thus have ensured its own destruction. The experience of these noble Reformers contains a lesson for all succeeding ages. Satan's manner of working against God and His word has not changed; he is still as much opposed to the Scriptures being made the guide of life as in the sixteenth century. In our time there is a wide departure from their doctrines and precepts, and there is need of a return to the great Protestant principle—the Bible, and the Bible only, as the rule of faith and duty. Satan is still working through every means which he can control to destroy religious liberty. The antichristian power which the protesters of Spires rejected is now with renewed vigor seeking to re-establish its lost supremacy. The same unswerving adherence to the word of God manifested at that crisis of the Reformation is the only hope of reform today.

There appeared tokens of danger to the Protestants; there were tokens, also, that the divine hand was stretched out to protect the faithful. It was about this time that "Melanchthon hastily conducted through the streets of Spires toward the Rhine his friend Simon Grynaeus, pressing him to cross the river. The latter was astonished at such precipitation. 'An old man of grave and solemn air, but who is unknown to me,' said Melanchthon, 'appeared before me and said, In a minute officers of justice will be sent by Ferdinand to arrest Grynaeus.'"

During the day, Grynaeus had been scandalized at a sermon by Faber, a leading papal doctor; and at the close, remonstrated with him for defending "certain detestable errors." "Faber dissembled his anger, but immediately after repaired to the king, from whom he had obtained an order against the importunate professor of Heidelberg. Melanchthon doubted not that God had saved his friend by sending one of His holy angels to forewarn him.

"Motionless on the banks of the Rhine, he waited until the waters of that stream had rescued Grynaeus from his persecutors. 'At last,' cried Melanchthon, as he saw him on the opposite side, 'at last he is torn from the cruel jaws of those who thirst for innocent blood.' When he returned to his house, Melanchthon was informed that officers in search of Grynaeus had ransacked it from top to bottom."—*Ibid.*, b. 13, ch. 6.

The Reformation was to be brought into greater prominence before the mighty ones of the earth. The evangelical princes had been denied a hearing by King Ferdinand; but they were to be granted an opportunity to present their cause in the presence of the emperor and the assembled dignitaries of church and state. To quiet the dissensions which disturbed the empire, Charles V, in the year following the Protest of Spires, convoked a diet at Augsburg, over which he announced his intention to preside in person. Thither the Protestant leaders were summoned.

Great dangers threatened the Reformation; but its advocates still trusted their cause with God, and pledged themselves to be firm to the gospel. The elector of Saxony was urged by his councilors not to appear at the Diet. The emperor, they said, required the attendance of the princes in order to draw them into a snare. "Is it not risking everything to go and shut oneself up within the walls of a city with a powerful enemy?" But others nobly declared, "Let the princes only comport themselves with courage, and God's cause is saved." "God is faithful; He will not abandon us," said Luther.—*Ibid.*, b. 14, ch. 2. The elector set out, with his retinue, for Augsburg. All were acquainted with the dangers that menaced him, and many went forward with gloomy countenance and troubled heart. But Luther, who accompanied them as far as Coburg, revived their sinking faith by singing the hymn, written on that journey, "A strong tower is our God." Many an anxious foreboding was banished, many a heavy heart lightened, at the sound of the inspiring strains.

The reformed princes had determined upon having a statement of their views in systematic form, with the evidence from the Scriptures, to present before the Diet; and the task of its preparation was committed to Luther, Melanchthon, and their associates. This Confession was accepted by the Protestants as an exposition of their faith, and they assembled to affix their names to the important document. It was a solemn and trying time. The Reformers were solicitous that their cause should not be confounded with political questions; they felt that the Reformation should exercise no other influence than that which proceeds from the word of God. As the Christian princes advanced to sign the Confession, Melanchthon interposed, saying: "It is for the theologians and ministers to propose these things; let us reserve for other matters the authority of the mighty ones of the earth." "God forbid," replied John of Saxony, "that you should exclude me. I am resolved to do what is right, without troubling myself about my crown. I desire to confess the Lord. My electoral hat and my ermine are not so precious to me as the cross of Jesus Christ." Having thus spoken, he wrote down his name. Said another of the princes as he took the pen: "If the honor of my Lord Jesus Christ requires it, I am ready . . . to leave my goods and life behind." "I would rather renounce my subjects and my states, rather quit the country of my fathers staff in hand," he continued, "than receive any other doctrine than that which is contained in this Confession."—*Ibid.*, b. 14, ch. 6. Such was the faith and daring of those men of God.

The appointed time came to appear before the emperor. Charles V, seated upon his throne, surrounded by the electors and the princes, gave audience to the Protestant Reformers. The confession of their faith was read. In that august assembly the truths of the gospel were clearly set forth, and the errors of the papal church were pointed out. Well has that day been pronounced "the greatest day of the Reformation, and one of the most glorious in the history of Christianity and of mankind."—*Ibid.*, b. 14, ch. 7.

But a few years had passed since the monk of Wittenberg stood alone at Worms before the national council. Now in his stead were the noblest and most powerful princes of the empire. Luther had been forbidden to appear at Augsburg, but he had been present by his words and prayers. "I am overjoyed," he wrote, "that I have lived until this hour, in which Christ has been publicly exalted by such illustrious confessors, and in so glorious an assembly."—*Ibid.*, b. 14, ch. 7. Thus was fulfilled what the Scripture says: "I will speak of Thy testimonies . . . before kings." Psalm 119:46.

208   In the days of Paul the gospel for which he was imprisoned was thus brought before the princes and nobles of the imperial city. So on this occasion, that which the emperor had forbidden to be preached from the pulpit was proclaimed from the palace; what many had regarded as unfit even for servants to listen to was heard with wonder by the masters and lords of the empire. Kings and great men were the auditory, crowned princes were the preachers, and the sermon was the royal truth of God. "Since the apostolic age," says a writer, "there has never been a greater work or a more magnificent confession."—D'Aubigné, b. 14, ch. 7.

"All that the Lutherans have said is true; we cannot deny it," declared a papist bishop. "Can you refute by sound reasons the Confession made by the elector and his allies?" asked another of Dr. Eck. "With the writings of the apostles and prophets—no!" was the reply; "but with those of the Fathers and of the councils—yes!" "I understand," responded the questioner. "The Lutherans, according to you, are in Scripture, and we are outside."—*Ibid.*, b. 14, ch. 8.

Some of the princes of Germany were won to the reformed faith. The emperor himself declared that the Protestant articles were but the truth. The Confession was translated into many languages and circulated through all Europe,

and it has been accepted by millions in succeeding generations as the expression of their faith.

God's faithful servants were not toiling alone. While principalities and powers and wicked spirits in high places were leagued against them, the Lord did not forsake His people. Could their eyes have been opened, they would have seen as marked evidence of divine presence and aid as was granted to a prophet of old. When Elisha's servant pointed his master to the hostile army surrounding them and cutting off all opportunity for escape, the prophet prayed: "Lord, I pray Thee, open his eyes, that he may see." 2 Kings 6:17. And, lo, the mountain was filled with chariots and horses of fire, the army of heaven stationed to protect the man of God. Thus did angels guard the workers in the cause of the Reformation.

One of the principles most firmly maintained 209 by Luther was that there should be no resort to secular power in support of the Reformation, and no appeal to arms for its defense. He rejoiced that the gospel was confessed by princes of the empire; but when they proposed to unite in a defensive league, he declared that "the doctrine of the gospel should be defended by *God* alone. . . . The less man meddled in the work, the more striking would be God's intervention in its behalf. All the politic precautions suggested were, in his view, attributable to unworthy fear and sinful mistrust."—D'Aubigné, London ed., b. 10, ch. 14.

When powerful foes were uniting to overthrow the reformed faith, and thousands of swords seemed about to be unsheathed against it, Luther wrote: "Satan is putting forth his fury; ungodly pontiffs are conspiring; and we are threatened with war. Exhort the people to contend valiantly before the throne of the Lord, by faith and prayer, so that our enemies, vanquished by the Spirit of God, may be constrained to peace. Our chief want, our chief labor, is prayer; let the people know that they are now exposed to the edge of the sword and to the rage of Satan, and let them pray."—D'Aubigné, b. 10, ch. 14.

Again, at a later date, referring to the league contemplated by the reformed princes, Luther declared that the only weapon employed in this warfare should be "the sword of the Spirit." He wrote to the elector of Saxony: "We cannot on our conscience approve the proposed alliance. We would rather die ten times than see our gospel cause one drop of blood to be shed. Our part is to be like lambs of the slaughter. The cross of Christ must be borne. Let your highness be without fear. We shall do more by our prayers than all our enemies by their boastings. Only let not your hands be stained with the blood of your brethren. If the emperor requires us to be given up to his tribunals, we are ready to appear. You cannot defend our faith: each one should believe at his own risk and peril."—*Ibid.*, b. 14, ch. 1.

210 From the secret place of prayer came the power that shook the world in the Great Reformation. There, with holy calmness, the servants of the Lord set their feet upon the rock of His promises. During the struggle at Augsburg, Luther "did not pass a day without devoting three hours at least to prayer, and they were hours selected from those the most favorable to study." In the privacy of his chamber he was heard to pour out his soul before God in words "full of adoration, fear, and hope, as when one speaks to a friend." "I know that Thou art our Father and our God," he said, "and that Thou wilt scatter the persecutors of Thy children; for Thou art Thyself endangered with us. All this matter is Thine, and it is only by Thy constraint that we have put our hands to it. Defend us, then, O Father!"—*Ibid.*, b. 14, ch. 6.

To Melanchthon, who was crushed under the burden of anxiety and fear, he wrote: "Grace and peace in Christ—in Christ, I say, and not in the world. Amen. I hate with exceeding hatred those extreme cares which consume you. If the cause is unjust, abandon it; if the cause is just, why should we belie the promises of Him who commands us to sleep without fear? . . . Christ will not be wanting to the work of justice and truth. He lives, He reigns; what fear, then, can we have?"—*Ibid.*, b. 14, ch. 6.

God did listen to the cries of His servants. He gave to princes and ministers grace and courage to maintain the truth against the rulers of the darkness of this world. Saith the Lord: "Behold, I lay in Zion a chief cornerstone, elect, precious: and he that believeth on Him shall not be confounded." 1 Peter 2:6. The Protestant Reformers had built on Christ, and the gates of hell could not prevail against them.

211

12

The French Reformation

The Protest of Spires and the Confession at Augsburg, which marked the triumph of the Reformation in Germany, were followed by years of conflict and darkness. Weakened by divisions among its supporters, and assailed by powerful foes, Protestantism seemed destined to be utterly destroyed. Thousands sealed their testimony with their blood. Civil war broke out; the Protestant cause was betrayed by one of its leading adherents; the noblest of the reformed princes fell into the hands of the emperor and were dragged as captives from town to town. But in the moment of his apparent triumph, the emperor was smitten with defeat. He saw the prey wrested from his grasp, and he was forced

at last to grant toleration to the doctrines which it had been the ambition of his life to destroy. He had staked his kingdom, his treasures, and life itself upon the crushing out of the heresy. Now he saw his armies wasted by battle, his treasuries drained, his many kingdoms threatened by revolt, while everywhere the faith which he had vainly endeavored to suppress, was extending. Charles V had been battling against omnipotent power. God had said, "Let there be light," but the emperor had sought to keep the darkness unbroken. His purposes had failed; and in premature old age, worn out with the long struggle, he abdicated the throne and buried himself in a cloister.

In Switzerland, as in Germany, there came dark days for the Reformation. While many cantons accepted the reformed faith, others 212 clung with blind persistence to the creed of Rome. Their persecution of those who desired to receive the truth finally gave rise to civil war. Zwingli and many who had united with him in reform fell on the bloody field of Cappel. Oecolampadius, overcome by these terrible disasters, soon after died. Rome was triumphant, and in many places seemed about to recover all that she had lost. But He whose counsels are from everlasting had not forsaken His cause or His people. His hand would bring deliverance for them. In other lands He had raised up laborers to carry forward the reform.

In France, before the name of Luther had been heard as a Reformer, the day had already begun to break. One of the first to catch the light was the aged Lefevre, a man of extensive learning, a professor in the University of Paris, and a sincere and zealous papist. In his researches into ancient literature his attention was directed to the Bible, and he introduced its study among his students.

Lefevre was an enthusiastic adorer of the saints, and he had undertaken to prepare a history of the saints and martyrs as given in the legends of the church. This was a work which involved great labor; but he had already made considerable progress in it, when, thinking that he might obtain useful assistance from the Bible, he began its study with this object. Here indeed he found saints brought to view, but not such as figured in the Roman calendar. A flood of divine light broke in upon his mind. In amazement and disgust he turned away from his self-appointed task and devoted himself to the word of God. The precious truths which he there discovered he soon began to teach.

In 1512, before either Luther or Zwingli had begun the work of reform, Lefevre wrote: "It is God who gives us, by faith, that righteousness which by grace alone justifies to eternal life."—Wylie, b. 13, ch. 1. Dwelling upon the mysteries of redemption, he exclaimed: "Oh, the unspeakable greatness of that exchange,—the Sinless

213 One is condemned, and he who is guilty goes free; the Blessing bears the curse, and the cursed is brought into blessing; the Life dies, and the dead live; the Glory is whelmed in darkness, and he who knew nothing but confusion of face is clothed with glory."—D'Aubigné, London ed., b. 12, ch. 2.

And while teaching that the glory of salvation belongs solely to God, he also declared that the duty of obedience belongs to man. "If thou art a member of Christ's church," he said, "thou art a member of His body; if thou art of His body, then thou art full of the divine nature. . . . Oh, if men could but enter into the understanding of this privilege, how purely, chastely, and holily would they live, and how contemptible, when compared with the glory within them,—that glory which the eye of flesh cannot see,—would they deem all the glory of this world."—*Ibid.*, b. 12, ch. 2.

There were some among Lefevre's students who listened eagerly to his words, and who, long after the teacher's voice should be silenced, were to continue to declare the truth. Such was William Farel. The son of pious parents, and educated to accept with implicit faith the teachings of the church, he might, with the apostle Paul, have declared concerning himself: "After the most straitest sect of our religion I lived a Pharisee." Acts 26:5. A devoted Romanist, he burned with zeal to destroy all who should dare to oppose the church. "I would gnash my teeth like a furious wolf," he afterward said, referring to this period of his life, "when I heard anyone speaking against the pope."—Wylie, b. 13, ch. 2. He had been untiring in his adoration of the saints, in company with Lefevre making the round of the churches of Paris, worshiping at the altars, and adorning with gifts the holy shrines. But these observances could not bring peace of soul. Conviction of sin fastened upon him, which all the acts of penance that he practiced failed to banish. As to a voice from heaven he listened to the Reformer's words: "Salvation is of grace." "The Innocent One is condemned, and the criminal is acquitted." "It is the cross of Christ alone that 214 openeth the gates of heaven, and shutteth the gates of hell."—*Ibid.*, b. 13, ch. 2.

Farel joyfully accepted the truth. By a conversion like that of Paul he turned from the bondage of tradition to the liberty of the sons of God. "Instead of the murderous heart of a ravening wolf," he came back, he says, "quietly like a meek and harmless lamb, having his heart entirely withdrawn from the pope, and given to Jesus Christ."—D'Aubigné, b. 12, ch. 3.

While Lefevre continued to spread the light among his students, Farel, as zealous in the cause of Christ as he had been in that of the pope, went forth to declare the truth in public. A dignitary of the church, the bishop of Meaux,

soon after united with them. Other teachers who ranked high for their ability and learning joined in proclaiming the gospel, and it won adherents among all classes, from the homes of artisans and peasants to the palace of the king. The sister of Francis I, then the reigning monarch, accepted the reformed faith. The king himself, and the queen mother, appeared for a time to regard it with favor, and with high hopes the Reformers looked forward to the time when France should be won to the gospel.

But their hopes were not to be realized. Trial and persecution awaited the disciples of Christ. This, however, was mercifully veiled from their eyes. A time of peace intervened, that they might gain strength to meet the tempest; and the Reformation made rapid progress. The bishop of Meaux labored zealously in his own diocese to instruct both the clergy and the people. Ignorant and immoral priests were removed, and, so far as possible, replaced by men of learning and piety. The bishop greatly desired that his people might have access to the word of God for themselves, and this was soon accomplished. Lefevre undertook the translation of the New Testament; and at the very time when Luther's German Bible was issuing from the press in Wittenberg, the French New Testament was published at Meaux. The bishop spared no labor or expense to circulate it in his parishes, and soon the peasants of Meaux were in possession of the Holy 215 Scriptures.

As travelers perishing from thirst welcome with joy a living water spring, so did these souls receive the message of heaven. The laborers in the field, the artisans in the workshop, cheered their daily toil by talking of the precious truths of the Bible. At evening, instead of resorting to the wineshops, they assembled in one another's homes to read God's word and join in prayer and praise. A great change was soon manifest in these communities. Though belonging to the humblest class, the unlearned and hard-working peasantry, the reforming, uplifting power of divine grace was seen in their lives. Humble, loving, and holy, they stood as witnesses to what the gospel will accomplish for those who receive it in sincerity.

The light kindled at Meaux shed its beams afar. Every day the number of converts was increasing. The rage of the hierarchy was for a time held in check by the king, who despised the narrow bigotry of the monks; but the papal leaders finally prevailed. Now the stake was set up. The bishop of Meaux, forced to choose between the fire and recantation, accepted the easier path; but notwithstanding the leader's fall, his flock remained steadfast. Many witnessed for the truth amid the flames. By their courage and fidelity at the stake, these humble Christians spoke to thousands who in days of peace had never heard their testimony.

It was not alone the humble and the poor that amid suffering and scorn dared to bear witness for Christ. In the lordly halls of the castle and the palace there were kingly souls by whom truth was valued above wealth or rank or even life. Kingly armor concealed a loftier and more steadfast spirit than did the bishop's robe and miter. Louis de Berquin was of noble birth. A brave and courtly knight, he was devoted to study, polished in manners, and of blameless morals. "He was," says a writer, "a great follower of the papistical constitutions, and a great hearer of masses and sermons; . . . and he crowned all his other virtues by holding Lutheranism in special abhorrence." But, like so many others, providentially guided to the Bible, he was amazed to find there, "not the doctrines of Rome, but the doctrines of Luther."—Wylie, b. 13, ch. 9. Henceforth he gave himself with entire devotion to the cause of the gospel.

"The most learned of the nobles of France," his genius and eloquence, his indomitable courage and heroic zeal, and his influence at court,—for he was a favorite with the king,—caused him to be regarded by many as one destined to be the Reformer of his country. Said Beza: "Berquin would have been a second Luther, had he found in Francis I a second elector." "He is worse than Luther," cried the papists.—*Ibid.*, b. 13, ch. 9. More dreaded he was indeed by the Romanists of France. They thrust him into prison as a heretic, but he was set at liberty by the king. For years the struggle continued. Francis, wavering between Rome and the Reformation, alternately tolerated and restrained the fierce zeal of the monks. Berquin was three times imprisoned by the papal authorities, only to be released by the monarch, who, in admiration of his genius and his nobility of character, refused to sacrifice him to the malice of the hierarchy.

Berquin was repeatedly warned of the danger that threatened him in France, and urged to follow the steps of those who had found safety in voluntary exile. The timid and time-serving Erasmus, who with all the splendor of his scholarship failed of that moral greatness which holds life and honor subservient to truth, wrote to Berquin: "Ask to be sent as ambassador to some foreign country; go and travel in Germany. You know Beda and such as he—he is a thousand-headed monster, darting venom on every side. Your enemies are named legion. Were your cause better than that of Jesus Christ, they will not let you go till they have miserably destroyed you. Do not trust too much to the king's protection. At all events, *do not compromise me* with the faculty of theology."—*Ibid.*, b. 13, ch. 9.

But as dangers thickened, Berquin's zeal only waxed the stronger. So far from adopting the politic and self-serving counsel of Erasmus, he

determined upon still bolder measures. He would not only stand in defense of the truth, but he would attack error. The charge of heresy which the Romanists were seeking to fasten upon him, he would rivet upon them. The most active and bitter of his opponents were the learned doctors and monks of the theological department in the great University of Paris, one of the highest ecclesiastical authorities both in the city and the nation. From the writings of these doctors, Berquin drew twelve propositions which he publicly declared to be "opposed to the Bible, and heretical;" and he appealed to the king to act as judge in the controversy.

The monarch, not loath to bring into contrast the power and acuteness of the opposing champions, and glad of an opportunity of humbling the pride of these haughty monks, bade the Romanists defend their cause by the Bible. This weapon, they well knew, would avail them little; imprisonment, torture, and the stake were arms which they better understood how to wield. Now the tables were turned, and they saw themselves about to fall into the pit into which they had hoped to plunge Berquin. In amazement they looked about them for some way of escape.

"Just at that time an image of the Virgin at the corner of one of the streets, was mutilated." There was great excitement in the city. Crowds of people flocked to the place, with expressions of mourning and indignation. The king also was deeply moved. Here was an advantage which the monks could turn to good account, and they were quick to improve it. "These are the fruits of the doctrines of Berquin," they cried. "All is about to be overthrown—religion, the laws, the throne itself—by this Lutheran conspiracy."—*Ibid.*, b. 13, ch. 9.

Again Berquin was apprehended. The king withdrew from Paris, and the monks were thus left free to work their will. The Reformer was tried and condemned to die, and lest Francis should even yet interpose to save him, the sentence was executed on the very day it was pronounced. At noon Berquin was conducted to the place of death. An immense throng gathered to witness the event, and there were many who saw with astonishment and misgiving that the victim had been chosen from the best and bravest of the noble families of France. Amazement, indignation, scorn, and bitter hatred darkened the faces of that surging crowd; but upon one face no shadow rested. The martyr's thoughts were far from that scene of tumult; he was conscious only of the presence of his Lord.

The wretched tumbrel upon which he rode, the frowning faces of his persecutors, the dreadful death to which he was going—these he heeded not; He who liveth and was dead, and is alive for evermore, and hath the keys of death and of hell, was beside him. Berquin's countenance was radiant with the light and peace of heaven. He had attired himself in goodly raiment, wearing "a cloak of velvet, a doublet of satin and damask, and golden hose."—D'Aubigné, *History of the Reformation in Europe in the Time of Calvin*, b. 2, ch. 16. He was about to testify to his faith in the presence of the King of kings and the witnessing universe, and no token of mourning should belie his joy.

As the procession moved slowly through the crowded streets, the people marked with wonder the unclouded peace, the joyous triumph, of his look and bearing. "He is," they said, "like one who sits in a temple, and meditates on holy things."—Wylie, b. 13, ch. 9.

At the stake, Berquin endeavored to address a few words to the people; but the monks, fearing the result, began to shout, and the soldiers to clash their arms, and their clamor drowned the martyr's voice. Thus in 1529 the highest literary and ecclesiastical authority of cultured Paris "set the populace of 1793 the base example of stifling on the scaffold the sacred words of the dying."—*Ibid.*, b. 13, ch. 9.

Berquin was strangled, and his body was consumed in the flames. The tidings of his death caused sorrow to the friends of the Reformation throughout France. But his example was not lost. "We, too, are ready," said the witnesses for the truth, "to meet death cheerfully, setting our eyes on the life that is to come."—D'Aubigné, *History of the Reformation in Europe in the Time of Calvin*, b. 2, ch. 16.

During the persecution at Meaux, the teachers of the reformed faith were deprived of their license to preach, and they departed to other fields. Lefevre after a time made his way to Germany. Farel returned to his native town in eastern France, to spread the light in the home of his childhood. Already tidings had been received of what was going on at Meaux, and the truth, which he taught with fearless zeal, found listeners. Soon the authorities were roused to silence him, and he was banished from the city. Though he could no longer labor publicly, he traversed the plains and villages, teaching in private dwellings and in secluded meadows, and finding shelter in the forests and among the rocky caverns which had been his haunts in boyhood. God was preparing him for greater trials. "The crosses, persecutions, and machinations of Satan, of which I was forewarned, have not been wanting," he said; "they are even much severer than I could have borne of myself; but God is my Father; He has provided and always will provide me the strength which I require."—D'Aubigné, *History of the Reformation of the Sixteenth Century*, b. 12, ch. 9.

As in apostolic days, persecution had "fallen out rather unto the furtherance of the gospel."

Philippians 1:12. Driven from Paris and Meaux, "they that were scattered abroad went everywhere preaching the word." Acts 8:4. And thus the light found its way into many of the remote provinces of France.

God was still preparing workers to extend His cause. In one of the schools of Paris was a thoughtful, quiet youth, already giving evidence of a powerful and penetrating mind, and no less marked for the blamelessness of his life than for intellectual ardor and religious devotion. His genius and application soon made him the pride of the college, and it was confidently anticipated that John Calvin would become one of the ablest and most honored defenders of the church. But a ray of divine light penetrated even within the walls of scholasticism and superstition by which Calvin was enclosed. He heard of the new doctrines with a shudder, nothing doubting that the heretics deserved the fire to which they were given. Yet all unwittingly he was brought face to face with the heresy and forced to test the power of Romish theology to combat the Protestant teaching.

A cousin of Calvin's, who had joined the Reformers, was in Paris. The two kinsmen often met and discussed together the matters that were disturbing Christendom. "There are but two religions in the world," said Olivetan, the Protestant. "The one class of religions are those which men have invented, in all of which man saves himself by ceremonies and good works; the other is that one religion which is revealed in the Bible, and which teaches man to look for salvation solely from the free grace of God."

"I will have none of your new doctrines," exclaimed Calvin; "think you that I have lived in error all my days?"—Wylie, b. 13, ch. 7.

But thoughts had been awakened in his mind which he could not banish at will. Alone in his chamber he pondered upon his cousin's words. Conviction of sin fastened upon him; he saw himself, without an intercessor, in the presence of a holy and just Judge. The mediation of saints, good works, the ceremonies of the church, all were powerless to atone for sin. He could see before him nothing but the blackness of eternal despair. In vain the doctors of the church endeavored to relieve his woe. Confession, penance, were resorted to in vain; they could not reconcile the soul with God.

While still engaged in these fruitless struggles, Calvin, chancing one day to visit one of the public squares, witnessed there the burning of a heretic. He was filled with wonder at the expression of peace which rested upon the martyr's countenance. Amid the tortures of that dreadful death, and under the more terrible condemnation of the church, he manifested a faith and courage which the young student painfully contrasted with his own despair and darkness, while living in strictest obedience to the church.

Upon the Bible, he knew, the heretics rested their faith. He determined to study it, and discover, if he could, the secret of their joy.

In the Bible he found Christ. "O Father," he cried, "His sacrifice has appeased Thy wrath; His blood has washed away my impurities; His cross has borne my curse; His death has atoned for me. We had devised for ourselves many useless follies, but Thou hast placed Thy word before me like a torch, and Thou hast touched my heart, in order that I may hold in abomination all other merits save those of Jesus."—Martyn, vol. 3, ch. 13.

Calvin had been educated for the priesthood. When only twelve years of age he had been appointed to the chaplaincy of a small church, and his head had been shorn by the bishop in accordance with the canon of the church. He did not receive consecration, nor did he fulfill the duties of a priest, but he became a member of the clergy, holding the title of his office, and receiving an allowance in consideration thereof.

Now, feeling that he could never become a priest, he turned for a time to the study of law, but finally abandoned this purpose and determined to devote his life to the gospel. But he hesitated to become a public teacher. He was naturally timid, and was burdened with a sense of the weighty responsibility of the position, and he desired still to devote himself to study. The earnest entreaties of his friends, however, at last won his consent. "Wonderful it is," he said, "that one of so lowly an origin should be exalted to so great a dignity."—Wylie, b. 13, ch. 9.

Quietly did Calvin enter upon his work, and his words were as the dew falling to refresh the earth. He had left Paris, and was now in a provincial town under the protection of the princess Margaret, who, loving the gospel, extended her protection to its disciples. Calvin 222 was still a youth, of gentle, unpretentious bearing. His work began with the people at their homes. Surrounded by the members of the household, he read the Bible and opened the truths of salvation. Those who heard the message carried the good news to others, and soon the teacher passed beyond the city to the outlying towns and hamlets. To both the castle and the cabin he found entrance, and he went forward, laying the foundation of churches that were to yield fearless witnesses for the truth.

A few months and he was again in Paris. There was unwonted agitation in the circle of learned men and scholars. The study of the ancient languages had led men to the Bible, and many whose hearts were untouched by its truths were eagerly discussing them and even giving battle to the champions of Romanism. Calvin, though an able combatant in the fields of theological controversy, had a higher mission to accomplish than that of these noisy schoolmen. The minds of men were stirred, and now was the time to open to them the truth. While the halls of the universities were filled with the clamor of theological disputation, Calvin was making his way from house to house, opening the Bible to the people, and speaking to them of Christ and Him crucified.

In God's providence, Paris was to receive another invitation to accept the gospel. The call of Lefevre and Farel had been rejected, but again the message was to be heard by all classes in that great capital. The king, influenced by political considerations, had not yet fully sided with Rome against the Reformation. Margaret still clung to the hope that Protestantism was to triumph in France. She resolved that the reformed faith should be preached in Paris. During the absence of the king, she ordered a Protestant minister to preach in the churches of the city. This being forbidden by the papal dignitaries, the princess threw open the palace. An apartment was fitted up as a chapel, and it was announced that every day, at a specified hour, a sermon would be preached, and the people of every rank and station were invited to attend. Crowds flocked to the service. Not only the 223 chapel, but the antechambers and halls were thronged. Thousands every day assembled—nobles, statesmen, lawyers, merchants, and artisans. The king, instead of forbidding the assemblies, ordered that two of the churches of Paris should be opened. Never before had the city been so moved by the word of God. The spirit of life from heaven seemed to be breathed upon the people. Temperance, purity, order, and industry were taking the place of drunkenness, licentiousness, strife, and idleness.

But the hierarchy were not idle. The king still refused to interfere to stop the preaching, and they turned to the populace. No means were spared to excite the fears, the prejudices, and the fanaticism of the ignorant and superstitious multitude. Yielding blindly to her false teachers, Paris, like Jerusalem of old, knew not the time of her visitation nor the things which belonged unto her peace. For two years the word of God was preached in the capital; but, while there were many who accepted the gospel, the majority of the people rejected it. Francis had made a show of toleration, merely to serve his own purposes, and the papists succeeded in regaining the ascendancy. Again the churches were closed, and the stake was set up.

Calvin was still in Paris, preparing himself by study, meditation, and prayer for his future labors, and continuing to spread the light. At last, however, suspicion fastened upon him. The authorities determined to bring him to the flames. Regarding himself as secure in his seclusion, he had no thought of danger, when friends came hurrying to his room with the news that officers were on their way to arrest him. At that instant a loud knocking was heard at the outer entrance. There was not a moment to be lost. Some of his friends detained the officers at the door, while others assisted the Reformer to let himself down from a window, and he rapidly made his way to the outskirts of the city. Finding shelter in the cottage of a laborer who was a friend to the reform, he disguised himself in the garments of his host, and, 224 shouldering a hoe, started on his journey. Traveling southward, he again found refuge in the dominions of Margaret. (See D'Aubigné, *History of the Reformation in Europe in the Time of Calvin*, b. 2, ch. 30.)

Here for a few months he remained, safe under the protection of powerful friends, and engaged as before in study. But his heart was set upon the evangelization of France, and he could not long remain inactive. As soon as the storm had somewhat abated, he sought a new field of labor in Poitiers, where was a university, and where already the new opinions had found favor. Persons of all classes gladly listened to the gospel. There was no public preaching, but in the home of the chief magistrate, in his own lodgings, and sometimes in a public garden, Calvin opened the words of eternal life to those who desired to listen. After a time, as the number of hearers increased, it was thought safer to assemble outside the city. A cave in the side of a deep and narrow gorge, where trees and overhanging rocks made the seclusion still more complete, was chosen as the place of meeting. Little companies, leaving the city by different routes, found their way hither. In this retired spot the Bible was read aloud and explained. Here the Lord's Supper was celebrated for the first time by the Protestants of France. From this little church several faithful evangelists were sent out.

Once more Calvin returned to Paris. He could not even yet relinquish the hope that France as a nation would accept the Reformation. But he found almost every door of labor closed. To teach the gospel was to take the direct road to the stake, and he at last determined to depart to Germany. Scarcely had he left France when a storm burst over the Protestants, that, had he remained, must surely have involved him in the general ruin.

The French Reformers, eager to see their country keeping pace with Germany and Switzerland, determined to strike a bold blow against the superstitions of Rome, that should arouse the whole nation. Accordingly placards 225 attacking the mass were in one night posted all over France. Instead of advancing the reform, this zealous but ill-judged movement brought ruin, not only upon its propagators, but upon the friends of the reformed faith throughout France. It gave the Romanists what they had long desired—a pretext for demanding the utter destruction of the heretics as agitators dangerous to the stability of the throne and the peace of the nation.

By some secret hand—whether of indiscreet friend or wily foe was never known—one of the placards was attached to the door of the king's private chamber. The monarch was filled with horror. In this paper, superstitions that had received the veneration of ages were attacked with an unsparing hand. And the unexampled boldness of obtruding these plain and startling utterances into the royal presence aroused the wrath of the king. In his amazement he stood for a little time trembling and speechless. Then his rage found utterance in the terrible words: "Let all be seized without distinction who are suspected of Lutheresy. I will exterminate them all."—*Ibid.*, b. 4, ch. 10. The die was cast. The king had determined to throw himself fully on the side of Rome.

Measures were at once taken for the arrest of every Lutheran in Paris. A poor artisan, an adherent of the reformed faith, who had been accustomed to summon the believers to their secret assemblies, was seized and, with the threat of instant death at the stake, was commanded to conduct the papal emissary to the home of every Protestant in the city. He shrank in horror from the base proposal, but at last fear of the flames prevailed, and he consented to become the betrayer of his brethren. Preceded by the host, and surrounded by a train of priests, incense bearers, monks, and soldiers, Morin, the royal detective, with the traitor, slowly and silently passed through the streets of the city. The demonstration was ostensibly in honor of the "holy sacrament," an act of expiation for the insult put upon the mass by the protesters. But beneath this pageant a deadly purpose was concealed. On arriving opposite the house of a 226 Lutheran, the betrayer made a sign, but no word was uttered. The procession halted, the house was entered, the family were dragged forth and chained, and the terrible company went forward in search of fresh victims. They "spared no house, great or small, not even the colleges of the University of Paris. . . . Morin made all the city quake. . . . It was a reign of terror."—*Ibid.*, b. 4, ch. 10.

The victims were put to death with cruel torture, it being specially ordered that the fire should be lowered in order to prolong their agony. But they died as conquerors. Their constancy was unshaken, their peace unclouded. Their persecutors, powerless to move their inflexible firmness, felt themselves defeated. "The scaffolds were distributed over all the quarters of Paris, and the burnings followed on successive days, the design being to spread the terror of heresy by spreading the executions. The advantage, however, in the end, remained with the gospel. All Paris was enabled to see what kind of men the new opinions could produce. There was no pulpit like the martyr's pile. The serene joy that lighted up the faces of these men as they passed along . . . to the place of execution, their heroism as they stood amid the bitter flames, their meek forgiveness of injuries, transformed, in instances not a few, anger into pity, and hate into love, and pleaded with resistless eloquence in behalf of the gospel."—Wylie, b. 13, ch. 20.

The priests, bent upon keeping the popular fury at its height, circulated the most terrible accusations against the Protestants. They were charged with plotting to massacre the Catholics, to overthrow the government, and to murder the king. Not a shadow of evidence could be produced in support of the allegations. Yet these prophecies of evil were to have a fulfillment; under far different circumstances, however, and from causes of an opposite character. The cruelties that were inflicted upon the innocent Protestants by the Catholics accumulated in a weight of retribution, and in after centuries wrought the very doom they had predicted to be impending, 227 upon the king, his government, and his subjects; but it was brought about by infidels and by the papists themselves. It was not the establishment, but the suppression, of Protestantism, that, three hundred years later, was to bring upon France these dire calamities.

Suspicion, distrust, and terror now pervaded all classes of society. Amid the general alarm it was seen how deep a hold the Lutheran teaching had gained upon the minds of men who stood highest for education, influence, and excellence of character. Positions of trust and honor were suddenly found vacant. Artisans, printers, scholars, professors in the universities, authors, and even courtiers, disappeared. Hundreds fled from Paris, self-constituted exiles from their native land, in many cases thus giving the first intimation that they favored the reformed faith. The papists looked about them in amazement at thought of the unsuspected heretics that had been tolerated among them. Their rage spent itself upon the multitudes of humbler victims who were within their power. The prisons were crowded, and the very air seemed darkened with the smoke of burning piles, kindled for the confessors of the gospel.

Francis I had gloried in being a leader in the great movement for the revival of learning which marked the opening of the sixteenth century. He had delighted to gather at his court men of letters from every country. To his love of learning and his contempt for the ignorance and superstition of the monks was due, in part at least, the degree of toleration that had been granted to the reform. But, inspired with zeal to stamp out heresy, this patron of learning issued an edict declaring printing abolished all over France! Francis I presents one among the many examples on record showing that intellectual culture is not a safeguard against religious intolerance and persecution.

France by a solemn and public ceremony was to commit herself fully to the destruction of Protestantism. The priests demanded that the affront offered to High Heaven in the condemnation of the mass be expiated in blood, and that the king, in behalf of his people, publicly give his sanction to the dreadful work.

The 21st of January, 1535, was fixed upon for 228 the awful ceremonial. The superstitious fears and bigoted hatred of the whole nation had been roused. Paris was thronged with the multitudes that from all the surrounding country crowded her streets. The day was to be ushered in by a vast and imposing procession. "The houses along the line of march were hung with mourning drapery, and altars rose at intervals." Before every door was a lighted torch in honor of the "holy sacrament." Before daybreak the procession formed at the palace of the king. "First came the banners and crosses of the several parishes; next appeared the citizens, walking two and two, and bearing torches." The four orders of friars followed, each in its own peculiar dress. Then came a vast collection of famous relics. Following these rode lordly ecclesiastics in their purple and scarlet robes and jeweled adornings, a gorgeous and glittering array.

"The host was carried by the bishop of Paris under a magnificent canopy, . . . supported by four princes of the blood. . . . After the host walked the king. . . . Francis I on that day wore no crown, nor robe of state." With "head uncovered, his eyes cast on the ground, and in his hand a lighted taper," the king of France appeared "in the character of a penitent."— *Ibid.*, b. 13, ch. 21. At every altar he bowed down in humiliation, not for the vices that defiled his soul, nor the innocent blood that stained his hands, but for the deadly sin of his subjects who had dared to condemn the mass. Following him came the queen and the dignitaries of state, also walking two and two, each with a lighted torch.

As a part of the services of the day the monarch himself addressed the high officials of the kingdom in the great hall of the bishop's palace. With a sorrowful countenance he appeared before them and in words of moving eloquence bewailed "the crime, the blasphemy, the day of sorrow and disgrace," that had come upon the nation. And he called upon every loyal subject to aid in the extirpation of the pestilent heresy that threatened France with ruin. "As true, messieurs, as I am your king," he said, "if I knew one of my own limbs spotted or infected 229 with this detestable rottenness, I would give it you to cut off. . . . And further, if I saw one of my children defiled by it, I would not spare him. . . . I would deliver him up myself, and would sacrifice him to God." Tears choked his utterance, and the whole assembly wept, with one accord exclaiming: "We will live and die for the Catholic religion!"—D'Aubigné, History of the Reformation in Europe in the Time of Calvin, b. 4, ch. 12.

Terrible had become the darkness of the nation that had rejected the light of truth. The grace "that bringeth salvation" had appeared; but France, after beholding its power and holiness, after thousands had been drawn by its divine beauty, after cities and hamlets had been illuminated by its radiance, had turned away, choosing darkness rather than light. They had put from them the heavenly gift when it was offered them. They had called evil good, and good evil, till they had fallen victims to their willful self-deception. Now, though they might actually believe that they were doing God service in persecuting His people, yet their sincerity did not render them guiltless. The light that would have saved them from deception, from staining their souls with bloodguiltiness, they had willfully rejected.

A solemn oath to extirpate heresy was taken in the great cathedral where, nearly three centuries later, the Goddess of Reason was to be enthroned by a nation that had forgotten the living God. Again the procession formed, and the representatives of France set out to begin the work which they had sworn to do. "At short distances scaffolds had been erected, on which certain Protestant Christians were to be burned alive, and it was arranged that the fagots should be lighted at the moment the king approached, and that the procession should halt to witness the execution."—Wylie, b. 13, ch. 21. The details of the tortures endured by these witnesses for Christ are too harrowing for recital; but there was no wavering on the part of the victims. On being urged to recant, one answered: "I only believe in what the prophets and the apostles formerly preached, and what all the company of saints believed. My faith has a confidence in God which will resist all the powers of hell."—D'Aubigné, *History of the Reformation in Europe in the Time of Calvin*, b. 4, ch. 12.

230

Again and again the procession halted at the places of torture. Upon reaching their starting point at the royal palace, the crowd dispersed, and the king and the prelates withdrew, well satisfied with the day's proceedings and congratulating themselves that the work now begun would be continued to the complete destruction of heresy.

The gospel of peace which France had rejected was to be only too surely rooted out, and terrible would be the results. On the 21st of January, 1793, two hundred and fifty-eight years from the very day that fully committed France to the persecution of the Reformers, another procession, with a far different purpose, passed through the streets of Paris. "Again the king was the chief figure; again there were tumult and shouting; again there was heard the cry for more victims; again there were black scaffolds; and again the scenes of the day were closed by horrid executions; Louis XVI, struggling hand to hand with his jailers and executioners, was dragged forward to the block, and there held down by main force till the ax had fallen, and his dissevered head rolled on the scaffold."—Wylie, b. 13, ch. 21. Nor was the king the only victim; near the same spot two thousand and eight hundred human beings perished by the guillotine during the bloody days of the Reign of Terror.

The Reformation had presented to the world an open Bible, unsealing the precepts of the law of God and urging its claims upon the consciences of the people. Infinite Love had unfolded to men the statutes and principles of heaven. God had said: "Keep therefore and do them; for this is your wisdom and your understanding in the sight of the nations, which shall hear all these statutes, and say, Surely this great nation is a wise and understanding people." Deuteronomy 4:6. When France rejected the gift of heaven, she sowed the seeds of anarchy and ruin; and the inevitable outworking of cause and effect resulted in the Revolution and the Reign of Terror.

Long before the persecution excited by the 231 placards, the bold and ardent Farel had been forced to flee from the land of his birth. He repaired to Switzerland, and by his labors, seconding the work of Zwingli, he helped to turn the scale in favor of the Reformation. His later years were to be spent here, yet he continued to exert a decided influence upon the reform in France. During the first years of his exile, his efforts were especially directed to spreading the gospel in his native country. He spent considerable time in preaching among his countrymen near the frontier, where with tireless vigilance he watched the conflict and aided by his words of encouragement and counsel. With the assistance of other exiles, the writings of the German Reformers were translated into the French language and, together with the French Bible, were printed in large quantities. By colporteurs these works were sold extensively in France. They were furnished to the colporteurs at a low price, and thus the profits of the work enabled them to continue it.

Farel entered upon his work in Switzerland in the humble guise of a schoolmaster. Repairing to a secluded parish, he devoted himself to the instruction of children. Besides the usual branches of learning, he cautiously introduced the truths of the Bible, hoping through the children to reach the parents. There were some who believed, but the priests came forward to stop the work, and the superstitious country people were roused to oppose it. "That cannot be the gospel of Christ," urged the priests, "seeing the preaching of it does not bring peace, but war."—Wylie, b. 14, ch. 3. Like the first disciples, when persecuted in one city he fled to another. From village to village, from city to city, he went, traveling on foot, enduring hunger, cold, and weariness, and everywhere in peril of his life. He preached in the market places, in the churches, sometimes in the pulpits of the cathedrals. Sometimes he found the church empty of hearers; at times his preaching was interrupted by shouts and jeers; again he was pulled violently out of the pulpit. More than once he was set upon by the rabble and beaten

232 almost to death. Yet he pressed forward. Though often repulsed, with unwearying persistence he returned to the attack; and, one after another, he saw towns and cities which had been strongholds of popery, opening their gates to the gospel. The little parish where he had first labored soon accepted the reformed faith. The cities of Morat and Neuchatel also renounced the Romish rites and removed the idolatrous images from their churches.

Farel had long desired to plant the Protestant standard in Geneva. If this city could be won, it would be a center for the Reformation in France, in Switzerland, and in Italy. With this object before him, he had continued his labors until many of the surrounding towns and hamlets had been gained. Then with a single companion he entered Geneva. But only two sermons was he permitted to preach. The priests, having vainly endeavored to secure his condemnation by the civil authorities, summoned him before an ecclesiastical council, to which they came with arms concealed under their robes, determined to take his life. Outside the hall, a furious mob, with clubs and swords, was gathered to make sure of his death if he should succeed in escaping the council. The presence of magistrates and an armed force, however, saved him. Early next morning he was conducted, with his companion, across the lake to a place of safety. Thus ended his first effort to evangelize Geneva.

For the next trial a lowlier instrument was chosen—a young man, so humble in appearance that he was coldly treated even by the professed friends of reform. But what could such a one do where Farel had been rejected? How could one of little courage and experience withstand the tempest before which the strongest and bravest had been forced to flee? "Not by might, nor by power, but by My Spirit, saith the Lord." Zechariah 4:6. "God hath chosen the weak things of the world to confound the things which are mighty." "Because the foolishness of God is wiser than men; and the weakness of God is stronger than men." 1 Corinthians 1:27, 25.

Froment began his work as a schoolmaster. The truths which he taught the children at school they repeated at their homes. Soon the 233 parents came to hear the Bible explained, until the schoolroom was filled with attentive listeners. New Testaments and tracts were freely distributed, and they reached many who dared not come openly to listen to the new doctrines. After a time this laborer also was forced to flee; but the truths he taught had taken hold upon the minds of the people. The Reformation had been planted, and it continued to strengthen and extend. The preachers returned, and through their labors the Protestant worship was finally established in Geneva.

The city had already declared for the Reformation when Calvin, after various wanderings and vicissitudes, entered its gates. Returning from a last visit to his birthplace, he was on his way to Basel, when, finding the direct road occupied by the armies of Charles V, he was forced to take the circuitous route by Geneva.

In this visit Farel recognized the hand of God. Though Geneva had accepted the reformed faith, yet a great work remained to be accomplished here. It is not as communities but as individuals that men are converted to God; the work of regeneration must be wrought in the heart and conscience by the power of the Holy Spirit, not by the decrees of councils. While the people of Geneva had cast off the authority of Rome, they were not so ready to renounce the vices that had flourished under her rule. To establish here the pure principles of the gospel and to prepare this people to fill worthily the position to which Providence seemed calling them were not light tasks.

Farel was confident that he had found in Calvin one whom he could unite with himself in this work. In the name of God he solemnly adjured the young evangelist to remain and labor here. Calvin drew back in alarm. Timid and peace-loving, he shrank from contact with the bold, independent, and even violent spirit of the Genevese. The feebleness of his health, together with his studious habits, led him to seek retirement. Believing that by his pen he could best serve the cause of reform, he desired to find a quiet retreat for study, and there, 234 through the press, instruct and build up the churches. But Farel's solemn admonition came to him as a call from Heaven, and he dared not refuse. It seemed to him, he said, "that the hand of God was stretched down from heaven, that it lay hold of him, and fixed him irrevocably to the place he was so impatient to leave."— D'Aubigné, *History of the Reformation in Europe in the Time of Calvin*, b. 9, ch. 17.

At this time great perils surrounded the Protestant cause. The anathemas of the pope thundered against Geneva, and mighty nations threatened it with destruction. How was this little city to resist the powerful hierarchy that had so often forced kings and emperors to submission? How could it stand against the armies of the world's great conquerors?

Throughout Christendom, Protestantism was menaced by formidable foes. The first triumphs of the Reformation past, Rome summoned new forces, hoping to accomplish its destruction. At this time the order of the Jesuits was created, the most cruel, unscrupulous, and powerful of all the champions of popery. Cut off from earthly ties and human interests, dead to the claims of natural affection, reason and conscience wholly silenced, they knew no rule, no tie, but that of their order, and no duty but to extend its power. (See Appendix.) The gospel of Christ had enabled its adherents to meet danger and endure suffering, undismayed by cold, hunger, toil, and poverty, to uphold the banner of truth in face of the rack, the dungeon, and the stake. To combat these forces, Jesuitism inspired its followers with a fanaticism that enabled them to endure like dangers, and to oppose to the power of truth all the weapons of deception. There was no crime too great for them to commit, no deception too base for them to practice, no disguise too difficult for them to assume. Vowed to perpetual poverty and humility, it was their studied aim to secure wealth and power, to be devoted to the overthrow of Protestantism, and the re-establishment of the papal supremacy.

235 When appearing as members of their order, they wore a garb of sanctity, visiting prisons and hospitals, ministering to the sick and the poor, professing to have renounced the world, and bearing the sacred name of Jesus, who went about doing good. But under this blameless exterior the most criminal and deadly purposes were often concealed. It was a fundamental principle of the order that the end justifies the means. By this code, lying, theft, perjury, assassination, were not only pardonable but commendable, when they served the interests of the church. Under various disguises the Jesuits worked their way into offices of state, climbing up to be the counselors of kings, and shaping the policy of nations. They became servants to act as spies upon their masters. They established colleges for the sons of princes and nobles, and schools for the common people; and the children of Protestant parents were drawn into an observance of popish rites. All the outward pomp and display of the Romish worship was brought to bear to confuse the mind and dazzle and captivate the imagination, and thus the liberty for which the fathers had toiled and bled was betrayed by the sons. The Jesuits rapidly spread themselves over Europe, and wherever they went, there followed a revival of popery.

To give them greater power, a bull was issued re-establishing the inquisition. (See Appendix.) Notwithstanding the general abhorrence with which it was regarded, even in Catholic countries, this terrible tribunal was again set up by popish rulers, and atrocities too terrible to bear the light of day were repeated in its secret dungeons. In many countries, thousands upon thousands of the very flower of the nation, the purest and noblest, the most intellectual and highly educated, pious and devoted pastors, industrious and patriotic citizens, brilliant scholars, talented artists, skillful artisans, were slain or forced to flee to other lands.

Such were the means which Rome had invoked to quench the light of the Reformation, to withdraw from men the Bible, and to restore the ignorance and superstition of the Dark Ages. 236 But under God's blessing and the labors of those noble men whom He had raised up to succeed Luther, Protestantism was not overthrown. Not to the favor or arms of princes was it to owe its strength. The smallest countries, the humblest and least powerful nations, became its strongholds. It was little Geneva in the midst of mighty foes plotting her destruction; it was Holland on her sandbanks by the northern sea, wrestling against the tyranny of Spain, then the greatest and most opulent of kingdoms; it was bleak, sterile Sweden, that gained victories for the Reformation.

For nearly thirty years Calvin labored at Geneva, first to establish there a church adhering to the morality of the Bible, and then for the advancement of the Reformation throughout Europe. His course as a public leader was not faultless, nor were his doctrines free from error. But he was instrumental in promulgating truths that were of special importance in his time, in maintaining the principles of Protestantism against the fast-returning tide of popery, and in promoting in the reformed churches simplicity and purity of life, in place of the pride and corruption fostered under the Romish teaching.

From Geneva, publications and teachers went out to spread the reformed doctrines. To this point the persecuted of all lands looked for instruction, counsel, and encouragement. The city of Calvin became a refuge for the hunted Reformers of all Western Europe. Fleeing from the awful tempests that continued for centuries, the fugitives came to the gates of Geneva. Starving, wounded, bereft of home and kindred, they were warmly welcomed and tenderly cared for; and finding a home here, they blessed the city of their adoption by their skill, their learning, and their piety. Many who sought here a refuge returned to their own countries to resist the tyranny of Rome. John Knox, the brave Scotch Reformer, not a few of the English Puritans, the Protestants of Holland and of Spain, and the Huguenots of France carried from Geneva the torch of truth to lighten the darkness of their native lands.

13

237

The Netherlands and
Scandinavia

In the Netherlands the papal tyranny very early called forth resolute protest. Seven hundred years before Luther's time the Roman pontiff was thus fearlessly impeached by two bishops, who, having been sent on an embassy to Rome, had learned the true character of the "holy see": God "has made His queen and spouse, the church, a noble and everlasting provision for her family, with a dowry that is neither fading nor corruptible, and given her an eternal crown and scepter; . . . all which benefits you like a thief intercept. You set up yourself in the temple of God; instead of a pastor, you are become a wolf to the sheep; . . . you would make us believe you are a supreme bishop, but you rather behave like a tyrant. . . . Whereas you ought to be a servant of servants, as you call yourself, you endeavor to become a lord of lords. . . . You bring the commands of God into contempt. . . . The Holy Ghost is the builder of all churches as far as the earth extends. . . . The city of our God, of which we are the citizens, reaches to all the regions of the heavens; and it is greater than the city, by the holy prophets named Babylon, which pretends to be divine, wins herself to heaven, and brags that her wisdom is immortal; and finally, though without reason, that she never did err, nor ever can."—Gerard Brandt, *History of the Reformation in and About the Low Countries*, b. 1, p. 6.

238   Others arose from century to century to echo this protest. And those early teachers who, traversing different lands and known by various names, bore the character of the Vaudois missionaries, and spread everywhere the knowledge of the gospel, penetrated to the Netherlands. Their doctrines spread rapidly. The Waldensian Bible they translated in verse into the Dutch language. They declared "that there was great advantage in it; no jests, no fables, no trifles, no deceits, but the words of truth; that indeed there was here and there a hard crust, but that the marrow and sweetness of what was good and holy might be easily discovered in it."—*Ibid.*, b. 1, p. 14. Thus wrote the friends of the ancient faith, in the twelfth century.

Now began the Romish persecutions; but in the midst of fagots and torture the believers continued to multiply, steadfastly declaring that the Bible is the only infallible authority in religion, and that "no man should be coerced to believe, but should be won by preaching."—Martyn, vol. 2, p. 87.

The teachings of Luther found a congenial soil in the Netherlands, and earnest and faithful men arose to preach the gospel. From one of the provinces of Holland came Menno Simons. Educated a Roman Catholic and ordained to the priesthood, he was wholly ignorant of the Bible, and he would not read it for fear of being beguiled into heresy. When a doubt concerning the doctrine of transubstantiation forced itself upon him, he regarded it as a temptation from Satan, and by prayer and confession sought to free himself from it; but in vain. By mingling in scenes of dissipation he endeavored to silence the accusing voice of conscience; but without avail. After a time he was led to the study of the New Testament, and this, with Luther's writings, caused him to accept the reformed faith. He soon after witnessed in a neighboring village the beheading of a man who was put to death for having been rebaptized. This led him to study the Bible in regard to infant baptism. He could find no evidence for it in the Scriptures, but saw that repentance and faith are every- 239 where required as the condition of receiving baptism.

Menno withdrew from the Roman Church and devoted his life to teaching the truths which he had received. In both Germany and the Netherlands a class of fanatics had risen, advocating absurd and seditious doctrines, outraging order and decency, and proceeding to violence and insurrection. Menno saw the horrible results to which these movements would inevitably lead, and he strenuously opposed the erroneous teachings and wild schemes of the fanatics. There were many, however, who had been misled by these fanatics, but who had renounced their pernicious doctrines; and there were still remaining many descendants of the ancient Christians, the fruits of the Waldensian teaching. Among these classes Menno labored with great zeal and success.

For twenty-five years he traveled, with his wife and children, enduring great hardships and privations, and frequently in peril of his life. He traversed the Netherlands and northern Germany, laboring chiefly among the humbler classes, but exerting a widespread influence. Naturally eloquent, though possessing a limited education, he was a man of unwavering integrity, of humble spirit and gentle manners, of sincere and earnest piety, exemplifying in his own life the precepts which he taught, and he commanded the confidence of the people. His followers were scattered and oppressed. They suffered greatly from being confounded with the fanatical Munsterites. Yet great numbers were converted under his labors.

Nowhere were the reformed doctrines more generally received than in the Netherlands. In few countries did their adherents endure more terrible persecution. In Germany Charles V had banned the Reformation, and he would gladly have brought all its adherents to the stake; but the princes stood up as a barrier against his tyranny. In the Netherlands his power was greater, and persecuting edicts followed each other in quick succession. To read the Bible, to hear or preach it, or even to speak concerning it, was to incur the penalty of death by the stake. To pray to God in secret, to refrain from bowing to an image, or to sing a psalm, was also punishable with death. Even those who should abjure their errors were condemned, if men, to die by the sword; if women, to be buried alive. Thousands perished under the reign of Charles and of Philip II.

At one time a whole family was brought before the inquisitors, charged with remaining away from mass and worshiping at home. On his examination as to their practices in secret the youngest son answered: "We fall on our knees, and pray that God may enlighten our minds and pardon our sins; we pray for our sovereign, that his reign may be prosperous and his life happy; we pray for our magistrates, that God may preserve them."—Wylie, b. 18, ch. 6. Some of the judges were deeply moved, yet the father and one of his sons were condemned to the stake.

The rage of the persecutors was equaled by the faith of the martyrs. Not only men but delicate women and young maidens displayed unflinching courage. "Wives would take their stand by their husband's stake, and while he was enduring the fire they would whisper words of solace, or sing psalms to cheer him." "Young maidens would lie down in their living grave as if they were entering into their chamber of nightly sleep; or go forth to the scaffold and the fire, dressed in their best apparel, as if they were going to their marriage."—*Ibid.*, b. 18, ch. 6.

As in the days when paganism sought to destroy the gospel, the blood of the Christians was seed. (See Tertullian, *Apology*, paragraph 50.) Persecution served to increase the number of witnesses for the truth. Year after year the monarch, stung to madness by the unconquerable determination of the people, urged on his cruel work; but in vain. Under the noble William of Orange the Revolution at last brought to Holland freedom to worship God.

In the mountains of Piedmont, on the plains of France and the shores of Holland, the progress of the gospel was marked with the blood of its disciples. But in the countries of the North it found a peaceful entrance. Students at Wittenberg, returning to their homes, carried the reformed faith to Scandinavia. The publication of Luther's writings also spread the light. The simple, hardy people of the North turned from the corruption, the pomp, and the superstitions of Rome, to welcome the purity, the simplicity, and the life-giving truths of the Bible.

Tausen, "the Reformer of Denmark," was a peasant's son. The boy early gave evidence of vigorous intellect; he thirsted for an education; but this was denied him by the circumstances of his parents, and he entered a cloister. Here the purity of his life, together with his diligence and fidelity, won the favor of his superior. Examination showed him to possess talent that promised at some future day good service to the church. It was determined to give him an education at some one of the universities of Germany or the Netherlands. The young student was granted permission to choose a school for himself, with one proviso, that he must not go to Wittenberg. The scholar of the church was not to be endangered by the poison of heresy. So said the friars.

Tausen went to Cologne, which was then, as now, one of the strongholds of Romanism. Here he soon became disgusted with the mysticisms of the schoolmen. About the same time he obtained Luther's writings. He read them with wonder and delight, and greatly desired to enjoy the personal instruction of the Reformer. But to do so he must risk giving offense to his monastic superior and forfeiting his support. His decision was soon made, and erelong he was enrolled as a student at Wittenberg.

On returning to Denmark, he again repaired to his cloister. No one as yet suspected him of Lutheranism; he did not reveal his secret, but endeavored, without exciting the prejudices of his companions, to lead them to a purer faith and a holier life. He opened the Bible, and explained its true meaning, and at last preached Christ to them as the sinner's righteousness and his only hope of salvation. Great was the wrath of the prior, who had built high hopes upon him as a valiant defender of Rome. He was at once removed from his own monastery to another and confined to his cell under strict supervision.

To the terror of his new guardians several of the monks soon declared themselves converts to Protestantism. Through the bars of his cell Tausen had communicated to his companions a knowledge of the truth. Had those Danish fathers been skilled in the church's plan of dealing with heresy, Tausen's voice would never again have been heard; but instead of consigning him to a tomb in some underground dungeon, they expelled him from the monastery. Now they were powerless. A royal edict, just issued, offered protection to the teachers of the new doctrine. Tausen began to preach. The churches were opened to him, and the people thronged to listen. Others also were preaching the word of God. The New Testament, translated into the Danish tongue, was widely circulated. The efforts made by the papists to overthrow the work resulted in extending it, and erelong Denmark declared its acceptance of the reformed faith.

In Sweden, also, young men who had drunk from the well of Wittenberg carried the water of life to their countrymen. Two of the leaders in the Swedish Reformation, Olaf and Laurentius Petri, the sons of a blacksmith of Orebro, studied under Luther and Melanchthon, and the truths which they thus learned they were diligent to teach. Like the great Reformer, Olaf aroused the people by his zeal and eloquence, while Laurentius, like Melanchthon, was learned, thoughtful, and calm. Both were men of ardent piety, of high theological attainments, and of unflinching courage in advancing the truth. Papist opposition was not lacking. The Catholic priests stirred up the ignorant and superstitious people. Olaf Petri was often assailed by the mob, and upon several occasions barely escaped with his life. These Reformers were, however, favored and protected by the king.

243   Under the rule of the Roman Church the people were sunken in poverty and ground down by oppression. They were destitute of the Scriptures; and having a religion of mere signs and ceremonies, which conveyed no light to the mind, they were returning to the superstitious beliefs and pagan practices of their heathen ancestors. The nation was divided into contending factions, whose perpetual strife increased the misery of all. The king determined upon a reformation in the state and the church, and he welcomed these able assistants in the battle against Rome.

In the presence of the monarch and the leading men of Sweden, Olaf Petri with great ability defended the doctrines of the reformed faith against the Romish champions. He declared that the teachings of the Fathers are to be received only when in accordance with the Scriptures; that the essential doctrines of the faith are presented in the Bible in a clear and simple manner, so that all men may understand them. Christ said, "My doctrine is not Mine, but His that sent Me" (John 7:16); and Paul declared that should he preach any other gospel than that which he had received, he would be accursed (Galatians 1:8). "How, then," said the Reformer, "shall others presume to enact dogmas at their pleasure, and impose them as things necessary to salvation?"—Wylie, b. 10, ch. 4. He showed that the decrees of the church are of no authority when in opposition to the commands of God, and maintained the great Protestant principle that "the Bible and the Bible only" is the rule of faith and practice.

This contest, though conducted upon a stage comparatively obscure, serves to show us "the sort of men that formed the rank and file of the army of the Reformers. They were not illiterate, sectarian, noisy controversialists—far from it; they were men who had studied the word of God, and knew well how to wield the weapons with which the armory of the Bible supplied them. In respect of erudition they were ahead of their age. When we confine our attention to such brilliant centers as Wittenberg and Zurich, and to such illustrious names as those of Luther 244 and Melanchthon, of Zwingli and Oecolampadius, we are apt to be told, these were the leaders of the movement, and we should naturally expect in them prodigious power and vast acquisitions; but the subordinates were not like these. Well, we turn to the obscure theater of Sweden, and the humble names of Olaf and Laurentius Petri—from the masters to the disciples—what do we find? . . . Scholars and theologians; men who have thoroughly mastered the whole system of gospel truth, and who win an easy victory over the sophists of the schools and the dignitaries of Rome."—Ibid., b. 10, ch. 4.

As the result of this disputation the king of Sweden accepted the Protestant faith, and not long afterward the national assembly declared in its favor. The New Testament had been translated by Olaf Petri into the Swedish language, and at the desire of the king the two brothers undertook the translation of the whole Bible. Thus for the first time the people of Sweden received the word of God in their native tongue. It was ordered by the Diet that throughout the kingdom, ministers should explain the Scriptures and that the children in the schools should be taught to read the Bible.

Steadily and surely the darkness of ignorance and superstition was dispelled by the blessed light of the gospel. Freed from Romish oppression, the nation attained to a strength and greatness it had never before reached. Sweden became one of the bulwarks of Protestantism. A century later, at a time of sorest peril, this small and hitherto feeble nation—the only one in Europe that dared lend a helping hand—came to the deliverance of Germany in the terrible struggle of the Thirty Years' War. All Northern Europe seemed about to be brought again under the tyranny of Rome. It was the armies of Sweden that enabled Germany to turn the tide of popish success, to win toleration for the Protestants,—Calvinists as well as Lutherans,—and to restore liberty of conscience to those countries that had accepted the Reformation.

14   245

Later English Reformers

While Luther was opening a closed Bible to the people of Germany, Tyndale was impelled by the Spirit of God to do the same for England. Wycliffe's Bible had been translated from the Latin text, which contained many errors. It had never been printed, and the cost of manuscript copies was so great that few but wealthy men or nobles could procure it; and, furthermore, being strictly proscribed by the church, it had had a comparatively narrow circulation. In 1516, a year before the appearance of Luther's theses, Erasmus had published his Greek and Latin version of the New Testament. Now for the first time the word of God was printed in the original tongue. In this work many errors of former versions were corrected, and the sense was more clearly rendered. It led many among the educated classes to a better knowledge of the truth, and gave a new impetus to the work of reform. But the common people were still, to a great extent, debarred from God's word. Tyndale was to complete the work of Wycliffe in giving the Bible to his countrymen.

A diligent student and an earnest seeker for truth, he had received the gospel from the Greek Testament of Erasmus. He fearlessly preached his convictions, urging that all doctrines be tested by the Scriptures. To the papist claim that the church had given the Bible, and the church alone could explain it, Tyndale responded: "Do 246 you know who taught the eagles to find their prey? Well, that same God teaches His hungry children to find their Father in His word. Far from having given us the Scriptures, it is you who have hidden them from us; it is you who burn those who teach them, and if you could, you would burn the Scriptures themselves."— D'Aubigné, *History of the Reformation of the Sixteenth Century*, b. 18, ch. 4.

Tyndale's preaching excited great interest; many accepted the truth. But the priests were on the alert, and no sooner had he left the field than they by their threats and misrepresentations endeavored to destroy his work. Too often they succeeded. "What is to be done?" he exclaimed. "While I am sowing in one place, the enemy ravages the field I have just left. I cannot be everywhere. Oh! if Christians possessed the Holy Scriptures in their own tongue, they could of themselves withstand these sophists. Without the Bible it is impossible to establish the laity in the truth."—*Ibid.*, b. 18, ch. 4.

A new purpose now took possession of his mind. "It was in the language of Israel," said he, "that the psalms were sung in the temple of Jehovah; and shall not the gospel speak the language of England among us? . . . Ought the church to have less light at noonday than at the dawn? . . . Christians must read the New Testament in their mother tongue." The doctors and teachers of the church disagreed among themselves. Only by the Bible could men arrive at the truth. "One holdeth this doctor, another that. . . . Now each of these authors contradicts the other. How then can we distinguish him who says right from him who says wrong? . . . How? . . . Verily by God's word."—*Ibid.*, b. 18, ch. 4.

It was not long after that a learned Catholic doctor, engaging in controversy with him,

exclaimed: "We were better to be without God's laws than the pope's." Tyndale replied: "I defy the pope and all his laws; and if God spare my life, ere many years I will cause a boy that driveth the plow to know more of the Scripture than you do."—Anderson, *Annals of the English Bible*, page 19.

The purpose which he had begun to cherish, of giving to the people the New Testament 247 Scriptures in their own language, was now confirmed, and he immediately applied himself to the work. Driven from his home by persecution, he went to London, and there for a time pursued his labors undisturbed. But again the violence of the papists forced him to flee. All England seemed closed against him, and he resolved to seek shelter in Germany. Here he began the printing of the English New Testament. Twice the work was stopped; but when forbidden to print in one city, he went to another. At last he made his way to Worms, where, a few years before, Luther had defended the gospel before the Diet. In that ancient city were many friends of the Reformation, and Tyndale there prosecuted his work without further hindrance. Three thousand copies of the New Testament were soon finished, and another edition followed in the same year.

With great earnestness and perseverance he continued his labors. Notwithstanding the English authorities had guarded their ports with the strictest vigilance, the word of God was in various ways secretly conveyed to London and thence circulated throughout the country. The papists attempted to suppress the truth, but in vain. The bishop of Durham at one time bought of a bookseller who was a friend of Tyndale his whole stock of Bibles, for the purpose of destroying them, supposing that this would greatly hinder the work. But, on the contrary, the money thus furnished, purchased material for a new and better edition, which, but for this, could not have been published. When Tyndale was afterward made a prisoner, his liberty was offered him on condition that he would reveal the names of those who had helped him meet the expense of printing his Bibles. He replied that the bishop of Durham had done more than any other person; for by paying a large price for the books left on hand, he had enabled him to go on with good courage.

Tyndale was betrayed into the hands of his enemies, and at one time suffered imprisonment for many months. He finally witnessed for his faith by a martyr's death; but the weapons which he prepared have enabled other soldiers to do battle through all the centuries even to our 248 time.

Latimer maintained from the pulpit that the Bible ought to be read in the language of the people. The Author of Holy Scripture, said he, "is God Himself;" and this Scripture partakes of the might and eternity of its Author. "There is no king, emperor, magistrate, and ruler . . . but are bound to obey . . . His holy word." "Let us not take any bywalks, but let God's word direct us: let us not walk after . . . our forefathers, nor seek not what they did, but what they should have done."—Hugh Latimer, "First Sermon Preached Before King Edward VI."

Barnes and Frith, the faithful friends of Tyndale, arose to defend the truth. The Ridleys and Cranmer followed. These leaders in the English Reformation were men of learning, and most of them had been highly esteemed for zeal or piety in the Romish communion. Their opposition to the papacy was the result of their knowledge of the errors of the "holy see." Their acquaintance with the mysteries of Babylon gave greater power to their testimonies against her.

"Now I would ask a strange question," said Latimer. "Who is the most diligent bishop and prelate in all England? . . . I see you listening and hearkening that I should name him. . . . I will tell you: it is the devil. . . . He is never out of his diocese; call for him when you will, he is ever at home; . . . he is ever at his plow. . . . Ye shall never find him idle, I warrant you. . . . Where the devil is resident, . . . there away with books, and up with candles; away with Bibles, and up with beads; away with the light of the gospel, and up with the light of candles, yea, at noondays; . . . down with Christ's cross, up with purgatory pickpurse; . . . away with clothing the naked, the poor, and impotent, up with decking of images and gay garnishing of stocks and stones; up with man's traditions and his laws, down with God's traditions and His most holy word. . . . O that our prelates would be as diligent to sow the corn of good doctrine, as Satan is to sow cockle and darnel!"—*Ibid.*, "Sermon of the Plough."

249 The grand principle maintained by these Reformers—the same that had been held by the Waldenses, by Wycliffe, by John Huss, by Luther, Zwingli, and those who united with them—was the infallible authority of the Holy Scriptures as a rule of faith and practice. They denied the right of popes, councils, Fathers, and kings, to control the conscience in matters of religion. The Bible was their authority, and by its teaching they tested all doctrines and all claims. Faith in God and His word sustained these holy men as they yielded up their lives at the stake. "Be of good comfort," exclaimed Latimer to his fellow martyr as the flames were about to silence their voices, "we shall this day light such a candle, by God's grace, in England, as I trust shall never be put out."—*Works of Hugh Latimer*, vol. 1, p. xiii.

In Scotland the seeds of truth scattered by Columba and his colaborers had never been wholly destroyed. For hundreds of years after the churches of England submitted to Rome,

those of Scotland maintained their freedom. In the twelfth century, however, popery became established here, and in no country did it exercise a more absolute sway. Nowhere was the darkness deeper. Still there came rays of light to pierce the gloom and give promise of the coming day. The Lollards, coming from England with the Bible and the teachings of Wycliffe, did much to preserve the knowledge of the gospel, and every century had its witnesses and martyrs.

With the opening of the Great Reformation came the writings of Luther, and then Tyndale's English New Testament. Unnoticed by the hierarchy, these messengers silently traversed the mountains and valleys, kindling into new life the torch of truth so nearly extinguished in Scotland, and undoing the work which Rome for four centuries of oppression had done.

Then the blood of martyrs gave fresh impetus to the movement. The papist leaders, suddenly awakening to the danger that threatened their cause, brought to the stake some of the noblest 250 and most honored of the sons of Scotland. They did but erect a pulpit, from which the words of these dying witnesses were heard throughout the land, thrilling the souls of the people with an undying purpose to cast off the shackles of Rome.

Hamilton and Wishart, princely in character as in birth, with a long line of humbler disciples, yielded up their lives at the stake. But from the burning pile of Wishart there came one whom the flames were not to silence, one who under God was to strike the death knell of popery in Scotland.

John Knox had turned away from the traditions and mysticisms of the church, to feed upon the truths of God's word; and the teaching of Wishart had confirmed his determination to forsake the communion of Rome and join himself to the persecuted Reformers.

Urged by his companions to take the office of preacher, he shrank with trembling from its responsibility, and it was only after days of seclusion and painful conflict with himself that he consented. But having once accepted the position, he pressed forward with inflexible determination and undaunted courage as long as life continued. This truehearted Reformer feared not the face of man. The fires of martyrdom, blazing around him, served only to quicken his zeal to greater intensity. With the tyrant's ax held menacingly over his head, he stood his ground, striking sturdy blows on the right hand and on the left to demolish idolatry.

When brought face to face with the queen of Scotland, in whose presence the zeal of many a leader of the Protestants had abated, John Knox bore unswerving witness for the truth. He was not to be won by caresses; he quailed not before threats. The queen charged him with heresy. He had taught the people to receive a religion prohibited by the state, she declared, and had thus transgressed God's command enjoining subjects to obey their princes. Knox answered firmly:

"As right religion took neither original strength nor authority from worldly princes, but from the eternal God alone, so are not subjects bound to frame their religion according to the appetites of their princes. For oft it is that princes are the most ignorant of all others in God's true religion. . . . If all the seed of Abraham had been of the religion of Pharaoh, whose subjects they long were, I pray you, madam, what religion would there have been in the world? Or if all men in the days of the apostles had been of the religion of the Roman emperors, what religion would there have been upon the face of the earth? . . . And so, madam, ye may perceive that subjects are not bound to the religion of their princes, albeit they are commanded to give them obedience."

Said Mary: "Ye interpret the Scriptures in one manner, and they [the Roman Catholic teachers] interpret in another; whom shall I believe, and who shall be judge?"

"Ye shall believe God, that plainly speaketh in His word," answered the Reformer; "and farther than the word teaches you, ye neither shall believe the one nor the other. The word of God is plain in itself; and if there appear any obscurity in one place, the Holy Ghost, which is never contrary to Himself, explains the same more clearly in other places, so that there can remain no doubt but unto such as obstinately remain ignorant."—David Laing, *The Collected Works of John Knox*, vol. 2, pp. 281, 284.

Such were the truths that the fearless Reformer, at the peril of his life, spoke in the ear of royalty. With the same undaunted courage he kept to his purpose, praying and fighting the battles of the Lord, until Scotland was free from popery.

In England the establishment of Protestantism as the national religion diminished, but did not wholly stop, persecution. While many of the doctrines of Rome had been renounced, not a few of its forms were retained. The supremacy of the pope was rejected, but in his place the monarch was enthroned as the head of the church. In the service of the church there was still a wide departure from the purity and simplicity of the gospel. The great principle of religious liberty was not yet understood. Though the horrible cruelties which Rome employed against heresy were resorted to but rarely by Protestant rulers, yet the right of every man to worship God according to the dictates of his own conscience was not acknowledged. All were required to accept the doctrines and observe the forms of worship prescribed by the established church. Dissenters suffered persecution, to a greater or less extent, for hundreds of years.

In the seventeenth century thousands of pastors were expelled from their positions. The people were forbidden, on pain of heavy fines, imprisonment, and banishment, to attend any religious meetings except such as were sanctioned by the church. Those faithful souls who could not refrain from gathering to worship God were compelled to meet in dark alleys, in obscure garrets, and at some seasons in the woods at midnight. In the sheltering depths of the forest, a temple of God's own building, those scattered and persecuted children of the Lord assembled to pour out their souls in prayer and praise. But despite all their precautions, many suffered for their faith. The jails were crowded. Families were broken up. Many were banished to foreign lands. Yet God was with His people, and persecution could not prevail to silence their testimony. Many were driven across the ocean to America and here laid the foundations of civil and religious liberty which have been the bulwark and glory of this country.

Again, as in apostolic days, persecution turned out to the furtherance of the gospel. In a loathsome dungeon crowded with profligates and felons, John Bunyan breathed the very atmosphere of heaven; and there he wrote his wonderful allegory of the pilgrim's journey from the land of destruction to the celestial city. For over two hundred years that voice from Bedford jail has spoken with thrilling power to the hearts of men. Bunyan's *Pilgrim's Progress and Grace Abounding to the Chief of Sinners* have guided many feet into the path of life.

Baxter, Flavel, Alleine, and other men of talent, education, and deep Christian experience stood up in valiant defense of the faith which was once delivered to the saints. The work accomplished by these men, proscribed and outlawed by the rulers of this world, can never perish. Flavel's *Fountain of Life* and *Method of Grace* have taught thousands how to commit the keeping of their souls to Christ. Baxter's *Reformed Pastor* has proved a blessing to many who desire a revival of the work of God, and his *Saints' Everlasting Rest* has done its work in leading souls to the "rest" that remaineth for the people of God.

A hundred years later, in a day of great spiritual darkness, Whitefield and the Wesleys appeared as light bearers for God. Under the rule of the established church the people of England had lapsed into a state of religious declension hardly to be distinguished from heathenism. Natural religion was the favorite study of the clergy, and included most of their theology. The higher classes sneered at piety, and prided themselves on being above what they called its fanaticism. The lower classes were grossly ignorant and abandoned to vice, while the church had no courage or faith any longer to support the downfallen cause of truth.

The great doctrine of justification by faith, so clearly taught by Luther, had been almost wholly lost sight of; and the Romish principle of trusting to good works for salvation, had taken its place. Whitefield and the Wesleys, who were members of the established church, were sincere seekers for the favor of God, and this they had been taught was to be secured by a virtuous life and an observance of the ordinances of religion.

When Charles Wesley at one time fell ill, and anticipated that death was approaching, he was asked upon what he rested his hope of eternal life. His answer was: "I have used my best endeavors to serve God." As the friend who had put the question seemed not to be fully satisfied with his answer, Wesley thought: "What! are not my endeavors a sufficient ground of hope? Would he rob me of my endeavors? I have nothing else to trust to."—John Whitehead, *Life of the Rev. Charles Wesley*, page 102. Such was 254 the dense darkness that had settled down on the church, hiding the atonement, robbing Christ of His glory, and turning the minds of men from their only hope of salvation—the blood of the crucified Redeemer.

Wesley and his associates were led to see that true religion is seated in the heart, and that God's law extends to the thoughts as well as to the words and actions. Convinced of the necessity of holiness of heart, as well as correctness of outward deportment, they set out in earnest upon a new life. By the most diligent and prayerful efforts they endeavored to subdue the evils of the natural heart. They lived a life of self-denial, charity, and humiliation, observing with great rigor and exactness every measure which they thought could be helpful to them in obtaining what they most desired—that holiness which could secure the favor of God. But they did not obtain the object which they sought. In vain were their endeavors to free themselves from the condemnation of sin or to break its power. It was the same struggle which Luther had experienced in his cell at Erfurt. It was the same question which had tortured his soul—"How should man be just before God?" Job 9:2.

The fires of divine truth, well-nigh extinguished upon the altars of Protestantism, were to be rekindled from the ancient torch handed down the ages by the Bohemian Christians. After the Reformation, Protestantism in Bohemia had been trampled out by the hordes of Rome. All who refused to renounce the truth were forced to flee. Some of these, finding refuge in Saxony, there maintained the ancient faith. It was from the descendants of these Christians that light came to Wesley and his associates.

John and Charles Wesley, after being ordained to the ministry, were sent on a mission to America. On board the ship was a company of Moravians. Violent storms were encountered on the passage, and John Wesley, brought face to face with death, felt that he had not the assurance of peace with God. The Germans, on the contrary, manifested a calmness and trust to which he was a stranger.

"I had long before," he says, "observed the 255 great seriousness of their behavior. Of their humility they had given a continual proof, by performing those servile offices for the other passengers which none of the English would undertake; for which they desired and would receive no pay, saying it was good for their proud hearts, and their loving Saviour had done more for them. And every day had given them occasion of showing a meekness which no injury could move. If they were pushed, struck, or thrown about, they rose again and went away; but no complaint was found in their mouth. There was now an opportunity of trying whether they were delivered from the spirit of fear, as well as from that of pride, anger, and revenge. In the midst of the psalm wherewith their service began, the sea broke over, split the mainsail in pieces, covered the ship, and poured in between the decks as if the great deep had already swallowed us up. A terrible screaming began among the English. The Germans calmly sang on. I asked one of them afterwards, 'Were you not afraid?' He answered, 'I thank God, no.' I asked, 'But were not your women and children afraid?' He replied mildly, 'No; our women and children are not afraid to die.'"—Whitehead, *Life of the Rev. John Wesley*, page 10.

Upon arriving in Savannah, Wesley for a short time abode with the Moravians, and was deeply impressed with their Christian deportment. Of one of their religious services, in striking contrast to the lifeless formalism of the Church of England, he wrote: "The great simplicity as well as solemnity of the whole almost made me forget the seventeen hundred years between, and imagine myself in one of those assemblies where form and state were not; but Paul, the tentmaker, or Peter, the fisherman, presided; yet with the demonstration of the Spirit and of power."—*Ibid.*, pages 11, 12.

On his return to England, Wesley, under the instruction of a Moravian preacher, arrived at a clearer understanding of Bible faith. He was convinced that he must renounce all dependence upon his own works for salvation and must trust wholly to "the Lamb of God, which taketh away 256 the sin of the world." At a meeting of the Moravian society in London a statement was read from Luther, describing the change which the Spirit of God works in the heart of the believer. As Wesley listened, faith was kindled in his soul. "I felt my heart strangely warmed," he says. "I felt I did trust in Christ, Christ alone, for salvation: and an assurance was given me, that

He had taken away *my* sins, even *mine*, and saved *me* from the law of sin and death."—*Ibid.*, page 52.

Through long years of wearisome and comfortless striving—years of rigorous self-denial, of reproach and humiliation—Wesley had steadfastly adhered to his one purpose of seeking God. Now he had found Him; and he found that the grace which he had toiled to win by prayers and fasts, by almsdeeds and self-abnegation, was a gift, "without money and without price."

Once established in the faith of Christ, his whole soul burned with the desire to spread everywhere a knowledge of the glorious gospel of God's free grace. "I look upon all the world as my parish," he said; "in whatever part of it I am, I judge it meet, right, and my bounden duty, to declare unto all that are willing to hear, the glad tidings of salvation."—*Ibid.*, page 74.

He continued his strict and self-denying life, not now as the *ground*, but the *result* of faith; not the root, but the *fruit* of holiness. The grace of God in Christ is the foundation of the Christian's hope, and that grace will be manifested in obedience. Wesley's life was devoted to the preaching of the great truths which he had received—justification through faith in the atoning blood of Christ, and the renewing power of the Holy Spirit upon the heart, bringing forth fruit in a life conformed to the example of Christ.

Whitefield and the Wesleys had been prepared for their work by long and sharp personal convictions of their own lost condition; and that they might be able to endure hardness as good soldiers of Christ, they had been subjected to the fiery ordeal of scorn, derision, and persecution, both in the university and as they were entering the ministry. They and a few others who sympathized with them were contemptuously called Methodists by their ungodly fellow students—a name which is at the present time regarded as honorable by one of the largest denominations in England and America.

As members of the Church of England they were strongly attached to her forms of worship, but the Lord had presented before them in His word a higher standard. The Holy Spirit urged them to preach Christ and Him crucified. The power of the Highest attended their labors. Thousands were convicted and truly converted. It was necessary that these sheep be protected from ravening wolves. Wesley had no thought of forming a new denomination, but he organized them under what was called the Methodist Connection.

Mysterious and trying was the opposition which these preachers encountered from the established church; yet God, in His wisdom, had overruled events to cause the reform to begin within the church itself. Had it come wholly from without, it would not have penetrated where it was so much needed. But as the revival preachers were churchmen, and labored within the pale of the church wherever they could find opportunity, the truth had an entrance where the doors would otherwise have remained closed. Some of the clergy were roused from their moral stupor and became zealous preachers in their own parishes. Churches that had been petrified by formalism were quickened into life.

In Wesley's time, as in all ages of the church's history, men of different gifts performed their work. They did not harmonize upon every point of doctrine, but all were moved by the Spirit of God, and united in the absorbing aim to win souls to Christ. The differences between Whitefield and the Wesleys threatened at one time to create alienation; but as they learned meekness in the school of Christ, mutual forbearance and charity reconciled them. They had no time to dispute, while error and iniquity were teeming everywhere, and sinners were going down to ruin.

The servants of God trod a rugged path. Men of influence and learning employed their powers against them. After a time many of the clergy manifested determined hostility, and the doors of the churches were closed against a pure faith and those who proclaimed it. The course of the clergy in denouncing them from the pulpit aroused the elements of darkness, ignorance, and iniquity. Again and again did John Wesley escape death by a miracle of God's mercy. When the rage of the mob was excited against him, and there seemed no way of escape, an angel in human form came to his side, the mob fell back, and the servant of Christ passed in safety from the place of danger.

Of his deliverance from the enraged mob on one of these occasions, Wesley said: "Many endeavored to throw me down while we were going down hill on a slippery path to the town; as well judging that if I was once on the ground, I should hardly rise any more. But I made no stumble at all, nor the least slip, till I was entirely out of their hands. . . . Although many strove to lay hold on my collar or clothes, to pull me down, they could not fasten at all: only one got fast hold of the flap of my waistcoat, which was soon left in his hand; the other flap, in the pocket of which was a bank note, was torn but half off. . . . A lusty man just behind, struck at me several times, with a large oaken stick; with which if he had struck me once on the back part of my head, it would have saved him all further trouble. But every time, the blow was turned aside, I know not how; for I could not move to the right hand or left. . . . Another came rushing through the press, and raising his arm to strike, on a sudden let it drop, and only stroked my head, saying, 'What soft hair he has!' . . . The very first men whose hearts were turned were

259 the heroes of the town, the captains of the rabble on all occasions, one of them having been a prize fighter at the bear gardens. . . .

"By how gentle degrees does God prepare us for His will! Two years ago, a piece of brick grazed my shoulders. It was a year after that the stone struck me between the eyes. Last month I received one blow, and this evening two, one before we came into the town, and one after we were gone out; but both were as nothing: for though one man struck me on the breast with all his might, and the other on the mouth with such force that the blood gushed out immediately, I felt no more pain from either of the blows than if they had touched me with a straw."—John Wesley, *Works*, vol. 3, pp. 297, 298.

The Methodists of those early days—people as well as preachers—endured ridicule and persecution, alike from church members and from the openly irreligious who were inflamed by their misrepresentations. They were arraigned before courts of justice—such only in name, for justice was rare in the courts of that time. Often they suffered violence from their persecutors. Mobs went from house to house, destroying furniture and goods, plundering whatever they chose, and brutally abusing men, women, and children. In some instances, public notices were posted, calling upon those who desired to assist in breaking the windows and robbing the houses of the Methodists, to assemble at a given time and place. These open violations of both human and divine law were allowed to pass without a reprimand. A systematic persecution was carried on against a people whose only fault was that of seeking to turn the feet of sinners from the path of destruction to the path of holiness.

Said John Wesley, referring to the charges against himself and his associates: "Some allege that the doctrines of these men are false, erroneous, and enthusiastic; that they are new and unheard-of till of late; that they are Quakerism, fanaticism, popery. This whole pretense has been already cut up by the roots, it having been shown at large that every branch of this doctrine 260 is the plain doctrine of Scripture interpreted by our own church. Therefore it cannot be either false or erroneous, provided the Scripture be true." "Others allege, 'Their doctrine is too strict; they make the way to heaven too narrow.' And this is in truth the original objection, (as it was almost the only one for some time,) and is secretly at the bottom of a thousand more, which appear in various forms. But do they make the way to heaven any narrower than our Lord and His apostles made it? Is their doctrine stricter than that of the Bible? Consider only a few plain texts: 'Thou shalt love the Lord thy God with all thy heart, and with all thy mind, and with all thy soul, and with all thy strength.' 'For every idle word which men shall speak, they shall give an account in the day of judg-

ment.' 'Whether ye eat, or drink, or whatever ye do, do all to the glory of God.'

"If their doctrine is stricter than this, they are to blame; but you know in your conscience it is not. And who can be one jot less strict without corrupting the word of God? Can any steward of the mysteries of God be found faithful if he change any part of that sacred depositum? No. He can abate nothing, he can soften nothing; he is constrained to declare to all men, 'I may not bring down the Scripture to your taste. You must come up to it, or perish forever.' This is the real ground of that other popular cry concerning 'the uncharitableness of these men.' Uncharitable, are they? In what respect? Do they not feed the hungry and clothe the naked? 'No; that is not the thing: they are not wanting in this: but they are so uncharitable in judging! they think none can be saved but those of their own way.'"—*Ibid.*, vol. 3, pp. 152, 153.

The spiritual declension which had been manifest in England just before the time of Wesley was in great degree the result of antinomian teaching. Many affirmed that Christ had abolished the moral law and that Christians are therefore under no obligation to observe it; that a believer is freed from the "bondage of good works." Others, though admitting the perpetuity 261 of the law, declared that it was unnecessary for ministers to exhort the people to obedience of its precepts, since those whom God had elected to salvation would, "by the irresistible impulse of divine grace, be led to the practice of piety and virtue," while those who were doomed to eternal reprobation "did not have power to obey the divine law."

Others, also holding that "the elect cannot fall from grace nor forfeit the divine favor," arrived at the still more hideous conclusion that "the wicked actions they commit are not really sinful, nor to be considered as instances of their violation of the divine law, and that, consequently, they have no occasion either to confess their sins or to break them off by repentance."— McClintock and Strong, *Cyclopedia*, art. "Antinomians." Therefore, they declared that even one of the vilest of sins, "considered universally an enormous violation of the divine law, is not a sin in the sight of God," if committed by one of the elect, "because it is one of the essential and distinctive characteristics of the elect, that they cannot do anything that is either displeasing to God or prohibited by the law."

These monstrous doctrines are essentially the same as the later teaching of popular educators and theologians—that there is no unchangeable divine law as the standard of right, but that the standard of morality is indicated by society itself, and has constantly been subject to change. All these ideas are inspired by the same master spirit—by him who, even among the sinless inhabitants of heaven, began his work of seeking to break down the righteous restraints of the law of God.

The doctrine of the divine decrees, unalterably fixing the character of men, had led many to a virtual rejection of the law of God. Wesley steadfastly opposed the errors of the antinomian teachers and showed that this doctrine which led to antinomianism was contrary to the Scriptures. "The grace of God that bringeth salvation hath appeared to *all men.*" "This is good and acceptable in the sight of God our Saviour; who will have *all men* to be saved, and to come unto the knowledge of the truth. For there is one God, and one mediator between God and men, the man Christ Jesus; who gave Himself a ransom for *all.*" Titus 2:11; 1 Timothy 2:3-6. The Spirit of God is freely bestowed to enable every man to lay hold upon the means of salvation. Thus Christ, "the true Light," "lighteth every man that cometh into the world." John 1:9. Men fail of salvation through their own willful refusal of the gift of life.

In answer to the claim that at the death of Christ the precepts of the Decalogue had been abolished with the ceremonial law, Wesley said: "The moral law, contained in the Ten Commandments and enforced by the prophets, He did not take away. It was not the design of His coming to revoke any part of this. This is a law which never can be broken, which 'stands fast as the faithful witness in heaven.' . . . This was from the beginning of the world, being 'written not on tables of stone,' but on the hearts of all the children of men, when they came out of the hands of the Creator. And however the letters once wrote by the finger of God are now in a great measure defaced by sin, yet can they not wholly be blotted out, while we have any consciousness of good and evil. Every part of this law must remain in force upon all mankind, and in all ages; as not depending either on time or place, or any other circumstances liable to change, but on the nature of God, and the nature of man, and their unchangeable relation to each other.

" 'I am not come to destroy, but to fulfill.' . . . Without question, His meaning in this place is (consistently with all that goes before and follows after),—I am come to establish it in its fullness, in spite of all the glosses of men: I am come to place in a full and clear view whatsoever was dark or obscure therein: I am come to declare the true and full import of every part of it; to show the length and breadth, the entire extent, of every commandment contained therein, and the height and depth, the inconceivable purity and spirituality of it in all its branches."—Wesley, sermon 25.

Wesley declared the perfect harmony of the law and the gospel. "There is, therefore, the closest connection that can be conceived, between the law and the gospel. On the one hand, the law continually makes way for, and points us to, the gospel; on the other, the gospel continually leads us to a more exact fulfilling of the law. The law, for instance, requires us to love God, to love our neighbor, to be meek, humble, or holy. We feel that we are not sufficient for these things; yea, that 'with man this is impossible;' but we see a promise of God to give us that love, and to make us humble, meek, and holy: we lay hold of this gospel, of these glad tidings; it is done unto us according to our faith; and 'the righteousness of the law is fulfilled in us,' through faith which is in Christ Jesus. . . .

"In the highest rank of the enemies of the gospel of Christ," said Wesley, "are they who openly and explicitly 'judge the law' itself, and 'speak evil of the law;' who teach men to break (to dissolve, to loose, to untie the obligation of) not one only, whether of the least or of the greatest, but all the commandments at a stroke. . . . The most surprising of all the circumstances that attend this strong delusion, is that they who are given up to it, really believe that they honor Christ by overthrowing His law, and that they are magnifying His office while they are destroying His doctrine! Yea, they honor Him just as Judas did when he said, 'Hail, Master, and kissed Him.' And He may as justly say to every one of them, 'Betrayest thou the Son of man with a kiss?' It is no other than betraying Him with a kiss, to talk of His blood, and take away His crown; to set light by any part of His law, under pretense of advancing His gospel. Nor indeed can anyone escape this charge, who preaches faith in any such a manner as either directly or indirectly tends to set aside any branch of obedience: who preaches Christ so as to disannul, or weaken in any wise, the least of the commandments of God."—*Ibid.*

To those who urged that "the preaching of the gospel answers all the ends of the law," Wesley replied: "This we utterly deny. It does not answer the very first end of the law, namely, the convincing men of sin, the awakening those who are still asleep on the brink of hell." The apostle Paul declares that "by the law is the knowledge of sin;" "and not until man is convicted of sin, will he truly feel his need of the atoning blood of Christ. . . . 'They that be whole,' as our Lord Himself observes, 'need not a physician, but they that are sick.' It is absurd, therefore, to offer a physician to them that are whole, or that at least imagine themselves so to be. You are first to convince them that they are sick; otherwise they will not thank you for your labor. It is equally absurd to offer Christ to them whose heart is whole, having never yet been broken."—*Ibid.*, sermon 35.

Thus while preaching the gospel of the grace of God, Wesley, like his Master, sought to "magnify the law, and make it honorable."

Faithfully did he accomplish the work given him of God, and glorious were the results which he was permitted to behold. At the close of his long life of more than fourscore years—above half a century spent in itinerant ministry—his avowed adherents numbered more than half a million souls. But the multitude that through his labors had been lifted from the ruin and degradation of sin to a higher and a purer life, and the number who by his teaching had attained to a deeper and richer experience, will never be known till the whole family of the redeemed shall be gathered into the kingdom of God. His life presents a lesson of priceless worth to every Christian. Would that the faith and humility, the untiring zeal, self-sacrifice, and devotion of this servant of Christ might be reflected in the churches of today!

265

15

The Bible and the French Revolution

In the sixteenth century the Reformation, presenting an open Bible to the people, had sought admission to all the countries of Europe. Some nations welcomed it with gladness, as a messenger of Heaven. In other lands the papacy succeeded to a great extent in preventing its entrance; and the light of Bible knowledge, with its elevating influences, was almost wholly excluded. In one country, though the light found entrance, it was not comprehended by the darkness. For centuries, truth and error struggled for the mastery. At last the evil triumphed, and the truth of Heaven was thrust out. "This is the condemnation, that light is come into the world, and men loved darkness rather than light." John 3:19. The nation was left to reap the results of the course which she had chosen. The restraint of God's Spirit was removed from a people that had despised the gift of His grace. Evil was permitted to come to maturity. And all the world saw the fruit of willful rejection of the light.

The war against the Bible, carried forward for so many centuries in France, culminated in the scenes of the Revolution. That terrible outbreaking was but the legitimate result of Rome's suppression of the Scriptures. (See Appendix.) It presented the most striking illustration which the world has ever witnessed of the working out of the papal policy—an illustration
266 of the results to which for more than a thousand years the teaching of the Roman Church had been tending.

The suppression of the Scriptures during the period of papal supremacy was foretold by the prophets; and the Revelator points also to the terrible results that were to accrue especially to France from the domination of the "man of sin."

Said the angel of the Lord: "The holy city shall they tread underfoot forty and two months. And I will give power unto My two witnesses, and they shall prophesy a thousand two hundred and threescore days, clothed in sackcloth. . . . And when they shall have finished their testimony, the beast that ascendeth out of the bottomless pit shall make war against them, and shall overcome them, and kill them. And their dead bodies shall lie in the street of the great city, which spiritually is called Sodom and Egypt, where also our Lord was crucified. . . . And they that dwell upon the earth shall rejoice over them, and make merry, and shall send gifts one to another; because these two prophets tormented them that dwelt on the earth. And after three days and a half the Spirit of life from God entered into them, and they stood upon their feet; and great fear fell upon them which saw them." Revelation 11:2-11.

The periods here mentioned—"forty and two months," and "a thousand two hundred and threescore days"—are the same, alike representing the time in which the church of Christ was to suffer oppression from Rome. The 1260 years of papal supremacy began in A.D. 538, and would therefore terminate in 1798. (See Appendix note for page 54.) At that time a French army entered Rome and made the pope a prisoner, and he died in exile. Though a new pope was soon afterward elected, the papal hierarchy has never since been able to wield the power which it before possessed.

The persecution of the church did not continue throughout the entire period of the 1260 years. God in mercy to His people cut short the time of their fiery trial. In foretelling the "great 267 tribulation" to befall the church, the Saviour said: "Except those days should be shortened, there should no flesh be saved: but for the elect's sake those days shall be shortened." Matthew 24:22. Through the influence of the Reformation the persecution was brought to an end prior to 1798.

Concerning the two witnesses the prophet declares further: "These are the two olive trees, and the two candlesticks standing before the God of the earth." "Thy word," said the psalmist, "is a lamp unto my feet, and a light unto my path." Revelation 11:4; Psalm 119:105. The two witnesses represent the Scriptures of the Old and the New Testament. Both are important testimonies to the origin and perpetuity of the law of God. Both are witnesses also to the plan of salvation. The types, sacrifices, and prophecies of the Old Testament point forward to a Saviour to come. The Gospels and Epistles of the New Testament tell of a Saviour who has come in the exact manner foretold by type and prophecy.

"They shall prophecy a thousand two hundred and threescore days, clothed in sackcloth." During the greater part of this period, God's witnesses remained in a state of obscurity. The papal power sought to hide from the people the word of truth, and set before them false witnesses to contradict its testimony. (See Appendix.) When the Bible was proscribed by religious and secular authority; when its testimony was perverted, and every effort made that men and demons could invent to turn the minds of the people from it; when those who dared proclaim its sacred truths were hunted, betrayed, tortured, buried in dungeon cells, martyred for their faith, or compelled to flee to mountain fastnesses, and to dens and caves of the earth—then the faithful witnesses prophesied in sackcloth. Yet they continued their testimony throughout the entire period of 1260 years. In the darkest times there were faithful men who loved God's word and were jealous for His honor. To these loyal servants were given wisdom, power, and authority to declare His truth during the whole of this time.

"And if any man will hurt them, fire proceedeth out of their mouth, and devoureth their enemies: and if any man will hurt them, he must in this manner be killed." Revelation 11:5. Men cannot with impunity trample upon the word of God. The meaning of this fearful denunciation is set forth in the closing chapter of the Revelation: "I testify unto every man that heareth the words of the prophecy of this book, If any man shall add unto these things, God shall add unto him the plagues that are written in this book: and if any man shall take away from the words of the book of this prophecy, God shall take away his part out of the book of life, and out of the holy city, and from the things which are written in this book." Revelation 22:18, 19.

Such are the warnings which God has given to guard men against changing in any manner that which He has revealed or commanded. These solemn denunciations apply to all who by their influence lead men to regard lightly the law of God. They should cause those to fear and tremble who flippantly declare it a matter of little consequence whether we obey God's law or not. All who exalt their own opinions above divine revelation, all who would change the plain meaning of Scripture to suit their own convenience, or for the sake of conforming to the world, are taking upon themselves a fearful responsibility. The written word, the law of God, will measure the character of every man and condemn all whom this unerring test shall declare wanting.

"When they shall have finished [are finishing] their testimony." The period when the two witnesses were to prophesy clothed in sackcloth, ended in 1798. As they were approaching the termination of their work in obscurity, war

was to be made upon them by the power represented as "the beast that ascendeth out of the bottomless pit." In many of the nations of Europe the powers that ruled in church and state had for centuries been controlled by Satan through the medium of the papacy. But here is brought to view a new manifestation of satanic power.

It had been Rome's policy, under a profession of reverence for the Bible, to keep it locked up in an unknown tongue and hidden away from the people. Under her rule the witnesses prophesied "clothed in sackcloth." But another power—the beast from the bottomless pit—was to arise to make open, avowed war upon the word of God.

"The great city" in whose streets the witnesses are slain, and where their dead bodies lie, is "spiritually" Egypt. Of all nations presented in Bible history, Egypt most boldly denied the existence of the living God and resisted His commands. No monarch ever ventured upon more open and highhanded rebellion against the authority of Heaven than did the king of Egypt. When the message was brought him by Moses, in the name of the Lord, Pharaoh proudly answered: "Who is Jehovah, that I should hearken unto His voice to let Israel go? I know not Jehovah, and moreover I will not let Israel go." Exodus 5:2, A.R.V. This is atheism, and the nation represented by Egypt would give voice to a similar denial of the claims of the living God and would manifest a like spirit of unbelief and defiance. "The great city" is also compared, "spiritually," to Sodom. The corruption of Sodom in breaking the law of God was especially manifested in licentiousness. And this sin was also to be a pre-eminent characteristic of the nation that should fulfill the specifications of this scripture.

According to the words of the prophet, then, a little before the year 1798 some power of satanic origin and character would rise to make war upon the Bible. And in the land where the testimony of God's two witnesses should thus be silenced, there would be manifest the atheism of the Pharaoh and the licentiousness of Sodom.

This prophecy has received a most exact and striking fulfillment in the history of France. During the Revolution, in 1793, "the world for the first time heard an assembly of men, born and educated in civilization, and assuming the right to govern one of the finest of the European nations, uplift their united voice to deny the most solemn truth which man's soul receives, and renounce unanimously the belief and worship of a Deity."—Sir Walter Scott, *Life of Napoleon,* vol. 1, ch. 17. "France is the only nation in the world concerning which the authentic record survives, that as a nation she lifted her hand in open rebellion against the Author of the universe. Plenty of blasphemers, plenty of infidels, there have been, and still continue to be, in England, Germany, Spain, and elsewhere; but France stands apart in the world's history as the single state which, by the decree of her Legislative Assembly, pronounced that there was no God, and of which the entire population of the capital, and a vast majority elsewhere, women as well as men, danced and sang with joy in accepting the announcement."—*Blackwood's Magazine*, November, 1870.

France presented also the characteristics which especially distinguished Sodom. During the Revolution there was manifest a state of moral debasement and corruption similar to that which brought destruction upon the cities of the plain. And the historian presents together the atheism and the licentiousness of France, as given in the prophecy: "Intimately connected with these laws affecting religion, was that which reduced the union of marriage—the most sacred engagement which human beings can form, and the permanence of which leads most strongly to the consolidation of society—to the state of a mere civil contract of a transitory character, which any two persons might engage in and cast loose at pleasure. . . . If fiends had set themselves to work to discover a mode of most effectually destroying whatever is venerable, graceful, or permanent in domestic life, and of obtaining at the same time an assurance that the mischief which it was their object to create should be perpetuated from one generation to another, they could not have invented a more effectual plan than the degradation of marriage. . . .

271 Sophie Arnoult, an actress famous for the witty things she said, described the republican marriage as 'the sacrament of adultery.'"—Scott, vol. 1, ch. 17.

"Where also our Lord was crucified." This specification of the prophecy was also fulfilled by France. In no land had the spirit of enmity against Christ been more strikingly displayed. In no country had the truth encountered more bitter and cruel opposition. In the persecution which France had visited upon the confessors of the gospel, she had crucified Christ in the person of His disciples.

Century after century the blood of the saints had been shed. While the Waldenses laid down their lives upon the mountains of Piedmont "for the word of God, and for the testimony of Jesus Christ," similar witness to the truth had been borne by their brethren, the Albigenses of France. In the days of the Reformation its disciples had been put to death with horrible tortures. King and nobles, highborn women and delicate maidens, the pride and chivalry of the nation, had feasted their eyes upon the agonies of the martyrs of Jesus. The brave Huguenots, battling for those rights which the human heart holds

most sacred, had poured out their blood on many a hard-fought field. The Protestants were counted as outlaws, a price was set upon their heads, and they were hunted down like wild beasts.

The "Church in the Desert," the few descendants of the ancient Christians that still lingered in France in the eighteenth century, hiding away in the mountains of the south, still cherished the faith of their fathers. As they ventured to meet by night on mountainside or lonely moor, they were chased by dragoons and dragged away to lifelong slavery in the galleys. The purest, the most refined, and the most intelligent of the French were chained, in horrible torture, amidst robbers and assassins. (See Wylie, b. 22, ch. 6.) Others, more mercifully dealt with, were shot down in cold blood, as, unarmed and helpless, they fell upon their knees in prayer. Hundreds 272 of aged men, defenseless women, and innocent children were left dead upon the earth at their place of meeting. In traversing the mountainside or the forest, where they had been accustomed to assemble, it was not unusual to find "at every four paces, dead bodies dotting the sward, and corpses hanging suspended from the trees." Their country, laid waste with the sword, the ax, the fagot, "was converted into one vast, gloomy wilderness." "These atrocities were enacted . . . in no dark age, but in the brilliant era of Louis XIV. Science was then cultivated, letters flourished, the divines of the court and of the capital were learned and eloquent men, and greatly affected the graces of meekness and charity."—*Ibid.*, b. 22, ch. 7.

But blackest in the black catalogue of crime, most horrible among the fiendish deeds of all the dreadful centuries, was the St. Bartholomew Massacre. The world still recalls with shuddering horror the scenes of that most cowardly and cruel onslaught. The king of France, urged on by Romish priests and prelates, lent his sanction to the dreadful work. A bell, tolling at dead of night, was a signal for the slaughter. Protestants by thousands, sleeping quietly in their homes, trusting to the plighted honor of their king, were dragged forth without a warning and murdered in cold blood.

As Christ was the invisible leader of His people from Egyptian bondage, so was Satan the unseen leader of his subjects in this horrible work of multiplying martyrs. For seven days the massacre was continued in Paris, the first three with inconceivable fury. And it was not confined to the city itself, but by special order of the king was extended to all the provinces and towns where Protestants were found. Neither age nor sex was respected. Neither the innocent babe nor the man of gray hairs was spared. Noble and peasant, old and young, mother and child, were cut down together. Throughout France the butchery continued for two months.

Seventy thousand of the very flower of the nation perished.

"When the news of the massacre reached Rome, the exultation among the clergy knew no bounds. The cardinal of Lorraine rewarded the messenger with a thousand crowns; the cannon of St. Angelo thundered forth a joyous salute; and bells rang out from every steeple; bonfires turned night into day; and Gregory XIII, attended by the cardinals and other ecclesiastical dignitaries, went in long procession to the church of St. Louis, where the cardinal of Lorraine chanted a *Te Deum*. . . . A medal was struck to commemorate the massacre, and in the Vatican may still be seen three frescoes of Vasari, describing the attack upon the admiral, the king in council plotting the massacre, and the massacre itself. Gregory sent Charles the Golden Rose; and four months after the massacre, . . . he listened complacently to the sermon of a French priest, . . . who spoke of 'that day so full of happiness and joy, when the most holy father received the news, and went in solemn state to render thanks to God and St. Louis.'"—Henry White, The Massacre of St. Bartholomew, ch. 14, par. 34.

The same master spirit that urged on the St. Bartholomew Massacre led also in the scenes of the Revolution. Jesus Christ was declared to be an impostor, and the rallying cry of the French infidels was, "Crush the Wretch," meaning Christ. Heaven-daring blasphemy and abominable wickedness went hand in hand, and the basest of men, the most abandoned monsters of cruelty and vice, were most highly exalted. In all this, supreme homage was paid to Satan; while Christ, in His characteristics of truth, purity, and unselfish love, was crucified.

"The beast that ascendeth out of the bottomless pit shall make war against them, and shall overcome them, and kill them." The atheistical power that ruled in France during the Revolution and the Reign of Terror, did wage such a war against God and His holy word as the world had never witnessed. The worship of the Deity was abolished by the National Assembly. Bibles were collected and publicly burned with every possible manifestation of scorn. The law of God was trampled underfoot. The institutions of the Bible were abolished. The weekly rest day was set aside, and in its stead every tenth day was devoted to reveling and blasphemy. Baptism and the Communion were prohibited. And announcements posted conspicuously over the burial places declared death to be an eternal sleep.

The fear of God was said to be so far from the beginning of wisdom that it was the beginning of folly. All religious worship was prohibited, except that of liberty and the country. The "constitutional bishop of Paris was brought forward to play the principal part in the most impu-

dent and scandalous farce ever acted in the face of a national representation. . . . He was brought forward in full procession, to declare to the Convention that the religion which he had taught so many years was, in every respect, a piece of priestcraft, which had no foundation either in history or sacred truth. He disowned, in solemn and explicit terms, the existence of the Deity to whose worship he had been consecrated, and devoted himself in future to the homage of liberty, equality, virtue, and morality. He then laid on the table his episcopal decorations, and received a fraternal embrace from the president of the Convention. Several apostate priests followed the example of this prelate."—Scott, vol. 1, ch. 17.

"And they that dwell upon the earth shall rejoice over them, and make merry, and shall send gifts one to another; because these two prophets tormented them that dwelt on the earth." Infidel France had silenced the reproving voice of God's two witnesses. The word of truth lay dead in her streets, and those who hated the restrictions and requirements of God's law were jubilant. Men publicly defied the King of heaven. Like the sinners of old, they cried: "How doth God know? and is there knowledge in the Most High?" Psalm 73:11.

With blasphemous boldness almost beyond belief, one of the priests of the new order said: "God, if You exist, avenge Your injured name. I bid You defiance! You remain silent; You dare not launch Your thunders. Who after this will believe in Your existence?"—Lacretelle, *History*, vol. 11, p. 309; in Sir Archibald Alison, *History of Europe*, vol. 1, ch. 10. What an echo is this of the Pharaoh's demand: "Who is Jehovah, that I should obey His voice?" "I know not Jehovah!"

"The fool hath said in his heart, There is no God." Psalm 14:1. And the Lord declares concerning the perverters of the truth: "Their folly shall be manifest unto all." 2 Timothy 3:9. After France had renounced the worship of the living God, "the high and lofty One that inhabiteth eternity," it was only a little time till she descended to degrading idolatry, by the worship of the Goddess of Reason, in the person of a profligate woman. And this in the representative assembly of the nation, and by its highest civil and legislative authorities! Says the historian: "One of the ceremonies of this insane time stands unrivaled for absurdity combined with impiety. The doors of the Convention were thrown open to a band of musicians, preceded by whom, the members of the municipal body entered in solemn procession, singing a hymn in praise of liberty, and escorting, as the object of their future worship, a veiled female, whom they termed the Goddess of Reason. Being brought within the bar, she was unveiled with great form, and placed on the right of the president, when she was generally recognized as a dancing girl of the opera, ... To this person, as the fittest representative of that reason whom they worshiped, the National Convention of France rendered public homage.

"This impious and ridiculous mummery had a certain fashion; and the installation of the Goddess of Reason was renewed and imitated throughout the nation, in such places where the inhabitants desired to show themselves equal to all the heights of the Revolution."—Scott, vol. 1, ch. 17.

Said the orator who introduced the worship of Reason: "Legislators! Fanaticism has given way to reason. Its bleared eyes could not endure the brilliancy of the light. This day an immense concourse has assembled beneath those gothic vaults, which, for the first time, re-echoed the 276 truth. There the French have celebrated the only true worship,—that of Liberty, that of Reason. There we have formed wishes for the prosperity of the arms of the Republic. There we have abandoned inanimate idols for Reason, for that animated image, the masterpiece of nature."—M. A. Thiers, History of the French Revolution, vol. 2, pp. 370, 371.

When the goddess was brought into the Convention, the orator took her by the hand, and turning to the assembly said: "Mortals, cease to tremble before the powerless thunders of a God whom your fears have created. Henceforth acknowledge no divinity but Reason. I offer you its noblest and purest image; if you must have idols, sacrifice only to such as this. . . . Fall before the august Senate of Freedom, oh! Veil of Reason!"

"The goddess, after being embraced by the president, was mounted on a magnificent car, and conducted, amid an immense crowd, to the cathedral of Notre Dame, to take the place of the Deity. There she was elevated on the high altar, and received the adoration of all present."—Alison, vol. 1, ch. 10.

This was followed, not long afterward, by the public burning of the Bible. On one occasion "the Popular Society of the Museum" entered the hall of the municipality, exclaiming, "Vive la Raison!" and carrying on the top of a pole the half-burned remains of several books, among others breviaries, missals, and the Old and New Testaments, which "expiated in a great fire," said the president, "all the fooleries which they have made the human race commit."—Journal of Paris, 1793, No. 318. Quoted in Buchez-Roux, Collection of Parliamentary History, vol. 30, pp. 200, 201.

It was popery that had begun the work which atheism was completing. The policy of Rome had wrought out those conditions, social, political, and religious, that were hurrying France on to ruin. Writers, in referring to the horrors of the Revolution, say that these excesses are to be charged upon the throne and the church. (See Appendix.) In strict justice they are to be charged 277 upon the church. Popery had poisoned the minds of kings against the Reformation, as an enemy to the crown, an element of discord that would be fatal to the peace and harmony of the nation. It was the genius of Rome that by this means inspired the direst cruelty and the most galling oppression which proceeded from the throne.

The spirit of liberty went with the Bible. Wherever the gospel was received, the minds of the people were awakened. They began to cast off the shackles that had held them bondslaves of ignorance, vice, and superstition. They began to think and act as men. Monarchs saw it and trembled for their despotism.

Rome was not slow to inflame their jealous fears. Said the pope to the regent of France in 1525: "This mania [Protestantism] will not only confound and destroy religion, but all principalities, nobility, laws, orders, and ranks besides."—G. de Felice, History of the Protestants of France, b. 1, ch. 2, par. 8. A few years later a papal nuncio warned the king: "Sire, be not deceived. The Protestants will upset all civil as well as religious order. . . . The throne is in as much danger as the altar. . . . The introduction of a new religion must necessarily introduce a new government."—D'Aubigné, History of the Reformation in Europe in the Time of Calvin, b. 2, ch. 36. And theologians appealed to the prejudices of the people by declaring that the Protestant doctrine "entices men away to novelties and folly; it robs the king of the devoted affection of his subjects, and devastates both church and state." Thus Rome succeeded in arraying France against the Reformation. "It was to uphold the throne, preserve the nobles, and maintain the laws, that the sword of persecution was first unsheathed in France."—Wylie, b. 13, ch. 4.

Little did the rulers of the land foresee the results of that fateful policy. The teaching of the Bible would have implanted in the minds and hearts of the people those principles of justice, temperance, truth, equity, and benevolence which are the very cornerstone of a nation's prosperity. "Righteousness exalteth a nation." Thereby "the throne is established." Proverbs 278 14:34; 16:12. "The work of righteousness shall be peace;" and the effect, "quietness and assurance forever." Isaiah 32:17. He who obeys the divine law will most truly respect and obey the laws of his country. He who fears God will honor the king in the exercise of all just and legitimate authority. But unhappy France prohibited the Bible and banned its disciples. Century after century, men of principle and integrity, men of intellectual acuteness and moral strength, who had the courage to avow their convictions and the faith to suffer for the truth—for centuries these men toiled as slaves in the galleys, perished at the stake, or rotted in dungeon cells. Thousands upon thousands found safety in flight; and this continued for two hundred and fifty years after the opening of the Reformation.

"Scarcely was there a generation of Frenchmen during that long period that did not witness the disciples of the gospel fleeing before the insane fury of the persecutor, and carrying with them the intelligence, the arts, the industry, the order, in which, as a rule, they pre-eminently excelled, to enrich the lands in which they found an asylum. And in proportion as they replenished other countries with these good gifts, did they empty their own of them. If all that was now driven away had been retained in France; if, during these three hundred years, the industrial skill of the exiles had been cultivating her soil; if, during these three hundred years, their artistic bent had been improving her manufactures; if, during these three hundred years, their creative genius and analytic power had been enriching her literature and cultivating her science; if their wisdom had been guiding her councils, their bravery fighting her battles, their equity framing her laws, and the religion of the Bible strengthening the intellect and governing the conscience of her people, what a glory would at this day have encompassed France! What a great, prosperous, and happy country—a pattern to the nations—would she have been!

279   "But a blind and inexorable bigotry chased from her soil every teacher of virtue, every champion of order, every honest defender of the throne; it said to the men who would have made their country a 'renown and glory' in the earth, Choose which you will have, a stake or exile. At last the ruin of the state was complete; there remained no more conscience to be proscribed; no more religion to be dragged to the stake; no more patriotism to be chased into banishment."—Wylie, b. 13, ch. 20. And the Revolution, with all its horrors, was the dire result.

"With the flight of the Huguenots a general decline settled upon France. Flourishing manufacturing cities fell into decay; fertile districts returned to their native wildness; intellectual dullness and moral declension succeeded a period of unwonted progress. Paris became one vast almshouse, and it is estimated that, at the breaking out of the Revolution, two hundred thousand paupers claimed charity from the hands of the king. The Jesuits alone flourished in the decaying nation, and ruled with dreadful tyranny over churches and schools, the prisons and the galleys."

The gospel would have brought to France the solution of those political and social problems that baffled the skill of her clergy, her king, and her legislators, and finally plunged the nation into anarchy and ruin. But under the domination of Rome the people had lost the Saviour's blessed lessons of self-sacrifice and unselfish love. They had been led away from the practice of self-denial for the good of others. The rich had found no rebuke for their oppression of the poor, the poor no help for their servitude and degradation. The selfishness of the wealthy and powerful grew more and more apparent and oppressive. For centuries the greed and profligacy of the noble resulted in grinding extortion toward the peasant. The rich wronged the poor, and the poor hated the rich.

In many provinces the estates were held by the nobles, and the laboring classes were only tenants; they were at the mercy of their landlords and were forced to submit to their exorbitant demands. The burden of supporting both the church and the state fell upon the middle and lower classes, who were heavily taxed by the civil authorities and by the clergy. "The pleasure of the nobles was considered the supreme law; the farmers and the peasants might starve, for aught their oppressors cared. . . . The people were compelled at every turn to consult the exclusive interest of the landlord. The lives of the agricultural laborers were lives of incessant work and unrelieved misery; their complaints, if they ever dared to complain, were treated with insolent contempt. The courts of justice would always listen to a noble as against a peasant; bribes were notoriously accepted by the judges; and the merest caprice of the aristocracy had the force of law, by virtue of this system of universal corruption. Of the taxes wrung from the commonalty, by the secular magnates on the one hand, and the clergy on the other, not half ever found its way into the royal or episcopal treasury; the rest was squandered in profligate self-indulgence. And the men who thus impoverished their fellow subjects were themselves exempt from taxation, and entitled by law or custom to all the appointments of the state. The privileged classes numbered a hundred and fifty thousand, and for their gratification millions were condemned to hopeless and degrading lives." (See Appendix.)   280

The court was given up to luxury and profligacy. There was little confidence existing between the people and the rulers. Suspicion fastened upon all the measures of the government as designing and selfish. For more than half a century before the time of the Revolution the throne was occupied by Louis XV, who, even in those evil times, was distinguished as an indolent, frivolous, and sensual monarch. With a depraved and cruel aristocracy and an impoverished and ignorant lower class, the state financially embarrassed and the people exasperated, it needed no prophet's eye to foresee a terrible impending outbreak. To the warnings of his counselors the king was accustomed to reply: "Try to make things go on as long as I am likely to live; after my death it may be as it will." It   281 was in vain that the necessity of reform was urged. He saw the evils, but had neither the courage nor the power to meet them. The doom awaiting France was but too truly pictured in his indolent and selfish answer, "After me, the deluge!"

By working upon the jealousy of the kings and the ruling classes, Rome had influenced them to keep the people in bondage, well knowing that the state would thus be weakened, and purposing by this means to fasten both rulers and people in her thrall. With farsighted policy she perceived that in order to enslave men effectually, the shackles must be bound upon their souls; that the surest way to prevent them from escaping their bondage was to render them incapable of freedom. A thousandfold more terrible than the physical suffering which resulted from her policy, was the moral degradation. Deprived of the Bible, and abandoned to the teachings of bigotry and selfishness, the people were shrouded in ignorance and superstition, and sunken in vice, so that they were wholly unfitted for self-government.

But the outworking of all this was widely different from what Rome had purposed. Instead of holding the masses in a blind submission to her dogmas, her work resulted in making them infidels and revolutionists. Romanism they despised as priestcraft. They beheld the clergy as a party to their oppression. The only god they knew was the god of Rome; her teaching was their only religion. They regarded her greed and cruelty as the legitimate fruit of the Bible, and they would have none of it.

Rome had misrepresented the character of God and perverted His requirements, and now men rejected both the Bible and its Author. She had required a blind faith in her dogmas, under the pretended sanction of the Scriptures. In the reaction, Voltaire and his associates cast aside God's word altogether and spread everywhere the poison of infidelity. Rome had ground down the people under her iron heel; and now the masses, degraded and brutalized, in their recoil 282 from her tyranny, cast off all restraint. Enraged at the glittering cheat to which they had so long paid homage, they rejected truth and falsehood together; and mistaking license for liberty, the slaves of vice exulted in their imagined freedom.

At the opening of the Revolution, by a concession of the king, the people were granted a representation exceeding that of the nobles and the clergy combined. Thus the balance of power was in their hands; but they were not prepared to use it with wisdom and moderation. Eager to redress the wrongs they had suffered, they determined to undertake the reconstruction of society. An outraged populace, whose minds were filled with bitter and long-treasured memories of wrong, resolved to revolutionize the state of misery that had grown unbearable and to avenge themselves upon those whom they regarded as the authors of their sufferings. The oppressed wrought out the lesson they had learned under tyranny and became the oppressors of those who had oppressed them.

Unhappy France reaped in blood the harvest she had sown. Terrible were the results of her submission to the controlling power of Rome. Where France, under the influence of Romanism, had set up the first stake at the opening of the Reformation, there the Revolution set up its first guillotine. On the very spot where the first martyrs to the Protestant faith were burned in the sixteenth century, the first victims were guillotined in the eighteenth. In repelling the gospel, which would have brought her healing, France had opened the door to infidelity and ruin. When the restraints of God's law were cast aside, it was found that the laws of man were inadequate to hold in check the powerful tides of human passion; and the nation swept on to revolt and anarchy. The war against the Bible inaugurated an era which stands in the world's history as the Reign of Terror. Peace and happiness were banished from the homes and hearts of men. No one was secure. He who triumphed today was suspected, condemned, tomorrow. Violence and lust held undisputed sway.

King, clergy, and nobles were compelled to 283 submit to the atrocities of an excited and maddened people. Their thirst for vengeance was only stimulated by the execution of the king; and those who had decreed his death soon followed him to the scaffold. A general slaughter of all suspected of hostility to the Revolution was determined. The prisons were crowded, at one time containing more than two hundred thousand captives. The cities of the kingdom were filled with scenes of horror. One party of revolutionists was against another party, and France became a vast field for contending masses, swayed by the fury of their passions. "In Paris one tumult succeeded another, and the citizens were divided into a medley of factions, that seemed intent on nothing but mutual extermination." And to add to the general misery, the nation became involved in a prolonged and devastating war with the great powers of Europe. "The country was nearly bankrupt, the armies were clamoring for arrears of pay, the Parisians were starving, the provinces were laid waste by brigands, and civilization was almost extinguished in anarchy and license."

All too well the people had learned the lessons of cruelty and torture which Rome had so diligently taught. A day of retribution at last had come. It was not now the disciples of Jesus that were thrust into dungeons and dragged to the stake. Long ago these had perished or been driven into exile. Unsparing Rome now felt the deadly power of those whom she had trained to delight in deeds of blood. "The example of persecution which the clergy of France had exhibited for so many ages, was now retorted upon them with signal vigor. The scaffolds ran red with the blood of the priests. The galleys and the prisons, once crowded with Huguenots, were now filled with their persecutors. Chained to the bench and toiling at the oar, the Roman Catholic clergy experienced all those woes which their church had so freely inflicted on the gentle heretics." (See Appendix.)

284 "Then came those days when the most barbarous of all codes was administered by the most barbarous of all tribunals; when no man could greet his neighbors or say his prayers . . . without danger of committing a capital crime; when spies lurked in every corner; when the guillotine was long and hard at work every morning; when the jails were filled as close as the holds of a slave ship; when the gutters ran foaming with blood into the Seine. . . . While the daily wagonloads of victims were carried to their doom through the streets of Paris, the proconsuls, whom the sovereign committee had sent forth to the departments, reveled in an extravagance of cruelty unknown even in the capital. The knife of the deadly machine rose and fell too slow for their work of slaughter. Long rows of captives were mowed down with grapeshot. Holes were made in the bottom of crowded barges. Lyons was turned into a desert. At Arras even the cruel mercy of a speedy death was denied to the prisoners. All down the Loire, from Saumur to the sea, great flocks of crows and kites feasted on naked corpses, twined together in hideous embraces. No mercy was shown to sex or age. The number of young lads and of girls of seventeen who were murdered by that execrable government, is to be reckoned by hundreds. Babies torn from the breast were tossed from pike to pike along the Jacobin ranks." (See Appendix.) In the short space of ten years, multitudes of human beings perished.

All this was as Satan would have it. This was what for ages he had been working to secure. His policy is deception from first to last, and his steadfast purpose is to bring woe and wretchedness upon men, to deface and defile the workmanship of God, to mar the divine purposes of benevolence and love, and thus cause grief in heaven. Then by his deceptive arts he blinds the minds of men, and leads them to throw back the blame of his work upon God, as if all this misery were the result of the Creator's plan. In like 285 manner, when those who have been degraded and brutalized through his cruel power achieve their freedom, he urges them on to excesses and atrocities. Then this picture of unbridled license is pointed out by tyrants and oppressors as an illustration of the results of liberty.

When error in one garb has been detected, Satan only masks it in a different disguise, and multitudes receive it as eagerly as at the first. When the people found Romanism to be a 319 deception, and he could not through this agency lead them to transgression of God's law, he urged them to regard all religion as a cheat, and the Bible as a fable; and, casting aside the divine statutes, they gave themselves up to unbridled iniquity.

The fatal error which wrought such woe for the inhabitants of France was the ignoring of this one great truth: that true freedom lies within the proscriptions of the law of God. "O that thou hadst hearkened to My commandments! then had thy peace been as a river, and thy righteousness as the waves of the sea." "There is no peace, saith the Lord, unto the wicked." "But whoso hearkeneth unto Me shall dwell safely, and shall be quiet from fear of evil." Isaiah 48:18, 22; Proverbs 1:33.

Atheists, infidels, and apostates oppose and denounce God's law; but the results of their influence prove that the well-being of man is bound up with his obedience of the divine statutes. Those who will not read the lesson from the book of God are bidden to read it in the history of nations.

When Satan wrought through the Roman Church to lead men away from obedience, his agency was concealed, and his work was so disguised that the degradation and misery which resulted were not seen to be the fruit of transgression. And his power was so far counteracted by the working of the Spirit of God that his purposes were prevented from reaching their full fruition. The people did not trace the effect to its cause and discover the source of their miseries. But in the Revolution the law of God was open- 286 ly set aside by the National Council. And in the Reign of Terror which followed, the working of cause and effect could be seen by all.

When France publicly rejected God and set aside the Bible, wicked men and spirits of darkness exulted in their attainment of the object so long desired—a kingdom free from the restraints of the law of God. Because sentence against an evil work was not speedily executed, therefore the heart of the sons of men was "fully set in them to do evil." Ecclesiastes 8:11. But the transgression of a just and righteous law must inevitably result in misery and ruin. Though not visited at once with judgments, the wickedness of men was nevertheless surely working out their doom. Centuries of apostasy and crime had been treasuring up wrath against the day of retribution; and when their iniquity was full, the despisers of God learned too late that it is a fearful thing to have worn out the divine patience. The restraining Spirit of God, which imposes a check upon the cruel power of Satan, was in a great measure removed, and he whose only delight is the wretchedness of men was permitted to work his will. Those who had chosen the service of rebellion were left to reap its fruits until the land was filled with crimes too horrible for pen to trace. From devastated provinces and ruined cities a terrible cry was heard—a cry of bitterest anguish. France was shaken as if by an earthquake. Religion, law, social order, the family, the state, and the church—all were smitten down by the impious hand that had been lifted against the law of God. Truly spoke the wise man: "The wicked shall fall by his own wickedness." "Though a sinner do evil a hundred times, and his days be prolonged, yet surely I know that it shall be well with them that fear God, which fear before Him: but it shall not be well with the wicked." Proverbs 11:5; Ecclesiastes 8:12, 13. "They hated knowledge, and did not choose the fear of the Lord;" "therefore shall they eat of the fruit of their own way, and be filled with their own devices." Proverbs 1:29, 31.

287   God's faithful witnesses, slain by the blasphemous power that "ascendeth out of the bottomless pit," were not long to remain silent. "After three days and a half the Spirit of life from God entered into them, and they stood upon their feet; and great fear fell upon them which saw them." Revelation 11:11. It was in 1793 that the decrees which abolished the Christian religion and set aside the Bible passed the French Assembly. Three years and a half later a resolution rescinding these decrees, thus granting toleration to the Scriptures, was adopted by the same body. The world stood aghast at the enormity of guilt which had resulted from a rejection of the Sacred Oracles, and men recognized the necessity of faith in God and His word as the foundation of virtue and morality. Saith the Lord: "Whom hast thou reproached and blasphemed? and against whom hast thou exalted thy voice, and lifted up thine eyes on high? even against the Holy One of Israel." Isaiah 37:23. "Therefore, behold, I will cause them to know, this once will I cause them to know My hand and My might; and they shall know that My name is Jehovah." Jeremiah 16:21, A.R.V.

Concerning the two witnesses the prophet declares further: "And they heard a great voice from heaven saying unto them, Come up hither. And they ascended up to heaven in a cloud; and their enemies beheld them." Revelation 11:12. Since France made war upon God's two witnesses, they have been honored as never before. In 1804 the British and Foreign Bible Society was organized. This was followed by similar organizations, with numerous branches, upon the continent of Europe. In 1816 the American Bible Society was founded. When the British Society was formed, the Bible had been printed and circulated in fifty tongues. It has since been translated into many hundreds of languages and dialects. (See Appendix.)

For the fifty years preceding 1792, little atten-

tion was given to the work of foreign missions. No new societies were formed, and there were but few churches that made any effort for the   288 spread of Christianity in heathen lands. But toward the close of the eighteenth century a great change took place. Men became dissatisfied with the results of rationalism and realized the necessity of divine revelation and experimental religion. From this time the work of foreign missions attained an unprecedented growth. (See Appendix.)

The improvements in printing have given an impetus to the work of circulating the Bible. The increased facilities for communication between different countries, the breaking down of ancient barriers of prejudice and national exclusiveness, and the loss of secular power by the pontiff of Rome have opened the way for the entrance of the word of God. For some years the Bible has been sold without restraint in the streets of Rome, and it has now been carried to every part of the habitable globe.

The infidel Voltaire once boastingly said: "I am weary of hearing people repeat that twelve men established the Christian religion. I will prove that one man may suffice to overthrow it." Generations have passed since his death. Millions have joined in the war upon the Bible. But it is so far from being destroyed, that where there were a hundred in Voltaire's time, there are now ten thousand, yes, a hundred thousand copies of the book of God. In the words of an early Reformer concerning the Christian church, "The Bible is an anvil that has worn out many hammers." Saith the Lord: "No weapon that is formed against thee shall prosper; and every tongue that shall rise against thee in judgment thou shalt condemn." Isaiah 54:17.

"The word of our God shall stand forever." "All His commandments are sure. They stand fast for ever and ever, and are done in truth and uprightness." Isaiah 40:8; Psalm 111:7, 8. Whatever is built upon the authority of man will be overthrown; but that which is founded upon the rock of God's immutable word shall stand forever.

16   289

The Pilgrim Fathers

The English Reformers, while renouncing the doctrines of Romanism, had retained many of its forms. Thus though the authority and the creed of Rome were rejected, not a few of her customs and ceremonies were incorporated into the worship of the Church of England. It was claimed that these things were not matters of conscience; that though they were not commanded in Scripture, and hence were nonessential, yet not being forbidden, they were not intrinsically evil. Their observance tended to narrow the gulf which separated the reformed churches from Rome, and it was urged that they would promote the acceptance of the Protestant faith by Romanists.

To the conservative and compromising, these arguments seemed conclusive. But there was another class that did not so judge. The fact that these customs "tended to bridge over the chasm between Rome and the Reformation" (Martyn, volume 5, page 22), was in their view a conclusive argument against retaining them. They looked upon them as badges of the slavery from which they had been delivered and to which they had no disposition to return. They reasoned that God has in His word established the regulations governing His worship, and that men are not at liberty to add to these or to detract from them. The very beginning of the great apostasy was in seeking to supplement the authority of God by that of the church. Rome began by enjoining what God had not forbidden, and she ended by forbidding what He had explicitly enjoined.

Many earnestly desired to return to the purity and simplicity which characterized the primitive church. They regarded many of the established customs of the English Church as monuments of idolatry, and they could not in conscience unite in her worship. But the church, being supported by the civil authority, would permit no dissent from her forms. Attendance upon her service was required by law, and unauthorized assemblies for religious worship were prohibited, under penalty of imprisonment, exile, and death.

At the opening of the seventeenth century the monarch who had just ascended the throne of England declared his determination to make the Puritans "conform, or . . . harry them out of the land, or else worse."—George Bancroft, *History of the United States of America*, pt. 1, ch. 12, par. 6. Hunted, persecuted, and imprisoned, they could discern in the future no promise of better days, and many yielded to the conviction that for such as would serve God according to the dictates of their conscience, "England was ceasing forever to be a habitable place."—J. G. Palfrey, *History of New England*, ch. 3, par. 43. Some at last determined to seek refuge in Holland. Difficulties, losses, and imprisonment were encountered. Their purposes were thwarted, and they were betrayed into the hands of their enemies. But steadfast perseverance finally conquered, and they found shelter on the friendly shores of the Dutch Republic.

In their flight they had left their houses, their goods, and their means of livelihood. They were strangers in a strange land, among a people of different language and customs. They were forced to resort to new and untried occupations to earn their bread. Middle-aged men, who had

spent their lives in tilling the soil, had now to learn mechanical trades. But they cheerfully accepted the situation and lost no time in idleness or repining. Though often pinched with poverty, they thanked God for the blessings which were still granted them and found their joy in unmolested spiritual communion. "They knew they were pilgrims, and looked not much on those things, but lifted up their eyes to heaven, their dearest country, and quieted their spirits."—Bancroft, pt. 1, ch. 12, par. 15.

In the midst of exile and hardship their love and faith waxed strong. They trusted the Lord's promises, and He did not fail them in time of need. His angels were by their side, to encourage and support them. And when God's hand seemed pointing them across the sea, to a land where they might found for themselves a state, and leave to their children the precious heritage of religious liberty, they went forward, without shrinking, in the path of providence.

God had permitted trials to come upon His people to prepare them for the accomplishment of His gracious purpose toward them. The church had been brought low, that she might be exalted. God was about to display His power in her behalf, to give to the world another evidence that He will not forsake those who trust in Him. He had overruled events to cause the wrath of Satan and the plots of evil men to advance His glory and to bring His people to a place of security. Persecution and exile were opening the way to freedom.

When first constrained to separate from the English Church, the Puritans had joined themselves together by a solemn covenant, as the Lord's free people, "to walk together in all His ways made known or to be made known to them."—J. Brown, The *Pilgrim Fathers*, page 74. Here was the true spirit of reform, the vital principle of Protestantism. It was with this purpose that the Pilgrims departed from Holland to find a home in the New World. John Robinson, their pastor, who was providentially prevented from accompanying them, in his farewell address to the exiles said:

"Brethren, we are now erelong to part asunder, and the Lord knoweth whether I shall live ever to see your faces more. But whether the Lord hath appointed it or not, I charge you before God and His blessed angels to follow me no farther than I have followed Christ. If God should reveal anything to you by any other instrument of His, be as ready to receive it as ever you were to receive any truth of my ministry; for I am very confident the Lord hath more truth and light yet to break forth out of His holy word."—Martyn, vol. 5, p. 70.

"For my part, I cannot sufficiently bewail the condition of the reformed churches, who are come to a period in religion, and will go at present no farther than the instruments of their reformation. The Lutherans cannot be drawn to go beyond what Luther saw; . . . and the Calvinists, you see, stick fast where they were left by that great man of God, who yet saw not all things. This is a misery much to be lamented; for though they were burning and shining lights in their time, yet they penetrated not into the whole counsel of God, but were they now living, would be as willing to embrace further light as that which they first received."—D. Neal, *History of the Puritans,* vol. 1, p. 269.

"Remember your church covenant, in which you have agreed to walk in all the ways of the Lord, made or to be made known unto you. Remember your promise and covenant with God and with one another, to receive whatever light and truth shall be made known to you from His written word; but withal, take heed, I beseech you, what you receive for truth, and compare it and weigh it with other scriptures of truth before you accept it; for it is not possible the Christian world should come so lately out of such thick antichristian darkness, and that full perfection of knowledge should break forth at once."—Martyn, vol. 5, pp. 70, 71.

It was the desire for liberty of conscience that inspired the Pilgrims to brave the perils of the long journey across the sea, to endure the hardships and dangers of the wilderness, and with God's blessing to lay, on the shores of America, the foundation of a mighty nation. Yet honest
293 and God-fearing as they were, the Pilgrims did not yet comprehend the great principle of religious liberty. The freedom which they sacrificed so much to secure for themselves, they were not equally ready to grant to others. "Very few, even of the foremost thinkers and moralists of the seventeenth century, had any just conception of that grand principle, the outgrowth of the New Testament, which acknowledges God as the sole judge of human faith."—*Ibid.,* vol. 5, p. 297. The doctrine that God has committed to the church the right to control the conscience, and to define and punish heresy, is one of the most deeply rooted of papal errors. While the Reformers rejected the creed of Rome, they were not entirely free from her spirit of intolerance. The dense darkness in which, through the long ages of her rule, popery had enveloped all Christendom, had not even yet been wholly dissipated. Said one of the leading ministers in the colony of Massachusetts Bay: "It was toleration that made the world antichristian; and the church never took harm by the punishment of heretics."—*Ibid.,* vol. 5, p. 335. The regulation was adopted by the colonists that only church members should have a voice in the civil government. A kind of state church was formed, all the people being required to contribute to the support of the clergy, and the magistrates being authorized to suppress heresy. Thus the secular power was in the hands of the church. It was not

long before these measures led to the inevitable result—persecution.

Eleven years after the planting of the first colony, Roger Williams came to the New World. Like the early Pilgrims he came to enjoy religious freedom; but, unlike them, he saw—what so few in his time had yet seen—that this freedom was the inalienable right of all, whatever might be their creed. He was an earnest seeker for truth, with Robinson holding it impossible that all the light from God's word had yet been received. Williams "was the first person in modern Christendom to establish civil government on the doctrine of the liberty of conscience, the equality of opinions before the law."—Bancroft, 294
pt. 1, ch. 15, par. 16. He declared it to be the duty of the magistrate to restrain crime, but never to control the conscience. "The public or the magistrates may decide," he said, "what is due from man to man; but when they attempt to prescribe a man's duties to God, they are out of place, and there can be no safety; for it is clear that if the magistrate has the power, he may decree one set of opinions or beliefs today and another tomorrow; as has been done in England by different kings and queens, and by different popes and councils in the Roman Church; so that belief would become a heap of confusion."—Martyn, vol. 5, p. 340.

Attendance at the services of the established church was required under a penalty of fine or imprisonment. "Williams reprobated the law; the worst statute in the English code was that which did but enforce attendance upon the parish church. To compel men to unite with those of a different creed, he regarded as an open violation of their natural rights; to drag to public worship the irreligious and the unwilling, seemed only like requiring hypocrisy. . . . 'No one should be bound to worship, or,' he added, 'to maintain a worship, against his own consent.' 'What!' exclaimed his antagonists, amazed at his tenets, 'is not the laborer worthy of his hire?' 'Yes,' replied he, 'from them that hire him.'"—Bancroft, pt. 1, ch. 15, par. 2.

Roger Williams was respected and beloved as a faithful minister, a man of rare gifts, of unbending integrity and true benevolence; yet his steadfast denial of the right of civil magistrates to authority over the church, and his demand for religious liberty, could not be tolerated. The application of this new doctrine, it was urged, would "subvert the fundamental state and government of the country."—*Ibid.,* pt. 1, ch. 15, par. 10. He was sentenced to banishment from the colonies, and, finally, to avoid arrest, he was forced to flee, amid the cold and storms of winter, into the unbroken forest.

"For fourteen weeks," he says, "I was sorely tossed in a bitter season, not knowing what bread or bed did mean." But "the ravens fed me 295
in the wilderness," and a hollow tree often

served him for a shelter.—Martyn, vol. 5, pp. 349, 350. Thus he continued his painful flight through the snow and the trackless forest, until he found refuge with an Indian tribe whose confidence and affection he had won while endeavoring to teach them the truths of the gospel.

Making his way at last, after months of change and wandering, to the shores of Narragansett Bay, he there laid the foundation of the first state of modern times that in the fullest sense recognized the right of religious freedom. The fundamental principle of Roger Williams's colony was "that every man should have liberty to worship God according to the light of his own conscience."—*Ibid.*, vol. 5, p. 354. His little state, Rhode Island, became the asylum of the oppressed, and it increased and prospered until its foundation principles—civil and religious liberty—became the cornerstones of the American Republic.

In that grand old document which our forefathers set forth as their bill of rights—the Declaration of Independence—they declared: "We hold these truths to be self-evident, that all men are created equal; that they are endowed by their Creator with certain unalienable rights; that among these are life, liberty, and the pursuit of happiness." And the Constitution guarantees, in the most explicit terms, the inviolability of conscience: "No religious test shall ever be required as a qualification to any office of public trust under the United States." "Congress shall make no law respecting an establishment of religion, or prohibiting the free exercise thereof."

"The framers of the Constitution recognized the eternal principle that man's relation with his God is above human legislation, and his rights of conscience inalienable. Reasoning was not necessary to establish this truth; we are conscious of it in our own bosoms. It is this consciousness which, in defiance of human laws, has sustained so many martyrs in tortures and flames. They felt that their duty to God was superior to human enactments, and that man 296 could exercise no authority over their consciences. It is an inborn principle which nothing can eradicate."—Congressional documents (U.S.A.), serial No. 200, document No. 271.

As the tidings spread through the countries of Europe, of a land where every man might enjoy the fruit of his own labor and obey the convictions of his own conscience, thousands flocked to the shores of the New World. Colonies rapidly multiplied. "Massachusetts, by special law, offered free welcome and aid, at the public cost, to Christians of any nationality who might fly beyond the Atlantic 'to escape from wars or famine, or the oppression of their persecutors.' Thus the fugitive and the downtrodden were, by statute, made the guests of the commonwealth."—Martyn, vol. 5, p. 417. In twenty years from the first landing at Plymouth, as many thousand Pilgrims were settled in New England.

To secure the object which they sought, "they were content to earn a bare subsistence by a life of frugality and toil. They asked nothing from the soil but the reasonable returns of their own labor. No golden vision threw a deceitful halo around their path. . . . They were content with the slow but steady progress of their social polity. They patiently endured the privations of the wilderness, watering the tree of liberty with their tears, and with the sweat of their brow, till it took deep root in the land."

The Bible was held as the foundation of faith, the source of wisdom, and the charter of liberty. Its principles were diligently taught in the home, in the school, and in the church, and its fruits were manifest in thrift, intelligence, purity, and temperance. One might be for years a dweller in the Puritan settlement, "and not see a drunkard, or hear an oath, or meet a beggar."—Bancroft, pt. 1, ch. 19, par. 25. It was demonstrated that the principles of the Bible are the surest safeguards of national greatness. The feeble and isolated colonies grew to a confederation of powerful states, and the world marked with wonder the peace and prosperity of "a church without a pope, and a state without a king."

But continually increasing numbers were attracted to the shores of America, actuated by 297 motives widely different from those of the first Pilgrims. Though the primitive faith and purity exerted a widespread and molding power, yet its influence became less and less as the numbers increased of those who sought only worldly advantage.

The regulation adopted by the early colonists, of permitting only members of the church to vote or to hold office in the civil government, led to most pernicious results. This measure had been accepted as a means of preserving the purity of the state, but it resulted in the corruption of the church. A profession of religion being the condition of suffrage and officeholding, many, actuated solely by motives of worldly policy, united with the church without a change of heart. Thus the churches came to consist, to a considerable extent, of unconverted persons; and even in the ministry were those who not only held errors of doctrine, but who were ignorant of the renewing power of the Holy Spirit. Thus again was demonstrated the evil results, so often witnessed in the history of the church from the days of Constantine to the present, of attempting to build up the church by the aid of the state, of appealing to the secular power in support of the gospel of Him who declared: "My kingdom is not of this world." John 18:36. The union of the church with the state, be the degree never so slight, while it may appear to bring the world nearer to the church, does in reality but bring the church nearer to the world.

The great principle so nobly advocated by Robinson and Roger Williams, that truth is progressive, that Christians should stand ready to accept all the light which may shine from God's holy word, was lost sight of by their descendants. The Protestant churches of America,—and those of Europe as well,—so highly favored in receiving the blessings of the Reformation, failed to press forward in the path of reform. Though a few faithful men arose, from time to time, to proclaim new truth and expose long-cherished error, the majority, like the Jews in Christ's day or the papists in the time of Luther, were content to believe as their fathers had believed and to live as they had lived. Therefore religion again degenerated into formalism; and errors and superstitions which would have been cast aside had the church continued to walk in the light of God's word, were retained and cherished. Thus the spirit inspired by the Reformation gradually died out, until there was almost as great need of reform in the Protestant churches as in the Roman Church in the time of Luther. There was the same worldliness and spiritual stupor, a similar reverence for the opinions of men, and substitution of human theories for the teachings of God's word.

The wide circulation of the Bible in the early part of the nineteenth century, and the great light thus shed upon the world, was not followed by a corresponding advance in knowledge of revealed truth, or in experimental religion. Satan could not, as in former ages, keep God's word from the people; it had been placed within the reach of all; but in order still to accomplish his object, he led many to value it but lightly. Men neglected to search the Scriptures, and thus they continued to accept false interpretations, and to cherish doctrines which had no foundation in the Bible.

Seeing the failure of his efforts to crush out the truth by persecution, Satan had again resorted to the plan of compromise which led to the great apostasy and the formation of the Church of Rome. He had induced Christians to ally themselves, not now with pagans, but with those who, by their devotion to the things of this world, had proved themselves to be as truly idolaters as were the worshipers of graven images. And the results of this union were no less pernicious now than in former ages; pride and extravagance were fostered under the guise of religion, and the churches became corrupted. Satan continued to pervert the doctrines of the Bible, and traditions that were to ruin millions were taking deep root. The church was upholding and defending these traditions, instead of contending for "the faith which was once delivered unto the saints." Thus were degraded the principles for which the Reformers had done and suffered so much.

17

Heralds of the Morning

One of the most solemn and yet most glorious truths revealed in the Bible is that of Christ's second coming to complete the great work of redemption. To God's pilgrim people, so long left to sojourn in "the region and shadow of death," a precious, joy-inspiring hope is given in the promise of His appearing, who is "the resurrection and the life," to "bring home again His banished." The doctrine of the second advent is the very keynote of the Sacred Scriptures. From the day when the first pair turned their sorrowing steps from Eden, the children of faith have waited the coming of the Promised One to break the destroyer's power and bring them again to the lost Paradise. Holy men of old looked forward to the advent of the Messiah in glory, as the consummation of their hope. Enoch, only the seventh in descent from them that dwelt in Eden, he who for three centuries on earth walked with his God, was permitted to behold from afar the coming of the Deliverer. "Behold," he declared, "the Lord cometh with ten thousands of His saints, to execute judgment upon all." Jude 14, 15. The patriarch Job in the night of his affliction exclaimed with unshaken trust: "I know that my Redeemer liveth, and that He shall stand at the latter day upon the earth: . . . in my flesh shall I see God: whom I shall see for myself, and mine eyes shall behold, and not another." Job 19:25-27.

The coming of Christ to usher in the reign of righteousness has inspired the most sublime and impassioned utterances of the sacred writers. The poets and prophets of the Bible have dwelt upon it in words glowing with celestial fire. The psalmist sang of the power and majesty of Israel's King: "Out of Zion, the perfection of beauty, God hath shined. Our God shall come, and shall not keep silence. . . . He shall call to the heavens from above, and to the earth, that He may judge His people." Psalm 50:2-4. "Let the heavens rejoice, and let the earth be glad . . . before the Lord: for He cometh, for He cometh to judge the earth: He shall judge the world with righteousness, and the people with His truth." Psalm 96:11-13.

Said the prophet Isaiah: "Awake and sing, ye that dwell in dust: for thy dew is as the dew of herbs, and the earth shall cast out the dead." "Thy dead men shall live, together with my dead body shall they arise." "He will swallow up death in victory; and the Lord God will wipe away tears from off all faces; and the rebuke of His people shall He take away from off all the earth: for the Lord hath spoken it. And it shall be said in that day, Lo, this is our God; we have waited for Him, and He will save us: this is the Lord; we have waited for Him, we will be glad and rejoice in His salvation." Isaiah 26:19; 25:8, 9.

And Habakkuk, rapt in holy vision, beheld His appearing. "God came from Teman, and the Holy One from Mount Paran. His glory covered the heavens, and the earth was full of His praise. And His brightness was as the light." "He stood, and measured the earth: He beheld, and drove asunder the nations; and the everlasting mountains were scattered, the perpetual hills did bow: His ways are everlasting." "Thou didst ride upon Thine horses and Thy chariots of salvation." "The mountains saw Thee, and they trembled: . . . the deep uttered his voice, and lifted up his hands on high. The sun and moon stood still in their habitation: at the light of Thine arrows they went, and at the shining of Thy glittering spear." "Thou wentest forth for the salvation of Thy people, even for salvation with Thine anointed." Habakkuk 3:3, 4, 6, 8, 10, 11, 13.

When the Saviour was about to be separated from His disciples, He comforted them in their sorrow with the assurance that He would come again: "Let not your heart be troubled. . . . In My Father's house are many mansions. . . . I go to prepare a place for you. And if I go and prepare a place for you, I will come again, and receive you unto Myself." John 14:1-3. "The Son of man shall come in His glory, and all the holy angels with Him." "Then shall He sit upon the throne of His glory: and before Him shall be gathered all nations." Matthew 25:31, 32.

The angels who lingered upon Olivet after Christ's ascension repeated to the disciples the promise of His return: "This *same* Jesus, which is taken up from you into heaven, shall *so* come in like manner as ye have seen Him go into heaven." Acts 1:11. And the apostle Paul, speaking by the Spirit of Inspiration, testified: "The Lord *Himself* shall descend from heaven with a shout, with the voice of the Archangel, and with the trump of God." 1 Thessalonians 4:16. Says the prophet of Patmos: "Behold, He cometh with clouds; and every eye shall see Him." Revelation 1:7.

About His coming cluster the glories of that "restitution of all things, which God hath spoken by the mouth of all His holy prophets since the world began." Acts 3:21. Then the long-continued rule of evil shall be broken; "the kingdoms of this world" will become "the kingdoms of our Lord, and of His Christ; and He shall reign for ever and ever." Revelation 11:15. "The glory of the Lord shall be revealed, and all flesh shall see it together." "The Lord God will cause righteousness and praise to spring forth before all the nations." He shall be "for a crown of glory, and for a diadem of beauty, unto the residue of His people." Isaiah 40:5; 61:11; 28:5.

It is then that the peaceful and long-desired kingdom of the Messiah shall be established under the whole heaven. "The Lord shall comfort Zion: He will comfort all her waste places; and He will make her wilderness like Eden, and her desert like the garden of the Lord." "The glory of Lebanon shall be given unto it, the excellency of Carmel and Sharon." "Thou shalt no more be termed Forsaken; neither shall thy land any more be termed Desolate: but thou shalt be called My Delight, and thy land Beulah." "As the bridegroom rejoiceth over the bride, so shall thy God rejoice over thee." Isaiah 51:3; 35:2; 62:4, 5, margin.

The coming of the Lord has been in all ages the hope of His true followers. The Saviour's parting promise upon Olivet, that He would come again, lighted up the future for His disciples, filling their hearts with joy and hope that sorrow could not quench nor trials dim. Amid suffering and persecution, the "appearing of the great God and our Saviour Jesus Christ" was the "blessed hope." When the Thessalonian Christians were filled with grief as they buried their loved ones, who had hoped to live to witness the coming of the Lord, Paul, their teacher, pointed them to the resurrection, to take place at the Saviour's advent. Then the dead in Christ should rise, and together with the living be caught up to meet the Lord in the air. "And so," he said, "shall we ever be with the Lord. Wherefore comfort one another with these words." 1 Thessalonians 4:16-18.

On rocky Patmos the beloved disciple hears the promise, "Surely I come quickly," and his longing response voices the prayer of the church in all her pilgrimage, "Even so, come, Lord Jesus." Revelation 22:20.

From the dungeon, the stake, the scaffold, where saints and martyrs witnessed for the truth, comes down the centuries the utterance of their faith and hope. Being "assured of His personal resurrection, and consequently of their own at His coming, for this cause," says one of these Christians, "they despised death, and were found to be above it."—Daniel T. Taylor, *The Reign of Christ on Earth: or, The Voice of the Church in All Ages*, page 33. They were willing to go down to the grave, that they might "rise free."—*Ibid.*, page 54. They looked for the "Lord to come from heaven in the clouds with the glory of His Father," "bringing to the just the times of the kingdom." The Waldenses cherished the same faith.—*Ibid.*, pages 129-132. Wycliffe looked forward to the Redeemer's appearing as the hope of the church.—*Ibid.*, pages 132-134.

Luther declared: "I persuade myself verily, that the day of judgment will not be absent full three hundred years. God will not, cannot, suffer this wicked world much longer." "The great day is drawing near in which the kingdom of abominations shall be overthrown."—*Ibid.*, pages 158, 134.

"This aged world is not far from its end," said Melanchthon. Calvin bids Christians "not to hesitate, ardently desiring the day of Christ's coming as of all events most auspicious;" and declares that "the whole family of the faithful will keep in view that day." "We must hunger after Christ, we must seek, contemplate," he says, "till the dawning of that great day, when our Lord will fully manifest the glory of His kingdom."—*Ibid.*, pages 158, 134.

"Has not the Lord Jesus carried up our flesh into heaven?" said Knox, the Scotch Reformer, "and shall He not return? We know that He shall return, and that with expedition." Ridley and Latimer, who laid down their lives for the truth, looked in faith for the Lord's coming. Ridley wrote: "The world without doubt—this I do believe, and therefore I say it—draws to an end. Let us with John, the servant of God, cry in our hearts unto our Saviour Christ, Come, Lord Jesus, come."—*Ibid.*, pages 151, 145.

"The thoughts of the coming of the Lord," said Baxter, "are most sweet and joyful to me."—Richard Baxter, *Works*, vol. 17, p. 555. "It is the work of faith and the character of His saints to love His appearing and to look for that blessed hope." "If death be the last enemy to be destroyed at the resurrection, we may learn how earnestly believers should long and pray for the second coming of Christ, when this full and final conquest shall be made."—*Ibid.*, vol. 17, p. 500. "This is the day that all believers should long, and hope, and wait for, as being the accomplishment of all the work of their redemption, and all the desires and endeavors of their souls." "Hasten, O Lord, this blessed day!"—*Ibid.*, vol. 17, pp. 182, 183. Such was the hope of the apostolic church, of the "church in the wilderness," and of the Reformers.

Prophecy not only foretells the manner and object of Christ's coming, but presents tokens by which men are to know when it is near. Said Jesus: "There shall be signs in the sun, and in the moon, and in the stars." Luke 21:25. "The sun shall be darkened, and the moon shall not give her light, and the stars of heaven shall fall, and the powers that are in heaven shall be shaken. And then shall they see the Son of man coming in the clouds with great power and glory." Mark 13:24-26. The revelator thus describes the first of the signs to precede the second advent: "There was a great earthquake; and the sun became black as sackcloth of hair, and the moon became as blood." Revelation 6:12.

These signs were witnessed before the opening of the nineteenth century. In fulfillment of this prophecy there occurred, in the year 1755, the most terrible earthquake that has ever been recorded. Though commonly known as the earthquake of Lisbon, it extended to the greater part of Europe, Africa, and America. It was felt in Greenland, in the West Indies, in the island of Madeira, in Norway and Sweden, Great Britain and Ireland. It pervaded an extent of not less than four million square miles. In Africa the shock was almost as severe as in Europe. A great part of Algiers was destroyed; and a short distance from Morocco, a village containing eight or ten thousand inhabitants was swallowed up. A vast wave swept over the coast of Spain and Africa engulfing cities and causing great destruction.

It was in Spain and Portugal that the shock manifested its extreme violence. At Cadiz the inflowing wave was said to be sixty feet high. Mountains, "some of the largest in Portugal, were impetuously shaken, as it were, from their very foundations, and some of them opened at their summits, which were split and rent in a wonderful manner, huge masses of them being thrown down into the adjacent valleys. Flames are related to have issued from these mountains."—Sir Charles Lyell, *Principles of Geology*, page 495.

At Lisbon "a sound of thunder was heard underground, and immediately afterwards a violent shock threw down the greater part of that city. In the course of about six minutes sixty thousand persons perished. The sea first retired, and laid the bar dry; it then rolled in, rising fifty feet or more above its ordinary level." "Among other extraordinary events related to have occurred at Lisbon during the catastrophe, was the subsidence of a new quay, built entirely of marble, at an immense expense. A great concourse of people had collected there for safety, as a spot where they might be beyond the reach of falling ruins; but suddenly the quay sank down with all the people on it, and not one of the dead bodies ever floated to the surface."—*Ibid.*, page 495.

"The shock" of the earthquake "was instantly followed by the fall of every church and convent, almost all the large public buildings, and more than one fourth of the houses. In about two hours after the shock, fires broke out in different quarters, and raged with such violence for the space of nearly three days, that the city was completely desolated. The earthquake happened on a holyday, when the churches and convents were full of people, very few of whom escaped."—*Encyclopedia Americana*, art. "Lisbon," note (ed. 1831). "The terror of the people was beyond description. Nobody wept; it was beyond tears. They ran hither and thither, delirious with horror and astonishment, beating their faces and breasts, crying, '*Misericordia! the world's at an end!*' Mothers forgot their children, and ran about loaded with crucifixed images. Unfortunately, many ran to the churches for protection; but in vain was the sacrament exposed; in vain did the poor creatures embrace the altars; images, priests, and people were buried in one common ruin." It has been estimated that ninety thousand persons lost their lives on that fatal day.

306   Twenty-five years later appeared the next sign mentioned in the prophecy—the darkening of the sun and moon. What rendered this more striking was the fact that the time of its fulfillment had been definitely pointed out. In the Saviour's conversation with His disciples upon Olivet, after describing the long period of trial for the church,—the 1260 years of papal persecution, concerning which He had promised that the tribulation should be shortened,—He thus mentioned certain events to precede His coming, and fixed the time when the first of these should be witnessed: "In those days, after that tribulation, the sun shall be darkened, and the moon shall not give her light." Mark 13:24. The 1260 days, or years, terminated in 1798. A quarter of a century earlier, persecution had almost wholly ceased. Following this persecution, according to the words of Christ, the sun was to be darkened. On the 19th of May, 1780, this prophecy was fulfilled.

"Almost, if not altogether alone, as the most mysterious and as yet unexplained phenomenon of its kind, . . . stands the dark day of May 19, 1780,—a most unaccountable darkening of the whole visible heavens and atmosphere in New England."—R. M. Devens, *Our First Century*, page 89.

An eyewitness living in Massachusetts describes the event as follows: "In the morning the sun rose clear, but was soon overcast. The clouds became lowery, and from them, black and ominous, as they soon appeared, lightning flashed, thunder rolled, and a little rain fell. Toward nine o'clock, the clouds became thinner, and assumed a brassy or coppery appearance, and earth, rocks, trees, buildings, water, and persons were changed by this strange, unearthly light. A few minutes later, a heavy black cloud spread over the entire sky except a narrow rim at the horizon, and it was as dark as it usually is at nine o'clock on a summer evening. . . .

"Fear, anxiety, and awe gradually filled the minds of the people. Women stood at the door, looking out upon the dark landscape; men 307 returned from their labor in the fields; the carpenter left his tools, the blacksmith his forge, the tradesman his counter. Schools were dismissed, and tremblingly the children fled homeward. Travelers put up at the nearest farmhouse. 'What is coming?' queried every lip and heart. It seemed as if a hurricane was about to dash across the land, or as if it was the day of the consummation of all things.

"Candles were used; and hearth fires shone as brightly as on a moonless evening in autumn. . .

. Fowls retired to their roosts and went to sleep, cattle gathered at the pasture bars and lowed, frogs peeped, birds sang their evening songs, and bats flew about. But the human knew that night had not come. . . .

"Dr. Nathanael Whittaker, pastor of the Tabernacle church in Salem, held religious services in the meetinghouse, and preached a sermon in which he maintained that the darkness was supernatural. Congregations came together in many other places. The texts for the extemporaneous sermons were invariably those that seemed to indicate that the darkness was consonant with Scriptural prophecy. . . . The darkness was most dense shortly after eleven o'clock."— *The Essex Antiquarian*, April, 1899, vol. 3, No. 4, pp. 53, 54. "In most parts of the country it was so great in the daytime, that the people could not tell the hour by either watch or clock, nor dine, nor manage their domestic business, without the light of candles. . . .

"The extent of this darkness was extraordinary. It was observed as far east as Falmouth. To the westward it reached to the farthest part of Connecticut, and to Albany. To the southward, it was observed along the seacoasts; and to the north as far as the American settlements extend."—William Gordon, *History of the Rise, Progress, and Establishment of the Independence of the U.S.A.*, vol. 3, p. 57.

The intense darkness of the day was succeeded, an hour or two before evening, by a partially clear sky, and the sun appeared, though it was still obscured by the black, heavy mist. "After sundown, the clouds came again overhead, and it grew dark very fast." "Nor was the darkness 308 of the night less uncommon and terrifying than that of the day; notwithstanding there was almost a full moon, no object was discernible but by the help of some artificial light, which, when seen from the neighboring houses and other places at a distance, appeared through a kind of Egyptian darkness which seemed almost impervious to the rays."—Isaiah Thomas, *Massachusetts Spy; or, American Oracle of Liberty*, vol. 10, No. 472 (May 25, 1780). Said an eyewitness of the scene: "I could not help conceiving at the time, that if every luminous body in the universe had been shrouded in impenetrable shades, or struck out of existence, the darkness could not have been more complete."—Letter by Dr. Samuel Tenney, of Exeter, New Hampshire, December, 1785 (in *Massachusetts Historical Society Collections*, 1792, 1st series, vol. 1, p. 97). Though at nine o'clock that night the moon rose to the full, "it had not the least effect to dispel the deathlike shadows." After midnight the darkness disappeared, and the moon, when first visible, had the appearance of blood.

May 19, 1780, stands in history as "The Dark Day." Since the time of Moses no period of darkness of equal density, extent, and duration, has ever been recorded. The description of this event, as given by eyewitnesses, is but an echo of the words of the Lord, recorded by the prophet Joel, twenty-five hundred years previous to their fulfillment: "The sun shall be turned into darkness, and the moon into blood, before the great and terrible day of the Lord come." Joel 2:31.

Christ had bidden His people watch for the signs of His advent and rejoice as they should behold the tokens of their coming King. "When these things begin to come to pass," He said, "then look up, and lift up your heads; for your redemption draweth nigh." He pointed His followers to the budding trees of spring, and said: "When they now shoot forth, ye see and know of your own selves that summer is now nigh at hand. So likewise ye, when ye see these things 309 come to pass, know ye that the kingdom of God is nigh at hand." Luke 21:28, 30, 31.

But as the spirit of humility and devotion in the church had given place to pride and formalism, love for Christ and faith in His coming had grown cold. Absorbed in worldliness and pleasure seeking, the professed people of God were blinded to the Saviour's instructions concerning the signs of His appearing. The doctrine of the second advent had been neglected; the scriptures relating to it were obscured by misinterpretation, until it was, to a great extent, ignored and forgotten. Especially was this the case in the churches of America. The freedom and comfort enjoyed by all classes of society, the ambitious desire for wealth and luxury, begetting an absorbing devotion to money-making, the eager rush for popularity and power, which seemed to be within the reach of all, led men to center their interests and hopes on the things of this life, and to put far in the future that solemn day when the present order of things should pass away.

When the Saviour pointed out to His followers the signs of His return, He foretold the state of backsliding that would exist just prior to His second advent. There would be, as in the days of Noah, the activity and stir of worldly business and pleasure seeking—buying, selling, planting, building, marrying, and giving in marriage—with forgetfulness of God and the future life. For those living at this time, Christ's admonition is: "Take heed to yourselves, lest at any time your hearts be overcharged with surfeiting, and drunkenness, and cares of this life, and so that day come upon you unawares." "Watch ye therefore, and pray always, that ye may be accounted worthy to escape all these things that shall come to pass, and to stand before the Son of man." Luke 21:34, 36.

The condition of the church at this time is pointed out in the Saviour's words in the Reve-310 lation: "Thou hast a name that thou livest, and art dead." And to those who refuse to arouse from their careless security, the solemn warning is addressed: "If therefore thou shalt not watch, I will come on thee as a thief, and thou shalt not know what hour I will come upon thee." Revelation 3:1, 3.

It was needful that men should be awakened to their danger; that they should be roused to prepare for the solemn events connected with the close of probation. The prophet of God declares: "The day of the Lord is great and very terrible; and who can abide it?" Who shall stand when He appeareth who is "of purer eyes than to behold evil," and cannot "look on iniquity"? Joel 2:11; Habakkuk 1:13. To them that cry, "My God, we know Thee," yet have transgressed His covenant, and hastened after another god, hiding iniquity in their hearts, and loving the paths of unrighteousness—to these the day of the Lord is "darkness, and not light, even very dark, and no brightness in it." Hosea 8:2, 1; Psalm 16:4; Amos 5:20. "It shall come to pass at that time," saith the Lord, "that I will search Jerusalem with candles, and punish the men that are settled on their lees: that say in their heart, The Lord will not do good, neither will He do evil." Zephaniah 1:12. "I will punish the world for their evil, and the wicked for their iniquity; and I will cause the arrogancy of the proud to cease, and will lay low the haughtiness of the terrible." Isaiah 13:11. "Neither their silver nor their gold shall be able to deliver them;" "their goods shall become a booty, and their houses a desolation." Zephaniah 1:18, 13.

The prophet Jeremiah, looking forward to this fearful time, exclaimed: "I am pained at my very heart. . . . I cannot hold my peace, because thou hast heard, O my soul, the sound of the trumpet, the alarm of war. Destruction upon destruction is cried." Jeremiah 4:19, 20.

"That day is a day of wrath, a day of trouble and distress, a day of wasteness and desolation, a day of darkness and gloominess, a day of clouds and thick darkness, a day of the trumpet and alarm." Zephaniah 1:15, 16. "Behold, the day of the Lord cometh, . . . to lay the land des-311 olate: and He shall destroy the sinners thereof out of it." Isaiah 13:9.

In view of that great day the word of God, in the most solemn and impressive language, calls upon His people to arouse from their spiritual lethargy and to seek His face with repentance and humiliation: "Blow ye the trumpet in Zion, and sound an alarm in My holy mountain: let all the inhabitants of the land tremble: for the day of the Lord cometh, for it is nigh at hand." "Sanctify a fast, call a solemn assembly: gather the people, sanctify the congregation, assemble the elders, gather the children: . . . let the bridegroom go forth of his chamber, and the bride out of her closet. Let the priests, the ministers of the Lord, weep between the porch and the altar." "Turn ye even to Me with all your heart, and with fasting, and with weeping, and with mourning: and rend your heart, and not your garments, and turn unto the Lord your God: for He is gracious and merciful, slow to anger, and of great kindness." Joel 2:1, 15-17, 12, 13.

To prepare a people to stand in the day of God, a great work of reform was to be accomplished. God saw that many of His professed people were not building for eternity, and in His mercy He was about to send a message of warning to arouse them from their stupor and lead them to make ready for the coming of the Lord.

This warning is brought to view in Revelation 14. Here is a threefold message represented as proclaimed by heavenly beings and immediately followed by the coming of the Son of man to reap "the harvest of the earth." The first of these warnings announces the approaching judgment. The prophet beheld an angel flying "in the midst of heaven, having the everlasting gospel to preach unto them that dwell on the earth, and to every nation, and kindred, and tongue, and people, saying with a loud voice, Fear God, and give glory to Him; for the hour of His judgment is come: and worship Him that made heaven, and earth, and the sea, and the fountains of waters." Revelation 14:6, 7.

312 This revelation is declared to be a part of "the everlasting gospel." The work of preaching the gospel has not been committed to angels, but has been entrusted to men. Holy angels have been employed in directing this work, they have in charge the great movements for the salvation of men; but the actual proclamation of the gospel is performed by the servants of Christ upon the earth.

Faithful men, who were obedient to the promptings of God's Spirit and the teachings of His word, were to proclaim this warning to the world. They were those who had taken heed to the "sure word of prophecy," the "light that shineth in a dark place, until the day dawn, and the daystar arise." 2 Peter 1:19. They had been seeking the knowledge of God more than all hid treasures, counting it "better than the merchandise of silver, and the gain thereof than fine gold." Proverbs 3:14. And the Lord revealed to them the great things of the kingdom. "The secret of the Lord is with them that fear Him; and He will show them His covenant." Psalm 25:14.

It was not the scholarly theologians who had an understanding of this truth, and engaged in its proclamation. Had these been faithful watchmen, diligently and prayerfully searching the Scriptures, they would have known the time of night; the prophecies would have opened to them the events about to take place. But they did not occupy this position, and the message was given by humbler men. Said Jesus: "Walk while ye have the light, lest darkness come upon you." John 12:35. Those who turn away from the light which God has given, or who neglect to seek it when it is within their reach, are left in darkness. But the Saviour declares: "He that followeth Me shall not walk in darkness, but shall have the light of life." John 8:12. Whoever is with singleness of purpose seeking to do God's will, earnestly heeding the light already given, will receive greater light; to that soul some star of heavenly radiance will be sent to guide him into all truth.

At the time of Christ's first advent the priests 313 and scribes of the Holy City, to whom were entrusted the oracles of God, might have discerned the signs of the times and proclaimed the coming of the Promised One. The prophecy of Micah designated His birthplace; Daniel specified the time of His advent. Micah 5:2; Daniel 9:25. God committed these prophecies to the Jewish leaders; they were without excuse if they did not know and declare to the people that the Messiah's coming was at hand. Their ignorance was the result of sinful neglect. The Jews were building monuments for the slain prophets of God, while by their deference to the great men of earth they were paying homage to the servants of Satan. Absorbed in their ambitious strife for place and power among men, they lost sight of the divine honors proffered them by the King of heaven.

With profound and reverent interest the elders of Israel should have been studying the place, the time, the circumstances, of the greatest event in the world's history—the coming of the Son of God to accomplish the redemption of man. All the people should have been watching and waiting that they might be among the first to welcome the world's Redeemer. But, lo, at Bethlehem two weary travelers from the hills of Nazareth traverse the whole length of the narrow street to the eastern extremity of the town, vainly seeking a place of rest and shelter for the night. No doors are open to receive them. In a wretched hovel prepared for cattle, they at last find refuge, and there the Saviour of the world is born.

Heavenly angels had seen the glory which the Son of God shared with the Father before the world was, and they had looked forward with intense interest to His appearing on earth as an event fraught with the greatest joy to all people. Angels were appointed to carry the glad tidings to those who were prepared to receive it and who would joyfully make it known to the inhabitants of the earth. Christ had stooped to take upon Himself man's nature; He was to bear an infinite weight of woe as He should make His 314 soul an offering for sin; yet angels desired that even in His humiliation the Son of the Highest might appear before men with a dignity and glory befitting His character. Would the great men of earth assemble at Israel's capital to greet His coming? Would legions of angels present Him to the expectant company?

An angel visits the earth to see who are prepared to welcome Jesus. But he can discern no tokens of expectancy. He hears no voice of praise and triumph that the period of Messiah's coming is at hand. The angel hovers for a time over the chosen city and the temple where the divine presence has been manifested for ages; but even here is the same indifference. The priests, in their pomp and pride, are offering polluted sacrifices in the temple. The Pharisees are with loud voices addressing the people or making boastful prayers at the corners of the streets. In the palaces of kings, in the assemblies of philosophers, in the schools of the rabbis, all are alike unmindful of the wondrous fact which has filled all heaven with joy and praise—that the Redeemer of men is about to appear upon the earth.

There is no evidence that Christ is expected, and no preparation for the Prince of life. In amazement the celestial messenger is about to return to heaven with the shameful tidings, when he discovers a group of shepherds who are watching their flocks by night, and, as they gaze into the starry heavens, are contemplating the prophecy of a Messiah to come to earth, and longing for the advent of the world's Redeemer. Here is a company that is prepared to receive the heavenly message. And suddenly the angel of the Lord appears, declaring the good tidings of great joy. Celestial glory floods all the plain, an innumerable company of angels is revealed, and as if the joy were too great for one messenger to bring from heaven, a multitude of voices break forth in the anthem which all the nations of the saved shall one day sing: "Glory to God in the highest, and on earth peace, good will toward men." Luke 2:14.

315 Oh, what a lesson is this wonderful story of Bethlehem! How it rebukes our unbelief, our pride and self-sufficiency. How it warns us to beware, lest by our criminal indifference we also fail to discern the signs of the times, and therefore know not the day of our visitation.

It was not alone upon the hills of Judea, not among the lowly shepherds only, that angels found the watchers for Messiah's coming. In the land of the heathen also were those that looked for Him; they were wise men, rich and noble, the philosophers of the East. Students of nature, the Magi had seen God in His handiwork. From the Hebrew Scriptures they had learned of the Star to arise out of Jacob, and with eager desire they awaited His coming, who should be not only the "Consolation of Israel," but a "Light to lighten the Gentiles," and "for salvation unto the ends of the earth." Luke 2:25, 32; Acts 13:47. They were seekers for light, and light from the throne of God illumined the path for their feet. While the priests and rabbis of Jerusalem, the appointed guardians and expounders of the truth, were shrouded in darkness, the Heaven-sent star guided these Gentile strangers to the birthplace of the newborn King.

It is "unto them that look for Him" that Christ is to "appear the second time without sin unto salvation." Hebrews 9:28. Like the tidings of the Saviour's birth, the message of the second advent was not committed to the religious leaders of the people. They had failed to preserve their connection with God, and had refused light from heaven; therefore they were not of the number described by the apostle Paul: "But ye, brethren, are not in darkness, that that day should overtake you as a thief. Ye are all the children of light, and the children of the day: we are not of the night, nor of darkness." 1 Thessalonians 5:4, 5.

The watchmen upon the walls of Zion should have been the first to catch the tidings of the Saviour's advent, the first to lift their voices to proclaim Him near, the first to warn the people to prepare for His coming. But they were at ease, dreaming of peace and safety, while the 316 people were asleep in their sins. Jesus saw His church, like the barren fig tree, covered with pretentious leaves, yet destitute of precious fruit. There was a boastful observance of the forms of religion, while the spirit of true humility, penitence, and faith—which alone could render the service acceptable to God—was lacking. Instead of the graces of the Spirit there were manifested pride, formalism, vainglory, selfishness, oppression. A backsliding church closed their eyes to the signs of the times. God did not forsake them, or suffer His faithfulness to fail; but they departed from Him, and separated themselves from His love. As they refused to comply with the conditions, His promises were not fulfilled to them.

Such is the sure result of neglect to appreciate and improve the light and privileges which God bestows. Unless the church will follow on in His opening providence, accepting every ray of light, performing every duty which may be revealed, religion will inevitably degenerate into the observance of forms, and the spirit of vital godliness will disappear. This truth has been repeatedly illustrated in the history of the church. God requires of His people works of faith and obedience corresponding to the blessings and privileges bestowed. Obedience requires a sacrifice and involves a cross; and this is why so many of the professed followers of Christ refused to receive the light from heaven, and, like the Jews of old, knew not the time of their visitation. Luke 19:44. Because of their pride and unbelief the Lord passed them by and revealed His truth to those who, like the shepherds of Bethlehem and the Eastern Magi, had given heed to all the light they had received.

317

18

An American Reformer

An upright, honest-hearted farmer, who had been led to doubt the divine authority of the Scriptures, yet who sincerely desired to know the truth, was the man specially chosen of God to lead out in the proclamation of Christ's second coming. Like many other reformers, William Miller had in early life battled with poverty and had thus learned the great lessons of energy and self-denial. The members of the family from which he sprang were characterized by an independent, liberty-loving spirit, by capability of endurance, and ardent patriotism—traits which were also prominent in his character. His father was a captain in the army of the Revolution, and to the sacrifices which he made in the struggles and sufferings of that stormy period may be traced the straitened circumstances of Miller's early life.

He had a sound physical constitution, and even in childhood gave evidence of more than ordinary intellectual strength. As he grew older, this became more marked. His mind was active and well developed, and he had a keen thirst for knowledge. Though he did not enjoy the advantages of a collegiate education, his love of study and a habit of careful thought and close criticism rendered him a man of sound judgment and comprehensive views. He possessed an irreproachable moral character and an enviable reputation, being generally esteemed for integrity, thrift, and benevolence. By dint of energy and
318 application he early acquired a competence, though his habits of study were still maintained. He filled various civil and military offices with credit, and the avenues to wealth and honor seemed wide open to him.

His mother was a woman of sterling piety, and in childhood, he had been subject to religious impressions. In early childhood, however, he was thrown into the society of deists, whose influence was the stronger from the fact that they were mostly good citizens and men of humane and benevolent disposition. Living, as they did, in the midst of Christian institutions, their characters had been to some extent molded by their surroundings. For the excellencies which won them respect and confidence they were indebted to the Bible; and yet these good gifts were so perverted as to exert an influence against the word of God. By association with these men, Miller was led to adopt their sentiments. The current interpretations of Scripture presented difficulties which seemed to him insurmountable; yet his new belief, while setting aside the Bible, offered nothing better to

take its place, and he remained far from satisfied. He continued to hold these views, however, for about twelve years. But at the age of thirty-four the Holy Spirit impressed his heart with a sense of his condition as a sinner. He found in his former belief no assurance of happiness beyond the grave. The future was dark and gloomy. Referring afterward to his feelings at this time, he said:

"Annihilation was a cold and chilling thought, and accountability was sure destruction to all. The heavens were as brass over my head, and the earth as iron under my feet. Eternity—what was it? And death—why was it? The more I reasoned, the further I was from demonstration. The more I thought, the more scattered were my conclusions. I tried to stop thinking, but my thoughts would not be controlled. I was truly wretched, but did not understand the cause. I murmured and complained, but knew not of whom. I knew that there was a wrong, but knew not how or where to find the right. I mourned, but without hope."

In this state he continued for some months. 319 "Suddenly," he says, "the character of a Saviour was vividly impressed upon my mind. It seemed that there might be a being so good and compassionate as to himself atone for our transgressions, and thereby save us from suffering the penalty of sin. I immediately felt how lovely such a being must be, and imagined that I could cast myself into the arms of, and trust in the mercy of, such a one. But the question arose, How can it be proved that such a being does exist? Aside from the Bible, I found that I could get no evidence of the existence of such a Saviour, or even of a future state. . . .

"I saw that the Bible did bring to view just such a Saviour as I needed; and I was perplexed to find how an uninspired book should develop principles so perfectly adapted to the wants of a fallen world. I was constrained to admit that the Scriptures must be a revelation from God. They became my delight; and in Jesus I found a friend. The Saviour became to me the chiefest among ten thousand; and the Scriptures, which before were dark and contradictory, now became the lamp to my feet and light to my path. My mind became settled and satisfied. I found the Lord God to be a Rock in the midst of the ocean of life. The Bible now became my chief study, and I can truly say, I searched it with great delight. I found the half was never told me. I wondered why I had not seen its beauty and glory before, and marveled that I could have ever rejected it. I found everything revealed that my heart could desire, and a remedy for every disease of the soul. I lost all taste for other reading, and applied my heart to get wisdom from God."—S. Bliss, *Memoirs of Wm. Miller*, pages 65-67.

Miller publicly professed his faith in the religion which he had despised. But his infidel associates were not slow to bring forward all those arguments which he himself had often urged against the divine authority of the Scriptures. He was not then prepared to answer them; but he reasoned that if the Bible is a revelation from God, it must be consistent with itself; and that as it was given for man's instruction, it must be adapted to his understanding. He determined to study the Scriptures for himself, and ascertain if every apparent contradiction could not be harmonized.

Endeavoring to lay aside all preconceived opinions, and dispensing with commentaries, he compared scripture with scripture by the aid of the marginal references and the concordance. He pursued his study in a regular and methodical manner; beginning with Genesis, and reading verse by verse, he proceeded no faster than the meaning of the several passages so unfolded as to leave him free from all embarrassment. When he found anything obscure, it was his custom to compare it with every other text which seemed to have any reference to the matter under consideration. Every word was permitted to have its proper bearing upon the subject of the text, and if his view of it harmonized with every collateral passage, it ceased to be a difficulty. Thus whenever he met with a passage hard to be understood he found an explanation in some other portion of the Scriptures. As he studied with earnest prayer for divine enlightenment, that which had before appeared dark to his understanding was made clear. He experienced the truth of the psalmist's words: "The entrance of Thy words giveth light; it giveth understanding unto the simple." Psalm 119:130.

With intense interest he studied the books of Daniel and the Revelation, employing the same principles of interpretation as in the other scriptures, and found, to his great joy, that the prophetic symbols could be understood. He saw that the prophecies, so far as they had been fulfilled, had been fulfilled literally; that all the various figures, metaphors, parables, similitudes, etc., were either explained in their immediate connection, or the terms in which they were expressed were defined in other scriptures, and when thus explained, were to be literally understood. "I was thus satisfied," he says, "that the Bible is a system of revealed truths, so clearly and simply given that the wayfaring man, though a fool, need not err therein."—Bliss, page 70. Link after link of the chain of truth rewarded his efforts, as step by step he traced down the great lines of prophecy. Angels of heaven were guiding his mind and opening the Scriptures to his understanding.

Taking the manner in which the prophecies had been fulfilled in the past as a criterion by which to judge of the fulfillment of those which were still future, he became satisfied that the popular view of the spiritual reign of Christ—a temporal millennium before the end of the world—was not sustained by the word of God. This doctrine, pointing to a thousand years of righteousness and peace before the personal coming of the Lord, put far off the terrors of the day of God. But, pleasing though it may be, it is contrary to the teachings of Christ and His apostles, who declared that the wheat and the tares are to grow together until the harvest, the end of the world; that "evil men and seducers shall wax worse and worse;" that "in the last days perilous times shall come;" and that the kingdom of darkness shall continue until the advent of the Lord and shall be consumed with the spirit of His mouth and be destroyed with the brightness of His coming. Matthew 13:30, 38-41; 2 Timothy 3:13, 1; 2 Thessalonians 2:8.

The doctrine of the world's conversion and the spiritual reign of Christ was not held by the apostolic church. It was not generally accepted by Christians until about the beginning of the eighteenth century. Like every other error, its results were evil. It taught men to look far in the future for the coming of the Lord and prevented them from giving heed to the signs heralding His approach. It induced a feeling of confidence and security that was not well founded and led many to neglect the preparation necessary in order to meet their Lord.

Miller found the literal, personal coming of Christ to be plainly taught in the Scriptures. Says Paul: "The Lord Himself shall descend from heaven with a shout, with the voice of the Archangel, and with the trump of God." 1 Thessalonians 4:16. And the Saviour declares: "They shall *see* the Son of man coming in the clouds of heaven with power and great glory." "For as the lightning cometh out of the east, and shineth even unto the west; so shall also the coming of the Son of man be." Matthew 24:30, 27. He is to be accompanied by all the hosts of heaven. "The Son of man shall come in His glory, and all the holy angels with Him." Matthew 25:31. "And He shall send His angels with a great sound of a trumpet, and they shall gather together His elect." Matthew 24:31.

At His coming the righteous dead will be raised, and the righteous living will be changed. "We shall not all sleep," says Paul, "but we shall all be changed, in a moment, in the twinkling of an eye, at the last trump: for the trumpet shall sound, and the dead shall be raised incorruptible, and we shall be changed. For this corruptible must put on incorruption, and this mortal must put on immortality." 1 Corinthians 15:51-53. And in his letter to the Thessalonians, after describing the coming of the Lord, he says: "The dead in Christ shall rise first: then we which are alive and remain shall be caught up together with them in the clouds, to meet the Lord in the air: and so shall we ever be with the

Lord." 1 Thessalonians 4:16, 17.

Not until the personal advent of Christ can His people receive the kingdom. The Saviour said: "When the Son of man shall come in His glory, and all the holy angels with Him, then shall He sit upon the throne of His glory: and before Him shall be gathered all nations: and He shall separate them one from another, as a shepherd divideth his sheep from the goats: and He shall set the sheep on His right hand, but the goats on the left. Then shall the King say unto them on His right hand, Come, ye blessed of My Father, inherit the kingdom prepared for you from the foundation of the world." Matthew 25:31-34. We have seen by the scriptures just given that when the Son of man comes, the dead are raised incorruptible and the living are 323 changed. By this great change they are prepared to receive the kingdom; for Paul says: "Flesh and blood cannot inherit the kingdom of God; neither doth corruption inherit incorruption." 1 Corinthians 15:50. Man in his present state is mortal, corruptible; but the kingdom of God will be incorruptible, enduring forever. Therefore man in his present state cannot enter into the kingdom of God. But when Jesus comes, He confers immortality upon His people; and then He calls them to inherit the kingdom of which they have hitherto been only heirs.

These and other scriptures clearly proved to Miller's mind that the events which were generally expected to take place before the coming of Christ, such as the universal reign of peace and the setting up of the kingdom of God upon the earth, were to be subsequent to the second advent. Furthermore, all the signs of the times and the condition of the world corresponded to the prophetic description of the last days. He was forced to the conclusion, from the study of Scripture alone, that the period allotted for the continuance of the earth in its present state was about to close.

"Another kind of evidence that vitally affected my mind," he says, "was the chronology of the Scriptures. . . . I found that predicted events, which had been fulfilled in the past, often occurred within a given time. The one hundred and twenty years to the flood (Genesis 6:3); the seven days that were to precede it, with forty days of predicted rain (Genesis 7:4); the four hundred years of the sojourn of Abraham's seed (Genesis 15:13); the three days of the butler's and baker's dreams (Genesis 40:12-20); the seven years of Pharaoh's (Genesis 41:28-54); the forty years in the wilderness (Numbers 14:34); the three and a half years of famine (1 Kings 17:1) [see Luke 4:25;] . . . the seventy years' captivity (Jeremiah 25:11); Nebuchadnezzar's seven times (Daniel 4:13-16); and the seven weeks, threescore and two weeks, and the one week, making seventy weeks, determined upon the Jews (Daniel 9:24-27),—the

events limited by these times were all once only a matter of prophecy, and were fulfilled in accordance with the predictions."—Bliss, pages 74, 75.

When, therefore, he found, in his study of the 324 Bible, various chronological periods that, according to his understanding of them, extended to the second coming of Christ, he could not but regard them as the "times before appointed," which God had revealed unto His servants. "The secret things," says Moses, "belong unto the Lord our God: but those things which are revealed belong unto us and to our children forever;" and the Lord declares by the prophet Amos, that He "will do nothing, but He revealeth His secret unto His servants the prophets." Deuteronomy 29:29; Amos 3:7. The students of God's word may, then, confidently expect to find the most stupendous event to take place in human history clearly pointed out in the Scriptures of truth.

"As I was fully convinced," says Miller, "that all Scripture given by inspiration of God is profitable (2 Timothy 3:16); that it came not at any time by the will of man, but was written as holy men were moved by the Holy Ghost (2 Peter 1:21), and was written 'for our learning, that we through patience and comfort of the Scriptures might have hope' (Romans 15:4), I could but regard the chronological portions of the Bible as being as much a portion of the word of God, and as much entitled to our serious consideration, as any other portion of the Scriptures. I therefore felt that in endeavoring to comprehend what God had in His mercy seen fit to reveal to us, I had no right to pass over the prophetic periods."—Bliss, page 75.

The prophecy which seemed most clearly to reveal the *time* of the second advent was that of Daniel 8:14: "Unto two thousand and three hundred days; then shall the sanctuary be cleansed." Following his rule of making Scripture its own interpreter, Miller learned that a day in symbolic prophecy represents a year (Numbers 14:34; Ezekiel 4:6); he saw that the period of 2300 prophetic days, or literal years, would extend far beyond the close of the Jewish dispensation, hence it could not refer to the sanctuary of that 325 dispensation. Miller accepted the generally received view that in the Christian age the earth is the sanctuary, and he therefore understood that the cleansing of the sanctuary foretold in Daniel 8:14 represented the purification of the earth by fire at the second coming of Christ. If, then, the correct starting point could be found for the 2300 days, he concluded that the time of the second advent could be readily ascertained. Thus would be revealed the time of that great consummation, the time when the present state, with "all its pride and power, pomp and vanity, wickedness and oppression, would come to an end;" when the curse would be "removed from off the earth, death be destroyed, reward be given to the servants of God, the prophets and saints, and them who fear His name, and those be destroyed that destroy the earth."—Bliss, page 76.

With a new and deeper earnestness, Miller continued the examination of the prophecies, whole nights as well as days being devoted to the study of what now appeared of such stupendous importance and all-absorbing interest. In the eighth chapter of Daniel he could find no clue to the starting point of the 2300 days; the angel Gabriel, though commanded to make Daniel understand the vision, gave him only a partial explanation. As the terrible persecution to befall the church was unfolded to the prophet's vision, physical strength gave way. He could endure no more, and the angel left him for a time. Daniel "fainted, and was sick certain days," he says, "but none understood it."

Yet God had bidden His messenger: "Make this man to understand the vision." That commission must be fulfilled. In obedience to it, the angel, some time afterward, returned to Daniel, saying: "I am now come forth to give thee skill and understanding;" "therefore understand the matter, and consider the vision." Daniel 8:27, 16; 9:22, 23, 25-27. There was one important point in the vision of chapter 8 which had been left unexplained, namely, that relating to time—the period of the 2300 days; therefore the angel, in resuming his explanation, dwells chiefly upon the subject of time:

326 "Seventy weeks are determined upon thy people and upon thy Holy City. . . . Know therefore and understand, that from the going forth of the commandment to restore and to build Jerusalem unto the Messiah the Prince shall be seven weeks, and threescore and two weeks: the street shall be built again, and the wall, even in troublous times. And after threescore and two weeks shall Messiah be cut off, but not for Himself. . . . And He shall confirm the covenant with many for one week: and in the midst of the week He shall cause the sacrifice and the oblation to cease."

The angel had been sent to Daniel for the express purpose of explaining to him the point which he had failed to understand in the vision of the eighth chapter, the statement relative to time—"unto two thousand and three hundred days; then shall the sanctuary be cleansed." After bidding Daniel "understand the matter, and consider the vision," the very first words of the angel are: "Seventy weeks are determined upon thy people and upon thy Holy City." The word here translated "determined" literally signifies "cut off." Seventy weeks, representing 490 years, are declared by the angel to be cut off, as specially pertaining to the Jews. But from what were they cut off? As the 2300 days was

the only period of time mentioned in chapter 8, it must be the period from which the seventy weeks were cut off; the seventy weeks must therefore be a part of the 2300 days, and the two periods must begin together. The seventy weeks were declared by the angel to date from the going forth of the commandment to restore and build Jerusalem. If the date of this commandment could be found, then the starting point for the great period of the 2300 days would be ascertained.

In the seventh chapter of Ezra the decree is found. Verses 12-26. In its completest form it was issued by Artaxerxes, king of Persia, 457 B.C. But in Ezra 6:14 the house of the Lord at Jerusalem is said to have been built "according to the commandment ["decree," margin] of Cyrus, and Darius, and Artaxerxes king of Persia." These three kings, in originating, reaffirm- 327 ing, and completing the decree, brought it to the perfection required by the prophecy to mark the beginning of the 2300 years. Taking 457 B.C., the time when the decree was completed, as the date of the commandment, every specification of the prophecy concerning the seventy weeks was seen to have been fulfilled.

"From the going forth of the commandment to restore and to build Jerusalem unto the Messiah the Prince shall be seven weeks, and threescore and two weeks"—namely, sixty-nine weeks, or 483 years. The decree of Artaxerxes went into effect in the autumn of 457 B.C. From this date, 483 years extend to the autumn of A.D. 27. (See Appendix.) At that time this prophecy was fulfilled. The word "Messiah" signifies "the Anointed One." In the autumn of A.D. 27 Christ was baptized by John and received the anointing of the Spirit. The apostle Peter testifies that "God anointed Jesus of Nazareth with the Holy Ghost and with power." Acts 10:38. And the Saviour Himself declared: "The Spirit of the Lord is upon Me, because He hath anointed Me to preach the gospel to the poor." Luke 4:18. After His baptism He went into Galilee, "preaching the gospel of the kingdom of God, and saying, *The time* is fulfilled." Mark 1:14, 15.

"And He shall confirm the covenant with many for one week." The "week" here brought to view is the last one of the seventy; it is the last seven years of the period allotted especially to the Jews. During this time, extending from A.D. 27 to A.D. 34, Christ, at first in person and afterward by His disciples, extended the gospel invitation especially to the Jews. As the apostles went forth with the good tidings of the kingdom, the Saviour's direction was: "Go not into the way of the Gentiles, and into any city of the Samaritans enter ye not: but go rather to the lost sheep of the house of Israel." Matthew 10:5, 6.

"In the midst of the week He shall cause the sacrifice and the oblation to cease." In A.D. 31, three and a half years after His baptism, our Lord was crucified. With the great sacrifice offered upon Calvary, ended that system of offerings which for four thousand years had pointed forward to the Lamb of God. Type had met antitype, and all the sacrifices and oblations of the ceremonial system were there to cease.

The seventy weeks, or 490 years, especially allotted to the Jews, ended, as we have seen, in A.D. 34. At that time, through the action of the Jewish Sanhedrin, the nation sealed its rejection of the gospel by the martyrdom of Stephen and the persecution of the followers of Christ. Then the message of salvation, no longer restricted to the chosen people, was given to the world. The disciples, forced by persecution to flee from Jerusalem, "went everywhere preaching the word." "Philip went down to the city of Samaria, and preached Christ unto them." Peter, divinely guided, opened the gospel to the centurion of Caesarea, the God-fearing Cornelius; and the ardent Paul, won to the faith of Christ, was commissioned to carry the glad tidings "far hence unto the Gentiles." Acts 8:4, 5; 22:21.

Thus far every specification of the prophecies is strikingly fulfilled, and the beginning of the seventy weeks is fixed beyond question at 457 B.C., and their expiration in A.D. 34. From this data there is no difficulty in finding the termination of the 2300 days. The seventy weeks—490 days—having been cut off from the 2300, there were 1810 days remaining. After the end of 490 days, the 1810 days were still to be fulfilled. From A.D. 34, 1810 years extend to 1844. Consequently the 2300 days of Daniel 8:14 terminate in 1844. At the expiration of this great prophetic period, upon the testimony of the angel of God, "the sanctuary shall be cleansed." Thus the time of the cleansing of the sanctuary—which was almost universally believed to take place at the second advent—was definitely pointed out.

Miller and his associates at first believed that the 2300 days would terminate in the *spring* of 1844, whereas the prophecy points to the *autumn* of that year. (See Appendix.) The misapprehension of this point brought disappointment and perplexity to those who had fixed upon the earlier date as the time of the Lord's coming. But this did not in the least affect the strength of the argument showing that the 2300 days terminated in the year 1844, and that the great event represented by the cleansing of the sanctuary must then take place.

Entering upon the study of the Scriptures as he had done, in order to prove that they were a revelation from God, Miller had not, at the outset, the slightest expectation of reaching the conclusion at which he had now arrived. He himself could hardly credit the results of his investigation. But the Scripture evidence was too clear and forcible to be set aside.

He had devoted two years to the study of the Bible, when, in 1818, he reached the solemn conviction that in about twenty-five years Christ would appear for the redemption of His people. "I need not speak," says Miller, "of the joy that filled my heart in view of the delightful prospect, nor of the ardent longings of my soul for a participation in the joys of the redeemed. The Bible was now to me a new book. It was indeed a feast of reason; all that was dark, mystical, or obscure to me in its teachings, had been dissipated from my mind before the clear light that now dawned from its sacred pages; and, oh, how bright and glorious the truth appeared! All the contradictions and inconsistencies I had before found in the word were gone; and although there were many portions of which I was not satisfied I had a full understanding, yet so much light had emanated from it to the illumination of my before darkened mind, that I felt a delight in studying the Scripture which I had not before supposed could be derived from its teachings."—*Bliss, pages 76, 77.*

"With the solemn conviction that such momentous events were predicted in the Scriptures to be fulfilled in so short a space of time, the question came home to me with mighty power regarding my duty to the world, in view of the evidence that had affected my own mind."—*Ibid.,* page 81. He could not but feel that it was his duty to impart to others the light which he had received. He expected to encounter opposition from the ungodly, but was confident that all Christians would rejoice in the hope of meeting the Saviour whom they professed to love. His only fear was that in their great joy at the prospect of glorious deliverance, so soon to be consummated, many would receive the doctrine without sufficiently examining the Scriptures in demonstration of its truth. He therefore hesitated to present it, lest he should be in error and be the means of misleading others. He was thus led to review the evidences in support of the conclusions at which he had arrived, and to consider carefully every difficulty which presented itself to his mind. He found that objections vanished before the light of God's word, as mist before the rays of the sun. Five years spent thus left him fully convinced of the correctness of his position.

And now the duty of making known to others what he believed to be so clearly taught in the Scriptures, urged itself with new force upon him. "When I was about my business," he said, "it was continually ringing in my ears, 'Go and tell the world of their danger.' This text was constantly occurring to me: 'When I say unto the wicked, O wicked man, thou shalt surely die; if thou dost not speak to warn the wicked from his way, that wicked man shall die in his iniquity; but his blood will I require at thine hand. Nevertheless, if thou warn the wicked of his way to turn from it; if he do not turn from his way, he shall die in his iniquity; but thou hast delivered thy soul.' Ezekiel 33:8, 9. I felt that if the wicked could be effectually warned, multitudes of them would repent; and that if they were not warned, their blood might be required at my hand."—Bliss, page 92.

He began to present his views in private as he had opportunity, praying that some minister might feel their force and devote himself to their 331 promulgation. But he could not banish the conviction that he had a personal duty to perform in giving the warning. The words were ever recurring to his mind: "Go and tell it to the world; their blood will I require at thy hand." For nine years he waited, the burden still pressing upon his soul, until in 1831 he for the first time publicly gave the reasons of his faith.

As Elisha was called from following his oxen in the field, to receive the mantle of consecration to the prophetic office, so was William Miller called to leave his plow and open to the people the mysteries of the kingdom of God. With trembling he entered upon his work, leading his hearers down, step by step, through the prophetic periods to the second appearing of Christ. With every effort he gained strength and courage as he saw the widespread interest excited by his words.

It was only at the solicitation of his brethren, in whose words he heard the call of God, that Miller consented to present his views in public. He was now fifty years of age, unaccustomed to public speaking, and burdened with a sense of unfitness for the work before him. But from the first his labors were blessed in a remarkable manner to the salvation of souls. His first lecture was followed by a religious awakening in which thirteen entire families, with the exception of two persons, were converted. He was immediately urged to speak in other places, and in nearly every place his labor resulted in a revival of the work of God. Sinners were converted, Christians were roused to greater consecration, and deists and infidels were led to acknowledge the truth of the Bible and the Christian religion. The testimony of those among whom he labored was: "A class of minds are reached by him not within the influence of other men."—Ibid., page 138. His preaching was calculated to arouse the public mind to the great things of religion and to check the growing worldliness and sensuality of the age.

In nearly every town there were scores, in some, hundreds, converted as a result of his 332 preaching. In many places Protestant churches of nearly all denominations were thrown open to him, and the invitations to labor usually came from the ministers of the several congregations. It was his invariable rule not to labor in any place to which he had not been invited, yet he soon found himself unable to comply with half the requests that poured in upon him. Many who did not accept his views as to the exact time of the second advent were convinced of the certainty and nearness of Christ's coming and their need of preparation. In some of the large cities his work produced a marked impression. Liquor dealers abandoned the traffic and turned their shops into meeting rooms; gambling dens were broken up; infidels, deists, Universalists, and even the most abandoned profligates were reformed, some of whom had not entered a house of worship for years. Prayer meetings were established by the various denominations, in different quarters, at almost every hour, businessmen assembling at midday for prayer and praise. There was no extravagant excitement, but an almost universal solemnity on the minds of the people. His work, like that of the early Reformers, tended rather to convince the understanding and arouse the conscience than merely to excite the emotions.

In 1833 Miller received a license to preach, 333 from the Baptist Church, of which he was a member. A large number of the ministers of his denomination also approved his work, and it was with their formal sanction that he continued his labors. He traveled and preached unceasingly, though his personal labors were confined principally to the New England and Middle States. For several years his expenses were met wholly from his own private purse, and he never afterward received enough to meet the expense of travel to the places where he was invited. Thus his public labors, so far from being a pecuniary benefit, were a heavy tax upon his property, which gradually diminished during this period of his life. He was the father of a large family, but as they were all frugal and industrious, his farm sufficed for their maintenance as well as his own.

In 1833, two years after Miller began to present in public the evidences of Christ's soon coming, the last of the signs appeared which were promised by the Saviour as tokens of His second advent. Said Jesus: "The stars shall fall from heaven." Matthew 24:29. And John in the Revelation declared, as he beheld in vision the scenes that should herald the day of God: "The stars of heaven fell unto the earth, even as a fig tree casteth her untimely figs, when she is shaken of a mighty wind." Revelation 6:13. This prophecy received a striking and impressive fulfillment in the great meteoric shower of November 13, 1833. That was the most extensive and wonderful display of falling stars which has ever been recorded; "the whole firmament, over all the United States, being then, for hours, in fiery commotion! No celestial phenomenon has ever occurred in this country, since its first settlement, which was viewed with such intense admiration by one class in the community, or with so much dread and alarm by another." "Its sublimity and awful beauty still linger in many minds. . . . Never did rain fall much thicker than the meteors fell toward the earth; east, west, north, and south, it was the same. In a word, the whole heavens seemed in motion. . . . The display, as described in Professor Silliman's *Journal*, was seen all over North America. . . . From two o'clock until broad daylight, the sky being perfectly serene and cloudless, an incessant play of dazzlingly brilliant luminosities was kept up in the whole heavens."—R. M. Devens, *American Progress; or, The Great Events of the Greatest Century*, ch. 28, pars. 1-5.

"No language, indeed, can come up to the splendor of that magnificent display; . . . no one who did not witness it can form an adequate conception of its glory. It seemed as if the whole starry heavens had congregated at one point near the zenith, and were simultaneously shooting forth, with the velocity of lightning, to every part of the horizon; and yet they were not exhausted—thousands swiftly followed in the tracks of thousands, as if created for the occasion."—F. Reed, in the *Christian Advocate and Journal*, Dec. 13, 1833. "A more correct picture of a fig tree casting its figs when blown by a mighty wind, it was not possible to behold." — "The Old Countryman," in Portland *Evening Advertiser*, Nov. 26, 1833.

In the New York *Journal of Commerce* of November 14, 1833, appeared a long article regarding this wonderful phenomenon, containing this statement: "No philosopher or scholar has told or recorded an event, I suppose, like that of yesterday morning. A prophet eighteen hundred years ago foretold it exactly, if we will be at the trouble of understanding stars falling to mean falling stars, . . . in the only sense in which it is possible to be literally true."

Thus was displayed the last of those signs of His coming, concerning which Jesus bade His disciples: "When ye shall see all these things, *know* that it is near, even at the doors." Matthew 24:33. After these signs, John beheld, as the great event next impending, the heavens departing as a scroll, while the earth quaked, mountains and islands removed out of their places, and the wicked in terror sought to flee from the presence of the Son of man. Revelation 6:12-17.

Many who witnessed the falling of the stars, looked upon it as a herald of the coming judgment, "an awful type, a sure forerunner, a merciful sign, of that great and dreadful day." — "The Old Countryman," in Portland *Evening Advertiser*, Nov. 26, 1833. Thus the attention of the people was directed to the fulfillment of prophecy, and many were led to give heed to the warning of the second advent.

In the year 1840 another remarkable fulfillment of prophecy excited widespread interest. Two years before, Josiah Litch, one of the leading ministers preaching the second advent, published an exposition of Revelation 9, predicting the fall of the Ottoman Empire. According to his calculations, this power was to be overthrown "in A.D. 1840, sometime in the month of August;" and only a few days previous to its accomplishment he wrote: "Allowing the first period, 150 years, to have been exactly fulfilled before Deacozes ascended the throne by permission of the Turks, and that the 391 years, fifteen days, commenced at the close of the first period, it will end on the 11th of August, 1840, when the Ottoman power in Constantinople may be expected to be broken. And this, I believe, will be found to be the case."—Josiah Litch, in *Signs of the Times, and Expositor of Prophecy*, Aug. 1, 1840.

At the very time specified, Turkey, through her ambassadors, accepted the protection of the allied powers of Europe, and thus placed herself under the control of Christian nations. The event exactly fulfilled the prediction. (See Appendix.) When it became known, multitudes were convinced of the correctness of the principles of prophetic interpretation adopted by Miller and his associates, and a wonderful impetus was given to the advent movement. Men of learning and position united with Miller, both in preaching and in publishing his views, and from 1840 to 1844 the work rapidly extended.

William Miller possessed strong mental powers, disciplined by thought and study; and he added to these the wisdom of heaven by connecting himself with the Source of wisdom. He was a man of sterling worth, who could not but command respect and esteem wherever integrity of character and moral excellence were valued. Uniting true kindness of heart with Christian humility and the power of self-control, he was attentive and affable to all, ready to listen to the opinions of others and to weigh their arguments. Without passion or excitement he tested all theories and doctrines by the word of God, and his sound reasoning and thorough knowledge of the Scriptures enabled him to refute error and expose falsehood.

Yet he did not prosecute his work without bitter opposition. As with earlier Reformers, the truths which he presented were not received with favor by popular religious teachers. As these could not maintain their position by the Scriptures, they were driven to resort to the sayings and doctrines of men, to the traditions of the Fathers. But the word of God was the only testimony accepted by the preachers of the advent truth. "The Bible, and the Bible only," was their watchword. The lack of Scripture argument on the part of their opponents was supplied by ridicule and scoffing. Time, means, and talents were employed in maligning those whose only offense was that they looked with joy for the return of their Lord and were striving to live holy lives and to exhort others to prepare for His appearing.

Earnest were the efforts put forth to draw away the minds of the people from the subject of the second advent. It was made to appear a sin, something of which men should be ashamed, to study the prophecies which relate to the coming of Christ and the end of the world. Thus the popular ministry undermined faith in the word of God. Their teaching made men infidels, and many took license to walk after their own ungodly lusts. Then the authors of the evil charged it all upon Adventists.

While drawing crowded houses of intelligent and attentive hearers, Miller's name was seldom mentioned by the religious press except by way of ridicule or denunciation. The careless and ungodly, emboldened by the position of religious teachers, resorted to opprobrious epithets, to base and blasphemous witticisms, in their efforts to heap contumely upon him and his work. The gray-headed man who had left a comfortable home to travel at his own expense from city to city, from town to town, toiling unceasingly to bear to the world the solemn warning of the judgment near, was sneeringly denounced as a fanatic, a liar, a speculating knave.

The ridicule, falsehood, and abuse heaped upon him called forth indignant remonstrance, even from the secular press. "To treat a subject of such overwhelming majesty and fearful consequences," with lightness and ribaldry was declared by worldly men to be "not merely to sport with the feelings of its propagators and advocates," but "to make a jest of the day of judgment, to scoff at the Deity Himself, and contemn the terrors of His judgment bar."—Bliss, page 183.

The instigator of all evil sought not only to counteract the effect of the advent message, but to destroy the messenger himself. Miller made a practical application of Scripture truth to the hearts of his hearers, reproving their sins and 337 disturbing their self-satisfaction, and his plain and cutting words aroused their enmity. The opposition manifested by church members toward his message emboldened the baser classes to go to greater lengths; and enemies plotted to take his life as he should leave the place of meeting. But holy angels were in the throng, and one of these, in the form of a man, took the arm of this servant of the Lord and led him in safety from the angry mob. His work was not yet done, and Satan and his emissaries were disappointed in their purpose.

Despite all opposition, the interest in the advent movement had continued to increase. From scores and hundreds, the congregations had grown to as many thousands. Large accessions had been made to the various churches,

but after a time the spirit of opposition was manifested even against these converts, and the churches began to take disciplinary steps with those who had embraced Miller's views. This action called forth a response from his pen, in an address to Christians of all denominations, urging that if his doctrines were false, he should be shown his error from the Scriptures.

"What have we believed," he said, "that we have not been commanded to believe by the word of God, which you yourselves allow is the rule, and only rule, of our faith and practice? What have we done that should call down such virulent denunciations against us from pulpit and press, and give you just cause to exclude us [Adventists] from your churches and fellowship?" "If we are wrong, pray show us wherein consists our wrong. Show us from the word of God that we are in error; we have had ridicule enough; that can never convince us that we are in the wrong; the word of God alone can change our views. Our conclusions have been formed deliberately and prayerfully, as we have seen the evidence in the Scriptures."—*Ibid.*, pages 250, 252.

From age to age the warnings which God has sent to the world by His servants have been received with like incredulity and unbelief. When the iniquity of the antediluvians moved 338 Him to bring a flood of waters upon the earth, He first made known to them His purpose, that they might have opportunity to turn from their evil ways. For a hundred and twenty years was sounded in their ears the warning to repent, lest the wrath of God be manifested in their destruction. But the message seemed to them an idle tale, and they believed it not. Emboldened in their wickedness they mocked the messenger of God, made light of his entreaties, and even accused him of presumption. How dare one man stand up against all the great men of the earth? If Noah's message were true, why did not all the world see it and believe it? One man's assertion against the wisdom of thousands! They would not credit the warning, nor would they seek shelter in the ark.

Scoffers pointed to the things of nature,—to the unvarying succession of the seasons, to the blue skies that had never poured out rain, to the green fields refreshed by the soft dews of night,—and they cried out: "Doth he not speak parables?" In contempt they declared the preacher of righteousness to be a wild enthusiast; and they went on, more eager in their pursuit of pleasure, more intent upon their evil ways, than before. But their unbelief did not hinder the predicted event. God bore long with their wickedness, giving them ample opportunity for repentance; but at the appointed time His judgments were visited upon the rejecters of His mercy.

Christ declares that there will exist similar

unbelief concerning His second coming. As the people of Noah's day "knew not until the Flood came, and took them all away; so," in the words of our Saviour, "shall also the coming of the Son of man be." Matthew 24:39. When the professed people of God are uniting with the world, living as they live, and joining with them in forbidden pleasures; when the luxury of the world becomes the luxury of the church; when the marriage bells are chiming, and all are looking forward to many years of worldly prosperity— 339 then, suddenly as the lightning flashes from the heavens, will come the end of their bright visions and delusive hopes.

As God sent His servant to warn the world of the coming Flood, so He sent chosen messengers to make known the nearness of the final judgment. And as Noah's contemporaries laughed to scorn the predictions of the preacher of righteousness, so in Miller's day many, even of the professed people of God, scoffed at the words of warning.

And why were the doctrine and preaching of Christ's second coming so unwelcome to the churches? While to the wicked the advent of the Lord brings woe and desolation, to the righteous it is fraught with joy and hope. This great truth had been the consolation of God's faithful ones through all the ages; why had it become, like its Author, "a stone of stumbling" and "a rock of offense" to His professed people? It was our Lord Himself who promised His disciples: "If I go and prepare a place for you, I will come again, and receive you unto Myself." John 14:3. It was the compassionate Saviour, who, anticipating the loneliness and sorrow of His followers, commissioned angels to comfort them with the assurance that He would come again in person, even as He went into heaven. As the disciples stood gazing intently upward to catch the last glimpse of Him whom they loved, their attention was arrested by the words: "Ye men of Galilee, why stand ye gazing up into heaven? this same Jesus, which is taken up from you into heaven, shall so come in like manner as ye have seen Him go into heaven." Acts 1:11. Hope was kindled afresh by the angels' message. The disciples "returned to Jerusalem with great joy: and were continually in the temple, praising and blessing God." Luke 24:52, 53. They were not rejoicing because Jesus had been separated from them and they were left to struggle with the trials and temptations of the world, but because of the angels' assurance that He would come again.

The proclamation of Christ's coming should now be, as when made by the angels to the 340 shepherds of Bethlehem, good tidings of great joy. Those who really love the Saviour cannot but hail with gladness the announcement founded upon the word of God that He in whom their hopes of eternal life are centered is coming

again, not to be insulted, despised, and rejected, as at His first advent, but in power and glory, to redeem His people. It is those who do not love the Saviour that desire Him to remain away, and there can be no more conclusive evidence that the churches have departed from God than the irritation and animosity excited by this Heaven-sent message.

Those who accepted the advent doctrine were roused to the necessity of repentance and humiliation before God. Many had long been halting between Christ and the world; now they felt that it was time to take a stand. "The things of eternity assumed to them an unwonted reality. Heaven was brought near, and they felt themselves guilty before God."—Bliss, page 146. Christians were quickened to new spiritual life. They were made to feel that time was short, that what they had to do for their fellow men must be done quickly. Earth receded, eternity seemed to open before them, and the soul, with all that pertained to its immortal weal or woe, was felt to eclipse every temporal object. The Spirit of God rested upon them and gave power to their earnest appeals to their brethren, as well as to sinners, to prepare for the day of God. The silent testimony of their daily life was a constant rebuke to formal and unconsecrated church members. These did not wish to be disturbed in their pursuit of pleasure, their devotion to money-making, and their ambition for worldly honor. Hence the enmity and opposition excited against the advent faith and those who proclaimed it.

As the arguments from the prophetic periods were found to be impregnable, opposers endeavored to discourage investigation of the subject by teaching that the prophecies were sealed. Thus Protestants followed in the steps of Romanists. While the papal church withholds the Bible (see Appendix) from the people, Protestant churches claimed that an important part of 341 the Sacred Word—and that the part which brings to view truths specially applicable to our time—could not be understood.

Ministers and people declared that the prophecies of Daniel and the Revelation were incomprehensible mysteries. But Christ directed His disciples to the words of the prophet Daniel concerning events to take place in their time, and said: "Whoso readeth, let him *understand*." Matthew 24:15. And the assertion that the Revelation is a mystery, not to be understood, is contradicted by the very title of the book: "The Revelation of Jesus Christ, which God gave unto Him, to show unto His servants things which must shortly come to pass. . . . *Blessed* is he that *readeth*, and they that *hear* the words of this prophecy, and *keep* those things which are written therein: for the time is at hand." Revelation 1:1-3.

Says the prophet: "Blessed is he that readeth"—there are those who will not read; the blessing is not for them. "And they that hear"—there are some, also, who refuse to hear anything concerning the prophecies; the blessing is not for this class. "And keep those things which are written therein"—many refuse to heed the warnings and instructions contained in the Revelation; none of these can claim the blessing promised. All who ridicule the subjects of the prophecy and mock at the symbols here solemnly given, all who refuse to reform their lives and to prepare for the coming of the Son of man, will be unblessed.

In view of the testimony of Inspiration, how dare men teach that the Revelation is a mystery beyond the reach of human understanding? It is a mystery revealed, a book opened. The study of the Revelation directs the mind to the prophecies of Daniel, and both present most important instruction, given of God to men, concerning events to take place at the close of this world's history.

To John were opened scenes of deep and thrilling interest in the experience of the church. He saw the position, dangers, conflicts, and final deliverance of the people of God. He 342 records the closing messages which are to ripen the harvest of the earth, either as sheaves for the heavenly garner or as fagots for the fires of destruction. Subjects of vast importance were revealed to him, especially for the last church, that those who should turn from error to truth might be instructed concerning the perils and conflicts before them. None need be in darkness in regard to what is coming upon the earth.

Why, then, this widespread ignorance concerning an important part of Holy Writ? Why this general reluctance to investigate its teachings? It is the result of a studied effort of the prince of darkness to conceal from men that which reveals his deceptions. For this reason, Christ the Revelator, foreseeing the warfare that would be waged against the study of the Revelation, pronounced a blessing upon all who should read, hear, and observe the words of the prophecy.

343

19
Light Through Darkness

The work of God in the earth presents, from age to age, a striking similarity in every great reformation or religious movement. The principles of God's dealing with men are ever the same. The important movements of the present have their parallel in those of the past, and the experience of the church in former ages has lessons of great value for our own time.

No truth is more clearly taught in the Bible than that God by His Holy Spirit especially directs His servants on earth in the great movements for the carrying forward of the work of salvation. Men are instruments in the hand of God, employed by Him to accomplish His purposes of grace and mercy. Each has his part to act; to each is granted a measure of light, adapted to the necessities of his time, and sufficient to enable him to perform the work which God has given him to do. But no man, however honored of Heaven, has ever attained to a full understanding of the great plan of redemption, or even to a perfect appreciation of the divine purpose in the work for his own time. Men do not fully understand what God would accomplish by the work which He gives them to do; they do not comprehend, in all its bearings, the message which they utter in His name.

"Canst thou by searching find out God? canst thou find out the Almighty unto perfection?" "My thoughts are not your thoughts, neither are your ways My ways, saith the Lord. For as the 344 heavens are higher than the earth, so are My ways higher than your ways, and My thoughts than your thoughts." "I am God, and there is none like Me, declaring the end from the beginning, and from ancient times the things that are not yet done." Job 11:7; Isaiah 55:8, 9; 46:9, 10.

Even the prophets who were favored with the special illumination of the Spirit did not fully comprehend the import of the revelations committed to them. The meaning was to be unfolded from age to age, as the people of God should need the instruction therein contained.

Peter, writing of the salvation brought to light through the gospel, says: Of this salvation "the prophets have inquired and searched diligently, who prophesied of the grace that should come unto you: searching what, or what manner of time the Spirit of Christ which was in them did signify, when it testified beforehand the sufferings of Christ, and the glory that should follow. Unto whom it was revealed, that not unto them-selves, but unto us they did minister." 1 Peter 1:10-12.

Yet while it was not given to the prophets to understand fully the things revealed to them, they earnestly sought to obtain all the light which God had been pleased to make manifest. They "inquired and searched diligently," "searching what, or what manner of time the Spirit of Christ which was in them did signify." What a lesson to the people of God in the Christian age, for whose benefit these prophecies were given to His servants! "Unto whom it was revealed, that not unto themselves, but unto us they did minister." Witness those holy men of God as they "inquired and searched diligently" concerning revelations given them for generations that were yet unborn. Contrast their holy zeal with the listless unconcern with which the favored ones of later ages treat this gift of Heaven. What a rebuke to the ease-loving, world-loving indifference which is content to declare that the prophecies cannot be understood!

Though the finite minds of men are inadequate to enter into the counsels of the Infinite One, or to understand fully the working out of His purposes, yet often it is because of some error or neglect on their own part that they so dimly comprehend the messages of Heaven. Not infrequently the minds of the people, and even of God's servants, are so blinded by human opinions, the traditions and false teaching of men, that they are able only partially to grasp the great things which He has revealed in His word. Thus it was with the disciples of Christ, even when the Saviour was with them in person. Their minds had become imbued with the popular conception of the Messiah as a temporal prince, who was to exalt Israel to the throne of the universal empire, and they could not understand the meaning of His words foretelling His sufferings and death.

Christ Himself had sent them forth with the message: "The time is fulfilled, and the kingdom of God is at hand: repent ye, and believe the gospel." Mark 1:15. That message was based on the prophecy of Daniel 9. The sixty-nine weeks were declared by the angel to extend to "the Messiah the Prince," and with high hopes and joyful anticipations the disciples looked forward to the establishment of Messiah's kingdom at Jerusalem to rule over the whole earth.

They preached the message which Christ had committed to them, though they themselves misapprehended its meaning. While their announcement was founded on Daniel 9:25, they did not see, in the next verse of the same chapter, that Messiah was to be cut off. From their very birth their hearts had been set upon the anticipated glory of an earthly empire, and this blinded their understanding alike to the specifications of the prophecy and to the words of Christ.

They performed their duty in presenting to the Jewish nation the invitation of mercy, and then, at the very time when they expected to see their Lord ascend the throne of David, they beheld Him seized as a malefactor, scourged, derided, and condemned, and lifted up on the cross of Calvary. What despair and anguish wrung the hearts of those disciples during the days while their Lord was sleeping in the tomb!

Christ had come at the exact time and in the manner foretold by prophecy. The testimony of Scripture had been fulfilled in every detail of His ministry. He had preached the message of salvation, and "His word was with power." The hearts of His hearers had witnessed that it was of Heaven. The word and the Spirit of God attested the divine commission of His Son.

The disciples still clung with undying affection to their beloved Master. And yet their minds were shrouded in uncertainty and doubt. In their anguish they did not then recall the words of Christ pointing forward to His suffering and death. If Jesus of Nazareth had been the true Messiah, would they have been thus plunged in grief and disappointment? This was the question that tortured their souls while the Saviour lay in His sepulcher during the hopeless hours of that Sabbath which intervened between His death and His resurrection.

Though the night of sorrow gathered dark about these followers of Jesus, yet were they not forsaken. Saith the prophet: "When I sit in darkness, the Lord shall be a light unto me. . . . He will bring me forth to the light, and I shall behold His righteousness." "Yea, the darkness hideth not from Thee; but the night shineth as the day: the darkness and the light are both alike to Thee." God hath spoken: "Unto the upright there ariseth light in the darkness." "I will bring the blind by a way that they knew not; I will lead them in paths that they have not known: I will make darkness light before them, and crooked things straight. These things will I do unto them, and not forsake them." Micah 7:8, 9; Psalms 139:12; 112:4; Isaiah 42:16.

The announcement which had been made by the disciples in the name of the Lord was in every particular correct, and the events to which it pointed were even then taking place. "The time is fulfilled, the kingdom of God is at hand," had been their message. At the expiration of "the time"—the sixty-nine weeks of Daniel 9, which were to extend to the Messiah, "the Anointed One"—Christ had received the anointing of the Spirit after His baptism by John in Jordan. And the "kingdom of God" which they had declared to be at hand was established by the death of Christ. This kingdom was not, as they had been taught to believe, an earthly empire. Nor was it that future, immortal kingdom which shall be set up when "the kingdom and dominion, and the greatness of the kingdom under the whole heaven, shall be given to the people of the saints of the Most High;" that everlasting kingdom, in which "all dominions shall serve and obey Him." Daniel 7:27. As used in the Bible, the expression "kingdom of God" is employed to designate both the kingdom of grace and the kingdom of glory. The kingdom of grace is brought to view by Paul in the Epistle to the Hebrews. After pointing to Christ, the compassionate intercessor who is "touched with the feeling of our infirmities," the apostle says: "Let us therefore come boldly unto *the throne of grace*, that we may obtain mercy, and find grace." Hebrews 4:15, 16. The throne of grace represents the kingdom of grace; for the existence of a throne implies the existence of a kingdom. In many of His parables Christ uses the expression "the kingdom of heaven" to designate the work of divine grace upon the hearts of men.

So the throne of glory represents the kingdom of glory; and this kingdom is referred to in the Saviour's words: "When the Son of man shall come in His glory, and all the holy angels with Him, then shall He sit upon the throne of His glory: and before Him shall be gathered all nations." Matthew 25:31, 32. This kingdom is yet future. It is not to be set up until the second advent of Christ.

The kingdom of grace was instituted immediately after the fall of man, when a plan was devised for the redemption of the guilty race. It then existed in the purpose and by the promise of God; and through faith, men could become its subjects. Yet it was not actually established 348 until the death of Christ. Even after entering upon His earthly mission, the Saviour, wearied with the stubbornness and ingratitude of men, might have drawn back from the sacrifice of Calvary. In Gethsemane the cup of woe trembled in His hand. He might even then have wiped the blood-sweat from His brow and have left the guilty race to perish in their iniquity. Had He done this, there could have been no redemption for fallen men. But when the Saviour yielded up His life, and with His expiring breath cried out, "It is finished," then the fulfillment of the plan of redemption was assured. The promise of salvation made to the sinful pair in Eden was ratified. The kingdom of grace, which had before existed by the promise of God, was then established.

Thus the death of Christ—the very event which the disciples had looked upon as the final destruction of their hope—was that which made it forever sure. While it had brought them a cruel disappointment, it was the climax of proof that their belief had been correct. The event that had filled them with mourning and despair was that which opened the door of hope to every child of Adam, and in which centered the future life and eternal happiness of all God's faithful ones in all the ages.

Purposes of infinite mercy were reaching their fulfillment, even through the disappointment of the disciples. While their hearts had been won by the divine grace and power of His teaching, who "spake as never man spake," yet intermingled with the pure gold of their love for Jesus, was the base alloy of worldly pride and selfish ambitions. Even in the Passover chamber, at that solemn hour when their Master was already entering the shadow of Gethsemane, there was "a strife among them, which of them should be accounted the greatest." Luke 22:24. Their vision was filled with the throne, the crown, and the glory, while just before them lay the shame and agony of the garden, the judgment hall, the cross of Calvary. It was their 349 pride of heart, their thirst for worldly glory, that

had led them to cling so tenaciously to the false teaching of their time, and to pass unheeded the Saviour's words showing the true nature of His kingdom, and pointing forward to His agony and death. And these errors resulted in the trial—sharp but needful—which was permitted for their correction. Though the disciples had mistaken the meaning of their message, and had failed to realize their expectations, yet they had preached the warning given them of God, and the Lord would reward their faith and honor their obedience. To them was to be entrusted the work of heralding to all nations the glorious gospel of their risen Lord. It was to prepare them for this work that the experience which seemed to them so bitter had been permitted.

After His resurrection Jesus appeared to His disciples on the way to Emmaus, and, "beginning at Moses and all the prophets, He expounded unto them in all the Scriptures the things concerning Himself." Luke 24:27. The hearts of the disciples were stirred. Faith was kindled. They were "begotten again into a lively hope" even before Jesus revealed Himself to them. It was His purpose to enlighten their understanding and to fasten their faith upon the "sure word of prophecy." He wished the truth to take firm root in their minds, not merely because it was supported by His personal testimony, but because of the unquestionable evidence presented by the symbols and shadows of the typical law, and by the prophecies of the Old Testament. It was needful for the followers of Christ to have an intelligent faith, not only in their own behalf, but that they might carry the knowledge of Christ to the world. And as the very first step in imparting this knowledge, Jesus directed the disciples to "Moses and all the prophets." Such was the testimony given by the risen Saviour to the value and importance of the Old Testament Scriptures.

What a change was wrought in the hearts of the disciples as they looked once more on the loved countenance of their Master! Luke 24:32. 350 In a more complete and perfect sense than ever before they had "found Him, of whom Moses in the law, and the prophets, did write." The uncertainty, the anguish, the despair, gave place to perfect assurance, to unclouded faith. What marvel that after His ascension they "were continually in the temple, praising and blessing God." The people, knowing only of the Saviour's ignominious death, looked to see in their faces the expression of sorrow, confusion, and defeat; but they saw there gladness and triumph. What a preparation these disciples had received for the work before them! They had passed through the deepest trial which it was possible for them to experience, and had seen how, when to human vision all was lost, the word of God had been triumphantly accomplished. Henceforward what could daunt their faith or chill the ardor of their love? In the keenest sorrow they had "strong consolation," a hope which was as "an anchor of the soul, both sure and steadfast." Hebrews 6:18, 19. They had been witness to the wisdom and power of God, and they were "persuaded, that neither death, nor life, nor angels, nor principalities, nor powers, nor things present, nor things to come, nor height, nor depth, nor any other creature," would be able to separate them from "the love of God, which is in Christ Jesus our Lord." "In all these things," they said, "we are more than conquerors through Him that loved us." Romans 8:38, 39, 37. "The word of the Lord endureth forever." 1 Peter 1:25. And "who is he that condemneth? It is Christ that died, yea rather, that is *risen again*, who is even at the right hand of God, who also maketh intercession for us." Romans 8:34.

Saith the Lord: "My people shall never be ashamed." Joel 2:26. "Weeping may endure for a night, but joy cometh in the morning." Psalm 30:5. When on His resurrection day these disciples met the Saviour, and their hearts burned within them as they listened to His words; when they looked upon the head and hands and feet that had been bruised for them; when, before His ascension, Jesus led them out as far as Bethany, and lifting up His hands in blessing, bade them, "Go ye into all the world, and preach the gospel," adding, "Lo, I am with you alway" (Mark 16:15; Matthew 28:20); when on the Day of Pentecost the promised Comforter descended and the power from on high was given and the souls of the believers thrilled with the conscious presence of their ascended Lord—then, even though, like His, their pathway led through sacrifice and martyrdom, would they have exchanged the ministry of the gospel of His grace, with the "crown of righteousness" to be received at His coming, for the glory of an earthly throne, which had been the hope of their earlier discipleship? He who is "able to do exceeding abundantly above all that we ask or think," had granted them, with the fellowship of His sufferings, the communion of His joy—the joy of "bringing many sons unto glory," joy unspeakable, an "eternal weight of glory," to which, says Paul, "our light affliction, which is but for a moment," is "not worthy to be compared."

The experience of the disciples who preached the "gospel of the kingdom" at the first advent of Christ, had its counterpart in the experience of those who proclaimed the message of His second advent. As the disciples went out preaching, "The time is fulfilled, the kingdom of God is at hand," so Miller and his associates proclaimed that the longest and last prophetic period brought to view in the Bible was about to expire, that the judgment was at hand, and the everlasting kingdom was to be ushered in. The preaching of the disciples in regard to time was

based on the seventy weeks of Daniel 9. The message given by Miller and his associates announced the termination of the 2300 days of Daniel 8:14, of which the seventy weeks form a part. The preaching of each was based upon the fulfillment of a different portion of the same great prophetic period.

Like the first disciples, William Miller and his associates did not, themselves, fully comprehend the import of the message which they bore. Errors that had been long established in the church prevented them from arriving at a correct interpretation of an important point in the prophecy. Therefore, though they proclaimed the message which God had committed to them to be given to the world, yet through a misapprehension of its meaning they suffered disappointment.

In explaining Daniel 8:14, "Unto two thousand and three hundred days; then shall the sanctuary be cleansed," Miller, as has been stated, adopted the generally received view that the earth is the sanctuary, and he believed that the cleansing of the sanctuary represented the purification of the earth by fire at the coming of the Lord. When, therefore, he found that the close of the 2300 days was definitely foretold, he concluded that this revealed the time of the second advent. His error resulted from accepting the popular view as to what constitutes the sanctuary.

In the typical system, which was a shadow of the sacrifice and priesthood of Christ, the cleansing of the sanctuary was the last service performed by the high priest in the yearly round of ministration. It was the closing work of the atonement—a removal or putting away of sin from Israel. It prefigured the closing work in the ministration of our High Priest in heaven, in the removal or blotting out of the sins of His people, which are registered in the heavenly records. This service involves a work of investigation, a work of judgment; and it immediately precedes the coming of Christ in the clouds of heaven with power and great glory; for when He comes, every case has been decided. Says Jesus: "My reward is with Me, to give every man according as his work shall be." Revelation 22:12. It is this work of judgment, immediately preceding the second advent, that is announced in the first angel's message of Revelation 14:7: "Fear God, and give glory to Him; for the hour of His judgment is come."

Those who proclaimed this warning gave the right message at the right time. But as the early disciples declared, "The time is fulfilled, and the kingdom of God is at hand," based on the prophecy of Daniel 9, while they failed to perceive that the death of the Messiah was foretold in the same scripture, so Miller and his associates preached the message based on Daniel 8:14 and Revelation 14:7, and failed to see that there were still other messages brought to view in Revelation 14, which were also to be given before the advent of the Lord. As the disciples were mistaken in regard to the kingdom to be set up at the end of the seventy weeks, so Adventists were mistaken in regard to the event to take place at the expiration of the 2300 days. In both cases there was an acceptance of, or rather an adherence to, popular errors that blinded the mind to the truth. Both classes fulfilled the will of God in delivering the message which He desired to be given, and both, through their own misapprehension of their message, suffered disappointment.

Yet God accomplished His own beneficent purpose in permitting the warning of the judgment to be given just as it was. The great day was at hand, and in His providence the people were brought to the test of a definite time, in order to reveal to them what was in their hearts. The message was designed for the testing and purification of the church. They were to be led to see whether their affections were set upon this world or upon Christ and heaven. They professed to love the Saviour; now they were to prove their love. Were they ready to renounce their worldly hopes and ambitions, and welcome with joy the advent of their Lord? The message was designed to enable them to discern their true spiritual state; it was sent in mercy to arouse them to seek the Lord with repentance and humiliation.

The disappointment also, though the result of their own misapprehension of the message which they gave, was to be overruled for good. It would test the hearts of those who had professed to receive the warning. In the face of their disappointment would they rashly give up their experience and cast away their confidence in God's word? or would they, in prayer and humility, seek to discern where they had failed to comprehend the significance of the prophecy? How many had moved from fear, or from impulse and excitement? How many were half-hearted and unbelieving? Multitudes professed to love the appearing of the Lord. When called to endure the scoffs and reproach of the world, and the test of delay and disappointment, would they renounce the faith? Because they did not immediately understand the dealings of God with them, would they cast aside truths sustained by the clearest testimony of His word?

This test would reveal the strength of those who with real faith had obeyed what they believed to be the teaching of the word and the Spirit of God. It would teach them, as only such an experience could, the danger of accepting the theories and interpretations of men, instead of making the Bible its own interpreter. To the children of faith the perplexity and sorrow resulting from their error would work the needed correction. They would be led to a closer study of the prophetic word. They would be taught to examine more carefully the foundation of their faith, and to reject everything, however widely accepted by the Christian world, that was not founded upon the Scriptures of truth.

With these believers, as with the first disciples, that which in the hour of trial seemed dark to their understanding would afterward be made plain. When they should see the "end of the Lord" they would know that, notwithstanding the trial resulting from their errors, His purposes of love toward them had been steadily fulfilling. They would learn by a blessed experience that He is "very pitiful, and of tender mercy;" that all His paths "are mercy and truth unto such as keep His covenant and His testimonies."

20

A Great Religious Awakening

A great religious awakening under the proclamation of Christ's soon coming is foretold in the prophecy of the first angel's message of Revelation 14. An angel is seen flying "in the midst of heaven, having the everlasting gospel to preach unto them that dwell on the earth, and to every nation, and kindred, and tongue, and people." "With a loud voice" he proclaims the message: "Fear God, and give glory to Him; for the hour of His judgment is come: and worship Him that made heaven, and earth, and the sea, and the fountains of waters." Verses 6, 7.

The fact that an angel is said to be the herald of this warning is significant. By the purity, the glory, and the power of the heavenly messenger, divine wisdom has been pleased to represent the exalted character of the work to be accomplished by the message and the power and glory that were to attend it. And the angel's flight "in the midst of heaven," the "loud voice" with which the warning is uttered, and its promulgation to all "that dwell on the earth," — "to every nation, and kindred, and tongue, and people," — give evidence of the rapidity and world-wide extent of the movement.

The message itself sheds light as to the time when this movement is to take place. It is declared to be a part of the "everlasting gospel;" and it announces the opening of the judgment. The message of salvation has been preached in all ages; but this message is a part of the gospel which could be proclaimed only in the last days, for only then would it be true that the hour of judgment *had come*. The prophecies present a succession of events leading down to the opening of the judgment. This is especially true of the book of Daniel. But that part of his prophecy which related to the last days, Daniel was bidden to close up and seal "to the time of the end."

Not till we reach this time could a message concerning the judgment be proclaimed, based on a fulfillment of these prophecies. But at the time of the end, says the prophet, "many shall run to and fro, and knowledge shall be increased." Daniel 12:4.

The apostle Paul warned the church not to look for the coming of Christ in his day. "That day shall not come," he says, "except there come a falling away first, and that man of sin be revealed." 2 Thessalonians 2:3. Not till after the great apostasy, and the long period of the reign of the "man of sin," can we look for the advent of our Lord. The "man of sin," which is also styled "the mystery of iniquity," "the son of perdition," and "that wicked," represents the papacy, which, as foretold in prophecy, was to maintain its supremacy for 1260 years. This period ended in 1798. The coming of Christ could not take place before that time. Paul covers with his caution the whole of the Christian dispensation down to the year 1798. It is this side of that time that the message of Christ's second coming is to be proclaimed.

No such message has ever been given in past ages. Paul, as we have seen, did not preach it; he pointed his brethren into the then far-distant future for the coming of the Lord. The Reformers did not proclaim it. Martin Luther placed the judgment about three hundred years in the future from his day. But since 1798 the book of Daniel has been unsealed, knowledge of the prophecies has increased, and many have proclaimed the solemn message of the judgment near.

357   Like the great Reformation of the sixteenth century, the advent movement appeared in different countries of Christendom at the same time. In both Europe and America men of faith and prayer were led to the study of the prophecies, and, tracing down the inspired record, they saw convincing evidence that the end of all things was at hand. In different lands there were isolated bodies of Christians who, solely by the study of the Scriptures, arrived at the belief that the Saviour's advent was near.

In 1821, three years after Miller had arrived at his exposition of the prophecies pointing to the time of the judgment, Dr. Joseph Wolff, "the missionary to the world," began to proclaim the Lord's soon coming. Wolff was born in Germany, of Hebrew parentage, his father being a Jewish rabbi. While very young he was convinced of the truth of the Christian religion. Of an active, inquiring mind, he had been an eager listener to the conversations that took place in his father's house as devout Hebrews daily assembled to recount the hopes and anticipations of their people, the glory of the coming Messiah, and the restoration of Israel. One day hearing Jesus of Nazareth mentioned, the boy inquired who He was. "A Jew of the greatest

talent," was the answer; "but as He pretended to be the Messiah, the Jewish tribunal sentenced Him to death." "Why," rejoined the questioner, "is Jerusalem destroyed, and why are we in captivity?" "Alas, alas!" answered his father, "because the Jews murdered the prophets." The thought was at once suggested to the child: "Perhaps Jesus was also a prophet, and the Jews killed Him when He was innocent."—*Travels and Adventures of the Rev. Joseph Wolff*, vol. 1, p. 6. So strong was this feeling that, though forbidden to enter a Christian church, he would often linger outside to listen to the preaching.

When only seven years old he was boasting to an aged Christian neighbor of the future triumph of Israel at the advent of the Messiah, when the old man said kindly: "Dear boy, I will tell you who the real Messiah was: He was Jesus of Nazareth, . . . whom your ancestors   358 have crucified, as they did the prophets of old. Go home and read the fifty-third chapter of Isaiah, and you will be convinced that Jesus Christ is the Son of God."—*Ibid.*, vol. 1, p. 7. Conviction at once fastened upon him. He went home and read the scripture, wondering to see how perfectly it had been fulfilled in Jesus of Nazareth. Were the words of the Christian true? The boy asked of his father an explanation of the prophecy, but was met with a silence so stern that he never again dared to refer to the subject. This, however, only increased his desire to know more of the Christian religion.

The knowledge he sought was studiously kept from him in his Jewish home; but, when only eleven years old, he left his father's house and went out into the world to gain for himself an education, to choose his religion and his lifework. He found a home for a time with kinsmen, but was soon driven from them as an apostate, and alone and penniless he had to make his own way among strangers. He went from place to place, studying diligently and maintaining himself by teaching Hebrew. Through the influence of a Catholic instructor he was led to accept the Romish faith and formed the purpose of becoming a missionary to his own people. With this object he went, a few years later, to pursue his studies in the College of the Propaganda at Rome. Here his habit of independent thought and candid speech brought upon him the imputation of heresy. He openly attacked the abuses of the church and urged the necessity of reform. Though at first treated with special favor by the papal dignitaries, he was after a time removed from Rome. Under the surveillance of the church he went from place to place, until it became evident that he could never be brought to submit to the bondage of Romanism. He was declared to be incorrigible and was left at liberty to go where he pleased. He now made his way to England and, professing the Protestant faith, united with the English Church. After two years' study he set out, in 1821, upon his mission.

359 While Wolff accepted the great truth of Christ's first advent as "a Man of Sorrows, and acquainted with grief," he saw that the prophecies bring to view with equal clearness His second advent with power and glory. And while he sought to lead his people to Jesus of Nazareth as the Promised One, and to point them to His first coming in humiliation as a sacrifice for the sins of men, he taught them also of His second coming as a king and deliverer.

"Jesus of Nazareth, the true Messiah," he said, "whose hands and feet were pierced, who was brought like a lamb to the slaughter, who was the Man of Sorrows and acquainted with grief, who after the scepter was taken from Judah, and the legislative power from between his feet, came the first time; shall come the second time in the clouds of heaven, and with the trump of the Archangel" (Joseph Wolff, Researches and Missionary Labors, page 62) "and shall stand upon the Mount of Olives; and that dominion, once consigned to Adam over the creation, and forfeited by him (Genesis 1:26; 3:17), shall be given to Jesus. He shall be king over all the earth. The groanings and lamentations of the creation shall cease, but songs of praises and thanksgivings shall be heard. . . . When Jesus comes in the glory of His Father, with the holy angels, . . . the dead believers shall rise first. 1 Thessalonians 4:16; 1 Corinthians 15:32. This is what we Christians call the first resurrection. Then the animal kingdom shall change its nature (Isaiah 11:6-9), and be subdued unto Jesus. Psalm 8. Universal peace shall prevail."—Journal of the Rev. Joseph Wolff, pages 378, 379. "The Lord again shall look down upon the earth, and say, 'Behold, it is very good.'"—Ibid., page 294.

Wolff believed the coming of the Lord to be at hand, his interpretation of the prophetic periods placing the great consummation within a very few years of the time pointed out by Miller. To those who urged from the scripture, "Of that day and hour knoweth no man," that men are to know nothing concerning the nearness of the advent, Wolff replied: "Did our Lord say that that day and hour should never be known? Did He not give us signs of the times, 360 in order that we may know at least the approach of His coming, as one knows the approach of the summer by the fig tree putting forth its leaves? Matthew 24:32. Are we never to know that period, whilst He Himself exhorteth us not only to read Daniel the prophet, but to understand it? and in that very Daniel, where it is said that the words were shut up to the time of the end (which was the case in his time), and that 'many shall run to and fro' (a Hebrew expression for observing and thinking upon the time), 'and knowledge' (regarding that time) 'shall be increased.' Daniel 12:4. Besides this, our Lord does not intend to say by this, that the approach of the time shall not be known, but that the exact 'day and hour knoweth no man.' Enough, He does say, shall be known by the signs of the times, to induce us to prepare for His coming, as Noah prepared the ark."—Wolff, Researches and Missionary Labors, pages 404, 405.

Concerning the popular system of interpreting, or misinterpreting, the Scriptures, Wolff wrote: "The greater part of the Christian church have swerved from the plain sense of Scripture, and have turned to the phantomizing system of the Buddhists, who believe that the future happiness of mankind will consist in moving about in the air, and suppose that when they are reading Jews they must understand Gentiles; and when they read Jerusalem, they must understand the church; and if it is said earth, it means sky; and for the coming of the Lord they must understand the progress of the missionary societies; and going up to the mountain of the Lord's house, signifies a grand class meeting of Methodists."—Journal of the Rev. Joseph Wolff, page 96.

During the twenty-four years from 1821 to 1845, Wolff traveled extensively: in Africa, visiting Egypt and Abyssinia; in Asia, traversing Palestine, Syria, Persia, Bokhara, and India. He also visited the United States, on the journey thither preaching on the island of Saint Helena. He arrived in New York in August, 1837; and, after speaking in that city, he preached in Philadelphia and Baltimore, and finally proceeded to Washington. Here, he says, "on a 361 motion brought forward by the ex-President, John Quincy Adams, in one of the houses of Congress, the House unanimously granted to me the use of the Congress Hall for a lecture, which I delivered on a Saturday, honored with the presence of all the members of Congress, and also of the bishop of Virginia, and of the clergy and citizens of Washington. The same honor was granted to me by the members of the government of New Jersey and Pennsylvania, in whose presence I delivered lectures on my researches in Asia, and also on the personal reign of Jesus Christ."—Ibid., pages 398, 399.

Dr. Wolff traveled in the most barbarous countries without the protection of any European authority, enduring many hardships and surrounded with countless perils. He was bastinadoed and starved, sold as a slave, and three times condemned to death. He was beset by robbers, and sometimes nearly perished from thirst. Once he was stripped of all that he possessed and left to travel hundreds of miles on foot through the mountains, the snow beating in his face and his naked feet benumbed by contact with the frozen ground.

When warned against going unarmed among savage and hostile tribes, he declared himself "provided with arms" — "prayer, zeal for Christ, and confidence in His help." "I am also," he said, "provided with the love of God and my neighbor in my heart, and the Bible is in my hand."—W. H. D. Adams, In Perils Oft, page 192. The Bible in Hebrew and English he carried with him wherever he went. Of one of his later journeys he says: "I . . . kept the Bible open in my hand. I felt my power was in the Book, and that its might would sustain me." — *Ibid.*, page 201.

Thus he persevered in his labors until the message of the judgment had been carried to a large part of the habitable globe. Among Jews, Turks, Parsees, Hindus, and many other nationalities and races he distributed the word of God in these various tongues and everywhere heralded the approaching reign of the Messiah.

In his travels in Bokhara he found the doctrine of the Lord's soon coming held by a
362 remote and isolated people. The Arabs of Yemen, he says, "are in possession of a book called *Seera*, which gives notice of the second coming of Christ and His reign in glory; and they expect great events to take place in the year 1840."—*Journal of the Rev. Joseph Wolff*, page 377. "In Yemen . . . I spent six days with the children of Rechab. They drink no wine, plant no vineyard, sow no seed, and live in tents, and remember good old Jonadab, the son of Rechab; and I found in their company children of Israel, of the tribe of Dan, . . . who expect, with the children of Rechab, the speedy arrival of the Messiah in the clouds of heaven."—*Ibid.*, page 389.

A similar belief was found by another missionary to exist in Tatary. A Tatar priest put the question to the missionary as to when Christ would come the second time. When the missionary answered that he knew nothing about it, the priest seemed greatly surprised at such ignorance in one who professed to be a Bible teacher, and stated his own belief, founded on prophecy, that Christ would come about 1844.

As early as 1826 the advent message began to be preached in England. The movement here did not take so definite a form as in America; the exact time of the advent was not so generally taught, but the great truth of Christ's soon coming in power and glory was extensively proclaimed. And this not among the dissenters and nonconformists only. Mourant Brock, an English writer, states that about seven hundred ministers of the Church of England were engaged in preaching "this gospel of the kingdom." The message pointing to 1844 as the time of the Lord's coming was also given in Great Britain. Advent publications from the United States were widely circulated. Books and journals were republished in England. And in 1842 Robert Winter, an Englishman by birth, who had received the advent faith in America,

returned to his native country to herald the coming of the Lord. Many united with him in the work, and the message of the judgment was proclaimed in various parts of England.

In South America, in the midst of barbarism 363 and priestcraft, Lacunza, a Spaniard and a Jesuit, found his way to the Scriptures and thus received the truth of Christ's speedy return. Impelled to give the warning, yet desiring to escape the censures of Rome, he published his views under the assumed name of "Rabbi Ben-Ezra," representing himself as a converted Jew. Lacunza lived in the eighteenth century, but it was about 1825 that his book, having found its way to London, was translated into the English language. Its publication served to deepen the interest already awakening in England in the subject of the second advent.

In Germany the doctrine had been taught in the eighteenth century by Bengel, a minister in the Lutheran Church and a celebrated Biblical scholar and critic. Upon completing his education, Bengel had "devoted himself to the study of theology, to which the grave and religious tone of his mind, deepened by his early training and discipline, naturally inclined him. Like other young men of thoughtful character, before and since, he had to struggle with doubts and difficulties of a religious nature, and he alludes, with much feeling, to the 'many arrows which pierced his poor heart, and made his youth hard to bear.'" Becoming a member of the consistory of Wurttemberg, he advocated the cause of religious liberty. "While maintaining the rights and privileges of the church, he was an advocate for all reasonable freedom being accorded to those who felt themselves bound, on grounds of conscience, to withdraw from her communion."— *Encyclopaedia Britannica*, 9th ed., art. "Bengel." The good effects of this policy are still felt in his native province.

It was while preparing a sermon from Revelation 21 for advent Sunday that the light of Christ's second coming broke in upon Bengel's mind. The prophecies of the Revelation unfolded to his understanding as never before. Overwhelmed with a sense of the stupendous importance and surpassing glory of the scenes presented by the prophet, he was forced to turn for a time from the contemplation of the subject. In the pulpit it again presented itself to him with all 364 its vividness and power. From that time he devoted himself to the study of the prophecies, especially those of the Apocalypse, and soon arrived at the belief that they pointed to the coming of Christ as near. The date which he fixed upon as the time of the second advent was within a very few years of that afterward held by Miller.

Bengel's writings have been spread throughout Christendom. His views of prophecy were quite generally received in his own state of

Wurttemberg, and to some extent in other parts of Germany. The movement continued after his death, and the advent message was heard in Germany at the same time that it was attracting attention in other lands. At an early date some of the believers went to Russia and there formed colonies, and the faith of Christ's soon coming is still held by the German churches of that country.

The light shone also in France and Switzerland. At Geneva where Farel and Calvin had spread the truth of the Reformation, Gaussen preached the message of the second advent. While a student at school, Gaussen had encountered that spirit of rationalism which pervaded all Europe during the latter part of the eighteenth and the opening of the nineteenth century; and when he entered the ministry he was not only ignorant of true faith, but inclined to skepticism. In his youth he had become interested in the study of prophecy. After reading Rollin's *Ancient History,* his attention was called to the second chapter of Daniel, and he was struck with the wonderful exactness with which the prophecy had been fulfilled, as seen in the historian's record. Here was a testimony to the inspiration of the Scriptures, which served as an anchor to him amid the perils of later years. He could not rest satisfied with the teachings of rationalism, and in studying the Bible and searching for clearer light he was, after a time, led to a positive faith.

As he pursued his investigation of the prophecies he arrived at the belief that the coming of the Lord was at hand. Impressed with the solemnity and importance of this great truth, he 365 desired to bring it before the people; but the popular belief that the prophecies of Daniel are mysteries and cannot be understood was a serious obstacle in his way. He finally determined—as Farel had done before him in evangelizing Geneva—to begin with the children, through whom he hoped to interest the parents.

"I desire this to be understood," he afterward said, speaking of his object in this undertaking, "it is not because of its small importance, but on the contrary because of its great value, that I wished to present it in this familiar form, and that I addressed it to the children. I desired to be heard, and I feared that I would not be if I addressed myself to the grown people first." "I determined therefore to go to the youngest. I gather an audience of children; if the group enlarges, if it is seen that they listen, are pleased, interested, that they understand and explain the subject, I am sure to have a second circle soon, and in their turn, grown people will see that it is worth their while to sit down and study. When this is done, the cause is gained."—L. Gaussen, *Daniel the Prophet,* vol. 2, Preface.

The effort was successful. As he addressed the children, older persons came to listen. The galleries of his church were filled with attentive hearers. Among them were men of rank and learning, and strangers and foreigners visiting Geneva; and thus the message was carried to other parts.

Encouraged by this success, Gaussen published his lessons, with the hope of promoting the study of the prophetic books in the churches of the French-speaking people. "To publish instruction given to the children," says Gaussen, "is to say to adults, who too often neglect such books under the false pretense that they are obscure, 'How can they be obscure, since your children understand them?'" "I had a great desire," he adds, "to render a knowledge of the prophecies popular in our flocks, if possible." "There is no study, indeed, which it seems to me answers the needs of the time better." "It is by this that we are to prepare for the tribulation near at hand, and watch and wait for Jesus Christ."

Though one of the most distinguished and 366 beloved of preachers in the French language, Gaussen was after a time suspended from the ministry, his principal offense being that instead of the church's catechism, a tame and rationalistic manual, almost destitute of positive faith, he had used the Bible in giving instruction to the youth. He afterward became teacher in a theological school, while on Sunday he continued his work as catechist, addressing the children and instructing them in the Scriptures. His works on prophecy also excited much interest. From the professor's chair, through the press, and in his favorite occupation as teacher of children he continued for many years to exert an extensive influence and was instrumental in calling the attention of many to the study of the prophecies which showed that the coming of the Lord was near.

In Scandinavia also the advent message was proclaimed, and a widespread interest was kindled. Many were roused from their careless security to confess and forsake their sins, and seek pardon in the name of Christ. But the clergy of the state church opposed the movement, and through their influence some who preached the message were thrown into prison. In many places where the preachers of the Lord's soon coming were thus silenced, God was pleased to send the message, in a miraculous manner, through little children. As they were under age, the law of the state could not restrain them, and they were permitted to speak unmolested.

The movement was chiefly among the lower class, and it was in the humble dwellings of the laborers that the people assembled to hear the warning. The child-preachers themselves were mostly poor cottagers. Some of them were not more than six or eight years of age; and while their lives testified that they loved the Saviour, and were trying to live in obedience to God's holy requirements, they ordinarily manifested only the intelligence and ability usually seen in children of that age. When standing before the 367 people, however, it was evident that they were moved by an influence beyond their own natural gifts. Tone and manner changed, and with solemn power they gave the warning of the judgment, employing the very words of Scripture: "Fear God, and give glory to Him; for the hour of His judgment is come." They reproved the sins of the people, not only condemning immorality and vice, but rebuking worldliness and backsliding, and warning their hearers to make haste to flee from the wrath to come.

The people heard with trembling. The convicting Spirit of God spoke to their hearts. Many were led to search the Scriptures with new and deeper interest, the intemperate and immoral were reformed, others abandoned their dishonest practices, and a work was done so marked that even ministers of the state church were forced to acknowledge that the hand of God was in the movement.

It was God's will that the tidings of the Saviour's coming should be given in the Scandinavian countries; and when the voices of His servants were silenced, He put His Spirit upon the children, that the work might be accomplished. When Jesus drew near to Jerusalem attended by the rejoicing multitudes that, with shouts of triumph and the waving of palm branches, heralded Him as the Son of David, the jealous Pharisees called upon Him to silence them; but Jesus answered that all this was in fulfillment of prophecy, and if these should hold their peace, the very stones would cry out. The people, intimidated by the threats of the priests and rulers, ceased their joyful proclamation as they entered the gates of Jerusalem; but the children in the temple courts afterward took up the refrain, and, waving their branches of palm, they cried: "Hosanna to the Son of David!" Matthew 21:8-16. When the Pharisees, sorely displeased, said unto Him, "Hearest Thou what these say?" Jesus answered, "Yea; have ye never read, Out of the mouth of babes and sucklings Thou hast perfected praise?" As God 368 wrought through children at the time of Christ's first advent, so He wrought through them in giving the message of His second advent. God's word must be fulfilled, that the proclamation of the Saviour's coming should be given to all peoples, tongues, and nations.

To William Miller and his colaborers it was given to preach the warning in America. This country became the center of the great advent movement. It was here that the prophecy of the first angel's message had its most direct fulfillment. The writings of Miller and his associates were carried to distant lands. Wherever missionaries had penetrated in all the world, were sent the glad tidings of Christ's speedy return. Far and wide spread the message of the everlasting gospel: "Fear God, and give glory to Him; for the hour of His judgment is come."

The testimony of the prophecies which seemed to point to the coming of Christ in the spring of 1844 took deep hold of the minds of the people. As the message went from state to state, there was everywhere awakened widespread interest. Many were convinced that the arguments from the prophetic periods were correct, and, sacrificing their pride of opinion, they joyfully received the truth. Some ministers laid aside their sectarian views and feelings, left their salaries and their churches, and united in proclaiming the coming of Jesus. There were comparatively few ministers, however, who would accept this message; therefore it was largely committed to humble laymen. Farmers left their fields, mechanics their tools, traders their merchandise, professional men their positions; and yet the number of workers was small in comparison with the work to be accomplished. The condition of an ungodly church and a world lying in wickedness, burdened the souls of the true watchmen, and they willingly endured toil, privation, and suffering, that they might call men to repentance unto salvation. Though opposed by Satan, the work went steadily forward, and the advent truth was accepted by many thousands.

Everywhere the searching testimony was 369 heard, warning sinners, both worldlings and church members, to flee from the wrath to come. Like John the Baptist, the forerunner of Christ, the preachers laid the ax at the root of the tree and urged all to bring forth fruit meet for repentance. Their stirring appeals were in marked contrast to the assurances of peace and safety that were heard from popular pulpits; and wherever the message was given, it moved the people. The simple, direct testimony of the Scriptures, set home by the power of the Holy Spirit, brought a weight of conviction that few were able wholly to resist. Professors of religion were roused from their false security. They saw their backslidings, their worldliness and unbelief, their pride and selfishness. Many sought the Lord with repentance and humiliation. The affections that had so long clung to earthly things they now fixed upon heaven. The Spirit of God rested upon them, and with hearts softened and subdued they joined to sound the cry: "Fear God, and give glory to Him; for the hour of His judgment is come."

Sinners inquired with weeping: "What must I do to be saved?" Those whose lives had been marked with dishonesty were anxious to make restitution. All who found peace in Christ longed to see others share the blessing. The hearts of parents were turned to their children, and the hearts of children to their parents. The barriers of pride and reserve were swept away. Heartfelt confessions were made, and the members of the household labored for the salvation of those who were nearest and dearest. Often was heard the sound of earnest intercession. Everywhere were souls in deep anguish pleading with God. Many wrestled all night in prayer for the assurance that their own sins were pardoned, or for the conversion of their relatives or neighbors.

All classes flocked to the Adventist meetings. Rich and poor, high and low, were, from various causes, anxious to hear for themselves the doctrine of the second advent. The Lord held the spirit of opposition in check while His ser-370 vants explained the reasons of their faith. Sometimes the instrument was feeble; but the Spirit of God gave power to His truth. The presence of holy angels was felt in these assemblies, and many were daily added to the believers. As the evidences of Christ's soon coming were repeated, vast crowds listened in breathless silence to the solemn words. Heaven and earth seemed to approach each other. The power of God was felt upon old and young and middle-aged. Men sought their homes with praises upon their lips, and the glad sound rang out upon the still night air. None who attended those meetings can ever forget those scenes of deepest interest.

The proclamation of a definite time for Christ's coming called forth great opposition from many of all classes, from the minister in the pulpit down to the most reckless, Heaven-daring sinner. The words of prophecy were fulfilled: "There shall come in the last days scoffers, walking after their own lusts, and saying, Where is the promise of His coming? for since the fathers fell asleep, all things continue as they were from the beginning of the creation." 2 Peter 3:3, 4. Many who professed to love the Saviour, declared that they had no opposition to the doctrine of the second advent; they merely objected to the definite time. But God's all-seeing eye read their hearts. They did not wish to hear of Christ's coming to judge the world in righteousness. They had been unfaithful servants, their works would not bear the inspection of the heart-searching God, and they feared to meet their Lord. Like the Jews at the time of Christ's first advent they were not prepared to welcome Jesus. They not only refused to listen to the plain arguments from the Bible, but ridiculed those who were looking for the Lord. Satan and his angels exulted, and flung the taunt in the face of Christ and holy angels that His professed people had so little love for Him that they did not desire His appearing.

"No man knoweth the day nor the hour" was the argument most often brought forward by rejecters of the advent faith. The scripture is: 371 "Of that day and hour knoweth no man, no not the angels of heaven, but My Father only."

Matthew 24:36. A clear and harmonious explanation of this text was given by those who were looking for the Lord, and the wrong use made of it by their opponents was clearly shown. The words were spoken by Christ in that memorable conversation with His disciples upon Olivet after He had for the last time departed from the temple. The disciples had asked the question: "What shall be the sign of Thy coming, and of the end of the world?" Jesus gave them signs, and said: "When ye shall see all these things, know that it is near, even at the doors." Verses 3, 33. One saying of the Saviour must not be made to destroy another. Though no man knoweth the *day* nor the *hour* of His coming, we are instructed and required to know when it is near. We are further taught that to disregard His warning, and refuse or neglect to know when His advent is near, will be as fatal for us as it was for those who lived in the days of Noah not to know when the flood was coming. And the parable in the same chapter, contrasting the faithful and the unfaithful servant, and giving the doom of him who said in his heart, "My Lord delayeth His coming," shows in what light Christ will regard and reward those whom He finds watching, and teaching His coming, and those denying it. "Watch therefore," He says. "Blessed is that servant, whom his Lord when He cometh shall find so doing." Verses 42, 46. "If therefore thou shalt not watch, I will come on thee as a thief, and thou shalt not know what hour I will come upon thee." Revelation 3:3.

Paul speaks of a class to whom the Lord's appearing will come unawares. "The day of the Lord so cometh as a thief in the night. For when they shall say, Peace and safety; then sudden destruction cometh upon them, . . . and they shall not escape." But he adds, to those who have given heed to the Saviour's warning: "Ye, brethren, are not in darkness, that that day should overtake you as a thief. Ye are all the children of light, and the children of the day: we are not of the night, nor of darkness." 1 Thessalonians 5:2-5.

Thus it was shown that Scripture gives no 372 warrant for men to remain in ignorance concerning the nearness of Christ's coming. But those who desired only an excuse to reject the truth closed their ears to this explanation, and the words "No man knoweth the day nor the hour" continued to be echoed by the bold scoffer and even by the professed minister of Christ. As the people were roused, and began to inquire the way of salvation, religious teachers stepped in between them and the truth, seeking to quiet their fears by falsely interpreting the word of God. Unfaithful watchmen united in the work of the great deceiver, crying, Peace, peace, when God had not spoken peace. Like the Pharisees in Christ's day, many refused to enter the kingdom of heaven themselves, and those who were entering in they hindered. The blood of these souls will be required at their hand.

The most humble and devoted in the churches were usually the first to receive the message. Those who studied the Bible for themselves could not but see the unscriptural character of the popular views of prophecy; and wherever the people were not controlled by the influence of the clergy, wherever they would search the word of God for themselves, the advent doctrine needed only to be compared with the Scriptures to establish its divine authority.

Many were persecuted by their unbelieving brethren. In order to retain their position in the church, some consented to be silent in regard to their hope; but others felt that loyalty to God forbade them thus to hide the truths which He had committed to their trust. Not a few were cut off from the fellowship of the church for no other reason than expressing their belief in the coming of Christ. Very precious to those who bore this trial of their faith were the words of the prophet: "Your brethren that hated you, that cast you out for My name's sake, said, Let the Lord be glorified: but He shall appear to your joy, and they shall be ashamed." Isaiah 66:5.

373 Angels of God were watching with the deepest interest the result of the warning. When there was a general rejection of the message by the churches, angels turned away in sadness. But there were many who had not yet been tested in regard to the advent truth. Many were misled by husbands, wives, parents, or children, and were made to believe it a sin even to listen to such heresies as were taught by the Adventists. Angels were bidden to keep faithful watch over these souls, for another light was yet to shine upon them from the throne of God.

With unspeakable desire those who had received the message watched for the coming of their Saviour. The time when they expected to meet Him was at hand. They approached this hour with a calm solemnity. They rested in sweet communion with God, an earnest of the peace that was to be theirs in the bright hereafter. None who experienced this hope and trust can forget those precious hours of waiting. For some weeks preceding the time, worldly business was for the most part laid aside. The sincere believers carefully examined every thought and emotion of their hearts as if upon their deathbeds and in a few hours to close their eyes upon earthly scenes. There was no making of "ascension robes" (see Appendix); but all felt the need of internal evidence that they were prepared to meet the Saviour; their white robes were purity of soul—characters cleansed from sin by the atoning blood of Christ. Would that there were still with the professed people of God the same spirit of heart searching, the same earnest, determined faith. Had they continued thus to humble themselves before the Lord and

press their petitions at the mercy seat they would be in possession of a far richer experience than they now have. There is too little prayer, too little real conviction of sin, and the lack of living faith leaves many destitute of the grace so richly provided by our Redeemer.

God designed to prove His people. His hand covered a mistake in the reckoning of the prophetic periods. Adventists did not discover 374 the error, nor was it discovered by the most learned of their opponents. The latter said: "Your reckoning of the prophetic periods is correct. Some great event is about to take place; but it is not what Mr. Miller predicts; it is the conversion of the world, and not the second advent of Christ." (See Appendix.)

The time of expectation passed, and Christ did not appear for the deliverance of His people. Those who with sincere faith and love had looked for their Saviour, experienced a bitter disappointment. Yet the purposes of God were being accomplished; He was testing the hearts of those who professed to be waiting for His appearing. There were among them many who had been actuated by no higher motive than fear. Their profession of faith had not affected their hearts or their lives. When the expected event failed to take place, these persons declared that they were not disappointed; they had never believed that Christ would come. They were among the first to ridicule the sorrow of the true believers.

But Jesus and all the heavenly host looked with love and sympathy upon the tried and faithful yet disappointed ones. Could the veil separating the visible from the invisible world have been swept back, angels would have been seen drawing near to these steadfast souls and shielding them from the shafts of Satan.

21

A Warning Rejected

375

In preaching the doctrine of the second advent, William Miller and his associates had labored with the sole purpose of arousing men to a preparation for the judgment. They had sought to awaken professors of religion to the true hope of the church and to their need of a deeper Christian experience; and they labored also to awaken the unconverted to the duty of immediate repentance and conversion to God. "They made no attempt to convert men to a sect or party in religion. Hence they labored among all parties and sects, without interfering with their organization or discipline."

"In all my labors," said Miller, "I never had the desire or thought to establish any separate interest from that of existing denominations, or to benefit one at the expense of another. I thought to benefit all. Supposing that all Christians would rejoice in the prospect of Christ's coming, and that those who could not see as I did would not love any the less those who should embrace this doctrine, I did not conceive there would ever be any necessity for separate meetings. My whole object was a desire to convert souls to God, to notify the world of a coming judgment, and to induce my fellow men to make that preparation of heart which will enable them to meet their God in peace. The great majority of those who were converted under my labors united with the various existing churches."—Bliss, page 328.

376   As his work tended to build up the churches, it was for a time regarded with favor. But as ministers and religious leaders decided against the advent doctrine and desired to suppress all agitation of the subject, they not only opposed it from the pulpit, but denied their members the privilege of attending preaching upon the second advent, or even of speaking of their hope in the social meetings of the church. Thus the believers found themselves in a position of great trial and perplexity. They loved their churches and were loath to separate from them; but as they saw the testimony of God's word suppressed and their right to investigate the prophecies denied they felt that loyalty to God forbade them to submit. Those who sought to shut out the testimony of God's word they could not regard as constituting the church of Christ, "the pillar and ground of the truth." Hence they felt themselves justified in separating from their former connection. In the summer of 1844 about fifty thousand withdrew from the churches.

About this time a marked change was apparent in most of the churches throughout the United States. There had been for many years a gradual but steadily increasing conformity to worldly practices and customs, and a corresponding decline in real spiritual life; but in that year there were evidences of a sudden and marked declension in nearly all the churches of the land. While none seemed able to suggest the cause, the fact itself was widely noted and commented upon by both the press and the pulpit.

At a meeting of the presbytery of Philadelphia, Mr. Barnes, author of a commentary widely used and pastor of one of the leading churches in that city, "stated that he had been in the ministry for twenty years, and never, till the last Communion, had he administered the ordinance without receiving more or less into the church. But now there are *no awakenings, no conversions*, not much apparent growth in grace in professors, and none come to his study to converse about the salvation of their souls. With the

377 increase of business, and the brightening prospects of commerce and manufacture, there is an increase of worldly-mindedness. *Thus it is with all the denominations.*"—*Congregational Journal,* May 23, 1844.

In the month of February of the same year, Professor Finney of Oberlin College said: "We have had the fact before our minds, that, in general, the Protestant churches of our country, as such, were either apathetic or hostile to nearly all the moral reforms of the age. There are partial exceptions, yet not enough to render the fact otherwise than general. We have also another corroborated fact: the almost universal absence of revival influence in the churches. The spiritual apathy is almost all-pervading, and is fearfully deep; so the religious press of the whole land testifies. . . . Very extensively, church members are becoming devotees of fashion,—join hands with the ungodly in parties of pleasure, in dancing, in festivities, etc. . . . But we need not expand this painful subject. Suffice it that the evidence thickens and rolls heavily upon us, to show that the *churches generally are becoming sadly degenerate.* They have gone very far from the Lord, and He has withdrawn Himself from them."

And a writer in the *Religious Telescope* testified: "We have never witnessed such a general declension of religion as at the present. Truly, the church should awake, and search into the cause of this affliction; for as an affliction everyone that loves Zion must view it. When we call to mind how 'few and far between' cases of true conversion are, and the almost unparalleled impertinence and hardness of sinners, we almost involuntarily exclaim, 'Has God forgotten to be gracious? or, Is the door of mercy closed?'"

Such a condition never exists without cause in the church itself. The spiritual darkness which falls upon nations, upon churches and individuals, is due, not to an arbitrary withdrawal of the succors of divine grace on the part of God, but to neglect or rejection of divine light on the part of men. A striking illustration of this 378 truth is presented in the history of the Jewish people in the time of Christ. By their devotion to the world and forgetfulness of God and His word, their understanding had become darkened, their hearts earthly and sensual. Thus they were in ignorance concerning Messiah's advent, and in their pride and unbelief they rejected the Redeemer. God did not even then cut off the Jewish nation from a knowledge of, or a participation in, the blessings of salvation. But those who rejected the truth lost all desire for the gift of Heaven. They had "put darkness for light, and light for darkness," until the light which was in them became darkness; and how great was that darkness!

It suits the policy of Satan that men should retain the forms of religion if but the spirit of vital godliness is lacking. After their rejection of the gospel, the Jews continued zealously to maintain their ancient rites, they rigorously preserved their national exclusiveness, while they themselves could not but admit that the presence of God was no longer manifest among them. The prophecy of Daniel pointed so unmistakably to the time of Messiah's coming, and so directly foretold His death, that they discouraged its study, and finally the rabbis pronounced a curse on all who should attempt a computation of the time. In blindness and impenitence the people of Israel during succeeding centuries have stood, indifferent to the gracious offers of salvation, unmindful of the blessings of the gospel, a solemn and fearful warning of the danger of rejecting light from heaven.

Wherever the cause exists, the same results will follow. He who deliberately stifles his convictions of duty because it interferes with his inclinations will finally lose the power to distinguish between truth and error. The understanding becomes darkened, the conscience callous, the heart hardened, and the soul is separated from God. Where the message of divine truth is spurned or slighted, there the church will be enshrouded in darkness; faith and love grow
379 cold, and estrangement and dissension enter. Church members center their interests and energies in worldly pursuits, and sinners become hardened in their impenitence.

The first angel's message of Revelation 14, announcing the hour of God's judgment and calling upon men to fear and worship Him, was designed to separate the professed people of God from the corrupting influences of the world and to arouse them to see their true condition of worldliness and backsliding. In this message, God had sent to the church a warning, which, had it been accepted, would have corrected the evils that were shutting them away from Him. Had they received the message from heaven, humbling their hearts before the Lord and seeking in sincerity a preparation to stand in His presence, the Spirit and power of God would have been manifested among them. The church would again have reached that blessed state of unity, faith, and love which existed in apostolic days, when the believers "were of one heart and of one soul," and "spake the word of God with boldness," when "the Lord added to the church daily such as should be saved." Acts 4:32, 31; 2:47.

If God's professed people would receive the light as it shines upon them from His word, they would reach that unity for which Christ prayed, that which the apostle describes, "the unity of the Spirit in the bond of peace." "There is," he says, "one body, and one Spirit, even as ye are called in one hope of your calling; one Lord, one faith, one baptism." Ephesians 4:3-5.

Such were the blessed results experienced by those who accepted the advent message. They came from different denominations, and their denominational barriers were hurled to the ground; conflicting creeds were shivered to atoms; the unscriptural hope of a temporal millennium was abandoned, false views of the second advent were corrected, pride and conformity to the world were swept away; wrongs were made right; hearts were united in the sweetest fellowship, and love and joy reigned supreme. If this doctrine did this for the few who did receive 380 it, it would have done the same for all if all had received it.

But the churches generally did not accept the warning. Their ministers, who, as watchmen "unto the house of Israel," should have been the first to discern the tokens of Jesus' coming, had failed to learn the truth either from the testimony of the prophets or from the signs of the times. As worldly hopes and ambitions filled the heart, love for God and faith in His word had grown cold; and when the advent doctrine was presented, it only aroused their prejudice and unbelief. The fact that the message was, to a great extent, preached by laymen, was urged as an argument against it. As of old, the plain testimony of God's word was met with the inquiry: "Have any of the rulers or of the Pharisees believed?" And finding how difficult a task it was to refute the arguments drawn from the prophetic periods, many discouraged the study of the prophecies, teaching that the prophetic books were sealed and were not to be understood. Multitudes, trusting implicitly to their pastors, refused to listen to the warning; and others, though convinced of the truth, dared not confess it, lest they should be "put out of the synagogue." The message which God had sent for the testing and purification of the church revealed all too surely how great was the number who had set their affections on this world rather than upon Christ. The ties which bound them to earth were stronger than the attractions heavenward. They chose to listen to the voice of worldly wisdom and turned away from the heart-searching message of truth.

In refusing the warning of the first angel, they rejected the means which Heaven had provided for their restoration. They spurned the gracious messenger that would have corrected the evils which separated them from God, and with greater eagerness they turned to seek the friendship of the world. Here was the cause of that fearful condition of worldliness, backsliding, and spiritual death which existed in the churches in 1844.

In Revelation 14 the first angel is followed by 381 a second proclaiming: "Babylon is fallen, is fallen, that great city, because she made all nations drink of the wine of the wrath of her fornication." Revelation 14:8. The term "Babylon" is derived from "Babel," and signifies confusion. It is employed in Scripture to designate the various forms of false or apostate religion. In Revelation 17 Babylon is represented as a woman—a figure which is used in the Bible as the symbol of a church, a virtuous woman representing a pure church, a vile woman an apostate church.

In the Bible the sacred and enduring character of the relation that exists between Christ and His church is represented by the union of marriage. The Lord has joined His people to Himself by a solemn covenant, He promising to be their God, and they pledging themselves to be His and His alone. He declares: "I will betroth thee unto Me forever; yea, I will betroth thee unto Me in righteousness, and in judgment, and in loving-kindness, and in mercies." Hosea 2:19. And, again: "I am married unto you." Jeremiah 3:14. And Paul employs the same figure in the New Testament when he says: "I have espoused you to one husband, that I may present you as a chaste virgin to Christ." 2 Corinthians 11:2.

The unfaithfulness of the church to Christ in permitting her confidence and affection to be turned from Him, and allowing the love of worldly things to occupy the soul, is likened to the violation of the marriage vow. The sin of Israel in departing from the Lord is presented under this figure; and the wonderful love of God which they thus despised is touchingly portrayed: "I sware unto thee, and entered into a covenant with thee, saith the Lord God, and thou becamest Mine." "And thou wast exceeding beautiful and thou didst prosper into a kingdom. And thy renown went forth among the heathen for thy beauty: for it was perfect through My comeliness, which I had put upon thee. . . . But thou didst trust in thine own beauty, and playedst the harlot because of thy renown." "As a wife treacherously departeth 382 from her husband, so have ye dealt treacherously with Me, O house of Israel, saith the Lord;" "as a wife that committeth adultery, which taketh strangers instead of her husband!" Ezekiel 16:8, 13-15, 32; Jeremiah 3:20.

In the New Testament, language very similar is addressed to professed Christians who seek the friendship of the world above the favor of God. Says the apostle James: "Ye adulterers and adulteresses, know ye not that the friendship of the world is enmity with God? whosoever therefore will be a friend of the world is the enemy of God."

The woman (Babylon) of Revelation 17 is described as "arrayed in purple and scarlet color, and decked with gold and precious stones and pearls, having a golden cup in her hand full of abominations and filthiness: . . . and upon her forehead was a name written, *Mystery, Babylon the Great, the mother of harlots.*" Says the prophet: "I saw the woman drunk with the blood of the saints, and with the blood of the martyrs of Jesus." Babylon is further declared to be "that great city, which reigneth over the kings of the earth." Revelation 17:4-6, 18. The power that for so many centuries maintained despotic sway over the monarchs of Christendom is Rome. The purple and scarlet color, the gold and precious stones and pearls, vividly picture the magnificence and more than kingly pomp affected by the haughty see of Rome. And no other power could be so truly declared "drunken with the blood of the saints" as that church which has so cruelly persecuted the followers of Christ. Babylon is also charged with the sin of unlawful connection with "the kings of the earth." It was by departure from the Lord, and alliance with the heathen, that the Jewish church became a harlot; and Rome, corrupting herself in like manner by seeking the support of worldly powers, receives a like condemnation.

Babylon is said to be "the *mother* of harlots." By her *daughters* must be symbolized churches that cling to her doctrines and traditions, and follow her example of sacrificing the truth and 383 the approval of God, in order to form an unlawful alliance with the world. The message of Revelation 14, announcing the *fall* of Babylon must apply to religious bodies that were once pure and have become corrupt. Since this message follows the warning of the judgment, it must be given in the last days; therefore it cannot refer to the Roman Church alone, for that church has been in a fallen condition for many centuries. Furthermore, in the eighteenth chapter of the Revelation the people of God are called upon to come out of Babylon. According to this scripture, many of God's people must still be in Babylon. And in what religious bodies are the greater part of the followers of Christ now to be found? Without doubt, in the various churches professing the Protestant faith. At the time of their rise these churches took a noble stand for God and the truth, and His blessing was with them. Even the unbelieving world was constrained to acknowledge the beneficent results that followed an acceptance of the principles of the gospel. In the words of the prophet to Israel: "Thy renown went forth among the heathen for thy beauty: for it was perfect through My comeliness, which I had put upon thee, saith the Lord God." But they fell by the same desire which was the curse and ruin of Israel—the desire of imitating the practices and courting the friendship of the ungodly. "Thou didst trust in thine own beauty, and playedst the harlot because of thy renown." Ezekiel 16:14, 15.

Many of the Protestant churches are following Rome's example of iniquitous connection with "the kings of the earth"—the state churches, by their relation to secular governments; and other denominations, by seeking the favor of the world. And the term "Babylon"—confusion—may be appropriately applied to these bodies, all professing to derive their doctrines from the Bible, yet divided into almost innumerable sects, with widely conflicting creeds and theories.

Besides a sinful union with the world, the churches that separated from Rome present other of her characteristics.

384 A Roman Catholic work argues that "if the Church of Rome were ever guilty of idolatry in relation to the saints, her daughter, the Church of England, stands guilty of the same, which has ten churches dedicated to Mary for one dedicated to Christ."—Richard Challoner, *The Catholic Christian Instructed, Preface*, pages 21, 22.

And Dr. Hopkins, in "A Treatise on the Millennium," declares: "There is no reason to consider the antichristian spirit and practices to be confined to that which is now called the Church of Rome. The Protestant churches have much of antichrist in them, and are far from being wholly reformed from . . . corruptions and wickedness."—Samuel Hopkins, *Works*, vol. 2, p. 328.

Concerning the separation of the Presbyterian Church from Rome, Dr. Guthrie writes: "Three hundred years ago, our church, with an open Bible on her banner, and this motto, 'Search the Scriptures,' on her scroll, marched out from the gates of Rome." Then he asks the significant question: "Did they come *clean* out of Babylon?"—Thomas Guthrie, T*he Gospel in Ezekiel,* page 237.

"The Church of England," says Spurgeon, "seems to be eaten through and through with sacramentarianism; but nonconformity appears to be almost as badly riddled with philosophical infidelity. Those of whom we thought better things are turning aside one by one from the fundamentals of the faith. Through and through, I believe, the very heart of England is honeycombed with a damnable infidelity which dares still go into the pulpit and call itself Christian."

What was the origin of the great apostasy? How did the church first depart from the simplicity of the gospel? By conforming to the practices of paganism, to facilitate the acceptance of Christianity by the heathen. The apostle Paul declared, even in his day, "The mystery of iniquity doth already work." 2 Thessalonians 2:7. During the lives of the apostles the church remained comparatively pure. But "toward the latter end of the second century most of the churches assumed a new form; the first simplic-385 ity disappeared, and insensibly, as the old disciples retired to their graves, their children, along with new converts, . . . came forward and new-modeled the cause."—Robert Robinson, *Ecclesiastical Researches*, ch. 6, par. 17, p. 51. To secure converts, the exalted standard of the Christian faith was lowered, and as the result "a pagan flood, flowing into the church, carried with it its customs, practices, and idols."—Gavazzi, *Lectures*, page 278. As the Christian religion secured the favor and support of secular rulers, it was nominally accepted by multitudes;

but while in appearance Christians, many "remained in substance pagans, especially worshiping in secret their idols."—*Ibid.*, page 278.

Has not the same process been repeated in nearly every church calling itself Protestant? As the founders, those who possessed the true spirit of reform, pass away, their descendants come forward and "new-model the cause." While blindly clinging to the creed of their fathers and refusing to accept any truth in advance of what they saw, the children of the reformers depart widely from their example of humility, self-denial, and renunciation of the world. Thus "the first simplicity disappears." A worldly flood, flowing into the church, carries "with it its customs, practices, and idols."

Alas, to what a fearful extent is that friendship of the world which is "enmity with God," now cherished among the professed followers of Christ! How widely have the popular churches throughout Christendom departed from the Bible standard of humility, self-denial, simplicity, and godliness! Said John Wesley, in speaking of the right use of money: "Do not waste any part of so precious a talent, merely in gratifying the desire of the eye, by superfluous or expensive apparel, or by needless ornaments. Waste no part of it in curiously adorning your houses; in superfluous or expensive furniture; in costly pictures, painting, gilding. . . . Lay out nothing to gratify the pride of life, to gain the admiration or praise of men. . . . 'So long as thou doest well unto thyself, men will speak good of thee.' So long as thou art 'clothed in purple and fine linen,' and farest 'sumptuously every day,' no doubt many will applaud thy ele-386 gance of taste, thy generosity and hospitality. But do not buy their applause so dear. Rather be content with the honor that cometh from God."—Wesley, *Works*, Sermon 50, "The Use of Money." But in many churches of our time such teaching is disregarded.

A profession of religion has become popular with the world. Rulers, politicians, lawyers, doctors, merchants, join the church as a means of securing the respect and confidence of society, and advancing their own worldly interests. Thus they seek to cover all their unrighteous transactions under a profession of Christianity. The various religious bodies, re-enforced by the wealth and influence of these baptized worldlings, make a still higher bid for popularity and patronage. Splendid churches, embellished in the most extravagant manner, are erected on popular avenues. The worshipers array themselves in costly and fashionable attire. A high salary is paid for a talented minister to entertain and attract the people. His sermons must not touch popular sins, but be made smooth and pleasing for fashionable ears. Thus fashionable sinners are enrolled on the church records, and fashionable sins are concealed under a pretense of godliness.

Commenting on the present attitude of professed Christians toward the world, a leading secular journal says: "Insensibly the church has yielded to the spirit of the age, and adapted its forms of worship to modern wants." "All things, indeed, that help to make religion attractive, the church now employs as its instruments." And a writer in the New York *Independent* speaks thus concerning Methodism as it is: "The line of separation between the godly and the irreligious fades out into a kind of penumbra, and zealous men on both sides are toiling to obliterate all difference between their modes of action and enjoyment." "The popularity of religion tends vastly to increase the number of those who would secure its benefits without squarely meeting its duties."

387 Says Howard Crosby: "It is a matter of deep concern that we find Christ's church so little fulfilling the designs of its Lord. Just as the ancient Jews let a familiar intercourse with the idolatrous nations steal away their hearts from God, . . . so the church of Jesus now is, by its false partnerships with an unbelieving world, giving up the divine methods of its true life, and yielding itself to the pernicious, though often plausible, habits of a Christless society, using the arguments and reaching the conclusions which are foreign to the revelation of God, and directly antagonistic to all growth in grace."— *The Healthy Christian: An Appeal to the Church,* pages 141, 142.

In this tide of worldliness and pleasure seeking, self-denial and self-sacrifice for Christ's sake are almost wholly lost. "Some of the men and women now in active life in our churches were educated, when children, to make sacrifices in order to be able to give or do something for Christ." But "if funds are wanted now, . . . nobody must be called on to give. Oh, no! have a fair, tableau, mock trial, antiquarian supper, or something to eat—anything to amuse the people."

Governor Washburn of Wisconsin in his annual message, January 9, 1873, declared: "Some law seems to be required to break up the schools where gamblers are made. These are everywhere. Even the church (unwittingly, no doubt) is sometimes found doing the work of the devil. Gift concerts, gift enterprises and raffles, sometimes in aid of religious or charitable objects, but often for less worthy purposes, lotteries, prize packages, etc., are all devices to obtain money without value received. Nothing is so demoralizing or intoxicating, particularly to the young, as the acquisition of money or property without labor. Respectable people engaging in these chance enterprises, and easing their consciences with the reflection that the money is to go to a good object, it is not strange that the youth of the state should so often fall

into the habits which the excitement of games of hazard is almost certain to engender."

The spirit of worldly conformity is invading the churches throughout Christendom. Robert 388 Atkins, in a sermon preached in London, draws a dark picture of the spiritual declension that prevails in England: "The truly righteous are diminished from the earth, and no man layeth it to heart. The professors of religion of the present day, in every church, are lovers of the world, conformers to the world, lovers of creature comfort, and aspirers after respectability. They are called to suffer with Christ, but they shrink from even reproach. . . . *Apostasy, apostasy, apostasy*, is engraven on the very front of every church; and did they know it, and did they feel it, there might be hope; but, alas! they cry, 'We are rich, and increased in goods, and stand in need of nothing.'"—Second Advent Library, tract No. 39.

The great sin charged against Babylon is that she "made all nations drink of the wine of the wrath of her fornication." This cup of intoxication which she presents to the world represents the false doctrines that she has accepted as the result of her unlawful connection with the great ones of the earth. Friendship with the world corrupts her faith, and in her turn she exerts a corrupting influence upon the world by teaching doctrines which are opposed to the plainest statements of Holy Writ.

Rome withheld the Bible from the people and required all men to accept her teachings in its place. It was the work of the Reformation to restore to men the word of God; but is it not too true that in the churches of our time men are taught to rest their faith upon their creed and the teachings of their church rather than on the Scriptures? Said Charles Beecher, speaking of the Protestant churches: "They shrink from any rude word against creeds with the same sensitiveness with which those holy fathers would have shrunk from a rude word against the rising veneration of saints and martyrs which they were fostering. . . . The Protestant evangelical denominations have so tied up one another's hands, and their own, that, between them all, a man cannot become a preacher at all, anywhere, without accepting some book besides the Bible. 389 . . . There is nothing imaginary in the statement that the creed power is now beginning to prohibit the Bible as really as Rome did, though in a subtler way."—Sermon on "The Bible a Sufficient Creed," delivered at Fort Wayne, Indiana, Feb. 22, 1846.

When faithful teachers expound the word of God, there arise men of learning, ministers professing to understand the Scriptures, who denounce sound doctrine as heresy, and thus turn away inquirers after truth. Were it not that the world is hopelessly intoxicated with the wine of Babylon, multitudes would be convicted and converted by the plain, cutting truths of the word of God. But religious faith appears so confused and discordant that the people know not what to believe as truth. The sin of the world's impenitence lies at the door of the church.

The second angel's message of Revelation 14 was first preached in the summer of 1844, and it then had a more direct application to the churches of the United States, where the warning of the judgment had been most widely proclaimed and most generally rejected, and where the declension in the churches had been most rapid. But the message of the second angel did not reach its complete fulfillment in 1844. The churches then experienced a moral fall, in consequence of their refusal of the light of the advent message; but that fall was not complete. As they have continued to reject the special truths for this time they have fallen lower and lower. Not yet, however, can it be said that "Babylon is fallen, . . . because she made *all nations* drink of the wine of the wrath of her fornication." She has not yet made all nations do this. The spirit of world conforming and indifference to the testing truths for our time exists and has been gaining ground in churches of the Protestant faith in all the countries of Christendom; and these churches are included in the solemn and terrible denunciation of the second angel. But the work of apostasy has not yet reached its culmination.

The Bible declares that before the coming of the Lord, Satan will work "with *all* power and 390 signs and lying wonders, and with all deceivableness of unrighteousness;" and they that "received not the love of the truth, that they might be saved," will be left to receive "strong delusion, that they should believe a lie." 2 Thessalonians 2:9-11. Not until this condition shall be reached, and the union of the church with the world shall be fully accomplished throughout Christendom, will the fall of Babylon be complete. The change is a progressive one, and the perfect fulfillment of Revelation 14:8 is yet future.

Notwithstanding the spiritual darkness and alienation from God that exist in the churches which constitute Babylon, the great body of Christ's true followers are still to be found in their communion. There are many of these who have never seen the special truths for this time. Not a few are dissatisfied with their present condition and are longing for clearer light. They look in vain for the image of Christ in the churches with which they are connected. As these bodies depart further and further from the truth, and ally themselves more closely with the world, the difference between the two classes will widen, and it will finally result in separation. The time will come when those who love God supremely can no longer remain in connec-tion with such as are "lovers of pleasures more than lovers of God; having a form of godliness, but denying the power thereof."

Revelation 18 points to the time when, as the result of rejecting the threefold warning of Revelation 14:6-12, the church will have fully reached the condition foretold by the second angel, and the people of God still in Babylon will be called upon to separate from her communion. This message is the last that will ever be given to the world; and it will accomplish its work. When those that "believed not the truth, but had pleasure in unrighteousness" (2 Thessalonians 2:12), shall be left to receive strong delusion and to believe a lie, then the light of truth will shine upon all whose hearts are open to receive it, and all the children of the Lord that remain in Babylon will heed the call: "Come out of her, My people" (Revelation 18:4).

22

391

Prophecies Fulfilled

When the time passed at which the Lord's coming was first expected,—in the spring of 1844,—those who had looked in faith for His appearing were for a season involved in doubt and uncertainty. While the world regarded them as having been utterly defeated and proved to have been cherishing a delusion, their source of consolation was still the word of God. Many continued to search the Scriptures, examining anew the evidences of their faith and carefully studying the prophecies to obtain further light. The Bible testimony in support of their position seemed clear and conclusive. Signs which could not be mistaken pointed to the coming of Christ as near. The special blessing of the Lord, both in the conversion of sinners and the revival of spiritual life among Christians, had testified that the message was of Heaven. And though the believers could not explain their disappointment, they felt assured that God had led them in their past experience.

Interwoven with prophecies which they had regarded as applying to the time of the second advent was instruction specially adapted to their state of uncertainty and suspense, and encouraging them to wait patiently in the faith that what was now dark to their understanding would in due time be made plain.

Among these prophecies was that of 392 Habakkuk 2:1-4: "I will stand upon my watch, and set me upon the tower, and will watch to see what He will say unto me, and what I shall answer when I am reproved. And the Lord answered me, and said, Write the vision, and make it plain upon tables, that he may run that readeth it. For the vision is yet for an appointed time, but at the end it shall speak, and not lie: though it tarry, wait for it; because it will surely come, it will not tarry. Behold, his soul which is lifted up is not upright in him: but the just shall live by his faith."

As early as 1842 the direction given in this prophecy to "write the vision, and make it plain upon tables, that he may run that readeth it," had suggested to Charles Fitch the preparation of a prophetic chart to illustrate the visions of Daniel and the Revelation. The publication of this chart was regarded as a fulfillment of the command given by Habakkuk. No one, however, then noticed that an apparent delay in the accomplishment of the vision—a tarrying time—is presented in the same prophecy. After the disappointment, this scripture appeared very significant: "The vision is yet for an appointed time, but at the end it shall speak, and not lie: though it tarry, wait for it; because it will surely come, it will not tarry. . . . The just shall live by his *faith.*"

A portion of Ezekiel's prophecy also was a source of strength and comfort to believers: "The word of the Lord came unto me, saying, Son of man, what is that proverb that ye have in the land of Israel, saying, The days are prolonged, and every vision faileth? Tell them therefore, Thus saith the Lord God. . . . The days are at hand, and the effect of every vision. . . . I will speak, and the word that I shall speak shall come to pass; it shall be no more prolonged." "They of the house of Israel say, The vision that he seeth is for many days to come, and he prophesieth of the times that are far off. Therefore say unto them, Thus saith the Lord God; There shall none of My words be pro393 longed any more, but the word which I have spoken shall be done." Ezekiel 12:21-25, 27, 28.

The waiting ones rejoiced, believing that He who knows the end from the beginning had looked down through the ages and, foreseeing their disappointment, had given them words of courage and hope. Had it not been for such portions of Scripture, admonishing them to wait with patience and to hold fast their confidence in God's word, their faith would have failed in that trying hour.

The parable of the ten virgins of Matthew 25 also illustrates the experience of the Adventist people. In Matthew 24, in answer to the question of His disciples concerning the sign of His coming and of the end of the world, Christ had pointed out some of the most important events in the history of the world and of the church from His first to His second advent; namely, the destruction of Jerusalem, the great tribulation of the church under the pagan and papal persecutions, the darkening of the sun and moon, and the falling of the stars. After this He spoke of His coming in His kingdom, and related the parable describing the two classes of servants

who look for His appearing. Chapter 25 opens with the words: "*Then* shall the kingdom of heaven be likened unto ten virgins." Here is brought to view the church living in the last days, the same that is pointed out in the close of chapter 24. In this parable their experience is illustrated by the incidents of an Eastern marriage.

"Then shall the kingdom of heaven be likened unto ten virgins, which took their lamps, and went forth to meet the bridegroom. And five of them were wise, and five were foolish. They that were foolish took their lamps, and took no oil with them: but the wise took oil in their vessels with their lamps. While the bridegroom tarried, they all slumbered and slept. And at midnight there was a cry made, Behold, the bridegroom cometh; go ye out to meet him."

The coming of Christ, as announced by the first angel's message, was understood to be represented by the coming of the bridegroom. The 394 widespread reformation under the proclamation of His soon coming, answered to the going forth of the virgins. In this parable, as in that of Matthew 24, two classes are represented. All had taken their lamps, the Bible, and by its light had gone forth to meet the Bridegroom. But while "they that were foolish took their lamps, and took no oil with them," "the wise took oil in their vessels with their lamps. The latter class had received the grace of God, the regenerating, enlightening power of the Holy Spirit, which renders His word a lamp to the feet and a light to the path. In the fear of God they had studied the Scriptures to learn the truth, and had earnestly sought for purity of heart and life. These had a personal experience, a faith in God and in His word, which could not be overthrown by disappointment and delay. Others "took their lamps, and took no oil with them." They had moved from impulse. Their fears had been excited by the solemn message, but they had depended upon the faith of their brethren, satisfied with the flickering light of good emotions, without a thorough understanding of the truth or a genuine work of grace in the heart. These had gone forth to meet the Lord, full of hope in the prospect of immediate reward; but they were not prepared for delay and disappointment. When trials came, their faith failed, and their lights burned dim.

"While the bridegroom tarried, they all slum- 443 bered and slept." By the tarrying of the bridegroom is represented the passing of the time when the Lord was expected, the disappointment, and the seeming delay. In this time of uncertainty, the interest of the superficial and halfhearted soon began to waver, and their efforts to relax; but those whose faith was based on a personal knowledge of the Bible had a rock beneath their feet, which the waves of disappointment could not wash away. "They all

slumbered and slept;" one class in unconcern and abandonment of their faith, the other class patiently waiting till clearer light should be
395 given. Yet in the night of trial the latter seemed to lose, to some extent, their zeal and devotion. The halfhearted and superficial could no longer lean upon the faith of their brethren. Each must stand or fall for himself.

About this time, fanaticism began to appear. Some who had professed to be zealous believers in the message rejected the word of God as the one infallible guide and, claiming to be led by the Spirit, gave themselves up to the control of their own feelings, impressions, and imaginations. There were some who manifested a blind and bigoted zeal, denouncing all who would not sanction their course. Their fanatical ideas and exercises met with no sympathy from the great body of Adventists; yet they served to bring reproach upon the cause of truth.

Satan was seeking by this means to oppose and destroy the work of God. The people had been greatly stirred by the advent movement, thousands of sinners had been converted, and faithful men were giving themselves to the work of proclaiming the truth, even in the tarrying time. The prince of evil was losing his subjects; and in order to bring reproach upon the cause of God, he sought to deceive some who professed the faith and to drive them to extremes. Then his agents stood ready to seize upon every error, every failure, every unbecoming act, and hold it up before the people in the most exaggerated light, to render Adventists and their faith odious. Thus the greater the number whom he could crowd in to make a profession of faith in the second advent while his power controlled their hearts, the greater advantage would he gain by calling attention to them as representatives of the whole body of believers.

Satan is "the accuser of the brethren," and it is his spirit that inspires men to watch for the errors and defects of the Lord's people, and to hold them up to notice, while their good deeds are passed by without a mention. He is always active when God is at work for the salvation of souls. When the sons of God come to present
396 themselves before the Lord, Satan comes also among them. In every revival he is ready to bring in those who are unsanctified in heart and unbalanced in mind. When these have accepted some points of truth, and gained a place with believers, he works through them to introduce theories that will deceive the unwary. No man is proved to be a true Christian because he is found in company with the children of God, even in the house of worship and around the table of the Lord. Satan is frequently there upon the most solemn occasions in the form of those whom he can use as his agents.

The prince of evil contests every inch of ground over which God's people advance in their journey toward the heavenly city. In all the history of the church no reformation has been carried forward without encountering serious obstacles. Thus it was in Paul's day. Wherever the apostle raised up a church, there were some who professed to receive the faith, but who brought in heresies, that, if received, would eventually crowd out the love of the truth. Luther also suffered great perplexity and distress from the course of fanatical persons who claimed that God had spoken directly through them, and who therefore set their own ideas and opinions above the testimony of the Scriptures. Many who were lacking in faith and experience, but who had considerable self-sufficiency, and who loved to hear and tell some new thing, were beguiled by the pretensions of the new teachers, and they joined the agents of Satan in their work of tearing down what God had moved Luther to build up. And the Wesleys, and others who blessed the world by their influence and their faith, encountered at every step the wiles of Satan in pushing overzealous, unbalanced, and unsanctified ones into fanaticism of every grade.

William Miller had no sympathy with those influences that led to fanaticism. He declared, with Luther, that every spirit should be tested by the word of God. "The devil," said Miller, "has great power over the minds of some at the pre-
397 sent day. And how shall we know what manner of spirit they are of? The Bible answers: 'By their fruits ye shall know them.' . . . There are many spirits gone out into the world; and we are commanded to try the spirits. The spirit that does not cause us to live soberly, righteously, and godly, in this present world, is not the Spirit of Christ. I am more and more convinced that Satan has much to do in these wild movements. . . . Many among us who pretend to be wholly sanctified, are following the traditions of men, and apparently are as ignorant of truth as others who make no such pretensions."—Bliss, pages 236, 237. "The spirit of error will lead us from the truth; and the Spirit of God will lead us into truth. But, say you, a man may be in an error, and think he has the truth. What then? We answer, The Spirit and word agree. If a man judges himself by the word of God, and finds a perfect harmony through the whole word, then he must believe he has the truth; but if he finds the spirit by which he is led does not harmonize with the whole tenor of God's law or Book, then let him walk carefully, lest he be caught in the snare of the devil."—*The Advent Herald and Signs of the Times Reporter,* vol. 8, No. 23 (Jan. 15, 1845). "I have often obtained more evidence of inward piety from a kindling eye, a wet cheek, and a choked utterance, than from all the noise in Christendom."—Bliss, page 282.

In the days of the Reformation its enemies charged all the evils of fanaticism upon the very ones who were laboring most earnestly against it. A similar course was pursued by the opposers of the advent movement. And not content with misrepresenting and exaggerating the errors of extremists and fanatics, they circulated unfavorable reports that had not the slightest semblance of truth. These persons were actuated by prejudice and hatred. Their peace was disturbed by the proclamation of Christ at the door. They feared it might be true, yet hoped it was not, and this was the secret of their warfare against Adventists and their faith.

398   The fact that a few fanatics worked their way into the ranks of Adventists is no more reason to decide that the movement was not of God than was the presence of fanatics and deceivers in the church in Paul's or Luther's day a sufficient excuse for condemning their work. Let the people of God arouse out of sleep and begin in earnest the work of repentance and reformation; let them search the Scriptures to learn the truth as it is in Jesus; let them make an entire consecration to God, and evidence will not be wanting that Satan is still active and vigilant. With all possible deception he will manifest his power, calling to his aid all the fallen angels of his realm.

It was not the proclamation of the second advent that caused fanaticism and division. These appeared in the summer of 1844, when Adventists were in a state of doubt and perplexity concerning their real position. The preaching of the first angel's message and of the "midnight cry" tended directly to repress fanaticism and dissension. Those who participated in these solemn movements were in harmony; their hearts were filled with love for one another and for Jesus, whom they expected soon to see. The one faith, the one blessed hope, lifted them above the control of any human influence, and proved a shield against the assaults of Satan.

"While the bridegroom tarried, they all slumbered and slept. And at midnight there was a cry made, Behold, the bridegroom cometh; go ye out to meet him. Then all those virgins arose, and trimmed their lamps." Matthew 25:5-7. In the summer of 1844, midway between the time when it had been first thought that the 2300 days would end, and the autumn of the same year, to which it was afterward found that they extended, the message was proclaimed in the very words of Scripture: "Behold, the Bridegroom cometh!"

That which led to this movement was the discovery that the decree of Artaxerxes for the restoration of Jerusalem, which formed the starting point for the period of the 2300 days, went into effect in the autumn of the year 457

399   B.C., and not at the beginning of the year, as had been formerly believed. Reckoning from the autumn of 457, the 2300 years terminate in the autumn of 1844. (See Appendix note for page 329.)

Arguments drawn from the Old Testament types also pointed to the autumn as the time when the event represented by the "cleansing of the sanctuary" must take place. This was made very clear as attention was given to the manner in which the types relating to the first advent of Christ had been fulfilled.

The slaying of the Passover lamb was a shadow of the death of Christ. Says Paul: "Christ our Passover is sacrificed for us." 1 Corinthians 5:7. The sheaf of first fruits, which at the time of the Passover was waved before the Lord, was typical of the resurrection of Christ. Paul says, in speaking of the resurrection of the Lord and of all His people: "Christ the first fruits; afterward they that are Christ's at His coming." 1 Corinthians 15:23. Like the wave sheaf, which was the first ripe grain gathered before the harvest, Christ is the first fruits of that immortal harvest of redeemed ones that at the future resurrection shall be gathered into the garner of God.

These types were fulfilled, not only as to the event, but as to the time. On the fourteenth day of the first Jewish month, the very day and month on which for fifteen long centuries the Passover lamb had been slain, Christ, having eaten the Passover with His disciples, instituted that feast which was to commemorate His own death as "the Lamb of God, which taketh away the sin of the world." That same night He was taken by wicked hands to be crucified and slain. And as the antitype of the wave sheaf our Lord was raised from the dead on the third day, "the first fruits of them that slept," a sample of all the resurrected just, whose "vile body" shall be changed, and "fashioned like unto His glorious body." Verse 20; Philippians 3:21.

In like manner the types which relate to the second advent must be fulfilled at the time pointed out in the symbolic service. Under the 400 Mosaic system the cleansing of the sanctuary, or the great Day of Atonement, occurred on the tenth day of the seventh Jewish month (Leviticus 16:29-34), when the high priest, having made an atonement for all Israel, and thus removed their sins from the sanctuary, came forth and blessed the people. So it was believed that Christ, our great High Priest, would appear to purify the earth by the destruction of sin and sinners, and to bless His waiting people with immortality. The tenth day of the seventh month, the great Day of Atonement, the time of the cleansing of the sanctuary, which in the year 1844 fell upon the twenty-second of October, was regarded as the time of the Lord's coming. This was in harmony with the proofs already presented that the 2300 days would terminate in the autumn, and the conclusion seemed irresistible.

In the parable of Matthew 25 the time of

waiting and slumber is followed by the coming of the bridegroom. This was in accordance with the arguments just presented, both from prophecy and from the types. They carried strong conviction of their truthfulness; and the "midnight cry" was heralded by thousands of believers.

Like a tidal wave the movement swept over the land. From city to city, from village to village, and into remote country places it went, until the waiting people of God were fully aroused. Fanaticism disappeared before this proclamation like early frost before the rising sun. Believers saw their doubt and perplexity removed, and hope and courage animated their hearts. The work was free from those extremes which are ever manifested when there is human excitement without the controlling influence of the word and Spirit of God. It was similar in character to those seasons of humiliation and returning unto the Lord which among ancient Israel followed messages of reproof from His servants. It bore the characteristics that mark the work of God in every age. There was little ecstatic joy, but rather deep searching of heart, confession of sin, and forsaking of the world. A 401 preparation to meet the Lord was the burden of agonizing spirits. There was persevering prayer and unreserved consecration to God.

Said Miller in describing that work: "There is no great expression of joy: that is, as it were, suppressed for a future occasion, when all heaven and earth will rejoice together with joy unspeakable and full of glory. There is no shouting: that, too, is reserved for the shout from heaven. The singers are silent: they are waiting to join the angelic hosts, the choir from heaven. . . . There is no clashing of sentiments: all are of one heart and of one mind."—Bliss, pages 270, 271.

Another who participated in the movement testified: "It produced everywhere the most deep searching of heart and humiliation of soul before the God of high heaven. It caused a weaning of affections from the things of this world, a healing of controversies and animosities, a confession of wrongs, a breaking down before God, and penitent, brokenhearted supplications to Him for pardon and acceptance. It caused self-abasement and prostration of soul, such as we never before witnessed. As God by Joel commanded, when the great day of God should be at hand, it produced a rending of hearts and not of garments, and a turning unto the Lord with fasting, and weeping, and mourning. As God said by Zechariah, a spirit of grace and supplication was poured out upon His children; they looked to Him whom they had pierced, there was a great mourning in the land, . . . and those who were looking for the Lord afflicted their souls before Him."—Bliss, in *Advent Shield and Review,* vol. 1, p. 271 (January, 1845).

Of all the great religious movements since the days of the apostles, none have been more free from human imperfection and the wiles of Satan than was that of the autumn of 1844. Even now, after the lapse of many years, all who shared in that movement and who have stood firm upon the platform of truth still feel the holy influence of that blessed work and bear witness that it was of God.

At the call, "The Bridegroom cometh; go ye 402 out to meet Him," the waiting ones "arose and trimmed their lamps;" they studied the word of God with an intensity of interest before unknown. Angels were sent from heaven to arouse those who had become discouraged and prepare them to receive the message. The work did not stand in the wisdom and learning of men, but in the power of God. It was not the most talented, but the most humble and devoted, who were the first to hear and obey the call. Farmers left their crops standing in the fields, mechanics laid down their tools, and with tears and rejoicing went out to give the warning. Those who had formerly led in the cause were among the last to join in this movement. The churches in general closed their doors against this message, and a large company of those who received it withdrew from their connection. In the providence of God this proclamation united with the second angel's message and gave power to that work.

The message, "Behold, the Bridegroom cometh!" was not so much a matter of argument, though the Scripture proof was clear and conclusive. There went with it an impelling power that moved the soul. There was no doubt, no questioning. Upon the occasion of Christ's triumphal entry into Jerusalem the people who were assembled from all parts of the land to keep the feast flocked to the Mount of Olives, and as they joined the throng that were escorting Jesus they caught the inspiration of the hour and helped to swell the shout: "Blessed is He that cometh in the name of the Lord!" Matthew 21:9. In like manner did unbelievers who flocked to the Adventist meetings—some from curiosity, some merely to ridicule—feel the convincing power attending the message: "Behold, the Bridegroom cometh!"

At that time there was faith that brought answers to prayer—faith that had respect to the recompense of reward. Like showers of rain upon the thirsty earth, the Spirit of grace descended upon the earnest seekers. Those who expected soon to stand face to face with their 403 Redeemer felt a solemn joy that was unutterable. The softening, subduing power of the Holy Spirit melted the heart as His blessing was bestowed in rich measure upon the faithful, believing ones.

Carefully and solemnly those who received the message came up to the time when they hoped to meet their Lord. Every morning they felt that it was their first duty to secure the evidence of their acceptance with God. Their hearts were closely united, and they prayed much with and for one another. They often met together in secluded places to commune with God, and the voice of intercession ascended to heaven from the fields and groves. The assurance of the Saviour's approval was more necessary to them than their daily food; and if a cloud darkened their minds, they did not rest until it was swept away. As they felt the witness of pardoning grace, they longed to behold Him whom their souls loved.

But again they were destined to disappointment. The time of expectation passed, and their Saviour did not appear. With unwavering confidence they had looked forward to His coming, and now they felt as did Mary when, coming to the Saviour's tomb and finding it empty, she exclaimed with weeping: "They have taken away my Lord, and I know not where they have laid Him." John 20:13.

A feeling of awe, a fear that the message might be true, had for a time served as a restraint upon the unbelieving world. After the passing of the time this did not at once disappear; at first they dared not triumph over the disappointed ones; but as no tokens of God's wrath were seen, they recovered from their fears and resumed their reproach and ridicule. A large class who had professed to believe in the Lord's soon coming, renounced their faith. Some who had been very confident were so deeply wounded in their pride that they felt like fleeing from the world. Like Jonah, they complained of God, 404 and chose death rather than life. Those who had based their faith upon the opinions of others, and not upon the word of God, were now as ready again to change their views. The scoffers won the weak and cowardly to their ranks, and all these united in declaring that there could be no more fears or expectations now. The time had passed, the Lord had not come, and the world might remain the same for thousands of years.

The earnest, sincere believers had given up all for Christ and had shared His presence as never before. They had, as they believed, given their last warning to the world; and, expecting soon to be received into the society of their divine Master and the heavenly angels, they had, to a great extent, withdrawn from the society of those who did not receive the message. With intense desire they had prayed: "Come, Lord Jesus, and come quickly." But He had not come. And now to take up again the heavy burden of life's cares and perplexities, and to endure the taunts and sneers of a scoffing world, was a terrible trial of faith and patience.

Yet this disappointment was not so great as was that experienced by the disciples at the time of Christ's first advent. When Jesus rode triumphantly into Jerusalem, His followers believed that He was about to ascend the throne of David and deliver Israel from her oppressors. With high hopes and joyful anticipations they vied with one another in showing honor to their King. Many spread their outer garments as a carpet in His path, or strewed before Him the leafy branches of the palm. In their enthusiastic joy they united in the glad acclaim: "Hosanna to the Son of David!" When the Pharisees, disturbed and angered by this outburst of rejoicing, wished Jesus to rebuke His disciples, He replied: "If these should hold their peace, He stones would immediately cry out." Luke 19:40. Prophecy must be fulfilled. The disciples were accomplishing the purpose of God; yet they were doomed to a bitter disappointment. But a few days had passed ere they witnessed the Saviour's agonizing death, and laid Him in the tomb. Their expectations had not been realized 405 in a single particular, and their hopes died with Jesus. Not till their Lord had come forth triumphant from the grave could they perceive that all had been foretold by prophecy, and "that Christ must needs have suffered, and risen again from the dead." Acts 17:3.

Five hundred years before, the Lord had declared by the prophet Zechariah: "Rejoice greatly, O daughter of Zion; shout, O daughter of Jerusalem: behold, thy King cometh unto thee: He is just, and having salvation; lowly, and riding upon an ass, and upon a colt the foal of an ass." Zechariah 9:9. Had the disciples realized that Christ was going to judgment and to death, they could not have fulfilled this prophecy.

In like manner Miller and his associates fulfilled prophecy and gave a message which Inspiration had foretold should be given to the world, but which they could not have given had they fully understood the prophecies pointing out their disappointment, and presenting another message to be preached to all nations before the Lord should come. The first and second angel's messages were given at the right time and accomplished the work which God designed to accomplish by them.

The world had been looking on, expecting that if the time passed and Christ did not appear, the whole system of Adventism would be given up. But while many, under strong temptation, yielded their faith, there were some who stood firm. The fruits of the advent movement, the spirit of humility and heart searching, of renouncing of the world and reformation of life, which had attended the work, testified that it was of God. They dared not deny that the power of the Holy Spirit had witnessed to the preaching of the second advent, and they could detect no error in their reckoning of the prophetic periods. The ablest of their opponents had not succeeded in overthrowing their system of prophetic interpretation. They could not consent, without Bible evidence, to renounce positions which had been reached through earnest, prayerful study of the Scriptures, by minds enlightened by the Spirit of God and hearts burning with its living power; positions which had withstood the most searching criticisms and the most bitter opposition of popular religious teachers and worldly-wise men, and which had stood firm against the combined forces of learning and eloquence, and the taunts and revilings alike of the honorable and the base.

True, there had been a failure as to the expected event, but even this could not shake their faith in the word of God. When Jonah proclaimed in the streets of Nineveh that within forty days the city would be overthrown, the Lord accepted the humiliation of the Ninevites and extended their period of probation; yet the message of Jonah was sent of God, and Nineveh was tested according to His will. Adventists believed that in like manner God had led them to give the warning of the judgment. "It has," they declared, "tested the hearts of all who heard it, and awakened a love for the Lord's appearing; or it has called forth a hatred, more or less perceivable, but known to God, of His coming. It has drawn a line, . . . so that those who will examine their own hearts, may know on which side of it they would have been found, had the Lord then come—whether they would have exclaimed, 'Lo! this is our God, we have waited for Him, and He will save us;' or whether they would have called to the rocks and mountains to fall on them to hide them from the face of Him that sitteth on the throne, and from the wrath of the Lamb. God thus, as we believe, has tested His people, has tried their faith, has proved them, and seen whether they would shrink, in the hour of trial, from the position in which He might see fit to place them; and whether they would relinquish this world and rely with implicit confidence in the word of God."—*The Advent Herald and Signs of the Times Reporter,* vol. 8, No. 14 (Nov. 13, 1844).

The feelings of those who still believed that God had led them in their past experience are expressed in the words of William Miller: "Were I to live my life over again, with the same evidence that I then had, to be honest with God and man I should have to do as I have done." "I hope that I have cleansed my garments from the blood of souls. I feel that, as far as it was in my power, I have freed myself from all guilt in their condemnation." "Although I have been twice disappointed," wrote this man of God, "I am not yet cast down or discouraged. . . . My hope in the coming of Christ is as strong as ever. I have done only what, after years of solemn consideration, I felt it my solemn duty to do. If I have erred, it has been on the side of

charity, love to my fellow men, and conviction of duty to God." "One thing I do know, I have preached nothing but what I believed; and God has been with me; His power has been manifested in the work, and much good has been effected." "Many thousands, to all human appearance, have been made to study the Scriptures by the preaching of the time; and by that means, through faith and the sprinkling of the blood of Christ, have been reconciled to God."—Bliss, pages 256, 255, 277, 280, 281. "I have never courted the smiles of the proud, nor quailed when the world frowned. I shall not now purchase their favor, nor shall I go beyond duty to tempt their hate. I shall never seek my life at their hands, nor shrink, I hope, from losing it, if God in His good providence so orders."—J. White, *Life of Wm. Miller,* page 315.

God did not forsake His people; His Spirit still abode with those who did not rashly deny the light which they had received, and denounce the advent movement. In the Epistle to the Hebrews are words of encouragement and warning for the tried, waiting ones at this crisis: "Cast not away therefore your confidence, which hath great recompense of reward. For ye have need of patience, that, after ye have done the will of God, ye might receive the promise. For yet a little while, and He that shall come will come, and will not tarry. Now the just shall live by faith: but if any man draw back, My soul shall have no pleasure in him. But we are not of them who draw back unto perdition; but of them that believe to the saving of the soul." Hebrews 10:35-39.

That this admonition is addressed to the church in the last days is evident from the words pointing to the nearness of the Lord's coming: "For yet a little while, and He that shall come will come and will not tarry." And it is plainly implied that there would be a seeming delay and that the Lord would appear to tarry. The instruction here given is especially adapted to the experience of Adventists at this time. The people here addressed were in danger of making shipwreck of faith. They had done the will of God in following the guidance of His Spirit and His word; yet they could not understand His purpose in their past experience, nor could they discern the pathway before them, and they were tempted to doubt whether God had indeed been leading them. At this time the words were applicable: "Now the just shall live by faith." As the bright light of the "midnight cry" had shone upon their pathway, and they had seen the prophecies unsealed and the rapidly fulfilling signs telling that the coming of Christ was near, they had walked, as it were, by sight. But now, bowed down by disappointed hopes, they could stand only by faith in God and in His word. The scoffing world were saying: "You have been deceived. Give up your faith, and say that the advent movement was of Satan." But God's word declared: "If any man draw back, My soul shall have no pleasure in him." To renounce their faith now, and deny the power of the Holy Spirit which had attended the message, would be drawing back toward perdition. They were encouraged to steadfastness by the words of Paul: "Cast not away therefore your confidence;" "ye have need of patience," "for yet a little while, and He that shall come will come, and will not tarry." Their only safe course was to cherish the light which they had already received of God, hold fast to His promises, and continue to search the Scriptures, and patiently wait and watch to receive further light.

23

What Is the Sanctuary?

The scripture which above all others had been both the foundation and the central pillar of the advent faith was the declaration: "Unto two thousand and three hundred days; then shall the sanctuary be cleansed." Daniel 8:14. These had been familiar words to all believers in the Lord's soon coming. By the lips of thousands was this prophecy repeated as the watchword of their faith. All felt that upon the events therein foretold depended their brightest expectations and most cherished hopes. These prophetic days had been shown to terminate in the autumn of 1844. In common with the rest of the Christian world, Adventists then held that the earth, or some portion of it, was the sanctuary. They understood that the cleansing of the sanctuary was the purification of the earth by the fires of the last great day, and that this would take place at the second advent. Hence the conclusion that Christ would return to the earth in 1844.

But the appointed time had passed, and the Lord had not appeared. The believers knew that God's word could not fail; their interpretation of the prophecy must be at fault; but where was the mistake? Many rashly cut the knot of difficulty by denying that the 2300 days ended in 1844. No reason could be given for this except that Christ had not come at the time they expected Him. They argued that if the prophetic days had ended in 1844, Christ would then have returned to cleanse the sanctuary by the purification of the earth by fire; and that since He had not come, the days could not have ended.

To accept this conclusion was to renounce the former reckoning of the prophetic periods. The 2300 days had been found to begin when the commandment of Artaxerxes for the restoration and building of Jerusalem went into effect, in the autumn of 457 B.C. Taking this as the starting point, there was perfect harmony in the application of all the events foretold in the explanation of that period in Daniel 9:25-27. Sixty-nine weeks, the first 483 of the 2300 years, were to reach to the Messiah, the Anointed One; and Christ's baptism and anointing by the Holy Spirit, A.D. 27, exactly fulfilled the specification. In the midst of the seventieth week, Messiah was to be cut off. Three and a half years after His baptism, Christ was crucified, in the spring of A.D. 31. The seventy weeks, or 490 years, were to pertain especially to the Jews. At the expiration of this period the nation sealed its rejection of Christ by the persecution of His disciples, and the apostles turned to the Gentiles, A.D. 34. The first 490 years of the 2300 having then ended, 1810 years would remain. From A.D. 34, 1810 years extend to 1844. "Then," said the angel, "shall the sanctuary be cleansed." All the preceding specifications of the prophecy had been unquestionably fulfilled at the time appointed.

With this reckoning, all was clear and harmonious, except that it was not seen that any event answering to the cleansing of the sanctuary had taken place in 1844. To deny that the days ended at that time was to involve the whole question in confusion, and to renounce positions which had been established by unmistakable fulfillments of prophecy.

But God had led His people in the great advent movement; His power and glory had attended the work, and He would not permit it to end in darkness and disappointment, to be reproached as a false and fanatical excitement. He would not leave His word involved in doubt and uncertainty. Though many abandoned their former reckoning of the prophetic periods and denied the correctness of the movement based thereon, others were unwilling to renounce points of faith and experience that were sustained by the Scriptures and by the witness of the Spirit of God. They believed that they had adopted sound principles of interpretation in their study of the prophecies, and that it was their duty to hold fast the truths already gained, and to continue the same course of Biblical research. With earnest prayer they reviewed their position and studied the Scriptures to discover their mistake. As they could see no error in their reckoning of the prophetic periods, they were led to examine more closely the subject of the sanctuary.

In their investigation they learned that there is no Scripture evidence sustaining the popular view that the earth is the sanctuary; but they found in the Bible a full explanation of the subject of the sanctuary, its nature, location, and services; the testimony of the sacred writers being so clear and ample as to place the matter beyond all question. The apostle Paul, in the Epistle to the Hebrews, says: "Then verily the first covenant had also ordinances of divine service, and a worldly sanctuary. For there was a tabernacle made; the first, wherein was the candlestick, and the table, and the shewbread; which is called the sanctuary. And after the second veil, the tabernacle which is called the holiest of all; which had the golden censer, and the ark of the covenant overlaid round about with gold, wherein was the golden pot that had manna, and Aaron's rod that budded, and the tables of the covenant; and over it the cherubim of glory shadowing the mercy seat." Hebrews 9:1-5.

The sanctuary to which Paul here refers was the tabernacle built by Moses at the command of God as the earthly dwelling place of the Most High. "Let them make Me a sanctuary; that I may dwell among them" (Exodus 25:8), was the direction given to Moses while in the mount with God. The Israelites were journeying through the wilderness, and the tabernacle was so constructed that it could be removed from place to place; yet it was a structure of great magnificence. Its walls consisted of upright boards heavily plated with gold and set in sockets of silver, while the roof was formed of a series of curtains, or coverings, the outer of skins, the innermost of fine linen beautifully wrought with figures of cherubim. Besides the outer court, which contained the altar of burnt offering, the tabernacle itself consisted of two apartments called the holy and the most holy place, separated by a rich and beautiful curtain, or veil; a similar veil closed the entrance to the first apartment.

In the holy place was the candlestick, on the south, with its seven lamps giving light to the sanctuary both by day and by night; on the north stood the table of shewbread; and before the veil separating the holy from the most holy was the golden altar of incense, from which the cloud of fragrance, with the prayers of Israel, was daily ascending before God.

In the most holy place stood the ark, a chest of precious wood overlaid with gold, the depository of the two tables of stone upon which God had inscribed the law of Ten Commandments. Above the ark, and forming the cover to the sacred chest, was the mercy seat, a magnificent piece of workmanship, surmounted by two cherubim, one at each end, and all wrought of solid gold. In this apartment the divine presence was manifested in the cloud of glory between the cherubim.

After the settlement of the Hebrews in Canaan, the tabernacle was replaced by the temple of Solomon, which, though a permanent structure and upon a larger scale, observed the same proportions, and was similarly furnished. In this form the sanctuary existed—except while it lay in ruins in Daniel's time—until its destruction by the Romans, in A.D. 70.

This is the only sanctuary that ever existed on the earth, of which the Bible gives any information. This was declared by Paul to be the sanctuary of the first covenant. But has the new covenant no sanctuary?

Turning again to the book of Hebrews, the seekers for truth found that the existence of a second, or new-covenant sanctuary, was implied in the words of Paul already quoted: "Then verily the first covenant had also ordinances of divine service, and a worldly sanctuary." And the use of the word "*also*" intimates that Paul has before made mention of this sanctuary. Turning back to the beginning of the previous chapter, they read: "Now of the things which we have spoken this is the sum: We have such an High Priest, who is set on the right hand of the throne of the Majesty in the heavens; a Minister of the sanctuary, and of the true tabernacle, which the Lord pitched, and not man." Hebrews 8:1, 2.

Here is revealed the sanctuary of the new covenant. The sanctuary of the first covenant was pitched by man, built by Moses; this is pitched by the Lord, not by man. In that sanctuary the earthly priests performed their service; in this, Christ, our great High Priest, ministers at God's right hand. One sanctuary was on earth, the other is in heaven.

Further, the tabernacle built by Moses was made after a pattern. The Lord directed him: "According to all that I show thee, after the pattern of the tabernacle, and the pattern of all the instruments thereof, even so shall ye make it." And again the charge was given, "Look that thou make them after their pattern, which was showed thee in the mount." Exodus 25:9, 40. And Paul says that the first tabernacle "was a figure for the time then present, in which were offered both gifts and sacrifices;" that its holy places were "patterns of things in the heavens;" that the priests who offered gifts according to the law served "unto the example and shadow of heavenly things," and that "Christ is not entered into the holy places made with hands, which are the figures of the true; but into heaven itself, now to appear in the presence of God for us." Hebrews 9:9, 23; 8:5; 9:24.

The sanctuary in heaven, in which Jesus ministers in our behalf, is the great original, of which the sanctuary built by Moses was a copy. God placed His Spirit upon the builders of the earthly sanctuary. The artistic skill displayed in its construction was a manifestation of divine wisdom. The walls had the appearance of massive gold, reflecting in every direction the light of the seven lamps of the golden candlestick. The table of shewbread and the altar of incense glittered like burnished gold. The gorgeous curtain which formed the ceiling, inwrought with figures of angels in blue and purple and scarlet, added to the beauty of the scene. And beyond the second veil was the holy Shekinah, the visible manifestation of God's glory, before which none but the high priest could enter and live.

The matchless splendor of the earthly tabernacle reflected to human vision the glories of that heavenly temple where Christ our forerunner ministers for us before the throne of God. The abiding place of the King of kings, where thousand thousands minister unto Him, and ten thousand times ten thousand stand before Him (Daniel 7:10); that temple, filled with the glory of the eternal throne, where seraphim, its shining guardians, veil their faces in adoration, could find, in the most magnificent structure ever reared by human hands, but a faint reflection of its vastness and glory. Yet important truths concerning the heavenly sanctuary and the great work there carried forward for man's redemption were taught by the earthly sanctuary and its services.

The holy places of the sanctuary in heaven are represented by the two apartments in the sanctuary on earth. As in vision the apostle John was granted a view of the temple of God in heaven, he beheld there "seven lamps of fire burning before the throne." Revelation 4:5. He saw an angel "having a golden censer; and there was given unto him much incense, that he should offer it with the prayers of all saints upon the golden altar which was before the throne." Revelation 8:3. Here the prophet was permitted 415 to behold the first apartment of the sanctuary in heaven; and he saw there the "seven lamps of fire" and "the golden altar," represented by the golden candlestick and the altar of incense in the sanctuary on earth. Again, "the temple of God was opened" (Revelation 11:19), and he looked within the inner veil, upon the holy of holies. Here he beheld "the ark of His testament," represented by the sacred chest constructed by Moses to contain the law of God.

Thus those who were studying the subject found indisputable proof of the existence of a sanctuary in heaven. Moses made the earthly sanctuary after a pattern which was shown him. Paul teaches that that pattern was the true sanctuary which is in heaven. And John testifies that he saw it in heaven.

In the temple in heaven, the dwelling place of God, His throne is established in righteousness and judgment. In the most holy place is His law, the great rule of right by which all mankind are tested. The ark that enshrines the tables of the law is covered with the mercy seat, before which Christ pleads His blood in the sinner's behalf. Thus is represented the union of justice and mercy in the plan of human redemption. This union infinite wisdom alone could devise and infinite power accomplish; it is a union that fills all heaven with wonder and adoration. The cherubim of the earthly sanctuary, looking reverently down upon the mercy seat, represent the interest with which the heavenly host contemplate the work of redemption. This is the mystery of mercy into which angels desire to look— that God can be just while He justifies the repenting sinner and renews His intercourse with the fallen race; that Christ could stoop to raise unnumbered multitudes from the abyss of ruin and clothe them with the spotless garments of His own righteousness to unite with angels who have never fallen and to dwell forever in the presence of God.

The work of Christ as man's intercessor is presented in that beautiful prophecy of Zechariah concerning Him "whose name is the Branch." Says the prophet: "He shall build the 416 temple of the Lord; and He shall bear the glory, and shall sit and rule upon His [the Father's] throne; and He shall be a priest upon His throne: and the *counsel of peace* shall be between Them both." Zechariah 6:12, 13.

"He shall build the temple of the Lord." By His sacrifice and mediation Christ is both the foundation and the builder of the church of God. The apostle Paul points to Him as "the chief Cornerstone; in whom all the building fitly framed together groweth into an holy temple in the Lord: in whom ye also," he says, "are builded together for an habitation of God through the Spirit." Ephesians 2:20-22.

"He shall bear the glory." To Christ belongs the glory of redemption for the fallen race. Through the eternal ages, the song of the ransomed ones will be: "Unto Him that loved us, and washed us from our sins in His own blood, . . . to Him be glory and dominion for ever and ever." Revelation 1:5, 6.

He "shall sit and rule upon His throne; and He shall be a priest upon His throne." Not now "upon the throne of His glory;" the kingdom of glory has not yet been ushered in. Not until His work as a mediator shall be ended will God "give unto Him the throne of His father David," a kingdom of which "there shall be no end." Luke 1:32, 33. As a priest, Christ is now set down with the Father in His throne. Revelation 3:21. Upon the throne with the eternal, self-existent One is He who "hath borne our griefs, and carried our sorrows," who "was in all points tempted like as we are, yet without sin," that He might be "able to succor them that are tempted." "If any man sin, we have an advocate with the Father." Isaiah 53:4; Hebrews 4:15; 2:18; 1 John 2:1. His intercession is that of a pierced and broken body, of a spotless life. The wounded hands, the pierced side, the marred feet, plead for fallen man, whose redemption was purchased at such infinite cost.

"And the counsel of peace shall be between Them both." The love of the Father, no less than of the Son, is the fountain of salvation for the lost race. Said Jesus to His disciples before He 417 went away: "I say not unto you, that I will pray the Father for you: for the Father Himself loveth you." John 16:26, 27. God was "in Christ, reconciling the world unto Himself." 2 Corinthians 5:19. And in the ministration in the sanctuary above, "the counsel of peace shall be between Them both." "God *so loved* the world, that He gave His only-begotten Son, that whosoever believeth in Him should not perish, but have everlasting life." John 3:16.

The question, What is the sanctuary? is clearly answered in the Scriptures. The term "sanctuary," as used in the Bible, refers, first, to the tabernacle built by Moses, as a pattern of heavenly things; and, secondly, to the "true tabernacle" in heaven, to which the earthly sanctuary pointed. At the death of Christ the typical service ended. The "true tabernacle" in heaven is the sanctuary of the new covenant. And as the prophecy of Daniel 8:14 is fulfilled in this dispensation, the sanctuary to which it refers must be the sanctuary of the new covenant. At the termination of the 2300 days, in 1844, there had been no sanctuary on earth for many centuries. Thus the prophecy, "Unto two thousand and three hundred days; then shall the sanctuary be cleansed," unquestionably points to the sanctuary in heaven.

But the most important question remains to be answered: What is the cleansing of the sanctuary? That there was such a service in connection with the earthly sanctuary is stated in the Old Testament Scriptures. But can there be anything in heaven to be cleansed? In Hebrews 9 the cleansing of both the earthly and the heavenly sanctuary is plainly taught. "Almost all things are by the law purged with blood; and without shedding of blood is no remission. It was therefore necessary that the patterns of things in the heavens should be purified with these [the blood of animals]; but the heavenly things themselves with better sacrifices than these" (Hebrews 9:22, 23), even the precious blood of Christ.

The cleansing, both in the typical and in the real service, must be accomplished with blood:
418 in the former, with the blood of animals; in the latter, with the blood of Christ. Paul states, as the reason why this cleansing must be performed with blood, that without shedding of blood is no *remission*. Remission, or putting away of sin, is the work to be accomplished. But how could there be sin connected with the sanctuary, either in heaven or upon the earth? This may be learned by reference to the symbolic service; for the priests who officiated on earth, served "unto the example and shadow of heavenly things." Hebrews 8:5.

The ministration of the earthly sanctuary consisted of two divisions; the priests ministered daily in the holy place, while once a year the high priest performed a special work of atonement in the most holy, for the cleansing of the sanctuary. Day by day the repentant sinner brought his offering to the door of the tabernacle and, placing his hand upon the victim's head, confessed his sins, thus in figure transferring them from himself to the innocent sacrifice. The animal was then slain. "Without shedding of blood," says the apostle, there is no remission of sin. "The life of the flesh is in the blood." Leviticus 17:11. The broken law of God demanded the life of the transgressor. The blood, representing the forfeited life of the sinner, whose guilt the victim bore, was carried by the priest into the holy place and sprinkled before the veil, behind which was the ark containing the law that the sinner had transgressed. By this ceremony the sin was, through the blood, transferred in figure to the sanctuary. In some cases the blood was not taken into the holy place; but the flesh was then to be eaten by the priest, as Moses directed the sons of Aaron, saying: "God hath given it you to bear the iniquity of the congregation." Leviticus 10:17. Both ceremonies alike symbolized the transfer of the sin from the penitent to the sanctuary.

Such was the work that went on, day by day, throughout the year. The sins of Israel were thus transferred to the sanctuary, and a special work became necessary for their removal. God commanded that an atonement be made for each of the sacred apartments. "He shall make an atone- 419 ment for the holy place, because of the uncleanness of the children of Israel, and because of their transgressions in all their sins: and so shall he do for the tabernacle of the congregation, that remaineth among them in the midst of their uncleanness." An atonement was also to be made for the altar, to "cleanse it, and hallow it from the uncleanness of the children of Israel." Leviticus 16:16, 19.

Once a year, on the great Day of Atonement, the priest entered the most holy place for the cleansing of the sanctuary. The work there performed completed the yearly round of ministration. On the Day of Atonement two kids of the goats were brought to the door of the tabernacle, and lots were cast upon them, "one lot for the Lord, and the other lot for the scapegoat." Verse 8. The goat upon which fell the lot for the Lord was to be slain as a sin offering for the people. And the priest was to bring his blood within the veil and sprinkle it upon the mercy seat and before the mercy seat. The blood was also to be sprinkled upon the altar of incense that was before the veil.

"And Aaron shall lay both his hands upon the head of the live goat, and confess over him all the iniquities of the children of Israel, and all their transgressions in all their sins, putting them upon the head of the goat, and shall send him away by the hand of a fit man into the wilderness: and the goat shall bear upon him all their iniquities unto a land not inhabited." Verses 21, 22. The scapegoat came no more into the camp of Israel, and the man who led him away was required to wash himself and his clothing with water before returning to the camp.

The whole ceremony was designed to impress the Israelites with the holiness of God and His abhorrence of sin; and, further, to show them that they could not come in contact with sin without becoming polluted. Every man was required to afflict his soul while this work of atonement was going forward. All business was to be laid aside, and the whole congregation of Israel were to spend the day in solemn humiliation before God, with prayer, fasting, and deep searching of heart.

Important truths concerning the atonement are taught by the typical service. A substitute was accepted in the sinner's stead; but the sin was not canceled by the blood of the victim. A means was thus provided by which it was transferred to the sanctuary. By the offering of blood the sinner acknowledged the authority of the law, confessed his guilt in transgression, and expressed his desire for pardon through faith in a Redeemer to come; but he was not yet entirely released from the condemnation of the law. On the Day of Atonement the high priest, having taken an offering from the congregation, went into the most holy place with the blood of this offering, and sprinkled it upon the mercy seat, directly over the law, to make satisfaction for its claims. Then, in his character of mediator, he took the sins upon himself and bore them from the sanctuary. Placing his hands upon the head of the scapegoat, he confessed over him all these sins, thus in figure transferring them from himself to the goat. The goat then bore them away, and they were regarded as forever separated from the people.

Such was the service performed "unto the example and shadow of heavenly things." And what was done in type in the ministration of the earthly sanctuary is done in reality in the ministration of the heavenly sanctuary. After His ascension our Saviour began His work as our high priest. Says Paul: "Christ is not entered into the holy places made with hands, which are the figures of the true; but into heaven itself, now to appear in the presence of God for us." Hebrews 9:24.

The ministration of the priest throughout the year in the first apartment of the sanctuary, "within the veil" which formed the door and separated the holy place from the outer court, represents the work of ministration upon which Christ entered at His ascension. It was the work of the priest in the daily ministration to present before God the blood of the sin offering, also the incense which ascended with the prayers of Israel. So did Christ plead His blood before the Father in behalf of sinners, and present before Him also, with the precious fragrance of His own righteousness, the prayers of penitent believers. Such was the work of ministration in the first apartment of the sanctuary in heaven.

Thither the faith of Christ's disciples followed Him as He ascended from their sight. Here their hopes centered, "which hope we have," said Paul, "as an anchor of the soul, both sure and steadfast, and which entereth into that within the veil; whither the forerunner is for us entered, even Jesus, made an high priest forever." "Neither by the blood of goats and calves, but by His own blood He entered in once into the holy place, having obtained eternal redemption for us." Hebrews 6:19, 20; 9:12.

For eighteen centuries this work of ministration continued in the first apartment of the sanctuary. The blood of Christ, pleaded in behalf of penitent believers, secured their pardon and acceptance with the Father, yet their sins still remained upon the books of record. As in the typical service there was a work of atonement at the close of the year, so before Christ's work for the redemption of men is completed there is a work of atonement for the removal of sin from the sanctuary. This is the service which began when the 2300 days ended. At that time, as foretold by Daniel the prophet, our High Priest entered the most holy, to perform the last division of His solemn work—to cleanse the sanctuary.

As anciently the sins of the people were by faith placed upon the sin offering and through its blood transferred, in figure, to the earthly sanctuary, so in the new covenant the sins of the repentant are by faith placed upon Christ and transferred, in fact, to the heavenly sanctuary. And as the typical cleansing of the earthly was accomplished by the removal of the sins by which it had been polluted, so the actual cleansing of the heavenly is to be accomplished by the removal, or blotting out, of the sins which are there recorded. But before this can be accomplished, there must be an examination of the books of record to determine who, through repentance of sin and faith in Christ, are entitled to the benefits of His atonement. The cleansing of the sanctuary therefore involves a work of investigation—a work of judgment. This work must be performed prior to the coming of Christ to redeem His people; for when He comes, His reward is with Him to give to every man according to his works. Revelation 22:12.

Thus those who followed in the light of the prophetic word saw that, instead of coming to the earth at the termination of the 2300 days in 1844, Christ then entered the most holy place of the heavenly sanctuary to perform the closing work of atonement preparatory to His coming.

It was seen, also, that while the sin offering pointed to Christ as a sacrifice, and the high priest represented Christ as a mediator, the scapegoat typified Satan, the author of sin, upon whom the sins of the truly penitent will finally be placed. When the high priest, by virtue of the blood of the sin offering, removed the sins from the sanctuary, he placed them upon the scapegoat. When Christ, by virtue of His own blood, removes the sins of His people from the heavenly sanctuary at the close of His ministration, He will place them upon Satan, who, in the execution of the judgment, must bear the final penalty. The scapegoat was sent away into a land not inhabited, never to come again into the congregation of Israel. So will Satan be forever banished from the presence of God and His people, and he will be blotted from existence in the final destruction of sin and sinners.

423

24
In the Holy of Holies

The subject of the sanctuary was the key which unlocked the mystery of the disappointment of 1844. It opened to view a complete system of truth, connected and harmonious, showing that God's hand had directed the great advent movement and revealing present duty as it brought to light the position and work of His people. As the disciples of Jesus after the terrible night of their anguish and disappointment were "glad when they saw the Lord," so did those now rejoice who had looked in faith for His second coming. They had expected Him to appear in glory to give reward to His servants. As their hopes were disappointed, they had lost sight of Jesus, and with Mary at the sepulcher they cried: "They have taken away my Lord, and I know not where they have laid Him." Now in the holy of holies they again beheld Him, their compassionate High Priest, soon to appear as their king and deliverer. Light from the sanctuary illumined the past, the present, and the future. They knew that God had led them by His unerring providence. Though, like the first disciples, they themselves had failed to understand the message which they bore, yet it had been in every respect correct. In proclaiming it they had fulfilled the purpose of God, and their labor had not been in vain in the Lord. Begotten "again unto a lively hope," they rejoiced "with joy unspeakable and full of glory."

424 Both the prophecy of Daniel 8:14, "Unto two thousand and three hundred days; then shall the sanctuary be cleansed," and the first angel's message, "Fear God, and give glory to Him; for the hour of His judgment is come," pointed to Christ's ministration in the most holy place, to the investigative judgment, and not to the coming of Christ for the redemption of His people and the destruction of the wicked. The mistake had not been in the reckoning of the prophetic periods, but in the *event* to take place at the end of the 2300 days. Through this error the believ-

ers had suffered disappointment, yet all that was foretold by the prophecy, and all that they had any Scripture warrant to expect, had been accomplished. At the very time when they were lamenting the failure of their hopes, the event had taken place which was foretold by the message, and which must be fulfilled before the Lord could appear to give reward to His servants.

Christ had come, not to the earth, as they expected, but, as foreshadowed in the type, to the most holy place of the temple of God in heaven. He is represented by the prophet Daniel as coming at this time to the Ancient of Days: "I saw in the night visions, and, behold, one like the Son of man came with the clouds of heaven, and came"—not to the earth, but—"to the Ancient of Days, and they brought Him near before Him." Daniel 7:13.

This coming is foretold also by the prophet Malachi: "The Lord, whom ye seek, shall suddenly come to His temple, even the Messenger of the covenant, whom ye delight in: behold, He shall come, saith the Lord of hosts." Malachi 3:1. The coming of the Lord to His temple was sudden, unexpected, to His people. They were not looking for Him *there*. They expected Him to come to earth, "in flaming fire taking vengeance on them that know not God, and that obey not the gospel." 2 Thessalonians 1:8.

But the people were not yet ready to meet their Lord. There was still a work of preparation to be accomplished for them. Light was to be 425 given, directing their minds to the temple of God in heaven; and as they should by faith follow their High Priest in His ministration there, new duties would be revealed. Another message of warning and instruction was to be given to the church.

Says the prophet: "Who may abide the day of His coming? and who shall stand when He appeareth? for He is like a refiner's fire, and like fullers' soap: and He shall sit as a refiner and purifier of silver: and He shall purify the sons of Levi, and purge them as gold and silver, that they may offer unto the Lord an offering in righteousness." Malachi 3:2, 3. Those who are living upon the earth when the intercession of Christ shall cease in the sanctuary above are to stand in the sight of a holy God without a mediator. Their robes must be spotless, their characters must be purified from sin by the blood of sprinkling. Through the grace of God and their own diligent effort they must be conquerors in the battle with evil. While the investigative judgment is going forward in heaven, while the sins of penitent believers are being removed from the sanctuary, there is to be a special work of purification, of putting away of sin, among God's people upon earth. This work is more clearly presented in the messages of Revelation 14.

When this work shall have been accomplished, the followers of Christ will be ready for His appearing. "Then shall the offering of Judah and Jerusalem be pleasant unto the Lord, as in the days of old, and as in former years." Malachi 3:4. Then the church which our Lord at His coming is to receive to Himself will be a "glorious church, not having spot, or wrinkle, or any such thing." Ephesians 5:27. Then she will look "forth as the morning, fair as the moon, clear as the sun, and terrible as an army with banners." Song of Solomon 6:10.

Besides the coming of the Lord to His temple, Malachi also foretells His second advent, His coming for the execution of the judgment, in these words: "And I will come near to you to judgment; and I will be a swift witness against the sorcerers, and against the adulterers, and against false swearers, and against those that oppress the hireling in his wages, the widow, and the fatherless, and that turn aside the stranger from his right, and fear not Me, saith the Lord of hosts." Malachi 3:5. Jude refers to the same scene when he says, "Behold, the Lord cometh with ten thousands of His saints, to execute judgment upon all, and to convince all that are ungodly among them of all their ungodly deeds." Jude 14, 15. This coming, and the coming of the Lord to His temple, are distinct and separate events.

The coming of Christ as our high priest to the most holy place, for the cleansing of the sanctuary, brought to view in Daniel 8:14; the coming of the Son of man to the Ancient of Days, as presented in Daniel 7:13; and the coming of the Lord to His temple, foretold by Malachi, are descriptions of the same event; and this is also represented by the coming of the bridegroom to the marriage, described by Christ in the parable of the ten virgins, of Matthew 25.

In the summer and autumn of 1844 the proclamation, "Behold, the Bridegroom cometh," was given. The two classes represented by the wise and foolish virgins were then developed—one class who looked with joy to the Lord's appearing, and who had been diligently preparing to meet Him; another class that, influenced by fear and acting from impulse, had been satisfied with a theory of the truth, but were destitute of the grace of God. In the parable, when the bridegroom came, "they that were ready went in with him to the marriage." The coming of the bridegroom, here brought to view, takes place before the marriage. The marriage represents the reception by Christ of His kingdom. The Holy City, the New Jerusalem, which is the capital and representative of the kingdom, is called "the bride, the Lamb's wife." Said the angel to John: "Come hither, I will show thee the bride, the Lamb's wife." "He carried me away in the spirit," says the prophet, "and showed me that great city, the holy Jerusalem, descending out of heaven from God." Revelation 21:9, 10. Clearly, then, the bride represents the Holy City, and the virgins that go out to meet the bridegroom are a symbol of the church. In the Revelation the people of God are said to be the guests at the marriage supper. Revelation 19:9. If *guests*, they cannot be represented also as the *bride*. Christ, as stated by the prophet Daniel, will receive from the Ancient of Days in heaven, "dominion, and glory, and a kingdom;" He will receive the New Jerusalem, the capital of His kingdom, "prepared as a bride adorned for her husband." Daniel 7:14; Revelation 21:2. Having received the kingdom, He will come in His glory, as King of kings and Lord of lords, for the redemption of His people, who are to "sit down with Abraham, and Isaac, and Jacob," at His table in His kingdom (Matthew 8:11; Luke 22:30), to partake of the marriage supper of the Lamb.

The proclamation, "Behold, the Bridegroom cometh," in the summer of 1844, led thousands to expect the immediate advent of the Lord. At the appointed time the Bridegroom came, not to the earth, as the people expected, but to the Ancient of Days in heaven, to the marriage, the reception of His kingdom. "They that were ready went in with Him to the marriage: and the door was shut." They were not to be present in person at the marriage; for it takes place in heaven, while they are upon the earth. The followers of Christ are to "wait for their Lord, when He will *return from* the wedding." Luke 12:36. But they are to understand His work, and to follow Him by faith as He goes in before God. It is in this sense that they are said to go in to the marriage.

In the parable it was those that had oil in their vessels with their lamps that went in to the marriage. Those who, with a knowledge of the truth from the Scriptures, had also the Spirit and grace of God, and who, in the night of their bitter trial, had patiently waited, searching the Bible for clearer light—these saw the truth concerning the sanctuary in heaven and the Saviour's change in ministration, and by faith they followed Him in His work in the sanctuary above. And all who through the testimony of the Scriptures accept the same truths, following Christ by faith as He enters in before God to perform the last work of mediation, and at its close to receive His kingdom—all these are represented as going in to the marriage.

In the parable of Matthew 22 the same figure of the marriage is introduced, and the investigative judgment is clearly represented as taking place before the marriage. Previous to the wedding the king comes in to see the guests, to see if all are attired in the wedding garment, the spotless robe of character washed and made white in the blood of the Lamb. Matthew 22:11; Revelation 7:14. He who is found wanting is cast out, but all who upon examination are seen to have the wedding garment on are accepted of God and accounted worthy of a share in His kingdom and a seat upon His throne. This work of examination of character, of determining who are prepared for the kingdom of God, is that of the investigative judgment, the closing work in the sanctuary above.

When the work of investigation shall be ended, when the cases of those who in all ages have professed to be followers of Christ have been examined and decided, then, and not till then, probation will close, and the door of mercy will be shut. Thus in the one short sentence, "They that were ready went in with Him to the marriage: and the door was shut," we are carried down through the Saviour's final ministration, to the time when the great work for man's salvation shall be completed.

In the service of the earthly sanctuary, which, as we have seen, is a figure of the service in the heavenly, when the high priest on the Day of Atonement entered the most holy place, the ministration in the first apartment ceased. God commanded: "There shall be no man in the tabernacle of the congregation when he goeth in to make an atonement in the holy place, until he comes out." Leviticus 16:17. So when Christ entered the holy of holies to perform the closing work of the atonement, He ceased His ministration in the first apartment. But when the ministration in the first apartment ended, the ministration in the second apartment began. When in the typical service the high priest left the holy on the Day of Atonement, he went in before God to present the blood of the sin offering in behalf of all Israel who truly repented of their sins. So Christ had only completed one part of His work as our intercessor, to enter upon another portion of the work, and He still pleaded His blood before the Father in behalf of sinners.

This subject was not understood by Adventists in 1844. After the passing of the time when the Saviour was expected, they still believed His coming to be near; they held that they had reached an important crisis and that the work of Christ as man's intercessor before God had ceased. It appeared to them to be taught in the Bible that man's probation would close a short time before the actual coming of the Lord in the clouds of heaven. This seemed evident from those scriptures which point to a time when men will seek, knock, and cry at the door of mercy, and it will not be opened. And it was a question with them whether the date to which they had looked for the coming of Christ might not rather mark the beginning of this period which was immediately to precede His coming. Having given the warning of the judgment near, they felt that their work for the world was done, and they lost their burden of soul for the salvation of sinners, while the bold and blasphemous scoffing of the ungodly seemed to them another evi-

dence that the Spirit of God had been withdrawn from the rejecters of His mercy. All this confirmed them in the belief that probation had ended, or, as they then expressed it, "the door of mercy was shut."

But clearer light came with the investigation of the sanctuary question. They now saw that they were correct in believing that the end of the 2300 days in 1844 marked an important crisis. But while it was true that that door of hope and mercy by which men had for eighteen hundred years found access to God, was closed, another door was opened, and forgiveness of sins was offered to men through the intercession of Christ in the most holy. One part of His ministration had closed, only to give place to another. There was still an "open door" to the heavenly sanctuary, where Christ was ministering in the sinner's behalf.

Now was seen the application of those words of Christ in the Revelation, addressed to the church at this very time: "These things saith He that is holy, He that is true, He that hath the key of David, He that openeth, and no man shutteth; and shutteth, and no man openeth; I know thy works: behold, I have set before thee an open door, and no man can shut it." Revelation 3:7, 8.

It is those who by faith follow Jesus in the great work of the atonement who receive the benefits of His mediation in their behalf, while those who reject the light which brings to view this work of ministration are not benefited thereby. The Jews who rejected the light given at Christ's first advent, and refused to believe on Him as the Saviour of the world, could not receive pardon through Him. When Jesus at His ascension entered by His own blood into the heavenly sanctuary to shed upon His disciples the blessings of His mediation, the Jews were left in total darkness to continue their useless sacrifices and offerings. The ministration of types and shadows had ceased. That door by which men had formerly found access to God was no longer open. The Jews had refused to seek Him in the only way whereby He could then be found, through the ministration in the sanctuary in heaven. Therefore they found no communion with God. To them the door was shut. They had no knowledge of Christ as the true sacrifice and the only mediator before God; hence they could not receive the benefits of His mediation.

The condition of the unbelieving Jews illustrates the condition of the careless and unbelieving among professed Christians, who are willingly ignorant of the work of our merciful High Priest. In the typical service, when the high priest entered the most holy place, all Israel were required to gather about the sanctuary and in the most solemn manner humble their souls before God, that they might receive the pardon of their sins and not be cut off from the congregation. How much more essential in this anti-typical Day of Atonement that we understand the work of our High Priest and know what duties are required of us.

Men cannot with impunity reject the warning which God in mercy sends them. A message was sent from heaven to the world in Noah's day, and their salvation depended upon the manner in which they treated that message. Because they rejected the warning, the Spirit of God was withdrawn from the sinful race, and they perished in the waters of the Flood. In the time of Abraham, mercy ceased to plead with the guilty inhabitants of Sodom, and all but Lot with his wife and two daughters were consumed by the fire sent down from heaven. So in the days of Christ. The Son of God declared to the unbelieving Jews of that generation: "Your house is left unto you desolate." Matthew 23:38. Looking down to the last days, the same Infinite Power declares, concerning those who "received not the love of the truth, that they might be saved": "For this cause God shall send them strong delusion, that they should believe a lie: that they all might be damned who believed not the truth, but had pleasure in unrighteousness." 2 Thessalonians 2:10-12. As they reject the teachings of His word, God withdraws His Spirit and leaves them to the deceptions which they love.

But Christ still intercedes in man's behalf, and light will be given to those who seek it. Though this was not at first understood by Adventists, it was afterward made plain as the Scriptures which define their true position began to open before them.

The passing of the time in 1844 was followed by a period of great trial to those who still held the advent faith. Their only relief, so far as 432 ascertaining their true position was concerned, was the light which directed their minds to the sanctuary above. Some renounced their faith in their former reckoning of the prophetic periods and ascribed to human or satanic agencies the powerful influence of the Holy Spirit which had attended the advent movement. Another class firmly held that the Lord had led them in their past experience; and as they waited and watched and prayed to know the will of God they saw that their great High Priest had entered upon another work of ministration, and, following Him by faith, they were led to see also the closing work of the church. They had a clearer understanding of the first and second angels' messages, and were prepared to receive and give to the world the solemn warning of the third angel of Revelation 14.

25 ⁴³³

God's Law Immutable

"The temple of God was opened in heaven, and there was seen in His temple the ark of His testament." Revelation 11:19. The ark of God's testament is in the holy of holies, the second apartment of the sanctuary. In the ministration of the earthly tabernacle, which served "unto the example and shadow of heavenly things," this apartment was opened only upon the great Day of Atonement for the cleansing of the sanctuary. Therefore the announcement that the temple of God was opened in heaven and the ark of His testament was seen points to the opening of the most holy place of the heavenly sanctuary in 1844 as Christ entered there to perform the closing work of the atonement. Those who by faith followed their great High Priest as He entered upon His ministry in the most holy place, beheld the ark of His testament. As they had studied the subject of the sanctuary they had come to understand the Saviour's change of ministration, and they saw that He was now officiating before the ark of God, pleading His blood in behalf of sinners.

The ark in the tabernacle on earth contained the two tables of stone, upon which were inscribed the precepts of the law of God. The ark was merely a receptacle for the tables of the law, and the presence of these divine precepts gave to it its value and sacredness. When the temple of God was opened in heaven, the ark of His testament was seen. Within the holy of ⁴³⁴ holies, in the sanctuary in heaven, the divine law is sacredly enshrined—the law that was spoken by God Himself amid the thunders of Sinai and written with His own finger on the tables of stone.

The law of God in the sanctuary in heaven is the great original, of which the precepts inscribed upon the tables of stone and recorded by Moses in the Pentateuch were an unerring transcript. Those who arrived at an understanding of this important point were thus led to see the sacred, unchanging character of the divine law. They saw, as never before, the force of the Saviour's words: "Till heaven and earth pass, one jot or one tittle shall in no wise pass from the law." Matthew 5:18. The law of God, being a revelation of His will, a transcript of His character, must forever endure, "as a faithful witness in heaven." Not one command has been annulled; not a jot or tittle has been changed. Says the psalmist: "Forever, O Lord, Thy word is settled in heaven." "All His commandments are sure. They stand fast for ever and ever." Psalms 119:89; 111:7, 8.

In the very bosom of the Decalogue is the fourth commandment, as it was first proclaimed: "Remember the Sabbath day, to keep it holy. Six days shalt thou labor, and do all thy work: but the seventh day is the Sabbath of the Lord thy God: in it thou shalt not do any work, thou, nor thy son, nor thy daughter, thy manservant, nor thy maidservant, nor thy cattle, nor thy stranger that is within thy gates: for in six days the Lord made heaven and earth, the sea, and all that in them is, and rested the seventh day: wherefore the Lord blessed the Sabbath day, and hallowed it." Exodus 20:8-11.

The Spirit of God impressed the hearts of those students of His word. The conviction was urged upon them that they had ignorantly transgressed this precept by disregarding the Creator's rest day. They began to examine the reasons for observing the first day of the week instead of the day which God had sanctified. 435 They could find no evidence in the Scriptures that the fourth commandment had been abolished, or that the Sabbath had been changed; the blessing which first hallowed the seventh day had never been removed. They had been honestly seeking to know and to do God's will; now, as they saw themselves transgressors of His law, sorrow filled their hearts, and they manifested their loyalty to God by keeping His Sabbath holy.

Many and earnest were the efforts made to overthrow their faith. None could fail to see that if the earthly sanctuary was a figure or pattern of the heavenly, the law deposited in the ark on earth was an exact transcript of the law in the ark in heaven; and that an acceptance of the truth concerning the heavenly sanctuary involved an acknowledgment of the claims of God's law and the obligation of the Sabbath of the fourth commandment. Here was the secret of the bitter and determined opposition to the harmonious exposition of the Scriptures that revealed the ministration of Christ in the heavenly sanctuary. Men sought to close the door which God had opened, and to open the door which He had closed. But "He that openeth, and no man shutteth; and shutteth, and no man openeth," had declared: "Behold, I have set before thee an open door, and no man can shut it." Revelation 3:7, 8. Christ had opened the door, or ministration, of the most holy place, light was shining from that open door of the sanctuary in heaven, and the fourth commandment was shown to be included in the law which is there enshrined; what God had established, no man could overthrow.

Those who had accepted the light concerning the mediation of Christ and the perpetuity of the law of God found that these were the truths presented in Revelation 14. The messages of this chapter constitute a threefold warning (see Appendix) which is to prepare the inhabitants of the earth for the Lord's second coming. The announcement, "The hour of His judgment is come," points to the closing work of Christ's ministration for the salvation of men. It heralds a truth which must be proclaimed until the Saviour's intercession shall cease and He shall 436 return to the earth to take His people to Himself. The work of judgment which began in 1844 must continue until the cases of all are decided, both of the living and the dead; hence it will extend to the close of human probation. That men may be prepared to stand in the judgment, the message commands them to "fear God, and give glory to Him," "and worship Him that made heaven, and earth, and the sea, and the fountains of waters." The result of an acceptance of these messages is given in the word: "Here are they that keep the commandments of God, and the faith of Jesus." In order to be prepared for the judgment, it is necessary that men should keep the law of God. That law will be the standard of character in the judgment. The apostle Paul declares: "As many as have sinned in the law shall be judged by the law, . . . in the day when God shall judge the secrets of men by Jesus Christ." And he says that "the doers of the law shall be justified." Romans 2:12-16. Faith is essential in order to the keeping of the law of God; for "without faith it is impossible to please Him." And "whatsoever is not of faith is sin." Hebrews 11:6; Romans 14:23.

By the first angel, men are called upon to "fear God, and give glory to Him" and to worship Him as the Creator of the heavens and the earth. In order to do this, they must obey His law. Says the wise man: "Fear God, and keep His commandments: for this is the whole duty of man." Ecclesiastes 12:13. Without obedience to His commandments no worship can be pleasing to God. "This is the love of God, that we keep His commandments." "He that turneth away his ear from hearing the law, even his prayer shall be abomination." 1 John 5:3; Proverbs 28:9.

The duty to worship God is based upon the fact that He is the Creator and that to Him all other beings owe their existence. And wherever, in the Bible, His claim to reverence and worship, above the gods of the heathen, is presented, there is cited the evidence of His creative 437 power. "All the gods of the nations are idols: but the Lord made the heavens." Psalm 96:5. "To whom then will ye liken Me, or shall I be equal? saith the Holy One. Lift up your eyes on high, and behold who hath created these things." "Thus saith the Lord that created the heavens; God Himself that formed the earth and made it: . . . I am the Lord; and there is none else." Isaiah 40:25, 26; 45:18. Says the psalmist: "Know ye that the Lord He is God: it is He that hath made us, and not we ourselves." "O come, let us worship and bow down: let us kneel before the Lord our Maker." Psalms 100:3; 95:6. And the holy beings who worship God in heaven state, as the reason why their homage is due to Him: "Thou art worthy, O Lord, to receive glory and honor and power: for Thou hast created all things." Revelation 4:11.

In Revelation 14, men are called upon to worship the Creator; and the prophecy brings to view a class that, as the result of the threefold message, are keeping the commandments of God. One of these commandments points directly to God as the Creator. The fourth precept declares: "The seventh day is the Sabbath of the Lord thy God: . . . for in six days the Lord made heaven and earth, the sea, and all that in them is, and rested the seventh day: wherefore the Lord blessed the Sabbath day, and hallowed it." Exodus 20:10, 11. Concerning the Sabbath, the Lord says, further, that it is "a sign, . . . that ye may know that I am the Lord your God." Ezekiel 20:20. And the reason given is: "For in six days the Lord made heaven and earth, and on the seventh day He rested, and was refreshed." Exodus 31:17.

"The importance of the Sabbath as the memorial of creation is that it keeps ever present the true reason why worship is due to God"— because He is the Creator, and we are His creatures. "The Sabbath therefore lies at the very foundation of divine worship, for it teaches this great truth in the most impressive manner, and no other institution does this. The true ground of divine worship, not of that on the seventh day merely, but of all worship, is found in the distinction between the Creator and His creatures. This great fact can never become obsolete, and must never be forgotten."—J. N. Andrews, *History of the Sabbath*, chapter 27. It was to keep this truth ever before the minds of men, that God instituted the Sabbath in Eden; and so long as the fact that He is our Creator continues to be a reason why we should worship Him, so long the Sabbath will continue as its sign and memorial. Had the Sabbath been universally kept, man's thoughts and affections would have been led to the Creator as the object of reverence and worship, and there would never have been an idolater, an atheist, or an infidel. The keeping of the Sabbath is a sign of loyalty to the true God, "Him that made heaven, and earth, and the sea, and the fountains of waters." It follows that the message which commands men to worship God and keep His commandments will especially call upon them to keep the fourth commandment.

In contrast to those who keep the commandments of God and have the faith of Jesus, the third angel points to another class, against whose errors a solemn and fearful warning is uttered: "If any man worship the beast and his image, and receive his mark in his forehead, or in his hand, the same shall drink of the wine of the wrath of God." Revelation 14:9, 10. A correct interpretation of the symbols employed is necessary to an understanding of this message. What is represented by the beast, the image, the mark?

The line of prophecy in which these symbols are found begins with Revelation 12, with the dragon that sought to destroy Christ at His birth. The dragon is said to be Satan (Revelation 12:9); he it was that moved upon Herod to put the Saviour to death. But the chief agent of Satan in making war upon Christ and His people during the first centuries of the Christian Era was the Roman Empire, in which paganism was the prevailing religion. Thus while the dragon, primarily, represents Satan, it is, in a secondary sense, a symbol of pagan Rome.

In chapter 13 (verses 1-10) is described another beast, "like unto a leopard," to which the dragon gave "his power, and his seat, and great authority." This symbol, as most Protestants have believed, represents the papacy, which succeeded to the power and seat and authority once held by the ancient Roman empire. Of the leopardlike beast it is declared: "There was given unto him a mouth speaking great things and blasphemies. . . . And he opened his mouth in blasphemy against God, to blaspheme His name, and His tabernacle, and them that dwell in heaven. And it was given unto him to make war with the saints, and to overcome them: and power was given him over all kindreds, and tongues, and nations." This prophecy, which is nearly identical with the description of the little horn of Daniel 7, unquestionably points to the papacy.

"Power was given unto him to continue forty and two months." And, says the prophet, "I saw one of his heads as it were wounded to death." And again: "He that leadeth into captivity shall go into captivity: he that killeth with the sword must be killed with the sword." The forty and two months are the same as the "time and times and the dividing of time," three years and a half, or 1260 days, of Daniel 7—the time during which the papal power was to oppress God's people. This period, as stated in preceding chapters, began with the supremacy of the papacy, A.D. 538, and terminated in 1798. At that time the pope was made captive by the French army, the papal power received its deadly wound, and the prediction was fulfilled, "He that leadeth into captivity shall go into captivity."

At this point another symbol is introduced. Says the prophet: "I beheld another beast coming up out of the earth; and he had two horns like a lamb." Verse 11. Both the appearance of this beast and the manner of its rise indicate that the nation which it represents is unlike those presented under the preceding symbols. The great kingdoms that have ruled the world were presented to the prophet Daniel as beasts of prey, rising when "the four winds of the heaven strove upon the great sea." Daniel 7:2. In Revelation 17 an angel explained that waters represent "peoples, and multitudes, and nations, and tongues." Revelation 17:15. Winds are a symbol of strife. The four winds of heaven striving upon the great sea represent the terrible scenes of conquest and revolution by which kingdoms have attained to power.

But the beast with lamblike horns was seen "coming up out of the earth." Instead of overthrowing other powers to establish itself, the nation thus represented must arise in territory previously unoccupied and grow up gradually and peacefully. It could not, then, arise among the crowded and struggling nationalities of the Old World—that turbulent sea of "peoples, and multitudes, and nations, and tongues." It must be sought in the Western Continent.

What nation of the New World was in 1798 rising into power, giving promise of strength and greatness, and attracting the attention of the world? The application of the symbol admits of no question. One nation, and only one, meets the specifications of this prophecy; it points unmistakably to the United States of America. Again and again the thought, almost the exact words, of the sacred writer has been unconsciously employed by the orator and the historian in describing the rise and growth of this nation. The beast was seen "coming up out of the earth;" and, according to the translators, the word here rendered "coming up" literally signifies "to grow or spring up as a plant." And, as we have seen, the nation must arise in territory previously unoccupied. A prominent writer, describing the rise of the United States, speaks of "*the mystery of her coming forth from vacancy,*" and says: "Like a *silent seed* we grew into empire."—G. A. Townsend, *The New World Compared With the Old,* page 462. A European journal in 1850 spoke of the United States as a wonderful empire, which was "emerging," and "*amid the silence of the earth* daily adding to its power and pride."—The *Dublin Nation.* Edward 441 Everett, in an oration on the Pilgrim founders of this nation, said: "Did they look for a retired spot, inoffensive for its obscurity, and safe in its remoteness, where the little church of Leyden might enjoy the freedom of conscience? Behold the *mighty regions* over which, in *peaceful conquest,* . . . they have borne the banners of the cross!"—Speech delivered at Plymouth, Massachusetts, Dec. 22, 1824, page 11.

"And he had two horns like a lamb." The lamblike horns indicate youth, innocence, and gentleness, fitly representing the character of the United States when presented to the prophet as "coming up" in 1798. Among the Christian exiles who first fled to America and sought an asylum from royal oppression and priestly intolerance were many who determined to establish a government upon the broad foundation of civil and religious liberty. Their views found place in the Declaration of Independence, which sets forth the great truth that "all men are created equal" and endowed with the inalienable right to "life, liberty, and the pursuit of happiness." And the Constitution guarantees to the people the right of self-government, providing that representatives elected by the popular vote shall enact and administer the laws. Freedom of religious faith was also granted, every man being permitted to worship God according to the dictates of his conscience. Republicanism and Protestantism became the fundamental principles of the nation. These principles are the secret of its power and prosperity. The oppressed and downtrodden throughout Christendom have turned to this land with interest and hope. Millions have sought its shores, and the United States has risen to a place among the most powerful nations of the earth.

But the beast with lamblike horns "spake as a dragon. And he exerciseth all the power of the first beast before him, and causeth the earth and them which dwell therein to worship the first beast, whose deadly wound was healed; . . . saying to them that dwell on the earth, that they should make an image to the beast, which had the wound by a sword, and did live." Revelation 13:11-14. 442

The lamblike horns and dragon voice of the symbol point to a striking contradiction between the professions and the practice of the nation thus represented. The "speaking" of the nation is the action of its legislative and judicial authorities. By such action it will give the lie to those liberal and peaceful principles which it has put forth as the foundation of its policy. The prediction that it will speak "as a dragon" and exercise "all the power of the first beast" plainly foretells a development of the spirit of intolerance and persecution that was manifested by the nations represented by the dragon and the leopardlike beast. And the statement that the beast with two horns "causeth the earth and them which dwell therein to worship the first beast" indicates that the authority of this nation is to be exercised in enforcing some observance which shall be an act of homage to the papacy.

Such action would be directly contrary to the principles of this government, to the genius of its free institutions, to the direct and solemn avowals of the Declaration of Independence, and to the Constitution. The founders of the nation wisely sought to guard against the employment of secular power on the part of the church, with its inevitable result—intolerance and persecution. The Constitution provides that "Congress shall make no law respecting an establishment of religion, or prohibiting the free exercise thereof," and that "no religious test shall ever be required as a qualification to any office of public trust under the United States." Only in flagrant violation of these safeguards to the nation's liberty, can any religious observance be enforced by civil authority. But the inconsistency of such action is no greater than is represented in the symbol. It is the beast with lamblike horns—in profession pure, gentle, and harmless—that speaks as a dragon.

443 "Saying to them that dwell on the earth, that they *should* make an image to the beast." Here is clearly presented a form of government in which the legislative power rests with the people, a most striking evidence that the United States is the nation denoted in the prophecy.

But what is the "image to the beast"? and how is it to be formed? The image is made by the two-horned beast, and is an image *to* the beast. It is also called an image *of* the beast. Then to learn what the image is like and how it is to be formed we must study the characteristics of the beast itself—the papacy.

When the early church became corrupted by departing from the simplicity of the gospel and accepting heathen rites and customs, she lost the Spirit and power of God; and in order to control the consciences of the people, she sought the support of the secular power. The result was the papacy, a church that controlled the power of the state and employed it to further her own ends, especially for the punishment of "heresy." In order for the United States to form an image of the beast, the religious power must so control the civil government that the authority of the state will also be employed by the church to accomplish her own ends.

Whenever the church has obtained secular power, she has employed it to punish dissent from her doctrines. Protestant churches that have followed in the steps of Rome by forming alliance with worldly powers have manifested a similar desire to restrict liberty of conscience. An example of this is given in the long-continued persecution of dissenters by the Church of England. During the sixteenth and seventeenth centuries, thousands of nonconformist ministers were forced to flee from their churches, and many, both of pastors and people, were subjected to fine, imprisonment, torture, and martyrdom.

It was apostasy that led the early church to seek the aid of the civil government, and this prepared the way for the development of the papacy—the beast. Said Paul: "There shall 444 "come a falling away, . . . and that man of sin be revealed." 2 Thessalonians 2:3. So apostasy in the church will prepare the way for the image to the beast.

The Bible declares that before the coming of the Lord there will exist a state of religious declension similar to that in the first centuries. "In the last days perilous times shall come. For men shall be *lovers of their own selves*, cov-

etous, boasters, proud, blasphemers, disobedient to parents, unthankful, unholy, without natural affection, trucebreakers, false accusers, incontinent, fierce, *despisers of those that are good*, traitors, heady, high-minded, *lovers of pleasures more than lovers of God*; *having a form of godliness*, but denying the power thereof." 2 Timothy 3:1-5. "Now the Spirit speaketh expressly, that in the latter times some shall depart from the faith, giving heed to seducing spirits, and doctrines of devils." 1 Timothy 4:1. Satan will work "with all power and signs and lying wonders, and with all deceivableness of unrighteousness." And all that "received not the love of the truth, that they might be saved," will be left to accept "strong delusion, that they should believe a lie." 2 Thessalonians 2:9-11. When this state of ungodliness shall be reached, the same results will follow as in the first centuries.

The wide diversity of belief in the Protestant churches is regarded by many as decisive proof that no effort to secure a forced uniformity can ever be made. But there has been for years, in churches of the Protestant faith, a strong and growing sentiment in favor of a union based upon common points of doctrine. To secure such a union, the discussion of subjects upon which all were not agreed—however important they might be from a Bible standpoint—must necessarily be waived.

Charles Beecher, in a sermon in the year 1846, declared that the ministry of "the evangelical Protestant denominations" is "not only formed all the way up under a tremendous pressure of merely human fear, but they live, and move, and breathe in a state of things radically corrupt, and appealing every hour to every baser element of their nature to hush up the 445 truth, and bow the knee to the power of apostasy. Was not this the way things went with Rome? Are we not living her life over again? And what do we see just ahead? Another general council! A world's convention! Evangelical alliance, and universal creed!"—Sermon on "The Bible a Sufficient Creed," delivered at Fort Wayne, Indiana, Feb. 22, 1846. When this shall be gained, then, in the effort to secure complete uniformity, it will be only a step to the resort to force.

When the leading churches of the United States, uniting upon such points of doctrine as are held by them in common, shall influence the state to enforce their decrees and to sustain their institutions, then Protestant America will have formed an image of the Roman hierarchy, and the infliction of civil penalties upon dissenters will inevitably result.

The beast with two horns "causeth [commands] all, both small and great, rich and poor, free and bond, to receive a mark in their right hand, or in their foreheads: and that no man might buy or sell, save he that had the mark, or the name of the beast, or the number of his name." Revelation 13:16, 17. The third angel's warning is: "If any man worship the beast and his image, and receive his mark in his forehead, or in his hand, the same shall drink of the wine of the wrath of God." "The beast" mentioned in this message, whose worship is enforced by the two-horned beast, is the first, or leopardlike beast of Revelation 13—the papacy. The "image to the beast" represents that form of apostate Protestantism which will be developed when the Protestant churches shall seek the aid of the civil power for the enforcement of their dogmas. The "mark of the beast" still remains to be defined.

After the warning against the worship of the beast and his image the prophecy declares: "Here are they that keep the commandments of God, and the faith of Jesus." Since those who keep God's commandments are thus placed in contrast with those that worship the beast and his image and receive his mark, it follows that 446 the keeping of God's law, on the one hand, and its violation, on the other, will make the distinction between the worshipers of God and the worshipers of the beast.

The special characteristic of the beast, and therefore of his image, is the breaking of God's commandments. Says Daniel, of the little horn, the papacy: "He shall think to change times and the law." Daniel 7:25, R.V. And Paul styled the same power the "man of sin," who was to exalt himself above God. One prophecy is a complement of the other. Only by changing God's law could the papacy exalt itself above God; whoever should understandingly keep the law as thus changed would be giving supreme honor to that power by which the change was made. Such an act of obedience to papal laws would be a mark of allegiance to the pope in the place of God.

The papacy has attempted to change the law of God. The second commandment, forbidding image worship, has been dropped from the law, and the fourth commandment has been so changed as to authorize the observance of the first instead of the seventh day as the Sabbath. But papists urge, as a reason for omitting the second commandment, that it is unnecessary, being included in the first, and that they are giving the law exactly as God designed it to be understood. This cannot be the change foretold by the prophet. An intentional, deliberate change is presented: "He shall *think* to change the times and the law." The change in the fourth commandment exactly fulfills the prophecy. For this the only authority claimed is that of the church. Here the papal power openly sets itself above God.

While the worshipers of God will be especially distinguished by their regard for the fourth commandment,—since this is the sign of His creative power and the witness to His claim upon man's reverence and homage,—the worshipers of the beast will be distinguished by their efforts to tear down the Creator's memorial, to exalt the institution of Rome. It was in behalf of the Sunday that popery first asserted 447 its arrogant claims (see Appendix); and its first resort to the power of the state was to compel the observance of Sunday as "the Lord's day." But the Bible points to the seventh day, and not to the first, as the Lord's day. Said Christ: "The Son of man is Lord also of the Sabbath." The fourth commandment declares: "The seventh day is the Sabbath of the Lord." And by the prophet Isaiah the Lord designates it: "My holy day." Mark 2:28; Isaiah 58:13.

The claim so often put forth that Christ changed the Sabbath is disproved by His own words. In His Sermon on the Mount He said: "Think not that I am come to destroy the law, or the prophets: I am not come to destroy, but to fulfill. For verily I say unto you, Till heaven and earth pass, one jot or one tittle shall in no wise pass from the law, till all be fulfilled. Whosoever therefore shall break one of these least commandments, and shall teach men so, he shall be called the least in the kingdom of heaven: but whosoever shall do and teach them, the same shall be called great in the kingdom of heaven." Matthew 5:17-19.

It is a fact generally admitted by Protestants that the Scriptures give no authority for the change of the Sabbath. This is plainly stated in publications issued by the American Tract Society and the American Sunday School Union. One of these works acknowledges "the complete silence of the New Testament so far as any explicit command for the Sabbath [Sunday, the first day of the week] or definite rules for its observance are concerned."—George Elliott, *The Abiding Sabbath*, page 184.

Another says: "Up to the time of Christ's death, no change had been made in the day;" and, "so far as the record shows, they [the apostles] did not . . . give any explicit command enjoining the abandonment of the seventh-day Sabbath, and its observance on the first day of the week."—A. E. Waffle, *The Lord's Day*, pages 186-188.

Roman Catholics acknowledge that the change of the Sabbath was made by their church, and declare that Protestants by observing the Sunday are recognizing her power. In 448 the *Catholic Catechism of Christian Religion*, in answer to a question as to the day to be observed in obedience to the fourth commandment, this statement is made: "During the old law, Saturday was the day sanctified; but *the church*, instructed by Jesus Christ, and directed by the Spirit of God, has substituted Sunday for Saturday; so now we sanctify the first, not the seventh day. Sunday means, and now is, the day of the Lord."

As the sign of the authority of the Catholic Church, papist writers cite "the very act of changing the Sabbath into Sunday, which Protestants allow of; . . . because by keeping Sunday, they acknowledge the church's power to ordain feasts, and to command them under sin."—Henry Tuberville, *An Abridgment of the Christian Doctrine*, page 58. What then is the change of the Sabbath, but the sign, or mark, of the authority of the Roman Church—"the mark of the beast"?

The Roman Church has not relinquished her claim to supremacy; and when the world and the Protestant churches accept a sabbath of her creating, while they reject the Bible Sabbath, they virtually admit this assumption. They may claim the authority of tradition and of the Fathers for the change; but in so doing they ignore the very principle which separates them from Rome—that "the Bible, and the Bible only, is the religion of Protestants." The papist can see that they are deceiving themselves, willingly closing their eyes to the facts in the case. As the movement for Sunday enforcement gains favor, he rejoices, feeling assured that it will eventually bring the whole Protestant world under the banner of Rome.

Romanists declare that "the observance of Sunday by the Protestants is an homage they pay, in spite of themselves, to the authority of the [Catholic] Church."—Mgr. Segur, *Plain Talk About the Protestantism of Today*, page 213. The enforcement of Sundaykeeping on the part of Protestant churches is an enforcement of the worship of the papacy—of the beast. Those who, understanding the claims of the fourth commandment, choose to observe the false instead of the true Sabbath are thereby paying homage to that power by which alone it is commanded. But in the very act of enforcing a religious duty by secular power, the churches would themselves form an image to the beast; hence the enforcement of Sundaykeeping in the United States would be an enforcement of the worship of the beast and his image.

But Christians of past generations observed the Sunday, supposing that in so doing they were keeping the Bible Sabbath; and there are now true Christians in every church, not excepting the Roman Catholic communion, who honestly believe that Sunday is the Sabbath of divine appointment. God accepts their sincerity of purpose and their integrity before Him. But when Sunday observance shall be enforced by law, and the world shall be enlightened concerning the obligation of the true Sabbath, then whoever shall transgress the command of God, to obey a precept which has no higher authority than that of Rome, will thereby honor popery above God. He is paying homage to Rome and to the power which enforces the institution ordained by Rome. He is worshiping the beast and his image. As men then reject the institution which God has declared to be the sign of His authority, and honor in its stead that which Rome has chosen as the token of her supremacy, they will thereby accept the sign of allegiance to Rome—"the mark of the beast." And it is not until the issue is thus plainly set before the people, and they are brought to choose between the commandments of God and the commandments of men, that those who continue in transgression will receive "the mark of the beast."

The most fearful threatening ever addressed to mortals is contained in the third angel's message. That must be a terrible sin which calls down the wrath of God unmingled with mercy. Men are not to be left in darkness concerning this important matter; the warning against this sin is to be given to the world before the visitation of God's judgments, that all may know why they are to be inflicted, and have opportunity to escape them. Prophecy declares that the first angel would make his announcement to "every nation, and kindred, and tongue, and people." The warning of the third angel, which forms a part of the same threefold message, is to be no less widespread. It is represented in the prophecy as being proclaimed with a loud voice, by an angel flying in the midst of heaven; and it will command the attention of the world.

In the issue of the contest all Christendom will be divided into two great classes—those who keep the commandments of God and the faith of Jesus, and those who worship the beast and his image and receive his mark. Although church and state will unite their power to compel "all, both small and great, rich and poor, free and bond" (Revelation 13:16), to receive "the mark of the beast," yet the people of God will not receive it. The prophet of Patmos beholds "them that had gotten the victory over the beast, and over his image, and over his mark, and over the number of his name, stand on the sea of glass, having the harps of God" and singing the song of Moses and the Lamb. Revelation 15:2, 3.

26

A Work of Reform

The work of Sabbath reform to be accomplished in the last days is foretold in the prophecy of Isaiah: "Thus saith the Lord, Keep ye judgment, and do justice: for My salvation is near to come, and My righteousness to be revealed. Blessed is the man that doeth this, and the son of man that layeth hold on it; that keepeth the Sabbath from polluting it, and keepeth his hand from doing any evil." "The sons of the stranger, that join themselves to the Lord, to serve Him, and to love the name of the Lord, to be His servants, everyone that keepeth the Sabbath from polluting it, and taketh hold of My covenant; even them will I bring to My holy mountain, and make them joyful in My house of prayer." Isaiah 56:1, 2, 6, 7.

These words apply in the Christian age, as shown by the context: "The Lord God which gathereth the outcasts of Israel saith, Yet will I gather others to him, beside those that are gathered unto him." Verse 8. Here is foreshadowed the gathering in of the Gentiles by the gospel. And upon those who then honor the Sabbath, a blessing is pronounced. Thus the obligation of the fourth commandment extends past the crucifixion, resurrection, and ascension of Christ, to the time when His servants should preach to all nations the message of glad tidings.

452 The Lord commands by the same prophet: "Bind up the testimony, seal the law among My disciples." Isaiah 8:16. The seal of God's law is found in the fourth commandment. This only, of all the ten, brings to view both the name and the title of the Lawgiver. It declares Him to be the Creator of the heavens and the earth, and thus shows His claim to reverence and worship above all others. Aside from this precept, there is nothing in the Decalogue to show by whose authority the law is given. When the Sabbath was changed by the papal power, the seal was taken from the law. The disciples of Jesus are called upon to restore it by exalting the Sabbath of the fourth commandment to its rightful position as the Creator's memorial and the sign of His authority.

"To the law and to the testimony." While conflicting doctrines and theories abound, the law of God is the one unerring rule by which all opinions, doctrines, and theories are to be tested. Says the prophet: "If they speak not according to this word, it is because there is no light in them." Verse 20.

Again, the command is given: "Cry aloud, spare not, lift up thy voice like a trumpet, and show My people their transgression, and the house of Jacob their sins." It is not the wicked world, but those whom the Lord designates as "My people," that are to be reproved for their transgressions. He declares further: "Yet they seek Me daily, and delight to know My ways, as a nation that did righteousness, and forsook not the ordinance of their God." Isaiah 58:1, 2. Here is brought to view a class who think themselves righteous and appear to manifest great interest in the service of God; but the stern and solemn rebuke of the Searcher of hearts proves them to be trampling upon the divine precepts.

The prophet thus points out the ordinance which has been forsaken: "Thou shalt raise up the foundations of many generations; and thou shalt be called, The repairer of the breach, the

restorer of paths to dwell in. If thou turn away thy foot from the Sabbath, from doing thy pleasure on My holy day; and call the Sabbath a delight, the holy of the Lord, honorable; and shalt honor Him, not doing thine own ways, nor finding thine own pleasure, nor speaking thine own words: then shalt thou delight thyself in the Lord." Verses 12-14. This prophecy also applies in our time. The breach was made in the law of God when the Sabbath was changed by the Roman power. But the time has come for that divine institution to be restored. The breach is to be repaired and the foundation of many generations to be raised up. 453

Hallowed by the Creator's rest and blessing, the Sabbath was kept by Adam in his innocence in holy Eden; by Adam, fallen yet repentant, when he was driven from his happy estate. It was kept by all the patriarchs, from Abel to righteous Noah, to Abraham, to Jacob. When the chosen people were in bondage in Egypt, many, in the midst of prevailing idolatry, lost their knowledge of God's law; but when the Lord delivered Israel, He proclaimed His law in awful grandeur to the assembled multitude, that they might know His will and fear and obey Him forever.

From that day to the present the knowledge of God's law has been preserved in the earth, and the Sabbath of the fourth commandment has been kept. Though the "man of sin" succeeded in trampling underfoot God's holy day, yet even in the period of his supremacy there were, hidden in secret places, faithful souls who paid it honor. Since the Reformation, there have been some in every generation to maintain its observance. Though often in the midst of reproach and persecution, a constant testimony has been borne to the perpetuity of the law of God and the sacred obligation of the creation Sabbath.

These truths, as presented in Revelation 14 in connection with "the everlasting gospel," will distinguish the church of Christ at the time of His appearing. For as the result of the threefold 454 message it is announced: "Here are they that keep the commandments of God, and the faith of Jesus." And this message is the last to be given before the coming of the Lord. Immediately following its proclamation the Son of man is seen by the prophet, coming in glory to reap the harvest of the earth.

Those who received the light concerning the sanctuary and the immutability of the law of God were filled with joy and wonder as they saw the beauty and harmony of the system of truth that opened to their understanding. They desired that the light which appeared to them so precious might be imparted to all Christians; and they could not but believe that it would be joyfully accepted. But truths that would place them at variance with the world were not welcome to many who claimed to be followers of

Christ. Obedience to the fourth commandment required a sacrifice from which the majority drew back.

As the claims of the Sabbath were presented, many reasoned from the worldling's standpoint. Said they: "We have always kept Sunday, our fathers kept it, and many good and pious men have died happy while keeping it. If they were right, so are we. The keeping of this new Sabbath would throw us out of harmony with the world, and we would have no influence over them. What can a little company keeping the seventh day hope to accomplish against all the world who are keeping Sunday?" It was by similar arguments that the Jews endeavored to justify their rejection of Christ. Their fathers had been accepted of God in presenting the sacrificial offerings, and why could not the children find salvation in pursuing the same course? So, in the time of Luther, papists reasoned that true Christians had died in the Catholic faith, and therefore that religion was sufficient for salvation. Such reasoning would prove an effectual barrier to all advancement in religious faith or practice.

Many urged that Sundaykeeping had been an established doctrine and a widespread custom of 455 the church for many centuries. Against this argument it was shown that the Sabbath and its observance were more ancient and widespread, even as old as the world itself, and bearing the sanction both of angels and of God. When the foundations of the earth were laid, when the morning stars sang together, and all the sons of God shouted for joy, then was laid the foundation of the Sabbath. Job 38:6, 7; Genesis 2:1-3. Well may this institution demand our reverence; it was ordained by no human authority and rests upon no human traditions; it was established by the Ancient of Days and commanded by His eternal word.

As the attention of the people was called to the subject of Sabbath reform, popular ministers perverted the word of God, placing such interpretations upon its testimony as would best quiet inquiring minds. And those who did not search the Scriptures for themselves were content to accept conclusions that were in accordance with their desires. By argument, sophistry, the traditions of the Fathers, and the authority of the church, many endeavored to overthrow the truth. Its advocates were driven to their Bibles to defend the validity of the fourth commandment. Humble men, armed with the word of truth alone, withstood the attacks of men of learning, who, with surprise and anger, found their eloquent sophistry powerless against the simple, straightforward reasoning of men who were versed in the Scriptures rather than in the subtleties of the schools.

In the absence of Bible testimony in their favor, many with unwearying persistence urged—forgetting how the same reasoning had been employed against Christ and His apostles: "Why do not our great men understand this Sabbath question? But few believe as you do. It cannot be that you are right and that all the men of learning in the world are wrong."

To refute such arguments it was needful only to cite the teachings of the Scriptures and the history of the Lord's dealings with His people in all ages. God works through those who hear and 456 obey His voice, those who will, if need be, speak unpalatable truths, those who do not fear to reprove popular sins. The reason why He does not oftener choose men of learning and high position to lead out in reform movements is that they trust to their creeds, theories, and theological systems, and feel no need to be taught of God. Only those who have a personal connection with the Source of wisdom are able to understand or explain the Scriptures. Men who have little of the learning of the schools are sometimes called to declare the truth, not because they are unlearned, but because they are not too self-sufficient to be taught of God. They learn in the school of Christ, and their humility and obedience make them great. In committing to them a knowledge of His truth, God confers upon them an honor, in comparison with which earthly honor and human greatness sink into insignificance.

The majority of Adventists rejected the truths concerning the sanctuary and the law of God, and many also renounced their faith in the advent movement and adopted unsound and conflicting views of the prophecies which applied to that work. Some were led into the error of repeatedly fixing upon a definite time for the coming of Christ. The light which was now shining on the subject of the sanctuary should have shown them that no prophetic period extends to the second advent; that the exact time of this advent is not foretold. But, turning from the light, they continued to set time after time for the Lord to come, and as often they were disappointed.

When the Thessalonian church received erroneous views concerning the coming of Christ, the apostle Paul counseled them to test their hopes and anticipations carefully by the word of God. He cited them to prophecies revealing the events to take place before Christ should come, and showed that they had no ground to expect Him in their day. "Let no man deceive you by any means" (2 Thessalonians 2:3), are his words of warning. Should they indulge expectations that were not sanctioned by the Scriptures, they would be led to a mistaken course of action; dis- 457 appointment would expose them to the derision of unbelievers, and they would be in danger of yielding to discouragement and would be tempted to doubt the truths essential for their salvation. The apostle's admonition to the Thessalonians contains an important lesson for those who live in the last days. Many Adventists have felt that unless they could fix their faith upon a definite time for the Lord's coming, they could not be zealous and diligent in the work of preparation. But as their hopes are again and again excited, only to be destroyed, their faith receives such a shock that it becomes well-nigh impossible for them to be impressed by the great truths of prophecy.

The preaching of a definite time for the judgment, in the giving of the first message, was ordered of God. The computation of the prophetic periods on which that message was based, placing the close of the 2300 days in the autumn of 1844, stands without impeachment. The repeated efforts to find new dates for the beginning and close of the prophetic periods, and the unsound reasoning necessary to sustain these positions, not only lead minds away from the present truth, but throw contempt upon all efforts to explain the prophecies. The more frequently a definite time is set for the second advent, and the more widely it is taught, the better it suits the purposes of Satan. After the time has passed, he excites ridicule and contempt of its advocates, and thus casts reproach upon the great advent movement of 1843 and 1844. Those who persist in this error will at last fix upon a date too far in the future for the coming of Christ. Thus they will be led to rest in a false security, and many will not be undeceived until it is too late.

The history of ancient Israel is a striking illustration of the past experience of the Adventist body. God led His people in the advent movement, even as He led the children of Israel from Egypt. In the great disappointment their faith was tested as was that of the Hebrews at the Red Sea. Had they still trusted to the guiding hand 458 that had been with them in their past experience, they would have seen the salvation of God. If all who had labored unitedly in the work in 1844, had received the third angel's message and proclaimed it in the power of the Holy Spirit, the Lord would have wrought mightily with their efforts. A flood of light would have been shed upon the world. Years ago the inhabitants of the earth would have been warned, the closing work completed, and Christ would have come for the redemption of His people.

It was not the will of God that Israel should wander forty years in the wilderness; He desired to lead them directly to the land of Canaan and establish them there, a holy, happy people. But "they could not enter in because of unbelief." Hebrews 3:19. Because of their backsliding and apostasy they perished in the desert, and others were raised up to enter the Promised Land. In like manner, it was not the will of God that the coming of Christ should be so long delayed and His people should remain so many years in this world of sin and sorrow. But unbelief separated them from God. As they refused to do the work which He had appointed them, others were raised up to proclaim the message. In mercy to the world, Jesus delays His coming, that sinners may have an opportunity to hear the warning and find in Him a shelter before the wrath of God shall be poured out.

Now as in former ages, the presentation of a truth that reproves the sins and errors of the times will excite opposition. "Everyone that doeth evil hateth the light, neither cometh to the light, lest his deeds should be reproved." John 3:20. As men see that they cannot maintain their position by the Scriptures, many determine to maintain it at all hazards, and with a malicious spirit they assail the character and motives of those who stand in defense of unpopular truth. It is the same policy which has been pursued in all ages. Elijah was declared to be a troubler in Israel, Jeremiah a traitor, Paul a polluter of the temple. From that day to this, those who would be loyal to truth have been denounced as seditious, heretical, or schismatic. Multitudes who 459 are too unbelieving to accept the sure word of prophecy will receive with unquestioning credulity an accusation against those who dare to reprove fashionable sins. This spirit will increase more and more. And the Bible plainly teaches that a time is approaching when the laws of the state will so conflict with the law of God that whosoever would obey all the divine precepts must brave reproach and punishment as an evildoer.

In view of this, what is the duty of the messenger of truth? Shall he conclude that the truth ought not to be presented, since often its only effect is to arouse men to evade or resist its claims? No; he has no more reason for withholding the testimony of God's word, because it excites opposition, than had earlier Reformers. The confession of faith made by saints and martyrs was recorded for the benefit of succeeding generations. Those living examples of holiness and steadfast integrity have come down to inspire courage in those who are now called to stand as witnesses for God. They received grace and truth, not for themselves alone, but that, through them, the knowledge of God might enlighten the earth. Has God given light to His servants in this generation? Then they should let it shine forth to the world.

Anciently the Lord declared to one who spoke in His name: "The house of Israel will not hearken unto thee; for they will not hearken unto Me." Nevertheless He said: "Thou shalt speak My words unto them, whether they will hear, or whether they will forbear." Ezekiel 3:7; 2:7. To the servant of God at this time is the command addressed: "Lift up thy voice like a trumpet, and show My people their transgression, and the house of Jacob their sins."

So far as his opportunities extend, everyone who has received the light of truth is under the same solemn and fearful responsibility as was the prophet of Israel, to whom the word of the Lord came, saying: "Son of man, I have set thee a watchman unto the house of Israel; therefore thou shalt hear the word at My mouth, and warn them from Me. When I say unto the wicked, O wicked man, thou shalt surely die; if thou dost not speak to warn the wicked from his way, that wicked man shall die in his iniquity; but his blood will I require at thine hand. Nevertheless, if thou warn the wicked of his way to turn from it; if he do not turn from his way, he shall die in his iniquity; but thou hast delivered thy soul." Ezekiel 33:7-9.

The great obstacle both to the acceptance and to the promulgation of truth is the fact that it involves inconvenience and reproach. This is the only argument against the truth which its advocates have never been able to refute. But this does not deter the true followers of Christ. These do not wait for truth to become popular. Being convinced of their duty, they deliberately accept the cross, with the apostle Paul counting that "our light affliction, which is but for a moment, worketh for us a far more exceeding and eternal weight of glory;" with one of old, "esteeming the reproach of Christ greater riches than the treasures in Egypt." 2 Corinthians 4:17; Hebrews 11:26.

Whatever may be their profession, it is only those who are world servers at heart that act from policy rather than principle in religious things. We should choose the right because it is right, and leave consequences with God. To men of principle, faith, and daring, the world is indebted for its great reforms. By such men the work of reform for this time must be carried forward.

Thus saith the Lord: "Hearken unto Me, ye that know righteousness, the people in whose heart is My law; fear ye not the reproach of men, neither be ye afraid of their revilings. For the moth shall eat them up like a garment, and the worm shall eat them like wool: but My righteousness shall be forever, and My salvation from generation to generation." Isaiah 51:7, 8.

27
Modern Revivals

Wherever the word of God has been faithfully preached, results have followed that attested its divine origin. The Spirit of God accompanied the message of His servants, and the word was with power. Sinners felt their consciences quickened. The "light which lighteth every man that cometh into the world" illumined the secret chambers of their souls, and the hidden things of darkness were made manifest. Deep conviction took hold upon their minds and hearts. They were convinced of sin and of righteousness and of judgment to come. They had a sense of the righteousness of Jehovah and felt the terror of appearing, in their guilt and uncleanness, before the Searcher of hearts. In anguish they cried out: "Who shall deliver me from the body of this death?" As the cross of Calvary, with its infinite sacrifice for the sins of men, was revealed, they saw that nothing but the merits of Christ could suffice to atone for their transgressions; this alone could reconcile man to God. With faith and humility they accepted the Lamb of God, that taketh away the sin of the world. Through the blood of Jesus they had "remission of sins that are past."

These souls brought forth fruit meet for repentance. They believed and were baptized, and rose to walk in newness of life—new creatures in Christ Jesus; not to fashion themselves according to the former lusts, but by the faith of the Son of God to follow in His steps, to reflect His character, and to purify themselves even as He is pure. The things they once hated they now loved, and the things they once loved they hated. The proud and self-assertive became meek and lowly of heart. The vain and supercilious became serious and unobtrusive. The profane became reverent, the drunken sober, and the profligate pure. The vain fashions of the world were laid aside. Christians sought not the "outward adorning of plaiting the hair, and of wearing of gold, or of putting on of apparel; but . . . the hidden man of the heart, in that which is not corruptible, even the ornament of a meek and quiet spirit, which is in the sight of God of great price." 1 Peter 3:3, 4.

Revivals brought deep heart searching and humility. They were characterized by solemn, earnest appeals to the sinner, by yearning compassion for the purchase of the blood of Christ. Men and women prayed and wrestled with God for the salvation of souls. The fruits of such revivals were seen in souls who shrank not at self-denial and sacrifice, but rejoiced that they were counted worthy to suffer reproach and trial for the sake of Christ. Men beheld a transformation in the lives of those who had professed the name of Jesus. The community was benefited by their influence. They gathered with Christ, and sowed to the Spirit, to reap life everlasting.

It could be said of them: "Ye sorrowed to repentance." "For godly sorrow worketh repentance to salvation not to be repented of: but the sorrow of the world worketh death. For behold this selfsame thing, that ye sorrowed after a godly sort, what carefulness it wrought in you, yea, what clearing of yourselves, yea, what indignation, yea, what fear, yea, what vehement desire, yea, what zeal, yea, what revenge! In all things ye have approved yourselves to be clear in this matter." 2 Corinthians 7:9-11.

This is the result of the work of the Spirit of God. There is no evidence of genuine repentance unless it works reformation. If he restore the pledge, give again that he had robbed, confess his sins, and love God and his fellow men, the sinner may be sure that he has found peace with God. Such were the effects that in former years followed seasons of religious awakening. Judged by their fruits, they were known to be blessed of God in the salvation of men and the uplifting of humanity.

But many of the revivals of modern times have presented a marked contrast to those manifestations of divine grace which in earlier days followed the labors of God's servants. It is true that a widespread interest is kindled, many profess conversion, and there are large accessions to the churches; nevertheless the results are not such as to warrant the belief that there has been a corresponding increase of real spiritual life. The light which flames up for a time soon dies out, leaving the darkness more dense than before.

Popular revivals are too often carried by appeals to the imagination, by exciting the emotions, by gratifying the love for what is new and startling. Converts thus gained have little desire to listen to Bible truth, little interest in the testimony of prophets and apostles. Unless a religious service has something of a sensational character, it has no attractions for them. A message which appeals to unimpassioned reason awakens no response. The plain warnings of God's word, relating directly to their eternal interests, are unheeded.

With every truly converted soul the relation to God and to eternal things will be the great topic of life. But where, in the popular churches of today, is the spirit of consecration to God? The converts do not renounce their pride and love of the world. They are no more willing to deny self, to take up the cross, and follow the meek and lowly Jesus, than before their conversion. Religion has become the sport of infidels and skeptics because so many who bear its name are ignorant of its principles. The power of godliness has well-nigh departed from many of the churches. Picnics, church theatricals, church fairs, fine houses, personal display, have banished thoughts of God. Lands and goods and worldly occupations engross the mind, and things of eternal interest receive hardly a passing notice.

Notwithstanding the widespread declension of faith and piety, there are true followers of Christ in these churches. Before the final visitation of God's judgments upon the earth there will be among the people of the Lord such a revival of primitive godliness as has not been witnessed since apostolic times. The Spirit and power of God will be poured out upon His children. At that time many will separate themselves from those churches in which the love of this world has supplanted love for God and His word. Many, both of ministers and people, will gladly accept those great truths which God has caused to be proclaimed at this time to prepare a people for the Lord's second coming. The enemy of souls desires to hinder this work; and before the time for such a movement shall come, he will endeavor to prevent it by introducing a counterfeit. In those churches which he can bring under his deceptive power he will make it appear that God's special blessing is poured out; there will be manifest what is thought to be great religious interest. Multitudes will exult that God is working marvelously for them, when the work is that of another spirit. Under a religious guise, Satan will seek to extend his influence over the Christian world.

In many of the revivals which have occurred during the last half century, the same influences have been at work, to a greater or less degree, that will be manifest in the more extensive movements of the future. There is an emotional excitement, a mingling of the true with the false, that is well adapted to mislead. Yet none need be deceived. In the light of God's word it is not difficult to determine the nature of these movements. Wherever men neglect the testimony of the Bible, turning away from those plain, soul-testing truths which require self-denial and renunciation of the world, there we may be sure that God's blessing is not bestowed. And by the rule which Christ Himself has given, "Ye shall know them by their fruits" (Matthew 7:16), it is evident that these movements are not the work of the Spirit of God.

In the truths of His word, God has given to men a revelation of Himself; and to all who accept them they are a shield against the deceptions of Satan. It is a neglect of these truths that has opened the door to the evils which are now becoming so widespread in the religious world. The nature and the importance of the law of God have been, to a great extent, lost sight of. A wrong conception of the character, the perpetuity, and the obligation of the divine law has led to errors in relation to conversion and sanctification, and has resulted in lowering the standard of piety in the church. Here is to be found the secret of the lack of the Spirit and power of God in the revivals of our time.

There are, in the various denominations, men eminent for their piety, by whom this fact is acknowledged and deplored. Professor Edwards A. Park, in setting forth the current religious perils, ably says: "One source of danger is the neglect of the pulpit to enforce the divine law. In former days the pulpit was an echo of the voice of conscience. . . . Our most illustrious preachers gave a wonderful majesty to their discourses by following the example of the Master, and giving prominence to the law, its precepts, and its threatenings. They repeated the two great maxims, that the law is a transcript of the divine perfections, and that a man who does not love the law does not love the gospel; for the law, as well as the gospel, is a mirror reflecting the true character of God. This peril leads to another, that of underrating the evil of sin, the extent of it, the demerit of it. In proportion to the rightfulness of the commandment is the wrongfulness of disobeying it. . . .

"Affiliated to the dangers already named is the danger of underestimating the justice of God. The tendency of the modern pulpit is to strain out the divine justice from the divine benevolence, to sink benevolence into a sentiment rather than exalt it into a principle. The new theological prism puts asunder what God has joined together. Is the divine law a good or an evil? It is a good. Then justice is good; for it is a disposition to execute the law. From the habit of underrating the divine law and justice, the extent and demerit of human disobedience, men easily slide into the habit of underestimating the grace which has provided an atonement for sin." Thus the gospel loses its value and importance in the minds of men, and soon they are ready practically to cast aside the Bible itself.

Many religious teachers assert that Christ by His death abolished the law, and men are henceforth free from its requirements. There are some who represent it as a grievous yoke, and in contrast to the bondage of the law they present the liberty to be enjoyed under the gospel.

But not so did prophets and apostles regard the holy law of God. Said David: "I will walk at liberty: for I seek Thy precepts." Psalm 119:45. The apostle James, who wrote after the death of Christ, refers to the Decalogue as "the royal law" and "the perfect law of liberty." James 2:8; 1:25. And the revelator, half a century after the crucifixion, pronounces a blessing upon them "that do His commandments, that they may have right to the tree of life, and may enter in through the gates into the city." Revelation 22:14.

The claim that Christ by His death abolished His Father's law is without foundation. Had it been possible for the law to be changed or set aside, then Christ need not have died to save man from the penalty of sin. The death of Christ, so far from abolishing the law, proves that it is immutable. The Son of God came to "magnify the law, and make it honorable." Isaiah 42:21. He said: "Think not that I am come to destroy the law;" "till heaven and earth pass, one jot or one tittle shall in no wise pass from the law." Matthew 5:17, 18. And concerning Himself He declares: "I delight to do Thy will, O my God: yea, Thy law is within My heart." Psalm 40:8.

The law of God, from its very nature, is unchangeable. It is a revelation of the will and the character of its Author. God is love, and His law is love. Its two great principles are love to God and love to man. "Love is the fulfilling of the law." Romans 13:10. The character of God is righteousness and truth; such is the nature of His law. Says the psalmist: "Thy law is the truth;" "all Thy commandments are righteousness." Psalm 119:142, 172. And the apostle Paul declares: "The law is holy, and the commandment holy, and just, and good." Romans 7:12. Such a law, being an expression of the mind and will of God, must be as enduring as its Author.

It is the work of conversion and sanctification to reconcile men to God by bringing them into accord with the principles of His law. In the beginning, man was created in the image of God. He was in perfect harmony with the nature and the law of God; the principles of righteousness were written upon his heart. But sin alienated him from his Maker. He no longer reflected the divine image. His heart was at war with the principles of God's law. "The carnal mind is enmity against God: for it is not subject to the law of God, neither indeed can be." Romans 8:7. But "God so loved the world, that He gave His only-begotten Son," that man might be reconciled to God. Through the merits of Christ he can be restored to harmony with his Maker. His heart must be renewed by divine grace; he must have a new life from above. This change is the new birth, without which, says Jesus, "he cannot see the kingdom of God."

The first step in reconciliation to God is the conviction of sin. "Sin is the transgression of the law." "By the law is the knowledge of sin." 1 John 3:4; Romans 3:20. In order to see his guilt, the sinner must test his character by God's great standard of righteousness. It is a mirror which shows the perfection of a righteous character and enables him to discern the defects in his own.

The law reveals to man his sins, but it provides no remedy. While it promises life to the obedient, it declares that death is the portion of the transgressor. The gospel of Christ alone can free him from the condemnation or the defilement of sin. He must exercise repentance toward God, whose law has been transgressed; and faith in Christ, his atoning sacrifice. Thus he obtains "remission of sins that are past" and becomes a partaker of the divine nature. He is a child of God, having received the spirit of adoption, whereby he cries: "Abba, Father!"

Is he now free to transgress God's law? Says Paul: "Do we then make void the law through faith? God forbid: yea, we establish the law." "How shall we, that are dead to sin, live any longer therein?" And John declares: "This is the love of God, that we keep His commandments: and His commandments are not grievous." Romans 3:31; 6:2; 1 John 5:3. In the new birth the heart is brought into harmony with God, as it is brought into accord with His law. When this mighty change has taken place in the sinner, he has passed from death unto life, from sin unto holiness, from transgression and rebellion to obedience and loyalty. The old life of alienation from God has ended; the new life of reconciliation, of faith and love, has begun. Then "the righteousness of the law" will "be fulfilled in us, who walk not after the flesh, but after the Spirit." Romans 8:4. And the language of the soul will be: "O how love I Thy law! it is my meditation all the day." Psalm 119:97.

"The law of the Lord is perfect, converting the soul." Psalm 19:7. Without the law, men have no just conception of the purity and holiness of God or of their own guilt and uncleanness. They have no true conviction of sin and feel no need of repentance. Not seeing their lost condition as violators of God's law, they do not realize their need of the atoning blood of Christ. The hope of salvation is accepted without a radical change of heart or reformation of life. Thus superficial conversions abound, and multitudes are joined to the church who have never been united to Christ.

469 Erroneous theories of sanctification, also, springing from neglect or rejection of the divine law, have a prominent place in the religious movements of the day. These theories are both false in doctrine and dangerous in practical results; and the fact that they are so generally finding favor, renders it doubly essential that all have a clear understanding of what the Scriptures teach upon this point.

True sanctification is a Bible doctrine. The apostle Paul, in his letter to the Thessalonian church, declares: "This is the will of God, even your sanctification." And he prays: "The very God of peace sanctify you wholly." 1 Thessalonians 4:3; 5:23. The Bible clearly teaches what sanctification is and how it is to be attained. The Saviour prayed for His disciples: "Sanctify them through Thy truth: Thy word is truth." John 17:17. And Paul teaches that believers are to be "sanctified by the Holy Ghost." Romans 15:16. What is the work of the Holy Spirit? Jesus told His disciples: "When He, the Spirit of truth, is come, He will guide you into all truth." John 16:13. And the psalmist says: "Thy law is the truth." By the word and the Spirit of God are opened to men the great principles of righteousness embodied in His law. And since the law of God is "holy, and just, and good," a transcript of the divine perfection, it follows that a character formed by obedience to that law will be holy. Christ is a perfect example of such a character. He says: "I have kept My Father's commandments." "I do always those things that please

Him." John 15:10; 8:29. The followers of Christ are to become like Him—by the grace of God to form characters in harmony with the principles of His holy law. This is Bible sanctification.

This work can be accomplished only through faith in Christ, by the power of the indwelling Spirit of God. Paul admonishes believers: "Work out your own salvation with fear and trembling. For it is God which worketh in you both to will and to do of His good pleasure." Philippians 2:12, 13. The Christian will feel the promptings of sin, but he will maintain a constant warfare against it. Here is where Christ's 470 help is needed. Human weakness becomes united to divine strength, and faith exclaims: "Thanks be to God, which giveth us the victory through our Lord Jesus Christ." 1 Corinthians 15:57.

The Scriptures plainly show that the work of sanctification is progressive. When in conversion the sinner finds peace with God through the blood of the atonement, the Christian life has but just begun. Now he is to "go on unto perfection;" to grow up "unto the measure of the stature of the fullness of Christ." Says the apostle Paul: "This one thing I do, forgetting those things which are behind, and reaching forth unto those things which are before, I press toward the mark for the prize of the high calling of God in Christ Jesus." Philippians 3:13, 14. And Peter sets before us the steps by which Bible sanctification is to be attained: "Giving all diligence, add to your faith virtue; and to virtue knowledge; and to knowledge temperance; and to temperance patience; and to patience godliness; and to godliness brotherly kindness; and to brotherly kindness charity. . . . If ye do these things, ye shall never fall." 2 Peter 1:5-10.

Those who experience the sanctification of the Bible will manifest a spirit of humility. Like Moses, they have had a view of the awful majesty of holiness, and they see their own unworthiness in contrast with the purity and exalted perfection of the Infinite One.

The prophet Daniel was an example of true sanctification. His long life was filled up with noble service for his Master. He was a man "greatly beloved" (Daniel 10:11) of Heaven. Yet instead of claiming to be pure and holy, this honored prophet identified himself with the really sinful of Israel as he pleaded before God in behalf of his people: "We do not present our supplications before Thee for our righteousnesses, but for Thy great mercies." "We have sinned, we have done wickedly." He declares: "I was speaking, and praying, and confessing my sin and the sin of my people." And when at a later time the Son of God appeared, to give 471 him instruction, Daniel says: "My comeliness was turned in me into corruption, and I retained no strength." Daniel 9:18, 15, 20; 10:8.

When Job heard the voice of the Lord out of

the whirlwind, he exclaimed: "I abhor myself, and repent in dust and ashes." Job 42:6. It was when Isaiah saw the glory of the Lord, and heard the cherubim crying, "Holy, holy, holy, is the Lord of hosts," that he cried out, "Woe is me! for I am undone." Isaiah 6:3, 5. Paul, after he was caught up into the third heaven and heard things which it was not possible for a man to utter, speaks of himself as "less than the least of all saints." 2 Corinthians 12:2-4, margin; Ephesians 3:8. It was the beloved John, who leaned on Jesus' breast and beheld His glory, that fell as one dead before the feet of the angel. Revelation 1:17.

There can be no self-exaltation, no boastful claim to freedom from sin, on the part of those who walk in the shadow of Calvary's cross. They feel that it was their sin which caused the agony that broke the heart of the Son of God, and this thought will lead them to self-abasement. Those who live nearest to Jesus discern most clearly the frailty and sinfulness of humanity, and their only hope is in the merit of a crucified and risen Saviour.

The sanctification now gaining prominence in the religious world carries with it a spirit of self-exaltation and a disregard for the law of God that mark it as foreign to the religion of the Bible. Its advocates teach that sanctification is an instantaneous work, by which, through faith alone, they attain to perfect holiness. "Only believe," say they, "and the blessing is yours." No further effort on the part of the receiver is supposed to be required. At the same time they deny the authority of the law of God, urging that they are released from obligation to keep the commandments. But is it possible for men to be holy, in accord with the will and character of God, without coming into harmony with the principles which are an expression of His nature and will, and which show what is well pleasing to Him?

472 The desire for an easy religion that requires no striving, no self-denial, no divorce from the follies of the world, has made the doctrine of faith, and faith only, a popular doctrine; but what saith the word of God? Says the apostle James: "What doth it profit, my brethren, though a man say he hath faith, and have not works? can faith save him? . . . Wilt thou know, O vain man, that faith without works is dead? Was not Abraham our father justified by works, when he had offered Isaac his son upon the altar? Seest thou how faith wrought with his works, and by works was faith made perfect? . . . Ye see then how that by works a man is justified, and not by faith only." James 2:14-24.

The testimony of the word of God is against this ensnaring doctrine of faith without works. It is not faith that claims the favor of Heaven without complying with the conditions upon which mercy is to be granted, it is presumption; for

genuine faith has its foundation in the promises and provisions of the Scriptures.

Let none deceive themselves with the belief that they can become holy while willfully violating one of God's requirements. The commission of a known sin silences the witnessing voice of the Spirit and separates the soul from God. "Sin is the transgression of the law." And "whosoever sinneth [transgresseth the law] hath not seen Him, neither known Him." 1 John 3:6. Though John in his epistles dwells so fully upon love, yet he does not hesitate to reveal the true character of that class who claim to be sanctified while living in transgression of the law of God. "He that saith, I know Him, and keepeth not His commandments, is a liar, and the truth is not in him. But whoso keepeth His word, in him verily is the love of God perfected." 1 John 2:4, 5. Here is the test of every man's profession. We cannot accord holiness to any man without bringing him to the measurement of God's only standard of holiness in heaven and in earth. If men feel no weight of the moral law, if they belittle and make light of God's precepts, if they break one of the least of these commandments, 473 and teach men so, they shall be of no esteem in the sight of Heaven, and we may know that their claims are without foundation.

And the claim to be without sin is, in itself, evidence that he who makes this claim is far from holy. It is because he has no true conception of the infinite purity and holiness of God or of what they must become who shall be in harmony with His character; because he has no true conception of the purity and exalted loveliness of Jesus, and the malignity and evil of sin, that man can regard himself as holy. The greater the distance between himself and Christ, and the more inadequate his conceptions of the divine character and requirements, the more righteous he appears in his own eyes.

The sanctification set forth in the Scriptures embraces the entire being—spirit, soul, and body. Paul prayed for the Thessalonians that their "whole spirit and soul and body be preserved blameless unto the coming of our Lord Jesus Christ." 1 Thessalonians 5:23. Again he writes to believers: "I beseech you therefore, brethren, by the mercies of God, that ye present your bodies a living sacrifice, holy, acceptable unto God." Romans 12:1. In the time of ancient Israel every offering brought as a sacrifice to God was carefully examined. If any defect was discovered in the animal presented, it was refused; for God had commanded that the offering be "without blemish." So Christians are bidden to present their bodies, "a living sacrifice, holy, acceptable unto God." In order to do this, all their powers must be preserved in the best possible condition. Every practice that weakens physical or mental strength unfits man for the service of his Creator. And will God be pleased with anything less than the best we can offer? Said Christ: "Thou shalt love the Lord thy God with all thy heart." Those who do love God with all the heart will desire to give Him the best service of their life, and they will be constantly seeking to bring every power of their being into harmony with the laws that will promote their ability to do His will. They will not, by the indulgence of appetite or passion, enfeeble or defile the offering which they present to their heavenly Father.

Peter says: "Abstain from fleshly lusts, which war against the soul." 1 Peter 2:11. Every sinful gratification tends to benumb the faculties and deaden the mental and spiritual perceptions, and the word or the Spirit of God can make but a feeble impression upon the heart. Paul writes to the Corinthians: "Let us cleanse ourselves from all filthiness of the flesh and spirit, perfecting holiness in the fear of God." 2 Corinthians 7:1. And with the fruits of the Spirit—"love, joy, peace, long-suffering, gentleness, goodness, faith, meekness"—he classes "temperance." Galatians 5:22, 23.

Notwithstanding these inspired declarations, how many professed Christians are enfeebling their powers in the pursuit of gain or the worship of fashion; how many are debasing their godlike manhood by gluttony, by wine drinking, by forbidden pleasure. And the church, instead of rebuking, too often encourages the evil by appealing to appetite, to desire for gain or love of pleasure, to replenish her treasury, which love for Christ is too feeble to supply. Were Jesus to enter the churches of today and behold the feasting and unholy traffic there conducted in the name of religion, would He not drive out those desecrators, as He banished the money-changers from the temple?

The apostle James declares that the wisdom from above is "first pure." Had he encountered those who take the precious name of Jesus upon lips defiled by tobacco, those whose breath and person are contaminated by its foul odor, and who pollute the air of heaven and force all about them to inhale the poison—had the apostle come in contact with a practice so opposed to the purity of the gospel, would he not have denounced it as "earthly, sensual, devilish"? Slaves of tobacco, claiming the blessing of entire sanctification, talk of their hope of heaven; but God's word plainly declares that "there shall in no wise enter into it anything that defileth." Revelation 21:27.

"Know ye not that your body is the temple of the Holy Ghost which is in you, which ye have of God, and ye are not your own? for ye are bought with a price: therefore glorify God in your body, and in your spirit, which are God's." 1 Corinthians 6:19, 20. He whose body is the temple of the Holy Spirit will not be enslaved by a pernicious habit. His powers belong to Christ, who has bought him with the price of blood. His property is the Lord's. How could he be guiltless in squandering this entrusted capital? Professed Christians yearly expend an immense sum upon useless and pernicious indulgences, while souls are perishing for the word of life. God is robbed in tithes and offerings, while they consume upon the altar of destroying lust more than they give to relieve the poor or for the support of the gospel. If all who profess to be followers of Christ were truly sanctified, their means, instead of being spent for needless and even hurtful indulgences, would be turned into the Lord's treasury, and Christians would set an example of temperance, self-denial, and self-sacrifice. Then they would be the light of the world.

The world is given up to self-indulgence. "The lust of the flesh, and the lust of the eyes, and the pride of life" control the masses of the people. But Christ's followers have a holier calling. "Come out from among them, and be ye separate, saith the Lord, and touch not the unclean." In the light of God's word we are justified in declaring that sanctification cannot be genuine which does not work this utter renunciation of the sinful pursuits and gratifications of the world.

To those who comply with the conditions, "Come out from among them, and be ye separate, ... and touch not the unclean," God's promise is, "I will receive you, and will be a Father unto you, and ye shall be My sons and daughters, saith the Lord Almighty." 2 Corinthians 6:17, 18. It is the privilege and the duty of every Christian to have a rich and abundant experience in the things of God. "I am the light of the world," said Jesus. "He that followeth Me shall not walk in darkness, but shall have the light of life." John 8:12. "The path of the just is as the shining light, that shineth more and more unto the perfect day." Proverbs 4:18. Every step of faith and obedience brings the soul into closer connection with the Light of the world, in whom there "is no darkness at all." The bright beams of the Sun of Righteousness shine upon the servants of God, and they are to reflect His rays. As the stars tell us that there is a great light in heaven with whose glory they are made bright, so Christians are to make it manifest that there is a God on the throne of the universe whose character is worthy of praise and imitation. The graces of His Spirit, the purity and holiness of His character, will be manifest in His witnesses.

Paul in his letter to the Colossians sets forth the rich blessings granted to the children of God. He says: We "do not cease to pray for you, and to desire that ye might be filled with the knowledge of His will in all wisdom and spiritual understanding; that ye might walk worthy of the Lord unto all pleasing, being fruitful in every good work, and increasing in the knowledge of God; strengthened with all might, according to His glorious power, unto all patience and long-suffering with joyfulness." Colossians 1:9-11.

Again he writes of his desire that the brethren at Ephesus might come to understand the height of the Christian's privilege. He opens before them, in the most comprehensive language, the marvelous power and knowledge that they might possess as sons and daughters of the Most High. It was theirs "to be strengthened with might by His Spirit in the inner man," to be "rooted and grounded in love," to "comprehend with all saints what is the breadth, and length, and depth, and height; and to know the love of Christ, which passeth knowledge." But the prayer of the apostle reaches the climax of privilege when he prays that "ye might be filled with all the fullness of God." Ephesians 3:16-19.

477 Here are revealed the heights of attainment that we may reach through faith in the promises of our heavenly Father, when we fulfill His requirements. Through the merits of Christ we have access to the throne of Infinite Power. "He that spared not His own Son, but delivered Him up for us all, how shall He not with Him also freely give us all things?" Romans 8:32. The Father gave His Spirit without measure to His Son, and we also may partake of its fullness. Jesus says, "If ye then, being evil, know how to give good gifts unto your children: how much more shall your heavenly Father give the Holy Spirit to them that ask Him?" Luke 11:13. "If ye shall ask anything in My name, I will do it." "Ask, and ye shall receive, that your joy may be full." John 14:14; 16:24.

While the Christian's life will be characterized by humility, it should not be marked with sadness and self-depreciation. It is the privilege of everyone so to live that God will approve and bless him. It is not the will of our heavenly Father that we should be ever under condemnation and darkness. There is no evidence of true humility in going with the head bowed down and the heart filled with thoughts of self. We may go to Jesus and be cleansed, and stand before the law without shame and remorse. "There is therefore now no condemnation to them which are in Christ Jesus, who walk not after the flesh, but after the Spirit." Romans 8:1.

Through Jesus the fallen sons of Adam become "sons of God." "Both He that sanctifieth and they who are sanctified are all of one: for which cause He is not ashamed to call them brethren." Hebrews 2:11. The Christian's life should be one of faith, of victory, and joy in God. "Whatsoever is born of God overcometh the world: and this is the victory that overcometh the world, even our faith." 1 John 5:4. Truly spoke God's servant Nehemiah: "The joy of the Lord is your strength." Nehemiah 8:10.

And Paul says: "Rejoice in the Lord alway: and again I say, Rejoice." "Rejoice evermore. Pray without ceasing. In everything give thanks: for this is the will of God in Christ Jesus concerning you." Philippians 4:4; 1 Thessalonians 5:16-18.

Such are the fruits of Bible conversion and sanctification; and it is because the great principles of righteousness set forth in the law of God are so indifferently regarded by the Christian world that these fruits are so rarely witnessed. This is why there is manifest so little of that deep, abiding work of the Spirit of God which marked revivals in former years.

It is by beholding that we become changed. And as those sacred precepts in which God has opened to men the perfection and holiness of His character are neglected, and the minds of the people are attracted to human teachings and theories, what marvel that there has followed a decline of living piety in the church. Saith the Lord: "They have forsaken Me the fountain of living waters, and hewed them out cisterns, broken cisterns, that can hold no water." Jeremiah 2:13.

"Blessed is the man that walketh not in the counsel of the ungodly. . . . But his delight is in the law of the Lord; and in His law doth he meditate day and night. And he shall be like a tree planted by the rivers of water, that bringeth forth his fruit in his season; his leaf also shall not wither; and whatsoever he doeth shall prosper." Psalm 1:1-3. It is only as the law of God is restored to its rightful position that there can be a revival of primitive faith and godliness among His professed people. "Thus saith the Lord, Stand ye in the ways, and see, and ask for the old paths, where is the good way, and walk therein, and ye shall find rest for your souls." Jeremiah 6:16.

28

479

Facing Life's Record

"I beheld," says the prophet Daniel, "till thrones were placed, and One that was Ancient of Days did sit: His raiment was white as snow, and the hair of His head like pure wool; His throne was fiery flames, and the wheels thereof burning fire. A fiery stream issued and came forth from before Him: thousand thousands ministered unto Him, and ten thousand times ten thousand stood before Him: the judgment was set, and the books were opened." Daniel 7:9, 10, R.V.

Thus was presented to the prophet's vision the great and solemn day when the characters and the lives of men should pass in review before the Judge of all the earth, and to every man should be rendered "according to his works." The Ancient of Days is God the Father. Says the psalmist: "Before the mountains were brought forth, or ever Thou hadst formed the earth and the world, even from everlasting to everlasting, Thou art God." Psalm 90:2. It is He, the source of all being, and the fountain of all law, that is to preside in the judgment. And holy angels as ministers and witnesses, in number "ten thousand times ten thousand, and thousands of thousands," attend this great tribunal.

"And, behold, one like the Son of man came with the clouds of heaven, and came to the Ancient of Days, and they brought Him near
480 before Him. And there was given Him dominion, and glory, and a kingdom, that all people, nations, and languages, should serve Him: His dominion is an everlasting dominion, which shall not pass away." Daniel 7:13, 14. The coming of Christ here described is not His second coming to the earth. He comes to the Ancient of Days in heaven to receive dominion and glory and a kingdom, which will be given Him at the close of His work as a mediator. It is this coming, and not His second advent to the earth, that was foretold in prophecy to take place at the termination of the 2300 days in 1844. Attended by heavenly angels, our great High Priest enters the holy of holies and there appears in the presence of God to engage in the last acts of His ministration in behalf of man—to perform the work of investigative judgment and to make an atonement for all who are shown to be entitled to its benefits.

In the typical service only those who had come before God with confession and repentance, and whose sins, through the blood of the sin offering, were transferred to the sanctuary, had a part in the service of the Day of Atonement. So in the great day of final atonement and investigative judgment the only cases considered are those of the professed people of God. The judgment of the wicked is a distinct and separate work, and takes place at a later period. "Judgment must begin at the house of God: and if it first begin at us, what shall the end be of them that obey not the gospel?" 1 Peter 4:17.

The books of record in heaven, in which the names and the deeds of men are registered, are to determine the decisions of the judgment. Says the prophet Daniel: "The judgment was set, and the books were opened." The revelator, describing the same scene, adds: "Another book was opened, which is the book of life: and the dead were judged out of those things which were written in the books, according to their works." Revelation 20:12.

The book of life contains the names of all who have ever entered the service of God. Jesus
481 bade His disciples: "Rejoice, because your names are written in heaven." Luke 10:20. Paul speaks of his faithful fellow workers, "whose names are in the book of life." Philippians 4:3. Daniel, looking down to "a time of trouble, such as never was," declares that God's people shall be delivered, "everyone that shall be found written in the book." And the revelator says that those only shall enter the city of God whose names "are written in the Lamb's book of life." Daniel 12:1; Revelation 21:27.

"A book of remembrance" is written before God, in which are recorded the good deeds of "them that feared the Lord, and that thought upon His name." Malachi 3:16. Their words of faith, their acts of love, are registered in heaven. Nehemiah refers to this when he says: "Remember me, O my God, . . . and wipe not out my good deeds that I have done for the house of my God." Nehemiah 13:14. In the book of God's remembrance every deed of righteousness is immortalized. There every temptation resisted, every evil overcome, every word of tender pity expressed, is faithfully chronicled. And every act of sacrifice, every suffering and sorrow endured for Christ's sake, is recorded. Says the psalmist: "Thou tellest my wanderings: put Thou my tears into Thy bottle: are they not in Thy book?" Psalm 56:8.

There is a record also of the sins of men. "For God shall bring every work into judgment, with every secret thing, whether it be good, or whether it be evil." "Every idle word that men shall speak, they shall give account thereof in the day of judgment." Says the Saviour: "By thy words thou shalt be justified, and by thy words thou shalt be condemned." Ecclesiastes 12:14; Matthew 12:36, 37. The secret purposes and motives appear in the unerring register; for God "will bring to light the hidden things of darkness, and will make manifest the counsels of the hearts." 1 Corinthians 4:5. "Behold, it is written before Me, . . . your iniquities, and the iniquities of your fathers together, saith the Lord." Isaiah 65:6, 7.

Every man's work passes in review before 482 God and is registered for faithfulness or unfaithfulness. Opposite each name in the books of heaven is entered with terrible exactness every wrong word, every selfish act, every unfulfilled duty, and every secret sin, with every artful dissembling. Heaven-sent warnings or reproofs neglected, wasted moments, unimproved opportunities, the influence exerted for good or for evil, with its far-reaching results, all are chronicled by the recording angel.

The law of God is the standard by which the characters and the lives of men will be tested in the judgment. Says the wise man: "Fear God, and keep His commandments: for this is the whole duty of man. For God shall bring every work into judgment." Ecclesiastes 12:13, 14. The apostle James admonishes his brethren: "So speak ye, and so do, as they that shall be judged by the law of liberty." James 2:12.

Those who in the judgment are "accounted worthy" will have a part in the resurrection of the just. Jesus said: "They which shall be accounted worthy to obtain that world, and the resurrection from the dead, . . . are equal unto the angels; and are the children of God, being the children of the resurrection." Luke 20:35, 36. And again He declares that "they that have done good" shall come forth "unto the resurrection of life." John 5:29. The righteous dead will not be raised until after the judgment at which they are accounted worthy of "the resurrection of life." Hence they will not be present in person at the tribunal when their records are examined and their cases decided.

Jesus will appear as their advocate, to plead in their behalf before God. "If any man sin, we have an advocate with the Father, Jesus Christ the righteous." 1 John 2:1. "For Christ is not entered into the holy places made with hands, which are the figures of the true; but into heaven itself, now to appear in the presence of God for us." "Wherefore He is able also to save them to the uttermost that come unto God by Him, seeing He ever liveth to make intercession for them." Hebrews 9:24; 7:25.

483   As the books of record are opened in the judgment, the lives of all who have believed on Jesus come in review before God. Beginning with those who first lived upon the earth, our Advocate presents the cases of each successive generation, and closes with the living. Every name is mentioned, every case closely investigated. Names are accepted, names rejected. When any have sins remaining upon the books of record, unrepented of and unforgiven, their names will be blotted out of the book of life, and the record of their good deeds will be erased from the book of God's remembrance. The Lord declared to Moses: "Whosoever hath sinned against Me, him will I blot out of My book." Exodus 32:33. And says the prophet Ezekiel: "When the righteous turneth away from his righteousness, and committeth iniquity, . . . all his righteousness that he hath done shall not be mentioned." Ezekiel 18:24.

All who have truly repented of sin, and by faith claimed the blood of Christ as their atoning sacrifice, have had pardon entered against their names in the books of heaven; as they have become partakers of the righteousness of Christ, and their characters are found to be in harmony with the law of God, their sins will be blotted out, and they themselves will be accounted worthy of eternal life. The Lord declares, by the prophet Isaiah: "I, even I, am He that blotteth out thy transgressions for Mine own sake, and will not remember thy sins." Isaiah 43:25. Said Jesus: "He that overcometh, the same shall be clothed in white raiment; and I will not blot out his name out of the book of life, but I will confess his name before My Father, and before His

angels." "Whosoever therefore shall confess Me before men, him will I confess also before My Father which is in heaven. But whosoever shall deny Me before men, him will I also deny before My Father which is in heaven." Revelation 3:5; Matthew 10:32, 33.

The deepest interest manifested among men in the decisions of earthly tribunals but faintly represents the interest evinced in the heavenly 484 courts when the names entered in the book of life come up in review before the Judge of all the earth. The divine Intercessor presents the plea that all who have overcome through faith in His blood be forgiven their transgressions, that they be restored to their Eden home, and crowned as joint heirs with Himself to "the first dominion." Micah 4:8. Satan in his efforts to deceive and tempt our race had thought to frustrate the divine plan in man's creation; but Christ now asks that this plan be carried into effect as if man had never fallen. He asks for His people not only pardon and justification, full and complete, but a share in His glory and a seat upon His throne.

While Jesus is pleading for the subjects of His grace, Satan accuses them before God as transgressors. The great deceiver has sought to lead them into skepticism, to cause them to lose confidence in God, to separate themselves from His love, and to break His law. Now he points to the record of their lives, to the defects of character, the unlikeness to Christ, which has dishonored their Redeemer, to all the sins that he has tempted them to commit, and because of these he claims them as his subjects.

Jesus does not excuse their sins, but shows their penitence and faith, and, claiming for them forgiveness, He lifts His wounded hands before the Father and the holy angels, saying: I know them by name. I have graven them on the palms of My hands. "The sacrifices of God are a broken spirit: a broken and a contrite heart, O God, Thou wilt not despise." Psalm 51:17. And to the accuser of His people He declares: "The Lord rebuke thee, O Satan; even the Lord that hath chosen Jerusalem rebuke thee: is not this a brand plucked out of the fire?" Zechariah 3:2. Christ will clothe His faithful ones with His own righteousness, that He may present them to His Father "a glorious church, not having spot, or wrinkle, or any such thing." Ephesians 5:27. Their names stand enrolled in the book of life, and concerning them it is written: "They shall walk with Me in white: for they are worthy." Revelation 3:4.

Thus will be realized the complete fulfillment 485 of the new-covenant promise: "I will forgive their iniquity, and I will remember their sin no more." "In those days, and in that time, saith the Lord, the iniquity of Israel shall be sought for, and there shall be none; and the sins of Judah, and they shall not be found." Jeremiah 31:34;

50:20. "In that day shall the branch of the Lord be beautiful and glorious, and the fruit of the earth shall be excellent and comely for them that are escaped of Israel. And it shall come to pass, that he that is left in Zion, and he that remaineth in Jerusalem, shall be called holy, even everyone that is written among the living in Jerusalem." Isaiah 4:2, 3.

The work of the investigative judgment and the blotting out of sins is to be accomplished before the second advent of the Lord. Since the dead are to be judged out of the things written in the books, it is impossible that the sins of men should be blotted out until after the judgment at which their cases are to be investigated. But the apostle Peter distinctly states that the sins of believers will be blotted out "when the times of refreshing shall come from the presence of the Lord; and He shall send Jesus Christ." Acts 3:19, 20. When the investigative judgment closes, Christ will come, and His reward will be with Him to give to every man as his work shall be.

In the typical service the high priest, having made the atonement for Israel, came forth and blessed the congregation. So Christ, at the close of His work as mediator, will appear, "without sin unto salvation" (Hebrews 9:28), to bless His waiting people with eternal life. As the priest, in removing the sins from the sanctuary, confessed them upon the head of the scapegoat, so Christ will place all these sins upon Satan, the originator and instigator of sin. The scapegoat, bearing the sins of Israel, was sent away "unto a land not inhabited" (Leviticus 16:22); so Satan, bearing the guilt of all the sins which he has caused God's people to commit, will be for a thousand years confined to the earth, which will then be desolate, without inhabitant, and he will at last 486 suffer the full penalty of sin in the fires that shall destroy all the wicked. Thus the great plan of redemption will reach its accomplishment in the final eradication of sin and the deliverance of all who have been willing to renounce evil.

At the time appointed for the judgment—the close of the 2300 days, in 1844—began the work of investigation and blotting out of sins. All who have ever taken upon themselves the name of Christ must pass its searching scrutiny. Both the living and the dead are to be judged "out of those things which were written in the books, according to their works."

Sins that have not been repented of and forsaken will not be pardoned and blotted out of the books of record, but will stand to witness against the sinner in the day of God. He may have committed his evil deeds in the light of day or in the darkness of night; but they were open and manifest before Him with whom we have to do. Angels of God witnessed each sin and registered it in the unerring records. Sin may be concealed, denied, covered up from

father, mother, wife, children, and associates; no one but the guilty actors may cherish the least suspicion of the wrong; but it is laid bare before the intelligences of heaven. The darkness of the darkest night, the secrecy of all deceptive arts, is not sufficient to veil one thought from the knowledge of the Eternal. God has an exact record of every unjust account and every unfair dealing. He is not deceived by appearances of piety. He makes no mistakes in His estimation of character. Men may be deceived by those who are corrupt in heart, but God pierces all disguises and reads the inner life.

How solemn is the thought! Day after day, passing into eternity, bears its burden of records for the books of heaven. Words once spoken, deeds once done, can never be recalled. Angels have registered both the good and the evil. The mightiest conqueror upon the earth cannot call back the record of even a single day. Our acts, our words, even our most secret motives, all have their weight in deciding our destiny for weal or woe. Though they may be forgotten by us, they will bear their testimony to justify or 487 condemn.

As the features of the countenance are reproduced with unerring accuracy on the polished plate of the artist, so the character is faithfully delineated in the books above. Yet how little solicitude is felt concerning that record which is to meet the gaze of heavenly beings. Could the veil which separates the visible from the invisible world be swept back, and the children of men behold an angel recording every word and deed, which they must meet again in the judgment, how many words that are daily uttered would remain unspoken, how many deeds would remain undone.

In the judgment the use made of every talent will be scrutinized. How have we employed the capital lent us of Heaven? Will the Lord at His coming receive His own with usury? Have we improved the powers entrusted us, in hand and heart and brain, to the glory of God and the blessing of the world? How have we used our time, our pen, our voice, our money, our influence? What have we done for Christ, in the person of the poor, the afflicted, the orphan, or the widow? God has made us the depositaries of His holy word; what have we done with the light and truth given us to make men wise unto salvation? No value is attached to a mere profession of faith in Christ; only the love which is shown by works is counted genuine. Yet it is love alone which in the sight of Heaven makes any act of value. Whatever is done from love, however small it may appear in the estimation of men, is accepted and rewarded of God.

The hidden selfishness of men stands revealed in the books of heaven. There is the record of unfulfilled duties to their fellow men, of forgetfulness of the Saviour's claims. There they will see how often were given to Satan the time, thought, and strength that belonged to Christ. Sad is the record which angels bear to heaven. Intelligent beings, professed followers of Christ, are absorbed in the acquirement of worldly possessions or the enjoyment of earthly pleasures. Money, time, and strength are sacrificed for display and self-indulgence; but few are the moments devoted to prayer, to the searching of the Scriptures, to humiliation of soul and confession of sin.

Satan invents unnumbered schemes to occupy our minds, that they may not dwell upon the very work with which we ought to be best acquainted. The archdeceiver hates the great truths that bring to view an atoning sacrifice and an all-powerful mediator. He knows that with him everything depends on his diverting minds from Jesus and His truth.

Those who would share the benefits of the Saviour's mediation should permit nothing to interfere with their duty to perfect holiness in the fear of God. The precious hours, instead of being given to pleasure, to display, or to gain seeking, should be devoted to an earnest, prayerful study of the word of truth. The subject of the sanctuary and the investigative judgment should be clearly understood by the people of God. All need a knowledge for themselves of the position and work of their great High Priest. Otherwise it will be impossible for them to exercise the faith which is essential at this time or to occupy the position which God designs them to fill. Every individual has a soul to save or to lose. Each has a case pending at the bar of God. Each must meet the great Judge face to face. How important, then, that every mind contemplate often the solemn scene when the judgment shall sit and the books shall be opened, when, with Daniel, every individual must stand in his lot, at the end of the days.

All who have received the light upon these subjects are to bear testimony of the great truths which God has committed to them. The sanctuary in heaven is the very center of Christ's work in behalf of men. It concerns every soul living upon the earth. It opens to view the plan of redemption, bringing us down to the very close of time and revealing the triumphant issue of the contest between righteousness and sin. It is of the utmost importance that all should thoroughly investigate these subjects and be able to give an answer to everyone that asketh them a reason of the hope that is in them.

The intercession of Christ in man's behalf in the sanctuary above is as essential to the plan of salvation as was His death upon the cross. By His death He began that work which after His resurrection He ascended to complete in heaven. We must by faith enter within the veil, "whither the forerunner is for us entered." Hebrews 6:20. There the light from the cross of Calvary is reflected. There we may gain a clearer insight into the mysteries of redemption. The salvation of man is accomplished at an infinite expense to heaven; the sacrifice made is equal to the broadest demands of the broken law of God. Jesus has opened the way to the Father's throne, and through His mediation the sincere desire of all who come to Him in faith may be presented before God.

"He that covereth his sins shall not prosper: but whoso confesseth and forsaketh them shall have mercy." Proverbs 28:13. If those who hide and excuse their faults could see how Satan exults over them, how he taunts Christ and holy angels with their course, they would make haste to confess their sins and to put them away. Through defects in the character, Satan works to gain control of the whole mind, and he knows that if these defects are cherished, he will succeed. Therefore he is constantly seeking to deceive the followers of Christ with his fatal sophistry that it is impossible for them to overcome. But Jesus pleads in their behalf His wounded hands, His bruised body; and He declares to all who would follow Him: "My grace is sufficient for thee." 2 Corinthians 12:9. "Take My yoke upon you, and learn of Me; for I am meek and lowly in heart: and ye shall find rest unto your souls. For My yoke is easy, and My burden is light." Matthew 11:29, 30. Let none, then, regard their defects as incurable. God will give faith and grace to overcome them.

We are now living in the great day of atonement. In the typical service, while the high priest was making the atonement for Israel, all were required to afflict their souls by repentance of sin and humiliation before the Lord, lest they be cut off from among the people. In like manner, all who would have their names retained in the book of life should now, in the few remaining days of their probation, afflict their souls before God by sorrow for sin and true repentance. There must be deep, faithful searching of heart. The light, frivolous spirit indulged by so many professed Christians must be put away. There is earnest warfare before all who would subdue the evil tendencies that strive for the mastery. The work of preparation is an individual work. We are not saved in groups. The purity and devotion of one will not offset the want of these qualities in another. Though all nations are to pass in judgment before God, yet He will examine the case of each individual with as close and searching scrutiny as if there were not another being upon the earth. Everyone must be tested and found without spot or wrinkle or any such thing.

Solemn are the scenes connected with the closing work of the atonement. Momentous are the interests involved therein. The judgment is now passing in the sanctuary above. For many years this work has been in progress.

Soon—none know how soon—it will pass to the cases of the living. In the awful presence of God our lives are to come up in review. At this time above all others it behooves every soul to heed the Saviour's admonition: "Watch and pray: for ye know not when the time is." Mark 13:33. "If therefore thou shalt not watch, I will come on thee as a thief, and thou shalt not know what hour I will come upon thee." Revelation 3:3.

When the work of the investigative judgment closes, the destiny of all will have been decided for life or death. Probation is ended a short time before the appearing of the Lord in the clouds of heaven. Christ in the Revelation, looking forward to that time, declares: "He that is unjust, let him be unjust still: and he which is filthy, let him be filthy still: and he that is righteous let
491 him be righteous still: and he that is holy, let him be holy still. And, behold, I come quickly; and My reward is with Me, to give every man according as his work shall be." Revelation 22:11, 12.

The righteous and the wicked will still be living upon the earth in their mortal state—men will be planting and building, eating and drinking, all unconscious that the final, irrevocable decision has been pronounced in the sanctuary above. Before the Flood, after Noah entered the ark, God shut him in and shut the ungodly out; but for seven days the people, knowing not that their doom was fixed, continued their careless, pleasure-loving life and mocked the warnings of impending judgment. "So," says the Saviour, "shall also the coming of the Son of man be." Matthew 24:39. Silently, unnoticed as the midnight thief, will come the decisive hour which marks the fixing of every man's destiny, the final withdrawal of mercy's offer to guilty men.

"Watch ye therefore: . . . lest coming suddenly He find you sleeping." Mark 13:35, 36. Perilous is the condition of those who, growing weary of their watch, turn to the attractions of the world. While the man of business is absorbed in the pursuit of gain, while the pleasure lover is seeking indulgence, while the daughter of fashion is arranging her adornments—it may be in that hour the Judge of all the earth will pronounce the sentence: "Thou art weighed in the balances, and art found wanting." Daniel 5:27.

492

29

The Origin of Evil

To many minds the origin of sin and the reason for its existence are a source of great perplexity. They see the work of evil, with its terrible results of woe and desolation, and they question how all this can exist under the sovereignty of One who is infinite in wisdom, in power, and in love. Here is a mystery of which they find no explanation. And in their uncertainty and doubt they are blinded to truths plainly revealed in God's word and essential to salvation. There are those who, in their inquiries concerning the existence of sin, endeavor to search into that which God has never revealed; hence they find no solution of their difficulties; and such as are actuated by a disposition to doubt and cavil seize upon this as an excuse for rejecting the words of Holy Writ. Others, however, fail of a satisfactory understanding of the great problem of evil, from the fact that tradition and misinterpretation have obscured the teaching of the Bible concerning the character of God, the nature of His government, and the principles of His dealing with sin.

It is impossible to explain the origin of sin so as to give a reason for its existence. Yet enough may be understood concerning both the origin and the final disposition of sin to make fully manifest the justice and benevolence of God in all His dealings with evil. Nothing is more plainly taught in Scripture than that God was in 493 no wise responsible for the entrance of sin; that there was no arbitrary withdrawal of divine grace, no deficiency in the divine government, that gave occasion for the uprising of rebellion. Sin is an intruder, for whose presence no reason can be given. It is mysterious, unaccountable; to excuse it is to defend it. Could excuse for it be found, or cause be shown for its existence, it would cease to be sin. Our only definition of sin is that given in the word of God; it is "the transgression of the law;" it is the outworking of a principle at war with the great law of love which is the foundation of the divine government.

Before the entrance of evil there was peace and joy throughout the universe. All was in perfect harmony with the Creator's will. Love for God was supreme, love for one another impartial. Christ the Word, the Only Begotten of God, was one with the eternal Father,—one in nature, in character, and in purpose,—the only being in all the universe that could enter into all the counsels and purposes of God. By Christ the Father wrought in the creation of all heavenly beings. "By Him were all things created, that are in heaven, . . . whether they be thrones, or dominions, or principalities, or powers" (Colossians 1:16); and to Christ, equally with the Father, all heaven gave allegiance.

The law of love being the foundation of the government of God, the happiness of all created beings depended upon their perfect accord with its great principles of righteousness. God desires from all His creatures the service of love—homage that springs from an intelligent appreciation of His character. He takes no pleasure in a forced allegiance, and to all He grants freedom of will, that they may render Him voluntary service.

But there was one that chose to pervert this freedom. Sin originated with him who, next to Christ, had been most honored of God and who stood highest in power and glory among the inhabitants of heaven. Before his fall, Lucifer was first of the covering cherubs, holy and undefiled. "Thus saith the Lord God; Thou sealest up the sum, full of wisdom, and perfect in beauty. Thou hast been in Eden the garden of God; every precious stone was thy covering. . . . Thou art the anointed cherub that covereth; and I have set thee so: thou wast upon the holy mountain of God; thou hast walked up and down in the midst of the stones of fire. Thou wast perfect in thy ways from the day that thou wast created, till iniquity was found in thee." Ezekiel 28:12-15.

Lucifer might have remained in favor with God, beloved and honored by all the angelic host, exercising his noble powers to bless others and to glorify his Maker. But, says the prophet, "Thine heart was lifted up because of thy beauty, thou hast corrupted thy wisdom by reason of thy brightness." Verse 17. Little by little, Lucifer came to indulge a desire for self-exaltation. "Thou hast set thine heart as the heart of God." "Thou hast said, . . . I will exalt my throne above the stars of God: I will sit also upon the mount of the congregation. . . . I will ascend above the heights of the clouds; I will be like the Most High." Verse 6; Isaiah 14:13, 14. Instead of seeking to make God supreme in the affections and allegiance of His creatures, it was Lucifer's endeavor to win their service and homage to himself. And coveting the honor which the infinite Father had bestowed upon His Son, this prince of angels aspired to power which it was the prerogative of Christ alone to wield.

All heaven had rejoiced to reflect the Creator's glory and to show forth His praise. And while God was thus honored, all had been peace and gladness. But a note of discord now marred the celestial harmonies. The service and exaltation of self, contrary to the Creator's plan, awakened forebodings of evil in minds to whom God's glory was supreme. The heavenly councils pleaded with Lucifer. The Son of God presented before him the greatness, the goodness, and the justice of the Creator, and the sacred, unchanging nature of His law. God Himself had established the order of heaven; and in departing from it, Lucifer would dishonor his Maker, and bring ruin upon himself. But the warning, given in infinite love and mercy, only aroused a spirit of resistance. Lucifer allowed jealousy of Christ to prevail, and he became the more determined.

Pride in his own glory nourished the desire for supremacy. The high honors conferred upon Lucifer were not appreciated as the gift of God and called forth no gratitude to the Creator. He gloried in his brightness and exaltation, and aspired to be equal with God. He was beloved and reverenced by the heavenly host. Angels delighted to execute his commands, and he was clothed with wisdom and glory above them all. Yet the Son of God was the acknowledged Sovereign of heaven, one in power and authority with the Father. In all the councils of God, Christ was a participant, while Lucifer was not permitted thus to enter into the divine purposes. "Why," questioned this mighty angel, "should Christ have the supremacy? Why is He thus honored above Lucifer?"

Leaving his place in the immediate presence of God, Lucifer went forth to diffuse the spirit of discontent among the angels. Working with mysterious secrecy, and for a time concealing his real purpose under an appearance of reverence for God, he endeavored to excite dissatisfaction concerning the laws that governed heavenly beings, intimating that they imposed an unnecessary restraint. Since their natures were holy, he urged that the angels should obey the dictates of their own will. He sought to create sympathy for himself by representing that God had dealt unjustly with him in bestowing supreme honor upon Christ. He claimed that in aspiring to greater power and honor he was not aiming at self-exaltation, but was seeking to secure liberty for all the inhabitants of heaven, that by this means they might attain to a higher state of existence.

God in His great mercy bore long with Lucifer. He was not immediately degraded from his exalted station when he first indulged the spirit of discontent, nor even when he began to present his false claims before the loyal angels. Long was he retained in heaven. Again and again he was offered pardon on condition of repentance and submission. Such efforts as only infinite love and wisdom could devise were made to convince him of his error. The spirit of discontent had never before been known in heaven. Lucifer himself did not at first see whither he was drifting; he did not understand the real nature of his feelings. But as his dissatisfaction was proved to be without cause, Lucifer was convinced that he was in the wrong, that the divine claims were just, and that he ought to acknowledge them as such before all heaven. Had he done this, he might have saved himself and many angels. He had not at this time fully cast off his allegiance to God. Though he had forsaken his position as covering cherub, yet if he had been willing to return to God, acknowledging the Creator's wisdom, and satisfied to fill the place appointed him in God's great plan, he would have been reinstated in his office. But pride forbade him to submit. He persistently defended his own course, maintained that he had no need of repentance, and fully committed himself, in the great controversy, against his Maker.

All the powers of his master mind were now bent to the work of deception, to secure the sympathy of the angels that had been under his command. Even the fact that Christ had warned and counseled him was perverted to serve his traitorous designs. To those whose loving trust bound them most closely to him, Satan had represented that he was wrongly judged, that his position was not respected, and that his liberty was to be abridged. From misrepresentation of the words of Christ he passed to prevarication and direct falsehood, accusing the Son of God of a design to humiliate him before the inhabitants of heaven. He sought also to make a false issue between himself and the loyal angels. All whom he could not subvert and bring fully to his side he accused of indifference to the interests of heavenly beings. The very work which he himself was doing he charged upon those 497 who remained true to God. And to sustain his charge of God's injustice toward him, he resorted to misrepresentation of the words and acts of the Creator. It was his policy to perplex the angels with subtle arguments concerning the purposes of God. Everything that was simple he shrouded in mystery, and by artful perversion cast doubt upon the plainest statements of Jehovah. His high position, in such close connection with the divine administration, gave greater force to his representations, and many were induced to unite with him in rebellion against Heaven's authority.

God in His wisdom permitted Satan to carry forward his work, until the spirit of disaffection ripened into active revolt. It was necessary for his plans to be fully developed, that their true nature and tendency might be seen by all. Lucifer, as the anointed cherub, had been highly exalted; he was greatly loved by the heavenly beings, and his influence over them was strong. God's government included not only the inhabitants of heaven, but of all the worlds that He had created; and Satan thought that if he could carry the angels of heaven with him in rebellion, he could carry also the other worlds. He had artfully presented his side of the question, employing sophistry and fraud to secure his objects. His power to deceive was very great, and by disguising himself in a cloak of falsehood he had gained an advantage. Even the loyal angels could not fully discern his character or see to what his work was leading.

Satan had been so highly honored, and all his acts were so clothed with mystery, that it was difficult to disclose to the angels the true nature of his work. Until fully developed, sin would not appear the evil thing it was. Heretofore it had had no place in the universe of God, and holy beings had no conception of its nature and malignity. They could not discern the terrible consequences that would result from setting aside the divine law. Satan had, at first, concealed his work under a specious profession of loyalty to God. He claimed to be seeking to promote the honor of God, the stability of His government, and the good of all the inhabitants of heaven. While instilling discontent into the 498 minds of the angels under him, he had artfully made it appear that he was seeking to remove dissatisfaction. When he urged that changes be made in the order and laws of God's government, it was under the pretense that these were necessary in order to preserve harmony in heaven.

In His dealing with sin, God could employ only righteousness and truth. Satan could use what God could not—flattery and deceit. He had sought to falsify the word of God and had misrepresented His plan of government before the angels, claiming that God was not just in laying laws and rules upon the inhabitants of heaven; that in requiring submission and obedience from His creatures, He was seeking merely the exaltation of Himself. Therefore it must be demonstrated before the inhabitants of heaven, as well as of all the worlds, that God's government was just, His law perfect. Satan had made it appear that he himself was seeking to promote the good of the universe. The true character of the usurper, and his real object, must be understood by all. He must have time to manifest himself by his wicked works.

The discord which his own course had caused in heaven, Satan charged upon the law and government of God. All evil he declared to be the result of the divine administration. He claimed that it was his own object to improve upon the statutes of Jehovah. Therefore it was necessary that he should demonstrate the nature of his claims, and show the working out of his proposed changes in the divine law. His own work must condemn him. Satan had claimed from the first that he was not in rebellion. The whole universe must see the deceiver unmasked.

Even when it was decided that he could no longer remain in heaven, Infinite Wisdom did not destroy Satan. Since the service of love can alone be acceptable to God, the allegiance of His creatures must rest upon a conviction of His justice and benevolence. The inhabitants of heaven and of other worlds, being unprepared to comprehend the nature or consequences of sin, could not then have seen the justice and mercy 499 of God in the destruction of Satan. Had he been immediately blotted from existence, they would have served God from fear rather than from love. The influence of the deceiver would not have been fully destroyed, nor would the spirit of rebellion have been utterly eradicated. Evil must be permitted to come to maturity. For the good of the entire universe through ceaseless ages Satan must more fully develop his principles, that his charges against the divine government might be seen in their true light by all created beings, that the justice and mercy of God and the immutability of His law might forever be placed beyond all question.

Satan's rebellion was to be a lesson to the universe through all coming ages, a perpetual testimony to the nature and terrible results of sin. The working out of Satan's rule, its effects upon both men and angels, would show what must be the fruit of setting aside the divine authority. It would testify that with the existence of God's government and His law is bound up the well-being of all the creatures He has made. Thus the history of this terrible experiment of rebellion was to be a perpetual safeguard to all holy intelligences, to prevent them from being deceived as to the nature of transgression, to save them from committing sin and suffering its punishments.

To the very close of the controversy in heaven the great usurper continued to justify himself. When it was announced that with all his sympathizers he must be expelled from the abodes of bliss, then the rebel leader boldly avowed his contempt for the Creator's law. He reiterated his claim that angels needed no control, but should be left to follow their own will, which would ever guide them right. He denounced the divine statutes as a restriction of their liberty and declared that it was his purpose to secure the abolition of law; that, freed from this restraint, the hosts of heaven might enter upon a more exalted, more glorious state of existence.

500 With one accord, Satan and his host threw the blame of their rebellion wholly upon Christ, declaring that if they had not been reproved, they would never have rebelled. Thus stubborn and defiant in their disloyalty, seeking vainly to overthrow the government of God, yet blasphemously claiming to be themselves the innocent victims of oppressive power, the archrebel and all his sympathizers were at last banished from heaven.

The same spirit that prompted rebellion in heaven still inspires rebellion on earth. Satan has continued with men the same policy which he pursued with the angels. His spirit now reigns in the children of disobedience. Like him they seek to break down the restraints of the law of God and promise men liberty through transgression of its precepts. Reproof of sin still arouses the spirit of hatred and resistance. When God's messages of warning are brought home to the conscience, Satan leads men to justify themselves and to seek the sympathy of others in their course of sin. Instead of correcting their errors, they excite indignation against the reprover, as if he were the sole cause of difficulty. From the days of righteous Abel to our own time such is the spirit which has been displayed toward those who dare to condemn sin.

By the same misrepresentation of the character of God as he had practiced in heaven, causing Him to be regarded as severe and tyrannical, Satan induced man to sin. And having succeeded thus far, he declared that God's unjust restrictions had led to man's fall, as they had led to his own rebellion.

But the Eternal One Himself proclaims His character: "The Lord God, merciful and gracious, long-suffering, and abundant in goodness and truth, keeping mercy for thousands, forgiving iniquity and transgression and sin, and that will by no means clear the guilty." Exodus 34:6, 7.

In the banishment of Satan from heaven, God declared His justice and maintained the honor of His throne. But when man had sinned through yielding to the deceptions of this apostate spirit, God gave an evidence of His love by yielding up His only-begotten Son to die for the fallen race. In the atonement the character of God is 501 revealed. The mighty argument of the cross demonstrates to the whole universe that the course of sin which Lucifer had chosen was in no wise chargeable upon the government of God.

In the contest between Christ and Satan, during the Saviour's earthly ministry, the character of the great deceiver was unmasked. Nothing could so effectually have uprooted Satan from the affections of the heavenly angels and the whole loyal universe as did his cruel warfare upon the world's Redeemer. The daring blasphemy of his demand that Christ should pay him homage, his presumptuous boldness in bearing Him to the mountain summit and the pinnacle of the temple, the malicious intent betrayed in urging Him to cast Himself down from the dizzy height, the unsleeping malice that hunted Him from place to place, inspiring the hearts of priests and people to reject His love, and at the last to cry, "Crucify Him! crucify Him!"—all this excited the amazement and indignation of the universe.

It was Satan that prompted the world's rejection of Christ. The prince of evil exerted all his power and cunning to destroy Jesus; for he saw that the Saviour's mercy and love, His compassion and pitying tenderness, were representing to the world the character of God. Satan contested every claim put forth by the Son of God and employed men as his agents to fill the Saviour's life with suffering and sorrow. The sophistry and falsehood by which he had sought to hinder the work of Jesus, the hatred manifested through the children of disobedience, his cruel accusations against Him whose life was one of unexampled goodness, all sprang from deep-seated revenge. The pent-up fires of envy and malice, hatred and revenge, burst forth on Calvary against the Son of God, while all heaven gazed upon the scene in silent horror.

When the great sacrifice had been consummated, Christ ascended on high, refusing the adoration of angels until He had presented the request: "I will that they also, whom Thou hast given Me, be with Me where I am." John 17:24.

502 Then with inexpressible love and power came forth the answer from the Father's throne: "Let all the angels of God worship Him." Hebrews 1:6. Not a stain rested upon Jesus. His humiliation ended, His sacrifice completed, there was given unto Him a name that is above every name.

Now the guilt of Satan stood forth without excuse. He had revealed his true character as a liar and a murderer. It was seen that the very same spirit with which he ruled the children of men, who were under his power, he would have manifested had he been permitted to control the inhabitants of heaven. He had claimed that the transgression of God's law would bring liberty and exaltation; but it was seen to result in bondage and degradation.

Satan's lying charges against the divine character and government appeared in their true light. He had accused God of seeking merely the exaltation of Himself in requiring submission and obedience from His creatures, and had declared that, while the Creator exacted self-denial from all others, He Himself practiced no self-denial and made no sacrifice. Now it was seen that for the salvation of a fallen and sinful race, the Ruler of the universe had made the greatest sacrifice which love could make; for "God was in Christ, reconciling the world unto Himself." 2 Corinthians 5:19. It was seen, also, that while Lucifer had opened the door for the entrance of sin by his desire for honor and supremacy, Christ had, in order to destroy sin, humbled Himself and become obedient unto death.

God had manifested His abhorrence of the principles of rebellion. All heaven saw His justice revealed, both in the condemnation of Satan and in the redemption of man. Lucifer had declared that if the law of God was changeless, and its penalty could not be remitted, every transgressor must be forever debarred from the Creator's favor. He had claimed that the sinful race were placed beyond redemption and were therefore his rightful prey. But the death of Christ was an argument in man's behalf that

503 could not be overthrown. The penalty of the law fell upon Him who was equal with God, and man was free to accept the righteousness of Christ and by a life of penitence and humiliation to triumph, as the Son of God had triumphed, over the power of Satan. Thus God is just and yet the justifier of all who believe in Jesus.

But it was not merely to accomplish the redemption of man that Christ came to the earth to suffer and to die. He came to "magnify the law" and to "make it honorable." Not alone that the inhabitants of this world might regard the law as it should be regarded; but it was to demonstrate to all the worlds of the universe that God's law is unchangeable. Could its claims have been set aside, then the Son of God need not have yielded up His life to atone for its transgression. The death of Christ proves it immutable. And the sacrifice to which infinite love impelled the Father and the Son, that sinners might be redeemed, demonstrates to all the universe—what nothing less than this plan of atonement could have sufficed to do—that justice and mercy are the foundation of the law and government of God.

In the final execution of the judgment it will be seen that no cause for sin exists. When the Judge of all the earth shall demand of Satan, "Why hast thou rebelled against Me, and robbed Me of the subjects of My kingdom?" the originator of evil can render no excuse. Every mouth will be stopped, and all the hosts of rebellion will be speechless.

The cross of Calvary, while it declares the law immutable, proclaims to the universe that the wages of sin is death. In the Saviour's expiring cry, "It is finished," the death knell of Satan was rung. The great controversy which had been so long in progress was then decided, and the final eradication of evil was made certain. The Son of God passed through the portals of the tomb, that "through death He might destroy him that had the power of death, that is, the devil." Hebrews 2:14. Lucifer's desire for self-exaltation had led him to say: "I will exalt my throne above the stars of God: . . . I will be like the Most High." God declares: "I will bring thee   504 to ashes upon the earth, . . . and never shalt thou be any more." Isaiah 14:13, 14; Ezekiel 28:18, 19. When "the day cometh, that shall burn as an oven; . . . all the proud, yea, and all that do wickedly, shall be stubble: and the day that cometh shall burn them up, saith the Lord of hosts, that it shall leave them neither root nor branch." Malachi 4:1.

The whole universe will have become witnesses to the nature and results of sin. And its utter extermination, which in the beginning would have brought fear to angels and dishonor to God, will now vindicate His love and establish His honor before the universe of beings who delight to do His will, and in whose heart is His law. Never will evil again be manifest. Says the word of God: "Affliction shall not rise up the second time." Nahum 1:9. The law of God, which Satan has reproached as the yoke of bondage, will be honored as the law of liberty. A tested and proved creation will never again be turned from allegiance to Him whose character has been fully manifested before them as fathomless love and infinite wisdom.

505

30

Enmity Between
Man and Satan

"I will put enmity between thee and the woman, and between thy seed and her seed; it shall bruise thy head, and thou shalt bruise his heel." Genesis 3:15. The divine sentence pronounced against Satan after the fall of man was also a prophecy, embracing all the ages to the close of time and foreshadowing the great conflict to engage all the races of men who should live upon the earth.

God declares: "I will put enmity." This enmity is not naturally entertained. When man transgressed the divine law, his nature became evil, and he was in harmony, and not at variance, with Satan. There exists naturally no enmity between sinful man and the originator of sin. Both became evil through apostasy. The apostate is never at rest, except as he obtains sympathy and support by inducing others to follow his example. For this reason fallen angels and wicked men unite in desperate companionship. Had not God specially interposed, Satan and man would have entered into an alliance against Heaven; and instead of cherishing enmity against Satan, the whole human family would have been united in opposition to God.

Satan tempted man to sin, as he had caused angels to rebel, that he might thus secure cooperation in his warfare against Heaven. There was no dissension between himself and the fall-506 en angels as regards their hatred of Christ; while on all other points there was discord, they were firmly united in opposing the authority of the Ruler of the universe. But when Satan heard the declaration that enmity should exist between himself and the woman, and between his seed and her seed, he knew that his efforts to deprave human nature would be interrupted; that by some means man was to be enabled to resist his power.

Satan's enmity against the human race is kindled because, through Christ, they are the objects of God's love and mercy. He desires to thwart the divine plan for man's redemption, to cast dishonor upon God, by defacing and defiling His handiwork; he would cause grief in heaven and fill the earth with woe and desolation. And he points to all this evil as the result of God's work in creating man.

It is the grace that Christ implants in the soul which creates in man enmity against Satan. Without this converting grace and renewing power, man would continue the captive of Satan, a servant ever ready to do his bidding. But the new principle in the soul creates conflict where hitherto had been peace. The power which Christ imparts enables man to resist the tyrant and usurper. Whoever is seen to abhor sin instead of loving it, whoever resists and conquers those passions that have held sway within, displays the operation of a principle wholly from above.

The antagonism that exists between the spirit of Christ and the spirit of Satan was most strikingly displayed in the world's reception of Jesus. It was not so much because He appeared without worldly wealth, pomp, or grandeur that the Jews were led to reject Him. They saw that He possessed power which would more than compensate for the lack of these outward advantages. But the purity and holiness of Christ called forth against Him the hatred of the ungodly. His life of self-denial and sinless devotion was a perpetual reproof to a proud, sensual people. It was this that evoked enmity against the Son of God. Satan and evil angels joined with evil men. All the energies of apostasy conspired against the Champion of truth.

The same enmity is manifested toward 507 Christ's followers as was manifested toward their Master. Whoever sees the repulsive character of sin, and in strength from above resists temptation, will assuredly arouse the wrath of Satan and his subjects. Hatred of the pure principles of truth, and reproach and persecution of its advocates, will exist as long as sin and sinners remain. The followers of Christ and the servants of Satan cannot harmonize. The offense of the cross has not ceased. "All that will live godly in Christ Jesus shall suffer persecution." 2 Timothy 3:12.

Satan's agents are constantly working under his direction to establish his authority and build up his kingdom in opposition to the government of God. To this end they seek to deceive Christ's followers and allure them from their allegiance. Like their leader, they misconstrue and pervert the Scriptures to accomplish their object. As Satan endeavored to cast reproach upon God, so do his agents seek to malign God's people. The spirit which put Christ to death moves the wicked to destroy His followers. All this is foreshadowed in that first prophecy: "I will put enmity between thee and the woman, and between thy seed and her seed." And this will continue to the close of time.

Satan summons all his forces and throws his whole power into the combat. Why is it that he meets with no greater resistance? Why are the soldiers of Christ so sleepy and indifferent? Because they have so little real connection with Christ; because they are so destitute of His Spirit. Sin is not to them repulsive and abhorrent, as it was to their Master. They do not meet it, as did Christ, with decisive and determined resistance. They do not realize the exceeding evil and malignity of sin, and they are blinded both to the character and the power of the prince of darkness. There is little enmity against Satan and his works, because there is so great ignorance concerning his power and malice, and the vast extent of his warfare against Christ and His church. Multitudes are deluded here. They do not know that their enemy is a mighty general who controls the minds of evil angels, and that with well-matured plans and skillful movements he is warring against Christ to prevent the salvation of souls. Among professed Christians, and even among ministers of the gospel, there is heard scarcely a reference to Satan, except perhaps an incidental mention in the pulpit. They overlook the evidences of his continual activity and success; they neglect the many warnings of his subtlety; they seem to ignore his very existence.

While men are ignorant of his devices, this vigilant foe is upon their track every moment. He is intruding his presence in every department of the household, in every street of our cities, in the churches, in the national councils, in the courts of justice, perplexing, deceiving, seducing, everywhere ruining the souls and bodies of men, women, and children, breaking up families, sowing hatred, emulation, strife, sedition, murder. And the Christian world seem to regard these things as though God had appointed them and they must exist.

Satan is continually seeking to overcome the people of God by breaking down the barriers which separate them from the world. Ancient Israel were enticed into sin when they ventured into forbidden association with the heathen. In a similar manner are modern Israel led astray. "The god of this world hath blinded the minds of them which believe not, lest the light of the glorious gospel of Christ, who is the image of God, should shine unto them." 2 Corinthians 4:4. All who are not decided followers of Christ are servants of Satan. In the unregenerate heart there is love of sin and a disposition to cherish and excuse it. In the renewed heart there is hatred of sin and determined resistance against it. When Christians choose the society of the ungodly and unbelieving, they expose themselves to temptation. Satan conceals himself from view and stealthily draws his deceptive covering over their eyes. They cannot see that such company is calculated to do them harm; and while all the time assimilating to the world in character, words, and actions, they are becoming more and more blinded.

Conformity to worldly customs converts the church to the world; it never converts the world to Christ. Familiarity with sin will inevitably cause it to appear less repulsive. He who chooses to associate with the servants of Satan will soon cease to fear their master. When in the way

of duty we are brought into trial, as was Daniel in the king's court, we may be sure that God will protect us; but if we place ourselves under temptation we shall fall sooner or later.

The tempter often works most successfully through those who are least suspected of being under his control. The possessors of talent and education are admired and honored, as if these qualities could atone for the absence of the fear of God or entitle men to His favor. Talent and culture, considered in themselves, are gifts of God; but when these are made to supply the place of piety, when, instead of bringing the soul nearer to God, they lead away from Him, then they become a curse and a snare. The opinion prevails with many that all which appears like courtesy or refinement must, in some sense, pertain to Christ. Never was there a greater mistake. These qualities should grace the character of every Christian, for they would exert a powerful influence in favor of true religion; but they must be consecrated to God, or they also are a power for evil. Many a man of cultured intellect and pleasant manners, who would not stoop to what is commonly regarded as an immoral act, is but a polished instrument in the hands of Satan. The insidious, deceptive character of his influence and example renders him a more dangerous enemy to the cause of Christ than are those who are ignorant and uncultured.

By earnest prayer and dependence upon God, Solomon obtained the wisdom which excited the wonder and admiration of the world. But when he turned from the Source of his strength, and went forward relying upon himself, he fell a prey to temptation. Then the marvelous powers bestowed on this wisest of kings only rendered him a more effective agent of the adversary of souls.

While Satan is constantly seeking to blind their minds to the fact, let Christians never forget that they "wrestle not against flesh and blood, but against principalities, against powers, against the rulers of the darkness of this world, against wicked spirits in high places." Ephesians 6:12, margin. The inspired warning is sounding down the centuries to our time: "Be sober, be vigilant; because your adversary the devil, as a roaring lion, walketh about, seeking whom he may devour." 1 Peter 5:8. "Put on the whole armor of God, that ye may be able to stand against the wiles of the devil." Ephesians 6:11.

From the days of Adam to our own time, our great enemy has been exercising his power to oppress and destroy. He is now preparing for his last campaign against the church. All who seek to follow Jesus will be brought into conflict with this relentless foe. The more nearly the Christian imitates the divine Pattern, the more surely will he make himself a mark for the attacks of Satan. All who are actively engaged in the cause of God, seeking to unveil the deceptions of the evil one and to present Christ before the people, will be able to join in the testimony of Paul, in which he speaks of serving the Lord with all humility of mind, with many tears and temptations.

Satan assailed Christ with his fiercest and most subtle temptations, but he was repulsed in every conflict. Those battles were fought in our behalf; those victories make it possible for us to conquer. Christ will give strength to all who seek it. No man without his own consent can be overcome by Satan. The tempter has no power to control the will or to force the soul to sin. He may distress, but he cannot contaminate. He can cause agony, but not defilement. The fact that Christ has conquered should inspire His followers with courage to fight manfully the battle against sin and Satan.

31

Agency of Evil Spirits

The connection of the visible with the invisible world, the ministration of angels of God, and the agency of evil spirits, are plainly revealed in the Scriptures, and inseparably interwoven with human history. There is a growing tendency to disbelief in the existence of evil spirits, while the holy angels that "minister for them who shall be heirs of salvation" (Hebrews 1:14) are regarded by many as spirits of the dead. But the Scriptures not only teach the existence of angels, both good and evil, but present unquestionable proof that these are not disembodied spirits of dead men.

Before the creation of man, angels were in existence; for when the foundations of the earth were laid, "the morning stars sang together, and all the sons of God shouted for joy." Job 38:7. After the fall of man, angels were sent to guard the tree of life, and this before a human being had died. Angels are in nature superior to men, for the psalmist says that man was made "a little lower than the angels." Psalm 8:5.

We are informed in Scripture as to the number, and the power and glory, of the heavenly beings, of their connection with the government of God, and also of their relation to the work of redemption. "The Lord hath prepared His throne in the heavens; and His kingdom ruleth over all." And, says the prophet, "I heard the voice of many angels round about the throne." In the presence chamber of the King of kings they wait—"angels, that excel in strength," "ministers of His, that do His pleasure," "hearkening unto the voice of His word." Psalm 103:19-21; Revelation 5:11. Ten thousand times ten thousand and thousands of thousands, were the heavenly messengers beheld by the prophet Daniel. The apostle Paul declared them "an innumerable company." Daniel 7:10; Hebrews 12:22. As God's messengers they go forth, like "the appearance of a flash of lightning," (Ezekiel 1:14), so dazzling their glory, and so swift their flight. The angel that appeared at the Saviour's tomb, his countenance "like lightning, and his raiment white as snow," caused the keepers for fear of him to quake, and they "became as dead men." Matthew 28:3, 4. When Sennacherib, the haughty Assyrian, reproached and blasphemed God, and threatened Israel with destruction, "it came to pass that night, that the angel of the Lord went out, and smote in the camp of the Assyrians an hundred fourscore and five thousand." There were "cut off all the mighty men of valor, and the leaders and captains," from the army of Sennacherib. "So he returned with shame of face to his own land." 2 Kings 19:35; 2 Chronicles 32:21.

Angels are sent on missions of mercy to the children of God. To Abraham, with promises of blessing; to the gates of Sodom, to rescue righteous Lot from its fiery doom; to Elijah, as he was about to perish from weariness and hunger in the desert; to Elisha, with chariots and horses of fire surrounding the little town where he was shut in by his foes; to Daniel, while seeking divine wisdom in the court of a heathen king, or abandoned to become the lions' prey; to Peter, doomed to death in Herod's dungeon; to the prisoners at Philippi; to Paul and his companions in the night of tempest on the sea; to open the mind of Cornelius to receive the gospel; to dispatch Peter with the message of salvation to the Gentile stranger—thus holy angels have, in all ages, ministered to God's people.

A guardian angel is appointed to every follower of Christ. These heavenly watchers shield the righteous from the power of the wicked one. This Satan himself recognized when he said: "Doth Job fear God for nought? Hast not Thou made an hedge about him, and about his house, and about all that he hath on every side?" Job 1:9, 10. The agency by which God protects His people is presented in the words of the psalmist: "The angel of the Lord encampeth round about them that fear Him, and delivereth them." Psalm 34:7. Said the Saviour, speaking of those that believe in Him: "Take heed that ye despise not one of these little ones; for I say unto you, That in heaven their angels do always behold the face of My Father." Matthew 18:10. The angels appointed to minister to the children of God have at all times access to His presence.

Thus God's people, exposed to the deceptive power and unsleeping malice of the prince of darkness, and in conflict with all the forces of evil, are assured of the unceasing guardianship of heavenly angels. Nor is such assurance given without need. If God has granted to His children promise of grace and protection, it is because there are mighty agencies of evil to be met—agencies numerous, determined, and untiring, of whose malignity and power none can safely be ignorant or unheeding.

Evil spirits, in the beginning created sinless, were equal in nature, power, and glory with the holy beings that are now God's messengers. But fallen through sin, they are leagued together for the dishonor of God and the destruction of men. United with Satan in his rebellion, and with him cast out from heaven, they have, through all succeeding ages, co-operated with him in his warfare against the divine authority. We are told in Scripture of their confederacy and government, of their various orders, of their intelligence and subtlety, and of their malicious designs against the peace and happiness of men.

Old Testament history presents occasional mention of their existence and agency; but it was during the time when Christ was upon the earth that evil spirits manifested their power in the most striking manner. Christ had come to 514 enter upon the plan devised for man's redemption, and Satan determined to assert his right to control the world. He had succeeded in establishing idolatry in every part of the earth except the land of Palestine. To the only land that had not fully yielded to the tempter's sway, Christ came to shed upon the people the light of heaven. Here two rival powers claimed supremacy. Jesus was stretching out His arms of love, inviting all who would to find pardon and peace in Him. The hosts of darkness saw that they did not possess unlimited control, and they understood that if Christ's mission should be successful, their rule was soon to end. Satan raged like a chained lion and defiantly exhibited his power over the bodies as well as the souls of men.

The fact that men have been possessed with demons, is clearly stated in the New Testament. The persons thus afflicted were not merely suffering with disease from natural causes. Christ had perfect understanding of that with which He was dealing, and He recognized the direct presence and agency of evil spirits.

A striking example of their number, power, and malignity, and also of the power and mercy of Christ, is given in the Scripture account of the healing of the demoniacs at Gadara. Those wretched maniacs, spurning all restraint, writhing, foaming, raging, were filling the air with their cries, doing violence to themselves, and endangering all who should approach them. Their bleeding and disfigured bodies and distracted minds presented a spectacle well pleasing to the prince of darkness. One of the demons controlling the sufferers declared: "My name is Legion: for we are many." Mark 5:9. In the Roman army a legion consisted of from three to five thousand men. Satan's hosts also are marshaled in companies, and the single company to which these demons belonged numbered no less than a legion.

At the command of Jesus the evil spirits departed from their victims, leaving them calmly sitting at the Saviour's feet, subdued, intelligent, and gentle. But the demons were permitted 515 to sweep a herd of swine into the sea; and to the dwellers of Gadara the loss of these outweighed the blessings which Christ had bestowed, and the divine Healer was entreated to depart. This was the result which Satan designed to secure. By casting the blame of their loss upon Jesus, he aroused the selfish fears of the people and prevented them from listening to His words. Satan is constantly accusing Christians as the cause of loss, misfortune, and suffering, instead of allowing the reproach to fall where it belongs—upon himself and his agents.

But the purposes of Christ were not thwarted. He allowed the evil spirits to destroy the herd of swine as a rebuke to those Jews who were raising these unclean beasts for the sake of gain. Had not Christ restrained the demons, they would have plunged into the sea, not only the swine, but also their keepers and owners. The preservation of both the keepers and the owners was due alone to His power, mercifully exercised for their deliverance. Furthermore, this event was permitted to take place that the disciples might witness the cruel power of Satan upon both man and beast. The Saviour desired His followers to have a knowledge of the foe whom they were to meet, that they might not be deceived and overcome by his devices. It was also His will that the people of that region should behold His power to break the bondage of Satan and release his captives. And though Jesus Himself departed, the men so marvelously delivered, remained to declare the mercy of their Benefactor.

Other instances of a similar nature are recorded in the Scriptures. The daughter of the Syrophoenician woman was grievously vexed with a devil, whom Jesus cast out by His word. Mark 7:26-30. "One possessed with a devil, blind, and dumb" (Matthew 12:22); a youth who had a dumb spirit, that ofttimes "cast him into the fire, and into the waters, to destroy him" (Mark 9:17-27); the maniac who, tormented by "a spirit of an unclean devil" (Luke 4:33-36), disturbed the Sabbath quiet of the synagogue at Capernaum—all were healed by the compas- 516 sionate Saviour. In nearly every instance, Christ addressed the demon as an intelligent entity, commanding him to come out of his victim and to torment him no more. The worshipers at Capernaum, beholding His mighty power, "were all amazed, and spake among themselves, saying, What a word is this! for with authority and power He commandeth the unclean spirits, and they come out." Luke 4:36.

Those possessed with devils are usually represented as being in a condition of great suffering; yet there were exceptions to this rule. For the sake of obtaining supernatural power, some welcomed the satanic influence. These of course had no conflict with the demons. Of this class were those who possessed the spirit of divination,—Simon Magus, Elymas the sorcerer, and the damsel who followed Paul and Silas at Philippi.

None are in greater danger from the influence of evil spirits than those who, notwithstanding the direct and ample testimony of the Scriptures, deny the existence and agency of the devil and his angels. So long as we are ignorant of their wiles, they have almost inconceivable advantage; many give heed to their suggestions while they suppose themselves to be following the dictates of their own wisdom. This is why, as we approach the close of time, when Satan is to work with greatest power to deceive and destroy, he spreads everywhere the belief that he does not exist. It is his policy to conceal himself and his manner of working.

There is nothing that the great deceiver fears so much as that we shall become acquainted with his devices. The better to disguise his real character and purposes, he has caused himself to be so represented as to excite no stronger emotion than ridicule or contempt. He is well pleased to be painted as a ludicrous or loathsome object, misshapen, half animal and half human. He is pleased to hear his name used in sport and mockery by those who think themselves intelligent and well informed.

517   It is because he has masked himself with consummate skill that the question is so widely asked: "Does such a being really exist?" It is an evidence of his success that theories giving the lie to the plainest testimony of the Scriptures are so generally received in the religious world. And it is because Satan can most readily control the minds of those who are unconscious of his influence, that the word of God gives us so many examples of his malignant work, unveiling before us his secret forces, and thus placing us on our guard against his assaults.

The power and malice of Satan and his host might justly alarm us were it not that we may find shelter and deliverance in the superior power of our Redeemer. We carefully secure our houses with bolts and locks to protect our property and our lives from evil men; but we seldom think of the evil angels who are constantly seeking access to us, and against whose attacks we have, in our own strength, no method of defense. If permitted, they can distract our minds, disorder and torment our bodies, destroy our possessions and our lives. Their only delight is in misery and destruction. Fearful is the condition of those who resist the divine claims and yield to Satan's temptations, until God gives them up to the control of evil spirits. But those

who follow Christ are ever safe under His watchcare. Angels that excel in strength are sent from heaven to protect them. The wicked one cannot break through the guard which God has stationed about His people.

32   518

Snares of Satan

The great controversy between Christ and Satan, that has been carried forward for nearly six thousand years, is soon to close; and the wicked one redoubles his efforts to defeat the work of Christ in man's behalf and to fasten souls in his snares. To hold the people in darkness and impenitence till the Saviour's mediation is ended, and there is no longer a sacrifice for sin, is the object which he seeks to accomplish.

When there is no special effort made to resist his power, when indifference prevails in the church and the world, Satan is not concerned; for he is in no danger of losing those whom he is leading captive at his will. But when the attention is called to eternal things, and souls are inquiring, "What must I do to be saved?" he is on the ground, seeking to match his power against the power of Christ and to counteract the influence of the Holy Spirit.

The Scriptures declare that upon one occasion, when the angels of God came to present themselves before the Lord, Satan came also among them (Job 1:6), not to bow before the Eternal King, but to further his own malicious designs against the righteous. With the same object he is in attendance when men assemble for the worship of God. Though hidden from sight, he is working with all diligence to control the minds of the worshipers. Like a skillful general he lays his plans beforehand. As he sees the messenger of God searching the Scriptures, he takes note of the subject to be presented to the   519 people. Then he employs all his cunning and shrewdness so to control circumstances that the message may not reach those whom he is deceiving on that very point. The one who most needs the warning will be urged into some business transaction which requires his presence, or will by some other means be prevented from hearing the words that might prove to him a savor of life unto life.

Again, Satan sees the Lord's servants burdened because of the spiritual darkness that enshrouds the people. He hears their earnest prayers for divine grace and power to break the spell of indifference, carelessness, and indolence. Then with renewed zeal he plies his arts. He tempts men to the indulgence of appetite or to some other form of self-gratification, and thus benumbs their sensibilities so that they fail to hear the very things which they most need to learn.

Satan well knows that all whom he can lead to neglect prayer and the searching of the Scriptures, will be overcome by his attacks. Therefore he invents every possible device to engross the mind. There has ever been a class professing godliness, who, instead of following on to know the truth, make it their religion to seek some fault of character or error of faith in those with whom they do not agree. Such are Satan's right-hand helpers. Accusers of the brethren are not few, and they are always active when God is at work and His servants are rendering Him true homage. They will put a false coloring upon the words and acts of those who love and obey the truth. They will represent the most earnest, zealous, self-denying servants of Christ as deceived or deceivers. It is their work to misrepresent the motives of every true and noble deed, to circulate insinuations, and arouse suspicion in the minds of the inexperienced. In every conceivable manner they will seek to cause that which is pure and righteous to be regarded as foul and deceptive.

But none need be deceived concerning them. It may be readily seen whose children they are, whose example they follow, and whose work 520 they do. "Ye shall know them by their fruits." Matthew 7:16. Their course resembles that of Satan, the envenomed slanderer, "the accuser of our brethren." Revelation 12:10.

The great deceiver has many agents ready to present any and every kind of error to ensnare souls—heresies prepared to suit the varied tastes and capacities of those whom he would ruin. It is his plan to bring into the church insincere, unregenerate elements that will encourage doubt and unbelief, and hinder all who desire to see the work of God advance and to advance with it. Many who have no real faith in God or in His word assent to some principles of truth and pass as Christians, and thus they are enabled to introduce their errors as Scriptural doctrines.

The position that it is of no consequence what men believe is one of Satan's most successful deceptions. He knows that the truth, received in the love of it, sanctifies the soul of the receiver; therefore he is constantly seeking to substitute false theories, fables, another gospel. From the beginning the servants of God have contended against false teachers, not merely as vicious men, but as inculcators of falsehoods that were fatal to the soul. Elijah, Jeremiah, Paul, firmly and fearlessly opposed those who were turning men from the word of God. That liberality which regards a correct religious faith as unimportant found no favor with these holy defenders of the truth.

The vague and fanciful interpretations of Scripture, and the many conflicting theories concerning religious faith, that are found in the Christian world are the work of our great adversary to confuse minds so that they shall not discern the truth. And the discord and division which exist among the churches of Christendom are in a great measure due to the prevailing custom of wresting the Scriptures to support a favorite theory. Instead of carefully studying God's word with humility of heart to obtain a knowledge of His will, many seek only to discover something odd or original.

In order to sustain erroneous doctrines or 521 unchristian practices, some will seize upon passages of Scripture separated from the context, perhaps quoting half of a single verse as proving their point, when the remaining portion would show the meaning to be quite the opposite. With the cunning of the serpent they entrench themselves behind disconnected utterances construed to suit their carnal desires. Thus do many willfully pervert the word of God. Others, who have an active imagination, seize upon the figures and symbols of Holy Writ, interpret them to suit their fancy, with little regard to the testimony of Scripture as its own interpreter, and then they present their vagaries as the teachings of the Bible.

Whenever the study of the Scriptures is entered upon without a prayerful, humble, teachable spirit, the plainest and simplest as well as the most difficult passages will be wrested from their true meaning. The papal leaders select such portions of Scripture as best serve their purpose, interpret to suit themselves, and then present these to the people, while they deny them the privilege of studying the Bible and understanding its sacred truths for themselves. The whole Bible should be given to the people just as it reads. It would be better for them not to have Bible instruction at all than to have the teaching of the Scriptures thus grossly misrepresented.

The Bible was designed to be a guide to all who wish to become acquainted with the will of their Maker. God gave to men the sure word of prophecy; angels and even Christ Himself came to make known to Daniel and John the things that must shortly come to pass. Those important matters that concern our salvation were not left involved in mystery. They were not revealed in such a way as to perplex and mislead the honest seeker after truth. Said the Lord by the prophet Habakkuk: "Write the vision, and make it plain, . . . that he may run that readeth it." Habakkuk 2:2. The word of God is plain to all who study it with a prayerful heart. Every truly honest soul 522 will come to the light of truth. "Light is sown for the righteous." Psalm 97:11. And no church can advance in holiness unless its members are earnestly seeking for truth as for hid treasure.

By the cry, Liberality, men are blinded to the devices of their adversary, while he is all the time working steadily for the accomplishment of his object. As he succeeds in supplanting the Bible by human speculations, the law of God is set aside, and the churches are under the bondage of sin while they claim to be free.

To many, scientific research has become a curse. God has permitted a flood of light to be poured upon the world in discoveries in science and art; but even the greatest minds, if not guided by the word of God in their research, become bewildered in their attempts to investigate the relations of science and revelation.

Human knowledge of both material and spiritual things is partial and imperfect; therefore many are unable to harmonize their views of science with Scripture statements. Many accept mere theories and speculations as scientific facts, and they think that God's word is to be tested by the teachings of "science falsely so called." 1 Timothy 6:20. The Creator and His works are beyond their comprehension; and because they cannot explain these by natural laws, Bible history is regarded as unreliable. Those who doubt the reliability of the records of the Old and New Testaments too often go a step further and doubt the existence of God and attribute infinite power to nature. Having let go their anchor, they are left to beat about upon the rocks of infidelity.

Thus many err from the faith and are seduced by the devil. Men have endeavored to be wiser than their Creator; human philosophy has attempted to search out and explain mysteries which will never be revealed through the eternal ages. If men would but search and understand what God has made known of Himself and His purposes, they would obtain such a view of the 523 glory, majesty, and power of Jehovah that they would realize their own littleness and would be content with that which has been revealed for themselves and their children.

It is a masterpiece of Satan's deceptions to keep the minds of men searching and conjecturing in regard to that which God has not made known and which He does not intend that we shall understand. It was thus that Lucifer lost his place in heaven. He became dissatisfied because all the secrets of God's purposes were not confided to him, and he entirely disregarded that which was revealed concerning his own work in the lofty position assigned him. By arousing the same discontent in the angels under his command, he caused their fall. Now he seeks to imbue the minds of men with the same spirit and to lead them also to disregard the direct commands of God.

Those who are unwilling to accept the plain, cutting truths of the Bible are continually seeking for pleasing fables that will quiet the conscience. The less spiritual, self-denying, and humiliating the doctrines presented, the greater the favor with which they are received. These persons degrade the intellectual powers to serve their carnal desires. Too wise in their own conceit to search the Scriptures with contrition of soul and earnest prayer for divine guidance, they have no shield from delusion. Satan is ready to supply the heart's desire, and he palms off his deceptions in the place of truth. It was thus that the papacy gained its power over the minds of men; and by rejection of the truth because it involves a cross, Protestants are following the same path. All who neglect the word of God to study convenience and policy, that they may not be at variance with the world, will be left to receive damnable heresy for religious truth. Every conceivable form of error will be accepted by those who willfully reject the truth. He who looks with horror upon one deception will readily receive another. The apostle Paul, speaking of a class who "received not the love of the truth, that they might be saved," declares: "For this cause God shall send them strong delusion, that they should believe a lie: that they all might be damned who believed not the truth, 524 but had pleasure in unrighteousness." 2 Thessalonians 2:10-12. With such a warning before us it behooves us to be on our guard as to what doctrines we receive.

Among the most successful agencies of the great deceiver are the delusive teachings and lying wonders of spiritualism. Disguised as an angel of light, he spreads his nets where least suspected. If men would but study the Book of God with earnest prayer that they might understand it, they would not be left in darkness to receive false doctrines. But as they reject the truth they fall a prey to deception.

Another dangerous error is the doctrine which denies the deity of Christ, claiming that He had no existence before His advent to this world. This theory is received with favor by a large class who profess to believe the Bible; yet it directly contradicts the plainest statements of our Saviour concerning His relationship with the Father, His divine character, and His pre-existence. It cannot be entertained without the most unwarranted wresting of the Scriptures. It not only lowers man's conceptions of the work of redemption, but undermines faith in the Bible as a revelation from God. While this renders it the more dangerous, it makes it also harder to meet. If men reject the testimony of the inspired Scriptures concerning the deity of Christ, it is in vain to argue the point with them; for no argument, however conclusive, could convince them. "The natural man receiveth not the things of the Spirit of God: for they are foolishness unto him: neither can he know them, because they are spiritually discerned." 1 Corinthians 2:14. None who hold this error can have a true conception of the character or the mission of Christ, or of the great plan of God for man's redemption.

Still another subtle and mischievous error is

the fast-spreading belief that Satan has no existence as a personal being; that the name is used in Scripture merely to represent men's evil thoughts and desires.

525   The teaching so widely echoed from popular pulpits, that the second advent of Christ is His coming to each individual at death, is a device to divert the minds of men from His personal coming in the clouds of heaven. For years Satan has thus been saying, "Behold, He is in the secret chambers" (Matthew 24:23-26); and many souls have been lost by accepting this deception.

Again, worldly wisdom teaches that prayer is not essential. Men of science claim that there can be no real answer to prayer; that this would be a violation of law, a miracle, and that miracles have no existence. The universe, say they, is governed by fixed laws, and God Himself does nothing contrary to these laws. Thus they represent God as bound by His own laws—as if the operation of divine laws could exclude divine freedom. Such teaching is opposed to the testimony of the Scriptures. Were not miracles wrought by Christ and His apostles? The same compassionate Saviour lives today, and He is as willing to listen to the prayer of faith as when He walked visibly among men. The natural cooperates with the supernatural. It is a part of God's plan to grant us, in answer to the prayer of faith, that which He would not bestow did we not thus ask.

Innumerable are the erroneous doctrines and fanciful ideas that are obtaining among the churches of Christendom. It is impossible to estimate the evil results of removing one of the landmarks fixed by the word of God. Few who venture to do this stop with the rejection of a single truth. The majority continue to set aside one after another of the principles of truth, until they become actual infidels.

The errors of popular theology have driven many a soul to skepticism who might otherwise have been a believer in the Scriptures. It is impossible for him to accept doctrines which outrage his sense of justice, mercy, and benevolence; and since these are represented as the teaching of the Bible, he refuses to receive it as the word of God.

526   And this is the object which Satan seeks to accomplish. There is nothing that he desires more than to destroy confidence in God and in His word. Satan stands at the head of the great army of doubters, and he works to the utmost of his power to beguile souls into his ranks. It is becoming fashionable to doubt. There is a large class by whom the word of God is looked upon with distrust for the same reason as was its Author—because it reproves and condemns sin. Those who are unwilling to obey its requirements endeavor to overthrow its authority. They read the Bible, or listen to its teachings as pre-sented from the sacred desk, merely to find fault with the Scriptures or with the sermon. Not a few become infidels in order to justify or excuse themselves in neglect of duty. Others adopt skeptical principles from pride and indolence. Too ease-loving to distinguish themselves by accomplishing anything worthy of honor, which requires effort and self-denial, they aim to secure a reputation for superior wisdom by criticizing the Bible. There is much which the finite mind, unenlightened by divine wisdom, is powerless to comprehend; and thus they find occasion to criticize. There are many who seem to feel that it is a virtue to stand on the side of unbelief, skepticism, and infidelity. But underneath an appearance of candor it will be found that such persons are actuated by self-confidence and pride. Many delight in finding something in the Scriptures to puzzle the minds of others. Some at first criticize and reason on the wrong side, from a mere love of controversy. They do not realize that they are thus entangling themselves in the snare of the fowler. But having openly expressed unbelief, they feel that they must maintain their position. Thus they unite with the ungodly and close to themselves the gates of Paradise.

God has given in His word sufficient evidence of its divine character. The great truths which concern our redemption are clearly presented. By the aid of the Holy Spirit, which is promised to all who seek it in sincerity, every man may understand these truths for himself. 527 God has granted to men a strong foundation upon which to rest their faith.

Yet the finite minds of men are inadequate fully to comprehend the plans and purposes of the Infinite One. We can never by searching find out God. We must not attempt to lift with presumptuous hand the curtain behind which He veils His majesty. The apostle exclaims: "How unsearchable are His judgments, and His ways past finding out!" Romans 11:33. We can so far comprehend His dealings with us, and the motives by which He is actuated, that we may discern boundless love and mercy united to infinite power. Our Father in heaven orders everything in wisdom and righteousness, and we are not to be dissatisfied and distrustful, but to bow in reverent submission. He will reveal to us as much of His purposes as it is for our good to know, and beyond that we must trust the Hand that is omnipotent, the Heart that is full of love.

While God has given ample evidence for faith, He will never remove all excuse for unbelief. All who look for hooks to hang their doubts upon will find them. And those who refuse to accept and obey God's word until every objection has been removed, and there is no longer an opportunity for doubt, will never come to the light.

Distrust of God is the natural outgrowth of

the unrenewed heart, which is at enmity with Him. But faith is inspired by the Holy Spirit, and it will flourish only as it is cherished. No man can become strong in faith without a determined effort. Unbelief strengthens as it is encouraged; and if men, instead of dwelling upon the evidences which God has given to sustain their faith, permit themselves to question and cavil, they will find their doubts constantly becoming more confirmed.

528 But those who doubt God's promises and distrust the assurance of His grace are dishonoring Him; and their influence, instead of drawing others to Christ, tends to repel them from Him. They are unproductive trees, that spread their dark branches far and wide, shutting away the sunlight from other plants, and causing them to droop and die under the chilling shadow. The lifework of these persons will appear as a never-ceasing witness against them. They are sowing seeds of doubt and skepticism that will yield an unfailing harvest.

There is but one course for those to pursue who honestly desire to be freed from doubts. Instead of questioning and caviling concerning that which they do not understand, let them give heed to the light which already shines upon them, and they will receive greater light. Let them do every duty which has been made plain to their understanding, and they will be enabled to understand and perform those of which they are now in doubt.

Satan can present a counterfeit so closely resembling the truth that it deceives those who are willing to be deceived, who desire to shun the self-denial and sacrifice demanded by the truth; but it is impossible for him to hold under his power one soul who honestly desires, at whatever cost, to know the truth. Christ is the truth and the "Light, which lighteth every man that cometh into the world." John 1:9. The Spirit of truth has been sent to guide men into all truth. And upon the authority of the Son of God it is declared: "Seek, and ye shall find." "If any man will do His will, he shall know of the doctrine." Matthew 7:7; John 7:17.

The followers of Christ know little of the plots which Satan and his hosts are forming against them. But He who sitteth in the heavens will overrule all these devices for the accomplishment of His deep designs. The Lord permits His people to be subjected to the fiery ordeal of temptation, not because He takes pleasure in their distress and affliction, but because this process is essential to their final victory. He could not, consistently with His own glory, shield them from temptation; for the very object of the trial is to prepare them to resist all the allurements of evil.

529 Neither wicked men nor devils can hinder the work of God, or shut out His presence from His people, if they will, with subdued, contrite hearts, confess and put away their sins, and in faith claim His promises. Every temptation, every opposing influence, whether open or secret, may be successfully resisted, "not by might, nor by power, but by My Spirit, saith the Lord of hosts." Zechariah 4:6.

"The eyes of the Lord are over the righteous, and His ears are open unto their prayers. . . . And who is he that will harm you, if ye be followers of that which is good?" 1 Peter 3:12, 13. When Balaam, allured by the promise of rich rewards, practiced enchantments against Israel, and by sacrifices to the Lord sought to invoke a curse upon His people, the Spirit of God forbade the evil which he longed to pronounce, and Balaam was forced to exclaim: "How shall I curse, whom God hath not cursed? or how shall I defy, whom the Lord hath not defied?" "Let me die the death of the righteous, and let my last end be like his!" When sacrifice had again been offered, the ungodly prophet declared: "Behold, I have received commandment to bless: and He hath blessed; and I cannot reverse it. He hath not beheld iniquity in Jacob, neither hath He seen perverseness in Israel: the Lord his God is with him, and the shout of a King is among them." "Surely there is no enchantment against Jacob, neither is there any divination against Israel: according to this time it shall be said of Jacob and of Israel, What hath God wrought!" Yet a third time altars were erected, and again Balaam essayed to secure a curse. But from the unwilling lips of the prophet, the Spirit of God declared the prosperity of His chosen, and rebuked the folly and malice of their foes: "Blessed is he that blesseth thee, and cursed is he that curseth thee." Numbers 23:8, 10, 20, 21, 23; 24:9.

The people of Israel were at this time loyal to God; and so long as they continued in obedience to His law, no power in earth or hell could prevail against them. But the curse which Balaam had not been permitted to pronounce against God's people, he finally succeeded in 530 bringing upon them by seducing them into sin. When they transgressed God's commandments, then they separated themselves from Him, and they were left to feel the power of the destroyer.

Satan is well aware that the weakest soul who abides in Christ is more than a match for the hosts of darkness, and that, should he reveal himself openly, he would be met and resisted. Therefore he seeks to draw away the soldiers of the cross from their strong fortification, while he lies in ambush with his forces, ready to destroy all who venture upon his ground. Only in humble reliance upon God, and obedience to all His commandments, can we be secure.

No man is safe for a day or an hour without prayer. Especially should we entreat the Lord for wisdom to understand His word. Here are revealed the wiles of the tempter and the means by which he may be successfully resisted. Satan is an expert in quoting Scripture, placing his own interpretation upon passages, by which he hopes to cause us to stumble. We should study the Bible with humility of heart, never losing sight of our dependence upon God. While we must constantly guard against the devices of Satan, we should pray in faith continually: "Lead us not into temptation."

33

The First Great Deception

With the earliest history of man, Satan began his efforts to deceive our race. He who had incited rebellion in heaven desired to bring the inhabitants of the earth to unite with him in his warfare against the government of God. Adam and Eve had been perfectly happy in obedience to the law of God, and this fact was a constant testimony against the claim which Satan had urged in heaven, that God's law was oppressive and opposed to the good of His creatures. And furthermore, Satan's envy was excited as he looked upon the beautiful home prepared for the sinless pair. He determined to cause their fall, that, having separated them from God and brought them under his own power, he might gain possession of the earth and here establish his kingdom in opposition to the Most High.

Had Satan revealed himself in his real character, he would have been repulsed at once, for Adam and Eve had been warned against this dangerous foe; but he worked in the dark, concealing his purpose, that he might more effectually accomplish his object. Employing as his medium the serpent, then a creature of fascinating appearance, he addressed himself to Eve: "Hath God said, Ye shall not eat of every tree of the garden?" Genesis 3:1. Had Eve refrained from entering into argument with the tempter, she would have been safe; but she ventured to parley with him and fell a victim to his wiles. It is thus that many are still overcome. They doubt and argue concerning the requirements of God; and instead of obeying the divine commands, they accept human theories, which but disguise the devices of Satan.

"The woman said unto the serpent, We may eat of the fruit of the trees of the garden: but of the fruit of the tree which is in the midst of the garden, God hath said, Ye shall not eat of it, neither shall ye touch it, lest ye die. And the serpent said unto the woman, Ye shall not surely die: for God doth know that in the day ye eat thereof, then your eyes shall be opened, and ye shall be as gods, knowing good and evil." Verses 2-5. He declared that they would become like God, possessing greater wisdom than before and being capable of a higher state of existence. Eve yielded to temptation; and through her influence, Adam was led into sin. They accepted the words of the serpent, that God did not mean what He said; they distrusted their Creator and imagined that He was restricting their liberty and that they might obtain great wisdom and exaltation by transgressing His law.

But what did Adam, after his sin, find to be the meaning of the words, "In the day that thou eatest thereof thou shalt surely die"? Did he find them to mean, as Satan had led him to believe, that he was to be ushered into a more exalted state of existence? Then indeed there was great good to be gained by transgression, and Satan was proved to be a benefactor of the race. But Adam did not find this to be the meaning of the divine sentence. God declared that as a penalty for his sin, man should return to the ground whence he was taken: "Dust thou art, and unto dust shalt thou return." Verse 19. The words of Satan, "Your eyes shall be opened," proved to be true in this sense only: After Adam and Eve had disobeyed God, their eyes were opened to discern their folly; they did know evil, and they tasted the bitter fruit of transgression.

In the midst of Eden grew the tree of life, whose fruit had the power of perpetuating life. Had Adam remained obedient to God, he would have continued to enjoy free access to this tree and would have lived forever. But when he sinned he was cut off from partaking of the tree of life, and he became subject to death. The divine sentence, "Dust thou art, and unto dust shalt thou return," points to the utter extinction of life.

Immortality, promised to man on condition of obedience, had been forfeited by transgression. Adam could not transmit to his posterity that which he did not possess; and there could have been no hope for the fallen race had not God, by the sacrifice of His Son, brought immortality within their reach. While "death passed upon all men, for that all have sinned," Christ "hath brought life and immortality to light through the gospel." Romans 5:12; 2 Timothy 1:10. And only through Christ can immortality be obtained. Said Jesus: "He that believeth on the Son hath everlasting life: and he that believeth not the Son shall not see life." John 3:36. Every man may come into possession of this priceless blessing if he will comply with the conditions. All "who by patient continuance in well-doing seek for glory and honor and immortality," will receive "eternal life." Romans 2:7.

The only one who promised Adam life in disobedience was the great deceiver. And the declaration of the serpent to Eve in Eden—"Ye shall not surely die"—was the first sermon ever preached upon the immortality of the soul. Yet this declaration, resting solely upon the authority of Satan, is echoed from the pulpits of Christendom and is received by the majority of mankind as readily as it was received by our first parents. The divine sentence, "The soul that sinneth, it shall die" (Ezekiel 18:20), is made to mean: The soul that sinneth, it shall not die, but live eternally. We cannot but wonder at the strange infatuation which renders men so credulous concerning the words of Satan and so unbelieving in regard to the words of God.

534 Had man after his fall been allowed free access to the tree of life, he would have lived forever, and thus sin would have been immortalized. But cherubim and a flaming sword kept "the way of the tree of life" (Genesis 3:24), and not one of the family of Adam has been permitted to pass that barrier and partake of the life-giving fruit. Therefore there is not an immortal sinner.

But after the Fall, Satan bade his angels make a special effort to inculcate the belief in man's natural immortality; and having induced the people to receive this error, they were to lead them on to conclude that the sinner would live in eternal misery. Now the prince of darkness, working through his agents, represents God as a revengeful tyrant, declaring that He plunges into hell all those who do not please Him, and causes them ever to feel His wrath; and that while they suffer unutterable anguish and writhe in the eternal flames, their Creator looks down upon them with satisfaction.

Thus the archfiend clothes with his own attributes the Creator and Benefactor of mankind. Cruelty is satanic. God is love; and all that He created was pure, holy, and lovely, until sin was brought in by the first great rebel. Satan himself is the enemy who tempts man to sin, and then destroys him if he can; and when he has made sure of his victim, then he exults in the ruin he has wrought. If permitted, he would sweep the entire race into his net. Were it not for the interposition of divine power, not one son or daughter of Adam would escape.

Satan is seeking to overcome men today, as he overcame our first parents, by shaking their confidence in their Creator and leading them to doubt the wisdom of His government and the justice of His laws. Satan and his emissaries represent God as even worse than themselves, in order to justify their own malignity and rebellion. The great deceiver endeavors to shift his own horrible cruelty of character upon our heavenly Father, that he may cause himself to appear as one greatly wronged by his expulsion from heaven because he would not submit to so 535 unjust a governor. He presents before the world the liberty which they may enjoy under his mild sway, in contrast with the bondage imposed by the stern decrees of Jehovah. Thus he succeeds in luring souls away from their allegiance to God.

How repugnant to every emotion of love and mercy, and even to our sense of justice, is the doctrine that the wicked dead are tormented with fire and brimstone in an eternally burning hell; that for the sins of a brief earthly life they are to suffer torture as long as God shall live. Yet this doctrine has been widely taught and is still embodied in many of the creeds of Christendom. Said a learned doctor of divinity: "The sight of hell torments will exalt the happiness of the saints forever. When they see others who are of the same nature and born under the same circumstances, plunged in such misery, and they so distinguished, it will make them sensible of how happy they are." Another used these words: "While the decree of reprobation is eternally executing on the vessels of wrath, the smoke of their torment will be eternally ascending in view of the vessels of mercy, who, instead of taking the part of these miserable objects, will say, Amen, Alleluia! praise ye the Lord!"

Where, in the pages of God's word, is such teaching to be found? Will the redeemed in heaven be lost to all emotions of pity and compassion, and even to feelings of common humanity? Are these to be exchanged for the indifference of the stoic or the cruelty of the savage? No, no; such is not the teaching of the Book of God. Those who present the views expressed in the quotations given above may be learned and even honest men, but they are deluded by the sophistry of Satan. He leads them to misconstrue strong expressions of Scripture, giving to the language the coloring of bitterness and malignity which pertains to himself, but not to our Creator. "As I live, saith the Lord God, I have no pleasure in the death of the wicked; but that the wicked turn from his way and live: turn ye, turn ye from your evil ways; for why will ye die?" Ezekiel 33:11.

What would be gained to God should we 536 admit that He delights in witnessing unceasing tortures; that He is regaled with the groans and shrieks and imprecations of the suffering creatures whom He holds in the flames of hell? Can these horrid sounds be music in the ear of Infinite Love? It is urged that the infliction of endless misery upon the wicked would show God's hatred of sin as an evil which is ruinous to the peace and order of the universe. Oh, dreadful blasphemy! As if God's hatred of sin is the reason why it is perpetuated. For, according to the teachings of these theologians, continued torture without hope of mercy maddens its wretched victims, and as they pour out their rage in curses and blasphemy, they are forever augmenting their load of guilt. God's glory is not enhanced by thus perpetuating continually increasing sin through ceaseless ages.

It is beyond the power of the human mind to estimate the evil which has been wrought by the heresy of eternal torment. The religion of the Bible, full of love and goodness, and abounding in compassion, is darkened by superstition and clothed with terror. When we consider in what false colors Satan has painted the character of God, can we wonder that our merciful Creator is feared, dreaded, and even hated? The appalling views of God which have spread over the world from the teachings of the pulpit have made thousands, yes, millions, of skeptics and infidels.

The theory of eternal torment is one of the false doctrines that constitute the wine of the abomination of Babylon, of which she makes all nations drink. Revelation 14:8; 17:2. That ministers of Christ should have accepted this heresy and proclaimed it from the sacred desk is indeed a mystery. They received it from Rome, as they received the false sabbath. True, it has been taught by great and good men; but the light on this subject had not come to them as it has come to us. They were responsible only for the light which shone in their time; we are accountable for that which shines in our day. If we turn from the testimony of God's word, and accept false doctrines because our fathers taught them, we fall under the condemnation pronounced upon Babylon; we are drinking of the wine of her abomination.

A large class to whom the doctrine of eternal torment is revolting are driven to the opposite error. They see that the Scriptures represent God as a being of love and compassion, and they cannot believe that He will consign His creatures to the fires of an eternally burning hell. But holding that the soul is naturally immortal, they see no alternative but to conclude that all mankind will finally be saved. Many regard the threatenings of the Bible as designed merely to frighten men into obedience, and not to be literally fulfilled. Thus the sinner can live in selfish pleasure, disregarding the requirements of God, and yet expect to be finally received into His favor. Such a doctrine, presuming upon God's mercy, but ignoring His justice, pleases the carnal heart and emboldens the wicked in their iniquity.

To show how believers in universal salvation wrest the Scriptures to sustain their soul-destroying dogmas, it is needful only to cite their own utterances. At the funeral of an irreligious young man, who had been killed instantly by an accident, a Universalist minister selected as his text the Scripture statement concerning David: "He was comforted concerning Amnon, seeing he was dead." 2 Samuel 13:39.

"I am frequently asked," said the speaker, "what will be the fate of those who leave the world in sin, die, perhaps, in a state of inebriation, die with the scarlet stains of crime unwashed from their robes, or die as this young man died, having never made a profession or enjoyed an experience of religion. We are content with the Scriptures; their answer shall solve the awful problem. Amnon was exceedingly

sinful; he was unrepentant, he was made drunk, and while drunk was killed. David was a prophet of God; he must have known whether it would be ill or well for Amnon in the world to come. What were the expressions of his heart? 'The soul of King David longed to go forth unto Absalom: for he was comforted concerning Amnon, seeing he was dead.' Verse 39.

"And what is the inference to be deduced from this language? Is it not that endless suffering formed no part of his religious belief? So we conceive; and here we discover a triumphant argument in support of the more pleasing, more enlightened, more benevolent hypothesis of ultimate universal purity and peace. He was comforted, seeing his son was dead. And why so? Because by the eye of prophecy he could look forward into the glorious future and see that son far removed from all temptations, released from the bondage and purified from the corruptions of sin, and after being made sufficiently holy and enlightened, admitted to the assembly of ascended and rejoicing spirits. His only comfort was that, in being removed from the present state of sin and suffering, his beloved son had gone where the loftiest breathings of the Holy Spirit would be shed upon his darkened soul, where his mind would be unfolded to the wisdom of heaven and the sweet raptures of immortal love, and thus prepared with a sanctified nature to enjoy the rest and society of the heavenly inheritance.

"In these thoughts we would be understood to believe that the salvation of heaven depends upon nothing which we can do in this life; neither upon a present change of heart, nor upon present belief, or a present profession of religion."

Thus does the professed minister of Christ reiterate the falsehood uttered by the serpent in Eden: "Ye shall not surely die." "In the day ye eat thereof, then your eyes shall be opened, and ye shall be as gods." He declares that the vilest of sinners—the murderer, the thief, and the adulterer—will after death be prepared to enter into immortal bliss.

And from what does this perverter of the Scriptures draw his conclusions? From a single sentence expressing David's submission to the dispensation of Providence. His soul "longed to go forth unto Absalom; for he was comforted concerning Amnon, seeing he was dead." The poignancy of his grief having been softened by time, his thoughts turned from the dead to the living son, self-banished through fear of the just punishment of his crime. And this is the evidence that the incestuous, drunken Amnon was at death immediately transported to the abodes of bliss, there to be purified and prepared for the companionship of sinless angels! A pleasing fable indeed, well suited to gratify the carnal heart! This is Satan's own doctrine, and it does his work effectually. Should we be surprised that, with such instruction, wickedness abounds?

The course pursued by this one false teacher illustrates that of many others. A few words of Scripture are separated from the context, which would in many cases show their meaning to be exactly opposite to the interpretation put upon them; and such disjointed passages are perverted and used in proof of doctrines that have no foundation in the word of God. The testimony cited as evidence that the drunken Amnon is in heaven is a mere inference directly contradicted by the plain and positive statement of the Scriptures that no drunkard shall inherit the kingdom of God. 1 Corinthians 6:10. It is thus that doubters, unbelievers, and skeptics turn the truth into a lie. And multitudes have been deceived by their sophistry and rocked to sleep in the cradle of carnal security.

If it were true that the souls of all men passed directly to heaven at the hour of dissolution, then we might well covet death rather than life. Many have been led by this belief to put an end to their existence. When overwhelmed with trouble, perplexity, and disappointment, it seems an easy thing to break the brittle thread of life and soar away into the bliss of the eternal world.

God has given in His word decisive evidence that He will punish the transgressors of His law. 540 Those who flatter themselves that He is too merciful to execute justice upon the sinner, have only to look to the cross of Calvary. The death of the spotless Son of God testifies that "the wages of sin is death," that every violation of God's law must receive its just retribution. Christ the sinless became sin for man. He bore the guilt of transgression, and the hiding of His Father's face, until His heart was broken and His life crushed out. All this sacrifice was made that sinners might be redeemed. In no other way could man be freed from the penalty of sin. And every soul that refuses to become a partaker of the atonement provided at such a cost must bear in his own person the guilt and punishment of transgression.

Let us consider what the Bible teaches further concerning the ungodly and unrepentant, whom the Universalist places in heaven as holy, happy angels.

"I will give unto him that is athirst of the fountain of the water of life freely." Revelation 21:6. This promise is only to those that thirst. None but those who feel their need of the water of life, and seek it at the loss of all things else, will be supplied. "He that overcometh shall inherit all things; and I will be his God, and he shall be My son." Verse 7. Here, also, conditions are specified. In order to inherit all things, we must resist and overcome sin.

The Lord declares by the prophet Isaiah: "Say ye to the righteous, that it shall be well with him." "Woe unto the wicked! it shall be ill with him: for the reward of his hands shall be given him." Isaiah 3:10, 11. "Though a sinner do evil an hundred times," says the wise man, "and his days be prolonged, yet surely I know that it shall be well with them that fear God, which fear before Him: but it shall not be well with the wicked." Ecclesiastes 8:12, 13. And Paul testifies that the sinner is treasuring up unto himself "wrath against the day of wrath and revelation of the righteous judgment of God; who will render to every man according to his deeds;" "tribulation and anguish upon every soul of man that doeth evil." Romans 2:5, 6, 9.

"No fornicator, nor unclean person, nor cov- 541 etous man, who is an idolater, hath any inheritance in the kingdom of Christ and God." Ephesians 5:5, A.R.V. "Follow peace with all men, and holiness, without which no man shall see the Lord." Hebrews 12:14. "Blessed are they that do His commandments, that they may have right to the tree of life, and may enter in through the gates into the city. For without are dogs, and sorcerers, and whoremongers, and murderers, and idolaters, and whosoever loveth and maketh a lie." Revelation 22:14, 15.

God has given to men a declaration of His character and of His method of dealing with sin. "The Lord God, merciful and gracious, long-suffering and abundant in goodness and truth, keeping mercy for thousands, forgiving iniquity and transgression and sin, and that will by no means clear the guilty." Exodus 34:6, 7. "All the wicked will He destroy." "The transgressors shall be destroyed together: the end of the wicked shall be cut off." Psalms 145:20; 37:38. The power and authority of the divine government will be employed to put down rebellion; yet all the manifestations of retributive justice will be perfectly consistent with the character of God as a merciful, long-suffering, benevolent being.

God does not force the will or judgment of any. He takes no pleasure in a slavish obedience. He desires that the creatures of His hands shall love Him because He is worthy of love. He would have them obey Him because they have an intelligent appreciation of His wisdom, justice, and benevolence. And all who have a just conception of these qualities will love Him because they are drawn toward Him in admiration of His attributes.

The principles of kindness, mercy, and love, taught and exemplified by our Saviour, are a transcript of the will and character of God. Christ declared that He taught nothing except that which He had received from His Father. The principles of the divine government are in perfect harmony with the Saviour's precept, "Love your enemies." God executes justice 542 upon the wicked, for the good of the universe, and even for the good of those upon whom His judgments are visited. He would make them happy if He could do so in accordance with the laws of His government and the justice of His character. He surrounds them with the tokens of His love, He grants them a knowledge of His law, and follows them with the offers of His mercy; but they despise His love, make void His law, and reject His mercy. While constantly receiving His gifts, they dishonor the Giver; they hate God because they know that He abhors their sins. The Lord bears long with their perversity; but the decisive hour will come at last, when their destiny is to be decided. Will He then chain these rebels to His side? Will He force them to do His will?

Those who have chosen Satan as their leader and have been controlled by his power are not prepared to enter the presence of God. Pride, deception, licentiousness, cruelty, have become fixed in their characters. Can they enter heaven to dwell forever with those whom they despised and hated on earth? Truth will never be agreeable to a liar; meekness will not satisfy self-esteem and pride; purity is not acceptable to the corrupt; disinterested love does not appear attractive to the selfish. What source of enjoyment could heaven offer to those who are wholly absorbed in earthly and selfish interests?

Could those whose lives have been spent in rebellion against God be suddenly transported to heaven and witness the high, the holy state of perfection that ever exists there,—every soul filled with love, every countenance beaming with joy, enrapturing music in melodious strains rising in honor of God and the Lamb, and ceaseless streams of light flowing upon the redeemed from the face of Him who sitteth upon the throne,—could those whose hearts are filled with hatred of God, of truth and holiness, mingle with the heavenly throng and join their songs of praise? Could they endure the glory of 543 God and the Lamb? No, no; years of probation were granted them, that they might form characters for heaven; but they have never trained the mind to love purity; they have never learned the language of heaven, and now it is too late. A life of rebellion against God has unfitted them for heaven. Its purity, holiness, and peace would be torture to them; the glory of God would be a consuming fire. They would long to flee from that holy place. They would welcome destruction, that they might be hidden from the face of Him who died to redeem them. The destiny of the wicked is fixed by their own choice. Their exclusion from heaven is voluntary with themselves, and just and merciful on the part of God.

Like the waters of the Flood the fires of the great day declare God's verdict that the wicked are incurable. They have no disposition to submit to divine authority. Their will has been exercised in revolt; and when life is ended, it is too late to turn the current of their thoughts in the opposite direction, too late to turn from transgression to obedience, from hatred to love.

In sparing the life of Cain the murderer, God gave the world an example of what would be the result of permitting the sinner to live to continue a course of unbridled iniquity. Through the influence of Cain's teaching and example, multitudes of his descendants were led into sin, until "the wickedness of man was great in the earth" and "every imagination of the thoughts of his heart was only evil continually." "The earth also was corrupt before God, and the earth was filled with violence." Genesis 6:5, 11.

In mercy to the world, God blotted out its wicked inhabitants in Noah's time. In mercy He destroyed the corrupt dwellers in Sodom. Through the deceptive power of Satan the workers of iniquity obtain sympathy and admiration, and are thus constantly leading others to rebellion. It was so in Cain's and in Noah's day, and in the time of Abraham and Lot; it is so in our time. It is in mercy to the universe that God will finally destroy the rejecters of His grace.

"The wages of sin is death; but the gift of 544 God is eternal life through Jesus Christ our Lord." Romans 6:23. While life is the inheritance of the righteous, death is the portion of the wicked. Moses declared to Israel: "I have set before thee this day life and good, and death and evil." Deuteronomy 30:15. The death referred to in these scriptures is not that pronounced upon Adam, for all mankind suffer the penalty of his transgression. It is "the second death" that is placed in contrast with everlasting life.

In consequence of Adam's sin, death passed upon the whole human race. All alike go down into the grave. And through the provisions of the plan of salvation, all are to be brought forth from their graves. "There shall be a resurrection of the dead, both of the just and unjust;" "for as in Adam all die, even so in Christ shall all be made alive." Acts 24:15; 1 Corinthians 15:22. But a distinction is made between the two classes that are brought forth. "All that are in the graves shall hear His voice, and shall come forth; they that have done good, unto the resurrection of life; and they that have done evil, unto the resurrection of damnation." John 5:28, 29. They who have been "accounted worthy" of the resurrection of life are "blessed and holy." "On such the second death hath no power." Revelation 20:6. But those who have not, through repentance and faith, secured pardon, must receive the penalty of transgression—"the wages of sin." They suffer punishment varying in duration and intensity, "according to their works," but finally ending in the second death. Since it is impossible for God, consistently with His justice and mercy, to save the sinner in his sins, He deprives him of the existence which his transgressions have forfeited and of which he has proved himself unworthy. Says an inspired writer: "Yet a little while, and the wicked shall not be: yea, thou shalt diligently consider his place, and it shall not be." And another declares: "They shall be as though they had not been." Psalm 37:10; Obadiah 16. Covered with infamy, they sink into hopeless, eternal oblivion.

Thus will be made an end of sin, with all the woe and ruin which have resulted from it. Says the psalmist: "Thou hast destroyed the wicked, Thou hast put out their name forever and ever. O thou enemy, destructions are come to a perpetual end." Psalm 9:5, 6. John, in the Revelation, looking forward to the eternal state, hears a universal anthem of praise undisturbed by one note of discord. Every creature in heaven and earth was heard ascribing glory to God. Revelation 5:13. There will then be no lost souls to blaspheme God as they writhe in never-ending torment; no wretched beings in hell will mingle their shrieks with the songs of the saved.

Upon the fundamental error of natural immortality rests the doctrine of consciousness in death—a doctrine, like eternal torment, opposed to the teachings of the Scriptures, to the dictates of reason, and to our feelings of humanity. According to the popular belief, the redeemed in heaven are acquainted with all that takes place on the earth and especially with the lives of the friends whom they have left behind. But how could it be a source of happiness to the dead to know the troubles of the living, to witness the sins committed by their own loved ones, and to see them enduring all the sorrows, disappointments, and anguish of life? How much of heaven's bliss would be enjoyed by those who were hovering over their friends on earth? And how utterly revolting is the belief that as soon as the breath leaves the body the soul of the impenitent is consigned to the flames of hell! To what depths of anguish must those be plunged who see their friends passing to the grave unprepared, to enter upon an eternity of woe and sin! Many have been driven to insanity by this harrowing thought.

What say the Scriptures concerning these things? David declares that man is not conscious in death. "His breath goeth forth, he returneth to his earth; in that very day his thoughts perish." Psalm 146:4. Solomon bears the same testimony: "The living know that they shall die: but the dead know not anything." "Their love, and their hatred, and their envy, is now perished; neither have they any more a portion forever in anything that is done under the sun." "There is no work, nor device, nor knowledge, nor wisdom, in the grave, whither thou goest." Ecclesiastes 9:5, 6, 10.

When, in answer to his prayer, Hezekiah's life was prolonged fifteen years, the grateful king rendered to God a tribute of praise for His great mercy. In this song he tells the reason why he thus rejoices: "The grave cannot praise Thee, death cannot celebrate Thee: they that go down into the pit cannot hope for Thy truth. The living, the living, he shall praise Thee, as I do this day." Isaiah 38:18, 19. Popular theology represents the righteous dead as in heaven, entered into bliss and praising God with an immortal tongue; but Hezekiah could see no such glorious prospect in death. With his words agrees the testimony of the psalmist: "In death there is no remembrance of Thee: in the grave who shall give Thee thanks?" "The dead praise not the Lord, neither any that go down into silence." Psalms 6:5; 115:17.

Peter on the Day of Pentecost declared that the patriarch David "is both dead and buried, and his sepulcher is with us unto this day." "For David is not ascended into the heavens." Acts 2:29, 34. The fact that David remains in the grave until the resurrection proves that the righteous do not go to heaven at death. It is only through the resurrection, and by virtue of the fact that Christ has risen, that David can at last sit at the right hand of God.

And said Paul: "If the dead rise not, then is not Christ raised: and if Christ be not raised, your faith is vain; ye are yet in your sins. Then they also which are fallen asleep in Christ are perished." 1 Corinthians 15:16-18. If for four thousand years the righteous had gone directly to heaven at death, how could Paul have said that if there is no resurrection, "they also which are fallen asleep in Christ are perished"? No resurrection would be necessary.

The martyr Tyndale, referring to the state of the dead, declared: "I confess openly, that I am not persuaded that they be already in the full glory that Christ is in, or the elect angels of God are in. Neither is it any article of my faith; for if it were so, I see not but then the preaching of the resurrection of the flesh were a thing in vain."—William Tyndale, Preface to New Testament (ed. 1534). Reprinted in *British Reformers—Tindal, Frith,* Barnes, page 349.

It is an undeniable fact that the hope of immortal blessedness at death has led to a widespread neglect of the Bible doctrine of the resurrection. This tendency was remarked by Dr. Adam Clarke, who said: "The doctrine of the resurrection appears to have been thought of much more consequence among the primitive Christians than it is *now*! How is this? The apostles were continually insisting on it, and exciting the followers of God to diligence, obedience, and cheerfulness through it. And their successors in the present day seldom mention it! So apostles preached, and so primitive Christians believed; so we preach, and so our hearers believe. There is not a doctrine in the gospel on which more stress is laid; and there is not a doctrine in the present system of preaching which is treated with more neglect!"—*Commentary,* remarks on 1 Corinthians 15, paragraph 3.

This has continued until the glorious truth of the resurrection has been almost wholly obscured and lost sight of by the Christian world. Thus a leading religious writer, commenting on the words of Paul in 1 Thessalonians 4:13-18, says: "For all practical purposes of comfort the doctrine of the blessed immortality of the righteous takes the place for us of any doubtful doctrine of the Lord's second coming. At our death the Lord comes for us. That is what we are to wait and watch for. The dead are already passed into glory. They do not wait for the trump for their judgment and blessedness."

548   But when about to leave His disciples, Jesus did not tell them that they would soon come to Him. "I go to prepare a place for you," He said. "And if I go and prepare a place for you, I will come again, and receive you unto Myself." John 14:2, 3. And Paul tells us, further, that "the Lord Himself shall descend from heaven with a shout, with the voice of the Archangel, and with the trump of God: and the dead in Christ shall rise first: then we which are alive and remain shall be caught up together with them in the clouds, to meet the Lord in the air: and so shall we ever be with the Lord." And he adds: "Comfort one another with these words." 1 Thessalonians 4:16-18. How wide the contrast between these words of comfort and those of the Universalist minister previously quoted! The latter consoled the bereaved friends with the assurance that, however sinful the dead might have been, when he breathed out his life here he was to be received among the angels. Paul points his brethren to the future coming of the Lord, when the fetters of the tomb shall be broken, and the "dead in Christ" shall be raised to eternal life.

Before any can enter the mansions of the blessed, their cases must be investigated, and their characters and their deeds must pass in review before God. All are to be judged according to the things written in the books and to be rewarded as their works have been. This judgment does not take place at death. Mark the words of Paul: "He hath appointed a day, in the which He will judge the world in righteousness by that Man whom He hath ordained; whereof He hath given assurance unto all men, in that He hath raised Him from the dead." Acts 17:31. Here the apostle plainly stated that a specified time, then future, had been fixed upon for the judgment of the world.

Jude refers to the same period: "The angels which kept not their first estate, but left their own habitation, He hath reserved in everlasting chains under darkness unto the judgment of the great day." And, again, he quotes the words of Enoch: "Behold, the Lord cometh with ten thou-

549   sands of His saints, to execute judgment upon all." Jude 6, 14, 15. John declares that he "saw

the dead, small and great, stand before God; and the books were opened: . . . and the dead were judged out of those things which were written in the books." Revelation 20:12.

But if the dead are already enjoying the bliss of heaven or writhing in the flames of hell, what need of a future judgment? The teachings of God's word on these important points are neither obscure nor contradictory; they may be understood by common minds. But what candid mind can see either wisdom or justice in the current theory? Will the righteous, after the investigation of their cases at the judgment, receive the commendation, "Well done, thou good and faithful servant: . . . *enter thou* into the joy of thy Lord," when they have been dwelling in His presence, perhaps for long ages? Are the wicked summoned from the place of torment to receive sentence from the Judge of all the earth: "Depart from Me, ye cursed, into everlasting fire"? Matthew 25:21, 41. Oh, solemn mockery! shameful impeachment of the wisdom and justice of God!

The theory of the immortality of the soul was one of those false doctrines that Rome, borrowing from paganism, incorporated into the religion of Christendom. Martin Luther classed it with the "monstrous fables that form part of the Roman dunghill of decretals."—E. Petavel, *The Problem of Immortality*, page 255. Commenting on the words of Solomon in Ecclesiastes, that the dead know not anything, the Reformer says: "Another place proving that the dead have no . . . feeling. There is, saith he, no duty, no science, no knowledge, no wisdom there. Solomon judgeth that the dead are asleep, and feel nothing at all. For the dead lie there, accounting neither days nor years, but when they are awaked, they shall seem to have slept scarce one minute."—Martin Luther, *Exposition of Solomon's Booke Called Ecclesiastes*, page 152.

Nowhere in the Sacred Scriptures is found the statement that the righteous go to their reward 550 or the wicked to their punishment at death. The patriarchs and prophets have left no such assurance. Christ and His apostles have given no hint of it. The Bible clearly teaches that the dead do not go immediately to heaven. They are represented as sleeping until the resurrection. 1 Thessalonians 4:14; Job 14:10-12. In the very day when the silver cord is loosed and the golden bowl broken (Ecclesiastes 12:6), man's thoughts perish. They that go down to the grave are in silence. They know no more of anything that is done under the sun. Job 14:21. Blessed rest for the weary righteous! Time, be it long or short, is but a moment to them. They sleep; they are awakened by the trump of God to a glorious immortality. "For the trumpet shall sound, and the dead shall be raised incorruptible. . . . So when this corruptible shall have put on incorruption, and this mortal shall have put on immortality, then shall be brought to pass the saying that is written, Death is swallowed up in victory." 1 Corinthians 15:52-54. As they are called forth from their deep slumber they begin to think just where they ceased. The last sensation was the pang of death; the last thought, that they were falling beneath the power of the grave. When they arise from the tomb, their first glad thought will be echoed in the triumphal shout: "O death, where is thy sting? O grave, where is thy victory?" Verse 55.

551

34
Can Our Dead Speak to Us?

The ministration of holy angels, as presented in the Scriptures, is a truth most comforting and precious to every follower of Christ. But the Bible teaching upon this point has been obscured and perverted by the errors of popular theology. The doctrine of natural immortality, first borrowed from the pagan philosophy, and in the darkness of the great apostasy incorporated into the Christian faith, has supplanted the truth, so plainly taught in Scripture, that "the dead know not anything." Multitudes have come to believe that it is spirits of the dead who are the "ministering spirits, sent forth to minister for them who shall be heirs of salvation." And this notwithstanding the testimony of Scripture to the existence of heavenly angels, and their connection with the history of man, before the death of a human being.

The doctrine of man's consciousness in death, especially the belief that spirits of the dead return to minister to the living, has prepared the way for modern spiritualism. If the dead are admitted to the presence of God and holy angels, and privileged with knowledge far exceeding what they before possessed, why should they not return to the earth to enlighten and instruct the living? If, as taught by popular theologians, spirits of the dead are hovering about their friends on earth, why should they not be permitted to communicate with them, to warn them against evil, or to comfort them in sorrow? How can 552 those who believe in man's consciousness in death reject what comes to them as divine light communicated by glorified spirits? Here is a channel regarded as sacred, through which Satan works for the accomplishment of his purposes. The fallen angels who do his bidding appear as messengers from the spirit world. While professing to bring the living into communication with the dead, the prince of evil exercises his bewitching influence upon their minds.

He has power to bring before men the appearance of their departed friends. The counterfeit is perfect; the familiar look, the words, the tone,

are reproduced with marvelous distinctness. Many are comforted with the assurance that their loved ones are enjoying the bliss of heaven, and without suspicion of danger, they give ear "to seducing spirits, and doctrines of devils."

When they have been led to believe that the dead actually return to communicate with them, Satan causes those to appear who went into the grave unprepared. They claim to be happy in heaven and even to occupy exalted positions there, and thus the error is widely taught that no difference is made between the righteous and the wicked. The pretended visitants from the world of spirits sometimes utter cautions and warnings which prove to be correct. Then, as confidence is gained, they present doctrines that directly undermine faith in the Scriptures. With an appearance of deep interest in the well-being of their friends on earth, they insinuate the most dangerous errors. The fact that they state some truths, and are able at times to foretell future events, gives to their statements an appearance of reliability; and their false teachings are accepted by the multitudes as readily, and believed as implicitly, as if they were the most sacred truths of the Bible. The law of God is set aside, the Spirit of grace despised, the blood of the covenant counted an unholy thing. The spirits deny the deity of Christ and place even the Creator on a level with themselves. Thus under a new disguise the great rebel still carries on his 553 warfare against God, begun in heaven and for nearly six thousand years continued upon the earth.

Many endeavor to account for spiritual manifestations by attributing them wholly to fraud and sleight of hand on the part of the medium. But while it is true that the results of trickery have often been palmed off as genuine manifestations, there have been, also, marked exhibitions of supernatural power. The mysterious rapping with which modern spiritualism began was not the result of human trickery or cunning, but was the direct work of evil angels, who thus introduced one of the most successful of soul-destroying delusions. Many will be ensnared through the belief that spiritualism is a merely human imposture; when brought face to face with manifestations which they cannot but regard as supernatural, they will be deceived, and will be led to accept them as the great power of God.

These persons overlook the testimony of the Scriptures concerning the wonders wrought by Satan and his agents. It was by satanic aid that Pharaoh's magicians were enabled to counterfeit the work of God. Paul testifies that before the second advent of Christ there will be similar manifestations of satanic power. The coming of the Lord is to be preceded by "the working of Satan with all power and signs and lying wonders, and with all deceivableness of unrighteousness." 2 Thessalonians 2:9, 10. And the apostle John, describing the miracle-working power that will be manifested in the last days, declares: "He doeth great wonders, so that he maketh fire come down from heaven on the earth in the sight of men, and deceiveth them that dwell on the earth by the means of those miracles which he had power to do." Revelation 13:13, 14. No mere impostures are here foretold. Men are deceived by the miracles which Satan's agents have power to do, not which they pretend to do.

The prince of darkness, who has so long bent the powers of his mastermind to the work of deception, skillfully adapts his temptations to men of all classes and conditions. To persons of culture and refinement he presents spiritualism in its more refined and intellectual aspects, and thus succeeds in drawing many into his snare. The wisdom which spiritualism imparts is that described by the apostle James, which "descendeth not from above, but is earthly, sensual, devilish." James 3:15. This, however, the great deceiver conceals when concealment will best suit his purpose. He who could appear clothed with the brightness of the heavenly seraphs before Christ in the wilderness of temptation, comes to men in the most attractive manner as an angel of light. He appeals to the reason by the presentation of elevating themes; he delights the fancy with enrapturing scenes; and he enlists the affections by his eloquent portrayals of love and charity. He excites the imagination to lofty flights, leading men to take so great pride in their own wisdom that in their hearts they despise the Eternal One. That mighty being who could take the world's Redeemer to an exceedingly high mountain and bring before Him all the kingdoms of the earth and the glory of them, will present his temptations to men in a manner to pervert the senses of all who are not shielded by divine power.

Satan beguiles men now as he beguiled Eve in Eden by flattery, by kindling a desire to obtain forbidden knowledge, by exciting ambition for self-exaltation. It was cherishing these evils that caused his fall, and through them he aims to compass the ruin of men. "Ye shall be as gods," he declares, "knowing good and evil." Genesis 3:5. Spiritualism teaches "that man is the creature of progression; that it is his destiny from his birth to progress, even to eternity, toward the Godhead." And again: "Each mind will judge itself and not another." "The judgment will be right, because it is the judgment of self. . . . The throne is within you." Said a spiritualistic teacher, as the "spiritual consciousness" awoke within him: "My fellow men, all were unfallen demigods." And another declares: "Any just and perfect being is Christ."

Thus, in place of the righteousness and perfection of the infinite God, the true object of

adoration; in place of the perfect righteousness of His law, the true standard of human attainment, Satan has substituted the sinful, erring nature of man himself as the only object of adoration, the only rule of judgment, or standard of character. This is progress, not upward, but downward.

It is a law both of the intellectual and the spiritual nature that by beholding we become changed. The mind gradually adapts itself to the subjects upon which it is allowed to dwell. It becomes assimilated to that which it is accustomed to love and reverence. Man will never rise higher than his standard of purity or goodness or truth. If self is his loftiest ideal, he will never attain to anything more exalted. Rather, he will constantly sink lower and lower. The grace of God alone has power to exalt man. Left to himself, his course must inevitably be downward.

To the self-indulgent, the pleasure-loving, the sensual, spiritualism presents itself under a less subtle disguise than to the more refined and intellectual; in its grosser forms they find that which is in harmony with their inclinations. Satan studies every indication of the frailty of human nature, he marks the sins which each individual is inclined to commit, and then he takes care that opportunities shall not be wanting to gratify the tendency to evil. He tempts men to excess in that which is in itself lawful, causing them, through intemperance, to weaken physical, mental, and moral power. He has destroyed and is destroying thousands through the indulgence of the passions, thus brutalizing the entire nature of man. And to complete his work, he declares, through the spirits that "true knowledge places man above all law;" that "whatever is, is right;" that "God doth not condemn;" and that "all sins which are committed are innocent." When the people are thus led to believe that desire is the highest law, that liberty is license, and that man is accountable only to himself, who can wonder that corruption and depravity teem on every hand? Multitudes eagerly accept teachings that leave them at liberty to obey the promptings of the carnal heart. The reins of self-control are laid upon the neck of lust, the powers of mind and soul are made subject to the animal propensities, and Satan exultingly sweeps into his net thousands who profess to be followers of Christ.

But none need be deceived by the lying claims of spiritualism. God has given the world sufficient light to enable them to discover the snare. As already shown, the theory which forms the very foundation of spiritualism is at war with the plainest statements of Scripture. The Bible declares that the dead know not anything, that their thoughts have perished; they have no part in anything that is done under the sun; they know nothing of the joys or sorrows of those who were dearest to them on earth.

Furthermore, God has expressly forbidden all pretended communication with departed spirits. In the days of the Hebrews there was a class of people who claimed, as do the spiritualists of today, to hold communication with the dead. But the "familiar spirits," as these visitants from other worlds were called, are declared by the Bible to be "the spirits of devils." (Compare Numbers 25:1-3; Psalm 106:28; 1 Corinthians 10:20; Revelation 16:14.) The work of dealing with familiar spirits was pronounced an abomination to the Lord, and was solemnly forbidden under penalty of death. Leviticus 19:31; 20:27. The very name of witchcraft is now held in contempt. The claim that men can hold intercourse with evil spirits is regarded as a fable of the Dark Ages. But spiritualism, which numbers its converts by hundreds of thousands, yea, by millions, which has made its way into scientific circles, which has invaded churches, and has found favor in legislative bodies, and even in the courts of kings—this mammoth deception is but a revival, in a new disguise, of the witchcraft condemned and prohibited of old.

If there were no other evidence of the real character of spiritualism, it should be enough 557 for the Christian that the spirits make no difference between righteousness and sin, between the noblest and purest of the apostles of Christ and the most corrupt of the servants of Satan. By representing the basest of men as in heaven, and highly exalted there, Satan says to the world: "No matter how wicked you are; no matter whether you believe or disbelieve God and the Bible. Live as you please; heaven is your home." The spiritualist teachers virtually declare: "Everyone that doeth evil is good in the sight of the Lord, and He delighteth in them; or, Where is the God of judgment?" Malachi 2:17. Saith the word of God: "Woe unto them that call evil good, and good evil; that put darkness for light, and light for darkness." Isaiah 5:20.

The apostles, as personated by these lying spirits, are made to contradict what they wrote at the dictation of the Holy Spirit when on earth. They deny the divine origin of the Bible, and thus tear away the foundation of the Christian's hope and put out the light that reveals the way to heaven. Satan is making the world believe that the Bible is a mere fiction, or at least a book suited to the infancy of the race, but now to be lightly regarded, or cast aside as obsolete. And to take the place of the word of God he holds out spiritual manifestations. Here is a channel wholly under his control; by this means he can make the world believe what he will. The Book that is to judge him and his followers he puts in the shade, just where he wants it; the Saviour of the world he makes to be no more than a common man. And as the Roman guard that watched the tomb of Jesus spread the lying report which the priests and elders put into their mouths to disprove His resurrection, so do the believers in spiritual manifestations try to make it appear that there is nothing miraculous in the circumstances of our Saviour's life. After thus seeking to put Jesus in the background, they call attention to their own miracles, declaring that these far exceed the works of Christ.

It is true that spiritualism is now changing its form and, veiling some of its more objectionable features, is assuming a Christian guise. But 558 its utterances from the platform and the press have been before the public for many years, and in these its real character stands revealed. These teachings cannot be denied or hidden.

Even in its present form, so far from being more worthy of toleration than formerly, it is really a more dangerous, because a more subtle, deception. While it formerly denounced Christ and the Bible, it now *professes* to accept both. But the Bible is interpreted in a manner that is pleasing to the unrenewed heart, while its solemn and vital truths are made of no effect. Love is dwelt upon as the chief attribute of God, but it is degraded to a weak sentimentalism, making little distinction between good and evil. God's justice, His denunciations of sin, the requirements of His holy law, are all kept out of sight. The people are taught to regard the Decalogue as a dead letter. Pleasing, bewitching fables captivate the senses and lead men to reject the Bible as the foundation of their faith. Christ is as verily denied as before; but Satan has so blinded the eyes of the people that the deception is not discerned.

There are few who have any just conception of the deceptive power of spiritualism and the danger of coming under its influence. Many tamper with it merely to gratify their curiosity. They have no real faith in it and would be filled with horror at the thought of yielding themselves to the spirits' control. But they venture upon the forbidden ground, and the mighty destroyer exercises his power upon them against their will. Let them once be induced to submit their minds to his direction, and he holds them captive. It is impossible, in their own strength, to break away from the bewitching, alluring spell. Nothing but the power of God, granted in answer to the earnest prayer of faith, can deliver these ensnared souls.

All who indulge sinful traits of character, or willfully cherish a known sin, are inviting the temptations of Satan. They separate themselves 559 from God and from the watchcare of His angels; as the evil one presents his deceptions, they are without defense and fall an easy prey. Those who thus place themselves in his power little realize where their course will end. Having achieved their overthrow, the tempter will employ them as his agents to lure others to ruin.

Says the prophet Isaiah: "When they shall say

unto you, Seek unto them that have familiar spirits, and unto wizards that peep, and that mutter: should not a people seek unto their God? for the living to the dead? To the law and to the testimony: if they speak not according to this word, it is because there is no light in them." Isaiah 8:19, 20. If men had been willing to receive the truth so plainly stated in the Scriptures concerning the nature of man and the state of the dead, they would see in the claims and manifestations of spiritualism the working of Satan with power and signs and lying wonders. But rather than yield the liberty so agreeable to the carnal heart, and renounce the sins which they love, multitudes close their eyes to the light and walk straight on, regardless of warnings, while Satan weaves his snares about them, and they become his prey. "Because they received not the love of the truth, that they might be saved," therefore "God shall send them strong delusion, that they should believe a lie." 2 Thessalonians 2:10, 11.

Those who oppose the teachings of spiritualism are assailing, not men alone, but Satan and his angels. They have entered upon a contest against principalities and powers and wicked spirits in high places. Satan will not yield one inch of ground except as he is driven back by the power of heavenly messengers. The people of God should be able to meet him, as did our Saviour, with the words: "It is written." Satan can quote Scripture now as in the days of Christ, and he will pervert its teachings to sustain his delusions. Those who would stand in this time of peril must understand for themselves the testimony of the Scriptures.

560 Many will be confronted by the spirits of devils personating beloved relatives or friends and declaring the most dangerous heresies. These visitants will appeal to our tenderest sympathies and will work miracles to sustain their pretensions. We must be prepared to withstand them with the Bible truth that the dead know not anything and that they who thus appear are the spirits of devils.

Just before us is "the hour of temptation, which shall come upon all the world, to try them that dwell upon the earth." Revelation 3:10. All whose faith is not firmly established upon the word of God will be deceived and overcome. Satan "works with all deceivableness of unrighteousness" to gain control of the children of men, and his deceptions will continually increase. But he can gain his object only as men voluntarily yield to his temptations. Those who are earnestly seeking a knowledge of the truth and are striving to purify their souls through obedience, thus doing what they can to prepare for the conflict, will find, in the God of truth, a sure defense. "Because thou hast kept the word of My patience, I also will keep thee" (verse 10), is the Saviour's promise. He would sooner send every angel out of heaven to protect His people than leave one soul that trusts in Him to be overcome by Satan.

The prophet Isaiah brings to view the fearful deception which will come upon the wicked, causing them to count themselves secure from the judgments of God: "We have made a covenant with death, and with hell are we at agreement; when the overflowing scourge shall pass through, it shall not come unto us: for we have made lies our refuge, and under falsehood have we hid ourselves." Isaiah 28:15. In the class here described are included those who in their stubborn impenitence comfort themselves with the assurance that there is to be no punishment for the sinner; that all mankind, it matters not how corrupt, are to be exalted to heaven, to become as the angels of God. But still more emphatically are those making a covenant with 561 death and an agreement with hell, who renounce the truths which Heaven has provided as a defense for the righteous in the day of trouble, and accept the refuge of lies offered by Satan in its stead—the delusive pretensions of spiritualism.

Marvelous beyond expression is the blindness of the people of this generation. Thousands reject the word of God as unworthy of belief and with eager confidence receive the deceptions of Satan. Skeptics and scoffers denounce the bigotry of those who contend for the faith of prophets and apostles, and they divert themselves by holding up to ridicule the solemn declarations of the Scriptures concerning Christ and the plan of salvation, and the retribution to be visited upon the rejecters of the truth. They affect great pity for minds so narrow, weak, and superstitious as to acknowledge the claims of God and obey the requirements of His law. They manifest as much assurance as if, indeed, they had made a covenant with death and an agreement with hell—as if they had erected an impassable, impenetrable barrier between themselves and the vengeance of God. Nothing can arouse their fears. So fully have they yielded to the tempter, so closely are they united with him, and so thoroughly imbued with his spirit, that they have no power and no inclination to break away from his snare.

Satan has long been preparing for his final effort to deceive the world. The foundation of his work was laid by the assurance given to Eve in Eden: "Ye shall not surely die." "In the day ye eat thereof, then your eyes shall be opened, and ye shall be as gods, knowing good and evil." Genesis 3:4, 5. Little by little he has prepared the way for his masterpiece of deception in the development of spiritualism. He has not yet reached the full accomplishment of his designs; but it will be reached in the last remnant of time. Says the prophet: "I saw three unclean spirits like frogs; . . . they are the spirits

562 of devils, working miracles, which go forth unto the kings of the earth and of the whole world, to gather them to the battle of that great day of God Almighty." Revelation 16:13, 14. Except those who are kept by the power of God, through faith in His word, the whole world will be swept into the ranks of this delusion. The people are fast being lulled to a fatal security, to be awakened only by the outpouring of the wrath of God.

Saith the Lord God: "Judgment also will I lay to the line, and righteousness to the plummet: and the hail shall sweep away the refuge of lies, and the waters shall overflow the hiding place. And your covenant with death shall be disannulled, and your agreement with hell shall not stand; when the overflowing scourge shall pass through, then ye shall be trodden down by it." Isaiah 28:17, 18.

563

35

Liberty of Conscience Threatened

Romanism is now regarded by Protestants with far greater favor than in former years. In those countries where Catholicism is not in the ascendancy, and the papists are taking a conciliatory course in order to gain influence, there is an increasing indifference concerning the doctrines that separate the reformed churches from the papal hierarchy; the opinion is gaining ground that, after all, we do not differ so widely upon vital points as has been supposed, and that a little concession on our part will bring us into a better understanding with Rome. The time was when Protestants placed a high value upon the liberty of conscience which had been so dearly purchased. They taught their children to abhor popery and held that to seek harmony with Rome would be disloyalty to God. But how widely different are the sentiments now expressed!

The defenders of the papacy declare that the church has been maligned, and the Protestant world are inclined to accept the statement. Many urge that it is unjust to judge the church of today by the abominations and absurdities that marked her reign during the centuries of ignorance and darkness. They excuse her horrible cruelty as the result of the barbarism of the times and plead that the influence of modern civilization has changed her sentiments.

564 Have these persons forgotten the claim of infallibility put forth for eight hundred years by this haughty power? So far from being relinquished, this claim was affirmed in the nineteenth century with greater positiveness than ever before. As Rome asserts that the "church never erred; nor will it, according to the Scriptures, ever err" (John L. von Mosheim, Institutes of Ecclesiastical History, book 3, century 11, part 2, chapter 2, section 9, note 17), how can she renounce the principles which governed her course in past ages?

The papal church will never relinquish her claim to infallibility. All that she has done in her persecution of those who reject her dogmas she holds to be right; and would she not repeat the same acts, should the opportunity be presented? Let the restraints now imposed by secular governments be removed and Rome be reinstated in her former power, and there would speedily be a revival of her tyranny and persecution.

A well-known writer speaks thus of the attitude of the papal hierarchy as regards freedom of conscience, and of the perils which especially threaten the United States from the success of her policy:

"There are many who are disposed to attribute any fear of Roman Catholicism in the United States to bigotry or childishness. Such see nothing in the character and attitude of Romanism that is hostile to our free institutions, or find nothing portentous in its growth. Let us, then, first compare some of the fundamental principles of our government with those of the Catholic Church.

"The Constitution of the United States guarantees liberty of conscience. Nothing is dearer or more fundamental. Pope Pius IX, in his Encyclical Letter of August 15, 1854, said: 'The absurd and erroneous doctrines or ravings in defense of liberty of conscience are a most pestilential error—a pest, of all others, most to be dreaded in a state.' The same pope, in his Encyclical Letter of December 8, 1864, anathematized 'those who assert the liberty of conscience and of religious worship,' also 'all such 565 as maintain that the church may not employ force.'

"The pacific tone of Rome in the United States does not imply a change of heart. She is tolerant where she is helpless. Says Bishop O'Connor: 'Religious liberty is merely endured until the opposite can be carried into effect without peril to the Catholic world.'. . . The archbishop of St. Louis once said: 'Heresy and unbelief are crimes; and in Christian countries, as in Italy and Spain, for instance, where all the people are Catholics, and where the Catholic religion is an essential part of the law of the land, they are punished as other crimes.'. . .

"Every cardinal, archbishop, and bishop in the Catholic Church takes an oath of allegiance to the pope, in which occur the following words: 'Heretics, schismatics, and rebels to our said lord (the pope), or his aforesaid successors, I will to my utmost persecute and oppose.'"— Josiah Strong, Our Country, ch. 5, pars. 2-4.

It is true that there are real Christians in the Roman Catholic communion. Thousands in that church are serving God according to the best light they have. They are not allowed access to His word, and therefore they do not discern the truth. *They have never seen the contrast between a living heart service and a round of mere forms and ceremonies. God looks with pitying tenderness upon these souls, educated as they are in a faith that is delusive and unsatisfying. He will cause rays of light to penetrate the dense darkness that surrounds them. He will reveal to them the truth as it is in Jesus, and many will yet take their position with His people.

But Romanism as a system is no more in harmony with the gospel of Christ now than at any former period in her history. The Protestant churches are in great darkness, or they would discern the signs of the times. The Roman Church is far-reaching in her plans and modes of operation. She is employing every device to extend her influence and increase her power in 566 preparation for a fierce and determined conflict to regain control of the world, to re-establish persecution, and to undo all that Protestantism has done. Catholicism is gaining ground upon every side. See the increasing number of her churches and chapels in Protestant countries. Look at the popularity of her colleges and seminaries in America, so widely patronized by Protestants. Look at the growth of ritualism in England and the frequent defections to the ranks of the Catholics. These things should awaken the anxiety of all who prize the pure principles of the gospel.

Protestants have tampered with and patronized popery; they have made compromises and concessions which papists themselves are surprised to see and fail to understand. Men are closing their eyes to the real character of Romanism and the dangers to be apprehended from her supremacy. The people need to be aroused to resist the advances of this most dangerous foe to civil and religious liberty.

Many Protestants suppose that the Catholic religion is unattractive and that its worship is a dull, meaningless round of ceremony. Here they mistake. While Romanism is based upon deception, it is not a coarse and clumsy imposture. The religious service of the Roman Church is a most impressive ceremonial. Its gorgeous display and solemn rites fascinate the senses of the people and silence the voice of reason and of conscience. The eye is charmed. Magnificent churches, imposing processions, golden altars, jeweled shrines, choice paintings, and exquisite sculpture appeal to the love of beauty. The ear also is captivated. The music is unsurpassed. The rich notes of the deep-toned organ, blending with the melody of many voices as it swells through the lofty domes and pillared aisles of her grand cathedrals, cannot fail to impress the mind with awe and reverence.

This outward splendor, pomp, and ceremony, that only mocks the longings of the sin-sick soul, is an evidence of inward corruption. The religion of Christ needs not such attractions to recommend it. In the light shining from the cross, true Christianity appears so pure and lovely that no external decorations can enhance 567 its true worth. It is the beauty of holiness, a meek and quiet spirit, which is of value with God.

Brilliancy of style is not necessarily an index of pure, elevated thought. High conceptions of art, delicate refinement of taste, often exist in minds that are earthly and sensual. They are often employed by Satan to lead men to forget the necessities of the soul, to lose sight of the future, immortal life, to turn away from their infinite Helper, and to live for this world alone.

A religion of externals is attractive to the unrenewed heart. The pomp and ceremony of the Catholic worship has a seductive, bewitching power, by which many are deceived; and they come to look upon the Roman Church as the very gate of heaven. None but those who have planted their feet firmly upon the foundation of truth, and whose hearts are renewed by the Spirit of God, are proof against her influence. Thousands who have not an experimental knowledge of Christ will be led to accept the forms of godliness without the power. Such a religion is just what the multitudes desire.

The church's claim to the right to pardon leads the Romanist to feel at liberty to sin; and the ordinance of confession, without which her pardon is not granted, tends also to give license to evil. He who kneels before fallen man, and opens in confession the secret thoughts and imaginations of his heart, is debasing his manhood and degrading every noble instinct of his soul. In unfolding the sins of his life to a priest,—an erring, sinful mortal, and too often corrupted with wine and licentiousness,—his standard of character is lowered, and he is defiled in consequence. His thought of God is degraded to the likeness of fallen humanity, for the priest stands as a representative of God. This degrading confession of man to man is the secret spring from which has flowed much of the evil that is defiling the world and fitting it for the final destruction. Yet to him who loves 568 self-indulgence, it is more pleasing to confess to a fellow mortal than to open the soul to God. It is more palatable to human nature to do penance than to renounce sin; it is easier to mortify the flesh by sackcloth and nettles and galling chains than to crucify fleshly lusts. Heavy is the yoke which the carnal heart is willing to bear rather than bow to the yoke of Christ.

There is a striking similarity between the Church of Rome and the Jewish Church at the

---

* Published in 1888 and 1911. See Appendix.

time of Christ's first advent. While the Jews secretly trampled upon every principle of the law of God, they were outwardly rigorous in the observance of its precepts, loading it down with exactions and traditions that made obedience painful and burdensome. As the Jews professed to revere the law, so do Romanists claim to reverence the cross. They exalt the symbol of Christ's sufferings, while in their lives they deny Him whom it represents.

Papists place crosses upon their churches, upon their altars, and upon their garments. Everywhere is seen the insignia of the cross. Everywhere it is outwardly honored and exalted. But the teachings of Christ are buried beneath a mass of senseless traditions, false interpretations, and rigorous exactions. The Saviour's words concerning the bigoted Jews, apply with still greater force to the leaders of the Roman Catholic Church: "They bind heavy burdens and grievous to be borne, and lay them on men's shoulders; but they themselves will not move them with one of their fingers." Matthew 23:4. Conscientious souls are kept in constant terror fearing the wrath of an offended God, while many of the dignitaries of the church are living in luxury and sensual pleasure.

The worship of images and relics, the invocation of saints, and the exaltation of the pope are devices of Satan to attract the minds of the people from God and from His Son. To accomplish their ruin, he endeavors to turn their attention from Him through whom alone they can find salvation. He will direct them to any object that can be substituted for the One who has said: 569 "Come unto Me, all ye that labor and are heavy-laden, and I will give you rest." Matthew 11:28.

It is Satan's constant effort to misrepresent the character of God, the nature of sin, and the real issues at stake in the great controversy. His sophistry lessens the obligation of the divine law and gives men license to sin. At the same time he causes them to cherish false conceptions of God so that they regard Him with fear and hate rather than with love. The cruelty inherent in his own character is attributed to the Creator; it is embodied in systems of religion and expressed in modes of worship. Thus the minds of men are blinded, and Satan secures them as his agents to war against God. By perverted conceptions of the divine attributes, heathen nations were led to believe human sacrifices necessary to secure the favor of Deity; and horrible cruelties have been perpetrated under the various forms of idolatry.

The Roman Catholic Church, uniting the forms of paganism and Christianity, and, like paganism, misrepresenting the character of God, has resorted to practices no less cruel and revolting. In the days of Rome's supremacy there were instruments of torture to compel assent to her doctrines. There was the stake for those who would not concede to her claims. There were massacres on a scale that will never be known until revealed in the judgment. Dignitaries of the church studied, under Satan their master, to invent means to cause the greatest possible torture and not end the life of the victim. In many cases the infernal process was repeated to the utmost limit of human endurance, until nature gave up the struggle, and the sufferer hailed death as a sweet release.

Such was the fate of Rome's opponents. For her adherents she had the discipline of the scourge, of famishing hunger, of bodily austerities in every conceivable, heart-sickening form. To secure the favor of Heaven, penitents violated the laws of God by violating the laws of nature. They were taught to sunder the ties which He has formed to bless and gladden man's earthly sojourn. The churchyard contains millions of victims who spent their lives in vain 570 endeavors to subdue their natural affections, to repress, as offensive to God, every thought and feeling of sympathy with their fellow creatures.

If we desire to understand the determined cruelty of Satan, manifested for hundreds of years, not among those who never heard of God, but in the very heart and throughout the extent of Christendom, we have only to look at the history of Romanism. Through this mammoth system of deception the prince of evil achieves his purpose of bringing dishonor to God and wretchedness to man. And as we see how he succeeds in disguising himself and accomplishing his work through the leaders of the church, we may better understand why he has so great antipathy to the Bible. If that Book is read, the mercy and love of God will be revealed; it will be seen that He lays upon men none of these heavy burdens. All that He asks is a broken and contrite heart, a humble, obedient spirit.

Christ gives no example in His life for men and women to shut themselves in monasteries in order to become fitted for heaven. He has never taught that love and sympathy must be repressed. The Saviour's heart overflowed with love. The nearer man approaches to moral perfection, the keener are his sensibilities, the more acute is his perception of sin, and the deeper his sympathy for the afflicted. The pope claims to be the vicar of Christ; but how does his character bear comparison with that of our Saviour? Was Christ ever known to consign men to the prison or the rack because they did not pay Him homage as the King of heaven? Was His voice heard condemning to death those who did not accept Him? When He was slighted by the people of a Samaritan village, the apostle John was filled with indignation, and inquired: "Lord, wilt Thou that we command fire to come down from heaven, and consume them, even as Elias did?" Jesus looked with pity upon His disciple, and rebuked his harsh spirit, saying: "The Son of man is not come to destroy men's lives, but to save them." Luke 9:54, 56. How different from 571 the spirit manifested by Christ is that of His professed vicar.

The Roman Church now presents a fair front to the world, covering with apologies her record of horrible cruelties. She has clothed herself in Christlike garments; but she is unchanged. Every principle of the papacy that existed in past ages exists today. The doctrines devised in the darkest ages are still held. Let none deceive themselves. The papacy that Protestants are now so ready to honor is the same that ruled the world in the days of the Reformation, when men of God stood up, at the peril of their lives, to expose her iniquity. She possesses the same pride and arrogant assumption that lorded it over kings and princes, and claimed the prerogatives of God. Her spirit is no less cruel and despotic now than when she crushed out human liberty and slew the saints of the Most High.

The papacy is just what prophecy declared that she would be, the apostasy of the latter times. 2 Thessalonians 2:3, 4. It is a part of her policy to assume the character which will best accomplish her purpose; but beneath the variable appearance of the chameleon she conceals the invariable venom of the serpent. "Faith ought not to be kept with heretics, nor persons suspected of heresy" (Lenfant, volume 1, page 516), she declares. Shall this power, whose record for a thousand years is written in the blood of the saints, be now acknowledged as a part of the church of Christ?

It is not without reason that the claim has been put forth in Protestant countries that Catholicism differs less widely from Protestantism than in former times. There has been a change; but the change is not in the papacy. Catholicism indeed resembles much of the Protestantism that now exists, because Protestantism has so greatly degenerated since the days of the Reformers.

As the Protestant churches have been seeking the favor of the world, false charity has blinded their eyes. They do not see but that it is right to believe good of all evil, and as the inevitable result they will finally believe evil of all good. 572 Instead of standing in defense of the faith once delivered to the saints, they are now, as it were, apologizing to Rome for their uncharitable opinion of her, begging pardon for their bigotry.

A large class, even of those who look upon Romanism with no favor, apprehend little danger from her power and influence. Many urge that the intellectual and moral darkness prevailing during the Middle Ages favored the spread of her dogmas, superstitions, and oppression, and that the greater intelligence of modern times, the general diffusion of knowledge, and the increasing liberality in matters of religion forbid a revival of intolerance and tyranny. The very thought that such a state of things will exist in this enlightened age is ridiculed. It is true that great light, intellectual, moral, and religious, is shining upon this generation. In the open pages of God's Holy Word, light from heaven has been shed upon the world. But it should be remembered that the greater the light bestowed, the greater the darkness of those who pervert and reject it.

A prayerful study of the Bible would show Protestants the real character of the papacy and would cause them to abhor and to shun it; but many are so wise in their own conceit that they feel no need of humbly seeking God that they may be led into the truth. Although priding themselves on their enlightenment, they are ignorant both of the Scriptures and of the power of God. They must have some means of quieting their consciences, and they seek that which is least spiritual and humiliating. What they desire is a method of forgetting God which shall pass as a method of remembering Him. The papacy is well adapted to meet the wants of all these. It is prepared for two classes of mankind, embracing nearly the whole world—those who would be saved by their merits, and those who would be saved in their sins. Here is the secret of its power.

A day of great intellectual darkness has been shown to be favorable to the success of the papacy. It will yet be demonstrated that a day of 573 great intellectual light is equally favorable for its success. In past ages, when men were without God's word and without the knowledge of the truth, their eyes were blindfolded, and thousands were ensnared, not seeing the net spread for their feet. In this generation there are many whose eyes become dazzled by the glare of human speculations, "science falsely so called;" they discern not the net, and walk into it as readily as if blindfolded. God designed that man's intellectual powers should be held as a gift from his Maker and should be employed in the service of truth and righteousness; but when pride and ambition are cherished, and men exalt their own theories above the word of God, then intelligence can accomplish greater harm than ignorance. Thus the false science of the present day, which undermines faith in the Bible, will prove as successful in preparing the way for the acceptance of the papacy, with its pleasing forms, as did the withholding of knowledge in opening the way for its aggrandizement in the Dark Ages.

In the movements now in progress in the United States to secure for the institutions and usages of the church the support of the state, Protestants are following in the steps of papists. Nay, more, they are opening the door for the papacy to regain in Protestant America the supremacy which she has lost in the Old World.

And that which gives greater significance to this movement is the fact that the principal object contemplated is the enforcement of Sunday observance—a custom which originated with Rome, and which she claims as the sign of her authority. It is the spirit of the papacy—the spirit of conformity to worldly customs, the veneration for human traditions above the commandments of God—that is permeating the Protestant churches and leading them on to do the same work of Sunday exaltation which the papacy has done before them.

If the reader would understand the agencies to be employed in the soon-coming contest, he has but to trace the record of the means which 574 Rome employed for the same object in ages past. If he would know how papists and Protestants united will deal with those who reject their dogmas, let him see the spirit which Rome manifested toward the Sabbath and its defenders.

Royal edicts, general councils, and church ordinances sustained by secular power were the steps by which the pagan festival attained its position of honor in the Christian world. The first public measure enforcing Sunday observance was the law enacted by Constantine. (A.D. 321; see Appendix.) This edict required townspeople to rest on "the venerable day of the sun," but permitted countrymen to continue their agricultural pursuits. Though virtually a heathen statute, it was enforced by the emperor after his nominal acceptance of Christianity.

The royal mandate not proving a sufficient substitute for divine authority, Eusebius, a bishop who sought the favor of princes, and who was the special friend and flatterer of Constantine, advanced the claim that Christ had transferred the Sabbath to Sunday. Not a single testimony of the Scriptures was produced in proof of the new doctrine. Eusebius himself unwittingly acknowledges its falsity and points to the real authors of the change. "All things," he says, "whatever that it was duty to do on the Sabbath, these we have transferred to the Lord's Day."—Robert Cox, *Sabbath Laws and Sabbath Duties*, page 538. But the Sunday argument, groundless as it was, served to embolden men in trampling upon the Sabbath of the Lord. All who desired to be honored by the world accepted the popular festival.

As the papacy became firmly established, the work of Sunday exaltation was continued. For a time the people engaged in agricultural labor when not attending church, and the seventh day was still regarded as the Sabbath. But steadily a change was effected. Those in holy office were forbidden to pass judgment in any civil controversy on the Sunday. Soon after, all persons, of whatever rank, were commanded to refrain from common labor on pain of a fine for freemen and 575 stripes in the case of servants. Later it was decreed that rich men should be punished with the loss of half of their estates; and finally, that if still obstinate they should be made slaves. The lower classes were to suffer perpetual banishment.

Miracles also were called into requisition. Among other wonders it was reported that as a husbandman who was about to plow his field on Sunday cleaned his plow with an iron, the iron stuck fast in his hand, and for two years he carried it about with him, "to his exceeding great pain and shame."—Francis West, *Historical and Practical Discourse on the Lord's Day*, page 174.

Later the pope gave directions that the parish priest should admonish the violators of Sunday and wish them to go to church and say their prayers, lest they bring some great calamity on themselves and neighbors. An ecclesiastical council brought forward the argument, since so widely employed, even by Protestants, that because persons had been struck by lightning while laboring on Sunday, it must be the Sabbath. "It is apparent," said the prelates, "how high the displeasure of God was upon their neglect of this day." An appeal was then made that priests and ministers, kings and princes, and all faithful people "use their utmost endeavors and care that the day be restored to its honor, and, for the credit of Christianity, more devoutly observed for the time to come."—Thomas Morer, *Discourse in Six Dialogues on the Name, Notion, and Observation of the Lord's Day*, page 271.

The decrees of councils proving insufficient, the secular authorities were besought to issue an edict that would strike terror to the hearts of the people and force them to refrain from labor on the Sunday. At a synod held in Rome, all previous decisions were reaffirmed with greater force and solemnity. They were also incorporated into the ecclesiastical law and enforced by the civil authorities throughout nearly all Christendom. (See Heylyn, *History of the Sabbath*, pt. 2, ch. 5, sec. 7.)

Still the absence of Scriptural authority for 576 Sundaykeeping occasioned no little embarrassment. The people questioned the right of their teachers to set aside the positive declaration of Jehovah, "The seventh day is the Sabbath of the Lord thy God," in order to honor the day of the sun. To supply the lack of Bible testimony, other expedients were necessary. A zealous advocate of Sunday, who about the close of the twelfth century visited the churches of England, was resisted by faithful witnesses for the truth; and so fruitless were his efforts that he departed from the country for a season and cast about him for some means to enforce his teachings. When he returned, the lack was supplied, and in his after labors he met with greater success. He brought with him a roll purporting to be from God Himself, which contained the needed command for Sunday observance, with awful threats to terrify the disobedient. This precious document—as base a counterfeit as the institution it supported—was said to have fallen from heaven and to have been found in Jerusalem, upon the altar of St. Simeon, in Golgotha. But, in fact, the pontifical palace at Rome was the source whence it proceeded. Frauds and forgeries to advance the power and prosperity of the church have in all ages been esteemed lawful by the papal hierarchy.

The roll forbade labor from the ninth hour, three o'clock, on Saturday afternoon, till sunrise on Monday; and its authority was declared to be confirmed by many miracles. It was reported that persons laboring beyond the appointed hour were stricken with paralysis. A miller who attempted to grind his corn, saw, instead of flour, a torrent of blood come forth, and the mill wheel stood still, notwithstanding the strong rush of water. A woman who placed dough in the oven found it raw when taken out, though the oven was very hot. Another who had dough prepared for baking at the ninth hour, but determined to set it aside till Monday, found, the next day, that it had been made into loaves and baked by divine power. A man who baked 577 bread after the ninth hour on Saturday found, when he broke it the next morning, that blood started therefrom. By such absurd and superstitious fabrications did the advocates of Sunday endeavor to establish its sacredness. (See Roger de Hoveden, *Annals,* vol. 2, pp. 528-530.)

In Scotland, as in England, a greater regard for Sunday was secured by uniting with it a portion of the ancient Sabbath. But the time required to be kept holy varied. An edict from the king of Scotland declared that "Saturday from twelve at noon ought to be accounted holy," and that no man, from that time till Monday morning, should engage in worldly business.—Morer, pages 290, 291.

But notwithstanding all the efforts to establish Sunday sacredness, papists themselves publicly confessed the divine authority of the Sabbath and the human origin of the institution by which it had been supplanted. In the sixteenth century a papal council plainly declared: "Let all Christians remember that the seventh day was consecrated by God, and hath been received and observed, not only by the Jews, but by all others who pretend to worship God; though we Christians have changed their Sabbath into the Lord's Day."—*Ibid.,* pages 281, 282. Those who were tampering with the divine law were not ignorant of the character of their work. They were deliberately setting themselves above God.

A striking illustration of Rome's policy toward those who disagree with her was given in the long and bloody persecution of the Waldenses, some of whom were observers of the Sabbath. Others suffered in a similar manner

for their fidelity to the fourth commandment. The history of the churches of Ethiopia and Abyssinia is especially significant. Amid the gloom of the Dark Ages, the Christians of Central Africa were lost sight of and forgotten by the world, and for many centuries they enjoyed freedom in the exercise of their faith. But at last Rome learned of their existence, and the emperor of Abyssinia was soon beguiled into an acknowledgment of the pope as the vicar of Christ. Other concessions followed. An edict 578 was issued forbidding the observance of the Sabbath under the severest penalties. (See Michael Geddes, *Church History of Ethiopia,* pages 311, 312.) But papal tyranny soon became a yoke so galling that the Abyssinians determined to break it from their necks. After a terrible struggle the Romanists were banished from their dominions, and the ancient faith was restored. The churches rejoiced in their freedom, and they never forgot the lesson they had learned concerning the deception, the fanaticism, and the despotic power of Rome. Within their solitary realm they were content to remain, unknown to the rest of Christendom.

The churches of Africa held the Sabbath as it was held by the papal church before her complete apostasy. While they kept the seventh day in obedience to the commandment of God, they abstained from labor on the Sunday in conformity to the custom of the church. Upon obtaining supreme power, Rome had trampled upon the Sabbath of God to exalt her own; but the churches of Africa, hidden for nearly a thousand years, did not share in this apostasy. When brought under the sway of Rome, they were forced to set aside the true and exalt the false sabbath; but no sooner had they regained their independence than they returned to obedience to the fourth commandment. (See Appendix.)

These records of the past clearly reveal the enmity of Rome toward the true Sabbath and its defenders, and the means which she employs to honor the institution of her creating. The word of God teaches that these scenes are to be repeated as Roman Catholics and Protestants shall unite for the exaltation of the Sunday.

The prophecy of Revelation 13 declares that the power represented by the beast with lamblike horns shall cause "the earth and them which dwell therein" to worship the papacy—there symbolized by the beast "like unto a leopard." The beast with two horns is also to say "to them that dwell on the earth, that they should make an image to the beast;" and, furthermore, it is to 579 command all, "both small and great, rich and poor, free and bond," to receive the mark of the beast. Revelation 13:11-16. It has been shown that the United States is the power represented by the beast with lamblike horns, and that this prophecy will be fulfilled when the United States shall enforce Sunday observance, which

Rome claims as the special acknowledgment of her supremacy. But in this homage to the papacy the United States will not be alone. The influence of Rome in the countries that once acknowledged her dominion is still far from being destroyed. And prophecy foretells a restoration of her power. "I saw one of his heads as it were wounded to death; and his deadly wound was healed: and all the world wondered after the beast." Verse 3. The infliction of the deadly wound points to the downfall of the papacy in 1798. After this, says the prophet, "his deadly wound was healed: and all the world wondered after the beast." Paul states plainly that the "man of sin" will continue until the second advent. 2 Thessalonians 2:3-8. To the very close of time he will carry forward the work of deception. And the revelator declares, also referring to the papacy: "All that dwell upon the earth shall worship him, whose names are not written in the book of life." Revelation 13:8. In both the Old and the New World, the papacy will receive homage in the honor paid to the Sunday institution, that rests solely upon the authority of the Roman Church.

Since the middle of the nineteenth century, students of prophecy in the United States have presented this testimony to the world. In the events now taking place is seen a rapid advance toward the fulfillment of the prediction. With Protestant teachers there is the same claim of divine authority for Sundaykeeping, and the same lack of Scriptural evidence, as with the papal leaders who fabricated miracles to supply the place of a command from God. The assertion that God's judgments are visited upon men for their violation of the Sunday-sabbath, will be repeated; already it is beginning to be urged. And a movement to enforce Sunday observance is fast gaining ground.

Marvelous in her shrewdness and cunning is the Roman Church. She can read what is to be. She bides her time, seeing that the Protestant churches are paying her homage in their acceptance of the false sabbath and that they are preparing to enforce it by the very means which she herself employed in bygone days. Those who reject the light of truth will yet seek the aid of this self-styled infallible power to exalt an institution that originated with her. How readily she will come to the help of Protestants in this work it is not difficult to conjecture. Who understands better than the papal leaders how to deal with those who are disobedient to the church?

The Roman Catholic Church, with all its ramifications throughout the world, forms one vast organization under the control, and designed to serve the interests, of the papal see. Its millions of communicants, in every country on the globe, are instructed to hold themselves as bound in allegiance to the pope. Whatever their nationality or their government, they are to regard the authority of the church as above all other. Though they may take the oath pledging their loyalty to the state, yet back of this lies the vow of obedience to Rome, absolving them from every pledge inimical to her interests.

History testifies of her artful and persistent efforts to insinuate herself into the affairs of nations; and having gained a foothold, to further her own aims, even at the ruin of princes and people. In the year 1204, Pope Innocent III extracted from Peter II, king of Arragon, the following extraordinary oath: "I, Peter, king of Arragonians, profess and promise to be ever faithful and obedient to my lord, Pope Innocent, to his Catholic successors, and the Roman Church, and faithfully to preserve my kingdom in his obedience, defending the Catholic faith, and persecuting heretical pravity."—John Dowling, The History of Romanism, b. 5, ch. 6, sec. 55. This is in harmony with the claims regarding the power of the Roman pontiff "that it is lawful for him to depose emperors" and "that he can absolve subjects from their allegiance to unrighteous rulers."—Mosheim, b. 3, cent. 11, pt. 2, ch. 2, sec. 9, note 17. (See also Appendix.)

And let it be remembered, it is the boast of Rome that she never changes. The principles of Gregory VII and Innocent III are still the principles of the Roman Catholic Church. And had she but the power, she would put them in practice with as much vigor now as in past centuries. Protestants little know what they are doing when they propose to accept the aid of Rome in the work of Sunday exaltation. While they are bent upon the accomplishment of their purpose, Rome is aiming to re-establish her power, to recover her lost supremacy. Let the principle once be established in the United States that the church may employ or control the power of the state; that religious observances may be enforced by secular laws; in short, that the authority of church and state is to dominate the conscience, and the triumph of Rome in this country is assured.

God's word has given warning of the impending danger; let this be unheeded, and the Protestant world will learn what the purposes of Rome really are, only when it is too late to escape the snare. She is silently growing into power. Her doctrines are exerting their influence in legislative halls, in the churches, and in the hearts of men. She is piling up her lofty and massive structures in the secret recesses of which her former persecutions will be repeated. Stealthily and unsuspectedly she is strengthening her forces to further her own ends when the time shall come for her to strike. All that she desires is vantage ground, and this is already being given her. We shall soon see and shall feel what the purpose of the Roman element is.

Whoever shall believe and obey the word of God will thereby incur reproach and persecution.

582

36

The Impending Conflict

From the very beginning of the great controversy in heaven it has been Satan's purpose to overthrow the law of God. It was to accomplish this that he entered upon his rebellion against the Creator, and though he was cast out of heaven he has continued the same warfare upon the earth. To deceive men, and thus lead them to transgress God's law, is the object which he has steadfastly pursued. Whether this be accomplished by casting aside the law altogether, or by rejecting one of its precepts, the result will be ultimately the same. He that offends "in one point," manifests contempt for the whole law; his influence and example are on the side of transgression; he becomes "guilty of all." James 2:10.

In seeking to cast contempt upon the divine statutes, Satan has perverted the doctrines of the Bible, and errors have thus become incorporated into the faith of thousands who profess to believe the Scriptures. The last great conflict between truth and error is but the final struggle of the long-standing controversy concerning the law of God. Upon this battle we are now entering—a battle between the laws of men and the precepts of Jehovah, between the religion of the Bible and the religion of fable and tradition.

The agencies which will unite against truth and righteousness in this contest are now actively at work. God's holy word, which has been 583 handed down to us at such a cost of suffering and blood, is but little valued. The Bible is within the reach of all, but there are few who really accept it as the guide of life. Infidelity prevails to an alarming extent, not in the world merely, but in the church. Many have come to deny doctrines which are the very pillars of the Christian faith. The great facts of creation as presented by the inspired writers, the fall of man, the atonement, and the perpetuity of the law of God, are practically rejected, wholly or in part, by a large share of the professedly Christian world. Thousands who pride themselves upon their wisdom and independence regard it as an evidence of weakness to place implicit confidence in the Bible; they think it a proof of superior talent and learning to cavil at the Scriptures and to spiritualize and explain away their most important truths. Many ministers are teaching their people, and many professors and teachers are instructing their students, that the law of God has been changed or abrogated; and those who

regard its requirements as still valid, to be literally obeyed, are thought to be deserving only of ridicule or contempt.

In rejecting the truth, men reject its Author. In trampling upon the law of God, they deny the authority of the Lawgiver. It is as easy to make an idol of false doctrines and theories as to fashion an idol of wood or stone. By misrepresenting the attributes of God, Satan leads men to conceive of Him in a false character. With many, a philosophical idol is enthroned in the place of Jehovah; while the living God, as He is revealed in His word, in Christ, and in the works of creation, is worshiped by but few. Thousands deify nature while they deny the God of nature. Though in a different form, idolatry exists in the Christian world today as verily as it existed among ancient Israel in the days of Elijah. The god of many professedly wise men, of philosophers, poets, politicians, journalists—the god of polished fashionable circles, of many colleges and universities, even of some theological institutions—is little better than Baal, the sun-god of Phoenicia.

No error accepted by the Christian world 584 strikes more boldly against the authority of Heaven, none is more directly opposed to the dictates of reason, none is more pernicious in its results, than the modern doctrine, so rapidly gaining ground, that God's law is no longer binding upon men. Every nation has its laws, which command respect and obedience; no government could exist without them; and can it be conceived that the Creator of the heavens and the earth has no law to govern the beings He has made? Suppose that prominent ministers were publicly to teach that the statutes which govern their land and protect the rights of its citizens were not obligatory—that they restricted the liberties of the people, and therefore ought not to be obeyed; how long would such men be tolerated in the pulpit? But is it a graver offense to disregard the laws of states and nations than to trample upon those divine precepts which are the foundation of all government?

It would be far more consistent for nations to abolish their statutes, and permit the people to do as they please, than for the Ruler of the universe to annul His law, and leave the world without a standard to condemn the guilty or justify the obedient. Would we know the result of making void the law of God? The experiment has been tried. Terrible were the scenes enacted in France when atheism became the controlling power. It was then demonstrated to the world that to throw off the restraints which God has imposed is to accept the rule of the cruelest of tyrants. When the standard of righteousness is set aside, the way is open for the prince of evil to establish his power in the earth.

Wherever the divine precepts are rejected, sin ceases to appear sinful or righteousness desir-

able. Those who refuse to submit to the government of God are wholly unfitted to govern themselves. Through their pernicious teachings the spirit of insubordination is implanted in the hearts of children and youth, who are naturally impatient of control; and a lawless, licentious state of society results. While scoffing at the credulity of those who obey the requirements of
585 God, the multitudes eagerly accept the delusions of Satan. They give the rein to lust and practice the sins which have called down judgments upon the heathen.

Those who teach the people to regard lightly the commandments of God sow disobedience to reap disobedience. Let the restraint imposed by the divine law be wholly cast aside, and human laws would soon be disregarded. Because God forbids dishonest practices, coveting, lying, and defrauding, men are ready to trample upon His statutes as a hindrance to their worldly prosperity; but the results of banishing these precepts would be such as they do not anticipate. If the law were not binding, why should any fear to transgress? Property would no longer be safe. Men would obtain their neighbor's possessions by violence, and the strongest would become richest. Life itself would not be respected. The marriage vow would no longer stand as a sacred bulwark to protect the family. He who had the power, would, if he desired, take his neighbor's wife by violence. The fifth commandment would be set aside with the fourth. Children would not shrink from taking the life of their parents if by so doing they could obtain the desire of their corrupt hearts. The civilized world would become a horde of robbers and assassins; and peace, rest, and happiness would be banished from the earth.

Already the doctrine that men are released from obedience to God's requirements has weakened the force of moral obligation and opened the floodgates of iniquity upon the world. Lawlessness, dissipation, and corruption are sweeping in upon us like an overwhelming tide. In the family, Satan is at work. His banner waves, even in professedly Christian households. There is envy, evil surmising, hypocrisy, estrangement, emulation, strife, betrayal of sacred trusts, indulgence of lust. The whole system of religious principles and doctrines, which should form the foundation and framework of social life, seems to be a tottering mass, ready to fall to ruin. The vilest of criminals, when thrown into prison for their offenses, are often
586 made the recipients of gifts and attentions as if they had attained an enviable distinction. Great publicity is given to their character and crimes. The press publishes the revolting details of vice, thus initiating others into the practice of fraud, robbery, and murder; and Satan exults in the success of his hellish schemes. The infatuation of vice, the wanton taking of life, the terrible

increase of intemperance and iniquity of every order and degree, should arouse all who fear God, to inquire what can be done to stay the tide of evil.

Courts of justice are corrupt. Rulers are actuated by desire for gain and love of sensual pleasure. Intemperance has beclouded the faculties of many so that Satan has almost complete control of them. Jurists are perverted, bribed, deluded. Drunkenness and revelry, passion, envy, dishonesty of every sort, are represented among those who administer the laws. "Justice standeth afar off: for truth is fallen in the street, and equity cannot enter." Isaiah 59:14.

The iniquity and spiritual darkness that prevailed under the supremacy of Rome were the inevitable result of her suppression of the Scriptures; but where is to be found the cause of the widespread infidelity, the rejection of the law of God, and the consequent corruption, under the full blaze of gospel light in an age of religious freedom? Now that Satan can no longer keep the world under his control by withholding the Scriptures, he resorts to other means to accomplish the same object. To destroy faith in the Bible serves his purpose as well as to destroy the Bible itself. By introducing the belief that God's law is not binding, he as effectually leads men to transgress as if they were wholly ignorant of its precepts. And now, as in former ages, he has worked through the church to further his designs. The religious organizations of the day have refused to listen to unpopular truths plainly brought to view in the Scriptures, and in combating them they have adopted interpretations and taken positions which have sown broadcast the seeds of skepticism. Clinging to the papal error of natural immortality and man's con- 587 sciousness in death, they have rejected the only defense against the delusions of spiritualism. The doctrine of eternal torment has led many to disbelieve the Bible. And as the claims of the fourth commandment are urged upon the people, it is found that the observance of the seventh-day Sabbath is enjoined; and as the only way to free themselves from a duty which they are unwilling to perform, many popular teachers declare that the law of God is no longer binding. Thus they cast away the law and the Sabbath together. As the work of Sabbath reform extends, this rejection of the divine law to avoid the claims of the fourth commandment will become well-nigh universal. The teachings of religious leaders have opened the door to infidelity, to spiritualism, and to contempt for God's holy law; and upon these leaders rests a fearful responsibility for the iniquity that exists in the Christian world.

Yet this very class put forth the claim that the fast-spreading corruption is largely attributable to the desecration of the so-called "Christian sabbath," and that the enforcement of Sunday observance would greatly improve the morals of society. This claim is especially urged in America, where the doctrine of the true Sabbath has been most widely preached. Here the temperance work, one of the most prominent and important of moral reforms, is often combined with the Sunday movement, and the advocates of the latter represent themselves as laboring to promote the highest interest of society; and those who refuse to unite with them are denounced as the enemies of temperance and reform. But the fact that a movement to establish error is connected with a work which is in itself good, is not an argument in favor of the error. We may disguise poison by mingling it with wholesome food, but we do not change its nature. On the contrary, it is rendered more dangerous, as it is more likely to be taken unawares. It is one of Satan's devices to combine with falsehood just enough truth to give it plausibility. The leaders of the Sunday movement may 588 advocate reforms which the people need, principles which are in harmony with the Bible; yet while there is with these a requirement which is contrary to God's law, His servants cannot unite with them. Nothing can justify them in setting aside the commandments of God for the precepts of men.

Through the two great errors, the immortality of the soul and Sunday sacredness, Satan will bring the people under his deceptions. While the former lays the foundation of spiritualism, the latter creates a bond of sympathy with Rome. The Protestants of the United States will be foremost in stretching their hands across the gulf to grasp the hand of spiritualism; they will reach over the abyss to clasp hands with the Roman power; and under the influence of this threefold union, this country will follow in the steps of Rome in trampling on the rights of conscience.

As spiritualism more closely imitates the nominal Christianity of the day, it has greater power to deceive and ensnare. Satan himself is converted, after the modern order of things. He will appear in the character of an angel of light. Through the agency of spiritualism, miracles will be wrought, the sick will be healed, and many undeniable wonders will be performed. And as the spirits will profess faith in the Bible, and manifest respect for the institutions of the church, their work will be accepted as a manifestation of divine power.

The line of distinction between professed Christians and the ungodly is now hardly distinguishable. Church members love what the world loves and are ready to join with them, and Satan determines to unite them in one body and thus strengthen his cause by sweeping all into the ranks of spiritualism. Papists, who boast of miracles as a certain sign of the true church, will be readily deceived by this wonder-working power; and Protestants, having cast away the shield of truth, will also be deluded. Papists, Protestants, and worldlings will alike accept the form of godliness without the power, and they will see in this union a grand movement for the 589 conversion of the world and the ushering in of the long-expected millennium.

Through spiritualism, Satan appears as a benefactor of the race, healing the diseases of the people, and professing to present a new and more exalted system of religious faith; but at the same time he works as a destroyer. His temptations are leading multitudes to ruin. Intemperance dethrones reason; sensual indulgence, strife, and bloodshed follow. Satan delights in war, for it excites the worst passions of the soul and then sweeps into eternity its victims steeped in vice and blood. It is his object to incite the nations to war against one another, for he can thus divert the minds of the people from the work of preparation to stand in the day of God.

Satan works through the elements also to garner his harvest of unprepared souls. He has studied the secrets of the laboratories of nature, and he uses all his power to control the elements as far as God allows. When he was suffered to afflict Job, how quickly flocks and herds, servants, houses, children, were swept away, one trouble succeeding another as in a moment. It is God that shields His creatures and hedges them in from the power of the destroyer. But the Christian world have shown contempt for the law of Jehovah; and the Lord will do just what He has declared that He would—He will withdraw His blessings from the earth and remove His protecting care from those who are rebelling against His law and teaching and forcing others to do the same. Satan has control of all whom God does not especially guard. He will favor and prosper some in order to further his own designs, and he will bring trouble upon others and lead men to believe that it is God who is afflicting them.

While appearing to the children of men as a great physician who can heal all their maladies, he will bring disease and disaster, until populous cities are reduced to ruin and desolation. Even now he is at work. In accidents and calamities by sea and by land, in great conflagrations, in fierce tornadoes and terrific hail- 590 storms, in tempests, floods, cyclones, tidal waves, and earthquakes, in every place and in a thousand forms, Satan is exercising his power. He sweeps away the ripening harvest, and famine and distress follow. He imparts to the air a deadly taint, and thousands perish by the pestilence. These visitations are to become more and more frequent and disastrous. Destruction will be upon both man and beast. "The earth mourneth and fadeth away," "the haughty people . . . . do languish. The earth also is defiled under the inhabitants thereof; because they have transgressed the laws, changed the ordinance, broken the everlasting covenant." Isaiah 24:4, 5.

And then the great deceiver will persuade men that those who serve God are causing these evils. The class that have provoked the displeasure of Heaven will charge all their troubles upon those whose obedience to God's commandments is a perpetual reproof to transgressors. It will be declared that men are offending God by the violation of the Sunday sabbath; that this sin has brought calamities which will not cease until Sunday observance shall be strictly enforced; and that those who present the claims of the fourth commandment, thus destroying reverence for Sunday, are troublers of the people, preventing their restoration to divine favor and temporal prosperity. Thus the accusation urged of old against the servant of God will be repeated and upon grounds equally well established: "And it came to pass, when Ahab saw Elijah, that Ahab said unto him, Art thou he that troubleth Israel? And he answered, I have not troubled Israel; but thou, and thy father's house, in that ye have forsaken the commandments of the Lord, and thou hast followed Baalim." 1 Kings 18:17, 18. As the wrath of the people shall be excited by false charges, they will pursue a course toward God's ambassadors very similar to that which apostate Israel pursued toward Elijah.

591   The miracle-working power manifested through spiritualism will exert its influence against those who choose to obey God rather than men. Communications from the spirits will declare that God has sent them to convince the rejecters of Sunday of their error, affirming that the laws of the land should be obeyed as the law of God. They will lament the great wickedness in the world and second the testimony of religious teachers that the degraded state of morals is caused by the desecration of Sunday. Great will be the indignation excited against all who refuse to accept their testimony.

Satan's policy in this final conflict with God's people is the same that he employed in the opening of the great controversy in heaven. He professed to be seeking to promote the stability of the divine government, while secretly bending every effort to secure its overthrow. And the very work which he was thus endeavoring to accomplish he charged upon the loyal angels. The same policy of deception has marked the history of the Roman Church. It has professed to act as the vicegerent of Heaven, while seeking to exalt itself above God and to change His law. Under the rule of Rome, those who suffered death for their fidelity to the gospel were denounced as evildoers; they were declared to be in league with Satan; and every possible means was employed to cover them with reproach, to cause them to appear in the eyes of the people and even to themselves as the

vilest of criminals. So it will be now. While Satan seeks to destroy those who honor God's law, he will cause them to be accused as lawbreakers, as men who are dishonoring God and bringing judgments upon the world.

God never forces the will or the conscience; but Satan's constant resort—to gain control of those whom he cannot otherwise seduce—is compulsion by cruelty. Through fear or force he endeavors to rule the conscience and to secure homage to himself. To accomplish this, he works through both religious and secular authorities, moving them to the enforcement of human laws in defiance of the law of God.

Those who honor the Bible Sabbath will be   592 denounced as enemies of law and order, as breaking down the moral restraints of society, causing anarchy and corruption, and calling down the judgments of God upon the earth. Their conscientious scruples will be pronounced obstinacy, stubbornness, and contempt of authority. They will be accused of disaffection toward the government. Ministers who deny the obligation of the divine law will present from the pulpit the duty of yielding obedience to the civil authorities as ordained of God. In legislative halls and courts of justice, commandment keepers will be misrepresented and condemned. A false coloring will be given to their words; the worst construction will be put upon their motives.

As the Protestant churches reject the clear, Scriptural arguments in defense of God's law, they will long to silence those whose faith they cannot overthrow by the Bible. Though they blind their own eyes to the fact, they are now adopting a course which will lead to the persecution of those who conscientiously refuse to do what the rest of the Christian world are doing, and acknowledge the claims of the papal sabbath.

The dignitaries of church and state will unite to bribe, persuade, or compel all classes to honor the Sunday. The lack of divine authority will be supplied by oppressive enactments. Political corruption is destroying love of justice and regard for truth; and even in free America, rulers and legislators, in order to secure public favor, will yield to the popular demand for a law enforcing Sunday observance. Liberty of conscience, which has cost so great a sacrifice, will no longer be respected. In the soon-coming conflict we shall see exemplified the prophet's words: "The dragon was wroth with the woman, and went to make war with the remnant of her seed, which keep the commandments of God, and have the testimony of Jesus Christ." Revelation 12:17.

593

37

The Scriptures a Safeguard

"To the law and to the testimony: if they speak not according to this word, it is because there is no light in them." Isaiah 8:20. The people of God are directed to the Scriptures as their safeguard against the influence of false teachers and the delusive power of spirits of darkness. Satan employs every possible device to prevent men from obtaining a knowledge of the Bible; for its plain utterances reveal his deceptions. At every revival of God's work the prince of evil is aroused to more intense activity; he is now putting forth his utmost efforts for a final struggle against Christ and His followers. The last great delusion is soon to open before us. Antichrist is to perform his marvelous works in our sight. So closely will the counterfeit resemble the true that it will be impossible to distinguish between them except by the Holy Scriptures. By their testimony every statement and every miracle must be tested.

Those who endeavor to obey all the commandments of God will be opposed and derided. They can stand only in God. In order to endure the trial before them, they must understand the will of God as revealed in His word; they can honor Him only as they have a right conception of His character, government, and purposes, and act in accordance with them. None but those who have fortified the mind with the truths of the Bible will stand through 594 the last great conflict. To every soul will come the searching test: Shall I obey God rather than men? The decisive hour is even now at hand. Are our feet planted on the rock of God's immutable word? Are we prepared to stand firm in defense of the commandments of God and the faith of Jesus?

Before His crucifixion the Saviour explained to His disciples that He was to be put to death and to rise again from the tomb, and angels were present to impress His words on minds and hearts. But the disciples were looking for temporal deliverance from the Roman yoke, and they could not tolerate the thought that He in whom all their hopes centered should suffer an ignominious death. The words which they needed to remember were banished from their minds; and when the time of trial came, it found them unprepared. The death of Jesus as fully destroyed their hopes as if He had not forewarned them. So in the prophecies the future is opened before us as plainly as it was opened to the disciples by the words of Christ. The events connected with the close of probation and the work of preparation for the time of trouble, are

clearly presented. But multitudes have no more understanding of these important truths than if they had never been revealed. Satan watches to catch away every impression that would make them wise unto salvation, and the time of trouble will find them unready.

When God sends to men warnings so important that they are represented as proclaimed by holy angels flying in the midst of heaven, He requires every person endowed with reasoning powers to heed the message. The fearful judgments denounced against the worship of the beast and his image (Revelation 14:9-11), should lead all to a diligent study of the prophecies to learn what the mark of the beast is, and how they are to avoid receiving it. But the masses of the people turn away their ears from hearing the truth and are turned unto fables. The apostle Paul declared, looking down to the last days: "The time will come when they will not endure sound doctrine." 2 Timothy 4:3. That 595 time has fully come. The multitudes do not want Bible truth, because it interferes with the desires of the sinful, world-loving heart; and Satan supplies the deceptions which they love.

But God will have a people upon the earth to maintain the Bible, and the Bible only, as the standard of all doctrines and the basis of all reforms. The opinions of learned men, the deductions of science, the creeds or decisions of ecclesiastical councils, as numerous and discordant as are the churches which they represent, the voice of the majority—not one nor all of these should be regarded as evidence for or against any point of religious faith. Before accepting any doctrine or precept, we should demand a plain "Thus saith the Lord" in its support.

Satan is constantly endeavoring to attract attention to man in the place of God. He leads the people to look to bishops, to pastors, to professors of theology, as their guides, instead of searching the Scriptures to learn their duty for themselves. Then, by controlling the minds of these leaders, he can influence the multitudes according to his will.

When Christ came to speak the words of life, the common people heard Him gladly; and many, even of the priests and rulers, believed on Him. But the chief of the priesthood and the leading men of the nation were determined to condemn and repudiate His teachings. Though they were baffled in all their efforts to find accusations against Him, though they could not but feel the influence of the divine power and wisdom attending His words, yet they incased themselves in prejudice; they rejected the clearest evidence of His Messiahship, lest they should be forced to become His disciples. These opponents of Jesus were men whom the people had been taught from infancy to reverence, to whose authority they had been accustomed implicitly to bow. "How is it," they asked, "that our rulers and learned scribes do not believe on Jesus? Would not these pious men receive Him if He were the Christ?" It was the influence of such teachers that led the Jewish nation to reject their Redeemer.

The spirit which actuated those priests and rulers is still manifested by many who make a high profession of piety. They refuse to examine the testimony of the Scriptures concerning the special truths for this time. They point to their own numbers, wealth, and popularity, and look with contempt upon the advocates of truth as few, poor, and unpopular, having a faith that separates them from the world.

Christ foresaw that the undue assumption of authority indulged by the scribes and Pharisees would not cease with the dispersion of the Jews. He had a prophetic view of the work of exalting human authority to rule the conscience, which has been so terrible a curse to the church in all ages. And His fearful denunciations of the scribes and Pharisees, and His warnings to the people not to follow these blind leaders, were placed on record as an admonition to future generations.

The Roman Church reserves to the clergy the right to interpret the Scriptures. On the ground that ecclesiastics alone are competent to explain God's word, it is withheld from the common people. *Though the Reformation gave the Scriptures to all, yet the selfsame principle which was maintained by Rome prevents multitudes in Protestant churches from searching the Bible for themselves. They are taught to accept its teachings *as interpreted by the church;* and there are thousands who dare receive nothing, however plainly revealed in Scripture, that is contrary to their creed or the established teaching of their church.

Notwithstanding the Bible is full of warnings against false teachers, many are ready thus to commit the keeping of their souls to the clergy. There are today thousands of professors of religion who can give no other reason for points of faith which they hold than that they were so instructed by their religious leaders. They pass by the Saviour's teachings almost unnoticed, and place implicit confidence in the words of the ministers. But are ministers infallible? How can we trust our souls to their guidance unless we know from God's word that they are light bearers? A lack of moral courage to step aside from the beaten track of the world leads many to follow in the steps of learned men; and by their reluctance to investigate for themselves, they are becoming hopelessly fastened in the chains of error. They see that the truth for this time is plainly brought to view in the Bible; and they feel the power of the Holy Spirit attending its proclamation; yet they allow the opposition of the clergy to turn them from the light.

Though reason and conscience are convinced, these deluded souls dare not think differently from the minister; and their individual judgment, their eternal interests, are sacrificed to the unbelief, the pride and prejudice, of another.

Many are the ways by which Satan works through human influence to bind his captives. He secures multitudes to himself by attaching them by the silken cords of affection to those who are enemies of the cross of Christ. Whatever this attachment may be, parental, filial, conjugal, or social, the effect is the same; the opposers of truth exert their power to control the conscience, and the souls held under their sway have not sufficient courage or independence to obey their own convictions of duty.

The truth and the glory of God are inseparable; it is impossible for us, with the Bible within our reach, to honor God by erroneous opinions. Many claim that it matters not what one believes, if his life is only right. But the life is molded by the faith. If light and truth is within our reach, and we neglect to improve the privilege of hearing and seeing it, we virtually reject it; we are choosing darkness rather than light.

"There is a way that seemeth right unto a man, but the end thereof are the ways of death." Proverbs 16:25. Ignorance is no excuse for error or sin, when there is every opportunity to know the will of God. A man is traveling and comes to a place where there are several roads and a guideboard indicating where each one leads. If he disregards the guideboard, and takes whichever road seems to him to be right, he may be ever so sincere, but will in all probability find himself on the wrong road.

God has given us His word that we may become acquainted with its teachings and know for ourselves what He requires of us. When the lawyer came to Jesus with the inquiry, "What shall I do to inherit eternal life?" the Saviour referred him to the Scriptures, saying: "What is written in the law? how readest thou?" Ignorance will not excuse young or old, nor release them from the punishment due for the transgression of God's law; because there is in their hands a faithful presentation of that law and of its principles and claims. It is not enough to have good intentions; it is not enough to do what a man thinks is right or what the minister tells him is right. His soul's salvation is at stake, and he should search the Scriptures for himself. However strong may be his convictions, however confident he may be that the minister knows what is truth, this is not his foundation. He has a chart pointing out every waymark on the heavenward journey, and he ought not to guess at anything.

It is the first and highest duty of every rational being to learn from the Scriptures what is truth, and then to walk in the light and encourage others to follow his example. We should day by day study the Bible diligently, weighing every thought and comparing scripture with scripture. With divine help we are to form our opinions for ourselves as we are to answer for ourselves before God.

The truths most plainly revealed in the Bible have been involved in doubt and darkness by learned men, who, with a pretense of great wisdom, teach that the Scriptures have a mystical, a secret, spiritual meaning not apparent in the language employed. These men are false teachers. It was to such a class that Jesus declared: "Ye know not the Scriptures, neither the power of God." Mark 12:24. The language of the Bible should be explained according to its obvious meaning, unless a symbol or figure is employed. Christ has given the promise: "If any man will do His will, he shall know of the doctrine." John 7:17. If men would but take the Bible as it reads, if there were no false teachers to mislead and confuse their minds, a work would be accomplished that would make angels glad and that would bring into the fold of Christ thousands upon thousands who are now wandering in error.

We should exert all the powers of the mind in the study of the Scriptures and should task the understanding to comprehend, as far as mortals can, the deep things of God; yet we must not forget that the docility and submission of a child is the true spirit of the learner. Scriptural difficulties can never be mastered by the same methods that are employed in grappling with philosophical problems. We should not engage in the study of the Bible with that self-reliance with which so many enter the domains of science, but with a prayerful dependence upon God and a sincere desire to learn His will. We must come with a humble and teachable spirit to obtain knowledge from the great I AM. Otherwise, evil angels will so blind our minds and harden our hearts that we shall not be impressed with the truth.

Many a portion of Scripture which learned men pronounce a mystery, or pass over as unimportant, is full of comfort and instruction to him who has been taught in the school of Christ. One reason why many theologians have no clearer understanding of God's word is, they close their eyes to truths which they do not wish to practice. An understanding of Bible truth depends not so much on the power of intellect brought to the search as on the singleness of purpose, the earnest longing after righteousness.

The Bible should never be studied without prayer. The Holy Spirit alone can cause us to feel the importance of those things easy to be understood, or prevent us from wresting truths difficult of comprehension. It is the office of heavenly angels to prepare the heart so to comprehend God's word that we shall be charmed with its beauty, admonished by its warnings, or

animated and strengthened by its promises. We should make the psalmist's petition our own: "Open Thou mine eyes, that I may behold wondrous things out of Thy law." Psalm 119:18. Temptations often appear irresistible because, through neglect of prayer and the study of the Bible, the tempted one cannot readily remember God's promises and meet Satan with the Scripture weapons. But angels are round about those who are willing to be taught in divine things; and in the time of great necessity they will bring to their remembrance the very truths which are needed. Thus "when the enemy shall come in like a flood, the Spirit of the Lord shall lift up a standard against him." Isaiah 59:19.

Jesus promised His disciples: "The Comforter, which is the Holy Ghost, whom the Father will send in My name, He shall teach you all things, and bring all things to your remembrance, whatsoever I have said unto you." John 14:26. But the teachings of Christ must previously have been stored in the mind in order for the Spirit of God to bring them to our remembrance in the time of peril. "Thy word have I hid in mine heart," said David, "that I might not sin against Thee." Psalm 119:11.

All who value their eternal interests should be on their guard against the inroads of skepticism. The very pillars of truth will be assailed. It is impossible to keep beyond the reach of the sarcasms and sophisms, the insidious and pestilent teachings, of modern infidelity. Satan adapts his temptations to all classes. He assails the illiterate with a jest or sneer, while he meets the educated with scientific objections and philosophical reasoning, alike calculated to excite distrust or contempt of the Scriptures. Even youth of little experience presume to insinuate doubts concerning the fundamental principles of Christianity. And this youthful infidelity, shallow as it is, has its influence. Many are thus led to jest at the faith of their fathers and to do despite to the Spirit of grace. Hebrews 10:29. Many a life that promised to be an honor to God and a blessing to the world has been blighted by the foul breath of infidelity. All who trust to the boastful decisions of human reason and imagine that they can explain divine mysteries and arrive at truth unaided by the wisdom of God are entangled in the snare of Satan.

We are living in the most solemn period of this world's history. The destiny of earth's teeming multitudes is about to be decided. Our own future well-being and also the salvation of other souls depend upon the course which we now pursue. We need to be guided by the Spirit of truth. Every follower of Christ should earnestly inquire: "Lord, what wilt Thou have me to do?" We need to humble ourselves before the Lord, with fasting and prayer, and to meditate much upon His word, especially upon the scenes of the judgment. We should now seek a deep and living experience in the things of God. We have not a moment to lose. Events of vital importance are taking place around us; we are on Satan's enchanted ground. Sleep not, sentinels of God; the foe is lurking near, ready at any moment, should you become lax and drowsy, to spring upon you and make you his prey.

Many are deceived as to their true condition before God. They congratulate themselves upon the wrong acts which they do not commit, and forget to enumerate the good and noble deeds which God requires of them, but which they have neglected to perform. It is not enough that they are trees in the garden of God. They are to answer His expectation by bearing fruit. He holds them accountable for their failure to accomplish all the good which they could have done, through His grace strengthening them. In the books of heaven they are registered as cumberers of the ground. Yet the case of even this class is not utterly hopeless. With those who have slighted God's mercy and abused His grace, the heart of long-suffering love yet pleads. "Wherefore He saith, Awake thou that sleepest, and arise from the dead, and Christ shall give thee light. See then that ye walk circumspectly, . . . redeeming the time, because the days are evil." Ephesians 5:14-16.

When the testing time shall come, those who have made God's word their rule of life will be revealed. In summer there is no noticeable difference between evergreens and other trees; but when the blasts of winter come, the evergreens remain unchanged, while other trees are stripped of their foliage. So the falsehearted professor may not now be distinguished from the real Christian, but the time is just upon us when the difference will be apparent. Let opposition arise, let bigotry and intolerance again bear sway, let persecution be kindled, and the half-hearted and hypocritical will waver and yield the faith; but the true Christian will stand firm as a rock, his faith stronger, his hope brighter, than in days of prosperity.

Says the psalmist: "Thy testimonies are my meditation." "Through Thy precepts I get understanding: therefore I hate every false way." Psalm 119:99, 104.

"Happy is the man that findeth wisdom." "He shall be as a tree planted by the waters, and that spreadeth out her roots by the river, and shall not see when heat cometh, but her leaf shall be green; and shall not be careful in the year of drought, neither shall cease from yielding fruit." Proverbs 3:13; Jeremiah 17:8.

38

The Final Warning

"I saw another angel come down from heaven, having great power; and the earth was lightened with his glory. And he cried mightily with a strong voice, saying, Babylon the great is fallen, is fallen, and is become the habitation of devils, and the hold of every foul spirit, and a cage of every unclean and hateful bird." "And I heard another voice from heaven, saying, Come out of her, My people, that ye be not partakers of her sins, and that ye receive not of her plagues." Revelation 18:1, 2, 4.

This scripture points forward to a time when the announcement of the fall of Babylon, as made by the second angel of Revelation 14 (verse 8), is to be repeated, with the additional mention of the corruptions which have been entering the various organizations that constitute Babylon, since that message was first given, in the summer of 1844. A terrible condition of the religious world is here described. With every rejection of truth the minds of the people will become darker, their hearts more stubborn, until they are entrenched in an infidel hardihood. In defiance of the warnings which God has given, they will continue to trample upon one of the precepts of the Decalogue, until they are led to persecute those who hold it sacred. Christ is set at nought in the contempt placed upon His word and His people. As the teachings of spiritualism are accepted by the churches, the restraint imposed upon the carnal heart is removed, and the profession of religion will become a cloak to conceal the basest iniquity. A belief in spiritual manifestations opens the door to seducing spirits and doctrines of devils, and thus the influence of evil angels will be felt in the churches.

Of Babylon, at the time brought to view in this prophecy, it is declared: "Her sins have reached unto heaven, and God hath remembered her iniquities." Revelation 18:5. She has filled up the measure of her guilt, and destruction is about to fall upon her. But God still has a people in Babylon; and before the visitation of His judgments these faithful ones must be called out, that they partake not of her sins and "receive not of her plagues." Hence the movement symbolized by the angel coming down from heaven, lightening the earth with his glory and crying mightily with a strong voice, announcing the sins of Babylon. In connection with his message the call is heard: "Come out of her, My people." These announcements, uniting with the third angel's message, constitute the final warning to be given to the inhabitants of the earth.

Fearful is the issue to which the world is to be brought. The powers of earth, uniting to war against the commandments of God, will decree that "all, both small and great, rich and poor, free and bond" (Revelation 13:16), shall conform to the customs of the church by the observance of the false sabbath. All who refuse compliance will be visited with civil penalties, and it will finally be declared that they are deserving of death. On the other hand, the law of God enjoining the Creator's rest day demands obedience and threatens wrath against all who transgress its precepts.

With the issue thus clearly brought before him, whoever shall trample upon God's law to obey a human enactment receives the mark of the beast; he accepts the sign of allegiance to the power which he chooses to obey instead of God. The warning from heaven is: "If any man worship the beast and his image, and receive his mark in his forehead, or in his hand, the same shall drink of the wine of the wrath of God, which is poured out without mixture into the cup of His indignation." Revelation 14:9, 10.

But not one is made to suffer the wrath of God until the truth has been brought home to his mind and conscience, and has been rejected. There are many who have never had an opportunity to hear the special truths for this time. The obligation of the fourth commandment has never been set before them in its true light. He who reads every heart and tries every motive will leave none who desire a knowledge of the truth, to be deceived as to the issues of the controversy. The decree is not to be urged upon the people blindly. Everyone is to have sufficient light to make his decision intelligently.

The Sabbath will be the great test of loyalty, for it is the point of truth especially controverted. When the final test shall be brought to bear upon men, then the line of distinction will be drawn between those who serve God and those who serve Him not. While the observance of the false sabbath in compliance with the law of the state, contrary to the fourth commandment, will be an avowal of allegiance to a power that is in opposition to God, the keeping of the true Sabbath, in obedience to God's law, is an evidence of loyalty to the Creator. While one class, by accepting the sign of submission to earthly powers, receive the mark of the beast, the other choosing the token of allegiance to divine authority, receive the seal of God.

Heretofore those who presented the truths of the third angel's message have often been regarded as mere alarmists. Their predictions that religious intolerance would gain control in the United States, that church and state would unite to persecute those who keep the commandments of God, have been pronounced groundless and absurd. It has been confidently declared that this land could never become other than what it has been—the defender of religious freedom. But as the question of enforcing Sunday observance is widely agitated, the event so long doubted and disbelieved is seen to be approaching, and the third message will produce an effect which it could not have had before.

In every generation God has sent His servants to rebuke sin, both in the world and in the church. But the people desire smooth things spoken to them, and the pure, unvarnished truth is not acceptable. Many reformers, in entering upon their work, determined to exercise great prudence in attacking the sins of the church and the nation. They hoped, by the example of a pure Christian life, to lead the people back to the doctrines of the Bible. But the Spirit of God came upon them as it came upon Elijah, moving him to rebuke the sins of a wicked king and an apostate people; they could not refrain from preaching the plain utterances of the Bible—doctrines which they had been reluctant to present. They were impelled to zealously declare the truth and the danger which threatened souls. The words which the Lord gave them they uttered, fearless of consequences, and the people were compelled to hear the warning.

Thus the message of the third angel will be proclaimed. As the time comes for it to be given with greatest power, the Lord will work through humble instruments, leading the minds of those who consecrate themselves to His service. The laborers will be qualified rather by the unction of His Spirit than by the training of literary institutions. Men of faith and prayer will be constrained to go forth with holy zeal, declaring the words which God gives them. The sins of Babylon will be laid open. The fearful results of enforcing the observances of the church by civil authority, the inroads of spiritualism, the stealthy but rapid progress of the papal power—all will be unmasked. By these solemn warnings the people will be stirred. Thousands upon thousands will listen who have never heard words like these. In amazement they hear the testimony that Babylon is the church, fallen because of her errors and sins, because of her rejection of the truth sent to her from heaven. As the people go to their former teachers with the eager inquiry, Are these things so? the ministers present fables, prophesy smooth things, to soothe their fears and quiet the awakened conscience. But since many refuse to be satisfied with the mere authority of men and demand a plain "Thus saith the Lord," the popular ministry, like the Pharisees of old, filled with anger as their authority is questioned, will denounce the message as of Satan and stir up the sin-loving multitudes to revile and persecute those who proclaim it.

As the controversy extends into new fields and the minds of the people are called to God's downtrodden law, Satan is astir. The power attending the message will only madden those who oppose it. The clergy will put forth almost superhuman efforts to shut away the light lest it should shine upon their flocks. By every means at their command they will endeavor to suppress the discussion of these vital questions. The church appeals to the strong arm of civil power, and, in this work, papists and Protestants unite. As the movement for Sunday enforcement becomes more bold and decided, the law will be invoked against commandment keepers. They will be threatened with fines and imprisonment, and some will be offered positions of influence, and other rewards and advantages, as inducements to renounce their faith. But their steadfast answer is: "Show us from the word of God our error"—the same plea that was made by Luther under similar circumstances. Those who are arraigned before the courts make a strong vindication of the truth, and some who hear them are led to take their stand to keep all the commandments of God. Thus light will be brought before thousands who otherwise would know nothing of these truths.

608 Conscientious obedience to the word of God will be treated as rebellion. Blinded by Satan, the parent will exercise harshness and severity toward the believing child; the master or mistress will oppress the commandment-keeping servant. Affection will be alienated; children will be disinherited and driven from home. The words of Paul will be literally fulfilled: "All that will live godly in Christ Jesus shall suffer persecution." 2 Timothy 3:12. As the defenders of truth refuse to honor the Sunday-sabbath, some of them will be thrust into prison, some will be exiled, some will be treated as slaves. To human wisdom all this now seems impossible; but as the restraining Spirit of God shall be withdrawn from men, and they shall be under the control of Satan, who hates the divine precepts, there will be strange developments. The heart can be very cruel when God's fear and love are removed.

As the storm approaches, a large class who have professed faith in the third angel's message, but have not been sanctified through obedience to the truth, abandon their position and join the ranks of the opposition. By uniting with the world and partaking of its spirit, they have come to view matters in nearly the same light; and when the test is brought, they are prepared to choose the easy, popular side. Men of talent and pleasing address, who once rejoiced in the truth, employ their powers to deceive and mislead souls. They become the most bitter enemies of their former brethren. When Sabbathkeepers are brought before the courts to answer for their faith, these apostates are the most efficient agents of Satan to misrepresent and accuse them, and by false reports and insinuations to stir up the rulers against them.

In this time of persecution the faith of the Lord's servants will be tried. They have faithfully given the warning, looking to God and to His word alone. God's Spirit, moving upon their hearts, has constrained them to speak. Stimulated with holy zeal, and with the divine impulse 609 strong upon them, they entered upon the performance of their duties without coldly calculating the consequences of speaking to the people the word which the Lord had given them. They have not consulted their temporal interests, nor sought to preserve their reputation or their lives. Yet when the storm of opposition and reproach bursts upon them, some, overwhelmed with consternation, will be ready to exclaim: "Had we foreseen the consequences of our words, we would have held our peace." They are hedged in with difficulties. Satan assails them with fierce temptations. The work which they have undertaken seems far beyond their ability to accomplish. They are threatened with destruction. The enthusiasm which animated them is gone; yet they cannot turn back. Then, feeling their utter helplessness, they flee to the Mighty One for strength. They remember that the words which they have spoken were not theirs, but His who bade them give the warning. God put the truth into their hearts, and they could not forbear to proclaim it.

The same trials have been experienced by men of God in ages past. Wycliffe, Huss, Luther, Tyndale, Baxter, Wesley, urged that all doctrines be brought to the test of the Bible and declared that they would renounce everything which it condemned. Against these men persecution raged with relentless fury; yet they ceased not to declare the truth. Different periods in the history of the church have each been marked by the development of some special truth, adapted to the necessities of God's people at that time. Every new truth has made its way against hatred and opposition; those who were blessed with its light were tempted and tried. The Lord gives a special truth for the people in an emergency. Who dare refuse to publish it? He commands His servants to present the last invitation of mercy to the world. They cannot remain silent, except at the peril of their souls. Christ's ambassadors have nothing to do with 610 consequences. They must perform their duty and leave results with God.

As the opposition rises to a fiercer height, the servants of God are again perplexed; for it seems to them that they have brought the crisis. But conscience and the word of God assure them that their course is right; and although the trials continue, they are strengthened to bear them. The contest grows closer and sharper, but their faith and courage rise with the emergency. Their testimony is: "We dare not tamper with God's word, dividing His holy law; calling one portion essential and another nonessential, to gain the favor of the world. The Lord whom we serve is able to deliver us. Christ has conquered the powers of earth; and shall we be afraid of a world already conquered?"

Persecution in its varied forms is the development of a principle which will exist as long as Satan exists and Christianity has vital power. No man can serve God without enlisting against himself the opposition of the hosts of darkness. Evil angels will assail him, alarmed that his influence is taking the prey from their hands. Evil men, rebuked by his example, will unite with them in seeking to separate him from God by alluring temptations. When these do not succeed, then a compelling power is employed to force the conscience.

But so long as Jesus remains man's intercessor in the sanctuary above, the restraining influence of the Holy Spirit is felt by rulers and people. It still controls to some extent the laws of the land. Were it not for these laws, the condition of the world would be much worse than it now is. While many of our rulers are active agents of Satan, God also has His agents among the leading men of the nation. The enemy moves upon his servants to propose measures that would greatly impede the work of God; but statesmen who fear the Lord are influenced by holy angels to oppose such propositions with unanswerable arguments. Thus a few men will hold in check a powerful current of evil. The opposition of the enemies of truth will be restrained that the third angel's message may do its work. When the final warning shall be given, it will arrest the attention of these leading men through whom the Lord is now working, and some of them will accept it, and will stand with the people of God through the time of trouble.

The angel who unites in the proclamation of the third angel's message is to lighten the whole earth with his glory. A work of world-wide extent and unwonted power is here foretold. The advent movement of 1840-44 was a glorious manifestation of the power of God; the first angel's message was carried to every missionary station in the world, and in some countries there was the greatest religious interest which has been witnessed in any land since the Reformation of the sixteenth century; but these are to be exceeded by the mighty movement under the last warning of the third angel.

The work will be similar to that of the Day of Pentecost. As the "former rain" was given, in the outpouring of the Holy Spirit at the opening of the gospel, to cause the upspringing of the precious seed, so the "latter rain" will be given at its close for the ripening of the harvest. "Then shall we know, if we follow on to know the Lord: His going forth is prepared as the morning; and He shall come unto us as the rain, as the latter and former rain unto the earth." Hosea 6:3. "Be glad then, ye children of Zion, and rejoice in the Lord

your God: for He hath given you the former rain moderately, and He will cause to come down for you the rain, the former rain, and the latter rain." Joel 2:23. "In the last days, saith God, I will pour out of My Spirit upon all flesh." "And it shall come to pass, that whosoever shall call on the name of the Lord shall be saved." Acts 2:17, 21.

The great work of the gospel is not to close with less manifestation of the power of God than marked its opening. The prophecies which were fulfilled in the outpouring of the former rain at the opening of the gospel are again to be fulfilled in the latter rain at its close. Here are "the times of refreshing" to which the apostle Peter looked forward when he said: "Repent ye therefore, and be converted, that your sins may be blotted out, when the times of refreshing shall come from the presence of the Lord; and He shall send Jesus." Acts 3:19, 20.

Servants of God, with their faces lighted up and shining with holy consecration, will hasten from place to place to proclaim the message from heaven. By thousands of voices, all over the earth, the warning will be given. Miracles will be wrought, the sick will be healed, and signs and wonders will follow the believers. Satan also works, with lying wonders, even bringing down fire from heaven in the sight of men. Revelation 13:13. Thus the inhabitants of the earth will be brought to take their stand.

The message will be carried not so much by argument as by the deep conviction of the Spirit of God. The arguments have been presented. The seed has been sown, and now it will spring up and bear fruit. The publications distributed by missionary workers have exerted their influence, yet many whose minds were impressed have been prevented from fully comprehending the truth or from yielding obedience. Now the rays of light penetrate everywhere, the truth is seen in its clearness, and the honest children of God sever the bands which have held them. Family connections, church relations, are powerless to stay them now. Truth is more precious than all besides. Notwithstanding the agencies combined against the truth, a large number take their stand upon the Lord's side.

39

The Time of Trouble

"At that time shall Michael stand up, the great Prince which standeth for the children of thy people: and there shall be a time of trouble, such as never was since there was a nation even to that same time: and at that time thy people shall be delivered, everyone that shall be found written in the book." Daniel 12:1.

When the third angel's message closes,

mercy no longer pleads for the guilty inhabitants of the earth. The people of God have accomplished their work. They have received "the latter rain," "the refreshing from the presence of the Lord," and they are prepared for the trying hour before them. Angels are hastening to and fro in heaven. An angel returning from the earth announces that his work is done; the final test has been brought upon the world, and all who have proved themselves loyal to the divine precepts have received "the seal of the living God." Then Jesus ceases His intercession in the sanctuary above. He lifts His hands and with a loud voice says, "It is done;" and all the angelic host lay off their crowns as He makes the solemn announcement: "He that is unjust, let him be unjust still: and he which is filthy, let him be filthy still: and he that is righteous, let him be righteous still: and he that is holy, let him be holy still." Revelation 22:11. Every case has been decided for life or death. Christ has 614 made the atonement for His people and blotted out their sins. The number of His subjects is made up; "the kingdom and dominion, and the greatness of the kingdom under the whole heaven," is about to be given to the heirs of salvation, and Jesus is to reign as King of kings and Lord of lords.

When He leaves the sanctuary, darkness covers the inhabitants of the earth. In that fearful time the righteous must live in the sight of a holy God without an intercessor. The restraint which has been upon the wicked is removed, and Satan has entire control of the finally impenitent. God's long-suffering has ended. The world has rejected His mercy, despised His love, and trampled upon His law. The wicked have passed the boundary of their probation; the Spirit of God, persistently resisted, has been at last withdrawn. Unsheltered by divine grace, they have no protection from the wicked one. Satan will then plunge the inhabitants of the earth into one great, final trouble. As the angels of God cease to hold in check the fierce winds of human passion, all the elements of strife will be let loose. The whole world will be involved in ruin more terrible than that which came upon Jerusalem of old.

A single angel destroyed all the first-born of the Egyptians and filled the land with mourning. When David offended against God by numbering the people, one angel caused that terrible destruction by which his sin was punished. The same destructive power exercised by holy angels when God commands, will be exercised by evil angels when He permits. There are forces now ready, and only waiting the divine permission, to spread desolation everywhere.

Those who honor the law of God have been accused of bringing judgments upon the world, and they will be regarded as the cause of the fearful convulsions of nature and the strife and bloodshed among men that are filling the earth with woe. The power attending the last warning has enraged the wicked; their anger is kindled against all who have received the message, and 615 Satan will excite to still greater intensity the spirit of hatred and persecution.

When God's presence was finally withdrawn from the Jewish nation, priests and people knew it not. Though under the control of Satan, and swayed by the most horrible and malignant passions, they still regarded themselves as the chosen of God. The ministration in the temple continued; sacrifices were offered upon its polluted altars, and daily the divine blessing was invoked upon a people guilty of the blood of God's dear Son and seeking to slay His ministers and apostles. So when the irrevocable decision of the sanctuary has been pronounced and the destiny of the world has been forever fixed, the inhabitants of the earth will know it not. The forms of religion will be continued by a people from whom the Spirit of God has been finally withdrawn; and the satanic zeal with which the prince of evil will inspire them for the accomplishment of his malignant designs, will bear the semblance of zeal for God.

As the Sabbath has become the special point of controversy throughout Christendom, and religious and secular authorities have combined to enforce the observance of the Sunday, the persistent refusal of a small minority to yield to the popular demand will make them objects of universal execration. It will be urged that the few who stand in opposition to an institution of the church and a law of the state ought not to be tolerated; that it is better for them to suffer than for whole nations to be thrown into confusion and lawlessness. The same argument eighteen hundred years ago was brought against Christ by the "rulers of the people." "It is expedient for us," said the wily Caiaphas, "that one man should die for the people, and that the whole nation perish not." John 11:50. This argument will appear conclusive; and a decree will finally be issued against those who hallow the Sabbath of the fourth commandment, denouncing them as deserving of the severest punishment and giving the people liberty, after a certain time, to 616 put them to death. Romanism in the Old World and apostate Protestantism in the New will pursue a similar course toward those who honor all the divine precepts.

The people of God will then be plunged into those scenes of affliction and distress described by the prophet as the time of Jacob's trouble. "Thus saith the Lord: We have heard a voice of trembling, of fear, and not of peace. . . . All faces are turned into paleness. Alas! for that day is great, so that none is like it: it is even the time of Jacob's trouble; but he shall be saved out of it." Jeremiah 30:5-7.

Jacob's night of anguish, when he wrestled in

prayer for deliverance from the hand of Esau (Genesis 32:24-30), represents the experience of God's people in the time of trouble. Because of the deception practiced to secure his father's blessing, intended for Esau, Jacob had fled for his life, alarmed by his brother's deadly threats. After remaining for many years an exile, he had set out, at God's command, to return with his wives and children, his flocks and herds, to his native country. On reaching the borders of the land, he was filled with terror by the tidings of Esau's approach at the head of a band of warriors, doubtless bent upon revenge. Jacob's company, unarmed and defenseless, seemed about to fall helpless victims of violence and slaughter. And to the burden of anxiety and fear was added the crushing weight of self-reproach, for it was his own sin that had brought this danger. His only hope was in the mercy of God; his only defense must be prayer. Yet he leaves nothing undone on his own part to atone for the wrong to his brother and to avert the threatened danger. So should the followers of Christ, as they approach the time of trouble, make every exertion to place themselves in a proper light before the people, to disarm prejudice, and to avert the danger which threatens liberty of conscience.

Having sent his family away, that they may not witness his distress, Jacob remains alone to 617 intercede with God. He confesses his sin and gratefully acknowledges the mercy of God toward him while with deep humiliation he pleads the covenant made with his fathers and the promises to himself in the night vision at Bethel and in the land of his exile. The crisis in his life has come; everything is at stake. In the darkness and solitude he continues praying and humbling himself before God. Suddenly a hand is laid upon his shoulder. He thinks that an enemy is seeking his life, and with all the energy of despair he wrestles with his assailant. As the day begins to break, the stranger puts forth his superhuman power; at his touch the strong man seems paralyzed, and he falls, a helpless, weeping suppliant, upon the neck of his mysterious antagonist. Jacob knows now that it is the Angel of the covenant with whom he has been in conflict. Though disabled and suffering the keenest pain, he does not relinquish his purpose. Long has he endured perplexity, remorse, and trouble for his sin; now he must have the assurance that it is pardoned. The divine visitant seems about to depart; but Jacob clings to Him, pleading for a blessing. The Angel urges, "Let Me go, for the day breaketh;" but the patriarch exclaims, "I will not let Thee go, except Thou bless me." What confidence, what firmness and perseverance, are here displayed! Had this been a boastful, presumptuous claim, Jacob would have been instantly destroyed; but his was the assurance of one who confesses his weakness

and unworthiness, yet trusts the mercy of a covenant-keeping God.

"He had power over the Angel, and prevailed." Hosea 12:4. Through humiliation, repentance, and self-surrender, this sinful, erring mortal prevailed with the Majesty of heaven. He had fastened his trembling grasp upon the promises of God, and the heart of Infinite Love could not turn away the sinner's plea. As an evidence of his triumph and an encouragement to others to imitate his example, his name was changed from one which was a reminder of his sin, to one that commemorated his victory. And the fact that Jacob had prevailed with God was 618 an assurance that he would prevail with men. He no longer feared to encounter his brother's anger, for the Lord was his defense.

Satan had accused Jacob before the angels of God, claiming the right to destroy him because of his sin; he had moved upon Esau to march against him; and during the patriarch's long night of wrestling, Satan endeavored to force upon him a sense of his guilt in order to discourage him and break his hold upon God. Jacob was driven almost to despair; but he knew that without help from heaven he must perish. He had sincerely repented of his great sin, and he appealed to the mercy of God. He would not be turned from his purpose, but held fast the Angel and urged his petition with earnest, agonizing cries until he prevailed.

As Satan influenced Esau to march against Jacob, so he will stir up the wicked to destroy God's people in the time of trouble. And as he accused Jacob, he will urge his accusations against the people of God. He numbers the world as his subjects; but the little company who keep the commandments of God are resisting his supremacy. If he could blot them from the earth, his triumph would be complete. He sees that holy angels are guarding them, and he infers that their sins have been pardoned; but he does not know that their cases have been decided in the sanctuary above. He has an accurate knowledge of the sins which he has tempted them to commit, and he presents these before God in the most exaggerated light, representing this people to be just as deserving as himself of exclusion from the favor of God. He declares that the Lord cannot in justice forgive their sins and yet destroy him and his angels. He claims them as his prey and demands that they be given into his hands to destroy.

As Satan accuses the people of God on account of their sins, the Lord permits him to try them to the uttermost. Their confidence in God, their faith and firmness, will be severely tested. As they review the past, their hopes sink; for in 619 their whole lives they can see little good. They are fully conscious of their weakness and unworthiness. Satan endeavors to terrify them with the thought that their cases are hopeless, that the stain of their defilement will never be washed away. He hopes so to destroy their faith that they will yield to his temptations and turn from their allegiance to God.

Though God's people will be surrounded by enemies who are bent upon their destruction, yet the anguish which they suffer is not a dread of persecution for the truth's sake; they fear that every sin has not been repented of, and that through some fault in themselves they will fail to realize the fulfillment of the Saviour's promise: I "will keep thee from the hour of temptation, which shall come upon all the world." Revelation 3:10. If they could have the assurance of pardon they would not shrink from torture or death; but should they prove unworthy, and lose their lives because of their own defects of character, then God's holy name would be reproached.

On every hand they hear the plottings of treason and see the active working of rebellion; and there is aroused within them an intense desire, an earnest yearning of soul, that this great apostasy may be terminated and the wickedness of the wicked may come to an end. But while they plead with God to stay the work of rebellion, it is with a keen sense of self-reproach that they themselves have no more power to resist and urge back the mighty tide of evil. They feel that had they always employed all their ability in the service of Christ, going forward from strength to strength, Satan's forces would have less power to prevail against them.

They afflict their souls before God, pointing to their past repentance of their many sins, and pleading the Saviour's promise: "Let him take hold of My strength, that he may make peace with Me; and he shall make peace with Me." Isaiah 27:5. Their faith does not fail because their prayers are not immediately answered. Though suffering the keenest anxiety, terror, and distress, they do not cease their intercessions. They lay hold of the strength of God as Jacob laid hold of the Angel; and the language of their souls is: "I will not let Thee go, except Thou bless me."

Had not Jacob previously repented of his sin in obtaining the birthright by fraud, God would not have heard his prayer and mercifully preserved his life. So, in the time of trouble, if the people of God had unconfessed sins to appear before them while tortured with fear and anguish, they would be overwhelmed; despair would cut off their faith, and they could not have confidence to plead with God for deliverance. But while they have a deep sense of their unworthiness, they have no concealed wrongs to reveal. Their sins have gone beforehand to judgment and have been blotted out, and they cannot bring them to remembrance.

Satan leads many to believe that God will overlook their unfaithfulness in the minor affairs of life; but the Lord shows in His dealings with Jacob that He will in no wise sanction or tolerate evil. All who endeavor to excuse or conceal their sins, and permit them to remain upon the books of heaven, unconfessed and unforgiven, will be overcome by Satan. The more exalted their profession and the more honorable the position which they hold, the more grievous is their course in the sight of God and the more sure the triumph of their great adversary. Those who delay a preparation for the day of God cannot obtain it in the time of trouble or at any subsequent time. The case of all such is hopeless.

Those professed Christians who come up to that last fearful conflict unprepared will, in their despair, confess their sins in words of burning anguish, while the wicked exult over their distress. These confessions are of the same character as was that of Esau or of Judas. Those who make them, lament the *result* of transgression, but not its guilt. They feel no true contrition, no abhorrence of evil. They acknowledge their sin, through fear of punishment; but, like Pharaoh of old, they would return to their defiance of Heaven should the judgments be removed.

Jacob's history is also an assurance that God will not cast off those who have been deceived and tempted and betrayed into sin, but who have returned unto Him with true repentance. While Satan seeks to destroy this class, God will send His angels to comfort and protect them in the time of peril. The assaults of Satan are fierce and determined, his delusions are terrible; but the Lord's eye is upon His people, and His ear listens to their cries. Their affliction is great, the flames of the furnace seem about to consume them; but the Refiner will bring them forth as gold tried in the fire. God's love for His children during the period of their severest trial is as strong and tender as in the days of their sunniest prosperity; but it is needful for them to be placed in the furnace of fire; their earthliness must be consumed, that the image of Christ may be perfectly reflected.

The season of distress and anguish before us will require a faith that can endure weariness, delay, and hunger—a faith that will not faint though severely tried. The period of probation is granted to all to prepare for that time. Jacob prevailed because he was persevering and determined. His victory is an evidence of the power of importunate prayer. All who will lay hold of God's promises, as he did, and be as earnest and persevering as he was, will succeed as he succeeded. Those who are unwilling to deny self, to agonize before God, to pray long and earnestly for His blessing, will not obtain it. Wrestling with God—how few know what it is! How few have ever had their souls drawn out after God with intensity of desire until every power is on the stretch. When waves of despair which no language can express sweep over the suppliant, how few cling with unyielding faith to the promises of God.

622   Those who exercise but little faith now, are in the greatest danger of falling under the power of satanic delusions and the decree to compel the conscience. And even if they endure the test they will be plunged into deeper distress and anguish in the time of trouble, because they have never made it a habit to trust in God. The lessons of faith which they have neglected they will be forced to learn under a terrible pressure of discouragement.

We should now acquaint ourselves with God by proving His promises. Angels record every prayer that is earnest and sincere. We should rather dispense with selfish gratifications than neglect communion with God. The deepest poverty, the greatest self-denial, with His approval, is better than riches, honors, ease, and friendship without it. We must take time to pray. If we allow our minds to be absorbed by worldly interests, the Lord may give us time by removing from us our idols of gold, of houses, or of fertile lands.

The young would not be seduced into sin if they would refuse to enter any path save that upon which they could ask God's blessing. If the messengers who bear the last solemn warning to the world would pray for the blessing of God, not in a cold, listless, lazy manner, but fervently and in faith, as did Jacob, they would find many places where they could say: "I have seen God face to face, and my life is preserved." Genesis 32:30. They would be accounted of heaven as princes, having power to prevail with God and with men.

The "time of trouble, such as never was," is soon to open upon us; and we shall need an experience which we do not now possess and which many are too indolent to obtain. It is often the case that trouble is greater in anticipation than in reality; but this is not true of the crisis before us. The most vivid presentation cannot reach the magnitude of the ordeal. In that time of trial, every soul must stand for himself before God. "Though Noah, Daniel, and Job" were in the land, "as I live, saith the Lord God, they shall deliver neither son nor daughter; they shall but deliver their own souls by their righteousness." Ezekiel 14:20.

623   Now, while our great High Priest is making the atonement for us, we should seek to become perfect in Christ. Not even by a thought could our Saviour be brought to yield to the power of temptation. Satan finds in human hearts some point where he can gain a foothold; some sinful desire is cherished, by means of which his temptations assert their power. But Christ declared of Himself: "The prince of this world cometh, and hath nothing in Me." John 14:30. Satan could find nothing in the Son of God that

would enable him to gain the victory. He had kept His Father's commandments, and there was no sin in Him that Satan could use to his advantage. This is the condition in which those must be found who shall stand in the time of trouble.

It is in this life that we are to separate sin from us, through faith in the atoning blood of Christ. Our precious Saviour invites us to join ourselves to Him, to unite our weakness to His strength, our ignorance to His wisdom, our unworthiness to His merits. God's providence is the school in which we are to learn the meekness and lowliness of Jesus. The Lord is ever setting before us, not the way we would choose, which seems easier and pleasanter to us, but the true aims of life. It rests with us to co-operate with the agencies which Heaven employs in the work of conforming our characters to the divine model. None can neglect or defer this work but at the most fearful peril to their souls.

The apostle John in vision heard a loud voice in heaven exclaiming: "Woe to the inhabiters of the earth and of the sea! for the devil is come down unto you, having great wrath, because he knoweth that he hath but a short time." Revelation 12:12. Fearful are the scenes which call forth this exclamation from the heavenly voice. The wrath of Satan increases as his time grows short, and his work of deceit and destruction will reach its culmination in the time of trouble.

Fearful sights of a supernatural character will   624 soon be revealed in the heavens, in token of the power of miracle-working demons. The spirits of devils will go forth to the kings of the earth and to the whole world, to fasten them in deception, and urge them on to unite with Satan in his last struggle against the government of heaven. By these agencies, rulers and subjects will be alike deceived. Persons will arise pretending to be Christ Himself, and claiming the title and worship which belong to the world's Redeemer. They will perform wonderful miracles of healing and will profess to have revelations from heaven contradicting the testimony of the Scriptures.

As the crowning act in the great drama of deception, Satan himself will personate Christ. The church has long professed to look to the Saviour's advent as the consummation of her hopes. Now the great deceiver will make it appear that Christ has come. In different parts of the earth, Satan will manifest himself among men as a majestic being of dazzling brightness, resembling the description of the Son of God given by John in the Revelation. Revelation 1:13-15. The glory that surrounds Him is unsurpassed by anything that mortal eyes have yet beheld. The shout of triumph rings out upon the air: "Christ has come! Christ has come!" The people prostrate themselves in adoration before him, while he lifts up his hands and pronounces a blessing upon them, as Christ blessed His disciples when He was upon the earth. His voice is soft and subdued, yet full of melody. In gentle, compassionate tones he presents some of the same gracious, heavenly truths which the Saviour uttered; he heals the diseases of the people, and then, in his assumed character of Christ, he claims to have changed the Sabbath to Sunday, and commands all to hallow the day which he has blessed. He declares that those who persist in keeping holy the seventh day are blaspheming his name by refusing to listen to his angels sent to them with light and truth. This is the strong, almost overmastering delusion. Like the Samaritans who were deceived by Simon Magus, the multitudes, from the least to the greatest, give heed to these sorceries, saying: This is "the great power of God." Acts 8:10.

But the people of God will not be misled. The teachings of this false christ are not in accordance with the Scriptures. His blessing is pronounced upon the worshipers of the beast and his image, the very class upon whom the Bible declares that God's unmingled wrath shall be poured out.

And, furthermore, Satan is not permitted to counterfeit the manner of Christ's advent. The Saviour has warned His people against deception upon this point, and has clearly foretold the manner of His second coming. "There shall arise false christs, and false prophets, and shall show great signs and wonders; insomuch that, if it were possible, they shall deceive the very elect. . . . Wherefore if they shall say unto you, Behold, He is in the desert; go not forth: behold, He is in the secret chambers; believe it not. For as the lightning cometh out of the east, and shineth even unto the west; so shall also the coming of the Son of man be." Matthew 24:24-27, 31; 25:31; Revelation 1:7; 1 Thessalonians 4:16, 17. This coming there is no possibility of counterfeiting. It will be universally known— witnessed by the whole world.

Only those who have been diligent students of the Scriptures and who have received the love of the truth will be shielded from the powerful delusion that takes the world captive. By the Bible testimony these will detect the deceiver in his disguise. To all the testing time will come. By the sifting of temptation the genuine Christian will be revealed. Are the people of God now so firmly established upon His word that they would not yield to the evidence of their senses? Would they, in such a crisis, cling to the Bible and the Bible only? Satan will, if possible, prevent them from obtaining a preparation to stand in that day. He will so arrange affairs as to hedge up their way, entangle them with earthly treasures, cause them to carry a heavy, wearisome burden, that their hearts may be overcharged with the cares of this life and the day of trial may come upon them as a thief.

As the decree issued by the various rulers of Christendom against commandment keepers shall withdraw the protection of government and abandon them to those who desire their destruction, the people of God will flee from the cities and villages and associate together in companies, dwelling in the most desolate and solitary places. Many will find refuge in the strongholds of the mountains. Like the Christians of the Piedmont valleys, they will make the high places of the earth their sanctuaries and will thank God for "the munitions of rocks." Isaiah 33:16. But many of all nations and of all classes, high and low, rich and poor, black and white, will be cast into the most unjust and cruel bondage. The beloved of God pass weary days, bound in chains, shut in by prison bars, sentenced to be slain, some apparently left to die of starvation in dark and loathsome dungeons. No human ear is open to hear their moans; no human hand is ready to lend them help.

Will the Lord forget His people in this trying hour? Did He forget faithful Noah when judgments were visited upon the antediluvian world? Did He forget Lot when the fire came down from heaven to consume the cities of the plain? Did He forget Joseph surrounded by idolaters in Egypt? Did He forget Elijah when the oath of Jezebel threatened him with the fate of the prophets of Baal? Did He forget Jeremiah in the dark and dismal pit of his prison house? Did He forget the three worthies in the fiery furnace? or Daniel in the den of lions?

"Zion said, The Lord hath forsaken me, and my Lord hath forgotten me. Can a woman forget her sucking child, that she should not have compassion on the son of her womb? yea, they may forget, yet will I not forget thee. Behold, I have graven thee upon the palms of My hands." Isaiah 49:14-16. The Lord of hosts has said: "He that toucheth you toucheth the apple of His eye." Zechariah 2:8.

Though enemies may thrust them into prison, yet dungeon walls cannot cut off the communication between their souls and Christ. One who sees their every weakness, who is acquainted with every trial, is above all earthly powers; and angels will come to them in lonely cells, bringing light and peace from heaven. The prison will be as a palace; for the rich in faith dwell there, and the gloomy walls will be lighted up with heavenly light as when Paul and Silas prayed and sang praises at midnight in the Philippian dungeon.

God's judgments will be visited upon those who are seeking to oppress and destroy His people. His long forbearance with the wicked emboldens men in transgression, but their punishment is nonetheless certain and terrible because it is long delayed. "The Lord shall rise up as in Mount Perazim, He shall be wroth as in the valley of Gibeon, that He may do His work,

His strange work; and bring to pass His act, His strange act." Isaiah 28:21. To our merciful God the act of punishment is a strange act. "As I live, saith the Lord God, I have no pleasure in the death of the wicked." Ezekiel 33:11. The Lord is "merciful and gracious, long-suffering, and abundant in goodness and truth, . . . forgiving iniquity and transgression and sin." Yet He will "by no means clear the guilty." "The Lord is slow to anger, and great in power, and will not at all acquit the wicked." Exodus 34:6, 7; Nahum 1:3. By terrible things in righteousness He will vindicate the authority of His downtrodden law. The severity of the retribution awaiting the transgressor may be judged by the Lord's reluctance to execute justice. The nation with which He bears long, and which He will not smite until it has filled up the measure of its iniquity in God's account, will finally drink the cup of wrath unmixed with mercy.

When Christ ceases His intercession in the sanctuary, the unmingled wrath threatened against those who worship the beast and his image and receive his mark (Revelation 14:9, 10), will be poured out. The plagues upon Egypt when God was about to deliver Israel were sim-

628 ilar in character to those more terrible and extensive judgments which are to fall upon the world just before the final deliverance of God's people. Says the revelator, in describing those terrific scourges: "There fell a noisome and grievous sore upon the men which had the mark of the beast, and upon them which worshiped his image." The sea "became as the blood of a dead man: and every living soul died in the sea." And "the rivers and fountains of waters . . . became blood." Terrible as these inflictions are, God's justice stands fully vindicated. The angel of God declares: "Thou art righteous, O Lord, . . . because Thou hast judged thus. For they have shed the blood of saints and prophets, and Thou hast given them blood to drink; for they are worthy." Revelation 16:2-6. By condemning the people of God to death, they have as truly incurred the guilt of their blood as if it had been shed by their hands. In like manner Christ declared the Jews of His time guilty of all the blood of holy men which had been shed since the days of Abel; for they possessed the same spirit and were seeking to do the same work with these murderers of the prophets.

In the plague that follows, power is given to the sun "to scorch men with fire. And men were scorched with great heat." Verses 8, 9. The prophets thus describe the condition of the earth at this fearful time: "The land mourneth; . . . because the harvest of the field is perished. . . . All the trees of the field are withered: because joy is withered away from the sons of men." "The seed is rotten under their clods, the garners are laid desolate. . . . How do the beasts groan! the herds of cattle are perplexed, because they

have no pasture. . . . The rivers of water are dried up, and the fire hath devoured the pastures of the wilderness." "The songs of the temple shall be howlings in that day, saith the Lord God: there shall be many dead bodies in every place; they shall cast them forth with silence." Joel 1:10-12, 17-20; Amos 8:3.

These plagues are not universal, or the inhabitants of the earth would be wholly cut off. Yet they will be the most awful scourges that have 629 ever been known to mortals. All the judgments upon men, prior to the close of probation, have been mingled with mercy. The pleading blood of Christ has shielded the sinner from receiving the full measure of his guilt; but in the final judgment, wrath is poured out unmixed with mercy.

In that day, multitudes will desire the shelter of God's mercy which they have so long despised. "Behold, the days come, saith the Lord God, that I will send a famine in the land, not a famine of bread, nor a thirst for water, but of hearing the words of the Lord: and they shall wander from sea to sea, and from the north even to the east, they shall run to and fro to seek the word of the Lord, and shall not find it." Amos 8:11, 12.

The people of God will not be free from suffering; but while persecuted and distressed, while they endure privation and suffer for want of food they will not be left to perish. That God who cared for Elijah will not pass by one of His self-sacrificing children. He who numbers the hairs of their head will care for them, and in time of famine they shall be satisfied. While the wicked are dying from hunger and pestilence, angels will shield the righteous and supply their wants. To him that "walketh righteously" is the promise: "Bread shall be given him; his waters shall be sure." "When the poor and needy seek water, and there is none, and their tongue faileth for thirst, I the Lord will hear them, I the God of Israel will not forsake them." Isaiah 33:15, 16; 41:17.

"Although the fig tree shall not blossom, neither shall fruit be in the vines; the labor of the olive shall fail, and the fields shall yield no meat; the flock shall be cut off from the fold, and there shall be no herd in the stalls;" yet shall they that fear Him "rejoice in the Lord" and joy in the God of their salvation. Habakkuk 3:17, 18.

"The Lord is thy keeper: the Lord is thy shade upon thy right hand. The sun shall not smite thee by day, nor the moon by night. The Lord shall preserve thee from all evil: He shall preserve thy soul." "He shall deliver thee from the 630 snare of the fowler, and from the noisome pestilence. He shall cover thee with His feathers, and under His wings shalt thou trust: His truth shall be thy shield and buckler. Thou shalt not be afraid for the terror by night; nor for the arrow that flieth by day; nor for the pestilence that walketh in darkness; nor for the destruction that wasteth at noonday. A thousand shall fall at thy side, and ten thousand at thy right hand; but it shall not come nigh thee. Only with thine eyes shalt thou behold and see the reward of the wicked. Because thou hast made the Lord, which is my refuge, even the Most High, thy habitation; there shall no evil befall thee, neither shall any plague come nigh thy dwelling." Psalms 121:5-7; 91:3-10.

Yet to human sight it will appear that the people of God must soon seal their testimony with their blood as did the martyrs before them. They themselves begin to fear that the Lord has left them to fall by the hand of their enemies. It is a time of fearful agony. Day and night they cry unto God for deliverance. The wicked exult, and the jeering cry is heard: "Where now is your faith? Why does not God deliver you out of our hands if you are indeed His people?" But the waiting ones remember Jesus dying upon Calvary's cross and the chief priests and rulers shouting in mockery: "He saved others; Himself He cannot save. If He be the King of Israel, let Him now come down from the cross, and we will believe Him." Matthew 27:42. Like Jacob, all are wrestling with God. Their countenances express their internal struggle. Paleness sits upon every face. Yet they cease not their earnest intercession.

Could men see with heavenly vision, they would behold companies of angels that excel in strength stationed about those who have kept the word of Christ's patience. With sympathizing tenderness, angels have witnessed their distress and have heard their prayers. They are waiting the word of their Commander to snatch them from their peril. But they must wait yet a 631 little longer. The people of God must drink of the cup and be baptized with the baptism. The very delay, so painful to them, is the best answer to their petitions. As they endeavor to wait trustingly for the Lord to work they are led to exercise faith, hope, and patience, which have been too little exercised during their religious experience. Yet for the elect's sake the time of trouble will be shortened. "Shall not God avenge His own elect, which cry day and night unto Him? . . . I tell you that He will avenge them speedily." Luke 18:7, 8. The end will come more quickly than men expect. The wheat will be gathered and bound in sheaves for the garner of God; the tares will be bound as fagots for the fires of destruction.

The heavenly sentinels, faithful to their trust, continue their watch. Though a general decree has fixed the time when commandment keepers may be put to death, their enemies will in some cases anticipate the decree, and before the time specified, will endeavor to take their lives. But none can pass the mighty guardians stationed about every faithful soul. Some are assailed in their flight from the cities and villages; but the swords raised against them break and fall powerless as a straw. Others are defended by angels in the form of men of war.

In all ages, God has wrought through holy angels for the succor and deliverance of His people. Celestial beings have taken an active part in the affairs of men. They have appeared clothed in garments that shone as the lightning; they have come as men in the garb of wayfarers. Angels have appeared in human form to men of God. They have rested, as if weary, under the oaks at noon. They have accepted the hospitalities of human homes. They have acted as guides to benighted travelers. They have, with their own hands, kindled the fires at the altar. They have opened prison doors and set free the servants of the Lord. Clothed with the panoply of heaven, they came to roll away the stone from the Saviour's tomb.

In the form of men, angels are often in the assemblies of the righteous; and they visit the assemblies of the wicked, as they went to Sodom, to make a record of their deeds, to determine whether they have passed the boundary of God's forbearance. The Lord delights in mercy; and for the sake of a few who really serve Him, He restrains calamities and prolongs the tranquillity of multitudes. Little do sinners against God realize that they are indebted for their own lives to the faithful few whom they delight to ridicule and oppress.

Though the rulers of this world know it not, yet often in their councils angels have been spokesmen. Human eyes have looked upon them; human ears have listened to their appeals; human lips have opposed their suggestions and ridiculed their counsels; human hands have met them with insult and abuse. In the council hall and the court of justice these heavenly messengers have shown an intimate acquaintance with human history; they have proved themselves better able to plead the cause of the oppressed than were their ablest and most eloquent defenders. They have defeated purposes and arrested evils that would have greatly retarded the work of God and would have caused great suffering to His people. In the hour of peril and distress "the angel of the Lord encampeth round about them that fear Him, and delivereth them." Psalm 34:7.

With earnest longing, God's people await the tokens of their coming King. As the watchmen are accosted, "What of the night?" the answer is given unfalteringly, " 'The morning cometh, and also the night.' Isaiah 21:11, 12. Light is gleaming upon the clouds above the mountaintops. Soon there will be a revealing of His glory. The Sun of Righteousness is about to shine forth. The morning and the night are both at hand— the opening of endless day to the righteous, the settling down of eternal night to the wicked."

632

As the wrestling ones urge their petitions before God, the veil separating them from the unseen seems almost withdrawn. The heavens glow with the dawning of eternal day, and like the melody of angel songs the words fall upon 633 the ear: "Stand fast to your allegiance. Help is coming." Christ, the almighty Victor, holds out to His weary soldiers a crown of immortal glory; and His voice comes from the gates ajar: "Lo, I am with you. Be not afraid. I am acquainted with all your sorrows; I have borne your griefs. You are not warring against untried enemies. I have fought the battle in your behalf, and in My name you are more than conquerors."

The precious Saviour will send help just when we need it. The way to heaven is consecrated by His footprints. Every thorn that wounds our feet has wounded His. Every cross that we are called to bear He has borne before us. The Lord permits conflicts, to prepare the soul for peace. The time of trouble is a fearful ordeal for God's people; but it is the time for every true believer to look up, and by faith he may see the bow of promise encircling him.

"The redeemed of the Lord shall return, and come with singing unto Zion; and everlasting joy shall be upon their head: they shall obtain gladness and joy; and sorrow and mourning shall flee away. I, even I, am He that comforteth you: who art thou, that thou shouldest be afraid of a man that shall die, and of the son of man which shall be made as grass; and forgettest the Lord thy Maker; . . . and hast feared continually every day because of the fury of the oppressor, as if he were ready to destroy? and where is the fury of the oppressor? The captive exile hasteneth that he may be loosed, and that he should not die in the pit, nor that his bread should fail. But I am the Lord thy God, that divided the sea, whose waves roared: The Lord of hosts is His name. And I have put My words in thy mouth, and I have covered thee in the shadow of Mine hand." Isaiah 51:11-16.

"Therefore hear now this, thou afflicted, and drunken, but not with wine: Thus saith thy Lord the Lord, and thy God that pleadeth the cause of His people, Behold, I have taken out of thine hand the cup of trembling, even the dregs of the cup of My fury; thou shalt no more drink it again: but I will put it into the hand of them that 634 afflict thee; which have said to thy soul, Bow down, that we may go over: and thou hast laid thy body as the ground, and as the street, to them that went over." Verses 21-23.

The eye of God, looking down the ages, was fixed upon the crisis which His people are to meet, when earthly powers shall be arrayed against them. Like the captive exile, they will be in fear of death by starvation or by violence. But the Holy One who divided the Red Sea before Israel, will manifest His mighty power and turn their captivity. "They shall be Mine, saith the Lord of hosts, in that day when I make up My jewels; and I will spare them, as a man spareth his own son that serveth him." Malachi 3:17. If the blood of Christ's faithful witnesses were shed at this time, it would not, like the blood of the martyrs, be as seed sown to yield a harvest for God. Their fidelity would not be a testimony to convince others of the truth; for the obdurate heart has beaten back the waves of mercy until they return no more. If the righteous were now left to fall a prey to their enemies, it would be a triumph for the prince of darkness. Says the psalmist: "In the time of trouble He shall hide me in His pavilion: in the secret of His tabernacle shall He hide me." Psalm 27:5. Christ has spoken: "Come, My people, enter thou into thy chambers, and shut thy doors about thee: hide thyself as it were for a little moment, until the indignation be overpast. For, behold, the Lord cometh out of His place to punish the inhabitants of the earth for their iniquity." Isaiah 26:20, 21. Glorious will be the deliverance of those who have patiently waited for His coming and whose names are written in the book of life.

40

635

God's People Delivered

When the protection of human laws shall be withdrawn from those who honor the law of God, there will be, in different lands, a simultaneous movement for their destruction. As the time appointed in the decree draws near, the people will conspire to root out the hated sect. It will be determined to strike in one night a decisive blow, which shall utterly silence the voice of dissent and reproof.

The people of God—some in prison cells, some hidden in solitary retreats in the forests and the mountains—still plead for divine protection, while in every quarter companies of armed men, urged on by hosts of evil angels, are preparing for the work of death. It is now, in the hour of utmost extremity, that the God of Israel will interpose for the deliverance of His chosen. Saith the Lord: "Ye shall have a song, as in the night when a holy solemnity is kept; and gladness of heart, as when one goeth . . . to come into the mountain of the Lord, to the Mighty One of Israel. And the Lord shall cause His glorious voice to be heard, and shall show the lighting down of His arm, with the indignation of His anger, and with the flame of a devouring fire, with scattering, and tempest, and hailstones." Isaiah 30:29, 30.

With shouts of triumph, jeering, and imprecation, throngs of evil men are about to rush upon their prey, when, lo, a dense blackness, deeper 636 than the darkness of the night, falls upon the earth. Then a rainbow, shining with the glory from the throne of God, spans the heavens and seems to encircle each praying company. The angry multitudes are suddenly arrested. Their mocking cries die away. The objects of their murderous rage are forgotten. With fearful forebodings they gaze upon the symbol of God's covenant and long to be shielded from its overpowering brightness.

By the people of God a voice, clear and melodious, is heard, saying, "Look up," and lifting their eyes to the heavens, they behold the bow of promise. The black, angry clouds that covered the firmament are parted, and like Stephen they look up steadfastly into heaven and see the glory of God and the Son of man seated upon His throne. In His divine form they discern the marks of His humiliation; and from His lips they hear the request presented before His Father and the holy angels: "I will that they also, whom Thou hast given Me, be with Me where I am." John 17:24. Again a voice, musical and triumphant, is heard, saying: "They come! they come! holy, harmless, and undefiled. They have kept the word of My patience; they shall walk among the angels;" and the pale, quivering lips of those who have held fast their faith utter a shout of victory.

It is at midnight that God manifests His power for the deliverance of His people. The sun appears, shining in its strength. Signs and wonders follow in quick succession. The wicked look with terror and amazement upon the scene, while the righteous behold with solemn joy the tokens of their deliverance. Everything in nature seems turned out of its course. The streams cease to flow. Dark, heavy clouds come up and clash against each other. In the midst of the angry heavens is one clear space of indescribable glory, whence comes the voice of God like the sound of many waters, saying: "It is done." Revelation 16:17.

637 That voice shakes the heavens and the earth. There is a mighty earthquake, "such as was not since men were upon the earth, so mighty an earthquake, and so great." Verses 17, 18. The firmament appears to open and shut. The glory from the throne of God seems flashing through. The mountains shake like a reed in the wind, and ragged rocks are scattered on every side. There is a roar as of a coming tempest. The sea is lashed into fury. There is heard the shriek of a hurricane like the voice of demons upon a mission of destruction. The whole earth heaves and swells like the waves of the sea. Its surface is breaking up. Its very foundations seem to be giving way. Mountain chains are sinking. Inhabited islands disappear. The seaports that have become like Sodom for wickedness are swallowed up by the angry waters. Babylon the great has come in remembrance before God, "to give unto her the cup of the wine of the fierceness of His wrath." Great hailstones, every one "about the weight of a talent," are doing their work of destruction. Verses 19, 21. The proudest cities of the earth are laid low. The lordly palaces, upon which the world's great men have lavished their wealth in order to glorify themselves, are crumbling to ruin before their eyes. Prison walls are rent asunder, and God's people, who have been held in bondage for their faith, are set free.

Graves are opened, and "many of them that sleep in the dust of the earth. . . awake, some to everlasting life, and some to shame and everlasting contempt." Daniel 12:2. All who have died in the faith of the third angel's message come forth from the tomb glorified, to hear God's covenant of peace with those who have kept His law. "They also which pierced Him" (Revelation 1:7), those that mocked and derided Christ's dying agonies, and the most violent opposers of His truth and His people, are raised to behold Him in His glory and to see the honor placed upon the loyal and obedient.

Thick clouds still cover the sky; yet the sun now and then breaks through, appearing like the avenging eye of Jehovah. Fierce lightnings leap 638 from the heavens, enveloping the earth in a sheet of flame. Above the terrific roar of thunder, voices, mysterious and awful, declare the doom of the wicked. The words spoken are not comprehended by all; but they are distinctly understood by the false teachers. Those who a little before were so reckless, so boastful and defiant, so exultant in their cruelty to God's commandment-keeping people, are now overwhelmed with consternation and shuddering in fear. Their wails are heard above the sound of the elements. Demons acknowledge the deity of Christ and tremble before His power, while men are supplicating for mercy and groveling in abject terror.

Said the prophets of old, as they beheld in holy vision the day of God: "Howl ye; for the day of the Lord is at hand; it shall come as a destruction from the Almighty." Isaiah 13:6. "Enter into the rock, and hide thee in the dust, for fear of the Lord, and for the glory of His majesty. The lofty looks of man shall be humbled, and the haughtiness of men shall be bowed down, and the Lord alone shall be exalted in that day. For the day of the Lord of hosts shall be upon everyone that is proud and lofty, and upon everyone that is lifted up; and he shall be brought low." "In that day a man shall cast the idols of his silver, and the idols of his gold, which they made each one for himself to worship, to the moles and to the bats; to go into the clefts of the rocks, and into the tops of the ragged rocks, for fear of the Lord, and for the glory of His majesty, when He ariseth to shake terribly the earth." Isaiah 2:10-12, 20, 21, margin.

Through a rift in the clouds there beams a star

whose brilliancy is increased fourfold in contrast with the darkness. It speaks hope and joy to the faithful, but severity and wrath to the transgressors of God's law. Those who have sacrificed all for Christ are now secure, hidden as in the secret of the Lord's pavilion. They have been tested, and before the world and the despisers of truth they have evinced their fidelity to Him who died for them. A marvelous change has come over those who have held fast their integrity in the very face of death. They have been suddenly delivered from the dark and terrible tyranny of men transformed to demons. Their faces, so lately pale, anxious, and haggard, are now aglow with wonder, faith, and love. Their voices rise in triumphant song: "God is our refuge and strength, a very present help in trouble. Therefore will not we fear, though the earth be removed, and though the mountains be carried into the midst of the sea; though the waters thereof roar and be troubled, though the mountains shake with the swelling thereof." Psalm 46:1-3.

While these words of holy trust ascend to God, the clouds sweep back, and the starry heavens are seen, unspeakably glorious in contrast with the black and angry firmament on either side. The glory of the celestial city streams from the gates ajar. Then there appears against the sky a hand holding two tables of stone folded together. Says the prophet: "The heavens shall declare His righteousness: for God is judge Himself." Psalm 50:6. That holy law, God's righteousness, that amid thunder and flame was proclaimed from Sinai as the guide of life, is now revealed to men as the rule of judgment. The hand opens the tables, and there are seen the precepts of the Decalogue, traced as with a pen of fire. The words are so plain that all can read them. Memory is aroused, the darkness of superstition and heresy is swept from every mind, and God's ten words, brief, comprehensive, and authoritative, are presented to the view of all the inhabitants of the earth.

It is impossible to describe the horror and despair of those who have trampled upon God's holy requirements. The Lord gave them His law; they might have compared their characters with it and learned their defects while there was yet opportunity for repentance and reform; but in order to secure the favor of the world, they set aside its precepts and taught others to transgress. They have endeavored to compel God's people to profane His Sabbath. Now they are condemned by that law which they have despised. With awful distinctness they see that they are without excuse. They chose whom they would serve and worship. "Then shall ye return, and discern between the righteous and the wicked, between him that serveth God and him that serveth Him not." Malachi 3:18.

The enemies of God's law, from the ministers down to the least among them, have a new conception of truth and duty. Too late they see that the Sabbath of the fourth commandment is the seal of the living God. Too late they see the true nature of their spurious sabbath and the sandy foundation upon which they have been building. They find that they have been fighting against God. Religious teachers have led souls to perdition while professing to guide them to the gates of Paradise. Not until the day of final accounts will it be known how great is the responsibility of men in holy office and how terrible are the results of their unfaithfulness. Only in eternity can we rightly estimate the loss of a single soul. Fearful will be the doom of him to whom God shall say: Depart, thou wicked servant.

The voice of God is heard from heaven, declaring the day and hour of Jesus' coming, and delivering the everlasting covenant to His people. Like peals of loudest thunder His words roll through the earth. The Israel of God stand listening, with their eyes fixed upward. Their countenances are lighted up with His glory, and shine as did the face of Moses when he came down from Sinai. The wicked cannot look upon them. And when the blessing is pronounced on those who have honored God by keeping His Sabbath holy, there is a mighty shout of victory.

Soon there appears in the east a small black cloud, about half the size of a man's hand. It is the cloud which surrounds the Saviour and which seems in the distance to be shrouded in darkness. The people of God know this to be the sign of the Son of man. In solemn silence they gaze upon it as it draws nearer the earth, becoming lighter and more glorious, until it is a great white cloud, its base a glory like consuming fire, and above it the rainbow of the covenant. Jesus rides forth as a mighty conqueror. Not now a "Man of Sorrows," to drink the bitter cup of shame and woe, He comes, victor in heaven and earth, to judge the living and the dead. "Faithful and True," "in righteousness He doth judge and make war." And "the armies which were in heaven" (Revelation 19:11, 14) follow Him. With anthems of celestial melody the holy angels, a vast, unnumbered throng, attend Him on His way. The firmament seems filled with radiant forms—"ten thousand times ten thousand, and thousands of thousands." No human pen can portray the scene; no mortal mind is adequate to conceive its splendor. "His glory covered the heavens, and the earth was full of His praise. And His brightness was as the light." Habakkuk 3:3, 4. As the living cloud comes still nearer, every eye beholds the Prince of life. No crown of thorns now mars that sacred head; but a diadem of glory rests on His holy brow. His countenance outshines the dazzling brightness of the noonday sun. "And He hath on His vesture and on His thigh a name written, *King of kings, and Lord of lords.*" Revelation 19:16.

Before His presence "all faces are turned into paleness;" upon the rejecters of God's mercy falls the terror of eternal despair. "The heart melteth, and the knees smite together, . . . and the faces of them all gather blackness." Jeremiah 30:6; Nahum 2:10. The righteous cry with trembling: "Who shall be able to stand?" The angels' song is hushed, and there is a period of awful silence. Then the voice of Jesus is heard, saying: "My grace is sufficient for you." The faces of the righteous are lighted up, and joy fills every heart. And the angels strike a note higher and sing again as they draw still nearer to the earth.

The King of kings descends upon the cloud, wrapped in flaming fire. The heavens are rolled together as a scroll, the earth trembles before 642 Him, and every mountain and island is moved out of its place. "Our God shall come, and shall not keep silence: a fire shall devour before Him, and it shall be very tempestuous round about Him. He shall call to the heavens from above, and to the earth, that He may judge His people." Psalm 50:3, 4.

"And the kings of the earth, and the great men, and the rich men, and the chief captains, and the mighty men, and every bondman, and every freeman, hid themselves in the dens and in the rocks of the mountains; and said to the mountains and rocks, Fall on us, and hide us from the face of Him that sitteth on the throne, and from the wrath of the Lamb: for the great day of His wrath is come; and who shall be able to stand?" Revelation 6:15-17.

The derisive jests have ceased. Lying lips are hushed into silence. The clash of arms, the tumult of battle, "with confused noise, and garments rolled in blood" (Isaiah 9:5), is stilled. Nought now is heard but the voice of prayer and the sound of weeping and lamentation. The cry bursts forth from lips so lately scoffing: "The great day of His wrath is come; and who shall be able to stand?" The wicked pray to be buried beneath the rocks of the mountains rather than meet the face of Him whom they have despised and rejected.

That voice which penetrates the ear of the dead, they know. How often have its plaintive, tender tones called them to repentance. How often has it been heard in the touching entreaties of a friend, a brother, a Redeemer. To the rejecters of His grace no other could be so full of condemnation, so burdened with denunciation, as that voice which has so long pleaded: "Turn ye, turn ye from your evil ways; for why will ye die?" Ezekiel 33:11. Oh, that it were to them the voice of a stranger! Says Jesus: "I have called, and ye refused; I have stretched out My hand, and no man regarded; but ye have set at nought all My counsel, and would none of My reproof." Proverbs 1:24, 25. That voice awakens memories which they would fain blot out—

warnings despised, invitations refused, privileges slighted.

There are those who mocked Christ in His 643 humiliation. With thrilling power come to their minds the Sufferer's words, when, adjured by the high priest, He solemnly declared: "Hereafter shall ye see the Son of man sitting on the right hand of power, and coming in the clouds of heaven." Matthew 26:64. Now they behold Him in His glory, and they are yet to see Him sitting on the right hand of power.

Those who derided His claim to be the Son of God are speechless now. There is the haughty Herod who jeered at His royal title and bade the mocking soldiers crown Him king. There are the very men who with impious hands placed upon His form the purple robe, upon His sacred brow the thorny crown, and in His unresisting hand the mimic scepter, and bowed before Him in blasphemous mockery. The men who smote and spit upon the Prince of life now turn from His piercing gaze and seek to flee from the overpowering glory of His presence. Those who drove the nails through His hands and feet, the soldier who pierced His side, behold these marks with terror and remorse.

With awful distinctness do priests and rulers recall the events of Calvary. With shuddering horror they remember how, wagging their heads in satanic exultation, they exclaimed: "He saved others; Himself He cannot save. If He be the King of Israel, let Him now come down from the cross, and we will believe Him. He trusted in God; let Him deliver Him now, if He will have Him." Matthew 27:42, 43.

Vividly they recall the Saviour's parable of the husbandmen who refused to render to their lord the fruit of the vineyard, who abused his servants and slew his son. They remember, too, the sentence which they themselves pronounced: The lord of the vineyard "will miserably destroy those wicked men." In the sin and punishment of those unfaithful men the priests and elders see their own course and their own just doom. And now there rises a cry of mortal agony. Louder than the shout, "Crucify Him, crucify Him," which rang through the streets of Jerusalem, swells the awful, despairing wail, 644 "He is the Son of God! He is the true Messiah!" They seek to flee from the presence of the King of kings. In the deep caverns of the earth, rent asunder by the warring of the elements, they vainly attempt to hide.

In the lives of all who reject truth there are moments when conscience awakens, when memory presents the torturing recollection of a life of hypocrisy and the soul is harassed with vain regrets. But what are these compared with the remorse of that day when "fear cometh as desolation," when "destruction cometh as a whirlwind"! Proverbs 1:27. Those who would have destroyed Christ and His faithful people now witness the glory which rests upon them. In the midst of their terror they hear the voices of the saints in joyful strains exclaiming: "Lo, this is our God; we have waited for Him, and He will save us." Isaiah 25:9.

Amid the reeling of the earth, the flash of lightning, and the roar of thunder, the voice of the Son of God calls forth the sleeping saints. He looks upon the graves of the righteous, then, raising His hands to heaven, He cries: "Awake, awake, awake, ye that sleep in the dust, and arise!" Throughout the length and breadth of the earth the dead shall hear that voice, and they that hear shall live. And the whole earth shall ring with the tread of the exceeding great army of every nation, kindred, tongue, and people. From the prison house of death they come, clothed with immortal glory, crying: "O death, where is thy sting? O grave, where is thy victory?" 1 Corinthians 15:55. And the living righteous and the risen saints unite their voices in a long, glad shout of victory.

All come forth from their graves the same in stature as when they entered the tomb. Adam, who stands among the risen throng, is of lofty height and majestic form, in stature but little below the Son of God. He presents a marked contrast to the people of later generations; in this one respect is shown the great degeneracy of the race. But all arise with the freshness and vigor of eternal youth. In the beginning, man 645 was created in the likeness of God, not only in character, but in form and feature. Sin defaced and almost obliterated the divine image; but Christ came to restore that which had been lost. He will change our vile bodies and fashion them like unto His glorious body. The mortal, corruptible form, devoid of comeliness, once polluted with sin, becomes perfect, beautiful, and immortal. All blemishes and deformities are left in the grave. Restored to the tree of life in the long-lost Eden, the redeemed will "grow up" (Malachi 4:2) to the full stature of the race in its primeval glory. The last lingering traces of the curse of sin will be removed, and Christ's faithful ones will appear in "the beauty of the Lord our God," in mind and soul and body reflecting the perfect image of their Lord. Oh, wonderful redemption! long talked of, long hoped for, contemplated with eager anticipation, but never fully understood.

The living righteous are changed "in a moment, in the twinkling of an eye." At the voice of God they were glorified; now they are made immortal and with the risen saints are caught up to meet their Lord in the air. Angels "gather together His elect from the four winds, from one end of heaven to the other." Little children are borne by holy angels to their mothers' arms. Friends long separated by death are united, nevermore to part, and with songs of gladness ascend together to the City of God.

On each side of the cloudy chariot are wings, and beneath it are living wheels; and as the chariot rolls upward, the wheels cry, "Holy," and the wings, as they move, cry, "Holy," and the retinue of angels cry, "Holy, holy, holy, Lord God Almighty." And the redeemed shout, "Alleluia!" as the chariot moves onward toward the New Jerusalem.

Before entering the City of God, the Saviour bestows upon His followers the emblems of victory and invests them with the insignia of their royal state. The glittering ranks are drawn up in the form of a hollow square about their King, whose form rises in majesty high above saint and angel, whose countenance beams upon 646 them full of benignant love. Throughout the unnumbered host of the redeemed every glance is fixed upon Him, every eye beholds His glory whose "visage was so marred more than any man, and His form more than the sons of men." Upon the heads of the overcomers, Jesus with His own right hand places the crown of glory. For each there is a crown, bearing his own "new name" (Revelation 2:17), and the inscription, "Holiness to the Lord." In every hand are placed the victor's palm and the shining harp. Then, as the commanding angels strike the note, every hand sweeps the harp strings with skillful touch, awaking sweet music in rich, melodious strains. Rapture unutterable thrills every heart, and each voice is raised in grateful praise: "Unto Him that loved us, and washed us from our sins in His own blood, and hath made us kings and priests unto God and His Father; to Him be glory and dominion for ever and ever." Revelation 1:5, 6.

Before the ransomed throng is the Holy City. Jesus opens wide the pearly gates, and the nations that have kept the truth enter in. There they behold the Paradise of God, the home of Adam in his innocency. Then that voice, richer than any music that ever fell on mortal ear, is heard, saying: "Your conflict is ended." "Come, ye blessed of My Father, inherit the kingdom prepared for you from the foundation of the world."

Now is fulfilled the Saviour's prayer for His disciples: "I will that they also, whom Thou hast given Me, be with Me where I am." "Faultless before the presence of His glory with exceeding joy" (Jude 24), Christ presents to the Father the purchase of His blood, declaring: "Here am I, and the children whom Thou hast given Me." "Those that Thou gavest Me I have kept." Oh, the wonders of redeeming love! the rapture of that hour when the infinite Father, looking upon the ransomed, shall behold His image, sin's discord banished, its blight removed, and the human once more in harmony with the divine!

With unutterable love, Jesus welcomes His 647 faithful ones to the joy of their Lord. The Saviour's joy is in seeing, in the kingdom of glory, the souls that have been saved by His agony and humiliation. And the redeemed will be sharers in His joy, as they behold, among the blessed, those who have been won to Christ through their prayers, their labors, and their loving sacrifice. As they gather about the great white throne, gladness unspeakable will fill their hearts, when they behold those whom they have won for Christ, and see that one has gained others, and these still others, all brought into the haven of rest, there to lay their crowns at Jesus' feet and praise Him through the endless cycles of eternity.

As the ransomed ones are welcomed to the City of God, there rings out upon the air an exultant cry of adoration. The two Adams are about to meet. The Son of God is standing with outstretched arms to receive the father of our race—the being whom He created, who sinned against his Maker, and for whose sin the marks of the crucifixion are borne upon the Saviour's form. As Adam discerns the prints of the cruel nails, he does not fall upon the bosom of his Lord, but in humiliation casts himself at His feet, crying: "Worthy, worthy is the Lamb that was slain!" Tenderly the Saviour lifts him up and bids him look once more upon the Eden home from which he has so long been exiled.

After his expulsion from Eden, Adam's life on earth was filled with sorrow. Every dying leaf, every victim of sacrifice, every blight upon the fair face of nature, every stain upon man's purity, was a fresh reminder of his sin. Terrible was the agony of remorse as he beheld iniquity abounding, and, in answer to his warnings, met the reproaches cast upon himself as the cause of sin. With patient humility he bore, for nearly a thousand years, the penalty of transgression. Faithfully did he repent of his sin and trust in the merits of the promised Saviour, and he died in the hope of a resurrection. The Son of God 648 redeemed man's failure and fall; and now, through the work of the atonement, Adam is reinstated in his first dominion.

Transported with joy, he beholds the trees that were once his delight—the very trees whose fruit he himself had gathered in the days of his innocence and joy. He sees the vines that his own hands have trained, the very flowers that he once loved to care for. His mind grasps the reality of the scene; he comprehends that this is indeed Eden restored, more lovely now than when he was banished from it. The Saviour leads him to the tree of life and plucks the glorious fruit and bids him eat. He looks about him and beholds a multitude of his family redeemed, standing in the Paradise of God. Then he casts his glittering crown at the feet of Jesus and, falling upon His breast, embraces the Redeemer. He touches the golden harp, and the vaults of heaven echo the triumphant song: "Worthy, worthy, worthy is the Lamb that was

slain, and lives again!" The family of Adam take up the strain and cast their crowns at the Saviour's feet as they bow before Him in adoration.

This reunion is witnessed by the angels who wept at the fall of Adam and rejoiced when Jesus, after His resurrection, ascended to heaven, having opened the grave for all who should believe on His name. Now they behold the work of redemption accomplished, and they unite their voices in the song of praise.

Upon the crystal sea before the throne, that sea of glass as it were mingled with fire,—so resplendent is it with the glory of God,—are gathered the company that have "gotten the victory over the beast, and over his image, and over his mark, and over the number of his name." With the Lamb upon Mount Zion, "having the harps of God," they stand, the hundred and forty and four thousand that were redeemed from among men; and there is heard, as the sound of many waters, and as the sound of a great thunder, "the voice of harpers harping with their harps." And they sing "a new song" 649 before the throne, a song which no man can learn save the hundred and forty and four thousand. It is the song of Moses and the Lamb—a song of deliverance. None but the hundred and forty-four thousand can learn that song; for it is the song of their experience—an experience such as no other company have ever had. "These are they which follow the Lamb whithersoever He goeth." These, having been translated from the earth, from among the living, are counted as "the first fruits unto God and to the Lamb." Revelation 15:2, 3; 14:1-5. "These are they which came out of great tribulation;" they have passed through the time of trouble such as never was since there was a nation; they have endured the anguish of the time of Jacob's trouble; they have stood without an intercessor through the final outpouring of God's judgments. But they have been delivered, for they have "washed their robes, and made them white in the blood of the Lamb." "In their mouth was found no guile: for they are without fault" before God. "Therefore are they before the throne of God, and serve Him day and night in His temple: and He that sitteth on the throne shall dwell among them." They have seen the earth wasted with famine and pestilence, the sun having power to scorch men with great heat, and they themselves have endured suffering, hunger, and thirst. But "they shall hunger no more, neither thirst any more; neither shall the sun light on them, nor any heat. For the Lamb which is in the midst of the throne shall feed them, and shall lead them unto living fountains of waters: and God shall wipe away all tears from their eyes." Revelation 7:14-17.

In all ages the Saviour's chosen have been educated and disciplined in the school of trial.

They walked in narrow paths on earth; they were purified in the furnace of affliction. For Jesus' sake they endured opposition, hatred, calumny. They followed Him through conflicts sore; they endured self-denial and experienced 650 bitter disappointments. By their own painful experience they learned the evil of sin, its power, its guilt, its woe; and they look upon it with abhorrence. A sense of the infinite sacrifice made for its cure humbles them in their own sight and fills their hearts with gratitude and praise which those who have never fallen cannot appreciate. They love much because they have been forgiven much. Having been partakers of Christ's sufferings, they are fitted to be partakers with Him of His glory.

The heirs of God have come from garrets, from hovels, from dungeons, from scaffolds, from mountains, from deserts, from the caves of the earth, from the caverns of the sea. On earth they were "destitute, afflicted, tormented." Millions went down to the grave loaded with infamy because they steadfastly refused to yield to the deceptive claims of Satan. By human tribunals they were adjudged the vilest of criminals. But now "God is judge Himself." Psalm 50:6. Now the decisions of earth are reversed. "The rebuke of His people shall He take away." Isaiah 25:8. "They shall call them, The holy people, The redeemed of the Lord." He hath appointed "to give unto them beauty for ashes, the oil of joy for mourning, the garment of praise for the spirit of heaviness." Isaiah 62:12; 61:3. They are no longer feeble, afflicted, scattered, and oppressed. Henceforth they are to be ever with the Lord. They stand before the throne clad in richer robes than the most honored of the earth have ever worn. They are crowned with diadems more glorious than were ever placed upon the brow of earthly monarchs. The days of pain and weeping are forever ended. The King of glory has wiped the tears from all faces; every cause of grief has been removed. Amid the waving of palm branches they pour forth a song of praise, clear, sweet, and harmonious; every voice takes up the strain, until the anthem swells through the vaults of heaven: "Salvation to our God which sitteth upon the throne, and unto the Lamb." And all the inhabitants of heaven respond in the ascription: "Amen: Blessing, 651 and glory, and wisdom, and thanksgiving, and honor, and power, and might, be unto our God for ever and ever." Revelation 7:10, 12.

In this life we can only begin to understand the wonderful theme of redemption. With our finite comprehension we may consider most earnestly the shame and the glory, the life and the death, the justice and the mercy, that meet in the cross; yet with the utmost stretch of our mental powers we fail to grasp its full significance. The length and the breadth, the depth and the height, of redeeming love are but dimly comprehended. The plan of redemption will not be fully understood, even when the ransomed see as they are seen and know as they are known; but through the eternal ages new truth will continually unfold to the wondering and delighted mind. Though the griefs and pains and temptations of earth are ended and the cause removed, the people of God will ever have a distinct, intelligent knowledge of what their salvation has cost.

The cross of Christ will be the science and the song of the redeemed through all eternity. In Christ glorified they will behold Christ crucified. Never will it be forgotten that He whose power created and upheld the unnumbered worlds through the vast realms of space, the Beloved of God, the Majesty of heaven, He whom cherub and shining seraph delighted to adore—humbled Himself to uplift fallen man; that He bore the guilt and shame of sin, and the hiding of His Father's face, till the woes of a lost world broke His heart and crushed out His life on Calvary's cross. That the Maker of all worlds, the Arbiter of all destinies, should lay aside His glory and humiliate Himself from love to man will ever excite the wonder and adoration of the universe. As the nations of the saved look upon their Redeemer and behold the eternal glory of the Father shining in His countenance; as they behold His throne, which is from everlasting to everlasting, and know that His kingdom is to have no end, they break forth in rapturous song: "Worthy, worthy is the Lamb that was slain, and hath redeemed us to God by 652 His own most precious blood!"

The mystery of the cross explains all other mysteries. In the light that streams from Calvary the attributes of God which had filled us with fear and awe appear beautiful and attractive. Mercy, tenderness, and parental love are seen to blend with holiness, justice, and power. While we behold the majesty of His throne, high and lifted up, we see His character in its gracious manifestations, and comprehend, as never before, the significance of that endearing title, "Our Father."

It will be seen that He who is infinite in wisdom could devise no plan for our salvation except the sacrifice of His Son. The compensation for this sacrifice is the joy of peopling the earth with ransomed beings, holy, happy, and immortal. The result of the Saviour's conflict with the powers of darkness is joy to the redeemed, redounding to the glory of God throughout eternity. And such is the value of the soul that the Father is satisfied with the price paid; and Christ Himself, beholding the fruits of His great sacrifice, is satisfied.

653

41
Desolation of the Earth

"Her sins have reached unto heaven, and God hath remembered her iniquities. . . . In the cup which she hath filled fill to her double. How much she hath glorified herself, and lived deliciously, so much torment and sorrow give her: for she saith in her heart, I sit a queen, and am no widow, and shall see no sorrow. Therefore shall her plagues come in one day, death, and mourning, and famine; and she shall be utterly burned with fire: for strong is the Lord God who judgeth her. And the kings of the earth, who have committed fornication and lived deliciously with her, shall bewail her, and lament for her, . . . saying, Alas, alas that great city Babylon, that mighty city! for in one hour is thy judgment come." Revelation 18:5-10.

"The merchants of the earth," that have "waxed rich through the abundance of her delicacies," "shall stand afar off for the fear of her torment, weeping and wailing, and saying, Alas, alas that great city, that was clothed in fine linen, and purple, and scarlet, and decked with gold, and precious stones, and pearls! For in one hour so great riches is come to nought." Revelation 18:11, 3, 15-17.

Such are the judgments that fall upon Babylon in the day of the visitation of God's wrath. She has filled up the measure of her iniquity; her time has come; she is ripe for destruction.

654   When the voice of God turns the captivity of His people, there is a terrible awakening of those who have lost all in the great conflict of life. While probation continued they were blinded by Satan's deceptions, and they justified their course of sin. The rich prided themselves upon their superiority to those who were less favored; but they had obtained their riches by violation of the law of God. They had neglected to feed the hungry, to clothe the naked, to deal justly, and to love mercy. They had sought to exalt themselves and to obtain the homage of their fellow creatures. Now they are stripped of all that made them great and are left destitute and defenseless. They look with terror upon the destruction of the idols which they preferred before their Maker. They have sold their souls for earthly riches and enjoyments, and have not sought to become rich toward God. The result is, their lives are a failure; their pleasures are now turned to gall, their treasures to corruption. The gain of a lifetime is swept away in a moment. The rich bemoan the destruction of their grand houses, the scattering of their gold and silver. But their lamentations are silenced by the fear that they themselves are to perish with their idols.

The wicked are filled with regret, not because of their sinful neglect of God and their fellow men, but because God has conquered. They lament that the result is what it is; but they do not repent of their wickedness. They would leave no means untried to conquer if they could.

The world see the very class whom they have mocked and derided, and desired to exterminate, pass unharmed through pestilence, tempest, and earthquake. He who is to the transgressors of His law a devouring fire, is to His people a safe pavilion.

The minister who has sacrificed truth to gain the favor of men now discerns the character and influence of his teachings. It is apparent that the omniscient eye was following him as he stood in the desk, as he walked the streets, as he mingled with men in the various scenes of life. Every emotion of the soul, every line written,   655 every word uttered, every act that led men to rest in a refuge of falsehood, has been scattering seed; and now, in the wretched, lost souls around him, he beholds the harvest.

Saith the Lord: "They have healed the hurt of the daughter of My people slightly, saying, Peace, peace; when there is no peace." "With lies ye have made the heart of the righteous sad, whom I have not made sad; and strengthened the hands of the wicked, that he should not return from his wicked way, by promising him life." Jeremiah 8:11; Ezekiel 13:22.

"Woe be unto the pastors that destroy and scatter the sheep of My pasture! . . . Behold, I will visit upon you the evil of your doings." "Howl, ye shepherds, and cry; and wallow yourselves in the ashes, ye principal of the flock: for your days for slaughter and of your dispersions are accomplished; . . . and the shepherds shall have no way to flee, nor the principal of the flock to escape." Jeremiah 23:1, 2; 25:34, 35, margin.

Ministers and people see that they have not sustained the right relation to God. They see that they have rebelled against the Author of all just and righteous law. The setting aside of the divine precepts gave rise to thousands of springs of evil, discord, hatred, iniquity, until the earth became one vast field of strife, one sink of corruption. This is the view that now appears to those who rejected truth and chose to cherish error. No language can express the longing which the disobedient and disloyal feel for that which they have lost forever—eternal life. Men whom the world has worshiped for their talents and eloquence now see these things in their true light. They realize what they have forfeited by transgression, and they fall at the feet of those whose fidelity they have despised and derided, and confess that God has loved them.

The people see that they have been deluded. They accuse one another of having led them to destruction; but all unite in heaping their bitterest condemnation upon the ministers. Unfaithful pastors have prophesied smooth things; they have led their hearers to make void the law of God and to persecute those who would keep it holy. Now, in their despair, these teachers confess before the world their work of deception. The multitudes are filled with fury. "We are lost!" they cry, "and you are the cause of our ruin;" and they turn upon the false shepherds. The very ones that once admired them most will pronounce the most dreadful curses upon them. The very hands that once crowned them with laurels will be raised for their destruction. The swords which were to slay God's people are now employed to destroy their enemies. Everywhere there is strife and bloodshed.

"A noise shall come even to the ends of the earth; for the Lord hath a controversy with the nations, He will plead with all flesh; He will give them that are wicked to the sword." Jeremiah 25:31. For six thousand years the great controversy has been in progress; the Son of God and His heavenly messengers have been in conflict with the power of the evil one, to warn, enlighten, and save the children of men. Now all have made their decisions; the wicked have fully united with Satan in his warfare against God. The time has come for God to vindicate the authority of His downtrodden law. Now the controversy is not alone with Satan, but with men. "The Lord hath a controversy with the nations;" "He will give them that are wicked to the sword."

The mark of deliverance has been set upon those "that sigh and that cry for all the abominations that be done." Now the angel of death goes forth, represented in Ezekiel's vision by the men with the slaughtering weapons, to whom the command is given: "Slay utterly old and young, both maids, and little children, and women: but come not near any man upon whom is the mark; and begin at My sanctuary." Says the prophet: "They began at the ancient men which were before the house." Ezekiel 9:1-6. The work of destruction begins among those who have professed to be the spiritual guardians of the people. The false watchmen are the first to fall. There are none to pity or to spare. Men, women, maidens, and little children perish together.

"The Lord cometh out of His place to punish the inhabitants of the earth for their iniquity: the earth also shall disclose her blood, and shall no more cover her slain." Isaiah 26:21. "And this shall be the plague wherewith the Lord will smite all the people that have fought against Jerusalem; Their flesh shall consume away while they stand upon their feet, and their eyes shall consume away in their holes, and their tongue shall consume away in their mouth. And it shall come to pass in that day, that a great tumult from the Lord shall be among them; and

they shall lay hold everyone on the hand of his neighbor, and his hand shall rise up against the hand of his neighbor." Zechariah 14:12, 13. In the mad strife of their own fierce passions, and by the awful outpouring of God's unmingled wrath, fall the wicked inhabitants of the earth—priests, rulers, and people, rich and poor, high and low. "And the slain of the Lord shall be at that day from one end of the earth even unto the other end of the earth: they shall not be lamented, neither gathered, nor buried." Jeremiah 25:33.

At the coming of Christ the wicked are blotted from the face of the whole earth—consumed with the spirit of His mouth and destroyed by the brightness of His glory. Christ takes His people to the City of God, and the earth is emptied of its inhabitants. "Behold, the Lord maketh the earth empty, and maketh it waste, and turneth it upside down, and scattereth abroad the inhabitants thereof." "The land shall be utterly emptied, and utterly spoiled: for the Lord hath spoken this word." "Because they have transgressed the laws, changed the ordinance, broken the everlasting covenant. Therefore hath the curse devoured the earth, and they that dwell therein are desolate: therefore the inhabitants of the earth are burned." Isaiah 24:1, 3, 5, 6.

The whole earth appears like a desolate wilderness. The ruins of cities and villages destroyed by the earthquake, uprooted trees, ragged rocks thrown out by the sea or torn out of the earth itself, are scattered over its surface, while vast caverns mark the spot where the mountains have been rent from their foundations.

Now the event takes place foreshadowed in the last solemn service of the Day of Atonement. When the ministration in the holy of holies had been completed, and the sins of Israel had been removed from the sanctuary by virtue of the blood of the sin offering, then the scapegoat was presented alive before the Lord; and in the presence of the congregation the high priest confessed over him "all the iniquities of the children of Israel, and all their transgressions in all their sins, putting them upon the head of the goat." Leviticus 16:21. In like manner, when the work of atonement in the heavenly sanctuary has been completed, then in the presence of God and heavenly angels and the hosts of the redeemed the sins of God's people will be placed upon Satan; he will be declared guilty of all the evil which he has caused them to commit. And as the scapegoat was sent away into a land not inhabited, so Satan will be banished to the desolate earth, an uninhabited and dreary wilderness.

The revelator foretells the banishment of Satan and the condition of chaos and desolation to which the earth is to be reduced, and he declares that this condition will exist for a thousand years. After presenting the scenes of the Lord's second coming and the destruction of the wicked, the prophecy continues: "I saw an angel come down from heaven, having the key of the bottomless pit and a great chain in his hand. And he laid hold on the dragon, that old serpent, which is the devil, and Satan, and bound him a thousand years, and cast him into the bottomless pit, and shut him up, and set a seal upon him, that he should deceive the nations no more, till the thousand years should be fulfilled: and after that he must be loosed a little season." Revelation 20:1-3.

That the expression "bottomless pit" represents the earth in a state of confusion and darkness is evident from other scriptures. Concerning the condition of the earth "in the beginning," the Bible record says that it "was without form, and void; and darkness was upon the face

659 of the deep."* Genesis 1:2. Prophecy teaches that it will be brought back, partially at least, to this condition. Looking forward to the great day of God, the prophet Jeremiah declares: "I beheld the earth, and, lo, it was without form, and void; and the heavens, and they had no light. I beheld the mountains, and, lo, they trembled, and all the hills moved lightly. I beheld, and, lo, there was no man, and all the birds of the heavens were fled. I beheld, and, lo, the fruitful place was a wilderness, and all the cities thereof were broken down." Jeremiah 4:23-26.

Here is to be the home of Satan with his evil angels for a thousand years. Limited to the earth, he will not have access to other worlds to tempt and annoy those who have never fallen. It is in this sense that he is bound: there are none remaining, upon whom he can exercise his power. He is wholly cut off from the work of deception and ruin which for so many centuries has been his sole delight.

The prophet Isaiah, looking forward to the time of Satan's overthrow, exclaims: "How art thou fallen from heaven, O Lucifer, son of the morning! how art thou cut down to the ground, which didst weaken the nations! . . . Thou hast said in thine heart, I will ascend into heaven, I will exalt my throne above the stars of God: . . . I will be like the Most High. Yet thou shalt be brought down to hell, to the sides of the pit. They that see thee shall narrowly look upon thee, and consider thee, saying, Is this the man that made the earth to tremble, that did shake kingdoms; that made the world as a wilderness, and destroyed the cities thereof; that *opened not the house of his prisoners?*" Isaiah 14:12-17.

For six thousand years, Satan's work of rebellion has "made the earth to tremble." He has "made the world as a wilderness, and destroyed the cities thereof." And he "opened not the house of his prisoners." For six thousand years his prison house has received God's people, and he would have held them captive forever; but

Christ has broken his bonds and set the prisoners free.

Even the wicked are now placed beyond the 660 power of Satan, and alone with his evil angels he remains to realize the effect of the curse which sin has brought. "The kings of the nations, even all of them, lie in glory, everyone in his own house [the grave]. But thou art cast out of thy grave like an abominable branch. . . . Thou shalt not be joined with them in burial, because thou hast destroyed thy land, and slain thy people." Isaiah 14:18-20.

For a thousand years, Satan will wander to and fro in the desolate earth to behold the results of his rebellion against the law of God. During this time his sufferings are intense. Since his fall his life of unceasing activity has banished reflection; but he is now deprived of his power and left to contemplate the part which he has acted since first he rebelled against the government of heaven, and to look forward with trembling and terror to the dreadful future when he must suffer for all the evil that he has done and be punished for the sins that he has caused to be committed.

To God's people the captivity of Satan will bring gladness and rejoicing. Says the prophet: "It shall come to pass in the day that Jehovah shall give thee rest from thy sorrow, and from thy trouble, and from the hard service wherein thou wast made to serve, that thou shalt take up this parable against the king of Babylon [here representing Satan], and say, How hath the oppressor ceased! . . . Jehovah hath broken the staff of the wicked, the scepter of the rulers; that smote the peoples in wrath with a continual stroke, that ruled the nations in anger, with a persecution that none restrained." Verses 3-6, R.V.

During the thousand years between the first and the second resurrection the judgment of the wicked takes place. The apostle Paul points to this judgment as an event that follows the second advent. "Judge nothing before the time, until the Lord come, who both will bring to light the hidden things of darkness, and will make manifest the counsels of the hearts." 1 Corinthi- 661 ans 4:5. Daniel declares that when the Ancient of Days came, "judgment was given to the saints of the Most High." Daniel 7:22. At this time the righteous reign as kings and priests unto God. John in the Revelation says: "I saw thrones, and they sat upon them, and judgment was given unto them." "They shall be priests of God and of Christ, and shall reign with Him a thousand years." Revelation 20:4, 6. It is at this time that, as foretold by Paul, "the saints shall judge the world." 1 Corinthians 6:2. In union with Christ they judge the wicked, comparing their acts with the statute book, the Bible, and deciding every case according to the deeds done in the body. Then the portion which the wicked

---

* The Hebrew word here translated "deep" is rendered in the Septuagint (Greek) translation of the Hebrew Old Testament by the same word rendered "bottomless pit" in Revelation 20:1-3.

must suffer is meted out, according to their works; and it is recorded against their names in the book of death.

Satan also and evil angels are judged by Christ and His people. Says Paul: "Know ye not that we shall judge angels?" Verse 3. And Jude declares that "the angels which kept not their first estate, but left their own habitation, He hath reserved in everlasting chains under darkness unto the judgment of the great day." Jude 6.

At the close of the thousand years the second resurrection will take place. Then the wicked will be raised from the dead and appear before God for the execution of "the judgment written." Thus the revelator, after describing the resurrection of the righteous, says: "The rest of the dead lived not again until the thousand years were finished." Revelation 20:5. And Isaiah declares, concerning the wicked: "They shall be gathered together, as prisoners are gathered in the pit, and shall be shut up in the prison, and *after many days shall they be visited.*" Isaiah 24:22.

662

42
The Controversy Ended

At the close of the thousand years, Christ again returns to the earth. He is accompanied by the host of the redeemed and attended by a retinue of angels. As He descends in terrific majesty He bids the wicked dead arise to receive their doom. They come forth, a mighty host, numberless as the sands of the sea. What a contrast to those who were raised at the first resurrection! The righteous were clothed with immortal youth and beauty. The wicked bear the traces of disease and death.

Every eye in that vast multitude is turned to behold the glory of the Son of God. With one voice the wicked hosts exclaim: "Blessed is He that cometh in the name of the Lord!" It is not love to Jesus that inspires this utterance. The force of truth urges the words from unwilling lips. As the wicked went into their graves, so they come forth with the same enmity to Christ and the same spirit of rebellion. They are to have no new probation in which to remedy the defects of their past lives. Nothing would be gained by this. A lifetime of transgression has not softened their hearts. A second probation, were it given them, would be occupied as was the first in evading the requirements of God and exciting rebellion against Him.

Christ descends upon the Mount of Olives, whence, after His resurrection, He ascended, and where angels repeated the promise of His return. Says the prophet: "The Lord my God shall come, and all the saints with Thee." "And

663

His feet shall stand in that day upon the Mount of Olives, which is before Jerusalem on the east, and the Mount of Olives shall cleave in the midst thereof, . . . and there shall be a very great valley." "And the Lord shall be king over all the earth: in that day shall there be one Lord, and His name one." Zechariah 14:5, 4, 9. As the New Jerusalem, in its dazzling splendor, comes down out of heaven, it rests upon the place purified and made ready to receive it, and Christ, with His people and the angels, enters the Holy City.

Now Satan prepares for a last mighty struggle for the supremacy. While deprived of his power and cut off from his work of deception, the prince of evil was miserable and dejected; but as the wicked dead are raised and he sees the vast multitudes upon his side, his hopes revive, and he determines not to yield the great controversy. He will marshal all the armies of the lost under his banner and through them endeavor to execute his plans. The wicked are Satan's captives. In rejecting Christ they have accepted the rule of the rebel leader. They are ready to receive his suggestions and to do his bidding. Yet, true to his early cunning, he does not acknowledge himself to be Satan. He claims to be the prince who is the rightful owner of the world and whose inheritance has been unlawfully wrested from him. He represents himself to his deluded subjects as a redeemer, assuring them that his power has brought them forth from their graves and that he is about to rescue them from the most cruel tyranny. The presence of Christ having been removed, Satan works wonders to support his claims. He makes the weak strong and inspires all with his own spirit and energy. He proposes to lead them against the camp of the saints and to take possession of the City of God. With fiendish exultation he points to the unnumbered millions who have been raised from the dead and declares that as their leader he is well able to overthrow the city and regain his throne and his kingdom.

In that vast throng are multitudes of the long- 664 lived race that existed before the Flood; men of lofty stature and giant intellect, who, yielding to the control of fallen angels, devoted all their skill and knowledge to the exaltation of themselves; men whose wonderful works of art led the world to idolize their genius, but whose cruelty and evil inventions, defiling the earth and defacing the image of God, caused Him to blot them from the face of His creation. There are kings and generals who conquered nations, valiant men who never lost a battle, proud, ambitious warriors whose approach made kingdoms tremble. In death these experienced no change. As they come up from the grave, they resume the current of their thoughts just where it ceased. They are actuated by the same desire to conquer that ruled them when they fell.

Satan consults with his angels, and then with these kings and conquerors and mighty men. They look upon the strength and numbers on their side, and declare that the army within the city is small in comparison with theirs, and that it can be overcome. They lay their plans to take possession of the riches and glory of the New Jerusalem. All immediately begin to prepare for battle. Skillful artisans construct implements of war. Military leaders, famed for their success, marshal the throngs of warlike men into companies and divisions.

At last the order to advance is given, and the countless host moves on—an army such as was never summoned by earthly conquerors, such as the combined forces of all ages since war began on earth could never equal. Satan, the mightiest of warriors, leads the van, and his angels unite their forces for this final struggle. Kings and warriors are in his train, and the multitudes follow in vast companies, each under its appointed leader. With military precision the serried ranks advance over the earth's broken and uneven surface to the City of God. By command of Jesus, the gates of the New Jerusalem are closed, and the armies of Satan surround the city and make ready for the onset.

665   Now Christ again appears to the view of His enemies. Far above the city, upon a foundation of burnished gold, is a throne, high and lifted up. Upon this throne sits the Son of God, and around Him are the subjects of His kingdom. The power and majesty of Christ no language can describe, no pen portray. The glory of the Eternal Father is enshrouding His Son. The brightness of His presence fills the City of God, and flows out beyond the gates, flooding the whole earth with its radiance.

Nearest the throne are those who were once zealous in the cause of Satan, but who, plucked as brands from the burning, have followed their Saviour with deep, intense devotion. Next are those who perfected Christian characters in the midst of falsehood and infidelity, those who honored the law of God when the Christian world declared it void, and the millions, of all ages, who were martyred for their faith. And beyond is the "great multitude, which no man could number, of all nations, and kindreds, and people, and tongues, . . . before the throne, and before the Lamb, clothed with white robes, and palms in their hands." Revelation 7:9. Their warfare is ended, their victory won. They have run the race and reached the prize. The palm branch in their hands is a symbol of their triumph, the white robe an emblem of the spotless righteousness of Christ which now is theirs.

The redeemed raise a song of praise that echoes and re-echoes through the vaults of heaven: "Salvation to our God which sitteth upon the throne, and unto the Lamb." Verse 10. And angel and seraph unite their voices in ado-

ration. As the redeemed have beheld the power and malignity of Satan, they have seen, as never before, that no power but that of Christ could have made them conquerors. In all that shining throng there are none to ascribe salvation to themselves, as if they had prevailed by their own power and goodness. Nothing is said of what they have done or suffered; but the burden of every song, the keynote of every anthem, is: Salvation to our God and unto the Lamb.

In the presence of the assembled inhabitants 666 of earth and heaven the final coronation of the Son of God takes place. And now, invested with supreme majesty and power, the King of kings pronounces sentence upon the rebels against His government and executes justice upon those who have transgressed His law and oppressed His people. Says the prophet of God: "I saw a great white throne, and Him that sat on it, from whose face the earth and the heaven fled away; and there was found no place for them. And I saw the dead, small and great, stand before God; and the books were opened: and another book was opened, which is the book of life: and the dead were judged out of those things which were written in the books, according to their works." Revelation 20:11, 12.

As soon as the books of record are opened, and the eye of Jesus looks upon the wicked, they are conscious of every sin which they have ever committed. They see just where their feet diverged from the path of purity and holiness, just how far pride and rebellion have carried them in the violation of the law of God. The seductive temptations which they encouraged by indulgence in sin, the blessings perverted, the messengers of God despised, the warnings rejected, the waves of mercy beaten back by the stubborn, unrepentant heart—all appear as if written in letters of fire.

Above the throne is revealed the cross; and like a panoramic view appear the scenes of Adam's temptation and fall, and the successive steps in the great plan of redemption. The Saviour's lowly birth; His early life of simplicity and obedience; His baptism in Jordan; the fast and temptation in the wilderness; His public ministry, unfolding to men heaven's most precious blessings; the days crowded with deeds of love and mercy, the nights of prayer and watching in the solitude of the mountains; the plottings of envy, hate, and malice which repaid His benefits; the awful, mysterious agony in Gethsemane beneath the crushing weight of the sins of the whole world; His betrayal into the hands of the murderous mob; the fearful events of that 667 night of horror—the unresisting prisoner, forsaken by His best-loved disciples, rudely hurried through the streets of Jerusalem; the Son of God exultingly displayed before Annas, arraigned in the high priest's palace, in the judgment hall of Pilate, before the cowardly and cruel Herod, mocked, insulted, tortured, and condemned to die—all are vividly portrayed.

And now before the swaying multitude are revealed the final scenes—the patient Sufferer treading the path to Calvary; the Prince of heaven hanging upon the cross; the haughty priests and the jeering rabble deriding His expiring agony; the supernatural darkness; the heaving earth, the rent rocks, the open graves, marking the moment when the world's Redeemer yielded up His life.

The awful spectacle appears just as it was. Satan, his angels, and his subjects have no power to turn from the picture of their own work. Each actor recalls the part which he performed. Herod, who slew the innocent children of Bethlehem that he might destroy the King of Israel; the base Herodias, upon whose guilty soul rests the blood of John the Baptist; the weak, timeserving Pilate; the mocking soldiers; the priests and rulers and the maddened throng who cried, "His blood be on us, and on our children!"—all behold the enormity of their guilt. They vainly seek to hide from the divine majesty of His countenance, outshining the glory of the sun, while the redeemed cast their crowns at the Saviour's feet, exclaiming: "He died for me!"

Amid the ransomed throng are the apostles of Christ, the heroic Paul, the ardent Peter, the loved and loving John, and their truehearted brethren, and with them the vast host of martyrs; while outside the walls, with every vile and abominable thing, are those by whom they were persecuted, imprisoned, and slain. There is Nero, that monster of cruelty and vice, beholding the joy and exaltation of those whom he once tortured, and in whose extremest anguish he found satanic delight. His mother is there to 668 witness the result of her own work; to see how the evil stamp of character transmitted to her son, the passions encouraged and developed by her influence and example, have borne fruit in crimes that caused the world to shudder.

There are papist priests and prelates, who claimed to be Christ's ambassadors, yet employed the rack, the dungeon, and the stake to control the consciences of His people. There are the proud pontiffs who exalted themselves above God and presumed to change the law of the Most High. Those pretended fathers of the church have an account to render to God from which they would fain be excused. Too late they are made to see that the Omniscient One is jealous of His law and that He will in no wise clear the guilty. They learn now that Christ identifies His interest with that of His suffering people; and they feel the force of His own words: "Inasmuch as ye have done it unto one of the least of these My brethren, ye have done it unto Me." Matthew 25:40.

The whole wicked world stand arraigned at the bar of God on the charge of high treason against the government of heaven. They have none to plead their cause; they are without excuse; and the sentence of eternal death is pronounced against them.

It is now evident to all that the wages of sin is not noble independence and eternal life, but slavery, ruin, and death. The wicked see what they have forfeited by their life of rebellion. The far more exceeding and eternal weight of glory was despised when offered them; but how desirable it now appears. "All this," cries the lost soul, "I might have had; but I chose to put these things far from me. Oh, strange infatuation! I have exchanged peace, happiness, and honor for wretchedness, infamy, and despair." All see that their exclusion from heaven is just. By their lives they have declared: "We will not have this Man [Jesus] to reign over us."

As if entranced, the wicked have looked upon the coronation of the Son of God. They see in His hands the tables of the divine law, the statutes which they have despised and trans- 669 gressed. They witness the outburst of wonder, rapture, and adoration from the saved; and as the wave of melody sweeps over the multitudes without the city, all with one voice exclaim, "Great and marvelous are Thy works, Lord God Almighty; just and true are Thy ways, Thou King of saints" (Revelation 15:3); and, falling prostrate, they worship the Prince of life.

Satan seems paralyzed as he beholds the glory and majesty of Christ. He who was once a covering cherub remembers whence he has fallen. A shining seraph, "son of the morning;" how changed, how degraded! From the council where once he was honored, he is forever excluded. He sees another now standing near to the Father, veiling His glory. He has seen the crown placed upon the head of Christ by an angel of lofty stature and majestic presence, and he knows that the exalted position of this angel might have been his.

Memory recalls the home of his innocence and purity, the peace and content that were his until he indulged in murmuring against God, and envy of Christ. His accusations, his rebellion, his deceptions to gain the sympathy and support of the angels, his stubborn persistence in making no effort for self-recovery when God would have granted him forgiveness—all come vividly before him. He reviews his work among men and its results—the enmity of man toward his fellow man, the terrible destruction of life, the rise and fall of kingdoms, the overturning of thrones, the long succession of tumults, conflicts, and revolutions. He recalls his constant efforts to oppose the work of Christ and to sink man lower and lower. He sees that his hellish plots have been powerless to destroy those who have put their trust in Jesus. As Satan looks upon his kingdom, the fruit of his toil, he sees only failure and ruin. He has led the multitudes to believe that the City of God would be an easy prey; but he knows that this is false. Again and again, in the progress of the great controversy, he has been defeated and compelled to yield. He knows too well the power and majesty of the Eternal.

670 The aim of the great rebel has ever been to justify himself and to prove the divine government responsible for the rebellion. To this end he has bent all the power of his giant intellect. He has worked deliberately and systematically, and with marvelous success, leading vast multitudes to accept his version of the great controversy which has been so long in progress. For thousands of years this chief of conspiracy has palmed off falsehood for truth. But the time has now come when the rebellion is to be finally defeated and the history and character of Satan disclosed. In his last great effort to dethrone Christ, destroy His people, and take possession of the City of God, the archdeceiver has been fully unmasked. Those who have united with him see the total failure of his cause. Christ's followers and the loyal angels behold the full extent of his machinations against the government of God. He is the object of universal abhorrence.

Satan sees that his voluntary rebellion has unfitted him for heaven. He has trained his powers to war against God; the purity, peace, and harmony of heaven would be to him supreme torture. His accusations against the mercy and justice of God are now silenced. The reproach which he has endeavored to cast upon Jehovah rests wholly upon himself. And now Satan bows down and confesses the justice of his sentence.

"Who shall not fear Thee, O Lord, and glorify Thy name? for Thou only art holy: for all nations shall come and worship before Thee; for Thy judgments are made manifest." Verse 4. Every question of truth and error in the long-standing controversy has now been made plain. The results of rebellion, the fruits of setting aside the divine statutes, have been laid open to the view of all created intelligences. The working out of Satan's rule in contrast with the government of God has been presented to the whole universe. Satan's own works have condemned him. God's wisdom, His justice, and His goodness stand fully vindicated. It is seen that all His dealings in the great controversy have been con-

671 ducted with respect to the eternal good of His people and the good of all the worlds that He has created. "All Thy works shall praise Thee, O Lord; and Thy saints shall bless Thee." Psalm 145:10. The history of sin will stand to all eternity as a witness that with the existence of God's law is bound up the happiness of all the beings He has created. With all the facts of the great controversy in view, the whole universe, both loyal and rebellious, with one accord declare: "Just and true are Thy ways, Thou King of saints."

Before the universe has been clearly presented the great sacrifice made by the Father and the Son in man's behalf. The hour has come when Christ occupies His rightful position and is glorified above principalities and powers and every name that is named. It was for the joy that was set before Him—that He might bring many sons unto glory—that He endured the cross and despised the shame. And inconceivably great as was the sorrow and the shame, yet greater is the joy and the glory. He looks upon the redeemed, renewed in His own image, every heart bearing the perfect impress of the divine, every face reflecting the likeness of their King. He beholds in them the result of the travail of His soul, and He is satisfied. Then, in a voice that reaches the assembled multitudes of the righteous and the wicked, He declares: "Behold the purchase of My blood! For these I suffered, for these I died, that they might dwell in My presence throughout eternal ages." And the song of praise ascends from the white-robed ones about the throne: "Worthy is the Lamb that was slain to receive power, and riches, and wisdom, and strength, and honor, and glory, and blessing." Revelation 5:12.

Notwithstanding that Satan has been constrained to acknowledge God's justice and to bow to the supremacy of Christ, his character remains unchanged. The spirit of rebellion, like a mighty torrent, again bursts forth. Filled with frenzy, he determines not to yield the great controversy. The time has come for a last desperate struggle against the King of heaven. He rushes 672 into the midst of his subjects and endeavors to inspire them with his own fury and arouse them to instant battle. But of all the countless millions whom he has allured into rebellion, there are none now to acknowledge his supremacy. His power is at an end. The wicked are filled with the same hatred of God that inspires Satan; but they see that their case is hopeless, that they cannot prevail against Jehovah. Their rage is kindled against Satan and those who have been his agents in deception, and with the fury of demons they turn upon them.

Saith the Lord: "Because thou hast set thine heart as the heart of God; behold, therefore I will bring strangers upon thee, the terrible of the nations: and they shall draw their swords against the beauty of thy wisdom, and they shall defile thy brightness. They shall bring thee down to the pit." "I will destroy thee, O covering cherub, from the midst of the stones of fire. . . . I will cast thee to the ground, I will lay thee before kings, that they may behold thee. . . . . I will bring thee to ashes upon the earth in the sight of all them that behold thee. . . . . Thou shalt be a terror, and never shalt thou be any more." Ezekiel 28:6-8, 16-19.

"Every battle of the warrior is with confused noise, and garments rolled in blood; but this shall be with burning and fuel of fire." "The indignation of the Lord is upon all nations, and His fury upon all their armies: He hath utterly destroyed them, He hath delivered them to the slaughter." "Upon the wicked He shall rain quick burning coals, fire and brimstone and an horrible tempest: this shall be the portion of their cup." Isaiah 9:5; 34:2; Psalm 11:6, margin. Fire comes down from God out of heaven. The earth is broken up. The weapons concealed in its depths are drawn forth. Devouring flames burst from every yawning chasm. The very rocks are on fire. The day has come that shall burn as an oven. The elements melt with fervent heat, the earth also, and the works that are therein are burned up. Malachi 4:1; 2 Peter 3:10. The earth's surface seems one molten mass—a vast, seething lake of fire. It is the time of the judgment and perdition of ungodly men—"the day of the Lord's vengeance, and the year of recompenses for the controversy of Zion." Isaiah 34:8.

The wicked receive their recompense in the earth. Proverbs 11:31. They "shall be stubble: and the day that cometh shall burn them up, saith the Lord of hosts." Malachi 4:1. Some are destroyed as in a moment, while others suffer many days. All are punished "according to their deeds." The sins of the righteous having been transferred to Satan, he is made to suffer not only for his own rebellion, but for all the sins which he has caused God's people to commit. His punishment is to be far greater than that of those whom he has deceived. After all have perished who fell by his deceptions, he is still to live and suffer on. In the cleansing flames the wicked are at last destroyed, root and branch—Satan the root, his followers the branches. The full penalty of the law has been visited; the demands of justice have been met; and heaven and earth, beholding, declare the righteousness of Jehovah.

Satan's work of ruin is forever ended. For six thousand years he has wrought his will, filling the earth with woe and causing grief throughout the universe. The whole creation has groaned and travailed together in pain. Now God's creatures are forever delivered from his presence and temptations. "The whole earth is at rest, and is quiet: they [the righteous] break forth into singing." Isaiah 14:7. And a shout of praise and triumph ascends from the whole loyal universe. "The voice of a great multitude," "as the voice of many waters, and as the voice of mighty thunderings," is heard, saying: "Alleluia: for the Lord God omnipotent reigneth." Revelation 19:6.

While the earth was wrapped in the fire of destruction, the righteous abode safely in the Holy City. Upon those that had part in the first resurrection, the second death has no power.

While God is to the wicked a consuming fire, He is to His people both a sun and a shield. Revelation 20:6; Psalm 84:11.

"I saw a new heaven and a new earth: for the first heaven and the first earth were passed away." Revelation 21:1. The fire that consumes the wicked purifies the earth. Every trace of the curse is swept away. No eternally burning hell will keep before the ransomed the fearful consequences of sin.

One reminder alone remains: Our Redeemer will ever bear the marks of His crucifixion. Upon His wounded head, upon His side, His hands and feet, are the only traces of the cruel work that sin has wrought. Says the prophet, beholding Christ in His glory: "He had bright beams coming out of His side: and there was the hiding of His power." Habakkuk 3:4, margin. That pierced side whence flowed the crimson stream that reconciled man to God—there is the Saviour's glory, there "the hiding of His power." "Mighty to save," through the sacrifice of redemption, He was therefore strong to execute justice upon them that despised God's mercy. And the tokens of His humiliation are His highest honor; through the eternal ages the wounds of Calvary will show forth His praise and declare His power.

"O Tower of the flock, the stronghold of the daughter of Zion, unto Thee shall it come, even the first dominion." Micah 4:8. The time has come to which holy men have looked with longing since the flaming sword barred the first pair from Eden, the time for "the redemption of the purchased possession." Ephesians 1:14. The earth originally given to man as his kingdom, betrayed by him into the hands of Satan, and so long held by the mighty foe, has been brought back by the great plan of redemption. All that was lost by sin has been restored. "Thus saith the Lord . . . that formed the earth and made it; He hath established it, He created it not in vain, He formed it to be inhabited." Isaiah 45:18. God's original purpose in the creation of the earth is fulfilled as it is made the eternal abode of the redeemed. "The righteous shall inherit the land, and dwell therein forever." Psalm 37:29.

A fear of making the future inheritance seem too material has led many to spiritualize away the very truths which lead us to look upon it as our home. Christ assured His disciples that He went to prepare mansions for them in the Father's house. Those who accept the teachings of God's word will not be wholly ignorant concerning the heavenly abode. And yet, "eye hath not seen, nor ear heard, neither have entered into the heart of man, the things which God hath prepared for them that love Him." 1 Corinthians 2:9. Human language is inadequate to describe the reward of the righteous. It will be known only to those who behold it. No finite mind can comprehend the glory of the Paradise of God.

In the Bible the inheritance of the saved is called "a country." Hebrews 11:14-16. There the heavenly Shepherd leads His flock to fountains of living waters. The tree of life yields its fruit every month, and the leaves of the tree are for the service of the nations. There are ever-flowing streams, clear as crystal, and beside them waving trees cast their shadows upon the paths prepared for the ransomed of the Lord. There the wide-spreading plains swell into hills of beauty, and the mountains of God rear their lofty summits. On those peaceful plains, beside those living streams, God's people, so long pilgrims and wanderers, shall find a home.

"My people shall dwell in a peaceable habitation, and in sure dwellings, and in quiet resting places." "Violence shall no more be heard in thy land, wasting nor destruction within thy borders; but thou shalt call thy walls Salvation, and thy gates Praise." "They shall build houses, and inhabit them; and they shall plant vineyards, and eat the fruit of them. They shall not build, and another inhabit; they shall not plant, and another eat: . . . Mine elect shall long enjoy the work of their hands." Isaiah 32:18; 60:18; 65:21, 22.

There, "the wilderness and the solitary place shall be glad for them; and the desert shall rejoice, and blossom as the rose." "Instead of the thorn shall come up the fir tree, and instead of the brier shall come up the myrtle tree." "The wolf also shall dwell with the lamb, and the 676 leopard shall lie down with the kid; . . . and a little child shall lead them." "They shall not hurt nor destroy in all My holy mountain," saith the Lord. Isaiah 35:1; 55:13; 11:6, 9.

Pain cannot exist in the atmosphere of heaven. There will be no more tears, no funeral trains, no badges of mourning. "There shall be no more death, neither sorrow, nor crying: . . . for the former things are passed away." "The inhabitant shall not say, I am sick: the people that dwell therein shall be forgiven their iniquity." Revelation 21:4; Isaiah 33:24.

There is the New Jerusalem, the metropolis of the glorified new earth, "a crown of glory in the hand of the Lord, and a royal diadem in the hand of thy God." "Her light was like unto a stone most precious, even like a jasper stone, clear as crystal." "The nations of them which are saved shall walk in the light of it: and the kings of the earth do bring their glory and honor into it." Saith the Lord: "I will rejoice in Jerusalem, and joy in My people." "The tabernacle of God is with men, and He will dwell with them, and they shall be His people, and God Himself shall be with them, and be their God." Isaiah 62:3; Revelation 21:11, 24; Isaiah 65:19; Revelation 21:3.

In the City of God "there shall be no night." None will need or desire repose. There will be no weariness in doing the will of God and offering praise to His name. We shall ever feel the freshness of the morning and shall ever be far from its close. "And they need no candle, neither light of the sun; for the Lord God giveth them light." Revelation 22:5. The light of the sun will be superseded by a radiance which is not painfully dazzling, yet which immeasurably surpasses the brightness of our noontide. The glory of God and the Lamb floods the Holy City with unfading light. The redeemed walk in the sunless glory of perpetual day.

"I saw no temple therein: for the Lord God Almighty and the Lamb are the temple of it." Revelation 21:22. The people of God are privileged to hold open communion with the Father and the Son. "Now we see through a glass, darkly." 1 Corinthians 13:12. We behold the 677 image of God reflected, as in a mirror, in the works of nature and in His dealings with men; but then we shall see Him face to face, without a dimming veil between. We shall stand in His presence and behold the glory of His countenance.

There the redeemed shall know, even as also they are known. The loves and sympathies which God Himself has planted in the soul shall there find truest and sweetest exercise. The pure communion with holy beings, the harmonious social life with the blessed angels and with the faithful ones of all ages who have washed their robes and made them white in the blood of the Lamb, the sacred ties that bind together "the whole family in heaven and earth" (Ephesians 3:15)—these help to constitute the happiness of the redeemed.

There, immortal minds will contemplate with never-failing delight the wonders of creative power, the mysteries of redeeming love. There will be no cruel, deceiving foe to tempt to forgetfulness of God. Every faculty will be developed, every capacity increased. The acquirement of knowledge will not weary the mind or exhaust the energies. There the grandest enterprises may be carried forward, the loftiest aspirations reached, the highest ambitions realized; and still there will arise new heights to surmount, new wonders to admire, new truths to comprehend, fresh objects to call forth the powers of mind and soul and body.

All the treasures of the universe will be open to the study of God's redeemed. Unfettered by mortality, they wing their tireless flight to worlds afar—worlds that thrilled with sorrow at the spectacle of human woe and rang with songs of gladness at the tidings of a ransomed soul. With unutterable delight the children of earth enter into the joy and the wisdom of unfallen beings. They share the treasures of knowledge and understanding gained through ages upon ages in contemplation of God's handiwork. With undimmed vision they gaze upon the glory of creation—suns and stars and systems, all in their appointed order circling the throne of 678

Deity. Upon all things, from the least to the greatest, the Creator's name is written, and in all are the riches of His power displayed.

And the years of eternity, as they roll, will bring richer and still more glorious revelations of God and of Christ. As knowledge is progressive, so will love, reverence, and happiness increase. The more men learn of God, the greater will be their admiration of His character. As Jesus opens before them the riches of redemption and the amazing achievements in the great controversy with Satan, the hearts of the ransomed thrill with more fervent devotion, and with more rapturous joy they sweep the harps of gold; and ten thousand times ten thousand and thousands of thousands of voices unite to swell the mighty chorus of praise.

"And every creature which is in heaven, and on the earth, and under the earth, and such as are in the sea, and all that are in them, heard I saying, Blessing, and honor, and glory, and power, be unto Him that sitteth upon the throne, and unto the Lamb for ever and ever." Revelation 5:13.

The great controversy is ended. Sin and sinners are no more. The entire universe is clean. One pulse of harmony and gladness beats through the vast creation. From Him who created all, flow life and light and gladness, throughout the realms of illimitable space. From the minutest atom to the greatest world, all things, animate and inanimate, in their unshadowed beauty and perfect joy, declare that God is love.

Appendix

General Notes

Page 50. TITLES.—In a passage which is included in the Roman Catholic Canon Law, or *Corpus Juris Canonici*, Pope Innocent III declares that the Roman pontiff is "the vicegerent upon earth, not of a mere man, but of very God;" and in a gloss on the passage it is explained that this is because he is the vicegerent of Christ, who is "very God and very man." See *Decretales Domini Gregorii Papae IX* (*Decretals of the Lord Pope Gregory IX*), liber 1, *de translatione Episcoporum*, (*on the transference of Bishops*), title 7, ch. 3; *Corpus Juris Canonici* (2d Leipzig ed., 1881), col. 99; (Paris, 1612), tom. 2, *Decretales*, col. 205. The documents which formed the Decretals were gathered by Gratian, who was teaching at the University of Bologna about the year 1140. His work was added to and re-edited by Pope Gregory IX in an edition issued in 1234. Other documents appeared in succeeding years from time to time including the *Extravagantes*, added toward the close of the fifteenth century. All of these, with Gratian's *Decretum*, were published as the *Corpus Juris Canonici* in 1582. Pope Pius X authorized the codification in Canon law in 1904, and the resulting code became effective in 1918.

For the title "Lord God the Pope" see a gloss on the *Extravagantes* of Pope John XXII, title 14, ch. 4, *Declaramus*. In an Antwerp edition of the *Extravagantes*, dated 1584, the words "*Dominum Deum nostrum Papam*" ("Our Lord God the Pope") occur in column 153. In a Paris edition, dated 1612, they occur in column 140. In several editions published since 1612 the word "*Deum*" ("God") has been omitted.

Page 50. INFALLIBILITY.—On the doctrine of infallibility as set forth at the Vatican Council of 1870-71, see Philip Schaff, *The Creeds of Christendom*, vol. 2, *Dogmatic Decrees of the Vatican Council*, pp. 234-271, where both the Latin and the English texts are given. For discussion see, for the Roman Catholic view, *The Catholic Encyclopedia*, vol. 7, art. "Infallibility," by Patrick J. Toner, p. 790 ff.; James Cardinal Gibbons, *The Faith of Our Fathers* (Baltimore: John Murphy Company, 110th ed., 1917), chs. 7, 11. For Roman Catholic opposition to the doctrine of papal infallibility, see Johann Joseph Ignaz von Döllinger (pseudonym "Janus") *The Pope and the Council* (New York: Charles Scribner's Sons, 1869); and W.J. Sparrow Simpson, *Roman Catholic Opposition to Papal Infallibility* (London: John Murray, 1909). For the non-Roman view, see George Salmon, *Infallibility of the Church* (London: John Murray, rev. ed., 1914).

Page 52. IMAGE WORSHIP.—"The worship of images . . . was one of those corruptions of Christianity which crept into the church stealthily and almost without notice or observation. This corruption did not, like other heresies, develop itself at once, for in that case it would have met with decided censure and rebuke: but, making its commencement under a fair disguise, so gradually was one practice after another introduced in connection with it, that the church had become deeply steeped in practical idolatry, not only without any efficient opposition, but almost without any decided remonstrance; and when at length an endeavor was made to root it out, the evil was found too deeply fixed to admit of removal. . . . It must be traced to the idolatrous tendency of the human heart, and its propensity to serve the creature more than the Creator. . . .

"Images and pictures were first introduced into churches, not to be worshiped, but either in the place of books to give instruction to those who could not read, or to excite devotion in the minds of others. How far they ever answered such a purpose is doubtful; but, even granting that this was the case for a time, it soon ceased to be so, and it was found that pictures and images brought into churches darkened rather than enlightened the minds of the ignorant—degraded rather than exalted the devotion of the worshiper. So that, however they might have been intended to direct men's minds to God, they ended in turning them from Him to the worship of created things."—J. Mendham, *The Seventh General Council, the Second of Nicaea*, Introduction, pages iii-vi.

For a record of the proceedings and decisions of the Second Council of Nicaea, A.D. 787, called to establish the worship of images, see Baronius, *Ecclesiastical Annals*, vol. 9, pp. 391-407 (Antwerp, 1612); J. Mendham, *The Seventh General Council, the Second of Nicaea*; Ed. Stillingfleet, *Defense of the Discourse Concerning the Idolatry Practiced in the Church of Rome* (London, 1686); *A Select Library of Nicene and Post-Nicene Fathers*, 2d series, vol. 14, pp. 521-587 (New York, 1900); Charles J. Hefele, *A History of the Councils of the Church, From the Original Documents*, b. 18, ch. 1, secs. 332, 333; ch. 2, secs. 345-352 (T. and T. Clark ed., 1896), vol. 5, pp. 260-304, 342-372.

Page 53. THE SUNDAY LAW OF CONSTANTINE.— The law issued by the emperor Constantine on the seventh of March, A.D. 321, regarding a day of rest from labor, reads thus:

"All judges and city people and the craftsmen shall rest upon the venerable Day of the Sun. Country people, however, may freely attend to the cultivation of the fields, because it frequently happens that no other days are better adapted for planting the grain in the furrows or the vines in trenches. So that the advantage given by heavenly providence may not for the occasion of a short time perish."—Joseph Cullen Ayer, *A Source Book for Ancient Church History* (New York: Charles Scribner's Sons, 1913), div. 2, per. 1, ch. 1, sec. 59, g, pp. 284, 285.

The Latin original is in the *Codex Justiniani* (*Codex of Justinian*), lib. 3, title 12, lex. 3. The law is given in Latin and in English translation in Philip Schaff's *History of the Christian Church*, vol. 3, 3d period, ch. 7, sec. 75, p. 380, footnote 1; and in James A. Hessey's *Bampton Lectures, Sunday*, lecture 3, par. 1, 3d ed., Murray's printing of 1866, p. 58. See discussion in Schaff, as above referred to; in Albert Henry Newman, *A Manual of Church History* (Philadelphia: The American Baptist Publication Society, printing of 1933), rev. ed., vol. 1, pp. 305-307; and in LeRoy E. Froom, *The Prophetic Faith of Our Fathers* (Washington, D.C.: Review and Herald Publishing Assn., 1950), vol. 1, pp. 376-381.

Page 54. PROPHETIC DATES.—An important principle in prophetic interpretation in connection with time prophecies is the year-day principle, under which a day of prophetic time is counted as a calendar year of historic time. Before the Israelites entered the land of Canaan they sent twelve spies ahead to investigate. The spies were gone forty days, and upon their return the Hebrews, frightened at their report, refused to go up and occupy the Promised Land. The result was a sentence the Lord passed upon them: "After the number of the days in which ye searched the land, even forty days, each day for a year, shall ye bear your iniquities, even forty years." Numbers 14:34. A similar method of computing future time is indicated through the prophet Ezekiel. Forty years of punishment for iniquities awaited the kingdom of Judah. The Lord said through the prophet: "Lie again on thy right side, and thou shalt bear the iniquity of the house of Judah forty days: I have appointed thee each day for a year." Ezekiel 4:6. This year-day principle has an important application in interpreting the time element of the prophecy of the "two thousand and three hundred evenings and mornings" (Daniel 8:14, R.V.) and the 1260-day period, variously indicated as "a time and times and the dividing of time" (Daniel 7:25), the "forty and two months" (Revelation 11:2; 13:5), and the "thousand two hundred and threescore days" (Revelation 11:3; 12:6).

Page 56. FORGED WRITINGS.—Among the documents that at the present time are generally admitted to be forgeries, the Donation of Constantine and the Pseudo-Isidorian Decretals are of primary importance. "The 'Donation of Constantine' is the name traditionally applied, since the later Middle Ages, to a document purporting to have been addressed by Constantine the Great to Pope Sylvester I, which is found first in a Parisian manuscript (*Codex lat.* 2777) of probably the beginning of the ninth century. Since the eleventh century it has been used as a powerful argument in favor of the papal claims, and consequently since the twelfth it has been the subject of a vigorous controversy. At the same time, by rendering it possible to regard the papacy as a middle term between the original and the medieval Roman Empire, and thus to form a theoretical basis of continuity for the reception of the Roman law in the Middle Ages, it has had no small influence upon secular
682 history."—*The New Schaff-Herzog Encyclopedia of Religious Knowledge*, vol. 3, art. "Donation of Constantine," pp. 484, 485.

The historical theory developed in the "Donation" is fully discussed in Henry E. Cardinal Manning's *The Temporal Power of the Vicar of Jesus Christ*, London, 1862. The arguments of the "Donation" were of a scholastic type, and the possibility of a forgery was not mentioned until the rise of historical criticism in the fifteenth century. Nicholas of Cusa was among the first to conclude that Constantine never made any such donation. Lorenza Valla in Italy gave a brilliant demonstration of its spuriousness in 1450. See Christopher B. Coleman's *Treatise of Lorenzo Valla on the Donation of Constantine* (New York, 1927). For a century longer, however, the belief in the authenticity of the "Donation" and of the *False Decretals* was kept alive. For example, Martin Luther at first accepted the decretals, but he soon said to Eck: "I impugn these decretals;" and to Spalatin: "He [the pope] does in his decretals corrupt and

crucify Christ, that is, the truth."

It is deemed established that the "Donation" is (1) a forgery, (2) the work of one man or period, (3) the forger has made use of older documents, (4) the forgery originated around 752 and 778. As for the Catholics, they abandoned the defense of the authenticity of the document with Baronius, *Ecclesiastical Annals*, in 1592. Consult for the best text, K. Zeumer, in the *Festgabe fur Rudolf von Gneist* (Berlin, 1888). Translated in Coleman's *Treatise*, referred to above, and in Ernest F. Henderson, *Select Historical Documents of the Middle Ages* (New York, 1892), p. 319; *Briefwechsel* (Weimar ed.), pp. 141, 161. See also The New *Schaff-Herzog Encyclopedia of Religious Knowledge* (1950), vol. 3, p. 484; F. Gregorovius, *Rome in the Middle Ages*, vol. 2, p. 329; and Johann Joseph Ignaz von Döllinger, *Fables Respecting the Popes of the Middle Ages* (London, 1871).

The "false writings" referred to in the text include also the Pseudo-Isidorian Decretals, together with other forgeries. The Pseudo-Isidorian Decretals are certain fictitious letters ascribed to early popes from Clement (A.D. 100) to Gregory the Great (A.D. 600), incorporated in a ninth century collection purporting to have been made by "Isidore Mercator." The name "Pseudo-Isidorian Decretals" has been in use since the advent of criticism in the fifteenth century.

Pseudo-Isidore took as the basis of his forgeries a collection of valid canons called the *Hispana Gallica Augustodunensis*, thus lessening the danger of detection, since collections of canons were commonly made by adding new matter to old. Thus his forgeries were less apparent when incorporated with genuine material. The falsity of the Pseudo-Isidorian fabrications is now incontestably admitted, being proved by internal evidence, investigation of the sources, the methods used, and the fact that this material was unknown before 852. Historians agree that 850 or 851 is the most probable date for the completion of the collection, since the document is first cited in the *Admonitio* of the capitulary of Quiercy, in 857.

The author of these forgeries is not known. It is probable that they emanated from the aggressive new church party 683 which formed in the ninth century at Rheims, France. It is agreed that Bishop Hincmar of Rheims used these Decretals in his deposition of Rothad of Soissons, who brought the Decretals to Rome in 864 and laid them before Pope Nicholas I.

Among those who challenged their authenticity were Nicholas of Cusa (1401-1464), Charles Dumoulin (1500-1566), and George Cassender (1513-1564). The irrefutable proof of their falsity was conveyed by David Blondel, 1628.

An early edition is given in *Migne Patrolgia Latina*, CXXX. For the oldest and best manuscript, see P. Hinschius, *Decretales Pseudo-Isidorianiae at capitula Angilramni* (Leipzig, 1863). Consult *The New Schaff-Herzog Encyclopedia of Religious Knowledge* (1950), vol. 9, pp. 343-345. See also H. H. Milman, *Latin Christianity* (9 vols.), vol. 3; Johann Joseph Ignaz von Döllinger, *The Pope and the Council* (1869); and Kenneth Scott Latourette, *A History of the Expansion of Christianity* (1939), vol. 3; *The Catholic Encyclopedia*, vol. 5, art. "False Decretals," and Fournier, "Etudes sure les Fausses Decretals," in *Revue d'Historique Ecclesiastique* (Louvain) vol. 7 (1906), and vol. 8 (1907).

Page 57. THE DICTATE OF HILDEBRAND (GRE-GORY VII).—For the original Latin version see Baronius, *Annales Ecclesiastici,* ann. 1076, vol. 17, pp. 405, 406 of the Paris printing of 1869; and the *Monumenta Germaniae Historica Selecta,* vol. 3, p. 17. For an English translation see Frederic A. Ogg, *Source Book of Medieval History* (New York: American Book Co., 1907), ch. 16, sec. 45, pp. 262-264; and Oliver J. Thatcher and Edgar H. McNeal, *Source Book for Medieval History* (New York: Charles Scribner's Sons, 1905), sec. 3, item 65, pp. 136-139.

For a discussion of the background of the *Dictate,* see James Bryce, *The Holy Roman Empire,* rev. ed., ch. 10; and James W. Thompson and Edgar N. Johnson, *An Introduction to Medieval Europe, 300-1500,* pages 377-380.

Page 59. PURGATORY.—Dr. Joseph Faa Di Bruno thus defines purgatory: "Purgatory is a state of suffering after this life, in which those souls are for a time detained, who depart this life after their deadly sins have been remitted as to the stain and guilt, and as to the ever-lasting pain that was due to them; but who have on account of those sins still some debt of temporal punish-ment to pay; as also those souls which leave this world guilty only of venial sins."—*Catholic Belief* (1884 ed.; imprimatur Archbishop of New York), page 196.

See also K. R. Hagenbach, *Compendium of the History of Doctrines* (T. and T. Clark ed.) vol. 1, pp. 234-237, 405, 408; vol. 2, pp. 135-150, 308, 309; Charles Elliott, *Delineation of Roman Catholicism,* b. 2, ch. 12; *The Catholic Encyclopedia,* vol. 12, art. "Purgatory."

Page 59. INDULGENCES.—For a detailed history of the doctrine of indulgences see Mandell Creighton, *A History of the Papacy From the Great Schism to the Sack* 684 *of Rome* (London: Longmans, Green and Co., 1911), vol. 5, pp. 56-64, 71; W.H. Kent, "Indulgences," *The Catholic Encyclopedia,* vol. 7, pp. 783-789; H. C. Lea, *A History of Auricular Confession and Indulgences in the Latin Church* (Philadelphia: Lea Brothers and Co., 1896); Thomas M. Lindsay, *A History of the Reformation* (New York: Charles Scribner's Sons, 1917), vol. 1, pp. 216-227; Albert Henry Newman, *A Manual of Church History* (Philadelphia: The American Baptist Publication Society, 1953), vol. 2, pp. 53, 54, 62; Leopold Ranke, *History of the Reformation in Germany* (2d London ed., 1845), translated by Sarah Austin, vol. 1, pp. 331, 335-337, 343-346; Preserved Smith, *The Age of the Reformation* (New York: Henry Holt and Company, 1920), pp. 23-25, 66.

On the practical outworkings of the doctrine of indul-gences during the period of the Reformation see a paper by Dr. H. C. Lea, entitled, "Indulgences in Spain," pub-lished in *Papers of the American Society of Church His-tory,* vol. 1, pp. 129-171. Of the value of this historical sidelight Dr. Lea says in his opening paragraph: "Unvexed by the controversy which raged between Luther and Dr. Eck and Silvester Prierias, Spain contin-ued tranquilly to follow in the old and beaten path, and furnishes us with the incontestable official documents which enable us to examine the matter in the pure light of history."

Page 59. THE MASS.—For the doctrine of the mass as set forth at the Council of Trent see *The Canons and Decrees of the Council of Trent* in Philip Schaff, *Creeds of Christendom,* vol. 2, pp. 126-139, where both Latin and English texts are given. See also H.G. Schroeder, *Canons and Decrees of the Council of Trent* (St. Louis, Missouri: B. Herder, 1941).

For a discussion of the mass see *The Catholic Ency-clopedia,* vol. 5, art. "Eucharist," by Joseph Pohle, page 572 ff.; Nikolaus Gihr, *Holy Sacrifice of the Mass, Dog-matically, Liturgically, Ascetically Explained,* 12th ed. (St. Louis, Missouri: B. Herder, 1937); Josef Andreas Jungmann, *The Mass of the Roman Rite, Its Origins and Development,* translated from the German by Francis A. Brunner (New York: Benziger Bros., 1951). For the non-Catholic view, see John Calvin, *Institutes of the Christ-ian Religion,* b. 4, chs. 17, 18; and Edward Bouverie Pusey, *The Doctrine of the Real Presence* (Oxford, Eng-land: John H. Parker, 1855).

Page 65. THE SABBATH AMONG THE WALDENSES.—There are writers who have maintained that the Waldenses made a general practice of observing the seventh-day Sabbath. This concept arose from sources which in the original Latin describe the Waldenses as keeping the *dies dominicalis,* or Lord's day (Sunday), but in which through a practice which dates from the Reformation, the word for "Sunday" has been translated "Sabbath."

But there is historical evidence of some observance of the seventh-day Sabbath among the Waldenses. A report of an inquisition before whom were brought some Waldenses of Moravia in the middle of the fifteenth cen-tury declares that among the Waldenses "not a few would celebrate the Sabbath with the Jews."—Johann Joseph 685 Ignaz von Döllinger, *Beitrage zur Sektengeschichte des Mittelalters* (*Reports on the History of the Sects of the Middle Ages*), Munich, 1890, 2d pt., p. 661. There can be no question that this source indicates the observance of the seventh-day Sabbath.

Page 65. WALDENSIAN VERSIONS OF THE BIBLE.—On recent discoveries of Waldensian manu-scripts see M. Esposito, "Sur quelques manuscrits de l'an-cienne littérature des Vaudois du Piemont," in *Revue d'Historique Ecclésiastique* (Louvain, 1951), p. 130 ff.; F. Jostes, "Die Waldenserbibeln," in *Historisches Jahrbuch,* 1894; D. Lortsch, *Histoire de la Bible en France* (Paris, 1910), ch. 10.

A classic written by one of the Waldensian "barbs" is jean Leger, *Histoire Générale des Eglises Evangéliques des Vallées de Piémont* (Leyden, 1669), which was writ-ten at the time of the great persecutions and contains firsthand information with drawings.

For the literature of Waldensian texts see A. deSte-fano, *Civilta Medioevale* (1944); and *Riformatori ed eretici nel medioeve* (Palermo, 1938); J. D. Bounous, *The Waldensian Patois of Pramol* (Nashville, 1936); and A. Dondaine, *Archivum Fratrum Praedicatorum* (1946).

For the history of the Waldenses some of the more recent, reliable works are: E. Comba, *History of the Waldenses in Italy* (see later Italian edition published in

Torre Pellice, 1934); E. Gebhart, *Mystics and Heretics* (Boston, 1927); G. Gonnet, *Il Valdismo Medioevale, Prolegomeni* (Torre Pellice, 1935); and Jalla, *Histoire des Vaudois et leurs colonies* (Torre Pellice, 1935).

Page 77. EDICT AGAINST THE WALDENSES.—A considerable portion of the text of the papal bull issued by Innocent VIII in 1487 against the Waldenses(the original of which is in the library of the University of Cambridge) is given, in an English translation, in John Dowling's *History of Romanism* (1871 ed.), b. 6, ch. 5, sec. 62.

Page 85. WYCLIFFE.—The historian discovers that the name of Wycliffe has many different forms of spelling. For a full discussion of these see J. Dahmus, *The Prosecution of John Wyclyf* (New Haven: Yale University Press, 1952), p. 7.

Page 86. INFALLIBILITY.—For the original text of the papal bulls issued against Wycliffe with English translation see J. Dahmus, *The Prosecution of John Wyclyf* (New Haven: Yale University Press, 1952), pp. 35-49; also John Foxe, *Acts and Monuments of the Church* (London: Pratt Townsend, 1870); vol. 3, pp. 4-13.

For a summary of these bulls sent to the archbishop of Canterbury, to King Edward, and to the chancellor of the University of Oxford, see Merle d'Aubigné, *The History of the Reformation in the Sixteenth Century* (London: Blackie and Son, 1885), vol. 4, div. 7, p. 93; August Neander, *General History of the Christian Church* (Boston: Crocker and Brester, 1862), vol. 5, pp. 146, 147; George Sargeant, *History of the Christian Church* (Dallas: Frederick Publishing House, 1948), p. 323; Gotthard V. Lechler, *John Wycliffe and His English Precursors* (London: The Religious Tract Society, 1878), pp. 162-164; Philip Schaff, *History of the Christian Church* (New York: Charles Scribner's Sons, 1915), vol. 5, pt. 2, p. 317.

Page 104. COUNCIL OF CONSTANCE.—A primary source on the Council of Constance is Richendal Ulrich, *Das Concilium so zu Constanz gehalten ist worden* (Augsburg, 1483, Incun.). An interesting, recent study of this text, based on the "Aulendorf Codex," is in the Spencer Collection of the New York Public Library, published by Karl Küp, *Ulrich von Richental's Chronicle of the Council of Constance* (New York, 1936). See also H. Finke (ed.), *Acta Concilii Constanciensis* (1896), vol. 1; Hefele, *Conciliengeschichte* (9 vols.), vols. 6, 7; L. Mirbt, *Quellen zur Geschichte des Papsttums* (1934); Milman, *Latin Christianity*, vol. 7, pp. 426-524; Pastor, *The History of the Popes* (34 vols.), vol. 1, p. 194 ff.

More recent publications on the council are K. Zähringer, *Das Kardinal Kollegium auf dem Konstanzer Konzil* (Munster, 1935); Th. F. Grogau, *The Conciliar Theory as It Manifested Itself at the Council of Constance* (Washington, 1949); Fred A. Kremple, *Cultural Aspects of the Council of Constance and Basel* (Ann Arbor, 1955); John Patrick McGowan, *d'Ailly and the Council of Constance* (Washington: Catholic University, 1936).

For John Huss see John Hus, *Letters*, 1904; E. J. Kitts,

Pope John XXIII and Master John Hus (London, 1910); D. S. Schaff, *John Hus* (1915); Schwarze, *John Hus* (1915); and Matthew Spinka, *John Hus and the Czech Reform* (1941).

Page 234. JESUITISM.—FOr a statement concerning the origin, the principles, and the purposes of the "Society of Jesus," as outlined by members of this Order, see a work entitled *Concerning Jesuits*, edited by the Rev. John Gerard, S.J., and published in London, 1902, by the Catholic Truth Society. In this work it is said, "The mainspring of the whole organization of the Society is a spirit of entire obedience: 'Let each one,' writes St. Ignatius, 'persuade himself that those who live under obedience ought to allow themselves to be moved and directed by divine Providence through their superiors, just as though they were a dead body, which allows itself to be carried anywhere and to be treated in any manner whatever, or as an old man's staff, which serves him who holds it in his hand in whatsoever way he will.'

"This absolute submission is ennobled by its motive, and should be, continues the . . . founder, 'prompt, joyous, and persevering; . . . the obedient religious accomplishes joyfully that which his superiors have confided to him for the general good, assured that thereby he corresponds truly with the divine will.'"—The Comtesse R. de Courson, in *Concerning Jesuits*, page 6.

See also L. E. Dupin, *A Compendious History of the Church*, cent. 16, ch. 33 (London, 1713, vol. 4, pp. 132-135); Mosheim, *Ecclesiastical History*, cent. 16, sec. 3, pt. 1, ch. 1, par. 10 (including notes); *The Encyclopedia Britannica* (9th ed.), art. "Jesuits"; C. Paroissen, *The Principles of the Jesuits, Developed in a Collection of Extracts From Their Own Authors* (London, 1860—an earlier edition appeared in 1839); W. C. Cartwright, *The Jesuits, Their Constitution and Teaching* (London, 1876); E. L. Taunton, *The History of the Jesuits in England*, 1580-1773 (London, 1901).

See also H. Boehmer, *The Jesuits* (translation from the German, Philadelphia, Castle Press, 1928); E. Goethein, *Ignatius Loyola and the Gegen-reformation* (Halle, 1895); T. Campbell, *The Jesuits, 1534-1921* (New York, 1922); E. L. Taunton, *The History of the Jesuits in England, 1580-1773* (London, 1901).

Page 235. THE INQUISITION.—For the Roman Catholic view see *The Catholic Encyclopedia*, vol. 8, art. "Inquisition" by Joseph Blötzer, p. 26 ff.; and E. Vacandard, *The Inquisition: A Critical and Historical Study of the Coercive Power of the Church* (New York: Longmans, Green and Company, 1908).

For an Anglo-Catholic view see Hoffman Nickerson, *The Inquisition: A Political and Military Study of Its Establishment*. For the non-Catholic view see Philip Van Limborch, *History of the Inquisition*; Henry Charles Lea, *A History of the Inquisition of the Middle Ages*, 3 vols.; *A History of the Inquisition of Spain*, 4 vols., and *The Inquisition in the Spanish Dependencies*; and H. S. Turberville, *Medieval Heresy and the Inquisition* (London: C. Lockwood and Son, 1920—a mediating view).

Page 265. CAUSES OF THE FRENCH REVOLUTION.—On the far-reaching consequences of the rejection of the Bible and of Bible religion, by the people of France, see H. von Sybel, *History of the French Revolution*, b. 5, ch. 1, pars. 3-7; Henry Thomas Buckle, *History of Civilization in England*, chs. 8, 12, 14 (New York, 1895, vol. 1, pp. 364-366, 369-371, 437, 540, 541, 550); *Blackwood's Magazine*, vol. 34, No. 215 (November, 1833), p. 739; J. G. Lorimer, *An Historical Sketch of the Protestant Church in France*, ch. 8, pars. 6, 7.

Page 267. EFFORTS TO SUPPRESS AND DESTROY THE BIBLE.—The Council of Toulouse, which met about the time of the crusade against the Albigenses, ruled: "We prohibit laymen possessing copies of the Old and New Testament. . . . We forbid them most severely to have the above books in the popular vernacular." "The lords of the districts shall carefully seek out the heretics in dwellings, hovels, and forests, and even their underground retreats shall be entirely wiped out."—*Council. Tolosanum, Pope Gregory IX, Anno. chr.* 1229. Canons 14 and 2. This Council sat at the time of the crusade against the Albigenses.

"This pest [the Bible] had taken such an extension that 688 some people had appointed priests of their own, and even some evangelists who distorted and destroyed the truth of the gospel and made new gospels for their own purpose . . . (they know that) the preaching and explanation of the Bible is absolutely forbidden to the lay members."—*Acts of Inquisition*, Philip van Limborch, *History of the Inquisition*, chapter 8.

The Council of Tarragona, 1234, ruled that: "No one may possess the books of the Old and New Testaments in the Romance language, and if anyone possesses them he must turn them over to the local bishop within eight days after promulgation of this decree, so that they may be burned lest, be he a cleric or a layman, he be suspected until he is cleared of all suspicion."—D. Lortsch, *Histoire de la Bible en France*, 1910, p. 14.

At the Council of Constance, in 1415, Wycliffe was posthumously condemned by Arundel, the archbishop of Canterbury, as "that pestilent wretch of damnable heresy who invented a new translation of the Scriptures in his mother tongue."

The opposition to the Bible by the Roman Catholic Church has continued through the centuries and was increased particularly at the time of the founding of Bible societies. On December 8, 1866, Pope Pius IX, in his encyclical *Quanta cura*, issued a syllabus of eighty errors under ten different headings. Under heading IV we find listed: "Socialism, communism, clandestine societies, Bible societies. . . . Pests of this sort must be destroyed by all possible means."

Page 276. THE REIGN OF TERROR.—For a reliable, brief introduction into the history of the French Revolution see L. Gershoy, *The French Revolution* (1932); G. Lefebvre, *The Coming of the French Revolution* (Princeton, 1947); and H. von Sybel, *History of the French Revolution* (1869), 4 vols.

The *Moniteur Officiel* was the government paper at the time of the Revolution and is a primary source, containing a factual account of actions taken by the Assemblies, full texts of the documents, etc. It has been reprinted. See also A. Aulard, *Christianity and the French Revolution*

(London, 1927), in which the account is carried through 1802—an excellent study; W. H. Jervis, *The Gallican Church and the Revolution* (London, 1882), a careful work by an Anglican, but shows preference for Catholicism.

On the relation of church and state in France during the French Revolution see Henry H. Walsh, *The Concordate of 1801: A Study of Nationalism in Relation to Church and State* (New York, 1933); Charles Ledre, *L'Englise de France souls la Revolution* (Paris, 1949).

Some contemporary studies on the religious significance of the Revolution are G. Chais de Sourcesol, *Le Livre des Manifestes* (Avignon, 1800), in which the author endeavored to ascertain the causes of the upheaval, and its religious significance, etc.; James Bicheno, *The Signs of the Times* (London, 1794); James Winthrop, *A Systematic Arrangement of Several Scripture Prophecies Relating to Antichrist; With Their Application to the Course of History* (Boston, 1795); and Lathrop, *The Prophecy of Daniel Relating to the Time of the End* 689 (Springfield, Massachusetts, 1811).

For the church during the Revolution see W. M. Sloan, *The French Revolution and Religious Reform* (1901); P. F. La Gorce, *Histoire Religieuse de la Révolution* (Paris, 1909).

On relations with the papacy see G. Bourgin, *La France et Rome de 1788-1797* (Paris, 1808), based on secret files in the Vatican; A. Latreille, *L'Eglise Catholique et la Révolution* (Paris, 1950), especially interesting on Pius VI and the religious crisis, 1775-1799.

For Protestants during the Revolution, see Pressensé (ed.), *The Reign of Terror* (Cincinnati, 1869).

Page 280. THE MASSES AND THE PRIVILEGED CLASSES.—On social conditions prevailing in France prior to the period of the Revolution, see H. von Holst, *Lowell Lectures on the French Revolution*, lecture 1; also Taine, *Ancien Régime*, and A. Young, *Travels in France*.

Page 283. RETRIBUTION.—For further details concerning the retributive character of the French Revolution see Thos. H. Gill, *The Papal Drama*, b. 10; Edmond de Pressensé, *The Church and the French Revolution*, b. 3, ch. 1.

Page 284. THE ATROCITIES OF THE REIGN OF TERROR.—See M. A. Thiers, *History of the French Revolution*, vol. 3, pp. 42-44, 62-74, 106 (New York, 1890, translated by F. Shoberl); F. A. Mignet, *History of the French Revolution*, ch. 9, par. 1 (Bohn, 1894); A. Alison, *History of Europe, 1789-1815*, vol. 1, ch. 14 (New York, 1872, vol. 1, pp. 293-312).

Page 287. THE CIRCULATION OF THE SCRIPTURES.—In 1804, according to Mr. William Canton of the British and Foreign Bible Society, "all the Bibles extant in the world, in manuscript or in print, counting every version in every land, were computed at not many more than four millions. . . . The various languages in which those four millions were written, including such bygone speech as the Moeso-Gothic of Ulfilas and the Anglo-Saxon of Bede, are set down as numbering about fifty."—*What Is the Bible Society?* rev. ed., 1904, p. 23.

The American Bible Society reported a distribution from 1816 through 1955 of 481,149,365 Bibles, Testaments, and portions of Testaments. To this may be added over 600,000,000 Bibles or Scripture portions distributed by the British and Foreign Bible Society. During the year 1955 alone the American Bible Society distributed a grand total of 23,819,733 Bibles, Testaments, and portions of Testaments throughout the world.

The Scriptures, in whole or in part, have been printed, as of December, 1955, in 1,092 languages; and new languages are constantly being added.

690 Page 288. FOREIGN MISSIONS.—The missionary activity of the early Christian church has not been duplicated until modern times. It had virtually died out by the year 1000, and was succeeded by the military campaigns of the Crusades. The Reformation era saw little foreign mission work, except on the part of the early Jesuits. The pietistic revival produced some missionaries. The work of the Moravian Church in the eighteenth century was remarkable, and there were some missionary societies formed by the British for work in colonized North America. But the great resurgence of foreign missionary activity begins around the year 1800, at "the time of the end." Daniel 12:4. In 1792 was formed the Baptist Missionary Society, which sent Carey to India. In 1795 the London Missionary Society was organized, and another society in 1799 which in 1812 became the Church Missionary Society. Shortly afterward the Wesleyan Missionary Society was founded. In the United States the American Board of Commissioners for Foreign Missions was formed in 1812, and Adoniram Judson was sent out that year to Calcutta. He established himself in Burma the next year. In 1814 the American Baptist Missionary Union was formed. The Presbyterian Board of Foreign Missions was formed in 1837.

"In A.D. 1800, . . . the overwhelming majority of Christians were the descendants of those who had been won before A.D. 1500. . . . Now, in the nineteenth century, came a further expansion of Christianity. Not so many continents or major countries were entered for the first time as in the preceding three centuries. That would have been impossible, for on all the larger land masses of the earth except Australia and among all the more numerous peoples and in all the areas of high civilization Christianity had been introduced before A.D. 1800. What now occurred was the acquisition of fresh footholds in regions and among peoples already touched, an expansion of unprecedented extent from both the newer bases and the older ones, and the entrance of Christianity into the large majority of such countries, islands, peoples, and tribes as had previously not been touched. . . .

"The nineteenth century spread of Christianity was due primarily to a new burst of religious life emanating from the Christian impulse. . . . Never in any corresponding length of time had the Christian impulse given rise to so many new movements. Never had it had quite so great an effect upon Western European peoples. It was from this abounding vigor that there issued the missionary enterprise which during the nineteenth century so augmented the numerical strength and the influence of Christianity."—Kenneth Scott Latourette, *A History of the Expansion of Christianity*, vol. IV, *The Great Century*

A.D. 1800-A.D. 1914 (New York: Harper & Brothers, 1941), pp. 2-4.

Pages 327, 329. PROPHETIC DATES.—According to Jewish reckoning the fifth month (Ab) of the seventh year of Artaxerxes' reign was from July 23 to August 21, 457 B.C. After Ezra's arrival in Jerusalem in the autumn of the year, the decree of the king went into effect. For the certainty of the date 457 B.C. being the seventh year of Artaxerxes, see S. H. Horn and L. H. Wood, *The Chronology of Ezra 7* (Washington, D.C.: 691 Review and Herald Publishing Assn., 1953); E. G. Kraeling, *The Brooklyn Museum Aramaic Papyri* (New Haven or London, 1953), pp. 191-193; *The Seventh-day Adventist Bible Commentary* (Washington, D.C.: Review and Herald Publishing Assn., 1954), vol. 3, pp. 97-110.

Page 335. FALL OF THE OTTOMAN EMPIRE.—The impact of Moslem Turkey upon Europe after the fall of Constantinople in 1453 was as severe as had been the catastrophic conquests of the Moslem Saracens, during the century and a half after the death of Mohammed, upon the Eastern Roman Empire. Throughout the Reformation era, Turkey was a continual threat at the eastern gates of European Christendom; the writings of the Reformers are full of condemnation of the Ottoman power. Christian writers since have been concerned with the role of Turkey in future world events, and commentators on prophecy have seen Turkish power and its decline forecast in Scripture.

For the latter chapter, under the "hour, day, month, year" prophecy, as part of the sixth trumpet, Josiah Litch worked out an application of the time prophecy, terminating Turkish independence in August, 1840. Litch's view can be found in full in his *The Probability of the Second Coming of Christ About A.D. 1843* (published in June, 1838); *An Address to the Clergy* (published in the spring of 1840; a second edition, with historical data in support of the accuracy of former calculations of the prophetic period extending to the fall of the Ottoman Empire, was published in 1841); and an article in *Signs of the Times and Expositor of Prophecy*, Aug. 1, 1840. See also article in *Signs of the Times and Expositor of Prophecy*, Feb. 1, 1841; and J. N. Loughborough, *The Great Advent Movement* (1905 ed.), pp. 129-132. The book by Uriah Smith, *Thoughts on Daniel and the Revelation*, rev. ed. of 1944, discusses the prophetic timing of this prophecy on pages 506-517.

For the earlier history of the Ottoman Empire and the decline of the Turkish power, see also William Miller, *The Ottoman Empire and Its Successors, 1801-1927* (Cambridge, England: University Press, 1936); George G. S. L. Eversley, *The Turkish Empire From 1288 to 1914* (London: T. Fisher Unwin, Ltd., 2d ed., 1923); Joseph von Hammer-Purgstall, *Geschichte des Osmannischen Reiches* (Pesth: C. A. Hartleben, 2d ed., 1834-36), 4 vols.; Herbert A. Gibbons, *Foundation of the Ottoman Empire, 1300-1403* (Oxford: University Press, 1916); Arnold J. Toynbee and Kenneth B. Kirkwood, *Turkey* (London, 1926).

Page 340. WITHHOLDING THE BIBLE FROM THE

PEOPLE.—The reader will recognize that the text of this volume was written prior to Vatican Council II, with its somewhat altered policies in regard to the reading of the Scriptures.

Through the centuries, the attitude of the Roman Catholic Church toward circulation of the Holy Scriptures in vernacular versions among the laity shows up as negative. See for example G. P. Fisher, *The Reformation*, ch. 15, par. 16 (1873 ed., pp. 530-532); J. Cardinal Gibbons, *The Faith of Our Fathers*, ch. 8 (49th ed., 1897), pp. 98-117; John Dowling, *History of Romanism*, b. 7, ch. 2, sec. 14; and b. 9, ch. 3, secs. 24-27 (1871 ed., pp. 491-496, 621-625); L. F. Bungener, *History of the Council of Trent*, pp. 101-110 (2d Edinburgh ed., 1853, translated by D. D. Scott); G. H. Putnam, *Books and Their Makers During the Middle Ages*, vol. 1, pt. 2, ch. 2, pars. 49, 54-56. See also *Index of Prohibited Books* (Vatican Polyglot Press, 1930), pp. ix, x; Timothy Hurley, *A Commentary on the Present Index Legislation* (New York: Benziger Brothers, 1908), p. 71; *Translation of the Great Encyclical Letters of Leo XIII* (New York: Benziger Brothers, 1903), p. 413.

But in recent years a dramatic and positive change has occurred in this respect. On the one hand, the church has approved several versions prepared on the basis of the original languages; on the other, it has promoted the study of the Holy Scriptures by means of free distribution and Bible institutes. The church, however, continues to reserve for herself the exclusive right to interpret the Bible in the light of her own tradition, thus justifying those doctrines that do not harmonize with biblical teachings.

Page 373. ASCENSION ROBES.—The story that the Adventists made robes with which to ascend "to meet the Lord in the air," was invented by those who wished to reproach the advent preaching. It was circulated so industriously that many believed it, but careful inquiry proved its falsity. For many years a substantial reward was offered for proof that one such instance ever occurred, but no proof has been produced. None who loved the appearing of the Saviour were so ignorant of the teachings of the Scriptures as to suppose that robes which they could make would be necessary for that occasion. The only robe which the saints will need to meet the Lord is the righteousness of Christ. See Isaiah 61:10; Revelation 19:8.

For a thorough refutation of the legend of ascension robes, see Francis D. Nichol, *Midnight Cry* (Washington, D.C.: Review and Herald Publishing Assn., 1944), chs. 25-27, and Appendices H-J. See also LeRoy Edwin Froom, *Prophetic Faith of Our Fathers* (Washington, D.C.: Review and Herald Publishing Assn., 1954), vol. 4, pp. 822-826.

Page 374. THE CHRONOLOGY OF PROPHECY.—Dr. George Bush, professor of Hebrew and Oriental Literature in the New York City University, in a letter addressed to William Miller and published in the *Advent Herald* and *Signs of the Times Reporter*, Boston, March 6 and 13, 1844, made some important admissions relative to his calculation of the prophetic times. Dr. Bush wrote:

"Neither is it to be objected, as I conceive, to yourself or your friends, that you have devoted much time and attention to the study of the *chronology* of prophecy, and have labored much to determine the commencing and closing dates of its great periods. If these periods are actually given by the Holy Ghost in the prophetic books, it was doubtless with the design that they Mede, Sir Isaac Newton, Bishop Newton, Kirby, Scott, Keith, and a host of others who have long since come to *substantially* your conclusions on this head. They all agree that the leading periods mentioned by Daniel and John, do actually expire *about this age of the world*, and it would be a strange logic that would convict you of heresy for holding in effect the same views which stand forth so prominent in the notices of these eminent divines." "Your results in this field of inquiry do not strike me so far out of the way as to affect any of the great interests of truth or duty." "Your error, as I apprehend, lies in another direction than your *chronology*." "You have entirely mistaken *the nature of the events* which are to occur when those periods have expired. This is the head and front of your expository offending." See also LeRoy Edwin Froom, *Prophetic Faith of Our Fathers* (Washington, D.C.: Review and Herald Publishing Assn., 1950), vol. 1, chs. 1, 2.

Page 435. A THREEFOLD MESSAGE.—Revelation 14:6, 7 foretells the proclamation of the first angel's message. Then the prophet continues: "There followed another angel, saying, Babylon is fallen, is fallen. . . . And the third angel followed them." The word here rendered "followed" means "to go along with," "to follow one," "go with him." See Henry George Liddell and Robert Scott, *Greek English Lexicon* (Oxford: Clarendon Press, 1940), vol. 1, p. 52. It also means "to accompany." See George Abbott-Smith, *A Manual Greek Lexicon of the New Testament* (Edinburgh: T. and T. Clark, 1950), page 17. It is the same word that is used in Mark 5:24, "Jesus went with him; and much people followed Him, and thronged Him." It is also used of the redeemed one hundred and forty-four thousand, Revelation 14:4, where it is said, "These are they which follow the Lamb whithersoever He goeth." In both these places it is evident that the idea intended to be conveyed is that of "going together," "in company with." So in 1 Corinthians 10:4, where we read of the children of Israel that "they drank of that spiritual Rock that followed them," the word "followed" is translated from the same Greek word, and the margin has it, "went with them." From this we learn that the idea in Revelation 14:8, 9 is not simply that the second and third angels followed the first in point of time, but that they went with him. The three messages are but one threefold message. They are *three* only in the order of their rise. But having risen, they go on together and are inseparable.

Page 447. SUPREMACY OF THE BISHOPS OF ROME.—For the leading circumstances in the assumption of supremacy by the bishops of Rome, see Robert Francis Cardinal Bellarmine, *Power of the Popes in Temporal Affairs* (there is an English translation in the Library of Congress, Washington, D.C.); Henry Edward Cardinal Manning, *The Temporal Power of the Vicar of*

694 *Jesus Christ* (London: Burns and Lambert, 2d ed., 1862); and James Cardinal Gibbons, *Faith of Our Fathers* (Baltimore: John Murphy Co., 110th ed., 1917), chs. 5, 9, 10, 12. For Protestant authors see Trevor Gervase Jalland, *The Church and the Papacy* (London: Society for Promoting Christian Knowledge, 1944, a Bamp (London: Burns and Lambert, 2d ed., 1862); and James Cardinal Gibbons, *Faith of Our Fathers* (Baltimore: John Murphy Co., 110th ed., 1917), chs. 5, 9, 10, 12. For Protestant authors see Trevor Gervase Jalland, *The Church and the Papacy* (London: Society for Promoting Christian Knowledge, 1944, a Bampton Lecture); and Richard Frederick Littledale, *Petrine Claims* (London: Society for Promoting Christian Knowledge, 1899). For sources of the early centuries of the Petrine theory, see James T. Shotwell and Louise Ropes Loomis, *The See of Peter* (New York: Columbia University Press, 1927). For the false "Donation of Constantine" see Christopher B. Coleman, *The Treatise of Lorenzo Valla on the Donation of Constantine* (New York, 1914), which gives the full Latin text and translation, and a complete criticism of the document and its thesis.

Page 565. WITHHOLDING THE BIBLE FROM THE PEOPLE.—See note for page 340.

Page 578. THE ETHIOPIAN CHURCH AND THE SABBATH.—Until rather recent years the Coptic Church of Ethiopia observed the seventh-day Sabbath. The Ethiopians also kept Sunday, the first day of the week, throughout their history as a Christian people. These days were marked by special services in the churches. The observance of the seventh-day Sabbath has, however, virtually ceased in modern Ethiopia. For eyewitness accounts of religious days in Ethiopia, see Pero Gomes de Teixeira, *The Discovery of Abyssinia by the Portuguese in 1520* (translated in English in London: British Museum, 1938), p. 79; Father Francisco Alverez, *Narrative of the Portuguese Embassy to Abyssinia During the Years 1520-1527*, in the Records of the Hakluyt Society (London, 1881), vol. 64, pp. 22-49; Michael Russell, *Nubia and Abyssinia* (quoting Father Lobo, Catholic missionary in Ethiopia in 1622) (New York: Harper & Brothers, 1837), pp. 226-229; S. Giacomo Baratti, *Late Travels Into the Remote Countries of Abyssinia* (London: Benjamin Billingsley, 1670), pp. 134-137; Job Ludolphus, *A New History for Ethiopia* (London: S. Smith, 1682), pp. 234-357; Samuel Gobat, *Journal of Three Years' Residence in Abyssinia* (New York: ed. of 1850), pp. 55-58, 83-98. For other works touching upon the question, see Peter Heylyn, *History of the Sabbath*, 2d ed., 1636, vol. 2, pp. 198-200; Arthur P. Stanley, *Lectures on the History of the Eastern Church* (New York: Charles Scribner's Sons, 1882), lecture 1, par. 1; C. F. Rey, *Romance of the Portuguese in Abyssinia* (London: F. H. and G. Witherley, 1929), pp. 59, 253-297.

8

INDEX

SUMMARY	PAGE	SUMMARY	PAGE

CONTENTS

1. God's Love for Man   1393

2. The Sinner's Need of Christ   1395

3. Repentance   1396

4. Confession   1400

5. Consecration   1402

6. Faith and Acceptance   1403

7. The Test of Discipleship   1405

8. Growing up Into Christ   1408

9. The Work and the Life   1410

10. A Knowledge of God   1412

11. The Privilege of Prayer   1414

12. What to Do With Doubt   1418

13. Rejoicing in the Lord   1420

1
God's Love for Man

Nature and revelation alike testify of God's love. Our Father in heaven is the source of life, of wisdom, and of joy. Look at the wonderful and beautiful things of nature. Think of their marvelous adaptation to the needs and happiness, not only of man, but of all living creatures. The sunshine and the rain, that gladden and refresh the earth, the hills and seas and plains, all speak to us of the Creator's love. It is God who supplies the daily needs of all His creatures. In the beautiful words of the psalmist—

"The eyes of all wait upon Thee;
And Thou givest them their meat in due season.
Thou openest Thine hand,
And satisfiest the desire of every living thing."

Psalm 145:15, 16.

God made man perfectly holy and happy; and the fair earth, as it came from the Creator's hand, bore no blight of decay or shadow of the curse. It is transgression of God's law—the law of love—that has brought woe and death. Yet even amid the suffering that results from sin, God's love is revealed. It is written that God cursed the ground for man's sake. Genesis 3:17. The thorn and the thistle—the difficulties and trials that make his life one of toil and care—were appointed for his good as a part of the training needful in God's plan for his uplifting from the ruin and degradation that sin has wrought. The world, though fallen, is not all sorrow and misery. In nature itself are messages of hope and comfort. There are flowers upon the thistles, and the thorns are covered with roses.

"God is love" is written upon every opening bud, upon every spire of springing grass. The lovely birds making the air vocal with their happy songs, the delicately tinted flowers in their perfection perfuming the air, the lofty trees of the forest with their rich foliage of living green—all testify to the tender, fatherly care of our God and to His desire to make His children happy.

The word of God reveals His character. He Himself has declared His infinite love and pity. When Moses prayed, "Show me Thy glory," the Lord answered, "I will make all My goodness pass before thee." Exodus 33:18, 19. This is His glory. The Lord passed before Moses, and proclaimed, "The Lord, The Lord God, merciful and gracious, long-suffering, and abundant in goodness and truth, keeping mercy for thousands, forgiving iniquity and transgression and sin." Exodus 34:6, 7. He is "slow to anger, and of great kindness," "because He delighteth in mercy." Jonah 4:2; Micah 7:18.

God has bound our hearts to Him by unnumbered tokens in heaven and in earth. Through the things of nature, and the deepest and tenderest earthly ties that human hearts can know, He has sought to reveal Himself to us. Yet these but imperfectly represent His love. Though all these evidences have been given, the enemy of good blinded the minds of men, so that they looked upon God with fear; they thought of Him as severe and unforgiving. Satan led men to conceive of God as a being whose chief attribute is stern justice,—one who is a severe judge, a harsh, exacting creditor. He pictured the Creator as a being who is watching with jealous eye to discern the errors and mistakes of men, that He may visit judgments upon them. It was to remove this dark shadow, by revealing to the world the infinite love of God, that Jesus came to live among men.

The Son of God came from heaven to make manifest the Father. "No man hath seen God at any time; the only begotten Son, which is in the bosom of the Father, He hath declared Him." John 1:18. "Neither knoweth any man the Father, save the Son, and he to whomsoever the Son will reveal Him." Matthew 11:27. When one of the disciples made the request, "Show us the Father," Jesus answered, "Have I been so long time with you, and yet hast thou not known Me, Philip? He that hath seen Me hath seen the Father; and how sayest thou then, Show us the Father?" John 14:8, 9.

In describing His earthly mission, Jesus said, The Lord "hath anointed Me to preach the gospel to the poor; He hath sent Me to heal the brokenhearted, to preach deliverance to the captives, and recovering of sight to the blind, to set at liberty them that are bruised." Luke 4:18. This was His work. He went about doing good and healing all that were oppressed by Satan. There were whole villages where there was not a moan of sickness in any house, for He had passed through them and healed all their sick. His work gave evidence of His divine anointing. Love, mercy, and compassion were revealed in every act of His life; His heart went out in tender sympathy to the children of men. He took man's nature, that He might reach man's wants. The poorest and humblest were not afraid to approach Him. Even little children were attracted to Him. They loved to climb upon His knees and gaze into the pensive face, benignant with love.

Jesus did not suppress one word of truth, but He uttered it always in love. He exercised the greatest tact and thoughtful, kind attention in His intercourse with the people. He was never rude, never needlessly spoke a severe word, never gave needless pain to a sensitive soul. He did not censure human weakness. He spoke the truth, but always in love. He denounced hypocrisy, unbelief, and iniquity; but tears were in His voice as He uttered His scathing rebukes. He wept over Jerusalem, the city He loved, which refused to receive Him, the way, the truth, and the life. They had rejected Him, the Saviour, but He regarded them with pitying tenderness. His life was one of self-denial and thoughtful care for others. Every soul was precious in His eyes. While He ever bore Himself with divine dignity, He bowed with the tenderest regard to every member of the family of God. In all men He saw fallen souls whom it was His mission to save.

Such is the character of Christ as revealed in His life. This is the character of God. It is from the Father's heart that the streams of divine compassion, manifest in Christ, flow out to the children of men. Jesus, the tender, pitying Saviour, was God "manifest in the flesh." 1 Timothy 3:16.

13   It was to redeem us that Jesus lived and suffered and died. He became "a Man of Sorrows," that we might be made partakers of everlasting joy. God permitted His beloved Son, full of grace and truth, to come from a world of indescribable glory, to a world marred and blighted with sin, darkened with the shadow of death and the curse. He permitted Him to leave the bosom of His love, the adoration of the angels, to suffer shame, insult, humiliation, hatred, and death. "The chastisement of our peace was upon Him; and with His stripes we are healed." Isaiah 53:5. Behold Him in the wilderness, in Gethsemane, upon the cross! The spotless Son of God took upon Himself the burden of sin. He who had been one with God, felt in His soul the awful separation that sin makes between God and man. This wrung from His lips the anguished cry, "My God, My God, why hast Thou forsaken Me?" Matthew 27:46. It was the burden of sin, the sense of its terrible enormity, of its separation of the soul from God—it was this that broke the heart of the Son of God.

But this great sacrifice was not made in order to create in the Father's heart a love for man, not to make Him willing to save. No, no! "God so loved the world, that He gave His only-begotten Son." John 3:16. The Father loves us, not because of the great propitiation, but He provided the propitiation because He loves us. Christ was the medium through which He could pour out His infinite love upon a fallen world. "God was in Christ, reconciling the world unto Himself." 2 Corinthians 5:19. God suffered with His Son. In the agony of Gethsemane, the death

14 of Calvary, the heart of Infinite Love paid the price of our redemption.

Jesus said, "Therefore doth My Father love Me, because I lay down My life, that I might take it again." John 10:17. That is, "My Father has so loved you that He even loves Me more for giving My life to redeem you. In becoming your Substitute and Surety, by surrendering My life, by taking your liabilities, your transgressions, I am endeared to My Father; for by My sacrifice, God can be just, and yet the Justifier of him who believeth in Jesus."

None but the Son of God could accomplish our redemption; for only He who was in the bosom of the Father could declare Him. Only He who knew the height and depth of the love of God could make it manifest. Nothing less than the infinite sacrifice made by Christ in behalf of fallen man could express the Father's love to lost humanity.

"God so loved the world, that He gave His only-begotten Son." He gave Him not only to live among men, to bear their sins, and die their sacrifice. He gave Him to the fallen race. Christ was to identify Himself with the interests and needs of humanity. He who was one with God has linked Himself with the children of men by ties that are never to be broken. Jesus is "not ashamed to call them brethren" (Hebrews 2:11); He is our Sacrifice, our Advocate, our Brother, bearing our human form before the Father's throne, and through eternal ages one with the race He has redeemed—the Son of man. And all this that man might be uplifted from the ruin and degradation of sin that he might reflect the love of God and share the joy of holiness.

The price paid for our redemption, the infinite 15 sacrifice of our heavenly Father in giving His Son to die for us, should give us exalted conceptions of what we may become through Christ. As the inspired apostle John beheld the height, the depth, the breadth of the Father's love toward the perishing race, he was filled with adoration and reverence; and, failing to find suitable language in which to express the greatness and tenderness of this love, he called upon the world to behold it. "Behold, what manner of love the Father hath bestowed upon us, that we should be called the sons of God." 1 John 3:1. What a value this places upon man! Through transgression the sons of man become subjects of Satan. Through faith in the atoning sacrifice of Christ the sons of Adam may become the sons of God. By assuming human nature, Christ elevates humanity. Fallen men are placed where, through connection with Christ, they may indeed become worthy of the name "sons of God."

Such love is without a parallel. Children of the heavenly King! Precious promise! Theme for the most profound meditation! The matchless love of God for a world that did not love

Him! The thought has a subduing power upon the soul and brings the mind into captivity to the will of God. The more we study the divine character in the light of the cross, the more we see mercy, tenderness, and forgiveness blended with equity and justice, and the more clearly we discern innumerable evidences of a love that is infinite and a tender pity surpassing a mother's yearning sympathy for her wayward child.

17

2
The Sinner's Need of Christ

Man was originally endowed with noble powers and a well-balanced mind. He was perfect in his being, and in harmony with God. His thoughts were pure, his aims holy. But through disobedience, his powers were perverted, and selfishness took the place of love. His nature became so weakened through transgression that it was impossible for him, in his own strength, to resist the power of evil. He was made captive by Satan, and would have remained so forever had not God specially interposed. It was the tempter's purpose to thwart the divine plan in man's creation, and fill the earth with woe and desolation. And he would point to all this evil as the result of God's work in creating man.

In his sinless state, man held joyful communion with Him "in whom are hid all the treasures of wisdom and knowledge." Colossians 2:3. But after his sin, he could no longer find joy in holiness, and he sought to hide from the presence of God. Such is still the condition of the unrenewed heart. It is not in harmony with God, and finds no joy in communion with Him. The sinner could not be happy in God's presence; he would shrink from the companionship of holy beings. Could he be permitted to enter heaven, it would have no joy for him. The spirit of unselfish love that reigns there — every heart responding to the heart of Infinite Love—would touch no answering chord in his soul. His thoughts, his interests, his motives, would be alien to those that actuate the sinless dwellers there. He would be a discordant note in the melody of heaven. Heaven would be to him a place of torture; he would long to be hidden from Him who is its light, and the center of its joy. It is no arbitrary decree on the part of God that excludes the wicked from heaven; they are shut out by their own unfitness for its companionship. The glory of God would be to them a consuming fire. They would welcome destruction, that they might be hidden from the face of Him who died to redeem them.

It is impossible for us, of ourselves, to escape

18

from the pit of sin in which we are sunken. Our hearts are evil, and we cannot change them. "Who can bring a clean thing out of an unclean? not one." "The carnal mind is enmity against God: for it is not subject to the law of God, neither indeed can be." Job 14:4; Romans 8:7. Education, culture, the exercise of the will, human effort, all have their proper sphere, but here they are powerless. They may produce an outward correctness of behavior, but they cannot change the heart; they cannot purify the springs of life. There must be a power working from within, a new life from above, before men can be changed from sin to holiness. That power is Christ. His grace alone can quicken the lifeless faculties of the soul, and attract it to God, to holiness.

The Saviour said, "Except a man be born from above," unless he shall receive a new heart, new desires, purposes, and motives, leading to a new life, "he cannot see the kingdom of God." John 3:3, margin. The idea that it is necessary only to develop the good that exists in man by nature, is a fatal deception. "The natural man receiveth not the things of the Spirit of God: for they are foolishness unto him: neither can he know them, because they are spiritually discerned." "Marvel not that I said unto thee, Ye must be born again." 1 Corinthians 2:14; John 3:7. Of Christ it is written, "In Him was life; and the life was the light of men"—the only "name under heaven given among men, whereby we must be saved." John 1:4; Acts 4:12.

19

It is not enough to perceive the loving-kindness of God, to see the benevolence, the fatherly tenderness, of His character. It is not enough to discern the wisdom and justice of His law, to see that it is founded upon the eternal principle of love. Paul the apostle saw all this when he exclaimed, "I consent unto the law that it is good." "The law is holy, and the commandment holy, and just, and good." But he added, in the bitterness of his soul-anguish and despair, "I am carnal, sold under sin." Romans 7:16, 12, 14. He longed for the purity, the righteousness, to which in himself he was powerless to attain, and cried out, "O wretched man that I am! who shall deliver me from this body of death?" Romans 7:24, margin. Such is the cry that has gone up from burdened hearts in all lands and in all ages. To all, there is but one answer, "Behold the Lamb of God, which taketh away the sin of the world." John 1:29.

Many are the figures by which the Spirit of God has sought to illustrate this truth, and make it plain to souls that long to be freed from the burden of guilt. When, after his sin in deceiving Esau, Jacob fled from his father's home, he was weighed down with a sense of guilt. Lonely and outcast as he was, separated from all that had made life dear, the one thought that above all

20

others pressed upon his soul, was the fear that his sin had cut him off from God, that he was forsaken of Heaven. In sadness he lay down to rest on the bare earth, around him only the lonely hills, and above, the heavens bright with stars. As he slept, a strange light broke upon his vision; and lo, from the plain on which he lay, vast shadowy stairs seemed to lead upward to the very gates of heaven, and upon them angels of God were passing up and down; while from the glory above, the divine voice was heard in a message of comfort and hope. Thus was made known to Jacob that which met the need and longing of his soul—a Saviour. With joy and gratitude he saw revealed a way by which he, a sinner, could be restored to communion with God. The mystic ladder of his dream represented Jesus, the only medium of communication between God and man.

This is the same figure to which Christ referred in His conversation with Nathanael, when He said, "Ye shall see heaven open, and the angels of God ascending and descending upon the Son of man." John 1:51. In the apostasy, man alienated himself from God; earth was cut off from heaven. Across the gulf that lay between, there could be no communion. But through Christ, earth is again linked with heaven. With His own merits, Christ has bridged the gulf which sin had made, so that the ministering angels can hold communion with man. Christ connects fallen man in his weakness and helplessness with the Source of infinite power.

21   But in vain are men's dreams of progress, in vain all efforts for the uplifting of humanity, if they neglect the one Source of hope and help for the fallen race. "Every good gift and every perfect gift" (James 1:17) is from God. There is no true excellence of character apart from Him. And the only way to God is Christ. He says, "I am the way, the truth, and the life: no man cometh unto the Father, but by Me." John 14:6.

The heart of God yearns over His earthly children with a love stronger than death. In giving up His Son, He has poured out to us all heaven in one gift. The Saviour's life and death and intercession, the ministry of angels, the pleading of the Spirit, the Father working above and through all, the unceasing interest of heavenly beings,—all are enlisted in behalf of man's redemption.

Oh, let us contemplate the amazing sacrifice that has been made for us! Let us try to appreciate the labor and energy that Heaven is expending to reclaim the lost, and bring them back to the Father's house. Motives stronger, and agencies more powerful, could never be brought into operation; the exceeding rewards for right-doing, the enjoyment of heaven, the society of the angels, the communion and love of God and His Son, the elevation and extension of all our

powers throughout eternal ages—are these not mighty incentives and encouragements to urge us to give the heart's loving service to our Creator and Redeemer?

And, on the other hand, the judgments of God pronounced against sin, the inevitable retribution, the degradation of our character, and the 22 final destruction, are presented in God's word to warn us against the service of Satan.

Shall we not regard the mercy of God? What more could He do? Let us place ourselves in right relation to Him who has loved us with amazing love. Let us avail ourselves of the means provided for us that we may be transformed into His likeness, and be restored to fellowship with the ministering angels, to harmony and communion with the Father and the Son.

3   23

Repentance

How shall a man be just with God? How shall the sinner be made righteous? It is only through Christ that we can be brought into harmony with God, with holiness; but how are we to come to Christ? Many are asking the same question as did the multitude on the Day of Pentecost, when, convicted of sin, they cried out, "What shall we do?" The first word of Peter's answer was, "Repent." Acts 2:37, 38. At another time, shortly after, he said, "Repent, . . . and be converted, that your sins may be blotted out." Acts 3:19.

Repentance includes sorrow for sin and a turning away from it. We shall not renounce sin unless we see its sinfulness; until we turn away from it in heart, there will be no real change in the life.

There are many who fail to understand the true nature of repentance. Multitudes sorrow that they have sinned and even make an outward reformation because they fear that their wrongdoing will bring suffering upon themselves. But this is not repentance in the Bible sense. They lament the suffering rather than the sin. Such was the grief of Esau when he saw that the birthright was lost to him forever. Balaam, terrified by the angel standing in his pathway with drawn sword, acknowledged his guilt lest he should lose his life; but there was no genuine repentance for sin, no conversion of purpose, no abhorrence of evil. Judas Iscariot, after betraying his Lord, exclaimed, "I have 24 sinned in that I have betrayed the innocent blood." Matthew 27:4.

The confession was forced from his guilty soul by an awful sense of condemnation and a fearful looking for of judgment. The consequences that were to result to him filled him with terror, but there was no deep, heartbreaking grief in his soul, that he had betrayed the spotless Son of God and denied the Holy One of Israel. Pharaoh, when suffering under the judgments of God, acknowledged his sin in order to escape further punishment, but returned to his defiance of Heaven as soon as the plagues were stayed. These all lamented the results of sin, but did not sorrow for the sin itself.

But when the heart yields to the influence of the Spirit of God, the conscience will be quickened, and the sinner will discern something of the depth and sacredness of God's holy law, the foundation of His government in heaven and on earth. The "Light, which lighteth every man that cometh into the world," illumines the secret chambers of the soul, and the hidden things of darkness are made manifest. John 1:9. Conviction takes hold upon the mind and heart. The sinner has a sense of the righteousness of Jehovah and feels the terror of appearing, in his own guilt and uncleanness, before the Searcher of hearts. He sees the love of God, the beauty of holiness, the joy of purity; he longs to be cleansed and to be restored to communion with Heaven.

The prayer of David after his fall, illustrates the nature of true sorrow for sin. His repentance was sincere and deep. There was no effort to palliate his guilt; no desire to escape the judgment threatened, inspired his prayer. David saw the enormity of his transgression; he saw the defilement of his soul; he loathed his sin. It was not for pardon only that he prayed, but for purity of heart. He longed for the joy of holiness—to be restored to harmony and communion with God. This was the language of his soul:

"Blessed is he whose transgression is forgiven, whose sin is covered.
Blessed is the man unto whom the Lord imputeth not iniquity,
And in whose spirit there is no guile."
Psalm 32:1, 2.

"Have mercy upon me, O God, according to Thy loving-kindness:
According unto the multitude of Thy tender mercies blot out my transgressions. . . .
For I acknowledge my transgressions: and my sin is ever before me. . . .
Purge me with hyssop, and I shall be clean: wash me, and I shall be whiter than snow. . . .
Create in me a clean heart, O God;
And renew a right spirit within me.
Cast me not away from Thy presence;
And take not Thy Holy Spirit from me.
Restore unto me the joy of Thy salvation;
And uphold me with Thy free spirit. . . .
Deliver me from bloodguiltiness, O God,

Thou God of my salvation:
And my tongue shall sing aloud of Thy righteousness."
Psalm 51:1-14.

A repentance such as this, is beyond the reach of our own power to accomplish; it is obtained only from Christ, who ascended up on high and has given gifts unto men.

Just here is a point on which many may err, **26** and hence they fail of receiving the help that Christ desires to give them. They think that they cannot come to Christ unless they first repent, and that repentance prepares for the forgiveness of their sins. It is true that repentance does precede the forgiveness of sins; for it is only the broken and contrite heart that will feel the need of a Saviour. But must the sinner wait till he has repented before he can come to Jesus? Is repentance to be made an obstacle between the sinner and the Saviour?

The Bible does not teach that the sinner must repent before he can heed the invitation of Christ, "Come unto Me, all ye that labor and are heavy-laden, and I will give you rest." Matthew 11:28. It is the virtue that goes forth from Christ, that leads to genuine repentance. Peter made the matter clear in his statement to the Israelites when he said, "Him hath God exalted with His right hand to be a Prince and a Saviour, for to give repentance to Israel, and forgiveness of sins." Acts 5:31. We can no more repent without the Spirit of Christ to awaken the conscience than we can be pardoned without Christ.

Christ is the source of every right impulse. He is the only one that can implant in the heart enmity against sin. Every desire for truth and purity, every conviction of our own sinfulness, is an evidence that His Spirit is moving upon our hearts.

Jesus has said, "I, if I be lifted up from the earth, will draw all men unto Me." John 12:32. Christ must be revealed to the sinner as the Saviour dying for the sins of the world; and as we behold the Lamb of God upon the cross of Calvary, the mystery of redemption begins to **27** unfold to our minds and the goodness of God leads us to repentance. In dying for sinners, Christ manifested a love that is incomprehensible; and as the sinner beholds this love, it softens the heart, impresses the mind, and inspires contrition in the soul.

It is true that men sometimes become ashamed of their sinful ways, and give up some of their evil habits, before they are conscious that they are being drawn to Christ. But whenever they make an effort to reform, from a sincere desire to do right, it is the power of Christ that is drawing them. An influence of which they are unconscious works upon the soul, and

25

the conscience is quickened, and the outward life is amended. And as Christ draws them to look upon His cross, to behold Him whom their sins have pierced, the commandment comes home to the conscience. The wickedness of their life, the deep-seated sin of the soul, is revealed to them. They begin to comprehend something of the righteousness of Christ, and exclaim, "What is sin, that it should require such a sacrifice for the redemption of its victim? Was all this love, all this suffering, all this humiliation, demanded, that we might not perish, but have everlasting life?"

The sinner may resist this love, may refuse to be drawn to Christ; but if he does not resist he will be drawn to Jesus; a knowledge of the plan of salvation will lead him to the foot of the cross in repentance for his sins, which have caused the sufferings of God's dear Son.

28 The same divine mind that is working upon the things of nature is speaking to the hearts of men and creating an inexpressible craving for something they have not. The things of the world cannot satisfy their longing. The Spirit of God is pleading with them to seek for those things that alone can give peace and rest—the grace of Christ, the joy of holiness. Through influences seen and unseen, our Saviour is constantly at work to attract the minds of men from the unsatisfying pleasures of sin to the infinite blessings that may be theirs in Him. To all these souls, who are vainly seeking to drink from the broken cisterns of this world, the divine message is addressed, "Let him that is athirst come. And whosoever will, let him take the water of life freely." Revelation 22:17.

You who in heart long for something better than this world can give, recognize this longing as the voice of God to your soul. Ask Him to give you repentance, to reveal Christ to you in His infinite love, in His perfect purity. In the Saviour's life the principles of God's law—love to God and man—were perfectly exemplified. Benevolence, unselfish love, was the life of His soul. It is as we behold Him, as the light from our Saviour falls upon us, that we see the sinfulness of our own hearts.

We may have flattered ourselves, as did Nicodemus, that our life has been upright, that our moral character is correct, and think that we need not humble the heart before God, like the common sinner: but when the light from Christ shines into our souls, we shall see how impure we are; we shall discern the selfishness of 29 motive, the enmity against God, that has defiled every act of life. Then we shall know that our own righteousness is indeed as filthy rags, and that the blood of Christ alone can cleanse us from the defilement of sin, and renew our hearts in His own likeness.

One ray of the glory of God, one gleam of the purity of Christ, penetrating the soul, makes every spot of defilement painfully distinct, and lays bare the deformity and defects of the human character. It makes apparent the unhallowed desires, the infidelity of the heart, the impurity of the lips. The sinner's acts of disloyalty in making void the law of God, are exposed to his sight, and his spirit is stricken and afflicted under the searching influence of the Spirit of God. He loathes himself as he views the pure, spotless character of Christ.

When the prophet Daniel beheld the glory surrounding the heavenly messenger that was sent unto him, he was overwhelmed with a sense of his own weakness and imperfection. Describing the effect of the wonderful scene, he says, "There remained no strength in me: for my comeliness was turned in me into corruption, and I retained no strength." Daniel 10:8. The soul thus touched will hate its selfishness, abhor its self-love, and will seek, through Christ's righteousness, for the purity of heart that is in harmony with the law of God and the character of Christ.

Paul says that as "touching the righteousness which is in the law"—as far as outward acts were concerned—he was "blameless" (Philippians 3:6); but when the spiritual character of the law was discerned, he saw himself a sinner. Judged by the letter of the law as men apply it 30 to the outward life, he had abstained from sin; but when he looked into the depths of its holy precepts, and saw himself as God saw him, he bowed in humiliation and confessed his guilt. He says, "I was alive without the law once: but when the commandment came, sin revived, and I died." Romans 7:9. When he saw the spiritual nature of the law, sin appeared in its true hideousness, and his self-esteem was gone.

God does not regard all sins as of equal magnitude; there are degrees of guilt in His estimation, as well as in that of man; but however trifling this or that wrong act may seem in the eyes of men, no sin is small in the sight of God. Man's judgment is partial, imperfect; but God estimates all things as they really are. The drunkard is despised and is told that his sin will exclude him from heaven; while pride, selfishness, and covetousness too often go unrebuked. But these are sins that are especially offensive to God; for they are contrary to the benevolence of His character, to that unselfish love which is the very atmosphere of the unfallen universe. He who falls into some of the grosser sins may feel a sense of his shame and poverty and his need of the grace of Christ; but pride feels no need, and so it closes the heart against Christ and the infinite blessings He came to give.

The poor publican who prayed, "God be merciful to me a sinner" (Luke 18:13), regarded himself as a very wicked man, and others

looked upon him in the same light; but he felt
31 his need, and with his burden of guilt and shame
he came before God, asking for His mercy. His
heart was open for the Spirit of God to do its
gracious work and set him free from the power
of sin. The Pharisee's boastful, self-righteous
prayer showed that his heart was closed against
the influence of the Holy Spirit. Because of his
distance from God, he had no sense of his own
defilement, in contrast with the perfection of the
divine holiness. He felt no need, and he received
nothing.

If you see your sinfulness, do not wait to
make yourself better. How many there are who
think they are not good enough to come to
Christ. Do you expect to become better through
your own efforts? "Can the Ethiopian change
his skin, or the leopard his spots? then may ye
also do good, that are accustomed to do evil."
Jeremiah 13:23. There is help for us only in
God. We must not wait for stronger persuasions,
for better opportunities, or for holier tempers.
We can do nothing of ourselves. We must come
to Christ just as we are.

But let none deceive themselves with the
thought that God, in His great love and mercy,
will yet save even the rejecters of His grace.
The exceeding sinfulness of sin can be estimated only in the light of the cross. When men
urge that God is too good to cast off the sinner,
let them look to Calvary. It was because there
was no other way in which man could be
saved, because without this sacrifice it was
impossible for the human race to escape from
the defiling power of sin, and be restored to
communion with holy beings,—impossible for
32 them again to become partakers of spiritual
life,—it was because of this that Christ took
upon Himself the guilt of the disobedient and
suffered in the sinner's stead. The love and
suffering and death of the Son of God all testify to the terrible enormity of sin and declare
that there is no escape from its power, no hope
of the higher life, but through the submission
of the soul to Christ.

The impenitent sometimes excuse themselves
by saying of professed Christians, "I am as good
as they are. They are no more self-denying,
sober, or circumspect in their conduct than I am.
They love pleasure and self-indulgence as well
as I do." Thus they make the faults of others an
excuse for their own neglect of duty. But the
sins and defects of others do not excuse anyone,
for the Lord has not given us an erring human
pattern. The spotless Son of God has been given
as our example, and those who complain of the
wrong course of professed Christians are the
ones who should show better lives and nobler
examples. If they have so high a conception of
what a Christian should be, is not their own sin
so much the greater? They know what is right,
and yet refuse to do it.

Beware of procrastination. Do not put off
the work of forsaking your sins and seeking
purity of heart through Jesus. Here is where
thousands upon thousands have erred to their
eternal loss. I will not here dwell upon the
shortness and uncertainty of life; but there is a
terrible danger—a danger not sufficiently
understood—in delaying to yield to the pleading voice of God's Holy Spirit, in choosing to
live in sin; for such this delay really is. Sin,
however small it may be esteemed, can be 33
indulged in only at the peril of infinite loss.
What we do not overcome, will overcome us
and work out our destruction.

Adam and Eve persuaded themselves that in
so small a matter as eating of the forbidden fruit
there could not result such terrible consequences
as God had declared. But this small matter was
the transgression of God's immutable and holy
law, and it separated man from God and opened
the floodgates of death and untold woe upon our
world. Age after age there has gone up from our
earth a continual cry of mourning, and the
whole creation groaneth and travaileth together
in pain as a consequence of man's disobedience.
Heaven itself has felt the effects of his rebellion
against God. Calvary stands as a memorial of
the amazing sacrifice required to atone for the
transgression of the divine law. Let us not
regard sin as a trivial thing.

Every act of transgression, every neglect or
rejection of the grace of Christ, is reacting upon
yourself; it is hardening the heart, depraving the
will, benumbing the understanding, and not
only making you less inclined to yield, but less
capable of yielding, to the tender pleading of
God's Holy Spirit.

Many are quieting a troubled conscience with
the thought that they can change a course of evil
when they choose; that they can trifle with the
invitations of mercy, and yet be again and again
impressed. They think that after doing despite to
the Spirit of grace, after casting their influence
on the side of Satan, in a moment of terrible
extremity they can change their course. But this
is not so easily done. The experience, the educa- 34
tion, of a lifetime, has so thoroughly molded the
character that few then desire to receive the
image of Jesus.

Even one wrong trait of character, one sinful
desire, persistently cherished, will eventually
neutralize all the power of the gospel. Every sinful indulgence strengthens the soul's aversion to
God. The man who manifests an infidel hardihood, or a stolid indifference to divine truth, is
but reaping the harvest of that which he has
himself sown. In all the Bible there is not a
more fearful warning against trifling with evil
than the words of the wise man that the sinner
"shall be holden with the cords of his sins."
Proverbs 5:22.

Christ is ready to set us free from sin, but He

does not force the will; and if by persistent transgression the will itself is wholly bent on evil, and we do not *desire* to be set free, if we *will* not accept His grace, what more can He do? We have destroyed ourselves by our determined rejection of His love. "Behold, now is the accepted time; behold, now is the day of salvation." "Today if ye will hear His voice, harden not your hearts." 2 Corinthians 6:2; Hebrews 3:7, 8.

"Man looketh on the outward appearance, but the Lord looketh on the heart"—the human heart, with its conflicting emotions of joy and sorrow; the wandering, wayward heart, which is the abode of so much impurity and deceit. 1 Samuel 16:7. He knows its motives, its very intents and purposes. Go to Him with your soul all stained as it is. Like the psalmist, throw its chambers open to the all-seeing eye, exclaiming, "Search me, O God, and know my heart: 35 try me, and know my thoughts: and see if there be any wicked way in me, and lead me in the way everlasting." Psalm 139:23, 24.

Many accept an intellectual religion, a form of godliness, when the heart is not cleansed. Let it be your prayer, "Create in me a clean heart, O God; and renew a right spirit within me." Psalm 51:10. Deal truly with your own soul. Be as earnest, as persistent, as you would be if your mortal life were at stake. This is a matter to be settled between God and your own soul, settled for eternity. A supposed hope, and nothing more, will prove your ruin.

Study God's word prayerfully. That word presents before you, in the law of God and the life of Christ, the great principles of holiness, without which "no man shall see the Lord." Hebrews 12:14. It convinces of sin; it plainly reveals the way of salvation. Give heed to it as the voice of God speaking to your soul.

As you see the enormity of sin, as you see yourself as you really are, do not give up to despair. It was sinners that Christ came to save. We have not to reconcile God to us, but—O wondrous love!—God in Christ is "reconciling the world unto Himself." 2 Corinthians 5:19. He is wooing by His tender love the hearts of His erring children. No earthly parent could be as patient with the faults and mistakes of his children, as is God with those He seeks to save. No one could plead more tenderly with the transgressor. No human lips ever poured out more tender entreaties to the wanderer than does He. All His promises, His warnings, are but the breathing of unutterable love.

When Satan comes to tell you that you are a 36 great sinner, look up to your Redeemer and talk of His merits. That which will help you is to look to His light. Acknowledge your sin, but tell the enemy that "Christ Jesus came into the world to save sinners" and that you may be saved by His matchless love. 1 Timothy 1:15. Jesus asked Simon a question in regard to two debtors. One owed his lord a small sum, and the other owed him a very large sum; but he forgave them both, and Christ asked Simon which debtor would love his lord most. Simon answered, "He to whom he forgave most." Luke 7:43. We have been great sinners, but Christ died that we might be forgiven. The merits of His sacrifice are sufficient to present to the Father in our behalf. Those to whom He has forgiven most will love Him most, and will stand nearest to His throne to praise Him for His great love and infinite sacrifice. It is when we most fully comprehend the love of God that we best realize the sinfulness of sin. When we see the length of the chain that was let down for us, when we understand something of the infinite sacrifice that Christ has made in our behalf, the heart is melted with tenderness and contrition.

4
Confession

37

"He that covereth his sins shall not prosper: but whoso confesseth and forsaketh them shall have mercy." Proverbs 28:13.

The conditions of obtaining mercy of God are simple and just and reasonable. The Lord does not require us to do some grievous thing in order that we may have the forgiveness of sin. We need not make long and wearisome pilgrimages, or perform painful penances, to commend our souls to the God of heaven or to expiate our transgression; but he that confesseth and forsaketh his sin shall have mercy.

The apostle says, "Confess your faults one to another, and pray one for another, that ye may be healed." James 5:16. Confess your sins to God, who only can forgive them, and your faults to one another. If you have given offense to your friend or neighbor, you are to acknowledge your wrong, and it is his duty freely to forgive you. Then you are to seek the forgiveness of God, because the brother you have wounded is the property of God, and in injuring him you sinned against his Creator and Redeemer. The case is brought before the only true Mediator, our great High Priest, who "was in all points tempted like as we are, yet without sin," and who is "touched with the feeling of our infirmities," and is able to cleanse from every stain of iniquity. Hebrews 4:15.

Those who have not humbled their souls before God in acknowledging their guilt, have not yet fulfilled the first condition of accep- 38 tance. If we have not experienced that repentance which is not to be repented of, and have not with true humiliation of soul and brokenness of spirit confessed our sins, abhorring our iniquity, we have never truly sought for the forgiveness of sin; and if we have never sought, we have never found the peace of God. The only reason why we do not have remission of sins that are past is that we are not willing to humble our hearts and comply with the conditions of the word of truth. Explicit instruction is given concerning this matter. Confession of sin, whether public or private, should be heartfelt and freely expressed. It is not to be urged from the sinner. It is not to be made in a flippant and careless way, or forced from those who have no realizing sense of the abhorrent character of sin. The confession that is the outpouring of the inmost soul finds its way to the God of infinite pity. The psalmist says, "The Lord is nigh unto them that are of a broken heart; and saveth such as be of a contrite spirit." Psalm 34:18.

True confession is always of a specific character, and acknowledges particular sins. They may be of such a nature as to be brought before God only; they may be wrongs that should be confessed to individuals who have suffered injury through them; or they may be of a public character, and should then be as publicly confessed. But all confession should be definite and to the point, acknowledging the very sins of which you are guilty.

In the days of Samuel the Israelites wandered from God. They were suffering the conse-
39 quences of sin; for they had lost their faith in God, lost their discernment of His power and wisdom to rule the nation, lost their confidence in His ability to defend and vindicate His cause. They turned from the great Ruler of the universe and desired to be governed as were the nations around them. Before they found peace they made this definite confession: "We have added unto all our sins this evil, to ask us a king." 1 Samuel 12:19. The very sin of which they were convicted had to be confessed. Their ingratitude oppressed their souls and severed them from God.

Confession will not be acceptable to God without sincere repentance and reformation. There must be decided changes in the life; everything offensive to God must be put away. This will be the result of genuine sorrow for sin. The work that we have to do on our part is plainly set before us: "Wash you, make you clean; put away the evil of your doings from before Mine eyes; cease to do evil; learn to do well; seek judgment, relieve the oppressed, judge the fatherless, plead for the widow." Isaiah 1:16, 17. "If the wicked restore the pledge, give again that he had robbed, walk in the statutes of life, without committing iniquity; he shall surely live, he shall not die." Ezekiel 33:15. Paul says, speaking of the work of repentance: "Ye sorrowed after a godly sort, what

carefulness it wrought in you, yea, what clearing of yourselves, yea, what indignation, yea, what fear, yea, what vehement desire, yea, what zeal, yea, what revenge! In all things ye have approved yourselves to be clear in this matter." 2 Corinthians 7:11.

When sin has deadened the moral percep- 40 tions, the wrongdoer does not discern the defects of his character nor realize the enormity of the evil he has committed; and unless he yields to the convicting power of the Holy Spirit he remains in partial blindness to his sin. His confessions are not sincere and in earnest. To every acknowledgment of his guilt he adds an apology in excuse of his course, declaring that if it had not been for certain circumstances he would not have done this or that for which he is reproved.

After Adam and Eve had eaten of the forbidden fruit, they were filled with a sense of shame and terror. At first their only thought was how to excuse their sin and escape the dreaded sentence of death. When the Lord inquired concerning their sin, Adam replied, laying the guilt partly upon God and partly upon his companion: "The woman whom Thou gavest to be with me, she gave me of the tree, and I did eat." The woman put the blame upon the serpent, saying, "The serpent beguiled me, and I did eat." Genesis 3:12, 13. Why did You make the serpent? Why did You suffer him to come into Eden? These were the questions implied in her excuse for her sin, thus charging God with the responsibility of their fall. The spirit of self-justification originated in the father of lies and has been exhibited by all the sons and daughters of Adam. Confessions of this order are not inspired by the divine Spirit and will not be acceptable to God. True repentance will lead a man to bear his guilt himself and acknowledge it without deception or hypocrisy. Like the poor publican, not lifting up so much as his eyes unto heaven, he will cry, "God be merciful to me a sinner," 41 and those who do acknowledge their guilt will be justified, for Jesus will plead His blood in behalf of the repentant soul.

The examples in God's word of genuine repentance and humiliation reveal a spirit of confession in which there is no excuse for sin or attempt at self-justification. Paul did not seek to shield himself; he paints his sin in its darkest hue, not attempting to lessen his guilt. He says, "Many of the saints did I shut up in prison, having received authority from the chief priests; and when they were put to death, I gave my voice against them. And I punished them oft in every synagogue, and compelled them to blaspheme; and being exceedingly mad against them, I persecuted them even unto strange cities." Acts 26:10, 11. He does not hesitate to declare that "Christ Jesus came into the world to save sinners; of whom I am chief." 1 Timothy

1:15.

The humble and broken heart, subdued by genuine repentance, will appreciate something of the love of God and the cost of Calvary; and as a son confesses to a loving father, so will the truly penitent bring all his sins before God. And it is written, "If we confess our sins, He is faithful and just to forgive us our sins, and to cleanse us from all unrighteousness." 1 John 1:9.

5

Consecration

God's promise is, "Ye shall seek Me, and find Me, when ye shall search for Me with all your heart." Jeremiah 29:13.

The whole heart must be yielded to God, or the change can never be wrought in us by which we are to be restored to His likeness. By nature we are alienated from God. The Holy Spirit describes our condition in such words as these: "Dead in trespasses and sins;" "the whole head is sick, and the whole heart faint;" "no soundness in it." We are held fast in the snare of Satan, "taken captive by him at his will." Ephesians 2:1; Isaiah 1:5, 6; 2 Timothy 2:26. God desires to heal us, to set us free. But since this requires an entire transformation, a renewing of our whole nature, we must yield ourselves wholly to Him.

The warfare against self is the greatest battle that was ever fought. The yielding of self, surrendering all to the will of God, requires a struggle; but the soul must submit to God before it can be renewed in holiness.

The government of God is not, as Satan would make it appear, founded upon a blind submission, an unreasoning control. It appeals to the intellect and the conscience. "Come now, and let us reason together" is the Creator's invitation to the beings He has made. Isaiah 1:18. God does not force the will of His creatures. He cannot accept an homage that is not willingly and intelligently given. A mere forced submission would prevent all real development of mind or character; it would make man a mere automaton. Such is not the purpose of the Creator. He desires that man, the crowning work of His creative power, shall reach the highest possible development. He sets before us the height of blessing to which He desires to bring us through His grace. He invites us to give ourselves to Him, that He may work His will in us. It remains for us to choose whether we will be set free from the bondage of sin, to share the glorious liberty of the sons of God.

In giving ourselves to God, we must necessarily give up all that would separate us from Him. Hence the Saviour says, "Whosoever he be of you that forsaketh not all that he hath, he cannot be My disciple." Luke 14:33. Whatever shall draw away the heart from God must be given up. Mammon is the idol of many. The love of money, the desire for wealth, is the golden chain that binds them to Satan. Reputation and worldly honor are worshiped by another class. The life of selfish ease and freedom from responsibility is the idol of others. But these slavish bands must be broken. We cannot be half the Lord's and half the world's. We are not God's children unless we are such entirely.

There are those who profess to serve God, while they rely upon their own efforts to obey His law, to form a right character, and secure salvation. Their hearts are not moved by any deep sense of the love of Christ, but they seek to perform the duties of the Christian life as that which God requires of them in order to gain heaven. Such religion is worth nothing. When Christ dwells in the heart, the soul will be so filled with His love, with the joy of communion with Him, that it will cleave to Him; and in the contemplation of Him, self will be forgotten. Love to Christ will be the spring of action. Those who feel the constraining love of God, do not ask how little may be given to meet the requirements of God; they do not ask for the lowest standard, but aim at perfect conformity to the will of their Redeemer. With earnest desire they yield all and manifest an interest proportionate to the value of the object which they seek. A profession of Christ without this deep love is mere talk, dry formality, and heavy drudgery.

Do you feel that it is too great a sacrifice to yield all to Christ? Ask yourself the question, "What has Christ given for me?" The Son of God gave all—life and love and suffering—for our redemption. And can it be that we, the unworthy objects of so great love, will withhold our hearts from Him? Every moment of our lives we have been partakers of the blessings of His grace, and for this very reason we cannot fully realize the depths of ignorance and misery from which we have been saved. Can we look upon Him whom our sins have pierced, and yet be willing to do despite to all His love and sacrifice? In view of the infinite humiliation of the Lord of glory, shall we murmur because we can enter into life only through conflict and self-abasement?

The inquiry of many a proud heart is, "Why need I go in penitence and humiliation before I can have the assurance of my acceptance with God?" I point you to Christ. He was sinless, and, more than this, He was the Prince of heaven; but in man's behalf He became sin for the race. "He was numbered with the transgressors; and He bare the sin of many, and made intercession for the transgressors." Isaiah 53:12.

But what do we give up, when we give all? A sin-polluted heart, for Jesus to purify, to cleanse by His own blood, and to save by His matchless love. And yet men think it hard to give up all! I am ashamed to hear it spoken of, ashamed to write it.

God does not require us to give up anything that it is for our best interest to retain. In all that He does, He has the well-being of His children in view. Would that all who have not chosen Christ might realize that He has something vastly better to offer them than they are seeking for themselves. Man is doing the greatest injury and injustice to his own soul when he thinks and acts contrary to the will of God. No real joy can be found in the path forbidden by Him who knows what is best and who plans for the good of His creatures. The path of transgression is the path of misery and destruction.

It is a mistake to entertain the thought that God is pleased to see His children suffer. All heaven is interested in the happiness of man. Our heavenly Father does not close the avenues of joy to any of His creatures. The divine requirements call upon us to shun those indulgences that would bring suffering and disappointment, that would close to us the door of happiness and heaven. The world's Redeemer accepts men as they are, with all their wants, imperfections, and weaknesses; and He will not only cleanse from sin and 47 grant redemption through His blood, but will satisfy the heart-longing of all who consent to wear His yoke, to bear His burden. It is His purpose to impart peace and rest to all who come to Him for the bread of life. He requires us to perform only those duties that will lead our steps to heights of bliss to which the disobedient can never attain. The true, joyous life of the soul is to have Christ formed within, the hope of glory.

Many are inquiring, "*How* am I to make the surrender of myself to God?" You desire to give yourself to Him, but you are weak in moral power, in slavery to doubt, and controlled by the habits of your life of sin. Your promises and resolutions are like ropes of sand. You cannot control your thoughts, your impulses, your affections. The knowledge of your broken promises and forfeited pledges weakens your confidence in your own sincerity, and causes you to feel that God cannot accept you; but you need not despair. What you need to understand is the true force of the will. This is the governing power in the nature of man, the power of decision, or of choice. Everything depends on the right action of the will. The power of choice God has given to men; it is theirs to exercise. You cannot change your heart, you cannot of yourself give to God its affections; but you can *choose* to serve Him.

You can give Him your will; He will then work in you to will and to do according to His good pleasure. Thus your whole nature will be brought under the control of the Spirit of Christ; your affections will be centered upon Him, your thoughts will be in harmony with Him.

Desires for goodness and holiness are right as far as they go; but if you stop here, they will 48 avail nothing. Many will be lost while hoping and desiring to be Christians. They do not come to the point of yielding the will to God. They do not now *choose* to be Christians.

Through the right exercise of the will, an entire change may be made in your life. By yielding up your will to Christ, you ally yourself with the power that is above all principalities and powers. You will have strength from above to hold you steadfast, and thus through constant surrender to God you will be enabled to live the new life, even the life of faith.

6

Faith and Acceptance

As your conscience has been quickened by the Holy Spirit, you have seen something of the evil of sin, of its power, its guilt, its woe; and you look upon it with abhorrence. You feel that sin has separated you from God, that you are in bondage to the power of evil. The more you struggle to escape, the more you realize your helplessness. Your motives are impure; your heart is unclean. You see that your life has been filled with selfishness and sin. You long to be forgiven, to be cleansed, to be set free. Harmony with God, likeness to Him—what can you do to obtain it?

It is peace that you need—Heaven's forgiveness and peace and love in the soul. Money cannot buy it, intellect cannot procure it, wisdom cannot attain to it; you can never hope, by your own efforts, to secure it. But God offers it to you as a gift, "without money and without price." Isaiah 55:1. It is yours if you will but reach out your hand and grasp it. The Lord says, "Though your sins be as scarlet, they shall be as white as snow; though they be red like crimson, they shall be as wool." Isaiah 1:18. "A new heart also will I give you, and a new spirit will I put within you." Ezekiel 36:26.

You have confessed your sins, and in heart put them away. You have resolved to give yourself to God. Now go to Him, and ask that He will wash away your sins and give you a new heart. Then believe that He does this *because* 50 *He has promised.* This is the lesson which Jesus taught while He was on earth, that the gift which God promises us, we must believe we do receive, and it is ours. Jesus healed the people of their diseases when they had faith in His power; He helped them in the things which they could see, thus inspiring them with confidence in Him concerning things which they could not see—leading them to believe in His power to forgive sins. This He plainly stated in the healing of the man sick with palsy: *"That ye may know that the Son of man hath power on earth to forgive sins,* (then saith He to the sick of the palsy,) Arise, take up thy bed, and go unto thine house." Matthew 9:6. So also John the evangelist says, speaking of the miracles of Christ, "These are written, that ye might believe that Jesus is the Christ, the Son of God; and that believing ye might have life through His name." John 20:31.

From the simple Bible account of how Jesus healed the sick, we may learn something about how to believe in Him for the forgiveness of sins. Let us turn to the story of the paralytic at Bethesda. The poor sufferer was helpless; he had not used his limbs for thirty-eight years. Yet Jesus bade him, "Rise, take up thy bed, and walk." The sick man might have said, "Lord, if Thou wilt make me whole, I will obey Thy word." But, no, he believed Christ's word, believed that he was made whole, and he made the effort at once; he *willed* to walk, and he did walk. He acted on the word of Christ, and God gave the power. He was made whole.

51   In like manner you are a sinner. You cannot atone for your past sins; you cannot change your heart and make yourself holy. But God promises to do all this for you through Christ. You *believe* that promise. You confess your sins and give yourself to God. You *will* to serve Him. Just as surely as you do this, God will fulfill His word to you. If you believe the promise,—believe that you are forgiven and cleansed,—God supplies the fact; you are made whole, just as Christ gave the paralytic power to walk when the man believed that he was healed. It *is* so if you believe it.

Do not wait to *feel* that you are made whole, but say, "I believe it; it *is* so, not because I feel it, but because God has promised."

Jesus says, "What things soever ye desire, when ye pray, believe that ye receive them, and ye shall have them." Mark 11:24. There is a condition to this promise—that we pray according to the will of God. But it is the will of God to cleanse us from sin, to make us His children, and to enable us to live a holy life. So we may ask for these blessings, and believe that we receive them, and thank God that we have received them. It is our privilege to go to Jesus and be cleansed, and to stand before the law without shame or remorse. "There is therefore now no condemnation to them which are in Christ Jesus, who walk not after the flesh, but after the Spirit." Romans 8:1.

Henceforth you are not your own; you are bought with a price. "Ye were not redeemed with corruptible things, as silver and gold; . . . but with the precious blood of Christ, as of a lamb without blemish and without spot." 1 Peter 52 1:18, 19. Through this simple act of believing God, the Holy Spirit has begotten a new life in your heart. You are as a child born into the family of God, and He loves you as He loves His Son.

Now that you have given yourself to Jesus, do not draw back, do not take yourself away from Him, but day by day say, "I am Christ's; I have given myself to Him;" and ask Him to give you His Spirit and keep you by His grace. As it is by giving yourself to God, and believing Him, that you become His child, so you are to live in Him. The apostle says, "As ye have therefore received Christ Jesus the Lord, so walk ye in Him." Colossians 2:6.

Some seem to feel that they must be on probation, and must prove to the Lord that they are reformed, before they can claim His blessing. But they may claim the blessing of God even now. They must have His grace, the Spirit of Christ, to help their infirmities, or they cannot resist evil. Jesus loves to have us come to Him just as we are, sinful, helpless, dependent. We may come with all our weakness, our folly, our sinfulness, and fall at His feet in penitence. It is His glory to encircle us in the arms of His love and to bind up our wounds, to cleanse us from all impurity.

Here is where thousands fail; they do not believe that Jesus pardons them personally, individually. They do not take God at His word. It is the privilege of all who comply with the conditions to know for themselves that pardon is freely extended for every sin. Put away the suspicion that God's promises are not meant for you. They are for every repentant transgressor. 53 Strength and grace have been provided through Christ to be brought by ministering angels to every believing soul. None are so sinful that they cannot find strength, purity, and righteousness in Jesus, who died for them. He is waiting to strip them of their garments stained and polluted with sin, and to put upon them the white robes of righteousness; He bids them live and not die.

God does not deal with us as finite men deal with one another. His thoughts are thoughts of mercy, love, and tenderest compassion. He says, "Let the wicked forsake his way, and the unrighteous man his thoughts: and let him return unto the Lord, and He will have mercy upon him; and to our God, for He will abundantly pardon." "I have blotted out, as a thick cloud, thy transgressions, and, as a cloud, thy sins." Isaiah 55:7; 44:22.

"I have no pleasure in the death of him that dieth, saith the Lord God: wherefore turn yourselves, and live ye." Ezekiel 18:32. Satan is ready to steal away the blessed assurances of God. He desires to take every glimmer of hope and every ray of light from the soul; but you must not permit him to do this. Do not give ear to the tempter, but say, "Jesus has died that I might live. He loves me, and wills not that I should perish. I have a compassionate heavenly Father; and although I have abused His love, though the blessings He has given me have been squandered, I will arise, and go to my Father, and say, 'I have sinned against heaven, and before Thee, and am no more worthy to be called Thy son: make me as one of Thy hired 54 servants.' " The parable tells you how the wanderer will be received: "*When he was yet a great way off*, his father saw him, and had compassion, and ran, and fell on his neck, and kissed him." Luke 15:18-20.

But even this parable, tender and touching as it is, comes short of expressing the infinite compassion of the heavenly Father. The Lord declares by His prophet, "I have loved thee with an everlasting love: *therefore with loving-kindness have I drawn thee*." Jeremiah 31:3. While the sinner is yet far from the Father's house, wasting his substance in a strange country, the Father's heart is yearning over him; and every longing awakened in the soul to return to God is but the tender pleading of His Spirit, wooing, entreating, drawing the wanderer to his Father's heart of love.

With the rich promises of the Bible before you, can you give place to doubt? Can you believe that when the poor sinner longs to return, longs to forsake his sins, the Lord sternly withholds him from coming to His feet in repentance? Away with such thoughts! Nothing can hurt your own soul more than to entertain such a conception of our heavenly Father. He hates sin, but He loves the sinner, and He gave Himself in the person of Christ, that all who would might be saved and have eternal blessedness in the kingdom of glory. What stronger or more tender language could have been employed than He has chosen in which to express His love toward us? He declares, "Can a woman forget her sucking child, that she should not have compassion on the son of her womb? yea, they may forget, yet will I not forget thee." Isaiah 49:15.

Look up, you that are doubting and trem- 55 bling; for Jesus lives to make intercession for us. Thank God for the gift of His dear Son and pray that He may not have died for you in vain. The Spirit invites you today. Come with your whole heart to Jesus, and you may claim His blessing.

As you read the promises, remember they are the expression of unutterable love and pity. The great heart of Infinite Love is drawn toward the sinner with boundless compassion. "We have

redemption through His blood, the forgiveness of sins." Ephesians 1:7. Yes, only believe that God is your helper. He wants to restore His moral image in man. As you draw near to Him with confession and repentance, He will draw near to you with mercy and forgiveness.

7   57

The Test of Discipleship

"If any man be in Christ, he is a new creature: old things are passed away; behold, all things are become new." 2 Corinthians 5:17.

A person may not be able to tell the exact time or place, or trace all the chain of circumstances in the process of conversion; but this does not prove him to be unconverted. Christ said to Nicodemus, "The wind bloweth where it listeth, and thou hearest the sound thereof, but canst not tell whence it cometh, and whither it goeth: so is everyone that is born of the Spirit." John 3:8. Like the wind, which is invisible, yet the effects of which are plainly seen and felt, is the Spirit of God in its work upon the human heart. That regenerating power, which no human eye can see, begets a new life in the soul; it creates a new being in the image of God. While the work of the Spirit is silent and imperceptible, its effects are manifest. If the heart has been renewed by the Spirit of God, the life will bear witness to the fact. While we cannot do anything to change our hearts or to bring ourselves into harmony with God; while we must not trust at all to ourselves or our good works, our lives will reveal whether the grace of God is dwelling within us. A change will be seen in the character, the habits, the pursuits. The contrast will be clear and decided between what they have been and what they are. The character is revealed, not by 58 occasional good deeds and occasional misdeeds, but by the tendency of the habitual words and acts.

It is true that there may be an outward correctness of deportment without the renewing power of Christ. The love of influence and the desire for the esteem of others may produce a well-ordered life. Self-respect may lead us to avoid the appearance of evil. A selfish heart may perform generous actions. By what means, then, shall we determine whose side we are on?

Who has the heart? With whom are our thoughts? Of whom do we love to converse? Who has our warmest affections and our best energies? If we are Christ's, our thoughts are with Him, and our sweetest thoughts are of Him. All we have and are is consecrated to Him. We long to bear His image, breathe His spirit, do His will, and please Him in all things.

Those who become new creatures in Christ Jesus will bring forth the fruits of the Spirit, "love, joy, peace, long-suffering, gentleness, goodness, faith, meekness, temperance." Galatians 5:22, 23. They will no longer fashion themselves according to the former lusts, but by the faith of the Son of God they will follow in His steps, reflect His character, and purify themselves even as He is pure. The things they once hated they now love, and the things they once loved they hate. The proud and self-assertive become meek and lowly in heart. The vain and supercilious become serious and unobtrusive. The drunken become sober, and the profligate pure. The vain customs and fashions of the world are laid aside. Christians will seek not the 59 "outward adorning," but "the hidden man of the heart, in that which is not corruptible, even the ornament of a meek and quiet spirit." 1 Peter 3:3, 4.

There is no evidence of genuine repentance unless it works reformation. If he restore the pledge, give again that he had robbed, confess his sins, and love God and his fellow men, the sinner may be sure that he has passed from death unto life.

When, as erring, sinful beings, we come to Christ and become partakers of His pardoning grace, love springs up in the heart. Every burden is light, for the yoke that Christ imposes is easy. Duty becomes a delight, and sacrifice a pleasure. The path that before seemed shrouded in darkness, becomes bright with beams from the Sun of Righteousness.

The loveliness of the character of Christ will be seen in His followers. It was His delight to do the will of God. Love to God, zeal for His glory, was the controlling power in our Saviour's life. Love beautified and ennobled all His actions. Love is of God. The unconsecrated heart cannot originate or produce it. It is found only in the heart where Jesus reigns. "We love, because He first loved us." 1 John 4:19, R.V. In the heart renewed by divine grace, love is the principle of action. It modifies the character, governs the impulses, controls the passions, subdues enmity, and ennobles the affections. This love, cherished in the soul, sweetens the life and sheds a refining influence on all around.

There are two errors against which the children of God—particularly those who have just come to trust in His grace—especially need to guard. The first, already dwelt upon, is that of 60 looking to their own works, trusting to anything they can do, to bring themselves into harmony with God. He who is trying to become holy by his own works in keeping the law, is attempting an impossibility. All that man can do without Christ is polluted with selfishness and sin. It is the grace of Christ alone, through faith, that can make us holy.

The opposite and no less dangerous error is that belief in Christ releases men from keeping the law of God; that since by faith alone we become partakers of the grace of Christ, our works have nothing to do with our redemption.

But notice here that obedience is not a mere outward compliance, but the service of love. The law of God is an expression of His very nature; it is an embodiment of the great principle of love, and hence is the foundation of His government in heaven and earth. If our hearts are renewed in the likeness of God, if the divine love is implanted in the soul, will not the law of God be carried out in the life? When the principle of love is implanted in the heart, when man is renewed after the image of Him that created him, the new-covenant promise is fulfilled, "I will put My laws into their hearts, and in their minds will I write them." Hebrews 10:16. And if the law is written in the heart, will it not shape the life? Obedience—the service and allegiance of love—is the true sign of discipleship. Thus the Scripture says, "This is the love of God, that we keep His commandments." "He that saith, I know Him, and keepeth not His commandments, is a liar, and the truth is not in him." 1 John 5:3; 2:4. Instead of releasing man from obedience, it is faith, and 61 faith only, that makes us partakers of the grace of Christ, which enables us to render obedience.

We do not earn salvation by our obedience; for salvation is the free gift of God, to be received by faith. But obedience is the fruit of faith. "Ye know that He was manifested to take away our sins; and in Him is no sin. Whosoever abideth in Him sinneth not: whosoever sinneth hath not seen Him, neither known Him." 1 John 3:5, 6. Here is the true test. If we abide in Christ, if the love of God dwells in us, our feelings, our thoughts, our purposes, our actions, will be in harmony with the will of God as expressed in the precepts of His holy law. "Little children, let no man deceive you: he that doeth righteousness is righteous, even as He is righteous." 1 John 3:7. Righteousness is defined by the standard of God's holy law, as expressed in the ten precepts given on Sinai.

That so-called faith in Christ which professes to release men from the obligation of obedience to God, is not faith, but presumption. "By grace are ye saved through faith." But "faith, if it hath not works, is dead." Ephesians 2:8; James 2:17. Jesus said of Himself before He came to earth, "I delight to do Thy will, O My God: yea, Thy law is within My heart." Psalm 40:8. And just before He ascended again to heaven He declared, "I have kept My Father's commandments, and abide in His love." John 15:10. The Scripture says, "Hereby we do know that we know Him, if we keep His commandments. . . . He that saith he abideth in Him ought himself

also so to walk even as He walked." 1 John 2:3-
6. "Because Christ also suffered for us, leaving
us an example, that ye should follow His steps."
1 Peter 2:21.

The condition of eternal life is now just what
it always has been,—just what it was in Paradise before the fall of our first parents,—perfect obedience to the law of God, perfect righteousness. If eternal life were granted on any
condition short of this, then the happiness of the
whole universe would be imperiled. The way
would be open for sin, with all its train of woe
and misery, to be immortalized.

It was possible for Adam, before the fall, to
form a righteous character by obedience to
God's law. But he failed to do this, and because
of his sin our natures are fallen and we cannot
make ourselves righteous. Since we are sinful,
unholy, we cannot perfectly obey the holy law.
We have no righteousness of our own with
which to meet the claims of the law of God. But
Christ has made a way of escape for us. He
lived on earth amid trials and temptations such
as we have to meet. He lived a sinless life. He
died for us, and now He offers to take our sins
and give us His righteousness. If you give yourself to Him, and accept Him as your Saviour,
then, sinful as your life may have been, for His
sake you are accounted righteous. Christ's character stands in place of your character, and you
are accepted before God just as if you had not
sinned.

More than this, Christ changes the heart. He
abides in your heart by faith. You are to maintain this connection with Christ by faith and the
continual surrender of your will to Him; and so
long as you do this, He will work in you to will
and to do according to His good pleasure. So
you may say, "The life which I now live in the
flesh I live by the faith of the Son of God, who
loved me, and gave Himself for me." Galatians
2:20. So Jesus said to His disciples, "It is not ye
that speak, but the Spirit of your Father which
speaketh in you." Matthew 10:20. Then with
Christ working in you, you will manifest the
same spirit and do the same good works—
works of righteousness, obedience.

So we have nothing in ourselves of which to
boast. We have no ground for self-exaltation.
Our only ground of hope is in the righteousness
of Christ imputed to us, and in that wrought by
His Spirit working in and through us.

When we speak of faith, there is a distinction that should be borne in mind. There is a
kind of belief that is wholly distinct from faith.
The existence and power of God, the truth of
His word, are facts that even Satan and his
hosts cannot at heart deny. The Bible says that
"the devils also believe, and tremble;" but this
is not faith. James 2:19. Where there is not
only a belief in God's word, but a submission
of the will to Him; where the heart is yielded

to Him, the affections fixed upon Him, there is
faith—faith that works by love and purifies the
soul. Through this faith the heart is renewed in
the image of God. And the heart that in its
unrenewed state is not subject to the law of
God, neither indeed can be, now delights in its
holy precepts, exclaiming with the psalmist,
"O how love I Thy law! it is my meditation all
the day." Psalm 119:97. And the righteousness
of the law is fulfilled in us, "who walk not
after the flesh, but after the Spirit." Romans
8:1.

There are those who have known the pardoning love of Christ and who really desire to
be children of God, yet they realize that their
character is imperfect, their life faulty, and
they are ready to doubt whether their hearts
have been renewed by the Holy Spirit. To such
I would say, Do not draw back in despair. We
shall often have to bow down and weep at the
feet of Jesus because of our shortcomings and
mistakes, but we are not to be discouraged.
Even if we are overcome by the enemy, we are
not cast off, not forsaken and rejected of God.
No; Christ is at the right hand of God, who
also maketh intercession for us. Said the
beloved John, "These things write I unto you,
that ye sin not. And if any man sin, we have an
advocate with the Father, Jesus Christ the
righteous." 1 John 2:1. And do not forget the
words of Christ, "The Father Himself loveth
you." John 16:27. He desires to restore you to
Himself, to see His own purity and holiness
reflected in you. And if you will but yield
yourself to Him, He that hath begun a good
work in you will carry it forward to the day of
Jesus Christ. Pray more fervently; believe
more fully. As we come to distrust our own
power, let us trust the power of our Redeemer,
and we shall praise Him who is the health of
our countenance.

The closer you come to Jesus, the more faulty
you will appear in your own eyes; for your
vision will be clearer, and your imperfections
will be seen in broad and distinct contrast to His
perfect nature. This is evidence that Satan's
delusions have lost their power; that the vivifying influence of the Spirit of God is arousing
you.

No deep-seated love for Jesus can dwell in
the heart that does not realize its own sinfulness.
The soul that is transformed by the grace of
Christ will admire His divine character; but if
we do not see our own moral deformity, it is
unmistakable evidence that we have not had a
view of the beauty and excellence of Christ.

The less we see to esteem in ourselves, the
more we shall see to esteem in the infinite purity
and loveliness of our Saviour. A view of our
sinfulness drives us to Him who can pardon;
and when the soul, realizing its helplessness,
reaches out after Christ, He will reveal Himself

in power. The more our sense of need drives us to Him and to the word of God, the more exalted views we shall have of His character, and the more fully we shall reflect His image.

67

8
Growing Up Into Christ

The change of heart by which we become children of God is in the Bible spoken of as birth. Again, it is compared to the germination of the good seed sown by the husbandman. In like manner those who are just converted to Christ are, "as new-born babes," to "grow up" to the stature of men and women in Christ Jesus. 1 Peter 2:2; Ephesians 4:15. Or like the good seed sown in the field, they are to grow up and bring forth fruit. Isaiah says that they shall "be called trees of righteousness, the planting of the Lord, that He might be glorified." Isaiah 61:3. So from natural life, illustrations are drawn, to help us better to understand the mysterious truths of spiritual life.

Not all the wisdom and skill of man can produce life in the smallest object in nature. It is only through the life which God Himself has imparted, that either plant or animal can live. So it is only through the life from God that spiritual life is begotten in the hearts of men. Unless a man is "born from above," he cannot become a partaker of the life which Christ came to give. John 3:3, margin.

As with life, so it is with growth. It is God who brings the bud to bloom and the flower to fruit. It is by His power that the seed develops, "first the blade, then the ear, after that the full corn in the ear." Mark 4:28. And the prophet Hosea says of Israel, that "he shall grow as the lily." "They shall revive as the corn, and grow as the vine." Hosea 14:5, 7. And Jesus bids us
68   "consider the lilies how they grow." Luke 12:27. The plants and flowers grow not by their own care or anxiety or effort, but by receiving that which God has furnished to minister to their life. The child cannot, by any anxiety or power of its own, add to its stature. No more can you, by anxiety or effort of yourself, secure spiritual growth. The plant, the child, grows by receiving from its surroundings that which ministers to its life—air, sunshine, and food. What these gifts of nature are to animal and plant, such is Christ to those who trust in Him. He is their "everlasting light," "a sun and shield." Isaiah 60:19; Psalm 84:11. He shall be as "the dew unto Israel." "He shall come down like rain upon the mown grass." Hosea 14:5; Psalm 72:6. He is the living water, "the Bread of God . . . which cometh down from heaven, and giveth life unto the world." John 6:33.

In the matchless gift of His Son, God has encircled the whole world with an atmosphere of grace as real as the air which circulates around the globe. All who choose to breathe this life-giving atmosphere will live and grow up to the stature of men and women in Christ Jesus.

As the flower turns to the sun, that the bright beams may aid in perfecting its beauty and symmetry, so should we turn to the Sun of Righteousness, that heaven's light may shine upon us, that our character may be developed into the likeness of Christ.

Jesus teaches the same thing when He says, "Abide in Me, and I in you. As the branch cannot bear fruit of itself, except it abide in the vine; no more can ye, except ye abide in Me. . . . Without Me ye can do nothing." John 15:4, 5. 69 You are just as dependent upon Christ, in order to live a holy life, as is the branch upon the parent stock for growth and fruitfulness. Apart from Him you have no life. You have no power to resist temptation or to grow in grace and holiness. Abiding in Him, you may flourish. Drawing your life from Him, you will not wither nor be fruitless. You will be like a tree planted by the rivers of water.

Many have an idea that they must do some part of the work alone. They have trusted in Christ for the forgiveness of sin, but now they seek by their own efforts to live aright. But every such effort must fail. Jesus says, "Without Me ye can do nothing." Our growth in grace, our joy, our usefulness,—all depend upon our union with Christ. It is by communion with Him, daily, hourly,—by abiding in Him,—that we are to grow in grace. He is not only the Author, but the Finisher of our faith. It is Christ first and last and always. He is to be with us, not only at the beginning and the end of our course, but at every step of the way. David says, "I have set the Lord always before me: because He is at my right hand, I shall not be moved." Psalm 16:8.

Do you ask, "How am I to abide in Christ?" In the same way as you received Him at first. "As ye have therefore received Christ Jesus the Lord, so walk ye in Him." "The just shall live by faith." Colossians 2:6; Hebrews 10:38. You gave yourself to God, to be His wholly, to serve and obey Him, and you took Christ as your Saviour. You could not yourself atone for your sins or change your heart; but having given yourself 70 to God, you believe that He for Christ's sake did all this for you. By faith you became Christ's, and by faith you are to grow up in Him—by giving and taking. You are to *give* all,—your heart, your will, your service,—give yourself to Him to obey all His requirements; and you must *take* all,—Christ, the fullness of all blessing, to abide in your heart, to be your strength, your righteousness, your everlasting helper,—to give you power to obey.

Consecrate yourself to God in the morning; make this your very first work. Let your prayer be, "Take me, O Lord, as wholly Thine. I lay all my plans at Thy feet. Use me today in Thy service. Abide with me, and let all my work be wrought in Thee." This is a daily matter. Each morning consecrate yourself to God for that day. Surrender all your plans to Him, to be carried out or given up as His providence shall indicate. Thus day by day you may be giving your life into the hands of God, and thus your life will be molded more and more after the life of Christ.

A life in Christ is a life of restfulness. There may be no ecstasy of feeling, but there should be an abiding, peaceful trust. Your hope is not in yourself; it is in Christ. Your weakness is united to His strength, your ignorance to His wisdom, your frailty to His enduring might. So you are not to look to yourself, not to let the mind dwell upon self, but look to Christ. Let the mind dwell upon His love, upon the beauty, the perfection, of His character. Christ in His self-denial, Christ in His humiliation, Christ in His purity and holiness, Christ in His matchless love—this is the subject for the soul's contemplation. It is by loving Him, copying Him, depending wholly upon Him, that you are to be transformed into His likeness.

Jesus says, "Abide in Me." These words convey the idea of rest, stability, confidence. Again He invites, "Come unto Me, . . . and I will give you rest." Matthew 11:28. The words of the psalmist express the same thought: "Rest in the Lord, and wait patiently for Him." And Isaiah gives the assurance, "In quietness and in confidence shall be your strength." Psalm 37:7; Isaiah 30:15. This rest is not found in inactivity; for in the Saviour's invitation the promise of rest is united with the call to labor: "Take My yoke upon you: . . . and ye shall find rest." Matthew 11:29. The heart that rests most fully upon Christ will be most earnest and active in labor for Him.

When the mind dwells upon self, it is turned away from Christ, the source of strength and life. Hence it is Satan's constant effort to keep the attention diverted from the Saviour and thus prevent the union and communion of the soul with Christ. The pleasures of the world, life's cares and perplexities and sorrows, the faults of others, or your own faults and imperfections—to any or all of these he will seek to divert the mind. Do not be misled by his devices. Many who are really conscientious, and who desire to live for God, he too often leads to dwell upon their own faults and weaknesses, and thus by separating them from Christ he hopes to gain the victory. We should not make self the center and indulge anxiety and fear as to whether we shall be saved. All this turns the soul away

from the Source of our strength. Commit the keeping of your soul to God, and trust in Him. Talk and think of Jesus. Let self be lost in Him. Put away all doubt; dismiss your fears. Say with the apostle Paul, "I live; yet not I, but Christ liveth in me: and the life which I now live in the flesh I live by the faith of the Son of God, who loved me, and gave Himself for me." Galatians 2:20. Rest in God. He is able to keep that which you have committed to Him. If you will leave yourself in His hands, He will bring you off more than conqueror through Him that has loved you.

When Christ took human nature upon Him, He bound humanity to Himself by a tie of love that can never be broken by any power save the choice of man himself. Satan will constantly present allurements to induce us to break this tie—to choose to separate ourselves from Christ. Here is where we need to watch, to strive, to pray, that nothing may entice us to *choose* another master; for we are always free to do this. But let us keep our eyes fixed upon Christ, and He will preserve us. Looking unto Jesus, we are safe. Nothing can pluck us out of His hand. In constantly beholding Him, we "are changed into the same image from glory to glory, even as by the Spirit of the Lord." 2 Corinthians 3:18.

It was thus that the early disciples gained their likeness to the dear Saviour. When those disciples heard the words of Jesus, they felt their need of Him. They sought, they found, they followed Him. They were with Him in the house, at the table, in the closet, in the field. They were with Him as pupils with a teacher, daily receiving from His lips lessons of holy truth. They looked to Him, as servants to their master, to learn their duty. Those disciples were men "subject to like passions as we are." James 5:17. They had the same battle with sin to fight. They needed the same grace, in order to live a holy life.

Even John, the beloved disciple, the one who most fully reflected the likeness of the Saviour, did not naturally possess that loveliness of character. He was not only self-assertive and ambitious for honor, but impetuous, and resentful under injuries. But as the character of the Divine One was manifested to him, he saw his own deficiency and was humbled by the knowledge. The strength and patience, the power and tenderness, the majesty and meekness, that he beheld in the daily life of the Son of God, filled his soul with admiration and love. Day by day his heart was drawn out toward Christ, until he lost sight of self in love for his Master. His resentful, ambitious temper was yielded to the molding power of Christ. The regenerating influence of the Holy Spirit renewed his heart. The power of the love of Christ wrought a transformation of character. This is the sure result of union with Jesus. When Christ abides in the heart, the whole nature is transformed. Christ's Spirit, His love, softens the heart, subdues the soul, and raises the thoughts and desires toward God and heaven.

When Christ ascended to heaven, the sense of His presence was still with His followers. It was a personal presence, full of love and light. Jesus, the Saviour, who had walked and talked and prayed with them, who had spoken hope and comfort to their hearts, had, while the message of peace was still upon His lips, been taken up from them into heaven, and the tones of His voice had come back to them, as the cloud of angels received Him—"Lo, I am with you alway, even unto the end of the world." Matthew 28:20. He had ascended to heaven in the form of humanity. They knew that He was before the throne of God, their Friend and Saviour still; that His sympathies were unchanged; that He was still identified with suffering humanity. He was presenting before God the merits of His own precious blood, showing His wounded hands and feet, in remembrance of the price He had paid for His redeemed. They knew that He had ascended to heaven to prepare places for them, and that He would come again and take them to Himself.

As they met together after the ascension they were eager to present their requests to the Father in the name of Jesus. In solemn awe they bowed in prayer, repeating the assurance, "Whatsoever ye shall ask the Father in My name, He will give it you. Hitherto have ye asked nothing in My name: ask, and ye shall receive, that your joy may be full." John 16:23, 24. They extended the hand of faith higher and higher with the mighty argument, "It is Christ that died, yea rather, that is risen again, who is even at the right hand of God, who also maketh intercession for us." Romans 8:34. And Pentecost brought them the presence of the Comforter, of whom Christ had said, He "shall be in you." And He had further said, "It is expedient for you that I go away: for if I go not away, the Comforter will not come unto you; but if I depart, I will send Him unto you." John 14:17; 16:7. Henceforth through the Spirit, Christ was to abide continually in the hearts of His children. Their union with Him was closer than when He was personally with them. The light, and love, and power of the indwelling Christ shone out through them, so that men, beholding, "marveled; and they took knowledge of them, that they had been with Jesus." Acts 4:13.

All that Christ was to the disciples, He desires to be to His children today; for in that last prayer, with the little band of disciples gathered about Him, He said, "Neither pray I for these alone, but for them also which shall believe on Me through their word." John 17:20.

Jesus prayed for us, and He asked that we might be one with Him, even as He is one with the Father. What a union is this! The Saviour has said of Himself, "The Son can do nothing of Himself;" "the Father that dwelleth in Me, He doeth the works." John 5:19; 14:10. Then if Christ is dwelling in our hearts, He will work in us "both to will and to do of His good pleasure." Philippians 2:13. We shall work as He worked; we shall manifest the same spirit. And thus, loving Him and abiding in Him, we shall "grow up into Him in all things, which is the head, even Christ." Ephesians 4:15.

9
The Work and the Life

God is the source of life and light and joy to the universe. Like rays of light from the sun, like the streams of water bursting from a living spring, blessings flow out from Him to all His creatures. And wherever the life of God is in the hearts of men, it will flow out to others in love and blessing.

Our Saviour's joy was in the uplifting and redemption of fallen men. For this He counted not His life dear unto Himself, but endured the cross, despising the shame. So angels are ever engaged in working for the happiness of others. This is their joy. That which selfish hearts would regard as humiliating service, ministering to those who are wretched and in every way inferior in character and rank, is the work of sinless angels. The spirit of Christ's self-sacrificing love is the spirit that pervades heaven and is the very essence of its bliss. This is the spirit that Christ's followers will possess, the work that they will do.

When the love of Christ is enshrined in the heart, like sweet fragrance it cannot be hidden. Its holy influence will be felt by all with whom we come in contact. The spirit of Christ in the heart is like a spring in the desert, flowing to refresh all and making those who are ready to perish, eager to drink of the water of life.

Love to Jesus will be manifested in a desire to work as He worked for the blessing and uplifting of humanity. It will lead to love, tenderness, and sympathy toward all the creatures of our heavenly Father's care.

The Saviour's life on earth was not a life of ease and devotion to Himself, but He toiled with persistent, earnest, untiring effort for the salvation of lost mankind. From the manger to Calvary He followed the path of self-denial and sought not to be released from arduous tasks, painful travels and exhausting care and labor. He said, "The Son of man came not to be ministered unto, but to minister, and to give His life a ransom for many." Matthew 20:28. This was the one great object of His life. Everything else was secondary and subservient. It was His meat and drink to do the will of God and to finish His work. Self and self-interest had no part in His labor.

So those who are the partakers of the grace of Christ will be ready to make any sacrifice, that others for whom He died may share the heavenly gift. They will do all they can to make the world better for their stay in it. This spirit is the sure outgrowth of a soul truly converted. No sooner does one come to Christ than there is born in his heart a desire to make known to others what a precious friend he has found in Jesus; the saving and sanctifying truth cannot be shut up in his heart. If we are clothed with the righteousness of Christ and are filled with the joy of His indwelling Spirit, we shall not be able to hold our peace. If we have tasted and seen that the Lord is good we shall have something to tell. Like Philip when he found the Saviour, we shall invite others into His presence. We shall

79 seek to present to them the attractions of Christ and the unseen realities of the world to come. There will be an intensity of desire to follow in the path that Jesus trod. There will be an earnest longing that those around us may "behold the Lamb of God, which taketh away the sin of the world." John 1:29.

And the effort to bless others will react in blessings upon ourselves. This was the purpose of God in giving us a part to act in the plan of redemption. He has granted men the privilege of becoming partakers of the divine nature and, in their turn, of diffusing blessings to their fellow men. This is the highest honor, the greatest joy, that it is possible for God to bestow upon men. Those who thus become participants in labors of love are brought nearest to their Creator.

God might have committed the message of the gospel, and all the work of loving ministry, to the heavenly angels. He might have employed other means for accomplishing His purpose. But in His infinite love He chose to make us co-workers with Himself, with Christ and the angels, that we might share the blessing, the joy, the spiritual uplifting, which results from this unselfish ministry.

We are brought into sympathy with Christ through the fellowship of His sufferings. Every act of self-sacrifice for the good of others strengthens the spirit of beneficence in the giver's heart, allying him more closely to the Redeemer of the world, who "was rich, yet for your sakes . . . became poor, that ye through His poverty might be rich." 2 Corinthians 8:9. And it is only as we thus fulfill the divine pur-

80 pose in our creation that life can be a blessing to us.

If you will go to work as Christ designs that His disciples shall, and win souls for Him, you will feel the need of a deeper experience and a greater knowledge in divine things, and will hunger and thirst after righteousness. You will plead with God, and your faith will be strengthened, and your soul will drink deeper drafts at the well of salvation. Encountering opposition and trials will drive you to the Bible and prayer. You will grow in grace and the knowledge of Christ, and will develop a rich experience.

The spirit of unselfish labor for others gives depth, stability, and Christlike loveliness to the character, and brings peace and happiness to its possessor. The aspirations are elevated. There is no room for sloth or selfishness. Those who thus exercise the Christian graces will grow and will become strong to work for God. They will have clear spiritual perceptions, a steady, growing faith, and an increased power in prayer. The Spirit of God, moving upon their spirit, calls forth the sacred harmonies of the soul in answer to the divine touch. Those who thus devote themselves to unselfish effort for the good of others are most surely working out their own salvation.

The only way to grow in grace is to be disinterestedly doing the very work which Christ has enjoined upon us—to engage, to the extent of our ability, in helping and blessing those who need the help we can give them. Strength comes by exercise; activity is the very condition of life. Those who endeavor to maintain Christian life by passively accepting the blessings that come through the means of grace, and doing nothing 81 for Christ, are simply trying to live by eating without working. And in the spiritual as in the natural world, this always results in degeneration and decay. A man who would refuse to exercise his limbs would soon lose all power to use them. Thus the Christian who will not exercise his God-given powers not only fails to grow up into Christ, but he loses the strength that he already had.

The church of Christ is God's appointed agency for the salvation of men. Its mission is to carry the gospel to the world. And the obligation rests upon all Christians. Everyone, to the extent of his talent and opportunity, is to fulfill the Saviour's commission. The love of Christ, revealed to us, makes us debtors to all who know Him not. God has given us light, not for ourselves alone, but to shed upon them.

If the followers of Christ were awake to duty, there would be thousands where there is one today proclaiming the gospel in heathen lands. And all who could not personally engage in the work, would yet sustain it with their means, their sympathy, and their prayers. And there would be far more earnest labor for souls in Christian countries.

We need not go to heathen lands, or even leave the narrow circle of the home, if it is there that our duty lies, in order to work for Christ. We can do this in the home circle, in the church, among those with whom we associate, and with whom we do business.

The greater part of our Saviour's life on earth was spent in patient toil in the carpenter's shop at Nazareth. Ministering angels attended the Lord of life as He walked side by side with peasants and laborers, unrecognized and unhonored. He was as faithfully fulfilling His mission while working at His humble trade as when He healed the sick or walked upon the storm-tossed waves of Galilee. So in the humblest duties and lowliest positions of life, we may walk and work with Jesus.

The apostle says, "Let every man, wherein he is called, therein abide with God." 1 Corinthians 7:24. The businessman may conduct his business in a way that will glorify his Master because of his fidelity. If he is a true follower of Christ he will carry his religion into everything that is done and reveal to men the spirit of Christ. The mechanic may be a diligent and faithful representative of Him who toiled in the lowly walks of life among the hills of Galilee. Everyone who names the name of Christ should so work that others, by seeing his good works, may be led to glorify their Creator and Redeemer.

Many have excused themselves from rendering their gifts to the service of Christ because others were possessed of superior endowments and advantages. The opinion has prevailed that only those who are especially talented are required to consecrate their abilities to the service of God. It has come to be understood by many that talents are given to only a certain favored class to the exclusion of others who of course are not called upon to share in the toils or the rewards. But it is not so represented in the parable. When the master of the house called his servants, he gave to every man *his* work.

With a loving spirit we may perform life's humblest duties "as to the Lord." Colossians 3:23. If the love of God is in the heart, it will be manifested in the life. The sweet savor of Christ will surround us, and our influence will elevate and bless.

You are not to wait for great occasions or to expect extraordinary abilities before you go to work for God. You need not have a thought of what the world will think of you. If your daily life is a testimony to the purity and sincerity of your faith, and others are convinced that you desire to benefit them, your efforts will not be wholly lost.

The humblest and poorest of the disciples of Jesus can be a blessing to others. They may not realize that they are doing any special good, but by their unconscious influence they may start waves of blessing that will widen and deepen, and the blessed results they may never know

until the day of final reward. They do not feel or know that they are doing anything great. They are not required to weary themselves with anxiety about success. They have only to go forward quietly, doing faithfully the work that God's providence assigns, and their life will not be in vain. Their own souls will be growing more and more into the likeness of Christ; they are workers together with God in this life and are thus fitting for the higher work and the unshadowed joy of the life to come.

10

A Knowledge of God

Many are the ways in which God is seeking to make Himself known to us and bring us into communion with Him. Nature speaks to our senses without ceasing. The open heart will be impressed with the love and glory of God as revealed through the works of His hands. The listening ear can hear and understand the communications of God through the things of nature. The green fields, the lofty trees, the buds and flowers, the passing cloud, the falling rain, the babbling brook, the glories of the heavens, speak to our hearts, and invite us to become acquainted with Him who made them all.

Our Saviour bound up His precious lessons with the things of nature. The trees, the birds, the flowers of the valleys, the hills, the lakes, and the beautiful heavens, as well as the incidents and surroundings of daily life, were all linked with the words of truth, that His lessons might thus be often recalled to mind, even amid the busy cares of man's life of toil.

God would have His children appreciate His works and delight in the simple, quiet beauty with which He has adorned our earthly home. He is a lover of the beautiful, and above all that is outwardly attractive He loves beauty of character; He would have us cultivate purity and simplicity, the quiet graces of the flowers.

If we will but listen, God's created works will teach us precious lessons of obedience and trust. From the stars that in their trackless courses through space follow from age to age their appointed path, down to the minutest atom, the things of nature obey the Creator's will. And God cares for everything and sustains everything that He has created. He who upholds the unnumbered worlds throughout immensity, at the same time cares for the wants of the little brown sparrow that sings its humble song without fear. When men go forth to their daily toil, as when they engage in prayer; when they lie down at night, and when they rise in the morning; when the rich man feasts in his palace, or when the poor man gathers his children about the scanty board, each is tenderly watched by the heavenly Father. No tears are shed that God does not notice. There is no smile that He does not mark.

If we would but fully believe this, all undue anxieties would be dismissed. Our lives would not be so filled with disappointment as now; for everything, whether great or small, would be left in the hands of God, who is not perplexed by the multiplicity of cares, or overwhelmed by their weight. We should then enjoy a rest of soul to which many have long been strangers.

As your senses delight in the attractive loveliness of the earth, think of the world that is to come, that shall never know the blight of sin and death; where the face of nature will no more wear the shadow of the curse. Let your imagination picture the home of the saved, and remember that it will be more glorious than your brightest imagination can portray. In the varied gifts of God in nature we see but the faintest
87 gleaming of His glory. It is written, "Eye hath not seen, nor ear heard, neither have entered into the heart of man, the things which God hath prepared for them that love Him." 1 Corinthians 2:9.

The poet and the naturalist have many things to say about nature, but it is the Christian who enjoys the beauty of the earth with the highest appreciation, because he recognizes his Father's handiwork and perceives His love in flower and shrub and tree. No one can fully appreciate the significance of hill and vale, river and sea, who does not look upon them as an expression of God's love to man.

God speaks to us through His providential workings and through the influence of His Spirit upon the heart. In our circumstances and surroundings, in the changes daily taking place around us, we may find precious lessons if our hearts are but open to discern them. The psalmist, tracing the work of God's providence, says, "The earth is full of the goodness of the Lord." "Whoso is wise, and will observe these things, even they shall understand the lovingkindness of the Lord." Psalm 33:5; 107:43.

God speaks to us in His word. Here we have in clearer lines the revelation of His character, of His dealings with men, and the great work of redemption. Here is open before us the history of patriarchs and prophets and other holy men of old. They were men "subject to like passions as we are." James 5:17. We see how they struggled through discouragements like our own, how they fell under temptation as we have done, and yet took heart again and conquered through the grace of God; and, beholding, we are
88 encouraged in our striving after righteousness. As we read of the precious experiences granted them, of the light and love and blessing it was

theirs to enjoy, and of the work they wrought through the grace given them, the spirit that inspired them kindles a flame of holy emulation in our hearts and a desire to be like them in character—like them to walk with God.

Jesus said of the Old Testament Scriptures,—and how much more is it true of the New,—"They are they which testify of Me," the Redeemer, Him in whom our hopes of eternal life are centered. John 5:39. Yes, the whole Bible tells of Christ. From the first record of creation—for "without Him was not anything made that was made"—to the closing promise, "Behold, I come quickly," we are reading of His works and listening to His voice. John 1:3; Revelation 22:12. If you would become acquainted with the Saviour, study the Holy Scriptures.

Fill the whole heart with the words of God. They are the living water, quenching your burning thirst. They are the living bread from heaven. Jesus declares, "Except ye eat the flesh of the Son of man, and drink His blood, ye have no life in you." And He explains Himself by saying, "The words that I speak unto you, they are spirit, and they are life." John 6:53, 63. Our bodies are built up from what we eat and drink; and as in the natural economy, so in the spiritual economy: it is what we meditate upon that will give tone and strength to our spiritual nature.

The theme of redemption is one that the angels desire to look into; it will be the science and the song of the redeemed throughout the ceaseless ages of eternity. Is it not worthy of 89 careful thought and study now? The infinite mercy and love of Jesus, the sacrifice made in our behalf, call for the most serious and solemn reflection. We should dwell upon the character of our dear Redeemer and Intercessor. We should meditate upon the mission of Him who came to save His people from their sins. As we thus contemplate heavenly themes, our faith and love will grow stronger, and our prayers will be more and more acceptable to God, because they will be more and more mixed with faith and love. They will be intelligent and fervent. There will be more constant confidence in Jesus, and a daily, living experience in His power to save to the uttermost all that come unto God by Him.

As we meditate upon the perfections of the Saviour, we shall desire to be wholly transformed and renewed in the image of His purity. There will be a hungering and thirsting of soul to become like Him whom we adore. The more our thoughts are upon Christ, the more we shall speak of Him to others and represent Him to the world.

The Bible was not written for the scholar alone; on the contrary, it was designed for the common people. The great truths necessary for salvation are made as clear as noonday; and none will mistake and lose their way except those who follow their own judgment instead of the plainly revealed will of God.

We should not take the testimony of any man as to what the Scriptures teach, but should study the words of God for ourselves. If we allow others to do our thinking, we shall have crippled energies and contracted abilities. The noble powers of the mind may be so dwarfed by lack of exercise on themes worthy of their concentration as to lose their ability to grasp the deep meaning of the word of God. The mind will enlarge if it is employed in tracing out the relation of the subjects of the Bible, comparing scripture with scripture and spiritual things with spiritual.

There is nothing more calculated to strengthen the intellect than the study of the Scriptures. No other book is so potent to elevate the thoughts, to give vigor to the faculties, as the broad, ennobling truths of the Bible. If God's word were studied as it should be, men would have a breadth of mind, a nobility of character, and a stability of purpose rarely seen in these times.

But there is but little benefit derived from a hasty reading of the Scriptures. One may read the whole Bible through and yet fail to see its beauty or comprehend its deep and hidden meaning. One passage studied until its significance is clear to the mind and its relation to the plan of salvation is evident, is of more value than the perusal of many chapters with no definite purpose in view and no positive instruction gained. Keep your Bible with you. As you have opportunity, read it; fix the texts in your memory. Even while you are walking the streets you may read a passage and meditate upon it, thus fixing it in the mind.

We cannot obtain wisdom without earnest attention and prayerful study. Some portions of Scripture are indeed too plain to be misunderstood, but there are others whose meaning does not lie on the surface to be seen at a glance. Scripture must be compared with scripture. There must be careful research and prayerful reflection. And such study will be richly repaid. As the miner discovers veins of precious metal concealed beneath the surface of the earth, so will he who perseveringly searches the word of God as for hid treasure find truths of the greatest value, which are concealed from the view of the careless seeker. The words of inspiration, pondered in the heart, will be as streams flowing from the fountain of life.

Never should the Bible be studied without prayer. Before opening its pages we should ask for the enlightenment of the Holy Spirit, and it will be given. When Nathanael came to Jesus, the Saviour exclaimed, "Behold an Israelite indeed, in whom is no guile!" Nathanael said,

"Whence knowest Thou me?" Jesus answered, "Before that Philip called thee, when thou wast under the fig tree, I saw thee." John 1:47, 48. And Jesus will see us also in the secret places of prayer if we will seek Him for light that we may know what is truth. Angels from the world of light will be with those who in humility of heart seek for divine guidance.

The Holy Spirit exalts and glorifies the Saviour. It is His office to present Christ, the purity of His righteousness, and the great salvation that we have through Him. Jesus says, "He shall receive of Mine, and shall show it unto you." John 16:14. The Spirit of truth is the only effectual teacher of divine truth. How must God esteem the human race, since He gave His Son to die for them and appoints His Spirit to be man's teacher and continual guide!

11

The Privilege of Prayer

Through nature and revelation, through His providence, and by the influence of His Spirit, God speaks to us. But these are not enough; we need also to pour out our hearts to Him. In order to have spiritual life and energy, we must have actual intercourse with our heavenly Father. Our minds may be drawn out toward Him; we may meditate upon His works, His mercies, His blessings; but this is not, in the fullest sense, communing with Him. In order to commune with God, we must have something to say to Him concerning our actual life.

Prayer is the opening of the heart to God as to a friend. Not that it is necessary in order to make known to God what we are, but in order to enable us to receive Him. Prayer does not bring God down to us, but brings us up to Him.

When Jesus was upon the earth, He taught His disciples how to pray. He directed them to present their daily needs before God, and to cast all their care upon Him. And the assurance He gave them that their petitions should be heard, is assurance also to us.

Jesus Himself, while He dwelt among men, was often in prayer. Our Saviour identified Himself with our needs and weaknesses, in that He became a suppliant, a petitioner, seeking from His Father fresh supplies of strength, that He might come forth braced for duty and trial. He is our example in all things. He is a brother in our infirmities, "in all points tempted like as we are;" but as the sinless one His nature recoiled from evil; He endured struggles and torture of soul in a world of sin. His humanity made prayer a necessity and a privilege. He found comfort and joy in communion with His Father. And if the Saviour of men, the Son of

God, felt the need of prayer, how much more should feeble, sinful mortals feel the necessity of fervent, constant prayer.

Our heavenly Father waits to bestow upon us the fullness of His blessing. It is our privilege to drink largely at the fountain of boundless love. What a wonder it is that we pray so little! God is ready and willing to hear the sincere prayer of the humblest of His children, and yet there is much manifest reluctance on our part to make known our wants to God. What can the angels of heaven think of poor helpless human beings, who are subject to temptation, when God's heart of infinite love yearns toward them, ready to give them more than they can ask or think, and yet they pray so little and have so little faith? The angels love to bow before God; they love to be near Him. They regard communion with God as their highest joy; and yet the children of earth, who need so much the help that God only can give, seem satisfied to walk without the light of His Spirit, the companionship of His presence.

The darkness of the evil one encloses those who neglect to pray. The whispered temptations of the enemy entice them to sin; and it is all because they do not make use of the privileges that God has given them in the divine appointment of prayer. Why should the sons and daughters of God be reluctant to pray, when prayer is the key in the hand of faith to unlock heaven's storehouse, where are treasured the boundless resources of Omnipotence? Without unceasing prayer and diligent watching we are in danger of growing careless and of deviating from the right path. The adversary seeks continually to obstruct the way to the mercy seat, that we may not by earnest supplication and faith obtain grace and power to resist temptation.

There are certain conditions upon which we may expect that God will hear and answer our prayers. One of the first of these is that we feel our need of help from Him. He has promised, "I will pour water upon him that is thirsty, and floods upon the dry ground." Isaiah 44:3. Those who hunger and thirst after righteousness, who long after God, may be sure that they will be filled. The heart must be open to the Spirit's influence, or God's blessing cannot be received.

Our great need is itself an argument and pleads most eloquently in our behalf. But the Lord is to be sought unto to do these things for us. He says, "Ask, and it shall be given you." And "He that spared not His own Son, but delivered Him up for us all, how shall He not with Him also freely give us all things?" Matthew 7:7; Romans 8:32.

If we regard iniquity in our hearts, if we cling to any known sin, the Lord will not hear us; but the prayer of the penitent, contrite soul is always accepted. When all known wrongs are righted, we may believe that God will answer our peti-

tions. Our own merit will never commend us to the favor of God; it is the worthiness of Jesus that will save us, His blood that will cleanse us; yet we have a work to do in complying with the conditions of acceptance.

Another element of prevailing prayer is faith. 96 "He that cometh to God must believe that He is, and that He is a rewarder of them that diligently seek Him." Hebrews 11:6. Jesus said to His disciples, "What things soever ye desire, when ye pray, believe that ye receive them, and ye shall have them." Mark 11:24. Do we take Him at His word?

The assurance is broad and unlimited, and He is faithful who has promised. When we do not receive the very things we asked for, at the time we ask, we are still to believe that the Lord hears and that He will answer our prayers. We are so erring and short-sighted that we sometimes ask for things that would not be a blessing to us, and our heavenly Father in love answers our prayers by giving us that which will be for our highest good—that which we ourselves would desire if with vision divinely enlightened we could see all things as they really are. When our prayers seem not to be answered, we are to cling to the promise; for the time of answering will surely come, and we shall receive the blessing we need most. But to claim that prayer will always be answered in the very way and for the particular thing that we desire, is presumption. God is too wise to err, and too good to withhold any good thing from them that walk uprightly. Then do not fear to trust Him, even though you do not see the immediate answer to your prayers. Rely upon His sure promise, "Ask, and it shall be given you."

If we take counsel with our doubts and fears, or try to solve everything that we cannot see clearly, before we have faith, perplexities will only increase and deepen. But if we come to 97 God, feeling helpless and dependent, as we really are, and in humble, trusting faith make known our wants to Him whose knowledge is infinite, who sees everything in creation, and who governs everything by His will and word, He can and will attend to our cry, and will let light shine into our hearts. Through sincere prayer we are brought into connection with the mind of the Infinite. We may have no remarkable evidence at the time that the face of our Redeemer is bending over us in compassion and love, but this is even so. We may not feel His visible touch, but His hand is upon us in love and pitying tenderness.

When we come to ask mercy and blessing from God we should have a spirit of love and forgiveness in our own hearts. How can we pray, "Forgive us our debts, as we forgive our debtors," and yet indulge an unforgiving spirit? Matthew 6:12. If we expect our own prayers to be heard we must forgive others in the same manner and to the same extent as we hope to be forgiven.

Perseverance in prayer has been made a condition of receiving. We must pray always if we would grow in faith and experience. We are to be "instant in prayer," to "continue in prayer, and watch in the same with thanksgiving." Romans 12:12; Colossians 4:2. Peter exhorts believers to be "sober, and watch unto prayer." 1 Peter 4:7. Paul directs, "In everything by prayer and supplication with thanksgiving let your requests be made known unto God." Philippians 4:6. "But ye, beloved," says Jude, "praying in the Holy Ghost, keep yourselves in the love of God." Jude 20, 21. Unceasing prayer is the unbroken union of the soul with God, so that life from God flows into our life; and from our life, purity and holiness flow back to God.

There is necessity for diligence in prayer; let nothing hinder you. Make every effort to keep open the communion between Jesus and your own soul. Seek every opportunity to go where prayer is wont to be made. Those who are really seeking for communion with God will be seen in the prayer meeting, faithful to do their duty and earnest and anxious to reap all the benefits they can gain. They will improve every opportunity of placing themselves where they can receive the rays of light from heaven.

We should pray in the family circle, and above all we must not neglect secret prayer, for this is the life of the soul. It is impossible for the soul to flourish while prayer is neglected. Family or public prayer alone is not sufficient. In solitude let the soul be laid open to the inspecting eye of God. Secret prayer is to be heard only by the prayer-hearing God. No curious ear is to receive the burden of such petitions. In secret prayer the soul is free from surrounding influences, free from excitement. Calmly, yet fervently, will it reach out after God. Sweet and abiding will be the influence emanating from Him who seeth in secret, whose ear is open to hear the prayer arising from the heart. By calm, simple faith the soul holds communion with God and gathers to itself rays of divine light to strengthen and sustain it in the conflict with Satan. God is our tower of strength.

Pray in your closet, and as you go about your daily labor let your heart be often uplifted to God. It was thus that Enoch walked with God. These silent prayers rise like precious incense before the throne of grace. Satan cannot overcome him whose heart is thus stayed upon God.

There is no time or place in which it is inappropriate to offer up a petition to God. There is nothing that can prevent us from lifting up our hearts in the spirit of earnest prayer. In the crowds of the street, in the midst of a business engagement, we may send up a petition to God and plead for divine guidance, as did Nehemiah when he made his request before King Artax-

erxes. A closet of communion may be found wherever we are. We should have the door of the heart open continually and our invitation going up that Jesus may come and abide as a heavenly guest in the soul.

Although there may be a tainted, corrupted atmosphere around us, we need not breathe its miasma, but may live in the pure air of heaven. We may close every door to impure imaginings and unholy thoughts by lifting the soul into the presence of God through sincere prayer. Those whose hearts are open to receive the support and blessing of God will walk in a holier atmosphere than that of earth and will have constant communion with heaven.

We need to have more distinct views of Jesus and a fuller comprehension of the value of eternal realities. The beauty of holiness is to fill the hearts of God's children; and that this may be accomplished, we should seek for divine disclosures of heavenly things.

Let the soul be drawn out and upward, that God may grant us a breath of the heavenly atmosphere. We may keep so near to God that in every unexpected trial our thoughts will turn to Him as naturally as the flower turns to the sun.

Keep your wants, your joys, your sorrows, your cares, and your fears before God. You cannot burden Him; you cannot weary Him. He who numbers the hairs of your head is not indifferent to the wants of His children. "The Lord is very pitiful, and of tender mercy." James 5:11. His heart of love is touched by our sorrows and even by our utterances of them. Take to Him everything that perplexes the mind. Nothing is too great for Him to bear, for He holds up worlds, He rules over all the affairs of the universe. Nothing that in any way concerns our peace is too small for Him to notice. There is no chapter in our experience too dark for Him to read; there is no perplexity too difficult for Him to unravel. No calamity can befall the least of His children, no anxiety harass the soul, no joy cheer, no sincere prayer escape the lips, of which our heavenly Father is unobservant, or in which He takes no immediate interest. "He healeth the broken in heart, and bindeth up their wounds." Psalm 147:3. The relations between God and each soul are as distinct and full as though there were not another soul upon the earth to share His watchcare, not another soul for whom He gave His beloved Son.

Jesus said, "Ye shall ask in My name: and I say not unto you, that I will pray the Father for you: for the Father Himself loveth you." "I have chosen you: . . . that whatsoever ye shall ask of the Father in My name, He may give it you." John 16:26, 27; 15:16. But to pray in the name of Jesus is something more than a mere mention of that name at the beginning and the ending of a prayer. It is to pray in the mind and spirit of

Jesus, while we believe His promises, rely upon His grace, and work His works.

God does not mean that any of us should become hermits or monks and retire from the world in order to devote ourselves to acts of worship. The life must be like Christ's life— between the mountain and the multitude. He who does nothing but pray will soon cease to pray, or his prayers will become a formal routine. When men take themselves out of social life, away from the sphere of Christian duty and cross bearing; when they cease to work earnestly for the Master, who worked earnestly for them, they lose the subject matter of prayer and have no incentive to devotion. Their prayers become personal and selfish. They cannot pray in regard to the wants of humanity or the upbuilding of Christ's kingdom, pleading for strength wherewith to work.

We sustain a loss when we neglect the privilege of associating together to strengthen and encourage one another in the service of God. The truths of His word lose their vividness and importance in our minds. Our hearts cease to be enlightened and aroused by their sanctifying influence, and we decline in spirituality. In our association as Christians we lose much by lack of sympathy with one another. He who shuts himself up to himself is not filling the position that God designed he should. The proper cultivation of the social elements in our nature brings us into sympathy with others and is a means of development and strength to us in the service of God.

If Christians would associate together, speaking to each other of the love of God and of the precious truths of redemption, their own hearts would be refreshed and they would refresh one another. We may be daily learning more of our heavenly Father, gaining a fresh experience of His grace; then we shall desire to speak of His love; and as we do this, our own hearts will be warmed and encouraged. If we thought and talked more of Jesus, and less of self, we should have far more of His presence.

If we would but think of God as often as we have evidence of His care for us we should keep Him ever in our thoughts and should delight to talk of Him and to praise Him. We talk of temporal things because we have an interest in them. We talk of our friends because we love them; our joys and our sorrows are bound up with them. Yet we have infinitely greater reason to love God than to love our earthly friends; it should be the most natural thing in the world to make Him first in all our thoughts, to talk of His goodness and tell of His power. The rich gifts He has bestowed upon us were not intended to absorb our thoughts and love so much that we should have nothing to give to God; they are constantly to remind us of Him and to bind us in bonds of love and gratitude to our heavenly

Benefactor. We dwell too near the lowlands of earth. Let us raise our eyes to the open door of the sanctuary above, where the light of the glory of God shines in the face of Christ, who "is able also to save them to the uttermost that come unto God by Him." Hebrews 7:25.

We need to praise God more "for His goodness, and for His wonderful works to the children of men." Psalm 107:8. Our devotional exercises should not consist wholly in asking and receiving. Let us not be always thinking of our wants and never of the benefits we receive. We do not pray any too much, but we are too sparing of giving thanks. We are the constant recipients of God's mercies, and yet how little gratitude we express, how little we praise Him for what He has done for us.

Anciently the Lord bade Israel, when they met together for His service, "Ye shall eat before the Lord your God, and ye shall rejoice in all that ye put your hand unto, ye and your households, wherein the Lord thy God hath blessed thee." Deuteronomy 12:7. That which is done for the glory of God should be done with cheerfulness, with songs of praise and thanksgiving, not with sadness and gloom.

Our God is a tender, merciful Father. His service should not be looked upon as a heart-saddening, distressing exercise. It should be a pleasure to worship the Lord and to take part in His work. God would not have His children, for whom so great salvation has been provided, act as if He were a hard, exacting taskmaster. He is their best friend; and when they worship Him, He expects to be with them, to bless and comfort them, filling their hearts with joy and love. The Lord desires His children to take comfort in His service and to find more pleasure than hardship in His work. He desires that those who come to worship Him shall carry away with them precious thoughts of His care and love, that they may be cheered in all the employments of daily life, that they may have grace to deal honestly and faithfully in all things.

We must gather about the cross. Christ and Him crucified should be the theme of contemplation, of conversation, and of our most joyful emotion. We should keep in our thoughts every blessing we receive from God, and when we realize His great love we should be willing to trust everything to the hand that was nailed to the cross for us.

The soul may ascend nearer heaven on the wings of praise. God is worshiped with song and music in the courts above, and as we express our gratitude we are approximating to the worship of the heavenly hosts. "Whoso offereth praise glorifieth" God. Psalm 50:23. Let us with reverent joy come before our Creator, with "thanksgiving, and the voice of melody." Isaiah 51:3.

105

12
What to Do With Doubt

Many, especially those who are young in the Christian life, are at times troubled with the suggestions of skepticism. There are in the Bible many things which they cannot explain, or even understand, and Satan employs these to shake their faith in the Scriptures as a revelation from God. They ask, "How shall I know the right way? If the Bible is indeed the word of God, how can I be freed from these doubts and perplexities?"

God never asks us to believe, without giving sufficient evidence upon which to base our faith. His existence, His character, the truthfulness of His word, are all established by testimony that appeals to our reason; and this testimony is abundant. Yet God has never removed the possibility of doubt. Our faith must rest upon evidence, not demonstration. Those who wish to doubt will have opportunity; while those who really desire to know the truth will find plenty of evidence on which to rest their faith.

It is impossible for finite minds fully to comprehend the character or the works of the Infinite One. To the keenest intellect, the most highly educated mind, that holy Being must ever remain clothed in mystery. "Canst thou by searching find out God? canst thou find out the Almighty unto perfection? It is as high as heaven; what canst thou do? deeper than hell; what canst thou know?" Job 11:7, 8.

106 The apostle Paul exclaims, "O the depth of the riches both of the wisdom and knowledge of God! how unsearchable are His judgments, and His ways past finding out!" Romans 11:33. But though "clouds and darkness are round about Him," "righteousness and judgment are the foundation of His throne." Psalm 97:2, R.V. We can so far comprehend His dealings with us, and the motives by which He is actuated, that we may discern boundless love and mercy united to infinite power. We can understand as much of His purposes as it is for our good to know; and beyond this we must still trust the hand that is omnipotent, the heart that is full of love.

The word of God, like the character of its divine Author, presents mysteries that can never be fully comprehended by finite beings. The entrance of sin into the world, the incarnation of Christ, regeneration, the resurrection, and many other subjects presented in the Bible, are mysteries too deep for the human mind to explain, or even fully to comprehend. But we have no reason to doubt God's word because we cannot understand the mysteries of His providence. In the natural world we are constantly surrounded with mysteries that we cannot fathom. The very humblest forms of life present a problem that the wisest of philosophers is powerless to explain. Everywhere are wonders beyond our ken. Should we then be surprised to find that in the spiritual world also there are mysteries that we cannot fathom? The difficulty lies solely in the weakness and narrowness of the human mind. God has given us in the Scriptures sufficient evidence of their divine character, and we are not to doubt His word because we cannot 107 understand all the mysteries of His providence.

The apostle Peter says that there are in Scripture "things hard to be understood, which they that are unlearned and unstable wrest . . . unto their own destruction." 2 Peter 3:16. The difficulties of Scripture have been urged by skeptics as an argument against the Bible; but so far from this, they constitute a strong evidence of its divine inspiration. If it contained no account of God but that which we could easily comprehend; if His greatness and majesty could be grasped by finite minds, then the Bible would not bear the unmistakable credentials of divine authority. The very grandeur and mystery of the themes presented should inspire faith in it as the word of God.

The Bible unfolds truth with a simplicity and a perfect adaptation to the needs and longings of the human heart, that has astonished and charmed the most highly cultivated minds, while it enables the humblest and uncultured to discern the way of salvation. And yet these simply stated truths lay hold upon subjects so elevated, so far-reaching, so infinitely beyond the power of human comprehension, that we can accept them only because God has declared them. Thus the plan of redemption is laid open to us, so that every soul may see the steps he is to take in repentance toward God and faith toward our Lord Jesus Christ, in order to be saved in God's appointed way; yet beneath these truths, so easily understood, lie mysteries that are the hiding of His glory—mysteries that overpower the mind in its research, yet inspire the sincere seeker for truth with reverence and faith. The more he searches the Bible, the deep- 108 er is his conviction that it is the word of the living God, and human reason bows before the majesty of divine revelation.

To acknowledge that we cannot fully comprehend the great truths of the Bible is only to admit that the finite mind is inadequate to grasp the infinite; that man, with his limited, human knowledge, cannot understand the purposes of Omniscience.

Because they cannot fathom all its mysteries, the skeptic and the infidel reject God's word; and not all who profess to believe the Bible are free from danger on this point. The apostle says, "Take heed, brethren, lest there be in any of you an evil heart of unbelief, in departing from the living God." Hebrews 3:12. It is right to study closely the teachings of the Bible and to search into "the deep things of God" so far as they are revealed in Scripture. 1 Corinthians 2:10. While "the secret things belong unto the Lord our God," "those things which are revealed belong unto us." Deuteronomy 29:29. But it is Satan's work to pervert the investigative powers of the mind. A certain pride is mingled with the consideration of Bible truth, so that men feel impatient and defeated if they cannot explain every portion of Scripture to their satisfaction. It is too humiliating to them to acknowledge that they do not understand the inspired words. They are unwilling to wait patiently until God shall see fit to reveal the truth to them. They feel that their unaided human wisdom is sufficient to enable them to comprehend the Scripture, and failing to do this, they virtually deny its authority. It is true that many theories and doctrines popularly supposed to be derived from the Bible have no foundation in its teaching, and indeed are contrary to the whole tenor of inspiration. These things have been a cause of doubt and perplexity to many minds. They are not, however, chargeable to God's word, but to man's perversion of it.

If it were possible for created beings to attain to a full understanding of God and His works, then, having reached this point, there would be for them no further discovery of truth, no growth in knowledge, no further development of mind or heart. God would no longer be supreme; and man, having reached the limit of knowledge and attainment, would cease to advance. Let us thank God that it is not so. God is infinite; in Him are "all the treasures of wisdom and knowledge." Colossians 2:3. And to all eternity men may be ever searching, ever learning, and yet never exhaust the treasures of His wisdom, His goodness, and His power.

God intends that even in this life the truths of His word shall be ever unfolding to His people. There is only one way in which this knowledge can be obtained. We can attain to an understanding of God's word only through the illumination of that Spirit by which the word was given. "The things of God knoweth no man, but the Spirit of God;" "for the Spirit searcheth all things, yea, the deep things of God." 1 Corinthians 2:11, 10. And the Saviour's promise to His followers was, "When He, the Spirit of truth, is come, He will guide you into all truth. . . . For He shall receive of Mine, and shall show it unto you." John 16:13, 14.

God desires man to exercise his reasoning powers; and the study of the Bible will strengthen and elevate the mind as no other study can. Yet we are to beware of deifying reason, which is subject to the weakness and infirmity of humanity. If we would not have the Scriptures clouded to our understanding, so that the plainest truths shall not be comprehended, we must have the simplicity and faith of a little child, ready to learn, and beseeching the aid of the Holy Spirit. A sense of the power and wisdom of God, and of our inability to comprehend His greatness, should inspire us with humility, and we should open His word, as we would enter His presence, with holy awe. When we come to the Bible, reason must acknowledge an authority superior to itself, and heart and intellect must bow to the great I AM.

There are many things apparently difficult or obscure, which God will make plain and simple to those who thus seek an understanding of them. But without the guidance of the Holy Spirit we shall be continually liable to wrest the Scriptures or to misinterpret them. There is much reading of the Bible that is without profit and in many cases a positive injury. When the word of God is opened without reverence and without prayer; when the thoughts and affections are not fixed upon God, or in harmony with His will, the mind is clouded with doubts; and in the very study of the Bible, skepticism strengthens. The enemy takes control of the thoughts, and he suggests interpretations that are not correct. Whenever men are not in word and deed seeking to be in harmony with God, then, however learned they may be, they are liable to err in their understanding of Scripture, and it is not safe to trust to their explanations. Those who look to the Scriptures to find discrepancies, have not spiritual insight. With distorted vision they will see many causes for doubt and unbelief in things that are really plain and simple.

Disguise it as they may, the real cause of doubt and skepticism, in most cases, is the love of sin. The teachings and restrictions of God's word are not welcome to the proud, sin-loving heart, and those who are unwilling to obey its requirements are ready to doubt its authority. In order to arrive at truth, we must have a sincere desire to know the truth and a willingness of heart to obey it. And all who come in this spirit to the study of the Bible will find abundant evidence that it is God's word, and they may gain an understanding of its truths that will make them wise unto salvation.

Christ has said, "If any man willeth to do His will, he shall know of the teaching." John 7:17, R.V. Instead of questioning and caviling concerning that which you do not understand, give heed to the light that already shines upon you, and you will receive greater light. By the grace of Christ, perform every duty that has been made plain to your understanding, and you will be enabled to understand and perform those of which you are now in doubt.

There is an evidence that is open to all,—the most highly educated, and the most illiterate,— the evidence of experience. God invites us to prove for ourselves the reality of His word, the truth of His promises. He bids us "taste and see that the Lord is good." Psalm 34:8. Instead of depending upon the word of another, we are to taste for ourselves. He declares, "Ask, and ye shall receive." John 16:24. His promises will be fulfilled. They have never failed; they never can fail. And as we draw near to Jesus, and rejoice in the fullness of His love, our doubt and darkness will disappear in the light of His presence.

The apostle Paul says that God "hath delivered us from the power of darkness, and hath translated us into the kingdom of His dear Son." Colossians 1:13. And everyone who has passed from death unto life is able to "set to his seal that God is true." John 3:33. He can testify, "I needed help, and I found it in Jesus. Every want was supplied, the hunger of my soul was satisfied; and now the Bible is to me the revelation of Jesus Christ. Do you ask why I believe in Jesus? Because He is to me a divine Saviour. Why do I believe the Bible? Because I have found it to be the voice of God to my soul." We may have the witness in ourselves that the Bible is true, that Christ is the Son of God. We know that we are not following cunningly devised fables.

Peter exhorts his brethren to "grow in grace, and in the knowledge of our Lord and Saviour Jesus Christ." 2 Peter 3:18. When the people of God are growing in grace, they will be constantly obtaining a clearer understanding of His word. They will discern new light and beauty in its sacred truths. This has been true in the history of the church in all ages, and thus it will continue to the end. "The path of the righteous is as the light of dawn, that shineth more and more unto the perfect day." Proverbs 4:18, R.V., margin.

By faith we may look to the hereafter and grasp the pledge of God for a growth of intellect, the human faculties uniting with the divine, and every power of the soul being brought into direct contact with the Source of light. We may rejoice that all which has perplexed us in the providences of God will then be made plain, things hard to be understood will then find an explanation; and where our finite minds discovered only confusion and broken purposes, we shall see the most perfect and beautiful harmony. "Now we see through a glass, darkly; but then face to face: now I know in part; but then shall I know even as also I am known." 1 Corinthians 13:12.

13
Rejoicing in the Lord

The children of God are called to be representatives of Christ, showing forth the goodness and mercy of the Lord. As Jesus has revealed to us the true character of the Father, so we are to reveal Christ to a world that does not know His tender, pitying love. "As Thou hast sent Me into the world," said Jesus, "even so have I also sent them into the world." "I in them, and Thou in Me; . . . that the world may know that Thou hast sent Me." John 17:18, 23. The apostle Paul says to the disciples of Jesus, "Ye are manifestly declared to be the epistle of Christ," "known and read of all men." 2 Corinthians 3:3, 2. In every one of His children, Jesus sends a letter to the world. If you are Christ's follower, He sends in you a letter to the family, the village, the street, where you live. Jesus, dwelling in you, desires to speak to the hearts of those who are not acquainted with Him. Perhaps they do not read the Bible, or do not hear the voice that speaks to them in its pages; they do not see the love of God through His works. But if you are a true representative of Jesus, it may be that through you they will be led to understand something of His goodness and be won to love and serve Him.

Christians are set as light bearers on the way to heaven. They are to reflect to the world the light shining upon them from Christ. Their life and character should be such that through them others will get a right conception of Christ and of His service.

If we do represent Christ, we shall make His service appear attractive, as it really is. Christians who gather up gloom and sadness to their souls, and murmur and complain, are giving to others a false representation of God and the Christian life. They give the impression that God is not pleased to have His children happy, and in this they bear false witness against our heavenly Father.

Satan is exultant when he can lead the children of God into unbelief and despondency. He delights to see us mistrusting God, doubting His willingness and power to save us. He loves to have us feel that the Lord will do us harm by His providences. It is the work of Satan to represent the Lord as lacking in compassion and pity. He misstates the truth in regard to Him. He fills the imagination with false ideas concerning God; and instead of dwelling upon the truth in regard to our heavenly Father, we too often fix our minds upon the misrepresentations of Satan and dishonor God by distrusting Him and murmuring against Him. Satan ever seeks to make the religious life one of gloom. He desires it to appear toilsome and difficult; and when the Christian presents in his own life this view of religion, he is, through his unbelief, seconding the falsehood of Satan.

Many, walking along the path of life, dwell upon their mistakes and failures and disappointments, and their hearts are filled with grief and discouragement. While I was in Europe, a sister who had been doing this, and who was in deep distress, wrote to me, asking for some word of encouragement. The night after I had read her letter I dreamed that I was in a garden, and one who seemed to be the owner of the garden was conducting me through its paths. I was gathering the flowers and enjoying their fragrance, when this sister, who had been walking by my side, called my attention to some unsightly briers that were impeding her way. There she was mourning and grieving. She was not walking in the pathway, following the guide, but was walking among the briers and thorns. "Oh," she mourned, "is it not a pity that this beautiful garden is spoiled with thorns?" Then the guide said, "Let the thorns alone, for they will only wound you. Gather the roses, the lilies, and the pinks."

Have there not been some bright spots in your experience? Have you not had some precious seasons when your heart throbbed with joy in response to the Spirit of God? When you look back into the chapters of your life experience do you not find some pleasant pages? Are not God's promises, like the fragrant flowers, growing beside your path on every hand? Will you not let their beauty and sweetness fill your heart with joy?

The briers and thorns will only wound and grieve you; and if you gather only these things, and present them to others, are you not, besides slighting the goodness of God yourself, preventing those around you from walking in the path of life?

It is not wise to gather together all the unpleasant recollections of a past life,—its iniquities and disappointments,—to talk over them and mourn over them until we are overwhelmed with discouragement. A discouraged soul is filled with darkness, shutting out the light of God from his own soul and casting a shadow upon the pathway of others.

Thank God for the bright pictures which He has presented to us. Let us group together the blessed assurances of His love, that we may look upon them continually: The Son of God leaving His Father's throne, clothing His divinity with humanity, that He might rescue man from the power of Satan; His triumph in our behalf, opening heaven to men, revealing to human vision the presence chamber where the Deity unveils His glory; the fallen race uplifted from the pit of ruin into which sin had plunged

it, and brought again into connection with the infinite God, and having endured the divine test through faith in our Redeemer, clothed in the righteousness of Christ, and exalted to His throne—these are the pictures which God would have us contemplate.

When we seem to doubt God's love and distrust His promises we dishonor Him and grieve His Holy Spirit. How would a mother feel if her children were constantly complaining of her, just as though she did not mean them well, when her whole life's effort had been to forward their interests and to give them comfort? Suppose they should doubt her love; it would break her heart. How would any parent feel to be thus treated by his children? And how can our heavenly Father regard us when we distrust His love, which has led Him to give His only-begotten Son that we might have life? The apostle writes, "He that spared not His own Son, but delivered Him up for us all, how shall He not with Him also freely give us all things?" Romans 8:32. And yet how many, by their actions, if not in word, are saying, "The Lord does not mean this for me. Perhaps He loves others, but He does not love me."

All this is harming your own soul; for every word of doubt you utter is inviting Satan's temptations; it is strengthening in you the tendency to doubt, and it is grieving from you the ministering angels. When Satan tempts you, breathe not a word of doubt or darkness. If you choose to open the door to his suggestions, your mind will be filled with distrust and rebellious questioning. If you talk out your feelings, every doubt you express not only reacts upon yourself, but it is a seed that will germinate and bear fruit in the life of others, and it may be impossible to counteract the influence of your words. You yourself may be able to recover from the season of temptation and from the snare of Satan, but others who have been swayed by your influence may not be able to escape from the unbelief you have suggested. How important that we speak only those things that will give spiritual strength and life!

Angels are listening to hear what kind of report you are bearing to the world about your heavenly Master. Let your conversation be of Him who liveth to make intercession for you before the Father. When you take the hand of a friend, let praise to God be on your lips and in your heart. This will attract his thoughts to Jesus.

All have trials; griefs hard to bear, temptations hard to resist. Do not tell your troubles to your fellow mortals, but carry everything to God in prayer. Make it a rule never to utter one word of doubt or discouragement. You can do much to brighten the life of others and strengthen their efforts, by words of hope and holy cheer.

There is many a brave soul sorely pressed by temptation, almost ready to faint in the conflict with self and with the powers of evil. Do not discourage such a one in his hard struggle. Cheer him with brave, hopeful words that shall urge him on his way. Thus the light of Christ may shine from you. "None of us liveth to himself." Romans 14:7. By our unconscious influence others may be encouraged and strengthened, or they may be discouraged, and repelled from Christ and the truth.

There are many who have an erroneous idea of the life and character of Christ. They think that He was devoid of warmth and sunniness, that He was stern, severe, and joyless. In many cases the whole religious experience is colored by these gloomy views.

It is often said that Jesus wept, but that He was never known to smile. Our Saviour was indeed a Man of Sorrows, and acquainted with grief, for He opened His heart to all the woes of men. But though His life was self-denying and shadowed with pain and care, His spirit was not crushed. His countenance did not wear an expression of grief and repining, but ever one of peaceful serenity. His heart was a wellspring of life, and wherever He went He carried rest and peace, joy and gladness.

Our Saviour was deeply serious and intensely in earnest, but never gloomy or morose. The life of those who imitate Him will be full of earnest purpose; they will have a deep sense of personal responsibility. Levity will be repressed; there 121 will be no boisterous merriment, no rude jesting; but the religion of Jesus gives peace like a river. It does not quench the light of joy; it does not restrain cheerfulness nor cloud the sunny, smiling face. Christ came not to be ministered unto but to minister; and when His love reigns in the heart, we shall follow His example.

If we keep uppermost in our minds the unkind and unjust acts of others we shall find it impossible to love them as Christ has loved us; but if our thoughts dwell upon the wondrous love and pity of Christ for us, the same spirit will flow out to others. We should love and respect one another, notwithstanding the faults and imperfections that we cannot help seeing. Humility and self-distrust should be cultivated, and a patient tenderness with the faults of others. This will kill out all narrowing selfishness and make us large-hearted and generous.

The psalmist says, "Trust in the Lord, and do good; so shalt thou dwell in the land, and verily thou shalt be fed." Psalm 37:3. "Trust in the Lord." Each day has its burdens, its cares and perplexities; and when we meet how ready we are to talk of our difficulties and trials. So many borrowed troubles intrude, so many fears are indulged, such a weight of anxiety is expressed, that one might suppose we had no pitying, loving Saviour ready to hear all our requests and to be to us a present help in every time of need.

Some are always fearing, and borrowing trouble. Every day they are surrounded with the tokens of God's love; every day they are enjoying the bounties of His providence; but they overlook these present blessings. Their minds 122 are continually dwelling upon something disagreeable which they fear may come; or some difficulty may really exist which, though small, blinds their eyes to the many things that demand gratitude. The difficulties they encounter, instead of driving them to God, the only source of their help, separate them from Him because they awaken unrest and repining.

Do we well to be thus unbelieving? Why should we be ungrateful and distrustful? Jesus is our friend; all heaven is interested in our welfare. We should not allow the perplexities and worries of everyday life to fret the mind and cloud the brow. If we do we shall always have something to vex and annoy. We should not indulge a solicitude that only frets and wears us, but does not help us to bear trials.

You may be perplexed in business; your prospects may grow darker and darker, and you may be threatened with loss; but do not become discouraged; cast your care upon God, and remain calm and cheerful. Pray for wisdom to manage your affairs with discretion, and thus prevent loss and disaster. Do all you can on your part to bring about favorable results. Jesus has promised His aid, but not apart from our effort. When, relying upon our Helper, you have done all you can, accept the result cheerfully.

It is not the will of God that His people should be weighed down with care. But our Lord does not deceive us. He does not say to us, "Do not fear; there are no dangers in your path." He knows there are trials and dangers, and He deals with us plainly. He does not propose to take His people out of a world of sin and evil, but He points them to a never-failing refuge. 123 His prayer for His disciples was, "I pray not that Thou shouldest take them out of the world, but that Thou shouldest keep them from the evil." "In the world," He says, "ye shall have tribulation: but be of good cheer; I have overcome the world." John 17:15, 16:33.

In His Sermon on the Mount, Christ taught His disciples precious lessons in regard to the necessity of trusting in God. These lessons were designed to encourage the children of God through all ages, and they have come down to our time full of instruction and comfort. The Saviour pointed His followers to the birds of the air as they warbled their carols of praise, unencumbered with thoughts of care, for "they sow not, neither do they reap." And yet the great Father provides for their needs. The Saviour asks, "Are ye not much better than they?" Matthew 6:26. The great Provider for man and beast opens His hand and supplies all His creatures. The birds of the air are not beneath His notice. He does not drop the food into their bills, but He makes provision for their needs. They must gather the grains He has scattered for them. They must prepare the material for their little nests. They must feed their young. They go forth singing to their labor, for "your heavenly Father feedeth them." And "are ye not much better than they?" Are not you, as intelligent, spiritual worshipers, of more value than the birds of the air? Will not the Author of our being, the Preserver of our life, the One who formed us in His own divine image, provide for our necessities if we but trust in Him?

124 Christ pointed His disciples to the flowers of the field, growing in rich profusion and glowing in the simple beauty which the heavenly Father had given them, as an expression of His love to man. He said, "Consider the lilies of the field, how they grow." The beauty and simplicity of these natural flowers far outrival the splendor of Solomon. The most gorgeous attire produced by the skill of art cannot bear comparison with the natural grace and radiant beauty of the flowers of God's creation. Jesus asks, "If God so clothe the grass of the field, which today is, and tomorrow is cast into the oven, shall He not much more clothe you, O ye of little faith?" Matthew 6:28, 30. If God, the divine Artist, gives to the simple flowers that perish in a day their delicate and varied colors, how much greater care will He have for those who are created in His own image? This lesson of Christ's is a rebuke to the anxious thought, the perplexity and doubt, of the faithless heart.

The Lord would have all His sons and daughters happy, peaceful, and obedient. Jesus says, "My peace I give unto you: not as the world giveth, give I unto you. Let not your heart be troubled, neither let it be afraid." "These things have I spoken unto you, that My joy might remain in you, and that your joy might be full." John 14:27; 15:11.

Happiness that is sought from selfish motives, outside of the path of duty, is ill-balanced, fitful, and transitory; it passes away, and the soul is filled with loneliness and sorrow; but there is joy and satisfaction in the service of God; the Christian is not left to walk in uncertain paths; he is not left to vain regrets and disappoint-

125 ments. If we do not have the pleasures of this life we may still be joyful in looking to the life beyond.

But even here Christians may have the joy of communion with Christ; they may have the light of His love, the perpetual comfort of His presence. Every step in life may bring us closer to Jesus, may give us a deeper experience of His love, and may bring us one step nearer to the

blessed home of peace. Then let us not cast away our confidence, but have firm assurance, firmer than ever before. "Hitherto hath the Lord helped us," and He will help us to the end. 1 Samuel 7:12. Let us look to the monumental pillars, reminders of what the Lord has done to comfort us and to save us from the hand of the destroyer. Let us keep fresh in our memory all the tender mercies that God has shown us,—the tears He has wiped away, the pains He has soothed, the anxieties removed, the fears dispelled, the wants supplied, the blessings bestowed,—thus strengthening ourselves for all that is before us through the remainder of our pilgrimage.

We cannot but look forward to new perplexities in the coming conflict, but we may look on what is past as well as on what is to come, and say, "Hitherto hath the Lord helped us." "As thy days, so shall thy strength be." Deuteronomy 33:25. The trial will not exceed the strength that shall be given us to bear it. Then let us take up our work just where we find it, believing that whatever may come, strength proportionate to the trial will be given.

And by and by the gates of heaven will be thrown open to admit God's children, and from the lips of the King of glory the benediction will fall on their ears like richest music, "Come, ye 126 blessed of My Father, inherit the kingdom prepared for you from the foundation of the world." Matthew 25:34.

Then the redeemed will be welcomed to the home that Jesus is preparing for them. There their companions will not be the vile of earth, liars, idolaters, the impure, and unbelieving; but they will associate with those who have overcome Satan and through divine grace have formed perfect characters. Every sinful tendency, every imperfection, that afflicts them here has been removed by the blood of Christ, and the excellence and brightness of His glory, far exceeding the brightness of the sun, is imparted to them. And the moral beauty, the perfection of His character, shines through them, in worth far exceeding this outward splendor. They are without fault before the great white throne, sharing the dignity and the privileges of the angels.

In view of the glorious inheritance that may be his, "what shall a man give in exchange for his soul?" Matthew 16:26. He may be poor, yet he possesses in himself a wealth and dignity that the world could never bestow. The soul redeemed and cleansed from sin, with all its noble powers dedicated to the service of God, is of surpassing worth; and there is joy in heaven in the presence of God and the holy angels over one soul redeemed, a joy that is expressed in songs of holy triumph.